HOLT SCIENCE & TECHNOLOGY

Earth Science

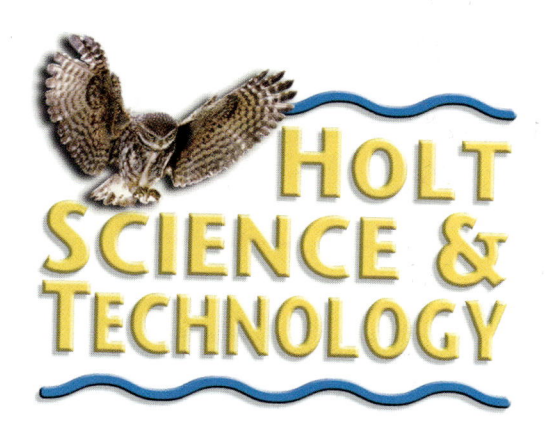

Contents in Brief

Teacher Edition WALK-THROUGH

Contents in Brief T1	Lab Materials Ordering T19
Program Overview T2	Meeting Individual Needs T20
Student Edition T4	Reading Skills T22
Teacher Edition T6	Cross-Disciplinary T24
Assessment Resources T8	Math and Science Skills Worksheets T26
Teaching Resources T10	Pacing Guide T34
Technology Resources T12	Safety Guidelines for Teachers T36
Online Resources T14	Correlation to the National Science Education Standards ... T42
Labs and Activities T16	

Student Edition CONTENTS IN BRIEF

Chapter 1	The World of Earth Science 4	Chapter 13	Exploring the Oceans 372
Chapter 2	Maps and Models of the Earth 34	Chapter 14	The Movement of Ocean Water 414
Chapter 3	Minerals of the Earth's Crust 64	Chapter 15	The Atmosphere 446
Chapter 4	Rocks: Mineral Mixtures 88	Chapter 16	Understanding Weather 480
Chapter 5	Energy Resources 120	Chapter 17	Climate 516
Chapter 6	The Rock and Fossil Record 150	Chapter 18	Studying Space 552
Chapter 7	Plate Tectonics 188	Chapter 19	Stars, Galaxies, and the Universe 580
Chapter 8	Earthquakes 222	Chapter 20	Formation of the Solar System 612
Chapter 9	Volcanoes 248	Chapter 21	Family of Planets 642
Chapter 10	Weathering and Soil Formation 276	Chapter 22	Exploring Space 682
Chapter 11	The Flow of Fresh Water 306	Appendix	 768
Chapter 12	Agents of Erosion and Deposition ... 340	Glossary	 804

HOLT, RINEHART AND WINSTON
A Harcourt Education Company

Orlando • Austin • New York • San Diego • Toronto • London

Designed to meet the needs of all students

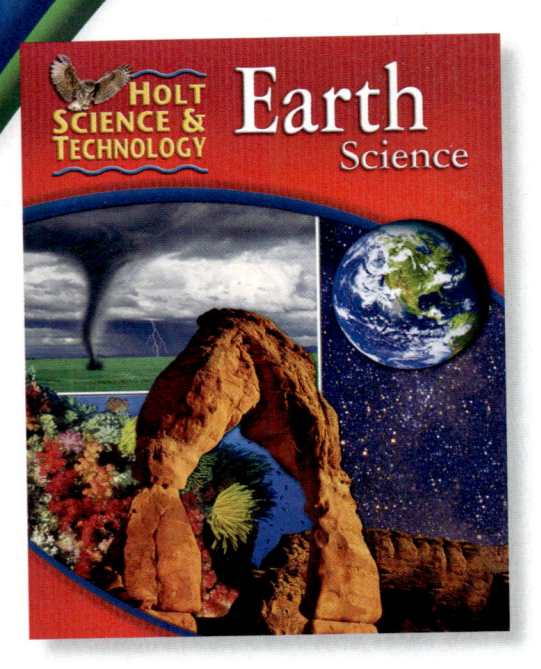

Holt Science & Technology reflects current curriculum developments and includes the strongest skills-development strand of any middle school science series. This comprehensive middle school program provides students with a solid foundation in life science, Earth science, and physical science fundamentals. Students of all abilities will develop skills that they can use both in science as well as in other courses.

STUDENTS OF ALL ABILITIES RECEIVE THE READING HELP AND TAILORED INSTRUCTION THEY NEED.

- The *Student Edition* is accessible with a clean, easy-to-follow design and highlighted vocabulary words.
- Inclusion strategies and different learning styles are addressed to support all learners.
- **Comprehensive Section** and **Chapter Reviews** and **Standardized Test Preparation** allow students to practice their test-taking skills.
- **Reading Comprehension Guide** and **Guided Reading Audio CDs** help students better understand the content.

CROSS-DISCIPLINARY CONNECTIONS LET STUDENTS SEE HOW SCIENCE RELATES TO OTHER DISCIPLINES.

- **Mathematics, reading, and writing skills** are integrated throughout the program.
- Cross-discipline **Connection To** features show students how science relates to language arts, social studies, and other sciences.

A FLEXIBLE LABORATORY PROGRAM HELPS STUDENTS BUILD IMPORTANT INQUIRY AND CRITICAL-THINKING SKILLS.

- The laboratory program includes labs in each chapter, labs in the **LabBook** at the end of the text, six different lab books, and **Video Labs**.
- All labs are teacher-tested and rated by difficulty in the *Teacher Edition,* so you can be sure the labs will be appropriate for your students.
- A variety of labs, from Inquiry Labs to Skills Practice Labs, helps you meet the needs of your curriculum and work within the time constraints of your teaching schedule.

INTEGRATED TECHNOLOGY AND ONLINE RESOURCES EXPAND LEARNING BEYOND CLASSROOM WALLS.

- An **Enhanced Online Edition** or **CD-ROM Version** of the student text lightens your students' load.

- **SciLinks,** a Web service developed and maintained by the National Science Teachers Association (NSTA), contains current prescreened links directly related to the textbook.

- **Brain Food Video Quizzes** on videotape and DVD are game-show style quizzes that assess students' progress and motivate them to study.

- The **One-Stop Planner®** CD-ROM with **ExamView®** Test Generator contains all of the resources you need including an *Interactive Teacher Edition*, worksheets, customizable lesson plans, **Holt Calendar Planner**, a powerful test generator, **Lab Materials QuickList Software,** and more.

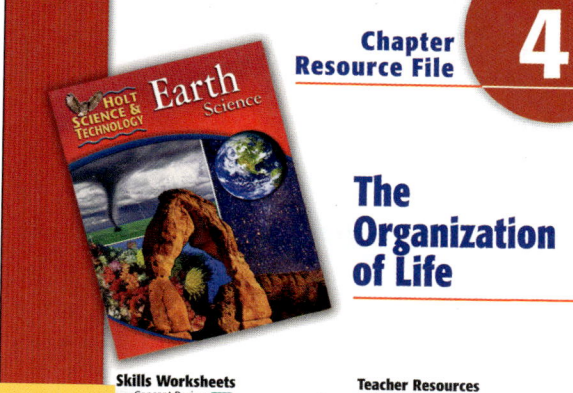

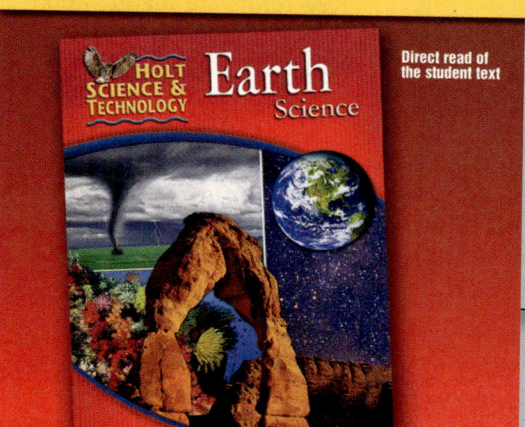

The skills students need for science success

A WELL-DESIGNED TEXT MAKES SCIENCE ENGAGING AND ACCESSIBLE.

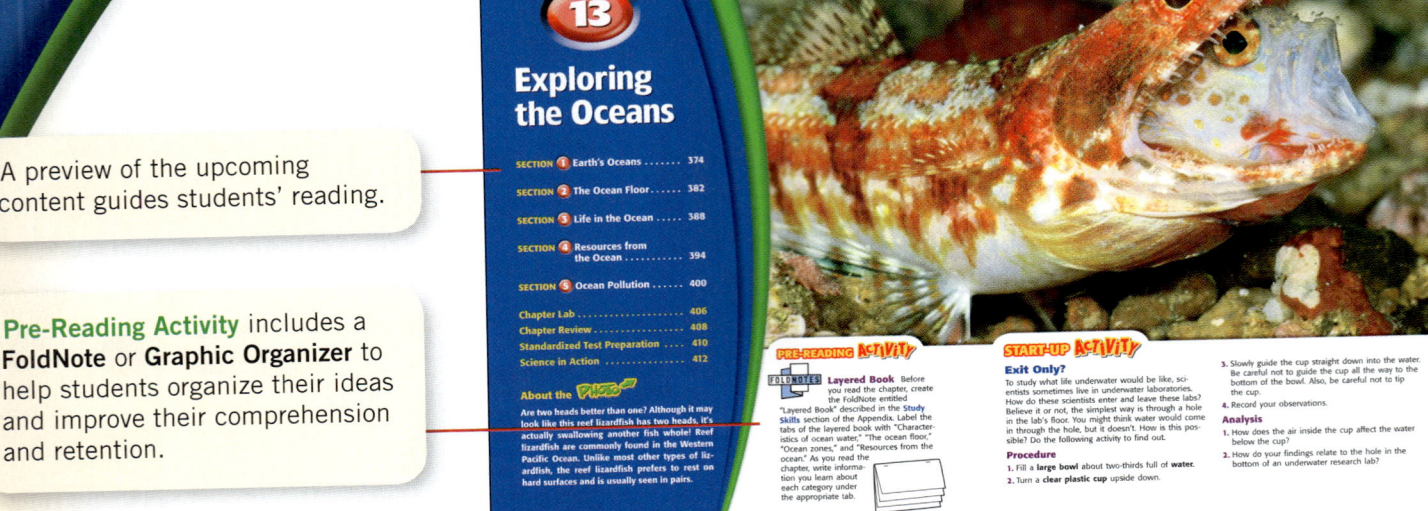

A preview of the upcoming content guides students' reading.

Pre-Reading Activity includes a **FoldNote** or **Graphic Organizer** to help students organize their ideas and improve their comprehension and retention.

Accessible navigation engages students with outline-style headings, content grouped into small chunks, and text that doesn't break between pages.

Reading Strategy gives students additional reading guidance with a **Reading Organizer, Prediction Guide, Discussion, Paired Summarizing, Brainstorming,** or **Mnemonics Tip.**

Visuals are engaging and closely related to the text narrative.

An engaging photo and hands-on **Start-Up Activity** motivate students.

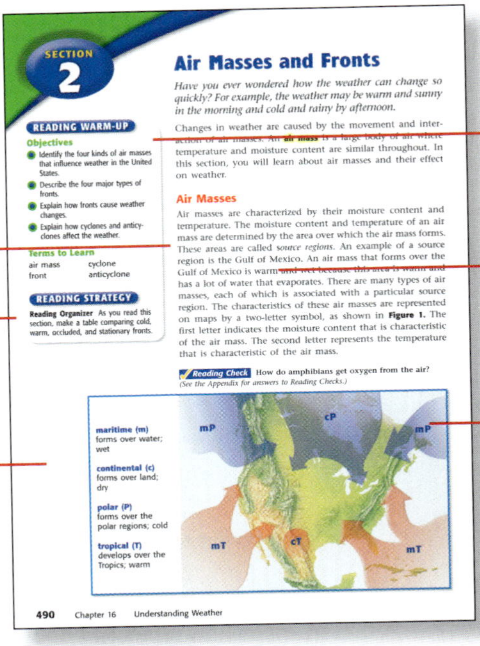

Objectives and **Terms to Learn** help focus students' attention and develop reading skills.

Key Terms are highlighted in yellow and defined in the margin to develop students' vocabulary skills.

Reading Check allows students to check their understanding at least once every two-page spread. Answers are found in the **Appendix.**

T4

RELEVANT AND EXCITING FEATURES PROMOTE STUDENTS' INTEREST.

Science in Action grabs students' attention with three short articles and online extensions.

Current Science connects students to interesting online articles from *Current Science*® magazine.

SciLinks refers students to the NSTA Web site for up-to-date links, information, and activities.

CROSS-DISCIPLINARY FEATURES CONNECT SCIENCE TO OTHER SUBJECTS.

Math Practice and **Math Focus** help build students' math skills.

Connection shows how science relates to social studies, language arts, or other sciences.

Writing skills are developed and highlighted throughout the program, including in the **Science Journal**.

Social Studies, Language Arts, and **Math Activity** are included in the **Science in Action** feature at the end of every chapter.

LABS AND ACTIVITIES MAKE LEARNING HANDS-ON.

Internet Activity sends students online for a variety of projects, such as creating scientist biographies and writing articles.

Quick Lab and **School to Home Activity** require few materials and reinforce science concepts.

Chapter Lab includes **Inquiry, Model-Making,** and **Skills Practice** labs. Additional labs are located in the **LabBook** at the end of the book.

REVIEW FOR TEST-READINESS

Section Review includes a comprehensive assessment of the section's **Objectives**.

Chapter Review checks students' understanding of all of the chapter **Objectives** with vocabulary, multiple-choice, short answer, **Critical Thinking,** and **Interpreting Graphics** questions.

Standardized Test Preparation gives students skill practice in reading, math, and interpreting graphics.

A Teacher Edition that is functional and easy-to-use

The **Chapter Organizer** is an easy-to-follow visual planning guide that provides the support you need to plan your lessons.

You'll be glad to know that we've included a convenient time-saving guide suggesting how to use the wealth of program resources. The **Chapter Organizer**:

- integrates all labs, technology, and print resources.
- is organized according to time requirements.
- includes section correlations to the National Science Education Standards.
- rates activities by ability level to help you select those that are appropriate for your class.

Chapter Resources and Worksheets are shown as reduced pages to make choosing appropriate worksheets easy. Available resources and worksheets are grouped by

- Visual Resources
- Meeting Individual Needs
- Review and Assessment
- Applications and Extensions

Chapter Enrichment provides additional information for each section in the chapter, including interesting facts that spark student interest. Also included is a selection of **SciLinks** for more information about the topics listed.

The **Lesson Cycle** provides a structure for the teaching strategies included in the Teacher's wrap. **Focus** uses objectives to focus student attention on the upcoming content; **Motivate** includes activities and discussions to get students excited about learning; **Teach** includes **Teaching** and **Reading Strategies**; and **Close** provides additional assessment including **Alternative Assessment**.

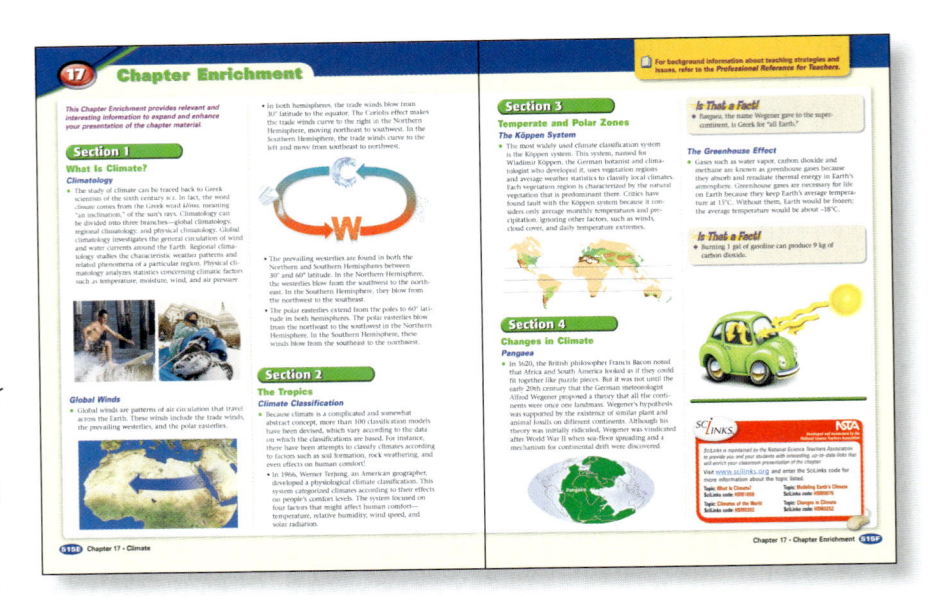

ACTIVITIES AND DEMONSTRATIONS FOR EVERY LEARNING LEVEL

Activities in the teacher's wrap are labeled by ability level—**Basic, General,** and **Advanced**—helping you choose appropriate activities for each student.

- **Basic** activities are designed to be accessible to all students.
- **General** activities are appropriate for most students and require more critical-thinking skills than Basic activities.
- **Advanced** activities are more challenging than General activities and can be used to extend learning.

Learning styles—**Interpersonal, Intrapersonal, Auditory, Kinesthetic, Logical, Visual,** and **Verbal**—are addressed throughout so you can adapt material to different ways of learning. In addition, some labels identify the activities that help with **Co-op Learning** and **English Language Learners.**

Bellringer activities begin each section with an activity designed to get students thinking. **Bellringers** are also available on transparency.

Bellringer
Ask students to think about how potholes form in paved roads. Have students write a few sentences that describe how water contributes to the formation of potholes. Students should illustrate how cycles of freezing and

Activity, Group Activity, Connection Activity, Demonstrations, and **Homework** provide more quick activities that you can integrate into your lesson.

ACTIVITY — BASIC
Plant Identification Have students work together in small groups to find pictures in magazines of ferns and flowering plants that grow in North America. Provide resource books for the students to use to identify the plants. Then, have students mount the plant pictures on poster board and label them.
LS Visual — English Language Learners

BRAIN FOOD
Mining on Other Planets
know that there are val of minerals on other bod system. Ask students to what issues should be co staking claims and mini

MISCONCEPTION ALERT
The Force of Water Students may think that it seems illogical that water makes magma more likely to explode. Explain that magma contains water and that the magma. When liquid to a gas, a increases e causes a

Teach, continued
READING STRATEGY — GENERAL
Mnemonics Have students think of some rhymes to help them remember key points about the projections discussed in the text. You might suggest the following to help students get started:
- "If you're traveling to the equator, you'll do well with Mercator."
- "For east to west, conic is best."
- "For a stroll at a pole, an azimuthal will help you stay in control."
LS Verbal/Auditory — English Language Learners

TEACHING TIPS AND ENGAGING FEATURES KEEP STUDENTS INTERESTED AND INVOLVED.

- Reading and Teaching Strategies
- Misconception Alert
- Cultural Awareness
- Scientists at Odds
- Weird Science
- Brain Food
- Connections to other disciplines and sciences
- Science Humor
- Is That a Fact!

INCLUSION STRATEGIES MAKE MATERIAL ACCESSIBLE TO ALL.

Written by professionals in the field of special needs education, **Inclusion Strategies** address many different learning exceptionalities in the classroom.

- Hearing Impaired
- Visually Impaired
- Developmentally Delayed
- Attention Deficit Disorder
- Behavior Control Issues
- Gifted and Talented

INCLUSION Strategies
- Visually Impaired
- Learning Disabled
- Behavior Control Issues

Organize students into small groups. Give each group colored modeling clay, a piece of cardboard, and self-stick notes. Have each group create a cross-section of a vol-

Complete assessment every step of the way

Holt Science & Technology provides many ways to accurately measure students' mastery of content.

CUSTOM ASSESSMENT WITH THE ONE-STOP PLANNER CD-ROM WITH TEST GENERATOR

With Holt's *One-Stop Planner CD-ROM* create, revise, and edit quizzes, section and chapter reviews, and chapter tests. Thousands of questions, organized by chapter and linked to chapter objectives, allow you to customize tests for your classroom. **Performance-Based Assessment** is also included.

SECTION ASSESSMENT

Reading Check is found at least once on each two-page spread. Students are encouraged to check their understanding of content by answering these questions found throughout the chapter and comparing their answers to the answer key in the **Appendix**.

Section Review provides a summary of the section and a comprehensive assessment of students' understanding of section **Objectives**. **Math, Interpreting Graphics,** and **Critical Thinking** questions are included.

Section Quiz in the *Teacher Edition* and the *Chapter Resource Files* provides additional questions to check students' understanding.

Alternative Assessment gives you different evaluation options, such as expository writing and concept mapping, to ensure a thorough assessment.

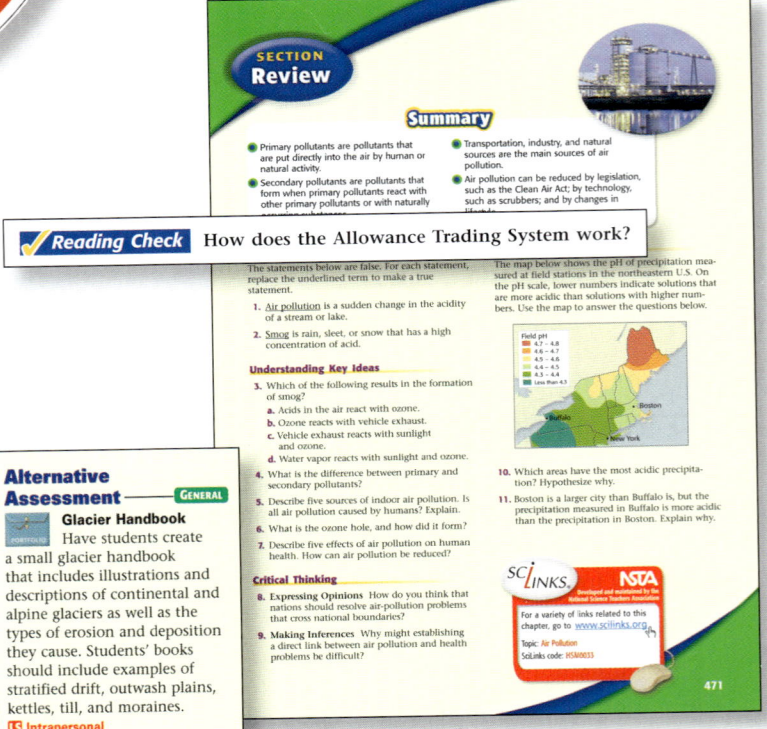

CHAPTER ASSESSMENT

Chapter Review checks students' understanding of all of the section **Objectives** with vocabulary, multiple-choice, short-answer, critical-thinking, and interpreting graphics questions. Question types are similar to those found on **Chapter Tests**, making this an excellent resource for pretest practice.

- **Assignment Guide** in the *Teacher Edition* lets you see which review questions correlate with a specific section's content.
- **Study Guide** provides blackline masters of the **Section** and **Chapter Reviews** to help students prepare for testing.

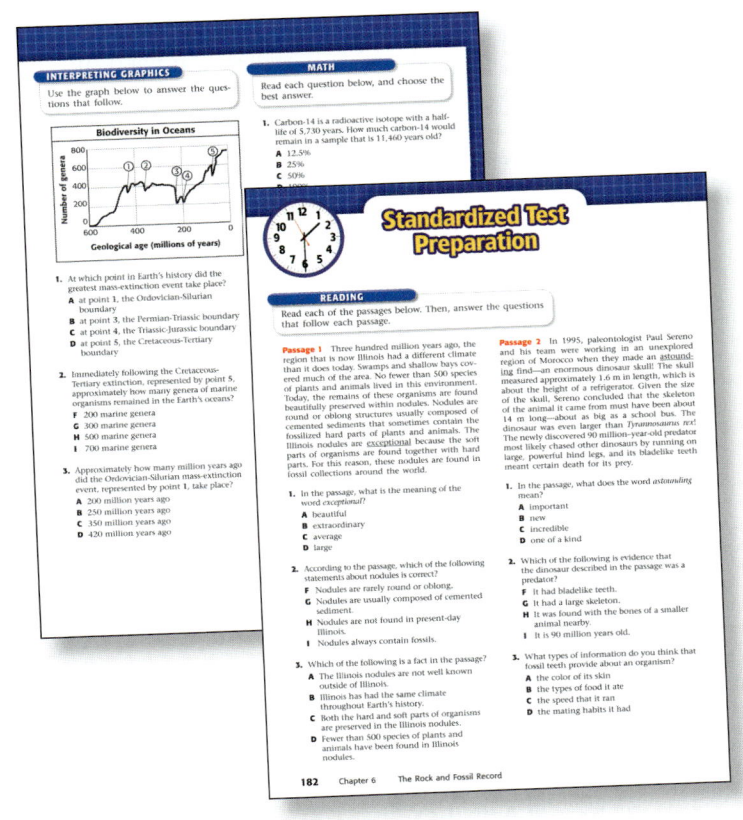

Standardized Test Preparation helps students prepare for testing with skill practice in reading, math, and interpreting graphics. There are two full pages of test preparation in the *Student Edition* and additional practice in the *Chapter Resource Files*.

Test Doctor in the *Teacher Edition* helps you diagnose why a student answered a **Standardized Test Preparation** question incorrectly.

Chapter Resource Files include **Performance-Based Assessment** plus three levels of **Chapter Tests** to meet the needs of your classroom—Special Needs, General, and Advanced. In addition, a **Test Item Listing** is available so you can quickly see all of the available test items located on the **One-Stop Planner CD-ROM**.

Assessment Checklists & Rubrics provide guidelines for evaluating your students' progress. You can create a customized checklist for each class to help you gather daily scores and determine grades.

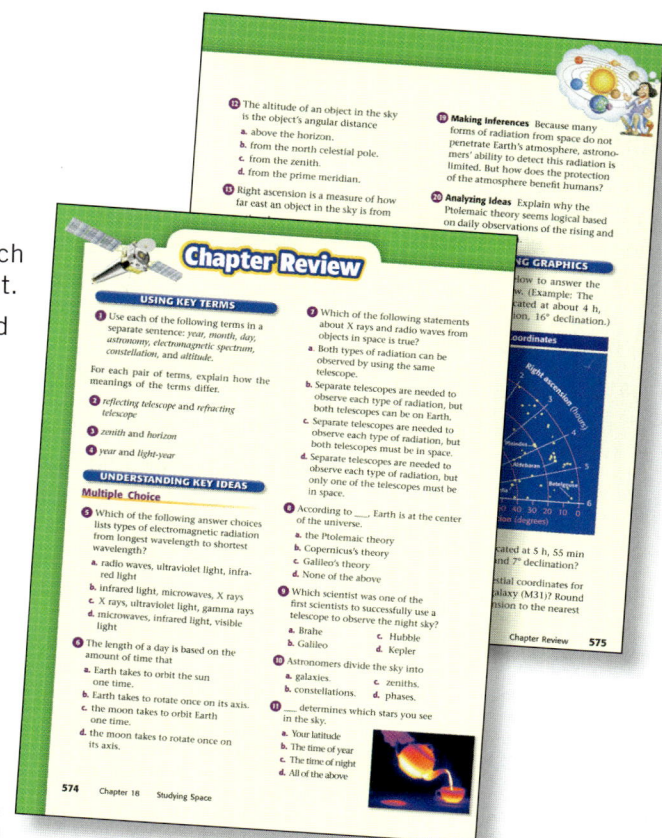

T9

Resources to make teaching easier

CHAPTER RESOURCE FILES

A *Chapter Resource File* is provided for each chapter of **Holt Science & Technology.** Each *Chapter Resource File* provides everything you need to plan and manage your lessons for the chapter in a convenient, time-saving format. Also included is a **Program Resource Introduction File,** your guide to the resources in each *Chapter Resource File. Chapter Resource Files* include the following:

Skills Worksheets
- Directed Reading A: Basic
- Directed Reading B: Special Needs
- Vocabulary and Section Summary
- Section Reviews
- Chapter Review
- Reinforcement
- Critical Thinking

Assessments
- Section Quizzes
- Chapter Test A: General
- Chapter Test B: Advanced
- Chapter Test C: Special Needs
- Performance-Based Assessment
- Standardized Test Preparation

Labs and Activities
- Datasheet for Chapter Lab
- Datasheets for Quick Labs
- Datasheets for LabBook Labs
- Vocabulary Activity
- SciLinks Activity

Teacher Resources
- Teacher Notes for Performance-Based Assessment
- Lab Notes and Answers
- Answer Keys
- Lesson Plans
- Test Item Listing for ExamView® Test Generator

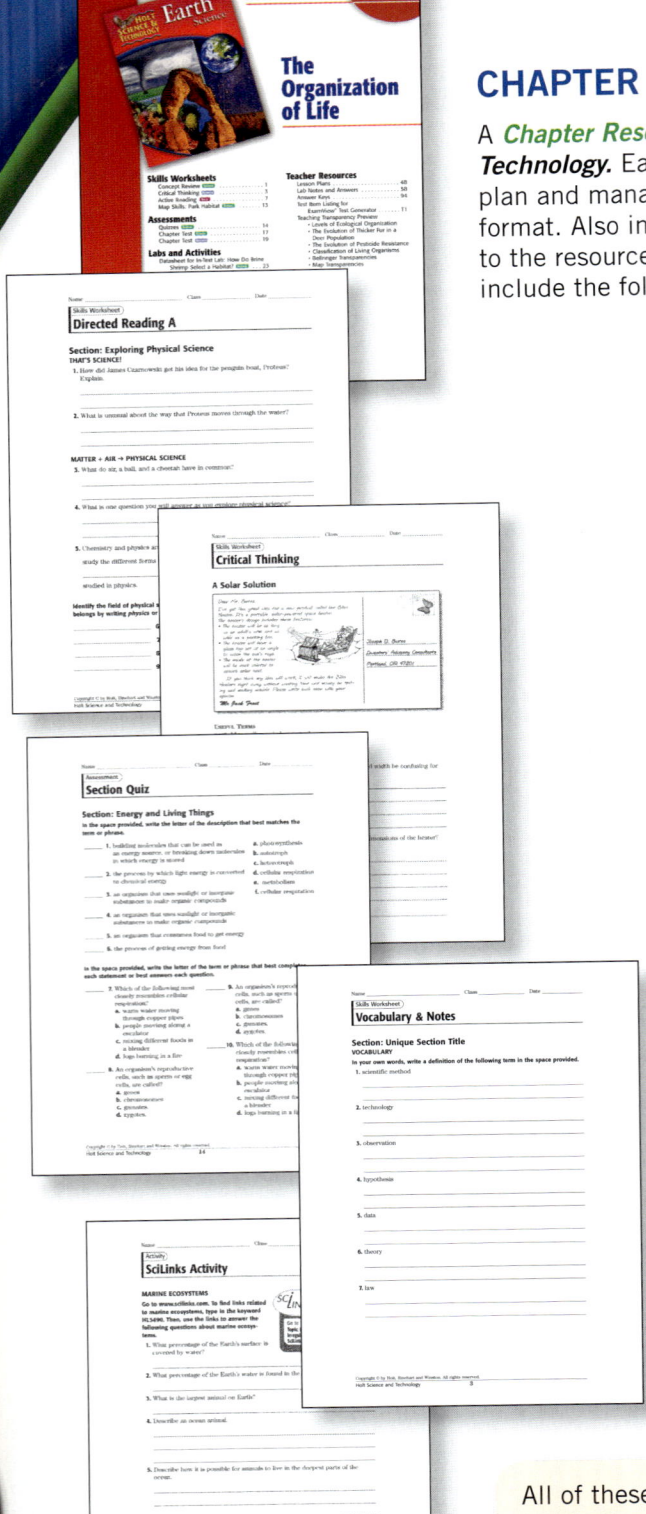

All of these additional resources can also be found in one place on Holt's **One-Stop Planner CD-ROM.** Also included on this CD-ROM is a **Test Generator** that allows you to customize your quizzes and tests.

Teaching Resources

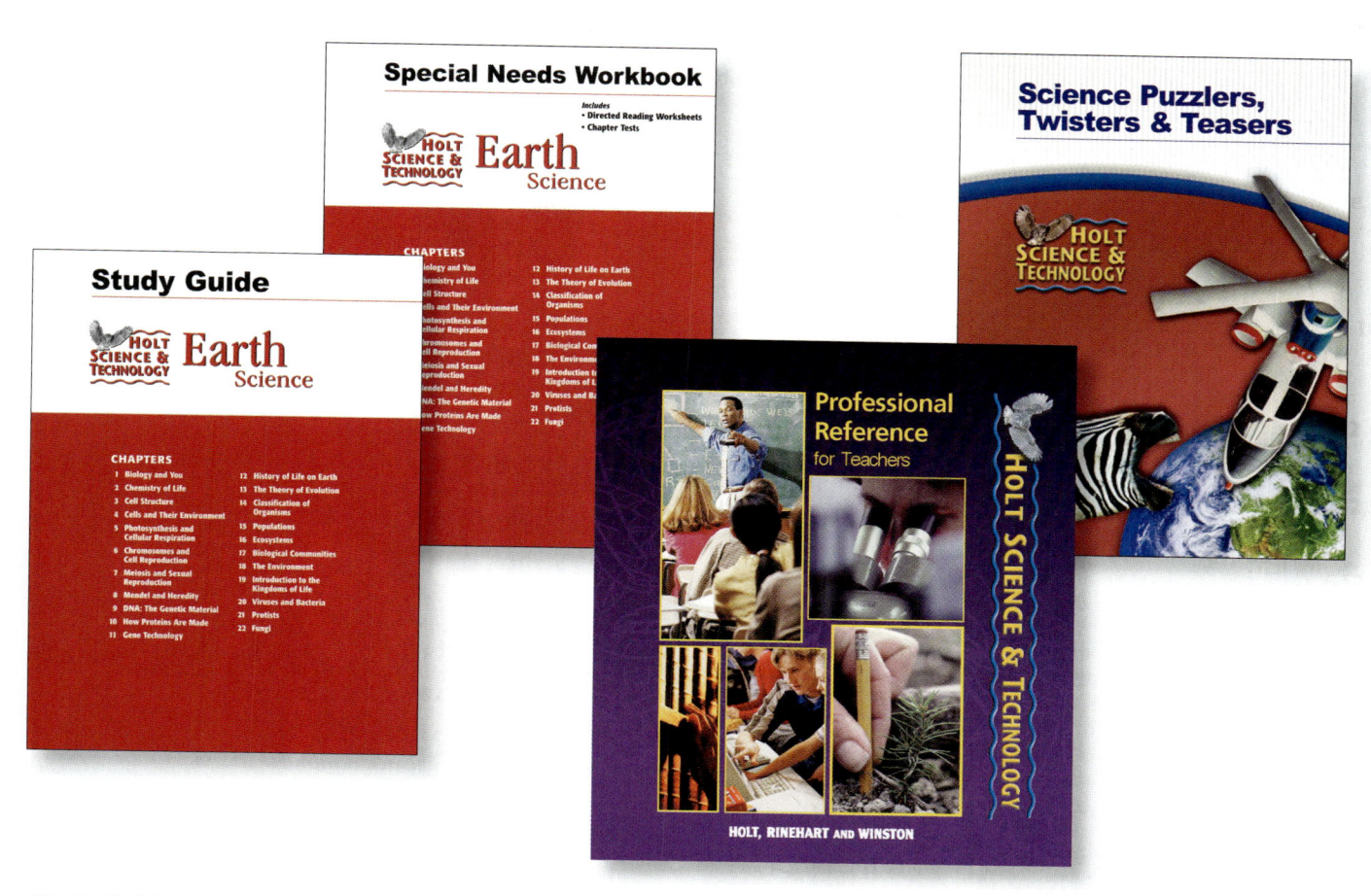

Study Guide contains **Section** and **Chapter Review Worksheets.** Answers are contained in the corresponding *Chapter Resource File.*

Reading Comprehension Guide includes **Directed Reading Worksheets** and **Vocabulary** and **Section Summary** worksheets to improve students' understanding of the text.

Special Needs Workbook includes **Special Needs Directed Reading Worksheets** and the **Special Needs Chapter Tests.**

Program Teaching Resources includes a variety of resources for additional skill development—*Science Puzzlers, Twisters & Teasers; Science Skills Worksheets; Math Skills for Science; Science Fair Guide; Assessment Checklists & Rubrics.*

Professional Reference for Teachers provides current information about issues in science education today. In professional articles, you can learn more about the National Education Standards, block scheduling, classroom management, and more.

Holt Science Posters includes seven colorful posters.

Holt Anthology of Science Fiction sparks your students' imaginations.

Holt Science Skills Workshop: Reading in the Content Area contains exercises that target key reading skills using excerpts from Holt's science textbooks.

Transparencies visually reinforce important science concepts with 300 *Teaching Transparencies* plus *Bellringer, Chapter Starter,* and *Concept Mapping Transparencies.*

SPANISH RESOURCES BRING HOLT SCIENCE & TECHNOLOGY TO ENGLISH-LANGUAGE LEARNERS.

These translations open the door to students who are frequently locked out.

- *Student Edition* in Spanish
- Spanish glossary in both the English and Spanish *Student Edition*
- **Study Guide** in Spanish
- **Reading Comprehension Guide** in Spanish
- **Assessments** in Spanish
- **Guided Reading Audio CD Program** in Spanish

T11

Technology Resources

Technology that expands your teaching options

One-Stop Planner CD-ROM® with Test Generator

Holt Science & Technology provides the correct combination of integrated technology resources—including CD-ROMs, videotapes, and DVD products—to make teaching more effective, efficient, and creative.

Planning and managing lessons has never been easier than with this convenient, all-in-one CD-ROM that includes the following time-saving features:

Printable:
- Teaching Resources
- Transparency Masters
- Special Needs Resources

Customizable:
- **Lesson Plans:** traditional and block-scheduling lesson plans in several word-processing formats
- **Holt Calendar Planner:** a tool that allows you to manage your time and resources by the day, week, month, or year
- **PowerPoint® LectureNotes:** graphic organizers and key concepts for each section that teachers can use to develop their own customized lectures

Powerful:
- **ExamView® Test Generator:** test items organized by chapter, plus thousands of editable questions, so you can put together your own tests and quizzes
- **Lab Materials QuickList Software:** a tool to easily create a customizable list of lab materials you need
- **Holt PuzzlePro:** an easy way to create crossword puzzles and word searches that make learning vocabulary fun
- **Interactive** *Teacher Edition:* the entire teacher text, with links to related Teaching Resources; planning has never been easier

T12

CD-ROM RESOURCES

Guided Reading Audio CD Program provides a direct reading of each chapter in English and in Spanish. This program helps struggling readers and English-language learners better understand the text.

Interactive Explorations CD-ROM turns a computer into a virtual laboratory where students help solve a selection of real-world problems.

Science Tutor CD-ROM serves as a personal tutor to help students practice what they learn. Immediate feedback is provided.

Student Edition on CD-ROM provides students with the entire textbook on a CD-ROM so that they have less to carry home.

Visual Concepts CD-ROM provides you with graphics, animations, and movie clips that demonstrate key chapter concepts. Visual Concepts work well as a student tutor or a teacher-presentation tool.

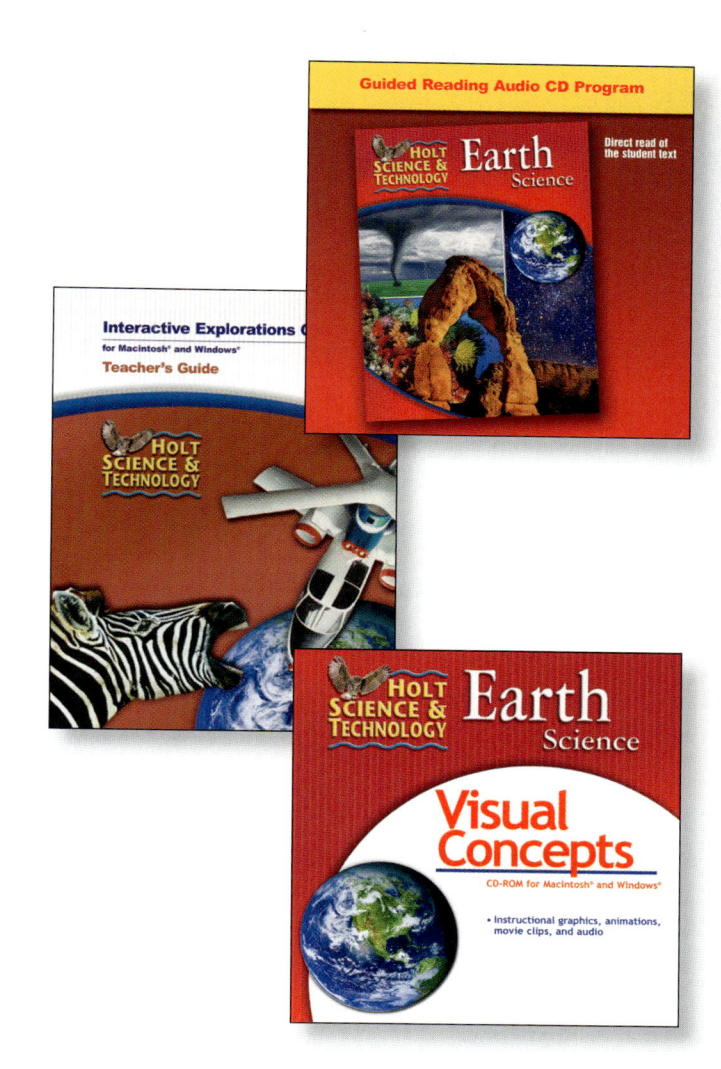

VIDEO RESOURCES

Lab Videos (on videotape or DVD) make it easier for you to integrate more experiments into your lessons without the preparation time and costs of a traditional laboratory setup.

Brain Food Video Quizzes (on videotape or DVD) are game-show style quizzes that assess students' progress and motivate students to study.

HRW Earth Science Videotape takes your students on a geology "field trip" with full-motion video.

CNN Presents Science in the News: Video Library allows your students to see the impact of science in their everyday lives with the following videos: Scientists in Action, Multicultural Connections, Science, Technology & Society, and Eye on the Environment. This program includes a **Teacher's Guide** and **Critical-Thinking Worksheets.**

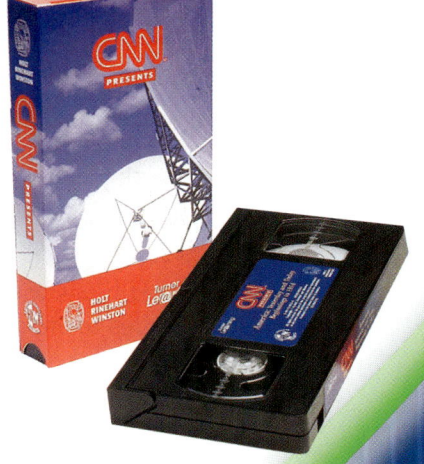

Online Resources

Online resources available anytime, anywhere!

ENHANCED ONLINE EDITIONS ARE PORTABLE, EXPANDABLE, AND INTERACTIVE, AND YET WEIGH NOTHING AT ALL.

Enhanced Online Editions of **Holt Science & Technology** engage students in ways that were never before possible. You'll find the following:

- Entire *Student Edition* online
- Interactive exercises, quizzes, and a science tutor with immediate feedback
- Web links
- **Visual Concepts** for student study or teacher presentation
- General tools, such as a glossary
- **Classroom Manager** and **One-Stop Planner** to create a lesson and manage resources.

This web service, developed and maintained by the National Science Teachers Association, contains a large collection of prescreened links that include current information and activities directly related to chapter topics.

- Prescreening saves you valuable time searching for relevant and up-to-date Web sites.
- Sites are reviewed by science-content experts and educators.
- **Internet Connect** boxes within each chapter offer opportunities to enrich, enhance, and extend learning.
- Each topic leads to many links.

Online Resources

Current Science

Current Science is a science magazine with articles that speak directly to middle school students and relate to students' lives. A collection of articles and activities have been placed online and are correlated to the text.

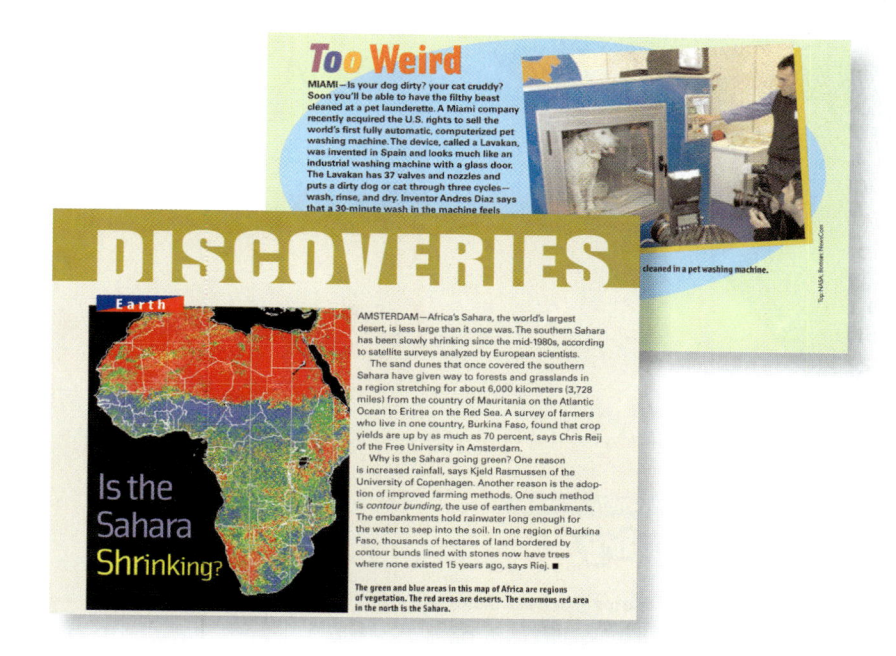

student CNN News

cnnstudentsnews.com is the ultimate news and information Web site for both teachers and students. The site includes news as it happens, classroom resources, activities, and lesson plans.

go.hrw.com

go.hrw.com enriches student learning with activities and resources keyed to the chapters in the textbook.

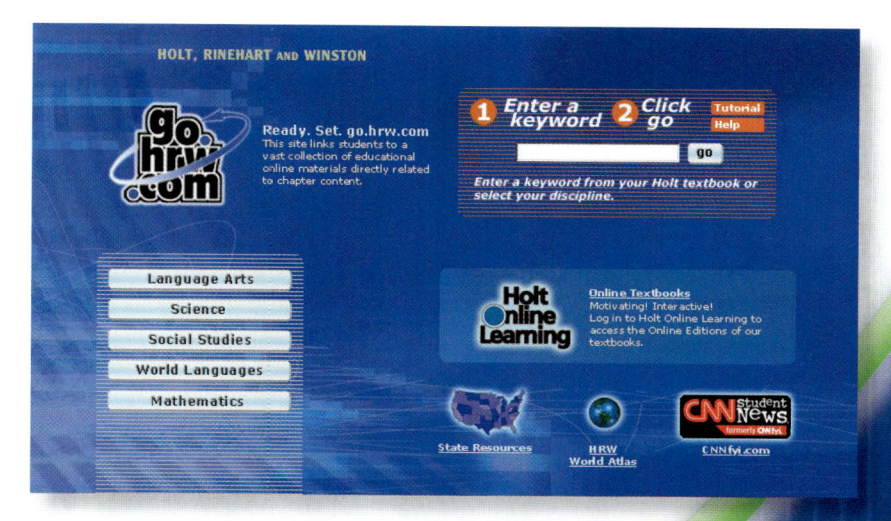

T15

A complete lab program that makes learning meaningful

Labs and Activities

Using Scientific Methods
Inquiry Lab

Water Rockets Save the Day!

Imagine that for the big Fourth of July celebration, you and your friends had planned a full day of swimming, volleyball, and fireworks at the lake. You've just learned, however, that the city passed a law that bans all fireworks within city limits. But you do not give up so easily on having fun. Last year at summer camp, you learned how to build water rockets. And you have kept the launcher in your garage since then. With a little bit of creativity, you and your friends are going to celebrate with a splash!

OBJECTIVES

Predict which design features would improve a rocket's flight.
Design and build a rocket that includes your design features.
Test your rocket design, and evaluate your results.

MATERIALS
- bottle, soda, 2 L
- clay, modeling
- foam board
- rocket launcher
- scissors
- tape, duct
- watch or clock that indicates seconds
- water

SAFETY

Ask a Question
1. What is the most efficient design for a water rocket?

Form a Hypothesis
2. Write a hypothesis that provides a possible answer to the question above.

Test the Hypothesis
3. Decide how your rocket will look, and then draw a sketch.
4. Using only the materials listed, decide how to build your rocket. Write a description of your plan, and have your teacher approve your plan. Keep in mind that you will need to leave the opening of your bottle clear. The bottle opening will be placed over a rubber stopper on the rocket launcher.
5. Fins are often used to stabilize rockets. Do you want fins on your water rocket? Decide on the best shape for the fins, and then decide how many fins your rocket needs. Use the foam board to construct the fins.
6. Your rocket must be heavy enough to fly in a controlled manner. Consider using clay in the body of your rocket to provide some additional weight and stability.
7. Pour water into your rocket until the rocket is one-third to one-half full.
8. Your teacher will provide the launcher and will assist you during blastoff. Attach your rocket to the launcher by placing the opening of the bottle on the rubber stopper.
9. When the rocket is in place, clear the immediate area and begin pumping air into your rocket. Watch the pump gauge, and take note of how much pressure is needed for liftoff.
Caution: Be sure to step back from the launch site. You should be several meters away from the bottle when you launch it.
10. Use the watch to time your rocket's flight. How long was your rocket in the air?
11. Make small changes in your rocket design that you think will improve the rocket's performance. Consider using different amounts of water and clay or experimenting with different fins. You may also want to compare your design with those of your classmates.

Analyze the Results
1. **Describing Events** How did your rocket perform? If you used fins, do you think they helped your flight? Explain your answer.
2. **Explaining Results** What do you think propelled your rocket? Use Newton's third law of motion to explain your answer.
3. **Analyzing Results** How did the amount of water in your rocket affect the launch?

Draw Conclusions
4. **Drawing Conclusions** What modifications made your rocket fly for the longest time? How did the design help the rockets fly so far?
5. **Evaluating Results** Which group's rocket was the most stable? How did the design help the rocket fly straight?
6. **Making Predictions** How can you improve your design to make your rocket perform even better?

706 Chapter 22 Exploring Space

Chapter Lab 707

Holt Science & Technology provides a strong and flexible lab program that meets lab science requirements, regardless of lab equipment limits or time restrictions.

Chapter Labs—Inquiry Labs, Skills Practice Labs, and **Model Making Labs**—include clear procedures, demonstrate scientific concepts, and help develop students' understanding of scientific methods. All labs have been classroom-tested and reviewed for reliability, safety, and efficiency. Labs are rated in the *Teacher Edition,* making it easy for you to select labs that are appropriate for your classroom.

Video Labs (on videotape or DVD) demonstrate the **Chapter Labs,** making it easy for you to integrate more experiments into your lessons without the preparation time and costs of a traditional laboratory setup. **Video Labs** can also provide reinforcement and reteaching opportunities for students.

LabBook provides additional experiments at the end of the *Student Edition,* giving you even more full-length labs to choose from.

Datasheets for all **Quick Labs, Chapter Labs,** and **LabBook Labs** are available in the *Chapter Resource Files.*

Labs and Activities

START-UP ACTIVITY
Making Fossils
How do scientists learn from fossils? In this activity, you will study "fossils" and identify the object that made each.
Procedure

Start-Up Activity is an engaging activity at the beginning of the chapter that motivates students to learn.

QUICK Lab
A Cool Breeze
1. Hold a **thermometer** next to the top edge of a **cup**

Quick Lab is easy to execute and requires minimal time and materials—great for an in-class activity, teacher demonstration, or group presentation.

School to Home
Water Conservation
Did you know that water use in the United States has been reduced by 15% in the

School-to-Home Activity provides an opportunity for parents or guardians to get involved with student learning. These activities require little or no equipment and do not require safety precautions.

INTERNET ACTIVITY
For another activity related to this chapter, go to **go.hrw.com** and type in the keyword **HZ5DEPW**.

Internet Activity sends students online for a variety of projects, such as creating scientist biographies and writing science articles.

Language Arts ACTIVITY
WRITING SKILL Write your own short story about

Social Studies ACTIVITY
WRITING SKILL Research a location where there

Math ACTIVITY
In space flight, astronauts experience changes in gravity that affect their bodies in several ways. Because of gravity, a person who has a mass of 50 kg weighs 110 pounds on Earth. But on the

Cross-Disciplinary Activity gives students the opportunity to see how science relates to social studies, language arts, or mathematics.

Group ACTIVITY — GENERAL
Classifying Divide the class into small groups. Ask them to classify as many items in the classroom as they can based on the following categories:

You can also integrate additional activities from the *Teacher Edition* into your lessons—**Activity, Group Activity, Connection Activity, Demonstration,** and **Homework.**

T17

Labs and Activities

Lab options for every need

Holt Science & Technology provides a variety of additional meaningful activities that are cost effective and fun. A variety of ancillary materials complement and complete your presentations.

Calculator-Based Labs integrate calculator use into science labs, providing a link to help students develop mathematics skills. **20 labs in all!**

Whiz-Bang Demonstrations include compelling demonstrations that students will enjoy—proving that learning science can be fun, as well as meaningful. **65 labs in all!**

Labs You Can Eat spark student interest, while explaining important scientific concepts. **25 labs in all!**

Inquiry Labs introduce students to the world of science inquiry and foster the skills necessary to develop hands-on science literacy. **23 labs in all!**

EcoLabs & Field Activities provide students with ideas for exploring the world of science outside the classroom. **23 labs in all!**

Long-Term Projects and Research Ideas help students think about science as a long-term process. Students are encouraged to study topics they find intriguing and to construct their own types of investigation. **2 for every chapter!**

Materials ordering made easy

LAB MATERIALS ORDERING

Now it's easier to order your laboratory materials!

Lab Materials QuickList Software saves you time:

- See all materials needed for in-text labs.
- Create a customized list of materials.
- Quickly create a list of the items you need.
- Find everything conveniently located on the *One-Stop Planner CD-ROM.*

Lab Materials Ordering

T19

Meeting Individual Needs

Students have a wide range of abilities and learning exceptionalities. These pages show you how *Holt Science & Technology* provides resources and strategies to help you tailor your instruction to engage every student in your classroom. Furthermore, activities in the *Teacher Edition* are labeled with one or more learning styles designed to engage a variety of skills and strengths in every student.

- **LS Visual** activities emphasize learning through pictures, colors, and shapes.
- **LS Verbal** activities emphasize learning through words.
- **LS Logical** activities emphasize learning through patterns, reason, or numbers.
- **LS Kinesthetic** activities emphasize learning through physical activity and touch.
- **LS Auditory** activities emphasize learning through sound.
- **LS Interpersonal** activities emphasize learning through interactions with others.
- **LS Intrapersonal** activities emphasize learning through independent work and reflection.

Learning exceptionality	Inclusion Strategies and Activities
Learning Disabilities and Slow Learners Students who have dyslexia or dysgraphia, students reading below grade level, students having difficulty understanding abstract or complex concepts, and slow learners	• Inclusion Strategies labeled *Learning Disabled* • Activities and Alternative Assessments labeled *Basic* • *Reteaching* activities • Activities labeled *Visual, Kinesthetic,* or *Auditory* • Hands-on activities or projects • Oral presentations instead of written tests or assignments
Developmental Delays Students who are functioning far below grade level because of mental retardation, autism, or brain injury; goals are to learn or retain basic concepts	• Inclusion Strategies labeled *Developmentally Delayed* • Activities and Alternative Assessments labeled *Basic* • *Reteaching* activities • Project-based activities
Attention Deficit Disorders Students experiencing difficulty completing a task that has multiple steps, difficulty handling long assignments, or difficulty concentrating without sensory input from physical activity	• Inclusion Strategies labeled *Attention Deficit Disorder* • Activities and Alternative Assessments labeled *Basic* • *Reteaching* activities • Activities labeled *Co-op Learning* • Activities labeled *Visual, Kinesthetic,* or *Auditory* • Concepts broken into small chunks • Oral presentations instead of written tests or assignments
English as a Second Language Students learning English	• Activities labeled *English-Language Learners* • Activities labeled *Basic* • *Reteaching* activities • Activities labeled *Visual*
Gifted and Talented Students who are performing above grade level and demonstrate aptitude in crosscurricular assignments	• Inclusion Strategies labeled *Gifted and Talented* • Activities and Alternative Assessments labeled *Advanced* • *Connection* activities • Activities that involve multiple tasks, a strong degree of independence, and student initiative
Hearing Impairments Students who are deaf or who have difficulty hearing	• Inclusion Strategies labeled *Hearing Impaired* • Activities labeled *Visual* • Activities labeled *Co-op Learning* • Assessments that use written presentations
Visual Impairments Students who are blind or who have difficulty seeing	• Inclusion strategies labeled *Visually Impaired* • Activities labeled *Auditory* • Activities labeled *Co-op Learning* • Assessments that use oral presentations
Behavior Control Issues Students learning to manage their behavior	• Inclusion Strategies labeled *Behavior Control Issues* • Activities labeled *Basic* • Assignments that actively involve students and help students develop confidence and improved behaviors

GENERAL INCLUSION STRATEGIES

The following strategies can help you modify instruction to help students who struggle with common classroom difficulties.

A student experiencing difficulty with...	May benefit if you...
Beginning assignments	• Assign work in small amounts • Have the student use cooperative or paired learning • Provide varied and interesting activities • Allow choice in assignments or projects • Reinforce participation • Seat the student closer to you
Following directions	• Gain the student's attention before giving directions • Break up the task into small steps • Give written directions rather than oral directions • Use short, simple phrases • Stand near the student when you are giving directions • Have the student repeat directions to you • Prepare the student for changes in activity • Give visual cues by posting general routines • Reinforce improvement in or approximation of following directions
Keeping track of assignments	• Have the student use folders for assignments • Have the student use assignment notebooks • Have the student keep a checklist of assignments and highlight assignments when they are turned in
Reading the textbook	• Provide outlines of the textbook content • Reduce the length of required reading • Allow extra time for reading • Have the students read aloud in small groups • Have the student use peer or mentor readers • Have the student use books on tape or CD • Discuss the content of the textbook in class after reading
Staying on task	• Reduce distracting elements in the classroom • Provide a task-completion checklist • Seat the student near you • Provide alternative ways to complete assignments, such as oral projects taped with a buddy
Behavioral or social skills	• Model the appropriate behaviors • Establish class rules, and reiterate them often • Reinforce positive behavior • Assign a mentor as a positive role model to the student • Contract with the student for expected behaviors • Reinforce the desired behaviors or any steps toward improvement • Separate the student from any peer who stimulates the inappropriate behavior • Provide a "cooling off" period before talking with the student • Address academic/instructional problems that may contribute to disruptive behaviors • Include parents in the problem-solving process through conferences, home visits, and frequent communication
Attendance	• Recognize and reinforce attendance by giving incentives or verbal praise • Emphasize the importance of attendance by letting the student know that he or she was missed when he or she was absent • Encourage the student's desire to be in school by planning activities that are likely to be enjoyable, giving the student a preferred responsibility to be performed in class, and involving the student in extracurricular activities • Schedule problem-solving meeting with parents, faculty, or both
Test-taking skills	• Prepare the student for testing by teaching ways to study in pairs, such as using flashcards, practice tests, and study guides, and by promoting adequate sleep, nourishment, and exercise • Decrease visual distraction by improving the visual design of the test through use of larger type, spacing, consistent layout, and shorter sentences • During testing, allow the student to respond orally on tape or to respond using a computer; to use notes; to take breaks; to take the test in another location; to work without time constraints; or to take the test in several short sessions

Meeting Individual Needs

Mastering Reading and Comprehension

Reading features that foster understanding

Holt Science & Technology makes instruction accessible to all students—advanced learners, students having difficulty mastering content, and those needing more practice or hands-on experiences.

Every page begins with a new head, making the text easy to navigate and more accessible.

Each section begins with a **Reading Warm-up** that lists objectives and terms covered in the section. This feature helps students focus on the content being presented and understand what they read.

Reading Strategy helps students better understand what they read. Strategies provided include the following: **Reading Organizer, Prediction Guide, Discussion, Paired Summarizing, Brainstorming,** and **Mnemonics.**

Key Terms are highlighted in yellow and defined in the margin, helping students increase their science vocabulary.

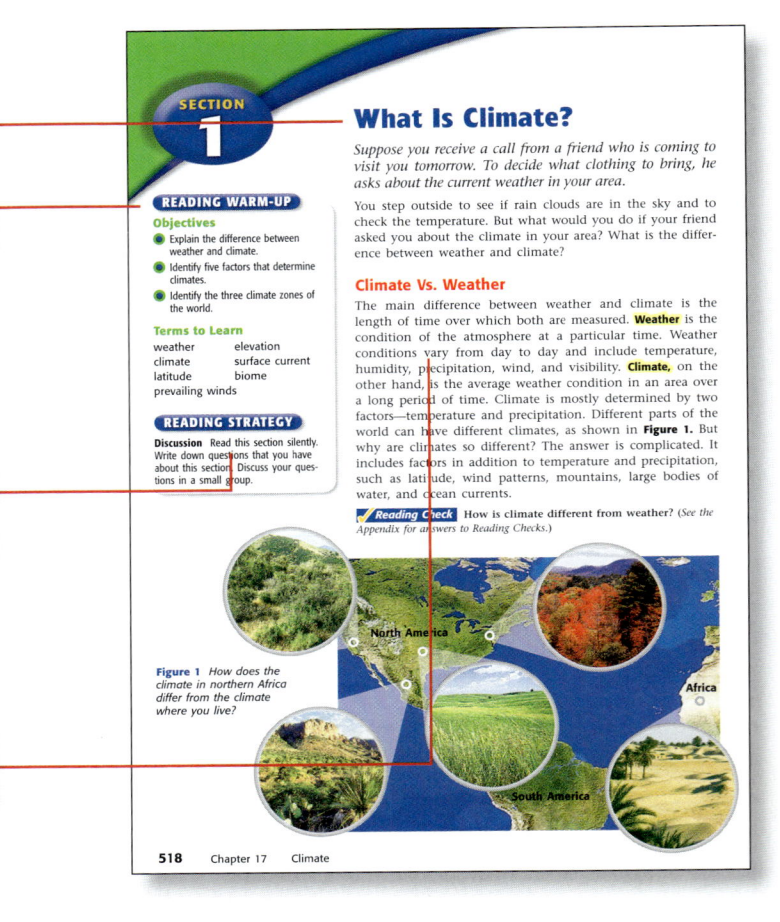

READ FOR UNDERSTANDING

Each chapter provides suggestions to help your students read for understanding.

- **Pre-Reading Activity** provides **FoldNotes** or **Graphic Organizer** activities to help students organize information presented in the chapter. Students are encouraged to take notes and then categorize what they read. In addition, the **Appendix** provides complete instruction on how to create and use the reading strategies suggested in pre-reading activities.

- **Reading Check** provides students with opportunities to check their comprehension as they read. Answers are included in the **Appendix.**

- Additional **Reading Strategies** in the *Teacher Edition* emphasize key concepts in order to guide reading and ensure comprehension.

- **Standardized Test Preparation** enables students to test their comprehension skills by reading a passage and answering a series of questions in a standardized test format. Practice is included at the end of each chapter and a blackline master of the test is located in the *Chapter Resource Files.*

ADDITIONAL RESOURCES HELP STUDENTS DEVELOP READING COMPREHENSION SKILLS.

Reading Comprehension Guide includes **Directed Reading Worksheets** and **Vocabulary** and **Section Summary Worksheets** that make reading an active process.

- **Directed Reading Worksheets** guide students through each section and focus their attention on key elements. Available in two levels: Basic and Special Needs.
- **Vocabulary** and **Section Summary** worksheets help students review vocabulary words and provide a bulleted list of main topics from each section.

Reinforcement Worksheets, found in the *Chapter Resource Files,* make reviewing and reinforcing chapter content easy.

Guided Reading Audio CD Program, a direct reading of the student text, is helpful to students who benefit from different learning modalities. Available in English and Spanish.

Special Needs Workbook provides special needs directed reading worksheets and special needs **Chapter Tests** to give special needs students additional practice opportunities.

HOLT SCIENCE SKILLS WORKSHOP: READING IN THE CONTENT AREA

Target the reading skills specific to the comprehension of science texts with these activities and exercises. Students learn to analyze text structures, recognize patterns, and organize information in ways that help them construct meaning.

Mastering Reading and Comprehension

T23

Linking science to other disciplines

Science does not occur in a vacuum. It is an integral part of the human quest to understand the world. Connection features help students become more aware of the interconnectedness of their school studies and prepare them for standardized testing.

Science in Action features provide short articles designed to spark students' interest in science topics. Cross-Disciplinary activities including social studies, language arts, and math activities are also included for each article. Students can extend their learning by visiting **go.hrw.com**.

Connection to Language Arts links science with various language arts skills.

Holt Anthology of Science Fiction connects science to literature with interesting and relevant stories.

Writing Skills icon occurs in any activity that requires students to practice their writing skills.

Connection to Social Studies links science to social studies, presenting students with opportunities to see how science relates to history, geography, and wider society concerns.

Connection to Science links various sciences to explain phenomena in the natural world. This feature provides students with opportunities to recognize and explore important links to sciences such as environmental science, geology, physics, and oceanography.

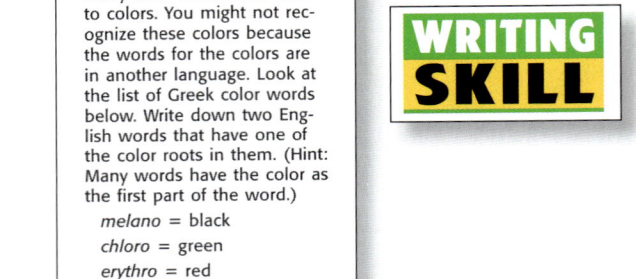

ADDITIONAL MATH CONNECTIONS

Math Practice provides practice in simple mathematical computations. Students can hone math skills by using the exercises provided in this feature.

> **MATH PRACTICE**
> **Averages**
> Finding the average, or mean, of a group of numbers is a common way to analyze data.
> For example, three seeds were kept at 25°C and sprouted in 8, 8, and 5 days. To find the average number of days that it took the seeds to sprout, add 8, 8, and 5

Math Focus feature links mathematics directly to the science being presented. Problems are solved to show students the natural links between these two disciplines. Following the solved problem, students are presented with an application that checks their understanding.

> **MATH FOCUS**
> **Probability** If you roll a pair of dice, what is the probability that you will roll 2 threes?
> **Step 1:** Count the number of faces on a single die. Put this number in the denominator: 6.
> **Step 2:** Count how many ways you can roll a three with one die. Put this number in the numerator: 1/6.
> **Step 3:** To find the probability that you will throw 2 threes, multiply the probability of throwing the first three by the probability of throwing the second three: 1/6 × 1/6 = 1/36.
>
> **Now It's Your Turn**
> If you roll a single die, what is the probability that you will roll an even number?

Math Activity in **Science in Action** provides additional integrated exposure to mathematics problems.

> **Math ACTIVITY**
> Suppose that each dolphin in the Navy's program is trained for 5 years and each trained dolphin works for 25 years. If 10 dolphins began training each year for 10 years, how many would be working at the end of those 10 years? How many would still be in training?

Math Skills problem is presented in most Section Reviews, providing additional math practice.

> **Math Skills**
> 9. A certain toad species spends 2 months of its life as a tadpole and 3 years of its life as an adult. What percentage of its life is spent in the water? What percentage is spent on land?

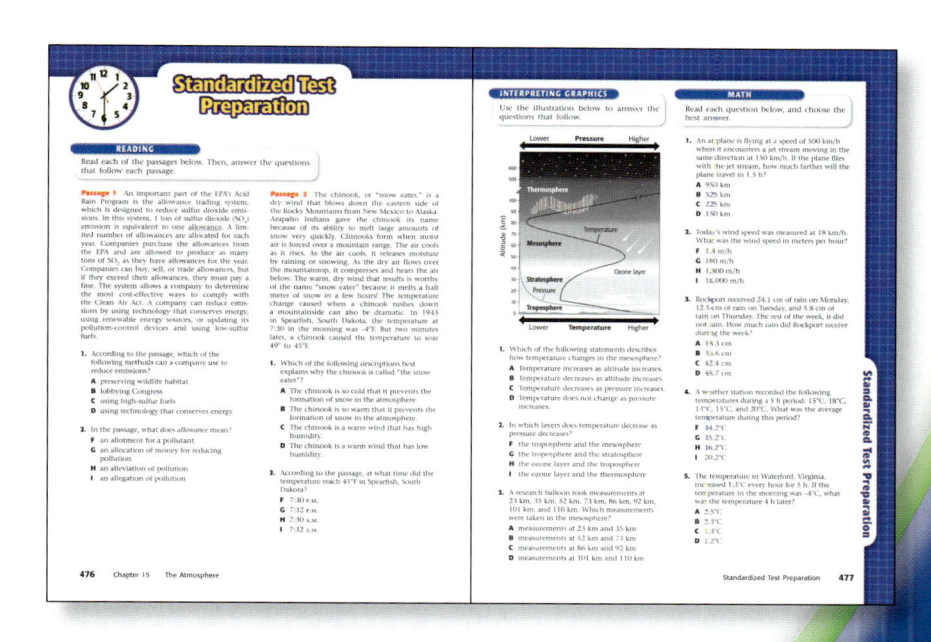

Standardized Test Preparation tests students' math abilities with questions in a standardized test format. Practice is included at the end of each chapter, and a blackline master is located in the *Chapter Resource Files*.

Math Refresher, found in the **Appendix,** reviews basic math skills such as averages, ratios, percentages, and more.

Math Skills for Science helps students develop and apply basic math skills to scientific problems.

T25

Science and Math Skills Worksheets

The **Holt Science & Technology** program helps you meet the needs of a wide variety of students, regardless of their skill level. The following pages provide examples of the worksheets available to improve your students' science and math skills whether they already have a strong science and math background or are weak in these areas. Samples of assessment checklists and rubrics are also provided.

In addition to the skills worksheets represented here, **Holt Science & Technology** provides a variety of worksheets that are correlated directly with each chapter of the program. Representations of these worksheets are found at the beginning of each chapter in this *Teacher Edition*.

Many worksheets are also available on the Holt Web site. The address is **go.hrw.com**.

Science Skills Worksheets: Thinking Skills

- BEING FLEXIBLE 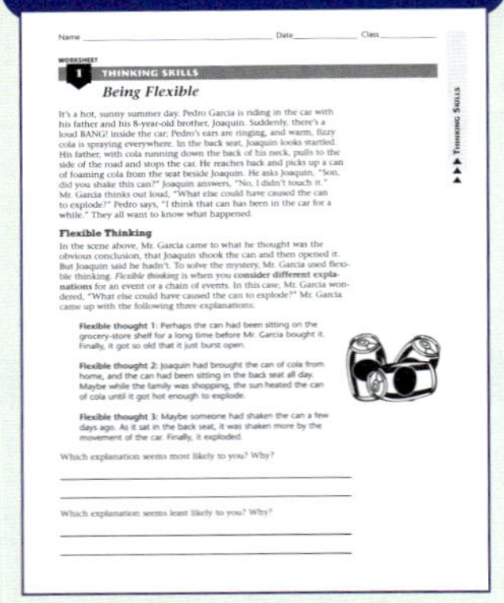
- USING YOUR SENSES 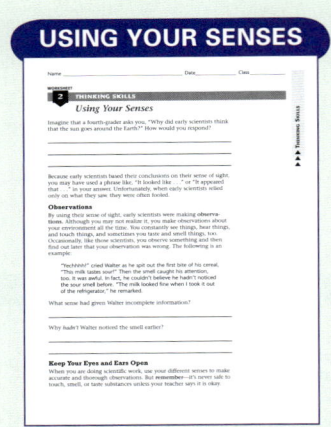
- THINKING OBJECTIVELY 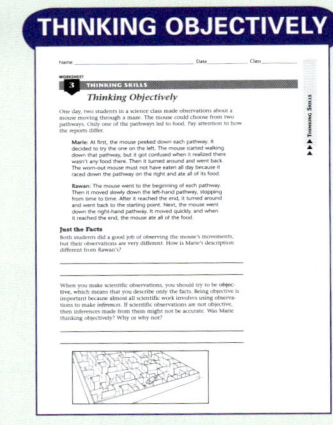
- UNDERSTANDING BIAS 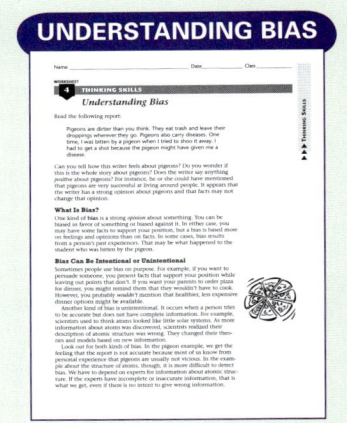
- USING LOGIC 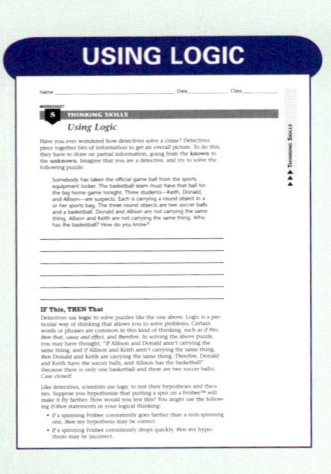
- BOOSTING YOUR MEMORY 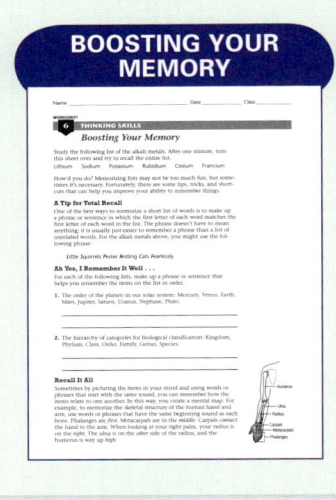
- IMPROVING YOUR STUDY HABITS 
- READING A SCIENCE TEXTBOOK

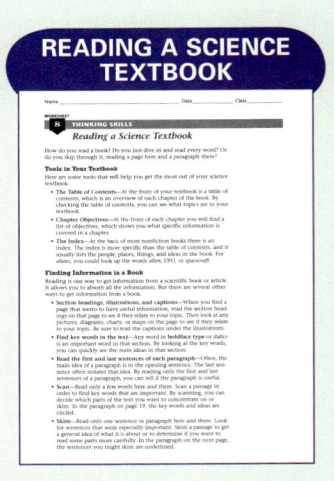

Science Skills Worksheets: Experimenting Skills

- SAFETY RULES! 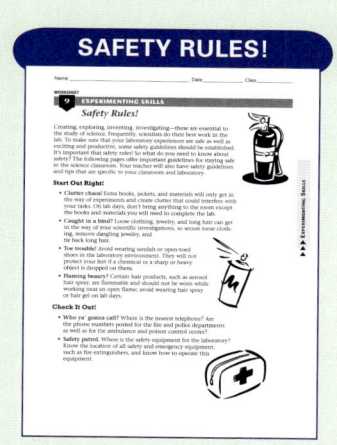
- DOING A LAB WRITE-UP 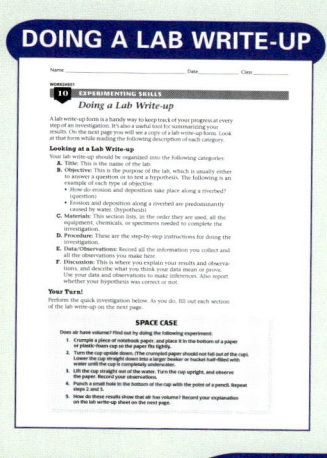
- UNDERSTANDING VARIABLES 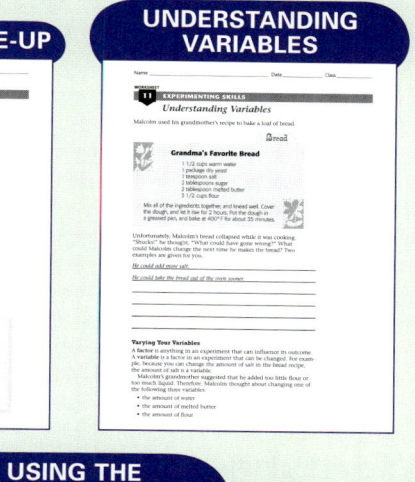
- WORKING WITH HYPOTHESES 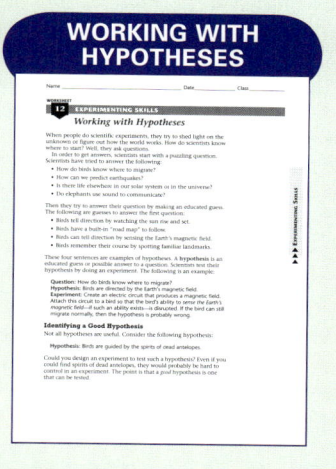
- DESIGNING AN EXPERIMENT 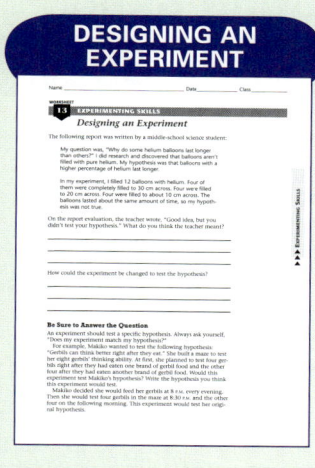
- USING THE INTERNATIONAL SYSTEM OF UNITS (SI) 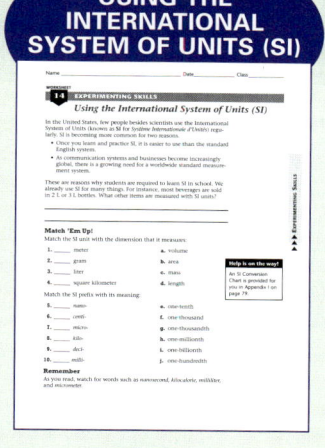
- MEASURING

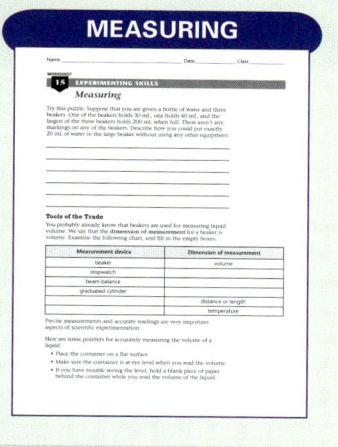

Science Skills Worksheets: Researching Skills

- CHOOSING YOUR TOPIC 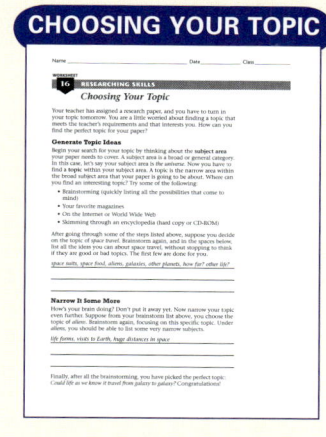
- ORGANIZING YOUR RESEARCH 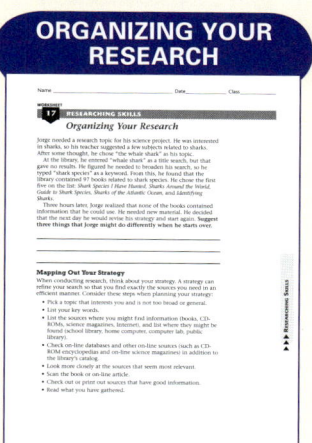
- FINDING USEFUL SOURCES 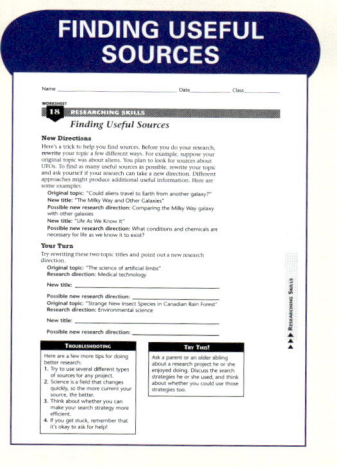
- RESEARCHING ON THE WEB

Science and Math Skills Worksheets

T27

Science Skills Worksheets: Researching Skills (continued)

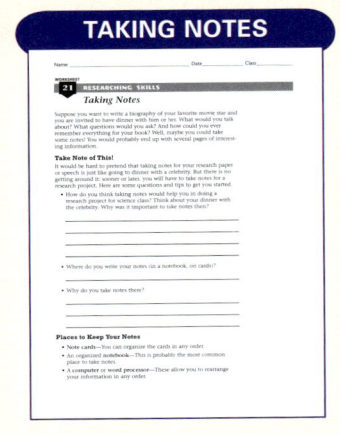

- IDENTIFYING BIAS
- TAKING NOTES

Science Skills Worksheets: Communicating Skills

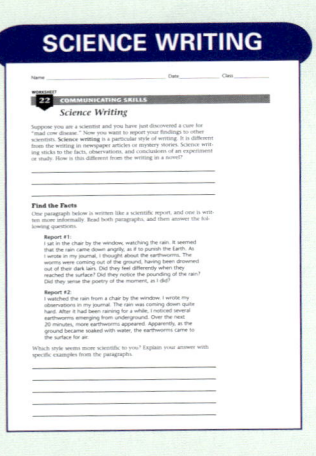

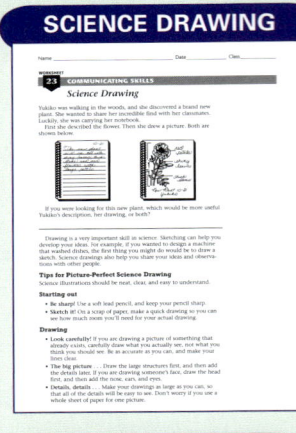

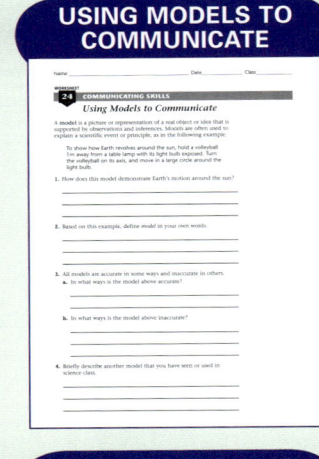

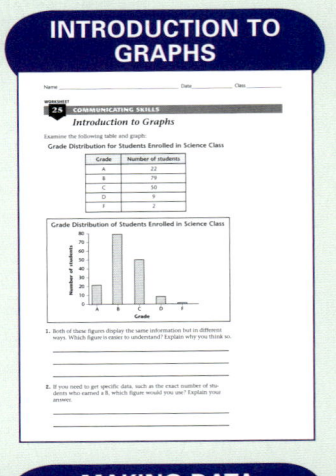

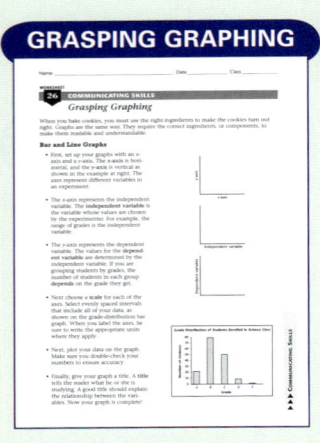

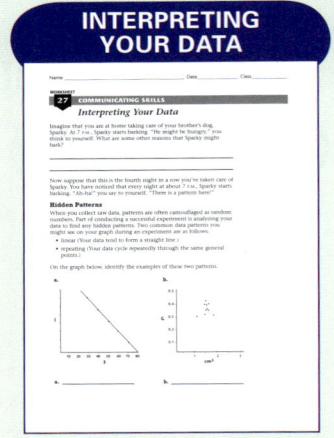

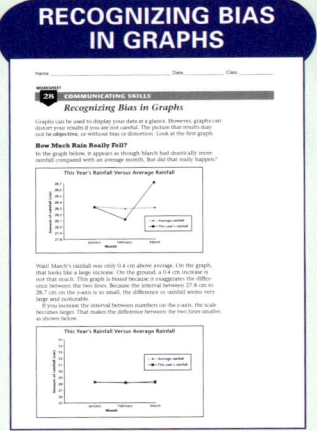

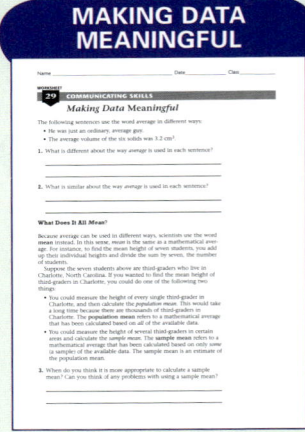

- SCIENCE WRITING
- SCIENCE DRAWING
- USING MODELS TO COMMUNICATE
- INTRODUCTION TO GRAPHS
- GRASPING GRAPHING
- INTERPRETING YOUR DATA
- RECOGNIZING BIAS IN GRAPHS
- MAKING DATA MEANINGFUL
- HINTS FOR ORAL PRESENTATIONS

Math Skills for Science

ADDITION AND SUBTRACTION
- Worksheet 1: Addition Review
- Worksheet 2: Subtraction Review

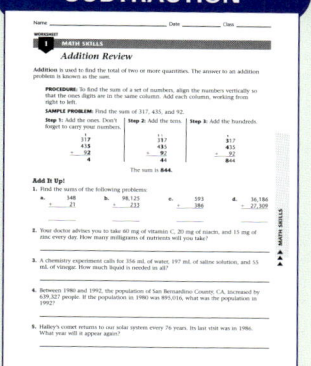

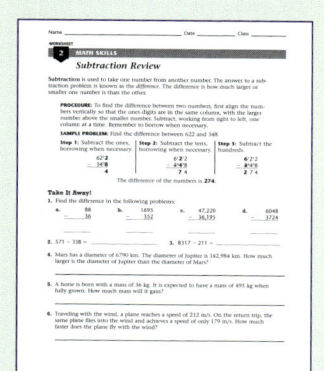

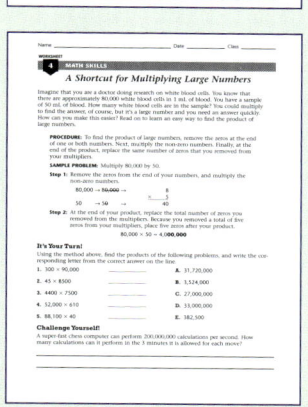

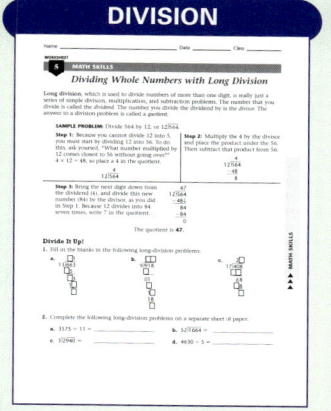

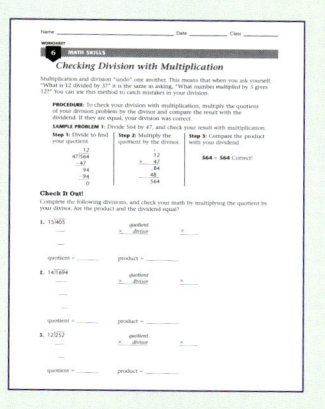

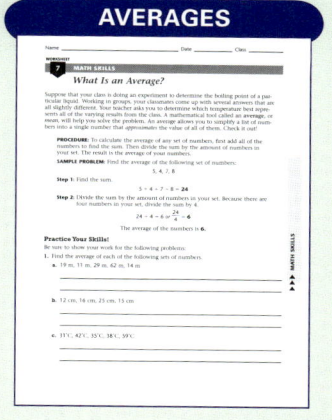

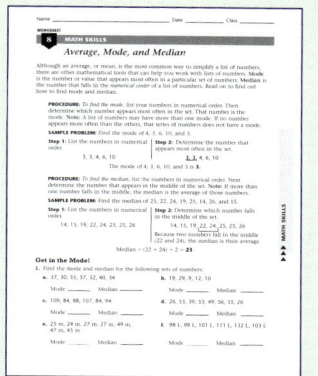

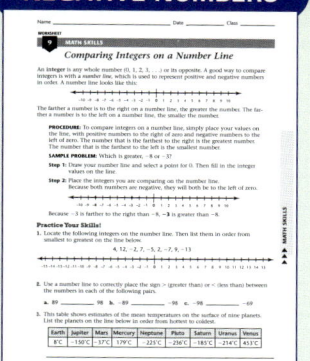

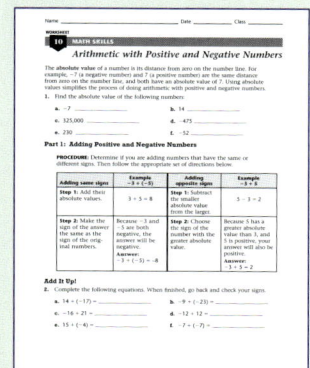

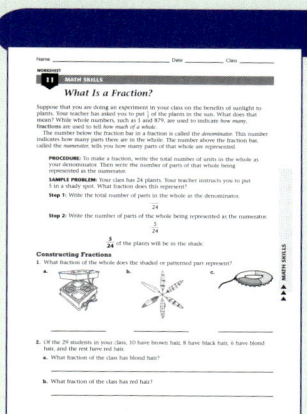

MULTIPLICATION
- Worksheet 3: Multiplying Whole Numbers
- Worksheet 4: A Shortcut for Multiplying Large Numbers

DIVISION
- Worksheet 5: Dividing Whole Numbers with Long Division
- Worksheet 6: Checking Division with Multiplication

AVERAGES
- Worksheet 7: What Is an Average?
- Worksheet 8: Average, Mode, and Median

POSITIVE AND NEGATIVE NUMBERS
- Worksheet 9: Comparing Integers on a Number Line
- Worksheet 10: Arithmetic with Positive and Negative Numbers

FRACTIONS
- Worksheet 11: What Is a Fraction?
- Worksheet 12: Reducing Fractions to Lowest Terms
- Worksheet 13: Improper Fractions and Mixed Numbers
- Worksheet 14: Adding and Subtracting Fractions
- Worksheet 15: Multiplying and Dividing Fractions

Science and Math Skills Worksheets

T29

Math Skills for Science (continued)

RATIOS AND PROPORTIONS
DECIMALS
PERCENTAGES
POWERS OF 10
SCIENTIFIC NOTATION
SI MEASUREMENT AND CONVERSION

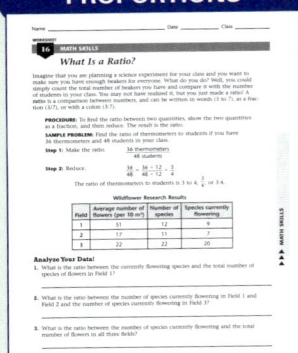

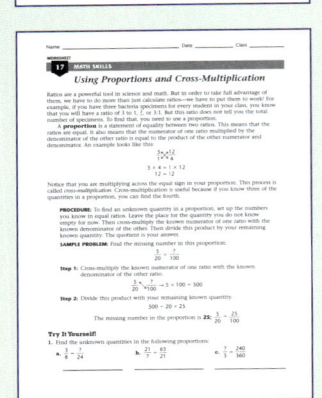

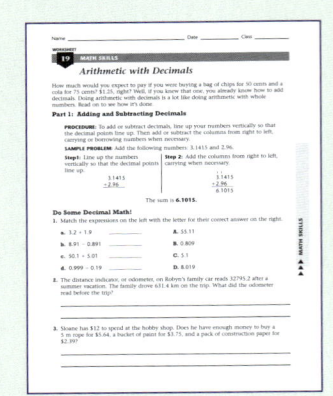

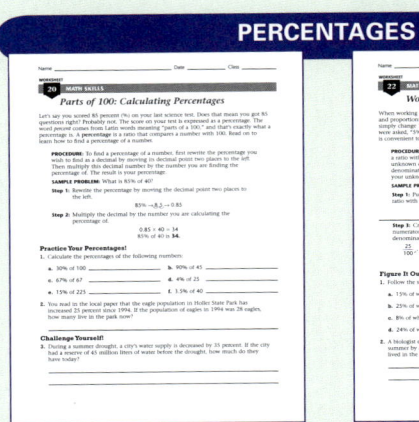

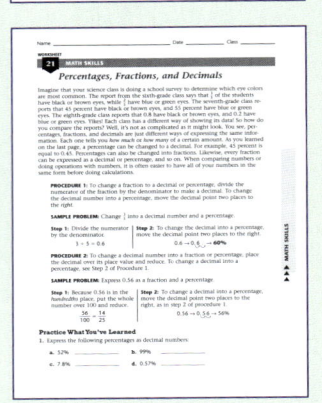

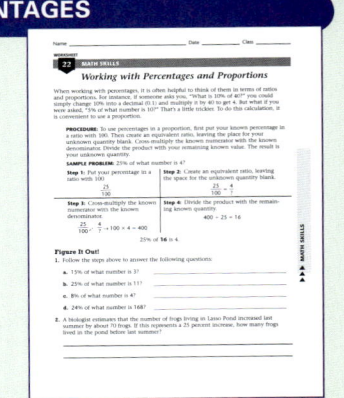

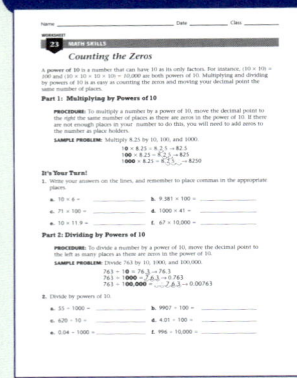

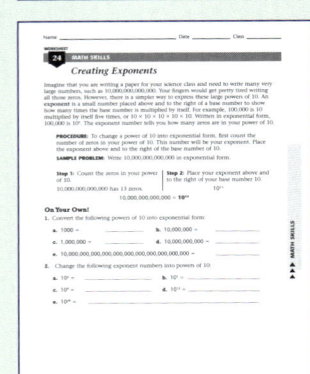

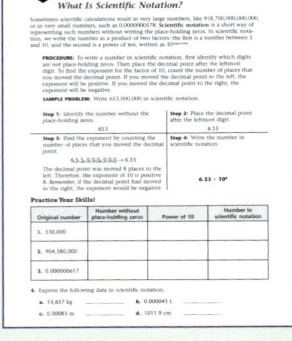

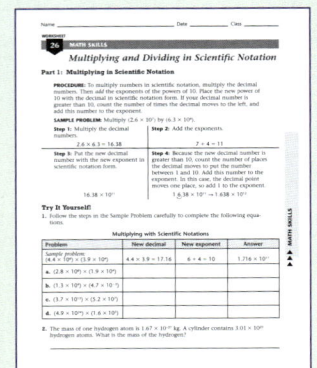

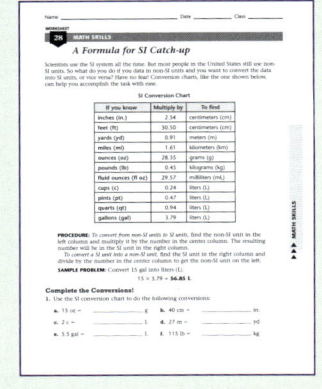

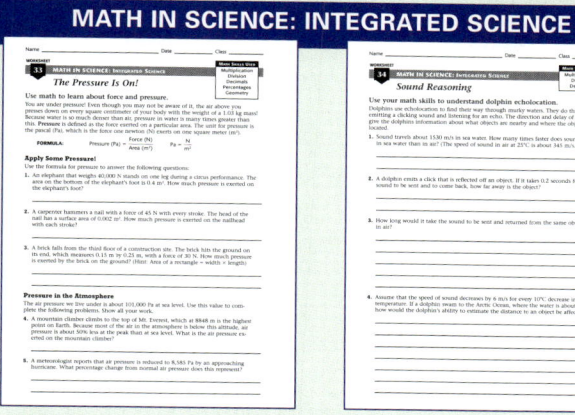

Math Skills for Science (continued)

GEOMETRY

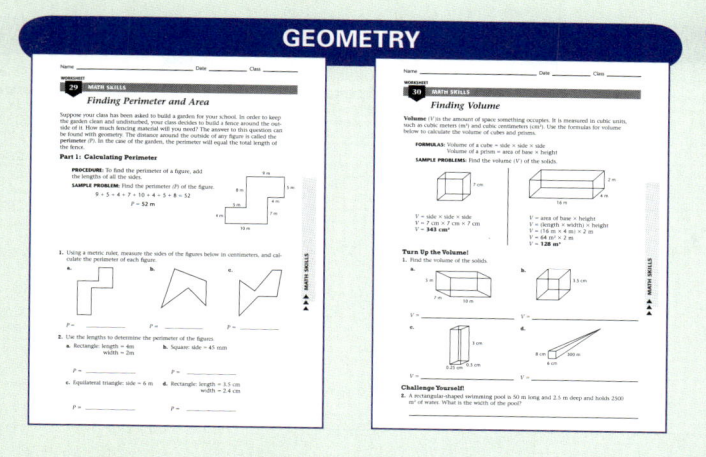

THE UNIT FACTOR AND DIMENSIONAL ANALYSIS

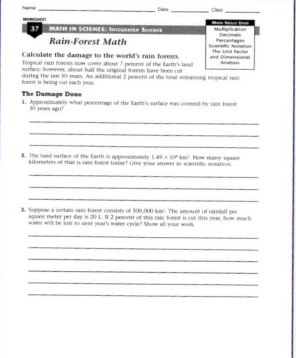

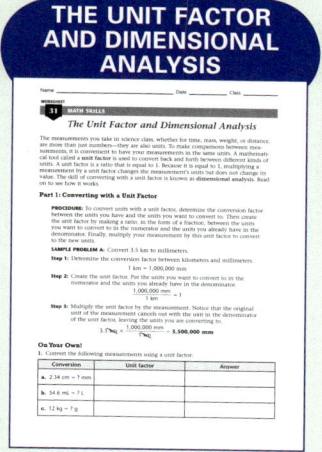

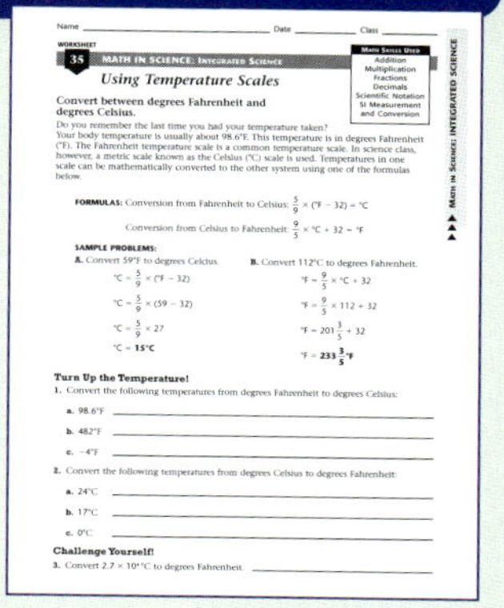

MATH IN SCIENCE: INTEGRATED SCIENCE

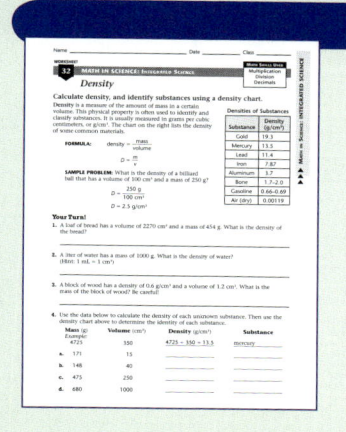

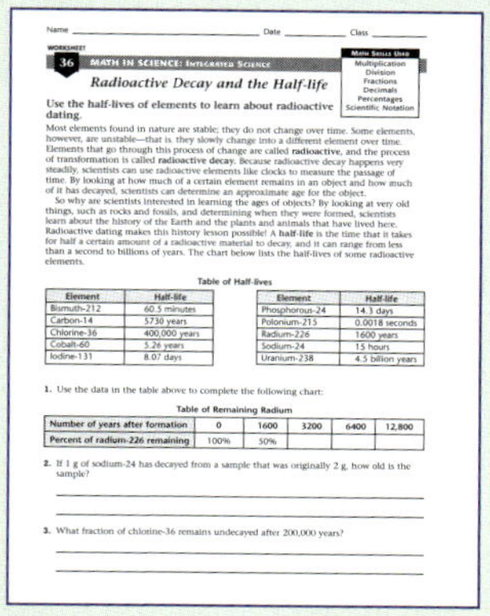

Math Skills for Science (continued)

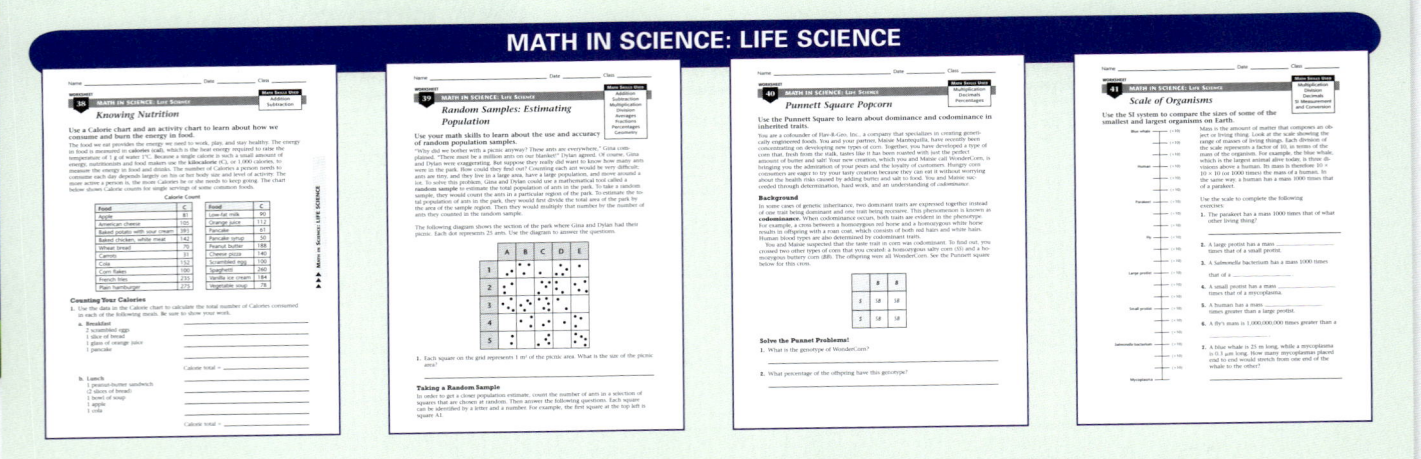

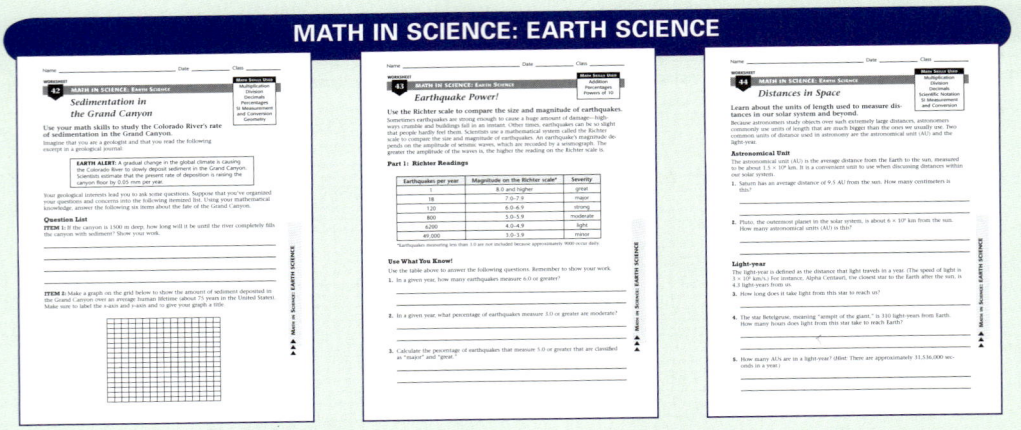

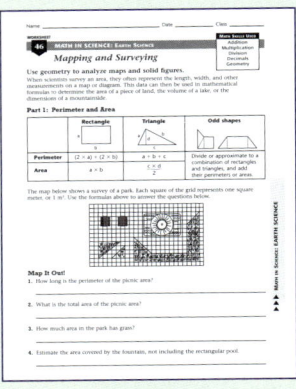

MATH IN SCIENCE: LIFE SCIENCE

MATH IN SCIENCE: EARTH SCIENCE

Math Skills for Science (continued)

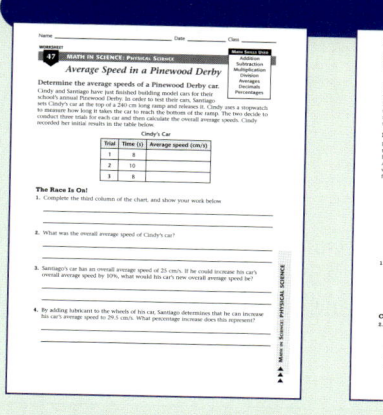

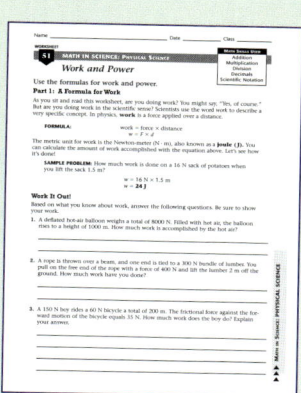

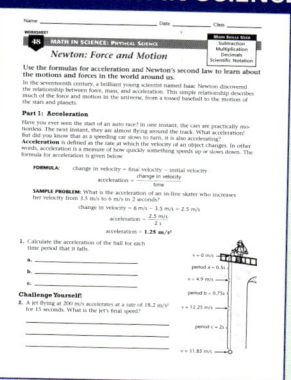

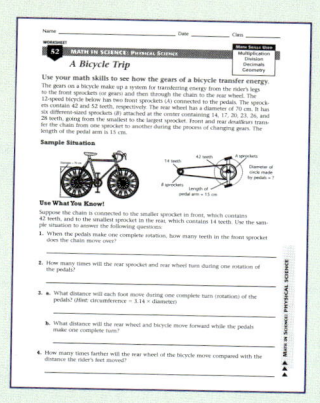

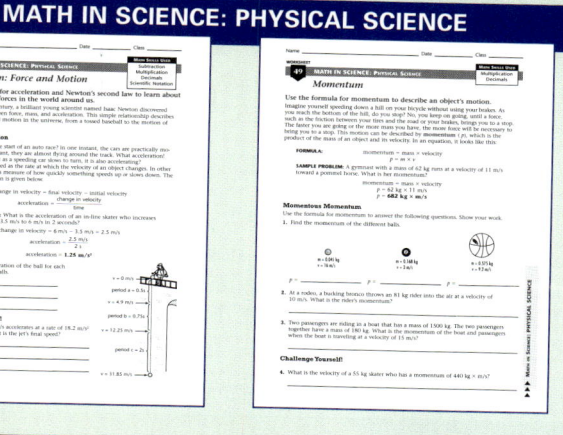

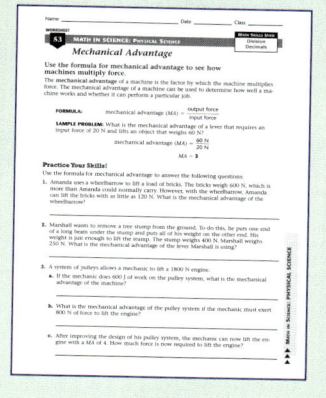

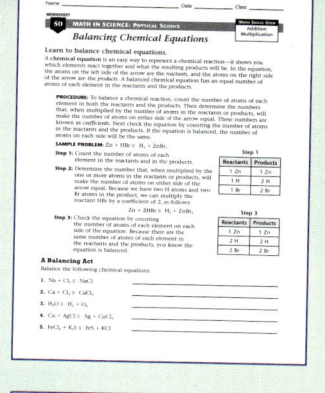

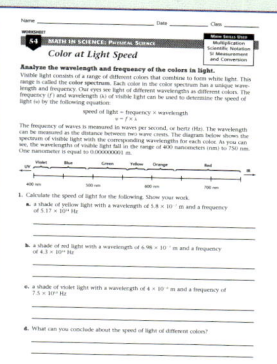

MATH IN SCIENCE: PHYSICAL SCIENCE

Assessment Checklist & Rubrics

The following is just a sample of over 50 checklists and rubrics contained in this booklet.

- **RUBRICS FOR WRITTEN WORK**
- **RUBRIC FOR EXPERIMENTS**
- **TEACHER EVALUATION OF COOPERATIVE LEARNING**
- **TEACHER EVALUATION OF STUDENT PROGRESS**

Pacing and Compression Guide

Pacing Each **Chapter Planning Guide** breaks down the chapter into instructional blocks. Each instructional block consists of sections and labs that you can cover in 45 or 90 minutes. The **Chapter Planning Guide** also lists activities, demonstrations, and resources that are available to accompany each section.

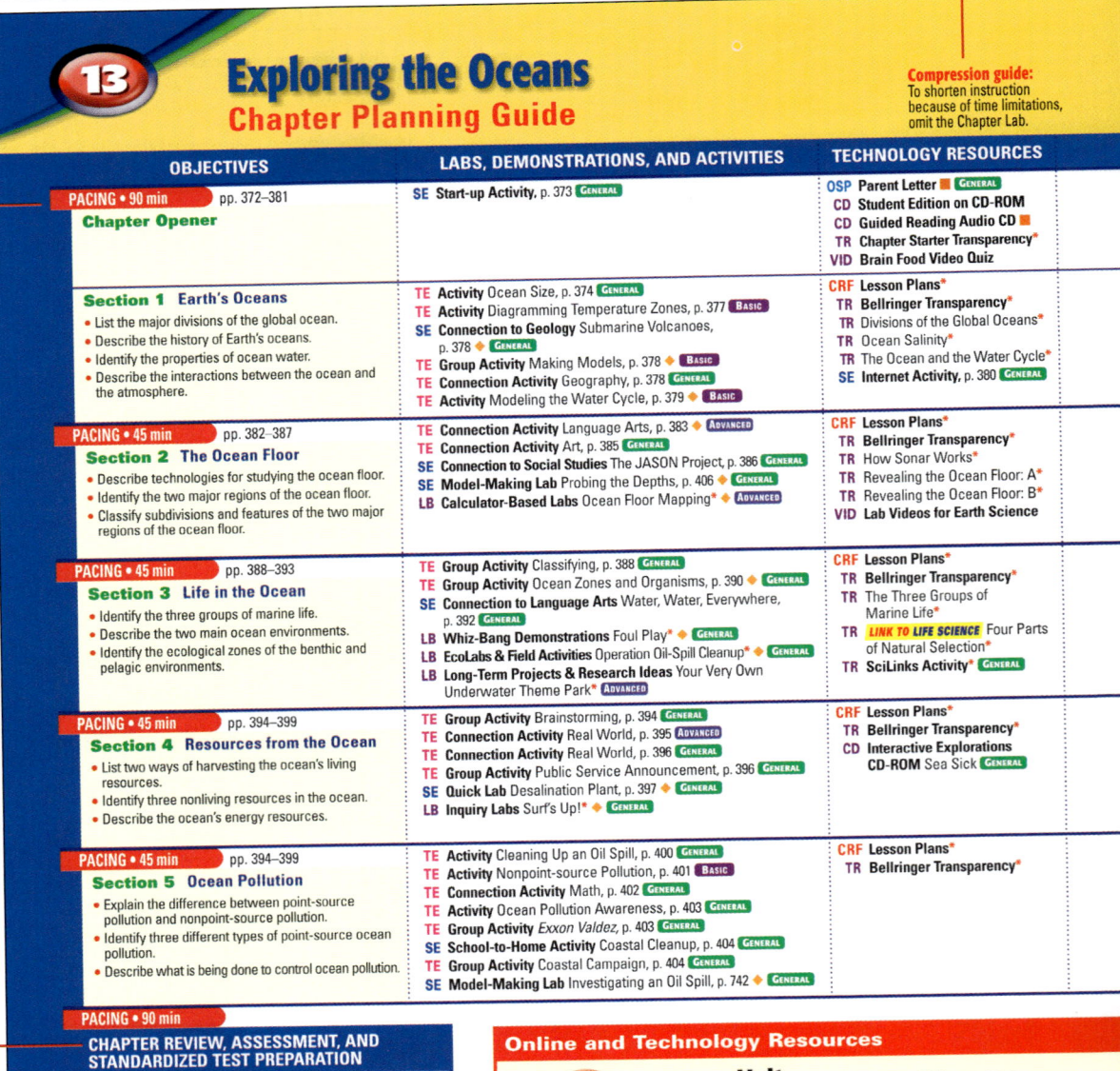

Assessment Each chapter includes enough chapter assessment material to fill two 45-minute periods.

Compression guide: To shorten instruction because of time limitations, omit the Chapter Lab.

13 Exploring the Oceans
Chapter Planning Guide

OBJECTIVES	LABS, DEMONSTRATIONS, AND ACTIVITIES	TECHNOLOGY RESOURCES
PACING • 90 min pp. 372–381 **Chapter Opener**	SE Start-up Activity, p. 373 GENERAL	OSP Parent Letter ■ GENERAL CD Student Edition on CD-ROM CD Guided Reading Audio CD ■ TR Chapter Starter Transparency* VID Brain Food Video Quiz
Section 1 Earth's Oceans • List the major divisions of the global ocean. • Describe the history of Earth's oceans. • Identify the properties of ocean water. • Describe the interactions between the ocean and the atmosphere.	TE Activity Ocean Size, p. 374 GENERAL TE Activity Diagramming Temperature Zones, p. 377 BASIC SE Connection to Geology Submarine Volcanoes, p. 378 ◆ GENERAL TE Group Activity Making Models, p. 378 ◆ BASIC TE Connection Activity Geography, p. 378 GENERAL TE Activity Modeling the Water Cycle, p. 379 ◆ BASIC	CRF Lesson Plans* TR Bellringer Transparency* TR Divisions of the Global Oceans* TR Ocean Salinity* TR The Ocean and the Water Cycle* SE Internet Activity, p. 380 GENERAL
PACING • 45 min pp. 382–387 **Section 2 The Ocean Floor** • Describe technologies for studying the ocean floor. • Identify the two major regions of the ocean floor. • Classify subdivisions and features of the two major regions of the ocean floor.	TE Connection Activity Language Arts, p. 383 ◆ ADVANCED TE Connection Activity Art, p. 385 GENERAL SE Connection to Social Studies The JASON Project, p. 386 GENERAL SE Model-Making Lab Probing the Depths, p. 406 ◆ GENERAL LB Calculator-Based Labs Ocean Floor Mapping* ◆ ADVANCED	CRF Lesson Plans* TR Bellringer Transparency* TR How Sonar Works* TR Revealing the Ocean Floor: A* TR Revealing the Ocean Floor: B* VID Lab Videos for Earth Science
PACING • 45 min pp. 388–393 **Section 3 Life in the Ocean** • Identify the three groups of marine life. • Describe the two main ocean environments. • Identify the ecological zones of the benthic and pelagic environments.	TE Group Activity Classifying, p. 388 GENERAL TE Group Activity Ocean Zones and Organisms, p. 390 ◆ GENERAL SE Connection to Language Arts Water, Water, Everywhere, p. 392 GENERAL LB Whiz-Bang Demonstrations Foul Play* ◆ GENERAL LB EcoLabs & Field Activities Operation Oil-Spill Cleanup* ◆ GENERAL LB Long-Term Projects & Research Ideas Your Very Own Underwater Theme Park* ADVANCED	CRF Lesson Plans* TR Bellringer Transparency* TR The Three Groups of Marine Life* TR LINK TO LIFE SCIENCE Four Parts of Natural Selection* TR SciLinks Activity* GENERAL
PACING • 45 min pp. 394–399 **Section 4 Resources from the Ocean** • List two ways of harvesting the ocean's living resources. • Identify three nonliving resources in the ocean. • Describe the ocean's energy resources.	TE Group Activity Brainstorming, p. 394 GENERAL TE Connection Activity Real World, p. 395 ADVANCED TE Connection Activity Real World, p. 396 GENERAL TE Group Activity Public Service Announcement, p. 396 GENERAL SE Quick Lab Desalination Plant, p. 397 ◆ GENERAL LB Inquiry Labs Surf's Up!* ◆ GENERAL	CRF Lesson Plans* TR Bellringer Transparency* CD Interactive Explorations CD-ROM Sea Sick GENERAL
PACING • 45 min pp. 394–399 **Section 5 Ocean Pollution** • Explain the difference between point-source pollution and nonpoint-source pollution. • Identify three different types of point-source ocean pollution. • Describe what is being done to control ocean pollution.	TE Activity Cleaning Up an Oil Spill, p. 400 GENERAL TE Activity Nonpoint-source Pollution, p. 401 BASIC TE Connection Activity Math, p. 402 GENERAL TE Activity Ocean Pollution Awareness, p. 403 GENERAL TE Group Activity Exxon Valdez, p. 403 GENERAL SE School-to-Home Activity Coastal Cleanup, p. 404 GENERAL TE Group Activity Coastal Campaign, p. 404 GENERAL SE Model-Making Lab Investigating an Oil Spill, p. 742 ◆ GENERAL	CRF Lesson Plans* TR Bellringer Transparency*

PACING • 90 min

CHAPTER REVIEW, ASSESSMENT, AND STANDARDIZED TEST PREPARATION
- CRF Vocabulary Activity* GENERAL
- SE Chapter Review, pp. 408–409 GENERAL
- CRF Chapter Review* ■ GENERAL
- CRF Chapter Tests A* ■ GENERAL, B* ◆ ADVANCED, C* SPECIAL NEEDS
- SE Standardized Test Preparation, pp. 410–411 GENERAL
- CRF Standardized Test Preparation* ■ GENERAL
- CRF Performance-Based Assessment* GENERAL
- OSP Test Generator GENERAL
- CRF Test Item Listing* ■ GENERAL

Online and Technology Resources

go.hrw.com
Visit go.hrw.com for a variety of free resources related to this textbook. Enter the keyword **HA5OCE**.

Holt Online Learning
Students can access interactive problem-solving help and active visual concept development with the Holt Science and Technology Online Edition available at www.hrw.com.

Guided Reading Audio CD
A direct reading of each chapter using instructional visuals as guideposts. For auditory learners, reluctant readers, and Spanish-speaking students. Available in English and Spanish.

371A Chapter 13 • Exploring the Oceans

Pacing and Compression

Compression In many cases, a chapter contains more material than you will have time to teach. The Compression Guide in each **Chapter Planning Guide** suggests sections or labs you can omit if you are short on time. The sections or labs that can be omitted often contain advanced material. You may wish to also consider using the material suggested for omission as extension material for advanced students.

KEY
- **SE** Student Edition
- **TE** Teacher Edition
- **CRF** Chapter Resource File
- **OSP** One-Stop Planner
- **LB** Lab Bank
- **TR** Transparencies
- **SS** Science Skills Worksheets
- **MS** Math Skills for Science Worksheets
- **CD** CD or CD-ROM
- **VID** Classroom Video/DVD
- ✱ Also on One-Stop Planner
- ◆ Requires advance prep
- ■ Also available in Spanish

SKILLS DEVELOPMENT RESOURCES	SECTION REVIEW AND ASSESSMENT	STANDARDS CORRELATIONS
SE Pre-Reading Activity, p. 372 GENERAL OSP Science Puzzlers, Twisters & Teasers* GENERAL		National Science Education Standards UCP 2, 5; SAI 1; ST 2; SPSP 5
CRF Directed Reading A* ■ BASIC, B* SPECIAL NEEDS CRF Vocabulary and Section Summary* ■ GENERAL SE Reading Strategy Discussion, p. 374 GENERAL TE Reading Strategy Mnemonics, p. 375 GENERAL TE Inclusion Strategies, p. 377 ◆	SE Reading Checks, pp. 375, 376, 378, 380 GENERAL TE Homework, p. 379 ADVANCED TE Reteaching, p. 380 BASIC TE Quiz, p. 380 GENERAL TE Alternative Assessment, p. 380 ADVANCED SE Section Review,* p. 381 ■ GENERAL CRF Section Quiz* ■ GENERAL	UCP 1, 2, 3; ES 1b, 1f, 1g, 1h, 1j, 2a
CRF Directed Reading A* ■ BASIC, B* SPECIAL NEEDS CRF Vocabulary and Section Summary* ■ GENERAL SE Reading Strategy Reading Organizer, p. 382 GENERAL MS Math Skills for Science Multiplying Whole Numbers* GENERAL MS Math Skills for Science Multiplying and Dividing Fractions* GENERAL	SE Reading Checks, pp. 383, 384, 385, 386 GENERAL TE Homework, p. 384 ADVANCED TE Reteaching, p. 386 BASIC TE Quiz, p. 386 GENERAL TE Alternative Assessment, p. 386 GENERAL SE Section Review,* p. 387 ■ GENERAL CRF Section Quiz* ■ GENERAL	UCP 2, 3; SAI 1, 2; ST 2; SPSP 5; HNS 1, 3; ES 1b, 1c; Chapter Lab: UCP 2, 3; SAI 1, 2; ST 2; SPSP 5; HNS 1
CRF Directed Reading A* ■ BASIC, B* SPECIAL NEEDS CRF Vocabulary and Section Summary* ■ GENERAL SE Reading Strategy Mnemonics, p. 388 GENERAL TE Inclusion Strategy Mnemonics, p. 391 CRF Reinforcement Worksheet The Ocean's Environment* BASIC	SE Reading Checks, pp. 389, 391, 392 GENERAL TE Homework, p. 389, 390 GENERAL TE Reteaching, p. 392 BASIC TE Quiz, p. 392 GENERAL TE Alternative Assessment, p. 392 GENERAL SE Section Review,* p. 393 ■ GENERAL CRF Section Quiz* ■ GENERAL	UCP 1
CRF Directed Reading A* ■ BASIC, B* SPECIAL NEEDS CRF Vocabulary and Section Summary* ■ GENERAL SE Reading Strategy Paired Summarizing, p. 394 GENERAL TE Reading Strategy Prediction Guide, p. 395 BASIC CRF Reinforcement Worksheet The Oceans and Us* BASIC CRF Critical Thinking Chain Reaction* ADVANCED	SE Reading Checks, pp. 395, 396, 397, 399 GENERAL TE Homework, p. 396 GENERAL TE Reteaching, p. 398 BASIC TE Quiz, p. 398 GENERAL TE Alternative Assessment, p. 398 GENERAL SE Section Review,* p. 399 ■ GENERAL CRF Section Quiz* ■ GENERAL	SAI 1; ST 2; SPSP 2, 4, 5; HNS 1
CRF Directed Reading A* ■ BASIC, B* SPECIAL NEEDS CRF Vocabulary and Section Summary* ■ GENERAL SE Reading Strategy Reading Organizer, p. 400 GENERAL	SE Reading Checks, pp. 395, 401, 403, 405 GENERAL TE Homework, p. 401 GENERAL TE Reteaching, p. 404 BASIC TE Quiz, p. 404 GENERAL TE Alternative Assessment, p. 404 GENERAL SE Section Review,* p. 405 ■ GENERAL CRF Section Quiz* ■ GENERAL	ST 2; SPSP 2, 4, 5; LabBook: UPC 2, 3; SAI 1; SPSP 2, 3, 4; HNS 1

One-Stop Planner® CD-ROM
This convenient CD-ROM includes:
- Lab Materials QuickList Software
- Holt Calendar Planner
- Customizable Lesson Plans
- Printable Worksheets
- ExamView® Test Generator

CNN Student News
cnnstudentnews.com
Find the latest news, lesson plans, and activities related to important scientific events.

SciLinks NSTA
www.scilinks.org
Maintained by the National Science Teachers Association. See Chapter Enrichment pages for a complete list of topics.

Current Science®
Check out **Current Science** articles and activities by visiting the HRW Web site at **go.hrw.com**. Just type in the keyword **HA5CS13T**.

Classroom Videos
- Lab Videos demonstrate the chapter lab.
- Brain Food Video Quizzes help students review the chapter material.

Chapter 13 • Chapter Planning Guide

Safety in your laboratory

RISK ASSESSMENT

MAKING YOUR LABORATORY A SAFE PLACE TO WORK AND LEARN

Concern for safety must begin before any activity in the classroom and before students enter the lab. A careful review of the facilities should be a basic part of preparation for each school term. You should investigate the physical environment, identify any safety risks, and inspect your work areas for compliance with safety regulations.

The review of the lab should be thorough, and all safety issues must be addressed immediately. Keep a file of your review, and add to the list each year. This will allow you to continue to raise the standard of safety in your lab and classroom.

Many classroom experiments, demonstrations, and other activities are classics that have been used for years. This familiarity may lead to a comfort that can obscure inherent safety concerns. Review all experiments, demonstrations, and activities for safety concerns before presenting them to the class. Identify and eliminate potential safety hazards.

1. **Identify the Risks**

   Before introducing any activity, demonstration, or experiment to the class, analyze it and consider what could possibly go wrong. Carefully review the list of materials to make sure they are safe. Inspect the equipment in your lab or classroom to make sure it is in good working order. Read the procedures to make sure they are safe. Record any hazards or concerns you identify.

2. **Evaluate the Risks**

   Minimize the risks you identified in the last step without sacrificing learning. Remember that no activity you perform in the lab or classroom is worth risking injury. Thus, extremely hazardous activities, or those that violate your school's policies, must be eliminated. For activities that present smaller risks, analyze each risk carefully to determine its likelihood. If the pedagogical value of the activity does not outweigh the risks, the activity must be eliminated.

3. **Select Controls to Address Risks**

   Even low-risk activities require controls to eliminate or minimize the risks. Make sure that in devising controls you do not substitute an equally or more hazardous alternative. Some control methods include the following:

   - Explicit verbal and written warnings may be added or posted.
   - Equipment may be rebuilt or relocated, parts may be replaced, or equipment be replaced entirely by safer alternatives.
   - Risky procedures may be eliminated.
   - Activities may be changed from student activities to teacher demonstrations.

4. **Implement and Review Selected Controls**

   Controls do not help if they are forgotten or not enforced. The implementation and review of controls should be as systematic and thorough as the initial analysis of safety concerns in the lab and laboratory activities.

SOME SAFETY RISKS AND PREVENTATIVE CONTROLS

The following list describes several possible safety hazards and controls that can be implemented to resolve them. This list is not complete, but it can be used as a starting point to identify hazards in your laboratory.

Identified risk	Preventative control
Facilities and Equipment	
Lab tables are in disrepair, room is poorly lighted and ventilated, faucets and electrical outlets do not work or are difficult to use because of their location.	Work surfaces should be level and stable. There should be adequate lighting and ventilation. Water supplies, drains, and electrical outlets should be in good working order. Any equipment in a dangerous location should not be used; it should be relocated or rendered inoperable.
Wiring, plumbing, and air circulation systems do not work or do not meet current specifications.	Specifications should be kept on file. Conduct a periodic review of all equipment, and document compliance. Damaged fixtures must be labeled as such and must be repaired as soon as possible.
Eyewash fountains and safety showers are present, but no one knows anything about their specifications.	Ensure that eyewash fountains and safety showers meet the requirements of the ANSI standard (Z358.1).
Eyewash fountains are checked and cleaned once at the beginning of each school year. No records are kept of routine checks and maintenance on the safety showers and eyewash fountains.	Flush eyewash fountains for 5 min. every month to remove any bacteria or other organisms from pipes. Test safety showers (measure flow in gallons per min.) and eyewash fountains every 6 months and keep records of the test results.
Labs are conducted in multipurpose rooms, and equipment from other courses remains accessible.	Only the items necessary for a given activity should be available to students. All equipment should be locked away when not in use.
Students are permitted to enter or work in the lab without teacher supervision.	Lock all laboratory rooms whenever a teacher is not present. Supervising teachers must be trained in lab safety and emergency procedures.
Safety equipment and emergency procedures	
Fire and other emergency drills are infrequent, and no records or measurements are made of the results of the drills.	Always carry out critical reviews of fire or other emergency drills. Be sure that plans include alternate routes. Don't wait until an emergency to find the flaws in your plans.
Emergency evacuation plans do not include instructions for securing the lab in the event of an evacuation during a lab activity.	Plan actions in case of emergency: establish what devices should be turned off, which escape route to use, and where to meet outside the building.
Fire extinguishers are in out-of-the-way locations, not on the escape route.	Place fire extinguishers near escape routes so that they will be of use during an emergency.
Fire extinguishers are not maintained. Teachers are not trained to use them.	Document regular maintenance of fire extinguishers. Train supervisory personnel in the proper use of extinguishers. Instruct students not to use an extinguisher but to call for a teacher.

Safety Guide

Identified risk	Preventative control
Safety equipment and emergency procedures, *continued*	
Teachers in labs and neighboring classrooms are not trained in CPR or first aid.	Teachers should receive training. The American Red Cross and other groups offer training. Certifications should be kept current with frequent refresher courses.
Teachers are not aware of their legal responsibilities in case of an injury or accident.	Review your faculty handbook for your responsibilities regarding safety in the classroom and laboratory. Contact the legal counsel for your school district to find out the extent of their support and any rules, regulations, or procedures you must follow.
Emergency procedures are not posted. Emergency numbers are kept only at the switchboard or main office. Instructions are given verbally only at the beginning of the year.	Emergency procedures should be posted at all exits and near all safety equipment. Emergency numbers should be posted at all phones, and a script should be provided for the caller to use. Emergency procedures must be reviewed periodically, and students should be reminded of them at the beginning of each activity.
Spills are handled on a case-by-case basis and are cleaned up with whatever materials happen to be on hand.	Have the appropriate equipment and materials available for cleaning up; replace them before expiration dates. Make sure students know to alert you to spilled chemicals, blood, and broken glass.
Work habits and environment	
Safety wear is only used for activities involving chemicals or hot plates.	Aprons and goggles should be worn in the lab at all times. Long hair, loose clothing, and loose jewelry should be secured.
There is no dress code established for the laboratory; students are allowed to wear sandals or open-toed shoes.	Open-toed shoes should never be worn in the laboratory. Do not allow any footwear in the lab that does not cover feet completely.
Students are required to wear safety gear, but teachers and visitors are not.	Always wear safety gear in the lab. Keep extra equipment on hand for visitors.
Safety is emphasized at the beginning of the term but is not mentioned later in the year.	Safety must be the first priority in all lab work. Students should be warned of risks and instructed in emergency procedures for each activity.
There is no assessment of students' knowledge and attitudes regarding safety.	Conduct frequent safety quizzes. Only students with perfect scores should be allowed to work in the lab.
You work alone during your preparation period to organize the day's labs.	Never work alone in a science laboratory or a storage area.
Safety inspections are conducted irregularly and are not documented. Teachers and administrators are unaware of what documentation will be necessary in case of a lawsuit.	Safety reviews should be frequent and regular. All reviews should be documented, and improvements must be implemented immediately. Contact legal counsel for your district to make sure your procedures will protect you in case of a lawsuit.

Safety Guide

Identified risk	Preventative control
Purchasing, storing, and using chemicals	
The storeroom is too crowded, so you decide to keep some equipment on the lab benches.	Do not store reagents or equipment on lab benches and keep shelves organized. Never place reactive chemicals (in bottles, beakers, flasks, wash bottles, etc.) near the edges of a lab bench.
You prepare solutions from concentrated stock to save money.	Reduce risks by ordering diluted instead of concentrated substances.
You purchase plenty of chemicals to be sure that you won't run out or to save money.	Purchase chemicals in class-size quantities. Do not purchase or have on hand more than one year's supply of each chemical.
You don't generally read labels on chemicals when preparing solutions for a lab because you already know about a chemical.	Read each label to be sure it states the hazards and describes the precautions and first aid procedures (when appropriate) that apply to the contents in case someone else has to deal with that chemical in an emergency.
You never read the Material Safety Data Sheets (MSDSs) that come with your chemicals.	Always read the Material Safety Data Sheet (MSDS) for a chemical before using it and follow the precautions described. File and organize MSDSs for all chemicals where they can be found easily in case of an emergency.
The main stockroom contains chemicals that haven't been used for years.	Do not leave bottles of chemicals unused on the shelves of the lab for more than one week or unused in the main stockroom for more than one year. Dispose of or use up any leftover chemicals.
No extra precautions are taken when flammable liquids are dispensed from their containers.	When transferring flammable liquids from bulk containers, ground the container, and before transferring to a smaller metal container, ground both containers.
Students are told to put their broken glass and solid chemical wastes in the trash can.	Have separate containers for trash, for broken glass, and for different categories of hazardous chemical wastes.
You store chemicals alphabetically instead of by hazard class. Chemicals are stored without consideration of possible emergencies (fire, earthquake, flood, etc.), which could compound the hazard.	Use MSDSs to determine which chemicals are incompatible. Store chemicals by the hazard class indicated on the MSDS. Store chemicals that are incompatible with common fire-fighting media like water (such as alkali metals) or carbon dioxide (such as alkali and alkaline-earth metals) under conditions that eliminate the possibility of a reaction with water or carbon dioxide if it is necessary to fight a fire in the storage area.
Corrosives are kept above eye level, out of reach from anyone who is not authorized to be in the storeroom.	Always store corrosive chemicals on shelves below eye level. Remember, fumes from many corrosives can destroy metal cabinets and shelving.
Chemicals are kept on the stockroom floor on the days that they will be used so that they are easy to find.	Never store chemicals or other materials on floors or in the aisles of the laboratory or storeroom, even for a few minutes.

Safety symbols and safety guidelines for students

EYE PROTECTION
- Wear safety goggles, and know where the eyewash station is located and how to use it.
- Avoid swinging objects, which can cause serious injury.
- Avoid directly looking at a light source, as this may cause permanent eye damage.

HAND SAFETY
- Wear latex or nitrile gloves to protect yourself from chemicals in the lab.
- Use a hot mitt to handle resistors, light sources, and other equipment that may be hot. Allow equipment to cool before handling it and storing it.

CLOTHING PROTECTION
- Wear a laboratory apron to protect your clothing.
- Tie back long hair, secure loose clothing, and remove loose jewelry to prevent their getting caught in moving parts or coming in contact with chemicals.

HEATING SAFETY
- When using a Bunsen burner or a hot plate, always wear safety goggles and a laboratory apron to protect your eyes and clothing. Tie back long hair, secure loose clothing, and remove loose jewelry.
- Never leave a hot plate unattended while it is turned on.
- If your clothing catches on fire, walk to the emergency lab shower, and use the shower to put out the fire.
- Wire coils may heat up rapidly during experiments. If heating occurs, open the switch immediately, and handle the equipment with a hot mitt.
- Allow all equipment to cool before storing it.

CHEMICAL SAFETY

- Do not eat or drink anything in the lab. Never taste chemicals.
- If a chemical gets on your skin or clothing or in your eyes, rinse it immediately with lukewarm water, and alert your teacher.
- If a chemical is spilled, tell your teacher, but do not clean it up yourself unless your teacher says it is OK to do so.

ELECTRICAL SAFETY

- Never close a circuit until it has been approved by your teacher. Never rewire or adjust any element of a closed circuit.
- Never work with electricity near water; be sure the floor and all work surfaces are dry.
- If the pointer of any kind of meter moves off the scale, open the circuit immediately by opening the switch.
- Light bulbs or wires that are conducting electricity can become very hot.
- Do not work with any batteries, electrical devices, or magnets other than those provided by your teacher.

ANIMAL SAFETY

- Handle animals only as directed by your teacher.
- Always treat animals carefully and with respect.
- Wash your hands thoroughly after handling any animal.

PLANT SAFETY

- Wash your hands thoroughly after handling any part of a plant.

SHARP/POINTED OBJECTS

- Use knives and other sharp instruments with extreme care.
- Do not cut an object while holding it in your hands. Instead, place it on a suitable work surface for cutting.

National Science Education Standards

The following lists show the chapter correlation of **Holt Science & Technology: Earth Science** with the **National Science Education Standards** (grades 5-8).

The chapter correlations for the Earth Science Content Standards begin on page T46.

Unifying Concepts and Processes

Standard	Chapter Correlation		
Systems, order, and organization Code: UCP 1	Chapter 3 — 3.1, 3.2 Chapter 4 — 4.1, 4.2, 4.3, 4.4 Chapter 6 — 6.2, 6.3, 6.4, 6.5 Chapter 11 — 11.1 Chapter 13 — 13.1, 13.3		Chapter 14 — 14.3 Chapter 19 — 19.1, 19.2, 19.3, 19.4 Chapter 20 — 20.1, 20.4 Chapter 21 — 21.1, 21.2, 21.3, 21.4
Evidence, models, and explanation Code: UCP 2	Chapter 1 — 1.3 Chapter 2 — 2.1, 2.2, 2.3 Chapter 4 — 4.2, 4.3, 4.4 Chapter 5 — 5.3 Chapter 6 — 6.1, 6.2, 6.4 Chapter 7 — 7.2, 7.3, 7.4 Chapter 8 — 8.1, 8.3 Chapter 10 — 10.1 Chapter 11 — 11.1, 11.4 Chapter 12 — 12.2, 12.3		Chapter 13 — 13.1, 13.2, 13.5 Chapter 14 — 14.1, 14.2, 14.3, 14.4 Chapter 15 — 15.2 Chapter 16 — 16.1 Chapter 17 — 17.2, 17.4 Chapter 18 — 18.1 Chapter 19 — 19.1, 19.2, 19.4 Chapter 20 — 20.1, 20.3, 20.4 Chapter 21 — 21.1, 21.4 Chapter 22 — 22.1, 22.2
Change, constancy, and measurement Code: UCP 3	Chapter 1 — 1.3 Chapter 2 — 2.1, 2.2, 2.3 Chapter 5 — 5.3 Chapter 6 — 6.3, 6.4, 6.5 Chapter 8 — 8.2, 8.3 Chapter 9 — 9.3 Chapter 11 — 11.4 Chapter 12 — 12.1, 12.2, 12.3 Chapter 13 — 13.1, 13.2, 13.5		Chapter 14 — 14.3 Chapter 16 — 16.1 Chapter 17 — 17.2, 17.4 Chapter 18 — 18.3 Chapter 19 — 19.1, 19.2, 19.4 Chapter 20 — 20.4 Chapter 21 — 21.1, 21.2, 21.3, 21.4 Chapter 22 — 22.1, 22.2
Evolution and equilibrium Code: UCP 4	Chapter 6 — 6.1, 6.4, 6.5 Chapter 20 — 20.1, 20.3		
Form and function Code: UCP 5	Chapter 2 — 2.1, 2.2, 2.3 Chapter 3 — 3.1, 3.2, 3.3 Chapter 5 — 5.3		Chapter 11 — 11.1 Chapter 19 — 19.2, 19.3, 19.4 Chapter 22 — 22.3, 22.4

National Science Education Standards

Science as Inquiry

Standard	Chapter Correlation			
Abilities necessary to do scientific inquiry Code: SAI 1	Chapter 1 Chapter 2 Chapter 3 Chapter 4 Chapter 5 Chapter 6 Chapter 7 Chapter 8 Chapter 9 Chapter 10 Chapter 11	1.1, 1.2, 1.3, 1.4 2.1, 2.2, 2.3 3.2, 3.3 4.1, 4.2, 4.3, 4.4 5.1, 5.2, 5.3 6.3, 6.4, 6.5 7.1, 7.2, 7.3, 7.4 8.1, 8.2, 8.3 9.1, 9.3 10.1, 10.2, 10.3, 10.4 11.4	Chapter 12 Chapter 13 Chapter 14 Chapter 15 Chapter 16 Chapter 17 Chapter 18 Chapter 19 Chapter 20 Chapter 21 Chapter 22	12.1, 12.2, 12.3, 12.4 13.2, 13.4, 13.5 14.1, 14.2, 14.3, 14.4 15.4 16.1, 16.4 17.1, 17.2, 17.3, 17.4 18.3 19.1, 19.2, 19.3, 19.4 20.3, 20.4 21.1, 21.2, 21.3, 21.4 22.2
Understandings about scientific inquiry Code: SAI 2	Chapter 1 Chapter 3 Chapter 4 Chapter 6 Chapter 7 Chapter 8 Chapter 10	1.2 3.2 4.1, 4.2, 4.3, 4.4 6.3, 6.4, 6.5 7.1, 7.2, 7.3 8.1, 8.2, 8.3 10.1, 10.2, 10.3	Chapter 13 Chapter 15 Chapter 17 Chapter 18 Chapter 19 Chapter 20	13.2 15.2 17.2, 17.3, 17.4 18.1 19.1 20.4

Science and Technology

Standard	Chapter Correlation			
Abilities of technological design Code: ST 1	Chapter 1 Chapter 2 Chapter 5 Chapter 11 Chapter 14	1.2, 1.3 2.1, 2.3 5.3 11.3 14.4	Chapter 16 Chapter 17 Chapter 19 Chapter 21	16.4 17.2 19.3 21.1, 21.4
Understandings about science and technology Code: ST 2	Chapter 1 Chapter 2 Chapter 4 Chapter 5 Chapter 6 Chapter 7 Chapter 8 Chapter 9 Chapter 10	1.2, 1.3 2.1, 2.2, 2.3 4.1 5.3 6.3 7.2, 7.3 8.1, 8.2, 8.3 9.2, 9.3 10.4	Chapter 11 Chapter 12 Chapter 13 Chapter 17 Chapter 18 Chapter 19 Chapter 20 Chapter 21 Chapter 22	11.4 12.2 13.2, 13.4, 13.5 17.4 18.3 19.3 20.1, 20.2, 20.4 21.1, 21.2, 21.3 22.2, 22.3, 23.4

T43

National Science Education Standards

Science in Personal Perspectives

Standard	Chapter Correlation			
Personal health Code: SPSP 1	Chapter 1 Chapter 5 Chapter 8	1.4 5.2 8.3	Chapter 15 Chapter 17	15.1 17.1, 17.4
Populations, resources, and environments Code: SPSP 2	Chapter 2 Chapter 3 Chapter 5 Chapter 10	2.3 3.3 5.1, 5.2, 5.3 10.4	Chapter 12 Chapter 13 Chapter 17	12.1, 12.2 13.4, 13.5 17.2, 17.3
Natural hazards Code: SPSP 3	Chapter 1 Chapter 5 Chapter 7 Chapter 8 Chapter 9 Chapter 10 Chapter 11	1.1, 1.3 5.2 7.3 8.1, 8.2, 8.3 9.2 10.4 11.2, 11.3, 11.4	Chapter 12 Chapter 13 Chapter 14 Chapter 15 Chapter 16 Chapter 17	12.1, 12.3, 12.4 13.5 14.3 15.1, 15.2, 15.4 16.1, 16.3, 16.4 17.1, 17.4
Risks and benefits Code: SPSP 4	Chapter 1 Chapter 3 Chapter 5 Chapter 7 Chapter 8 Chapter 9 Chapter 10	1.1, 1.3 3.3 5.1, 5.2, 5.3 7.3 8.1, 8.2, 8.3 9.2 10.3, 10.4	Chapter 11 Chapter 12 Chapter 13 Chapter 14 Chapter 15 Chapter 16 Chapter 17	11.2 12.4 13.4, 13.5 14.3 15.1, 15.2, 15.4 16.3, 16.4 17.4
Science and technology in society Code: SPSP 5	Chapter 2 Chapter 3 Chapter 4 Chapter 5 Chapter 6 Chapter 7 Chapter 8 Chapter 10	2.1, 2.2, 2.3 3.3 4.1 5.2, 5.3 6.1, 6.3, 6.4 7.2, 7.3 8.3 10.4	Chapter 11 Chapter 13 Chapter 17 Chapter 18 Chapter 19 Chapter 20 Chapter 21 Chapter 22	11.4 13.2, 13.4, 135 17.4 18.1, 18.3 19.1, 19.3 20.1, 20.2, 20.4 21.1, 21.2, 21.3 22.2, 22.4

National Science Education Standards

History and Nature of Science

Standard	Chapter Correlation			
Science as a human endeavor Code: HNS 1	Chapter 1 Chapter 2 Chapter 4 Chapter 6 Chapter 7 Chapter 8 Chapter 10 Chapter 12	1.1 2.1, 2.3 4.1 6.1, 6.3 7.2 8.2 10.4 12.2	Chapter 13 Chapter 14 Chapter 17 Chapter 18 Chapter 19 Chapter 20 Chapter 21 Chapter 22	13.2, 13.4, 13.5 14.1, 14.4 17.2, 17.3, 17.4 18.1, 18.3 19.2, 19.3 20.2, 20.4 21.1, 21.2, 21.3, 21.4 22.1, 22.4
Nature of science Code: HNS 2	Chapter 1 Chapter 6 Chapter 7 Chapter 8	1.2, 1.3 6.1, 6.2, 6.3, 6.5 7.2, 7.3 8.3	Chapter 9 Chapter 18 Chapter 19 Chapter 20	9.1 18.1 19.2, 19.3 20.1, 20.2, 20.4
History of science Code: HNS 3	Chapter 1 Chapter 2 Chapter 6 Chapter 7 Chapter 8 Chapter 13 Chapter 14	1.4 2.1, 2.2 6.1, 6.3 7.2 8.2 13.2 14.1, 14.4	Chapter 16 Chapter 17 Chapter 18 Chapter 20 Chapter 21 Chapter 22	16.2 17.2, 17.3 18.1 20.1, 20.2, 20.4 21.1, 21.2, 21.3, 21.4 22.1, 22.4

National Science Education Standards

Earth Science Content Standards

Structure of the Earth System

Standard	Chapter Correlation
The solid earth is layered with a lithosphere; hot, convecting mantle; and dense metallic core. Code: ES 1a	Chapter 1 1.3 Chapter 8 8.1 Chapter 21 21.4
Lithospheric plates on the scales of continents and oceans constantly move at rates of centimeters per year in response to movements in the mantle. Major geological events, such as earthquakes, volcanic eruptions, and mountain building result from these plate motions. Code: ES 1b	Chapter 7 7.2, 7.3, 7.4 Chapter 8 8.1, 8.2, 8.3 Chapter 9 9.3 Chapter 13 13.1, 13.2 Chapter 14 14.3
Land forms are the result of a combination of constructive and destructive forces. Constructive forces include crustal deformation, volcanic eruption, and deposition of sediment, while destructive forces include weathering and erosion. Code: ES 1c	Chapter 4 4.1, 4.2, 4.3, 4.4 Chapter 9 9.1, 9.2, 9.3 Chapter 10 10.1, 10.2, 10.3 Chapter 11 11.1, 11.2, 11.3 Chapter 12 12.1, 12.2, 12.3, 12.4 Chapter 21 21.1, 21.2, 21.3
Some changes in the solid earth can be described as the "rock cycle." Old rocks at the earth's surface weather, forming sediments that are buried, then compacted, heated, and often recrystallized into new rock. Eventually, those new rocks may be brought to the earth's surface by the forces that drive plate motions, and the rock cycle continues. Code: ES 1d	Chapter 4 4.1, 4.2, 4.3 Chapter 5 5.2 Chapter 10 10.1, 10.2
Soil consists of weathered rocks and decomposed organic material from dead plants, animals, and bacteria. Soils are often found in layers, with each having a different chemical composition and texture. Code: ES 1e	Chapter 5 5.2 Chapter 10 10.3
Water, which covers the majority of the earth's surface, circulates through the crust, oceans, and atmosphere in what is known as the "water cycle." Water evaporates from the earth's surface, rises and cools as it moves to higher elevations, condenses as rain or snow, and falls to the surface where it collects in lakes, oceans soil, and in rocks underground. Code: ES 1f	Chapter 11 11.1 Chapter 13 13.1 Chapter 16 16.1 Chapter 17 17.1

Structure of the Earth System (cont.)

Standard	Chapter Correlation
Water is a solvent. As it passes through the water cycle it dissolves minerals and gases and carries them to the oceans. Code: ES 1g	**Chapter 10** 10.3 **Chapter 13** 13.1
The atmosphere is a mixture of nitrogen, oxygen, and trace gases that include water vapor. The atmosphere has different properties at different elevations. Code: ES 1h	**Chapter 13** 13.1 **Chapter 15** 15.1
Clouds, formed by the condensation of water vapor, affect weather and climate. Code: ES 1i	**Chapter 16** 16.1, 16.3, 16.4
Global patterns of atmospheric movement influence local weather. Oceans have a major effect on climate, because water in the oceans holds a large amount of heat. Code: ES 1j	**Chapter 13** 13.1 **Chapter 14** 14.1, 14.2 **Chapter 15** 15.3 **Chapter 16** 16.2, 16.3, 16.4 **Chapter 17** 17.1
Living organisms have played many roles in the earth system, including affecting the composition of the atmosphere, producing some types of rocks, and contributing to the weathering of rocks. Code: ES 1k	**Chapter 4** 4.3 **Chapter 5** 5.2 **Chapter 6** 6.4 **Chapter 10** 10.1, 10.3 **Chapter 17** 17.4

Earth's History

Standard	Chapter Correlation
The earth processes we see today, including erosion, movement of lithospheric plates, and changes in atmospheric composition, are similar to those that occurred in the past. Earth history is also influenced by occasional catastrophes, such as the impact of an asteroid or comet. Code: ES 2a	**Chapter 6** 6.1 **Chapter 7** 7.2, 7.3, 7.4 **Chapter 12** 12.2, 12.3 **Chapter 13** 13.1 **Chapter 17** 17.4
Fossils provide important evidence of how life and environmental conditions have changed. Code: ES 2b	**Chapter 4** 4.3 **Chapter 6** 6.1, 6.2, 6.3, 6.4, 6.5 **Chapter 20** 20.3

National Science Education Standards

Earth in the Solar System

Standard	Chapter Correlation
The earth is the third planet from the sun in a system that includes the moon, the sun, eight other planets and their moons, and smaller objects, such as asteroids and comets. The sun, an average star, is the central and largest body in the solar system. Code: ES 3a	**Chapter 18** 18.1 **Chapter 20** 20.1, 20.2 **Chapter 21** 21.1, 21.2, 21.3, 21.4
Most objects in the solar system are in regular and predictable motion. Those motions explain such phenomena as the day, the year, phases of the moon, and eclipses. Code: ES 3b	**Chapter 18** 18.1 **Chapter 20** 20.1, 20.4 **Chapter 21** 21.1, 21.2, 21.3, 21.4
Gravity is the force that keeps planets in orbit around the sun and governs the rest of the motion in the solar system. Gravity alone holds us to the earth's surface and explains the phenomena of the tides. Code: ES 3c	**Chapter 14** 14.4 **Chapter 18** 18.1 **Chapter 20** 20.1 **Chapter 21** 21.1, 21.4
The sun is the major source of energy for phenomena on the earth's surface, such as growth of plants, winds, ocean currents, and the water cycle. Seasons result from variations in the amount of the sun's energy hitting the surface, due to the tilt of the earth's rotation on its axis and the length of the day. Code: ES 3d	**Chapter 5** 5.1, 5.2, 5.3 **Chapter 17** 17.1

HOLT SCIENCE & TECHNOLOGY

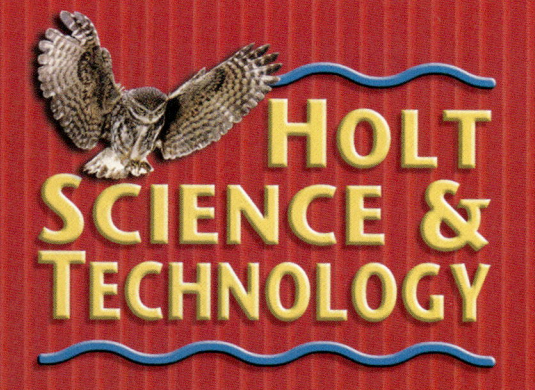

Earth Science

HOLT, RINEHART AND WINSTON
A Harcourt Education Company
Orlando • Austin • New York • San Diego • Toronto • London

Acknowledgments

Contributing Authors

Kathleen Meehan Berry
Science Chairman
Canon-McMillan School District
Canonsburg, Pennsylvania

Robert H. Fronk, Ph.D.
Professor
Science and Mathematics Education Department
Florida Institute of Technology
Melbourne, Florida

Mary Kay Hemenway, Ph.D.
Research Associate and Senior Lecturer
Department of Astronomy
The University of Texas at Austin
Austin, Texas

Kathleen Kaska
Former Life and Earth Science Teacher and Science Department Chair

Peter E. Malin, Ph.D.
Professor of Geology
Division of Earth and Ocean Sciences
Duke University
Durham, North Carolina

Karen J. Meech, Ph.D.
Astronomer
Institute for Astronomy
University of Hawaii
Honolulu, Hawaii

Robert J. Sager, M.S., J.D., L.G.
Coordinator and Professor of Earth Science
Pierce College
Lakewood, Washington

Inclusion Specialist

Karen Clay
Inclusion Specialist Consultant
Boston, Massachusetts

Safety Reviewer

Jack Gerlovich, Ph.D.
Associate Professor
School of Education
Drake University
Des Moines, Iowa

Academic Reviewers

David M. Armstrong, Ph.D.
Professor
Ecology and Evolutionary Biology
University of Colorado
Boulder, Colorado

Kenneth H. Brink, Ph.D.
Senior Scientist and Physical Oceanography Director
Coastal Ocean Institute and Rinehart Coastal Research Center
Woods Hole Oceanographic Institution
Woods Hole, Massachusetts

John Brockhaus, Ph.D.
Professor of Geospatial Information Science and Director of Geospatial Information Science Program
Department of Geography and Environmental Engineering
United States Military Academy
West Point, New York

Dan Bruton, Ph.D.
Associate Professor
Department of Physics and Astronomy
Stephen F. Austin State University
Nacogdoches, Texas

Wesley N. Colley, Ph.D.
Lecturer
Department of Astronomy
University of Virginia
Charlottesville, Virginia

Roger J. Cuffey, Ph.D.
Professor of Paleontology
Department of Geosciences
Pennsylvania State University
University Park, Pennsylvania

Turgay Ertekin, Ph.D.
Professor and Chairman of Petroleum and Natural Gas Engineering
Energy and Geo-Environmental Engineering
Pennsylvania State University
University Park, Pennsylvania

Deborah Hanley, Ph.D.
Meteorologist
State of Florida
Department of Agriculture and Consumer Services
Division of Forestry
Tallahassee, Florida

Mary Kay Hemenway, Ph.D.
Research Associate and Senior Lecturer
Astronomy Department
The University of Texas
Austin, Texas

Richard N. Hey, Ph.D.
Professor of Geophysics
Department of Geophysics & Planetology
University of Hawaii at Manoa
Honolulu, Hawaii

Ken Hon, Ph.D.
Associate Professor of Volcanology
Geology Department
University of Hawaii at Hilo
Hilo, Hawaii

Susan Hough, Ph.D.
Scientist
United States Geological Survey (USGS)
Pasadena, California

Steven A. Jennings, Ph.D.
Associate Professor
Geography and Environmental Studies
University of Colorado at Colorado Springs
Colorado Springs, Colorado

Acknowledgments *continued on page 846*

Copyright © 2005 by Holt, Rinehart and Winston

All rights reserved. No part of this publication may be reproduced or transmitted in any form or by any means, electronic or mechanical, including photocopy, recording, or any information storage and retrieval system, without permission in writing from the publisher.

Requests for permission to make copies of any part of the work should be mailed to the following address: Permissions Department, Holt, Rinehart and Winston, 10801 N. MoPac Expressway, Building 3, Austin, Texas 78759.

ONE-STOP PLANNER is a trademark licensed to Holt, Rinehart and Winston, registered in the United States of America and/or other jurisdictions.

SciLINKS is a registered trademark owned and provided by the National Science Teachers Association. All rights reserved.

CNN is a registered trademark and CNN STUDENT NEWS is a trademark of Cable News Network LP, LLLP, an AOL Time Warner Company.

Current Science is a registered trademark of Weekly Reader Corporation.

Printed in the United States of America

ISBN 0-03-066479-9

2 3 4 5 6 7 048 08 07 06 05 04

Contents in Brief

UNIT 1 **Introduction to Earth Science** — 2
- Chapter 1 The World of Earth Science — 4
- Chapter 2 Maps as Models of the Earth — 34

UNIT 2 **Earth's Resources** — 62
- Chapter 3 Minerals of the Earth's Crust — 64
- Chapter 4 Rocks: Mineral Mixtures — 88
- Chapter 5 Energy Resources — 120
- Chapter 6 The Rock and Fossil Record — 150

UNIT 3 **The Restless Earth** — 186
- Chapter 7 Plate Tectonics — 188
- Chapter 8 Earthquakes — 222
- Chapter 9 Volcanoes — 248

UNIT 4 **Reshaping the Land** — 274
- Chapter 10 Weathering and Soil Formation — 276
- Chapter 11 The Flow of Fresh Water — 306
- Chapter 12 Agents of Erosion and Deposition — 340

UNIT 5 **Oceanography** — 370
- Chapter 13 Exploring the Oceans — 372
- Chapter 14 The Movement of Ocean Water — 414

UNIT 6 **Weather and Climate** — 444
- Chapter 15 The Atmosphere — 446
- Chapter 16 Understanding Weather — 480
- Chapter 17 Climate — 516

UNIT 7 **Astronomy** — 550
- Chapter 18 Studying Space — 552
- Chapter 19 Stars, Galaxies, and the Universe — 580
- Chapter 20 Formation of the Solar System — 612
- Chapter 21 A Family of Planets — 642
- Chapter 22 Exploring Space — 682

Contents

Safety First! xxvi

UNIT 1 ··· **Introduction to Earth Science**
TIMELINE 2

CHAPTER 1 The World of Earth Science 4
- **SECTION 1** Branches of Earth Science 6
- **SECTION 2** Scientific Methods in Earth Science 12
- **SECTION 3** Scientific Models 18
- **SECTION 4** Measurement and Safety 22

Chapter Lab Model Making Using Scientific Methods 26
Chapter Review 28
Standardized Test Preparation 30
Science in Action 32
  Science, Technology, and Society A "Ship" That Flips?
  Weird Science It's Raining Fish and Frogs
  Careers Sue Hendrickson: Paleontologist

CHAPTER 2 Maps as Models of the Earth 34
- **SECTION 1** You Are Here 36
- **SECTION 2** Mapping the Earth's Surface 42
- **SECTION 3** Topographic Maps 50

Chapter Lab Skills Practice Round or Flat? 54
Chapter Review 56
Standardized Test Preparation 58
Science in Action 60
  Science, Technology, and Society Geocaching
  Scientific Discoveries The Lost City of Ubar
  People in Science Matthew Henson: Arctic Explorer

LabBook Inquiry Orient Yourself! 716
  Skills Practice Topographic Tuber 718

iv Contents

UNIT 2 — Earth's Resources

TIMELINE **62**

CHAPTER 3 Minerals of the Earth's Crust 64

- **SECTION 1** What Is a Mineral? 66
- **SECTION 2** Identifying Minerals 70
- **SECTION 3** The Formation, Mining, and Use of Minerals .. 74

Chapter Lab Skills Practice Is It Fool's Gold? A Dense Situation 80
Chapter Review 82
Standardized Test Preparation 84
Science in Action 86
 Science Fiction "The Metal Man"
 Weird Science Wieliczka Salt Mine
 People in Science Jamie Hill: The Emerald Man

LabBook Skills Practice Mysterious Minerals 720

CHAPTER 4 Rocks: Mineral Mixtures 88

- **SECTION 1** The Rock Cycle 90
- **SECTION 2** Igneous Rock 98
- **SECTION 3** Sedimentary Rock 102
- **SECTION 4** Metamorphic Rock 106

Chapter Lab Skills Practice Let's Get Sedimental 112
Chapter Review 114
Standardized Test Preparation 116
Science in Action 118
 Science, Technology, and Society The Moai of Easter Island
 Scientific Discoveries Shock Metamorphism
 Careers Robert L. Folk: Petrologist

LabBook Skills Practice Crystal Growth 722
 Model Making Metamorphic Mash 725

v

CHAPTER 5 Energy Resources 120

SECTION 1 Natural Resources 122
SECTION 2 Fossil Fuels 126
SECTION 3 Alternative Resources 134

Chapter Lab Model Making Make a Water Wheel 142
Chapter Review 144
Standardized Test Preparation 146
Science in Action 148
   Science, Technology, and Society Hybrid Cars
   Scientific Debate The Three Gorges Dam
   Careers Fred Begay: Nuclear Physicist

LabBook Skills Practice Power of the Sun 726

CHAPTER 6 The Rock and Fossil Record 150

SECTION 1 Earth's Story and Those Who First Listened ... 152
SECTION 2 Relative Dating: Which Came First? 156
SECTION 3 Absolute Dating: A Measure of Time 162
SECTION 4 Looking at Fossils 166
SECTION 5 Time Marches On 172

Chapter Lab Model Making How Do You Stack Up? 178
Chapter Review 180
Standardized Test Preparation 182
Science in Action 184
   Science, Technology, and Society DNA and a Mammoth Discovery
   Scientific Debate Feathered Dinosaurs
   People in Science Lizzie May: Amateur Paleontologist

Contents

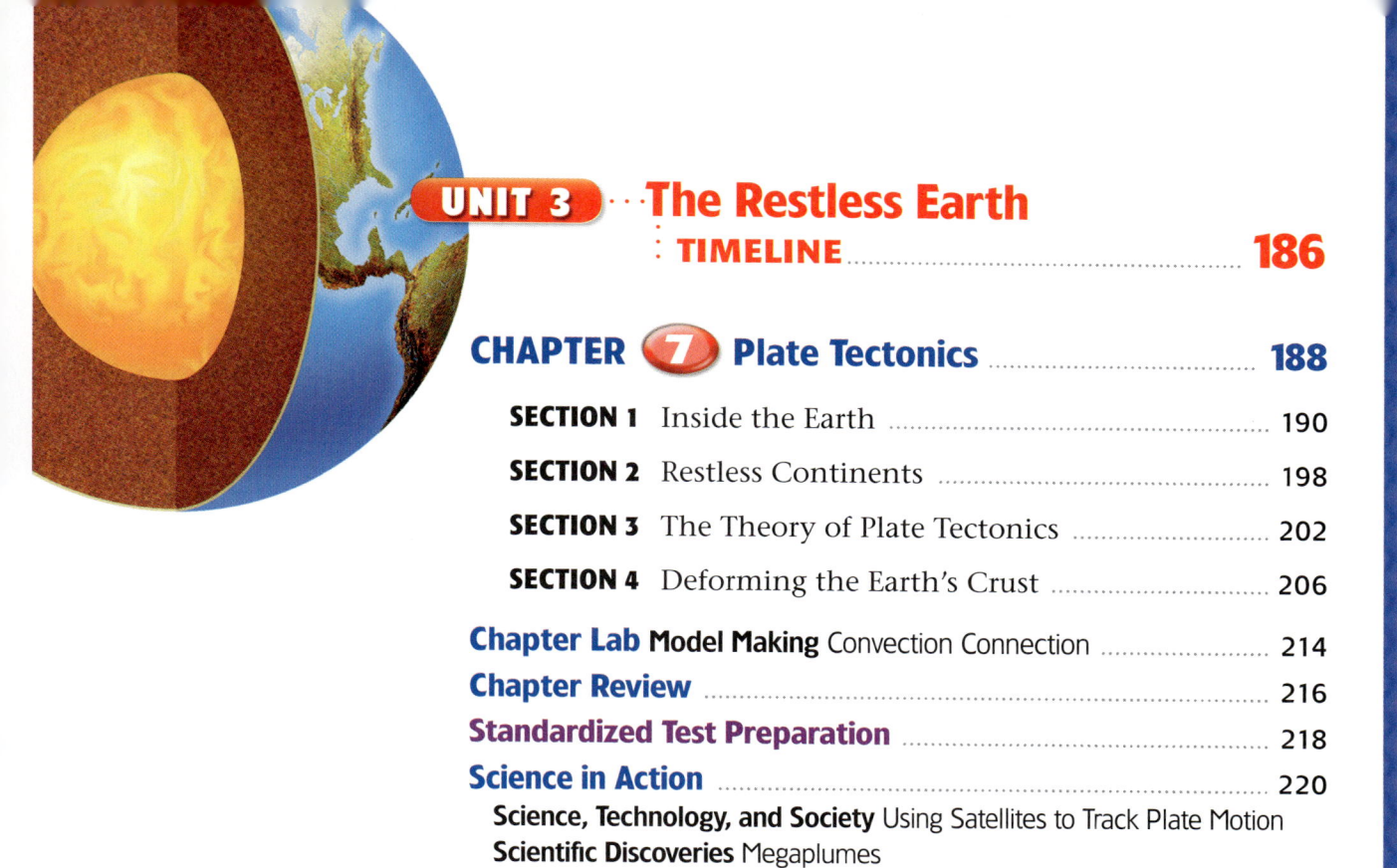

UNIT 3 · The Restless Earth
TIMELINE ... 186

CHAPTER 7 Plate Tectonics ... 188
- **SECTION 1** Inside the Earth ... 190
- **SECTION 2** Restless Continents ... 198
- **SECTION 3** The Theory of Plate Tectonics ... 202
- **SECTION 4** Deforming the Earth's Crust ... 206

Chapter Lab Model Making Convection Connection ... 214
Chapter Review ... 216
Standardized Test Preparation ... 218
Science in Action ... 220
  Science, Technology, and Society Using Satellites to Track Plate Motion
  Scientific Discoveries Megaplumes
  People in Science Alfred Wegener: Continental Drift

LabBook Model Making Oh, the Pressure! ... 728

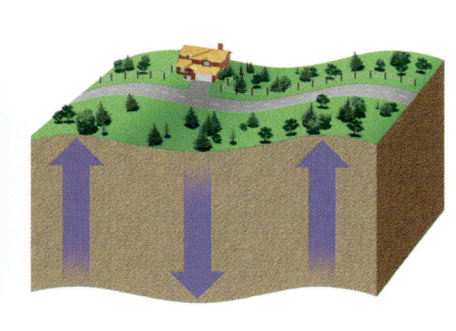

CHAPTER 8 Earthquakes ... 222
- **SECTION 1** What Are Earthquakes? ... 224
- **SECTION 2** Earthquake Measurement ... 230
- **SECTION 3** Earthquakes and Society ... 234

Chapter Lab Inquiry Quake Challenge ... 240
Chapter Review ... 242
Standardized Test Preparation ... 244
Science in Action ... 246
  Science, Technology, and Society San Andreas Fault Observatory at Depth (SAFOD)
  Weird Science Can Animals Predict Earthquakes?
  Careers Hiroo Kanamori: Seismologist

LabBook Skills Practice Earthquake Waves ... 731

Contents

CHAPTER 9 Volcanoes 248

- **SECTION 1** Volcanic Eruptions 250
- **SECTION 2** Effects of Volcanic Eruptions 256
- **SECTION 3** Causes of Volcanic Eruptions 260

Chapter Lab Skills Practice Volcano Verdict 266
Chapter Review 268
Standardized Test Preparation 270
Science in Action 272
  Science, Technology, and Society Fighting Lava with Fire Hoses
  Weird Science Pele's Hair
  Careers Tina Neal: Volcanologist

LabBook Skills Practice Some Go "Pop," Some Do Not 733

UNIT 4 — Reshaping the Land
TIMELINE 274

CHAPTER 10 Weathering and Soil Formation 276

- **SECTION 1** Weathering 278
- **SECTION 2** Rates of Weathering 284
- **SECTION 3** From Bedrock to Soil 288
- **SECTION 4** Soil Conservation 294

Chapter Lab Model Making Rockin' Through Time 298
Chapter Review 300
Standardized Test Preparation 302
Science in Action 304
  Science, Technology, and Society Flying Fertilizer
  Scientific Discoveries Strange Soil
  People in Science J. David Bamberger: Habitat Restoration

LabBook Skills Practice Great Ice Escape 735

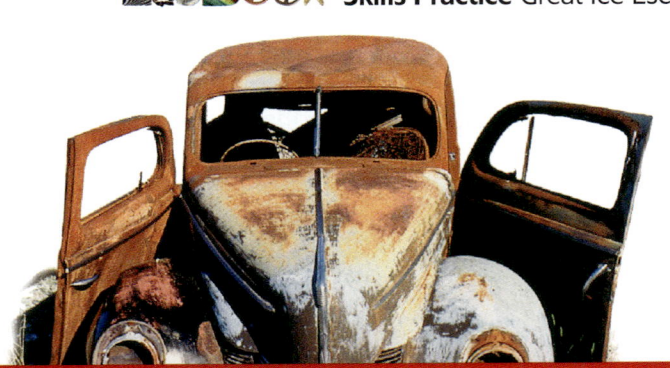

CHAPTER 11 The Flow of Fresh Water ... 306

- **SECTION 1** The Active River ... 308
- **SECTION 2** Stream and River Deposits ... 316
- **SECTION 3** Water Underground ... 320
- **SECTION 4** Using Water Wisely ... 326

Chapter Lab Model Making Water Cycle—What Goes Up... ... 332
Chapter Review ... 334
Standardized Test Preparation ... 336
Science in Action ... 338
- Weird Science Secret Lake
- Scientific Discoveries Sunken Forests
- People in Science Rita Colwell: A Water Filter for All

LabBook Skills Practice Clean Up Your Act ... 736

CHAPTER 12 Agents of Erosion and Deposition ... 340

- **SECTION 1** Shoreline Erosion and Deposition ... 342
- **SECTION 2** Wind Erosion and Deposition ... 348
- **SECTION 3** Erosion and Deposition by Ice ... 352
- **SECTION 4** The Effect of Gravity on Erosion and Deposition ... 358

Chapter Lab Model Making Gliding Glaciers ... 362
Chapter Review ... 364
Standardized Test Preparation ... 366
Science in Action ... 368
- Weird Science Long-Runout Landslides
- Scientific Discoveries The Lost Squadron
- Careers Johan Reinhard: High-Altitude Anthropologist

LabBook Model Making Dune Movement ... 740
Skills Practice Creating a Kettle ... 741

UNIT 5 Oceanography
TIMELINE ... 370

CHAPTER 13 Exploring the Oceans ... 372
- **SECTION 1** Earth's Oceans ... 374
- **SECTION 2** The Ocean Floor ... 382
- **SECTION 3** Life in the Ocean ... 388
- **SECTION 4** Resources from the Ocean ... 394
- **SECTION 5** Ocean Pollution ... 400

Chapter Lab Model Making Probing the Depths ... 406
Chapter Review ... 408
Standardized Test Preparation ... 410
Science in Action ... 412
  Scientific Discoveries In Search of the Giant Squid
  Science, Technology, and Society Creating Artificial Reefs
  People in Science Jacques Cousteau: Ocean Explorer

LabBook Skills Practice Investigating an Oil Spill ... 742

CHAPTER 14 The Movement of Ocean Water ... 414
- **SECTION 1** Currents ... 416
- **SECTION 2** Currents and Climate ... 422
- **SECTION 3** Waves ... 426
- **SECTION 4** Tides ... 432

Chapter Lab Skills Practice Up from the Depths ... 436
Chapter Review ... 438
Standardized Test Preparation ... 440
Science in Action ... 442
  Weird Science Using Toy Ducks to Track Ocean Currents
  Science, Technology, and Society Red Tides
  Careers Cristina Castro: Marine Biologist

LabBook Model Making Turning the Tides ... 744

Contents

UNIT 6 — Weather and Climate
TIMELINE ... 444

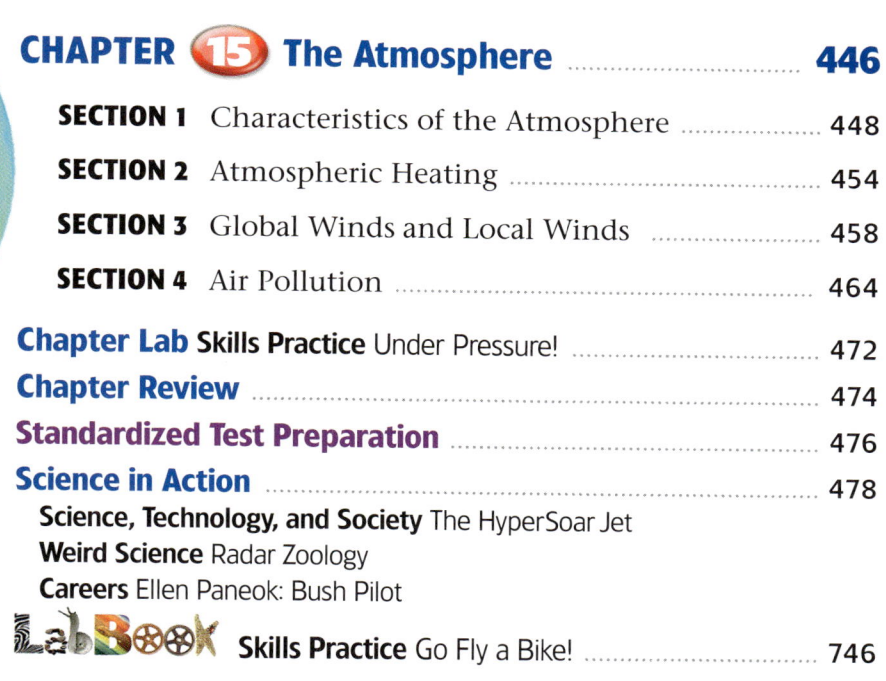

CHAPTER 15 The Atmosphere ... 446
- **SECTION 1** Characteristics of the Atmosphere ... 448
- **SECTION 2** Atmospheric Heating ... 454
- **SECTION 3** Global Winds and Local Winds ... 458
- **SECTION 4** Air Pollution ... 464

Chapter Lab Skills Practice Under Pressure! ... 472
Chapter Review ... 474
Standardized Test Preparation ... 476
Science in Action ... 478
  Science, Technology, and Society The HyperSoar Jet
  Weird Science Radar Zoology
  Careers Ellen Paneok: Bush Pilot

LabBook Skills Practice Go Fly a Bike! ... 746

CHAPTER 16 Understanding Weather ... 480
- **SECTION 1** Water in the Air ... 482
- **SECTION 2** Air Masses and Fronts ... 490
- **SECTION 3** Severe Weather ... 496
- **SECTION 4** Forecasting the Weather ... 504

Chapter Lab Inquiry Boiling Over! ... 508
Chapter Review ... 510
Standardized Test Preparation ... 512
Science in Action ... 514
  Science Fiction "All Summer in a Day"
  Weird Science Can Animals Forecast the Weather?
  Careers Cristy Mitchell: Meteorologist

LabBook Skills Practice Watching the Weather ... 748
Skills Practice Let It Snow! ... 751
Model Making Gone with the Wind ... 752

Contents   xi

CHAPTER 17	**Climate**	**516**
SECTION 1	What Is Climate?	518
SECTION 2	The Tropics	526
SECTION 3	Temperate and Polar Zones	530
SECTION 4	Changes in Climate	536

Chapter Lab Skills Practice Biome Business ... 542
Chapter Review ... 544
Standardized Test Preparation ... 546
Science in Action ... 548
  Scientific Debate Global Warming
  Science, Technology, and Society Ice Cores
  People in Science Mercedes Pascual: Climate Change and Disease

LabBook Skills Practice Global Impact ... 754
  Skills Practice For the Birds ... 755

UNIT 7 ··· Astronomy
TIMELINE ... 550

CHAPTER 18	**Studying Space**	**552**
SECTION 1	Astronomy: The Original Science	554
SECTION 2	Telescopes	558
SECTION 3	Mapping the Stars	564

Chapter Lab Skills Practice Through the Looking Glass ... 572
Chapter Review ... 574
Standardized Test Preparation ... 576
Science in Action ... 578
  Science Fiction "Why I Left Harry's All-Night Hamburgers"
  Science, Technology, and Society Light Pollution
  People in Science Neil deGrasse Tyson: A Star Writer

LabBook Skills Practice The Sun's Yearly Trip
  Through the Zodiac ... 758

CHAPTER 19 Stars, Galaxies, and the Universe 580

SECTION 1 Stars 582
SECTION 2 The Life Cycle of Stars 590
SECTION 3 Galaxies 596
SECTION 4 Formation of the Universe 600

Chapter Lab Skills Practice Red Hot, or Not? 604
Chapter Review 606
Standardized Test Preparation 608
Science in Action 610
  Weird Science Holes Where Stars Once Were
  Scientific Discoveries Eta Carinae: The Biggest Star Ever Discovered
  Careers Jocelyn Bell-Burnell: Astrophysicist

LabBook Skills Practice I See the Light! 760

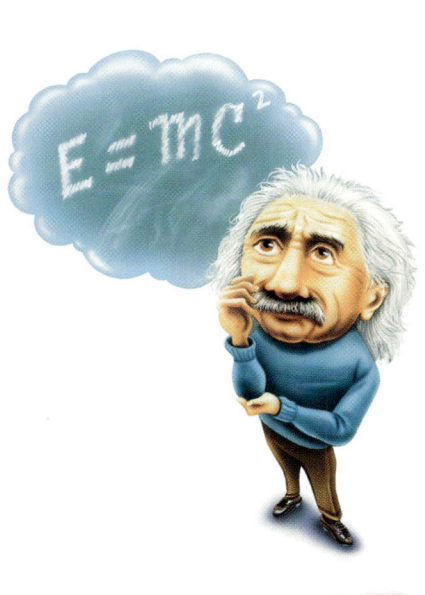

CHAPTER 20 Formation of the Solar System ... 612

SECTION 1 A Solar System Is Born 614
SECTION 2 The Sun: Our Very Own Star 618
SECTION 3 The Earth Takes Shape 624
SECTION 4 Planetary Motion 630

Chapter Lab Skills Practice How Far Is the Sun? 634
Chapter Review 636
Standardized Test Preparation 638
Science in Action 640
  Science, Technology, and Society Don't Look at the Sun!
  Scientific Discoveries The Oort Cloud
  People in Science Subrahmanyan Chandrasekhar: From White Dwarfs to Black Holes

CHAPTER 21   A Family of Planets **642**

    SECTION 1 The Nine Planets 644
    SECTION 2 The Inner Planets 648
    SECTION 3 The Outer Planets 654
    SECTION 4 Moons 660
    SECTION 5 Small Bodies in the Solar System 668

Chapter Lab Inquiry Create a Calendar 674
Chapter Review 676
Standardized Test Preparation 678
Science in Action 680
    Science Fiction "The Mad Moon"
    Scientific Debate Is Pluto a Planet?
    Careers Adriana C. Ocampo: Planetary Geologist

LabBook   **Model Making** Why Do They Wander? 762
    Model Making Eclipses 764
    Skills Practice Phases of the Moon 765

CHAPTER 22   Exploring Space **682**

    SECTION 1 Rocket Science 684
    SECTION 2 Artificial Satellites 688
    SECTION 3 Space Probes 694
    SECTION 4 People in Space 700

Chapter Lab Inquiry Water Rockets Save the Day! 706
Chapter Review 708
Standardized Test Preparation 710
Science in Action 712
    Science, Technology, and Society Mission to Mars
    Weird Science Flashline Mars Arctic Research Station
    Careers Franklin Chang-Diaz: Astronaut

LabBook   **Model Making** Reach for the Stars 766

LabBook 714

Appendix 768

Reading Check Answers 769
Study Skills 776
SI Measurement 782
Temperature Scales 783
Measuring Skills 784
Scientific Methods 785
Making Charts and Graphs 787
Math Refresher 790
Periodic Table of the Elements 794
Physical Science Refresher 796
Physical Science Laws and Equations 798
Properties of Common Minerals 800
Sky Maps 802

Glossary 804

Spanish Glossary 813

Index 824

Chapter Labs and LabBook

Safety First! xxvi

CHAPTER 1 — The World of Earth Science
Chapter Lab
Model Making Using Scientific Methods ... 26

CHAPTER 2 — Maps as Models of the Earth
Chapter Lab
Skills Practice Round or Flat? 54
LabBook
Inquiry Orient Yourself! 716
Skills Practice Topographic Tuber 718

CHAPTER 3 — Minerals of the Earth's Crust
Chapter Lab
Skills Practice Is It Fool's Gold? A Dense Situation 80
LabBook
Skills Practice Mysterious Minerals 720

CHAPTER 4 — Rocks: Mineral Mixtures
Chapter Lab
Skills Practice Let's Get Sedimental 112
LabBook
Skills Practice Crystal Growth 722
Model Making Metamorphic Mash 725

CHAPTER 5 — Energy Resources
Chapter Lab
Model Making Make a Water Wheel 142
LabBook
Skills Practice Power of the Sun 726

CHAPTER 6 — The Rock and Fossil Record
Chapter Lab
Model Making How Do You Stack Up? ... 178

CHAPTER 7 — Plate Tectonics
Chapter Lab
Model Making Convection Connection ... 214
LabBook
Model Making Oh, the Pressure! 728

CHAPTER 8 — Earthquakes
Chapter Lab
Inquiry Quake Challenge 240
LabBook
Skills Practice Earthquake Waves 731

CHAPTER 9 — Volcanoes
Chapter Lab
Skills Practice Volcano Verdict 266
LabBook
Skills Practice Some Go "Pop," Some Do Not 733

CHAPTER 10 — Weathering and Soil Formation
Chapter Lab
Model Making Rockin' Through Time 298
LabBook
Skills Practice Great Ice Escape 735

CHAPTER 11 — The Flow of Fresh Water
Chapter Lab
Model Making Water Cycle—What Goes Up. 332
LabBook
Skills Practice Clean Up Your Act 736

The more labs, the better!
Take a minute to browse the variety of exciting **labs** in this textbook. Labs appear within the chapters and in a special LabBook in the back of the textbook. All labs are designed to help you experience science firsthand. But please don't forget to be safe. Read the Safety First! section before starting any of the labs.

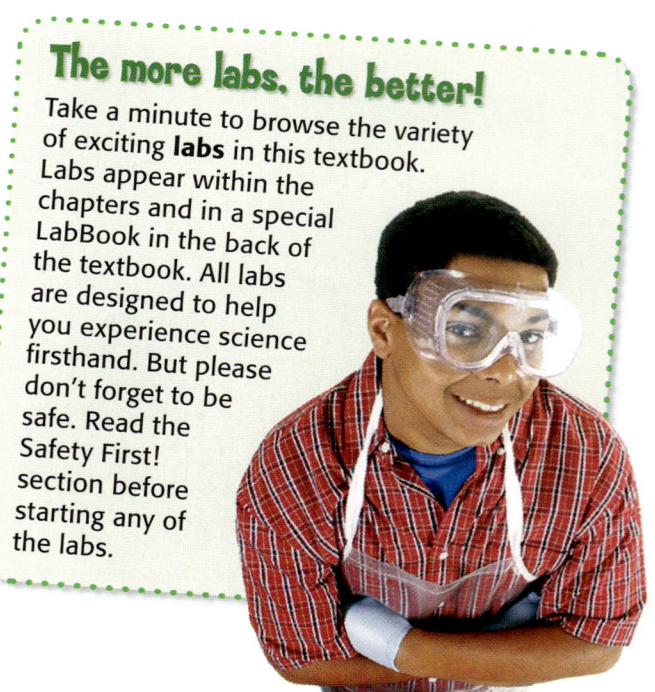

CHAPTER 12 Agents of Erosion and Deposition
Chapter Lab
Model Making Gliding Glaciers 362
LabBook
Model Making Dune Movement 740
Skills Practice Creating a Kettle 741

CHAPTER 13 Exploring the Oceans
Chapter Lab
Model Making Probing the Depths 406
LabBook
Skills Practice Investigating an Oil Spill ... 742

CHAPTER 14 The Movement of Ocean Water
Chapter Lab
Skills Practice Up from the Depths 436
LabBook
Model Making Turning the Tides 744

CHAPTER 15 The Atmosphere
Chapter Lab
Skills Practice Under Pressure! 472
LabBook
Skills Practice Go Fly a Bike! 746

CHAPTER 16 Understanding Weather
Chapter Lab
Inquiry Boiling Over! 508
LabBook
Skills Practice Watching the Weather 748
Skills Practice Let It Snow! 751
Model Making Gone with the Wind 752

CHAPTER 17 Climate
Chapter Lab
Skills Practice Biome Business 542
LabBook
Skills Practice Global Impact 754
Skills Practice For the Birds 755

CHAPTER 18 Studying Space
Chapter Lab
Skills Practice Through the Looking Glass 572
LabBook
Skills Practice The Sun's Yearly Trip Through the Zodiac 758

CHAPTER 19 Stars, Galaxies, and the Universe
Chapter Lab
Skills Practice Red Hot, or Not? 604
LabBook
Skills Practice I See the Light! 760

CHAPTER 20 Formation of the Solar System
Chapter Lab
Skills Practice How Far Is the Sun? 634

CHAPTER 21 A Family of Planets
Chapter Lab
Inquiry Create a Calendar 674
LabBook
Model Making Why Do They Wander? ... 762
Model Making Eclipses 764
Skills Practice Phases of the Moon 765

CHAPTER 22 Exploring Space
Chapter Lab
Inquiry Water Rockets Save the Day! 706
LabBook
Model Making Reach for the Stars 766

Contents xvii

Start your engines with an activity!

Get motivated to learn by doing the two activities at the beginning of each chapter. The **Pre-Reading Activity** helps you organize information as you read the chapter. The **Start-up Activity** helps you gain scientific understanding of the topic through hands-on experience.

PRE-READING ACTIVITY

FOLDNOTES

Key-Term Fold	4
Three-Panel Flip Chart	34
Layered Book	150
Key-Term Fold	188
Layered Book	248
Key-Term Fold	276
Booklet	306
Layered Book	340
Layered Book	372
Booklet	446
Four-Corner Fold	480
Pyramid	516
Three-Panel Flip Chart	552
Three-Panel Flip Chart	580
Booklet	642

Graphic Organizer

Concept Map	64
Spider Map	88
Comparison Table	120
Spider Map	222
Concept Map	414
Chain-of-Events Chart	612
Chain-of-Events Chart	682

START-UP ACTIVITY

Mission Impossible?	5
Follow the Yellow Brick Road	35
What Is Your Classroom Made Of?	65
Classifying Objects	89
What Is the Sun's Favorite Color?	121
Making Fossils	151
Continental Collisions	189
Bend, Break, or Shake	223
Anticipation	249
What's the Difference?	277
Stream Weavers	307
Making Waves	341
Exit Only?	373
When Whirls Collide	415
Does Air Have Mass?	447
Meeting of the Masses	481
What's Your Angle?	517
Making an Astrolabe	553
Exploring the Movement of Galaxies in the Universe	581
Strange Gravity	613
Measuring Space	643
Balloon Rockets	683

Contents

READING STRATEGY

Brainstorming
Chapter 5 126
Chapter 6 172
Chapter 7 202

Discussion
Chapter 1 6
Chapter 2 42
Chapter 3 74
Chapter 4 106
Chapter 7 206
Chapter 8 234
Chapter 11 320
Chapter 12 352
Chapter 13 374
Chapter 14 432
Chapter 17 518
Chapter 20 624
Chapter 21 668
Chapter 22 684

Mnemonics
Chapter 1 12
Chapter 13 388
Chapter 15 448
Chapter 18 558

Paired Summarizing
Chapter 2 50
Chapter 3 66
Chapter 5 134
Chapter 7 198
Chapter 8 224
Chapter 9 256
Chapter 10 278
Chapter 11 326
Chapter 13 394
Chapter 14 422

Chapter 16 482
Chapter 17 536
Chapter 18 564
Chapter 19 590
Chapter 20 630
Chapter 21 644

Prediction Guide
Chapter 10 288
Chapter 11 316
Chapter 12 358
Chapter 14 426
Chapter 15 458
Chapter 19 582
Chapter 19 600
Chapter 21 654

Reading Organizer— Concept Map
Chapter 5 122
Chapter 6 162
Chapter 22 694

Reading Organizer— Flowchart
Chapter 4 90
Chapter 9 260
Chapter 18 554
Chapter 20 614
Chapter 22 700

Reading Organizer— Outline
Chapter 1 22
Chapter 2 36
Chapter 3 70
Chapter 4 102
Chapter 6 156

Chapter 6 166
Chapter 7 190
Chapter 8 230
Chapter 10 284
Chapter 11 308
Chapter 12 342
Chapter 13 382
Chapter 13 400
Chapter 14 416
Chapter 16 496
Chapter 17 530
Chapter 20 618
Chapter 21 648

Reading Organizer—Table
Chapter 1 18
Chapter 4 98
Chapter 6 152
Chapter 9 250
Chapter 10 294
Chapter 12 348
Chapter 15 454
Chapter 15 464
Chapter 16 490
Chapter 16 504
Chapter 17 526
Chapter 19 596
Chapter 21 660
Chapter 22 688

Remembering what you read doesn't have to be hard!
A **Reading Strategy** at the beginning of every section provides tips to help you remember and/or organize the information covered in the section.

Quick Lab

How Hot Is 300°C?	7
Making a Compass	38
Scratch Test	72
Stretching Out	107
Rock Sponge	129
Make a Fossil	169
Tectonic Ice Cubes	195
Modeling Strike-Slip Faults	209
Modeling Seismic Waves	228
Modeling an Explosive Eruption	254
Reaction to Stress	261
Acids React!	282
Measuring Alkalinity	327
Making Desert Pavement	349
The Desalination Plant	397
Doing the Wave	428
Testing for Particulates	467
Out of Thin Air	485
A Cool Breeze	521
Using a Sky Map	565
Not All Thumbs!	587
Staying in Focus	632
Clever Insight	663
Modeling LEO and GEO	689

School to Home

Taking Measurements	23
Columbus's Voyage	37
Recycling Minerals at Home	77
Making a Rock Collection	108
Renewable?	124
Fossil Hunt	170
Build a Seismograph	196
Disaster Planning	239
Tectonic Models	263
Ice Wedging	286
Floating down the River	310
Water Conservation	322
The *Titanic*	353
Coastal Cleanup	404
Coriolis Effect in Your Sink?	418
Air Pollution Awareness	470
Natural Disaster Plan	501
Using a Map	522
Your Biome	534
Reducing Pollution	541
Stargazing	585
Comets and Meteors	627
Surviving Space	659
Tracking Satellites	691

ACTIVITY

Science brings you closer together! Bring science into your home by doing **School-to-Home Activities** with a parent or another adult in your household.

Internet Activity

CHAPTER 1	The World of Earth Science	**HZ5WESW**
CHAPTER 2	Maps as Models of the Earth	**HZ5MAPW**
CHAPTER 3	Minerals of the Earth's Crust	**HZ5MINW**
CHAPTER 4	Rocks: Mineral Mixtures	**HZ5RCKW**
CHAPTER 5	Energy Resources	**HZ5ENRW**
CHAPTER 6	The Rock and Fossil Record	**HZ5FOSW**
CHAPTER 7	Plate Tectonics	**HZ5TECW**
CHAPTER 8	Earthquakes	**HZ5EQKW**
CHAPTER 9	Volcanoes	**HZ5VOLW**
CHAPTER 10	Weathering and Soil Formation	**HZ5WSFW**
CHAPTER 11	The Flow of Fresh Water	**HZ5DEPW**
CHAPTER 12	Agents of Erosion and Deposition	**HZ5ICEW**
CHAPTER 13	Exploring the Oceans	**HZ5OCEW**
CHAPTER 14	The Movement of Ocean Water	**HZ5H2OW**
CHAPTER 15	The Atmosphere	**HZ5ATMW**
CHAPTER 16	Understanding Weather	**HZ5WEAW**
CHAPTER 17	Climate	**HZ5CLMW**
CHAPTER 18	Studying Space	**HZ5OBSW**
CHAPTER 19	Stars, Galaxies, and the Universe	**HZ5UNVW**
CHAPTER 20	Formation of the Solar System	**HZ5SOLW**
CHAPTER 21	A Family of Planets	**HZ5FAMW**
CHAPTER 22	Exploring Space	**HZ5EXPW**

Get caught in the Web!
Go to **go.hrw.com** for **Internet Activities** related to each chapter. To find the Internet Activity for a particular chapter, just type in the keyword listed below.

Math Practice

Lots of Zeros!	9
Earth Shaker!	16
Surface Coal Mining	76
Miles per Acre	139
Using Models	192
How Hot Is Hot?	262
Making Soil	295
Calculating a Stream's Gradient	311
Agriculture in Israel	330
Counting Waves	343
Speed of a Glacier	354
Modeling the Atmosphere	450
Relative Humidity	483
The Ride to School	540
Starlight, Star Bright	586
Kepler's Formula	631
Triangulation	690

Math Focus

Finding Area	24

Science and math go hand in hand.
The **Math Focus** and **Math Practice** items show you many ways that math applies directly to science and vice versa.

Contents   xxi

Connection to...

Astronomy
Storms on Jupiter 495
Sunspots 539
Long Live the Sun 591

Biology
Magnetite 68
Metamorphosis 110
Darwin and Lyell 153
Cleaning the Air with Plants 466
Predicting the Weather 506
Animal and Plant Adaptations 528
Rods, Cones, and Stars 584
Mass Extinctions 672
Effects of Weightlessness 702

Chemistry
Hydrocarbons 128
Acidity of Precipitation 281
Atoms 620

Environmental Science
Endangered Species 53
Preservation in Ice 167
Bat Environmentalists 324
El Niño and Coral Reefs 424
The Greenhouse Effect 626
Space Junk 692

Geology
Submarine Volcanoes 378

Language Arts
Salty Expressions 103
Resources of the Future 136
Huckleberry Finn 313
The Dust Bowl 350
Water, Water, Everywhere 392
Mont-Saint-Michel Is Sometimes
   an Island? 433
Cloud Clues 486
Alien Observer 597
Eyewitness Account 617
Interplanetary Journalist 669

Oceanography
Making Hypotheses 15
Mapping the Ocean Floor 51

Physics
Earthquake-Proof Buildings 238
Convection Currents 419
Air-Pressure Experiment 449
Hot Roofs! 535
Detecting Infrared Radiation 562
Fingerprinting Cars 583
Origin of the Universe 603
Boiling Point on Mars 652

Social Studies
The Spread of Disease 20
Global Addresses 40
Mapmaking and Ship Navigation .. 44
The Naming of the Appalachian
   Mountains 211
New Madrid Earthquakes 232
Fertile Farmlands 253
Deforestation in Brazil 291
The Jason Project 386
Local Breezes 463
Living in the Tropics 527
Cosmic Message in a Bottle 698
Oral Histories 703

One subject leads to another.
You may not realize it at first, but different subjects are related to each other in many ways. Each **Connection** explores a topic from the viewpoint of another discipline. In this way, all of the subjects you learn about in school merge to improve your understanding of the world around you.

Science in Action

Science moves beyond the classroom!
Read **Science in Action** articles to learn more about science in the real world. These articles will give you an idea of how interesting, strange, helpful, and action packed science is. At the end of each chapter, you will find three short articles. And if your thirst is still not quenched, go to **go.hrw.com** for in-depth coverage.

Science Fiction
"The Metal Man" 86
"All Summer in a Day" 514
"Why I Left Harry's
 All-Night Hamburgers" 578
"The Mad Moon" 680

Science, Technology, and Society
A "Ship" That Flips? 32
Geocaching 60
The Moai of Easter Island 118
Hybrid Cars 148
DNA and a Mammoth Discovery 184
Using Satellites to Track Plate Motion 220
San Andreas Fault Observatory
 at Depth (SAFOD) 246
Fighting Lava with Fire Hoses 272
Flying Fertilizer 304
Creating Artificial Reefs 412
Red Tides 442
The HyperSoar Jet 478
Ice Cores 548
Light Pollution 578
Don't Look at the Sun! 640
Mission to Mars 712

Scientific Debate
The Three Gorges Dam 148
Feathered Dinosaurs 184
Global Warming 548
Is Pluto a Planet? 680

Scientific Discoveries
The Lost City of Ubar 60
Shock Metamorphism 118
Megaplumes 220
Strange Soil 304
Sunken Forests 338
The Lost Squadron 368
In Search of the Giant Squid 412
Eta Carinae: The Biggest Star
 Ever Discovered 610
The Oort Cloud 640

Weird Science
It's Raining Fish and Frogs 32
Wieliczka Salt Mine 86
Can Animals Predict Earthquakes? 246
Pele's Hair 272
Secret Lake 338
Long-Runout Landslides 368
Using Toy Ducks to Track
 Ocean Currents 442
Radar Zoology 478
Can Animals Forecast the Weather? 514
Holes Where Stars Once Were 610
Flashline Mars Arctic Research Station ... 712

Careers
Sue Hendrickson Paleontologist 33
Robert L. Folk Petrologist 119
Fred Begay Nuclear Physicist 149
Hiroo Kanamori Seismologist 247
Tina Neal Volcanologist 273
Johan Reinhard High-Altitude
 Anthropologist 369
Cristina Castro Marine Biologist 443
Ellen Paneok Bush Pilot 479
Cristy Mitchell Meteorologist 515
Jocelyn Bell-Burnell Astrophysicist 611
Adriana C. Ocampo Planetary Geologist .. 681
Franklin Chang-Diaz Astronaut 713

People in Science
Matthew Henson Arctic Explorer 61
Jamie Hill The Emerald Man 87
Lizzie May Amateur Paleontologist 185
Alfred Wegener Continental Drift 221
J. David Bamberger Habitat Restoration .. 305
Rita Colwell A Water Filter for All 339
Jacques Cousteau Ocean Explorer 413
Mercedes Pascual Climate Change
 and Disease 549
Neil deGrasse Tyson A Star Writer 579
Subrahmanyan Chandrasekhar
 From White Dwarfs to Black Holes 641

Contents **xxiii**

How to Use Your Textbook

Your Roadmap for Success with Holt Science and Technology

Reading Warm-Up
A Reading Warm-Up at the beginning of every section provides you with the section's objectives and key terms. The objectives tell you what you'll need to know after you finish reading the section.

Key terms are listed for each section. Learn the definitions of these terms because you will most likely be tested on them. Each key term is highlighted in the text and is defined at point of use and in the margin. You can also use the glossary to locate definitions quickly.

STUDY TIP Reread the objectives and the definitions to the key terms when studying for a test to be sure you know the material.

Get Organized
A Reading Strategy at the beginning of every section provides tips to help you organize and remember the information covered in the section. Keep a science notebook so that you are ready to take notes when your teacher reviews the material in class. Keep your assignments in this notebook so that you can review them when studying for the chapter test.

Be Resourceful — Use the Web

Internet Connect boxes in your textbook take you to resources that you can use for science projects, reports, and research papers. Go to scilinks.org, and type in the SciLinks code to get information on a topic.

Visit go.hrw.com Find worksheets, Current Science® magazine articles online, and other materials that go with your textbook at **go.hrw.com.** Click on the textbook icon and the table of contents to see all of the resources for each chapter.

xxiv   How to Use Your Textbook

Use the Illustrations and Photos

Art shows complex ideas and processes. Learn to analyze the art so that you better understand the material you read in the text.

Tables and graphs display important information in an organized way to help you see relationships.

A picture is worth a thousand words. Look at the photographs to see relevant examples of science concepts that you are reading about.

Answer the Section Reviews

Section Reviews test your knowledge of the main points of the section. Critical Thinking items challenge you to think about the material in greater depth and to find connections that you infer from the text.

STUDY TIP When you can't answer a question, reread the section. The answer is usually there.

Do Your Homework

Your teacher may assign worksheets to help you understand and remember the material in the chapter.

STUDY TIP Don't try to answer the questions without reading the text and reviewing your class notes. A little preparation up front will make your homework assignments a lot easier. Answering the items in the Chapter Review will help prepare you for the chapter test.

Visit Holt Online Learning
If your teacher gives you a special password to log onto the Holt Online Learning site, you'll find your complete textbook on the Web. In addition, you'll find some great learning tools and practice quizzes. You'll be able to see how well you know the material from your textbook.

Visit CNN Student News
You'll find up-to-date events in science at **cnnstudentnews.com.**

How to Use Your Textbook   XXV

SAFETY FIRST!

Exploring, inventing, and investigating are essential to the study of science. However, these activities can also be dangerous. To make sure that your experiments and explorations are safe, you must be aware of a variety of safety guidelines. You have probably heard of the saying, "It is better to be safe than sorry." This is particularly true in a science classroom where experiments and explorations are being performed. Being uninformed and careless can result in serious injuries. Don't take chances with your own safety or with anyone else's.

The following pages describe important guidelines for staying safe in the science classroom. Your teacher may also have safety guidelines and tips that are specific to your classroom and laboratory. Take the time to be safe.

Safety Rules!

Start Out Right

Always get your teacher's permission before attempting any laboratory exploration. Read the procedures carefully, and pay particular attention to safety information and caution statements. If you are unsure about what a safety symbol means, look it up or ask your teacher. You cannot be too careful when it comes to safety. If an accident does occur, inform your teacher immediately regardless of how minor you think the accident is.

If you are instructed to note the odor of a substance, wave the fumes toward your nose with your hand. Never put your nose close to the source.

Safety Symbols

All of the experiments and investigations in this book and their related worksheets include important safety symbols to alert you to particular safety concerns. Become familiar with these symbols so that when you see them, you will know what they mean and what to do. It is important that you read this entire safety section to learn about specific dangers in the laboratory.

Eye protection

Clothing protection

Hand safety

Heating safety

Electric safety

Chemical safety

Animal safety

Sharp object

Plant safety

xxvi

Eye Safety

Wear safety goggles when working around chemicals, acids, bases, or any type of flame or heating device. Wear safety goggles any time there is even the slightest chance that harm could come to your eyes. If any substance gets into your eyes, notify your teacher immediately and flush your eyes with running water for at least 15 minutes. Treat any unknown chemical as if it were a dangerous chemical. Never look directly into the sun. Doing so could cause permanent blindness.

Avoid wearing contact lenses in a laboratory situation. Even if you are wearing safety goggles, chemicals can get between the contact lenses and your eyes. If your doctor requires that you wear contact lenses instead of glasses, wear eye-cup safety goggles in the lab.

Safety Equipment

Know the locations of the nearest fire alarms and any other safety equipment, such as fire blankets and eyewash fountains, as identified by your teacher, and know the procedures for using the equipment.

Neatness

Keep your work area free of all unnecessary books and papers. Tie back long hair, and secure loose sleeves or other loose articles of clothing, such as ties and bows. Remove dangling jewelry. Don't wear open-toed shoes or sandals in the laboratory. Never eat, drink, or apply cosmetics in a laboratory setting. Food, drink, and cosmetics can easily become contaminated with dangerous materials.

Certain hair products (such as aerosol hair spray) are flammable and should not be worn while working near an open flame. Avoid wearing hair spray or hair gel on lab days.

Sharp/Pointed Objects

Use knives and other sharp instruments with extreme care. Never cut objects while holding them in your hands. Place objects on a suitable work surface for cutting.

Be extra careful when using any glassware. When adding a heavy object to a graduated cylinder, tilt the cylinder so that the object slides slowly to the bottom.

Safety First!

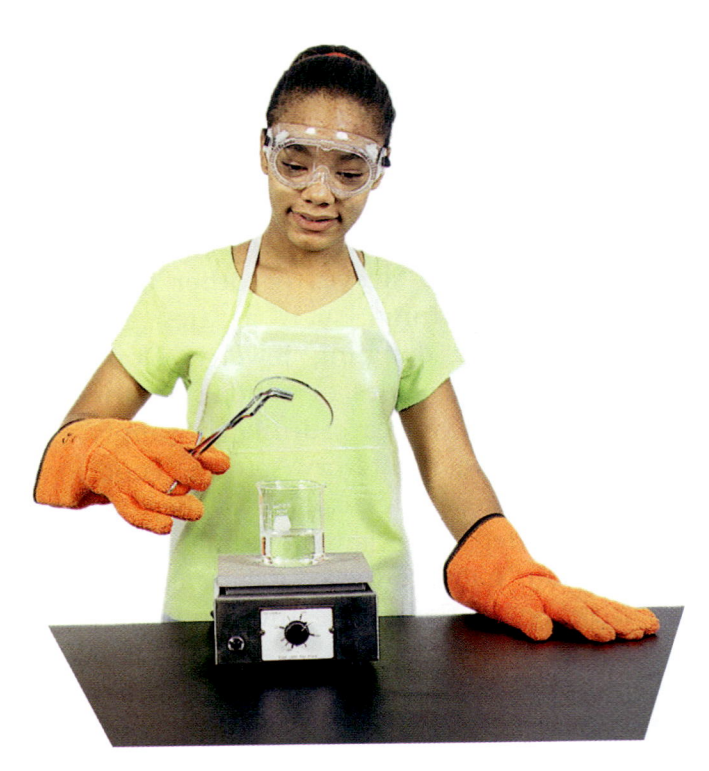

Heat

Wear safety goggles when using a heating device or a flame. Whenever possible, use an electric hot plate as a heat source instead of using an open flame. When heating materials in a test tube, always angle the test tube away from yourself and others. To avoid burns, wear heat-resistant gloves whenever instructed to do so.

Electricity

Be careful with electrical cords. When using a microscope with a lamp, do not place the cord where it could trip someone. Do not let cords hang over a table edge in a way that could cause equipment to fall if the cord is accidentally pulled. Do not use equipment with damaged cords. Be sure that your hands are dry and that the electrical equipment is in the "off" position before plugging it in. Turn off and unplug electrical equipment when you are finished.

Chemicals

Wear safety goggles when handling any potentially dangerous chemicals, acids, or bases. If a chemical is unknown, handle it as you would a dangerous chemical. Wear an apron and protective gloves when you work with acids or bases or whenever you are told to do so. If a spill gets on your skin or clothing, rinse it off immediately with water for at least 5 minutes while calling to your teacher.

Never mix chemicals unless your teacher tells you to do so. Never taste, touch, or smell chemicals unless you are specifically directed to do so. Before working with a flammable liquid or gas, check for the presence of any source of flame, spark, or heat.

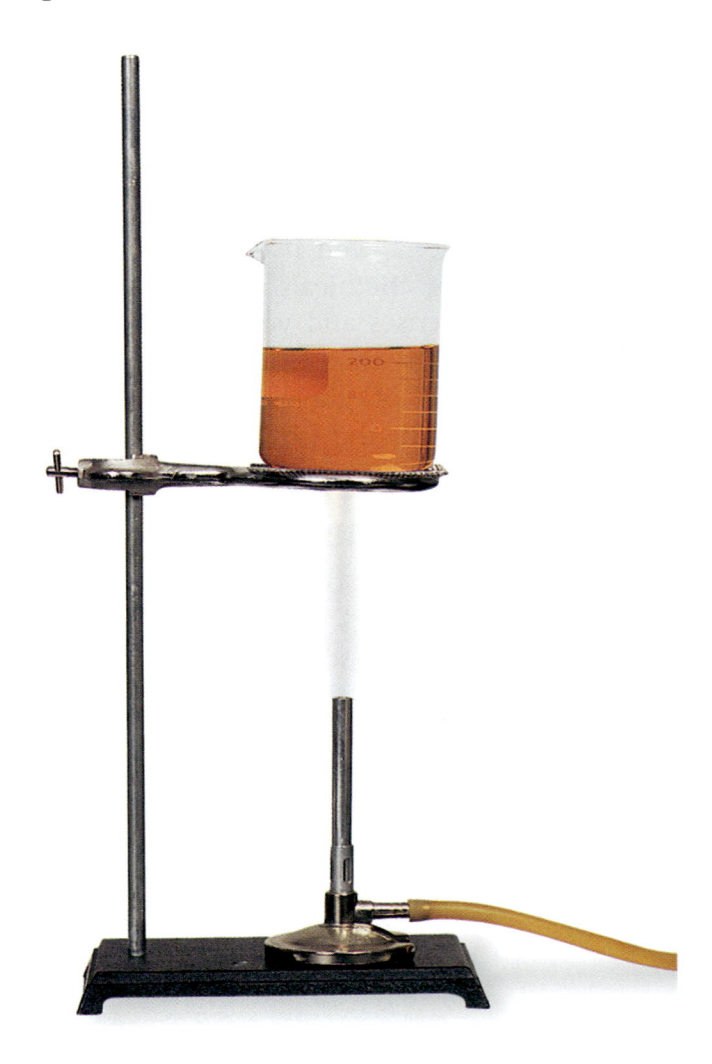

xxviii   Safety First!

Animal Safety

Always obtain your teacher's permission before bringing any animal into the school building. Handle animals only as your teacher directs. Always treat animals carefully and respectfully. Wash your hands thoroughly after handling any animal.

Plant Safety

Do not eat any part of a plant or plant seed used in the laboratory. Wash your hands thoroughly after handling any part of a plant. When in nature, do not pick any wild plants unless your teacher instructs you to do so.

Glassware

Examine all glassware before use. Be sure that glassware is clean and free of chips and cracks. Report damaged glassware to your teacher. Glass containers used for heating should be made of heat-resistant glass.

Safety First!

UNIT 1

TIMELINE

Introduction to Earth Science

In this unit, you will start your own investigation of the planet Earth and of the regions of space beyond it. But first you should prepare yourself by learning about the tools and methods used by Earth scientists. As you can imagine, it is not easy to study something as large as the Earth or as far away as Venus. Yet Earth scientists study these planets and more. The timeline shown here identifies a few of the events that have helped shape our understanding of the Earth.

1669
Nicolaus Steno accurately describes the process by which living organisms become fossils.

1904
Roald Amundsen determines the position of the magnetic north pole.

1922
Roy Chapman Andrews discovers fossilized dinosaur eggs in the Gobi Desert. They are the first such eggs to be found.

fossilized dinosaur eggs in the Gobi Desert

1962
By reaching an altitude of over 95 km, the *X-15* becomes the first fixed-wing plane to reach space.

2 Unit 1

1758
Halley's comet makes a reappearance, which confirms Edmond Halley's 1705 prediction. The comet reappeared 16 years after Halley's death.

1799
The Rosetta stone is discovered in Egypt. It enables scholars to decipher Egyptian hieroglyphics.

1896
The first modern Olympic Games are held in Athens, Greece.

1943
The volcano Paricutín grows more than 200 m tall during its first two weeks of eruption.

Paricutín Volcano

1960
The first weather satellite, *TIROS I*, is launched by the United States.

1970
The first Earth Day is celebrated in the United States on April 22.

1990
The Hubble Space Telescope is launched into orbit. Three years later, faulty optics are repaired during a space walk.

Hubble Space Telescope

1994
China begins construction of Three Gorges Dam, the world's largest dam. Designed to control the Yangtze River, the dam will supply an estimated 84 billion kilowatt-hours of hydroelectric power per year.

2002
A new order of insects—*Mantophasmatodea*—is found both preserved in 45 million-year-old amber and living in southern Africa.

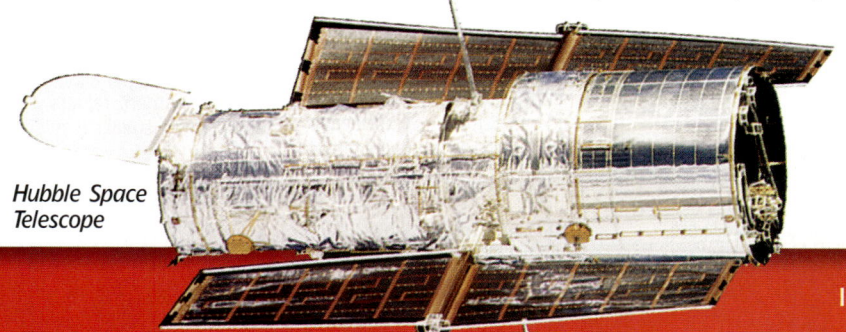

Introduction to Earth Science

1 The World of Earth Science
Chapter Planning Guide

Compression guide: To shorten instruction because of time limitations, omit Section 1.

OBJECTIVES	LABS, DEMONSTRATIONS, AND ACTIVITIES	TECHNOLOGY RESOURCES
PACING • 90 min pp. 4–11 **Chapter Opener**	SE Start-up Activity, p. 5 GENERAL	OSP Parent Letter ■ GENERAL CD Student Edition on CD-ROM CD Guided Reading Audio CD ■ TR Chapter Starter Transparency* VID Brain Food Video Quiz
Section 1 Branches of Earth Science • Describe the four major branches of Earth science. • Identify four examples of Earth science that are linked to other areas of science.	TE Activity Using Prefixes and Suffixes, p. 6 GENERAL SE Quick Lab How Hot is 300°C?, p. 7 GENERAL CRF Datasheet for Quick Lab* TE Connection Activity History, p. 7 GENERAL TE Activity Current Events Scrapbook, p. 8 GENERAL TE Connection Activity Math, p. 9 ADVANCED	CRF Lesson Plans* TR Bellringer Transparency*
PACING • 90 min pp. 12–17 **Section 2 Scientific Methods in Earth Science** • Explain how scientists begin to learn about the natural world. • Explain what scientific methods are and how scientists use them. • Identify the importance of communicating the results of a scientific investigation. • Describe how scientific investigations often lead to new investigations.	TE Connection Activity Language Arts, p. 12 ADVANCED TE Group Activity Solving a Problem, p. 13 GENERAL SE Connection to Oceanography Making Hypotheses, p. 15 GENERAL TE Connection Activity Language Arts, p. 16 GENERAL SE Skills Practice Lab Using Scientific Methods, p. 26 ◆ GENERAL CRF Datasheet for Chapter Lab* LB Whiz-Bang Demonstrations Tubby Terra* GENERAL	CRF Lesson Plans* TR Bellringer Transparency* TR Scientific Methods* SE Internet Activity, p. 14 GENERAL
PACING • 45 min pp. 18–21 **Section 3 Scientific Models** • Explain how models are used in science. • Describe the three types of models. • Identify which types of models are best for certain topics. • Describe the climate model as an example of a mathematical model.	TE Activity Modeling an Airplane, p. 18 GENERAL TE Connection Activity Math, p. 19 ADVANCED SE Connection to Social Studies The Spread of Disease, p. 20 GENERAL SE Science in Action Math, Social Studies, and Language Arts Activities, pp. 32–33	CRF Lesson Plans* TR Bellringer Transparency* CRF SciLinks Activity* GENERAL
PACING • 45 min pp. 22–25 **Section 4 Measurement and Safety** • Explain the importance of the International System of Units. • Determine appropriate units to use for particular measurements. • Identify lab safety symbols, and determine what they mean.	SE School-to-Home Activity Taking Measurements, p. 23 GENERAL TE Connection Activity Math, p. 23 GENERAL TE Activity SI Note Cards, p. 23 BASIC LB Long-Term Projects & Research Ideas How Big Is the Earth?* ADVANCED	CRF Lesson Plans* TR Bellringer Transparency* TR Common SI Units* TR **LINK TO PHYSICAL SCIENCE** Differences Between Mass and Weight

PACING • 90 min

CHAPTER REVIEW, ASSESSMENT, AND STANDARDIZED TEST PREPARATION

CRF Vocabulary Activity* GENERAL
SE Chapter Review, pp. 28–29 GENERAL
CRF Chapter Review* ■ GENERAL
CRF Chapter Tests A* ■ GENERAL, B* ADVANCED, C* SPECIAL NEEDS
SE Standardized Test Preparation, pp. 30–31 GENERAL
CRF Standardized Test Preparation* GENERAL
CRF Performance-Based Assessment* GENERAL
OSP Test Generator GENERAL
CRF Test Item Listing* GENERAL

Online and Technology Resources

go.hrw.com
Visit **go.hrw.com** for a variety of free resources related to this textbook. Enter the keyword **HZ5WES**.

Holt Online Learning
Students can access interactive problem-solving help and active visual concept development with the *Holt Science and Technology* Online Edition available at **www.hrw.com**.

Guided Reading Audio CD
Also in Spanish
A direct reading of each chapter for auditory learners, reluctant readers, and Spanish-speaking students.

Science Tutor CD-ROM
Excellent for remediation and test practice.

Chapter 1 • The World of Earth Science

KEY

SE Student Edition	**CRF** Chapter Resource File	**SS** Science Skills Worksheets
TE Teacher Edition	**OSP** One-Stop Planner	**MS** Math Skills for Science Worksheets
	LB Lab Bank	**CD** CD or CD-ROM
	TR Transparencies	**VID** Classroom Video/DVD

* Also on One-Stop Planner
♦ Requires advance prep
■ Also available in Spanish

SKILLS DEVELOPMENT RESOURCES	SECTION REVIEW AND ASSESSMENT	STANDARDS CORRELATIONS
SE Pre-Reading Activity, p. 4 GENERAL **OSP** Science Puzzlers, Twisters & Teasers* GENERAL		National Science Education Standards SAI 1; HNS 2
CRF Directed Reading A* ■, BASIC, B* SPECIAL NEEDS **CRF** Vocabulary and Section Summary* ■ GENERAL **SE** Reading Strategy Discussion, p. 6 GENERAL **SE** Math Practice Lots of Zeros!, p. 9 GENERAL **TE** Inclusion Strategies, p. 10 ♦ **MS** Math Skills for Science Counting the Zeros* GENERAL **MS** Math Skills for Science What is Scientific Notation?* GENERAL **CRF** Reinforcement Worksheet Scenes from the Earth* BASIC	**SE** Reading Checks, pp. 7, 9, 11 GENERAL **TE** Homework, p. 8 GENERAL **TE** Homework, p. 9 GENERAL **TE** Reteaching, p. 10 BASIC **TE** Quiz, p. 10 GENERAL **TE** Alternative Assessment, p. 10 GENERAL **SE** Section Review,* p. 11 ■ GENERAL **CRF** Section Quiz* ■ GENERAL	SAI 1; ST 2; SPSP 3, 4; HNS 1
CRF Directed Reading A* ■ BASIC, B* SPECIAL NEEDS **CRF** Vocabulary and Section Summary* ■ GENERAL **SE** Reading Strategy Mnemonics, p. 12 GENERAL **SE** Math Practice Earth Shaker!, p. 16 GENERAL **CRF** Critical Thinking Kryptonite!* ADVANCED	**SE** Reading Checks, pp. 12, 15, 16 GENERAL **TE** Homework, p. 15 BASIC **TE** Reteaching, p. 16 BASIC **TE** Quiz, p. 16 GENERAL **TE** Alternative Assessment, p. 16 GENERAL **SE** Section Review,* p. 17 ■ GENERAL **CRF** Section Quiz* ■ GENERAL	SAI 1, 2; ST 1; HNS 2; *Chapter Lab:* UCP 2; SAI 1; ST 2
CRF Directed Reading A* ■ BASIC, B* SPECIAL NEEDS **CRF** Vocabulary and Section Summary* ■ GENERAL **SE** Reading Strategy Reading Organizer, p. 18 GENERAL **MS** Math Skills for Science Using Proportions and Cross-Multiplication* GENERAL **SS** Science Skills Measuring* GENERAL	**SE** Reading Checks, pp. 19, 21 GENERAL **TE** Homework, p. 19 GENERAL **TE** Reteaching, p. 20 BASIC **TE** Quiz, p. 20 GENERAL **TE** Alternative Assessment, p. 20 GENERAL **SE** Section Review,* p. 21 ■ GENERAL **CRF** Section Quiz* ■ GENERAL	UCP 2; SAI 1; ST 1; SPSP 3, 4; HNS 2; ES 1a
CRF Directed Reading A* ■ BASIC, B* SPECIAL NEEDS **CRF** Vocabulary and Section Summary* ■ GENERAL **SE** Reading Strategy Reading Organizer, p. 22 GENERAL **SE** Math Focus Finding Area, p. 24 GENERAL **TE** Inclusion Strategies, p. 24 ♦ **MS** Math Skills for Science What Is SI?* GENERAL **SS** Science Skills Safety Rules!* GENERAL	**SE** Reading Checks, pp. 22, 25 GENERAL **TE** Reteaching, p. 24 BASIC **TE** Quiz, p. 24 GENERAL **TE** Alternative Assessment, p. 24 GENERAL **SE** Section Review,* p. 25 ■ GENERAL **TE** Homework, p. 25 GENERAL **CRF** Section Quiz* ■ GENERAL	UCP 3; SAI 1; SPSP 1; HNS 3

One-Stop Planner® CD-ROM

This convenient CD-ROM includes:
- Lab Materials QuickList Software
- Holt Calendar Planner
- Customizable Lesson Plans
- Printable Worksheets
- ExamView® Test Generator

CNN Student News

cnnstudentnews.com

Find the latest news, lesson plans, and activities related to important scientific events.

SciLinks NSTA

www.scilinks.org

Maintained by the **National Science Teachers Association**. See Chapter Enrichment pages for a complete list of topics.

Current Science®

Check out *Current Science* articles and activities by visiting the HRW Web site at **go.hrw.com**. Just type in the keyword **HZ5CS01T**.

Classroom Videos

- **Lab Videos** demonstrate the chapter lab.
- **Brain Food Video Quizzes** help students review the chapter material.
- **CNN Videos** bring science into your students' daily life.

Chapter 1 • Chapter Planning Guide

Chapter 1 Chapter Resources

Visual Resources

- **CHAPTER STARTER TRANSPARENCY**
- **BELLRINGER TRANSPARENCIES**
- **TEACHING TRANSPARENCIES**
- **TEACHING TRANSPARENCIES**
- **CONCEPT MAPPING TRANSPARENCY**

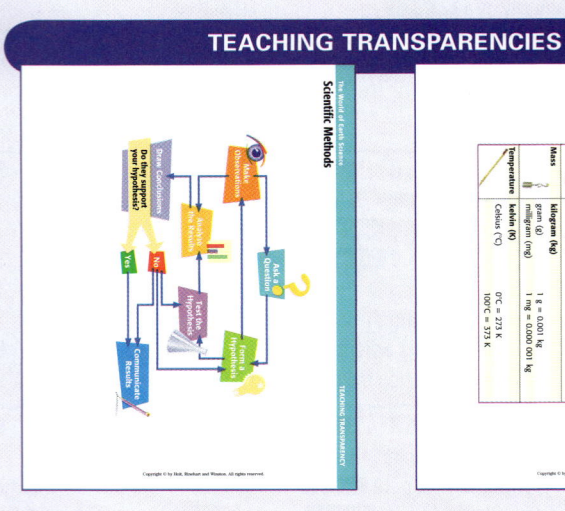

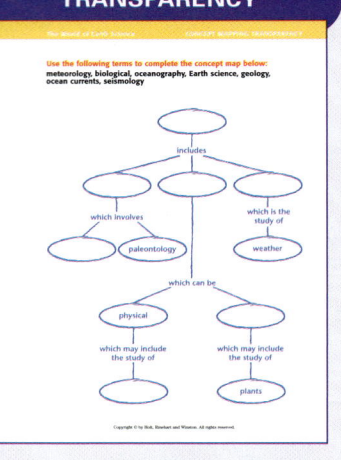

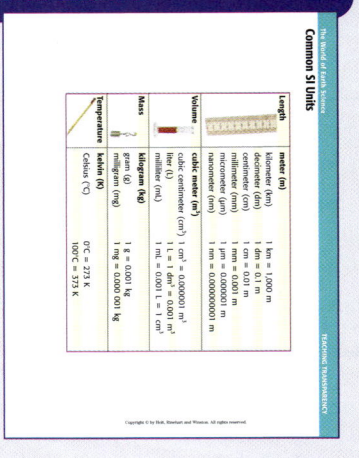

Planning Resources

- **LESSON PLANS**
- **PARENT LETTER**
- **TEST ITEM LISTING**

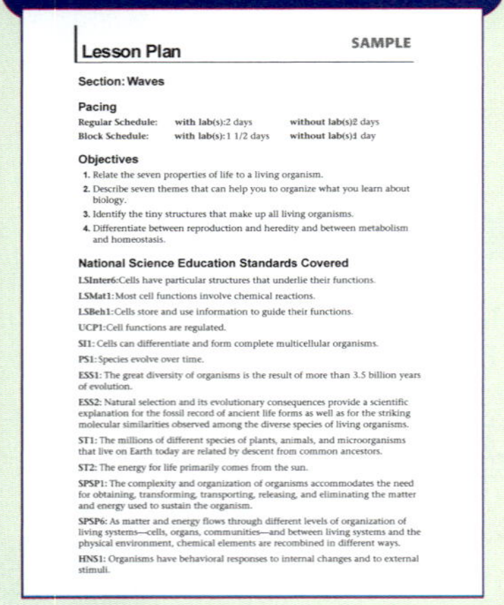

One-Stop Planner® CD-ROM

This CD-ROM includes all of the resources shown here and the following time-saving tools:

- Lab Materials QuickList Software
- Customizable lesson plans
- Holt Calendar Planner
- The powerful ExamView® Test Generator

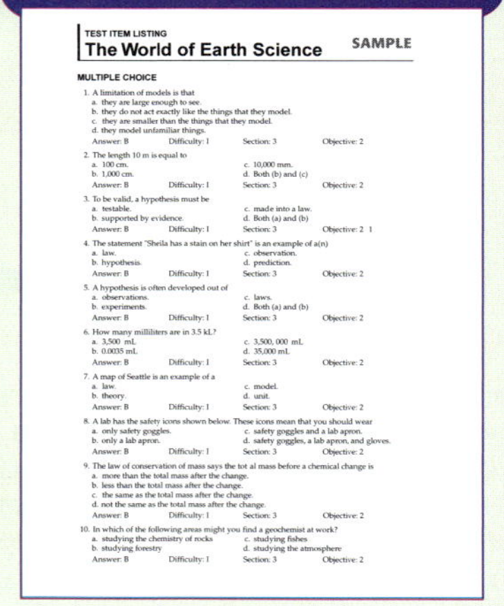

3C Chapter 1 • The World of Earth Science

For a preview of available worksheets covering math and science skills, see pages T26–T33. All of these resources are also on the One-Stop Planner®.

Meeting Individual Needs

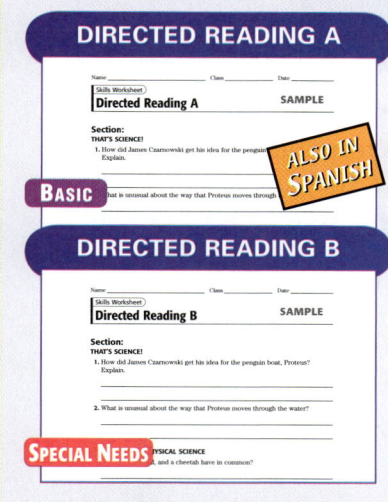

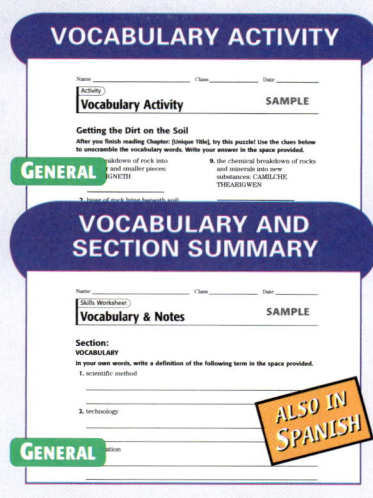

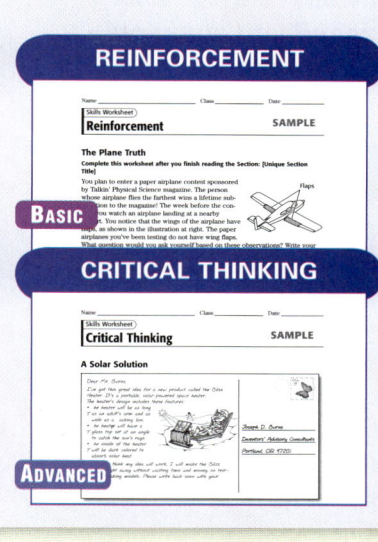

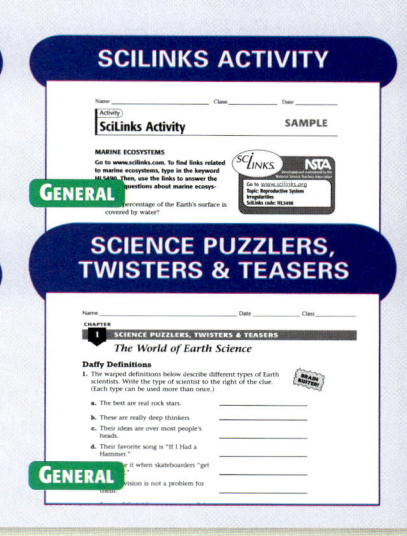

- **DIRECTED READING A** — Basic (Also in Spanish)
- **DIRECTED READING B** — Special Needs
- **VOCABULARY ACTIVITY** — General
- **VOCABULARY AND SECTION SUMMARY** — General (Also in Spanish)
- **REINFORCEMENT** — Basic
- **CRITICAL THINKING** — Advanced
- **SCILINKS ACTIVITY** — General
- **SCIENCE PUZZLERS, TWISTERS & TEASERS** — General

Labs and Activities

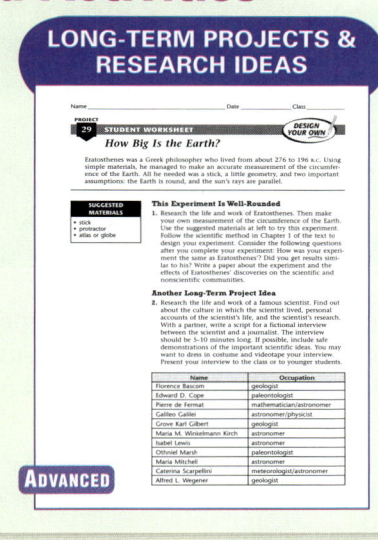

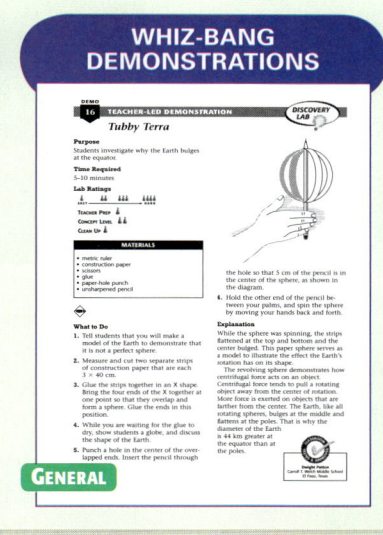

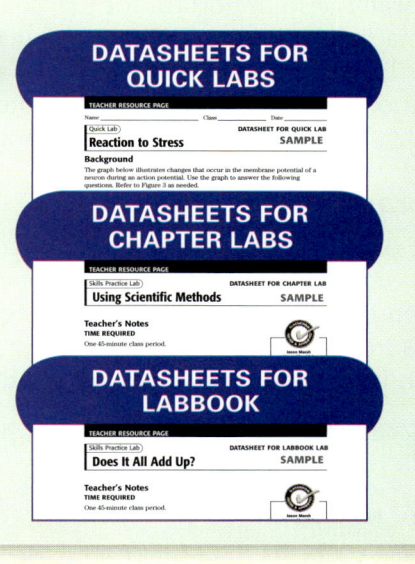

- **LONG-TERM PROJECTS & RESEARCH IDEAS** — Advanced
- **WHIZ-BANG DEMONSTRATIONS** — General
- **DATASHEETS FOR QUICK LABS**
- **DATASHEETS FOR CHAPTER LABS**
- **DATASHEETS FOR LABBOOK**

Review and Assessments

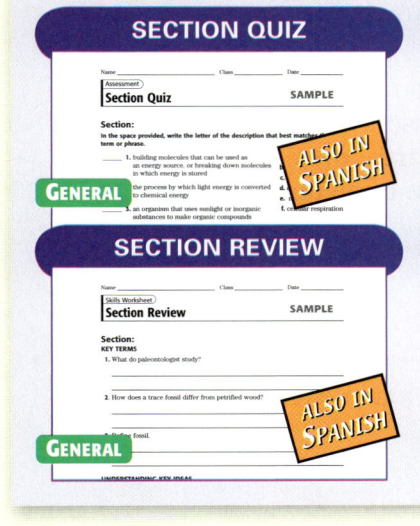

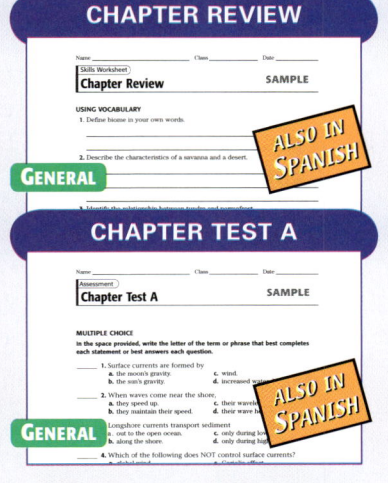

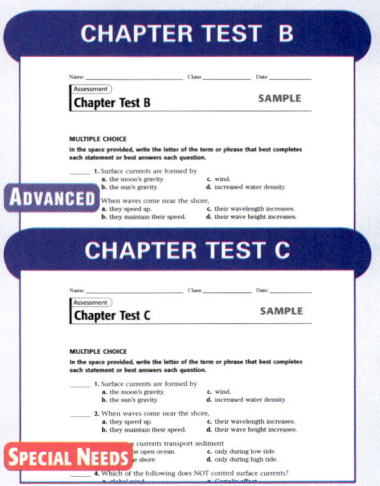

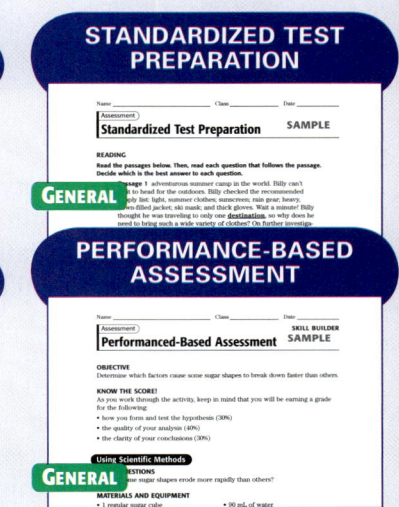

- **SECTION QUIZ** — General (Also in Spanish)
- **SECTION REVIEW** — General (Also in Spanish)
- **CHAPTER REVIEW** — General (Also in Spanish)
- **CHAPTER TEST A** — General (Also in Spanish)
- **CHAPTER TEST B** — Advanced
- **CHAPTER TEST C** — Special Needs
- **STANDARDIZED TEST PREPARATION** — General
- **PERFORMANCE-BASED ASSESSMENT** — General

Chapter 1 • Chapter Resources   3D

1 Chapter Enrichment

This Chapter Enrichment provides relevant and interesting information to expand and enhance your presentation of the chapter material.

Section 1

Branches of Earth Science

Volcanology and Seismology
- Seismology and volcanology are separate branches of Earth science but often are studied together under the heading of geology. Earthquakes and volcanic activity are often connected. Earthquakes may give clues to impending eruptions, and movements of magma sometimes produce tremors.

Hydrology
- Because water is so important for life, society, and industry, a special branch of Earth science is devoted to water. There are many regional, state, and federal organizations involved in evaluating water quantity and quality and in delivering water to society.

Oceanography
- Research organizations and industrial firms interested in the ocean employ many oceanographers. These scientists must have at least a bachelor's degree with emphasis in geology, physics, chemistry, and biology. Most also have some specialized postgraduate training.

Meteorology and Doppler Radar
- The National Weather Service has greatly improved the quality and reliability of forecasting with the use of Doppler weather surveillance radar. The radar bounces an electromagnetic signal off particles of water, ice, or dust in the atmosphere and measures the time that the signal takes to return. If objects are moving, their speed can be determined by analyzing variations in the signal. Doppler technology can calculate both the direction and speed of severe storms. It also can identify the conditions leading to severe weather.

Section 2

Scientific Methods in Earth Science

Cooperation Between the Sciences
- Before David Gillette and his team broke ground on their historic *Seismosaurus* dig, they used exhaustive high-tech sensing and mapping technology to locate the best places to dig. Gillette's team was helped by the technology and expertise of the Los Alamos National Laboratory in New Mexico. The Los Alamos technology was developed for use in other fields of science, but paleontologists and physicists cooperated to make Gillette's dig a success.

- The ground-penetrating radar that helped paleontologists locate the bones of *Seismosaurus* was originally developed to locate 55 gal drums of hazardous waste beneath the soil.
- Magnetometry helped scientists identify the subtle variations in Earth's magnetic field that could be caused by buried bone.
- Radiation detectors measured radiation levels below the surface. Dinosaur bone can have as much as 100,000 times the uranium content of the surrounding rock.
- The underground location of the dinosaur bones was mapped by using seismic waves. First, a shotgun was fired into the Earth; then, the time that the waves took to reach a receiving station was recorded.

Is That a Fact!
◆ A dowser also visited the *Seismosaurus* dig site and tried his hand with a more traditional version of remote sensing.

Chapter 1 • The World of Earth Science

> For background information about teaching strategies and issues, refer to the *Professional Reference for Teachers*.

Section 3
Scientific Models

Revising the Model of the Solar System

- Ptolemy (second century CE) is credited with developing the solar system model in which Earth is at the center. The sun, moon, and five visible planets moved around Earth in circular orbits. This model worked so well that astronomers used it to predict the positions of the known planets for many centuries.

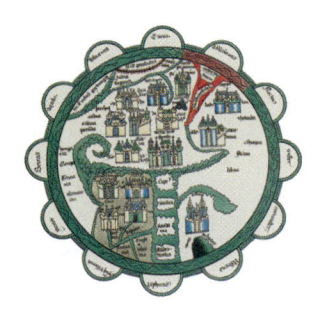

- Nicolaus Copernicus (1473–1543) challenged Ptolemy's theory that Earth was the center of the solar system and developed a model in which the sun was at the center. In this model, only the moon orbited Earth. Copernicus first presented his theory to friends in 1513. Only 30 years later, at the very end of his life, did Copernicus publish his complete theory.

Is That a Fact!
◆ Although Copernicus's model made it easier to explain the observed changes in the positions of the sun, moon, and planets, many people resisted the idea that the model represented. They would not believe that Earth was not the center of *everything*.

Early Flying Models

- Some of the earliest pioneers in flight attempted to model the flight of birds. In the 13th century, Roger Bacon (c. 1220–1292) suggested that people could use wings like those of birds to fly. Two hundred years later, following Bacon's suggestions, Leonardo da Vinci (1452–1519) drew plans for a craft that had flapping wings and that would be operated by hand. The machine was referred to as an *ornithopter*. No one ever developed a successful ornithopter.

- The first successful glider flight was made in 1855 by Jean-Marie le Bris. The glider that he designed was inspired by the albatross, a bird capable of soaring over the ocean for many hours without flapping its wings.

Section 4
Measurement and Safety

Early Systems of Measurement

- For many centuries, measurement was based on the human body. Egyptians defined a cubit as the distance between the elbow and the tip of the middle finger. A yard was the distance from the nose to the middle fingertip of an extended arm. The standard yard, still used today, was based on a measurement established by England's King Henry I (1068–1135).

The International System of Units

- In 1840, the metric system was established as the legal system of measurement in France. In 1960, the International System of Units, which is based almost entirely on the metric system, was adopted by the General Conference on Weights and Measures.

SciLinks is maintained by the National Science Teachers Association to provide you and your students with interesting, up-to-date links that will enrich your classroom presentation of the chapter.

Visit www.scilinks.org and enter the SciLinks code for more information about the topic listed.

Topic: Branches of Earth Science
SciLinks code: HSM0191

Topic: Using Models
SciLinks code: HSM1588

Topic: Scientific Methods
SciLinks code: HSM1359

Topic: Systems of Measurement
SciLinks code: HSM1490

Chapter 1 • Chapter Enrichment **3F**

Overview

This chapter introduces Earth science. Students learn about the branches of Earth science, and careers available in Earth science. Then, students explore scientific methods and follow David Gillette's discovery of *Seismosaurus*. Students also learn about the use of models in Earth science. The chapter concludes with a discussion of measurement and safety.

Assessing Prior Knowledge

Students should be familiar with the following topics:
- measurement
- basic math skills

Identifying Misconceptions

Students may think of laboratories, bubbling test tubes, flashing screens, and white coats when they hear the word *experiment*. However, in Earth science, the laboratory is often outdoors. Often, Earth-science phenomena cannot be observed under controlled conditions—you can't make a volcano erupt at will. In these cases, scientists make many observations and use statistics and long-term records to predict when an event, such as an eruption, will occur.

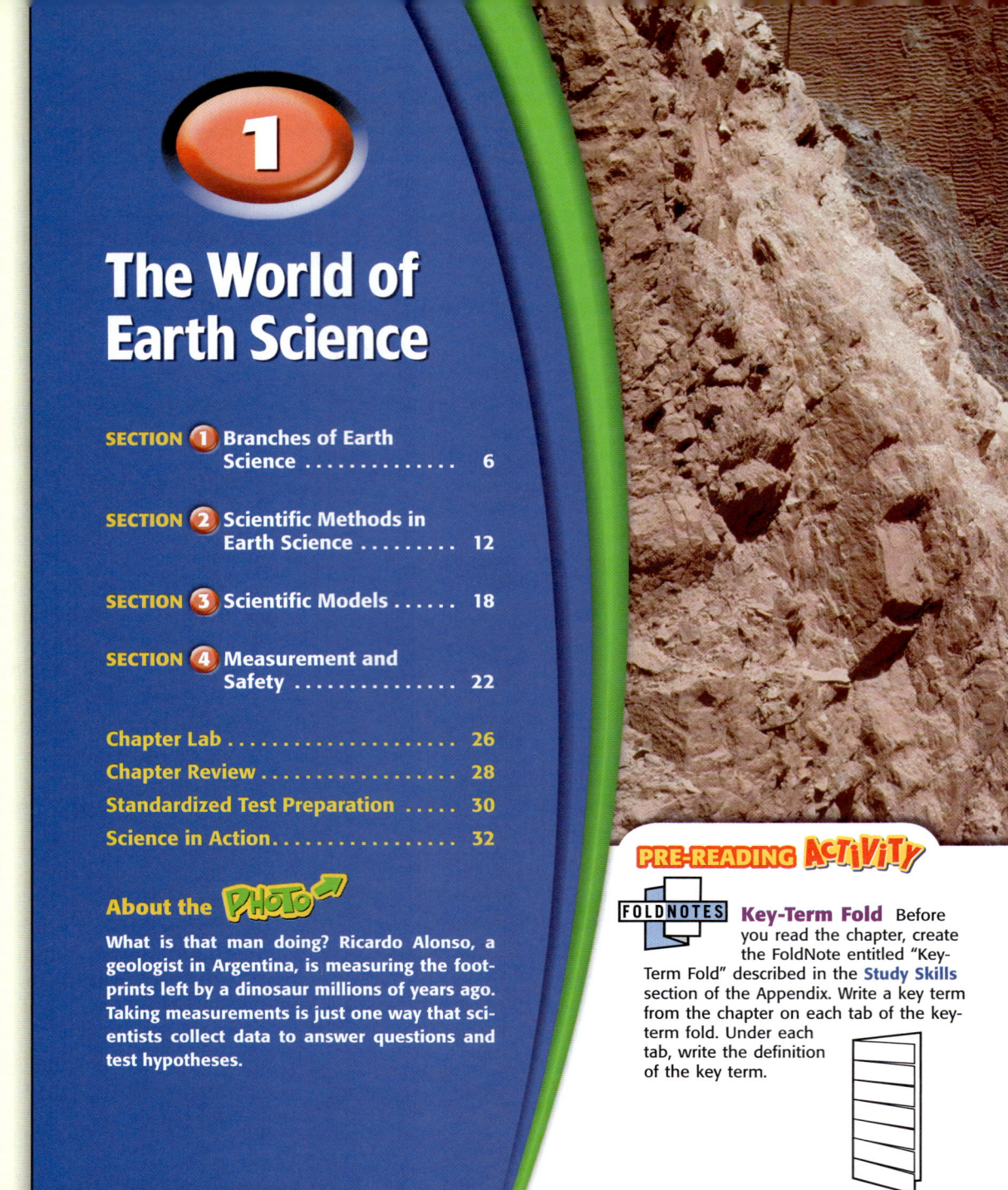

The World of Earth Science

SECTION 1 Branches of Earth Science 6

SECTION 2 Scientific Methods in Earth Science 12

SECTION 3 Scientific Models 18

SECTION 4 Measurement and Safety 22

Chapter Lab 26
Chapter Review 28
Standardized Test Preparation 30
Science in Action................ 32

About the PHOTO

What is that man doing? Ricardo Alonso, a geologist in Argentina, is measuring the footprints left by a dinosaur millions of years ago. Taking measurements is just one way that scientists collect data to answer questions and test hypotheses.

PRE-READING ACTIVITY

FOLDNOTES **Key-Term Fold** Before you read the chapter, create the FoldNote entitled "Key-Term Fold" described in the **Study Skills** section of the Appendix. Write a key term from the chapter on each tab of the key-term fold. Under each tab, write the definition of the key term.

Standards Correlations

National Science Education Standards

The following codes indicate the National Science Education Standards that correlate to this chapter. The full text of the standards are at the front of the book.

Chapter Opener
HNS 2; SAI 1

Section 1 Branches of Earth Science
SAI 1; ST 2; SPSP 3, 4; HNS 1

Section 2 Scientific Methods in Earth Science
SAI 1, 2; HNS 2

Section 3 Scientific Models
UCP 2; SAI 1; SPSP 3, 4; HNS 2; ES 1a

Section 4 Measurement and Safety
UCP 3; SAI 1; SPSP 1; HNS 3

Chapter Lab
UCP 2; SAI 1; ST 2

START-UP ACTIVITY

MATERIALS

For Each Pair of Students
- index card, 3 × 5

Safety Caution: If students need a hint, suggest that they consider using a combination of folds and tears to accomplish their task. (The solution is to fold the card in half lengthwise. Students should tear or cut a slit along the fold that does not quite reach either end of the card. Then students should carefully make very thin tears or cuts perpendicular to the original tear or cut. These tears or cuts should alternate direction as shown below.)

Answers

1. Answers may vary. Students should indicate that developing a plan helped them cooperate and be more efficient.
2. Answers may vary. Students may indicate that testing the plan was similar to testing a scientific hypothesis.
3. Answers may vary. Students should indicate that communication helped the class determine the solution to the problem.

START-UP ACTIVITY

Mission Impossible?

In this activity, you will do some creative thinking to solve what might seem like an impossible problem.

Procedure

1. Examine an **index card.** Your mission is to fit yourself through the card. You can only tear and fold the card. You cannot use tape, glue, or anything else to hold the card together.
2. Brainstorm with a partner ways to complete your mission. Then, record your plan.
3. Test your plan. Did it work? If necessary, get **another index card** and try again. Record your new plan and the results.
4. Share your plans and results with your classmates.

Analysis

1. Why was it helpful to come up with a plan in advance?
2. How did testing your plan help you complete your mission?
3. How did sharing your ideas with your classmates help you complete your mission? What did your classmates do differently?

Chapter Review
UCP 2, 3; SAI 2; SPSP 3, 4

Science in Action
UCP 5; ST 2; SPSP 5; HNS 1; ES 1i, 2b

Chapter Starter Transparency
Use this transparency to help students begin thinking about the role of serendipity in scientific discoveries.

CHAPTER RESOURCES

Technology
- **Transparencies**
  - Chapter Starter Transparency **READING SKILLS**
- **Student Edition on CD-ROM**
- **Guided Reading Audio CD**
  - English or Spanish
- **Classroom Videos**
  - Brain Food Video Quiz

Workbooks
- **Science Puzzlers, Twisters & Teasers**
  - The World of Earth Science **GENERAL**

Chapter 1 • The World of Earth Science   5

SECTION 1

Focus

Overview
This section explores the branches of Earth science. It examines the fields of geology, oceanography, meteorology, astronomy, environmental science, ecology, geochemistry, geography, and cartography.

🔔 Bellringer
Tell students the following: "Imagine that you are an Earth scientist and can travel wherever you want to on Earth. Describe the aspects or features of Earth that you would like to study. Explain where you would go and what you would do." Have students write and illustrate their answers in their **science journal.**

Motivate

ACTIVITY — GENERAL

Using Prefixes and Suffixes
Have students use dictionaries to determine the meaning of the following prefixes: *geo-, volcan-, paleo-, meteor-, ocean-,* and *astro-*. Ask students to build scientists' names by adding suffixes such as *-nomer, -ologist,* and *-ographer.* Have students describe what they think each scientist does. **English Language Learners**
LS Verbal

SECTION 1

READING WARM-UP

Objectives
- Describe the four major branches of Earth science.
- Identify four examples of Earth science that are linked to other areas of science.

Terms to Learn
geology
oceanography
meteorology
astronomy

READING STRATEGY

Discussion Read this section silently. Write down questions that you have about this section. Discuss your questions in a small group.

geology the study of the origin, history, and structure of the Earth and the processes that shape the Earth

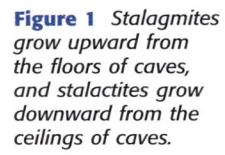

Figure 1 *Stalagmites grow upward from the floors of caves, and stalactites grow downward from the ceilings of caves.*

CHAPTER RESOURCES

Chapter Resource File
- Lesson Plan
- Directed Reading A BASIC
- Directed Reading B SPECIAL NEEDS

Technology
- Transparencies
  - Bellringer

Workbooks
- Science Skills
  - Reading a Science Textbook GENERAL

Branches of Earth Science

Planet Earth! How can anyone study something as large and complicated as our planet?

One way is to divide the study of the Earth into smaller areas of study. In this section, you will learn about some of the most common areas of study. You will also learn about some of the people that work within these areas.

Geology—Science That Rocks

The study of the origin, history, and structure of the Earth and the processes that shape the Earth is called **geology.** Everything that has to do with the solid Earth is part of geology.

Most geologists specialize in a particular aspect of the Earth. For example, a *volcanologist* is a geologist who studies volcanoes. Are earthquakes more to your liking? Then, you could be a *seismologist,* a geologist who studies earthquakes. How about digging up dinosaurs? You could be a *paleontologist,* a geologist who studies fossils. These are only a few of the careers you could have as a geologist.

Some geologists become highly specialized. For example, geologist Robert Fronk, at the Florida Institute of Technology, explores the subsurface of Earth by scuba diving in underwater caves in Florida and the Bahamas. Underwater caves often contain evidence that sea level was once much lower than it is now. The underwater caves shown in **Figure 1** contain *stalagmites* and *stalactites.* These formations develop from minerals in water that drips in air-filled caves. When Fronk sees these kinds of geologic formations in underwater caves, he knows that the caves were once above sea level.

Is That a Fact!

Earth is estimated to be 4.6 billion years old. It travels around the sun at 29.79 km/s (18.5 mi/s). Earth is not round; it is an oblate spheroid—flattened at the poles and bulging at the equator.

---

6 Chapter 1 • The World of Earth Science

Oceanography—Water, Water Everywhere

The scientific study of the sea is called **oceanography**. Special areas of oceanography include physical oceanography, biological oceanography, geological oceanography, and chemical oceanography. Physical oceanographers study physical features of the ocean such as waves and currents to see how they affect weather patterns and aquatic life. Biological oceanographers study the plants and animals that live in the ocean. Geological oceanographers study and explore the ocean floor for clues to the Earth's history. Chemical oceanographers study amounts and distributions of natural and human-made chemicals in the ocean.

Reading Check Describe four special areas of oceanography. *(See the Appendix for answers to Reading Checks.)*

oceanography the scientific study of the sea

Exploring the Ocean Floor

Not long ago, people studied the ocean only from the surface. But as technology has advanced, scientists have worked with engineers to build miniature research submarines to go practically anywhere in the oceans.

John Trefry is an oceanographer who studies the ocean floor in a minisub called *Alvin*. Using the *Alvin*, Trefry can travel 2.4 km below the surface of the ocean. At this depth, Trefry can explore an interesting new world. One of the most exciting sights Trefry has seen is a black smoker. As shown in **Figure 2**, *black smokers* are rock chimneys on the ocean floor that spew black clouds of minerals. Black smokers are a kind of *hydrothermal vent*, which is a crack in the ocean floor that releases very hot water from beneath the Earth's surface. The minerals and hot water from these vents support a beautiful and exotic biological community. The aquatic life includes blood-red tube worms that are 3.5 m long, clams that are 30 cm in diameter, and blind white crabs.

Quick Lab

How Hot Is 300°C?

1. Use a **thermometer** to measure the air temperature in the room in degrees Celsius. Record your reading.
2. Hold the thermometer near a **heat source** in the room, such as a light bulb or a heating vent. Be careful not to burn yourself. Record your reading.
3. How do the temperatures you recorded compare with the 300°C temperature of the water from a black smoker?

Figure 2 Black smokers, such as this one seen through the window of *Alvin*, can reach temperatures up to 300°C!

CONNECTION ACTIVITY
History — GENERAL

Earth Scientists Help students research the lives and contributions of the following Earth or space scientists:

- Hipparchus (developed the first system for identifying stars)
- James Hutton (father of modern geology)
- Galileo Galilei (refined the scientific method and studied astronomy)
- Inge Lehman (discovered the Earth's inner core)
- Robert Goddard (advanced rocket science)
- Johannes Kepler (discovered elliptical orbits in the solar system)
- Marie Curie (studied radioactive decay)
- George E. Hale (developed the Hale reflecting telescope)
- Florence Bascom (a distinguished American geologist)

Intrapersonal

Teach

Discussion — GENERAL

What Kind of Ologist? Invite students to speculate about what kind of scientist might answer each of the following questions. Discuss ways that scientists find answers to these questions.

- How can you tell when a volcano is going to erupt? (volcanologist)
- What life-forms dwell on the ocean floor, 9.5 km below the ocean surface? (biological oceanographer)
- Is Earth's atmosphere becoming warmer? If so, how will humans be affected? (climatologist or meteorologist)
- Are there deposits of oil, gas, gold, and silver still undiscovered in Earth's crust? How can they be reached? (geologist)
- How many stars are there? Is there life on other planets? (astronomer)

Have students add their own questions to the discussion.
Verbal

Answer to Quick Lab

3. Answers may vary, but students should recognize that the temperature of the water around a black smoker is much hotter than the temperatures that they measured. Encourage students to speculate how the water temperature around a black smoker can be 200°C above the boiling point of water at sea level. Students might conclude that the tremendous pressure at that depth raises the boiling point of water.

Answer to Reading Check

Four areas of oceanography are physical oceanography, biological oceanography, geological oceanography, and chemical oceanography.

Section 1 • Branches of Earth Science

Teach, continued

Cultural Awareness — GENERAL

Studying Animal Behavior to Predict Weather Cultures all over the world observe animal behavior to predict the weather. Chinese farmers use this formula: If frogs croak on a fine day, it will rain in two days. If frogs croak after rain, there will be fine weather. Rain will continue if frogs do not croak after many overcast days. Other cultures observe insect behavior: It will rain if ants travel in a straight line; it will be clear if the ants are scattered. Students may be surprised to learn that counting cricket chirps is an accurate way to measure ambient temperature. Have students find out how other cultures observe animal behavior to predict the weather, and have students use these methods for one week. **LS Intrapersonal**

ACTiViTY — GENERAL

Current Events Scrapbook Have students create an Earth Science Current Events scrapbook. Encourage students to be creative as they incorporate articles, illustrations, photographs, and original entries. The book can be organized by category in a three-ring binder, and students can add pages throughout the school year. **English Language Learners** **LS Kinesthetic**

Figure 3 *This image, made from several satellite photos, traces Hurricane Andrew's path at three locations from the Atlantic Ocean (right) to the Gulf of Mexico (left).*

meteorology the scientific study of the Earth's atmosphere, especially in relation to weather and climate

Figure 4 *These meteorologists are risking their lives to gather data about tornadoes.*

Is That a Fact!

Earth has some extreme temperatures. A world-record high temperature of 58°C (136°F) was recorded in El Azizia, Libya, in 1922. In Vostok, Antarctica, a world-record low temperature of −89°C (−128.2°F) was recorded in 1983.

Meteorology—It's a Gas!

The study of the Earth's atmosphere, especially in relation to weather and climate, is called **meteorology**. When you ask, "Is it going to rain today?" you are asking a meteorological question. One of the most common careers in meteorology is weather forecasting. Sometimes, knowing what the weather will be like makes our lives more comfortable. Sometimes, our lives depend on these forecasts.

Hurricanes

In 1928, a major hurricane hit Florida and killed 1,836 people. In contrast, a hurricane of similar strength—Hurricane Andrew, shown in **Figure 3**—hit Florida in 1992 and killed 48 people. Why were there far fewer deaths in 1992? Two major reasons were hurricane tracking and weather forecasting.

Meteorologists began tracking Hurricane Andrew on Monday, August 17, 1992. By the following Sunday morning, most people in southern Florida had left the coast. The National Hurricane Center had warned them that Andrew was headed their way. The hurricane caused a lot of damage. However, it killed very few people, thanks to meteorologists' warnings.

Tornadoes

An average of 780 tornadoes touch down each year in the United States. What do you think about a meteorologist who chases tornadoes as a career? Howard Bluestein does just that. He predicts where tornadoes are likely to form. He then drives to within a couple of kilometers of the site to gather data, as shown in **Figure 4**. By gathering data this way, scientists such as Bluestein hope to understand tornadoes better. The better scientists understand tornadoes, the better scientists can predict how tornadoes will behave.

Homework — GENERAL

A Day in the Life Ask students to imagine an exciting day in the life of an astronomer, a volcanologist, a meteorologist, or an oceanographer. Have students write a **science journal** entry from the perspective of the scientist describing what happened to make the day exciting and why the scientist enjoys his or her job. **LS Intrapersonal**

---

8 Chapter 1 • The World of Earth Science

Astronomy—Far, Far Away

How do you study things that are beyond Earth? Astronomers can answer this question. **Astronomy** is the study of the universe. Astronomers study stars, asteroids, planets, and everything else in space.

Because most things in space are too far away to study directly, astronomers depend on technology to help them study objects in space. Optical telescopes are one way astronomers study objects in space. Optical telescopes have been used for hundreds of years. Galileo built an optical telescope in 1609. But optical telescopes are not the only kind of telescope astronomers use.

Optical telescopes need light to see objects, such as planets and comets. However, some objects do not give off light or are too far away to be seen with an optical telescope. Instead of detecting the visible light waves, radio telescopes, such as the one in **Figure 5,** detect radio waves. Radio waves are not visible like light waves are, but data from radio waves form patterns. From these patterns, astronomers can make images to learn more about the objects in space.

astronomy the study of the universe

Star Struck

Astronomers spend much of their time studying stars. Astronomers estimate that there are more than 100 billion billion stars—that is a lot of stars! The most familiar star in the universe is the sun. The sun is the closest star to the Earth. For this reason, astronomers have studied the sun more than other stars.

✓ **Reading Check** What do astronomers study?

Figure 5 Radio telescopes receive radio waves from objects in space.

MATH PRACTICE

Lots of Zeros!
Astronomers estimate that there are more than 100 billion billion stars! One billion written out in numerals looks like this: 1,000,000,000.

How many zeros do you need in order to write 100 billion billion in numerals? To find out, multiply 1 billion by 1 billion, and then multiply your answer by 100. Count the zeros in the final answer.

Now, time how long it takes you to count to 100. How long would it take you to count to 100 a billion billion times?

Answer to Reading Check
Astronomers study stars, asteroids, planets, and everything else in space.

CHAPTER RESOURCES
Workbooks
Math Skills for Science
• Counting the Zeros GENERAL
• What Is Scientific Notation? GENERAL

CONNECTION ACTIVITY
Math — ADVANCED

Scientific Notation Explain that space science involves measuring extremely large distances. To express these enormous numbers, scientists use *scientific notation,* or powers of 10. Write the following on the board:

$$10 = 10^1$$
$$100 = 10^2$$
$$1,000 = 10^3$$

Have students continue the table and explain the pattern. Ask students to express the following numbers in scientific notation:

1. 10,000°C (1.0×10^{4}°C)
2. 1,497,000 km (1.497×10^6 km)
3. 4,600,000,000 years (4.6×10^9 years)

LS Logical

Answer to Math Practice
20 zeros; Answers may vary, but if one number per second is counted, it will take 1.0×10^{20} seconds, or more than 3 trillion years, to count to 100 a billion, billion times! The universe is thought to be only about 13.7 billion years old.

Homework — GENERAL

Finding Out About Telescopes
Ask students to research a type of telescope and share their findings with the class. Students could research optical telescopes, liquid mirror telescopes, X-ray telescopes, gamma ray telescopes, or radio telescopes. Have students draw the telescope and show its working parts. Ask students to write a brief explanation of how the telescope works and how it is used. **LS** Visual

Section 1 • Branches of Earth Science 9

Close

Reteaching — BASIC

Concept Mapping Have students create concept-map posters for the four branches of Earth and space science and their subdivisions. Have students add illustrations, symbols, and photographs or headlines clipped from articles to provide visual information about each field. **LS Visual/Logical**

Quiz — GENERAL

1. Describe three areas of specialization in geology. (Sample answer: Volcanology is the study of volcanoes, seismology is the study of earthquakes, and paleontology is the study of fossils.)

2. What new technology has expanded the study of the oceans in recent years? (submersibles)

3. What tasks is a meteorologist likely to perform? (weather forecasting, hurricane tracking, and tornado research)

Alternative Assessment — BASIC

Career Posters Have students work in small groups to prepare a poster ad to persuade classmates to choose one of the Earth or space sciences as a career. Posters should include an explanation of the field of study, a description of a job that scientists in the field might tackle, and illustrations that show why the career is exciting. **LS Visual/Kinesthetic**

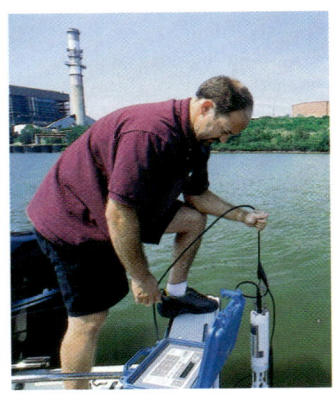

Special Branches of Earth Science

In addition to the main branches of Earth science, there are branches that depend heavily on other areas of science. Earth scientists often find themselves in careers that rely on life science, chemistry, physics, and many other areas of science.

Environmental Science

The study of how humans interact with the environment is called *environmental science*. As shown in **Figure 6**, one task of an environmental scientist is to determine how humans affect the environment. Environmental science relies on geology, life science, chemistry, and physics to help preserve Earth's resources and to teach others how to use them wisely.

Figure 6 This environmental scientist is measuring chemicals in the water to look for traces of urban or industrial pollution.

Ecology

By studying the relationships between organisms and their surroundings, scientists can better understand the behavior of these organisms. An *ecologist* is a person who studies a community of organisms and their nonliving environment. Ecologists work in many fields, such as wildlife management, agriculture, forestry, and conservation.

Geochemistry

Geochemistry combines the studies of geology and chemistry. *Geochemists*, such as the one in **Figure 7**, specialize in the chemistry of rocks, minerals, and soil. By studying the chemistry of these materials, geochemists can determine the economic value of the materials. Geochemists also can determine what the environment was like when the rocks first formed. Additionally, geochemists study the distribution and effect of chemicals added to the environment by human activity.

Figure 7 This geochemist is taking rock samples from the field so she can perform chemical analyses of them in a laboratory.

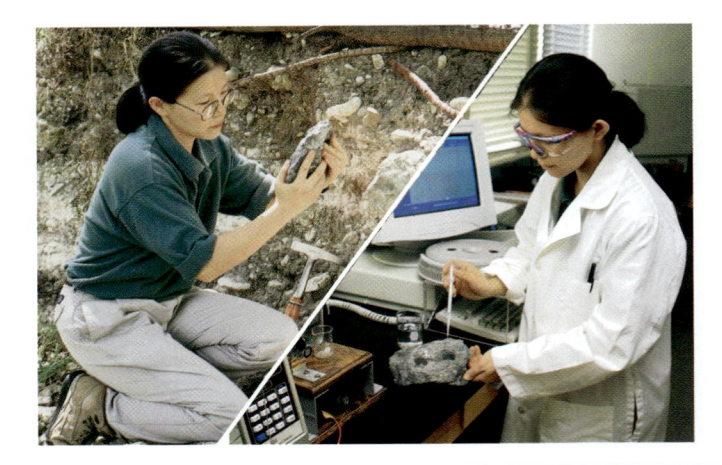

INCLUSION Strategies

- Learning Disabled
- Attention Deficit Disorder
- Gifted and Talented

Students might enjoy researching their "universal address." Provide reference materials, and have students work in groups of four students. Try to place one gifted and talented student in each group. Give each group a worksheet that has three columns titled "Place," "Unit of measurement," and "Travel time." Under "Place," students should write their room number, school name, school address, state, country, planet, solar system, galaxy (Orion arm of the Milky Way), galaxy group (local group), and universe. Ask students to estimate how long it would take to travel across the room, across the school, and across the state. Have students identify the units commonly used to measure the other items on the list. **LS Logical/Interpersonal**

10 Chapter 1 • The World of Earth Science

Geography and Cartography

Physical geographers, who are educated in geology, biology, and physics, study the surface features of Earth. *Cartographers* make maps of those features by using aerial and satellite photos, and computer mapping systems. Have you ever wondered why cities are located where they are? Often, the location of a city is determined by geography. Many cities, such as the one in **Figure 8,** were built near bodies of water because boats were used for transporting people and trade items. Rivers and lakes also provide communities with water for drinking and for raising crops and animals.

Reading Check What do cartographers do?

Figure 8 *The Mississippi River helped St. Louis become the large city it is today.*

SECTION Review

Summary

- The four major branches of Earth science are geology, oceanography, meteorology, and astronomy.
- Other areas of science that are linked to Earth science are environmental science, geochemistry, ecology, geography, and cartography.
- Some careers that are associated with branches of Earth science are volcanologist, seismologist, paleontologist, oceanographer, meteorologist, and astronomer.

Using Key Terms

1. Use each of the following terms in a separate sentence: *geology, oceanography,* and *astronomy.*

Understanding Key Ideas

2. Which of the following Earth scientists would study tornadoes?
    a. a geologist
    b. an oceanographer
    c. a meteorologist
    d. an astronomer

3. On which major branch of Earth science does geochemistry rely?
    a. geology
    b. oceanography
    c. meteorology
    d. astronomy

4. List the major branches of Earth science.

5. In which major branch of Earth science would a scientist study black smokers?

6. List two branches of Earth science that rely heavily on other areas of science. Explain how the branches rely on the other areas of science.

7. List and describe three Earth science careers.

Math Skills

8. Each week, a volcanologist reads 80 pages in a book about volcanoes. In a 4-week period, how many pages will the volcanologist read?

Critical Thinking

9. **Making Inferences** If you were a *hydrogeologist,* what kind of work would you do?

10. **Identifying Relationships** Explain why an ecologist might need to understand geology.

11. **Applying Concepts** Explain how an airline pilot would use Earth science in his or her career.

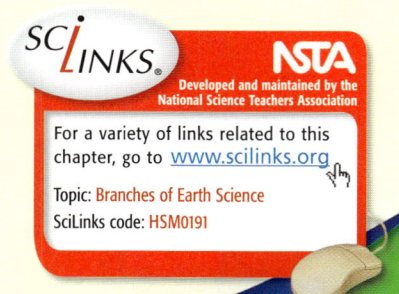

For a variety of links related to this chapter, go to www.scilinks.org
Topic: Branches of Earth Science
SciLinks code: HSM0191

Answer to Reading Check
Cartographers make maps.

CHAPTER RESOURCES
Chapter Resource File
- Section Quiz GENERAL
- Section Review GENERAL
- Vocabulary and Section Summary GENERAL
- Reinforcement Worksheet BASIC
- Datasheet for Quick Lab

Answers to Section Review

1. Sample answer: Geology is the study of the structure of Earth and the processes that shape Earth. Oceanography is the study of the oceans. Astronomy is the study of the universe.
2. c
3. a
4. The major branches of Earth science are geology, oceanography, meteorology, and astronomy.
5. oceanography
6. Answers may vary. Branches listed in the text include environmental science, ecology, geochemistry, geography, and cartography. Other branches not mentioned in the text are acceptable answers at the teacher's discretion. If branches are chosen from the text, explanations of how the branches rely on other areas should reflect the information given in the text.
7. Answers may vary. Any of the careers listed in the text are acceptable. Descriptions should match the text. Other careers may be accepted.
8. 80 pages per week × 4 weeks = 320 pages
9. A hydrogeologist is a geologist who studies water. (The prefix *hydro-* refers to water.)
10. Answers may vary. An ecologist studies the relationships between organisms and their environment. Part of an organism's environment is the physical environment, which includes geologic structures, such as landforms.
11. Answers may vary. An airline pilot must understand the characteristics of the atmosphere and weather patterns. The study of the atmosphere is a branch of Earth science called *meteorology.*

Section 1 • Branches of Earth Science

SECTION 2

Focus

Overview
This section introduces scientific methods. Students learn how paleontologist David Gillette applied scientific methods as he discovered and studied *Seismosaurus*.

🔔 Bellringer
Pose the following question to students: "How can a paleontologist know what a dinosaur looked like, how it behaved, and what it ate by studying fossils?"

Motivate

Discussion — GENERAL

Scientific Detectives Ask students to consider how scientific methods are like detective work. Have students match the stages of a robbery investigation to the steps of scientific methods. (Sample answer: Realizing that a crime has taken place and wondering who did it involve asking a question. Gathering clues is making observations. Determining suspects is forming hypotheses. Interrogating suspects is testing the hypothesis. Solving the crime is drawing a conclusion.) **LS** Logical

Answer to Reading Check
Scientists begin to learn about things by asking questions.

SECTION 2

Scientific Methods in Earth Science

READING WARM-UP

Objectives
- Explain how scientists begin to learn about the natural world.
- Explain what scientific methods are and how scientists use them.
- Identify the importance of communicating the results of a scientific investigation.
- Describe how scientific investigations often lead to new investigations.

Terms to Learn
scientific methods
hypothesis

READING STRATEGY

Mnemonics As you read this section, create a mnemonic device to help you remember the steps of scientific methods.

Imagine that you are standing in a thick forest on the bank of a river. Suddenly, you hear a booming noise, and you feel the ground begin to shake.

You notice a creature's head looming over the treetops. The creature's head is so high that its neck must be 20 m long! Then, the entire animal comes into view. You now understand why the ground is shaking. The giant animal is *Seismosaurus hallorum* (SIEZ moh SAWR uhs hah LOHR uhm), the "earth shaker," illustrated in **Figure 1**.

Learning About the Natural World

The description of the *Seismosaurus hallorum* is not based on imagination alone. Scientists have been studying dinosaurs since the 1800s. Scientists gather bits and pieces of information about dinosaurs and their environment. Then, they re-create what dinosaurs might have been like 150 million years ago. But how do scientists put it all together? How do they know if they have discovered a new species? Asking questions like these is the beginning of a process scientists use to learn more about the natural world.

✓ **Reading Check** How do scientists begin to learn about the natural world? (*See the Appendix for answers to Reading Checks.*)

Figure 1 *Seismosaurus hallorum* is one of the largest dinosaurs known.

CHAPTER RESOURCES

Chapter Resource File
- Lesson Plan
- Directed Reading A BASIC
- Directed Reading B SPECIAL NEEDS

Technology
- Transparencies
  - Bellringer
  - Scientific Methods

CONNECTION ACTIVITY
Language Arts — ADVANCED

Jurassic Description As students read the description of a Jurassic period environment, have them pay particular attention to the language used to describe the scene. Ask them to analyze the description and hypothesize how scientists might have discovered what this environment was like. For example, what parts of the description could be learned from the fossil record? What parts are inferred from observations of living things today? **LS** Intrapersonal

---

12 Chapter 1 • The World of Earth Science

Figure 2 Steps of scientific methods are illustrated in this flowchart. Notice that there are several ways to follow the paths.

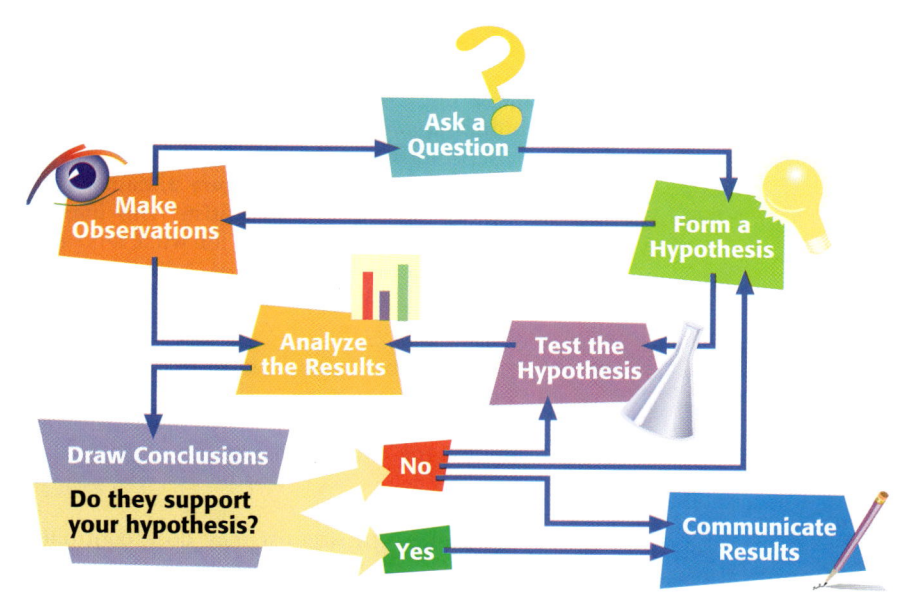

What Are Scientific Methods?

When scientists observe the natural world, they often think of a question or problem. But scientists don't just guess answers. Instead, they follow a series of steps called *scientific methods*. **Scientific methods** are a series of steps that scientists use to answer questions and solve problems. The most basic steps are shown in **Figure 2**.

Although scientific methods have several steps, there is not a set procedure. Scientists may use all of the steps or just some of the steps. They may even repeat some of the steps or do them in a different order. The goal of scientific methods is to come up with reliable answers and solutions. Scientists use scientific methods to gain insight into the problems they investigate.

scientific methods a series of steps followed to solve problems

Ask a Question

Asking a question helps focus the purpose of an investigation. For example, David D. Gillette, a scientist who studies fossils, examined some bones found by hikers in New Mexico in 1979. He could tell they were bones of a dinosaur. But he didn't know what kind of dinosaur. Gillette may have asked, "What kind of dinosaur did these bones come from?" Gillette knew that in order to answer this question, he would have to use scientific methods.

MISCONCEPTION ALERT

To Err Can Be Useful When experimental results do not match a hypothesis, the experiment was not necessarily a failure. Emphasize to students that unexpected results can be as useful as results that support a hypothesis. Sometimes, scientists make new and unexpected observations or discoveries while testing a hypothesis. Many people confuse hypotheses with predictions. Explain that a hypothesis is a general statement that offers an explanation of a problem that has been observed. Hypotheses can generally be supported or contradicted by experimentation. Point out that a prediction is based on a hypothesis. A prediction is meant to explain what will happen in a specific situation if the hypothesis is correct. Reinforce this distinction by having students form hypotheses and then form predictions based on the hypotheses.

Teach

Using the Figure — GENERAL

Scientific Methods Have students examine **Figure 2,** and then ask them the following questions:

- Is there a definite starting point? How can you tell? (no; There is no step that has only arrows pointing away from it.)
- Can a person use the steps more than once? (Yes, most steps can be used several times.)
- Does every person always follow the same steps in the same order? Explain your answer. (No, there is not a single series of steps but many possible paths, as shown by all of the arrows in the figure.)
- What value does reporting your results have if they do not support your hypothesis? (The results may be important to other scientists studying the same problem.)

LS Visual/Logical

Group Activity — GENERAL

Solving a Problem Have students work in small groups to solve an everyday problem by using scientific methods. For example, students might devise a way to keep sandwiches in a sack lunch from being squashed in a backpack. In each group, one or two students should design and perform experiments, one student should record the information gathered, and one student should prepare a report to communicate the results to the class. The report should describe how the group used scientific methods and should describe the steps the group followed. After the reports are done, have students point out different ways in which groups approached each step.

LS Verbal/Interpersonal Co-op Learning

Section 2 • Scientific Methods in Earth Science   **13**

Teach, continued

Discussion — BASIC

Everyday Science Ask students to think about "discoveries" that they have made in their lives. Students may be surprised to learn that they make scientific discoveries every day. A student might say, for example, "I found out that if my brother sat on the seesaw opposite from me, I would go flying off." Tell students that discoveries are often made accidentally but that a controlled experiment using scientific methods is necessary to explain observations. Have students identify the steps of the scientific method in their discoveries. **LS Logical**

CONNECTION to Physical Science — GENERAL

Radar Paleontology Unearthing *Seismosaurus* took seven years. The fossil bones were so deeply embedded in the sandstone that David Gillette asked for help from the Los Alamos National Laboratory. The lab staff devised an experimental way to use ground-penetrating radar and magnetometers to pinpoint the location of bone inside solid rock. Although the laboratory helped locate the dinosaur, Gillette's team still put in many hard days excavating the fossil by using hammers, picks, and shovels.

---

hypothesis an explanation that is based on prior scientific research or observations and that can be tested

Form a Hypothesis

When scientists want to investigate a question, they form a hypothesis (hie PAHTH uh sis). A **hypothesis** is a possible explanation or answer to a question that can be tested. Based on his observations and on what he already knew, Gillette said that the bones, shown in **Figure 3**, came from a kind of dinosaur not yet known to scientists. This hypothesis was Gillette's best testable explanation for what kind of dinosaur the bones came from.

Test the Hypothesis

Once a hypothesis is formed, it must be tested. Scientists test hypotheses by gathering data. The data can help scientists tell if the hypotheses are valid or not. To test his hypothesis, Gillette studied the dinosaur bones.

Controlled Experiments

To test a hypothesis, a scientist may do a controlled experiment. A *controlled experiment* is an experiment that tests only one factor, or *variable*, at a time. All other variables remain constant. By changing only one variable, scientists can see the results of just that one change. If more than one variable is changed, scientists cannot easily determine which variable caused the outcome. For example, let's say you tried to make a gelatin fruit mold, but the gelatin would not harden. The next time you made the gelatin fruit mold, you take out the oranges and pineapples. The gelatin might harden this time, but you won't know whether the pineapples or the oranges caused the gelatin not to harden the first time.

INTERNET ACTIVITY
For another activity related to this chapter, go to **go.hrw.com** and type in the keyword **HZ5WESW**.

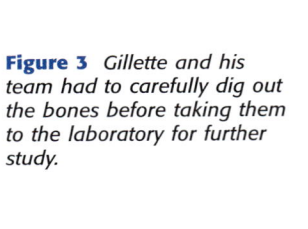

Figure 3 Gillette and his team had to carefully dig out the bones before taking them to the laboratory for further study.

Science Bloopers

Cold Fusion In 1989, two scientists from the University of Utah held a press conference to announce that they accomplished nuclear fusion using a method called *cold fusion*. They claimed this method would offer the world cheap, clean, and unlimited energy. Without having their work reviewed by other scientists, the two scientists presented their results at a press conference. Within five weeks, scientists around the world discredited their work because the results could not be duplicated. Because the two scientists were unable to provide data on how their apparatus achieved cold fusion, their results were rejected for publication by a prestigious journal.

Chapter 1 • The World of Earth Science

Making Observations

Controlled experiments are important for testing hypotheses. Some scientists, however, often depend more on observations than experiments to test their hypotheses. Because scientists cannot always control all variables, some scientists often observe nature and collect large amounts of data. Gillette took hundreds of measurements of the dinosaur bones, as illustrated in **Figure 4.** He compared his measurements with those of bones from known dinosaurs. He also visited museums and talked with other scientists.

Keeping Accurate Records

When testing a hypothesis, a scientist's expectations can affect what he or she actually observes. For this reason, it is important for scientists to keep clear, honest, and accurate records of their experiments and observations. Scientists should present findings supported by scientific data, not by opinions. When possible, scientists will repeat experiments to verify their findings. A hypothesis cannot be examined usefully in a scientific way without enough data. Just one example is never enough to prove something true. However, one example could prove that something is not true.

Analyze the Results

Once scientists finish their tests, they must analyze the results. Scientists often make tables and graphs to organize and summarize their data. When Gillette analyzed his results, he found that the bones of the mystery dinosaur did not match the bones of any known dinosaur. The bones were either too large or too different in shape.

Reading Check Why would scientists create graphs and tables of their data?

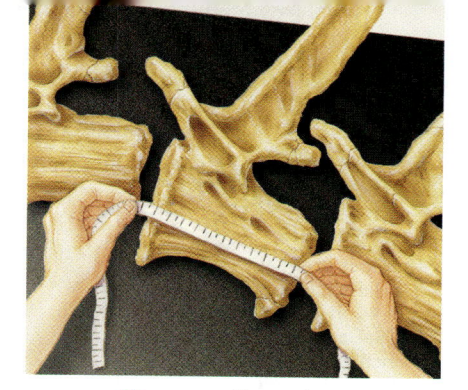

Figure 4 Gillette observed and measured the dinosaur bones to test his hypothesis.

CONNECTION TO Oceanography

WRITING SKILL **Making Hypotheses** Scientists exploring the Texas Gulf Coast have discovered American Indian artifacts that are thousands of years old. The odd thing is that the artifacts were buried in the sea floor several meters below sea level. These artifacts had not been moved since they were originally buried. If American Indian artifacts are several meters below sea level, the question to ask is, "Why are they there?" In your **science journal,** form a hypothesis that answers this question. Remember, your hypothesis must be stated in such a way that it can be tested using scientific methods.

Discussion — GENERAL

Kinds of Observations Discuss the difference between qualitative and quantitative observations. Qualitative observations use adjectives to describe things. Examples of qualitative observations include "blue eyed" or "brown haired." Quantitative observations use numbers and units to describe things. Examples of quantitative descriptions include "1.5 m high" or "a mass of 200 kg." Have students brainstorm examples of both kinds of observations. **LS Verbal**

MISCONCEPTION ALERT

Observations Ask students to define the term *observation*. Many students may assume that observations include only phenomena that they can see. In fact, observations are made by using all the senses as well as by using scientific instruments. Point out that many scientific observations must be made indirectly: for example, when studying movements of magma within volcanoes, when measuring the strength of earthquake tremors, or when determining the temperature on the surface of the sun.

Answer to Reading Check
Scientists create graphs and tables to organize and summarize their data.

Answer to Connection to Oceanography
Answers may vary. The most accepted hypothesis is that the sea level has risen since the artifacts were originally placed. This hypothesis is testable through the analysis of other evidence suggesting that the sea level was once lower than it is now. For example, old river channels have been found below sea level in the same area that the artifacts have been found.

Homework — BASIC

Hypothesizing Ask students to think of a question that is related to their daily lives and that they can answer by forming a hypothesis, making observations, recording data, and analyzing results. Possibilities could include "How much television do I watch?" "How many soft drinks do I consume?" or "How do I spend my allowance?" Establish a time limit of a week for students' observations, and then have students share what they learned in a written or oral report. **LS Verbal/Intrapersonal**

Section 2 • Scientific Methods in Earth Science

Close

Reteaching — BASIC

Scientific Methods Review
Reproduce **Figure 2** on the board. Then, ask students to help you navigate through the flowchart using examples for each step. After repeating this review several times, ask students to create their own scientific methods flowchart in their **science journal**. **LS** Logical

Quiz — GENERAL

1. Why is a hypothesis sometimes called an educated guess? Why must it be testable? (A hypothesis is a possible solution based on previous knowledge, so it is an educated guess. No conclusion can be reached if the hypothesis cannot be tested.)

2. What would happen if scientists kept their experimental results secret? (Efforts and mistakes would be duplicated, and there would be less scientific progress.)

Alternative Assessment — GENERAL

Writing a Story Have students write a detective story in which the detective solves a mystery by using scientific methods. Encourage students to make the story flow naturally and to avoid merely listing steps in the process. Have students exchange stories and identify each of the steps used. **LS** Verbal/Intrapersonal

---

MATH PRACTICE

Earth Shaker!
One foot is equal to 0.305 m. If a *Seismosaurus hallorum* was 45 m long, how long is the *Seismosaurus hallorum* in inches?

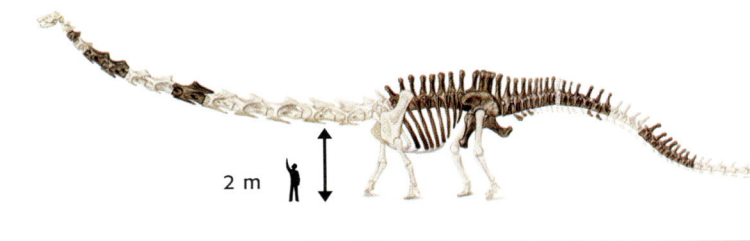

Figure 5 This model of the skeleton of *Seismosaurus hallorum* is based on Gillette's research. The darker-colored bones are those that have been found so far.

2 m

Answer to Math Practice
45 m ÷ 0.305 m/ft = 147.5 ft;
147.5 ft × 12 in./ft = 1,770.5 in.

Answer to Reading Check
It is important for the scientific community to review new evidence so that scientists can evaluate and question the evidence for accuracy.

Draw Conclusions

After carefully analyzing the results of their tests, scientists must conclude whether the results supported the hypothesis. Hypotheses are valuable even if they turn out not to be true. If a hypothesis is not supported by the tests, scientists may repeat the investigation to check for errors. Or they may ask new questions and form new hypotheses.

Based on all his studies, Gillette concluded that the bones found in New Mexico were indeed from an unknown dinosaur. This dinosaur, shown in **Figure 5,** was probably 45 m long and weighed between 60 and 100 tons. The creature certainly fit the name Gillette gave it—*Seismosaurus hallorum*, the "earth shaker."

Communicate Results

After finishing an investigation, scientists communicate their results. In this way, scientists share with others what they have learned. Science depends on the sharing of information. Scientists share information by writing reports for scientific journals and giving lectures on their results.

Gillette shared his discovery of *Seismosaurus* at a press conference at the New Mexico Museum of Natural History and Science. He later sent a report that described his investigation to the *Journal of Vertebrate Paleontology*.

When a scientist reveals new evidence, other scientists will evaluate the evidence. They will review the experimental procedure, the data from the experiments, and the reasoning behind explanations. This questioning of evidence and explanations is part of scientific inquiry. Scientists know that their results may be questioned by other scientists. They also understand that data aren't always interpreted the same way by two people. In some cases, another scientist may have published different results on the same topic. In this case, scientists may come to different conclusions. When there is disagreement, scientists will further investigate to find the truth.

✓ **Reading Check** Why is it important for the scientific community to review new evidence?

CONNECTION ACTIVITY
Language Arts — GENERAL

Communication Communicating results is an important part of science. Have students choose a scientific discovery and then present the related findings to their fellow scientists in class as if they were the discoverer. Students should write and read a brief speech describing their accomplishment. Encourage students to be creative as well as concise and clear. Other students should prepare questions about the discovery. **LS** Verbal

---

Chapter 1 • The World of Earth Science

Case Closed?

Even after results are reviewed and accepted by the scientific community for publication, the investigation of the topic may not be finished. New evidence may become available. The scientist may change the hypothesis based on the new evidence. In other cases, the scientist may have more questions that arise from the original evidence. For example, with the discovery of the *Seismosaurus*, Gillette may have wondered what the *Seismosaurus* ate. What environment did it live in? How did it become extinct? As shown in **Figure 6**, Gillette continues to use scientific methods to answer these questions.

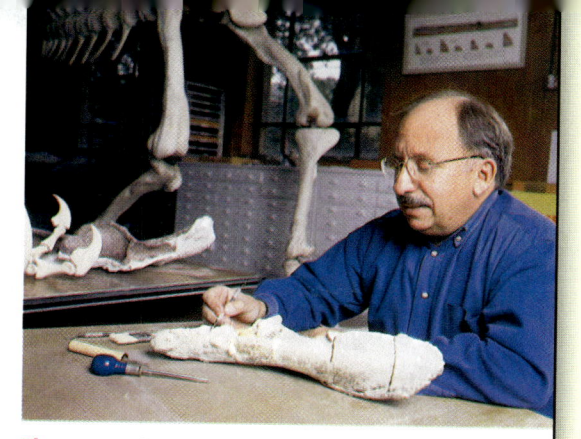

Figure 6 Gillette continues to study the bones of Seismosaurus for new insights into the past.

SECTION Review

Summary

- Scientists begin to learn about the natural world by asking questions.
- The steps of scientific methods are to ask a question, form a hypothesis, test the hypothesis, analyze the results, draw conclusions, and communicate results.
- Communicating results allows the evidence to be reviewed for accuracy by other scientists.
- Scientific investigations often lead people to ask new questions about the topic.

Using Key Terms

1. Use the following terms in the same sentence: *scientific method* and *hypothesis*.

Understanding Key Ideas

2. Which of the following is NOT part of scientific methods?
    a. ask a question
    b. test the hypothesis
    c. analyze results
    d. close the case

3. Which of the following is the step in scientific methods in which a scientist uses a controlled experiment?
    a. form a hypothesis
    b. test the hypothesis
    c. analyze results
    d. communicate results

4. Explain how scientists use more than imagination to form answers about the natural world.

5. Why do scientists communicate the results of their investigations?

6. For what reason might a scientist change his or her hypothesis after it has already been accepted?

Math Skills

7. If the *Seismosaurus*'s neck is 20 m long and the scientist studying *Seismosaurus* is 2 m long, how many scientists, lined up head to toe, would it take to equal the length of a *Seismosaurus* neck?

Critical Thinking

8. **Applying Concepts** Why might two scientists develop different hypotheses based on the same observations? Explain.

9. **Evaluating Hypotheses** Explain why Gillette's hypothesis—that the bones came from a kind of dinosaur unknown to science—is a testable hypothesis.

For a variety of links related to this chapter, go to www.scilinks.org
Topic: Scientific Methods
SciLinks code: HSM1359

Answers to Section Review

1. Sample answer: Forming a hypothesis is an important part of using scientific methods.
2. d
3. b
4. Answers may vary. Scientists perform controlled experiments and make observations to study the natural world.
5. Scientists communicate the results of their investigations because scientific progress depends on the exchange of information.
6. Answers may vary. A scientist could change his or her hypothesis because subsequent observations or experiments provide new data.
7. 20 m ÷ 2 m per scientist = 10 scientists
8. Answers may vary. A hypothesis is a possible explanation for observations that have been made. It is possible that two scientists have different explanations for the same data.
9. Sample answer: Gillette's hypothesis was testable because he could compare the discovered bones with the bones of known dinosaurs.

WEIRD SCIENCE

In addition to finding bones, Gillette found many *gastroliths*, or large stones found in the digestive system of some animals, particularly birds. *Seismosaurus* apparently swallowed the stones; once inside the digestive system, the stones ground up plant material that *Seismosaurus* would not have been able to digest!

CHAPTER RESOURCES

Chapter Resource File
- Section Quiz GENERAL
- Section Review GENERAL
- Vocabulary and Section Summary GENERAL
- Critical Thinking ADVANCED

Section 2 • Scientific Methods in Earth Science

SECTION 3

Focus

Overview
This section discusses the importance of models in science. Students learn about physical, mathematical, and conceptual models.

Bellringer
Ask students the following questions:

- How is an airplane flight simulator a kind of model? (Sample answer: A flight simulator models how an airplane performs.)

- What are some advantages to training pilots in a flight simulator rather than in a real airplane? (Sample answer: The simulator allows pilots to train in a safe environment.)

Motivate

ACTiViTY — GENERAL

Modeling an Airplane Give each student a piece of paper. Ask students to use the paper to make a paper airplane that can fly. Conduct trials to see whose airplane can fly the farthest and whose airplane can stay in the air the longest. Then, ask students the following questions:

- How are your model and an actual airplane alike?
- How are they different?

LS Kinesthetic/Verbal

SECTION 3

READING WARM-UP

Objectives
- Explain how models are used in science.
- Describe the three types of models.
- Identify which types of models are best for certain topics.
- Describe the climate model as an example of a mathematical model.

Terms to Learn
model
theory

READING STRATEGY

Reading Organizer As you read this section, make a table comparing the three types of models.

model a pattern, plan, representation, or description designed to show the structure or workings of an object, system, or concept

Figure 1 The model volcano looks a little bit like the real volcano, but the model cannot destroy acres of forests with hot lava!

CHAPTER RESOURCES

Chapter Resource File
- Lesson Plan
- Directed Reading A BASIC
- Directed Reading B SPECIAL NEEDS

Technology
- Transparencies
  - Bellringer

Workbooks
- Math Skills for Science
  - Using Proportions and Cross-Multiplication GENERAL
  - Measuring GENERAL

Scientific Models

For your next science project, you will be studying volcanoes. To help you learn more about volcanoes, your teacher suggests using baking soda, vinegar, and clay. How can this help you learn about volcanoes?

Baking soda, vinegar, and clay were the materials used to make the model of the volcano shown in **Figure 1.** By building a model, you can learn more about how volcanoes work.

Types of Scientific Models

A pattern, plan, representation, or description designed to show the structure or workings of an object, system, or concept is a **model**. Models are used to help us understand the natural world. With a model, a scientist can explain or analyze an object, system, or concept in more detail. Models can be used to represent things that are too small to see, such as atoms, or too large to completely see, such as the Earth or the solar system. Models can also be used to explain the past and present and to predict the future. There are three major types of scientific models—physical, mathematical, and conceptual.

Physical Models

Physical models are models that you can touch. Model airplanes, cars, and dolls are all physical models. Physical models often look like the real thing. However, physical models have limitations. For example, a doll is a model of a baby, but a doll does not act like a baby.

Is That a Fact!

One of the biggest volcanic eruptions on Earth occurred around 130 CE in New Zealand. Geologists estimate that 33 billion tons of pumice was thrown from the volcano and covered more than 51,813 km^2 (20,000 mi^2) of Earth's surface. No written accounts of the eruption exist, but scientists were able to learn about the eruption by studying the landforms and the layers of rock in the area.

---

18   Chapter 1 • The World of Earth Science

World Population

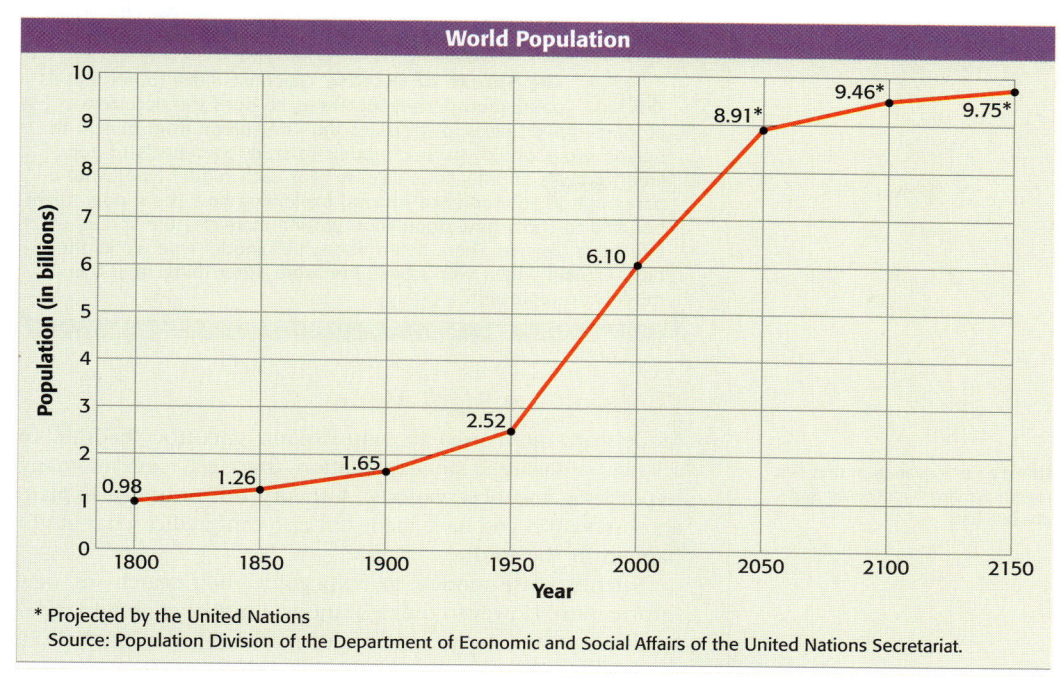

Figure 2 This graph shows human population growth predicted by a mathematical model run on a computer.

Data points shown on graph:
- 1800: 0.98
- 1850: 1.26
- 1900: 1.65
- 1950: 2.52
- 2000: 6.10
- 2050: 8.91*
- 2100: 9.46*
- 2150: 9.75*

* Projected by the United Nations
Source: Population Division of the Department of Economic and Social Affairs of the United Nations Secretariat.

Mathematical Models

A *mathematical model* is made up of mathematical equations and data. Some mathematical models are simple. These models allow you to calculate things such as how far a car will go in an hour or how much you would weigh on the moon. Other models are so complex that computers are needed to process them. Look at **Figure 2.** Scientists used a mathematical model to predict population growth in the world. There are many variables that affect population growth. A computer helped process these variables into a model scientists could use.

Conceptual Models

The third type of model is a *conceptual model*. Some conceptual models are systems of ideas. Others are based on making comparisons with familiar things to help illustrate or explain an idea. One example of a conceptual model is the big bang theory. The *big bang theory* is an explanation of the structure of the universe. Conceptual models are composed of many hypotheses. Each hypothesis is supported through scientific methods.

Reading Check What is the big bang theory? (See the Appendix for answers to Reading Checks.)

Teach

Discussion — GENERAL

Model Practice Use a model car or a map to discuss with students what a scale model is. A unit of measure in the model is equivalent to a larger or smaller unit of measure in the original. For example, in a model car, 1 cm might equal 1 m on the actual vehicle. Point out the legend of a map, and ask students to explain how distance on the map relates to actual miles and kilometers. **LS Verbal**

CONNECTION ACTIVITY
Math — ADVANCED

Scale Models Assign students to groups. Have each group select a large object and measure and record its dimensions. Have each group plan a scale model of the object (suggest a one-tenth scale), calculate the dimensions of the scale model, and draw it. Discuss the methods that students used to create their scale drawings. Have students devise strategies for creating more-accurate scale models, and have them work individually to create their own scale models. **LS Visual/Logical**

Answer to Reading Check
The big bang theory is an explanation of the creation of the universe.

Homework — GENERAL

Identifying Models Have students use the weather section of the newspaper to identify uses of models. For example, a mathematical model may be used to predict the likelihood of rain. A physical model, such as a map, may be used to show where pressure fronts are. A conceptual model may be used to explain long-term trends in the weather. **LS Logical**

Is That a Fact!
The big bang theory is also a mathematical model because it is partially based on mathematical equations developed by Albert Einstein.

Section 3 • Scientific Models **19**

Close

Reteaching — BASIC
Reviewing Models Have students work independently to come up with three examples of each type of model. Students should also identify a use and a limitation of each example.
LS Logical

Quiz — GENERAL
1. What three types of models are discussed in this section? (physical, mathematical, and conceptual models)
2. What is the difference between a physical model and a conceptual model? (A physical model is a model that you can touch. A conceptual model is a system of ideas or comparisons that support an idea.)

Alternative Assessment — ADVANCED
Critiquing Models Many advertisements feature models. Ask each student to find an example of one type of model in a magazine. Then, have students write a critique of the model. (Emphasize that students should not critique human models.) Have students consider the following questions: "How useful is the model? What has been left out or exaggerated? How could the model be improved?" **LS Visual/Verbal**

Answer to Connection to Social Studies
Answers may vary. Accept any well-supported answer.

CONNECTION TO Social Studies

WRITING SKILL **The Spread of Disease** Scientists have found that as population density increases, so does the occurrence of infectious diseases, or diseases that are spread from person to person. How would you use models to study the effects of population growth on infectious disease? For each model type, write a paragraph in your **science journal** explaining how the model might be used to show how population growth increases the spread of infectious disease. Then, determine which model type works the best. Explain why it works best. Are there other things that this model can represent?

theory an explanation that ties together many hypotheses and observations

Choosing the Right Model

Models are often used to help explain scientific theories. In science, a **theory** is an explanation that ties together many hypotheses and observations. A theory not only can explain an observation you have made but also can predict what might happen in the future.

Scientists use models to help guide their search for new information. However, the right model must be chosen in order for the scientist to be able to learn from it. For example, a physical model is useful to understand objects that are too small or too large to see completely. In these cases, a model can help you picture the thing in your mind.

The information that scientists gather by using models can help support a theory or show it to be wrong. Models can be changed or replaced. These changes happen when new observations are made that lead scientists to change their theories. For example, **Figure 3** shows that as scientists' knowledge of the Earth changed, so did the Earth's model.

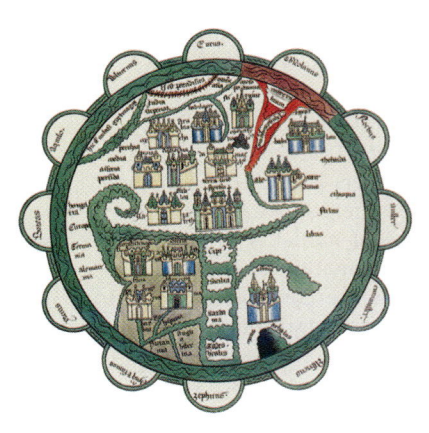

Figure 3 Scientists' model of Earth changed as new information was gathered.

MISCONCEPTION ALERT

Laws and Theories Many students believe that if a theory is accepted for a long period of time, it will "grow up" to be a law. Emphasize to students that both laws and theories are correct but serve different functions. A law, such as the law of gravity, is a concise statement of fact that is accepted as true and universal. Theories, such as the theory of evolution, are statements that are products of many scientific observations and may encompass numerous hypotheses or laws. Like laws, theories are accepted as true, but theories are much more complex. A law can be compared to a rubber ball. When dropped under constant conditions, the ball will always bounce exactly as predicted. On the other hand, a theory can be compared to a car. A part of the car may be improved, such as the brakes, but the general function of the car does not change.

Chapter 1 • The World of Earth Science

Climate Models

Scientists who study the Earth's atmosphere have developed mathematical climate models to try to imitate Earth's climate. A climate model is like a complicated recipe with thousands of ingredients. One important ingredient is the level of carbon dioxide in the atmosphere. Other ingredients are land and ocean-water temperatures around the globe as well as information about clouds, cloud cover, snow, ice cover, and ocean currents.

You may be wondering how a model can be created with so much data. Because of the development of more powerful computers, scientists are able to process large amounts of data from many different variables, as shown in **Figure 4**. These mathematical models do not make exact predictions about future climates, but they do estimate what might happen. Someday, these models may help scientists prevent serious climate problems, such as global warming or another ice age.

Figure 4 This meteorologist is using a high-speed supercomputer to do climate modeling.

Reading Check Why is a climate model complicated?

SECTION Review

Summary

- Models are used to help us understand the natural world.
- There are three types of models: physical models, mathematical models, and conceptual models.
- Scientists must choose the right type of model to learn about a topic.
- A climate model is a mathematical model with so many variables that powerful computers are needed to process the data.

Using Key Terms

1. In your own words, write a definition for each of the following terms: *model* and *theory*.

Understanding Key Ideas

2. Which of the following types of models are systems of ideas?
   a. physical models
   b. mathematical models
   c. conceptual models
   d. climate models

3. Why do scientists use models?

4. Describe the three types of models.

5. Which type of model would you use to study objects that are too small to be seen? Explain.

6. Describe why the climate model is a mathematical model.

Math Skills

7. A model of a bridge is 1 m long and 2.5% of the actual size of the bridge. How long is the actual bridge?

Critical Thinking

8. **Analyzing Ideas** Describe one advantage of physical models.

9. **Applying Concepts** What type of model would you use to study an earthquake? Explain.

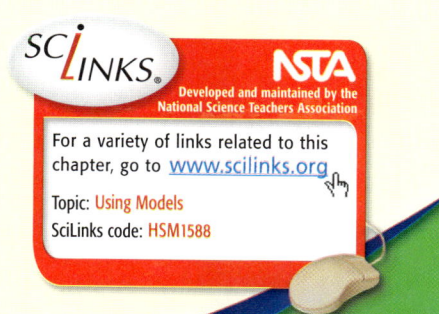

Answers to Section Review

1. Sample answer: A model is a representation of an object, system, or process. A theory is an explanation that ties together many observations and hypotheses.
2. c
3. Answers may vary. Scientists use models to study objects, systems, and concepts. They also use models to communicate results.
4. Answers may vary. Physical models are models that you can touch. Mathematical models are made of data and equations. Conceptual models comprise ideas and hypotheses supported by observation and data.
5. Answers may vary. All three types of models could be used to study objects that are too small to be seen.
6. Answers may vary. A climate model is a mathematical model that comprises a vast amount of data. Equations help predict the consequences of changes in the data.
7. 1 m ÷ 0.025 = 40 m
8. Answers may vary. One advantage of physical models is that they often look like the object or system that they are intended to model.
9. Answers may vary. Students may choose any of the models described in the section.

Answer to Reading Check

A climate model is complicated because there are so many variables that affect climate.

CHAPTER RESOURCES

Chapter Resource File
- Section Quiz GENERAL
- Section Review GENERAL
- Vocabulary and Section Summary GENERAL
- SciLinks Activity GENERAL

Section 3 • Scientific Models

SECTION 4

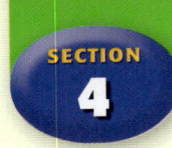

Focus

Overview
This section describes the International System of Units (SI), which is a unified global measurement system. Students also learn about measurement and safety.

Bellringer
Write the following questions on the board or an overhead projector.
- What can be measured in centimeters, meters, or kilometers? (distance and length)
- What can be measured in liters or milliliters? (volume)
- What can be measured in milligrams, grams, or kilograms? (mass and weight)

Motivate

Discussion — GENERAL
Hey Buddy, Can You Spare a Decidollar? Tell students that like our monetary system, the SI is based on the decimal system. Ask students the following questions: "How many pennies equal one dime?" (10) "How many dimes equal $1?" (10) Explain that the SI uses prefixes to signify larger or smaller units. Have students identify the prefixes in **Table 1.** LS Logical

---

SECTION 4

READING WARM-UP

Objectives
- Explain the importance of the International System of Units.
- Determine appropriate units to use for particular measurements.
- Identify lab safety symbols, and determine what they mean.

Terms to Learn
meter   temperature
volume   area
mass   density

READING STRATEGY

Reading Organizer As you read this section, create an outline of the section. Use the headings from the section in your outline.

CHAPTER RESOURCES

Chapter Resource File
- Lesson Plan
- Directed Reading A BASIC
- Directed Reading B SPECIAL NEEDS

Technology

Transparencies
- Bellringer
- Common SI Units
- LINK TO PHYSICAL SCIENCE Differences Between Mass and Weight

Workbooks

Math Skills for Science
- What Is SI? GENERAL

Measurement and Safety

Have you ever used your hand or your foot to measure the length of an object?

At one time, standardized units were based on parts of the body. Long ago, in England, the standard for an inch was three grains of barley. Using such units was not a very accurate way to measure things because they were based on objects that varied in size. Recognizing the need for a global measurement system, the French Academy of Sciences developed a system in the late 1700s. Over the next 200 years, the metric system, now called the *International System of Units* (SI), was refined.

Using the International System of Units

Today, most scientists and other people in almost all countries use the International System of Units. One advantage of using SI measurements is that all scientists can share and compare their observations and results. Another advantage of the SI is that all units are based on the number 10, which is a number that is easy to use in calculations. **Table 1** contains the commonly used SI units.

✓ **Reading Check** Why was the International System of Units developed? (*See the Appendix for answers to Reading Checks.*)

Table 1	Common SI Units and Conversions	
Length	meter (m)	
	kilometer (km)	1 km = 1,000 m
	decimeter (dm)	1 dm = 0.1 m
	centimeter (cm)	1 cm = 0.01 m
	millimeter (mm)	1 mm = 0.001 m
	micrometer (µm)	1 µm = 0.000001 m
	nanometer (nm)	1 nm = 0.000000001 m
Volume	cubic meter (m^3)	
	cubic centimeter (cm^3)	1 cm^3 = 0.000001 m^3
	liter (L)	1 L = 1 dm^3 = 0.001 m^3
	milliliter (mL)	1 mL = 0.001 L = 1 cm^3
Mass	kilogram (kg)	
	gram (g)	1 g = 0.001 kg
	milligram (mg)	1 mg = 0.000 001 kg
Temperature	kelvin (K)	
	Celsius (°C)	0°C = 273 K
		100°C = 373 K

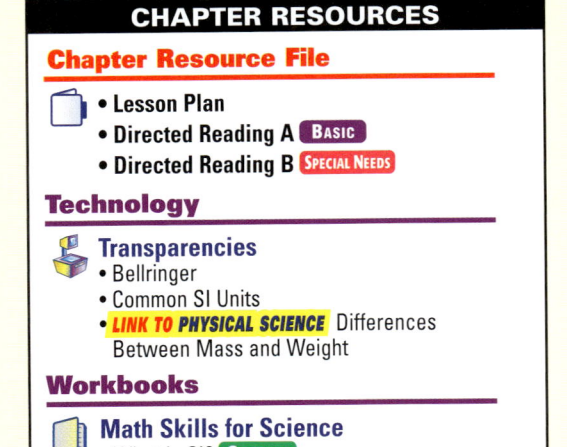

Answer to Reading Check
The International System of Units was developed to create a standard measurement system.

---

22 Chapter 1 • The World of Earth Science

Length

To measure length, a scientist uses meters (m). A **meter** is the basic SI unit of length. You may remember that SI units are based on the number 10. If you divide 1 m into 100 parts, for example, each part equals 1 cm. In other words, a centimeter equals one-hundredth of a meter. Some objects are so tiny that smaller units must be used. To describe the length of microscopic objects, scientists use micrometers (μm) or nanometers (nm). To describe the length of larger objects, scientists use kilometers (km).

Volume

Imagine that you are a scientist who needs to move some fossils to a museum. How many fossils will fit into a crate? The answer depends on the volume of the crate and the volume of each fossil. **Volume** is the measure of the size of a body or region in three-dimensional space.

The volume of a liquid is often given in liters (L). Liters are based on the meter. A cubic meter (1 m^3) is equal to 1,000 L. So, 1,000 L will fit into a box measuring 1 m on each side. The volume of a large, solid object is given in cubic meters. The volumes of smaller objects can be given in cubic centimeters (cm^3) or cubic millimeters (mm^3). To calculate the volume of a box-shaped object, multiply the object's length by its width and then multiply by its height.

The length, height, and width of irregularly shaped objects, such as rocks and fossils, are difficult to measure accurately. However, the volume of an irregularly shaped object can be determined by measuring the volume of liquid that the object displaces. The student in **Figure 1** is using a graduated cylinder to measure the volume of water a rock displaces.

meter the basic unit of length in the SI (symbol, m)

volume a measure of the size of a body or region in three-dimensional space

School to Home

Taking Measurements
With a parent, measure the width of your kitchen table, using your hands as a unit of measure. First, use your own hand to determine the width of the table. Then, have your parent use his or her hand to measure the width of the table. Compare your measurement with that of your parent. Was the number of units the same? Explain why it is important to use standard units of measurement.

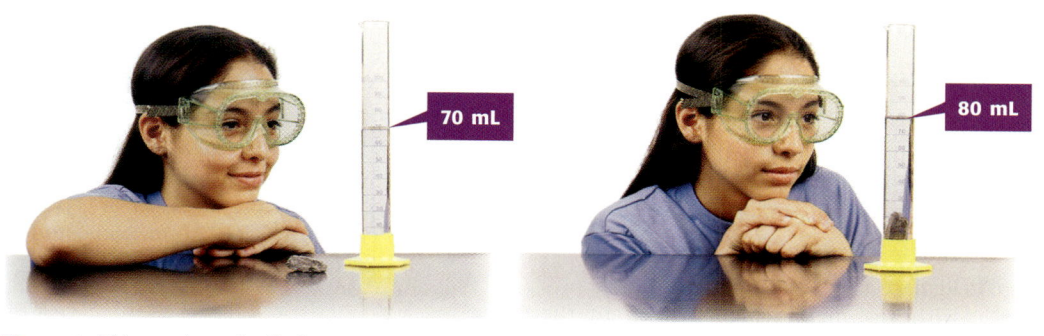

Figure 1 This graduated cylinder contains 70 mL of water. After the rock was added, the water level moved to 80 mL. Because the rock displaced 10 mL of water and because 1 mL = 1 cm^3, the volume of the rock is 10 cm^3.

CONNECTION ACTIVITY
Math — GENERAL

Area Practice Ask these questions:

1. What is the area of a field that measures 20 m by 40 m? (20 m × 40 m = 800 m^2)

2. A rectangle has an area of 45 mm^2 and a width of 5 mm. What is its length? (45 mm^2 ÷ 5 mm = 9 mm)

3. A piece of paper has an area of 120 cm^2 and a length of 15 cm. What is its width? (120 cm^2 ÷ 15 cm = 8 cm)

LS Logical

Science Bloopers

The meter was originally defined as one ten-millionth of the distance along the meridian running from the North Pole to the equator through Dunkirk, France, and Barcelona, Spain. French surveyors determined this length in 1798. Almost 100 years later, a tiny error of about 3.2 km was discovered in the surveyors' measurement. Today, a meter is defined as the distance that light travels in 1/299,792,458 of a second in a vacuum.

Teach

CONNECTION to Physical Science — GENERAL

Mass and Weight Students often confuse mass and weight. Explain that mass is measured in units such as grams, and it is a measure of the amount of matter that makes up an object. Weight is expressed in newtons, and it measures the gravitational force between objects. The mass of a given object will be the same anywhere in the universe. The weight of an object, however, varies with gravitational attraction. Use the transparency entitled "Differences Between Mass and Weight" to reinforce this distinction.

ACTIVITY — BASIC

SI Note Cards Have students make cards containing SI prefixes on one side and the values that the prefixes designate on the other (for example, *deci-* = 1/10 and *kilo-* = 1,000). Have students arrange the following measurements in sequence from the shortest to the longest:

- 3,000 mm, 15,000 cm, 12 m, 0.5 km (3,000 mm, 12 m, 15,000 cm, 0.5 km)

- 8,500 cm, 250,000 mm, 18 m, 0.45 km (18 m, 8,500 cm, 250,000 mm, 0.45 km)

You may wish to provide similar practice using mass and volume.

LS Logical

Answer to School-to-Home Activity

Because people's hands vary in size, it would take fewer large hands to measure the width of the table. If "hand" were a unit of measure, the width of the table would vary depending on whose hand was used to measure it.

Section 4 • Measurement and Safety 23

Close

Reteaching — BASIC

SI Equivalents Ask students to choose familiar objects and measure their mass, size, and volume in SI units. For example, students can measure the area of a CD jewel case, the weight of a paper clip, or the volume of a soda can. Students can use these measurements throughout the year as reference points.
LS Logical

Quiz — GENERAL

1. What is the basic SI unit for length? for mass? (meter; kilogram)
2. Why is volume measured in both cubic meters and in milliliters? (The volume of solid objects is often measured in cubic meters, and the volume of fluids is usually measured in milliliters.)

Alternative Assessment — GENERAL

Public Safety Announcements Have groups of students work together to prepare a presentation on lab safety for younger students. Encourage students to be creative, engaging, and safe in their presentations. Groups can use posters, skits, and visual aids to make their presentations dynamic. **LS Kinesthetic/Verbal**

Answers to Math Focus

1. $5 m \times 5 m = 25 m^2$
2. $22 cm \times 28 cm = 616 cm^2$

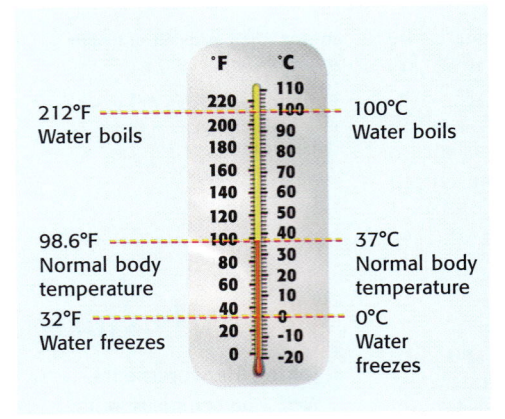

Figure 2 *This thermometer shows the relationship between degrees Fahrenheit and degrees Celsius.*

mass a measure of the amount of matter in an object

temperature a measure of how hot (or cold) something is

area a measure of the size of a surface or a region

Mass
A measure of the amount of matter in an object is **mass**. The kilogram (kg) is the basic unit for mass. The kilogram is used to describe the mass of things such as boulders. But many common objects are not so large. Grams (g) are used to describe the mass of smaller objects, such as an apple. One thousand grams equals 1 kg. The mass of large objects, such as an elephant, is given in metric tons. A metric ton equals 1,000 kg.

Temperature
Temperature is the measure of how hot (or cold) something is. You are probably used to describing temperature with degrees Fahrenheit (°F). For example, if your body temperature is 101°F, you have a fever. Scientists, however, usually use degrees Celsius (°C). The thermometer in **Figure 2** shows the relationship between degrees Fahrenheit and degrees Celsius. The kelvin, the SI base unit for temperature, is also used in science.

Area
How much paper would you need to cover the top of your desk? To answer this question, you must find the area of the desk. **Area** is a measure of how much surface an object has. The units for area are square units, such as square meters (m^2), square centimeters (cm^2), and square kilometers (km^2). To calculate the area of a square or rectangle, first measure the length and width. Then, use the following equation:

$$area = length \times width$$

MATH FOCUS

Finding Area What is the area of a rectangle that has a length of 4 cm and a width of 5 cm?

Step 1: Write the equation for area.
$area = length \times width$

Step 2: Replace the length and width with the measurements given in the problem, and solve.
$area = 4 cm \times 5 cm = 20 cm^2$

Now It's Your Turn
1. What is the area of a square whose sides measure 5 m?
2. What is the area of a book cover that is 22 cm wide and 28 cm long?

INCLUSION Strategies

• Learning Disabled • Visually Impaired

Organize students into groups of four students. Give each group a cup with the same amount of warm water and a medium-sized wooden block. First, ask groups to determine how much water is in the cup. Tell them to be creative in thinking about how to measure without using proper instruments. Next, ask students to estimate the temperature of the water. Then, ask them to estimate the mass of the wooden block. Finally, ask students to determine the length of the classroom. Have them record their data in their **science journal.** Repeat the activity but use tools such as a thermometer, a graduated cylinder, a scale, and a meterstick. Have students compare their measurements with their estimates. If necessary, repeat this activity with different objects until student estimates are reasonably accurate. **LS Kinesthetic/Logical**

24 Chapter 1 • The World of Earth Science

Density

The ratio of the mass of a substance to the volume of the substance is the substance's **density**. Because density is the ratio of mass to volume, units often used for density are grams per milliliter (g/mL) and grams per cubic centimeter (g/cm³). You can calculate density by using the following equation:

$$\text{density} = \frac{\text{mass}}{\text{volume}}$$

Safety Rules!

Science is exciting and fun, but it can also be dangerous. Always follow your teacher's instructions. Before starting any scientific investigation, obtain your teacher's permission. Read the lab procedures completely and carefully before you start. Pay attention to safety information and caution statements. **Figure 3** shows the safety symbols that are used in this book.

✓ **Reading Check** What should you do before you start a scientific investigation?

Figure 3 Safety Symbols

Eye protection | Clothing protection | Hand safety
Heating safety | Electric safety | Sharp object
Chemical safety | Animal safety | Plant safety

density the ratio of the mass of a substance to the volume of the substance

SECTION Review

Summary

- The SI is the standard system of measurement used by scientists around the world.
- The basic SI units of measurement for length, volume, mass, and temperature are the meter, liter, kilogram, and kelvin, respectively.
- Safety rules must be followed at all times during a scientific investigation.

Using Key Terms

The statements below are false. For each statement, replace the underlined term to make a true statement.

1. The length multiplied by the width of an object is the <u>density</u> of the object.
2. The measure of the amount of matter in an object is the <u>area</u>.

Understanding Key Ideas

3. Which of the following SI units is most often used to measure length?
   a. meter
   b. liter
   c. gram
   d. degrees Celsius
4. What are two benefits of using the International System of Units?
5. At what temperature in degrees Celsius does water freeze?
6. Why is it important to follow safety rules?

Math Skills

7. Find the density of an object that has a mass of 34 g and a volume of 14 mL.

Critical Thinking

8. **Making Comparisons** Which weighs more: a pound of feathers or a pound of lead? Explain.

For a variety of links related to this chapter, go to www.scilinks.org
Topic: Systems of Measurement
SciLinks code: HSM1490

Answer to Reading Check

Before you start a science investigation, obtain your teacher's permission and read the lab procedures carefully.

Answers to Section Review

1. area
2. mass
3. a
4. Answers may vary. Students should mention that the SI is used by scientists throughout the world. Students may also note the advantages of using a system of units that is based on 10.
5. 0 C
6. Answers may vary. Sample answer: Safety rules are created to minimize risks associated with some experiments.
7. 34 g ÷ 14 mL = 2.43 g/mL
8. Students should recognize that both materials weigh 1 lb.

Homework — GENERAL

Finding Safety Risks Have students choose five photographs from magazines and label each photograph with appropriate safety cautions. Students should use the safety symbols shown in this section. Ask students to explain to the class how each photo depicts a safety risk. **LS** Visual/Verbal

CHAPTER RESOURCES

Chapter Resource File
- Section Quiz GENERAL
- Section Review GENERAL
- Vocabulary and Section Summary GENERAL

Workbooks
- Science Skills
  - Safety Rules! GENERAL

Section 4 • Measurement and Safety

Model-Making Lab

Using Scientific Methods

Teacher's Notes

Time Required
One 45-minute class period

Lab Ratings
EASY — HARD

Teacher Prep ▲▲
Student Set-Up ▲▲▲
Concept Level ▲▲
Clean Up ▲▲

MATERIALS
The materials listed on the student page are enough for a pair of students. Students can also work in groups of four. In that case, two students should assume the role of model builders, and two other students should assume the role of core samplers.

Safety Caution
Remind students to review all safety cautions and icons before beginning this lab activity.

Lab Notes
Provide each student group with three pieces of 1/2 in. PVC pipe cut slightly longer than the height of the models. A small amount of vegetable oil may help the PVC pipes glide smoothly through the clay.

Model-Making Lab

Using Scientific Methods

OBJECTIVES

Design a model to demonstrate core sampling.

Create a diagram of a classmate's model by using the core sample method.

MATERIALS

- knife, plastic
- modeling clay, three or four colors
- pan or box, opaque
- pencil, unsharpened
- pencils or markers, three or four colors
- PVC pipe, 1/2 in.

SAFETY

Using Scientific Methods

Geologists often use a technique called core sampling to learn what underground rock layers look like. This technique involves drilling several holes in the ground in different places and taking samples of the underground rock or soil. Geologists then compare the samples from each hole at each depth to construct a diagram that shows the bigger picture.

In this activity, you will model the process geologists use to diagram underground rock layers. You will first use modeling clay to form a rock-layer model. You will then exchange models with a classmate, take core samples, and draw a diagram of your classmate's rock layers.

- Form a plan for your rock layers. Make a sketch of the layers. Your sketch should include the colors of clay in several layers of varying thicknesses. Note: Do not let the classmates who will be using your model see your plan.

- In the pan or box, mold the clay into the shape of the lowest layer in your sketch.

- Repeat the procedure described in the second bullet for each additional layer of clay. Exchange your rock-layer model with a classmate.

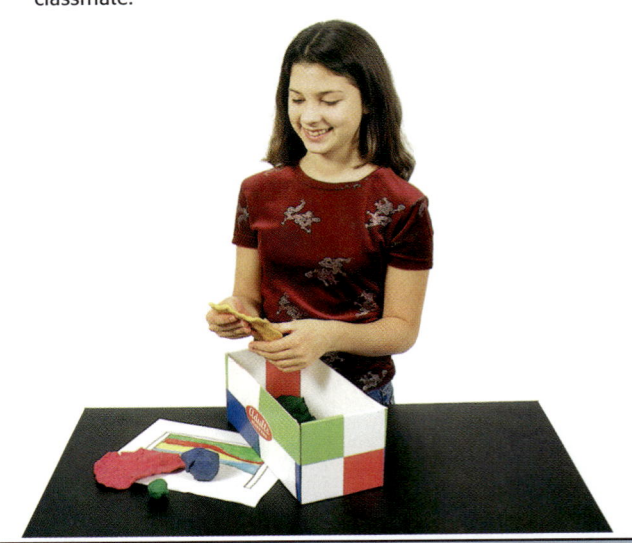

Jan Nelson
East Valley Middle School
East Helena, Montana

CHAPTER RESOURCES

Chapter Resource File
- Datasheet for Chapter Lab
- Lab Notes and Answers

Technology
- Classroom Videos
  - Lab Video

Chapter 1 • The World of Earth Science

Ask a Question

1. Can unseen features be revealed by sampling parts of the whole?

Form a Hypothesis

2. Form a hypothesis about whether taking core samples from several locations will give a good indication of the entire hidden feature.

Test the Hypothesis

3. Choose three places on the surface of the clay to drill holes. The holes should be far apart and in a straight line. (Do not remove the clay from the pan or box.)

4. Slowly push the PVC pipe through all the layers of clay. Slowly remove the pipe.

5. Gently push the clay out of the pipe with an unsharpened pencil. This clay is a core sample.

6. Draw the core sample, and record your observations. Be sure to use a different color of pencil or marker for each layer.

7. Repeat steps 4–6 for the next two core samples. Make sure your drawings are side by side and in the same order as the samples in the model.

Analyze the Results

1. **Examining Data** Look at the pattern of rock layers in each of your core samples. Think about how the rock layers between the core samples might look. Then, make a diagram of the rock layers.

2. **Organizing Data** Complete your diagram by coloring the rest of each rock layer.

Draw Conclusions

3. **Evaluating Data** Use the plastic knife to cut the clay model along a line connecting the three holes. Remove one side of the model so that you can see the layers.

4. **Evaluating Models** How well does your rock-layer diagram match the model? Explain.

5. **Evaluating Methods** What are some limitations of your diagram as a model of the rock layers?

6. **Drawing Conclusions** Do your conclusions support your hypothesis? Explain your answer.

Applying Your Data

List two ways that the core-sampling method could be improved.

Analyze the Results
1. Diagrams may vary.
2. Diagrams may vary.

Draw Conclusions
4. Sample answer: The rock-layer diagram provides a general overview of the layers. It may not be as specific as the model or provide all of the details from the model.
5. Answers may vary. Sample answer: My model would not allow me to see all of the details of the rock.
6. Answers may vary depending on students' hypotheses.

Applying Your Data
Answers may vary. Sample answers: More core samples could be taken, or the core samples could be taken at standard increments. The core samples could be larger or closer together, or smaller areas could be combined for an overall picture of the layers.

CHAPTER RESOURCES
Workbooks

- **Whiz-Bang Demonstrations**
  - Tubby Terra GENERAL
- **Long-Term Projects & Research Ideas**
  - How Big Is the Earth? ADVANCED

Chapter 1 • Chapter Lab   27

Chapter Review

Assignment Guide

Section	Questions
1	1, 4, 19
2	2–3, 8–9, 12, 15–18
3	7, 10–11, 20–23
4	5–6, 13–14

ANSWERS

Using Key Terms

1. geology
2. hypothesis
3. Scientific methods

Understanding Key Ideas

4. b
5. b
6. b
7. b
8. a
9. Students should recognize that observations and data gathered during a scientific investigation can lead to new questions, which lead to new investigations.
10. Answers may vary. Scientists use models to represent things that are too small or too large to see, to test designs and hypotheses, to explain the past, and to predict the future.

Chapter Review

USING KEY TERMS

Complete each of the following sentences by choosing the correct term from the word bank.

geology astronomy
scientific methods hypothesis

1. The study of the origin, history, and structure of the Earth and the processes that shape the Earth is called ___.

2. An explanation that is based on prior scientific research or observations and that can be tested is called a(n) ___.

3. ___ are a series of steps followed to solve problems.

UNDERSTANDING KEY IDEAS

Multiple Choice

4. The science that uses geology to study how humans affect the natural environment is
   a. paleontology.
   b. environmental science.
   c. cartography.
   d. volcanology.

5. A pencil measures 14 cm long. How many millimeters long is it?
   a. 1.4 mm   c. 1,400 mm
   b. 140 mm   d. 1,400,000 mm

6. Which of the following is NOT an SI unit?
   a. meter   c. liter
   b. foot   d. degrees Celsius

7. Which of the following is a limitation of models?
   a. They are large enough to be seen.
   b. They do not act exactly like the thing they model.
   c. They are smaller than the thing they model.
   d. They use familiar things to model unfamiliar things.

8. Gillette's hypothesis was
   a. supported by his results.
   b. not supported by his results.
   c. based only on observations.
   d. based only on what he already knew.

Short Answer

9. Why would scientific investigations lead to new scientific investigations?

10. How and why do scientists use models?

11. What are three types of models? Give an example of each.

12. What problems could occur if scientists didn't communicate the results of their investigations?

13. What problems could occur if there were not an International System of Units?

14. Which safety symbols would you expect to see for an experiment that requires the use of acid?

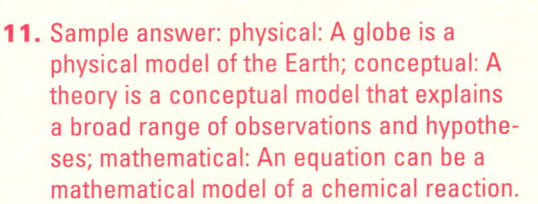

---

11. Sample answer: physical: A globe is a physical model of the Earth; conceptual: A theory is a conceptual model that explains a broad range of observations and hypotheses; mathematical: An equation can be a mathematical model of a chemical reaction.

12. Answers may vary. Students may suggest that if the results of an investigation are not communicated, scientists could not build on each other's knowledge and science could not advance as quickly.

13. Answers may vary. Students should note that it would be difficult for scientists to share data.

14. eye protection, chemical safety, clothing protection, and hand safety

28   Chapter 1 • The World of Earth Science

CRITICAL THINKING

15. Concept Mapping Use the following terms to create a concept map: *Earth science, scientific methods, hypothesis, problem, question, experiment,* and *observations.*

16. Analyzing Processes Why do you not need to complete the steps of scientific methods in a specific order?

17. Evaluating Conclusions Why might two scientists working on the same problem draw different conclusions?

18. Analyzing Methods Scientific methods often begin with observation. How does observation limit what scientists can study?

19. Making Comparisons A rock that contains fossil seashells might be studied by scientists in at least two branches of Earth science. Name those branches. Why did you choose those two branches?

INTERPRETING GRAPHICS

Use the graph below to answer the questions that follow.

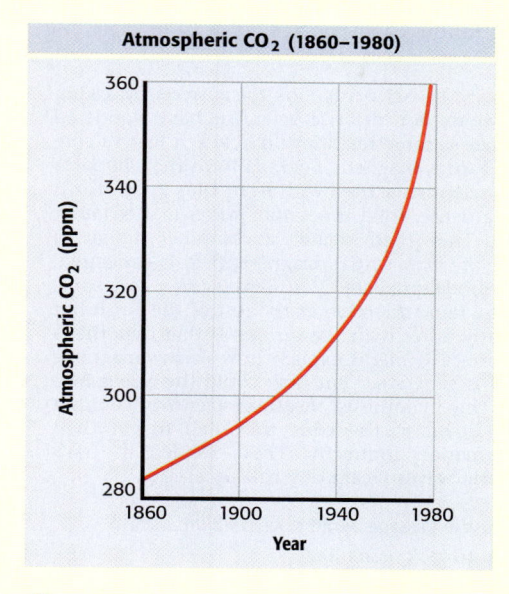

Atmospheric CO_2 (1860–1980)

20. Has the amount of CO_2 in the atmosphere increased or decreased since 1860?

21. The line on the graph is curved. What does this curve indicate?

22. Was the rate of change in the level of CO_2 between 1940 and 1960 higher or lower than it was between 1880 and 1900? How can you tell?

23. What conclusions can you draw from reading this graph?

Critical Thinking

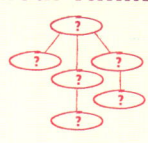

15. An answer to this exercise can be found at the end of this book.

16. Answers may vary. Students should note that each step of scientific methods can lead to other steps. For example, observations might lead a researcher to develop a new hypothesis.

17. Sample answer: The scientists may make different observations, form different hypotheses, test the same hypothesis differently, or analyze the results of their tests differently.

18. Answers may vary. Observation can limit what scientists can study because some objects and phenomena cannot be observed easily.

19. Sample answer: geology and paleontology; A geologist might be interested in studying how the rock formed and how it relates to other rock formations in the area. A paleontologist might study the rock because it contains fossils of ancient life.

Interpreting Graphics

20. The amount of CO_2 has increased.

21. The rate at which the amount of CO_2 in the atmosphere increased has also increased over time.

22. higher; The line in the graph curves more steeply between 1940 and 1960 than it does between 1880 and 1900.

23. Answers may vary. Sample answer: The rate at which CO_2 has been added to the atmosphere has increased over time.

CHAPTER RESOURCES

Chapter Resource File
- Chapter Review **GENERAL**
- Chapter Test A **GENERAL**
- Chapter Test B **ADVANCED**
- Chapter Test C **SPECIAL NEEDS**
- Vocabulary Activity **GENERAL**

Workbooks
- Study Guide
  - Assessment resources are also available in Spanish.

Chapter 1 • Chapter Review

Standardized Test Preparation

Teacher's Note
To provide practice under more realistic testing conditions, give students 20 minutes to answer all of the questions in this Standardized Test Preparation.

MISCONCEPTION ALERT
Answers to the standardized test preparation can help you identify student misconceptions and misunderstandings.

READING

Passage 1
1. A
2. G
3. C

TEST DOCTOR

Question 1: All of the answer choices may appear correct. Tell students that standardized test questions often have several answer choices that appear to be correct. In this case, one way to determine the correct answer is to substitute each answer choice for the underlined word in the passage.

Standardized Test Preparation

READING
Read each of the passages below. Then, answer the questions that follow each passage.

Passage 1 Scientists look for answers by asking questions. For instance, scientists have wondered if there is some relationship between Earth's core and Earth's magnetic field. To form their hypothesis, scientists started with what they knew: Earth has a dense, solid inner core and a molten outer core. They then created a computer model to <u>simulate</u> how Earth's magnetic field is generated. The model predicted that Earth's inner core spins in the same direction as the rest of the Earth but slightly faster than the surface. If that hypothesis is correct, it might explain how Earth's magnetic field is generated. But how could the researchers test the hypothesis? Because scientists couldn't drill down to the core, they had to get their information indirectly. They decided to track seismic waves created by earthquakes.

1. In the passage, what does *simulate* mean?
   A to look or act like
   B to process
   C to calculate
   D to predict

2. According to the passage, what do scientists wonder?
   F if the Earth's inner core was molten
   G if there was a relationship between Earth's core and Earth's magnetic field
   H if the Earth had a solid outer core
   I if computers could model the Earth's core

3. What did the model predict?
   A The Earth's outer core is molten.
   B The Earth's inner core is molten.
   C The Earth's inner core spins in the same direction as the rest of the Earth.
   D The Earth's outer core spins in the same direction as the rest of the Earth.

Passage 2 Scientists analyzed seismic data for a 30-year period. They knew that seismic waves traveling through the inner core along a north-south path travel faster than waves passing through it along an east-west line. Scientists searched seismic data records to see if the <u>orientation</u> of the "fast path" for seismic waves changed over time. They found that in the last 30 years, the direction of the "fast path" for seismic waves had indeed shifted. This is strong evidence that Earth's core does travel faster than the surface, and it strengthens the hypothesis that the spinning core creates Earth's magnetic field.

1. In the passage, what does *orientation* mean?
   A speed
   B direction
   C magnetic field
   D intensity

2. What evidence did scientists find?
   F The Earth's core does travel faster than the surface.
   G The "fast path" does not change.
   H Seismic waves travel faster along an east-west line.
   I The spinning core does not create the Earth's magnetic field.

3. What do scientists hypothesize about the Earth's magnetic field?
   A It was found in the last 30 years.
   B It travels faster along a north-south path.
   C It is losing its strength.
   D It is created by the spinning core.

Passage 2
1. B
2. F
3. D

TEST DOCTOR

Question 1: The correct answer is B. Students may choose answer A because the speed of the inner core differs from the speed at the surface. They may choose answer C because the phrase *magnetic field* is used in the passage. Students may choose answer D because the passage describes the difference between seismic waves traveling north-south and seismic waves traveling east-west. They may conclude that the north-south waves are more intense, but this is not a fact in the passage.

Chapter 1 • The World of Earth Science

INTERPRETING GRAPHICS

The table below contains data that shows the relationship between volume and pressure. Use the table to answer the questions that follow.

Volume (L)	Pressure (kPa)
0.5	4,960
1.0	2,480
2.0	1,240
3.0	827

1. What is the pressure when the volume is 2.0 L?
   A 4,960 kPa
   B 2,480 kPa
   C 1,240 kPa
   D 827 kPa

2. What is the volume when the pressure is 827 kPa?
   F 0.5 L
   G 1.0 L
   H 2.0 L
   I 3.0 L

3. What is the change in pressure when the volume is increased from 0.5 L to 1.0 L?
   A 4,960 kPa
   B 2,480 kPa
   C 1,240 kPa
   D 0.50 kPa

4. Which of the following patterns best describes the data?
   F When the volume is doubled, the pressure is tripled.
   G When the volume is tripled, the pressure is cut in half.
   H As the volume increases, the pressure remains the same.
   I As the volume increases, the pressure decreases.

MATH

Read each question below, and choose the best answer.

1. The original design for a boat shows a rectangular shape that is 5 m long and 1.5 m wide. If the design is reduced to 3.4 m long and 1 m wide, by how much does the area of the boat decrease?
   A 1.7 m^2
   B 4.1 m^2
   C 7.5 m^2
   D 9.2 m^2

2. If *density = mass/volume*, what is the density of an object that has a mass of 50 g and a volume of 2.6 cm^3?
   F 0.052 cm^3/g
   G 19.2 g/cm^3
   H 47.4 g/cm^3
   I 130 g/cm^3

3. During a chemical change, two separate pieces of matter combined into one. The mass of the final product is 82 g. The masses of the original pieces must equal the final product's mass. What are the possible masses of the original pieces of matter?
   A 2 g and 18 g
   B 2 g and 41 g
   C 12 g and 8 g
   D 42 g and 40 g

4. An adult *Seismosaurus hallorum* weighs 82 tons. A baby *Seismosaurus hallorum* weighs 46 tons. The weight of the baby *Seismosaurus hallorum* is what percentage of the weight of the adult *Seismosaurus hallorum*?
   F 24%
   G 44%
   H 56%
   I 98%

INTERPRETING GRAPHICS
1. C
2. I
3. B
4. I

TEST DOCTOR

Question 4: Although answer choices F and G are more specific than answer I, answers F and G are incorrect. Answer I is correct—pressure decreases as volume increases.

MATH
1. B
2. G
3. D
4. H

TEST DOCTOR

Question 3: If students multiplied the masses, they may have chosen answer B, because 2 g × 41 g = 82 g^2. The correct answer is obtained by adding the masses in answer D.

CHAPTER RESOURCES

Chapter Resource File
- Standardized Test Preparation GENERAL

State Resources

For specific resources for your state, visit **go.hrw.com** and type in the keyword **HSMSTR**.

Chapter 1 • Standardized Test Preparation

Science in Action

Science, Technology, and Society

Background

More than 40 years ago, two scientists named Fred Fisher and Fred Spiess were studying the behavior of sound waves underwater. They needed to study sound waves in a setting that was quieter and more stable than a traditional research ship. So, they created the *Floating Instrument Platform* (FLIP). Since then, the physical behavior of ocean waves and currents has been studied extensively aboard *FLIP*. The platform is amazingly stable—according to one scientist aboard *FLIP* during a hurricane, the platform barely moved. *FLIP* is operated by the Scripps Institute of Oceanography.

Weird Science

Teaching Strategy — GENERAL

Reports of organisms falling with precipitation are not uncommon. Thousands of maggots fell in Acapulco in 1968. In 2000, a heavy rainstorm in the town of Great Yarmouth, located about half a mile from the east coast of England, dropped 2 in. fish with the rain. Have students research other instances of organisms falling with precipitation.

Science in Action

Science, Technology, and Society

A "Ship" That Flips?

Does your school's laboratory have doors on the floor or tables bolted sideways to the walls? A lab like this exists, and you can find it floating in the ocean. *FLIP*, or *Floating Instrument Platform*, is a 108 m long ocean research vessel that can tilt 90°. *FLIP* is towed to an area that scientists want to study. To flip the vessel, empty chambers within the vessel are filled with water. The *FLIP* begins tilting until almost all of the vessel is underwater. Having most of the vessel below the ocean's surface stabilizes the vessel against wind and waves. Scientists can collect accurate data from the ocean, even during a hurricane!

Social Studies ACTIVITY

Design your own *FLIP*. Make a map on poster board. Draw the layout of a living room, bathroom, and bedroom before your *FLIP* is tilted 90°. Include entrances and walkways to use when *FLIP* is not flipped.

Weird Science

It's Raining Fish and Frogs

What forms of precipitation have you seen fall from the sky? Rain, snow, hail, sleet, or fish? Wait a minute! Fish? Fish and frogs might not be a form of precipitation, but as early as the second century, they have been reported to fall from the sky during rainstorms. Scientists theorize that tornadoes or waterspouts that suck water into clouds can also suck up unsuspecting fish, frogs, or tadpoles that are near the surface of the water. After being sucked up into the clouds and carried a few miles, these reluctant travelers then rain down from the sky.

Language Arts ACTIVITY

WRITING SKILL You are a reporter for your local newspaper. On a rainy day in spring, while driving to work, you witness a downpour of frogs and fish. You pull off to the side of the road and interview other witnesses. Write an article describing this event for your local newspaper.

Answer to Social Studies Activity
Answers may vary.

Answer to Language Arts Activity
Answers may vary.

32 Chapter 1 • The World of Earth Science

Careers

Sue Hendrickson

Paleontologist Could you imagine having a job in which you spent all day digging in the dirt? This is just one of Sue Hendrickson's job descriptions. But Hendrickson does not dig up flowers. Hendrickson is a paleontologist, and she digs up dinosaurs! Her most famous discovery is the bones of a *Tyrannosaurus rex*. *T. rex* is one of the largest meat-eating dinosaurs. It lived between 65 million and 85 million years ago. Walking tall at 6 m, *T. rex* was approximately 12.4 m long and weighed between 5 and 7 tons. Hendrickson's discovery is the most complete set of bones ever found of the *T. rex*. The dinosaur was named Sue to honor Hendrickson for her important find. From these bones, Hendrickson and other scientists have been able to learn more about the dinosaur, including how it lived millions of years ago. For example, Hendrickson and her team of scientists found the remains of Sue's last meal, part of a duck-billed, plant-eating dinosaur called *Edmontosaurus* that weighed approximately 3.5 tons!

Math Activity

The *T. rex* named Sue weighed 7 tons and the *Edmontosaurus* weighed 3.5 tons. How much smaller is *Edmontosaurus* than Sue? Express your answer as a percentage.

To learn more about these Science in Action topics, visit go.hrw.com and type in the keyword **HZ5WESF**.

Current Science
Check out Current Science® articles related to this chapter by visiting go.hrw.com. Just type in the keyword **HZ5CS01**.

Answer to Math Activity
3.5 tons ÷ 7.0 tons × 100 = 50% smaller

Is That a Fact!

Shortly after Sue Hendrickson's discovery, a lawsuit that involved The Black Hills Institute, the U.S. government, Maurice Williams (the owner of the land on which the fossil was found), and the Sioux Indian tribe began. The National Guard removed "Sue" from the Black Hills Institute, and kept her for seven years until the matter was settled. The fossil later sold for over $8 million to the Field Museum in Chicago.

Careers

Background

Sue Hendrickson was on an archeological dig in the badlands of South Dakota when she stumbled upon a scientific treasure. She had separated from the rest of her team for a short hike when she discovered a giant vertebra sticking out of a boulder. No stranger to thrilling discoveries, Hendrickson had a pretty good hunch that the vertebra belonged to a *Tyrannosaurus Rex* dinosaur! In a state of disbelief, she removed a few pieces of bone and ran to show her boss what she had found. Sure enough, her hunch was correct! Only 25 *T. rex* fossils had been discovered up to that point, and none were as complete as the fossil that Hendrickson found. It took more than 20 days for a crew to remove the 1,200 tons of dirt that encased the 67 million-year-old fossil. Later, this *T. rex* was named Sue in honor of the woman who discovered her. Even before that fateful day, Hendrickson lived a life of adventure and exploration. A professional diver since 1971, she has recovered long-lost ships such as Napoleon's shipwrecked *L'Orent* and a Chinese trader ship from the 1500's. She dives for everything from lobsters to ancient archeological treasures and has unearthed pearls, gold, and ancient butterflies fossilized in amber. This modern-day explorer loves every minute of her work. "I'm like a kid who didn't grow up. I love to look for and find things."

Chapter 1 • Science in Action   **33**

2 Maps as Models of the Earth
Chapter Planning Guide

Compression guide: To shorten instruction because of time limitations, omit the Chapter Lab.

OBJECTIVES	LABS, DEMONSTRATIONS, AND ACTIVITIES	TECHNOLOGY RESOURCES
PACING • 90 min pp. 34–41 **Chapter Opener**	SE Start-up Activity, p. 35 GENERAL	OSP Parent Letter ■ GENERAL CD Student Edition on CD-ROM CD Guided Reading Audio CD ■ TR Chapter Starter Transparency* VID Brain Food Video Quiz
Section 1 You Are Here • Explain how a magnetic compass can be used to find directions on Earth. • Explain the difference between true north and magnetic north. • Compare latitude and longitude. • Explain how latitude and longitude are used to locate places on Earth.	TE Group Activity Using Directions, p. 36 GENERAL SE School-to-Home Activity Columbus's Voyage, p. 37 GENERAL SE Quick Lab Making a Compass, p. 38 ◆ GENERAL CRF Datasheet for Quick Lab* TE Group Activity Finding True North, p. 39 GENERAL SE Connection to Social Studies Global Addresses, p. 40 GENERAL SE Skills Practice Lab Round or Flat?, p. 54 ◆ GENERAL CRF Datasheet for Chapter Lab*	CRF Lesson Plans* TR Bellringer Transparency* TR The North and South Poles* TR Lines of Longitude; Lines of Latitude* VID Lab Videos for Earth Science
PACING • 45 min pp. 42–49 **Section 2 Mapping the Earth's Surface** • Explain why maps of the Earth show distortion. • Describe four types of map projections. • Identify five pieces of information that should be shown on a map. • Describe four methods modern mapmakers use to make accurate maps.	SE Science in Action Math, Social Studies, and Language Arts Activities, pp. 60–61 GENERAL TE Group Activity Comparing Map Projections, p. 45 BASIC TE Connection Activity Math, p. 46 GENERAL TE Connection Activity Language Arts, p. 47 ADVANCED TE Activity Remote-Sensing Technology, p. 47 GENERAL	CRF Lesson Plans* TR Bellringer Transparency* TR Cylindrical Projection; Conic Projection; Azimuthal Projection* TR LINK TO PHYSICAL SCIENCE The Electromagnetic Spectrum* TE Internet Activity, p. 43 CRF SciLinks Activity* GENERAL
PACING • 45 min pp. 50–53 **Section 3 Topographic Maps** • Explain how contour lines show elevation and landforms on a map. • Explain how the relief of an area determines the contour interval used on a map. • List the rules of contour lines.	TE Activity Investigate Your Area, p. 50 ◆ GENERAL TE Group Activity Model Terrain, p. 51 BASIC SE Skills Practice Lab Topographic Tuber, p. 718 GENERAL CRF Datasheet for LabBook* LB Inquiry Labs Looking for Buried Treasure* ADVANCED LB Long-Term Projects & Research Ideas Globe Trotting* ADVANCED	CRF Lesson Plans* CRF Bellringer Transparency*

PACING • 90 min

CHAPTER REVIEW, ASSESSMENT, AND STANDARDIZED TEST PREPARATION

- CRF Vocabulary Activity* GENERAL
- SE Chapter Review, pp. 56–57 GENERAL
- CRF Chapter Review* ■ GENERAL
- CRF Chapter Tests A* ■ GENERAL, B* ADVANCED, C* SPECIAL NEEDS
- SE Standardized Test Preparation, pp. 58–59 GENERAL
- CRF Standardized Test Preparation* GENERAL
- CRF Performance-Based Assessment* GENERAL
- OSP Test Generator GENERAL
- CRF Test Item Listing* GENERAL

Online and Technology Resources

Visit **go.hrw.com** for a variety of free resources related to this textbook. Enter the keyword **HZ5MAP**.

Holt Online Learning
Students can access interactive problem-solving help and active visual concept development with the *Holt Science and Technology* Online Edition available at **www.hrw.com**.

Guided Reading Audio CD Also in Spanish
A direct reading of each chapter for auditory learners, reluctant readers, and Spanish-speaking students.

Science Tutor CD-ROM
Excellent for remediation and test practice.

KEY			
SE Student Edition	**CRF** Chapter Resource File	**SS** Science Skills Worksheets	***** Also on One-Stop Planner
TE Teacher Edition	**OSP** One-Stop Planner	**MS** Math Skills for Science Worksheets	**♦** Requires advance prep
	LB Lab Bank	**CD** CD or CD-ROM	**■** Also available in Spanish
	TR Transparencies	**VID** Classroom Video/DVD	

SKILLS DEVELOPMENT RESOURCES	SECTION REVIEW AND ASSESSMENT	STANDARDS CORRELATIONS
SE Pre-Reading Activity, p. 34 GENERAL **OSP** Science Puzzlers, Twisters & Teasers GENERAL		National Science Education Standards UCP 2, 3, 5; ST 1, 2; SAI 1; SPSP 5; HNS 1, 3
CRF Directed Reading A* BASIC, B* SPECIAL NEEDS **CRF** Vocabulary and Section Summary* GENERAL **SE** Reading Strategy Reading Organizer, p. 36 GENERAL **TE** Reading Strategy Prediction Guide, p. 38 GENERAL **TE** Inclusion Strategies, p. 39 ♦ **CRF** Reinforcement Worksheet Where on Earth?* BASIC	**SE** Reading Checks, pp. 37, 38, 40 GENERAL **TE** Reteaching, p. 40 BASIC **TE** Quiz, p. 40 GENERAL **TE** Alternative Assessment, p. 40 GENERAL **SE** Section Review,* p. 41 GENERAL **CRF** Section Quiz* GENERAL	UCP 2, 3, 5; SAI 1; ST 1, 2; SPSP 5; HNS 1, 3 *Chapter Lab:* UCP 2, 3; SAI 1; HNS 3
CRF Directed Reading A* BASIC, B* SPECIAL NEEDS **CRF** Vocabulary and Section Summary* GENERAL **SE** Reading Strategy Discussion, p. 42 GENERAL **SE** Connection to Social Studies Mapmaking and Ship Navigation, p. 44 GENERAL **TE** Reading Strategy Making an Outline, p. 43 BASIC **TE** Reading Strategy Mnemonics, p. 44 GENERAL **TE** Inclusion Strategies, p. 46 ♦ **MS** Math Skills for Science Using Proportions and Cross-Multiplication* GENERAL **CRF** Critical Thinking Shaping the World* ADVANCED	**SE** Reading Checks, pp. 42, 45, 46, 48 GENERAL **TE** Homework, p. 44 GENERAL **TE** Homework, p. 45 ADVANCED **TE** Reteaching, p. 48 BASIC **TE** Quiz, p. 48 GENERAL **TE** Alternative Assessment, p. 48 GENERAL **SE** Section Review,* p. 49 GENERAL **CRF** Section Quiz* GENERAL	UCP 2, 3, 5; SAI 1; ST 2; SPSP 5; HNS 3
CRF Directed Reading A* BASIC, B* SPECIAL NEEDS **CRF** Vocabulary and Section Summary* GENERAL **SE** Reading Strategy Paired Summarizing, p. 50 GENERAL **SE** Connection to Oceanography Mapping the Ocean Floor, p. 51 GENERAL **SE** Connection to Environmental Science Endangered Species, p. 53 GENERAL **CRF** Reinforcement Worksheet Interpreting a Topographic Map* BASIC **MS** Math Skills for Science Mapping and Surveying GENERAL	**SE** Reading Checks, p. 51 GENERAL **TE** Homework, p. 51 ADVANCED **TE** Reteaching, p. 52 BASIC **TE** Quiz, p. 52 GENERAL **TE** Alternative Assessment, p. 52 GENERAL **SE** Section Review,* p. 53 GENERAL **CRF** Section Quiz* GENERAL	UCP 2, 3, 5; SAI 1; ST 2; SPSP 2, 5; HNS 1 *LabBook:* UCP 2, 3; SAI 1; ST 1

One-Stop Planner® CD-ROM

This convenient CD-ROM includes:
- Lab Materials QuickList Software
- Holt Calendar Planner
- Customizable Lesson Plans
- Printable Worksheets
- ExamView® Test Generator

CNN student News

cnnstudentnews.com

Find the latest news, lesson plans, and activities related to important scientific events.

SciLinks NSTA

www.scilinks.org

Maintained by the **National Science Teachers Association.** See Chapter Enrichment pages for a complete list of topics.

Current Science®

Check out *Current Science* articles and activities by visiting the HRW Web site at **go.hrw.com.** Just type in the keyword **HZ5CS02T.**

Classroom Videos

- **Lab Videos** demonstrate the chapter lab.
- **Brain Food Video Quizzes** help students review the chapter material.
- **CNN Videos** bring science into your students' daily life.

Chapter 2 • Chapter Planning Guide

Chapter Resources

Visual Resources

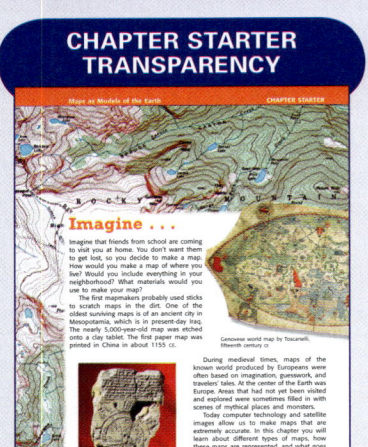

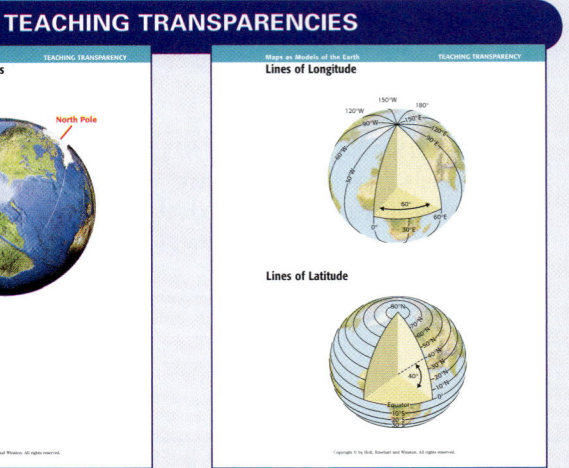

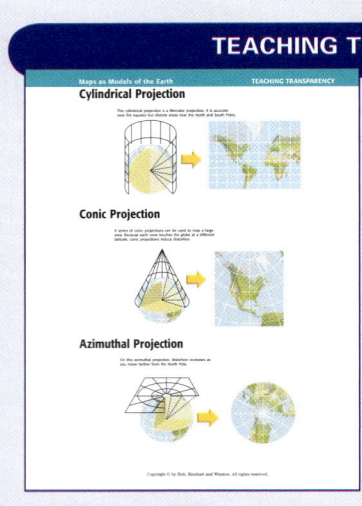

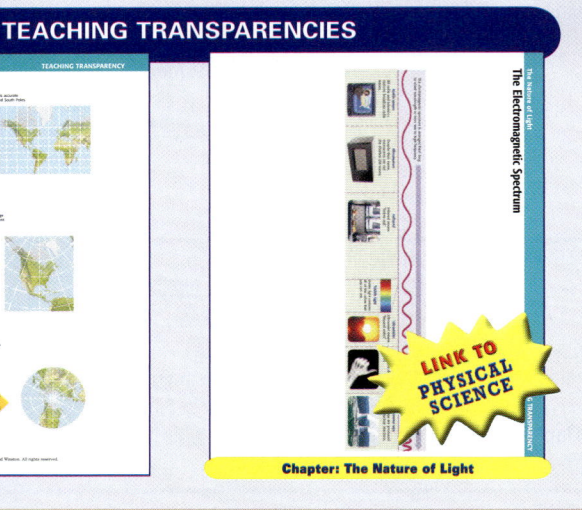

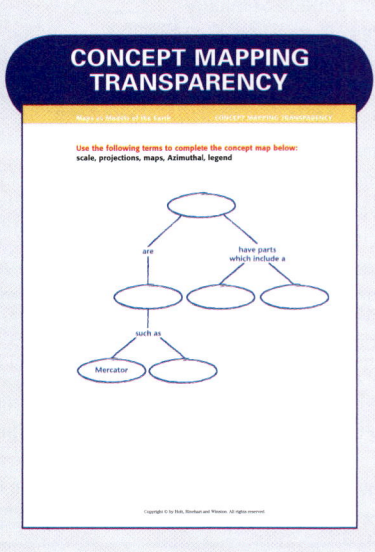

CHAPTER STARTER TRANSPARENCY

BELLRINGER TRANSPARENCIES

TEACHING TRANSPARENCIES

TEACHING TRANSPARENCIES

CONCEPT MAPPING TRANSPARENCY

Planning Resources

LESSON PLANS

PARENT LETTER

TEST ITEM LISTING

One-Stop Planner® CD-ROM

This CD-ROM includes all of the resources shown here and the following time-saving tools:

- *Lab Materials QuickList Software*
- *Customizable lesson plans*
- *Holt Calendar Planner*
- *The powerful ExamView® Test Generator*

33C Chapter 2 • Maps as Models of the Earth

For a preview of available worksheets covering math and science skills, see pages T26–T33. All of these resources are also on the One-Stop Planner®.

Meeting Individual Needs

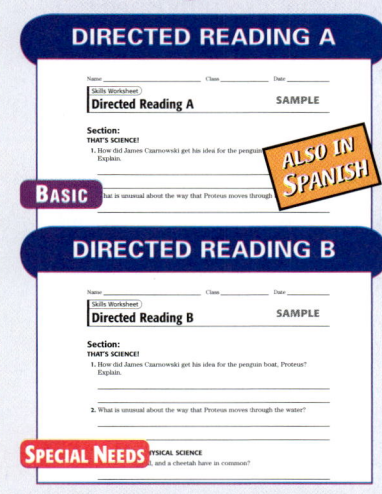

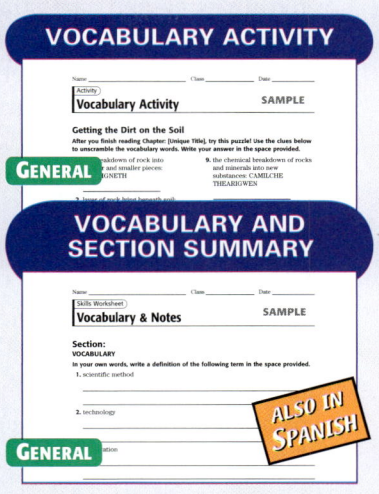

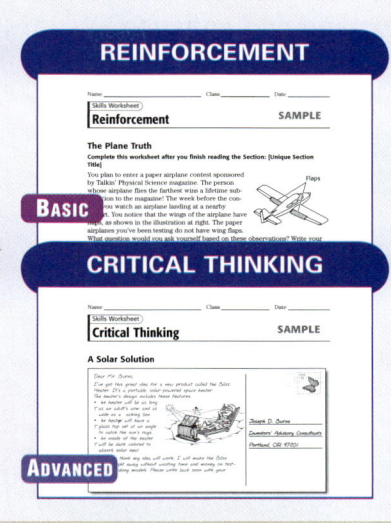

- **DIRECTED READING A** — BASIC — ALSO IN SPANISH
- **DIRECTED READING B** — SPECIAL NEEDS
- **VOCABULARY ACTIVITY** — GENERAL
- **VOCABULARY AND SECTION SUMMARY** — GENERAL — ALSO IN SPANISH
- **REINFORCEMENT** — BASIC
- **CRITICAL THINKING** — ADVANCED
- **SCILINKS ACTIVITY** — GENERAL
- **SCIENCE PUZZLERS, TWISTERS & TEASERS** — GENERAL

Labs and Activities

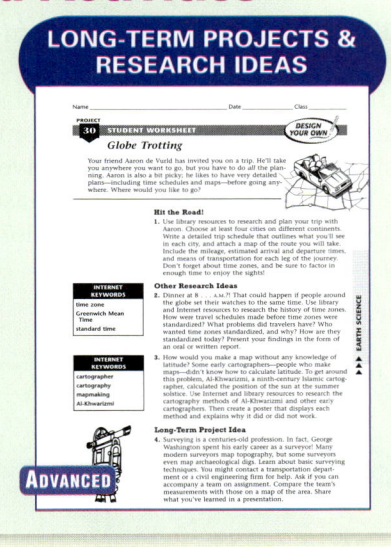

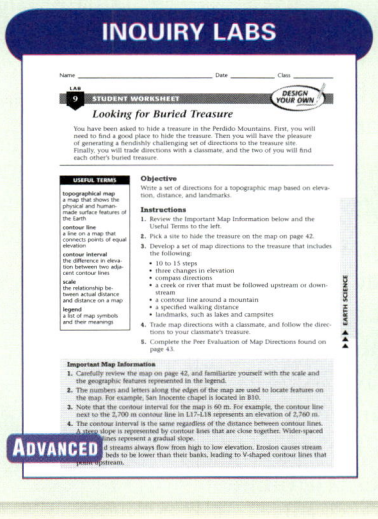

- **LONG-TERM PROJECTS & RESEARCH IDEAS** — ADVANCED
- **INQUIRY LABS** — ADVANCED
- **DATASHEETS FOR QUICK LABS**
- **DATASHEETS FOR CHAPTER LABS**
- **DATASHEETS FOR LABBOOK**

Review and Assessments

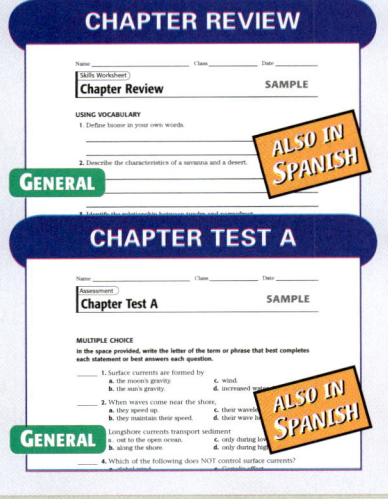

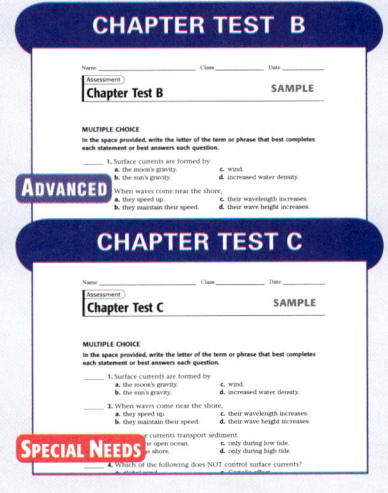

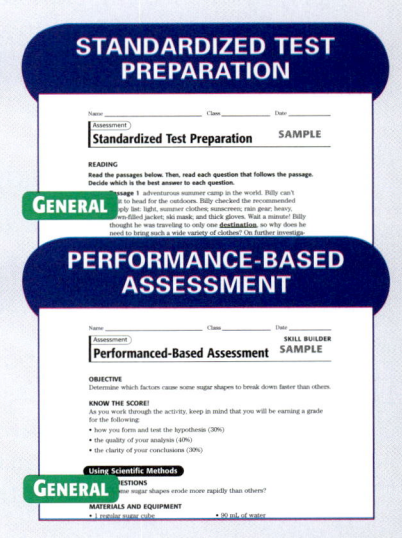

- **SECTION QUIZ** — GENERAL — ALSO IN SPANISH
- **SECTION REVIEW** — GENERAL — ALSO IN SPANISH
- **CHAPTER REVIEW** — GENERAL — ALSO IN SPANISH
- **CHAPTER TEST A** — GENERAL
- **CHAPTER TEST B** — ADVANCED
- **CHAPTER TEST C** — SPECIAL NEEDS
- **STANDARDIZED TEST PREPARATION** — GENERAL
- **PERFORMANCE-BASED ASSESSMENT** — GENERAL

Chapter 2 • Chapter Resources 33D

2 Chapter Enrichment

This Chapter Enrichment provides relevant and interesting information to expand and enhance your presentation of the chapter material.

Section 1

You Are Here
Longitude

- Because Earth rotates 360° every 24 h, it turns 15° every hour. Therefore, longitude can be determined at any place on the globe if the local time and the time at the prime meridian are known. Before the mid-18th century, the unreliability of clocks—especially those aboard ships, where motion, temperature variation, and moisture could wreak havoc with a timepiece's workings—thwarted calculations of longitude. Many shipwrecks occurred because the ship captains could not accurately calculate their location.

- In 1707, inaccurate longitudinal information caused four ships in a British fleet to run aground, and 2,000 sailors died. The British Parliament addressed the problem by offering a large reward to anyone who could develop a method to accurately calculate longitude within half a degree. John Harrison (1693–1776), a self-taught clockmaker, developed a chronometer that remained accurate on rough seas, and he won the prize in 1763. More than 200 years later, astronaut Neil Armstrong gave credit to Harrison for the role he played in enabling exploration of Earth and in inspiring future generations to venture toward exploration of the moon.

Section 2

Mapping the Earth's Surface
Gerardus Mercator

- Gerardus Mercator was born Gerhard Kremer in 1512 in Rupelmonde, Flanders (present-day Belgium). At age 24, Mercator was a highly skilled engraver, calligrapher, and scientific-instrument maker. With two of his teachers, he made the first globe of the Earth in 1536–1537. A true Renaissance man, Mercator was a highly esteemed cartographer, who also published a treatise on italic lettering, designed a grammar-school curriculum, taught mathematics, and conducted genealogical research for his patron, Duke Wilhelm of Cleve. He even attempted to write a chronology of the history of the world from the formation of Earth to 1568.

Is That a Fact!

♦ In 1544, Gerardus Mercator was imprisoned on charges of treason. Apparently, his frequent absences from Flanders to gather map data aroused the suspicions of authorities. He remained imprisoned for 7 months before his friends succeeded in clearing his name.

The Global Positioning System

- During the 1970s, the U.S. Department of Defense developed the Global Positioning System (GPS) for use in aircraft navigation and missile guidance. The system uses a network of satellites that continuously transmit positioning information to receivers on Earth. The distance between a receiver and at least four satellites is used to compute the latitude and longitude coordinates of the receiver's position.

- In 1983, the system was made available to the public and has since been used for land, sea, and air navigation, surveying, and geophysical exploration. The system can be highly accurate, making it possible to determine a position within less than 1 m. As the prices of some of the receivers have plummeted, the use of the GPS for recreational activities, such as boating, hiking, and hunting, has increased. Most receivers used by the public for recreational purposes are accurate only to about 10 m.

33E Chapter 2 • Maps as Models of the Earth

For background information about teaching strategies and issues, refer to the *Professional Reference for Teachers*.

Landsat

- Since the Landsat program began in 1972, a number of satellites have been deployed that carry remote-sensing equipment. The equipment is designed to detect radiation in different bands of the electromagnetic spectrum. The most recent satellites, *Landsat 4, 5,* and *7,* orbit Earth from pole to pole every 16 days. Landsat data are particularly useful for thematic mapping. For example, data from the blue-green spectral region are useful for distinguishing between coniferous and deciduous plants, and data from the thermal infrared range supply information about soil moisture.

Section 3

Topographic Maps

Inuit Relief Maps

- The Inuit of Baffin Island were skilled mapmakers. They made permanent relief maps by carving coastal features into pieces of wood and walrus ivory. The Inuit also sewed small pieces of fur or driftwood to sealskin to represent islands. They measured distance on their maps not by miles but by "sleeps." The distance to a hunting ground, for example, would be measured by how many rest stops would be taken before reaching it.

John Wesley Powell (1834–1902)

- American geologist and surveyor John Wesley Powell headed an official expedition to the Grand Canyon in 1871. His purpose was to conduct a topographic survey to map "as broad a belt of country as it was possible" on both sides of the Colorado and Green Rivers. The expedition yielded meticulously detailed topographic maps for an area that had previously been described as the "great unknown." Those maps were instrumental to Powell's appointment in 1881 as director of the U.S. Geological Survey (USGS).

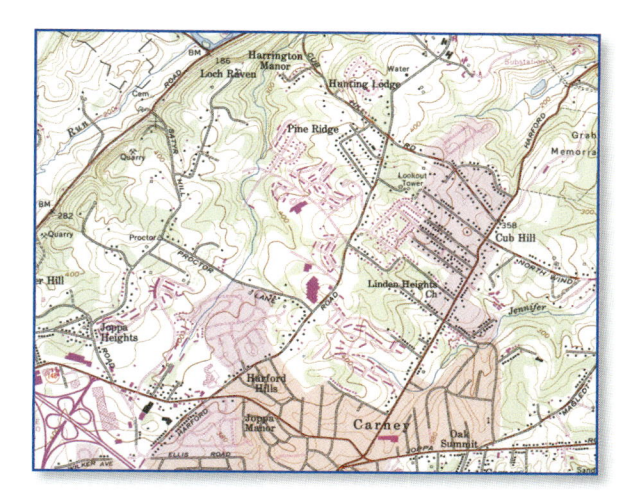

- As director, Powell aimed to create topographic maps for the entire country by using large scales, ranging from 1:250,000 for desert regions to 1:62,500 for densely populated areas. Powell insisted on including data concerning soils, springs, and other natural resources, which he felt were essential for making land-use decisions. The high-quality topographical maps created during Powell's administration set the standard for published topographic maps in the United States for many years to come.

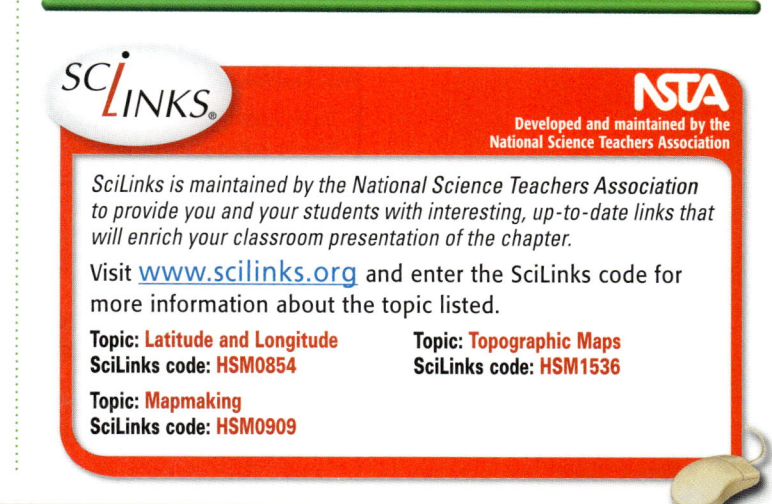

SciLinks — Developed and maintained by the National Science Teachers Association

SciLinks is maintained by the National Science Teachers Association to provide you and your students with interesting, up-to-date links that will enrich your classroom presentation of the chapter.

Visit www.scilinks.org and enter the SciLinks code for more information about the topic listed.

Topic: Latitude and Longitude
SciLinks code: HSM0854

Topic: Topographic Maps
SciLinks code: HSM1536

Topic: Mapmaking
SciLinks code: HSM0909

Chapter 2 • Chapter Enrichment   **33F**

Overview
This chapter will help students learn basic map-reading skills. Students will also learn how a compass is used to find directions and how lines of latitude and longitude are used to identify points on the Earth's surface.

Assessing Prior Knowledge
Students should be familiar with the following topic:
- scientific models

Identifying Misconceptions
As students learn the material in this chapter, some of them may be confused about how a compass is used to determine direction. Some students may think that a compass can keep a person from getting lost. Stress to students that a compass is usually used in conjunction with a map. Also, some students may be confused about the distortion that occurs when information on a sphere is transferred to a flat surface. Students may not recognize that all maps have some degree of distortion.

2
Maps as Models of the Earth

SECTION 1 You Are Here 36

SECTION 2 Mapping the Earth's Surface 42

SECTION 3 Topographic Maps 50

Chapter Lab 54
Chapter Review 56
Standardized Test Preparation 58
Science in Action 60

About the PHOTO
No ordinary camera took this picture! In fact, a camera wasn't used at all. This image is a radar image of a mountainous area of Tibet. It was taken from the space shuttle. Radar imaging is a method that scientists use to map areas of the Earth from far above the Earth's surface.

PRE-READING ACTIVITY

FOLDNOTES **Three-Panel Flip Chart**
Before you read the chapter, create the FoldNote entitled "Three-Panel Flip Chart" described in the **Study Skills** section of the Appendix. Label the flaps of the three-panel flip chart with "Cylindrical projection," "Conical projection," and "Azimuthal projection." As you read the chapter, write information you learn about each category under the appropriate flap.

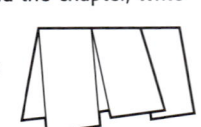

Standards Correlations
The following codes indicate the National Science Education Standards that correlate to this chapter. The full text of the standards is at the front of the book.

Chapter Opener
SAI 1; SPSP 5; HNS 1, 3

Section 1 You Are Here
UCP 2, 3, 5; SAI 1; ST 1, 2; SPSP 5; HNS 1, 3

Section 2 Mapping Earth's Surface
UCP 2, 3, 5; SAI 1; ST 2; SPSP 5; HNS 3

Section 3 Topographic Maps
UCP 2, 3, 5; SAI 1; ST 2; SPSP 2, 5; HNS 1; *LabBook:* UCP 2, 3; SAI 1; ST 1

Chapter Lab
UCP 2, 3; SAI 1; ST 1; HNS 1

Chapter Review
UCP 2; SAI 2; HNS 3

Science in Action
ST1; SPSP 5; HNS 1, 3

34 Chapter 2 • Maps as Models of the Earth

START-UP ACTIVITY

MATERIALS

FOR EACH STUDENT
- computer (optional)
- paper
- pencils, colored

Teacher's Note: Before students start their maps, have them brainstorm a list of school landmarks, and suggest that they use the location of these landmarks as reference points in their maps.

Answers
1. Answers may vary. Accept all reasonable responses.
2. Answers may vary. Accept all reasonable responses.
3. Answers may vary.

START-UP ACTIVITY

Follow the Yellow Brick Road

In this activity, you will not only learn how to read a map but you will also make a map that someone else can read.

Procedure
1. Use a **computer drawing program or colored pencils and paper** to draw a map that shows how to get from your classroom to another place in your school, such as the gym. Make sure you include enough information for someone unfamiliar with your school to find his or her way.
2. After you finish drawing your map, switch maps with a partner. Examine your classmate's map, and try to figure out where the map is leading you.

Analysis
1. Is your map an accurate picture of your school? Explain your answer.
2. What could you do to make your map better? What are some limitations of your map?
3. Compare your map with your partner's map. How are your maps alike? How are they different?

Chapter Starter Transparency
Use this transparency to help students begin thinking about the history of mapmaking.

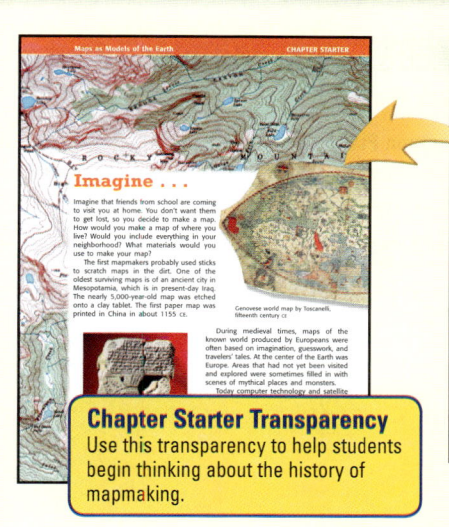

CHAPTER RESOURCES

Technology
- **Transparencies** — READING SKILLS
  - Chapter Starter Transparency
- **Student Edition on CD-ROM**
- **Guided Reading Audio CD**
  - English or Spanish
- **Classroom Videos**
  - Brain Food Video Quiz

Workbooks
- **Science Puzzlers, Twisters & Teasers**
  - Maps as Models of the Earth GENERAL

Chapter 2 • Maps as Models of the Earth   35

SECTION 1

Focus

Overview

This section opens with a discussion of the history of mapmaking. Students learn how to find directions on a globe by using reference points such as the North and South Poles. Students learn how a compass is used to find directions and how true north differs from magnetic north. The section closes with a discussion of lines of latitude and longitude and the way they can be used to locate points on the Earth's surface.

Bellringer

Ask students to draw a map from their home to one of their favorite places. Have them clearly label all landmarks and include information that might be useful to someone using the map.

Motivate

Group Activity — GENERAL

Using Directions Have students write a description of the route they take as they travel between home and school. Then, have them rewrite the description using cardinal directions. Have pairs of students trade descriptions and use a map to check the accuracy of each other's maps. **English Language Learners** **LS Verbal**

SECTION 1

READING WARM-UP

Objectives
- Explain how a magnetic compass can be used to find directions on Earth.
- Explain the difference between true north and magnetic north.
- Compare latitude and longitude.
- Explain how latitude and longitude is used to locate places on Earth.

Terms to Learn

map
true north
magnetic declination
latitude
equator
longitude
prime meridian

READING STRATEGY

Reading Organizer As you read this section, create an outline of the section. Use the headings from the section in your outline.

map a representation of the features of a physical body such as Earth

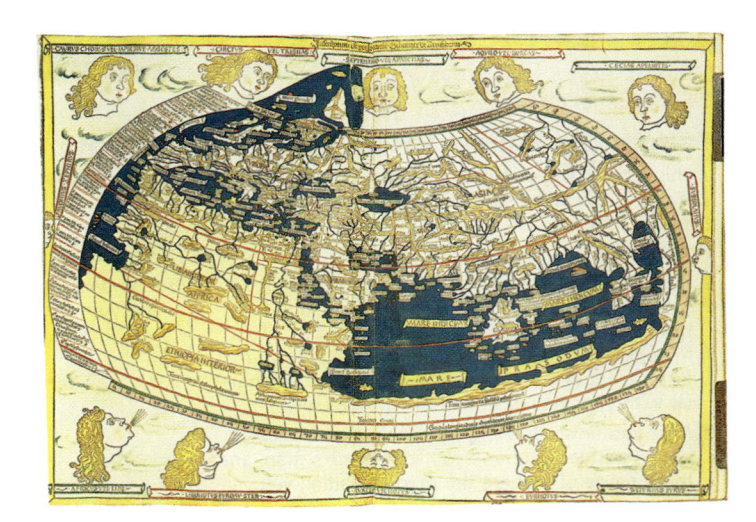

Figure 1 This map shows what explorers thought the world looked like 1,800 years ago.

CHAPTER RESOURCES

Chapter Resource File
- Lesson Plan
- Directed Reading A BASIC
- Directed Reading B SPECIAL NEEDS

Technology
- Transparencies
  - Bellringer
  - The North and South Poles

You Are Here

Have you ever noticed the curve of the Earth's surface? You probably haven't. When you walk across the Earth, it does not appear to be curved. It looks flat.

Over time, ideas about Earth's shape have changed. Maps reflected how people saw the world and what technology was available. A **map** is a representation of the features of a physical body such as Earth. If you look at Ptolemy's (TAHL uh meez) world map from the second century, as shown in **Figure 1**, you might not know what you are looking at. Today satellites give us more accurate images of the Earth. In this section, you will learn how early scientists knew Earth was round long before pictures from space were taken. You will also learn how to find location and direction on Earth's surface.

What Does Earth Really Look Like?

The Greeks thought of Earth as a sphere almost 2,000 years before Christopher Columbus made his voyage in 1492. The observation that a ship sinks below the horizon as it sails into the distance supported the idea of a spherical Earth. If Earth were flat, the ship would not sink below the horizon.

Eratosthenes (ER uh TAHS thuh NEEZ), a Greek mathematician, wanted to know the size of Earth. In about 240 BCE, he calculated Earth's circumference using math and observations of the sun. There were no satellites or computers back then. We now know his calculation was wrong by only 6,250 km!

Is That a Fact!

The orientation of maps with north at the top is arbitrary. For many centuries, European maps placed east at the top to emphasize the importance of Jerusalem to the Europeans' faith. The Chinese put south at the top of their maps because nothing to the north held any interest for them.

---

36 Chapter 2 • Maps as Models of the Earth

Figure 2 *The North Pole is a good reference point for describing locations in North America.*

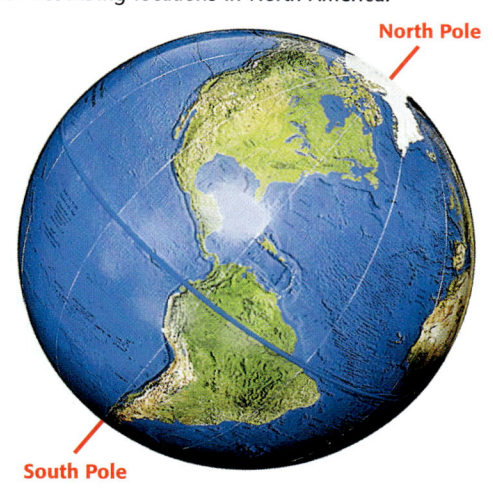

SCHOOL to HOME

WRITING SKILL Columbus's Voyage

Did Christopher Columbus discover that Earth was a sphere only after he completed his voyage in 1492? Or did he know before he left? With a parent, use the Internet or the library to find out more information about Columbus's voyage. Then, write a paragraph describing what you learned.

ACTIVITY

Finding Direction on Earth

When giving directions to your home, you might name a landmark, such as a grocery store, as a reference point. A *reference point* is a fixed place on the Earth's surface from which direction and location can be described.

The Earth is spherical, so it has no top, bottom, or sides for people to use as reference points for determining locations on its surface. However, the Earth does rotate, or spin, on its axis. The Earth's axis is an imaginary line that runs through the Earth. At either end of the axis is a geographic pole. The North and South Poles are used as reference points when describing direction and location on the Earth, as shown in **Figure 2**.

✓ **Reading Check** What is a reference point? (*See the Appendix for answers to Reading Checks.*)

Cardinal Directions

A reference point alone will not help you give good directions. You will need to be able to describe how to get to your home from the reference point. You will need to use the directions north, south, east, and west. These directions are called *cardinal directions*. Using cardinal directions is much more precise than saying "Turn left," "Go straight," or "Turn right." So, you may tell a friend to walk a block north of the gas station to get to your home. To use cardinal directions properly, you will need a compass, shown in **Figure 3**.

Figure 3 *A compass shows the cardinal directions north, south, east and west, as well as combinations of these directions.*

Teach

MISCONCEPTION ALERT

Christopher Columbus Students may be under the impression that Christopher Columbus discovered that Earth was round only after he safely made his voyage in 1492 without sailing off the edge of the world. In fact, Columbus, like most other educated people of his time, was well aware before he set out that Earth was not flat.

CONNECTION to Life Science — GENERAL

Magnetic Bacteria Magnetotactic bacteria use magnetic particles in their cytoplasm to align themselves with the Earth's magnetic field. North of the equator, the bacteria are north-seeking travelers. South of the equator, they are south-seeking travelers. At the equator, where the magnetic fields are at their weakest, the populations are mixed between north- and south-seeking bacteria.

Answer to Reading Check

A reference point is a fixed place on the Earth's surface from which direction and location can be described.

Cultural Awareness — GENERAL

Chinese Compasses The Chinese invented the magnetic compass in the third century BCE. The magnetic properties of lodestone, known today as magnetite, were well known to the Chinese. Early compasses consisted of a piece of lodestone on a card that was balanced on a pivot. The scale of the compass was marked with compass points at 15° increments. By the 10th century, the compass was standard equipment on Chinese sailing ships.

Section 1 • You Are Here

Teach, continued

READING STRATEGY — GENERAL

Prediction Guide Before students read these pages, ask them if the following statements are true or false:

- Earth has four poles. (true)
- A compass is the only thing you need to find a location. (false)
- Imaginary lines drawn around Earth can be used to pinpoint locations. (true)

English Language Learners

LS **Verbal**

Quick Lab

MATERIALS

FOR EACH STUDENT
- compass
- magnet
- needle, sewing, steel
- paper, tissue, 1 cm × 3 cm
- water, in a bowl

Answers

4. Answers may vary. Both compasses should be pointing in the same direction.
5. Answers may vary.

Answer to Reading Check

True north is the direction to the geographic North Pole.

Using a Compass

A magnetic compass will show you which direction is north. A *compass* is a tool that uses the natural magnetism of the Earth to show direction. A compass needle points to the magnetic north pole. Earth has two different sets of poles—the geographic poles and the magnetic poles, as shown in **Figure 4**.

True North and Magnetic Declination

Remember that the Earth's geographic poles are on either end of the Earth's axis. Earth has its own magnetic field, which produces magnetic poles. Earth's magnetic poles are not lined up exactly with Earth's axis. So, there is a difference between the locations of Earth's magnetic and geographic poles. **True north** is the direction to the geographic North Pole. When using a compass, you need to make a correction for the difference between the geographic North Pole and the magnetic north pole. The angle of correction is called **magnetic declination**.

✓ **Reading Check** What is true north?

true north the direction to the geographic North Pole

magnetic declination the difference between the magnetic north and the true north

Figure 4 Unlike the geographic poles, which are always in the same place, the magnetic poles have changed location throughout the history of the Earth.

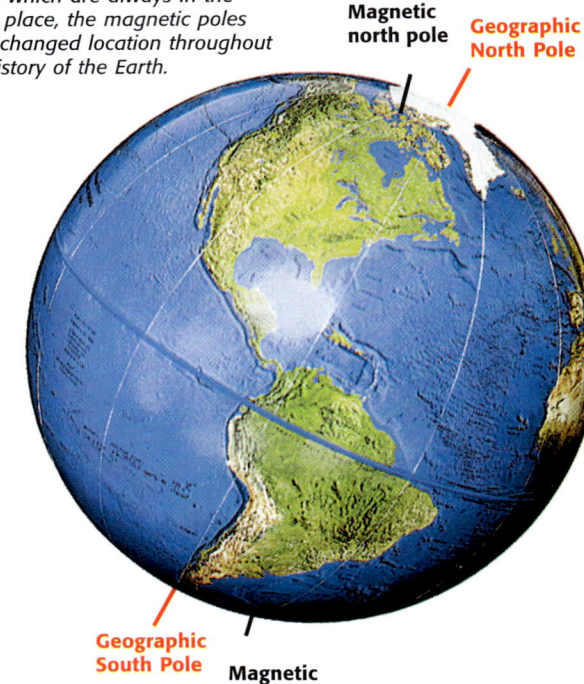

- Magnetic north pole
- Geographic North Pole
- Geographic South Pole
- Magnetic south pole

Quick Lab

Making a Compass

1. Do this lab outside. Carefully rub a **steel sewing needle** against a **magnet** in the same direction 40 times.
2. Float a **1 cm × 3 cm piece of tissue paper** in a **bowl of water.**
3. Place the needle in the center of the tissue paper.
4. Compare your compass with a **regular compass.** Are both compasses pointing in the same direction?
5. How would you improve your compass?

SCIENCE HUMOR

Before the 17th century, many sailors refused to transport onions and garlic because they believed that these items would destroy a compass's magnetic properties. In 1600, English physician and scientist William Gilbert set out to test this belief. He ate a large quantity of garlic and then belched on a compass needle that he had also rubbed with garlic juice. The compass's magnetic properties remained intact, and Gilbert proved, at least to himself, that the notion was unfounded.

Chapter 2 • Maps as Models of the Earth

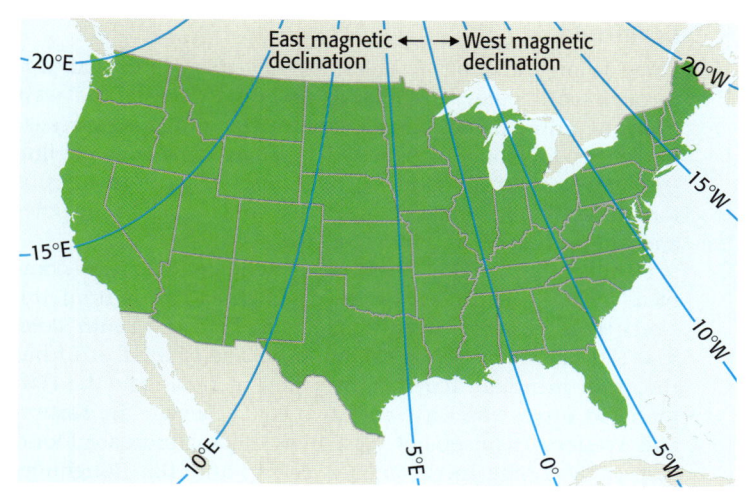

Figure 5 The blue lines on the map connect points that have the same magnetic declination.

Using Magnetic Declination

Magnetic declination is measured in degrees east or west of true north. Magnetic declination has been determined for different points on the Earth's surface. Once you know the declination for your area, you can use a compass to determine true north. This correction is like the correction you would make to the handlebars of a bike with a bent front wheel. You have to turn the handlebars a certain amount to make the bicycle go straight. **Figure 5** shows a map of the magnetic declination of the United States. What is the approximate magnetic declination of your city or town?

Finding Locations on the Earth

All of the houses and buildings in your neighborhood have addresses that give their location. But how would you find the location of something such as a city or an island? These places can be given an "address" using *latitude* and *longitude*. Latitude and longitude are shown by intersecting lines on a globe or map that allow you to find exact locations.

Latitude

Imaginary lines drawn around the Earth parallel to the equator are called lines of latitude, or *parallels*. **Latitude** is the distance north or south from the equator. Latitude is expressed in degrees, as shown in **Figure 6**. The **equator** is a circle halfway between the North and South Poles that divides the Earth into the Northern and Southern Hemispheres. The equator represents 0° latitude. The North Pole is 90° north latitude, and the South Pole is 90° south latitude.

latitude the distance north or south from the equator; expressed in degrees

equator the imaginary circle halfway between the poles that divides the Earth into the Northern and Southern Hemispheres

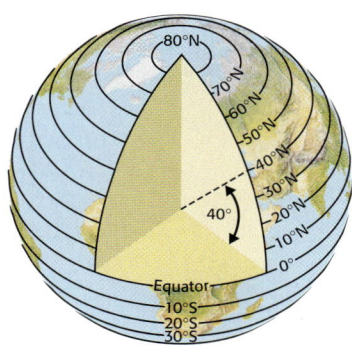

Figure 6 Degrees latitude are a measure of the angle made by the equator and the location on the Earth's surface, as measured from the center of the Earth.

WEIRD SCIENCE

As the Earth rotates, both the geographic North Pole and the magnetic north pole move constantly. The geographic North Pole moves about 6 m on a 435-day cycle. This movement results from a wobble in the Earth's rotation. The magnetic north pole wanders because of changes in Earth's rotating iron core. The magnetic pole is currently moving northwest at an average rate of 10 km per year.

CHAPTER RESOURCES

Technology

Transparencies
• Lines of Longitude; Lines of Latitude

Group ACTIVITY — GENERAL

Finding True North For thousands of years, people have used the sun to determine true north. This activity is most accurate at midday, when the sun is at its southernmost point.

• At 11:30 A.M., have students insert a ruler in the ground and a pencil at the tip of the ruler's shadow.

• After 1 h, have students insert another pencil at the tip of the ruler's new shadow.

• Have students place a piece of string between the two pencils. The string will be an east-west line. Viewed with your back to the sun, the first pencil indicates west, and the second indicates east.

Students can then use a protractor to position a north-south string perpendicular to the east-west string. **LS Visual/Kinesthetic**

INCLUSION Strategies

• Learning Disabled
• Developmentally Delayed
• Hearing Impaired

Tell students that they are going to create a "human globe." You will need a variety of colored yarns. Establish direction in the classroom by hanging place cards marked North, South, East, and West. Have students form a circle around the room. Ask them to use red yarn to mark the equator, using the place cards as reference. Next, ask students to begin to mark some additional parallels of latitude with black yarn. Next, create the prime meridian. Finally, use the black yarn to add more lines of longitude. Have tall students push up on the center of the circle to create the rounded effect you see on a globe. **English Language Learners**
LS Kinesthetic

Section 1 • You Are Here

Close

Reteaching — BASIC

Latitude and Longitude On the board, draw two columns. Label one column "Latitude" and the other column "Longitude." Ask students to call out characteristics of latitude and longitude as you write their answers on the board. Students can copy the information on the board and use it as a study tool. **LS** Verbal

Quiz — GENERAL

1. List two reference points that can be used to describe direction and location on Earth. (Sample answer: North Pole, South Pole)

2. What are lines of latitude and lines of longitude? (Lines of latitude are imaginary lines around Earth parallel to the equator that are used to measure a location's distance north or south of the equator. Lines of longitude are imaginary lines that run between the Earth's geographic poles, and they are used to measure a location's distance east or west of the prime meridian.)

Alternative Assessment — GENERAL

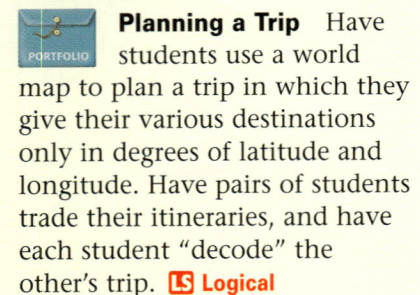

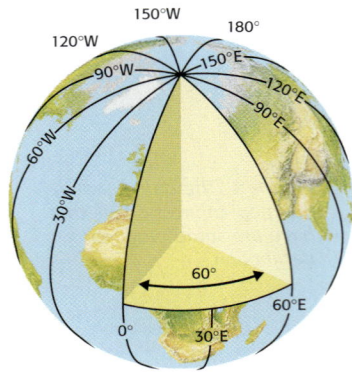

Planning a Trip Have students use a world map to plan a trip in which they give their various destinations only in degrees of latitude and longitude. Have pairs of students trade their itineraries, and have each student "decode" the other's trip. **LS** Logical

Figure 7 Degrees longitude are a measure of the angle made by the prime meridian and the location on the Earth's surface, as measured from the center of the Earth.

longitude the distance east and west from the prime meridian; expressed in degrees

prime meridian the meridian, or line of longitude, that is designated as 0° longitude

Longitude

Lines of longitude, or *meridians*, are imaginary lines that pass through both poles. **Longitude** is the distance east and west from the prime meridian. Like latitude, longitude is expressed in degrees, as shown in **Figure 7**. The **prime meridian** is the line that represents 0° longitude. Unlike lines of latitude, lines of longitude are not parallel. Lines of longitude touch at the poles and are farthest apart at the equator.

Unlike the equator, the prime meridian does not completely circle the globe. The prime meridian runs from the North Pole through Greenwich, England, to the South Pole. The 180° meridian lies on the opposite side of the Earth from the prime meridian. Together, the prime meridian and the 180° meridian divide the Earth into two equal halves—the Eastern and Western Hemispheres. East lines of longitude are found east of the prime meridian, between 0° and 180° longitude. West lines of longitude are found west of the prime meridian, between 0° and 180° longitude.

Using Latitude and Longitude

Points on the Earth's surface can be located by using latitude and longitude. Lines of latitude and lines of longitude cross and form a grid system on globes and maps. This grid system can be used to find locations north or south of the equator and east or west of the prime meridian.

Figure 8 shows you how latitude and longitude can be used to find the location of your state capital. First, locate the star representing your state capital on the appropriate map. Then, use the lines of latitude and longitude closest to your state capital to estimate its approximate latitude and longitude.

Reading Check Which set of imaginary lines are referred to as meridians: lines of latitude or lines of longitude?

CONNECTION TO Social Studies

Global Addresses You can find the location of any place on Earth by finding the coordinates of the place, or latitude and longitude, on a globe or a map. Using a globe or an atlas, find the coordinates of the following cities:

New York, New York
Sao Paulo, Brazil
Sydney, Australia
Madrid, Spain
Paris, France
Cairo, Egypt

Then, find the latitude and longitude coordinates of your own city. Can you find another city that shares the same latitude as your city? Can you find another city that shares the same longitude?

ACTIVITY

Answer to Connection to Social Studies
New York, New York: 40°N, 74°W
Sao Paulo, Brazil: 23°S, 47°W
Sydney, Australia: 33°S, 151°E
Madrid, Spain: 40°N, 4°W
Paris, France: 42°N, 2°E
Cairo, Egypt: 30°N, 31°E

Answer to Reading Check
lines of longitude

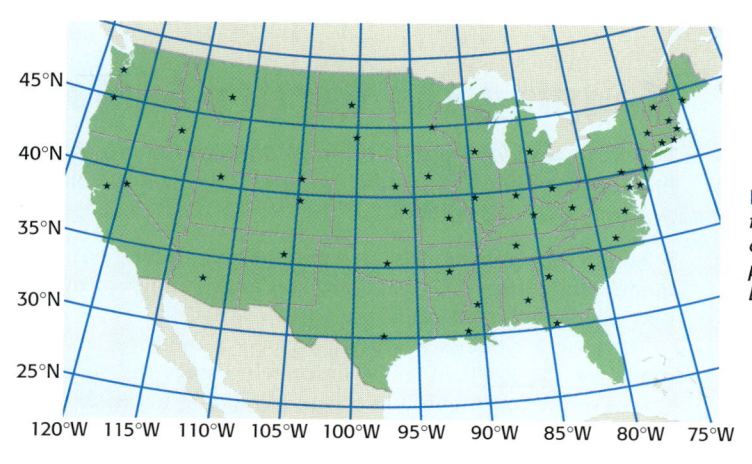

Figure 8 The grid pattern formed by lines of latitude and longitude allows you to pinpoint any location on the Earth's surface.

SECTION Review

Summary

- Magnetic compasses are used to find direction on Earth's surface. A compass needle points to the magnetic north pole.
- True north is the direction to the geographic North Pole, which never changes. The magnetic north pole may change over time. Magnetic declination is the difference between true north and magnetic north.
- Latitude and longitude help you find locations on a map or a globe. Lines of latitude run east and west. Lines of longitude run north and south through the poles. These lines cross and form a grid system on globes and maps.

Using Key Terms

1. Use each of the following terms in a separate sentence: *latitude*, *longitude*, *equator*, and *prime meridian*.

2. In your own words, write a definition for the term *true north*.

Understanding Key Ideas

3. The geographic poles are
   a. used as reference points when describing direction and location on Earth.
   b. formed because of the Earth's magnetic field.
   c. at either end of the Earth's axis.
   d. Both (a) and (c)

4. How are lines of latitude and lines of longitude alike? How are they different?

5. How can you use a magnetic compass to find directions on Earth?

6. What is the difference between true north and magnetic north?

7. How do lines of latitude and longitude help you find locations on the Earth's surface?

Math Skills

8. The distance between 40°N latitude and 41°N latitude is 69 mi. What is this distance in km? (Hint: 1 km = 0.621 mi)

Critical Thinking

9. **Applying Concepts** While exploring the attic, you find a treasure map. The map shows that the treasure is buried at 97°N and 188°E. Explain why this location is incorrect.

10. **Making Inferences** When using a compass to explore an area, why do you need to know an area's magnetic declination?

Answers to Section Review

1. Sample answer: Lines of latitude are also referred to as parallels. Lines of longitude are also known as meridians. The equator is an imaginary circle that divides the Earth into the Northern and Southern Hemispheres. The prime meridian is the line that represents 0° longitude.

2. Sample answer: True north is the direction to the Earth's geographic North Pole.

3. d

4. Lines of latitude and lines of longitude are alike because they are both used to describe locations on Earth. Lines of latitude are different from lines of longitude because lines of latitude are parallel to the equator, whereas lines of longitude pass through the poles.

5. Sample answer: A compass needle will point in the direction of the magnetic north pole. You can use this information to find general directions on Earth.

6. True north is the direction to the geographic North Pole. Magnetic north is the direction to the Earth's magnetic north pole. True north and magnetic north have different locations.

7. Lines of latitude and longitude form a grid system that can be used to find locations on the Earth's surface.

8. (69 mi ÷ 0.621 mi) × 1 km = 111.11 km

9. This location is impossible because the greatest measure of latitude is 90° and the greatest measure of longitude is 180°.

10. Because the compass points to magnetic north, it is important to know the magnetic declination at your location. This will help you make corrections to adjust for the difference between true north and magnetic north.

MISCONCEPTION ALERT

Compasses and GPS Students may believe that a compass or GPS is all you need to keep from getting lost outdoors. Point out that compasses and GPS are useful only when combined with the ability to read maps and to observe land features. Compasses and GPS can be used for orienting oneself and for taking bearings on landmarks for map triangulation.

CHAPTER RESOURCES

Chapter Resource File
- Section Quiz GENERAL
- Section Review GENERAL
- Vocabulary and Section Summary GENERAL
- Reinforcement Worksheet BASIC
- Datasheet for Quick Lab

Section 1 • You Are Here 41

SECTION 2

Focus

Overview
In this section, students compare maps and globes as models of the Earth and identify their limitations. Students explore the features of four common map projections. In addition, they discover some of the technological advances that have influenced recent trends in cartography.

🔔 Bellringer
Display a world map, a map of your state, and a map of your community. Have students make a chart in which they list the similarities and differences between each map. Then, have them suggest three uses and three improvements for each map.

Motivate

Discussion — GENERAL
Map Distortion Have students examine a globe and a Mercator projection of a world map. Tell students that both are representations of Earth. Ask students to find ways in which the two representations differ. Point out the difference in the size and shape of Greenland. Ask students how they might account for the discrepancies. Tell them that in this section they will learn about the difficulties involved in making flat representations of Earth's curved surface. **LS Visual/Verbal**

SECTION 2

READING WARM-UP

Objectives
- Explain why maps of the Earth show distortion.
- Describe four types of map projections.
- Identify five pieces of information that should be shown on a map.
- Describe four methods modern mapmakers use to make accurate maps.

Terms to Learn
cylindrical projection
conic projection
azimuthal projection
remote sensing

READING STRATEGY

Discussion Read this section silently. Write down questions that you have about this section. Discuss your questions in a small group.

Mapping the Earth's Surface

What do a teddy bear, a toy airplane, and a plastic doll have in common besides being toys? They are all models that represent real things.

Scientists also use models to represent real things, but their models are not toys. Globes and maps are examples of models that scientists use to study the Earth's surface.

Because a globe is a sphere, a globe is the most accurate model of the Earth. A globe accurately shows the sizes and shapes of the continents and oceans in relation to one another. But a globe is not always the best model to use when studying the Earth's surface. A globe is too small to show many details, such as roads and rivers. It is much easier to show details on maps. But how do you show the Earth's curved surface on a flat surface? Keep reading to find out.

A Flat Sphere?

A map is a flat representation of the Earth's curved surface. However, when you move information from a curved surface to a flat surface, you lose some accuracy. Changes called *distortions* happen in the shapes and sizes of landmasses and oceans on maps. Direction and distance can also be distorted. Consider the example of the orange peel shown in **Figure 1**.

✓ **Reading Check** What are distortions on maps? (*See the Appendix for answers to Reading Checks.*)

Figure 1 If you remove and flatten the peel from an orange, the peel will stretch and tear. Notice how shapes as well as distances between points on the peel are distorted.

CHAPTER RESOURCES

Chapter Resource File
- Lesson Plan
- Directed Reading A BASIC
- Directed Reading B SPECIAL NEEDS

Technology
- Transparencies
  - Bellringer
  - Cylindrical Projection; Conic Projection; Azimuthal Projection

Answer to Reading Check
Distortions are inaccuracies produced when information is transferred from a curved surface to a flat surface.

---

42 Chapter 2 • Maps as Models of the Earth

Map Projections

Mapmakers use map projections to move the image of Earth's curved surface onto a flat surface. No map projection of Earth can show the surface of a sphere in the correct proportions. All flat maps have distortion. However, a map showing a smaller area, such as a city, has less distortion than a map showing a larger area, such as the world.

To understand how map projections are made, think of Earth as a translucent globe that has a light inside. If you hold a piece of paper against the globe, shadows appear on the paper. These shadows show marks on the globe, such as continents, oceans, and lines of latitude and longitude. The way the paper is held against the globe determines the kind of map projection that is made. The most common map projections are based on three shapes—cylinders, cones, and planes.

Cylindrical Projection

A map projection that is made when the contents of the globe are moved onto a cylinder of paper is called a **cylindrical projection** (suh LIN dri kuhl proh JEK shuhn). The most common cylindrical projection is called a *Mercator projection* (muhr KAYT uhr proh JEK shuhn). The Mercator projection shows the globe's latitude and longitude lines as straight lines. Equal amounts of space are used between longitude lines. Latitude lines are spaced farther apart north and south of the equator. Because of the spacing, areas near the poles look wider and longer on the map than they look on the globe. In **Figure 2**, Greenland appears almost as large as Africa!

cylindrical projection a map projection that is made by moving the surface features of the globe onto a cylinder

Figure 2 Cylindrical Projection

This cylindrical projection is a Mercator projection. It is accurate near the equator but distorts areas near the North and South Poles.

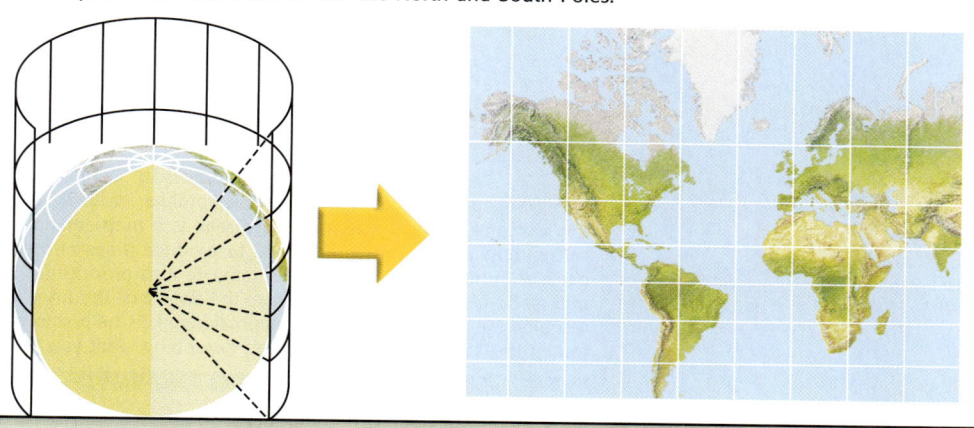

INTERNET ACTIVITY
Short Story — GENERAL

For an internet activity related to this chapter, have students go to **go.hrw.com** and type in the keyword **HZ5MAPW**.

SCIENCE HUMOR

Q: What do you get when you cross a cowboy with a mapmaker?

A: a cowtographer

Teach

READING STRATEGY — BASIC

Making an Outline As students read about map projections, have them write down the name of each type of projection and a brief description of how the projection is made. Have students list the advantages or disadvantages of each type of projection. **English Language Learners**
LS Verbal

MISCONCEPTION ALERT

Map Inaccuracies The distortions of landmasses are not the only inaccuracies that occur on maps. When making maps, such as road maps, for popular use, mapmakers routinely generalize them for both practical and aesthetic reasons. For example, when the size of a map's scale is reduced, two features (such as two lakes or two towns) might appear to be adjacent to each other. In this case, the mapmaker might move them slightly apart. Mapmakers sometimes also add details that may not really exist; for instance, meander loops might be added to a river or stream to make it look more realistic. Topographic maps, however, are made from aerial photographs and are extremely accurate.

Section 2 • Mapping the Earth's Surface

Teach, continued

READING STRATEGY — GENERAL

Mnemonics Have students think of some rhymes to help them remember key points about the projections discussed in the text. You might suggest the following to help students get started:

- "If you're traveling to the equator, you'll do well with Mercator."
- "For east to west, conic is best."
- "For a stroll at a pole, an azimuthal will help you stay in control."

English Language Learners
LS Verbal/Auditory

Homework — GENERAL

Map Projections Have students make a chart listing the strengths and weaknesses of cylindrical, conic, azimuthal, and equal-area projections. Then, have students research another projection, such as the Robinson projection. Have them add the strengths and weaknesses of that projection to their charts. Have them explain at the bottom of the chart why none of the projections is entirely free of distortions and inaccuracies. **LS** Verbal

---

Figure 3 Conic Projection

A series of conic projections can be used to map a large area. Because each cone touches the globe at a different latitude, conic projections reduce distortion.

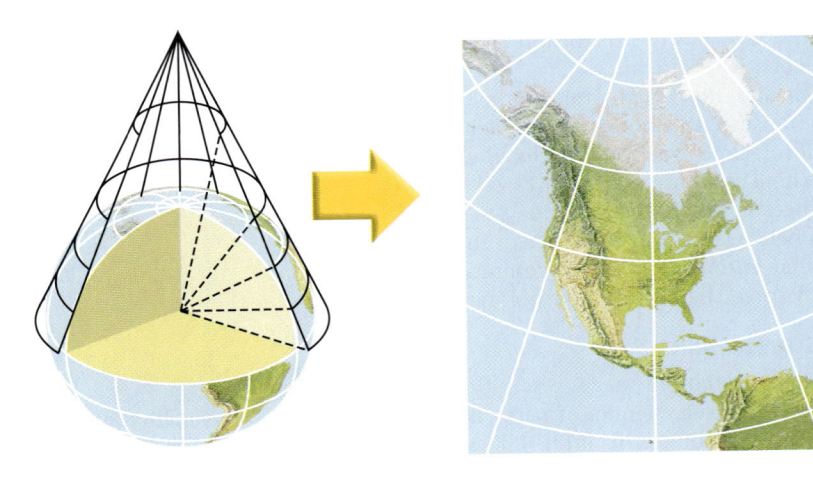

conic projection a map projection that is made by moving the surface features of the globe onto a cone

Conic Projection

A map projection that is made by moving the contents of the globe onto a cone is a **conic projection**, shown in **Figure 3**. This cone is then unrolled to form a flat plane.

The cone touches the globe at each line of longitude but at only one line of latitude. There is no distortion along the line of latitude where the globe touches the cone. Areas near this line of latitude are distorted less than other areas are. Because the cone touches many lines of longitude and only one line of latitude, conic projections are best for mapping large masses of land that have more area east to west. For example, a conic projection is often used to map the United States.

CONNECTION TO Social Studies

WRITING SKILL **Mapmaking and Ship Navigation** Gerardus Mercator is the cartographer (or mapmaker) who developed the Mercator projection. During his career as a mathematician and cartographer, Mercator worked hard to produce maps of many parts of Europe, including Great Britain. He also produced a terrestrial globe and a celestial globe. Use the library or the Internet to research Mercator. How did his mapmaking skills help ship navigators in the 1500s? Write a paragraph describing what you learn.

Science Bloopers

During the process of compiling data from a number of different sources, mistakes are sometimes made. Cartographers have wiped entire cities off maps accidentally! For example, Canada's capital, Ottawa, was once omitted from a Canadian tourist-office map. An official explanation was that there was no direct air service between New York City and Ottawa failed to satisfy one Ottawa tourist bureau executive, who remarked irately, "Ottawa should be shown in any case, even if the only point of entry was by two-man kayak."

---

44 Chapter 2 • Maps as Models of the Earth

Figure 4 Azimuthal Projection

On this azimuthal projection, distortion increases as you move farther from the North Pole.

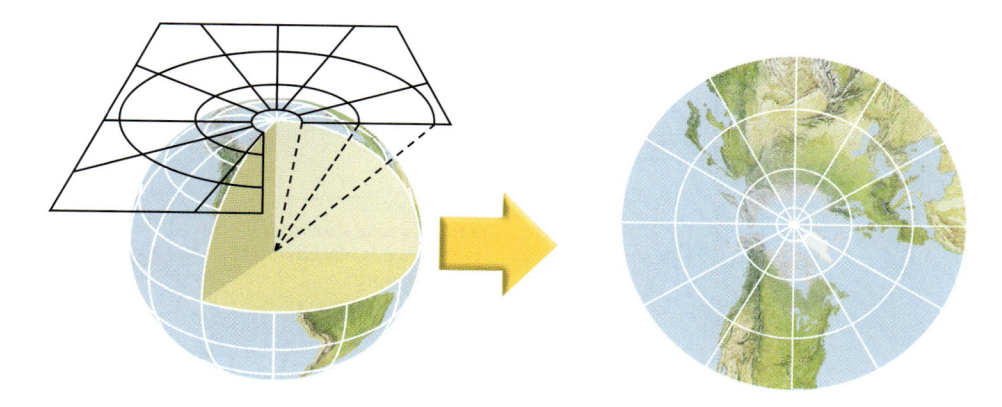

Azimuthal Projection

An **azimuthal projection** (AZ uh MYOOTH uhl proh JEK shuhn) is a map projection that is made by moving the contents of the globe onto a flat plane. Look at **Figure 4.** On an azimuthal projection, the plane touches the globe at only one point. There is little distortion at this point of contact. The point of contact for an azimuthal projection is usually one of the poles. However, distortion of direction, distance, and shape increases as you move away from the point of contact. Azimuthal projections are most often used to map areas of the globe that are near the North and South Poles.

azimuthal projection a map projection that is made by moving the surface features of the globe onto a plane

✓ **Reading Check** How are azimuthal and conic projections alike? How are they different?

Equal-Area Projection

A map projection that shows the area between the latitude and longitude lines the same size as that area on a globe is called an *equal-area projection*. Equal-area projections can be made by using cylindrical, conic, or azimuthal projections. Equal-area projections are often used to map large land areas, such as continents. The shapes of the continents and oceans are distorted on equal-area projections. But because the scale used on equal-area projections is constant throughout the map, this type of projection is good for determining distance on a map. **Figure 5** is an example of an equal-area projection.

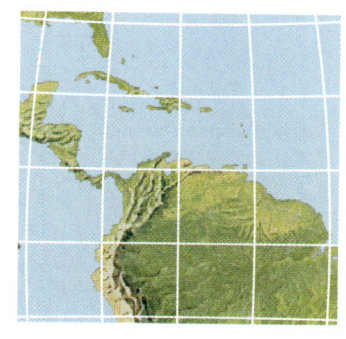

Figure 5 Equal-area projections are useful for determining distance on a map.

Group Activity — BASIC

Comparing Map Projections As a class, review the characteristics of cylindrical, conic, and azimuthal map projections. Display a globe at the front of the classroom, and have a piece of paper large enough to encircle it at hand. Call on volunteers to demonstrate how each type of map projection is made by wrapping the paper around the globe in the appropriate fashion.
LS Visual/Kinesthetic

Homework — ADVANCED

Equal-Area Projections Equal-area projections represent the area between the lines of latitude and longitude as equal to the area as shown on a globe. Have interested students find examples of equal-area map projections. Ask students to find out if the equal-area projection is based on a cylindrical, conic, or azimuthal projection. Then, ask students if the equal-area maps they found have common characteristics. (Students may find that maps made from equal-area projections are often used to map large landmasses.) **LS** Logical

---

Answer to Reading Check

Azimuthal and conic projections are similar because they are both ways to represent the curved surface of the Earth on a flat map. Azimuthal projections show the surface of a globe transferred to a flat plane, whereas conic projections show the surface of a globe transferred to a cone.

Section 2 • Mapping the Earth's Surface

Teach, continued

INCLUSION Strategies

- Learning Disabled
- Attention Deficit Disorder
- Gifted and Talented

Organize students into pairs or groups of three. Hand out to each group a map of their town or city and brightly colored sticky dots. Ask students to identify and mark with sticky dots on the map the title of the map, map scale, compass rose, and legend. Ask them to find their school, home, and an additional landmark and indicate these sites as well. Next, ask each team to calculate the distance from their school to the various landmarks. For gifted and talented students, ask them to do additional calculations, such as distance between points and direction in degrees using a compass. **English Language Learners**
LS Visual

Answer to Reading Check

Every map should have a title, a compass rose, a scale, the date, and a legend.

Information Shown on Maps

Regardless of the kind of map you are reading, the map should contain the information shown in **Figure 6**. This information includes a title, a compass rose, a scale, a legend, and a date. Unfortunately, not all maps have all this information. The more of this information a map has, the more reliable the map is.

Reading Check What information should every map have?

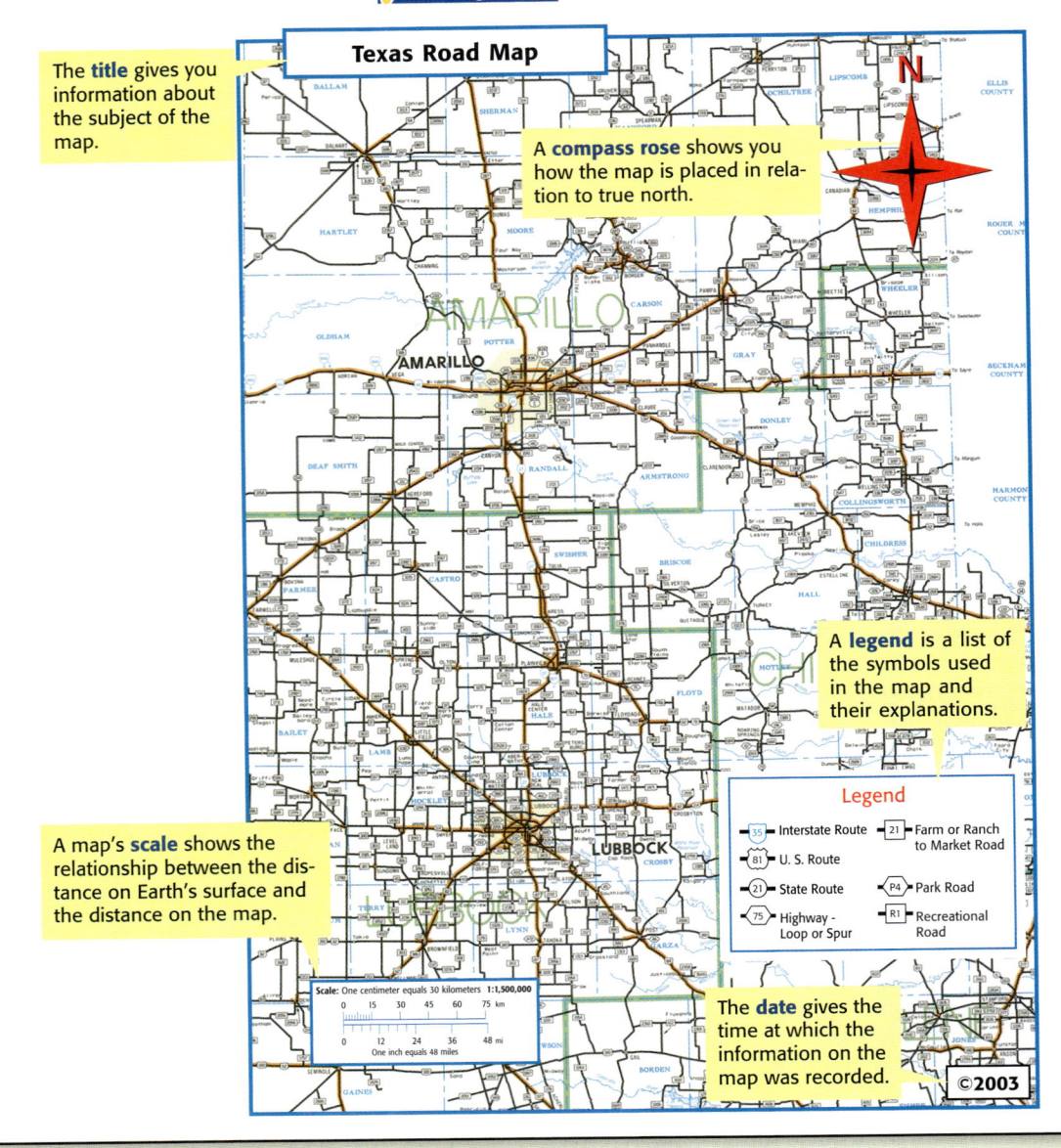

Figure 6 This Texas road map includes all of the information that a map should contain.

The **title** gives you information about the subject of the map.

A **compass rose** shows you how the map is placed in relation to true north.

A **legend** is a list of the symbols used in the map and their explanations.

A map's **scale** shows the relationship between the distance on Earth's surface and the distance on the map.

The **date** gives the time at which the information on the map was recorded.

CONNECTION ACTIVITY
Math — GENERAL

Taking a Hike Have students imagine that they want to use a map with a scale of 1:24,000 to estimate the length of a hike. On the map, the route measures 20 cm. Have students calculate the length of the hike in kilometers.
(20 cm × 24,000 = 480,000 cm;
480,000 cm ÷ 100 cm/m = 4,800 m;
4,800 ÷ 1,000 m/km = 4.8 km)
LS Logical

Is That a Fact!

In an attempt to keep foreigners and even Soviet citizens from knowing the exact geography of their country, mapmakers in the Soviet Union printed maps with deliberate mistakes. Roads, rivers, and even cities would be misplaced or omitted. These revisions were especially true of Moscow street maps. Although these maps were made with national security in mind, the end result was that the country operated much less efficiently.

Modern Mapmaking

For many centuries mapmakers relied on the observations of explorers to make maps. Today, however, mapmakers have far more technologically advanced tools for mapmaking.

Many of today's maps are made by remote sensing. **Remote sensing** is a way to collect information about something without physically being there. Remote sensing can be as basic as putting cameras on airplanes. However, many mapmakers rely on more sophisticated technology, such as satellites.

remote sensing the process of gathering and analyzing information about an object without physically being in touch with the object

Remote Sensing and Satellites

The image shown in **Figure 7** is a photograph taken by a satellite. Satellites can also detect energy that your eyes cannot. Remote sensors gather data about energy coming from Earth's surface and send the data back to receiving stations on Earth. A computer is then used to process the information to make a picture you can see.

Remote Sensing Using Radar

Radar is a tool that uses waves of energy to map Earth's surface. Waves of energy are sent from a satellite to the area being observed. The waves are then reflected from the area to a receiver on the satellite. The distance and the speed in which the waves travel to the area and back are measured and analyzed to create a map of the area. The waves used in radar can move through clouds and water. Because of this ability, radar has been used to map the surface of Venus, whose atmosphere is thick and cloudy.

Figure 7 Satellites can produce very detailed images of the Earth's surface. The satellite that took this picture was 423 mi above the Earth's surface!

ACTIVITY — GENERAL

Remote-Sensing Technology To give students an idea of the different types of remote-sensing tools used to analyze the surface of the Earth, download photographs and images obtained by remote-sensing technology from the NASA Web site. Have students compare the images and photographs from different remote-sensing technologies. Ask students to write a paragraph describing what they have learned. **LS Visual**

CONNECTION to Physical Science — ADVANCED

Landsat Satellites Data collected by remote-sensing devices on satellites in the Landsat program are useful not only for making maps of landforms but also for determining the type and amount of vegetation in a certain area. Explain to students that Landsat satellites analyze the infrared range of the electromagnetic spectrum as well as visible light. Have interested students find out how remote sensors reveal vegetative cover and how they have been useful in the study of deforestation. Use the teaching transparency "The Electromagnetic Spectrum" to discuss the types of energy that remote-sensing satellites detect. **LS Logical**

CONNECTION ACTIVITY
Language Arts — ADVANCED

Imaginary Places Famous writers such as Anne McCaffrey, Thomas Hardy, Sinclair Lewis, J.R.R. Tolkien, and Bernard Cornwall all drew maps to illustrate their works. Ask students to create a detailed map of an imaginary place. The maps must use all of the map elements shown in the road map. Students' maps can serve as inspiration for the setting of a short story. **LS Intrapersonal**

CHAPTER RESOURCES

Technology

Transparencies
- **LINK TO PHYSICAL SCIENCE** The Electromagnetic Spectrum

Section 2 • Mapping the Earth's Surface   **47**

Close

Reteaching — BASIC

Demonstration To reinforce students' understanding of GPS technology, show students how a GPS unit operates. Using a hand-held GPS unit, take students to various locations outside, and have them observe the unit as it updates the coordinates of your location. **LS** Visual

Quiz — GENERAL

1. Equal-area projections are used to map what type of area? (Equal-area projections are used to map large areas of land.)

2. How has remote-sensing technology contributed to the science of mapmaking? (Remote sensing has allowed people to view Earth's surface from above, which enables mapmakers to make more accurate maps.)

3. Why is it important for a road map to show the date the map was made? (The date allows the user to determine if the map is accurate because the location and names of streets and roads may change over time.)

Alternative Assessment — GENERAL

Analyzing Maps Maps made by a noncartographer using a computer often omit crucial elements, such as a scale, a date, or a compass rose. Have students bring in a map from a newspaper, a magazine, or an advertisement, and have them write a critique of the map. **LS** Visual

Figure 8 This tiny GPS unit may come in handy if you are ever lost.

Global Positioning System

Did you know that satellite technology can actually help you from getting lost? The *global positioning system* (GPS) can help you find where you are on Earth. GPS is a system of orbiting satellites that send radio signals to receivers on Earth. The receivers calculate a given place's latitude, longitude, and elevation.

GPS was invented in the 1970s by the U.S. Department of Defense for military use. However, during the last 30 years, GPS has made its way into people's daily lives. Mapmakers use GPS to verify the location of boundary lines between countries and states. Airplane and boat pilots use GPS for navigation. Businesses and state agencies use GPS for mapping and environmental planning. Many new cars have GPS units that show information on a screen on the dashboard. Some GPS units are small enough to wear on your wrist, as shown in **Figure 8,** so you can know your location anywhere you go!

Geographic Information Systems

Mapmakers now use geographic information systems to store, use, and view geographic information. A *geographic information system*, or GIS, is a computerized system that allows a user to enter different types of information about an area. This information is entered and stored as layers. The user can then use the stored information to make complex analyses or display maps. **Figure 9** shows three GIS images of Seattle, Washington.

✓ **Reading Check** Explain how information is stored using GIS.

Figure 9 The images at right show the location of sewer lines, roads, and parks in Seattle, Washington.

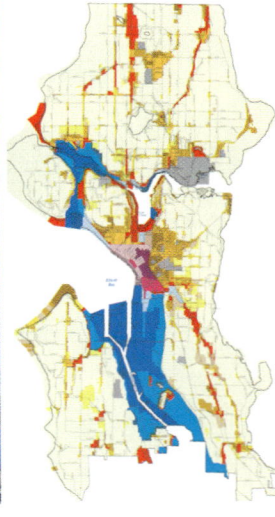

Answer to Reading Check
A GIS system stores information in layers.

48 Chapter 2 • Maps as Models of the Earth

SECTION Review

Summary

- When information is moved from a curved surface to a flat surface, distortion occurs.
- Three main types of projections are used to show Earth's surface on a flat map: cylindrical, conic, and azimuthal projections.
- Equal-area maps are used to show the area of a piece of land in relation to the area of other landmasses and oceans.
- Maps should contain a title, a scale, a legend, a compass rose, and a date.
- Modern mapmakers use remote sensing technology, such as satellites and radar.
- The Global positioning system, or GPS, is a system of satellites that can help you determine your location no matter where you are.
- Geographical information systems, or GIS, are computerized systems that allow mapmakers to store and use many types of data about an area.

Using Key Terms

1. In your own words, write a definition for each of the following terms: *cylindrical projection, azimuthal projection,* and *conic projection.*

Understanding Key Ideas

2. Which of the following map projections is most often used to map the United States?
   a. cylindrical projection
   b. conic projection
   c. azimuthal projection
   d. equal-area projection

3. List five things found on maps. Explain how each thing is important to reading a map.

4. Describe how GPS can help you find your location on Earth.

5. Why is radar useful when mapping areas that tend to be covered in clouds?

Critical Thinking

6. **Analyzing Ideas** Imagine you are a mapmaker. You have been asked to map a landmass that has more area from east to west than from north to south. What type of map projection would you use? Explain.

7. **Making Inferences** Imagine looking at a map of North America. Would this map have a large scale or a small scale? Would a map of your city have a large scale or a small scale? Explain.

Interpreting Graphics

Use the map below to answer the questions that follow.

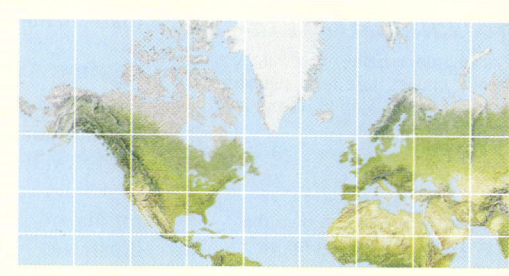

8. What type of projection was used to make this map?

9. Which areas of this map are the most distorted? Explain.

10. Which areas of this map are the least distorted? Explain.

Answers to Section Review

1. Sample answer: A cylindrical projection transfers information from a curved surface onto a cylinder. An azimuthal projection transfers information from a curved surface onto a flat plane. A conic projection transfers information from a curved surface onto a cone.
2. b
3. Maps should include a title, a scale, a legend, a compass rose, and a date. The title describes the subject of the map; the scale, legend, and compass rose help the reader use the map; and the date describes the age of the map.
4. A GPS unit uses satellite technology to pinpoint the latitude, longitude, and elevation of the area you are in.
5. Radar is useful when mapping cloudy areas because radar waves can travel through clouds.
6. Sample answer: A conic projection would be the best map projection to use when mapping a landmass that has more area from east to west than from north to south.
7. Sample answer: A map of North America would most likely have a small scale, because a map of a large area would not show much detail. A map of my city would have a larger scale, because this map would show more detail.
8. cylindrical projection
9. The areas near the North Pole are most distorted.
10. The areas nearest the equator is the least distorted.

CHAPTER RESOURCES

Chapter Resource File
- Section Quiz GENERAL
- Section Review GENERAL
- Vocabulary and Section Summary GENERAL
- Critical Thinking ADVANCED
- SciLinks Activity GENERAL

SciLinks
Developed and maintained by the National Science Teachers Association
For a variety of links related to this chapter, go to www.scilinks.org
Topic: Mapmaking
SciLinks code: HSM0909

Section 2 • Mapping the Earth's Surface

SECTION 3

Focus

Overview
In this section, students investigate how contour lines are used to show elevation and landforms on a topographic map. In addition, they learn how to read and interpret the features of a topographic map.

🔔 Bellringer
Have students examine the topographic map shown on this page. Have them imagine that they are standing on the top of Campbell Hill. Students should describe in their **science journal** what they see in each direction. Tell students that they will learn to read topographic maps, such as the ones in this section.

Motivate

ACTIVITY — GENERAL

Investigate Your Area If possible, obtain topographic maps of your area. You may be able to find these maps at camping stores or on the Internet. As a class, locate different landforms in your area. Discuss with students how contour intervals indicate changes in elevation. If possible, take a class field trip to one of the areas. **LS Visual** English Language Learners

---

SECTION 3

READING WARM-UP

Objectives
- Explain how contour lines show elevation and landforms on a map.
- Explain how the relief of an area determines the contour interval used on a map.
- List the rules of contour lines.

Terms to Learn
topographic map
elevation
contour line
contour interval
relief
index contour

READING STRATEGY

Paired Summarizing Read this section silently. In pairs, take turns summarizing the material. Stop to discuss ideas that seem confusing.

topographic map a map that shows the surface features of Earth

elevation the height of an object above sea level

contour line a line that connects points of equal elevation

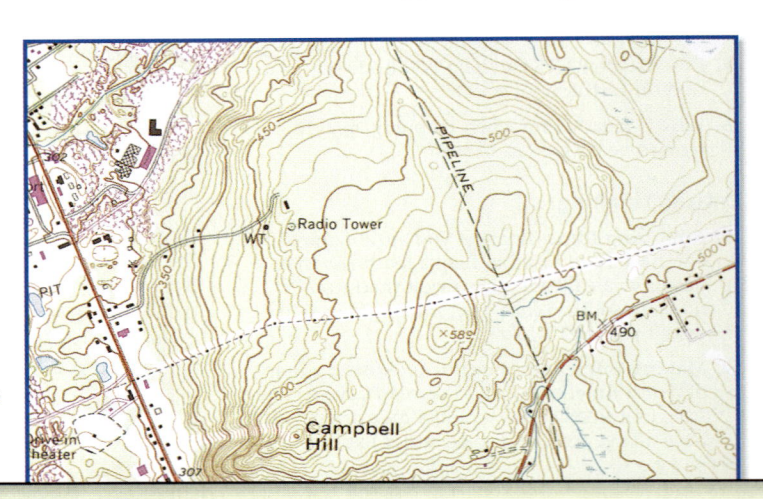

Figure 1 Because contour lines connect points of equal elevation, the shape of the contour lines reflects the shape of the land.

CHAPTER RESOURCES

Chapter Resource File
- Lesson Plan
- Directed Reading A BASIC
- Directed Reading B SPECIAL NEEDS

Technology
- Transparencies
  - Bellringer

Topographic Maps

Imagine you are going on a camping trip in the wilderness. To be prepared, you want to take a compass and a map. But what kind of map should you take? Because there won't be any roads in the wilderness, you can forget about a road map. Instead, you will need a topographic map.

A **topographic map** (TAHP uh GRAF ik MAP) is a map that shows surface features, or topography (tuh PAHG ruh fee), of the Earth. Topographic maps show both natural features, such as rivers, lakes, and mountains, and features made by humans, such as cities, roads, and bridges. Topographic maps also show elevation. **Elevation** is the height of an object above sea level. The elevation at sea level is 0. In this section, you will learn how to read a topographic map.

Elements of Elevation

The United States Geological Survey (USGS), a federal government agency, has made topographic maps for most of the United States. These maps show elevation in feet (ft) rather than in meters, the SI unit usually used by scientists.

Contour Lines

On a topographic map, *contour lines* are used to show elevation. **Contour lines** are lines that connect points of equal elevation. For example, one contour line would connect points on a map that have an elevation of 100 ft. Another line would connect points on a map that have an elevation of 200 ft. **Figure 1** illustrates how contour lines appear on a map.

Is That a Fact!

The Ordnance Survey of Great Britain produces topographic maps with very large scales, ranging from 1:10,000 to 1:1,250. Such large scales permit a level of detail that shows the location of public telephones, windmills, and even large boulders!

---

50 Chapter 2 • Maps as Models of the Earth

Figure 2 The portion of the topographic map on the left shows Pikes Peak in Colorado. The map above shows a valley in Big Bend Ranch State Park in Texas.

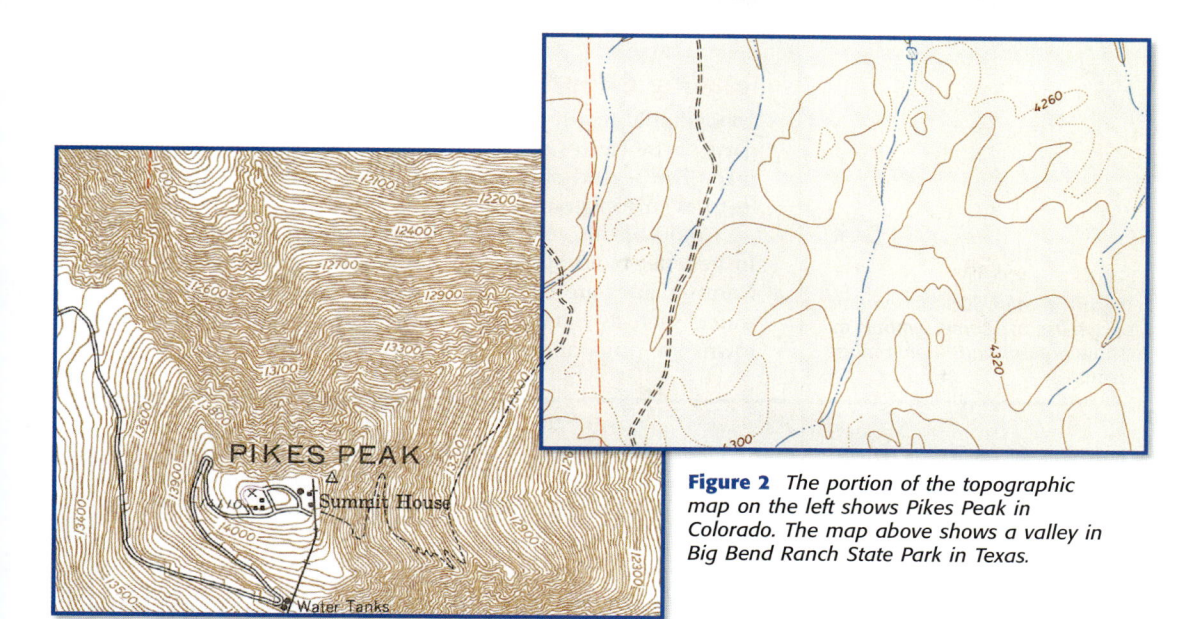

Contour Interval

The difference in elevation between one contour line and the next is called the **contour interval**. For example, a map with a contour interval of 20 ft would have contour lines every 20 ft of elevation change, such as 0 ft, 20 ft, 40 ft, and 60 ft. A mapmaker chooses a contour interval based on the area's relief. **Relief** is the difference in elevation between the highest and lowest points of the area being mapped. Because the relief of an area with mountains is large, the relief might be shown on a map using a large contour interval, such as 100 ft. However, a flat area has small relief and might be shown on a map by using a small contour interval, such as 10 ft.

The spacing of contour lines also indicates slope, as shown in **Figure 2**. Contour lines that are close together show a steep slope. Contour lines that are spaced far apart show a gentle slope.

contour interval the difference in elevation between one contour line and the next

relief the variations in elevation of a land surface

index contour on a map, a darker, heavier contour line that is usually every fifth line and that indicates a change in elevation

Index Contour

On USGS topographic maps, an index contour is used to make reading the map easier. An **index contour** is a darker, heavier contour line that is usually every fifth line and that is labeled by elevation. Find an index contour on both of the topographic maps shown in **Figure 2**.

✓ **Reading Check** What is an index contour? (See the Appendix for answers to Reading Checks.)

CONNECTION TO Oceanography

Mapping the Ocean Floor
Oceanographers use topographic maps to map the topography of the ocean floor. Use the Internet or the library to find a topographic map of the ocean floor. How are maps of the ocean floor similar to maps of the continents? How are they different?

Teach

Discussion — BASIC

Contour Maps On the board, reproduce Campbell Hill, shown on the previous page. Discuss with students where the steepest slopes are (where the lines are closest together). Ask students to think about what the map would look like with a larger contour interval. Discuss the advantages and the disadvantages of a map with a larger contour interval. *(The map may seem easier to read with a larger contour interval, but detail is lost.)* **LS** Visual

Group Activity — BASIC

Model Terrain If students are having trouble understanding contour lines, use some modeling clay to make a landform. Ask a volunteer to hold a ruler vertically next to the landform while you use a plastic knife to mark off contour intervals around the landform. When you are finished, have students view the landform from the side so that they can see the uniformity of the contour intervals. Next, have students view the landform from above so that they can see how the intervals would appear on a topographic map. Then, ask pairs of students to try the same activity themselves. **LS** Visual — English Language Learners

Answer to Reading Check

An index contour is a darker contour line that is usually every fifth line. Index contours make it easier to read a map.

Homework — ADVANCED

Expedition Journal Have students write a fictitious journal from the perspective of a member of an expedition team. Every journal entry should include a description of the topography the team encountered. Students should include a map in which they use the appropriate symbols and contour lines to show their route. This activity will take several days to complete. After the student explorers have "returned" from their expedition, they should display their journals. **LS** Visual

CONNECTION to Oceanography — BASIC

Maps of the Ocean Floor Oceanographers use contour maps to map the topography of the ocean floor. Traditionally, darker colors represent deeper depths, and lighter colors represent areas closer to the surface of the water. If possible, display an oceanographic map. Students should find similarities between the topography of the ocean floor and that of continental landmasses. **LS** Visual

Section 3 • Topographic Maps

Close

Reteaching — BASIC

Rules of Contour Lines Using a topographic map, show students examples of the rules of contour lines. Discuss how contour lines never cross, and show specific areas of steep slope, gentle slope, rivers or streams, and hills and depressions. **LS** Visual

Quiz — GENERAL

1. What is a contour interval on a topographic map? (the difference in elevation between one contour line and the next)
2. What do closely spaced contour lines on a topographic map indicate? (a steep area)
3. How does a topographic map indicate the direction that a stream flows? (Streams flow downhill, or in the direction that elevation decreases. The Vs point toward higher elevations.)

Alternative Assessment — GENERAL

Using Maps Photocopy a portion of a topographic map that shows a mountain. Indicate the scale of the map on the photocopy. Distribute copies to students, and ask them to trace a route to the top. Then, have them write a description of their "trail" that includes the length of the hike, the elevations where the trail is the steepest, and the points where the slope is gentle. Have students also note other features, such as streams, power lines, or road crossings. **LS** Verbal

Reading a Topographic Map

Topographic maps, like other maps, use symbols to represent parts of the Earth's surface. **Figure 3** shows a USGS topographic map. The legend shows some of the symbols that represent features in topographic maps.

Colors are also used to represent features of Earth's surface. In general, buildings, roads, bridges, and railroads are black. Contour lines are brown. Major highways are red. Bodies of water, such as rivers, lakes, and oceans are blue. Cities and towns are pink, and wooded areas are green.

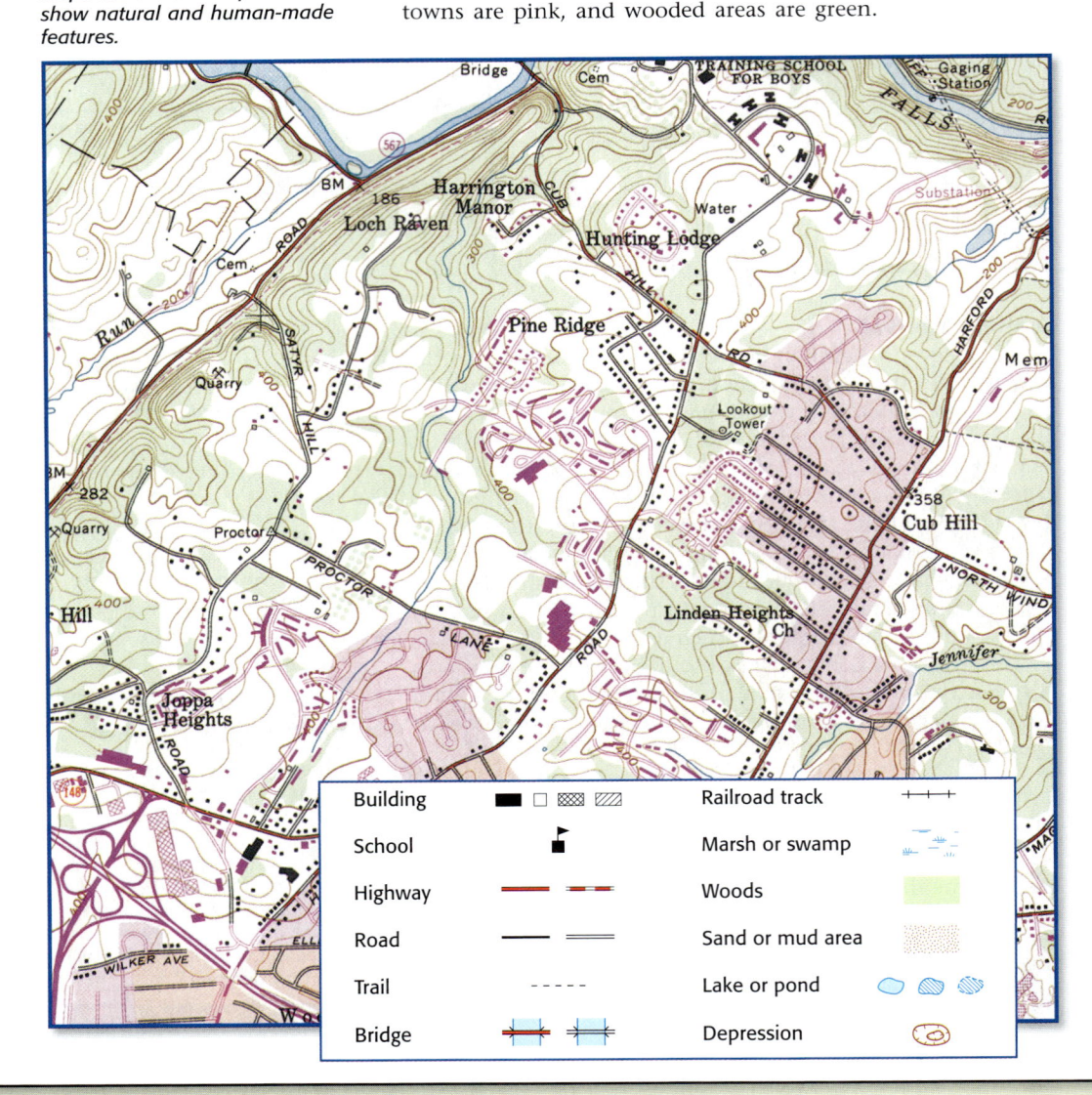

Figure 3 All USGS topographic maps use the same symbols to show natural and human-made features.

52 Chapter 2 • Maps as Models of the Earth

The Golden Rules of Contour Lines

Contour lines are the key to explaining the size and shape of landforms on a topographic map. Reading a topographic map takes training and practice. The following rules will help you understand how to read topographic maps:

- Contour lines never cross. All points along a contour line represent one elevation.
- The spacing of contour lines depends on slope characteristics. Contour lines that are close together show a steep slope. Contour lines that are far apart show a gentle slope.
- Contour lines that cross a valley or stream are V shaped. The V points toward the area of highest elevation. If a stream or river flows through the valley, the V points upstream.
- The tops of hills, mountains, and depressions are shown by closed circles. Depressions are marked with short, straight lines inside the circle that point downslope to the depression.

CONNECTION TO Environmental Science

Endangered Species State agencies, such as the Texas Parks and Wildlife Department, use topographic maps to mark where endangered plant and animal species are. By marking the location of the endangered plants and animals, these agencies can record and protect these places. Use the Internet or another source to find out if there is an agency in your state that tracks endangered species by using topographic maps.

SECTION Review

Summary

- Contour lines are used to show elevation and landforms by connecting points of equal elevation.
- The contour interval is determined by the relief of an area.
- Contour lines never cross. Contour lines that cross a valley or a stream are V shaped and point upstream. The tops of hills, mountains, and depressions are shown by closed circles.

Using Key Terms

1. In your own words, write a definition for each of the following terms: *topographic map, contour interval,* and *relief.*

Understanding Key Ideas

2. An index contour
   a. is a heavier contour line that shows a change in elevation.
   b. points in the direction of higher elevation.
   c. indicates a depression.
   d. indicates a hill.

3. How do topographic maps represent the Earth's surface?

4. How does the relief of an area determine the contour interval used on a map?

5. What are the rules of contour lines?

Math Skills

6. The contour line at the base of a hill reads 90 ft. There are five contour lines between the base of the hill and the top of the hill. If the contour interval is 30 ft, what is the elevation of the highest contour line?

Critical Thinking

7. **Making Inferences** Why isn't the highest point on a hill represented by a contour line?

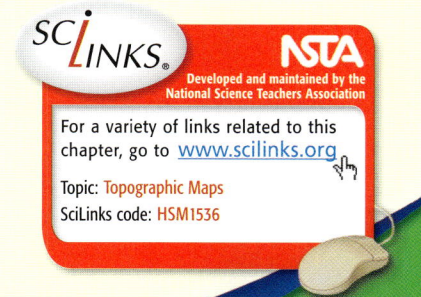

For a variety of links related to this chapter, go to www.scilinks.org
Topic: Topographic Maps
SciLinks code: HSM1536

Answers to Section Review

1. Sample answer: A topographic map shows the surface features of the Earth. A contour interval is the difference in elevation between two adjacent contour lines. Relief is the difference in elevation between the highest and lowest points of the area being mapped.
2. a
3. Topographic maps use contour lines to show the surface features of Earth. Symbols indicate other features.
4. If the relief of an area is large, a topographic map of the area will have a large contour interval. If the relief of an area is small, a topographic map of the area will have a small contour interval.
5. Contour lines never cross. The spacing of contour lines depends on the slope characteristics of an area. Contour lines that cross a valley or a stream are V shaped, and the V points upstream. The tops of mountains and the bottoms of depressions are shown by closed circles. Depressions are marked with short, straight lines inside the circle that point downslope.
6. 30 ft × 5 = 150 ft; 90 ft + 150 ft = 240 ft
7. The highest point on a hill or mountain is a single point, not a group of points with the same elevation.

CHAPTER RESOURCES

Chapter Resource File
- Section Quiz GENERAL
- Section Review GENERAL
- Vocabulary and Section Summary GENERAL
- Reinforcement Worksheet BASIC

Workbooks
- Math Skills for Science
  - Mapping and Surveying GENERAL

Section 3 • Topographic Maps

Skills Practice Lab

Round or Flat?

Teacher's Notes

Time Required
One 45-minute class period

Lab Ratings

EASY —————— HARD

Teacher Prep 🧪🧪
Student Set-Up 🧪🧪🧪
Concept Level 🧪🧪🧪
Clean Up 🧪

MATERIALS
The materials listed on the student page are enough for a group of 3 or 4 students.

Safety Caution
Remind students to review all safety cautions and icons before beginning this lab activity.

Preparation Notes
Obtain inflated basketballs from your school's physical education instructor. Asking students to bring basketballs from home may be necessary. Begin the activity by reminding students that circumference is the distance around a circle or sphere.

You may also need to review the use of protractors with students before performing this activity.

Using Scientific Methods
Skills Practice Lab

OBJECTIVES

Construct a tool to measure the circumference of the Earth.

Calculate the circumference of the Earth.

MATERIALS
- basketball
- books or notebooks (2)
- calculator (optional)
- clay, modeling
- flashlight or small lamp
- meterstick
- pencils, unsharpened (2)
- protractor
- ruler, metric
- string, 10 cm long
- tape, masking
- tape measure

SAFETY

Round or Flat?

Eratosthenes thought of a way to measure the circumference of Earth. He came up with the idea when he read that a well in southern Egypt was entirely lit by the sun at noon once each year. He realized that to shine on the entire surface of the well water, the sun must be directly over the well. At the same time, in a city just north of the well, a tall monument cast a shadow. Thus, Eratosthenes reasoned that the sun could not be directly over both the monument and the well at noon on the same day. In this experiment, you will see how Eratosthenes' way of measuring works.

Ask a Question

1. How could I use Eratosthenes' method of investigation to measure the size of the Earth?

Form a Hypothesis

2. Formulate a hypothesis that answers the question above. Record your hypothesis.

Test the Hypothesis

3. Set the basketball on a table. Place a book or notebook on either side of the basketball to hold the ball in place. The ball represents Earth.

Lab Notes
Explain that Eratosthenes' experiment worked because he set up a ratio. It may be necessary to review ratios before performing this activity. The formula Eratosthenes used is as follows:

$$\frac{\text{distance around ball}}{\text{distance between sticks}} = \frac{360° \text{ in the sphere}}{\text{angle of shadow with stick}}$$

Students may be interested to learn that they can calculate the circumference of the Earth by performing Eratosthenes' experiment in partnership with other schools around the world. The experiment is conducted twice a year during the fall and spring equinoxes. To find out more, have students search for "Eratosthenes' experiment" on the Internet.

54 Chapter 2 • Maps as Models of the Earth

4. Use modeling clay to attach a pencil to the "equator" of the ball so that the pencil points away from the ball.

5. Attach the second pencil to the ball at a point that is 5 cm above the first pencil. This second pencil should also point away from the ball.

6. Use a meterstick to measure 1 m away from the ball. Mark the 1 m position with masking tape. Label the position "Sun." Hold the flashlight so that its front edge is above the masking tape.

7. When your teacher turns out the lights, turn on your flashlight and point it so that the pencil on the equator does not cast a shadow. Ask a partner to hold the flashlight in this position. The second pencil should cast a shadow on the ball.

8. Tape one end of the string to the top of the second pencil. Hold the other end of the string against the ball at the far edge of the shadow. Make sure that the string is tight. But be careful not to pull the pencil over.

9. Use a protractor to measure the angle between the string and the pencil. Record this angle.

10. Use the following formula to calculate the experimental circumference of the ball.

$$Circumference = \frac{360° \times 5\ cm}{\text{angle between pencil and string}}$$

11. Record the experimental circumference you calculated in step 10. Wrap the tape measure around the ball's equator to measure the actual circumference of the ball. Record this circumference.

Analyze the Results

1. **Examining Data** Compare the experimental circumference with the actual circumference.

2. **Analyzing Data** What could have caused your experimental circumference to differ from the actual circumference?

3. **Analyzing Data** What are some of the advantages and disadvantages of taking measurements this way?

Draw Conclusions

4. **Evaluating Methods** Was Eratosthenes' method an effective way to measure Earth's circumference? Explain your answer.

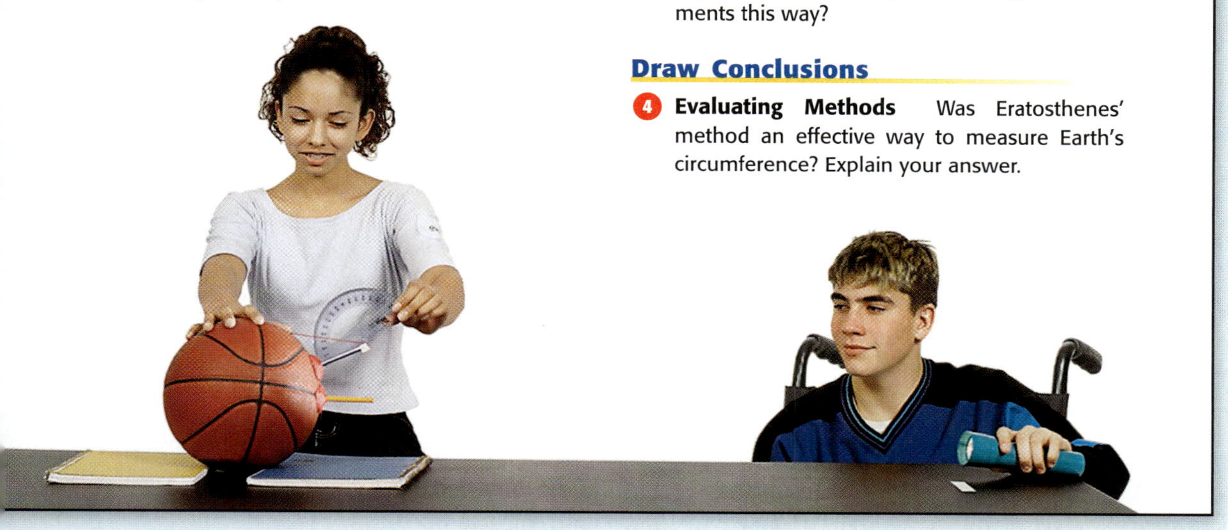

Analyze the Results

1. Students will likely find that the experimental and actual circumferences are not equal. The two values should be close, however.

2. Answers may vary. Factors that affect this measurement include the angle of the pencils and human error.

3. Sample answer: Because it is impossible to use a tape measure to determine the circumference of the Earth, this procedure offers a good approximation. One disadvantage is that the measurements are not exact.

Draw Conclusions

4. Sample answers: yes; It gives a value that is close to the actual value.

CHAPTER RESOURCES

Chapter Resource File
- Datasheet for Chapter Lab
- Lab Notes and Answers

Technology
- Classroom Videos
  • Lab Video

LabBook
- Topographic Tuber

CHAPTER RESOURCES

Workbooks
- Inquiry Labs
  • Looking for Buried Treasure GENERAL
- Long-Term Projects & Research Ideas
  • Globe Trotting ADVANCED

Barry L. Bishop
San Rafael Junior High
Ferron, Utah

Chapter 2 • Chapter Lab

Chapter Review

Assignment Guide

Section	Questions
1	1–3, 7, 8
2	4, 6, 10, 11, 12, 14–16, 18–22, 24
3	5, 9, 13, 17, 23, 25–29

ANSWERS

Using Key Terms

1. Sample answer: True north is the geographic North Pole. Magnetic north refers to the magnetic north pole, which changes.

2. Sample answer: Latitude is the distance north or south from the equator. Longitude is the distance east and west from the prime meridian. Both latitude and longitude are measured in degrees.

3. Sample answer: The equator is the imaginary circle halfway between the poles that divides the Earth into Northern and Southern Hemispheres and represents 0° latitude. The prime meridian represents 0° longitude. It runs from the North to South Poles through Greenwich, England.

4. Sample answer: A cylindrical projection is a map projection made by transferring the surface of the globe onto a cylinder. An azimuthal projection is a map projection made by projecting the surface of the globe onto a plane.

5. Sample answer: Contour interval is the difference in elevation between one contour line and the next. An index contour is a darker, heavier contour line that usually occurs every fifth line.

6. Sample answer: The global positioning system is a system of satellites that send radio signals to receivers on Earth. The receivers calculate a given place's latitude, longitude, and elevation. A geographic information system is a computer system that stores data about an area in layers.

Understanding Key Ideas

7. b
8. c
9. b
10. b
11. b
12. d
13. b

Chapter Review

USING KEY TERMS

For each pair of terms, explain how the meanings of the terms differ.

1. *true north* and *magnetic north*
2. *latitude* and *longitude*
3. *equator* and *prime meridian*
4. *cylindrical projection* and *azimuthal projection*
5. *contour interval* and *index contour*
6. *global positioning system* and *geographic information system*

UNDERSTANDING KEY IDEAS

Multiple Choice

7. A point whose latitude is 0° is located on the
   a. North Pole.
   b. equator.
   c. South Pole.
   d. prime meridian.

8. The distance in degrees east or west of the prime meridian is
   a. latitude.
   b. declination.
   c. longitude.
   d. projection.

9. Widely spaced contour lines indicate a
   a. steep slope.
   b. gentle slope.
   c. hill.
   d. river.

10. The most common map projections are based on three geometric shapes. Which of the following geometric shapes is NOT one of the three geometric shapes?
    a. cylinder
    b. square
    c. cone
    d. plane

11. A cylindrical projection is distorted near the
    a. equator.
    b. poles.
    c. prime meridian.
    d. date line.

12. What is the relationship between the distance on a map and the actual distance on Earth called?
    a. legend
    b. elevation
    c. relief
    d. scale

13. ___ is the height of an object above sea level.
    a. Contour interval
    b. Elevation
    c. Declination
    d. Index contour

Short Answer

14. List four methods that modern mapmakers use to make accurate maps.

15. Why is a map legend important?

16 Why does Greenland appear so large in relation to other landmasses on a map made using a cylindrical projection?

17 What is the function of contour lines on a topographic map?

18 How can GPS help you find your location on Earth?

19 What is GIS?

CRITICAL THINKING

20 Concept Mapping Use the following terms to create a concept map: *maps, legend, map projection, map parts, scale, cylinder, title, cone, plane, date,* and *compass rose*.

21 Making Inferences One of the important parts of a map is its date. Why is the date important?

22 Analyzing Ideas Why is it important for maps to have scales?

23 Applying Concepts Imagine that you are looking at a topographic map of the Grand Canyon. Would the contour lines be spaced close together or far apart? Explain your answer.

24 Analyzing Processes How would a GIS system help a team of engineers plan a new highway system for a city?

25 Making Inferences If you were stranded in a national park, what kind of map of the park would you want to have with you? Explain your answer.

INTERPRETING GRAPHICS

Use the topographic map below to answer the questions that follow.

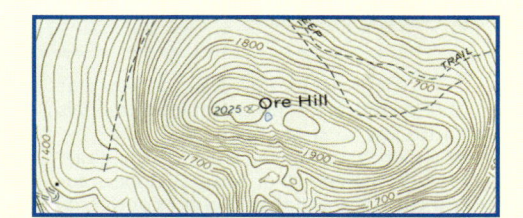

26 What is the elevation change between two adjacent lines on this map?

27 What type of relief does this area have?

28 What surface features are shown on this map?

29 What is the elevation at the top of Ore Hill?

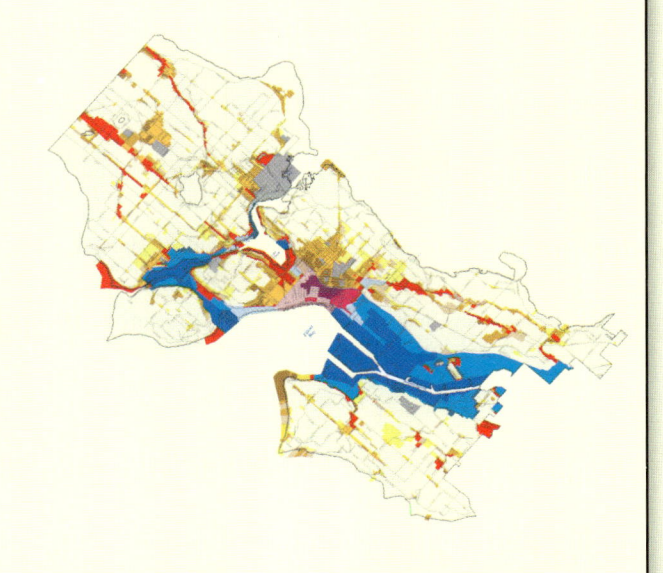

---

18. A GPS unit receives signals from a system of satellites and then calculates the latitude and longitude of your location.

19. GIS is a computerized system that allows a user to enter different types of information about an area, this information is then stored in layers.

Critical Thinking

20. An answer to this exercise can be found at the end of this book.

21. Sample answer: A date on a map is important because the Earth's surface is constantly changing. The date shows you how old the information is.

22. Sample answer: It is important that maps have scales because a map scale allows the user to determine distances on the map.

23. Sample answer: A topographic map of the Grand Canyon would show contour lines close together, indicating steep slopes.

24. Sample answer: A GIS system would allow the team of engineers to access information about current roads and streets, as well as power lines, sewer lines, natural features, and any other information they may need when building a highway.

25. Sample answer: I would want to have a topographic map because this type of map shows the relief of the area rather than only roads and streets.

Interpreting Graphics

26. 20 ft

27. It has very large relief.

28. Answers may vary. Sample answer: Two hills are shown on this map.

29. 2,025 ft

---

14. Modern mapmakers use satellite and radar technology, GPS, and GIS to make accurate maps.

15. A map legend is important because it defines the set of symbols used in the map.

16. Greenland appears large on a map created with a cylindrical projection because of distortion. Maps created with a cylindrical projection are increasingly distorted as the distance from the equator increases.

17. Contour lines on a topographic map show the elevation, the relief, and the shape of landforms.

CHAPTER RESOURCES

Chapter Resource File
- Chapter Review GENERAL
- Chapter Test A GENERAL
- Chapter Test B ADVANCED
- Chapter Test C SPECIAL NEEDS
- Vocabulary Activity GENERAL

Workbooks

Study Guide
- Assessment resources are also available in Spanish.

Chapter 2 • Chapter Review

Standardized Test Preparation

Teacher's Note

To provide practice under more realistic testing conditions, give students 20 minutes to answer all of the questions in this Standardized Test Preparation.

MISCONCEPTION ALERT

Answers to the standardized test preparation can help you identify student misconceptions and misunderstandings.

READING

Passage 1
1. C
2. F
3. C

TEST DOCTOR

Question 1: Students may think that the last sentence means that maps can show accurate sizes of Earth's oceans as well as show a lot of detail. However, the passage states in the second sentence that globes and maps are both models of Earth.

Question 3: Some students may misunderstand the idea that globes show less detail than maps. Therefore, some students may choose one of the answer choices concerning details found mainly on maps rather than on globes.

Standardized Test Preparation

READING

Read each of the passages below. Then, answer the questions that follow each passage.

Passage 1 Scientists use models to represent things. Globes and maps are examples of models that scientists use to study Earth's surface.

Because a globe is a sphere, as Earth is, a globe is the most accurate model of Earth. A globe accurately shows the sizes and shapes of the continents and oceans in relation to one another. But a globe is not always the best model to use when studying Earth's surface. For example, a globe is too small to show a lot of detail, such as roads and rivers. It is much easier to show details on maps. Maps can show the whole Earth or parts of it.

1. According to the passage, how are a globe and a map alike?
   A Both show a lot of detail.
   B Both are used to study the size of Earth's oceans.
   C Both are models used to the study Earth's surface.
   D Both show one part of Earth.

2. How are a globe and Earth alike?
   F Both are spheres.
   G Both represent real things.
   H Both are flat surfaces.
   I Both are models.

3. According to the passage, examining a globe would help you answer which of the following questions?
   A How many highways are in Michigan?
   B Where are the streams in my state?
   C Which continents border the Indian Ocean?
   D What is the exact length of the Nile River?

Passage 2 The names of many geographic locations in the United States are <u>rich</u> in description and national history. Names such as Adirondack and Chesapeake come from Native American languages. Some names, such as New London, Baton Rouge, and San Francisco, reflect European naming traditions. Other names, such as Stone Mountain and Long Island, provide a description of the area. The mapping efforts in the United States that took place after the Civil War often led to multiple names for one location. But mapmakers and scientists needed consistent names of locations for their studies. In 1890, the U.S. Board on Geographic Names was formed. This board determines and maintains location names.

1. In the passage, what does *rich* mean?
   A wealthy
   B abundant
   C incomplete
   D thick

2. Which of the following statements is true?
   F Mapmakers enjoyed using multiple names for the same location.
   G The U.S. Board on Geographic Names determines the name for an area.
   H Names such as Baton Rouge and San Francisco describe the physical area.
   I All geographic names came from Native American languages.

3. What can you infer from the passage?
   A Mapmakers name locations after themselves.
   B Scientists used descriptions of the physical area as names for locations.
   C The U.S. Board on Geographic Names now determines the names for locations.
   D Today, many locations in the United States have several names.

Passage 2
1. B
2. G
3. C

TEST DOCTOR

Question 1: Some students may interpret the meaning of the word *rich* to mean "wealthy" in this context. Therefore, students may choose answer A. However, in this passage, the meaning of the word *rich* is "abundant."

INTERPRETING GRAPHICS

Use each figure below to answer the question that follows each figure.

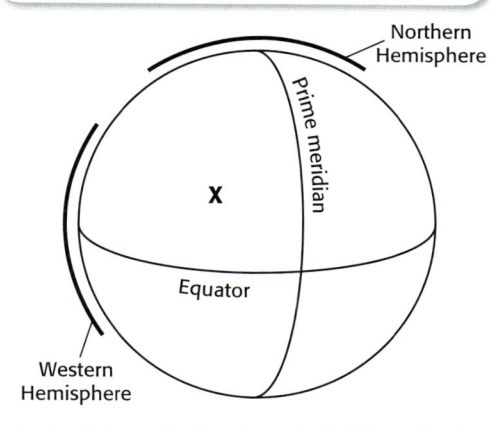

1. An X shows the location of a field investigation study site. Which of the following pairs of terms accurately describes the location of the X on the map?

A Northern Hemisphere; Western Hemisphere
B Northern Hemisphere; Eastern Hemisphere
C Southern Hemisphere; Eastern Hemisphere
D Southern Hemisphere; Western Hemisphere

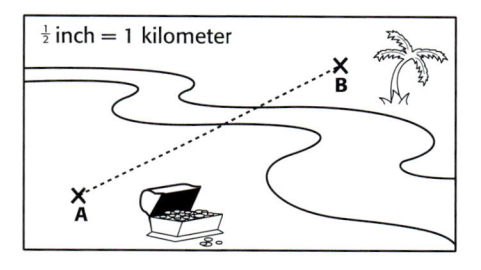

2. The map above shows the distance from point A to point B. According to this map, what is the actual distance from point A to point B?

F 1 km
G 2 km
H 4 km
I 6 km

MATH

Read each question below, and choose the best answer.

1. Greenland's area is approximately 2 million square kilometers. The area of Africa is approximately 15 times the area of Greenland. What is the approximate area of Africa?

A 30 million square kilometers
B 17 million square kilometers
C 13 million square kilometers
D 7.5 million square kilometers

2. A satellite is 264 km above Earth's surface. What is this measurement expressed in meters?

F 264,000 m
G 26,400 m
H 2,640 m
I 0.264 m

3. On a topographic map, every fifth contour line is a darker line, or *index contour*. How many index contours are there in a series of 50 contour lines?

A 8
B 9
C 10
D 11

4. Juan and Maria hike up a mountain. Maria is at an elevation of 4.3 km. Juan is at an elevation of 2.7 km. What is the difference between their elevations?

F 1.6 km
G 2.6 km
H 6.0 km
I 7.0 km

5. The North Pole is 90°N latitude. If you drew a line from the North Pole to the center of Earth and a line from a point on the equator to the center of Earth, what kind of angle would the two lines form at Earth's center?

A acute
B obtuse
C equilateral
D right

INTERPRETING GRAPHICS

1. A
2. H

TEST DOCTOR

Question 2: Students must be able to estimate the length of an inch in order to answer this question. Some students may not estimate this distance correctly.

MATH

1. A
2. F
3. C
4. F
5. D

TEST DOCTOR

Question 1: Students may mistakenly add or subtract the estimated areas of Greenland and Africa. Students must multiply the estimated areas of Greenland and Africa in order to arrive at the correct answer.

Question 5: Students must have some prior knowledge of basic geometry in order to recognize that a 90° angle is a right angle. In addition, some students may not recognize the equator as being 0° latitude and therefore may answer incorrectly.

CHAPTER RESOURCES

Chapter Resource File
• Standardized Test Preparation GENERAL

State Resources
For specific resources for your state, visit go.hrw.com and type in the keyword **HSMSTR**.

Chapter 2 • Standardized Test Preparation

Science in Action

Science, Technology, and Society

ACTIVITY — GENERAL

If you have access to a GPS unit, try taking your class on a geocache treasure hunt. You can find geocaches posted at many different sites on the Internet. Simply enter in the keyword *geocaching*. Choose a geocache that is relatively easy to find. You may want to find the cache first before taking your class with you to ensure that the cache is still there and that your students can safely access the area.

Scientific Discoveries

Background

According to legend, Allah became displeased with the wickedness of the citizens of Ubar and buried the city under a wave of sand. Ubar was lost for millennia until filmmaker Nicholas Clapp, NASA scientist Dr. Ronald Blom, and a team of explorers uncovered the ruins in 1991.

Discussion — GENERAL

Discuss with students the myth of the lost city of Atlantis. Have students suggest different ways that archeologists might search for a city that was covered by water instead of by sand.

Science in Action

Scientific Discoveries

The Lost City of Ubar

According to legend, the city of Ubar was a prosperous ancient city. Ubar was most famous for its frankincense, a tree sap that had many uses. As Ubar was in its decline, however, something strange happened. The city disappeared! It was a great myth that Ubar was swallowed up by the desert. It wasn't until present-day scientists used information from a Shuttle Imaging Radar system aboard the space shuttle that this lost city was found! Using radar, scientists were able to "see" beneath the huge dunes of the desert, where they finally found the lost city of Ubar.

Roads appear as purple lines on this computer-generated remote-sensing image.

Science, Technology, and Society

Geocaching

Wouldn't it be exciting to go on a hunt for buried treasure? Thousands of people around the world participate in geocaching, which is an adventure game for GPS users. In this adventure game, individuals and groups of people put caches, or hidden treasures, in places all over the world. Once the cache is hidden, the coordinates of the cache's location are posted on the Internet. Then, geocaching teams compete to find the cache. Geocaching should only be attempted with parental supervision.

Language Arts ACTIVITY

Why was the word *geocaching* chosen for this adventure game? Use the Internet or another source to find the origin and meaning of the word *geocaching*.

Social Studies ACTIVITY

WRITING SKILL Ubar was once a very wealthy, magnificent city. Its riches were built on the frankincense trade. Research the history of frankincense, and write a paragraph describing how frankincense was used in ancient times and how it is used today.

Answer to Language Arts Activity
The word *geocaching* comes from the Greek root *geo*, meaning "Earth," and the word *cache*, which is a type of hiding place for money, food, or other necessities.

Answer to Social Studies Activity
Sample answer: Frankincense was used to treat illnesses and disguise body odor. Ancient civilizations from Rome to India treasured frankincense. Today, frankincense is used mainly as an incense or an herbal scent in some commercial products.

60   Chapter 2 • Maps as Models of the Earth

People in Science

Matthew Henson

Arctic Explorer Matthew Henson was born in Maryland in 1866. His parents were freeborn sharecroppers. When Henson was a young boy, his parents died. He then went to look for work as a cabin boy on a ship. Several years later, Henson had traveled around the world and had become educated in the areas of geography, history, and mathematics. In 1898, Henson met U.S. Naval Lieutenant Robert E. Peary. Peary was the leader of Arctic expeditions between 1886 and 1909.

Peary asked Henson to accompany him as a navigator on several trips, including trips to Central America and Greenland. One of Peary's passions was to be the first person to reach the North Pole. It was Henson's vast knowledge of mathematics and carpentry that made Peary's trek to the North Pole possible. In 1909, Henson was the first person to reach the North Pole. Part of Henson's job as navigator was to drive ahead of the party and blaze the first trail. As a result, he often arrived ahead of everyone else. On April 6, 1909, Henson reached the approximate North Pole 45 minutes ahead of Peary. Upon his arrival, he exclaimed, "I think I'm the first man to sit on top of the world!"

Math Activity

On the last leg of their journey, Henson and Peary traveled 664.5 km in 16 days! On average, how far did Henson and Peary travel each day?

To learn more about these Science in Action topics, visit **go.hrw.com** and type in the keyword **HZ5MAPF**.

Current Science Check out *Current Science®* articles related to this chapter by visiting **go.hrw.com**. Just type in the keyword **HZ5CS02**.

Answer to Math Activity
664.5 km ÷ 16 days = 41.53 km/day.

People in Science

Background

Apart from enduring subfreezing temperatures, sudden snowstorms, and slow starvation, Peary's team had to deal with the unique conditions of ice sheets that cover the Arctic Ocean. Movements of water currents under the ice cause constant changes on its surface. These changes include "pressure ridges," or small, steep mountains of ice that well up on the surface, and "leads," or open lanes of water caused from drifts or rents in the ice. Twice, Henson saved Peary's life by pulling him out of the freezing water of a suddenly formed lead.

Activity — GENERAL

The Explorers Club has been an international meeting place for explorers and scientists since 1904. Some of the most famous and influential field researchers in the world have been invited to join its ranks. Have students research past members of this organization. Then, have them plot on a map all the places these members have explored or discovered. (Students will find that some of the famous members of the Explorers Club include Tenzing Norgay and Sir Edmund Hillary, the first people to climb Mount Everest, Theodore Roosevelt, 26th President and founding member, Roald Amundsen, the first to reach the South Pole and sail the Northwest Passage, Herbert Hoover, 34th President, and Richard Byrd, the first aviator to fly over the Antarctic.)

Chapter 2 • Science in Action

UNIT 2

TIMELINE

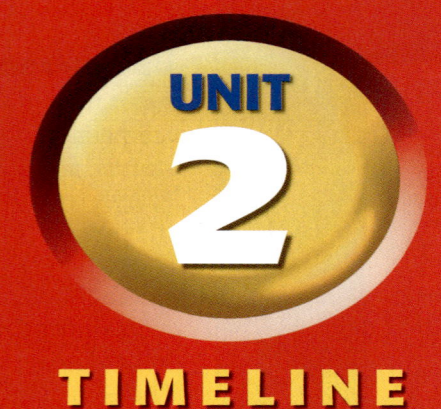

Earth's Resources

In this unit, you will learn about the basic components of the solid Earth—rocks and the minerals from which they are made. You will also learn about other resources the Earth contains. The ground beneath your feet is a treasure-trove of interesting materials, some of which are very valuable. Secrets of Earth's history are also hidden within the ground's depths. This timeline shows some of the events that have occurred through human history as scientists have come to understand more about our planet.

1543
Nicolaus Copernicus argues that the sun rather than the Earth is the center of the universe.

1860
Fossil remains of *Archaeopteryx*, a species that may link reptiles and birds, are discovered in Germany.

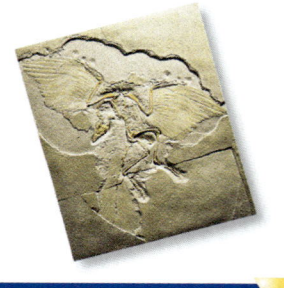

1936
Hoover Dam is completed. This massive hydroelectric dam, standing more than 221 m, required 3.25 million cubic yards of concrete to build.

1975
Tabei Junko of Japan becomes the first woman to successfully climb Mount Everest, 22 years after Edmund Hillary and Tenzing Norgay first conquered the mountain in 1953.

1681
The dodo, a flightless bird, is driven to extinction by the actions of humans.

1739
Georg Brandt identifies a new element and names it cobalt.

1848
James Marshall discovers gold at Sutter's Mill, in California, beginning the California gold rush. Prospectors during the gold rush of the following year are referred to as "forty-niners."

1947
Willard F. Libby develops a method of dating prehistoric objects by using radioactive carbon.

1955
Using 1 million pounds of pressure per square inch and temperatures of more than 1,700°C, General Electric creates the first artificial diamonds from graphite.

1969
Apollo 11 astronauts Neil Armstrong and Edwin "Buzz" Aldrin bring 22 kg of moon rocks and soil back to the Earth.

1989
Russian engineers drill a borehole 12 km into the Earth's crust. The borehole is more than 3 times deeper than the deepest mine shaft.

1997
Sojourner, a roving probe on Mars, investigates a Martian boulder nicknamed Yogi.

1999
A Japanese automaker introduces the first hybrid car into the U.S. market.

Earth's Resources

3 Minerals of the Earth's Crust
Chapter Planning Guide

Compression guide: To shorten instruction because of time limitations, omit the Chapter Lab.

OBJECTIVES	LABS, DEMONSTRATIONS, AND ACTIVITIES	TECHNOLOGY RESOURCES
PACING • 90 min pp. 64–69 **Chapter Opener**	SE Start-up Activity, p. 65 GENERAL	OSP Parent Letter ■ GENERAL CD Student Edition on CD-ROM CD Guided Reading Audio CD ■ TR Chapter Starter Transparency* VID Brain Food Video Quiz
Section 1 What Is a Mineral? • Describe the structure of minerals. • Describe the two major groups of minerals.	TE Group Activity Identifying Minerals, p. 66 ◆ GENERAL TE Group Activity Mineral Identification, p. 67 GENERAL SE Science in Action Math, Social Studies, and Language Arts Activities, pp. 86–87 GENERAL	CRF Lesson Plans* TR Bellringer Transparency*
PACING • 90 min pp. 70–73 **Section 2 Identifying Minerals** • Identify seven ways to determine the identity of minerals. • Explain special properties of minerals.	TE Group Activity Mineral Classification, p. 70 GENERAL TE Connection Activity Real World, p. 71 ◆ GENERAL TE Demonstration Applying the Scientific Method, p. 71 GENERAL SE Quick Lab Scratch Test, p. 72 GENERAL CRF Datasheet for Quick Lab* SE Skills Practice Lab Is It Fool's Gold?—A Dense Situation, p. 80 GENERAL CRF Datasheet for Chapter Lab* SE Skills Practice Lab Mysterious Minerals, p. 720 GENERAL CRF Datasheet for LabBook*	CRF Lesson Plans* TR Bellringer Transparency* TR LINK TO PHYSICAL SCIENCE The Three Major Categories of Elements* TR Mohs' Hardness Scale* TR Special Properties of Some Minerals* CRF SciLinks Activity* GENERAL VID Lab Videos for Earth Science
PACING • 45 min pp. 74–79 **Section 3 The Formation, Mining, and Use of Minerals** • Describe the environments in which minerals form. • Compare the two types of mining. • Describe two ways to reduce the effects of mining. • Describe different uses for metallic and nonmetallic minerals.	TE Connection Activity History, p. 75 GENERAL SE School-to-Home Activity Recycling Minerals at Home, p. 77 GENERAL TE Connection Activity Life Science, p. 78 GENERAL LB Long-Term Projects & Research Ideas What's Yours is Mined* ADVANCED	CRF Lesson Plans* TR Bellringer Transparency* SE Internet Activity, p. 75 GENERAL

PACING • 90 min

CHAPTER REVIEW, ASSESSMENT, AND STANDARDIZED TEST PREPARATION
- CRF Vocabulary Activity* GENERAL
- SE Chapter Review, pp. 82–83 GENERAL
- CRF Chapter Review* ■ GENERAL
- CRF Chapter Tests A* ■ GENERAL, B* ADVANCED, C* SPECIAL NEEDS
- SE Standardized Test Preparation, pp. 84–85 GENERAL
- CRF Standardized Test Preparation* GENERAL
- CRF Performance-Based Assessment* GENERAL
- OSP Test Generator GENERAL
- CRF Test Item Listing* GENERAL

Online and Technology Resources

Visit **go.hrw.com** for a variety of free resources related to this textbook. Enter the keyword **HZ5MIN**.

Holt Online Learning
Students can access interactive problem-solving help and active visual concept development with the *Holt Science and Technology* Online Edition available at **www.hrw.com**.

Guided Reading Audio CD
Also in Spanish
A direct reading of each chapter for auditory learners, reluctant readers, and Spanish-speaking students.

Science Tutor CD-ROM
Excellent for remediation and test practice.

Chapter 3 • Minerals of the Earth's Crust

KEY

SE Student Edition	**CRF** Chapter Resource File	**SS** Science Skills Worksheets
TE Teacher Edition	**OSP** One-Stop Planner	**MS** Math Skills for Science Worksheets
	LB Lab Bank	**CD** CD or CD-ROM
	TR Transparencies	**VID** Classroom Video/DVD

* Also on One-Stop Planner
♦ Requires advance prep
■ Also available in Spanish

SKILLS DEVELOPMENT RESOURCES	SECTION REVIEW AND ASSESSMENT	STANDARDS CORRELATIONS
SE Pre-Reading Activity, p. 64 GENERAL **OSP** Science Puzzlers, Twisters & Teasers GENERAL		**National Science Education Standards** UCP 5; SAI 1
CRF Directed Reading A* ■ BASIC, B* SPECIAL NEEDS **CRF** Vocabulary and Section Summary* GENERAL **SE** Reading Strategy Paired Summarizing, p. 66 GENERAL **SE** Connection to Biology Magnetite, p. 68 GENERAL **TE** Inclusion Strategies, p. 68 ♦ **CRF** Reinforcement Worksheet Mystery Mineral* BASIC **CRF** Reinforcement Worksheet The Mineral Quiz Show* BASIC	**TE** Homework, p. 66 GENERAL **SE** Reading Checks, pp. 67, 68 GENERAL **TE** Reteaching, p. 68 BASIC **TE** Quiz, p. 68 GENERAL **TE** Alternative Assessment, p. 68 GENERAL **SE** Section Review,* p. 69 ■ GENERAL **CRF** Section Quiz* ■ GENERAL	UCP 1, 5
CRF Directed Reading A* ■ BASIC, B* GENERAL **CRF** Vocabulary and Section Summary* GENERAL **SE** Reading Strategy Reading Organizer, p. 70 GENERAL **MS** Math Skills for Science Percentages, Fractions, and Decimals* GENERAL **CRF** Critical Thinking Mineral Hunt* ADVANCED	**SE** Reading Checks, pp. 71, 72 GENERAL **TE** Reteaching, p. 72 BASIC **TE** Quiz, p. 72 GENERAL **TE** Alternative Assessment, p. 72 GENERAL **SE** Section Review,* p. 73 ■ GENERAL **CRF** Section Quiz* ■ GENERAL	UCP 1, 5; SAI 1, 2; *LabBook:* SAI 1
CRF Directed Reading A* ■ BASIC, B* SPECIAL NEEDS **CRF** Vocabulary and Section Summary* GENERAL **SE** Reading Strategy Discussion, p. 74 GENERAL **SE** Math Practice Surface Coal Mining, p. 76 GENERAL **TE** Inclusion Strategies, p. 75	**SE** Reading Checks, pp. 77, 79 GENERAL **TE** Reteaching, p. 78 BASIC **TE** Quiz, p. 78 GENERAL **TE** Alternative Assessment, p. 78 GENERAL **SE** Section Review,* p. 79 ■ GENERAL **CRF** Section Quiz* ■ GENERAL	UCP 5; SAI 1; SPSP 2, 4, 5

One-Stop Planner® CD-ROM

This convenient CD-ROM includes:
- Lab Materials QuickList Software
- Holt Calendar Planner
- Customizable Lesson Plans
- Printable Worksheets
- ExamView® Test Generator

CNN Student News
cnnstudentnews.com

Find the latest news, lesson plans, and activities related to important scientific events.

SciLinks NSTA
www.scilinks.org

Maintained by the **National Science Teachers Association.** See Chapter Enrichment pages for a complete list of topics.

Current Science®

Check out *Current Science* articles and activities by visiting the HRW Web site at **go.hrw.com.** Just type in the keyword **HZ5CS03T.**

Classroom Videos

- **Lab Videos** demonstrate the chapter lab.
- **Brain Food Video Quizzes** help students review the chapter material.
- **CNN Videos** bring science into your students' daily life.

Chapter 3 • Chapter Planning Guide

Chapter 3 Chapter Resources

Visual Resources

CHAPTER STARTER TRANSPARENCY

BELLRINGER TRANSPARENCIES

TEACHING TRANSPARENCIES

TEACHING TRANSPARENCIES

CONCEPT MAPPING TRANSPARENCY

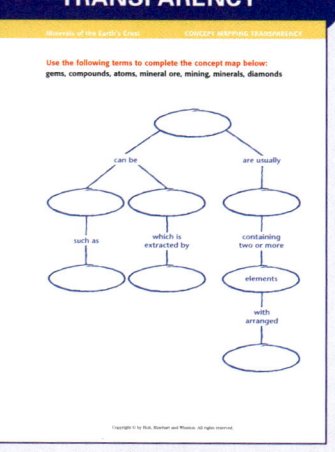

Planning Resources

LESSON PLANS

PARENT LETTER — ALSO IN SPANISH

TEST ITEM LISTING

One-Stop Planner® CD-ROM

This CD-ROM includes all of the resources shown here and the following time-saving tools:

- *Lab Materials QuickList Software*
- *Customizable lesson plans*
- *Holt Calendar Planner*
- *The powerful ExamView® Test Generator*

63C   Chapter 3 • Minerals of the Earth's Crust

For a preview of available worksheets covering math and science skills, see pages T26–T33. All of these resources are also on the One-Stop Planner®.

Meeting Individual Needs

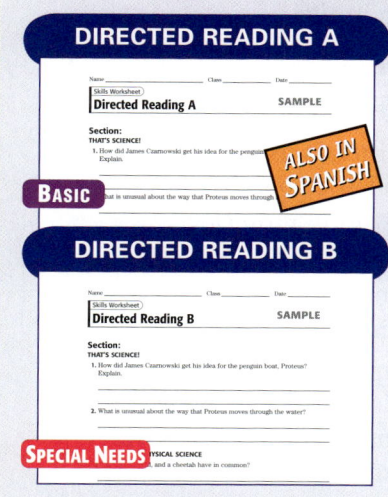

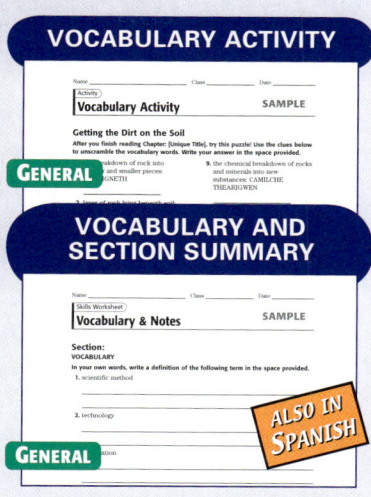

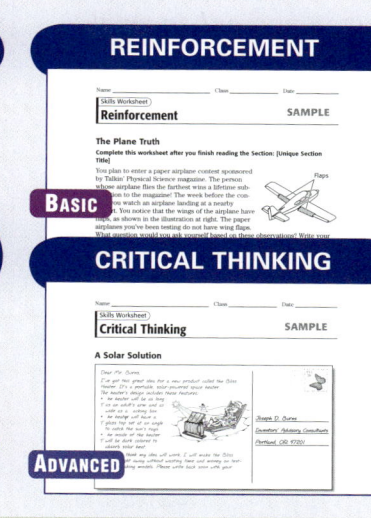

DIRECTED READING A — BASIC (ALSO IN SPANISH)

DIRECTED READING B — SPECIAL NEEDS

VOCABULARY ACTIVITY — GENERAL

VOCABULARY AND SECTION SUMMARY — GENERAL (ALSO IN SPANISH)

REINFORCEMENT — BASIC

CRITICAL THINKING — ADVANCED

SCILINKS ACTIVITY — GENERAL

SCIENCE PUZZLERS, TWISTERS & TEASERS — GENERAL

Labs and Activities

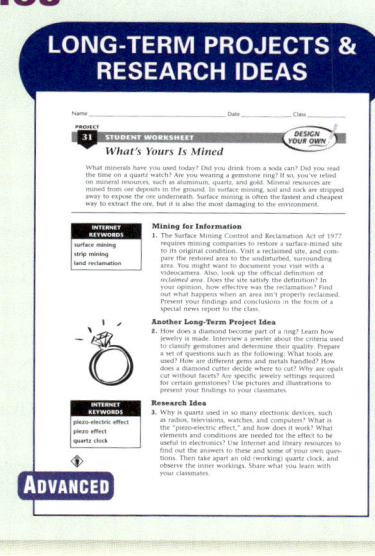

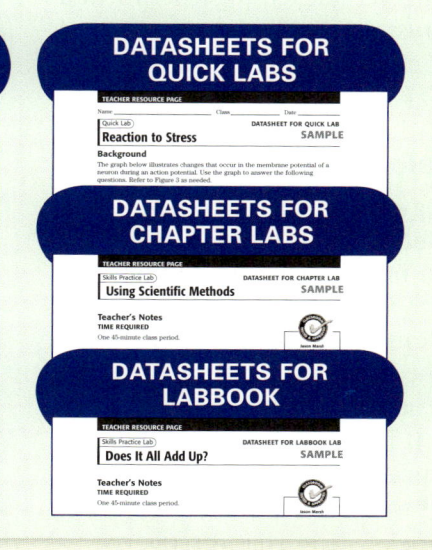

LONG-TERM PROJECTS & RESEARCH IDEAS — ADVANCED

DATASHEETS FOR QUICK LABS

DATASHEETS FOR CHAPTER LABS

DATASHEETS FOR LABBOOK

Review and Assessments

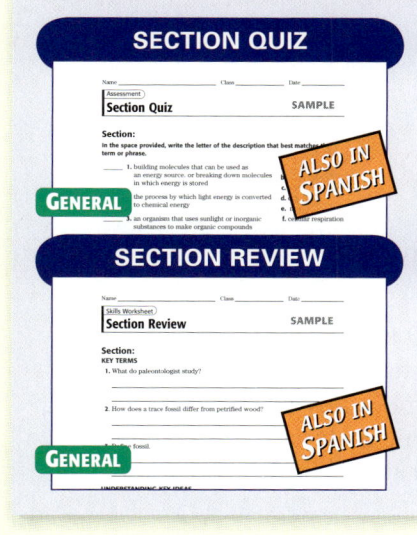

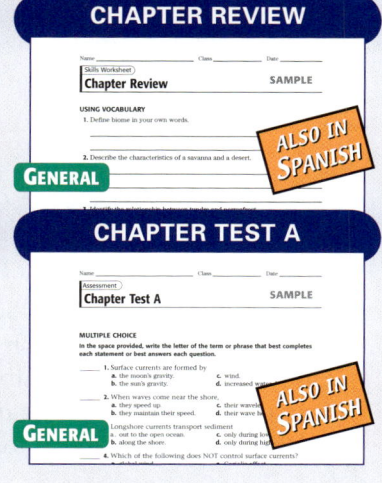

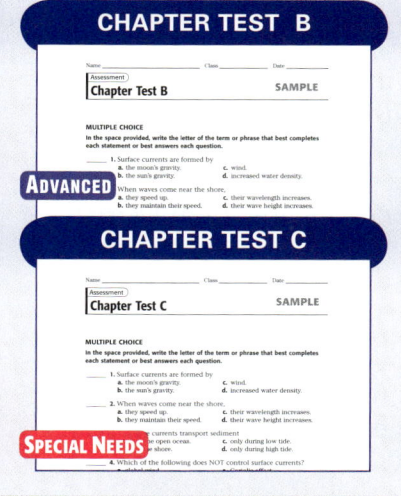

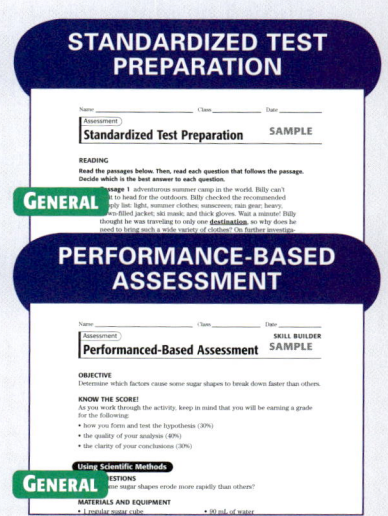

SECTION QUIZ — GENERAL (ALSO IN SPANISH)

SECTION REVIEW — GENERAL (ALSO IN SPANISH)

CHAPTER REVIEW — GENERAL (ALSO IN SPANISH)

CHAPTER TEST A — GENERAL (ALSO IN SPANISH)

CHAPTER TEST B — ADVANCED

CHAPTER TEST C — SPECIAL NEEDS

STANDARDIZED TEST PREPARATION — GENERAL

PERFORMANCE-BASED ASSESSMENT — GENERAL

Chapter 3 • Chapter Resources **63D**

Chapter 3 Enrichment

This Chapter Enrichment provides relevant and interesting information to expand and enhance your presentation of the chapter material.

Section 1

What Is a Mineral?

Crystal Structures

- Minerals are composed of atoms that are arranged in repeating three-dimensional patterns. The basic building block of a mineral crystal is called a unit cell. A *unit cell* is the smallest three-dimensional arrangement of atoms that displays the basic form, or symmetry, of the crystal. Many unit cells stacked together form a crystal. For example, a crystal of halite is composed of unit cells of sodium and chlorine atoms arranged in a unique three-dimensional structure.

The Origins of Mineralogy

- The founder of mineralogy is considered to be Georgius Agricola. His treatise on minerals, *De Re Metallica* (1556), recorded most of what was known about minerals at that time. The science of mineralogy advanced greatly when Romé de l'Isle, a French scientist, proposed the concept of the unit cell in 1772. He argued that the characteristics of mineral crystals could be explained only if they were composed of identical unit cells organized in a predictable way. Crystals are composed of unit cells much like a wall might be composed of bricks. After that discovery, the composition of mineral crystals was actively studied by many scientists.

Industrial Uses of Crystals

- The properties of crystals make crystals useful in many ways. The electronics industry uses quartz in the manufacture of radios, watches, microphones, and sonar transducers. Rubies are used in lasers and as styluses in record players, and diamonds are used in industrial drills and saws.

Is That a Fact!

♦ Currently, about 4,000 minerals have been identified, and 50 to 100 new minerals are discovered each year.

Section 2

Identifying Minerals

Methods of Identifying Minerals

- Scientists usually identify minerals using a petrographic microscope, the hand-specimen method, X-ray diffraction, or an electron microprobe.
  - The hand-specimen method involves determining the color, luster, streak, cleavage, hardness, density, fluorescence, and magnetic qualities of a mineral.
  - When geologists take samples back to the lab, they often use petrographic microscopes to identify minerals. These microscopes make it easier to identify minerals by the optical properties of their crystals.
  - Geologists can analyze minerals at the atomic level by using X-ray diffraction, which measures the way crystal structures diffract X rays. The chemical composition of minerals can also be determined by using an electron microprobe. An electron microprobe produces a beam of electrons that focuses on a sample diameter that may be as small as .001 to .002 mm.

Mohs Hardness Scale

- Friedrich Mohs (1773–1839) was a mineralogist who lived in Vienna, Austria. In 1812, Mohs developed a method for identifying minerals based on their relative hardness. He proposed that a mineral's identity can be determined by comparing the mineral with several minerals of known hardness. A mineral can scratch another mineral of equal or lesser hardness, but it cannot scratch a mineral of greater hardness.

Gemstones

- Of the approximately 4,000 known minerals, only about 100 are cut and polished to become gemstones. One definition of a gemstone is any naturally occurring mineral, rock, or organic material that, when cut and polished, is suitable for use as jewelry.

Chapter 3 • Minerals of the Earth's Crust

- Diamond, emerald, ruby, and topaz are usually referred to as precious stones. Amethyst, garnet, and jade are considered semiprecious. Materials such as coral, pearls, and amber are also considered gemstones, even though they form by organic processes.

- Many gems used in jewelry are imitations. For example, glass can be colored green to look like an emerald. Scientists also create some gems artificially. Synthetic rubies, for example, have the same chemical structure as natural rubies. However, a gemologist can identify synthetic rubies by the presence of curved growth striations and air pockets, which do not occur in natural rubies.

Is That a Fact!

◆ The Cullinan diamond is the world's largest diamond. It was found in the Premier mine in Pretoria, Transvaal in 1905. Before being cut, the Cullinan weighed 3,106 carats, or a little more than .5 kg.

◆ The largest gold nugget ever found was the "Welcome Stranger." It had a mass of 71 kg (156.5 pounds) and was found in Australia on February 5, 1869.

Section 3

The Formation, Mining, and Use of Minerals

Ancient Mines

- The earliest evidence of mining dates to a 43,000-year-old iron mine in South Africa. Early miners were probably interested in the pigments associated with iron ores. The earliest metals used by neolithic people were probably gold and copper. Archaeological evidence indicates that the Egyptians mined copper and turquoise around 3400 BCE. Although most of the earliest mining was conducted on the surface, underground mining did occur by 1300 BCE in Africa.

Intrusions and Mineral Formation

- Plutons are intrusive bodies of igneous rock that cool beneath the Earth's surface. A large body of exposed intrusive rock (greater than 100 km²) is called a *batholith*. Large batholiths occur in British Columbia, Alaska, and in the Sierra Nevada.

- A pegmatite is a very coarse-grained intrusive rock formed from the fluid-rich magma that remains after the rest of a pluton has solidified. Pegmatites may contain minerals such as tourmaline, topaz, or beryl.

The Hope Diamond

- The Hope diamond is a 45.5-carat blue diamond owned by the Smithsonian Institution since 1958. The gem was thought to be cursed because it was allegedly stolen from a statue of the Hindu goddess Sita. Misfortune and tragedy seemed to befall those who came in contact with the stone. The fabled gem was originally 112 carats. It was sold to King Louis XIV in 1668, and named the French Blue. The French Blue was stolen in 1792 from Louis XVI and may have been depicted in an 1800 portrait of a Spanish queen. In 1830, a 45.5-carat cut diamond surfaced in London. Experts declared that it was the French Blue recut to hide its identity. The American Henry Hope bought it, and it has since been called the Hope diamond.

Is That a Fact!

◆ At 215 m deep and 1.6 km in circumference, the Kimberley Mine in Kimberley, Union of South Africa, is the largest hand-dug excavation in the world.

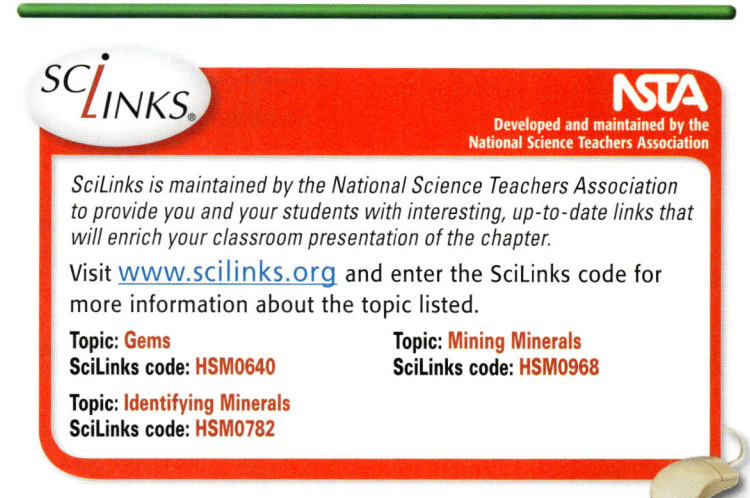

SciLinks is maintained by the National Science Teachers Association to provide you and your students with interesting, up-to-date links that will enrich your classroom presentation of the chapter.

Visit www.scilinks.org and enter the SciLinks code for more information about the topic listed.

Topic: Gems
SciLinks code: HSM0640

Topic: Mining Minerals
SciLinks code: HSM0968

Topic: Identifying Minerals
SciLinks code: HSM0782

Overview
Tell students that this chapter will help them learn about the minerals found in the rocks of the Earth's crust. The chapter describes the structure of minerals, mineral identification, environments in which minerals form, the mining of minerals, and mineral uses.

Assessing Prior Knowledge
Students should be familiar with the following topics:
- fundamental geologic processes
- the periodic table

Identifying Misconceptions
Before teaching the material in this chapter, make sure that students understand the difference between minerals and rocks. Often, these two words are used interchangeably. Emphasize that minerals are the building blocks of rocks and that different rocks are composed of different minerals or different combinations of minerals. For example, the sedimentary rock limestone is composed mostly of calcium carbonate in the form of the mineral calcite. The igneous rock granite is composed of a combination of the minerals quartz, orthoclase, and mica, and often has accessory minerals.

3
Minerals of the Earth's Crust

SECTION 1 What Is a Mineral? 66

SECTION 2 Identifying Minerals ... 70

SECTION 3 The Formation, Mining, and Use of Minerals ... 74

Chapter Lab 80
Chapter Review 82
Standardized Test Preparation 84
Science in Action 86

About the PHOTO
Fluorescence is the ability that some minerals have to glow under ultraviolet light. The beauty of mineral fluorescence is well represented at the Sterling Hill Mine in Franklin, New Jersey. In this picture taken at the mine, minerals in the rock glow as brightly as if they had been freshly painted by an artist.

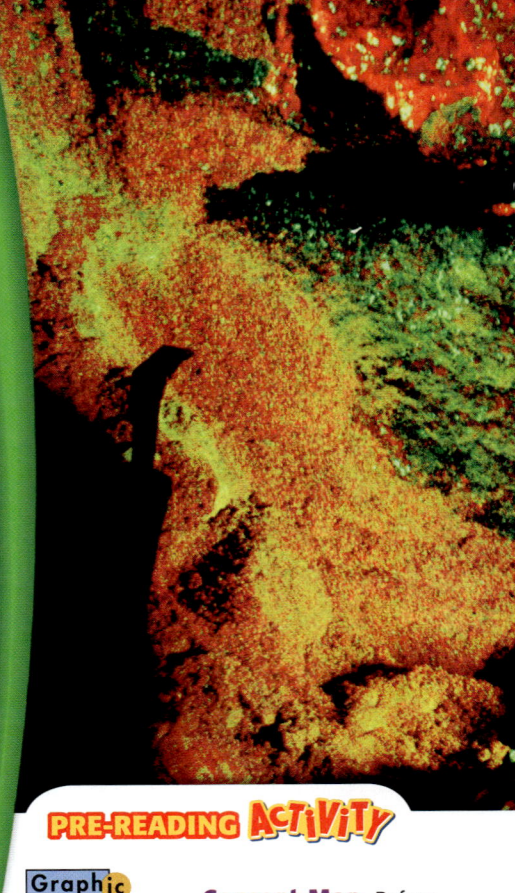

PRE-READING ACTIVITY

Graphic Organizer

Concept Map Before you read the chapter, create the graphic organizer entitled "Concept Map" described in the **Study Skills** section of the Appendix. As you read the chapter, fill in the concept map with details about minerals.

Standards Correlations

National Science Education Standards
The following codes indicate the National Science Education Standards that correlate to this chapter. The full text of the standards is at the front of the book.

Chapter Opener
SAI 1; UCP 5

Section 1 What Is a Mineral?
UCP 1, 5

Section 2 Identifying Minerals
SAI 1; UCP 1, 5; LabBook: SAI 1

Section 3 The Formation, Mining, and Use of Minerals
SAI 1; UCP 5; SPSP 2, 4

Chapter Lab
SAI 1, 2

Chapter Review
SAI 1; UCP 1, 5; SPSP 2, 4

Science in Action
HNS 1

START-UP ACTIVITY

MATERIALS

FOR EACH GROUP
- paper, notebook (one sheet)

Teacher's Notes: Make students aware that most of the materials in the classroom will be made from nonliving things. Exceptions are items that are made of wood or plant fiber and items that are made of plastic, which are made from petroleum. You may want to go further and have students attempt to differentiate between items that are made of metallic minerals and those made of nonmetallic minerals.

Answers

1. Most of the materials in the classroom will most likely be made of nonliving materials. Materials that are made of minerals include graphite in pencils, clay in paper products, metal in desks, gypsum in wallboard, silica in glass, and cement (calcite) in the concrete-slab foundation.

START-UP ACTIVITY

What Is Your Classroom Made Of?

One of the properties of minerals is that minerals are made from nonliving material. Complete the following activity to see if you can determine whether items in your classroom are made from living or nonliving materials.

Procedure

1. On a **sheet of paper,** make two columns. Label one column "Materials made from living things." Label the second column "Materials made from nonliving things."

2. Look around your classroom. Choose a variety of items to put on your list. Some items that you might select are your clothing, your desk, books, notebook paper, pencils, the classroom windows, doors, walls, the ceiling, and the floor.

3. With a partner, discuss each item that you have chosen. Decide into which column each item should be placed. Write down the reason for your decision.

Analysis

1. Are most of the items that you chose made of living or nonliving materials?

Chapter Starter Transparency
Use this transparency to help students begin thinking about the diversity of minerals.

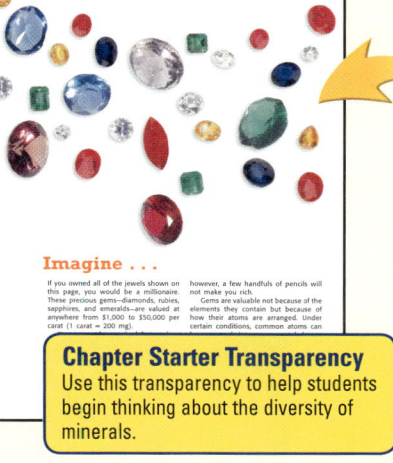

CHAPTER RESOURCES

Technology

- **Transparencies**
  - Chapter Starter Transparency **READING SKILLS**
- **Student Edition on CD-ROM**
- **Guided Reading Audio CD**
  - English or Spanish
- **Classroom Videos**
  - Brain Food Video Quiz

Workbooks

- **Science Puzzlers, Twisters & Teasers**
  - Minerals of the Earth's Crust **GENERAL**

Chapter 3 • **Minerals of the Earth's Crust**   **65**

SECTION 1

Focus

Overview
This section explores the nature of minerals by describing their four characteristics. Students learn that mineral crystals are generated by atomic structures, and they learn how to classify minerals into two major compositional groups—silicates and nonsilicates.

Bellringer
Display a piece of pencil lead (graphite) and a photograph of a diamond. Explain that both substances are composed of carbon. Ask students to brainstorm how two substances with such different properties can form from atoms of the same element.

Motivate

Group Activity — GENERAL

Identifying Minerals Place an assortment of objects on a table. Possibilities include a piece of wood, a fossil, a piece of bone, a piece of granite, and a quartz crystal. Organize the class into groups of two or three students. Tell the students to examine the objects and to determine which ones are minerals by using the four questions in **Figure 1** on this page. **LS** Logical/Verbal

---

SECTION 1

READING WARM-UP

Objectives
- Describe the structure of minerals.
- Describe the two major groups of minerals.

Terms to Learn
mineral
element
compound
crystal
silicate mineral
nonsilicate mineral

READING STRATEGY

Paired Summarizing Read this section silently. In pairs, take turns summarizing the material. Stop to discuss ideas that seem confusing.

What Is a Mineral?

You may think that all minerals look like gems. But, in fact, most minerals look more like rocks. Does this mean that minerals are the same as rocks? Well, not really. So, what's the difference?

For one thing, rocks are made of minerals, but minerals are not made of rocks. A **mineral** is a naturally formed, inorganic solid that has a definite crystalline structure.

Mineral Structure

By answering the four questions in **Figure 1**, you can tell whether an object is a mineral. If you cannot answer "yes" to all four questions, you don't have a mineral. Three of the four questions may be easy to answer. The question about crystalline structure may be more difficult. To understand what crystalline structure is, you need to know a little about the elements that make up a mineral. **Elements** are pure substances that cannot be broken down into simpler substances by ordinary chemical means. All minerals contain one or more of the 92 naturally occurring elements.

Is it nonliving material?
A mineral is inorganic, meaning it isn't made of living things.

Is it a solid?
Minerals can't be gases or liquids.

Does it have a crystalline structure?
Minerals are crystals, which have a repeating inner structure that is often reflected in the shape of the crystal. Minerals generally have the same chemical composition throughout.

Is it formed in nature?
Crystalline materials made by people aren't classified as minerals.

Figure 1 The answers to these four questions will determine whether an object is a mineral.

CHAPTER RESOURCES

Chapter Resource File
- Lesson Plan
- Directed Reading A BASIC
- Directed Reading B SPECIAL NEEDS

Technology
- Transparencies
  • Bellringer

Homework — GENERAL

At Home with Minerals Ask students to find four items in their home that are derived from minerals. Have them add labels to identify the minerals that are contained in different products. Have students share their findings with the class. (Examples include table salt, which is composed of halite; pencil lead, which is composed of graphite; and cooking pots, which are composed of iron, copper, or aluminum.) **LS** Visual

---

66 Chapter 3 • Minerals of the Earth's Crust

Atoms and Compounds

Each element is made of only one kind of atom. An *atom* is the smallest part of an element that has all the properties of that element. Like other substances, minerals are made up of atoms of one or more elements.

Most minerals are made of compounds of several different elements. A **compound** is a substance made of two or more elements that have been chemically joined, or bonded. Halite, NaCl, for example, is a compound of sodium, Na, and chlorine, Cl, as shown in **Figure 2**. A few minerals, such as gold and silver, are composed of only one element. A mineral that is composed of only one element is called a *native element*.

Reading Check How does a compound differ from an element? (*See the Appendix for answers to Reading Checks.*)

Crystals

Solid, geometric forms of minerals produced by a repeating pattern of atoms that is present throughout the mineral are called **crystals**. A crystal's shape is determined by the arrangement of the atoms within the crystal. The arrangement of atoms in turn is determined by the kinds of atoms that make up the mineral. Each mineral has a definite crystalline structure. All minerals can be grouped into crystal classes according to the kinds of crystals they form. **Figure 3** shows how the atomic structure of gold gives rise to cubic crystals.

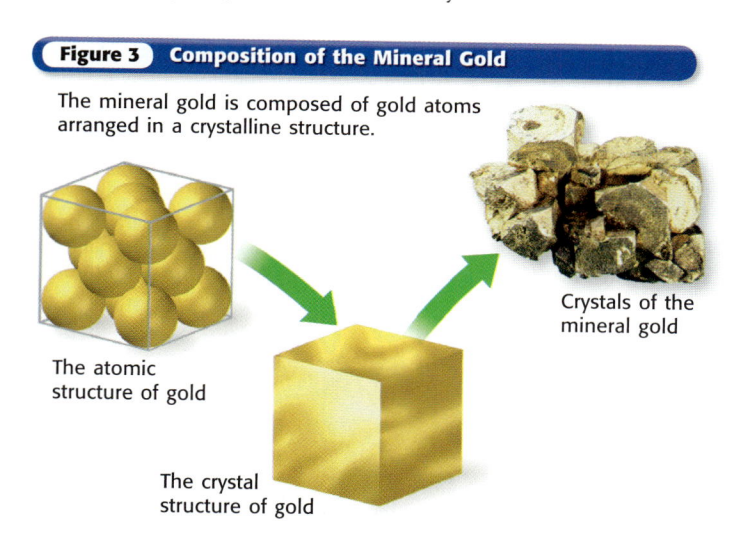

Figure 2 When atoms of sodium (purple) and chlorine (green) join, they form a compound commonly known as rock salt, or the mineral halite.

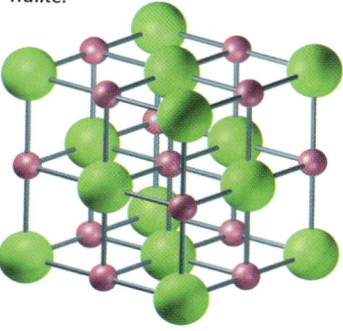

mineral a naturally formed, inorganic solid that has a definite crystalline structure

element a substance that cannot be separated or broken down into simpler substances by chemical means

compound a substance made up of atoms of two or more different elements joined by chemical bonds

crystal a solid whose atoms, ions, or molecules are arranged in a definite pattern

Figure 3 Composition of the Mineral Gold

The mineral gold is composed of gold atoms arranged in a crystalline structure.

The atomic structure of gold

The crystal structure of gold

Crystals of the mineral gold

MISCONCEPTION ALERT

Crystal Form and Mineral Identification In much the same way that color is a deceptive guide to identifying minerals, crystal form is often a misleading physical property. The unit cells of halite and gold are shown in **Figure 2** and **Figure 3**. When different unit cells are combined, however, they can generate crystal forms that look nothing like their atomic structure. A large variety of complex crystal shapes can be generated by starting with a simple polyhedron, such as a cube. For example, the mineral fluorite belongs in the isometric (cubic) class but commonly forms octahedral-shaped crystals.

Teach

Discussion — GENERAL

Rocks and Minerals Students may benefit from a discussion of the differences between rocks and minerals. Emphasize that rocks are composed of minerals but that minerals are not composed of rock. It is possible for a rock to be made of one mineral or of many. Minerals should also not be confused with mineraloids. Mineraloids are similar to minerals, but mineraloids have no crystalline structure. Some common mineraloids are obsidian, limonite, flint, and opal. **LS Verbal**

Group Activity — GENERAL

Writing **Mineral Identification** When you begin teaching this section, give pairs of students an unknown mineral. Tell students that their goal will be to identify the mineral by the time the class finishes studying the chapter and to present a short report on the mineral to the class. Their reports should include the chemical formula of the mineral, detail the mineral's uses and properties, and explain how the mineral was formed and the type of rock in which the mineral occurs. Student reports can also include the location of mines where the mineral is found. **LS Verbal/Logical**

Answer to Reading Check

An element is a pure substance that cannot be broken down into simpler substances by ordinary chemical means. A compound is a substance made of two or more elements that have been chemically bonded.

Section 1 • What Is a Mineral?

Close

Reteaching — BASIC

Elements and Compounds Have students prepare a set of cards for 10 common minerals. Give students the chemical formula for each mineral, and have them write the chemical formula next to the mineral name. This exercise will reinforce the difference between minerals that are composed of a single element and minerals that are composed of multiple elements. **LS Visual**

Quiz — GENERAL

1. What is a mineral? (a naturally formed, inorganic solid that has a crystalline structure)
2. What does a crystal's shape depend on? (the arrangement of the atoms within the crystal)

Alternative Assessment — GENERAL

Classifying Minerals Write the following mineral-group names on the board: silicates, native elements, carbonates, halides, oxides, sulfates, and sulfides. Have students match the following items with the mineral group from which they are derived: a copper penny (native elements); cement (carbonates); rock salt (halides); toothpaste (sulfates); batteries (sulfides); sand (silicates). **LS Logical**

Answer to Reading Check

Answers may vary. Silicate minerals contain a combination of silicon and oxygen; nonsilicate minerals do not contain a combination of silicon and oxygen.

CONNECTION TO Biology

WRITING SKILL

Magnetite The mineral magnetite has a special property—it is magnetic. Scientists have found that some animals' brains contain magnetite. And scientists have shown that certain fish can sense magnetic fields because of the magnetite in the brains of these fish. The magnetite gives the fish a sense of direction. Using the Internet or another source, research other animals that have magnetite in their brains. Summarize your findings in a short essay.

silicate mineral a mineral that contains a combination of silicon, oxygen, and one or more metals

nonsilicate mineral a mineral that does not contain compounds of silicon and oxygen

---

Two Groups of Minerals

The most common classification of minerals is based on chemical composition. Minerals are divided into two groups based on their chemical composition. These groups are the silicate minerals and the nonsilicate minerals.

Silicate Minerals

Silicon and oxygen are the two most common elements in the Earth's crust. Minerals that contain a combination of these two elements are called **silicate minerals.** Silicate minerals make up more than 90% of the Earth's crust. The rest of the Earth's crust is made up of nonsilicate minerals. Silicon and oxygen usually combine with other elements, such as aluminum, iron, magnesium, and potassium, to make up silicate minerals. Some of the more common silicate minerals are shown in **Figure 4.**

Nonsilicate Minerals

Minerals that do not contain a combination of the elements silicon and oxygen form a group called the **nonsilicate minerals.** Some of these minerals are made up of elements such as carbon, oxygen, fluorine, and sulfur. **Figure 5** on the following page shows the most important classes of nonsilicate minerals.

✓ **Reading Check** How do silicate minerals differ from nonsilicate minerals?

Figure 4 Common Silicate Minerals

Quartz is the basic building block of many rocks.

Feldspar minerals are the main component of most rocks on the Earth's surface.

Mica minerals separate easily into sheets when they break. Biotite is one of several kinds of mica.

INCLUSION Strategies

- Learning Disabilities
- Developmentally Delayed

Organize students into pairs or groups of three. Give each group some common mineral samples. Pass out paint sample strips from a hardware store, and have students identify each mineral's color. Students should record their observations in their **science journal.** Next, hand out materials that serve as examples of luster. A candle could demonstrate waxy luster, and a jar top is an example of metallic luster. Have students use these examples to determine the luster of each mineral sample. The teams should perform all of the mineral tests in a similar way and share their findings with the class. **LS Visual/Kinesthetic** **English Language Learners**

Chapter 3 • Minerals of the Earth's Crust

Figure 5 Classes of Nonsilicate Minerals

Native elements are minerals that are composed of only one element. Some examples are copper, Cu, gold, Au, and silver, Ag. Native elements are used in communications and electronics equipment.

Copper

Oxides are compounds that form when an element, such as aluminum or iron, combines chemically with oxygen. Oxide minerals are used to make abrasives, aircraft parts, and paint.

Corundum

Carbonates are minerals that contain combinations of carbon and oxygen in their chemical structure. We use carbonate minerals in cement, building stones, and fireworks.

Calcite

Sulfates are minerals that contain sulfur and oxygen, SO_4. Sulfates are used in cosmetics, toothpaste, cement, and paint.

Gypsum

Halides are compounds that form when fluorine, chlorine, iodine, or bromine combine with sodium, potassium, or calcium. Halide minerals are used in the chemical industry and in detergents.

Fluorite

Sulfides are minerals that contain one or more elements, such as lead, iron, or nickel, combined with sulfur. Sulfide minerals are used to make batteries, medicines, and electronic parts.

Galena

SECTION Review

Summary

- A mineral is a naturally formed, inorganic solid that has a definite crystalline structure.
- Minerals may be either elements or compounds.
- Mineral crystals are solid, geometric forms that are produced by a repeating pattern of atoms.
- Minerals are classified as either silicate minerals or nonsilicate minerals based on the elements of which they are composed.

Using Key Terms

1. In your own words, write a definition for each of the following terms: *element*, *compound*, and *mineral*.

Understanding Key Ideas

2. Which of the following minerals is a nonsilicate mineral?
   a. mica
   b. quartz
   c. gypsum
   d. feldspar

3. What is a crystal, and what determines a crystal's shape?

4. Describe the two major groups of minerals.

Math Skills

5. If there are approximately 3,600 known minerals and about 20 of the minerals are native elements, what percentage of all minerals are native elements?

Critical Thinking

6. **Applying Concepts** Explain why each of the following is not considered a mineral: water, oxygen, honey, and teeth.

7. **Applying Concepts** Explain why scientists consider ice to be a mineral.

8. **Making Comparisons** In what ways are sulfate and sulfide minerals the same. In what ways are they different?

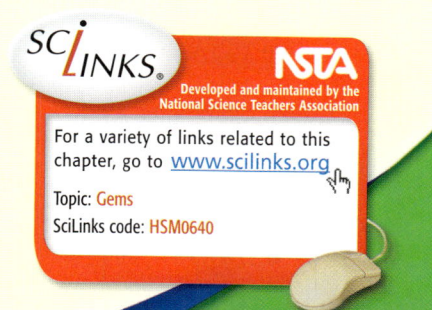

SciLinks
Developed and maintained by the National Science Teachers Association
For a variety of links related to this chapter, go to www.scilinks.org
Topic: Gems
SciLinks code: HSM0640

Answers to Section Review

1. Sample answer: Pure substances that cannot be broken down into simpler substances are called elements. Compounds are two or more elements bonded together. A mineral is a naturally formed, inorganic solid that has a crystalline structure.

2. c

3. A crystal is a solid, geometric form of mineral produced by a repeating pattern of atoms that is present throughout the mineral. The shape of a crystal is determined by the arrangement of atoms within the crystal.

4. The two major groups of minerals are silicate and nonsilicate minerals. Silicate minerals contain a combination of silicon and oxygen. Nonsilicate minerals do not contain a combination of silicon and oxygen.

5. $20 \div 3{,}600 \times 100 = .55\%$

6. Water is not a mineral because it does not have a crystalline structure and it is a liquid, not a solid. Oxygen is not a mineral because oxygen atoms by themselves do not have a crystalline structure. Teeth are not minerals because they are living parts of your body. Honey is not a mineral because it is made of organic substances.

7. Ice is considered to be a mineral because it is a solid, it is a nonliving material, it is formed in nature, and it has a definite crystalline structure.

8. Sulfate minerals are similar to sulfide minerals because both contain the element sulfur. Sulfate minerals and sulfide minerals are different because sulfide minerals contain one or more elements combined with sulfur, whereas sulfate minerals contain one or more elements combined with sulfur and oxygen.

CHAPTER RESOURCES

Chapter Resource File
- Section Quiz GENERAL
- Section Review GENERAL
- Vocabulary and Section Summary GENERAL
- Reinforcement Worksheet BASIC

Section 1 • What Is a Mineral?

SECTION 2

Focus

Overview
In this section, students will learn common techniques used to identify minerals. They will also examine some of the interesting properties of minerals, such as fluorescence, radioactivity, and magnetism.

🔔 Bellringer
Show students a variety of mineral samples. Have students list as many phrases as they can to describe each sample. Have students organize these phrases into categories. Students can use these categories to determine whether or not each sample is a different mineral.

Motivate

Group Activity — GENERAL

Mineral Classification Have students develop a classification system for minerals based on observable physical properties. Give groups a variety of minerals or photographs of minerals. Students should create a classification system based on observable differences and similarities between the samples. After the groups have developed a classification system, give them several new samples. Have them place the samples in their classification scheme.
LS Visual/Logical

SECTION 2

READING WARM-UP

Objectives
- Identify seven ways to determine the identity of minerals.
- Explain special properties of minerals.

Terms to Learn
luster   fracture
streak   hardness
cleavage   density

READING STRATEGY

Reading Organizer As you read this section, create an outline of the section. Use the headings from the section in your outline.

luster the way in which a mineral reflects light

CHAPTER RESOURCES

Chapter Resource File
- Lesson Plan
- Directed Reading A **BASIC**
- Directed Reading B **SPECIAL NEEDS**

Technology
- Transparencies
  - Bellringer
  - **LINK TO PHYSICAL SCIENCE** The Three Major Categories of Elements

---

Identifying Minerals

If you closed your eyes and tasted different foods, you could probably determine what the foods are by noting properties such as saltiness or sweetness. You can also determine the identity of a mineral by noting different properties.

In this section, you will learn about the properties that will help you identify minerals.

Color

The same mineral can come in a variety of colors. For example, in its purest state quartz is clear. Samples of quartz that contain various types of and various amounts of impurities, however, can be a variety of colors.

Besides impurities, other factors can change the appearance of minerals. The mineral pyrite, often called fool's gold, normally has a golden color. But if pyrite is exposed to air and water for a long period, it can turn brown or black. Because of factors such as impurities, color usually is not the best way to identify a mineral.

Luster

The way a surface reflects light is called **luster**. When you say an object is shiny or dull, you are describing its luster. Minerals have metallic, submetallic, or nonmetallic luster. If a mineral is shiny, it has a metallic luster. If the mineral is dull, its luster is either submetallic or nonmetallic. The different types of lusters are shown in **Figure 1**.

Figure 1 Types of Mineral Luster

Metallic
bright, reflective

Submetallic
dull, reflective

Nonmetallic

Vitreous
glassy, brilliant

Waxy
greasy, oily

Silky
fibrous

Pearly
creamy

Resinous
plastic

Earthy
rough, dull

WEIRD SCIENCE

How can you tell a real diamond from a fake? A gem specialist uses specialized tools to distinguish real diamonds from impostors. But there are some tests that even an untrained person can conduct. One of the simplest tests is to try to pick up the stone in question with a moistened fingertip. Diamonds can be picked up this way; most other stones cannot.

Chapter 3 • Minerals of the Earth's Crust

Streak

The color of a mineral in powdered form is called the mineral's **streak**. A mineral's streak can be found by rubbing the mineral against a piece of unglazed porcelain called a *streak plate*. The mark left on the streak plate is the streak. The streak is a thin layer of powdered mineral. The color of a mineral's streak is not always the same as the color of the mineral sample. The difference between color and streak is shown in **Figure 2**. Unlike the surface of a mineral sample, the streak is not affected by air or water. For this reason, using streak is more reliable than using color in identifying a mineral.

Reading Check Why is using streak more reliable in identifying a mineral than using color is? *(See the Appendix for answers to Reading Checks.)*

Figure 2 The color of the mineral hematite may vary, but hematite's streak is always red-brown.

Cleavage and Fracture

Different types of minerals break in different ways. The way a mineral breaks is determined by the arrangement of its atoms. **Cleavage** is the tendency of some minerals to break along smooth, flat surfaces. **Figure 3** shows the cleavage patterns of the minerals mica and halite.

Fracture is the tendency of some minerals to break unevenly along curved or irregular surfaces. One type of fracture is shown in **Figure 4**.

streak the color of the powder of a mineral

cleavage the splitting of a mineral along smooth, flat surfaces

fracture the manner in which a mineral breaks along either curved or irregular surfaces

Figure 3 Cleavage varies with mineral type.

▶ Mica breaks easily into distinct sheets.

Halite breaks at 90° angles in three directions. ▼

Figure 4 This sample of quartz shows a curved fracture pattern called conchoidal fracture (kahn KOYD uhl FRAK chuhr).

Answer to Reading Check
A mineral's streak is not affected by air or water, but a mineral's color may be affected by air or water.

CONNECTION ACTIVITY
Real World — GENERAL

Class Visit Invite a jeweler to visit the class, and ask the jeweler to explain how gemstones are made into jewelry. The jeweler could bring in visual aids to help students understand how gems are located, mined, and prepared for commercial use. **LS Visual**

Teach

Demonstration — GENERAL
Applying the Scientific Method
Before allowing students to test minerals, demonstrate how each step is performed. Use a few common minerals that have distinct characteristics, such as talc and quartz. Show students how each test is conducted, and discuss with them why every step is necessary to identify a mineral. Tell students that a systematic approach to testing the minerals is important. Students should perform the same steps, in order, to each unknown sample. Caution students not to taste mineral samples. **LS Visual/Kinesthetic**

MISCONCEPTION ALERT
Color in Minerals Students may think that a given mineral is easy to identify because it is always the same color. Explain to students that a mineral can occur in a range of colors. For example, labradorite can be yellow or dull gray. Quartz crystals range from clear to purple and from brown to rose. Purple quartz is the gemstone amethyst, and yellow quartz is the gemstone citrine. Remind students that they must test all of a mineral's characteristics—color, luster, hardness, streak, cleavage and fracture, density, and special properties to determine its identity.

Section 2 • Identifying Minerals **71**

Close

Reteaching — BASIC

Mnemonics Have students create a mnemonic device that will help them learn the Mohs hardness scale. One example is **T**errible **G**iants **C**an **F**ind **A**lligators **O**r **Q**uaint **T**igers **C**onveniently **D**igestible. This will help students remember the minerals in order of hardness: talc, gypsum, calcite, fluorite, apatite, orthoclase, quartz, topaz, corundum, and diamond. **LS Auditory**

Quiz — GENERAL

1. Why is color not always a reliable way of identifying a mineral? (Factors such as weathering and the inclusion of impurities can affect the mineral's color.)

2. What property do minerals that glow under ultraviolet light display? (fluorescence)

Alternative Assessment — GENERAL

Mineral Identification Cards Have students prepare mineral identification cards for some of the most common minerals. They can list the words color, luster, hardness, streak, cleavage and fracture, and density on each card. For each card, ask them to fill in the properties of a common mineral. Students should write the name of the mineral on the back of the card and use the cards as study aids or assessment tools. **LS Visual**

Figure 5 Mohs Hardness Scale

A mineral's number indicates its relative hardness. The scale ranges from 1, which is the softest, to 10, which is the hardest. A mineral of a given hardness will scratch any mineral that is softer than it is.

1. Talc
2. Gypsum
3. Calcite
4. Fluorite
5. Apatite
6. Orthoclase
7. Quartz
8. Topaz
9. Corundum
10. Diamond

hardness a measure of the ability of a mineral to resist scratching

density the ratio of the mass of a substance to the volume of the substance

Hardness

A mineral's resistance to being scratched is called **hardness**. To determine the hardness of minerals, scientists use *Mohs hardness scale*, shown in **Figure 5**. Notice that talc has a rating of 1 and diamond has a rating of 10. The greater a mineral's resistance to being scratched is, the higher the mineral's rating is. To identify a mineral by using Mohs scale, try to scratch the surface of a mineral with the edge of one of the 10 reference minerals. If the reference mineral scratches your mineral, the reference mineral is harder than your mineral.

Reading Check How would you determine the hardness of an unidentified mineral sample?

Density

If you pick up a golf ball and a table-tennis ball, which will feel heavier? Although the balls are of similar size, the golf ball will feel heavier because it is denser. **Density** is the measure of how much matter is in a given amount of space. In other words, density is a ratio of an object's mass to its volume. Density is usually measured in grams per cubic centimeter. Because water has a density of 1 g/cm^3, it is used as a reference point for other substances. The ratio of an object's density to the density of water is called the object's *specific gravity*. The specific gravity of gold, for example, is 19. So, gold has a density of 19 g/cm^3. In other words, there is 19 times more matter in 1 cm^3 of gold than in 1 cm^3 of water.

Quick Lab

Scratch Test

1. You will need a **penny**, a **pencil**, and your **fingernail**. Which one of these three materials is the hardest?
2. Use your fingernail to try to scratch the graphite at the tip of a pencil.
3. Now try to scratch the penny with your fingernail.
4. Rank the three materials in order from softest to hardest.

Answer to Reading Check
Scratch the mineral with a series of 10 reference minerals. If the reference mineral scratches the unidentified mineral, the reference mineral is harder than the unidentified mineral.

Quick Lab

MATERIALS

FOR EACH GROUP
- pencil
- penny

Answers

4. The penny is the hardest material of the three, followed by the fingernail and then the graphite.

---

72 Chapter 3 • Minerals of the Earth's Crust

Special Properties

Some properties are particular to only a few types of minerals. The properties shown in **Figure 6** can help you quickly identify the minerals shown. To identify some properties, however, you will need specialized equipment.

Figure 6 Special Properties of Some Minerals

Fluorescence
Calcite and fluorite glow under ultraviolet light. The same fluorite sample is shown in ultraviolet light (top) and in white light (bottom).

Chemical Reaction
Calcite will become bubbly, or "fizz," when a drop of weak acid is placed on it.

Optical Properties
A thin, clear piece of calcite placed over an image will cause a double image.

Magnetism
Both magnetite and pyrrhotite are natural magnets that attract iron.

Taste
Halite has a salty taste.

Radioactivity
Minerals that contain radium or uranium can be detected by a Geiger counter.

SECTION Review

Summary

- Properties that can be used to identify minerals are color, luster, streak, cleavage, fracture, hardness, and density.
- Some minerals can be identified by special properties they have, such as taste, magnetism, fluorescence, radioactivity, chemical reaction, and optical properties.

Using Key Terms

1. Use each of the following terms in a separate sentence: *luster*, *streak*, and *cleavage*.

Understanding Key Ideas

2. Which of the following properties of minerals is expressed in numbers?
   a. fracture
   b. cleavage
   c. hardness
   d. streak

3. How do you determine a mineral's streak?

4. Briefly describe the special properties of minerals.

Math Skills

5. If a mineral has a specific gravity of 5.5, how much more matter is there in 1 cm³ of this mineral than in 1 cm³ of water?

Critical Thinking

6. **Applying Concepts** What properties would you use to determine whether two mineral samples are different minerals?

7. **Applying Concepts** If a mineral scratches calcite but is scratched by apatite, what is the mineral's hardness?

8. **Analyzing Methods** What would be the easiest way to identify calcite?

For a variety of links related to this chapter, go to www.scilinks.org
Topic: Identifying Minerals
SciLinks code: HSM0782

Answers to Section Review

1. Sample answer: Luster is the way the surface of a mineral reflects light. Streak is the thin layer of powder that a mineral leaves when rubbed against a streak plate. If a mineral has cleavage, it breaks along flat surfaces.

2. c

3. The streak of a mineral is determined by rubbing the mineral against a streak plate. The thin layer of powder left on the streak plate is the mineral's streak.

4. The special properties of minerals include fluorescence (glowing under ultraviolet light), chemical reaction, optical properties (such as producing a double image), magnetism, taste, and radioactivity.

5. There is 5.5 times more matter in 1 cm³ of this mineral than in 1 cm³ of water.

6. Properties that would be useful to determine whether two mineral samples are different include color, luster, streak, cleavage and fracture, hardness, density, or any of the special properties listed in the text.

7. The hardness would be 4 on the Mohs hardness scale.

8. The easiest way to identify calcite would be to place a drop of weak acid on the sample to see if the acid produces bubbles.

CHAPTER RESOURCES

Chapter Resource File

- Section Quiz GENERAL
- Section Review GENERAL
- Vocabulary and Section Summary GENERAL
- Datasheet for Quick Lab
- SciLinks Activity GENERAL
- Critical Thinking ADVANCED

Technology

Transparencies
- Mohs Hardness Scale
- Special Properties of Some Minerals

Section 2 • Identifying Minerals

SECTION 3

Focus

Overview
This section discusses how minerals form deep within Earth's crust and how they form at or close to the Earth's surface. Students will learn about different techniques used to mine minerals. This section concludes with a discussion of the value of mineral resources and the importance of environmentally responsible mining and reclamation.

🔔 **Bellringer**
Show students a mineral resource map of your state. Have students locate mines that are closest to where they live and discuss the mineral commodities that are mined at these locations.

Motivate

Discussion — GENERAL
Simulating a Gold Rush To simulate the excitement of the gold rush of 1849, make up a flyer that tells of a rich gold deposit found in a nearby area. Make copies, and pass them out to students. Have students discuss their reactions to such an announcement. Then, discuss the chaotic enthusiasm of the gold rush. Note that from 1848 to 1860, the population in California grew from 14,000 to 380,000 people! LS Visual/Verbal

---

SECTION 3

The Formation, Mining, and Use of Minerals

If you wanted to find a mineral, where do you think you would look?

Minerals form in a variety of environments in the Earth's crust. Each of these environments has a different set of physical and chemical conditions. Therefore, the environment in which a mineral forms determines the mineral's properties. Environments in which minerals form may be on or near the Earth's surface or deep beneath the Earth's surface.

READING WARM-UP

Objectives
- Describe the environments in which minerals form.
- Compare the two types of mining.
- Describe two ways to reduce the effects of mining.
- Describe different uses for metallic and nonmetallic minerals.

Terms to Learn
ore
reclamation

READING STRATEGY

Discussion Read this section silently. Write down questions that you have about this section. Discuss your questions in a small group.

Evaporating Salt Water When a body of salt water dries up, minerals such as gypsum and halite are left behind. As the salt water evaporates, these minerals crystallize.

Limestones Surface water and groundwater carry dissolved materials into lakes and seas, where they crystallize on the bottom. Minerals that form in this environment include calcite and dolomite.

Metamorphic Rocks When changes in pressure, temperature, or chemical makeup alter a rock, *metamorphism* takes place. Minerals that form in metamorphic rock include calcite, garnet, graphite, hematite, magnetite, mica, and talc.

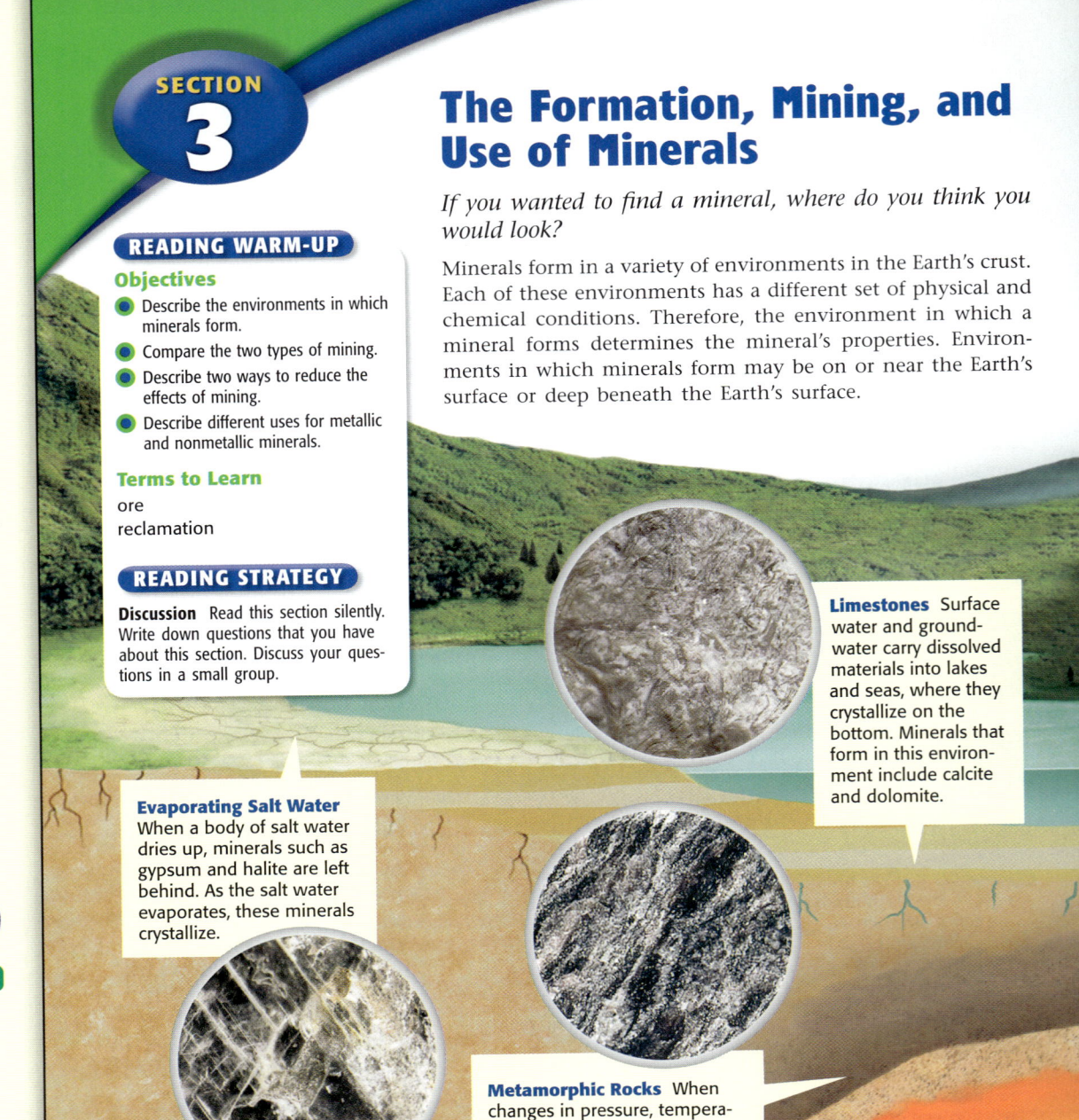

CHAPTER RESOURCES

Chapter Resource File
- Lesson Plan
- Directed Reading A BASIC
- Directed Reading B SPECIAL NEEDS

Technology
- Transparencies
 • Bellringer

WEIRD SCIENCE

Some of the greatest untapped sources of minerals are hydrothermal vents deep under the sea. These hydrothermal vents are called *black smokers* because they spew out hot, mineral-rich water that is almost black. As the hot water mixes with the cool ocean water, minerals crystallize on the ocean floor. But no one has found an economical way to mine them yet.

74 Chapter 3 • Minerals of the Earth's Crust

INTERNET ACTIVITY

For another activity related to this chapter, go to go.hrw.com and type in the keyword **HZ5MINW**.

Hot-Water Solutions Groundwater works its way downward and is heated by magma. It then reacts with minerals to form a hot liquid solution. Dissolved metals and other elements crystallize out of the hot fluid to form new minerals. Gold, copper, sulfur, pyrite, and galena form in such hot-water environments.

Pegmatites As magma moves upward, it can form teardrop-shaped bodies called *pegmatites*. The mineral crystals in pegmatites become extremely large, sometimes growing to several meters across! Many gemstones, such as topaz and tourmaline, form in pegmatites.

Plutons As magma rises upward through the crust, it sometimes stops moving before it reaches the surface and cools slowly, forming millions of mineral crystals. Eventually, the entire magma body solidifies to form a *pluton*. Mica, feldspar, magnetite, and quartz are some of the minerals that form from magma.

INCLUSION Strategies

- Learning Disabled
- Attention Deficit Disorder
- Behavior Control Issues

Organize students into small teams to play a mineral quiz game. Each team should choose a category that relates to a heading in the section and write five questions and answers for the category on separate index cards. The difficulty and point value of the questions should increase incrementally. Review each team's questions and answers before you start the game. If a team cannot answer a question, the team should work with another team to answer the question. If teams cooperate, they should share the points earned. When the game is over, hand out a review sheet that contains the questions and answers. **LS Interpersonal** **English Language Learners**

Teach

CONNECTION ACTIVITY
History —————— GENERAL

The History of Mining Communities

Encourage students to learn more about the social and environmental effects of mining by having each student create a scrapbook detailing the history of a mining community. Students should research the history of a community from the discovery of ore to the present. Students' scrapbooks should include drawings and photographs showing changes in the community as well as text describing the history of the area. Have students focus on the types of ore extracted, the use and value of the ore in the world market, and the impact mining has had on the people and environment of the area. Possible communities include the following: Bodie, California; Calico, California; Johannesburg, California; Randsburg, California; Bullfrog, Nevada; Goldfield, Nevada; Manhattan, Nevada; Rhyolite, Nevada; Tonopah, Nevada; Silver City, Utah; Bisbee, Arizona; Gleeson, Arizona; Silverbell, Arizona; Tombstone, Arizona; Kelly, New Mexico; Terlingua, Texas; Leadville, Colorado; Butte, Montana; and the Yanomami Indian tribes of Brazil and Venezuela. Have students share their scrapbooks with the class. **LS Visual/Intrapersonal**

Section 3 • The Formation, Mining, and Use of Minerals 75

Teach, continued

Answer to Math Practice
30 metric tons × 50,000 metric tons = 1,500,000 metric tons of earth

Debate — GENERAL

Surface Versus Subsurface Mining Tell the class that both surface and subsurface mining have positive and negative aspects. Divide the class into two groups. Assign each group a type of mining, and ask the students in the groups to list the advantages of their type of mining. Also have the groups list the disadvantages of the other group's type of mining. Then, have the groups debate their points. (Some advantages of surface mining include that miners are safer when working above ground and have easier access to ore. On the other hand, surface mining alters the landscape and has a greater potential for contaminating the environment. Subsurface mining does not necessarily affect the landscape, and with this type of mining, it is easier to contain potentially harmful wastes. However, subsurface mining has a greater potential for miners to be trapped underground and has the possibility of underground fires and explosions.) Ask each student to write a brief summary of his or her team's viewpoint. Students should include reasons they personally agree or disagree with the opinion. **LS Verbal/Interpersonal**
Co-op Learning

MATH PRACTICE

Surface Coal Mining
Producing 1 metric ton of coal requires that up to 30 metric tons of earth be removed first. Some surface coal mines produce up to 50,000 metric tons of coal per day. How many metric tons of earth might have to be removed in order to mine 50,000 metric tons of coal?

ore a natural material whose concentration of economically valuable minerals is high enough for the material to be mined profitably

---

Mining

Many kinds of rocks and minerals must be mined to extract the valuable elements they contain. Geologists use the term **ore** to describe a mineral deposit large enough and pure enough to be mined for profit. Rocks and minerals are removed from the ground by one of two methods—surface mining or subsurface mining. The method miners choose depends on how close to the surface or how far down in the Earth the mineral is located.

Surface Mining

When mineral deposits are located at or near the surface of the Earth, surface-mining methods are used to remove the minerals. Types of surface mines include open pits, surface coal mines, and quarries.

Open-pit mining is used to remove large, near-surface deposits of economically important minerals such as gold and copper. As shown in **Figure 1,** ore is mined downward, layer by layer, in an open-pit mine. Explosives are often used to break up the ore. The ore is then loaded into haul trucks and transported from the mine for processing. Quarries are open pits that are used to mine building stone, crushed rock, sand, and gravel. Coal that is near the surface is removed by surface coal mining. Surface coal mining is sometimes known as strip mining because the coal is removed in strips that may be as wide as 50 m and as long as 1 km.

Figure 1 In open-pit mines, the ore is mined downward in layers. The stair-step excavation of the walls keeps the sides of the mine from collapsing. Giant haul trucks (inset) are used to transport ore from the mine.

Cultural Awareness — GENERAL

The Empire of Great Zimbabwe The mining of gold, copper, and iron in southeastern Africa helped build the empire of Great Zimbabwe, which arose during the mid-thirteenth century and lasted until about the middle of the fifteenth century. Invite students to find out more about mining techniques in Great Zimbabwe and about the Karanga people who ruled the empire. **LS Logical**

BRAIN FOOD

Mining on Other Planets Some scientists speculate that there are valuable deposits of minerals on other bodies in our solar system. Ask students to think about what issues should be considered before staking claims and mining other planets.

---

76 Chapter 3 • Minerals of the Earth's Crust

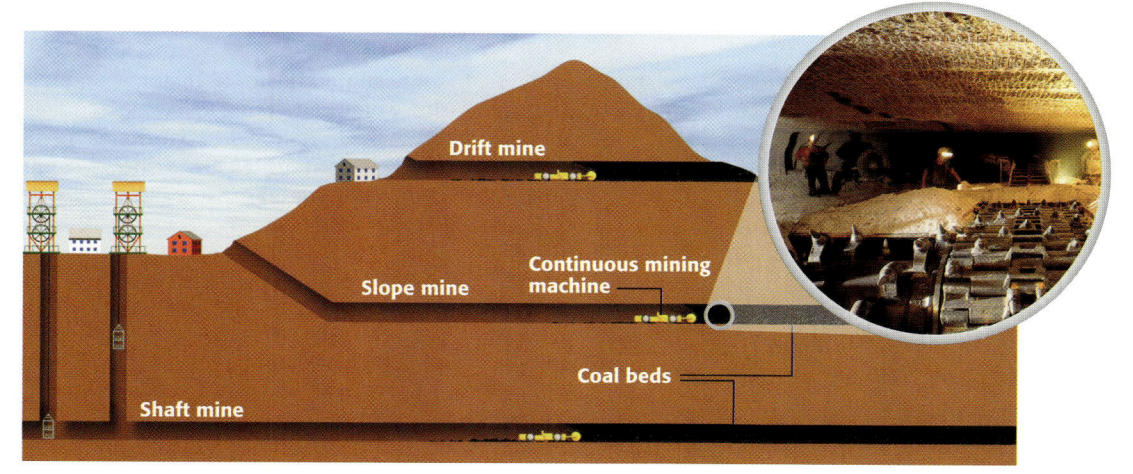

Subsurface Mining

Subsurface mining methods are used when mineral deposits are located too deep within the Earth to be surface mined. Subsurface mining often requires that passageways be dug into the Earth to reach the ore. As shown in **Figure 2,** these passageways may be dug horizontally or at an angle. If a mineral deposit extends deep within the Earth, however, a vertical shaft is sunk. This shaft may connect a number of passageways that intersect the ore at different levels.

Reading Check Compare surface and subsurface mining.
(See the Appendix for answers to Reading Checks.)

Responsible Mining

Mining gives us the minerals we need, but it may also create problems. Mining can destroy or disturb the habitats of plants and animals. Also, the waste products from a mine may get into water sources, which pollutes surface water and groundwater.

Mine Reclamation

One way to reduce the potential harmful effects of mining is to return the land to its original state after the mining is completed. The process by which land used for mining is returned to its original state or better is called **reclamation.** Reclamation of mined public and private land has been required by law since the mid-1970s. Another way to reduce the effects of mining is to reduce our need for minerals. We reduce our need for minerals by recycling many of the mineral products that we currently use, such as aluminum.

Figure 2 *Subsurface mining is the removal of minerals or other materials from deep within the Earth. Passageways must be dug underground to reach the ore. Machines such as continuous mining machines (inset) are used to mine ore in subsurface mines.*

reclamation the process of returning land to its original condition after mining is completed

School to Home

Recycling Minerals at Home

With your parent, locate products in your home that are made of minerals. Decide which of these products could be recycled. In your **science journal,** make a list of the products that could be recycled to save minerals.

Discussion — GENERAL

Mine Reclamation Download photographs of reclaimed mine land from the Internet. Discuss the photos. Ask students, "Can mined land be returned to its original condition? Can mined land be returned to a condition that is better than the original one?" Ask students to think of some techniques that might be used to reclaim mined land.
LS Verbal/Visual

CONNECTION to Real Life — GENERAL

Mineral Collecting Mineral collecting is a popular pastime for many people around the world. The practitioners are commonly referred to as "rockhounds." The tools of the mineral-collecting trade include pickaxes, sledgehammers, pry bars, chisels, hand lenses, and paint brushes. Mineral collectors are often members of local mineralogical societies. Contact a mineralogical society that is located near you, and find out if one of its members can speak to your class about different aspects of mineralogy.

Answer to Reading Check

Surface mining is used to remove mineral deposits that are at or near the Earth's surface. Subsurface mining is used to remove mineral deposits that are too deep to be removed by surface mining.

MISCONCEPTION ALERT

What Is a Carat? The mass of a gem is measured using a unit called the *carat*. This should not be confused with the karat used to measure the purity of gold. A 1-carat diamond crystal has a mass of 200 mg. This is approximately the same as the mass of one children's aspirin. A 1-karat gold nugget is 1/24 pure gold.

Section 3 • The Formation, Mining, and Use of Minerals

Close

Reteaching — BASIC

Concept Mapping Have students make a concept map in their **science journal** of one mining process discussed in this section. Make sure students include each step in the mining process. The first step should be the search for mineral or ore deposits. The final step should include information about the products that are manufactured from the mineral and information about the cleanup of the mine wastes. **LS Visual**

Quiz — GENERAL

1. List three minerals that form in metamorphic rock. (sample answers: garnet, mica, and talc)

2. What is ore? (mineral deposits large enough and pure enough to be mined for profit)

3. How can mining cause water pollution? (The waste products from a mine can introduce toxic concentrations of elements into rivers, lakes, and groundwater.)

Alternative Assessment — GENERAL

Designing a Spacecraft Tell students to design a spacecraft that will carry astronauts to another planet in our solar system. Have students create a diagram of their spacecraft that includes labels that indicate the minerals used to make the spacecraft.
LS Logical

Table 1	Common Uses of Minerals
Mineral	**Uses**
Copper	electrical wire, plumbing, coins
Diamond	jewelry, cutting tools, drill bits
Galena	batteries, ammunition
Gibbsite	cans, foil, appliances, utensils
Gold	jewelry, computers, spacecraft, dentistry
Gypsum	wallboards, plaster, cement
Halite	nutrition, highway de-icer, water softener
Quartz	glass, computer chips
Silver	photography, electronics products, jewelry
Sphalerite	jet aircraft, spacecraft, paints

The Use of Minerals

As shown in **Table 1**, some minerals are of major economic and industrial importance. Some minerals can be used just as they are. Other minerals must be processed to get the element or elements that the minerals contain. **Figure 3** shows some processed minerals used to make the parts of a bicycle.

Metallic Minerals

Some minerals are metallic. Metallic minerals have shiny surfaces, do not let light pass through them, and are good conductors of heat and electricity. Metallic minerals can be processed into metals that are strong and do not rust. Other metals can be pounded or pressed into various shapes or stretched thinly without breaking. These properties make metals desirable for use in aircraft, automobiles, computers, communications and electronic equipment, and spacecraft. Examples of metallic minerals that have many industrial uses are gold, silver, and copper.

Nonmetallic Minerals

Other minerals are nonmetals. Nonmetallic minerals have shiny or dull surfaces, may let light pass through them, and are good insulators of electricity. Nonmetallic minerals are some of the most widely used minerals in industry. For example, calcite is a major component of concrete, which is used in building roads, buildings, bridges, and other structures. Industrial sand and gravel, or silica, have uses that range from glassmaking to producing computer chips.

Figure 3 Some Materials Used in the Parts of a Bicycle

Handlebars titanium from ilmenite

Frame aluminum from bauxite

Spokes iron from magnetite

Pedals beryllium from beryl

CONNECTION ACTIVITY
Life Science — GENERAL

The SEAM Project The Surface Environment and Mining (SEAM) program was established by the U.S. Forest Service in 1973 to address the issue of land reclamation in the wake of mining operations. Since then, this highly successful program has returned vast areas of land formerly used for mining to its original condition. The most recent SEAM projects can be researched on the Internet. To research local reclamation efforts, students could contact mining companies and local conservation groups listed in the phone directory. **LS Logical**

Chapter 3 • Minerals of the Earth's Crust

Gemstones

Some nonmetallic minerals, called *gemstones*, are highly valued for their beauty and rarity rather than for their usefulness. Important gemstones include diamond, ruby, sapphire, emerald, aquamarine, topaz, and tourmaline. An example of a diamond is shown in **Figure 4**. Color is the most important characteristic of a gemstone. The more attractive the color is, the more valuable the gem is. Gemstones must also be durable. That is, they must be hard enough to be cut and polished. The mass of a gemstone is expressed in a unit known as a *carat*. One carat is equal to 200 mg.

Reading Check In your own words, define the term *gemstone*.

Figure 4 The Cullinan diamond, at the center of this scepter, is part of the largest diamond ever found.

SECTION Review

Summary

- Environments in which minerals form may be located at or near the Earth's surface or deep below the surface.
- The two types of mining are surface mining and subsurface mining.
- Two ways to reduce the effects of mining are the reclamation of mined land and the recycling of mineral products.
- Some metallic and nonmetallic minerals have many important economic and industrial uses.

Using Key Terms

Complete each of the following sentences by choosing the correct term from the word bank.

ore   reclamation

1. ____ is the process of returning land to its original condition after mining is completed.

2. ____ is the term used to describe a mineral deposit that is large enough and pure enough to be mined for profit.

Understanding Key Ideas

3. Which of the following conditions is NOT important in the formation of minerals?
   a. presence of groundwater
   b. evaporation
   c. volcanic activity
   d. wind

4. What are the two main types of mining, and how do they differ?

5. List some uses of metallic minerals.

6. List some uses of nonmetallic minerals.

Math Skills

7. A diamond cutter has a raw diamond that weighs 19.5 carats and from which two 5-carat diamonds will be cut. How much did the raw diamond weigh in milligrams? How much will each of the two cut diamonds weigh in milligrams?

Critical Thinking

8. **Analyzing Ideas** How does reclamation protect the environment around a mine?

9. **Applying Concepts** Suppose you find a mineral crystal that is as tall as you are. What kinds of environmental factors would cause such a crystal to form?

For a variety of links related to this chapter, go to www.scilinks.org
Topic: Mining Minerals
SciLinks code: HSM0968

Answers to Section Review

1. Reclamation
2. Ore
3. d
4. The two main types of mining are surface mining and subsurface mining. Surface mining methods are used when mineral deposits are located at or near the Earth's surface. Subsurface methods are used when mineral deposits are located too deep within the Earth to be surface mined. Surface mining usually requires some form of open-pit mining. Subsurface mines feature shafts and passageways that are excavated to reach the ore.
5. Sample answer: Metallic minerals are used in aircraft, automobiles, computers, communications and electronic equipment, and spacecraft.
6. Sample answer: Nonmetallic minerals are used to make concrete, glass, and computer chips.
7. The raw diamond weighed 3,900 mg (19.5 carats × 200 mg = 3,900 mg). Each cut diamond will weigh 1,000 mg (5 carats × 200 mg = 1,000 mg).
8. Sample answer: Reclamation reduces the harmful effects of mining by returning the land to its original state.
9. Sample answer: The crystal could have formed in a slow-cooling magma body surrounded by rock.

Answer to Reading Check

Sample answer: Gemstones are nonmetallic minerals that are valued for their beauty and rarity rather than for their usefulness.

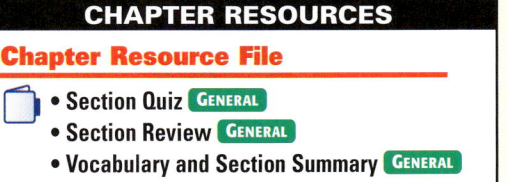

CHAPTER RESOURCES

Chapter Resource File
- Section Quiz GENERAL
- Section Review GENERAL
- Vocabulary and Section Summary GENERAL

Section 3 • The Formation, Mining, and Use of Minerals

Skills Practice Lab

Is It Fool's Gold? A Dense Situation

Teacher's Notes

Time Required
One 45-minute class period

Lab Ratings

EASY — HARD

Teacher Prep 🧪🧪
Student Set-Up 🧪🧪🧪
Concept Level 🧪🧪
Clean Up 🧪🧪

MATERIALS

Materials listed on the student page are sufficient for a group of 2 to 4 students. If your mineral samples are small, the change in volume may be difficult to detect. In that case, replace the beaker in steps 7–10 with a graduated cylinder.

Safety Caution
Remind students to review all safety cautions and icons before beginning this lab activity.

Preparation Notes
Students may need to review the concepts of density and specific gravity prior to performing this activity.

Norman Holcomb
Marion Local Schools
Maria Stein, Ohio

Skills Practice Lab
Using Scientific Methods

Is It Fool's Gold? A Dense Situation

Have you heard of fool's gold? Maybe you've seen a piece of it. This mineral is actually pyrite, and it was often passed off as real gold. However, there are simple tests that you can do to keep from being tricked. Minerals can be identified by their properties. Some properties, such as color, vary from sample to sample. Other properties, such as density and specific gravity, remain consistent across samples. In this activity, you will try to verify the identity of some mineral samples.

OBJECTIVES

Calculate the density and specific gravity of a mineral.

Explain how density and specific gravity can be used to identify a mineral specimen.

MATERIALS
- balance
- beaker, 400 mL
- galena sample
- pyrite sample
- ring stand
- spring scale
- string
- water, 400 mL

SAFETY

Ask a Question

1. How can I determine if an unknown mineral is not gold or silver?

Form a Hypothesis

2. Write a hypothesis that is a possible answer to the question above. Explain your reasoning.

Test the Hypothesis

3. Copy the data table. Use it to record your observations.

Observation Chart		
Measurement	Galena	Pyrite
Mass in air (g)		
Weight in air (N)		
Volume of mineral (mL)	DO NOT WRITE IN BOOK	
Weight in water (N)		

4. Find the mass of each sample by laying the mineral on the balance. Record the mass of each sample in your data table.

5. Attach the spring scale to the ring stand.

6. Tie a string around the sample of galena, and leave a loop at the loose end. Suspend the galena from the spring scale, and find its mass and weight in air. Do not remove the sample from the spring scale yet. Enter these data in your data table.

CHAPTER RESOURCES

Chapter Resource File
- Datasheet for Chapter Lab
- Lab Notes and Answers

Technology

Classroom Videos
- Lab Video

LabBook
- Mysterious Minerals

80 Chapter 3 • Minerals of the Earth's Crust

7 Fill a beaker halfway with water. Record the beginning volume of water in your data table.

8 Carefully lift the beaker around the galena until the mineral is completely submerged. Be careful not to splash any water out of the beaker! Do not allow the mineral to touch the beaker.

9 Record the new volume and weight in your data table.

10 Subtract the original volume of water from the new volume to find the amount of water displaced by the mineral. This is the volume of the mineral sample itself. Record this value in your data table.

11 Repeat steps 6–10 for the sample of pyrite.

Analyze the Results

1 **Constructing Tables** Copy the data table below. (Note: 1 mL = 1 cm³)

Density Data Table

Mineral	Density (g/cm³)	Specific gravity
Silver	10.5	10.5
Galena	DO NOT WRITE IN BOOK	
Pyrite		
Gold	19.0	19.0

2 **Organizing Data** Use the following equations to calculate the density and specific gravity of each mineral, and record your answers in your data table.

$$\text{density} = \frac{\text{mass in air}}{\text{volume}}$$

$$\text{specific gravity} = \frac{\text{weight in air}}{\text{weight in air} - \text{weight in water}}$$

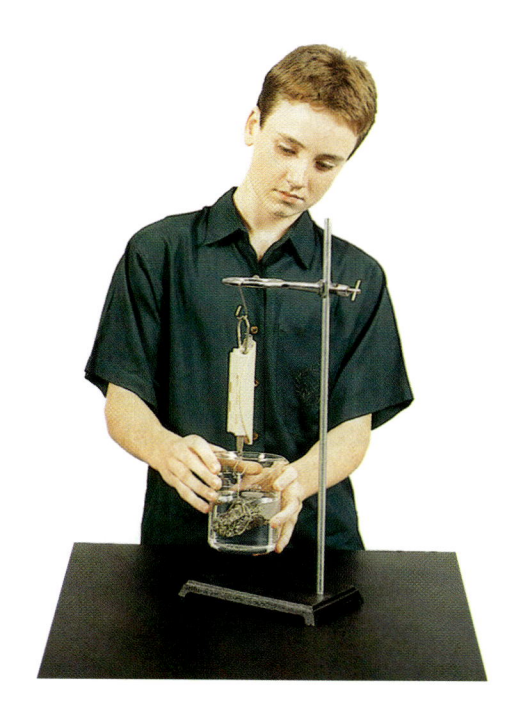

Draw Conclusions

3 **Drawing Conclusions** The density of pure gold is 19 g/cm³. How can you use this information to prove that your sample of pyrite is not gold?

4 **Drawing Conclusions** The density of pure silver is 10.5 g/cm³. How can you use this information to prove that your sample of galena is not silver?

5 **Applying Conclusions** If you found a gold-colored nugget, how could you find out if the nugget was real gold or fool's gold?

CHAPTER RESOURCES

Workbooks

📖 Long-Term Projects & Research Ideas
  • What's Yours Is Mined **ADVANCED**

Analyze the Results

2.

Mineral	Density (g/cm³)	Specific gravity
Silver	10.5	10.5
Galena	7.4 to 7.6	7.4 to 7.6
Pyrite	5.0	5.0
Gold	19.0	19.0

Lab Notes

- Density is conventionally described as g/cm³, not g/mL.
- Because specific gravity is the ratio of a substance's density to the density of water (1 g/cm³), the value will be the same for density. The difference is that specific gravity is a number, and density is a number with the units grams per cubic centimeter (g/cm³).
- Because of impurities, the density of some minerals is given in ranges. The density of pure gold is 19.0 g/cm³; lower numbers indicate the presence of impurities. The density of pure silver is 10.5 g/cm³; depending on impurities, that number can be higher or lower.
- Ideally, the values for specific gravity and density obtained in this lab will be identical. Discrepancies will likely result from differences in precision. Students should learn that all scientific measurements involve some margin of error.

Draw Conclusions

3. Because the density of the sample is not 19.0 g/cm³, the sample is not gold.

4. Because the density of the sample is not 10.5 g/cm³, the sample is not pure silver. (The sample could contain silver mixed with other minerals.)

5. Sample answer: You could find the density and specific gravity of the nugget. If it was pure gold, the density would be 19.0 g/cm³ and the specific gravity would be 19.0, but you would have to perform more tests. If the sample had a density of 5.0 g/cm³ and a specific gravity of 5.0, then it would likely be pyrite (fool's gold).

Chapter Review

Assignment Guide

Section	Questions
1	1, 4, 6, 8, 12, 19
2	2, 5, 7, 16, 18–20, 22–25
3	9–11, 13–15, 21
1 and 3	3

ANSWERS

Using Key Terms

1. Sample answer: An element is a pure substance that cannot be broken into simpler substances by normal chemical means. A compound is a substance made of two or more bonded elements. A mineral is an inorganic solid that formed naturally and has a crystalline structure.
2. Sample answer: Streak is the color of a mineral in powdered form. The color of a mineral may change due to air or water, but the mineral's streak is always the same.
3. Sample answer: A mineral is a naturally formed, inorganic solid with a crystalline structure. An ore is a deposit of minerals that is large enough and pure enough to be mined for a profit.
4. Sample answer: Silicate minerals contain compounds of silicon and oxygen; nonsilicate minerals do not contain compounds of silicon and oxygen.

Chapter Review

USING KEY TERMS

1. Use each of the following terms in a separate sentence: *element*, *compound*, and *mineral*.

For each pair of terms, explain how the meanings of the terms differ.

2. *color* and *streak*
3. *mineral* and *ore*
4. *silicate mineral* and *nonsilicate mineral*

UNDERSTANDING KEY IDEAS

Multiple Choice

5. Which of the following properties of minerals does Mohs scale measure?
   a. luster
   b. hardness
   c. density
   d. streak

6. Pure substances that cannot be broken down into simpler substances by ordinary chemical means are called
   a. molecules.
   b. elements.
   c. compounds.
   d. crystals.

7. Which of the following properties is considered a special property that applies to only a few minerals?
   a. luster
   b. hardness
   c. taste
   d. density

8. Silicate minerals contain a combination of the elements
   a. sulfur and oxygen.
   b. carbon and oxygen.
   c. iron and oxygen.
   d. silicon and oxygen.

9. The process by which land used for mining is returned to its original state is called
   a. recycling.
   b. regeneration.
   c. reclamation.
   d. renovation.

10. Which of the following minerals is an example of a gemstone?
    a. mica
    b. diamond
    c. gypsum
    d. copper

Short Answer

11. Compare surface and subsurface mining.
12. Explain the four characteristics of a mineral.
13. Describe two environments in which minerals form.
14. List two uses for metallic minerals and two uses for nonmetallic minerals.
15. Describe two ways to reduce the effects of mining.
16. Describe three special properties of minerals.

Understanding Key Ideas

5. b
6. b
7. c
8. d
9. c
10. b
11. Surface mining is used to mine mineral deposits that are at or near the Earth's surface. Subsurface mining is used to mine mineral deposits that are too deep in the Earth to be surface mined.
12. A mineral is inorganic, meaning its origin is not living things. A mineral is a solid, not a liquid or gas. A mineral is formed in nature and is not made by people. A mineral has a crystalline structure and has the same chemical structure throughout.
13. Sample answer: Two environments in which minerals form are plutons, in which a magma body solidifies before it reaches the Earth's surface, and hot-water solutions, from which dissolved metals and other elements crystallize out of a hot fluid to form minerals.

82 Chapter 3 • Minerals of the Earth's Crust

CRITICAL THINKING

17. Concept Mapping Use the following terms to create a concept map: *minerals, calcite, silicate minerals, gypsum, carbonates, nonsilicate minerals, quartz,* and *sulfates.*

18. Making Inferences Imagine that you are trying to determine the identity of a mineral. You decide to do a streak test. You rub the mineral across the streak plate, but the mineral does not leave a streak. Has your test failed? Explain your answer.

19. Applying Concepts Why would cleavage be important to gem cutters, who cut and shape gemstones?

20. Applying Concepts Imagine that you work at a jeweler's shop and someone brings in some gold nuggets for sale. You are not sure if the nuggets are real gold. Which identification tests would help you decide whether the nuggets are gold?

21. Identifying Relationships Suppose you are in a desert. You are walking across the floor of a dry lake, and you see crusts of cubic halite crystals. How do you suppose the halite crystals formed? Explain your answer.

INTERPRETING GRAPHICS

The table below shows the temperatures at which various minerals melt. Use the table below to answer the questions that follow.

Melting Points of Various Minerals	
Mineral	Melting Point (°C)
Mercury	−39
Sulfur	+113
Halite	801
Silver	961
Gold	1,062
Copper	1,083
Pyrite	1,171
Fluorite	1,360
Quartz	1,710
Zircon	2,500

22. According to the table, what is the approximate difference in temperature between the melting points of the mineral that has the lowest melting point and the mineral that has the highest melting point?

23. Which of the minerals listed in the table do you think is a liquid at room temperature?

24. Pyrite is often called *fool's gold*. Using the information in the table, how could you determine if a mineral sample is pyrite or gold?

25. Convert the melting points of the minerals shown in the table from degrees Celsius to degrees Fahrenheit. Use the formula °F = (9/5 × °C) + 32.

---

14. Sample answer: Metallic minerals such as gold are used in the manufacture of computers and spacecraft. Nonmetallic minerals such as quartz are used to manufacture computer chips and glass.

15. Two ways to reduce the effects of mining are the reclamation of mined land and the recycling of mineral products.

16. Sample answer: chemical reaction: some minerals, such as calcite, bubble when a drop of weak acid is placed on them; fluorescence: some minerals glow under ultraviolet light; radioactivity: minerals that contain radium or uranium can be detected by a Geiger counter

Critical Thinking

17. 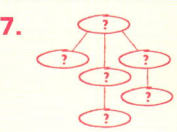 An answer to this exercise can be found at the end of this book.

18. No, the test was successful. I learned that the unknown mineral has no streak and that the mineral is harder than the streak plate. This clue will help me identify the mineral.

19. Sample answer: Gem cutters can cut along cleavage surfaces to shape gemstones. Gem cutters also want to avoid cutting across cleavage surfaces.

20. Students should suggest performing several tests to see whether the mineral is gold. Gold is very dense and soft, so one would start with density and hardness tests.

21. Sample answer: Because halite is salt (sodium chloride), the crusts of halite crystals formed when a body of salt water evaporated and left the halite behind.

Interpreting Graphics

22. The difference between the highest and lowest melting points is 2,539°C, the difference between the melting points of mercury and zircon. (2,500°C − −39°C = 2,539°C)

23. Mercury would be a liquid at room temperature because its melting point is −39°C.

24. Pyrite has a higher melting point than gold does (1,171°C > 1,062°C).

25. mercury: −38°F; sulfur: 235°F; halite: 1,474°F; silver: 1,762°F; gold: 1,944°F; copper: 1,981°F; pyrite: 2,140°F; fluorite: 2,480°F; quartz: 3,110°F; zircon: 4,532°F (Answers are rounded.)

CHAPTER RESOURCES

Chapter Resource File
- Chapter Review GENERAL
- Chapter Test A GENERAL
- Chapter Test B ADVANCED
- Chapter Test C SPECIAL NEEDS
- Vocabulary Activity GENERAL

Workbooks
- Study Guide
  - Assessment resources are also available in Spanish.

Standardized Test Preparation

Teacher's Note

To provide practice under more realistic testing conditions, give students 20 minutes to answer all of the questions in this Standardized Test Preparation.

MISCONCEPTION ALERT

Answers to the standardized test preparation can help you identify student misconceptions and misunderstandings.

READING

Passage 1
1. D
2. H
3. A

TEST DOCTOR

Question 2: Answer H is correct. Because the ancient copper miners traded copper and these artifacts appear to be widespread across North America, answers F and I are incorrect. Rock was heated, not cooled, to make the copper easier to extract. Therefore, answer G is incorrect.

Passage 2
1. B
2. H
3. A

Standardized Test Preparation

READING

Read each of the passages below. Then, answer the questions that follow each passage.

Passage 1 In North America, copper was mined at least 6,700 years ago by the ancestors of the Native Americans who live on Michigan's upper peninsula. Much of this mining took place on Isle Royale, an island in Lake Superior. These ancient people removed copper from the rock by using stone hammers and wedges. The rock was sometimes heated first to make breaking it up easier. Copper that was mined was used to make jewelry, tools, weapons, fish hooks, and other objects. These objects were often marked with designs. The Lake Superior copper was traded over long distances along ancient trade routes. Copper objects have been found in Ohio, Florida, the Southwest, and the Northwest.

1. In the passage, what does *ancient* mean?
   A young
   B future
   C modern
   D early

2. According to the passage, what did the ancient copper miners do?
   F They mined copper in Ohio, Florida, the Southwest, and the Northwest.
   G They mined copper by cooling the rock in which the copper was found.
   H They mined copper by using stone tools.
   I They mined copper for their use only.

3. Which of the following statements is a fact according to the passage?
   A Copper could be shaped into different objects.
   B Copper was unknown outside of Michigan's upper peninsula.
   C Copper could be mined easily from the rock in which it was found.
   D Copper could not be marked with designs.

Passage 2 Most mineral names end in *-ite*. The practice of so naming minerals dates back to the ancient Romans and Greeks, who added *-ites* and *-itis* to common words to indicate a color, a use, or the chemistry of a mineral. More recently, mineral names have been used to honor people, such as scientists, mineral collectors, and even rulers of countries. Other minerals have been named after the place where they were discovered. These place names include mines, quarries, hills, mountains, towns, regions, and even countries. Finally, some minerals have been named after gods in Greek, Roman, and Scandinavian mythology.

1. In the passage, what does *practice* mean?
   A skill
   B custom
   C profession
   D use

2. According to the passage, the ancient Greeks and Romans did not name minerals after what?
   F colors
   G chemical properties
   H people
   I uses

3. Which of the following statements is a fact according to the passage?
   A Minerals are sometimes named for the country in which they are discovered.
   B Minerals are never named after their collectors.
   C All mineral names end in *-ite*.
   D All of the known minerals were named by the Greeks and Romans.

TEST DOCTOR

Question 3: Answer A is correct. Answer B is incorrect, because modern practice includes naming minerals after people. Because most, but not all, mineral names end in *-ite*, answer C is incorrect. Answer D is incorrect, because it is clear that the practice of naming minerals has continued since the time of the ancient Greeks and Romans.

Chapter 3 • Minerals of the Earth's Crust

INTERPRETING GRAPHICS

A sample of feldspar was analyzed to find out what it was made of. The graph below shows the results of the analysis. Use the graph below to answer the questions that follow.

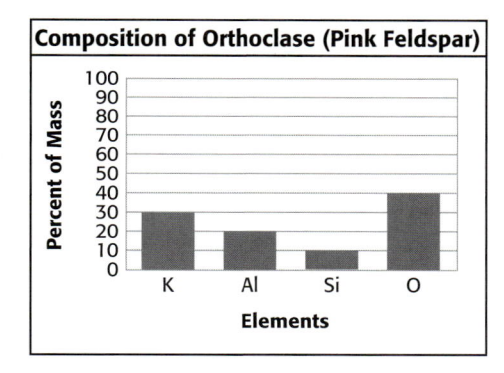

Composition of Orthoclase (Pink Feldspar)

[Bar graph showing Percent of Mass on y-axis (0-100) and Elements on x-axis: K (~30), Al (~20), Si (~10), O (~40)]

1. The sample consists of four elements: potassium, K, aluminum, Al, silicon, Si, and oxygen, O. Which element makes up the largest percentage of your sample?
   A potassium
   B aluminum
   C silicon
   D oxygen

2. Silicate minerals, such as feldspar, contain a combination of silicon and oxygen. What percentage of your sample is composed of silicon and oxygen combined?
   F 30%
   G 40%
   H 50%
   I 70%

3. If your sample has a mass of 10 g, how many grams of oxygen does it contain?
   A 1 g
   B 2 g
   C 4 g
   D 8 g

4. Your sample of orthoclase has a hardness of 6. Which of the following minerals will scratch your sample?
   F gypsum
   G corundum
   H calcite
   I apatite

MATH

Read each question below, and choose the best answer.

1. Gold classified as 24-karat is 100% gold. Gold classified as 18-karat is 18 parts gold and 6 parts another, similar metal. The gold is therefore 18/24, or 3/4, pure. What is the percentage of pure gold in 18-karat gold?
   A 10%
   B 25%
   C 50%
   D 75%

2. Gold's specific gravity is 19. Pyrite's specific gravity is 5. What is the difference in the specific gravities of gold and pyrite?
   F 8 g/cm^3
   G 10 g/cm^3
   H 12 g/cm^3
   I 14 g/cm^3

3. In a quartz crystal, there is one silicon atom for every two oxygen atoms. So, the ratio of silicon atoms to oxygen atoms is 1:2. If there were 8 million oxygen atoms in a sample of quartz, how many silicon atoms would there be in the sample?
   A 2 million
   B 4 million
   C 8 million
   D 16 million

INTERPRETING GRAPHICS

1. D
2. H
3. C
4. G

TEST DOCTOR

Question 4: Answer G is correct. Corundum has a hardness of 7, which is greater than 6. Gypsum, calcite, and apatite all have hardnesses less than 6, so answers F, H, and I are incorrect.

MATH

1. D
2. I
3. B

TEST DOCTOR

Question 3: Answer B is correct. In the mineral quartz, the ratio of silicon atoms to oxygen atoms is 1:2. Therefore, there are twice as many oxygen atoms as silicon atoms in a sample of quartz. Inversely, there are half as many silicon atoms as oxygen atoms in a sample of quartz. If there are 8 million oxygen atoms in a sample of quartz, then there are half as many, or 4 million, silicon atoms in the sample. Students who misread the question and reverse the ratio of silicon atoms to oxygen atoms might incorrectly answer D.

CHAPTER RESOURCES

Chapter Resource File
- Standardized Test Preparation GENERAL

State Resources

For specific resources for your state, visit **go.hrw.com** and type in the keyword **HSMSTR**.

Chapter 3 • Standardized Test Preparation

Science in Action

Science Fiction

Background

Few people have had as long-lasting an impact on science fiction as Jack Williamson. This story, "The Metal Man," was first published in 1928—over 70 years ago! Although it was his very first short story, it is still a classic. Since then, Williamson has written dozens of science fiction novels, short-stories, other novels, and books about writing. The term *science fiction* did not exist when Williamson began writing. Known as one of the great pioneers of science fiction, Williamson was the first to write about antimatter. And, he coined the terms *terraform* (in 1941) and *genetic engineering* (in 1951). Williamson is also credited for making science fiction a field worthy of literary attention. For this accomplishment, Williamson has received several awards. In 1976, he became the second person to win the Grand Nebula Award. In 1994, he earned a lifetime achievement award from World Fantasy.

Science in Action

Science Fiction

"The Metal Man" by Jack Williamson

In a dark, dusty corner of Tyburn College Museum stands a life-sized statue of a man. Except for its strange greenish color, the statue looks quite ordinary. But if you look closely, you will see the perfect detail of the hair and skin. On the statue's chest, you will also see a strange mark—a dark crimson shape with six sides. No one knows how the statue ended up in the dark corner. But most people in Tyburn believe that the metal man is, or once was, Professor Thomas Kelvin of Tyburn College's geology department. Read for yourself the strange story of Professor Kelvin and the Metal Man, which is in the *Holt Anthology of Science Fiction*.

Language Arts ACTIVITY

WRITING SKILL Read "The Metal Man" by Jack Williamson. Write a short essay explaining how the ideas in the story are related to what you are learning.

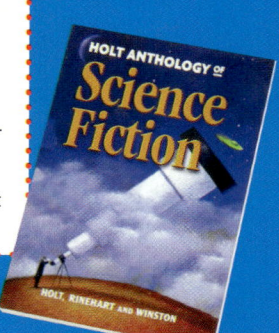

Weird Science

Wieliczka Salt Mine

Imagine an underground city that is made entirely of salt. Within the city are churches, chapels, rooms of many kinds, and salt lakes. Sculptures of biblical scenes, saints, and famous historical figures carved from salt are found throughout the city. Even chandeliers of salt hang from the ceilings. Such a city is located 16 km southeast of Krakow, Poland, inside the Wieliczka (VEE uh LEETS kuh) Salt Mine. As the mine grew over the past 700 years, it turned into an elaborate underground city. Miners constructed chapels to patron saints so they could pray for a safe day in the mine. Miners also developed superstitions about the mine. So, images that were meant to bring good luck were carved in salt. In 1978, the mine was added to UNESCO's list of endangered world heritage sites. Many of the sculptures in the mine have begun to dissolve because of the humidity in the air. Efforts to save the treasures in the mine from further damage were begun in 1996.

Social Studies ACTIVITY

WRITING SKILL Research some aspect of the role of salt in human history. For example, subjects might include the Saharan and Tibetan salt trade or the use of salt as a form of money in ancient Poland. Report your findings in a one-page essay.

Answer to Language Arts Activity
Have students present short essays on "The Metal Man" in front of the class.

Answer to Social Studies Activity
Answers may vary.

86 Chapter 3 • Minerals of Earth's Crust

People in Science

Jamie Hill

The Emerald Man Jamie Hill was raised in the Brushy Mountains of North Carolina. While growing up, Hill gained firsthand knowledge of the fabulous green crystals that could be found in the mountains. These green crystals were emeralds. Emerald is the green variety of the silicate mineral beryl and is a valuable gemstone. Emerald crystals form in pockets, or openings, in rock known as *pegmatite*.

Since 1985, Hill has been searching for pockets containing emeralds in rock near the small town of Hiddenite, North Carolina. He has been amazingly successful. Hill has discovered some spectacular emerald crystals. The largest of these crystals weighs 858 carats and is on display at the North Carolina Museum of Natural Science. Estimates of the total value of the emeralds that Hill has discovered so far are well in the millions of dollars. Hill's discoveries have made him a celebrity, and he has appeared both on national TV and in magazines.

Math Activity

An emerald discovered by Jamie Hill in 1999 was cut into a 7.85-carat stone that sold for $64,000 per carat. What was the total value of the cut stone?

go.hrw.com
To learn more about these Science in Action topics, visit go.hrw.com and type in the keyword **HZ5MINF**.

Current Science
Check out Current Science® articles related to this chapter by visiting go.hrw.com. Just type in the keyword **HZ5CS03**.

Answer to Math Activity
$64,000 \times 7.85 = $502,400

Weird Science
Background
On September 9, 1978, the Wieliczka Salt Mine was entered into UNESCO's 1st World List of Cultural and Natural Heritage. An important reason for the mine's inclusion in the list was the fact that the mine illustrates most of the stages of the development of mining technology over time. This developmental progression began in the Middle Ages, when salt was obtained from brine springs by the process of heating the brine and vaporizing the water. During the 14th and early 15th centuries, technological developments included the sinking of shafts and the use of pulley systems to transport salt to the surface. By the mid-15th century, horse gear was used to transport salt to the surface. In the 18th century, steam lifts began to be used for transporting salt. Similarly, the excavation of the salt progressed from the use of simple hand-tools to hand drills and then to pneumatic drills.

People in Science
Teaching Strategy — BASIC
Have students research minerals that can be found in the area in which they live. This information may be obtained from the United States Geological Survey or from a state entity, such as a state bureau of mines and geology. Have students put together a mineral list and, if possible, locations where specific minerals might be found.

If the option is practical, you may wish to lead the class on a rock hunt around the schoolyard. Have students discuss which minerals they think make up the rocks they found.

Chapter 3 • Science in Action **87**

4 Rocks: Mineral Mixtures
Chapter Planning Guide

Compression guide: To shorten instruction because of time limitations, omit the Chapter Lab.

OBJECTIVES	LABS, DEMONSTRATIONS, AND ACTIVITIES	TECHNOLOGY RESOURCES
PACING • 90 min pp. 88–97 **Chapter Opener**	SE Start-up Activity, p. 89 ◆ GENERAL	OSP Parent Letter ■ GENERAL CD Student Edition on CD-ROM CD Guided Reading Audio CD ■ TR Chapter Starter Transparency* VID Brain Food Video Quiz
Section 1 The Rock Cycle • Describe two ways rocks have been used by humans. • Describe four processes that shape Earth's features. • Describe how each type of rock changes into another type as it moves through the rock cycle. • List two characteristics of rock that are used to help classify it.	TE Group Activity Rates of Weathering, p. 91 GENERAL TE Activity Rock Dictionary, p. 93 BASIC TE Connection Activity Language Arts, p. 93 BASIC TE Group Activity Describing Rocks, p. 95 BASIC LB Labs You Can Eat Famous Rock Groups* ◆ GENERAL LB Calculator-Based Labs A Hot and Cool Lab ◆ ADVANCED	CRF Lesson Plans* TR Bellringer Transparency* TR The Rock Cycle* TR LINK TO LIFE SCIENCE The Water Cycle*
PACING • 45 min pp. 98–101 **Section 2 Igneous Rock** • Describe three ways that igneous rock forms. • Explain how the cooling rate of magma affects the texture of igneous rock. • Distinguish between igneous rock that cools within Earth's crust and igneous rock that cools at Earth's surface.	SE Science in Action Math, Social Studies, and Language Arts Activities, pp. 118–119 GENERAL SE Skills Practice Lab Crystal Growth, p. 722 ◆ GENERAL	CRF Lesson Plans* TR Bellringer Transparency* TR Intrusive Igneous Rock Bodies* SE Internet Activity, p. 100 GENERAL
PACING • 45 min pp. 102–105 **Section 3 Sedimentary Rock** • Describe the origin of sedimentary rock. • Describe the three main categories of sedimentary rock. • Describe three types of sedimentary structures.	TE Demonstration Dissolution of Minerals, p. 102 GENERAL SE Connection to Language Arts Salty Expressions, p. 103 GENERAL TE Activity Sedimentary Rock, p. 103 BASIC TE Connection Activity Real World, p. 104 GENERAL SE Skills Practice Lab Let's Get Sedimental, p. 112 ◆ GENERAL LB Whiz-Bang Demonstrations Settling Down* ◆ BASIC	CRF Lesson Plans* TR Bellringer Transparency* VID Lab Videos for Earth Science
PACING • 45 min pp. 106–111 **Section 4 Metamorphic Rock** • Describe two ways a rock can undergo metamorphism. • Explain how the mineral composition of rock changes as the rocks undergo metamorphism. • Describe the difference between foliated and nonfoliated metamorphic rock. • Explain how metamorphic rock structures are related to deformation.	TE Activity Modeling Metamorphism, p. 106 GENERAL SE Quick Lab Stretching Out, p. 107 GENERAL SE School-to-Home Activity Making a Rock Collection, p. 108 GENERAL TE Connection Activity Real World, p. 109 ADVANCED SE Connection to Biology Metamorphosis, p. 110 GENERAL SE Model-Making Lab Metamorphic Mash, p. 725 ◆ GENERAL LB Long-Term Projects & Research Ideas Home-Grown Crystals* ADVANCED	CRF Lesson Plans* TR Bellringer Transparency* TR Regional and Contact Metamorphism* CD Interactive Explorations CD-ROM "Rock On!"* GENERAL

PACING • 90 min

CHAPTER REVIEW, ASSESSMENT, AND STANDARDIZED TEST PREPARATION

- CRF Vocabulary Activity* GENERAL
- SE Chapter Review, pp. 114–115 GENERAL
- CRF Chapter Review* ■ GENERAL
- CRF Chapter Tests A* ■ GENERAL, B* ADVANCED, C* SPECIAL NEEDS
- SE Standardized Test Preparation, pp. 116–117 GENERAL
- CRF Standardized Test Preparation* GENERAL
- CRF Performance-Based Assessment* GENERAL
- OSP Test Generator GENERAL
- CRF Test Item Listing* GENERAL

Online and Technology Resources

go.hrw.com — Visit go.hrw.com for a variety of free resources related to this textbook. Enter the keyword **HZ5RCK**.

Holt Online Learning — Students can access interactive problem-solving help and active visual concept development with the Holt Science and Technology Online Edition available at www.hrw.com.

Guided Reading Audio CD Also in Spanish — A direct reading of each chapter for auditory learners, reluctant readers, and Spanish-speaking students.

Science Tutor CD-ROM — Excellent for remediation and test practice.

KEY			
SE Student Edition **TE** Teacher Edition	**CRF** Chapter Resource File **OSP** One-Stop Planner **LB** Lab Bank **TR** Transparencies	**SS** Science Skills Worksheets **MS** Math Skills for Science Worksheets **CD** CD or CD-ROM **VID** Classroom Video/DVD	***** Also on One-Stop Planner **◆** Requires advance prep **■** Also available in Spanish

SKILLS DEVELOPMENT RESOURCES	SECTION REVIEW AND ASSESSMENT	STANDARDS CORRELATIONS
SE Pre-Reading Activity, p. 88 GENERAL **OSP** Science Puzzlers, Twisters & Teasers* GENERAL		National Science Education Standards SAI 1, 2
CRF Directed Reading A* ■ BASIC, B* SPECIAL NEEDS **CRF** Vocabulary and Section Summary* ■ GENERAL **SE** Reading Strategy Reading Organizer, p. 90 GENERAL **TE** Inclusion Strategies, p. 92 ◆ **SE** Math Practice What's In It?, p. 95 GENERAL **MS** Math Skills for Science Parts of 100: Calculating Percentages* GENERAL **CRF** SciLinks Activity, The Rock Cycle* GENERAL		**SE** Reading Checks, pp. 90, 94, 95, 96 GENERAL **TE** Homework, p. 93 GENERAL **TE** Reteaching, p. 96 BASIC **TE** Quiz, p. 96 GENERAL **TE** Alternative Assessment, p. 96 GENERAL
CRF Directed Reading A* ■ BASIC, B* SPECIAL NEEDS **CRF** Vocabulary and Section Summary* ■ GENERAL **SE** Reading Strategy Reading Organizer, p. 98 GENERAL	**SE** Reading Checks, pp. 99, 101 GENERAL **TE** Reteaching, p. 100 BASIC **TE** Quiz, p. 100 GENERAL **TE** Alternative Assessment, p. 100 GENERAL **TE** Homework, p. 100 ADVANCED **SE** Section Review,* p. 101 ■ GENERAL **CRF** Section Quiz* ■ GENERAL	UCP 1, 2; SAI 1 2; ES 1c, 1d; *LabBook:* SAI 1, 2
CRF Directed Reading A* ■ BASIC, B* SPECIAL NEEDS **CRF** Vocabulary and Section Summary* ■ GENERAL **SE** Reading Strategy Reading Organizer, p. 102 GENERAL	**SE** Reading Checks, pp. 103, 105 GENERAL **TE** Reteaching, p. 104 BASIC **TE** Quiz, p. 104 GENERAL **TE** Alternative Assessment, p. 104 GENERAL **SE** Section Review,* p. 105 ■ GENERAL **CRF** Section Quiz* ■ GENERAL	UCP 1, 2; SAI 1, 2; ES 1c, 1d, 1k, 2b; *Chapter Lab:* SAI 1, 2
CRF Directed Reading A* ■ BASIC, B* SPECIAL NEEDS **CRF** Vocabulary and Section Summary* ■ GENERAL **SE** Reading Strategy Discussion, p. 106 GENERAL **TE** Inclusion Strategies, p. 109 **MS** Math Skills for Science The Unit Factor and Dimensional Analysis* GENERAL **CRF** Reinforcement Worksheet What Is It?* BASIC **CRF** Critical Thinking Between a Rock and a Hard Place* ADVANCED	**SE** Reading Checks, pp. 107, 108, 111 GENERAL **TE** Homework, p. 108 GENERAL **TE** Reteaching, p. 110 BASIC **TE** Quiz, p. 110 GENERAL **TE** Alternative Assessment, p. 110 GENERAL **TE** Homework, p. 110 ADVANCED **SE** Section Review,* p. 111 ■ GENERAL **CRF** Section Quiz* ■ GENERAL	UCP 1, 2; SAI 1 2; ES 1c; *LabBook:* SAI 1, 2

One-Stop Planner® CD-ROM

This convenient CD-ROM includes:
- Lab Materials QuickList Software
- Holt Calendar Planner
- Customizable Lesson Plans
- Printable Worksheets
- ExamView® Test Generator

CNN Student News

cnnstudentnews.com

Find the latest news, lesson plans, and activities related to important scientific events.

SciLinks NSTA

www.scilinks.org

Maintained by the **National Science Teachers Association.** See Chapter Enrichment pages for a complete list of topics.

Current Science®

Check out *Current Science* articles and activities by visiting the HRW Web site at **go.hrw.com.** Just type in the keyword **HZ5CS04T.**

Classroom Videos

- **Lab Videos** demonstrate the chapter lab.
- **Brain Food Video Quizzes** help students review the chapter material.
- **CNN Videos** bring science into your students' daily life.

Chapter 4 • Chapter Planning Guide

4 Chapter Resources

Visual Resources

CHAPTER STARTER TRANSPARENCY

BELLRINGER TRANSPARENCIES

TEACHING TRANSPARENCIES

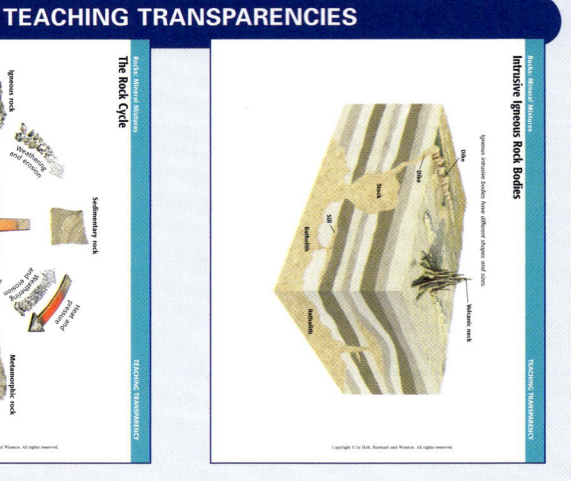

TEACHING TRANSPARENCIES

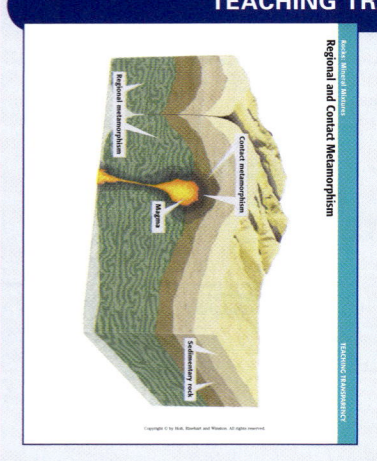

CONCEPT MAPPING TRANSPARENCY

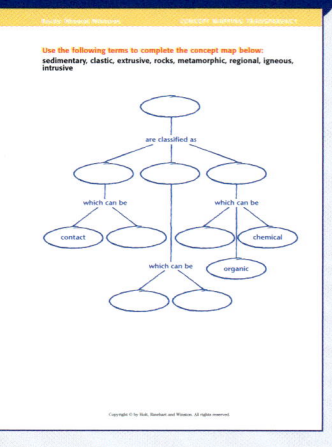

Planning Resources

LESSON PLANS

PARENT LETTER

TEST ITEM LISTING

One-Stop Planner® CD-ROM

This CD-ROM includes all of the resources shown here and the following time-saving tools:

- *Lab Materials QuickList Software*
- *Customizable lesson plans*
- *Holt Calendar Planner*
- *The powerful ExamView® Test Generator*

87C Chapter 4 • Rocks: Mineral Mixtures

For a preview of available worksheets covering math and science skills, see pages T26–T33. All of these resources are also on the One-Stop Planner®.

Meeting Individual Needs

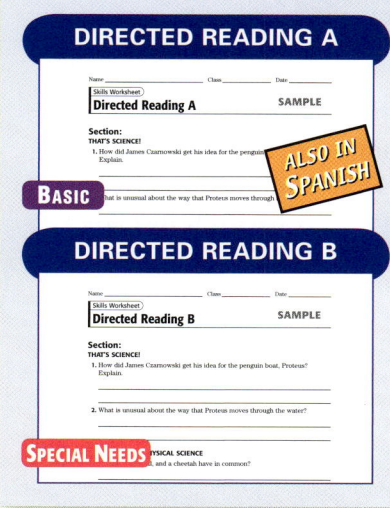

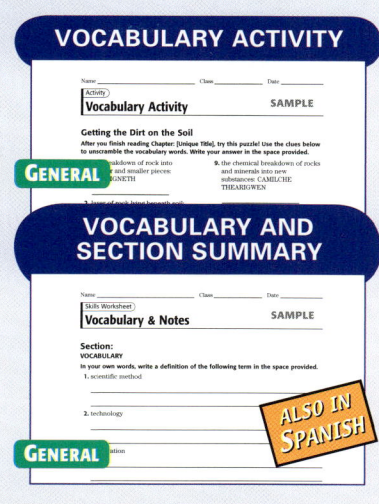

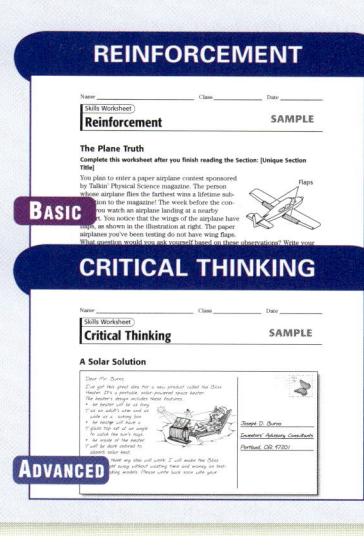

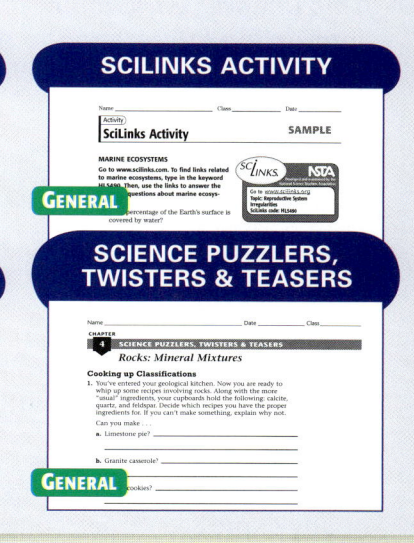

- **DIRECTED READING A** — BASIC (ALSO IN SPANISH)
- **DIRECTED READING B** — SPECIAL NEEDS
- **VOCABULARY ACTIVITY** — GENERAL
- **VOCABULARY AND SECTION SUMMARY** — GENERAL (ALSO IN SPANISH)
- **REINFORCEMENT** — BASIC
- **CRITICAL THINKING** — ADVANCED
- **SCILINKS ACTIVITY** — GENERAL
- **SCIENCE PUZZLERS, TWISTERS & TEASERS** — GENERAL

Labs and Activities

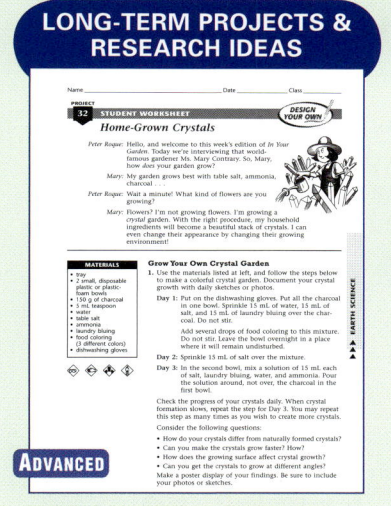

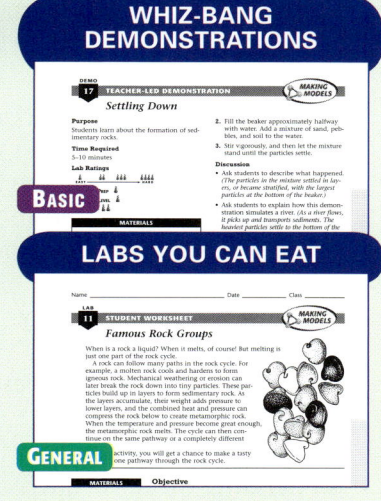

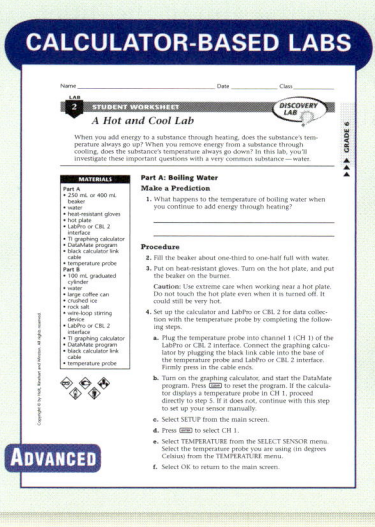

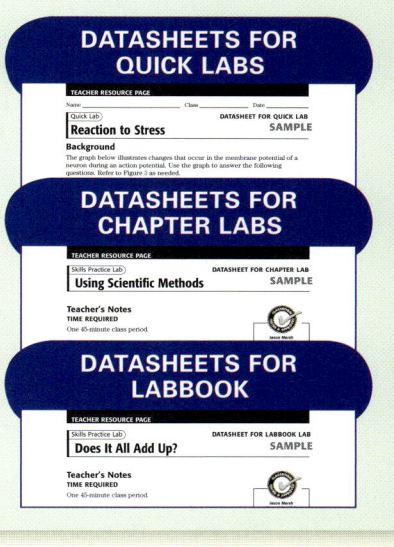

- **LONG-TERM PROJECTS & RESEARCH IDEAS** — ADVANCED
- **WHIZ-BANG DEMONSTRATIONS** — BASIC
- **LABS YOU CAN EAT** — GENERAL
- **CALCULATOR-BASED LABS** — ADVANCED
- **DATASHEETS FOR QUICK LABS**
- **DATASHEETS FOR CHAPTER LABS**
- **DATASHEETS FOR LABBOOK**

Review and Assessments

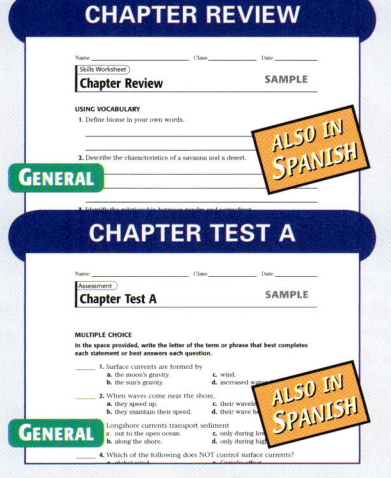

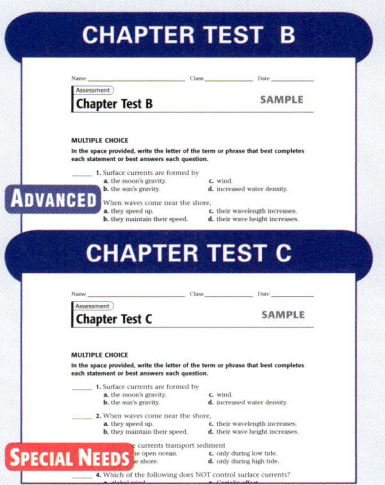

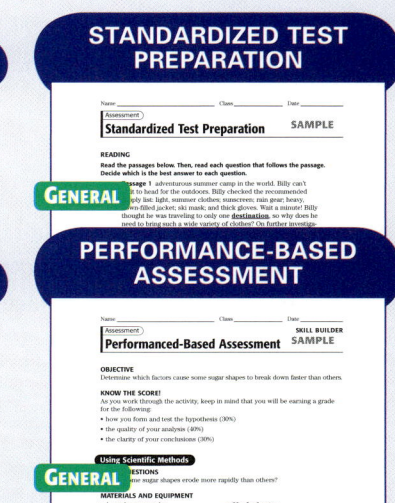

- **SECTION QUIZ** — GENERAL (ALSO IN SPANISH)
- **SECTION REVIEW** — GENERAL (ALSO IN SPANISH)
- **CHAPTER REVIEW** — GENERAL (ALSO IN SPANISH)
- **CHAPTER TEST A** — GENERAL
- **CHAPTER TEST B** — ADVANCED
- **CHAPTER TEST C** — SPECIAL NEEDS
- **STANDARDIZED TEST PREPARATION** — GENERAL
- **PERFORMANCE-BASED ASSESSMENT** — GENERAL

Chapter 4 • Chapter Resources   87D

4 Chapter Enrichment

This Chapter Enrichment provides relevant and interesting information to expand and enhance your presentation of the chapter material.

Section 1

The Rock Cycle

Rock Composition

- This chapter focuses on the mineral composition of rock, not its bulk composition. These are two very different means of measuring rock composition.

- The *mineral composition* of a rock refers to the proportions of the different minerals in the rock and is usually expressed in percentages by volume. Even coal, a sedimentary rock made of organic matter, contains clay minerals or pyrite.

- The *bulk composition* of a rock is the sum of the different elements that make up the rock and is usually expressed in percentages by weight. Mineral composition is affected by bulk composition.

Is That a Fact!

- Although rocks contain many elements, the rocks in Earth's crust are nearly 94% oxygen by number of atoms.

- Approximately 92% of the Earth's crust is igneous and metamorphic rock.

- Although sedimentary rock makes up about 8% of the Earth's crust, it is spread thinly over much of the planet's surface. Sedimentary rock covers 75% of the Earth's continental surfaces!

Section 2

Igneous Rock

The Great Dike of Zimbabwe

- Dikes can range in width from a few millimeters to many kilometers. The Great Dike of Zimbabwe, in Africa, is the largest known dike on Earth. It has an average width of 6 to 8 km and extends for almost 500 km across Zimbabwe.

Pumice

- Some magmas contain dissolved gases, such as carbon dioxide. When these gases come out of magma in the form of small bubbles, the magma greatly increases its volume, causing an enormous buildup of pressure. This can result in an explosive volcanic eruption. The result can be a frothy-looking rock called *pumice*. Pumice is full of small holes, called *vesicles*, where the trapped gases used to be. Depending on how much space is taken up by vesicles, some types of pumice can float in water!

Is That a Fact!

- Igneous rocks that form deep underground are called plutonic rocks, after Pluto, the god of the underworld in Roman mythology. Volcanic rocks are named after Vulcan, the Roman god of metalworking and fire.

- Although many people think of lava as a thin and runny liquid, lava flows are often quite viscous. Usually, the temperature has cooled enough for crystals to begin forming, which can give lava a consistency similar to that of thick oatmeal.

Section 3
Sedimentary Rock
Working with Clay
- Clay is composed primarily of silicate minerals. Clays are easy to work with when they are wet because the tiny plate-shaped silicate crystals are surrounded by water molecules. As the water evaporates, the silicates are cemented into place, and the clay becomes brittle and difficult to work with.

Is That a Fact!
◆ Bentonite, a form of clay composed of very fine silicate crystals, has a wide variety of industrial applications. Some forms of bentonite can expand as much as 300% when mixed with water. Bentonite is used to make cat litter, to line artificial ponds, to remove impurities from wines and juices, to treat wastewater, and in a variety of applications for oil drilling.

Section 4
Metamorphic Rock
Metamorphosis in a Lab
- Geologists can estimate the temperature and pressure that metamorphosed a rock by simulating the process of metamorphosis in a laboratory. When geologists know the chemical composition of certain minerals within a rock, they can subject a similar compound to a range of temperatures and pressures. By observing the laboratory results, they can make predictions about how similar materials behave in metamorphic environments. Geologists can determine the temperature at which metamorphism occurred within 20°C and the pressure within a fraction of a kilobar.

Carrara Marble
- In the mountains around Carrara, Italy, a marble prized for its purity and beauty has been quarried for at least 2,000 years. Its whiteness is due to the lack of organic materials in the limestone from which it recrystallized. Carrara marble was used in the interior of the Pantheon, in Rome. It is also found in the Leaning Tower of Pisa, in the pavement of Saint Peter's Basilica, in Vatican City, and in the Kennedy Center, in Washington, D.C.

Is That a Fact!
◆ Metamorphic rocks are a challenge to study because they form within a wide range of temperature and pressure. Scientists must distinguish between the geologic history of the metamorphic rock and the history of the igneous, sedimentary, or previously metamorphosed rocks it formed from. For the same reason, however, metamorphic rocks offer many important clues about tectonic activity in the Earth's past.

◆ Metamorphism occurs quickly at high temperatures, but it also occurs at temperatures that are surprisingly low. For example, clay minerals in mudstone and shale can begin to metamorphose at temperatures as low as 50°C! This reaction, however, takes many millions of years to occur.

SciLinks is maintained by the National Science Teachers Association to provide you and your students with interesting, up-to-date links that will enrich your classroom presentation of the chapter.

Visit www.scilinks.org and enter the SciLinks code for more information about the topic listed.

Topic: Composition of Rock
SciLinks code: HSM0327

Topic: Igneous Rock
SciLinks code: HSM0783

Topic: Sedimentary Rock
SciLinks code: HSM1365

Topic: Metamorphic Rock
SciLinks code: HSM0949

Overview
Tell students that this chapter will teach them about the rock cycle. They will learn about igneous, sedimentary, and metamorphic rocks. Students will find out how each rock type is formed and how each rock type is classified.

Assessing Prior Knowledge
Students should be familiar with the following topics:
- mineral environments

Identifying Misconceptions
Students may not realize that rock, like other substances on Earth, is part of a cycle. Within this cycle, a variety of geological processes act on rock to change and ultimately recycle it. These processes occur on the Earth's surface, in the shallow subsurface, or deep within the Earth and may be continuous or occur in a series of steps. The time in which processes act to change or recycle rock often happen over millions or tens of millions of years.

Rocks: Mineral Mixtures

SECTION 1 The Rock Cycle	90
SECTION 2 Igneous Rock	98
SECTION 3 Sedimentary Rock	102
SECTION 4 Metamorphic Rock	106
Chapter Lab	112
Chapter Review	114
Standardized Test Preparation	116
Science in Action	118

About the PHOTO
Irish legend claims that the mythical hero Finn MacCool built the Giant's Causeway, shown here. But this rock formation is the result of the cooling of huge amounts of molten rock. As the molten rock cooled, it formed tall pillars separated by cracks called *columnar joints*.

PRE-READING ACTIVITY
Graphic Organizer

Spider Map Before you read the chapter, create the graphic organizer entitled "Spider Map" described in the **Study Skills** section of the Appendix. Label the circle "Rock." Create a leg for each of the sections in this chapter. As you read the chapter, fill in the map with details about the material presented in each section of the chapter.

Standards Correlations

National Science Education Standards
The following codes indicate the National Science Education Standards that correlate to this chapter. The full text of the standards is at the front of the book.

Chapter Opener
SAI 1, 2

Section 1 The Rock Cycle
ES 1c, 1d; HNS 1; SAI 1, 2; SPSP 5; ST 2; UCP 1

Section 2 Igneous Rock
ES 1c, 1d; SAI 1, 2; UCP 1, 2; LabBook: SAI 1, 2

Section 3 Sedimentary Rock
ES 1c, 1d, 1k, 2b; SAI 1, 2: UCP 1, 2

Section 4 Metamorphic Rock
ES 1c; SAI 1, 2; UCP 1, 2; LabBook: SAI 1, 2

Chapter Lab
SAI 1, 2

Chapter Review
ES 1c, 1d, 2b; HNS 1; SAI 1, 2; SPSP 5; ST 2; UCP 1, 2

Science in Action
ES 1c, 2a; HNS 1, 2, 3; SAI 1, 2; SPSP 3, 5; ST 2

START-UP ACTIVITY

MATERIALS

FOR EACH GROUP
- bag containing several different and varied objects

Answers

1. Answers may vary. Sample answer: I sorted the objects by color, size, and composition.
2. Answers may vary. Sample answer: Yes, there were objects that could fit into more than one group. I solved this problem by deciding which characteristics were more important and then sorting the object into a corresponding group.
3. Answers may vary. Accept all reasonable responses. Students may mention color, texture, composition, and hardness.

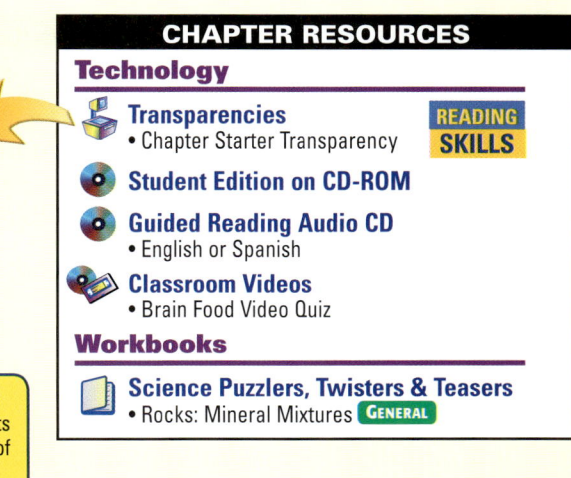

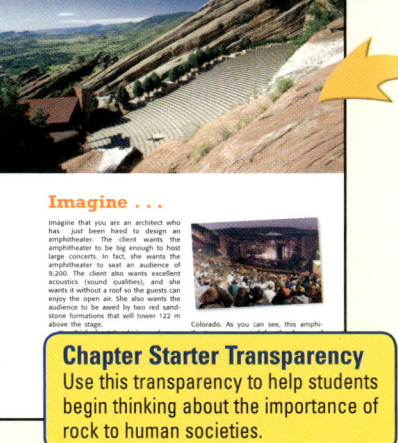

START-UP ACTIVITY

Classifying Objects

Scientists use the physical and chemical properties of rocks to classify rocks. Classifying objects such as rocks requires looking at many properties. Do this exercise for some classification practice.

Procedure

1. Your teacher will give you a **bag** containing **several objects.** Examine the objects, and note features such as size, color, shape, texture, smell, and any unique properties.
2. Develop three different ways to sort these objects.
3. Create a chart that organizes objects by properties.

Analysis

1. What properties did you use to sort the items?
2. Were there any objects that could fit into more than one group? How did you solve this problem?
3. Which properties might you use to classify rocks? Explain your answer.

Chapter Starter Transparency
Use this transparency to help students begin thinking about the importance of rock to human societies.

CHAPTER RESOURCES

Technology

Transparencies
- Chapter Starter Transparency

READING SKILLS

Student Edition on CD-ROM

Guided Reading Audio CD
- English or Spanish

Classroom Videos
- Brain Food Video Quiz

Workbooks

Science Puzzlers, Twisters & Teasers
- Rocks: Mineral Mixtures GENERAL

Chapter 4 • Rocks: Mineral Mixtures   **89**

SECTION 1

Focus

Overview
This section introduces the rock cycle and the processes that shape the surface of the Earth. The processes of weathering, erosion, deposition, uplift, melting, cooling, and metamorphism are explained, in the context of the rock cycle.

🔔 Bellringer
Pose the following questions to students:
- How can rock be recycled?
- How long would recycling a rock take?
- What would the rock look like before, during, and after the process of recycling?

Motivate

Discussion — GENERAL

Geologic Time Some students may not realize how long changes in the rock cycle take. The processes that shape rock can take millions to tens of millions of years. Discuss the geologic time scale with students to give them a perspective of how long the Earth has existed and how long these processes have been affecting the Earth.
LS Logical

SECTION 1

READING WARM-UP

Objectives
- Describe two ways rocks have been used by humans.
- Describe four processes that shape Earth's features.
- Describe how each type of rock changes into another type as it moves through the rock cycle.
- List two characteristics of rock that are used to help classify it.

Terms to Learn
rock cycle   deposition
rock   composition
erosion   texture

READING STRATEGY

Reading Organizer As you read this section, make a flowchart of the steps of the rock cycle.

The Rock Cycle

You know that paper, plastic, and aluminum can be recycled. But did you know that the Earth also recycles? And one of the things that Earth recycles is rock.

Scientists define **rock** as a naturally occurring solid mixture of one or more minerals and organic matter. It may be hard to believe, but rocks are always changing. The continual process by which new rock forms from old rock material is called the **rock cycle**.

The Value of Rock

Rock has been an important natural resource as long as humans have existed. Early humans used rocks as hammers to make other tools. They discovered that they could make arrowheads, spear points, knives, and scrapers by carefully shaping rocks such as chert and obsidian.

Rock has also been used for centuries to make buildings, monuments, and roads. **Figure 1** shows how rock has been used as a construction material by both ancient and modern civilizations. Buildings have been made out of granite, limestone, marble, sandstone, slate, and other rocks. Modern buildings also contain concrete and plaster, in which rock is an important ingredient.

✓ **Reading Check** Name some types of rock that have been used to construct buildings. *(See the Appendix for answers to Reading Checks.)*

Figure 1 *The ancient Egyptians used a sedimentary rock called* limestone *to construct the pyramids at Giza (left). Granite, an igneous rock, was used to construct the Texas state capitol building in Austin (right).*

CHAPTER RESOURCES

Chapter Resource File
- Lesson Plan
- Directed Reading A [BASIC]
- Directed Reading B [SPECIAL NEEDS]

Technology
- Transparencies
  - Bellringer

Answer to Reading Check
Types of rock that have been used by humans to construct buildings include granite, limestone, marble, sandstone, and slate.

---

90 Chapter 4 • Rocks: Mineral Mixtures

Processes That Shape the Earth

Certain geological processes make and destroy rock. These processes shape the features of our planet. These processes also influence the type of rock that is found in a certain area of Earth's surface.

Weathering, Erosion, and Deposition

The process in which water, wind, ice, and heat break down rock is called *weathering*. Weathering is important because it breaks down rock into fragments. These rock and mineral fragments are the sediment of which much sedimentary rock is made.

The process by which sediment is removed from its source is called **erosion.** Water, wind, ice, and gravity can erode and move sediments and cause them to collect. **Figure 2** shows an example of the way land looks after weathering and erosion.

The process in which sediment moved by erosion is dropped and comes to rest is called **deposition.** Sediment is deposited in bodies of water and other low-lying areas. In those places, sediment may be pressed and cemented together by minerals dissolved in water to form sedimentary rock.

Heat and Pressure

Sedimentary rock made of sediment can also form when buried sediment is squeezed by the weight of overlying layers of sediment. If the temperature and pressure are high enough at the bottom of the sediment, the rock can change into metamorphic rock. In some cases, the rock gets hot enough to melt. This melting creates the magma that eventually cools to form igneous rock.

How the Cycle Continues

Buried rock is exposed at the Earth's surface by a combination of uplift and erosion. *Uplift* is movement within the Earth that causes rocks inside the Earth to be moved to the Earth's surface. When uplifted rock reaches the Earth's surface, weathering, erosion, and deposition begin.

rock a naturally occurring solid mixture of one or more minerals or organic matter

rock cycle the series of processes in which a rock forms, changes from one type to another, is destroyed, and forms again by geological processes

erosion the process by which wind, water, ice, or gravity transports soil and sediment from one location to another

deposition the process in which material is laid down

Figure 2 Bryce Canyon, in Utah, is an excellent example of how the processes of weathering and erosion shape the face of our planet.

MISCONCEPTION ALERT

Weathering, Erosion, and Deposition
Some students may be confused by weathering, erosion, and deposition. Explain that weathering is the process that actually breaks down rock, whereas erosion is the removal and transport of the sediment that is formed by weathering. Deposition is the process by which sediments are dropped in a new location. The processes of weathering and erosion are not easy to separate because they happen simultaneously.

Teach

Group Activity — GENERAL

Rates of Weathering
Tombstones can be used to determine rates of weathering. In the 1960s, professor E. M. Winkler calculated the weathering rate for a marble marker in Indiana to be 1.5 mm in 43 y. In 1916, American geologist D. C. Barton estimated the weathering rate for granite monuments near the Nile River to be only 1 to 2 mm per millennium! With your students, visit a cemetery, and measure weathering rates of grave markers. Quartz veins in marble markers do not erode easily. Students can measure how much the marble has eroded relative to a quartz vein. By dividing the amount that a grave marker has eroded by the number of years the stone has been standing (the date of death), students can calculate the rate of weathering.
LS Visual/Kinesthetic

Cultural Awareness — GENERAL

Stone Cities Between 900 and 1400 CE, the Anasazi Indians of the American Southwest carved small towns in cliff sides. In what is now Cambodia, a vast temple complex called Angkor was carved from clay, sandstone, and laterite in the 12th century. In the 1300s, African traders built the Great Zimbabwe, a walled city guarded by huge monoliths. Have students write a report or build a model of one of these ancient sites.
LS Logical/Kinesthetic

Section 1 • The Rock Cycle **91**

Teach, continued

Using the Figure — GENERAL

Diagramming the Rock Cycle Ask students to use the information in the rock-cycle illustration to draw a diagram of the rock cycle in their **science journal**. The first step in the illustration is the formation of sedimentary rock; ask students to begin their rock cycle with a different step. Encourage them to write a descriptive caption for every stage of the rock cycle. **LS Visual**

MISCONCEPTION ALERT

Rock Cycle Misconceptions Rocks rarely undergo the complete process shown in the rock-cycle diagram. Sedimentary rocks can become igneous rocks, and metamorphic rocks can become sedimentary rocks. Also, some students may not realize the length of time it takes for changes to occur in the rock cycle. The process shown in the diagram can take millions to tens of millions of years.

Illustrating the Rock Cycle

You have learned about various geological processes, such as weathering, erosion, heat, and pressure, that create and destroy rock. The diagram on these two pages illustrates one way that sand grains can change as different geological processes act on them. In the following steps, you will see how these processes change the original sand grains into sedimentary rock, metamorphic rock, and igneous rock.

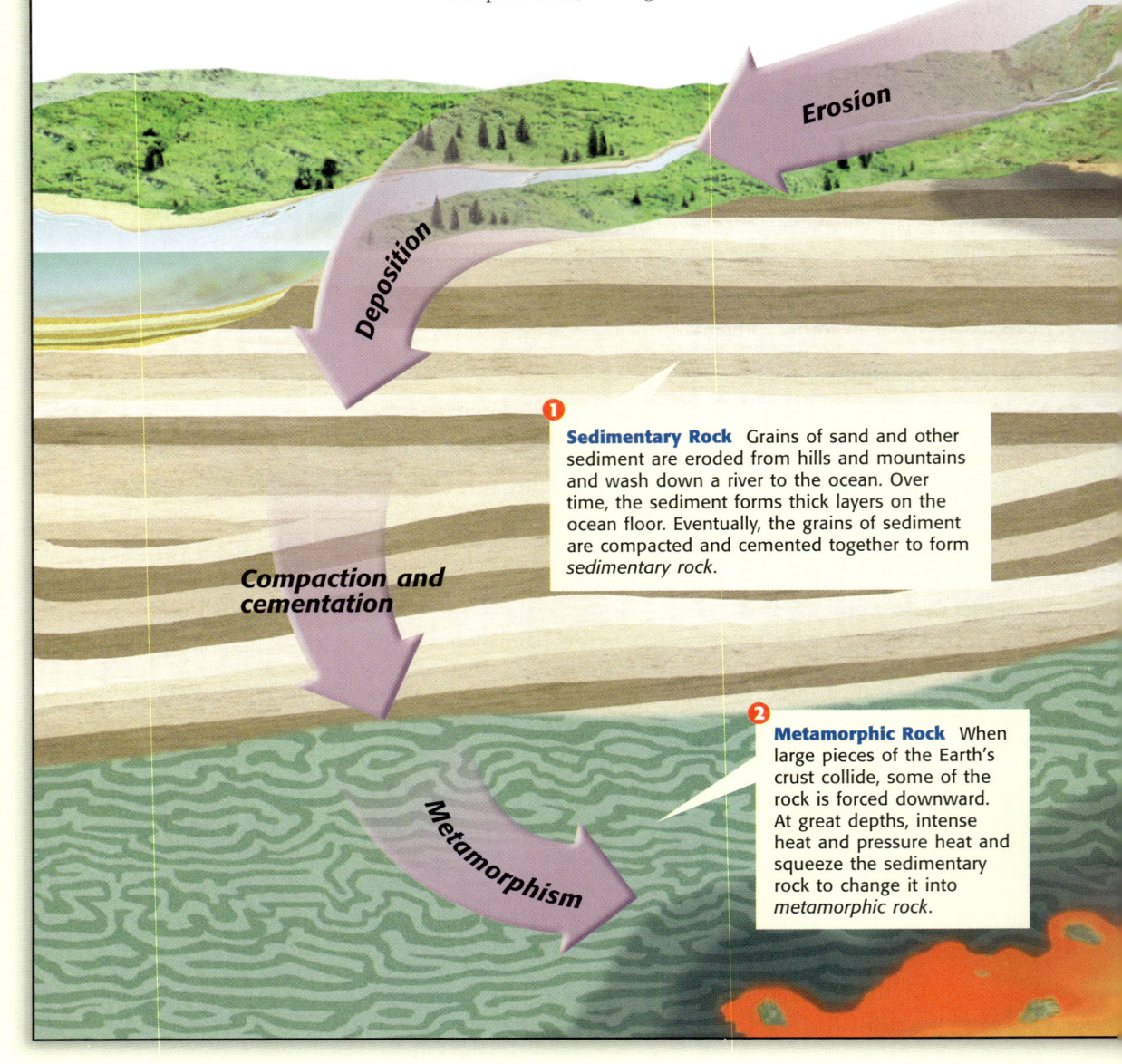

① Sedimentary Rock Grains of sand and other sediment are eroded from hills and mountains and wash down a river to the ocean. Over time, the sediment forms thick layers on the ocean floor. Eventually, the grains of sediment are compacted and cemented together to form *sedimentary rock*.

② Metamorphic Rock When large pieces of the Earth's crust collide, some of the rock is forced downward. At great depths, intense heat and pressure heat and squeeze the sedimentary rock to change it into *metamorphic rock*.

INCLUSION Strategies

- Learning Disabled
- Hearing Impaired
- Attention Deficit Disorder

Groups will use different foods to model sedimentary, metamorphic, and igneous rocks and minerals. Have real rock samples available (enough for each group). Organize students into groups of three or four students. Give students a chocolate-chip cookie to model granite (igneous), a sugar cube to model marble (metamorphic), a brownie to model shale (sedimentary), a magnifying glass, a large sheet of paper, and magic markers. Ask students to describe and sketch their three samples. To describe each sample, students should note the sample's texture, color, and composition. On the board, compile descriptions for each "rock" from each group. Pass real rock samples to each group, and have the groups match their samples to the real rocks. **LS Visual** **English Language Learners**

Chapter 4 • Rocks: Mineral Mixtures

Weathering

Solidification

⑤ **Sediment** Uplift and erosion expose the igneous rock at the Earth's surface. The igneous rock then weathers and wears away into grains of sand and clay. These grains of sediment are then transported and deposited elsewhere, and the cycle begins again.

④ **Igneous Rock** The sand grains from step 1 have changed a lot, but they will change more! Magma is usually less dense than the surrounding rock, so magma tends to rise to higher levels of the Earth's crust. Once there, the magma cools and solidifies to become *igneous rock*.

Cooling

Melting

③ **Magma** The hot liquid that forms when rock partially or completely melts is called *magma*. Where the metamorphic rock comes into contact with magma, the rock tends to melt. The material that began as a collection of sand grains now becomes part of the magma.

Is That a Fact!
Geologists can use the Earth's magnetic field to determine the approximate age of rocks. They examine both igneous and sedimentary rocks to determine the pattern of magnetic reversals. When these rocks form, the magnetic minerals they contain orient with the direction of the Earth's magnetic field. The pattern of magnetic reversals allows scientists to date the rock layers.

CHAPTER RESOURCES

Technology
Transparencies
• The Rock Cycle

ACTIVITY — BASIC

Rock Dictionary Have students prepare a *Rock Dictionary*. Ask them to list the three types of rock and the processes that occur in the rock cycle. Ask students to record the dictionary definition for each rock type or rock-cycle process and then define it in their own words. Encourage students to make up mnemonic devices, such as jokes or rhymes, to help them remember the meaning of each term.
LS Logical *English Language Learners*

CONNECTION ACTIVITY
Language Arts — BASIC

Writing **Passing Through** Ask students to imagine being an ancient grain of sand on a beach. Have them write a letter describing their lifetime in the rock cycle. The grain of sand should pass through several processes in the rock cycle during its lifetime. Students can share their letters with the class.
LS Intrapersonal *English Language Learners*

Homework — GENERAL

Illustration Have students make a poster that illustrates the rock cycle. Encourage them to cut out pictures from magazines of the different types of rock and processes in the rock cycle. For example, marble is a metamorphic rock that could be represented by a picture of a marble statue.
LS Visual *English Language Learners*

Section 1 • The Rock Cycle   93

Teach, continued

Cultural Awareness — GENERAL

Avicenna The Persian scholar Avicenna (980–1037) contributed immensely to our knowledge of medicine, astronomy, mathematics, and geology. In the *Book of Minerals,* he described how rivers and seas laid down sediment that eventually became rock. Avicenna's theories contributed to the foundations of Western geology. Many of his controversial ideas did not gain acceptance in Europe until the 1600s. Encourage students to learn more about Avicenna. Have them come to class as Avicenna and act out his life story. **LS Logical**

CONNECTION to Environmental Science — ADVANCED

Cycles in Nature Many important substances on Earth follow cycles. Examples include water, carbon, and rock. Use the teaching transparency entitled "The Water Cycle" to lead a discussion about the ways that the water cycle and the rock cycle interact with each other. **LS Visual**

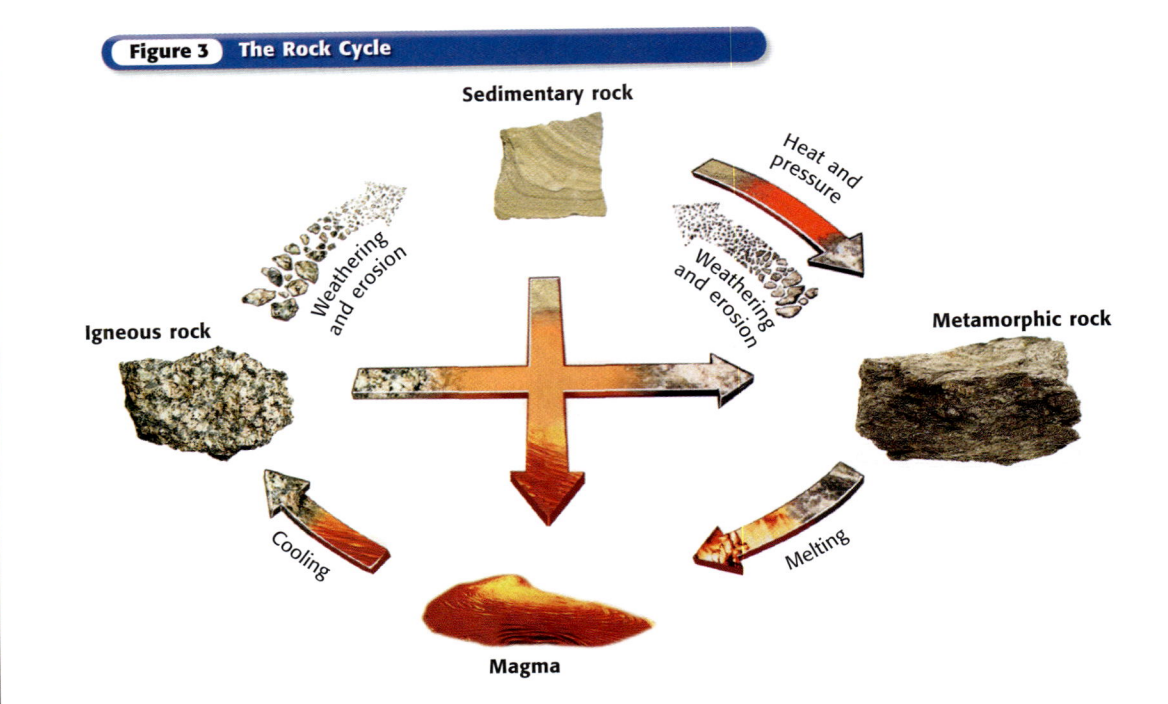

Figure 3 The Rock Cycle

Sedimentary rock

Heat and pressure

Weathering and erosion

Igneous rock

Weathering and erosion

Metamorphic rock

Cooling

Melting

Magma

Round and Round It Goes

You have seen how different geological processes can change rock. Each rock type can change into one of the three types of rock. For example, igneous rock can change into sedimentary rock, metamorphic rock, or even back into igneous rock. This cycle, in which rock is changed by geological processes into different types of rock, is known as the rock cycle.

Rocks may follow various pathways in the rock cycle. As one rock type is changed to another type, several variables, including time, heat, pressure, weathering, and erosion may alter a rock's identity. The location of a rock determines which natural forces will have the biggest impact on the process of change. For example, rock at the Earth's surface is primarily affected by forces of weathering and erosion, whereas deep inside the Earth, rocks change because of extreme heat and pressure. **Figure 3** shows the different ways rock may change when it goes through the rock cycle and the different forces that affect rock during the cycle.

✓ **Reading Check** What processes change rock deep within the Earth?

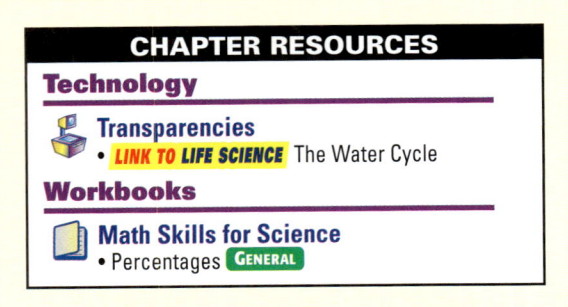

CHAPTER RESOURCES

Technology

Transparencies
• **LINK TO LIFE SCIENCE** The Water Cycle

Workbooks

Math Skills for Science
• Percentages **GENERAL**

Answer to Reading Check
Rock within the Earth is affected by temperature and pressure.

---

94 Chapter 4 • Rocks: Mineral Mixtures

Rock Classification

You have already learned that scientists divide all rock into three main classes based on how the rock formed: igneous, sedimentary, and metamorphic. But did you know that each class of rock can be divided further? These divisions are also based on differences in the way rocks form. For example, all igneous rock forms when magma cools and solidifies. But some igneous rocks form when magma cools *on* the Earth's surface, and others form when magma cools deep *beneath* the surface. Therefore, igneous rock can be divided again based on how and where it forms. Sedimentary and metamorphic rocks are also divided into groups. How do scientists know how to classify rocks? They study rocks in detail using two important criteria—composition and texture.

Composition

The minerals a rock contains determine the **composition** of that rock, as shown in **Figure 4.** For example, a rock made of mostly the mineral quartz will have a composition very similar to that of quartz. But a rock made of 50% quartz and 50% feldspar will have a very different composition than quartz does.

composition the chemical makeup of a rock; describes either the minerals or other materials in the rock

Reading Check What determines a rock's composition?

MATH PRACTICE

What's in It?
Assume that a granite sample you are studying is made of 30% quartz and 55% feldspar by volume. The rest is made of biotite mica. What percentage of the sample is biotite mica?

Figure 4 Two Examples of Rock Composition

The composition of a rock depends on the minerals the rock contains.

Limestone
95% Calcite
5% Aragonite

Granite
10% Biotite mica
35% Quartz
55% Feldspar

CONNECTION to Math — GENERAL

Percentages A percentage is a ratio that is expressed in terms of hundredths. When analyzing pure substances, percentage composition remains the same at any mass. For example, in terms of atomic mass, the percentage of oxygen by weight in water is 88.8%, whether you are describing a single raindrop or an entire ocean. **LS Logical**

Answer to Math Practice
100% of rock − (30% quartz + 55% feldspar) = 15% biotite mica

Group ACTIVITY — BASIC

Describing Rocks Organize the class into small groups. Give each group samples of sandstone, limestone, and conglomerate. Number the samples. Provide a magnifying lens, a mineral identification key, a small dental pick, and paper towels (to capture any pieces of rock that break off during the activity). Write the following instructions on the board:

1. Describe the color and texture of each rock.

2. Using your unaided eye, examine the grains that make up each rock. Describe what you see.

3. Using the magnifying lens, try to identify the mineral composition of each rock.

4. Use the dental pick to test how well each rock is cemented, and record what you discover.

5. Classify each rock by grain size as fine grained, medium grained, or coarse grained.

After groups have analyzed the rocks, have group members discuss their findings. **English Language Learners**
LS Logical/Kinesthetic

Answer to Reading Check
The minerals that a rock contains determine a rock's composition.

Section 1 • The Rock Cycle

Close

Reteaching — BASIC
Diagramming the Rock Cycle
Have students create a diagram of the processes that shape Earth's surface. The diagram should be a simplified version of the rock cycle. The diagram should include the processes of weathering, erosion, deposition, and uplift. **LS Visual**

Quiz — GENERAL

1. List four processes that change rock from one type to another. (weathering, changes in pressure, melting, and cooling)
2. What are the three main classes of rock? (igneous, sedimentary, and metamorphic)
3. How is a brick similar to a metamorphic rock? (Bricks are made from clay and then baked to become strong and resistant to weathering. Bricks are "metamorphosed" by high temperatures.)

Alternative Assessment — GENERAL
Rock Cycle Skit Have students write a skit portraying the rock cycle. Roles can include the minerals that make up rock and the forces that affect them. To represent the forces—heat, pressure, erosion, and weathering—suggest that students create special costumes. **LS Kinesthetic**

Figure 5 Three Examples of Sedimentary Rock Texture

Fine-grained — Siltstone
Medium-grained — Sandstone
Coarse-grained — Conglomerate

texture the quality of a rock that is based on the sizes, shapes, and positions of the rock's grains

Texture

The size, shape, and positions of the grains that make up a rock determine a rock's **texture.** Sedimentary rock can have a fine-grained, medium-grained, or coarse-grained texture, depending on the size of the grains that make up the rock. Three samples of textures are shown in **Figure 5.** The texture of igneous rock can be fine-grained or coarse-grained, depending on how much time magma has to cool. Based on the degree of temperature and pressure a rock is exposed to, metamorphic rock can also have a fine-grained or coarse-grained texture.

The texture of a rock can provide clues as to how and where the rock formed. Look at the rocks shown in **Figure 6.** The rocks look different because they formed in very different ways. The texture of a rock can reveal the process that formed it.

✓ Reading Check Give three examples of sedimentary rock textures.

Figure 6 Texture and Rock Formation

Basalt, a fine-grained igneous rock, forms when lava that erupts onto Earth's surface cools rapidly.

Sandstone, a medium-grained sedimentary rock, forms when sand grains deposited in dunes, on beaches, or on the ocean floor are buried and cemented.

Answer to Reading Check
Fine-grained rocks are made of small grains, such as silt or clay particles. Medium-grained rocks are made of medium-sized grains, such as sand. Coarse-grained rocks are made of large grains, such as pebbles.

Chapter 4 • Rocks: Mineral Mixtures

SECTION Review

Summary

- Rock has been an important natural resource for as long as humans have existed. Early humans used rock to make tools. Ancient and modern civilizations have used rock as a construction material.
- Weathering, erosion, deposition, and uplift are all processes that shape the surface features of the Earth.
- The rock cycle is the continual process by which new rock forms from old rock material.
- The sequence of events in the rock cycle depends on processes, such as weathering, erosion, deposition, pressure, and heat, that change the rock material.
- Composition and texture are two characteristics that scientists use to classify rocks.
- The composition of a rock is determined by the minerals that make up the rock.
- The texture of a rock is determined by the size, shape, and positions of the grains that make up the rock.

Using Key Terms

Complete each of the following sentences by choosing the correct term from the word bank.

rock   composition
rock cycle   texture

1. The minerals that a rock is made of determine the ___ of that rock.
2. ___ is a naturally occurring, solid mixture of crystals of one or more minerals.

Understanding Key Ideas

3. Sediments are transported or moved from their original source by a process called
   a. deposition.
   b. erosion.
   c. uplift.
   d. weathering.

4. Describe two ways that rocks have been used by humans.

5. Name four processes that change rock inside the Earth.

6. Describe four processes that shape Earth's surface.

7. Give an example of how texture can provide clues as to how and where a rock formed.

Critical Thinking

8. **Making Comparisons** Explain the difference between texture and composition.

9. **Analyzing Processes** Explain how rock is continually recycled in the rock cycle.

Interpreting Graphics

10. Look at the table below. Sandstone is a type of sedimentary rock. If you had a sample of sandstone that had an average particle size of 2 mm, what texture would your sandstone have?

Classification of Clastic Sedimentary Rocks

Texture	Particle size
coarse grained	> 2 mm
medium grained	0.06 to 2 mm
fine grained	< 0.06 mm

For a variety of links related to this chapter, go to www.scilinks.org
Topic: Composition of Rock
SciLinks code: HSM0327

CHAPTER RESOURCES

Chapter Resource File
- Section Quiz GENERAL
- Section Review GENERAL
- Vocabulary and Section Summary GENERAL

Answers to Section Review

1. composition
2. Rock
3. b
4. Rocks have been used by humans to make tools and weapons and to construct buildings.
5. Four processes that change rock inside the Earth are compaction and cementation, metamorphism, melting, and cooling.
6. Weathering is the process by which water, wind, ice, and heat break down rock. Erosion is the process by which sediment is removed from its source. Deposition is the process by which sediment moved by erosion is laid down. Uplift is the process by which rock within the Earth moves to Earth's surface.
7. Answers may vary. Sample answer: Fine grains in an igneous rock indicate that the rock cooled quickly, which means it was likely to have formed at Earth's surface.
8. Composition is the percent of elements that make up a rock. Texture is a quality of a rock that is based on the size, shape, and position of its grains.
9. Answers may vary. Sample answer: Rock is continually recycled by different processes in the rock cycle. Melting of sedimentary, metamorphic, or igneous rock creates new igneous rock. The weathering, erosion, deposition, burial, compression, and cementation of igneous, metamorphic, or sedimentary rock creates new sedimentary rock. Igneous, sedimentary, or metamorphic rock that is subjected to increased heat and pressure can be metamorphosed.
10. a medium-grained texture

Section 1 • The Rock Cycle

SECTION 2

Focus

Overview
This section discusses the formation of igneous rock from the cooling of magma. Students learn about the difference between intrusive and extrusive igneous rock. Students also learn about the difference between felsic and mafic igneous rock and how the rate of cooling affects the texture of igneous rock.

Bellringer
Pose the following question to students: "Do you think rocks that cooled and solidified from lava on Earth's surface would look different from those that cooled and solidified from magma inside the Earth? Why?"

Motivate

Discussion — GENERAL

Volcanoes Ask students to discuss how volcanoes affect people. Discuss eruptions, lava flows, and ash clouds. Then, ask students about the benefits of volcanoes. Explain that lava and magma form land. Explain that volcanic soil is some of the most fertile soil in the world, which is why many populations are willing to live alongside potentially dangerous volcanoes. **LS Logical**

SECTION 2

READING WARM-UP

Objectives
- Describe three ways that igneous rock forms.
- Explain how the cooling rate of magma affects the texture of igneous rock.
- Distinguish between igneous rock that cools within Earth's crust and igneous rock that cools at Earth's surface.

Terms to Learn
intrusive igneous rock
extrusive igneous rock

READING STRATEGY

Reading Organizer As you read this section, make a table comparing intrusive rock and extrusive rock.

Igneous Rock

Where do igneous rocks come from? Here's a hint: The word igneous *comes from a Latin word that means "fire."*

Igneous rock forms when hot, liquid rock, or *magma*, cools and solidifies. The type of igneous rock that forms depends on the composition of the magma and the amount of time it takes the magma to cool.

Origins of Igneous Rock

Igneous rock begins as magma. As shown in **Figure 1**, there are three ways magma can form: when rock is heated, when pressure is released, or when rock changes composition.

When magma cools enough, it solidifies to form igneous rock. Magma solidifies in much the same way that water freezes. But there are also differences between the way magma freezes and the way water freezes. One main difference is that water freezes at 0°C. Magma freezes between 700°C and 1,250°C. Also, liquid magma is a complex mixture containing many melted minerals. Because these minerals have different melting points, some minerals in the magma will freeze or become solid before other minerals do.

Figure 1 The Formation of Magma

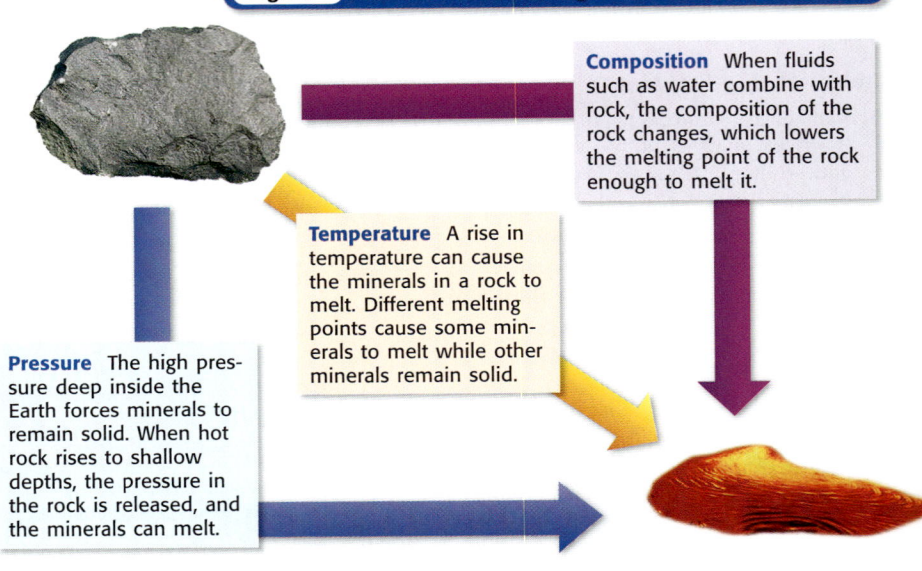

Composition When fluids such as water combine with rock, the composition of the rock changes, which lowers the melting point of the rock enough to melt it.

Temperature A rise in temperature can cause the minerals in a rock to melt. Different melting points cause some minerals to melt while other minerals remain solid.

Pressure The high pressure deep inside the Earth forces minerals to remain solid. When hot rock rises to shallow depths, the pressure in the rock is released, and the minerals can melt.

CHAPTER RESOURCES

Chapter Resource File
- Lesson Plan
- Directed Reading A BASIC
- Directed Reading B SPECIAL NEEDS

Technology
Transparencies
- Bellringer

WEIRD SCIENCE

Surtsey is a volcanic island south of Iceland that people actually saw being born! In 1963, fishermen saw jets of spray, steam, and lava shooting more than 30 m out of the ocean. One month later, the volcano broke through the surface to form an island. By the time the eruptions ended, Surtsey covered an area of approximately 2.8 km².

---

98 Chapter 4 • Rocks: Mineral Mixtures

Figure 2 Igneous Rock Texture

	Coarse-grained	Fine-grained
Felsic	Granite	Rhyolite
Mafic	Gabbro	Basalt

Composition and Texture of Igneous Rock

Look at the rocks in **Figure 2.** All of the rocks are igneous rocks even though they look different from one another. These rocks differ from one another in what they are made of and how fast they cooled.

The light-colored rocks are less dense than the dark-colored rocks are. The light-colored rocks are rich in elements such as aluminum, potassium, silicon, and sodium. These rocks are called *felsic rocks.* The dark-colored rocks, called *mafic rocks,* are rich in calcium, iron, and magnesium, and poor in silicon.

Figure 3 shows what happens to magma when it cools at different rates. The longer it takes for the magma or lava to cool, the more time mineral crystals have to grow. The more time the crystals have to grow, the larger the crystals are and the coarser the texture of the resulting igneous rock is.

In contrast, the less time magma takes to cool, the less time crystals have to grow. Therefore, the rock that is formed will be fine grained. Fine-grained igneous rock contains very small crystals, or if the cooling is very rapid, it contains no crystals.

✓ **Reading Check** Explain the difference between felsic rock and mafic rock. (*See the Appendix for answers to Reading Checks.*)

Figure 3 *The amount of time it takes for magma or lava to cool determines the texture of igneous rock.*

- Fast-cooling lava
- Fine-grained igneous rock
- Magma
- Slow-cooling magma
- Coarse-grained igneous rock

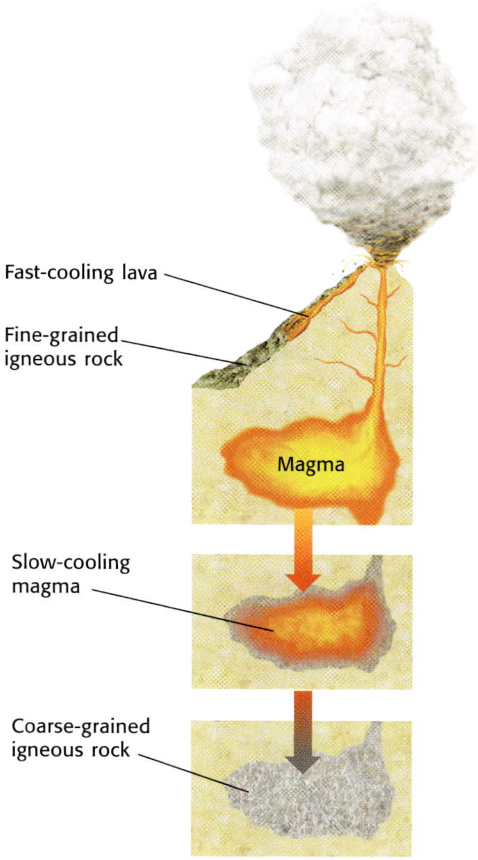

Teach

Using the Figure — BASIC
Making Inferences Have students rank the rocks shown in **Figure 2** by how fast they cooled. Tell students to pay careful attention to the grain size of each rock. (From fastest cooled to slowest cooled, the rocks are basalt, rhyolite, gabbro, and granite.) **LS** Visual/Logical

CONNECTION to Life Science — ADVANCED
Life Along a Rift Until 1977, biologists thought few life-forms lived at ocean depths where sunlight does not reach. When scientists in the submersible *Alvin* explored the bottom of a deep ocean trench called the Galápagos Rift, they discovered structures called black smokers that release dissolved mineral compounds and heat the water. Scientists were amazed to discover an entire ecosystem that did not depend on photosynthesis for energy. This discovery has led some scientists to speculate that life may also have originated in the outer solar system—particularly in the oceans that may exist under the surface of Europa, one of Jupiter's moons. Have students research the bizarre life-forms that scientists found living around black smokers. **LS** Logical

Answer to Reading Check
Felsic rocks are light-colored igneous rocks rich in aluminum, potassium, silicon, and sodium. Mafic rocks are dark-colored igneous rocks rich in calcium, iron, and magnesium.

Is That a Fact!
The Deccan Traps of India Between 68 and 64 million years ago, a hot spot under western India erupted over 1 million km^3 of basaltic lava. These lava flows, called the Deccan Traps, are more than 2 km thick in some places. Mathematicians calculate that if the lava from the eruptions in western India were spread evenly over the entire Earth, it would cover the Earth with a layer more than 2 m thick!

Section 2 • Igneous Rock

Close

Reteaching — BASIC

Word Meanings Compare the words *intrusive* and *extrusive* with the words *interior* and *exterior*. Have students brainstorm other words that use the prefixes *in-* and *ex-* to help them remember the meanings of the terms *intrusive* and *extrusive*. **English Language Learners** **LS Logical**

Quiz — GENERAL

1. Name five types of bodies of intrusive igneous rock. (batholiths, stocks, dikes, sills, and volcanic necks)
2. What is a fissure? (A fissure is a long crack in the Earth's crust through which lava erupts and flows.)

Alternative Assessment — GENERAL

Modeling Igneous Rock Bodies Have students create a model cross section that shows the formation of both intrusive and extrusive igneous rock. Students can use **Figure 4** as a basis for their models. Supply students with several different colors of clay so that they can color-code different bodies, such as the magma source, dikes, sills, plutons, and the lava that forms extrusive rock. **English Language Learners** **LS Kinesthetic/Visual**

INTERNET ACTIVITY

For another activity related to this chapter, go to **go.hrw.com** and type in the keyword **HZ5RCKW**.

intrusive igneous rock rock formed from the cooling and solidification of magma beneath the Earth's surface

Figure 4 Igneous intrusive bodies have different shapes and sizes.

Igneous Rock Formations

Igneous rock formations are located above and below the surface of the Earth. You may be familiar with igneous rock formations that were caused by lava cooling on the Earth's surface, such as volcanoes. But not all magma reaches the surface. Some magma cools and solidifies deep within the Earth's crust.

Intrusive Igneous Rock

When magma *intrudes*, or pushes, into surrounding rock below the Earth's surface and cools, the rock that forms is called **intrusive igneous rock.** Intrusive igneous rock usually has a coarse-grained texture because it is well insulated by surrounding rock and cools very slowly. The minerals that form are large, visible crystals.

Masses of intrusive igneous rock are named for their size and shape. Common intrusive shapes are shown in **Figure 4**. *Plutons* are large, irregular-shaped intrusive bodies. The largest of all igneous intrusions are *batholiths*. *Stocks* are intrusive bodies that are exposed over smaller areas than batholiths. Sheetlike intrusions that cut across previous rock units are called *dikes*, whereas *sills* are sheetlike intrusions that are oriented parallel to previous rock units.

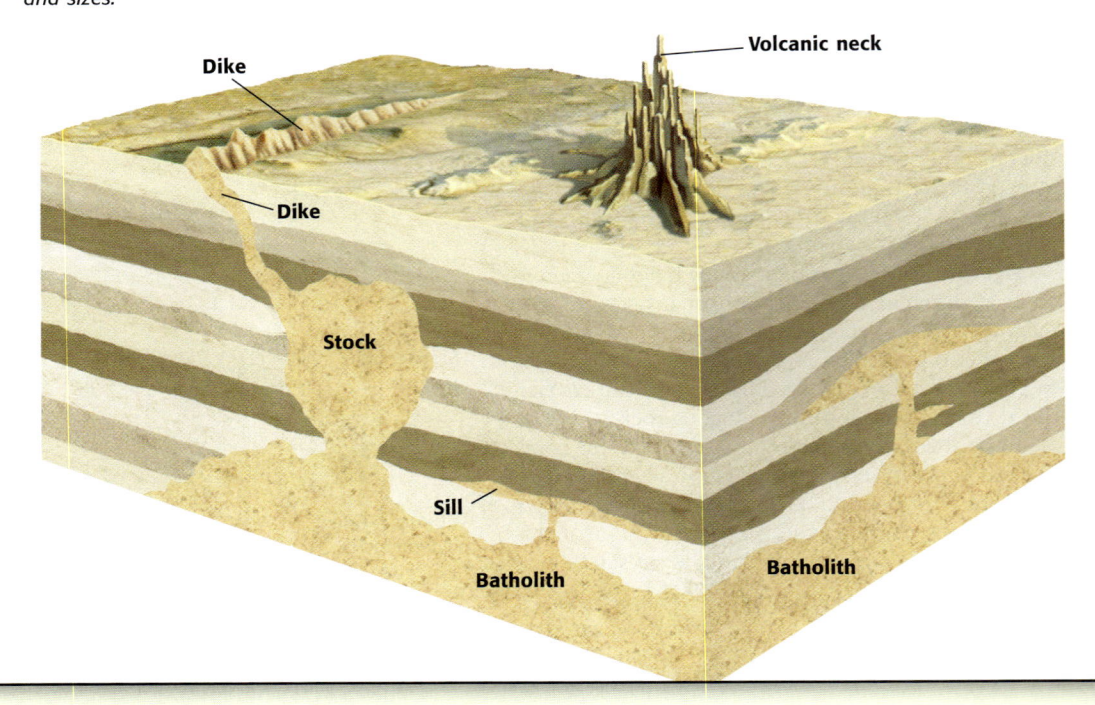

Homework — ADVANCED

Volcanic Necks A volcanic neck is the hardened core of a volcano that is left behind after the volcano erodes away. Ship Rock, a volcanic neck on a Navajo reservation in New Mexico, soars 518 m above the desert. Devils Tower National Monument, in Wyoming, rises 386 m. Have students research one of these formations to learn how it formed. **LS Logical**

---

100   Chapter 4 • Rocks: Mineral Mixtures

Extrusive Igneous Rock

Igneous rock that forms from magma that erupts, or extrudes, onto the Earth's surface is called **extrusive igneous rock.** Extrusive rock is common around volcanoes. It cools quickly on the surface and contains very small crystals or no crystals.

When lava erupts from a volcano, a *lava flow* forms. **Figure 5** shows an active lava flow. Lava does not always flow from volcanoes. Sometimes lava erupts and flows from long cracks in the Earth's crust called *fissures*. Lava flows from fissures on the ocean floor at places where tension is causing the ocean floor to be pulled apart. This lava cools to form new ocean floor. When a large amount of lava flows out of fissures onto land, the lava can cover a large area and form a plain called a *lava plateau*. Pre-existing landforms are often buried by these lava flows.

✓ **Reading Check** How does new ocean floor form?

Figure 5 An active lava flow is shown in this photo. When exposed to Earth's surface conditions, lava quickly cools and solidifies to form a fine-grained igneous rock.

extrusive igneous rock rock that forms as a result of volcanic activity at or near the Earth's surface

SECTION Review

Summary

- Igneous rock forms when magma cools and hardens.
- The texture of igneous rock is determined by the rate at which the rock cools.
- Igneous rock that solidifies at Earth's surface is extrusive. Igneous rock that solidifies within Earth's surface is intrusive.
- Shapes of common igneous intrusive bodies include batholiths, stocks, sills, and dikes.

Using Key Terms

1. In your own words, write a definition for each of the following terms: *intrusive igneous rock* and *extrusive igneous rock*.

Understanding Key Ideas

2. ___ is an example of a coarse-grained, felsic, igneous rock.
   a. Basalt
   b. Gabbro
   c. Granite
   d. Rhyolite

3. Explain three ways in which magma can form.

4. What determines the texture of igneous rocks?

Math Skills

5. The summit of a granite batholith has an elevation of 1,825 ft. What is the height of the batholith in meters?

Critical Thinking

6. **Making Comparisons** Dikes and sills are both types of igneous intrusive bodies. What is the difference between a dike and a sill?

7. **Predicting Consequences** An igneous rock forms from slow-cooling magma deep beneath the surface of the Earth. What type of texture is this rock most likely to have? Explain.

For a variety of links related to this chapter, go to www.scilinks.org
Topic: Igneous Rock
SciLinks code: HSM0783

Answers to Section Review

1. Sample answer: Intrusive igneous rock forms from magma that solidifies underground. Extrusive igneous rock forms from magma that solidifies after it has reached the surface.

2. c

3. Temperature, pressure, and a change in the composition of a rock can cause magma to form. A rise in temperature can cause minerals in a rock to melt, forming magma. When pressure in a rock that is hot is released, the minerals in that rock can melt, forming magma. When fluids such as water combine with rock, the composition of the rock changes. This change in composition lowers the melting point of the rock enough to melt it, forming magma.

4. When magma cools slowly, crystals have a longer time to grow, so the igneous rock that forms is coarse grained. When magma cools quickly, crystals have a short time to grow, so the igneous rock that forms is fine grained.

5. 1,825 ft ÷ 3.28 ft/m = 556.4 ft/m

6. A sill intrudes rock parallel to the surrounding rock layers. A dike cuts across the surrounding rock layers.

7. Because the rock formed from slowly cooling magma deep inside the Earth, the crystals had more time to grow. Therefore, the texture of the rock would most likely be coarse grained.

Answer to Reading Check

New sea floor forms when lava that flows from fissures on the ocean floor cools and hardens.

CHAPTER RESOURCES

Chapter Resource File
- Section Quiz GENERAL
- Section Review GENERAL
- Vocabulary and Section Summary GENERAL

Technology

Transparencies
- Intrusive Igneous Rock Bodies

SECTION 3

Focus

Overview
This section explores how sedimentary rock forms and how it accumulates in layers, or strata. Students distinguish between clastic, chemical, and organic sedimentary rocks and learn how each rock type forms.

Bellringer
Ask students to write about how layers in sedimentary rock are like the rings in a tree. How are they different? What information can geologists infer by examining sedimentary layers?

Motivate

Demonstration — GENERAL

Dissolution of Minerals Limestone forms when calcium carbonate crystallizes out of ocean water. Students may not believe that water contains the chemical components of dissolved minerals. If you live in an area with hard water, have students observe ice melting in warm water. After the ice melts, there is a layer of fluffy calcium carbonate that forms at the bottom of the glass. If you live in an area with soft water, make hard water by dissolving a little baking soda and calcium chloride in water. Then, freeze the water into ice cubes. Use these ice cubes for the demonstration. **LS Visual**

SECTION 3

READING WARM-UP

Objectives
- Describe the origin of sedimentary rock.
- Describe the three main categories of sedimentary rock.
- Describe three types of sedimentary structures.

Terms to Learn
strata
stratification

READING STRATEGY

Reading Organizer As you read this section, create an outline of this section. Use the headings from the section in your outline.

Figure 1 The red sandstone "monuments" for which Monument Valley in Arizona has been named are the products of millions of years of erosion.

Sedimentary Rock

Have you ever tried to build a sand castle at the beach? Did you ever wonder where the sand came from?

Sand is a product of weathering, which breaks rock into pieces. Over time, sand grains may be compacted, or compressed, and then cemented together to form a rock called *sandstone*. Sandstone is just one of many types of sedimentary rock.

Origins of Sedimentary Rock

Wind, water, ice, sunlight, and gravity all cause rock to physically weather into fragments. Through the process of erosion, these rock and mineral fragments, called *sediment*, are moved from one place to another. Eventually, the sediment is deposited in layers. As new layers of sediment are deposited, they cover older layers. Older layers become compacted. Dissolved minerals, such as calcite and quartz, separate from water that passes through the sediment to form a natural cement that binds the rock and mineral fragments together into sedimentary rock.

Sedimentary rock forms at or near the Earth's surface. It forms without the heat and pressure that are involved in the formation of igneous and metamorphic rocks.

The most noticeable feature of sedimentary rock is its layers, or **strata.** A single, horizontal layer of rock is sometimes visible for many miles. Road cuts are good places to observe strata. **Figure 1** shows the spectacular views that sedimentary rock formations carved by erosion can provide.

CHAPTER RESOURCES

Chapter Resource File
- Lesson Plan
- Directed Reading A BASIC
- Directed Reading B SPECIAL NEEDS

Technology
- Transparencies
  • Bellringer

WEIRD SCIENCE

The Bonneville Salt Flats, in Utah, are the remnants of a vast lake called Lake Bonneville. After the last ice age, most of the lake drained quickly, but much of the remaining water slowly evaporated, which left behind the salt flats. The Great Salt Lake is the largest of the lakes left after Lake Bonneville evaporated.

102 Chapter 4 • Rocks: Mineral Mixtures

Figure 2 Classification of Clastic Sedimentary Rock

Conglomerate — Sandstone — Siltstone — Shale

Coarse grained ⟶ Fine grained

Composition of Sedimentary Rock

Sedimentary rock is classified by the way it forms. *Clastic sedimentary rock* forms when rock or mineral fragments, called *clasts,* are cemented together. *Chemical sedimentary rock* forms when minerals crystallize out of a solution, such as sea water, to become rock. *Organic sedimentary rock* forms from the remains of once-living plants and animals.

Clastic Sedimentary Rock

Clastic sedimentary rock is made of fragments of rocks cemented together by a mineral such as calcite or quartz. **Figure 2** shows how clastic sedimentary rock is classified according to the size of the fragments from which the rock is made. Clastic sedimentary rocks can have coarse-grained, medium-grained, or fine-grained textures.

Chemical Sedimentary Rock

Chemical sedimentary rock forms from solutions of dissolved minerals and water. As rainwater slowly makes its way to the ocean, it dissolves some of the rock material it passes through. Some of this dissolved material eventually crystallizes and forms the minerals that make up chemical sedimentary rock. Halite, one type of chemical sedimentary rock, is made of sodium chloride, NaCl, or table salt. Halite forms when sodium ions and chlorine ions in shallow bodies of water become so concentrated that halite crystallizes from solution.

Reading Check How does a chemical sedimentary rock such as halite form? (*See the Appendix for answers to Reading Checks.*)

strata layers of rock (singular, *stratum*)

CONNECTION TO Language Arts

WRITING SKILL **Salty Expressions** The word *salt* is used in many expressions in the English language. Some common examples include "the salt of the earth," "taken with a grain of salt," "not worth his salt," "the salt of truth," "rubbing salt into a wound," and "old salt." Use the Internet or another source to research one these expressions. In your research, attempt to find the origin of the expression. Write a short paragraph that summarizes what you found.

Answer to Reading Check
Halite forms when sodium ions and chlorine ions in shallow bodies of water become so concentrated that halite crystallizes from solution.

Teach

ACTIVITY — BASIC

Sedimentary Rock Organize students into three groups to investigate sandstone, shale, and limestone. The first group should work together to learn how the rocks form. The second group should investigate how the rocks are used in industry, architecture, or the arts. The third group should investigate rock formations that have become tourist attractions. Members of each group should prepare exhibits, posters, or models to demonstrate what they have learned.
LS Logical/Visual Co-op Learning

CONNECTION to Life Science — BASIC

Calcium Carbonate Critters Calcium carbonate is an important compound for many different animals. Many mollusks remove calcium and carbonate from sea water and combine them in special tissues that then harden to form a calcium carbonate shell. When the mollusk dies, its shell either dissolves back into the water or becomes part of the sediment on the bottom of the ocean. If the shell is part of deposited sediment, it may become a fossil. Have students research a fossil locality in their state (for example, the Mazon Creek deposits, in Illinois) to learn more about fossils. **LS** Logical

Section 3 • Sedimentary Rock

Close

Reteaching — BASIC

Creating a Diagram Have students select one of the three types of sedimentary rock. Ask students to create a diagram that illustrates all of the processes that occur in the formation of the rock type they have selected. **LS** Visual

Quiz — GENERAL

1. How does halite form? (It forms when sodium ions and chlorine ions become so concentrated in ocean water that halite crystallizes out of the water.)
2. What is stratification, and why is it important to Earth scientists? (Stratification is the layering of rock. It is important because it records many events in Earth's history, as well as erosion and deposition rates.)

Alternative Assessment — GENERAL

Depositional Environments To review sedimentary rock formation, have students draw a picture of an environment that shows where the sediments come from and where they are deposited. A second drawing should show what the environment might look like millions of years later after sedimentary rock has formed. **LS** Visual

Organic Sedimentary Rock

Most limestone forms from the remains, or *fossils*, of animals that once lived in the ocean. For example, some limestone is made of the skeletons of tiny organisms called *coral*. Coral are very small, but they live in huge colonies called *reefs*, shown in **Figure 3**. Over time, the skeletons of these sea animals, which are made of calcium carbonate, collect on the ocean floor. These animal remains eventually become cemented together to form *fossiliferous limestone* (FAH suhl IF uhr uhs LIEM STOHN).

Corals are not the only animals whose remains are found in fossiliferous limestone. The shells of mollusks, such as clams and oysters, commonly form fossiliferous limestone. An example of fossiliferous limestone that contains mollusks is shown in **Figure 4**.

Another type of organic sedimentary rock is *coal*. Coal forms underground when partially decomposed plant material is buried beneath sediment and is changed into coal by increasing heat and pressure. This process occurs over millions of years.

Figure 3 *Ocean animals called* coral *create huge deposits of limestone. As they die, their skeletons collect on the ocean floor.*

Figure 4 The Formation of Organic Sedimentary Rock

Marine organisms, such as brachiopods, get the calcium carbonate for their shells from ocean water. When these organisms die, their shells collect on the ocean floor and eventually form fossiliferous limestone (inset). Over time, huge rock formations that contain the remains of large numbers of organisms, such as brachiopods, form.

CONNECTION ACTIVITY Real World — GENERAL

Uses of Organic Sedimentary Rock Chalk is a sedimentary rock formed from the shells of tiny marine creatures, including diatoms. The shells of diatoms contain silica, which can be used as an abrasive to clean teeth. Have students divide into groups and research other uses of organic sedimentary rock. Have each group prepare a class presentation in which they discuss the benefits and ingredients of a product made from sedimentary rock. **LS** Logical

Is That a Fact!

The Great Barrier Reef, a long coral reef that lies off the northeastern coast of Australia, is the most massive structure ever built by living creatures. It is more than 2,000 km long and covers an area of 207,000 km².

104 Chapter 4 • Rocks: Mineral Mixtures

Sedimentary Rock Structures

Many features can tell you about the way sedimentary rock formed. The most important feature of sedimentary rock is stratification. **Stratification** is the process in which sedimentary rocks are arranged in layers. Strata differ from one another depending on the kind, size, and color of their sediment.

Sedimentary rocks sometimes record the motion of wind and water waves on lakes, oceans, rivers, and sand dunes in features called *ripple marks*, as shown in **Figure 5**. Structures called *mud cracks* form when fine-grained sediments at the bottom of a shallow body of water are exposed to the air and dry out. Mud cracks indicate the location of an ancient lake, stream, or ocean shoreline. Even raindrop impressions can be preserved in fine-grained sediments, as small pits with raised rims.

✓ **Reading Check** What are ripple marks?

Figure 5 *These ripple marks were made by flowing water and were preserved when the sediments became sedimentary rock. Ripple marks can also form from the action of wind.*

stratification the process in which sedimentary rocks are arranged in layers

SECTION Review

Summary

- Sedimentary rock forms at or near the Earth's surface.
- Clastic sedimentary rock forms when rock or mineral fragments are cemented together.
- Chemical sedimentary rock forms from solutions of dissolved minerals and water.
- Organic limestone forms from the remains of plants and animals.
- Sedimentary structures include ripple marks, mud cracks, and raindrop impressions.

Using Key Terms

1. In your own words, write a definition for each of the following terms: *strata* and *stratification*.

Understanding Key Ideas

2. Which of the following is an organic sedimentary rock?
   a. chemical limestone
   b. shale
   c. fossiliferous limestone
   d. conglomerate

3. Explain the process by which clastic sedimentary rock forms.

4. Describe the three main categories of sedimentary rock.

Math Skills

5. A layer of a sedimentary rock is 2 m thick. How many years did it take for this layer to form if an average of 4 mm of sediment accumulated per year?

Critical Thinking

6. **Identifying Relationships** Rocks are classified based on texture and composition. Which of these two properties would be more important for classifying clastic sedimentary rock?

7. **Analyzing Processes** Why do you think raindrop impressions are more likely to be preserved in fine-grained sedimentary rock rather than in coarse-grained sedimentary rock?

SciLinks
Topic: Sedimentary Rock
SciLinks code: HSM1365

Answer to Reading Check

Ripple marks are the marks left by wind and water waves on lakes, seas, rivers, and sand dunes.

CHAPTER RESOURCES

Chapter Resource File
- Section Quiz GENERAL
- Section Review GENERAL
- Vocabulary and Section Summary GENERAL

Answers to Section Review

1. Sample answer: Strata are layers in sedimentary rock. Stratification is the process in which layers are arranged into sedimentary rock.

2. c

3. Clastic sedimentary rock is formed by the processes of weathering, erosion, deposition, compaction, and cementation. Rocks are physically weathered into fragments called sediment. Sediment is transported by erosion and is deposited in layers. Older layers of sediments are compacted by younger layers of sediments. Sediments in layers that have been compacted are cemented together by minerals that are dissolved in water, such as calcite and quartz, forming clastic sedimentary rock.

4. Clastic sedimentary rock forms when sediments are compacted and cemented together. Chemical sedimentary rock forms when dissolved minerals separate out of solution and crystallize. Organic sedimentary rock is made from the remains of animals that once lived in the ocean.

5. 2 m = 2,000 mm;
   2,000 mm ÷ 4 mm/year = 500 years

6. Texture is more useful in classifying clastic sedimentary rock because the size of the grain can provide clues to where and how the rock was formed.

7. Answers may vary. Sample answer: The finer the grains of sediment are, the more likely delicate structures such as raindrop impressions will be preserved in them.

Section 3 • Sedimentary Rock

SECTION 4

Focus

Overview
This section examines what happens when rock metamorphoses. Changes in heat or pressure can alter a rock's chemical nature and physical structure. Students will learn how different types of metamorphism cause changes in rock texture.

🔔 Bellringer
Ask students to write a brief description of how cookies are made. Ask them to consider how the mixture of raw ingredients is like sedimentary rock. Ask them to describe how cookie dough metamorphoses when it is baked in an oven.

Motivate

ACTIVITY — GENERAL

Modeling Metamorphism
Provide each student with pieces of red, yellow, green, and purple modeling clay. Have students flatten each piece, pile the pieces on top of each other, and press down on them firmly. Then, have students push inward on opposite sides of the stack or pull the stack gently so that the clay doesn't break apart. Explain that they will be learning how intense pressure and heat can cause rock to behave in similar ways. **LS** Visual/Kinesthetic

---

SECTION 4

READING WARM-UP

Objectives
- Describe two ways a rock can undergo metamorphism.
- Explain how the mineral composition of rocks changes as the rocks undergo metamorphism.
- Describe the difference between foliated and nonfoliated metamorphic rock.
- Explain how metamorphic rock structures are related to deformation.

Terms to Learn
foliated
nonfoliated

READING STRATEGY

Discussion Read this section silently. Write down questions that you have about this section. Discuss your questions in a small group.

CHAPTER RESOURCES

Chapter Resource File
- Lesson Plan
- Directed Reading A BASIC
- Directed Reading B SPECIAL NEEDS

Technology
- Transparencies
  - Bellringer
  - Regional and Contact Metamorphism

Metamorphic Rock

Have you ever watched a caterpillar change into a butterfly? Some caterpillars go through a biological process called metamorphosis in which they completely change their shape.

Rocks can also go through a process called *metamorphism*. The word *metamorphism* comes from the Greek words *meta*, which means "changed," and *morphos*, which means "shape." Metamorphic rocks are rocks in which the structure, texture, or composition of the rock have changed. All three types of rock can be changed by heat, pressure, or a combination of both.

Origins of Metamorphic Rock

The texture or mineral composition of a rock can change when its surroundings change. If the temperature or pressure of the new environment is different from the one in which the rock formed, the rock will undergo metamorphism.

The temperature at which most metamorphism occurs ranges from 50°C to 1,000°C. However, the metamorphism of some rocks takes place at temperatures above 1,000°C. It seems that at these temperatures the rock would melt, but this is not true of metamorphic rock. It is the depth and pressure at which metamorphic rocks form that allows the rock to heat to this temperature and maintain its solid nature. Most metamorphic change takes place at depths greater than 2 km. But at depths greater than 16 km, the pressure can be 4,000 times greater than the pressure of the atmosphere at Earth's surface.

Large movements within the crust of the Earth cause additional pressure to be exerted on a rock during metamorphism. This pressure can cause the mineral grains in rock to align themselves in certain directions. The alignment of mineral grains into parallel bands is shown in the metamorphic rock in **Figure 1**.

Figure 1 This metamorphic rock is an example of how mineral grains were aligned into distinct bands when the rock underwent metamorphism.

WEIRD SCIENCE

When rocks metamorphose under high temperature and pressure, they become plastic and can be easily deformed. It is not unusual for spherical pebbles in a conglomerate to be stretched into ellipses more than 30 times their original diameter!

---

106 Chapter 4 • Rocks: Mineral Mixtures

Figure 2 Metamorphism occurs over small areas, such as next to bodies of magma, and over large areas, such as mountain ranges.

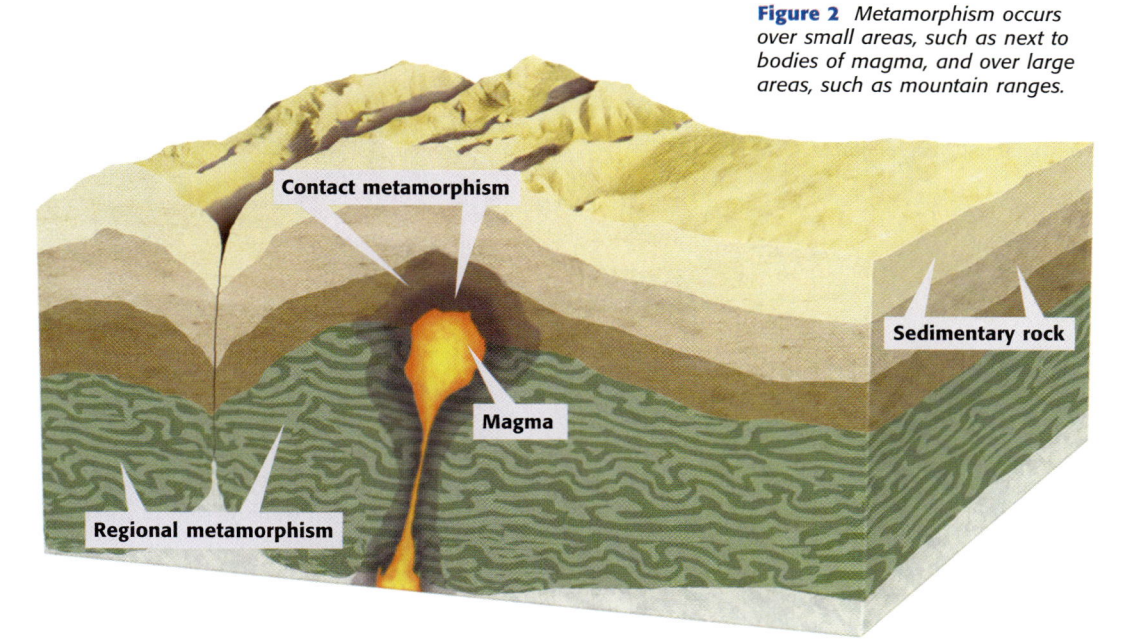

Contact Metamorphism

One way rock can undergo metamorphism is by being heated by nearby magma. When magma moves through the crust, the magma heats the surrounding rock and changes it. Some minerals in the surrounding rock are changed into other minerals by this increase in temperature. The greatest change takes place where magma comes into direct contact with the surrounding rock. The effect of heat on rock gradually decreases as the rock's distance from the magma increases and as temperature decreases. *Contact metamorphism* occurs near igneous intrusions, as shown in **Figure 2**.

Regional Metamorphism

When pressure builds up in rock that is buried deep below other rock formations or when large pieces of the Earth's crust collide with each other, *regional metamorphism* occurs. The increased pressure and temperature causes rock to become deformed and chemically changed. Unlike contact metamorphism, which happens near bodies of magma, regional metamorphism occurs over thousands of cubic kilometers deep within Earth's crust. Rocks that have undergone regional metamorphism are found beneath most continental rock formations.

Reading Check Explain how and where regional metamorphism takes place. *(See the Appendix for answers to Reading Checks.)*

Quick Lab

Stretching Out

1. Sketch the crystals in granite rock on a **piece of paper** with a **black-ink pen.** Be sure to include the outline of the rock, and fill it in with different crystal shapes.
2. Flatten some **plastic play putty** over your drawing, and slowly peel it off.
3. After making sure that the outline of your granite has been transferred to the putty, squeeze and stretch the putty. What happened to the crystals in the granite? What happened to the granite?

Answer to Reading Check

Regional metamorphism occurs when pressure builds up in rock that is buried deep below other rock formations or when large pieces of the Earth's crust collide. The increased pressure can cause thousands of square miles of rock to become deformed and chemically changed.

Is That a Fact!

The largest expanse of exposed metamorphic rock in the world is the Canadian Shield, a huge horseshoe-shaped region encircling Hudson Bay. Covering about half of Canada, it is about 4,586,900 km² and is the source of more than 70% of the minerals mined in Canada.

Teach

Using the Figure — BASIC

Analogies Ask students to think of some analogies for contact metamorphism (for example, an egg frying in a skillet). Have students draw a diagram of the process of contact metamorphism. Have the class think of some analogies for regional metamorphism (for example, making toast). Then, have students draw a diagram of the process of regional metamorphism. **LS Logical/Visual**

Quick Lab

MATERIALS

FOR EACH STUDENT
- black ink pen
- paper
- plastic play putty

Answer

3. The "crystals" become stretched and deformed. The "granite" changes its shape because of the force applied to it.

MISCONCEPTION ALERT

Metamorphism As you discuss **Figure 2**, be sure students understand that the composition of a metamorphic rock and the heat and pressure it is subjected to determine how much it deforms. Students should understand that the bulk composition of rock does not change during metamorphism unless fluids are introduced into the rock. However, the mineral composition of the rock may change as heat and pressure change.

Section 4 • Metamorphic Rock **107**

Teach, continued

Research — GENERAL

Metamorphic Minerals Several types of minerals found in metamorphic rock, such as garnet, tourmaline, and serpentine, are used in sculpture and in jewelry making. Encourage students to choose one of these minerals, research it, and create a poster illustrating how it forms and what its uses are. **LS Visual**

MISCONCEPTION ALERT

Heat and Temperature Heat and temperature are not the same thing. Heat is the transfer of thermal energy from one object to another. Temperature is a measure of how hot (or cold) something is. Temperature is not a form of energy. When a rock comes into contact with magma, thermal energy is transferred from the magma to the rock because the magma is at a higher temperature than the rock. As a result, the temperature of the rock increases while the temperature of the magma decreases. But heating a rock does not always raise its temperature. If the rock is already so hot that it is on the verge of melting, additional heat will cause the rock to melt (and change state), but will not change the rock's temperature.

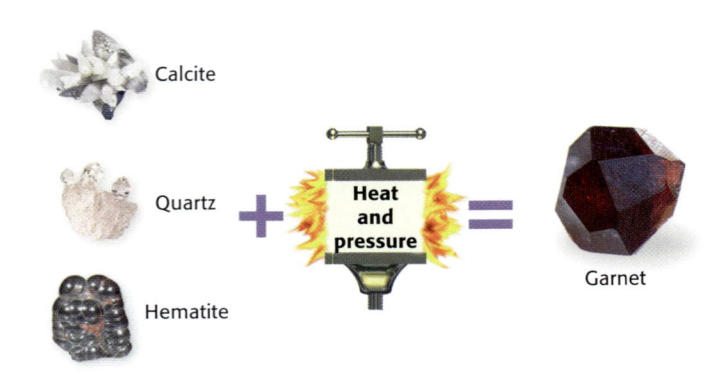

Figure 3 The minerals calcite, quartz, and hematite combine and recrystallize to form the metamorphic mineral garnet.

Calcite + Quartz + Hematite + Heat and pressure = Garnet

SCHOOL to HOME

Making a Rock Collection With a parent, try to collect a sample of each class of rock described in this chapter. You may wish to collect rocks from road cuts or simply collect pebbles from your garden or driveway. Try to collect samples that show the composition and texture of each rock. Classify the rocks in your collection, and bring it to class. With other members of the class, discuss your rock samples and see if they are accurately identified.

ACTIVITY

Composition of Metamorphic Rock

Metamorphism occurs when temperature and pressure inside the Earth's crust change. Minerals that were present in the rock when it formed may not be stable in the new temperature and pressure conditions. The original minerals change into minerals that are more stable in these new conditions. Look at **Figure 3** to see an example of how this change happens.

Many of these new minerals form only in metamorphic rock. As shown in **Figure 4**, some metamorphic minerals form only at certain temperatures and pressures. These minerals, known as *index minerals,* are used to estimate the temperature, depth, and pressure at which a rock undergoes metamorphism. Index minerals include biotite mica, chlorite, garnet, kyanite, muscovite mica, sillimanite, and staurolite.

✓ Reading Check What is an index mineral?

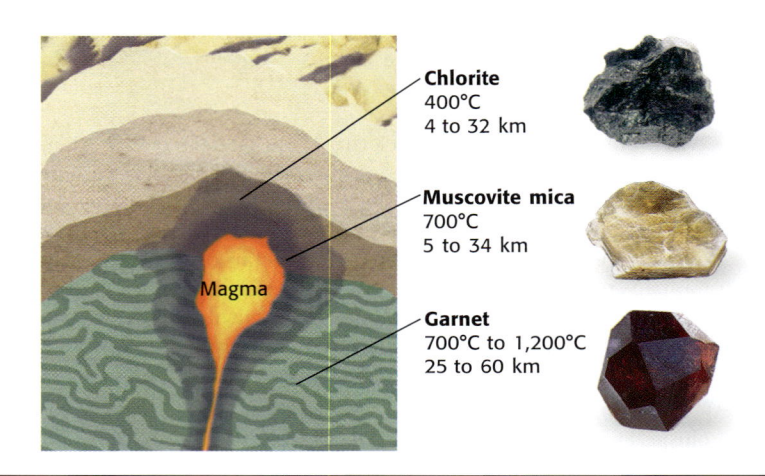

Figure 4 Scientists can understand a metamorphic rock's history by observing the minerals the rock contains. For example, a metamorphic rock that contains garnet formed at a greater depth and under greater heat and pressure than a rock that contains only chlorite.

Chlorite 400°C, 4 to 32 km
Muscovite mica 700°C, 5 to 34 km
Garnet 700°C to 1,200°C, 25 to 60 km

Magma

Answer to Reading Check

An index mineral is a metamorphic mineral that forms only at certain temperatures and pressures and therefore can be used by scientists to estimate the temperature, pressure, and depth at which a rock undergoes metamorphosis.

Homework — GENERAL

Making Models Have students make a model cross section of the Earth's crust. The model should include materials that represent magma, contact and regional metamorphic rocks, and sedimentary strata. **English Language Learners**
LS Kinesthetic/Visual

---

108 Chapter 4 • Rocks: Mineral Mixtures

Textures of Metamorphic Rock

You have learned that texture helps scientists classify igneous and sedimentary rock. The same is true of metamorphic rock. All metamorphic rock has one of two textures—foliated or nonfoliated. Take a closer look at each of these types of metamorphic rock to find out how each type forms.

Foliated Metamorphic Rock

The texture of metamorphic rock in which the mineral grains are arranged in planes or bands is called **foliated**. Foliated metamorphic rock usually contains aligned grains of flat minerals, such as biotite mica or chlorite. Look at **Figure 5**. Shale is a sedimentary rock made of layers of clay minerals. When shale is exposed to slight heat and pressure, the clay minerals change into mica minerals. The shale becomes a foliated metamorphic rock called *slate*.

Metamorphic rocks can become other metamorphic rocks if the environment changes again. If slate is exposed to more heat and pressure, the slate can change into rock called *phyllite*. When phyllite is exposed to heat and pressure, it can change into *schist*.

If metamorphism continues, the arrangement of minerals in the rock changes. More heat and pressure cause minerals to separate into distinct bands in a metamorphic rock called *gneiss* (NIES).

foliated the texture of metamorphic rock in which the mineral grains are arranged in planes or bands

Figure 5 The effects of metamorphism depend on the heat and pressure applied to the rock. Here you can see what happens to shale, a sedimentary rock, when it is exposed to more and more heat and pressure.

Sedimentary shale → Slate → Phyllite → Schist → Gneiss

Discussion — BASIC

Predicting Patterns Display metamorphic rocks in groups of foliated rocks (slate, phyllite, schist, and gneiss) and nonfoliated rocks (quartzite, marble, hornfels, and soapstone). Have students compare the rocks according to color, appearance, and composition. Explain that the temperature and pressure of regional metamorphism tend to produce foliated rocks, whereas the temperature of contact metamorphism tends to produce nonfoliated rocks. Ask students to predict what the terms *foliated* and *nonfoliated* mean and then read further to see if they were correct. **LS** Visual/Logical

CONNECTION ACTIVITY Real World — ADVANCED

Asbestos Removal Asbestos is an informal name for a group of fibrous minerals usually found in regionally metamorphosed rock. Manufacturers value these minerals because minerals resist burning and don't readily conduct thermal energy or electric current. However, some kinds of asbestos fracture into tiny needles that can become airborne. This dust is linked to a lung disease called *asbestosis*. As a result, asbestos has been removed from many public places at great expense. Have students find out about the many uses for asbestos and any cleanup projects that are occurring in your area. Have students summarize their findings in the form of a poster.
LS Logical

INCLUSION Strategies

- Behavior Control
- Attention Deficit Disorder
- Gifted and Talented

Have students conduct a scavenger hunt in their classroom to identify minerals that are used to make items that we use every day. Organize students into groups of 3 to 4 students. Assign each group an area of the classroom, and provide each group with self-stick labels to mark items made out of minerals. Each group should try to label the mineral(s) that make up each item. Items made of minerals that students may identify include light bulbs, electrical wiring, door knobs, locks, hinges, windows, plumbing fixtures, and pencils. Ask students what additional items made of minerals may be found in their homes. Talented and gifted students can do additional research on minerals used to make a light bulb and/or a computer. **LS** Visual/Logical **English Language Learners**

Section 4 • Metamorphic Rock 109

Close

Reteaching — BASIC

Creating an Outline Have students select a type of foliated or nonfoliated metamorphic rock. Ask students to create an outline of the steps that occur in the formation of the rock. Some students may want to write their outline in the form of a recipe for making a metamorphic rock. **LS Logical**

Quiz — GENERAL

1. Why is marble considered a nonfoliated metamorphic rock? (Its mineral grains are not arranged in planes or bands.)
2. What does the composition of a metamorphic rock tell you about the rock's origin and formation? (Different metamorphic minerals indicate the temperature and pressure conditions that existed when the rock formed.)

Alternative Assessment — GENERAL

Preparing a Lesson Have students prepare a lesson about this chapter to present to a second-grade class. They will need to prepare vocabulary lists, illustrations, and worksheets to help the younger students understand the types of rock, the uses of rock, and the way rocks form. **LS Logical/Visual**

CONNECTION TO Biology

WRITING SKILL **Metamorphosis** The term *metamorphosis* means "change in form." When some animals undergo a dramatic change in the shape of their body, they are said to have undergone a metamorphosis. As part of their natural life cycle, moths and butterflies go through four stages. After they hatch from an egg, they are in the larval stage in the form of a caterpillar. In the next stage, they build a cocoon or become a chrysalis. This stage is called the *pupal stage*. They finally emerge into the adult stage of their life, in which they have wings, antennae, and legs! Research other animals that undergo a metamorphosis, and summarize your findings in a short essay.

nonfoliated the texture of metamorphic rock in which the mineral grains are not arranged in planes or bands

---

Nonfoliated Metamorphic Rock

The texture of metamorphic rock in which the mineral grains are not arranged in planes or bands is called **nonfoliated**. Notice that the rocks shown in **Figure 6** do not have mineral grains that are aligned. This lack of aligned mineral grains is the reason these rocks are called *nonfoliated rocks*.

Nonfoliated rocks are commonly made of one or only a few minerals. During metamorphism, the crystals of these minerals may change in size or the mineral may change in composition in a process called *recrystallization*. The quartzite and marble shown in **Figure 6** are examples of sedimentary rocks that have recrystallized during metamorphism.

Quartz sandstone is a sedimentary rock made of quartz sand grains that have been cemented together. When quartz sandstone is exposed to the heat and pressure, the spaces between the sand grains disappear as the grains recrystallize to form quartzite. Quartzite has a shiny, glittery appearance. Like quartz sandstone, it is made of quartz. But during recrystallization, the mineral grains have grown larger than the original grains in the sandstone.

When limestone undergoes metamorphism, the same process that happened to the quartz happens to the calcite, and the limestone becomes marble. The calcite crystals in the marble are larger than the calcite grains in the original limestone.

Figure 6 *Two Examples of Nonfoliated Metamorphic Rock*

Marble and quartzite are nonfoliated metamorphic rocks. As you can see in the views through a microscope, the mineral crystals are not well aligned.

Marble

Quartzite

Homework — ADVANCED

Investigate Your Area Have students look at stone buildings and houses around their town. Ask students to identify the rock used in construction as igneous, sedimentary, or metamorphic. Ask students to consider the following questions: Which rock type was most commonly used? Which rock type was used least? Why was a specific rock type used for a particular application? Encourage students to find out the origin of rock used in buildings in your community. **LS Visual**

Metamorphic Rock Structures

Like igneous and sedimentary rock, metamorphic rock also has features that tell you about its history. In metamorphic rocks, these features are caused by deformation. *Deformation* is a change in the shape of a rock caused by a force placed on it. These forces may cause a rock to be squeezed or stretched.

Folds, or bends, in metamorphic rock are structures that indicate that a rock has been deformed. Some folds are not visible to the naked eye. But, as shown in **Figure 7**, some folds may be kilometers or even hundreds of kilometers in size.

Reading Check How are metamorphic rock structures related to deformation?

Figure 7 These large folds occur in metamorphosed sedimentary rock along Saglet Fiord in Labrador, Canada.

SECTION Review

Summary

- Metamorphic rocks are rocks in which the structure, texture, or composition has changed.
- Two ways rocks can undergo metamorphism are by contact metamorphism and regional metamorphism.
- As rocks undergo metamorphism, the original minerals in a rock change into new minerals that are more stable in new pressure and temperature conditions.
- Foliated metamorphic rock has mineral crystals aligned in planes or bands, whereas nonfoliated rocks have unaligned mineral crystals.
- Metamorphic rock structures are caused by deformation.

Using Key Terms

1. In your own words, define the following terms: *foliated* and *nonfoliated*.

Understanding Key Ideas

2. Which of the following is not a type of foliated metamorphic rock?
   a. gneiss
   b. slate
   c. marble
   d. schist

3. Explain the difference between contact metamorphism and regional metamorphism.

4. Explain how index minerals allow a scientist to understand the history of a metamorphic rock.

Math Skills

5. For every 3.3 km a rock is buried, the pressure placed upon it increases 0.1 gigapascal (100 million pascals). If rock undergoing metamorphosis is buried at 16 km, what is the pressure placed on that rock? (Hint: The pressure at Earth's surface is .101 gigapascal.)

Critical Thinking

6. **Making Inferences** If you had two metamorphic rocks, one that has garnet crystals and the other that has chlorite crystals, which one could have formed at a deeper level in the Earth's crust? Explain your answer.

7. **Applying Concepts** Which do you think would be easier to break, a foliated rock, such as slate, or a nonfoliated rock, such as quartzite? Explain.

8. **Analyzing Processes** A mountain range is located at a boundary where two tectonic plates are colliding. Would most of the metamorphic rock in the mountain range be a product of contact metamorphism or regional metamorphism? Explain.

SCLINKS
Developed and maintained by the National Science Teachers Association

For a variety of links related to this chapter, go to www.scilinks.org
Topic: Metamorphic Rock
SciLinks code: HSM0949

Answer to Reading Check
Deformation causes metamorphic structures such as folds.

CHAPTER RESOURCES

Chapter Resource File
- Section Quiz GENERAL
- Section Review GENERAL
- Vocabulary and Section Summary GENERAL
- Reinforcement Worksheet BASIC
- Critical Thinking ADVANCED

Technology
- Interactive Explorations CD-ROM
  - "Rock On!" GENERAL

Answers to Section Review

1. Sample answer: Foliated metamorphic rock consists of minerals that are arranged in planes or bands. The minerals in nonfoliated metamorphic rock do not appear to be arranged in a pattern.

2. c

3. Contact metamorphism is a type of metamorphism that occurs near igneous intrusions, where magma comes into direct contact with surrounding rock. Regional metamorphism is a type of metamorphism that occurs when large pieces of Earth's crust collide, causing rock to become deformed and chemically changed over large areas.

4. Because index minerals form only at certain temperatures and pressures, index minerals indicate the temperature, pressure, and depth at which a rock metamorphosed.

5. 16 km ÷ 3.3 km = 4.84 km × 0.1 gigapascal = 0.484 gigapascal + .101 gigapascal (atmospheric pressure) = .585 gigapascal

6. The rock with garnet crystals would probably have formed deeper in the Earth because the mineral garnet forms at a higher temperature and higher pressure than the mineral chlorite.

7. Because the grains in a foliated metamorphic rock are arranged in parallel bands, foliated metamorphic rock would be easier to break than a nonfoliated metamorphic rock.

8. Rock becomes deformed and chemically changed over large areas of Earth's crust by increases in temperature and pressure that occur when tectonic plates collide. Therefore, most of the rock in the mountain range would be the product of regional metamorphism.

Section 4 • Metamorphic Rock

Skills Practice Lab

Let's Get Sedimental

Teacher's Notes

Time Required
Two 45-minute class periods

Lab Ratings
EASY —————→ HARD

Teacher Prep – 1
Student Set-Up – 2
Concept Level – 2
Clean Up – 2

MATERIALS
The materials listed are enough for a group of three or four students. You may substitute smaller plastic bottles. The amount of sand, gravel, and soil depends on the size of the jar. Each group will need enough of these materials to fill the bottle two-thirds full with a mixture of sand, gravel, and soil.

Safety Caution
Students should be extremely careful when cutting the sides from the plastic bottles.

Preparation Notes
If the students use larger plastic bottles, the sediment may take several days to dry completely. It may be a good idea to ask the students to follow steps 1–5 as an introduction to the chapter. The class can then finish the procedure when the sediment has dried.

Skills Practice Lab

OBJECTIVES
Model the process of sedimentation.

Determine whether sedimentary rock layers are undisturbed.

MATERIALS
- clay
- dropper pipet
- gravel
- magnifying lens
- mixing bowl, 2 qt
- sand
- scissors
- soda bottle with a cap, plastic, 2 L
- soil, clay rich, if available
- water

SAFETY

Let's Get Sedimental

How do we determine if sedimentary rock layers are undisturbed? The best way to do this is to be sure that fine-grained sediments near the top of a layer lie above coarse-grained sediments near the bottom of the layer. This lab activity will show you how to read rock features that will help you distinguish individual sedimentary rock layers. Then, you can look for the features in real rock layers.

Procedure

1. In a mixing bowl, thoroughly mix the sand, gravel, and soil. Fill the soda bottle about one-third full of the mixture.

2. Add water to the soda bottle until the bottle is two-thirds full. Twist the cap back onto the bottle, and shake the bottle vigorously until all of the sediment is mixed in the rapidly moving water.

3. Place the bottle on a tabletop. Using the scissors, carefully cut the top off the bottle a few centimeters above the water, as shown. The open bottle will allow water to evaporate.

4. Immediately after you set the bottle on the tabletop, describe what you see from above and through the sides of the bottle.

5. Do not disturb the container. Allow the water to evaporate. (You may speed up the process by carefully using the dropper pipet to siphon off some of the clear water after you allow the container to sit for at least 24 hours.) You may also set the bottle in the sun or under a desk lamp to speed up evaporation.

6. After the sediment has dried and hardened, describe its surface.

7. Carefully lay the container on its side, and cut a wide, vertical strip of plastic down the length of the bottle to expose the sediments in the container. You may find it easier if you place pieces of clay on either side of the container to stabilize it. (If the bottle is clear along its length, this step may not be required.)

8. Brush away the loose material from the sediment, and gently blow on the surface until it is clean. Examine the surface, and record your observations.

Lab Notes
This lab illustrates the sedimentary (depositional) process of sorting. When sediment is suspended in water, the largest, heaviest particles will settle out first, followed by the finer, lighter particles. This process can allow scientists and students studying sedimentary rock layers to determine the original orientation of the rock.

CHAPTER RESOURCES

Chapter Resource File
- Datasheet for Chapter Lab
- Lab Notes and Answers

Technology

Classroom Videos
- Lab Video

LabBook
- Crystal Growth
- Metamorphic Mash

Analyze the Results

1. **Identifying Patterns** Do you see anything through the side of the bottle that could help you determine if a sedimentary rock is undisturbed? Explain your answer.

2. **Identifying Patterns** Can you observe a pattern of deposition? If so, describe the pattern of deposition of sediment that you observe from top to bottom.

3. **Explaining Events** Explain how these features might be used to identify the top of a sedimentary layer in real rock and to decide if the layer has been disturbed.

4. **Identifying Patterns** Do you see any structures through the side of the bottle that might indicate which direction is up, such as a change in particle density or size?

5. **Identifying Patterns** Use the magnifying lens to examine the boundaries between the gravel, sand, and silt. Do the size of the particles and the type of sediment change dramatically in each layer?

Draw Conclusions

6. **Making Predictions** Imagine that a layer was deposited directly above the sediment in your bottle. Describe the composition of this new layer. Will it have the same composition as the mixture in steps 1–5 in the Procedure?

Applying Your Data

With your class or with a parent, visit an outcrop of sedimentary rock. Apply the information that you have learned in this lab to see if you can determine whether the sedimentary rock layers are disturbed or undisturbed.

Analyze the Results

1. Answers may vary. Students should understand that the finest sediments should be at the top. This sequence can indicate the top of a layer in a sedimentary outcrop. If the layers are not in this order, the rock may have been disturbed.

2. Students should indicate that in the sorting process, gravel settled out first, followed by sand, and then soil.

3. If features that geologists expect to find only in the top layer are found elsewhere, this finding indicates that the column has been disturbed. Geologists carefully study the layers for these features so that they can determine the original order of the layers.

4. Each layer should show finer particles at the top. This pattern can be seen only from the side.

5. Students should see the same grading effect at the boundaries. The changes within each layer will be gradual, but the changes between layers may be more dramatic.

Draw Conclusions

6. If sediment having the same particle sizes as the mixture in steps 1-5 is deposited on top of the sediment in the bottle, the new layer should have the same composition as the layer in the bottle.

CHAPTER RESOURCES

Workbooks

- **Whiz-Bang Demonstrations**
  • Settling Down BASIC
- **Labs You Can Eat**
  • Famous Rock Groups GENERAL
- **Long-Term Projects & Research Ideas**
  • Home-Grown Crystals ADVANCED
- **Calculator-Based Labs**
  • A Hot and Cool Lab ADVANCED

CLASSROOM TESTED & APPROVED

Helen Schiller
Northwood Middle School
Taylors, South Carolina

Chapter Review

Assignment Guide

Section	Questions
1	1, 2, 10, 12, 15–16, 21–25
2	5, 7, 8, 11, 19
3	4, 6
4	3, 9, 13–14, 18, 20
2, 3, and 4	17

ANSWERS

Using Key Terms

1. Sample answer: The rock cycle is the process in which one rock type changes into another rock type. In this process, rock is continuously recycled.
2. texture
3. Foliated
4. stratification
5. Extrusive igneous rock

Understanding Key Ideas

6. c
7. d
8. c
9. b
10. b
11. d
12. Scientists use differences in composition, or the minerals a rock is made up of, to classify rock. Scientists use differences in texture—the sizes, shapes, and positions of the grains a rock is made up of—to further classify rocks.

13. Two ways in which a rock can undergo metamorphism is by contact metamorphism and regional metamorphism. Contact metamorphism occurs near igneous intrusions, where magma comes in direct contact with the surrounding rock. Regional metamorphism occurs when pressure builds up in deep rock or when large pieces of Earth's crust collide, deforming and chemically changing rock over large areas.

14. Some minerals can form only at specific pressures and temperatures present during metamorphism.

15. Sample answer: When rocks are buried, they are heated and squeezed to create metamorphic rock. Sometimes, the heat is enough to melt the rock and create magma, which cools to form igneous rock. Buried rocks are uplifted, and when rocks at the Earth's surface are eroded, sediments are created. These sediments are buried and later harden into sedimentary rock.

Chapter Review

USING KEY TERMS

1 In your own words, write a definition for the term *rock cycle*.

Complete each of the following sentences by choosing the correct term from the word bank.

stratification   foliated
extrusive igneous rock   texture

2 The ___ of a rock is determined by the sizes, shapes, and positions of the minerals the rock contains.

3 ___ metamorphic rock contains minerals that are arranged in plates or bands.

4 The most characteristic property of sedimentary rock is ___.

5 ___ forms plains called *lava plateaus*.

UNDERSTANDING KEY IDEAS

Multiple Choice

6 Sedimentary rock is classified into all of the following main categories except
a. clastic sedimentary rock.
b. chemical sedimentary rock.
c. nonfoliated sedimentary rock.
d. organic sedimentary rock.

7 An igneous rock that cools very slowly has a ___ texture.
a. foliated
b. fine-grained
c. nonfoliated
d. coarse-grained

8 Igneous rock forms when
a. minerals crystallize from a solution.
b. sand grains are cemented together.
c. magma cools and solidifies.
d. mineral grains in a rock recrystallize.

9 A ___ is a common structure found in metamorphic rock.
a. ripple mark   c. sill
b. fold   d. layer

10 The process in which sediment is removed from its source and transported is called
a. deposition.   c. weathering.
b. erosion.   d. uplift.

11 Mafic rocks are
a. light-colored rocks rich in calcium, iron, and magnesium.
b. dark-colored rocks rich in aluminum, potassium, silica, and sodium.
c. light-colored rocks rich in aluminum, potassium, silica, and sodium.
d. dark-colored rocks rich in calcium, iron, and magnesium.

Short Answer

12 Explain how composition and texture are used by scientists to classify rocks.

13 Describe two ways a rock can undergo metamorphism.

14 Explain why some minerals only occur in metamorphic rocks.

15 Describe how each type of rock changes as it moves through the rock cycle.

Chapter 4 • Rocks: Mineral Mixtures

16 Describe two ways rocks were used by early humans and ancient civilizations.

CRITICAL THINKING

17 **Concept Mapping** Use the following terms to construct a concept map: *rocks, metamorphic, sedimentary, igneous, foliated, nonfoliated, organic, clastic, chemical, intrusive,* and *extrusive*.

18 **Making Inferences** If you were looking for fossils in the rocks around your home and the rock type that was closest to your home was metamorphic, do you think that you would find many fossils? Explain your answer.

19 **Applying Concepts** Imagine that you want to quarry, or mine, granite. You have all of the equipment, but you have two pieces of land to choose from. One area has a granite batholith underneath it. The other has a granite sill. If both intrusive bodies are at the same depth, which one would be the better choice for you to quarry? Explain your answer.

20 **Applying Concepts** The sedimentary rock coquina is made up of pieces of seashells. Which of the three kinds of sedimentary rock could coquina be? Explain your answer.

21 **Analyzing Processes** If a rock is buried deep inside the Earth, which geological processes cannot change the rock? Explain your answer.

INTERPRETING GRAPHICS

The bar graph below shows the percentage of minerals by mass that compose a sample of granite. Use the graph below to answer the questions that follow.

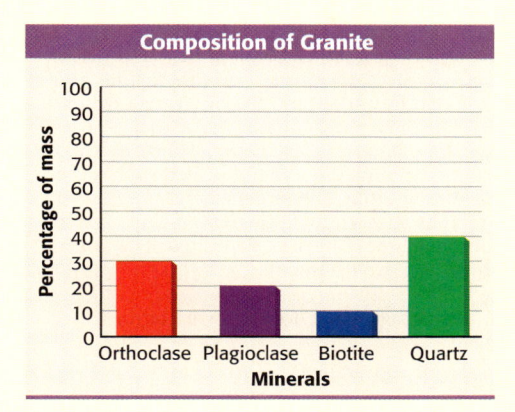

Composition of Granite

(Bar graph: Orthoclase ≈ 30%, Plagioclase ≈ 20%, Biotite ≈ 10%, Quartz ≈ 40%; y-axis: Percentage of mass 0–100; x-axis: Minerals)

22 Your rock sample is made of four minerals. What percentage of each mineral makes up your sample?

23 Both plagioclase and orthoclase are feldspar minerals. What percentage of the minerals in your sample of granite are not feldspar minerals?

24 If your rock sample has a mass of 10 g, how many grams of quartz does it contain?

25 Use paper, a compass, and a protractor or a computer to make a pie chart. Show the percentage of each of the four minerals your sample of granite contains. (Look in the Appendix of this book for help on making a pie chart.)

---

16. Two ways rocks were used by early humans and ancient civilizations were as tools and as building materials.

Critical Thinking

17. 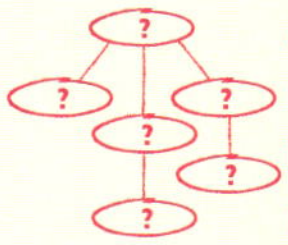 An answer to this exercise can be found at the end of this book.

18. You would not find many—or any—fossils where you live because fossils are usually found in sedimentary rock, not metamorphic rock. (Occasionally, fossils are preserved in metamorphic rock that was once sedimentary rock.)

19. The property with the batholith would be a better buy because batholiths are much bigger than sills.

20. The seashells that make up coquina are made up of the remains of once-living organisms, so coquina is an organic sedimentary rock. (The shells are technically clasts, because they are particles that have been deposited.)

21. A rock buried deep beneath the surface cannot be changed by weathering and erosion, which are geological processes that change Earth's surface features.

Interpreting Graphics

22. orthoclase = 30%, plagioclase = 20%, biotite = 10%, quartz = 40%

23. plagioclase + orthoclase = 30% + 20% = 50%
100% − 50% = 50%
Fifty percent of the minerals in the granite are not feldspars.

24. 10 g × 0.40 = 4 g

25. Accept all reasonable responses. Charts should show the correct percentages of the minerals.

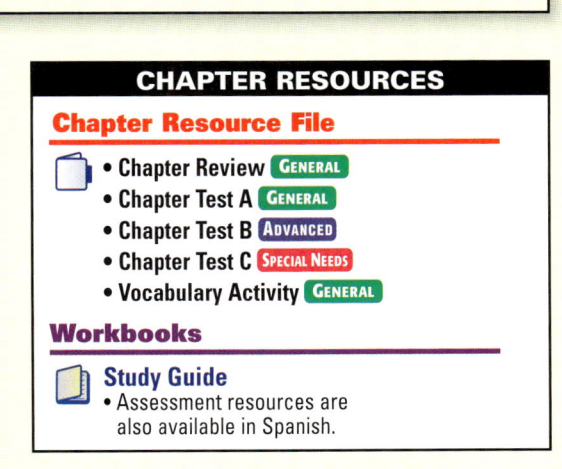

CHAPTER RESOURCES

Chapter Resource File
- Chapter Review GENERAL
- Chapter Test A GENERAL
- Chapter Test B ADVANCED
- Chapter Test C SPECIAL NEEDS
- Vocabulary Activity GENERAL

Workbooks

Study Guide
- Assessment resources are also available in Spanish.

Chapter 4 • Chapter Review

Standardized Test Preparation

Teacher's Note

To provide practice under more realistic testing conditions, give students 20 minutes to answer all of the questions in this Standardized Test Preparation.

MISCEPTION ALERT

Answers to the standardized test preparation can help you identify student misconceptions and misunderstandings.

READING

Passage 1
1. D
2. G
3. B

TEST DOCTOR

Question 3: The correct answer is B. Some students who have not read the passage carefully may choose answer D. Although this statement is correct, it is not the main idea of the passage, which is elucidated in the opening sentence.

Standardized Test Preparation

READING

Read each of the passages below. Then, answer the questions that follow each passage.

Passage 1 The texture and composition of a rock can provide good clues about how and where the rock formed. Scientists use both texture and composition to understand the origin and history of rocks. For example, marble is a rock that is made when limestone is metamorphosed. Only limestone contains the mineral—calcite—that can change into marble. Therefore, wherever scientists find marble, they know the sediment that created the original limestone was deposited in a warm ocean or lake environment.

1. In the passage, what does the word *origin* mean?
   A size or appearance
   B age
   C location or surroundings
   D source or formation

2. Based on the passage, what can the reader conclude?
   F Marble is a sedimentary rock.
   G Limestone is created by sediments deposited in warm ocean or lake environments.
   H Marble is a rock that is made when sandstone has undergone metamorphism.
   I In identifying a rock, the texture of a rock is more important than the composition of the rock.

3. What is the main idea of the passage?
   A Scientists believe marble is the most important rock type to study.
   B Scientists study the composition and texture of a rock to determine how the rock formed and what happened after it formed.
   C Some sediments are deposited in warm oceans and lakes.
   D When limestone undergoes metamorphism, it creates marble.

Passage 2 Fulgurites are a rare type of natural glass found in areas that have quartz-rich sediments, such as beaches and deserts. A tubular fulgurite forms when a lightning bolt strikes material such as sand and melts the quartz into a liquid. The liquid quartz cools and solidifies quickly, and a thin, glassy tube is left behind. Fulgurites usually have a rough outer surface and a smooth inner surface. Underground, a fulgurite may be shaped like the roots of a tree. The fulgurite branches out with many arms that trace the zigzag path of the lightning bolt. Some fulgurites are as short as your little finger, but others stretch 20 m into the ground.

1. In the passage, what does the word *tubular* mean?
   A flat and sharp
   B round and long
   C funnel shaped
   D pyramid shaped

2. From the information in the passage, what can the reader conclude?
   F Fulgurites are formed above ground.
   G Sand contains a large amount of quartz.
   H Fulgurites are most often very small.
   I Fulgurites are easy to find in sandy places.

3. Which of the following statements best describes a fulgurite?
   A Fulgurites are frozen lightning bolts.
   B Fulgurites are rootlike rocks.
   C Fulgurites are glassy tubes found in deserts.
   D Fulgurites are natural glass tubes formed by lightning bolts.

Passage 2
1. B
2. G
3. D

TEST DOCTOR

Question 2: The correct answer is G. Some students who have not read the passage carefully may choose answer F. Although lightning strikes the ground surface, the vast majority of a fulgurite is located underground, which gives little or no evidence of its existence.

Question 3: The correct answer is D. Some students may choose answer C. Although this answer may appear correct, it does not contain the necessary modifier *natural*, nor does it describe how fulgurites form.

116 Chapter 4 • Rocks: Mineral Mixtures

INTERPRETING GRAPHICS

Use the diagram below to answer the questions that follow.

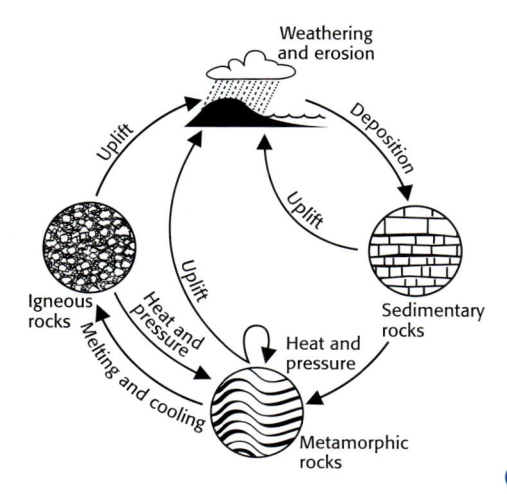

[Rock cycle diagram showing Weathering and erosion, Deposition, Uplift, Heat and pressure, Melting and cooling between Igneous rocks, Sedimentary rocks, and Metamorphic rocks]

1. According to the rock cycle diagram, which of the following statements is true?
   A Only sedimentary rock gets weathered and eroded.
   B Sedimentary rocks are made from metamorphic, igneous, and sedimentary rock fragments and minerals.
   C Heat and pressure create igneous rocks.
   D Metamorphic rocks are created by melting and cooling.

2. A rock exists at the surface of the Earth. What would be the next step in the rock cycle?
   F cooling
   G weathering
   H melting
   I metamorphism

3. Which of the following processes brings rocks to Earth's surface, where they can be eroded?
   A burial
   B deposition
   C uplift
   D weathering

4. Which of the following is the best summary of the rock cycle?
   F Each type of rock gets melted. Then the magma turns into igneous, sedimentary, and metamorphic rock.
   G Magma cools to form igneous rock. Then, the igneous rock becomes sedimentary rock. Sedimentary rock is heated and forms metamorphic rock. Metamorphic rock melts to form magma.
   H All three rock types weather to create sedimentary rock. All three rock types melt to form magma. Magma forms igneous rock. All three types of rock form metamorphic rock because of heat and pressure.
   I Igneous rock is weathered to create sedimentary rock. Sedimentary rock is melted to form igneous rock. Metamorphic rock is weathered to form igneous rock.

MATH

Read each question below, and choose the best answer.

1. Eric has 25 rocks he has collected as a science project for class. Nine rocks are sedimentary, 10 are igneous, and 6 are metamorphic. If Eric chooses a rock at random, what is the probability that he will choose an igneous rock?
   A 1/2
   B 2/5
   C 3/8
   D 1/15

2. At a mineral and fossil show, Elizabeth bought two quartz crystals that cost $2.00 each and four trilobite fossils that cost $3.50 each. Which equation can be used to describe c, the total cost of her purchase?
   F $c = (2 \times 4) + (2.00 \times 3.50)$
   G $c = (2 \times 2.00) + (4 \times 3.50)$
   H $c = (4 \times 2.00) + (2 \times 3.50)$
   I $c = (2 + 2.00) + (4 + 3.50)$

INTERPRETING GRAPHICS
1. B
2. G
3. C
4. H

TEST DOCTOR

Question 1: The correct answer is B. Some students may select answer A, incorrectly believing that sedimentary rock forms during the processes of weathering and erosion rather than as a result of it.

Question 4: The correct answer is H. Answers F, G, and I incorrectly describe one or more processes that are part of the rock cycle. (Helpful hint: When describing the rock cycle to students, make them aware that the three classes of rock can be involved in each process in the cycle.)

MATH
1. B
2. G

TEST DOCTOR

Question 2: The correct answer is G. Answer F incorrectly multiplies the numbers of objects with each other and the prices with each other, then adds the totals together. Answer H incorrectly matches the prices with the objects and adds the totals together. Answer I incorrectly adds the number of objects to the prices.

CHAPTER RESOURCES

Chapter Resource File
• Standardized Test Preparation GENERAL

State Resources
For specific resources for your state, visit go.hrw.com and type in the keyword HSMSTR.

Chapter 4 • Standardized Test Preparation 117

Science in Action

Science, Technology, and Society

Background
Archaeologists estimate that Easter Island was first settled sometime between 400 CE and 700 CE. The first inhabitants arrived from Polynesia. This was confirmed in 1994, when DNA extracted from 12 Easter Island skeletons was found to be Polynesian. Either Tahiti or the Marquesas islands, which had been reached by Melanesian seafarers by at least 300 CE, were the most likely starting point for these voyages.

Scientific Discoveries

Background
Sixty-five million years ago, an asteroid at least 10 km wide struck the Earth near Yucatán, Mexico. Some scientists think the collision caused the extinction of approximately 15% to 20% of life on Earth, including the dinosaurs. Today, the crater is buried beneath 1,100 m of limestone, so there are few clues to the crater's existence. As scientists drilled into the impact site, they found mineral evidence of shock metamorphism. They confirmed that rocks in the area had been subjected to a high-pressure event.

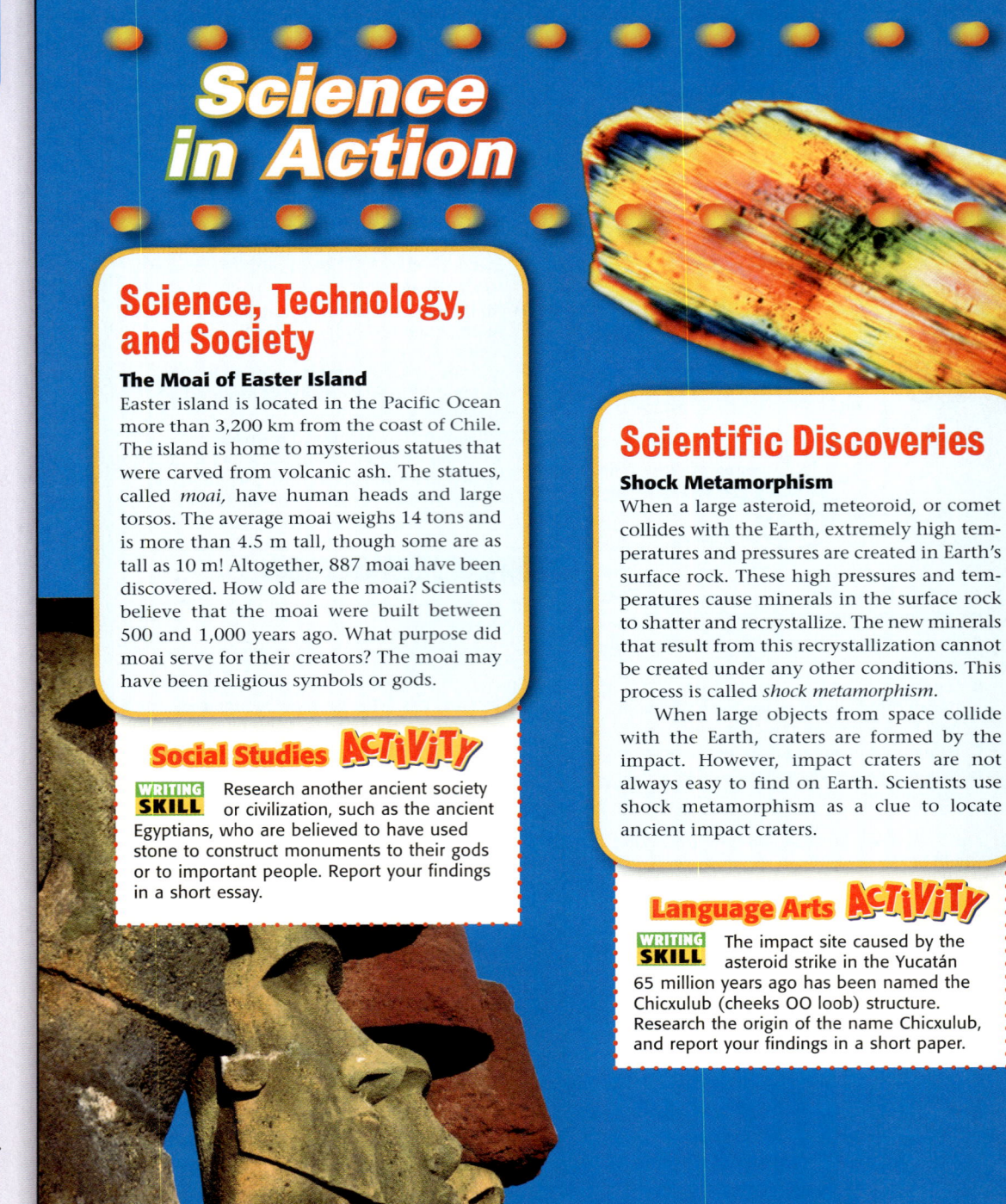

Science in Action

Science, Technology, and Society

The Moai of Easter Island
Easter island is located in the Pacific Ocean more than 3,200 km from the coast of Chile. The island is home to mysterious statues that were carved from volcanic ash. The statues, called *moai*, have human heads and large torsos. The average moai weighs 14 tons and is more than 4.5 m tall, though some are as tall as 10 m! Altogether, 887 moai have been discovered. How old are the moai? Scientists believe that the moai were built between 500 and 1,000 years ago. What purpose did moai serve for their creators? The moai may have been religious symbols or gods.

Social Studies ACTIVITY
WRITING SKILL Research another ancient society or civilization, such as the ancient Egyptians, who are believed to have used stone to construct monuments to their gods or to important people. Report your findings in a short essay.

Scientific Discoveries

Shock Metamorphism
When a large asteroid, meteoroid, or comet collides with the Earth, extremely high temperatures and pressures are created in Earth's surface rock. These high pressures and temperatures cause minerals in the surface rock to shatter and recrystallize. The new minerals that result from this recrystallization cannot be created under any other conditions. This process is called *shock metamorphism*.

When large objects from space collide with the Earth, craters are formed by the impact. However, impact craters are not always easy to find on Earth. Scientists use shock metamorphism as a clue to locate ancient impact craters.

Language Arts ACTIVITY
WRITING SKILL The impact site caused by the asteroid strike in the Yucatán 65 million years ago has been named the Chicxulub (cheeks OO loob) structure. Research the origin of the name Chicxulub, and report your findings in a short paper.

Answer to Social Studies Activity
Have students report their findings to the class. While reporting their findings, students should pinpoint the location of the monuments they are discussing on a world map.

Answer to Language Arts Activity
Hold a short discussion with the class about the meaning of the name *Chicxulub* (in the local Mayan dialect, *Chicxulub* means "the devil's tail") and the importance of the Chicxulub impact structure. While doing so, point out the location of the Chicxulub impact site on a map. You may also want to discuss other large North American impact structures, such as Sudbury in Ontario, Canada, Manicouagan in Quebec, Canada, and the impact structure in Chesapeake Bay, in Virginia, USA.

118 Chapter 4 • Rocks: Mineral Mixtures

Careers

Robert L. Folk

Petrologist For Dr. Robert Folk, the study of rock takes place on the microscopic level. Dr. Folk is searching for tiny life-forms he has named nannobacteria, or dwarf bacteria, in rock. *Nannobacteria* may also be spelled *nanobacteria*. Because nannobacteria are so incredibly small, only 0.05 to 0.2 µm in diameter, Folk must use an extremely powerful 100,000× microscope, called a *scanning electron microscope,* to see the shape of the bacteria in rock. Folk's research had already led him to discover that a certain type of Italian limestone is produced by bacteria. The bacteria were consuming the minerals, and the waste of the bacteria was forming the limestone. Further research led Folk to the discovery of the tiny nannobacteria. The spherical or oval-shaped nannobacteria appeared as chains and grapelike clusters. From his research, Folk hypothesized that nannobacteria are responsible for many inorganic reactions that occur in rock. Many scientists are skeptical of Folk's nannobacteria. Some skeptics believe that the tiny size of nannobacteria makes the bacteria simply too small to contain the chemistry of life. Others believe that nannobacteria actually represent structures that do not come from living things.

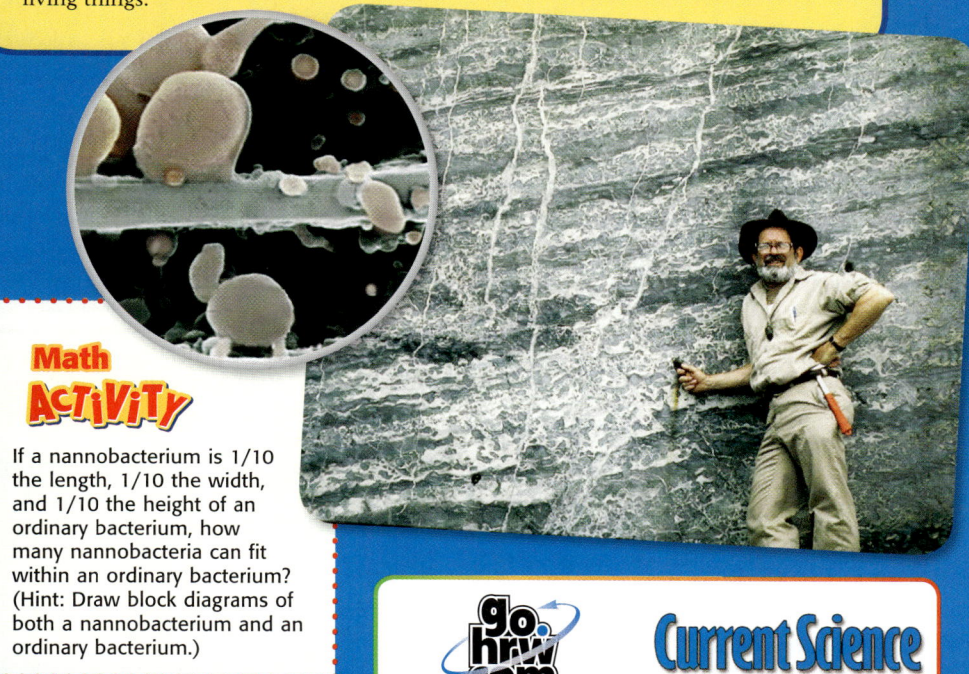

Math Activity

If a nannobacterium is 1/10 the length, 1/10 the width, and 1/10 the height of an ordinary bacterium, how many nannobacteria can fit within an ordinary bacterium? (Hint: Draw block diagrams of both a nannobacterium and an ordinary bacterium.)

To learn more about these Science in Action topics, visit go.hrw.com and type in the keyword HZ5RCKF.

Current Science
Check out Current Science® articles related to this chapter by visiting go.hrw.com. Just type in the keyword HZ5CS04.

Answer to Math Activity
$10 \times 10 \times 10 = 10^3 = 1,000$ nannobacteria can fit within a normal bacterium.

Careers

Background

Dr. Robert L. Folk is currently Professor Emeritus in the Department of Geology at the University of Texas at Austin, where he taught sedimentary geology from 1953 to 1988. His classification system of sediments, proposed in 1954, is still used by some sedimentary petrologists. In 1962, Dr. Folk's *The Classification of Sedimentary Rocks* was published. This work is considered a classic text in the field of sedimentary petrology. Dr. Folk was the recipient of the Twenhofel Medal for excellence in sedimentary petrology in 1979 and was awarded the Penrose Medal in 2000 for outstanding original contributions or achievements that mark a major advance in the science of geology. In addition, Dr. Folk has received two national teaching awards. In 1980, he first became interested in the role of bacteria in forming materials, and, in 1990, he discovered the first mineralized nannobacteria. Dr. Folk's research involving nannobacteria is still very controversial.

MISCONCEPTION ALERT

Nannobacteria or Nanobacteria? In 1988, the term *nanobacteria* was first applied to the controversial microscopic spheres and rods that Dr. Folk is studying. Since the first use of term, *nanobacteria* (with the prefix *nano-*) has become the preferred spelling of the term in the scientific literature. Dr. Folk prefers to spell the same term *nannobacteria* (with the prefix *nanno-*). His contention is that this is the preferred geological spelling. In point of fact, both prefixes come from the Greek *nannos*, meaning "dwarf."

Chapter 4 • Science in Action 119

5 Energy Resources
Chapter Planning Guide

Compression guide: To shorten instruction because of time limitations, omit the Chapter Lab.

OBJECTIVES	LABS, DEMONSTRATIONS, AND ACTIVITIES	TECHNOLOGY RESOURCES
PACING • 90 min pp. 120–125 **Chapter Opener**	SE Start-up Activity, p. 121 ◆ GENERAL	OSP Parent Letter ■ GENERAL CD Student Edition on CD-ROM CD Guided Reading Audio CD ■ TR Chapter Starter Transparency* VID Brain Food Video Quiz
Section 1 Natural Resources • Describe how humans use natural resources. • Compare renewable resources with nonrenewable resources. • Explain three ways that humans can conserve natural resources.	TE Connection Activity Real World, p. 123 GENERAL SE School-to-Home Activity Renewable?, p. 124 GENERAL SE Science in Action Math, Social Studies, and Language Arts Activities, pp. 148–149	CRF Lesson Plans* TR Bellringer Transparency*
PACING • 45 min pp. 126–133 **Section 2 Fossil Fuels** • Describe what energy resources are. • Identify three different forms of fossil fuels. • Explain how fossil fuels form. • Describe how fossil fuels are found and obtained. • Identify four problems with fossil fuels.	TE Connection Activity Language Arts, p. 127 ADVANCED SE Connection to Chemistry Hydrocarbons, p. 128 GENERAL TE Connection Activity Real World, p. 128 ADVANCED SE Quick Lab Rock Sponge, p. 129 ◆ GENERAL CRF Datasheet for Quick Lab* TE Demonstration Simulating Reservoirs, p. 129 ◆ GENERAL TE Connection Activity Math, p. 130 BASIC	CRF Lesson Plans* TR Bellringer Transparency* TR LINK TO PHYSICAL SCIENCE Energy Conversions in a Car Engine* TR Porous Rocks as Reservoirs for Fossil Fuels* SE Internet Activity, p. 128 GENERAL CRF SciLinks Activity* GENERAL
PACING • 90 min pp. 134–141 **Section 3 Alternative Resources** • Describe alternatives to the use of fossil fuels. • List advantages and disadvantages of using alternative energy resources.	TE Connection Activity History, p. 135 GENERAL SE Connection to Language Arts Resources of the Future, p. 136 GENERAL TE Group Activity Building a Solar Cooker, p. 136 GENERAL TE Activity Problems with Burning Biomass, p. 139 ADVANCED SE Skills Practice Lab Make a Water Wheel, p. 142 ◆ GENERAL CRF Datasheet for Chapter Lab* SE Model-Making Lab Power of the Sun, p. 726 ◆ GENERAL CRF Datasheet for LabBook* LB Long-Term Projects & Research Ideas Build a City—Save a World!* ADVANCED LB Calculator Based Labs Solar Homes ◆ ADVANCED	CRF Lesson Plans* TR Bellringer Transparency* TR Fission* TR Fusion* CD Interactive Explorations CD-ROM The Generation Gap GENERAL VID Lab Videos for Earth Science

PACING • 90 min

CHAPTER REVIEW, ASSESSMENT, AND STANDARDIZED TEST PREPARATION

- CRF Vocabulary Activity* GENERAL
- SE Chapter Review, pp. 144–145 GENERAL
- CRF Chapter Review* ■ GENERAL
- CRF Chapter Tests A* ■ GENERAL, B* ADVANCED, C* SPECIAL NEEDS
- SE Standardized Test Preparation, pp. 146–147 GENERAL
- CRF Standardized Test Preparation* GENERAL
- CRF Performance-Based Assessment* GENERAL
- OSP Test Generator GENERAL
- CRF Test Item Listing* GENERAL

Online and Technology Resources

go.hrw.com — Visit go.hrw.com for a variety of free resources related to this textbook. Enter the keyword **HZ5ENR**.

Holt Online Learning — Students can access interactive problem-solving help and active visual concept development with the *Holt Science and Technology* Online Edition available at **www.hrw.com**.

Guided Reading Audio CD — Also in Spanish. A direct reading of each chapter for auditory learners, reluctant readers, and Spanish-speaking students.

Science Tutor CD-ROM — Excellent for remediation and test practice.

Chapter 5 • Energy Resources

KEY					
SE Student Edition	CRF Chapter Resource File	SS Science Skills Worksheets	* Also on One-Stop Planner		
TE Teacher Edition	OSP One-Stop Planner	MS Math Skills for Science Worksheets	♦ Requires advance prep		
	LB Lab Bank	CD CD or CD-ROM	■ Also available in Spanish		
	TR Transparencies	VID Classroom Video/DVD			

SKILLS DEVELOPMENT RESOURCES	SECTION REVIEW AND ASSESSMENT	STANDARDS CORRELATIONS
SE Pre-Reading Activity, p. 120 GENERAL OSP Science Puzzlers, Twisters & Teasers* GENERAL		National Science Education Standards SAI 1; ST 2; SPSP 5
CRF Directed Reading A* BASIC, B* SPECIAL NEEDS CRF Vocabulary and Section Summary* GENERAL SE Reading Strategy Reading Organizer, p. 122 GENERAL CRF Reinforcement Worksheet What Are My Resources?* GENERAL	SE Reading Checks, pp. 123, 125 GENERAL TE Homework, p. 123 BASIC TE Reteaching, p. 124 BASIC TE Quiz, p. 124 GENERAL TE Alternative Assessment, p. 124 GENERAL SE Section Review,* p. 125 GENERAL CRF Section Quiz* GENERAL	SAI 1; SPSP 2, 4; ES 3d
CRF Directed Reading A* BASIC, B* SPECIAL NEEDS CRF Vocabulary and Section Summary* GENERAL SE Reading Strategy Brainstorming, p. 126 GENERAL TE Inclusion Strategies, p. 128 MS Math Skills for Science Parts of 100: Calculating Percentages* GENERAL CRF Reinforcement Worksheet If It's a Fossil, How Is It a Fuel?* BASIC	SE Reading Checks, pp. 127, 128, 131, 132 GENERAL TE Homework, p. 130 ADVANCED TE Reteaching, p. 132 BASIC TE Quiz, p. 132 GENERAL TE Alternative Assessment, p. 132 GENERAL SE Section Review,* p. 133 GENERAL CRF Section Quiz* GENERAL	SAI 1; SPSP 1, 2, 4, 5; ES 1d, 1e, 1k, 3d
CRF Directed Reading A* BASIC, B* SPECIAL NEEDS CRF Vocabulary and Section Summary* GENERAL SE Reading Strategy Paired Summarizing, p. 134 GENERAL TE Reading Strategy Mnemonics, p. 135 BASIC TE Inclusion Strategies, p. 137 ♦ GENERAL TE Reading Strategy Prediction Guide, p. 138 BASIC SE Math Practice Miles per Acre, p. 139 GENERAL MS Math Skills for Science Radioactive Decay and the Half-Life* GENERAL CRF Critical Thinking Nature's Gold* ADVANCED	SE Reading Checks, pp. 135, 136, 138, 140 GENERAL TE Homework, p. 135 ADVANCED TE Homework, p. 138 GENERAL TE Reteaching, p. 140 BASIC TE Quiz, p. 140 GENERAL TE Alternative Assessment, p. 140 BASIC SE Section Review,* p. 141 GENERAL CRF Section Quiz* GENERAL	UCP 5; ST 2; SPSP 2, 4, 5; ES 3d; *LabBook:* UCP 2, 3; SAI 1; ST 1; *Chapter Lab:* UCP 2, 3; SAI 1; ST 1

One-Stop Planner® CD-ROM

This convenient CD-ROM includes:
- Lab Materials QuickList Software
- Holt Calendar Planner
- Customizable Lesson Plans
- Printable Worksheets
- ExamView® Test Generator

CNN Student News

cnnstudentnews.com

Find the latest news, lesson plans, and activities related to important scientific events.

SciLinks NSTA

www.scilinks.org

Maintained by the **National Science Teachers Association**. See Chapter Enrichment pages for a complete list of topics.

Current Science®

Check out *Current Science* articles and activities by visiting the HRW Web site at **go.hrw.com**. Just type in the keyword **HZ5CS05T**.

Classroom Videos

- **Lab Videos** demonstrate the chapter lab.
- **Brain Food Video Quizzes** help students review the chapter material.
- **CNN Videos** bring science into your students' daily life.

Chapter 5 • Chapter Planning Guide

5 Chapter Resources

Visual Resources

CHAPTER STARTER TRANSPARENCY

BELLRINGER TRANSPARENCIES

TEACHING TRANSPARENCIES

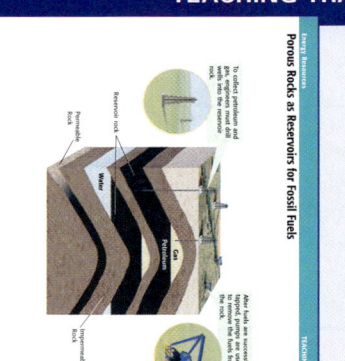

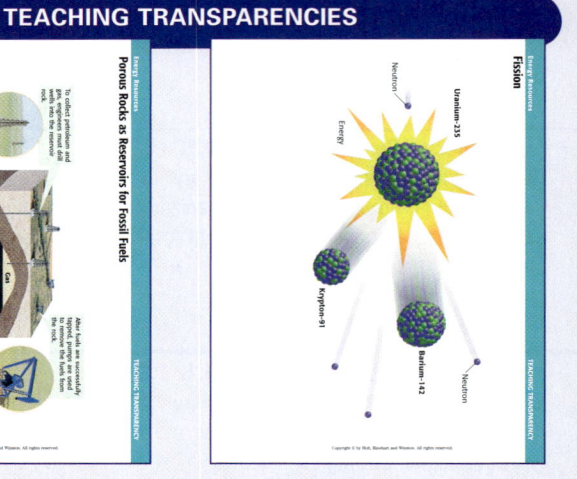

TEACHING TRANSPARENCIES

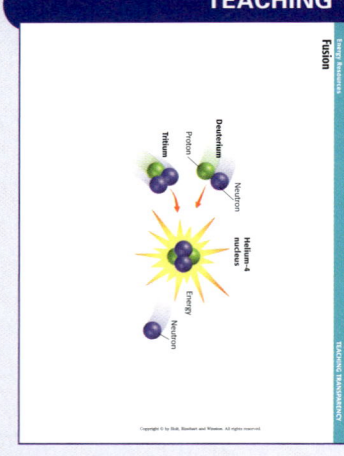

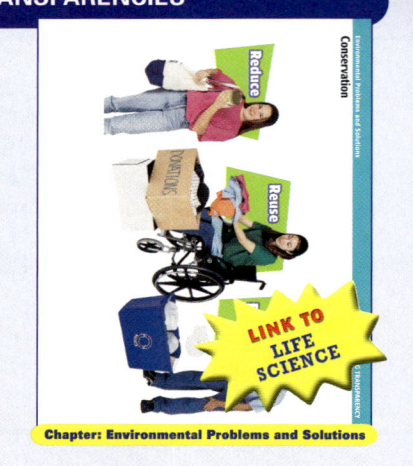

CONCEPT MAPPING TRANSPARENCY

Planning Resources

LESSON PLANS

PARENT LETTER

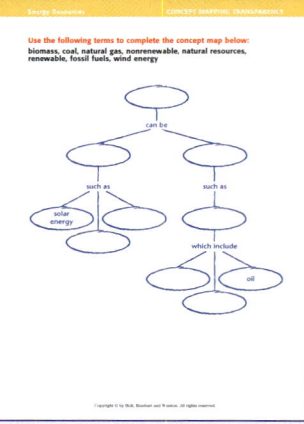

TEST ITEM LISTING

One-Stop Planner® CD-ROM

This CD-ROM includes all of the resources shown here and the following time-saving tools:

- *Lab Materials QuickList Software*
- *Customizable lesson plans*
- *Holt Calendar Planner*
- *The powerful ExamView® Test Generator*

119C Chapter 5 • Energy Resources

For a preview of available worksheets covering math and science skills, see pages T26–T33. All of these resources are also on the One-Stop Planner®.

Meeting Individual Needs

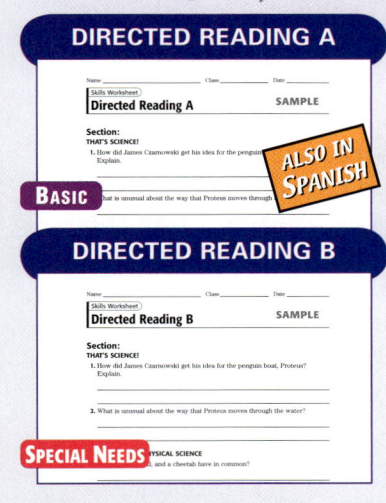

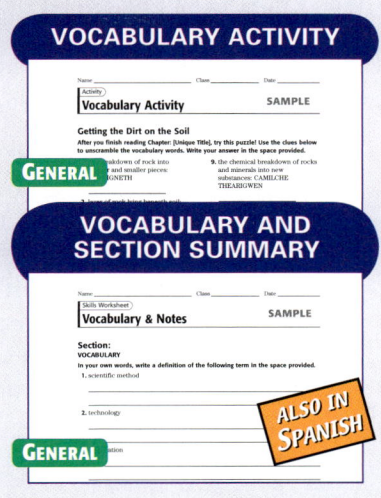

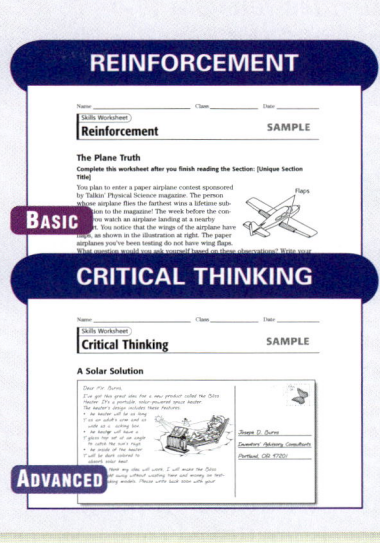

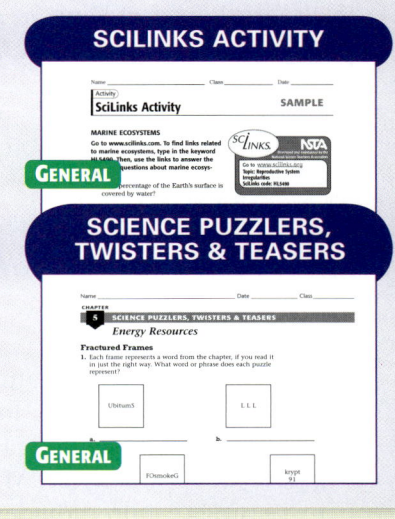

- **DIRECTED READING A** — BASIC / ALSO IN SPANISH
- **DIRECTED READING B** — SPECIAL NEEDS
- **VOCABULARY ACTIVITY** — GENERAL
- **VOCABULARY AND SECTION SUMMARY** — GENERAL / ALSO IN SPANISH
- **REINFORCEMENT** — BASIC
- **CRITICAL THINKING** — ADVANCED
- **SCILINKS ACTIVITY** — GENERAL
- **SCIENCE PUZZLERS, TWISTERS & TEASERS** — GENERAL

Labs and Activities

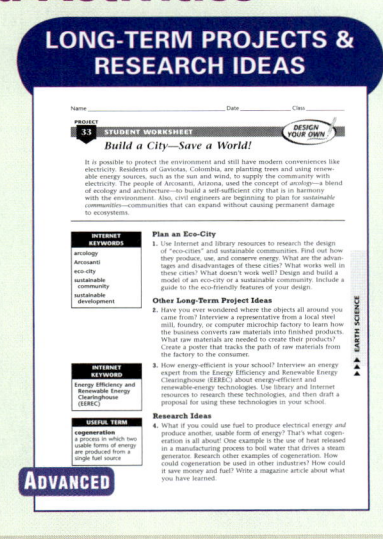

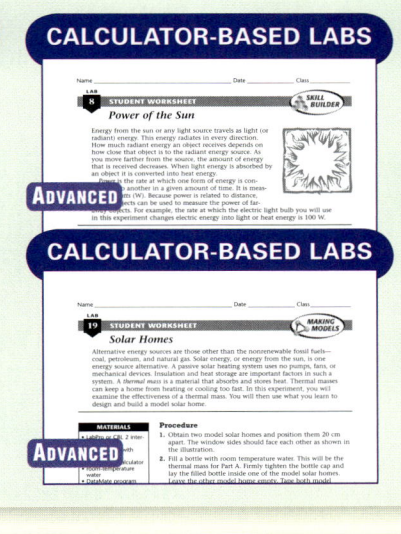

- **LONG-TERM PROJECTS & RESEARCH IDEAS** — ADVANCED
- **CALCULATOR-BASED LABS** — ADVANCED
- **CALCULATOR-BASED LABS** — ADVANCED
- **DATASHEETS FOR QUICK LABS**
- **DATASHEETS FOR CHAPTER LABS**
- **DATASHEETS FOR LABBOOK**

Review and Assessments

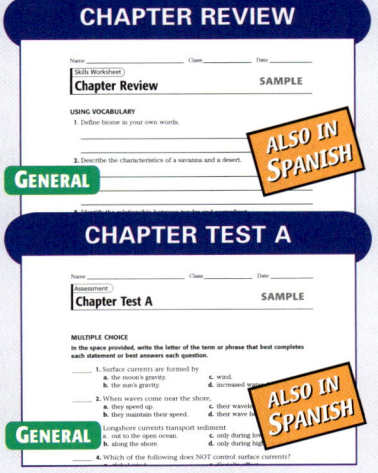

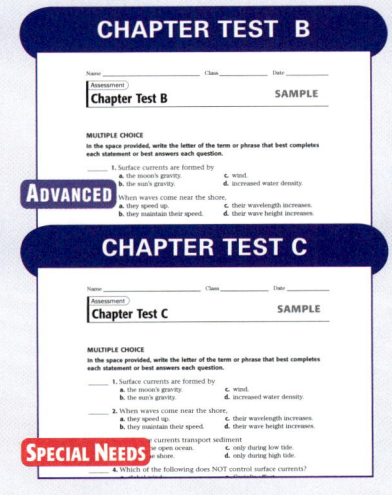

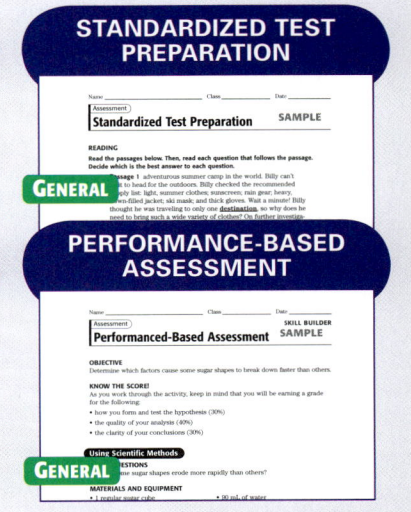

- **SECTION QUIZ** — GENERAL / ALSO IN SPANISH
- **SECTION REVIEW** — GENERAL / ALSO IN SPANISH
- **CHAPTER REVIEW** — GENERAL / ALSO IN SPANISH
- **CHAPTER TEST A** — GENERAL / ALSO IN SPANISH
- **CHAPTER TEST B** — ADVANCED
- **CHAPTER TEST C** — SPECIAL NEEDS
- **STANDARDIZED TEST PREPARATION** — GENERAL
- **PERFORMANCE-BASED ASSESSMENT** — GENERAL

Chapter 5 • Chapter Resources 119D

5 Chapter Enrichment

This Chapter Enrichment provides relevant and interesting information to expand and enhance your presentation of the chapter material.

Section 1

Natural Resources

Interconnected Resources

- The Earth's resources are intricately linked. For example, clearing trees from a forest affects the water quality downstream. The use of fossil fuels offers another example: fossil-fuel combustion adds enormous quantities of carbon dioxide, a greenhouse gas, to the atmosphere. Many scientists think that increasing carbon dioxide levels are linked to the rising temperatures on the Earth in recent years.

The Three Rs

- Over the past three decades, environmentalists have encouraged consumers to consider the three Rs—reduce, reuse, and recycle—to conserve Earth's natural resources.

- When buying new items, consumers should buy in bulk or purchase products that have minimal packaging. Reusing plastic bags is another way to conserve petroleum-based natural resources. Use of cloth rags and napkins instead of paper towels and paper napkins is one way to reduce paper consumption. Donating used items to charities and friends and family members is one way to recycle clothes, shoes, appliances, books, toys, and other such items.

Section 2

Fossil Fuels

Light Up Your Life

- Before electricity was discovered, one of the primary functions of fossil fuels was to provide light. Kerosene lamps became popular in the United States after the first oil well was drilled in 1859 in Pennsylvania. Coal gas had been used in lamps as early as 1784. By the early 1800s, most cities in the United States and Europe had coal-gas street lights. Electric lamps did not replace the gaslights until the early 1900s.

Is That a Fact!

♦ Ancient fossil reefs buried underground make excellent oil and gas reservoirs because the reefs are very porous. The productivity of the oil fields in Alberta, Canada, is due to the presence of Devonian reefs that are 408 million to 360 million years old.

Rigs-to-Reefs Program

- Environmentalists usually consider offshore oil rigs to be detrimental to marine ecosystems. However, obsolete oil rigs have become a welcome addition to many areas. In 1979, the Rigs-to-Reefs Program was initiated when an oil rig was moved from off the coast of Louisiana to a site off the coast of Florida to become an artificial reef. During the next 20 years, more than 500 platforms were relocated for the same purpose.

- Within six months of placement in a suitable marine area, a platform is covered with invertebrates and plants. These organisms attract other invertebrates and fish and form the basis of a complex food chain. The open framework of the rig allows water to circulate and fish to swim freely through the structure. Some people remain concerned, however, about residual pollution from the submerged rigs.

Section 3

Alternative Resources

Chernobyl

- The radioactive fallout from the 1986 Chernobyl nuclear accident affected people, livestock, and crops.

- Although only 31 people died from direct exposure, about 600,000 people were significantly exposed to the fallout. About 10,000 people were exposed to at least 100 rads and suffered from radiation sickness. For comparison, a person undergoing a chest X ray is exposed to a maximum of 1 rad.

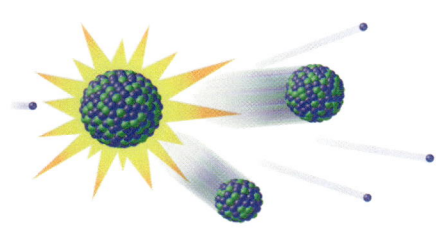

- Livestock also suffered from the fallout. At least 86,000 head of cattle were evacuated from the area immediately after the accident. The sale of milk, meat, and many fruits and vegetables was banned in 1986 and 1987 in cities near Chernobyl.

Concentrating Solar Power Systems

- Concentrating solar power systems harness solar energy by focusing reflected sunlight onto a receiver. The receiver absorbs the light and converts it into thermal energy, which is then used to generate electricity.

  - **Solar trough systems** consist of parabolic, mirrored troughs that focus sunlight onto oil-filled tubes at the troughs' focal points.
  - **Solar power towers** use thousands of mirrors to reflect sunlight onto a receiver that is mounted on a tall tower.
  - **Solar dish systems** use circular mirrors arranged into the shape of a dish to concentrate solar energy onto a receiver.

Geothermal Energy

- Geothermal energy is tapped at places in the Earth's crust that are heated by underground bodies of magma. Geothermal energy is currently used in Japan, in parts of Russia, in Iceland, in Italy, in New Zealand, and on the western coast of the United States.

- Iceland is the world leader in using geothermal energy for space heating. More than 85% of Icelanders use geothermal energy to warm their homes! The cost of heating is only about one-third of the cost of burning oil to power electric heaters. Industries in Iceland use geothermal energy because it is inexpensive, widely available, and very reliable.

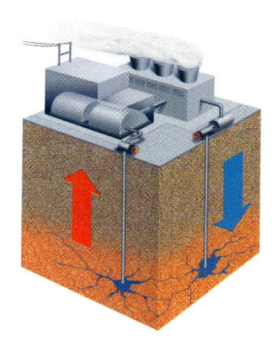

Is That a Fact!

◆ Traditional fuels, such as wood and animal dung, are used to meet one-quarter of India's energy needs.

SciLinks is maintained by the National Science Teachers Association to provide you and your students with interesting, up-to-date links that will enrich your classroom presentation of the chapter.

Visit www.scilinks.org and enter the SciLinks code for more information about the topic listed.

Topic: Natural Resources
SciLinks code: HSM1015

Topic: Fossil Fuels
SciLinks code: HSM0614

Topic: Renewable Resources
SciLinks code: HSM1291

Topic: Nuclear Energy
SciLinks code: HSM1047

Topic: Nonrenewable Resources
SciLinks code: HSM1044

Chapter 5 • Chapter Enrichment

Overview

This chapter introduces renewable and nonrenewable energy resources. Students will learn about how fossil fuels form and how they are obtained. The chapter also discusses the environmental effects of fossil fuel use. Finally, students will explore alternatives to fossil fuels. They will compare advantages and disadvantages of using alternative energy resources.

Assessing Prior Knowledge

Students should be familiar with the following topics:
- minerals
- rocks

Identifying Misconceptions

Students may be confused about the difference between the nuclear energy released from nuclear power plants and the nuclear energy released from nuclear weapons. Explain to students that nuclear energy from nuclear power plants and nuclear weapons is energy from fission. Fission is the process by which a nucleus splits into two or more nuclei and releases and energy. The rate of fission in a nuclear power plant is carefully controlled. However, fission occurs at an unregulated rate in a nuclear weapon.

5 Energy Resources

SECTION 1	Natural Resources	122
SECTION 2	Fossil Fuels	126
SECTION 3	Alternative Resources	134

Chapter Lab 142
Chapter Review 144
Standardized Test Preparation 146
Science in Action 148

About the PHOTO

Would you believe that this house is made from empty soda cans and old tires? Well, it is! *The Castle,* named by its designer, architect Mike Reynolds, and located in Taos, New Mexico, not only uses recycled materials but also saves Earth's energy resources. All of the energy used to run this house comes directly from the sun, and the water used for household activities is rainwater.

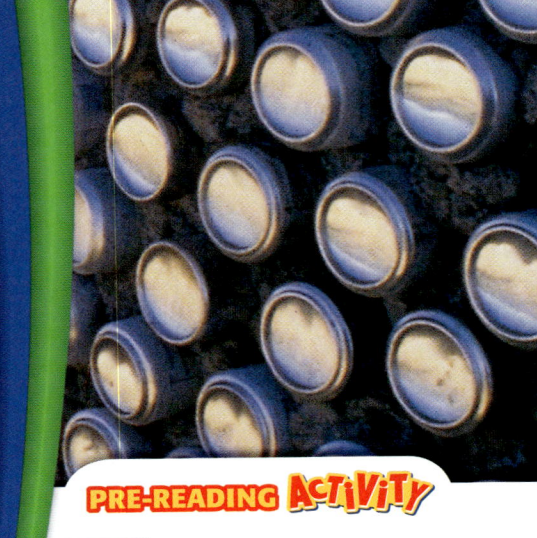

PRE-READING ACTIVITY

Graphic Organizer — **Comparison Table** Before you read the chapter, create the graphic organizer entitled "Comparison Table" described in the **Study Skills** section of the Appendix. Label the columns with an energy resource from the chapter. Label the rows with "Pros" and "Cons." As you read the chapter, fill in the table with details about the pros and cons of each energy resource.

Standards Correlations

National Science Education Standards

The following codes indicate the National Science Education Standards that correlate to this chapter. The full text of the standards is at the front of the book.

Chapter Opener
SAI 1; ST 2; SPSP 5

Section 1 Natural Resources
SAI 1; SPSP 2, 4; ES 3d

Section 2 Fossil Fuels
SAI 1; SPSP 1, 2, 4, 5; ES 1d, 1e, 1k, 3d

Section 3 Alternative Resources
UCP 5; ST 2; SPSP 2, 4, 5; ES 3d; *LabBook:* UCP 2, 3; SAI 1; ST 1

Chapter Lab
UCP 2, 3; SAI 1; ST 1

Chapter Review
UCP 2, 3; ST 2; SPSP 5; ES 1d, 1e

Science in Action
ST 2; SPSP 3, 5; HNS 1

START-UP ACTIVITY

What Is the Sun's Favorite Color?
Try the following activity to see which colors are better than others at absorbing the sun's energy.

Procedure
1. Obtain **at least five balloons** that are different colors but the same size and shape. One of the balloons should be white, and one should be black. Do not inflate the balloons.
2. Place **several small ice cubes** in each balloon. Each balloon should contain the same amount of ice.
3. Line up the balloons on a flat, uniformly colored surface that receives direct sunlight. Make sure that all of the balloons receive the same amount of sunlight and that the openings in the balloons are not facing directly toward the sun.
4. Record the time that it takes the ice to melt completely in each of the balloons. You can tell how much ice has melted in each balloon by pinching the balloons open and then gently squeezing the balloon.

Analysis
1. In which balloon did the ice melt first? Why?
2. What color would you paint a device used to collect solar energy? Explain your answer.

START-UP ACTIVITY

MATERIALS
For Each Group
- balloons, different-colored, (5)
- ice cubes
- scissors
- watch or clock with a second hand

Teacher's Notes: Balloons must be identical except for color. Also, note that one balloon in each group must be black and that one must be white.

One large ice cube or several small cubes are enough for each balloon. Stress to students that they should not use too much ice or it will take too long to obtain the desired results. You might have students mark their balloons with permanent markers before they add the ice so that groups can identify their balloons.

Answers
1. Students should observe that the ice in the black balloon melted first. The darker an object is, the more light energy it will absorb.
2. Sample answer: black; A device used to collect solar energy should be black because the dark-colored object would collect more energy than an object of any other color.

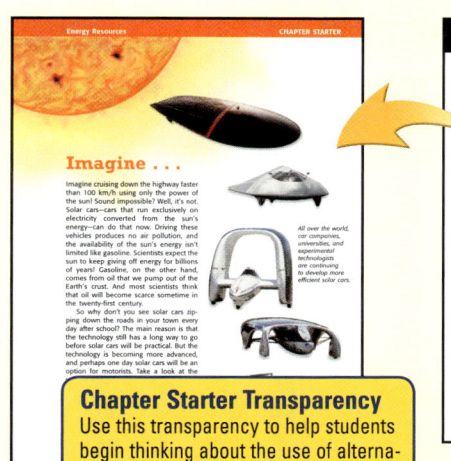

Chapter Starter Transparency
Use this transparency to help students begin thinking about the use of alternative energy sources.

CHAPTER RESOURCES

Technology
- **Transparencies**
  - Chapter Starter Transparency
- **Student Edition on CD-ROM**
- **Guided Reading Audio CD**
  - English or Spanish
- **Classroom Videos**
  - Brain Food Video Quiz

READING SKILLS

Workbooks
- **Science Puzzlers, Twisters & Teasers**
  - Energy Resources GENERAL

Chapter 5 • Energy Resources   **121**

SECTION 1

Focus

Overview
In this section, students will learn about Earth's natural resources. They will explore the difference between renewable resources and nonrenewable resources. Students will also learn why conservation and recycling are important.

🔔 **Bellringer**
Display the following items: a plastic sandwich bag, a piece of paper, a pencil, a glass of water, 1 qt of motor oil, an empty aluminum can, a wooden match, salt, and some aquarium charcoal. Challenge students to determine what these items have in common. Help students conclude that all of these items are made from natural resources. Have students make a list of resources that are renewable and are resources that nonrenewable.

Motivate

Discussion — GENERAL
Kinds of Energy Have students brainstorm a list of different sources of energy, such as oil, coal, sunlight, and wind. Ask students to discuss which sources are nonrenewable resources and why.
LS Interpersonal

SECTION 1

READING WARM-UP

Objectives
- Describe how humans use natural resources.
- Compare renewable resources with nonrenewable resources.
- Explain three ways that humans can conserve natural resources.

Terms to Learn
natural resource
renewable resource
nonrenewable resource
recycling

READING STRATEGY

Reading Organizer As you read this section, make a concept map by using the terms above.

Natural Resources

What does the water you drink, the paper you write on, the gasoline used in the cars you ride in, and the air you breathe have in common?

Water, trees used to make paper, crude oil used to make gasoline, and air are just a few examples of Earth's resources. Can you think of other examples of Earth's resources?

Earth's Resources

The Earth provides almost everything needed for life. For example, the Earth's atmosphere provides the air you breathe, maintains air temperatures, and produces rain. The oceans and other waters of the Earth give you food and needed water. The solid part of the Earth gives nutrients, such as potassium, to the plants you eat. These resources that the Earth provides for you are called natural resources.

A **natural resource** is any natural material that is used by humans. Examples of natural resources are water, petroleum, minerals, forests, and animals. Most resources are changed and made into products that make people's lives more comfortable and convenient, as shown in **Figure 1**. The energy we get from many of these resources, such as gasoline and wind, ultimately comes from the sun's energy.

Figure 1 Natural Resources

This pile of lumber is made of wood, which comes from trees.

The gasoline in this can is made from oil pumped from the Earth's crust.

Electrical energy generated by these wind turbines ultimately comes from the sun's energy.

CHAPTER RESOURCES

Chapter Resource File
- Lesson Plan
- Directed Reading A [BASIC]
- Directed Reading B [SPECIAL NEEDS]

Technology
- Transparencies
  • Bellringer

CONNECTION to Environmental Science — GENERAL

Volunteering Have your class learn what volunteer opportunities related to the environment exist in your area. Students may be interested in a beach or river cleanup, tree planting, or a public outreach program for resource conservation. Suggest that students volunteer two weekends as they study this chapter. At the end of the chapter, have students share their volunteer experiences with the class. LS Intrapersonal

122 Chapter 5 • Energy Resources

Renewable Resources

Some natural resources can be renewed. A **renewable resource** is a natural resource that can be replaced at the same rate at which the resource is used. **Figure 2** shows two examples of renewable resources. Although many resources are renewable, they still can be used up before they can be renewed. Trees, for example, are renewable. However, some forests are being cut down faster than new forests can grow to replace them.

Reading Check What is a renewable resource? *(See the Appendix for answers to Reading Checks.)*

Nonrenewable Resources

Not all of Earth's natural resources are renewable. A **nonrenewable resource** is a resource that forms at a rate that is much slower than the rate at which it is consumed. Coal, shown in **Figure 3**, is an example of a nonrenewable resource. It takes millions of years for coal to form. Once coal is used up, it is no longer available. Petroleum and natural gas are other examples of nonrenewable resources. When these resources become scarce, humans will have to find other resources to replace them.

Figure 2 Trees and fresh water are just a few of the renewable resources available on Earth.

natural resource any natural material that is used by humans, such as water, petroleum, minerals, forests, and animals

renewable resource a natural resource that can be replaced at the same rate at which the resource is consumed

nonrenewable resource a resource that forms at a rate that is much slower than the rate at which it is consumed

Figure 3 The coal used in the industrial process shown here is not quickly replaced by natural processes.

Answer to Reading Check
A renewable resource is a natural resource that can be replaced at the same rate at which the resource is used.

Homework — BASIC
A Resourceful Project Provide students a large piece of poster board, scissors, glue, and magazines. Have them attach pictures of products made from renewable and nonrenewable resources on each side of the poster board. Beside each type of resource, have students describe its origin, how it is obtained, and the environmental effects of extracting and using it. Have students suggest ways the resource can be conserved or recycled. **LS Visual**

Teach

Discussion — BASIC
The Three Rs Complete your discussion of nonrenewable resources by reviewing with students the three Rs of conservation: reducing, reusing, and recycling. Have students list as many examples as possible of reducing, reusing, and recycling. **LS Verbal**

CONNECTION ACTIVITY
Real World — GENERAL

The Costs of Aluminum
Aluminum is refined from the ore bauxite, which is deposited in a thin layer at the Earth's surface. Bauxite strip mines cover more of the Earth's surface than any other type of metal ore mine. Aluminum production uses so much electrical energy that the metal has been referred to as *congealed electricity*. The energy of 1 L of gasoline is needed to produce six aluminum cans. For this reason, aluminum smelters are located close to cheap and reliable energy sources, such as the hydroelectric dams in the Pacific Northwest, Quebec, and the Amazon. When the environmental damage caused by producing new aluminum is considered, the importance of recycling becomes clear. Recycling one aluminum can saves enough energy to run a television set for 4 hours! Currently, the United States obtains about 20% of its aluminum from recycling. Have students write a persuasive letter explaining why that percentage should increase. Gather students' letters, and mail them to your state or federal representative. **LS Intrapersonal**

Section 1 • Natural Resources **123**

Close

Reteaching — BASIC
Reviewing the Three R's Draw a table that has three columns on the board. Label one "Reduce," one "Reuse," and one "Recycle." Have students list examples of each type of conservation to fill in the table. **LS Verbal/Visual**

Quiz — GENERAL
1. List three renewable and three nonrenewable natural resources. (Sample answer: renewable: trees, wind, and water; nonrenewable: coal, oil, and natural gas)
2. Explain the difference between conserving a resource and recycling it. (Conserving a resource is using it sparingly and not wasting it. Recycling is reusing natural resources to make new products.)

Alternative Assessment — GENERAL
Concept Mapping Have students use the following terms to construct a concept map: *use, disposal, recycling, nonrenewable resource, reuse, production, renewable resource,* and *conserving*. **LS Visual**

SCHOOL to HOME

Renewable?

WRITING SKILL With a parent, find five products in your home that were made from natural resources. List the resource or resources from which each product was made. Label each resource as renewable or nonrenewable. What can you do to help conserve the resources you listed? In your **science journal,** describe a personal action plan to conserve some of the resources you rely on every day.

ACTIVITY

Conserving Natural Resources

Whether the natural resources you use are renewable or nonrenewable, you should be careful how you use them. To conserve natural resources, you should try to use them only when necessary. For example, leaving the faucet on while brushing your teeth wastes clean water. Turning the faucet on only to rinse your brush saves water that you may need for other uses.

Conserving resources also means taking care of the resources even when you are not using them. For example, it is important to keep lakes, rivers, and other water resources free of pollution. Polluted lakes and rivers can affect the water you drink. Also, polluted water resources can harm the plants and animals, including humans, that depend on them to survive.

Energy Conservation

The energy we use to heat our homes, drive our cars, and run our computers comes from natural resources. The way in which we choose to use energy on a daily basis affects the availability of the natural resources. Most of the natural resources that provide us energy are nonrenewable resources. So, if we don't limit our use of energy now, the resources may not be available in the future.

As with all natural resources, conserving energy is important. You can conserve energy by being careful to use only the resources that you need. For example, turn lights off when you are not using them. And make sure the washing machine is full before you start it, as shown in **Figure 4.** You can also ride a bike, walk, or take a bus because these methods use fewer resources than a car does.

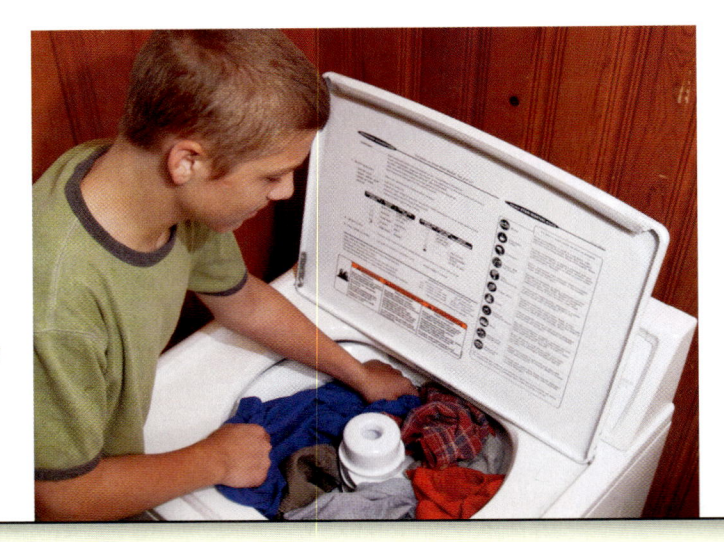

Figure 4 *Making sure the washing machine is full before running it is one way you can avoid wasting natural resources.*

Chapter 5 • Energy Resources

Reduce, Reuse, Recycle

Another way to conserve natural resources is to recycle, as shown in **Figure 5**. **Recycling** is the process of reusing materials from waste or scrap. Recycling reduces the amount of natural resources that must be obtained from the Earth. For example, recycling paper reduces the number of trees that must be cut down to make new paper products. Recycling also conserves energy. Though energy is required to recycle materials, it takes less energy to recycle an aluminum can than it does to make a new one!

Newspaper, aluminum cans, most plastic containers, and cardboard boxes can be recycled. Most plastic containers have a number on them. This number informs you whether the item can be recycled. Plastic products with the numbers 1 and 2 can be recycled in most communities. Check with your community's recycling center to see what kinds of materials the center recycles.

✓ **Reading Check** What are some kinds of products that can be recycled?

recycling the process of recovering valuable or useful materials from waste or scrap; the process of reusing some items

Figure 5 You can recycle many household items to help conserve natural resources.

SECTION Review

Summary

- We use natural resources such as water, petroleum, and lumber to make our lives more comfortable and convenient.
- Renewable resources can be replaced within a relatively short period of time, but nonrenewable resources may take thousands or even millions of years to form.
- Natural resources can be conserved by using only what is needed, taking care of resources, and recycling.

Using Key Terms

1. Use each of the following terms in a separate sentence: *natural resource, renewable resource, nonrenewable resource,* and *recycling*.

Understanding Key Ideas

2. How do humans use most natural resources?

3. Which of the following is a renewable resource?
   a. oil
   b. water
   c. coal
   d. natural gas

4. Describe three ways to conserve natural resources.

Math Skills

5. If a faucet dripped for 8.6 h and 3.3 L of water dripped out every hour, how many liters of water dripped out altogether?

Critical Thinking

6. **Making Inferences** How does human activity affect Earth's renewable and nonrenewable resources?

7. **Applying Concepts** List five products you regularly use that can be recycled.

8. **Making Inferences** Why is the availability of some renewable resources more of a concern now than it was 100 years ago?

SciLinks
For a variety of links related to this chapter, go to www.scilinks.org
Topic: Natural Resources
SciLinks code: HSM1015

Answer to Reading Check
Answers may vary. Sample answer: newspapers, plastic containers, and cardboard boxes

Answers to Section Review

1. Sample answer: A natural resource is any natural material that is used by humans. Renewable resources can be replaced at the same rate at which they are consumed. Nonrenewable resources form at a rate much slower than the rate at which they are consumed. Recycling is the process of recovering valuable materials from waste or scrap.

2. Humans consume most natural resources by using products made from the resources.

3. b

4. Sample answer: We can conserve natural resources by using them only when necessary, by reusing them whenever possible, and by recycling them.

5. 3.3 L/h × 8.6 h = 28.38 L

6. Answers may vary. Students should note that most human activity affects Earth's resources.

7. Sample answer: aluminum cans, milk jugs, glass bottles, paper, and plastic bottles

8. Sample answer: The population is significantly larger now than it was 100 years ago, so many nonrenewable resources are being used at a much faster rate than they were used in the past. As these resources become harder to find, people may begin to use renewable resources.

CHAPTER RESOURCES
Chapter Resource File
- Section Quiz GENERAL
- Section Review GENERAL
- Vocabulary and Section Summary GENERAL
- Reinforcement Worksheet BASIC

Section 1 • Natural Resources

SECTION 2

Focus

Overview
In this section, students will learn how fossil fuels, such as petroleum, natural gas, and coal, form. Students will also learn where fossil-fuel deposits are found in the United States. The section discusses some of the ways we obtain fossil fuels and the environmental problems associated with obtaining and using fossil fuels.

🔔 Bellringer
Pose this question on the board: "What does the term *fossil fuels* imply about the source of these fuels?" (The term *fossil fuels* implies that these fuels are derived from the remains of ancient life.)

Motivate

Discussion — GENERAL

Fossil-Fuel Use Lead students in a discussion about why fossil fuels are so widely used as energy resources. (Answers may include the cost, availability, amount of stored energy, and ease of use.) Challenge students to think about qualities an ideal fuel should have. (Sample answer: It should be abundant, be affordable, be easy to obtain, and produce little waste.) **LS** Verbal

---

SECTION 2

READING WARM-UP

Objectives
- Describe what energy resources are.
- Identify three different forms of fossil fuels.
- Explain how fossil fuels form.
- Describe how fossil fuels are found and obtained.
- Identify four problems with fossil fuels.

Terms to Learn
fossil fuel
petroleum
natural gas
coal
acid precipitation
smog

READING STRATEGY

Brainstorming The key idea of this section is fossil fuels. Brainstorm words and phrases related to fossil fuels.

fossil fuel a nonrenewable energy resource formed from the remains of organisms that lived long ago; examples include oil, coal, and natural gas

Figure 1 Light produced from electrical energy can be seen in this satellite image taken from space.

CHAPTER RESOURCES

Chapter Resource File
- Lesson Plan
- Directed Reading A BASIC
- Directed Reading B SPECIAL NEEDS

Technology
- Transparencies
  - Bellringer
  - LINK TO PHYSICAL SCIENCE Energy Conversions in a Car Engine
  - Porous Rocks as Reservoirs for Fossil Fuels

Fossil Fuels

How does a sunny day 200 million years ago relate to your life today?

Chances are that if you traveled to school today or used a product made of plastic, you used some of the energy from sunlight that fell on Earth several hundred million years ago. Life as you know it would be very different without the fuels or products formed from plants and animals that lived alongside the dinosaurs.

Energy Resources

The fuels we use to run cars, ships, planes, and factories and to generate electrical energy, shown in **Figure 1,** are energy resources. *Energy resources* are natural resources that humans use to generate energy. Most of the energy we use comes from a group of natural resources called fossil fuels. A **fossil fuel** is a nonrenewable energy resource formed from the remains of plants and animals that lived long ago. Examples of fossil fuels include petroleum, coal, and natural gas.

Energy is released from fossil fuels when they are burned. For example, the energy from burning coal in a power plant is used to produce electrical energy. However, because fossil fuels are a nonrenewable resource, once they are burned, they are gone. Therefore, like other resources, fossil fuels need to be conserved. In the 21st century, societies will continue to explore alternatives to fossil fuels. But they will also focus on developing more-efficient ways to use these fuels.

Science Bloopers

Fossil-Fuel Fountain On January 10, 1901, oil from the famous Spindletop well near Beaumont, Texas, began to flow. In fact, the crude oil spewed higher than 90 m into the air! Drillers were caught off guard by the tremendous volume of petroleum—100,000 barrels per day. And drillers took 9 days to cap the well.

126 Chapter 5 • Energy Resources

Figure 2 *Some refineries use a process called* distillation *to separate petroleum into various types of petroleum products.*

Types of Fossil Fuels

All living things are made up of the element carbon. Because fossil fuels are formed from the remains of plants and animals, all fossil fuels are made of carbon, too. Most of the carbon in fossil fuels exists as hydrogen-carbon compounds called *hydrocarbons*. But different fossil fuels have different forms. Fossil fuels may exist as liquids, gases, or solids.

Liquid Fossil Fuels: Petroleum

A liquid mixture of complex hydrocarbon compounds is called **petroleum.** Petroleum is also commonly known as *crude oil*. Petroleum is separated into several kinds of products in refineries, such as the one shown in **Figure 2**. Examples of fossil fuels separated from petroleum are gasoline, jet fuel, kerosene, diesel fuel, and fuel oil.

More than 40% of the world's energy comes from petroleum products. Petroleum products are the main fuel for forms of transportation, such as airplanes, trains, boats, and ships. Crude oil is so valuable that it is often called *black gold*.

Gaseous Fossil Fuels: Natural Gas

A gaseous mixture of hydrocarbons is called **natural gas.** Most natural gas is used for heating, but it is also used for generating electrical energy. Your kitchen stove may be powered by natural gas. Some motor vehicles, such as the van in **Figure 3**, use natural gas as fuel. An advantage of using natural gas is that using it causes less air pollution than using oil does. However, natural gas is very flammable. Gas leaks can lead to fires or deadly explosions.

Methane, CH_4, is the main component of natural gas. But other components, such as butane and propane, can be separated from natural gas, too. Butane and propane are often used as fuel for camp stoves and outdoor grills.

✓ **Reading Check** What is natural gas most often used for? *(See the Appendix for answers to Reading Checks.)*

petroleum a liquid mixture of complex hydrocarbon compounds; used widely as a fuel source

natural gas a mixture of gaseous hydrocarbons located under the surface of the Earth, often near petroleum deposits; used as a fuel

Figure 3 *Vehicles powered by natural gas are becoming more common.*

Answer to Reading Check
Natural gas is most often used for heating and generating electrical energy.

Teach

CONNECTION to Physical Science — GENERAL

How Car Engines Work Use the teaching transparency entitled "Energy Conversions in a Car Engine" to show students how car engines convert the chemical energy of gasoline into thermal energy and kinetic energy through combustion. **LS** Visual

BRAIN FOOD

The Origin of Fossil Fuels
One characteristic all fossil fuels share is that they formed from the remains of organisms that lived long ago. Over millions of years, these remains are buried by sediment and rock. Rising pressure and temperature cause slow chemical changes that cause the formation of coal, petroleum, or natural gas. When hydrocarbons combust, or combine rapidly with oxygen, they release the energy stored in the carbon-carbon and carbon-hydrogen bonds made by organisms when they were alive.

CONNECTION ACTIVITY
Language Arts — ADVANCED

Creative Writing Petroleum is more than a fuel source; it is refined to make plastics and other petrochemical products we use every day. Petrochemicals are used to create medicines, inks, solvents, clothing, fertilizers, and many other products. Have students make a list of 20 products made from petroleum. Then, have students write a story about a world without petroleum products. **LS** Verbal

Section 2 • Fossil Fuels

Teach, continued

CONNECTION ACTIVITY
Real World — ADVANCED

Electrical Energy in Your Community Have students find out what fuel sources are used to produce electrical energy in their community. Have students create a list of 15 ways electrical energy consumption in your community can be reduced. Have students create an anonymous survey to find out how many people would follow their 15-step energy conservation plan.
LS Interpersonal

Cultural Awareness — GENERAL

Ancient Wells Natural gas seeps were first discovered in ancient Persia (now Iran) between 6000 and 2000 BCE. Records from China indicate that natural gas was used beginning about 900 BCE. The Chinese drilled the first known natural gas well by using bamboo poles and primitive drill bits. The well was 140 m deep. In Europe, natural gas was first discovered in England in 1659.

Answer to Reading Check
Coal was most commonly used to power trains.

Figure 4 This coal is being gathered so that it may be burned in the power plant shown in the background.

coal a fossil fuel that forms underground from partially decomposed plant material

INTERNET ACTIVITY

For another activity related to this chapter, go to **go.hrw.com** and type in the keyword **HZ5ENRW**.

Solid Fossil Fuels: Coal

The solid fossil fuel that humans use most is coal. **Coal** is a fossil fuel that is formed underground from partially decomposed plant material. Coal was once the major source of energy in the United States. People burned coal in stoves to heat their homes. They also used coal in transportation. Many trains in the 1800s and early 1900s were powered by coal-burning steam locomotives.

As cleaner energy resources became available, people reduced their use of coal. People began to use coal less because burning coal produces large amounts of air pollution. Now, people use forms of transportation that use oil instead of coal as fuel. In the United States, coal is now rarely used as a fuel for heating. However, many power plants, such as the one shown in **Figure 4,** burn coal to generate electrical energy.

✓ **Reading Check** In the 1800s and early 1900s, what was coal most commonly used for?

CONNECTION TO Chemistry

Hydrocarbons Both petroleum and natural gas are made of compounds called *hydrocarbons*. A hydrocarbon is an organic compound that contains only carbon and hydrogen. A molecule of propane, C_3H_8, a gaseous fossil fuel, contains three carbons and eight hydrogens. Using a molecular model set, create a model of a propane molecule. (Hint: Each carbon atom should have four bonds, and each hydrogen atom should have one bond.)
ACTIVITY

INCLUSION Strategies

- Learning Disabled
- Attention Deficit Disorder
- Developmentally Delayed

Have students identify three fossil fuels on separate index cards. On the back of each card, students should describe the uses of the fuel and the advantages and disadvantages of using it. Students may also list ways to conserve the fuel. Have students trade cards with a partner and quiz each other about the content of their cards. Encourage English language learners to write the information on their flash cards in English and in their first language. The cards can be used for studying or for a class presentation. **LS Verbal/Visual**   **English Language Learners**

---

128 Chapter 5 • Energy Resources

How Do Fossil Fuels Form?

All fossil fuels form from the buried remains of ancient organisms. But different kinds of fossil fuels form in different ways and from different kinds of organisms.

Petroleum and Natural Gas Formation

Petroleum and natural gas form mainly from the remains of microscopic sea organisms. When these organisms die, their remains settle on the ocean floor. There, the remains decay, are buried, and become part of the ocean sediment. Over time, the sediment slowly becomes rock, trapping the decayed remains. Through physical and chemical changes over millions of years, the remains become petroleum and gas. Gradually, more rocks form above the rocks that contain the fossil fuels. Under the pressure of overlying rocks and sediments, the fossil fuels can move through permeable rocks. *Permeable rocks* are rocks that allow fluids, such as petroleum and gas, to move through them. As shown in **Figure 5,** these permeable rocks become reservoirs that hold petroleum and natural gas.

The formation of petroleum and natural gas is an ongoing process. Part of the remains of today's sea life will become petroleum and natural gas millions of years from now.

Figure 5 *Petroleum and gas move through permeable rock. Eventually, these fuels are collected in reservoirs. Rocks that are folded upward are excellent fossil-fuel traps.*

To collect petroleum and gas, engineers must drill wells into the reservoir rock.

After fuels are successfully tapped, pumps are used to remove the fuels from the rock.

Gas
Petroleum
Reservoir rock
Water
Permeable Rock
Impermeable Rock

Quick Lab
Rock Sponge
1. Place **samples of sandstone, limestone,** and **shale** in separate **Petri dishes.**
2. Place **five drops of light machine oil** on each rock sample.
3. Observe and record the time required for the oil to be absorbed by each of the rock samples.
4. Which rock sample absorbed the oil fastest? Why?
5. Based on your findings, describe a property that allows fossil fuels to be easily removed from reservoir rock.

Quick Lab

MATERIALS
FOR EACH STUDENT
- machine oil, light
- Petri dishes (3)
- samples of sandstone, limestone, and shale

Teacher's Note: Use a light-colored shale. Shale has 2% or more organic matter, which will quickly soak up the oil.

Answers
4. Answers may vary. The rock sample that has the highest percentage of interconnected pore space should soak up the oil the fastest. Most reservoir rock is limestone, which has many connected pores.
5. Oil and gas move easily through reservoir rock that has a high percentage of interconnected pore space. This space allows for the easy removal of liquid fossil fuels.

Demonstration — GENERAL

MATERIALS
- food coloring, red and blue
- jar, glass, clean, empty
- rubbing alcohol, 100 mL
- water, 100 mL
- vegetable oil, 100 mL

Simulating Reservoirs Natural gas often accumulates above an oil deposit, as shown in **Figure 5.** Use rubbing alcohol to represent natural gas and cooking oil to represent petroleum. Add a few drops of blue food coloring to the water and a few drops of red food coloring to the alcohol. Ask students to determine the correct order to add the liquids to the jar to match the layers in **Figure 5. Note:** Rubbing alcohol is being used here to represent natural gas because it is less dense than cooking oil. However, when found underground, natural gas is in a gaseous state. **LS Visual**   *English Language Learners*

Section 2 • Fossil Fuels

Teach, continued

CONNECTION ACTIVITY
Math — BASIC

Percentage of Carbon A grade of coal contains a high percentage of carbon, such as anthracite, contains more usable energy and releases less pollution than a grade of coal that contains a low percentage of carbon, such as lignite. To find the percentage of carbon in a coal sample divide the mass of carbon by the total mass of the sample and multiply the result by 100. Have students answer the following questions:

- What is the percentage of carbon in a 10 g coal sample if the mass of carbon is 6.5 g? **(65%)**

- What is the percentage of carbon in a 15 g coal sample if the mass of carbon is 9.2 g? **(61%)**

- What is the percentage of carbon in an 8 g coal sample if the mass of carbon is 5.6 g? **(70%)**

LS Logical

Using the Figure — BASIC

Coal Formation Have students answer the following questions:

- What kinds of organisms play an important role in coal formation? **(bacteria, plants, and fungi)**

- In a given area, which would be older: peat or lignite deposits? **(lignite, because peat is an earlier stage of coal formation)**

LS Visual

Coal Formation

Coal forms differently from the way petroleum and natural gas form. Coal forms underground from decayed swamp plants over millions of years. When the plants die, they sink to the bottom of the swamp. This begins the process of coal formation.

The four stages of coal formation, as shown in **Figure 6**, are peat, lignite, bituminous coal, and anthracite. Peat is a form of coal in which the remains of plants are only partially decomposed. Over time, the peat is buried under sediment. Water and gases are squeezed out of the peat. Pressure and high temperature then turn the peat into lignite. The process by which pressure and temperature increase due to the deposition of sediment creates different forms of coal. The percentage of carbon increases with each stage of coal formation. The higher the carbon content is, the more cleanly the material burns. Pollution controls can remove most of the pollutants produced by burning coal. However, when burned, all grades of coal pollute the air.

Figure 6 Coal Formation

Stage 1: Peat
Bacteria and fungi change sunken swamp plants into peat. Peat is about **60% carbon**.

Stage 2: Lignite
Sediment buries the peat, which increases the pressure and temperature. The peat slowly changes into lignite, which is about **70% carbon**.

Stage 3: Bituminous Coal
As the lignite becomes more buried, the temperature and pressure continue to increase. Eventually, lignite turns into bituminous coal, which is about **80% carbon**.

Stage 4: Anthracite
As bituminous coal becomes more buried, the temperature and pressure continue to increase. Bituminous coal turns into anthracite, which is about **90% carbon**.

Homework — ADVANCED

Fuel-Efficient Cars In 1998, the United States consumed nearly 583 billion liters of liquid fossil fuels. More than 460 billion liters of this total was gasoline. After an average-sized car is driven 11,000 m, it has released its weight in carbon dioxide. Have students compare the fuel efficiency of commercially available cars and calculate the annual carbon dioxide reduction and fuel savings of a fuel-efficient car.

LS Logical

Figure 7 Most of the petroleum and natural gas produced in the continental United States comes from areas that were prehistoric oceans. Coal comes from areas that were swamps and bogs.

- Petroleum
- Natural gas
- Coal

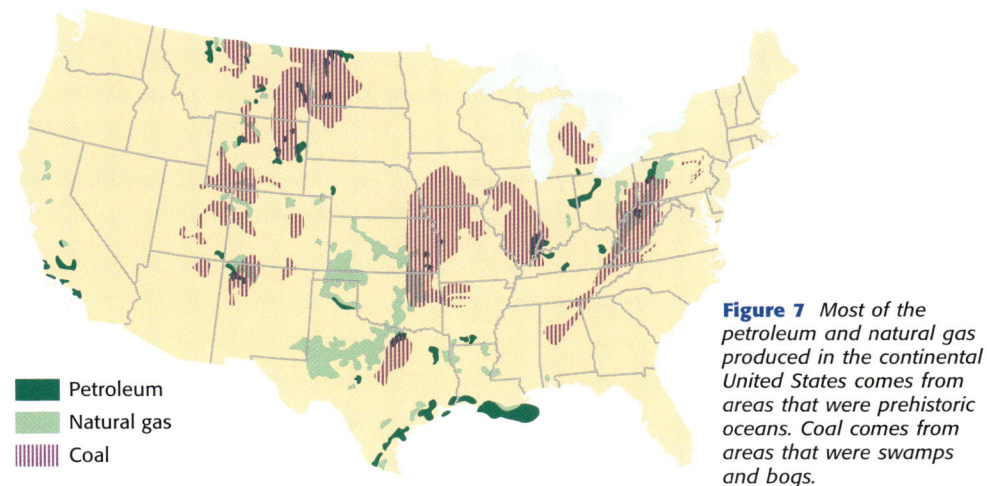

Where Are Fossil Fuels Found?

Fossil fuels are found in many parts of the world. Some fossil fuels are found on land, while other fossil fuels are found beneath the ocean. As shown in **Figure 7,** the United States has large reserves of petroleum, natural gas, and coal. Despite its large reserves of petroleum, the United States imports petroleum as well. About one-half of the petroleum used by the United States is imported from the Middle East, South America, Africa, Canada, and Mexico.

How Do We Obtain Fossil Fuels?

Humans use several methods to remove fossil fuels from the Earth's crust. The kind and location of fuel determine the method used to remove the fuel. People remove petroleum and natural gas from Earth by drilling wells into rock that contains these resources. Oil wells exist on land and in the ocean. For offshore drilling, engineers mount drills on platforms that are secured to the ocean floor or that float at the ocean's surface. **Figure 8** shows an offshore oil rig.

People obtain coal either by mining deep beneath Earth's surface or by surface mining. Surface mining, also known as *strip mining,* is the process by which soil and rock are stripped from the Earth's surface to expose the underlying coal that is to be mined.

Reading Check How are natural gas and petroleum removed from Earth?

Figure 8 Large oil rigs, some of which are more than 300 m tall, operate offshore in many places, such as the Gulf of Mexico and the North Sea.

Debate — ADVANCED
Drilling in a Wildlife Refuge
The U.S. Fish and Wildlife Service, which administers Alaska's Arctic National Wildlife Refuge, states that its primary mandate is "to protect the wildlife and habitats of this area for the benefit of people now and in the future." The refuge's coastal plain is the calving ground for the porcupine caribou herd, the most important land-based denning area for the entire Beaufort Sea polar bear population, home for 350 reintroduced musk oxen, and an important habitat for more than 180 bird species.

Encourage students to research the current status of the oil exploration and drilling projects in the Arctic National Wildlife Refuge. Divide the class into two teams, and assign one team the pros and assign one team the cons of drilling in the Arctic National Wildlife Refuge. Have the teams research and then debate the issue. **LS Verbal**

Answer to Reading Check
Natural gas and petroleum are removed from the Earth by drilling wells into rock that contains these resources.

CONNECTION to Climatology — ADVANCED

Writing **Carbon Dioxide and the Greenhouse Effect** One of the products of burning fossil fuels is carbon dioxide. Scientists recognize carbon dioxide as a greenhouse gas—a gas that traps thermal energy and increases the temperature of the Earth's atmosphere. Scientists have determined that both carbon dioxide levels and global temperatures are increasing. However, they have different opinions about the many possible ways increasing levels of carbon dioxide may be affecting the Earth's climate. Have students find newspaper and magazine articles that give examples of climate change. Have students write an essay discussing their predictions about greenhouse gases and climate change. **LS Intrapersonal**

Section 2 • Fossil Fuels

Close

Reteaching — BASIC

Resource Map Display a map of the United States. Have students use **Figure 7** to take turns marking the fossil fuel deposits in the United States and telling how these resources are extracted, how they are used, and what environmental problems are associated with them. **Verbal**

Quiz — GENERAL

1. Explain why we use different methods to extract fossil fuels from the Earth's crust. (We use different methods because fossil fuels are found in different locations and have different compositions.)

2. When an oil and gas reservoir is drilled, which substance is generally encountered first—oil or natural gas? Why? (natural gas; because it is less dense than oil and migrates to the top of the reservoir)

Alternative Assessment — GENERAL

Concept Mapping Have students construct concept maps that compare different fossil fuels. Their maps should include the formation of the fuel, the location of the fuel, and the extraction method. One type of fuel may have two or more locations and extraction methods. **Visual**

Figure 9 Notice how this statue looked before the effects of acid precipitation.

acid precipitation precipitation, such as rain, sleet, or snow, that contains a high concentration of acids, often because of the pollution of the atmosphere

smog photochemical haze that forms when sunlight acts on industrial pollutants and burning fuels

Figure 10 The oil spilled from the carrier, Treasure, endangered the lives of many animals including the blackfooted penguins.

Problems with Fossil Fuels

Although fossil fuels provide the energy we need, the methods of obtaining and using them can have negative effects on the environment. For example, when coal is burned without pollution controls, sulfur dioxide is released. Sulfur dioxide combines with moisture in the air to produce sulfuric acid. Sulfuric acid is one of the acids in acid precipitation. **Acid precipitation** is rain, sleet, or snow that has a high concentration of acids, often because of air pollutants. Acid precipitation negatively affects wildlife, plants, buildings, and statues, as shown in **Figure 9**.

✓ **Reading Check** How can the burning of fossil fuels affect rain?

Coal Mining

The mining of coal can also create environmental problems. Surface mining removes soil, which some plants need for growth and some animals need for shelter. If land is not properly restored afterward, surface mining can destroy wildlife habitats. Coal mining can also lower water tables and pollute water supplies. The potential for underground mines to collapse endangers the lives of miners.

Petroleum Problems

Producing, transporting, and using petroleum can cause environmental problems and endanger wildlife. In June 2000, the carrier, *Treasure*, sank off the coast of South Africa and spilled more than 400 tons of oil. The toxic oil coated thousands of blackfooted penguins, as shown in **Figure 10**. The oil hindered the penguins from swimming and catching fish for food.

Smog

Burning petroleum products causes an environmental problem called smog. **Smog** is photochemical haze that forms when sunlight acts on industrial pollutants and burning fuels. Smog is particularly serious in cities such as Houston and Los Angeles as a result of millions of automobiles that burn gasoline. Also, mountains that surround Los Angeles prevent the wind from blowing pollutants away.

Answer to Reading Check

The sulfur dioxide released from the burning coal combines with moisture in the air to produce acid rain.

132 Chapter 5 • Energy Resources

SECTION Review

Summary

- Energy resources are resources that humans use to produce energy.
- Petroleum is a liquid fossil fuel that is made of hydrocarbon compounds.
- Natural gas is a gaseous fossil fuel that is made of hydrocarbon compounds.
- Coal is a solid fossil fuel that forms from decayed swamp plants.
- Petroleum and natural gas form from decayed sea life on the ocean floor.
- Fossil fuels are found all over the world. The United States imports half of the petroleum it uses from the Middle East, South America, Africa, Mexico, and Canada.
- Fossil fuels are obtained by drilling oil wells, mining below Earth's surface, and strip mining.
- Acid precipitation, smog, water pollution, and the destruction of wildlife habitat are some of the environmental problems that are created by the use of fossil fuels.

Using Key Terms

1. Use each of the following terms in a separate sentence: *energy resource*, *fossil fuel*, *petroleum*, *natural gas*, *coal*, *acid precipitation*, and *smog*.

Understanding Key Ideas

2. Which of the following stages of coal formation contains the highest carbon content?
   a. lignite
   b. anthracite
   c. peat
   d. bituminous coal

3. Name a solid fossil fuel, a liquid fossil fuel, and a gaseous fossil fuel.

4. Briefly describe how petroleum and natural gas form.

5. How do we obtain petroleum and natural gas?

6. Describe the advantages and disadvantages of fossil fuel use.

Critical Thinking

7. **Making Comparisons** What is the difference between the organic material from which coal forms and the organic material from which petroleum and natural gas form?

8. **Making Inferences** Why can't carpooling and using mass-transit systems eliminate the problems associated with fossil fuels?

Interpreting Graphics

Use the pie chart below to answer the questions that follow.

Oil Production by Region
- North America 6%
- Europe and former Soviet Union 8%
- South America 9%
- Asia 4%
- Africa 7%
- Middle East 66%

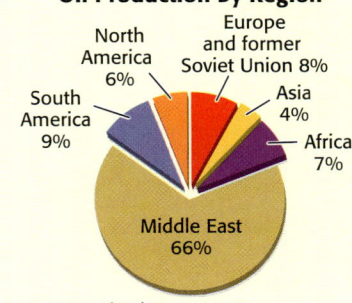

Source: International Energy Agency.

9. Which region produces the most oil?

10. If the total sales of oil in 2002 were $500 billion, what was the value of the oil produced in North America?

Answers to Section Review

1. Sample answer: An energy resource is a resource that humans use to produce energy. Fossil fuels are formed from the remains of organisms that lived long ago. Petroleum is a liquid mixture of complex hydrocarbon compounds. Natural gas is a mixture of gaseous hydrocarbons. Coal is formed from partially decomposed plant material. The combination of sulfur dioxide and water vapor produces acid precipitation. Smog is a petrochemical haze that forms when sunlight acts on industrial pollutants and burning fuels.

2. b

3. Coal is a solid fossil fuel, petroleum is a liquid fossil fuel, and natural gas is a gaseous fossil fuel.

4. Sample answer: Petroleum and natural gas both form when microscopic sea organisms die, settle to the ocean floor, and decay. The remains of organisms are buried, and after millions of years of pressure and heat they become natural gas and petroleum.

5. We obtain petroleum and natural gas by drilling wells into rock formations that contain these resources.

6. Answers may vary. Students may mention oil spills, loss of soil from strip mining coal, acid rain, the production of smog due to burning fossil fuels, and increasing atmospheric CO_2.

7. Petroleum and natural gas form underwater from the decayed remains of aquatic microorganisms. Coal forms on land from partially decayed plant matter.

8. Answers may vary. Accept any well supported answer.

9. the Middle East

10. $\$500{,}000{,}000{,}000 \times 0.06 = \$30{,}000{,}000{,}000$

CHAPTER RESOURCES

Chapter Resource File
- Section Quiz GENERAL
- Section Review GENERAL
- Vocabulary and Section Summary GENERAL
- Reinforcement Worksheet BASIC
- SciLinks Activity GENERAL

Workbooks
Math Skills for Science
- Parts of 100: Calculating Percentages GENERAL

Section 2 • Fossil Fuels

SECTION 3

Focus

Overview
In this section, students will learn about some of the alternatives to fossil fuels. The section also includes a discussion of the advantages and disadvantages of alternative energy sources.

🔔 Bellringer
Show students a picture of a wind farm, a solar energy facility, and a hydroelectric dam. Ask them which, if any, of these alternative energy facilities might work well in their community. Ask them to support their choice with three reasons.

Motivate

Discussion — GENERAL
Nuclear Energy Use the following questions to start a discussion about nuclear energy:

- What is nuclear fission? (splitting of nuclei) How does it generate electrical energy? (by producing heat)

- What are the advantages and disadvantages of nuclear fission? (advantages: no fossil fuels needed and no CO_2 or smog produced; disadvantages: high technology required and storage of nuclear waste difficult)
LS Verbal

SECTION 3

READING WARM-UP

Objectives
- Describe alternatives to the use of fossil fuels.
- List advantages and disadvantages of using alternative energy resources.

Terms to Learn
nuclear energy
chemical energy
solar energy
wind power
hydroelectric energy
biomass
gasohol
geothermal energy

READING STRATEGY
Paired Summarizing Read this section silently. In pairs, take turns summarizing the material. Stop to discuss ideas that seem confusing.

Alternative Resources

What would your life be like if you couldn't play video games, turn on lights, microwave your dinner, take a hot shower, or take the bus to school?

Most of your energy needs and the energy needs of others are met by the use of fossil fuels. Yet, there are two main problems with fossil fuels. First, the availability of fossil fuels is limited. Fossil fuels are nonrenewable resources. Once fossil fuels are used up, new supplies won't be available for thousands—or even millions—of years.

Second, obtaining and using fossil fuels has environmental consequences. To continue to have access to energy and to overcome pollution, we must find alternative sources of energy.

Splitting the Atom: Fission

The energy released by a fission or fusion reaction is **nuclear energy**. *Fission* is a process in which the nuclei of radioactive atoms are split into two or more smaller nuclei, as shown in **Figure 1**. When fission takes place, a large amount of energy is released. This energy can be used to generate electrical energy. The SI unit for all forms of energy is the joule. However, electrical energy and nuclear energy is often measured in megawatts (MW).

Figure 1 Fission
A neutron from a uranium-235 atom splits the nucleus into two smaller nuclei called *fission products* and two or more neutrons.

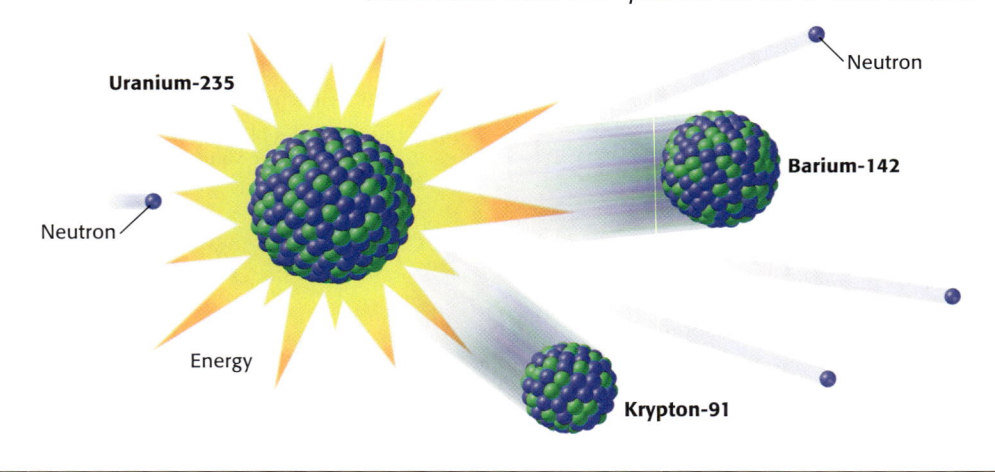

CHAPTER RESOURCES

Chapter Resource File
- Lesson Plan
- Directed Reading A **BASIC**
- Directed Reading B **SPECIAL NEEDS**

Technology
Transparencies
- Bellringer
- Fission
- Fusion

Is That a Fact!

Uncontrolled Fusion The text states that controlled fusion reactions have taken place only in labs. Other fusion reactions have taken place when hydrogen bombs have been detonated as part of a test. Neither lab experiments nor bomb tests have resulted in a fusion reaction that could be harnessed as an economically efficient and practical source of energy.

---

134 Chapter 5 • Energy Resources

Pros and Cons of Fission

Nuclear power plants provide alternative sources of energy that do not have the problems that fossil fuels do. So, why don't we use nuclear energy more instead of using fossil fuels? Nuclear power plants produce dangerous radioactive wastes. Radioactive wastes must be removed from the plant and stored until their radioactivity decreases to a harmless level. But nuclear wastes can remain dangerously radioactive for thousands of years. These wastes must be stored in an isolated place where the radiation that they emit cannot harm anyone.

Another problem with nuclear power plants is the potential for accidental release of radiation into the environment. A release could happen if the plant overheats. If a plant's cooling system were to stop working, the plant would overheat. Then, its reactor could melt, and a large amount of radiation could escape into the environment. In addition, towers like the one shown in **Figure 2,** keep hot water from potentially disrupting the local ecosystem.

Figure 2 Cooling towers are used to cool water leaving a nuclear power plant before the water is released into the environment.

nuclear energy the energy released by a fission or fusion reaction; the binding energy of the atomic nucleus

Combining Atoms: Fusion

Another method of getting energy from nuclei is fusion, shown in **Figure 3.** *Fusion* is the joining of two or more nuclei to form a larger nucleus. This process releases a large amount of energy and happens naturally in the sun.

The main advantage of fusion is that it produces few dangerous wastes. The main disadvantage of fusion is that very high temperatures are required for the reaction to take place. No known material can withstand such high temperatures. Therefore, the reaction must happen within a special environment, such as a magnetic field. Controlled fusion reactions have been limited to laboratory experiments.

Reading Check What is the advantage of producing energy through fusion? *(See the Appendix for answers to Reading Checks.)*

Figure 3 Fusion

During nuclear fusion, the nuclei of two forms of hydrogen, such as deuterium and tritium, join to form helium. The joining of nuclei releases large amounts of energy.

Answer to Reading Check
Fusion produces few dangerous wastes.

Homework — ADVANCED

The Aftermath of Chernobyl In 1991, the International Atomic Energy Agency issued a report on the Chernobyl accident that concluded that "future increases over the natural incidence of cancers or heredity effects would be difficult to discern." In 1996, however, some incidences of cancers were 100 to 200 times higher than normal in areas contaminated by fallout from the accident. Have students research the current status of the Chernobyl area and present an oral report to the class. **LS Verbal**

Teach

READING STRATEGY — BASIC

Mnemonics Use the following mnemonic device to help students remember the difference between fission and fusion. Atomic nuclei sp**li**t during f**i**ssion and **u**nite during f**u**sion.
LS Verbal

CONNECTION ACTIVITY
History — GENERAL

The History of Nuclear Energy Since the age of nuclear energy began in the early 1960s, support for nuclear power has shifted many times. By the mid-1970s, it was clear that nuclear power was not the ideal fuel promised by its proponents. The construction of new reactors had become so costly that the electrical energy generated by nuclear plants was often more expensive than the electrical energy generated by coal-fired power plants. Public concern about safety and waste disposal grew; in addition, the demand for electrical energy increased less than expected. Since 1977, no orders have been placed for nuclear plants in the United States. Encourage students to research the history of nuclear power in the United States and other countries. **LS Intrapersonal**

Section 3 • Alternative Resources **135**

Teach, continued

Group Activity — GENERAL

Building a Solar Cooker Solar cookers have been used successfully in many developing countries where deforestation is a problem. There are many different designs for solar cookers available on the Internet. Have groups of students research, build, and test their own solar cookers. Consider organizing a contest to see which group can build the most efficient solar cooker.

Safety Caution: Warn students not to look at reflected sunlight.

LS Interpersonal/Kinesthetic

MISCONCEPTION ALERT

Solar Energy Students may think that solar energy is an inexhaustible source of energy. However, it is important to note that the sun doesn't shine 24 hours a day in most areas and that the sun is not always directly overhead. Using solar energy efficiently depends on the time of day, local weather conditions, the time of year, and an area's latitude. To solve some of these problems, solar power systems use batteries to store the electrical energy they generate.

Answer to Reading Check

The energy of fossil fuels comes from the sun.

Figure 4 This image shows a prototype of a fuel-cell car. Power from fuel cells may be commonly used in the future.

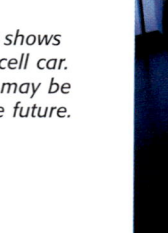

chemical energy the energy released when a chemical compound reacts to produce new compounds

solar energy the energy received by the Earth from the sun in the form of radiation

CONNECTION TO Language Arts

WRITING SKILL **Resources of the Future** In 100 years from now do you think humans will still be using fossil fuels to power their cars? Maybe humans will be using alternative energy resources. Maybe humans won't even be driving cars! Write a short, creative, science fiction story describing the energy use of humans 100 years from now.

Chemical Energy

When you think of fuel for an automobile, you most likely think of gasoline. However, not all vehicles are fueled by gasoline. Some vehicles, such as the one shown in **Figure 4**, are powered by energy that is generated by fuel cells. Fuel cells power automobiles by converting **chemical energy** into electrical energy by reacting hydrogen and oxygen into water. One advantage of using fuel cells as energy sources is that fuel cells do not create pollution. The only byproduct of fuel cells is water. Fuel cells are also more efficient than internal combustion engines are.

The United States has been using fuel cells in space travel since the 1960s. Fuel cells have provided space crews with electrical energy and drinking water. One day, fuel-cell technology may be used to generate electrical energy in buildings, ships, and submarines, too.

Solar Energy

Almost all forms of energy, such as the energy of fossil fuels, come from the sun. The energy received by the Earth from the sun in the form of radiation is **solar energy.** The Earth receives more than enough solar energy to meet all of our energy needs. And because the Earth continuously receives solar energy, this energy is a renewable resource. Solar energy can be used directly to heat buildings and to generate electrical energy. However, we do not yet have the technology to generate the amount of electrical energy we need from solar energy.

Sunlight can be changed into electrical energy through the use of solar cells or photovoltaic cells. You may have used a calculator that is powered by solar cells. *Solar panels* are large panels made up of many solar cells wired together. Solar panels mounted on the roofs of some homes and businesses provide some of the electrical energy used in the buildings.

✓ **Reading Check** Where does the energy of fossil fuels come from?

CONNECTION to Astronomy — ADVANCED

Conserving Energy in Space In space, conserving natural resources is very important. Many of the innovations in alternative energy research began in the space program. For example, NASA scientists have created solar panels that use solar energy as efficiently as possible and have developed materials that insulate space probes from the temperature extremes of space. Have students research contributions that NASA has made to alternative energy technology. Students may be interested in aerogel, the lightest solid on Earth. Aerogel, a nearly transparent substance, is only 3 times as dense as air and has 20 times the insulating power of window glass.

LS Intrapersonal

---

136 Chapter 5 • Energy Resources

Solar Heating

Solar energy is also used for direct heating through solar collectors. *Solar collectors* are dark-colored boxes that have glass or plastic tops. A common use of solar collectors is to heat water, as shown in **Figure 5.** More than 1 million solar water heaters have been installed in the United States. Solar water heaters are especially common in Florida and California.

Pros and Cons of Solar Energy

One of the best things about solar energy is that it doesn't produce pollution. Also, solar energy is renewable, because it comes from the sun. However, some climates don't have enough sunny days to benefit from solar energy. Also, although solar energy is free, solar cells and solar collectors are more expensive to make than other energy systems are. The cost of installing a complete solar-power system in a house can be one-third of the total cost of the house.

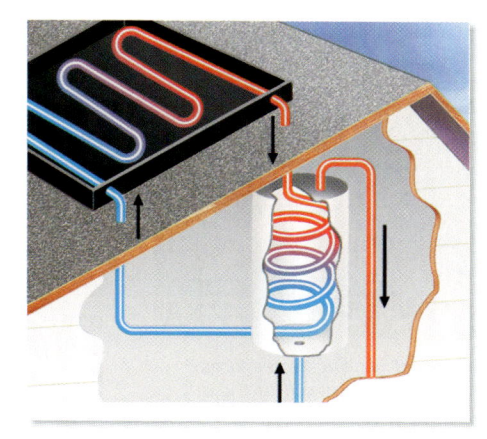

Figure 5 *The liquid in the solar collector is heated by the sun. Then, the liquid is pumped through tubes that run through a water heater, which causes the temperature of the water to increase.*

Wind Power

Wind is made indirectly by solar energy through the uneven heating of air. Energy can be harnessed from wind. **Wind power** is the use of a windmill to drive an electric generator. Clusters of wind turbines, like the ones shown in **Figure 6,** can generate a significant amount of electrical energy. Wind energy is renewable, and it doesn't cause any pollution. However, in many areas, the wind isn't strong enough or frequent enough to create energy on a large scale.

wind power the use of a windmill to drive an electric generator

Figure 6 *Wind turbines take up only a small part of the ground's surface. As a result, the land on wind farms can be used for more than one purpose.*

INCLUSION Strategies

• **Learning Disabled** • **Attention Deficit Disorder**

Have students work in small groups to construct simple wind speed indicators (anemometers). Supply each group with four paper cups, two pieces of stiff wire, a twist tie, a pushpin, and a dowel rod. Have students color one of the cups red. Then, have students connect the wire pieces with the twist tie to form an ×. Next, have students attach the cups to the wire so that all the cups face away from the center of the ×. Finally, have students attach the center of the wire × to the dowel rod with the pushpin so that the wire spins freely. Students can measure relative wind speed by counting the number of times the colored cup goes around in 1 min. Have students measure the wind speed at various locations around your school. Ask students which location would be the best place to set up a wind generator. **LS Kinesthetic**

BRAIN FOOD

Wind Power Generating electrical energy from wind energy has evolved from an experimental technology to a practical energy source in some places; revenues from wind energy projects exceed $1 billion annually. Wind turbines in the United States currently produce about 3 billion kilowatt-hours of electrical energy per year. Texas is becoming a leader in wind energy. From 1995 to 2000, enough wind turbines were installed in Texas to provide electrical energy for 40,000 homes! Have students prepare a class exhibit on the history and future of wind power in the United States.

CONNECTION to History — BASIC

Windmill History Humans have harnessed the energy of the wind to perform mechanical tasks for more than 1,000 years. Windmills were common in ancient China and Persia and were used primarily for grinding grain and pumping water. Windmills were introduced in Europe in the 12th century, and by the 18th century, they reached levels of incredible sophistication. The invention of coal-powered steam engines in the 1760s caused the demise of many windmills. But windmills remained the most efficient way to pump water—they played a key role in the settlement of the American West. In fact, many ranchers still use windmills to pump water for cattle and for irrigation.

Section 3 • Alternative Resources

Teach, continued

READING STRATEGY — BASIC

Prediction Guide Have students predict whether the following statements are true or false:

- Moving water can be used to produce electrical energy. (true)
- Water wheels were once used to power cars. (false)
- Hydroelectric energy is non-renewable. (false)
- Large hydroelectric dams can cause many ecological problems. (true)

Verbal

Cultural Awareness — ADVANCED

The Pros and Cons of Hydroelectrical Energy
Hydroelectric dams bring electrical energy to many communities around the world. Unfortunately, the construction of hydroelectric dams has displaced many indigenous cultures and disrupted traditional ways of life. The land that is flooded by the construction of dams is often the most fertile, and land downstream from a dam can become much less productive because it is deprived of flood sediments. Encourage students to report on the positive and negative effects of a hydropower project in China, South Africa, India, Thailand, or Brazil. **Intrapersonal**

Figure 7 Falling water turns water wheels, which turn giant millstones used to grind grain into flour.

hydroelectric energy electrical energy produced by falling water

Figure 8 Falling water turns turbines inside hydroelectric dams and generates electrical energy for millions of people.

Homework — GENERAL

Research Have students research how ocean waves and tides can be used to generate electrical energy. Have students present their information as a poster with labeled diagrams. **Visual**

Hydroelectric Energy

Humans have used the energy of falling water for thousands of years. Water wheels, such as the one shown in **Figure 7**, have been around since ancient times. In the early years of the Industrial Revolution, water wheels provided energy for many factories. Today, the energy of falling water is used to generate electrical energy. Electrical energy produced by falling water is called **hydroelectric energy.**

Pros and Cons of Hydroelectric Energy

After the dam is built, hydroelectric energy is inexpensive and causes little pollution. It is renewable because water constantly cycles from water sources to the air, to the land, and back to the water source. But like wind energy, hydroelectric energy is not available everywhere. It can be produced only where large volumes of falling water can be harnessed. Huge dams, such as the one in **Figure 8,** must be built on major rivers to capture enough water to generate significant amounts of electrical energy.

Using more hydroelectric energy could reduce the demand for fossil fuels, but there are trade-offs. Building the large dams necessary for hydroelectric power plants often destroys other resources, such as forests and wildlife habitats. For example, hydroelectric dams on the lower Snake and Columbia Rivers in Washington state disrupt the migratory paths of local populations of salmon and steelhead. Large numbers of these fish die each year because their migratory path is disrupted. Dams can also decrease water quality and create erosion problems.

Reading Check Why is hydroelectric energy renewable?

Answer to Reading Check

Hydroelectric energy is renewable because water is constantly recycled.

138 Chapter 5 • Energy Resources

Power from Plants

Plants are similar to solar collectors. Both absorb energy from the sun and store it for later use. Leaves, wood, and other parts of plants contain the stored energy. Even the dung of plant-grazing animals is high in stored energy. These sources of energy are called biomass. **Biomass** is organic matter that can be a source of energy.

Burning Biomass

Biomass energy can be released in several ways. The most common way is to burn biomass. Approximately 70% of people living in developing countries, about half the world population, burn wood or charcoal to heat their homes and cook their food. In contrast, about 5% of the people in the United States heat and cook this way. Scientists estimate that the burning of wood and animal dung accounts for approximately 14% of the world's total energy use. **Figure 9** shows a woman who is preparing cow dung that will be dried and used for fuel.

Gasohol

Biomass material can also be changed into liquid fuel. Plants that contain sugar or starch can be made into alcohol. The alcohol can be burned as a fuel. Or alcohol can be mixed with gasoline to make a fuel called **gasohol.** More than 1,000 L of alcohol can be made from 1 acre of corn. But people in the United States use a large amount of fuel for their cars. And the alcohol produced from about 40% of one corn harvest in the United States would provide only 10% of the fuel used in our cars! Biomass is a renewable source of energy. However, producing biomass requires land that could be used for growing food.

biomass organic matter that can be a source of energy

gasohol a mixture of gasoline and alcohol that is used as a fuel

MATH PRACTICE

Miles per Acre
Imagine that you own a car that runs on alcohol made from corn that you grow. You drive your car about 15,000 mi per year, and you get 240 gal of alcohol from each acre of corn that you process. If your car has a gas mileage of 25 mi/gal, how many acres of corn must you process to fuel your car for a year?

Figure 9 In many parts of the world where firewood is scarce, people burn animal dung for energy.

Cultural Awareness — GENERAL

Alternative Biomass Fuels
Given that 70% of people in developing countries burn wood and charcoal for heating and cooking fuel, the use of alternative biomass fuels is crucial to slowing rates of deforestation. In the Bolivian highlands of South America, the llama's dung is an important source of biomass fuel. In India, cow dung is used in many rural areas for heating and cooking fuel. In the deserts of Arabia, the nomadic Bedouin use camel dung as fuel, and many people in Tibet and Nepal use yak dung as fuel. In China and other countries, methane produced from composting pig manure is used to generate electrical energy.

Answer to Math Practice
15,000 mi/yr ÷ 25 mi/gal = 600 gal/yr
600 gal/yr ÷ 240 gal/acre = 2.5 acres/yr

ACTIVITY — ADVANCED

Problems with Burning Biomass Have students research biomass fuels and prepare reports. Students might choose to research the use of lumber industry wastes, agricultural wastes, organic municipal wastes, food processing wastes, aquatic plants and algae, and municipal sewage.
LS Intrapersonal

CONNECTION to Physical Science — GENERAL

Generators Hydroelectric dams and wind turbines supply electrical energy using a device called a *generator*. Generators convert kinetic energy (the energy of motion) into electrical energy (the energy of moving electrons). A generator contains a large magnet that spins rapidly within thousands of tiny wire coils. As the magnet spins, electric current is generated in the wire coils. Students can model a generator by wrapping 1 m of thin-gauge wire around a cardboard tube. Have them attach both ends of the wire to a galvanometer and pass a bar magnet quickly through the tube. **LS Kinesthetic**

Section 3 • Alternative Resources

Close

Reteaching — BASIC
Reviewing Fission and Fusion
Have students reproduce **Figure 1** and **Figure 3** and make their own labels to reinforce the difference between fission and fusion. **LS Visual**

Quiz — GENERAL
1. How are plants used to produce energy? (Plant biomass can be burned, and alcohol made from plants can be burned to produce energy.)
2. How are water wheels like hydroelectric dams? (Both devices harness energy from falling water.)

Alternative Assessment — BASIC
Conservation Task Force
Have students compile a table that lists each fuel mentioned in this chapter and compares the advantages and disadvantages of each. Have students use what they have learned in this chapter to compile a list of suggestions for conserving natural resources in their home, school, or classroom. **LS Intrapersonal**

Energy from Within Earth

If you have ever seen a volcanic eruption, you know how powerful the Earth can be. The energy produced by the heat within Earth is called **geothermal energy**.

geothermal energy the energy produced by heat within the Earth

Geothermal Energy

In some areas, groundwater is heated by *magma*, or melted rock. Often, the heated groundwater becomes steam. *Geysers* are natural vents that discharge this steam or water in a column into the air. The steam and hot water can also escape through wells drilled into the rock. From these wells, geothermal power plants can harness the energy from within Earth by pumping the steam and hot water, as shown in **Figure 10**. The world's largest geothermal power plant in California, called *The Geysers*, produces electrical energy for 1.7 million households.

Geothermal energy can also be used to heat buildings. In this process, hot water and steam are used to heat a fluid. Then, this fluid is pumped through a building in order to heat the building. Buildings in Iceland are heated from the country's many geothermal sites in this way.

Reading Check How do geothermal power plants obtain geothermal energy from the Earth?

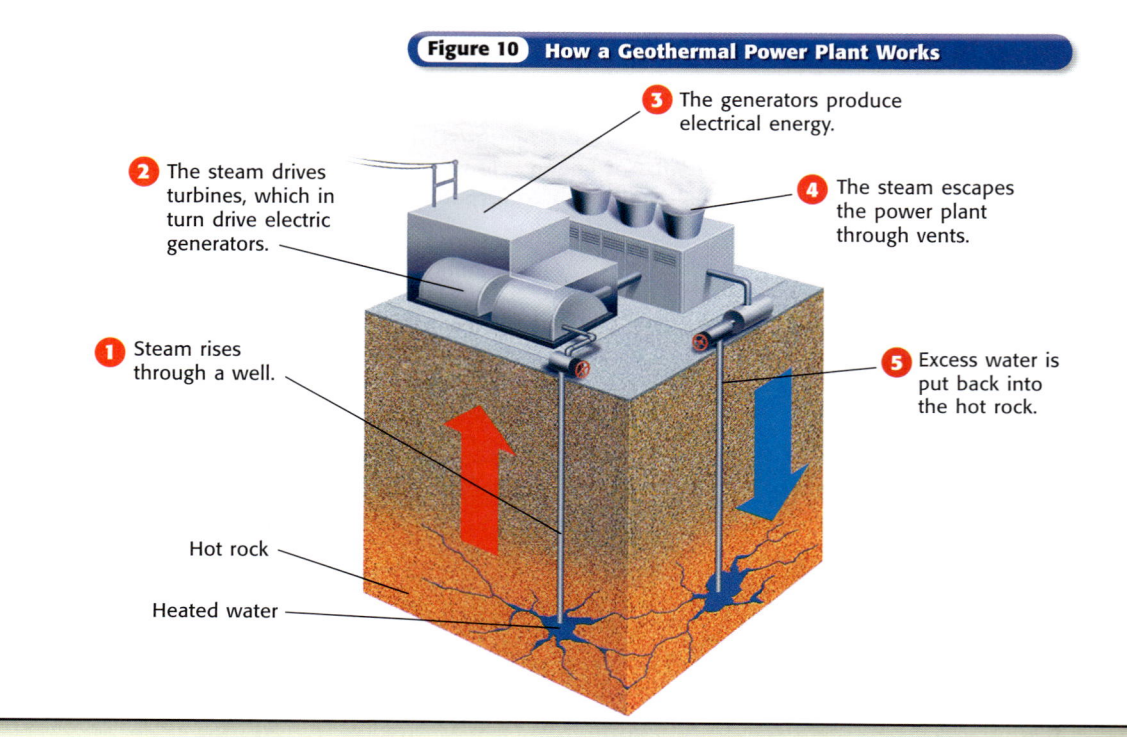

Figure 10 How a Geothermal Power Plant Works

1. Steam rises through a well.
2. The steam drives turbines, which in turn drive electric generators.
3. The generators produce electrical energy.
4. The steam escapes the power plant through vents.
5. Excess water is put back into the hot rock.

Hot rock
Heated water

Answer to Reading Check
Geothermal power plants obtain energy from the Earth by pumping steam and hot water from wells drilled into the rock.

Chapter 5 • Energy Resources

SECTION Review

Summary

- Nuclear energy can be released by fission, and or fusion. The byproduct of fission is radioactive waste.
- For fusion to take place, extremely high temperatures are required.
- Fuel cells combine hydrogen and oxygen to produce electrical energy. Fuel cells release water as a byproduct.
- Solar energy is a renewable resource that doesn't emit pollution. However, solar panels and solar collectors are expensive.
- Wind power is a renewable resource that doesn't emit pollution. However, wind energy cannot be generated in all areas.
- Hydroelectric energy is a cheap, renewable resource that causes little pollution. However, it is available only in some areas.
- Burning biomass and gasohol can release energy, but not enough to meet all of our energy needs.
- Geothermal energy comes from the Earth but is available only in certain areas.

Using Key Terms

1. In your own words, write a definition for each of the following terms: *nuclear energy, solar energy, wind power, hydroelectric energy, biomass, gasohol,* and *geothermal energy.*

Understanding Key Ideas

2. Which of the following alternative resources requires hydrogen and oxygen to produce energy?
   a. fuel cells
   b. solar energy
   c. nuclear energy
   d. geothermal energy

3. Describe two ways of using solar energy.

4. Where is the production of hydroelectric energy practical?

5. Describe two ways to release biomass energy.

6. Describe two ways to use geothermal energy.

Critical Thinking

7. **Analyzing Methods** If you were going to build a nuclear power plant, why wouldn't you build it in the middle of a desert?

8. **Predicting Consequences** If an alternative resource could successfully replace crude oil, how might the use of that resource affect the environment?

Interpreting Graphics

Use the graph below to answer the questions that follow.

How Energy Is Used in the United States

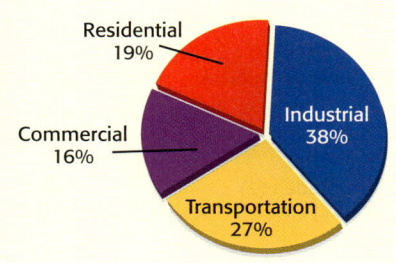

- Residential 19%
- Industrial 38%
- Commercial 16%
- Transportation 27%

Source: International Energy Agency.

9. What is the total percentage of energy that is used for commercial and industrial purposes?

10. What is the total percentage of energy that is not used for residential purposes?

Answer to Section Review

1. Sample answer: The energy released by fission or fusion is nuclear energy. Solar energy is produced by the sun. Using a windmill to drive an electric generator is called wind power. Electrical energy produced by falling water is hydroelectric energy. Biomass is organic matter that can be used as a source of energy. Gasohol is a combination of alcohol and gasoline. Geothermal energy is produced by using heat within the Earth to produce hot water or steam.

2. a

3. Solar energy can be used for heating or used to produce electricity.

4. Hydroelectric energy production is practical in areas in which there are large rivers.

5. Sample answer: Burning biomass and converting plant material to alcohol that can be burned are two ways to release biomass energy.

6. Steam and water heated by geothermal energy can be used to generate electrical energy. Water heated by geothermal energy can also be used as a direct heat source.

7. Nuclear power plants require large volumes of water to prevent overheating and to generate steam. There is little water in the desert.

8. Answers may vary. Accept any well supported answer.

9. $16\% + 38\% = 54\%$

10. $16\% + 27\% + 38\% = 81\%$

CHAPTER RESOURCES

Chapter Resource File
- Section Quiz GENERAL
- Section Review GENERAL
- Vocabulary and Section Summary GENERAL
- Critical Thinking ADVANCED

Technology
- Interactive Explorations CD-ROM
  - The Generation Gap GENERAL

Workbooks
- Math Skills for Science
  - Radioactive Decay and the Half-life GENERAL

Section 3 • Alternative Resources 141

Model-Making Lab

Make a Water Wheel

Teacher's Notes

Time Required
One or two 45-minute class periods

Lab Ratings

EASY →→→ HARD

Teacher Prep — easy
Student Set-Up — medium
Concept Level — easy
Clean Up — easy-medium

MATERIALS
The materials listed are best for a group of 3 or 4 students.

Safety Caution
Remind students to review all safety cautions and icons before beginning this lab activity.

Preparation Notes
One week before the activity, have students bring in empty, plastic, 1 gal milk and water jugs. (Be sure that the milk jugs are thoroughly rinsed.) Also, have students bring in empty 2 L soda bottles. Obtain corks from a craft store. You may wish to have extra corks on hand. Skewers can be obtained at a grocery store; they usually come in packages of 200 and are inexpensive. Remove any rough fibers to reduce friction.

Using Scientific Methods

Model-Making Lab

Make a Water Wheel

Lift Enterprises is planning to build a water wheel that will lift objects like a crane does. The president of the company has asked you to modify the basic water wheel design so that the water wheel will lift objects more quickly.

Ask a Question

1. What factors influence the rate at which a water wheel lifts a weight?

Form a Hypothesis

2. Change the question above into a statement to formulate a testable hypothesis.

Test the Hypothesis

3. Build a water wheel model. Measure and mark a 5 × 5 cm square on an index card. Cut the square out of the card. Fold the square in half to form a triangle.

4. Measure and mark a line 8 cm from the bottom of the plastic jug. Use scissors to cut along this line. (Your teacher may need to use a safety razor to start this cut for you.)

5. Use the paper triangle you made in step 3 as a template. Use a permanent marker to trace four triangles onto the flat parts of the top section of the plastic jug. Cut the triangles out of the plastic to form four fins.

6. Use a thumbtack to attach one corner of each plastic fin to the round edge of the cork, as shown below. Make sure the fins are equally spaced around the cork.

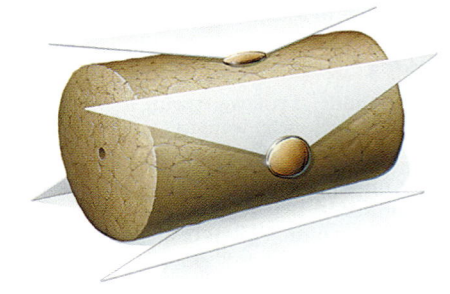

OBJECTIVES

Create a model of a water wheel.

Determine factors that influence the rate at which a water wheel lifts a weight.

MATERIALS

- bottle, soda, 2 L, filled with water
- card, index, 3 × 5 in.
- clay, modeling
- coin
- cork
- glue
- hole punch
- jug, milk, plastic
- marker, permanent, black
- meterstick
- safety razor (for teacher)
- scissors
- skewers, wooden (2)
- tape, transparent
- thread, 20 cm
- thumbtacks (5)
- watch or clock that indicates seconds

SAFETY

Tracy Jahn
Berkshire Junior-Senior High School
Canaan, New York

CHAPTER RESOURCES

Chapter Resource File
- Datasheet for Chapter Lab
- Lab Notes and Answers

Technology
- Classroom Videos
  - Lab Video

LabBook
- Power of the Sun

---

142 Chapter 5 • Energy Resources

7. Press a thumbtack into one of the flat sides of the cork. Jiggle the thumbtack to widen the hole in the cork, and then remove the thumbtack. Repeat on the other side of the cork.

8. Place a drop of glue on one end of each skewer. Insert the first skewer into one of the holes in the end of the cork. Insert the second skewer into the hole in the other end of the cork.

9. Use a hole punch to carefully punch two holes in the bottom section of the plastic jug. Punch each hole 1 cm from the top edge of the jug, directly across from one another.

10. Carefully push the skewers through the holes, and suspend the cork in the center of the jug. Attach a small ball of clay to the end of each skewer. The balls should be the same size.

11. Tape one end of the thread to one skewer on the outside of the jug, next to the clay ball. Wrap the thread around the clay ball three times. (As the water wheel turns, the thread should wrap around the clay. The other ball of clay balances the weight and helps to keep the water wheel turning smoothly.)

12. Tape the free end of the thread to a coin. Wrap the thread around the coin, and tape it again.

13. Slowly pour water from the 2 L bottle onto the fins so that the water wheel spins. What happens to the coin? Record your observations.

14. Lower the coin back to the starting position. Add more clay to the skewer to increase the diameter of the wheel. Repeat step 13. Did the coin rise faster or slower this time?

15. Lower the coin back to the starting position. Modify the shape of the clay, and repeat step 13. Does the shape of the clay affect how quickly the coin rises? Explain your answer.

16. What happens if you remove two of the fins from opposite sides? What happens if you add more fins?

17. Experiment with another fin shape. How does a different fin shape affect how quickly the coin rises?

Analyze the Results

1. **Examining Data** What factors influence how quickly you can lift the coin? Explain.

Draw Conclusions

2. **Drawing Conclusions** What recommendations would you make to the president of Lift Enterprises to improve the water wheel?

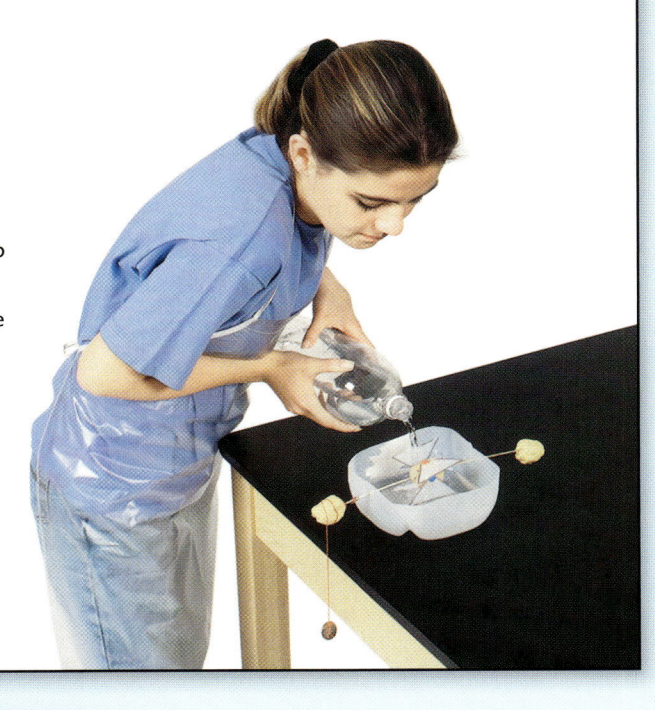

Lab Notes

If the coin is lowered instead of raised in step 13, instruct students to unwrap the thread, wrap it in the other direction around the clay, and repeat step 13. You may wish to have a class competition to see which wheel can lift the weight the fastest.

Test the Hypothesis

13. The coin rises.
14. The coin rises faster when there is more clay on the skewer.
15. If the clay is shaped so that the thread has to wrap around a bulge, the coin will rise faster. If the clay is shaped so that the thread has to wrap around a narrow part, the coin will rise more slowly.
16. Fewer fins cause the wheel to turn more slowly and the coin to rise more slowly. More fins cause the wheel to turn faster and the coin to rise faster.
17. Generally, fins that catch more water will cause the wheel to turn faster and the coin to rise faster.

Analyze the Results

1. The shape and amount of clay as well as and the number and shape of the fins influence how quickly the wheel lifts the coin.

Draw Conclusions

2. Answers may vary. Recommendations could include the following: using more fins, designing fins that catch more water, and wrapping the rope or cable around a wheel that has a large diameter.

CHAPTER RESOURCES

Workbooks

- **Long-Term Projects & Research Ideas**
  • Build a City—Save a World! GENERAL
- **Calculator-Based Labs**
  • Power of the Sun ADVANCED

Chapter Review

Assignment Guide

Section	Questions
1	5, 14, 19, 21, 22, 25, 26, 27
2	1, 6–8, 12, 15, 17, 18, 23,
3	2–4, 9–11, 13, 20, 24
1, 2, and 3	16

ANSWERS

Using Key Terms

1. petroleum
2. chemical energy
3. Sample answer: Solar energy is energy from the sun. Wind power uses a windmill to drive an electric generator.
4. Sample answer: Biomass is organic matter that contains stored energy. Gasohol is a fuel made from plant biomass and petroleum.

Understanding Key Ideas

5. b
6. b
7. c
8. d
9. a
10. a
11. d
12. Air pollutants mix with moisture in the air and produce acids. These acids fall with rain or snow as acid precipitation.
13. Solar cells are relatively expensive to make.

Chapter Review

USING KEY TERMS

The statements below are false. For each statement, replace the underlined term to make a true statement.

1 A liquid mixture of complex hydrocarbon compounds is called <u>natural gas</u>.

2 Energy that is released when a chemical compound reacts to produce a new compound is called <u>nuclear energy</u>.

For each pair of terms, explain how the meanings of the terms differ.

3 *solar energy* and *wind power*

4 *biomass* and *gasohol*

UNDERSTANDING KEY IDEAS

Multiple Choice

5 Which of the following resources is a renewable resource?
a. coal
b. trees
c. oil
d. natural gas

6 Which of the following fuels is NOT made from petroleum?
a. jet fuel
b. lignite
c. kerosene
d. fuel oil

7 Peat, lignite, and anthracite are all forms of
a. petroleum.
b. natural gas.
c. coal.
d. gasohol.

8 Which of the following factors contributes to smog?
a. automobiles
b. sunlight
c. mountains surrounding urban areas
d. All of the above

9 Which of the following resources is produced by fusion?
a. solar energy
b. natural gas
c. nuclear energy
d. petroleum

10 To produce energy, nuclear power plants use a process called
a. fission.
b. fusion.
c. fractionation.
d. None of the above

11 A solar-powered calculator uses
a. solar collectors.
b. solar panels.
c. solar mirrors.
d. solar cells.

Short Answer

12 How does acid precipitation form?

13 If sunlight is free, why is electrical energy from solar cells expensive?

14 Describe three ways that humans use natural resources.

15 Explain how fossil fuels are found and obtained.

14. Sample answer: Humans use natural resources to produce electrical energy, heat, food, and products.

15. Some fossil fuels are found underground on land, and others are found under the ocean. The type and location of fuel determine the method used to remove the fuel. Petroleum and natural gas are removed by drilling wells into rock that contains these resources. Coal is obtained either by mining deep into the Earth or by surface mining.

144 Chapter 5 • Energy Resources

CRITICAL THINKING

16. Concept Mapping Use the following terms to create a concept map: *fossil fuels, wind energy, energy resources, biomass, renewable resources, solar energy, nonrenewable resources, natural gas, gasohol, coal,* and *oil*.

17. Predicting Consequences How would your life be different if fossil fuels were less widely available?

18. Evaluating Assumptions Are fossil fuels nonrenewable? Explain.

19. Evaluating Assumptions Why do we need to conserve renewable resources even though they can be replaced?

20. Evaluating Data What might limit the productivity of a geothermal power plant?

21. Identifying Relationships Explain why the energy we get from many of our resources ultimately comes from the sun.

22. Applying Concepts Describe the different ways you can conserve natural resources at home.

23. Identifying Relationships Explain why coal usually forms in different locations from where petroleum and natural gas form.

24. Applying Concepts Choose an alternative energy resource that you think should be developed more. Explain the reason for your choice.

INTERPRETING GRAPHICS

Use the graph below to answer the questions that follow.

Energy Consumption and Population Growth in the United States

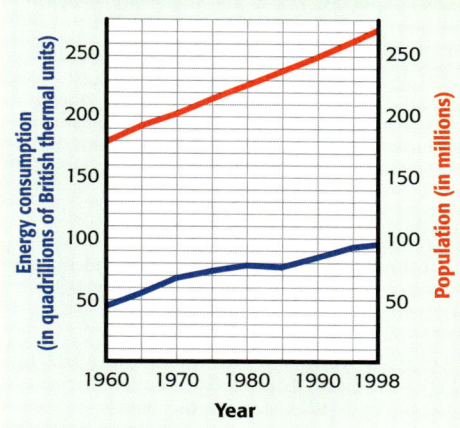

Source: U.S. Department of Energy.

25. How many British thermal units were consumed in 1970?

26. In what year was the most energy consumed?

27. Why do you think that energy consumption has not increased at the same rate as the population has increased?

Critical Thinking

16.  An answer to this exercise can be found at the end of this book.

17. Answers may vary. Accept all reasonable answers.

18. Answers may vary. We label certain resources as nonrenewable because it takes a long time for them to be replenished. Fossil fuels are renewable in the sense that they will be renewed in millions of years. But they form at a rate that is much slower than the rate at which they are used.

19. Sample answer: It is important to conserve renewable natural resources so that we don't use them up faster than they can be replenished.

20. Answers may vary. Students may discuss the amount of geothermal energy available. Geothermal energy can be exhausted in a particular location.

21. Sample answer: The sun provides energy for photosynthesis. Photosynthetic organisms use this energy to build their tissues. The tissues of dead plants and sea organisms form fossil fuels.

22. Sample answer: You can reduce the use of electrical energy and water. You can reuse products whenever possible. You can recycle things that cannot be reused.

23. Sample answer: Coal forms mainly from partly decayed plant matter. Petroleum and natural gas form from sea organisms. Therefore, they are generally found in different locations.

24. Answers may vary. Accept any well supported answer.

Interpreting Graphics

25. approximately 70 quadrillion BTU

26. 1998

27. Answers may vary. Students may state that a population increase would create a greater demand for resources.

CHAPTER RESOURCES

Chapter Resource File
- Chapter Review GENERAL
- Chapter Test A GENERAL
- Chapter Test B ADVANCED
- Chapter Test C SPECIAL NEEDS
- Vocabulary Activity GENERAL

Workbooks
- Study Guide
  - Assessment resources are also available in Spanish.

Standardized Test Preparation

Teacher's Note
To provide practice under more realistic testing conditions, give students 20 minutes to answer all of the questions in this Standardized Test Preparation.

MISCONCEPTION ALERT

Answers to the standardized test preparation can help you identify student misconceptions and misunderstandings.

READING

Passage 1
1. B
2. F
3. C

TEST DOCTOR

Question 2: Students who choose answer I may be relying on their previous knowledge, rather than reading the passage. The passage does not state that plastics cause environmental problems. However, the passage does state that plastics can be recycled into highchairs.

Standardized Test Preparation

READING
Read each of the passages below. Then, answer the questions that follow each passage.

Passage 1 Did you know that the average person creates about 2 kg of garbage every day? About 7% of this waste is <u>composed</u> of plastic products that can be recycled. Instead of adding to the landfill problem, you can recycle your plastic trash so that you can sit on it. Today, plastic is recycled into items such as park benches and highchairs. However, before plastic can be made into new products, it must be sorted. Plastic is sorted according to the resin codes that are printed on every recyclable plastic product. The resin code tells you the type of plastic that was used to make the product. The plastic most often recycled to make furniture includes the polyethylene plastic called high-density polyethylene, or HDPE, and low-density polyethylene, or LDPE. Both HDPE and LDPE are used to make items such as milk jugs, detergent bottles, and plastic bags.

1. In the passage, what does *composed* mean?
   A processed into
   B formed
   C crushed
   D melted

2. According to the passage, plastic products
   F can be recycled into highchairs.
   G can be recycled into cars.
   H cannot be recycled.
   I cause environmental problems.

3. According to the passage, which of the following statements is a fact?
   A The average person creates 7 kg of waste every day.
   B The average person weighs 7 kg.
   C LDPE can be used to make milk jugs, detergent bottles, plastic bags, and grocery bags.
   D Recycled plastics are too weak to be made into furniture.

Passage 2 You may have heard of the great California gold rush. In 1849, thousands of people moved west to California hoping to strike gold. But you may not have heard about another rush, which occurred 10 years later. What lured people to northwestern Pennsylvania in 1859? The thrill of striking oil did! However, people were using oil long before 1859. People started using oil as early as 3000 BCE. In Mesopotamia, oil was used to waterproof ships. The Egyptians and Chinese <u>utilized</u> oil as a medicine. It was not until the late 1700s and early 1800s that people began to use oil as a fuel for lamps to light homes and factories. Today, oil is most commonly used in transportation.

1. In the passage, what does *utilized* mean?
   A processed
   B drank
   C burned
   D used

2. According to the passage, which of the following statements is true?
   F Oil can be used to waterproof ships.
   G Oil wasn't discovered until 3000 BCE.
   H Oil was first used in Pennsylvania as a medicine.
   I Oil was used in transportation as early as 1849.

3. According to the passage, which of the following statements is a fact?
   A In 1849, people moved to Pennsylvania for a gold rush.
   B In 1649, people used oil to light homes and factories.
   C In 1849, people moved to California to find gold.
   D In 1849, people did not have any use for oil.

Passage 2
1. D
2. F
3. C

TEST DOCTOR

Question 2: Students may choose answer G, because the passage states that people started using oil as early as 3000 BCE. However, one cannot infer that oil was discovered in 3000 BCE. Answer F is the only statement that is true based on the passage.

146 Chapter 5 • Energy Resources

INTERPRETING GRAPHICS

Below is a pie chart of how various energy resources meet the world's energy needs. Use this pie chart to answer the questions that follow.

World Usage of Energy Resources

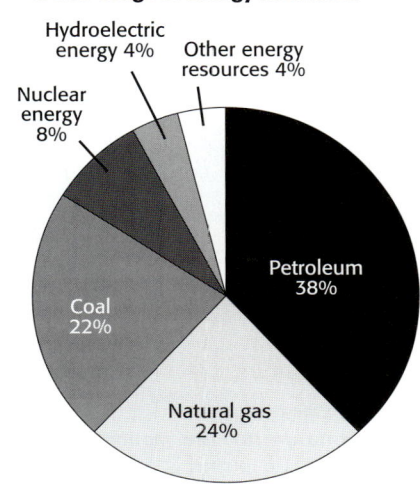

- Petroleum 38%
- Natural gas 24%
- Coal 22%
- Nuclear energy 8%
- Hydroelectric energy 4%
- Other energy resources 4%

1. What percentage of the energy used in the world comes from coal?
   - **A** 22%
   - **B** 24%
   - **C** 28%
   - **D** 38%

2. What percentage of the energy used in the world comes from fossil fuels?
   - **F** 54%
   - **G** 84%
   - **H** 96%
   - **I** 100%

3. What is the total percentage of energy used for resources that do not include fossil fuels?
   - **A** 3%
   - **B** 16%
   - **C** 24%
   - **D** 64%

MATH

Read each question below, and choose the best answer.

1. The ratio of the number of kilograms of aluminum recycled to the number of kilograms of newspaper recycled by a seventh-grade class is 34 to 170. What is this ratio written as a decimal?
   - **A** 0.02
   - **B** 0.2
   - **C** 0.5
   - **D** 5

2. Peat is about 60% carbon. Approximately how many kilograms of carbon would a 130 kg sample of peat contain?
   - **F** 7.8 kg
   - **G** 52 kg
   - **H** 78 kg
   - **I** 780 kg

3. If a 24 kg sample of anthracite is examined and 21.6 kg of carbon is found in the sample, what percentage of the sample is carbon?
   - **A** 90%
   - **B** 10%
   - **C** 9%
   - **D** 2.4%

4. Cora's car runs on alcohol made from corn. Cora drives her car 12,000 km per year, and her car's gas mileage is 30 km/L. If 200 L of alcohol can be obtained from each acre of corn that is processed, about how many acres of corn would Cora have to process to fuel her car for a year?
   - **F** 1 acre
   - **G** 2 acres
   - **H** 8 acres
   - **I** 50 acres

INTERPRETING GRAPHICS

1. A
2. G
3. B

TEST DOCTOR

Question 3: In order to get the correct answer, students should add the percentages for nuclear energy, hydroelectric energy, and other energy resources.

8% + 4% + 4% = 16%

MATH

1. B
2. H
3. A
4. G

TEST DOCTOR

Question 3: This question requires that a student is able to calculate percentages. If necessary, review ratios and percentages in class.

CHAPTER RESOURCES

Chapter Resource File
- Standardized Test Preparation GENERAL

State Resources
For specific resources for your state, visit **go.hrw.com** and type in the keyword **HSMSTR**.

Chapter 5 • Standardized Test Preparation

Science in Action

Scientific Debate

Group ACTIVITY — GENERAL

Have groups of students work together to create a model of a hydroelectric dam. As a class, find a flowing water source. Then, have groups compete to design a dam that will produce the most energy. Have students use small weights to measure the amount of energy produced by their dam. The group that creates a dam that can lift the most weight will win.

Science, Technology, and Society

Background

Hybrid cars are not the first alternative to gasoline-powered cars. As concerns grew about air pollution in the late 20th century, engineers developed cars that ran only on batteries. However, these battery powered cars were not very practical. Their batteries were heavy, expensive, and needed to be charged every 50 to 100 miles. Because of these limitations, battery powered cars did not sell very well.

Science in Action

Scientific Debate

The Three Gorges Dam

Dams provide hydroelectric energy, drinking water, and food for crops. Unfortunately, massive dam projects flood scenic landscapes and disrupt the environment around the dam. For example, the Three Gorges dam in China has displaced almost 2 million people living in the project area. Opponents of the project claim that the dam will also increase pollution levels in the Yangtze River. However, supporters of the dam say it will control flooding and provide millions of people with hydroelectric power. Engineers estimate that the dam's turbines will produce enough electrical energy to power a city 10 times the size of Los Angeles, California.

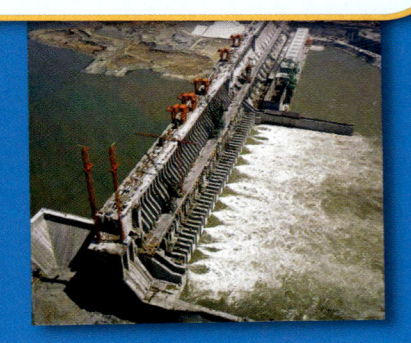

Language Arts ACTIVITY

WRITING SKILL Find out more about another dam project. Develop your own opinion on the project. What do you think the best outcome would be? Create a fictional story that expresses this outcome.

Science, Technology, and Society

Hybrid Cars

One solution to the pollution problem caused by the burning of fossil fuels for transportation purposes is to develop cars that depend less on fossil fuels. One such car is called a *hybrid*. Instead of using only gasoline for energy, a hybrid car uses gasoline and electricity. Because of its special batteries, the hybrid needs less gasoline to run than a car powered only by gasoline does. Some hybrids can have a gas mileage of as much as 45 mi/gal! Already, there are several models on the market to choose from. In the near future, you might see more hybrid cars on the roads.

Math ACTIVITY

Charlie's truck has a gas mileage of 17 mi/gal. Charlie drives his truck an average of 12,000 mi per year. Then, he sells the truck and buys a new hybrid car that has a gas mileage of 45 mi/gal. If gasoline costs $1.40 per gallon, how much money will Charlie save in a year by driving the hybrid car instead of his truck?

Answer to Language Arts Activity
Answers may vary. Accept any reasonable answer.

Answer to Math Activity
12,000 m/year ÷ 17 m/gal = 706 gallons/year
706 gal/year × $1.40/gal = $988/year of gasoline
12,000 m/year ÷ 45 m/gal = 267 gallons/year
267 gal/year × $1.40/gal = $374/year of gasoline
$988 − $374 = $614 saved

Careers

Fred Begay

Nuclear Physicist Generating energy by combining atoms is called *fusion*. This process is being developed by nuclear physicists, such as Dr. Fred Begay, at the Department of Energy's Los Alamos National Laboratory. Begay hopes to someday make fusion an alternative energy resource. Because fusion is the process that generates energy in the sun, Begay uses NASA satellites to study the sun. Begay explains that it is necessary to develop skills in abstract reasoning to study fusion. As a Navajo, Begay developed these skills while growing up at his Navajo home in Towaoc, Colorado, where his family taught him about nature. Today, Begay uses his skills not only to help develop a new energy resource but also to mentor Native American and minority students. In 1999, Begay won the Distinguished Scientist Award from the Society for Advancement of Chicanos and Native Americans in Science.

Social Studies ACTiViTY

Research the lifestyle of Native Americans before 1900. Then, create a poster that compares resources that Native Americans used before 1900 with resources that many people use today.

go.hrw.com
To learn more about these Science in Action topics, visit go.hrw.com and type in the keyword **HZ5ENRF**.

Current Science
Check out Current Science® articles related to this chapter by visiting go.hrw.com. Just type in the keyword **HZ5CS05**.

Careers

Background

When Fred Begay was growing up on the Navajo Reservation, he never dreamed that he would become the first Navajo to earn a Ph.D. in physics. At the age of 10, he was sent to the Bureau of Indian Affairs school in Colorado to learn farming. After serving in the Korean War, he was given an opportunity to study physics in college. He excelled in math and physics. His hard work earned him a Ph.D., and he never even received a high school diploma!

Begay regularly visits middle schools on the Navajo Reservation to educate and inspire the students. He draws on the geometric designs found in traditional Navajo art to teach about fractal geometry, which Begay uses in his laser research. He feels that the Navajo culture helped prepare him for life as a physicist, although he didn't know it at the time. For example, Navajo math is base-8, a type of math commonly used in computer science. Also, his parents were traditional healers, and Begay believes they helped to develop the abstract reasoning skills that are important to his work.

Answer to Social Studies Activity
Answers may vary depending on which Native American tribe the students choose to research. Sample answer: Resources used by Native Americans include native plants, such as yucca or pine, animal resources, such as deer and buffalo, and mineral resources, such as clay, turquoise, and silver.

6 The Rock and Fossil Record
Chapter Planning Guide

Compression guide: To shorten instruction because of time limitations, omit Section 1.

OBJECTIVES	LABS, DEMONSTRATIONS, AND ACTIVITIES	TECHNOLOGY RESOURCES
PACING • 90 min pp. 150–155 **Chapter Opener**	SE **Start-up Activity**, p. 151 GENERAL	OSP **Parent Letter** GENERAL CD **Student Edition on CD-ROM** CD **Guided Reading Audio CD** CRF **Chapter Starter Transparency*** VID **Brain Food Video Quiz**
Section 1 Earth's Story and Those Who First Listened • Compare uniformitarianism and catastrophism. • Describe how the science of geology has changed over the past 200 years. • Explain the role of paleontology in the study of Earth's history.	TE **Activity** Debate Posters, p. 152 GENERAL SE **Connection to Biology** Darwin and Lyell, p. 153 GENERAL TE **Connection Activity** Language Arts, p. 153 GENERAL LB **Inquiry Labs** A Penny for Your Thoughts* GENERAL	CRF **Lesson Plans*** TR **Bellringer Transparency*** TR **Hutton and the Principle of Uniformitarianism***
PACING • 45 min pp. 156–161 **Section 2 Relative Dating: Which Came First?** • Explain how relative dating is used in geology. • Explain the principle of superposition. • Describe how the geologic column is used in relative dating. • Identify two events and two features that disrupt rock layers. • Explain how physical features are used to determine relative ages.	TE **Demonstration** Superposition, p. 156 GENERAL TE **Activity** Modeling Faults and Intrusions, p. 158 GENERAL TE **Group Activity** Field Trip, p. 158 TE **Activity** Unconformities, p. 159 BASIC SE **Skills Practice Lab** How Do You Stack Up?, p. 178 GENERAL	CRF **Lesson Plans*** TR **Bellringer Transparency*** TR **Constructing the Geologic Column*** VID **Lab Videos for Earth Science**
PACING • 45 min pp. 162–165 **Section 3 Absolute Dating: A Measure of Time** • Describe how radioactive decay occurs. • Explain how radioactive decay relates to radiometric dating. • Identify four types of radiometric dating. • Determine the best type of radiometric dating to use to date an object.	TE **Activity** Absolute Dating Skit, p. 162 GENERAL TE **Connection Activity** Math, p. 162 GENERAL LB **Long-Term Projects & Research Ideas** The Hard Rock Chronicles* ADVANCED LB **Labs You Can Eat** Geopancakes* BASIC	CRF **Lesson Plans*** TR **Bellringer Transparency*** TR **LINK TO PHYSICAL SCIENCE** Radioactive Decay and Half-Life*
PACING • 45 min pp. 166–171 **Section 4 Looking at Fossils** • Describe five ways that different types of fossils form. • List three types of fossils that are not part of organisms. • Explain how fossils can be used to determine the history of changes in environments and organisms. • Explain how index fossils can be used to date rock layers.	TE **Group Activity** Carbon Impressions, p. 166 GENERAL SE **Connection to Environmental Science** Preservation in Ice, p. 167 GENERAL TE **Activity** Making Fossils, p. 167 GENERAL TE **Group Activity** Imagining Environmental Change, p. 169 GENERAL SE **Quick Lab** Make a Fossil, p. 169 GENERAL SE **School-to-Home Activity** Fossil Hunt, p. 170 GENERAL	CRF **Lesson Plans*** TR **Bellringer Transparency***
PACING • 45 min pp. 172–177 **Section 5 Time Marches On** • Explain how geologic time is recorded in rock layers. • Identify important dates on the geologic time scale. • Explain how environmental changes resulted in the extinction of some species.	TE **Connection Activity** Math, p. 172 GENERAL TE **Activity** Learning About the Eons, p. 173 BASIC TE **Connection Activity** Language Arts, p. 174 GENERAL TE **Activity** Prehistoric Illustrations, p. 176 ADVANCED LB **EcoLabs & Field Activities** Rock of Ages* ADVANCED SE **Science in Action** Math, Social Studies, and Language Arts Activities, p. 174 GENERAL	CRF **Lesson Plans*** TR **Bellringer Transparency*** TR **LINK TO LIFE SCIENCE** The Seven Levels of Classification* TR **The Geologic Time Scale*** SE **Internet Activity**, p. 173 GENERAL CRF **SciLinks Activity*** GENERAL

PACING • 90 min

CHAPTER REVIEW, ASSESSMENT, AND STANDARDIZED TEST PREPARATION
- CRF **Vocabulary Activity*** GENERAL
- SE **Chapter Review**, pp. 180–181 GENERAL
- CRF **Chapter Review*** GENERAL
- CRF **Chapter Tests** A* GENERAL, B* ADVANCED, C* SPECIAL NEEDS
- SE **Standardized Test Preparation**, pp. 182–183 GENERAL
- CRF **Standardized Test Preparation*** GENERAL
- CRF **Performance-Based Assessment*** GENERAL
- OSP **Test Generator** GENERAL
- CRF **Test Item Listing*** GENERAL

Online and Technology Resources

go.hrw.com
Visit go.hrw.com for a variety of free resources related to this textbook. Enter the keyword HZ5FOS.

Holt Online Learning
Students can access interactive problem-solving help and active visual concept development with the *Holt Science and Technology* Online Edition available at **www.hrw.com**.

Guided Reading Audio CD
Also in Spanish
A direct reading of each chapter for auditory learners, reluctant readers, and Spanish-speaking students.

Science Tutor CD-ROM
Excellent for remediation and test practice.

Chapter 6 • The Rock and Fossil Record

KEY

SE	Student Edition	**CRF**	Chapter Resource File	**SS**	Science Skills Worksheets	*	Also on One-Stop Planner
TE	Teacher Edition	**OSP**	One-Stop Planner	**MS**	Math Skills for Science Worksheets	♦	Requires advance prep
		LB	Lab Bank	**CD**	CD or CD-ROM	■	Also available in Spanish
		TR	Transparencies	**VID**	Classroom Video/DVD		

SKILLS DEVELOPMENT RESOURCES	SECTION REVIEW AND ASSESSMENT	STANDARDS CORRELATIONS
SE Pre-Reading Activity, p. 150 GENERAL OSP Science Puzzlers, Twisters & Teasers* GENERAL		National Science Education Standards SAI 1, 2
CRF Directed Reading A* ■ BASIC, B* SPECIAL NEEDS CRF Vocabulary and Section Summary* GENERAL SE Reading Strategy Reading Organizer, p. 152 GENERAL	SE Reading Checks, pp. 153, 154 GENERAL TE Reteaching, p. 154 BASIC TE Quiz, p. 154 GENERAL TE Alternative Assessment, p. 154 GENERAL SE Section Review,* p. 155 ■ GENERAL CRF Section Quiz* GENERAL	UCP 2, 4; SAI 1, 2; SPSP 5; HNS 1, 2, 3; ES 2a
CRF Directed Reading A* ■ BASIC, B* SPECIAL NEEDS CRF Vocabulary and Section Summary* GENERAL SE Reading Strategy Reading Organizer, p. 156 GENERAL TE Reading Strategy Prediction Guide, p. 158 BASIC CRF Reinforcement Worksheet A Geologic Column Sandwich* GENERAL	SE Reading Checks, pp. 157, 159, 160 GENERAL TE Reteaching, p. 160 BASIC TE Quiz, p. 160 GENERAL TE Alternative Assessment, p. 160 GENERAL SE Section Review,* p. 161 ■ GENERAL CRF Section Quiz* GENERAL	UCP 1, 2; HNS 2; ES 2b
CRF Directed Reading A* ■ BASIC, B* SPECIAL NEEDS CRF Vocabulary and Section Summary* GENERAL SE Reading Strategy Reading Organizer, p. 162 GENERAL TE Reading Strategy Activity, p. 163 GENERAL TE Inclusion Strategies, p. 163	SE Reading Checks, pp. 163, 164 GENERAL TE Reteaching, p. 164 BASIC TE Quiz, p. 164 GENERAL TE Alternative Assessment, p. 164 GENERAL SE Section Review,* p. 165 ■ GENERAL CRF Section Quiz* GENERAL	UCP 1, 3; SAI 1, 2; ST 2; SPSP 5; HNS 1, 2, 3; ES 2b
CRF Directed Reading A* ■ BASIC, B* SPECIAL NEEDS CRF Vocabulary and Section Summary* GENERAL SE Reading Strategy Reading Organizer, p. 166 GENERAL TE Reading Strategy Activity, p. 167 GENERAL CRF Critical Thinking Adiós Alamosaurus* ADVANCED	SE Reading Checks, pp. 166, 168, 170, 171 GENERAL TE Homework, p. 169 GENERAL TE Reteaching, p. 170 BASIC TE Quiz, p. 170 GENERAL TE Alternative Assessment, p. 170 ADVANCED TE Homework, p. 170 GENERAL SE Section Review,* p. 171 ■ GENERAL CRF Section Quiz* GENERAL	UCP 1, 2, 3, 4; SAI 1, 2; SPSP 5; ES 1k, 2b
CRF Directed Reading A* ■ BASIC, B* SPECIAL NEEDS CRF Vocabulary and Section Summary* GENERAL SE Reading Strategy Brainstorming, p. 172 GENERAL TE Reading Strategy Mnemonics, p. 174 GENERAL TE Inclusion Strategies, p. 175	SE Reading Checks, pp. 173, 174, 176 GENERAL TE Homework, p. 173 ADVANCED TE Reteaching, p. 176 BASIC TE Quiz, p. 176 GENERAL TE Alternative Assessment, p. 176 GENERAL SE Section Review,* p. 177 ■ GENERAL TE Homework, p. 177 GENERAL CRF Section Quiz* GENERAL	UCP 1, 3; SAI 1, 2; ES 2b

One-Stop Planner® CD-ROM

This convenient CD-ROM includes:
- Lab Materials QuickList Software
- Holt Calendar Planner
- Customizable Lesson Plans
- Printable Worksheets
- ExamView® Test Generator

CNN Student News

cnnstudentnews.com

Find the latest news, lesson plans, and activities related to important scientific events.

SciLinks NSTA

www.scilinks.org

Maintained by the **National Science Teachers Association.** See Chapter Enrichment pages for a complete list of topics.

Current Science®

Check out *Current Science* articles and activities by visiting the HRW Web site at **go.hrw.com.** Just type in the keyword **HZ5CS06T.**

Classroom Videos

- **Lab Videos** demonstrate the chapter lab.
- **Brain Food Video Quizzes** help students review the chapter material.
- **CNN Videos** bring science into your students' daily life.

Chapter 6 • Chapter Planning Guide

6 Chapter Resources

Visual Resources

CHAPTER STARTER TRANSPARENCY
BELLRINGER TRANSPARENCIES
TEACHING TRANSPARENCIES
TEACHING TRANSPARENCIES
CONCEPT MAPPING TRANSPARENCY

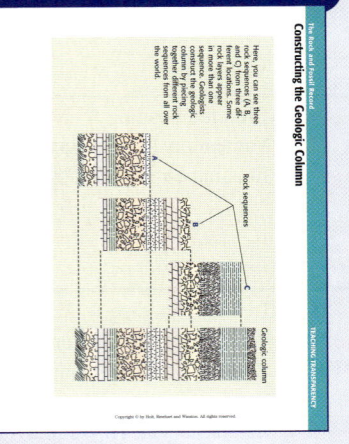

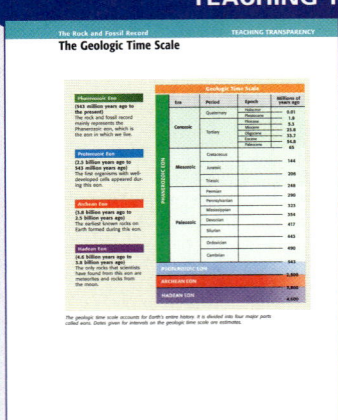

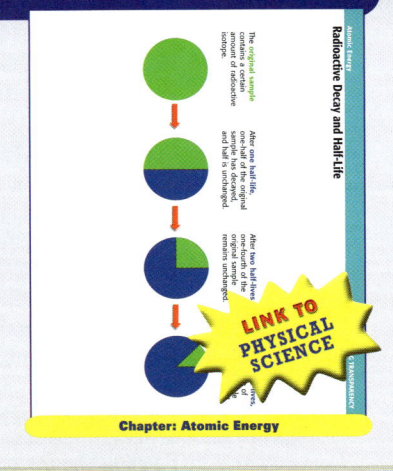

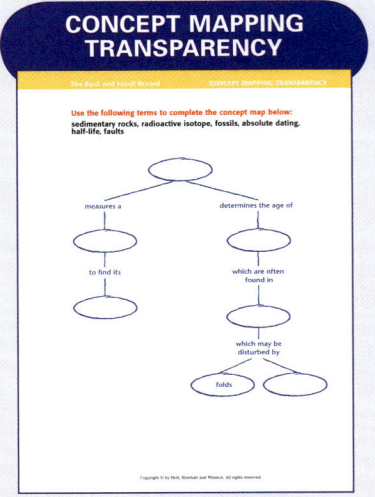

Planning Resources

LESSON PLANS
PARENT LETTER
TEST ITEM LISTING

One-Stop Planner® CD-ROM

This CD-ROM includes all of the resources shown here and the following time-saving tools:

- Lab Materials QuickList Software
- Customizable lesson plans
- Holt Calendar Planner
- The powerful ExamView® Test Generator

149C Chapter 6 • The Rock and Fossil Record

For a preview of available worksheets covering math and science skills, see pages T26–T33. All of these resources are also on the One-Stop Planner®.

Meeting Individual Needs

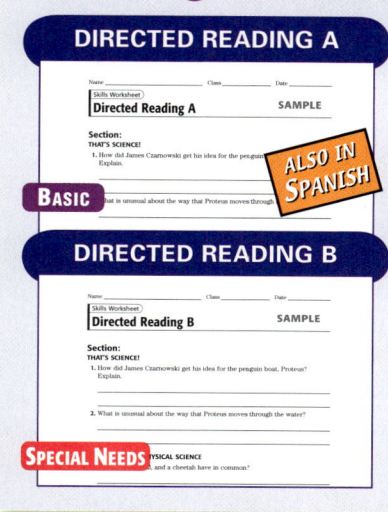

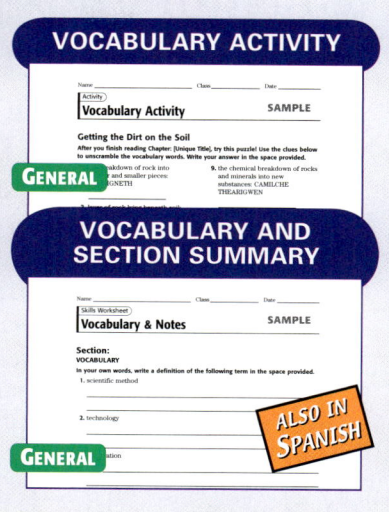

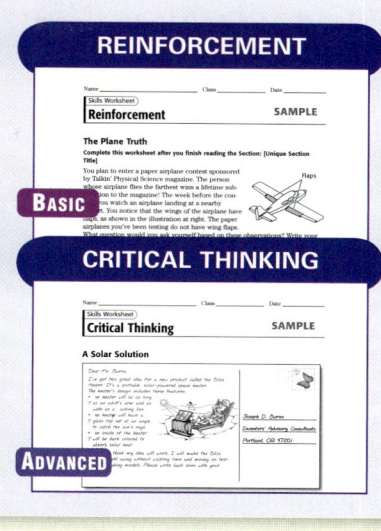

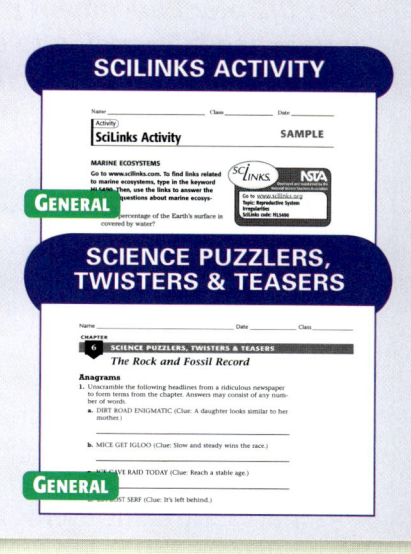

- **DIRECTED READING A** — BASIC — ALSO IN SPANISH
- **DIRECTED READING B** — SPECIAL NEEDS
- **VOCABULARY ACTIVITY** — GENERAL
- **VOCABULARY AND SECTION SUMMARY** — GENERAL — ALSO IN SPANISH
- **REINFORCEMENT** — BASIC
- **CRITICAL THINKING** — ADVANCED
- **SCILINKS ACTIVITY** — GENERAL
- **SCIENCE PUZZLERS, TWISTERS & TEASERS** — GENERAL

Labs and Activities

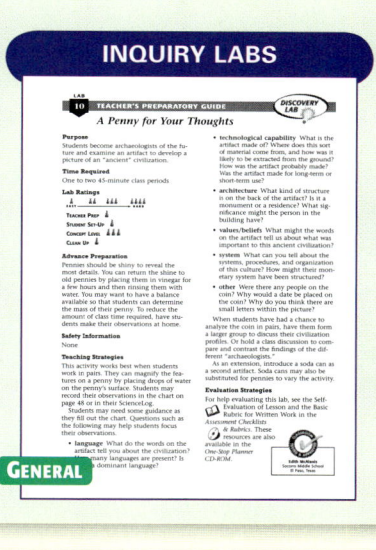

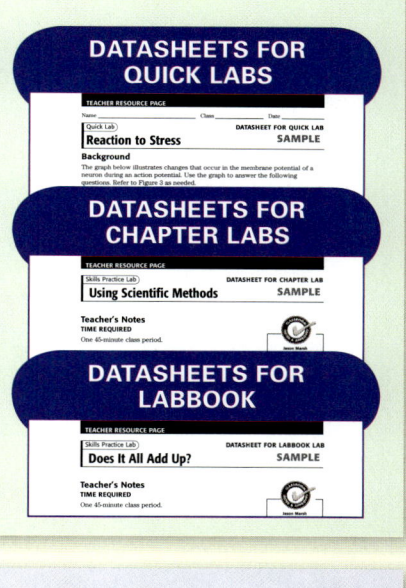

- **ECOLABS & FIELD ACTIVITIES** — ADVANCED
- **LONG-TERM PROJECTS & RESEARCH IDEAS** — ADVANCED
- **LABS YOU CAN EAT** — BASIC
- **INQUIRY LABS** — GENERAL
- **DATASHEETS FOR QUICK LABS**
- **DATASHEETS FOR CHAPTER LABS**
- **DATASHEETS FOR LABBOOK**

Review and Assessments

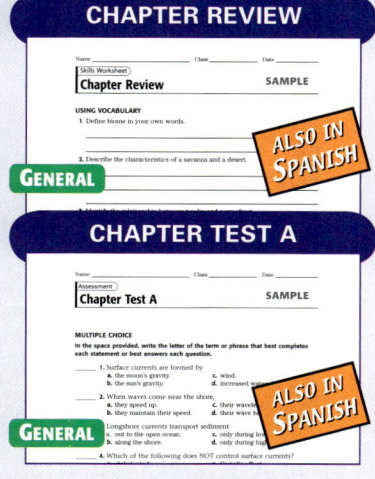

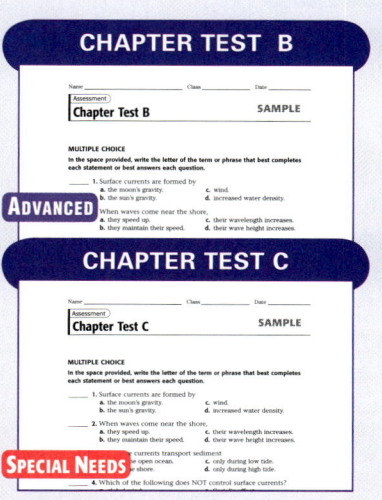

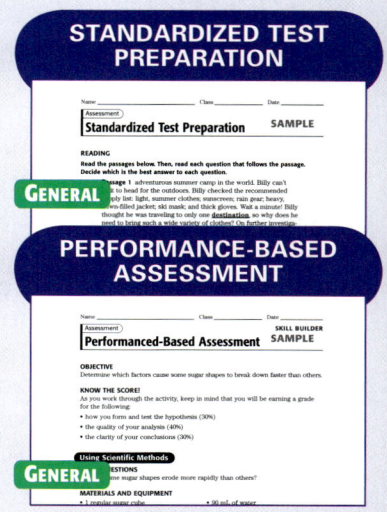

- **SECTION QUIZ** — GENERAL — ALSO IN SPANISH
- **SECTION REVIEW** — GENERAL — ALSO IN SPANISH
- **CHAPTER REVIEW** — GENERAL — ALSO IN SPANISH
- **CHAPTER TEST A** — GENERAL — ALSO IN SPANISH
- **CHAPTER TEST B** — ADVANCED
- **CHAPTER TEST C** — SPECIAL NEEDS
- **STANDARDIZED TEST PREPARATION** — GENERAL
- **PERFORMANCE-BASED ASSESSMENT** — GENERAL

Chapter 6 • Chapter Resources 149D

6 Chapter Enrichment

This Chapter Enrichment provides relevant and interesting information to expand and enhance your presentation of the chapter material.

Section 1

Earth's Story and Those Who First Listened

Actualism

- Although James Hutton was the first to introduce the principles of uniformitarianism, he is considered an actualist, not a strict uniformitarianist. He recognized that while many geologic processes happen slowly, some catastrophic events do play a role in the formation of the Earth. Today, geologists accept actualism as a more logical explanation of Earth's history.

Section 2

Relative Dating: Which Came First?

Nicolaus Steno

- Credit for discovering the principles of superposition and original horizontality is given to Niels Stensen (also known as Nicolaus Steno), born in Denmark in 1638. Though originally trained in anatomy and medicine, Steno became interested in geology while serving as the house physician to Grand Duke Ferdinand II of Tuscany. During this period, Steno made significant geologic discoveries. In addition to establishing the principles of superposition and original horizontality, Steno was one of the first Western scientists to argue that fossils are organic.

Section 3

Absolute Dating: A Measure of Time

Marie and Pierre Curie

- The Curies met in spring 1894 while Marie was studying mathematics and physics at the Sorbonne, in Paris. They married in 1895 and worked together in Pierre's laboratory. Marie began work on her doctoral thesis shortly after 1896, the year Henri Becquerel discovered that a strange radiation was emitted by uranium. Marie continued Becquerel's work, obtained her doctorate on radioactive substances in 1903, and won the Nobel Prize for physics with her husband and Becquerel.

- In 1906, Pierre Curie was killed in a wagon accident in Paris. Marie Curie was grief-stricken and dedicated the rest of her life to the work she and her husband had begun. She headed his laboratory at the Sorbonne and became the first woman lecturer at the university. In 1911, Marie received her second Nobel Prize, this time in chemistry for isolating pure radium. She died on July 4, 1934, of leukemia, which was probably caused by her prolonged exposure to radiation.

Radiometric Age-Dating

- The work of Becquerel and the Curies eventually changed the fields of archeology, geology, and paleontology. Before their work, geologists were restricted to using relative methods of dating when trying to determine the age of rocks and minerals. However, after scientists discovered that radioactive elements decay at a constant rate, physicists used this rate to calculate the ages of the rocks that contain these elements.

Chapter 6 • The Rock and Fossil Record

Section 4

Looking at Fossils

Prehistoric Weevil DNA

- In 1993, research in fossil DNA took a tremendous leap forward when Dr. George Poinar, of the University of California at Berkeley, successfully extracted fragmented DNA from the tissue of a weevil that is 125 million years old and was encased in amber found in Lebanon. In almost all fossils, the DNA has decayed and can no longer be analyzed.

Coelacanths: Living Fossils

- Coelacanths are large, carnivorous, lobe-finned fish. Their fossil record dates back to more than 350 million years ago and, until the 20th century, they were believed to have become extinct about 65 million years ago. In 1938, Marjorie Courtenay-Latimer, a museum curator in a small port village near Cape Town, South Africa, noticed an unusual blue-finned fish among the day's catch at the local docks—it was a coelacanth! A second coelacanth was recovered in 1952 by anglers, again off the African coast. Scientists believe that only a small number of the fish still survive, and in 1995, researchers declared the animal to be in danger of extinction.

- In 1998, Dr. Mark Erdmann confirmed at least two coelacanth specimens from North Sulawesi, Indonesia, 10,000 km from the African coast. The coelacanths were discovered living in volcanic caves below sea level.

Is That a Fact!

◆ The largest coprolite ever found is a mound of feces that is 65 million years old and was probably left by a *Tyrannosaurus rex*. It is 43 cm across and 15 cm high.

Section 5

Time Marches On

Life in the Precambrian Era

- The period of time from the formation of Earth 4.6 billion years ago to 543 million years ago is called the Precambrian era. Until the discovery of soft-bodied organisms in Australia in 1947, paleontologists believed that only single-celled microorganisms and blue-green algae lived during this period. Now scientists know that a wide variety of animals resembling jellyfish, annelids, and even arthropods evolved in Precambrian seas between 590 million and 700 million years ago. These animals are so far the oldest known multicellular organisms, although traces of possibly earlier ones date back to 1.2 billion years.

SciLinks is maintained by the National Science Teachers Association to provide you and your students with interesting, up-to-date links that will enrich your classroom presentation of the chapter.

Visit www.scilinks.org and enter the SciLinks code for more information about the topic listed.

Topic: Earth's Story
SciLinks code: HSM0450

Topic: Looking at Fossils
SciLinks code: HSM0886

Topic: Relative Dating
SciLinks code: HSM1288

Topic: Geologic Time
SciLinks code: HSM0668

Topic: Absolute Dating
SciLinks code: HSM0003

Chapter 6 • Chapter Enrichment 149F

Overview
Tell students that this chapter will help them learn about the history of the Earth. The chapter describes ways in which scientists use the rock and fossil record to decipher Earth's history.

Assessing Prior Knowledge
Students should be familiar with the following topics:
- basic geological processes
- the classification of life

Identifying Misconceptions
When students think of fossils, they probably think of body fossils—the hard parts of organisms most commonly preserved in rock. Make students aware that organisms can also be preserved in such substances as amber, asphalt, and ice, some of which may preserve soft tissues. The soft tissues of plants and animals can also be replaced by minerals, but this replacement rarely happens. Also inform students that the tracks, trails, and burrows made by organisms are considered fossils.

6 The Rock and Fossil Record

SECTION 1	Earth's Story and Those Who First Listened 152
SECTION 2	Relative Dating: Which Came First? 156
SECTION 3	Absolute Dating: A Measure of Time ... 162
SECTION 4	Looking at Fossils 166
SECTION 5	Time Marches On 172

Chapter Lab 178
Chapter Review 180
Standardized Test Preparation 182
Science in Action............. 184

About the PHOTO
This extremely well preserved crocodile fossil has been out of water for 49 million years. Its skeleton was collected in an abandoned mine pit in Messel, Germany.

PRE-READING ACTIVITY
FOLDNOTES **Layered Book** Before you read the chapter, create the FoldNote entitled "Layered Book" described in the **Study Skills** section of the Appendix. Label the tabs of the layered book with "Earth's history," "Relative dating," "Absolute dating," "Fossils," and "Geologic time." As you read the chapter, write information you learn about each category under the appropriate tab.

Standards Correlations

National Science Education Standards
The following codes indicate the National Science Education Standards that correlate to this chapter. The full text of the standards is in the front of the book.

Chapter Opener
SAI 1, 2

Section 1 Earth's Story and Those Who First Listened
UCP 2, 4; SAI 1, 2; SPSP 5; HNS 1, 2, 3; ES 2a

Section 2 Relative Dating: Which Came First?
UCP 1, 2; HNS 2; ES 2b

Section 3 Absolute Dating: A Measure of Time
UCP 1, 3; SAI 1, 2; ST 2; SPSP 5; HNS 1, 2, 3; ES 2b

Section 4 Looking at Fossils
UCP 1, 2, 3, 4; SAI 1, 2; SPSP 5; ES 1k, 2b

Section 5 Time Marches On
UCP 1, 3; SAI 1, 2; HNS 2; ES 2b

150 Chapter 6 • The Rock and Fossil Record

START-UP ACTIVITY

MATERIALS

FOR EACH GROUP
- clay, modeling
- paper sack containing a few small objects, such as shells, coins, paper clips, buttons, toys, or any other objects that have recognizable textures or shapes

Answers

1. Sample answer: Textures and shapes were useful in identifying the model fossils. Small details, colors, and the internal structure of the objects were not preserved.

2. Sample answer: Scientists carefully study fossil remains to determine the characteristics of the organism that became fossilized.

START-UP ACTIVITY

Making Fossils

How do scientists learn from fossils? In this activity, you will study "fossils" and identify the object that made each.

Procedure

1. You and three or four of your classmates will be given **several pieces** of **modeling clay** and a **paper sack** containing a few **small objects.**
2. Press each object firmly into a piece of clay. Try to leave a "fossil" imprint showing as much detail as possible.
3. After you have made an imprint of each object, exchange your model fossils with another group.
4. On a **sheet of paper,** describe the fossils you have received. List as many details as possible. What patterns and textures do you observe?
5. Work as a group to identify each fossil, and check your results. Were you right?

Analysis

1. What kinds of details were important in identifying your fossils? What kinds of details were not preserved in the imprints? For example, can you tell the materials from which the objects are made or their color?
2. Explain how scientists follow similar methods when studying fossils.

Chapter Lab
SAI 1, 2

Chapter Review
UCP 1, 2, 3, 4; ST 2; HNS 2; ES 1k, 2a, 2b

Science in Action
UCP 2, 3, 4, 5; ST 2; SPSP 5; HNS 1, 2, 3; ES 2b

Chapter Starter Transparency
Use this transparency to help students begin thinking about the excitement of discovering and studying fossils.

CHAPTER RESOURCES

Technology

- **Transparencies**
  - Chapter Starter Transparency **READING SKILLS**
- **Student Edition on CD-ROM**
- **Guided Reading Audio CD**
  - English or Spanish
- **Classroom Videos**
  - Brain Food Video Quiz

Workbooks

- **Science Puzzlers, Twisters & Teasers**
  - The Rock and Fossil Record GENERAL

Chapter 6 • The Rock and Fossil Record   **151**

SECTION 1

Focus

Overview

In this section, students will explore the origins of modern geology by comparing and contrasting uniformitarianism and catastrophism. Students will learn that modern geology is a synthesis of both theories and that the forces that shaped the Earth around them are still at work today.

Bellringer

On the board, write the following: "The present is the key to the past." Tell students that this phrase was the cornerstone of the uniformitarianist theory. Have students write a few sentences about how studying the present could reveal the story of Earth's history.

Motivate

ACTIVITY — GENERAL

Debate Posters Have students design a poster announcing a debate between a catastrophist and a uniformitarian. Encourage students to use phrases and illustrations that would attract supporters from both sides. Have them summarize the major points of both sides, and display the finished posters in the classroom. **LS** Visual — English Language Learners

---

SECTION 1

READING WARM-UP

Objectives
- Compare uniformitarianism and catastrophism.
- Describe how the science of geology has changed over the past 200 years.
- Explain the role of paleontology in the study of Earth's history.

Terms to Learn
uniformitarianism
catastrophism
paleontology

READING STRATEGY

Reading Organizer As you read this section, make a table comparing uniformitarianism and catastrophism.

CHAPTER RESOURCES

Chapter Resource File
- Lesson Plan
- Directed Reading A BASIC
- Directed Reading B SPECIAL NEEDS

Technology
- Transparencies
  - Bellringer
  - Hutton and the Principle of Uniformitarianism

Earth's Story and Those Who First Listened

How do mountains form? How is new rock created? How old is the Earth? Have you ever asked these questions? Nearly 250 years ago, a Scottish farmer and scientist named James Hutton did.

Searching for answers to his questions, Hutton spent more than 30 years studying rock formations in Scotland and England. His observations led to the foundation of modern geology.

The Principle of Uniformitarianism

In 1788, James Hutton collected his notes and wrote *Theory of the Earth*. In *Theory of the Earth*, he stated that the key to understanding Earth's history was all around us. In other words, processes that we observe today—such as erosion and deposition—remain uniform, or do not change, over time. This assumption is now called uniformitarianism. **Uniformitarianism** is the idea that the same geologic processes shaping the Earth today have been at work throughout Earth's history. **Figure 1** shows how Hutton developed the idea of uniformitarianism.

Figure 1 *Hutton observed gradual, uniform geologic change.*

1. Hutton observed that rock is broken down into smaller particles.
2. He watched as these rock particles were carried downstream.
3. He saw that rock particles are deposited and that they form new layers of sediment. He predicted that these deposits would form new rock over time.
4. Hutton thought that in time, the new rock would be raised, creating new landforms, and that the cycle would begin again.

Is That a Fact!

James Hutton's colleague, Sir James Hall, dramatically demonstrated Hutton's theories by melting rock in a furnace and letting it cool, which showed how the rock changed from one form to another form. This demonstration struck a major blow against the catastrophists.

---

152 Chapter 6 • The Rock and Fossil Record

Figure 2 This photograph shows Siccar Point on the coast of Scotland. Siccar Point is one of the places where Hutton observed results of geologic processes that would lead him to form his principle of uniformitarianism.

Uniformitarianism Versus Catastrophism

Hutton's theories sparked a scientific debate by suggesting that Earth was much older than previously thought. In Hutton's time, most people thought that Earth was only a few thousand years old. A few thousand years was not nearly enough time for the gradual geologic processes that Hutton described to have shaped our planet. The rocks that he observed at Siccar Point, shown in **Figure 2**, were deposited and folded, indicating a long geological history. To explain Earth's history, most scientists supported catastrophism. **Catastrophism** is the principle that states that all geologic change occurs suddenly. Supporters of catastrophism thought that Earth's features, such as its mountains, canyons, and seas, formed during rare, sudden events called *catastrophes*. These unpredictable events caused rapid geologic change over large areas—sometimes even globally.

✓ **Reading Check** According to catastrophists, what was the rate of geologic change? (*See the Appendix for answers to Reading Checks.*)

uniformitarianism a principle that states that geologic processes that occurred in the past can be explained by current geologic processes

catastrophism a principle that states that geologic change occurs suddenly

A Victory for Uniformitarianism

Despite Hutton's work, catastrophism remained geology's guiding principle for decades. Only after the work of British geologist Charles Lyell did people seriously consider uniformitarianism as geology's guiding principle.

From 1830 to 1833, Lyell published three volumes, collectively titled *Principles of Geology*, in which he reintroduced uniformitarianism. Armed with Hutton's notes and new evidence of his own, Lyell successfully challenged the principle of catastrophism. Lyell saw no reason to doubt that major geologic change happened at the same rate in the past as it happens in the present—gradually.

CONNECTION TO Biology

WRITING SKILL

Darwin and Lyell The theory of evolution was developed soon after Lyell introduced his ideas, which was no coincidence. Lyell and Charles Darwin were good friends, and their talks greatly influenced Darwin's theories. Similar to uniformitarianism, Darwin's theory of evolution proposes that changes in species occur gradually over long periods of time. Write a short essay comparing uniformitarianism and evolution.

Teach

Debate — ADVANCED

Uniformitarianism Versus Catastrophism Ask students to engage in a debate that might have taken place between James Hutton and the catastrophists. Emphasize to students representing the catastrophists that the catastrophists' argument had a strong theological base and was the accepted geologic theory of the time. Help students imagine the opposition Hutton probably faced when he introduced his ideas. Students can advertise their debates with the posters they made in the Activity entitled "Debate Posters" under the Motivate head. **LS Interpersonal**

CONNECTION ACTIVITY
Language Arts — GENERAL

A Conversation Between Darwin and Lyell Although Charles Darwin and Charles Lyell were avid correspondents and good friends, they did not agree on everything. Darwin was quick to accept the principle of uniformitarianism; he read Lyell's *Principles of Geology* before his famous 1831 voyage on HMS *Beagle*. However, Lyell did not readily embrace Darwin's theories of natural selection. It was not until much later in life that Charles Lyell vigorously supported Darwin's ideas. Ask students to write a script for a conversation that the two scientists might have had. Have them imagine that Darwin has just returned from his journey aboard the HMS *Beagle*. Ask students what questions might Darwin and Lyell have exchanged. Students can present the conversations as short skits. **LS Verbal**

Answer to Connection to Biology
Student essays should include the idea that changes due to uniformitarianism or evolution may occur over very long periods of time.

Answer to Reading Check
Catastrophists believed that all geologic change occurs rapidly.

Section 1 • Earth's Story and Those Who First Listened   153

Close

Reteaching — BASIC
Summarizing Modern Geology Have students write a one-paragraph essay that explains how modern geology incorporates catastrophism and uniformitarianism. **LS Verbal**

Quiz — GENERAL
1. What is catastrophism? (Catastrophism is the idea that geologic change occurred suddenly as a result of infrequent, disastrous events.)
2. Describe uniformitarianism. (Uniformitarianism is the principle that the Earth has been shaped by gradual changes throughout history and is shaped by gradual changes that are still occurring today.)

Alternative Assessment — GENERAL
Writing **Addressing Mr. Hutton or Mr. Lyell** Have students write a letter to Charles Lyell or James Hutton. The letter should explain why the student agrees or disagrees with the scientist's theories. Suggest that students end the letter with at least two questions that they would like to ask the scientist. Have students exchange letters and answer each other's questions. **LS Verbal/Interpersonal**

Modern Geology—A Happy Medium
During the late 20th century, scientists such as Stephen J. Gould challenged Lyell's uniformitarianism. They believed that catastrophes do, at times, play an important role in shaping Earth's history.

Today, scientists realize that neither uniformitarianism nor catastrophism accounts for all geologic change throughout Earth's history. Although most geologic change is gradual and uniform, catastrophes that cause geologic change have occurred during Earth's long history. For example, huge craters have been found where asteroids and comets are thought to have struck Earth in the past. Some scientists think one such asteroid strike, approximately 65 million years ago, may have caused the dinosaurs to become extinct. **Figure 3** is an imaginary re-creation of the asteroid strike that is thought to have caused the extinction of the dinosaurs. The impact of this asteroid is thought to have thrown debris into the atmosphere. The debris spread around the entire planet and rained down on Earth for decades. This global debris cloud may have blocked the sun's rays, causing major changes in the global climate that doomed the dinosaurs.

✓ **Reading Check** How can a catastrophe affect life on Earth?

Figure 3 Today, scientists think that sudden events are responsible for some changes during Earth's past. An asteroid hitting Earth, for example, may have led to the extinction of the dinosaurs about 65 million years ago.

Answer to Reading Check
A global catastrophe can cause the extinction of species.

Paleontology—The Study of Past Life

The history of the Earth would be incomplete without a knowledge of the organisms that have inhabited our planet and the conditions under which they lived. The science involved with the study of past life is called **paleontology**. Scientists who study this life are called *paleontologists*. The data paleontologists use are fossils. Fossils are the remains of organisms preserved by geologic processes. Some paleontologists specialize in the study of particular organisms. Invertebrate paleontologists study animals without backbones, whereas vertebrate paleontologists, such as the scientist in **Figure 4,** study animals with backbones. Paleobotanists study fossils of plants. Other paleontologists reconstruct past ecosystems, study the traces left behind by animals, and piece together the conditions under which fossils were formed. As you see, the study of past life is as varied and complex as Earth's history itself.

Figure 4 Edwin Colbert was a 20th-century vertebrate paleontologist who made important contributions to the study of dinosaurs.

paleontology the scientific study of fossils

SECTION Review

Summary

- Uniformitarianism assumes that geologic change is gradual. Catastrophism is based on the idea that geologic change is sudden.
- Modern geology is based on the idea that gradual geologic change is interrupted by catastrophes.
- Using fossils to study past life is called *paleontology*.

Using Key Terms

1. Use each of the following terms in a separate sentence: *uniformitarianism, catastrophism,* and *paleontology*.

Understanding Key Ideas

2. Which of the following words describes change according to the principle of uniformitarianism?
   a. sudden
   b. rare
   c. global
   d. gradual

3. What is the difference between uniformitarianism and catastrophism?

4. Describe how the science of geology has changed.

5. Give one example of catastrophic global change.

6. Describe the work of three types of paleontologists.

Math Skills

7. An impact crater left by an asteroid strike has a radius of 85 km. What is the area of the crater? (Hint: The area of a circle is πr^2.)

Critical Thinking

8. **Analyzing Ideas** Why is uniformitarianism considered to be the foundation of modern geology?

9. **Applying Concepts** Give an example of a type of recent catastrophe.

For a variety of links related to this chapter, go to www.scilinks.org
Topic: Earth's Story
SciLinks code: HSM0450

Answers to Section Review

1. Sample answer: Uniformitarianism is the idea that the same gradual, uniform geologic processes that shape the Earth today have been at work throughout Earth's history. Catastrophism is the idea that all geologic processes that have shaped the Earth throughout Earth's history have been sudden and catastrophic. Paleontology is the scientific study of the history of life using the remains of organisms preserved by geologic processes.

2. d

3. The principle of uniformitarianism states that all geologic processes that shape the Earth are gradual and uniform. The principle of catastrophism states that all geologic processes that shape the Earth are sudden and catastrophic.

4. Catastrophism dominated geologic thinking until it was replaced by Hutton and Lyell's theories of uniformitarianism in the 1800s. Modern geology is based on uniformitarianism, but modern geology recognizes the role of catastrophism in geologic history.

5. Sample answer: One example of catastrophic global change would be a global climate change caused by an asteroid striking Earth.

6. Vertebrate paleontologists study fossils of animals that have backbones. Invertebrate paleontologists study fossils of animals that do not have backbones. Paleobotanists study plant fossils.

7. area = $\pi(85 \text{ km})^2$
   $3.1416 \times 85 \text{ km} \times 85 \text{ km} = 22,698 \text{ km}^2$

8. Uniformitarianism is considered to be the foundation of modern geology because most geologic change is gradual and uniform rather than sudden and catastrophic.

9. Answers may vary. An example of a recent catastrophe is the eruption of Mount Pinatubo in the Philippines in 1991.

CHAPTER RESOURCES

Chapter Resource File
- Section Quiz GENERAL
- Section Review GENERAL
- Vocabulary and Section Summary GENERAL

Section 1 • Earth's Story and Those Who First Listened

SECTION 2

Focus

Overview
In this section, students learn about relative dating techniques and how the geologic column is used to determine the sequence of rock formations.

🔔 Bellringer
Ask students to arrange the following sentences in a logical order to make a short story:

1. I stood in the checkout line.
2. I selected two apples.
3. I walked home from the store.
4. I gave the cashier money.
5. I went to the store.
6. The cashier gave me change.
7. I was hungry.

(7, 5, 2, 1, 4, 6, 3)

Motivate

Demonstration — GENERAL

Superposition Stack several books on your desk. Tell students that the books represent layers of rock that were deposited at different times. Ask students which layer is the oldest. **(the one on the bottom)** Ask which rock layer is the youngest. **(the one on top)** Ask students to explain their answers, and tell them that they have just applied a basic geologic concept—the principle of superposition.

LS Visual

SECTION 2

READING WARM-UP

Objectives
- Explain how relative dating is used in geology.
- Explain the principle of superposition.
- Describe how the geologic column is used in relative dating.
- Identify two events and two features that disrupt rock layers.
- Explain how physical features are used to determine relative ages.

Terms to Learn
relative dating
superposition
geologic column
unconformity

READING STRATEGY

Reading Organizer As you read this section, create an outline of the section. Use the headings from the section in your outline.

Relative Dating: Which Came First?

Imagine that you are a detective investigating a crime scene. What is the first thing you would do?

You might begin by dusting the scene for fingerprints or by searching for witnesses. As a detective, you must figure out the sequence of events that took place before you reached the crime scene.

Geologists have a similar goal when investigating the Earth. They try to determine the order in which events have happened during Earth's history. But instead of relying on fingerprints and witnesses, geologists rely on rocks and fossils to help them in their investigation. Determining whether an object or event is older or younger than other objects or events is called **relative dating**.

The Principle of Superposition

Suppose that you have an older brother who takes a lot of photographs of your family and piles them in a box. Over the years, he keeps adding new photographs to the top of the stack. Think about the family history recorded in those photos. Where are the oldest photographs—the ones taken when you were a baby? Where are the most recent photographs—those taken last week?

Layers of sedimentary rock, such as the ones shown in **Figure 1**, are like stacked photographs. As you move from top to bottom, the layers are older. The principle that states that younger rocks lie above older rocks in undisturbed sequences is called **superposition**.

Figure 1 Rock layers are like photos stacked over time—the younger ones lie above the older ones.

CHAPTER RESOURCES

Chapter Resource File
- Lesson Plan
- Directed Reading A **BASIC**
- Directed Reading B **SPECIAL NEEDS**

Technology

Transparencies
- Bellringer
- Constructing the Geologic Column

---

156 Chapter 6 • The Rock and Fossil Record

Disturbing Forces

Not all rock sequences are arranged with the oldest layers on the bottom and the youngest layers on top. Some rock sequences are disturbed by forces within the Earth. These forces can push other rocks into a sequence, tilt or fold rock layers, and break sequences into movable parts. Sometimes, geologists even find rock sequences that are upside down! The disruptions of rock sequences pose a challenge to geologists trying to determine the relative ages of rocks. Fortunately, geologists can get help from a very valuable tool—the geologic column.

The Geologic Column

To make their job easier, geologists combine data from all the known undisturbed rock sequences around the world. From this information, geologists create the geologic column, as illustrated in **Figure 2**. The **geologic column** is an ideal sequence of rock layers that contains all the known fossils and rock formations on Earth, arranged from oldest to youngest.

Geologists rely on the geologic column to interpret rock sequences. Geologists also use the geologic column to identify the layers in puzzling rock sequences.

Reading Check List two ways in which geologists use the geologic column. (*See the Appendix for answers to Reading Checks.*)

relative dating any method of determining whether an event or object is older or younger than other events or objects

superposition a principle that states that younger rocks lie above older rocks if the layers have not been disturbed

geologic column an arrangement of rock layers in which the oldest rocks are at the bottom

Figure 2 Constructing the Geologic Column

Here, you can see three rock sequences (A, B, and C) from three different locations. Some rock layers appear in more than one sequence. Geologists construct the geologic column by piecing together different rock sequences from all over the world.

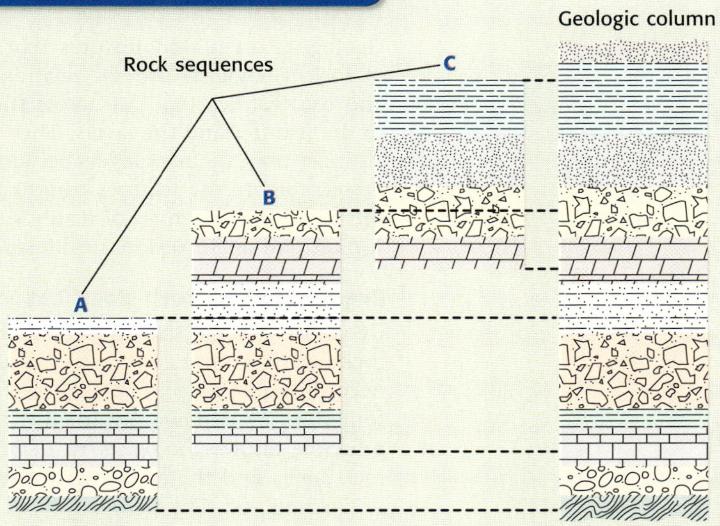

Teach

Using the Figure — BASIC
Geologic Column Practice
The geologic column is an easy concept for students to understand if they get some hands-on practice. Before the lesson, you may wish to make photocopies of **Figure 2**. Cut out the columns, and have students work independently to piece them together correctly. **English Language Learners**
LS Visual/Logical

MISCONCEPTION ALERT

The Geologic Column
Students may think that there is a place on Earth that has a continuous sequence of all the rocks formed throughout history. Emphasize to students that no single location on Earth has a continuous sequence of all of the rocks formed throughout geologic history. The geologic column is an idealized sequence of rock layers that have formed around the world since the Earth formed. The geologic column was first pieced together in the mid-19th century, and it is continually being revised as geologists map more of the Earth's rock layers.

Answer to Reading Check
Geologists use the geologic column to interpret rock sequences and to identify layers in puzzling rock sequences.

Section 2 • Relative Dating: Which Came First?

Teach, continued

READING STRATEGY — BASIC

Prediction Guide As students explore this section, ask them to answer the following questions:

- If a fault is observed in rock layers, are the rock layers or is the fault older? (the layers)
- If rock layers are deposited horizontally but you see them sharply tilted, did the deposition happen first or did the tilting happen first? (the deposition)

LS Logical

ACTIVITY — GENERAL

Modeling Faults and Intrusions
Show how intrusions and faults disturb rock layers by doing this simple demonstration. Glue several different-colored sponges together to form a model rock sequence. To show a fault, make a straight, diagonal cut through all of the sponge layers. Demonstrate fault movement by sliding the two sponge sections alongside each other. Have students work together to demonstrate intrusions, folding, and tilting. As an extension, have students create a permanent display by gluing their examples to a piece of poster board. **LS** Visual

---

Figure 3 How Rock Layers Become Disturbed

Fault A *fault* is a break in the Earth's crust along which blocks of the crust slide relative to one another.

Intrusion An *intrusion* is molten rock from the Earth's interior that squeezes into existing rock and cools.

Folding *Folding* occurs when rock layers bend and buckle from Earth's internal forces.

Tilting *Tilting* occurs when internal forces in the Earth slant rock layers.

Disturbed Rock Layers

Geologists often find features that cut across existing layers of rock. Geologists use the relationships between rock layers and the features that cut across them to assign relative ages to the features and the layers. They know that the features are younger than the rock layers because the rock layers had to be present before the features could cut across them. Faults and intrusions are examples of features that cut across rock layers. A fault and an intrusion are illustrated in **Figure 3**.

Events That Disturb Rock Layers

Geologists assume that the way sediment is deposited to form rock layers—in horizontal layers—has not changed over time. According to this principle, if rock layers are not horizontal, something must have disturbed them after they formed. This principle allows geologists to determine the relative ages of rock layers and the events that disturbed them.

Folding and tilting are two types of events that disturb rock layers. These events are always younger than the rock layers they affect. The results of folding and tilting are shown in **Figure 3**.

MISCONCEPTION ALERT

Intrusions Students may think that intrusions are vertical penetrations of rock layers. Point out to students that magma, like water, always follows the path of least resistance. Often, intrusions occur at angles or horizontally, between rock layers.

Group ACTIVITY — GENERAL

Field Trip Arrange a field trip to a local area that has exposed rock strata. If possible, contact a geologist from a local university or a museum to accompany the group. In small groups, have students try to locate unconformities and explain the origins of the unconformities. Encourage students to make drawings of the rock formations that they observe, and have them label the features that are described in this chapter.

LS Visual

Gaps in the Record—Unconformities

Faults, intrusions, and the effects of folding and tilting can make dating rock layers a challenge. Sometimes, layers of rock are missing altogether, creating a gap in the geologic record. To think of this another way, let's say that you stack your newspapers every day after reading them. Now, let's suppose you want to look at a paper you read 10 days ago. You know that the paper should be 10 papers deep in the stack. But when you look, the paper is not there. What happened? Perhaps you forgot to put the paper in the stack. Now, imagine a missing rock layer instead of a missing newspaper.

Missing Evidence

Missing rock layers create breaks in rock-layer sequences called unconformities. An **unconformity** is a surface that represents a missing part of the geologic column. Unconformities also represent missing time—time that was not recorded in layers of rock. When geologists find an unconformity, they must question whether the "missing layer" was never present or whether it was somehow removed. **Figure 4** shows how *nondeposition*, or the stoppage of deposition when a supply of sediment is cut off, and *erosion* create unconformities.

unconformity a break in the geologic record created when rock layers are eroded or when sediment is not deposited for a long period of time

✓ **Reading Check** Define the term unconformity.

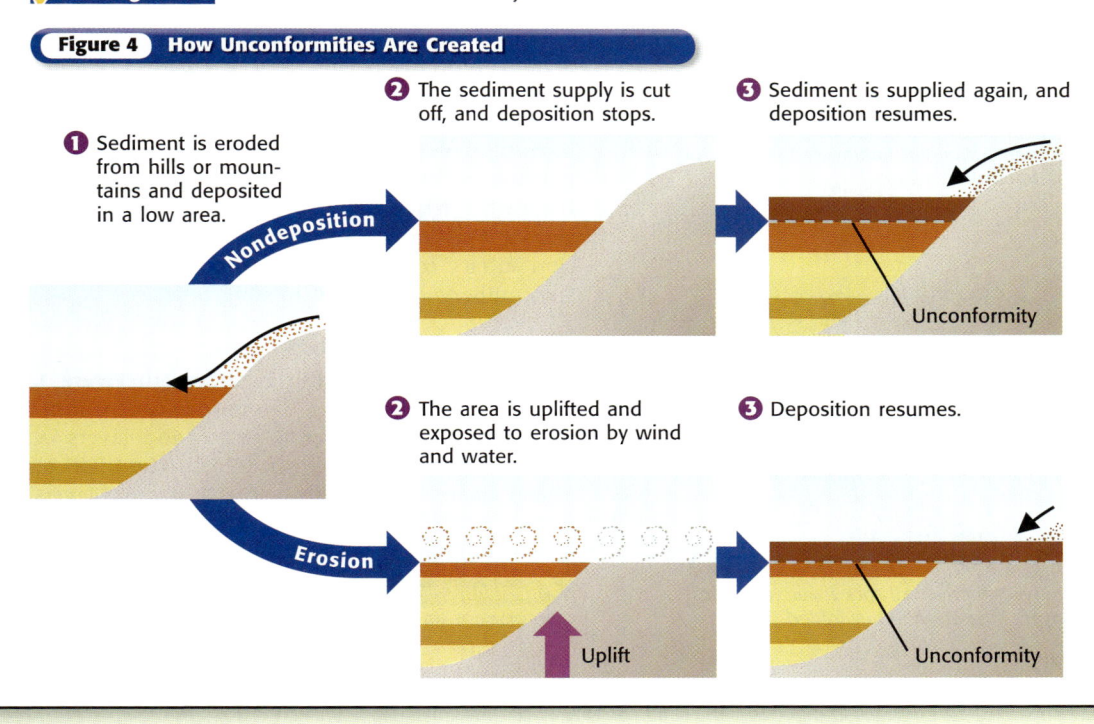

Figure 4 How Unconformities Are Created

❶ Sediment is eroded from hills or mountains and deposited in a low area.

Nondeposition

❷ The sediment supply is cut off, and deposition stops.

❸ Sediment is supplied again, and deposition resumes.

Unconformity

Erosion

❷ The area is uplifted and exposed to erosion by wind and water.

Uplift

❸ Deposition resumes.

Unconformity

Answer to Reading Check
An unconformity is a surface that represents a missing part of the geologic column.

Using the Figure—ADVANCED

Geologic History Comic Strip Have students study **Figure 4** and then work independently to create a comic strip that continues the sequence of images in the figure. Students can illustrate geologic events such as intrusions, tilting, folding, faulting, volcanic deposition, or unconformities. Have students share their illustrations with the class and explain the geologic history of their comic strip.
LS Visual

ACTIVITY — BASIC

Unconformities On the board or overhead projector, use different colors to create a rock formation that consists of five rock layers, an angular unconformity, a nonconformity, and two different fossils located in different layers. Ask students the following:

- Where is the angular unconformity and the nonconformity? How are they different? (An angular unconformity exists between layers that were tilted and horizontal rock layers. The nonconformity is found where nonlayered rock has eroded and where sedimentary rock has been deposited on its surface.)

- Partially erase the top layer of rock; then add two more layers of deposition. Ask students to name this type of unconformity. (disconformity)
LS Visual

Is That a Fact!
Unconformities can represent a short gap or a very long gap in the geologic record. The time gap can be as little as a few hundred years or as much as several billion years. Geologists must analyze many different variables to determine the amount of time an unconformity represents.

Section 2 • Relative Dating: Which Came First?

Close

Reteaching — BASIC
Unconformity Review Have students draw a diagram of each type of unconformity on a separate index card. Students can also depict folds, faults, tilting, and intrusions on separate index cards. Have students exchange cards and then try to guess the geologic concept shown on each card. Students can use the index cards as study aids. **LS Visual**

Quiz — GENERAL

1. What is an unconformity? Name some types of unconformities. (Unconformities are gaps in an area's geologic column. Examples include disconformities, nonconformities, and angular unconformities.)

2. If a folded outcrop features an undeformed intrusion that is interrupted by faulting, in what order did the folding, the faulting, and the intrusion occur? (folding, intrusion, faulting)

Alternative Assessment — GENERAL
Making Models Have students draw and label disconformities, nonconformities, and angular unconformities in their **science journal**. Ask them to identify the youngest and the oldest rocks and include examples of intrusions, folds, and faults. **LS Visual**

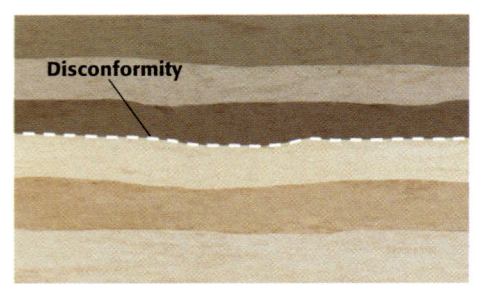

Figure 5 A disconformity exists where part of a sequence of parallel rock layers is missing.

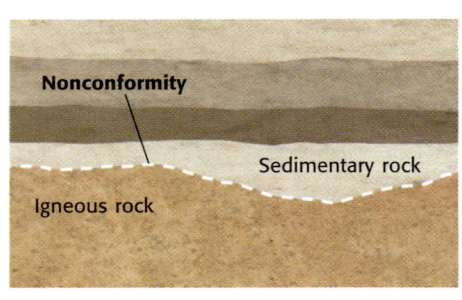

Figure 6 A nonconformity exists where sedimentary rock layers lie on top of an eroded surface of nonlayered igneous or metamorphic rock.

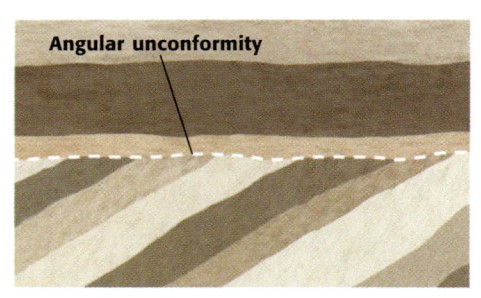

Figure 7 An angular unconformity exists between horizontal rock layers and rock layers that are tilted or folded.

Types of Unconformities
Most unconformities form by both erosion and nondeposition. But other factors can complicate matters. To simplify the study of unconformities, geologists place them into three major categories: disconformities, nonconformities, and angular unconformities. The three diagrams at left illustrate these three categories.

Disconformities
The most common type of unconformity is a disconformity, which is illustrated in **Figure 5**. *Disconformities* are found where part of a sequence of parallel rock layers is missing. A disconformity can form in the following way. A sequence of rock layers is uplifted. Younger layers at the top of the sequence are removed by erosion, and the eroded material is deposited elsewhere. At some future time, deposition resumes, and sediment buries the old erosion surface. The disconformity that results shows where erosion has taken place and rock layers are missing. A disconformity represents thousands to many millions of years of missing time.

Nonconformities
A nonconformity is illustrated in **Figure 6**. *Nonconformities* are found where horizontal sedimentary rock layers lie on top of an eroded surface of older intrusive igneous or metamorphic rock. Intrusive igneous and metamorphic rocks form deep within the Earth. When these rocks are raised to Earth's surface, they are eroded. Deposition causes the erosion surface to be buried. Nonconformities represent millions of years of missing time.

Angular Unconformities
An angular unconformity is shown in **Figure 7**. *Angular unconformities* are found between horizontal layers of sedimentary rock and layers of rock that have been tilted or folded. The tilted or folded layers were eroded before horizontal layers formed above them. Angular unconformities represent millions of years of missing time.

Reading Check Describe each of the three major categories of unconformities.

Answer to Reading Check
A disconformity is found where part of a sequence of parallel rock layers is missing. A nonconformity is found where horizontal sedimentary rock layers lie on top of an eroded surface of igneous or metamorphic rock. Angular unconformities are found between horizontal sedimentary rock layers and rock layers that have been tilted or folded.

Rock-Layer Puzzles

Geologists often find rock-layer sequences that have been affected by more than one of the events and features mentioned in this section. For example, as shown in **Figure 8**, intrusions may squeeze into rock layers that contain an unconformity. Determining the order of events that led to such a sequence is like piecing together a jigsaw puzzle. Geologists must use their knowledge of the events that disturb or remove rock-layer sequences to help piece together the history of Earth as told by the rock record.

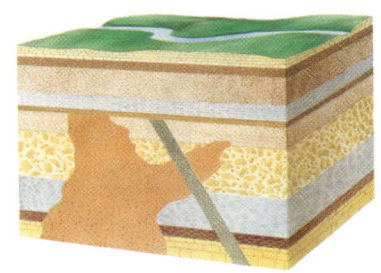

Figure 8 *Rock-layer sequences are often disturbed by more than one rock-disturbing feature.*

SECTION Review

Summary

- Geologists use relative dating to determine the order in which events happen.
- The principle of superposition states that in undisturbed rock sequences, younger layers lie above older layers.
- Folding and tilting are two events that disturb rock layers. Faults and intrusions are two features that disturb rock layers.
- The known rock and fossil record is indicated by the geologic column.
- Geologists examine the relationships between rock layers and the structures that cut across them in order to determine relative ages.

Using Key Terms

1. In your own words, write a definition for each of the following terms: *relative dating, superposition,* and *geologic column*.

Understanding Key Ideas

2. Molten rock that squeezes into existing rock and cools is called a(n)
   a. fold.
   b. fault.
   c. intrusion.
   d. unconformity.

3. List two events and two features that can disturb rock-layer sequences.

4. Explain how physical features are used to determine relative ages.

Critical Thinking

5. **Analyzing Concepts** Is there a place on Earth that has all the layers of the geologic column? Explain.

6. **Analyzing Ideas** Disconformities are hard to recognize because all of the layers are horizontal. How does a geologist know when he or she is looking at a disconformity?

Interpreting Graphics

Use the illustration below to answer the question that follows.

7. If the top rock layer were eroded and deposition later resumed, what type of unconformity would mark the boundary between older rock layers and the newly deposited rock layers?

SciLinks
For a variety of links related to this chapter, go to www.scilinks.org
Topic: Relative Dating
SciLinks code: HSM1288

Answers to Section Review

1. Sample answer: Relative dating is a method of determining whether an event or object is older or younger than other events or objects. Superposition is a principle that states that younger rocks lie above older rocks in undisturbed rock sequences. The geologic column is an ideal sequence of rock layers that contains all known rock and fossil formations on Earth, arranged from oldest to youngest.

2. c

3. Two events that can disturb rock layers are folding and tilting. Two features that disturb rock layers are faults and intrusions.

4. Geologists can use their knowledge of how physical features form to determine the order in which events occurred and thereby determine relative ages.

5. The geologic column is an ideal sequence of all the rock formations and fossils on Earth. No single location contains all of Earth's rock formations and fossils.

6. Disconformities represent a gap in the geologic column. If part of the column is missing from the layers, then the geologist could be observing a disconformity.

7. an angular unconformity

CHAPTER RESOURCES

Chapter Resource File
- Section Quiz GENERAL
- Section Review GENERAL
- Vocabulary and Section Summary GENERAL
- Reinforcement Worksheet BASIC

Section 2 • Relative Dating: Which Came First?

SECTION 3

Focus

Overview
This section explains how absolute dating can be used to determine the actual age of a fossil or a rock. Students will be able to explain the nature of radioactive decay and describe how radiometric dating measures the radioactive decay of different isotopes to calculate the age of the parent material.

🔔 Bellringer
Ask students to write a short paragraph explaining why geologists use both absolute and relative dating to interpret the past.

Motivate

ACTIVITY — GENERAL

Absolute Dating Skit Ask two students to be the geologists in this activity. The rest of the class will be radioactive isotopes in a newly formed rock sample. Tell the isotopes to stand up and that they have a half-life of 1 min. Have the geologists go outside the classroom and wait. After 1 min, tell half of the isotopes to sit down. Continue this pattern until one student remains standing. Ask the geologists to determine the age of the sample based on the number of original isotopes and the length of a half-life. **LS** Visual/Logical

---

SECTION 3

READING WARM-UP

Objectives
- Describe how radioactive decay occurs.
- Explain how radioactive decay relates to radiometric dating.
- Identify four types of radiometric dating.
- Determine the best type of radiometric dating to use to date an object.

Terms to Learn
absolute dating
isotope
radioactive decay
radiometric dating
half-life

READING STRATEGY

Reading Organizer As you read this section, make a concept map by using the terms above.

Absolute Dating: A Measure of Time

Have you ever heard the expression "turning back the clock"? With the discovery of the natural decay of uranium in 1896, French physicist Henri Becquerel provided a means of doing just that. Scientists could use radioactive elements as clocks to measure geologic time.

The process of establishing the age of an object by determining the number of years it has existed is called **absolute dating**. In this section, you will learn about radiometric dating, which is the most common method of absolute dating.

Radioactive Decay

To determine the absolute ages of fossils and rocks, scientists analyze isotopes of radioactive elements. Atoms of the same element that have the same number of protons but have different numbers of neutrons are called **isotopes**. Most isotopes are stable, meaning that they stay in their original form. But some isotopes are unstable. Scientists call unstable isotopes *radioactive*. Radioactive isotopes tend to break down into stable isotopes of the same or other elements in a process called **radioactive decay**. **Figure 1** shows an example of how radioactive decay occurs. Because radioactive decay occurs at a steady rate, scientists can use the relative amounts of stable and unstable isotopes present in an object to determine the object's age.

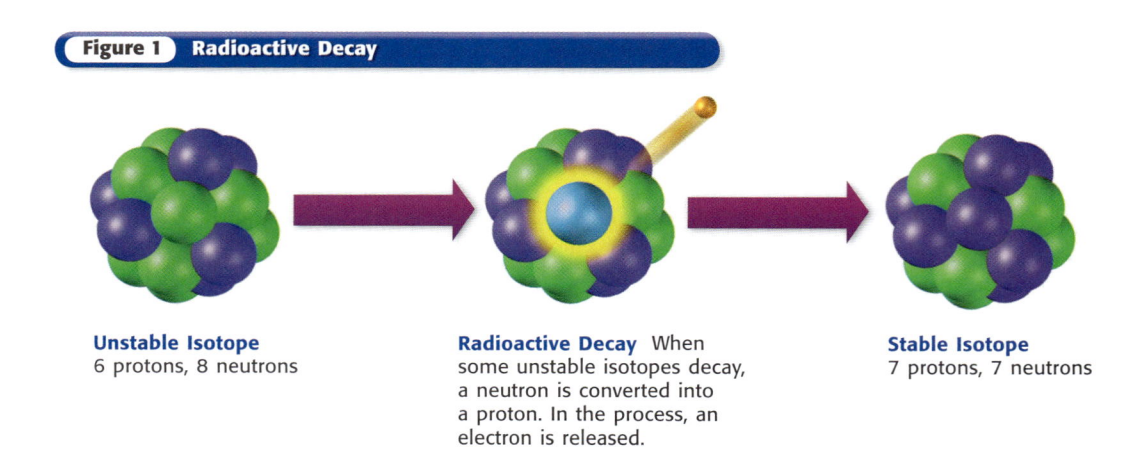

Figure 1 Radioactive Decay

Unstable Isotope
6 protons, 8 neutrons

Radioactive Decay When some unstable isotopes decay, a neutron is converted into a proton. In the process, an electron is released.

Stable Isotope
7 protons, 7 neutrons

CHAPTER RESOURCES

Chapter Resource File
- Lesson Plan
- Directed Reading A **BASIC**
- Directed Reading B **SPECIAL NEEDS**

Technology
- Transparencies
  - Bellringer
  - **LINK TO PHYSICAL SCIENCE** Radioactive Decay and Half-Life

---

CONNECTION ACTIVITY
Math — GENERAL

Calculating Half-Life To help students understand the concept of a half-life, use the transparency entitled "Radioactive Decay and Half-Life." Then, assess the comprehension of the students by asking them to calculate how old an object is when 1/4, 1/8, 1/32, and 1/64 of its carbon-14 remains. The half-life for carbon-14 is 5,730 years. (11,460 years; 17,190 years; 28,650 years; 34,380 years) **LS** Logical

---

162 Chapter 6 • The Rock and Fossil Record

Dating Rocks—How Does It Work?

In the process of radioactive decay, an unstable radioactive isotope of one element breaks down into a stable isotope. The stable isotope may be of the same element or, more commonly, a different element. The unstable radioactive isotope is called the *parent isotope*. The stable isotope produced by the radioactive decay of the parent isotope is called the *daughter isotope*. The radioactive decay of a parent isotope into a stable daughter isotope can occur in a single step or a series of steps. In either case, the rate of decay is constant. Therefore, to date rock, scientists compare the amount of parent material with the amount of daughter material. The more daughter material there is, the older the rock is.

Radiometric Dating

If you know the rate of decay for a radioactive element in a rock, you can figure out the absolute age of the rock. Determining the absolute age of a sample, based on the ratio of parent material to daughter material, is called **radiometric dating.** For example, let's say that a rock sample contains an isotope with a half-life of 10,000 years. A **half-life** is the time that it takes one-half of a radioactive sample to decay. So, for this rock sample, in 10,000 years, half the parent material will have decayed and become daughter material. You analyze the sample and find equal amounts of parent material and daughter material. This means that half the original radioactive isotope has decayed and that the sample must be about 10,000 years old.

What if one-fourth of your sample is parent material and three-fourths is daughter material? You would know that it took 10,000 years for half the original sample to decay and another 10,000 years for half of what remained to decay. The age of your sample would be 2 × 10,000, or 20,000, years. **Figure 2** shows how this steady decay happens.

✓ **Reading Check** What is a half-life? (*See the Appendix for answers to Reading Checks.*)

absolute dating any method of measuring the age of an event or object in years

isotope an atom that has the same number of protons (or the same atomic number) as other atoms of the same element do but that has a different number of neutrons (and thus a different atomic mass)

radioactive decay the process in which a radioactive isotope tends to break down into a stable isotope of the same element or another element

radiometric dating a method of determining the age of an object by estimating the relative percentages of a radioactive (parent) isotope and a stable (daughter) isotope

half-life the time needed for half of a sample of a radioactive substance to undergo radioactive decay

Figure 2 After every half-life, the amount of parent material decreases by one-half.

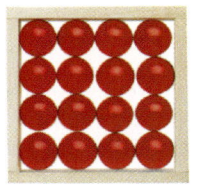

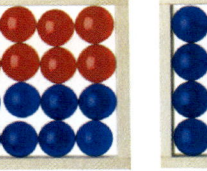

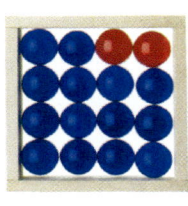

1/1	1/2	1/4	1/8	1/16
0 years	10,000 years	20,000 years	30,000 years	40,000 years

Teach

READING STRATEGY — GENERAL

Activity After students read the passage about radiometric dating, have them work together to define the terms *isotope*, *parent material*, *daughter material*, and *half-life*. Ask students to reproduce **Figure 2** in their **science journal** and have them calculate the percentage of isotope remaining in each box. (100%, 50%, 25%, 12.5%, and 6.25%) **LS Logical**

CONNECTION to Life Science — GENERAL

Carbon-14 Carbon-14 is continuously created in the atmosphere by cosmic radiation. There is one atom of radioactive carbon-14 for every trillion atoms of carbon-12 in the atmosphere. Plants absorb carbon-14 directly through their leaves in the form of carbon dioxide. Animals take in carbon-14 indirectly when they eat plants. Although carbon-14 disintegrates at a constant rate, it is continuously renewed as long as an organism remains alive. When an organism dies, it stops absorbing new carbon-14 and its radiocarbon "clock" is set.

Answer to Reading Check
A half-life is the time it takes one-half of a radioactive sample to decay.

INCLUSION Strategies

- Learning Disabled
- Hearing Impaired

Organize students into groups of three to five students. Give each group a stopwatch, a sheet of ruled notebook paper, and scissors. Tell students that this activity will simulate the radioactive decay of a substance. Begin by asking groups to record the time in their **science journal.** Instruct them to wait 1 min and then cut the paper in half. Have them select one piece, and set the other piece aside. Have students wait another minute and then cut the selected piece in half and select one piece. Students should continue this exercise until nine 1-min intervals have elapsed. Ask each group to estimate the age of the paper (10 min). Extra credit may be given to students who can tell you how old the paper is if 1 min represents 100 years (1,000 years). Have them share their answers with the class. **LS Kinesthetic**

Section 3 • Absolute Dating: A Measure of Time 163

Close

Reteaching — BASIC

Modeling Have students use two different colors of modeling clay to construct the nuclei of other unstable isotopes. Ask students to identify the protons and neutrons in each model. Discuss the difference between atomic mass and atomic number. Ask students to identify isotopes of the same element, and help them explain radioactive decay by using their model.
LS Logical/Kinesthetic

Quiz — GENERAL

1. When using the carbon-14 dating method, which sample would be older, a sample with a ratio of carbon-14 to carbon-12 of 2 to 1 or a sample with a ratio of 3 to 1? (the sample with a 2 to 1 ratio)

2. What is a half-life? (the time it takes for one-half of a radioactive isotope to decay)

Alternative Assessment — GENERAL

Absolute Dating Display three images of fossils. Tell students that the first fossil is about 30,000 years old, the second is about 1 million years old, and the last came from the Paleozoic era, around 400 million years ago. Ask students to describe how they would determine the absolute age of each fossil.
LS Verbal

Answer to Reading Check
strontium-87

Figure 3 This burial mound at Effigy Mounds resembles a snake.

Types of Radiometric Dating

Imagine traveling back through the centuries to a time before Columbus arrived in America. You are standing along the bluffs of what will one day be called the Mississippi River. You see dozens of people building large mounds. Who are these people, and what are they building?

The people you saw in your time travel were Native Americans, and the structures they were building were burial mounds. The area you imagined is now an archaeological site called Effigy Mounds National Monument. **Figure 3** shows one of these mounds.

According to archaeologists, people lived at Effigy Mounds from 2,500 years ago to 600 years ago. How do archaeologists know these dates? They have dated bones and other objects in the mounds by using radiometric dating. Scientists use different radiometric-dating techniques based on the estimated age of an object. As you read on, think about how the half-life of an isotope relates to the age of the object being dated. Which technique would you use to date the burial mounds?

Potassium-Argon Method

One isotope that is used for radiometric dating is potassium-40. Potassium-40 has a half-life of 1.3 billion years, and it decays to argon and calcium. Geologists measure argon as the daughter material. This method is used mainly to date rocks older than 100,000 years.

Uranium-Lead Method

Uranium-238 is a radioactive isotope that decays in a series of steps to lead-206. The half-life of uranium-238 is 4.5 billion years. The older the rock is, the more daughter material (lead-206) there will be in the rock. Uranium-lead dating can be used for rocks more than 10 million years old. Younger rocks do not contain enough daughter material to be accurately measured by this method.

Rubidium-Strontium Method

Through radioactive decay, the unstable parent isotope rubidium-87 forms the stable daughter isotope strontium-87. The half-life of rubidium-87 is 49 billion years. This method is used to date rocks older than 10 million years.

✓ Reading Check What is the daughter isotope of rubidium-87?

MISCONCEPTION ALERT

Atomic Decay Students may think that atomic decay is similar to other types of organic decay that they know about. Explain that some elements have forms called *isotopes*. Some isotopes have unstable atomic nuclei that tend to change, or decay. The chance that an atom will decay at any given moment is very small, but that chance is constant. Unstable atoms do not "wear out" or "grow old." From the moment these atoms form to the moment they decay, they always have the same probability of decaying. For example, every potassium-40 atom in a sample has a 50:50 chance of decaying during the course of 1.3 billion years. After 1.3 billion years, half the K-40 atoms will have decayed. Every unstable isotope has a characteristic half-life. Some half-lives are only a ten-thousandth of a second!

---

164   Chapter 6 • The Rock and Fossil Record

Carbon-14 Method

The element carbon is normally found in three forms, the stable isotopes carbon-12 and carbon-13 and the radioactive isotope carbon-14. These carbon isotopes combine with oxygen to form the gas carbon dioxide, which is taken in by plants during photosynthesis. As long as a plant is alive, new carbon dioxide with a constant carbon-14 to carbon-12 ratio is continually taken in. Animals that eat plants contain the same ratio of carbon isotopes.

Once a plant or an animal dies, however, no new carbon is taken in. The amount of carbon-14 begins to decrease as the plant or animal decays, and the ratio of carbon-14 to carbon-12 decreases. This decrease can be measured in a laboratory, such as the one shown in **Figure 4**. Because the half-life of carbon-14 is only 5,730 years, this dating method is used mainly for dating things that lived within the last 50,000 years.

Figure 4 *Some samples containing carbon must be cleaned and burned before their age can be determined.*

SECTION Review

Summary

- During radioactive decay, an unstable isotope decays at a constant rate and becomes a stable isotope of the same or a different element.
- Radiometric dating, based on the ratio of parent to daughter material, is used to determine the absolute age of a sample.
- Methods of radiometric dating include potassium-argon, uranium-lead, rubidium-strontium, and carbon-14 dating.

Using Key Terms

1. Use each of the following terms in a separate sentence: *absolute dating, isotope,* and *half-life.*

Understanding Key Ideas

2. Rubidium-87 has a half-life of
   a. 5,730 years.
   b. 4.5 billion years.
   c. 49 billion years.
   d. 1.3 billion years.

3. Explain how radioactive decay occurs.

4. How does radioactive decay relate to radiometric dating?

5. List four types of radiometric dating.

Math Skills

6. A radioactive isotope has a half-life of 1.3 billion years. After 3.9 billion years, how much of the parent material will be left?

Critical Thinking

7. **Analyzing Methods** Explain why radioactive decay must be constant in order for radiometric dating to be accurate.

8. **Applying Concepts** Which radiometric-dating method would be most appropriate for dating artifacts found at Effigy Mounds? Explain.

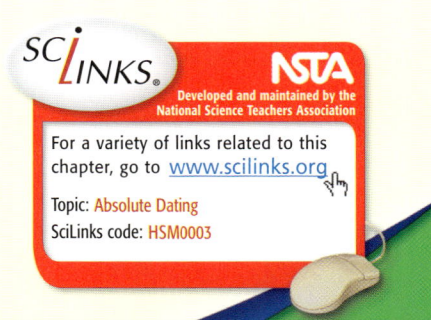

BRAIN FOOD

The oldest rock sample on record is a metamorphic gneiss from northern Canada, which is dated at 3.9 billion years old. Zircon crystals from Australia were found to be 4.2 billion years old, but they are part of much younger rock.

Answers to Section Review

1. Sample answers: Absolute dating is the process of establishing the age of an object by determining the number of years it has existed. An isotope is an atom that has the same number of protons as other atoms of the same element but has a different number of neutrons. A half-life is the time it takes one-half of a radioactive sample to decay.

2. c

3. Radioactive decay occurs as a radioactive isotope breaks down into a stable isotope. This change happens as the isotope loses an electron and a neutron becomes a proton.

4. Radioactive decay occurs at a constant rate. By determining the ratio between the parent material and the daughter material in an object, scientists can determine how old an object is.

5. potassium-argon, uranium-lead, strontium-rubidium, and carbon-14

6. One-eighth of the parent material will be left. After one half-life, 1/2 of the sample is left. After two half-lives, 1/4 of the sample is left. After three half-lives, 1/8 of the sample is left.

7. If decay rates were inconsistent, scientists would not have a specific half-life number to compare with an object's ratio of parent material to daughter material. Therefore, a precise age could never be determined.

8. Carbon-14 would be the best method to date artifacts from Effigy Mounds. This method is best because carbon-14 has a relatively short half-life of 5,730 years.

CHAPTER RESOURCES

Chapter Resource File
- Section Quiz GENERAL
- Section Review GENERAL
- Vocabulary and Section Summary GENERAL

Section 3 • Absolute Dating: A Measure of Time

SECTION 4

Focus

Overview
This section describes the formation and preservation of fossils. Students will learn how fossils are used to interpret the past and to date rock layers.

🔔 Bellringer
Ask students to write a few sentences to describe the fossil record of their own lives that might be found 65 million years from now. Tell students that fossils must be naturally preserved.

Motivate

Group Activity — GENERAL

Carbon Impressions Carbon impressions of plants can form when the plants are buried in sediment. As plants decay, a thin film of carbon is left behind. Have students work in groups to make carbon "fossil" imprints. Using plaster of Paris, have students place a flat leaf on the plaster surface. Then, after the plaster has dried, they should cover it with a second layer of plaster. When the plaster has dried, have students split the layers apart. Have students observe the leaf impression. Have them note that a bit of the leaf material sticks to the impression made in the hard material. **LS Visual/Kinesthetic**

SECTION 4

READING WARM-UP

Objectives
- Describe five ways that different types of fossils form.
- List three types of fossils that are not part of organisms.
- Explain how fossils can be used to determine the history of changes in environments and organisms.
- Explain how index fossils can be used to date rock layers.

Terms to Learn
fossil
trace fossil
mold
cast
index fossil

READING STRATEGY

Reading Organizer As you read this section, create an outline of the section. Use the headings from this section in your outline.

Figure 1 These insects are preserved in amber.

CHAPTER RESOURCES

Chapter Resource File
- Lesson Plan
- Directed Reading A BASIC
- Directed Reading B SPECIAL NEEDS

Technology
- Transparencies
  • Bellringer

Looking at Fossils

Descending from the top of a ridge in the badlands of Argentina, your expedition team suddenly stops. You look down and realize that you are walking on eggshells—dinosaur eggshells!

A paleontologist named Luis Chiappe had this experience. He had found an enormous dinosaur nesting ground.

Fossilized Organisms

The remains or physical evidence of an organism preserved by geologic processes is called a **fossil**. Fossils are most often preserved in sedimentary rock. But as you will see, other materials can also preserve evidence of past life.

Fossils in Rocks

When an organism dies, it either immediately begins to decay or is consumed by other organisms. Sometimes, however, organisms are quickly buried by sediment when they die. The sediment slows down decay. Hard parts of organisms, such as shells and bones, are more resistant to decay than soft tissues are. So, when sediments become rock, the hard parts of animals are much more commonly preserved than are soft tissues.

Fossils in Amber

Imagine that an insect is caught in soft, sticky tree sap. Suppose that the insect gets covered by more sap, which quickly hardens and preserves the insect inside. Hardened tree sap is called *amber*. Some of our best insect fossils are found in amber, as shown in **Figure 1**. Frogs and lizards have also been found in amber.

✓ **Reading Check** Describe how organisms are preserved in amber. (See the Appendix for answers to Reading Checks.)

Answer to Reading Check

An organism is caught in soft, sticky tree sap, which hardens and preserves the organism.

---

166   Chapter 6 • The Rock and Fossil Record

Figure 2 *Scientist Vladimir Eisner studies the upper molars of a 20,000-year-old woolly mammoth found in Siberia, Russia. The almost perfectly preserved male mammoth was excavated from a block of ice in October 1999.*

Petrifaction

Another way that organisms are preserved is by petrifaction. *Petrifaction* is a process in which minerals replace an organism's tissues. One form of petrifaction is called permineralization. *Permineralization* is a process in which the pore space in an organism's hard tissue—for example, bone or wood—is filled up with mineral. Another form of petrifaction is called *replacement*, a process in which the organism's tissues are completely replaced by minerals. For example, in some specimens of petrified wood, all of the wood has been replaced by minerals.

fossil the remains or physical evidence of an organism preserved by geological processes

Fossils in Asphalt

There are places where asphalt wells up at the Earth's surface in thick, sticky pools. The La Brea asphalt deposits in Los Angeles, California, for example, are at least 38,000 years old. These pools of thick, sticky asphalt have trapped and preserved many kinds of organisms for the past 38,000 years. From these fossils, scientists have learned about the past environment in southern California.

Frozen Fossils

In October 1999, scientists removed a 20,000-year-old woolly mammoth frozen in the Siberian tundra. The remains of this mammoth are shown in **Figure 2**. Woolly mammoths, relatives of modern elephants, became extinct approximately 10,000 years ago. Because cold temperatures slow down decay, many types of frozen fossils are preserved from the last ice age. Scientists hope to find out more about the mammoth and the environment in which it lived.

CONNECTION TO Environmental Science

WRITING SKILL **Preservation in Ice** Subfreezing climates contain almost no decomposing bacteria. The well-preserved body of John Torrington, a member of an expedition that explored the Northwest Passage in Canada in the 1840s, was uncovered in 1984. His body appeared much as it did at the time he died, more than 160 years earlier. Research another well-preserved discovery, and write a report for your class.

Teach

READING STRATEGY — GENERAL

Activity Ask students to write short paragraphs exploring possible scenarios for each type of fossilization described in this section. Encourage students to illustrate each scenario and to include details of the paleo-environment at the time of fossilization. **English Language Learners**
LS Logical/Visual

ACTIVITY — GENERAL

Making Fossils Distribute the following materials to groups of students: several leaves or small shells, a small amount of petroleum jelly, plaster of Paris, water, waxed paper, a square of heavy cardboard, and a milk carton. Have each group fill the carton halfway with plaster. Have groups add some water, and stir the mixture to form a smooth, thick paste. Have students pour the plaster mixture onto the cardboard square covered by waxed paper. Then, have them coat the leaves or the shells with petroleum jelly, and place the items jelly side down into the plaster. Have students allow the plaster to dry for 24 h before removing the leaves or the shells. Groups may wish to create a fossil record of a mystery environment. Have students exchange and interpret records of other groups. **LS Kinesthetic/Visual**

MISCONCEPTION ALERT

Rancho La Brea Asphalt Pits Students may refer to the Rancho La Brea asphalt pits in Los Angeles, California, as tar pits. Explain to students that the material seeping to the surface is asphalt, not tar. Asphalt is a type of bitumen found in a natural state or obtained by evaporating petroleum. Tar is obtained by the distillation of coal, wood, or shale.

Teach, continued

Debate — ADVANCED

Amateur Fossil Collecting
Have students debate the pros and cons of amateur fossil collecting. They should understand that amateur fossil collectors have made some amazing discoveries and have helped to advance the field of paleontology. On the other hand, amateur fossil collectors have lost important information by improperly removing fossils, by not recording data about locations or associated fossils, and by failing to donate specimens to research institutions for study. Point out that it is illegal to collect fossils from state or national parks without a permit that allows you to do so. It is also illegal to remove vertebrate fossils from public lands without a permit. Have students conclude the debate by writing a handbook for amateur fossil collectors.
LS Interpersonal

Answer to Reading Check
A mold is a cavity in rock where a plant or an animal was buried. A cast is an object created when sediment fills a mold and becomes rock.

Figure 3 These dinosaur tracks are located in Arizona. They leave a trace of a dinosaur that had longer legs than humans do.

trace fossil a fossilized mark that is formed in soft sediment by the movement of an animal

mold a mark or cavity made in a sedimentary surface by a shell or other body

cast a type of fossil that forms when sediments fill in the cavity left by a decomposed organism

Figure 4 This photograph shows two molds from an ammonite. The image on the left is the internal mold of the ammonite, which formed when sediment filled the ammonite's shell, which later dissolved away. The image on the right is the external mold of the ammonite, which preserves the external features of the shell.

Other Types of Fossils
Besides their hard parts—and in rare cases their soft parts—do organisms leave behind any other clues about their existence? What other evidence of past life do paleontologists look for?

Trace Fossils
Any naturally preserved evidence of animal activity is called a **trace fossil**. Tracks like the ones shown in **Figure 3** are a fascinating example of a trace fossil. These fossils form when animal footprints fill with sediment and are preserved in rock. Tracks reveal a lot about the animal that made them, including how big it was and how fast it was moving. Parallel trackways showing dinosaurs moving in the same direction have led paleontologists to hypothesize that dinosaurs moved in herds.

Burrows are another trace fossil. Burrows are shelters made by animals, such as clams, that bury in sediment. Like tracks, burrows are preserved when they are filled in with sediment and buried quickly. A *coprolite* (KAHP roh LIET), a third type of trace fossil, is preserved animal dung.

Molds and Casts
Molds and casts are two more examples of fossils. A cavity in rock where a plant or animal was buried is called a **mold**. A **cast** is an object created when sediment fills a mold and becomes rock. A cast shows what the outside of the organism looked like. **Figure 4** shows two types of molds from the same organism—and internal mold and an external mold.

Reading Check How are a cast and a mold different?

MISCONCEPTION ALERT

Museum Displays Many people assume that when they see dinosaur bones in a museum, they are looking at the actual bones that made up the dinosaur. In older museums, this may be the case. However, point out that many newer museums do not display the actual fossilized dinosaur bones. They make casts of the bones. Using the casts, they make fiberglass reproductions of the bones. The fiberglass bones are much lighter than the original bones and can stand without support.

Figure 5 This scientist has found marine fossils on mountaintops in the Yoho National Park in Canada. The fossil of Marrella, shown above, tells the scientist that these rocks were pushed up from below sea level millions of years ago.

Using Fossils to Interpret the Past

Think about your favorite outdoor place. Now, imagine that you are a paleontologist at the same site 65 million years from now. What types of fossils would you dig up? Based on the fossils you found, how would you reconstruct this place?

The Information in the Fossil Record

The fossil record offers only a rough sketch of the history of life on Earth. Some parts of this history are more complete than others. For example, scientists know more about organisms that had hard body parts than about organisms that had soft body parts. Scientists also know more about organisms that lived in environments that favored fossilization. The fossil record is incomplete because most organisms never became fossils. And of course, many fossils have yet to be discovered.

History of Environmental Changes

Would you expect to find marine fossils on the mountaintop shown in **Figure 5**? The presence of marine fossils means that the rocks of these mountaintops in Canada formed in a totally different environment—at the bottom of an ocean.

The fossil record reveals a history of environmental change. For example, marine fossils help scientists reconstruct ancient coastlines and the deepening and shallowing of ancient seas. Using the fossils of plants and land animals, scientists can reconstruct past climates. They can tell whether the climate in an area was cooler or wetter than it is at present.

Quick Lab

Make a Fossil

1. Find a **common object**, such as a shell, a button, or a pencil, to use to make a mold. Keep the object hidden from your classmates.
2. To create a mold, press the items down into **modeling clay** in a **shallow pan or tray.**
3. Trade your tray with a classmate's tray, and try to identify the item that made the mold.
4. Describe how a cast could be formed from your mold.

Group Activity — GENERAL

Imagining Environmental Change
Have small groups search in magazines for photographs representing five different biomes. Then, have the groups place the five photographs in a sequence. Tell them to imagine that they are paleontologists and that this sequence represents roughly 300 million years in the geologic history of a single location. Have them study their photographs and brainstorm about what the fossil record for each biome might contain. Ask students, "How would the fossil record indicate the environmental changes that occurred between each photograph in the sequence?" Have the group members work together to write a press release announcing their great discovery—a continuous record of 300 million years of environmental change! Students can describe how they made their discovery and what field techniques they used. They can show illustrations of the fossils they found and should explain why these fossils suggest the environmental changes shown in the sequence of photographs.
LS Visual/Logical

Quick Lab

MATERIALS

FOR EACH GROUP
- clay, modeling
- common object (such as a coin)
- pan or tray, shallow

Answer

4. Answers may vary. A cast could be formed by filling the mold with a substance such as plaster of Paris.

Homework — GENERAL

Tools of the Trade Have students research the methods used by paleontologists to excavate fossils. Show students a collection of tools that might be used by paleontologists, and ask them to think about the purpose of each item. Tools include picks, hammers, chisels, brushes, trowels, stakes and string, a tape measure, a compass, plaster, and sifting screens. Organize a dig, or have students demonstrate some paleontological techniques in class. **LS** Visual/Logical

Section 4 • Looking at Fossils

Close

Reteaching — BASIC

Section Review Have students write two questions for each heading in the section. Then, have students exchange questions and attempt to answer the questions. **LS Verbal**

Quiz — GENERAL

1. Would a shark tooth make a good index fossil? Why or why not? *(A shark tooth could make an excellent index fossil if the shark tooth came from a shark that lived during a relatively short, well-defined geologic time span.)*

2. Why do the frigid temperatures of Siberia and the sticky asphalt of the La Brea tar pits preserve fossils well? *(Both environments slow down the decay of an organism and help preserve it.)*

Alternative Assessment — ADVANCED

How-To Guide Have students prepare a how-to guide for the fossilization processes described in this section. Students should imagine that they are teaching an untrained person how to preserve an organism using sedimentation, amber, tar, ice, and petrifaction. Emphasize that this assignment should read like a recipe, so details are important. **LS Intrapersonal**

SCHOOL to HOME

Fossil Hunt
Go on a fossil hunt with your family. Find out what kinds of rocks in your local area might contain fossils. Take pictures or draw sketches of your trip and any fossils that you find.

ACTIVITY

index fossil a fossil that is found in the rock layers of only one geologic age and that is used to establish the age of the rock layers

Figure 6 *Tropites* is a genus of coiled ammonites. *Tropites* existed for only about 20 million years, which makes this genus a good index fossil.

Homework — GENERAL

Modern Index Fossils Which organisms would make good index fossils for marking the end of the 21st century? Have students research species that have become extinct during the last 100 years and illustrate what the fossils of these species might look like. **LS Logical**

History of Changing Organisms

By studying the relationships between fossils, scientists can interpret how life has changed over time. For example, older rock layers contain organisms that often differ from the organisms found in younger rock layers.

Only a small fraction of the organisms that have existed in Earth's history have been fossilized. Because the fossil record is incomplete, it does not provide paleontologists with a continuous record of change. Instead, they look for similarities between fossils, or between fossilized organisms and their closest living relatives, and try to fill in the blanks in the fossil record.

✓ Reading Check How do paleontologists fill in missing information about changes in organisms in the fossil record?

Using Fossils to Date Rocks

Scientists have found that particular types of fossils appear only in certain layers of rock. By dating the rock layers above and below these fossils, scientists can determine the time span in which the organisms that formed the fossils lived. If a type of organism existed for only a short period of time, its fossils would show up in a limited range of rock layers. These types of fossils are called index fossils. **Index fossils** are fossils of organisms that lived during a relatively short, well-defined geologic time span.

Ammonites

To be considered an index fossil, a fossil must be found in rock layers throughout the world. One example of an index fossil is the fossil of a genus of ammonites (AM uh NIETS) called *Tropites*, shown in **Figure 6**. *Tropites* was a marine mollusk similar to a modern squid. It lived in a coiled shell. *Tropites* lived between 230 million and 208 million years ago and is an index fossil for that period of time.

Answer to Reading Check

To fill in missing information about changes in organisms in the fossil record, paleontologists look for similarities between fossilized organisms or between fossilized organisms and their closest living relatives.

Trilobites

Fossils of a genus of trilobites (TRIE loh BIETS) called *Phacops* are another example of an index fossil. Trilobites are extinct. Their closest living relative is the horseshoe crab. Through the dating of rock, paleontologists have determined that *Phacops* lived approximately 400 million years ago. So, when scientists find *Phacops* in rock layers anywhere on Earth, they assume that these rock layers are also approximately 400 million years old. An example of a *Phacops* fossil is shown in **Figure 7**.

Reading Check Explain how fossils of *Phacops* can be used to establish the age of rock layers.

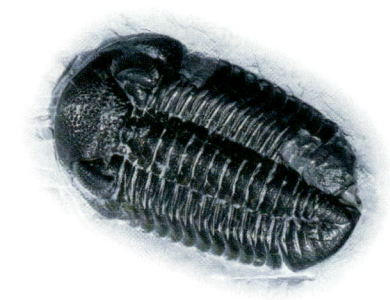

Figure 7 Paleontologists assume that any rock layer containing a fossil of the trilobite Phacops is about 400 million years old.

SECTION Review

Summary

- Fossils are the remains or physical evidence of an organism preserved by geologic processes.
- Fossils can be preserved in rock, amber, asphalt, and ice and by petrifaction.
- Trace fossils are any naturally preserved evidence of animal activity. Tracks, burrows, and coprolites are examples of trace fossils.
- Scientists study fossils to determine how environments and organisms have changed over time.
- An index fossil is a fossil of an organism that lived during a relatively short, well-defined time span. Index fossils can be used to establish the age of rock layers.

Using Key Terms

Complete each of the following sentences by choosing the correct term from the word bank.

cast   index fossils
mold   trace fossils

1. A ___ is a cavity in rock where a plant or animal was buried.
2. ___ can be used to establish the age of rock layers.

Understanding Key Ideas

3. Fossils are most often preserved in
   a. ice.
   b. amber.
   c. asphalt.
   d. rock.
4. Describe three types of trace fossils.
5. Explain how an index fossil can be used to date rock.
6. Explain why the fossil record contains an incomplete record of the history of life on Earth.
7. Explain how fossils can be used to determine the history of changes in environments and organisms.

Math Skills

8. If a scientist finds the remains of a plant between a rock layer that contains 400 million–year-old *Phacops* fossils and a rock layer that contains 230 million–year-old *Tropites* fossils, how old could the plant fossil be?

Critical Thinking

9. **Making Inferences** If you find rock layers containing fish fossils in a desert, what can you infer about the history of the desert?
10. **Identifying Bias** Because information in the fossil record is incomplete, scientists are left with certain biases concerning fossil preservation. Explain two of these biases.

SciLinks
Developed and maintained by the National Science Teachers Association
For a variety of links related to this chapter, go to www.scilinks.org
Topic: Looking at Fossils
SciLinks code: HSM0886

Answer to Reading Check

Phacops can be used to establish the age of rock layers because *Phacops* lived during a relatively short, well-defined time span and is found in rock layers throughout the world.

Answers to Section Review

1. mold
2. Index fossils
3. d
4. Three types of trace fossils are tracks, burrows, and coprolites.
5. Because index fossils are fossils of organisms that lived during a relatively short, well-defined time span, index fossils can be used to obtain relative dates for rock layers.
6. The fossil record is incomplete because most organisms, such as organisms that have soft body parts, did not become fossils, and many fossils have yet to be discovered.
7. Scientists can examine fossils of plants and animals in different rock layers to see how these organisms or their environment have changed over time.
8. Scientists can infer that the plant existed sometime between 400 million to 230 million years ago.
9. Answers may vary. The desert was once an aquatic environment, such as an ocean, lake, or stream.
10. Scientists know more about organisms that had hard body parts than organisms that had soft body parts. Scientists also know more about organisms that lived in environments that favored fossilization than in environments that did not favor fossilization.

CHAPTER RESOURCES

Chapter Resource File
- Section Quiz GENERAL
- Section Review GENERAL
- Vocabulary and Section Summary GENERAL
- Critical Thinking ADVANCED
- Datasheet for Quick Lab

Section 4 • Looking at Fossils

SECTION 5

Focus

Overview
In this section, students will be introduced to the geologic time scale. The section discusses some important biological and geological events that occurred during each geologic era. The section also informs students about events that result in the sudden appearance or disappearance of species.

🔔 Bellringer
Ask students the following question: "If the history of Earth were the length of 1 calendar year, on what date did modern humans arrive?" (December 31)

Motivate

Discussion — GENERAL

Geologic Time After students study the photographs in **Figure 1** and **Figure 2**, ask them how rock layers and fossils record Earth's history. Ask students what kinds of changes in Earth's history might be preserved in the rock and fossil records. Have students summarize their answers in a short essay. **LS** Logical

---

SECTION 5

READING WARM-UP

Objectives
- Explain how geologic time is recorded in rock layers.
- Identify important dates on the geologic time scale.
- Explain how environmental changes resulted in the extinction of some species.

Terms to Learn
geologic time scale
eon
era
period
epoch
extinction

READING STRATEGY

Brainstorming The key idea of this section is the geologic time scale. Brainstorm words and phrases related to the geologic time scale.

Figure 1 Bones of dinosaurs that lived about 150 million years ago are exposed in the quarry wall at Dinosaur National Monument in Utah.

Time Marches On

How old is the Earth? Well, if the Earth celebrated its birthday every million years, there would be 4,600 candles on its birthday cake! Humans have been around only long enough to light the last candle on the cake.

Try to think of the Earth's history in "fast-forward." If you could watch the Earth change from this perspective, you would see mountains rise up like wrinkles in fabric and quickly wear away. You would see life-forms appear and then go extinct. In this section, you will learn that geologists must "fast-forward" the Earth's history when they write or talk about it. You will also learn about some incredible events in the history of life on Earth.

Geologic Time

Shown in **Figure 1** is the rock wall at the Dinosaur Quarry Visitor Center in Dinosaur National Monument, Utah. Contained within this wall are approximately 1,500 fossil bones that have been excavated by paleontologists. These are the remains of dinosaurs that inhabited the area about 150 million years ago. Granted, 150 million years seems to be an incredibly long period of time. However, in terms of the Earth's history, 150 million years is little more than 3% of the time our planet has existed. It is a little less than 4% of the time represented by the Earth's oldest known rocks.

CHAPTER RESOURCES

Chapter Resource File
- Lesson Plan
- Directed Reading A BASIC
- Directed Reading B SPECIAL NEEDS

Technology
- Transparencies
  - Bellringer

CONNECTION ACTIVITY
Math — GENERAL

Calculating Percentage The dinosaur that had the smallest ratio of brain size to body size was the stegosaurus. The 30 ft long, 3,800 lb stegosaurus had a 2.5 oz brain. Have students calculate the percentage of the stegosaurus's total body weight that its brain represents. (The brain represents 0.004% of its total body weight.) **LS** Logical

---

172 Chapter 6 • The Rock and Fossil Record

Figure 2 Well-preserved plant and animal fossils are common in the Green River formation. Clockwise from the upper right are a fossil leaf, a dragonfly, a fish, and a turtle.

The Rock Record and Geologic Time

One of the best places in North America to see the Earth's history recorded in rock layers is in Grand Canyon National Park. The Colorado River has cut the canyon nearly 2 km deep in some places. Over the course of 6 million years, the river has eroded countless layers of rock. These layers represent almost half, or nearly 2 billion years, of Earth's history.

✓ **Reading Check** How much geologic time is represented by the rock layers in the Grand Canyon? (*See the Appendix for answers to Reading Checks.*)

The Fossil Record and Geologic Time

Figure 2 shows sedimentary rocks that belong to the Green River formation. These rocks, which are found in parts of Wyoming, Utah, and Colorado, are thousands of meters thick. These rocks were once part of a system of ancient lakes that existed for a period of millions of years. Fossils of plants and animals are common in these rocks and are very well preserved. Burial in the fine-grained lake-bed sediments preserved even the most delicate structures.

INTERNET ACTIVITY

For another activity related to this chapter, go to **go.hrw.com** and type in the keyword **HZ5FOSW**.

Teach

CONNECTION to Life Science — ADVANCED

Paleobotany The study of Earth's history has given rise to highly specific subdivisions of Earth science. Paleobotany, for example, is the study of the history of the plant kingdom. Have interested students find out how plant and pollen fossils can provide clues about past environments and tell how these environments have changed over time. **LS Verbal**

ACTIVITY — BASIC

Learning About the Eons As you begin to discuss the geologic time scale, write the names of the four eons on the board. Ask students to use what they have learned to help you list the characteristics of each eon. Have students find the dates of each eon, the biological events that define each eon, and other facts. You may wish to continue this activity with the eras and periods. Have students copy the information in their **science journal** for future study and review. **LS Logical** — English Language Learners

Answer to Reading Check
approximately 2 billion years

Homework — ADVANCED

Research Before the development of the theory of plate tectonics and the invention of radiometric dating, scientists developed many elaborate experiments to determine the age of the Earth. In the mid-1700s, a French scientist estimated that the Earth was 75,000 years old. He based his estimate on the cooling rate of iron cannonballs. By the 1930s, the estimated age of Earth reached 1 billion years, but it was not until the middle of the 20th century that the current estimate of 4.6 billion years was determined. Have interested students research the different methods that were used in the past to estimate the age of the Earth. **LS Verbal**

Section 5 • Time Marches On

Teach, continued

READING STRATEGY — GENERAL

Mnemonics Help students devise mnemonic sentences to learn and remember the eons of geologic history. For example, "**H**appy **A**ardvarks **Pr**ance for **Ph**otographers" could be used to recall the **H**adean, **A**rchean, **Pr**oterozoic, and **Ph**anerozoic eons. **LS** Auditory *English Language Learners*

CONNECTION ACTIVITY
Language Arts — GENERAL

Writing

Geologic Newspapers
As students read about the geologic time scale, encourage them to consider why scientists chose to divide geologic time in this way. Have them think about the important biological, climatological, and geological differences between each era. After students finish reading about each era, have them work independently to write the front-page headlines for an imaginary newspaper printed at the close of each era. The headlines should detail the important events and characteristics of the era. For example, the front page of the *Mesozoic Times* might herald, "Mammals Appear—Warmblooded" and "Hairy Critters—Can We Trust Them?" If students wish to research more about geologic history, they can write creative articles under each headline.
LS Visual

Phanerozoic Eon
(543 million years ago to the present)
The rock and fossil record mainly represents the Phanerozoic eon, which is the eon in which we live.

Proterozoic Eon
(2.5 billion years ago to 543 million years ago)
The first organisms with well-developed cells appeared during this eon.

Archean Eon
(3.8 billion years ago to 2.5 billion years ago)
The earliest known rocks on Earth formed during this eon.

Hadean Eon
(4.6 billion years ago to 3.8 billion years ago)
The only rocks that scientists have found from this eon are meteorites and rocks from the moon.

Figure 3 *The geologic time scale accounts for Earth's entire history. It is divided into four major parts called* eons. *Dates given for intervals on the geologic time scale are estimates.*

Geologic Time Scale

Era	Period	Epoch	Millions of years ago
Cenozoic	Quaternary	Holocene	0.01
		Pleistocene	1.8
	Tertiary	Pliocene	5.3
		Miocene	23.8
		Oligocene	33.7
		Eocene	54.8
		Paleocene	65
Mesozoic	Cretaceous		144
	Jurassic		206
	Triassic		248
Paleozoic	Permian		290
	Pennsylvanian		323
	Mississippian		354
	Devonian		417
	Silurian		443
	Ordovician		490
	Cambrian		543

PHANEROZOIC EON
PROTEROZOIC EON — 2,500
ARCHEAN EON — 3,800
HADEAN EON — 4,600

The Geologic Time Scale

The geologic column represents the billions of years that have passed since the first rocks formed on Earth. Altogether, geologists study 4.6 billion years of Earth's history! To make their job easier, geologists have created the geologic time scale. The **geologic time scale**, which is shown in **Figure 3**, is a scale that divides Earth's 4.6 billion–year history into distinct intervals of time.

✓**Reading Check** Define the term *geologic time scale*.

Answer to Reading Check
The geologic time scale is a scale that divides Earth's 4.6 billion–year history into distinct intervals of time.

CHAPTER RESOURCES

Technology
- Transparencies
  • The Geologic Time Scale

Divisions of Time

Geologists have divided Earth's history into sections of time, as shown on the geologic time scale in **Figure 3.** The largest divisions of geologic time are **eons** (EE AHNZ). There are four eons—the Hadean eon, the Archean eon, the Proterozoic eon, and the Phanerozoic eon. The Phanerozoic eon is divided into three **eras,** which are the second-largest divisions of geologic time. The three eras are further divided into **periods,** which are the third-largest divisions of geologic time. Periods are divided into **epochs** (EP uhks), which are the fourth-largest divisions of geologic time.

The boundaries between geologic time intervals represent shorter intervals in which visible changes took place on Earth. Some changes are marked by the disappearance of index fossil species, while others are recognized only by detailed paleontological studies.

geologic time scale the standard method used to divide the Earth's long natural history into manageable parts

eon the largest division of geologic time

era a unit of geologic time that includes two or more periods

period a unit of geologic time into which eras are divided

epoch a subdivision of a geologic period

extinction the death of every member of a species

The Appearance and Disappearance of Species

At certain times during Earth's history, the number of species has increased or decreased dramatically. An increase in the number of species often comes as a result of either a relatively sudden increase or decrease in competition among species. *Hallucigenia,* shown in **Figure 4,** appeared during the Cambrian period, when the number of marine species greatly increased. On the other hand, the number of species decreases dramatically over a relatively short period of time during a mass extinction event. **Extinction** is the death of every member of a species. Gradual events, such as global climate change and changes in ocean currents, can cause mass extinctions. A combination of these events can also cause mass extinctions.

Figure 4 Hallucigenia, named for its "bizarre and dreamlike quality," was one of numerous marine organisms to make its appearance during the early Cambrian period.

CONNECTION to Life Science — GENERAL

Biological Classification Review Students may benefit from a review of the levels of biological classification. Point out that fossil species are not the same as living species. While scientists can group organisms together based on structural similarities, scientists cannot tell whether similar fossil species could interbreed. **LS Visual/Logical**

MISCONCEPTION ALERT

Illustrations Based on the Fossil Record Students may think that illustrations of dinosaurs and ancient environments are completely accurate. But make students aware that that illustrations of dinosaurs and ancient environments are based partly on artists' interpretations. For example, scientists are sure about the skeletal structure of many dinosaurs, but features such as skin type and skin color are open to interpretation. Artists have drawn these types of features on dinosaurs to make the dinosaurs look familiar. In addition, most if not all movies and popular episodic TV programs about prehistoric life are full of paleontological inaccuracies. An obvious example is the depiction of prehistoric humans and dinosaurs coexisting.

INCLUSION Strategies

- **Developmentally Delayed**
- **Behavior Control Issues**
- **Attention Deficit Disorder**

Introduce the concept of deep time by creating a timeline of Earth's history and having students label the timeline. A timeline can be made out of adding machine tape or strips of vinyl glued together. You will need a length of 25.5 yards. Prepare the timeline using a scale of 1 in. is equal to 5 million years, and begin at 4.6 billion years ago (bya). Mark this beginning at one end of the timeline. Organize students into four groups, and assign each group an eon or combination of eons and eras. Give each group sticky notes and a marker. Ask groups to identify two events that occurred during their time period. Next, ask each group to identify and place a sticky note at the beginning of their time period on the timeline as well as add the two events they identified. **LS Visual**

Section 5 • Time Marches On **175**

Close

Reteaching — BASIC

Geologic Time Scale Have students reproduce **Figure 3** in their **science journal.** Students should leave enough space so that they can add details about the history of life on Earth for each eon and era. **LS Verbal**

Quiz — GENERAL

1. What are the largest divisions of time in the geologic time scale? (eons)
2. During which era did plants start to appear on land? (Paleozoic era)

Alternative Assessment — GENERAL

Making a Geologic History Book Have students work independently to make construction-paper cutouts of fossils that might be found in each era of Earth's history. Encourage students to create both plant and animal fossils. Students should then paste each era's fossils on rock layers made from construction paper. Students should create five layers for each era and attach all of the layers together so that they fold like an accordion. Students can then annotate each layer by describing the time period the rocks and fossils were deposited, and they can paste in small illustrations of what the environment was like during that time period. Students can display their accordion books for the class to enjoy. **LS Visual**

Figure 5 Jungles were present during the Paleozoic era, but there were no birds singing in the trees and no monkeys swinging from the branches. Birds and mammals didn't evolve until much later.

Figure 6 Imagine walking in the desert and bumping into these fierce creatures! It's a good thing humans didn't evolve in the Mesozoic era, which was dominated by dinosaurs.

ACTIVITY — ADVANCED

Prehistoric Illustrations Encourage advanced learners to use the Internet to research illustrations of prehistoric eras. Students can print the pictures and share them with the class, or students can create their own dioramas. As an extension, challenge students to find inaccuracies in the illustrations. **LS Visual**

The Paleozoic Era—Old Life

The Paleozoic era lasted from about 543 million to 248 million years ago. It is the first era well represented by fossils.

Marine life flourished at the beginning of the Paleozoic era. The oceans became home to a diversity of life. However, there were few land organisms. By the middle of the Paleozoic, all modern groups of land plants had appeared. By the end of the era, amphibians and reptiles lived on the land, and insects were abundant. **Figure 5** shows what the Earth might have looked like late in the Paleozoic era. The Paleozoic era came to an end with the largest mass extinction in Earth's history. Some scientists believe that ocean changes were a likely cause of this extinction, which killed nearly 90% of all species.

The Mesozoic Era—The Age of Reptiles

The Mesozoic era began about 248 million years ago. The Mesozoic is known as the *Age of Reptiles* because reptiles, such as the dinosaurs shown in **Figure 6,** inhabited the land.

During this time, reptiles dominated. Small mammals appeared about the same time as dinosaurs, and birds appeared late in the Mesozoic era. Many scientists think that birds evolved directly from a type of dinosaur. At the end of the Mesozoic era, about 15% to 20% of all species on Earth, including the dinosaurs, became extinct. Global climate change may have been the cause.

✓ **Reading Check** Why is the Mesozoic known as the *Age of Reptiles*?

Answer to Reading Check

The Mesozoic era is known as the Age of Reptiles because reptiles, including the dinosaurs, were the dominant organisms on land.

176 Chapter 6 • The Rock and Fossil Record

The Cenozoic Era—The Age of Mammals

The Cenozoic era, as shown in **Figure 7,** began about 65 million years ago and continues to the present. This era is known as the *Age of Mammals*. During the Mesozoic era, mammals had to compete with dinosaurs and other animals for food and habitat. After the mass extinction at the end of the Mesozoic era, mammals flourished. Unique traits, such as regulating body temperature internally and bearing young that develop inside the mother, may have helped mammals survive the environmental changes that probably caused the extinction of the dinosaurs.

Figure 7 Thousands of species of mammals evolved during the Cenozoic era. This scene shows species from the early Cenozoic era that are now extinct.

SECTION Review

Summary

- The geologic time scale divides Earth's 4.6 billion–year history into distinct intervals of time. Divisions of geologic time include eons, eras, periods, and epochs.
- The boundaries between geologic time intervals represent visible changes that have taken place on Earth.
- The rock and fossil record represents mainly the Phanerozoic eon, which is the eon in which we live.
- At certain times in Earth's history, the number of life-forms has increased or decreased dramatically.

Using Key Terms

1. Use each of the following terms in the same sentence: *era, period,* and *epoch.*

Understanding Key Ideas

2. The unit of geologic time that began 65 million years ago and continues to the present is the
   a. Holocene epoch.
   b. Cenozoic era.
   c. Phanerozoic eon.
   d. Quaternary period.

3. What are the major time intervals represented by the geologic time scale?

4. Explain how geologic time is recorded in rock layers.

5. What kinds of environmental changes cause mass extinctions?

Critical Thinking

6. **Making Inferences** What future event might mark the end of the Cenozoic era?

7. **Identifying Relationships** How might a decrease in competition between species lead to the sudden appearance of many new species?

Interpreting Graphics

8. Look at the illustration below. On the Earth-history clock shown, 1 h equals 383 million years, and 1 min equals 6.4 million years. In millions of years, how much more time is represented by the Proterozoic eon than by the Phanerozoic eon?

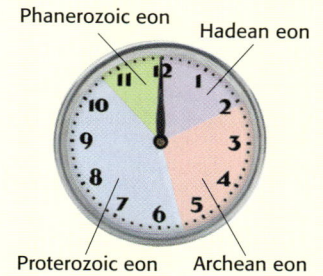

Phanerozoic eon — Hadean eon
Proterozoic eon — Archean eon

For a variety of links related to this chapter, go to www.scilinks.org
Topic: Geologic Time
SciLinks code: HSM0668

Answers to Section Review

1. Sample answer: Eras are divisions of geologic time that are divided into periods, and periods are units of geologic time that are divided into epochs.
2. b
3. The major time intervals represented by the geologic time scale are eons, eras, periods, and epochs.
4. Geologic time is recorded in rock layers by the differences in the fossils they contain.
5. Environmental changes that cause mass extinctions include global climate change, changes in oceans currents, and possibly asteroid strikes.
6. Answers may vary. Sample answer: a major change in the Earth's climate
7. A decrease in competition between species allows species to move into new parts of the environment and to adapt to use new resources.
8. 25 × 6.4 million years = 160 million years; 7 × 6.4 million years = 44.8 million years; 160 million years − 44.8 million years = 115.2 million years

Homework — GENERAL

Prehistoric Animals Ask each student to choose a favorite prehistoric animal. Then, have students find information about that animal and the time period in which it lived. University Web sites are an excellent place to look for this information. Students can present their information as an oral presentation or on a poster. **LS Visual**

CHAPTER RESOURCES

Chapter Resource File
- Section Quiz GENERAL
- Section Review GENERAL
- Vocabulary and Section Summary GENERAL

Model-Making Lab

How Do You Stack Up?

Teacher's Notes

Time Required
Two 45-minute class periods

Lab Ratings
EASY → HARD
Teacher Prep 🧪
Student Set-Up 🧪🧪
Concept Level 🧪🧪🧪
Clean Up 🧪

MATERIALS

The activity works best if the class is divided into four groups. The materials listed on the student page are enough for each group.

Preparation Notes

Students may need to review the geologic column and the principle of superposition before performing this activity. Also, be certain that your students understand what an index fossil is.

Thicknesses of layers given in the lab are the thicknesses of only the stratigraphic sections. The rock layers represented by the sections would probably be much thicker. However, the relative thicknesses of the layers are represented in the measurements given (i.e., a layer that is 4 cm thick is twice as thick as a layer that is 2 cm thick).

Lab Notes

Explain that the geologic column for the entire Earth is constructed from smaller columns that are similar to the hypothetical column in this lab. Stratigraphic sections are pieced together to form short columns, and short columns are pieced together to form longer columns. All columns put together make up the geologic column for the entire Earth.

Model-Making Lab

How Do You Stack Up?

OBJECTIVES

Make a model of a geologic column.

Interpret the geologic history represented by the geologic column you have made.

MATERIALS
- paper, white
- pencil
- pencils or crayons, assorted colors
- ruler, metric
- scissors
- tape, transparent

SAFETY

According to the principle of superposition, in undisturbed sequences of sedimentary rock, the oldest layers are on the bottom. Geologists use this principle to determine the relative age of the rocks in a small area. In this activity, you will model what geologists do by drawing sections of different rock outcrops. Then, you will create a part of the geologic column, showing the geologic history of the area that contains all of the outcrops.

Procedure

1. Use a metric ruler and a pencil to draw four boxes on a blank piece of paper. Each box should be 3 cm wide and at least 6 cm tall. (You can trace the boxes shown on the next page.)

2. With colored pencils, copy the illustrations of the four outcrops on the next page. Copy one illustration in each of the four boxes. Use colors and patterns similar to those shown.

3. Pay close attention to the contact between layers—straight or wavy. Straight lines represent bedding planes, where deposition was continuous. Wavy lines represent unconformities, where rock layers may be missing. The top of each outcrop is incomplete, so it should be a jagged line. (Assume that the bottom of the lowest layer is a bedding plane.)

4. Use a black crayon or pencil to add the symbols representing fossils to the layers in your drawings. Pay attention to the shapes of the fossils and the layers that they are in.

5. Write the outcrop number on the back of each section.

6. Carefully cut the outcrops out of the paper, and lay the individual outcrops next to each other on your desk or table.

7. Find layers that have the same rocks and contain the same fossils. Move each outcrop up or down to line up similar layers next to each other.

8. If unconformities appear in any of the outcrops, there may be rock layers missing. You may need to examine other sections to find out what fits between the layers above and below the unconformities. Leave room for these layers by cutting the outcrops along the unconformities (wavy lines).

CHAPTER RESOURCES

Chapter Resource File
- Datasheet for Chapter Lab
- Lab Notes and Answers

Technology
- Classroom Videos
  - Lab Video

Chapter 6 • The Rock and Fossil Record

9. Eventually, you should be able to make a geologic column that represents all four of the outcrops. It will show rock types and fossils for all the known layers in the area.

10. Tape the pieces of paper together in a pattern that represents the complete geologic column.

Analyze the Results

1. **Examining Data** How many layers are in the part of the geologic column that you modeled?

2. **Examining Data** Which is the oldest layer in your column? Which rock layer is the youngest? How do you know? Describe these layers in terms of rock type or the fossils they contain.

3. **Classifying** List the fossils in your column from oldest to youngest. Label the youngest and oldest fossils.

4. **Analyzing Data** Look at the unconformity in outcrop 2. Which rock layers are partially or completely missing? How do you know?

Draw Conclusions

5. **Drawing Conclusions** Which (if any) fossils can be used as index fossils for a single layer? Why are these fossils considered index fossils? What method(s) would be required to determine the absolute age of these fossils?

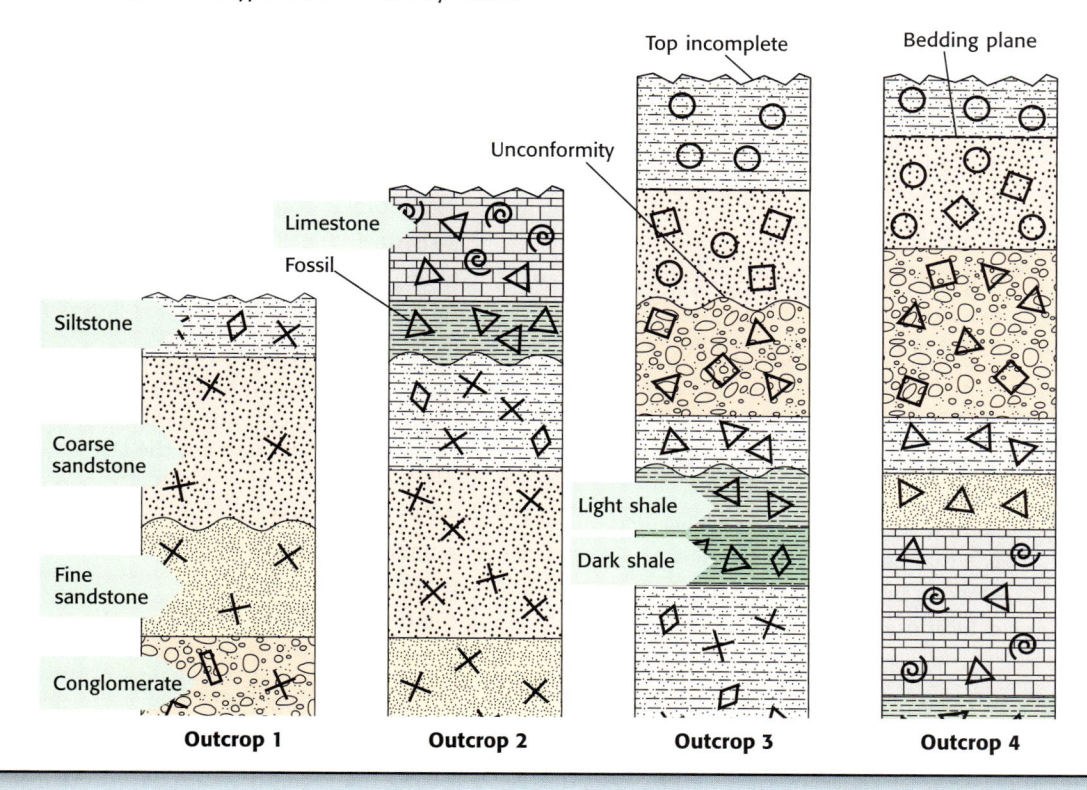

Analyze the Results

1. There are 12 layers in this part of the geologic column.

2. The conglomerate that contains rectangles and X fossils is the oldest. The siltstone that contains circle fossils is the youngest.

3. The relative age of the fossils from oldest to youngest is rectangles, X's, diamonds, triangles, spirals, squares, and circles.

4. In Outcrop 2, part of the siltstone and all of the dark shale are missing. This information can be determined by comparing the outcrop with the geologic column.

Draw Conclusions

5. Index fossils include the spirals in the limestone and the rectangles in the conglomerate. These fossils are considered index fossils because they existed for a short range of geologic time. To determine the absolute age of the fossils, you would need to use radiometric dating.

CHAPTER RESOURCES

Workbooks

- **Labs You Can Eat**
  - GeoPancakes BASIC
- **Inquiry Labs**
  - A Penny for Your Thoughts GENERAL
- **EcoLabs & Field Activities**
  - Rock of Ages ADVANCED
- **Long-Term Projects & Research Ideas**
  - The Hard Rock Chronicles ADVANCED

CLASSROOM TESTED & APPROVED

Dwight Patton
Carroll T. Welch Middle School
Horizon City, Texas

Chapter Review

Assignment Guide

Section	Questions
1	2, 5, 14, 17
2	6, 9, 11, 22–25
3	10, 12, 15
4	4, 7, 13, 16, 20, 21
5	8, 19
2 and 3	3, 18
2 and 5	1

ANSWERS

Using Key Terms

1. Sample answer: Superposition is the principle that states that younger rocks lie above older rocks in undisturbed sequences. The geologic column is an ideal sequence of rock layers that contains all the known fossil and rock layers on Earth, arranged from oldest to youngest. The geologic time scale is a scale that divides Earth's 4.6 billion year history into distinct intervals of time.

2. Sample answer: Uniformitarianism is the theory that gradual geologic processes that we observe in the present were also active in the past. This theory argues that slow gradual change shapes the Earth. Catastrophism is the theory that past episodes of sudden and drastic change are responsible for the major geologic features that change the Earth.

3. Sample answer: Relative dating is a method of comparing rocks or fossils to each other to determine which ones are older. Absolute dating is a method of determining the age of something in years.

4. Sample answer: A trace fossil is any naturally preserved evidence of animal activity. An index fossil is a fossil of an organism that lived during a relatively short, well-defined geologic time span. It is used to establish the age of rock layers.

Chapter Review

USING KEY TERMS

1. In your own words, write a definition for each of the following terms: *superposition*, *geologic column*, and *geologic time scale*.

For each pair of terms, explain how the meanings of the terms differ.

2. *uniformitarianism* and *catastrophism*

3. *relative dating* and *absolute dating*

4. *trace fossil* and *index fossil*

UNDERSTANDING KEY IDEAS

Multiple Choice

5. Which of the following does not describe catastrophic change?
   a. widespread
   b. sudden
   c. rare
   d. gradual

6. Scientists assign relative ages by using
   a. absolute dating.
   b. the principle of superposition.
   c. radioactive half-lives.
   d. carbon-14 dating.

7. Which of the following is a trace fossil?
   a. an insect preserved in amber
   b. a mammoth frozen in ice
   c. wood replaced by minerals
   d. a dinosaur trackway

8. The largest divisions of geologic time are called
   a. periods.
   b. eras.
   c. eons.
   d. epochs.

9. Rock layers cut by a fault formed
   a. after the fault.
   b. before the fault.
   c. at the same time as the fault.
   d. There is not enough information to determine the answer.

10. Of the following isotopes, which is stable?
    a. uranium-238
    b. potassium-40
    c. carbon-12
    d. carbon-14

11. A surface that represents a missing part of the geologic column is called a(n)
    a. intrusion.
    b. fault.
    c. unconformity.
    d. fold.

12. Which method of radiometric dating is used mainly to date the remains of organisms that lived within the last 50,000 years?
    a. carbon-14 dating
    b. potassium-argon dating
    c. uranium-lead dating
    d. rubidium-strontium dating

Understanding Key Ideas

5. d
6. b
7. d
8. c
9. b
10. c
11. c
12. a

180 Chapter 6 • The Rock and Fossil Record

Short Answer

13 Describe three processes by which fossils form.

14 Identify the role of uniformitarianism in Earth science.

15 Explain how radioactive decay occurs.

16 Describe two ways in which scientists use fossils to determine environmental change.

17 Explain the role of paleontology in the study of Earth's history.

CRITICAL THINKING

18 Concept Mapping Use the following terms to create a concept map: *age, half-life, absolute dating, radioactive decay, radiometric dating, relative dating, superposition, geologic column,* and *isotopes.*

19 Applying Concepts Identify how changes in environmental conditions can affect the survival of a species. Give two examples.

20 Identifying Relationships Why do paleontologists know more about hard-bodied organisms than about soft-bodied organisms?

21 Analyzing Processes Why isn't a 100 million–year-old fossilized tree made of wood?

INTERPRETING GRAPHICS

Use the diagram below to answer the questions that follow.

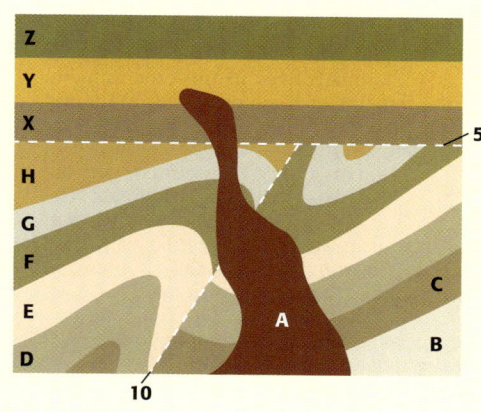

22 Is intrusion A younger or older than layer X? Explain.

23 What feature is marked by 5?

24 Is intrusion A younger or older than fault 10? Explain.

25 Other than the intrusion and faulting, what event happened in layers B, C, D, E, F, G, and H? Number this event, the intrusion, and the faulting in the order that they happened.

---

13. Sample answer: Fossils are formed by the process of petrifaction, in which minerals replace an organism's tissue. Fossils are formed when organisms become trapped in hardened tree sap, or amber. Fossils are formed when an organism is preserved by sediment that slows decay.

14. Uniformitarianism is the guiding principle in Earth science. The geologic processes shaping the Earth today have been at work throughout Earth's history.

15. Radioactive decay occurs as an unstable isotope breaks down into a stable isotope. This change happens as the isotope loses an electron and as a neutron becomes a proton.

16. Paleontologists use fossils to reconstruct past climates and to determine water depth in the oceans.

17. Paleontologists piece together the history of life on Earth by using fossils as their data.

Critical Thinking

18. An answer to this exercise can be found at the end of this book.

19. Changes in environmental conditions can change or eliminate a species' habitat, so a species cannot meet its basic needs. Both global climate change and changes in ocean currents can cause the extinction of species.

20. Hard-bodied organisms are more easily preserved, so more of these organisms have been studied.

21. The tree is not made of wood because the wood tissue in the tree was completely replaced by minerals.

Interpreting Graphics

22. younger

23. an angular unconformity

24. Intrusion A is younger than fault 10 because the intrusion is not disturbed by the fault.

25. folding; Folding occurred, and then the fault occurred. After erosion and deposition of layers X and Y, the intrusion occurred.

CHAPTER RESOURCES

Chapter Resource File
- Chapter Review GENERAL
- Chapter Test A GENERAL
- Chapter Test B ADVANCED
- Chapter Test C SPECIAL NEEDS
- Vocabulary Activity GENERAL

Workbooks
- Study Guide
- Assessment resources are also available in Spanish.

Chapter 6 • Chapter Review

Standardized Test Preparation

Teacher's Note
To provide practice under more realistic testing conditions, give students 20 minutes to answer all of the questions in this Standardized Test Preparation.

MISCONCEPTION ALERT

Answers to the standardized test preparation can help you identify student misconceptions and misunderstandings.

READING

Passage 1
1. B
2. G
3. C

TEST DOCTOR

Question 1: Although the word *exceptional* can describe something beautiful (choice A), the passage indicates that the nodules are exceptional because they are out of the ordinary, or extraordinary (choice B).

Passage 2
1. C
2. F
3. B

Standardized Test Preparation

READING
Read each of the passages below. Then, answer the questions that follow each passage.

Passage 1 Three hundred million years ago, the region that is now Illinois had a different climate than it does today. Swamps and shallow bays covered much of the area. No fewer than 500 species of plants and animals lived in this environment. Today, the remains of these organisms are found beautifully preserved within nodules. Nodules are round or oblong structures usually composed of cemented sediments that sometimes contain the fossilized hard parts of plants and animals. The Illinois nodules are <u>exceptional</u> because the soft parts of organisms are found together with hard parts. For this reason, these nodules are found in fossil collections around the world.

1. In the passage, what is the meaning of the word *exceptional*?
   A beautiful
   B extraordinary
   C average
   D large

2. According to the passage, which of the following statements about nodules is correct?
   F Nodules are rarely round or oblong.
   G Nodules are usually composed of cemented sediment.
   H Nodules are not found in present-day Illinois.
   I Nodules always contain fossils.

3. Which of the following is a fact in the passage?
   A The Illinois nodules are not well known outside of Illinois.
   B Illinois has had the same climate throughout Earth's history.
   C Both the hard and soft parts of organisms are preserved in the Illinois nodules.
   D Fewer than 500 species of plants and animals have been found in Illinois nodules.

Passage 2 In 1995, paleontologist Paul Sereno and his team were working in an unexplored region of Morocco when they made an <u>astounding</u> find—an enormous dinosaur skull! The skull measured approximately 1.6 m in length, which is about the height of a refrigerator. Given the size of the skull, Sereno concluded that the skeleton of the animal it came from must have been about 14 m long—about as big as a school bus. The dinosaur was even larger than *Tyrannosaurus rex*! The newly discovered 90 million–year-old predator most likely chased other dinosaurs by running on large, powerful hind legs, and its bladelike teeth meant certain death for its prey.

1. In the passage, what does the word *astounding* mean?
   A important
   B new
   C incredible
   D one of a kind

2. Which of the following is evidence that the dinosaur described in the passage was a predator?
   F It had bladelike teeth.
   G It had a large skeleton.
   H It was found with the bones of a smaller animal nearby.
   I It is 90 million years old.

3. What types of information do you think that fossil teeth provide about an organism?
   A the color of its skin
   B the types of food it ate
   C the speed that it ran
   D the mating habits it had

TEST DOCTOR

Question 3: Only choice B could be correct. Speed (choice C) could be determined by fossilized footprints. Color of skin (choice A) would require a frozen sample, but this would still be difficult to determine. Mating habits (choice D) would also be difficult to determine.

Chapter 6 • The Rock and Fossil Record

INTERPRETING GRAPHICS

Use the graph below to answer the questions that follow.

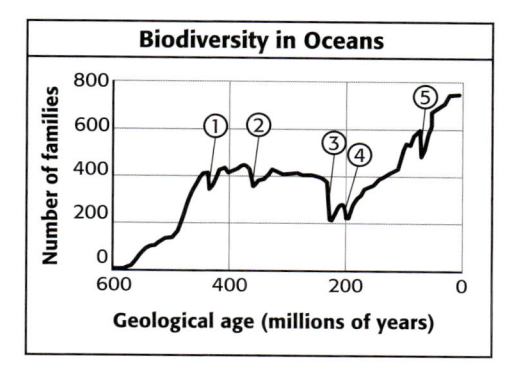

Biodiversity in Oceans

[Graph showing Number of families (0-800) vs Geological age (600-0 millions of years), with points 1, 2, 3, 4, 5 marked]

1. At which point in Earth's history did the greatest mass-extinction event take place?
   A at point 1, the Ordovician-Silurian boundary
   B at point 3, the Permian-Triassic boundary
   C at point 4, the Triassic-Jurassic boundary
   D at point 5, the Cretaceous-Tertiary boundary

2. Immediately following the Cretaceous-Tertiary extinction, represented by point 5, approximately how many families of marine organisms remained in the Earth's oceans?
   F 200 marine families
   G 300 marine families
   H 500 marine families
   I 700 marine families

3. Approximately how many million years ago did the Ordovician-Silurian mass-extinction event, represented by point 1, take place?
   A 200 million years ago
   B 250 million years ago
   C 350 million years ago
   D 420 million years ago

MATH

Read each question below, and choose the best answer.

1. Carbon-14 is a radioactive isotope with a half-life of 5,730 years. How much carbon-14 would remain in a sample that is 11,460 years old?
   A 12.5%
   B 25%
   C 50%
   D 100%

2. If a sample contains an isotope with a half-life of 10,000 years, how old would the sample be if 1/8 of the original isotope remained in the sample?
   F 20,000 years
   G 30,000 years
   H 40,000 years
   I 50,000 years

3. If a sample contains an isotope with a half-life of 5,000 years, how old would the sample be if 1/4 of the original isotope remained in the sample?
   A 10,000 years
   B 20,000 years
   C 30,000 years
   D 40,000 years

4. If Earth history spans 4.6 billion years and the Phanerozoic eon was 543 million years, what percentage of Earth history does the Phanerozoic eon represent?
   F about 6%
   G about 12%
   H about 18%
   I about 24%

5. Humans live in the Holocene epoch. If the Holocene epoch has lasted approximately 10,000 years, what percentage of the Quaternary period, which began 1.8 million years ago, is represented by the Holocene?
   A about 0.0055%
   B about 0.055%
   C about 0.55%
   D about 5.5%

INTERPRETING GRAPHICS
1. B
2. H
3. D

TEST DOCTOR

Question 2: Choice H is the correct answer. Students may choose choice G or F if they mistakenly look at points 3 or 4. If they look at the point of recovery after the Cretaceous-Tertiary extinction, they may choose choice I.

MATH
1. B
2. G
3. A
4. G
5. C

TEST DOCTOR

Question 1: To determine the correct percentage, students should assume that a new fossil has all of its carbon-14 (100%) and that it loses half of its carbon-14 every 5,730 years. After 11,460 years, half of half of the original carbon-14 would be left. So, 1/2 × 1/2 = 1/4 = 25% (choice B).

CHAPTER RESOURCES

Chapter Resource File
- Standardized Test Preparation GENERAL

State Resources

For specific resources for your state, visit go.hrw.com and type in the keyword **HSMSTR**.

Chapter 6 • Standardized Test Preparation **183**

Science in Action

Scientific Debate

Background
Since the 1990s, well-preserved fossils of dinosaurs that have featherlike structures have been found in northern China. For many vertebrate paleontologists, these fossils provide support for the theory that birds are descended from theropods, a group of dinosaurs that include *Tyrannosaurus* and *Velociraptor*. Paleontologists think that the "feathered" dinosaurs were flightless and that the feathers were used for warmth or display.

Science, Technology, and Society

Background
Movies such as *Jurassic Park* may lead some students to believe that DNA extracted from the preserved remains of organisms that have died a long time ago will tell us everything about ancient life. In reality, it is difficult to obtain and study DNA. Large, complex molecules such as DNA are broken down by bacteria and enzymes soon after the death of an organism. The DNA becomes fragmented and cannot be pieced together again. Even the DNA of organisms such as mammoths that have been preserved in ice becomes fragmented.

Science in Action

Scientific Debate

Feathered Dinosaurs
One day in 1996, a Chinese farmer broke open a rock he found in the bed of an ancient dry lake. What he found inside the rock became one of the most exciting paleontological discoveries of the 20th century. Preserved inside were the remains of a dinosaur. The dinosaur had a large head; powerful jaws; sharp, jagged teeth; and, most important of all, a row of featherlike structures along the backbone. Scientists named the dinosaur *Sinosauropteryx*, or "Chinese dragon wing." *Sinosauropteryx* and the remains of other "feathered" dinosaurs recently discovered in China have led some scientists to hypothesize that feathers evolved through theropod (three-toed) dinosaurs. Other paleontologists disagree. They believe the structures along the backbone of these dinosaurs are not feathers but the remains of elongated spines, like those that run down the head and back of an iguana.

Language Arts ACTIVITY
Paleontologists often give dinosaurs names that describe something unusual about the animal's head, body, feet, or size. These names have Greek or Latin roots. Research the names of some dinosaurs, and find out what the names mean. Create a list of dinosaur names and their meanings.

Science, Technology, and Society

DNA and a Mammoth Discovery
In recent years, scientists have unearthed several mammoths that had been frozen in ice in Siberia and other remote northern locations. Bones, fur, food in the stomach, and even dung have all been found in good condition. Some scientists hoped that DNA extracted from the mammoths might lead to the cloning of this animal, which became extinct about 10,000 years ago. But the DNA might not be able to be duplicated by scientists. However, DNA samples may nevertheless help scientists understand why mammoths became extinct. One theory about why mammoths became extinct is that they were killed off by disease. Using DNA taken from fossilized mammoth bone, hair, or dung, scientists can check to see if it contains the DNA of a disease-causing pathogen that led to the extinction of the mammoths.

Math ACTIVITY
The male Siberian mammoth reached a height of about 3 m at the shoulder. Females reached a height of about 2.5 m at the shoulder. What is the ratio of the maximum height of a female Siberian mammoth to the height of a male Siberian mammoth?

Answer to Language Arts Activity
Answers may vary.

Answer to Math Activity
2.5:3.0

184 Chapter 6 • The Rock and Fossil Record

People in Science

Lizzie May

Amateur Paleontologist For Lizzie May, summer vacations have meant trips into the Alaskan wilderness with her stepfather, geologist/paleontologist Kevin May. The purpose of these trips has not been for fun. Instead, Kevin and Lizzie have been exploring the Alaskan wilderness for the remains of ancient life—dinosaurs, in particular.

At age 18, Lizzie May has gained the reputation of being Alaska's most famous teenage paleontologist. It is a reputation that is well deserved. To date, Lizzie has collected hundreds of dinosaur bones and located important sites of dinosaur, bird, and mammal tracks. In her honor and as a result of her hard work in the field, scientists named the skeleton of a dinosaur discovered by the Mays "Lizzie." "Lizzie" is a duck-bill dinosaur, or hadrosaur, that lived approximately 90 million years ago. "Lizzie" is the oldest dinosaur ever found in Alaska and one of the earliest known duckbill dinosaurs in North America.

The Mays have made other, equally exciting discoveries. On one summer trip, Kevin and Lizzie located six dinosaur and bird track sites that dated back 97 million to 144 million years. On another trip, the Mays found a fossil marine reptile more than 200 million years old—an ichthyosaur—that had to be removed with the help of a military helicopter. You have to wonder what other exciting adventures are in store for Lizzie and Kevin!

Social Studies ACTIVITY

WRITING SKILL Lizzie May is not the only young person to have made a mark in dinosaur paleontology. Using the Internet or another source, research people such as Bucky Derflinger, Johnny Maurice, Brad Riney, and Wendy Sloboda, who as young people made contributions to the field of dinosaur study. Write a short essay summarizing your findings.

To learn more about these Science in Action topics, visit go.hrw.com and type in the keyword **HZ5FOSF**.

Current Science Check out Current Science® articles related to this chapter by visiting go.hrw.com. Just type in the keyword **HZ5CS06**.

People in Science

Teaching Strategy—GENERAL

Lizzie May shares the following fossil-hunting tips:

- If you are interested in finding bones, figure out in advance what the bones look like. This advice sounds obvious, but it's really helpful to know exactly what you are looking for.
- Bones are usually a different color from the dirt around them. So, you can look for white objects in the middle of the brown and black dirt. Sometimes, the bone will be the same color as the dirt, but as you sift through dirt, the inner portion of bones will stand out because the inner portion will be white.
- To find tracks, you need to be in the right place at the right time. Learn the kind of lighting that is right for finding tracks. Then, go out at that time to look for depressions in the Earth.
- Here's a clue for finding the right place to locate tracks. Tracks are often preserved in sedimentary rock near rivers. Being able to tell where the river channel is and has been is helpful.
- Stay in good shape—you don't want anything to slow you down when you are out in the field. It's hard work but is really fun!
- Volunteer at a museum!

Answer to Social Studies Activity
Answers may vary.

Chapter 6 • Science in Action   **185**

UNIT 3

TIMELINE

The Restless Earth

In this unit, you will learn what a dynamic planet the Earth is. Earth's landmasses are changing position continuously as they travel across Earth's surface on tremendous blocks of rock. As these blocks collide with each other, mountain ranges are formed. As these blocks pull apart, magma is released from below, sometimes explosively in volcanic eruptions. When these blocks grind slowly past one another, long breaks in the Earth are created, where devastating earthquakes can take place. This timeline shows some of the events that have occurred as scientists have tried to understand our dynamic Earth.

1864
Jules Verne's *A Journey to the Center of the Earth* is published. In this fictional story, the heroes enter and exit the Earth through volcanoes.

1912
Alfred Wegener proposes his theory of continental drift.

1979
Volcanoes are discovered on Io, one of Jupiter's moons.

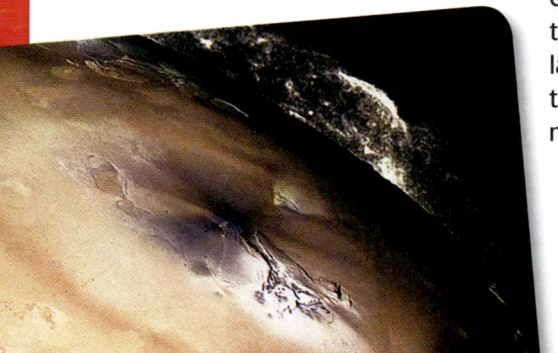

1980
Mount St. Helens erupts after an earthquake triggers a landslide on the volcano's north face.

Io, one of Jupiter's moons

1883
When Krakatau erupts, more than 36,000 people are killed.

1896
Henry Ford builds his first car.

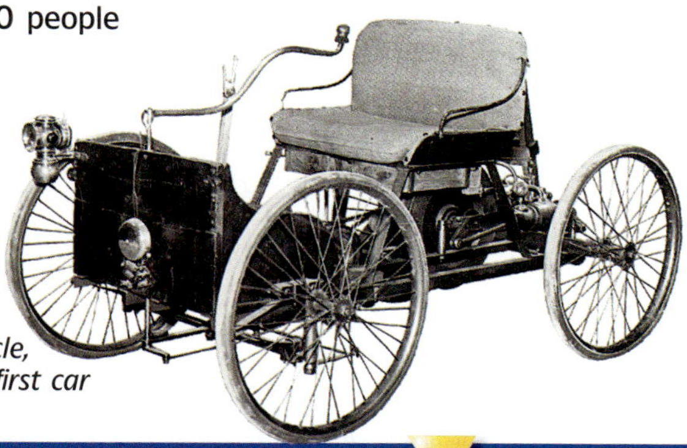

The Quadricycle, Henry Ford's first car

1906
San Francisco burns in the aftermath of an earthquake.

1935
Charles Richter devises a system of measuring the magnitude of earthquakes.

1951
Color television programming is introduced in the United States.

1962
A worldwide network of seismographs is established.

1982
Compact discs (CDs) and compact-disc players are made available to the public.

1994
An eight-legged robot named Dante II descends into the crater of an active volcano in Alaska.

1997
The population of the Caribbean island of Montserrat dwindles to less than half its original size as frequent eruptions of the Soufriere Hills volcano force evacuations.

2003
An earthquake of magnitude 4.6 strikes Alabama. It is one of the largest earthquakes ever recorded for this area.

Dante II

The Restless Earth 187

7 Plate Tectonics
Chapter Planning Guide

Compression guide: To shorten instruction because of time limitations, omit Section 4.

OBJECTIVES	LABS, DEMONSTRATIONS, AND ACTIVITIES	TECHNOLOGY RESOURCES
PACING • 90 min pp. 188–197 **Chapter Opener**	SE Start-up Activity, p. 189 GENERAL	OSP Parent Letter ■ GENERAL CD Student Edition on CD-ROM CD Guided Reading Audio CD ■ TR Chapter Starter Transparency* VID Brain Food Video Quiz
Section 1 Inside the Earth • Identify the layers of the Earth by their composition. • Identify the layers of the Earth by their physical properties. • Describe a tectonic plate. • Explain how scientists know about the structure of Earth's interior.	TE Activity Earth Models, p. 190 GENERAL TE Connection Activity Math, p. 191 GENERAL TE Connection Activity Language Arts, p. 194 GENERAL SE Quick Lab Tectonic Ice Cubes, p. 195 ◆ GENERAL CRF Datasheet for Quick Lab* TE Group Activity Modeling a Tectonic Plate, p. 195 ◆ GENERAL SE School-to-Home Activity Build a Seismograph, p. 196 GENERAL LB Labs You Can Eat Rescue Near the Center of the Earth* ◆ GENERAL	CRF Lesson Plans* TR Bellringer Transparency* TR The Composition of the Earth* TR The Earth's Lithosphere and Asthenosphere* TR The Earth's Mesosphere, Outer Core, and Inner Core* TR The Tectonic Plates; Close-Up of a Tectonic Plate* TR Discoveries of the Earth's Interior*
PACING • 45 min pp. 198–201 **Section 2 Restless Continents** • Describe Wegener's hypothesis of continental drift. • Explain how sea-floor spreading provides a way for continents to move. • Describe how new oceanic lithosphere forms at mid-ocean ridges. • Explain how magnetic reversals provide evidence for sea-floor spreading.	SE Science in Action Math, Social Studies, and Language Arts Activities, pp. 220–221 GENERAL LB Labs You Can Eat Cracks in the Hard-Boiled Earth* ◆ BASIC LB Whiz-Bang Demonstrations Thar She Blows!* ◆ GENERAL LB Long-Term Projects & Research Ideas Legend Has It* ADVANCED	CRF Lesson Plans* TR Bellringer Transparency* TR The Breakup of Pangaea* TR LINK TO LIFE SCIENCE Evolution of the Galápagos Finches* TR Sea-Floor Spreading*
PACING • 90 min pp. 202–205 **Section 3 The Theory of Plate Tectonics** • Describe the three types of tectonic plate boundaries. • Describe the three forces thought to move tectonic plates. • Explain how scientists measure the rate at which tectonic plates move.	TE Group Activity Plate Movements, p. 203 ADVANCED TE Activity Geologic Features at Tectonic Plate Boundaries, p. 203 GENERAL SE Model-Making Lab Convection Connection, p. 214 ◆ GENERAL CRF Datasheet for Chapter Lab* LB Labs You Can Eat Dough Fault of Your Own* ◆ ADVANCED	CRF Lesson Plans* TR Bellringer Transparency* TR Tectonic Plate Boundaries: A TR Tectonic Plate Boundaries: B TR Possible Causes of Tectonic Plate Motion* CRF SciLinks Activity* GENERAL VID Lab Videos for Earth Science
PACING • 45 min pp. 206–213 **Section 4 Deforming the Earth's Crust** • Describe two types of stress that deform rocks. • Describe three major types of folds. • Explain the differences between the three major types of faults. • Identify the most common types of mountains. • Explain the difference between uplift and subsidence.	TE Demonstration Modeling Deformation, p. 206 GENERAL TE Activity Folds that Trap Natural Gas, p. 207 ADVANCED TE Activity Hanging Walls Versus Footwalls, p. 208 BASIC SE Quick Lab Modeling Strike-Slip Faults, p. 209 GENERAL CRF Datasheet for Quick Lab* TE Activity Making Models, p. 209 GENERAL TE Activity Mountain-Building Gallery, p. 211 GENERAL SE Model-Making Lab Oh, the Pressure!, p. 728 GENERAL CRF Datasheet for LabBook*	CRF Lesson Plans* TR Bellringer Transparency* SE Internet Activity, p. 212 GENERAL

PACING • 90 min

CHAPTER REVIEW, ASSESSMENT, AND STANDARDIZED TEST PREPARATION

- CRF Vocabulary Activity* GENERAL
- SE Chapter Review, pp. 216–217 GENERAL
- CRF Chapter Review* ■ GENERAL
- CRF Chapter Tests A* ■ GENERAL, B* ADVANCED, C* SPECIAL NEEDS
- SE Standardized Test Preparation, pp. 218–219 GENERAL
- CRF Standardized Test Preparation* GENERAL
- CRF Performance-Based Assessment* GENERAL
- OSP Test Generator GENERAL
- CRF Test Item Listing* GENERAL

Online and Technology Resources

go.hrw.com
Visit go.hrw.com for a variety of free resources related to this textbook. Enter the keyword HZ5TEC.

Holt Online Learning
Students can access interactive problem-solving help and active visual concept development with the *Holt Science and Technology* Online Edition available at www.hrw.com.

Guided Reading Audio CD
Also in Spanish
A direct reading of each chapter for auditory learners, reluctant readers, and Spanish-speaking students.

Science Tutor CD-ROM
Excellent for remediation and test practice.

	KEY	CRF Chapter Resource File	SS Science Skills Worksheets	* Also on One-Stop Planner
	SE Student Edition	OSP One-Stop Planner	MS Math Skills for Science Worksheets	♦ Requires advance prep
	TE Teacher Edition	LB Lab Bank	CD CD or CD-ROM	■ Also available in Spanish
		TR Transparencies	VID Classroom Video/DVD	

SKILLS DEVELOPMENT RESOURCES	SECTION REVIEW AND ASSESSMENT	STANDARDS CORRELATIONS
SE Pre-Reading Activity, p. 188 GENERAL OSP Science Puzzlers, Twisters & Teasers GENERAL		National Science Education Standards SAI 1, SAI 2; ES 1b, 2a
CRF Directed Reading A* ■ BASIC, B* SPECIAL NEEDS CRF Vocabulary and Section Summary* ■ GENERAL SE Reading Strategy Reading Organizer, p. 190 GENERAL SE Math Practice Using Models, p. 192 GENERAL TE Reading Strategy Prediction Guide, p. 192 GENERAL TE Inclusion Strategies, p. 193 TE Reading Strategy Activity, p. 193 GENERAL CRF Reinforcement Worksheet The Layered Earth* BASIC CRF Critical Thinking Planet of Waves* ADVANCED	SE Reading Checks, pp. 191, 192, 195, 196 GENERAL TE Reteaching, p. 196 BASIC TE Quiz, p. 196 GENERAL TE Alternative Assessment, p. 196 GENERAL SE Section Review,* p. 197 ■ GENERAL CRF Section Quiz* ■ GENERAL	UCP 2; SAI 1, 2; ST 2; ES 1a
CRF Directed Reading A* ■ BASIC, B* SPECIAL NEEDS CRF Vocabulary and Section Summary* ■ GENERAL SE Reading Strategy Paired Summarizing, p. 198 GENERAL	SE Reading Checks, pp. 198, 201 GENERAL TE Reteaching, p. 200 BASIC TE Homework, p. 200 GENERAL TE Quiz, p. 200 GENERAL TE Alternative Assessment, p. 200 GENERAL SE Section Review,* p. 201 ■ GENERAL CRF Section Quiz* ■ GENERAL	UCP 2; SAI 1, 2; ST 2; SPSP 5; HNS 1, 2, 3; ES 1b, 2a
CRF Directed Reading A* ■ BASIC, B* SPECIAL NEEDS CRF Vocabulary and Section Summary* ■ GENERAL SE Reading Strategy Brainstorming, p. 202 GENERAL MS Math Skills for Science A Shortcut for Multiplying Large Numbers* GENERAL CRF Reinforcement Worksheet A Moving Jigsaw Puzzle* BASIC	SE Reading Checks, pp. 203, 204 GENERAL TE Homework, p. 204 ADVANCED TE Reteaching, p. 204 BASIC TE Quiz, p. 204 GENERAL TE Alternative Assessment, p. 204 GENERAL SE Section Review,* p. 205 ■ GENERAL CRF Section Quiz* ■ GENERAL	UCP 2; SAI 1, 2; ST 2; SPSP 3–5; HNS 1; ES 1b, 2a
CRF Directed Reading A* ■ BASIC, B* SPECIAL NEEDS CRF Vocabulary and Section Summary* ■ GENERAL SE Reading Strategy Discussion, p. 206 GENERAL TE Reading Strategy Sketching Folds and Faults, p. 207 GENERAL SE Connection to Social Studies The Naming of the Appalachian Mountains, p. 211 GENERAL TE Inclusion Strategies, p. 212 ♦	SE Reading Checks, pp. 206, 208, 210 GENERAL TE Homework, p. 207 GENERAL TE Reteaching, p. 212 BASIC TE Quiz, p. 212 GENERAL TE Alternative Assessment, p. 212 GENERAL SE Section Review,* p. 213 ■ GENERAL CRF Section Quiz* ■ GENERAL	UCP 2; SAI 1, 2; ES 1b, 1c, 1d, 2a

One-Stop Planner® CD-ROM

This convenient CD-ROM includes:
- Lab Materials QuickList Software
- Holt Calendar Planner
- Customizable Lesson Plans
- Printable Worksheets
- ExamView® Test Generator

CNN Student News

cnnstudentnews.com

Find the latest news, lesson plans, and activities related to important scientific events.

SCLINKS NSTA

www.scilinks.org

Maintained by the **National Science Teachers Association.** See Chapter Enrichment pages for a complete list of topics.

Current Science®

Check out *Current Science* articles and activities by visiting the HRW Web site at **go.hrw.com.** Just type in the keyword **HZ5CS07T.**

Classroom Videos

- **Lab Videos** demonstrate the chapter lab.
- **Brain Food Video Quizzes** help students review the chapter material.
- **CNN Videos** bring science into your students' daily life.

Chapter 7 • Chapter Planning Guide

7 Chapter Resources

Visual Resources

CHAPTER STARTER TRANSPARENCY

BELLRINGER TRANSPARENCIES

TEACHING TRANSPARENCIES

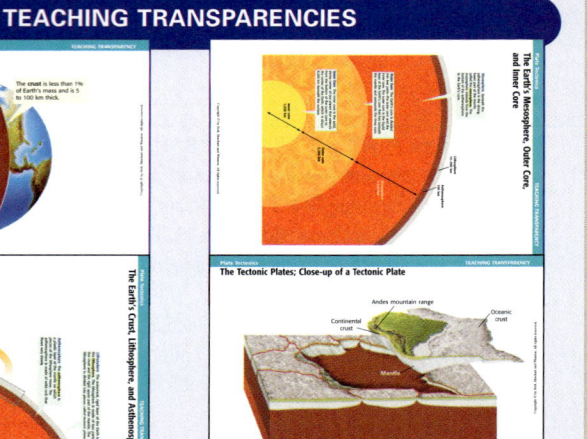

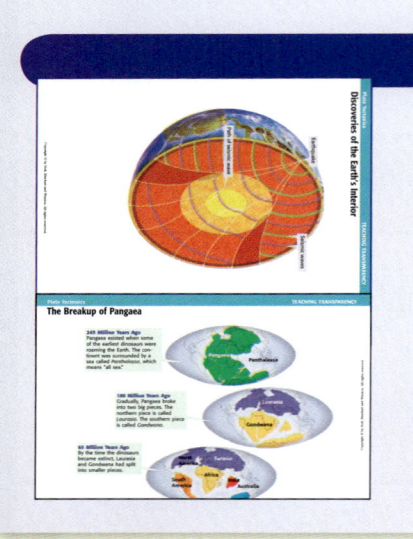

TEACHING TRANSPARENCIES

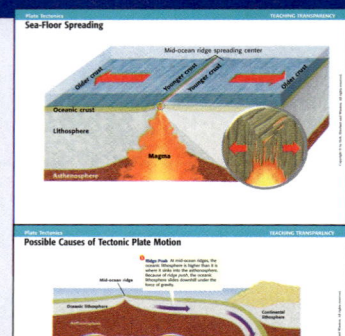

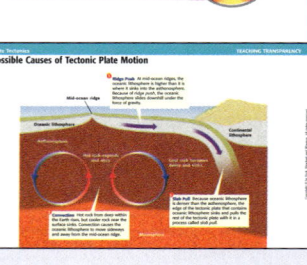

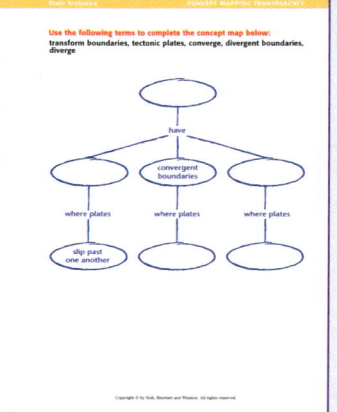

CONCEPT MAPPING TRANSPARENCY

Planning Resources

LESSON PLANS

PARENT LETTER — ALSO IN SPANISH

TEST ITEM LISTING

One-Stop Planner® CD-ROM

This CD-ROM includes all of the resources shown here and the following time-saving tools:

- Lab Materials QuickList Software
- Customizable lesson plans
- Holt Calendar Planner
- The powerful ExamView® Test Generator

187C   Chapter 7 • Plate Tectonics

For a preview of available worksheets covering math and science skills, see pages T26–T33. All of these resources are also on the One-Stop Planner®.

Meeting Individual Needs

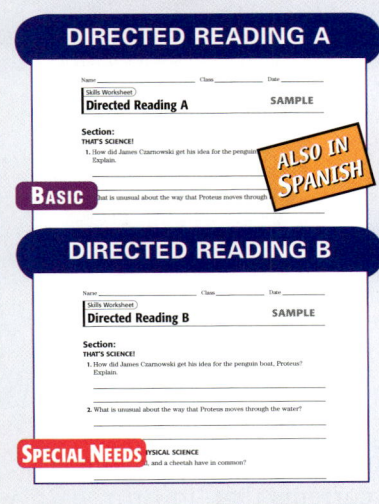

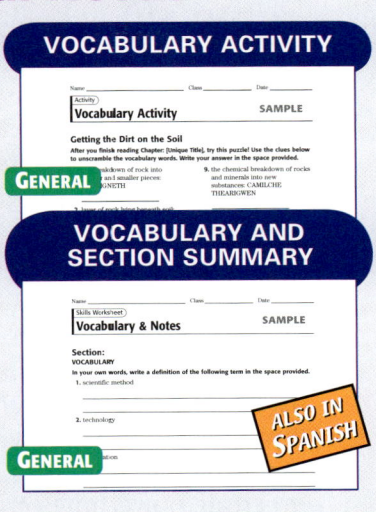

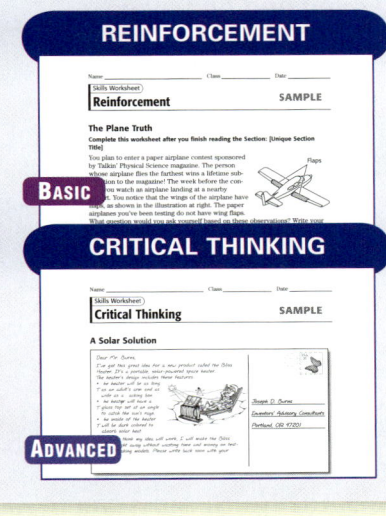

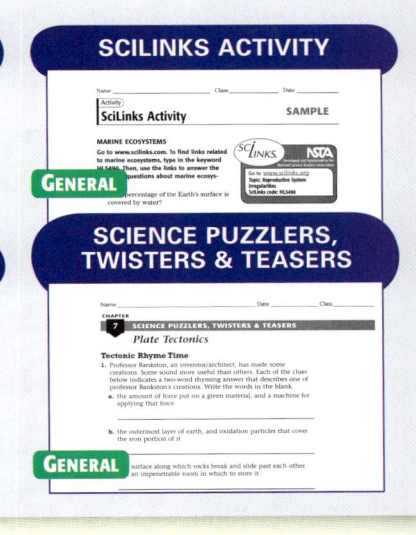

- **DIRECTED READING A** — BASIC (Also in Spanish)
- **DIRECTED READING B** — SPECIAL NEEDS
- **VOCABULARY ACTIVITY** — GENERAL
- **VOCABULARY AND SECTION SUMMARY** — GENERAL (Also in Spanish)
- **REINFORCEMENT** — BASIC
- **CRITICAL THINKING** — ADVANCED
- **SCILINKS ACTIVITY** — GENERAL
- **SCIENCE PUZZLERS, TWISTERS & TEASERS** — GENERAL

Labs and Activities

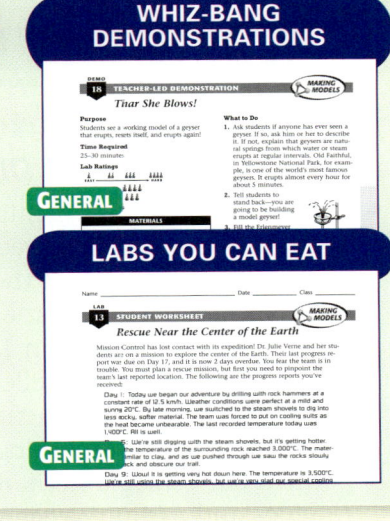

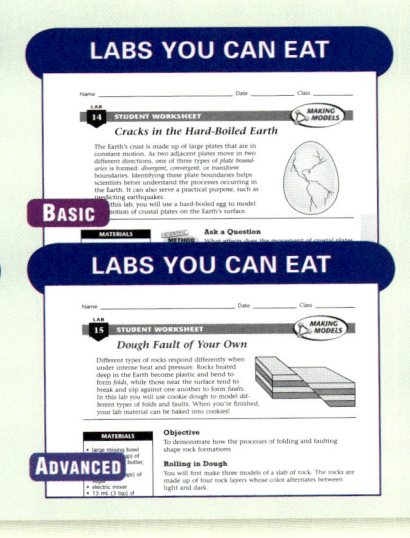

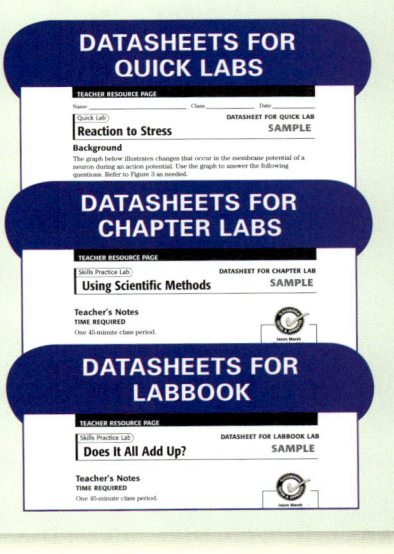

- **LONG-TERM PROJECTS & RESEARCH IDEAS** — ADVANCED
- **WHIZ-BANG DEMONSTRATIONS** — GENERAL
- **LABS YOU CAN EAT** — GENERAL
- **LABS YOU CAN EAT** — BASIC
- **LABS YOU CAN EAT** — ADVANCED
- **DATASHEETS FOR QUICK LABS**
- **DATASHEETS FOR CHAPTER LABS**
- **DATASHEETS FOR LABBOOK**

Review and Assessments

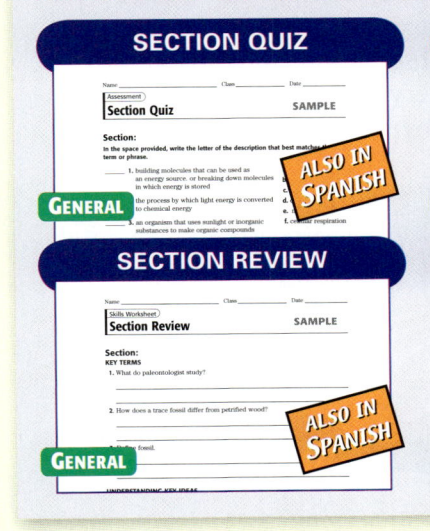

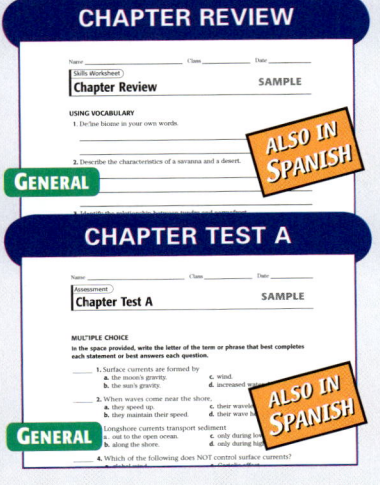

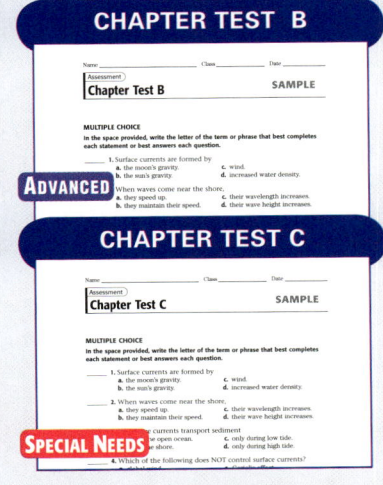

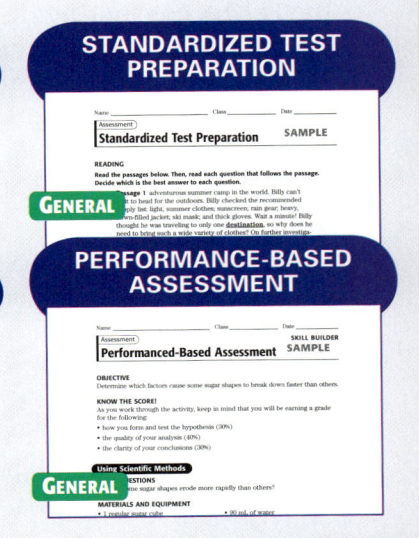

- **SECTION QUIZ** — GENERAL (Also in Spanish)
- **SECTION REVIEW** — GENERAL (Also in Spanish)
- **CHAPTER REVIEW** — GENERAL (Also in Spanish)
- **CHAPTER TEST A** — GENERAL (Also in Spanish)
- **CHAPTER TEST B** — ADVANCED
- **CHAPTER TEST C** — SPECIAL NEEDS
- **STANDARDIZED TEST PREPARATION** — GENERAL
- **PERFORMANCE-BASED ASSESSMENT** — GENERAL

Chapter 7 • Chapter Resources 187D

7 Chapter Enrichment

This Chapter Enrichment provides relevant and interesting information to expand and enhance your presentation of the chapter material.

Section 1

Inside the Earth

Continents and the Earth's Crust

- Continents are large, continuous landmasses composed of crust that is generally much older than the surrounding oceanic crust. The core or central, older, stabler part of a continent, called a *craton,* is generally composed of ancient, crystalline igneous and metamorphic rock. Cratons range from 3.9 billion to 200 million years old. Rocks of the North American craton are exposed more or less without interruption in the eastern two-thirds of Canada, along the U.S. margins of Lake Superior, and in most of Greenland.

Heat Within the Earth

- The Earth's internal heat contributes to the process of differentiation—the division of the Earth into layers that have distinct characteristics. This heat has three main sources: the decay of radioactive elements, which is a continuous process; the collapse of iron into the Earth's core during the process of differentiation 4.5 billion years ago; and leftover energy from the accretion and compression of particles that coalesced to form Earth 4.6 billion years ago.

Is That a Fact!

◆ Earth's magnetic poles have reversed more than 177 times in the last 85 million years. The most recent reversal occurred within the last 600,000 years. By using complex computer models, scientists are beginning to understand how this process happens, but they are unable to predict when the poles will reverse again or how life on Earth will be affected by this reversal.

Earth's Inner Core

- Research conducted in 1996 suggests that the solid inner core of the Earth spins faster than the rest of the planet. This 2,456 km wide sphere of hot iron moves at a speed that would allow it to lap Earth's surface once every 400 years. This information may give scientists clues about how the Earth formed.

- The Earth's outer core is a hot, electrically conducting liquid that is thought to be continuously moved by convection. This layer's conductivity combines with the differential spin of the Earth's inner core to create powerful electric currents that, in turn, generate the Earth's magnetic field.

Section 2

Restless Continents

Continental Drift: An Old Idea

- The idea that the continents were once joined together was not a new idea in Alfred Wegener's time. In 1620, Francis Bacon noted that the continents seemed to fit together like a jigsaw puzzle, but no one could understand how they moved. In 1858, a French scientist named Antonio Snider-Pellegrini cited fossil evidence that suggested the continents had been joined. In 1910, an American geologist named Frank Taylor pointed out geologic similarities between South America and Africa. Wegener's studies in 1915 were the first exhaustive research on the topic and combined evidence from many disciplines. Neither Wegener nor Taylor could explain how the continents had separated, and their observations were dismissed. It was not until the discovery of sea-floor spreading that the continental drift hypothesis was accepted.

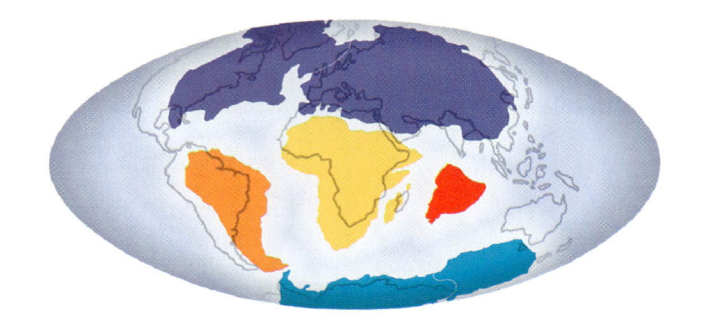

187E Chapter 7 • Plate Tectonics

For background information about teaching strategies and issues, refer to the *Professional Reference for Teachers*.

Testing the Continental Drift Hypothesis

- After sea-floor spreading was discovered in the 1960s, research groups tested Wegener's hypothesis using as many methods as possible:
  - The edges of continental slopes were mapped with sonar and have been shown to fit together even better than the coastlines do.
  - New radiometric dating methods showed that rocks in corresponding parts of Africa and South America formed at the same time.
  - The dating of igneous rocks around mid-ocean ridges showed a symmetrical pattern, in which older rocks were located farther away from the rifts. Few rocks older than 180 million years were discovered on the ocean floor. This discovery indicates that the oceanic lithosphere is continuously recycled.
  - Scientists found that zones of magnetic reversals also followed a symmetrical pattern on either side of mid-ocean ridges. The pattern of reversals matched the pattern revealed by the ages of the rocks.
  - The horizontal magnetic reversals recorded in the ocean floor matched those recorded in vertical sequences of lava flows on continents.

Section 3

The Theory of Plate Tectonics
Trenches

- Where an oceanic plate subducts under another tectonic plate, a long, steep-sided trench forms on the sea floor. On average, subduction trenches are 2,000 to 4,000 m deeper than the rest of the ocean floor. Nevertheless, some animals, including species of sea cucumbers, sea anemones, and marine worms, are capable of living in the cold, pressurized depths of ocean trenches.

Is That a Fact!

◆ The Mariana Trench, which is 2,500 km long and 11,033 m below sea level at its deepest point, is the deepest known place on Earth.

Section 4

Deforming the Earth's Crust
Fault Versus Fold

- Tectonic activity exerts a tremendous amount of pressure on crustal rocks. Whether they bend or break depends on several factors:
  - **Type of Stress** If stress is applied gradually, rocks often fold; if stress is applied suddenly, rocks tend to fault.
  - **Composition of Rock** Brittle rocks, such as sandstone, tend to break; ductile rocks, such as shale, tend to fold.
  - **Temperature** As the temperature at the point of stress increases, rocks are more likely to fold rather than fault.

SciLinks — Developed and maintained by the National Science Teachers Association

SciLinks is maintained by the National Science Teachers Association to provide you and your students with interesting, up-to-date links that will enrich your classroom presentation of the chapter.

Visit www.scilinks.org and enter the SciLinks code for more information about the topic listed.

Topic: **Composition of the Earth**	Topic: **Plate Tectonics**
SciLinks code: HSM0329	SciLinks code: HSM1171
Topic: **Structure of the Earth**	Topic: **Faults**
SciLinks code: HSM1468	SciLinks code: HSM0566
Topic: **Tectonic Plates**	Topic: **Mountain Building**
SciLinks code: HSM1497	SciLinks code: HSM0999

Chapter 7 • Chapter Enrichment   187F

Overview

Tell students that this chapter will help them learn about the structure of the Earth and the forces that continually reshape the crust of our planet.

Assessing Prior Knowledge

Students should be familiar with the following topics:
- the principle of uniformitarianism
- the geologic time scale

Identifying Misconceptions

Students may think that the theory of plate tectonics was developed a long time ago. Stress that this key concept in geology was accepted in the mainstream of geologic thought less than 50 years ago. Parents and teachers may remember learning alternative theories in Earth science classes. Even today, scientists have still not fully identified the mechanisms of tectonic plate movement. Although the theory of plate tectonics was accepted in relatively recent times, it is still the best explanation for many different lines of geologic evidence and observations.

7

Plate Tectonics

SECTION 1	Inside the Earth	190
SECTION 2	Restless Continents	198
SECTION 3	The Theory of Plate Tectonics	202
SECTION 4	Deforming the Earth's Crust	206

Chapter Lab 214
Chapter Review 216
Standardized Test Preparation 218
Science in Action 220

About the PHOTO

The San Andreas fault stretches across the California landscape like a giant wound. The fault, which is 1,000 km long, breaks the Earth's crust from Northern California to Mexico. Because the North American plate and Pacific plate are slipping past one another along the fault, many earthquakes happen.

PRE-READING ACTIVITY

FOLDNOTES **Key-Term Fold** Before you read the chapter, create the FoldNote entitled "Key-Term Fold" described in the **Study Skills** section of the Appendix. Write a key term from the chapter on each tab of the key-term fold. Under each tab, write the definition of the key term.

Standards Correlations

National Science Education Standards

The following codes indicate the National Science Education Standards that correlate to this chapter. The full text of the standards is at the front of the book.

Chapter Opener
SAI 1, 2; ES 1a, 2a

Section 1 Inside the Earth
UCP 2; SAI 1, 2; ST 2; ES 1a

Section 2 Restless Continents
UCP 2; HNS 1, 2, 3; ES 1b, 2a; SPSP 5; ST 2; SAI 1, 2

Section 3 The Theory of Plate Tectonics
UCP 2; HNS 2; ES 1b, 2a; SPSP 3, 4, 5; *LabBook:* SAI 1, 2

Section 4 Deforming the Earth's Crust
UCP 2; SAI 1; ES 1b, 2a; SAI 1, 2

Chapter Lab
SAI 1, 2

Chapter Review
UCP 2; SAI 1, 2; HNS 2; ES 1a, 1b, 2a; ST 2

Science in Action
UCP 2; ES 1b, 2a; HNS 1, 2, 3; ST 2; SAI 1, 2

188 Chapter 7 • Plate Tectonics

START-UP ACTIVITY

MATERIALS

FOR EACH STUDENT
- flat surface
- paper (2 stacks)

Answers

1. Sample answer: The stacks of paper buckle and fold over. Some of the paper in one stack slid under the paper in the other stack.
2. Sample answer: No, some pieces of paper slid under the opposite stack. Other pieces of paper slid into the other stack.
3. Sample answer: Continental collisions form high mountain ranges, such as the Himalayas.

START-UP ACTIVITY

Continental Collisions

As you can see, continents not only move but can also crash into each other. In this activity, you will model the collision of two continents.

Procedure

1. Obtain **two stacks of paper** that are each about 1 cm thick.
2. Place the two stacks of paper on a **flat surface**, such as a desk.
3. Very slowly, push the stacks of paper together so that they collide. Continue to push the stacks until the paper in one of the stacks folds over.

Analysis

1. What happens to the stacks of paper when they collide with each other?
2. Are all of the pieces of paper pushed upward? If not, what happens to the pieces that are not pushed upward?
3. What type of landform will most likely result from this continental collision?

Chapter Starter Transparency
Use this transparency to help students begin thinking about how tectonic forces have created tall mountains.

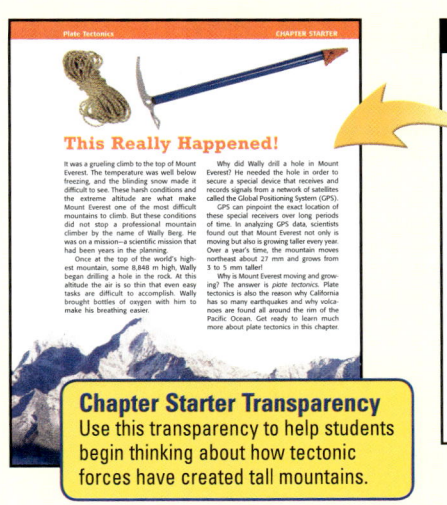

CHAPTER RESOURCES

Technology

- **Transparencies** — READING SKILLS
  - Chapter Starter Transparency
- **Student Edition on CD-ROM**
- **Guided Reading Audio CD**
  - English or Spanish
- **Classroom Videos**
  - Brain Food Video Quiz

Workbooks

- **Science Puzzlers, Twisters & Teasers**
  - Plate Tectonics GENERAL

Chapter 7 • Plate Tectonics 189

SECTION 1

Focus

Overview

This section describes the classification of the Earth according to composition (crust, mantle, and core) and according to physical structure (lithosphere, asthenosphere, mesosphere, outer core, and inner core). This section also describes tectonic plates. The section concludes with a discussion of how scientists study seismic waves to map the Earth's interior.

Bellringer

Ask students, "If you journeyed to the center of the Earth, what do you think you would observe along the way?" Have students draw an illustration of their journey in their **science journal**.

Motivate

ACTIVITY — GENERAL

Earth Models Have groups of students use materials of their choice to build a cutaway scale model of the Earth based on the dimensions shown in **Figure 3**. Encourage students to be creative. For example, they could use a chain of paperclips 64 clips long (34 clips for the core, 29 clips for the mantle, and 1 clip for the crust). **Kinesthetic/Visual**

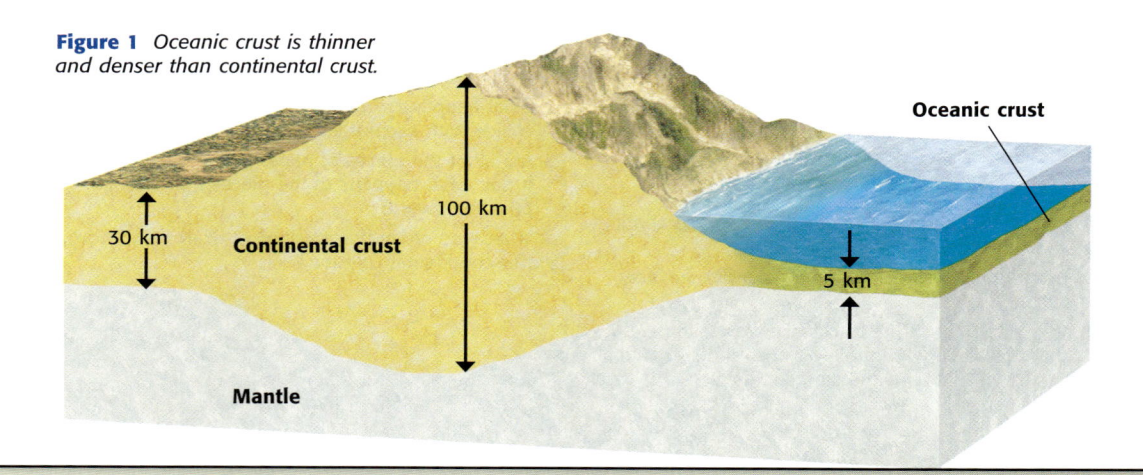

CHAPTER RESOURCES

Chapter Resource File
- Lesson Plan
- Directed Reading A BASIC
- Directed Reading B SPECIAL NEEDS

Technology
- Transparencies
  - Bellringer
  - The Composition of the Earth

190 Chapter 7 • Plate Tectonics

SECTION 1

READING WARM-UP

Objectives
- Identify the layers of the Earth by their composition.
- Identify the layers of the Earth by their physical properties.
- Describe a tectonic plate.
- Explain how scientists know about the structure of Earth's interior.

Terms to Learn

crust   asthenosphere
mantle   mesosphere
core   tectonic plate
lithosphere

READING STRATEGY

Reading Organizer As you read this section, create an outline of the section. Use the headings from the section in your outline.

Inside the Earth

If you tried to dig to the center of the Earth, what do you think you would find? Would the Earth be solid or hollow? Would it be made of the same material throughout?

Actually, the Earth is made of several layers. Each layer is made of different materials that have different properties. Scientists think about physical layers in two ways—by their composition and by their physical properties.

The Composition of the Earth

The Earth is divided into three layers—the crust, the mantle, and the core—based on the compounds that make up each layer. A *compound* is a substance composed of two or more elements. The less dense compounds make up the crust and mantle, and the densest compounds make up the core. The layers form because heavier elements are pulled toward the center of the Earth by gravity, and elements of lesser mass are found farther from the center.

The Crust

The outermost layer of the Earth is the **crust.** The crust is 5 to 100 km thick. It is the thinnest layer of the Earth.

As **Figure 1** shows, there are two types of crust—continental and oceanic. Both continental crust and oceanic crust are made mainly of the elements oxygen, silicon, and aluminum. However, the denser oceanic crust has almost twice as much iron, calcium, and magnesium, which form minerals that are denser than those in the continental crust.

Figure 1 Oceanic crust is thinner and denser than continental crust.

Is That a Fact!

Two lines of evidence indicate that Earth's core is a mixture of iron and nickel. The core's density, which is similar to a mixture of iron and nickel, was determined by studying the way seismic waves travel through it. The Earth's magnetic field also suggests this composition.

The Mantle

The layer of the Earth between the crust and the core is the **mantle**. The mantle is much thicker than the crust and contains most of the Earth's mass.

No one has ever visited the mantle. The crust is too thick to drill through to reach the mantle. Scientists must draw conclusions about the composition and other physical properties of the mantle from observations made on the Earth's surface. In some places, mantle rock pushes to the surface, which allows scientists to study the rock directly.

As you can see in **Figure 2,** another place scientists look for clues about the mantle is the ocean floor. Magma from the mantle flows out of active volcanoes on the ocean floor. These underwater volcanoes have given scientists many clues about the composition of the mantle. Because the mantle has more magnesium and less aluminum and silicon than the crust does, the mantle is denser than the crust.

The Core

The layer of the Earth that extends from below the mantle to the center of the Earth is the **core.** Scientists think that the Earth's core is made mostly of iron and contains smaller amounts of nickel but almost no oxygen, silicon, aluminum, or magnesium. As shown in **Figure 3,** the core makes up roughly one-third of the Earth's mass.

Reading Check Briefly describe the layers that make up the Earth. (*See the Appendix for answers to Reading Checks.*)

Figure 2 *Volcanic vents on the ocean floor, such as this vent off the coast of Hawaii, allow magma to rise up through the crust from the mantle.*

crust the thin and solid outermost layer of the Earth above the mantle

mantle the layer of rock between the Earth's crust and core

core the central part of the Earth below the mantle

The **mantle** is 67% of Earth's mass and is 2,900 km thick.

The **crust** is less than 1% of Earth's mass and is 5 to 100 km thick.

The **core** is 33% of Earth's mass and has a radius of 3,430 km.

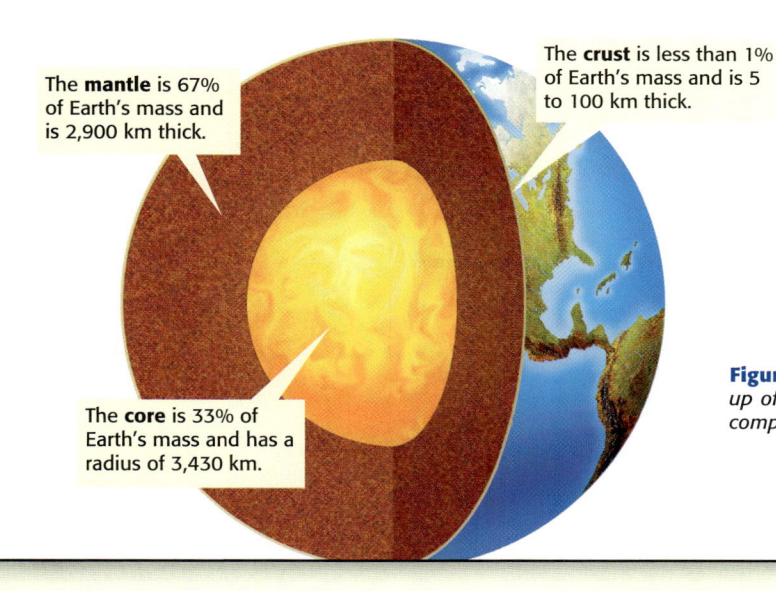

Figure 3 *The Earth is made up of three layers based on the composition of each layer.*

Teach

CONNECTION ACTIVITY
Math —— GENERAL

Comparing the Mantle and Crust Tell students to assume that the average thickness for the crust is 50 km, and have them calculate how much thicker the mantle is than the crust. Invite volunteers to write their calculations on the board. (2,900 km ÷ 50 km = 58; The mantle is 58 times thicker than the crust.) You may want to have students compare thicknesses for all of Earth's compositional and physical layers. **LS** Logical

CONNECTION to
Physical Science — GENERAL

Mass, Volume, and Density Use **Figure 3** to discuss the relationship between mass, volume, and density. Point out that although the core is 33% of Earth's mass, the core is only 10% of Earth's volume. The Earth's core is composed mostly of iron, which is much denser than the mantle and crustal rocks that make up the rest of the Earth. Ask students to speculate why density increases with depth. **LS** Logical

---

Answer to Reading Check

The crust is the thin, outermost layer of the Earth. It is 5 km to 100 km thick and is mainly made up of the elements oxygen, silicon, and aluminum. The mantle is the layer between the crust and core. It is 2,900 km thick, is denser than the crust, and contains most of the Earth's mass. The core is the Earth's innermost layer. The core has a radius of 3,430 km and is made mostly of iron.

MISCONCEPTION ALERT

Measuring Earth's Layers Students may think that the crust, mantle, and core are all measured by their thickness. Explain that the core is a sphere, so it is measured by its diameter or radius. Some students may think that the crust is the same as the lithosphere. Explain that the crust is the outermost compositional layer of the Earth. The lithosphere is the outermost layer of the Earth and is made up of the crust and the upper part of the mantle.

Section 1 • Inside the Earth **191**

Teach, continued

Answers to Math Practice
150 km ÷ 6,380 km = 0.0235 = 2.35%

2.35% × 1.00 m = 0.0235 m, or 2.35 cm

READING STRATEGY — GENERAL

Prediction Guide Before students read this page, ask them the following question: "If you could burrow to the center of the Earth, what would you expect to happen to the pressure, the temperature, and the physical state of matter?" (Each successive layer will become hotter and have higher pressure. The solidity of layers will depend on temperature, pressure, and chemical composition.) **LS Logical**

Discussion — BASIC

The Plastic Asthenosphere
Students may be confused by the use of the word *plastic* in the description of the asthenosphere. Remind students that plastic has two meanings. In this case, *plastic* means "malleable." **English Language Learners** **LS Verbal**

Answer to Reading Check
The five physical layers of the Earth are the lithosphere, asthenosphere, mesosphere, outer core, and inner core.

MATH PRACTICE

Using Models
Imagine that you are building a model of the Earth that will have a radius of 1 m. You find out that the average radius of the Earth is 6,380 km and that the thickness of the lithosphere is about 150 km. What percentage of the Earth's radius is the lithosphere? How thick (in centimeters) would you make the lithosphere in your model?

The Physical Structure of the Earth

Another way to look at the Earth is to examine the physical properties of its layers. The Earth is divided into five physical layers—the lithosphere, asthenosphere, mesosphere, outer core, and inner core. As shown in the figure below, each layer has its own set of physical properties.

✓ **Reading Check** What are the five physical layers of the Earth?

Lithosphere The outermost, rigid layer of the Earth is the **lithosphere.** The lithosphere is made of two parts—the crust and the rigid upper part of the mantle. The lithosphere is divided into pieces called *tectonic plates*.

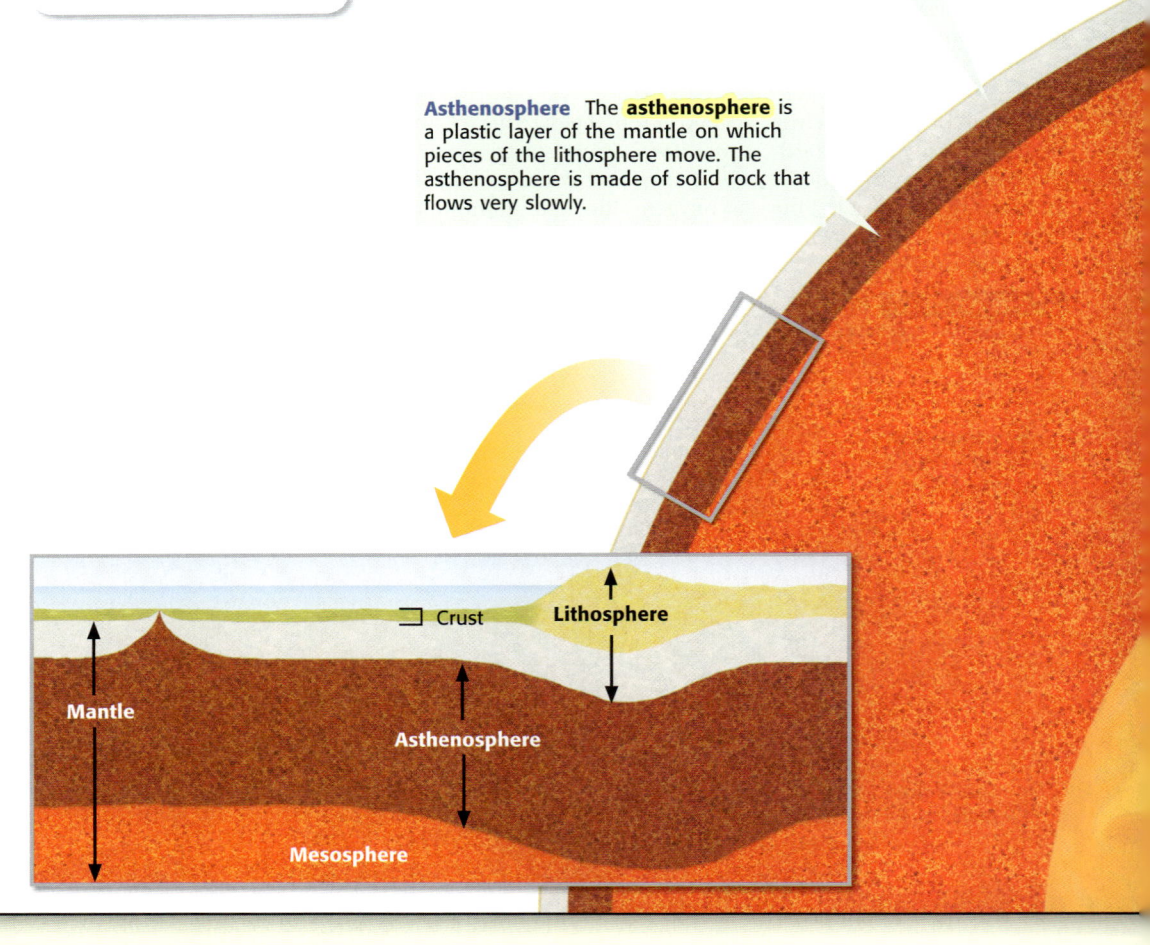

Asthenosphere The **asthenosphere** is a plastic layer of the mantle on which pieces of the lithosphere move. The asthenosphere is made of solid rock that flows very slowly.

CHAPTER RESOURCES

Technology
- **Transparencies**
  - The Earth's Lithosphere and Asthenosphere
  - The Earth's Mesosphere, Outer Core, and Inner Core

MISCONCEPTION ALERT

Chemical and Physical Properties
Some students may not understand that the two systems of naming Earth's layers describe different properties. *Crust, mantle,* and *core* describe differences in chemical composition; *lithosphere, asthenosphere, mesosphere, outer core,* and *inner core* describe differences in the response of the material to stress caused by differences in temperature and pressure.

lithosphere the solid, outer layer of the Earth that consists of the crust and the rigid upper part of the mantle

asthenosphere the soft layer of the mantle on which the tectonic plates move

mesosphere the strong, lower part of the mantle between the asthenosphere and the outer core

Mesosphere Beneath the asthenosphere is the strong, lower part of the mantle called the **mesosphere.** The mesosphere extends from the bottom of the asthenosphere to the Earth's core.

Lithosphere 15–300 km
Asthenosphere 250 km
Mesosphere 2,550 km
Outer core 2,200 km
Inner core 1,230 km

Outer Core The Earth's core is divided into two parts—the outer core and the inner core. The outer core is the liquid layer of the Earth's core that lies beneath the mantle and surrounds the inner core.

Inner Core The inner core is the solid, dense center of our planet that extends from the bottom of the outer core to the center of the Earth, which is about 6,380 km beneath the surface.

READING STRATEGY — GENERAL

Activity Encourage students to look up and learn the meanings of the following prefixes and terms: *litho-* and *lithosphere*; *astheno-* and *asthenosphere*; and *meso-* and *mesosphere*. (The prefix *litho-* means "rock." The lithosphere is the Earth's outermost rigid layer. The prefix *astheno-* means "weak." The asthenosphere is a layer of slowly flowing rock beneath the lithosphere. The prefix *meso-* means "middle." The mesosphere lies between the asthenosphere and the core.) If students know the meaning of the prefix, they may find it easier to remember the physical characteristics and locations of the Earth's layers. **English Language Learners**
LS Verbal

Using the Figure — GENERAL

Physical Structure of the Earth Define the term *viscous,* and have students read about each layer in the illustration on these two pages. Ask students to sketch a simple model of the Earth's physical layers in their **science journals** and label each layer "Solid," "Liquid," or "Viscous." Ask students what pattern they notice as they work from the outside of the model to the inside. (The lithosphere is solid. The asthenosphere is viscous. The mesosphere is viscous. The outer core is liquid. The inner core is solid.) Ask students to explain why the inner core is not liquid. (Although the inner core is very hot, it is solid because of the pressure exerted on it.) **LS Visual/Logical**

INCLUSION Strategies

- Learning Disabled
- Visually Impaired
- Attention Deficit Disorder

Organize students into groups. Give each group modeling clay in three colors, a piece of cardboard, and self-stick notes. Ask each group to use the clay to create a model of the Earth's layers. After groups create their model, ask each group to label each layer with a self-stick note. Next, ask each group to write two facts about each layer on individual self-stick notes and apply them to the appropriate place on the model. Have each group share their model and facts with the class. **English Language Learners**
LS Kinesthetic/Logical

Section 1 • Inside the Earth   **193**

Teach, continued

CONNECTION ACTIVITY
Language Arts —— GENERAL

Tectonic Essay *Tectonic* comes from the Greek word *tektonikos*, which means "of a builder." Ask students to consider how this meaning is appropriate for tectonic plates. Ask students, "In what ways are tectonic plates responsible for building features on the Earth's surface?" Have students write a short essay that describes how the movement of tectonic plates slowly shapes the landscape around us. **LS Verbal**

BRAIN FOOD

The Deepest Hole The deepest hole ever drilled into the continental crust was in the Kola Peninsula, in Russia, in 1984. It was 12,226 m deep! Because the temperature of the crust increases with depth, it is impossible to drill much deeper into crust. Hot rock flows around the drill bit and fills the hole faster than the hole can be drilled. Ask students, "How deep is the hole compared to the height of Mount Everest? Did it extend to the mantle?" (12,226 m − 8,850 m = 3,376 m; no)

---

tectonic plate a block of lithosphere that consists of the crust and the rigid, outermost part of the mantle

Tectonic Plates

Pieces of the lithosphere that move around on top of the asthenosphere are called **tectonic plates**. But what exactly does a tectonic plate look like? How big are tectonic plates? How and why do they move around? To answer these questions, begin by thinking of the lithosphere as a giant jigsaw puzzle.

A Giant Jigsaw Puzzle

All of the tectonic plates have names, some of which you may already know. Some of the major tectonic plates are named on the map in **Figure 4**. Notice that each tectonic plate fits together with the tectonic plates that surround it. The lithosphere is like a jigsaw puzzle, and the tectonic plates are like the pieces of a jigsaw puzzle.

Notice that not all tectonic plates are the same. For example, compare the size of the South American plate with that of the Cocos plate. Tectonic plates differ in other ways, too. For example, the South American plate has an entire continent on it and has oceanic crust, but the Cocos plate has only oceanic crust. Some tectonic plates, such as the South American plate, include both continental and oceanic crust.

Major Tectonic Plates
1. Pacific plate
2. North American plate
3. Cocos plate
4. Nazca plate
5. South American plate
6. African plate
7. Eurasian plate
8. Indian plate
9. Australian plate
10. Antarctic plate

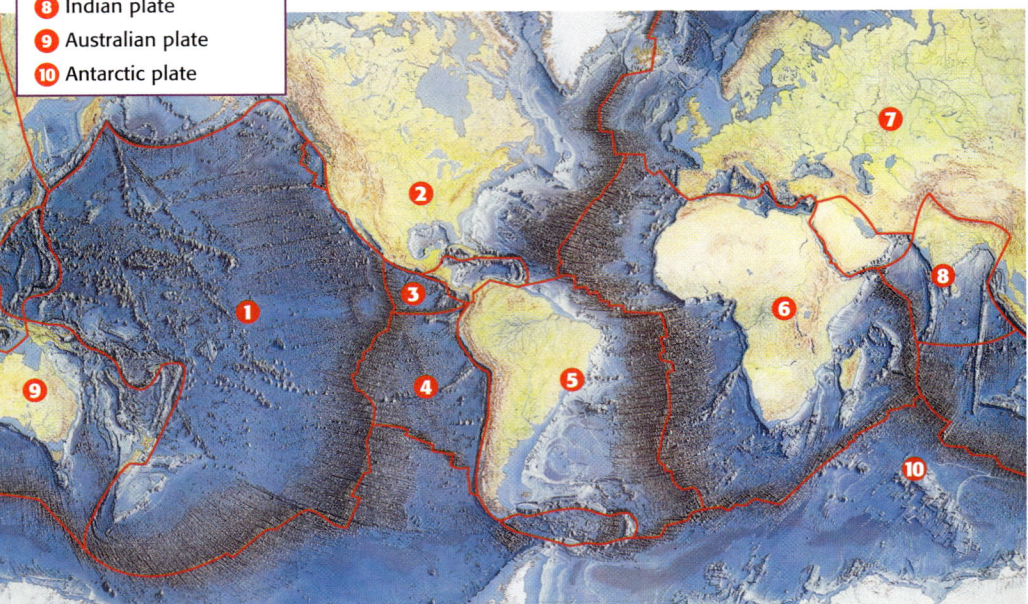

Figure 4 *Tectonic plates fit together like the pieces of a giant jigsaw puzzle.*

MISCONCEPTION ALERT

Tectonic Plates Students may think that tectonic plates are always neatly divided along continental lines, but the lines are not so neat. For example, the North American plate includes the North American continent, Greenland, half of Iceland, and part of Eurasia. All six of the Earth's large continental plates contain a continent and a large section of oceanic crust. Some of the 10 other small tectonic plates contain only oceanic crust.

Figure 5 The South American Plate

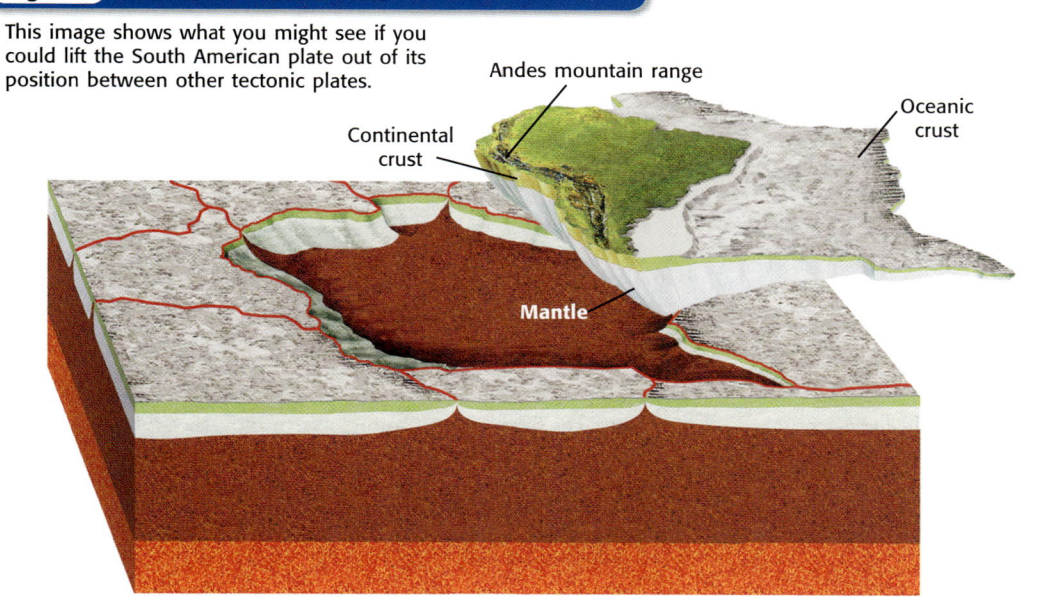

This image shows what you might see if you could lift the South American plate out of its position between other tectonic plates.

- Andes mountain range
- Continental crust
- Oceanic crust
- Mantle

A Tectonic Plate Close-Up

What would a tectonic plate look like if you could lift it out of its place? **Figure 5** shows what the South American plate might look like if you could. Notice that this tectonic plate not only consists of the upper part of the mantle but also consists of both oceanic crust and continental crust. The thickest part of the South American plate is the continental crust. The thinnest part of this plate is in the mid-Atlantic Ocean.

Like Ice Cubes in a Bowl of Punch

Think about ice cubes floating in a bowl of punch. If there are enough cubes, they will cover the surface of the punch and bump into one another. Parts of the ice cubes are below the surface of the punch and displace the punch. Large pieces of ice displace more punch than small pieces of ice. Tectonic plates "float" on the asthenosphere in a similar way. The plates cover the surface of the asthenosphere, and they touch one another and move around. The lithosphere displaces the asthenosphere. Thick tectonic plates, such as those made of continental crust, displace more asthenosphere than do thin plates, such as those made of oceanic lithosphere.

Reading Check Why do tectonic plates made of continental lithosphere displace more asthenosphere than tectonic plates made of oceanic lithosphere do?

Quick Lab

Tectonic Ice Cubes

1. Take the bottom half of a clear, **2 L soda bottle** that has been cut in half. Make sure that the label has been removed.
2. Fill the bottle with **water** to about 1 cm below the top edge of the bottle.
3. Get **three pieces of irregularly shaped ice** that are small, medium, and large.
4. Float the ice in the water, and note how much of each piece is below the surface of the water.
5. Do all pieces of ice float mostly below the surface? Which piece is mostly below the surface? Why?

Group Activity — GENERAL

Modeling a Tectonic Plate Pair students, and have them plan and build a three-dimensional model of a tectonic plate. Students might use materials such as cardboard, wood, and clay. Remind students to label the continental crust, oceanic crust, and lithosphere, as well as any surface topographical features, such as mountain ranges. When the models are complete, have students display them and give a brief presentation to the class. Students can use their models later in this chapter to simulate convergent, divergent, and transform motion.
LS Visual/Kinesthetic — English Language Learners

Quick Lab

MATERIALS

For Each Group
- ice, irregular shape
- soda bottle, 2 L
- water

Answer
5. All pieces of ice have the same density. Large, irregularly shaped pieces of ice have a greater weight and will therefore displace more water than smaller pieces of ice displace.

Answer to Reading Check

Although continental lithosphere is less dense than oceanic lithosphere is, continental lithosphere has a greater mass because of its greater thickness and will displace more asthenosphere than oceanic lithosphere.

CHAPTER RESOURCES

Technology

Transparencies
- The Tectonic Plates; Close-Up of a Tectonic Plate

Section 1 • Inside the Earth

Close

Reteaching — BASIC

Putting the Layers in Order
List Earth's physical layers on the board in random order. Have students arrange the list in the correct order. Then, have students help you write the compositional layers beside the physical layers (using brackets to indicate overlaps). Then, have students help you describe the characteristics of each layer.
LS Logical

Quiz — GENERAL

Ask students whether each of the statements below is true or false. Have students correct false statements.

1. The inner core of the Earth is solid and made primarily of iron. (true)
2. The asthenosphere is the thinnest physical layer. (false, the lithosphere is the thinnest layer)

Alternative Assessment — GENERAL

Journey to the Center of the Earth Have students write a story describing their "journey to the center of the Earth," or have them write a travel guide that describes the experience of traveling through Earth's different layers. Have them draw and color-code a model of Earth to include with their project. Emphasize that this model must show layers defined by chemical composition and by physical properties. **LS** Visual

SCHOOL to HOME

Build a Seismograph
Seismographs are instruments that seismologists, scientists who study earthquakes, use to detect seismic waves. Research seismograph designs with your parent. For example, a simple seismograph can be built by using a weight suspended by a spring next to a ruler. With your parent, attempt to construct a home seismograph based on a design you have selected. Outline each of the steps used to build your seismograph, and present the written outline to your teacher.

ACTIVITY

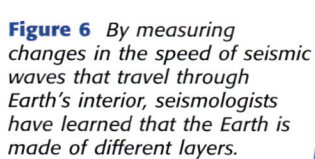

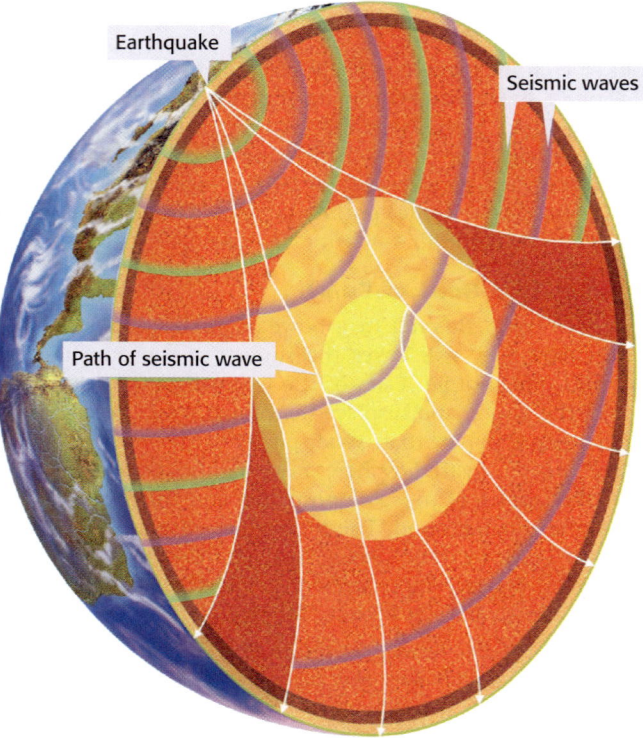

Figure 6 By measuring changes in the speed of seismic waves that travel through Earth's interior, seismologists have learned that the Earth is made of different layers.

CHAPTER RESOURCES

Technology

Transparencies
• Discoveries of the Earth's Interior

Mapping the Earth's Interior

How do scientists know things about the deepest parts of the Earth, where no one has ever been? Scientists have never even drilled through the crust, which is only a thin skin on the surface of the Earth. So, how do we know so much about the mantle and the core?

Would you be surprised to know that some of the answers come from earthquakes? When an earthquake happens, vibrations called *seismic waves* are produced. Seismic waves travel at different speeds through the Earth. Their speed depends on the density and composition of material that they pass through. For example, a seismic wave traveling through a solid will go faster than a seismic wave traveling through a liquid.

When an earthquake happens, machines called *seismographs* measure the times at which seismic waves arrive at different distances from an earthquake. Seismologists can then use these distances and travel times to calculate the density and thickness of each physical layer of the Earth. **Figure 6** shows how seismic waves travel through the Earth.

Reading Check What are some properties of seismic waves?

Answer to Reading Check
Answers may vary. A seismic wave traveling through a solid will go faster than a seismic wave traveling through a liquid.

SECTION Review

Summary

- The Earth is made up of three layers—the crust, the mantle, and the core—based on chemical composition. Less dense compounds make up the crust and mantle. Denser compounds make up the core.
- The Earth is made up of five main physical layers: the lithosphere, the asthenosphere, the mesosphere, the outer core, and the inner core.
- Tectonic plates are large pieces of the lithosphere that move around on the Earth's surface.
- The crust in some tectonic plates is mainly continental. Other plates have only oceanic crust. Still other plates include both continental and oceanic crust.
- Thick tectonic plates, such as those in which the crust is mainly continental, displace more asthenosphere than do thin plates, such as those in which the crust is mainly oceanic.
- Knowledge about the layers of the Earth comes from the study of seismic waves caused by earthquakes.

Using Key Terms

For each pair of terms, explain how the meanings of the terms differ.

1. *crust* and *mantle*
2. *lithosphere* and *asthenosphere*

Understanding Key Ideas

3. The part of the Earth that is molten is the
   a. crust.
   b. mantle.
   c. outer core.
   d. inner core.

4. The part of the Earth on which the tectonic plates move is the
   a. lithosphere.
   b. asthenosphere.
   c. mesosphere.
   d. crust.

5. Identify the layers of the Earth by their chemical composition.

6. Identify the layers of the Earth by their physical properties.

7. Describe a tectonic plate.

8. Explain how scientists know about the structure of the Earth's interior.

Interpreting Graphics

9. According to the wave speeds shown in the table below, which two physical layers of the Earth are densest?

Speed of Seismic Waves in Earth's Interior

Physical layer	Wave speed
Lithosphere	7 to 8 km/s
Asthenosphere	7 to 11 km/s
Mesosphere	11 to 13 km/s
Outer core	8 to 10 km/s
Inner core	11 to 12 km/s

Critical Thinking

10. **Making Comparisons** Explain the difference between the crust and the lithosphere.

11. **Analyzing Ideas** Why does a seismic wave travel faster through solid rock than through water?

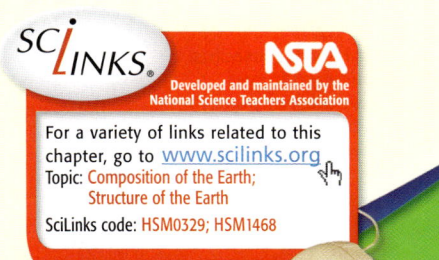

Answers to Section Review

1. Sample answer: The crust is the thin, outermost layer of the Earth. It is made mainly of less dense compounds and is less than 1% of the Earth's mass. The mantle is a thick layer beneath the crust. The mantle is made of dense compounds and is 67% of the Earth's mass.
2. Sample answer: The lithosphere is rigid and is divided into tectonic plates. The asthenosphere is a layer of soft mantle material that flows very slowly.
3. c
4. b
5. The crust is made mainly of the elements oxygen, silicon, and aluminum. The mantle has more magnesium and less aluminum and silicon than the crust has. The core is made mostly of iron.
6. The lithosphere is the outermost, rigid layer of the Earth. Beneath the lithosphere is the asthenosphere, a plastic layer of the mantle on which the lithosphere moves. The mesosphere is the strong, lower part of the mantle. The outer core is the liquid layer of the Earth's core that lies between the mantle and the inner core. The solid, dense center of our planet is the inner core.
7. A tectonic plate is a large piece of the Earth's lithosphere that moves slowly on top of the asthenosphere. Tectonic plates are composed of continental crust, oceanic crust, and both continental and oceanic crust.
8. Scientists can measure the speeds at which seismic waves travel through different parts of the Earth. This measurement helps them calculate the density and thickness of each layer the waves pass through.
9. According to the wave speeds in the table, the mesosphere and the inner core are the two densest physical layers. (In reality, the outer core and inner core are the two densest layers. Because the outer core is liquid, wave speed through the outer core is slower than it is in the mesosphere.)
10. The crust is the thin, outermost layer of the Earth that is compositionally different than the mantle. The lithosphere is a thick layer containing both the crust and upper mantle but which is rigid compared to the underlying asthenosphere.
11. Seismic waves travel through solid rock faster than they do through water because solid rock is denser than water.

CHAPTER RESOURCES

Chapter Resource File
- Section Quiz GENERAL
- Section Review GENERAL
- Vocabulary and Section Summary GENERAL
- Reinforcement Worksheet BASIC
- Critical Thinking ADVANCED
- Datasheet for Quick Lab

SECTION 2

Focus

Overview
This section explains the continental drift hypothesis and how the continents have moved to their present locations. Students will learn that support for this hypothesis came when mid-ocean ridges were discovered. They will also learn that sea-floor spreading was supported by the record of reversals of the Earth's magnetic field present in oceanic crust.

🔔 Bellringer
Ask students to explain why the following statement is true or false: "The North American continent is moving westward." (true; The plate that North America sits on is moving to the west.)

Motivate

ACTIVITY — GENERAL

Reconstructing Pangaea Have students work in small groups to create a model of Pangaea. Provide each group with two world maps. Have the groups cut the continents out of one map and treat them as puzzle pieces by seeing how they best fit together. Refer to both the complete and the altered maps, and help students explain and demonstrate how each continent moved from its original position. **English Language Learners**
LS Visual

SECTION 2

READING WARM-UP

Objectives
- Describe Wegener's hypothesis of continental drift.
- Explain how sea-floor spreading provides a way for continents to move.
- Describe how new oceanic lithosphere forms at mid-ocean ridges.
- Explain how magnetic reversals provide evidence for sea-floor spreading.

Terms to Learn
continental drift
sea-floor spreading

READING STRATEGY
Paired Summarizing Read this section silently. In pairs, take turns summarizing the material. Stop to discuss ideas that seem confusing.

Restless Continents

Have you ever looked at a map of the world and noticed how the coastlines of continents on opposite sides of the oceans appear to fit together like the pieces of a puzzle? Is it just coincidence that the coastlines fit together well? Is it possible that the continents were actually together sometime in the past?

Wegener's Continental Drift Hypothesis

One scientist who looked at the pieces of this puzzle was Alfred Wegener (VAY guh nuhr). In the early 1900s, he wrote about his hypothesis of *continental drift*. **Continental drift** is the hypothesis that states that the continents once formed a single landmass, broke up, and drifted to their present locations. This hypothesis seemed to explain a lot of puzzling observations, including the observation of how well continents fit together.

Continental drift also explained why fossils of the same plant and animal species are found on continents that are on different sides of the Atlantic Ocean. Many of these ancient species could not have crossed the Atlantic Ocean. As you can see in **Figure 1**, without continental drift, this pattern of fossils would be hard to explain. In addition to fossils, similar types of rock and evidence of the same ancient climatic conditions were found on several continents.

✓ **Reading Check** How did fossils provide evidence for Wegener's hypothesis of continental drift? *(See the Appendix for answers to Reading Checks.)*

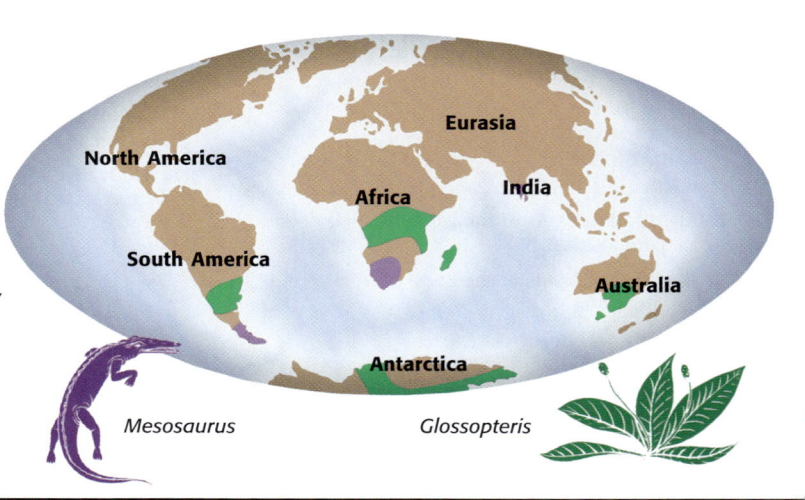

Figure 1 Fossils of Mesosaurus, *a small, aquatic reptile, and* Glossopteris, *an ancient plant species, have been found on several continents.*

CHAPTER RESOURCES

Chapter Resource File
- Lesson Plan
- Directed Reading A BASIC
- Directed Reading B SPECIAL NEEDS

Technology
- Transparencies
  - Bellringer
  - The Breakup of Pangaea
  - LINK TO LIFE SCIENCE The Evolution of the Galápagos Finches

Answer to Reading Check
Similar fossils were found on landmasses that are very far apart. The best explanation for this phenomenon is that the landmasses were once joined.

198 Chapter 7 • Plate Tectonics

Figure 2 The Drifting Continents

245 Million Years Ago
Pangaea existed when some of the earliest dinosaurs were roaming the Earth. The continent was surrounded by a sea called *Panthalassa*, which means "all sea."

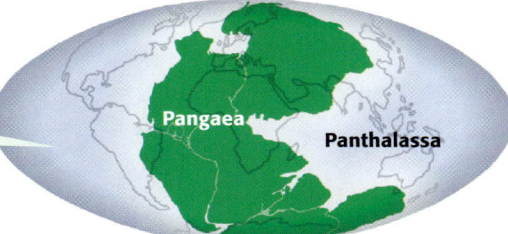

180 Million Years Ago
Gradually, Pangaea broke into two big pieces. The northern piece is called *Laurasia*. The southern piece is called *Gondwana*.

65 Million Years Ago
By the time the dinosaurs became extinct, Laurasia and Gondwana had split into smaller pieces.

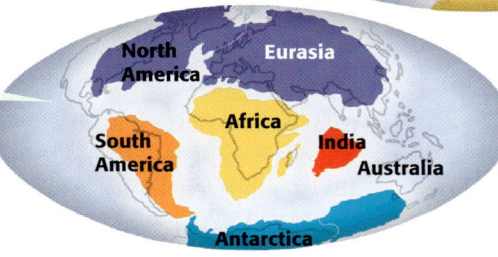

The Breakup of Pangaea

Wegener made many observations before proposing his hypothesis of continental drift. He thought that all of the present continents were once joined in a single, huge continent. Wegener called this continent *Pangaea* (pan JEE uh), which is Greek for "all earth." We now know from the hypothesis of plate tectonics that Pangaea existed about 245 million years ago. We also know that Pangaea further split into two huge continents—Laurasia and Gondwana—about 180 million years ago. As shown in **Figure 2,** these two continents split again and formed the continents we know today.

continental drift the hypothesis that states that the continents once formed a single landmass, broke up, and drifted to their present locations

Sea-Floor Spreading

When Wegener put forth his hypothesis of continental drift, many scientists would not accept his hypothesis. From the calculated strength of the rocks, it did not seem possible for the crust to move in this way. During Wegener's life, no one knew the answer. It wasn't until many years later that evidence provided some clues to the forces that moved the continents.

MISCONCEPTION ALERT

Supercontinents Past and Future
About 500 million years before Pangaea began to form, another supercontinent dominated the globe—Rodinia. Some scientists speculate that the formation of supercontinents occurs as a cycle of accretion and breakup.

Teach

CONNECTION to Life Science — GENERAL

The Breakup of Pangaea and Dinosaur Evolution Before Pangaea broke up, dinosaurs roamed the entire continent. The populations were very widespread. As Pangaea began to break up, the populations of dinosaurs were fragmented and isolated on the new continents. Scientists think a greater number of dinosaur species then evolved. Use the teaching transparency entitled "The Evolution of the Galápagos Finches" to discuss natural selection and the breakup of Pangaea. Have groups of students research different dinosaurs that lived after the breakup of Pangaea and speculate why these dinosaurs seemed to evolve the way they did. (Possible reasons include available food and type of climate.) **LS** Logical

---

MISCONCEPTION ALERT

Geographic Versus Geologic Divisions of Continents
Students may think that there are seven continents instead of six. Explain that geographers divide the landmass of Eurasia into Europe and Asia. Asia includes the countries of the former Soviet Union and the Middle East. Geologists call the entire landmass of Europe and Asia the continent of Eurasia. In addition, point out that the Arctic icecap is an ice sheet, not a landmass.

Section 2 • Restless Continents

Close

Reteaching — BASIC
Evidence for Continental Drift
Organize the class into groups of three. Ask each group to choose one of the following lines of evidence that support the continental drift hypothesis: fossil similarities, landform similarities, and sea-floor spreading. Have each group work for 20 min to gather evidence for the continental drift hypothesis, and then ask groups to share their findings with the class.
LS Logical Co-op Learning

Quiz — GENERAL
1. What material creates new lithosphere at a mid-ocean ridge? (solidified magma)
2. What was Pangaea? (the large landmass that later broke up to form two supercontinents and then fragmented further to form the six continents that exist today)

Alternative Assessment — GENERAL
Writing Sea-Floor Spreading
Have students write a paragraph explaining how sea-floor spreading causes continents to move apart. Students should also include a diagram of this process. **LS** Logical/Visual

---

Figure 3 Sea-Floor Spreading
Sea-floor spreading creates new oceanic lithosphere at mid-ocean ridges.

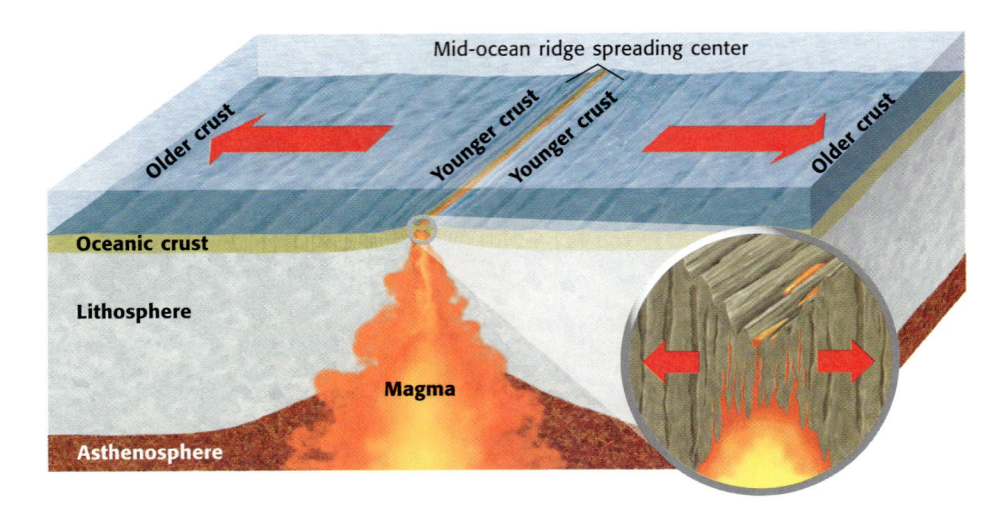

sea-floor spreading the process by which new oceanic lithosphere forms as magma rises toward the surface and solidifies

Mid-Ocean Ridges and Sea-Floor Spreading
A chain of submerged mountains runs through the center of the Atlantic Ocean. The chain is part of a worldwide system of mid-ocean ridges. Mid-ocean ridges are underwater mountain chains that run through Earth's ocean basins.

Mid-ocean ridges are places where sea-floor spreading takes place. **Sea-floor spreading** is the process by which new oceanic lithosphere forms as magma rises toward the surface and solidifies. As the tectonic plates move away from each other, the sea floor spreads apart and magma fills in the gap. As this new crust forms, the older crust gets pushed away from the mid-ocean ridge. As **Figure 3** shows, the older crust is farther away from the mid-ocean ridge than the younger crust is.

Evidence for Sea-Floor Spreading: Magnetic Reversals
Some of the most important evidence of sea-floor spreading comes from magnetic reversals recorded in the ocean floor. Throughout Earth's history, the north and south magnetic poles have changed places many times. When the poles change places, the polarity of Earth's magnetic poles changes, as shown in **Figure 4**. When Earth's magnetic poles change places, this change is called a *magnetic reversal*.

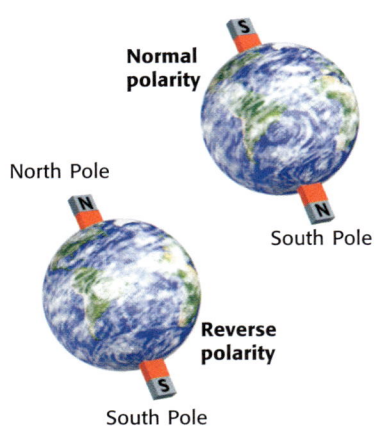

Figure 4 The polarity of Earth's magnetic field changes over time.

CONNECTION to Physical Science — GENERAL
Sonar Researchers used sonar to discover that the ocean floor is not flat. In the 1950s, scientists broadcast sound waves toward the sea floor and measured how long it took the waves to return. The echoes revealed valleys and mountains. Scientists were amazed to find a chain of undersea mountains snaking thousands of kilometers around the globe—the mid-ocean ridges.

Homework — GENERAL
Mid-Ocean Ridges Have students research and answer the following questions about **Figure 3**:
- Why does molten rock from the mantle come to the surface at the ridges?
- Why does the ocean floor spread apart at the ridges?
- Why is rock formed at the ridges called *new rock*?

Emphasize that mid-ocean ridges are not always in the middle of an ocean. **LS** Verbal

200 Chapter 7 • Plate Tectonics

Magnetic Reversals and Sea-Floor Spreading

The molten rock at the mid-ocean ridges contains tiny grains of magnetic minerals. These mineral grains contain iron and are like compasses. They align with the magnetic field of the Earth. When the molten rock cools, the record of these tiny compasses remains in the rock. This record is then carried slowly away from the spreading center of the ridge as sea-floor spreading occurs.

As you can see in **Figure 5,** when the Earth's magnetic field reverses, the magnetic mineral grains align in the opposite direction. The new rock records the direction of the Earth's magnetic field. As the sea floor spreads away from a mid-ocean ridge, it carries with it a record of magnetic reversals. This record of magnetic reversals was the final proof that sea-floor spreading does occur.

✓ **Reading Check** How is a record of magnetic reversals recorded in molten rock at mid-ocean ridges?

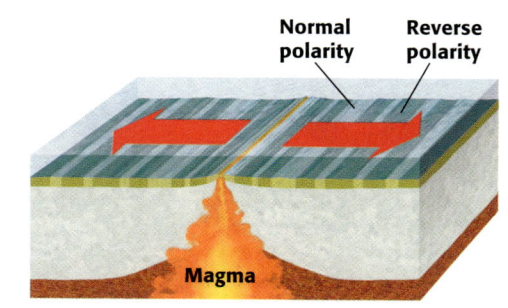

Figure 5 Magnetic reversals in oceanic crust are shown as bands of light blue and dark blue oceanic crust. Light blue bands indicate normal polarity, and dark blue bands indicate reverse polarity.

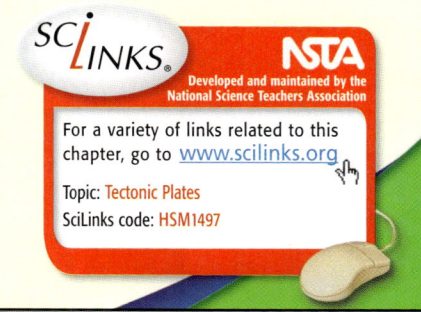

SECTION Review

Summary

- Wegener hypothesized that continents drift apart from one another and have done so in the past.
- The process by which new oceanic lithosphere forms at mid-ocean ridges is called sea-floor spreading.
- As tectonic plates separate, the sea floor spreads apart and magma fills in the gap.
- Magnetic reversals are recorded over time in oceanic crust.

Using Key Terms

1. In your own words, write a definition for each of the following terms: *continental drift* and *sea-floor spreading*.

Understanding Key Ideas

2. At mid-ocean ridges,
   a. the crust is older.
   b. sea-floor spreading occurs.
   c. oceanic lithosphere is destroyed.
   d. tectonic plates are colliding.

3. Explain how oceanic lithosphere forms at mid-ocean ridges.

4. What is magnetic reversal?

Math Skills

5. If a piece of sea floor has moved 50 km in 5 million years, what is the yearly rate of sea-floor motion?

Critical Thinking

6. **Identifying Relationships** Explain how magnetic reversals provide evidence for sea-floor spreading.

7. **Applying Concepts** Why do bands indicating magnetic reversals appear to be of similar width on both sides of a mid-ocean ridge?

8. **Applying Concepts** Why do you think that old rocks are rare on the ocean floor?

SECTION 3

Focus

Overview
This section discusses the theory of plate tectonics. Students will learn about possible causes of some plate movements. Students will also learn about types of plate boundaries.

🔔 Bellringer
Have students calculate the number of years that New York and the northwest coast of Africa took to reach their current locations, 6,760 km apart, if the sea floor is spreading at an average of 4 cm per year. (6,760 km = 676,000,000 cm ÷ 4 cm = 169,000,000 y. Point out that this number is fairly close to the estimate of when the breakup of Pangaea began 180 million years ago.)

Motivate

Discussion — GENERAL
A Preposterous Theory Write the word "preposterous" on the board. Then, discuss its meaning. Students may not realize how controversial and revolutionary the theory of plate tectonics was. Discuss why the idea that the enormous landmasses could "slide" across the asthenosphere seemed preposterous to most people. **LS Verbal**

SECTION 3

READING WARM-UP

Objectives
- Describe the three types of tectonic plate boundaries.
- Describe the three forces thought to move tectonic plates.
- Explain how scientists measure the rate at which tectonic plates move.

Terms to Learn
plate tectonics
convergent boundary
divergent boundary
transform boundary

READING STRATEGY

Brainstorming The key idea of this section is plate tectonics. Brainstorm words and phrases related to plate tectonics.

The Theory of Plate Tectonics

It takes an incredible amount of force to move a tectonic plate! But where does this force come from?

As scientists' understanding of mid-ocean ridges and magnetic reversals grew, scientists formed a theory to explain how tectonic plates move. **Plate tectonics** is the theory that the Earth's lithosphere is divided into tectonic plates that move around on top of the asthenosphere. In this section, you will learn what causes tectonic plates to move. But first you will learn about the different types of tectonic plate boundaries.

Tectonic Plate Boundaries

A boundary is a place where tectonic plates touch. All tectonic plates share boundaries with other tectonic plates. These boundaries are divided into three types: convergent, divergent, and transform. The type of boundary depends on how the tectonic plates move relative to one another. Tectonic plates can collide, separate, or slide past each other. Earthquakes can occur at all three types of plate boundaries. The figure below shows examples of tectonic plate boundaries.

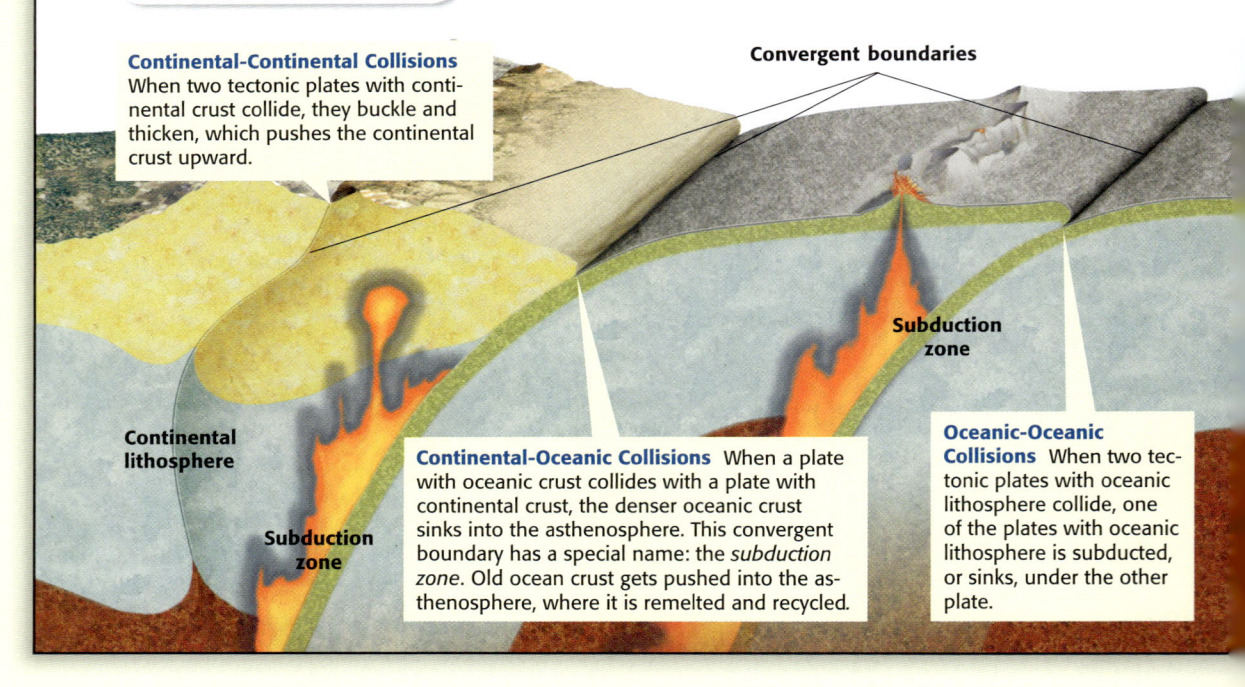

Convergent boundaries

Continental-Continental Collisions When two tectonic plates with continental crust collide, they buckle and thicken, which pushes the continental crust upward.

Continental lithosphere

Subduction zone

Continental-Oceanic Collisions When a plate with oceanic crust collides with a plate with continental crust, the denser oceanic crust sinks into the asthenosphere. This convergent boundary has a special name: the *subduction zone*. Old ocean crust gets pushed into the asthenosphere, where it is remelted and recycled.

Subduction zone

Oceanic-Oceanic Collisions When two tectonic plates with oceanic lithosphere collide, one of the plates with oceanic lithosphere is subducted, or sinks, under the other plate.

CHAPTER RESOURCES

Chapter Resource File
- Lesson Plan
- Directed Reading A BASIC
- Directed Reading B SPECIAL NEEDS

Technology
- Transparencies
  - Bellringer
  - Tectonic Plate Boundaries: A and B

Workbooks
- Math Skills for Science
  - A Shortcut for Multiplying Large Numbers GENERAL

CONNECTION to Physical Science — GENERAL

Temperature and Density Point out how the movement of tectonic plates is driven by differences in temperature and density. In slab pull and ridge push, gravity pulls the oceanic plate downward because the oceanic plate is denser than the continental lithosphere. In convection, hot material rises because it is less dense than cooler material, which sinks.

202   Chapter 7 • Plate Tectonics

Convergent Boundaries

When two tectonic plates collide, the boundary between them is a **convergent boundary.** What happens at a convergent boundary depends on the kind of crust at the leading edge of each tectonic plate. The three types of convergent boundaries are continental-continental boundaries, continental-oceanic boundaries, and oceanic-oceanic boundaries.

Divergent Boundaries

When two tectonic plates separate, the boundary between them is called a **divergent boundary.** New sea floor forms at divergent boundaries. Mid-ocean ridges are the most common type of divergent boundary.

Transform Boundaries

When two tectonic plates slide past each other horizontally, the boundary between them is a **transform boundary.** The San Andreas Fault in California is a good example of a transform boundary. This fault marks the place where the Pacific and North American plates are sliding past each other.

Reading Check Define the term *transform boundary*. (See the Appendix for answers to Reading Checks.)

plate tectonics the theory that explains how large pieces of the Earth's outermost layer, called *tectonic plates,* move and change shape

convergent boundary the boundary formed by the collision of two lithospheric plates

divergent boundary the boundary between two tectonic plates that are moving away from each other

transform boundary the boundary between tectonic plates that are sliding past each other horizontally

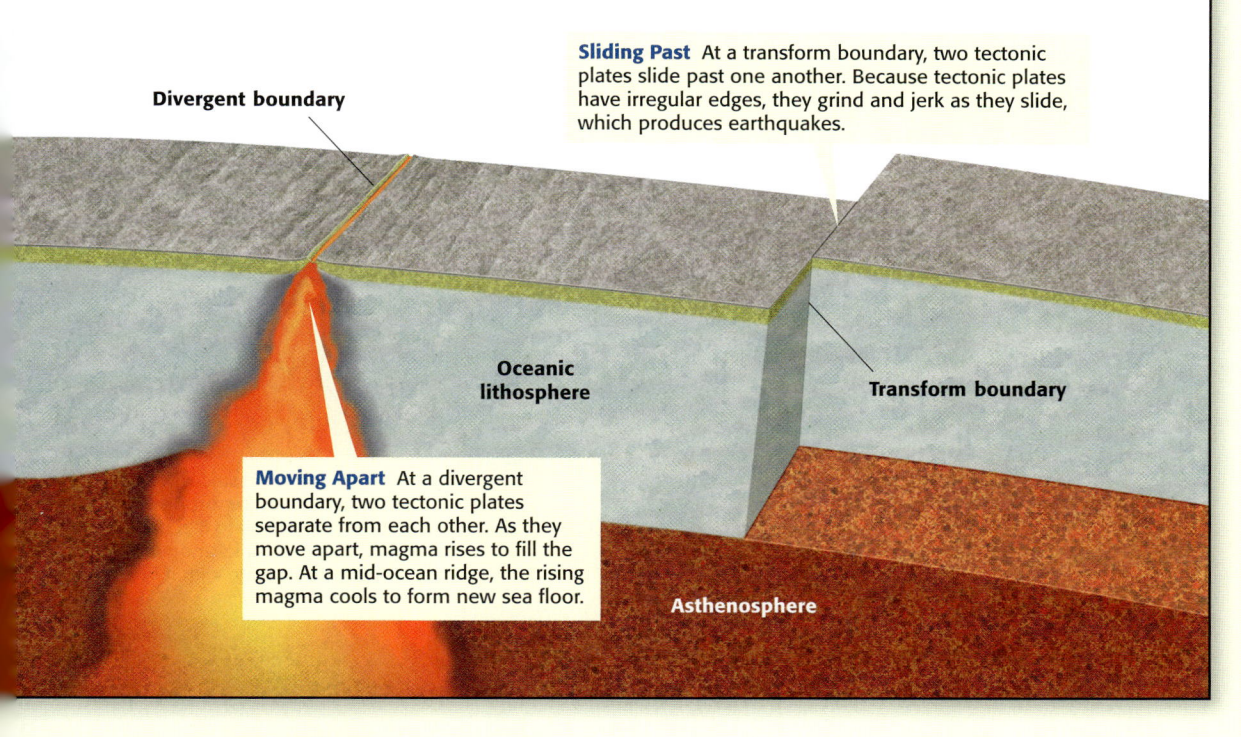

Sliding Past At a transform boundary, two tectonic plates slide past one another. Because tectonic plates have irregular edges, they grind and jerk as they slide, which produces earthquakes.

Divergent boundary

Oceanic lithosphere

Transform boundary

Moving Apart At a divergent boundary, two tectonic plates separate from each other. As they move apart, magma rises to fill the gap. At a mid-ocean ridge, the rising magma cools to form new sea floor.

Asthenosphere

Group Activity — Advanced

Plate Movements Ask groups of students to explain why continental-oceanic convergent boundaries and oceanic-oceanic convergent boundaries result in subduction, whereas continental-continental convergent boundaries do not. Then, have students do the following: create an illustrated chart showing the five types of boundary movements, and write captions explaining both how the boundaries move and what forces are responsible for their movement.

Logical/Visual

Answer to Reading Check

A transform boundary forms when two tectonic plates slide past each other horizontally.

Teach

Activity — General

Geologic Features at Tectonic Plate Boundaries Ask students to form hypotheses about what kinds of geologic features exist at different types of plate boundaries. Then, have them compare a topographic world map with a world map of tectonic plates. Help students conduct library and Internet research to find out if their hypotheses were correct.
Logical/Visual

Misconception Alert

Laws and Theories Students may think that if a theory is accepted by enough people for a long enough period of time, the theory will become a scientific law. Emphasize that scientific laws and theories are both correct and useful but that they serve different functions. A scientific law is a concise statement of fact that is accepted as true and universal. Theories are statements that are products of many scientific observations and may encompass numerous hypotheses or laws. Like a scientific law, a theory is accepted as true, but theories are much more complex than laws. A scientific law can be compared to an observation of a rubber ball. When dropped under constant conditions, the ball will always bounce as predicted. Bouncing is the only action the ball performs. On the other hand, a theory can be compared to a car. A car has many components that perform different tasks and work in unison. A part of the car may be improved, but the general function of the car is unchanged. **Logical**

Section 3 • The Theory of Plate Tectonics

Close

Reteaching — BASIC

Boundary Review On the board, write the names of the five types of boundaries. Then, have student volunteers draw each boundary on the board. As a class, discuss the landforms that result from each type of boundary. **LS Verbal**

Quiz — GENERAL

1. Why are there several categories of convergent plate boundaries? (Continental and oceanic plates behave differently when they are pushed together because their composition and density differs.)

2. Explain the process of subduction. (A denser oceanic plate is forced beneath a less dense oceanic or continental plate at a convergent boundary. Gravity pulls the denser oceanic plate into the hot asthenosphere, which causes melting.)

Alternative Assessment — GENERAL

Modeling Plate Boundaries Challenge students to model plate movement at each type of tectonic boundary. Have them work in pairs with materials they have chosen. As students demonstrate plate movements, they should be prepared to explain the composition of each plate and the differences between the forces at work. **English Language Learners**
LS Kinesthetic/Logical

Possible Causes of Tectonic Plate Motion

You have learned that plate tectonics is the theory that the lithosphere is divided into tectonic plates that move around on top of the asthenosphere. What causes the motion of tectonic plates? Remember that the solid rock of the asthenosphere flows very slowly. This movement occurs because of changes in density within the asthenosphere. These density changes are caused by the outward flow of thermal energy from deep within the Earth. When rock is heated, it expands, becomes less dense, and tends to rise to the surface of the Earth. As the rock gets near the surface, the rock cools, becomes more dense, and tends to sink. **Figure 1** shows three possible causes of tectonic plate motion.

✓ **Reading Check** What causes changes in density in the asthenosphere?

Figure 1 Three Possible Driving Forces of Plate Tectonics

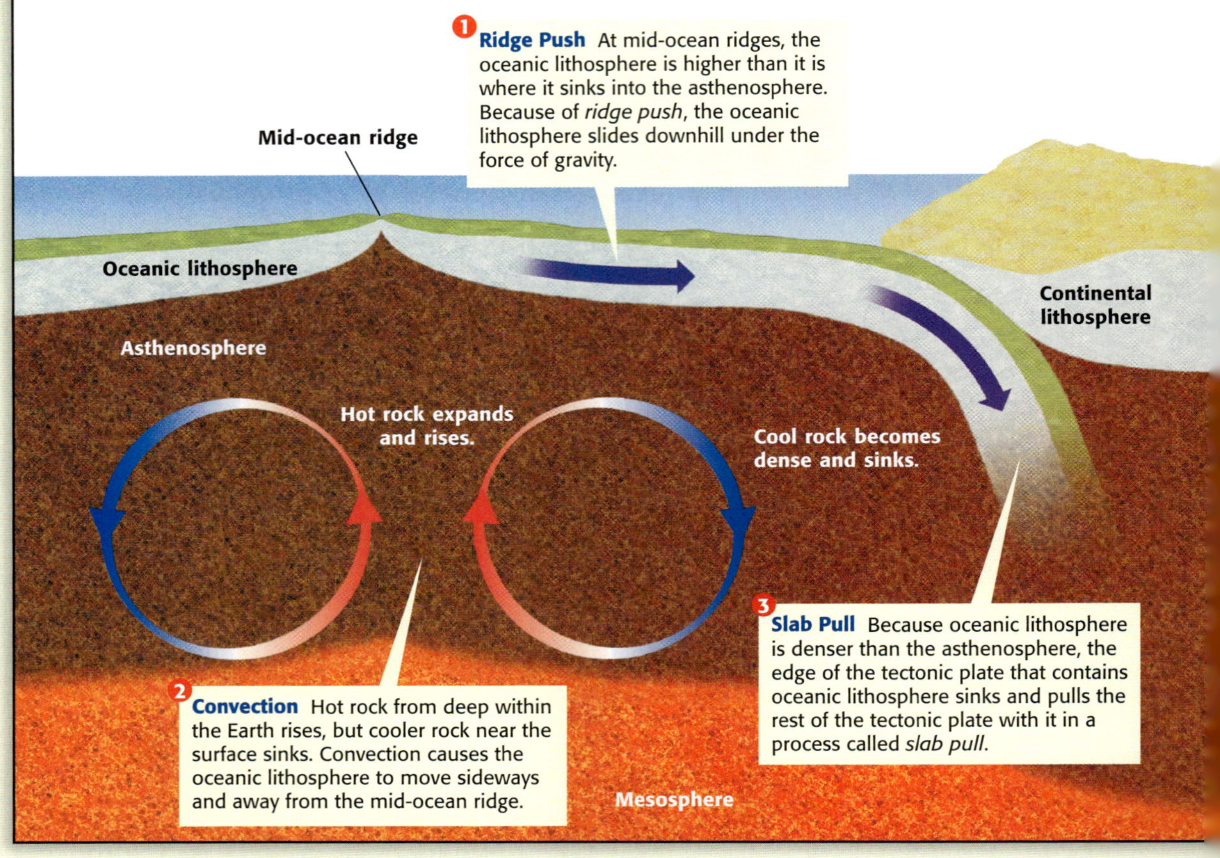

❶ **Ridge Push** At mid-ocean ridges, the oceanic lithosphere is higher than it is where it sinks into the asthenosphere. Because of *ridge push*, the oceanic lithosphere slides downhill under the force of gravity.

❷ **Convection** Hot rock from deep within the Earth rises, but cooler rock near the surface sinks. Convection causes the oceanic lithosphere to move sideways and away from the mid-ocean ridge.

❸ **Slab Pull** Because oceanic lithosphere is denser than the asthenosphere, the edge of the tectonic plate that contains oceanic lithosphere sinks and pulls the rest of the tectonic plate with it in a process called *slab pull*.

Answer to Reading Check
The circulation of thermal energy causes changes in density in the asthenosphere. As rock is heated, it expands, becomes less dense, and rises. As rock cools, it contracts, becomes denser, and sinks.

Homework — ADVANCED

Controversial Theories Alfred Wegener wrote, "If it turns out that sense and meaning are now becoming evident in the whole history of the Earth's development, why should we hesitate to toss the old views overboard?" Ask students to think about why the acceptance of new ideas in science is a slow process. Ask students to explain why continental drift and other controversial theories took a long time to be accepted.
LS Logical

Chapter 7 • Plate Tectonics

Tracking Tectonic Plate Motion

How fast do tectonic plates move? The answer to this question depends on many factors, such as the type and shape of the tectonic plate and the way that the tectonic plate interacts with the tectonic plates that surround it. Tectonic plate movements are so slow and gradual that you can't see or feel them—the movement is measured in centimeters per year.

The Global Positioning System

Scientists use a system of satellites called the *global positioning system* (GPS), shown in **Figure 2,** to measure the rate of tectonic plate movement. Radio signals are continuously beamed from satellites to GPS ground stations, which record the exact distance between the satellites and the ground station. Over time, these distances change slightly. By recording the time it takes for the GPS ground stations to move a given distance, scientists can measure the speed at which each tectonic plate moves.

GPS satellite

Figure 2 *The image above shows the orbits of the GPS satellites.*

SECTION Review

Summary

- Boundaries between tectonic plates are classified as convergent, divergent, or transform.
- Ridge push, convection, and slab pull are three possible driving forces of plate tectonics.
- Scientists use data from a system of satellites called the global positioning system to measure the rate of motion of tectonic plates.

Using Key Terms

1. In your own words, write a definition for the term *plate tectonics*.

Understanding Key Ideas

2. The speed a tectonic plate moves per year is best measured in
   a. kilometers per year.
   b. centimeters per year.
   c. meters per year.
   d. millimeters per year.

3. Briefly describe three possible driving forces of tectonic plate movement.

4. Explain how scientists use GPS to measure the rate of tectonic plate movement.

Math Skills

5. If an orbiting satellite has a diameter of 60 cm, what is the total surface area of the satellite? (Hint: *surface area* = $4\pi r^2$)

Critical Thinking

6. **Identifying Relationships** When convection takes place in the mantle, why does cool rock material sink and warm rock material rise?

7. **Analyzing Processes** Why does oceanic crust sink beneath continental crust at convergent boundaries?

SciLinks
Developed and maintained by the National Science Teachers Association

For a variety of links related to this chapter, go to www.scilinks.org
Topic: Plate Tectonics
SciLinks code: HSM1171

Answers to Section Review

1. Sample answer: Plate tectonics is the theory that the lithosphere is divided into tectonic plates that move slowly across the asthenosphere.
2. b
3. Three possible driving forces of tectonic plate movement are ridge push, slab pull, and convection. Ridge push occurs when an oceanic plate slides down the boundary between the lithosphere and asthenosphere because of gravity. Slab pull occurs when the sinking edge of an oceanic plate pulls the rest of the plate down with it into the subduction zone. Convection occurs when hot mantle material in the asthenosphere convects and causes the tectonic plate to move sideways.
4. In the GPS process, radio signals are beamed from satellites to ground stations. The distance between the satellites and a ground station is recorded. Over time, these distances change slightly. Scientists can measure the rate at which tectonic plates move by recording the time it takes for ground stations to move a given distance.
5. $(4 \times 3.1416 \times 30\,cm^2) = 11,310\,cm^2$
6. During the convection process in the mantle, cooler material sinks because it is denser than warmer material.
7. Oceanic crust sinks beneath continental crust at convergent boundaries because oceanic crust is denser than continental crust.

CHAPTER RESOURCES

Chapter Resource File
- Section Quiz GENERAL
- Section Review GENERAL
- Vocabulary and Section Summary GENERAL
- Reinforcement Worksheet BASIC
- SciLinks Activity GENERAL

Technology
- Transparencies
  - Possible Causes of Tectonic Plate Motion

Section 3 • The Theory of Plate Tectonics

SECTION 4

Focus

Overview

This section explores effects of tectonic forces on the Earth's crust. Students will learn how stress on rock causes it to fold or fault in various ways. The section also discusses how different types of mountains form from the action of tectonic forces and volcanic activity.

🔔 Bellringer

Display photographs of each type of mountain discussed in this section. Have students write a description of each example and suggest how each might have formed.

Motivate

Demonstration — GENERAL

Modeling Deformation Display two thin strips of modeling clay, one frozen and one at room temperature. Have a volunteer demonstrate what happens when the warm clay is bent. (It folds.)

Ask students to predict what will happen to the frozen clay when a force is applied to it. Provide protective gloves, and have a second volunteer attempt to bend the frozen clay. (It should break.) **Ⓛ Kinesthetic/Visual**

SECTION 4

READING WARM-UP

Objectives

- Describe two types of stress that deform rocks.
- Describe three major types of folds.
- Explain the differences between the three major types of faults.
- Identify the most common types of mountains.
- Explain the difference between uplift and subsidence.

Terms to Learn

compression   fault
tension   uplift
folding   subsidence

READING STRATEGY

Discussion Read this section silently. Write down questions that you have about this section. Discuss your questions in a small group.

Figure 1 When a small amount of stress is placed on uncooked spaghetti, the spaghetti bends. Additional stress causes the spaghetti to break.

CHAPTER RESOURCES

Chapter Resource File

- Lesson Plan
- Directed Reading A **BASIC**
- Directed Reading B **SPECIAL NEEDS**

Technology

- Transparencies
  - Bellringer

Deforming the Earth's Crust

Have you ever tried to bend something, only to have it break? Take long, uncooked pieces of spaghetti, and bend them very slowly but only a little. Now, bend them again, but this time, bend them much farther and faster. What happened?

How can a material bend at one time and break at another time? The answer is that the stress you put on the material was different each time. *Stress* is the amount of force per unit area on a given material. The same principle applies to the rocks in the Earth's crust. Different things happen to rock when different types of stress are applied.

Deformation

The process by which the shape of a rock changes because of stress is called *deformation*. In the example above, the spaghetti deformed in two different ways—by bending and by breaking. **Figure 1** illustrates this concept. The same thing happens in rock layers. Rock layers bend when stress is placed on them. But when enough stress is placed on rocks, they can reach their elastic limit and break.

Compression and Tension

The type of stress that occurs when an object is squeezed, such as when two tectonic plates collide, is called **compression**. When compression occurs at a convergent boundary, large mountain ranges can form.

Another form of stress is *tension*. **Tension** is stress that occurs when forces act to stretch an object. As you might guess, tension occurs at divergent plate boundaries, such as mid-ocean ridges, when two tectonic plates pull away from each other.

✔ **Reading Check** How do the forces of plate tectonics cause rock to deform? *(See the Appendix for answers to Reading Checks.)*

Answer to Reading Check

Compression can cause rocks to be pushed into mountain ranges as tectonic plates collide at convergent boundaries. Tension can pull rocks apart as tectonic plates separate at divergent boundaries.

---

206 Chapter 7 • Plate Tectonics

Figure 2 Folding: When Rock Layers Bend Because of Stress

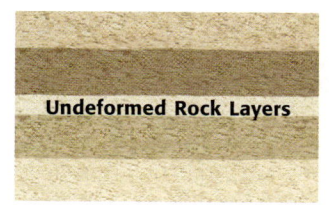

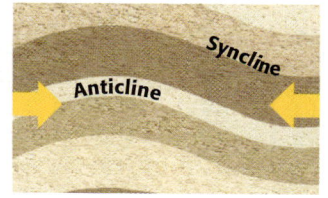

Unstressed — Undeformed Rock Layers

Horizontal stress — Anticline, Syncline

Vertical stress — Monocline

Folding

The bending of rock layers because of stress in the Earth's crust is called **folding**. Scientists assume that all rock layers started as horizontal layers. So, when scientists see a fold, they know that deformation has taken place.

Types of Folds

Depending on how the rock layers deform, different types of folds are made. **Figure 2** shows the two most common types of folds—*anticlines*, or upward-arching folds, and *synclines*, downward, troughlike folds. Another type of fold is a *monocline*. In a monocline, rock layers are folded so that both ends of the fold are horizontal. Imagine taking a stack of paper and laying it on a table. Think of the sheets of paper as different rock layers. Now put a book under one end of the stack. You can see that both ends of the sheets are horizontal, but all of the sheets are bent in the middle.

Folds can be large or small. The largest folds are measured in kilometers. Other folds are also obvious but are much smaller. These small folds can be measured in centimeters. **Figure 3** shows examples of large and small folds.

compression stress that occurs when forces act to squeeze an object

tension stress that occurs when forces act to stretch an object

folding the bending of rock layers due to stress

Figure 3 The large photo shows mountain-sized folds in the Rocky Mountains. The small photo shows a rock that has folds smaller than a penknife.

Teach

READING STRATEGY — GENERAL

Sketching Folds and Faults As students read this section, have them sketch the following examples in their **science journal**:

- folds that illustrate anticlines and synclines
- a fold that illustrates a monocline
- a normal fault
- a reverse fault
- a strike-slip fault

Have students label each sketch clearly, provide a caption, and draw arrows showing the direction of the forces causing the deformation. **English Language Learners**
LS Visual/Logical

Homework — GENERAL

Making Models Have students select a topographic feature in your state, or a state nearby, that resulted from the deformation of the Earth's crust and find out about how it formed. Tell them to choose appropriate materials and create a model of the formation. Point out that they may need to create a cross-section view to show layers within the formation. Finally, ask students to write labels explaining the formation's features and the tectonic forces that caused the features. **LS Kinesthetic/Visual**

ACTIVITY — ADVANCED

Folds That Trap Natural Gas Have students imagine that they are geologists who are exploring for trapped pockets of natural gas. Tell students that natural gas forms from plant matter that drifts to the ocean bottom and is covered by sediment. The pressure and temperature created over large amounts of time by overlying sediments cause the plant matter to be compressed and to decompose to natural gas. Explain to students that natural gas travels upward through rock layers until it hits a layer through which it cannot travel and becomes trapped. Ask students if they would expect to find these layers associated with anticlines or synclines. Ask students to explain their answer in their **science journal**. Have them include drawings in their explanation. (Pockets of natural gas would tend to get trapped in anticlines, because impermeable layers in these structures can seal off the upward movement of gas. In a syncline, the natural gas will still travel upward below an impermeable layer.) **LS Logical/Visual**

Section 4 • Deforming the Earth's Crust

Teach, continued

ACTIVITY — BASIC
Hanging Walls Versus Footwalls
Have students refer to **Figure 4** while you give the following explanation of hanging walls and footwalls: "When a fault occurs at an angle, the hanging wall is the block above the fault surface and the footwall is the block beneath the fault surface." Have students identify the hanging walls and footwalls in **Figure 5**. Have students do hand motions as they explain so that they can feel compression and tension. **Visual/Kinesthetic**

Discussion — GENERAL
Forces that Cause Faults Have students look at **Figure 5**, and point out that in a normal fault the hanging wall moves downward. Ask students to describe the tectonic force that causes this type of fault movement. *(tension or stretching from plate movements pulling rocks apart)* Have a student volunteer to use **Figure 5** to discuss the forces that cause reverse faults. *(When plate movements squeeze rocks, compression forces the hanging wall up and the footwall down.)* **English Language Learners**
Visual/Logical

Figure 4 *The position of a fault block determines whether it is a hanging wall or a footwall.*

fault a break in a body of rock along which one block slides relative to another

Faulting
Some rock layers break when stress is applied to them. The surface along which rocks break and slide past each other is called a **fault**. The blocks of crust on each side of the fault are called *fault blocks*.

When a fault is not vertical, understanding the difference between its two sides—the *hanging wall* and the *footwall*—is useful. **Figure 4** shows the difference between a hanging wall and a footwall. Two main types of faults can form. The type of fault that forms depends on how the hanging wall and footwall move in relationship to each other.

Normal Faults
A *normal fault* is shown in **Figure 5**. When a normal fault moves, it causes the hanging wall to move down relative to the footwall. Normal faults usually occur when tectonic forces cause tension that pulls rocks apart.

Reverse Faults
A *reverse fault* is shown in **Figure 5**. When a reverse fault moves, it causes the hanging wall to move up relative to the footwall. This movement is the reverse of a normal fault. Reverse faults usually happen when tectonic forces cause compression that pushes rocks together.

✓ **Reading Check** How does the hanging wall in a normal fault move in relation to a reverse fault?

Figure 5 Normal and Reverse Faults

Normal Fault When rocks are pulled apart because of tension, normal faults often form.

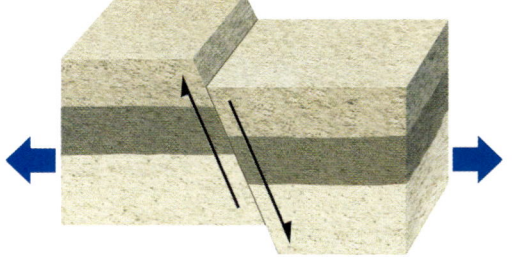

Reverse Fault When rocks are pushed together by compression, reverse faults often form.

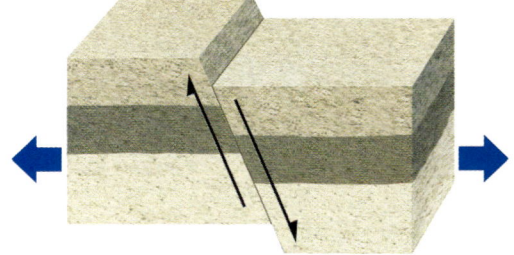

Answer to Reading Check
In a normal fault, the hanging wall moves down. In a reverse fault, the hanging wall moves up.

Is That a Fact!
Thrust faults are large-scale, low-angle, reverse faults caused by the collision of tectonic plates. They are an example of what can happen when stress (compression) is applied to the crust. An important example of thrust faulting in the United States is the Idaho-Wyoming thrust belt. Large-scale folding can also result from compression.

208 Chapter 7 • Plate Tectonics

Figure 6 *The photo at left is a normal fault. The photo at right is a reverse fault.*

Telling the Difference Between Faults

It's easy to tell the difference between a normal fault and a reverse fault in drawings with arrows. But what types of faults are shown in **Figure 6**? You can certainly see the faults, but which one is a normal fault, and which one is a reverse fault? In the top left photo in **Figure 6,** one side has obviously moved relative to the other side. You can tell this fault is a normal fault by looking at the order of sedimentary rock layers. If you compare the two dark layers near the surface, you can see that the hanging wall has moved down relative to the footwall.

Strike-Slip Faults

A third major type of fault is called a *strike-slip fault*. An illustration of a strike-slip fault is shown in **Figure 7**. *Strike-slip faults* form when opposing forces cause rock to break and move horizontally. If you were standing on one side of a strike-slip fault looking across the fault when it moved, the ground on the other side would appear to move to your left or right. The San Andreas Fault in California is a spectacular example of a strike-slip fault.

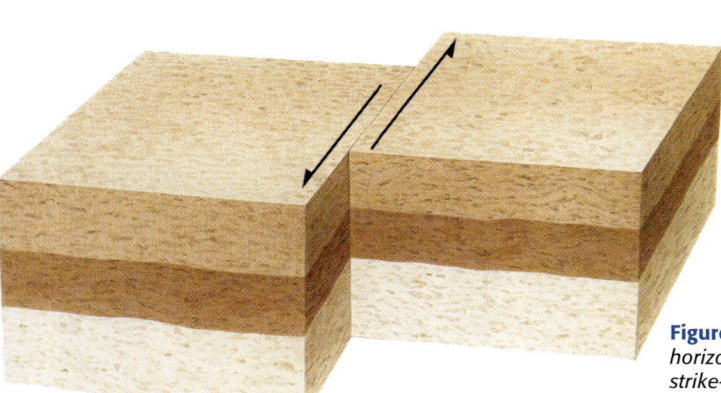

Figure 7 *When rocks are moved horizontally by opposing forces, strike-slip faults often form.*

Quick Lab

Modeling Strike-Slip Faults

1. Use **modeling clay** to construct a box that is 6 in. × 6 in. × 4 in. Use different colors of clay to represent different horizontal layers.
2. Using **scissors,** cut the box down the middle. Place **two 4 in. × 6 in. index cards** inside the cut so that the two sides of the box slide freely.
3. Using gentle pressure, slide the two sides horizontally past one another.
4. How does this model illustrate the motion that occurs along a strike-slip fault?

Teach, continued

BRAIN FOOD

The "Solid" Earth Ask students to write a one-page paper explaining their thoughts about the following quote from *Planet Earth* by Jonathan Weiner: "What we have been pleased to call 'solid Earth' is not as solid as we thought. It is energetic, dynamic, and fundamentally restless."
LS Logical

CONNECTION to Astronomy — GENERAL

Extraterrestrial Mountains and Mountain Ranges Earth is not the only place with mountains. Astronomers give extraterrestrial mountains the name *mons*, and extraterrestrial mountain ranges are called either *montes* or *highlands*. Encourage students to find out more about the formation of mountains on Mercury, Venus, Mars, Earth's moon, or on one of the moons of Jupiter or Saturn. Have students compare the mountains they study with mountains on Earth.
LS Logical

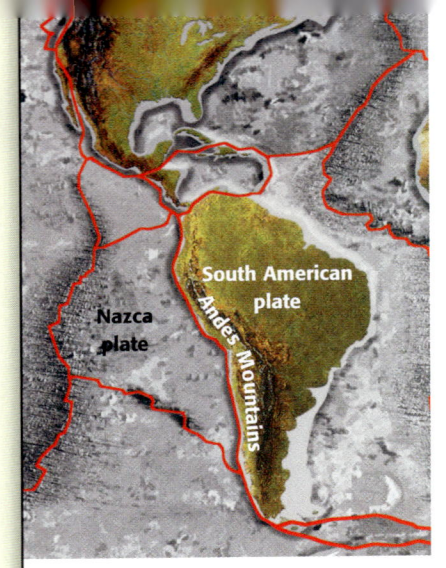

Figure 8 The Andes Mountains formed on the edge of the South American plate where it converges with the Nazca plate.

Figure 9 The Appalachian Mountains were once as tall as the Himalaya Mountains but have been worn down by hundreds of millions of years of weathering and erosion.

Plate Tectonics and Mountain Building

You have just learned about several ways the Earth's crust changes because of the forces of plate tectonics. When tectonic plates collide, land features that start as folds and faults can eventually become large mountain ranges. Mountains exist because tectonic plates are continually moving around and colliding with one another. As shown in **Figure 8,** the Andes Mountains formed above the subduction zone where two tectonic plates converge.

When tectonic plates undergo compression or tension, they can form mountains in several ways. Take a look at three of the most common types of mountains—folded mountains, fault-block mountains, and volcanic mountains.

Folded Mountains

The highest mountain ranges in the world are made up of folded mountains. These ranges form at convergent boundaries where continents have collided. *Folded mountains* form when rock layers are squeezed together and pushed upward. If you place a pile of paper on a table and push on opposite edges of the pile, you will see how folded mountains form.

An example of a folded mountain range that formed at a convergent boundary is shown in **Figure 9.** About 390 million years ago, the Appalachian Mountains formed when the landmasses that are now North America and Africa collided. Other examples of mountain ranges that consist of very large and complex folds are the Alps in central Europe, the Ural Mountains in Russia, and the Himalayas in Asia.

✓ **Reading Check** Explain how folded mountains form.

Answer to Reading Check
Folded mountains form when rock layers are squeezed together and pushed upward.

Is That a Fact!
The Sierra Nevada mountain range, in California, and the Teton Range, in Wyoming, are examples of fault-block mountains. The Appalachian Mountains, in eastern North America, are an example of folded mountains.

Chapter 7 • Plate Tectonics

Figure 10 *When the crust is subjected to tension, the rock can break along a series of normal faults, which creates fault-block mountains.*

Fault-Block Mountains

When tectonic forces put enough tension on the Earth's crust, a large number of normal faults can result. *Fault-block mountains* form when this tension causes large blocks of the Earth's crust to drop down relative to other blocks. **Figure 10** shows one way that fault-block mountains form.

When sedimentary rock layers are tilted up by faulting, they can produce mountains that have sharp, jagged peaks. As shown in **Figure 11,** the Tetons in western Wyoming are a spectacular example of fault-block mountains.

Volcanic Mountains

Most of the world's major volcanic mountains are located at convergent boundaries where oceanic crust sinks into the asthenosphere at subduction zones. The rock that is melted in subduction zones forms magma, which rises to the Earth's surface and erupts to form *volcanic mountains*. Volcanic mountains can also form under the sea. Sometimes these mountains can rise above the ocean surface to become islands. The majority of tectonically active volcanic mountains on the Earth have formed around the tectonically active rim of the Pacific Ocean. The rim has become known as the *Ring of Fire*.

CONNECTION TO Social Studies

WRITING SKILL — The Naming of the Appalachian Mountains How did the Appalachian Mountains get their name? It is believed that the Appalachian Mountains were named by Spanish explorers in North America during the 16th century. It is thought that the name was taken from a Native American tribe called *Appalachee*, who lived in northern Florida. Research other geological features in the United States, including mountains and rivers, whose names are of Native American origin. Write the results of your research in a short essay.

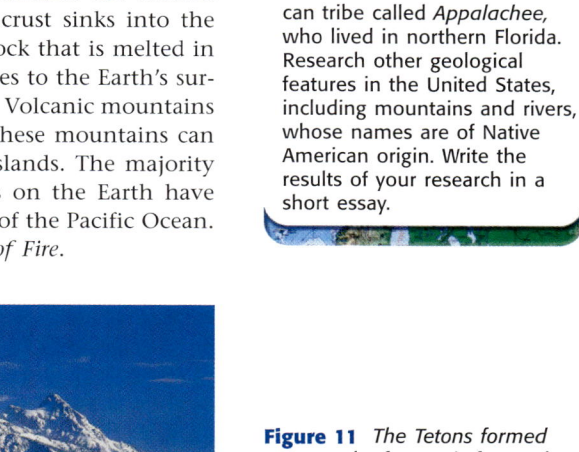

Figure 11 *The Tetons formed as a result of tectonic forces that stretched the Earth's crust and caused it to break in a series of normal faults.*

ACTIVITY — GENERAL

Mountain-Building Gallery Tell students to locate photographs of mountains in magazines, books, or on the Internet. Have them cut out, copy, or print these images and mount them on paper. Then, have them write the type of mountain, a description of how the mountains formed, and the location of the mountains relative to tectonic plates on a card and tape the card to the back of the photo. Number and post the photos around the room so that students can view the gallery and write their own guesses as to which type of mountain each is. Have students check their guesses against the cards.
LS Visual/Logical

Cultural Awareness — GENERAL

Mountain Cultures Although people living in mountainous regions are part of some of the world's most impoverished populations, they inhabit diverse ecosystems and have developed innovative technologies to live at high altitudes, where resources may be scarce. Encourage students to learn about the cultures living in the Andes, the Himalayas, or the Alps. Students should give a presentation about the culture they researched and hold a round-table discussion of the problems and opportunities people of these cultures face. The Mountain Institute in Washington, D.C. offers information about natural resource management issues in mountain environments.
LS Interpersonal/Verbal

CONNECTION to Life Science — GENERAL

Adaptations for High-Altitude Living Point out that living at high altitudes places stress on organisms. Organisms that live at these elevations have adaptations that help them survive. For example, some animals that live on mountains produce more red blood cells. This makes the blood able to deliver more oxygen to body tissues. Have students find out about the adaptations of other organisms, including humans, that live in high-altitude environments. **LS** Logical

Is That a Fact!

When the Appalachian Mountains formed, they were probably very similar to the Himalayas. But the Appalachians are about 350 million years older than the Himalayas. The Appalachians have been worn down by weathering and erosion over hundreds of millions of years, forming the Atlantic coastal plain and the continental shelf along the Atlantic seaboard.

Section 4 • Deforming the Earth's Crust

Close

Reteaching — BASIC
Review of Mountain Building
After students have read this section, invite volunteers to sketch examples of each type of mountain on the board. Ask other students to explain how each mountain type forms by referring to the diagram and by adding labels and arrows to show the direction of forces at work. **English Language Learners**
LS Visual

Quiz — GENERAL
1. What three features form when rock layers bend?
   (anticlines, synclines, and monoclines)
2. Why are the Appalachian Mountains no longer located at the edge of the North American plate?
   (The Appalachians formed when North America and Africa collided. In time, the plates separated and so much new crust was created that the mountains were no longer at the plate boundary.)

Alternative Assessment — GENERAL
Identifying the Forces That Create Mountains
Have students choose a mountain range to research. Then, ask students to identify in writing the relationship between the mountain range and the forces that created it. **LS Logical**

INTERNET ACTIVITY

For another activity related to this chapter, go to **go.hrw.com** and type in the keyword **HZ5TECW**.

uplift the rising of regions of the Earth's crust to higher elevations

subsidence the sinking of regions of the Earth's crust to lower elevations

---

Uplift and Subsidence
Vertical movements in the crust are divided into two types—uplift and subsidence. The rising of regions of Earth's crust to higher elevations is called **uplift**. Rocks that are uplifted may or may not be highly deformed. The sinking of regions of Earth's crust to lower elevations is known as **subsidence** (suhb SIED'ns). Unlike some uplifted rocks, rocks that subside do not undergo much deformation.

Uplifting of Depressed Rocks
The formation of mountains is one type of uplift. Uplift can also occur when large areas of land rise without deforming. One way areas rise without deforming is a process known as *rebound*. When the crust rebounds, it slowly springs back to its previous elevation. Uplift often happens when a weight is removed from the crust.

Subsidence of Cooler Rocks
Rocks that are hot take up more space than cooler rocks. For example, the lithosphere is relatively hot at mid-ocean ridges. The farther the lithosphere is from the ridge, the cooler and denser the lithosphere becomes. Because the oceanic lithosphere now takes up less volume, the ocean floor subsides.

Tectonic Letdown
Subsidence can also occur when the lithosphere becomes stretched in rift zones. A *rift zone* is a set of deep cracks that forms between two tectonic plates that are pulling away from each other. As tectonic plates pull apart, stress between the plates causes a series of faults to form along the rift zone. As shown in **Figure 12**, the blocks of crust in the center of the rift zone subside.

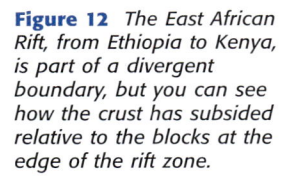

Figure 12 The East African Rift, from Ethiopia to Kenya, is part of a divergent boundary, but you can see how the crust has subsided relative to the blocks at the edge of the rift zone.

INCLUSION Strategies

- Learning Disabled
- Behavior Control Issues

Organize students into groups of four. Hand out a deck of cards that contain terms and concepts from this section. A different-colored set of cards should contain the definitions for the terms and concepts. Ask each group to match the terms to the correct definition. Have the groups work as a team when reviewing definitions. Students can use their textbooks as a resource if necessary. Next, ask groups to separate terms and definitions into two decks. A team of two students should choose from the term deck and attempt to give the definition without looking at the card. The other two members can give clues if requested. Ask students to write down terms they have difficulty remembering in their **science journal**. **LS Logical**

Chapter 7 • Plate Tectonics

SECTION Review

Summary

- Compression and tension are two forces of plate tectonics that can cause rock to deform.
- Folding occurs when rock layers bend because of stress.
- Faulting occurs when rock layers break because of stress and then move on either side of the break.
- Mountains are classified as either folded, fault-block, or volcanic depending on how they form.
- Mountain building is caused by the movement of tectonic plates. Folded mountains and volcanic mountains form at convergent boundaries. Fault-block mountains form at divergent boundaries.
- Uplift and subsidence are the two types of vertical movement in the Earth's crust. Uplift occurs when regions of the crust rise to higher elevations. Subsidence occurs when regions of the crust sink to lower elevations.

Using Key Terms

For each pair of key terms, explain how the meanings of the terms differ.

1. *compression* and *tension*
2. *uplift* and *subsidence*

Understanding Key Ideas

3. The type of fault in which the hanging wall moves up relative to the footwall is called a
   a. strike-slip fault.
   b. fault-block fault.
   c. normal fault.
   d. reverse fault.
4. Describe three types of folds.
5. Describe three types of faults.
6. Identify the most common types of mountains.
7. What is rebound?
8. What are rift zones, and how do they form?

Critical Thinking

9. **Predicting Consequences** If a fault occurs in an area where rock layers have been folded, which type of fault is it likely to be? Why?
10. **Identifying Relationships** Would you expect to see a folded mountain range at a mid-ocean ridge? Explain your answer.

Interpreting Graphics

Use the diagram below to answer the questions that follow.

11. What type of fault is shown in the diagram?
12. At what kind of tectonic boundary would you most likely find this fault?

For a variety of links related to this chapter, go to www.scilinks.org
Topic: Faults; Mountain Building
SciLinks code: HSM0566; HSM0999

Answers to Section Review

1. Sample answer: Compression is stress that occurs when forces act to squeeze an object. Tension is stress that occurs when forces act to stretch an object.
2. Sample answer: Uplift is the rising of Earth's crust to higher elevations. Subsidence is the sinking of Earth's crust to lower elevations.
3. d
4. The three types of folds include anticlines, which are upward-arching folds; synclines, which are downward-arching folds; and monoclines, in which rock layers are folded so that both ends of the fold are horizontal.
5. The three types of faults include normal faults, in which the hanging wall moves down relative to the footwall; reverse faults, in which the hanging wall moves up relative to the footwall; and strike-slip faults, in which opposing forces cause rock to break and move horizontally.
6. The most common types of mountains are folded mountains, fault-block mountains, and volcanic mountains.
7. Rebound is a process in which Earth's crust slowly springs back to its previous elevation.
8. Rift zones are a set of deep cracks in the Earth's crust that form when two tectonic plates are pulling away from each other. As tectonic plates pull apart, stress builds up between the plates. This stress causes strain in the Earth's crust, and a series of faults forms along the rift zone.
9. A reverse fault is likely to form because both reverse faults and folding occur in areas where compression takes place.
10. No, you would be more likely to see volcanic mountains where magma is rising along the mid-ocean ridge spreading center.
11. a reverse fault
12. a convergent boundary

CHAPTER RESOURCES

Chapter Resource File
- Section Quiz GENERAL
- Section Review GENERAL
- Vocabulary and Section Summary GENERAL
- Datasheet for Quick Lab

Section 4 • Deforming the Earth's Crust

Model-Making Lab

Convection Connection

Teacher's Notes

Time Required
One 45-minute class period

Lab Ratings
EASY ———— HARD

Teacher Prep 🧪
Student Set-Up 🧪🧪🧪
Concept Level 🧪🧪
Clean Up 🧪🧪

MATERIALS
The materials listed on the student page are enough for a group of 2 or 3 students.

Safety Caution
Remind students to review all safety cautions and icons before beginning this lab activity.

Preparation Notes
Because of the volume of water being used, you may wish to set up the blocks and hot plates ahead of time. Also, breezes and drafts may move the craft sticks, so eliminate or reduce as many of these variables as possible.

Using Scientific Methods
Model-Making Lab

OBJECTIVES

Model convection currents to simulate plate tectonic movement.

Draw conclusions about the role of convection in plate tectonics.

MATERIALS

- craft sticks (2)
- food coloring
- gloves, heat-resistant
- hot plates, small (2)
- pan, aluminum, rectangular
- pencil
- ruler, metric
- thermometers (3)
- water, cold
- wooden blocks

SAFETY

Convection Connection

Some scientists think that convection currents within the Earth's mantle cause tectonic plates to move. Because these convection currents cannot be observed directly, scientists use models to simulate the process. In this activity, you will make your own model to simulate tectonic plate movement.

Ask a Question

1. How can I make a model of convection currents in the Earth's mantle?

Form a Hypothesis

2. Turn the question above into a statement in which you give your best guess about what factors will have the greatest effect on your convection model.

Test the Hypothesis

3. Place two hot plates side by side in the center of your lab table. Be sure that they are away from the edge of the table.

4. Place the pan on top of the hot plates. Slide the wooden blocks under the pan to support the ends. Make sure that the pan is level and secure.

5. Fill the pan with cold water. The water should be at least 4 cm deep. Turn on the hot plates, and put on your gloves.

6. After a minute or two, tiny bubbles will begin to rise in the water above the hot plates. Gently place two craft sticks on the water's surface.

7. Use the pencil to align the sticks parallel to the short ends of the pan. The sticks should be about 3 cm apart and near the center of the pan.

8. As soon as the sticks begin to move, place a drop of food coloring in the center of the pan. Observe what happens to the food coloring.

Terry J. Rakes
Elmwood Jr. High
Rogers, Arkansas

CHAPTER RESOURCES

Chapter Resource File
- Datasheet for Chapter Lab
- Lab Notes and Answers

Technology
Classroom Videos
- Lab Video

LabBook
- Oh, the Pressure!

Chapter 7 • Plate Tectonics

⑨ With the help of a partner, hold one thermometer bulb just under the water at the center of the pan. Hold the other two thermometers just under the water near the ends of the pan. Record the temperatures.

⑩ When you are finished, turn off the hot plates. After the water has cooled, carefully empty the water into a sink.

Analyze the Results

① **Explaining Events** Based on your observations of the motion of the food coloring, how does the temperature of the water affect the direction in which the craft sticks move?

Draw Conclusions

② **Drawing Conclusions** How does the motion of the craft sticks relate to the motion of the water?

③ **Applying Conclusions** How does this model relate to plate tectonics and the movement of the continents?

④ **Applying Conclusions** Based on your observations, what can you conclude about the role of convection in plate tectonics?

Applying Your Data

Suggest a substance other than water that might be used to model convection in the mantle. Consider using a substance that flows more slowly than water.

CHAPTER RESOURCES

Workbooks

📘 **Whiz-Bang Demonstrations**
• Thar She Blows! GENERAL

📘 **Labs You Can Eat**
• Rescue Near the Center of the Earth GENERAL
• Cracks in the Hard-Boiled Earth BASIC
• Dough Fault of Your Own ADVANCED

📘 **Long-Term Projects & Research Ideas**
• To Complicate Things ADVANCED

Analyze the Results

1. Based on the motion of the food coloring, the warmer water rises and the cooler water sinks. Therefore, as the water warms, the craft sticks should move in a direction away from the center of the pan.

Draw Conclusions

2. The hot water flowed outward from the center of the pan. This movement pushed the sticks away from each other and toward the edges of the pan. (In some cases, the sticks may move together.)

3. Convection currents within the Earth's mantle may move tectonic plates in the same way that the convecting water moved the craft sticks. The convection currents in this model were created by the hot plates warming the water. In the mantle, convection currents are caused by thermal energy from deep within the Earth.

4. Answers will vary but should include a description of how convection may be at least partially responsible for the movement of tectonic plates.

Applying Your Data

Suggestions for improving the model will vary. Students may suggest increasing the size of the model or using model tectonic plates that have differing sizes and densities. Students may also suggest incorporating the processes of ridge push or slab pull into the model.

Chapter 7 • Chapter Lab   **215**

Chapter Review

Assignment Guide

Section	Questions
1	1, 3, 6, 11, 12, 21–24
2	2, 13, 14
3	7, 16, 18, 19
4	4, 5, 8–10, 15, 20
1, 2, and 3	17

ANSWERS

Using Key Terms

1. Sample answer: Scientists divide the Earth into the crust, mantle, and core based on the chemical elements that make up each of these layers.
2. continental drift
3. asthenosphere
4. Tension
5. uplift

Understanding Key Ideas

6. b
7. c
8. b
9. d
10. a
11. c
12. Scientists can measure the differences in the speeds of seismic waves that travel through the Earth's interior to calculate the density and thickness of each of the Earth's physical layers.

Chapter Review

USING KEY TERMS

1 Use the following terms in the same sentence: *crust, mantle,* and *core.*

Complete each of the following sentences by choosing the correct term from the word bank.

asthenosphere   uplift
tension   continental drift

2 The hypothesis that continents can drift apart and have done so in the past is known as ___.

3 The ___ is the soft layer of the mantle on which the tectonic plates move.

4 ___ is stress that occurs when forces act to stretch an object.

5 The rising of regions of the Earth's crust to higher elevations is called ___.

UNDERSTANDING KEY IDEAS

Multiple Choice

6 The strong, lower part of the mantle is a physical layer called the
  a. lithosphere.
  b. mesosphere.
  c. asthenosphere.
  d. outer core.

7 The type of tectonic plate boundary that forms from a collision between two tectonic plates is a
  a. divergent plate boundary.
  b. transform plate boundary.
  c. convergent plate boundary.
  d. normal plate boundary.

8 The bending of rock layers due to stress in the Earth's crust is known as
  a. uplift.
  b. folding.
  c. faulting.
  d. subsidence.

9 The type of fault in which the hanging wall moves up relative to the footwall is called a
  a. strike-slip fault.
  b. fault-block fault.
  c. normal fault.
  d. reverse fault.

10 The type of mountain that forms when rock layers are squeezed together and pushed upward is the
  a. folded mountain.
  b. fault-block mountain.
  c. volcanic mountain.
  d. strike-slip mountain.

11 Scientists' knowledge of the Earth's interior has come primarily from
  a. studying magnetic reversals in oceanic crust.
  b. using a system of satellites called the *global positioning system.*
  c. studying seismic waves generated by earthquakes.
  d. studying the pattern of fossils on different continents.

Short Answer

12 Explain how scientists use seismic waves to map the Earth's interior.

13 How do magnetic reversals provide evidence of sea-floor spreading?

---

13. As oceanic crust spreads away from a mid-ocean ridge, the crust carries bands that contain minerals that were aligned with Earth's magnetic field when the crust was formed. The similar sequence of bands on both sides of a mid-ocean ridge, even at a large distance from the ridge, indicates that the sea floor is spreading away from a center.

Chapter 7 • Plate Tectonics

14. Explain how sea-floor spreading provides a way for continents to move.

15. Describe two types of stress that deform rock.

16. What is the global positioning system (GPS), and how does GPS allow scientists to measure the rate of motion of tectonic plates?

CRITICAL THINKING

17. **Concept Mapping** Use the following terms to create a concept map: *sea-floor spreading, convergent boundary, divergent boundary, subduction zone, transform boundary,* and *tectonic plates.*

18. **Applying Concepts** Why does oceanic lithosphere sink at subduction zones but not at mid-ocean ridges?

19. **Identifying Relationships** New tectonic material continually forms at divergent boundaries. Tectonic plate material is also continually destroyed in subduction zones at convergent boundaries. Do you think that the total amount of lithosphere formed on the Earth is about equal to the amount destroyed? Why?

20. **Applying Concepts** Folded mountains usually form at the edge of a tectonic plate. How can you explain folded mountain ranges located in the middle of a tectonic plate?

INTERPRETING GRAPHICS

Imagine that you could travel to the center of the Earth. Use the diagram below to answer the questions that follow.

Composition	Structure
Crust (50 km)	Lithosphere (150 km)
Mantle (2,900 km)	Asthenosphere (250 km)
	Mesosphere (2,550 km)
Core (3,430 km)	Outer core (2,200 km)
	Inner core (1,228 km)

21. How far beneath the Earth's surface would you have to go before you were no longer passing through rock that had the composition of granite?

22. How far beneath the Earth's surface would you have to go to find liquid material in the Earth's core?

23. At what depth would you find mantle material but still be within the lithosphere?

24. How far beneath the Earth's surface would you have to go to find solid iron and nickel in the Earth's core?

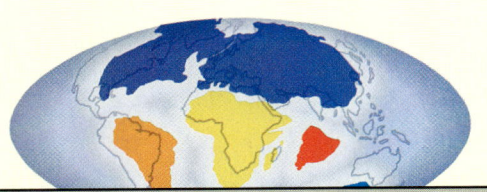

---

16. The global positioning system is a system of satellites that orbit the Earth. Radio signals are continuously beamed from these satellites to ground stations. The distance between satellites and ground stations is recorded. By recording the time it takes for ground stations to move a given distance, scientists can measure the rate at which tectonic plates move.

Critical Thinking

17. An answer to this exercise can be found at the back of this book.

18. Answers may vary. At a subduction zone, the lithosphere is denser than it is at a mid-ocean ridge. Convection causes oceanic lithosphere to move away from the mid-ocean ridge. Oceanic lithosphere is also higher at a mid-ocean ridge, so oceanic lithosphere moves down toward the subduction zone because of gravity.

19. Answers may vary. The amount of crust formed is roughly equal to the amount of crust destroyed. If this were not true, the Earth would either be expanding or shrinking.

20. At the time they formed, the folded mountains must have been on the edge of a tectonic plate. New material was later added to the tectonic plate, causing the folded mountains to be located closer to the center of the continent.

Interpreting Graphics

21. 50 km

22. 150 km + 250 km + 2,550 km = 2,950 km

23. between 50 km and 150 km

24. 150 km + 250 km + 2,550 km + 2,200 km = 5,150 km

---

14. As new crust forms at mid-ocean ridges, plates on either side of the ridge move away from the ridge. Therefore, continents on those plates also move.

15. Compression and tension are two types of stress that deform rock. Compression squeezes rock at convergent plate boundaries; tension stretches rock at divergent plate boundaries.

CHAPTER RESOURCES

Chapter Resource File
- Chapter Review GENERAL
- Chapter Test A GENERAL
- Chapter Test B ADVANCED
- Chapter Test C SPECIAL NEEDS
- Vocabulary Activity GENERAL

Workbooks
- Study Guide
  - Assessment resources are also available in Spanish.

Chapter 7 • Chapter Review 217

Standardized Test Preparation

Teacher's Note

To provide practice under more realistic testing conditions, give students 20 minutes to answer all of the questions in this Standardized Test Preparation.

MISCONCEPTION ALERT

Answers to the standardized test preparation can help you identify student misconceptions and misunderstandings.

READING

Passage 1
1. C
2. H
3. B

TEST DOCTOR

Question 3: Answer B is correct. The *Glomar Challenger* drilled into the ocean floor to obtain cores that contained fossils that would enable scientists on board the vessel to determine the relative age of the sea floor at various distances from mid-ocean ridges.

Standardized Test Preparation

READING

Read each of the passages below. Then, answer the questions that follow each passage.

Passage 1 The Deep Sea Drilling Project was a program to retrieve and research rocks below the ocean to test the hypothesis of sea-floor spreading. For 15 years, scientists studying sea-floor spreading conducted research aboard the ship *Glomar Challenger*. Holes were drilled in the sea floor from the ship. Long, cylindrical lengths of rock, called *cores*, were obtained from the drill holes. By examining fossils in the cores, scientists discovered that rock closest to mid-ocean ridges was the youngest. The farther from the ridge the holes were drilled, the older the rock in the cores was. This evidence supported the idea that sea-floor spreading creates new lithosphere at mid-ocean ridges.

1. In the passage, what does *conducted* mean?
   A directed
   B led
   C carried on
   D guided

2. Why were cores drilled in the sea floor from the *Glomar Challenger*?
   F to determine the depth of the crust
   G to find minerals in the sea-floor rock
   H to examine fossils in the sea-floor rock
   I to find oil and gas in the sea-floor rock

3. Which of the following statements is a fact according to the passage?
   A Rock closest to mid-ocean ridges is older than rock at a distance from mid-ocean ridges.
   B One purpose of scientific research on the *Glomar Challenger* was to gather evidence for sea-floor spreading.
   C Fossils examined by scientists came directly from the sea floor.
   D Evidence gathered by scientists did not support sea-floor spreading.

Passage 2 The Himalayas are a range of mountains that is 2,400 km long and that arcs across Pakistan, India, Tibet, Nepal, Sikkim, and Bhutan. The Himalayas are the highest mountains on Earth. Nine mountains, including Mount Everest, the highest mountain on Earth, are more than 8,000 m tall. The formation of the Himalaya Mountains began about 80 million years ago. A tectonic plate carrying the Indian subcontinent collided with the Eurasian plate. The Indian plate was driven beneath the Eurasian plate. This collision caused the uplift of the Eurasian plate and the formation of the Himalayas. This process is continuing today.

1. In the passage, what does the word *arcs* mean?
   A forms a circle
   B forms a plane
   C forms a curve
   D forms a straight line

2. According to the passage, which geologic process formed the Himalaya Mountains?
   F divergence
   G subsidence
   H strike-slip faulting
   I convergence

3. Which of the following statements is a fact according to the passage?
   A The nine tallest mountains on Earth are located in the Himalaya Mountains.
   B The Himalaya Mountains are located within six countries.
   C The Himalaya Mountains are the longest mountain range on Earth.
   D The Himalaya Mountains formed more than 80 million years ago.

Passage 2
1. C
2. I
3. B

TEST DOCTOR

Question 2: Convergence is the logical answer to this question. The Himalayas are the product of the continent-continent collision of the tectonic plate carrying the Indian subcontinent and the Eurasian plate.

Chapter 7 • Plate Tectonics

INTERPRETING GRAPHICS

The illustration below shows the relative velocities (in centimeters per year) and directions in which tectonic plates are separating and colliding. Arrows that point away from one another indicate plate separation. Arrows that point toward one another indicate plate collision. Use the illustration below to answer the questions that follow.

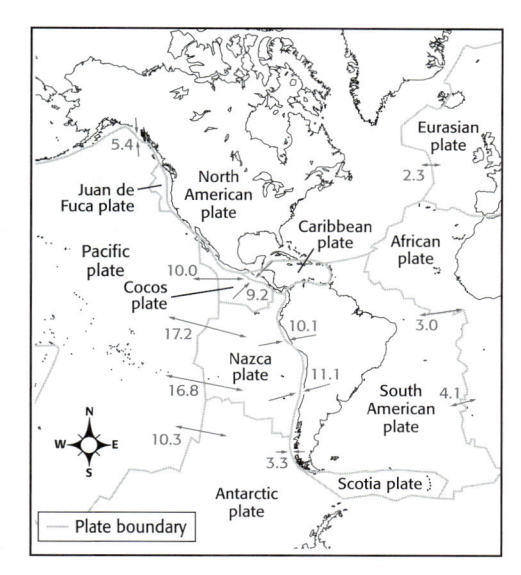

1. Between which two tectonic plates does spreading appear to be the fastest?
   - **A** the Australian plate and the Pacific plate
   - **B** the Antarctic plate and the Pacific plate
   - **C** the Nazca plate and the Pacific plate
   - **D** the Cocos plate and the Pacific plate

2. Where do you think mountain building is taking place?
   - **F** between the African plate and the South American plate
   - **G** between the Nazca plate and the South American plate
   - **H** between the North American plate and the Eurasian plate
   - **I** between the African plate and the North American plate

MATH

Read each question below, and choose the best answer.

1. The mesosphere is 2,550 km thick, and the asthenosphere is 250 km thick. If you assume that the lithosphere is 150 km thick and that the crust is 50 km thick, how thick is the mantle?
   - **A** 2,950 km
   - **B** 2,900 km
   - **C** 2,800 km
   - **D** 2,550 km

2. If a seismic wave travels through the mantle at an average velocity of 8 km/s, how many seconds will the wave take to travel through the mantle?
   - **F** 318.75 s
   - **G** 350.0 s
   - **H** 362.5 s
   - **I** 368.75 s

3. If the crust in a certain area is subsiding at the rate of 2 cm per year and has an elevation of 1,000 m, what elevation will the crust have in 10,000 years?
   - **A** 500 m
   - **B** 800 m
   - **C** 1,200 m
   - **D** 2,000 m

4. Assume that a very small oceanic plate is located between a mid-ocean ridge and a subduction zone. At the ridge, the plate is growing at a rate of 5 km every 1 million years. At the subduction zone, the plate is being destroyed at a rate of 10 km every 1 million years. If the oceanic plate is 100 km across, how long will it take the plate to disappear?
   - **F** 100 million years
   - **G** 50 million years
   - **H** 20 million years
   - **I** 5 million years

INTERPRETING GRAPHICS

1. C
2. G

TEST DOCTOR

Question 2: G is the only logical answer. Mountain building takes place at convergent boundaries. The Nazca plate and the South American plate are the only two plates that are converging.

MATH

1. B
2. H
3. B
4. H

TEST DOCTOR

Question 1: B is the correct answer. Obtaining the correct answer requires adding the thicknesses of the mesosphere, the asthenosphere, and the lithosphere and subtracting the thickness of the crust as follows: 2,550 km + 250 km + (150 km − 50 km) = 2,900 km.

Question 2: H is the correct answer. (2,900 km ÷ 8 km/s = 362.5 s, or a little more than 6 min)

Question 3: B is the correct answer. If the crust is subsiding at the rate of 2 cm/y, it will subside 200 m in 10,000 y (.02 m × 10,000 y = 200 m). If the current elevation is 1,000 m, the elevation will be 800 m (1,000 m − 200 m = 800 m) in 10,000 y.

Question 4: H is the correct answer. There is a net loss of 5 km of crust every 1 million years. If the plate is 100 km across, it will take 20 million years (100 km ÷ 5 km × 1,000,000 y) for the plate to disappear.

Science in Action

Science, Technology, and Society

Background
In addition to GPS satellites, satellite laser ranging (SLR) satellites are used to track the motion of tectonic plates. The *LAGEOS II SLR* satellite (pictured at right) is 60 cm in diameter and weighs approximately 405 kg. Imbedded in the surface of the satellite are 426 three-dimensional prisms. These prisms reflect laser beams directly back to their source.

Scientific Discoveries

Background
Megaplumes are giant, rotating disks of hot water that drift horizontally through the ocean. Megaplumes form at mid-ocean ridges during underwater volcanic eruptions. During an eruption, a column of boiling seawater rises upward from the volcano and expands until it forms a disk. The disks of megaplumes can drift through the oceans for hundreds of kilometers over a period of months. The first megaplume was discovered in 1986 along the Juan de Fuca Ridge, which is located approximately 300 miles off the northwest coast of the United States. Since 1986, at least seven more megaplumes have been recorded along the ridge.

Science in Action

Science, Technology, and Society

Using Satellites to Track Plate Motion
When you think of laser beams firing, you may think of science fiction movies. However, scientists use laser beams to determine the rate and direction of motion of tectonic plates. From ground stations on Earth, laser beams are fired at several small satellites orbiting 5,900 km above Earth. From the satellites, the laser beams are reflected back to ground stations. Differences in the time it takes signals to be reflected from targets are measured over a period of time. From these differences, scientists can determine the rate and direction of plate motion.

Social Studies ACTIVITY
WRITING SKILL Research a society that lives at an active plate boundary. Find out how the people live with dangers such as volcanoes and earthquakes. Include your findings in a short report.

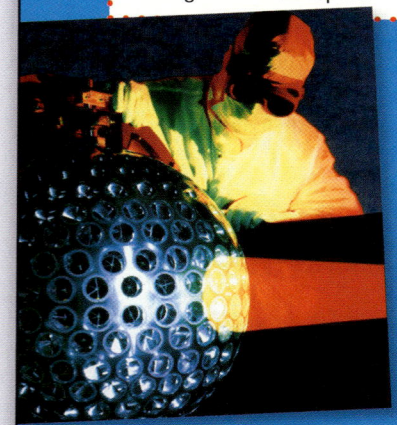

This scientist is using a laser to test one of the satellites that will be used to track plate motion.

Scientific Discoveries

Megaplumes
Eruptions of boiling water from the sea floor form giant, spiral disks that twist through the oceans. Do you think it's impossible? Oceanographers have discovered these disks at eight locations at mid-ocean ridges over the past 20 years. These disks, which may be tens of kilometers across, are called *megaplumes*. Megaplumes are like blenders. They mix hot water with cold water in the oceans. Megaplumes can rise hundreds of meters from the ocean floor to the upper layers of the ocean. They carry gases and minerals and provide extra energy and food to animals in the upper layers of the ocean.

Language Arts ACTIVITY
WRITING SKILL Did you ever wonder about the origin of the name *Himalaya*? Research the origin of the name *Himalaya*, and write a short report about what you find.

Answers to Social Studies Activity
Have students give a short report on the society they researched. Before each report, have students find the geographical location of that society on a tectonic map of the world.

Answers to Language Arts Activity
Students should include in their report that the name *Himalaya* comes from the Sanskrit word *hima*, which means "snow," and *alaya*, which means "abode." Therefore, the word *Himalaya* means "the abode of snow."

220 Chapter 7 • Plate Tectonics

People in Science

Alfred Wegener

Continental Drift Alfred Wegener's greatest contribution to science was the hypothesis of continental drift. This hypothesis states that continents drift apart from one another and have done so in the past. To support his hypothesis, Wegener used geologic, fossil, and glacial evidence gathered on both sides of the Atlantic Ocean. For example, Wegener recognized similarities between rock layers in North America and Europe and between rock layers in South America and Africa. He believed that these similarities could be explained only if these geologic features were once part of the same continent.

Although continental drift explained many of his observations, Wegener could not find scientific evidence to develop a complete explanation of how continents move. Most scientists were skeptical of Wegener's hypothesis and dismissed it as foolishness. It was not until the 1950s and 1960s that the discoveries of magnetic reversals and sea-floor spreading provided evidence of continental drift.

Math Activity

The distance between South America and Africa is 7,200 km. As new crust is created at the mid-ocean ridge, South America and Africa are moving away from each other at a rate of about 3.5 cm per year. How many millions of years ago were South America and Africa joined?

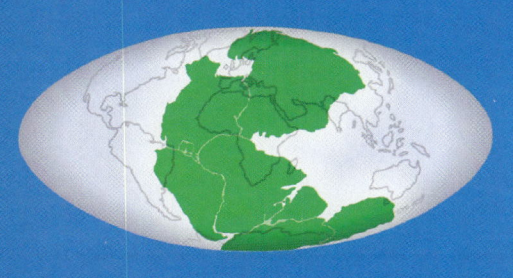

To learn more about these Science in Action topics, visit **go.hrw.com** and type in the keyword **HZ5TECF**.

Current Science Check out Current Science® articles related to this chapter by visiting go.hrw.com. Just type in the keyword **HZ5CS07**.

People in Science

Teaching Strategy — GENERAL

Many geologists ridiculed Wegener's hypothesis because they had been taught that continents and ocean basins were in fixed positions. These scientists knew of no force that could move an entire continent, and they discounted the evidence that continental drift had occurred.

The formation of a new hypothesis is an essential part of scientific inquiry. Yet, scientists are often met with opposition when they challenge conventional theories. Encourage students to investigate other scientists whose hypotheses were rejected during their lifetime but later were accepted. Students may want to explore the controversial hypotheses of Copernicus, Mendel, or Darwin or explore some modern controversies in the scientific community.

CONNECTION ACTIVITY
Math — BASIC

Breaking Up Is Hard to Do
The distance between New York and Paris increases every year. Currently, the two cities are moving apart by about 2 cm per year. Have students calculate the increase in distance in 1 million years. **(20 km)** Ask students how much the distance will increase in 100 million years. **(2,000 km)**
LS Logical

Answers to Math Activity
7,200 km = 720,000,000 cm;
720,000,000 cm ÷ 3.5 cm/y = 206,000,000 years ago

8 Earthquakes
Chapter Planning Guide

Compression guide: To shorten instruction because of time limitations, omit the Chapter Lab.

OBJECTIVES	LABS, DEMONSTRATIONS, AND ACTIVITIES	TECHNOLOGY RESOURCES
PACING • 90 min pp. 222–229 **Chapter Opener**	SE Start-up Activity, p. 223 ◆ GENERAL	OSP Parent Letter ■ GENERAL CD Student Edition on CD-ROM CD Guided Reading Audio CD ■ TR Chapter Starter Transparency* VID Brain Food Video Quiz
Section 1 What Are Earthquakes? • Explain where earthquakes take place. • Explain what causes earthquakes. • Identify three different types of faults that occur at plate boundaries. • Describe how energy from earthquakes travels through the Earth.	TE Demonstration Faults and Earthquakes, p. 225 ◆ BASIC SE Quick Lab Modeling Seismic Waves, p. 228 GENERAL CRF Datasheet for Quick Lab* SE Science in Action Math, Social Studies, and Language Arts Activities, pp. 246–247 GENERAL	CRF Lesson Plans* TR Bellringer Transparency* TR Elastic Rebound* TR LINK TO PHYSICAL SCIENCE Comparing Transverse and Longitudinal Waves* TR Primary Waves; Secondary Waves; Surface Waves* CRF SciLinks Activity* GENERAL
PACING • 45 min pp. 230–233 **Section 2 Earthquake Measurement** • Explain how earthquakes are detected. • Describe how to locate an earthquake's epicenter. • Explain how the strength of an earthquake is measured. • Explain how the intensity of an earthquake is measured.	TE Activity Exploring a Seismic Network, p. 230 GENERAL SE Skills Practice Lab Earthquake Waves, p. 729 GENERAL CRF Datasheet for LabBook* LB Long-Term Projects & Research Ideas A Whole Lotta Shakin'* ADVANCED	CRF Lesson Plans* TR Bellringer Transparency* TR Finding an Earthquake's Epicenter*
PACING • 90 min pp. 234–239 **Section 3 Earthquakes and Society** • Explain how earthquake-hazard level is determined. • Compare methods of earthquake forecasting. • Describe five ways to safeguard buildings against earthquakes. • Outline earthquake safety procedures.	TE Connection Activity Art, p. 234 GENERAL TE Connection Activity Math, p. 235 GENERAL TE Activity Tools of the Trade, p. 236 ADVANCED TE Demonstration Flexible Buildings, p. 237 BASIC TE Connection Activity Real Life, p. 237 ◆ GENERAL SE Connection to Physics Earthquake Proof Buildings, p. 238 GENERAL SE School-to-Home Activity Disaster Planning, p. 239 GENERAL SE Inquiry Lab Quake Challenge, p. 240 ◆ GENERAL CRF Datasheet for Chapter Lab* LB Whiz-Bang Demonstrations When Buildings Boogie* ◆ GENERAL	CRF Lesson Plans* TR Bellringer Transparency* SE Internet Activity, p. 235 GENERAL VID Lab Videos for Earth Science

PACING • 90 min

CHAPTER REVIEW, ASSESSMENT, AND STANDARDIZED TEST PREPARATION

- CRF Vocabulary Activity* GENERAL
- SE Chapter Review, pp. 242–243 GENERAL
- CRF Chapter Review* ■ GENERAL
- CRF Chapter Tests A* ■ GENERAL, B* ADVANCED, C* SPECIAL NEEDS
- SE Standardized Test Preparation, pp. 244–245 GENERAL
- CRF Standardized Test Preparation* GENERAL
- CRF Performance-Based Assessment* GENERAL
- OSP Test Generator GENERAL
- CRF Test Item Listing* GENERAL

Online and Technology Resources

go.hrw.com
Visit go.hrw.com for a variety of free resources related to this textbook. Enter the keyword HZ5EQK.

Holt Online Learning
Students can access interactive problem-solving help and active visual concept development with the Holt Science and Technology Online Edition available at www.hrw.com.

Guided Reading Audio CD
Also in Spanish
A direct reading of each chapter for auditory learners, reluctant readers, and Spanish-speaking students.

Science Tutor CD-ROM
Excellent for remediation and test practice.

KEY						
SE	Student Edition	CRF	Chapter Resource File	SS	Science Skills Worksheets	* Also on One-Stop Planner
TE	Teacher Edition	OSP	One-Stop Planner	MS	Math Skills for Science Worksheets	◆ Requires advance prep
		LB	Lab Bank	CD	CD or CD-ROM	■ Also available in Spanish
		TR	Transparencies	VID	Classroom Video/DVD	

SKILLS DEVELOPMENT RESOURCES	SECTION REVIEW AND ASSESSMENT	STANDARDS CORRELATIONS
SE Pre-Reading Activity, p. 222 GENERAL OSP Science Puzzlers, Twisters & Teasers GENERAL		National Science Education Standards SAI 1, 2
CRF Directed Reading A* ■ BASIC, B* SPECIAL NEEDS CRF Vocabulary and Section Summary* ■ GENERAL SE Reading Strategy Paired Summarizing, p. 224 GENERAL TE Inclusion Strategies, p. 228	SE Reading Checks, pp. 225, 227, 229 GENERAL TE Homework, p. 225 ADVANCED TE Homework, p. 226 GENERAL TE Reteaching, p. 228 BASIC TE Quiz, p. 228 GENERAL TE Alternative Assessment, p. 228 GENERAL SE Section Review,* p. 229 ■ GENERAL CRF Section Quiz* ■ GENERAL	UCP 2; SAI 1, 2; SPSP 3, 4; ES 1b
CRF Directed Reading A* ■ BASIC, B* SPECIAL NEEDS CRF Vocabulary and Section Summary* ■ GENERAL SE Reading Strategy Reading Organizer, p. 230 GENERAL SE Connection to Social Studies New Madrid Earthquakes, p. 232 GENERAL CRF Reinforcement Worksheet Complete a Seismic Story* BASIC MS Math Skills for Science Earthquake Power!* GENERAL CRF Critical Thinking Nearthlings Unite!* ADVANCED	SE Reading Checks, pp. 230, 232 GENERAL TE Reteaching, p. 232 BASIC TE Quiz, p. 232 GENERAL TE Alternative Assessment, p. 232 GENERAL SE Section Review,* p. 233 ■ GENERAL CRF Section Quiz* ■ GENERAL	UCP 3; SAI 1, 2; ST 2; ES 1b; *LabBook:* UCP 3; SAI 2; SPSP 3, 4; HNS 1, 3
CRF Directed Reading A* ■ BASIC, B* SPECIAL NEEDS CRF Vocabulary and Section Summary* ■ GENERAL TE Reading Strategy Discussion, p. 234 GENERAL TE Reading Strategy Prediction Guide, p. 235 GENERAL TE Inclusion Strategies, p. 238 ◆ MS Math Skills for Science Dividing Whole Numbers with Long Division* GENERAL	SE Reading Checks, pp. 235, 236, 238 GENERAL TE Homework, p. 236 GENERAL TE Reteaching, p. 238 BASIC TE Quiz, p. 238 GENERAL TE Alternative Assessment, p. 238 GENERAL SE Section Review,* p. 239 ■ GENERAL CRF Section Quiz* ■ GENERAL	UCP 2, 3; SAI 1; ST 2; SPSP 1, 3, 4, 5; ES 1b; *Chapter Lab:* UCP 2, 5; SAI 1; ST 1; SPSP 5

One-Stop Planner® CD-ROM

This convenient CD-ROM includes:
- Lab Materials QuickList Software
- Holt Calendar Planner
- Customizable Lesson Plans
- Printable Worksheets
- ExamView® Test Generator

CNN Student News

cnnstudentnews.com

Find the latest news, lesson plans, and activities related to important scientific events.

SciLinks NSTA

www.scilinks.org

Maintained by the **National Science Teachers Association**. See Chapter Enrichment pages for a complete list of topics.

Current Science®

Check out *Current Science* articles and activities by visiting the HRW Web site at **go.hrw.com.** Just type in the keyword **HZ5CS08T.**

Classroom Videos

- **Lab Videos** demonstrate the chapter lab.
- **Brain Food Video Quizzes** help students review the chapter material.
- **CNN Videos** bring science into your students' daily life.

8 Chapter Resources

Visual Resources

CHAPTER STARTER TRANSPARENCY

BELLRINGER TRANSPARENCIES

TEACHING TRANSPARENCIES

TEACHING TRANSPARENCIES

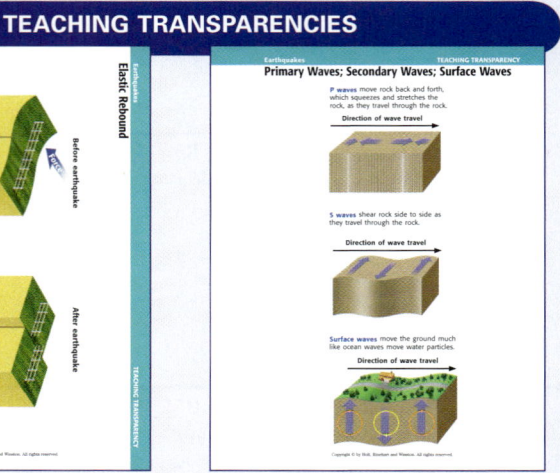

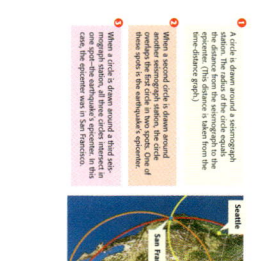

CONCEPT MAPPING TRANSPARENCY

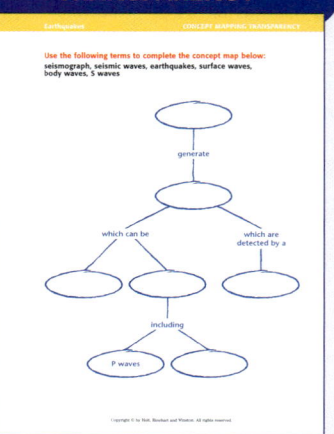

Planning Resources

LESSON PLANS

PARENT LETTER

TEST ITEM LISTING

One-Stop Planner® CD-ROM

This CD-ROM includes all of the resources shown here and the following time-saving tools:

- Lab Materials QuickList Software
- Customizable lesson plans
- Holt Calendar Planner
- The powerful ExamView® Test Generator

221C Chapter 8 • Earthquakes

For a preview of available worksheets covering math and science skills, see pages T26–T33. All of these resources are also on the One-Stop Planner®.

Meeting Individual Needs

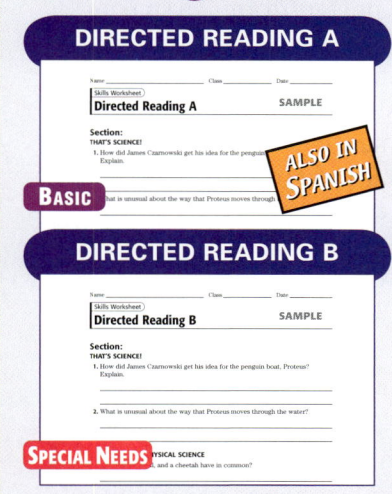

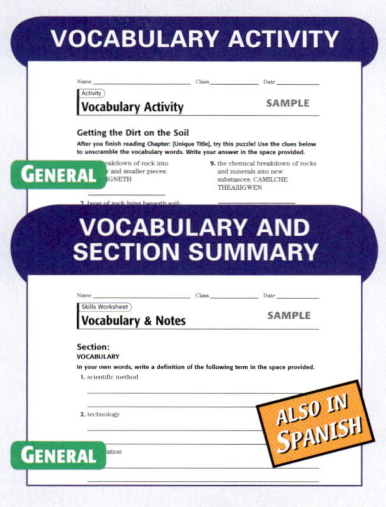

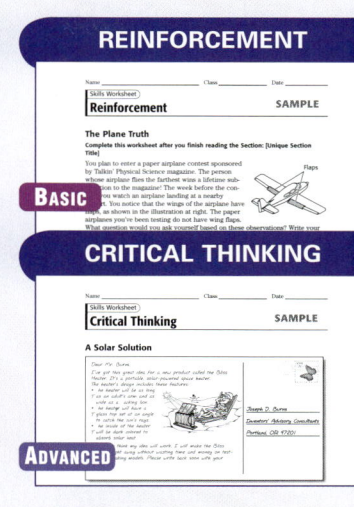

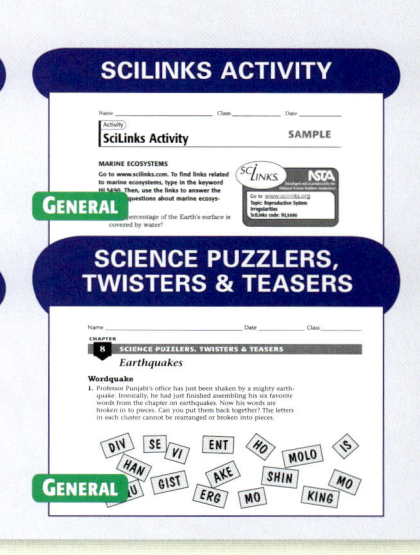

- **DIRECTED READING A** — BASIC / ALSO IN SPANISH
- **DIRECTED READING B** — SPECIAL NEEDS
- **VOCABULARY ACTIVITY** — GENERAL
- **VOCABULARY AND SECTION SUMMARY** — GENERAL / ALSO IN SPANISH
- **REINFORCEMENT** — BASIC
- **CRITICAL THINKING** — ADVANCED
- **SCILINKS ACTIVITY** — GENERAL
- **SCIENCE PUZZLERS, TWISTERS & TEASERS** — GENERAL

Labs and Activities

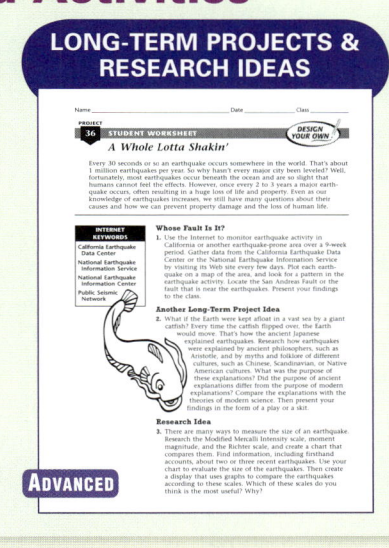

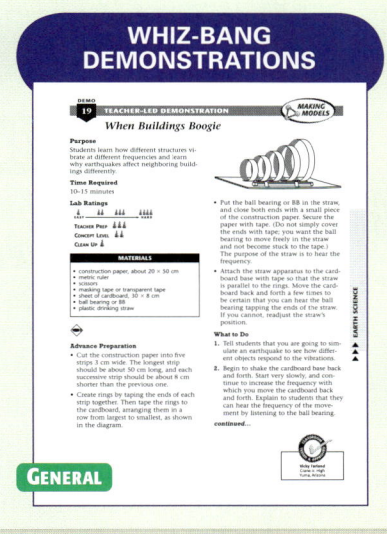

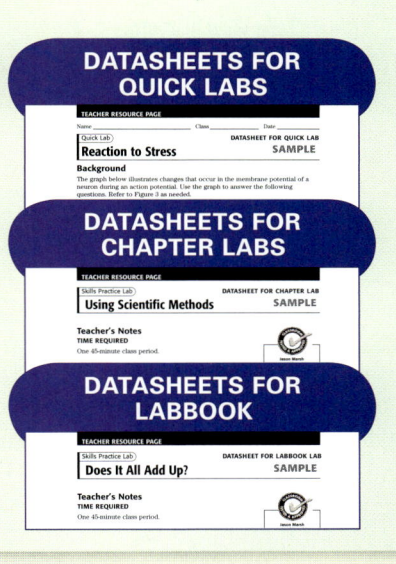

- **LONG-TERM PROJECTS & RESEARCH IDEAS** — ADVANCED
- **WHIZ-BANG DEMONSTRATIONS** — GENERAL
- **DATASHEETS FOR QUICK LABS**
- **DATASHEETS FOR CHAPTER LABS**
- **DATASHEETS FOR LABBOOK**

Review and Assessments

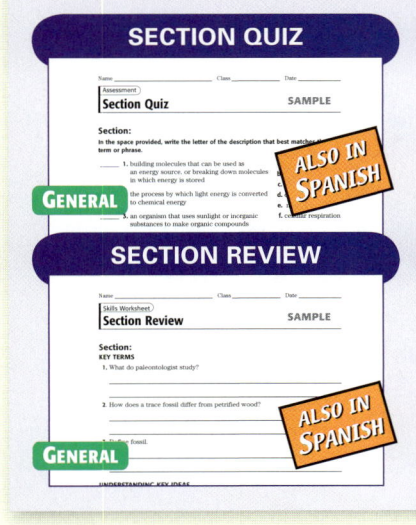

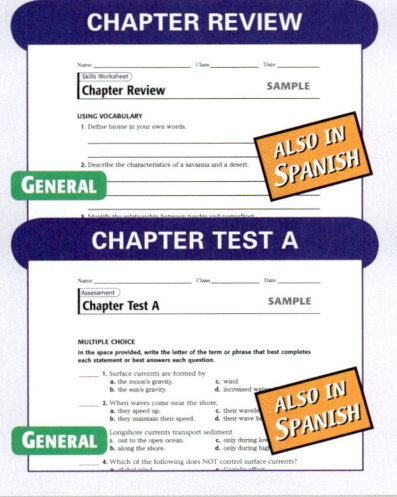

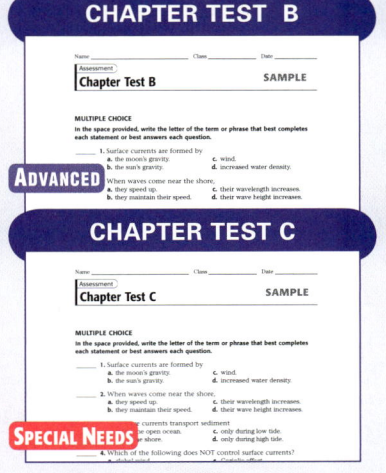

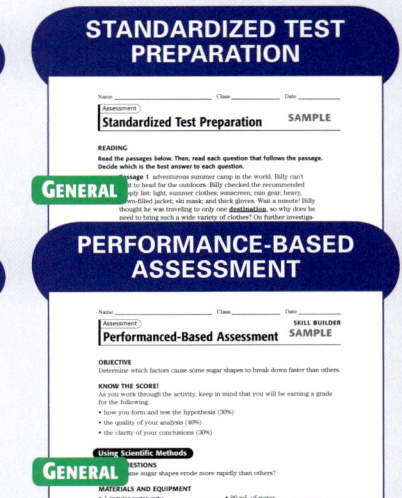

- **SECTION QUIZ** — GENERAL / ALSO IN SPANISH
- **SECTION REVIEW** — GENERAL / ALSO IN SPANISH
- **CHAPTER REVIEW** — GENERAL / ALSO IN SPANISH
- **CHAPTER TEST A** — GENERAL / ALSO IN SPANISH
- **CHAPTER TEST B** — ADVANCED
- **CHAPTER TEST C** — SPECIAL NEEDS
- **STANDARDIZED TEST PREPARATION** — GENERAL
- **PERFORMANCE-BASED ASSESSMENT** — GENERAL

Chapter 8 • Chapter Resources   221D

8 Chapter Enrichment

This Chapter Enrichment provides relevant and interesting information to expand and enhance your presentation of the chapter material.

Section 1

What Are Earthquakes?

Earthquake Origins

- Earthquakes originate at different depths. Shallow earthquakes are those that originate within about 60 km of Earth's surface. Intermediate-depth earthquakes originate between depths of about 60 km and 300 km. Deep earthquakes originate below 300 km.

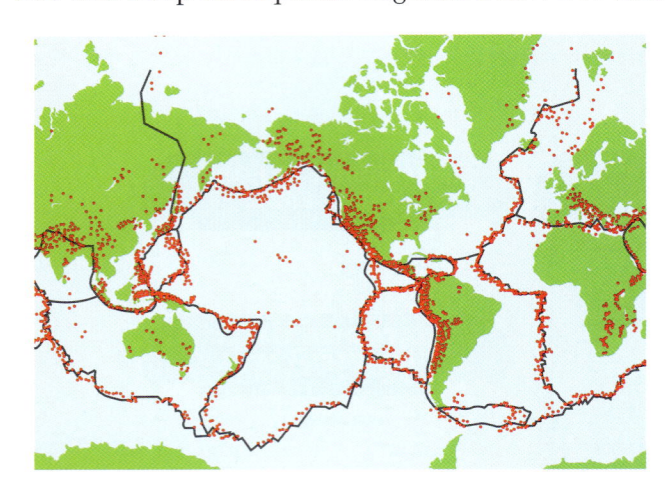

- Tectonic activity is not the only source of earthquakes. Earthquakes can also be caused by volcanic eruptions and by the impacts of cosmic bodies. These earthquakes, however, are less common than those occurring along faults.

The New Madrid Earthquakes

- Eyewitnesses to the 1811–1812 earthquakes in New Madrid, Missouri, reported seeing bright flashes of light and a dull glow in the sky over a wide area. Reeking sulfurous odors also accompanied the quakes. Many survivors were convinced that the quakes were a heavenly sign meant to frighten the local citizens back to church. As a result, church attendance in the area rose between 1811 and 1812!

The Punishment of Loki

- In Scandinavian mythology, earthquakes are believed to be caused by the clever prankster Loki. The gods decided to punish Loki when they discovered that he had killed Balder, the god of light and joy. Loki was chained in a deep cave, and a huge, poisonous snake was hung above him. As the poison from the snake's fangs dripped down, Loki's sister tried to protect him by catching the poison in a cup. Sometimes, however, a drop of poison would splash Loki, causing him unbearable pain. At those times, he would pull so violently on his chains that the ground above would tremble.

Is That a Fact!

- In 1755, in Lisbon, Portugal, an earthquake occurred that killed an estimated 60,000 people. Because it happened near midday on a religious holiday, many fatalities occurred when churches collapsed on churchgoers. This tragedy resulted in an analytic and systematic approach to studying earthquakes, the basis of seismology.

Section 2

Earthquake Measurement

Chinese Earthquake Measurement

- A Chinese man named Chang Heng designed the first known "earthquake detector" around 132 CE. Heng's earthquake detector was a bronze urn decorated with six dragons' heads. Each head held a bronze ball in its mouth. A pendulum was suspended inside the urn. During a tremor, the pendulum would strike the urn, causing one of the balls to drop into the mouth of a bronze toad below. The ball would make a loud noise, signaling the occurrence of an earthquake. By noting which ball fell, people could supposedly determine the direction of the earthquake's epicenter.

Magnitude Versus Intensity

- Earthquakes can be measured by magnitude or intensity. An earthquake's magnitude is a quantitative measurement of its strength. The Richter scale, and other, more modern scales, are used to measure magnitude. Intensity is a qualitative measurement of an earthquake's effect in a particular area. The Modified Mercalli Intensity Scale is used to assess shaking. This scale incorporates observations of the earthquake's effects at a particular location. Although an earthquake may have different intensities at different locations, it has only one magnitude.

Is That a Fact!

◆ The strongest earthquake recorded since the invention of seismographs occurred in Chile in 1960. It measured 9.5 on the Richter scale. This magnitude is equivalent to detonating more than 1 billion tons of TNT!

Section 3
Earthquakes and Society

Magnetometers

- Magnetometers are devices that measure changes in the Earth's magnetic field. Some theories suggest that changes in the Earth's magnetic field might be indicative of an upcoming earthquake, although such theories are controversial.

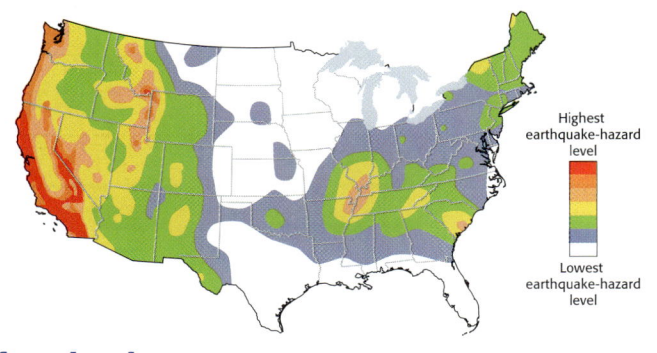

Aftershocks

- Aftershocks occur in sequences that take place within a particular time frame. They are most numerous after an earthquake and decrease with time. The largest aftershocks often occur within hours of an earthquake. These aftershocks can be the same size or smaller than the earthquake they follow. However, seismologists have found that the number of aftershocks decreases, but their magnitude does not necessarily decrease. Therefore, large aftershocks can occur months after an earthquake. Aftershocks may also produce their own subsequences, with an aftershock generating other aftershocks.

Survival of Structures

- The ability of a structure to withstand a quake depends on a variety of factors, including the composition of the ground on which the structure stands. Structures built on waterlogged or unconsolidated sediment, such as sand, are more likely to suffer intense damage than structures built on bedrock.

Is That a Fact!

◆ Sand boils are common during earthquakes that occur in areas with unconsolidated sediments. Loose, sandy sediments behave as fluids do as the ground moves. This condition can create a miniature "geyser" that spews buried debris from beneath the Earth's surface.

◆ One of the best structures for resisting damage from earthquakes is a wood-framed building. Wood-framed buildings are not very rigid and can therefore flex quite a bit without collapsing.

SciLinks — Developed and maintained by the National Science Teachers Association

SciLinks is maintained by the National Science Teachers Association to provide you and your students with interesting, up-to-date links that will enrich your classroom presentation of the chapter.

Visit www.scilinks.org and enter the SciLinks code for more information about the topic listed.

Topic: What Is an Earthquake?
SciLinks code: HSM1658

Topic: Earthquakes and Society
SciLinks code: HSM0455

Topic: Earthquake Measurement
SciLinks code: HSM0452

Chapter 8 • Chapter Enrichment **221F**

Overview

Tell students that this chapter will help them learn about earthquakes. The chapter is an introduction to the geophysical concepts that seismologists use in the study of earthquakes.

Assessing Prior Knowledge

Students should be familiar with the following topics:
- plate tectonics
- faults

Identifying Misconceptions

Students often assume that earthquakes are relatively rare phenomena. Point out that thousands of small earthquakes happen every day. Also, students may assume that earthquakes occur only near plate boundaries, in areas such as southern California. Point out that earthquakes can happen far from plate boundaries, for example, in places such as Charleston, South Carolina. Finally, students may think that the loss of life that occurs during an earthquake is a direct result of Earth movement. Point out that the majority of deaths are caused by the collapse of buildings and the disease and famine that may result from the disruption of infrastructure.

8 Earthquakes

SECTION 1	What Are Earthquakes?	224
SECTION 2	Earthquake Measurement	230
SECTION 3	Earthquakes and Society	234

Chapter Lab 240
Chapter Review 242
Standardized Test Preparation 244
Science in Action 246

About the PHOTO

On January 17, 1995, an earthquake of magnitude 7.0 shook the area in and around Kobe, Japan. Though the earthquake lasted for less than a minute, more than 5,000 people lost their lives and another 300,000 people were left homeless. More than 200,000 buildings were damaged or destroyed. Large sections of the elevated Hanshin Expressway, shown in the photo, toppled when the columns supporting the expressway failed. The expressway passed over ground that was soft and wet, where the shaking was stronger and longer lasting.

PRE-READING ACTIVITY

Spider Map Before you read the chapter, create the graphic organizer entitled "Spider Map" described in the **Study Skills** section of the Appendix. Label the circle "Earthquakes." Create a leg for each of the sections in this chapter. As you read the chapter, fill in the map with details about the material presented in each section of the chapter.

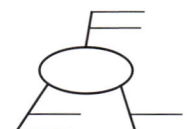

Standards Correlations

National Science Education Standards

The following codes indicate the National Science Education Standards that correlate to this chapter. The full text of the standards is at the front of the book.

Chapter Opener
SAI 1, 2

Section 1 What Are Earthquakes?
UCP 2; SAI 1, 2; SPSP 3, 4; ES 1b

Section 2 Earthquake Measurement
UCP 3; HNS 1, 3; SPSP 3,4; ST 2; SAI 1, 2; *LabBook:* SAI 1, SAI 2

Section 3 Earthquakes and Society
UCP 2, 3; SAI 1; ST 2; SPSP 1, 3, 4, 5; ES 1b; HNS 2

Chapter Lab
SAI 1, 2

Chapter Review
UCP 2, 3; ES 1b; ST 2; SPSP 1, 3, 4; HNS 2; SAI 1, 2

Science in Action
UCP 2; ES 1b; ST 2; SPSP 3, 5; HNS 1, 2, 3; SAI 1, 2

222 Chapter 8 • Earthquakes

START-UP ACTIVITY

Bend, Break, or Shake

In this activity, you will test different materials in a model earthquake setting.

Procedure

1. Gather a **small wooden stick**, a **wire clothes hanger**, and a **plastic clothes hanger**.
2. Draw a straight line on a **sheet of paper**. Use a **protractor** to measure and draw the following angles from the line: 20°, 45°, and 90°.
3. Put on your **safety goggles**. Using the angles that you drew as a guide, try bending each item 20° and then releasing it. What happens? Does it break? If it bends, does it return to its original shape?
4. Repeat step 3, but bend each item 45°. Repeat the test again, but bend each item 90°.

Analysis

1. How do the different materials' responses to bending compare?
2. Where earthquakes happen, engineers use building materials that are flexible but that do not break or stay bent. Which materials from this experiment would you want building materials to behave like? Explain your answer.

START-UP ACTIVITY

MATERIALS

FOR EACH GROUP
- clothes hanger, plastic
- clothes hanger, wire
- goggles, safety
- paper (1 per student)
- protractor (1 per student)
- stick, wooden, small

Safety Caution: Remind students to review all safety cautions and icons before beginning this lab activity.

Teacher's Note: Assist students who have difficulty using the protractors. You may want to provide them with paper on which the angles have already been drawn.

Answers

1. Answers may vary depending on the materials used and on the strength of the materials. The wooden stick would most likely break at greater angles, the wire hanger would bend, and the plastic hanger would bend but return to its original shape.
2. Answers may vary. Desirable building materials would behave in the same way as the materials that did not break or bend permanently.

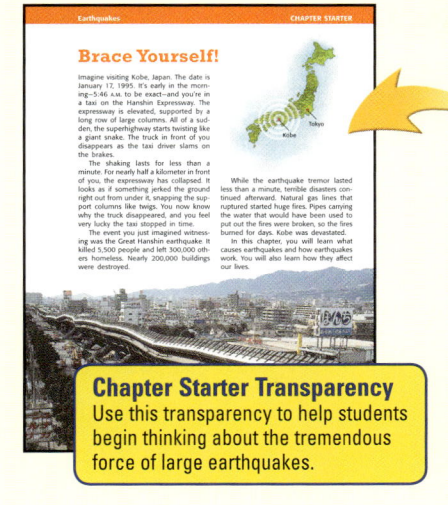

Chapter Starter Transparency
Use this transparency to help students begin thinking about the tremendous force of large earthquakes.

CHAPTER RESOURCES

Technology

- **Transparencies** — READING SKILLS
  - Chapter Starter Transparency
- **Student Edition on CD-ROM**
- **Guided Reading Audio CD**
  - English or Spanish
- **Classroom Videos**
  - Brain Food Video Quiz

Workbooks

- **Science Puzzlers, Twisters & Teasers**
  - Earthquakes GENERAL

Chapter 8 • Earthquakes

SECTION 1

Focus

Overview
This section discusses the seismic events known as earthquakes. Students learn where earthquakes most commonly occur and what causes them. The section also covers different kinds of faults and discusses how earthquakes travel as waves of energy through the Earth.

🔔 Bellringer
Ask students to write a few sentences describing what they think an earthquake is. Ask students to review what they wrote after completing this section.

Motivate

Discussion — GENERAL
Seismic Definitions Explain to students that *seismos* is a Greek word that means "to shake." Have students make a list of all the words that contain the root *seis-*. (These include *seismology, seismologist, seismic, seismograph, Seismosaurus,* and *seismogram.*) Have students copy the words onto a sheet of paper and consult a dictionary to divide each word into its proper parts. Then, have students define each word part and write a definition of each complete term using the meanings of its parts. **LS Logical** English Language Learners

SECTION 1

What Are Earthquakes?

Have you ever felt the earth move under your feet? Many people have. Every day, somewhere within this planet, an earthquake is happening.

READING WARM-UP

Objectives
- Explain where earthquakes take place.
- Explain what causes earthquakes.
- Identify three different types of faults that occur at plate boundaries.
- Describe how energy from earthquakes travels through the Earth.

Terms to Learn
seismology
deformation
elastic rebound
seismic waves
P waves
S waves

READING STRATEGY
Paired Summarizing Read this section silently. In pairs, take turns summarizing the material. Stop to discuss ideas that seem confusing.

The word *earthquake* defines itself fairly well. But there is more to earthquakes than just the shaking of the ground. An entire branch of Earth science, called **seismology** (siez MAHL uh jee), is devoted to studying earthquakes. Earthquakes are complex, and they present many questions for *seismologists*, the scientists who study earthquakes.

Where Do Earthquakes Occur?
Most earthquakes take place near the edges of tectonic plates. *Tectonic plates* are giant pieces of Earth's thin, outermost layer. Tectonic plates move around on top of a layer of plastic rock. **Figure 1** shows the Earth's tectonic plates and the locations of recent major earthquakes.

Tectonic plates move in different directions and at different speeds. Two plates can push toward or pull away from each other. They can also slip slowly past each other. As a result of these movements, numerous features called faults exist in the Earth's crust. A *fault* is a break in the Earth's crust along which blocks of the crust slide relative to one another. Earthquakes occur along faults because of this sliding.

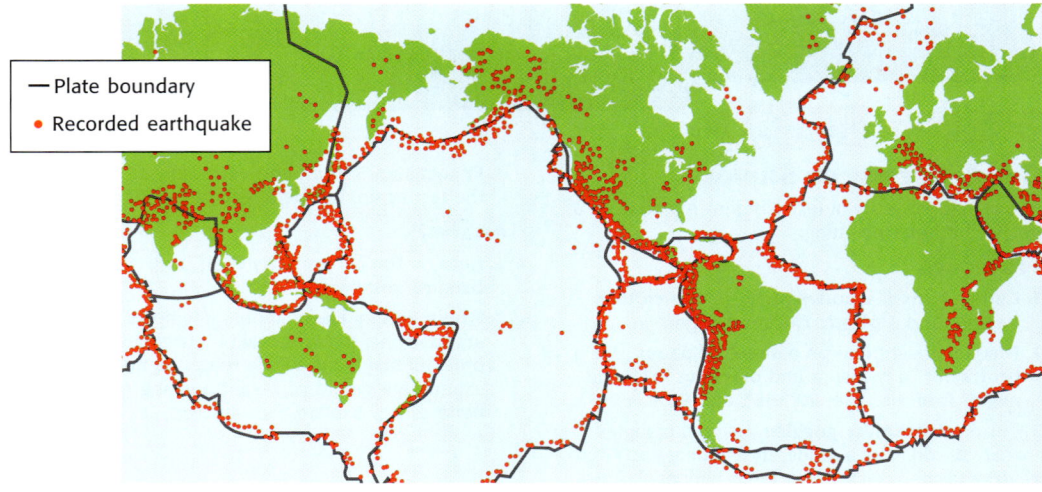

Figure 1 The largest and most active earthquake zone lies along the plate boundaries surrounding the Pacific Ocean.

— Plate boundary
• Recorded earthquake

CHAPTER RESOURCES

Chapter Resource File
- Lesson Plan
- Directed Reading A BASIC
- Directed Reading B SPECIAL NEEDS

Technology
- Transparencies
  - Bellringer
  - Elastic Rebound

MISCONCEPTION ALERT
Earthquake Frequency Earthquakes are not a rare phenomenon. In fact, more than 3 million earthquakes with Richter magnitudes of 1 or more happen each year—about one every 10 seconds! Most earthquakes are too weak to be felt by humans. The Ring of Fire, a volcanic zone that lies along the plate boundaries surrounding the Pacific Ocean, is the world's largest and most active earthquake zone.

224 Chapter 8 • Earthquakes

What Causes Earthquakes?

As tectonic plates push, pull, or slip past each other, stress increases along faults near the plates' edges. In response to this stress, rock in the plates deforms. **Deformation** is the change in the shape of rock in response to stress. Rock along a fault deforms in mainly two ways. It deforms in a plastic manner, like a piece of molded clay, or in an elastic manner, like a rubber band. *Plastic deformation*, which is shown in **Figure 2**, does not lead to earthquakes.

Elastic deformation, however, does lead to earthquakes. Rock can stretch farther without breaking than steel can, but rock will break at some point. Think of elastically deformed rock as a stretched rubber band. You can stretch a rubber band only so far before it breaks. When the rubber band breaks, it releases energy. Then, the broken pieces return to their unstretched shape.

Figure 2 This road cut is adjacent to the San Andreas Fault in southern California. The rocks in the cut have undergone deformation because of the continuous motion of the fault.

Elastic Rebound

The sudden return of elastically deformed rock to its original shape is called **elastic rebound.** Elastic rebound is like the return of the broken rubber-band pieces to their unstretched shape. Elastic rebound occurs when more stress is applied to rock than the rock can withstand. During elastic rebound, energy is released. Some of this energy travels as seismic waves. These seismic waves cause an earthquake, as shown in **Figure 3**.

seismology the study of earthquakes

deformation the bending, tilting, and breaking of the Earth's crust; the change in the shape of rock in response to stress

elastic rebound the sudden return of elastically deformed rock to its undeformed shape

✓ **Reading Check** How does elastic rebound relate to earthquakes? (*See the Appendix for answers to Reading Checks.*)

Figure 3 Elastic Rebound and Earthquakes

Before earthquake

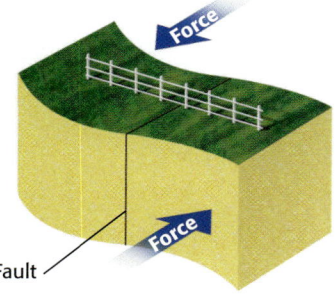

After earthquake

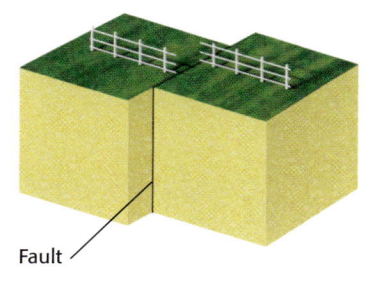

Fault

Fault

❶ Tectonic forces push rock on either side of the fault in opposite directions, but the rock is locked together and does not move. The rock deforms in an elastic manner.

❷ When enough stress is applied, the rock slips along the fault and releases energy.

Answer to Reading Check
During elastic rebound, rock releases energy. Some of this energy travels as seismic waves that cause earthquakes.

Homework — ADVANCED

Mapping Have students create an earthquake map using data from Internet sites that contain a log of the time and location of earthquakes around the world. This activity will help students understand that earthquakes occur every day, mainly near tectonic plate boundaries. This activity can become an ongoing investigation in which students keep records of earthquakes during the school year. **LS Visual**

Teach

Demonstration — BASIC

Faults and Earthquakes Use two smooth wooden blocks to demonstrate how blocks of crust move along a fault. Glue coarse sandpaper onto one side of each block. Firmly slide the sandpaper-covered sides against each other until there is a sudden movement. Explain that this model shows how rock slides along a fault during elastic rebound. As the rock slides, it releases energy that travels as waves. **LS Visual** — English Language Learners

Cultural Awareness — GENERAL

Earthquake Mythology Many different cultures have myths about earthquakes. According to Japanese mythology, earthquakes are caused by the *namazu*, a giant catfish that lives in mud beneath the Earth. *Kamisha*, a brave warrior, protects Japan from earthquakes by using divine powers to trap the *namazu* under an enormous rock. Earthquakes occur when *Kamisha* lets his guard down and allows the *namazu* to thrash about. Encourage students to research other cultural myths about earthquakes and to share their research with the class. Students can also write their own legend about the origin of earthquakes. **LS Verbal**

Section 1 • What Are Earthquakes?

Teach, continued

Using the Figure —GENERAL

Faults and Tectonics Each circle in the figure is a magnified view of a fault at the edge of a tectonic plate. In fact, large systems of multiple faults define the boundaries between plates. The sliding of crust along these faults and the overall movement of crust along plate boundaries are similar. For example, the block of crust to the right of the reverse fault moves down relative to the block to the left of the fault. Similarly, the plate to the right of the convergent plate boundary moves down relative to the plate to the left of the boundary. **LS Visual/Logical**

Homework —GENERAL

Illustrating Faults Ask students to draw the three types of faults illustrated on these pages. Students should label each fault and state the type of plate motion that creates each fault. Encourage students to locate an example of each type of tectonic plate boundary on a map. (An example of a transform plate boundary is the San Andreas Fault in California; an example of a convergent plate boundary is off the west coast of South America; an example of a divergent plate boundary is the Mid-Atlantic Ridge, on the bottom of the Atlantic Ocean.) **LS Visual** **English Language Learners**

Faults at Tectonic Plate Boundaries

A specific type of plate motion takes place at different tectonic plate boundaries. Each type of motion creates a particular kind of fault that can produce earthquakes. Examine **Table 1** and the diagram below to learn more about plate motion.

Table 1 **Plate Motion and Fault Types**

Plate motion	Major fault type
Transform	strike-slip fault
Convergent	reverse fault
Divergent	normal fault

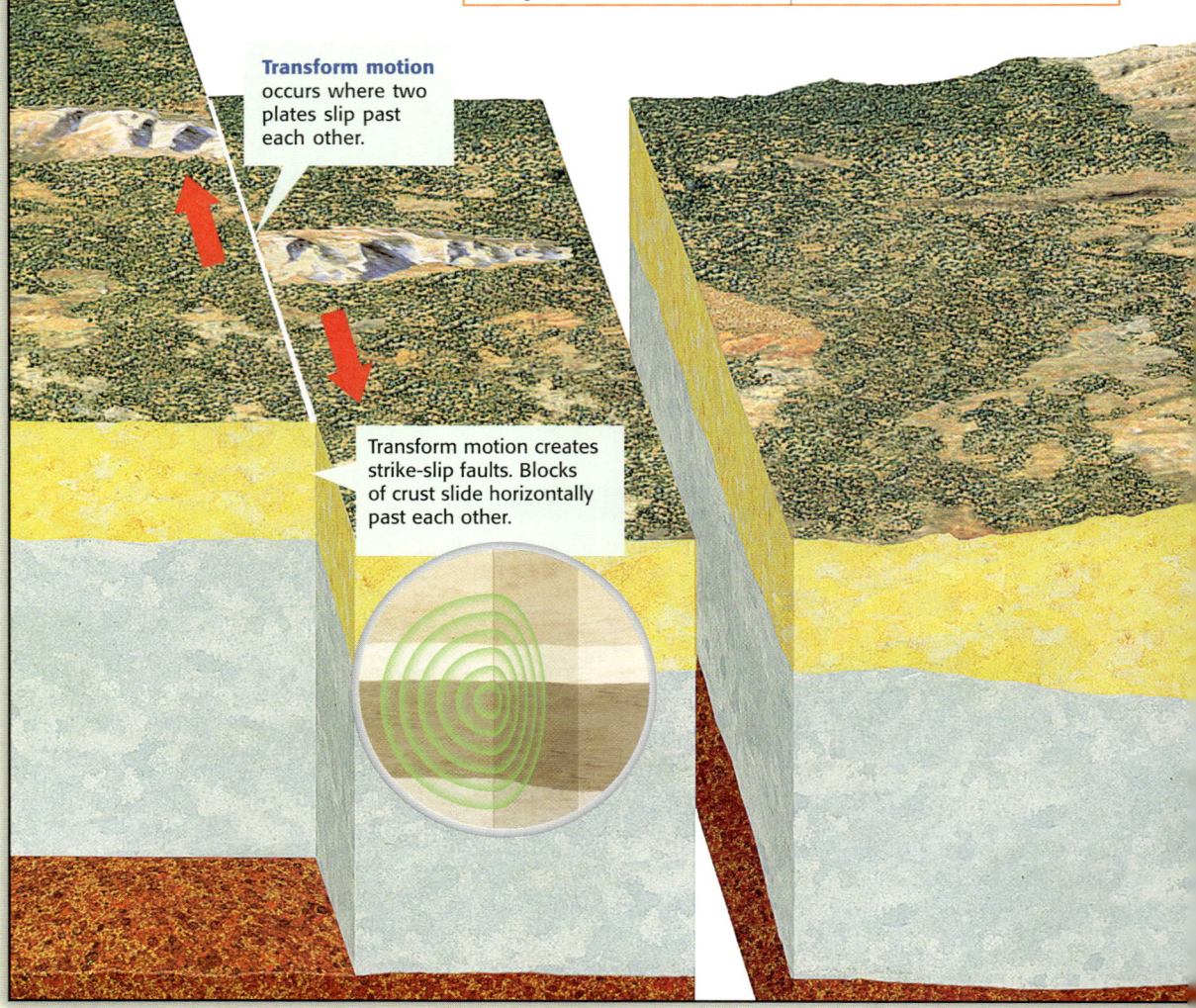

Transform motion occurs where two plates slip past each other.

Transform motion creates strike-slip faults. Blocks of crust slide horizontally past each other.

MISCONCEPTION ALERT

Aftershocks A general misconception is that aftershocks do not present the same level of danger as the earthquake, or mainshock, that they follow. Seismological evidence has proven that the opposite can be true. Aftershocks can be powerful earthquakes. An aftershock of magnitude 6.5 followed 3 hours after the 1992 magnitude 7.3 Landers earthquake! Aftershocks can be as damaging as, or even more damaging than, a mainshock. The reasons are that building damage is cumulative and aftershocks vary in location and in the pattern of radiation from the mainshock.

226 Chapter 8 • Earthquakes

Earthquake Zones

Earthquakes can happen both near Earth's surface or far below it. Most earthquakes happen in the earthquake zones along tectonic plate boundaries. Earthquake zones are places where a large number of faults are located. The San Andreas Fault Zone in California is an example of an earthquake zone. But not all faults are located at tectonic plate boundaries. Sometimes, earthquakes happen along faults in the middle of tectonic plates.

Reading Check Where are earthquake zones located?

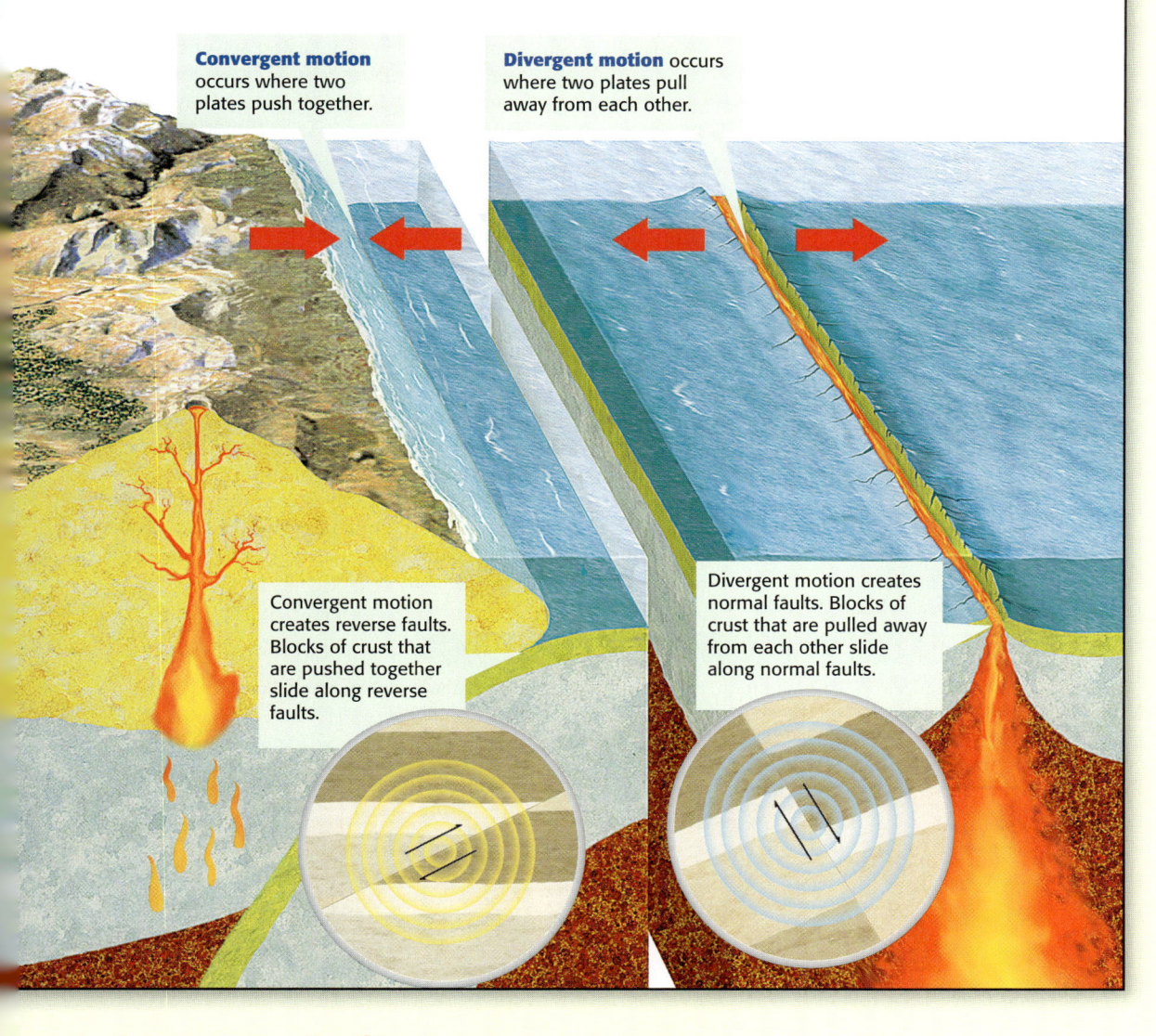

Convergent motion occurs where two plates push together.

Divergent motion occurs where two plates pull away from each other.

Convergent motion creates reverse faults. Blocks of crust that are pushed together slide along reverse faults.

Divergent motion creates normal faults. Blocks of crust that are pulled away from each other slide along normal faults.

MISCONCEPTION ALERT

Earthquakes in the Continental Interior
Many people assume that major earthquakes in the United States occur only on the West Coast. However, major quakes have occurred in South Carolina and Missouri—far from any active plate boundaries. The three major tremors of the 1811–1812 earthquakes in New Madrid, Missouri, were so intense that, according to reports, they altered the flow of the Mississippi River! In the late 1970s, scientists found a series of faults deep beneath sediment deposited by the Mississippi River. The area is still seismically active, and large earthquakes may still occur.

Answer to Reading Check
Earthquake zones are usually located along tectonic plate boundaries.

Section 1 • What Are Earthquakes?

Close

Answers to Quick Lab

4. P waves are represented in step 2; S waves are represented in step 3.

Reteaching — BASIC

P and S Waves Tell students that the *P* in P waves and the *S* in S waves each stand for two descriptive words. The letters describe how each type of wave affects rock—P stands for *pressure,* and S stands for *shear.* P also stands for *primary,* and S stands for *secondary.* This scheme describes the arrival times of each type of wave— P waves always arrive first, and S waves always arrive second. **LS** Logical

Quiz — GENERAL

1. What is a fault? (A fault is a break in the Earth's crust along which blocks of the crust slide relative to one another.)

2. How does rock that is along a fault deform in response to a decrease in stress? (Rock deforms in an elastic manner, as a rubber band does, by snapping back to its original shape.)

Alternative Assessment — GENERAL

Concept Mapping Have students create a concept map explaining the relationship between tectonic plate motion and fault types. **LS** Visual

Quick Lab

Modeling Seismic Waves

1. Stretch a **spring toy** lengthwise on a **table.**
2. Hold one end of the spring while a partner holds the other end. Push your end toward your partner's end, and observe what happens.
3. Repeat step 2, but this time shake the spring from side to side.
4. Which type of seismic wave is represented in step 2? in step 3?

seismic wave a wave of energy that travels through the Earth, away from an earthquake in all directions

P wave a seismic wave that causes particles of rock to move in a back-and-forth direction

S wave a seismic wave that causes particles of rock to move in a side-to-side direction

How Do Earthquake Waves Travel?

Waves of energy that travel through the Earth are called **seismic waves.** Seismic waves that travel through the Earth's interior are called *body waves.* There are two types of body waves: P waves and S waves. Seismic waves that travel along the Earth's surface are called *surface waves.* Each type of seismic wave travels through Earth's layers in a different way and at a different speed. Also, the speed of a seismic wave depends on the kind of material the wave travels through.

P Waves

Waves that travel through solids, liquids, and gases are called **P waves** (pressure waves). They are the fastest seismic waves, so P waves always travel ahead of other seismic waves. P waves are also called *primary waves,* because they are always the first waves of an earthquake to be detected. To understand how P waves affect rock, imagine a cube of gelatin sitting on a plate. Like most solids, gelatin is an elastic material. It wiggles if you tap it. Tapping the cube of gelatin changes the pressure inside the cube, which momentarily deforms the cube. The gelatin then reacts by springing back to its original shape. This process is how P waves affect rock, as shown in **Figure 4.**

S Waves

Rock can also be deformed from side to side. After being deformed from side to side, the rock springs back to its original position and S waves are created. **S waves,** or shear waves, are the second-fastest seismic waves. S waves shear rock side to side, as shown in **Figure 4,** which means they stretch the rock sideways. Unlike P waves, S waves cannot travel through parts of the Earth that are completely liquid. Also, S waves are slower than P waves and always arrive later. Thus, another name for S waves is *secondary waves.*

Figure 4 Body Waves

P waves move rock back and forth, which squeezes and stretches the rock, as they travel through the rock.

Direction of wave travel →

S waves shear rock side to side as they travel through the rock.

Direction of wave travel →

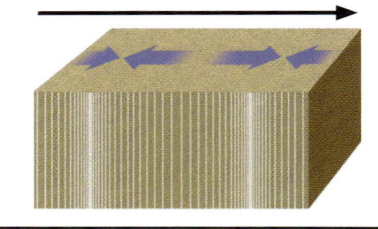

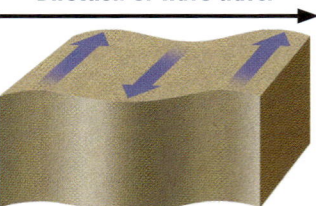

INCLUSION Strategies

- *Hearing Impaired*
- *Attention Deficit Disorder*
- *Learning Disabled*

Student groups will model pressure, shear, and surface waves. Organize students into groups of six or seven students. Move the furniture back to classroom walls. Have each group stand side by side and hold hands. Tell students that each group will have 15 seconds to gently model a P wave. Ask groups to plan their approach first, and then time them as they model a P wave. Repeat for an S wave and for a surface wave. Finally, assign three groups each one of the three waves, and have them model an earthquake. Allow them 30 seconds to complete their demonstration. **English Language Learners**
LS Interpersonal/Kinesthetic

228 Chapter 8 • Earthquakes

Surface Waves

Surface waves move along the Earth's surface and produce motion mostly in the upper few kilometers of Earth's crust. There are two types of surface waves. One type of surface wave produces motion up, down, and around, as shown in **Figure 5**. The other type produces back-and-forth motion like the motion produced by S waves. Surface waves are different from body waves in that surface waves travel more slowly and are more destructive.

Reading Check Explain the differences between surface waves and body waves.

Figure 5 Surface Waves
Surface waves move the ground much like ocean waves move water particles.

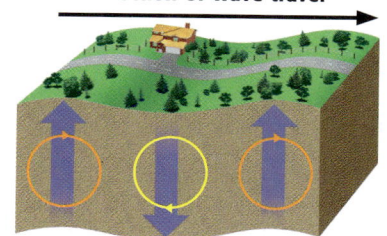

Direction of wave travel

SECTION Review

Summary

- Earthquakes occur mainly near the edges of tectonic plates.
- Elastic rebound is the direct cause of earthquakes.
- Three major types of faults occur at tectonic plate boundaries: normal faults, reverse faults, and strike-slip faults.
- Earthquake energy travels as body waves through the Earth's interior or as surface waves along the surface of the Earth.

Using Key Terms

Complete each of the following sentences by choosing the correct term from the word bank.

Deformation   P waves
Elastic rebound   S waves

1. ____ is the change in shape of rock due to stress.
2. ____ always travel ahead of other waves.

Understanding Key Ideas

3. Seismic waves that shear rock side to side are called
   a. surface waves.
   b. S waves.
   c. P waves.
   d. Both (b) and (c)
4. Where do earthquakes occur?
5. What is the direct cause of earthquakes?
6. Describe the three types of plate motion and the faults that are characteristic of each type of motion.
7. What is an earthquake zone?

Math Skills

8. A seismic wave is traveling through the Earth at an average rate of speed of 8 km/s. How long will it take the wave to travel 480 km?

Critical Thinking

9. **Applying Concepts** Given what you know about elastic rebound, why do you think some earthquakes are stronger than others?
10. **Identifying Relationships** Why are surface waves more destructive to buildings than P waves or S waves are?
11. **Identifying Relationships** Why do you think the majority of earthquake zones are located at tectonic plate boundaries?

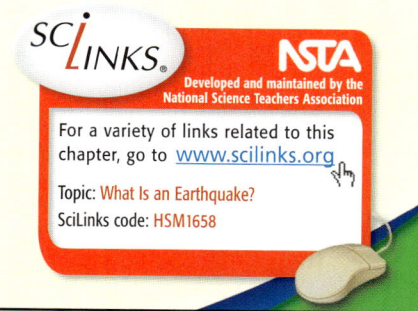

SciLinks

Developed and maintained by the National Science Teachers Association

For a variety of links related to this chapter, go to www.scilinks.org
Topic: What Is an Earthquake?
SciLinks code: HSM1658

Answers to Section Review

1. Deformation
2. P waves
3. b
4. The majority of earthquakes occur in earthquake zones along tectonic plate boundaries.
5. Earthquakes are caused by elastic rebound. When enough stress is applied to an elastically deformed rock, the rock along a fault slips and releases energy. Some of the energy travels as seismic waves, which cause an earthquake.
6. Sample answer: Convergent plate motion occurs where two plates are pushed together. It creates reverse faults. Divergent plate motion occurs where two plates pull away from each other. It creates normal faults. Transform motion occurs where two plates slip past each other. It creates strike-slip faults.
7. An earthquake zone is an area of Earth's crust where a large number of faults are located.
8. 480 km ÷ 8 km/s = 60 s = 1 min
9. Sample answer: Some earthquakes are stronger than others because a greater amount of energy is released when elastically deformed rock slips.
10. Sample answer: Surface waves are more destructive than P waves and S waves because surface waves produce ground motion in the upper few kilometers of the Earth's crust.
11. Sample answer: At tectonic plate boundaries, different types of plate motion all cause faulting.

Answer to Reading Check

Surface waves travel more slowly than body waves but are more destructive.

CONNECTION to Physical Science—ADVANCED

Seismic Waves Use the teaching transparency "Comparing Transverse and Longitudinal Waves" to discuss the differences between P waves (longitudinal) and S waves (transverse). P waves travel faster than S waves. P waves travel through solids, liquids, and gases; S waves cannot travel through materials that are completely liquid. P waves move rock back and forth between a squeezed and stretched position, and S waves shear rock back and forth.

CHAPTER RESOURCES

Chapter Resource File
- Section Quiz GENERAL
- Section Review GENERAL
- Vocabulary and Section Summary GENERAL
- SciLinks Activity GENERAL
- Datasheet for Quick Lab

Technology

Transparencies
- **LINK TO PHYSICAL SCIENCE** Comparing Transverse and Longitudinal Waves
- Primary Waves; Secondary Waves; Surface Waves

Section 1 • What Are Earthquakes?

SECTION 2

Focus

Overview
In this section, students learn how seismographs are used to detect and locate earthquakes. This section explains the difference between an earthquake's focus and epicenter. Students will also learn how the Richter scale is used to measure the magnitude of earthquakes.

🔔 Bellringer
Ask students to create a qualitative scale for gauging earthquake intensity. Students should use brief phrases to describe the effects of very minor to extreme earthquakes. Discuss the advantages and disadvantages of their finished scale.

Motivate

ACTIVITY — GENERAL

Exploring a Seismic Network
Have students locate a map on the Internet that shows worldwide seismic stations. Students should select an earthquake of magnitude 5.5 or greater that has been recorded at one of these stations during the past month. Have students find press releases that relate to the earthquake they have selected and then write a short report on the quake. **LS** Visual/Logical

---

SECTION 2

READING WARM-UP

Objectives
- Explain how earthquakes are detected.
- Describe how to locate an earthquake's epicenter.
- Explain how the strength of an earthquake is measured.
- Explain how the intensity of an earthquake is measured.

Terms to Learn
seismograph   epicenter
seismogram   focus

READING STRATEGY

Reading Organizer As you read this section, create an outline of the section. Use the headings from the section in your outline.

seismograph an instrument that records vibrations in the ground and determines the location and strength of an earthquake

seismogram a tracing of earthquake motion that is created by a seismograph

epicenter the point on Earth's surface directly above an earthquake's starting point, or focus

focus the point along a fault at which the first motion of an earthquake occurs

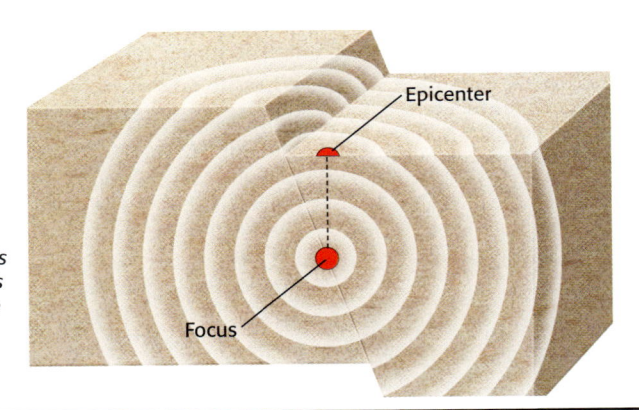

CHAPTER RESOURCES

Chapter Resource File
- Lesson Plan
- Directed Reading A BASIC
- Directed Reading B SPECIAL NEEDS

Technology
- Transparencies
  • Bellringer
  • Finding an Earthquake's Epicenter

Earthquake Measurement

Imagine walls shaking, windows rattling, and glassware and dishes clinking and clanking. After only seconds, the vibrating stops and the sounds die away.

Within minutes, news reports give information about the strength, the time, and the location of the earthquake. You are amazed at how scientists could have learned this information so quickly.

Locating Earthquakes

How do seismologists know when and where earthquakes begin? They depend on earthquake-sensing instruments called seismographs. **Seismographs** are instruments located at or near the surface of the Earth that record seismic waves. When the waves reach a seismograph, the seismograph creates a seismogram. A **seismogram** is a tracing of earthquake motion and is created by a seismograph.

Determining Time and Location of Earthquakes

Seismologists use seismograms to calculate when an earthquake began. Seismologists find an earthquake's start time by comparing seismograms and noting the differences in arrival times of P waves and S waves. Seismologists also use seismograms to find an earthquake's epicenter. An **epicenter** is the point on the Earth's surface directly above an earthquake's starting point. A **focus** is the point inside the Earth where an earthquake begins. **Figure 1** shows the location of an earthquake's epicenter and its focus.

✓ **Reading Check** How do seismologists determine an earthquake's start time? (*See the Appendix for answers to Reading Checks.*)

Figure 1 An earthquake's epicenter is on the Earth's surface directly above the earthquake's focus.

Answer to Reading Check
Seismologists determine an earthquake's start time by comparing seismograms and noting differences in arrival times of P waves and S waves.

230   Chapter 8 • Earthquakes

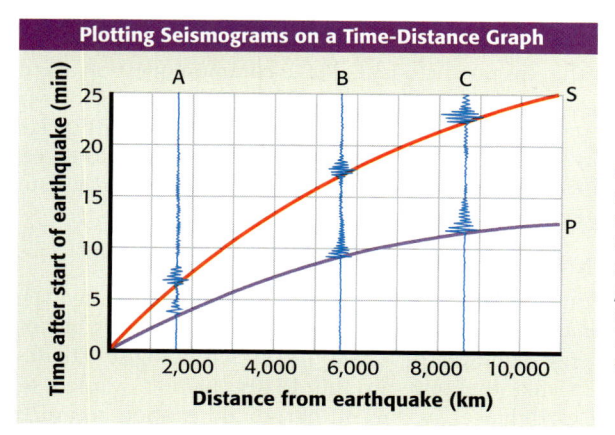

Plotting Seismograms on a Time-Distance Graph

Figure 2 After identifying P and S waves, seismologists can use the time difference to determine an earthquake's start time and the distance from the epicenter to each station. The vertical axis tells how much time passed between the start of the earthquake and the arrival of seismic waves at a station. The horizontal axis tells the distance between a station and the earthquake's epicenter.

The S-P Time Method

Perhaps the simplest method by which seismologists find an earthquake's epicenter is the *S-P time method*. The first step in this method is to collect several seismograms of the same earthquake from different locations. Then, the seismograms are placed on a time-distance graph. The seismogram tracing of the first P wave is lined up with the P-wave time-distance curve, and the tracing of the first S wave is lined up with the S-wave curve, as shown in **Figure 2**. The distance of each station from the earthquake can be found by reading the horizontal axis. After finding out the distances, a seismologist can locate an earthquake's epicenter, as shown in **Figure 3**.

Figure 3 Finding an Earthquake's Epicenter

❶ A circle is drawn around a seismograph station. The radius of the circle equals the distance from the seismograph to the epicenter. (This distance is taken from the time-distance graph.)

❷ When a second circle is drawn around another seismograph station, the circle overlaps the first circle in two spots. One of these spots is the earthquake's epicenter.

❸ When a circle is drawn around a third seismograph station, all three circles intersect in one spot—the earthquake's epicenter. In this case, the epicenter was in San Francisco.

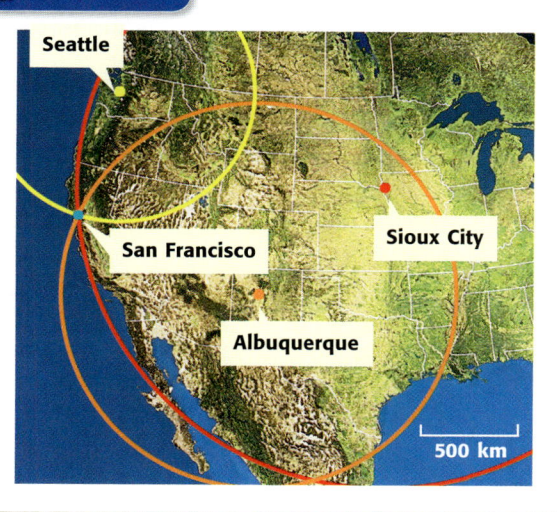

Teach

Using the Figure — GENERAL
Interpreting Seismograms
Explain to students that in **Figure 2**, the seismograms are the blue, wavy lines that extend vertically. Seismic activity at the bottom of a seismogram was recorded before seismic activity at the top. The large "wiggles" that line up with the P-wave curve are P waves, and the large "wiggles" that line up with the S-wave curve are S waves. Ask students to note the difference in time between the moment P waves reached station A and the moment S waves reached station A. (3 minutes)

Have students compare this time difference with the measurements recorded at station C. (The time difference at station C is around 10 or 11 minutes.)

Have students explain why the difference was greater at a station farther away from the epicenter. (P waves travel faster than S waves, so as the distance traveled by both waves increases, the difference in their arrival times also increases.) **LS** Logical

CONNECTION to History — GENERAL

The Richter Magnitude Scale In the 1920s, when Charles Richter was a graduate student, he was working on a catalog of earthquakes in southern California. He wanted to find an objective way to compare earthquakes. Up to that point, geologists used the Mercalli scale to classify earthquakes. The Mercalli scale was based on the observations of people who witnessed an earthquake and on the damage it caused. Richter wanted to devise a more quantitative measure of earthquake strength. This desire led him to develop what is now called the Richter scale in 1935, which is based on measurements of ground motion.

Section 2 • Earthquake Measurement

Close

Reteaching — BASIC

Defining Terms Have students help you come up with definitions for the following terms: *seismograph, seismogram, epicenter, focus, S-P time method, Richter magnitude scale,* and *Modified Mercalli Intensity Scale.*

English Language Learners

LS Logical

Quiz — GENERAL

1. How is an earthquake's epicenter related to its focus?
   (The epicenter is the point on the Earth's surface directly above the focus, which is where the earthquake originates.)

2. As seismic waves travel farther, what happens to the difference in arrival times of P waves and S waves?
   (It increases.)

Alternative Assessment — GENERAL

Recent Earthquakes Have students identify 10 recent earthquakes with a magnitude greater than 5.0 on the Richter scale. Students can compile their findings in a table that includes the epicenter and the magnitude of the quake, the damage it caused, and any other interesting information about the quake. Challenge students to find trends in the data.

LS Logical

CONNECTION TO Social Studies

WRITING SKILL New Madrid Earthquakes

During the winter of 1811–1812, three of the most powerful earthquakes in U.S. history were centered near New Madrid, Missouri, thousands of miles from the nearest tectonic plate boundary. Research the New Madrid earthquakes, and summarize your findings in a one-page essay.

Measuring Earthquake Strength and Intensity

"How strong was the earthquake?" is a common question asked of seismologists. This question is not easy to answer. But it is an important question for anyone living near an earthquake zone. Fortunately, seismograms can be used not only to determine an earthquake's epicenter and its start time but also to find out an earthquake's strength.

The Richter Magnitude Scale

Throughout much of the 20th century, seismologists used the *Richter magnitude scale*, commonly called the Richter scale, to measure the strength of earthquakes. Seismologist Charles Richter created the scale in the 1930s. Richter wanted to compare earthquakes by measuring ground motion recorded by seismograms at seismograph stations.

Earthquake Ground Motion

A measure of the strength of an earthquake is called *magnitude*. The Richter scale measures the ground motion from an earthquake and adjusts for distance to find its strength. Each time the magnitude increases by one unit, the measured ground motion becomes 10 times larger. For example, an earthquake with a magnitude of 5.0 on the Richter scale will produce 10 times as much ground motion as an earthquake with a magnitude of 4.0. Furthermore, an earthquake with a magnitude of 6.0 will produce 100 times as much ground motion (10 × 10) as an earthquake with a magnitude of 4.0. **Table 1** shows the differences in the estimated effects of earthquakes with each increase of one unit of magnitude.

✓ Reading Check How are magnitude and ground motion related in the Richter scale?

Table 1 Effects of Different-Sized Earthquakes

Magnitude	Estimated effects
2.0	can be detected only by seismograph
3.0	can be felt at epicenter
4.0	can be felt by most people in the area
5.0	causes damage at epicenter
6.0	can cause widespread damage
7.0	can cause great, widespread damage

Answer to Reading Check
Each time the magnitude increases by 1 unit, the amount of ground motion increases by 10 times.

Answer to Social Studies Activity
Have students present their one-page summary to the class. Encourage students to use visual aids, such as maps of the earthquake area, in their presentations. A variety of books have been written on the New Madrid earthquakes, and accounts are also available on the Internet.

Modified Mercalli Intensity Scale

A measure of the degree to which an earthquake is felt by people and the amount of damage caused by the earthquake, if any, is called *intensity*. Currently, seismologists in the United States use the Modified Mercalli Intensity Scale to measure earthquake intensity. This scale is a numerical scale that uses Roman numerals from I to XII to describe increasing earthquake intensity levels. An intensity level of I describes an earthquake that is not felt by most people. An intensity level of XII indicates total damage of an area. **Figure 4** shows the type of damage caused by an earthquake that has a Modified Mercalli intensity level of XI.

Because the effects of an earthquake vary from place to place, any earthquake will have more than one intensity value. Intensity values are usually higher near an earthquake's epicenter.

Figure 4 Intensity values for the 1906 San Francisco earthquake varied from place to place. The maximum intensity level was XI.

SECTION Review

Summary

- Seismologists detect seismic waves and record them as seismograms.
- The S-P time method is the simplest method to use to find an earthquake's epicenter.
- Seismologists use the Richter scale to measure an earthquake's strength.
- Seismologists use the Modified Mercalli Intensity Scale to measure an earthquake's intensity.

Using Key Terms

1. In your own words, write a definition for each of the following terms: *epicenter* and *focus*.

Understanding Key Ideas

2. What is the difference between a seismograph and a seismogram?

3. Explain how earthquakes are detected.

4. Briefly explain the steps of the S-P time method for locating an earthquake's epicenter.

5. Why might an earthquake have more than one intensity value?

Math Skills

6. How much more ground motion is produced by an earthquake of magnitude 7.0 than by an earthquake of magnitude 4.0?

Critical Thinking

7. **Making Inferences** Why is a 6.0 magnitude earthquake so much more destructive than a 5.0 magnitude earthquake?

8. **Identifying Bias** Which do you think is the more important measure of earthquakes, strength or intensity? Explain.

9. **Making Inferences** Do you think an earthquake of moderate magnitude can produce high Modified Mercalli intensity values?

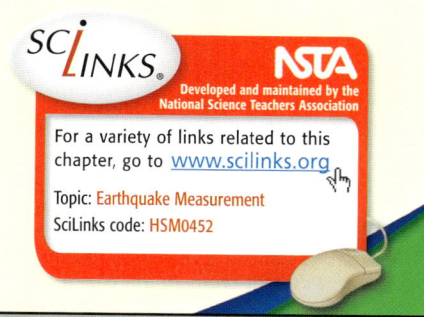

SciLinks
For a variety of links related to this chapter, go to www.scilinks.org
Topic: Earthquake Measurement
SciLinks code: HSM0452

SECTION 3

Focus

Overview
In this section, students learn how earthquake hazard is determined. The section explores the methods seismologists use to make forecasts about earthquakes. Students learn about the technologies used to reinforce buildings against earthquakes. The section concludes with a discussion of earthquake safety procedures.

🔔 Bellringer

If any of your students have experienced an earthquake, have them write a short paragraph describing how they felt and what they did to protect themselves during the earthquake. Have students who have not experienced an earthquake write a paragraph describing what they think they would do during a moderate earthquake.

Motivate

Discussion — GENERAL

Hazard Levels Have students examine **Figure 1**. Challenge them to explain why the West Coast has such high levels of earthquake hazard. If they need a hint, have them look again at **Figure 1** in Section 1. (There is a tectonic plate boundary along the western coast of the United States.) **LS Logical/Visual**

234 Chapter 8 • Earthquakes

SECTION 3

Earthquakes and Society

Imagine that you are in class and the ground begins to shake beneath your feet. What do you do?

Seismologists are not able to predict the exact time when and place where an earthquake will occur. They can, at best, make forecasts based on the frequency with which earthquakes take place. Therefore, seismologists are always looking for better ways to forecast when and where earthquakes will happen. In the meantime, it is important for people in earthquake zones to be prepared before an earthquake strikes.

Earthquake Hazard

Earthquake hazard is a measurement of how likely an area is to have damaging earthquakes in the future. An area's earthquake-hazard level is determined by past and present seismic activity. The map in **Figure 1** shows that some areas of the United States have a higher earthquake-hazard level than others do. This variation is caused by differences in seismic activity. The greater the seismic activity, the higher the earthquake-hazard level. The West Coast, for example, has a very high earthquake-hazard level because it has a lot of seismic activity.

Look at the map. What earthquake-hazard level or levels are shown in the area in which you live? How do the hazard levels of nearby areas compare with your area's hazard level?

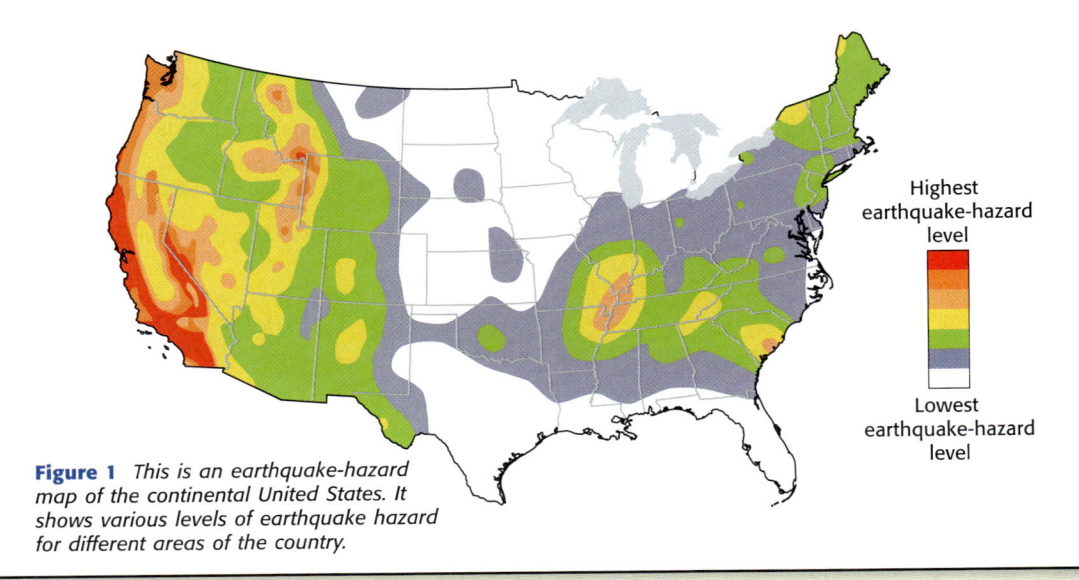

READING WARM-UP

Objectives
- Explain how earthquake-hazard level is determined.
- Compare methods of earthquake forecasting.
- Describe five ways to safeguard buildings against earthquakes.
- Outline earthquake safety procedures.

Terms to Learn
gap hypothesis
seismic gap

READING STRATEGY

Discussion Read this section silently. Write down questions that you have about this section. Discuss your questions in a small group.

Figure 1 This is an earthquake-hazard map of the continental United States. It shows various levels of earthquake hazard for different areas of the country.

CHAPTER RESOURCES

Chapter Resource File
- Lesson Plan
- Directed Reading A BASIC
- Directed Reading B SPECIAL NEEDS

Technology
- Transparencies
  • Bellringer

CONNECTION ACTIVITY
Art — GENERAL

The Protection of Art Treasures Have students find out what has been done to protect sculptures from earthquake damage at the J. Paul Getty Museum in Pacific Palisades, California, or at another museum in an earthquake-prone area. **LS Logical**

Table 1 Worldwide Earthquake Frequency (Based on Observations Since 1900)

Descriptor	Magnitude	Average number annually
Great	8.0 and higher	1
Major	7.0–7.9	18
Strong	6.0–6.9	120
Moderate	5.0–5.9	800
Light	4.0–4.9	about 6,200
Minor	3.0–3.9	about 49,000
Very minor	2.0–2.9	about 365,000

Earthquake Forecasting

Forecasting when and where earthquakes will occur and their strength is difficult. By looking carefully at areas of seismic activity, seismologists have discovered some patterns in earthquakes that allow them to make some general predictions.

Strength and Frequency

Earthquakes vary in strength. And you can probably guess that earthquakes don't occur on a set schedule. But what you may not know is that the strength of earthquakes is related to how often they occur. **Table 1** provides more detail about this relationship worldwide.

The relationship between earthquake strength and frequency is also at work on a local scale. For example, each year approximately 1.6 earthquakes with a magnitude of 4.0 on the Richter scale occur in the Puget Sound area of Washington State. Over this same time period, approximately 10 times as many earthquakes with a magnitude of 3.0 occur in this area. Scientists use these statistics to make forecasts about the strength, location, and frequency of future earthquakes.

Reading Check What is the relationship between the strength of earthquakes and earthquake frequency? *(See the Appendix for answers to Reading Checks.)*

The Gap Hypothesis

Another method of forecasting an earthquake's strength, location, and frequency is based on the gap hypothesis. The **gap hypothesis** is a hypothesis that states that sections of active faults that have had relatively few earthquakes are likely to be the sites of strong earthquakes in the future. The areas along a fault where relatively few earthquakes have occurred are called **seismic gaps.**

Internet Activity
For another activity related to this chapter, go to go.hrw.com and type in the keyword HZ5EQKW.

gap hypothesis a hypothesis that is based on the idea that a major earthquake is more likely to occur along the part of an active fault where no earthquakes have occurred for a certain period of time

seismic gap an area along a fault where relatively few earthquakes have occurred recently but where strong earthquakes have occurred in the past

Answer to Reading Check
With a decrease of 1 unit in earthquake magnitude, the number of earthquakes occurring annually increases by about 10 times.

Is That a Fact!
On March 27, 1964, an earthquake with a magnitude of 9.2 occurred in southern Alaska. The earthquake, which is the strongest recorded earthquake in North America, lasted for about 4 minutes. The port on Montague Island was raised 10 m, which stranded ships that had been docked in the port. After the earthquake, a devastating tsunami swept along the Pacific Northwest coastline.

Teach

READING STRATEGY — GENERAL

Prediction Guide Have students determine whether the following statements are true or false before they read the rest of this section:

- Hundreds of thousands of earthquakes that occur each year are not felt by people. (true)
- During an earthquake, rigid pipelines for natural gas and water are more resistant to damage than flexible pipelines are. (false)
- Because earthquakes are unpredictable, people cannot prepare for them. (false)

LS Logical

CONNECTION ACTIVITY
Math — GENERAL

Calculating Earthquake Frequency Have students use **Table 1** to convert the average number of minor earthquakes that occur each year to the number of minor earthquakes that occur each day. (49,000 minor earthquakes per year ÷ 365 days per year = 134 minor earthquakes per day) **LS** Logical

Section 3 • Earthquakes and Society **235**

Teach, continued

ACTIVITY — ADVANCED

Tools of the Trade Have interested students research the various types of instruments used to detect seismic activity, including tiltmeters, gravimeters, strainmeters, magnetometers, and laser range finders. Students' findings should include illustrations and detailed descriptions of how the instruments work.
LS Logical/Visual

Debate — GENERAL

Nuclear Waste Disposal? Scientists must consider the geologic stability of potential sites for nuclear waste facilities. Have students research and debate the issue of nuclear waste disposal. Have them consider that there are few viable options for the disposal of the world's nuclear waste. Remind them that no one can be sure that an area will be stable over the thousands of years it takes for nuclear waste to decay. **LS Interpersonal**

Homework — GENERAL

Presentation Have students create a poster to promote earthquake safety. Posters should focus on one of the following: how to prepare for an earthquake, what to do during an earthquake, or what to do after an earthquake. Students can create a display to educate the school about earthquake safety. **LS Visual**

Figure 2 A Seismic Gap on the San Andreas Fault

This diagram shows a cross section of the San Andreas Fault. Note how the seismic gap was filled by the 1989 Loma Prieta earthquake and its aftershocks. *Aftershocks* are weaker earthquakes that follow a stronger earthquake.

- Earthquakes prior to 1989 earthquake
- 1989 earthquake and aftershocks

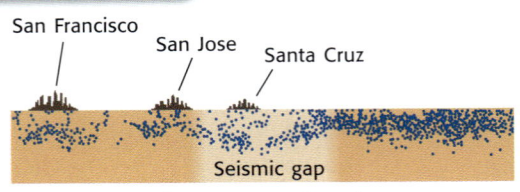

Before 1989 earthquake

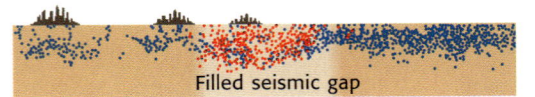

After 1989 earthquake

Using the Gap Hypothesis

Not all seismologists believe the gap hypothesis is an accurate method of forecasting earthquakes. But some seismologists think the gap hypothesis helped forecast the approximate location and strength of the 1989 Loma Prieta earthquake in the San Francisco Bay area. The seismic gap that they identified is illustrated in **Figure 2.** In 1988, these seismologists predicted that over the next 30 years there was a 30% chance that an earthquake with a magnitude of at least 6.5 would fill this seismic gap. Were they correct? The Loma Prieta earthquake, which filled in the seismic gap in 1989, measured 6.9 on the Richter scale. Their prediction was very close, considering how complicated the forecasting of earthquakes is.

Figure 3 During the January 17, 1995, earthquake, the fronts of entire buildings collapsed into the streets of Kobe, Japan.

Earthquakes and Buildings

Figure 3 shows what can happen to buildings during an earthquake. These buildings were not designed or constructed to withstand the forces of an earthquake.

Today, older structures in seismically active places, such as California, are being made more earthquake resistant. The process of making older structures more earthquake resistant is called *retrofitting*. A common way to retrofit an older home is to securely fasten it to its foundation. Steel can be used to strengthen structures made of brick.

✓ **Reading Check** Explain the meaning of the term *retrofitting*.

WEIRD SCIENCE

Engineers have devised giant shock absorbers for buildings. The shock absorbers contain a ferrofluid solution that becomes rigid in a magnetic field. When an earthquake occurs, a computer controls electromagnets in the shock absorbers to damp the vibrations!

Answer to Reading Check

Retrofitting is the process of making older structures more earthquake resistant.

Earthquake-Resistant Buildings

A lot has been learned from building failure during earthquakes. Armed with this knowledge, architects and engineers use the newest technology to design and construct buildings and bridges to better withstand earthquakes. Carefully study **Figure 4** to learn more about this modern technology.

Figure 4 — Earthquake-Resistant Building Technology

The **mass damper** is a weight placed in the roof of a building. Motion sensors detect building movement during an earthquake and send messages to a computer. The computer then signals controls in the roof to shift the mass damper to counteract the building's movement.

The **active tendon system** works much like the mass damper system in the roof. Sensors notify a computer that the building is moving. Then, the computer activates devices to shift a large weight to counteract the movement.

Base isolators act as shock absorbers during an earthquake. They are made of layers of rubber and steel wrapped around a lead core. Base isolators absorb seismic waves, preventing them from traveling through the building.

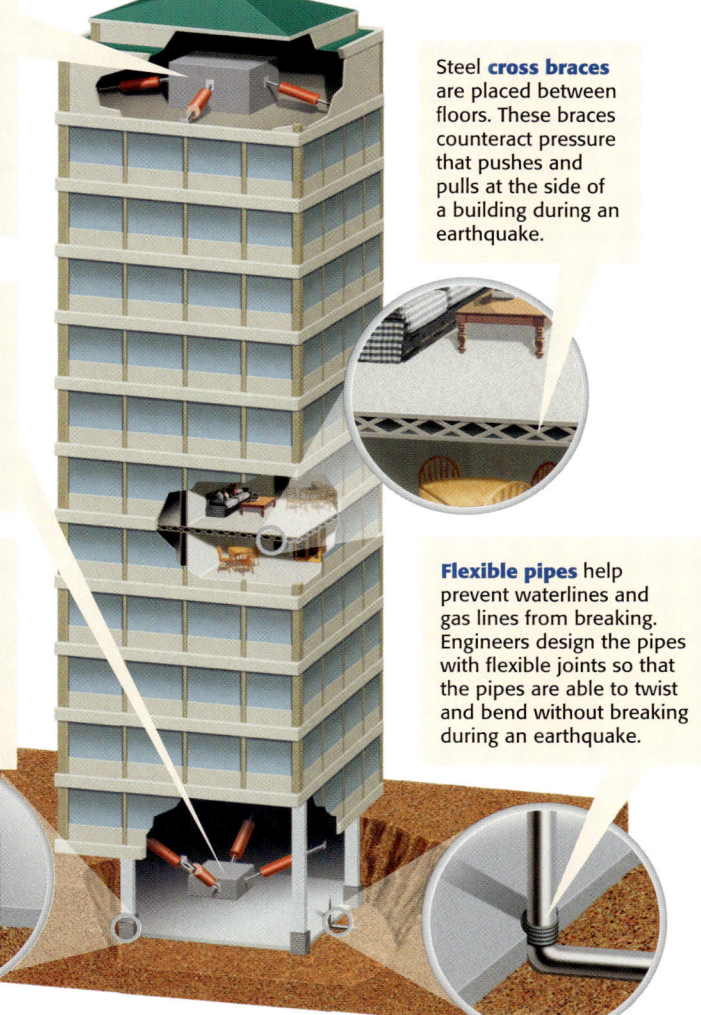

Steel **cross braces** are placed between floors. These braces counteract pressure that pushes and pulls at the side of a building during an earthquake.

Flexible pipes help prevent waterlines and gas lines from breaking. Engineers design the pipes with flexible joints so that the pipes are able to twist and bend without breaking during an earthquake.

Using the Figure — GENERAL

Have students answer the following questions by using **Figure 4**:

- How are the mass damper system and the active tendon system alike? (In both systems, motion sensors detect movement and send this information to a computer. The computer signals devices that counteract the movement of the structure.)
- What is a base isolator? (a shock absorber that prevents seismic waves from traveling through a structure)
- What advantage do flexible pipes have over rigid metal pipes during an earthquake? (Flexible pipes twist and bend more readily than metal pipes, which tend to snap when subjected to significant seismic tremors.)

LS Logical

Demonstration — BASIC

Flexible Buildings People on the highest floors of tall buildings often feel minor tremors that go unnoticed by people on the ground. The reason is that tall buildings intensify minor tremors. Demonstrate this concept by holding a meterstick upright by the end and shaking it back and forth. Tell students to observe the difference in movement between the top and the bottom of the meterstick. **LS** Visual/Kinesthetic

CONNECTION ACTIVITY
Real Life — GENERAL

Earthquake Kit Collect the following items: bottled water, nonperishable foods, a flashlight, batteries, a bucket, rubber gloves, safety goggles, a first-aid kit, money, an electric can opener, a few perishable food items, a small TV (not battery operated), a battery-operated radio, clean rags, tissues and toilet paper, a deck of playing cards, and a blanket. Have students take turns deciding which items would be useful if a severe earthquake occurred in your area. Ask questions to help students realize that electricity and fresh water may not be available for some time after the earthquake. Suggest that students use the Internet to find ways to prepare for an earthquake.

LS Interpersonal/Visual

Section 3 • Earthquakes and Society

Close

Reteaching — BASIC

Earthquake Hazards Ask students to write a description of the hazards they might face if an earthquake occurred when they were in each of the following situations:

- asleep in bed (collapsing building)
- at the beach (tsunamis)
- snow skiing (avalanche)

LS Logical

Quiz — GENERAL

1. What is the gap hypothesis? (The gap hypothesis states that sections of active faults that have had relatively few earthquakes are likely to be the sites of strong earthquakes in the future.)

2. Why should you lie under a table or desk during an earthquake? (The table or desk might prevent falling objects from hitting you and causing injury.)

3. What are aftershocks? (They are generally weaker quakes that follow stronger earthquakes.)

Alternative Assessment — GENERAL

Earthquake Safety Guidelines Have students work together to create a pamphlet that instructs the general public what to do when an earthquake occurs.

LS Visual

Answer to Reading Check

You should crouch or lie face down under a table or desk.

CONNECTION TO Physics

WRITING SKILL **Earthquake Proof Buildings** During earthquakes, buildings often sway from side to side when the ground beneath them moves. This swaying can cause structural damage to buildings. Scientists and engineers are developing computer-controlled systems that counteract the swaying of buildings during earthquakes. Research a computer-controlled system that uses mass dampers or active tendons to reduce damage to buildings. Summarize your research in a short essay.

Figure 5 These students are participating in an earthquake drill.

INCLUSION Strategies

- Developmentally Delayed
- Behavior Control Issues
- Attention Deficit Disorder

Have students create models of transform, divergent, and convergent tectonic plate motion. A large world map with areas marked that illustrate different tectonic plate motion should be visible in the classroom. Organize students into groups of four. Hand out six plastic foam blocks (edges should meet on an angle) and magic markers. Ask students to use the blocks to model transform, divergent, and convergent tectonic plate motion. Students should use the magic marker to put arrows signifying what direction the plates are moving and to label the model with a "T" for transform, "D" for divergent, and "C" for convergent. Next, ask students to look at the map and review where these types of tectonic plate motion occur, and the landforms that are associated with them. **LS** Visual/Logical

English Language Learners

Are You Prepared for an Earthquake?

If you live in an area where earthquakes are common, there are many things you can do to protect yourself and your property from earthquakes. Plan ahead so that you will know what to do before, during, and after an earthquake. Stick to your plan as closely as possible.

Before the Shaking Starts

The first thing you should do is safeguard your home against earthquakes. You can do so by putting heavier objects on lower shelves so that they do not fall during the earthquake. You can also talk to a parent about having your home strengthened. Next, you should find safe places within each room of your home and outside of your home. Then, make a plan with others (your family, neighbors, or friends) to meet in a safe place after the earthquake is over. This plan ensures that you will all know who is safe. During the earthquake, waterlines, power lines, and roadways may be damaged. So, you should store water, nonperishable food, a fire extinguisher, a flashlight with batteries, a portable radio, medicines, and a first-aid kit in a place you can access after the earthquake.

When the Shaking Starts

The best thing to do if you are indoors when an earthquake begins is to crouch or lie face down under a table or desk in the center of a room, as shown in **Figure 5**. If you are outside, lie face down away from buildings, power lines, and trees and cover your head with your hands. If you are in a car on an open road, you should stop the car and remain inside.

✓ **Reading Check** Explain what you would do if you were in class and an earthquake began to shake the ground.

---

238   Chapter 8 • Earthquakes

After the Shaking Stops

Being in an earthquake is a startling and often frightening experience for most people. After being in an earthquake, you should not be surprised to find yourself and others puzzled about what took place. You should try to calm down and get your bearings as quickly as possible. Then, remove yourself from immediate danger, such as downed power lines, broken glass, and fire hazards. Always stay out of damaged buildings, and return home only when you are told that it is safe to do so by someone in authority. Be aware that there may be aftershocks, which may cause more damage to structures. Recall your earthquake plan, and follow it.

School to Home

Disaster Planning
With your parent, create a plan that will protect your family in the event of a natural disaster, such as an earthquake. The plan should include steps to take before, during, and after a disaster. Present your disaster plan in the form of an oral report to your class.

SECTION Review

Summary

- Earthquake hazard is a measure of how likely an area is to have earthquakes in the future.
- Seismologists use their knowledge of the relationship between earthquake strength and frequency and of the gap hypothesis to forecast earthquakes.
- Homes and buildings and bridges can be strengthened to decrease earthquake damage.
- People who live in earthquake zones should safeguard their home against earthquakes.

Using Key Terms

1. In your own words, write a definition for each of the following terms: *gap hypothesis* and *seismic gap*.

Understanding Key Ideas

2. A weight that is placed on a building to make the building earthquake resistant is called a(n)
   a. active tendon system.
   b. cross brace.
   c. mass damper.
   d. base isolator.

3. How is an area's earthquake-hazard level determined?

4. Compare the strength and frequency method with the gap hypothesis method for predicting earthquakes.

5. What is a common way of making homes more earthquake resistant?

6. Describe four pieces of technology that are designed to make buildings earthquake resistant.

7. Name five items that you should store in case of an earthquake.

Math Skills

8. Of the approximately 420,000 earthquakes recorded each year, about 140 have a magnitude greater than 6.0. What percentage of total earthquakes have a magnitude greater than 6.0?

Critical Thinking

9. **Evaluating Hypotheses** Seismologists predict that there is a 20% chance that an earthquake of magnitude 7.0 or greater will fill a seismic gap during the next 50 years. Is the hypothesis incorrect if the earthquake does not happen? Explain your answer.

10. **Applying Concepts** Why is a large earthquake often followed by numerous aftershocks?

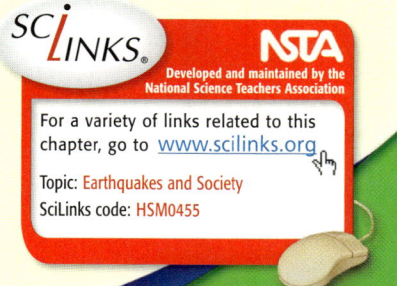

Answers to Section Review

1. Sample answer: According to the gap hypothesis, strong earthquakes are likely to occur along sections of active faults that have had relatively few earthquakes. A seismic gap is an area along an active fault where relatively few earthquakes have occurred.

2. c

3. The earthquake hazard level of a particular area is determined by the amount of past and present seismic activity that has occurred in the area.

4. Sample answer: According to the strength and frequency method, earthquake strength is related to how often earthquakes occur. The gap hypothesis predicts an earthquake's strength and location by finding out the parts of an active fault where no earthquakes have recently occurred.

5. Sample answer: A common way of making a home more earthquake resistant is to securely fasten it to its foundation.

6. Answers may vary. Sample answer: Flexible pipes that are able to twist and bend during earthquakes prevent water and gas lines from breaking. A base isolator made of rubber and steel wrapped around lead absorbs seismic waves. A mass damper placed in the roof of a building counteracts the movement of the building during an earthquake. Cross braces placed between floors in a building counteract pressure that pushes and pulls at the side of a building.

7. Answers may vary. Sample answer: nonperishable food, a flashlight, a portable radio, a fire extinguisher, and a first-aid kit

8. $140 \div 420{,}000 \times 100 = .03\%$

9. The hypothesis is not incorrect because there was only a 20% probability an earthquake would fill the seismic gap.

10. Aftershocks follow a large earthquake because the earthquake causes elastically deformed rock along other nearby faults to break.

CHAPTER RESOURCES

Chapter Resource File
- Section Quiz GENERAL
- Section Review GENERAL
- Vocabulary and Section Summary GENERAL
- Critical Thinking ADVANCED

Inquiry Lab

Quake Challenge

Teacher's Notes

Time Required
One 45-minute class period

Lab Ratings
EASY →→→ HARD

Teacher Prep 🧪🧪
Student Set-Up 🧪
Concept Level 🧪🧪
Clean Up 🧪🧪

MATERIALS
The materials listed on the student page are enough for 2 students.

Safety Caution
Remind students to review all safety cautions and icons before beginning this lab activity.

Preparation Notes
Make the gelatin 24 hours in advance. When making the gelatin, experiment with the ratio of water to gelatin. The more water you use, the more "wiggly" your gelatin will be. Cut the gelatin squares ahead of time, and place each square on a piece of wax paper. For steps 8 and 9, you will need to create a gelatin square large enough to place all the student structures on. This allows each group's structure to be evaluated on its own merit.

CLASSROOM TESTED & APPROVED

Helen Schiller
Northwood Middle School
Taylors, South Carolina

Using Scientific Methods

Inquiry Lab

OBJECTIVES

Build a model of a structure that can withstand a simulated earthquake.

Evaluate ways in which you can strengthen your model.

MATERIALS

- gelatin, square, approximately 8 × 8 cm
- marshmallows (10)
- paper plate
- toothpicks (10)

SAFETY

Quake Challenge

In many parts of the world, people must have earthquakes in mind when they construct buildings. Each building must be designed so that the structure is protected during an earthquake. Architects have greatly improved the design of buildings since 1906, when an earthquake and the fires it caused destroyed much of San Francisco. In this activity, you will use marshmallows and toothpicks to build a structure that can withstand a simulated earthquake. In the process, you will discover some of the ways a building can be built to withstand an earthquake.

Ask a Question

1. What features help a building withstand an earthquake? How can I use this information to build my structure?

Form a Hypothesis

2. Brainstorm with a classmate to design a structure that will resist the simulated earthquake. Write two or three sentences to describe your design. Explain why you think your design will be able to withstand a simulated earthquake.

Test the Hypothesis

3. Follow your design to build a structure using the toothpicks and marshmallows.

4. Set your structure on a square of gelatin, and place the gelatin on a paper plate.

5. Shake the square of gelatin to test whether your building will remain standing during a quake. Do not pick up the gelatin.

6. If your first design does not work well, change it until you find a design that does. Try to determine why your building is falling so that you can improve your design each time.

7. Sketch your final design.

CHAPTER RESOURCES

Chapter Resource File
- Datasheet for Chapter Lab
- Lab Notes and Answers

Technology
- **Classroom Videos**
  - Lab Video

LabBook
- Earthquake Waves

240 Chapter 8 • Earthquakes

❽ After you have tested your final design, place your structure on the gelatin square on your teacher's desk.

❾ When every group has added a structure to the teacher's gelatin, your teacher will simulate an earthquake by shaking the gelatin. Watch to see which buildings withstand the most severe quake.

Analyze the Results

❶ **Explaining Events** Which buildings were still standing after the final earthquake? What features made them more stable?

❷ **Analyzing Results** How would you change your design in order to make your structure more stable?

Draw Conclusions

❸ **Evaluating Models** This was a simple model of a real-life problem for architects. Based on this activity, what advice would you give to architects who design buildings in earthquake zones?

❹ **Evaluating Models** What are some limitations of your earthquake model?

❺ **Making Predictions** How could your research have an impact on society?

Analyze the Results

1. Answers may vary. Sample answer: Structures that had a wide base generally withstood the earthquake. Structures that used triangles in the design also were successful.
2. Answers may vary. Sample answer: By experimenting with different design shapes, such as cubes or triangles, we could find the most stable structure.

Draw Conclusions

3. Buildings designed in earthquake zones should have wide and flexible foundations. The buildings should also be reinforced to prevent collapse.
4. Answers may vary. Accept all reasonable answers. Sample answer: Rocks and gelatin have very different physical properties, such as hardness and density. Seismic waves may have different effects on rock than shaking does on gelatin.
5. Answers may vary. Accept all reasonable answers. Sample answer: By changing the design of our marshmallow-and-toothpick building, we can come up with better designs for buildings.

CHAPTER RESOURCES

Workbooks

Whiz-Bang Demonstrations
• When Buildings Boogie GENERAL

Long-Term Projects & Research Ideas
• A Whole Lotta Shakin' ADVANCED

Chapter 8 • Chapter Lab

Chapter Review

Assignment Guide

SECTION	QUESTIONS
1	1, 5–7, 14, 18, 20
2	2, 3, 11, 12, 21–23
3	4, 8–10, 13, 15, 17, 19
1 and 2	16

ANSWERS

Using Key Terms

1. Sample answer: A seismic wave is released when elastically deformed rock along a fault slips. A P wave is the fastest seismic wave and can move through all parts of the Earth. An S wave moves rock from side to side as the wave travels through the Earth.

2. Sample answer: A seismograph is an instrument that is used to record seismic waves. A seismogram is the tracing of earthquake motion created by a seismograph.

3. Sample answer: A focus is the point along a fault where an earthquake starts. An epicenter is the point on Earth's surface above the focus.

4. Sample answer: The gap hypothesis states that strong earthquakes are likely to occur along sections of active faults that have had relatively few earthquakes. Seismic gaps are areas along active faults where relatively few earthquakes have occurred.

Chapter Review

USING KEY TERMS

1. Use each of the following terms in a separate sentence: *seismic wave*, *P wave*, and *S wave*.

For each pair of terms, explain how the meanings of the terms differ.

2. *seismograph* and *seismogram*

3. *epicenter* and *focus*

4. *gap hypothesis* and *seismic gap*

UNDERSTANDING KEY IDEAS

Multiple Choice

5. When rock is ___, energy builds up in it. Seismic waves occur as this energy is ___.
   a. plastically deformed, increased
   b. elastically deformed, released
   c. plastically deformed, released
   d. elastically deformed, increased

6. Reverse faults are created
   a. by divergent plate motion.
   b. by convergent plate motion.
   c. by transform plate motion.
   d. All of the above

7. The last seismic waves to arrive are
   a. P waves.
   b. body waves.
   c. S waves.
   d. surface waves.

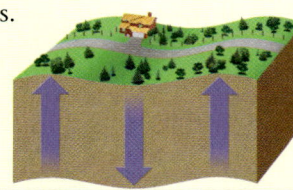

8. If an earthquake begins while you are in a building, the safest thing for you to do is
   a. to run out into an open space.
   b. to get under the strongest table, chair, or other piece of furniture.
   c. to call home.
   d. to crouch near a wall.

9. How many major earthquakes (magnitude 7.0 to 7.9) happen on average in the world each year?
   a. 1
   b. 18
   c. 120
   d. 800

10. ___ counteract pressure that pushes and pulls at the side of a building during an earthquake.
    a. Base isolators
    b. Mass dampers
    c. Active tendon systems
    d. Cross braces

Short Answer

11. Can the S-P time method be used with one seismograph station to locate the epicenter of an earthquake? Explain your answer.

12. Explain how the Richter scale and the Modified Mercalli Intensity Scale are different.

13. What is the relationship between the strength of earthquakes and earthquake frequency?

Understanding Key Ideas

5. b
6. b
7. d
8. b
9. b
10. d

11. No, a minimum of three seismograph stations are needed to find an earthquake's epicenter using the S-P time method.

12. The Richter magnitude scale measures the ground motion from an earthquake and adjusts for distance to find earthquake strength. The Modified Mercalli Intensity Scale measures the degree to which an earthquake is felt by people and the amount of damage caused by an earthquake.

13. With each step down in earthquake strength or magnitude, the number of earthquakes per year is greater.

242 Chapter 8 • Earthquakes

14. Explain the way that different seismic waves affect rock as they travel through it.

15. Describe some steps you can take to protect yourself and your property from earthquakes.

CRITICAL THINKING

16. **Concept Mapping** Use the following terms to create a concept map: *focus, epicenter, earthquake start time, seismic waves, P waves,* and *S waves*.

17. **Identifying Relationships** Would a strong or light earthquake be more likely to happen along a major fault where there have not been many recent earthquakes? Explain. (Hint: Think about the average number of earthquakes of different magnitudes that occur annually.)

18. **Applying Concepts** Japan is located near a point where three tectonic plates converge. What would you imagine the earthquake-hazard level in Japan to be? Explain why.

19. **Applying Concepts** You learned that if you are in a car during an earthquake and are out in the open, it is best to stay in the car. Can you think of any situation in which you might want to leave a car during an earthquake?

20. **Identifying Relationships** You use gelatin to simulate rock in an experiment in which you are investigating the way different seismic waves affect rock. In what ways is your gelatin model limited?

INTERPRETING GRAPHICS

The graph below illustrates the relationship between earthquake magnitude and the height of tracings on a seismogram. Charles Richter initially formed his magnitude scale by comparing the heights of seismogram readings for different earthquakes. Use the graph below to answer the questions that follow.

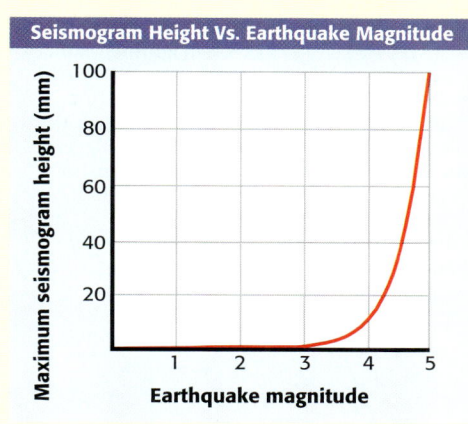

Seismogram Height Vs. Earthquake Magnitude

21. According to the graph, what would the magnitude of an earthquake be if its maximum seismograph height is 10 mm?

22. According to the graph, what is the difference in maximum seismogram height (in mm) between an earthquake of magnitude 4.0 and an earthquake of magnitude 5.0?

23. Look at the shape of the curve on the graph. What does this tell you about the relationship between seismogram heights and earthquake magnitudes? Explain.

---

14. P waves move rock back and forth, squeezing and stretching the rock. S waves stretch rock sideways as well as back and forth. Surface waves move rock up, down, and around, or in a back-and-forth motion.

15. Answers may vary. Sample answer: You should protect yourself and your property against earthquakes by creating an earthquake kit of items you may need after a strong, damaging earthquake. You should put heavy items closer to the floor so that they do not fall during earthquakes. You should find safe places within each room of your home or outdoors in the event there is an earthquake.

Critical Thinking

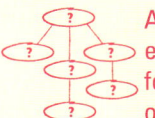

16. An answer to this exercise can be found at the end of this book.

17. Answers may vary. Sample answer: Based on the average number of earthquakes of different magnitudes that happen annually, a light earthquake would be more likely to happen along a major fault where there have not been many major earthquakes.

18. Because most earthquakes occur at tectonic plate boundaries, the earthquake-hazard level in Japan would be high.

19. Answers may vary. Sample answer: You might want to leave your car if it was stranded on or beneath a highway overpass.

20. A gelatin model is limited because it does not have the same properties as rock, such as density and hardness.

Interpreting Graphics

21. 4
22. 100 mm − 10 mm = 90 mm
23. Students should recognize that seismogram heights increase at a greater rate with each increase in earthquake magnitude. The relationship is logarithmic, not linear.

CHAPTER RESOURCES

Chapter Resource File
- Chapter Review GENERAL
- Chapter Test A GENERAL
- Chapter Test B ADVANCED
- Chapter Test C SPECIAL NEEDS
- Vocabulary Activity GENERAL

Workbooks
- Study Guide
  • Assessment resources are also available in Spanish.

Chapter 8 • Chapter Review

Standardized Test Preparation

Teacher's Note

To provide practice under more realistic testing conditions, give students 20 minutes to answer all of the questions in this Standardized Test Preparation.

MISCONCEPTION ALERT

Answers to the standardized test preparation can help you identify student misconceptions and misunderstandings.

READING

Passage 1

1. B
2. H
3. D

TEST DOCTOR

Question 2: The correct answer is H. In the passage, it is stated that the earthquake lasted 20 s. Students may think answer H is true because the passage describes changes that happened between 5:04 P.M. and 5:05 P.M.

Question 3: The correct answer is D. In the passage, it is stated that the earthquake happened during the 1989 World Series. Students are incorrect if they think that answer C is correct, because the earthquake, at magnitude 6.9, was a strong earthquake, not light to moderate.

Standardized Test Preparation

READING

Read each of the passages below. Then, answer the questions that follow each passage.

Passage 1 At 5:04 P.M. on October 14, 1989, life in California's San Francisco Bay area seemed normal. While 62,000 fans filled Candlestick Park to watch the third game of the World Series, other people were rushing home from a day's work. By 5:05 P.M., the area had changed drastically. The area was rocked by the 6.9 magnitude Loma Prieta earthquake, which lasted 20 s and caused 68 deaths, 3,757 injuries, and the destruction of more than 1,000 homes. Considering that the earthquake was of such a high magnitude and that the earthquake happened during rush hour, it is amazing that more people did not die.

1. In the passage, what does the word *drastically* mean?
   A continuously
   B severely
   C gradually
   D not at all

2. Which of the following statements about the Loma Prieta earthquake is false?
   F The earthquake happened during rush hour.
   G The earthquake destroyed more than 1,000 homes.
   H The earthquake lasted for 1 min.
   I The earthquake had a magnitude of 6.9.

3. Which of the following statements is a fact in the passage?
   A Thousands of people were killed in the Loma Prieta earthquake.
   B The Loma Prieta earthquake happened during the morning rush hour.
   C The Loma Prieta earthquake was a light to moderate earthquake.
   D The Loma Prieta earthquake occurred during the 1989 World Series.

Passage 2 In the United States, seismologists use the Modified Mercalli Intensity Scale to measure the intensity of earthquakes. Japanese seismologists, however, use the Shindo scale to measure earthquake intensity. Earthquakes are assigned a number between 1 and 7 on the scale. Shindo 1 indicates a slight earthquake. Such an earthquake is felt by few people, usually people who are sitting. Shindo 7 indicates a severe earthquake. An earthquake that causes great destruction, such as the earthquake that struck Kobe, Japan, in January 1995, would be classified as Shindo 7.

1. In the passage, what does the word *assigned* mean?
   A named
   B voted
   C given
   D chosen

2. Which of the following statements about the Shindo scale is true?
   F The Shindo scale is used to measure earthquake strength.
   G The Shindo scale, which ranges from 1 to 7, is used to rank earthquake intensity.
   H The Shindo scale is the same as the Modified Mercalli Intensity Scale.
   I Seismologists all over the world use the Shindo scale.

3. Which of the following is a fact in the passage?
   A American seismologists use the Richter scale instead of the Shindo scale.
   B Japanese seismologists measure the intensity of large earthquakes only.
   C The Kobe earthquake was too destructive to be given a Shindo number.
   D Shindo 1 indicates a slight earthquake.

Passage 2

1. C
2. G
3. D

TEST DOCTOR

Question 2: The correct answer is G. The passage explicitly states that Japanese seismologists use the Shindo scale to rate earthquake intensity on a scale of 1 to 7. Students may think answer F is correct if they confuse the concepts of strength and intensity.

Question 3: The correct answer is D. In the passage, it is stated that Japanese seismologists use Shindo 1 to indicate a slight earthquake. Students may think A is the correct answer if they confuse the Richter magnitude scale with the Shindo scale of earthquake intensity.

INTERPRETING GRAPHICS

Use the graph below to answer the questions that follow.

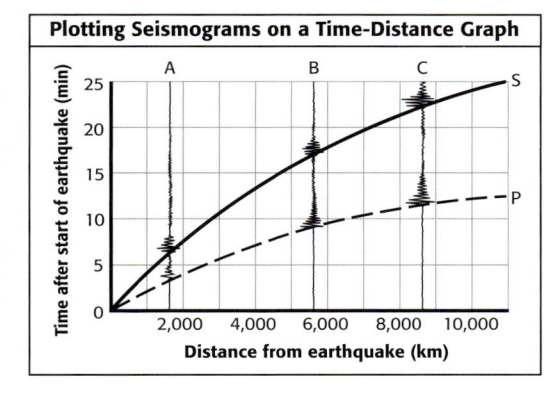

Plotting Seismograms on a Time-Distance Graph

1. According to the seismogram, which waves travel the **fastest**?
   A P waves travel the fastest.
   B S waves travel the fastest.
   C P waves and S waves travel at the same speed.
   D The graph does not show how fast P waves and S waves travel.

2. What is the approximate difference in minutes between the time the first P waves arrived at station B and the time the first S waves arrived at station B?
   F 22 1/2 min
   G 10 1/2 min
   H 8 min
   I 3 min

3. Station A is approximately how much closer to the epicenter than station B is?
   A 1,800 km
   B 4,000 km
   C 5,800 km
   D 8,600 km

MATH

Read each question below, and choose the best answer.

1. If a seismic wave travels at a rate of 12 km/s, how far will it travel away from the earthquake in 1 min?
   A 7,200 km
   B 720 km
   C 72 km
   D 7.2 km

2. If a P wave travels a distance of 70 km in 10 s, what is its speed?
   F 700 km/s
   G 70 km/s
   H 7 km/s
   I 0.7 km/s

3. Each time the magnitude of an earthquake increases by 1 unit, the amount of energy released is 31.7 times greater. How much greater is the energy for a magnitude 7.0 earthquake than a magnitude 5.0 earthquake?
   A 31,855 times as strong
   B 63.4 times as strong
   C 634 times as strong
   D 1,005 times as strong

4. An approximate relationship between earthquake magnitude and frequency is that when magnitude increases by 1.0, 10 times fewer earthquakes occur. Thus, if 150 earthquakes of magnitude 2.0 happen in your area this year, about how many 4.0 magnitude earthquakes will happen in your area this year?
   F 50
   G 10
   H 2
   I 0

5. If an average of 421,140 earthquakes occur annually, what percentage of these earthquakes are minor earthquakes if 49,000 minor earthquakes occur annually?
   A approximately .01%
   B approximately .12%
   C approximately 12%
   D approximately 86%

INTERPRETING GRAPHICS

1. A
2. H
3. B

TEST DOCTOR

Question 2: The correct answer is H. Students may think answer I is correct if they use station A to obtain the answer instead of station B. They may think answer G is correct if they use station C to obtain the answer instead of station B.

Question 3: The correct answer is B. The graph indicates that recording station A is approximately 4,000 km closer to the epicenter than recording station B.

MATH

1. B
2. H
3. D
4. H
5. C

TEST DOCTOR

Question 3: The correct answer is D. An earthquake of magnitude 7.0 is approximately 1,005 times (31.7^2) as strong as an earthquake of magnitude 5.0. Students may obtain an incorrect answer if they multiply 31.7 times 2 or by 20, or cube 31.7 instead of squaring it.

Question 4: The correct answer is H. With each increase of 1.0 unit of magnitude, there is a decrease in earthquake frequency of 10 times. Because $150 \div 10^2 = 1.5$, 2 is the only logical answer. Students may think answer F is correct if they divide 150 by 2. Students may think answer G is correct if they divide 150 by 20.

CHAPTER RESOURCES

Chapter Resource File
• Standardized Test Preparation GENERAL

State Resources
For specific resources for your state, visit go.hrw.com and type in the keyword **HSMSTR**.

Chapter 8 • Standardized Test Preparation

Science in Action

Weird Science

Background
There have been many studies on the different types of animal responses to the geophysical environment. Most of these studies indicate that the behavior of living organisms is affected by electromagnetic fields. Studies have been performed on how migrating birds find their way and how fish navigate. Fish such as catfish and sharks use electroreceptors to detect objects around them and to communicate. Even earthworms respond to changes in Earth's magnetic field.

Science, Technology, and Society

Background
During the summer of 2002, a pilot hole 2 km in depth was drilled at the SAFOD site. When drilling concluded, seismometers were placed in the drill hole to locate the microearthquakes that will be targeted with SAFOD.

Science in Action

Weird Science

Can Animals Predict Earthquakes?
Is it possible that animals close to the epicenter of an earthquake are able to sense changes in their environment? And should we be paying attention to such animal behavior? As long ago as the 1700s, unusual animal activity prior to earthquakes has been recorded. Examples include domestic cattle seeking higher ground and zoo animals refusing to enter their shelters at night. Other animals, such as lizards, snakes, and small mammals, evacuate their underground burrows, and wild birds leave their usual habitats. These events occur days, hours, or even minutes before an earthquake.

Language Arts ACTIVITY
WRITING SKILL Create an illustrated field guide of animal activity to show how animal activity can predict earthquakes. Each illustration must have a paragraph that describes the activity of a specific animal.

Science, Technology, and Society

San Andreas Fault Observatory at Depth (SAFOD)
Seismologists are creating an underground observatory in Parkfield, California, to study earthquakes along the San Andreas Fault. The observatory will be named the San Andreas Fault Observatory at Depth (SAFOD). A deep hole will be drilled directly into the fault zone near a point where earthquakes of magnitude 6.0 have been recorded. Instruments will be placed at the bottom of the hole, 3 to 4 km beneath Earth's surface. These instruments will make seismological measurements of earthquakes and measure the deformation of rock.

Social Studies ACTIVITY
Research the great San Francisco earthquake of 1906. Find images of the earthquake on the Internet and download them, or cut them out of old magazines. Create a photo collage of the earthquake that shows San Francisco before and after the earthquake.

Answer to Language Arts Activity
Have students bring their field guides to class. In the classroom, have students play the role of scientists who are discussing how animal behavior might be used to forecast earthquakes. Students should use facts taken from their field guides to discuss animal behavior that might be useful in earthquake forecasting.

Answer to Social Studies Activity
Have students bring their montages to class. Create a classroom exhibit using the student montages. Use the exhibit to stimulate a discussion about the type of damage that can be caused by a major earthquake, such as the earthquake that struck San Francisco in 1906.

Careers

Hiroo Kanamori

Seismologist Hiroo Kanamori is a seismologist at the California Institute of Technology in Pasadena, California. Dr. Kanamori studies how earthquakes occur and tries to reduce their impact on our society. He also analyzes what the effects of earthquakes on oceans are and how earthquakes create giant ocean waves called *tsunamis* (tsoo NAH meez). Tsunamis are very destructive to life and property when they reach land. Kanamori has discovered that even some weak earthquakes can cause powerful tsunamis. He calls these events *tsunami earthquakes,* and he has learned to predict when tsunamis will form. In short, when tectonic plates grind together slowly, special waves called *long-period seismic waves* are created. When Kanamori sees a long-period wave recorded on a seismogram, he knows a tsunami will form. Because long-period waves travel faster than tsunamis, they arrive at recording stations earlier. When an earthquake station records an earthquake, information about that earthquake is provided to a tsunami warning center. The center determines if the earthquake may cause a tsunami and, if so, issues a tsunami warning to areas that may be affected.

Math Activity

An undersea earthquake causes a tsunami to form. The tsunami travels across the open ocean at 800 km/h. How long will the tsunami take to travel from the point where it formed to a coastline 3,600 km away?

To learn more about these Science in Action topics, visit **go.hrw.com** and type in the keyword **HZ5EQKF**.

Current Science Check out Current Science® articles related to this chapter by visiting **go.hrw.com**. Just type in the keyword **HZ5CS08**.

Careers

Background

In 1996, Dr. Kanamori received the Bucher Medal for his outstanding achievements in seismology. He and his colleague Tom Hanks bridged the gap between seismology and physics by developing an earthquake scale called the "moment magnitude scale." It rates earthquakes by the minimum energy released and is consistent with the Richter scale.

Answer to Math Activity

The speed of the tsunami in the open ocean is 800 km/h. It will take the tsunami 4.5 h to travel the 3,600 km distance to the coastline (3,600 km ÷ 800 km/h = 4.5 h).

9 Volcanoes
Chapter Planning Guide

Compression guide: To shorten instruction because of time limitations, omit the Chapter Lab.

OBJECTIVES	LABS, DEMONSTRATIONS, AND ACTIVITIES	TECHNOLOGY RESOURCES
PACING • 45 min pp. 248–255 **Chapter Opener**	SE **Start-up Activity**, p. 249 GENERAL	OSP **Parent Letter** GENERAL CD **Student Edition on CD-ROM** CD **Guided Reading Audio CD** TR **Chapter Starter Transparency*** VID **Brain Food Video Quiz**
Section 1 Volcanic Eruptions • Distinguish between nonexplosive and explosive volcanic eruptions. • Identify the features of a volcano. • Explain how the composition of magma affects the type of volcanic eruption that will occur. • Describe four types of lava and four types of pyroclastic material.	TE **Activity** Volcano Pen Pals, p. 250 GENERAL TE **Group Activity** Volcanic Radio Show, p. 251 GENERAL SE **Connection to Social Studies** Fertile Farmlands, p. 253 GENERAL TE **Group Activity** Describing Viscosity, p. 253 GENERAL SE **Quick Lab** Modeling an Explosive Eruption, p. 254 GENERAL CRF **Datasheet for Quick Lab***	CRF **Lesson Plans*** TR **Bellringer Transparency*** TR **LINK TO PHYSICAL SCIENCE** Models of a Solid, a Liquid, and a Gas* TR **Four Types of Lava***
PACING • 45 min pp. 256–259 **Section 2 Effects of Volcanic Eruptions** • Explain how volcanic eruptions can affect climate. • Compare the three types of volcanoes. • Compare craters, calderas, and lava plateaus.	TE **Connection Activity** History, p. 257 GENERAL TE **Activity** Classifying Volcanoes, p. 257 BASIC TE **Activity** Book Report, p. 257 ADVANCED TE **Connection Activity** Astronomy, p. 258 ADVANCED SE **Skills Practice Lab** Some Go "Pop," Some Do Not, p. 733 GENERAL CRF **Datasheet for LabBook*** LB **Whiz-Bang Demonstrations** How's Your Lava Life?* GENERAL CD **Interactive Explorations CD-Rom**, What's the Matter? ADVANCED	CRF **Lesson Plans*** TR **Bellringer Transparency*** TR **Three Types of Volcanoes*** TR **The Formation of a Caldera***
PACING • 90 min pp. 260–265 **Section 3 Causes of Volcanic Eruptions** • Describe the formation and movement of magma. • Explain the relationship between volcanoes and plate tectonics. • Summarize the methods scientists use to predict volcanic eruptions.	SE **Quick Lab** Reaction to Stress, p. 261 GENERAL CRF **Datasheet for Quick Lab*** TE **Connection Activity** Math, p. 262 GENERAL SE **School-to-Home Activity** Tectonic Models, p. 263 GENERAL TE **Group Activity** Preparing for an Eruption, p. 263 ADVANCED SE **Skills Practice Lab** Volcano Verdict, p. 266 GENERAL CRF **Datasheet for Chapter Lab*** LB **Labs You Can Eat** Hot Spots* GENERAL LB **Whiz-Bang Demonstrations** What Makes a Vent Event?* GENERAL LB **Long-Term Projects & Research Ideas** A City Lost and Found* ADVANCED SE **Science In Action** Math, Social Studies, and Language Arts Activities, pp. 272–273 GENERAL	CRF **Lesson Plans*** TR **Bellringer Transparency*** TR **The Location of Major Volcanoes*** TR **How Magma Forms at a Divergent Boundary*** TR **How Magma Forms at a Convergent Boundary*** SE **Internet Activity**, p. 265 GENERAL CRF **SciLinks Activity*** GENERAL VID **Lab Videos for Earth Science**

PACING • 90 min

CHAPTER REVIEW, ASSESSMENT, AND STANDARDIZED TEST PREPARATION
- CRF **Vocabulary Activity*** GENERAL
- SE **Chapter Review**, pp. 268–269 GENERAL
- CRF **Chapter Review*** GENERAL
- CRF **Chapter Tests A*** GENERAL, **B*** ADVANCED, **C*** SPECIAL NEEDS
- SE **Standardized Test Preparation**, pp. 270–271 GENERAL
- CRF **Standardized Test Preparation*** GENERAL
- CRF **Performance-Based Assessment*** GENERAL
- OSP **Test Generator** GENERAL
- CRF **Test Item Listing*** GENERAL

Online and Technology Resources

go.hrw.com
Visit go.hrw.com for a variety of free resources related to this textbook. Enter the keyword **HZ5VOL**.

Holt Online Learning
Students can access interactive problem-solving help and active visual concept development with the *Holt Science and Technology* Online Edition available at **www.hrw.com**.

Guided Reading Audio CD
Also in Spanish
A direct reading of each chapter for auditory learners, reluctant readers, and Spanish-speaking students.

Science Tutor CD-ROM
Excellent for remediation and test practice.

KEY						
SE Student Edition	**CRF** Chapter Resource File	**SS** Science Skills Worksheets	* Also on One-Stop Planner
TE Teacher Edition	**OSP** One-Stop Planner	**MS** Math Skills for Science Worksheets	♦ Requires advance prep
	LB Lab Bank	**CD** CD or CD-ROM	■ Also available in Spanish
	TR Transparencies	**VID** Classroom Video/DVD	

SKILLS DEVELOPMENT RESOURCES	SECTION REVIEW AND ASSESSMENT	STANDARDS CORRELATIONS
SE Pre-Reading Activity, p. 248 GENERAL **OSP** Science Puzzlers, Twisters & Teasers GENERAL		National Science Education Standards SAI 1; ST 1; SPSP 3
CRF Directed Reading A* ■ BASIC, B* SPECIAL NEEDS **CRF** Vocabulary and Section Summary* ■ GENERAL **SE** Reading Strategy Reading Organizer, p. 250 GENERAL **TE** Inclusion Strategies, p. 253 **CRF** Critical Thinking Eruption Disruption* BASIC	**SE** Reading Checks, pp. 251, 252, 254 GENERAL **TE** Reteaching, p. 254 BASIC **TE** Quiz, p. 254 GENERAL **TE** Alternative Assessment, p. 254 BASIC **SE** Section Review,* p. 255 ■ GENERAL **TE** Homework, p. 255 GENERAL **CRF** Section Quiz* ■ GENERAL	SAI 1; HNS 2; ES 1c
CRF Directed Reading A* ■ BASIC, B* SPECIAL NEEDS **CRF** Vocabulary and Section Summary* ■ GENERAL **SE** Reading Strategy Paired Summarizing, p. 256 GENERAL **CRF** Reinforcement Worksheet A Variety of Volcanoes* BASIC	**SE** Reading Checks, pp. 256, 258 GENERAL **TE** Reteaching, p. 258 BASIC **TE** Quiz, p. 258 GENERAL **TE** Alternative Assessment, p. 258 GENERAL **SE** Section Review,* p. 259 ■ GENERAL **CRF** Section Quiz* ■ GENERAL	ST 2; SPSP 3, 4; ES 1c; *LabBook:* SAI 1
CRF Directed Reading A* ■ BASIC, B* SPECIAL NEEDS **CRF** Vocabulary and Section Summary* ■ GENERAL **SE** Reading Strategy Reading Organizer, p. 260 GENERAL **SE** Math Practice How Hot is Hot?, p. 262 GENERAL **TE** Inclusion Strategies, p. 263 **MS** Math Skills for Science Using Temperature Scales* GENERAL **CRF** Reinforcement Worksheet Tectonic Plate Movement* BASIC	**SE** Reading Checks, pp. 261, 263, 264 GENERAL **TE** Reteaching, p. 264 BASIC **TE** Quiz, p. 264 GENERAL **TE** Alternative Assessment, p. 264 ADVANCED **TE** Homework, p. 264 GENERAL **SE** Section Review,* p. 265 ■ GENERAL **CRF** Section Quiz* ■ GENERAL	UCP 3; SAI 1; ST 2; ES 1b, 1c; *Chapter Lab:* SAI 1

One-Stop Planner® CD-ROM

This convenient CD-ROM includes:
- Lab Materials QuickList Software
- Holt Calendar Planner
- Customizable Lesson Plans
- Printable Worksheets
- ExamView® Test Generator

CNN Student News

cnnstudentnews.com

Find the latest news, lesson plans, and activities related to important scientific events.

SciLinks NSTA

www.scilinks.org

Maintained by the **National Science Teachers Association**. See Chapter Enrichment pages for a complete list of topics.

Current Science®

Check out *Current Science* articles and activities by visiting the HRW Web site at **go.hrw.com.** Just type in the keyword **HZ5CS09T.**

Classroom Videos

- **Lab Videos** demonstrate the chapter lab.
- **Brain Food Video Quizzes** help students review the chapter material.
- **CNN Videos** bring science into your students' daily life.

Chapter 9 • Chapter Planning Guide 247B

Chapter 9 — Chapter Resources

Visual Resources

- **Chapter Starter Transparency**
- **Bellringer Transparencies**
- **Teaching Transparencies**
- **Concept Mapping Transparency**

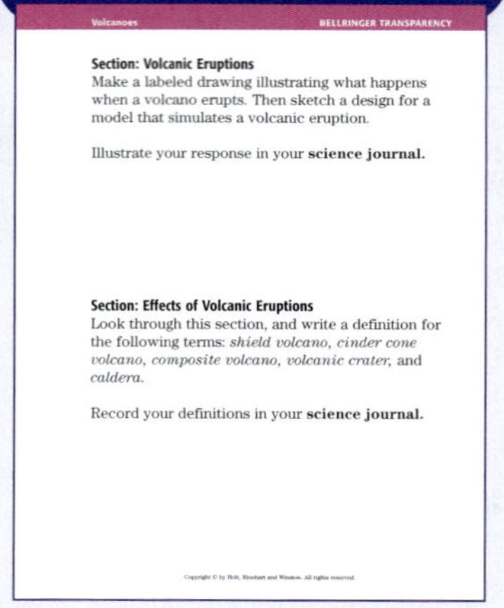

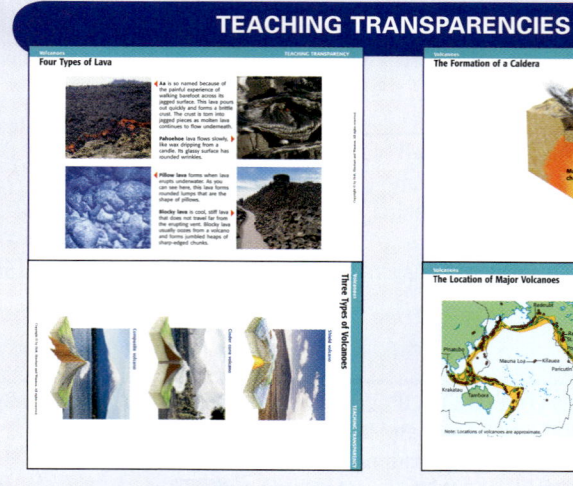

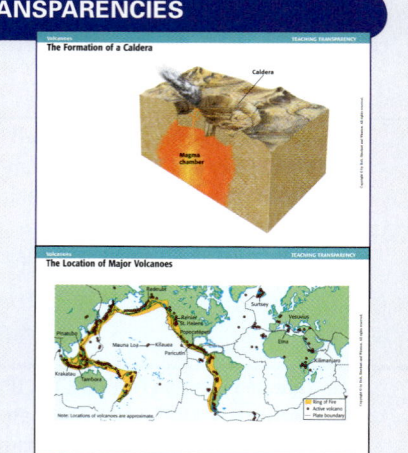

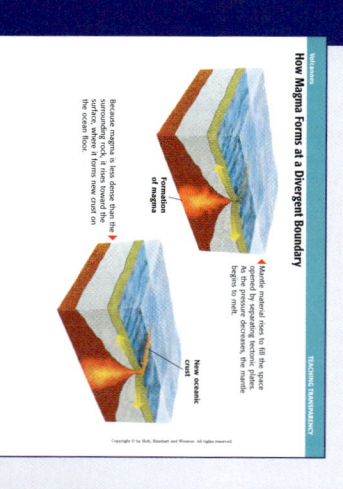

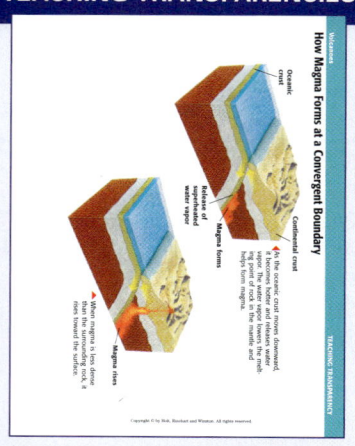

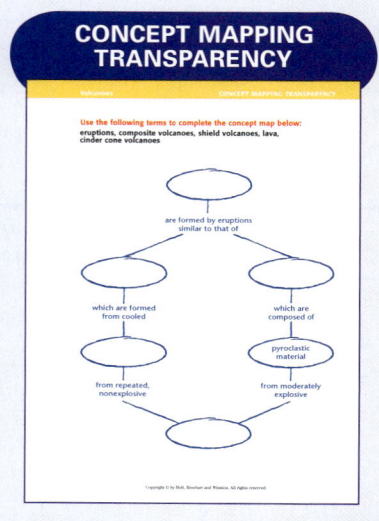

Planning Resources

- **Lesson Plans**
- **Parent Letter** (Also in Spanish)
- **Test Item Listing**

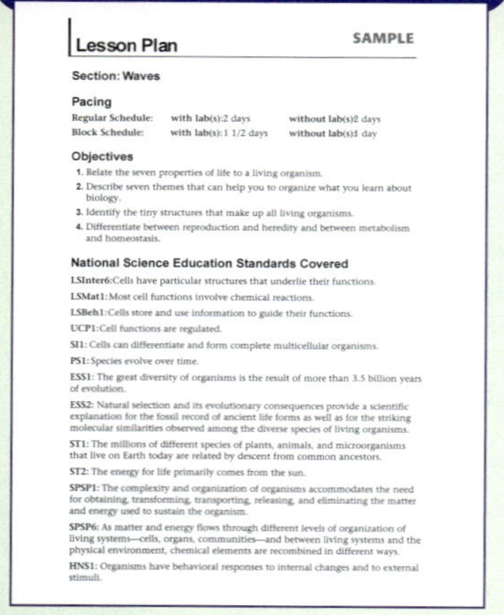

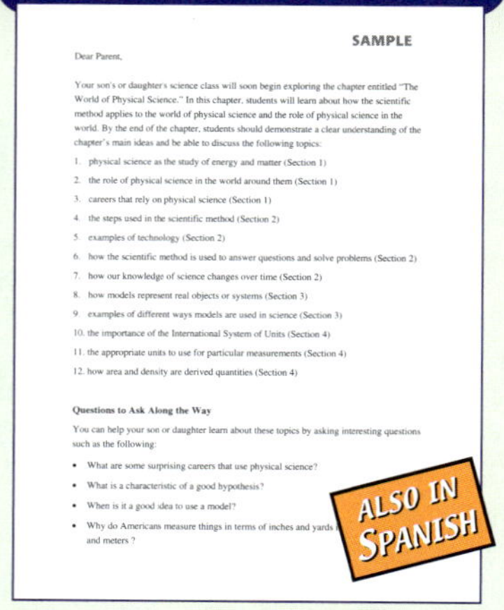

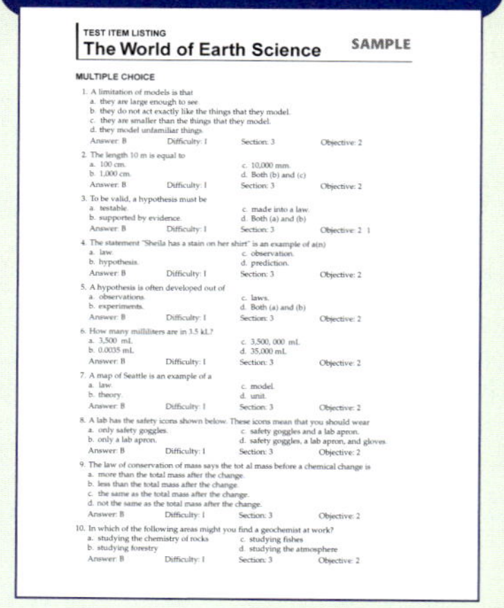

One-Stop Planner® CD-ROM

This CD-ROM includes all of the resources shown here and the following time-saving tools:

- Lab Materials QuickList Software
- Customizable lesson plans
- Holt Calendar Planner
- The powerful ExamView® Test Generator

247C Chapter 9 • Volcanoes

For a preview of available worksheets covering math and science skills, see pages T26–T33. All of these resources are also on the One-Stop Planner®.

Meeting Individual Needs

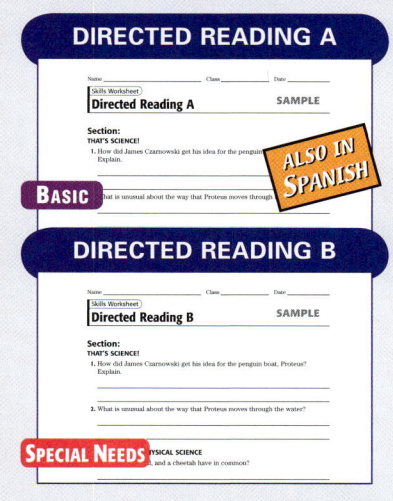

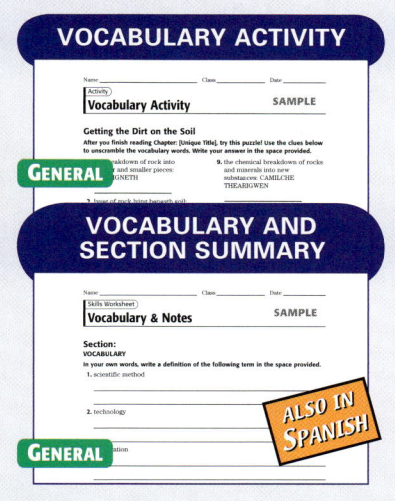

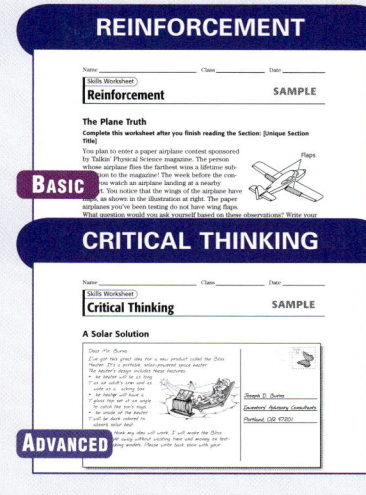

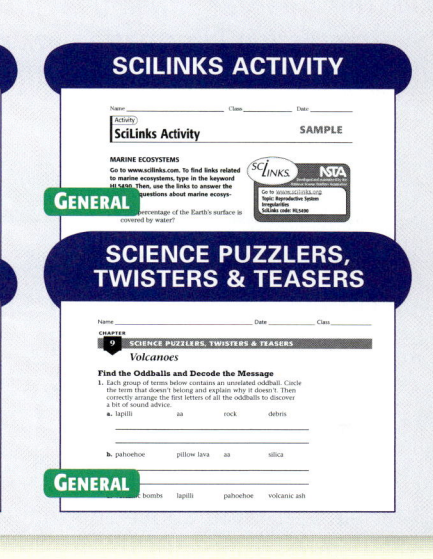

- **DIRECTED READING A** — BASIC — ALSO IN SPANISH
- **DIRECTED READING B** — SPECIAL NEEDS
- **VOCABULARY ACTIVITY** — GENERAL
- **VOCABULARY AND SECTION SUMMARY** — GENERAL — ALSO IN SPANISH
- **REINFORCEMENT** — BASIC
- **CRITICAL THINKING** — ADVANCED
- **SCILINKS ACTIVITY** — GENERAL
- **SCIENCE PUZZLERS, TWISTERS & TEASERS** — GENERAL

Labs and Activities

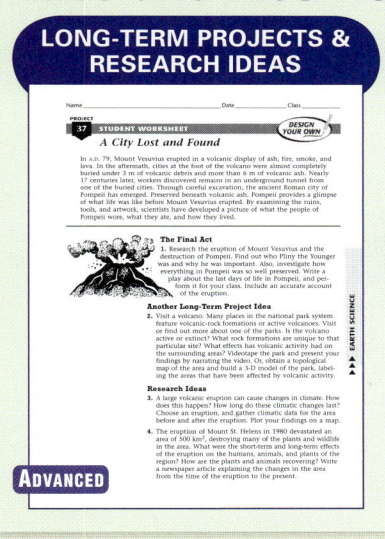

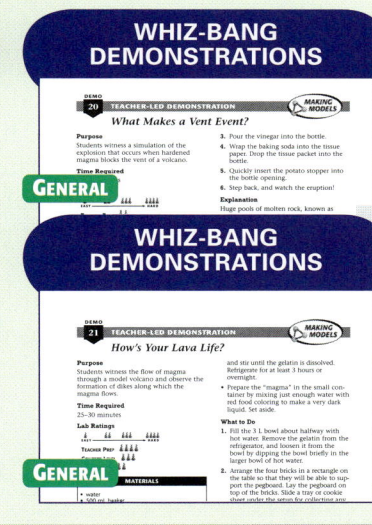

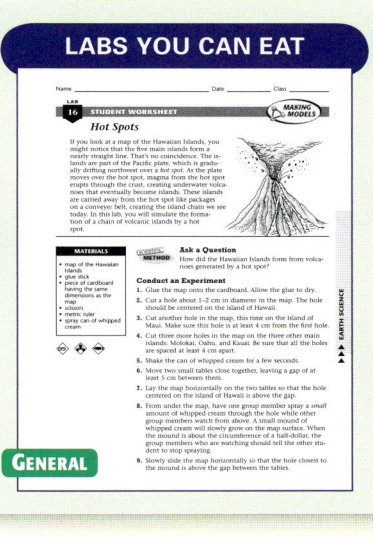

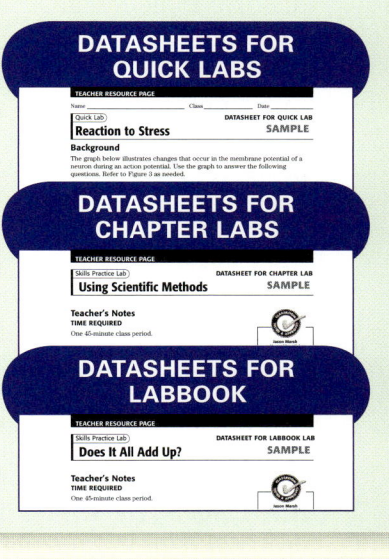

- **LONG-TERM PROJECTS & RESEARCH IDEAS** — ADVANCED
- **WHIZ-BANG DEMONSTRATIONS** — GENERAL
- **WHIZ-BANG DEMONSTRATIONS** — GENERAL
- **LABS YOU CAN EAT** — GENERAL
- **DATASHEETS FOR QUICK LABS**
- **DATASHEETS FOR CHAPTER LABS**
- **DATASHEETS FOR LABBOOK**

Review and Assessments

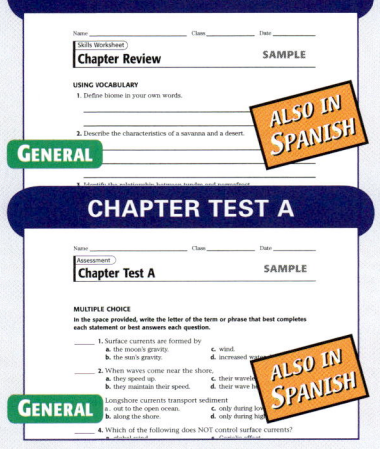

- **SECTION QUIZ** — GENERAL
- **SECTION REVIEW** — GENERAL
- **CHAPTER REVIEW** — GENERAL — ALSO IN SPANISH
- **CHAPTER TEST A** — GENERAL — ALSO IN SPANISH
- **CHAPTER TEST B** — ADVANCED
- **CHAPTER TEST C** — SPECIAL NEEDS
- **STANDARDIZED TEST PREPARATION** — GENERAL
- **PERFORMANCE-BASED ASSESSMENT** — GENERAL

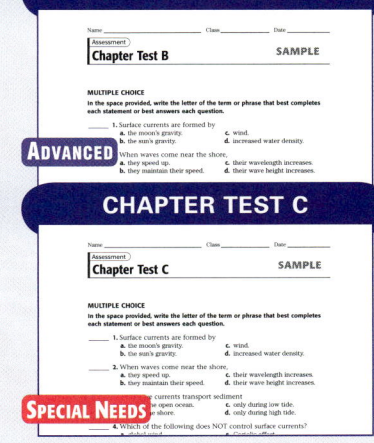

Chapter 9 • Chapter Resources 247D

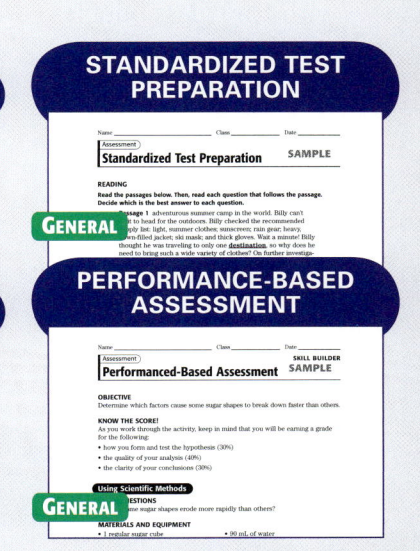

9 Chapter Enrichment

This Chapter Enrichment provides relevant and interesting information to expand and enhance your presentation of the chapter material.

Section 1

Volcanic Eruptions

Mineral Formation in Subduction Zones

- The formation of commercially valuable minerals is common in areas where subduction creates volcanoes. As magma that is formed from subducted crust rises, the magma heats the surrounding rocks, which causes the fluids the rocks contain to circulate around and above the magma body. The hot fluids react with the magma and surrounding rocks and dissolve some metals (including iron, lead, silver, and gold). As the water-rich fluid rises through Earth's crust, mineral precipitation occurs at points where the fluid cools. This process can form rich mineral veins.

The Origin of Volcanic Terms

- Many terms for nonexplosive eruptions are Hawaiian. For example, lava that blows into fine, spiky strands are called *Pele's hair,* for the Hawaiian goddess of fire. *Limu o Pele,* which means "Pele's seaweed," is the term for delicate, translucent sheets of spatter filled with tiny glass bubbles.

- The terms for explosive eruptions, however, are generally not Hawaiian. For example, *nuée ardente,* a French term that means "burning cloud," is a hot mass of volcanic gases, ash, and debris that is expelled explosively and then travels at tremendous speeds down a mountainside.

Is That a Fact!

- The Tambora eruption in Indonesia was the largest in the last 200 years. The eruption and the resulting tsunamis killed more than 10,000 people. Ash covered so much land that farmland was devastated; disease and famine killed 80,000 more people.

- During the Tambora eruption, so much ash was thrown into the atmosphere that weather patterns were affected worldwide. Scholars believe the eruption caused the "Year Without a Summer" in 1816, when snow fell in New England in July.

Section 2

Effects of Volcanic Eruptions

Islands of Survival

- Nonexplosive volcanoes, such as Kilauea, on the island of Hawaii, may produce many different lava flows during an eruption. If these flows surround an area of forest, they create an island in a sea of lava. Hawaiians call such areas *kipukas,* which means "islands of survival." Over the last 20 years, biologists have studied populations of animals isolated in kipukas and have found interesting evidence to support evolution. Picture-wing drosophila flies have exhibited changes that ultimately could produce new species.

Is That a Fact!

- In the Caribbean, a submarine volcano named Kick'em Jenny is gaining a very bad reputation. As one sailboat captain said, "Kick'em Jenny . . . has a reputation of kicking up a nasty sea." Between 1986 and 1996, the volcano grew more than 50 m; its top is now only 200 m below sea level. It's close enough to the surface that eruptions can cause waves and turbulence in the sea. Volcanologists are concerned that a large eruption could cause devastating tsunamis throughout the Caribbean.

- When lava flows in a defined channel, a crust eventually forms on the surface of the lava. If the crust remains stationary while the lava below is still flowing, a lava tube or a lava cave several kilometers long may form.

Section 3

Causes of Volcanic Eruptions

Merapi, "Mountain of Fire"

- There are more active volcanoes in Indonesia than anywhere on Earth—130! One of the most dangerous volcanoes is called Merapi, or "Mountain of Fire," on the island of Java. Since 1548, Merapi has erupted violently 68 times. In 1998, it became active again, and people began to evacuate the area. Scientists are worried about the city of Yogyakarta, which is 70 km north of the volcano and is home to about 500,000 people. A large eruption could destroy the city.

Predicting the Mount Pinatubo Eruptions

- Perhaps the most successful prediction of a volcanic eruption was on Mount Pinatubo, in the Philippines. When Pinatubo became active in March and April 1991, scientists rushed to the area and quickly established monitoring systems. Scientists from the Philippines and the United States distributed a five-level alert system to civil defense and local officials. Evacuations began when an eruption appeared imminent (level 4 alert); more than 250,000 people evacuated the area. The eruption caused enormous losses of land, housing, and crops, but because of the preparations and warnings, only 300 people died during the eruption. Lahars killed an additional 500 people.

- Most volcanic eruptions are not as predictable as those of Mount Pinatubo. For example, the monitoring methods used at Pinatubo have been much less successful on Montserrat, in the Caribbean.

Predicting the Eruption of Mount St. Helens

- Earthquake tremors are often a sign that a volcano is about to erupt. In the months before the eruption of Mount St. Helens, small earthquakes, which grew in number and intensity, shook the area. On March 27, 1980, the volcano began venting steam and ash. Geologists had set up seismometers to record the frequency, location, and magnitude of the quakes. Electronic surveying equipment employed laser beams to measure ground swelling as the lava dome rose. Tiltmeters measured changes in the mountain's slope. Stream gauges recorded water temperatures, pH levels, and amounts of dissolved minerals in the waters around the volcano. Gas sensors on the ground and in aircraft monitored hydrogen, carbon dioxide, and sulfur dioxide levels that might signal the movement of magma toward the surface.

Is That a Fact!

- The youngest Hawaiian "island," Loihi, is 3,500 m above the ocean floor. But it must grow almost 1 km before coming out of the ocean, which, scientists say, could take more than 20,000 years. However, it is difficult to predict when the volcano will become an island. For example, during a 1997 eruption the summit of Loihi sank by 50 to 100 m!

SciLinks is maintained by the National Science Teachers Association to provide you and your students with interesting, up-to-date links that will enrich your classroom presentation of the chapter.

Visit www.scilinks.org and enter the SciLinks code for more information about the topic listed.

Topic: Volcanic Eruptions
SciLinks code: HSM1616

Topic: What Causes Volcanoes?
SciLinks code: HSM1654

Topic: Volcanic Effects
SciLinks code: HSM1615

Chapter 9 • Chapter Enrichment   247F

9 Volcanoes

Overview
This chapter discusses volcanoes, the effects of eruptions, and how eruptions are predicted. About 500 million people live near active volcanoes. Volcanoes are carefully studied so that eruptions may be predicted.

Assessing Prior Knowledge
Students should be familiar with the following topics:
- the rock cycle
- plate tectonics
- changes of state

Identifying Misconceptions
Students may think that all volcanic eruptions are explosive and destructive. Point out that the majority of volcanic activity is nonexplosive. Also, reinforce the idea that volcanic activity plays a major role in forming the Earth's crust and in creating fertile land. Students may also think that volcanoes are uncommon and that volcanic activity is rare. Point out that the Earth has more than 1,300 active volcanoes and that at any moment, between 1 and 20 volcanoes are erupting on land. Many more volcanoes are erupting on the ocean floor. Volcano World is a Website that has updates on volcanoes that are currently erupting.

SECTION 1 Volcanic Eruptions 250

SECTION 2 Effects of Volcanic Eruptions 256

SECTION 3 Causes of Volcanic Eruptions 260

Chapter Lab 266
Chapter Review 268
Standardized Test Preparation 270
Science in Action............ 272

About the PHOTO
When you think of a volcanic eruption, you probably think of a cone-shaped mountain exploding and sending huge clouds of ash into the air. Some volcanic eruptions do just that! Most volcanic eruptions, such as the one shown here, which is flowing over a road in Hawaii, are slow and quiet. Volcanic eruptions happen throughout the world, and they play a major role in shaping the Earth's surface.

PRE-READING ACTIVITY
FOLDNOTES **Layered Book** Before you read the chapter, create the FoldNote entitled "Layered Book" described in the **Study Skills** section of the Appendix. Label the tabs of the layered book with "Volcanic eruptions," "Effects of eruptions," and "Causes of eruptions." As you read the chapter, write information you learn about each category under the appropriate tab.

Standards Correlations

National Science Education Standards
The following codes indicate the National Science Education Standards that correlate to this chapter. The full text of the standards is at the front of the book.

Chapter Opener
SAI 1; ST 1; SPSP 3, 4

Section 1 Volcanic Eruptions
SAI 1; HNS 2; ES 1c

Section 2 Effects of Volcanic Eruptions
ST 2; SPSP 3, 4; ES 1c; *LabBook:* SAI 1

Section 3 Causes of Volcanic Eruptions
UCP 3; SAI 1; ST 2; ES 1b, 1c

Chapter Lab
SAI 1; ST 2

Chapter Review
ES 1b, 1c

Science In Action
SPSP 3, SPSP 5; HNS 1, 2

248 Chapter 9 • Volcanoes

START-UP ACTIVITY

MATERIALS
FOR EACH GROUP
- baking soda, 10 mL
- bathroom tissue
- beaker or measuring cup, 200 mL
- clay, modeling
- dish soap, liquid
- funnel
- plate or pan, large
- stirring rod
- stopwatch
- vinegar, 50 mL

Safety Caution: Students should wear safety goggles and aprons during this activity.

Answers

1. Sample answer: The reaction between vinegar and baking soda produced CO_2 gas. The formation of gas bubbles caused the "magma" to increase in volume. Then, the "magma" erupted from the model volcano.
2. Answers may vary.
3. If the size of the funnel opening is smaller, the eruption may happen more quickly. If the amount of baking soda and vinegar is increased, the eruption will also happen more quickly.

START-UP ACTIVITY

Anticipation
In this activity, you will build a simple model of a volcano and you will try to predict an eruption.

Procedure
1. Place **10 mL of baking soda** on a **sheet of tissue.** Fold the corners of the tissue over the baking soda, and place the tissue packet in a **large pan.**
2. Put **modeling clay** around the top edge of a **funnel.** Press that end of the funnel over the tissue packet to make a tight seal.
3. After you put on **safety goggles**, add **50 mL of vinegar** and **several drops of liquid dish soap** to a **200 mL beaker** and stir.
4. Predict how long it will take the volcano to erupt after the liquid is poured into the funnel. Then, carefully pour the liquid into the funnel, and use a **stopwatch** to measure how long the volcano takes to begin erupting.

Analysis
1. Based on your observations, explain what happened to cause the eruption.
2. How accurate was your prediction? By how many seconds did the class predictions vary?
3. How do the size of the funnel opening and the amount of baking soda and vinegar affect the amount of time that the volcano takes to erupt?

Chapter Starter Transparency
Use this transparency to help students begin thinking about the effects of volcanic eruptions on human societies.

CHAPTER RESOURCES

Technology
- **Transparencies**
  - Chapter Starter Transparency *READING SKILLS*
- **Student Edition on CD-ROM**
- **Guided Reading Audio CD**
  - English or Spanish
- **Classroom Videos**
  - Brain Food Video Quiz

Workbooks
- **Science Puzzlers, Twisters & Teasers**
  - Volcanoes *GENERAL*

Chapter 9 • Volcanoes **249**

SECTION 1

Focus

Overview
In this section, students will learn how the composition of magma affects volcanic eruptions. Students will also learn to identify the internal structure of a volcano and the types of lava and pyroclastic material released during an eruption.

🔔 Bellringer
Have students create in their **science journal** a labeled drawing that illustrates what happens when a volcano erupts. Then, have students describe the photographs shown on this page and the next. Ask them to think about why the characteristics of volcanic eruptions vary.

Motivate

ACTIVITY — GENERAL

Writing **Volcano Pen Pals** Have students write a letter to a friend from a fictional survivor of a volcanic eruption. Have students describe the volcano hours before the eruption, during the eruption, and after the eruption. Students can then exchange letters and read the letters to the class. 🗣 **Verbal**

SECTION 1

Volcanic Eruptions

Think about the force released when the first atomic bomb exploded during World War II. Now imagine an explosion 10,000 times stronger, and you will get an idea of how powerful a volcanic eruption can be.

The explosive pressure of a volcanic eruption can turn an entire mountain into a billowing cloud of ash and rock in a matter of seconds. But eruptions are also creative forces—they help form fertile farmland. They also create some of the largest mountains on Earth. During an eruption, molten rock, or *magma*, is forced to the Earth's surface. Magma that flows onto the Earth's surface is called *lava*. **Volcanoes** are areas of Earth's surface through which magma and volcanic gases pass.

Nonexplosive Eruptions

At this moment, volcanic eruptions are occurring around the world—on the ocean floor and on land. Nonexplosive eruptions are the most common type of eruption. These eruptions produce relatively calm flows of lava, such as those shown in **Figure 1**. Nonexplosive eruptions can release huge amounts of lava. Vast areas of the Earth's surface, including much of the sea floor and the Northwest region of the United States, are covered with lava from nonexplosive eruptions.

READING WARM-UP

Objectives
- Distinguish between nonexplosive and explosive volcanic eruptions.
- Identify the features of a volcano.
- Explain how the composition of magma affects the type of volcanic eruption that will occur.
- Describe four types of lava and four types of pyroclastic material.

Terms to Learn
volcano   vent
magma chamber

READING STRATEGY

Reading Organizer As you read this section, make a table comparing types of lava and pyroclastic material.

volcano a vent or fissure in the Earth's surface through which magma and gases are expelled

▶ Sometimes, nonexplosive eruptions can spray lava into the air. Lava fountains, such as this one, pulse with the pressure of escaping gases.

Figure 1 Examples of Nonexplosive Eruptions

▲ The speed of a lava flow can range from a slow creep to as fast as 60 km/h.

CHAPTER RESOURCES

Chapter Resource File
- Lesson Plan
- Directed Reading A **BASIC**
- Directed Reading B **SPECIAL NEEDS**

Technology
- Transparencies
  • Bellringer

MISCONCEPTION ALERT

Nonexplosive Eruptions Although explosive volcanoes get the most attention, nonexplosive eruptions play a much more significant role in shaping our world. For instance, much of the ocean floor is basaltic pillow lava, and nonexplosive volcanoes formed many of the islands in the Pacific Ocean.

---

250 Chapter 9 • Volcanoes

Explosive Eruptions

Explosive eruptions, such as the one shown in **Figure 2,** are much rarer than nonexplosive eruptions. However, the effects of explosive eruptions can be incredibly destructive. During an explosive eruption, clouds of hot debris, ash, and gas rapidly shoot out from a volcano. Instead of producing lava flows, explosive eruptions cause molten rock to be blown into tiny particles that harden in the air. The dust-sized particles, called *ash,* can reach the upper atmosphere and can circle the Earth for years. Larger pieces of debris fall closer to the volcano. An explosive eruption can also blast millions of tons of lava and rock from a volcano. In a matter of seconds, an explosive eruption can demolish an entire mountainside, as shown in **Figure 3.**

Reading Check List two differences between explosive and nonexplosive eruptions. (*See the Appendix for answers to Reading Checks.*)

Figure 2 *In what resembles a nuclear explosion, volcanic ash rockets skyward during the 1990 eruption of Mount Redoubt in Alaska.*

Figure 3 *Within seconds, the 1980 eruption of Mount St. Helens in Washington State caused the side of the mountain to collapse. The blast scorched and flattened 600 km^2 of forest.*

Teach

Group Activity — GENERAL

Volcanic Radio Show Have groups prepare and present a mock radio program about a volcanic eruption of one of the following volcanoes:

Mount St. Helens, Nevado del Ruiz, Vesuvius, Mount Pinatubo

Have group members research the event together. Two students could write the script. One student could produce sound effects. One student could be the moderator, and two could be on-site reporters. The remaining students could be people directly affected by the eruption (teachers, students, store owners, and rescue personnel). Make sure students describe the event from the first signs of volcanic activity to the aftermath.
LS Verbal   **English Language Learners**
Co-op Learning

Answer to Reading Check
Nonexplosive eruptions are common, and they feature relatively calm flows of lava. Explosive eruptions are less common and produce large, explosive clouds of ash and gases.

Cultural Awareness — GENERAL

Volcano Legends The Klickitats of the Pacific Northwest had two names for Mount St. Helens. The first name was *Loo-Wit,* which referred to a lovely maiden who changed into a beautiful, white mountain. The other name was *Tah-one-lat-clah,* which means "fire mountain" and indicates the tribe's knowledge that the volcano was prone to eruptions. Ask students why they think the Klickitats had two very different names for Mount St. Helens. Have students research other American Indian names and legends for volcanic peaks in North America.

Section 1 • Volcanic Eruptions **251**

Teach, continued

CONNECTION to Physical Science — ADVANCED

States of Matter Use the teaching transparency entitled "Models of a Solid, a Liquid, and a Gas" to discuss changes of state in magma. When water or carbon dioxide is a part of the crystal structure of minerals in a rock, these compounds are in the solid state. When rock melts to form magma, the water or carbon dioxide is released into the molten liquid. In other words, the water or carbon dioxide is dissolved in the magma. When temperature and pressure conditions are right, water and carbon dioxide in the magma solution *exsolve*, or vaporize, changing from liquid to gas. The exsolution of gases forms bubbles that greatly increase the volume of the magma. When the magma erupts on the surface, it cools and solidifies, changing from a liquid to a solid. The gases escape into the air, but they leave distinctive round holes called *vesicles*. **LS Visual**

Answer to Reading Check

Because silica-rich magma has a high viscosity, it tends to trap gases and plug volcanic vents. This causes pressure to build up and can result in an explosive eruption.

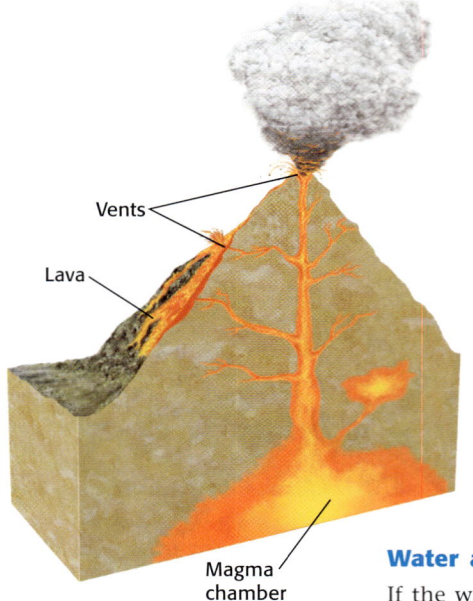

Figure 4 Volcanoes form when lava is released from vents.

Labels: Vents, Lava, Magma chamber

magma chamber the body of molten rock that feeds a volcano

vent an opening at the surface of the Earth through which volcanic material passes

---

What Is Inside a Volcano?

If you could look inside an erupting volcano, you would see the features shown in **Figure 4**. A **magma chamber** is a body of molten rock deep underground that feeds a volcano. Magma rises from the magma chamber through cracks in the Earth's crust to openings called **vents**. Magma is released from the vents during an eruption.

What Makes Up Magma?

By comparing the composition of magma from different eruptions, scientists have made an important discovery. The composition of the magma affects how explosive a volcanic eruption is. The key to whether an eruption will be explosive lies in the silica, water, and gas content of the magma.

Water and Magma Are an Explosive Combination

If the water content of magma is high, an explosive eruption is more likely. Because magma is underground, it is under intense pressure and water stays dissolved in the magma. If the magma quickly moves to the surface, the pressure suddenly decreases and the water and other compounds, such as carbon dioxide, become gases. As the gases expand rapidly, an explosion can result. This process is similar to what happens when you shake a can of soda and open it. When a can of soda is shaken, the CO_2 dissolved in the soda is released and pressure builds up. When the can is opened, the soda shoots out, just as lava shoots out of a volcano during an explosive eruption. In fact, some lava is so frothy with gas when it reaches the surface that its solid form, called *pumice*, can float in water!

Silica-Rich Magma Traps Explosive Gases

Magma that has a high silica content also tends to cause explosive eruptions. Silica-rich magma has a stiff consistency. It flows slowly and tends to harden in a volcano's vents. As a result, it plugs the vent. As more magma pushes up from below, pressure increases. If enough pressure builds up, an explosive eruption takes place. Stiff magma also prevents water vapor and other gases from easily escaping. Gas bubbles trapped in magma can expand until they explode. When they explode, the magma shatters and ash and pumice are blasted from the vent. Magma that contains less silica has a more fluid, runnier consistency. Because gases escape this type of magma more easily, explosive eruptions are less likely to occur.

✓ **Reading Check** How do silica levels affect an eruption?

CHAPTER RESOURCES

Technology

Transparencies
- **LINK TO PHYSICAL SCIENCE** Models of a Solid, a Liquid, and a Gas
- Four Types of Lava

WEIRD SCIENCE

Lava cools very slowly not only because it is very hot to start with but also because it is a good insulator. When a lava flow in Mexico in 1952 stopped, the flow was 10 m thick. Four years later, in 1956, the lava still steamed when it rained.

What Erupts from a Volcano?

Magma erupts as either lava or pyroclastic (PIE roh KLAS tik) material. *Lava* is liquid magma that flows from a volcanic vent. *Pyroclastic material* forms when magma is blasted into the air and hardens. Nonexplosive eruptions produce mostly lava. Explosive eruptions produce mostly pyroclastic material. Over many years—or even during the same eruption—a volcano's eruptions may alternate between lava and pyroclastic eruptions.

Types of Lava

The viscosity of lava, or how lava flows, varies greatly. To understand viscosity, remember that a milkshake has high viscosity and a glass of milk has low viscosity. Lava that has high viscosity is stiff. Lava that has low viscosity is more fluid. The viscosity of lava affects the surface of a lava flow in different ways, as shown in **Figure 5**. *Blocky lava* and *pahoehoe* (puh HOY HOY) have a high viscosity and flow slowly. Other types of lava flows, such as *aa* (AH AH) and *pillow lava*, have lower viscosities and flow more quickly.

CONNECTION TO Social Studies

Fertile Farmlands Volcanic ash helps create some of the most fertile farmland in the world. Use a world map and reference materials to find the location of volcanoes that have helped create farmland in Italy, Africa, South America, and the United States. Make an illustrated map on a piece of poster board to share your findings.

ACTIVITY

Figure 5 Four Types of Lava

Aa is so named because of the painful experience of walking barefoot across its jagged surface. This lava pours out quickly and forms a brittle crust. The crust is torn into jagged pieces as molten lava continues to flow underneath.

Pahoehoe lava flows slowly, like wax dripping from a candle. Its glassy surface has rounded wrinkles.

Pillow lava forms when lava erupts underwater. As you can see here, this lava forms rounded lumps that are the shape of pillows.

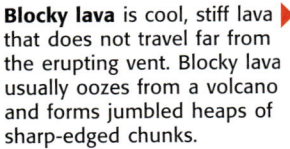

Blocky lava is cool, stiff lava that does not travel far from the erupting vent. Blocky lava usually oozes from a volcano and forms jumbled heaps of sharp-edged chunks.

Group ACTIVITY — GENERAL

Describing Viscosity Introduce the concept of viscosity by having students describe the observable differences in flow rate as you pour molasses or honey, vegetable oil, and water down a gently sloping cookie sheet. (They should observe that the molasses or honey flows slowest, oil flows somewhat faster, and water flows very fast.) Explain that viscosity is a liquid's resistance to flow. Honey has a high viscosity, so it flows very slowly. Water has a low viscosity, so it flows quickly. Ask the students how magma's composition affects its viscosity. (The more silica that is present in magma, the greater the viscosity of the magma.) **LS** Logical

INCLUSION Strategies

- Visually Impaired
- Learning Disabled
- Behavior Control Issues

Organize students into small groups. Give each group colored modeling clay, a piece of cardboard, and self-stick notes. Have each group create a cross-section of a volcano on the cardboard using the modeling clay. Next, students should label the parts of their model using the self-stick notes. After the volcano is labeled, students should add notes with three facts they have learned about volcanoes and attach the notes to the base of their model. **LS** Kinesthetic

---

MISCONCEPTION ALERT

The Force of Water Students may think that it seems illogical that water makes magma more likely to explode. Explain that magma contains water and that the water is dissolved in the magma. When the water changes from a liquid to a gas, the volume of the magma increases dramatically. This change causes a pressure increase that can generate a large explosive force. Discuss with students what would happen if water is boiled in a pot with a tight lid. Then, have students think of other examples in which water can have an explosive force, such as in a car's radiator or in popcorn.

Section 1 • Volcanic Eruptions

Close

Reteaching — BASIC

Volcano Field Guide Have students make an illustrated field guide to volcanic eruptions and types of lava. Students can add to the field guides as they read other sections in this chapter.
LS Visual

Quiz — GENERAL

1. Describe the lava flow from a nonexplosive eruption. (a calm stream of magma that flows out of a vent onto Earth's surface)
2. Describe an explosive eruption. (Ash, hot debris, gases, and chunks of rock spew from a volcano.)
3. Define *blocky lava, pahoehoe*, and *aa*. (Blocky lava is cool, stiff lava that doesn't travel far from the erupting vent. Pahoehoe is lava that flows slowly and forms a wrinkled surface. Aa is lava that flows more quickly than pahoehoe and that forms a brittle, jagged crust.)

Alternative Assessment — BASIC

Making Lava Provide students with cornstarch, salt, and water to make a paste. Then, have students experiment with the ingredients to create representations of the types of lava discussed in this section. Have students work independently to describe the eruptions that would produce each lava type.
LS Kinesthetic

Figure 6 Four Types of Pyroclastic Material

◀ **Volcanic bombs** are large blobs of magma that harden in the air. The shape of this bomb was caused by the magma spinning through the air as it cooled.

▼ **Volcanic blocks**, the largest pieces of pyroclastic material, are pieces of solid rock erupted from a volcano.

◀ **Lapilli**, which means "little stones" in Italian, are pebblelike bits of magma that hardened before they hit the ground.

◀ **Volcanic ash** forms when the gases in stiff magma expand rapidly and the walls of the gas bubbles explode into tiny, glasslike slivers. Ash makes up most of the pyroclastic material in an eruption.

Types of Pyroclastic Material

Pyroclastic material forms when magma explodes from a volcano and solidifies in the air. This material also forms when powerful eruptions shatter existing rock. The size of pyroclastic material ranges from boulders that are the size of houses to tiny particles that can remain suspended in the atmosphere for years. **Figure 6** shows four types of pyroclastic material: volcanic bombs, volcanic blocks, lapilli (lah PIL IE), and volcanic ash.

✓ **Reading Check** Describe four types of pyroclastic material.

Quick Lab

Modeling an Explosive Eruption

1. Inflate a **large balloon**, and place it in a **cardboard box**.
2. Spread a **sheet** on the floor. Place the box in the middle of the sheet. Mound a thin layer of **sand** over the balloon to make a volcano that is taller than the edges of the box.
3. Lightly mist the volcano with **water**. Sprinkle **tempera paint** on the volcano until the volcano is completely covered.
4. Place **small objects** such as **raisins** randomly on the volcano. Draw a sketch of the volcano.
5. Put on your **safety goggles**. Pop the balloon with a **pin**.
6. Use a **metric ruler** to calculate the average distance that 10 grains of sand and 10 raisins traveled.
7. How did the relative weight of each type of material affect the average distance that the material traveled?
8. Draw a sketch of the exploded volcano.

Answers to Quick Lab

7. Sample answer: Lighter materials such as sand traveled farther than heavier materials such as raisins.
8. Sketches may vary.

Teacher's Notes: This activity will work best if students use a very large balloon and if they cover the top of the balloon with a minimal amount of sand. Placing a few tablespoons of talcum powder inside the balloon will create a more dramatic effect when the balloon is popped. This activity models caldera formation as well. Students who have asthma or allergies to airborne particles should wear a filter mask for this activity.

Answer to Reading Check

Volcanic bombs are large blobs of magma that harden in the air. Lapilli are small pieces of magma that harden in the air. Volcanic blocks are pieces of solid rock erupted from a volcano. Ash forms when gases in stiff magma expand rapidly and the walls of the gas bubbles shatter into tiny glasslike slivers.

254 Chapter 9 • Volcanoes

Pyroclastic Flows

One particularly dangerous type of volcanic flow is called a *pyroclastic flow*. Pyroclastic flows are produced when enormous amounts of hot ash, dust, and gases are ejected from a volcano. This glowing cloud of pyroclastic material can race downhill at speeds of more than 200 km/h—faster than most hurricane-force winds! The temperature at the center of a pyroclastic flow can exceed 700°C. A pyroclastic flow from the eruption of Mount Pinatubo is shown in **Figure 7**. Fortunately, scientists were able to predict the eruption and a quarter of a million people were evacuated before the eruption.

Figure 7 The 1991 eruption of Mount Pinatubo in the Philippines released terrifying pyroclastic flows.

SECTION Review

Summary

- Volcanoes erupt both explosively and nonexplosively.
- Magma that has a high level of water, CO_2, or silica tends to erupt explosively.
- Lava can be classified by its viscosity and by the surface texture of lava flows.
- Pyroclastic material, such as ash and volcanic bombs, forms when magma solidifies as it travels through the air.

Using Key Terms

1. In your own words, write a definition for each of the following terms: *volcano, magma chamber,* and *vent.*

Understanding Key Ideas

2. Which of the following factors influences whether a volcano erupts explosively?
   a. the concentration of volcanic bombs in the magma
   b. the concentration of phosphorus in the magma
   c. the concentration of aa in the magma
   d. the concentration of water in the magma

3. How are lava and pyroclastic material classified? Describe four types of lava.

4. Which produces more pyroclastic material: an explosive eruption or a nonexplosive eruption?

5. Explain how the presence of silica and water in magma increases the chances of an explosive eruption.

6. What is a pyroclastic flow?

Math Skills

7. A sample of magma is 64% silica. Express this percentage as a simplified fraction.

Critical Thinking

8. **Analyzing Ideas** How is an explosive eruption similar to opening a can of soda that has been shaken? Be sure to describe the role of carbon dioxide.

9. **Making Inferences** Predict the silica content of aa, pillow lava, and blocky lava.

10. **Making Inferences** Explain why the names of many types of lava are Hawaiian but the names of many types of pyroclastic material are Italian and Indonesian.

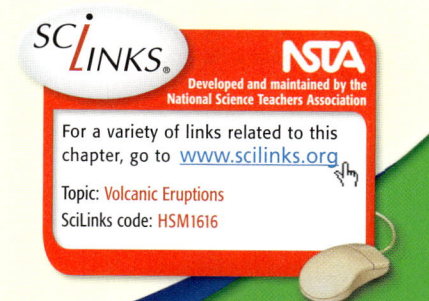

SciLinks
Developed and maintained by the National Science Teachers Association
For a variety of links related to this chapter, go to www.scilinks.org
Topic: Volcanic Eruptions
SciLinks code: HSM1616

Answers to Section Review

1. Sample answer: A volcano is a landform created by repeated eruptions of lava. A magma chamber is an underground body of magma that feeds a volcano. A vent is an opening through which lava or pyroclastic material passes.
2. d
3. Lava is classified by its surface texture. The way that lava flows may also be used to help classify it. Pyroclastic material is classified by size and how it forms. Four types of lava are aa, pahoehoe, blocky lava, and pillow lava. Aa flows quickly and has a jagged crust. Pahoehoe flows slowly and has a wrinkled surface. Pillow lava erupts underwater and forms rounded lumps. Blocky lava is cool, stiff lava that does not travel far from the erupting vent.
4. an explosive eruption
5. The presence of water increases the chance of an explosive eruption because as the magma body moves toward the surface, the water changes to a gas and expands rapidly. This rapid expansion causes an explosion. Silica-rich magma tends to trap volcanic gases and plug vents. The resulting pressure increase can cause an explosive eruption.
6. A pyroclastic flow is a cloud of very hot ash, dust, and gases that flows from a volcano.
7. $64/100 = 32/50 = 16/25$
8. Magma and soda have carbon dioxide dissolved in them. When the pressure on the magma and the soda is reduced, the carbon dioxide becomes a gas and expands rapidly.
9. Aa and pillow lava have a low viscosity, so they have a low silica content. Blocky lava has a high viscosity, so it has a high silica content.
10. Students should conclude that Indonesian and Italian volcanoes are more likely to erupt explosively than Hawaiian volcanoes.

Homework — GENERAL

Deadly Mudflows *Lahar* is an Indonesian term for a particularly deadly kind of volcanic mudflow. A lahar is a flow of water-saturated volcanic debris that races down the slope of a volcano with the consistency of wet cement. Volcanic debris can be saturated by the melting of ice or snow during an eruption, or by rain afterwards. When Nevado del Ruiz erupted in Colombia, its lahar killed more than 25,000 people. Have students research lahars from two eruptions. **LS Intrapersonal**

CHAPTER RESOURCES

Chapter Resource File
- Section Quiz GENERAL
- Section Review GENERAL
- Vocabulary and Section Summary GENERAL
- Datasheet for Quick Lab

Section 1 • Volcanic Eruptions **255**

SECTION 2

Focus

Overview
This section explores the effects of volcanic eruptions on Earth. Students will learn to identify different types of volcanoes and physical features created by volcanic activity, such as craters and calderas.

Bellringer
Write the following terms on the board:

composite volcano, shield volcano, cinder cone volcano, volcanic crater, caldera

Group students in teams of three, and have the groups look through the section to come up with a definition for each of the terms. Have them record their definitions and revise the definitions after they read the section.

Motivate

Discussion — GENERAL
Student Impressions of Eruptions Have students discuss the most exciting images they've seen in movies and television programs featuring volcanoes. Have them describe what they think about volcanic eruptions in their **science journal** so that they can revisit these impressions after reading this section. **LS Verbal**

SECTION 2

READING WARM-UP

Objectives
- Explain how volcanic eruptions can affect climate.
- Compare the three types of volcanoes.
- Compare craters, calderas, and lava plateaus.

Terms to Learn
crater
caldera
lava plateau

READING STRATEGY
Paired Summarizing Read this section silently. In pairs, take turns summarizing the material. Stop to discuss ideas that seem confusing.

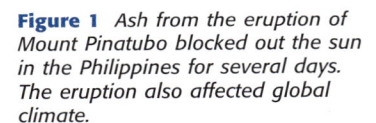

Figure 1 Ash from the eruption of Mount Pinatubo blocked out the sun in the Philippines for several days. The eruption also affected global climate.

CHAPTER RESOURCES

Chapter Resource File
- Lesson Plan
- Directed Reading A BASIC
- Directed Reading B SPECIAL NEEDS

Technology
- Transparencies
  - Bellringer
  - Three Types of Volcanoes

Effects of Volcanic Eruptions

In 1816, Chauncey Jerome, a resident of Connecticut, wrote that the clothes his wife had laid out to dry the day before had frozen during the night. This event would not have been unusual except that the date was June 10!

At that time, residents of New England did not know that the explosion of a volcanic island on the other side of the world had severely changed the global climate and was causing "The Year Without a Summer."

Volcanic Eruptions and Climate Change

The explosion of Mount Tambora in 1815 blanketed most of Indonesia in darkness for three days. It is estimated that 12,000 people died directly from the explosion and 80,000 people died from the resulting hunger and disease. The global effects of the eruption were not felt until the next year, however. During large-scale eruptions, enormous amounts of volcanic ash and gases are ejected into the upper atmosphere.

As volcanic ash and gases spread throughout the atmosphere, they can block enough sunlight to cause global temperatures to drop. The Tambora eruption affected the global climate enough to cause food shortages in North America and Europe. More recently, the eruption of Mount Pinatubo, shown in **Figure 1,** caused average global temperatures to drop by as much as 0.5°C. Although this may seem insignificant, such a shift can disrupt climates all over the world.

✓ **Reading Check** How does a volcanic eruption affect climate? (*See the Appendix for answers to Reading Checks.*)

Answer to Reading Check
Eruptions release large quantities of ash and gases, which can block sunlight and cause global temperatures to drop.

256 Chapter 9 • Volcanoes

Different Types of Volcanoes

Volcanic eruptions can cause profound changes in climate. But the changes to Earth's surface caused by eruptions are probably more familiar. Perhaps the best known of all volcanic landforms are the volcanoes themselves. The three basic types of volcanoes are illustrated in **Figure 2**.

Shield Volcanoes

Shield volcanoes are built of layers of lava released from repeated nonexplosive eruptions. Because the lava is very runny, it spreads out over a wide area. Over time, the layers of lava create a volcano that has gently sloping sides. Although their sides are not very steep, shield volcanoes can be enormous. Hawaii's Mauna Kea, the shield volcano shown here, is the tallest mountain on Earth. Measured from its base on the sea floor, Mauna Kea is taller than Mount Everest.

Cinder Cone Volcanoes

Cinder cone volcanoes are made of pyroclastic material usually produced from moderately explosive eruptions. The pyroclastic material forms steep slopes, as shown in this photo of the Mexican volcano Paricutín. Cinder cones are small and usually erupt for only a short time. Paricutín appeared in a cornfield in 1943 and erupted for only nine years before stopping at a height of 400 m. Cinder cones often occur in clusters, commonly on the sides of other volcanoes. They usually erode quickly because the pyroclastic material is not cemented together.

Composite Volcanoes

Composite volcanoes, sometimes called *stratovolcanoes,* are one of the most common types of volcanoes. They form from explosive eruptions of pyroclastic material followed by quieter flows of lava. The combination of both types of eruptions forms alternating layers of pyroclastic material and lava. Composite volcanoes, such as Japan's Mount Fuji (shown here), have broad bases and sides that get steeper toward the top. Composite volcanoes in the western region of the United States include Mount Hood, Mount Rainier, Mount Shasta, and Mount St. Helens.

Figure 2 Three Types of Volcanoes

Shield volcano

Cinder cone volcano

Composite volcano

Teach

ACTIVITY — BASIC

Classifying Volcanoes Have students write descriptive phrases about the three types of volcanoes in their **science journal**. Have them draw a cross section of each type of volcano beside the appropriate entry. Students should find an example of each volcano type and write three paragraphs about each type. The paragraphs should describe how the volcano fits its category, detail its last eruption, and explain how the volcano's shape is related to the way the volcano erupted. **Visual** *English Language Learners*

ACTIVITY — ADVANCED

Book Report In 1943, Dominic Pulido, a farmer in central Mexico, was working in his cornfield when the ground began to tremble and a noise like thunder filled the air. Pulido discovered a fissure in the field about 0.5 m wide. The ground began to swell and formed a mound 2.5 m high! A volcano named Paricutín was being born. In 1 year, the cinder cone volcano grew to 334 m high! Encourage students to read *Hill of Fire*, by Thomas Page Lewis, and to write a book report about it. **Intrapersonal**

CONNECTION ACTIVITY
History — GENERAL

The Battle of Iwo Jima One of World War II's fiercest battles was fought on the volcanic island of Iwo Jima. More than 6,000 Allied soldiers and 20,000 Japanese soldiers died fighting for an island that is about 8 km long and 4 km wide. Have students research the battle of Iwo Jima and prepare a map to show why this volcanic island was difficult to capture. **Visual**

Is That a Fact!

Measured from the seafloor, the volcano Mauna Kea, shown in **Figure 2,** is the tallest mountain in the world. It rises 4 km above sea level, and its slopes descend 5 km below the ocean. Hawaii's mass depresses the ocean floor another 8 km. So, the volcano is 17 km tall, almost twice as tall as Mount Everest!

Section 2 • Effects of Volcanic Eruptions

Close

Reteaching — BASIC
Section Quizzes Have students write five quiz questions based on the section. Students should exchange questions and then grade each other's work. Collect the quizzes, and use the best questions in an open-book quiz.

Quiz — GENERAL
1. Describe the shapes of shield, cinder cone, and composite volcanoes. (shield volcano: broad with gentle, shallow slopes; cinder cone volcano: generally smaller and steeper with more angled sides; composite volcano: high, covers less area than shield volcanoes, and has sides that are steeper near the peak)
2. What is a lava plateau? (It is a wide, flat landform that is formed from repeated nonexplosive eruptions of lava that spread over a large area.)

Alternative Assessment — GENERAL
Volcano Poster Have students draw a poster of each type of volcano. Students must label and write a caption for all of the volcano's parts. Students should also create a cartoon-panel illustration of how craters and calderas form. **LS** Visual

Answer to Reading Check
Calderas form when a magma chamber partially empties and the roof overlying the chamber collapses.

Figure 3 A crater, such as this one in Kamchatka, Russia, forms around the central vent of a volcano.

crater a funnel-shaped pit near the top of the central vent of a volcano

caldera a large, semicircular depression that forms when the magma chamber below a volcano partially empties and causes the ground above to sink

Other Types of Volcanic Landforms
In addition to volcanoes, other landforms are produced by volcanic activity. These landforms include craters, calderas, and lava plateaus. Read on to learn more about these landforms.

Craters
Around the central vent at the top of many volcanoes is a funnel-shaped pit called a **crater.** An example of a crater is shown in **Figure 3.** During less explosive eruptions, lava flows and pyroclastic material can pile up around the vent creating a cone with a central crater. As the eruption stops, the lava that is left in the crater often drains back underground. The vent may then collapse to form a larger crater. If the lava hardens in the crater, the next eruption may blast it away. In this way, a crater becomes larger and deeper.

Calderas
Calderas can appear similar to craters, but they are many times larger. A **caldera** is a large, semicircular depression that forms when the chamber that supplies magma to a volcano partially empties and the chamber's roof collapses. As a result, the ground above the magma chamber sinks, as shown in **Figure 4.** Much of Yellowstone Park is made up of three large calderas that formed when volcanoes collapsed between 1.9 million and 0.6 million years ago. Today, hot springs, such as Old Faithful, are heated by the thermal energy left over from those events.

✓ Reading Check How do calderas form?

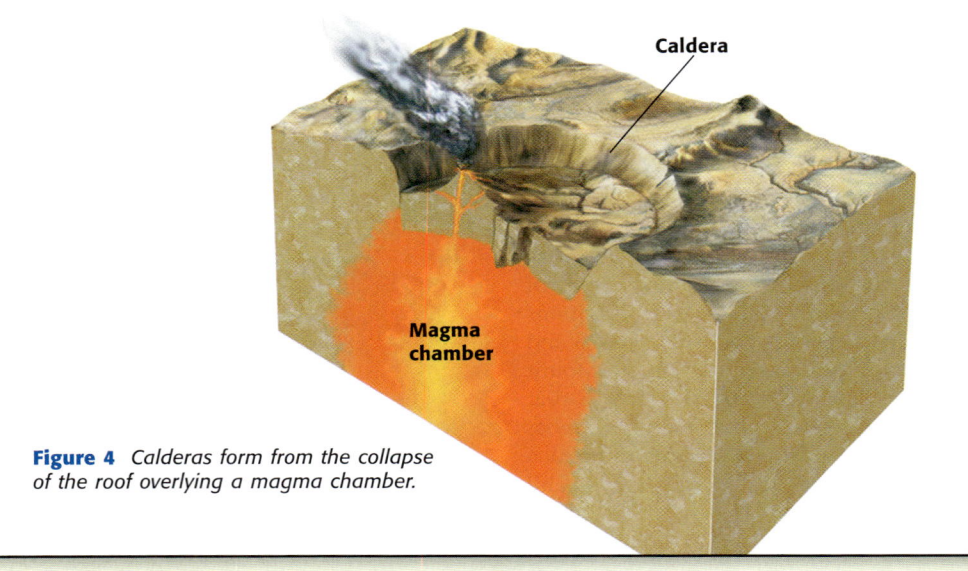

Figure 4 Calderas form from the collapse of the roof overlying a magma chamber.

CONNECTION ACTIVITY
Astronomy — ADVANCED
Lunar Maria Early astronomers thought that the dark patches on the moon were lunar seas. Thus, the areas were called *maria*, which is Latin for "seas." Today, we know that the dark patches are basins filled with basaltic lava that erupted after the moon's formation. Most of the lunar maria are on the side of the moon that faces Earth. Scientists think that after the moon's formation, the tidal attraction of Earth caused volcanic eruptions on the side of the moon that faces Earth. Like the jelly that comes out of a donut when it is squeezed, lava was pushed out of the moon by the Earth's gravitational force deforming the moon's suface more on the side closer to Earth. Have students research volcanism on another planet or moon in our solar system and report their findings to the class. **LS** Logical

258   Chapter 9 • Volcanoes

Lava Plateaus

The most massive outpourings of lava do not come from individual volcanoes. Most of the lava on Earth's surface erupted from long cracks, or *rifts*, in the crust. In this type of eruption, runny lava can pour out for millions of years and spread over huge areas. A landform that results from repeated eruptions of lava spread over a large area is called a **lava plateau**. The Columbia River Plateau, part of which is shown in **Figure 5**, is a lava plateau that formed between 17 million and 14 million years ago in the northwestern region of the United States. In some places, the Columbia River Plateau is 3 km thick.

Figure 5 The Columbia River Plateau formed from a massive outpouring of lava that began 17 million years ago.

lava plateau a wide, flat landform that results from repeated nonexplosive eruptions of lava that spread over a large area

SECTION Review

Summary

- The large volumes of gas and ash released from volcanic eruptions can affect climate.
- Shield volcanoes result from many eruptions of relatively runny lava.
- Cinder cone volcanoes result from mildly explosive eruptions of pyroclastic material.
- Composite volcanoes result from alternating explosive and nonexplosive eruptions.
- Craters, calderas, and lava plateaus are volcanic landforms.

Using Key Terms

Complete each of the following sentences by choosing the correct term from the word bank.

caldera   crater

1. A ___ is a funnel-shaped hole around the central vent.
2. A ___ results when a magma chamber partially empties.

Understanding Key Ideas

3. Which type of volcano results from alternating explosive and nonexplosive eruptions?
   a. composite volcano
   b. cinder cone volcano
   c. rift-zone volcano
   d. shield volcano
4. Why do cinder cone volcanoes have narrower bases and steeper sides than shield volcanoes do?
5. Why does a volcano's crater tend to get larger over time?

Math Skills

6. The fastest lava flow recorded was 60 km/h. A horse can gallop as fast as 48 mi/h. Could a galloping horse outrun the fastest lava flow? (Hint: 1 km = 0.621 mi)

Critical Thinking

7. **Making Inferences** Why did it take a year for the effects of the Tambora eruption to be experienced in New England?

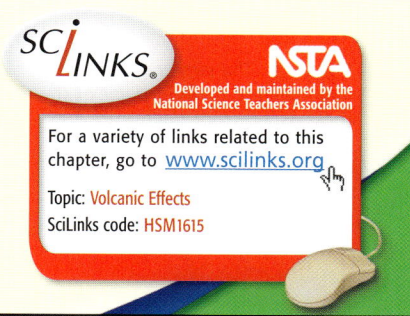

SciLinks
Developed and maintained by the National Science Teachers Association
For a variety of links related to this chapter, go to www.scilinks.org
Topic: Volcanic Effects
SciLinks code: HSM1615

Answers to Section Review

1. crater
2. caldera
3. a
4. Cinder cone volcanoes are made of pyroclastic material, which is thick and piles up like sand around the volcano. Shield volcanoes are made from lava that is thin and runny and that spreads out over large areas.
5. A volcano's crater tends to get larger over time because the vent may collapse after an eruption. In addition, if the lava hardens in the crater after an eruption, the next eruption may blast the hardened lava away, making the crater larger and deeper.
6. Yes, the horse could outrun the lava flow.
   60 km/h × 0.621 mi/km = 37.26 mi/h
   48 mi/h > 37.26 mi/h
7. It took a year for the effects of the Tambora eruption to be experienced in New England because the ash and gases from the eruption had to be circulated by global winds.

SCIENTISTS AT ODDS

Did Volcanism Play a Role in Dinosaur Extinctions? Most scientists think that the dinosaurs became extinct 65 million years ago when a large asteroid struck Earth. However, some scientists think that climatic changes caused by a period of catastrophic volcanism that occurred before and after the impact may have been a factor in the extinctions. Encourage students to find out more about these scientific hypotheses.

CHAPTER RESOURCES

Chapter Resource File
- Section Quiz GENERAL
- Section Review GENERAL
- Vocabulary and Section Summary GENERAL
- Reinforcement Worksheet BASIC
- Critical Thinking ADVANCED

Technology
- Transparencies
  - The Formation of a Caldera

Section 2 • Effects of Volcanic Eruptions

SECTION 3

Focus

Overview
In this section, students will learn how magma forms and how pressure affects the temperature at which rocks melt. The section draws a connection between volcanic activity and tectonic movement and concludes with a discussion of the challenges involved in predicting eruptions.

🔔 **Bellringer**
Ask students to imagine that they live on a volcanic island. Have them list in their **science journal** the signals that would tell them the volcano was about to erupt.

Motivate

Discussion — GENERAL
Volcano Safety Have students brainstorm measures a community could take to protect citizens from a volcanic eruption and then write their ideas in their **science journal.** Have them compare their suggestions with the information they learn in the chapter. **LS** *Logical*

SECTION 3

READING WARM-UP

Objectives
- Describe the formation and movement of magma.
- Explain the relationship between volcanoes and plate tectonics.
- Summarize the methods scientists use to predict volcanic eruptions.

Terms to Learn
rift zone
hot spot

READING STRATEGY
Reading Organizer As you read this section, make a flowchart of the steps of magma formation in different tectonic environments.

Figure 1 The curved line indicates the melting point of a rock. As pressure decreases and temperature increases, the rock begins to melt.

Causes of Volcanic Eruptions

More than 2,000 years ago, Pompeii was a busy Roman city near the sleeping volcano Mount Vesuvius. People did not see Vesuvius as much of a threat. Everything changed when Vesuvius suddenly erupted and buried the city in a deadly blanket of ash that was almost 20 ft thick!

Today, even more people are living on and near active volcanoes. Scientists closely monitor volcanoes to avoid this type of disaster. They study the gases coming from active volcanoes and look for slight changes in the volcano's shape that could indicate that an eruption is near. Scientists know much more about the causes of eruptions than the ancient Pompeiians did, but there is much more to be discovered.

The Formation of Magma
Understanding how magma forms helps explain why volcanoes erupt. Magma forms in the deeper regions of the Earth's crust and in the uppermost layers of the mantle where the temperature and pressure are very high. Changes in pressure and temperature cause magma to form.

Pressure and Temperature
Part of the upper mantle is made of very hot, puttylike rock that flows slowly. The rock of the mantle is hot enough to melt at Earth's surface, but it remains a puttylike solid because of pressure. This pressure is caused by the weight of the rock above the mantle. In other words, the rock above the mantle presses the atoms of the mantle so close together that the rock cannot melt. As **Figure 1** shows, rock melts when its temperature increases or when the pressure on the rock decreases.

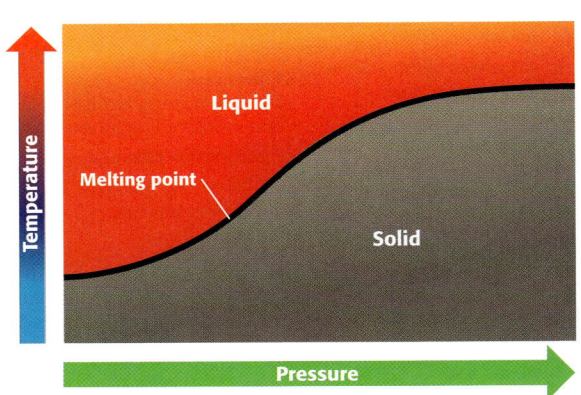

CHAPTER RESOURCES

Chapter Resource File
- Lesson Plan
- Directed Reading A BASIC
- Directed Reading B SPECIAL NEEDS

Technology

Transparencies
- Bellringer
- The Location of Major Volcanoes

---

260 Chapter 9 • Volcanoes

Magma Formation in the Mantle

Because the temperature of the mantle is fairly constant, a decrease in pressure is the most common cause of magma formation. Magma often forms at the boundary between separating tectonic plates, where pressure is decreased. Once formed, the magma is less dense than the surrounding rock, so the magma slowly rises toward the surface like an air bubble in a jar of honey.

Where Volcanoes Form

The locations of volcanoes give clues about how volcanoes form. The map in **Figure 2** shows the location of some of the world's major active volcanoes. The map also shows the boundaries between tectonic plates. A large number of volcanoes lie directly on tectonic plate boundaries. In fact, the plate boundaries surrounding the Pacific Ocean have so many volcanoes that the area is called the *Ring of Fire*.

Tectonic plate boundaries are areas where tectonic plates either collide, separate, or slide past one another. At these boundaries, it is possible for magma to form and travel to the surface. About 80% of active volcanoes on land form where plates collide, and about 15% form where plates separate. The remaining few occur far from tectonic plate boundaries.

Reading Check Why are most volcanoes on plate boundaries? *(See the Appendix for answers to Reading Checks.)*

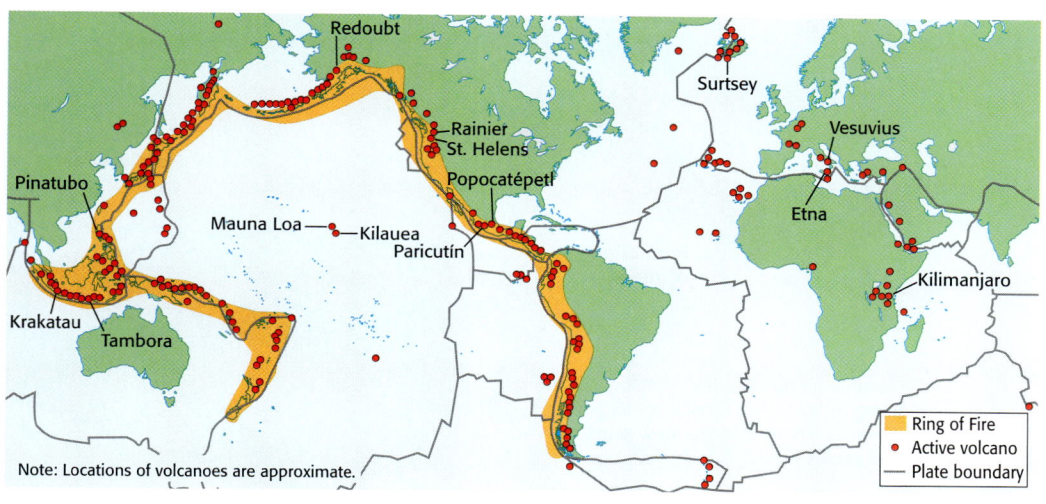

Figure 2 Tectonic plate boundaries are likely places for volcanoes to form. The Ring of Fire contains nearly 75% of the world's active volcanoes on land.

Quick Lab
Reaction to Stress

1. Make a pliable "rock" by pouring **60 mL of water** into a **plastic cup** and adding **150 mL of cornstarch**, 15 mL at a time. Stir well each time.
2. Pour half of the cornstarch mixture into a **clear bowl**. Carefully observe how the "rock" flows. Be patient—this process is slow!
3. Scrape the rest of the "rock" out of the cup with a **spoon**. Observe the behavior of the "rock" as you scrape.
4. What happened to the "rock" when you let it flow by itself? What happened when you put stress on the "rock"?
5. How is this pliable "rock" similar to the rock of the upper part of the mantle?

Teach

Quick Lab
MATERIALS

FOR EACH GROUP
- bowl, clear
- cornstarch, 150 mL
- cup, plastic
- spoon
- water, 60 mL

Answers

4. When left alone, the "rock" flowed like a liquid does, but flowed very slowly. When stress was applied by the spoon, the "rock" broke like a solid does.
5. Sample answer: The artificial rock is like the mantle because the artificial rock is a puttylike solid that flows very slowly.

Answer to Reading Check
Volcanic activity is common at tectonic plate boundaries because magma tends to form at plate boundaries.

BRAIN FOOD

Rates of Cooling Affect Crystal Size
Igneous rocks form when magma cools and solidifies either at or beneath Earth's surface. Magma that solidifies deep underground usually cools much more slowly than magma that solidifies closer to the surface. The difference in the rate of cooling affects the texture of the igneous rock that forms. Rocks that form from magma that cools slowly contain larger crystals than rocks that form from magma that cools quickly. Ask students how scientists could use information about crystal size to study an igneous outcrop. (By studying mineral type and crystal size, scientists can determine the origin of igneous rock.)

Section 3 • Causes of Volcanic Eruptions

Teach, continued

Answer to Math Practice

9/5 × 1,400°C + 32 = 2,552°F

Using the Figure — GENERAL

Plate Tectonics Have students study **Figure 4**, in which a continental plate and an oceanic plate converge.

- Ask students which plate is more dense. (oceanic)

- Explain that when an oceanic plate sinks, or *subducts,* beneath another tectonic plate, the scraping, pushing, and jostling may cause earthquakes and tsunamis.

- Ask students what kind of tectonic plate contains more water. (oceanic)

- Have students explain how water content in mantle rock affects magma formation. (The more water that is present in mantle rock, the more likely the rock is to melt.)

- Have students explain how magma forms when these two tectonic plates converge. (The subducted oceanic plate moves downward, and the high water content and increased temperature cause the rock to melt and form magma.)

- Ask students if they think that explosive eruptions tend to occur near convergent or divergent boundaries. (They tend to occur near convergent boundaries because the water and silica content of the magma is higher near convergent boundaries.)

LS Logical/Visual

MATH PRACTICE

How Hot Is Hot?
Inside the Earth, magma can reach a burning-hot 1,400°C! You may be more familiar with Fahrenheit temperatures, so convert 1,400°C to degrees Fahrenheit by using the formula below.

°F = (°C ÷ 5 × 9) + 32

What is the temperature in degrees Fahrenheit?

rift zone an area of deep cracks that forms between two tectonic plates that are pulling away from each other

When Tectonic Plates Separate

At a *divergent boundary,* tectonic plates move away from each other. As tectonic plates separate, a set of deep cracks called a **rift zone** forms between the plates. Mantle rock then rises to fill in the gap. When mantle rock gets closer to the surface, the pressure decreases. The pressure decrease causes the mantle rock to melt and form magma. Because magma is less dense than the surrounding rock, it rises through the rifts. When the magma reaches the surface, it spills out and hardens, creating new crust, as shown in **Figure 3**.

Mid-Ocean Ridges Form at Divergent Boundaries

Lava that flows from undersea rift zones produces volcanoes and mountain chains called *mid-ocean ridges.* Just as a baseball has stitches, the Earth is circled with mid-ocean ridges. At these ridges, lava flows out and creates new crust. Most volcanic activity on Earth occurs at mid-ocean ridges. While most mid-ocean ridges are underwater, Iceland, with its volcanoes and hot springs, was created by lava from the Mid-Atlantic Ridge. In 1963, enough lava poured out of the Mid-Atlantic Ridge near Iceland to form a new island called *Surtsey.* Scientists watched this new island being born!

Figure 3 How Magma Forms at a Divergent Boundary

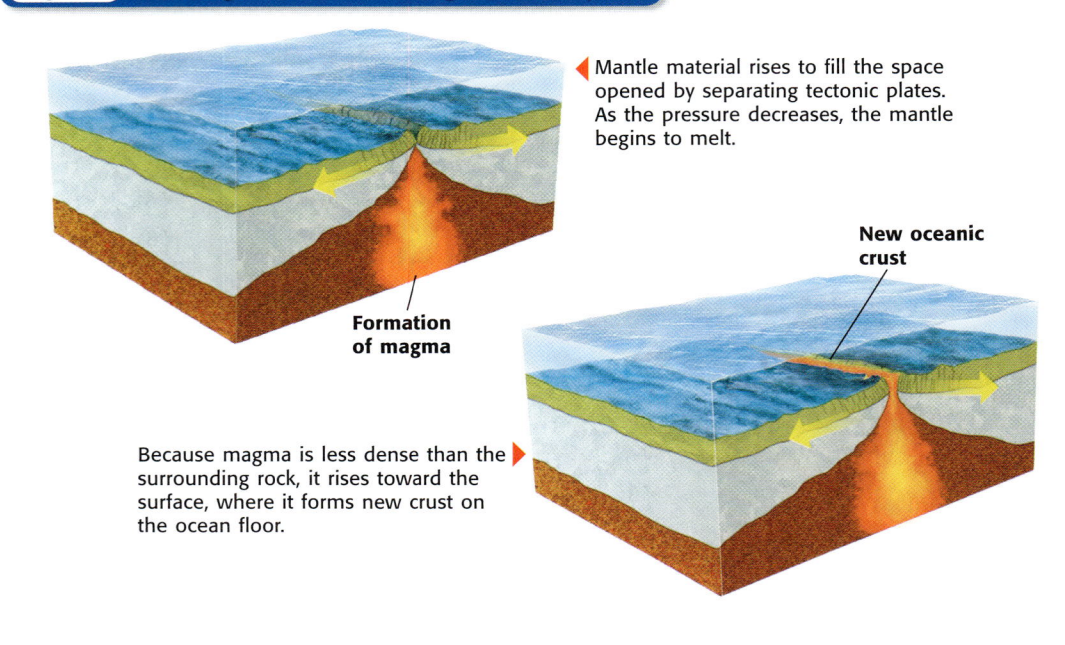

Mantle material rises to fill the space opened by separating tectonic plates. As the pressure decreases, the mantle begins to melt.

Formation of magma

Because magma is less dense than the surrounding rock, it rises toward the surface, where it forms new crust on the ocean floor.

New oceanic crust

CONNECTION ACTIVITY
Math — GENERAL

Kilauea Kilauea, in Hawaii, is one of the most studied volcanoes in the world. It has been erupting regularly since 1983. Every day, enough lava to pave a two-lane road 32 km long pours from the volcano. Have students calculate how long this lava "road" would be if the volcano erupted at that rate for 40 years.

(365 days/y × 32 km/day = 11,680 km/y; 11,680 km/y × 40 y = 467,200 km, more than 10 times the Earth's circumference) **LS** Logical

CHAPTER RESOURCES

Technology

Transparencies
- How Magma Forms at a Divergent Boundary
- How Magma Forms at a Convergent Boundary

Figure 4 How Magma Forms at a Convergent Boundary

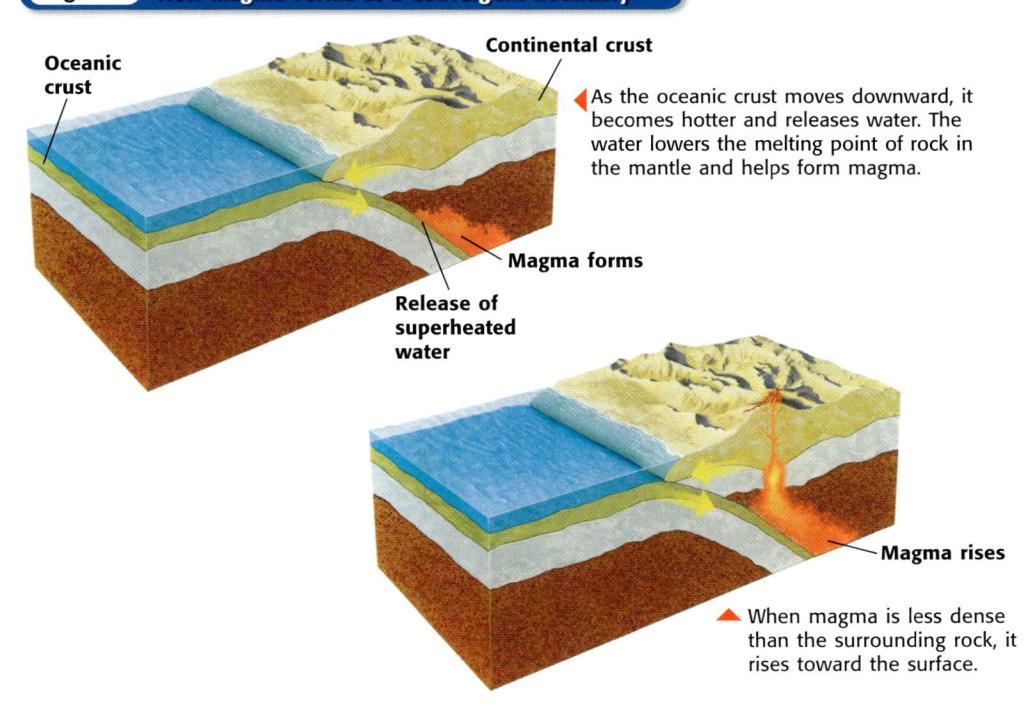

As the oceanic crust moves downward, it becomes hotter and releases water. The water lowers the melting point of rock in the mantle and helps form magma.

When magma is less dense than the surrounding rock, it rises toward the surface.

When Tectonic Plates Collide

If you slide two pieces of notebook paper into one another on a flat desktop, the papers will either buckle upward or one piece of paper will move under the other. This is similar to what happens at a convergent boundary. A *convergent boundary* is a place where tectonic plates collide. When an oceanic plate collides with a continental plate, the oceanic plate usually slides underneath the continental plate. The process of *subduction,* the movement of one tectonic plate underneath another, is shown in **Figure 4**. Oceanic crust is subducted because it is denser and thinner than continental crust.

Subduction Produces Magma

As the descending oceanic crust scrapes past the continental crust, the temperature and pressure increase. The combination of increased heat and pressure causes the water contained in the oceanic crust to be released. The water then mixes with the mantle rock, which lowers the rock's melting point, causing it to melt. This body of magma can rise to form a volcano.

✓ **Reading Check** How does subduction produce magma?

School to Home

Tectonic Models
Create models of convergent and divergent boundaries by using materials of your choice. Have your teacher approve your list before you start building your model at home with a parent. In class, use your model to explain how each type of boundary leads to the formation of magma.

ACTIVITY

Group ACTIVITY — ADVANCED

Preparing for an Eruption More than 30 earthquakes per year are caused by the movement of magma beneath Mount Rainier, in Washington State. Mount Rainier is the most seismically active volcano in the Cascade Range after Mount St. Helens. Because the area around Mount Rainier is heavily populated, an eruption would endanger thousands of people and destroy property worth millions of dollars. Many groups of people are studying Mount Rainier and are preparing for a possible eruption. Divide the class into groups, and give the following assignments:

- **Research Group** Members investigate the volcano's history to determine why the volcano has been ranked as a "decade volcano."
- **Early-Warning Group** Members research how the volcano's activity is being monitored with scientific equipment and other methods.
- **Washington State Emergency Management Agency (WaSEMA) Group** Members find out how this state organization plans to help people in case of an eruption.
- **Schools, Police, and Fire Group** Members investigate how local agencies would design a plan for warning people of an eruption and a plan for coping with the aftermath of an eruption.

After the groups do research, have them make presentations using posters, models, maps, and graphs. **LS Interpersonal**
Co-op Learning

Answer to Reading Check
When a tectonic plate subducts, it becomes hotter and releases water. The water lowers the melting point of the rock above the plate, causing magma to form.

INCLUSION Strategies

- Learning Disabled
- Gifted and Talented
- Attention Deficit Disorder

Organize students into small teams to play a volcano quiz game. Each team should choose a category that relates to a heading in the section and write five questions and answers for the category on separate index cards. The difficulty and point value of the questions should increase incrementally. Review each team's questions and answers before you start the game. If a team cannot answer a question, the team should work with another team to answer the question. If teams cooperate, they should share the points. **LS Interpersonal**

Section 3 • Causes of Volcanic Eruptions

Close

Reteaching — BASIC

Mantle Plumes Compare a mantle plume to a candle flame and a tectonic plate to a piece of paper passing over the flame. The point on Earth's surface above the mantle plume is called a hot spot. **LS Visual** — English Language Learners

Quiz — GENERAL

1. What conditions make magma rise? (when magma is less dense than the surrounding rock and when magma has a pathway to the surface)
2. Define a rift zone. (an area of deep cracks that forms at a divergent boundary)

Alternative Assessment — ADVANCED

Tectonics and Volcanoes Post on the bulletin board a map of the world that shows the location of tectonic plates. Have volunteers use pins and string to outline the plates on the map. Have other students use flagged pins to mark the location of the volcanoes they learned about in this chapter. Then, pair students. Have partners explain how tectonic plate boundaries and volcanoes are related. Each partner should evaluate the other partner's understanding by assessing his or her descriptions of rifts, converging tectonic plates, diverging tectonic plates, subduction, hot spots, and magma formation. **LS Visual** Co-op Learning

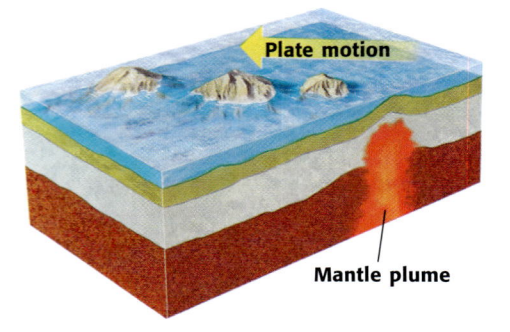

Figure 5 According to one theory, a string of volcanic islands forms as a tectonic plate passes over a mantle plume.

hot spot a volcanically active area of Earth's surface far from a tectonic plate boundary

Figure 6 As if being this close to an active volcano is not dangerous enough, the gases being collected are extremely poisonous.

Answer to Reading Check

According to one theory, a rising body of magma, called a mantle plume, causes a chain of volcanoes to form on a moving tectonic plate. According to another theory, a chain of volcanoes forms along cracks in the Earth's crust.

Hot Spots

Not all magma develops along tectonic plate boundaries. For example, the Hawaiian Islands, some of the most well-known volcanoes on Earth, are nowhere near a plate boundary. The volcanoes of Hawaii and several other places on Earth are known as *hot spots*. **Hot spots** are volcanically active places on the Earth's surface that are far from plate boundaries. Some scientists think that hot spots are directly above columns of rising magma, called *mantle plumes*. Other scientists think that hot spots are the result of cracks in the Earth's crust.

A hot spot often produces a long chain of volcanoes. One theory is that the mantle plume stays in the same spot while the tectonic plate moves over it, as shown in **Figure 5**. Another theory argues that hot-spot volcanoes occur in long chains because they form along the cracks in the Earth's crust. Both theories may be correct.

✓ **Reading Check** Describe two theories that explain the existence of hot spots.

Predicting Volcanic Eruptions

You now understand some of the processes that produce volcanoes, but how do scientists predict when a volcano is going to erupt? Volcanoes are classified in three categories. *Extinct volcanoes* have not erupted in recorded history and probably never will erupt again. *Dormant volcanoes* are currently not erupting, but the record of past eruptions suggests that they may erupt again. *Active volcanoes* are currently erupting or show signs of erupting in the near future. Scientists study active and dormant volcanoes for signs of a future eruption.

Measuring Small Quakes and Volcanic Gases

Most active volcanoes produce small earthquakes as the magma within them moves upward and causes the surrounding rock to shift. Just before an eruption, the number and intensity of the earthquakes increase and the occurrence of quakes may be continuous. Monitoring these quakes is one of the best ways to predict an eruption.

As **Figure 6** shows, scientists also study the volume and composition of volcanic gases. The ratio of certain gases, especially that of sulfur dioxide, SO_2, to carbon dioxide, CO_2, may be important in predicting eruptions. Changes in this ratio may indicate changes in the magma chamber below.

Homework — GENERAL

Hot Spots There are volcanic hot spots in Yellowstone Park, Easter Island, Hawaii, the Marquesas, the Canary Islands, Cameroon, Iceland, the Galápagos Islands, and the Samoan Islands. Have each student prepare a report on a hot spot, using maps, models, and details of the hot spot's history. **LS Visual**

Measuring Slope and Temperature

As magma moves upward prior to an eruption, it can cause the Earth's surface to swell. The side of a volcano may even bulge as the magma moves upward. An instrument called a *tiltmeter* helps scientists detect small changes in the angle of a volcano's slope. Scientists also use satellite technology such as the Global Positioning System (GPS) to detect the changes in a volcano's slope that may signal an eruption.

One of the newest methods for predicting volcanic eruptions includes using satellite images. Infrared satellite images record changes in the surface temperature and gas emissions of a volcano over time. If the site is getting hotter, the magma below is probably rising!

INTERNET ACTIVITY

For another activity related to this chapter, go to **go.hrw.com** and type in the keyword **HZ5VOLW**.

SECTION Review

Summary

- Temperature and pressure influence magma formation.
- Most volcanoes form at tectonic boundaries.
- As tectonic plates separate, magma rises to fill the cracks, or rifts, that develop.
- As oceanic and continental plates collide, the oceanic plate tends to subduct and cause the formation of magma.
- To predict eruptions, scientists study the frequency and type of earthquakes associated with the volcano as well as changes in slope, changes in the gases released, and changes in the volcano's surface temperature.

Using Key Terms

1. Use each of the following terms in a separate sentence: *hot spot* and *rift zone*.

Understanding Key Ideas

2. If the temperature of a rock remains constant but the pressure on the rock decreases, what tends to happen?
   a. The temperature increases.
   b. The rock becomes liquid.
   c. The rock becomes solid.
   d. The rock subducts.

3. Which of the following words is a synonym for *dormant*?
   a. predictable
   b. active
   c. dead
   d. sleeping

4. What is the Ring of Fire?

5. Explain how convergent and divergent plate boundaries cause magma formation.

6. Describe four methods that scientists use to predict volcanic eruptions.

7. Why does a oceanic plate tend to subduct when it collides with a continental plate?

Math Skills

8. If a tectonic plate moves at a rate of 2 km every 1 million years, how long would it take a hot spot to form a chain of volcanoes 100 km long?

Critical Thinking

9. **Making Inferences** New crust is constantly being created at mid-ocean ridges. So, why is the oldest oceanic crust only about 150 million years old?

10. **Identifying Relationships** If you are studying a volcanic deposit, would the youngest layers be more likely to be found on the top or on the bottom? Explain your answer.

SCLINKS NSTA
Developed and maintained by the National Science Teachers Association

For a variety of links related to this chapter, go to www.scilinks.org
Topic: What Causes Volcanoes?
SciLinks code: HSM1654

Answers to Section Review

1. Sample answer: A hot spot may form above a mantle plume. A rift zone is a series of cracks that form along a divergent plate boundary.
2. b
3. d
4. The Ring of Fire is a group of volcanoes that are located on convergent plate boundaries in the Pacific Ocean.
5. At convergent boundaries a plate is subducted. The subducted plate is heated and releases water. The water causes the melting point of the rock to decrease, forming magma. At divergent boundaries, mantle rock rises to fill the gap created by separating tectonic plates. As the rock rises, pressure decreases and the rock melts, forming magma.
6. Scientists monitor seismic activity associated with the volcano. If seismic activity increases, magma might be moving in the magma chamber. Scientists study the composition and volume of gases released from the volcano. If the composition of gases changes, an eruption may be imminent. Scientists also study the slope and temperature of volcanoes. If the slope or surface temperature change, an eruption might be imminent.
7. Oceanic plates tend to subduct because they are denser than continental plates.
8. 100 km ÷ 2 km/million years = 50 million years
9. New crust is constantly being created, but it is also being subducted at convergent boundaries.
10. The youngest layers would most likely be at the top because they were deposited over the older layers.

CHAPTER RESOURCES

Chapter Resource File
- Section Quiz GENERAL
- Section Review GENERAL
- Vocabulary Section Summary GENERAL
- Reinforcement Worksheet BASIC
- Scilinks Activity GENERAL
- Datasheet for Quick Lab

Technology
- Interactive Explorations CD-ROM
  - What's the Matter? GENERAL

Section 3 • Causes of Volcanic Eruptions

Skills Practice Lab

Volcano Verdict

Teacher's Notes

Time Required
One 45-minute class period

Lab Ratings
EASY ———— HARD
Teacher Prep
Student Set-Up
Concept Level
Clean Up

MATERIALS
The materials listed on the student page are sufficient for a pair of students.

Safety Caution
Remind students to review all safety cautions and icons before beginning this activity.

Preparation Notes
You may want to combine this activity with an activity involving a tiltmeter. Emphasize to students that a gas-emissions tester is just one tool used by volcanologists. These scientists must compare the data gathered through many tests before drawing any conclusions.

In this experiment, 10 mL of bromothymol blue may be substituted for limewater. Bromothymol blue changes from blue to yellow-green when carbon dioxide is present.

Skills Practice Lab

OBJECTIVES
Build a working apparatus to test carbon dioxide levels.
Test the levels of carbon dioxide emitted from a model volcano.

MATERIALS
- baking soda, 15 mL
- bottle, drinking, 16 oz
- box or stand for plastic cup
- clay, modeling
- coin
- cup, clear plastic, 9 oz
- graduated cylinder
- limewater, 1 L
- straw, drinking, flexible
- tissue, bathroom (2 sheets)
- vinegar, white, 140 mL
- water, 100 mL

SAFETY

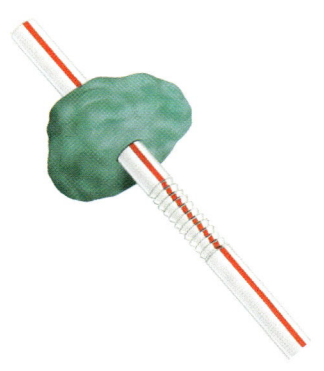

Volcano Verdict

You will need to pair up with a partner for this exploration. You and your partner will act as geologists who work in a city located near a volcano. City officials are counting on you to predict when the volcano will erupt next. You and your partner have decided to use limewater as a gas-emissions tester. You will use this tester to measure the levels of carbon dioxide emitted from a simulated volcano. The more active the volcano is, the more carbon dioxide it releases.

Procedure

1. Put on your safety goggles, and carefully pour limewater into the plastic cup until the cup is three-fourths full. You have just made your gas-emissions tester.

2. Now, build a model volcano. Begin by pouring 50 mL of water and 70 mL of vinegar into the drink bottle.

3. Form a plug of clay around the short end of the straw, as shown at left. The clay plug must be large enough to cover the opening of the bottle. Be careful not to get the clay wet.

4. Sprinkle 5 mL of baking soda along the center of a single section of bathroom tissue. Then, roll the tissue, and twist the ends so that the baking soda can't fall out.

CLASSROOM TESTED & APPROVED

Gordon Zibelman
Drexel Hill Middle School
Drexel Hill, Pennsylvania

CHAPTER RESOURCES

Chapter Resource File
- Datasheet for Chapter Lab
- Lab Notes and Answers

Technology
- Classroom Videos
  - Lab Video

LabBook
- Some Go "Pop," Some Do Not

Chapter 9 • Volcanoes

5 Drop the tissue into the drink bottle, and immediately put the short end of the straw inside the bottle to make a seal with the clay.

6 Put the other end of the straw into the lime-water, as shown at right.

7 You have just taken your first measurement of gas levels from the volcano. Record your observations.

8 Imagine that it is several days later and you need to test the volcano again to collect more data. Before you continue, toss a coin. If it lands heads up, go to step 9. If it lands tails up, go to step 10. Write down the step that you follow.

9 Repeat steps 1–7. This time, add 2 mL of baking soda to the vinegar and water. (Note: You must use fresh water, vinegar, and limewater.) Write down your observations. Go to step 11.

10 Repeat steps 1–7. This time, add 8 mL of baking soda to the vinegar and water. (Note: You must use fresh water, vinegar, and limewater.) Write down your observations. Go to step 11.

11 Return to step 8 once. Then, answer the questions below.

Analyze the Results

1 **Explaining Events** How do you explain the difference in the appearance of the limewater from one trial to the next?

2 **Recognizing Patterns** What does the data that you collected indicate about the activity in the volcano?

Draw Conclusions

3 **Evaluating Results** Based on your results, do you think it would be necessary to evacuate the city?

4 **Applying Conclusions** How would a geologist use a gas-emissions tester to predict volcanic eruptions?

Analyze the Results

1. Students should realize that carbon dioxide made the limewater cloudy. If more carbon dioxide is released, the limewater becomes cloudier.

2. The answer to this question depends on which steps students followed. If students performed step 9 twice, they should conclude that the volcano is not likely to erupt in the immediate future. (The volcano released less gas in the second and third trials). If students performed step 10 twice, they should conclude that the volcano is likely to erupt. (More gas was released in the second and third trials; and therefore the pressure must be building.) If students performed step 9 and then step 10, an eruption would be likely. If students performed step 10 and then step 9 an eruption would not be likely.

Draw Conclusions

3. Answers may vary. If an eruption appears imminent, the city should be evacuated.

4. A geologist would use a gas-emissions tester in conjunction with other tests to determine if pressure is building within a volcano. As the pressure builds, the volcano is more likely to erupt.

CHAPTER RESOURCES
Workbooks

- **Whiz-Bang Demonstrations**
  - How's Your Lava Life? GENERAL
  - What Makes a Vent Event? GENERAL
- **Labs You Can Eat**
  - Hot Spots GENERAL
- **Long-Term Projects & Research Ideas**
  - A City Lost and Found ADVANCED

MISCONCEPTION ALERT

Predicting Volcanic Eruptions
Scientists base their predictions of eruptions on several different kinds of evidence. If many types of evidence indicate that an eruption is imminent, they will recommend evacuation. They are much less likely to recommend evacuation if only one kind of evidence suggests that an eruption is imminent.

Chapter Review

Assignment Guide

Section	Questions
1	2, 3, 6, 7, 13, 17, 18,
2	1, 5, 10, 15, 16
3	8, 9, 11, 12, 14, 19, 20
1 and 3	4

ANSWERS

Using Key Terms

1. Sample answer: A caldera forms when the roof of a magma chamber collapses. A crater forms when the material above the main vent of a volcano is blasted out.
2. Sample answer: Magma is hot, liquid rock material beneath Earth's surface. Lava is magma that flows onto Earth's surface.
3. Sample answer: Lava is liquid magma that flows out of a volcanic vent onto the ground. Pyroclastic material is mostly ash and solid rock that is blasted into the air during an explosive volcanic eruption.
4. Sample answer: A vent is a spot in Earth's surface through which lava or pyroclastic material passes. A rift is a long crack in Earth's crust.
5. Sample answer: A cinder cone volcano forms when pyroclastic material erupts and piles up around a volcanic vent. A shield volcano forms when lava spreads out over large areas.

Chapter Review

USING KEY TERMS

For each pair of terms, explain how the meanings of the terms differ.

1. *caldera* and *crater*
2. *lava* and *magma*
3. *lava* and *pyroclastic material*
4. *vent* and *rift*
5. *cinder cone volcano* and *shield volcano*

UNDERSTANDING KEY IDEAS

Multiple Choice

6. The type of magma that tends to cause explosive eruptions has a
   a. high silica content and high viscosity.
   b. high silica content and low viscosity.
   c. low silica content and low viscosity.
   d. low silica content and high viscosity.

7. Lava that flows slowly to form a glassy surface with rounded wrinkles is called
   a. aa lava.
   b. pahoehoe lava.
   c. pillow lava.
   d. blocky lava.

8. Magma forms within the mantle most often as a result of
   a. high temperature and high pressure.
   b. high temperature and low pressure.
   c. low temperature and high pressure.
   d. low temperature and low pressure.

9. What causes an increase in the number and intensity of small earthquakes before an eruption?
   a. the movement of magma
   b. the formation of pyroclastic material
   c. the hardening of magma
   d. the movement of tectonic plates

10. If volcanic dust and ash remain in the atmosphere for months or years, what do you predict will happen?
    a. Solar reflection will decrease, and temperatures will increase.
    b. Solar reflection will increase, and temperatures will increase.
    c. Solar reflection will decrease, and temperatures will decrease.
    d. Solar reflection will increase, and temperatures will decrease.

11. At divergent plate boundaries,
    a. heat from Earth's core causes mantle plumes.
    b. oceanic plates sink, which causes magma to form.
    c. tectonic plates move apart.
    d. hot spots cause volcanoes.

12. A theory that helps explain the causes of both earthquakes and volcanoes is the theory of
    a. pyroclastics.
    b. plate tectonics.
    c. climatic fluctuation.
    d. mantle plumes.

Understanding Key Ideas

6. a
7. b
8. b
9. a
10. d
11. c
12. b

Short Answer

13. How does the presence of water in magma affect a volcanic eruption?

14. Describe four clues that scientists use to predict eruptions.

15. Identify the characteristics of the three types of volcanoes.

16. Describe the positive effects of volcanic eruptions.

CRITICAL THINKING

17. **Concept Mapping** Use the following terms to create a concept map: *volcanic bombs*, *aa*, *pyroclastic material*, *pahoehoe*, *lapilli*, *lava*, and *volcano*.

18. **Identifying Relationships** You are exploring a volcano that has been dormant for some time. You begin to keep notes on the types of volcanic debris that you see as you walk. Your first notes describe volcanic ash. Later, your notes describe lapilli. In what direction are you most likely traveling—toward the crater or away from the crater? Explain your answer.

19. **Making Inferences** Loihi is a submarine Hawaiian volcano that might grow to form a new island. The Hawaiian Islands are located on the Pacific plate, which is moving northwest. Considering how this island chain may have formed, where do you think the new volcanic island will be located? Explain your answer.

20. **Evaluating Hypotheses** What evidence could confirm the existence of mantle plumes?

INTERPRETING GRAPHICS

The graph below illustrates the average change in temperature above or below normal for a community over several years. Use the graph below to answer the questions that follow.

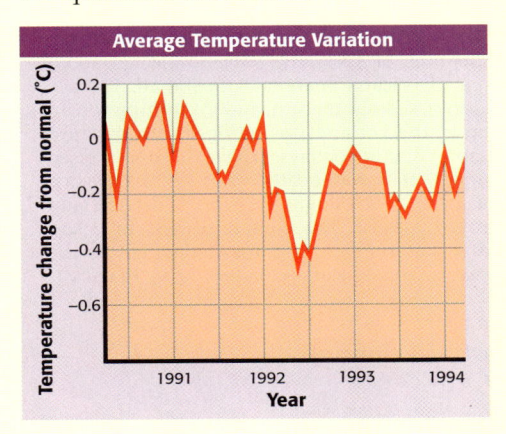

Average Temperature Variation

21. If the variation in temperature over the years was influenced by a major volcanic eruption, when did the eruption most likely take place? Explain.

22. If the temperature were measured only once each year (at the beginning of the year), how would your interpretation be different?

---

13. The presence of water in magma tends to cause explosive eruptions.

14. Earthquakes may indicate the movement of magma. Changes in the composition of volcanic gases may indicate changes in the magma chamber that may precede an eruption. Changes in the slope of a volcano may indicate that magma is rising. Finally, satellite data can reveal changes in surface temperature that may indicate that magma is rising.

15. Cinder cones are made from eruptions of pyroclastic materials. They are small and have steep sides. Shield volcanoes are made of lava that spreads over large distances before it solidifies, making very large, gently sloped volcanoes. Composite volcanoes are made of both lava and pyroclastic material. Composite volcanoes have large, gently sloping bases and steep sides.

16. Sample answer: Volcanoes form new crust and help create fertile soil.

Critical Thinking

17. An answer to this exercise can be found at the end of this book.

18. You would be traveling toward the volcano because the larger the pyroclastic material is, the closer it will be to the vent. It takes more energy to move larger particles than it does to move smaller particles.

19. The new island will be located southeast of Hawaii because the Pacific plate is moving toward the northwest.

20. Answers may vary. Students may suggest studying the composition and temperature of rock in the area where a mantle plume is thought to be.

Interpreting Graphics

21. The eruption probably happened in 1992 because that year had the lowest below-normal temperature. The volcanic ash that erupted into the atmosphere blocked the sunlight and lowered the temperature.

22. If the temperature was measured once a year, the graph would indicate that 1991 had the lowest temperature. This would indicate that the eruptions happened in 1991 instead of 1992.

CHAPTER RESOURCES

Chapter Resource File
- Chapter Review GENERAL
- Chapter Test A GENERAL
- Chapter Test B ADVANCED
- Chapter Test C SPECIAL NEEDS
- Vocabulary Activity GENERAL

Workbooks
- Study Guide
- Assessment resources are also available in Spanish.

Standardized Test Preparation

Teacher's Note

To provide practice under more realistic testing conditions, give students 20 minutes to answer all of the questions in this Standardized Test Preparation.

MISCONCEPTION ALERT

Answers to the standardized test preparation can help you identify student misconceptions and misunderstandings.

READING

Passage 1
1. C
2. I
3. B

TEST DOCTOR

Question 1: Earthquakes can cause tsunamis, but earthquakes are not tsunamis. A shock wave was produced by the explosion, but a shock wave is not a tsunami. A tsunami is an ocean wave produced by an earthquake, volcanic explosion, or asteroid impact.

Standardized Test Preparation

READING

Read each of the passages below. Then, answer the questions that follow each passage.

Passage 1 When the volcanic island of Krakatau in Indonesia exploded in 1883, a shock wave sped around the world seven times. The explosion was probably the loudest sound in recorded human history. What caused this enormous explosion? Most likely, the walls of the volcano ruptured, and ocean water flowed into the magma chamber of the volcano. The water instantly turned into steam, and the volcano exploded with the force of 100 million tons of TNT. The volcano ejected about 18 km³ of volcanic material into the air. The ash clouds blocked out the sun, and everything within 80 km of the volcano was plunged into darkness for more than two days. The explosion caused a tsunami that was nearly 40 m high. Detected as far away as the English Channel, the tsunami destroyed almost 300 coastal towns. In 1928, another volcano rose from the caldera left by the explosion. This volcano is called Anak Krakatau.

1. In the passage, what does *tsunami* mean?
   A a large earthquake
   B a shock wave
   C a giant ocean wave
   D a cloud of gas and dust

2. According to the passage, what was the size of the Krakatau explosion probably the result of?
   F pyroclastic material rapidly mixing with air
   G 100 million tons of TNT
   H an ancient caldera
   I the flow of water into the magma chamber

3. What does the Indonesian word *anak* probably mean?
   A father
   B child
   C mother
   D grandmother

Passage 2 Yellowstone National Park in Montana and Wyoming contains three overlapping calderas and evidence of the cataclysmic ash flows that erupted from them. The oldest eruption occurred 1.9 million years ago, the second eruption happened 1.3 million years ago, and the most recent eruption occurred 0.6 million years ago. Seismographs regularly detect the movement of magma beneath the caldera, and the hot springs and geysers of the park indicate that a large body of magma lies beneath the park. The geology of the area shows that major eruptions occurred about once every 0.6 or 0.7 million years. Thus, a devastating eruption is long overdue. People living near the park should be evacuated immediately.

1. In the passage, what does *cataclysmic* mean?
   A nonexplosive
   B ancient
   C destructive
   D characterized by ash flows

2. Which of the following clues are evidence of an active magma body beneath the park?
   F cataclysmic ash flows
   G the discovery of seismoclasts
   H minor eruptions
   I seismograph readings

3. Which of the following contradicts the author's conclusion that an eruption is "long overdue"?
   A Magma has been detected beneath the park.
   B With a variation of 0.1 million years, an eruption may occur in the next 100,000 years.
   C The composition of gases emitted indicates that an eruption is near.
   D Seismographs have detected the movement of magma.

Passage 2
1. C
2. I
3. B

TEST DOCTOR

Question 2: The ash flows are not evidence of an active magma body beneath the park because they happened 0.6 million years ago. *Seismoclast* is not a word. There have been no recent eruptions in the park. However, seismograph readings indicate that magma is moving underneath the park.

Question 3: Remind students that this passage expresses an author's opinion and that being able to distinguish fact from opinion is an important skill. The author gives no evidence to substantiate the opinion that a devastating eruption is "long overdue."

270   Chapter 9 • Volcanoes

INTERPRETING GRAPHICS

The map below shows some of the Earth's major volcanoes and the tectonic plate boundaries. Use the map below to answer the questions that follow.

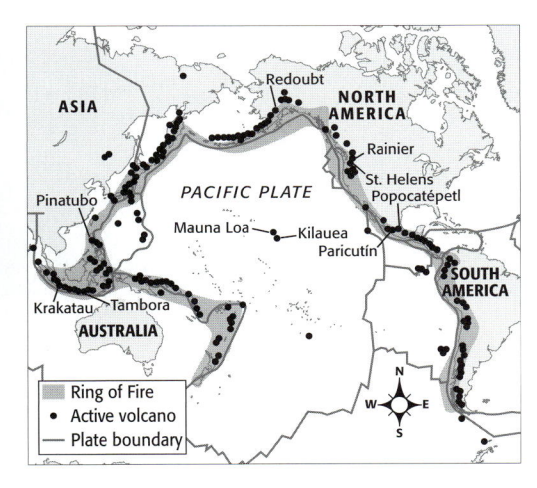

1. If ash from Popocatépetl landed on the west coast of the United States, what direction did the ash travel?
   A northeast
   B northwest
   C southeast
   D southwest

2. Why aren't there any active volcanoes in Australia?
   F Australia is not located on a plate boundary.
   G Australia is close to Krakatau and Tambora.
   H Australia is near a plate boundary.
   I Australia is near a rift zone.

3. If a scientist traveled along the Ring of Fire from Mt. Redoubt to Krakatau, which of the following most accurately describes the directions in which she traveled?
   A west, southeast, east
   B west, southeast, west
   C west, southwest, east
   D west, southwest, west

MATH

Read each question below, and choose the best answer.

1. Midway Island is 1,935 km northwest of Hawaii. If the Pacific plate is moving to the northwest at a rate of 9 cm per year, how long ago was Midway Island over the hot spot that formed the island?
   A 215,000 years
   B 2,150,000 years
   C 21,500,000 years
   D 215,000,000 years

2. In the first year that the Mexican volcano Paricutín appeared in a cornfield, it grew 360 m. The volcano stopped growing at about 400 m. What percentage of the volcano's total growth occurred in the first year?
   F 67%
   G 82%
   H 90%
   I 92%

3. A pyroclastic flow is moving down a hill at 120 km/h. If you lived in a town 5 km away, how much time would you have before the flow reached your town?
   A 2 min and 30 s
   B 1 min and 21 s
   C 3 min and 12 s
   D 8 min and 3 s

4. The Columbia River plateau is a lava plateau that contains 350,000 km^3 of solidified lava. The plateau took 3 million years to form. What was the average rate of lava deposition each century?
   F 0.116 km^3
   G 11.6 km^3
   H 116 km^3
   I 11,600 km^3

INTERPRETING GRAPHICS
1. B
2. F
3. D

TEST DOCTOR

Question 1: Students may choose answer C because the volcano is southeast of the west coast of the United States. However, if ash landed on the west coast of the United States, the ash traveled northwest.

MATH
1. C
2. H
3. A
4. G

TEST DOCTOR

Question 4: Remind students that they should multiply the rate of deposition per year by 100 to arrive at the rate of deposition per century.

CHAPTER RESOURCES

Chapter Resource File
- Standardized Test Preparation GENERAL

State Resources

For specific resources for your state, visit go.hrw.com and type in the keyword **HSMSTR**.

Chapter 9 • Standardized Test Preparation   271

Science in Action

Weird Science
Background
According to native Hawaiian mythology, Pele lives in the active crater of Kilauea. If Pele is angered, she stamps her feet, causing earthquakes and lava flows. Hawaiian myth states that she appears as an old woman just before an eruption. To prevent eruptions, villagers sometimes made sacrifices to appease her. Typically they sacrificed a pig, but if no pigs were available, a thick skinned fish called *Humu-humu-nuku-nuku-a-puaa* (which grunts like a pig) would suffice. Have students research myths about volcanoes and share their findings with the class.

Science, Technology, and Society
Background
The villagers in Heimaey lost about a third of their village to the Eldfell eruption but succeeded in protecting their harbor. If the eruption had flowed its course, lava would have filled in the harbor of one of Iceland's most profitable fishing communities. After the eruption was over, villagers constructed a geothermal power plant to take advantage of the thermal energy of the lava flow.

Science in Action

Weird Science
Pele's Hair
It is hard to believe that the fragile specimen shown below is a volcanic rock. This strange type of lava, called *Pele's hair*, forms when volcanic gases spray molten rock high into the air. When conditions are right, the lava can harden into strands of volcanic glass as thin as a human hair. This type of lava is named after Pele, the Hawaiian goddess of volcanoes. Several other types of lava are named in Pele's honor. Pele's tears are tear-shaped globs of volcanic glass often found at the end of strands of Pele's hair. Pele's diamonds are green, gemlike stones found in hardened lava flows.

Language Arts ACTIVITY
Volcanic terms come from many languages. Research some volcanic terms on the Internet, and create an illustrated volcanic glossary to share with your class.

Science, Technology, and Society
Fighting Lava with Fire Hoses
What would you do if a 60 ft wall of lava was advancing toward your home? Most people would head for safety. But when an eruption threatened to engulf the Icelandic fishing village of Heimaey in 1973, some villagers held their ground and fought back. Working 14-hour days in conditions so hot that their boots would catch on fire, villagers used fire-hoses to spray sea water on the lava flow. For several weeks, the lava advanced toward the town, and it seemed as if there was no hope. But the water eventually cooled the lava fast enough to divert the flow and save the village. It took 5 months and about 1.5 billion gallons of water to fight the lava flow. When the eruption stopped, villagers found that the island had grown by 20%!

Social Studies ACTIVITY
WRITING SKILL To try to protect the city of Hilo, Hawaii, from an eruption in 1935, planes dropped bombs on the lava. Find out if this mission was successful, and write a report about other attempts to stop lava flows.

Answer to Language Arts Activity
Answers may vary.

Answer to Social Studies Activity
B-3 and B-4 bombers tried to stop the flow of lava into the city of Hilo. The mission was unsuccessful. Ground-based explosives have been more successful. In 1996, the Italian army detonated 15,000 pounds of explosives to stop a lava flow. They also built earthen walls to dam the lava.

272   Chapter 9 • Volcanoes

Careers

Tina Neal

Volcanologist Would you like to study volcanoes for a living? Tina Neal is a volcanologist at the Alaska Volcano Observatory in Anchorage, Alaska. Her job is to monitor and study some of Alaska's 41 active volcanoes. Much of her work focuses on studying volcanoes in order to protect the public. According to Neal, being near a volcano when it is erupting is a wonderful adventure for the senses. "Sometimes you can get so close to an erupting volcano that you can feel the heat, hear the activity, and smell the lava. It's amazing! In Alaska, erupting volcanoes are too dangerous to get very close to, but they create a stunning visual display even from a distance."

Neal also enjoys the science of volcanoes. "It's fascinating to be near an active volcano and become aware of all the chemical and physical processes taking place. When I'm watching a volcano, I think about everything we understand and don't understand about what is happening. It's mind-boggling!" Neal says that if you are interested in becoming a volcanologist, it is important to be well rounded as a scientist. So, you would have to study math, geology, chemistry, and physics. Having a good understanding of computer tools is also important because volcanologists use computers to manage a lot of data and to create models. Neal also suggests learning a second language, such as Spanish. In her spare time, Neal is learning Russian so that she can better communicate with research partners in Kamchatka, Siberia.

Math Activity

The 1912 eruption of Mt. Katmai in Alaska could be heard 5,620 km away in Atlanta, Georgia. If the average speed of sound in the atmosphere is 342 m/s, how many hours after the eruption did the citizens of Atlanta hear the explosion?

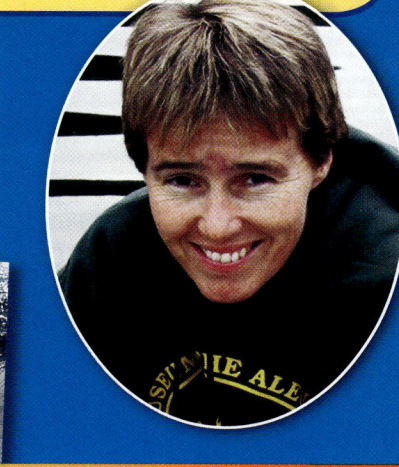

Current Science
Check out *Current Science®* articles related to this chapter by visiting go.hrw.com. Just type in the keyword **HZ5CS09**.

To learn more about these Science in Action topics, visit **go.hrw.com** and type in the keyword **HZ5VOLF**.

Careers

Background

Tina Neal always wanted to be an astronaut. She heard space programs needed medical doctors, so she decided to follow a pre-med track in college. But then she went to a fascinating lecture on the geology of Mars. Soon, she had enrolled in her first geology course and discovered that volcanoes are a common link among the planets. When Neal got a chance to see Mt. St. Helen's erupt, that was it. She was hooked on the field of volcanology—and the idea of staying on Earth!

Tina Neal received a degree in Geology from Brown University and an M.S. in Geology from Arizona State University. She has done additional graduate studies in Geology at the University of California at Santa Barbara.

She now works for the United States Geological Survey (USGS) as a physical volcanologist specializing in the study of young, active volcanoes.

Answer to Math Activity

342 m/s × 60 s/min × 60 m/h = 1,231,200 m/h
1,231,200 m/h ÷ 1000 m/km = 1231 km/h
5620 km ÷ 1231 km/h = 4.6 h

Homework — ADVANCED

USAID Between 1999 and 2000, Neal served a two-year detail with the United States Agency for International Development (USAID) in Washington, D.C. Through USAID, Neal worked with the Office of U.S. Foreign Disaster Assistance to help other nations prevent or cope with natural disasters. In this role, Neal visited Nepal, Colombia, Ecuador, Kazakhstan, and other countries. Have students find out more about how USAID employs Earth scientists in international programs.

Chapter 9 • Science in Action   273

UNIT 4 TIMELINE

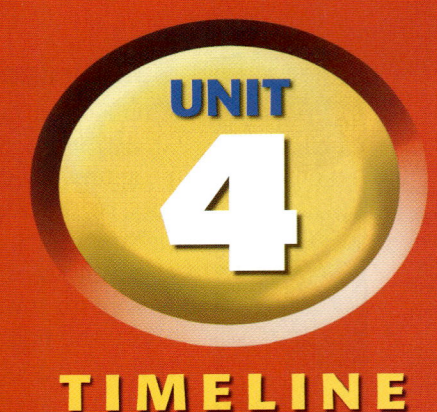

Reshaping the Land

In this unit, you will learn about how the surface of the Earth is continuously reshaped. There is a constant struggle between the forces that build up the Earth's land features and the forces that break them down. This timeline shows some of the events that have occurred in this struggle as natural changes in the Earth's features took place.

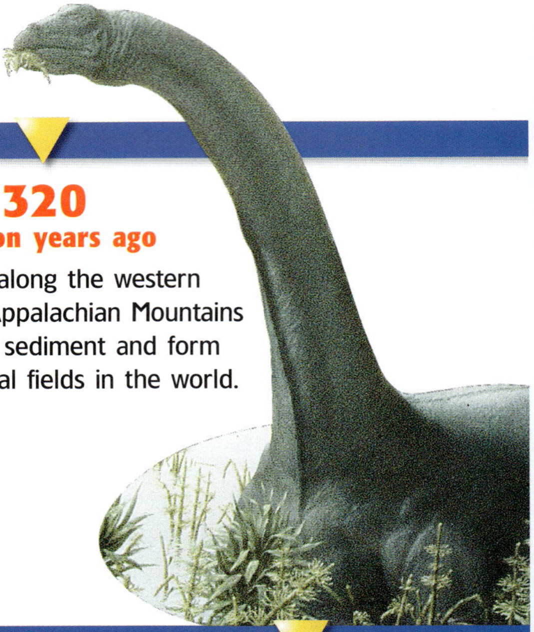

320 Million years ago
Vast swamps along the western edge of the Appalachian Mountains are buried by sediment and form the largest coal fields in the world.

6 Million years ago
The Colorado River begins to carve the Grand Canyon, which is roughly 2 km deep today.

10,000 years ago
The Great Lakes form at the end of the last Ice Age.

1930
Carlsbad Caverns National Park is established. It features the nation's deepest limestone cave and one of the largest underground chambers in the world.

Carlsbad Caverns

280 Million years ago
The shallow inland sea that covered much of what is now the upper midwestern United States fills with sediment and disappears.

140 Million years ago
The mouth of the Mississippi River is near present-day Cairo, Illinois.

65 Million years ago
Dinosaurs become extinct.

1775
The Battle of Bunker Hill, a victory for the Colonials, takes place on a drumlin, a tear-shaped mound of sediment that was formed by an ice-age glacier 10,000 years earlier.

1879
Cleopatra's Needle, a granite obelisk, is moved from Egypt to New York City. Within the next 100 years, the weather and pollution severely damage the 3,000-year-old monument.

1987
An iceberg twice the size of Rhode Island breaks off the edge of Antarctica's continental glacier.

1998
Hong Kong opens a new airport on an artificially enlarged island. Almost 350 million cubic meters of rock and soil were deposited in the South China Sea to form the over 3,000-acre island.

2002
A NASA study finds that the arctic ice cap is melting at a rate of 9% per decade. At this rate, the ice cap could melt during this century.

Reshaping the Land

10 Weathering and Soil Formation
Chapter Planning Guide

Compression guide: To shorten instruction because of time limitations, omit the Chapter Lab.

OBJECTIVES	LABS, DEMONSTRATIONS, AND ACTIVITIES	TECHNOLOGY RESOURCES
PACING • 90 min pp. 276–283 **Chapter Opener**	SE Start-up Activity, p. 277 ◆ GENERAL	OSP Parent Letter ■ GENERAL CD Student Edition on CD-ROM CD Guided Reading Audio CD ■ TR Chapter Starter Transparency* VID Brain Food Video Quiz
Section 1 Weathering • Describe how ice, water, wind, gravity, plants, and animals cause mechanical weathering. • Describe how water, acids, and air cause chemical weathering of rocks.	TE Group Activity Identifying Weathering, p. 278 GENERAL TE Group Activity Acid Precipitation, p. 281 ADVANCED TE Activity CO₂ and Rain, p. 280 GENERAL SE Quick Lab Acids React!, p. 282 ◆ GENERAL CRF Datasheet for Quick Lab* SE Model-Making Lab Rockin' Through Time, p. 298 ◆ GENERAL CRF Datasheet for Chapter Lab* LB Whiz-Bang Demonstrations When it Rains, It Fizzes* ◆ GENERAL LB EcoLabs & Field Activities Whether It Weathers (or Not)* ◆ GENERAL	CRF Lesson Plans* TR Bellringer Transparency* TR Chemical Weathering of Granite* TR LINK TO PHYSICAL SCIENCE pH Values of Common Materials* VID Lab Videos for Earth Science
PACING • 45 min pp. 284–287 **Section 2 Rates of Weathering** • Explain how the composition of rock affects the rate of weathering. • Describe how a rock's total surface area affects the rate at which the rock weathers. • Describe how differences in elevation and climate affect the rate of weathering.	TE Group Activity Surface Area and Weathering, p. 284 GENERAL SE School-to-Home Activity Ice Wedging, p. 286 GENERAL LB Calculator-Based Labs How Low Can You Go?* ◆ ADVANCED TE Activity Differential Weathering, p. 285 ◆ ADVANCED	CRF Lesson Plans* TR Bellringer Transparency* TR Total Surface Area to Volume*
PACING • 45 min pp. 288–293 **Section 3 From Bedrock to Soil** • Describe the source of soil. • Explain how the different properties of soil affect plant growth. • Describe how various climates affect soil.	TE Group Activity Describing Soil, p. 288 ◆ GENERAL TE Connection Activity Environmental Science, p. 289 GENERAL TE Group Activity Living Soil, p. 290 ◆ ADVANCED LB Calculator-Based Labs A Hot and Cool Lab* ADVANCED LB Calculator-Based Labs A Soil Study* ◆ ADVANCED TE Connection Activity Biology, p. 290 GENERAL TE Activity Soil Layers, p. 291 ◆ GENERAL	CRF Lesson Plans* TR Bellringer Transparency* TR Soil Horizons* SE Internet Activity, p. 292 GENERAL
PACING • 45 min pp. 294–297 **Section 4 Soil Conservation** • Describe three important benefits that soil provides. • Describe four methods of preventing soil damage and loss.	TE Activity Uses of Soil, p. 295 ◆ BASIC TE Connection Activity Math, p. 295 GENERAL SE Science in Action Math, Social Studies, and Language Arts Activities, pp. 304–305 GENERAL LB Long-Term Projects & Research Ideas Precious Soil* ADVANCED	CRF Lesson Plans* TR Bellringer Transparency* CRF SciLinks Activity* GENERAL

PACING • 90 min

CHAPTER REVIEW, ASSESSMENT, AND STANDARDIZED TEST PREPARATION
- CRF Vocabulary Activity* GENERAL
- SE Chapter Review, pp. 300–301 GENERAL
- CRF Chapter Review* ■ GENERAL
- CRF Chapter Tests A* ■ GENERAL, B* ADVANCED, C* SPECIAL NEEDS
- SE Standardized Test Preparation, pp. 302–303 GENERAL
- CRF Standardized Test Preparation* GENERAL
- CRF Performance-Based Assessment* GENERAL
- OSP Test Generator GENERAL
- CRF Test Item Listing* GENERAL

Online and Technology Resources

go.hrw.com — Visit go.hrw.com for a variety of free resources related to this textbook. Enter the keyword HZ5WSF.

Holt Online Learning — Students can access interactive problem-solving help and active visual concept development with the Holt Science and Technology Online Edition available at www.hrw.com.

Guided Reading Audio CD — Also in Spanish. A direct reading of each chapter for auditory learners, reluctant readers, and Spanish-speaking students.

Science Tutor CD-ROM — Excellent for remediation and test practice.

KEY

SE Student Edition	**CRF** Chapter Resource File	**SS** Science Skills Worksheets	* Also on One-Stop Planner
TE Teacher Edition	**OSP** One-Stop Planner	**MS** Math Skills for Science Worksheets	♦ Requires advance prep
	LB Lab Bank	**CD** CD or CD-ROM	■ Also available in Spanish
	TR Transparencies	**VID** Classroom Video/DVD	

SKILLS DEVELOPMENT RESOURCES	SECTION REVIEW AND ASSESSMENT	STANDARDS CORRELATIONS
SE Pre-Reading Activity, p. 276 GENERAL **OSP** Science Puzzlers, Twisters & Teasers GENERAL		National Science Education Standards UCP 2; SAI 1; SPSP 5; ES 2a
CRF Directed Reading A* ■ BASIC, B* SPECIAL NEEDS **CRF** Vocabulary and Section Summary* ■ GENERAL **SE** Reading Strategy Paired Summarizing, p. 278 GENERAL **SE** Connection to Chemistry Acidity of Precipitation, p. 281 GENERAL **TE** Inclusion Strategies, p. 281 ♦ **CRF** Reinforcement Worksheet Autobiography of a Rock* BASIC	**SE** Reading Checks, pp. 279, 280, 283 GENERAL **TE** Reteaching, p. 282 BASIC **TE** Quiz, p. 282 GENERAL **TE** Alternative Assessment, p. 282 GENERAL **SE** Section Review,* p. 283 GENERAL **CRF** Section Quiz* ■ GENERAL	SAI 1, 2; ES 1c, 1d, 1k; *Chapter Lab:* UCP 2; *LabBook:* UCP 2; SAI 1
CRF Directed Reading A* ■ BASIC, B* SPECIAL NEEDS **CRF** Vocabulary and Section Summary* ■ GENERAL **SE** Reading Strategy Reading Organizer, p. 284 GENERAL	**SE** Reading Checks, pp. 285, 286, 287 GENERAL **TE** Reteaching, p. 286 BASIC **TE** Quiz, p. 286 GENERAL **TE** Alternative Assessment, p. 286 GENERAL **SE** Section Review,* p. 287 ■ GENERAL **CRF** Section Quiz* ■ GENERAL	SAI 1, 2; ES 1c, 1d
CRF Directed Reading A* ■ BASIC, B* SPECIAL NEEDS **CRF** Vocabulary and Section Summary* ■ GENERAL **SE** Reading Strategy Prediction Guide, p. 288 GENERAL **TE** Inclusion Strategies, p. 289 ♦ **SE** Connection to Social Studies Deforestation in Brazil, p. 291 GENERAL	**SE** Reading Checks, pp. 288, 291, 292 GENERAL **TE** Reteaching, p. 292 BASIC **TE** Quiz, p. 292 GENERAL **TE** Alternative Assessment, p. 292 GENERAL **SE** Section Review,* p. 293 ■ GENERAL **CRF** Section Quiz* ■ GENERAL	SAI 1, 2; SPSP 4; ES 1c, 1e, 1g, 1k
CRF Directed Reading A* ■ BASIC, B* SPECIAL NEEDS **CRF** Vocabulary and Section Summary* ■ GENERAL **SE** Reading Strategy Reading Organizer, p. 294 GENERAL **SE** Math Practice Making Soil, p. 295 GENERAL **CRF** Reinforcement Worksheet Where the Tall Corn Grows* BASIC **CRF** Critical Thinking Buying the Farm* ADVANCED	**SE** Reading Checks, pp. 294, 297 GENERAL **TE** Homework, p. 296 ADVANCED **TE** Reteaching, p. 296 BASIC **TE** Quiz, p. 296 GENERAL **TE** Alternative Assessment, p. 296 GENERAL **SE** Section Review,* p. 297 ■ GENERAL **CRF** Section Quiz* ■ GENERAL	SAI 1; SPSP 2, 4, 5; ST 2; HNS 1

One-Stop Planner® CD-ROM

This convenient CD-ROM includes:
- Lab Materials QuickList Software
- Holt Calendar Planner
- Customizable Lesson Plans
- Printable Worksheets
- ExamView® Test Generator

CNN Student News

cnnstudentnews.com

Find the latest news, lesson plans, and activities related to important scientific events.

SciLinks NSTA

www.scilinks.org

Maintained by the **National Science Teachers Association**. See Chapter Enrichment pages for a complete list of topics.

Current Science®

Check out *Current Science* articles and activities by visiting the HRW Web site at **go.hrw.com.** Just type in the keyword **HZ5CS10T**.

Classroom Videos

- **Lab Videos** demonstrate the chapter lab.
- **Brain Food Video Quizzes** help students review the chapter material.
- **CNN Videos** bring science into your students' daily life.

Chapter 10 • Chapter Planning Guide

10 Chapter Resources

Visual Resources

CHAPTER STARTER TRANSPARENCY

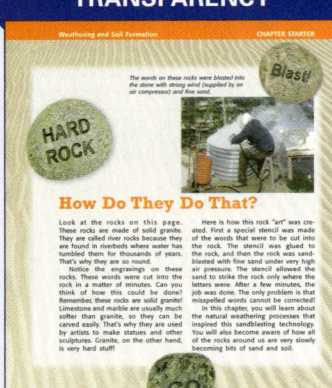

BELLRINGER TRANSPARENCIES

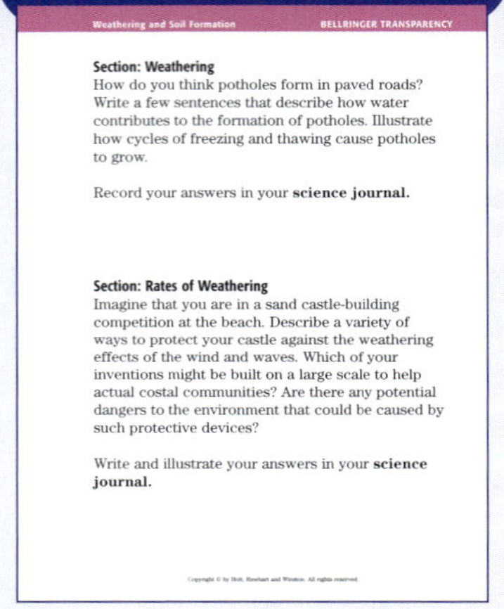

TEACHING TRANSPARENCIES

TEACHING TRANSPARENCIES

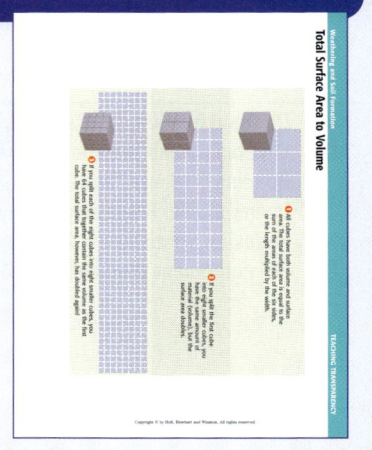

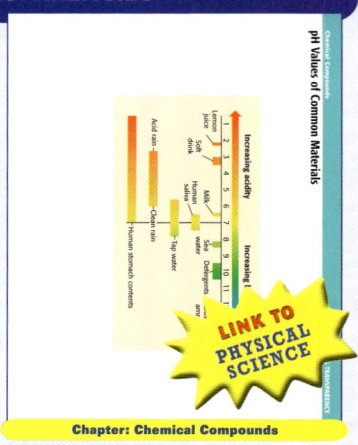

CONCEPT MAPPING TRANSPARENCY

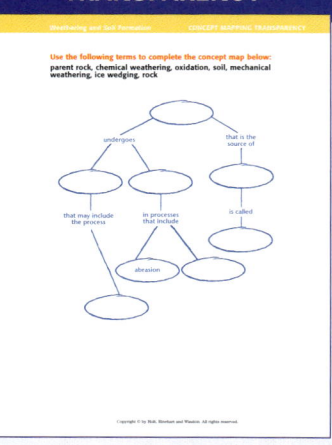

Planning Resources

LESSON PLANS

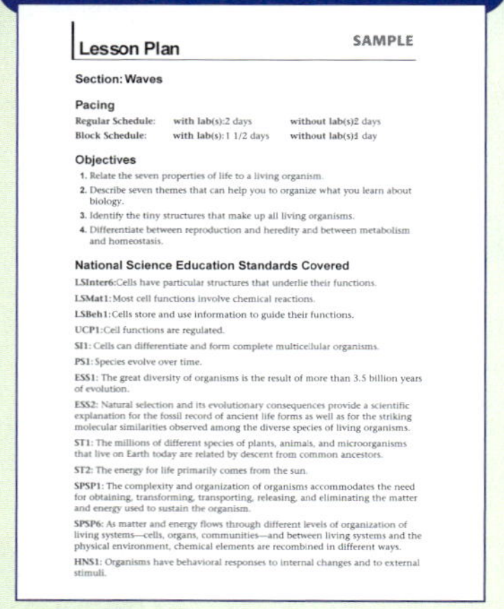

PARENT LETTER — ALSO IN SPANISH

TEST ITEM LISTING

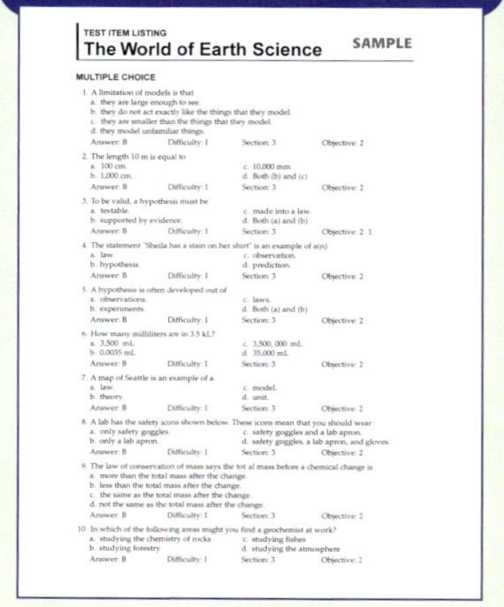

One-Stop Planner® CD-ROM

This CD-ROM includes all of the resources shown here and the following time-saving tools:

- Lab Materials QuickList Software
- Customizable lesson plans
- Holt Calendar Planner
- The powerful ExamView® Test Generator

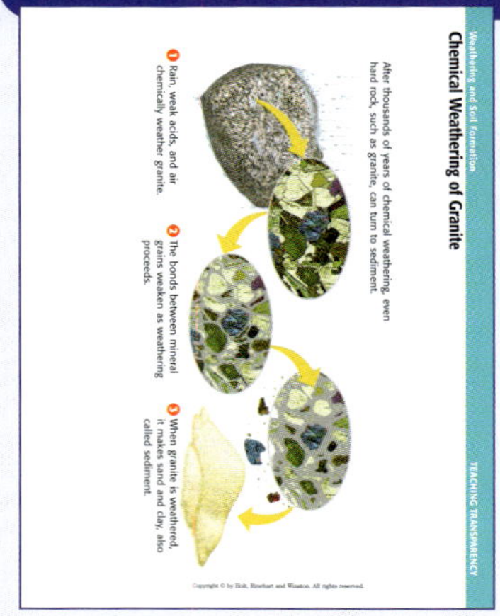

275C Chapter 10 • Weathering and Soil Formation

For a preview of available worksheets covering math and science skills, see pages T26–T33. All of these resources are also on the One-Stop Planner®.

Meeting Individual Needs

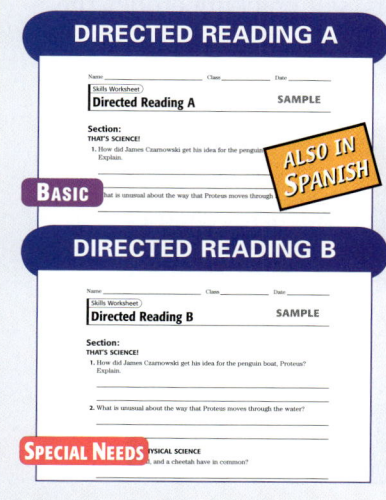

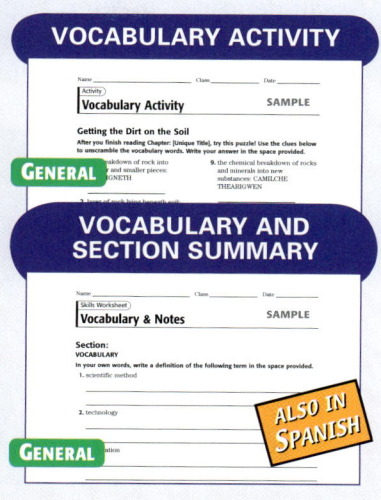

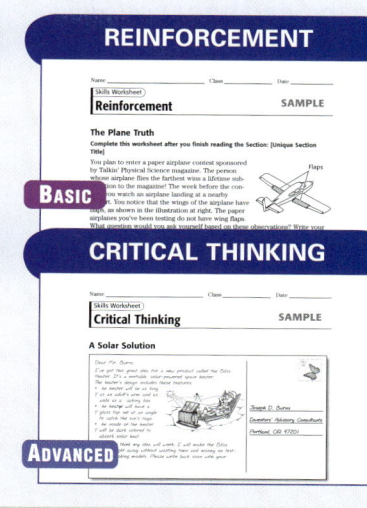

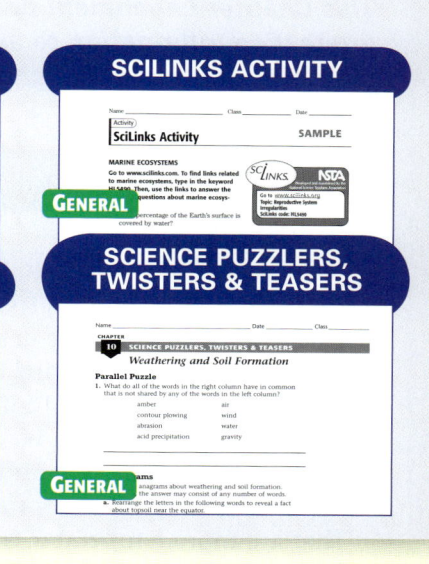

- **DIRECTED READING A** — BASIC — ALSO IN SPANISH
- **DIRECTED READING B** — SPECIAL NEEDS
- **VOCABULARY ACTIVITY** — GENERAL
- **VOCABULARY AND SECTION SUMMARY** — GENERAL — ALSO IN SPANISH
- **REINFORCEMENT** — BASIC
- **CRITICAL THINKING** — ADVANCED
- **SCILINKS ACTIVITY** — GENERAL
- **SCIENCE PUZZLERS, TWISTERS & TEASERS** — GENERAL

Labs and Activities

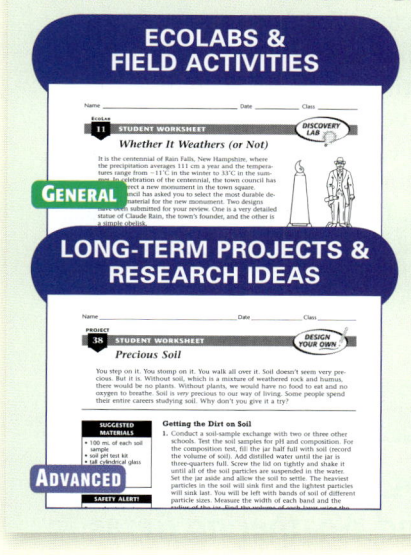

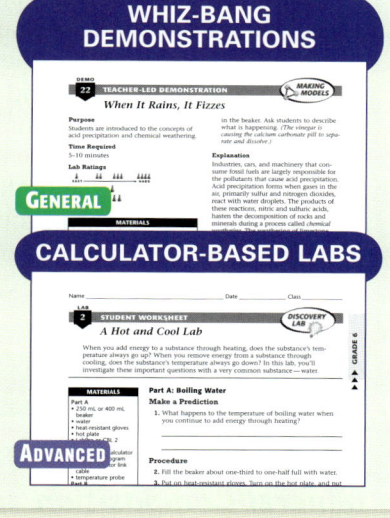

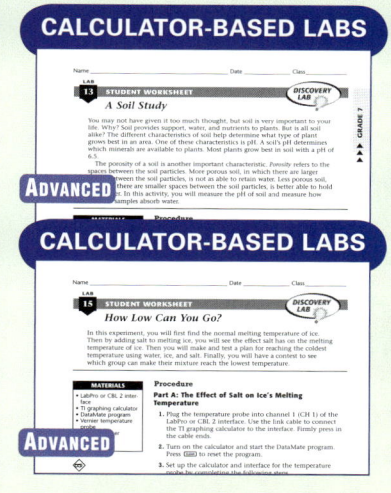

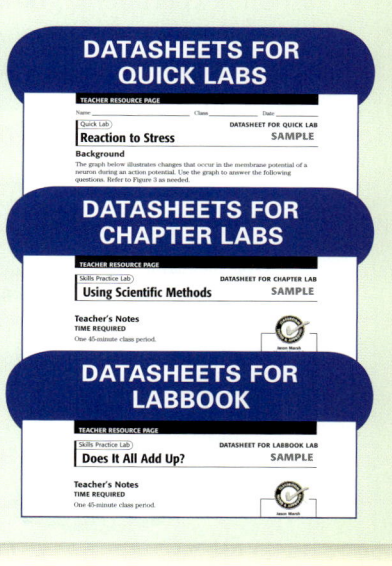

- **ECOLABS & FIELD ACTIVITIES** — GENERAL
- **LONG-TERM PROJECTS & RESEARCH IDEAS** — ADVANCED
- **WHIZ-BANG DEMONSTRATIONS** — GENERAL
- **CALCULATOR-BASED LABS** — ADVANCED
- **CALCULATOR-BASED LABS** — ADVANCED
- **CALCULATOR-BASED LABS** — ADVANCED
- **DATASHEETS FOR QUICK LABS**
- **DATASHEETS FOR CHAPTER LABS**
- **DATASHEETS FOR LABBOOK**

Review and Assessments

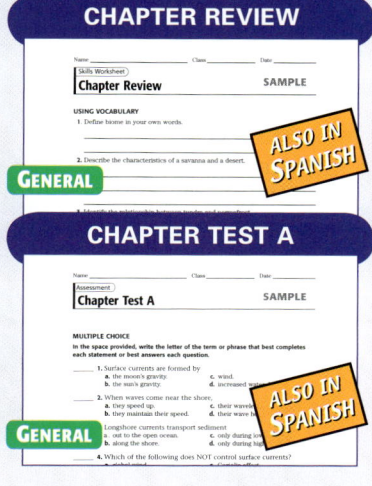

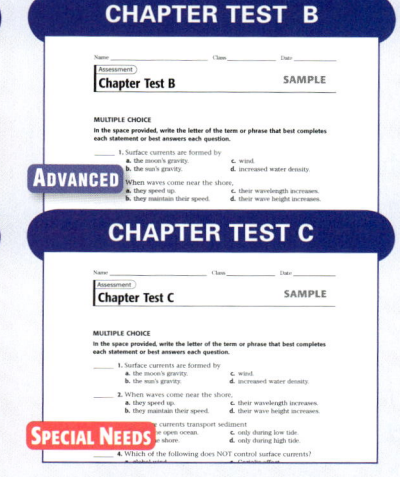

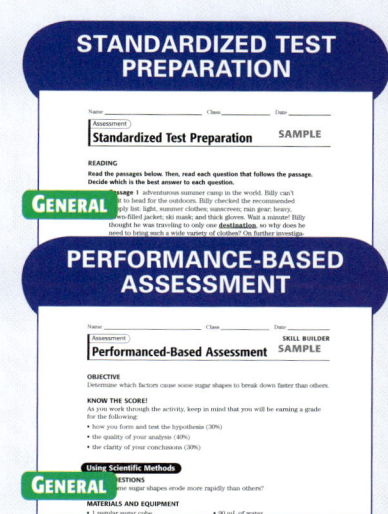

- **SECTION QUIZ** — GENERAL — ALSO IN SPANISH
- **SECTION REVIEW** — GENERAL — ALSO IN SPANISH
- **CHAPTER REVIEW** — GENERAL — ALSO IN SPANISH
- **CHAPTER TEST A** — GENERAL — ALSO IN SPANISH
- **CHAPTER TEST B** — ADVANCED
- **CHAPTER TEST C** — SPECIAL NEEDS
- **STANDARDIZED TEST PREPARATION** — GENERAL
- **PERFORMANCE-BASED ASSESSMENT** — GENERAL

Chapter 10 • Chapter Resources 275D

10 Chapter Enrichment

This Chapter Enrichment provides relevant and interesting information to expand and enhance your presentation of the chapter material.

Section 1

Weathering

Thermal Contraction and Expansion

- There is much scientific debate over whether the daily and seasonal heating and cooling of rocks cause wide-scale weathering. In desert environments, where temperature ranges can be extreme, small rocks can shatter from expansion and contraction. But does this type of weathering occur in larger rocks and in climates that are more temperate? Geologists attempting to replicate this process in a lab have had little success. In one experiment, granite samples were repeatedly heated and cooled by more than 100°C, and no fracturing was observed. This suggests that if thermal expansion and contraction weathers rock, it may do so over the course of hundreds of thousands of years.

Is That a Fact!

- Before the invention of power drills and saws, stonemasons sometimes filled existing joints and cracks in rocks with water and waited for ice wedging to split the rocks. Obviously, this method was effective only in areas where temperatures dropped to freezing or below.

Salt Cracking

- In places where groundwater contains dissolved salts, salt water seeps into bedrock. When the water evaporates, the dissolved salts crystallize, and the growing crystals can exert enough force to fracture rock. This process, known as *salt cracking,* can be seen at the ocean, where sea cliffs become pitted and cracked from salt deposits. In desert regions, salt cracking erodes the base of some sandstone formations, which leaves an unweathered rock balancing on an eroded pedestal.

Weathered Mountain

- Mount Fuji is a dormant volcano that is a source of national pride among the Japanese. Unfortunately, the forces of mechanical weathering threaten to change the volcano's conical shape and near-perfect symmetry. To preserve the mountain's shape, the Japanese government built a 17 m–long concrete brace over a widening crevice near the mountain's summit. Before action was taken, as much as 300,000 tons of rock and soil had fallen down the mountainside every year.

Section 2

Rates of Weathering

Mineral Composition and Weathering Rates

- The order in which minerals crystallize from magma is nearly the same as the order in which they weather. Minerals that form quickly and at high temperatures and pressures within Earth, such as olivine and pyroxene, tend to be unstable at the surface and are less resistant to chemical weathering. Minerals that form slowly and at lower temperatures are much more resistant to the effects of weathering.

> For background information about teaching strategies and issues, refer to the *Professional Reference for Teachers*.

Section 3

From Bedrock to Soil

Types of Soil in the United States

- The soils of the mainland United States can be divided into two major types—pedocal and pedalfer. Pedocal is a calcium-rich soil that covers most of the western United States. Pedocal gets its name from the Latin *ped*, meaning "soil," joined with *cal*, representing *calcium*. Pedalfer is an iron- and aluminum-rich soil that covers most of the eastern half of the country. The *al* in *pedalfer* stands for *aluminum*; the *fer* stands for *ferrum* (iron).

Salinization

- All groundwater contains small concentrations of salts. If arid or semiarid soil is intensively irrigated, it can accumulate so much salt that it cannot support plant life. This process, called *salinization*, can ruin croplands. Some historical scholars argue that salinization contributed to the decline and fall of many ancient societies, including the Babylonian civilization.

Is That a Fact!

◆ *Regolith* is a term that describes all of the weathered material that lies over the bedrock. Soil refers to the upper layers of the regolith that supports plant life.

◆ The term regolith is derived from the Greek word *rhegos*, meaning "blanket," and the Greek word *lithos* meaning "stone." This derivation is important because it denotes the protective qualities of soil. Like a blanket, the soil protects the rock below from weathering. In mountain regions where soil is easily eroded, bedrock weathers much more quickly.

Section 4

Soil Conservation

Farming in the Imperial Valley

- Although desert soils are low in organic matter, they are not necessarily poor soils. Desert soil such as that of the Imperial Valley in California is actually quite rich with the minerals needed for plant growth. Water diverted from the Colorado River is used to irrigate the valley, which is now one of the nation's major farming regions, where crops such as alfalfa, cotton, and sugar beets are grown. While the Imperial Valley is incredibly productive, agriculture in the region relies heavily on the use of fertilizers. There is also much debate over whether the Imperial Valley diverts too much water from the Colorado River.

Federal Soil Conservation Service

- In response to the devastating windstorms that swept across the Great Plains, the U.S. Department of Agriculture formed the Soil Conservation Service in 1935. Working with ranchers and farmers, conservationists instituted strategies such as contour plowing and terracing, planting trees as windbreaks, allowing land to lie fallow, and planting drought-resistant crops.

SciLinks — Developed and maintained by the National Science Teachers Association

SciLinks is maintained by the National Science Teachers Association to provide you and your students with interesting, up-to-date links that will enrich your classroom presentation of the chapter.

Visit www.scilinks.org and enter the SciLinks code for more information about the topic listed.

Topic: Weathering
SciLinks code: HSM1648

Topic: Soil Types
SciLinks code: HSM1412

Topic: Rates of Weathering
SciLinks code: HSM1269

Topic: Soil Conservation
SciLinks code: HSM1409

Topic: Soil and Climate
SciLinks code: HSM1408

Chapter 10 • Chapter Enrichment

10

Overview
Tell students that this chapter will help them learn about the process of weathering, including factors that cause weathering and factors that effect the rate of weathering. Students will learn about how soil is formed and how the properties of soil affect plant growth. They will also learn about the effect of climate on soil. Finally students will learn about soil conservation.

Assessing Prior Knowledge
Students should be familiar with the following topics:
- acids in precipitation, in groundwater, and in vegetation
- various types of rocks
- chemical reactions

Identifying Misconceptions
As students learn the material in this chapter, some of them may associate soil formation with deposits by rivers. Other students may think that the soil has existed since the Earth formed. Discuss the components of soil, and discuss where those components came from.

10
Weathering and Soil Formation

SECTION **1** Weathering 278

SECTION **2** Rates of Weathering .. 284

SECTION **3** From Bedrock to Soil .. 288

SECTION **4** Soil Conservation 294

Chapter Lab 298
Chapter Review 300
Standardized Test Preparation 302
Science in Action............. 304

About the PHOTO

Need a nose job, Mr. President? The carving of Thomas Jefferson that is part of the Mount Rushmore National Memorial is having its nose inspected by a National Parks worker. The process of weathering has caused cracks to form in the carving of President Jefferson. National Parks workers use a sealant to protect the memorial from moisture, which can cause further cracking.

PRE-READING ACTIVITY

FOLDNOTES **Key-Term Fold** Before you read the chapter, create the FoldNote entitled "Key-Term Fold" described in the **Study Skills** section of the Appendix. Write a key term from the chapter on each tab of the key-term fold. Under each tab, write the definition of the key term.

Standards Correlations

National Science Education Standards

The following codes indicate the National Science Education Standards that correlate to this chapter. The full text of the standards is at the front of the book.

Chapter Opener
UCP 2; SAI 1; SPSP 5; ES 2a

Section 1 Weathering
SAI 1; ES 1c, 1k; *LabBook*: UCP 2; SAI 1

Section 2 Rates of Weathering
SAI 1; ES 1c

Section 3 From Bedrock to Soil
ES 1e, 1k

Section 4 Soil Conservation
SPSP 2, 4, 5

Chapter Lab
UCP 2; SAI 1

Chapter Review
UCP 1; SPSP 2; HNS 1; ES 1c, 1e, 1k

Science in Action
ST 2; HNS 3; ES 1k

276 Chapter 10 • Weathering and Soil Formation

START-UP ACTIVITY

What's the Difference?

In this chapter, you will learn about the processes and rates of weathering. Complete this activity to learn about how the size and surface area of a substance affects how quickly the substance breaks down.

Procedure

1. Fill **two small containers** about half full with **water**.
2. Add **one sugar cube** to one container.
3. Add **1 tsp of granulated sugar** to the other container.
4. Using **one spoon for each container,** stir the water and sugar in each container at the same rate.
5. Using a **stopwatch,** measure how long it takes for the sugar to dissolve in each container.

Analysis

1. Did the sugar dissolve at the same rate in both containers? Explain why or why not.
2. Do you think one large rock or several smaller rocks would wear away faster? Explain your answer.

START-UP ACTIVITY

MATERIALS

FOR EACH GROUP
- container, small (2)
- spoon (2)
- stopwatch or timepiece with second hand
- sugar, granulated (1 tsp)
- sugar cube
- water

Teacher's Notes: The size of sugar cubes may vary, so students may obtain more accurate results if they use two sugar cubes rather than 1 sugar cube and 1 tsp of granulated sugar. Students can crush one of the sugar cubes between two spoons and then compare the rate at which both sugar samples dissolve.

Answers

1. Sample answer: The granulated sugar dissolved faster than the sugar cube because the grains of sugar had more surface area than the sugar cube did. Therefore, the water could come into contact with and dissolve the granulated sugar more quickly.
2. Sample answer: Several smaller rocks would wear away faster because they have more surface area than a large rock does.

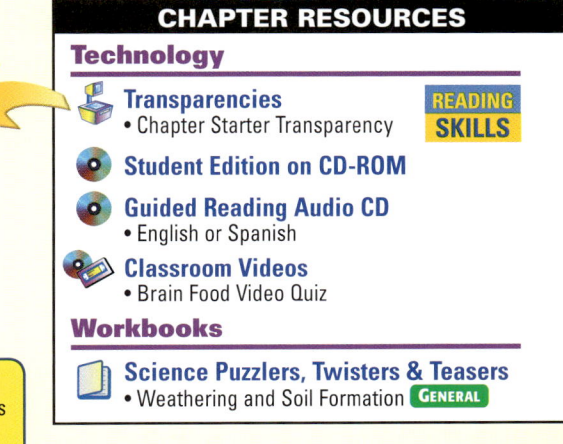

Chapter Starter Transparency
Use this transparency to help students begin thinking about the processes that weather rock.

CHAPTER RESOURCES

Technology

Transparencies
- Chapter Starter Transparency READING SKILLS

Student Edition on CD-ROM

Guided Reading Audio CD
- English or Spanish

Classroom Videos
- Brain Food Video Quiz

Workbooks

Science Puzzlers, Twisters & Teasers
- Weathering and Soil Formation GENERAL

Chapter 10 • Weathering and Soil Formation   **277**

SECTION 1

Focus

Overview
In this section, students will learn how processes such as ice wedging and abrasion and plant and animal activities contribute to the mechanical weathering of rock. Students will also learn how water and acids cause chemical weathering of rock.

🔔 Bellringer
Ask students to think about how potholes form in paved roads. Have students write a few sentences that describe how water contributes to the formation of potholes. Students should illustrate how cycles of freezing and thawing help cause potholes to grow.

Motivate

Group ACTIVITY — GENERAL
Identifying Weathering Have groups of students find photographs in magazines that illustrate weathering. Examples may include rusted cars or bikes, sidewalks or walls that have been cracked by plant roots, potholes, and weathered statues. Ask the class to help you group the photographs into examples of mechanical weathering and chemical weathering. **LS Logical**

SECTION 1

READING WARM-UP

Objectives
- Describe how ice, water, wind, gravity, plants, and animals cause mechanical weathering.
- Describe how water, acids, and air cause chemical weathering of rocks.

Terms to Learn
weathering
mechanical weathering
abrasion
chemical weathering
acid precipitation

READING STRATEGY

Paired Summarizing Read this section silently. In pairs, take turns summarizing the material. Stop to discuss ideas that seem confusing.

weathering the process by which rock materials are broken down by the action of physical and chemical processes

mechanical weathering the breakdown of rock into smaller pieces by physical means

---

Weathering

If you have ever walked along a trail, you might have noticed small rocks lying around. Where did these rocks come from?

These smaller rocks came from larger rocks that were broken down. **Weathering** is the process by which rock materials are broken down by the action of physical or chemical processes.

Mechanical Weathering

If you were to crush one rock with another rock, you would be demonstrating one type of mechanical weathering. **Mechanical weathering** is the breakdown of rock into smaller pieces by physical means. Agents of mechanical weathering include ice, wind, water, gravity, plants, and even animals.

Ice

The alternate freezing and thawing of soil and rock, called *frost action*, is a form of mechanical weathering. One type of frost action, *ice wedging*, is shown in **Figure 1**. Ice wedging starts when water seeps into cracks during warm weather. When temperatures drop, the water freezes and expands. The ice then pushes against the sides of the crack. This causes the crack to widen.

Figure 1 Ice Wedging
The granite in the photo has been broken down by repeated ice wedging, which is shown below.

Water   Ice   Water   Ice

CHAPTER RESOURCES

Chapter Resource File
- Lesson Plan
- Directed Reading A [BASIC]
- Directed Reading B [SPECIAL NEEDS]

Technology
Transparencies
- Bellringer

---

278 Chapter 10 • Weathering and Soil Formation

Figure 2 Three Forms of Abrasion

These river rocks are rounded because they have been tumbled in the riverbed by fast-moving water for many years.

This rock has been shaped by blowing sand. Such rocks are called ventifacts.

Rocks grind against each other in a rock slide, which creates smaller and smaller rock fragments.

Abrasion

As you scrape a piece of chalk against a board, particles of the chalk rub off to make a line on the board and the piece of chalk wears down and becomes smaller. The same process, called *abrasion,* happens with rocks. **Abrasion** is the grinding and wearing away of rock surfaces through the mechanical action of other rock or sand particles.

abrasion the grinding and wearing away of rock surfaces through the mechanical action of other rock or sand particles

Wind, Water, and Gravity

Abrasion can happen in many ways, as shown in **Figure 2.** When rocks and pebbles roll along the bottom of swiftly flowing rivers, they bump into and scrape against each other. The weathering that occurs eventually causes these rocks to become rounded and smooth.

Wind also causes abrasion. When wind blows sand and silt against exposed rock, the sand eventually wears away the rock's surface. The figure above (center) shows what this kind of sandblasting can do to a rock.

Abrasion also occurs when rocks fall on one another. You can imagine the forces rocks exert on each other as they tumble down a mountainside. In fact, anytime one rock hits another, abrasion takes place.

✓ **Reading Check** Name three things that can cause abrasion. (*See the Appendix for answers to Reading Checks.*)

Teach

CONNECTION to Physical Science—ADVANCED

Exfoliation Another process of mechanical weathering is called *exfoliation*. As overlying rock is removed by uplift and erosion, the pressure on the rock is reduced. As the pressure is reduced, the rock expands in volume and long, curved cracks develop parallel to the rock's surface. In this way, an outcrop "sheds" layers of rock. Exfoliation can often be observed in granite outcrops. Ask students to describe why granite formations are prone to exfoliation. (Granite forms underground, so it forms under a great deal of pressure from the rock above. A granite pluton 15 km underground forms at 5,000 times the pressure at Earth's surface. As the granite is pushed toward the surface and the overlying rock is weathered away, the pressure on the rock is reduced and the granite exfoliates.) **LS** Verbal

Answer to Reading Check

Wind, water, and gravity can cause abrasion.

Cultural Awareness — GENERAL

The Ajanta Caves In the second century BCE, Buddhist monks began carving an intricate system of caves in a massive basalt flow in central India. The Ajanta caves comprised a complex of monasteries, temples, and living quarters. The caves were adorned with beautiful frescoes and carvings and then were mysteriously abandoned in the seventh century CE. They were rediscovered by British game hunters less than 200 years ago. The Ajanta caves are notable not only for their artwork but also for the manner in which they were carved. The monks cut channels in the rock first and then jammed dry logs into the crevices. They poured water on top of the logs and waited for the expanding wood to shatter the rock. In this way, they carved 30 caves out of solid rock.

Section 1 • Weathering

Teach, continued

MISCONCEPTION ALERT

Humans Cause Weathering
Students may be surprised to learn that animals such as earthworms, coyotes, and rabbits play significant roles in weathering rock. Human activity also contributes to the weathering of rock. People move large amounts of soil and rock whenever they farm, build, or drive off-road vehicles. In addition, people blast rock to make tunnels, roads, mines, and quarries.

CONNECTION to Life Science — GENERAL

Gold Bugs As ground-dwelling termites construct their homes, they excavate an enormous amount of soil and rock fragments. Occasionally, the termites strike it rich. Geochemical prospectors have learned from indigenous cultures in Africa, Asia, Australia, and South America to analyze termite mounds for ore deposits such as tin, silver, gold, diamond, and uranium. In some parts of Africa, gold concentrations in termite mounds are rich enough that people earn money by panning gold from the mounds.

Answer to Reading Check
Answers may vary. Sample answer: ants, worms, mice, coyotes, and rabbits.

Plants

You may not think of plants as being strong, but some plants can easily break rocks. Have you ever seen sidewalks and streets that are cracked because of tree roots? Roots don't grow fast, but they certainly are powerful! Plants often send their roots into existing cracks in rocks. As the plant grows, the force of the expanding root becomes so strong that the crack widens. Eventually, the entire rock can split apart, as shown in **Figure 3**.

Animals

Believe it or not, earthworms cause a lot of weathering! They burrow through the soil and move soil particles around. This exposes fresh surfaces to continued weathering. Would you believe that some kinds of tropical worms move an estimated 100 metric tons of soil per acre every year? Almost any animal that burrows causes mechanical weathering. Ants, worms, mice, coyotes, and rabbits are just some of the animals that contribute to weathering. **Figure 4** shows some of these animals in action. The mixing and digging that animals do often contribute to another type of weathering, called *chemical weathering*. You will learn about this type of weathering next.

Reading Check List three animals that can cause weathering.

Figure 3 Although they grow slowly, tree roots are strong enough to break solid rock.

Figure 4 Animals that live in the soil, such as moles, prairie dogs, insects, worms, and gophers, cause a lot of weathering. When the animals burrow in the ground, they break up soil and loosen rocks to be exposed to further weathering.

CHAPTER RESOURCES

Technology

Transparencies
- Chemical Weathering of Granite
- **LINK TO PHYSICAL SCIENCE** pH Values of Common Materials

ACTIVITY — GENERAL

CO_2 and Rain Have students try this activity to learn how CO_2 combines with water in the atmosphere to form a slightly acidic solution. Fill a test tube halfway with water. Add a few drops of universal indicator solution. Have a student exhale through a straw into the water. As the CO_2 combines with the water, carbonic acid forms and the color of the solution changes. This color change indicates an acidic solution. **LS Visual/Kinesthetic**

280 Chapter 10 • Weathering and Soil Formation

Figure 5 Chemical Weathering of Granite

After thousands of years of chemical weathering, even hard rock, such as granite, can turn to sediment.

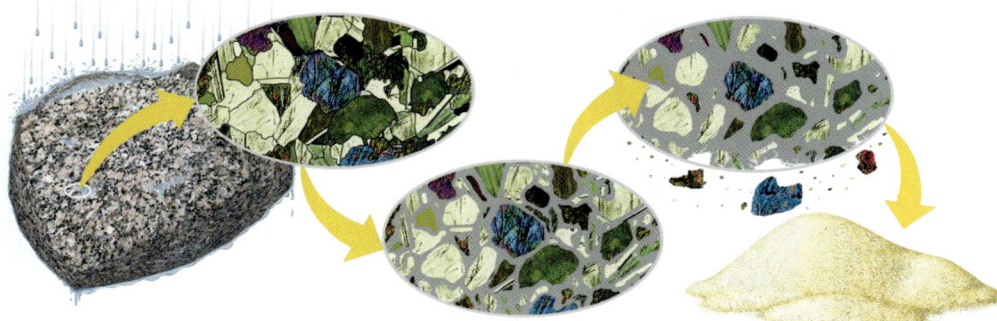

❶ Rain, weak acids, and air chemically weather granite.

❷ The bonds between mineral grains weaken as weathering proceeds.

❸ When granite is weathered, it makes sand and clay, also called sediment.

Chemical Weathering

The process by which rocks break down as a result of chemical reactions is called **chemical weathering.** Common agents of chemical weathering are water, weak acids, and air.

Water

If you drop a sugar cube into a glass of water, the sugar cube will dissolve after a few minutes. This process is an example of chemical weathering. Even hard rock, such as granite, can be broken down by water. But, it just may take thousands of years. **Figure 5** shows how granite is chemically weathered.

Acid Precipitation

Rain, sleet, or snow, that contains a high concentration of acids is called **acid precipitation.** Precipitation is naturally acidic. However, acid precipitation contains more acid than normal precipitation. The high level of acidity can cause very rapid weathering of rock. Small amounts of sulfuric and nitric acids from natural sources, such as volcanoes, can make precipitation acidic. However, acid precipitation can also be caused by air pollution from the burning of fossil fuels, such as coal and oil. When these fuels are burned, they give off gases, including sulfur oxides, nitrogen oxides, and carbon oxides. When these compounds combine with water in the atmosphere, they form weak acids, which then fall back to the ground in rain and snow. When the acidity is too high, acid precipitation can be harmful to plants and animals.

chemical weathering the process by which rocks break down as a result of chemical reactions

acid precipitation rain, sleet, or snow, that contains a high concentration of acids

CONNECTION TO Chemistry

Acidity of Precipitation
Acidity is measured by using a pH scale, the units of which range from 0 to 14. Solutions that have a pH of less than 7 are acidic. Research some recorded pH levels of acid rain. Then, compare these pH levels with the pH levels of other common acids, such as lemon juice and acetic acid.

INCLUSION Strategies

- Attention Deficit Disorder
- Developmentally Delayed
- Learning Disabled

Organize students into small groups. To each group, hand out a cork, sandpaper, and a small plastic container with a lid such as a margarine container. Ask students to abrade their "rock" by sanding away some of the cork. Next, students should completely fill the plastic containers with water. Place the containers in a freezer until the next class. Students should predict what will happen to the water-filled containers in their **science journal.** The next class, ask students to relate this experiment to the real world and discuss how they modeled two forms of mechanical weathering. **LS Kinesthetic**

Group ACTIVITY — ADVANCED

Acid Precipitation Have students study acid precipitation by dividing the class into the two groups described below. Have each group present its findings to the class.

- The monitoring group can test the pH of precipitation in your area by using a pH test kit. Students can also test the pH of tap water, surface runoff, rivers, and lakes. Have students contact the local weather service to find records of the pH of precipitation in your area over several decades. The monitoring group can present its findings in graphs and other visual displays.

- The research group can prepare a presentation on the causes and effects of acid precipitation. This group should also focus on legislation and other solutions for the air pollution problems that contribute to acid precipitation.

LS Visual

MISCONCEPTION ALERT

The pH Scale Students are often confused by the pH scale. The term *pH* is French and translates as "power of hydrogen." It refers to the concentration of hydronium ions in a solution. In a measurement of the pH of an acid, a decrease of one number on the pH scale represents an increase in the concentration of hydronium ions by a power of ten. Thus an acid with a pH of 2 is 100 times as concentrated as an acid with a pH of 4. Remind students that acidic solutions have a pH less than 7, and basic solutions have a pH greater than 7. Show students the teaching transparency entitled "pH Values of Common Materials" to learn more about the pH scale.

Section 1 • Weathering

Close

Reteaching — BASIC
Mechanical or Chemical?
To reinforce the difference between chemical and mechanical weathering, have students decide whether each of the following phenomena is an example of mechanical or chemical weathering:

- a rock fall on a mountainside (mechanical)
- a rusty bridge (chemical)
- lichens and mosses growing on a boulder (chemical)
- an alpine glacier advancing down a valley (mechanical)

English Language Learners
LS Verbal

Quiz — GENERAL
1. How do earthworms aid in weathering? (When earthworms burrow, they move soil particles around and expose fresh surfaces to weathering.)
2. What human activities can increase the acidity of precipitation? (activities that burn fossil fuels, such as coal)

Alternative Assessment — GENERAL
Trivia Challenge Divide students into small groups. Have each group research the process of weathering. Ask each group to create five multiple-choice trivia cards for a game that tests the players' knowledge of weathering. **LS Kinesthetic**

Figure 6 Acid in groundwater has weathered limestone to form Carlsbad Caverns, in New Mexico.

Acids in Groundwater

In certain places groundwater contains weak acids, such as carbonic or sulfuric acid. These acids react with rocks in the ground, such as limestone. When groundwater comes in contact with limestone, a chemical reaction occurs. Over a long period of time, the dissolving of limestone forms karst features, such as caverns. The caverns, like the one shown in **Figure 6,** form from the eating away of the limestone.

Acids in Living Things

Another source of acids that cause weathering might surprise you. Take a look at the lichens in **Figure 7.** Lichens produce acids that can slowly break down rock. If you have ever taken a walk in a park or forest, you have probably seen lichens growing on the sides of trees or rocks. Lichens can also grow in places where some of the hardiest plants cannot. For example, lichens can grow in deserts, in arctic areas, and in areas high above timberline, where even trees don't grow.

Figure 7 Lichens, which consist of fungi and algae living together, contribute to chemical weathering.

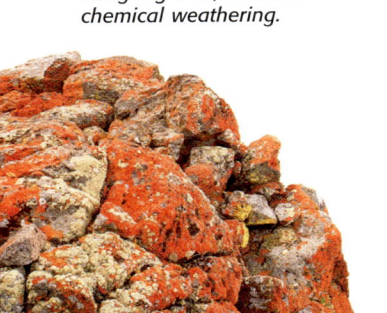

Quick Lab

Acids React!
1. Ketchup is one example of a food that contains weak acids, which react with certain substances. Take a **penny** that has a dull appearance, rub **ketchup** on it for several minutes.
2. Rinse the penny.
3. Where did all the grime on the penny go?
4. How is this process similar to what happens to a rock when it is exposed to natural acids during weathering?

Quick Lab

MATERIALS
FOR EACH GROUP
- ketchup
- penny

Safety Caution: Students who are allergic to tomatoes should use a cotton swab to apply the ketchup.

Answers
3. Answers may vary. Students might note that the grime on the surface of the penny reacted chemically with the acid in the ketchup and dissolved.
4. Answers may vary. Students should note that the way that rocks react with acids is similar to the way that the grime on the surface of the penny reacted with the ketchup.

282 Chapter 10 • Weathering and Soil Formation

Air

The car shown in **Figure 8** is undergoing chemical weathering due to the air. The oxygen in the air is reacting with the iron in the car, causing the car to rust. Water speeds up the process. But the iron would rust even if no water were present. Scientists call this process oxidation.

Oxidation is a chemical reaction in which an element, such as iron, combines with oxygen to form an oxide. This common form of chemical weathering is what causes rust. Old cars, aluminum cans, and your bike can experience oxidation if left exposed to air and rain for long periods of time.

Reading Check What can cause oxidation?

Figure 8 Rust is a result of chemical weathering.

SECTION Review

Summary

- Ice wedging is a form of mechanical weathering in which water seeps into rock cracks and then freezes and expands.
- Wind, water, and gravity cause mechanical weathering by abrasion.
- Animals and plants cause mechanical weathering by turning the soil and breaking apart rocks.
- Water, acids, and air chemically weather rock by weakening the bonds between mineral grains of the rock.

Using Key Terms

1. In your own words, write a definition for each of the following terms: *weathering, mechanical weathering, abrasion, chemical weathering* and *acid precipitation.*

Understanding Key Ideas

2. Which of the following things cannot cause mechanical weathering?
   a. water
   b. acid
   c. wind
   d. animals

3. List three things that cause chemical weathering of rocks.

4. Describe three ways abrasion occurs in nature.

5. Describe the similarity in the ways tree roots and ice mechanically weather rock.

6. Describe five sources of chemical weathering.

Critical Thinking

7. **Making Inferences** Why does acid precipitation weather rocks faster than normal precipitation?

8. **Making Comparisons** Compare the weather processes that affect a rock on top of a mountain and a rock buried beneath the ground.

Math Skills

9. Substances that have a pH of less than 7 are acidic. For each pH unit lower, the acidity is ten times greater. For example, normal precipitation is slightly acidic at a 5.6 pH. If acid precipitation were measured at 4.6 pH, it would be 10 times more acidic than normal precipitation. How many times more acidic would precipitation at 3.6 pH be than normal precipitation?

SciLinks
Developed and maintained by the National Science Teachers Association

For a variety of links related to this chapter, go to www.scilinks.org
Topic: Weathering
SciLinks code: HSM1648

Answers to Section Review

1. Sample answer: Weathering is the breakdown of rock by physical and chemical processes. Mechanical weathering is the breakdown of rock into smaller pieces by physical means. Abrasion is the grinding and wearing away of rock surfaces through mechanical action of other rock or sand particles. Chemical weathering is a process by which rocks break down because of chemical reactions. Acid precipitation is rain, sleet, or snow that has a high concentration of acid.
2. b
3. water, acids, and air
4. Sample answer: Abrasion can be caused by wind, water, and gravity.
5. Both tree roots and ice can force cracks in rocks to expand.
6. water, acid precipitation, acids in groundwater, acids in living things, and air
7. Acid precipitation is more acidic than natural precipitation. Stronger acids break down rocks faster.
8. A rock on top of a mountain tends to be weathered more because it is exposed to wind, precipitation, and the effects of gravity. A rock buried underground does not experience weathering from wind, precipitation, or gravity.
9. $10 \times 10 = 100$ times more acidic

Answer to Reading Check
Oxidation occurs when oxygen combines with an element to form an oxide.

CHAPTER RESOURCES

Chapter Resource File
- Section Quiz GENERAL
- Section Review GENERAL
- Vocabulary and Section Summary GENERAL
- Reinforcement Worksheet BASIC
- Datasheet for Quick Lab

Section 1 • Weathering 283

SECTION 2

Focus

Overview
This section explores how different types of rock, climate, and elevation affect weathering rates.

🔔 **Bellringer**
Ask students to imagine that they are in a sand castle–building competition at the beach. Ask them to come up with ways to protect their castle against the weathering effects of the wind and waves. Students can share their ideas with the class.

Motivate

Group Activity — GENERAL

Surface Area and Weathering
Supply each group with a clear glass that contains a calcium antacid tablet and a second glass that contains a calcium antacid tablet cut into quarters. Tell students that both antacid tablets and limestone contain calcium carbonate, which dissolves in acidic solutions. Have students pour enough vinegar into the glasses to cover the tablets. Ask students which of the tablets "weathers" more rapidly. (The tablet cut into quarters weathers more rapidly.) Lead students to conclude that surface area affects the rate at which materials weather. **LS** Logical

SECTION 2

READING WARM-UP

Objectives
- Explain how the composition of rock affects the rate of weathering.
- Describe how a rock's total surface area affects the rate at which the rock weathers.
- Describe how differences in elevation and climate affect the rate of weathering.

Terms to Learn
differential weathering

READING STRATEGY

Reading Organizer As you read this section, create an outline of the section. Use the headings from the section in your outline.

Rates of Weathering

Have you ever seen a cartoon in which a character falls off a cliff and lands on a ledge? Ledges exist in nature because the rock that the ledge is made of weathers more slowly than the surrounding rock.

Weathering is a process that takes a long time. However, some rock will weather faster than other rock. The rate at which a rock weathers depends on climate, elevation, and the makeup of the rock.

Differential Weathering

Hard rocks, such as granite, weather more slowly than softer rocks, such as limestone. **Differential weathering** is a process by which softer, less weather resistant rocks wear away and leave harder, more weather resistant rocks behind.

Figure 1 shows a landform that has been shaped by differential weathering. Devils Tower was once a mass of molten rock deep inside an active volcano. When the molten rock cooled and hardened, it was protected from weathering by the outer rock of the volcano. After thousands of years of weathering, the soft outer parts of the volcano have worn away. The harder, more resistant rock is all that remains.

Figure 1 The illustration is an artist's idea of how the original volcano may have looked. The photo inset shows Devils Tower as it appears today.

CHAPTER RESOURCES

Chapter Resource File
- Lesson Plan
- Directed Reading A BASIC
- Directed Reading B SPECIAL NEEDS

Technology
- Transparencies
  - Bellringer
  - Total Surface Area to Volume

Chapter 10 • Weathering and Soil Formation

The Shape of Rocks

Weathering takes place on the outer surface of rocks. Therefore, the more surface area that is exposed to weathering, the faster the rock will be worn down. A large rock has a large surface area. But a large rock also has a large volume. Because of the large rock's volume, the large rock will take a long time to wear down.

If a large rock is broken into smaller fragments, weathering of the rock happens much more quickly. The rate of weathering increases because a smaller rock has more surface area to volume than a larger rock has. So, more of a smaller rock is exposed to the weathering process. **Figure 2** shows this concept in detail.

differential weathering the process by which softer, less weather resistant rocks wear away and leave harder, more weather resistant rocks behind

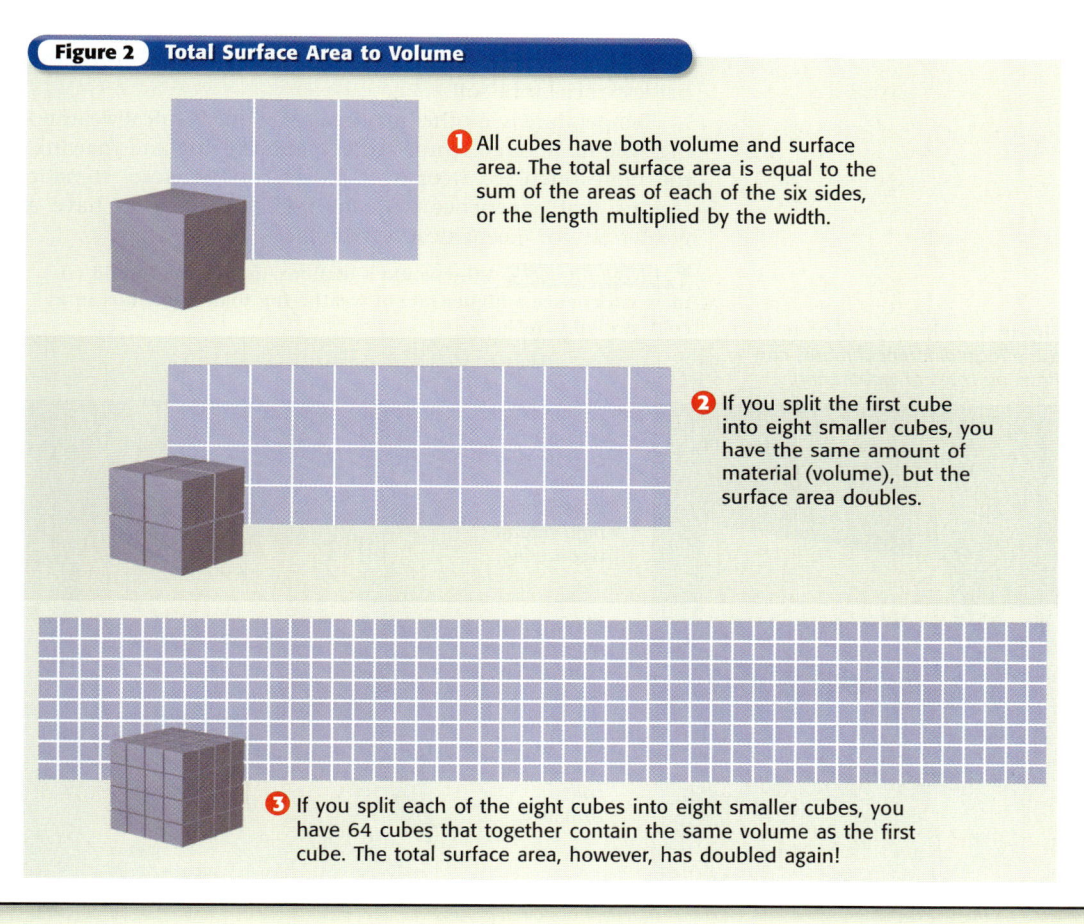

Reading Check How does an increase in surface area affect the rate of weathering? (*See the Appendix for answers to Reading Checks.*)

Figure 2 Total Surface Area to Volume

1. All cubes have both volume and surface area. The total surface area is equal to the sum of the areas of each of the six sides, or the length multiplied by the width.

2. If you split the first cube into eight smaller cubes, you have the same amount of material (volume), but the surface area doubles.

3. If you split each of the eight cubes into eight smaller cubes, you have 64 cubes that together contain the same volume as the first cube. The total surface area, however, has doubled again!

CONNECTION to Geology — GENERAL

Weathering Devils Tower Why is the intrusive volcanic rock that makes up Devils Tower more resistant to weathering than was the extrusive volcanic rock of the former volcano? Both rock types had the same composition. The difference is their cohesiveness. The intrusive rock cooled more slowly than the extrusive rock. As the rock cooled, it formed large crystals that interlocked like a 3-D jigsaw puzzle. As a result, the volcanic neck was more resistant to weathering. In contrast, the rock that made up the outside of the volcano cooled quickly. This rock was made of much smaller crystals and groundmass material—material that cooled so fast that it did not form crystals.

Teach

ACTIVITY — ADVANCED

Differential Weathering Have students use the Internet to learn more about how differential weathering created landforms in the United States. Students could investigate certain locations where differential weathering has created spectacular landforms, such as Good City of Rocks in Gooding, Idaho, and The Window in Big Bend National Park, Texas. **LS Visual**

MISCONCEPTION ALERT

Weathering of Hard Rocks Students may assume that some types of rock, such as granite, do not weather. Emphasize that all rocks weather, but different kinds of rock weather at different rates. The granite that is used in buildings and monuments is often polished. Polishing the surface slows the weathering process because less surface area is exposed.

Answer to Reading Check
As the surface area increases, the rate of weathering also increases.

Section 2 • Rates of Weathering **285**

Close

Reteaching — BASIC
Weathering Rates Show students a variety of rocks. Ask students what they could do to increase the rate of weathering of the rocks. (Sample answer: The rocks could be on top of a high mountain; the rocks could be put in a warm, humid climate; and the rocks could be crushed to increase the surface area.) **LS Visual**

Quiz — GENERAL
1. Do different types of rock weather at different rates? (yes)
2. Does chemical weathering affect the rate of mechanical weathering. (yes)
3. What factors contribute to accelerated weathering rates at high elevations? (wind, precipitation, and gravity)

Alternative Assessment — GENERAL
Investigate Your Area A cemetery is a great place to observe the effects of differential weathering because several kinds of rock are used to make headstones and most of the headstones are dated. Schedule a field trip to a cemetery, or encourage interested students to visit a cemetery on their own. Have them compare the dates and types of rock used to determine which kinds of rock are most susceptible to weathering. **LS Kinesthetic**

SCHOOL to HOME

Ice Wedging

WRITING SKILL To understand ice wedging, try this activity at home with a parent. Fill a small, plastic water bottle with water. Plug the opening with a piece of putty. Place the bottle in the freezer overnight. Describe in your **science journal** what happened to the putty.

ACTIVITY

Figure 3 These photos show the effects different climates can have on rates of weathering.

◀ This mailbox is in a dry climate and does not experience a high rate of weathering.

This mailbox ▶ is in a warm, humid climate. It experiences a high rate of chemical weathering called oxidation.

Answer to School-to-Home Activity
Sample answer: The putty was pushed out of the opening of the bottle when the water in the bottle froze and expanded.

Weathering and Climate

The rate of weathering in an area is greatly affected by the climate of that area. *Climate* is the average weather condition in an area over a long period of time. For example, the two mailboxes shown in **Figure 3** are in two different climates. The mailbox on the left is in a dry climate. The mailbox on the right is in a warm, humid climate. As you can see, the mailbox in the warm, humid climate is rusty.

Temperature and Water

The rate of chemical weathering happens faster in warm, humid climates. The rusty mailbox has experienced a type of chemical weathering called oxidation. Oxidation, like other chemical reactions, happens at a faster rate when temperatures are higher and when water is present.

Water also increases the rate of mechanical weathering. The freezing of water that seeps into the cracks of rocks is the process of ice wedging. Ice wedging causes rocks to break apart. Over time, this form of weathering can break down even the hardest rocks into soil.

Temperature is another major factor in mechanical weathering. The more often temperatures cause freezing and thawing, the more often ice wedging takes place. Therefore, climatic regions that experience frequent freezes and thaws have a greater rate of mechanical weathering.

✓ **Reading Check** Why would a mailbox in a warm, humid climate experience a higher rate of weathering than a mailbox in a cold, dry climate?

Answer to Reading Check
Warm, humid climates have higher rates of weathering because oxidation happens faster when temperatures are higher and when water is present.

Weathering and Elevation

Just like everything else, mountains are exposed to air and water. As a result, mountain ranges are weathered down. Weathering happens on mountains in the same way it does everywhere else. However, as shown in **Figure 4,** rocks at higher elevations, as on a mountain, are exposed to more wind, rain, and ice than the rocks at lower elevations are. This increase in wind, rain, and ice at higher elevations causes the peaks of mountains to weather faster.

Gravity affects weathering, too. The steepness of mountain slopes increases the effects of mechanical and chemical weathering. Steep slopes cause rainwater to quickly run off the sides of mountains. The rainwater carries the sediment down the mountain's slope. This continual removal of sediment exposes fresh rock surfaces to the effects of weathering. New rock surfaces are also exposed to weathering when gravity causes rocks to fall away from the sides of mountains. The increased surface area means weathering happens at a faster rate.

✓ **Reading Check** Why do mountaintops weather faster than rocks at sea level?

Figure 4 The ice, rain, and wind that these mountain peaks are exposed to cause them to weather at a fast rate.

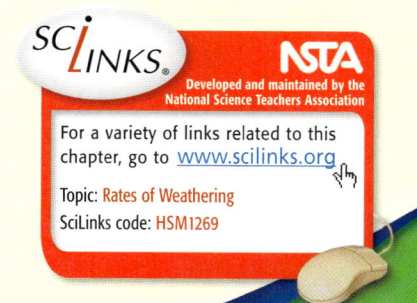

SECTION Review

Summary

- Hard rocks weather more slowly than softer rocks.
- The more surface area of a rock that is exposed to weathering, the faster the rock will be worn down.
- Chemical weathering occurs faster in warm, humid climates.
- Weathering occurs faster at high elevations because of an increase in ice, rain, and wind.

Using Key Terms

1. In your own words, write a definition for the term *differential weathering*.

Understanding Key Ideas

2. A rock will have a lower rate of weathering when the rock
   a. is in a humid climate.
   b. is a very hard rock, such as granite.
   c. is at a high elevation.
   d. has more surface area exposed to weathering.

3. How does surface area affect the rate of weathering?

4. How does climate affect the rate of weathering?

5. Why does the peak of a mountain weather faster than the rocks at the bottom of the mountain?

Math Skills

6. The surface area of an entire cube is 96 cm². If the length and width of each side are equal, what is the length of one side of the cube?

Critical Thinking

7. **Making Inferences** Does the rate of chemical weathering increase or stay the same when a rock becomes more mechanically weathered? Why?

SECTION 3

Focus

Overview
In this section, students will learn about sources for soil formation, the various properties of soil, and the effects of climate on soil type.

🔔 Bellringer

Have students answer the following questions:

- Has there always been soil on Earth? (No, soil did not exist until the parent rock of the early Earth was weathered.)
- What makes soil valuable to humans? (Answers may vary. Soil supports the growth of plants, which provide humans with oxygen and food.)

Motivate

Group ACTiViTY — GENERAL

Describing Soil Provide small groups of students with magnifying lenses and samples of several types of local soil. Have students empty each sample onto a piece of white paper and examine it. Have students record their observations about each sample's composition, color, particle size, texture, and moisture content. Ask groups to hypothesize how each soil type formed and what type of plant life might grow in the soil. **LS Kinesthetic Co-op Learning**

SECTION 3

READING WARM-UP

Objectives
- Describe the source of soil.
- Explain how the different properties of soil affect plant growth.
- Describe how various climates affect soil.

Terms to Learn

soil	soil structure
parent rock	humus
bedrock	leaching
soil texture	

READING STRATEGY

Prediction Guide Before you read this section, write the title of each heading in this section. Next, under each heading, write what you think you will learn.

---

soil a loose mixture of rock fragments, organic material, water, and air that can support the growth of vegetation

parent rock a rock formation that is the source of soil

bedrock the layer of rock beneath soil

CHAPTER RESOURCES

Chapter Resource File
- Lesson Plan
- Directed Reading A **BASIC**
- Directed Reading B **SPECIAL NEEDS**

Technology
- Transparencies
  - Bellringer

From Bedrock to Soil

Most plants need soil to grow. But what exactly is soil? Where does it come from?

The Source of Soil

To a scientist, **soil** is a loose mixture of small mineral fragments, organic material, water, and air that can support the growth of vegetation. But not all soils are the same. Because soils are made from weathered rock fragments, the type of soil that forms depends on the type of rock that weathers. The rock formation that is the source of mineral fragments in the soil is called **parent rock.**

Bedrock is the layer of rock beneath soil. In this case, the bedrock is the parent rock because the soil above it formed from the bedrock below. Soil that remains above its parent rock is called *residual soil*.

Soil can be blown or washed away from its parent rock. This soil is called *transported soil*. **Figure 1** shows one way that soil is moved from one place to another. Both wind and the movement of glaciers are also responsible for transporting soil.

✓ **Reading Check** What is soil formed from? *(See the Appendix for answers to Reading Checks.)*

Figure 1 Transported soil may be moved long distances from its parent rock by rivers, such as this one.

Answer to Reading Check

Soil is formed from parent rock, organic material, water, and air.

---

288 Chapter 10 • Weathering and Soil Formation

Figure 2 Soil Texture

The proportion of these different-sized particles in soil determine the soil's texture.

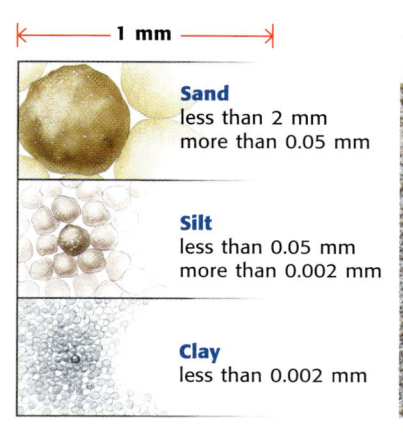

|←— 1 mm —→|

Sand less than 2 mm more than 0.05 mm

Silt less than 0.05 mm more than 0.002 mm

Clay less than 0.002 mm

This callout shows the makeup of sandy loam. It is made of
Sand 60%
Silt 30%
Clay 10%

Soil Properties

Some soils are great for growing plants. Other soils can't support the growth of plants. To better understand soil, you will next learn about its properties, such as soil texture, soil structure, and soil fertility.

Soil Texture and Soil Structure

Soil is made of different-sized particles. These particles can be as large as 2 mm, such as sand. Other particles can be too small to see without a microscope. **Soil texture** is the soil quality that is based on the proportions of soil particles. **Figure 2** shows the soil texture for a one type of soil.

Soil texture affects the soil's consistency. Consistency describes a soil's ability to be worked and broken up for farming. For example, soil texture that has a large proportion of clay can be hard and difficult for farmers to break up.

Soil texture influences the *infiltration*, or ability of water to move through soil. Soil should allow water to get to the plants' roots without causing the soil to be completely saturated.

Water and air movement through soil is also influenced by soil structure. **Soil structure** is the arrangement of soil particles. Soil particles are not always evenly spread out. Often, one type of soil particle will clump in an area. A clump of one type of soil can either block water flow or help water flow, which affects soil moisture.

soil texture the soil quality that is based on the proportions of soil particles.

soil structure the arrangement of soil particles

Teach

INCLUSION Strategies

- Hearing Impaired
- Visually Impaired
- Developmentally Delayed

Organize students into pairs or groups of three. Give each group three paper cups. Have the students fill the first paper cup with silt, the second with clay, and the third with sand. Make sure all three cups are filled to the same level. Have students use a sharp pencil to poke a small hole at the bottom of each cup. Make sure the hole is the same size for each cup. While holding the cup over a large bowl, students should pour half a cup of water into each cup of soil, one at a time. Using a stopwatch, students should determine the amount of time it takes the water to pass through each cup of soil. Have students record the times. Ask students, "Which type of soil did the water pass through the quickest?" (Water will pass through the sand fastest. Water will pass through the clay slowest.)
LS Kinesthetic
Co-op Learning
English Language Learners

CONNECTION ACTIVITY
Environmental Science — GENERAL

Writing

Persuasive Essay Some wind-swept deserts have very little surface soil because wind has carried off most of the smaller particles. This leaves an exposed layer of pebbles and gravel too heavy to be moved by the wind. This layer, called desert pavement, may take hundreds of years to form, but once established, it protects the desert from further erosion. Desert pavement is easily destroyed by off-road vehicles. Ask students to write a persuasive essay arguing that such sensitive desert areas should or should not be off limits to vehicles. **LS Verbal**

Section 3 • From Bedrock to Soil

Teach, continued

Group Activity — ADVANCED

MATERIALS

FOR EACH GROUP
- bag, plastic, resealable
- bread, without preservatives (several slices)
- soil samples (including potting soil)
- spatula and tongs

Living Soil Bacteria and fungi are the major decomposers of organic material in soil. These decomposers break down organic matter into simpler substances that plants can absorb. Have groups bring in several types of soil. Have students put 20 to 30 drops of distilled water on each of the bread slices. Using the spatula, students should then sprinkle onto each slice of bread a small amount of each soil sample. Next, students should use the tongs to place each slice of bread in a separate, labeled plastic bag. One slice of bread on which there is no soil should be used as a control. Place the bags in a dark box or drawer. After five to seven days, students may observe, describe, and analyze the patterns of mold grown in each sample by using a hand lens. Remind students that the bags must remain sealed during the observation period. Finally, ask the students to draw conclusions based on the data that they have recorded for each sample. **LS** Kinesthetic

humus the dark, organic material formed in soil from the decayed remains of plants and animals

leaching the removal of substances that can be dissolved from rock, ore, or layers of soil due to the passing of water

Soil Fertility

Nutrients in soil, such as iron, are necessary for plants to grow. Some soils are rich in nutrients. Other soils may not have many nutrients or are not able to supply the nutrients to the plants. A soil's ability to hold nutrients and to supply nutrients to a plant is described as *soil fertility*. Many nutrients in soil come from the parent rock. Other nutrients come from **humus,** which is the organic material formed in soil from the decayed remains of plants and animals. These remains are broken down into nutrients by decomposers, such as bacteria and fungi.

Soil Horizons

Because of the way soil forms, soil often ends up in a series of layers, with humus-rich soil on top, sediment below that, and bedrock on the bottom. Geologists call these layers *horizons*. The word *horizon* tells you that the layers are horizontal. **Figure 3** shows what these horizons can look like. You can see these layers in some road cuts.

The top layer of soil is often called the *topsoil*. Topsoil contains more humus than the layers below it. The humus is rich in the nutrients plants need to be healthy. This is why good topsoil is necessary for farming.

Figure 3 Soil Horizons

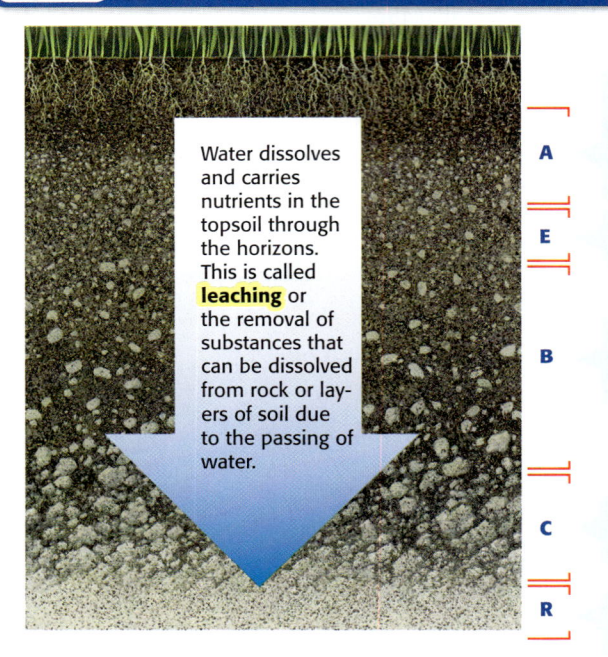

Water dissolves and carries nutrients in the topsoil through the horizons. This is called **leaching** or the removal of substances that can be dissolved from rock or layers of soil due to the passing of water.

A This horizon consists of the topsoil. Topsoil contains more humus than any other soil horizon. Soil in forests often has a O horizon. This layer is made up of litter from dead plants and animals.

E This horizon experiences intense leaching of nutrients.

B This horizon collects the dissolved substances and nutrients deposited from the upper horizons.

C This horizon is made of partially weathered bedrock.

R This horizon is made of bedrock that has little or no weathering.

Is That a Fact!

Where do soda cans and airplanes come from? They come from the soil, of course! In tropical areas, the process of soil leaching produces concentrated bauxite deposits in a thin layer at the Earth's surface. Bauxite is the ore that is refined to produce aluminum.

CONNECTION ACTIVITY
Biology — GENERAL

Berlese Funnels Students may be surprised to learn that soil is a thriving ecosystem. In 1 m³ of soil, there may be 10 million roundworms and 50,000 small insects and mites. In a single gram of fertile soil, there may be 50,000 algae, 400,000 fungi, and 2.5 million bacteria. Have students construct a Berlese funnel to collect small organisms from soil. Designs for Berlese funnels are available on the Internet. **LS** Kinesthetic

Soil pH

Soils can be acidic or basic. The pH scale is used to measure how acidic or basic a soil is and ranges from 0 to 14. The midpoint, which is 7, is neutral. Soil that has a pH below 7 is acidic. Soil that has a pH above 7 is basic.

The pH of a soil influences how nutrients dissolve in the soil. For example, plants are unable to take up certain nutrients from soils that are basic, or that have a high pH. Soils that have a low pH can restrict other important nutrients from hungry plants. Because different plants need different nutrients, the right pH for a soil depends on the plants growing in it.

Soil and Climate

Soil types vary from place to place. One reason for this is the differences in climate. As you read on, you will see that climate can make a difference in the types of soils that develop around the world.

Tropical Rain Forest Climates

Take a look at **Figure 4.** In tropical rain forest climates, the air is very humid and the land receives a large amount of rain. Because of warm temperatures, crops can be grown year-round. The warm soil temperature also allows dead plants and animals to decay easily. This provides rich humus to the soil.

Because of the lush plant growth, you may think that tropical rain forest soils are the most nutrient-rich in the world. However, tropical rain forest soils are nutrient poor. The heavy rains in this climate leach precious nutrients from the topsoil into deeper layers of soil. The result is that tropical topsoil is very thin. Another reason tropical rain forest soil is nutrient poor is that the lush vegetation has a great demand for nutrients. The nutrients that aren't leached away are quickly taken up by plants and trees that live off the soil.

Reading Check Why is the topsoil in tropical rain forests thin?

Figure 4 Lush tropical rain forests have surprisingly thin topsoil.

CONNECTION TO Social Studies

WRITING SKILL **Deforestation in Brazil** In Brazil, rain forests have been cut down at an alarmingly high rate, mostly by farmers. However, tropical rain forest topsoil is very thin and is not suitable for long-term farming. Research the long-term effects of deforestation on the farmers and indigenous people of Brazil. Then, write a one page report on your findings.

Cultural Awareness — GENERAL

Sustainable Farming The Lacandon Maya of Mexico have developed sustainable farming methods that do not destroy the fragile soil of the tropical rain forest. On a small piece of land, they grow both food crops and tree crops, a practice known as *agroforestry*. After a few years, they let the farmland recover by allowing it to become a forest again. The Lacandon Maya's approach to farming is recognized for its ecological soundness and has been replicated in many countries. Have students research sustainable farming techniques and create a model or poster to share with the class. **Visual**

Answer to Reading Check

Heavy rains leach precious nutrients into deeper layers of soil, resulting in a very thin layer of topsoil.

ACTIVITY — GENERAL

Soil Layers Have student groups collect two soil samples from the same area, one from the surface and one from 16 to 20 cm below the surface. Groups should fill two test tubes about one-quarter full with each soil sample and should add water until the tubes are three-quarters full. Have students gently shake the covered tubes for several minutes. Place the test tubes in a rack, and leave them overnight. Students should be able to observe the different compositions of layers that formed in the two test tubes. Soil components will settle according to weight. Have students measure the depth of each layer in the test tube and observe the color and size of the grains. Then, have students draw and label the soil layers. The surface soil will probably contain noticeably more humus than the below-surface soil will. **Kinesthetic**

Close

Reteaching — BASIC
Factors That Affect Soil Ask students to think of factors that influence the characteristics of soil. How does climate affect soil? Write factors on the board. (Factors might include parent rock, sources of organic material, and rainfall.) Be sure that students understand how these characteristics affect the soil's ability to sustain vegetation. **LS Verbal**

Quiz — GENERAL
1. What is the source of mineral fragments in soil? (parent rock)
2. What is the organic part of soil called? (humus)
3. What causes topsoil in tropical climates to be thin? (Sample answer: leaching from heavy rains)

Alternative Assessment — GENERAL
Making Postcards Have students imagine that they are on a world trip during which they travel to every climate mentioned in the section. Tell them to write a series of postcards in which they describe what the soil is like in each climate. The picture on each card should be a magazine photograph that illustrates the soil in that climate. **LS Visual**

Answer to Reading Check
Temperate climates have the most productive soil.

Desert Climates
While tropical climates get a lot of rain, deserts get less than 25 cm a year. Leaching of nutrients is not a problem in desert soils. But the lack of rain causes many other problems, such as very low rates of chemical weathering and less ability to support plant and animal life. A low rate of weathering means soil is created at a slower rate.

Some water is available from groundwater. Groundwater can trickle in from surrounding areas and seep to the surface. But as soon as the water is close to the surface, it evaporates. So, any materials that were dissolved in the water are left behind in the soil. Without the water to dissolve the minerals, the plants are unable to take them up. Often, the chemicals left behind are various types of salts. These salts can sometimes become so concentrated that the soil becomes toxic, or poisonous, even to desert plants! Death Valley, shown in **Figure 5,** is a desert that has toxic levels of salt in the soil.

Figure 5 *The salty conditions of desert soils make it difficult for many plants to survive.*

Temperate Forest and Grassland Climates
Much of the continental United States has a temperate climate. An abundance of weathering occurs in temperate climates. Temperate areas get enough rain to cause a high level of chemical weathering, but not so much that the nutrients are leached out of the soil. Frequent changes in temperature lead to frost action. As a result, thick, fertile soils develop, as shown in **Figure 6.**

Temperate soils are some of the most-productive soils in the world. In fact, the midwestern part of the United States has earned the nickname "breadbasket" for the many crops the region's soil supports.

✓ **Reading Check** Which climate has the most-productive soil?

INTERNET ACTIVITY
For another activity related to this chapter, go to go.hrw.com and type in the keyword **HZ5WSFW**.

Figure 6 *The rich soils in areas that have a temperate climate support a vast farming industry.*

BRAIN FOOD

Cryptogamic Soil In some desert areas, a special type of soil called *cryptogamic soil* is actually alive! This soil is composed of different species of mosses, lichens, fungi, and algae. Cryptogamic soil is sometimes known as "brown sugar soil" because it is dark brown and crusty. The spongy soil absorbs moisture readily and, when disturbed by freezing, it uplifts and cracks. The cracks are important to desert ecosystems because plant seeds get lodged in the cracks. The moisture allows the seeds to germinate. Cryptogamic soils can be severely damaged if they are walked on. Ask students to find out why walking on cryptogamic soil could damage the soil, and have them write a paragraph about it.

Arctic Climates

Arctic areas have so little precipitation that they are like cold deserts. In arctic climates, as in desert climates, chemical weathering occurs very slowly. So, soil formation also occurs slowly. Slow soil formation is why soil in arctic areas, as shown in **Figure 7**, is thin and unable to support many plants.

Arctic climates also have low soil temperatures. At low temperatures, decomposition of plants and animals happens more slowly or stops completely. Slow decomposition limits the amount of humus in the soil, which limits the nutrients available. These nutrients are necessary for plant growth.

Figure 7 Arctic soils, such as the soil along Denali Highway, in Alaska, cannot support lush vegetation.

SECTION Review

Summary

- Soil is formed from the weathering of bedrock.
- Soil texture affects how soil can be worked for farming and how well water passes through it.
- The ability of soil to provide nutrients so that plants can survive and grow is called *soil fertility*.
- The pH of a soil influences which nutrients plants can take up from the soil.
- Different climates have different types of soil, depending on the temperature and rainfall.

Using Key Terms

1. Use each of the following terms in a separate sentence: *soil, parent rock, bedrock, soil texture, soil structure, humus,* and *leaching*.

Understanding Key Ideas

2. Which of the following soil properties influences soil moisture?
   a. soil horizon
   b. soil fertility
   c. soil structure
   d. soil pH

3. Which of the following soil properties influences how nutrients can be dissolved in soil?
   a. soil texture
   b. soil fertility
   c. soil structure
   d. soil pH

4. When is parent rock the same as bedrock?

5. What is the difference between residual and transported soils?

6. Which climate has the most thick, fertile soil?

7. How does soil temperature influence arctic soil?

Math Skills

8. If a soil sample is 60% sand particles and has 30 million particles of soil, how many of those soil particles are sand?

Critical Thinking

9. **Identifying Relationships** In which type of climate would leaching be more common—tropical rain forest or desert?

10. **Making Comparisons** Although arctic climates are extremely different from desert climates, their soils may be somewhat similar. Explain why.

Topic: Soil and Climate
SciLinks code: HSM1408

Answers to Section Review

1. Sample answer: Soil is made up of minerals, water, organic material, and air. Soil is formed from parent rock. Bedrock is the layer of rock under soil. Soil texture affects a soil's ability to be worked. Soil structure affects water and air movement through the soil. Humus helps make soil rich in nutrients. Leaching from heavy rains can remove important nutrients from the soil.
2. c
3. d
4. when the rock formation below the soil is also the source of mineral fragments in the soil
5. Residual soil remains above its parent rock. Transported soil is blown or washed away from its parent rock.
6. temperate forest and grassland climates
7. Low temperatures slow down decomposition, which limits the amount of humus in the soil.
8. 30 million × 60% = 18 million
9. tropical rain forests
10. Both are dry climates. Chemical weathering occurs more slowly in dry climates; therefore, both deserts and arctic climates experience less chemical weathering.

CHAPTER RESOURCES

Chapter Resource File

- Section Quiz GENERAL
- Section Review GENERAL
- Vocabulary and Section Summary GENERAL

Section 3 • From Bedrock to Soil

SECTION 4

Focus

Overview
In this section, students will learn the importance of soil. Students will then learn about the methods used to prevent nutrient loss and erosion of soil.

🔔 Bellringer
Tell students Franklin D. Roosevelt's quote: "The nation that destroys its soil destroys itself." Lead a discussion on the meaning of this quote.

Motivate

Discussion — GENERAL

Soil Engineering Students may think that all soils are merely dirt. Soils have different characteristics, which depend on soil composition. Engineers study soil types when planning roads and buildings. Different types of soils require different engineering considerations. For example, soils high in clay swell when they are wet and contract when they dry. The expanding and contracting can cause shifting and cracking in roadbeds and building foundations. Arrange for an engineer, contractor, or geologist to speak with the class about the importance of understanding soil types. Have students prepare questions to ask the guest speaker. **LS Auditory**

SECTION 4

READING WARM-UP

Objectives
- Describe three important benefits that soil provides.
- Describe four methods of preventing soil damage and loss.

Terms to Learn
soil conservation
erosion

READING STRATEGY

Reading Organizer As you read this section, make a table comparing the four methods of preventing soil damage and loss.

soil conservation a method to maintain the fertility of the soil by protecting the soil from erosion and nutrient loss

Figure 1 Both of these photos show the same crop, but the soil in the photo on the right is poor in nutrients.

CHAPTER RESOURCES

Chapter Resource File
- Lesson Plan
- Directed Reading A BASIC
- Directed Reading B SPECIAL NEEDS

Technology
- Transparencies
  - Bellringer

Soil Conservation

Believe it or not, soil can be endangered, just like plants and animals. Because soil takes thousands of years to form, it is not easy to replace.

If we do not take care of our soils, we can ruin them or even lose them. Soil is a resource that must be conserved. **Soil conservation** is a method to maintain the fertility of the soil by protecting the soil from erosion and nutrient loss.

The Importance of Soil

Soil provides minerals and other nutrients for plants. If the soil loses these nutrients, then plants will not be able to grow. Take a look at the plants shown in **Figure 1**. The plants on the right look unhealthy because they are not getting enough nutrients. There is enough soil to support the plant's roots, but the soil is not providing them with the food they need. The plants on the left are healthy because the soil they live in is rich in nutrients.

All animals get their energy from plants. The animals get their energy either by eating the plants or by eating animals that have eaten plants. So, if plants can't get their nutrients from the soil, animals can't get their nutrients from plants.

✓ **Reading Check** Why is soil important? *(See the Appendix for answers to Reading Checks.)*

Housing

Soil also provides a place for animals to live. The region where a plant or animal lives is called its *habitat*. Earthworms, grubs, spiders, ants, moles, and prairie dogs all live in soil. If the soil disappears, so does the habitat for these animals.

Answer to Reading Check
Soil provides nutrients to plants, houses for animals, and stores water.

---

294 Chapter 10 • Weathering and Soil Formation

Water Storage

Soil is also extremely important to plants for water storage. Without soil to hold water, plants would not get the moisture or the nutrients they need. Soil also keeps water from running off, flowing elsewhere, and possibly causing flooding.

Soil Damage and Loss

What would happen if there were no soil? Soil loss is a serious problem around the world. Soil damage can lead to soil loss. Soil can be damaged from overuse by poor farming techniques or by overgrazing. Overused soil can lose its nutrients and become infertile. Plants can't grow in soil that is infertile. Without plants to hold and help cycle water, the area can become a desert. This process, formally known as *desertification*, is called *land degradation*. Without plants and moisture, the soil can be blown or washed away.

Soil Erosion

When soil is left unprotected, it can be exposed to erosion. **Erosion** is the process by which wind, water, or gravity transport soil and sediment from one location to another. **Figure 2** shows Providence Canyon, which was formed from the erosion of soil when trees were cut down to clear land for farming. Roots from plants and trees are like anchors to the soil. Roots keep topsoil from being eroded. Therefore, plants and trees protect the soil. By taking care of the vegetation, you also take care of the soil.

MATH PRACTICE

Making Soil

Suppose it takes 500 years for 2 cm of new soil to form in a certain area. But the soil is eroding at a rate of 1 mm per year. Is the soil eroding faster than it can be replaced? Explain.

erosion the process by which wind, water, ice, or gravity transport soil and sediment from one location to another

Figure 2 Providence Canyon has suffered soil erosion from the cutting of forests for farmland.

CONNECTION to Life Science — GENERAL

Soil for Plants Loam is a type of soil that, depending on the amount of humus, is best for plant growth. Because loam contains an ideal balance of varied soil particles (sand, silt, and clay), the soil can retain the air and water in the pore spaces between the particles. The air and water stored in these pore spaces are essential for plant growth. Have students research plants that have adapted to live in less hospitable soils.

CONNECTION ACTIVITY Math — GENERAL

All soils contain varying amounts of water, air, minerals, and organic matter. A 200 cm^3 soil sample ideal for plant growth may contain 40 cm^3 of water, 50 cm^3 of air, 70 cm^3 of mineral fragments, and 40 cm^3 of humus. Have students create a pie chart showing this composition by percentage. **LS Logical**

Teach

Answer to Math Practice
1 mm/y × 500 y = 500 mm
500 mm = 50 cm
50 cm > 2 cm
Thus, the soil is eroding faster than it is forming.

ACTIVITY — BASIC

Uses of Soil Obtain three 4 in. flowerpots. Fill one with gravel, one with clay, and one with potting soil. Place the pots on a plank of wood over a sink. Have three students slowly pour 500 mL of water into each pot simultaneously. Ask students to note which pot begins to leak first. Explain that the gravel started to leak first because the pores or spaces between pieces of gravel are too large to hold the water. The potting soil has much smaller spaces, where water can be stored. The clay has very small spaces between the soil particles and does not allow water to pass through. Have students then explain in writing which material they would choose for the following activities:

- lining the foundation of a house so that it drains quickly **(gravel)**
- sowing grass seed **(potting soil)**
- lining the bottom of an artificial pond so that it doesn't leak **(clay)**

LS Kinesthetic   **English Language Learners**

Section 4 • Soil Conservation

Close

Reteaching — BASIC

Soil Conservation On the board, write the headings "Soil erosion" on one side and "Nutrient depletion" on the other. Ask students to suggest different soil conservation methods, and have them state which problem (soil erosion or nutrient depletion) the method of conservation addresses. After a brief discussion of each method, write the method under the appropriate head. **LS** *Verbal*

Quiz — GENERAL

1. What is one way that nutrients are removed from soil? (Sample answer: by planting the same crops every year)
2. How do contour plowing and terracing help prevent soil erosion? (by interrupting water flow across the topsoil)

Alternative Assessment — GENERAL

Raising Awareness Declare "Soil Conservation Awareness Week." Have students create posters that alert your school to the importance of soil and that highlight some ways to protect and conserve soil. **LS** *Visual*

Figure 3 Soil Conservation Techniques

Contour plowing helps prevent erosion from heavy rains.

Terracing prevents erosion from heavy rains on steep hills.

No-till farming prevents erosion by providing cover that reduces water runoff.

Soybeans are a **cover crop** which restores nutrients to soil.

Contour Plowing and Terracing

If farmers plowed rows so that they ran up and down hills, what might happen during a heavy rain? The rows would act as river valleys and channel the rainwater down the hill, which would erode the soil. To prevent erosion in this way, a farmer could plow across the slope of the hills. This is called contour plowing. In *contour plowing,* the rows act as a series of dams instead of a series of rivers. **Figure 3** shows contour plowing and three other methods of soil conservation. If the hills are really steep, farmers can use *terracing*. Terracing changes one steep field into a series of smaller, flatter fields. *No-till farming,* which is the practice of leaving old stalks, provides cover from rain. The cover reduces water runoff and slows soil erosion.

CHAPTER RESOURCES

Technology

Transparencies
- Soil Horizons

Homework — ADVANCED

Indigenous Agriculture The ancient Maya of Central America used specialized agricultural techniques to maximize their corn crops. The Maya intentionally planted their crops over sinkholes. Soil over sinkholes is ideal because it is rich and all surface water drains into the sinkhole. Have students find out more about the agricultural innovations of other indigenous cultures and prepare a five-minute speech on the topic. Ask students if any of these techniques are still being used today. **LS** *Verbal*

Cover Crop and Crop Rotation

In the southern United States, during the early 1900s, the soil had become nutrient poor by the farming of only one crop, cotton. George Washington Carver, the scientist shown in **Figure 4**, urged farmers to plant soybeans and peanuts instead of cotton. Some plants, such as soybeans and peanuts, helped to restore important nutrients to the soil. These plants are called cover crops. *Cover crops* are crops that are planted between harvests to replace certain nutrients and prevent erosion. Cover crops prevent erosion by providing cover from wind and rain.

Another way to slow down nutrient depletion is through *crop rotation*. If the same crop is grown year after year in the same field, certain nutrients become depleted. To slow this process, a farmer can plant different crops. A different crop will use up less nutrients or different nutrients from the soil.

✓ **Reading Check** What can soybeans and peanuts do for nutrient-poor soil?

Figure 4 *George Washington Carver taught soil conservation techniques to farmers.*

SECTION Review

Summary

- Soil is important for plants to grow, for animals to live in, and for water to be stored.
- Soil erosion and soil damage can be prevented by contour plowing, terracing, using cover crop, and practicing crop rotation.

Using Key Terms

1. In your own words, write a definition for each of the following terms: *soil conservation* and *erosion*.

Understanding Key Ideas

2. What are three important benefits that soil provides?

3. Practicing which of the following soil conservation techniques will replace nutrients in the soil?
   a. cover crop use
   b. no-till farming
   c. terracing
   d. contour plowing

4. How does crop rotation benefit soil?

5. List four methods of soil conservation, and describe how each helps prevent the loss of soil.

Math Skills

6. Suppose it takes 500 years to form 2 cm of new soil without erosion. If a farmer needs at least 35 cm of soil to plant a particular crop, how many years will the farmer need to wait before planting his or her crop?

Critical Thinking

7. **Applying Concepts** Why do land animals, even meat eaters, depend on soil to survive?

SciLinks
For a variety of links related to this chapter, go to www.scilinks.org
Topic: Soil Conservation
SciLinks code: HSM1409

CONNECTION to History — GENERAL

George Washington Carver By the early 20th century, Southern cotton cultivation had so depleted soil nutrients that the area faced an agricultural crisis. George Washington Carver convinced farmers to plant peanuts and soybeans instead of cotton. These crops helped restore nitrogen to the soil. The soil recovered, and Carver's work helped revitalize the agricultural economy of the South. Ask students to learn more about the life of this remarkable scientist.

CHAPTER RESOURCES

Chapter Resource File
- Section Quiz GENERAL
- Section Review GENERAL
- Vocabulary and Section Summary GENERAL
- Reinforcement Worksheet BASIC
- Critical Thinking ADVANCED
- SciLinks Activity GENERAL

Answer to Reading Check
They restore important nutrients to the soil and provide cover to prevent erosion.

Answers to Section Review

1. Sample answer: Soil conservation is a method used to protect soil from erosion and nutrient depletion. Erosion is a process by which soil is moved from one location to another by wind, water, ice, or gravity.

2. Sample answer: Soil supplies support and nutrients to plants, provides housing for animals, and stores water.

3. a

4. Crop rotation helps prevent soil nutrients from being depleted. Alternation of crops in the same soil reduces nutrient loss.

5. Contour plowing prevents erosion by plowing across a slope so that plowed rows act like a series of dams to prevent erosion by rain. Terracing prevents erosion by dividing a hillside into a series of flat fields. No-till farming prevents erosion from water runoff by leaving cover over the soil. Cover crops prevent erosion from water runoff by providing cover for the soil.

6. 500 y ÷ 2 cm = 1 cm/250 y
   1 cm/250 y × 35 cm = 8,750 years

7. Land animals depend on the soil to support and grow plants. Animals get their energy by eating the plants or by eating the animals that eat the plants.

Section 4 • Soil Conservation

Model-Making Lab

Rockin' Through Time

Teacher's Notes

Time Required
One 45-minute class period

Lab Ratings

EASY ——————→ HARD

Teacher Prep ▲▲
Student Set-Up ▲
Concept Level ▲▲
Clean Up ▲

MATERIALS

The materials listed on the student page are adequate for groups of 4–5 students.

Safety Caution

Remind students to review all safety cautions and icons before beginning this lab activity. Be sure to use plastic bottles in this activity.

Using Scientific Methods
Model-Making Lab

Rockin' Through Time

Wind, water, and gravity constantly change rocks. As wind and water rush over the rocks, the rocks may be worn smooth. As rocks bump against one another, their shapes change. The form of mechanical weathering that occurs as rocks collide and scrape together is called *abrasion*. In this activity, you will shake some pieces of limestone to model the effects of abrasion.

Ask a Question

1. How does abrasion break down rocks? How can I use this information to identify rocks that have been abraded in nature?

Form a Hypothesis

2. Formulate a hypothesis that answers the questions above.

Test the Hypothesis

3. Copy the chart on the next page onto a piece of poster board. Allow enough space to place rocks in each square.

4. Lay three of the limestone pieces on the poster board in the area marked "0 shakes." Be careful not to bump the poster board after you have added the rocks.

5. Place the remaining 21 rocks in the 3 L bottle. Then, fill the bottle halfway with water.

6. Close the lid of the bottle securely. Shake the bottle vigorously 100 times.

7. Remove three rocks from the bottle, and place them on the poster board in the box that indicates the number of times the rocks have been shaken.

8. Repeat steps 6 and 7 six times until all of the rocks have been added to the board.

OBJECTIVES

Design a model to understand how abrasion breaks down rocks.

Evaluate the effects of abrasion.

MATERIALS

- bottle, plastic, wide-mouthed, with lid, 3 L
- graph paper or computer
- markers
- pieces of limestone, all about the same size (24)
- poster board
- tap water

SAFETY

Larry Tackett
Andrew Jackson Middle School
Cross Lanes, West Virginia

CHAPTER RESOURCES

Chapter Resource File
- Datasheet for Chapter Lab
- Lab Notes and Answers

Technology

Classroom Videos
- Lab Video

LabBook
- Great Ice Escape

---

298 Chapter 10 • Weathering and Soil Formation

Analyze the Results

1. **Examining Data** Describe the surface of the rocks that you placed in the area marked "0 shakes." Are they smooth or rough?

2. **Describing Events** How did the shape of the rocks change as you performed this activity?

3. **Constructing Graphs** Using graph paper or a computer, construct a graph, table, or chart that describes how the shapes of the rocks changed as a result of the number of times they were shaken.

Rocks Table	
0 shakes	100 shakes
200 shakes	300 shakes
400 shakes	500 shakes
600 shakes	700 shakes

Draw Conclusions

4. **Drawing Conclusions** Why did the rocks change?

5. **Evaluating Results** How did the water change during the activity? Why did it change?

6. **Making Predictions** What would happen if you used a much harder rock, such as granite, for this experiment?

7. **Interpreting Information** How do the results of this experiment compare with what happens in a river?

Analyze the Results

1. Sample answer: The surfaces of the rocks are rough and jagged.
2. Sample answer: As the rocks were shaken more, they became much smoother.
3. Student data may vary.

Draw Conclusions

4. Sample answer: The rocks became smoother because the edges broke off when they collided with the jar and with each other.
5. Sample answer: At the beginning of this activity, the water was clear. As the activity progressed, the water became increasingly dirty because particles broke away from the rocks and were suspended in the water.
6. Sample answer: If a harder rock were used, it would require longer and harder shaking to obtain similar results.
7. Sample answer: As a river carries pebbles and small particles, they bounce and grind against other rocks. Eventually, the rocks become smooth.

CHAPTER RESOURCES

Workbooks

- **Whiz-Bang Demonstrations**
  - When It Rains, It Fizzes GENERAL
- **EcoLabs & Field Activities**
  - Whether It Weathers (or Not) GENERAL
- **Long-Term Projects & Research Ideas**
  - Precious Soil ADVANCED
- **Calculator-Based Labs**
  - A Hot and Cool Lab ADVANCED
  - A Soil Study ADVANCED
  - How Low Can You Go? ADVANCED

Chapter Review

Assignment Guide	
SECTION	QUESTIONS
1	1, 3, 5, 11, 17, 21, 24–26
2	6, 12, 18, 19, 21, 23
3	4, 7, 8, 13, 20
4	2, 9, 10, 14, 15, 16, 22

ANSWERS

Using Key Terms

1. Sample answer: Abrasion is the grinding and wearing away of rock surfaces through the mechanical action of other rock or sand particles. Soil texture is the soil quality that is based on the proportions of soil particles.

2. Sample answer: Soil conservation can help ensure that there will be enough fertile soil in which to plant crops. Erosion may occur if the soil is not covered with vegetation.

3. Sample answer: Mechanical weathering is the breaking down of rock by physical means. Chemical weathering is the process by which rocks break down as a result of chemical reactions.

4. Sample answer: Soil is a mixture of organic material, water, minerals and air that support the growth of vegetation. Parent rock is the rock formation that is the source of mineral fragments in the soil.

Chapter Review

USING KEY TERMS

1. In your own words, write a definition for each of the following terms: *abrasion* and *soil texture*.

2. Use each of the following terms in a separate sentence: *soil conservation* and *erosion*.

For each pair of terms, explain how the meanings of the terms differ.

3. *mechanical weathering* and *chemical weathering*

4. *soil* and *parent rock*

UNDERSTANDING KEY IDEAS

Multiple Choice

5. Which of the following processes is a possible effect of water?
   a. mechanical weathering
   b. chemical weathering
   c. abrasion
   d. All of the above

6. In which climate would you find the fastest rate of chemical weathering?
   a. a warm, humid climate
   b. a cold, humid climate
   c. a cold, dry climate
   d. a warm, dry climate

7. Which of the following properties does soil texture affect?
   a. soil pH
   b. soil temperature
   c. soil consistency
   d. None of the above

8. Which of the following properties describes a soil's ability to supply nutrients?
   a. soil structure
   b. infiltration
   c. soil fertility
   d. consistency

9. Soil is important because it provides
   a. housing for animals.
   b. nutrients for plants.
   c. storage for water.
   d. All of the above

10. Which of the following soil conservation techniques prevents erosion?
    a. contour plowing
    b. terracing
    c. no-till farming
    d. All of the above

Short Answer

11. Describe the two major types of weathering.

12. Why is Devils Tower higher than the surrounding area?

13. Why is soil in temperate forests thick and fertile?

14. What can happen to soil when soil conservation is not practiced?

15. Describe the process of land degradation.

16. How do cover crops help prevent soil erosion?

Understanding Key Ideas

5. d
6. a
7. c
8. c
9. d
10. d

11. Mechanical weathering is the physical process of breaking down rock and minerals into smaller pieces. Chemical weathering is a chemical reaction that breaks down rock and minerals by chemical reactions.

12. The less resistant rock surrounding the original volcano weathered faster than the more resistant rock of Devils Tower.

13. Soil in temperate forests experiences high rates of weathering, which increases the rate of soil production.

14. Soil can be eroded or damaged if soil conservation is not practiced.

15. Overused soil loses its nutrients. Plants are unable to grow in this soil without nutrients. Without plants, water cannot be held and cycled, and the area can become a desert.

16. Cover crops protect the soil from wind, rain, and other agents of erosion.

300   Chapter 10 • Weathering and Soil Formation

CRITICAL THINKING

17 **Concept Mapping** Use the following terms to create a concept map: *weathering, chemical weathering, mechanical weathering, abrasion, ice wedging, oxidation,* and *soil*.

18 **Analyzing Processes** Heat generally speeds up chemical reactions. But weathering, including chemical weathering, is usually slowest in hot, dry climates. Why?

19 **Making Inferences** Mechanical weathering, such as ice wedging, increases surface area by breaking larger rocks into smaller rocks. Draw conclusions about how mechanical weathering can affect the rate of chemical weathering.

20 **Evaluating Data** A scientist has a new theory. She believes that climates that receive heavy rains all year long have thin topsoil. Given what you have learned, decide if the scientist's theory is correct. Explain your answer.

21 **Analyzing Processes** What forms of mechanical and chemical weathering would be most common in the desert? Explain your answer.

22 **Applying Concepts** If you had to plant a crop on a steep hill, what soil conservation techniques would you use to prevent erosion?

23 **Making Comparisons** Compare the weathering processes in a warm, humid climate with those in a dry, cold climate.

INTERPRETING GRAPHICS

The graph below shows how the density of water changes when temperature changes. The denser a substance is, the less volume it occupies. In other words, as most substances get colder, they contract and become denser. But water is unlike most other substances. When water freezes, it expands and becomes less dense. Use the graph below to answer the questions that follow.

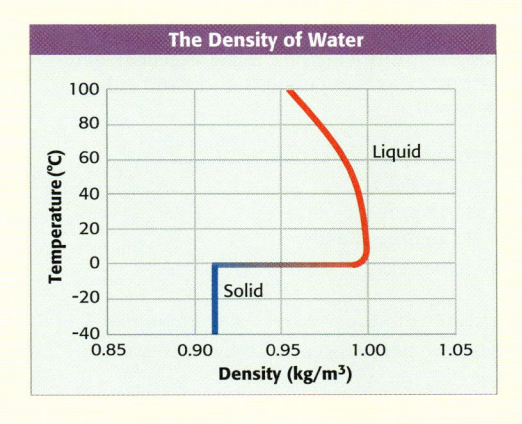

The Density of Water

[Graph showing Temperature (°C) on y-axis from -40 to 100, Density (kg/m³) on x-axis from 0.85 to 1.05, with Liquid and Solid regions labeled]

24 Which has the greater density: water at 40°C or water at –20°C?

25 How would the line in the graph look if water behaved like most other liquids?

26 Which substance would be a more effective agent of mechanical weathering: water or another liquid? Why?

---

19. Mechanical weathering increases the surface area of rock, which exposes more of the rock to the effects of chemical weathering and increases the rate of weathering.

20. Sample answer: The scientist's theory is correct because heavy rain will leach the nutrients out of the soil, which will make the topsoil thin.

21. Abrasion and oxidation would probably be the most common in desert climates. Although the rate of oxidation and abrasion may increase with the presence of water, both processes may occur when little or no water is present.

22. Terracing and planting a cover crop between harvests would help prevent erosion on a steep slope.

23. Warm, humid climates have a higher rate of weathering than cold, dry climates do because the warmer temperature and moisture speed up chemical and mechanical weathering processes.

Interpreting Graphics

24. water at 40°C

25. The line would slope downward from left to right because most other liquids would have an increase in density as they became colder.

26. Water is more effective than other liquids because it expands when it freezes.

Critical Thinking

17. An answer to this exercise can be found at the end of this book.

18. Hot, dry climates generally have less precipitation than more temperate climates. Moisture enables chemical weathering to occur more quickly. The lack of moisture inhibits all processes of mechanical weathering except abrasion.

CHAPTER RESOURCES

Chapter Resource File
- Chapter Review GENERAL
- Chapter Test A GENERAL
- Chapter Test B ADVANCED
- Chapter Test C SPECIAL NEEDS
- Vocabulary Activity GENERAL

Workbooks

Study Guide
- Assessment resources are also available in Spanish.

Chapter 10 • Chapter Review **301**

Standardized Test Preparation

Teacher's Note

To provide practice under more realistic testing conditions, give students 20 minutes to answer all of the questions in this Standardized Test Preparation.

MISCONCEPTION ALERT

Answers to the standardized test preparation can help you identify student misconceptions and misunderstandings.

READING

Passage 1
1. B
2. F
3. C

TEST DOCTOR

Question 1: If students misinterpret the passage, they may think that castings have negative effect on plant growth. Therefore, they might conclude that the word *enhance* means "to weaken" or "to decrease." However, as it is used in the sentence, *enhance* means "to improve."

Passage 2
1. C
2. F
3. D

Standardized Test Preparation

READING

Read each of the passages below. Then, answer the questions that follow each passage.

Passage 1 Earthworms are very important for forming soil. As they search for food by digging tunnels in the soil, they expose rocks and minerals to the effects of weathering. Over time, this process makes new soil. And as the worms dig tunnels, they mix the soil, which allows air and water and smaller organisms to move deeper into the soil. Worms have huge appetites. They eat organic matter and other materials in the soil. One earthworm can eat an amount equal to about half its body weight each day! Eating all of that food means that earthworms leave behind a lot of waste. Earthworm wastes, called *castings,* are very high in nutrients and make excellent natural fertilizer. Castings enrich the soil and <u>enhance</u> plant growth.

1. In the passage, what does *enhance* mean?
   A to weaken
   B to improve
   C to smooth out
   D to decrease

2. According to the passage, the earthworms
   F eat organic matter and other materials in soil.
   G do not have much of an appetite.
   H love to eat castings.
   I cannot digest organic matter in soil.

3. Which of the following statements is a fact according to the passage?
   A Earthworms are not important for forming soil.
   B Earthworms only eat organic matter in the soil.
   C An earthworm can eat an amount that equals half its body weight each day.
   D Earthworms eat little food but leave behind a lot of waste.

Passage 2 Worms are not the only living things that help create soil. Plants also play a part in the weathering process. As the roots of plants grow and seek out water and nutrients, they help break large rock fragments into smaller ones. Have you ever seen a plant growing in a crack in the sidewalk? As the plant grows, its roots spread into tiny cracks in the sidewalk. These roots apply pressure to the cracks, and over time, the cracks get bigger. As the plants make the cracks bigger, ice wedging can occur more readily. As the cracks expand, more water runs into them. When the water freezes, it expands and presses against the walls of the crack, which makes the crack even larger. Over time, the weathering caused by water, plants, and worms helps break down rock to form soil.

1. How do plants make it easier for ice wedging to occur?
   A Plant roots block the cracks and don't allow water to enter.
   B Plant roots provide moisture to cracks.
   C Plant roots make the cracks larger, which allows more water to enter the cracks.
   D Plants absorb excess water from cracks.

2. For ice wedging to occur,
   F water in cracks must freeze.
   G plant roots must widen cracks.
   H acid is needed.
   I water is not needed.

3. Which of the following statements is a fact according to the passage?
   A Plant roots can strangle earthworms.
   B Earthworms eat plant roots.
   C Plant roots cannot crack sidewalks.
   D Plant roots break large rock fragments into smaller ones.

TEST DOCTOR

Question 2: The second half of the passage describes ice wedging: "When the water freezes, it expands and presses against the walls of the crack, which makes the crack even larger." However, because the beginning of the passage describes how the roots of plants can widen cracks, students may associate plants with ice wedging.

302 Chapter 10 • Weathering and Soil Formation

INTERPRETING GRAPHICS

The graph below shows the average yearly rainfall in five locations. Use the graph below to answer the questions that follow.

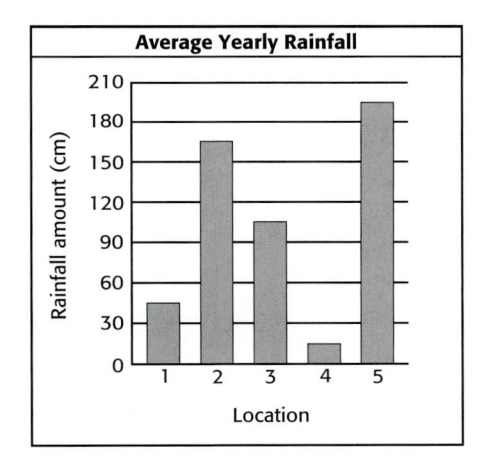

Average Yearly Rainfall

(bar graph showing rainfall amount in cm for locations 1–5)

1. Which location has the **most** average yearly rainfall?
   - A 1
   - B 2
   - C 4
   - D 5

2. At which location would you expect to find the **most** chemical weathering?
   - F 1
   - G 3
   - H 4
   - I 5

3. At which location would you expect to find the **least** amount of chemical weathering?
   - A 2
   - B 3
   - C 4
   - D 5

MATH

Read each question below, and choose the best answer.

1. If an earthworm that weighs 1.5 g eats an amount equal to half its body weight in a day, how much does the earthworm eat in 1 week?
   - A 10.5 g
   - B 7 g
   - C 5.25 g
   - D 1.5 g

2. Calculate the surface area of a cube that measures 3 cm by 3 cm.
   - F 9 cm
   - G 9 cm^2
   - H 54 cm
   - I 54 cm^2

3. If a mountain peak weathers away 2 cm every 6 years, how many years will the mountain peak take to weather away 1 m?
   - A 8 years
   - B 12 years
   - C 180 years
   - D 300 years

4. The rock ledge that lies under a waterfall erodes about 3 cm each year. How much of the rock will erode over a period of 18 months?
   - F 4.5 cm
   - G 6 cm
   - H 21 cm
   - I 54 cm

5. A garden shop charges $0.30 for each ground-cover seedling. How many seedlings can you buy for $6.00?
   - A 5 seedlings
   - B 18 seedlings
   - C 20 seedlings
   - D 200 seedlings

INTERPRETING GRAPHICS
1. D
2. I
3. C

TEST DOCTOR
Question 2: Water can increase the rate of chemical weathering. Students must know and apply this information to answer the question correctly.

MATH
1. C
2. I
3. D
4. F
5. C

TEST DOCTOR
Question 2: The question asks for the surface area of the entire cube, not one side of the cube. After calculating the surface area of one side of the cube, students must then multiply by 6 to obtain the correct answer.

CHAPTER RESOURCES

Chapter Resource File
- Standardized Test Preparation GENERAL

State Resources
For specific resources for your state, visit **go.hrw.com** and type in the keyword **HSMSTR**.

Chapter 10 • Standardized Test Preparation

Science in Action

Science, Technology, and Society
Background
Earth is not the only planet that experiences dust storms. NASA's *Mars Global Surveyor* and *Hubble Space Telescope* have given scientists amazing views of dust storms in the Martian atmosphere. Martian dust storms are far larger than those experienced on Earth. Martian dust storms can engulf the entire planet and last for months at a time. Students can find images of global dust storms online.

Scientific Discovery
Background
Brad Werner and Mark Kessler, the scientists who studied the soil patterns in Alaska and on the Norwegian Islands applied the principle of *self-organization* to their work. Self-organization looks for an explanation of change on a large scale. For example, it looks beyond the physics of a single grain of soil or an individual rock and looks at a system as a whole. According to the theory of self-organization, many phenomena on the Earth's surface, such as the soil patterns in Alaska, are responsible for their own development and maintenance over long periods of time.

Science in Action

Science, Technology, and Society

Flying Fertilizer
Would you believe that dust from storms in large deserts can be transported over the oceans to different continents? Dust from the Gobi Desert in China has traveled all the way to Hawaii! In many cases, the dust is a welcome guest. Iron in dust from the Sahara, a desert in Africa, fertilizes the canopies of South American rain forests. In fact, research has shown that the canopies of Central and South American rain forests get much of their nutrients from dust from the Sahara!

Social Studies ACTIVITY
Find pictures on the Internet or in magazines that show how people in rain forests live. Make a poster by using the pictures you find.

Scientific Discoveries

Strange Soil
Mysterious patterns of circles, polygons, and stripes were discovered in the soil in remote areas in Alaska and the Norwegian islands. At first, scientists were puzzled by these strange designs in remote areas. Then, the scientists discovered that these patterns were created by the area's weathering process, which includes cycles of freezing and thawing. When the soil freezes, the soil expands. When the soil thaws, the soil contracts. This process moves and sorts the particles of the soil into patterns.

Language Arts ACTIVITY
WRITING SKILL Write a creative short story describing what life would be like if you were a soil circle on one of these remote islands.

Answer to Social Studies Activity
Students' posters should include adaptive activities specific to the people who live in a tropical rain forest. For example, a student may include a picture of Fijians building a traditional house with high ceilings that allows the air to circulate in the house such that the air won't become stuffy in warm, humid climates.

Answer to Language Arts Activity
Students' stories should include a description of the freezing and thawing climate on the remote island. Encourage students to conduct more research about the climate, plants, and animals of these islands.

People in Science

J. David Bamberger

Habitat Restoration J. David Bamberger knows how important taking care of the environment is. Therefore, he has turned his ranch into the largest habitat restoration project in Texas. For Bamberger, restoring the habitat started with restoring the soil. One way Bamberger restored the soil was to manage the grazing of the grasslands and to make sure that grazing animals didn't expose the soil. Overgrazing causes soil erosion. When cattle clear the land of its grasses, the soil is exposed to wind and rain, which can wash the topsoil away.

Bamberger also cleared his land of most of the shrub, *juniper*. Juniper requires so much water per day that it leaves little water in the soil for the grasses and wildflowers. The change in the ranch since Bamberger first bought it in 1959 is most obvious at the fence-line border of his ranch. Beyond the fence is a small forest of junipers and little other vegetation. On Bamberger's side, the ranch is lush with grasses, wildflowers, trees, and shrubs.

Math Activity

Bamberger's ranch is 2,300 hectares. There are 0.405 hectares in 1 acre. How many acres is Bamberger's ranch?

Current Science
To learn more about these Science in Action topics, visit **go.hrw.com** and type in the keyword **HZ5WSFF**.

Check out Current Science® articles related to this chapter by visiting **go.hrw.com**. Just type in the keyword **HZ5CS10**.

People in Science

Teaching Strategy — GENERAL

Habitat restoration shows us what the land was like before the settlers arrived. It also shows us how much the land has changed under human management. Ask students to think of any habitat in their area that could be restored. How would they go about restoring it? What do they think it would look like after restoration?

Answer to Math Activity
2,300 hectares ÷ 0.405 hectares/acre = 5,700 acres

11 The Flow of Fresh Water
Chapter Planning Guide

Compression guide: To shorten instruction because of time limitations, omit Section 2.

OBJECTIVES	LABS, DEMONSTRATIONS, AND ACTIVITIES	TECHNOLOGY RESOURCES
PACING • 90 min pp. 306–315 **Chapter Opener**	SE Start-up Activity, p. 307 ◆ GENERAL	OSP Parent Letter ■ GENERAL CD Student Edition on CD-ROM CD Guided Reading Audio CD ■ TR Chapter Starter Transparency* VID Brain Food Video Quiz
Section 1 The Active River • Describe how moving water shapes the surface of the Earth by the process of erosion. • Explain how water moves through the water cycle. • Describe a watershed. • Explain three factors that affect the rate of stream erosion. • Identify four ways that rivers are described.	TE Demonstration Streams Carry Fertile Sediment, p. 308 ◆ GENERAL TE Activity Water Re-Cycle, p. 309 BASIC SE School-to-Home Activity Floating Down the River, p. 310 GENERAL TE Group Activity Mapping River Systems, p. 310 GENERAL TE Connection Activity Real World, p. 311 GENERAL TE Group Activity Stream Load, p. 312 ◆ BASIC TE Activity River Field Guide, p. 312 ADVANCED SE Connection to Language Arts Huckleberry Finn, p. 313 GENERAL TE Activity Illustrating River Stages, p. 313 GENERAL TE Connection Activity History, p. 313 ADVANCED SE Model-Making Labs Water Cycle—What Goes Up…, p. 332 GENERAL	CRF Lesson Plans* TR Bellringer Transparency* TR The Water Cycle* TR LINK TO LIFE SCIENCE Rivers* VID Lab Videos for Earth Science
PACING • 45 min pp. 316–319 **Section 2 Stream and River Deposits** • Describe the four different types of stream deposits. • Describe how the deposition of sediment affects the land.	TE Demonstration Modeling Deposition, p. 316 ◆ GENERAL TE Group Activity Gold Rush, p. 317 ADVANCED SE Science in Action Math, Social Studies, and Language Arts Activities, pp. 338–339 GENERAL LB Long-Term Projects & Research Ideas Canyon Controversy* ADVANCED	CRF Lesson Plans* TR Bellringer Transparency*
PACING • 45 min pp. 320–325 **Section 3 Water Underground** • Identify and describe the location of the water table. • Describe an aquifer. • Explain the difference between a spring and a well. • Explain how caves and sinkholes form as a result of erosion and deposition.	TE Demonstration Groundwater Model, p. 320 ◆ GENERAL TE Connection Activity Real World, p. 321 ADVANCED TE Group Activity Labeling Storm Drains, p. 321 ◆ GENERAL SE School-to-Home Activity Water Conservation, p. 322 GENERAL SE Connection to Environmental Science Bat Environmentalists, p. 324 GENERAL	CRF Lesson Plans* TR Bellringer Transparency* TR The Water Table and Wells* CRF SciLinks Activity* GENERAL SE Internet Activity p. 321 GENERAL
PACING • 45 min pp. 326–331 **Section 4 Using Water Wisely** • Identify two forms of water pollution. • Explain how the properties of water influence the health of a water system. • Describe two ways that wastewater can be treated. • Describe how water is used and how water can be conserved in industry, in agriculture, and at home.	SE Quick Lab Measuring Alkalinity, p. 327 GENERAL TE Group Activity Putting Pollution in its Place, p. 328 ADVANCED TE Connection Activity Math, p. 329 GENERAL TE Group Activity A Call for Conservation, p. 330 GENERAL SE Skills Practice Lab Clean Up Your Act, p. 736 GENERAL LB EcoLabs & Field Activities The Frogs Are Off Course* ◆ ADVANCED	CRF Lesson Plans* TR Bellringer Transparency* CD Interactive Explorations CD-ROM Flood Bank GENERAL

PACING • 90 min

CHAPTER REVIEW, ASSESSMENT, AND STANDARDIZED TEST PREPARATION

CRF Vocabulary Activity* GENERAL
SE Chapter Review, pp. 334–335 GENERAL
CRF Chapter Review* ■ GENERAL
CRF Chapter Tests A* ■ GENERAL, B* ADVANCED, C* SPECIAL NEEDS
SE Standardized Test Preparation, pp. 336–337 GENERAL
CRF Standardized Test Preparation* GENERAL
CRF Performance-Based Assessment* GENERAL
OSP Test Generator GENERAL
CRF Test Item Listing* GENERAL

Online and Technology Resources

Visit **go.hrw.com** for a variety of free resources related to this textbook. Enter the keyword **HZ5DEP**.

Holt Online Learning
Students can access interactive problem-solving help and active visual concept development with the *Holt Science and Technology* Online Edition available at **www.hrw.com**.

Guided Reading Audio CD
Also in Spanish
A direct reading of each chapter for auditory learners, reluctant readers, and Spanish-speaking students.

Science Tutor CD-ROM
Excellent for remediation and test practice.

Chapter 11 • The Flow of Fresh Water

KEY

SE	Student Edition	**CRF**	Chapter Resource File	**SS**	Science Skills Worksheets	*	Also on One-Stop Planner
TE	Teacher Edition	**OSP**	One-Stop Planner	**MS**	Math Skills for Science Worksheets	♦	Requires advance prep
		LB	Lab Bank	**CD**	CD or CD-ROM	■	Also available in Spanish
		TR	Transparencies	**VID**	Classroom Video/DVD		

SKILLS DEVELOPMENT RESOURCES	SECTION REVIEW AND ASSESSMENT	STANDARDS CORRELATIONS
SE Pre-Reading Activity, p. 306 GENERAL **OSP** Science Puzzlers, Twisters & Teasers GENERAL		National Science Education Standards SAI 1
CRF Directed Reading A* ■ BASIC, B* SPECIAL NEEDS **CRF** Vocabulary and Section Summary* ■ GENERAL **SE** Reading Strategy Reading Organizer, p. 308 GENERAL **TE** Math Practice Calculating a Stream's Gradient, p. 311 GENERAL **TE** Reading Strategy Prediction Guide, p. 313 GENERAL **MS** Math Skills for Science Checking Division with Multiplication* GENERAL **SE** Connection to Language Arts Huckleberry Finn, p. 313 GENERAL	**SE** Reading Checks, pp. 308, 310, 311, 313, 314 GENERAL **TE** Homework, p. 309 ADVANCED **TE** Reteaching, p. 314 BASIC **TE** Quiz, p. 314 GENERAL **TE** Alternative Assessment, p. 314 GENERAL **SE** Section Review,* p. 315 ■ GENERAL **CRF** Section Quiz* ■ GENERAL	UCP 1, 2, 5; ES 1c, 1f; *Chapter Lab:* SAI 1
CRF Directed Reading A* ■ BASIC, B* SPECIAL NEEDS **CRF** Vocabulary and Section Summary* ■ GENERAL **SE** Reading Strategy Prediction Guide, p. 316 GENERAL **CRF** Reinforcement Worksheet Fresh Water in the United States* BASIC **CRF** SciLinks Activity GENERAL	**SE** Reading Checks, pp. 317, 319 GENERAL **TE** Reteaching, p. 318 BASIC **TE** Quiz, p. 318 GENERAL **TE** Alternative Assessment, p. 318 GENERAL **SE** Section Review,* p. 319 ■ GENERAL **CRF** Section Quiz* ■ GENERAL	SPSP 3, 4; ES 1c
CRF Directed Reading A* ■ BASIC, B* SPECIAL NEEDS **CRF** Vocabulary and Section Summary* ■ GENERAL **SE** Reading Strategy Discussion, p. 320 GENERAL **TE** Inclusion Strategies, p. 322 **CRF** Reinforcement Worksheet Dig It!* GENERAL **CRF** Critical Thinking Water Crisis at Happy Acres* ADVANCED	**SE** Reading Checks, pp. 320, 322, 323, 324 GENERAL **TE** Reteaching, p. 324 BASIC **TE** Quiz, p. 324 GENERAL **TE** Alternative Assessment, p. 324 GENERAL **SE** Section Review,* p. 325 ■ GENERAL **CRF** Section Quiz* ■ GENERAL	ST 1; SPSP 3; ES 1c
CRF Directed Reading A* ■ BASIC, B* SPECIAL NEEDS **CRF** Vocabulary and Section Summary* ■ GENERAL **SE** Reading Strategy Paired Summarizing, p. 326 GENERAL **SE** Math Practice Agriculture in Israel, p. 330 GENERAL **MS** Math Skills for Science Multiplying Whole Numbers* GENERAL	**SE** Reading Checks, pp. 326, 329, 330, 331 GENERAL **TE** Homework, p. 327 GENERAL **TE** Reteaching, p. 330 BASIC **TE** Quiz, p. 330 GENERAL **TE** Alternative Assessment, p. 330 GENERAL **SE** Section Review,* p. 331 ■ GENERAL **CRF** Section Quiz* ■ GENERAL	UCP 2, 3; SAI 1; SPSP 3; *LabBook:* UCP 2, 3; ST 2; SAI 1; SPSP 5

One-Stop Planner® CD-ROM

This convenient CD-ROM includes:
- Lab Materials QuickList Software
- Holt Calendar Planner
- Customizable Lesson Plans
- Printable Worksheets
- ExamView® Test Generator

CNN Student News

cnnstudentnews.com

Find the latest news, lesson plans, and activities related to important scientific events.

SciLinks NSTA

www.scilinks.org

Maintained by the **National Science Teachers Association.** See Chapter Enrichment pages for a complete list of topics.

Current Science®

Check out *Current Science* articles and activities by visiting the HRW Web site at **go.hrw.com.** Just type in the keyword **HZ5CS11T.**

Classroom Videos

- **Lab Videos** demonstrate the chapter lab.
- **Brain Food Video Quizzes** help students review the chapter material.
- **CNN Videos** bring science into your students' daily life.

Chapter 11 • Chapter Planning Guide

11 Chapter Resources

Visual Resources

CHAPTER STARTER TRANSPARENCY

BELLRINGER TRANSPARENCIES

TEACHING TRANSPARENCIES

TEACHING TRANSPARENCIES

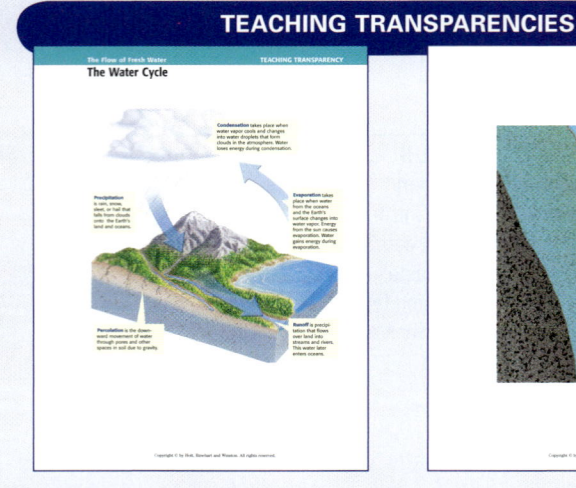

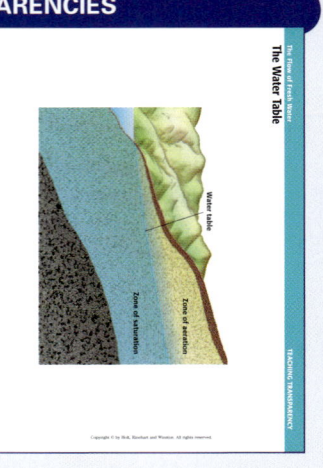

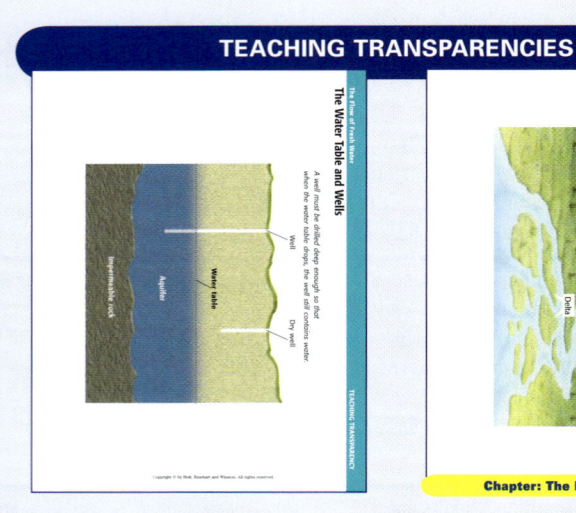

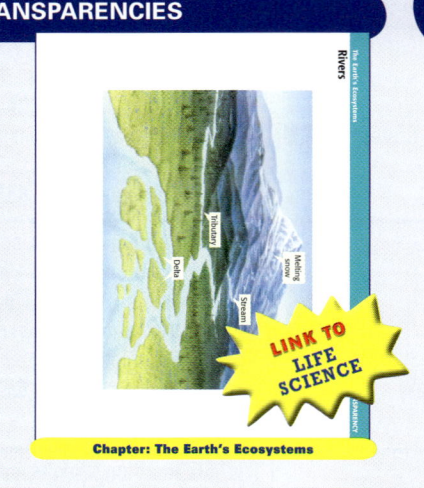

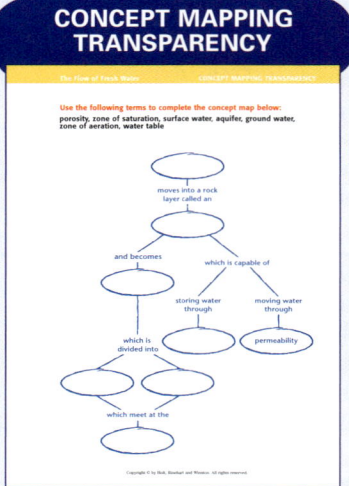

CONCEPT MAPPING TRANSPARENCY

Planning Resources

LESSON PLANS

PARENT LETTER — ALSO IN SPANISH

TEST ITEM LISTING

One-Stop Planner® CD-ROM

This CD-ROM includes all of the resources shown here and the following time-saving tools:

- Lab Materials QuickList Software
- Customizable lesson plans
- Holt Calendar Planner
- The powerful ExamView® Test Generator

305C Chapter 11 • The Flow of Fresh Water

For a preview of available worksheets covering math and science skills, see pages T26–T33. All of these resources are also on the One-Stop Planner®.

Meeting Individual Needs

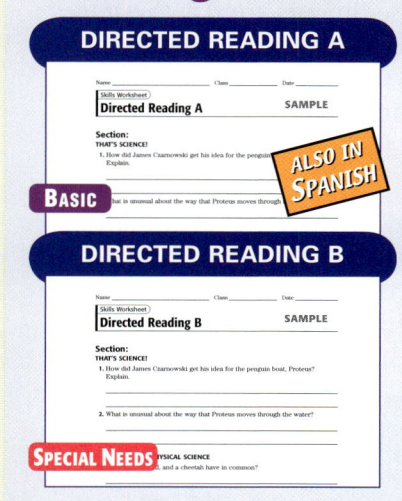

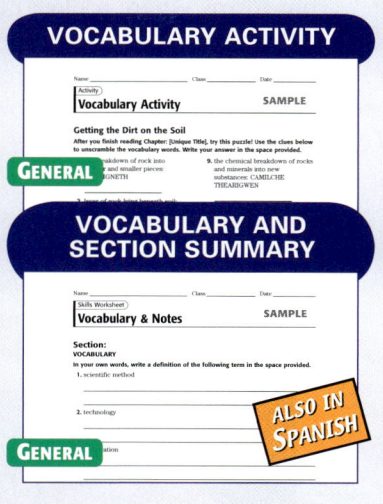

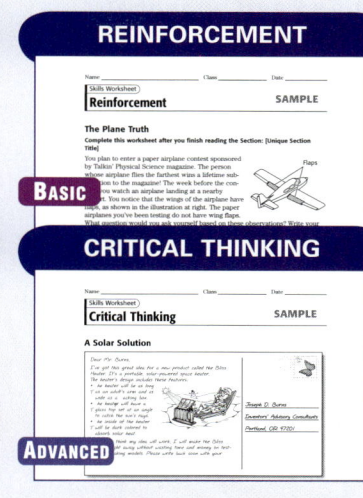

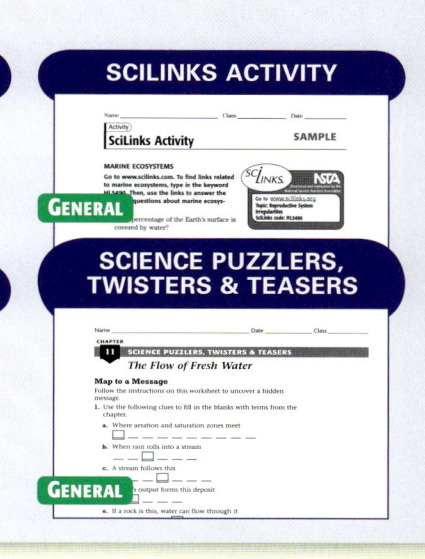

- **DIRECTED READING A** — BASIC (ALSO IN SPANISH)
- **VOCABULARY ACTIVITY** — GENERAL
- **REINFORCEMENT** — BASIC
- **SCILINKS ACTIVITY** — GENERAL
- **DIRECTED READING B** — SPECIAL NEEDS
- **VOCABULARY AND SECTION SUMMARY** — GENERAL (ALSO IN SPANISH)
- **CRITICAL THINKING** — ADVANCED
- **SCIENCE PUZZLERS, TWISTERS & TEASERS** — GENERAL

Labs and Activities

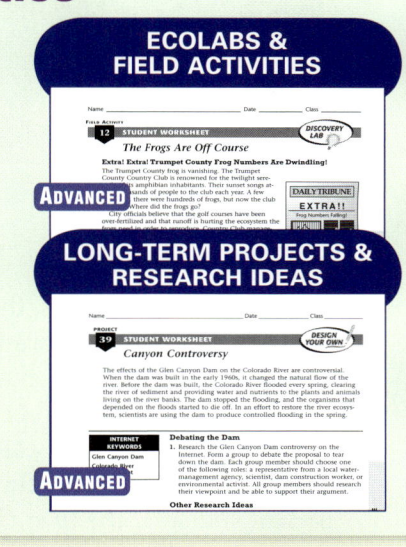

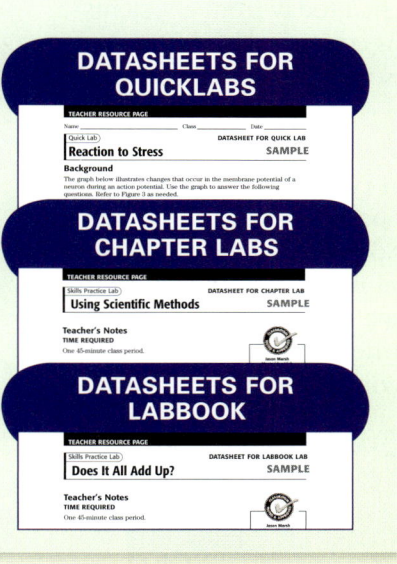

- **ECOLABS & FIELD ACTIVITIES** — ADVANCED
- **DATASHEETS FOR QUICKLABS**
- **LONG-TERM PROJECTS & RESEARCH IDEAS** — ADVANCED
- **DATASHEETS FOR CHAPTER LABS**
- **DATASHEETS FOR LABBOOK**

Review and Assessments

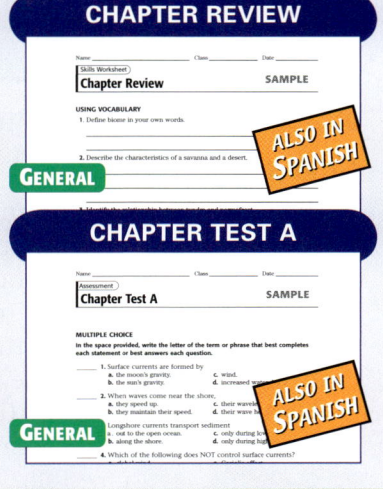

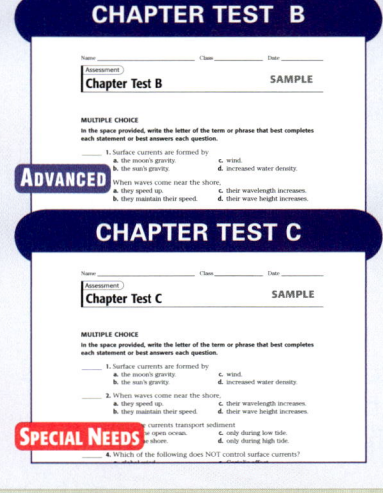

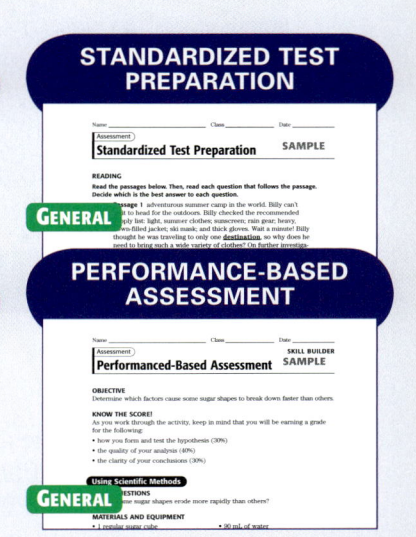

- **SECTION QUIZ** — GENERAL (ALSO IN SPANISH)
- **CHAPTER REVIEW** — GENERAL (ALSO IN SPANISH)
- **CHAPTER TEST B** — ADVANCED
- **STANDARDIZED TEST PREPARATION** — GENERAL
- **SECTION REVIEW** — GENERAL (ALSO IN SPANISH)
- **CHAPTER TEST A** — GENERAL (ALSO IN SPANISH)
- **CHAPTER TEST C** — SPECIAL NEEDS
- **PERFORMANCE-BASED ASSESSMENT** — GENERAL

Chapter 11 • Chapter Resources **305D**

11 Chapter Enrichment

This Chapter Enrichment provides relevant and interesting information to expand and enhance your presentation of the chapter material.

Section 1

The Active River

William Morris Davis

- William Morris Davis (1850–1934) was a famous American geographer who was the first to propose the erosion cycle. Davis theorized that landscapes are initially uplifted. Streams flow rapidly from the uplifted land and cut into the landscape. Gradually, the landscape's slope is reduced. Eventually, the landscape changes into an old erosional surface that is fairly flat. Davis's theory is not supported by scientists today, however. The process of river erosion is approached today from a systems perspective. Each system is composed of different parts that vary from landscape to landscape.

Stream Flow

- Streams have two general types of flow—laminar and turbulent. Laminar flow occurs when the stream load moves in a generally parallel flow. This movement occurs where the channel is smooth. Streams with a greater velocity experience turbulent flow. The stream load generally is rolled, lifted, and bounced along, causing much more erosion in the stream channel.

Section 2

Stream and River Deposits

Drainage Patterns

- A drainage pattern is the arrangement of river channels in a drainage basin. A drainage pattern is determined by an area's geology and climate. One of the most common patterns, called *dendritic*, is a treelike pattern that forms where rocks and sediments are flat. A *parallel* pattern forms where there are valleys and ridges. And a *radial* pattern forms when streams flow from a central peak, such as a volcanic mountain.

Deltas

- The word *delta* was first used by the Greek historian Herodotus to describe the mouth of a river. In the fifth century BCE, Herodotus was traveling in Egypt when he saw the triangular mouth of the Nile River and named the shape after the Greek letter, delta.

Is That a Fact!

◆ Over the last 6,000 years, the Mississippi River delta has shifted from east to west several times. Today, the river empties to the east, but scientists think that if left alone the river would change its course and head toward a swampy region called the Atchafalaya Basin. Only massive dams keep the Mississippi River on its present course. If the river channel changes, the river may no longer pass through New Orleans.

Section 3

Water Underground

Caves as Shelters

- The flow of fresh water underground created caves that were just as important to the development of human civilizations as fertile flood plains were. Humans have used caves as shelters for hundreds of thousands of years. Evidence suggests that the use of caves for shelter coincides with the first controlled use of fire. Hearths that may be 750,000 years old have been found in the cave of l'Escale, in southeastern France.

For background information about teaching strategies and issues, refer to the *Professional Reference for Teachers*.

...a cave called Chou-k'ou-tien
...year-old fossilized remains of
...e of charred animal bones sug-
...itants may have cooked their food.

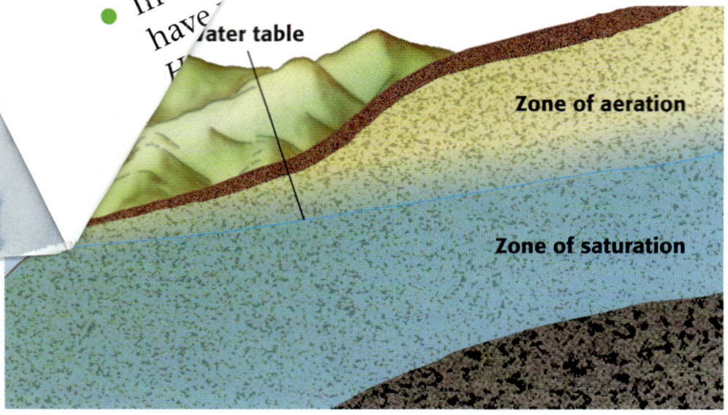

- In China...
  have...
  H...

Water table
Zone of aeration
Zone of saturation

Is That a Fact!
◆ The largest cave chamber in the world is the Sarawak chamber, in Malaysia. The chamber is 600 m long and has an average width of 450 m.

Section 4
Using Water Wisely
Aquifers
- There are two types of aquifers. The first forms in *consolidated formations*, which are formed from solid rock overlaid with permeable rock that is saturated with water. The second kind of aquifer forms in *unconsolidated formations*—loose sand, soil, and gravel. The amount of water contained in an unconsolidated aquifer depends on how tightly the materials are packed. Because of this, sand and gravel, which are coarse-grained, are usually high-yield aquifers, while formations that are finer-grained tend to hold less water.

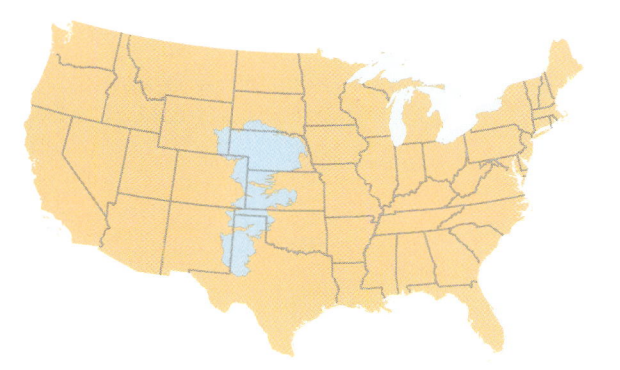

Acequias in New Mexico
- New Mexico receives very little rain each year, so water conservation is critical. Because wide irrigation ditches lose a great deal of water to evaporation, New Mexicans have relied for centuries on shallow earthen ditches fed by local rivers to supply growing plants with water. Each ditch, called an *acequia*, provides water to a small area. Acequias allow for water to seep into the ground, minimizing evaporation and allowing water to reach plant roots. Water that isn't absorbed by the soil returns to the river and provide water to people downstream to irrigate their fields.

Is That a Fact!
◆ When ground water is depleted so quickly that the system cannot recharge, there can be dramatic consequences. At Edwards Air Force Base, in California, the aquifer has lost water so quickly that ground settling has led to sinks and fissures. One of the fissures is about 625 m long!

SCLINKS — Developed and maintained by the National Science Teachers Association

SciLinks is maintained by the National Science Teachers Association to provide you and your students with interesting, up-to-date links that will enrich your classroom presentation of the chapter.

Visit www.scilinks.org and enter the SciLinks code for more information about the topic listed.

Topic: Rivers and Streams
SciLinks code: **HSM1316**

Topic: Stream Deposits
SciLinks code: **HSM1458**

Topic: Water Underground
SciLinks code: **HSM1633**

Topic: Water Erosion
SciLinks code: **HSM1627**

Topic: Water Pollution and Conservation
SciLinks code: **HSM1630**

Chapter 11 • Chapter Enrichment

Overview
Tell students that this chapter will help them learn about the movement of fresh water on the Earth's surface and undergound. The chapter describes the water cycle, erosion and deposition by rivers, and the characteristics of water underground. The chapter also discusses water pollution, wastewater treatment, and water conservation.

Assessing Prior Knowledge
Students should be familiar with the following topics:
- erosion and deposition
- states of matter

Identifying Misconceptions
Students may be confused about how water is stored underground. Explain to students that groundwater is usually not stored in giant underground caves. Rather, spaces between and within rocks fill with water. In this way, an aquifer is much like a sponge.

11
The Flow of Fresh Water

SECTION 1 The Active River 308

SECTION 2 Stream and River Deposits 316

SECTION 3 Water Underground ... 320

SECTION 4 Using Water Wisely ... 326

Chapter Lab 332
Chapter Review 334
Standardized Test Preparation 336
Science in Action 338

About the PHOTO
You can hear the roar of Iguaçu (EE gwah SOO) Falls for miles. The Iguaçu River travels more than 500 km across Brazil before it tumbles off the edge of a volcanic plateau in a series of 275 individual waterfalls. Over the past 20,000 years, erosion has caused the falls to move 28 km upstream.

PRE-READING ACTIVITY

FOLDNOTES **Booklet** Before you read the chapter, create the FoldNote entitled "Booklet" described in the **Study Skills** section of the Appendix. Label each page of the booklet with a main idea from the chapter. As you read the chapter, write what you learn about each main idea on the appropriate page of the booklet.

Standards Correlations

National Science Education Standards

The following codes indicate the National Science Education Standards that correlate to this chapter. The full text of the standards is at the front of the book.

Chapter Opener
SAI 1

Section 1 The Active River
UCP 1, 2, 5; ES 1c, 1f

Section 2 Stream and River Deposits
ES 1c; SPSP 3, 4

Section 3 Water Underground
ST1; ES 1c; SPSP 3

Section 4 Using Water Wisely
UCP 2, 3; SAI 1; SPSP 3; *LabBook:* UCP 2, 3; ST 2; SAI 1; SPSP 5

Chapter Lab
SAI 1

Chapter Review
ES 1c, 1f

Science in Action
SPSP 5

START-UP ACTIVITY

Stream Weavers
Do the following activity to learn how streams and river systems develop.

Procedure
1. Begin with enough **sand** and **gravel** to fill the bottom of a **rectangular plastic washtub.**
2. Spread the gravel in a layer at the bottom of the washtub. On top of the gravel, place a layer of sand that is 4 cm to 6 cm deep. Add more sand to one end of the washtub to form a slope.
3. Make a small hole in the bottom of a **paper cup.** Attach the cup to the inside wall of the tub with a **clothespin.** The cup should be placed at the end that has more sand.
4. Fill the cup with **water,** and observe the water as it moves over the sand. Use a **magnifying lens** to observe features of the stream more closely.
5. Record your observations.

Analysis
1. At the start of your experiment, how did the moving water affect the sand?
2. As time passed, how did the moving water affect the sand?
3. Explain how this activity modeled the development of streams. In what ways was the model accurate? How was it inaccurate?

START-UP ACTIVITY

MATERIALS
FOR EACH GROUP
- clothespin
- cup, paper
- gravel
- magnifying lens
- sand, bucket of
- washtub, plastic, rectangular
- water

Teacher's Notes: Students can tilt the tub by placing a block of wood or a book under one end.

Answers
1. Answers may vary. The moving water cut into the sand and formed a small groove.
2. Answers may vary. As time passed, the moving water cut deeper into the sand and created a wider groove.
3. Accept all reasonable responses. Sample answer: Runoff (water) moves over the land, cutting a gully into the soil. At first the gully is shallow and narrow, but over time the gully widens and becomes deeper. If there is enough water, the gully eventually becomes a river. (Students should note that the model is accurate in that moving water does produce similar landforms. The model is inaccurate for several reasons, including its scale and the fact that rivers flow over varied terrain, not just over uniform sand deposits.)

Chapter Starter Transparency
Use this transparency to help students begin thinking about how rivers can affect the Earth's surface.

CHAPTER RESOURCES
Technology
- **Transparencies**
  - Chapter Starter Transparency READING SKILLS
- **Student Edition on CD-ROM**
- **Guided Reading Audio CD**
  - English or Spanish
- **Classroom Videos**
  - Brain Food Video Quiz

Workbooks
- **Science Puzzlers, Twisters & Teasers**
  - The Flow of Fresh Water GENERAL

Chapter 11 • The Flow of Fresh Water   **307**

SECTION 1

Focus

Overview
This section introduces the water cycle and discusses the role that rivers play in the movement of fresh water. Students will learn that rivers are changing, dynamic systems that continually shape the land. The section discusses the factors that contribute to rates of stream erosion and concludes with descriptions of various types of rivers.

🔔 Bellringer
Ask students to discuss whether a river can be said to have a source and describe what a river's source might look like.
LS Verbal/Interpersonal

Motivate

Demonstration — GENERAL
Streams Carry Fertile Sediment
Add a teaspoon of brightly colored tempera paint to half a cup of soil. Place the soil in a funnel lined with filter paper, and place the funnel over a large jar. Tell students that the paint represents nutrients in the soil. Ask students to predict what will happen when it rains. Demonstrate rain by pouring water into the funnel. Discuss the role that rivers play in distributing soil nutrients. **LS Visual**

SECTION 1

READING WARM-UP

Objectives
- Describe how moving water shapes the surface of the Earth by the process of erosion.
- Explain how water moves through the water cycle.
- Describe a watershed.
- Explain three factors that affect the rate of stream erosion.
- Identify four ways that rivers are described.

Terms to Learn
erosion   divide
water cycle   channel
tributary   load
watershed

READING STRATEGY
Reading Organizer As you read this section, create an outline of the section. Use the headings from the section in your outline.

erosion the process by which wind, water, ice, or gravity transports soil and sediment from one location to another

Figure 1 The Grand Canyon is located in northwestern Arizona. The canyon formed over millions of years as running water eroded the rock layers. (In some places, the canyon is now 29 km wide.)

CHAPTER RESOURCES

Chapter Resource File
- Lesson Plan
- Directed Reading A BASIC
- Directed Reading B SPECIAL NEEDS

Technology
- Transparencies
  - Bellringer
  - The Water Cycle

The Active River

If you had fallen asleep with your toes dangling in the Colorado River 6 million years ago and you had woken up today, your toes would be hanging about 1.6 km (about 1 mi) above the river!

The Colorado River carved the Grand Canyon, shown in **Figure 1**, by washing billions of tons of soil and rock from its riverbed. The Colorado River made the Grand Canyon by a process that can take millions of years.

Rivers: Agents of Erosion
Six million years ago, the area now known as the Grand Canyon was nearly as flat as a pancake. The Colorado River cut down into the rock and formed the Grand Canyon over millions of years through a process called erosion. **Erosion** is the process by which soil and sediment are transported from one location to another. Rivers are not the only agents of erosion. Wind, rain, ice, and snow can also cause erosion.

Because of erosion caused by water, the Grand Canyon is now about 1.6 km deep and 446 km long. In this section, you will learn about stream development, river systems, and the factors that affect the rate of stream erosion.

✓ **Reading Check** Describe the process that created the Grand Canyon. *(See the Appendix for answers to Reading Checks.)*

Answer to Reading Check
The Colorado River eroded the rock over millions of years.

---

308 Chapter 11 • The Flow of Fresh Water

The Water Cycle

Have you ever wondered how rivers keep flowing? Where do rivers get their water? Learning about the water cycle, shown in **Figure 2,** will help you answer these questions. The **water cycle** is the continuous movement of Earth's water from the ocean to the atmosphere to the land and back to the ocean. The water cycle is driven by energy from the sun.

water cycle the continuous movement of water from the ocean to the atmosphere to the land and back to the ocean

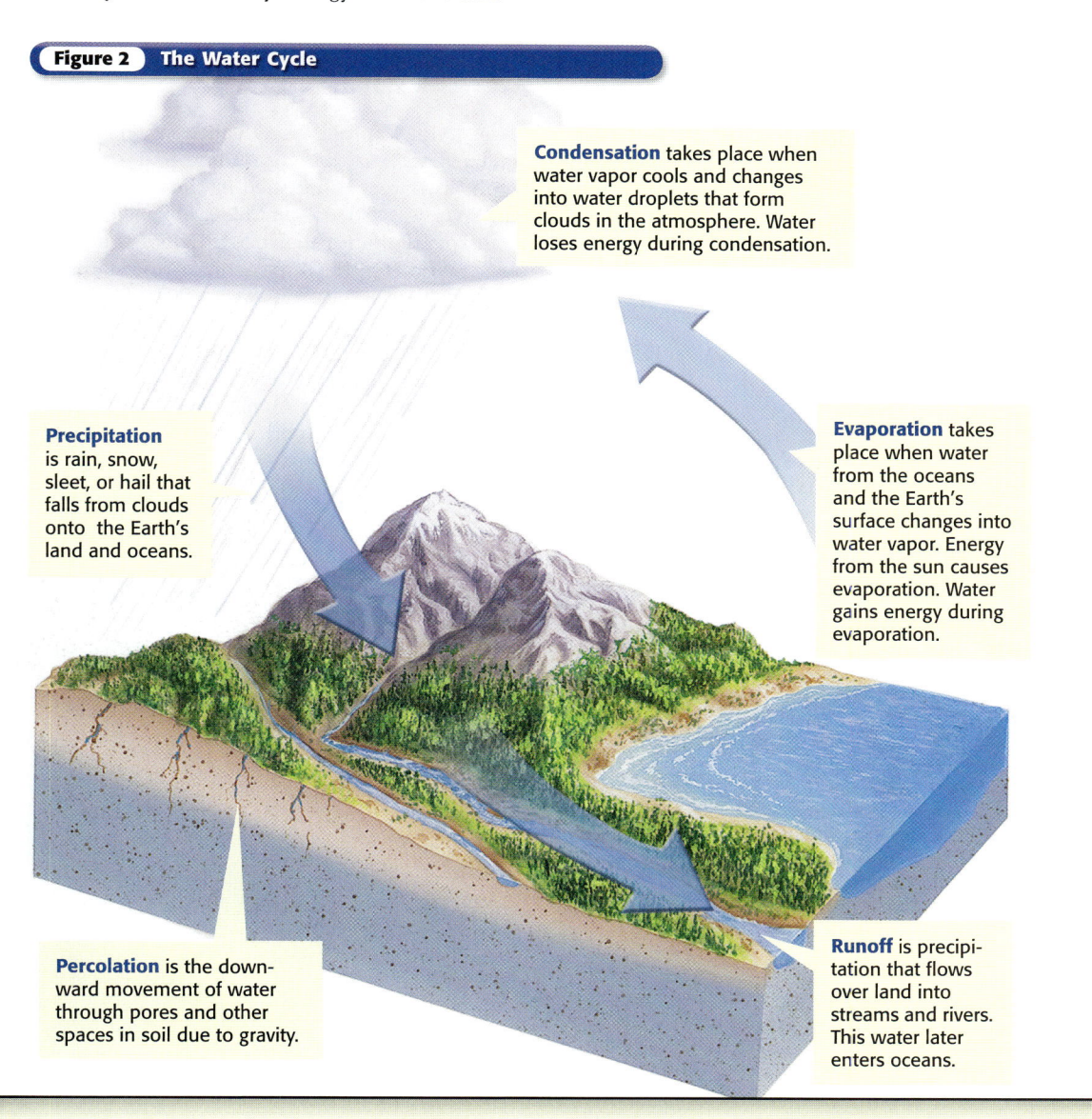

Figure 2 The Water Cycle

Condensation takes place when water vapor cools and changes into water droplets that form clouds in the atmosphere. Water loses energy during condensation.

Precipitation is rain, snow, sleet, or hail that falls from clouds onto the Earth's land and oceans.

Evaporation takes place when water from the oceans and the Earth's surface changes into water vapor. Energy from the sun causes evaporation. Water gains energy during evaporation.

Percolation is the downward movement of water through pores and other spaces in soil due to gravity.

Runoff is precipitation that flows over land into streams and rivers. This water later enters oceans.

Teach

ACTIVITY — BASIC

Water Re-Cycle Have students reproduce the water-cycle diagram and rewrite the labels in their own words. Have students exchange diagrams and review each other's work. **LS Visual**

CONNECTION to Environmental Science — ADVANCED

Large Dam Projects Damming and controlling rivers creates usable farmland, allows settlement in flood plains, and powers industry. Beginning in the 1930s, massive hydroelectric dams were built across many western rivers. Many developing nations are now following this example.

While dams provide many benefits, large dam projects face increasing criticism. Around the world, as many as 60 million people have been displaced by dams. Even more people have suffered from the effects of being downstream from dams: farmland is deprived of flood sediments and water for irrigation becomes unusable, fisheries become less productive, and epidemics of waterborne disease often follow large dam projects. Have students research large dam projects and debate this question: "After the industrialized world has benefited so much from damming its rivers, can industrialized nations ask developing countries not to exploit their water resources?" **LS Logical/Interpersonal**

Homework — ADVANCED

World River Scrapbook Beginning with early Mesopotamian cultures of the Tigris and Euphrates River valleys, river systems have been centers of human civilization. Have students choose an important world river and create a scrapbook in which they explore the cultural, ecological, and economic significance of the river. Students should apply concepts from each section as they create the scrapbooks. When they finish the chapter, have students present their scrapbooks to the class. **LS Visual/Kinesthetic**

MISCONCEPTION ALERT

Evaporation Everywhere Students may think that water evaporates only from rivers and other bodies of water, not from soil. Display the transparency entitled "The Water Cycle." Explain to students that water also evaporates from soil during the water cycle and that plants contribute to the water cycle. They draw liquid water from the ground and transpire, or release water vapor through leaf pores.

Section 1 • The Active River

Teach, continued

Answers to Activity
Missouri, Ohio, and Arkansas; Minneapolis, St. Paul, St. Louis, Memphis, Baton Rouge, and New Orleans; approximately 3,700 km (Hint: Measure the distance using a piece of thread, and then find the actual distance traveled by using the map's scale.)

Group Activity — GENERAL
Mapping River Systems
Have pairs of students use a map or atlas to create a poster that illustrates the river systems and drainage basins of North America. Encourage them to use arrows indicating the direction of flow in major rivers and to draw the divides that separate each drainage basin. Working independently, students could make a map that shows the river systems of your county or state. **LS Interpersonal**

SCHOOL to HOME
Floating down the River
Study a map of the United States at home with a parent. Find the Mississippi River. Imagine that you are planning a rafting trip down the river. On the map, trace the route of your trip from Lake Itasca, Minnesota to the mouth of the river in Louisiana. If you were floating on a raft down the Mississippi River, what major tributaries would you pass? What cities would you pass? Mark them on the map. How many kilometers would you travel on this trip?

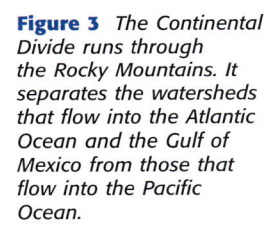

CONNECTION to History — GENERAL
Mono Reservoir In 1935, a dam was built in California to prevent sediment from filling Gibraltar Reservoir. This dam created Mono Reservoir. The watershed above Mono Reservoir was burned by forest fires, and people worried that sediment would fill the reservoirs before plants could regrow to hold the soil. Unfortunately, the next 2 years saw record rainfall. Sediment filled Mono Reservoir and half-filled Gibraltar Reservoir.

River Systems

The next time you take a shower, notice that individual drops of water join together to become small streams. These streams join other small streams and form larger ones. Eventually, all of the water flows down the drain. Every time you shower, you create a model river system—a network of streams and rivers that drains an area of its runoff. Just as the shower forms a network of flowing water, streams and rivers form a network of flowing water on land. A stream that flows into a lake or into a larger stream is called a **tributary.**

Watersheds

River systems are divided into regions called watersheds. A **watershed,** or *drainage basin,* is the area of land that is drained by a water system. The largest watershed in the United States is the Mississippi River watershed. The Mississippi River watershed has hundreds of tributaries that extend from the Rocky Mountains, in the West, to the Appalachian Mountains, in the East.

The satellite image in **Figure 3** shows that the Mississippi River watershed covers more than one-third of the United States. Other major watersheds in the United States are the Columbia River, Rio Grande, and Colorado River watersheds. Watersheds are separated from each other by an area of higher ground called a **divide.**

Reading Check Describe the difference between a watershed and a divide.

Figure 3 The Continental Divide runs through the Rocky Mountains. It separates the watersheds that flow into the Atlantic Ocean and the Gulf of Mexico from those that flow into the Pacific Ocean.

Answer to Reading Check
A divide is the boundary that separates drainage areas, whereas a watershed is the area of land that is drained by a water system.

Chapter 11 • The Flow of Fresh Water

Figure 4 *A mountain stream, such as the one at left, at Kenai Peninsula in Alaska, flows rapidly and has more erosive energy. A river on a flat plain, such as the Kuskowin River in Alaska, shown below, flows slowly and has less erosive energy.*

Stream Erosion

As a stream forms, it erodes soil and rock to make a channel. A **channel** is the path that a stream follows. When a stream first forms, its channel is usually narrow and steep. Over time, the stream transports rock and soil downstream and makes the channel wider and deeper. When streams become longer and wider, they are called *rivers*. A stream's ability to erode is influenced by three factors: gradient, discharge, and load.

Gradient

Figure 4 shows two photos of rivers with very different gradients. *Gradient* is the measure of the change in elevation over a certain distance. A high gradient gives a stream or river more erosive energy to erode rock and soil. A river or stream that has a low gradient has less energy for erosion.

Discharge

The amount of water that a stream or river carries in a given amount of time is called *discharge*. The discharge of a stream increases when a major storm occurs or when warm weather rapidly melts snow. As the stream's discharge increases, its erosive energy and speed and the amount of materials that the stream can carry also increase.

Reading Check What factors cause a stream to flow faster?

tributary a stream that flows into a lake or into a larger stream

watershed the area of land that is drained by a water system

divide the boundary between drainage areas that have streams that flow in opposite directions

channel the path that a stream follows

MATH PRACTICE

Calculating a Stream's Gradient

If a stream starts at an elevation of 4,900 m and travels 450 km downstream to a lake that is at an elevation of 400 m, what is the stream's gradient? (Hint: Subtract the final elevation from the starting elevation, and divide by 450. Don't forget to keep track of the units.)

Answer to Reading Check
An increase in a stream's gradient and discharge can cause the stream to flow faster.

WEIRD SCIENCE

Stream piracy occurs when one river "captures" another. If the land dividing two streams is eroded, one stream can "capture" the headwaters of the other stream. The eroding stream eventually pirates all of the water from the other stream.

CONNECTION to Physical Science — BASIC

Kinetic and Potential Energy
Discuss the difference between kinetic and potential energy by using the following example: "The reservoir of a hydroelectric dam has tremendous potential energy. When the gates are open, that potential energy is converted into kinetic energy that spins a turbine. The turbine then generates electrical energy." Ask students to list other devices that use the potential energy of water. (Examples include a flush toilet with a water tank.) **LS** Verbal

CONNECTION ACTIVITY Real World — GENERAL

Water Safety Meteorologists recognize the power of moving water, and they issue special warnings when there is a danger of floods. Ask students to guess how much moving water it takes to knock an adult off his or her feet: 15 cm, 30 cm, or 1 m. (15 cm) Ask students how deep the water would have to be to sweep away a car: more than 2 m, at least 1.5 m, or less than 1 m. (less than 1 m) Use a meterstick to demonstrate these water depths, and caution students to be careful around flowing water. **LS** Logical

Answer to Math Practice
4,900 m − 400 m = 4,500 m
4,500 m ÷ 450 km = 10 m/km

Section 1 • The Active River

Teach, continued

Group Activity — BASIC

Stream Load To help students learn the differences between the types of loads that streams carry, have them do the activity in groups of four. Have groups fill a plastic jar three-quarters full of water. Provide a few small pebbles, a 1/4 cup of soil, and 3 Tbsp of salt for each group. Have students choose which material best represents a stream's bed load (the pebbles), suspended load (the soil), and dissolved load (the salt).

Have students add all three materials to the jar and then shake it carefully to simulate a stream's load. After the contents have been thoroughly mixed, ask students to hypothesize how they could remove each material from the jar. (The pebbles settle to the bottom and can be picked out easily. If the water remains still long enough, the sediment will settle to the bottom of the jar. The salt can be removed if the water is evaporated.) **LS Kinesthetic**

load the materials carried by a stream

Load

The materials carried by a stream are called the stream's **load**. The size of a stream's load is affected by the stream's speed. Fast-moving streams can carry large particles. Rocks and pebbles bounce and scrape along the bottom and sides of the stream bed. Thus, the size of a stream's load also affects its rate of erosion. The illustration below shows the three ways that a stream can carry its load.

A stream can bounce large materials, such as pebbles and boulders, along the stream bed. These rocks are called the **bed load**.

A stream can carry small rocks and soil in suspension. These materials, called the **suspended load**, make the river look muddy.

The **dissolved load** is material carried in solution, which means that the material is dissolved in the water. Sodium and calcium are some of the materials in the dissolved load.

Activity — ADVANCED

River Field Guide Have students make a field guide for rivers. Suggest that they include photos of streams and rivers and write captions to describe each photo. The captions should incorporate terms such as *gradient, erosion, load, channel,* and *meanders*. Finally, have students hypothesize the river's speed, load, and erosional capacity. **LS Visual** English Language Learners

CONNECTION to Geography — GENERAL

Amazon Tours Web Page The Amazon River basin is the world's largest watershed. It has an area of about 6 million square kilometers, which is almost twice as big as the Mississippi River watershed! Have students work in groups to design a Web page that describes the people, plants, and animals of the Amazon River basin.
LS Verbal/Visual

312 Chapter 11 • The Flow of Fresh Water

The Stages of a River

In the early 1900s, William Morris Davis developed a model for the stages of river development. According to his model, rivers evolve from a youthful stage to an old-age stage. He thought that all rivers erode in the same way and at the same rate.

Today, scientists support a different model that considers factors of stream development that differ from those considered in Davis's model. For example, because different materials erode at different rates, one river may develop more quickly than another river. Many factors, including climate, gradient, and load, influence the development of a river. Scientists no longer use Davis's model to explain river development, but they still use many of his terms to describe a river. These terms describe a river's general features, not a river's actual age.

Youthful Rivers

A youthful river, such as the one shown in **Figure 5,** erodes its channel deeper rather than wider. The river flows quickly because of its steep gradient. Its channel is narrow and straight. The river tumbles over rocks in rapids and waterfalls. Youthful rivers have very few tributaries.

Mature Rivers

A mature river, as shown in **Figure 6,** erodes its channel wider rather than deeper. The gradient of a mature river is not as steep as that of a youthful river. Also, a mature river has fewer falls and rapids. A mature river is fed by many tributaries. Because of its good drainage, a mature river has more discharge than a youthful river.

Reading Check What are the characteristics of a mature river?

CONNECTION TO Language Arts

Huckleberry Finn Mark Twain's famous book, *The Adventures of Huckleberry Finn,* describes the life of a boy who lived on the Mississippi River. Mark Twain's real name was Samuel Clemens. Do research to find out why Clemens chose to use the name Mark Twain and how the name relates to the Mississippi River.

Figure 5 This youthful river is located in Yellowstone National Park in Wyoming. Rapids and falls are found where the river flows over hard, resistant rock.

Figure 6 A mature river, such as this one in the Amazon basin of Peru, curves back and forth. The bends in the river's channel are called meanders.

READING STRATEGY — GENERAL

Prediction Guide Write "Young," "Mature," "Old," and "Rejuvenated" on the board. Have students brainstorm concepts, words, or images related to these terms, and write their suggestions below the terms. Next, add the dictionary definitions of the terms. Then, discuss how the terms might describe a river. Have students compare their ideas with the descriptions in the text. Remind students that these terms do not describe the age of a river; the terms describe only a river's features. **English Language Learners**
LS Verbal

ACTIVITY — GENERAL

Illustrating River Stages As students read the section on the stages of a river, have them illustrate the stages. Encourage students to draw a cross section of the river channel and valley. Students should label the parts of their diagrams and should write a brief description of each stage of river development.
LS Visual/Verbal

Answer to Reading Check
A mature river erodes its channel wider rather than deeper. It is not steep and has fewer falls and rapids. It also has good drainage and more discharge than a youthful river does.

CONNECTION to History — ADVANCED

Rolling on the River In the eighteenth and nineteenth centuries, the Mississippi River served as an important trade route for the Midwest. Riverboats carried people and resources, such as grains, meat, and animal skins, down the river. Have interested students research how the Mississippi River influenced the history of the Midwest. **LS Verbal**

Section 1 • The Active River

Close

Reteaching — BASIC

Photo Opportunity Have students look through nature magazines to find photos illustrating river features discussed in this chapter, such as flood plains, deltas, and alluvial fans. **Visual**

Quiz — GENERAL

1. How does rainfall or snowmelt affect a river's discharge and ability to cause erosion? (Rainfall and snowmelt increase both a river's discharge and the amount of erosion the river can cause.)

2. Explain the three types of materials carried by a river. (bed load: large materials that roll or bounce along a riverbed; suspended load: materials that float suspended in a river; dissolved load: materials dissolved in a river)

Alternative Assessment — GENERAL

Modeling River Features Display the teaching transparency entitled "Rivers," and discuss the labeled features. Then, divide students into groups, and have each group use modeling clay to make a model of a river. The model should incorporate the concepts they have learned in this chapter. Students can use pins with attached labels to indicate river features. **Kinesthetic**

Figure 7 This old river is located in New Zealand.

Old Rivers

An old river has a low gradient and little erosive energy. Instead of widening and deepening its banks, the river deposits rock and soil in and along its channel. Old rivers, such as the one in **Figure 7,** are characterized by wide, flat *flood plains*, or valleys, and many bends. Also, an old river has fewer tributaries than a mature river because the smaller tributaries have joined together.

Rejuvenated Rivers

Rejuvenated (ri JOO vuh NAYT ed) rivers are found where the land is raised by tectonic activity. When land rises, the river's gradient becomes steeper, and the river flows more quickly. The increased gradient of a rejuvenated river allows the river to cut more deeply into the valley floor. Steplike formations called *terraces* often form on both sides of a stream valley as a result of rejuvenation. Can you find the terraces in **Figure 8**?

✓ **Reading Check** How do rejuvenated rivers form?

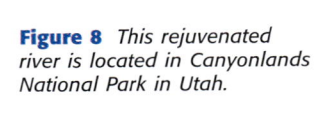

Figure 8 This rejuvenated river is located in Canyonlands National Park in Utah.

Answer to Reading Check
Rejuvenated rivers form when the land is raised by tectonic forces.

BRAIN FOOD

Most river water comes from rainfall and melted snow that flow down from mountains. Ask students, "Why do some rivers continue to flow during a severe drought?"

(These rivers are probably lower than the water table, so their flow is maintained by seepage from groundwater.)

Chapter 11 • The Flow of Fresh Water

SECTION Review

Summary

- Rivers cause erosion by removing and transporting soil and rock from the riverbed.
- The water cycle is the movement of Earth's water from the ocean to the atmosphere to the land and back to the ocean.
- A river system is made up of a network of streams and rivers.
- A watershed is a region that collects runoff water that then becomes part of a river or a lake.
- A stream with a high gradient has more energy for eroding soil and rock.
- When a stream's discharge increases, its erosive energy also increases.
- A stream with a load of large particles has a higher rate of erosion than a stream with a dissolved load.
- A developing river can be described as youthful, mature, old, or rejuvenated.

Using Key Terms

1. Use each of the following terms in a separate sentence: *erosion, water cycle, tributary, watershed, divide, channel,* and *load.*

Understanding Key Ideas

2. Which of the following drains a watershed?
   a. a divide
   b. a drainage basin
   c. a tributary
   d. a water system

3. Describe how the Grand Canyon was formed.

4. Draw the water cycle. In your drawing, label *condensation, precipitation,* and *evaporation.*

5. What are three factors that affect the rate of stream erosion?

6. Which stage of river development is characterized by flat flood plains?

Critical Thinking

7. **Making Inferences** How does the water cycle help develop river systems?

8. **Making Comparisons** How do youthful rivers, mature rivers, and old rivers differ?

Interpreting Graphics

Use the pie graph below to answer the questions that follow.

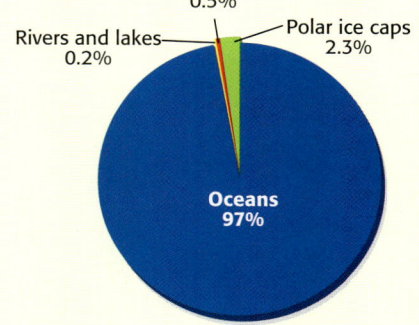

Distribution of Water in the World

- Water underground, in soil, and in air 0.5%
- Rivers and lakes 0.2%
- Polar ice caps 2.3%
- Oceans 97%

9. Where is most of the water in the world found?

10. In what form is the majority of the world's fresh water?

For a variety of links related to this chapter, go to www.scilinks.org
Topic: Rivers and Streams
SciLinks code: HSM1316

Answers to Section Review

1. Sample answer: The Grand Canyon was formed by erosion. Rain is a part of the water cycle. A tributary joins a larger river. A watershed can also be called a drainage basin. Watersheds are separated by a divide. A channel is a path that a stream follows. A river's load often includes rocks and pebbles.
2. d
3. The Grand Canyon was formed by erosion caused by the Colorado River washing away soil and rock from the riverbed.
4. Answers may vary. The drawing should resemble Figure 2.
5. gradient, discharge, and load
6. old rivers
7. Answers may vary. The water cycle causes continuous movement of water between the Earth's surface and the atmosphere. The flow of water to the oceans creates river systems.
8. Answers may vary. Youthful rivers erode deep channels. Mature rivers erode wide channels. Old rivers deposit sediment in their channels and along their banks. Rejuvenated rivers form terraces in the river valley.
9. Most of the world's water is found in the oceans.
10. The majority of fresh water is in the form of ice.

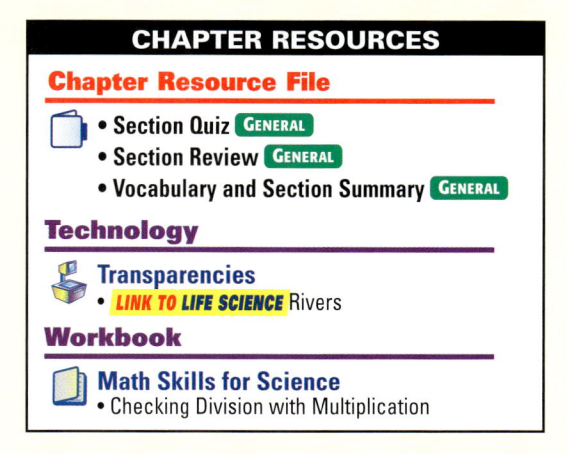

CHAPTER RESOURCES

Chapter Resource File
- Section Quiz GENERAL
- Section Review GENERAL
- Vocabulary and Section Summary GENERAL

Technology
- Transparencies
  - LINK TO LIFE SCIENCE Rivers

Workbook
- Math Skills for Science
  - Checking Division with Multiplication

Section 1 • The Active River

SECTION 2

Focus

Overview
This section describes the variety of ways that the load carried by a river can be deposited. Students will learn about the different landforms created by river deposits, and they will explore the connections between river deposits, floods, and agriculture.

🔔 Bellringer
Post the following question on the board or overhead projector: "Even though flooding along rivers is potentially harmful, many farms are located near rivers. Why do people build farms along rivers?" (The flood waters deposit sediments that contribute to the land's fertility.)

Motivate

Demonstration — GENERAL
Modeling Deposition To show students how sediment tends to sort according to particle size, place a handful of soil, sand, and small gravel in a large plastic jar filled with water. Shake the jar vigorously, and then place it on your desk. Ask students to describe what happens to the different-sized particles in the jar as time passes. **LS** Visual

SECTION 2

READING WARM-UP

Objectives
- Describe the four different types of stream deposits.
- Describe how the deposition of sediment affects the land.

Terms to Learn
deposition   alluvial fan
delta   floodplain

READING STRATEGY

Prediction Guide Before reading this section, write the title of each heading in this section. Next, under each heading, write what you think you will learn.

CHAPTER RESOURCES

Chapter Resource File
- Lesson Plan
- Directed Reading A BASIC
- Directed Reading B SPECIAL NEEDS

Technology
- Transparencies
- Bellringer

Stream and River Deposits

If your job were to carry millions of tons of soil across the United States, how would you do it? You might use a bulldozer or a dump truck, but it would still take you a long time. Did you know that rivers do this job every day?

Rivers erode and move enormous amounts of material, such as soil and rock. Acting as liquid conveyor belts, rivers often carry fertile soil to farmland and wetlands. Although erosion is a serious problem, rivers also renew soils and form new land. As you will see in this section, rivers create some of the most impressive landforms on Earth.

Deposition in Water

You have learned how flowing water erodes the Earth's surface. After rivers erode rock and soil, they drop, or *deposit*, their load downstream. **Deposition** is the process in which material is laid down or dropped. Rock and soil deposited by streams are called *sediment*. Rivers and streams deposit sediment where the speed of the water current decreases. **Figure 1** shows this type of deposition.

Figure 1 This photo shows erosion and deposition at a bend, or meander, of a river in Alaska.

Deposition occurs along the inside bank of the bend, where the water flows slower.

Erosion occurs along the outside bank of the bend, where the water flows faster.

WEIRD SCIENCE

The Okavango River, in Africa, flows approximately 1,600 km through Angola, Namibia, and Botswana before it empties into the middle of the Kalahari Desert, where the river evaporates! The river's alluvial fan provides a haven for the desert's plants and animals.

316 Chapter 11 • The Flow of Fresh Water

Placer Deposits

Heavy minerals are sometimes deposited at places in a river where the current slows down. This kind of sediment is called a *placer deposit* (PLAS uhr dee PAHZ it). Some placer deposits contain gold. During the California gold rush, which began in 1849, many miners panned for gold in the placer deposits of rivers, as shown in **Figure 2.**

Delta

A river's current slows when a river empties into a large body of water, such as a lake or an ocean. As its current slows, a river often deposits its load in a fan-shaped pattern called a **delta.** In **Figure 3,** you can see an astronaut's view of the Nile Delta. A delta usually forms on a flat surface and is made mostly of mud. These mud deposits form new land and cause the coastline to grow. The world's deltas are home to a rich diversity of plant and animal life.

If you look back at the map of the Mississippi River watershed, you can see where the Mississippi Delta has formed. It has formed where the Mississippi River flows into the Gulf of Mexico. Each of the fine mud particles in the delta began its journey far upstream. Parts of Louisiana are made up of particles that were transported from places as far away as Montana, Minnesota, Ohio, and Illinois!

Reading Check What are deltas made of? (*See the Appendix for answers to Reading Checks.*)

Figure 2 Miners rushed to California in the 1850s to find gold. They often found it in the bends of rivers in placer deposits.

deposition the process in which material is laid down

delta a fan-shaped mass of material deposited at the mouth of a stream

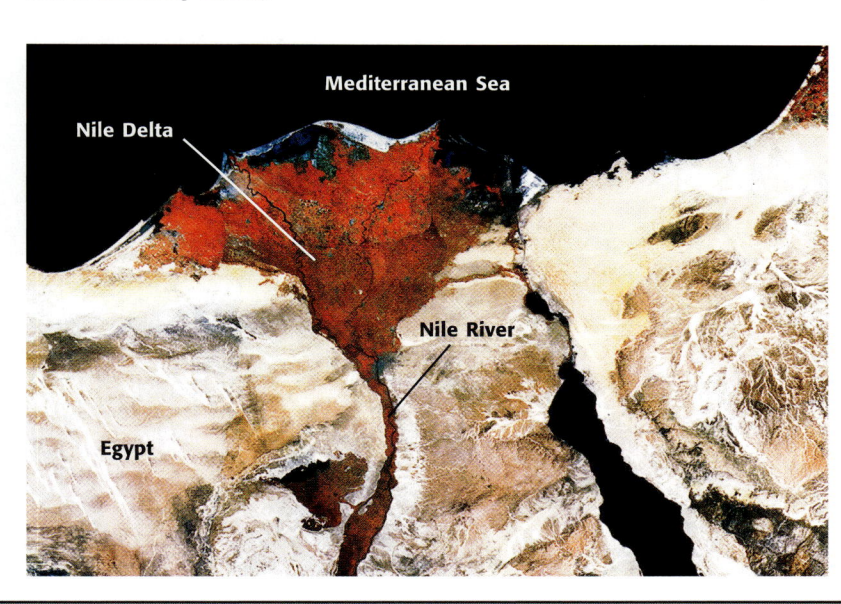

Figure 3 As sediment is dropped at the mouth of the Nile River, in Egypt, a delta forms.

Answer to Reading Check
Deltas are made of the deposited load of the river, which is mostly mud.

Is That a Fact!
Under average conditions, the Mississippi River carries about 17,000 m³ of water by a given point every second. A small carry-on suitcase is about 0.03 m³, so watching the river go by on an average day is equivalent to watching about 566,666 water-filled suitcases pass by you every second!

Teach

BRAIN FOOD
Rivers Make Political Borders Ask students to examine a map of the United States and note that rivers often serve as state borders. For instance, the Ohio River is the border between Indiana and Kentucky. But meanders can sometimes shift the course of the river. Does the state border then change? To prevent feuding between states, the courts have declared that state boundaries do not change when a river shifts.

Group ACTIVITY—ADVANCED
Gold Rush Between 1870 and 1898, many prospectors discovered gold in Canada's Yukon Territory. Dreams of getting rich overnight lured people to the Klondike River area in vast numbers.

Have students research the Yukon gold rush. Divide the class into three groups. Have group 1 prepare a presentation on how the gold deposits formed. Have group 2 prepare a presentation on how the gold ore became placer deposits in the Klondike River. Have group 3 prepare a presentation on the geography of the Yukon's river systems. Students can also find out about life in the gold fields and present their findings using models or posters. **LS Verbal** Co-op Learning

Section 2 • Stream and River Deposits

Close

Reteaching — BASIC
Prospecting Using a large map of a local river, have students label areas that are likely to have placer deposits or flood plains. Also, have students identify areas where the river's channel might be likely to shift over time. **LS Visual**

Quiz — GENERAL
1. A river runs down a rapids, eases through a valley for about 3 km, and then tumbles down a waterfall into a lake. Where along this path would you most likely find a placer deposit? Why? *(in the valley, because heavy minerals are often deposited where currents are slow)*

2. Define flood plain. *(land that is periodically flooded when a river overflows its banks)*

Alternative Assessment — GENERAL
Where the River Ends Have students use modeling clay to create a model of a delta and an alluvial fan. They should also model the immediate environment around each river feature and use pins with labels to identify the processes involved in the formation of each feature. **LS Kinesthetic**

Figure 4 An alluvial fan, like this one at Death Valley in California, forms when an eroding stream changes rapidly into a depositing stream.

alluvial fan a fan-shaped mass of material deposited by a stream when the slope of the land decreases sharply

floodplain an area along a river that forms from sediments deposited when the river overflows its banks

Deposition on Land
When a fast-moving mountain stream flows onto a flat plain, the stream slows down very quickly. As the stream slows down, it deposits sediment. The sediment forms an alluvial fan, such as the one shown in **Figure 4**. **Alluvial fans** are fan-shaped deposits that, unlike deltas, form on dry land.

Floodplains
During periods of high rainfall or rapid snow melt, a sudden increase in the volume of water flowing into a stream can cause the stream to overflow its banks. The area along a river that forms from sediment deposited when a river overflows its banks is called a **floodplain**. When a stream floods, a layer of sediment is deposited across the flood plain. Each flood adds another layer of sediment.

Flood plains are rich farming areas because periodic flooding brings new soil to the land. However, flooding can cause damage, too. When the Mississippi River flooded in 1993, farms were destroyed, and entire towns were evacuated. **Figure 5** shows an area north of St. Louis, Missouri, that was flooded.

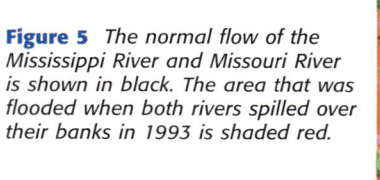

Figure 5 The normal flow of the Mississippi River and Missouri River is shown in black. The area that was flooded when both rivers spilled over their banks in 1993 is shaded red.

SCIENCE HUMOR

Q: What is a flood?
A: It's a river that's too big for its bridges.

Chapter 11 • The Flow of Fresh Water

Flooding Dangers

The flooding of the Mississippi River in 1993 caused damage in nine states. But floods can damage more than property. Many people have lost their lives to powerful floods. As shown in **Figure 6,** flash flooding can take a driver by surprise. However, there are ways that floods can be controlled.

One type of barrier that can be built to help control flooding is called a *dam*. A dam is a barrier that can redirect the flow of water. A dam can prevent flooding in one area and create an artificial lake in another area. The water stored in the artificial lake can be used to irrigate farmland during droughts and provide drinking water to local towns and cities. The stored water can also be used to generate electricity.

Overflow from a river can also be controlled by a barrier called a *levee*. A levee is the buildup of sediment deposited along the channel of a river. This buildup helps keep the river inside its banks. People often use sandbags to build artificial levees to control water during serious flooding.

Reading Check List two ways that the flow of water can be controlled.

Figure 6 *Cars driven on flooded roads can easily be carried down to deeper, more dangerous water.*

SECTION Review

Summary

- Sediment forms several types of deposits.
- Sediments deposited where a river's current slows are called *placer deposits*.
- A delta is a fan-shaped deposit of sediment where a river meets a large body of water.
- Alluvial fans can form when a river deposits sediment on land.
- Flooding brings rich soil to farmland but can also lead to property damage and death.

Using Key Terms

1. In your own words, write a definition for each of the following terms: *deposition* and *flood plain*.

Understanding Key Ideas

2. Which of the following forms at places in a river where the current slows?
   a. a placer deposit
   b. a delta
   c. a flood plain
   d. a levee

3. Which of the following can help to prevent a flood?
   a. a placer deposit
   b. a delta
   c. a flood plain
   d. a levee

4. Where do alluvial fans form?

5. Explain why flood plains are both good and bad areas for farming.

Math Skills

6. A river flows at a speed of 8 km/h. If you floated on a raft in this river, how far would you have traveled after 5 h?

Critical Thinking

7. **Identifying Relationships** What factors increase the likelihood that sediment will be deposited?

8. **Making Comparisons** How are alluvial fans and deltas similar?

For a variety of links related to this chapter, go to **www.scilinks.org**
Topic: Stream Deposits
SciLinks code: HSM1458

Answers to Section Review

1. Sample answer: Deposition is material being laid down or dropped. Flood plains are areas where sediment is deposited when a river overflows its banks.
2. a
3. d
4. Alluvial fans form where a fast-moving mountain stream flows onto a flat plain and deposits sediment in a fan-shaped pattern.
5. Answers may vary. Flood plains form fertile farmland because flood waters periodically deposit new soil on the land. However, flooding can damage crops.
6. 8 km/h × 5 h = 40 km
7. Answers may vary. Factors that reduce a river's speed increase the chance that a river's load will be deposited.
8. Answers may vary. Both deltas and alluvial fans are fan-shaped deposits formed when a stream slows. Deltas form as rivers enter larger bodies of water, and alluvial fans form on dry land.

Answer to Reading Check

The flow of water can be controlled by dams and levees.

CHAPTER RESOURCES

Chapter Resource File

- Section Quiz GENERAL
- Section Review GENERAL
- Vocabulary and Section Summary GENERAL
- Reinforcement Worksheet BASIC

Section 2 • Stream and River Deposits

SECTION 3

Focus

Overview
In this section, students will learn about groundwater. The section discusses the formation of aquifers and how surface water enters them. Students will learn how wells and springs bring groundwater to the surface. Finally, the section discusses how the movement of groundwater forms caves.

🔔 Bellringer
Ask students "A family lives 50 km from the nearest stream or lake and gets water from a well. Where does the water in the well come from?" (It comes from water stored underground.)

Motivate

Demonstration — GENERAL
Groundwater Model Layer an aquarium half full with gravel, sand, and potting soil. Pack the material firmly. Add water until you can clearly see areas of aeration and saturation. Ask students to compare this model to **Figure 1**. Using a marker, draw a line for the water table on the glass. Introduce the terms *zone of saturation* and *zone of aeration*. Discuss the difference between the terms. **LS Visual**

CHAPTER RESOURCES

Chapter Resource File
- Lesson Plan
- Directed Reading A BASIC
- Directed Reading B SPECIAL NEEDS

Technology
- Transparencies
  - Bellringer
  - The Water Table and Wells

SECTION 3

READING WARM-UP

Objectives
- Identify and describe the location of the water table.
- Describe an aquifer.
- Explain the difference between a spring and a well.
- Explain how caves and sinkholes form as a result of erosion and deposition.

Terms to Learn
water table
aquifer
porosity
permeability
recharge zone
artesian spring

READING STRATEGY
Discussion Read this section silently. Write down questions that you have about this section. Discuss your questions in a small group.

water table the upper surface of underground water; the upper boundary of the zone of saturation

Figure 1 The water table is the upper surface of the zone of saturation.

Water Underground

Imagine that instead of turning on a faucet to get a glass of water, you pour water from a chunk of solid rock! This idea may sound crazy, but millions of people get their water from within rock that is deep underground.

Although you can see some of Earth's water in streams and lakes, you cannot see the large amount of water that flows underground. The water located within the rocks below the Earth's surface is called *groundwater*. Groundwater not only is an important resource but also plays an important role in erosion and deposition.

The Location of Groundwater

Surface water seeps underground into the soil and rock. This underground area is divided into two zones. Rainwater passes through the upper zone, called the *zone of aeration*. Farther down, the water collects in an area called the *zone of saturation*. In this zone, the spaces between the rock particles are filled with water.

These two zones meet at a boundary known as the **water table**, shown in **Figure 1**. The water table rises during wet seasons and falls during dry seasons. In wet regions, the water table can be at or just beneath the soil's surface. In dry regions, such as deserts, the water table may be hundreds of meters beneath the ground.

✓ **Reading Check** Describe where the zone of aeration is located. *(See the Appendix for answers to Reading Checks.)*

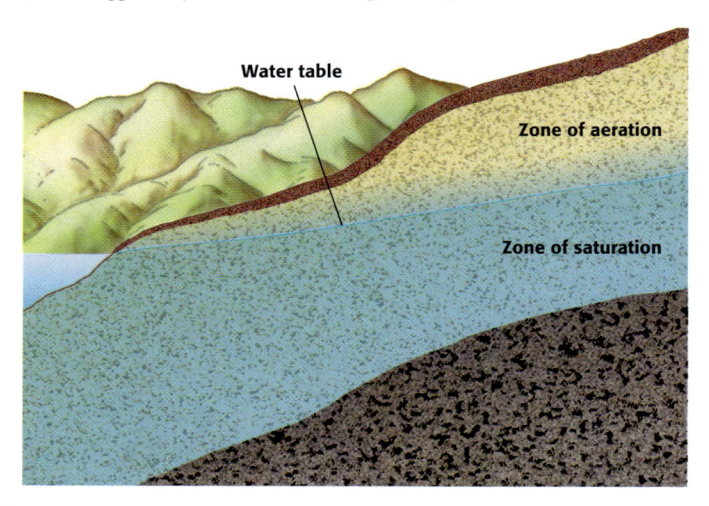

Answer to Reading Check
The zone of aeration is located underground. It is the area above the water table.

---

320   Chapter 11 • The Flow of Fresh Water

Aquifers

A rock layer that stores groundwater and allows the flow of groundwater is called an **aquifer**. An aquifer can be described by its ability to hold water and its ability to allow water to pass freely through it.

Porosity

The more open spaces, or pores, between particles in an aquifer, the more water the aquifer can hold. The percentage of open space between individual rock particles in a rock layer is called **porosity**.

Porosity is influenced by the differences in sizes of the particles in the rock layer. If a rock layer contains many particles of different sizes, it is likely that small particles will fill up the different-sized empty spaces between large particles. Therefore, a rock layer with particles of different sizes has a low percentage of open space between particles and has low porosity. On the other hand, a rock layer containing same-sized particles has high porosity. This rock layer has high porosity because smaller particles are not present to fill the empty space between particles. So, there is more open space between particles.

Permeability

If the pores of a rock layer are connected, groundwater can flow through the rock layer. A rock's ability to let water pass through is called **permeability**. A rock that stops the flow of water is *impermeable*.

The larger the particles are, the more permeable the rock layer is. Because large particles have less surface area relative to their volume than small particles do, large particles cause less friction. *Friction* is a force that causes moving objects to slow down. Less friction allows water to flow more easily through the rock layer, as shown in **Figure 2**.

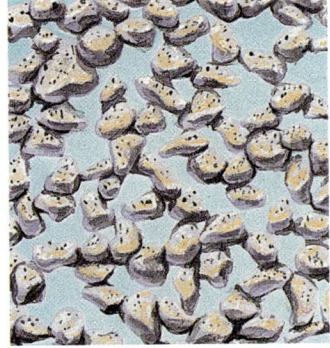

aquifer a body of rock or sediment that stores groundwater and allows the flow of groundwater

porosity the percentage of the total volume of a rock or sediment that consists of open spaces

permeability the ability of a rock or sediment to let fluids pass through its open spaces, or pores

INTERNET ACTIVITY

For another activity related to this chapter, go to **go.hrw.com** and type in the keyword **HZ5DEPW**.

Figure 2 Large particles, shown at left, have less total surface area—and so cause less friction—than small particles, shown at right, do.

Teach

CONNECTION ACTIVITY
Real World — ADVANCED

Investigating Your Area Groundwater is a source of drinking water for about 60% of the population of the United States. Encourage students to find out where their drinking water comes from. Students can do research in local newspapers to learn about issues affecting the quality of their drinking water and can prepare a poster illustrating the path that local groundwater follows from a rain cloud to a faucet. If there is time, arrange for a tour of a local water treatment plant. **LS Verbal**

Group ACTIVITY — GENERAL

Labeling Storm Drains Many people do not realize that storm drains often drain directly into local waterways. Many conservation groups and city corps of engineers have programs that can help your class label storm drains in your community. Invite a speaker from your city's corps of engineers to come speak to the class about city planning for channeling runoff, protecting groundwater, and preventing flooding. **LS Verbal**

Cultural Awareness — ADVANCED

Mayan Rain Myths The Maya, one of the early civilizations of the Americas, believed that rain clouds formed in caves and then rose to the sky. Elaborate ceremonies were performed in caves for the rain god. Have interested students find out more about how caves and water were important to early Mesoamerican civilizations. **LS Verbal**

WEIRD SCIENCE

Recently scientists have discovered that much fresh water flows into the oceans from groundwater. When the tide comes in, sea water seeps into the sediments of coastal land, mixes with the groundwater, and then is drawn out when the tide recedes. Many freshwater aquifers also drain directly into the ocean. These findings are significant because they suggest that groundwater pollution can affect the oceans.

Section 3 • Water Underground

Teach, continued

MISCONCEPTION ALERT

Water Pockets? Students may think that groundwater creates vast underground lakes or rivers. This rarely happens. Most groundwater is stored in spaces in rock and soil similar to the way water is stored in a sponge.

BRAIN FOOD

The Great Artesian Basin
Much of Australia's groundwater is stored in artesian formations that are fed by a vast underground aquifer called the Great Artesian Basin. Unfortunately, most of the water is too salty for people to drink or use for irrigation. Have students find out how this water could be processed in a desalination plant.

Answer to Reading Check
The size of the recharge zone depends on how permeable rock is at the surface.

Figure 3 This map shows aquifers in the United States (excluding Alaska and Hawaii).

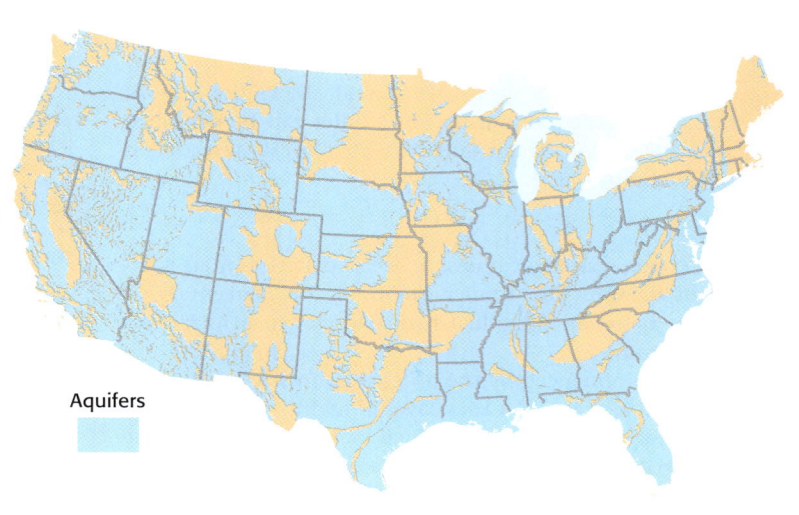

Aquifers

recharge zone an area in which water travels downward to become part of an aquifer

SCHOOL to HOME

Water Conservation
Did you know that water use in the United States has been reduced by 15% in the last 20 years? This decrease is due in part to the conservation efforts of people like you. Work with a parent to create a water budget for your household. Figure out how much water your family uses every day. Identify ways to reduce your water use, and then set a goal to limit your water use over the course of a week.

ACTIVITY

Aquifer Geology and Geography

The best aquifers usually form in permeable materials, such as sandstone, limestone, or layers of sand and gravel. Some aquifers cover large underground areas and are an important source of water for cities and agriculture. The map in **Figure 3** shows the location of the major aquifers in the United States.

Recharge Zones

Like rivers, aquifers depend on the water cycle to maintain a constant flow of water. The ground surface where water enters an aquifer is called the **recharge zone.** The size of the recharge zone depends on how permeable rock is at the surface. If the surface rock is permeable, water can seep down into the aquifer. If the aquifer is covered by an impermeable rock layer, water cannot reach the aquifer. Construction of buildings on top of the recharge zone can also limit the amount of water that enters an aquifer.

✓ **Reading Check** What factors affect the size of the recharge zone?

Springs and Wells

Groundwater movement is determined by the slope of the water table. Like surface water, groundwater tends to move downslope, toward lower elevations. If the water table reaches the Earth's surface, water will flow out from the ground and will form a *spring*. Springs are an important source of drinking water. In areas where the water table is higher than the Earth's surface, lakes will form.

INCLUSION Strategies

- Attention Deficit Disorder
- English Language Learners
- Learning Disabled

Have students play a card game to help them learn the vocabulary in this section. Organize students into groups of three. Have one student in the group write one vocabulary term on each card. Have another student make cards with one definition per card. Have the third student in the group draw an illustration for each vocabulary term on a card. When students are finished, have them exchange their cards with another group and try to match the term with the definition and illustration.
LS Verbal/Visual Co-op Learning English Language Learners

Chapter 11 • The Flow of Fresh Water

Artesian Springs

A sloping layer of permeable rock sandwiched between two layers of impermeable rock is called an *artesian formation*. The permeable rock is an aquifer, and the top layer of impermeable rock is called a *cap rock*, as shown in **Figure 4**. Artesian formations are the source of water for artesian springs. An **artesian spring** is a spring whose water flows from a crack in the cap rock of the aquifer. Artesian springs are sometimes found in deserts, where they are often the only source of water.

Most springs have cool water. However, some springs have hot water. The water becomes hot when it flows deep in the Earth, because Earth's temperature increases with depth. The temperature of some hot springs can reach 50°C!

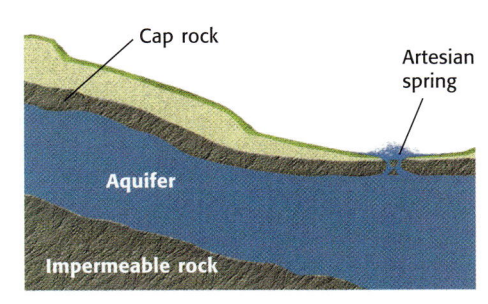

Figure 4 Artesian springs form when water from an aquifer flows through cracks in the cap rock of an artesian formation.

Wells

A human-made hole that is deeper than the level of the water table is called a *well*. If a well is not deep enough, as shown in **Figure 5**, it will dry up when the water table falls below the bottom of the well. Also, if an area has too many wells, groundwater can be removed too rapidly. If groundwater is removed too rapidly, the water table will drop, and all of the wells will run dry.

Reading Check How deep must a well be to reach water?

artesian spring a spring whose water flows from a crack in the cap rock over the aquifer

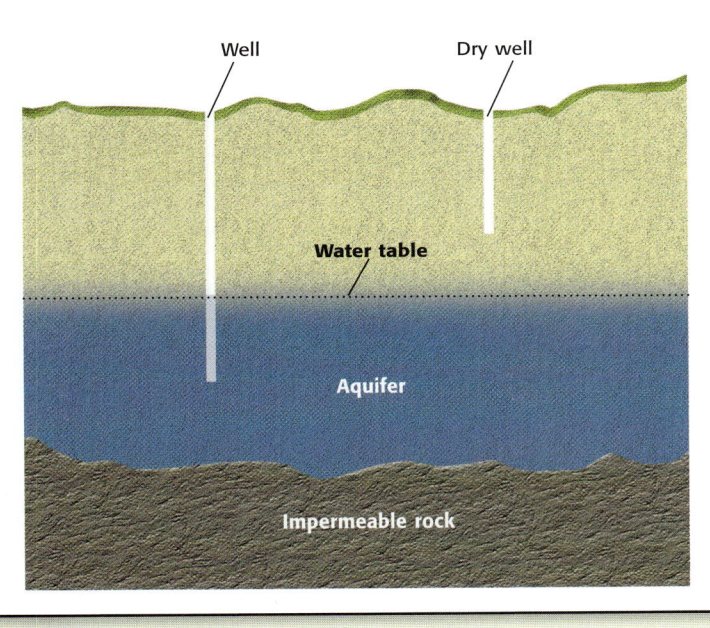

Figure 5 A well must be drilled deep enough so that when the water table drops, the well still contains water.

CONNECTION to Life Science — GENERAL

Life in the Desert Elephants that live in the desert of Namibia may travel four days to find a water hole. Once there, they might have to dig a meter into the sand to reach water. Antelopes, such as springbok and eland, and other desert animals depend on the elephants to penetrate the water table. Have students research ways in which desert plants and animals have adapted to regions that have little surface water. **LS Verbal**

Using the Figure — ADVANCED

Wells and Artesian Springs Guide students through **Figure 4**. List the labels on the board, and help students define each term. Explain that artesian springs are driven by hydraulic pressure. Artesian springs are found in areas where the water table is above the outlet for the spring. If students have ever siphoned a liquid, they have applied the principle that causes artesian springs to flow. Challenge students to demonstrate an artesian spring using a water-filled container and a length of tubing. **LS Visual** **English Language Learners**

Answer to Reading Check
A well must be deeper than the water table for it to be able to reach water.

Is That a Fact!
Geologists estimate that aquifers hold 50 million cubic kilometers of fresh water worldwide. There is about 20 times more water underground than in the atmosphere and in all of the rivers and lakes combined.

Section 3 • Water Underground

Close

Reteaching — BASIC

Spring Model Give students a large piece of floral foam and a plastic container with a lid. Have students soak the foam with water and place it in the container. Tell students to cut a small hole in the plastic lid and cut the edge off the lid so that it fits just inside the container. Then, have students press the lid down onto the foam. Ask students, "What happens?" (Water is forced up through the hole by the pressure from the lid.) **LS Visual/Kinesthetic**

Quiz — GENERAL

1. Define porosity and permeability. (Porosity is the amount of space between rock particles. Permeability is the ability of rock to allow water to flow.)

2. What is a spring? What is a well? (A spring forms where the water table reaches the surface and water flows out. A well is a human construction that extends below the water table.)

Alternative Assessment — GENERAL

Cave Tours Have students research a cave system in the United States. Then, help students construct a virtual cave. Have them create models of the cave's formations using modeling clay. Students can also make an audio tape tour of the cave that tells visitors about the cave's features and how the features formed. **LS Kinesthetic**

CONNECTION TO Environmental Science

Bat Environmentalists Most bat species live in caves. Bats are night-flying mammals that play an important role in the environment. Bats eat vast quantities of insects. Many bat species also pollinate plants and distribute seeds? Can you think of other animals that eat insects, pollinate plants, and distribute seeds? Create a poster that includes pictures of these other animals.

ACTIVITY

Figure 6 At Carlsbad Caverns in New Mexico, underground passages and enormous "rooms" have been eroded below the surface of the Earth.

Underground Erosion and Deposition

As you have learned, rivers cause erosion when water removes and transports rock and soil from its banks. Groundwater can also cause erosion. However, groundwater causes erosion by dissolving rock. Some groundwater contains weak acids, such as carbonic acid, that dissolve the rock. Also, some types of rock, such as limestone, dissolve in groundwater more easily than other types do.

When underground erosion happens, caves can form. Most of the world's caves formed over thousands of years as groundwater dissolved the limestone of the cave sites. Some caves, such as the one shown in **Figure 6,** reach spectacular proportions.

Cave Formations

Although caves are formed by erosion, they also show signs of deposition. Water that drips from a crack in a cave's ceiling leaves behind deposits of calcium carbonate. Sharp, icicle-shaped features that form on cave ceilings are known as *stalactites* (stuh LAK tiets). Water that falls to the cave's floor adds to cone-shaped features known as *stalagmites* (stuh LAG MIETS). If water drips long enough, the stalactites and stalagmites join to form a *dripstone column*.

✓ **Reading Check** What process causes the formation of stalactites and stalagmites?

Answer to Reading Check
Deposition is the process that causes the formation of stalactites and stalagmites.

Chapter 11 • The Flow of Fresh Water

Sinkholes

When the water table is lower than the level of a cave, the cave is no longer supported by the water underneath. The roof of the cave can then collapse, which leaves a circular depression called a *sinkhole*. Surface streams can "disappear" into sinkholes and then flow through underground caves. Sinkholes often form lakes in areas where the water table is high. Central Florida is covered with hundreds of round sinkhole lakes. **Figure 7** shows how the collapse of an underground cave can affect a landscape.

Figure 7 *The damage to this city block shows the effects of a sinkhole in Winter Park, Florida.*

SECTION Review

Summary

- The water table is the boundary between the zone of aeration and the zone of saturation.
- Porosity and permeability describe an aquifer's ability to hold water and ability to allow water to flow through.
- Springs are a natural way that water reaches the surface. Wells are made by humans.
- Caves and sinkholes form from the erosion of limestone by groundwater.

Using Key Terms

1. Use the following terms in the same sentence: *water table, aquifer, porosity,* and *artesian spring.*

Understanding Key Ideas

2. Which of the following describes an aquifer's ability to allow water to flow through?
   a. porosity
   b. permeability
   c. geology
   d. recharge zone

3. What is the water table?

4. Describe how particles affect the porosity of an aquifer.

5. Explain the difference between an artesian spring and other springs.

6. Name a feature that is formed by underground erosion.

7. Name two features that are formed by underground deposition.

8. What type of weathering process causes underground erosion?

Math Skills

9. Groundwater in an area flows at a speed of 4 km/h. How long would it take the water to flow 10 km to its spring?

Critical Thinking

10. **Predicting Consequences** Explain how urban growth might affect the recharge zone of an aquifer.

11. **Making Comparisons** Explain the difference between a spring and a well.

12. **Analyzing Relationships** What is the relationship between the zone of aeration, the zone of saturation, and the water table?

SciLinks
Topic: Water Underground
SciLinks code: HSM1633

Answers to Section Review

1. Sample answer: Depending on the porosity of the ground and the level of the water table, groundwater can exist in formations such as aquifers or artesian springs.
2. b
3. A water table is the upper surface of the zone of saturation.
4. Answers may vary. A rock layer that contains different-sized particles has less open space between particles and is less porous than a rock layer that contains same-sized particles.
5. Answers may vary. An artesian spring occurs if water flows upward through the cap rock and flows out at the surface. Other springs do not have a layer of cap rock.
6. Caves form by underground erosion.
7. Stalagmites, stalactites, and dripstone columns form by underground deposition.
8. Groundwater causes erosion by dissolving rock.
9. 10 km ÷ 4 km/h = 2.5 h
10. Answers may vary. Surface water in a watershed enters the ground in the recharge zone. A parking lot is an impermeable surface layer, so it could reduce or prevent the flow of water into the recharge zone.
11. Answers may vary. A spring is a place where the water table reaches the surface. A well is a human-made hole dug deeper than the level of the water table.
12. Sample answer: The zone of aeration is above the water table. The zone of saturation is below the water table, and the spaces between the rocks are filled with water.

CHAPTER RESOURCES

Chapter Resource File

- Section Quiz GENERAL
- Section Review GENERAL
- Vocabulary and Section Summary GENERAL
- Reinforcement Worksheet BASIC
- Critical Thinking ADVANCED
- SciLinks Activity GENERAL

SECTION 4

Focus

Overview
This section discusses water pollution, overuse, and treatment. Students will learn about the difference between point-source and nonpoint-source pollution and explore different methods for treating polluted water. The section discusses trends in domestic, industrial, and agricultural water use and conservation.

🔔 Bellringer
Write the following scenario on the board or overhead projector: "While hiking, you realize your canteen is almost empty." Then ask, "Why should you not fill the canteen with water from the nearby stream?" (Even though the water may look clean, it might contain pollutants or bacteria.)

Motivate

Discussion — GENERAL
Watching Water Use Ask students to list ways that people use water. Write the responses on the board. Ask students to track the amount of water they use during the week. Have them use this number to estimate how much water they will use in their lifetime. **LS Verbal**

SECTION 4

READING WARM-UP

Objectives
- Identify two forms of water pollution.
- Explain how the properties of water influence the health of a water system.
- Describe two ways that wastewater can be treated.
- Describe how water is used and how water can be conserved in industry, in agriculture, and at home.

Terms to Learn
point-source pollution
nonpoint-source pollution
sewage treatment plant
septic tank

READING STRATEGY

Paired Summarizing Read this section silently. In pairs, take turns summarizing the material. Stop to discuss ideas that seem confusing.

point-source pollution pollution that comes from a specific site

nonpoint-source pollution pollution that comes from many sources rather than from a single, specific site

Figure 1 The runoff from this irrigation system could collect pesticides and other pollutants. The result would be nonpoint-source pollution.

Using Water Wisely

Did you know that you are almost 65% water? You depend on clean, fresh drinking water to maintain that 65% of you. But there is a limited amount of fresh water available on Earth. Only 3% of Earth's water is drinkable.

And of the 3% of Earth's water that is drinkable, 75% is frozen in the polar icecaps. This frozen water is not readily available for our use. Therefore, it is important that we protect our water resources.

Water Pollution
Surface water, such as the water in rivers and lakes, and groundwater can be polluted by waste from cities, factories, and farms. Pollution is the introduction of harmful substances into the environment. Water can become so polluted that it can no longer be used or can even be deadly.

Point-Source and Nonpoint-Source Pollution
Pollution that comes from one specific site is called **point-source pollution**. For example, a leak from a sewer pipe is point-source pollution. In most cases, this type of pollution can be controlled because its source can be identified.

Nonpoint-source pollution, another type of pollution, is pollution that comes from many sources. This type of pollution is much more difficult to control because it does not come from a single source. Most nonpoint-source pollution reaches bodies of water by runoff. The main sources of nonpoint-source pollution are street gutters, fertilizers, eroded soils and silt from farming and logging, drainage from mines, and salts from irrigation. **Figure 1** shows an example of a source of nonpoint-source pollution.

✓ **Reading Check** What type of pollution is the hardest to control? (See the Appendix for answers to Reading Checks.)

CHAPTER RESOURCES

Chapter Resource File
- Lesson Plan
- Directed Reading A BASIC
- Directed Reading B SPECIAL NEEDS

Technology
- Transparencies
  - Bellringer

Answer to Reading Check
Nonpoint-source pollution is hardest to control.

---

326 Chapter 11 • The Flow of Fresh Water

Figure 2 Waste from farm animals can seep into groundwater and cause nitrate pollution.

Health of a Water System

You might not realize it, but water quality affects your quality of life as well as other organisms that depend on water. Therefore, it is important to understand how the properties of water influence water quality.

Dissolved Oxygen

Just as you need oxygen to live, so do fish and other organisms that live in lakes and streams. The oxygen dissolved in water is called *dissolved oxygen,* or DO. Levels of DO that are below 4.0 mg/L in fresh water can cause stress and possibly death for organisms in the water.

Pollutants such as sewage, fertilizer runoff, and animal waste can decrease DO levels. Temperature changes also affect DO levels. For example, cold water holds more oxygen than warm water does. Facilities such as nuclear power plants can increase the temperature of lakes and rivers when they use the water as a cooling agent. Such an increase in water temperature is called *thermal pollution,* which causes a decrease in DO levels.

Nitrates

Nitrates are naturally occurring compounds of nitrogen and oxygen. Small amounts of nitrates in water are normal. However, elevated nitrate levels in water can be harmful to organisms. An excess of nitrates in lakes and rivers can also lower DO levels. As shown in **Figure 2,** nitrate pollution can come from animal wastes or fertilizers that seep into groundwater.

Alkalinity

Alkalinity refers to the water's ability to neutralize acid. Acid rain and other acid wastes can harm aquatic life. A pH below 6.0 is too acidic for most aquatic life. Water with a higher alkalinity can better protect organisms from acid.

Quick Lab

Measuring Alkalinity

1. Identify two water sources from which to collect water samples.
2. Fill a **plastic cup** with water from one source. Fill a **second plastic cup** with water from the second source. Label each cup with its source.
3. Using a **pH test kit,** test the pH of each sample.
4. Follow the instructions in the test kit, and determine the pH of each of the two samples. Record your observations.
5. What did the results for the two samples indicate about the two sources?
6. Use **water test kits** to measure DO and nitrate levels in the two water samples, and discuss your results.

Homework — GENERAL

Presentation Have students research sources of nonpoint-source pollution. Ask them to make posters for a community action campaign to reduce nonpoint-source pollution. Display students' posters in the classroom or around the school.
LS Visual/Kinesthetic

Is That a Fact!

According to a 1998 U.S. Geological Survey report, water use in the United States has decreased 2% since 1990 and almost 10% since 1980, despite an increase in population. The report attributes this to public awareness and conservation efforts.

Teach

Cultural Awareness — ADVANCED

Sharing Our Resources Encourage students to use library or Internet resources to investigate traditional American Indian beliefs about the Earth, including rivers. Students may also be interested to find out about controversies involving American Indian tribes and the use of water resources, such as salmon fisheries in Alaska. Ask students to write a brief report summarizing their findings. **LS** Verbal

Quick Lab

MATERIALS

FOR EACH GROUP
- cups, plastic (2)
- pH test kit
- water, samples (2)

Teacher's Note: Cover the work area with plastic, and have students wear lab aprons and plastic gloves.

Low pH could indicate to students that the rainwater is polluted with acid precipitation. A very high pH would indicate a high mineral content in the water. **LS** Visual/Kinesthetic

MISCONCEPTION ALERT

A Drop in the Ocean Students may think that they cannot do anything to conserve water and prevent pollution. Point out to students that there are many things they can do to conserve water. Tell students that by changing a few habits, they can greatly reduce their water consumption and reduce water pollution.

Section 4 • Using Water Wisely

Teach, continued

Group Activity — Advanced

Putting Pollution in its Place
Organize the class into small groups, and challenge each group to create a board game. Tell students that the object of the game is to be the first player to successfully travel through a sewage treatment plant. Provide each group with poster board, plain index cards, and markers. Direct them to create a game board that leads players through the plant and incorporates the concepts they have learned in this section. On the index cards, have them write clues and questions directing players' movements through the sewage treatment process. For example, they might write, "If you can define primary treatment, advance to the aeration tank." Have students create written rules, and allow time for the game to be played. **LS Visual/Kinesthetic**

Cleaning Polluted Water

When you flush the toilet or watch water go down the shower drain, do you ever wonder where the water goes? If you live in a city or large town, the water flows through sewer pipes to a sewage treatment plant. **Sewage treatment plants** are facilities that clean the waste materials out of water. These plants help protect the environment from water pollution. They also protect us from diseases that are easily transmitted through dirty water.

sewage treatment plant a facility that cleans the waste materials found in water that comes from sewers or drains

Primary Treatment

When water reaches a sewage treatment plant, it is cleaned in two ways. First, it goes through a series of steps known as *primary treatment*. In primary treatment, dirty water is passed through a large screen to catch solid objects, such as paper, rags, and bottle caps. The water is then placed in a large tank, where smaller particles, or sludge, can sink and be filtered out. These particles include things such as food, coffee grounds, and soil. Any floating oils and scum are skimmed off the surface.

Secondary Treatment

After undergoing primary treatment, the water is ready for *secondary treatment*. In secondary treatment, the water is sent to an aeration tank, where it is mixed with oxygen and bacteria. The bacteria feed on the wastes and use the oxygen. The water is then sent to another settling tank, where chlorine is added to disinfect the water. The water is finally released into a water source—a river, a lake, or the ocean. **Figure 3** shows the major components of a sewage treatment plant.

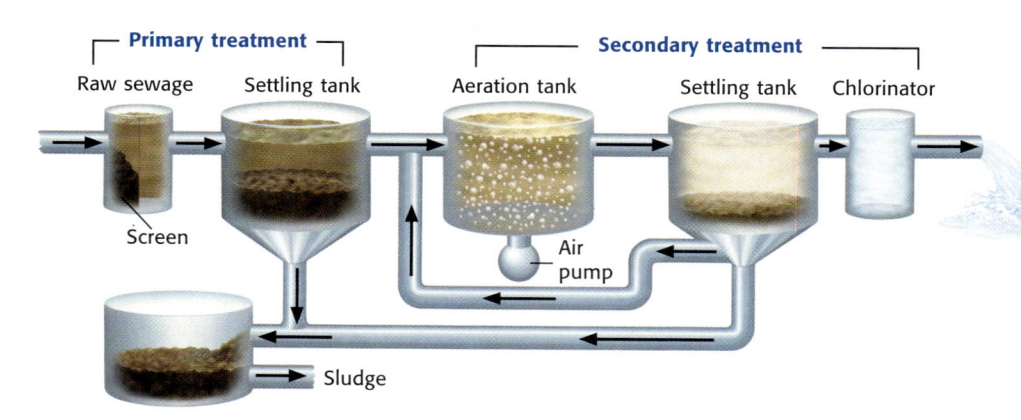

Figure 3 If you live in a city, the water used in your home most likely ends up at a sewage treatment plant, where the water is cleaned.

Primary treatment: Raw sewage — Screen — Settling tank — Sludge
Secondary treatment: Aeration tank — Air pump — Settling tank — Chlorinator

---

MISCONCEPTION ALERT

Waterborne Disease in North America
Most people in the United States and many students may think that waterborne diseases are a problem only in developing countries. But despite elaborate wastewater purification systems, outbreaks still occur. In 1993, the same year in which the *Cryptosporidium* outbreak affected 400,000 people in Milwaukee, a similar outbreak occurred in Round Rock, Texas. In 1993 and 1994, an epidemic of another, deadlier waterborne illness—cholera—swept through Latin America as far north as northern Mexico. The epidemic raised fears that the United States could eventually be affected.

---

328 Chapter 11 • The Flow of Fresh Water

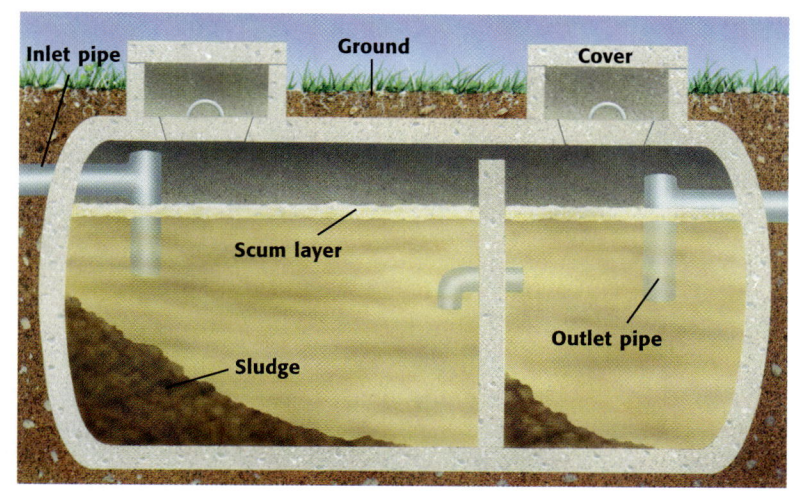

Figure 4 Most septic tanks must be cleaned out every few years in order to work properly.

Another Way to Clean Wastewater

If you live in an area that does not have a sewage treatment plant, your house probably uses a septic tank. **Figure 4** shows an example of a septic tank. A **septic tank** is a large underground tank that cleans the wastewater from a household. Wastewater flows from the house into the tank, where the solids sink to the bottom. Bacteria break down these wastes on the bottom of the tank. The water flows from the tank into a group of buried pipes. Then, the buried pipes, called a *drain field*, distribute the water. Distributing the water enables the water to soak into the ground.

septic tank a tank that separates solid waste from liquids and that has bacteria that break down the solid waste

Where the Water Goes

Think of some ways that you use water in your home. Do you water the lawn? Do you do the dishes? The graph in **Figure 5** shows how an average household in the United States uses water. Notice that less than 8% of the water we use in our homes is used for drinking. The rest is used for flushing toilets, doing laundry, bathing, and watering lawns and plants.

The water we use in our homes is not the only way water is used. More water is used in industry and agriculture than in homes.

Reading Check What percentage of water in our homes is used for drinking?

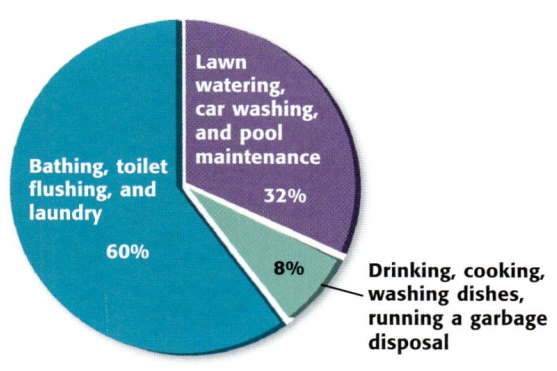

- Lawn watering, car washing, and pool maintenance 32%
- Bathing, toilet flushing, and laundry 60%
- Drinking, cooking, washing dishes, running a garbage disposal 8%

Figure 5 The average household in the United States uses about 100 gal of water per day. This pie graph shows some common uses of these 100 gal.

CONNECTION ACTIVITY
Math — GENERAL

Flushing Conservation Low-flush toilets use about 6 L of water per flush. Standard toilets use 19 L of water per flush. How much water is saved in a week by replacing a standard toilet with a low-flush toilet? Assume the toilet is flushed 10 times per day. (19 L − 6 L = 13 L; 13 L × 10 flushes/day × 7 days = 910 L/week)

How much water would be saved in a year? (910 L/week × 52 weeks/year = 47,320 L/year)
LS Logical

Debate — GENERAL

Should Water Conservation Be Enforced? Point out to students that many communities are enacting mandatory water conservation measures. For example, Albuquerque, New Mexico, has adopted a water-conservation policy in an effort to reduce per capita water use by 30%. However, some people are opposed to government regulation of water use. Divide the class into two groups, and assign each group a position in the debate. Have students use library or Internet resources to research their position. Then have students debate their positions in class. **LS** Verbal/Logical

---

Answer to Reading Check

Less than 8% of water in our homes is used for drinking.

Close

Reteaching — BASIC
Saving Water at Home Have students brainstorm ways they can conserve water at home. Consolidate students' lists on the board. The list may include the following: I will be sure the dishwasher is full before it is used. If I'm washing dishes in the sink, I won't let the water run continuously. I'll turn off the water while I brush my teeth. I won't do several small loads of laundry if I can do fewer large loads instead. **LS** Verbal

Quiz — GENERAL
1. What are two sources of nonpoint-source pollution? (Sample answer: street gutters, fertilizers, eroded soils and silt from farming and logging, drainage from mines)
2. Which states get some of their groundwater from the Ogallala Aquifer? (South Dakota, Wyoming, Colorado, New Mexico, Oklahoma, Texas, Nebraska, and Kansas)

Alternative Assessment — GENERAL
Pollution Posters
Provide students with poster board and markers. Direct them to create posters illustrating how nonpoint-source pollution can cause contamination of both surface water and ground water. Their diagrams should reflect the understanding that pollution of surface water can spread to groundwater. **English Language Learners** **LS** Verbal

MATH PRACTICE
Agriculture in Israel
From 1950 to 1980, Israel reduced the amount of water used in agriculture from 83% to 5%. Israel did so primarily by switching from overhead sprinklers to drip irrigation. A small farm uses 10,000 L of water per day for overhead sprinkler irrigation. How much water would the farm save in 1 year by using a drip irrigation system that uses 75% less water than a sprinkler system?

Group Activity — GENERAL
A Call for Conservation Divide the class into small groups. Challenge each group to write a public-service announcement to educate the public about the need to conserve water and to avoid polluting groundwater. The announcements should include definitions of point-source and nonpoint-source pollution and outline practical steps that everyone can take to protect water resources. **English Language Learners** **LS** Verbal

Water in Industry
About 19% of water used in the world is used for industrial purposes. Water is used to manufacture goods, cool power stations, clean industrial products, extract minerals, and generate energy for factories.

Because water resources have become expensive, many industries are trying to conserve, or use less, water. One way industries conserve water is by recycling it. In the United States, most of the water used in factories is recycled at least once. At least 90% of this recycled water can be treated and returned to surface water.

Water in Agriculture
The Ogallala aquifer is the largest known aquifer in North America. The map in **Figure 6** shows that the Ogallala aquifer runs beneath the ground through eight states, from South Dakota to Texas. The Ogallala aquifer provides water for approximately one-fifth of the cropland in the United States. Farming is the largest user of water in the Western United States. Recently, the water table in the aquifer has dropped so low that some scientists say that it would take at least 1,000 years to replenish the aquifer if it were no longer used.

Most of the water that is lost during farming is lost through evaporation and runoff. New technology, such as drip irrigation systems, has helped conserve water in agriculture. A drip irrigation system delivers small amounts of water directly to plant roots. This system allows plants to absorb the water before the water has a chance to evaporate or become runoff.

✓ **Reading Check** How does the drip irrigation system help conserve water?

Figure 6 Because the Ogallala aquifer has been such a good source of groundwater, it has become overused. The water table has dropped more than 30 m in some areas.

Answer to Reading Check
Drip irrigation systems deliver small amounts of water directly to the roots of the plant so that the plant absorbs the water before it can evaporate or run off.

Conserving Water at Home

There are many ways that people can conserve water at home. For example, many people save water by installing low-flow shower heads and low-flush toilets, because these items use much less water. To avoid watering lawns, some people plant only native plants in their yards. Native plants grow well in the local climate and don't need extra watering.

Your behavior can also help you conserve water. For example, you can take shorter showers. You can avoid running the water while brushing your teeth. And when you run the dishwasher, make sure it is full, as shown in **Figure 7**.

Reading Check List ways in which you can conserve water in your home.

Figure 7 Run the dishwasher only when it is full.

SECTION Review

Summary

- Point-source pollution and nonpoint-source pollution are two kinds of water pollution.
- Pollutants can decrease oxygen levels and increase nitrate levels in water. These changes can cause harm to plants, animals, and humans.
- Wastewater can be treated by sewage treatment plants and septic systems.
- Water can be conserved by using only the water that is needed, by recycling water, and by using drip irrigation systems.

Using Key Terms

1. Use each of the following terms in a separate sentence: *point-source pollution, nonpoint-source pollution, sewage treatment plant,* and *septic tank*.

Understanding Key Ideas

2. Which of the following can help protect fish from acid rain?
   a. dissolved oxygen
   b. nitrates
   c. alkalinity
   d. point-source pollution

3. What type of wastewater treatment can be used for an individual home?
   a. sewage treatment plant
   b. primary treatment
   c. secondary treatment
   d. septic tank

4. Which kind of water pollution is often caused by runoff of fertilizers?

5. Describe what DO is.

6. What factors affect the level of dissolved oxygen in water?

7. Describe how water is conserved in industry.

Math Skills

8. If 25% of water used in your home is used to water the lawn and you used a total of 95 gal of water today, how many gallons of water did you use to water the lawn?

Critical Thinking

9. **Making Inferences** How do bacteria help break down the waste in water treatment plants?

10. **Applying Concepts** Other than examples listed in this section, what are some ways you can conserve water?

11. **Making Inferences** Why is it better to water your lawn at night instead of during the day?

SciLinks — Developed and maintained by the National Science Teachers Association

For a variety of links related to this chapter, go to **www.scilinks.org**
Topic: Water Pollution and Conservation
SciLinks code: HSM1630

Answers to Review

1. Sample answers: Point-source pollution comes from a single source. Nonpoint-source pollution is difficult to control. Sewage treatment plants clean waste materials out of water. It is important to properly maintain a septic tank.
2. c
3. d
4. nitrates
5. DO is the amount of dissolved oxygen in water.
6. Temperature, nitrates, and other pollutants are factors that can affect DO.
7. Sample answer: Many industries have begun recycling water to conserve it.
8. 95 gal × 0.25 = 23.75 gal
9. Answers may vary. Students should mention that bacteria feed on the wastes during secondary treatment.
10. Sample answer: repairing dripping faucets and collecting rain water for use in watering plants
11. Answers may vary. Students should mention that less water is lost to evaporation at night than is lost during the day.

Answer to Reading Check

Answers may vary. Sample answer: taking shorter showers, avoiding running water while brushing your teeth, and using the dishwasher only when it is full

CHAPTER RESOURCES

Chapter Resource File
- Section Quiz GENERAL
- Section Review GENERAL
- Vocabulary and Section Summary GENERAL
- Datasheet for Quick Lab

Technology
- Interactive Explorations CD-ROM
  - Flood Bank GENERAL

Workbook
- Math Skills for Science
  - Multiplying Whole Numbers

Section 4 • Using Water Wisely

Model-Making Lab

Water Cycle— What Goes Up . . .

Teacher's Notes

Time Required
One 45-minute class period

Lab Ratings
EASY ———— HARD

Teacher Prep
Student Set-Up
Concept Level
Clean Up

MATERIALS
The materials listed on the student page are enough for a group of 4 or 5 students.

Safety Caution
Remind students to review all safety cautions and icons before beginning this lab activity. Students should be cautioned when using a hot plate. Care should also be exercised in using the glassware. Appropriate methods should be used to dispose of broken glass.

Model-Making Lab

OBJECTIVES

Design a model that follows the same processes as those of the water cycle.

Identify each stage of the water cycle in the model.

MATERIALS
- beaker
- gloves, heat-resistant
- graduated cylinder
- hot plate
- plate, glass, or watch glass
- tap water, 50 mL
- tongs or forceps

SAFETY

Water Cycle—What Goes Up . . .

Why does a bathroom mirror fog up? Where does water go when it dries up? Where does rain come from? These questions relate to the major parts of the water cycle—condensation, evaporation, and precipitation. In this activity, you will make a model of the water cycle.

Procedure

1. Use the graduated cylinder to pour 50 mL of water into the beaker. Note the water level in the beaker.

2. Put on your safety goggles and gloves. Place the beaker securely on the hot plate. Turn the heat to medium, and bring the water to a boil.

3. While waiting for the water to boil, practice picking up and handling the glass plate or watch glass with the tongs. Hold the glass plate a few centimeters above the beaker, and tilt it so that the lowest edge of the glass is still above the beaker.

4. Observe the glass plate as the water in the beaker boils. Record the changes you see in the beaker, in the air above the beaker, and on the glass plate held over the beaker. Write down any changes you see in the water.

CLASSROOM TESTED & APPROVED

Norman Holcomb
Marion Local Schools
Maria Stein, Ohio

CHAPTER RESOURCES

Chapter Resource File
- Datasheet for Chapter Lab
- Lab Notes and Answers

Technology
- Classroom Videos
  - Lab Video

LabBook
- Clean Up Your Act

5. Continue until you have observed steam rising off the water, the glass plate becoming foggy, and water dripping from the glass plate.

6. Carefully set the glass plate on a counter or other safe surface as directed by your teacher.

7. Turn off the hot plate, and allow the beaker to cool. Move the hot beaker with gloves or tongs if you are directed to do so by your teacher.

Analyze the Results

1. **Constructing Charts** Copy the illustration shown above. On your sketch, draw and label the water cycle as it happened in your model. Include arrows and labels for *evaporation, condensation,* and *precipitation*.

2. **Analyzing Results** Compare the water level in the beaker now with the water level at the beginning of the experiment. Was there a change? Explain why or why not.

Draw Conclusions

3. **Making Predictions** If you had used a scale or a balance to measure the mass of the water in the beaker before and after this activity, would the mass have changed? Explain.

4. **Analyzing Charts** How is your model similar to the Earth's water cycle? On your sketch of the illustration, label where the processes shown in the model reflect the Earth's water cycle.

5. **Drawing Conclusions** When you finished this experiment, the water in the beaker was still hot. What stores much of the energy in the Earth's water cycle?

Applying Your Data

As rainwater runs over the land, the water picks up minerals and salts. Do these minerals and salts evaporate, condense, and precipitate as part of the water cycle? Where do they go?

CHAPTER RESOURCES
Workbooks

- **EcoLabs & Field Activities**
  - The Frogs Are Off Course **ADVANCED**
- **Long-Term Projects & Research Ideas**
  - Canyon Controversy **ADVANCED**

Students' sketches should resemble the water cycle illustrated here:

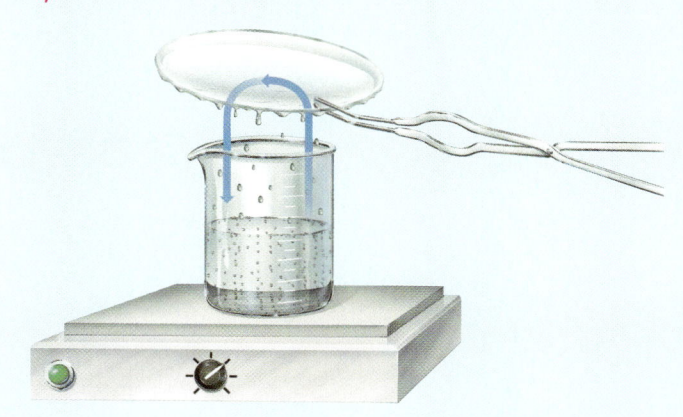

Analyze the Results

1. Sketches should resemble the illustration of the water cycle at the bottom of this page. Students should include labels for condensation, evaporation, and precipitation.

2. Sample answer: The water level is lower at the end of the experiment because some of the water evaporated.

Draw Conclusions

3. Sample answer: The mass would have changed slightly. Because some of the steam escaped, the mass of the water in the beaker would decrease.

4. Sample answer: The model is similar to the Earth's water cycle because evaporation, condensation, and precipitation occurred. Accept all reasonable depictions of the water cycle.

5. Sample answer: Much of the energy in the water cycle is stored in bodies of water, such as the oceans. Thermal energy is also stored in the atmosphere and the Earth's land surface.

Applying Your Data

No, minerals and salts are not part of the water cycle. As water evaporates, minerals and salts are left behind as deposits.

Chapter 11 • Chapter Lab

Chapter Review

Assignment Guide

Section	Questions
1	1, 4, 7–8, 18, 21–24
2	2, 9
3	3, 5, 10, 13–16
4	6, 11–12, 19–20
1 and 2	17

ANSWERS

Using Key Terms

1. A stream that flows into a lake or into a larger stream is a tributary.
2. The area along a river that forms from sediment deposited when the river overflows is a floodplain.
3. A rock's ability to let water through it is called permeability.
4. Sample answer: A divide is the boundary between two drainage areas. A watershed is a drainage area.
5. Sample answer: An artesian spring is a spring that flows through a natural crack in the cap rock. A well is a human made hole that reaches below the water table.
6. Sample answer: Point-source pollution is pollution that enters the water from a known single source, such as a factory. Nonpoint-source pollution is pollution that comes from many sources, such as a combination of fertilizer and pesticide in groundwater.

Chapter Review

USING KEY TERMS

The statements below are false. For each statement, replace the underlined term to make a true statement.

1. A stream that flows into a lake or into a larger stream is a <u>water cycle</u>.
2. The area along a river that forms from sediment deposited when the river overflows is a <u>delta</u>.
3. A rock's ability to let water pass through it is called <u>porosity</u>.

For each pair of terms, explain how the meanings of the terms differ.

4. *divide* and *watershed*
5. *artesian springs* and *wells*
6. *point-source pollution* and *nonpoint-source pollution*

UNDERSTANDING KEY IDEAS

Multiple Choice

7. Which of the following processes is not part of the water cycle?
   a. evaporation
   b. percolation
   c. condensation
   d. deposition

8. Which features are common in youthful river channels?
   a. meanders
   b. flood plains
   c. rapids
   d. sandbars

9. Which depositional feature is found at the coast?
   a. delta
   b. flood plain
   c. alluvial fan
   d. placer deposit

10. Caves are mainly a product of
    a. erosion by rivers.
    b. river deposition.
    c. water pollution.
    d. erosion by groundwater.

11. Which of the following is necessary for aquatic life to survive?
    a. dissolved oxygen
    b. nitrates
    c. alkalinity
    d. point-source pollution

12. During primary treatment at a sewage treatment plant,
    a. water is sent to an aeration tank.
    b. water is mixed with bacteria and oxygen.
    c. dirty water is passed through a large screen.
    d. water is sent to a settling tank where chlorine is added.

Short Answer

13. Identify and describe the location of the water table.
14. Explain how surface water enters an aquifer.
15. Why are caves usually found in limestone-rich regions?

Understanding Key Ideas

7. d
8. c
9. a
10. d
11. a
12. c
13. A water table is the upper surface of underground water and the upper boundary of the zone of saturation.
14. Aquifers are replenished in the recharge zone. The recharge zone is an area where a permeable rock layer allows water to percolate into the aquifer.
15. Limestone is made of calcium carbonate, which dissolves easily in water. Groundwater dissolves the limestone and produces caves.

334 Chapter 11 • The Flow of Fresh Water

CRITICAL THINKING

16. Concept Mapping Use the following terms to create a concept map: *zone of aeration, zone of saturation, water table, gravity, porosity,* and *permeability*.

17. Identifying Relationships What is water's role in erosion and deposition?

18. Analyzing Processes What are the features of a river channel that has a steep gradient?

19. Analyzing Processes Why is groundwater hard to clean?

20. Evaluating Conclusions How can water be considered both a renewable and a nonrenewable resource? Give an example of each case.

21. Analyzing Processes Does water vapor lose or gain energy during the process of condensation? Explain.

INTERPRETING GRAPHICS

The hydrograph below illustrates data collected on river flow during field investigations over a period of 1 year. The discharge readings are from the Yakima River, in Washington. Use the hydrograph below to answer the questions that follow.

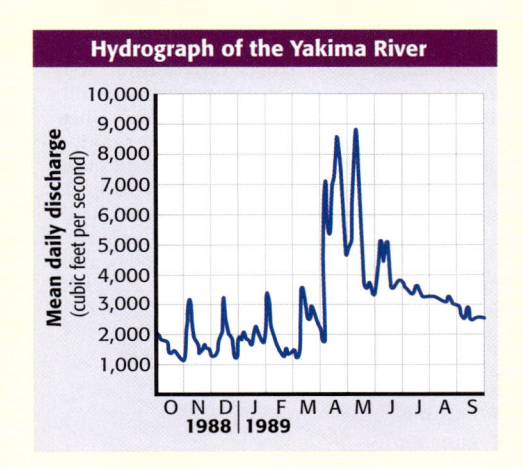

Hydrograph of the Yakima River

(Mean daily discharge in cubic feet per second, from O N D 1988 through J F M A M J J A S 1989; values range from about 1,000 to nearly 9,000, with a peak around April–May.)

22. In which months is there the highest river discharge?

23. Why is there such a high river discharge during these months?

24. What might cause the peaks in river discharge between November and March?

Critical Thinking

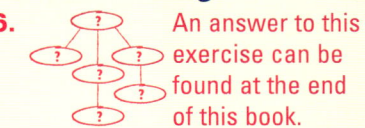

16. An answer to this exercise can be found at the end of this book.

17. Water flows across a landscape, eroding, transporting, and depositing material. Water is an agent of erosion and deposition.

18. A river channel that has a steep gradient is straight and narrow with rapids, waterfalls, and V-shaped valleys.

19. Once groundwater becomes polluted, it is hard to clean because it is not at the surface. Also, it moves very slowly and will therefore take a long time to clean.

20. Water is a renewable resource when it can be replaced or recycled. Rain is a renewable resource. Water is nonrenewable when it is consumed faster than it can be replenished. An example is the Ogallala aquifer.

21. Answers may vary. Students should conclude that water loses energy during the process of condensation. As water cools and condenses it loses heat energy.

Interpreting Graphics

22. April and May

23. Accept all reasonable responses. Sample answer: spring snowmelt from the mountains and high rainfall

24. Accept all reasonable responses. Sample answer: winter storms or thaws

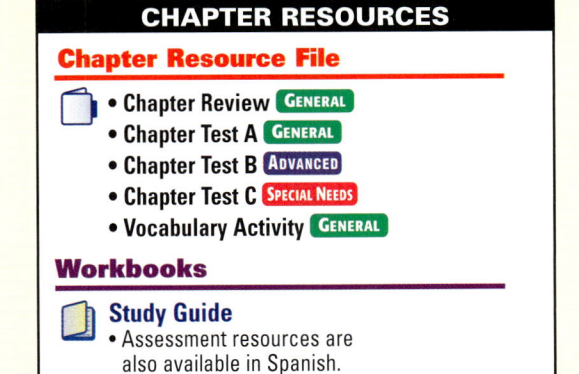

CHAPTER RESOURCES

Chapter Resource File
- Chapter Review GENERAL
- Chapter Test A GENERAL
- Chapter Test B ADVANCED
- Chapter Test C SPECIAL NEEDS
- Vocabulary Activity GENERAL

Workbooks
- Study Guide
  - Assessment resources are also available in Spanish.

Chapter 11 • Chapter Review   335

Standardized Test Preparation

Teacher's Note

To provide practice under more realistic testing conditions, give students 20 minutes to answer all of the questions in this Standardized Test Preparation.

MISCONCEPTION ALERT

Answers to the standardized test preparation can help you identify student misconceptions and misunderstandings.

READING

Passage 1
1. B
2. F
3. B

TEST DOCTOR

Question 3: Students may choose answer A because the text mentions that Old Faithful erupts every 60 to 70 minutes. However, the time in the text is approximate, and the statement in answer A indicates that the eruption takes place every 60 minutes exactly, which is not true.

Standardized Test Preparation

READING

Read each of the passages below. Then, answer the questions that follow each passage.

Passage 1 In parts of Yellowstone National Park, boiling water from deep in the ground blasts into the sky. These blasts of steam come from lakes of strange-colored boiling mud that gurgle and hiss. These features are called geysers. Yellowstone's most popular geyser is named Old Faithful. It is given this name because it erupts every 60 min to 70 min without fail. A geyser is formed when a narrow vent connects one or more underground chambers to Earth's surface. These underground chambers are heated by nearby molten rock. As underground water flows into the vent and chambers, it is heated above 100°C. This superheated water quickly turns to steam and explodes, projecting scalding water 60 m into the air. And Old Faithful erupts right on schedule!

1. In the passage, what does *scalding* mean?
   A muddy
   B burning
   C gurgling
   D steaming

2. According to the passage, what happens to underground water when geysers form?
   F It is heated by molten rock.
   G It is cycled to Earth's center.
   H It travels 60 m through vents.
   I It is poured into volcanoes.

3. Which of the following is a fact in the passage?
   A Old Faithful erupts every 60 min.
   B Old Faithful is located in Yellowstone National Park.
   C There are six geysers at Yellowstone National Park.
   D Molten rock explodes from geysers.

Passage 2 In the Mississippi Delta, long-legged birds step lightly through the marsh and hunt fish or frogs for breakfast. Hundreds of species of plants and animals start another day in this fragile ecosystem. This delta ecosystem is in danger of being destroyed. The threat comes from efforts to make the river more useful. Large portions of the river bottom were dredged to deepen the river for ship traffic. Underwater channels were built to control flooding. What no one realized was that sediments that once formed new land now passed through the channels and flowed out into the ocean. Those river sediments had once replaced the land that was lost every year to erosion. Without them, the river can't replace land lost to erosion. So, the Mississippi River Delta is shrinking. By 1995, more than half of the wetlands were already gone—swept out to sea by waves along the Louisiana coast.

1. In the passage, what does *dredged* mean?
   A moved to the side
   B circulated
   C cleaned
   D scooped up

2. Based on the passage, which of the following statements about the Mississippi River is true?
   F The river never floods.
   G The river is not wide enough for ships.
   H The river's delicate ecosystem is in danger.
   I The river is disappearing.

3. Which of the following is a fact in the passage?
   A By 1995, more than half of the Mississippi River was gone.
   B Underwater channels controlled flooding.
   C Channels help form new land.
   D Sediment cannot replace lost land.

Passage 2
1. D
2. H
3. B

Question 3: Students who do not thoroughly read the passage may choose answer A. They may incorrectly think that half the river system and not the wetlands has been lost.

336 Chapter 11 • The Flow of Fresh Water

INTERPRETING GRAPHICS

The chart below shows four wells drilled at different depths. Use the chart below to answer the questions that follow.

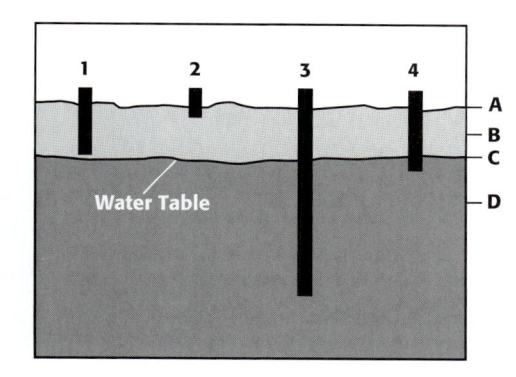

1. A well-drilling company offers the four types of wells shown in the chart. Which well is most likely to be a reliable source of groundwater?
   A 1
   B 2
   C 3
   D 4

2. If the area experienced heavy rains, toward which level would the water table move?
   F The water table would move toward level B.
   G The water table would move toward level D.
   H The water table would stay at level C.
   I The water table will be gone.

3. If the water table moves to level D, which wells will still be able to provide water?
   A all wells
   B wells 1 and 2
   C well 3
   D wells 3 and 4

4. Which well is most likely to be an unreliable source of groundwater?
   F 1
   G 2
   H 3
   I 4

MATH

Read each question below, and choose the best answer.

1. A river flows at a speed of 10 km/h. If a boat travels upstream at a speed of 15 km/h, how far will it travel in 3 h?
   A 10 km
   B 15 km
   C 20 km
   D 25 km

2. Water contamination is often measured in parts per million (ppm). If the concentration of a pollutant is 5 ppm, there are 5 parts of the pollutant in 1 million parts of water. If the concentration of gasoline is 3 ppm in 2,000,000 L of water, how many liters of gasoline are in the water?
   F 3 L
   G 6 L
   H 9 L
   I 10 L

3. One family uses 70 L of water a day for showering. If everyone in the family agreed to shorten his or her shower from 10 min to 5 min, how many liters of water would be saved each day?
   A 5 L
   B 10 L
   C 35 L
   D 70 L

4. A family uses 800 L of water per day. Of those 800 L, 200 L are used for flushing the toilet. Calculate the percentage of water that the family uses to flush the toilet.
   F 25%
   G 30%
   H 50%
   I 60%

5. A river flows at a speed of 8 km/h. If you floated on a raft in this river, how far will you have traveled after 5 h?
   A 5 km
   B 16 km
   C 40 km
   D 80 km

INTERPRETING GRAPHICS

1. C
2. F
3. C
4. G

TEST DOCTOR

Question 2: Students should understand that the water table is the upper surface of the groundwater. When it rains, the ground absorbs more water, and the water level rises, so the water table goes up.

MATH

1. B
2. G
3. C
4. F
5. C

TEST DOCTOR

Question 2: When measuring in parts per million, the units of the solute is the same as the units of the solvent. In this case, the solvent is water, and pollutants are present at 3 ppm in 2,000,000 L of water. So, there are 6 L of pollutant in 2,000,000 L of water.

CHAPTER RESOURCES

Chapter Resource File
- Standardized Test Preparation GENERAL

State Resources
For specific resources for your state, visit go.hrw.com and type in the keyword HSMSTR.

Chapter 11 • Standardized Test Preparation

Science in Action

Weird Science
Discussion — GENERAL

Scientists can learn alot by studying samples of water from Lake Vostok. However, investigating the lake will come with a price: damage to a completely untouched environment. It is currently impossible to avoid contaminating Lake Vostok in the process of gathering samples. Have students debate whether the information gained by studying Lake Vostok is worth the risk of contaminating the lake. **LS Verbal**

Scientific Discoveries
Background

Ankarana is a limestone formation known as karst topography. Karst topography describes a region where the effects of chemical weathering due to groundwater are clearly visible at the surface. Groundwater has carved long, mostly unexplored caves into the rock. There are human bones that date back as far as 750 CE in the caves. Some of these bones belong to Antakarana kings. The Antakarana people consider the caves sacred. They will not enter the caves except to conduct annual ceremonies in honor of the kings.

Science in Action

Weird Science
Secret Lake

Would you believe there is a freshwater lake more than 3 km below an Antarctic glacier near the South Pole? It is surprising that Lake Vostok can remain in a liquid state at a place where the temperature can fall below −50°C. Scientists believe that the intense pressure from the overlying ice heats the lake and keeps it from freezing. Geothermal energy, which is the energy within the surface of the Earth, also contributes to warmer temperatures. The other unique thing about Lake Vostok is the discovery of living microbes under the glacier that covers the lake!

Language Arts ACTIVITY

Look up the word *geothermal* in the dictionary. What is the meaning of the roots *geo-* and *-thermal*? Find other words in the dictionary that begin with the root *geo-*.

Vostok Station
Drilled core (3,623 m down)
Glacial ice
Lake ice
Lake Vostok (at least 500 m deep)
Sediment

Scientific Discoveries
Sunken Forests

Imagine having your own little secret forest. In Ankarana National Park, in Madagascar, there are plenty of them. Within the limestone mountain of the park, caves have formed from the twisting path of the flowing groundwater. In many places in the caves, the roof has collapsed to form a sinkhole. The light that now shines through the collapsed roof of the cave has allowed miniature sunken forests to grow. Each sunken forest has unique characteristics. Some have crocodiles. Others have blind cavefish. You can even find some species that can't be found anywhere else in the world!

Social Studies ACTIVITY

Find out how Madagascar's geography contributes to the biodiversity of the island nation. Make a map of the island that highlights some of the unique forms of life found there.

Answer to Language Arts Activity
The root *geo-* means "earth," and *-thermal* means "heat." Other words that begin with the prefix *geo-* include *geology* and *geometry*. *Geology* is the study of the Earth. *Geometry* literally means "to measure the Earth."

Answer to Social Studies Activity
Answers may vary. Accept any reasonable depiction of Madagascar's biodiversity. Answers should include many species of lemur and a wide variety of flora.

People in Science

Rita Colwell

A Water Filter for All Did you ever drink a glass of water through a piece of cloth? Dr. Rita Colwell, director of the National Science Foundation, has found that filtering drinking water through a cloth can actually decrease the number of disease-causing bacteria in the water. This discovery is very important for the people of Bangladesh, where deadly outbreaks of cholera are frequent. People are usually infected by the cholera bacteria by drinking contaminated water. Colwell knew that filtering the water would remove the bacteria. The water would then be safe to drink. Unfortunately, filters were too expensive for most of the people to buy. Colwell tried filtering the water with a sari. A sari is a long piece of colorful cloth that many women in Bangladesh wear as skirtlike cloth. Filtering the water with the sari cloth did the trick. The amount of cholera bacteria in the water was reduced. Fewer people contracted cholera, and many lives were saved!

Math Activity

With the cloth water-filter method, there was a 48% reduction in the occurrence of cholera. If there were 125 people out of 100,000 who contracted cholera before the cloth-filter method was used, how many people per 100,000 contracted cholera after using the cloth-filter method?

To learn more about these Science in Action topics, visit **go.hrw.com** and type in the keyword **HZ5DEPF**.

Current Science Check out Current Science® articles related to this chapter by visiting go.hrw.com. Just type in the keyword **HZ5CS11**.

People in Science
Teaching Strategy—BASIC

Demonstrate the way Dr. Colwell's cloth-filter method works by filtering a sample of pond water. Remind students not to drink this water, even after filtration. Use a 1 yard square of smooth sari cloth (or other smooth, tightly woven thin cloth). Fasten the cloth over the mouth of a jar with a rubber band. Pour the pond water through the cloth, and then have students examine the water and cloth. Ask them, "Does the water appear to be cleaner? Are filtered sediments visible on the cloth?"

(Answers may vary. The water should appear cleaner. Students should be able to see that the cloth filtered out large particles, such as duckweed or algae.)

Have students make a slide by wiping a cotton swab over the filter cloth to pick up some microorganisms. Allow students to view the sample under a microscope. Ask students, "Did the cloth filter anything that was not visible to the unaided eye?"

(Answers may vary. Students may be able to see microorganisms filtered out by the cloth.)

LS Visual/Kinesthetic

Answer to Math Activity

First students need to find 48% of 125 people.

$0.48 \times 125 = 60$

So, there were 60 fewer people who contracted cholera than before using cloth filters.

$125 - 60 = 65$

Therefore, 65 out of 100,000 people contracted cholera after using the cloth-filter method.

12 Agents of Erosion and Deposition
Chapter Planning Guide

Compression guide: To shorten instruction because of time limitations, omit the Chapter Lab.

OBJECTIVES	LABS, DEMONSTRATIONS, AND ACTIVITIES	TECHNOLOGY RESOURCES
PACING • 90 min pp. 340–347 **Chapter Opener**	SE Start-up Activity, p. 341 ◆ GENERAL	OSP Parent Letter ■ GENERAL CD Student Edition on CD-ROM CD Guided Reading Audio CD ■ TR Chapter Starter Transparency* VID Brain Food Video Quiz
Section 1 Shoreline Erosion and Deposition • Explain how energy from waves affects a shoreline. • Identify six shoreline features created by wave erosion. • Explain how wave deposits form beaches. • Describe how sand moves along a beach.	TE Activity Illustrating Beach Erosion, p. 342 BASIC TE Connection Activity Math, p. 343 BASIC TE Group Activity Coastal Features Board Game, p. 344 GENERAL LB Whiz-Bang Demonstrations Between a Rock and a Hard Place* ◆ BASIC LB Whiz-Bang Demonstrations Rising Mountains* ◆ GENERAL	CRF Lesson Plans* TR Bellringer Transparency* TR Coastal Landforms Created by Wave Erosion A* TR Coastal Landforms Created by Wave Erosion B*
PACING • 45 min pp. 348–351 **Section 2 Wind Erosion and Deposition** • Explain why some areas are more affected by wind erosion than other areas are. • Describe the process of saltation. • Identify three landforms that result from wind erosion and deposition. • Explain how dunes move.	SE Quick Lab Making Desert Pavement, p. 349 ◆ GENERAL CRF Datasheet for Quick Lab* SE Connection to Language Arts The Dust Bowl, p. 350 GENERAL TE Connection Activity Life Science, p. 350 BASIC SE Model-Making Lab Dune Movement, p. 740 GENERAL CRF Datasheet for LabBook*	CRF Lesson Plans* TR Bellringer Transparency*
PACING • 90 min pp. 352–357 **Section 3 Erosion and Deposition by Ice** • Explain the difference between alpine glaciers and continental glaciers. • Describe two ways in which glaciers move. • Identify five landscape features formed by alpine glaciers. • Identify four types of moraines.	TE Group Activity No Glaciers?, p. 352 GENERAL SE School-to-Home Activity The *Titanic*, p. 353 GENERAL TE Activity Describing Glacier Formation, p. 353 BASIC TE Demonstration Glacier Movement, p. 353 ◆ BASIC TE Connection Activity Environmental Science, p. 354 GENERAL TE Group Activity Making Models, p. 355 GENERAL TE Connection Activity Language Arts, p. 355 ADVANCED SE Model-Making Lab Gliding Glaciers, p. 362 ◆ GENERAL CRF Datasheet for Chapter Lab* SE Skills Practice Lab Creating a Kettle, p. 741 GENERAL CRF Datasheet for LabBook*	CRF Lesson Plans* TR Bellringer Transparency* TR Landscape Features Carved by Alpine Glaciers* VID Lab Videos for Earth Science
PACING • 45 min pp. 358–361 **Section 4 The Effect of Gravity on Erosion and Deposition** • Explain the role of gravity as an agent of erosion and deposition. • Explain how angle of repose is related to mass movement. • Describe four types of rapid mass movement. • Describe three factors that affect creep.	TE Activity Demonstrating Mass Movement, p. 359 ◆ BASIC TE Connection Activity Environmental Science, p. 359 GENERAL LB Long-Term Projects & Research Ideas Deep in the Mud* ADVANCED SE Science in Action Math, Social Studies, and Language Arts Activities, pp. 368–369 GENERAL	CRF Lesson Plans* TR Bellringer Transparency* TR LINK TO PHYSICAL SCIENCE Gravitational Force Depends on Mass* TE Internet Activity, p. 361 GENERAL CRF SciLinks Activity* GENERAL

PACING • 90 min

CHAPTER REVIEW, ASSESSMENT, AND STANDARDIZED TEST PREPARATION

- CRF Vocabulary Activity* GENERAL
- SE Chapter Review, pp. 364–365 GENERAL
- CRF Chapter Review* ■ GENERAL
- CRF Chapter Tests A* ■ GENERAL, B* ADVANCED, C* SPECIAL NEEDS
- SE Standardized Test Preparation, pp. 366–367 GENERAL
- CRF Standardized Test Preparation* GENERAL
- CRF Performance-Based Assessment* GENERAL
- OSP Test Generator GENERAL
- CRF Test Item Listing* GENERAL

Online and Technology Resources

go.hrw.com
Visit go.hrw.com for a variety of free resources related to this textbook. Enter the keyword HZ5ICE.

Holt Online Learning
Students can access interactive problem-solving help and active visual concept development with the *Holt Science and Technology* Online Edition available at www.hrw.com.

Guided Reading Audio CD
Also in Spanish
A direct reading of each chapter for auditory learners, reluctant readers, and Spanish-speaking students.

Science Tutor CD-ROM
Excellent for remediation and test practice.

KEY					
SE Student Edition	CRF Chapter Resource File	SS Science Skills Worksheets	* Also on One-Stop Planner		
TE Teacher Edition	OSP One-Stop Planner	MS Math Skills for Science Worksheets	♦ Requires advance prep		
	LB Lab Bank	CD CD or CD-ROM	■ Also available in Spanish		
	TR Transparencies	VID Classroom Video/DVD			

SKILLS DEVELOPMENT RESOURCES	SECTION REVIEW AND ASSESSMENT	STANDARDS CORRELATIONS
SE Pre-Reading Activity, p. 340 GENERAL OSP Science Puzzlers, Twisters & Teasers GENERAL		National Science Education Standards SAI 1; ES 2a
CRF Directed Reading A* ■ BASIC, B* SPECIAL NEEDS CRF Vocabulary and Section Summary* GENERAL SE Reading Strategy Reading Organizer, p. 342 GENERAL SE Math Practice Counting Waves, p. 343 GENERAL MS Math Skills for Science The Unit Factor and Dimensional Analysis* GENERAL SS Science Skills Using Your Senses* GENERAL	SE Reading Checks, pp. 343, 345, 346 GENERAL TE Reteaching, p. 346 BASIC TE Quiz, p. 346 GENERAL TE Alternative Assessment, p. 346 GENERAL SE Section Review,* p. 347 GENERAL CRF Section Quiz* GENERAL	UCP 3, SAI 1, SPSP 2, 3, ES 1c
CRF Directed Reading A* ■ BASIC, B* SPECIAL NEEDS CRF Vocabulary and Section Summary* GENERAL SE Reading Strategy Reading Organizer, p. 348 GENERAL TE Inclusion Strategies, p. 349 ♦ SE Connection to Language Arts The Dust Bowl, p. 350 GENERAL CRF Critical Thinking A Future in Sand* ADVANCED	SE Reading Checks, pp. 349, 351 GENERAL TE Reteaching, p. 350 ♦ BASIC TE Quiz, p. 350 GENERAL TE Alternative Assessment, p. 350 GENERAL SE Section Review,* p. 351 ■ GENERAL CRF Section Quiz* GENERAL	SAI 1; ST 2; SPSP 2; HNS 1; ES 1c, 2a; LabBook: UCP 2, 3; SAI 1
CRF Directed Reading A* ■ BASIC, B* SPECIAL NEEDS CRF Vocabulary and Section Summary* GENERAL SE Reading Strategy Discussion, p. 352 GENERAL SE Math Practice Speed of a Glacier, p. 354 GENERAL TE Reading Strategy Preparing Tables, p. 355 BASIC TE Inclusion Strategies, p. 356 ♦ MS Math Skills for Science Using Proportions and Cross-Multiplication* GENERAL CRF Reinforcement Worksheet An Alpine Vacation* BASIC	SE Reading Checks, pp. 352, 357 GENERAL TE Reteaching, p. 356 BASIC TE Quiz, p. 356 GENERAL TE Alternative Assessment, p. 356 GENERAL SE Section Review,* p. 357 ■ GENERAL CRF Section Quiz* GENERAL	UCP 2, 3; SAI 1; SPSP 3; ES 1c, 2a; Chapter Lab: UCP 2; SAI 1; ST 1; LabBook: UCP 2, SAI 1, ES 1c
CRF Directed Reading A* ■ BASIC, B* SPECIAL NEEDS CRF Vocabulary and Section Summary* ■ GENERAL SE Reading Strategy Prediction Guide, p. 358 GENERAL	SE Reading Checks, pp. 359, 360 GENERAL TE Reteaching, p. 360 BASIC TE Quiz, p. 360 GENERAL TE Alternative Assessment, p. 360 GENERAL SE Section Review,* p. 361 ■ GENERAL CRF Section Quiz* ■ GENERAL	SAI 1; SPSP 3, 4; ES 1c

One-Stop Planner® CD-ROM

This convenient CD-ROM includes:
- Lab Materials QuickList Software
- Holt Calendar Planner
- Customizable Lesson Plans
- Printable Worksheets
- ExamView® Test Generator

CNN Student News

cnnstudentnews.com

Find the latest news, lesson plans, and activities related to important scientific events.

SciLinks NSTA

www.scilinks.org

Maintained by the National Science Teachers Association. See Chapter Enrichment pages for a complete list of topics.

Current Science®

Check out *Current Science* articles and activities by visiting the HRW Web site at **go.hrw.com**. Just type in the keyword **HZ5CS12T**.

Classroom Videos

- **Lab Videos** demonstrate the chapter lab.
- **Brain Food Video Quizzes** help students review the chapter material.
- **CNN Videos** bring science into your students' daily life.

Chapter 12 • Chapter Planning Guide

12 Chapter Resources

Visual Resources

CHAPTER STARTER TRANSPARENCY

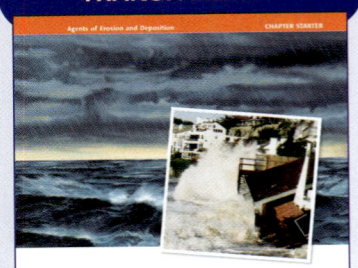

BELLRINGER TRANSPARENCIES

TEACHING TRANSPARENCIES

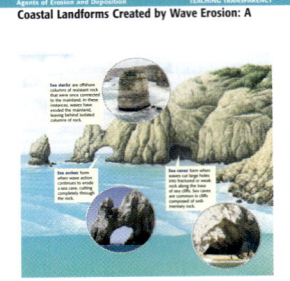

TEACHING TRANSPARENCIES

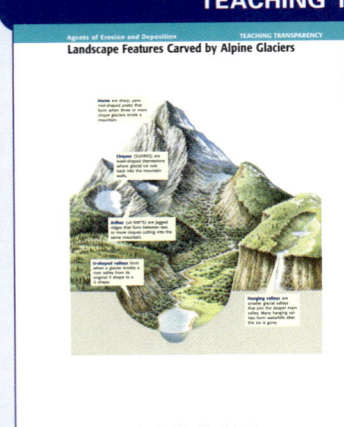

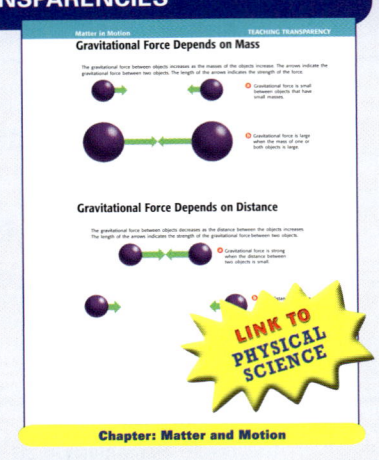

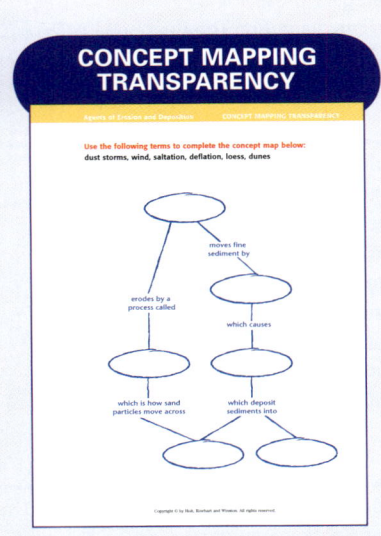

CONCEPT MAPPING TRANSPARENCY

Planning Resources

LESSON PLANS

PARENT LETTER

TEST ITEM LISTING

One-Stop Planner® CD-ROM

This CD-ROM includes all of the resources shown here and the following time-saving tools:

- *Lab Materials QuickList Software*
- *Customizable lesson plans*
- *Holt Calendar Planner*
- *The powerful ExamView® Test Generator*

339C Chapter 12 • Agents of Erosion and Deposition

For a preview of available worksheets covering math and science skills, see pages T26–T33. All of these resources are also on the One-Stop Planner®.

Meeting Individual Needs

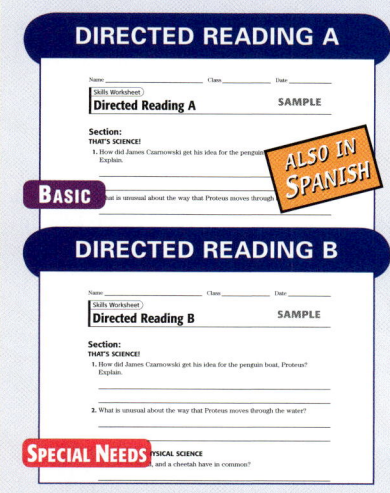

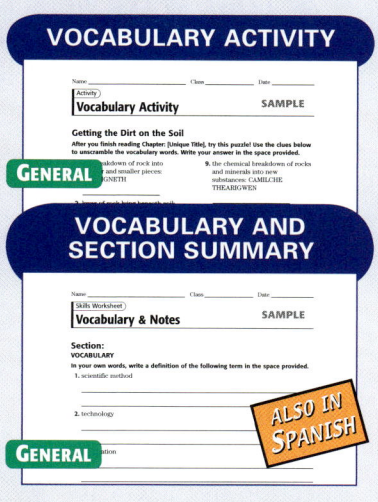

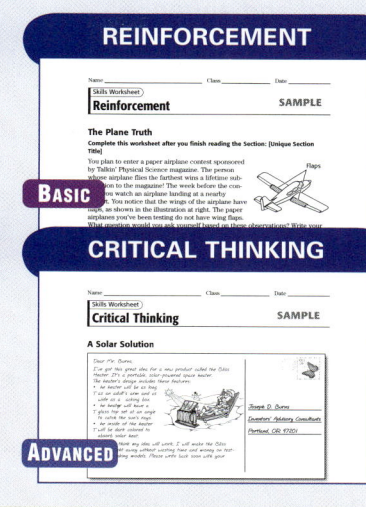

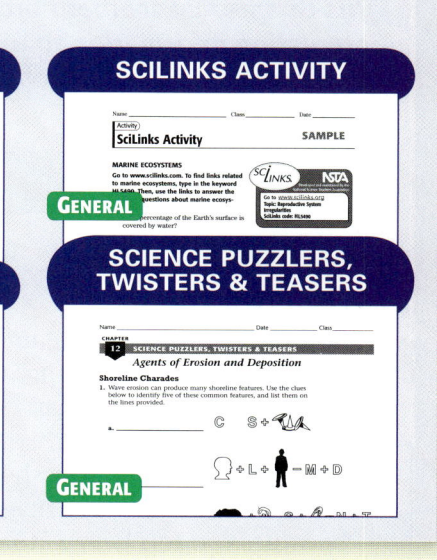

- **DIRECTED READING A** — BASIC
- **DIRECTED READING B** — SPECIAL NEEDS
- **VOCABULARY ACTIVITY** — GENERAL
- **VOCABULARY AND SECTION SUMMARY** — GENERAL
- **REINFORCEMENT** — BASIC
- **CRITICAL THINKING** — ADVANCED
- **SCILINKS ACTIVITY** — GENERAL
- **SCIENCE PUZZLERS, TWISTERS & TEASERS** — GENERAL

Labs and Activities

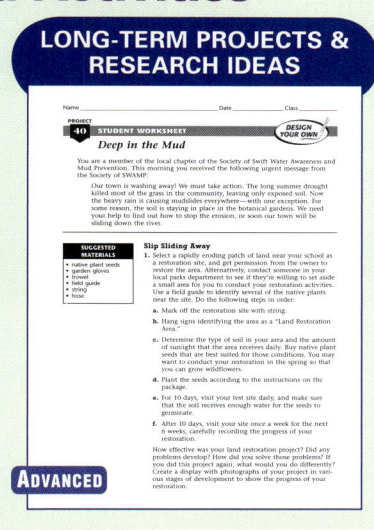

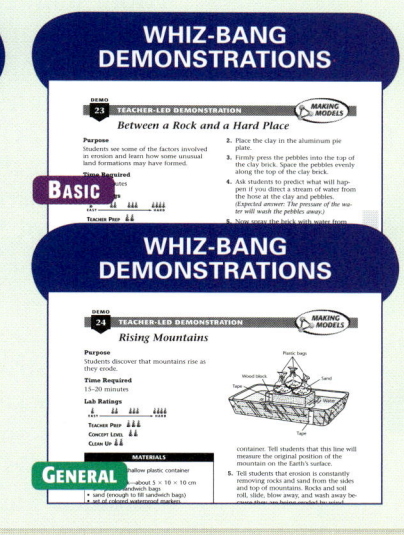

- **LONG-TERM PROJECTS & RESEARCH IDEAS** — ADVANCED
- **WHIZ-BANG DEMONSTRATIONS** — BASIC
- **WHIZ-BANG DEMONSTRATIONS** — GENERAL
- **DATASHEETS FOR QUICKLABS**
- **DATASHEETS FOR CHAPTER LABS**
- **DATASHEETS FOR LABBOOK**

Review and Assessments

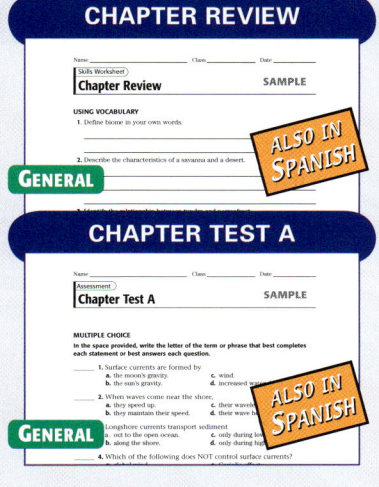

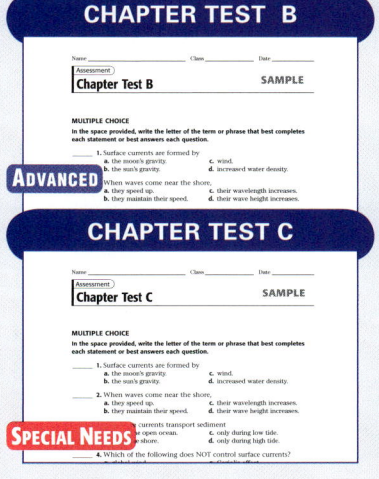

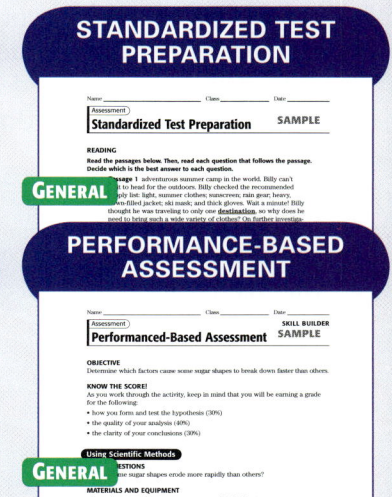

- **SECTION QUIZ** — GENERAL
- **SECTION REVIEW** — GENERAL
- **CHAPTER REVIEW** — GENERAL
- **CHAPTER TEST A** — GENERAL
- **CHAPTER TEST B** — ADVANCED
- **CHAPTER TEST C** — SPECIAL NEEDS
- **STANDARDIZED TEST PREPARATION** — GENERAL
- **PERFORMANCE-BASED ASSESSMENT** — GENERAL

Chapter 12 • Chapter Resources **339D**

12 Chapter Enrichment

This Chapter Enrichment provides relevant and interesting information to expand and enhance your presentation of the chapter material.

Is That a Fact!
- Scientists predict that if erosion continues at the current rate, Cape Cod will be completely reclaimed by the ocean in 4,000 to 5,000 years.

Section 1

Shoreline Erosion and Deposition

Acrobatic Waves
- To understand shoreline erosion, students may find it helpful to understand the forces acting in a breaking wave. Breaking waves can be thought of as somersaulting water. As waves move toward shallow coastal waters, the wavelengths shorten, the crests crowd together, and the wave heights grow. When a wave becomes too top heavy, it falls forward and rushes onto the shore. As the water flows back into the ocean, it carries sand and sediment with it.

The Origins of Cape Cod
- At the end of the last glacial period—10,000 years ago—glaciers receding across North America helped form Cape Cod, Massachusetts. Cape Cod was initially mounds of outwash, or debris left behind by the glaciers. These mounds of debris were then surrounded by the rising sea. Over time, currents eroded land and filled in depressions between the island mounds. Sandbars connected the islands to each other and to the mainland. Since its formation, Cape Cod has lost 3.2 km of coastline because of ocean erosion.

Section 2

Wind Erosion and Deposition

The Dust Bowl
- The Dust Bowl was a section of the Great Plains of the United States that extended from southeastern Colorado and southwestern Kansas to the panhandles of Texas and Oklahoma and to northeastern New Mexico. In the early 1930s, following years of overcultivation, the region suffered a severe drought. Exposed topsoil was carried away by strong spring winds. Windblown soil sometimes blocked out the sun, and the dirt piled up in drifts like snow. Occasionally, huge dust storms blew across the country and reached the East Coast. The wind erosion was gradually halted when the federal government planted windbreaks, and large areas of grasslands were restored. The area had mostly recovered by the early 1940s.

Lost Cities of the Takla Makan Desert
- The Takla Makan desert in China's arid northwest is so inhospitable that its name in the local language means "Go in, and you don't come out." The desert is covered with treacherous dunes of fine, dry sand. Buried under those dunes are the remains of cities that prospered along the ancient Silk Road. The Silk Road was a trade route that connected China to civilizations in the West. NASA's Spaceborne Imaging Radar (SIR-C), which flew on space shuttles twice in 1994, is being used to examine the desert. The radar-imaging technology has already helped archeologists locate some cities and promises to help them find other ruins.

Chapter 12 • Agents of Erosion and Deposition

For background information about teaching strategies and issues, refer to the *Professional Reference for Teachers*.

Section 3

Erosion and Deposition by Ice

Glaciers and Drinking Water

- Arapaho Glacier, a small, perennial ice sheet in Colorado, provides water to more than 75,000 people living in Boulder, Colorado. Many countries have explored the possibility of obtaining drinking water from glaciers. Some countries have even proposed towing icebergs into their harbors!

Is That a Fact!

- Glaciers flow at different rates. Most glaciers flow at an average rate of 20 cm/day or less, but some flow much faster. In 1936, the Black Rapids Glacier, in Alaska, was measured to flow at a rate of 30 m/day.

- If all of Earth's glaciers simultaneously melted, global sea levels would rise more than 65 m and would submerge coastal cities all over the world.

Battles on Siachen Glacier

- At 70 km long, the Siachen Glacier is one of the world's longest glaciers. The glacier is in the Karakoram Range, on the India-Pakistan border. The Siachen Glacier is also the site of the world's highest battles. Indian and Pakistani soldiers have fought over this disputed territory of Kashmir on peaks as high as 6,400 m (almost 21,000 ft).

The Great Lakes

- The Great Lakes were formed by the movement of ice sheets during the Pleistocene epoch. These glaciers advanced over the land and gouged out a series of deep basins. As the glaciers melted, the basins filled with meltwater, and the five Great Lakes were formed.

Section 4

The Effect of Gravity on Erosion and Deposition

Scree

- Stones and boulders loosened by weathering and carried downward by gravity may be deposited in long, loose heaps called *scree* at the base of a mountain.

Is That a Fact!

- When an earthquake that measured 5.0 on the Richter scale occurred near Mount St. Helens on May 18, 1980, it triggered a landslide of more than 2 km^3 of rock and ice. Immediately afterward, the eruption of Mount St. Helens began, and an explosion of steam and volcanic gases produced a lahar that raced down the mountain at speeds of up to 250 km/h.

SciLinks is maintained by the National Science Teachers Association to provide you and your students with interesting, up-to-date links that will enrich your classroom presentation of the chapter.

Visit www.scilinks.org and enter the SciLinks code for more information about the topic listed.

Topic: Wave Erosion
SciLinks code: HSM1638

Topic: Glaciers
SciLinks code: HSM0675

Topic: Wind Erosion
SciLinks code: HSM1669

Topic: Mass Movements
SciLinks code: HSM5295

Overview
Tell students that this chapter will help them learn about the processes of erosion and deposition by water, wind, ice, and gravity.

Assessing Prior Knowledge
Students should be familiar with the following topics:
- weathering
- soil formation

Identifying Misconceptions
Some students may be confused about the way that waves move. You may want to explain to students that as wave energy moves through water, the water itself does not travel very far toward the shore. When a wave passes through water, the water moves up and down. It is only when waves reach the shore and wave height exceeds the depth of the water, that water tumbles forward. In addition, students may not realize how much of the United States was shaped by glacial erosion. Use a map to show students how much of the northern United States was covered by glaciers during the last glacial period.

12
Agents of Erosion and Deposition

SECTION 1 Shoreline Erosion and Deposition 342

SECTION 2 Wind Erosion and Deposition 348

SECTION 3 Erosion and Deposition by Ice 352

SECTION 4 The Effect of Gravity on Erosion and Deposition 358

Chapter Lab 362
Chapter Review 364
Standardized Test Preparation 366
Science in Action 368

About the PHOTO
The results of erosion can often be dramatic. For example, this sinkhole formed in a parking lot in Atlanta, Georgia, when water running underground eventually caused the surface of the land to collapse.

PRE-READING ACTIVITY
FOLDNOTES Layered Book Before you read the chapter, create the FoldNote entitled "The Layered Book" described in the **Study Skills** section of the Appendix. Label the tabs of the layered book with "Shoreline erosion and deposition," "Wind erosion and deposition," and "Erosion and deposition by ice." As you read the chapter, write information you learn about each category under the appropriate tab.

Standards Correlations

National Science Education Standards
The following codes indicate the National Science Education Standards that correlate to this chapter. The full text of the standards is at the front of the book.

Chapter Opener
SAI 1; ES 2a

Section 1 Shoreline Erosion and Deposition
UCP 3, SAI 1, SPSP 2, 3, ES 1c

Section 2 Wind Erosion and Deposition
SAI 1; ST 2; SPSP 2; HNS 1; ES 1c, 2a; *LabBook*: UCP 2, 3; SAI 1

Section 3 Erosion and Deposition by Ice
UCP 2, 3; SAI 1; SPSP 3; ES 1c, 2a; *LabBook*: UCP 2, SAI 1, ES 1c

Section 4 The Effect of Gravity on Erosion and Deposition
SAI 1; SPSP 3, 4; ES 1c

Chapter Lab
UCP 2; SAI 1; ST 1

340 Chapter 12 • Agents of Erosion and Deposition

START-UP ACTIVITY

MATERIALS
FOR EACH GROUP
- block, wooden or plastic
- sand
- washtub
- water

Answers
1. Sample answer: The shoreline is slowly receding, or eroding.
2. Small waves erode less shoreline than large waves do. Therefore, large waves have a greater impact on the shoreline.

START-UP ACTIVITY

Making Waves
Above ground or below, water plays an important role in the erosion and deposition of rock and soil. A shoreline is a good example of how water shapes the Earth's surface by erosion and deposition. Did you know that shorelines are shaped by crashing waves? Build a model shoreline, and see for yourself!

Procedure
1. Make a shoreline by adding **sand** to one end of a **washtub**. Fill the washtub with **water** to a depth of 5 cm. Sketch the shoreline profile (side view), and label it "A."
2. Place a **block** at the end of the washtub opposite the beach.
3. Move the block up and down very slowly to create small waves for 2 min. Sketch the new shoreline profile, and label it "B."
4. Now, move the block up and down more rapidly to create large waves for 2 min. Sketch the new shoreline profile, and label it "C."

Analysis
1. Compare the three shoreline profiles. What is happening to the shoreline?
2. How do small waves and large waves erode the shoreline differently?

Chapter Review
UCP 2, 3; SAI 1; SPSP 3, 4, 5; ES 1c, 2a

Science in Action
SPSP 3; HNS 1, 3

Chapter Starter Transparency
Use this transparency to help students begin thinking about the erosive force of breaking waves.

CHAPTER RESOURCES

Technology
- Transparencies
  - Chapter Starter Transparency **READING SKILLS**
- Student Edition on CD-ROM
- Guided Reading Audio CD
  - English or Spanish
- Classroom Videos
  - Brain Food Video Quiz

Workbooks
- Science Puzzlers, Twisters & Teasers
  - Agents of Erosion and Deposition **GENERAL**

Chapter 12 • Agents of Erosion and Deposition **341**

SECTION 1

Focus

Overview
This section explores how wave erosion and deposition shape shorelines. Students explore coastal landforms created by wave erosion, such as sea cliffs, sea stacks, sea arches, sea caves, headlands, and wave-cut terraces. Students also learn about the formation of beaches and offshore landforms by deposition.

Bellringer
Ask students to think about where sand comes from. Have them write a short poem about how ocean waves create sand from rock.

Motivate

ACTIVITY — GENERAL

Illustrating Beach Erosion
Explain to students that shorelines are dynamic, changing environments because ocean waves and currents continually erode and redeposit sand. Have each student draw a "filmstrip" illustrating the changes that could occur in the history of a beach. Have students illustrate the processes that cause these changes and write a caption that explains each frame of the film strip. **English Language Learners**
LS Visual

SECTION 1

READING WARM-UP

Objectives
- Explain how energy from waves affects a shoreline.
- Identify six shoreline features created by wave erosion.
- Explain how wave deposits form beaches.
- Describe how sand moves along a beach.

Terms to Learn
shoreline
beach

READING STRATEGY

Reading Organizer As you read this section, create an outline of the section. Use the headings from the section in your outline.

Shoreline Erosion and Deposition

Think about the last time you were at a beach. Where did all of the sand come from?

Two basic ingredients are necessary to make sand: rock and energy. The rock is usually available on the shore. The energy is provided by waves that travel through water. When waves crash into rocks over long periods of time, the rocks are broken down into smaller and smaller pieces until they become sand.

As you read on, you will learn how wave erosion and deposition shape the shoreline. A **shoreline** is simply the place where land and a body of water meet. Waves usually play a major role in building up and breaking down the shoreline.

Wave Energy

As the wind moves across the ocean surface, it produces ripples called *waves*. The size of a wave depends on how hard the wind is blowing and how long the wind blows. The harder and longer the wind blows, the bigger the wave.

The wind that results from summer hurricanes and severe winter storms produces large waves that cause dramatic shoreline erosion. Waves may travel hundreds or even thousands of kilometers from a storm before reaching the shoreline. Some of the largest waves to reach the California coast are produced by storms as far away as Australia. So, the California surfer in **Figure 1** can ride a wave that formed on the other side of the Pacific Ocean!

Figure 1 Waves produced by storms on the other side of the Pacific Ocean propel this surfer toward a California shore.

CHAPTER RESOURCES

Chapter Resource File
- Lesson Plan
- Directed Reading A **BASIC**
- Directed Reading B **SPECIAL NEEDS**

Technology
- Transparencies
  • Bellringer

Workbooks
- Math Skills for Science
  • The Unit Factor and Dimensional Analysis **GENERAL**

MISCONCEPTION ALERT

Wave Movement A popular misconception is that a wave is a moving wall of water. Water actually moves up and down rather than forward as wave energy travels through it. When waves break, however, they do carry water with them.

---

342 Chapter 12 • Agents of Erosion and Deposition

Wave Trains

When you drop a pebble into a pond, is there just one ripple? Of course not. Waves, like ripples, don't move alone. As shown in **Figure 2,** waves travel in groups called *wave trains*. As wave trains move away from their source, they travel through the ocean water uninterrupted. But when waves reach shallow water, the bottom of the wave drags against the sea floor, slowing the wave down. The upper part of the wave moves more rapidly and grows taller. When the top of the wave becomes so tall that it cannot support itself, it begins to curl and break. These breaking waves are known as *surf*. Now you know how surfers got their name. The *wave period* is the time interval between breaking waves. Wave periods are usually 10 to 20 s long.

The Pounding Surf

Look at **Figure 3,** and you will get an idea of how sand is made. A tremendous amount of energy is released when waves break. A crashing wave can break solid rock and throw broken rocks back against the shore. As the rushing water in breaking waves enters cracks in rock, it helps break off large boulders and wash away fine grains of sand. The loose sand picked up by waves wears down and polishes coastal rocks. As a result of these actions, rock is broken down into smaller and smaller pieces that eventually become sand.

Reading Check How do waves help break down rock into sand? *(See the Appendix for answers to Reading Checks.)*

Figure 2 Because waves travel in wave trains, they break at regular intervals.

shoreline the boundary between land and a body of water

MATH PRACTICE

Counting Waves

If the wave period is 10 s, approximately how many waves reach a shoreline in a day? (Hint: Calculate how many waves occur in an hour, and multiply that number by the number of hours in a day.)

Figure 3 Breaking waves crash against the rocky shore, releasing their energy.

Answer to Reading Check
The amount of energy released from breaking waves causes rock to break down, eventually forming sand. Water from breaking waves also rushes into cracks in rocks, helping break them, and washes away fine grains of sand.

Teach

CONNECTION to Physical Science — GENERAL

Learning About Waves The waves in lakes and oceans are a form of energy traveling through a medium—water. Other energy waves, such as sound waves, also require a medium through which to travel. However, some waves, such as light and radio waves, can travel through a vacuum. Have students research a wave type of their choice and create a poster-board display illustrating the wave's characteristics. If possible, students can also plan a demonstration to educate the class about the wave they studied. **LS Visual**

Answer to Math Practice
In 1 min, six waves occur.
In 1 h, 360 waves occur.
In 1 day, 8,640 waves occur.
60 s ÷ 10 s/wave = 6 waves/min
6 waves/min × 60 min/h = 360 waves/h
360 waves/h × 24 h = 8,640 waves

CONNECTION ACTIVITY Math — BASIC

Wave Period Ask students to calculate the following:

How many waves reach a shoreline in 24 hours if the wave period is 15 s? 20 s?

(With a 15 s period, 5,760 waves would reach the shore. With a 20 s period, 4,320 waves would reach the shore.)

LS Logical

Section 1 • Shoreline Erosion and Deposition **343**

Teach, continued

Group Activity — GENERAL

Coastal Features Board Game
To reinforce section concepts, divide the class into small groups, and challenge each group to create a board game. Tell students that the object of the game is for players to visit as many coastal landforms as they can. Provide each group with poster board, plain index cards, and markers. Direct groups to create a game board that leads players along a "coastline" and allows them to encounter the features they have learned about. Have students use the index cards to write questions and clues to direct players' movements along the coast. For example, students might write, "If you can describe how a sea arch forms, you may move ahead to the sea stack. If not, you lose a turn." Have groups create written game rules, exchange games, and play their games. (**Note:** It might be helpful to brainstorm chapter concepts on the board before students create their games.) **LS Logical/Kinesthetic** **English Language Learners**

Wave Erosion

Wave erosion produces a variety of features along a shoreline. *Sea cliffs* are formed when waves erode and undercut rock to produce steep slopes. Waves strike the base of the cliff, which wears away the soil and rock and makes the cliff steeper. The rate at which the sea cliffs erode depends on the hardness of the rock and the energy of the waves. Sea cliffs made of hard rock, such as granite, erode very slowly. Sea cliffs made of soft rock, such as shale, erode more rapidly, especially during storms.

Figure 4 Coastal Landforms Created by Wave Erosion

Sea stacks are offshore columns of resistant rock that were once connected to the mainland. In these instances, waves have eroded the mainland, leaving behind isolated columns of rock.

Sea arches form when wave action continues to erode a sea cave, cutting completely through the rock.

Sea caves form when waves cut large holes into fractured or weak rock along the base of sea cliffs. Sea caves are common in cliffs composed of sedimentary rock.

Cultural Awareness — ADVANCED

Polynesian Cultures The Polynesians are considered to have been some of the greatest navigators of the ancient world. Polynesians visited and inhabited more than 10,000 islands throughout the South Pacific. They navigated not by using maps but by carefully observing stars, winds, and waves. On cloudy nights, they listened to the way the waves rocked and slapped against their dugout canoes. The Polynesians understood how wave patterns could indicate the direction of land or the presence of dangerous reefs or sandbars. Encourage students to discover more about Polynesian cultures of the past and present.

344 Chapter 12 • Agents of Erosion and Deposition

Shaping a Shoreline

Much of the erosion responsible for landforms you might see along the shoreline takes place during storms. Large waves generated by storms release far more energy than normal waves do. This energy is so powerful that it is capable of removing huge chunks of rock. **Figure 4** shows some of the major landscape features that result from wave erosion.

Reading Check Why are large waves more capable of removing large chunks of rock from a shoreline than normal waves are?

Headlands are finger-shaped projections that form when cliffs made of hard rock erode more slowly than surrounding rock. On many shorelines, hard rock will form headlands, and the softer rock will form beaches or bays.

Wave-cut terraces form when a sea cliff is worn back, producing a nearly level platform beneath the water at the base of the cliff.

Answer to Reading Check
Large waves are more capable of removing large rocks on a shoreline because they have more energy than normal waves do.

CHAPTER RESOURCES

Technology

Transparencies
- Coastal Landforms Created by Wave Erosion: A
- Coastal Landforms Created by Wave Erosion: B

Workbooks

Science Skills
- Using Your Senses GENERAL

CONNECTION to Life Science — GENERAL

Life on the Shore
Beaches and intertidal zones can be challenging places for organisms to live. Beaches offer little protection from predators, and intertidal zones are periodically pounded by waves and exposed to the sun. Most of the organisms that live in these areas have special adaptations for survival. Have students research how different organisms are adapted for living in these environments. Suggest that students use their research to create a diorama that illustrates an intertidal zone.
LS Verbal/Visual

BRAIN FOOD

Insuring Ocean Properties
Despite the numerous changes wrought by the ocean, people still live and vacation as close to the water as possible. Inevitably, property is damaged. Government loan subsidies to these property owners can cost taxpayers millions of dollars each year. Encourage students to consider the costs and benefits of erosion prevention. What solutions to the erosion problem would students propose? How would they finance their plans? Allow time for students to share their ideas with the class. **LS Logical**

Section 1 • Shoreline Erosion and Deposition

Close

Reteaching — BASIC
Wave Review Draw a profile of a new shore environment on the board. Have a student volunteer add a diagram of wave energy traveling toward the shore. Ask students to help you identify wave length, wave height, and wave period. Then have students help you illustrate what happens to a wave as it approaches the shore and breaks. Review the movement of water in each part of the diagram. **LS Visual**

Quiz — GENERAL
1. What is a wave period? (It is the time interval between breaking waves.)
2. What determines the way sand moves on a beach? (the direction at which waves strike the shore)

Alternative Assessment — GENERAL
Modeling Coastal Features Have students work independently to make a model of several land features created by waves. Ask students to present their models to the class and explain how the water strikes the shore to create the landforms. Have students brainstorm what organisms, if any, would live on the landforms they modeled. **LS Visual**

England

U.S. Virgin Islands

Hawaii

Figure 5 Beaches are made of different types of material deposited by waves.

beach an area of the shoreline made up of material deposited by waves

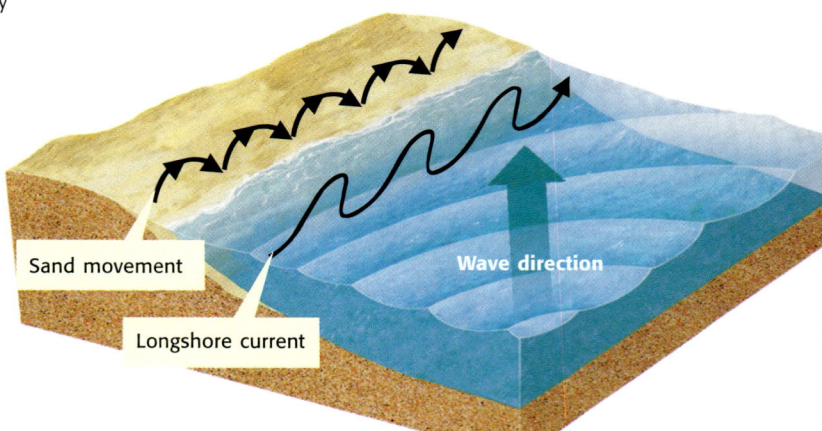

Figure 6 When waves strike the shoreline at an angle, sand migrates along the beach in a zigzag path.

Answer to Reading Check
Beach material comes from quartz, coral, broken seashells, lava, pebbles, and boulders.

Wave Deposits
Waves carry a variety of materials, including sand, rock fragments, dead coral, and shells. Often, this material is deposited on a shoreline, where it forms a beach.

Beaches
You would probably recognize a beach if you saw one. However, scientifically speaking, a **beach** is any area of the shoreline made up of material deposited by waves. Some beach material is also deposited by rivers.

Compare the beaches shown in **Figure 5**. Notice that the colors and textures vary. They vary because the type of material found on a beach depends on its source. Light-colored sand is the most common beach material. Much of this sand comes from the mineral quartz. But not all beaches are made of light-colored sand. For example, on many tropical islands, such as the Virgin Islands, beaches are made of fine, white coral material. Some Florida beaches are made of tiny pieces of broken seashells. Black sand beaches in Hawaii are made of eroded volcanic lava. In areas where stormy seas are common, beaches are made of pebbles and boulders.

Reading Check Where does beach material come from?

Wave Angle and Sand Movement
The movement of sand along a beach depends on the angle at which the waves strike the shore. Most waves approach the beach at a slight angle and retreat in a direction more perpendicular to the shore. This movement of water is called a longshore current. A *longshore current* is a water current that moves the sand in a zigzag pattern along the beach, as you can see in **Figure 6**.

Sand movement

Wave direction

Longshore current

WEIRD SCIENCE
Sometimes, even when the weather is clear and calm, huge waves, called *rogue waves*, appear unexpectedly. These waves are responsible for damaging or sinking several ships each year. Rogue waves are a poorly understood phenomenon of the high seas. One reason so little is known about rogue waves is that their random nature makes them hard to study.

346 Chapter 12 • Agents of Erosion and Deposition

Offshore Deposits

Waves moving at an angle to the shoreline push water along the shore and create longshore currents. When waves erode material from the shoreline, longshore currents can transport and deposit this material offshore, which creates landforms in open water. A *sandbar* is an underwater or exposed ridge of sand, gravel, or shell material. A *barrier spit* is an exposed sandbar that is connected to the shoreline. Cape Cod, Massachusetts, shown in **Figure 7**, is an example of a barrier spit. A barrier island is a long, narrow island usually made of sand that forms offshore parallel to the shoreline.

Figure 7 A barrier spit, such as Cape Cod, Massachusetts, occurs when an exposed sandbar is connected to the shoreline.

SECTION Review

Summary

- As waves break against a shoreline, rock is broken down into sand.
- Six shoreline features created by wave erosion include sea cliffs, sea stacks, sea caves, sea arches, headlands, and wave-cut terraces.
- Beaches are made from material deposited by waves.
- Longshore currents cause sand to move in a zigzag pattern along the shore.

Using Key Terms

Complete each of the following sentences by choosing the correct term from the word bank.

shoreline   beach

1. A ___ is an area made up of material deposited by waves.
2. An area in which land and a body of water meet is a ___.

Understanding Key Ideas

3. Which of the following is a result of wave deposition?
   a. sea arch
   b. sea cave
   c. barrier spit
   d. headland
4. How do wave deposits affect a shoreline?
5. Describe how sand moves along a beach.
6. What are six shoreline features created by wave erosion?
7. How can the energy of waves traveling through water affect a shoreline?
8. Would a small wave or a large wave have more energy? Explain your answer.

Math Skills

9. Imagine that there is a large boulder on the edge of a shoreline. If the wave period is 15 s long, how many times is the boulder hit in a year?

Critical Thinking

10. **Applying Concepts** Not all beaches are made from light-colored sand. Explain why this statement is true.
11. **Making Inferences** How can severe storms over the ocean affect shoreline erosion and deposition?
12. **Making Predictions** How could a headland change in 250 years? Describe some of the features that may form.

Answers to Section Review

1. beach
2. shoreline
3. c
4. Wave deposits often form beaches along shorelines.
5. Sand moves along a beach in a zigzag pattern because of the longshore current caused by waves breaking at an angle along the shore.
6. Six shoreline features created by wave erosion include sea stacks, sea arches, sea caves, headlands, sea cliffs, and wave-cut terraces.
7. The energy from waves can erode a shoreline.
8. Sample answer: A large wave would have more energy because larger waves are formed during storms and carry much of the energy from the storm.
9. 60 s/min × 15 s/wave = 4 waves/min
   4 waves/min × 60 min/h = 240 waves/h × 24 h/day = 5,760 waves/day × 365 days/year = 2,102,400 waves/year
   The boulder is hit by the waves 5,760 times a day and 2,102,400 times a year.
10. Beaches vary because the type of material found on a beach depends on the source of the material. For example, light-colored sand comes from the mineral quartz, but black sand beaches are made of eroded volcanic lava.
11. The winds that result from storms over the ocean form waves that carry a large amount of energy. In turn, these waves crash against the shoreline and can cause significant erosion. They can also transport and deposit larger materials, such as boulders.
12. Sample answer: Over 250 years, landforms such as sea arches and sea caves might begin to form along the wave-swept portion of the headland.

CHAPTER RESOURCES

Chapter Resource File
- Section Quiz GENERAL
- Section Review GENERAL
- Vocabulary and Section Summary GENERAL

SciLinks
Topic: Wave Erosion
SciLinks code: HSM1638

Section 1 • Shoreline Erosion and Deposition

SECTION 2

Focus

Overview

In this section, students learn about the effects of wind erosion. They explore the three major processes of wind erosion: saltation, deflation, and abrasion. Students also learn about the ways that the wind shapes and moves sand dunes.

🔔 Bellringer

Ask students to answer the following question in their **science journal:**

What causes wind? *(Students should understand that wind is caused by energy from the sun. The unequal heating of the Earth by the sun causes temperature and pressure differences, which in turn cause air to move.)*

Motivate

Discussion — GENERAL

Wind Erosion Engage students in a discussion about the ways that wind shapes the Earth's surface. Encourage them to compare wind with waves. Ask students to think of examples of the wind's effect on landscapes. *(Students should recognize that both wind and waves change the Earth's surface by erosion and deposition. Examples of the wind's effect on landscapes may include dunes and wind-weathered surfaces.)* **LS Verbal**

SECTION 2

READING WARM-UP

Objectives
- Explain why some areas are more affected by wind erosion than other areas are.
- Describe the process of saltation.
- Identify three landforms that result from wind erosion and deposition.
- Explain how dunes move.

Terms to Learn

saltation   loess
deflation   dune
abrasion

READING STRATEGY

Reading Organizer As you read this section, make a table comparing deflation and abrasion.

Wind Erosion and Deposition

Have you ever been working outside and had a gusty wind blow an important stack of papers all over the place?

Do you remember how fast and far the papers traveled and how long it took to pick them up? Every time you caught up with them, they were on the move again. If this has happened to you, then you have seen how wind erosion works. As an agent of erosion, the wind removes soil, sand, and rock particles and transports them from one place to another.

Certain locations are more vulnerable to wind erosion than others. An area with little plant cover can be severely affected by wind erosion because plant roots anchor sand and soil in place. Deserts and coastlines that are made of fine, loose rock material and have little plant cover are shaped most dramatically by the wind.

The Process of Wind Erosion

Wind moves material in different ways. In areas where strong winds occur, material is moved by saltation. **Saltation** is the skipping and bouncing movement of sand-sized particles in the direction the wind is blowing. As you can see in **Figure 1,** the wind causes the particles to bounce. When moving sand grains knock into one another, some grains bounce up in the air, fall forward, and strike other sand grains. These impacts cause other grains to roll and bounce forward.

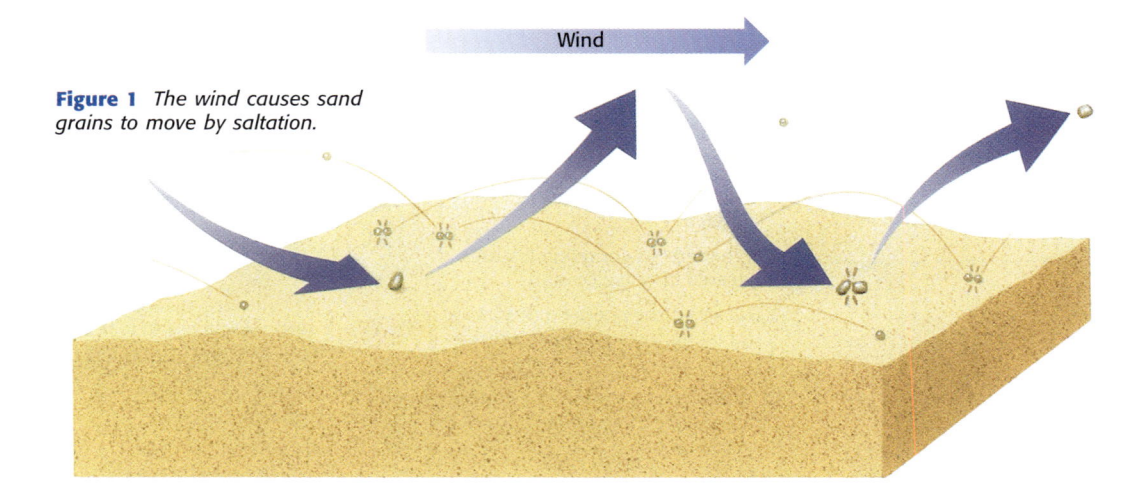

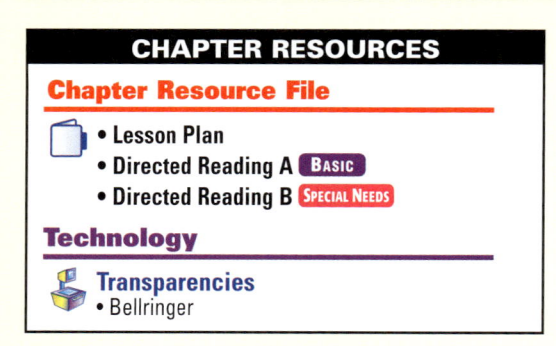

Figure 1 The wind causes sand grains to move by saltation.

CHAPTER RESOURCES

Chapter Resource File
- Lesson Plan
- Directed Reading A BASIC
- Directed Reading B SPECIAL NEEDS

Technology
- Transparencies
  - Bellringer

---

348 Chapter 12 • Agents of Erosion and Deposition

Figure 2 Desert pavement, such as that found in the Painted Desert in Arizona, forms when wind removes all the fine materials.

Deflation

The removal of fine sediment by wind is called **deflation.** During deflation, wind removes the top layer of fine sediment or soil and leaves behind rock fragments that are too heavy to be lifted by the wind. Deflation may cause *desert pavement*, which is a surface consisting of pebbles and small broken rocks. An example of desert pavement is shown in **Figure 2.**

Have you ever blown on a layer of dust while cleaning off a dresser? If you have, you may have noticed that in addition to your face getting dirty, a little scooped-out depression formed in the dust. Similarly, in areas where there is little vegetation, the wind may scoop out depressions in the landscape. These depressions are called *deflation hollows*.

✓ **Reading Check** Where do deflation hollows form? (*See the Appendix for answers to Reading Checks.*)

Abrasion

The grinding and wearing down of rock surfaces by other rock or sand particles is called **abrasion.** Abrasion commonly happens in areas where there are strong winds, loose sand, and soft rocks. The blowing of millions of sharp sand grains creates a sandblasting effect. This effect helps to erode, smooth, and polish rocks.

saltation the movement of sand or other sediments by short jumps and bounces that is caused by wind or water

deflation a form of wind erosion in which fine, dry soil particles are blown away

abrasion the grinding and wearing away of rock surfaces through the mechanical action of other rock or sand particles

Quick Lab
Making Desert Pavement

1. Spread a mixture of **dust, sand,** and **gravel** on an **outdoor table.**
2. Place an **electric fan** at one end of the table.
3. Put on **safety goggles** and a **filter mask.** Aim the fan across the sediment. Start the fan on its lowest speed. Record your observations.
4. Turn the fan to a medium speed. Record your observations.
5. Finally, turn the fan to a high speed to imitate a desert windstorm. Record your observations.
6. What is the relationship between the wind speed and the size of the sediment that is moved?
7. Does the remaining sediment fit the definition of desert pavement?

CONNECTION to Life Science — GENERAL

Dust in the Wind Each year, equatorial trade winds carry millions of tons of reddish brown dust from the Sahara to Florida. Sahara dust causes hazy skies in Florida and travels as far as South America. The dust provides nutrients for organisms that live in the rain-forest canopies. Traveling over the Pacific Ocean, yellow dust from Mongolia's Gobi Desert reaches Hawaii and fertilizes iron-deficient regions of the Pacific Ocean. In places where the dust settles, plankton populations increase and enrich the food chain. One researcher has tried to link this phenomenon to global climate change. According to this theory, desertification increases during glacial periods, so more sediment is deposited in the oceans. This deposition encourages plankton growth, which removes CO_2 from the atmosphere and further cools the planet.

Teach

INCLUSION Strategies

- Hearing Impaired
- Learning Disabled
- Attention Deficit Disorder

Demonstrate deflation for students using a large, shallow pan, large rocks, and plastic foam packing material. Line the bottom of the pan with rocks. Then pour the foam packing material into the pan with the rocks. Gently shake the pan so the packing fills the spaces between the rocks. Then use a blow drier to blow the foam packing out of the pan. Explain to students that this is similar to the effect deflation has on dry landscapes.
LS Visual — English Language Learners

Answer to Reading Check
Deflation hollows form in areas where there is little vegetation.

Quick Lab
MATERIALS

For Each Group
- fan, electric
- filter mask
- mixture of dust, sand, and gravel
- outdoor table
- safety goggles

Safety Caution: Because of the risk of eye injury and particle inhalation, students must wear both protective goggles and a filter mask during this lab.

Answers
6. The faster the wind speed is, the larger the sediment that can be moved.
7. Answers may vary. Accept all reasonable responses.

Section 2 • Wind Erosion and Deposition 349

Close

Reteaching — BASIC
Modeling Abrasion
Demonstrate the abrasiveness of sand by briskly rubbing quartz sandpaper on a soft rock specimen, and allow students to observe the changes. Remind students that sandblasting is used in many industrial applications to "erode" hard surfaces. **LS** Visual

Quiz — GENERAL

1. Why is sand more likely than silt to move by saltation?
   (Sand is heavier than dust and silt, so as sand moves, it tends to bounce along the ground. Silt is light enough to be carried by the wind.)

2. How can the process of deflation form desert pavement?
   (Deflation lifts and carries away lighter materials, while the heavier stones remain as desert pavement.)

3. Describe how dunes form.
   (When wind encounters an obstacle, the wind slows down and deposits some of the heavier material it is carrying. Gradually, this material collects, becoming a mound and then a dune.)

Alternative Assessment — GENERAL
Concept Mapping Have students use section vocabulary and concepts to construct a concept map that explores the ways wind can shape the Earth's surface. **LS** Logical

---

CONNECTION TO Language Arts

WRITING SKILL
The Dust Bowl During the 1930s, a severe drought occurred in a section of the Great Plains that became known as the *Dust Bowl*. The wind carried so much dust that some cities left street lights on during the day. Research the Dust Bowl, and describe it in a series of three journal entries written from the perspective of a farmer.

loess very fine sediments deposited by the wind

dune a mound of wind-deposited sand that keeps its shape even though it moves

Figure 3 Dunes migrate in the direction of the wind.

CONNECTION to Life Science — BASIC

Life in the Desert Point out to students that many desert animals have special adaptations to protect themselves from windblown sand. For example, some lizards have transparent eyelids that shield their eyes from blowing sand while still allowing them to see. Encourage students to use library or Internet resources to investigate the organisms that make deserts their home. Have students select one plant or animal and write a brief report describing its habitat, its predators and/or prey, and the adaptations it has developed to live in the desert environment. **English Language Learners**
LS Intrapersonal

Wind-Deposited Materials

Much like rivers, the wind also carries sediment. And just as rivers deposit their loads, the wind eventually drops all the material it carries. The amount and the size of particles the wind can carry depend on the wind speed. The faster the wind blows, the more material and the heavier the particles it can carry. As wind speed slows, heavier particles are deposited first.

Loess

Wind can deposit extremely fine material. Thick deposits of this windblown, fine-grained sediment are known as **loess** (LOH ES). Loess feels like the talcum powder a person may use after a shower.

Because wind carries fine-grained material much higher and farther than it carries sand, loess deposits are sometimes found far away from their source. Many loess deposits came from glacial sources during the last Ice Age. In the United States, loess is present in the Midwest, along the eastern edge of the Mississippi Valley, and in eastern Oregon and Washington.

Dunes

When the wind hits an obstacle, such as a plant or a rock, the wind slows down. As it slows, the wind deposits, or drops, the heavier material. The material collects, which creates an additional obstacle. This obstacle causes even more material to be deposited, forming a mound. Eventually, the original obstacle becomes buried. The mounds of wind-deposited sand are called **dunes.** Dunes are common in sandy deserts and along the sandy shores of lakes and oceans. **Figure 3** shows a large dune in a desert area.

---

350 Chapter 12 • Agents of Erosion and Deposition

The Movement of Dunes

Dunes tend to move in the direction of strong winds. Different wind conditions produce dunes in various shapes and sizes. A dune usually has a gently sloped side and a steeply sloped side, or *slip face,* as shown in **Figure 4.** In most cases, the gently sloped side faces the wind. The wind is constantly transporting material up this side of the dune. As sand moves over the crest, or peak, of the dune, it slides down the slip face, creating a steep slope.

✓ **Reading Check** In what direction do dunes move?

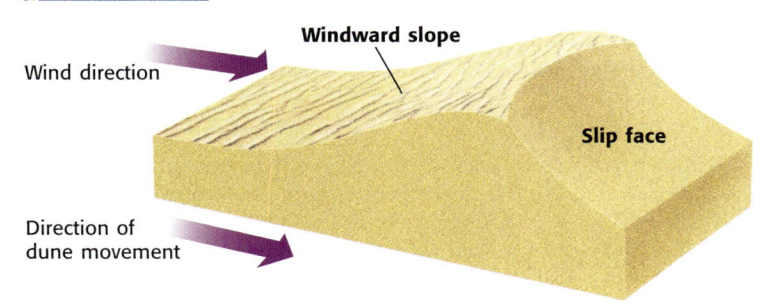

Figure 4 Dunes are formed from material deposited by wind.

SECTION Review

Summary

- Areas with little plant cover and desert areas covered with fine rock material are more vulnerable than other areas to wind erosion.
- Saltation is the process in which sand-sized particles move in the direction of the wind.
- Three landforms that are created by wind erosion and deposition are desert pavement, deflation hollows, and dunes.
- Dunes move in the direction of the wind.

Using Key Terms

In each of the following sentences, replace the incorrect term with the correct term from the word bank.

dune   saltation
deflation   abrasion

1. <u>Deflation hollows</u> are mounds of wind-deposited sand.
2. The removal of fine sediment by wind is called <u>abrasion</u>.

Understanding Key Ideas

3. Which of the following landforms is the result of wind deposition?
   a. deflation hollow
   b. desert pavement
   c. dune
   d. abrasion
4. Describe how material is moved in areas where strong winds blow.
5. Explain the process of abrasion.

Math Skills

6. If a dune moves 40 m per year, how far does it move in 1 day?

Critical Thinking

7. **Identifying Relationships** Explain the relationship between plant cover and wind erosion.
8. **Applying Concepts** If you climbed up the steep side of a sand dune, is it likely that you traveled in the direction the wind was blowing?

SciLinks
For a variety of links related to this chapter, go to www.scilinks.org
Topic: Wind Erosion
SciLinks code: HSM1669

Answer to Reading Check
Dunes move in the direction of strong winds.

Answers to Section Review

1. Dunes are mounds of wind-deposited sand.
2. The removal of fine sediment by wind is called *deflation.*
3. c
4. Sample answer: In areas where strong winds occur, material is moved by saltation. Saltation is the movement of sand-sized particles by bouncing and skipping in the direction that the wind is blowing. The wind lifts sand particles into the air. When the particles land, they hit other particles, which causes them to bounce forward.
5. Sample answer: Abrasion is the grinding and wearing down of rock surfaces by other rock or sand particles. In areas where there are strong winds and loose sand, the blowing of millions of sharp sand grains grinds and wears down rock surfaces.
6. 40 m/year ÷ 365 days/year = 0.11 m/day
7. Sample answer: Vegetation protects areas against the effects of wind erosion. In areas where there is little vegetation, the potential for wind erosion is great.
8. No. The gently sloped side generally faces the wind. The steep side, or slip face, generally faces away from the wind. If you climb up the steep slope, you will generally be climbing against the wind.

CHAPTER RESOURCES

Chapter Resource File
- Section Quiz GENERAL
- Section Review GENERAL
- Vocabulary and Section Summary GENERAL
- Critical Thinking ADVANCED
- Datasheet for Quick Lab

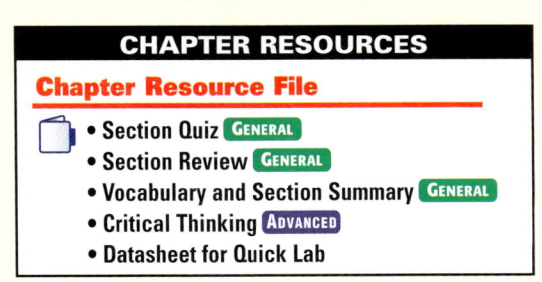

SECTION 3

Focus

Overview
This section examines how glaciers form and how they shape the Earth's surface. Students learn to identify different types of glaciers and learn how they move. Students also focus on how glacial erosion and deposition change the Earth's surface.

🔔 Bellringer
Tell students that 14,000 years ago, much of North America was covered in a thick layer of ice called a *continental glacier*, which moved as far south as southern Illinois. Humans were living in North America at the time. Have students imagine that they encounter this glacier as an early human, and have them write a paragraph about the experience.

Motivate

Group Activity — GENERAL
No Glaciers? Divide the class into small groups, and ask the class to imagine an Earth untouched by glaciers. Have the group members work together to make a poster showing such a planet. Encourage them to consider not only Earth's landscape but also the living things inhabiting it. **LS** Visual

---

SECTION 3

READING WARM-UP

Objectives
- Explain the difference between alpine glaciers and continental glaciers.
- Describe two ways in which glaciers move.
- Identify five landscape features formed by alpine glaciers.
- Identify four types of moraines.

Terms to Learn
glacier   till
glacial drift   stratified drift

READING STRATEGY

Discussion Read this section silently. Write down questions that you have about this section. Discuss your questions in a small group.

glacier a large mass of moving ice

Erosion and Deposition by Ice

Can you imagine an ice cube that is the size of a football stadium? Well, glaciers can be even bigger than that.

A **glacier** is an enormous mass of moving ice. Because glaciers are very heavy and have the ability to move across the Earth's surface, they are capable of eroding, moving, and depositing large amounts of rock materials. And while you will never see a glacier chilling a punch bowl, you might one day visit some of the spectacular landscapes carved by glacial activity!

Glaciers—Rivers of Ice

Glaciers form in areas so cold that snow stays on the ground year-round. In polar regions and at high elevations, snow piles up year after year. Over time, the weight of the snow on top causes the deep-packed snow to become ice crystals. These ice crystals eventually form a giant ice mass. Because glaciers are so massive, the pull of gravity causes them to flow slowly, like "rivers of ice." In this section, you will learn about two main types of glaciers, alpine and continental.

Alpine Glaciers

Alpine glaciers form in mountainous areas. One common type of alpine glacier is a valley glacier. Valley glaciers form in valleys originally created by stream erosion. As these glaciers slowly flow downhill, they widen and straighten the valleys into broad U shapes as shown in **Figure 1**.

✓ **Reading Check** Where do alpine glaciers form? (*See the Appendix for answers to Reading Checks.*)

Figure 1 Alpine glaciers start as snowfields in mountainous areas.

CHAPTER RESOURCES

Chapter Resource File
- Lesson Plan
- Directed Reading A **BASIC**
- Directed Reading B **SPECIAL NEEDS**

Technology
- Transparencies
  - Bellringer

Answer to Reading Check
Alpine glaciers form in mountainous areas.

352   Chapter 12 • Agents of Erosion and Deposition

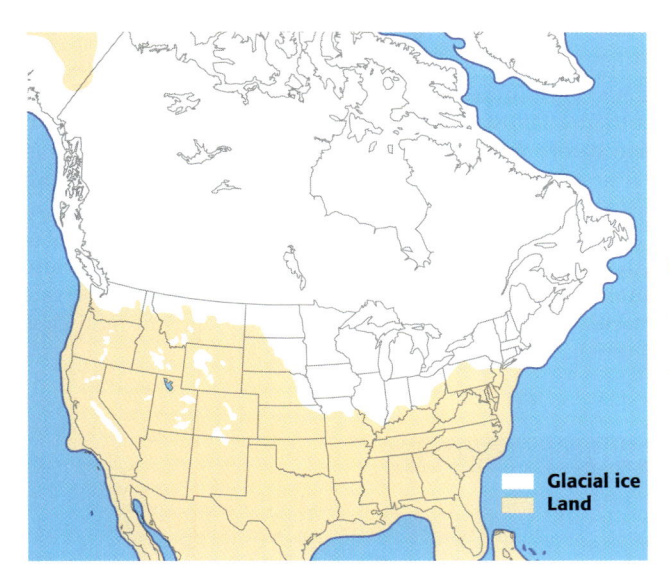

Figure 2 Eleven U.S. states were covered by ice during the last glacial ice period. Because much of the Earth's water was frozen in glaciers, sea levels fell. Blue lines show the coastline at that time.

☐ Glacial ice
☐ Land

Continental Glaciers

Not all glaciers are true "rivers of ice." In fact, some glaciers spread across entire continents. These glaciers, called *continental glaciers*, are huge, continuous masses of ice. The largest continental glacier in the world covers almost all of Antarctica. This ice sheet is approximately one and a half times the size of the United States. It is so thick—more than 4,000 m in places—that it buries everything but the highest mountain peaks.

Glaciers on the Move

When enough ice builds up on a slope, the ice begins to move downhill. Thick glaciers move faster than thin glaciers, and the steeper the slope is, the faster the glaciers will move. Glaciers move in two ways: by sliding and by flowing. A glacier slides when its weight causes the ice at the bottom of the glacier to melt. As the water from a melting ice cube causes the ice cube to travel across a table, the water from the melting ice causes a glacier to move forward. A glacier also flows slowly as ice crystals within the glacier slip over each other. Think of placing a deck of cards on a table and then tilting the table. The top cards will slide farther than the lower cards. Similarly, the upper part of the glacier flows faster than the base.

Glacier movement is affected by climate. As the Earth cools, glaciers grow. About 10,000 years ago, a continental glacier covered most of North America, as shown in **Figure 2**. In some places, the ice sheet was several kilometers thick!

School to Home

The *Titanic*

WRITING SKILL An area where an ice sheet is resting on open water is called an *ice shelf*. When pieces of the ice shelf break off, they are called *icebergs*. How far do you think the iceberg that struck the *Titanic* drifted before the two met that fateful night in 1912? Together with a parent, plot on a map of the North Atlantic Ocean the route of the *Titanic* from Southampton, England, to New York. Then, plot a possible route of the drifting iceberg from Greenland to where the ship sank, just south of the Canadian island province of Newfoundland. Describe your findings in your **science journal**.

Teach

ACTIVITY — BASIC

Describing Glacier Formation
Have students compare in writing the process of making a snowball with the process of forming glacial ice. Students should understand that snowflakes are compressed together when both snowballs and glaciers form. When a snowball is made, heat and pressure from a person's hands partially melt the snow. As the snowball is squeezed, the snowball becomes denser and harder. Alpine glaciers form in a similar way, but pressure comes from the snowpack above. A cycle of freezing and thawing causes the snow to gradually become glacial ice. Because temperatures always remain below freezing in Antarctica, ice sheets form as lower layers of snow are compressed by the weight of overlying layers. **English Language Learners**
LS Verbal

Demonstration — BASIC

Glacier Movement You may wish to demonstrate for students the comparison made on this page between a sliding deck of cards and one type of glacial flow. This process is called *internal plastic flow*. LS Visual

---

Is That a Fact!

How do snowflakes become massive blocks of glacial ice? As snow melts and is compacted, the grains become denser. As snow packs to a greater density, the air spaces between ice crystals are pressed out. Eventually, the ice recrystallizes to a stage between flakes and ice called *firn*. Over time, with more pressure from overlying layers of snow, the firn will recrystallize again to become glacial ice.

Weird Science

Glaciers can be very noisy. As they move and stretch, they howl, shriek, pop, groan, and make explosive noises. These sounds are so loud that they have kept high-altitude mountaineers awake at night!

Section 3 • Erosion and Deposition by Ice

Teach, continued

Answer to Math Practice
0.5 km = 500 m
500 m ÷ 5 m/day = 100 days

CONNECTION ACTIVITY
Environmental Science — GENERAL

Glaciers in the Water Cycle
Glaciers throughout the world provide fresh water that helps regulate the flow of large rivers and recharge aquifers. Scientists are concerned, however, that a permanent increase in global temperatures would alter this naturally controlled process. If the 13,800,000 km² Antarctic ice sheet melted, global sea level could rise 60 m, which would have devastating effects. Coastal towns and cities would be flooded, and some islands would disappear. Have students draw a map of what the coastline of the United States would look like if global sea level rose 60 m. **LS** Visual

MATH PRACTICE

Speed of a Glacier
An alpine glacier is estimated to be moving forward at 5 m per day. Calculate how long the ice will take to reach a road and campground located 0.5 km from the front of the advancing glacier. (Hint: 1 km = 1,000 m)

Landforms Carved by Glaciers

Continental glaciers and alpine glaciers produce landscapes that are very different from one another. Continental glaciers smooth the landscape by scraping and eroding features that existed before the ice appeared. Alpine glaciers carve out rugged features in the mountain rocks through which they flow. **Figure 3** shows the very different landscapes that each type of glacier produces.

Alpine glaciers, such as those in the Rocky Mountains and the Alps, carve out large amounts of rock material and create spectacular landforms. **Figure 4** shows the kinds of landscape features that are sculpted by alpine glaciers.

Figure 3 Landscapes Created by Glaciers

◀ Continental glaciers smooth and flatten the landscape.

Alpine glaciers carved out this rugged landscape. ▶

Is That a Fact!

When metal pipes are drilled through a glacier's layers, they eventually bend in the direction of flow, which demonstrates that glacial layers tend to move at different speeds. One cause of this phenomenon is friction—layers in closest contact with the Earth are often slowed by friction.

CONNECTION to Physical Science — GENERAL

Glacier Movement Point out to students that certain conditions can cause glacial surge. When glaciers surge, or flow rapidly, they may travel 30 m in a day. Explain to students that before and during a glacial surge, meltwater does not drain away from the glacier but builds up beneath the ice, which decreases the friction between the glacier and the land below, permitting the glacier to flow more rapidly.

Chapter 12 • Agents of Erosion and Deposition

Figure 4 Landscape Features Carved by Alpine Glaciers

Horns are sharp, pyramid-shaped peaks that form when three or more cirque glaciers erode a mountain.

Cirques (SUHRKS) are bowl-shaped depressions where glacial ice cuts back into the mountain walls.

Arêtes (uh RAYTS) are jagged ridges that form between two or more cirques cutting into the same mountain.

U-shaped valleys form when a glacier erodes a river valley from its original V shape to a U shape.

Hanging valleys are smaller glacial valleys that join the deeper main valley. Many hanging valleys form waterfalls after the ice is gone.

SCIENCE HUMOR

As glaciers travel downward and form U-shaped valleys, outcrops of hard rock may remain on the valley floor. These smooth rocks are called *roches moutonnees*. This French term meaning "sheep rocks" comically describes the rounded outcroppings, which look like sheep grazing in the valley.

CHAPTER RESOURCES

Technology

Transparencies
• Landscape Features Carved by Alpine Glaciers

Workbooks

Math Skills for Science
• Using Proportions and Cross-Multiplication GENERAL

READING STRATEGY — BASIC

Preparing Tables Have students work independently to create tables summarizing the characteristics and formation of the following landforms: arêtes, horns, hanging valleys, U-shaped valleys, and cirques. Have students keep the tables to use as study guides.
LS Visual/Verbal

Group ACTIVITY — GENERAL

Making Models Divide the class into pairs, and ask each pair to select a landscape feature created by glaciers. Provide modeling clay for students to make a model of the feature. Have each pair present its model to the class and demonstrate how the feature was formed, using another color of clay to represent the glacier. **English Language Learners**
LS Visual

CONNECTION ACTIVITY
Language Arts — ADVANCED

Glacial Explorers Students will enjoy reading about the adventures of high-altitude mountaineers and polar explorers. Have students read selections from the accounts of Antarctic explorers such as Robert Falcon Scott, Ernest Shackleton, or Richard Byrd. Students may also enjoy reading about mountaineers such as Reinhold Messner, Sir Edmund Hillary, or Dr. Johan Reinhard. Students should prepare a presentation for the class about the person they studied and should discuss the explorer's description of glaciers. **LS** Verbal

Section 3 • Erosion and Deposition by Ice

Close

Reteaching — BASIC
Landscape Features Have students create descriptions in their own words for each landscape feature carved by glaciers. Have students exchange descriptions and quiz each other. **LS Verbal**

Quiz — GENERAL
1. How are the landscape features formed by continental glaciers different from landscape features formed by alpine glaciers? (Continental glaciers tend to smooth the landscape, whereas alpine glaciers carve out rugged features.)
2. Why is the study of glaciers important? (Answers may vary. Students may note that many of Earth's landforms were created by glacial movement, that glaciers contain much of Earth's fresh water, and that melting glaciers can cause sea levels to rise.)

Alternative Assessment — GENERAL
Glacier Handbook Have students create a small glacier handbook that includes illustrations and descriptions of continental and alpine glaciers as well as the types of erosion and deposition they cause. Students' books should include examples of stratified drift, outwash plains, kettles, till, and moraines. **LS Intrapersonal**

---

glacial drift the rock material carried and deposited by glaciers

till unsorted rock material that is deposited directly by a melting glacier

stratified drift a glacial deposit that has been sorted and layered by the action of streams or meltwater

Types of Glacial Deposits
As a glacier melts, it drops all the material it is carrying. **Glacial drift** is the general term used to describe all material carried and deposited by glaciers. Glacial drift is divided into two main types, *till* and *stratified drift*.

Till Deposits
Unsorted rock material that is deposited directly by the ice when it melts is called **till.** *Unsorted* means that the till is made up of rock material of different sizes—from large boulders to fine sediment. When the glacier melts, the unsorted material is deposited on the surface of the ground.

The most common till deposits are *moraines*. Moraines generally form ridges along the edges of glaciers. Moraines are produced when glaciers carry material to the front of and along the sides of the ice. As the ice melts, the sediment and rock it is carrying are dropped, which forms different types of moraines. The various types of moraines are shown in **Figure 5.**

Figure 5 Types of Moraines

Lateral moraines form along each side of a glacier.

Medial moraines form when valley glaciers with lateral moraines meet.

Ground moraines form from unsorted materials left beneath a glacier.

Terminal moraines form when sediment is dropped at the front of the glacier.

INCLUSION Strategies

- **Behavior Control Issues**
- **Developmentally Delayed**
- **Learning Disabled**

Organize students in groups of three to four students to make a mini-glacier. You will need to have access to a freezer. Hand out to each group a plastic cup, gravel, tap water, plastic wrap, strong electrical tape, a paper plate, and a smooth, soft piece of wood. Have each group fill the plastic cup halfway with gravel and then cover the gravel with an inch of water. Carefully tape plastic wrap over the top, and flip the cup over onto the paper plate. Put the cups in the freezer overnight. During the next class, each group should peel off the paper plate and scrape the "glacier" gravel side down across the wood. Ask students what scientists can determine by studying the marks left by the gravel on the wood. Tell students these marks are called *striations* and have students sketch the striation pattern of the glacier in their **science journals.** **LS Visual/Kinesthetic**

---

356 Chapter 12 • Agents of Erosion and Deposition

Stratified Drift

When a glacier melts, streams form that carry rock material away from the shrinking glacier. A glacial deposit that is sorted into layers based on the size of the rock material is called **stratified drift**. Streams carry sorted material and deposit it in front of the glacier in a broad area called an *outwash plain*. Sometimes, a block of ice is left in the outwash plain when a glacier retreats. As the ice melts, sediment builds up around the block of ice, and a depression called a *kettle* forms. Kettles commonly fill with water to form lakes or ponds, as **Figure 6** shows.

Reading Check Explain the difference between a till deposit and stratified drift.

Figure 6 Kettle lakes form in outwash plains and are common in states such as Minnesota.

SECTION Review

Summary

- Alpine glaciers form in mountainous areas. Continental glaciers spread across entire continents.
- Glaciers can move by sliding or by flowing.
- Alpine glaciers can carve cirques, arêtes, horns, U-shaped valleys, and hanging valleys.
- Two types of glacial drift are till and stratified drift.
- Four types of moraines are lateral, medial, ground, and terminal moraines.

Using Key Terms

Complete each of the following sentences by choosing the correct term from the word bank.

glacial drift   glacier
stratified drift   till

1. A glacial deposit that is sorted into layers based on the size of the rock material is called ___.
2. ___ is all of the material carried and deposited by glaciers.
3. Unsorted rock material that is deposited directly by the ice when it melts is ___.
4. A ___ is an enormous mass of moving ice.

Understanding Key Ideas

5. Which of the following is not a type of moraine?
   a. lateral
   b. horn
   c. ground
   d. medial
6. Explain the difference between alpine and continental glaciers.
7. Name five landscape features formed by alpine glaciers.
8. Describe two ways in which glaciers move.

Math Skills

9. A recent study shows that a glacier in Alaska is melting at a rate of 23 ft per year. At what rate is the glacier melting in meters? (Hint: 1 ft = 0.3 m)

Critical Thinking

10. **Analyzing Ideas** Explain why continental glaciers smooth the landscape and alpine glaciers create a rugged landscape.
11. **Applying Concepts** How can a glacier deposit both sorted and unsorted material?
12. **Applying Concepts** Why are glaciers such effective agents of erosion and deposition?

For a variety of links related to this chapter, go to www.scilinks.org
Topic: Glaciers
SciLinks code: HSM0675

Answer to Reading Check

A till deposit is made up of unsorted material, while stratified drift is made up of layers of rock, sorted by size.

Answers to Section Review

1. stratified drift
2. Glacial drift
3. till
4. glacier
5. b
6. Continental glaciers are very large and tend to expand across entire continents. Alpine glaciers are smaller and form in mountainous regions.
7. Five landscape features formed by alpine glaciers include horns, cirques, arêtes, hanging valleys, and broad, U-shaped valleys.
8. Glaciers can move by either sliding or flowing.
9. 23 ft/year × 0.3 m/ft = 6.9 m/year
10. Continental glaciers smooth the landscape because they cover it entirely and scrape away older surface features. Alpine glaciers create rugged landscapes because they cover only portions of mountains. As alpine glaciers move downhill, they cut into the mountains and create dramatic features that were not there before.
11. Meltwater streams flowing through a glacier carry sorted material. Unsorted material is deposited when a glacier melts entirely.
12. Glaciers are effective agents of erosion and deposition because they are very heavy and move across the Earth's surface.

CHAPTER RESOURCES

Chapter Resource File
- Section Quiz GENERAL
- Section Review GENERAL
- Vocabulary and Section Summary GENERAL
- Reinforcement Worksheet BASIC

Section 3 • Erosion and Deposition by Ice

SECTION 4

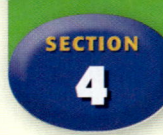

Focus

Overview
This section introduces gravity as an agent of erosion and deposition. Students learn that mass movements caused by gravity are affected by the material's size, weight, shape, and by the slope on which the material rests. Students then learn about rapid mass movements, such as landslides, mudflows, and volcanic lahars. This section also examines the effect of slow mass movements, such as creep.

🔔 Bellringer
Write the following sentence on the board or overhead projector:

Watch for falling rocks!

Ask students to describe places where a warning sign like this would be necessary. Ask students to consider what factors contribute to make a rock-fall zone.

Motivate

Discussion — GENERAL
Erosion by Gravity Ask students to review the three agents of erosion and deposition that they have learned about so far: waves, wind, and glaciers. Then discuss as a class how these types of erosion and deposition compare with erosion and deposition by gravity. **LS Verbal**

SECTION 4

READING WARM-UP

Objectives
- Explain the role of gravity as an agent of erosion and deposition.
- Explain how angle of repose is related to mass movement.
- Describe four types of rapid mass movement.
- Describe three factors that affect creep.

Terms to Learn
mass movement   mudflow
rock fall   creep
landslide

READING STRATEGY
Prediction Guide Before reading this section, write the title of each heading in this section. Next, under each heading, write what you think you will learn.

The Effect of Gravity on Erosion and Deposition

Did you know that the Appalachian Mountains may have once been almost five times as tall as they are now? Why are they shorter now? Part of the answer lies in the effect that gravity has on all objects on Earth.

Although you can't see it, the force of gravity is also an agent of erosion and deposition. Gravity not only influences the movement of water and ice but also causes rocks and soil to move downslope. **Mass movement** is the movement of any material, such as rock, soil, or snow, downslope. Whether mass movement happens rapidly or slowly, it plays a major role in shaping the Earth's surface.

Angle of Repose

If dry sand is piled up, it will move downhill until the slope becomes stable. The *angle of repose* is the steepest angle, or slope, at which loose material will not slide downslope. This is demonstrated in **Figure 1**. The angle of repose is different for each type of surface material. Characteristics of the surface material, such as its size, weight, shape, and moisture level, determine at what angle the material will move downslope.

mass movement a movement of a section of land down a slope

Figure 1 If the slope on which material rests is less than the angle of repose, the material will stay in place. If the slope is greater than the angle of repose, the material will move downslope.

CHAPTER RESOURCES

Chapter Resource File
- Lesson Plan
- Directed Reading A **BASIC**
- Directed Reading B **SPECIAL NEEDS**

Technology
- Transparencies
  - Bellringer
  - **LINK TO PHYSICAL SCIENCE** Gravitational Force Depends on Mass

---

358 Chapter 12 • Agents of Erosion and Deposition

Rapid Mass Movement

The most destructive mass movements happen suddenly and rapidly. Rapid mass movement can be very dangerous and can destroy everything in its path.

Rock Falls

While driving along a mountain road, you may have noticed signs along the road that warn of falling rocks. A **rock fall** happens when loose rocks fall down a steep slope. Steep slopes are sometimes created to make room for a road in mountainous areas. Loosened and exposed rocks above the road tend to fall as a result of gravity. The rocks in a rock fall can range in size from small fragments to large boulders.

Landslides

Another type of rapid mass movement is a landslide. A **landslide** is the sudden and rapid movement of a large amount of material downslope. A *slump,* shown in **Figure 2,** is the most common type of landslide. Slumping occurs when a block of material moves downslope over a curved surface. Heavy rains, deforestation, construction on unstable slopes, and earthquakes increase the chances that a landslide will happen. **Figure 3** shows a landslide in India.

Reading Check What is a slump? (*See the Appendix for answers to Reading Checks.*)

Figure 2 A slump is a type of landslide that occurs when a block of land becomes detached and slides downhill.

rock fall a group of loose rocks that fall down a steep slope

landslide the sudden movement of rock and soil down a slope

Figure 3 This landslide in Bombay, India, happened after heavy monsoon rains.

CONNECTION to Physical Science — BASIC

Gravity and Mass Use the teaching transparency "Gravitational Force Depends on Mass" to help explain the force of gravity to students. Explain to students that gravity is a force of attraction between two masses. The larger the masses are and the closer they are to one another, the stronger gravitational attraction is. Because Earth is so massive, it exerts a strong gravitational pull on objects near its surface. **LS Visual**

Answer to Reading Check

A slump is the result of a landslide in which a block of material moves downslope over a curved surface.

Teach

ACTIVITY — BASIC

Demonstrating Mass Movement
Ask students to prepare a demonstration that compares mass movements of different materials on varying slopes. Provide a cookie sheet, dry sand, potting soil, and gravel. Have students raise one end of the cookie sheet about 2 cm. Ask them to use a protractor to measure the angle of repose for each material. Have students repeat the procedure after moistening the materials, and ask them to make conclusions about the effect of water saturation on mass movement. Display the transparency entitled "Gravitational Force Depends on Mass" to help students understand how mass and gravity are related. **English Language Learners**
LS Visual/Kinesthetic

CONNECTION ACTIVITY
Environmental Science — GENERAL

Deforestation and Mudslides
Lack of vegetative cover contributes to the frequency and severity of mudslides. Tree roots stabilize the soil and absorb groundwater. Deforestation accelerates erosion of slopes. In 1995, there were 260 landslides in British Columbia's Clayquot Sound region during the rainy season. Only 33 landslides were in unlogged areas. As a class, find out more about the connections between large-scale logging operations and recent mudslides. Students may wish to investigate the relationship between deforestation in Central America and the devastating mudslides that followed Hurricane Mitch in 1998.
LS Verbal

Section 4 • The Effect of Gravity on Erosion and Deposition

Close

Reteaching — BASIC

Flashcards Have students label index cards with the five types of mass movement discussed in this section. On the reverse side of the index cards, have students write details about each type of mass movement. Students can use these flashcards as a study tool. **LS Verbal**

Quiz — GENERAL

1. Name four characteristics of surface material that affect its angle of repose. (size, weight, shape, and moisture level)
2. What is creep? (Creep is the slow movement of surface material downslope.)
3. What are four types of rapid mass movement? (rock falls, landslides, mudflows, and lahars)

Alternative Assessment — GENERAL

Public-Service Announcements Organize the class into groups. Have each group write a public-service announcement designed to educate the public about the dangers of one form of mass movement. Instruct students to focus on the causes and consequences of these phenomena. Have each group present its announcement for the class. **LS Verbal/Kinesthetic**

Figure 4 This photo shows one of the many mudflows that have occurred in California during rainy winters.

mudflow the flow of a mass of mud or rock and soil mixed with a large amount of water

Figure 5 This lahar overtook the city of Kyushu in Japan.

Mudflows

A rapid movement of a large mass of mud is a **mudflow.** Mudflows happen when a large amount of water mixes with soil and rock. The water causes the slippery mass of mud to flow rapidly downslope. Mudflows commonly happen in mountainous regions when a long dry season is followed by heavy rains. Deforestation and the removal of ground cover can often result in devastating mudflows. As you can see in **Figure 4,** a mudflow can carry trees, houses, cars, and other objects that lie in its path.

Lahars

Volcanic eruptions or heavy rains on volcanic ash can produce some of the most dangerous mudflows. Mudflows of volcanic origin are called *lahars*. Lahars can travel at speeds greater than 80 km/h and can be as thick as cement. On volcanoes with snowy peaks, an eruption can suddenly melt a great amount of ice. The water from the ice liquefies the soil and volcanic ash to produce a hot mudflow that rushes downslope. **Figure 5** shows the effects of a massive lahar in Japan.

Reading Check Explain how a lahar occurs.

Answer to Reading Check
A lahar is caused by the eruption of an ice-covered volcano, which melts ice and causes a hot mudflow.

CONNECTION to Life Science — GENERAL

Mudflows in California In 1980, six successive storms caused devastating mudflows in California. The storms dropped 33 cm of rain, which transformed the soil into mud. Soil on slopes oozed out from under the foundations of houses, which sent the houses tumbling into canyons and valleys, killing 24 people and causing millions of dollars in damage. Many believe that the mudflows were so massive because the area was recently logged.

Chapter 12 • Agents of Erosion and Deposition

Slow Mass Movement

Sometimes, you don't even notice mass movement happening. Although rapid mass movements are visible and dramatic, slow mass movements happen a little at a time. However, because slow mass movements occur more frequently, more material is moved collectively over time.

Creep

Even though most slopes appear to be stable, they are actually undergoing slow mass movement, as shown in **Figure 6**. The extremely slow movement of material downslope is called **creep**. Many factors contribute to creep. Water loosens soil and allows it to move freely. In addition, plant roots act as a wedge that forces rocks and soil particles apart. Burrowing animals, such as gophers and groundhogs, also loosen rock and soil particles. In fact, rock and soil on every slope travels slowly downhill.

Figure 6 Bent tree trunks are evidence that creep is happening.

creep the slow downhill movement of weathered rock material

SECTION Review

Summary

- Gravity causes rocks and soil to move downslope.
- If the slope on which material rests is greater than the angle of repose, mass movement will occur.
- Four types of rapid mass movement are rock falls, landslides, mudflows, and lahars.
- Water, plant roots, and burrowing animals can cause creep.

Using Key Terms

Complete each of the following sentences by choosing the correct term from the word bank.

creep   mass movement
mudflow   rock fall

1. A ___ occurs when a large amount of water mixes with soil and rock.
2. The extremely slow movement of material downslope is called ___.

Understanding Key Ideas

3. Which of the following is a factor that affects creep?
   a. water
   b. burrowing animals
   c. plant roots
   d. All of the above.
4. How is the angle of repose related to mass movement?

Math Skills

5. If a lahar is traveling at 80 km/h, how long will it take the lahar to travel 20 km?

Critical Thinking

6. **Identifying Relationships** Which types of mass movement are most dangerous to humans? Explain your answer.
7. **Making Inferences** How does deforestation increase the likelihood of mudflows?

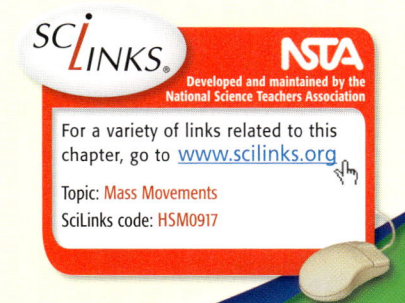

For a variety of links related to this chapter, go to **www.scilinks.org**
Topic: Mass Movements
SciLinks code: HSM0917

Answers to Section Review
1. mudflow
2. creep
3. d
4. Mass movement will occur if the slope of the material is steeper than the angle of repose.
5. 20 km ÷ 80 km/hr = 0.25 hr
6. Rapid mass movements are the most dangerous type of mass movement because a large amount of material moves rapidly and without warning.
7. Sample answer: Deforestation increases the likelihood of mudflows because root systems hold the soil in place.

INTERNET ACTIVITY
Essay — GENERAL

For an internet activity related to this chapter, have students go to **go.hrw.com** and type in the keyword **HZ5ICEW**.

CHAPTER RESOURCES
Chapter Resource File
- Section Quiz GENERAL
- Section Review GENERAL
- Vocabulary and Section Summary GENERAL
- SciLinks Activity GENERAL

Section 4 • The Effect of Gravity on Erosion and Deposition

Model-Making Lab

Gliding Glaciers

Teacher's Notes

Time Required
Two 45-minute class periods plus a 15-minute preparation activity

Lab Ratings
EASY —————→ HARD

Teacher Prep 🧪🧪
Student Set-Up 🧪🧪
Concept Level 🧪🧪
Clean Up 🧪🧪

MATERIALS
The materials listed on the student page are enough for one student or a pair of students. These materials could also be used in larger groups. To reduce the amount of materials, students could use ice cubes and smaller amounts of clay, sand, and gravel.

Preparation Notes
Students should review the entire section on glaciers in this chapter prior to performing this activity. For the second part of the lab, students might have to refreeze ice blocks overnight or make three more ice blocks. If new ice blocks are made, the sand and gravel can be omitted.

Model-Making Lab

OBJECTIVES
Build a model of a glacier.
Demonstrate the effects of glacial erosion by various materials.
Observe the effect of pressure on the melting rate of a glacier.

MATERIALS
- brick (3)
- clay, modeling (2 lb)
- container, empty large margarine (3)
- freezer
- graduated cylinder, 50 mL
- gravel (1 lb)
- pan, aluminum rectangular (3)
- rolling pin, wood
- ruler, metric
- sand (1 lb)
- stopwatch
- towel, small hand
- water

Gliding Glaciers

A glacier is a large, moving mass of ice. Glaciers are responsible for shaping many of Earth's natural features. Glaciers are set in motion by the pull of gravity and by the gradual melting of the glacier. As a glacier moves, it changes the landscape by eroding the surface over which it passes.

Part A: Getting in the Groove

Procedure
The material that is carried by a glacier erodes Earth's surface by gouging out grooves called *striations*. Different materials have varying effects on the landscape. In this activity, you will create a model glacier with which to demonstrate the effects of glacial erosion by various materials.

1. Fill one margarine container with sand to a depth of 1 cm. Fill another margarine container with gravel to a depth of 1 cm. Leave the third container empty. Fill the containers with water.

2. Put the three containers in a freezer, and leave them there overnight.

3. Retrieve the containers from the freezer, and remove the three ice blocks from the containers.

4. Use a rolling pin to flatten the modeling clay.

5. Hold the ice block from the third container firmly with a towel, and press as you move the ice along the length of the clay. Do this three times. In a notebook, sketch the pattern that the ice block makes in the clay.

CLASSROOM TESTED & APPROVED

Bert Sherwood
Socorro Middle School
El Paso, Texas

CHAPTER RESOURCES

Chapter Resource File
- Datasheet for Chapter Lab
- Lab Notes and Answers

Technology

Classroom Videos
- Lab Video

LabBook
- Dune Movement
- Creating a Kettle

362   Chapter 12 • Agents of Erosion and Deposition

6. Repeat steps 4 and 5 using the ice block that contains sand.

7. Repeat steps 4 and 5 using the ice block that contains gravel.

Analyze the Results

1. **Describing Events** Did any material from the clay become mixed with the material in the ice blocks? Explain.

2. **Describing Events** Was any material from the ice blocks deposited on the clay surface? Explain.

3. **Examining Data** What glacial features are represented in your clay model?

Draw Conclusions

4. **Evaluating Data** Compare the patterns formed by the three model glaciers. Do the patterns look like features carved by alpine glaciers or by continental glaciers? Explain.

Part B: Melting Away

Procedure

As the layers of ice build up and a glacier gets larger, a glacier will eventually begin to melt. The water from the melted ice allows a glacier to move forward. In this activity, you'll explore the effect of pressure on the melting rate of a glacier.

1. If possible, make three identical ice blocks without any sand or gravel in them. If that is not possible, use the ice blocks from Part A. Place one ice block upside down in each pan.

2. Place one brick on top of one of the ice blocks. Place two bricks on top of another ice block. Do not put any bricks on the third ice block.

3. After 15 min, remove the bricks from the ice blocks.

4. Using the graduated cylinder, measure the amount of water that has melted from each ice block.

5. Observe and record your findings.

Analyze the Results

1. **Analyzing Data** Which ice block produced the most water?

2. **Explaining Events** What did the bricks represent?

3. **Analyzing Results** What part of the ice blocks melted first? Explain.

Draw Conclusions

4. **Interpreting Information** How could you relate this investigation to the melting rate of glaciers? Explain.

Applying Your Data

Replace the clay with different materials, such as soft wood or sand. How does each ice block affect the different surface materials? What types of surfaces do the different materials represent?

CHAPTER RESOURCES
Workbooks

- **Whiz-Bang Demonstrations**
  - Between a Rock and a Hard Place BASIC
  - Rising Mountains GENERAL
- **Long-Term Projects & Research Ideas**
  - Deep in the Mud ADVANCED

Lab Notes

This part of the lab models how the weight of glacial ice causes the ice at the bottom of the glacier to melt. This is one way that glaciers move. You may wish to explain this concept by discussing how ice skates work. Ice skates glide smoothly because they distribute a skater's weight on two thin blades. The weight of a skater applied to such a small surface area causes the ice beneath the blades of the skate to melt and quickly re-freeze. Like glaciers, ice skaters glide on a thin layer of water.

Part A: Analyze the Results

1. Answers may vary. Small amounts of the surface material may become mixed with the ice.

2. Answers may vary. Small amounts of the material in the ice may be deposited on the clay surface.

3. Answers may vary. Answers may include moraines, striations, and outwash plains.

Part A: Draw Conclusions

4. Answers may vary. Alpine glaciers leave rugged features behind as they flow. Continental glaciers smooth the landscape.

Part B: Analyze the Results

1. The ice block with two bricks on it produced the most water.

2. The bricks represented layers of ice.

3. The bottom of the ice block melted first because of the weight of the bricks on top of the ice block.

Part B: Draw Conclusions

4. Students should conclude that glaciers that are heavier melt faster. This, in turn, causes glaciers to move faster.

Chapter 12 • Chapter Lab

Chapter Review

Assignment Guide

Section	Questions
1	1, 2, 7–9, 15, 24–27
2	3, 10, 16, 18, 20, 21
3	4, 5, 11, 12, 19, 22, 23
4	6, 13, 14, 17

ANSWERS

Using Key Terms

1. Sample answer: The shoreline is the area where land and a body of water meet. A longshore current is a movement of water close to the shoreline that moves sand in a zigzag pattern.
2. Sample answer: Beaches are areas of the shoreline made up of material deposited by waves. Dunes are deposits of windblown sand that can be found on a beach.
3. Sample answer: Deflation is the lifting and removal of material by the wind. Saltation is the movement of sand by a skipping and bouncing action in the direction the wind is blowing.
4. Sample answer: A continental glacier is a large, continuous mass of ice that can spread across an entire continent. Alpine glaciers form in mountainous areas, and they are much smaller than continental glaciers. Continental glaciers tend to smooth out the landscape, while alpine glaciers tend to carve rugged features in mountains.

Chapter Review

USING KEY TERMS

For each pair of terms, explain how the meanings of the terms differ.

1. *shoreline* and *longshore current*
2. *beaches* and *dunes*
3. *deflation* and *saltation*
4. *continental glacier* and *alpine glacier*
5. *stratified drift* and *till*
6. *mudflow* and *creep*

UNDERSTANDING KEY IDEAS

Multiple Choice

7. *Surf* refers to
   a. large storm waves in the open ocean.
   b. giant waves produced by hurricanes.
   c. breaking waves near the shoreline.
   d. small waves on a calm sea.

8. When waves cut completely through a headland, a ___ is formed.
   a. sea cave
   b. sea arch
   c. wave-cut terrace
   d. sandbar

9. A narrow strip of sand that is formed by wave deposition and is connected to the shore is called a
   a. barrier spit.
   b. sandbar.
   c. wave-cut terrace.
   d. headland.

10. A wind-eroded depression is called a
    a. deflation hollow.
    b. desert pavement.
    c. dune.
    d. dust bowl.

11. What term describes all types of glacial deposits?
    a. glacial drift
    b. dune
    c. till
    d. outwash

12. Which of the following is NOT a landform created by an alpine glacier?
    a. cirque
    b. deflation hollow
    c. horn
    d. arête

13. What is the term for a mass movement that is of volcanic origin?
    a. lahar
    b. slump
    c. creep
    d. rock fall

14. Which of the following is a slow mass movement?
    a. mudflow
    b. landslide
    c. creep
    d. rock fall

Short Answer

15. Why do waves break when they near the shore?

16. Why are some areas more affected by wind erosion than other areas are?

---

5. Sample answer: Stratified drift is sorted glacial drift. Till is unsorted glacial drift.
6. Sample answer: A mudflow is a rapid mass movement. Creep is a slow mass movement.

Understanding Key Ideas

7. c
8. b
9. a
10. a
11. a
12. b
13. a
14. c

15. When waves reach shallow water, the lower part of the wave is crowded by the ocean floor. The wave becomes taller and eventually grows so tall that it cannot support itself. When the wave reaches this point, it curls and breaks.

16. Areas with little vegetation, deserts, and coastlines are more affected by wind erosion than other areas because there are few plant roots to anchor the sand and soil in place.

364 Chapter 12 • Agents of Erosion and Deposition

17 What kind of mass movement happens continuously, day after day?

18 In what direction do sand dunes move?

19 Describe the different types of glacial moraines.

CRITICAL THINKING

20 **Concept Mapping** Use the following terms to create a concept map: *deflation, strong winds, saltation, dune,* and *desert pavement.*

21 **Making Inferences** How do humans increase the likelihood that wind erosion will occur?

22 **Identifying Relationships** If the large ice sheet covering Antarctica were to melt completely, what type of landscape would you expect Antarctica to have?

23 **Applying Concepts** You are a geologist who is studying rock to determine the direction of flow of an ancient glacier. What clues might help you determine the glacier's direction of flow?

24 **Applying Concepts** You are interested in purchasing a home that overlooks the ocean. The home that you want to buy sits atop a steep sea cliff. Given what you have learned about shoreline erosion, what factors would you take into consideration when deciding whether to buy the home?

INTERPRETING GRAPHICS

The graph below illustrates coastal erosion and deposition at an imaginary beach over a period of 8 years. Use the graph below to answer the questions that follow.

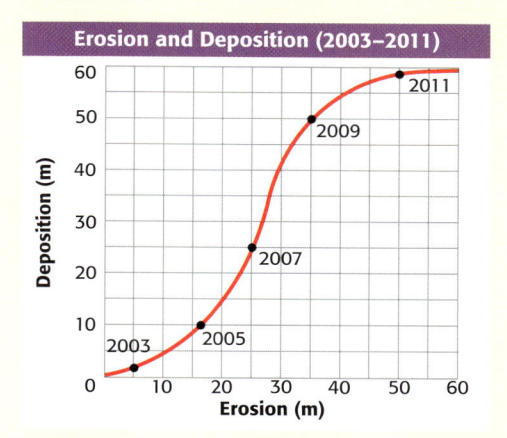

Erosion and Deposition (2003–2011)

25 What is happening to the beach over time?

26 In what year does the amount of erosion equal the amount of deposition?

27 Based on the erosion and deposition data for 2005, what might happen to the beach in the years that follow 2005?

Critical Thinking

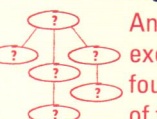

20. An answer to this exercise can be found at the end of this book.

21. Answers may vary. Sample answer: Sometimes people remove native vegetation from an area to make room for agricultural land. Plants anchor the soil in place. By removing them, people make the area more vulnerable to wind erosion.

22. Answers may vary. Sample answer: Because the ice sheet covering Antarctica is a continental glacier, one would expect the landscape of Antarctica to be smooth and flat.

23. Answers may vary. Students could study maps of rock formations to see which direction the rocks in the glacial drift came from. Students could also look for evidence of outwash plains, which would indicate deposits in front of the glacier.

24. Answers may vary. Sample answer: Factors to consider include the frequency of strong storms in the area, and the rate that the surrounding shoreline is eroding.

Interpreting Graphics

25. Sample answer: At first, more soil is being eroded than deposited. The beach is getting smaller. After 2007, more soil is being deposited than eroded. The beach is getting larger.

26. 2007

27. Sample answer: In 2005, more sand is being eroded than deposited. The coastline is losing land. This pattern would lead you to believe that the coastline would continue shrinking. But after 2007, the coastline stops losing land and begins growing.

---

17. Creep is the extremely slow mass movement of material downslope.

18. Sand dunes move in the direction of the strong winds.

19. Lateral moraines form along each side of a glacier. Medial moraines form when valley glaciers meet. Ground moraines form from unsorted materials left beneath a glacier. Terminal moraines form when sediment is dropped at the front of a glacier.

CHAPTER RESOURCES

Chapter Resource File
- Chapter Review GENERAL
- Chapter Test A GENERAL
- Chapter Test B ADVANCED
- Chapter Test C SPECIAL NEEDS
- Vocabulary Activity GENERAL

Workbooks

Study Guide
- Assessment resources are also available in Spanish.

Chapter 12 • Chapter Review

Standardized Test Preparation

Teacher's Note

To provide practice under more realistic testing conditions, give students 20 minutes to answer all of the questions in this Standardized Test Preparation.

MISCONCEPTION ALERT

Answers to the standardized test preparation can help you identify student misconceptions and misunderstandings.

READING

Passage 1
1. B
2. H
3. A
4. I

TEST DOCTOR

Question 3: Some students may think that taller waves are formed in the deeper water because the depth allows for larger waves. However, as the passage explains, waves become crowded as they reach the shore and therefore get taller.

Question 4: Some students may misinterpret short waves that are far apart as the waves that break on the shore. However, the passage implies that in the deep ocean water, waves have more room and are therefore shorter and farther apart than waves that are moving closer to the shore.

Passage 2
1. B
2. I
3. A

Standardized Test Preparation

READING

Read each of the passages below. Then, answer the questions that follow each passage.

Passage 1 When you drop a pebble into a pond, is there just one ripple? Of course not. Waves, like ripples, don't move alone. Waves travel in groups called wave trains. As wave trains move away from their sources, they travel through the ocean water uninterrupted. But when waves reach shallow water, they change form because the ocean floor crowds the lower part of the wave. As a result, the waves get closer together and taller.

1. In this passage, what does the word *uninterrupted* mean?
   A not continuous
   B not broken
   C broken again
   D not interpreted

2. In this passage, what does the word *train* mean?
   F to teach someone a skill
   G the part of a gown that trails behind the person who is wearing the gown
   H a series of moving things
   I a series of railroad cars

3. According to the passage, what is the cause of taller waves?
   A shallow water
   B deep ocean water
   C rippling
   D wave trains

4. If certain waves are short and far apart, which of the following can be concluded?
   F The waves are approaching the shore.
   G The waves are moving toward their source.
   H The waves were interrupted.
   I The waves are in deep ocean water.

Passage 2 Winter storms create powerful waves that crash into cliffs and break off pieces of rock that fall into the ocean. On February 8, 1998, unusually large waves crashed against the cliffs along Broad Beach Road in Malibu, California. Eventually, the ocean-eroded cliffs buckled, which caused a landslide. One house collapsed into the ocean, and two more houses dangled on the edge of the cliff's newly eroded face. Powerful waves, buckled cliffs, and landslides are part of the ongoing natural process of coastal erosion that is taking place along the California shoreline and along similar shorelines throughout the world.

1. In this passage, what does *buckled* mean?
   A tightened
   B collapsed
   C formed
   D heated up

2. Which of the following describes how this coastal area was damaged?
   F The area was damaged by collapsing houses.
   G The area was damaged an earthquake.
   H The area was damaged by ocean currents.
   I The area was damaged by unusually large waves produced by a winter storm.

3. Which of the following can be concluded from this passage?
   A This area may have landslides in the future.
   B This area is safe from future landslides.
   C This type of landslide is common only to the California coastline.
   D Erosion in this area happens very rarely.

TEST DOCTOR

Question 3: Some students may think because this area was severely eroded from the storm and landslide discussed in the passage, the area may be safe from future landslides. In fact, the passage infers that the area is susceptible to future landslides because of its location along the shoreline.

366 Chapter 12 • Agents of Erosion and Deposition

INTERPRETING GRAPHICS

Use each figure below to answer the questions that follow each figure.

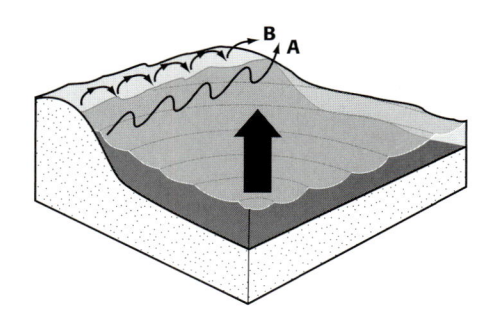

1. In the illustration, what does A label?
   - A wave direction
   - B wave amplitude
   - C wavelength
   - D a longshore current

2. In the illustration, what does B label?
   - F wave direction
   - G wave period
   - H the movement of sand
   - I a longshore current

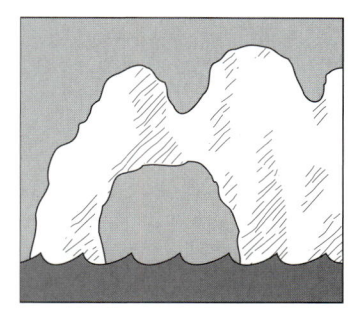

3. What process created the landform in the illustration above?
   - A erosion by waves
   - B saltation
   - C abrasion
   - D deposition by waves

MATH

Read each question below, and choose the best answer.

1. Wind erosion caused a deflation hollow that was circular in shape. The hollow is 100 m wide. What is the circumference of this deflation hollow?
   - A 31.4 m
   - B 62.8 m
   - C 314 m
   - D 628 m

2. A homeowner needs to buy and plant 28 trees to prevent wind erosion. Each tree costs $29.99. What is a reasonable estimate for the total cost of these trees before tax?
   - F a little more than $200
   - G a little less than $600
   - H a little less than $900
   - I a little more than $1,000

Use the equation below to answer the questions that follow.

$$\frac{\text{number of waves}}{\text{per minute}} = \frac{60 \text{ s}}{\text{wave period (s)}}$$

3. If the wave period is 15 s, how many waves occur in 1 min?
   - A 4
   - B 60
   - C 75
   - D 240

4. If the wave period is 30 s, how many waves occur in 1 min?
   - F 1
   - G 2
   - H 3
   - I 5

5. If 480 waves broke in 40 min, what is the wave period?
   - A 5 s
   - B 12 s
   - C 15 s
   - D 20 s

INTERPRETING GRAPHICS
1. D
2. H
3. A

TEST DOCTOR

Question 3: Saltation refers to the movement of sand along the shoreline. Abrasion refers to a form of wind erosion that smooths and polishes rock. This diagram shows a sea arch, which is formed by wave erosion rather than deposition, so answer A is correct.

MATH
1. C
2. I
3. A
4. G
5. A

TEST DOCTOR

Question 3: Answer B is the number of waves that would occur in 15 minutes. Answer C is the number of waves that would occur in 19 minutes. Answer D is the number of waves that would occur in 1 hour. So, answer A is the correct answer.

CHAPTER RESOURCES

Chapter Resource File
- Standardized Test Preparation GENERAL

State Resources
For specific resources for your state, visit go.hrw.com and type in the keyword HSMSTR.

Chapter 12 • Standardized Test Preparation

Science in Action

Weird Science

Long-Runout Landslides

At 4:10 A.M. on April 29, 1903, the town of Frank, Canada, was changed forever when disaster struck without warning. An enormous chunk of limestone fell suddenly from the top of nearby Turtle Mountain. In less than two minutes, the huge mass of rock buried most of the town! Landslides such as the Frank landslide are now known as *long-runout landslides*. Most landslides travel a horizontal distance that is less than twice the vertical distance that they have fallen. But long-runout landslides carry enormous amounts of rock and thus can travel many times farther than they fall. The physics of long-runout landslides are still a mystery to scientists.

Scientific Discoveries

The Lost Squadron

During World War II, an American squadron of eight planes crash-landed on the ice of Greenland. The crew was rescued, but the planes were lost. After the war, several people tried to find the "Lost Squadron." Finally, in 1988, a team of adventurers found the planes by using radar. The planes were buried by 40 years of snowfall and had become part of the Greenland ice sheet! When the planes were found, they were buried under 80 m of glacial ice. Incredibly, the team tunneled down through the ice and recovered a plane. The plane is now named Glacier Girl, and it still flies today!

Language Arts Activity

WRITING SKILL The crew of the Lost Squadron had to wait 10 days to be rescued by dog sled. Imagine that you were part of the crew—what would you have done to survive? Write a short story describing your adventure on the ice sheet of Greenland.

Math Activity

The Frank landslide traveled 4 km in 100 s. Calculate this speed in meters per second.

Teacher Notes

Weird Science
Background
Friction calculations predict that the ratio of a landslide's vertical drop to the horizontal distance it travels should be about 0.6 to 1. For some rare, giant landslides of rock, however, this ratio can be as low as 0.1 to 1. These long-runout landslides are also known as "sturzstroms," which is German for "fall streams."

Scientific Discoveries
Background
The recovery team looked at the ice near the surface and saw about 30 cm of ice between each year's summer melt. The team also reasoned that global warming may have increased melting and slowed the rate of deposition. With this information, they expected the planes to be buried under 12 m of ice. So why were they so far off?

Studies over the last few decades show a slight rise in global temperatures, but the area of the crash site has actually been cooling. This means less melting each summer, so more snow is added to the growing layers of ice. Also, rising global temperatures may be causing more snowfall in some parts of Greenland.

Answer to Math Activity
4 km = 4,000 m
4,000 m ÷ 100 s = 40 m/s

Answer to Language Arts Activity
Answers may vary. Students' stories should describe harsh weather conditions, similar to the conditions that the Lost Squadron crew encountered, and the stories could provide a description of the survival techniques the students depended upon until their crew was rescued.

Chapter 12 • Agents of Erosion and Deposition

Careers

Johan Reinhard

High-Altitude Anthropologist Imagine discovering the mummified body of a girl from 500 years ago! In 1995, while climbing Mount Ampato, one of the tallest mountains in the Andes, Johan Reinhard made an incredible discovery—the well-preserved mummy of a young Inca girl. The recent eruption of a nearby volcano had caused the snow on Mount Ampato to melt and uncover the mummy. The discovery of the "Inca Ice Maiden" gave scientists a wealth of new information about Incan culture. Today, Reinhard considers the discovery of the Inca Ice Maiden his most exciting moment in the field.

Johan Reinhard is an anthropologist. Anthropologists study the physical and cultural characteristics of human populations. Reinhard studied anthropology at the University of Arizona and at the University of Vienna, in Austria. Early in his career, Reinhard worked on underwater archeology projects in Austria and Italy and on projects in the mountains of Nepal and Tibet. He soon made mountains and mountain peoples the focus of his career as an anthropologist. Reinhard spent 10 years in the highest mountains on Earth, the Himalayas. There, he studied the role of sacred mountains in Tibetan religions. Now, Reinhard studies the culture of the ancient Inca in the Andes of South America.

Social Studies ACTIVITY

Find out more about the Inca Ice Maiden or about Ötzi, a mummy that is more than 5,000 years old that was found in a glacier in Italy. Create a poster that summarizes what scientists have learned from these discoveries.

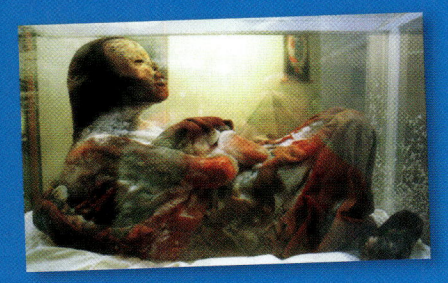

The Inca Ice Maiden was buried under ice and snow for more than 500 years.

To learn more about these Science in Action topics, visit go.hrw.com and type in the keyword HZ5ICEF.

Current Science Check out Current Science® articles related to this chapter by visiting go.hrw.com. Just type in the keyword HZ5CS12.

Careers

ACTIVITY — GENERAL

Discovering the Ice Maiden
Students can accompany Johan Reinhard as he discovers the Inca Ice Maiden! Reinhard catalogued his journey in an article, a book, and on the Internet. Go to your local library and check out the June 1996 *National Geographic* and Reinhard's book, *Discovering the Inca Ice Maiden: My Adventures on Ampato*. Then have the entire class participate in the journey on the Internet, through an interactive feature on *National Geographic*'s Web site. Have the class discuss what scientists can learn about Incan culture and the Andes from Reinhard's discovery.

LS Intrapersonal

Answer to Social Studies Activity
Answers may vary.

Chapter 12 • Science in Action

UNIT 5 TIMELINE

Oceanography

In this unit, you will learn about the Earth's oceans and the physical environments that they contain. Together, the oceans form the largest single feature on the Earth. In fact, they cover approximately 70% of the Earth's surface. The oceans not only serve as home for countless living organisms but also affect life on land. This timeline presents some milestones in the exploration of Earth's oceans. Take a deep breath, and dive in!

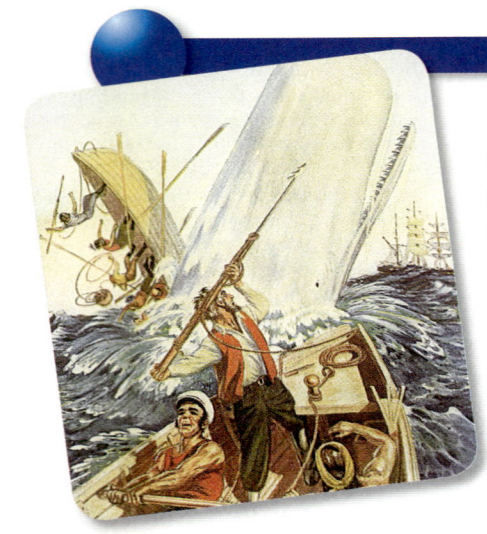

1851
Herman Melville's novel *Moby Dick* is published.

1938
A coelacanth is discovered in the Indian Ocean near South Africa. Called a fossil fish, the coelacanth was thought to have been extinct for 60 million years.

1978
Louise Brown, the first "test-tube baby," is born in England.

1986
Commercial whaling is temporarily stopped by the International Whaling Commission, but some whaling continues.

1872
The *HMS Challenger* begins its four-year voyage. Its discoveries lay the foundation for the science of oceanography.

1914
The Panama Canal, which links the Atlantic Ocean with the Pacific Ocean, is completed.

1927
Charles Lindbergh completes the first nonstop solo airplane flight over the Atlantic Ocean.

1943
Jacques Cousteau and Émile Gagnan invent the aqualung, a breathing device that allows divers to freely explore the silent world of the oceans.

1960
Jacques Piccard and Don Walsh dive to a record 10,916 m below sea level in their bathyscaph *Trieste*.

1977
Thermal vent communities of organisms that exist without sunlight are discovered on the ocean floor.

1994
The completion of the tunnel under the English Channel makes train and auto travel between Great Britain and France possible.

1998
Ben Lecomte of Austin, Texas, successfully swims across the Atlantic Ocean from Massachusetts to France, a distance of 5,980 km. His record-breaking feat takes 73 days.

2001
Researchers find that dolphins, like humans and the great apes, can recognize themselves in mirrors.

13 Exploring the Oceans
Chapter Planning Guide

Compression guide: To shorten instruction because of time limitations, omit the Chapter Lab.

OBJECTIVES	LABS, DEMONSTRATIONS, AND ACTIVITIES	TECHNOLOGY RESOURCES
PACING • 90 min pp. 372–381 **Chapter Opener**	SE Start-up Activity, p. 373 GENERAL	OSP Parent Letter ■ GENERAL CD Student Edition on CD-ROM CD Guided Reading Audio CD ■ TR Chapter Starter Transparency* VID Brain Food Video Quiz
Section 1 Earth's Oceans • List the major divisions of the global ocean. • Describe the history of Earth's oceans. • Identify the properties of ocean water. • Describe the interactions between the ocean and the atmosphere.	TE Activity Ocean Size, p. 374 GENERAL TE Activity Diagramming Temperature Zones, p. 377 BASIC SE Connection to Geology Submarine Volcanoes, p. 378 ◆ GENERAL TE Group Activity Making Models, p. 378 BASIC TE Connection Activity Geography, p. 378 GENERAL TE Activity Modeling the Water Cycle, p. 379 ◆ BASIC	CRF Lesson Plans* TR Bellringer Transparency* TR Divisions of the Global Ocean* TR Ocean Salinity* TR The Ocean and the Water Cycle* SE Internet Activity, p. 380 GENERAL
PACING • 45 min pp. 382–387 **Section 2 The Ocean Floor** • Describe technologies for studying the ocean floor. • Identify the two major regions of the ocean floor. • Classify subdivisions and features of the two major regions of the ocean floor.	TE Connection Activity Language Arts, p. 383 ◆ ADVANCED TE Connection Activity Art, p. 385 GENERAL SE Connection to Social Studies The JASON Project, p. 386 GENERAL SE Model-Making Lab Probing the Depths, p. 406 ◆ GENERAL LB Calculator-Based Labs Ocean Floor Mapping* ◆ ADVANCED	CRF Lesson Plans* TR Bellringer Transparency* TR How Sonar Works* TR Revealing the Ocean Floor: A* TR Revealing the Ocean Floor: B* VID Lab Videos for Earth Science
PACING • 45 min pp. 388–393 **Section 3 Life in the Ocean** • Identify the three groups of marine life. • Describe the two main ocean environments. • Identify the ecological zones of the benthic and pelagic environments.	TE Group Activity Classifying, p. 388 GENERAL TE Group Activity Ocean Zones and Organisms, p. 390 ◆ GENERAL SE Connection to Language Arts Water, Water, Everywhere, p. 392 GENERAL LB Whiz-Bang Demonstrations Foul Play* ◆ GENERAL LB EcoLabs & Field Activities Operation Oil-Spill Cleanup* ◆ GENERAL LB Long-Term Projects & Research Ideas Your Very Own Underwater Theme Park* ADVANCED	CRF Lesson Plans* TR Bellringer Transparency* TR The Three Groups of Marine Life* TR LINK TO LIFE SCIENCE Four Parts of Natural Selection* CRF SciLinks Activity* GENERAL CD Interactive Explorations CD-ROM Sea Sick GENERAL
PACING • 45 min pp. 394–399 **Section 4 Resources from the Ocean** • List two ways of harvesting the ocean's living resources. • Identify three nonliving resources in the ocean. • Describe the ocean's energy resources.	TE Group Activity Brainstorming, p. 394 GENERAL TE Connection Activity Real World, p. 395 ADVANCED TE Connection Activity Real World, p. 396 GENERAL TE Group Activity Public Service Announcement, p. 396 GENERAL SE Quick Lab Desalination Plant, p. 397 ◆ GENERAL LB Inquiry Labs Surf's Up!* ◆ GENERAL	CRF Lesson Plans* TR Bellringer Transparency*
PACING • 45 min pp. 394–399 **Section 5 Ocean Pollution** • Explain the difference between point-source pollution and nonpoint-source pollution. • Identify three different types of point-source ocean pollution. • Describe what is being done to control ocean pollution.	TE Activity Cleaning Up an Oil Spill, p. 400 GENERAL TE Activity Nonpoint-source Pollution, p. 401 BASIC TE Connection Activity Math, p. 402 GENERAL TE Activity Ocean Pollution Awareness, p. 403 GENERAL TE Group Activity Exxon Valdez, p. 403 GENERAL SE School-to-Home Activity Coastal Cleanup, p. 404 GENERAL TE Group Activity Coastal Campaign, p. 404 GENERAL SE Model-Making Lab Investigating an Oil Spill, p. 742 ◆ GENERAL	CRF Lesson Plans* TR Bellringer Transparency*

PACING • 90 min

CHAPTER REVIEW, ASSESSMENT, AND STANDARDIZED TEST PREPARATION
- CRF Vocabulary Activity* GENERAL
- SE Chapter Review, pp. 408–409 GENERAL
- CRF Chapter Review* ■ GENERAL
- CRF Chapter Tests A* ■ GENERAL, B* ADVANCED, C* SPECIAL NEEDS
- SE Standardized Test Preparation, pp. 410–411 GENERAL
- CRF Standardized Test Preparation* GENERAL
- CRF Performance-Based Assessment* GENERAL
- OSP Test Generator GENERAL
- CRF Test Item Listing* GENERAL

Online and Technology Resources

go.hrw.com
Visit go.hrw.com for a variety of free resources related to this textbook. Enter the keyword HA5OCE.

Holt Online Learning
Students can access interactive problem-solving help and active visual concept development with the Holt Science and Technology Online Edition available at www.hrw.com.

Guided Reading Audio CD
Also in Spanish
A direct reading of each chapter for auditory learners, reluctant readers, and Spanish-speaking students.

Science Tutor CD-ROM
Excellent for remediation and test practice.

371A Chapter 13 • Exploring the Oceans

KEY

SE Student Edition	**CRF** Chapter Resource File	**SS** Science Skills Worksheets	* Also on One-Stop Planner
TE Teacher Edition	**OSP** One-Stop Planner	**MS** Math Skills for Science Worksheets	♦ Requires advance prep
	LB Lab Bank	**CD** CD or CD-ROM	■ Also available in Spanish
	TR Transparencies	**VID** Classroom Video/DVD	

SKILLS DEVELOPMENT RESOURCES	SECTION REVIEW AND ASSESSMENT	STANDARDS CORRELATIONS
SE Pre-Reading Activity, p. 372 GENERAL OSP Science Puzzlers, Twisters & Teasers* GENERAL		National Science Education Standards UCP 2, 5; SAI 1; ST 2; SPSP 5
CRF Directed Reading A* ■ BASIC, B* SPECIAL NEEDS CRF Vocabulary and Section Summary* ■ GENERAL SE Reading Strategy Discussion, p. 374 GENERAL TE Reading Strategy Mnemonics, p. 375 GENERAL TE Inclusion Strategies, p. 377 ♦	SE Reading Checks, pp. 375, 376, 378, 380 GENERAL TE Homework, p. 379 ADVANCED TE Reteaching, p. 380 BASIC TE Quiz, p. 380 GENERAL TE Alternative Assessment, p. 380 ADVANCED SE Section Review,* p. 381 ■ GENERAL CRF Section Quiz* ■ GENERAL	UCP 1, 2, 3; ES 1b, 1f, 1g, 1h, 1j, 2a
CRF Directed Reading A* ■ BASIC, B* SPECIAL NEEDS CRF Vocabulary and Section Summary* ■ GENERAL SE Reading Strategy Reading Organizer, p. 382 GENERAL MS Math Skills for Science Multiplying Whole Numbers* GENERAL MS Math Skills for Science Multiplying and Dividing Fractions* GENERAL	SE Reading Checks, pp. 383, 384, 385, 386 GENERAL TE Homework, p. 384 ADVANCED TE Reteaching, p. 386 BASIC TE Quiz, p. 386 GENERAL TE Alternative Assessment, p. 386 GENERAL SE Section Review,* p. 387 ■ GENERAL CRF Section Quiz* ■ GENERAL	UCP 2, 3; SAI 1, 2; ST 2; SPSP 5; HNS 1, 3; ES 1b, 1c; *Chapter Lab:* UCP 2, 3; SAI 1, 2; ST 2; SPSP 5; HNS 1
CRF Directed Reading A* ■ BASIC, B* SPECIAL NEEDS CRF Vocabulary and Section Summary* ■ GENERAL SE Reading Strategy Mnemonics, p. 388 GENERAL TE Inclusion Strategy p. 391 CRF Reinforcement Worksheet The Ocean's Environment* BASIC	SE Reading Checks, pp. 389, 391, 392 GENERAL TE Homework, p. 389, 390 GENERAL TE Reteaching, p. 392 BASIC TE Quiz, p. 392 GENERAL TE Alternative Assessment, p. 392 GENERAL SE Section Review,* p. 393 ■ GENERAL CRF Section Quiz* ■ GENERAL	UCP 1
CRF Directed Reading A* ■ BASIC, B* SPECIAL NEEDS CRF Vocabulary and Section Summary* ■ GENERAL SE Reading Strategy Paired Summarizing, p. 394 GENERAL TE Reading Strategy Prediction Guide, p. 395 BASIC CRF Reinforcement Worksheet The Oceans and Us* BASIC CRF Critical Thinking Chain Reaction* ADVANCED	SE Reading Checks, pp. 395, 396, 397, 399 GENERAL TE Homework, p. 396 GENERAL TE Reteaching, p. 398 BASIC TE Quiz, p. 398 GENERAL TE Alternative Assessment, p. 398 GENERAL SE Section Review,* p. 399 ■ GENERAL CRF Section Quiz* ■ GENERAL	SAI 1; ST 2; SPSP 2, 4, 5; HNS 1
CRF Directed Reading A* ■ BASIC, B* SPECIAL NEEDS CRF Vocabulary and Section Summary* ■ GENERAL SE Reading Strategy Reading Organizer, p. 400 GENERAL	SE Reading Checks, pp. 401, 403, 405 GENERAL TE Homework, p. 401 GENERAL TE Reteaching, p. 404 BASIC TE Quiz, p. 404 GENERAL TE Alternative Assessment, p. 404 GENERAL SE Section Review,* p. 405 ■ GENERAL CRF Section Quiz* ■ GENERAL	ST 2; SPSP 2, 4, 5; *LabBook:* UPC 2, 3; SAI 1; SPSP 2, 3, 4; HNS 1

One-Stop Planner® CD-ROM

This convenient CD-ROM includes:
- Lab Materials QuickList Software
- Holt Calendar Planner
- Customizable Lesson Plans
- Printable Worksheets
- ExamView® Test Generator

CNN Student News

cnnstudentnews.com

Find the latest news, lesson plans, and activities related to important scientific events.

SciLinks NSTA

www.scilinks.org

Maintained by the **National Science Teachers Association.** See Chapter Enrichment pages for a complete list of topics.

Current Science®

Check out **Current Science** articles and activities by visiting the HRW Web site at **go.hrw.com.** Just type in the keyword **HZ5CS13T.**

Classroom Videos

- **Lab Videos** demonstrate the chapter lab.
- **Brain Food Video Quizzes** help students review the chapter material.
- **CNN Videos** bring science into your students' daily life.

Chapter 13 • Chapter Planning Guide

13 Chapter Resources

Visual Resources

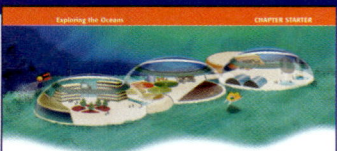

CHAPTER STARTER TRANSPARENCY

BELLRINGER TRANSPARENCIES

TEACHING TRANSPARENCIES

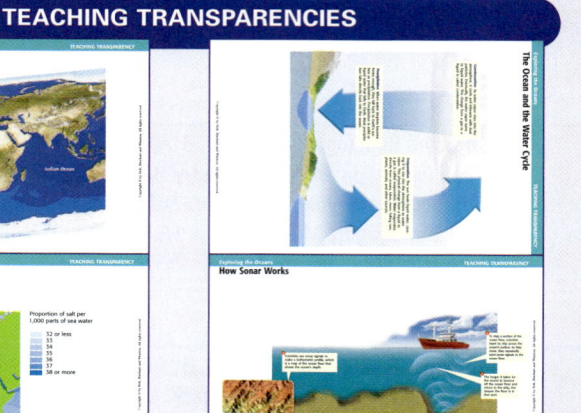

TEACHING TRANSPARENCIES

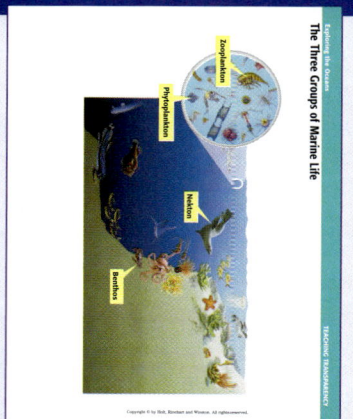

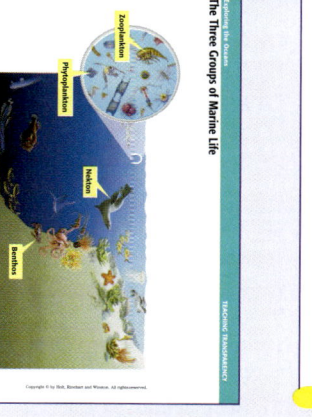

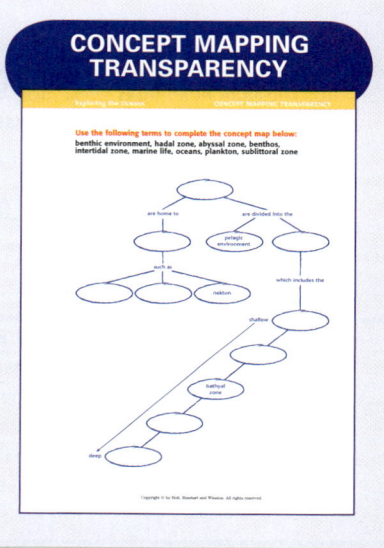

CONCEPT MAPPING TRANSPARENCY

Planning Resources

LESSON PLANS

PARENT LETTER

ALSO IN SPANISH

TEST ITEM LISTING

One-Stop Planner® CD-ROM

This CD-ROM includes all of the resources shown here and the following time-saving tools:

- Lab Materials QuickList Software
- Customizable lesson plans
- Holt Calendar Planner
- The powerful ExamView® Test Generator

371C Chapter 13 • Exploring the Oceans

For a preview of available worksheets covering math and science skills, see pages T26–T33. All of these resources are also on the One-Stop Planner®.

Meeting Individual Needs

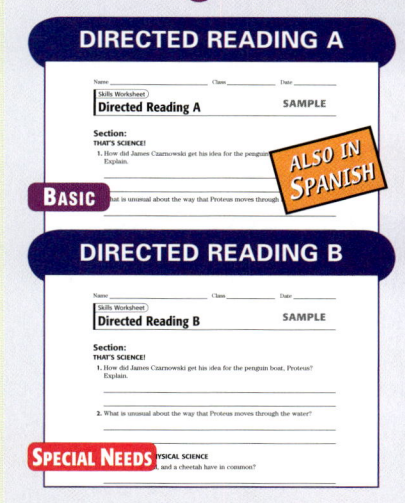

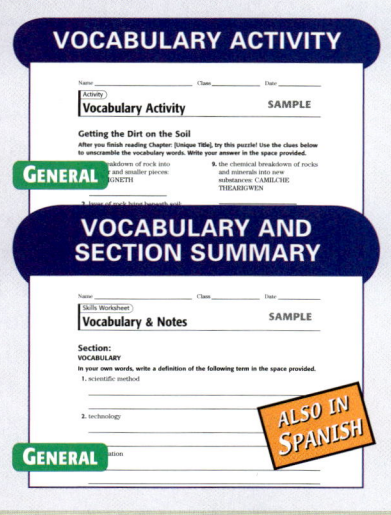

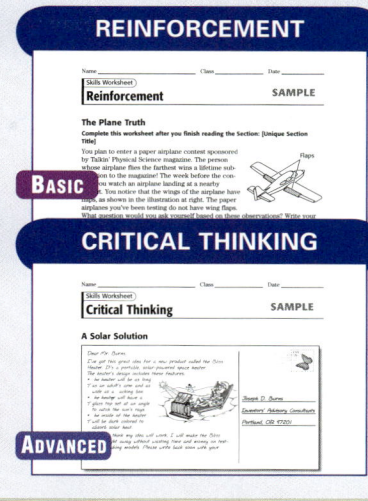

- **DIRECTED READING A** — BASIC / ALSO IN SPANISH
- **DIRECTED READING B** — SPECIAL NEEDS
- **VOCABULARY ACTIVITY** — GENERAL
- **VOCABULARY AND SECTION SUMMARY** — GENERAL / ALSO IN SPANISH
- **REINFORCEMENT** — BASIC
- **CRITICAL THINKING** — ADVANCED
- **SCILINKS ACTIVITY** — GENERAL
- **SCIENCE PUZZLERS, TWISTERS & TEASERS** — GENERAL

Labs and Activities

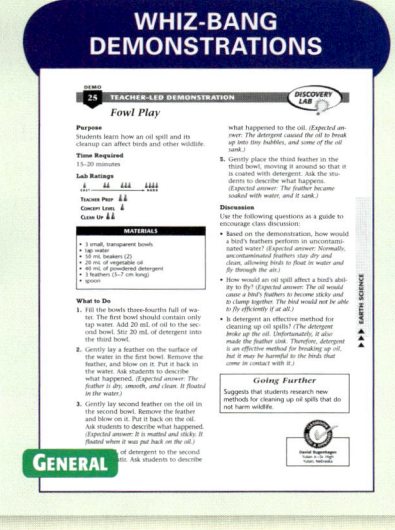

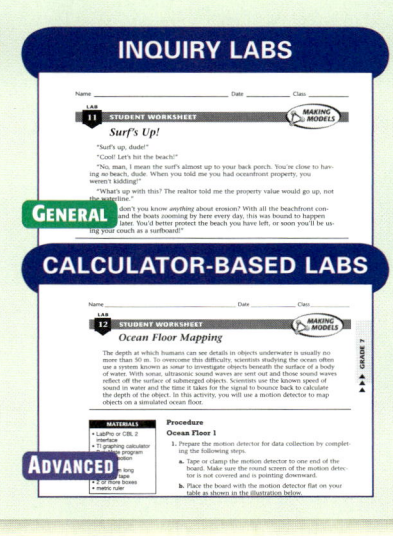

- **ECOLABS & FIELD ACTIVITIES** — ADVANCED
- **LONG-TERM PROJECTS & RESEARCH IDEAS** — ADVANCED
- **WHIZ-BANG DEMONSTRATIONS** — GENERAL
- **INQUIRY LABS** — GENERAL
- **CALCULATOR-BASED LABS** — ADVANCED
- **DATASHEETS FOR QUICKLABS**
- **DATASHEETS FOR CHAPTER LABS**
- **DATASHEETS FOR LABBOOK**

Review and Assessments

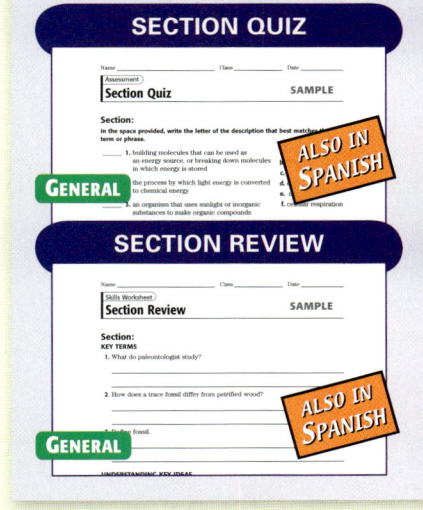

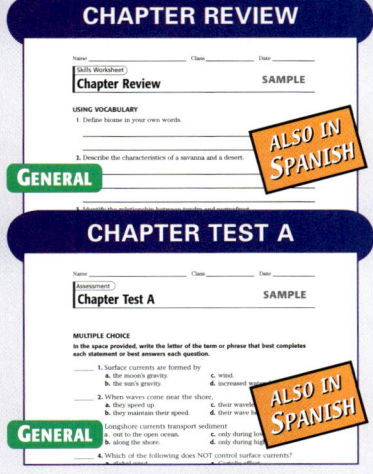

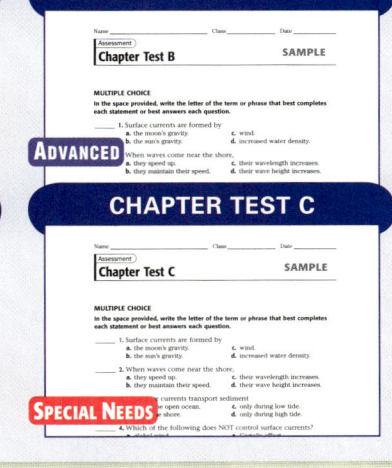

- **SECTION QUIZ** — GENERAL / ALSO IN SPANISH
- **SECTION REVIEW** — GENERAL / ALSO IN SPANISH
- **CHAPTER REVIEW** — GENERAL / ALSO IN SPANISH
- **CHAPTER TEST A** — GENERAL / ALSO IN SPANISH
- **CHAPTER TEST B** — ADVANCED
- **CHAPTER TEST C** — SPECIAL NEEDS
- **STANDARDIZED TEST PREPARATION** — GENERAL
- **PERFORMANCE-BASED ASSESSMENT** — GENERAL

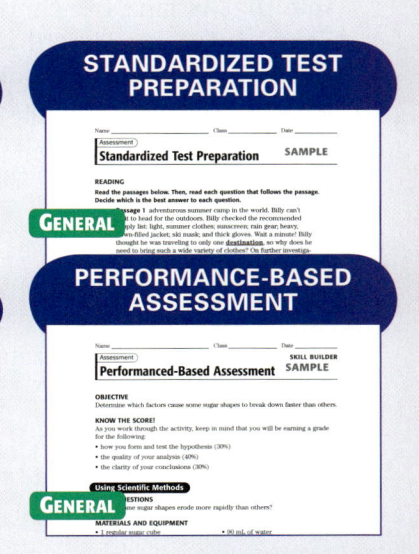

Chapter 13 • Chapter Resources 371D

13 Chapter Enrichment

This Chapter Enrichment provides relevant and interesting information to expand and enhance your presentation of the chapter material.

Section 1

Earth's Oceans
The Global Ocean
- Historically, the global ocean was divided into five oceans: the Atlantic, Pacific, Indian, Arctic, and Antarctic Oceans. Today, most oceanographers agree that the Antarctic Ocean is actually the southernmost section of the Atlantic, Pacific, and Indian Oceans.

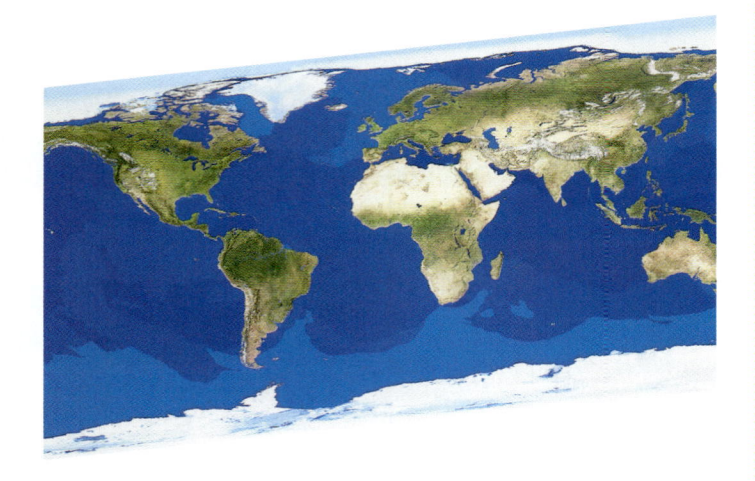

The Mariana Trench
- In 1960, the *Trieste*, a small submersible designed to explore the ocean to great depths, set out on a voyage that until then had only been imagined: it descended into the Mariana Trench, the deepest known place on Earth. As Jacques Piccard and a companion descended in the *Treiste*, they were surprised to feel abrupt changes between the ocean's temperature layers. Every time the vessel reached the boundary between two layers, the *Trieste* seemed to stop as though it had reached the ocean floor.

Is That a Fact!
- The average depth of each ocean is as follows: Arctic: 1,038 m; Atlantic: 3,735 m; Indian: 3,872 m; and Pacific: 4,188 m.
- The average depth for all the oceans is about 3,800 m.

Section 2

The Ocean Floor
The Renewal of a Planet
- Submersible missions such as those of *Alvin* have enabled oceanographers to witness the creation of oceanic crust and the forces that drive tectonic plate movement. By observing molten rock welling up into the ocean, they have seen how new sea floor forms and have gained a better understanding of how the continents drift apart. Trained to "read" rock formations, these scientists use their observations to reconstruct Earth's history.

Is That a Fact!
- The oceans' deep-water sound channels carry sound waves for hundreds of kilometers. Whales and other marine animals take advantage of these properties to communicate over long ranges and to search for food. Whales communicate with clicks, whistles, squeaks, and songs that convey information. Scientists aren't sure what these songs mean but do know that whales can communicate at distances as great as 1,600 km!

Section 3

Life in the Ocean
A World of Its Own
- In 1977, scientists aboard *Alvin* witnessed an astonishing new world around deep-sea vents. Exploring hydrothermal vents 320 km off the Galápagos Islands, these explorers saw an amazing multitude of unusual marine populations—giant clams and worms, fish, and crabs—gathered in an abyssal oasis.

371E Chapter 13 • Exploring the Oceans

- Using a special claw attachment, scientists harvested samples of the marine life they found. When they analyzed their specimens, they were in for a surprise— the water from around the specimans smelled like rotten eggs! This smell came from hydrogen sulfide dissolved in the water around the vents.
- The scientists discovered that certain marine bacteria thrive on the hydrogen sulfide released by vents in the ocean floor. These bacteria are food for the other marine creatures, and they are part of a food chain that does not rely on photosynthesis for energy.

Section 4

Resources from the Ocean

Food for Thought

- Fish are an invaluable ocean resource, providing a significant percentage of the world's protein needs every year. About 75 million tons of fish are harvested from the ocean each year. But many fish populations have been depleted by overfishing.

- Concerned that too few fish will remain to breed, scientists determine the maximum sustainable yield, or the amount of fish that can be harvested each year without jeopardizing future catches. Using the scientists' guidelines, governments sometimes impose fishing restrictions to manage fish populations. Many people are working to ensure that the world can continue to count on fish for food.

Sea Thermal Energy

- Harnessing tidal and wave energy is not the only way to get electrical power from the ocean. Since 1979, the United States government has operated an Ocean Thermal Energy Conversion (OTEC) plant off the coast of Hawaii, where the temperature differential between surface and deeper water layers is converted into electrical energy.

Section 5

Ocean Pollution

Thermal Pollution

- Pesticides, oil, sludge, and trash are not the only harmful pollutants released into our oceans. Power plants can cause thermal pollution by releasing heated water into the sea. Thermal pollution may result in only a one- or two-degree temperature increase in the area near the heat source, but that can have profound effects on the ecology. Fish populations may migrate away from the affected area, and overgrowth of other organisms, or "algal blooms," may occur.

Close Quarters

- Seas that are surrounded by land are particularly vulnerable to damage from ocean pollution. The shores and adjacent waters of the Mediterranean, Baltic, and Adriatic Seas have been fouled with city sewage, factory waste, and fertilizer and pesticide runoff from farms. Their open waters have also been affected by dumping and oil spills.

SciLinks
Developed and maintained by the National Science Teachers Association

SciLinks is maintained by the National Science Teachers Association to provide you and your students with interesting, up-to-date links that will enrich your classroom presentation of the chapter.

Visit www.scilinks.org and enter the SciLinks code for more information about the topic listed.

Topic: Exploring Earth's Oceans
SciLinks code: HSM0557

Topic: Ocean Floor
SciLinks code: HSM1062

Topic: Life in the Oceans
SciLinks code: HSM0874

Topic: Ocean Resources
SciLinks code: HSM1065

Topic: Ocean Pollution
SciLinks code: HSM1063

Chapter 13 • Chapter Enrichment

Overview

Tell students that this chapter will help them learn about the Earth's oceans. The chapter describes ocean characteristics, the ocean floor, life in the ocean, resources from the ocean, and ocean pollution.

Assessing Prior Knowledge

Students should be familiar with the following topics:
- plate tectonics
- the water cycle

Identifying Misconceptions

As students learn about the ocean as a resource, some of them may think that the oceans are a limitless resource. It may be helpful to review the definitions of *renewable resource* and *nonrenewable resource* before teaching about the resources from the ocean. Students may also think that vast bodies of water, such as the oceans, cannot be polluted. When teaching about ocean pollution, remind students that even though the oceans are very large, they are also susceptible to pollution.

13 Exploring the Oceans

SECTION 1	Earth's Oceans	374
SECTION 2	The Ocean Floor	382
SECTION 3	Life in the Ocean	388
SECTION 4	Resources from the Ocean	394
SECTION 5	Ocean Pollution	400

Chapter Lab 406
Chapter Review 408
Standardized Test Preparation 410
Science in Action 412

About the PHOTO

Are two heads better than one? Although it may look like this reef lizardfish has two heads, it's actually swallowing another fish whole! Reef lizardfish are commonly found in the Western Pacific Ocean. Unlike most other types of lizardfish, the reef lizardfish prefers to rest on hard surfaces and is usually seen in pairs.

PRE-READING ACTIVITY

FOLDNOTES **Layered Book** Before you read the chapter, create the FoldNote entitled "Layered Book" described in the **Study Skills** section of the Appendix. Label the tabs of the layered book with "Characteristics of ocean water," "The ocean floor," "Ocean zones," and "Resources from the ocean." As you read the chapter, write information you learn about each category under the appropriate tab.

Standards Correlations

National Science Education Standards

The following codes indicate the National Science Education Standards that correlate to this chapter. The full text of the standards is at the front of the book.

Chapter Opener
UCP 2, 5; SAI 1; ST 2; SFSP 5

Section 1 Earth's Oceans
UCP 1, 2, 3; ES 1b, 1f, 1g. 1h, 1j, 2a

Section 2 The Ocean Floor
UCP 2, 3; SAI 1, 2; ST 2; SPSP 5; HNS 1, 3; ES 1b, 1c

Section 3 Life in the Ocean
UCP 1

Section 4 Resources from the Ocean
SAI 1; ST 2; SPSP 2, 4, 5, HNS 1

Section 5 Ocean Pollution
ST 2; SPSP 2, 4, 5; *LabBook:* UCP 2, 3; SAI 1; SPSP 2, 3, 4; HNS 1

START-UP ACTIVITY

MATERIALS
FOR EACH GROUP
- bowl, large
- cup, plastic, small, clear
- water

Teacher's Notes: A cylindrical cup (one that does not taper) is best for this activity.

Answers
1. Sample answer: The air inside the cup prevented the water below it from filling the space inside the cup.
2. Sample answer: The air in the cup keeps the water from filling the cup. Likewise, the air in an underwater research lab keeps water from coming through the hole in the bottom of the lab.

START-UP ACTIVITY

Exit Only?
To study what life underwater would be like, scientists sometimes live in underwater laboratories. How do these scientists enter and leave these labs? Believe it or not, the simplest way is through a hole in the lab's floor. You might think water would come in through the hole, but it doesn't. How is this possible? Do the following activity to find out.

Procedure
1. Fill a **large bowl** about two-thirds full of **water**.
2. Turn a **clear plastic cup** upside down.
3. Slowly guide the cup straight down into the water. Be careful not to guide the cup all the way to the bottom of the bowl. Also, be careful not to tip the cup.
4. Record your observations.

Analysis
1. How does the air inside the cup affect the water below the cup?
2. How do your findings relate to the hole in the bottom of an underwater research lab?

Chapter Lab
UCP 2, 3; SAI 1, 2; ST 2; SPSP 5; HNS 1

Chapter Review
UCP 1, 2, 3; SAI 2; ST 2; SPSP 5; HNS 1, 2; ES 1b, 1c, 1f, 1g, 1h, 1j

Science in Action
UCP 2; SAI 2; ST 2; SPSP 5; HNS 1, 2, 3

Chapter Starter Transparency
Use this transparency to help students begin thinking about exploring the oceans.

CHAPTER RESOURCES
Technology
- Transparencies
  - Chapter Starter Transparency
- Student Edition on CD-ROM
- Guided Reading Audio CD
  - English or Spanish
- Classroom Videos
  - Brain Food Video Quiz

READING SKILLS

Workbooks
- Science Puzzlers, Twisters & Teasers
  - Exploring the Oceans GENERAL

Chapter 13 • Exploring the Oceans

SECTION 1

Focus

Overview
This section discusses how the oceans formed and how the global ocean is divided. It explores the properties of ocean water, including factors that affect salinity, temperature zones, and surface temperature changes.

Bellringer
Show students a photo of Earth from space, and predict the percentage of land and water on Earth. (Liquid water covers 71% of Earth's surface.)

Motivate

ACTIVITY — GENERAL

Ocean Size Discuss the divisions of the global ocean, and note that the volume of the Pacific Ocean is 724 million cubic kilometers. The volume of the Atlantic Ocean is about 322 million cubic kilometers, the volume of the Indian Ocean is about 292 million cubic kilometers, and the volume of the Arctic Ocean is about 12 million cubic kilometers. Have students fill graduated cylinders with water to demonstrate these ratios. (The Pacific Ocean would be 724 mL, the Atlantic Ocean would be 322 mL, the Indian Ocean would be 292 mL, and the Arctic Ocean would be 12 mL.) **LS** Visual

---

SECTION 1

READING WARM-UP

Objectives
- List the major divisions of the global ocean.
- Describe the history of Earth's oceans.
- Identify the properties of ocean water.
- Describe the interactions between the ocean and the atmosphere.

Terms to Learn
salinity
water cycle

READING STRATEGY

Discussion Read this section silently. Write down questions that you have about this section. Discuss your questions in a small group.

CHAPTER RESOURCES

Chapter Resource File
- Lesson Plan
- Directed Reading A BASIC
- Directed Reading B SPECIAL NEEDS

Technology
- Transparencies
  - Bellringer
  - Divisions of the Global Ocean

Earth's Oceans

What makes Earth so different from Mars? What does Earth have that Mercury doesn't?

Earth stands out from the other planets in our solar system primarily for one reason—71% of the Earth's surface is covered with water. Most of Earth's water is found in the global ocean. The global ocean is divided by the continents into four main oceans. The divisions of the global ocean are shown in **Figure 1**. The ocean is a unique body of water that plays many parts in regulating Earth's environment.

Divisions of the Global Ocean

The largest ocean is the *Pacific Ocean*. It flows between Asia and the Americas. The volume of the *Atlantic Ocean*, the second-largest ocean, is about half the volume of the Pacific. The *Indian Ocean* is the third-largest ocean. The *Arctic Ocean* is the smallest ocean. This ocean is unique because much of its surface is covered by ice. Therefore, the Arctic Ocean has not been fully explored.

Figure 1 The global ocean is divided by the continents into four main oceans.

Is That a Fact!

The global ocean covers nearly 376 million square kilometers. The entire North American continent, by comparison, covers only a little more than 24 million square kilometers.

374 Chapter 13 • Exploring the Oceans

Figure 2 The History of Earth's Oceans

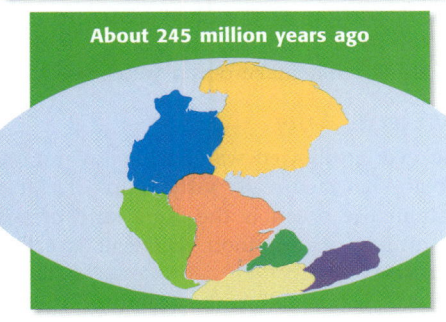

About 245 million years ago

The continents were one giant landmass called Pangaea. The oceans were one giant body of water called Panthalassa.

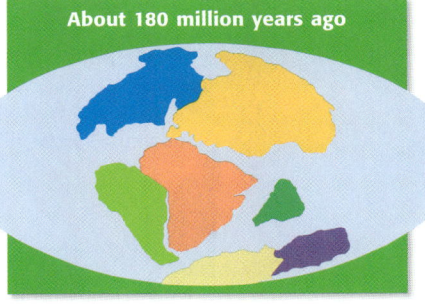

About 180 million years ago

As Pangaea broke apart, the North Atlantic Ocean and the Indian Ocean began to form.

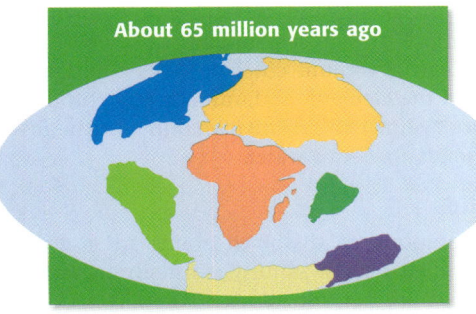

About 65 million years ago

The South Atlantic Ocean was much smaller than it is today.

Today

The continents continue to move at a rate of 1 to 10 cm per year. The Pacific Ocean is getting smaller. However, the other oceans are growing.

How Did the Oceans Form?

About 4.5 billion years ago, Earth was a very different place. There were no oceans. Volcanoes spewed lava, ash, and gases all over the planet. The volcanic gases began to form Earth's atmosphere. Meanwhile, Earth was cooling. Sometime before 4 billion years ago, Earth cooled enough for water vapor to condense. This water began to fall as rain. The rain filled the deeper levels of Earth's surface, and the first oceans began to form.

The shape of the Earth's oceans has changed a lot over time. Much has been learned about the oceans' history. Some of this history is shown in **Figure 2**.

✔ **Reading Check** How did the first oceans begin to form on Earth? (See the Appendix for answers to Reading Checks.)

MISCONCEPTION ALERT

Sea or Ocean? Students might find the terms *sea* and *ocean* confusing. In some cases, the words are interchangeable, but the terms can also mean different things. Parts of the global ocean that are partly surrounded by land are known as *seas*. The Mediterranean Sea is an example of a sea that is part of the global ocean. Seas that are completely landlocked, such as the Caspian Sea, are not part of the global ocean. Have students identify on a map landlocked seas and seas that are part of the global ocean.

Teach

READING STRATEGY — GENERAL

Mnemonics Encourage students to create a mnemonic device that will help them remember the names of the world's oceans. For example, they might write "**A**unt **P**atty **A**te **I**nchworms" in order to recall **A**tlantic, **P**acific, **A**rctic, and **I**ndian. **LS** Verbal — English Language Learners

CONNECTION to Physical Science — GENERAL

Condensation Explain to students that condensation is a physical change from a gas to a liquid. In the atmosphere, the amount of water vapor that the air can hold depends on temperature. As temperature decreases, the air can hold less water vapor, and the water vapor condenses to form clouds. Ask students to think of other examples of condensation. (Examples might include condensation on the side of a soda can, dew in the morning, or a foggy mirror in the bathroom.) **LS** Logical

Answer to Reading Check

The first oceans began to form sometime before 4 billion years ago as the Earth cooled enough for water vapor to condense and fall as rain.

Section 1 • Earth's Oceans

Teach, continued

SCIENTISTS AT ODDS

Long Rainy Days When Earth cooled about 4 billion years ago, the rains that resulted probably lasted for thousands of years. But some scientists do not believe all the water on Earth came from condensation as Earth cooled. Instead, they argue that some of the water came from "cosmic rain"—comets that struck Earth in its early history. Encourage students to find out more about this debate.

MISCONCEPTION ALERT

The Composition of Ocean Water In **Figure 3,** students may notice that the percentages of some of the elements dissolved in ocean water are particularly low. This fact does not necessarily mean that these elements are not abundant in the ocean. Organisms, such as diatoms (phytoplankton) and coral, remove dissolved minerals containing some of these elements and use them to make hard body parts.

Ask students to note the two elements that are most abundant. **(sodium and chlorine)**

Ask students what these elements form when they are combined. **(sodium chloride, or salt)**

Percentages of Dissolved Solids in Ocean Water

- Chlorine = 55.0%
- Sodium = 30.6%
- Magnesium = 7.7%
- Sulfur = 3.7%
- Calcium = 1.2%
- Potassium = 1.1%
- Others = 0.7%

Figure 3 This pie graph shows the relative percentages of dissolved solids (by mass) in ocean water.

salinity a measure of the amount of dissolved salts in a given amount of liquid

CHAPTER RESOURCES

Technology

Transparencies
• Ocean Salinity

Characteristics of Ocean Water

You know that ocean water is different from the water that flows from your sink at home. For one thing, ocean water is not safe to drink. But there are other things that make ocean water special.

Ocean Water Is Salty

Have you ever swallowed water while swimming in the ocean? It tasted really salty, didn't it? Most of the salt in the ocean is the same kind of salt that we sprinkle on our food. This salt is called *sodium chloride.*

Salts have been added to the ocean for billions of years. As rivers and streams flow toward the oceans, they dissolve various minerals on land. The running water carries these dissolved minerals to the ocean. At the same time, water is *evaporating* from the ocean and is leaving the dissolved solids behind. The most abundant dissolved solid in the ocean is sodium chloride. This compound consists of the elements sodium, Na, and chlorine, Cl. **Figure 3** shows the relative amounts of the dissolved solids in ocean water.

Chock-Full of Solids

A measure of the amount of dissolved solids in a given amount of liquid is called **salinity.** Salinity is usually measured as grams of dissolved solids per kilogram of water. Think of it this way: 1 kg (1,000 g) of ocean water can be evaporated to 35 g of dissolved solids, on average. Therefore, if you evaporated 1 kg of ocean water, 965 g of fresh water would be removed and 35 g of solids would remain.

Climate Affects Salinity

Some parts of the ocean are saltier than others. Coastal water in places with hotter, drier climates typically has a higher salinity. Coastal water in cooler, more humid places typically has a lower salinity. One reason for this difference is that heat increases the evaporation rate. Evaporation removes water but leaves salts and other dissolved solids behind. Salinity levels are also lower in coastal areas that have a cooler, more humid climate because more fresh water from streams and rivers runs into the ocean in these areas.

✓ **Reading Check** Why does coastal water in places with hotter, drier climates typically have a higher salinity than coastal water in places with cooler, more humid climates?

Answer to Reading Check

Coastal water in places with hotter, drier climates has a higher salinity because less fresh water flows into the ocean in drier areas and because heat increases the evaporation rate.

376 Chapter 13 • Exploring the Oceans

Figure 4 Salinity varies in different parts of the ocean because of variations in evaporation, circulation, and freshwater inflow.

Water Movement Affects Salinity

Another factor that affects ocean salinity is water movement. Some parts of the ocean, such as bays, gulfs, and seas, move less than other parts. Parts of the open ocean that do not have currents running through them can also be slow moving. Slower-moving areas of water develop higher salinity. **Figure 4** shows salinity differences in different parts of the ocean.

Temperature Zones

The temperature of ocean water decreases as depth increases. However, this temperature change does not happen gradually from the ocean's surface to its bottom. Water in the ocean can be divided into three layers by temperature. As **Figure 5** shows, the temperature at the surface is much warmer than the average temperature of ocean water.

Figure 5 Temperature Zones in the Ocean

Surface zone The *surface zone* is the warm, top layer of ocean water. It can extend to 300 m below sea level. Sunlight heats the top 100 m of the surface zone. Surface currents mix the heated water with cooler water below.

Thermocline The *thermocline* is the second layer of ocean water. It can extend from 300 m below sea level to about 700 m below sea level. In the thermocline, temperature drops with increased depth faster than it does in the other two zones.

Deep zone The *deep zone* is the bottom layer that extends from the base of the thermocline to the bottom of the ocean. The temperature in this zone can range from 1°C to 3°C.

ACTIVITY — BASIC

Diagramming Temperature Zones To help students visualize the temperature zones of the ocean, ask them to make cross-sectional diagrams of the ocean. They should label the surface zone, thermocline, and deep zone. They should also write captions that explain the relationship between temperature and depth. **English Language Learners**
LS Visual

CONNECTION to Physical Science — GENERAL

Sound Waves in the Ocean Sound waves travel faster in warm water than in cold water. A technique called *Acoustic Thermometry of Ocean Climate* (ATOC) measures the time sound takes to travel a known distance through the ocean. Using this method, oceanographers can determine the average temperature of areas of the ocean with great accuracy.
LS Verbal

MISCONCEPTION ALERT

Less Than Zero The deepest water in the Arctic Ocean is colder than 0°C, but it remains liquid because of its salinity.

INCLUSION Strategies

- Learning Disabled
- Attention Deficit Disorder
- Gifted and Talented

Organize students into groups of three or four. Give each group a labeled cup ¾ full with clear water, a labeled cup ¾ full with very salty water, a labeled cup ¼ full with very salty green water, a labeled cup ¼ full with blue tap water, and two medicine droppers. First, ask students to fill a dropper with green water and to place one drop of it into the cup of clear water. Have students record their observations in their **science journal.** Next, have students fill the second dropper with blue water, and place one drop of it into the cup with clear salt water. Have students record their observations. Ask groups to develop a hypothesis about why salty water sinks below fresh water. Have groups share their hypotheses with the class. **LS Visual/Interpersonal**

Section 1 • Earth's Oceans

Teach, continued

Group Activity —BASIC

Making Models Using balloons and permanent markers, students can model how latitude affects ocean surface temperatures. Have students clearly label the poles and equator on their balloons and indicate surface water temperatures. Have them use colored pens to draw bands around their balloons. They should construct a key for their colors, correlating warmer temperatures with the colors closest to the equator. After they color in the shapes of the continents, students can present their models to the class. **LS** Visual/Logical

CONNECTION ACTIVITY
Geography —GENERAL

Comparing the Oceans Encourage students to use atlases or globes to locate the four main oceans. Suggest that students draw a map of the oceans that indicates modern or ancient trade routes, and suggest that they illustrate the map with drawings of animals that are unique to each ocean. Students might also make a chart in which they compare all of the oceans by size, average temperature, depth, and other characteristics. **LS** Visual

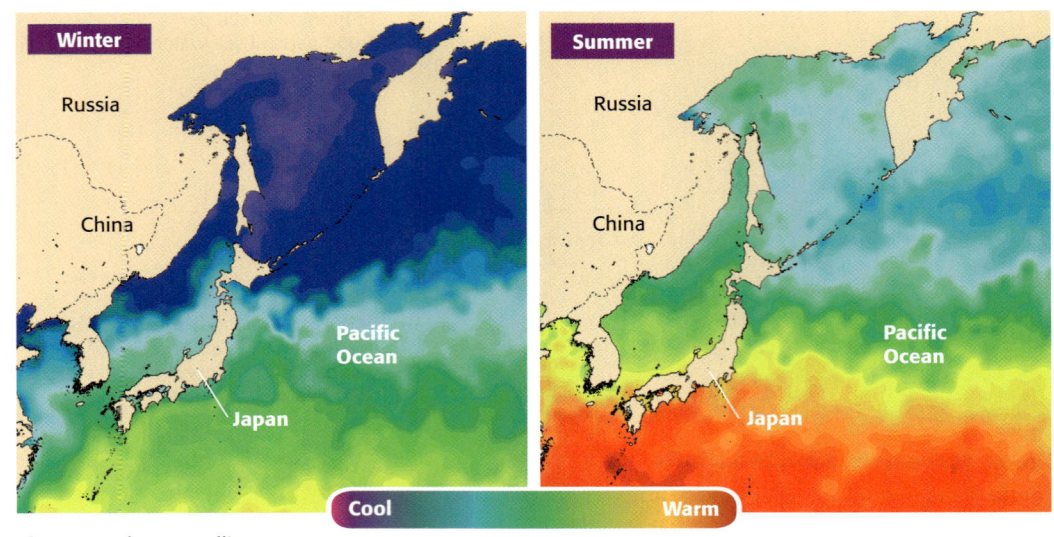

Figure 6 These satellite images show that the surface temperatures in the northern Pacific Ocean change with the seasons.

Surface Temperature Changes

If you live near the coast, you may know how different a swim in the ocean feels in December than it feels in July. Temperatures in the surface zone vary with latitude and the time of year. Surface temperatures range from 1°C near the poles to about 24°C near the equator. Parts of the ocean along the equator are warmer because they receive more direct sunlight per year than areas closer to the poles. However, both hemispheres receive more direct sunlight during their summer seasons. Therefore, the surface zone is heated more in the summer. **Figure 6** shows how surface-zone temperatures vary depending on the time of year.

✓ **Reading Check** Why are parts of the ocean along the equator warmer than those closer to the poles?

CONNECTION TO Geology

Submarine Volcanoes Geologists estimate that approximately 80% of the volcanic activity on Earth takes place on the ocean floor. Most of the volcanic activity occurs as magma slowly flows onto the ocean floor where tectonic plates pull away from each other. Other volcanic activity is the result of volcanoes that are located on the ocean floor. Both of these types of volcanoes are called *submarine volcanoes*. Submarine volcanoes behave differently than volcanoes on land do. Research how submarine volcanoes behave underwater. Then, create a model of a submarine volcano based on the information you find. **ACTIVITY**

Answer to Reading Check
Parts of the ocean along the equator are warmer because they receive more sunlight per year.

Is That a Fact!
Eighteen thousand years ago, much more of Earth's ocean water was frozen in glaciers and icecaps, and the Atlantic coast was miles farther out than it is today due to lower sea levels. Modern-day divers exploring the Chesapeake Bay found a mound of oyster shells— the remains of a long-ago picnic— 40 m below present sea levels!

378 Chapter 13 • Exploring the Oceans

The Ocean and the Water Cycle

If you could sit on the moon and look down at Earth, what would you see? You would notice that Earth's surface is made up of three basic components—water, land, and clouds (air). All three are part of a process called the water cycle, as shown in **Figure 7**. The **water cycle** is the continuous movement of water from the ocean to the atmosphere to the land and back to the ocean. The ocean is an important part of the water cycle because nearly all of Earth's water is in the ocean.

water cycle the continuous movement of water from the ocean to the atmosphere to the land and back to the ocean

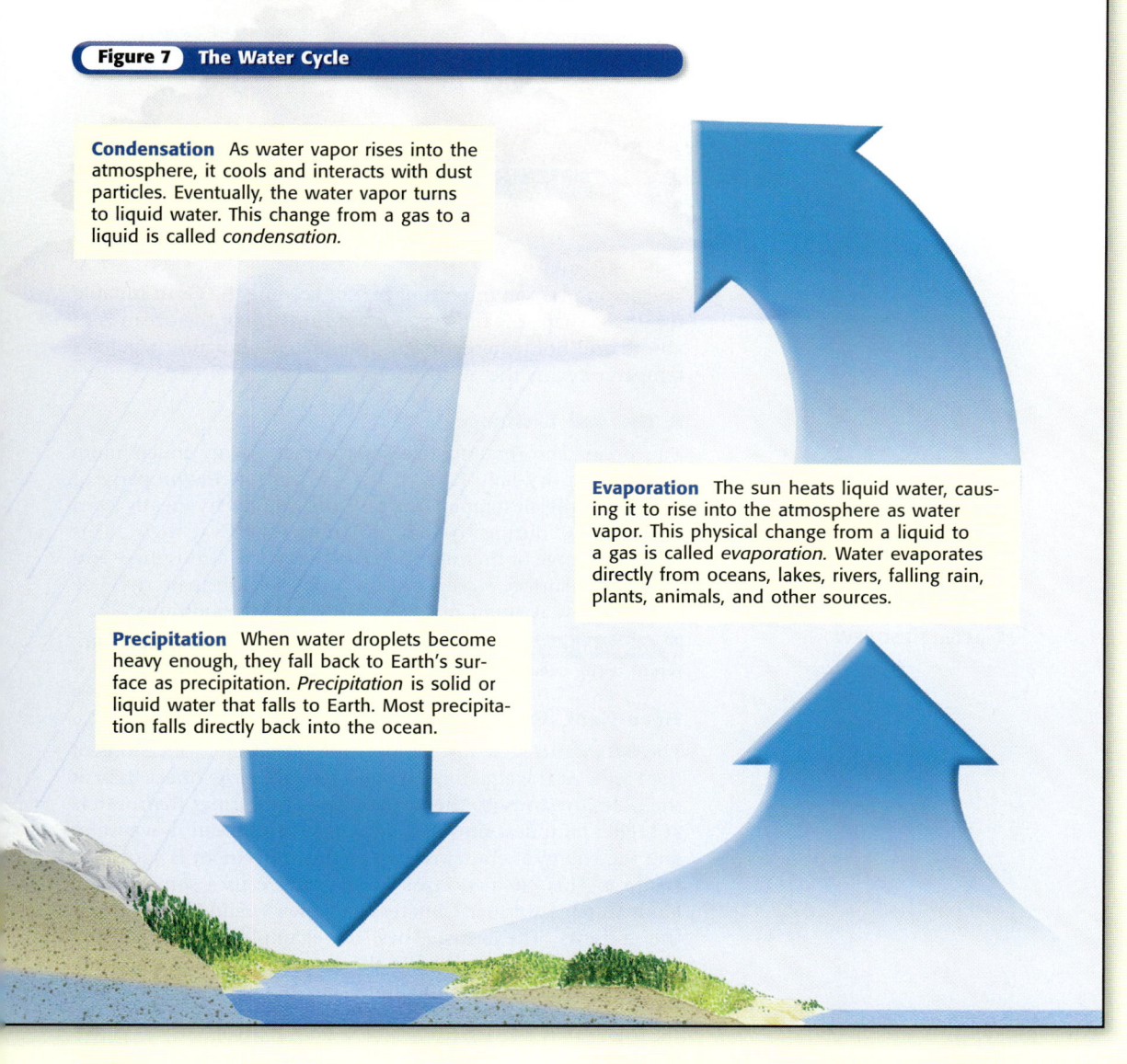

Figure 7 The Water Cycle

Condensation As water vapor rises into the atmosphere, it cools and interacts with dust particles. Eventually, the water vapor turns to liquid water. This change from a gas to a liquid is called *condensation*.

Evaporation The sun heats liquid water, causing it to rise into the atmosphere as water vapor. This physical change from a liquid to a gas is called *evaporation*. Water evaporates directly from oceans, lakes, rivers, falling rain, plants, animals, and other sources.

Precipitation When water droplets become heavy enough, they fall back to Earth's surface as precipitation. *Precipitation* is solid or liquid water that falls to Earth. Most precipitation falls directly back into the ocean.

ACTIVITY — BASIC

Modeling the Water Cycle Divide the class into small groups, and provide each group with a small dish or bowl, a plastic bag with a twist tie, and water. Challenge students to create a model demonstrating the water cycle. (Students might place the dish, filled with water, into the bag, seal it and put it in a window or on a table in the sun. As water evaporates from the dish, it will condense on the inner surface of the bag and will eventually fall as "rain." Allow time for each group to explain its model to the class.) **LS Visual/Verbal**

Cultural Awareness — GENERAL

Greek Maps About 3,000 years ago, Greek maps of the world had the Mediterranean Sea in the center of a flat world. Oceans surrounded the lands around the Mediterranean Sea. Ask students: Why do you think the Greeks drew the Mediterranean Sea at the center of their maps?" (Their known world centered around it.)

Have students collect replicas of ancient maps from different cultures and have students critique the strengths and weaknesses of the maps. **LS Visual/Verbal**

Homework — ADVANCED

The Oceans and Weather Challenge students to explain why the oceans are an important influence on the world's weather. (The oceans receive and absorb a large portion of the sun's energy. This energy raises the temperature of the oceans, which influences the atmosphere. Ocean currents carry warm water to colder areas, and vice versa, affecting local climates. Finally, solar energy evaporates an enormous amount of ocean water, which eventually returns to Earth as precipitation.) **LS Verbal**

CHAPTER RESOURCES

Technology
- **Transparencies**
  - The Ocean and the Water Cycle

Section 1 • Earth's Oceans

Close

Reteaching — BASIC
The Water Cycle List the steps of the water cycle on the board, and ask students to describe what happens at each step.
LS Verbal

Quiz — GENERAL
1. Which ocean is the largest? Which ocean is the smallest? (the Pacific Ocean; the Arctic Ocean)
2. How do scientists think the oceans are likely to change in the future? (They predict that the oceans will change in size and shape as the continents change position.)

Alternative Assessment — ADVANCED
Ocean Timeline Encourage students to examine **Figure 2**. Ask students to prepare a timeline detailing the history of Earth's oceans. Challenge students to predict how the oceans will change during the next 150 million years. Students can illustrate their timelines with drawings of each stage of Earth's history.
LS Visual

Figure 8 *This infrared satellite image shows the Gulf Stream moving warm water from lower latitudes to higher latitudes.*

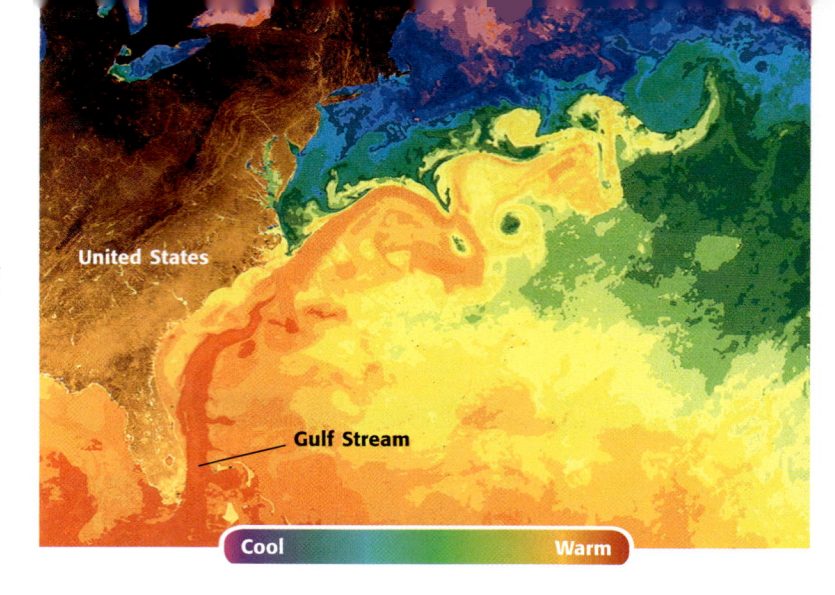

INTERNET ACTIVITY
For another activity related to this chapter, go to **go.hrw.com** and type in the keyword **HZ5OCEW**.

A Global Thermostat
The ocean plays an important part in keeping the Earth suitable for life. Perhaps the most important function of the ocean is to absorb and hold energy from sunlight. This function regulates temperatures in the atmosphere.

A Thermal Exchange
The ocean absorbs and releases thermal energy much more slowly than dry land does. If it were not for this property of the ocean, the air temperature on Earth could vary greatly from above 100°C during the day to below –100°C at night. This rapid exchange of thermal energy between the atmosphere and the Earth's surface would cause violent weather patterns. Life as you know it could not exist under these conditions.

✔**Reading Check** How would the air temperature on land be different if the ocean did not release thermal energy so slowly?

Have Heat, Will Travel
The ocean also regulates temperatures at different locations of the Earth. At the equator, the sun's rays are more direct than at the poles. As a result, the waters there are warmer than waters at higher latitudes. However, currents in the ocean move water and the energy it contains. Part of this movement is shown in **Figure 8**. This circulation of warm water causes some coastal lands to have warmer climates than they would have without the currents. The British Isles, for example, have a warmer climate than most regions at the same latitude. This warmer climate is due to the warm water of the Gulf Stream.

Answer to Reading Check
If the ocean did not release thermal energy so slowly, the air temperature on land would vary greatly from above 100°C during the day to below -100°C at night.

MISCONCEPTION ALERT
Sea Level Students may think that sea level is the same worldwide. Tides and winds alter the ocean's depth constantly. Pacific Ocean trade winds blow westward, causing the ocean level to be about a half meter higher on the western side of the Pacific. Sea level is higher at the equator than at the poles because the equatorial waters expand and the centrifugal force of Earth's rotation causes the middle of the planet to bulge.

380 Chapter 13 • Exploring the Oceans

SECTION Review

Summary

- The global ocean is divided by the continents into four main oceans: Pacific Ocean, Atlantic Ocean, Indian Ocean, and Arctic Ocean.
- The four oceans as we know them today formed within the last 300 million years.
- Salts have been added to the ocean for billions of years. Salinity is a measure of the amount of dissolved salts in a given weight or mass of liquid.
- The three temperature zones of ocean water are the surface zone, the thermocline, and the deep zone.
- The water cycle is the continuous movement of water from the ocean to the atmosphere to the land and back to the ocean. The ocean plays the largest role in the water cycle.
- The ocean stabilizes Earth's weather conditions by absorbing and holding thermal energy.

Using Key Terms

1. In your own words, write a definition for each of the following terms: *salinity* and *water cycle*.

Understanding Key Ideas

2. The top layer of ocean water that extends to 300 m below sea level is called the
   a. deep zone.
   b. surface zone.
   c. Gulf Stream.
   d. thermocline.
3. Name the major divisions of the global ocean.
4. Explain how Earth's first oceans formed.
5. Why is the ocean an important part of the water cycle?
6. Between which two steps of the water cycle does the ocean fit?

Critical Thinking

7. **Making Inferences** Describe how the ocean plays a role in stabilizing Earth's weather conditions.
8. **Identifying Relationships** List one factor that affects salinity in the ocean and one factor that affects ocean temperatures. Explain how each factor affects salinity or temperature.

Interpreting Graphics

Use the image below to answer the questions that follow.

2 Condensation
1 Evaporation
3 Precipitation

9. At which stage would solid or liquid water fall to the Earth?
10. At which stage would the sun's energy cause liquid to rise into the atmosphere as water vapor?

SciLinks
Developed and maintained by the National Science Teachers Association
For a variety of links related to this chapter, go to www.scilinks.org
Topic: Exploring Earth's Oceans
SciLinks code: HSM0557

SCIENCE HUMOR
Q: Why is the ocean salty?
A: because fish don't like pepper

CHAPTER RESOURCES
Chapter Resource File
- Section Quiz GENERAL
- Section Review GENERAL
- Vocabulary and Section Summary GENERAL

Answers to Section Review

1. Sample answer: Salinity is a measure of the amount of dissolved salts in a given amount of liquid. The water cycle is the continuous movement of water from the ocean to the atmosphere to the land and back to the ocean.
2. b
3. The major divisions of the global ocean are the Pacific Ocean, the Atlantic Ocean, the Indian Ocean, and the Arctic Ocean.
4. Sample answer: Sometime before 4 billion years ago, Earth cooled enough for water vapor to condense. This water began to fall as rain. The rain filled the deeper levels of Earth's surface, and the first oceans began to form.
5. Sample answer: The ocean is an important part of the water cycle because nearly all of Earth's water is found in the ocean and the ocean absorbs the majority of the solar radiation that reaches the Earth.
6. The ocean fits between precipitation and evaporation in the water cycle.
7. The ocean helps to stabilize Earth's weather conditions because it absorbs and releases thermal energy from sunlight slowly. This function regulates temperatures in the atmosphere.
8. Sample answer: Evaporation affects salinity in the ocean, and depth affects the temperature of the ocean. When water evaporates from the ocean, dissolved solids are left behind. Therefore, high rates of evaporation leave the ocean saltier. The temperature of ocean water decreases as depth increases. Therefore, the temperature at the surface is much warmer than the average temperature of the ocean.
9. precipitation
10. evaporation

Section 1 • Earth's Oceans

SECTION 2

Focus

Overview

This section discusses how technology has facilitated exploration of the ocean floor and the methods used to survey the ocean floor, including sonar and satellites. This section also discusses the regional divisions of the ocean floor and the geographical features of each division.

🔔 **Bellringer**

Have students pretend that they have walked off the edge of North America and into the depths of the Atlantic Ocean. As they walk along the ocean floor toward Europe, what would they see? Have students make a drawing of the ocean floor that they would see along the way.

Motivate

Discussion — GENERAL

The Ocean Floor It has been said that scientists know more about the surface of the moon than about the ocean floor. Most of what scientists know about the ocean floor comes from sonar readings and sample dredging. Ask students to think about why the ocean is so difficult to study and what kinds of technology would help scientists learn more about the deep-ocean floor. **LS Verbal**

SECTION 2

READING WARM-UP

Objectives
- Describe technologies for studying the ocean floor.
- Identify the two major regions of the ocean floor.
- Classify subdivisions and features of the two major regions of the ocean floor.

Terms to Learn

continental shelf • rift valley
continental slope • seamount
continental rise • ocean trench
abyssal plain
mid-ocean ridge

READING STRATEGY

Reading Organizer As you read this section, create an outline of the section. Use the headings from the section in your outline.

CHAPTER RESOURCES

Chapter Resource File
- Lesson Plan
- Directed Reading A BASIC
- Directed Reading B SPECIAL NEEDS

Technology

Transparencies
- Bellringer
- How Sonar Works

The Ocean Floor

What lies at the bottom of the ocean? How deep is the ocean?

These questions were once unanswerable. By using new technology, scientists have learned a lot about the ocean floor. Scientists have discovered landforms on the ocean floor and have measured depths for almost the entire ocean floor.

Studying the Ocean Floor

Sending people into deep water to study the ocean floor can be risky. Fortunately, there are other ways to study the deep ocean. These ways include surveying from the ocean surface and from high above in space.

Seeing by Sonar

Sonar stands for *sound navigation and ranging*. This technology is based on the echo-ranging behavior of bats. Scientists use sonar to determine the ocean's depth by sending sound pulses from a ship down into the ocean. The sound moves through the water, bounces off the ocean floor, and returns to the ship. The deeper the water is, the longer the round trip takes. Scientists then calculate the depth by multiplying half the travel time by the speed of sound in water (about 1,500 m/s). This process is shown in **Figure 1**.

Figure 1 Ocean Floor Mapping with Sonar

❸ Scientists use sonar signals to make a *bathymetric profile*, which is a map of the ocean floor that shows the ocean's depth.

WEIRD SCIENCE

Although many people know that whales and dolphins communicate by sound, few people are aware that shrimp do the same thing. To locate food sources and other shrimp, they emit a sound similar to the sound of bacon frying!

---

382 Chapter 13 • Exploring the Oceans

Oceanography via Satellite

In the 1970s, scientists began studying Earth from satellites in orbit around the Earth. In 1978, scientists launched the satellite *Seasat*. This satellite focused on the ocean, sending images back to Earth that allowed scientists to measure the direction and speed of ocean currents.

Studying the Ocean with *Geosat*

Geosat, once a top-secret military satellite, has been used to measure slight changes in the height of the ocean's surface. Different underwater features, such as mountains and trenches, affect the height of the water above them. Scientists measure the different heights of the ocean surface and use the measurements to make detailed maps of the ocean floor. Maps made using satellite measurements, such as the map in **Figure 2**, can cover much more territory than maps made using ship-based sonar readings.

Reading Check How do scientists use satellites to make detailed maps of the ocean floor? (*See the Appendix for answers to Reading Checks.*)

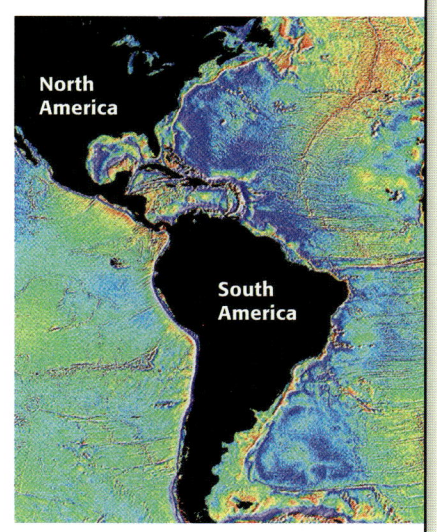

Figure 2 *This map was generated by satellite measurements of different heights of the ocean surface.*

1. To map a section of the ocean floor, scientists travel by ship across the ocean's surface. As they move, they repeatedly send sonar signals to the ocean floor.

2. The longer it takes for the sound to bounce off the ocean floor and return to the ship, the deeper the floor is in that spot.

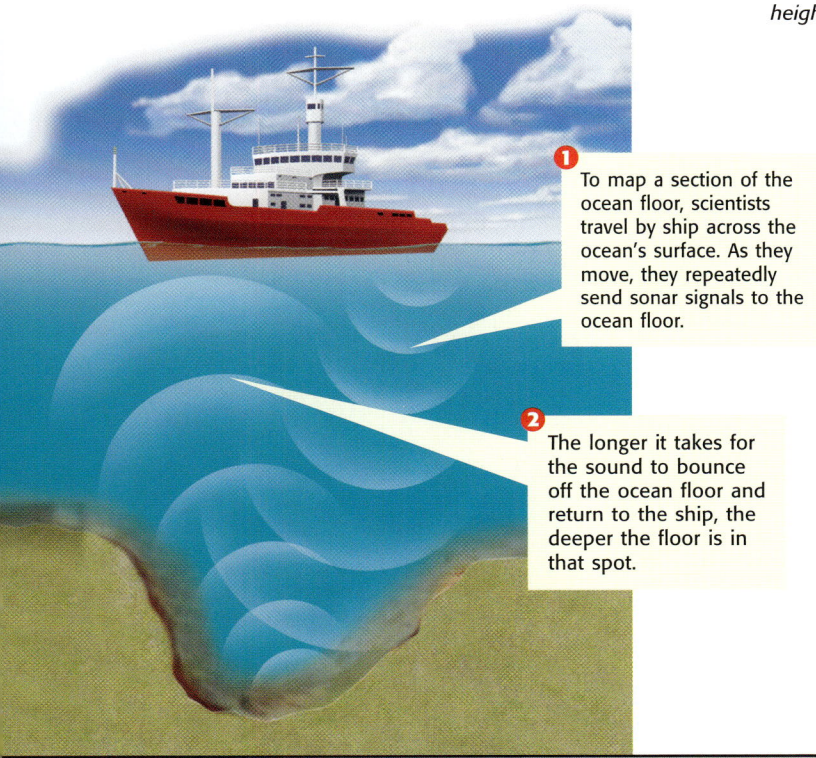

Answer to Reading Check
Satellite photos from *Seasat* send images of the ocean back to Earth. These images allow scientists to measure the direction and speed of ocean currents. Satellite photos and information from *Geosat* have been used to measure slight changes in the height of the ocean's surface.

Teach

CONNECTION ACTIVITY
Language Arts — ADVANCED

Undersea Exploration Tell students that the 1870 publication of *Twenty Thousand Leagues Under the Sea*, by Jules Verne, revived an interest in undersea exploration. Have students read sections of Verne's book aloud in class. Point out that the story inspired engineers to solve the problems plaguing submarines, which enabled scientists to reach greater depths in their exploration of the sea. **LS Verbal**

BRAIN FOOD

The Ocean Floor Affects Sea Level Students may be surprised to learn that underwater features such as seamounts and trenches affect the height of the ocean above them. Interestingly, the topography and composition of the ocean floor cause differences in gravity that are pronounced enough to affect sea level. For example, the mass of a seamount creates enough gravitational attraction to cause a 5 m bulge of water above it. Similarly, the sea level above a deep-sea trench can be depressed by as much as 60 m!

Section 2 • The Ocean Floor

Teach, continued

CONNECTION to Physical Science — BASIC

Water Pressure To show how water pressure changes with depth, punch three holes in the side of a milk carton: one near the top, one halfway down the side, and one near the bottom. Put one piece of tape over all three holes, and fill the carton with water. Remove the tape quickly. Have students observe the streams of water and explain what they see. **(The water stream at the bottom of the carton will shoot out the farthest and with the greatest force. The reason is that the water at the top of the carton exerted pressure on the water at the bottom of the carton.)**
LS Visual/Kinesthetic

Homework — ADVANCED

Concept Mapping
Remind students that volcanic seamounts that rise above the ocean surface become volcanic islands. The Hawaiian Islands formed this way. Have students research other ways islands form and then prepare a concept map of the different ways that islands form. They should find that some islands form by the growth of coral, some form by deposition (barrier islands), and some are continental islands (for example, Great Britain and Madagascar). **LS** Visual

continental shelf the gently sloping section of the continental margin located between the shoreline and the continental slope

continental slope the steeply inclined section of the continental margin located between the continental rise and the continental shelf

continental rise the gently sloping section of the continental margin located between the continental slope and the abyssal plain

abyssal plain a large, flat, almost level area of the deep-ocean basin

Answer to Reading Check
64,000 km; on the ocean floor

Revealing the Ocean Floor

Can you imagine being an explorer assigned to map uncharted areas on the planet? You might think that there are not many uncharted areas left because most of the land has already been explored. But what about the bottom of the ocean?

The ocean floor is not a flat surface. If you could go to the bottom of the ocean, you would see a number of impressive features. You would see the world's longest mountain chain, which is about 64,000 km (40,000 mi) long as well as canyons deeper than the Grand Canyon. And because it is underwater and some areas are so deep, much of the ocean floor is still not completely explored.

✓ **Reading Check** How long is the longest mountain chain in the world? Where is it located?

Figure 3 The Ocean Floor

The **continental shelf** begins at the shoreline and slopes gently toward the open ocean. It continues until the ocean floor begins to slope more steeply downward. The depth of the continental shelf can reach 200 m.

The **continental slope** begins at the edge of the continental shelf. It continues down to the flattest part of the ocean floor. The depth of the continental slope ranges from about 200 m to about 4,000 m.

The **continental rise,** which is the base of the continental slope, is made of large piles of sediment. The boundary between the continental margin and the deep-ocean basin lies underneath the continental rise.

The **abyssal plain** is the broad, flat part of the deep-ocean basin. It is covered by mud and the remains of tiny marine organisms. The average depth of the abyssal plain is about 4,000 m.

SCIENCE HUMOR

Q: What lies on the bottom of the ocean and trembles?
A: a nervous wreck

Chapter 13 • Exploring the Oceans

Regions of the Ocean Floor

If you journeyed to the ocean floor, you would first notice two major regions. The *continental margin* is made of continental crust, and the *deep-ocean basin* is made of oceanic crust. Imagine that the ocean is a giant swimming pool. The continental margin is the shallow end of the pool, and the deep-ocean basin is the deep end of the pool. The figure below shows how these two regions are subdivided.

Underwater Real Estate

As you can see in **Figure 3** below, the continental margin is subdivided into the continental shelf, the continental slope, and the continental rise. These divisions are based on depth and changes in slope. The deep-ocean basin consists of the abyssal (uh BIS uhl) plain, mid-ocean ridges, rift valleys, and ocean trenches. All of these features form near the boundaries of Earth's *tectonic plates*. On parts of the deep-ocean basin that are not near plate boundaries, there are thousands of seamounts. Seamounts are submerged volcanic mountains on the ocean floor.

Reading Check What are the subdivisions of the continental margin?

mid-ocean ridge a long, undersea mountain chain that forms along the floor of the major oceans

rift valley a long, narrow valley that forms as tectonic plates separate

seamount a submerged mountain on the ocean floor that is at least 1,000 m high and that has a volcanic origin

ocean trench a steep, long depression in the deep-sea floor that runs parallel to a chain of volcanic islands or a continental margin

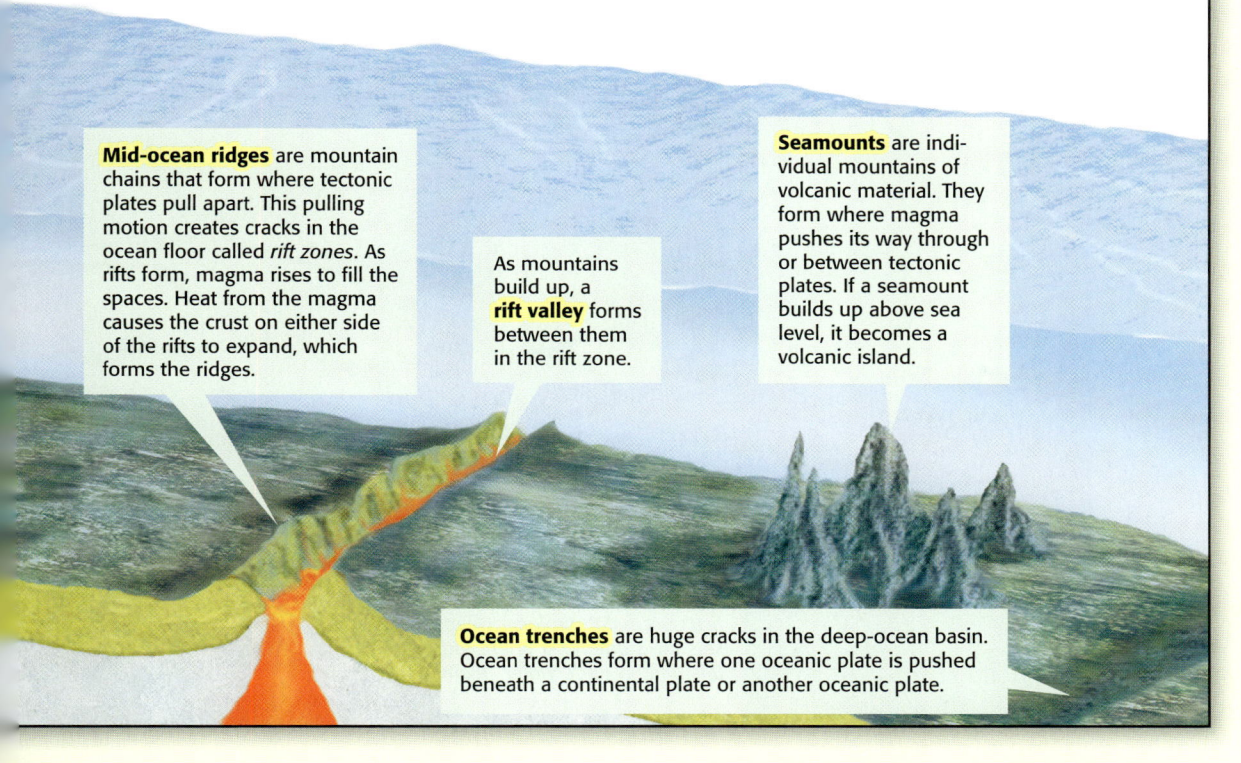

Mid-ocean ridges are mountain chains that form where tectonic plates pull apart. This pulling motion creates cracks in the ocean floor called *rift zones*. As rifts form, magma rises to fill the spaces. Heat from the magma causes the crust on either side of the rifts to expand, which forms the ridges.

As mountains build up, a **rift valley** forms between them in the rift zone.

Seamounts are individual mountains of volcanic material. They form where magma pushes its way through or between tectonic plates. If a seamount builds up above sea level, it becomes a volcanic island.

Ocean trenches are huge cracks in the deep-ocean basin. Ocean trenches form where one oceanic plate is pushed beneath a continental plate or another oceanic plate.

Answer to Reading Check
continental shelf, continental slope, and continental rise

CHAPTER RESOURCES

Technology

Transparencies
- Revealing the Ocean Floor: A
- Revealing the Ocean Floor: B

Using the Figure — GENERAL

Mid-Ocean Ridges Draw students' attention to the mid-ocean ridges in **Figure 3**. Below the rift zones that characterize mid-ocean ridges, magma rises from beneath the crust and erupts as lava. The lava cools when it enters the water and forms new oceanic crust. Point out that ocean trenches formed by the subduction of plates are some of the deepest places on Earth and often support a diversity of life. **LS Verbal**

CONNECTION ACTIVITY
Art — GENERAL

Illustrating the Ocean Floor Draw students' attention to **Figure 3**, and have them draw, label, and color their own illustration of the depth zones of the ocean floor. Point out the canyon in the continental slope. This canyon is a submarine canyon. Most of the sediment that makes up the continental rise travels down from the continental shelf through submarine canyons. Be sure that students have divided the continental margin into the continental shelf, continental slope, and continental rise. They should identify the features of the deep-ocean basin as mid-ocean ridges, seamounts, rift valleys, and ocean trenches. In addition, students can indicate the temperature of the ocean water at each depth by using different colors. **LS Visual** — English Language Learners

Section 2 • The Ocean Floor

Close

Reteaching — BASIC

The Ocean Floor Have students review the regions and features of the ocean floor. Ask students to choose any two regions or features and to describe them in their own words. If describing features, students should include how the features form.
LS Verbal

Quiz — GENERAL

1. Which features of the abyssal plain form at the boundaries of tectonic plates? (mid-ocean ridges, rift valleys, and ocean trenches)

2. How is the depth of the ocean measured? (It is measured using sonar. Scientists calculate the depth by multiplying half the time a sound wave takes to hit the ocean floor and return to the surface by the speed of sound in water.)

Alternative Assessment — GENERAL

Modeling the Ocean Floor Encourage students to imagine that they are oceanographers on a deep-sea mission aboard a piloted vessel. Have them work in groups to make a model of the ocean floor, including all the features from this section. The model can be a cross section similar to **Figure 3** or a view from above.

English Language Learners
LS Visual/Verbal

CONNECTION TO Social Studies

The JASON Project The JASON project, started by oceanographer Dr. Robert Ballard, allows students and teachers to take part in virtual field trips to some of the most exotic locations on Earth. Using satellite links and the Internet, students around the world have participated in scientific expeditions to places such as the Galápagos Islands, the Sea of Cortez, and deep-sea hydrothermal vents. Using the Internet, research where the JASON project is headed to next!

Answer to Reading Check

It is unique because some of the organisms living around the vent do not rely on photosynthesis for energy.

Exploring the Ocean with Underwater Vessels

Just as astronauts explore space with rockets, scientists explore the oceans with underwater vessels. These vessels contain the air that the explorers need to breathe and all of the scientific instruments that the explorers need to study the oceans.

Piloted Vessels: *Alvin* and *Deep Flight*

One research vessel used to travel to the deep ocean is called *Alvin*. *Alvin* is 7 m long and can reach some of the deepest parts of the ocean. Scientists have used *Alvin* for many underwater missions, including searches for sunken ships, the recovery of a lost hydrogen bomb, and explorations of the sea floor. In 1977, scientists aboard *Alvin* discovered an oasis of life around hydrothermal vents near the Galápagos Islands. Ecosystems near hydrothermal vents are unique because some organisms living around the vent do not rely on photosynthesis for energy. Instead, these organisms rely on chemicals in the water as their source of energy.

Another modern vessel that scientists use to explore the deep ocean is an underwater airplane called *Deep Flight*. This vessel, shown in **Figure 4**, moves through the water in much the same way that an airplane moves through the air. Future models of *Deep Flight* will be designed to transport pilots to the deepest parts of the ocean, which are more than 11,000 m deep.

✓ **Reading Check** Why is the ecosystem discovered by *Alvin* unique?

Figure 4 Like the Wright brothers' first successful airplane, Deep Flight sets the stage for a bright future—this time in underwater "flight."

Is That a Fact!

The same explorer who led the first voyage around the world also attempted to determine the depth of the ocean. In 1520, Ferdinand Magellan weighted a 370 m rope with lead and lowered it into the ocean. But, his rope was not long enough to reach the ocean floor! The first successful measurement was made in 1773. Using Magellan's techniques, explorers found that the depth of the ocean near Norway is about 1,250 m.

Robotic Vessels: *JASON II* and *Medea*

Exploring the deep ocean by using piloted vessels is expensive and can be very dangerous. For these reasons, scientists use robotic vessels to explore the ocean. One interesting robot team consists of *JASON II* and *Medea*. These robots are designed to withstand pressures much greater than those found in the deepest parts of the ocean. *JASON II* is "flown" by a pilot at the surface and is used to explore the ocean floor. *Medea* is attached to *JASON II* with a tether and explores above the sea floor. In the future, unpiloted "drone" robots shaped like fish may be used. Another robot under development uses the ocean's thermal energy for power. These robots could explore the ocean for years and send data to scientists at the surface.

SECTION Review

Summary

- Scientists study the ocean floor from the surface using sonar and satellites.
- The ocean floor is divided into two regions—the continental margin and the deep-ocean basin.
- The continental margin consists of the continental shelf, the continental slope, and the continental rise.
- The deep-ocean basin consists of the abyssal plain, mid-ocean ridges, rift valleys, seamounts, and ocean trenches.
- Scientists explore the ocean from below the surface by using piloted vessels and robotic vessels.

Using Key Terms

For each pair of terms, explain how the meanings of the terms differ.

1. *continental shelf* and *continental slope*
2. *abyssal plain* and *ocean trench*
3. *mid-ocean ridge* and *seamount*

Understanding Key Ideas

4. Sonar is a technology based on the
   a. *Geosat* satellite.
   b. surface currents in the ocean.
   c. zones of the ocean floor.
   d. echo-ranging behavior of bats.
5. List the two major regions of the ocean floor.
6. Describe the subdivisions of the continental margin.
7. List three technologies for studying the ocean floor, and explain how they are used.
8. List three underwater missions that *Alvin* has been used for.
9. Explain how *Jason II* and *Medea* are used to explore the ocean.
10. Describe how a bathymetric profile is made.

Math Skills

11. Air pressure at sea level is 1 atmosphere (atm). Underwater, pressure increases by 1 atm every 10 m of depth. For example, at a depth of 10 m, water pressure is 2 atm. What is the pressure at 100 m?

Critical Thinking

12. **Making Comparisons** How is exploring the oceans similar to exploring space?
13. **Applying Concepts** Is the ocean floor a flat surface? Explain your answer.

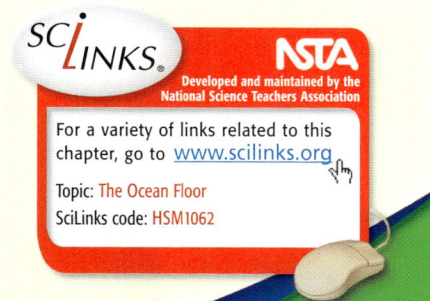

Answers to Section Review

1. Sample answer: The continental shelf is the gently sloping section of the continental margin. The continental slope is the steeply inclined section of the continental margin.
2. Sample answer: The abyssal plain is a large, flat, almost-level area of the deep-ocean basin. An ocean trench is a steep, long depression in the deep-sea floor.
3. Sample answer: A midocean ridge is a long, undersea mountain chain that forms along the floor of the major oceans. A seamount is a submerged mountain on the ocean floor.
4. d
5. continental margin and deep-ocean basin
6. The continental shelf is the gently sloping section located between the shoreline and the continental slope. The continental slope is the steeply inclined section of the continental margin. The continental rise is the gently sloping section located between the continental slope and the abyssal plain.
7. Sample answer: sonar, *Geosat*, and underwater vessels; Sonar is used to determine the ocean's depth by sending sound pulses from a ship down into the ocean. *Geosat* is a satellite that is used to measure the different heights of the ocean's surface, which can help detect mountains and trenches on the ocean floor. Underwater vessels (both piloted and robotic) are used to travel to the deepest parts of the ocean.
8. searches for sunken ships, the recovery of a lost hydrogen bomb, and explorations of the sea floor
9. Sample answer: *Jason II* is "flown" by a pilot at the surface and is used to explore the ocean floor. *Medea* is attached to *Jason II* with a tether and explores above the sea floor.
10. Scientists use sonar signals to make a bathymetric profile.
11. 11 atm
12. Sample answer: Exploring the oceans is similar to exploring space because it can be dangerous to explore both and much is still unknown about the ocean and about space.
13. Sample answer: no; The ocean floor is not a flat surface because it has many features, including the world's longest mountain chain.

CHAPTER RESOURCES

Chapter Resource File
- Section Quiz GENERAL
- Section Review GENERAL
- Vocabulary and Section Summary GENERAL

SECTION 3

Focus

Overview
This section introduces a system for classifying marine organisms based on where they live and how they move. Students also learn to describe ecological zones of the ocean and give examples of organisms inhabiting each zone.

Bellringer
Before they read this section, have students imagine they are marine biologists who must classify marine life into three groups. Challenge them to identify the criteria they would use in their classification systems.

Motivate

Group Activity — GENERAL
Classifying Divide the class into small groups. Ask them to classify as many items in the classroom as they can based on the following categories:
- height at which the items are located
- ways the items are used

LS Visual/Verbal

SECTION 3

Life in the Ocean

In which part of the ocean does an octopus live? And where do dolphins spend most of their time?

Just as armadillos and birds occupy very different places on Earth, octopuses and dolphins live in very different parts of the ocean. Trying to study life in the oceans can be a challenge for scientists. The oceans are so large that many forms of marine life have not been discovered, and there are many more organisms that scientists know little about. To make things easier, scientists classify marine organisms into three main groups.

READING WARM-UP

Objectives
- Identify the three groups of marine life.
- Describe the two main ocean environments.
- Identify the ecological zones of the benthic and pelagic environments.

Terms to Learn
plankton
nekton
benthos
benthic environment
pelagic environment

READING STRATEGY

Mnemonics As you read this section, create a mnemonic device to help you remember the ecological zones of the ocean.

The Three Groups of Marine Life

The three main groups of marine life, as shown in **Figure 1,** are plankton, nekton, and benthos. Marine organisms are placed into one of these three groups according to where they live and how they move.

Organisms that float or drift freely near the ocean's surface are called **plankton**. Most plankton are microscopic. Plankton are divided into two groups—those that are plant-like (*phytoplankton*) and those that are animal-like (*zooplankton*). Organisms that swim actively in the open ocean are called **nekton**. Types of nekton include mammals, such as whales, dolphins, and sea lions, as well as many varieties of fish. **Benthos** are organisms that live on or in the ocean floor. There are many types of benthos, such as crabs, starfish, worms, coral, sponges, seaweed, and clams.

Figure 1 Plankton, nekton, and benthos are the three groups of organisms that live in the ocean.

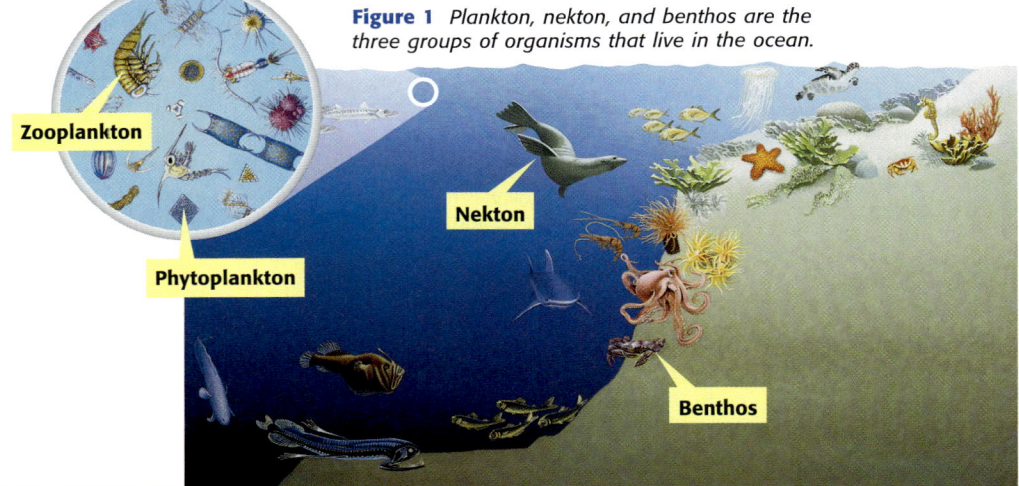

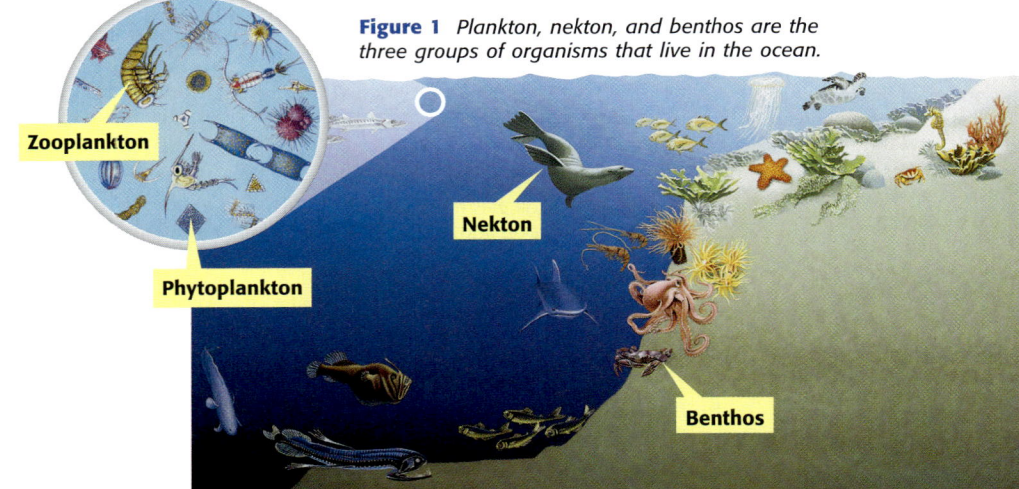

CHAPTER RESOURCES

Chapter Resource File
- Lesson Plan
- Directed Reading A BASIC
- Directed Reading B SPECIAL NEEDS

Technology
- Transparencies
  - Bellringer
  - The Three Groups of Marine Life

Is That a Fact!

The word *plankton* comes from the Greek *planktos,* meaning "wandering." Because plankton float at or near the ocean's surface, they "wander" with the ocean currents. Interestingly, tiny plankton are the sole sustenance of two of the largest marine animals—the blue whale and the basking shark. The word *planets* is also derived from the same root and refers to the observation that planets appear to wander among the stars.

388 Chapter 13 • Exploring the Oceans

The Benthic Environment

In addition to being divided into zones based on depth, the ocean floor is divided into ecological zones based on where different types of benthos live. These zones are grouped into one major marine environment—the benthic environment. The **benthic environment,** or bottom environment, is the region near the ocean floor and all the organisms that live on or in it.

The Intertidal Zone

The shallowest benthic zone, called the *intertidal zone,* is located between the low-tide and high-tide limits. Twice a day, the intertidal zone changes. As the tide flows in, the zone is covered with ocean water. Then, as the tide flows out, the intertidal zone is exposed to the air and sun.

Because of the change in tides, intertidal organisms must be able to live both underwater and on exposed land. Some organisms, such as the sea anemones and starfish shown in **Figure 2,** attach themselves to rocks and reefs to avoid being washed out to sea during low tide. Other organisms, such as clams, oysters, barnacles, and crabs, have tough shells that give them protection against strong waves during high tide and against harsh sunlight during low tide. Some animals can burrow in sand or between rocks to avoid harsh conditions. Plants also protect themselves from being washed away by strong waves. Plants such as seaweed have strong *holdfasts* (rootlike structures) that allow them to grow in this zone.

Reading Check How do clams and oysters survive in the intertidal zone during high tide and low tide? *(See the Appendix for answers to Reading Checks.)*

Figure 2 *Organisms such as sea anemones and starfish attach themselves to rocks and reefs. These organisms must be able to survive both wet and dry conditions.*

plankton the mass of mostly microscopic organisms that float or drift freely in freshwater and marine environments

nekton all organisms that swim actively in open water, independent of currents

benthos the organisms that live at the bottom of the sea or ocean

benthic environment the region near the bottom of a pond, lake, or ocean

SCIENTISTS AT ODDS

The Azoic Theory Before the late 1870s, scientists widely believed the "azoic theory" of James Forbes and Alexander Agassiz. This theory argued that no life existed below shallow depths in the oceans. Sir Wyville Thomson disputed this theory, and in 1872, he embarked on a three-and-a-half year voyage to prove his point. The HMS *Challenger* voyage, which established oceanography as a modern science, collected ocean-floor samples from deeper than 8,000 m. Thomson's evidence disproved the azoic theory and greatly expanded our knowledge of the world's oceans. He published his results in *The Depths of the Sea,* the first general textbook on oceanography.

Teach

MISCONCEPTION ALERT

Ocean Phytoplankton Many people think that rain forests produce most of Earth's oxygen. Actually, ocean phytoplankton are the most productive photosynthesizers on the planet. Because phytoplankton consume the greenhouse gas CO_2 during photosynthesis, many scientists think that phytoplankton populations play a significant role in global climate patterns.

Homework —— GENERAL

Odd Organisms Have students draw five imaginary organisms, each inhabiting a different benthic zone. Students should describe each plant or animal and explain its particular adaptations for living in that zone. Their drawings and descriptions should include the following:

- how the organisms obtain food
- how they avoid predation
- how they withstand the water pressure and temperature at the depth where they live

Encourage students to share their drawings and explanations with the class.

LS Visual/Verbal   **English Language Learners**

Answer to Reading Check
The tough shells of clams and oysters protect the organisms against strong waves and harsh sunlight.

Section 3 • Life in the Ocean   **389**

Teach, continued

Group Activity —GENERAL

Ocean Zones and Organisms
Divide the class into groups of five, and provide each group with poster board and markers. Ask groups to draw a cross-sectional illustration of the ocean and label the following features: benthic environment, intertidal zone, sublittoral zone, bathyal zone, abyssal zone, and hadal zone.

Have each group member illustrate the organisms found in one of the five zones. (Each group should illustrate all of the five zones.) Instruct each group to elect a spokesperson to present the poster to the class.
LS Visual/Intrapersonal

Homework —GENERAL

Benthic Research
Have students select one of the benthic zones to investigate further. Ask them to focus on the adaptations that organisms living there have developed that enable them to exist in that zone. Students can present their findings in a concept map, poster, or comic book. **English Language Learners**
LS Interpersonal

Figure 3 Corals, like many other types of organisms, can live in both the sublittoral zone and the intertidal zone. However, they are more common in the sublittoral zone.

The Sublittoral Zone

The *sublittoral zone* begins where the intertidal zone ends, at the low-tide limit, and extends to the edge of the continental shelf. This zone of the benthic environment is more stable than the intertidal zone. The temperature, water pressure, and amount of sunlight remain fairly constant in the sublittoral zone. Sublittoral organisms, such as corals, shown in **Figure 3,** do not have to cope with as much change as intertidal organisms do. Although the sublittoral zone extends down 200 m below sea level, plants and most animals stay in the upper 100 m, where small amounts of sunlight reaches the ocean floor.

The Bathyal Zone

The *bathyal* (BATH ee uhl) *zone* extends from the edge of the continental shelf to the abyssal plain. The depth of this zone ranges from 200 m to 4,000 m below sea level. Because of the lack of sunlight at these depths, plant life is scarce in this part of the benthic environment. Animals in this zone include sponges, brachiopods, sea stars, echinoids, and octopuses, such as the one shown in **Figure 4.**

Figure 4 Octopuses are one of the animals common to the bathyal zone.

Cultural Awareness —GENERAL

Sea Stories Stories of mermaids and sea monsters are a part of many cultures. In some legends, mermaids were good and helped shipwrecked sailors. In others, mermaids lured ships and sailors into dangerous waters. Sea monsters were always bad, sinking ships and killing sailors. Ask students why they think these legends were told. Have them research a legend and write one of their own. **LS** Interpersonal

SCIENCE HUMOR

Q: What's the best way to catch a fish?
A: Have someone throw it to you.

390 Chapter 13 • Exploring the Oceans

Figure 5 Tube worms can tolerate higher temperatures than most other organisms can. These animals survive in water as hot as 81°C.

Abyssal zone

The Abyssal Zone

No plants and very few animals live in the *abyssal zone*, which is on the abyssal plain. The abyssal zone is the largest ecological zone of the ocean and can reach 4,000 m in depth. Animals such as crabs, sponges, worms, and sea cucumbers live within the abyssal zone. Many of these organisms, such as the tube worms shown in **Figure 5**, live around hot-water vents called *black smokers*. Scientists know very little about this benthic environment because it is so deep and dark.

✓ **Reading Check** What types of animals live in the abyssal zone?

The Hadal Zone

The deepest benthic zone is the *hadal* (HAYD'l) *zone*. This zone consists of the floor of the ocean trenches and any organisms found there. The hadal zone can reach from 6,000 m to 7,000 m in depth. Scientists know even less about the hadal zone than they do about the abyssal zone. So far, scientists have discovered a type of sponge, a few species of worms, and a type of clam, which is shown in **Figure 6**.

Hadal zone

Figure 6 These clams are one of the few types of organisms known to live in the hadal zone.

CONNECTION to Life Science — GENERAL

Survival of the Fittest Because food is so scarce in the deeper parts of the ocean, its inhabitants have special adaptations to ensure their survival. Some gulper eels, for example, have huge jaws and elastic stomachs that allow them to eat fish larger than themselves. Show students photographs of some of these organisms, and use the teaching transparency entitled "Four Parts of Natural Selection" to discuss the process of natural selection. **LS Visual**

CONNECTION to Life Science — GENERAL

Sea Skaters Sea skaters are the only insects known to live directly on the surface of the open ocean. The insects have waxy hairs on their feet that repel water and help them travel on the surface of the water. They are predators that hunt prey swimming beneath the surface by spearing them with sharp mouth parts. Ask students to list reasons why other insects do not live in the open ocean. **LS Verbal**

INCLUSION Strategies

- Learning Disabled
- Attention Deficit Disorder
- Developmentally Delayed

Ask students to create a mnemonic device that will remind them of the zones of the benthic environment. For example, they might write "**I**sabel **S**ent **B**art **A**way from **H**ome" to remind them that the zones are **I**ntertidal, **S**ublittoral, **B**athyal, **A**byssal, and **H**adal. Ask them to share their mnemonic devices with the class. **LS Verbal**

Answer to Reading Check
crabs, sponges, worms, and sea cucumbers

CHAPTER RESOURCES

Technology

Transparencies
- **LINK TO LIFE SCIENCE** Four Parts of Natural Selection

Section 3 • Life in the Ocean **391**

Close

Reteaching — BASIC
Concept Mapping Have students create a concept map linking the two ocean environments and the ocean zones that make up each environment. **LS Verbal**

Quiz — GENERAL
1. Why do scientists know little about the abyssal and hadal zones? (Because these zones are so deep and dark, scientists know very little about them.)
2. Where do most marine organisms live? (in the neritic zone)

Alternative Assessment — GENERAL
PORTFOLIO **Exploring the Abyssal Zone** Challenge students to write science-fiction stories about exploring the abyssal zone of the benthic environment. Have them describe the difficulties of exploring that zone, and encourage them to use their imagination to describe creatures they might find there. **LS Interpersonal**

Figure 7 Many marine animals, such as these dolphins, live in the neritic zone.

pelagic environment in the ocean, the zone near the surface or at middle depths, beyond the sublittoral zone and above the abyssal zone

The Pelagic Environment
The zone near the ocean's surface and at the middle depths of the ocean is called the **pelagic environment**. It is beyond the sublittoral zone and above the abyssal zone. There are two major zones in the pelagic environment—the neritic zone and the oceanic zone.

The Neritic Zone
The *neritic zone* covers the continental shelf. This warm, shallow zone contains the largest concentration of marine life. Fish, plankton, and marine mammals, such as the dolphins in **Figure 7**, are just a few of the animal groups found in this zone. The neritic zone contains diverse marine life because it receives more sunlight than the other zones in the ocean. Sunlight allows plankton, which are food for other marine organisms, to grow. The many animals in the benthic zone below the neritic zone also serve as a food supply.

✓ **Reading Check** Why does the neritic zone contain the largest concentration of marine life in the ocean?

CONNECTION TO Language Arts

WRITING SKILL **Water, Water, Everywhere** Samuel Taylor Coleridge wrote "The Rime of the Ancient Mariner" in 1798. The following is an excerpt from the poem:

Water, water, everywhere, / And all the boards did shrink / Water, water, everywhere, / Nor any drop to drink . . . / And every tongue through utter drought, / Was withered at the root; / We could not speak, no more than if / We had been choked with soot.

What do you think this excerpt means? Write a short essay describing the meaning of this passage.

Answer to Reading Check
The neritic zone contains the largest concentration of marine life in the ocean because it receives more sunlight than the other zones in the ocean.

Answer to Connection to Language Arts
Suggest that students use library resources or the Internet to help them research the meaning of the passage.

Chapter 13 • Exploring the Oceans

The Oceanic Zone

The *oceanic zone* includes the volume of water that covers the entire sea floor except for the continental shelf. In the deeper parts of the oceanic zone, the water temperature is colder and the pressure is much greater than in the neritic zone. Also, organisms are more spread out in the oceanic zone than in the neritic zone. Although many of the same organisms that live in the neritic zone are found throughout the upper regions, some strange animals lurk in the darker depths, as shown in **Figure 8**. Other animals in the deeper parts of this zone include giant squids and some whale species.

Figure 8 The angler fish is a predator that uses a wormlike lure attached to its head to attract prey.

SECTION Review

Summary

- The three main groups of marine life are plankton, nekton, and benthos.
- The two main ocean environments are the benthic environment and the pelagic environment.
- The ecological zones of the benthic environment include the intertidal zone, sublittoral zone, bathyal zone, abyssal zone, and hadal zone.
- The ecological zones of the pelagic environment include the neritic zone and the oceanic zone.

Using Key Terms

The statements below are false. For each statement, replace the underlined term to make a true statement.

1. <u>Plankton</u> are organisms that swim actively in ocean water.
2. The intertidal zone is part of the <u>pelagic zone</u>.
3. Dolphins live in the <u>benthic environment</u>.

Understanding Key Ideas

4. The deepest benthic zone is the
   a. pelagic environment.
   b. hadal zone.
   c. oceanic zone.
   d. abyssal zone.
5. List and briefly describe the three main groups of marine organisms.
6. Name the two ocean environments. In your own words, describe where they are located in the ocean.

Critical Thinking

7. **Making Inferences** Describe why organisms in the intertidal zone must be able to live underwater and on exposed land.

8. **Applying Concepts** How would the ocean's ecological zones change if sea level dropped 300 m?

Interpreting Graphics

Use the diagram below to answer the following question.

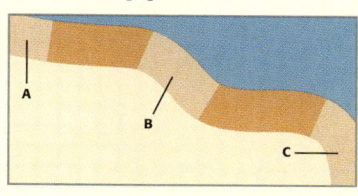

9. Identify the names of the ecological zones of the benthic environment shown above.

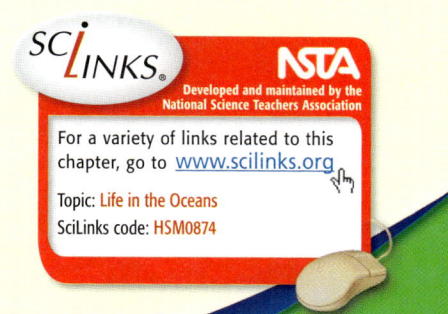

SECTION 4

Focus

Overview
This section discusses the ocean's living and nonliving resources and focuses on the methods used to obtain them. Students are asked to consider the importance of the ocean resources and to explore ways to conserve them.

🔔 Bellringer
Write the following sentences on the board, and challenge students to identify four items or activities that involve ocean resources.

- Tabitha drove her car to the market to buy a tuna steak for dinner. When she got home, she poured herself a glass of water, then fired up her gas grill, and cooked the tuna.

Motivate

Group Activity — GENERAL
Brainstorming Divide the class into small groups. Have students imagine a world without ocean resources. Ask them to brainstorm a list of activities that would no longer be possible. Examples might include eating seafood, shipping goods by sea, or deep-sea diving. Have each group share its list with the class and discuss the importance of ocean resources. **LS Verbal**

READING WARM-UP

Objectives
- List two ways of harvesting the ocean's living resources.
- Identify three nonliving resources in the ocean.
- Describe the ocean's energy resources.

Terms to Learn
desalination

READING STRATEGY
Paired Summarizing Read this section silently. In pairs, take turns summarizing the material. Stop to discuss ideas that seem confusing.

CHAPTER RESOURCES

Chapter Resource File
- Lesson Plan
- Directed Reading A BASIC
- Directed Reading B SPECIAL NEEDS

Technology
- Transparencies
  - Bellringer

Resources from the Ocean

The next time you enjoy your favorite ice cream, remember that without seaweed, it would be a runny mess!

The ocean offers a vast supply of resources. These resources are put to a number of uses. For example, a seaweed called *kelp* is used as a thickener for many food products, including ice cream. Food, raw materials, energy, and drinkable water are all harvested from the ocean. And there are probably more resources in unexplored parts of the ocean. As human populations have grown, however, the demand for these resources has increased, while the availability has decreased.

Living Resources
People have been harvesting plants and animals from the ocean for thousands of years. Many civilizations formed in coastal regions where the ocean offered plenty of food for a growing population. Today, harvesting food from the ocean is a multi-billion-dollar industry.

Fishing the Ocean
Of all the marine organisms, fish are the largest group of organisms that are taken from the ocean. Almost 75 million tons of fish are harvested each year. With improved technology, such as drift nets, fishers have become better at taking fish from the ocean. **Figure 1** shows the large number of fish that can be caught using a drift net. In recent years, many people have become concerned that we are overfishing the ocean. We are taking more fish than can be naturally replaced. Also, animals other than fish, especially dolphins and turtles, can be accidentally caught in drift nets. Today, the fishing industry is making efforts to prevent overfishing and damage to other wildlife from drift nets.

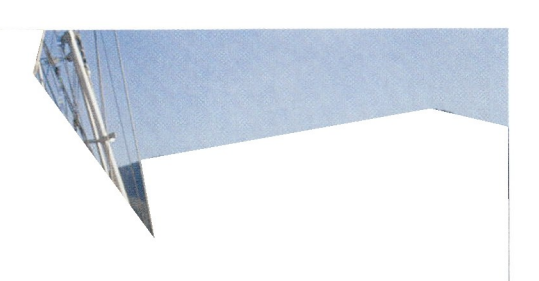

Figure 1 Drift nets are fishing nets that cover kilometers of ocean. Whole schools of fish can be caught with a single drift net.

Farming the Ocean

Overfishing reduces fish populations. Recently, laws regulating fishing have become stricter. As a result, it is becoming more difficult to supply our demand for fish. Many people have begun to raise ocean fish in fish farms to help meet the demand. Fish farming requires several holding ponds. Each pond contains fish at a certain level of development. **Figure 2** shows a holding pond in a fish farm. When the fish are old enough, they are harvested and packaged for shipping.

Fish are not the only seafood harvested in a farmlike setting. Shrimp, oysters, crabs, and mussels are raised in enclosed areas near the shore. Mussels and oysters are grown attached to ropes. Huge nets line the nursery area, preventing the animals from being eaten by their natural predators.

Reading Check How can fish farms help reduce overfishing? (See the Appendix for answers to Reading Checks.)

Figure 2 Eating fish raised in a fish farm helps lower the number of fish harvested from the ocean.

Savory Seaweed

Many types of seaweed, which are species of alga, are harvested from the ocean. For example, kelp, shown in **Figure 3**, is a seaweed that grows as much as 33 cm a day. Kelp is harvested and used as a thickener in jellies, ice cream, and similar products. Seaweed is rich in protein. In fact, several species of seaweed are staples of the Japanese diet. For example, some kinds of sushi, a Japanese dish, are wrapped in seaweed.

Figure 3 Kelp, a type of alga, can grow up to 33 cm a day. It is harvested and used in a number of products, including ice cream.

Teach

READING STRATEGY — BASIC

Prediction Guide Before students read the passage about living ocean resources, ask them to write an answer for the following question: "What are two problems you think might be associated with fishing the oceans?" (Sample answer: overfishing, accidentally catching other animals in drift nets) **Verbal**

CONNECTION ACTIVITY
Real World — ADVANCED

Writing **Fish Story** In the United States, more than 50% of the population lives and works within 80 km of the sea even though coastal areas account for only 11% of the nation's land area. Have students write a short story that accurately describes the route that a fish takes from the ocean to the dinner table. Encourage them to focus on the human characters in their story. Ask students to consider how this ocean resource benefits the people who catch, process, ship, sell, and eat it. **Interpersonal**

Answer to Reading Check

Fish farms can help reduce overfishing because the fish are raised instead of fished directly out of the ocean.

CONNECTION ACTIVITY
Environmental Science — ADVANCED

Factory Trawlers Factory trawlers are enormous boats that pull nets as large as four football fields and can harvest 400 tons of fish in a single haul. They can stay at sea for months catching, processing, freezing, and packaging fish. Because of their incredible cost (as much as $40 million), they must catch vast quantities of fish to remain operational. Factory trawlers threaten marine ecosystems because the trawlers can deplete an entire local fish population and quickly move on. They are also criticized for netting large quantities of *bycatch*, unwanted fish and sea life that are caught and thrown overboard, often dead or dying. However, fish are an important source of protein. Also, fishing is a major source of employment in the world, but many scientists agree that strong restrictions limiting fishing are important. Have students find out more about these ships and the environmental controversies that surround them. **Verbal**

Section 4 • Resources from the Ocean   **395**

Teach, continued

CONNECTION ACTIVITY
Real World —— GENERAL

Petroleum Dependence
Have students make a list of all their daily activities that rely on petroleum. (Answers might include taking a hot shower, using a hair dryer, cooking breakfast, driving to school, turning on lights, and washing and drying clothes.) Allow time for students to share their lists with classmates, and then encourage them to brainstorm ways they might reduce their reliance on fossil fuels.

Group ACTIVITY —— GENERAL

Writing — Public Service Announcement
Divide the class into small groups, and encourage each group to select a different ocean resource. Have students work together to write a public service announcement designed to convince the public of the resource's value to people. Have them include ways people can help conserve the resource. Ask students to present their announcements to the class.
LS Verbal/Intrapersonal

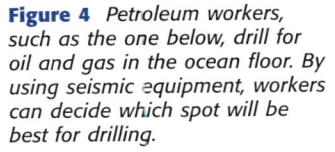

Homework —— GENERAL

Graphing Ocean Resources Help students use references to find out how much of the world's energy needs are met by the following: oil, natural gas, coal, tidal energy, geothermal energy, wave energy, hydroelectric energy, solar energy, and wind energy. Have students prepare pie graphs or bar graphs of their findings. **LS Visual/Interpersonal**

Nonliving Resources

Humans also harvest many nonliving resources from the ocean. These resources provide raw materials, drinkable water, and energy for our growing population. Some resources are easy to get, while others are very difficult to harvest.

Oil and Natural Gas

Modern civilization continues to be very dependent on oil and natural gas for energy. Oil and natural gas are *nonrenewable resources*. They are used up faster than they can be replenished naturally. Both oil and natural gas are found under layers of impermeable rock. Petroleum engineers must drill through this rock in order to reach these resources.

✓ **Reading Check** What are nonrenewable resources? Give an example of a nonrenewable resource.

Searching for Oil

How do engineers know where to drill for oil and natural gas? They use seismic equipment. Special devices send powerful pulses of sound to the ocean floor. The pulses move through the water and penetrate the rocks and sediment below. The pulses are then reflected back toward the ship, where they are recorded by electronic equipment and analyzed by a computer. The computer readings indicate how rock layers are arranged below the ocean floor. Petroleum workers, such as the one in **Figure 4,** use these readings to locate a promising area to drill.

Figure 4 Petroleum workers, such as the one below, drill for oil and gas in the ocean floor. By using seismic equipment, workers can decide which spot will be best for drilling.

Answer to Reading Check
Nonrenewable resources are resources that cannot be replenished. Oil and natural gas are nonrenewable resources.

396 Chapter 13 • Exploring the Oceans

Figure 5 Most desalination plants, like this one in Kuwait, use evaporation to separate ocean water from the salt it contains.

Fresh Water and Desalination

In parts of the world where fresh water is limited, people desalinate ocean water. **Desalination** (DEE SAL uh NAY shuhn) is the process of removing salt from sea water. After the salt is removed, the fresh water is then collected for human use. But desalination is not as simple as it sounds, and it is very expensive. Countries with enough annual rainfall rely on the fresh water provided by precipitation and do not need costly desalination plants. Some countries located in drier parts of the world must build desalination plants to provide enough fresh water. One of these plants is shown in **Figure 5**. Saudi Arabia, located in the desert region of the Middle East, has one of the largest desalination plants in the world.

desalination a process of removing salt from ocean water

✓ **Reading Check** Explain where desalination plants are most likely to be built.

Quick Lab

The Desalination Plant

1. Measure **1,000 mL of warm water** in a **graduated cylinder.** Pour the water in a **large pot.**
2. Carefully, add **35 g of table salt.** Stir the water until all of the salt is dissolved.
3. Place the pot on a **hot plate,** and allow all of the water to boil away.
4. Using a **wooden spoon,** scrape the salt residue from the bottom of the pot.
5. Measure the mass of the salt that was left in the bottom of the pot. How much salt did you separate from the water?
6. How does this activity model what happens in a desalination plant? What would be done differently in a desalination plant?

BRAIN FOOD

Desalination The most common method of desalination involves both evaporation and condensation. This method usually relies on fossil fuels. Other methods of desalination exist, but they require more energy and are thus more expensive. In one method, sea water is frozen to separate most of the salt from the water. The ice is then removed and melted for use. This method is not widely used. Another method forces water through a semipermeable membrane. The pore spaces in the membrane are large enough to allow water molecules to pass through, but they do not allow salt molecules to pass through. Encourage students to find out more about desalination and to make a poster that shows how one method works.

Answer to Reading Check
Desalination plants are most likely to be built in drier parts of the world, and where governments can afford to buy expensive equipment. Most desalination plants are in the Middle East where the fuel needed to run the plants is relatively inexpensive.

Quick Lab

MATERIALS

FOR EACH GROUP
- graduated cylinder
- hot plate
- pot, large
- spoon, wooden
- table salt, 35 g
- water, warm, 1,000 mL

Safety Caution: Remind students to review all safety cautions and icons before beginning this lab activity.

Answers

5. Answers may vary.

6. Sample answer: In this activity, salt was separated from salt water by evaporation, just as in a desalination plant. In a desalination plant, the evaporating water would have been collected.

Section 4 • Resources from the Ocean

Close

Reteaching — BASIC
Using Ocean Resources Ask students to describe three ways in which we can conserve ocean resources. **Verbal**

Quiz — GENERAL
1. Why are oil and natural gas considered nonrenewable resources? (because they can be used up faster than they can be replenished naturally)
2. Why does tidal energy generate a large amount of energy? (The motion of tides moves an enormous mass of water, which generates a large amount of energy.)

Alternative Assessment — GENERAL
Depending on Ocean Resources Ask students to consider the ways in which their lives depend on ocean resources. Have students write a short essay about how their lives would be different if ocean resources did not exist. **Verbal/Interpersonal**

Figure 6 Manganese nodules are difficult to mine because they are located on the deep ocean floor.

Sea-Floor Minerals

Mining companies are interested in mineral nodules that are lying on the ocean floor. These nodules are made mostly of manganese, which can be used to make certain types of steel. They also contain iron, copper, nickel, and cobalt. Other nodules are made of phosphates, which are used to make fertilizer.

Nodules are formed from dissolved substances in sea water that stick to solid objects, such as pebbles. As more substances stick to the coated pebble, a nodule begins to grow. Manganese nodules can be as small as a marble or as large as a soccer ball. The photograph in **Figure 6** shows a number of nodules on the ocean floor. Scientists estimate that 15% of the ocean floor is covered with these nodules. However, these nodules are located in the deeper parts of the ocean, and mining them is costly and difficult.

Tidal Energy

The ocean generates a great deal of energy simply because of its constant movement. The gravitational pulls of the sun and moon cause the ocean to rise and fall as tides. *Tidal energy* is energy generated from the movement of tides. Tidal energy can be an excellent source of power. If the water during high tide can be rushed through a narrow coastal passageway, the water's force can be powerful enough to generate electrical energy. **Figure 7** shows how this process works. Tidal energy is a clean, inexpensive, and renewable resource. A *renewable resource* can be replenished, in time, after being used. Unfortunately, tidal energy is practical only in a few parts of the world. These areas must have a coastline with shallow, narrow channels. For example, the coastline at Cook Inlet, in Alaska, is ideal for generating electrical energy.

Figure 7 Using Tides to Generate Electrical Energy

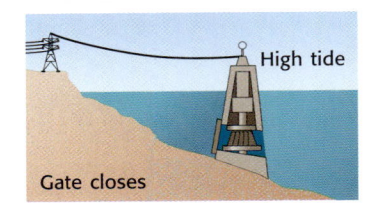

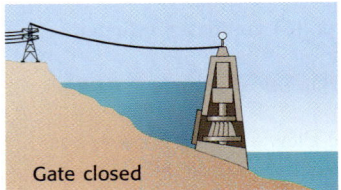

❶ As the tide rises, water enters a bay behind a dam. The gate then closes at high tide.

❷ The gate remains closed as the tide lowers.

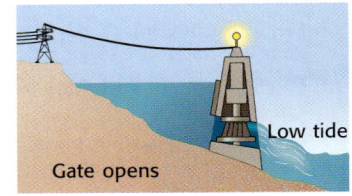

❸ At low tide, the gate opens, and the water rushes through the dam and moves the turbines, which, in turn, generate electrical energy.

CONNECTION to Geology — GENERAL

Nodule Formation Explain that the mineral nodules shown in **Figure 6** form much as pearls or rock candy forms—a solid precipitates out of a chemical solution and adheres to a particle. This particle could be a small pebble or even a piece of shell. In a process called *accretion*, the nodules grow larger as more solids precipitate out. Students could model accretion by making rock candy with a supersaturated sugar solution and a piece of string. **Verbal**

398 Chapter 13 • Exploring the Oceans

Wave Energy

Have you ever stood on the beach and watched as waves crashed on the shore? This constant motion is an energy resource. Wave energy, like tidal energy, is a clean, renewable resource. Recently, computer programs have been developed to analyze wave energy. Researchers have found certain areas of the world where wave energy can generate enough electrical energy to make building power plants worthwhile. Wave energy in the North Sea is strong enough to produce power for parts of Scotland and England.

Reading Check Why would wave energy be a good alternative energy resource?

SECTION Review

Summary

- Humans depend on the ocean for living and nonliving resources.
- Fish and other marine life are being raised in ocean farms to help feed growing human populations.
- Nonliving ocean resources include oil and natural gas, water, minerals, and tidal and wave energy.

Using Key Terms

1. In your own words, write a definition for the term *desalination*.

Understanding Key Ideas

2. Mineral nodules on the ocean floor are
   a. renewable resources.
   b. easily mined.
   c. used during the process of desalination.
   d. nonliving resources.

3. List two ways of harvesting the ocean's living resources.

4. Name four nonliving resources in the ocean.

5. Explain how fish farms help meet the demand for fish.

6. Explain how engineers decide where to drill for oil and natural gas in the ocean.

Math Skills

7. A kelp plant is 5 cm tall. If it grows an average of 29 cm per day, how tall will the kelp plant be after 2 weeks?

Critical Thinking

8. **Analyzing Processes** Explain why tidal energy and wave energy are considered renewable resources.

9. **Predicting Consequences** Define the term *overfishing* in your own words. What would happen to the population of fish in the ocean if laws did not regulate overfishing? What would happen to the ocean ecosystem?

10. **Analyzing Ideas** What is one benefit and one consequence of building a desalination plant? Would a desalination plant be beneficial to your local area? Explain why or why not.

SciLinks
For a variety of links related to this chapter, go to www.scilinks.org
Topic: Ocean Resources
SciLinks code: HSM1065

Answers to Section Review

1. Sample answer: Desalination is a process for removing salt from ocean water.
2. d
3. Sample answer: Two ways of harvesting the ocean's living resources include fishing the ocean for marine organisms and farming the ocean by raising marine organisms in fish or seaweed farms.
4. oil, fresh water, sea-floor minerals, and energy
5. Sample answer: Fish farms help meet the demand for fish by breeding fish in farms instead of fishing them directly from the ocean.
6. Sample answer: Engineers decide where to drill for oil and natural gas in the ocean by using seismic equipment. This equipment sends powerful pulses of sound from a ship to the ocean floor and then back to the ship. These pulses are then analyzed by a computer. The pulses indicate how rock layers are arranged below the ocean floor and therefore where there are good locations for drilling.
7. (14 days × 29 cm) = 406 cm, (406 cm + 5 cm) = 411 cm
8. Sample answer: Tidal energy and wave energy are renewable resources because tides and waves are naturally occurring movements of water. Therefore, as long as tides and waves continue to occur on Earth, energy can be harnessed from the movement of tides and waves.
9. Sample answer: Overfishing occurs when we take more fish from the ocean than can be naturally replaced; If laws did not regulate overfishing, the fish population would continue to decrease; If overfishing continued, ocean food chains, food webs, and ocean ecosystems would eventually collapse.
10. Answers may vary. Sample answer: One benefit of building a desalination plant is that it allows an area that is very dry to have a supply of fresh water. One consequence is that it is very expensive.

Answer to Reading Check

Wave energy would be a good alternative energy resource because it is a clean and renewable resource.

CHAPTER RESOURCES

Chapter Resource File
- Section Quiz GENERAL
- Section Review GENERAL
- Vocabulary and Section Summary GENERAL
- Reinforcement Worksheet BASIC
- Critical Thinking ADVANCED
- Datasheet for Quick Lab

Section 4 • Resources from the Ocean **399**

SECTION 5

Focus

Overview
In this section, students learn about the sources and effects of ocean pollution. They also learn about some of the strategies that are used to minimize ocean pollution.

🔔 Bellringer
Ask students to write a few sentences about how ocean pollution could affect their lives. Then, have students list the ways they contribute to ocean pollution in their daily lives. Ask groups to brainstorm about the ways they could reduce ocean pollution.

Motivate

ACTIVITY — GENERAL

Cleaning Up an Oil Spill
Give each pair of students a pan with water. Pour about 5 mL of vegetable oil into each pan. Have students think of ways to remove the oil from the pan *without pouring out the water.* Students can experiment with methods such as absorbing the oil with a paper towel or scooping it out with a spoon. Discuss the results of students' efforts. Tell them that this problem is similar to dealing with a petroleum spill in the ocean. **LS Visual**

SECTION 5

READING WARM-UP

Objectives
- Explain the difference between point-source pollution and nonpoint-source pollution.
- Identify three different types of point-source ocean pollution.
- Describe what is being done to control ocean pollution.

Terms to Learn
nonpoint-source pollution
point-source pollution

READING STRATEGY

Reading Organizer As you read this section, create an outline of the section. Use the headings from the section in your outline.

Ocean Pollution

It's a hot summer day at the beach. You can hardly wait to swim in the ocean. You run to the surf only to be met by piles of trash washed up on the shore. Where did all that trash come from?

Humans have thrown their trash in the ocean for hundreds, if not thousands, of years. This trash has harmed the plants and animals that live in the oceans, as well as the people and animals that depend on them. Fortunately, we are becoming more aware of ocean pollution, and we are learning from our mistakes.

Nonpoint-Source Pollution

There are many sources of ocean pollution. Some of these sources are easily identified, but others are more difficult to pinpoint. **Nonpoint-source pollution** is pollution that comes from many sources rather than just from a single site. Some common sources of nonpoint-source pollutants are shown in **Figure 1**. Most ocean pollution is nonpoint-source pollution. Human activities on land can pollute streams and rivers, which then flow into the ocean and bring the pollutants they carry with them. Because nonpoint-source pollutants can enter bodies of water in many different ways, they are very hard to regulate and control. Nonpoint-source pollution can be reduced by using less lawn chemicals and disposing of used motor oil properly.

Figure 1 Examples of Nonpoint-Source Pollution

Oil and gasoline that have leaked from cars onto streets can wash into storm sewers and then drain into waterways.

Thousands of watercraft, such as boats and jet skis can leak gasoline and oil directly into bodies of water.

Pesticides, herbicides, and fertilizer from residential lawns, golf courses, and farmland can wash into waterways.

CHAPTER RESOURCES

Chapter Resource File
- Lesson Plan
- Directed Reading A BASIC
- Directed Reading B SPECIAL NEEDS

Technology
- Transparencies
  - Bellringer

SCIENCE HUMOR

Huntsville, Alabama, hairdresser Phil McCrory has patented a way to use discarded human hair to clean up oil spills. He tested the idea in his son's wading pool by using a pair of pantyhose filled with hair. The idea works so well that McCrory has attracted the attention of NASA!

400 Chapter 13 • Exploring the Oceans

Figure 2 This barge is headed out to the open ocean, where it will dump the trash it carries.

Point-Source Pollution

Water pollution caused by a leaking oil tanker, a factory, or a wastewater treatment plant is one type of point-source pollution. **Point-source pollution** is pollution that comes from a specific site. Even when the source of pollution is known, cleanup of the pollution is difficult.

nonpoint-source pollution pollution that comes from many sources rather than from a single, specific site

point-source pollution pollution that comes from a specific site

Trash Dumping

People dump trash in many places, including the ocean. In the 1980s, scientists became alarmed by the kinds of trash that were washing up on beaches. Bandages, vials of blood, and syringes (needles) were found among the waste. Some of the blood in the vials even contained the AIDS virus. The Environmental Protection Agency (EPA) began an investigation and discovered that hospitals in the United States produce an average of 3 million tons of medical waste each year. Because of stricter laws, much of this medical waste is now buried in sanitary landfills. However, dumping trash in the deeper part of the ocean is still a common practice in many countries. The barge in **Figure 2** will dump the trash it carries into the open ocean.

Figure 3 Marine animals can be strangled by plastic trash or can choke if they mistake the plastic for food.

Effects of Trash Dumping

Trash thrown into the ocean can affect the organisms that live in the ocean and those organisms that depend on the ocean for food. Trash such as plastic can be particularly harmful to ocean organisms. This is because most plastic materials do not break down for thousands of years. Marine animals can mistake plastic materials for food and choke or become strangled. The sea gull in **Figure 3** is tangled up in a piece of plastic trash.

Reading Check What is one effect of trash dumping? (See the Appendix for answers to Reading Checks.)

Answer to Reading Check
One effect of trash dumping is that plastic materials may harm and kill marine animals because these animals may mistake the trash for food.

Is That a Fact!
The world's first major oil spill occurred on March 18, 1967. The tanker *Torrey Canyon* ran aground off the coast near Cornwall, England. The ship spilled about 870,000 barrels of oil, more than 3 times the oil spilled by the *Exxon Valdez*.

Teach

ACTIVITY — BASIC
Nonpoint-Source Pollution
Draw students' attention to the photographs of nonpoint-source pollutants in **Figure 1**. Ask them to think about their daily lives and to list ways they might be contributing to nonpoint-source pollution. Ask them to help you list ways that they could reduce their contribution to nonpoint-source pollution. **LS Verbal** — English Language Learners

Homework — GENERAL
Investigate Your Area Inform students that many companies are creating products that are marketed to be less harmful to the environment. These claims have varying degrees of truth. Have groups choose a product and investigate the environmental statements that are used to market it. For example, a group could visit the detergent aisle of a grocery store to compare products. Have students prepare a list of products claiming to be environmentally friendly and their primary ingredients. Encourage students to use Internet or library resources to determine whether the ingredients listed could be harmful to the environment. Another group could compare the percentage of postconsumer waste in recycled paper products. Have groups present their findings to the class. **LS Intrapersonal**

Section 5 • Ocean Pollution

Teach, continued

CONNECTION ACTIVITY
Math ——————— GENERAL

Global Ocean Pollution Challenge students to use the Internet or library resources to find out which nations contribute the most to ocean pollution. Have students construct pie graphs to show their results and write a short essay explaining the trends they observe. **LS Visual**

Discussion ——————— GENERAL

Nuclear Waste and the Ocean Remind students that the ocean tends to separate into layers because temperature and salinity differences create layers with different densities.

Point out that the world community is confronted with the dilemma of nuclear waste disposal. One proposed solution is to bury weighted barrels of waste in the sediment of the ocean floor. Encourage students to consider the implications of such a strategy. As nuclear waste decays, it releases heat energy. What would happen if water contaminated by nuclear waste heated the deep zone? **LS Verbal**

Figure 4 Sludge is the solid part of waste matter and often carries bacteria. Sludge makes beaches dirty and kills marine animals.

Sludge Dumping

By 1990, the United States alone had discharged 38 trillion liters of treated sludge into the waters along its coasts. Sludge is part of raw sewage. *Raw sewage* is all the liquid and solid wastes that are flushed down toilets and poured down drains. After collecting in sewer drains, raw sewage is sent through a treatment plant, where it undergoes a cleaning process that removes solid waste. The solid waste is called *sludge*, as shown in **Figure 4**. In many areas, people dump sludge into the ocean several kilometers offshore, intending for it to settle and stay on the ocean floor. Unfortunately, currents can stir the sludge up and move it closer to shore. This sludge can pollute beaches and kill marine life. Many countries have banned sludge dumping, but it continues to occur in many areas of the world.

Oil Spills

Because oil is in such high demand across the world, large tankers must transport billions of barrels of it across the oceans. If not handled properly, these transports can turn disastrous and cause oil spills. **Figure 5** shows some of the major oil spills that have occurred off the coast of North America.

Figure 5 This map shows some of the major oil spills that have occurred off the coast of North America in the last 30 years.

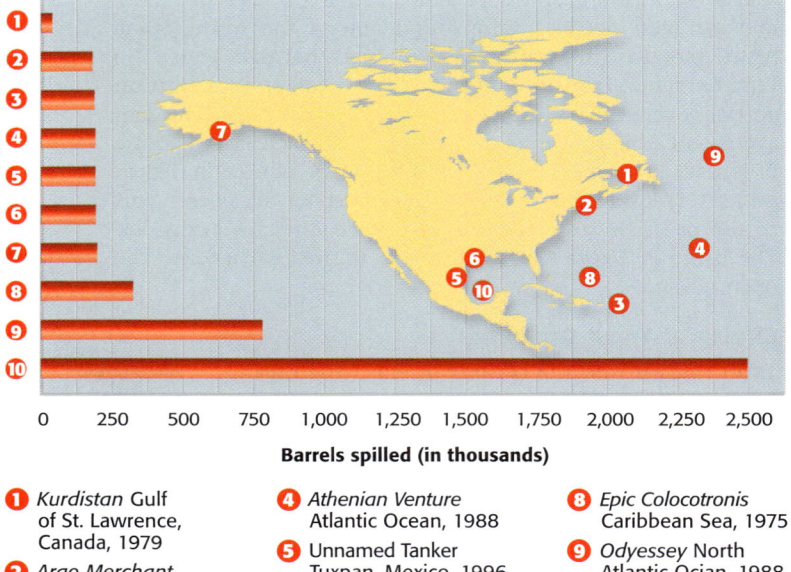

Barrels spilled (in thousands)

❶ **Kurdistan** Gulf of St. Lawrence, Canada, 1979
❷ **Argo Merchant** Nantucket, MA, 1976
❸ **Storage Tank** Benuelan, Puerto Rico, 1978
❹ **Athenian Venture** Atlantic Ocean, 1988
❺ **Unnamed Tanker** Tuxpan, Mexico, 1996
❻ **Burmah Agate** Galveston Bay, TX, 1979
❼ **Exxon Valdez** Prince William Sound, AK, 1989
❽ **Epic Colocotronis** Caribbean Sea, 1975
❾ **Odyessey** North Atlantic Ocian, 1988
❿ **Exploratory Well** Bay of Campeche, 1979

Homework ——————— GENERAL

Environmental Impacts Help students find information to investigate the environmental impact of one of the following: developing areas where salt marshes once were, draining mangrove swamps for development, polluting of ocean waters with agricultural runoff, damming rivers and streams that flow into the ocean, using dynamite to catch fish (common in the Pacific and particularly harmful to coral reefs), or destroying coral reefs to obtain construction materials. Encourage students to focus on the effects of these human behaviors on other organisms, and challenge them to suggest alternatives **LS Verbal**

Effects of Oil Spills

One of the oil spills shown on the map in **Figure 5** occurred in Prince William Sound, Alaska, in 1989. The supertanker *Exxon Valdez* struck a reef and spilled more than 260,000 barrels of crude oil along the shorelines of Alaska. The amount of spilled oil is roughly equivalent to 125 olympic-sized swimming pools.

Although some animals were saved, such as the bird in **Figure 6,** many plants and animals died as a result of the spill. Alaskans who made their living from fishing lost their businesses. The Exxon Oil Company spent $2.1 billion to try to clean up the mess. But Alaska's wildlife and economy will continue to suffer for decades.

While oil spills can harm plants, animals, and people, they are responsible for only about 5% of oil pollution in the oceans. Most of the oil that pollutes the oceans is caused by nonpoint-source pollution on land from cities and towns.

Figure 6 Many oil-covered animals were rescued and cleaned after the *Exxon Valdez* spill.

Preventing Oil Spills

Today, many oil companies are using new technology to safeguard against oil spills. Tankers are now being built with two hulls instead of one. The inner hull prevents oil from spilling into the ocean if the outer hull of the ship is damaged. **Figure 7** shows the design of a double-hulled tanker.

Reading Check How can two hulls on an oil tanker help prevent an oil spill?

Figure 7 If the outer hull of a double-hulled tanker is punctured, the oil will still be contained within the inner hull.

CONNECTION to Environmental Science — GENERAL

Double-Hulled Tankers The Oil Pollution Act of 1990 was a direct response to the *Exxon Valdez* oil spill. The controversial bill had been debated for 14 years; it passed swiftly in the aftermath of the disaster. Under the law, all oil tankers operating in United States waters must be double-hulled by 2015. Compliance has been slow, however; many oil companies have been reluctant to replace the aging boats in their fleets with hundred-million-dollar double-hulled ships. As of 1999, of the 3,294 oil tankers operating worldwide, only 876 were double hulled.

ACTIVITY — GENERAL

Ocean Pollution Awareness Divide the class into small groups. Provide each group with poster board and markers. Direct each group to work together to create a poster designed to educate the public about the need for clean water. Ask groups to focus on ways people can minimize the pollution of our oceans. Consider displaying the posters around the school to educate students and teachers. As an extension, have students draft a letter to a United States Congress member that outlines each group's ideas. **English Language Learners**
LS Intrapersonal

Group ACTIVITY — GENERAL

Exxon Valdez Have student groups report on the current status of the communities and ecosystems of Prince William Sound in the wake of the *Exxon Valdez* oil spill. Ask students to consider questions such as the following: "How has the ecosystem recovered? Do fishing communities feel that they have been compensated?"
LS Intrapersonal

Answer to Reading Check

An oil tanker that has two hulls can prevent an oil spill, because if the outer hull is damaged, the inner hull will prevent oil from spilling into the ocean.

Section 5 • Ocean Pollution

Close

Reteaching — BASIC
Effects of Ocean Pollution
Have students list one type of pollution they saw on the way to school today. Ask them if this type of pollution affects the ocean. **LS Verbal**

Quiz — GENERAL
1. Why do oil spills pose a long-term risk? (Sample answer: Organisms living in the ocean are part of a complex web of relationships. If one group of organisms is affected, many other groups could be threatened. In addition, the oil tends to concentrate in the tissues of living organisms and can persist long after the spill has been cleaned up.)
2. Why is sludge dumping a threat to marine and human life? (Sludge dumping can cause diseases, kill marine organisms, and pollute beaches.)

Alternative Assessment — GENERAL
Concept Mapping Have students recall the sources of ocean pollution discussed in this section, the effects of pollution on oceans and wildlife, and the actions being taken by nations and individuals to limit and reduce pollution. Ask them to prepare a concept map that organizes and compares this information. Challenge students to propose additional suggestions for pollution prevention. **LS Visual/Verbal**

SCHOOL to HOME
Coastal Cleanup
WRITING SKILL You can be a part of a coastal cleanup. Every September, people from all over the world set aside one day to help clean up trash and debris from beaches. You can join this international effort! With a parent, write a letter to the Ocean Conservancy to see what you can do to help clean up coastal areas.
ACTIVITY

Figure 8 Making an effort to pick up trash on a beach can help make the beach safer for plants, animals, and people.

Group ACTIVITY — GENERAL
Coastal Campaign Divide the class into small groups. Ask groups to imagine that they are the campaign managers for a candidate trying to become the city manager of a coastal town. Tell them that they must convince voters that the groups' candidates are concerned for the environmental health of the ocean and have a realistic plan to preserve the beaches and marine life. Have them write a campaign speech outlining the sources of pollution and the solutions they propose. Ask one student from each group to present the speech to the class. Allow the class to vote for the most convincing candidate. **LS Verbal**

Saving Our Ocean Resources
Although humans have done much to harm the ocean's resources, we have also begun to do more to save them. From international treaties to volunteer cleanups, efforts to conserve the ocean's resources are making an impact around the world.

Nations Take Notice
When ocean pollution reached an all-time high, many countries recognized the need to work together to solve the problem. In 1989, a treaty was passed by 64 countries that prohibits the dumping of certain metals, plastics, oil, and radioactive wastes into the ocean. Even though many other international agreements and laws restricting ocean pollution have been made, waste dumping and oil spills still occur. Therefore, waste continues to wash ashore, as shown in **Figure 8**. Enforcing pollution-preventing laws at all times is often difficult.

Citizens Taking Charge
Citizens of many countries have demanded that their governments do more to solve the growing problem of ocean pollution. Because of public outcry, the United States now spends more than $130 million each year to protect the oceans and beaches. United States citizens have also begun to take the matter into their own hands. In the early 1980s, citizens began organizing beach cleanups. One of the largest cleanups is the semiannual Adopt-a-Beach program, shown in **Figure 8,** which originated with the Texas Coastal Cleanup campaign. Millions of tons of trash have been gathered from the beaches, and people are being educated about the hazards of ocean dumping.

---

404 Chapter 13 • Exploring the Oceans

Action in the United States

The United States, like many other countries, has taken additional measures to control local pollution. For example, in 1972, Congress passed the Clean Water Act, which put the Environmental Protection Agency in charge of issuing permits for any dumping of trash into the ocean. Later that year, a stricter law—the U.S. Marine Protection, Research, and Sanctuaries Act—was passed. This act prohibits the dumping of any material that would affect human health or welfare, the marine environment or ecosystems, or businesses that depend on the ocean.

Reading Check What is the U.S. Marine Protection, Research, and Sanctuaries Act?

SECTION Review

Summary

- The two main types of ocean pollution are non-point-source pollution and point-source pollution.
- Types of nonpoint-source pollution include oil and gasoline from cars, trucks, and watercraft, as well as the use of pesticides, herbicides, and fertilizers.
- Types of point-source ocean pollution include trash dumping, sludge dumping, and oil spills.
- Efforts to save ocean resources include international treaties and volunteer cleanups.

Using Key Terms

1. Use the following terms in the same sentence: *point-source pollution* and *nonpoint-source pollution*.

Understanding Key Ideas

2. Which of the following is an example of nonpoint-source pollution?
   a. a leak from an oil tanker
   b. a jet ski
   c. an unlined landfill
   d. water discharged by industries

3. List three types of ocean pollution. How can each of these types be prevented or minimized?

4. Which part of raw sewage is a type of ocean pollution?

Math Skills

5. Only 3% of Earth's water is drinkable. What portion of Earth's water is not drinkable?

6. A ship spilled 750,000 barrels of oil when it accidentally struck a reef. The oil company was able to recover 65% of the oil spilled. How many barrels of oil were not recovered?

Critical Thinking

7. **Identifying Relationships** List and describe three measures that governments have taken to control ocean pollution.

8. **Evaluating Data** What were two effects of the *Exxon Valdez* oil spill? Describe two ways in which oil spills can be prevented.

9. **Applying Concepts** List two examples of nonpoint-source pollution that occur in your area. Explain why they are nonpoint-source pollution.

10. **Predicting Consequences** How can trash dumping and sludge dumping affect food chains in the ocean?

SciLinks / **NSTA**
Developed and maintained by the National Science Teachers Association

For a variety of links related to this chapter, go to www.scilinks.org
Topic: Ocean Pollution
SciLinks code: HSM1063

Answers to Section Review

1. Sample answer: Trash dumping is an example of point-source pollution, and the use of pesticides is an example of nonpoint-source pollution.

2. d

3. Sample answer: trash dumping, sludge dumping, and oil spills; Trash can be dumped in sanitary landfills, sludge can be used to make compost, and tankers with double hulls can be used to transport oil. All of these types of pollution can be prevented or minimized through legislation, education, and actions by citizens.

4. sludge

5. 97%

6. (750,000 barrels × 0.65) = 487,500 barrels, (750,000 barrels − 487,500 barrels) = 262,500 barrels were not recovered

7. Three measures taken by governments to control ocean pollution include passing laws that prohibit the dumping of radioactive wastes into the ocean, that prohibit the dumping of trash into the ocean, and that prohibits dumping of any material that would affect any organism that depends on the ocean.

8. Two effects of the *Exxon Valdez* oil spill were that many plants and animals died and that many Alaskans, who made their living from fishing, lost their businesses. Two ways in which oil spills can be prevented are to reduce shipping oil by sea and to build oil tankers with two hulls.

9. Sample answer: using watercraft such as boats and jet skis and using pesticides on lawns; The use of watercraft can be minimized, and humans can use cleaner fuels to operate their watercraft. The use of pesticides on lawns can be reduced, and humans can use more environmentally friendly ways of pest control.

10. Trash dumping and sludge dumping can affect a food chain because both trash and toxic materials from sludge can make organisms sick or die. Therefore, if organisms eat other organisms that are sick, they will likely become sick, too. Also, if organisms die, animals that depend on those animals for food may starve.

Answer to Reading Check

The U.S. Marine Protection, Research, and Sanctuaries Act prohibits the dumping of any material that would affect human health or welfare, the marine environment or ecosystems, or businesses that depend on the ocean.

CHAPTER RESOURCES

Chapter Resource File
- Section Quiz GENERAL
- Section Review GENERAL
- Vocabulary and Section Summary GENERAL

Section 5 • Ocean Pollution

Model-Making Lab

Probing the Depths

Teacher's Notes

Time Required
One 45-minute class period

Lab Ratings

EASY —————— HARD

Teacher Prep 🧪
Student Set-Up 🧪🧪
Concept Level 🧪🧪
Clean Up 🧪

MATERIALS
The materials listed on the student page are enough for each student or for a group of 2 to 4 students.

Safety Caution
Remind students to review all safety cautions and icons before beginning this lab activity.

Preparation Notes
You may wish to ask students to provide their own shoe boxes. Punch the holes along the center of the lids for the students prior to class. You may use corrugated cardboard instead of modeling clay. If you do, shape the cardboard into steps and ridges to model changes in depth. With this type of model, students should use the eraser end of an unsharpened pencil to measure depths.

Model-Making Lab

OBJECTIVES

Model a method of mapping the ocean floor.

Construct a map of an ocean-floor model.

MATERIALS

- clay, modeling (1 lb)
- pencil, unsharpened (8 of equal length)
- ruler, metric
- scissors
- shoe box with lid

SAFETY

Probing the Depths

In the 1870s, the crew of the ship the HMS *Challenger* used a wire and a weight to discover and map some of the deepest places in the world's oceans. The crew members tied a wire to a weight and dropped the weight overboard. When the weight reached the bottom of the ocean, they hauled the weight back up to the surface and measured the length of the wet wire. In this way, they were eventually able to map the ocean floor. In this activity, you will model this method of mapping by making a map of an ocean-floor model.

Procedure

1. Use the clay to make a model ocean floor in the shoe box. The model ocean floor should have some mountains and valleys.

2. Cut eight holes in a line along the center of the lid. The holes should be just big enough for a pencil to slide through. Place the lid on the box.

3. Exchange boxes with another student or group of students. Do not look into the box.

4. Copy the table shown on the facing page onto a piece of paper. Also, copy the graph shown on the facing page.

5. Measure the length of the probe (pencil) in centimeters. Record the length in your data table.

6. Gently insert the probe into the first hole position in the box until the probe touches the model ocean floor. Do not push the probe down. Pushing the probe down could affect your reading.

7. Make sure that the probe is straight up and down, and measure the length of probe showing above the lid. Record your data in the data table.

8. Use the formula below to calculate the depth in centimeters.

$$\text{length of probe} - \text{length of probe showing (cm)} = \text{depth (cm)}$$

Tracy Jahn
Berkshire Junior-Senior High School
Canaan, New York

CHAPTER RESOURCES

Chapter Resource File
- Datasheet for Chapter Lab
- Lab Notes and Answers

Technology
- Classroom Videos
  - Lab Video

LabBook
- Investigating an Oil Spill

Chapter 13 • Exploring the Oceans

Ocean Depth Table

Hole position	Length of probe	Length of probe showing (cm)	Depth (cm)	Depth (m) scale of 1cm = 200m
1				
2				
3				
4				
5				
6				
7				
8				

DO NOT WRITE IN BOOK

9. To better represent real ocean depths, use the scale 1 cm = 200 m to convert the depth in centimeters to depth in meters. Add the data to your table.

10. Plot the depth in meters for hole position 1 on your graph.

11. Repeat steps 6–10 for the other hole positions.

12. After plotting the data for the eight hole positions, connect the plotted points with a smooth curve.

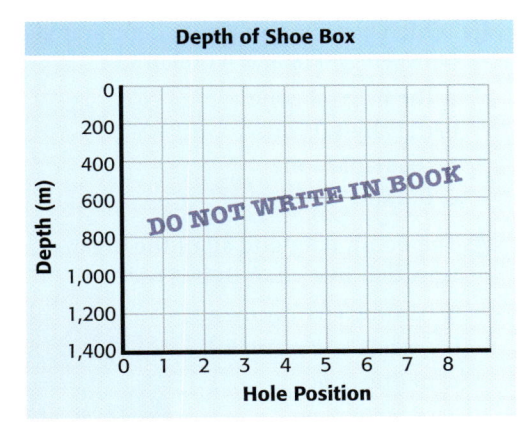

13. Put a pencil in each of the holes in the shoe box. Compare the rise and fall of the eight pencils with the shape of your graph.

Analyze the Results

1. **Describing Events** How deep was the deepest point of your ocean-floor model? How deep was the shallowest point of your ocean-floor model?

2. **Explaining Events** Did your graph resemble the ocean-floor model, as shown by the pencils in step 13? If not, why not?

Draw Conclusions

3. **Applying Conclusions** Why is measuring the real ocean floor difficult? Explain your answer.

Depth of Shoe Box graph (Depth (m) 0–1,400 vs Hole Position 0–8)

DO NOT WRITE IN BOOK

Analyze the Results
1. Answers may vary.
2. Answers may vary. Discrepancies between the model and the graph may be attributed to plotting the points incorrectly, failing to keep the probe vertical, or pushing the probe into the clay.

Draw Conclusions
3. Scientists may encounter many difficulties in measuring the ocean floor. Students may note that the extreme depths of the ocean make it difficult to map the ocean floor accurately. Students may also note that scientists are often unable to "open the box" to check their measurements; that is, the ocean is too deep in places and too vast to explore fully.

CHAPTER RESOURCES

Workbooks

- **Whiz-Bang Demonstrations**
  - Foul Play GENERAL
- **Inquiry Labs**
  - Surf's Up! GENERAL
- **EcoLabs & Field Activities**
  - Rescue Near the Center of the Earth GENERAL
- **Long-Term Projects & Research Ideas**
  - Your Very Own Underwater Theme Park ADVANCED
- **Calculator-Based Labs**
  - Ocean Floor Mapping ADVANCED

Chapter Review

Assignment Guide

SECTION	QUESTIONS
1	3, 7–10, 14, 19
2	1, 4, 15–16, 21
3	5, 12–13, 17, 23–26
4	2, 11, 18, 20
5	6, 22

ANSWERS

Using Key Terms
1. continental shelf
2. Desalination
3. Salinity
4. abyssal plain
5. benthic environment
6. nonpoint-source pollution

Understanding Key Ideas
7. b
8. c
9. d
10. c
11. c
12. a
13. a

Chapter Review

USING KEY TERMS

Complete each of the following sentences by choosing the correct term from the word bank.

- continental shelf
- abyssal plain
- salinity
- nonpoint-source pollution
- continental slope
- desalination
- benthic environment
- point-source pollution

1. The region of the ocean floor that is closest to the shoreline is the ___.

2. ___ is the process of removing salt from sea water.

3. ___ is a measure of the amount of dissolved salts in a liquid.

4. The ___ is the broad, flat part of the deep-ocean basin.

5. The region near the bottom of a pond, lake, or ocean is called the ___.

6. Pollution that comes from many sources rather than a single specific source is called ___.

UNDERSTANDING KEY IDEAS

Multiple Choice

7. The largest ocean is the
   a. Indian Ocean.
   b. Pacific Ocean.
   c. Atlantic Ocean.
   d. Arctic Ocean.

8. One of the most abundant elements in the ocean is
   a. potassium.
   b. calcium.
   c. chlorine.
   d. magnesium.

9. Which of the following affects the ocean's salinity?
   a. fresh water added by rivers
   b. currents
   c. evaporation
   d. All of the above

10. Most precipitation falls
    a. on land.
    b. into lakes and rivers.
    c. into the ocean.
    d. in rain forests.

11. Which of the following is a nonrenewable resource in the ocean?
    a. fish
    b. tidal energy
    c. oil
    d. All of the above

12. Which benthic zone has a depth range between 200 m and 4,000 m?
    a. the bathyal zone
    b. the abyssal zone
    c. the hadal zone
    d. the sublittoral zone

13. The ocean floor and all of the organisms that live on or in it is the
    a. benthic environment.
    b. pelagic environment.
    c. neritic zone.
    d. oceanic zone.

14. Coastal water in hotter, drier climates typically has higher salinity because less fresh water runs into the ocean in drier areas and because heat increases the evaporation rate.

15. Answers may vary. Sample answer: Technology used to study the ocean floor includes sonar and piloted vessels. *Sonar* stands for "sound navigation and ranging" and is used to determine the ocean's depth by sending sound pulses from a ship down into the ocean. Piloted vessels such as *Alvin* and *Deep Flight* are research vessels used to explore the ocean floor.

16. Sample answer: The two major regions of the ocean floor include the continental margin and the deep-ocean basin. The continental shelf, the continental slope, and the continental rise are sections of the continental margin based on depth and changes in slope.

Short Answer

14 Why does coastal water in areas that have hotter, drier climates typically have a higher salinity than coastal water in cooler, more humid areas does?

15 Describe two technologies used for studying the ocean floor.

16 Identify the two major regions of the ocean floor, and describe how the continental shelf, the continental slope, and the continental rise are related.

17 In your own words, write a definition for each of the following terms: *plankton*, *nekton*, and *benthos*. Give two examples of each.

18 List two living resources and two nonliving resources that are harvested from the ocean.

CRITICAL THINKING

19 Concept Mapping Use the following terms to create a concept map: *water cycle*, *evaporation*, *condensation*, *precipitation*, *atmosphere*, and *oceans*.

20 Making Inferences What benefit other than being able to obtain fresh water from salt water comes from desalination?

21 Making Comparisons Explain the difference between a bathymetric profile and a seismic reading.

22 Analyzing Ideas In your own words, define *nonpoint-source pollution* and *point-source pollution*. Give an example of each. What is being done to control ocean pollution?

INTERPRETING GRAPHICS

The graph below shows the ecological zones of the ocean. Use the graph below to answer the questions that follow.

Ecological Zones of the Ocean

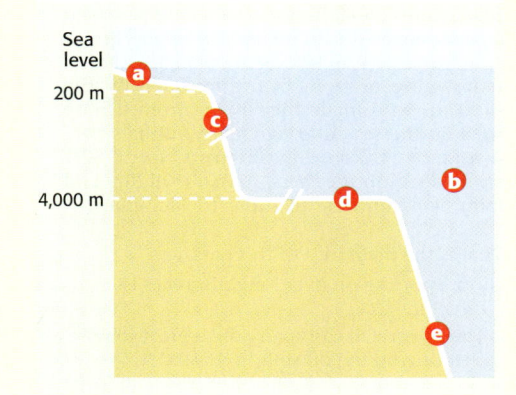

[Diagram showing depth zones from sea level to below 4,000 m with labeled points a, b, c, d, e]

23 At which point would you most likely find an anglerfish?

24 At which point would you most likely find tube worms?

25 Which ecological zone is shown at point c? Which depth zone is shown at point c?

26 Name an organism that you might find at point e.

---

17. Sample answer: Plankton are microscopic organisms that float freely in freshwater and marine environments. Examples of plankton are phytoplankton and zooplankton. Nekton are organisms that swim actively in open water and include sea lions and whales. Benthos are the organisms that live at the bottom of the ocean, such as crabs and starfish.

18. Sample answer: Two living resources that are harvested from the ocean include fish and seaweed. Two nonliving resources that are harvested from the ocean include oil and sea-floor minerals.

CHAPTER RESOURCES

Chapter Resource File
- Chapter Review GENERAL
- Chapter Test A GENERAL
- Chapter Test B ADVANCED
- Chapter Test C SPECIAL NEEDS
- Vocabulary Activity GENERAL

Workbooks
- Study Guide
  - Assessment resources are also available in Spanish.

Critical Thinking

19. An answer to this exercise can be found at the end of this book.

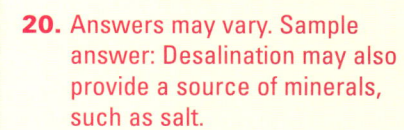

20. Answers may vary. Sample answer: Desalination may also provide a source of minerals, such as salt.

21. Answers may vary. Sample answer: A bathymetric profile shows what the contour of the ocean floor looks like. A seismic reading can show what the contour of the ocean floor and what rocks beneath the ocean floor look like.

22. Sample answer: Nonpoint-source pollution is pollution that comes from many sources rather than from a single, specific site. Point-source pollution is pollution that comes from a specific site; An example of nonpoint-source pollution includes oil and gasoline that have leaked from cars onto streets. An example of point-source pollution is trash dumping from barges; Controlling ocean pollution is difficult, but many countries have taken legal action to protect oceans. For example, the United States passed the U.S. Marine Protection, Research, and Sanctuaries Act, which prohibits harmful dumping in the ocean. Beach cleanups run by citizens, such as the Adopt-a-Beach program, have been very successful in cleaning up polluted beaches.

Interpreting Graphics

23. b

24. d

25. bathyal zone; continental slope from 200 m to 4,000 m below sea level

26. Sample answer: clams

Chapter 13 • Chapter Review

Standardized Test Preparation

Teacher's Note

To provide practice under more realistic testing conditions, give students 20 minutes to answer all of the questions in this Standardized Test Preparation.

MISCONCEPTION ALERT

Answers to the standardized test preparation can help you identify student misconceptions and misunderstandings.

READING

Passage 1
1. C
2. I

TEST DOCTOR

Question 1: Answer A is incorrect because this problem is not mentioned in the passage. Answer B is incorrect because the passage implies that the cleanup was less than successful. Answer D is incorrect because Alaska's economy will suffer because of damage caused by the spill, not because of lost oil.

Passage 2
1. D
2. G

Standardized Test Preparation

READING

Read each of the passages below. Then, answer the questions that follow each passage.

Passage 1 Because oil is in such high demand across the world, large tankers must transport billions of barrels of it across the oceans. If not handled properly, these transports can quickly turn disastrous. In 1989, the supertanker *Exxon Valdez* struck a reef and spilled more than 260,000 barrels of crude oil. The effect of this accident on wildlife was catastrophic. Within the first few weeks of the *Exxon Valdez* oil spill, more than half a million birds, including 109 endangered bald eagles, were covered with oil and drowned. Almost half the sea otters in the area also died, either from drowning or from being poisoned by the oil. Alaskans who made their living from fishing lost their businesses. Although many animals were saved and the Exxon Oil Company spent $2.1 billion to clean up the mess, Alaska's wildlife and economy will continue to suffer for decades.

1. What is the main idea of this passage?
   A Transporting oil over long distances is difficult.
   B The Exxon Oil Company did a great job of cleaning up the oil spill in Alaska.
   C Oil spills such as the *Exxon Valdez* spill can create huge problems.
   D Alaska's economy will suffer because so much oil was lost.

2. In the passage, which of the following problems was said to be a result of the *Exxon Valdez* oil spill?
   F The beach became too slippery to walk on.
   G Many people in Alaska had no oil for their cars.
   H Exxon had to build a new tanker.
   I Many Alaskan fishers lost their businesses.

Passage 2 Whales, dolphins, and porpoises are mammals that belong to the order Cetacea (suh TAY shuh). Cetaceans live throughout the global ocean. They have fishlike bodies and forelimbs called *flippers*. Cetaceans lack hind limbs but have broad, flat tails that help them swim through the water. Cetaceans breathe through blowholes located on the top of the head. They are completely hairless except for a few bristles on their snout. A thick layer of blubber below the skin helps insulate cetaceans against cold temperatures. Cetaceans are divided into two groups: toothed whales and baleen whales. Toothed whales include sperm whales, beluga whales, narwhals, killer whales, dolphins, and porpoises. Baleen whales, such as blue whales, lack teeth. They filter food from the water by using a meshlike net of baleen that hangs from the roof of their mouth.

1. How are organisms that make up the order Cetacea divided?
   A They are divided into cetaceans that have hair and cetaceans that do not have hair.
   B They are divided into cetaceans that have flippers and cetaceans that do not have flippers.
   C They are divided into cetaceans that have blowholes and cetaceans that do not have blowholes.
   D They are divided into cetaceans that have teeth and cetaceans that do not have teeth.

2. Which of the following statements lists characteristics of all cetaceans?
   F Cetaceans have fur and claws and live in rivers.
   G Cetaceans have flippers and bristles on the snout and live in oceans.
   H Cetaceans have blowholes and flippers and live in lakes.
   I Cetaceans have fur, bristles on the snout, and flippers.

TEST DOCTOR

Question 1: Answer A is incorrect because according to the passage, cetaceans are completely hairless. Answer B is incorrect because according to the passage, all cetaceans have flippers. Answer C is incorrect because according to the passage, all cetaceans breathe through blowholes located on the top of the head. Answer D is correct because the fact is mentioned in the passage that cetaceans are divided into two groups: toothed whales and baleen whales. The passage states that baleen whales lack teeth.

INTERPRETING GRAPHICS

Use the image of the ocean floor below to answer the questions that follow.

1. At which point are two tectonic plates separating?
   A 1
   B 2
   C 3
   D 4

2. Which point shows an ocean trench?
   F 1
   G 2
   H 3
   I 4

3. Which feature might eventually become a volcanic island?
   A 1
   B 2
   C 3
   D 4

4. Which features are part of the deep-ocean basin?
   F 2, 3, and 4
   G 1, 2, and 3
   H 1, 3, and 4
   I 1, 2, and 4

5. Which feature is part of the continental margin?
   A 1
   B 2
   C 3
   D 4

MATH

Read each question below, and choose the best answer.

1. Imagine that you are in the kelp-farming business and your kelp grows 33 cm per day. You begin harvesting when your plants are 50 cm tall. During the first 7 days of harvest, you cut 10 cm off the top of your kelp plants each day. How tall will your kelp plants be after the seventh day of harvesting?
   A 80 cm
   B 130 cm
   C 210 cm
   D 211 cm

2. A sample of ocean water contains 36 g of dissolved solids per 1,000 g of water. So, how many grams of dissolved solids will be in 4 kg of ocean water?
   F 36,000 g
   G 360 g
   H 250 g
   I 144 g

3. If the average depth of the Pacific Ocean is 4,250 m and the average depth of the Atlantic Ocean is 4,000 m, what is the average depth of the two oceans?
   A 4,250 m
   B 4,150 m
   C 4,125 m
   D 4,000 m

4. *Alvin*, a minisub, starts at −300 m, then rises 20 m, then drops 150 m, and finally reaches the ocean floor by dropping another 218 m. At what depth is *Alvin* when it reaches the ocean floor?
   F −648 m
   G −88 m
   H 88 m
   I 648 m

5. The speed of sound in water is 1,500 m/s. How far will sound travel in water in 1 min?
   A 25 m
   B 1,500 m
   C 9,000 m
   D 90,000 m

INTERPRETING GRAPHICS

1. D
2. G
3. C
4. F
5. A

TEST DOCTOR

Question 1: Answer D is correct because number 4 is pointing to a mid-ocean ridge. Mid-ocean ridges are mountain chains that form where tectonic plates pull apart and create a series of cracks in the ocean floor. Number 4 is the only part of the image that shows a separation in the ocean floor.

Question 5: Answer A is correct because number 1 is pointing to the continental slope of the ocean floor. The continental slope is one division of the continental margin. Answers B through D are all features of the deep-ocean basin.

MATH

1. D
2. I
3. C
4. F
5. D

TEST DOCTOR

Question 2: Students may arrive at the incorrect answer F by multiplying 36 by 1,000 instead of multiplying 36 by 4. Students may arrive at the incorrect answer H by dividing 1,000 by 4 instead of multiplying 36 by 4. Answer I is correct because if there is 36 g of dissolved solids in each kilogram of ocean water, then 4 kg of ocean water should contain 144 g of dissolved solids (36 × 4 = 144).

CHAPTER RESOURCES

Chapter Resource File
- Standardized Test Preparation GENERAL

State Resources
For specific resources for your state, visit go.hrw.com and type in the keyword HSMSTR.

Chapter 13 • Standardized Test Preparation

Science in Action

Scientific Discoveries
Background
According to accounts, the giant squid can put up quite a fight against a whale. Lighthouse keepers in South Africa claim to have seen a giant squid attack and subsequently drown a baby southern whale after an intense battle that lasted for more than an hour.

Researchers do know that squids have excellent eyesight and some of the largest eyes in the animal kingdom. They also have one of the most highly developed brains of any invertebrate.

Science, Technology, and Society
Background
Artificial reefs are usually constructed of materials that are environmentally friendly. The most ideal materials are concrete and steel. It is important to use materials that do not break down and cause pollution. Old ships and planes make ideal artificial reefs because of the materials from which they are constructed. Before the plane or ship is sunk to make a reef, all fuel and oil are removed so that they do not leak out and pollute the area. Other structures that are good for artificial reefs are retired oil rigs and pieces of old concrete foundations.

Science in Action

Scientific Discoveries
In Search of the Giant Squid
You might think that giant squids exist only in science fiction novels. You aren't alone, because many people have never seen a giant squid or do not know that giant squids exist. Scientists have not been able to study giant squids in the ocean. They have been able to study only dead or dying squids that have washed ashore or that have been trapped in fishing nets. As the largest of all invertebrates, giant squids range from 8 to 25 m long and have a mass of as much as 2,000 kg. Giant squids are very similar to smaller squids. But a giant squid's body parts are much larger. For example, a giant squid's eye may be as large as a volleyball! Because of the size of giant squids, you may think that they don't have any enemies in the ocean, but they do. They are usually eaten by sperm whales that can weigh 20 tons!

Math ACTIVITY
A giant squid that washed ashore has a mass of 900 kg. A deep-sea squid that washed ashore has a mass that is 93% smaller than the mass of the giant squid. What is the mass in kilograms of the deep-sea squid?

Science, Technology, and Society
Creating Artificial Reefs
If you found a sunken ship, would you look for hidden treasure? Treasure is not the only thing that sunken ships are known for. Hundreds of years ago, people found that the fishing is often good over a sunken ship. The fishing is good because many marine organisms, such as seaweed, corals, and oysters, live only where they can attach to a hard surface in clear water. They attract other organisms to the sunken ship and eventually form a reef community. Thus, in recent years, many human communities have created artificial reefs by sinking objects such as warships, barges, concrete, airplanes, and school buses in the ocean. Like natural reefs, artificial reefs provide a home for organisms and protect organisms from predators.

Social Studies ACTIVITY
WRITING SKILL Research how some artificial reefs are created off the coast of some states in the United States. Write a report that describes some of the objects used to create artificial reefs. In your report also include what countries other than the United States create artificial reefs and what are the benefits and disadvantages of creating artificial reefs.

Answer to Math Activity
(900 kg × 0.93) = 837 kg,
(900 kg − 837 kg) = 63 kg

Answer to Social Studies Activity
Suggest that students research library resources or the Internet to answer the questions. Artificial reefs benefit organisms by giving them a place to live, feed, and breed. Artificial reefs may be beneficial in any aquatic ecosystem because they can replace lost habitat that is needed by the organisms living there. Artificial reefs are not entirely problem free. Artificial reefs must be built safely so that they do not interfere with the movement of ships, they do not entangle divers, and do not pollute the water or fall apart.

People in Science

Jacques Cousteau

Ocean Explorer Jacques Cousteau was born in France in 1910. Cousteau performed his first underwater diving mission at age 10 and became very fascinated with the possibilities of seeing and breathing underwater. As a result, in 1943, Cousteau and Emile Gagnan developed the first aqualung, a self-contained breathing system for underwater exploration. Using the aqualung and other underwater equipment that he developed, Cousteau began making underwater films. In 1950, Cousteau transformed the *Calypso*, a retired minesweeper boat, into an oceanographic vessel and laboratory. For the next 40 years, Cousteau sailed with the *Calypso* around the world to explore and film the world's oceans. Cousteau produced more than 115 films, many of which have won awards.

Jacques Cousteau opened the eyes of countless people to the sea. During his long life, Cousteau explored Earth's oceans and documented the amazing variety of life that they contain. He was an environmentalist, inventor, and teacher who inspired millions with his joy and wonder of the ocean. Cousteau was an outspoken defender of the environment. He campaigned vigorously to protect the oceans and environment. Cousteau died in 1997 at age 87. Before his death, he dedicated the *Calypso II*, a new research vessel, to the children of the world.

Language Arts ACTIVITY

WRITING SKILL Ocean pollution and overfishing are subjects of intense debate. Think about these issues, and discuss them with your classmates. Take notes on what you discuss with your classmates. Then, write an essay in which you try to convince readers of your point of view.

Cousteau sailed his ship, the Calypso, around the world exploring and filming the world's oceans.

go.hrw.com
To learn more about these Science in Action topics, visit **go.hrw.com** and type in the keyword **HZ5OCEF**.

Current Science
Check out *Current Science®* articles related to this chapter by visiting **go.hrw.com**. Just type in the keyword **HZ5CS13**.

People in Science
Teaching Strategy—GENERAL

In addition to being an inventor and an explorer, Jacques Cousteau was a commentator on the 20th century and its environmental problems. He was criticized as being a populist because he brought information to the public in common language instead of in academic terms. Help the class find information about his condemnation of French nuclear testing or his controversial opinions on overpopulation and animal testing.

You may want to show your students some of Cousteau's inspiring documentaries. Some of his full-length features include *The Silent World*, *World Without Sun*, and *Voyage to the Edge of the World*. Tapes of his many television series (*The Undersea World of Jacques Cousteau*, *Cousteau Odyssey*, and *Cousteau Amazon*) may also be available at a public library.

Answer to Language Arts Activity
Encourage students to research ocean pollution and overfishing by using library resources or the Internet before they discuss the issues with each other.

Chapter 13 • Science in Action

14 The Movement of Ocean Water
Chapter Planning Guide

Compression guide: To shorten instruction because of time limitations, omit the Chapter Lab.

OBJECTIVES	LABS, DEMONSTRATIONS, AND ACTIVITIES	TECHNOLOGY RESOURCES
PACING • 90 min pp. 414–421 **Chapter Opener**	SE **Start-up Activity**, p. 415 ◆ GENERAL	OSP **Parent Letter** ■ GENERAL CD **Student Edition on CD-ROM** CD **Guided Reading Audio CD** ■ TR **Chapter Starter Transparency*** VID **Brain Food Video Quiz**
Section 1 Currents • Describe surface currents. • List the three factors that control surface currents. • Describe deep currents. • Identify the three factors that form deep currents.	SE **School-to-Home Activity** Coriolis Effect in Your Sink?, p. 418 GENERAL TE **Activity** The Coriolis Effect ◆ BASIC TE **Connection Activity** Life Science, p. 417 ADVANCED TE **Activity** Differences in Currents, p. 419 BASIC TE **Connection Activity** Math, p. 421 GENERAL SE **Skills Practice Lab** Up From the Depths, p. 436 ◆ GENERAL CRF **Datasheet for Chapter Lab*** LB **Whiz-Bang Demonstrations** Spin Cycle* ◆ ADVANCED	CRF **Lesson Plans*** TR **Bellringer Transparency*** TR **Earth's Surface Currents*** TR **How Deep Currents Form*** CRF **SciLinks Activity*** GENERAL CD **Interactive Explorations CD-ROM** Latitude Attitude GENERAL VID **Lab Videos for Earth Science**
PACING • 45 min pp. 422–425 **Section 2 Currents and Climate** • Explain how currents affect climate. • Describe the effects of El Niño. • Explain how scientists study and predict the pattern of El Niño.	TE **Activity** Graphing Temperatures, p. 423 GENERAL SE **Connection to Environmental Science** El Niño and Coral Reefs, p. 424 GENERAL TE **Connection Activity** Real World, p. 424 GENERAL	SE **Internet Activity**, p. 425 GENERAL CRF **Lesson Plans*** TR **Bellringer Transparency*** TR **Upwelling***
PACING • 45 min pp. 426–431 **Section 3 Waves** • Identify the parts of a wave. • Explain how the parts of a wave relate to wave movement. • Describe how ocean waves form and move. • Classify types of waves.	TE **Demonstration** Making Waves, p. 426 ◆ GENERAL TE **Group Activity** Modeling Waves, p. 427 BASIC TE **Connection Activity** Math, p. 427 GENERAL SE **Quick Lab** Doing the Wave, p. 428 GENERAL CRF **Datasheet for Quick Lab*** TE **Connection Activity** Real World, p. 428 GENERAL TE **Connection Activity** Math, p. 429 GENERAL	CRF **Lesson Plans*** TR **Bellringer Transparency*** TR **How Deep-Water Waves Become Shallow-Water Waves*** TR **LINK TO PHYSICAL SCIENCE** Measuring Wavelength; Measuring Frequency*
PACING • 45 min pp. 432–435 **Section 4 Tides** • Explain tides and their relationship with the Earth, sun, and moon. • Describe four different types of tides. • Analyze the relationship between tides and coastal land.	TE **Activity** Intertidal Zones, p. 432 ◆ GENERAL SE **Model-Making Lab** Turning the Tides, p. 744 GENERAL CRF **Datasheet for LabBook*** LB **Long-Term Projects & Research Ideas** An Ocean Commotion* ADVANCED SE **Science in Action** Math, Social Studies, and Language Arts Activities, pp. 442–443 GENERAL	CRF **Lesson Plans*** TR **Bellringer Transparency*** TR **Tidal Variations: Spring Tides; Neap Tides***

PACING • 90 min

CHAPTER REVIEW, ASSESSMENT, AND STANDARDIZED TEST PREPARATION

CRF **Vocabulary Activity*** GENERAL
SE **Chapter Review**, pp. 438–439 GENERAL
CRF **Chapter Review*** ■ GENERAL
CRF **Chapter Tests A*** ■ GENERAL, **B*** ADVANCED, **C*** SPECIAL NEEDS
SE **Standardized Test Preparation**, pp. 440–441 GENERAL
CRF **Standardized Test Preparation*** GENERAL
CRF **Performance-Based Assessment*** GENERAL
OSP **Test Generator** GENERAL
CRF **Test Item Listing*** GENERAL

Online and Technology Resources

Visit **go.hrw.com** for a variety of free resources related to this textbook. Enter the keyword **HZ5H2O**.

Holt Online Learning
Students can access interactive problem-solving help and active visual concept development with the *Holt Science and Technology* Online Edition available at **www.hrw.com**.

Guided Reading Audio CD Also in Spanish
A direct reading of each chapter for auditory learners, reluctant readers, and Spanish-speaking students.

Science Tutor CD-ROM
Excellent for remediation and test practice.

Chapter 14 • The Movement of Ocean Water

KEY			
SE Student Edition	**CRF** Chapter Resource File	**SS** Science Skills Worksheets	* Also on One-Stop Planner
TE Teacher Edition	**OSP** One-Stop Planner	**MS** Math Skills for Science Worksheets	♦ Requires advance prep
	LB Lab Bank	**CD** CD or CD-ROM	■ Also available in Spanish
	TR Transparencies	**VID** Classroom Video/DVD	

SKILLS DEVELOPMENT RESOURCES	SECTION REVIEW AND ASSESSMENT	STANDARDS CORRELATIONS
SE Pre-Reading Activity, p. 414 GENERAL **OSP** Science Puzzlers, Twisters & Teasers GENERAL		National Science Education Standards UCP 1, 2; SAI 1
CRF Directed Reading A* ■ BASIC, B* SPECIAL NEEDS **CRF** Vocabulary and Section Summary* ■ GENERAL **SE** Reading Strategy Reading Organizer, p. 416 GENERAL **TE** Reading Strategy Prediction Guide, p. 417 GENERAL **TE** Inclusion Strategies, p. 417 ♦ **MS** Math Skills for Science What Is Scientific Notation?* GENERAL **SE** Connection to Physics Convection Currents, p. 419 GENERAL **TE** Connection to Language Arts Endurance: Shackleton's Incredible Voyage, p. 419 ADVANCED	**SE** Reading Checks, pp. 416, 418, 419, 420 GENERAL **TE** Homework, p. 419 GENERAL **TE** Reteaching, p. 420 BASIC **TE** Quiz, p. 420 GENERAL **TE** Alternative Assessment, p. 420 GENERAL **SE** Section Review,* p. 421 ■ GENERAL **CRF** Section Quiz* ■ GENERAL	UCP 2; SAI 1; HNS 1, 3; ES 1j; *Chapter Lab:* UCP 2; SAI 1
CRF Directed Reading A* ■ BASIC, B* SPECIAL NEEDS **CRF** Vocabulary and Section Summary* ■ GENERAL **SE** Reading Strategy Paired Summarizing, p. 422 GENERAL **TE** Connection to History Benjamin Franklin's Navigation Charts, p. 422 GENERAL	**SE** Reading Checks, pp. 423, 425 GENERAL **TE** Reteaching, p. 424 BASIC **TE** Quiz, p. 424 GENERAL **TE** Alternative Assessment, p. 424 GENERAL **SE** Section Review,* p. 425 ■ GENERAL **CRF** Section Quiz* ■ GENERAL	UCP 2; SAI 1; ES 1j
CRF Directed Reading A* ■ BASIC, B* SPECIAL NEEDS **CRF** Vocabulary and Section Summary* ■ GENERAL **SE** Reading Strategy Prediction Guide, p. 426 GENERAL **TE** Inclusion Strategies, p. 427 ♦ **TE** Reading Strategy Types of Waves, p. 428 BASIC **MS** Math Skills for Science What is a Fraction?* GENERAL **TE** Connection to Environmental Science Beach Nourishment, p. 429 GENERAL **TE** Connection to Meteorology NOAA, p. 430 ADVANCED **CRF** Reinforcement Worksheet Waves to Your Pen Pal* BASIC	**SE** Reading Checks, pp. 426, 428, 431 GENERAL **TE** Homework, p. 429 ADVANCED **TE** Reteaching, p. 430 BASIC **TE** Quiz, p. 430 GENERAL **TE** Alternative Assessment, p. 430 GENERAL **TE** Homework, p. 430 GENERAL **SE** Section Review,* p. 431 ■ GENERAL **CRF** Section Quiz* ■ GENERAL	UCP 1, 2, 3; SAI 1; SPSP 3, 4; ES 1b
CRF Directed Reading A* ■ BASIC, B* SPECIAL NEEDS **CRF** Vocabulary and Section Summary* ■ GENERAL **SE** Reading Strategy Discussion, p. 432 GENERAL **SE** Connection to Language Arts Mont-St-Michel Is Sometimes an Island?, p. 433 GENERAL **CRF** Reinforcement Worksheet But What About the Tides?* BASIC **CRF** Critical Thinking Tides of Trouble* ADVANCED	**SE** Reading Checks, pp. 432, 434 GENERAL **TE** Reteaching, p. 434 BASIC **TE** Quiz, p. 434 GENERAL **TE** Alternative Assessment, p. 434 GENERAL **TE** Homework, p. 434 GENERAL **SE** Section Review,* p. 435 ■ GENERAL **CRF** Section Quiz* ■ GENERAL	SAI 1; ST 1; HNS 1, 3; ES 3c; *LabBook:* UCP 2; SAI 1; ST 1; ES 3c

One-Stop Planner® CD-ROM

This convenient CD-ROM includes:
- Lab Materials QuickList Software
- Holt Calendar Planner
- Customizable Lesson Plans
- Printable Worksheets
- ExamView® Test Generator

CNN Student News

cnnstudentnews.com

Find the latest news, lesson plans, and activities related to important scientific events.

SciLinks NSTA

www.scilinks.org

Maintained by the **National Science Teachers Association**. See Chapter Enrichment pages for a complete list of topics.

Current Science®

Check out *Current Science* articles and activities by visiting the HRW Web site at **go.hrw.com**. Just type in the keyword **HZ5CS14T**.

Classroom Videos

- **Lab Videos** demonstrate the chapter lab.
- **Brain Food Video Quizzes** help students review the chapter material.
- **CNN Videos** bring science into your students' daily life.

Chapter 14 • Chapter Planning Guide   413B

14 Chapter Resources

Visual Resources

CHAPTER STARTER TRANSPARENCY

BELLRINGER TRANSPARENCIES

TEACHING TRANSPARENCIES

TEACHING TRANSPARENCIES

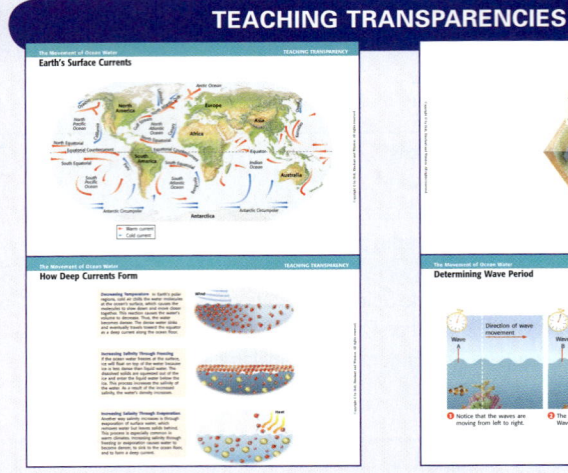

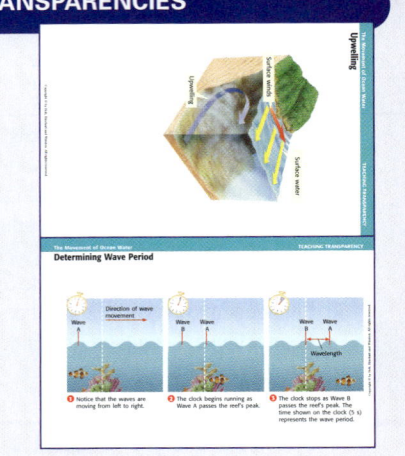

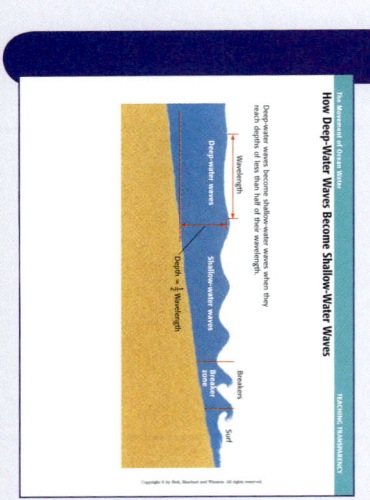

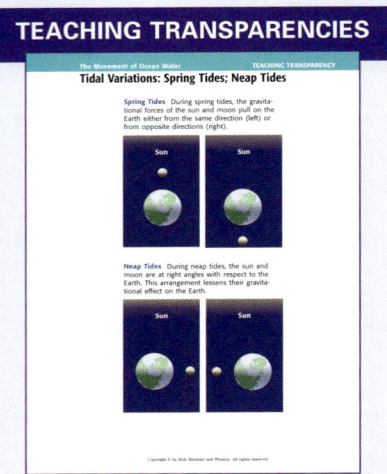

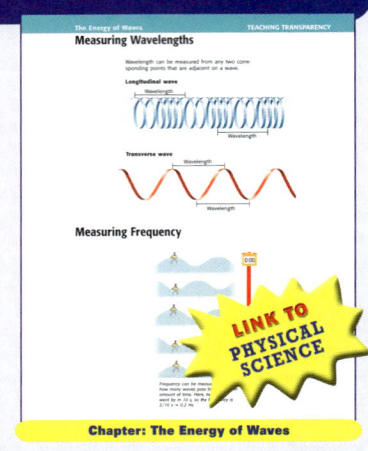

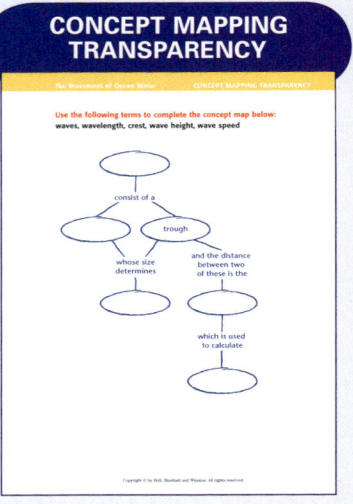

CONCEPT MAPPING TRANSPARENCY

Planning Resources

LESSON PLANS

PARENT LETTER

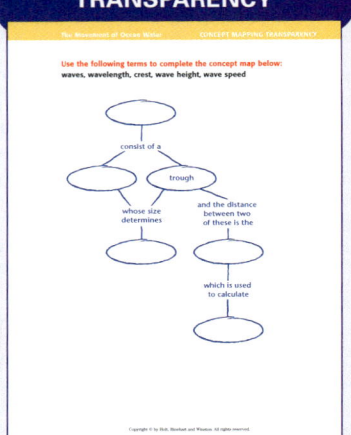

ALSO IN SPANISH

TEST ITEM LISTING

One-Stop Planner® CD-ROM

This CD-ROM includes all of the resources shown here and the following time-saving tools:

- **Lab Materials QuickList Software**
- **Customizable lesson plans**
- **Holt Calendar Planner**
- **The powerful ExamView® Test Generator**

413C Chapter 14 • The Movement of Ocean Water

For a preview of available worksheets covering math and science skills, see pages T26–T33. All of these resources are also on the One-Stop Planner®.

Meeting Individual Needs

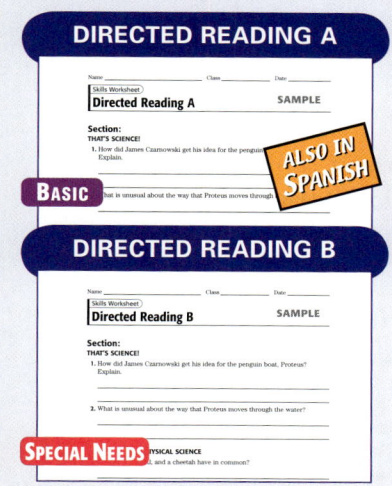

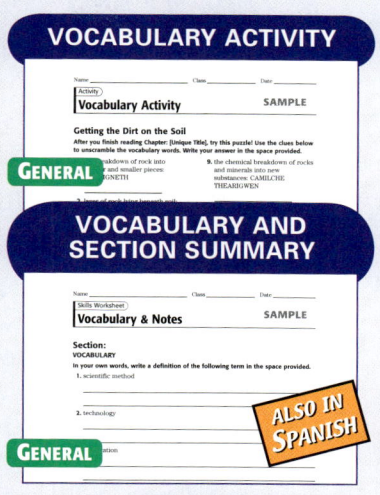

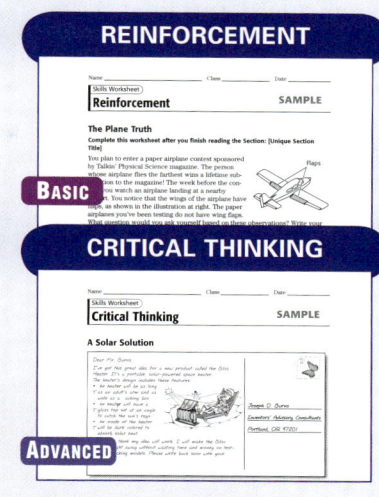

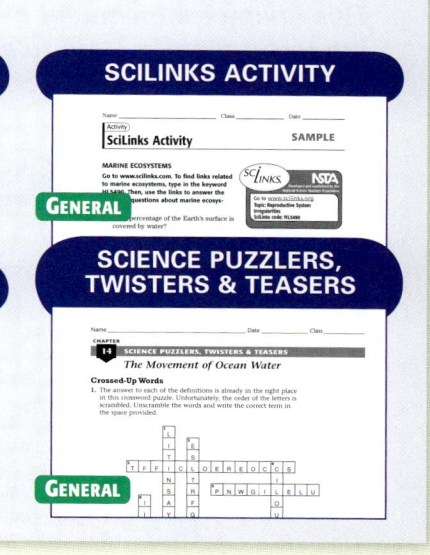

- **DIRECTED READING A** — BASIC — ALSO IN SPANISH
- **DIRECTED READING B** — SPECIAL NEEDS
- **VOCABULARY ACTIVITY** — GENERAL
- **VOCABULARY AND SECTION SUMMARY** — GENERAL — ALSO IN SPANISH
- **REINFORCEMENT** — BASIC
- **CRITICAL THINKING** — ADVANCED
- **SCILINKS ACTIVITY** — GENERAL
- **SCIENCE PUZZLERS, TWISTERS & TEASERS** — GENERAL

Labs and Activities

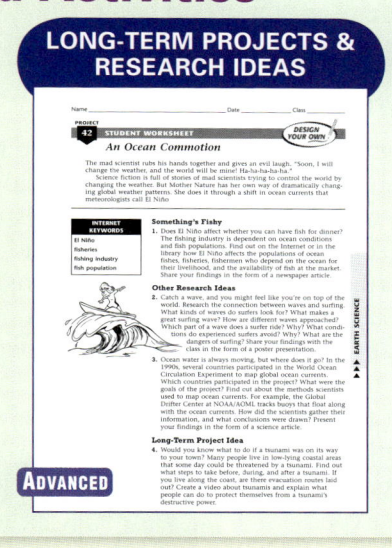

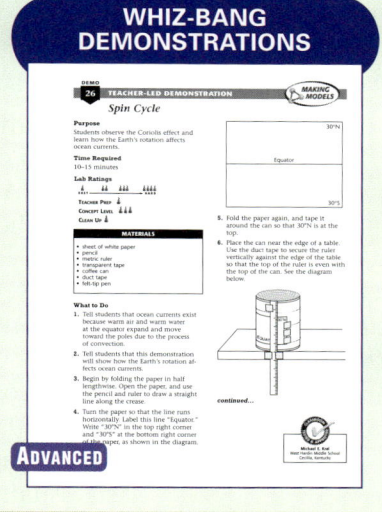

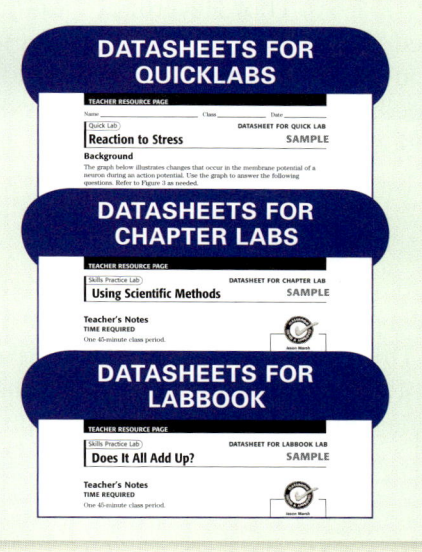

- **LONG-TERM PROJECTS & RESEARCH IDEAS** — ADVANCED
- **WHIZ-BANG DEMONSTRATIONS** — ADVANCED
- **DATASHEETS FOR QUICKLABS**
- **DATASHEETS FOR CHAPTER LABS**
- **DATASHEETS FOR LABBOOK**

Review and Assessments

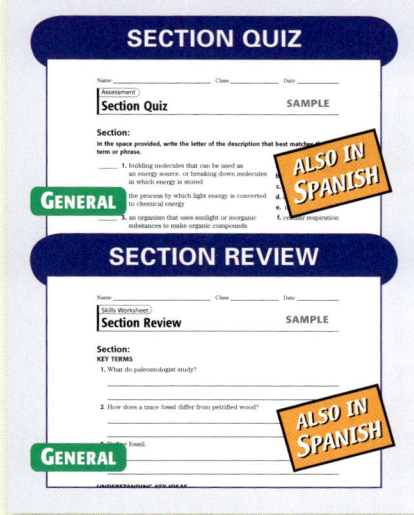

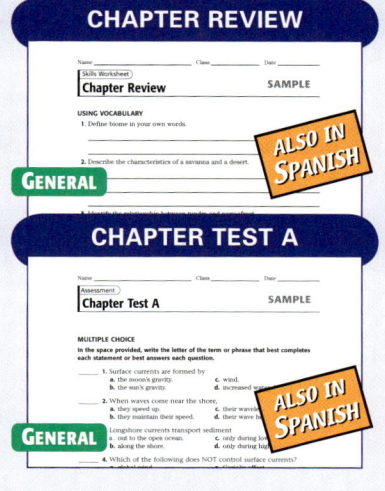

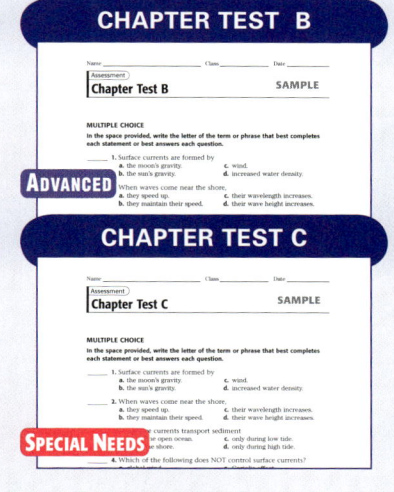

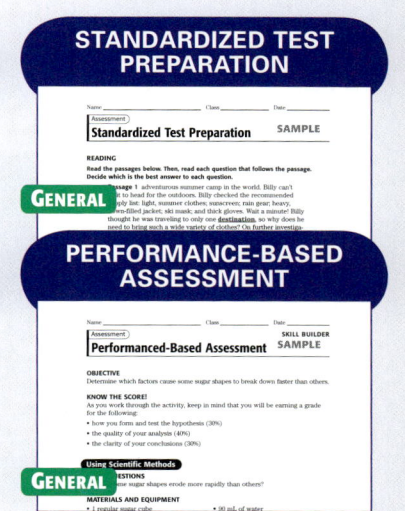

- **SECTION QUIZ** — GENERAL — ALSO IN SPANISH
- **SECTION REVIEW** — GENERAL — ALSO IN SPANISH
- **CHAPTER REVIEW** — GENERAL — ALSO IN SPANISH
- **CHAPTER TEST A** — GENERAL — ALSO IN SPANISH
- **CHAPTER TEST B** — ADVANCED
- **CHAPTER TEST C** — SPECIAL NEEDS
- **STANDARDIZED TEST PREPARATION** — GENERAL
- **PERFORMANCE-BASED ASSESSMENT** — GENERAL

Chapter 14 • Chapter Resources   413D

14 Chapter Enrichment

This Chapter Enrichment provides relevant and interesting information to expand and enhance your presentation of the chapter material.

Section 1

Currents

Solar Radiation

- One of the fundamental energy sources for all ocean currents is solar radiation. Uneven heating of the Earth by the sun creates differences in air pressure. These differences create wind, which drives surface currents. The sun's energy also creates temperature differences in ocean water, driving deep currents.

The *Ra II* Expedition

- On May 17, 1970, Thor Heyerdahl's *Ra II* expedition attempted to demonstrate that mariners from ancient Egypt could have reached the New World. The eight-man expedition successfully reached its destination in Barbados on July 12, 1970.

Is That a Fact!

◆ In addition to the westward surface currents that form along the equator, a strong eastward current forms. This current, called the *equatorial countercurrent,* flows alongside or just beneath the westward equatorial currents at depths of up to 100 m.

Is That a Fact!

◆ The strongest and largest ocean current is the Antarctic Circumpolar Current, which is estimated to flow at a rate of 125 million cubic meters per second.

◆ One of the fastest ocean currents is the Somali Current, in the western Indian Ocean, which flows at a speed of 14.5 km/h.

◆ The Weddell Sea, where the Antarctic Bottom Water is thought to originate, has the clearest water of any sea. Its clarity has been recorded to a depth of nearly 80 m. In other words, water collected from the upper 80 m of the Weddell Sea is as clear as you would find in a glass of distilled water.

Section 2

Currents and Climate

Global Weather Effects of El Niño

- El Niño affects almost every region of the world. El Niño can cause flooding, landslides, erosion, and drought. Areas that receive excessive moisture, such as the coastal regions of Ecuador and northern Peru, can experience infestations of insects. California usually experiences heavy rainfall throughout the winter. The storms associated with the 1997–1998 El Niño cost northern California more than $150 million in landslide damage. Southeast Asia usually experiences drought and forest fires, which affect the agricultural industry.

Section 3

Waves

Swells

- Swells are generated in the open ocean by wind and can travel thousands of kilometers to shore. These long-wavelength waves have periods of 10 to 30 s. When swells reach shallower water, their height increases, so they fall forward. When this occurs, the waves are called *breakers.*

413E Chapter 14 • The Movement of Ocean Water

Tsunamis

● *Tsunami* is a Japanese word that means "harbor wave." Japan has experienced many devastating tsunamis throughout history. The subduction of tectonic plates off the coast of Japan generates the seismic energy necessary to cause tsunamis. Because the Japanese islands are on the edge of deep water and the coastline is rugged with many small harbors, tsunamis have been particularly destructive. The deep water close to the Japanese islands keeps tsunami wave heights short until the waves are very close to shore; when the waves enter shallow water, they suddenly grow taller. The narrow shape of many Japanese harbors causes tsunamis to grow even taller.

Is That a Fact!

◆ Tsunamis have the potential to be the most destructive ocean waves. Their speed averages 500 km/h, and their period ranges from 5 to 60 min. Because the wave height of a tsunami is usually less than 2 m in the open ocean, they often pass unnoticed beneath ships.

◆ The earthquakes that produce destructive tsunamis are generally greater than 6.5 on the Richter scale. Most occur in the Pacific Ocean, where there is a high level of seismic activity near plate boundaries.

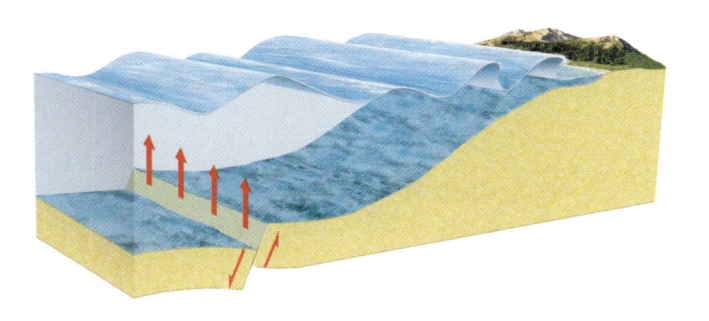

Section 4

Tides

The Bay of Fundy

● The Bay of Fundy experiences the greatest tidal range in the world. The Bay of Fundy is located between New Brunswick and Nova Scotia in Canada and has an average tidal range of 12 m. The primary cause of the extreme tidal range is the Bay of Fundy–Gulf of Maine system. The Atlantic tides push water into the Bay of Fundy–Gulf of Maine basin, which causes the large back-and-forth motion of the tides. A tiny portion of energy from the tides at the Bay of Fundy is being converted into commercial electrical energy.

Is That a Fact!

◆ The sun exerts only about half the tidal force on Earth that the moon does. The reason is that the distance between Earth and the sun is much greater than the distance between Earth and the moon.

◆ The Great Lakes also experience tides. Although the tidal range is smaller than that of the oceans.

SCILINKS

SciLinks is maintained by the National Science Teachers Association to provide you and your students with interesting, up-to-date links that will enrich your classroom presentation of the chapter.

Visit www.scilinks.org and enter the SciLinks code for more information about the topic listed.

Topic: Ocean Currents
SciLinks code: HSM1061

Topic: Ocean Waves
SciLinks code: HSM1066

Topic: El Niño
SciLinks code: HSM0468

Topic: Tides
SciLinks code: HSM1525

Chapter 14 • Chapter Enrichment

Overview

Tell students that this chapter will help them learn about the different factors that affect the movement of ocean water. The chapter describes the different movements of ocean water, including currents, waves, and tides. It also describes how these movements affect land, climate, and organisms.

Assessing Prior Knowledge

Students should be familiar with the following topics:
- ocean-floor topography
- plate tectonics

Identifying Misconceptions

Students tend to confuse the movement of a wave with the movement of the medium (water). Tell students that waves travel through water, the water itself remains basically stationary. You may want to demonstrate this phenomenon using a string tied to a doorknob. Have students snap the string to create a wave that travels the length of the string. Explain that the wave moves from the hand to the doorknob, but the string does not move horizontally.

14
The Movement of Ocean Water

SECTION 1	Currents	416
SECTION 2	Currents and Climate	422
SECTION 3	Waves	426
SECTION 4	Tides	432

Chapter Lab	436
Chapter Review	438
Standardized Test Preparation	440
Science in Action	442

About the PHOTO

No, this isn't a traffic jam or the result of careless navigation. Hurricane Hugo is to blame for this major boat pile up. When Hurricane Hugo hit South Carolina's coast in 1989, the hurricane's strong winds created large ocean waves. These ocean waves carried these boats right onto the shore.

PRE-READING ACTIVITY

Graphic Organizer

Concept Map Before you read the chapter, create the graphic organizer entitled "Concept Map" described in the **Study Skills** section of the Appendix. As you read the chapter, fill in the concept map with details about each type of ocean water movement.

Standards Correlations

National Science Education Standards

The following codes indicate the National Science Education Standards that correlate to this chapter. The full text of the standards is at the front of the book.

Chapter Opener
UCP 1, 2; SAI 1

Section 1 Currents
UCP 2; SAI 1; HNS 1, 3; ES 1j

Section 2 Currents and Climate
UCP 2; SAI 1; ES 1j

Section 3 Waves
UCP 1, 2, 3; SAI 1; SPSP 3, 4; ES 1b

Section 4 Tides
SAI 1; ST 1; HNS 1, 3; ES 3c; *LabBook:* UCP 2; SAI 1; ST 1; ES 3c

Chapter Lab
UCP 2; SAI 1

Chapter Review
SAI 1; ST 2; SPSP 2, 5; HNS 1; ES 1b, 1j, 3c

Science in Action
SAI 1; ST 2; SPSP 5; HNS 1

414 Chapter 14 • The Movement of Ocean Water

START-UP ACTIVITY

When Whirls Collide

Some ocean currents flow in a clockwise direction, while other ocean currents flow in a counterclockwise direction. Sometimes these currents collide. In this activity, you and your lab partner will demonstrate how two currents flowing in opposite directions affect one another.

Procedure

1. Fill a large **tub** with **water** 5 cm deep.
2. Add **10 drops of red food coloring** to the water at one end of the tub.
3. Add **10 drops of blue food coloring** to the water at the other end of the tub.
4. Using a **pencil**, quickly stir the water at one end of the tub in a clockwise direction while your partner stirs the water at the other end in a counterclockwise direction. Stir both ends for 5 s.
5. Draw what you see happening in the tub immediately after you stop stirring. (Both ends should be swirling.)

Analysis

1. How did the blue water and the red water interact?
2. How does this activity relate to how ocean currents interact?

START-UP ACTIVITY

MATERIALS
FOR EACH GROUP
- food coloring, blue
- food coloring, red
- pencils (2)
- tub, large
- water

Teacher's Notes: To avoid spilling water after the tub is filled, put the tub in position before adding water. Although food coloring is nontoxic, students should be careful not to spill the food coloring on their skin or clothes.

A large cake pan can be used for this activity. Water depth should be about 5 cm. Advise students to observe the experiment closely—the desired result happens quickly and lasts only a few seconds. Explore what happens with different sizes and shapes of tubs.

Answers

1. Sample answer: When the blue water left the current in which it was circulating, it crossed the middle of the tub and began circling in the opposite direction. The red water followed the same pattern.
2. Answers may vary. Currents circulate in the Northern and Southern Hemispheres. When a current crosses the equator, it joins other currents and eventually circulates in the direction that they are moving.

Chapter Starter Transparency
Use this transparency to help students begin thinking about the factors that make the Bermuda Triangle dangerous.

CHAPTER RESOURCES

Technology
- **Transparencies**
  - Chapter Starter Transparency   READING SKILLS
- **Student Edition on CD-ROM**
- **Guided Reading Audio CD**
  - English or Spanish
- **Classroom Videos**
  - Brain Food Video Quiz

Workbooks
- **Science Puzzlers, Twisters & Teasers**
  - The Movement of Ocean Water GENERAL

Chapter 14 • The Movement of Ocean Water

SECTION 1

Focus

Overview
This section discusses the causes and characteristics of surface currents and deep currents.

🔔 Bellringer
Pass out excerpts from Thor Heyerdahl's *Kon-Tiki* (1950) or *The Ra Expeditions* (1971) to students. Display a large map of the world that shows the different ocean currents. After showing students the departure and destination points for Heyerdahl's voyages, have them hypothesize which currents Heyerdahl would have used to reach his destinations. Point out that DNA testing later showed that Polynesians did not originate in Peru. Have students write about how a scientific model can be plausible but incorrect.

Motivate

Discussion — GENERAL

Rivers and Surface Currents
Ask students to compare rivers and surface currents. Explain that rivers and surface currents are similar because both are long, moving bodies of water. However, rivers flow because of the pull of gravity, while surface currents are driven by the wind and the rotation of the Earth.
LS Verbal

SECTION 1

READING WARM-UP

Objectives
- Describe surface currents.
- List the three factors that control surface currents.
- Describe deep currents.
- Identify the three factors that form deep currents.

Terms to Learn
ocean current
surface current
Coriolis effect
deep current

READING STRATEGY
Reading Organizer As you read this section, create an outline of the section. Use the headings from the section in your outline.

ocean current a movement of ocean water that follows a regular pattern

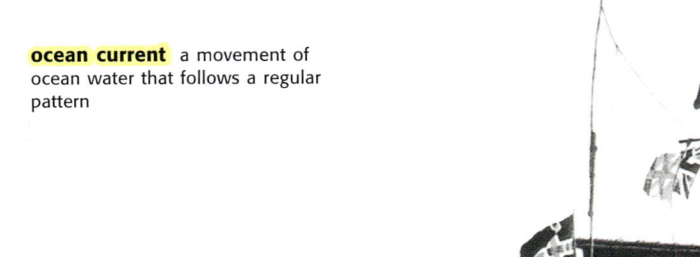

Figure 1 The handcrafted Kon-Tiki was made mainly from materials that would have been available to ancient Peruvians.

CHAPTER RESOURCES

Chapter Resource File
- Lesson Plan
- Directed Reading A BASIC
- Directed Reading B SPECIAL NEEDS

Technology
- Transparencies
  • Bellringer

Currents

Imagine that you are stranded on a desert island. You stuff a distress message into a bottle and throw it into the ocean. Is there any way to predict where your bottle may land?

Actually, there is a way to predict where the bottle will end up. Ocean water contains streamlike movements of water called **ocean currents**. Currents are influenced by a number of factors, including weather, the Earth's rotation, and the position of the continents. With knowledge of ocean currents, people are able to predict where objects in the open ocean will be carried.

One Way to Explore Currents
In the 1940s, a Norwegian explorer named Thor Heyerdahl tried to answer questions about human migration across the ocean. Heyerdahl theorized that the inhabitants of Polynesia originally sailed from Peru on rafts powered only by the wind and ocean currents. In 1947, Heyerdahl and a crew of five people set sail from Peru on a raft, which is shown in **Figure 1**.

On the 97th day of their expedition, Heyerdahl and his crew landed on an island in Polynesia. Currents had carried the raft westward more than 6,000 km across the South Pacific. This landing supported Heyerdahl's theory that ocean currents carried the ancient Peruvians across the Pacific to Polynesia.

✓ **Reading Check** What was Heyerdahl's theory, and how did he prove it? (*See the Appendix for answers to Reading Checks.*)

Answer to Reading Check
Heyerdahl theorized that the inhabitants of Polynesia originally sailed from Peru on rafts powered only by the wind and ocean currents. Heyerdahl proved his theory by sailing from Peru to Polynesia on a raft powered only by wind and ocean currents.

---

416 Chapter 14 • The Movement of Ocean Water

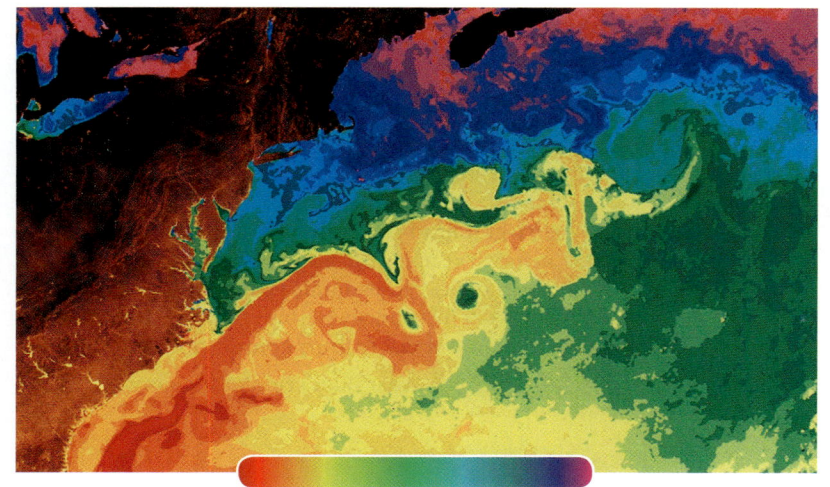

Figure 2 This infrared satellite image shows the Gulf Stream current moving warm water from lower latitudes to higher latitudes.

Warm — Cool

Surface Currents

Horizontal, streamlike movements of water that occur at or near the surface of the ocean are called **surface currents.** Surface currents can reach depths of several hundred meters and lengths of several thousand kilometers and can travel across oceans. The Gulf Stream, shown in **Figure 2,** is one of the longest surface currents—it transports 25 times more water than all the rivers in the world.

Surface currents are controlled by three factors: global winds, the Coriolis effect, and continental deflections. These three factors keep surface currents flowing in distinct patterns around the Earth.

Global Winds

Have you ever blown gently on a cup of hot chocolate? You may have noticed ripples moving across the surface, as in **Figure 3.** These ripples are caused by a tiny surface current created by your breath. In much the same way that you create ripples, winds that blow across the Earth's surface create surface currents in the ocean.

Different winds cause currents to flow in different directions. Near the equator, the winds blow ocean water east to west, but closer to the poles, ocean water is blown west to east. Merchant ships often use these currents to travel more quickly back and forth across the oceans.

surface current a horizontal movement of ocean water that is caused by wind and that occurs at or near the ocean's surface

Figure 3 Winds form surface currents in the ocean, much like blowing on a cup of hot chocolate forms ripples.

Teach

READING STRATEGY — GENERAL

Prediction Guide Before students read the passage describing the three causes of surface currents, ask them what they think might cause currents on the surface of oceans. Students will discover the answers as they continue reading this section.
LS Logical

CONNECTION ACTIVITY
Life Science — ADVANCED

Writing **Current Colonies** Ocean currents help animals and plants colonize new islands. The Galápagos Islands are 1,100 km west of South America. Of the 22 species of reptiles on the islands, 20 are found nowhere else in the world. Scientists speculate that the ancestors of these reptiles found their way from South America to the islands on natural rafts carried by the Humbolt and South Equatorial Currents (the same currents that carried Thor Heyerdahl to Polynesia). Have interested students find out more about the unique plants and animals of the Galápagos Islands. Then, have each student create a poster to showcase his or her research.
LS Visual/Intrapersonal

Is That a Fact!

No metal was used in the construction of the *Kon-Tiki*. The wood raft was made of thick Peruvian balsa logs and featured a bamboo cabin set in the center, a large steering oar at the stern, and five centerboards. Two masts were used to support the rectangular sail. Although it crashed into a reef when it finally reached Polynesia, the *Kon-Tiki* was restored and is currently on display at a museum in Oslo, Norway.

INCLUSION Strategies

- Learning Disabled • Attention Deficit Disorder
- Hearing Impaired

Sprinkle pepper on top of the surface of water in a shallow pan. Then, turn on a blow dryer, and blow the pepper across the surface of the water. Organize students into small groups, and ask them to brainstorm how the demonstration is similar to what happens in oceans. Have students share their ideas with the rest of the class. **LS** Visual/Interpersonal

Section 1 • Currents **417**

Teach, continued

ACTIVITY — BASIC

The Coriolis Effect For students having difficulty understanding the Coriolis effect, use a turntable to demonstrate the concept.

1. Cover the entire surface of the turntable with a circle of paper.
2. Spin the turntable platter, and explain that it represents the rotating Earth.
3. Instruct a student to attempt to draw a straight line from the center of the turntable to the edge. A curved line will be formed. The curved line represents the curved path of surface currents due to Earth's rotation.

LS Visual/Kinesthetic   English Language Learners

Answer to Reading Check
The Earth's rotation causes surface currents to move in curved paths rather than in straight lines.

Answer to School-to-Home Activity
Students should find that the Coriolis effect does not influence the direction in which water drains from a sink.

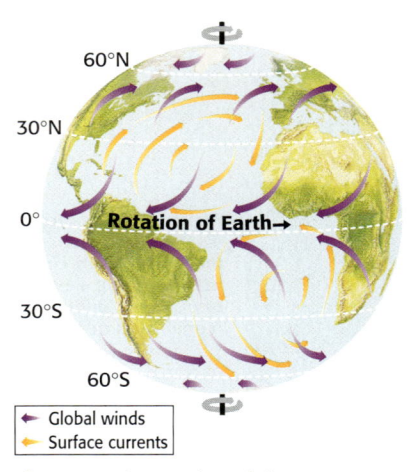

Figure 4 The rotation of the Earth causes surface currents (yellow arrows) and global winds (purple arrows) to curve as they move across the Earth's surface.

→ Global winds
→ Surface currents

Coriolis effect the apparent curving of the path of a moving object from an otherwise straight path due to the Earth's rotation

School to Home

Coriolis Effect in Your Sink?

WRITING SKILL Some people think the Coriolis effect can be seen in sinks. Does water draining from sinks turns clockwise in the Northern Hemisphere and counterclockwise in the Southern Hemisphere? Research this question at the library, on the Internet, and in your sink at home with a parent. Write what you learn in your **science journal**.

ACTIVITY

The Coriolis Effect

The Earth's rotation causes wind and surface currents to move in curved paths rather than in straight lines. The apparent curving of moving objects from a straight path due to the Earth's rotation is called the **Coriolis effect.** To understand the Coriolis effect, imagine trying to roll a ball straight across a turning merry-go-round. Because the merry-go-round is spinning, the path of the ball will curve before it reaches the other side. **Figure 4** shows how the Coriolis effect causes surface currents in the Northern Hemisphere to turn clockwise, and surface currents in the Southern Hemisphere to turn counterclockwise.

✓ **Reading Check** What causes currents to move in curved paths instead of straight lines?

Continental Deflections

If the Earth's surface were covered only with water, surface currents would travel freely across the globe in a very uniform pattern. However, you know that water does not cover the entire surface of the Earth. Continents rise above sea level over roughly one-third of the Earth's surface. When surface currents meet continents, the currents *deflect*, or change direction. Notice in **Figure 5** how the Brazil Current deflects southward as it meets the east coast of South America.

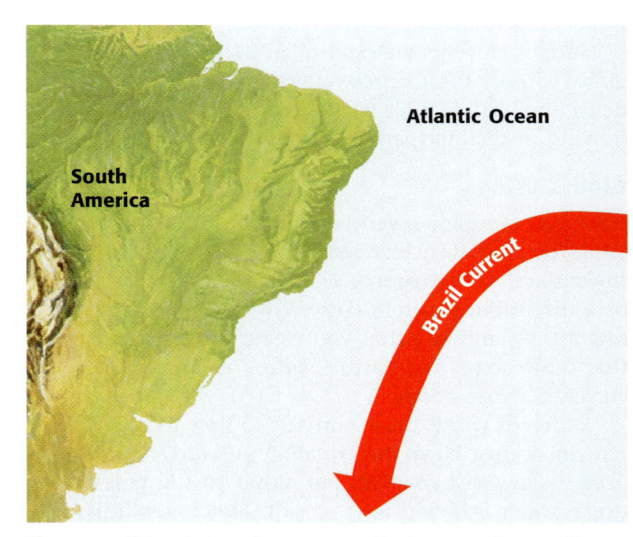

Figure 5 If South America were not in the way, the Brazil Current would probably flow farther west.

CHAPTER RESOURCES

Technology

Transparencies
- Earth's Rotation and the Coriolis Effect
- Earth's Surface Currents

Is That a Fact!
The Earth's rotation affects ocean currents directly by causing currents to circle in opposite directions on either side of the equator. Earth's rotation also affects the wind patterns, which in turn drive surface currents.

418   Chapter 14 • The Movement of Ocean Water

Figure 6 *This map shows Earth's surface currents. Warm-water currents are shown as red arrows, and cold-water currents are shown as blue arrows.*

Taking Temperatures

All three factors—global winds, the Coriolis effect, and continental deflections—work together to form a pattern of surface currents on Earth. But currents are also affected by the temperature of the water in which they form. Warm-water currents begin near the equator and carry warm water to other parts of the ocean. Cold-water currents begin closer to the poles and carry cool water to other parts of the ocean. As you can see on the map in **Figure 6,** all the oceans are connected and both warm-water and cold-water currents travel from one ocean to another.

Reading Check What three factors form a pattern of surface currents on Earth?

Deep Currents

Streamlike movements of ocean water located far below the surface are called **deep currents.** Unlike surface currents, deep currents are not directly controlled by wind. Instead, deep currents form in parts of the ocean where water density increases. *Density* is the amount of matter in a given space, or volume. The density of ocean water is affected by temperature and *salinity*—a measure of the amount of dissolved salts or solids in a liquid. Both decreasing the temperature of ocean water and increasing the water's salinity increase the water's density.

deep current a streamlike movement of ocean water far below the surface

CONNECTION TO Physics

Convection Currents While winds are often responsible for ocean currents, the sun is the initial energy source of the winds and currents. Because the sun heats the Earth more in some places than in others, convection currents are formed. These currents transfer thermal energy. Which ocean currents do you think carry more thermal energy, currents located near the equator or currents located near the poles?

CONNECTION to Language Arts — ADVANCED

Endurance: Shackleton's Incredible Voyage In 1914, British explorer Ernest Shackleton attempted to reach the South Pole in his ship *Endurance*. Just one day's sail from Antarctica, *Endurance* became trapped in sea ice and was frozen for 10 months. Pressure from the ice eventually crushed the ship, and Shackleton and his crew were forced to spend 5 months camping on ice floes. At the end of this 5-month period, Shackleton made a daring attempt to seek help and organize a team to rescue the crew that he was forced to leave behind by crossing 800 miles of open ocean to South Georgia Island. After crossing the mountains of South Georgia, Shackleton was able to reach the island's whaling station. There, he assembled the rescue team that would return to Antarctica to save all of the men he had left behind. This heroic epic is documented in the book *Endurance: Shackleton's Incredible Voyage* by Alfred Lansing, which is available in a print version, an audio book, and a documentary.

ACTIVITY — BASIC

Differences in Currents Refer to **Figure 6** to point out that the currents in the Southern Hemisphere turn counterclockwise and the currents in the Northern Hemisphere turn clockwise. Using a globe, show the direction of ocean currents in various areas around the world. Note that a current in the South Atlantic Ocean crosses the equator and joins the clockwise-turning currents. Discuss how this process was modeled in the Start-up Activity at the beginning of this chapter. **English Language Learners**
Visual

Homework — GENERAL

Research Have students choose four coastal cities that are separated by oceans. Ask students to describe in their **science journal** the currents they would use to sail from one city to the next. Students should use **Figure 6** as a reference for determining which currents they would use. For further details on the names of ocean currents, students can use an atlas or another reference tool. They can write their entries in the form of a ship's log.
Visual/Intrapersonal

Answer to Reading Check
The three factors that form a pattern of surface currents on Earth are global winds, the Coriolis effect, and continental deflections.

Answer to Connection to Physics
Currents located near the equator carry more thermal energy.

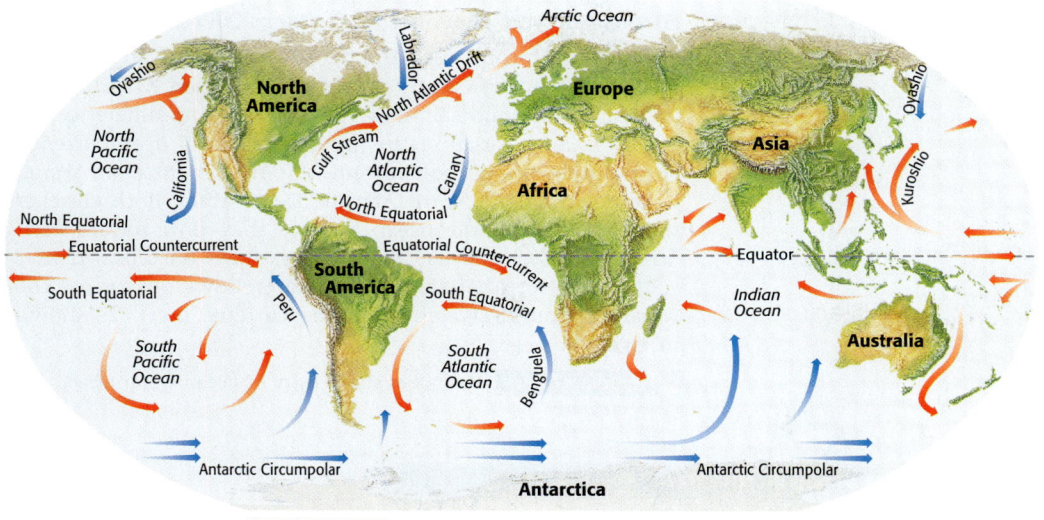

Section 1 • Currents   **419**

Close

Reteaching — BASIC
Movement of Ocean Currents
Ask students to list the three factors that control surface currents. Then, ask students to list the factors that cause deep currents to form. **LS Verbal**

Quiz — GENERAL
1. Give two characteristics and one example of each type of current. (Sample answer: Surface currents occur at the surface of the ocean and are directly influenced by the wind, continental deflections, and the Coriolis effect. The Gulf Stream is an example of a surface current. Deep currents occur deep in the ocean and are influenced by differences in water density. The Antarctic Bottom Water is an example of a deep current.)

Alternative Assessment — GENERAL
Sailing with the Currents Ask students to imagine that they are planning a voyage around the world. They can choose any route they wish, but they must sail with the currents. Have them map out their selected route and show the names of the currents, their point of origin, and their point of destination. **LS Logical**

Formation and Movement of Deep Currents

The relationship between the density of ocean water and the formation of deep currents is shown in **Figure 7**. Differences in temperature and salinity—and the resulting differences in density—cause variations in the movement of deep currents. For example, the deepest current, the Antarctic Bottom Water, is denser than the North Atlantic Deep Water. Both currents spread out across the ocean floor as they flow toward each other. Because less-dense water always flows on top of denser water, the North Atlantic Deep Water flows on top of the Antarctic Bottom Water when the currents meet, as shown in **Figure 8**.

✓ **Reading Check** How does the density of ocean water affect deep currents?

Figure 7 How Deep Currents Form

Decreasing Temperature In Earth's polar regions, cold air chills the water molecules at the ocean's surface, which causes the molecules to slow down and move closer together. This reaction causes the water's volume to decrease. Thus, the water becomes denser. The dense water sinks and eventually travels toward the equator as a deep current along the ocean floor.

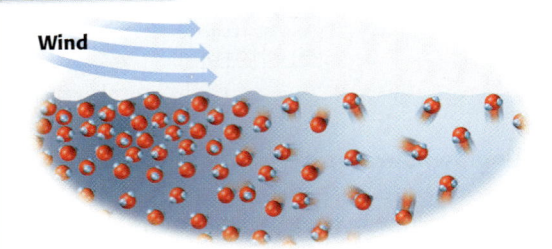

Increasing Salinity Through Freezing If the ocean water freezes at the surface, ice will float on top of the water because ice is less dense than liquid water. The dissolved solids are squeezed out of the ice and enter the liquid water below the ice. This process increases the salinity of the water. As a result of the increased salinity, the water's density increases.

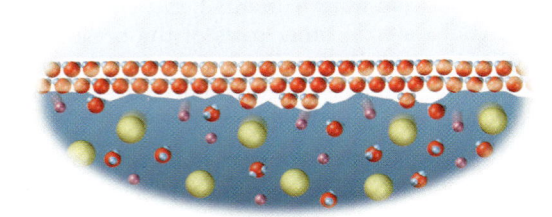

Increasing Salinity Through Evaporation Another way salinity increases is through evaporation of surface water, which removes water but leaves solids behind. This process is especially common in warm climates. Increasing salinity through freezing or evaporation causes water to become denser, to sink to the ocean floor, and to form a deep current.

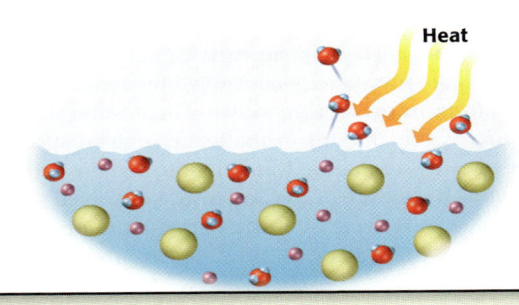

Answer to Reading Check
Density causes variations in the movement of deep currents.

MISCONCEPTION ALERT
Models of Molecules Remind students that molecules aren't made of little colored balls—the balls in the illustration on this page are models that represent molecules. The red and blue balls that are attached to one another represent water molecules, and the yellow balls represent dissolved solids.

Figure 8 *The warmer, less-dense water in surface currents cools and becomes the colder, denser water in deep currents.*

Polar regions

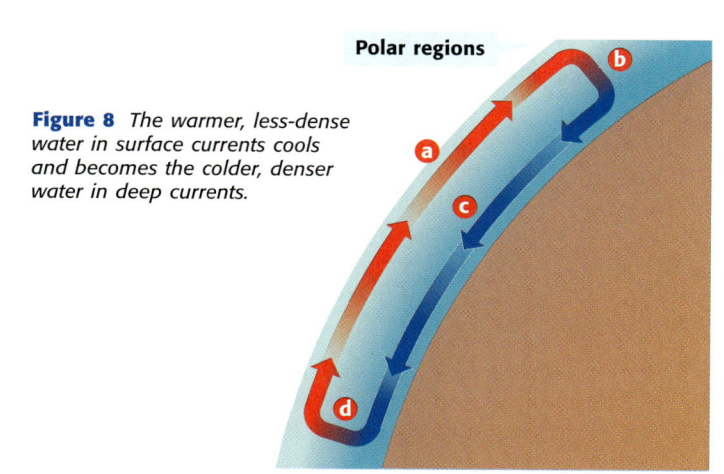

ⓐ Surface currents carry the warmer, less-dense water from other ocean regions to polar regions.

ⓑ Warm water from surface currents replaces colder, denser water that sinks to the ocean floor.

ⓒ Deep currents carry colder, denser water along the ocean floor from polar regions to other ocean regions.

ⓓ Water from deep currents rises to replace water leaving surface currents.

SECTION Review

Summary

- Surface currents are streamlike movements of water at or near the surface of the ocean.
- Surface currents are controlled by three factors: global winds, the Coriolis effect, and continental deflections.
- Deep currents are streamlike movements of ocean water located far below the surface.
- Deep currents form where the density of ocean water increases. Water density depends on temperature and salinity.

Using Key Terms

The statements below are false. For each statement, replace the underlined word to make a true statement.

1. <u>Deep currents</u> are directly controlled by wind.
2. An increase in density in parts of the ocean can cause <u>surface currents</u> to form.

Understanding Key Ideas

3. Surface currents
   a. are formed by wind.
   b. are streamlike movements of water.
   c. can travel across entire oceans.
   d. All of the above
4. List three factors that control surface currents.
5. How does a continent affect the movement of a surface current?
6. Explain how temperature and salinity affect the formation of deep currents.

Math Skills

7. The Gulf Stream flows along the North Carolina coast at 90 million cubic meters per second and at 40 million cubic meters per second when it turns eastward. How much faster is the Gulf Stream flowing along the coast than when it turns eastward?

Critical Thinking

8. **Evaluating Conclusions** If there were no land on Earth's surface, what would the pattern of surface currents look like? Explain your answer.
9. **Making Comparisons** Compare the factors that contribute to the formation of surface currents and deep currents.

SciLinks
Developed and maintained by the National Science Teachers Association
For a variety of links related to this chapter, go to www.scilinks.org
Topic: Ocean Currents
SciLinks code: HSM1061

Answers to Section Review

1. Surface currents
2. deep currents
3. d
4. global winds, the Coriolis effect, and continental deflections
5. When a surface current meets a continent, the surface current will *deflect*, or change direction.
6. Decreasing the water's temperature or increasing its salinity will increase its density. As water becomes denser, it sinks and becomes a deep current that moves along the ocean floor.
7. 90,000,000 mi³/s − 40,000,000 mi³/s = 50,000,000 mi³/s
8. Sample answer: If there were no land on Earth's surface, surface currents would not deflect sharply, as they do when they encounter continents.
9. Sample answer: Surface currents are streamlike movements of water at or near the surface of the ocean. Deep currents are streamlike movements of ocean water located far below the surface. Global winds, the Coriolis effect, and continental deflections contribute to the formation of surface currents. Deep currents form where the density of ocean water increases.

CONNECTION ACTIVITY
Math — GENERAL

Scientific Notation Review scientific notation with students. Tell them that there are approximately 1.7×10^{20} water molecules in one drop of sea water and 4×10^{43} water molecules in the Mediterranean Sea. Have students help you write these two numbers to show how large they are. For reference, tell students that there are approximately 17 times as many molecules in a drop of water as there are insects on Earth. **LS** Visual/Logical

CHAPTER RESOURCES

Chapter Resource File
- Section Quiz GENERAL
- Section Review GENERAL
- Vocabulary and Section Summary GENERAL
- SciLinks Activity GENERAL

Technology
- **Transparencies**
  - How Deep Currents Form
- **Interactive Explorations CD-ROM**
  - Latitude Attitude GENERAL

Section 1 • Currents

SECTION 2

Focus

Overview

This section discusses how currents affect climate. Students will learn about the effects of El Niño and ways in which scientists study El Niño.

Bellringer

Find the average yearly temperatures for the Scilly Isles in England and the average yearly temperatures for Newfoundland, Canada, and display them on the board or an overhead projector. Then, show students where those places are located on a map or globe. Ask students to compare the temperatures of the two locations. Then, explain that surface currents contribute to the different temperatures of the two locations. **LS Visual/Verbal**

Motivate

Discussion — GENERAL

The Effects of Currents Ask students to think of ways in which currents affect climate. Ask students to think about how climate changes in areas that are close to bodies of water.
LS Verbal

SECTION 2

READING WARM-UP

Objectives
- Explain how currents affect climate.
- Describe the effects of El Niño.
- Explain how scientists study and predict the pattern of El Niño.

Terms to Learn
upwelling
El Niño
La Niña

READING STRATEGY

Paired Summarizing Read this section silently. In pairs, take turns summarizing the material. Stop to discuss ideas that seem confusing.

CHAPTER RESOURCES

Chapter Resource File
- Lesson Plan
- Directed Reading A BASIC
- Directed Reading B SPECIAL NEEDS

Technology
- Transparencies
  - Bellringer
  - Upwelling

Currents and Climate

The Scilly Isles in England are located as far north as Newfoundland in northeast Canada. But the Scilly Isles experience warm temperatures almost all year long, while Newfoundland has long winters of frost and snow. How can two places at similar latitudes have completely different climates? This difference in climate is caused by surface currents.

Surface Currents and Climate

Surface currents greatly affect the climate in many parts of the world. Some surface currents warm or cool coastal areas year-round. Other surface currents sometimes change their circulation pattern. Changes in circulation patterns cause changes in atmosphere that affect the climate in many parts of the world.

Warm-Water Currents and Climate

Although surface currents are generally much warmer than deep currents, the temperatures of surface currents do vary. Surface currents are classified as warm-water currents or cold-water currents. Warm-water currents create warmer climates in coastal areas that would otherwise be much cooler. **Figure 1** shows how the Gulf Stream carries warm water from the Tropics to the North Atlantic Ocean. The Gulf Stream flows to the British Isles and creates a relatively mild climate for land at such high latitude. The Gulf Stream is the same current that makes the climate of the Scilly Isles very different from the climate of Newfoundland.

Figure 1 How Warm-Water Currents Affect Climate

Warm-water currents, such as the Gulf Stream, can affect the climate of coastal regions.

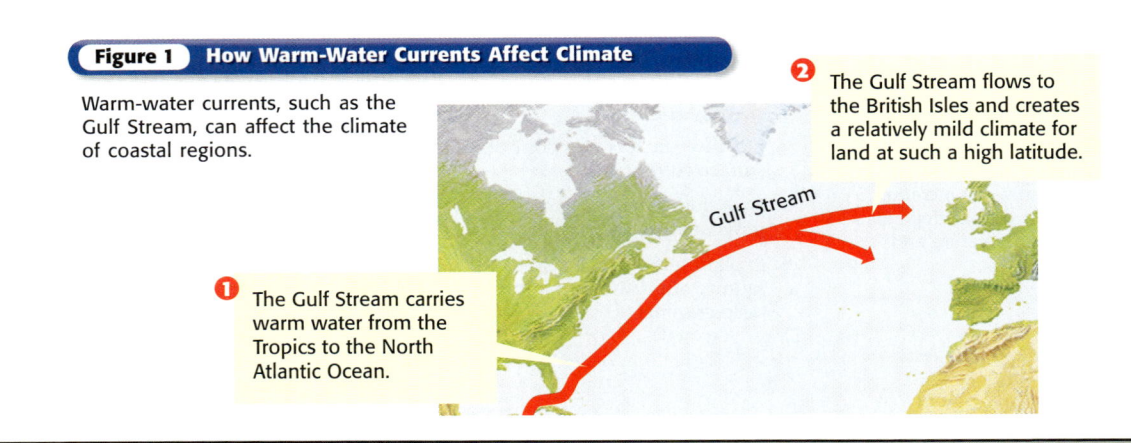

❶ The Gulf Stream carries warm water from the Tropics to the North Atlantic Ocean.

❷ The Gulf Stream flows to the British Isles and creates a relatively mild climate for land at such a high latitude.

CONNECTION to History — GENERAL

Benjamin Franklin's Navigation Charts Early in U.S. history, Benjamin Franklin noticed that mail ships took much longer to travel from England to the United States than from United States to England. He then discovered that ships from England were sailing against the Gulf Stream. Franklin revolutionized ocean navigation by designing charts that helped sailors avoid sailing against major surface currents.

422 Chapter 14 • The Movement of Ocean Water

Figure 2 How Cold-Water Currents Affect Climate

Cold-water currents, such as the California Current, can affect the climate of coastal regions.

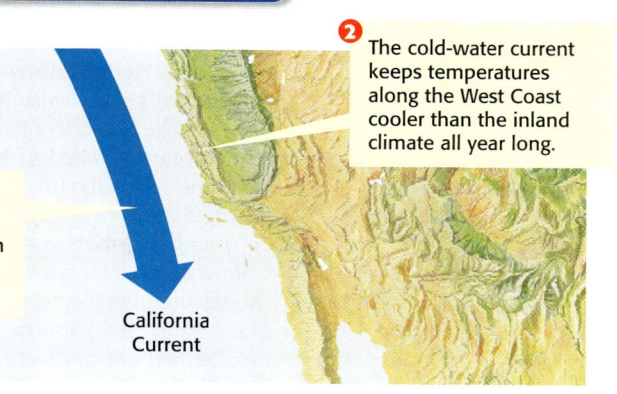

❶ Cold water from the northern Pacific Ocean is carried south to Mexico by the California Current.

❷ The cold-water current keeps temperatures along the West Coast cooler than the inland climate all year long.

California Current

Cold-Water Currents and Climate

Cold-water currents also affect the climate of the land near where they flow. **Figure 2** shows how the California Current carries cold water from the North Pacific Ocean southward to Mexico. The cold-water California Current keeps the climate along the West Coast cooler than the inland climate year-round.

upwelling the movement of deep, cold, and nutrient-rich water to the surface

✓ **Reading Check** How do cold-water currents affect coastal regions?

Upwelling

When local wind patterns blow along the northwest coast of South America, they cause local surface currents to move away from the shore. This warm water is then replaced by deep, cold water. This movement causes upwelling to occur in the eastern Pacific. **Upwelling** is a process in which cold, nutrient-rich water from the deep ocean rises to the surface and replaces warm surface water, as shown in **Figure 3**. The nutrients from the deep ocean are made up of elements and chemicals, such as iron and nitrate. When these chemicals are brought to the sunny surface, they help tiny plants grow through the process of photosynthesis.

The process of upwelling is extremely important to organisms. The nutrients that are brought to the surface of the ocean support the growth of phytoplankton and zooplankton. These tiny plants and animals support other organisms such as fish and seabirds.

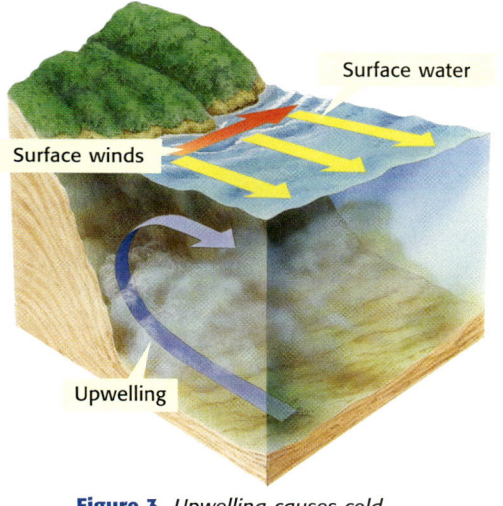

Figure 3 Upwelling causes cold, nutrient-rich water from the deep ocean to rise to the surface.

Teach

ACTIVITY — GENERAL

Graphing Temperatures Have students select two pairs of cities on opposite sides of a continent. All of the cities should be at approximately the same latitude. One city from each pair should be located on the coast, and the other city from each pair should be less than 300 km inland. For example, students could choose San Francisco and Fresno, California, and Norfolk and Roanoke, Virginia. Have students find the average high and low temperatures for each city. Next, have students find the average ocean temperature at the coastal cities. Have students plot the temperatures on a bar graph. Ask students to explain how ocean temperature affects the climate of the coastal cities. **LS Visual**

Answer to Reading Check

Cold-water currents keep coastal climates cooler than inland climates all year long.

BRAIN FOOD

Surface Currents and Hurricanes
Hurricanes are large tropical storms that originate over large bodies of warm water, such as the Caribbean Sea. Hurricanes are created when warm water builds storm clouds, resulting in a massive low-pressure cell. In North America, hurricanes generally make landfall on the East Coast of the United States or on the coast of the Gulf of Mexico, and they have reached as far north as Maine. On the West Coast, a hurricane has never made landfall in California, because the water off the coast of California is not warm enough to generate storm clouds or a low-pressure cell.

Section 2 • Currents and Climates

Close

Reteaching — BASIC

Effects of Currents Ask students to describe the effects of currents on climate, land, and organisms. Students can use these notes as a study aid.

LS Logical

Quiz — GENERAL

Ask students whether each of the statements below is true or false.

1. Upwelling is a process in which warm, nutrient-rich water from the deep ocean rises to the surface. (false)
2. El Niño occurs every 2 to 12 years. (true)
3. During an El Niño, California usually experiences a drought. (false)
4. Surface currents greatly affect the climate in many parts of the world. (true)

Alternative Assessment — GENERAL

Studying El Niño Ask students to research how scientists study El Niño. Then, ask students to write a report explaining how the data that scientists collect about El Niño can help prevent future disasters caused by El Niño.

LS Intrapersonal

CONNECTION TO Environmental Science

El Niño and Coral Reefs
The increase of surface water temperatures during El Niño can destroy coral reefs. *Coral reefs* are fragile limestone ridges built by tiny coral animals. An increase in surface water temperature and exposure to the sun (due to a decrease in sea level) can cause corals to become bleached and die. Coral reefs support a diverse community of marine life. Create a world map that shows the locations of the coral reefs.

ACTIVITY

El Niño a change in the water temperature in the Pacific Ocean that produces a warm current

La Niña a change in the eastern Pacific Ocean in which the surface water temperature becomes unusually cool

Figure 4 This damage in Southern California was the result of excessive rain caused by El Niño in 1997.

El Niño

Every 2 to 12 years, the South Pacific trade winds move less warm water to the western Pacific than they usually do. Thus, surface-water temperatures along the coast of South America rise. Gradually, this warming spreads westward. This periodic change in the location of warm and cool surface waters in the Pacific Ocean is called **El Niño**. El Niño can last for a year or longer and not only affects the surface waters but also changes the interaction of the ocean and the atmosphere, which in turn changes global weather patterns.

Sometimes, El Niño is followed by La Niña. **La Niña** is a periodic change in the eastern Pacific Ocean in which the surface-water temperature becomes unusually cool. Like El Niño, La Niña also affects weather patterns.

Effects of El Niño

El Niño alters weather patterns enough to cause disasters. These disasters include flash floods and mudslides in areas of the world that usually receive little rain, such as the southern half of the United States and Peru. **Figure 4** shows homes in Southern California destroyed by a mudslide caused by El Niño. While some regions flood, regions that usually get a lot of rain may experience *droughts,* an unusually long period during which rainfall is below average. During El Niño, severe droughts can occur in Indonesia and Australia. Periods of severe drought can lead to crop failure.

During El Niño, the upwelling of nutrient-rich water does not occur off the coast of South America, which affects the organisms that depend on the nutrients for food.

CONNECTION ACTIVITY Real World — GENERAL

El Niño El Niño has far-reaching effects on many countries. Many areas have been devastated as a result of El Niño–related floods, storms, and droughts. Have students search for news stories describing some of the effects of El Niño in recent years. Encourage students to contrast these negative effects with the positive effects of El Niño, such as extended growing seasons. **LS** Intrapersonal

Studying and Predicting El Niño

Because El Niño occurs every 2 to 12 years, studying and predicting it can be difficult. However, it is important for scientists to learn as much as possible about El Niño because of its effects on organisms and land.

One way scientists collect data to predict an El Niño is through a network of buoys operated by the National Oceanic and Atmospheric Administration (NOAA). The buoys, some of which are anchored to the ocean floor, are located along the Earth's equator. The buoys record data about surface temperature, air temperature, currents, and winds. The buoys transmit some of the data on a daily basis to NOAA through a satellite in space.

When the buoys report that the South Pacific trade winds are not as strong as they usually are or that the surface temperatures of the tropical oceans have risen, scientists can predict that an El Niño is likely to occur.

✓ **Reading Check** Why is it important to study El Niño? Describe one way scientists study El Niño.

INTERNET ACTIVITY

For another activity related to this chapter, go to **go.hrw.com** and type in the keyword **HZ5H20W**.

SECTION Review

Summary

- Surface currents affect the climate of the land near which they flow.
- Warm-water currents bring warmer climates to coastal regions.
- Cold-water currents bring cooler climates to coastal regions.
- During El Niño, warm and cool surface waters change locations.
- El Niño can cause floods, mudslides, and drought.

Using Key Terms

1. Use each of the following terms in a separate sentence: *upwelling*, *El Niño*, and *La Niña*.

Understanding Key Ideas

2. The Gulf Stream carries warm water to the North Atlantic Ocean, which contributes to
   a. a harsh winter in the British Isles.
   b. a cold-water surface current that flows to the British Isles.
   c. a mild climate for the British Isles.
   d. a warm-water surface current that flows along the coast of California.

3. Why might the climate in Scotland be relatively mild even though the country is located at a high latitude?

4. Name two disasters caused by El Niño.

Math Skills

5. A fisher usually catches 540 kg of anchovies off the coast of Peru. During El Niño, the fisher caught 85% less fish. How many kilograms of fish did the fisher catch during El Niño?

Critical Thinking

6. **Applying Concepts** Many marine organisms depend on upwelling to bring nutrients to the surface. How might El Niño affect a fisher's way of life?

SCILINKS

For a variety of links related to this chapter, go to www.scilinks.org
Topic: El Niño
SciLinks code: HSM0468

Answer to Reading Check

Sample answer: Answers may vary. It is important to study El Niño because El Niño can greatly affect organisms and land. One way that scientists study El Niño is through a network of buoys located along the equator. These buoys record information that helps scientists predict when an El Niño is likely to occur.

CHAPTER RESOURCES

Chapter Resource File
- Section Quiz GENERAL
- Section Review GENERAL
- Vocabulary and Section Summary GENERAL

Answers to Section Review

1. Sample answer: Upwelling is a process in which cold, nutrient-rich water from the deep ocean rises to the surface. El Niño can alter weather patterns enough to cause disasters. La Niña can cause surface-water temperatures to become unusually cool.

2. c

3. Even though Scotland is located at a high latitude, its climate is relatively mild because the Gulf Stream carries warm water from the Tropics to the North Atlantic Ocean.

4. El Niño can cause flash floods and landslides.

5. 540 kg × 0.85 = 459 kg; 540 kg − 459 kg = 81 kg

6. Sample answer: During El Niño, upwelling does not occur along the coast of Peru. When upwelling does not occur, nutrients from deep water do not rise to the surface. Marine organisms that depend on the nutrients for food may die or move to other areas in search of food. Fishers who depend on these organisms may have reduced catch, which will negatively affect fishers' way of life.

SECTION 3

Focus

Overview
This section describes the characteristics of waves. Students will learn about wave formation and movement, ways to identify different types of waves, and ways to measure different wave features. The section also discusses dangerous movements of ocean water.

🔔 Bellringer
Describe the following scenario to students: "You are floating in the ocean 1 km from shore, which is north of you. A surface current is flowing east. Are you more likely to travel north with the waves toward the shore or east with the surface current?"
(east, because wave energy travels through the water, but the water doesn't travel with the waves)

Motivate

Demonstration — GENERAL
Making Waves Fill a large tub with water, and place it at the front of the classroom. Ask students to suggest ways to produce waves in the tub without touching the water. Demonstrate the suggestions. Discuss whether each method of producing waves is similar to any of the ways that ocean waves are naturally produced. **LS** Visual

---

SECTION 3

READING WARM-UP

Objectives
- Identify the parts of a wave.
- Explain how the parts of a wave relate to wave movement.
- Describe how ocean waves form and move.
- Classify types of waves.

Terms to Learn
undertow
longshore current
whitecap
swell
tsunami
storm surge

READING STRATEGY
Prediction Guide Before reading this section, write the title of each heading in this section. Next, write what you think you will learn under each heading.

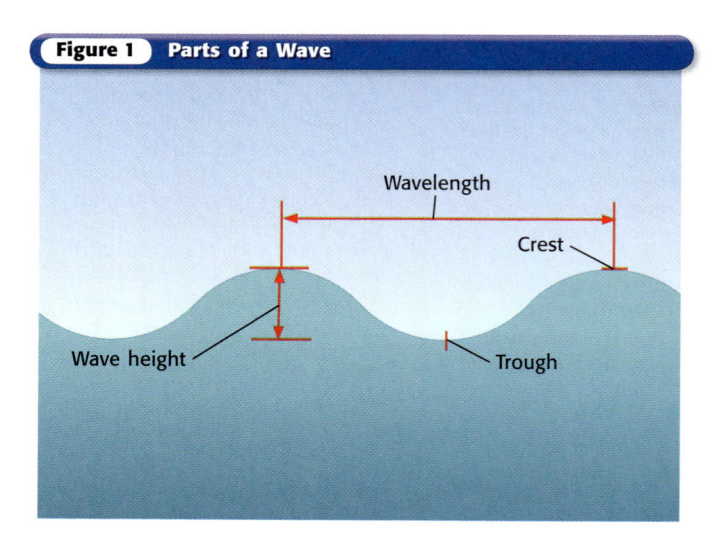

CHAPTER RESOURCES

Chapter Resource File
- Lesson Plan
- Directed Reading A BASIC
- Directed Reading B SPECIAL NEEDS

Technology
- Transparencies
  - Bellringer
  - Determining Wave Period

Waves

Have you ever seen a surfer riding waves? Did you ever wonder where the waves come from? And why are some waves big, while others are small?

We all know what ocean waves look like. Even if you've never been to the seashore, you've most likely seen waves on TV. But how do waves form and move? Waves are affected by a number of different factors. They can be formed by something as simple as wind or by something as violent as an earthquake. Ocean waves can travel through water slowly or incredibly quickly. Read on to discover the many forces that affect the formation and movement of ocean waves.

Anatomy of a Wave
Waves are made up of two main parts—crests and troughs. A *crest* is the highest point of a wave. A *trough* is the lowest point of a wave. Imagine a roller coaster designed with many rises and dips. The top of a rise on a roller-coaster track is similar to the crest of a wave, and the bottom of a dip in the track resembles the trough of a wave. The distance between two adjacent wave crests or wave troughs is a *wavelength*. The vertical distance between the crest and trough of a wave is called the *wave height*. **Figure 1** shows the parts of a wave.

✓ **Reading Check** What is the lowest point of a wave called? *(See the Appendix for answers to Reading Checks.)*

Figure 1 Parts of a Wave

Answer to Reading Check
The lowest point of a wave is called a *trough*.

426 Chapter 14 • The Movement of Ocean Water

Wave Formation and Movement

If you have watched ocean waves before, you may have noticed that water appears to move across the ocean's surface. However, this movement is only an illusion. Most waves form as wind blows across the water's surface and transfers energy to the water. As the energy moves through the water, so do the waves. But the water itself stays behind, rising and falling in circular movements. Notice in **Figure 2** that the floating bottle remains in the same spot as the waves travel from left to right. This circular motion gets smaller as the water depth increases, because wave energy decreases as the water depth increases. Wave energy reaches only a certain depth. Below that depth, the water is not affected by wave energy.

Specifics of Wave Movement

Waves not only come in different sizes but also travel at different speeds. To calculate wave speed, scientists must know the wavelength and the wave period. *Wave period* is the time between the passage of two wave crests (or troughs) at a fixed point, as shown in **Figure 3**. Dividing wavelength by wave period gives you wave speed, as shown below.

$$\frac{\text{wavelength (m)}}{\text{wave period (s)}} = \text{wave speed (m/s)}$$

For any given wavelength, an increase in the wave period will decrease the wave speed and a decrease in the wave period will increase the wave speed.

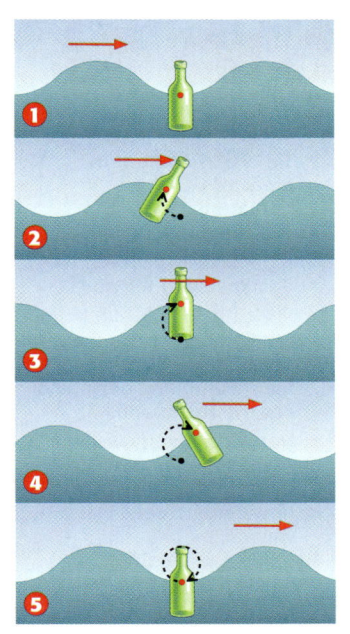

Figure 2 Like the bottle in this figure, water remains in the same place as waves travel through it.

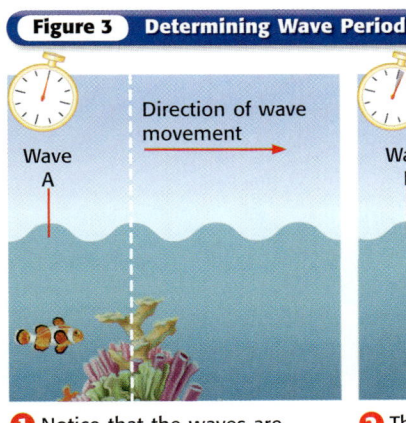

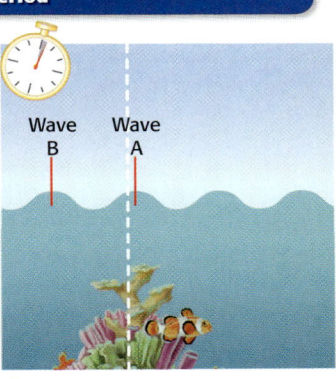

Figure 3 Determining Wave Period

❶ Notice that the waves are moving from left to right.

❷ The clock begins running as Wave A passes the reef's peak.

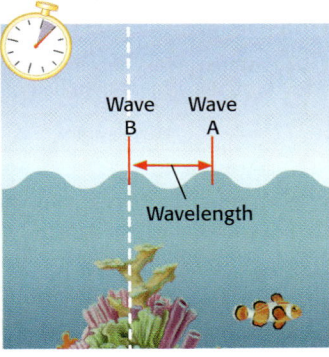

❸ The clock stops as Wave B passes the reef's peak. The time shown on the clock (5 s) represents the wave period.

Teach

Group ACTIVITY — BASIC

Modeling Waves Arrange chairs in a long row, and have students sit in the chairs. Then, have the students stand and sit in succession to form a "human wave." Ask students to discuss and then demonstrate how the shape and motion of the wave could be changed. (Examples include standing and sitting more quickly to decrease the wave period or stretching their arms over their heads as they stand and bringing their arms down to their sides as they sit to increase the wave height.) **LS** Kinesthetic/Interpersonal

CONNECTION ACTIVITY
Math — GENERAL

Wavelength and Wave Period Ask students how they would estimate wavelength and wave period if they were in a boat at sea. What visual marks might they use? Make sure students understand that wave period and wave speed are inversely proportional. That is, for a given wavelength, an increase in wave period means a decrease in wave speed. Have students work through several examples in their **science journal** to explore the relationships between wave measurements.
LS Logical

INCLUSION Strategies

- **Learning Disabled**
- **Attention Deficit Disorder**

Organize students into small groups. Tell them that they are going to create a wave bottle. Give each group a 1 L bottle, water, vegetable oil, food coloring, and a funnel. Ask students to use the funnel to fill the bottle two-thirds full with water. Next, they should add a few drops of food coloring to the water. Finally, they should fill the bottle to the top with oil (using the funnel) and screw the top on tightly. Students should turn the bottle on its side and gently tip it back and forth to make waves. In their **science journal**, they should draw and record the types of waves they see and anything they notice about the movement of the waves. Ask students, "What is the difference between the internal waves in the bottle and wind-driven waves on a beach?" Groups should share their observations with the class. **LS** Visual English Language Learners

Section 3 • Waves **427**

Teach, continued

READING STRATEGY — BASIC

Types of Waves Have students reproduce **Figures 4** and **5**. As you read the section, have students label their diagrams. Use the teaching transparency entitled "Measuring Wavelength; Measuring Frequency" to review these concepts.

English Language Learners
LS Visual/Intrapersonal

BRAIN FOOD

Offshore Breakers Ask the class why sighting a line of offshore breakers might cause sailors to consider turning their boats around. (As water becomes shallower, the wave height increases and the waves may break. Breaking waves could indicate a submerged sandbar or reef.)

CONNECTION ACTIVITY
Real World — GENERAL

Water Safety Discuss with students what they should do if they are ever caught in a rip current. Explain that instead of trying to swim against the current, they should signal for help and swim parallel to the shore. This will get them out of the rip current. They can then swim to shore with the waves. Diagram this scenario for students, and have them show you the proper direction to swim. **LS Verbal**

Quick Lab

Doing the Wave

1. Tie one end of a **thin piece of rope** to a doorknob.
2. Tie a **ribbon** around the rope halfway between the doorknob and the other end of the rope.
3. Holding the rope at the untied end, quickly move the rope up and down and observe the ribbon.
4. How does the movement of the rope and ribbon relate to the movement of water and deep-water waves?
5. Repeat step 3, but move the rope higher and lower this time.
6. How does this affect the waves in the rope?

Types of Waves

As you learned earlier in this section, wind forms most ocean waves. Waves can also form by other mechanisms. Underwater earthquakes and landslides as well as impacts by cosmic bodies can form different types of waves. Most waves move in one way regardless of how they are formed. Depending on their size and the angle at which they hit the shore, waves can generate a variety of near-shore events, some of which can be dangerous to humans.

Deep-Water Waves and Shallow-Water Waves

Have you ever wondered why waves increase in height as they approach the shore? The answer has to do with the depth of the water. *Deep-water waves* are waves that move in water deeper than one-half their wavelength. When the waves reach water shallower than one-half their wavelength, they begin to interact with the ocean floor. These waves are called *shallow-water waves*. **Figure 4** shows how deep-water waves become shallow-water waves as they move toward the shore.

As deep-water waves become shallow-water waves, the water particles slow down and build up. This change forces more water between wave crests and increases wave height. Gravity eventually pulls the high wave crests down, which causes them to crash into the ocean floor as *breakers*. The area where waves first begin to tumble downward, or break, is called the *breaker zone*. Waves continue to break as they move from the breaker zone to the shore. The area between the breaker zone and the shore is called the *surf*.

✓ **Reading Check** How do deep-water waves become shallow-water waves?

Figure 4 Deep-Water and Shallow-Water Waves
Deep-water waves become shallow-water waves when they reach depths of less than half of their wavelength.

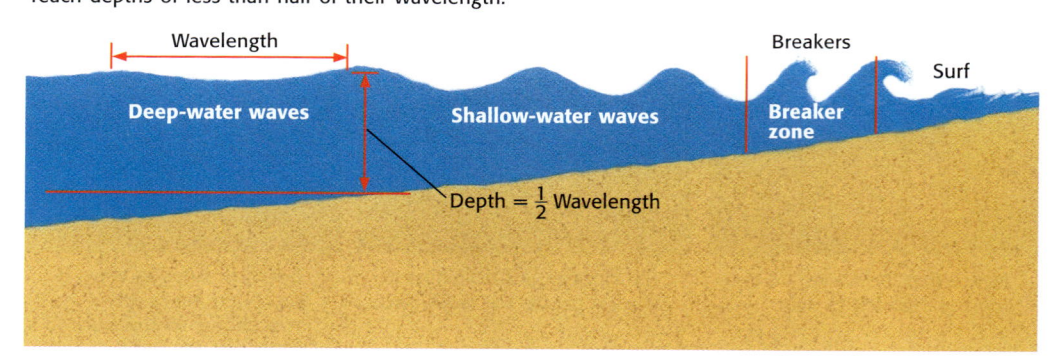

Wavelength | Deep-water waves | Shallow-water waves | Breaker zone | Breakers | Surf
Depth = $\frac{1}{2}$ Wavelength

Answer to Reading Check
Deep-water waves become shallow-water waves as they move toward the shore and reach water that is shallower than one-half their wavelength.

Answer to Quick Lab
4. Sample answer: As wave energy passed through the rope, the ribbon moved up and down, but it did not move closer to the doorknob. Similarly, as wave energy passes through water, it moves it up and down but does not transport water.
6. Sample answer: The wave height increased.

428 Chapter 14 • The Movement of Ocean Water

Figure 5 Formation of an Undertow

Head-on waves create an undertow.

Direction of wave movement

Undertow

Shore Currents

When waves crash on the beach head-on, the water they moved through flows back to the ocean underneath new incoming waves. This movement of water, which carries sand, rock particles, and plankton away from the shore, is called an **undertow**. **Figure 5** illustrates the back-and-forth movement of water at the shore.

Longshore Currents

When waves hit the shore at an angle, they cause water to move along the shore in a current called a **longshore current,** which is shown in **Figure 6**. Longshore currents transport most of the sediment in beach environments. This movement of sand and other sediment both tears down and builds up the coastline. Unfortunately, longshore currents also carry and spread trash and other types of ocean pollution along the shore.

undertow a subsurface current that is near shore and that pulls objects out to sea

longshore current a water current that travels near and parallel to the shoreline

Figure 6 Longshore currents form where waves approach beaches at an angle.

Longshore current

Homework — GENERAL

Writing **Surfing Report** Surfing originated in the South Seas about 2,500 years ago. Polynesian sailors who couldn't get their boats through the rough waves near the shore would surf to land. Surfing is now a recreational sport practiced all over the world. Have students write a report about the history of surfing. Their report should include an explanation of the characteristics that make specific locations around the world ideal for the sport. **LS Intrapersonal**

CHAPTER RESOURCES

Technology
- Transparencies
  • Deep-Water Waves Become Shallow-Water Waves
  • **LINK TO PHYSICAL SCIENCE** Measuring Wavelength; Measuring Frequency

Workbooks
- Math Skills for Science
  • What Is a Fraction?

CONNECTION ACTIVITY
Math — GENERAL

Whitecap Math Whitecaps are usually caused by strong winds. When the wind blows more than 13 km/h, wave height increases faster than wavelength. When wave height is more than one-seventh of the wavelength, whitecaps form. If the wavelength is 3 m, what is the minimum wave height needed for whitecaps to form? (about 43 cm)

If the wavelength is 10 m, what is the minimum wave height needed for whitecaps to form? (about 1.43 m)

If whitecaps begin to form when the wave height reaches 4 m, what is the wavelength? (about 28 m) **LS Verbal**

CONNECTION to
Environmental Science — GENERAL

Beach Nourishment Beach nourishment involves dredging enormous amounts of sand from the ocean floor and pumping the sand back onto the shoreline to rebuild beaches that have been eroded by longshore currents. This practice is common along the Atlantic coast, but it is controversial. Some people think the natural erosion of beaches should not be disrupted. Beach erosion is influenced by other human activities, however. For example, artificial dams prevent sediment from reaching protective barrier islands, and the dredging of ship channels disrupts the natural movement of sediment along the coast. Encourage students to investigate this issue and form their own opinions. **LS Intrapersonal**

Section 3 • Waves **429**

Close

Reteaching — BASIC
Wave Components Ask students to describe in their own words the four components of a wave. **LS Verbal**

Quiz — GENERAL
Have students create a concept map linking section concepts and vocabulary.

Alternative Assessment — GENERAL
Diagraming Waves Have students use the wave characteristics described in this section to construct diagrams of different types of waves with various characteristics. The diagrams should be made on poster board so that they can be shared with the class and displayed in the classroom. **LS Visual**

Homework — GENERAL
Tsunamis Have students research a tsunami that occurred and write a brief newspaper-style article about it. The articles should explain the cause and effects of the tsunami. Students could learn about the tsunami that struck the Pacific coast of Nicaragua in 1992 or the one that devastated Papua New Guinea in 1998. Encourage students to read their articles to the class. **LS Verbal/Intrapersonal**

Figure 7 Whitecaps (left) break in the open ocean, while swells, (right), roll gently in the open ocean.

whitecap the bubbles in the crest of a breaking wave

swell one of a group of long ocean waves that have steadily traveled a great distance from their point of generation

tsunami a giant ocean wave that forms after a volcanic eruption, submarine earthquake, or landslide

Open-Ocean Waves

Sometimes waves called *whitecaps* form in the open ocean. **Whitecaps** are white, foaming waves with very steep crests that break in the open ocean before the waves get close to the shore. These waves usually form during stormy weather, and they are usually short-lived. Winds that are far away from the shore form waves called *swells*. **Swells** are rolling waves that move steadily across the ocean. Swells have longer wavelengths than whitecaps and can travel for thousands of kilometers. **Figure 7** shows how whitecaps and swells differ.

Tsunamis

Professional surfers often travel to Hawaii to catch some of the highest waves in the world. But even the best surfers would not be able to handle a tsunami. **Tsunamis** are waves that form when a large volume of ocean water is suddenly moved up or down. This movement can be caused by underwater earthquakes, volcanic eruptions, landslides, underwater explosions, or the impact of a meteorite or comet. The majority of tsunamis occur in the Pacific Ocean because of the large number of earthquakes in that region. **Figure 8** shows how an earthquake can generate a tsunami.

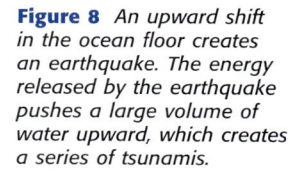

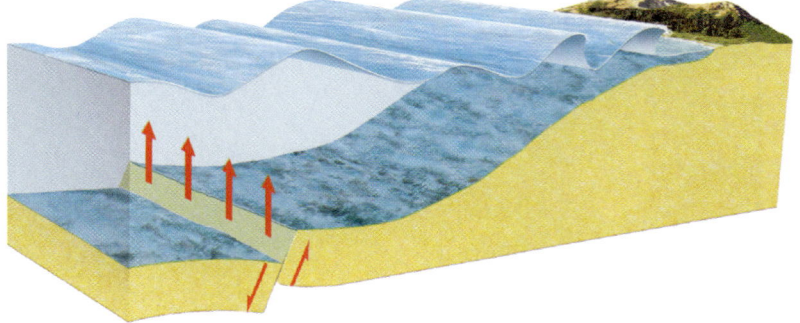

Figure 8 An upward shift in the ocean floor creates an earthquake. The energy released by the earthquake pushes a large volume of water upward, which creates a series of tsunamis.

Answer to Reading Check
A storm surge is a local rise in sea level near the shore and is caused by strong winds from a storm, such as a hurricane. Storm surges are difficult to study because they disappear as quickly as they form.

CONNECTION to Meteorology — ADVANCED
NOAA The National Oceanic and Atmospheric Administration (NOAA) studies oceanography and meteorology. Founded in 1970, this federal agency forecasts weather and monitors potentially destructive natural events, such as hurricanes, floods, and tsunamis. Interested students can write to NOAA or visit its Web site for more information.

430 Chapter 14 • The Movement of Ocean Water

Storm Surges

A local rise in sea level near the shore that is caused by strong winds from a storm, such as a hurricane, is called a **storm surge**. Winds form a storm surge by blowing water into a big pile under the storm. As the storm moves onto shore, so does the giant mass of water beneath it. Storm surges often disappear as quickly as they form, which makes them difficult to study. Storm surges contain a lot of energy and can reach about 8 m in height. Their size and power often make them the most destructive part of hurricanes.

storm surge a local rise in sea level near the shore that is caused by strong winds from a storm, such as those from a hurricane

✓ **Reading Check** What is a storm surge? Why are storm surges difficult to study?

SECTION Review

Summary

- Waves are made up of two main parts—crests and troughs.
- Waves are usually created by the transfer of the wind's energy across the surface of the ocean.
- Waves travel through water near the water's surface, while the water itself rises and falls in circular movements.
- Wind-generated waves are classified as deep-water or shallow-water waves.
- When waves hit the shore at a certain angle, they can create either an undertow or a longshore current.
- Tsunamis are dangerous waves that can be very destructive to coastal communities.

Using Key Terms

For each pair of terms, explain how the meanings of the terms differ.

1. *whitecap* and *swell*
2. *undertow* and *longshore current*
3. *tsunami* and *storm surge*

Understanding Key Ideas

4. Longshore currents transport sediment
   a. to the open ocean.
   b. along the shore.
   c. only during low tide.
   d. only during high tide.
5. Where do deep-water waves become shallow-water waves?
6. Explain how water moves as waves travel through it.
7. Name five events that can cause a tsunami.
8. Describe the two parts of a wave.

Math Skills

9. If a barrier island that is 1 km wide and 10 km long loses 1.5 m of its width per year to erosion by a longshore current, how long will the island take to lose one-fourth of its width?

Critical Thinking

10. **Analyzing Processes** How would you explain a bottle moving across the water in the same direction that the waves are traveling? Make a drawing of the bottle's movement.
11. **Analyzing Processes** Describe the motion of a wave as it approaches the shore.
12. **Applying Concepts** Explain how energy plays a role in the creation of ocean waves.
13. **Making Comparisons** How does the formation of an undertow differ from the formation of a longshore current? How is sand on the beach affected by each?

SciLinks
Developed and maintained by the National Science Teachers Association
For a variety of links related to this chapter, go to www.scilinks.org
Topic: Ocean Waves
SciLinks code: HSM1066

Answers to Section Review

1. Sample answer: A whitecap is a wave that is white and foamy and has very steep crests that break in the open ocean. Swells are rolling waves that move steadily across the ocean.
2. Sample answer: An undertow is a movement of water that carries sand, rock particles, and plankton away from the shoreline. A longshore current is a water current that travels near and parallel to the shoreline.
3. Sample answer: A tsunami is a giant ocean wave that forms after a volcanic eruption, submarine earthquake, or landslide. A storm surge is a local rise in sea level near the shore and is caused by a storm, such as a hurricane.
4. b
5. Deep-water waves become shallow-water waves as they move toward the shore.
6. Water at and near the surface rises and falls in circular movements as waves move through it.
7. underwater earthquakes, volcanic eruptions, landslides, underwater explosions, and the impact of a meteorite or comet
8. The crest is the highest point of a wave, and the trough is the lowest point.
9. $1/4 \times 1$ km $= 0.25$ km; 1.5 m/year $\div$ 1000 m/km $= 0.0015$ km/year; 0.25 km $\div$ 0.0015 km/year $=$ about 167 years
10. A floating bottle remains in the same spot as waves travel from left to right. If the bottle moves in the same direction as the waves, it is moving because of a surface current. Student drawings should look similar to **Figure 2** but should include a surface current.
11. As a wave approaches the shore, wave height increases and causes the wave to crash into the ocean floor. Then, wave height decreases as the wave continues to break until it reaches the shore.
12. Waves are created when energy is transferred to the water as wind blows across the water's surface.
13. An undertow forms when waves crash on the beach head-on. A longshore current forms when waves hit the shore at an angle. An undertow carries sand away from the shoreline, and a longshore current carries sand along the shoreline.

CHAPTER RESOURCES

Chapter Resource File
- Section Quiz GENERAL
- Section Review GENERAL
- Vocabulary and Section Summary GENERAL
- Reinforcement Worksheet BASIC
- Datasheet for Quick Lab

Section 3 • Waves **431**

SECTION 4

Focus

Overview
Students will learn how the position of Earth in relation to the moon and the sun creates different kinds of tides. They will also learn about the effects of coastal topography on tidewaters.

🔔 Bellringer
Show students a golf ball. Tell them that if the moon had the mass of a golf ball, the sun would have the mass of approximately 110 school buses. Ask students why they think that the moon exerts more influence over tides on Earth than the sun does. Tell students to write their guesses on a sheet of paper. (Gravitational force decreases with distance. The sun is almost 150 million kilometers from the Earth, but the moon is only 385,000 km away.)

Motivate

ACTIVITY — GENERAL

Intertidal Zones If possible, plan a visit to a coastal area. Beforehand, have the class research intertidal zones and the organisms that inhabit these areas. If a visit to the coast is not possible, have students research intertidal organisms and their survival strategies. Students should share their findings with the class. **LS Interpersonal**

SECTION 4

READING WARM-UP

Objectives
- Explain tides and their relationship with the Earth, sun, and moon.
- Describe four different types of tides.
- Analyze the relationship between tides and coastal land.

Terms to Learn
tide
tidal range
spring tide
neap tide

READING STRATEGY

Discussion Read this section silently. Write down questions that you have about this section. Discuss your questions in a small group.

tide the periodic rise and fall of the water level in the oceans and other large bodies of water

CHAPTER RESOURCES

Chapter Resource File
- Lesson Plan
- Directed Reading A BASIC
- Directed Reading B SPECIAL NEEDS

Technology
- Transparencies
  - Bellringer

Tides

If you stand at some ocean shores long enough, you will see the edge of the ocean shrink away from you. Wait longer, and you will see it return to its original place on the shore. Would you believe the moon causes this movement?

You have learned how winds and earthquakes can move ocean water. But less obvious forces move ocean water in regular patterns called tides. **Tides** are daily changes in the level of ocean water. Tides are influenced by the sun and the moon, as shown in **Figure 1,** and they occur in a variety of cycles.

The Lure of the Moon

The phases of the moon and their relationship to the tides were first discovered more than 2,000 years ago by a Greek explorer named *Pytheas*. But Pytheas and other early investigators could not explain the relationship. A scientific explanation was not given until 1687, when Sir Isaac Newton's theories on the principle of gravitation were published.

The gravity of the moon pulls on every particle of the Earth. But the pull on liquids is much more noticeable than on solids, because liquids move more easily. Even the liquid in an open soft drink is slightly pulled by the moon's gravity.

✓ **Reading Check** How does the moon affect Earth's particles? *(See the Appendix for answers to Reading Checks.)*

High Tide and Low Tide

How often tides occur and the difference in tidal levels depend on the position of the moon as it revolves around the Earth. The moon's pull is strongest on the part of the Earth directly facing the moon.

Figure 1 Although gravitational forces from both the sun and moon continuously pull on the Earth, the moon's gravity is the dominant force on Earth's tides.

Answer to Reading Check
The gravity of the moon pulls on every particle of the Earth.

432 Chapter 14 • The Movement of Ocean Water

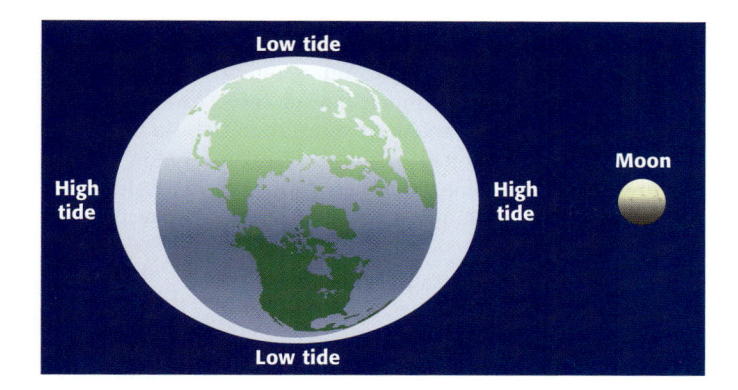

Figure 2 High tide occurs on the part of Earth that is closest to the moon. At the same time, high tide also occurs on the opposite side of Earth.

Battle of the Bulge

When part of the ocean is directly facing the moon, the water there bulges toward the moon. At the same time, water on the opposite side of the Earth bulges because of the rotation of the Earth and the motion of the moon around the Earth. These bulges are called *high tides*. Notice in **Figure 2** how the position of the moon causes the water to bulge. Also notice that when high tides occur, water is drawn away from the area between the high tides, which causes *low tides* to form.

Timing the Tides

The rotation of the Earth and the moon's revolution around the Earth determine when tides occur. If the Earth rotated at the same speed that the moon revolves around the Earth, the tides would not alternate between high and low. But the moon revolves around the Earth much more slowly than the Earth rotates. As **Figure 3** shows, a spot on Earth that is facing the moon takes 24 h and 50 m to rotate and face the moon again.

Figure 3 Tides occur at different locations on Earth because the Earth rotates more quickly than the moon revolves around the Earth.

CONNECTION TO Language Arts

WRITING SKILL **Mont-St-Michel Is Sometimes an Island?** Mont-St-Michel is located off the coast of France. Mont-St-Michel experiences extreme tides. The tides are so extreme that during high tide, it is an island and during low tide, it is connected to the mainland. Research the history behind Mont-St-Michel and then write a short story describing what it would be like to live there for a day. Be sure to include a description of Mont-St-Michel at high tide and at low tide.

Teach

Using the Figure — GENERAL

Earth's Rotation Remind students that Earth rotates much faster than the moon orbits. In **Figure 3,** point out that the distance that the moon traveled is much shorter than the distance the spot on Earth that faces the moon traveled. The spot on Earth made more than a full rotation around Earth's axis. **LS Visual**

Discussion — BASIC

Tide Discussion Help students understand the hypothetical scenario discussed in the text (in which the moon orbits Earth at the same speed that Earth rotates). Have students imagine that the moon is attached to a pole that is anchored to Earth. In this scenario, the moon would turn with Earth as Earth rotates. The moon would always be facing the same spot on Earth, so high tide would always occur at that spot and at the spot on the opposite side of Earth. In other words, the moon would orbit the Earth every 24 hours. Make sure students realize that this is not the case and that the location of tides varies constantly because the moon's revolution and the Earth's rotation occur at different speeds. **LS Verbal**

SCIENTISTS AT ODDS

Galileo Versus Kepler The cause of tides was a debated topic in the 16th and 17th centuries. Galileo suggested that there was a connection between tides and Earth's motion. To Galileo, tides proved beyond all doubt that Earth was moving. He argued that because Earth's waters are moving, Earth must be moving too. Johannes Kepler, another prominent scientist of the time, argued that the tides were linked to the moon's phases. Galileo made such a convincing argument that Kepler's ideas were dismissed. It was not until after Newton that scientists accepted that the gravitational forces exerted by the moon and the sun, as well as the rotation of Earth, are responsible for the tides.

Section 4 • Tides **433**

Close

Reteaching — BASIC
Spring Tides and Neap Tides
Have students reproduce **Figure 4** in their **science journal.** Then, have students write a definition for *spring tides* and *neap tides* in their own words. **English Language Learners**
LS Visual

Quiz — GENERAL
1. Why do spring tides exhibit such extremes of range? (because the gravitational force is greater than when neap tides occur)
2. What is a tidal bore? (a body of water that rushes up through a narrow bay, estuary, or river)

Alternative Assessment — GENERAL
Illustrating Tidal Relationships
Draw a random configuration of the sun, the moon, and Earth. Have students copy the drawing onto a sheet of paper. Then, ask them to draw the tidal bulges caused by that configuration. Finally, have students draw the positions of the sun, the moon, and Earth during spring and neap tides. **LS** Visual/Verbal

---

tidal range the difference in levels of ocean water at high tide and low tide

spring tide a tide of increased range that occurs two times a month, at the new and full moons

neap tide a tide of minimum range that occurs during the first and third quarters of the moon

---

Tidal Variations

The sun also affects tides. The sun is much larger than the moon, but the sun is also much farther away. As a result, the sun's influence on tides is less powerful than the moon's influence. The combined forces of the sun and the moon on the Earth result in tidal ranges that vary based on the positions of all three bodies. A **tidal range** is the difference between levels of ocean water at high tide and low tide.

✓ **Reading Check** What is a tidal range?

Spring Tides
When the sun, Earth, and moon are aligned, spring tides occur. **Spring tides** are tides with the largest daily tidal range and occur during the new and full moons, or every 14 days. The first time spring tides occur is when the moon is between the sun and Earth. The second time spring tides occur is when the moon and the sun are on opposite sides of the Earth. **Figure 4** shows the positions of the sun, Earth, and moon during spring tides.

Neap Tides
When the sun, Earth, and moon form a 90° angle, neap tides occur. **Neap tides** are tides with the smallest daily tidal range and occur during the first and third quarters of the moon. Neap tides occur halfway between the occurrence of spring tides. When neap tides occur, the gravitational forces on the Earth by the sun and moon work against each other. **Figure 4** shows the positions of the sun, Earth, and moon during neap tides.

Figure 4 Spring Tides and Neap Tides

Spring Tides During spring tides, the gravitational forces of the sun and moon pull on the Earth either from the same direction (left) or from opposite directions (right).

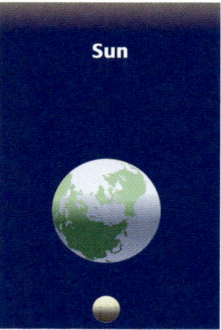

Neap Tides During neap tides, the sun and moon are at right angles with respect to the Earth. This arrangement lessens their gravitational effect on the Earth.

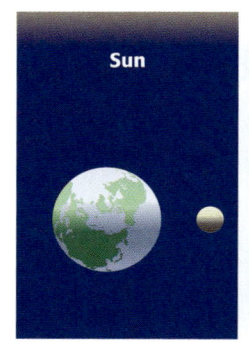

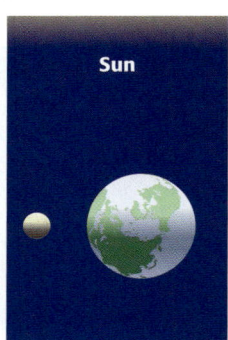

Answer to Reading Check
A tidal range is the difference between levels of ocean water at high tide and low tide.

Homework — GENERAL
Graphing Help students look in the newspaper or on the Internet to find daily tidal information for a certain area for 1 month. Record the high- and low-tide measurements on a large chart that can be displayed in the classroom. At the end of the month, determine when spring tide and neap tide occurred. Compare these dates with the full-, new-, and quarter-moon dates on a calendar, and explain why the dates correspond. **LS** Visual

Tides and Topography

After a tidal range has been measured, the times that tides occur can be accurately predicted. This information can be useful for people who live near or visit the coast, as shown in **Figure 5**. In some coastal areas that have narrow inlets, movements of water called tidal bores occur. A *tidal bore* is a body of water that rushes up through a narrow bay, estuary, or river channel during the rise of high tide and causes a very sudden tidal rise. Tidal bores occur in coastal areas of China, the British Isles, France, and Canada.

Figure 5 It's a good thing the people on this beach (left) knew when high tide occurred (right). These photos show the Bay of Fundy, in New Brunswick, Canada. The Bay of Fundy has the greatest tidal range on Earth.

SECTION Review

Summary

- Tides are caused by the gravitational forces of the moon and sun on the Earth.
- The moon's gravity is the main force behind the tides.
- The positions of the sun and moon relative to the position of the Earth cause tidal ranges.
- The four different types of tides are: high tides, low tides, spring tides, and neap tides.

Using Key Terms

1. In your own words, write a definition for each of the following terms: *spring tides* and *neap tides*.

Understanding Key Ideas

2. Tides are at their highest during
   a. spring tide.
   b. neap tide.
   c. a tidal bore.
   d. the daytime.

3. Which tides have minimum tidal range? Which tides have maximum tidal range?

4. What causes tidal ranges?

Math Skills

5. If it takes 24 h and 50 min for a spot on Earth that is facing the moon to rotate to face the moon again, how many minutes does it take?

Critical Thinking

6. **Applying Concepts** How many days pass between the minimum and the maximum of the tidal range in any given area? Explain your answer.

7. **Analyzing Processes** Explain how the position of the moon relates to the occurrence of high tides and low tides.

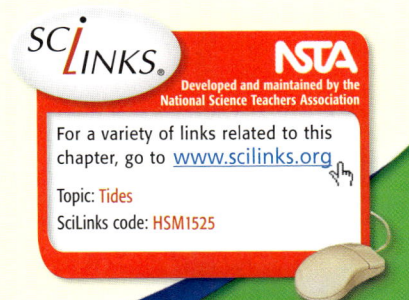

WEIRD SCIENCE

The moon also creates tides in our atmosphere that are called *lunar winds*. Lunar winds move eastward in the morning and westward in the evening. Although these tides travel only 0.08 km/h, they can be detected by studying slight fluctuations in weather patterns.

Answers to Section Review

1. Sample answer: Spring tides have maximum tidal range and occur every 14 days. Neap tides have minimum tidal range and occur during the first and third quarters of the moon.
2. a
3. Neap tides have minimum tidal range, and spring tides have maximum tidal range.
4. The combined forces of the sun and the moon on Earth result in tidal ranges that vary based on the positions of all three bodies.
5. 24 h × 60 min = 1440 min; 1440 min − 50 min = 1,490 min
6. Seven days pass between the maximum and minimum tidal ranges in any given area. Both spring tides and neap tides occur every 14 days. Neap tides occur midway between the occurrence of spring tides and vice versa. Therefore, the two types of tides alternate every 7 days.
7. High tides occur on the side of Earth facing the moon and on the side of Earth opposite the moon. When high tides occur, low tides form on the sides of Earth that are not facing or opposite the moon.

CHAPTER RESOURCES

Chapter Resource File
- Section Quiz GENERAL
- Section Review GENERAL
- Vocabulary and Section Summary GENERAL
- Critical Thinking ADVANCED

Technology
- Transparencies
  - Spring Tides and Neap Tides

Skills Practice Lab

Up from the Depths

Teacher's Notes

Time Required
One 45-minute class period

Lab Ratings

EASY ———————→ HARD

Teacher Prep 🧪
Student Set-Up 🧪🧪
Concept Level 🧪🧪
Clean Up 🧪🧪

MATERIALS

The materials listed on the student page are enough for a group of 4 to 5 students. Note that the food coloring is used only to distinguish the water layers. Any two colors will work. You may find it simpler to make a roll of plastic wrap available to the class. Groups can then take a piece when they reach the appropriate steps.

Safety Caution

Remind students to review all safety cautions and icons before beginning this lab activity.

Using Scientific Methods
Skills Practice Lab

OBJECTIVES

Demonstrate the effects of temperature and salinity on the density of water.

Describe why some parts of the ocean turn over, while others do not.

MATERIALS

- beakers, 400 mL (5)
- blue and red food coloring
- bucket of ice
- gloves, heat-resistant
- hot plate
- plastic wrap, 4 pieces, approximately 30 cm × 20 cm
- salt
- spoon
- tap water
- watch or clock

SAFETY

Up from the Depths

Every year, the water in certain parts of the ocean "turns over." That is, the water at the bottom rises to the top and the water at the top falls to the bottom. This yearly change brings fresh nutrients from the bottom of the ocean to the fish living near the surface. However, the water in some parts of the ocean never turns over. By completing this activity, you will find out why not.

Keep in mind that some parts of the ocean are warmer at the bottom, and some are warmer at the top. And sometimes the saltiest water is at the bottom and sometimes not. As you complete this activity, you will investigate how these factors help determine whether the water will turn over.

Ask a Question

1. Why do some parts of the ocean turn over and not others?

Form a Hypothesis

2. Write a hypothesis that is a possible answer to the question above. Explain your reasoning.

Test the Hypothesis

3. Label the beakers 1 through 5. Fill beakers 1 through 4 with tap water.

4. Add a drop of blue food coloring to the water in beakers 1 and 2, and stir with the spoon.

5. Place beaker 1 in the bucket of ice for 10 min.

6. Add a drop of red food coloring to the water in beakers 3 and 4, and stir with the spoon.

7. Set beaker 3 on a hot plate turned to a low setting for 10 min.

8. Add one spoonful of salt to the water in beaker 4, and stir with the spoon.

Gordon Zibelman
Drexel Hill Middle School
Drexel Hill, Pennsylvania

CHAPTER RESOURCES

Chapter Resource File
- Datasheet for Chapter Lab
- Lab Notes and Answers

Technology

Classroom Videos
- Lab Videos for Earth Science

LabBook
- Turning the Tides

---

436 Chapter 14 • The Movement of Ocean Water

9. While beaker 1 is cooling and beaker 3 is heating, copy the observations table below on a sheet of paper.

Observations Table

Mixture of water	Observations
Warm water placed above cold water	
Cold water placed above warm water	DO NOT WRITE IN BOOK
Salty water placed above fresh water	
Fresh water placed above salty water	

10. Pour half of the water in beaker 1 into beaker 5. Return beaker 1 to the bucket of ice.

11. Tuck a sheet of plastic wrap into beaker 5 so that the plastic rests on the surface of the water and lines the upper half of the beaker.

12. Put on your gloves. Slowly pour half of the water in beaker 3 into the plastic-lined upper half of beaker 5 to form two layers of water. Return beaker 3 to the hot plate, and remove your gloves.

13. Very carefully, pull on one edge of the plastic wrap and remove it so that the warm, red water rests on the cold, blue water.
Caution: The plastic wrap may be warm.

14. Wait about 5 minutes, and then observe the layers in beaker 5. Did one layer remain on top of the other? Was there any mixing or turning over? Record your observations in your observations table.

15. Empty beaker 5, and rinse it with clean tap water.

16. Repeat the procedure used in steps 10–15. This time, pour warm, red water from beaker 3 on the bottom and cold, blue water from beaker 1 on top. (Use gloves when pouring warm water.)

17. Again, repeat the procedure used in steps 10–15. This time, pour blue tap water from beaker 2 on the bottom and red, salty water from beaker 4 on top.

18. Repeat the procedure used in steps 10–15 a third time. This time, pour red, salty water from beaker 4 on the bottom and blue tap water from beaker 2 on top.

Analyze the Results

1. **Analyzing Data** Compare the results of all four trials. Explain why the water turned over in some of the trials but not in all of them.

Draw Conclusions

2. **Evaluating Results** What is the effect of temperature and salinity on the density of water?

3. **Drawing Conclusions** What makes the temperature of ocean water decrease? What could make the salinity of ocean water increase?

4. **Drawing Conclusions** What reasons can you give to explain why some parts of the ocean do not turn over in the spring while some do?

Applying Your Data

Suggest a method for setting up a model that tests the combined effects of temperature and salinity on the density of water. Consider using more than two water samples and dyes.

CHAPTER RESOURCES

Workbooks

- **Whiz-Bang Demonstrations**
  - Spin Cycle ADVANCED
- **Long-Term Projects & Research Ideas**
  - An Ocean Commotion ADVANCED

Procedure

14. The warm, red water remained on top of the cold, blue water. There was very little mixing (if any) and no turning over.

16. The cold, blue water did not remain on top of the warm, red water. There was very little mixing (if any), and the water turned over.

17. The red, salty water did not remain on top of the blue tap water. There was little mixing, and the water turned over.

18. The blue tap water remained on top of the red, salty water. There was little mixing, and the water did not turn over.

Analyze the Results

1. In each case, the denser water sank to the bottom. Cold water is denser than warm water. When put in a beaker with warm water, the cold water either stayed at the bottom or sank to the bottom. Salt water is denser than fresh water. When put in a beaker with fresh water, the salt water either stayed at the bottom or sank to the bottom.

Draw Conclusions

2. The density of water increases as the water's temperature decreases—cold water is denser than warm water. The density of water increases as the water's salinity increases—salt water is denser than fresh water.

3. The temperature of water can decrease because of seasonal temperature fluctuations or cold wind blowing across the water's surface. Currents can also carry cooler water to an area. The salinity of water can increase when evaporation occurs or when ice forms on the water's surface. These processes leave salts behind and make the remaining water denser.

4. Parts of the ocean that turn over do so because their density changes because of variations in salinity or temperature.

Applying Your Data

The following combinations could be used:

Top	Bottom
salt/cold	fresh/warm
salt/warm	fresh/cold
fresh/cold	salt/warm
fresh/warm	salt/cold

Chapter Review

Assignment Guide

SECTION	QUESTIONS
1	1, 5, 15, 16, 18, 21–23
2	2, 10, 11, 19
3	6, 7, 12, 14
4	3, 4, 8, 9, 13, 20
1, 3, 4	17

ANSWERS

Using Key Terms

1. Sample answer: Surface currents are streamlike movements of water that occur at or near the surface of the ocean. Deep currents are streamlike movements of ocean water far below the surface.

2. Sample answer: El Niño is a change in the water temperature in the Pacific Ocean that produces a warm current. La Niña is a change in the eastern Pacific Ocean in which the surface water temperature becomes unusually cool.

3. Sample answer: A spring tide is a tide of increased range that occurs during the full and new moons. A neap tide is a tide of minimum tidal range that occurs during the first and third quarters of the moon.

4. Sample answer: A tide is the periodic rise and fall of the water level in the oceans and other large bodies of water. Tidal range is the difference in levels of ocean water at high tide and low tide.

USING KEY TERMS

For each pair of terms, explain how the meanings of the terms differ.

1. *surface current* and *deep current*
2. *El Niño* and *La Niña*
3. *spring tide* and *neap tide*
4. *tide* and *tidal range*

UNDERSTANDING KEY IDEAS

Multiple Choice

5. Deep currents form when
   a. cold air decreases water density.
   b. warm air increases water density.
   c. the ocean surface freezes and solids from the water underneath are removed.
   d. salinity increases.

6. When waves come near the shore,
   a. they speed up.
   b. they maintain their speed.
   c. their wavelength increases.
   d. their wave height increases.

7. Whitecaps break
   a. in the surf.
   b. in the breaker zone.
   c. in the open ocean.
   d. as their wavelength increases.

8. Tidal range is greatest during
   a. spring tide.
   b. neap tide.
   c. a tidal bore.
   d. the daytime.

9. Tides alternate between high and low because the moon revolves around the Earth
   a. at the same speed the Earth rotates.
   b. at a much faster speed than the Earth rotates.
   c. at a much slower speed than the Earth rotates.
   d. at different speeds.

10. El Niño can cause
    a. droughts to occur in Indonesia and Australia.
    b. upwelling to occur off the coast of South America.
    c. earthquakes.
    d. droughts to occur in the southern half of the United States.

Short Answer

11. Explain the relationship between upwelling and El Niño.

12. Describe the two parts of a wave. Describe how these two parts relate to wavelength and wave height.

13. Compare the relative positions of the Earth, moon, and sun during the spring and neap tides.

14. Explain the difference between the breaker zone and the surf.

15. Describe how warm-water currents affect the climate in the British Isles.

16. Describe the factors that form deep currents.

Understanding Key Ideas

5. d
6. d
7. c
8. a
9. c
10. a
11. When El Niño occurs, warm surface water remains along the Pacific coast of South America. Therefore, upwelling does not occur along the coast.
12. A crest is the highest point of a wave, and a trough is the lowest point of a wave. The wavelength of a wave is the distance between two adjacent wave crests or wave troughs. Wave period is the time between the passage of two wave crests or troughs. Wavelength divided by wave period yields wave speed.
13. During neap tide, the sun, the moon, and Earth form a right angle, with Earth in the middle. During spring tide, the sun, moon, and Earth align in a straight line.

438 Chapter 14 • The Movement of Ocean Water

CRITICAL THINKING

17. **Concept Mapping** Use the following terms to create a concept map: *wind, deep currents, sun's gravity, types of ocean-water movement, surface currents, tides, increasing water density, waves,* and *moon's gravity.*

18. **Identifying Relationships** Why are tides more noticeable in Earth's oceans than on its land?

19. **Expressing Opinions** Explain why it's important to study El Niño and La Niña.

20. **Applying Concepts** Suppose you and a friend are planning a fishing trip to the ocean. Your friend tells you that the fish bite more in his secret fishing spot during low tide. If low tide occurred at the spot at 7 a.m. today and you are going to fish there in 1 week, at what time will low tide occur in that spot?

21. **Identifying Relationships** Describe how global winds, the Coriolis Effect, and continental deflections form a pattern of surface currents on Earth.

INTERPRETING GRAPHICS

The diagram below shows some of Earth's major surface currents that flow in the Western Hemisphere. Use the diagram to answer the questions that follow.

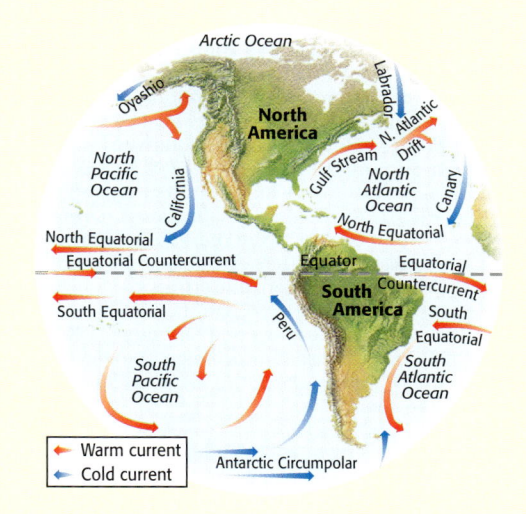

22. List two warm-water currents and two cold-water currents.

23. How do you think the Labrador Current affects the climate of Canada and Greenland?

Critical Thinking

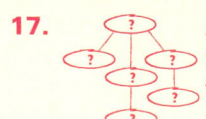

17. An answer to this exercise can be found at the end of this book.

18. Because the oceans are liquid, they flow more easily than land.

19. It is important to study El Niño and La Niña because both affect climate, land, and organisms.

20. 12:50 P.M. (The answer 1:15 A.M. is also acceptable.)

21. Global winds blow across Earth's surface, which creates surface currents in the ocean. The Coriolis effect is the apparent curving of moving objects from a straight path due to Earth's rotation. Therefore, the rotation of the Earth causes ocean currents to curve as they move across Earth's surface. Continental deflections occur when a surface current comes into contact with a continent. As a result, surface currents deflect, or change direction.

Interpreting Graphics

22. Answers may vary. Any two currents marked by red arrows are acceptable as warm-water currents. Any two currents marked by blue arrows are acceptable as cold-water currents.

23. Sample answer: Because it is a cold-water current, the Labrador Current would most likely bring a cool climate to Canada and Greenland.

---

14. The breaker zone is the zone where waves first begin to tumble downward. The surf is the zone between the breaker zone and the shore. In the surf, water moves toward the shore.

15. The Gulf Stream, which is a warm-water current, creates a relatively mild climate for the British Isles.

16. Deep currents form where the density of ocean water increases. Water density depends on temperature and salinity.

CHAPTER RESOURCES

Chapter Resource File
- Chapter Review GENERAL
- Chapter Test A GENERAL
- Chapter Test B ADVANCED
- Chapter Test C SPECIAL NEEDS
- Vocabulary Activity GENERAL

Workbooks
- Study Guide
- Assessment resources are also available in Spanish.

Chapter 14 • Chapter Review **439**

Standardized Test Preparation

Teacher's Note
To provide practice under more realistic testing conditions, give students 20 minutes to answer all of the questions in this Standardized Test Preparation.

MISCONCEPTION ALERT

Answers to the standardized test preparation can help you identify student misconceptions and misunderstandings.

READING
Passage 1
1. B
2. I

TEST DOCTOR

Question 1: Although the term *red tides* was used to describe algal blooms, the abbreviation HABs is more accurate because algal blooms are not always red and are not directly related to tides. This fact is mentioned in the first paragraph.

Question 2: The fact is mentioned in the last paragraph: "Unfortunately, seafood contamination is not noticeable without testing..." Although HABs are reddish in color, contaminated seafood does not appear different physically.

Standardized Test Preparation

READING
Read each of the passages below. Then, answer the questions that follow each passage.

Passage 1 When certain algae grow rapidly, they clump together on the ocean's surface in an algal bloom that changes the color of the water. Because these algal blooms often turn the water red or reddish brown and tidal conditions were believed to cause the blooms, people called these blooms *red tides*. However, algal blooms are not always red and are not directly related to tides. Scientists now call these algae clusters harmful algal blooms (HABs). HABs are considered harmful because the species of algae that makes up the blooms produces toxins that can poison fish and shellfish, which in turn can poison people.

Unfortunately, seafood contamination is not noticeable without testing and is not easily eliminated. The toxins don't change the flavor of the seafood, and cooking the seafood doesn't eliminate the toxins.

1. Why did scientists start calling red tides *HABs*?
   A The name *HABs* is easier to remember.
   B The name *red tides* was not accurate in describing the phenomenon.
   C The algal blooms are actually green.
   D The term *red tides* did not reflect the danger of the blooms.

2. How can a person tell if seafood has been contaminated by HABs?
   F Contaminated seafood has a reddish color.
   G HABs change the flavor of the seafood.
   H Seafood contaminated by HABs has a strange smell.
   I Unfortunately, there is no easy way to tell.

Passage 2 Tsunamis are the most destructive waves in the ocean. Most tsunamis are caused by earthquakes on the ocean floor, but some can be caused by volcanic eruptions and underwater landslides. Tsunamis are sometimes called *tidal waves*, which is misleading because tsunamis have no connection with tides.

Tsunamis commonly have a wave period of about 15 min and a wave speed of about 725 km/h, which is about as fast as a jet airliner. By the time a tsunami reaches the shore, its height may be 30 to 40 m.

In 1960, a tsunami was triggered by an earthquake off the coast of South America. The tsunami was so powerful that it crossed the Pacific Ocean and hit the city of Hilo, on the coast of Hawaii, approximately 10,000 km away. The same tsunami then continued on to strike Japan.

1. The word *misleading* was used in this passage to describe the use of the term *tidal waves* because
   A tsunamis are related to tides.
   B tsunamis can cause extensive damage to shores.
   C tsunamis are related to earthquakes.
   D tsunamis are not related to tides.

2. Which of the following statements is a fact from the passage?
   F All tsunamis are caused by earthquakes.
   G A tsunami can travel as fast as a jet airliner.
   H The tsunami of 1960 caused destruction only in Japan.
   I Tsunamis are caused by surface currents.

Passage 2
1. D
2. G

TEST DOCTOR

Question 2: This fact is mentioned in the second paragraph. Students may choose answer F because most tsunamis are caused by earthquakes. However, some tsunamis can be caused by events such as volcanic eruptions and underwater landslides. Answer H is incorrect because the last paragraph states that the tsunami of 1960 caused destruction in both Hawaii and Japan. Answer I is incorrect because surface currents are not related to tsunamis and are not mentioned in the passage.

440   Chapter 14 • The Movement of Ocean Water

INTERPRETING GRAPHICS

The diagram below shows the possible positions of the moon relative to the Earth and sun during different tidal ranges. Use the diagram below to answer the questions that follow.

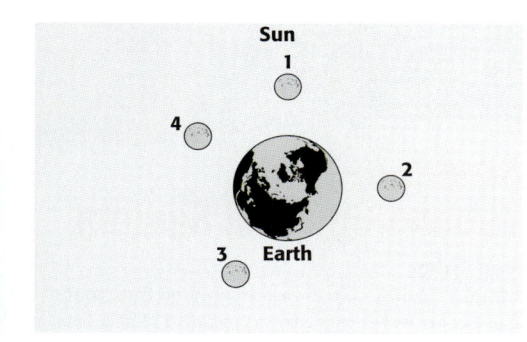

1. At which position would the moon be during a neap tide?
   A 1
   B 2
   C 3
   D 4

2. At which position would the moon be during a spring tide?
   F 1
   G 2
   H 3
   I 4

3. The tidal range would be greater when the moon is at position 3 than when the moon is at position 4 because
   A position 4 forms a 90° angle with the sun and the Earth.
   B position 3 is very near a neap-tide position.
   C position 3 is very near a spring-tide position.
   D position 4 is very near a spring-tide position.

MATH

Read each question below, and choose the best answer.

1. If a wave has a speed of 3 m/s and a wavelength of 12 m, what is its period? Use the following equation to answer the question above:

$$\frac{\text{wavelength (m)}}{\text{wave period (s)}} = \text{wave speed (m/s)}$$

   A 36 s
   B 4 m
   C 24 s
   D 4 s

2. Antarctic Bottom Water takes 750 years to move from the Antarctic coast to the equator. If the distance between the equator and the Antarctic coast is about 10,000 km, approximately how many kilometers does the bottom water move each year?
   F 13 km
   G 200 km
   H 75 km
   I 1 km

3. A boat is traveling north at 20 km/h against a current that is moving south at 12 km/h. What is the overall speed and direction of the boat?
   A 8 km/h north
   B 8 km/h south
   C 32 km/h north
   D 32 km/h south

4. Imagine that you are in a rowboat on the open ocean. You count 2 waves traveling right under your boat in 10 seconds. You estimate the wavelength to be 3 m. What is the wave speed?
   F 0.6 m/s
   G 6.0 m/s
   H 0.3 m/s
   I 3.0 m/s

INTERPRETING GRAPHICS

1. B
2. F
3. C

TEST DOCTOR

Question 3: Spring tides are tides with the largest daily tidal range. Spring tides occur when the sun and the moon pull on Earth from either the same direction or from opposite directions. Therefore, the moon at position 3 has the greatest tidal range—it is very near a spring-tide position because it is almost at a position opposite the sun.

MATH

1. D
2. F
3. A
4. F

TEST DOCTOR

Question 1: The first answer, 36 s, is incorrect because students would arrive at this answer by multiplying 3 by 12 rather than dividing 12 by 3. Answer B is incorrect because wave periods are measured in seconds, not in meters. Answer C is incorrect because it is too high. Answer D is correct because the wave period is 4 s; therefore, 12 m/ 4 s = 3 m/s.

Question 4: The first answer, F, is correct because students would arrive at this answer by first calculating the wave period by dividing 10 s by 2. Then, students would divide 3 m by 5 s to arrive at 0.6 m/s as the wave speed. Answer G is incorrect because the wave speed is too high. Answer H is incorrect because students would arrive at this answer by dividing 3 by 10 rather than dividing 3 by 5. Answer I is incorrect because the wave speed is too high.

CHAPTER RESOURCES

Chapter Resource File
- Standardized Test Preparation GENERAL

State Resources
For specific resources for your state, visit go.hrw.com and type in the keyword HSMSTR.

Chapter 14 • Standardized Test Preparation **441**

Science in Action

Weird Science

ACTIVITY — GENERAL

Surface currents move in large, slow circles called *gyres*. In 1990, a Korean ship carrying a load of athletic shoes was bound for the United States. During a storm in the North Pacific Ocean, 80,000 shoes were washed overboard. Six months later, the shoes began to wash up on North American shores from Oregon to British Columbia. This accident turned out to be an advantage to oceanographers. They created a computer model to predict where the gyres would carry the shoes next. True to the model, the shoes began to wash up in Hawaii three years later. With the help of dedicated beachcombers, this accident has enabled oceanographers to create a detailed map of surface currents in the Pacific Ocean. Have students look at a map of global ocean currents and identify the currents that carried the shoes.

Answer to Math Activity
The average distance traveled by the toys per day was 10.7 km (3,220 km ÷ 301 days = 10.7 km).

Science in Action

Weird Science
Using Toy Ducks to Track Ocean Currents
Accidents can sometimes lead to scientific discovery. For example, on January 10, 1992, 29,000 plastic tub toys spilled overboard when a container ship traveling northwest of Hawaii ran into a storm. In November of that year, those toys began washing up on Alaskan beaches. When oceanographers heard about this, they placed advertisements in newspapers along the Alaskan coast asking people who found the toys to call them. Altogether, hundreds of toys were recovered. Using recovery dates and locations and computer models, oceanographers were able to re-create the toys' drift and figure out which currents carried the toys. As for the remaining toys, currents may carry them to a number of different destinations. Some may travel through the Arctic Ocean and eventually reach Europe!

Math ACTIVITY
Between January 10, 1992, and November 16, 1992, some of the toys were carried approximately 3,220 km from the cargo-spill site to the coast of Alaska. Calculate the average distance traveled by these toys per day. (Hint: The year 1992 was a leap year.)

Science, Technology, and Society
Red Tides
Imagine going to the beach only to find that the ocean water has turned red and that a lot of fish are floating belly up. What could cause such damage to the ocean? It may surprise you to find that the answer is single-celled algae. When certain algae grow rapidly, they clump together on the ocean's surface in what are known as algal blooms. These algal blooms have been commonly called *red tides* because the blooms often turn the water red or reddish-brown. The term scientists use for these sudden explosions in algae growth is *harmful algal blooms* (HABs). The blooms are harmful because certain species of algae produce toxins that can poison fish, shellfish, and people who eat poisoned fish or shellfish. Toxic blooms can be carried hundreds of miles on ocean currents. HABs can ride into an area on an ocean current and cause fish to die and people who eat the poisoned fish or shellfish to become ill.

Social Studies ACTIVITY
Some scientists think that factors related to human activities, such as agricultural runoff into the ocean, are causing more HABs than occurred in the past. Other scientists disagree. Find out more about this issue, and have a class debate about the roles humans play in creating HABs.

Science, Technology, and Society
Background
Of the 4,400 phytoplankton species, a mere 50 to 60 can produce toxins. Even a small dose of the toxin of certain species can prove fatal. The best way for consumers to reduce the chances of buying poisoned seafood is to shop at a reputable seafood store. Seafood purchased at reputable supermarkets, restaurants, and seafood stores.

Answer to Social Studies Activity
At present, no definitive study links HABs to human activities; all information is still speculation. Activities considered to be either directly or indirectly related to the cause of HABs include overfishing, global warming, and ocean-nutrient fluctuations due to coastal development and water runoff.

442 Chapter 14 • The Movement of Ocean Water

Careers

Cristina Castro

Marine Biologist Have you ever imagined watching whales for a living? Cristina Castro does. Castro works as a marine biologist with the Pacific Whale Foundation in Ecuador. She is studying the migratory patterns of a whale species known as the *humpback whale*. Each year, the humpback whale migrates from feeding grounds in the Antarctic to the warm waters off Ecuador, where the whales breed. Her studies take place largely in the Machalilla National Park. The park is a two-mile stretch of beach that is protected by the government of Ecuador.

In her research, Cristina Castro focuses on the connection between El Niño events and the number of humpback whales in the waters off Ecuador. Castro believes that during an El Niño event, the waters off Ecuador are too hot for the whales. When the whales get hot, they have a difficult time cooling off because they have a thick coat of blubber that provides insulation. So, Castro believes that the whales stay in colder waters during an El Niño event.

Language Arts ACTIVITY

WRITING SKILL Research the humpback whale's migratory route from Antarctica to Ecuador. Write a short story in which you tell of the migration from the point of view of a young whale.

To learn more about these Science in Action topics, visit go.hrw.com and type in the keyword **HZ5H2OF**.

Current Science Check out Current Science® articles related to this chapter by visiting go.hrw.com. Just type in the keyword **HZ5CS14**.

Career in Science

Background

Cristina Castro earned a bachelor's degree in Biology and Chemistry from the Central University in Ecuador in 1996. She went on to earn a doctorate degree in Biology there in 2001. Castro directs an environmental education program that teaches kids how to protect the local marine ecosystem through performing arts and training workshops. Castro has written two books: Elana la Ballena (*Elena the Whale*) and Los Riqueza Del Mar (*The Riches of the Sea*). Her books are designed for the children living in the jungles and along the coast of Ecuador.

Answer to Language Arts Activity
Students can research information about the migration route of humpback whales by using the Internet or library resources. Encourage students to be creative when they write their short stories. Also, encourage students to read their short stories to the class.

UNIT 6

TIMELINE

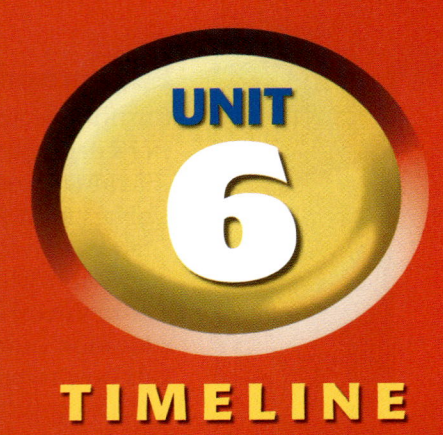

Weather and Climate

In this unit, you will learn about Earth's atmosphere, including how it affects conditions on the Earth's surface. The constantly changing weather is always a good topic for conversation, but forecasting the weather is not an easy task. Climate, on the other hand, is much more predictable. This timeline shows some of the events that have occurred as scientists have tried to better understand Earth's atmosphere, weather, and climate.

1281
A sudden typhoon destroys a fleet of Mongolian ships about to reach Japan. This "divine wind," or *kamikaze* in Japanese, saves the country from invasion and conquest.

1778
Carl Scheele concludes that air is mostly made of nitrogen and oxygen.

1838
John James Audubon publishes *The Birds of America*.

1974
Chlorofluorocarbons (CFCs) are recognized as harmful to the ozone layer.

1982
Weather information becomes available 24 hours a day, 7 days a week, on commercial TV.

1655
Saturn's rings are recognized as such. Galileo Galilei had seen them in 1610, but his telescope was not strong enough to show that they were rings.

1718
Gabriel Fahrenheit builds the first mercury thermometer.

1749
Benjamin Franklin explains how updrafts of air are caused by the sun's heating of the local atmosphere.

1920
Serbian scientist Milutin Milankovitch determines that over tens of thousands of years, changes in the Earth's motion through space have profound effects on climate.

1945
The first atmospheric test of an atomic bomb takes place near Alamogordo, New Mexico.

1985
Scientists discover an ozone hole over Antarctica.

1986
The world's worst nuclear accident takes place at Chernobyl, Ukraine, and spreads radiation through the atmosphere as far as the western United States.

1999
The first nonstop balloon trip around the world is successfully completed when Brian Jones and Bertrand Piccard land in Egypt.

2003
A record 393 tornadoes are observed in the United States during one week in May.

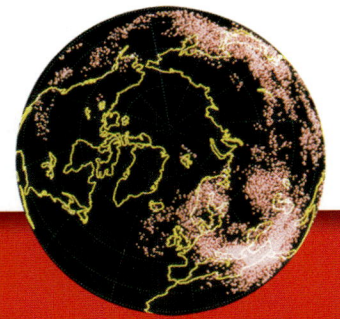

The path of radioactive material released from Chernobyl

The Breitling Orbiter 3 lands in Egypt on March 21, 1999.

Weather and Climate 445

15 The Atmosphere
Chapter Planning Guide

Compression guide: To shorten instruction because of time limitations, omit the Chapter Lab.

OBJECTIVES	LABS, DEMONSTRATIONS, AND ACTIVITIES	TECHNOLOGY RESOURCES
PACING • 90 min pp. 446–453 **Chapter Opener**	SE **Start-up Activity,** p. 447 GENERAL	OSP **Parent Letter** GENERAL CD **Student Edition on CD-ROM** CD **Guided Reading Audio CD** TR **Chapter Starter Transparency*** VID **Brain Food Video Quiz**
Section 1 Characteristics of the Atmosphere • Describe the composition of Earth's atmosphere. • Explain why air pressure changes with altitude. • Explain how air temperature changes with atmospheric composition. • Describe the layers of the atmosphere.	SE **Connection to Physics** Air-Pressure Experiment, p. 449 GENERAL TE **Group Activity** It's a Gas!, p. 449 ADVANCED SE **Skills Practice Lab** Under Pressure! p. 472 GENERAL CRF **Datasheet for Chapter Lab*** LB **Whiz-Bang Demonstrations** Blue Sky* ADVANCED	CRF **Lesson Plans*** TR **Bellringer Transparency*** TR **Layers of the Atmosphere*** TR **LINK TO LIFE SCIENCE** The Connection Between Photosynthesis and Respiration* VID **Lab Videos for Earth Science**
PACING • 90 min pp. 454–457 **Section 2 Atmospheric Heating** • Describe what happens to solar energy that reaches Earth. • Summarize the processes of radiation, conduction, and convection. • Explain the relationship between the greenhouse effect and global warming.	TE **Activity** Popcorn, p. 454 BASIC TE **Connection to Environmental Science,** p. 455 GENERAL TE **Group Activity** Model Greenhouses, p. 456 BASIC LB **Inquiry Labs** Boiling Over!* GENERAL LB **EcoLabs & Field Activities** That Greenhouse Effect!* GENERAL LB **Calculator-Based Lab** The Greenhouse Effect* ADVANCED LB **Calculator-Based Lab** Heating of Land and Water* ADVANCED	CRF **Lesson Plans*** TR **Bellringer Transparency*** TR **Scattering, Absorption, and Reflection*** TR **Radiation, Conduction, and Convection*** TR **The Greenhouse Effect***
PACING • 45 min pp. 458–463 **Section 3 Global Winds and Local Winds** • Explain the relationship between air pressure and wind direction. • Describe global wind patterns. • Explain the causes of local wind patterns.	TE **Demonstration** Air Movement, p. 458 GENERAL TE **Activity** Coriolis Effect, p. 460 BASIC SE **Connection to Social Studies** Local Breezes, p. 463 GENERAL SE **Skills Practice Lab** Go Fly a Bike!, p. 746 GENERAL CRF **Datasheet for LabBook*** SE **Science in Action** Math, Social Studies, and Language Arts, pp. 478–479 GENERAL	CRF **Lesson Plans*** TR **Bellringer Transparency*** TR **Pressure Belts*** TR **The Coriolis Effect*** TR **Global Winds*** TR **Sea and Land Breezes***
PACING • 45 min pp. 464–471 **Section 4 Air Pollution** • Compare primary and secondary air pollutants. • Identify the major sources of air pollution. • Explain the effects of an ozone hole. • List five effects of air pollution on the human body. • Identify ways to reduce air pollution.	SE **Connection to Biology** Cleaning the Air with Plants, p. 466 GENERAL TE **Connection Activity** Real World, p. 466 GENERAL SE **Quick Lab** Testing for Particulates, p. 467 GENERAL CRF **Datasheet for Quick Lab*** TE **Demonstration** Acid Rain, p. 467 BASIC TE **Connection Activity** Health, p. 469 GENERAL SE **School-to-Home Activity** Air Pollution Awareness, p. 470 GENERAL TE **Internet Activity,** p. 470 GENERAL LB **Long-Term Projects & Research Ideas** A Breath of Fresh Ether?* ADVANCED	CRF **Lesson Plans*** TR **Bellringer Transparency*** TR **The Formation of Smog*** TR **Sources of Indoor Air Pollution*** CRF **SciLinks Activity*** GENERAL CD **Interactive Explorations CD-ROM** Moose Malady GENERAL

PACING • 90 min

CHAPTER REVIEW, ASSESSMENT, AND STANDARDIZED TEST PREPARATION
- CRF **Vocabulary Activity*** GENERAL
- SE **Chapter Review,** pp. 474–475 GENERAL
- CRF **Chapter Review*** GENERAL
- CRF **Chapter Tests A*** GENERAL, **B*** ADVANCED, **C*** SPECIAL NEEDS
- SE **Standardized Test Preparation,** pp. 476–477 GENERAL
- CRF **Standardized Test Preparation*** GENERAL
- CRF **Performance-Based Assessment*** GENERAL
- OSP **Test Generator** GENERAL
- CRF **Test Item Listing*** GENERAL

Online and Technology Resources

Visit go.hrw.com for a variety of free resources related to this textbook. Enter the keyword **HZ5ATM**.

Holt Online Learning — Students can access interactive problem-solving help and active visual concept development with the *Holt Science and Technology* Online Edition available at **www.hrw.com**.

Guided Reading Audio CD Also in Spanish
A direct reading of each chapter for auditory learners, reluctant readers, and Spanish-speaking students.

Science Tutor CD-ROM
Excellent for remediation and test practice.

KEY

SE Student Edition	**CRF** Chapter Resource File	**SS** Science Skills Worksheets	***** Also on One-Stop Planner
TE Teacher Edition	**OSP** One-Stop Planner	**MS** Math Skills for Science Worksheets	♦ Requires advance prep
	LB Lab Bank	**CD** CD or CD-ROM	■ Also available in Spanish
	TR Transparencies	**VID** Classroom Video/DVD	

SKILLS DEVELOPMENT RESOURCES	SECTION REVIEW AND ASSESSMENT	STANDARDS CORRELATIONS
SE Pre-Reading Activity, p. 446 GENERAL **OSP** Science Puzzlers, Twisters & Teasers GENERAL		National Science Education Standards SAI 1
CRF Directed Reading A* ■ BASIC, B* SPECIAL NEEDS **CRF** Vocabulary and Section Summary* GENERAL **SE** Reading Strategy Mnemonics, p. 448 GENERAL **TE** Reading Strategy Reading Organizer, p. 449 BASIC **SE** Math Practice Modeling the Atmosphere, p. 450 GENERAL **TE** Inclusion Strategies, p. 451 **CRF** Reinforcement Worksheet Earth's Amazing Atmosphere* BASIC	**SE** Reading Checks, pp. 448, 450, 452 GENERAL **TE** Reteaching, p. 452 BASIC **TE** Quiz, p. 452 GENERAL **TE** Alternative Assessment, p. 452 GENERAL **SE** Section Review,* p. 453 ■ GENERAL **CRF** Section Quiz* ■ GENERAL	SPSP 1,3,4; ES 1h
CRF Directed Reading A* ■ BASIC, B* SPECIAL NEEDS **CRF** Vocabulary and Section Summary* GENERAL **SE** Reading Strategy Reading Organizer, p. 454 GENERAL **TE** Inclusion Strategies, p. 455 ♦	**SE** Reading Checks, pp. 455, 457 GENERAL **TE** Reteaching, p. 456 BASIC **TE** Quiz, p. 456 GENERAL **TE** Alternative Assessment, p. 456 GENERAL **SE** Section Review,* p. 457 ■ GENERAL **CRF** Section Quiz* ■ GENERAL	UCP 2 ; SAI 2; SPSP 3, 4
CRF Directed Reading A* ■ BASIC, B* SPECIAL NEEDS **CRF** Vocabulary and Section Summary* GENERAL **SE** Reading Strategy Prediction Guide, p. 458 GENERAL	**SE** Reading Checks, pp. 459, 460, 463 GENERAL **TE** Homework, p. 460 GENERAL **TE** Reteaching, p. 462 BASIC **TE** Quiz, p. 462 GENERAL **TE** Alternative Assessment, p. 462 ♦ GENERAL **SE** Section Review,* p. 463 ■ GENERAL **CRF** Section Quiz* ■ GENERAL	ES 1j; *LabBook:* UCP 2; SAI 1; ST 1
CRF Directed Reading A* ■ BASIC, B* SPECIAL NEEDS **CRF** Vocabulary and Section Summary* GENERAL **SE** Reading Strategy Reading Organizer, p. 464 GENERAL **CRF** Critical Thinking The Extraordinary GBG5K* ADVANCED	**SE** Reading Checks, pp. 464, 467, 468, 470 GENERAL **TE** Homework, p. 468 GENERAL **TE** Homework, p. 469 ADVANCED **TE** Reteaching, p. 470 BASIC **TE** Quiz, p. 470 GENERAL **TE** Alternative Assessment, p. 470 BASIC **SE** Section Review,* p. 471 ■ GENERAL **CRF** Section Quiz* ■ GENERAL	SAI 1; SPSP 3, 4; *Chapter Lab:* SAI 1

One-Stop Planner® CD-ROM

This convenient CD-ROM includes:
- Lab Materials QuickList Software
- Holt Calendar Planner
- Customizable Lesson Plans
- Printable Worksheets
- ExamView® Test Generator

CNN Student News

cnnstudentnews.com

Find the latest news, lesson plans, and activities related to important scientific events.

SciLinks NSTA

www.scilinks.org

Maintained by the **National Science Teachers Association**. See Chapter Enrichment pages for a complete list of topics.

Current Science®

Check out *Current Science* articles and activities by visiting the HRW Web site at **go.hrw.com**. Just type in the keyword **HZ5CS15T**.

Classroom Videos

- **Lab Videos** demonstrate the chapter lab.
- **Brain Food Video Quizzes** help students review the chapter material.
- **CNN Videos** bring science into your students' daily life.

Chapter 15 • Chapter Planning Guide

15 Chapter Resources

Visual Resources

CHAPTER STARTER TRANSPARENCY

BELLRINGER TRANSPARENCIES

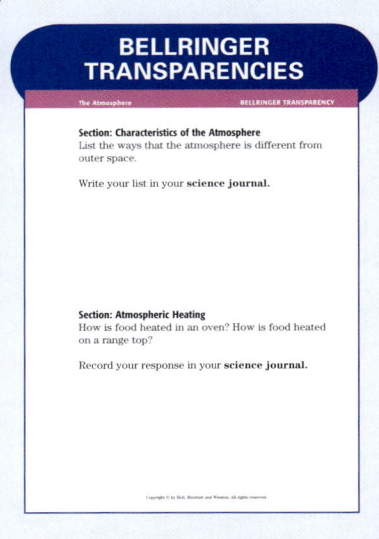

Section: Characteristics of the Atmosphere
List the ways that the atmosphere is different from outer space.

Write your list in your **science journal**.

Section: Atmospheric Heating
How is food heated in an oven? How is food heated on a range top?

Record your response in your **science journal**.

TEACHING TRANSPARENCIES

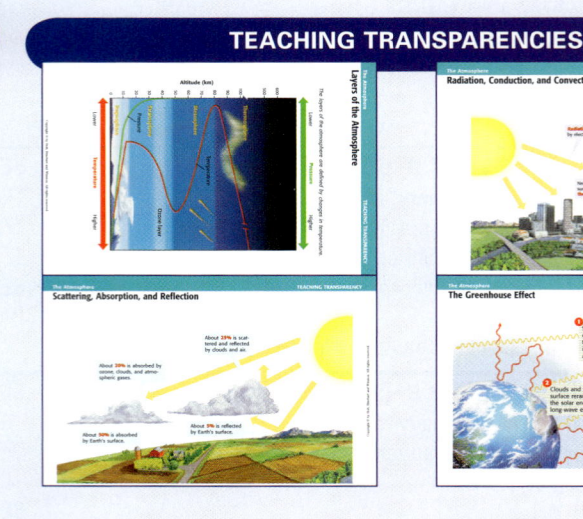

- Layers of the Atmosphere
- Radiation, Conduction, and Convection
- Scattering, Absorption, and Reflection
- The Greenhouse Effect

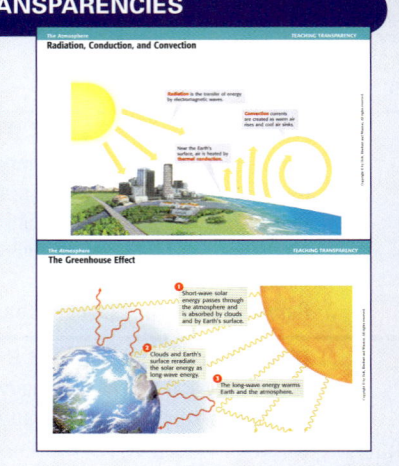

TEACHING TRANSPARENCIES

- Pressure Belts
- Global Winds
- The Coriolis Effect
- Sea and Land Breezes
- The Connection Between Photosynthesis and Respiration — **LINK TO LIFE SCIENCE** — Chapter: The Cell in Action

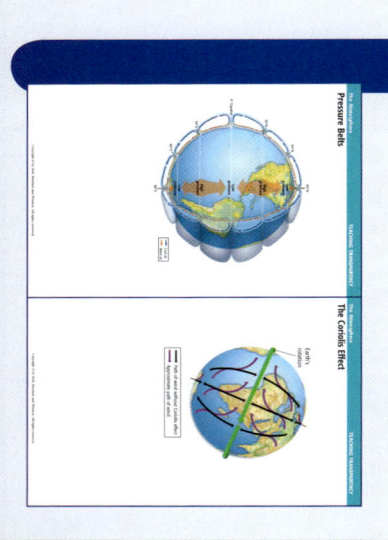

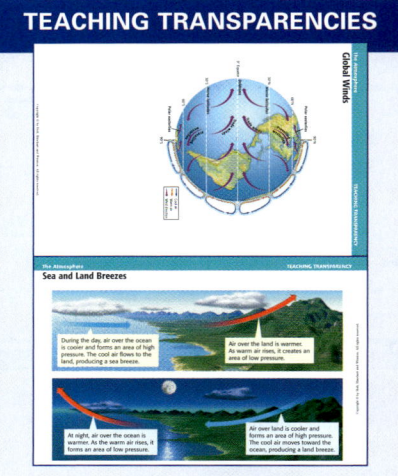

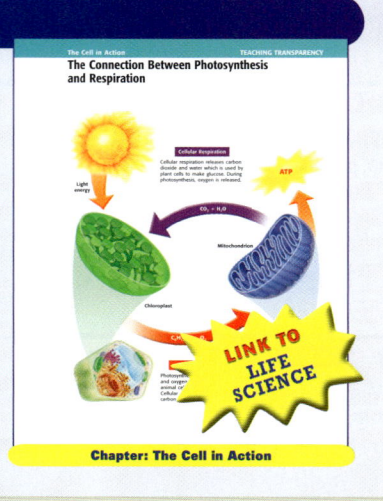

CONCEPT MAPPING TRANSPARENCY

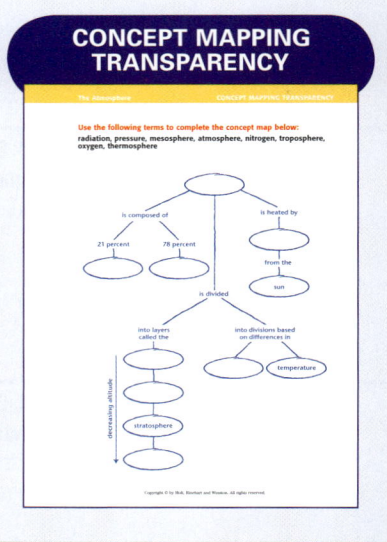

Use the following terms to complete the concept map below: radiation, pressure, mesosphere, atmosphere, nitrogen, troposphere, oxygen, thermosphere

Planning Resources

LESSON PLANS

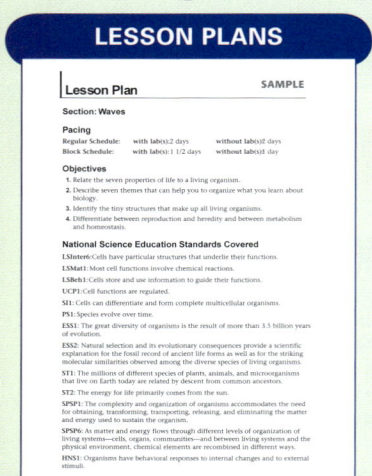

PARENT LETTER
ALSO IN SPANISH

TEST ITEM LISTING

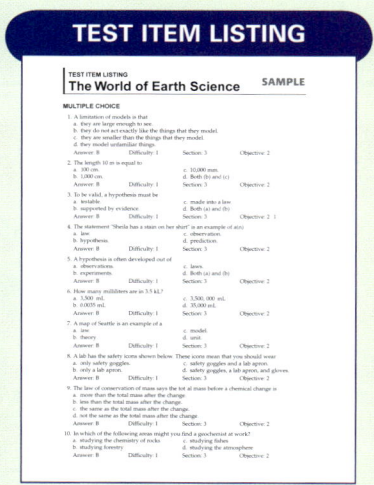

One-Stop Planner® CD-ROM

This CD-ROM includes all of the resources shown here and the following time-saving tools:

- **Lab Materials QuickList Software**
- **Customizable lesson plans**
- **Holt Calendar Planner**
- **The powerful ExamView® Test Generator**

445C Chapter 15 • The Atmosphere

For a preview of available worksheets covering math and science skills, see pages T26–T33. All of these resources are also on the One-Stop Planner®.

Meeting Individual Needs

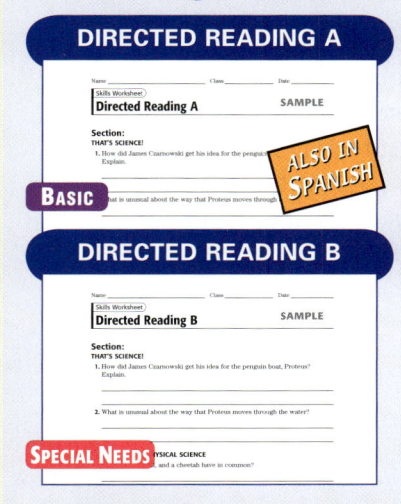

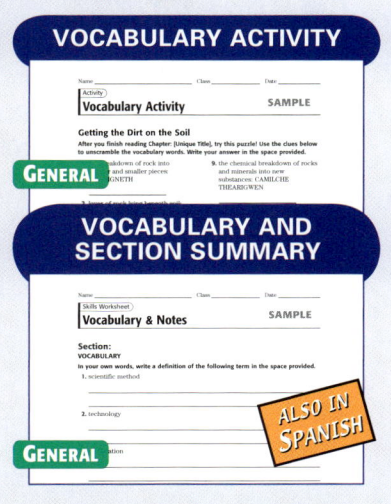

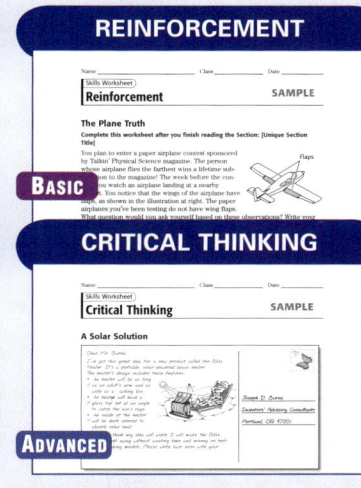

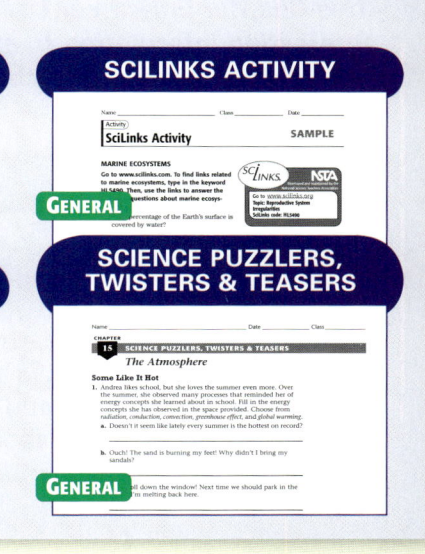

- **DIRECTED READING A** — BASIC (ALSO IN SPANISH)
- **DIRECTED READING B** — SPECIAL NEEDS
- **VOCABULARY ACTIVITY** — GENERAL
- **VOCABULARY AND SECTION SUMMARY** — GENERAL (ALSO IN SPANISH)
- **REINFORCEMENT** — BASIC
- **CRITICAL THINKING** — ADVANCED
- **SCILINKS ACTIVITY** — GENERAL
- **SCIENCE PUZZLERS, TWISTERS & TEASERS** — GENERAL

Labs and Activities

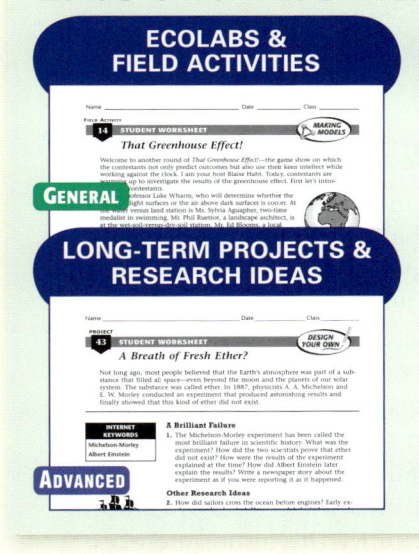

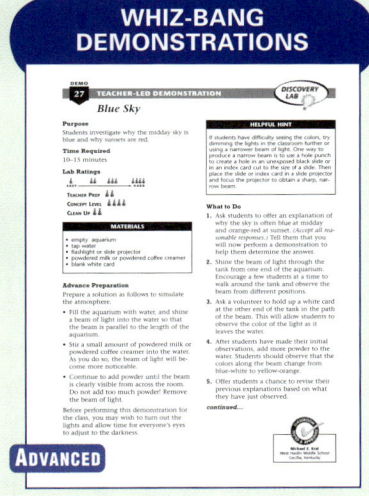

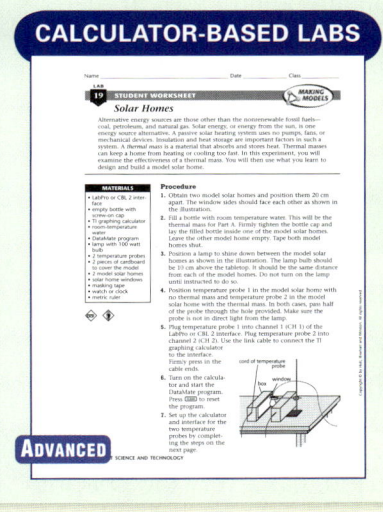

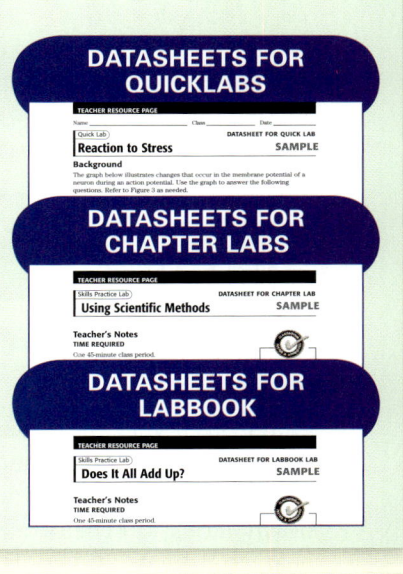

- **ECOLABS & FIELD ACTIVITIES** — GENERAL
- **LONG-TERM PROJECTS & RESEARCH IDEAS** — ADVANCED
- **WHIZ-BANG DEMONSTRATIONS** — ADVANCED
- **CALCULATOR-BASED LABS** — ADVANCED
- **DATASHEETS FOR QUICKLABS**
- **DATASHEETS FOR CHAPTER LABS**
- **DATASHEETS FOR LABBOOK**

Review and Assessments

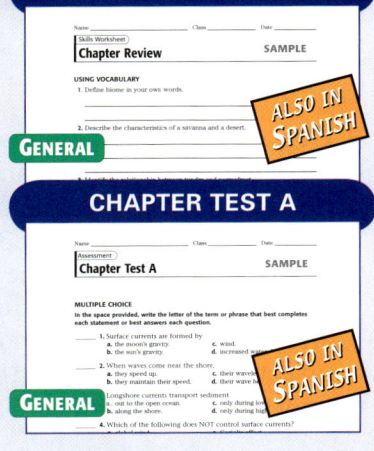

- **SECTION QUIZ** — GENERAL (ALSO IN SPANISH)
- **SECTION REVIEW** — GENERAL
- **CHAPTER REVIEW** — GENERAL (ALSO IN SPANISH)
- **CHAPTER TEST A** — GENERAL (ALSO IN SPANISH)
- **CHAPTER TEST B** — ADVANCED
- **CHAPTER TEST C** — SPECIAL NEEDS
- **STANDARDIZED TEST PREPARATION** — GENERAL
- **PERFORMANCE-BASED ASSESSMENT** — GENERAL

Chapter 15 • Chapter Resources 445D

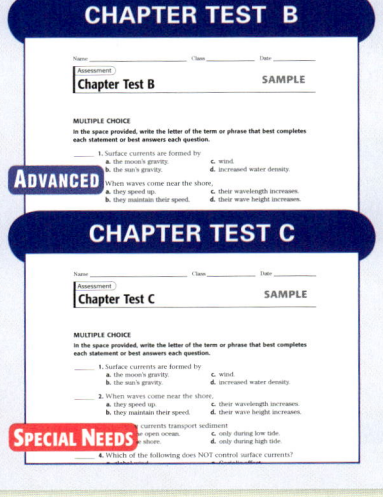

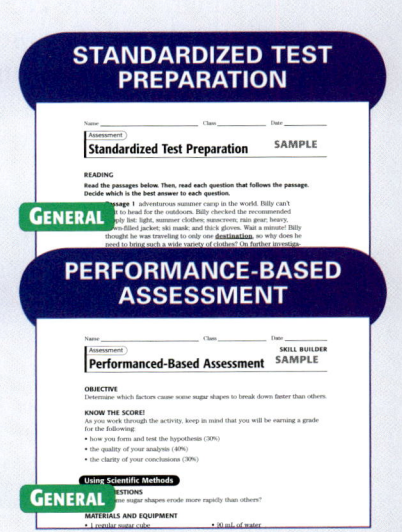

15 Chapter Enrichment

This Chapter Enrichment provides relevant and interesting information to expand and enhance your presentation of the chapter material.

Section 1

Characteristics of the Atmosphere

Take a Deep Breath!

- Near the Earth's surface, the atmosphere consists of 78.08% nitrogen, 20.95% oxygen, 0.93% argon, 0.03% carbon dioxide, and traces of water vapor. Scientists theorize that about 95% of the oxygen present in today's atmosphere formed as a byproduct of photosynthesis.

Is That a Fact!

◆ The Earth's troposphere contains almost 90% of the atmosphere's total mass. In the troposphere, temperature decreases at an average rate of 6.4°C/km as altitude increases.

Section 2

Atmospheric Heating

Specific Heat

- Water has a very high *specific heat,* which means that a great deal of thermal energy is needed to increase the temperature of water. Thus, water heats and cools very slowly. Rock, on the other hand, has a very low specific heat, so it heats and cools more quickly. For this reason, areas of high pressure (anticyclones) form over bodies of water, and areas of low pressure (cyclones) form over landmasses during the summer months. During the winter months, cyclones tend to form over bodies of water, and anticyclones tend to form over landmasses.

Is That a Fact!

◆ The summer monsoon in Asia is caused because central Asia heats up more quickly than the Indian Ocean. As the air above central Asia warms, it rises, creating an area of low pressure that draws moisture-laden air toward central Asia. When this moist air encounters the Himalayas, it cools quickly and releases its moisture in the form of torrential rains.

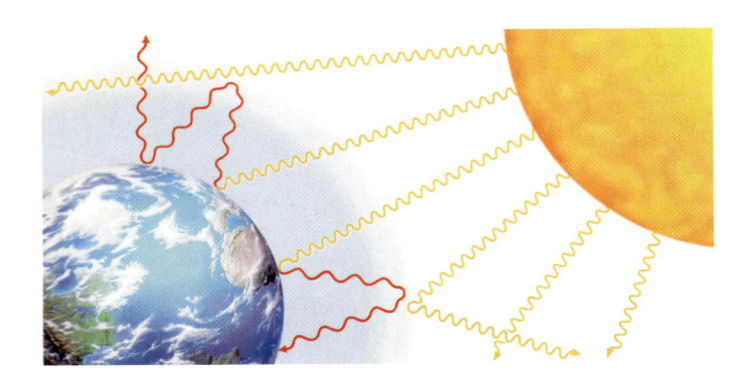

Global Warming—An Idea Before Its Time!

- Since the 1970s, global warming has been a topic of concern. However, a global warming model was proposed as early as 1896 by a Swedish physicist and chemist named Svante Arrhenius. Arrhenius theorized that the carbon dioxide released from burning coal would increase the intensity of Earth's greenhouse effect and lead to global warming. In 1954, it was first suggested that deforestation increases the amount of CO_2 in the atmosphere. Since then, numerous scientific studies have examined the effects of carbon dioxide on the temperature of Earth's atmosphere.

Section 3

Global Winds and Local Winds

Gustave Coriolis

- Gustave Gaspard Coriolis was a French mathematician and engineer who lived and worked in Paris from 1792 to 1843. His most well-known contribution to science is a paper published in 1835 that introduces the Coriolis effect. In "On the Equations of Relative Motion of Systems of Bodies," Coriolis argued that an inertial force (the Coriolis force) acts on a rotating object at a right angle to the object's motion. We now know that the "Coriolis force" is an apparent force.

445E Chapter 15 • The Atmosphere

- The rotation of the Earth causes matter in motion to appear to be deflected from its path. The Coriolis effect influences the general direction of global winds and open-ocean circulation, as well as the rotational movements of weather systems, such as cyclones and anticyclones.

Is That a Fact!
♦ When airplanes fly north or south, pilots have to make corrections to counteract the Coriolis effect.

Convection Cells
- The major convection cells on the Earth's surface have specific names. The cells that circulate between 30° north latitude and 30° south latitude are called *Hadley cells* after an English meteorologist. The cells that circulate between 30° north latitude and 60° north latitude and between 30° south latitude and 60° south latitude are called *Ferrel cells* after an American meteorologist. The cells that circulate between 90° and 60° are called *polar cells* because they are closest to the poles.

Jet Streaks
- Jet streaks are winds within jet streams that flow faster than the adjacent winds. Jet streaks influence storm formation and associated precipitation. Rising jet streaks and the low-pressure area that forms beneath them present favorable conditions for storms to form. Sinking jet streaks inhibit storm formation and precipitation.

Section 4
Air Pollution
Global Distillation
- Scientists have found high levels of airborne contaminants in the breast milk of Inuit women in Greenland and Arctic Canada. Researchers think the contaminants arrived in these remote areas by a process called global distillation. In this process, contaminants are redistributed around the globe by atmospheric currents. Contaminants tend to concentrate in polar areas for the same reason that water vapor condenses on cold glass: gaseous substances tend to condense at colder temperatures.

SciLinks

SciLinks is maintained by the National Science Teachers Association to provide you and your students with interesting, up-to-date links that will enrich your classroom presentation of the chapter.

Visit www.scilinks.org and enter the SciLinks code for more information about the topic listed.

Topic: Composition of the Atmosphere
SciLinks code: HSM0328

Topic: Energy in the Atmosphere
SciLinks code: HSM0512

Topic: Greenhouse Effect
SciLinks code: HSM0694

Topic: Atmospheric Pressure and Winds
SciLinks code: HSM0115

Topic: Air Pollution
SciLinks code: HSM0033

Chapter 15 • Chapter Enrichment

Overview

Tell students that this chapter will help them learn about the atmosphere. They will study the circulation of energy in the atmosphere and the greenhouse effect. They will also learn about global winds and air pollution.

Assessing Prior Knowledge

Students should be familiar with the following topics:

- changes of state
- radiation, conduction, and convection

Identifying Misconceptions

Because air cannot be seen, students may assume that the atmosphere has no mass and is therefore not subject to the physical laws that affect matter. Point out that air, like water, is a fluid. A *fluid* is any material that can flow and that takes the shape of its container. Students may find it easier to visualize wind if they think of air flowing like water. For example, the Coriolis effect affects the ocean currents as well as the global winds. Similarly, the convection of gases in the atmosphere is similar to the convection of bodies of water in the ocean. Be sure to explain that all fluids move according to specific laws of fluid dynamics.

15
The Atmosphere

SECTION 1	Characteristics of the Atmosphere	448
SECTION 2	Atmospheric Heating	454
SECTION 3	Global Winds and Local Winds	458
SECTION 4	Air Pollution	464

Chapter Lab 472
Chapter Review 474
Standardized Test Preparation 476
Science in Action 478

About the PHOTO

Imagine climbing a mountain and taking only one out of three breaths! As altitude increases, the density of the atmosphere decreases. At the heights shown in this picture, the atmosphere is so thin that it contains only 30% of the amount of oxygen found in the atmosphere at sea level. So, most mountaineers carry part of their atmosphere with them—in the form of oxygen tanks.

PRE-READING ACTIVITY

FOLDNOTES Booklet Before you read the chapter, create the FoldNote entitled "Booklet" described in the **Study Skills** section of the Appendix. Label each page of the booklet with a main idea from the chapter. As you read the chapter, write what you learn about each main idea on the appropriate page of the booklet.

Standards Correlations

National Science Education Standards

The following codes indicate the National Science Education Standards that correlate to this chapter. The full text of the standards is at the front of the book.

Chapter Opener
SAI 1

Section 1 Characteristics of the Atmosphere
SPSP 1, 3, 4; ES 1h

Section 2 Atmospheric Heating
UCP 2 ; SAI 2; SPSP 3, 4; ES 2a; *LabBook:* SAI 1; ST 1

Section 3 Global Winds and Local Winds
ES 1j, 3d; *LabBook:* UCP 3; SAI 1; ST 1

Section 4 Air Pollution
SAI 1; SPSP 3, 4

Chapter Lab
SAI 1; ST 1

446   Chapter 15 • The Atmosphere

START-UP ACTIVITY

Does Air Have Mass?

In this activity, you will compare an inflated balloon with a deflated balloon to find out if air has mass.

Procedure

1. In a **notebook,** answer the following questions: Does air have mass? Will an inflated balloon weigh more than a deflated balloon?
2. Inflate **two large balloons,** and tie the balloons closed. Attach each balloon to opposite ends of a **meterstick** using identical **pushpins.** Balance the meterstick on a **pencil** held by a volunteer. Check that the meterstick is perfectly balanced.
3. Predict what will happen when you pop one balloon. Record your predictions.
4. Put on **safety goggles,** and carefully pop one of the balloons with a **pushpin.**
5. Record your observations.

Analysis

1. Explain your observations. Was your prediction correct?
2. Based on your results, does air have mass? If air has mass, is the atmosphere affected by Earth's gravity? Explain your answers.

Chapter Review
ES 1h, 1j, 2a, 3d

Science in Action
HNS 1; SPSP 5

Chapter Starter Transparency
Use this transparency to help students begin thinking about the atmosphere.

START-UP ACTIVITY

MATERIALS

FOR THE CLASS
- balloon, large (2)
- meterstick
- notebook
- pencil
- pushpins (3)
- safety goggles

Teacher's Note: This activity may work best as a demonstration. You may find it easier to balance the meterstick yourself, or to create a stand on which to balance the meterstick.

Answers

1. Answers may vary. Students should note that the meterstick became unbalanced when the balloon was popped. The reason for this change is that the popped balloon contained air, which has mass.
2. Sample answer: Yes, air has mass. Because air has mass, it is subject to the gravitational attraction of the Earth. The atmosphere is held around the Earth by gravity.

CHAPTER RESOURCES

Technology
- **Transparencies**
  - Chapter Starter Transparency READING SKILLS
- **Student Edition on CD-ROM**
- **Guided Reading Audio CD**
  - English or Spanish
- **Classroom Videos**
  - Brain Food Video Quiz

Workbooks
- **Science Puzzlers, Twisters & Teasers**
  - The Atmosphere GENERAL

Chapter 15 • The Atmosphere   447

SECTION 1

Focus

Overview
This section defines the atmosphere and explains its basic characteristics. It describes the atmosphere's composition and explains how pressure and temperature are related to altitude. The section also discusses the four layers of the Earth's atmosphere.

🔔 Bellringer
Have students list the ways that the atmosphere is different from outer space. Tell students that a little more than a century ago, many scientists believed that the Earth's atmosphere blended with a hypothetical substance called *ether* that filled the entire universe. In 1887, the physicist A. A. Michelson demonstrated that the universe is not filled with ether.

Motivate

Identifying Preconceptions — GENERAL

Atmospheric Composition
Before students read the section, ask them these questions:

- What is the most common gas in the atmosphere? (nitrogen)
- Does air contain anything other than gases? (solids, such as dust, and liquids, such as water)

LS Logical

SECTION 1

READING WARM-UP

Objectives
- Describe the composition of Earth's atmosphere.
- Explain why air pressure changes with altitude.
- Explain how air temperature changes with atmospheric composition.
- Describe the layers of the atmosphere.

Terms to Learn
atmosphere
air pressure
troposphere
stratosphere
mesosphere
thermosphere

READING STRATEGY
Mnemonics As you read this section, create a mnemonic device to help you remember the layers of the Earth's atmosphere.

CHAPTER RESOURCES

Chapter Resource File
- Lesson Plan
- Directed Reading A BASIC
- Directed Reading B SPECIAL NEEDS

Technology
- Transparencies
  - Bellringer
  - **LINK TO LIFE SCIENCE** The Connection Between Photosynthesis and Respiration

---

Characteristics of the Atmosphere

If you were lost in the desert, you could survive for a few days without food and water. But you wouldn't last more than five minutes without the atmosphere.

The **atmosphere** is a mixture of gases that surrounds Earth. In addition to containing the oxygen you need to breathe, the atmosphere protects you from the sun's damaging rays. The atmosphere is always changing. Every breath you take, every tree that is planted, and every vehicle you ride in affects the atmosphere's composition.

The Composition of the Atmosphere

As you can see in **Figure 1**, the atmosphere is made up mostly of nitrogen gas. The oxygen you breathe makes up a little more than 20% of the atmosphere. In addition to containing nitrogen and oxygen, the atmosphere contains small particles, such as dust, volcanic ash, sea salt, dirt, and smoke. The next time you turn off the lights at night, shine a flashlight, and you will see some of these tiny particles floating in the air.

Water is also found in the atmosphere. Liquid water (water droplets) and solid water (snow and ice crystals) are found in clouds. But most water in the atmosphere exists as an invisible gas called *water vapor*. When atmospheric conditions change, water vapor can change into solid or liquid water, and rain or snow might fall from the sky.

✓ **Reading Check** Describe the three physical states of water in the atmosphere. (*See the Appendix for answers to Reading Checks.*)

Figure 1 Composition of the Atmosphere

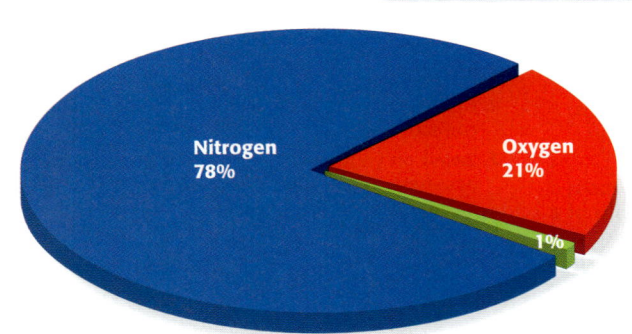

Nitrogen 78%
Oxygen 21%
1%

Nitrogen, the most common atmospheric gas, is released when dead plants and dead animals break down and when volcanoes erupt.

Oxygen, the second most common atmospheric gas, is made by phytoplankton and plants.

The **remaining 1%** of the atmosphere is made up of argon, carbon dioxide, water vapor, and other gases.

Answer to Reading Check
Water can be liquid (rain), solid (snow or ice), or gas (water vapor).

---

448 Chapter 15 • The Atmosphere

Atmospheric Pressure and Temperature

What would carrying a column of air that is 700 km high feel like? You may be surprised to learn that you carry this load every day. While air is not very heavy, its weight adds up. At sea level, a square inch of surface area is under almost 15 lb of air. Carrying that much air on such a small surface area is like carrying a large bowling ball on the tip of your finger!

As Altitude Increases, Air Pressure Decreases

The atmosphere is held around the Earth by gravity. Gravity pulls gas molecules in the atmosphere toward the Earth's surface, causing air pressure. **Air pressure** is the measure of the force with which air molecules push on a surface. Air pressure is strongest at the Earth's surface because more air is above you. As you move farther away from the Earth's surface, fewer gas molecules are above you. So, as altitude (distance from sea level) increases, air pressure decreases. Think of air pressure as a human pyramid, as shown in **Figure 2**. The people at the bottom of the pyramid can feel all the weight and pressure of the people on top. Air pressure works in a similar way.

Atmospheric Composition Affects Air Temperature

Air temperature also changes as altitude increases. The temperature differences result mainly from the way solar energy is absorbed as it moves through the atmosphere. Some parts of the atmosphere are warmer because they contain a high percentage of gases that absorb solar energy. Other parts of the atmosphere contain less of these gases and are cooler.

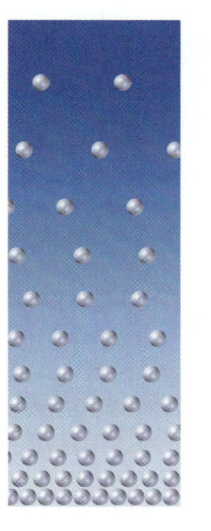

CONNECTION TO Physics

Air-Pressure Experiment Does air pressure push only downward? Try this experiment to find out. Fill a plastic cup to the brim with water. Firmly hold a piece of cardboard over the mouth of the cup. Quickly invert the glass over a sink, and observe what happens. How do the effects of air pressure explain your observations?

ACTIVITY

atmosphere a mixture of gases that surrounds a planet or moon

air pressure the measure of the force with which air molecules push on a surface

Lower pressure

Higher pressure

Figure 2 As in a human pyramid, air pressure increases closer to the Earth's surface.

MISCONCEPTION ALERT

Water Vapor Is a Gas Make sure students realize that water vapor is an invisible gas. The steam they observe coming out of a pot of boiling water is composed of water droplets that form as water vapor cools and condenses on particles in the air. Similarly, clouds appear in the sky when the air cools enough for water vapor to condense and form liquid droplets.

WEIRD SCIENCE

An experiment in 1664 demonstrated the force exerted by air pressure. Most of the air was removed from a hollow sphere whose halves had been sealed together with an airtight gasket. Sixteen horses were needed to pull the metal hemispheres apart!

Teach

Answer to Connection to Physics

Students should see that the cardboard stays on the cup after it is inverted. This is because air pressure exerts force in every direction.

READING STRATEGY — BASIC

Reading Organizer Have students survey the chapter and note the headings and subheadings. Then, ask them to create a outline using the headings and subheadings. As students read the chapter, have them fill in at least two points beneath each heading and subheading. **English Language Learners**
LS Interpersonal

Group ACTIVITY — ADVANCED

It's a Gas! Have small groups demonstrate how oxygen enters the atmosphere. Suggested materials include a freshwater plant, such as *Elodea*, a small, plastic storage beaker, a glass funnel, a test tube, and water. Tell students to immerse the plant in the water-filled beaker and then cover the plant with the inverted funnel. Have them place a water-filled test tube over the funnel's spout and let the setup sit in a well-lighted area for a few days. After this time, students will observe gas bubbles in the test tube. Inform them that the bubbles they see are made of oxygen gas released during the process of photosynthesis.

Use the teaching transparency entitled "The Connection Between Photosynthesis and Respiration" to discuss how the process of photosynthesis produces oxygen. **English Language Learners**
LS Visual

Section 1 • Characteristics of the Atmosphere **449**

Teach, continued

Using the Figure — BASIC

Atmospheric Layers Have students refer to **Figure 3** to answer these questions:

- Which layer of the atmosphere is closest to Earth? (the troposphere)

- How does temperature change within the stratosphere? (For the first few kilometers, the temperature remains fairly constant. Then, the temperature begins rising steeply and levels off again toward the top of the layer.)

- Which atmospheric layer has the greatest range of temperatures? (the thermosphere)

Students may notice that the iridescent cloud in the thermosphere is an aurora and that the white layer near the top of the stratosphere represents the ozone layer. The space shuttles orbit at an altitude of about 300 km. **Visual**

Answer to Reading Check

The troposphere is the layer of turning or change. The stratosphere is the layer in which gases are layered and do not mix vertically. The mesosphere is the middle layer. The thermosphere is the layer in which temperatures are highest.

MATH PRACTICE

Modeling the Atmosphere
In teams, use a metric ruler to create an illustrated scale model of the atmosphere similar to the one shown on this page. Assume that the atmosphere is about 700 km high. If you reduced the height of the atmosphere by a factor of 100,000, your scale model would be 7 m long, and the troposphere would be 16 cm long. Think of a creative way to display your model. You could use sidewalk chalk, stakes and string, poster board, or other materials approved by your teacher. Do some research to add interesting information about each layer.

ACTIVITY

Figure 3 The layers of the atmosphere are defined by changes in temperature.

Layers of the Atmosphere

Based on temperature changes, the Earth's atmosphere is divided into four layers, as shown in **Figure 3**. These layers are the *troposphere, stratosphere, mesosphere,* and *thermosphere.* Although these words might sound complicated, the name of each layer gives you clues about its features.

For example, *-sphere* means "ball," which suggests that each layer of the atmosphere surrounds the Earth like a hollow ball. *Tropo-* means "turning" or "change," and the troposphere is the layer where gases turn and mix. *Strato-* means "layer," and the stratosphere is the sphere where gases are layered and do not mix very much. *Meso-* means "middle," and the mesosphere is the middle layer. Finally, *thermo-* means "heat," and the thermosphere is the sphere where temperatures are highest.

✓ **Reading Check** What does the name of each atmospheric layer mean?

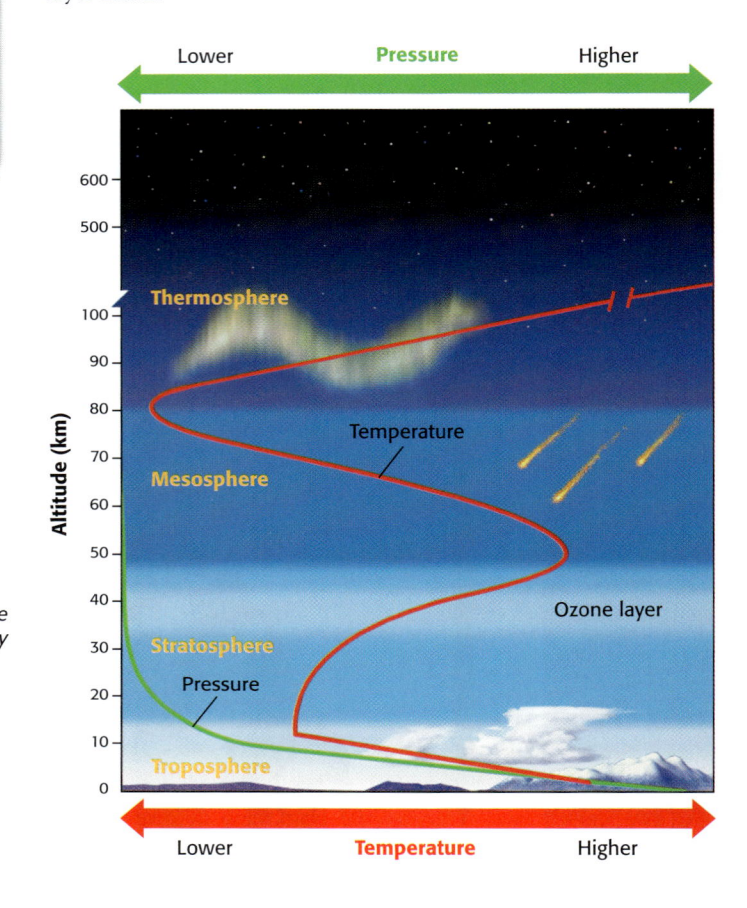

CHAPTER RESOURCES

Technology

Transparencies
- Layers of the Atmosphere

Is That a Fact!

The oxygen in the Earth's current atmosphere is produced primarily by phytoplankton (tiny, drifting sea plants) and land plants that release oxygen during photosynthesis.

The Troposphere: The Layer in Which We Live

The lowest layer of the atmosphere, which lies next to the Earth's surface, is called the **troposphere.** The troposphere is also the densest atmospheric layer. It contains almost 90% of the atmosphere's total mass! Almost all of the Earth's carbon dioxide, water vapor, clouds, air pollution, weather, and life-forms are in the troposphere. As shown in **Figure 4,** temperatures vary greatly in the troposphere. Differences in air temperature and density cause gases in the troposphere to mix continuously.

The Stratosphere: Home of the Ozone Layer

The atmospheric layer above the troposphere is called the **stratosphere. Figure 5** shows the boundary between the stratosphere and the troposphere. Gases in the stratosphere are layered and do not mix as much as gases in the troposphere. The air is also very thin in the stratosphere and contains little moisture. The lower stratosphere is extremely cold. Its temperature averages –60°C. But temperature rises as altitude increases in the stratosphere. This rise happens because ozone in the stratosphere absorbs ultraviolet radiation from the sun, which warms the air. Almost all of the ozone in the stratosphere is contained in the ozone layer. The *ozone layer* protects life on Earth by absorbing harmful ultraviolet radiation.

The Mesosphere: The Middle Layer

Above the stratosphere is the mesosphere. The **mesosphere** is the middle layer of the atmosphere. It is also the coldest layer. As in the troposphere, the temperature decreases as altitude increases in the mesosphere. Temperatures can be as low as –93°C at the top of the mesosphere.

Figure 4 As altitude increases in the troposphere, temperature decreases. Snow remains all year on this mountaintop.

troposphere the lowest layer of the atmosphere, in which temperature decreases at a constant rate as altitude increases

stratosphere the layer of the atmosphere that is above the troposphere and in which temperature increases as altitude increases

mesosphere the layer of the atmosphere between the stratosphere and the thermosphere and in which temperature decreases as altitude increases

Figure 5 This photograph of Earth's atmosphere was taken from space. The troposphere is the yellow layer; the stratosphere is the white layer.

Discussion — ADVANCED

Air Density Remind students that cold air is denser than warm air. This fact is important for pilots to know. Ask students to think about why the Wright brothers tested their biplane early in the morning. (The air is colder and denser in the morning. Dense air provides more lift to a plane's wings, which enables shorter takeoffs. In addition, controls respond more quickly in dense air, and landing speeds are decreased.)

Ask students to apply this logic to explain why people driving jet-powered rocket cars attempt to break the land-speed record at midday on hot salt flats. (The hot air of the salt flats at midday is not very dense, which reduces drag.) **LS Verbal/Logical**

INCLUSION Strategies

- Learning Disabled
- Visually Impaired
- Behavior Control Issues

Organize students into groups of four. Give each group a large piece of poster board, a ruler, magic markers, and self-stick notes. Have groups use a ruler to draw a scale representation of the atmosphere on the poster board. The illustration should be unlabeled. Then, have students label the layers of the atmosphere with self-stick notes. Check the accuracy of the label on each drawing before students proceed. Then, ask each student to write information about each layer on a separate self-stick note. Have them read the fact aloud to the group, and have the rest of the group members attempt to identify the correct layer on which to place the self-stick note. When they have finished, have groups share their models with the rest of the class.
LS Visual/Interpersonal

Section 1 • Characteristics of the Atmosphere   **451**

Close

Reteaching — BASIC

Describing the Atmosphere
On the board, make a table entitled "The Atmosphere." Include the following headings:

"Layer," "Altitude range," "Temperature range," and "Other features."

Have volunteers contribute information for each section of the table.
LS Verbal   English Language Learners

Quiz — GENERAL

1. List the layers of the atmosphere, starting with the one closest to Earth. (troposphere, stratosphere, mesosphere, thermosphere)

2. Explain how density affects the transfer of thermal energy in the air. (The less dense the air is, the less effective it is at transferring thermal energy. Particles must collide with one another to transfer energy. Particles that are farther apart are less likely to collide with other particles.)

Alternative Assessment — GENERAL

Writing **Poetry** Have each student write a poem that creatively yet accurately describes each layer of Earth's atmosphere. Allow time for volunteers to read their poem aloud or to display the poem for others to read on their own.
LS Intrapersonal

---

thermosphere the uppermost layer of the atmosphere, in which temperature increases as altitude increases

The Thermosphere: The Edge of the Atmosphere

The uppermost atmospheric layer is called the **thermosphere.** In the thermosphere, temperature again increases with altitude. Atoms of nitrogen and oxygen absorb high-energy solar radiation and release thermal energy, which causes temperatures in the thermosphere to be 1,000°C or higher.

When you think of an area that has high temperatures, you probably think of a place that is very hot. Although the thermosphere has very high temperatures, it does not feel hot. Temperature is different from heat. Temperature is a measure of the average energy of particles in motion. The high temperature of the thermosphere means that particles in that layer are moving very fast. Heat, however, is the transfer of thermal energy between objects of different temperatures. Particles must touch one another to transfer thermal energy. The space between particles in the thermosphere is so great that particles do not transfer much energy. In other words, the density of the thermosphere is so low that particles do not often collide and transfer energy. **Figure 6** shows how air density affects the heating of the troposphere and the thermosphere.

✓ **Reading Check** Why doesn't the thermosphere feel hot?

Figure 6 Temperature in the Troposphere and the Thermosphere

The **thermosphere** is less dense than the troposphere. So, although particles are moving very fast, they do not transfer much thermal energy.

The **troposphere** is denser than the thermosphere. So, although particles in the troposphere are moving much slower than particles in the thermosphere, they can transfer much more thermal energy.

Answer to Reading Check
The thermosphere does not feel hot because air molecules are spaced far apart and cannot collide to transfer much thermal energy.

CONNECTION to Physical Science — BASIC

Thermal Energy Have students imagine a sink full of hot water. Ask them to pretend that they have removed a cup of the hot water from the sink. Students should agree that both volumes of water have the same temperature at this point. Explain that the sink has more thermal energy than the cup because the sink contains more water (and therefore more particles in motion) than the cup. Ask students to help you come up with other examples to explain these ideas.

452 Chapter 15 • The Atmosphere

The Ionosphere: Home of the Auroras

In the upper mesosphere and the lower thermosphere, nitrogen and oxygen atoms absorb harmful solar energy. As a result, the thermosphere's temperature rises, and gas particles become electrically charged. Electrically charged particles are called *ions*. Therefore, this part of the thermosphere is called the *ionosphere*. As shown in **Figure 7,** in polar regions these ions radiate energy as shimmering lights called *auroras*. The ionosphere also reflects AM radio waves. When conditions are right, an AM radio wave can travel around the world by reflecting off the ionosphere. These radio signals bounce off the ionosphere and are sent back to Earth.

Figure 7 Charged particles in the ionosphere cause auroras, or northern and southern lights.

SECTION Review

Summary

- Nitrogen and oxygen make up most of Earth's atmosphere.
- Air pressure decreases as altitude increases.
- The composition of atmospheric layers affects their temperature.
- The troposphere is the lowest atmospheric layer. It is the layer in which we live.
- The stratosphere contains the ozone layer, which protects us from harmful UV radiation.
- The mesosphere is the coldest atmospheric layer.
- The thermosphere is the uppermost layer of the atmosphere.

Using Key Terms

1. Use each of the following terms in a separate sentence: *air pressure, atmosphere, troposphere, stratosphere, mesosphere,* and *thermosphere*.

Understanding Key Ideas

2. Why does the temperature of different layers of the atmosphere vary?
   a. because air temperature increases as altitude increases
   b. because the amount of energy radiated from the sun varies
   c. because of interference by humans
   d. because of the composition of gases in each layer

3. Why does air pressure decrease as altitude increases?

4. How can the thermosphere have high temperatures but not feel hot?

5. What determines the temperature of atmospheric layers?

6. What two gases make up most of the atmosphere?

Math Skills

7. If an average cloud has a density of 0.5 g/m^3 and has a volume of 1,000,000,000 m^3, what is the weight of an average cloud?

Critical Thinking

8. **Applying Concepts** Apply what you know about the relationship between altitude and air pressure to explain why rescue helicopters have a difficult time flying at altitudes above 6,000 m.

9. **Making Inferences** If the upper atmosphere is very thin, why do space vehicles heat up as they enter the atmosphere?

10. **Making Inferences** Explain why gases such as helium can escape Earth's atmosphere.

SCLINKS. NSTA
Developed and maintained by the National Science Teachers Association

For a variety of links related to this chapter, go to www.scilinks.org
Topic: Composition of the Atmosphere
SciLinks code: HSM0328

Cultural Awareness — GENERAL

The Auroras Different cultures have different explanations for the shimmering lights known as *auroras*. Inuit groups thought of the aurora borealis as the torches of spirits that guided souls from Earth to paradise. Have students find out about other myths concerning the auroras. **LS Intrapersonal**

CHAPTER RESOURCES

Chapter Resource File
- Section Quiz GENERAL
- Section Review GENERAL
- Vocabulary and Section Summary GENERAL
- Reinforcement Worksheet BASIC

Answers to Section Review

1. Sample answer: Air pressure is caused by gravity pulling air molecules in the atmosphere toward the Earth. The atmosphere is a mixture of gases that surrounds the Earth. The troposphere is the layer where most weather occurs. The stratosphere is where the ozone layer is located. The mesosphere is the middle atmospheric layer. The thermosphere is the atmospheric layer with the highest temperatures.

2. d

3. Air pressure decreases as altitude increases because the atmosphere is less dense at higher altitudes.

4. Temperatures in the thermosphere are high because particles are moving quickly in the thermosphere. The thermosphere does not feel hot because it is not very dense, so particles cannot collide to transfer much thermal energy.

5. The temperature of atmospheric layers varies because of the way solar energy is absorbed by different gases.

6. nitrogen and oxygen

7. 0.5 g/m^3 × 1,000,000,000 m^3 = 500,000,000 g, or 500,000 kg

8. Answers may vary. Students should recognize that air density is lower at higher altitudes. Helicopters need air to provide lift. At altitudes higher than 6,000 m, air density is so low that it is difficult for helicopters to fly.

9. Answers may vary. Space vehicles reenter the atmosphere at a very high rate of speed. Although the atmosphere is not very dense at the altitude that space vehicles reenter, the vehicles are traveling fast enough to compress air in front of them. This layer of air transfers thermal energy to the spacecraft's exterior.

10. Answers may vary. Helium does not have enough mass to be held by the Earth's gravitational attraction.

Section 1 • Characteristics of the Atmosphere

SECTION 2

Focus

Overview

This section discusses how the atmosphere is heated by energy from the sun. Thermal energy is transferred by radiation, thermal conduction, and convection. The section concludes with a discussion of the greenhouse effect and global warming.

🔔 Bellringer

Ask students to explain how food is heated in an oven. (The heating coil heats the air in the oven by radiation and thermal conduction. The hot air circulates by convection and heats the food and its container. The hot container heats the food by thermal conduction.)

Motivate

ACTIVITY — BASIC

Popcorn Make some popcorn the "old-fashioned" way—use a hot plate or stove top, a pan with a lid, oil, and popcorn kernels. Have volunteers explain how the processes of convection, conduction, and radiation are involved. Explain that a kernel pops when the water stored inside changes to water vapor and expands suddenly. Share the treat with students if time allows. **LS Kinesthetic**

SECTION 2

READING WARM-UP

Objectives
- Describe what happens to solar energy that reaches Earth.
- Summarize the processes of radiation, conduction, and convection.
- Explain the relationship between the greenhouse effect and global warming.

Terms to Learn
radiation
thermal conduction
convection
global warming
greenhouse effect

READING STRATEGY

Reading Organizer As you read this section, make a table comparing radiation, conduction, and convection.

Atmospheric Heating

You are lying in a park. Your eyes are closed, and you feel the warmth of the sun on your face. You may have done this before, but have you ever stopped to think that it takes a little more than eight minutes for the energy that warms your face to travel from a star that is 149,000,000 km away?

Energy in the Atmosphere

In the scenario above, your face was warmed by energy from the sun. Earth and its atmosphere are also warmed by energy from the sun. In this section, you will find out what happens to solar energy as it enters the atmosphere.

Radiation: Energy Transfer by Waves

The Earth receives energy from the sun by radiation. **Radiation** is the transfer of energy as electromagnetic waves. Although the sun radiates a huge amount of energy, Earth receives only about two-billionths of this energy. But this small fraction of energy is enough to drive the weather cycle and make Earth habitable. **Figure 1** shows what happens to solar energy once it enters the atmosphere.

Figure 1 Energy from the sun is absorbed by the atmosphere, land, and water and is changed into thermal energy.

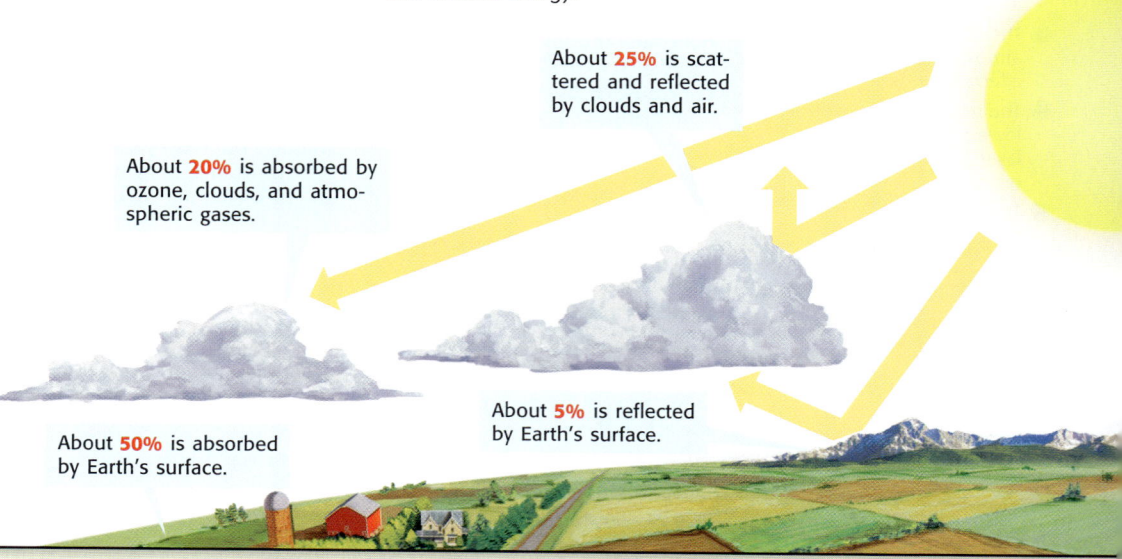

About **25%** is scattered and reflected by clouds and air.

About **20%** is absorbed by ozone, clouds, and atmospheric gases.

About **5%** is reflected by Earth's surface.

About **50%** is absorbed by Earth's surface.

CHAPTER RESOURCES

Chapter Resource File
- Lesson Plan
- Directed Reading A **BASIC**
- Directed Reading B **SPECIAL NEEDS**

Technology
- Transparencies
  - Bellringer
  - Scattering, Absorption, and Reflection
  - Radiation, Conduction, and Convection

MISCONCEPTION ALERT

Thermal Conduction Point out that compared with radiation and convection, thermal conduction plays a relatively minor role in heating the atmosphere. Only the thin layer of air that comes in contact with the Earth's surface is heated by thermal conduction. However, thermal energy that is absorbed and reradiated by the land and oceans play a major role in heating the atmosphere.

---

454 Chapter 15 • The Atmosphere

Conduction: Energy Transfer by Contact

If you have ever touched something hot, you have experienced the process of conduction. **Thermal conduction** is the transfer of thermal energy through a material. Thermal energy is always transferred from warm to cold areas. When air molecules come into direct contact with the warm surface of Earth, thermal energy is transferred to the atmosphere.

Convection: Energy Transfer by Circulation

If you have ever watched a pot of water boil, you have observed convection. **Convection** is the transfer of thermal energy by the circulation or movement of a liquid or gas. Most thermal energy in the atmosphere is transferred by convection. For example, as air is heated, it becomes less dense and rises. Cool air is denser, so it sinks. As the cool air sinks, it pushes the warm air up. The cool air is eventually heated by the Earth's surface and begins to rise again. This cycle of warm air rising and cool air sinking causes a circular movement of air, called a *convection current,* as shown in **Figure 2.**

Reading Check How do differences in air density cause convection currents? (*See the Appendix for answers to Reading Checks.*)

radiation the transfer of energy as electromagnetic waves

thermal conduction the transfer of energy as heat through a material

convection the transfer of thermal energy by the circulation or movement of a liquid or gas

Figure 2 *The processes of radiation, thermal conduction, and convection heat Earth and its atmosphere.*

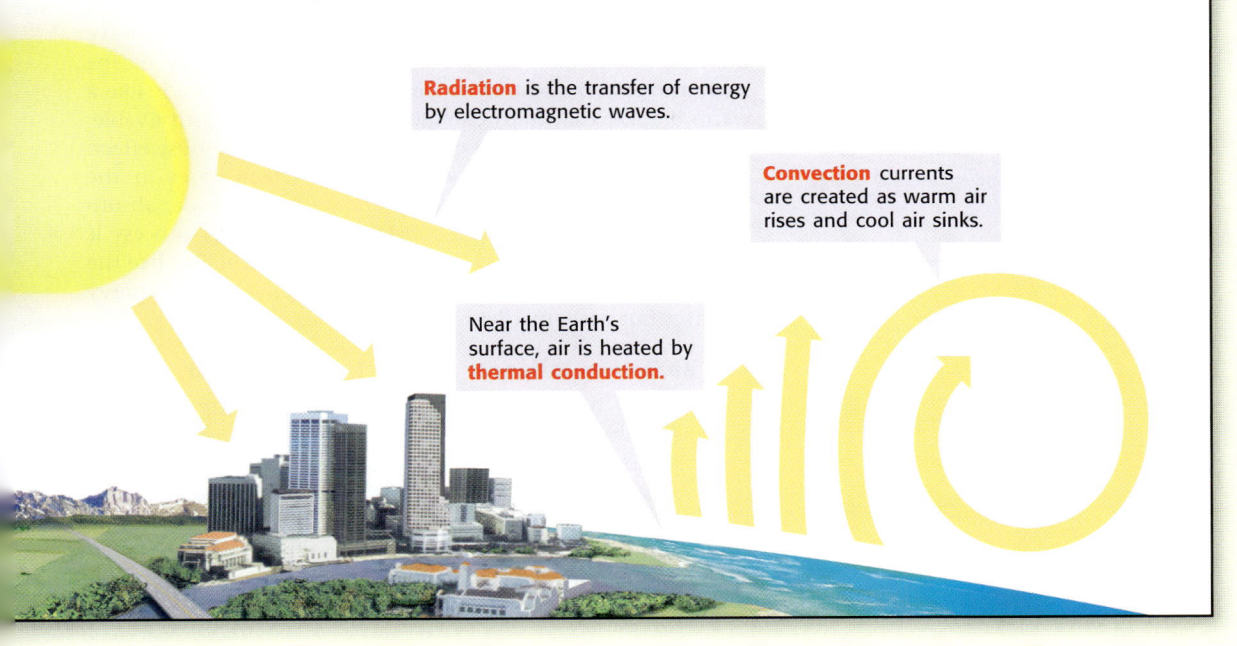

Radiation is the transfer of energy by electromagnetic waves.

Convection currents are created as warm air rises and cool air sinks.

Near the Earth's surface, air is heated by **thermal conduction.**

CONNECTION ACTIVITY
Environmental Science — GENERAL

The Heat Island Effect Cities that have few green spaces and a lot of asphalt can have temperatures 10°C higher than surrounding rural areas do. This phenomenon is called the *heat island effect.* The heat island effect occurs because concrete buildings and asphalt absorb solar radiation and reradiate thermal energy, which elevates temperatures and increases the production of smog. The effect is worse in urban areas that have little surface water and few trees because the evaporation of water and plant transpiration cool the air. To counteract the heat island effect, cities have begun to preserve green spaces and plant trees. Some cities are beginning to use construction materials that have a higher reflectivity, such as white rooftops and concrete streets. Have groups of students create a model city in a large box or aquarium. Using two light bulbs and a thermometer, students should test strategies to reduce the heat island effect. **LS Logical**

Teach

INCLUSION Strategies

- **Developmentally Delayed**
- **Hearing Impaired**

This activity will demonstrate how different colors absorb different amounts of solar energy. Obtain two 2 L soda bottles. Paint one bottle white and the other bottle black. Place the open end of a small, prestretched balloon on the mouth of both bottles. Make sure the balloons form an airtight seal.

Organize students into pairs, and ask them to observe the bottles. If possible, pass the bottles around. Ask students to predict what will happen when the bottles are placed in bright sunlight. Ask students to write their predictions in their **science journal.** Now, place both bottles in bright sunlight. Within a few minutes, the students will notice that the balloon on the black bottle starts to expand. The balloon of the white bottle remains limp. Have student pairs record their observations. **English Language Learners**
LS Logical

Answer to Reading Check

Cold air is more dense than warm air, so cold air sinks and warm air rises. This produces convection currents.

Section 2 • Atmospheric Heating

Close

Reteaching — BASIC

Greenhouse Review Reproduce **Figure 3** on the board, and ask student volunteers to explain how the greenhouse effect works. **LS Visual/Verbal**

Quiz — GENERAL

1. A metal spoon left in a bowl of hot soup feels hot. Which process—radiation, thermal conduction, or convection—is mainly responsible for heating the spoon? (thermal conduction)

2. What is a convection current? (the circular movement of warm and cool particles in a liquid or gas)

3. How does a greenhouse stay warm? (Sunlight passes through the glass. Objects in the structure absorb some of the radiant energy. In turn, the objects radiate this energy as thermal energy. The glass prevents the thermal energy from escaping, which warms the greenhouse.)

Alternative Assessment — GENERAL

Writing Have students write a two-paragraph essay that explains the concepts in this section. The essay should contain the following terms: *radiation, thermal conduction, convection, greenhouse gas, greenhouse effect, global warming,* and *radiation balance*. Student volunteers can read their essays to the class. **LS Verbal**

Figure 3 The Greenhouse Effect

1. Short-wave solar energy passes through the atmosphere and is absorbed by clouds and by Earth's surface.
2. Clouds and Earth's surface reradiate the solar energy as long-wave energy.
3. The long-wave energy warms Earth and the atmosphere.

greenhouse effect the warming of the surface and lower atmosphere of Earth that occurs when water vapor, carbon dioxide, and other gases absorb and reradiate thermal energy

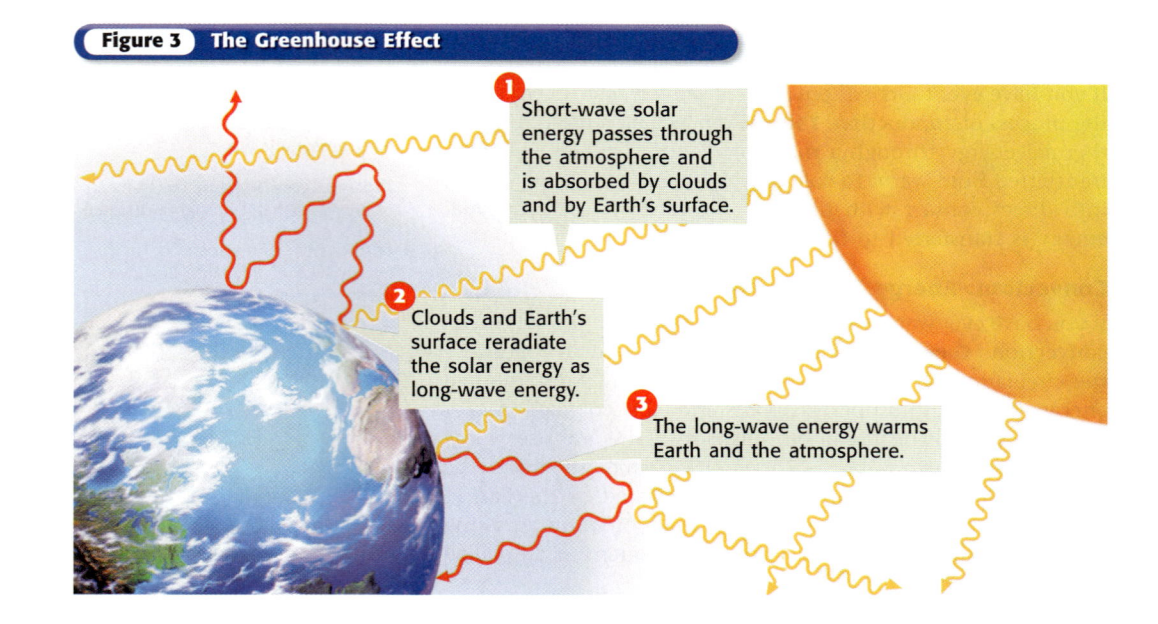

The Greenhouse Effect and Life on Earth

As you have learned, about 70% of the radiation that enters Earth's atmosphere is absorbed by clouds and by the Earth's surface. This energy is converted into thermal energy that warms the planet. In other words, short-wave visible light is absorbed and reradiated into the atmosphere as long-wave thermal energy. So, why doesn't this thermal energy escape back into space? Most of it does, but the atmosphere is like a warm blanket that traps enough energy to make Earth livable. This process, shown in **Figure 3,** is called the greenhouse effect. The **greenhouse effect** is the process by which gases in the atmosphere, such as water vapor and carbon dioxide, absorb thermal energy and radiate it back to Earth. This process is called the greenhouse effect because the gases function like the glass walls and roof of a greenhouse, which allow solar energy to enter but prevent thermal energy from escaping.

The Radiation Balance: Energy In, Energy Out

For Earth to remain livable, the amount of energy received from the sun and the amount of energy returned to space must be approximately equal. Solar energy that is absorbed by the Earth and its atmosphere is eventually reradiated into space as thermal energy. Every day, the Earth receives more energy from the sun. The balance between incoming energy and outgoing energy is known as the *radiation balance*.

Group ACTIVITY — BASIC

Model Greenhouses Have students work in groups to make model greenhouses by placing a thermometer inside a jar and anchoring the thermometer with modeling clay. Next, have students seal each jar with a lid. Have each group put its model in a different sunny spot. Students should observe and record changes in temperature every day for 1 week. Students can compare the temperatures recorded with the temperatures in a control jar that lacks a lid. Help students infer that solar energy enters a greenhouse and is converted to thermal energy and that the glass prevents most of the thermal energy from escaping. **English Language Learners** **LS Kinesthetic**

456 Chapter 15 • The Atmosphere

Greenhouse Gases and Global Warming

Many scientists have become concerned about data that show that average global temperatures have increased in the past 100 years. Such an increase in average global temperatures is called **global warming**. Some scientists have hypothesized that an increase of greenhouse gases in the atmosphere may be the cause of this warming trend. Greenhouse gases are gases that absorb thermal energy in the atmosphere.

Human activity, such as the burning of fossil fuels and deforestation, may be increasing levels of greenhouse gases, such as carbon dioxide, in the atmosphere. If this hypothesis is correct, increasing levels of greenhouse gases may cause average global temperatures to continue to rise. If global warming continues, global climate patterns could be disrupted. Plants and animals that are adapted to live in specific climates would be affected. However, climate models are extremely complex, and scientists continue to debate whether the global warming trend is the result of an increase in greenhouse gases.

global warming a gradual increase in average global temperature

Reading Check What is a greenhouse gas?

SECTION Review

Summary

- Energy from the sun is transferred through the atmosphere by radiation, thermal conduction, and convection.
- Radiation is energy transfer by electromagnetic waves. Thermal conduction is energy transfer by direct contact. Convection is energy transfer by circulation.
- The greenhouse effect is Earth's natural heating process. Increasing levels of greenhouse gases could cause global warming.

Using Key Terms

1. Use each of the following terms in a separate sentence: *thermal conduction, radiation, convection, greenhouse effect,* and *global warming.*

Understanding Key Ideas

2. Which of the following is the best example of thermal conduction?
   a. a light bulb warming a lampshade
   b. an egg cooking in a frying pan
   c. water boiling in a pot
   d. gases circulating in the atmosphere

3. Describe three ways that energy is transferred in the atmosphere.

4. What is the difference between the greenhouse effect and global warming?

5. What is the radiation balance?

Math Skills

6. Find the average of the following temperatures: 73.2°F, 71.1°F, 54.6°F, 65.5°F, 78.2°F, 81.9°F, and 82.1°F.

Critical Thinking

7. **Identifying Relationships** How does the process of convection rely on radiation?

8. **Applying Concepts** Describe global warming in terms of the radiation balance.

For a variety of links related to this chapter, go to www.scilinks.org
Topic: Energy in the Atmosphere
SciLinks code: HSM0512

Answer to Reading Check

A greenhouse gas is a gas that absorbs thermal energy in the atmosphere.

Answers to Section Review

1. Sample answer: Thermal conduction is the transfer of thermal energy as heat through a material. Radiation is the transfer of energy by electromagnetic waves. Convection is the transfer of energy by circulation in a fluid. The greenhouse effect is Earth's natural warming process. Global warming is a gradual increase in average global temperature.

2. b

3. Sample answer: Energy from the sun warms the atmosphere by radiation. The Earth reradiates energy from the sun, which warms the atmosphere. The air directly above the Earth's surface is also heated by conduction. Warm air is then circulated through the atmosphere by convection currents.

4. The greenhouse effect is the Earth's natural heating process by which gases in the atmosphere trap reradiated energy, which heats the atmosphere. Global warming is the rise in average global temperature and may be caused by an increase in the greenhouse effect.

5. The radiation balance is the balance between incoming solar energy and thermal energy that the Earth radiates into space.

6. 506.6°F ÷ 7 = 72.4°F

7. Convection in the atmosphere relies on radiation from the sun. If radiation from the sun stopped, air would not be warmed and convection currents would eventually stop circulating.

8. Answers may vary. Global warming occurs when the radiation balance is upset and more energy is coming in than is going out.

CHAPTER RESOURCES

Chapter Resource File
- Section Quiz GENERAL
- Section Review GENERAL
- Vocabulary and Section Summary GENERAL

Technology

Transparencies
- The Greenhouse Effect

Section 2 • Atmospheric Heating

SECTION 3

Focus

Overview
This section explains what wind is and describes how differences in atmospheric pressure cause air to move. Students will also learn about global and local winds.

Bellringer
Have students write a poem about moving air. The poem should include an explanation of why air moves.

Motivate

Demonstration — GENERAL

Air Movement Create an area of high pressure by filling a plastic container with ice. Create an area of low pressure by heating a hot plate. Place the container of ice and the hot plate approximately 30 cm from each other. Make sure the container of ice is slightly higher than the hot plate. Light a splint or long match, and let it burn for a few seconds. Extinguish the splint or match over the ice, and place the smoking end close to the ice. Ask students to observe the movement of the smoke. The smoke should move from the ice to the hot plate (from an area of high pressure to an area of low pressure). **LS Visual**

SECTION 3

Global Winds and Local Winds

If you open the valve on a bicycle tube, the air rushes out. Why? The air inside the tube is at a higher pressure than the air is outside the tube. In effect, letting air out of the tube created a wind.

READING WARM-UP

Objectives
- Explain the relationship between air pressure and wind direction.
- Describe global wind patterns.
- Explain the causes of local wind patterns.

Terms to Learn
wind
Coriolis effect
polar easterlies
westerlies
trade winds
jet stream

READING STRATEGY

Prediction Guide Before reading this section, write the title of each heading in this section. Next, under each heading, write what you think you will learn.

wind the movement of air caused by differences in air pressure

Why Air Moves

The movement of air caused by differences in air pressure is called **wind.** The greater the pressure difference, the faster the wind moves. The devastation shown in **Figure 1** was caused by winds that resulted from extreme differences in air pressure.

Air Rises at the Equator and Sinks at the Poles

Differences in air pressure are generally caused by the unequal heating of the Earth. The equator receives more direct solar energy than other latitudes, so air at the equator is warmer and less dense than the surrounding air. Warm, less dense air rises and creates an area of low pressure. This warm, rising air flows toward the poles. At the poles, the air is colder and denser than the surrounding air, so it sinks. As the cold air sinks, it creates areas of high pressure around the poles. This cold polar air then flows toward the equator.

Figure 1 In 1992, Hurricane Andrew became the most destructive hurricane in U.S. history. The winds from the hurricane reached 264 km/h.

CHAPTER RESOURCES

Chapter Resource File
- Lesson Plan
- Directed Reading A BASIC
- Directed Reading B SPECIAL NEEDS

Technology
- Transparencies
  - Bellringer
  - Pressure Belts

Cultural Awareness — GENERAL

Animals and Air Pressure Changes in atmospheric pressure are often said to affect fish. Egyptian fishers notice that mullet move with the wind to prevent getting stuck in muddy water. According to Caribbean lore, a container of shark oil will grow cloudy when a hurricane is imminent. Have students find out about other organisms that might indicate changes in air pressure and other atmospheric phenomena. **LS Intrapersonal**

Chapter 15 • The Atmosphere

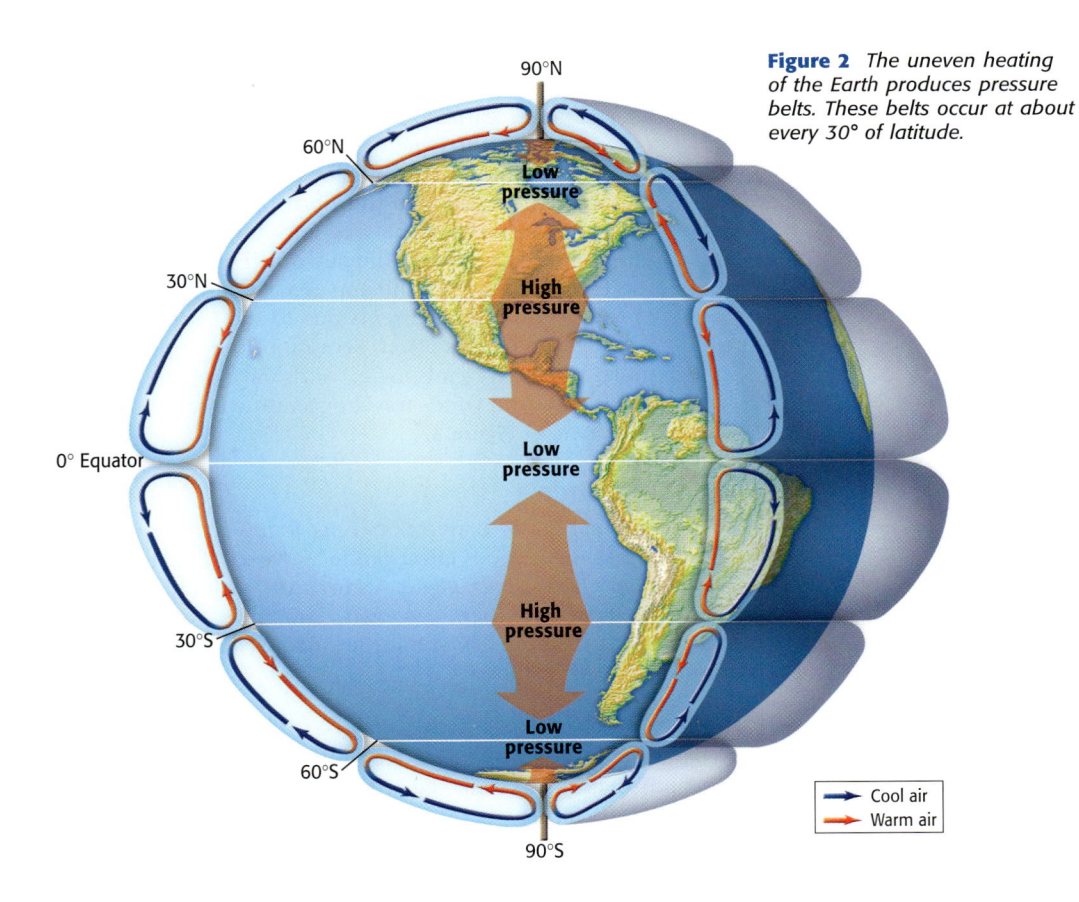

Figure 2 The uneven heating of the Earth produces pressure belts. These belts occur at about every 30° of latitude.

→ Cool air
→ Warm air

Pressure Belts Are Found Every 30°

You may imagine that wind moves in one huge, circular pattern from the poles to the equator. In fact, air travels in many large, circular patterns called *convection cells*. Convection cells are separated by *pressure belts*, bands of high pressure and low pressure found about every 30° of latitude, as shown in **Figure 2**. As warm air rises over the equator and moves toward the poles, the air begins to cool. At about 30° north and 30° south latitude, some of the cool air begins to sink. Cool, sinking air causes high pressure belts near 30° north and 30° south latitude. This cool air flows back to the equator, where it warms and rises again. At the poles, cold air sinks and moves toward the equator. Air warms as it moves away from the poles. Around 60° north and 60° south latitude, the warmer air rises, which creates a low pressure belt. This air flows back to the poles.

Reading Check Why does sinking air cause areas of high pressure? *(See the Appendix for answers to Reading Checks.)*

Teach

MISCONCEPTION ALERT

What Causes Wind? Make sure students understand that air circulates because of temperature differences that cause pressure differences in the atmosphere. The sun heats the Earth, which heats the air above it by radiation and conduction. This warm air is less dense than the colder air above it, so the warm air rises, while the cold, denser air sinks. Air is colder near the poles because less solar energy reaches the ground at the poles than at the equator. Because air is warmer and less dense at the equator, air tends to rise and circulate toward the poles.

Answer to Reading Check
Sinking air causes areas of high pressure because sinking air presses down on the air beneath it.

CONNECTION to Physical Science — ADVANCED

Katabatic Winds A katabatic wind is the movement of air due to the influence of gravity. This flow can range from a gentle breeze to gale-force winds. The world's strongest katabatic winds occur in Antarctica because there is plenty of cold air and the highest spot is near the center of the continent. Because the continent is basically cone shaped, winds radiate from the South Pole, accelerating like a car rolling down a hill. Cold, dense air rushes down mountainsides, tumbles across the ice sheets, and spills out over the ocean. The winds can blow for months, and they sometimes reach speeds as fast as 320 km/h! Use dry ice and a modeling-clay mountain to demonstrate this phenomenon. **LS Kinesthetic**

Section 3 • Global Winds and Local Winds

Teach, continued

ACTIVITY — BASIC

Coriolis Effect Try the following activity to help students who have problems understanding the Coriolis effect. You will need a globe, some flour, an eyedropper, red food coloring, and water. Mix a few drops of food coloring with water, and fill the eyedropper with the solution. Dust the globe thoroughly with flour. If the flour doesn't stick, mist the globe lightly with water, and sprinkle the flour over the globe. Enlist a volunteer to slowly spin the globe counterclockwise to simulate Earth's rotation. Have another volunteer slowly drop water from the dropper at the top of the globe, at the North Pole. Students will observe that the water is deflected westward in the Northern Hemisphere. **English Language Learners**
Ⓛ Kinesthetic

Answer to Reading Check
the westerlies

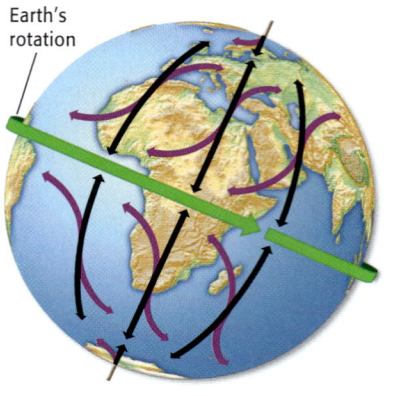

Earth's rotation

➡ Path of wind without Coriolis effect
➡ Approximate path of wind

Figure 3 *The Coriolis effect in the Northern Hemisphere causes winds traveling north to appear to curve to the east and winds traveling south to appear to curve to the west.*

Coriolis effect the apparent curving of the path of a moving object from an otherwise straight path due to the Earth's rotation

polar easterlies prevailing winds that blow from east to west between 60° and 90° latitude in both hemispheres

westerlies prevailing winds that blow from west to east between 30° and 60° latitude in both hemispheres

trade winds prevailing winds that blow northeast from 30° north latitude to the equator and that blow southeast from 30° south latitude to the equator

The Coriolis Effect

As you have learned, pressure differences cause air to move between the equator and the poles. But try spinning a globe and using a piece of chalk to trace a straight line from the equator to the North Pole. The chalk line curves because the globe was spinning. Like the chalk line, winds do not travel directly north or south, because the Earth is rotating. The apparent curving of the path of winds and ocean currents due to the Earth's rotation is called the **Coriolis effect.** Because of the Coriolis effect in the Northern Hemisphere, winds traveling north curve to the east, and winds traveling south curve to the west, as shown in **Figure 3**.

Global Winds

The combination of convection cells found at every 30° of latitude and the Coriolis effect produces patterns of air circulation called *global winds*. **Figure 4** shows the major global wind systems: polar easterlies, westerlies, and trade winds. Winds such as easterlies and westerlies are named for the direction from which they blow.

Polar Easterlies

The wind belts that extend from the poles to 60° latitude in both hemispheres are called the **polar easterlies.** The polar easterlies are formed as cold, sinking air moves from the poles toward 60° north and 60° south latitude. In the Northern Hemisphere, polar easterlies can carry cold arctic air over the United States, producing snow and freezing weather.

Westerlies

The wind belts found between 30° and 60° latitude in both hemispheres are called the **westerlies.** The westerlies flow toward the poles from west to east. The westerlies can carry moist air over the United States, producing rain and snow.

Trade Winds

In both hemispheres, the winds that blow from 30° latitude almost to the equator are called **trade winds.** The Coriolis effect causes the trade winds to curve to the west in the Northern Hemisphere and to the east in the Southern Hemisphere. Early traders used the trade winds to sail from Europe to the Americas. As a result, the winds became known as "trade winds."

✓**Reading Check** If the trade winds carried traders from Europe to the Americas, what wind system carried traders back to Europe?

Homework — GENERAL

The Coriolis Effect Many people often assume that the Coriolis effect affects the direction that water drains from sink basins or toilet bowls. Challenge students to devise an experiment to test this assumption. Students should record their data and present their data to the class. If time allows, graph the class results, and discuss any trends that appear.
Ⓛ Intrapersonal

CHAPTER RESOURCES

Technology

📀 **Transparencies**
• The Coriolis Effect
• Global Winds

The Doldrums

The trade winds of the Northern and Southern Hemispheres meet in an area around the equator called the *doldrums*. In the doldrums, there is very little wind because the warm, rising air creates an area of low pressure. The name *doldrums* means "dull" or "sluggish."

The Horse Latitudes

At about 30° north and 30° south latitude, sinking air creates an area of high pressure. The winds at these locations are weak. These areas are called the *horse latitudes*. According to legend, this name was given to these areas when sailing ships carried horses from Europe to the Americas. When the ships were stuck in this windless area, horses were sometimes thrown overboard to save drinking water for the sailors. Most of the world's deserts are located in the horse latitudes because the sinking air is very dry.

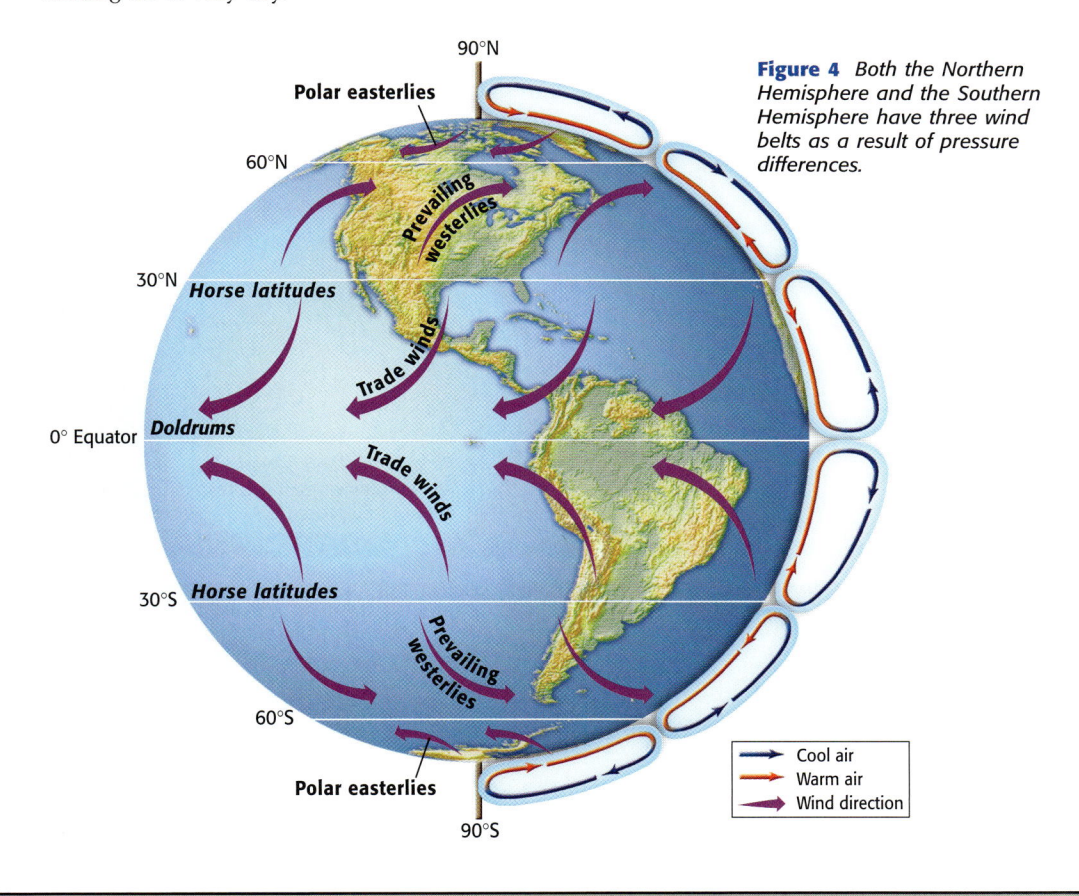

Figure 4 Both the Northern Hemisphere and the Southern Hemisphere have three wind belts as a result of pressure differences.

Using the Figure — BASIC

Wind Systems Have students use **Figure 4** to answer the following questions:

- Where are the trade winds? (The trade winds blow from 30° north and south latitudes to the equator.)
- Describe the motion of the trade winds in the Southern Hemisphere. (They move from the southeast to the northwest.)
- How do the westerlies flow in the Northern Hemisphere? (The westerlies flow from the southwest to the northeast.)

LS Logical

MISCONCEPTION ALERT

The Coriolis "Force" The Coriolis effect is not a force. When an object appears to be deflected from its path, it is not the object that is deflected but the Earth that has moved. Because the Earth is rotating, the Earth moves out from under the object that is passing over the surface. The change of the Earth's position gives the path traveled by the object the appearance of being curved. However, the Coriolis "force" can be used in mathematical equations to predict the movement of objects.

Science Bloopers

The Coriolis Effect During a World War I naval engagement off the Falkland Islands, British gunners were astonished to see that their artillery shells were landing 100 yd to the left of German ships. The gunners had made corrections for the Coriolis effect at 50° north latitude, not 50° south of the equator. Consequently, their shells fell at a distance from the target equal to twice the Coriolis deflection!

Is That a Fact!

Because the air descending over the horse latitudes has lost most of its moisture, the land around these latitudes receives very little precipitation. In fact, the Earth's largest deserts are in these areas.

Section 3 • Global Winds and Local Winds

Close

Reteaching — BASIC
Concept Mapping Have students create a concept map using the vocabulary and concepts in this section. **LS Visual**

Quiz — GENERAL
1. How does air temperature over landmasses and adjacent bodies of water change between day and night? (During the day, the air is cooler over water. At night, the air is cooler over land.)
2. List two kinds of breezes that result from local topography. (mountain and valley breezes)

Alternative Assessment — GENERAL
Modeling Sea and Land Breezes Give each group two baking pans—one filled with sand and the other filled with ice. Groups should carefully warm the sand in an oven until the sand is very warm. Have the groups place the pans side by side. Then, they should fold a cardboard wind screen in three places so that it surrounds both pans. As they hold a burning splint at the boundary between the pans, students should see smoke travel toward the hot sand in the same way that the wind blows toward the beach during the daytime. Ask them to explain their observations and try to simulate a land breeze. (They could simulate a land breeze by letting the sand cool and replacing the ice with warm water.) **LS Kinesthetic**

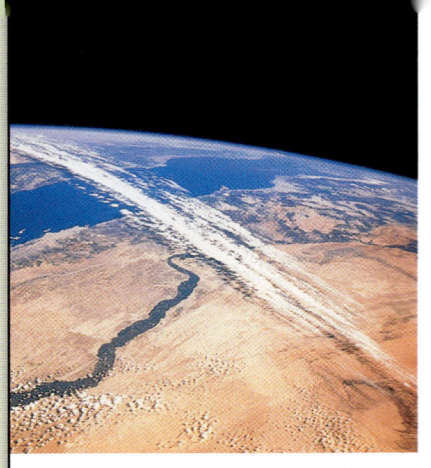

Figure 5 The jet stream forms this band of clouds as it flows above the Earth.

jet stream a narrow belt of strong winds that blow in the upper troposphere

Jet Streams: Atmospheric Conveyor Belts

The flight from Seattle to Boston can be 30 minutes faster than the flight from Boston to Seattle. Why? Pilots take advantage of a jet stream similar to the one shown in **Figure 5**. The **jet streams** are narrow belts of high-speed winds that blow in the upper troposphere and lower stratosphere. These winds can reach maximum speeds of 400 km/h. Unlike other global winds, the jet streams do not follow regular paths around the Earth. Knowing the path of a jet stream is important not only to pilots but also to meteorologists. Because jet streams affect the movement of storms, meteorologists can track a storm if they know the location of a jet stream.

Local Winds

Local winds generally move short distances and can blow from any direction. Local geographic features, such as a shoreline or a mountain, can produce temperature differences that cause local winds. For example, the formation of sea and land breezes is shown in **Figure 6**. During the day, the land heats up faster than the water, so the air above the land becomes warmer than the air above the ocean. The warm land air rises, and the cold ocean air flows in to replace it. At night, the land cools faster than water, so the wind blows toward the ocean.

Figure 6 Sea and Land Breezes

During the day, air over the ocean is cooler and forms an area of high pressure. The cool air flows to the land, producing a sea breeze.

Air over the land is warmer. As warm air rises, it creates an area of low pressure.

At night, air over the ocean is warmer. As the warm air rises, it forms an area of low pressure.

Air over land is cooler and forms an area of high pressure. The cool air moves toward the ocean, producing a land breeze.

CONNECTION to Life Science — GENERAL

High-Altitude Highway Migrating birds use jet streams and local winds as aerial highways to reach their destinations. Insects and spiders also take advantage of wind currents. Glider plane pilots have reported seeing air so thick with spiders that it looked like snow, and ships 800 km out at sea have been deluged with spiders falling from the sky! Dangling from the end of long, silk streamers, spiders ride updrafts until they reach a wind current. They occasionally reach altitudes of 4 km. There they can travel for weeks, rolling in their streamers and dropping from the sky after covering up to 300 km. Students might enjoy finding radar entomology Internet sites for people who track traveling insects.

Mountain Breezes and Valley Breezes

Mountain and valley breezes are other examples of local winds caused by an area's geography. Campers in mountainous areas may feel a warm afternoon quickly change into a cold night soon after the sun sets. During the day, the sun warms the air along the mountain slopes. This warm air rises up the mountain slopes, creating a valley breeze. At nightfall, the air along the mountain slopes cools. This cool air moves down the slopes into the valley, producing a mountain breeze.

Reading Check Why does the wind tend to blow down from mountains at night?

CONNECTION TO Social Studies

Local Breezes The chinook, the shamal, the sirocco, and the Santa Ana are all local winds. Find out about an interesting local wind, and create a poster-board display that shows how the wind forms and how it affects human cultures.

ACTIVITY

SECTION Review

Summary

- Winds blow from areas of high pressure to areas of low pressure.
- Pressure belts are found approximately every 30° of latitude.
- The Coriolis effect causes wind to appear to curve as it moves across the Earth's surface.
- Global winds include the polar easterlies, the westerlies, and the trade winds.
- Local winds include sea and land breezes and mountain and valley breezes.

Using Key Terms

1. In your own words, write a definition for each of the following terms: *wind, Coriolis effect, jet stream, polar easterlies, westerlies,* and *trade winds.*

Understanding Key Ideas

2. Why does warm air rise and cold air sink?
   a. because warm air is less dense than cold air
   b. because warm air is denser than cold air
   c. because cold air is less dense than warm air
   d. because warm air has less pressure than cold air does

3. What are pressure belts?
4. What causes winds?
5. How does the Coriolis effect affect wind movement?
6. How are sea and land breezes similar to mountain and valley breezes?
7. Would there be winds if the Earth's surface were the same temperature everywhere? Explain your answer.

Math Skills

8. Flying an airplane at 500 km/h, a pilot plans to reach her destination in 5 h. But she finds a jet stream moving 250 km/h in the direction she is traveling. If she gets a boost from the jet stream for 2 h, how long will the flight last?

Critical Thinking

9. **Making Inferences** In the Northern Hemisphere, why do westerlies flow from the west but trade winds flow from the east?

10. **Applying Concepts** Imagine you are near an ocean in the daytime. You want to go to the ocean, but you don't know how to get there. How might a local wind help you find the ocean?

SciLinks

For a variety of links related to this chapter, go to www.scilinks.org
Topic: Atmospheric Pressure and Winds
SciLinks code: HSM0115

Answers to Section Review

1. Sample answer: Wind is the movement of air from areas of high pressure to areas of low pressure. The Coriolis effect is the apparent deflection of a moving object due to Earth's rotation. Jet streams are high altitude belts of strong winds. Polar easterlies are global winds that blow from the poles toward 60° north and 60° south latitude. Westerlies are global winds that blow between 30° and 60° latitude in both hemispheres. Trade winds are global winds that blow between 30° latitude and the equator in both hemispheres.

2. a
3. Pressure belts are bands of high and low pressure that are found about every 30° of latitude.
4. Winds are caused by the unequal heating of the Earth's surface, which causes pressure differences.
5. The Coriolis effect causes winds to appear to be deflected to the east or west depending on the direction that the winds are traveling in each hemisphere. Because of the Coriolis effect, winds in the Northern Hemisphere appear to curve to the right, and winds in the Southern Hemisphere appear to curve to the left.
6. Both types of breezes result from pressure differences caused by unequal heating of materials.
7. Because unequal heating of the Earth's surface causes winds, there would probably not be winds near Earth's surface if Earth's surface were the same temperature everywhere.
8. 500 km/h × 5 h = 2,500 km
   (500 km/h + 250 km/h) × 2 h = 1,500 km
   2,500 km − 1,500 km = 1,000 km
   1,000 km ÷ 500 km = 2 h
   2 h + 2 h = 4 h
9. Both winds are affected by the Coriolis effect. In the Northern Hemisphere, the westerlies travel in a northerly direction. They appear to be deflected to the northeast by the Coriolis effect. In contrast, in the Northern Hemisphere, the trade winds blow in a southerly direction, so they appear to be deflected to the southwest.
10. During the day, a sea breeze is caused by cooler air over the water moving toward the land. Walking toward the sea breeze would lead you to the ocean.

Answer to Reading Check

At night, the air along the mountain slopes cools. This cool air moves down the slopes into the valley and produces a mountain breeze.

CHAPTER RESOURCES

Chapter Resource File
- Section Quiz GENERAL
- Section Review GENERAL
- Vocabulary and Section Summary GENERAL

Technology
- Transparencies
- Sea and Land Breezes

Section 3 • Global Winds and Local Winds

SECTION 4

Focus

Overview
This section discusses the causes and effects of air pollution. Students learn the difference between primary and secondary pollutants and about acid precipitation and the ozone hole. The section concludes with a discussion about reducing air pollution.

🔔 Bellringer
Bring a filter mask to class. Have each student make a list of three situations in which one might wear such a mask. For example, surgeons wear such masks to prevent the transfer of disease-causing microbes, and sandblasters wear masks to avoid inhaling dust and paint chips. Tell students that some people living in areas with heavily polluted air wear such masks to protect themselves from impurities in the air they breathe.

SECTION 4

READING WARM-UP

Objectives
- Compare primary and secondary air pollutants.
- Identify the major sources of air pollution.
- Explain the effects of an ozone hole.
- List five effects of air pollution on the human body.
- Identify ways to reduce air pollution.

Terms to Learn
air pollution
acid precipitation

READING STRATEGY

Reading Organizer As you read this section, make a table that identifies major sources of air pollution and that suggests ways to reduce pollution from each source.

air pollution the contamination of the atmosphere by the introduction of pollutants from human and natural sources

Air Pollution

In December 1952, one of London's dreaded "pea souper" fogs settled on the city. But this was no ordinary fog—it was thick with coal smoke and air pollution. It burned people's lungs, and the sky grew so dark that people could not see their hands in front of their faces. When the fog lifted four days later, thousands of people were dead!

London's killer fog shocked the world and caused major changes in England's air-pollution laws. People began to think that air pollution was not simply a part of urban life that had to be endured. Air pollution had to be reduced. Although this event is an extreme example, air pollution is common in many parts of the world. However, nations are taking major steps to reduce air pollution. But what is air pollution? **Air pollution** is the contamination of the atmosphere by the introduction of pollutants from human and natural sources. Air pollutants are classified according to their source as either primary pollutants or secondary pollutants.

Primary Pollutants

Pollutants that are put directly into the air by human or natural activity are *primary pollutants*. Primary pollutants from natural sources include dust, sea salt, volcanic gases and ash, smoke from forest fires, and pollen. Primary pollutants from human sources include carbon monoxide, dust, smoke, and chemicals from paint and other substances. In urban areas, vehicle exhaust is a common source of primary pollutants. Examples of primary pollutants are shown in **Figure 1**.

✓ **Reading Check** List three primary pollutants from natural sources. (*See the Appendix for answers to Reading Checks.*)

Figure 1 Examples of Primary Pollutants

Industrial emissions   Vehicle exhaust   Volcanic ash

CHAPTER RESOURCES

Chapter Resource File
- Lesson Plan
- Directed Reading A BASIC
- Directed Reading B SPECIAL NEEDS

Technology
- Transparencies
  - Bellringer
  - The Formation of Smog

Answer to Reading Check
Sample answer: smoke, dust, and sea salt

---

464   Chapter 15 • The Atmosphere

Secondary Pollutants

Pollutants that form when primary pollutants react with other primary pollutants or with naturally occurring substances, such as water vapor, are *secondary pollutants*. Ozone and smog are examples of secondary pollutants. Ozone is produced when sunlight reacts with vehicle exhaust and air. You may have heard of "Ozone Action Day" warnings in your community. When such a warning is issued, people are discouraged from outdoor physical activity because ozone can damage their lungs. In the stratosphere, ozone forms a protective layer that absorbs harmful radiation from the sun. Near the Earth's surface, however, ozone is a dangerous pollutant that negatively affects the health of organisms.

The Formation of Smog

Smog forms when ozone and vehicle exhaust react with sunlight, as shown in **Figure 2**. Local geography and weather patterns can also contribute to smog formation. Los Angeles, shown in **Figure 3**, is almost completely surrounded by mountains that trap pollutants and contribute to smog formation. Although pollution controls have reduced levels of smog in Los Angeles, smog remains a problem for Los Angeles and many other large cities.

❷ Ozone reacts with vehicle exhaust to form smog.

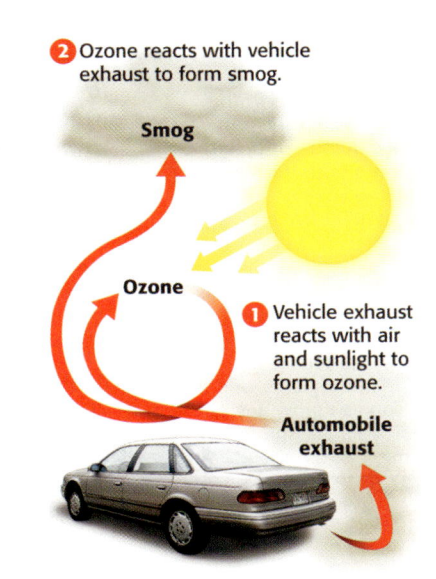

❶ Vehicle exhaust reacts with air and sunlight to form ozone.

Figure 2 *Smog forms when sunlight reacts with ozone and vehicle exhaust.*

Figure 3 *Smog levels in Los Angeles can vary dramatically. During summer, a layer of warm air can trap smog near the ground. However, in the winter, a storm can quickly clear the air.*

MISCONCEPTION ALERT

Invisible Air Pollutants Many people believe that polluted air must be visibly smoky or must be brown or black in color. Stress that some of the most dangerous air pollutants are those that can't be seen with the naked eye. Challenge students to use the Internet to find out about the various pollutants monitored by the Environmental Protection Agency and other organizations that monitor air quality. Have students compile their results in a table that lists the acceptable amounts allowed in the air, the levels in your community, and the health problems associated with each pollutant. Students should also be encouraged to monitor pollen counts and fungal spore counts in the newspaper or on local television news programs.

Motivate

Identifying Preconceptions — GENERAL

Indoor Air Pollution Ask students whether indoor air can be polluted. Explain that the air inside buildings may be polluted by a variety of sources. Ask students to list possible sources of indoor air pollution. If students have difficulty coming up with examples, tell them that air pollution is often invisible. Chalk dust, cooking oils, carpets, insulation, tobacco smoke, paints, glues, copier machines, space heaters, gas appliances, and fireplaces are just a few sources of indoor air pollution. **LS Verbal**

Teach

ACTIVITY — BASIC

Classifying Pollutants List the following pollutants on the board or on an overhead projector:

> smog, house dust, acid rain, pollen, soot, ground-level ozone, volcanic ash, acid rain

Beside the list, make a two-column table with the following column headings: "Primary pollutants" and "Secondary pollutants."

Help students classify each pollutant as either a primary pollutant (house dust, pollen, volcanic ash, and soot) or a secondary pollutant (ground-level ozone, smog, and acid rain). **LS Verbal**

Section 4 • Air Pollution

Teach, continued

Answer to Connection to Biology Activity

Plants that are effective at removing indoor air pollutants include: philodendrons, spider plants, golden pothos, gerbera daisies, chrysanthemums, corn plant, peace lily, and English ivy.

CONNECTION to Physical Science — GENERAL

Incomplete Combustion

Explain to students that much of the human-caused air pollution results from incomplete combustion. Combustion, another word for burning, is the process by which substances combine with oxygen rapidly, producing thermal energy. Byproducts are produced when a substance does not burn completely, as in an automobile engine. Many of these byproducts, such as carbon monoxide, are harmful to living organisms.

CONNECTION TO Biology

Cleaning the Air with Plants Did you know that common houseplants can help fight indoor air pollution? Some houseplants are so effective at removing air pollutants that NASA might use them as part of the life-support system in future space stations. Back on Earth, you can use plants to clean the air in your school or home. Research the top 10 air-cleaning houseplants, and find out if you can grow any of them in your classroom or home. **ACTIVITY**

Figure 4 There are many sources of indoor air pollution. Indoor air pollution can be difficult to detect because it is often invisible.

- **Nitrogen oxides** from unvented gas stove, wood stove, or kerosene heater
- **Chlorine and ammonia** from household cleaners
- **Chemicals** from dry cleaning
- **Formaldehyde** from furniture, carpeting, particleboard, and foam insulation
- **Fungi and bacteria** from dirty heating and air conditioning ducts
- **Carbon monoxide** from faulty furnace and car left running
- **Solvents** from paint strippers and thinners
- **Gasoline** from car and lawn mower

Sources of Human-Caused Air Pollution

Human-caused air pollution comes from a variety of sources. A major source of air pollution today is transportation. Cars contribute about 10% to 20% of the human-caused air pollution in the United States. Vehicle exhaust contains nitrogen oxide, which contributes to smog formation and acid precipitation. However, pollution controls and cleaner gasoline have greatly reduced air pollution from vehicles.

Industrial Air Pollution

Many industrial plants and electric power plants burn fossil fuels, such as coal, to produce energy. Burning some types of coal without pollution controls can release large amounts of air pollutants. Some industries also produce chemicals that can pollute the air. Oil refineries, chemical manufacturing plants, dry-cleaning businesses, furniture refinishers, and auto body shops are all potential sources of air pollution.

Indoor Air Pollution

Sometimes, the air inside a building can be more polluted than the air outside. Some sources of indoor air pollution are shown in **Figure 4.** *Ventilation,* or the mixing of indoor air with outdoor air, can reduce indoor air pollution. Another way to reduce indoor air pollution is to limit the use of chemical solvents and cleaners.

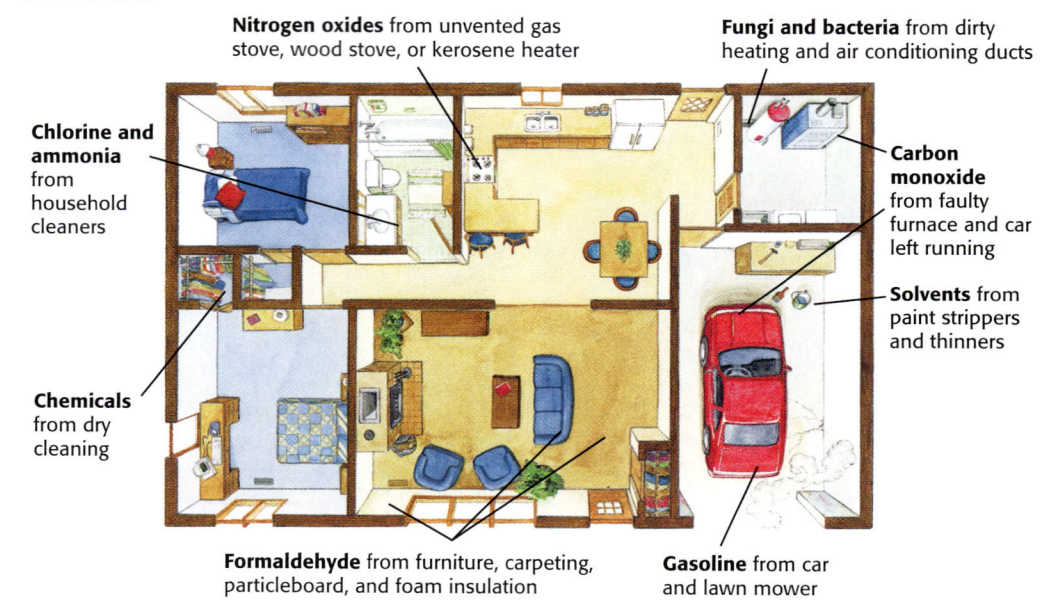

CHAPTER RESOURCES

Technology

📀 **Transparencies**
- Sources of Indoor Air Pollution

CONNECTION ACTIVITY
Real World — GENERAL

Local Air Pollution and Weather Air quality varies greatly from place to place. Even in one location, air quality can change seasonally or from day to day. Have students research the air quality where they live. Ask students to consider the following questions: "What are the sources of air pollution where you live? What are the weather conditions that lead to the worst and best air quality in your area?" **LS Interpersonal**

Chapter 15 • The Atmosphere

Acid Precipitation

Precipitation such as rain, sleet, or snow that contains acids from air pollution is called **acid precipitation.** When fossil fuels are burned, they can release sulfur dioxide and nitrogen oxide into the atmosphere. When these pollutants combine with water in the atmosphere, they form sulfuric acid and nitric acid. Precipitation is naturally acidic, but sulfuric acid and nitric acid can make it so acidic that it can negatively affect the environment. In most areas of the world, pollution controls have helped reduce acid precipitation.

Acid Precipitation and Plants

Plant communities have adapted over long periods of time to the natural acidity of the soil in which they grow. Acid precipitation can cause the acidity of soil to increase. This process, called *acidification*, changes the balance of a soil's chemistry in several ways. When the acidity of soil increases, some nutrients are dissolved. Nutrients that plants need for growth get washed away by rainwater. Increased acidity also causes aluminum and other toxic metals to be released. Some of these toxic metals are absorbed by the roots of plants.

Reading Check How does acid precipitation affect plants?

The Effects of Acid Precipitation on Forests

Forest ecology is complex. Scientists are still trying to fully understand the long-term effects of acid precipitation on groups of plants and their habitats. In some areas of the world, however, acid precipitation has damaged large areas of forest. The effects of acid precipitation are most noticeable in Eastern Europe, as shown in **Figure 5.** Forests in the northeastern United States and in eastern Canada have also been affected by acid precipitation.

acid precipitation rain, sleet, or snow that contains a high concentration of acids

Quick Lab

Testing for Particulates

1. Particulates are pollutants such as dust that are extremely small. In this lab, you will measure the amount of particulates in the air. Begin by covering **ten 5 in. × 7 in. index cards** with a thin coat of **petroleum jelly.**
2. Hang the cards in various locations inside and outside your school.
3. One day later, use a **magnifying lens** to count the number of particles on the cards. Which location had the fewest number of particulates? Which location had the highest number of particulates? Hypothesize why.

Figure 5 This forest in Poland was damaged by acid precipitation.

Is That a Fact!

Ozone can form during thunderstorms. Lightning provides the energy to change O_2 to O_3. In fact, the distinct smell that people notice after an intense thunderstorm is probably the smell of ozone.

Answer to Reading Check
Answers may vary. Acid precipitation may decrease the soil nutrients that are available to plants.

Demonstration — BASIC

Acid Rain Demonstrate how acid rain affects limestone or marble. Put some limestone or marble chips into a beaker of vinegar. Let the chips sit a few days, and have students note any differences in the surface of the chips and in the acid solution. (Students should observe that the surface of the chips is pitted. The solution will be cloudy.) **LS Visual** **English Language Learners**

Quick Lab

Teacher's Notes: As an extension, students can conduct a more thorough test for particulate matter. First, have students remove the protective backing from an 8 1/2 × 11 in. sheet of clear contact paper and place it over a sheet of graph paper with the sticky side up. Then, have them pin the papers to a piece of cardboard. Have students attach a note identifying the collector as a part of a student project. Students should make at least five collectors and place them where they will be undisturbed for 1 day. Students can collect the contact paper and can use the grids on the graph paper and a magnifying lens to count the number of particles they collected. Students should also note particle sizes. Try this experiment at different times of the year and in different locations in your community. **English Language Learners**

Section 4 • Air Pollution

Teach, continued

MISCONCEPTION ALERT

The Ozone Layer The amount of stratospheric ozone protecting Earth is less than most people realize. If the ozone layer were brought to sea-level pressure and temperature, it would range from 2.5 to 3.5 mm thick! (There is a range because the ozone layer is thinner above the poles than above the equator.)

Homework — GENERAL

The Ozone Holes Remind students that there are two ozone holes—the large Antarctic ozone hole and the smaller Arctic ozone hole. Although the Arctic ozone hole is smaller, it has a more direct effect on North America. Have interested students find out how the ozone holes have changed since they were first measured. Have students graph the values on both a yearly and seasonal basis, and have them describe any trends they see. Have them compile their findings into a short report. **LS Intrapersonal**

Figure 6 Polar weather conditions cause the size of the ozone hole (shown in blue) to vary. In the 2001 image, the ozone hole is larger than North America. One year later, it was 40% smaller.

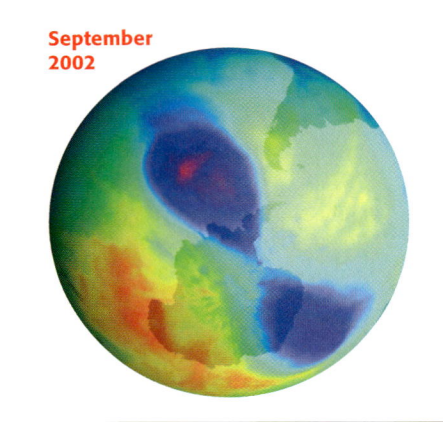

September 2001

September 2002

WEIRD SCIENCE

Ice core samples from Greenland show large-scale lead pollution in the atmosphere more than 2,000 years ago. The pollution can be traced to Roman silver mines in southern Spain. Large amounts of lead were released into the atmosphere during the smelting of silver ore.

Acid Precipitation and Aquatic Ecosystems

Aquatic organisms have adapted to live in water with a particular range of acidity. If acid precipitation increases the acidity of a lake or stream, aquatic plants, fish, and other aquatic organisms may die. The effects of acid precipitation on lakes and rivers are worst in the spring, when the acidic snow that built up in the winter melts and acidic water flows into lakes and rivers. A rapid change in a body of water's acidity is called *acid shock*. Acid shock can cause large numbers of fish to die. Acid shock can also affect the delicate eggs of fish and amphibians.

To reduce the effects of acid precipitation on aquatic ecosystems, some communities spray powdered lime on acidified lakes in the spring, which reduces the acidity of the lakes. Lime, a base, neutralizes the acid in the water. Unfortunately, lime cannot be spread to offset all acid damage to lakes.

✓ **Reading Check** Why is powdered lime sprayed on lakes in the spring instead of the fall?

The Ozone Hole

In 1985, scientists reported an alarming discovery about the Earth's protective ozone layer. Over the Antarctic regions, the ozone layer was thinning, particularly during the spring. This change was also noted over the Arctic. Chemicals called *CFCs* were causing ozone to break down into oxygen, which does not block the sun's harmful ultraviolet (UV) rays. The thinning of the ozone layer creates an ozone hole, shown in **Figure 6**. The ozone hole allows more UV radiation to reach the Earth's surface. UV radiation is dangerous to organisms because it damages genes and can cause skin cancer.

Cooperation to Reduce the Ozone Hole

In 1987, a group of nations met in Canada and agreed to take action against ozone depletion. Agreements were made to reduce and eventually ban CFC use, and CFC alternatives were quickly developed. Because many countries agreed to take swift action to control CFC use, and because a technological solution was quickly found, many people consider ozone protection an environmental success story. The battle to protect the ozone layer is not over, however. CFC molecules can remain active in the stratosphere for 60 to 120 years. So, CFCs released 30 years ago are still destroying ozone today. Thus, it will take many years for the ozone layer to completely recover.

Answer to Reading Check

Powdered lime is used to counteract the effects of acidic snowmelt from snow that accumulated during the winter.

Air Pollution and Human Health

Daily exposure to small amounts of air pollution can cause serious health problems. Children, elderly people, and people with asthma, allergies, lung problems, and heart problems are especially vulnerable to the effects of air pollution. **Table 1** shows some of the effects of air pollution on the human body. The short-term effects of air pollution are immediately noticeable. Coughing, headaches, and increase in asthma-related problems are only a few short-term effects. The long-term effects of air pollution, such as lung cancer, are more dangerous because they may not be noticed until many years after an individual has been exposed to pollutants.

Table 1 Effects of Air Pollution on Human Health

Short-term effects	headache; nausea; irritation of eyes, nose, and throat; coughing; upper respiratory infections; worsening of asthma and emphysema
Long-term effects	emphysema; lung cancer; permanent lung damage; heart disease

Cleaning Up Air Pollution

Much progress has been made in reducing air pollution. For example, in the United States the Clean Air Act was passed by Congress in 1970. The Clean Air Act is a law that gives the Environmental Protection Agency (EPA) the authority to control the amount of air pollutants that can be released from any source, such as cars and factories. The EPA also checks air quality. If air quality worsens, the EPA can set stricter standards. The Clean Air Act was strengthened in 1990.

Controlling Air Pollution from Industry

The Clean Air Act requires many industries to use pollution-control devices such as scrubbers. A *scrubber* is a device that is used to remove some pollutants before they are released by smokestacks. Scrubbers in coal-burning power plants remove particles such as ash from the smoke. Other industrial plants, such as the power plant shown in **Figure 7,** focus on burning fuel more efficiently so that fewer pollutants are released.

Figure 7 This power plant in Florida is leading the way in clean-coal technology. The plant turns coal into a gas before it is burned, so fewer pollutants are released.

Homework — ADVANCED

Radon Radon is a naturally occurring gas that results from the decay of uranium, particularly in igneous rocks such as granite. Have students use the Internet to research the health problems associated with radon. Have students assess the potential for significant radon concentrations in your community and write a short informative essay based on their findings. **LS Intrapersonal**

CONNECTION ACTIVITY
Health — GENERAL

Respiratory Diseases Have students find out about respiratory diseases, such as asthma, that can be aggravated by air pollution. Have students compile their findings into tables that list the diseases, their symptoms, the ways they are treated, the age groups most commonly afflicted, and the relationship between the diseases and the air pollutants. **LS Logical**

Discussion — BASIC

Pollutant Review Have students try to answer the questions below without referring to their textbook.

- How do primary air pollutants differ from secondary ones? (Primary pollutants enter the atmosphere from human activities and natural events. Secondary pollutants form when primary pollutants react with other primary pollutants or with naturally occurring substances in the air.)

- How does smog form? (Sunlight reacts with automobile exhaust to create ozone. Ozone then reacts with automobile exhaust to create smog.)

- How does acid precipitation form? (Acid precipitation forms when fossil fuels are burned, releasing oxides of nitrogen and sulfur into the air. These oxides combine with moisture in the air to form acids that fall to Earth in rain, snow, sleet, and hail.) **LS Verbal** **English Language Learners**

Section 4 • Air Pollution **469**

Close

Reteaching — BASIC

Pollution Terms Have students use each of the following terms in a sentence that correctly conveys the meaning of the term: *scrubber, smog, acid precipitation, industrial pollutants, ozone hole,* and *air quality.* **LS Visual**

Quiz — GENERAL

1. Classify each of the following as either a primary or secondary air pollutant: smog, tobacco smoke, chalk dust, and acid rain. **(Sample answer: Tobacco smoke and chalk dust are primary pollutants. Smog and acid rain are secondary pollutants.)**

2. What are two health problems that can result from breathing polluted air? **(Sample answer: dizziness; headaches; burning, itchy eyes; runny nose; coughing; shortness of breath; sore throat; lung cancer and other respiratory diseases; chest pain; colds; and allergies)**

Alternative Assessment — BASIC

Writing **Critical Reading** Have students find an article about air pollution in a popular periodical or newspaper. Students should photocopy the article on 11 × 17 paper. Then, ask students to critique the article's strengths and weaknesses and write comments on the margin of the paper. **LS Verbal**

SCHOOL to HOME

Air Pollution Awareness

Work at home with a parent to develop a presentation for an "Air Pollution Awareness Day" at school. Develop a unique way to educate the public about air pollution, but have your presentation approved by your teacher before working on it. On "Air Pollution Awareness Day," your teacher might decide to invite students from another grade or a parent to come see the exhibits.

ACTIVITY

Figure 8 *In Copenhagen, Denmark, companies loan free bicycles in exchange for publicity. The program helps reduce air pollution and auto traffic.*

Answer to Reading Check

Allowance trading establishes allowances for a certain type of pollutant. Companies are permitted to release their allowance of the pollutant, but if they exceed the allowance, they must buy additional allowances or pay a fine.

The Allowance Trading System

The Allowance Trading System is another initiative to reduce air pollution. In this program, the EPA establishes allowances for the amount of a pollutant that companies can release. If a company exceeds their allowance, they must pay a fine. A company that releases less than its allowance can sell some of its allowance to a company that releases more. Allowances are also available for the public to buy. So, organizations seeking to reduce air pollution can buy an allowance of 1,000 tons of sulfur dioxide, thus reducing the total amount of sulfur dioxide released by industries.

✓ **Reading Check** How does the Allowance Trading System work?

Reducing Air Pollution from Vehicles

A large percentage of air pollution in the United States comes from the vehicles we drive. To reduce air pollution from vehicles, the EPA requires car makers to meet a certain standard for vehicle exhaust. Devices such as catalytic converters remove many pollutants from exhaust and help cars meet this standard. Cleaner fuels and more-efficent engines have also helped reduce air pollution from vehicles. Car manufacturers are also making cars that run on fuels other than gasoline. Some of these cars run on hydrogen or natural gas. Hybrid cars, which are becoming more common, use gasoline and electric power to reduce emissions. Another way to reduce air pollution is to carpool, use public transportation, or bike or walk to your destination, as shown in **Figure 8**.

INTERNET ACTIVITY

Short Story — GENERAL

For an internet activity related to this chapter, have students go to **go.hrw.com** and type in the keyword **HZ5ATMW**.

---

470 Chapter 15 • The Atmosphere

SECTION Review

Summary

- Primary pollutants are pollutants that are put directly into the air by human or natural activity.
- Secondary pollutants are pollutants that form when primary pollutants react with other primary pollutants or with naturally occurring substances.
- Transportation, industry, and natural sources are the main sources of air pollution.
- Air pollution can be reduced by legislation, such as the Clean Air Act; by technology, such as scrubbers; and by changes in lifestyle.

Using Key Terms

The statements below are false. For each statement, replace the underlined term to make a true statement.

1. <u>Air pollution</u> is a sudden change in the acidity of a stream or lake.
2. <u>Smog</u> is rain, sleet, or snow that has a high concentration of acid.

Understanding Key Ideas

3. Which of the following results in the formation of smog?
   a. Acids in the air react with ozone.
   b. Ozone reacts with vehicle exhaust.
   c. Vehicle exhaust reacts with sunlight and ozone.
   d. Water vapor reacts with sunlight and ozone.
4. What is the difference between primary and secondary pollutants?
5. Describe five sources of indoor air pollution. Is all air pollution caused by humans? Explain.
6. What is the ozone hole, and why does it form?
7. Describe five effects of air pollution on human health. How can air pollution be reduced?

Critical Thinking

8. **Expressing Opinions** How do you think that nations should resolve air-pollution problems that cross national boundaries?
9. **Making Inferences** Why might establishing a direct link between air pollution and health problems be difficult?

Interpreting Graphics

The map below shows the pH of precipitation measured at field stations in the northeastern U.S. On the pH scale, lower numbers indicate solutions that are more acidic than solutions with higher numbers. Use the map to answer the questions below.

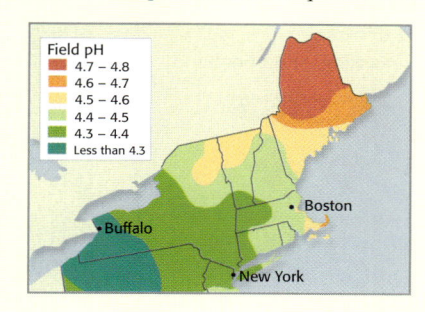

Field pH
- 4.7 – 4.8
- 4.6 – 4.7
- 4.5 – 4.6
- 4.4 – 4.5
- 4.3 – 4.4
- Less than 4.3

10. Which areas have the most acidic precipitation? Hypothesize why.
11. Boston is a larger city than Buffalo is, but the precipitation measured in Buffalo is more acidic than the precipitation in Boston. Explain why.

Answers to Section Review

1. Acid shock
2. Acid precipitation
3. c
4. Primary pollutants are pollutants that are put into the air directly by human or natural activity. Secondary pollutants form when primary pollutants react with other substances.
5. Answers may vary. Household cleaners, paint products, dirty air heating and air conditioning vents, furniture and carpeting, heaters, and stoves can all be sources of indoor air pollution. There are many natural sources of air pollution, including dust, ash from volcanoes, pollen, and smoke.
6. The ozone hole is a thinning of the ozone layer in polar regions, particularly the Antarctic. Levels of ozone vary seasonally, but the ozone hole is caused primarily by CFCs that were released into the atmosphere by human activity.
7. Answers may vary. Accept any of the effects of air pollution on human health mentioned in this section. There are many ways that air pollution can be reduced. Legislation, such as the Clean Air Act, gives the Environmental Protection Agency the power to control the amount of air pollutants released from most sources. In addition, new technology has helped create cars that release fewer pollutants and devices, such as scrubbers, that reduce industrial air pollution.
8. Answers may vary. Cooperation is important to reducing air pollution problems that cross national boundaries.
9. Answers may vary. Students should note that it can take a long time before the effects of air pollution on an individual's health can be observed.
10. western New York and Pennsylvania; Answers may vary. Students may suggest that the prevailing winds concentrate the pollutants that contribute to acid precipitation on the Eastern seaboard.
11. Students may note that the prevailing winds and topographic features such as the Adirondack mountains concentrate acid precipitation over Buffalo.

CHAPTER RESOURCES

Chapter Resource File
- Section Quiz GENERAL
- Section Review GENERAL
- Vocabulary and Section Summary GENERAL
- Critical Thinking ADVANCED
- SciLinks Activity GENERAL
- Datasheet for Quick Lab

Technology
- Interactive Explorations CD-ROM
  - Moose Malady GENERAL

Section 4 • Air Pollution

Skills Practice Lab

Under Pressure!

Teacher's Notes

Time Required
One 45-minute class period plus 15 minutes each day for 3 or 4 days

Lab Ratings
EASY →→→ HARD

Teacher Prep – 2
Student Set-Up – 4
Concept Level – 2
Clean Up – 2

MATERIALS
The materials listed on the student page are enough for a group of 2–4 students.

Safety Caution
Remind students to review all safety cautions and icons before beginning this lab activity.

Preparation Notes
A week before the activity, have students bring in large coffee cans. Jars can substitute for coffee cans in this experiment. For more-accurate results, make sure students place their barometers in a shaded area. As students work on this lab in class, have them collect newspaper clippings of daily weather reports.

Using Scientific Methods
Skills Practice Lab

Under Pressure!

Imagine that you are planning a picnic with your friends, so you look in the newspaper for the weather forecast. The temperature this afternoon should be in the low 80s. This temperature sounds quite comfortable! But you notice that the newspaper's forecast also includes the barometer reading. What's a barometer? And what does the reading tell you? In this activity, you will build your own barometer and will discover what this tool can tell you.

OBJECTIVES
Predict how changes in air pressure affect a barometer.
Build a barometer to test your hypothesis.

MATERIALS
- balloon
- can, coffee, large, empty, 10 cm in diameter
- card, index
- scissors
- straw, drinking
- tape, masking, or rubber band

SAFETY

Ask a Question
❶ How can I use a barometer to detect changes in air pressure?

Form a Hypothesis
❷ Write a few sentences that answer the question above.

Test the Hypothesis
❸ Stretch the balloon a few times. Then, blow up the balloon, and let the air out. This step will make your barometer more sensitive to changes in atmospheric pressure.

❹ Cut off the open end of the balloon. Next, stretch the balloon over the open end of the coffee can. Then, attach the balloon to the can with masking tape or a rubber band.

CLASSROOM TESTED & APPROVED

Terry J. Rakes
Elmwood Jr. High
Rogers, Arkansas

CHAPTER RESOURCES

Chapter Resource File
- Datasheet for Chapter Lab
- Lab Notes and Answers

Technology
- Classroom Videos
  • Lab Video

LabBook
• Go Fly a Bike!

---

472 Chapter 15 • The Atmosphere

5. Cut one end of the straw at an angle to make a pointer.

6. Place the straw on the stretched balloon so that the pointer is directed away from the center of the balloon. Five centimeters of the end of the straw should hang over the edge of the can. Tape the straw to the balloon as shown in the illustration at right.

7. Tape the index card to the side of the can as shown in the illustration at right. Congratulations! You have just made a barometer!

8. Now, use your barometer to collect and record information about air pressure. Place the barometer outside for 3 or 4 days. On each day, mark on the index card where the tip of the straw points.

Analyze the Results

1. **Explaining Events** What atmospheric factors affect how your barometer works? Explain your answer.

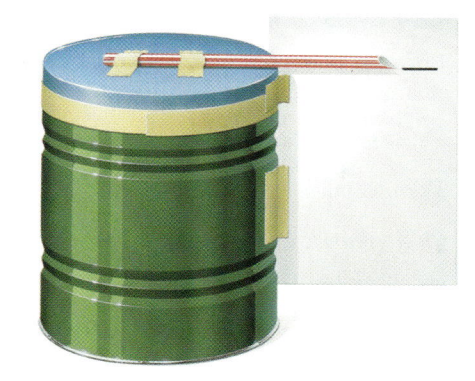

2. **Recognizing Patterns** What does it mean when the straw moves up?

3. **Recognizing Patterns** What does it mean when the straw moves down?

Draw Conclusions

4. **Applying Conclusions** Compare your results with the barometric pressures listed in your local newspaper. What kind of weather is associated with high pressure? What kind of weather is associated with low pressure?

5. **Evaluating Results** Does the barometer you built support your hypothesis? Explain your answer.

Applying Your Data

Now, you can use your barometer to measure the actual air pressure! Get the weather section from your local newspaper for the same 3 or 4 days that you were testing your barometer. Find the barometer reading in the newspaper for each day, and record the reading beside that day's mark on your index card. Use these markings on your card to create a scale with marks at regular intervals. Transfer this scale to a new card and attach it to your barometer.

Analyze the Results

1. A change in air pressure will affect how the barometer works. Temperature changes may also affect the barometer.

2. An upward movement of the straw indicates that the atmospheric pressure is increasing. Air pressure is pushing on the balloon, which causes the pointer to rise.

3. A downward movement of the straw indicates that the atmospheric pressure is decreasing. Less air pressure causes the pointer to dip downward.

Draw Conclusions

4. Clear, dry days are associated with high pressure. Cloudy, rainy, or humid days are associated with low pressure. A sudden drop in air pressure usually indicates that a storm is on the way.

5. Answers will vary depending on the hypothesis. Students should explain how their barometer was affected by atmospheric pressure and why the experiment supported or disproved their hypothesis.

Applying Your Data

Make sure students are aware that barometric pressure changes throughout the day. Students should try to get recorded pressures for the same time of day that they were testing their barometer. Some Internet sites provide weather reports that are updated hourly. Be sure to tell students that their barometric measurements will be approximate.

CHAPTER RESOURCES

Workbooks

- **Whiz-Bang Demonstrations**
  - Blue Sky ADVANCED
- **EcoLabs & Field Activities**
  - That Greenhouse Effect! GENERAL
- **Long-Term Projects & Research Ideas**
  - A Breath of Fresh Ether? ADVANCED
- **Calculator-Based Labs**
  - Heating of Land and Water ADVANCED
  - The Greenhouse Effect ADVANCED

Chapter 15 • Chapter Lab   473

Chapter Review

Assignment Guide

Section	Questions
1	2, 6, 7–9, 11, 17–19, 21
2	3, 4, 12, 13, 22, 24
3	5, 14, 23, 25, 26
4	15, 16, 20
1 and 3	1

ANSWERS

Using Key Terms

1. Sample answer: Air pressure is the measure of the force with which air molecules are pushing on a surface. Wind is the movement of air caused by differences in air pressure.
2. Sample answer: The troposphere is the lowest layer of the Earth's atmosphere. The thermosphere is the uppermost layer of the Earth's atmosphere.
3. Sample answer: The greenhouse effect is the Earth's natural heating process, by which gases in the atmosphere absorb and reradiate thermal energy. Global warming is a rise in average global temperature.
4. Sample answer: Convection is the transfer of thermal energy by the circulation of a liquid or gas. Thermal conduction is the transfer of thermal energy through a material.
5. Sample answer: A global wind is a large-scale pattern of air circulation in the atmosphere. A local wind generally flows short distances and can blow from any direction.
6. Sample answer: The stratosphere is the atmospheric layer above the troposphere, where temperature rises with altitude. The mesosphere is between the stratosphere and thermosphere, where temperature decreases with increasing altitude.

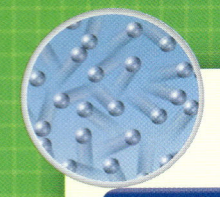

Chapter Review

USING KEY TERMS

For each pair of terms, explain how the meanings of the terms differ.

1. *air pressure* and *wind*
2. *troposphere* and *thermosphere*
3. *greenhouse effect* and *global warming*
4. *convection* and *thermal conduction*
5. *global wind* and *local wind*
6. *stratosphere* and *mesosphere*

UNDERSTANDING KEY IDEAS

Multiple Choice

7. What is the most abundant gas in the atmosphere?
    a. oxygen
    b. hydrogen
    c. nitrogen
    d. carbon dioxide

8. A major source of oxygen for the Earth's atmosphere is
    a. sea water.
    b. the sun.
    c. plants.
    d. animals.

9. The bottom layer of the atmosphere, where almost all weather occurs, is the
    a. stratosphere.
    b. troposphere.
    c. thermosphere.
    d. mesosphere.

10. What percentage of the solar energy that reaches the outer atmosphere is absorbed at the Earth's surface?
    a. 20%
    b. 30%
    c. 50%
    d. 70%

11. The ozone layer is located in the
    a. stratosphere.
    b. troposphere.
    c. thermosphere.
    d. mesosphere.

12. By which method does most thermal energy in the atmosphere circulate?
    a. conduction
    b. convection
    c. advection
    d. radiation

13. The balance between incoming and outgoing energy is called
    a. the convection balance.
    b. the conduction balance.
    c. the greenhouse effect.
    d. the radiation balance.

14. In which wind belt is most of the United States located?
    a. westerlies
    b. northeast trade winds
    c. southeast trade winds
    d. doldrums

15. Which of the following pollutants is NOT a primary pollutant?
    a. car exhaust
    b. acid precipitation
    c. smoke from a factory
    d. fumes from burning plastic

Understanding Key Ideas

7. c
8. c
9. b
10. c
11. a
12. b
13. d
14. a
15. b
16. d

474 Chapter 15 • The Atmosphere

16 The Clean Air Act
   a. controls the amount of air pollutants that can be released from many sources.
   b. requires cars to run on fuels other than gasoline.
   c. requires many industries to use scrubbers.
   d. Both (a) and (c)

Short Answer

17 Why does the atmosphere become less dense as altitude increases?

18 Explain why air rises when it is heated.

19 What is the main cause of temperature changes in the atmosphere?

20 What are secondary pollutants, and how do they form? Give an example of a secondary pollutant.

CRITICAL THINKING

21 **Concept Mapping** Use the following terms to create a concept map: *mesosphere, stratosphere, layers, temperature, troposphere,* and *atmosphere.*

22 **Identifying Relationships** What is the relationship between the greenhouse effect and global warming?

23 **Applying Concepts** How do you think the Coriolis effect would change if the Earth rotated twice as fast as it does? Explain.

24 **Making Inferences** The atmosphere of Venus has a very high level of carbon dioxide. How might this fact influence the greenhouse effect on Venus?

INTERPRETING GRAPHICS

Use the diagram below to answer the questions that follow. When answering the questions that follow, assume that ocean currents do not affect the path of the boats.

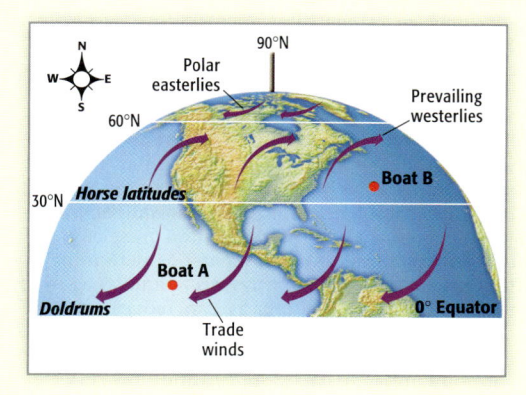

25 If Boat A traveled to 50°N, from which direction would the prevailing winds blow?

26 If Boat B sailed with the prevailing westerlies in the Northern Hemisphere, in which direction would the boat be traveling?

---

17. As altitude increases, there are fewer gas molecules. Gravity pulls most of the atmosphere's gas molecules close to the Earth's surface, which makes the lower layers more dense than the upper layers.

18. Air rises as it is heated because it becomes less dense.

19. The temperature differences in the atmosphere result mainly from the way solar energy is absorbed. Some layers are warmer because they contain gases that absorb solar energy.

20. Secondary pollutants form when primary pollutants react with other primary pollutants or with other naturally occurring substances. Acid rain is an example of a secondary pollutant.

Critical Thinking

21. An answer to this exercise can be found at the end of this book.

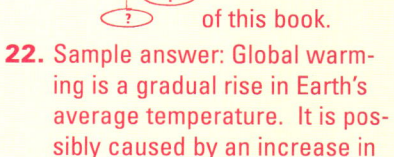

22. Sample answer: Global warming is a gradual rise in Earth's average temperature. It is possibly caused by an increase in the greenhouse effect.

23. The Coriolis effect would be greater if the Earth rotated twice as fast. The apparent deflection of winds is caused by the Earth's rotation.

24. Answers may vary. The greater concentration of carbon dioxide in Venus's atmosphere causes the greenhouse effect to be more extreme on Venus than on Earth.

Interpreting Graphics

25. The prevailing winds would be blowing east.

26. The boat would be traveling northeast.

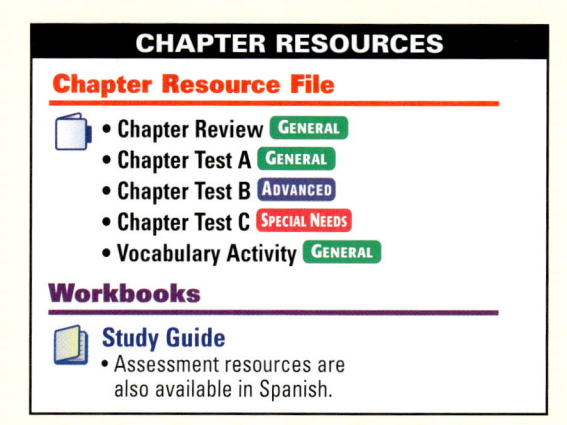

CHAPTER RESOURCES

Chapter Resource File
- Chapter Review GENERAL
- Chapter Test A GENERAL
- Chapter Test B ADVANCED
- Chapter Test C SPECIAL NEEDS
- Vocabulary Activity GENERAL

Workbooks
- Study Guide
- Assessment resources are also available in Spanish.

Standardized Test Preparation

Teacher's Note

To provide practice under more realistic testing conditions, give students 20 minutes to answer all of the questions in this Standardized Test Preparation.

MISCONCEPTION ALERT

Answers to the standardized test preparation can help you identify student misconceptions and misunderstandings.

READING

Passage 1
1. D
2. F

TEST DOCTOR

Question 2: All of the answer options may appear similar. Remind students that they must read the passage carefully to discover the correct answer choice.

Passage 2
1. D
2. I

Standardized Test Preparation

READING

Read each of the passages below. Then, answer the questions that follow each passage.

Passage 1 An important part of the EPA's Acid Rain Program is the allowance trading system, which is designed to reduce sulfur dioxide emissions. In this system, 1 ton of sulfur dioxide (SO_2) emission is equivalent to one <u>allowance</u>. A limited number of allowances are allocated for each year. Companies purchase the allowances from the EPA and are allowed to produce as many tons of SO_2 as they have allowances for the year. Companies can buy, sell, or trade allowances, but if they exceed their allowances, they must pay a fine. The system allows a company to determine the most cost-effective ways to comply with the Clean Air Act. A company can reduce emissions by using technology that conserves energy, using renewable energy sources, or updating its pollution-control devices and using low-sulfur fuels.

1. According to the passage, which of the following methods can a company use to reduce emissions?
   A preserving wildlife habitat
   B lobbying Congress
   C using high-sulfur fuels
   D using technology that conserves energy

2. In the passage, what does *allowance* mean?
   F an allotment for a pollutant
   G an allocation of money for reducing pollution
   H an alleviation of pollution
   I an allegation of pollution

Passage 2 The chinook, or "snow eater," is a dry wind that blows down the eastern side of the Rocky Mountains from New Mexico to Alaska. Arapaho Indians gave the chinook its name because of its ability to melt large amounts of snow very quickly. Chinooks form when moist air is forced over a mountain range. The air cools as it rises. As the air cools, it releases moisture by raining or snowing. As the dry air flows over the mountaintop, it compresses and heats the air below. The warm, dry wind that results is worthy of the name "snow eater" because it melts a half meter of snow in a few hours! The temperature change caused when a chinook rushes down a mountainside can also be dramatic. In 1943 in Spearfish, South Dakota, the temperature at 7:30 in the morning was –4°F. But two minutes later, a chinook caused the temperature to soar 49° to 45°F.

1. Which of the following descriptions best explains why the chinook is called "the snow eater"?
   A The chinook is so cold that it prevents the formation of snow in the atmosphere.
   B The chinook is so warm that it prevents the formation of snow in the atmosphere.
   C The chinook is a warm wind that has high humidity.
   D The chinook is a warm wind that has low humidity.

2. According to the passage, at what time did the temperature reach 45°F in Spearfish, South Dakota?
   F 7:30 P.M.
   G 7:32 P.M.
   H 7:30 A.M.
   I 7:32 A.M.

TEST DOCTOR

Question 2: Students may see the time *7:30* in the text and conclude that H is the answer to Question 2. Remind students to read the passage thoroughly. The most obvious answer is not always the correct choice.

INTERPRETING GRAPHICS

Use the illustration below to answer the questions that follow.

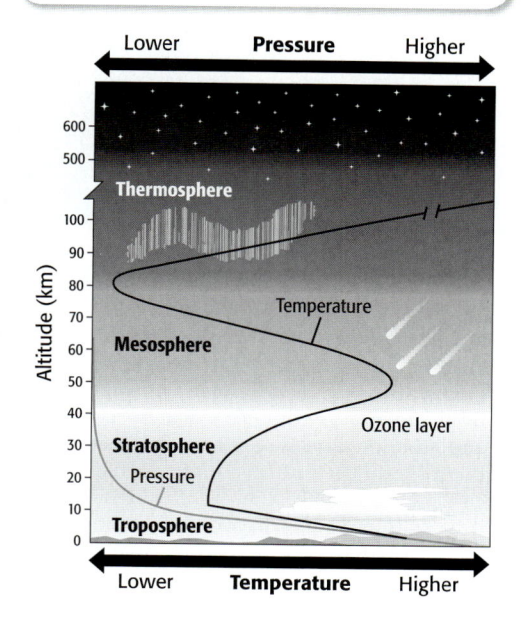

1. Which of the following statements describes how temperature changes in the mesosphere?
   A Temperature increases as altitude increases.
   B Temperature decreases as altitude increases.
   C Temperature decreases as pressure increases.
   D Temperature does not change as pressure increases.

2. In which layers does temperature decrease as pressure decreases?
   F the troposphere and the mesosphere
   G the troposphere and the stratosphere
   H the ozone layer and the troposphere
   I the ozone layer and the thermosphere

3. A research balloon took measurements at 23 km, 35 km, 52 km, 73 km, 86 km, 92 km, 101 km, and 110 km. Which measurements were taken in the mesosphere?
   A measurements at 23 km and 35 km
   B measurements at 52 km and 73 km
   C measurements at 86 km and 92 km
   D measurements at 101 km and 110 km

MATH

Read each question below, and choose the best answer.

1. An airplane is flying at a speed of 500 km/h when it encounters a jet stream moving in the same direction at 150 km/h. If the plane flies with the jet stream, how much farther will the plane travel in 1.5 h?
   A 950 km
   B 525 km
   C 225 km
   D 150 km

2. Today's wind speed was measured at 18 km/h. What was the wind speed in meters per hour?
   F 1.8 m/h
   G 180 m/h
   H 1,800 m/h
   I 18,000 m/h

3. Rockport received 24.1 cm of rain on Monday, 12.5 cm of rain on Tuesday, and 5.8 cm of rain on Thursday. The rest of the week, it did not rain. How much rain did Rockport receive during the week?
   A 18.3 cm
   B 36.6 cm
   C 42.4 cm
   D 45.7 cm

4. A weather station recorded the following temperatures during a 5 h period: 15°C, 18°C, 13°C, 15°C, and 20°C. What was the average temperature during this period?
   F 14.2°C
   G 15.2°C
   H 16.2°C
   I 20.2°C

5. The temperature in Waterford, Virginia, increased 1.3°C every hour for 5 h. If the temperature in the morning was −4°C, what was the temperature 4 h later?
   A 2.5°C
   B 2.3°C
   C 1.3°C
   D 1.2°C

INTERPRETING GRAPHICS

1. B
2. F
3. B

TEST DOCTOR

Question 1: This is a complex graphic that may appear intimidating to students at first. The illustration synthesizes three types of data: altitude, temperature, and pressure. To help students answer this question, have them analyze each statement and eliminate the incorrect statements until they are left with the correct choice.

MATH

1. C
2. I
3. C
4. H
5. D

TEST DOCTOR

Question 4: Students may choose answer choice I if they divide the total temperature by 4 instead of 5. Remind students to always double-check the number of numbers that they are asked to average. If scrap paper is available during the test, it is a good strategy to write down all of the numbers given in a test question before solving a problem.

Chapter 15 • Standardized Test Preparation

Science in Action

Science, Technology, and Society

ACTIVITY — BASIC

The HyperSoar jet looks like a giant paper airplane. This design makes the jet more aerodynamic, so it is able to glide for long distances. Organize students into small groups, and have them design and test paper airplanes for gliding ability. Have a contest, and give a prize for the best glider.

Weird Science

ACTIVITY — GENERAL

Students can learn a lot about NEXRAD radar and animal migrations by visiting the Clemson University Radar Ornithology Web Site. The Web Site has NEXRAD images of bird, bat, and insect migrations. Images of bat migrations are especially interesting. When bats leave their roosts in the evening, they usually fly in a spiral pattern. This pattern is shown as a crescent shape in the radar images. Insects are indicated by a dotted pattern that is similar to the pattern that birds make but insects have a lower reflectivity because they are less dense.

Science in Action

Science, Technology, and Society

The HyperSoar Jet
Imagine traveling from Chicago to Tokyo in 72 minutes. If the HyperSoar jet becomes a reality, you may be able to travel to the other side of the world in less time than it takes to watch a movie! To accomplish this amazing feat, the jet would "skip" across the upper stratosphere. To begin skipping, the jet would climb above the stratosphere, turn off its engines, and glide for about 60 km. Then, gravity would pull the jet down to where the air is denser. The denser air would cause the jet to soar upward. In this way, the jet would skip across a layer of dense air until it was ready to land. Each 2-minute skip would cover about 450 km, and the HyperSoar would be able to fly at Mach 10—a speed of 3 km/s!

Math ACTIVITY

A trip on the HyperSoar from Chicago to Tokyo would require about 18 "skips." Each skip is 450 km. If the trip is 10,123 km, how many kilometers will the jet travel when it is not skipping?

Weird Science

Radar Zoology
"For tonight's forecast, expect a light shower of mayflies. A wave of warblers will approach from the south. Tomorrow will be cloudy, and a band of free-tailed bats will move to the south in the early evening." Such a forecast may not make the evening news, but it is a familiar scenario for radar zoologists. Radar zoologists use a type of radar called *NEXRAD* to track migrating birds, bands of bats, and swarms of insects. NEXRAD tracks animals in the atmosphere in the same way that it tracks storms. The system sends out a microwave signal. If the signal hits an object, some of the energy reflects back to a receiver. NEXRAD has been especially useful to scientists who study bird migration. Birds tend to migrate at night, when the atmosphere is more stable, so until now, nighttime bird migration has been difficult to observe. NEXRAD has also helped identify important bird migration routes and critical stopovers. For example, scientists have discovered that many birds migrate over the Gulf of Mexico instead of around it.

Social Studies ACTIVITY

Geography plays an important role in bird migration. Many birds ride the "thermals" produced by mountain ranges. Find out what thermals are, and create a map of bird migration routes over North America.

Answer to Math Activity
10,123 km − (18 skips × 450 km) = 2023 km

Answer to Social Studies Activity
Thermals are strong updrafts created by rising columns of warm air. When warm air encounters a mountain or ridge, it may rise sharply upward. Birds take advantage of thermals to conserve energy. Maps of bird migration routes are available on the Internet. The four major migratory routes in North America are the Central Flyway, the Mississippi Flyway, the Atlantic Flyway, and the Pacific Flyway.

Careers

Ellen Paneok

Bush Pilot For Ellen Paneok, understanding weather patterns is a matter of life and death. As a bush pilot, she flies mail, supplies, and people to remote villages in Alaska that can be reached only by plane. Bad weather is one of the most serious challenges Paneok faces. "It's beautiful up here," she says, "but it can also be harsh." One dangerous situation is landing a plane in mountainous regions. "On top of a mountain you can't tell which way the wind is blowing," Paneok says. In this case, she flies in a rectangular pattern to determine the wind direction. Landing a plane on the frozen Arctic Ocean is also dangerous. In white-out conditions, the horizon can't be seen because the sky and the ground are the same color. "It's like flying in a milk bottle full of milk," Paneok says. In these conditions, she fills black plastic garbage bags and drops them from the plane to help guide her landing.

Paneok had to overcome many challenges to become a pilot. As a child, she lived in seven foster homes before being placed in an all-girls' home at the age of 14. In the girls' home, she read a magazine about careers in aviation and decided then and there that she wanted to become a pilot. At first, she faced a lot of opposition from people telling her that she wouldn't be able to become a pilot. Now, she encourages young people to pursue their goals. "If you decide you want to go for it, go for it. There may be obstacles in your way, but you've just got to find a way to go over them, get around them, or dig under them," she says.

Language Arts Activity

Beryl Markham lived an exciting life as a bush pilot delivering mail and supplies to remote areas of Africa. Read about her life or the life of Bessie Coleman, one of the most famous African American women in the history of flying.

Ellen Paneok is shown at right with two of her Inupiat passengers.

go.hrw.com
To learn more about these Science in Action topics, visit **go.hrw.com** and type in the keyword **HZ5ATMF**.

Current Science
Check out Current Science® articles related to this chapter by visiting **go.hrw.com**. Just type in the keyword **HZ5CS15**.

Careers

Background
Ellen Paneok is a native Alaskan Eskimo who has been flying for 26 years. She says that the biggest personal reward of working as a bush pilot is the opportunity to interact with the people in the bush, many of whom are her relatives or close friends. In addition to working as a commercial pilot, Paneok serves as a board member of an air museum. In this role, she flies antique airplanes at air shows and other exhibitions. She has also written several magazine articles and creates and sells Indian art. She has illustrated a book and is also interested in photography.

Answer to Language Arts Activity
Beryl Markham's autobiography *West with the Night* is often found on high school reading lists. Advanced students may enjoy reading about her life.

Science Humor

Ellen Paneok has had many exciting adventures during her years of flying in Alaska. When the weather turns bad, she sometimes has to spend the night in small villages where the only available bed is in the jail house. Once, she had to chase two polar bears off the runway before she could land. After she landed, Paneok was starting to unload the plane when she realized that she didn't know exactly where the polar bears had gone. "You've never seen anyone unload a thousand pounds off an airplane so fast," she laughs.

Chapter 15 • Science in Action   479

16 Understanding Weather
Chapter Planning Guide

Compression guide: To shorten instruction because of time limitations, omit the Chapter Lab.

OBJECTIVES	LABS, DEMONSTRATIONS, AND ACTIVITIES	TECHNOLOGY RESOURCES
PACING • 90 min pp. 480–489 **Chapter Opener**	SE Start-up Activity, p. 481 ◆ GENERAL	OSP Parent Letter ■ GENERAL CD Student Edition on CD-ROM CD Guided Reading Audio CD ■ TR Chapter Starter Transparency* VID Brain Food Video Quiz
Section 1 Water in the Air • Explain how water moves through the water cycle. • Describe how relative humidity is affected by temperature and levels of water vapor. • Describe the relationship between dew point and condensation. • List three types of cloud forms. • Identify four kinds of precipitation.	TE Group Activity Air Molecules, p. 482 GENERAL TE Demonstration Water in Air, p. 483 ◆ BASIC TE Activity Sentence Completion, p. 484 GENERAL SE Quick Lab Out of Thin Air, p. 485 GENERAL SE Connection to Language Arts Cloud Clues, p. 486 GENERAL TE Activity Naming Clouds, p. 487 BASIC TE Connection Activity Language Arts, p. 487 GENERAL SE Inquiry Lab Boiling Over!, p. 508 ◆ GENERAL SE Skills Practice Lab Let It Snow!, p. 751 GENERAL LB Whiz-Bang Demonstrations It's Raining Again* ◆ GENERAL LB Calculator-Based Lab Relative Humidity* ◆ GENERAL	CRF Lesson Plans* TR Bellringer Transparency* TR The Water Cycle* TR Cloud Types Based on Form and Altitude* SE Internet Activity, p. 484 GENERAL CRF SciLinks Activity GENERAL VID Lab Videos for Earth Science
PACING • 45 min pp. 490–495 **Section 2 Air Masses and Fronts** • Identify the four kinds of air masses that influence weather in the United States. • Describe the four major types of fronts. • Explain how fronts cause weather changes. • Explain how cyclones and anticyclones affect the weather.	TE Demonstration Density, p. 491 ◆ GENERAL TE Activity Using Maps, p. 493 BASIC LB Whiz-Bang Demonstrations When Air Bags Collide* ◆ GENERAL LB Long-Term Projects & Research Ideas A Storm on the Horizon* ADVANCED SE Science in Action Math, Social Studies, and Language Arts Activities, pp. 514–515	CRF Lesson Plans* TR Bellringer Transparency* TR Cold and Warm Fronts* TR Occluded and Stationary Fronts*
PACING • 45 min pp. 496–503 **Section 3 Severe Weather** • Describe how lightning forms. • Describe the formation of thunderstorms, tornadoes, and hurricanes. • Describe the characteristics of thunderstorms, tornadoes, and hurricanes. • Explain how to stay safe during severe weather.	TE Demonstration Modeling Thunder, p. 496 ◆ GENERAL TE Connection Activity Math, p. 497 GENERAL TE Connection Activity Real World, p. 498 GENERAL TE Activity Weather and Energy, p. 500 GENERAL TE Group Activity Hurricane Newscast, p. 500 GENERAL SE School-to-Home Activity Natural Disaster Plan, p. 501 GENERAL TE Connection Activity Meteorology, p. 501 ADVANCED LB Inquiry Labs When Disaster Strikes* BASIC	CRF Lesson Plans* TR Bellringer Transparency* CRF SciLinks Activity* GENERAL TR LINK TO PHYSICAL SCIENCE How Lightning Forms
PACING • 45 min pp. 504–507 **Section 4 Forecasting the Weather** • Describe the different types of instruments used to take weather measurements. • Explain how radar and weather satellites help meteorologists forecast the weather. • Explain how to interpret a weather map.	TE Demonstration Air Pressure and Barometers, p. 504 ◆ GENERAL TE Connection Activity Real World, p. 505 GENERAL TE Connection Activity Math, p. 506 GENERAL SE Skills Practice Lab Watching the Weather, p. 748 GENERAL SE Model-Making Lab Gone With the Wind, p. 752 ◆ GENERAL LB EcoLabs & Field Activities Rain Maker or Rain Faker?* ◆ ADVANCED	CRF Lesson Plans* TR Bellringer Transparency*

PACING • 90 min

CHAPTER REVIEW, ASSESSMENT, AND STANDARDIZED TEST PREPARATION
- CRF Vocabulary Activity* GENERAL
- SE Chapter Review, pp. 510–511 GENERAL
- CRF Chapter Review* ■ GENERAL
- CRF Chapter Tests A* ■ GENERAL, B* ADVANCED, C* SPECIAL NEEDS
- SE Standardized Test Preparation, pp. 512–513 GENERAL
- CRF Standardized Test Preparation* GENERAL
- CRF Performance-Based Assessment* GENERAL
- OSP Test Generator GENERAL
- CRF Test Item Listing* GENERAL

Online and Technology Resources

Visit **go.hrw.com** for a variety of free resources related to this textbook. Enter the keyword **HZ5WEA**.

Holt Online Learning — Students can access interactive problem-solving help and active visual concept development with the *Holt Science and Technology* Online Edition available at **www.hrw.com**.

Guided Reading Audio CD Also in Spanish — A direct reading of each chapter for auditory learners, reluctant readers, and Spanish-speaking students.

Science Tutor CD-ROM — Excellent for remediation and test practice.

KEY

SE Student Edition	**CRF** Chapter Resource File	**SS** Science Skills Worksheets	∗ Also on One-Stop Planner
TE Teacher Edition	**OSP** One-Stop Planner	**MS** Math Skills for Science Worksheets	♦ Requires advance prep
	LB Lab Bank	**CD** CD or CD-ROM	■ Also available in Spanish
	TR Transparencies	**VID** Classroom Video/DVD	

SKILLS DEVELOPMENT RESOURCES	SECTION REVIEW AND ASSESSMENT	STANDARDS CORRELATIONS
SE Pre-Reading Activity, p. 480 GENERAL OSP Science Puzzlers, Twisters & Teasers* GENERAL		National Science Education Standards UCP 2; SAI 1; SPSP 3, 4; ES 1f, 1i, 1j
CRF Directed Reading A* ■ BASIC, B* SPECIAL NEEDS CRF Vocabulary and Section Summary* GENERAL SE Reading Strategy Paired Summarizing, p. 482 GENERAL SE Math Practice Relative Humidity, p. 483 GENERAL TE Inclusion Strategies, p. 484 ♦ TE Reading Strategy Sequencing, p. 486 GENERAL	SE Reading Checks, pp. 482, 484, 485, 487 GENERAL TE Homework, p. 486 BASIC TE Reteaching, p. 488 BASIC TE Quiz, p. 488 GENERAL TE Alternative Assessment, p. 488 ADVANCED TE Homework, p. 488 ADVANCED SE Section Review,* p. 489 GENERAL CRF Section Quiz* ■ GENERAL	UCP 2, 3; SAI 1; SPSP 3; ES 1f, 1i; *Chapter Lab:* UCP 2, 3; SAI 1, 2; ST 1; HNS 2; *LabBook:* UCP 3; SAI 1
CRF Directed Reading A* ■ BASIC, B* SPECIAL NEEDS CRF Vocabulary and Section Summary* GENERAL SE Reading Strategy Reading Organizer, p. 490 GENERAL	SE Reading Checks, pp. 491, 493, 495 GENERAL TE Homework, p. 490 GENERAL TE Reteaching, p. 494 BASIC TE Quiz, p. 494 GENERAL TE Alternative Assessment, p. 494 GENERAL SE Section Review,* p. 495 ■ GENERAL CRF Section Quiz* ■ GENERAL	HNS 3; ES 1j
CRF Directed Reading A* ■ BASIC, B* SPECIAL NEEDS CRF Vocabulary and Section Summary* GENERAL SE Reading Strategy Reading Organizer, p. 496 GENERAL TE Inclusion Strategies, p. 498 ♦ CRF Reinforcement Worksheet Precipitation Situations* BASIC	SE Reading Checks, pp. 497, 499, 500 GENERAL TE Homework, p. 499 ADVANCED TE Reteaching, p. 502 BASIC TE Quiz, p. 502 GENERAL TE Alternative Assessment, p. 502 GENERAL SE Section Review,* p. 503 ■ GENERAL CRF Section Quiz* ■ GENERAL	SPSP 3, 4; ES 1i, 1j
CRF Directed Reading A* ■ BASIC, B* SPECIAL NEEDS CRF Vocabulary and Section Summary* GENERAL SE Reading Strategy Reading Organizer, p. 504 GENERAL MS Math Skills for Science Using Temperature Scales* GENERAL CRF Critical Thinking Commanding the Sky* ADVANCED	SE Reading Checks, p. 504 GENERAL TE Reteaching, p. 506 BASIC TE Quiz, p. 506 GENERAL TE Alternative Assessment, p. 506 GENERAL SE Section Review,* p. 507 ■ GENERAL CRF Section Quiz* ■ GENERAL	SPSP 3, 4; ES 1i, 1j; *LabBook:* SAI 1; ST 1

One-Stop Planner® CD-ROM

This convenient CD-ROM includes:
- Lab Materials QuickList Software
- Holt Calendar Planner
- Customizable Lesson Plans
- Printable Worksheets
- ExamView® Test Generator

CNN Student News

cnnstudentnews.com

Find the latest news, lesson plans, and activities related to important scientific events.

SciLinks NSTA

www.scilinks.org

Maintained by the **National Science Teachers Association.** See Chapter Enrichment pages for a complete list of topics.

Current Science®

Check out **Current Science** articles and activities by visiting the HRW Web site at **go.hrw.com**. Just type in the keyword **HZ5CS16T**.

Classroom Videos

- **Lab Videos** demonstrate the chapter lab.
- **Brain Food Video Quizzes** help students review the chapter material.
- **CNN Videos** bring science into your students' daily life.

Chapter 16 • Chapter Planning Guide

16 Chapter Resources

Visual Resources

CHAPTER STARTER TRANSPARENCY

BELLRINGER TRANSPARENCIES

TEACHING TRANSPARENCIES

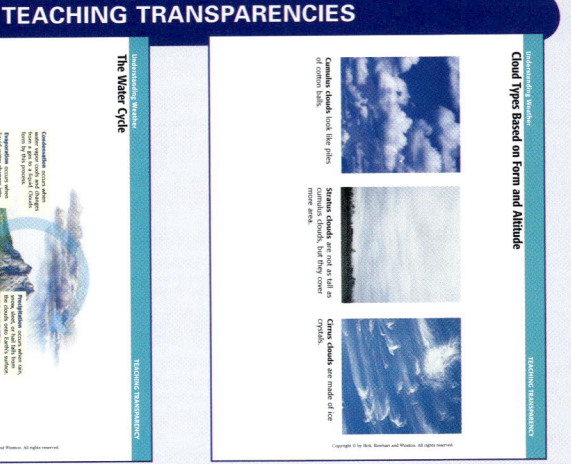

TEACHING TRANSPARENCIES

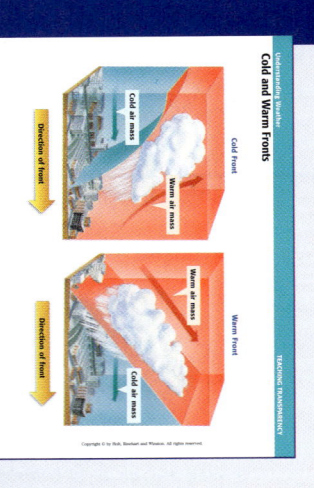

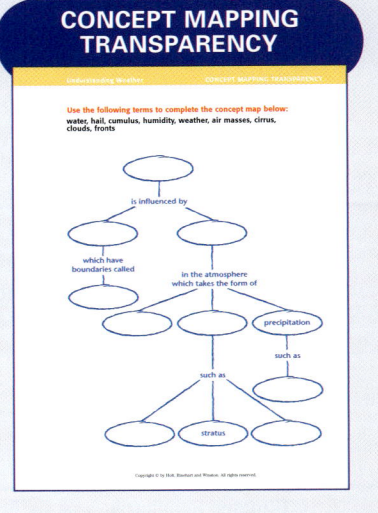

CONCEPT MAPPING TRANSPARENCY

Planning Resources

LESSON PLANS

PARENT LETTER — ALSO IN SPANISH

TEST ITEM LISTING

One-Stop Planner® CD-ROM

This CD-ROM includes all of the resources shown here and the following time-saving tools:

- **Lab Materials QuickList Software**
- **Customizable lesson plans**
- **Holt Calendar Planner**
- **The powerful ExamView® Test Generator**

479C Chapter 16 • Understanding Weather

For a preview of available worksheets covering math and science skills, see pages T26–T33. All of these resources are also on the One-Stop Planner®.

Meeting Individual Needs

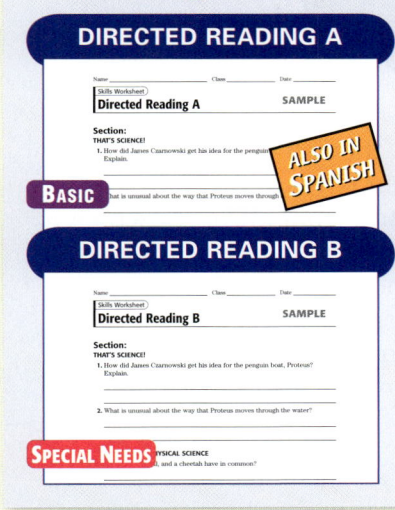

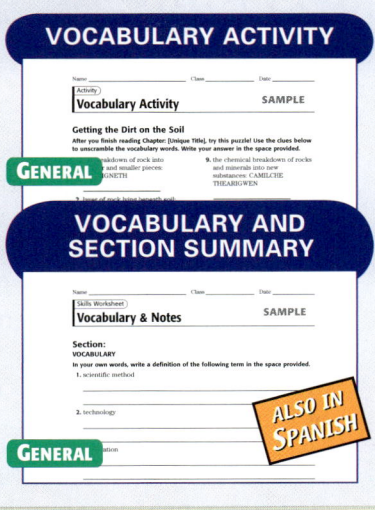

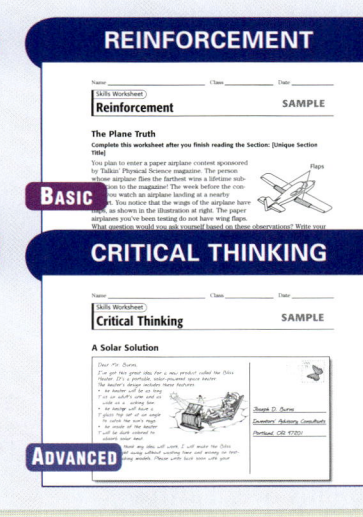

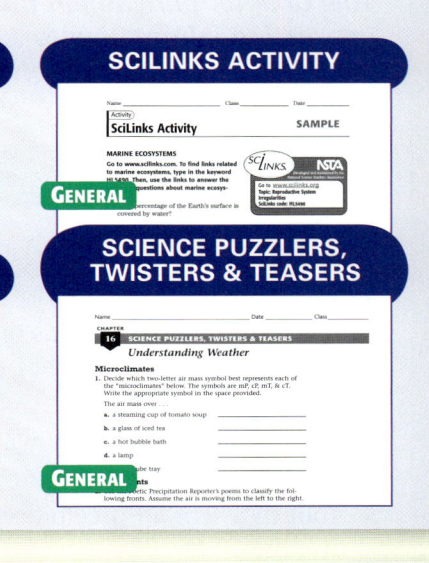

- **DIRECTED READING A** — BASIC (ALSO IN SPANISH)
- **DIRECTED READING B** — SPECIAL NEEDS
- **VOCABULARY ACTIVITY** — GENERAL
- **VOCABULARY AND SECTION SUMMARY** — GENERAL (ALSO IN SPANISH)
- **REINFORCEMENT** — BASIC
- **CRITICAL THINKING** — ADVANCED
- **SCILINKS ACTIVITY** — GENERAL
- **SCIENCE PUZZLERS, TWISTERS & TEASERS** — GENERAL

Labs and Activities

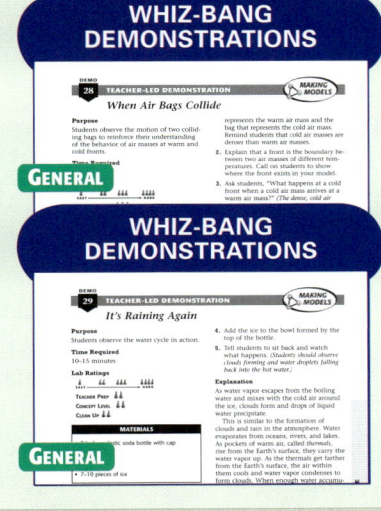

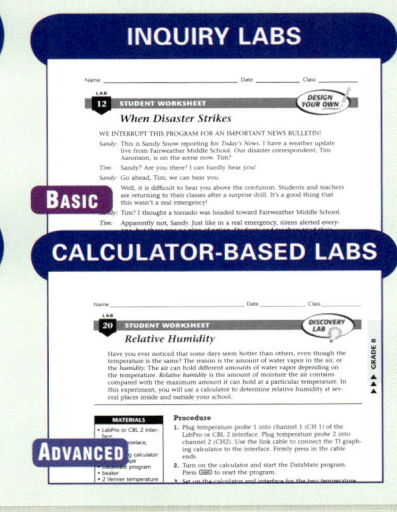

- **ECOLABS & FIELD ACTIVITIES** — GENERAL
- **LONG-TERM PROJECTS & RESEARCH IDEAS** — ADVANCED
- **WHIZ-BANG DEMONSTRATIONS** — GENERAL
- **WHIZ-BANG DEMONSTRATIONS** — GENERAL
- **INQUIRY LABS** — BASIC
- **CALCULATOR-BASED LABS** — ADVANCED
- **DATASHEETS FOR QUICKLABS**
- **DATASHEETS FOR CHAPTER LABS**
- **DATASHEETS FOR LABBOOK**

Review and Assessments

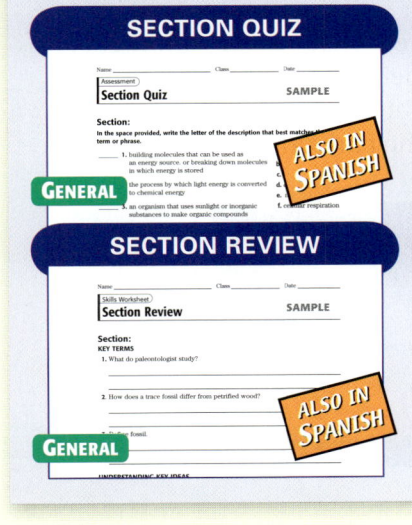

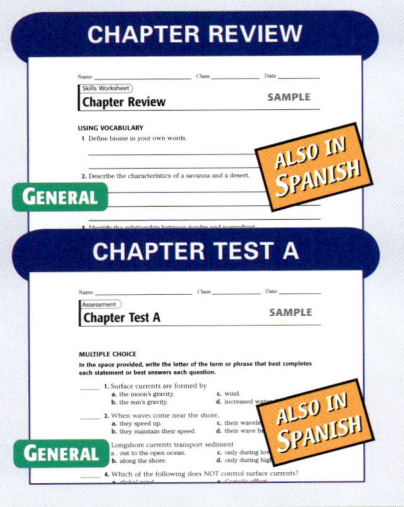

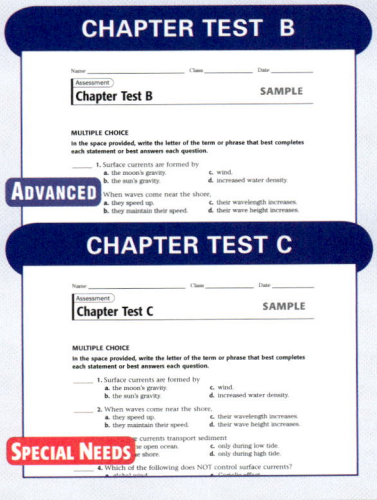

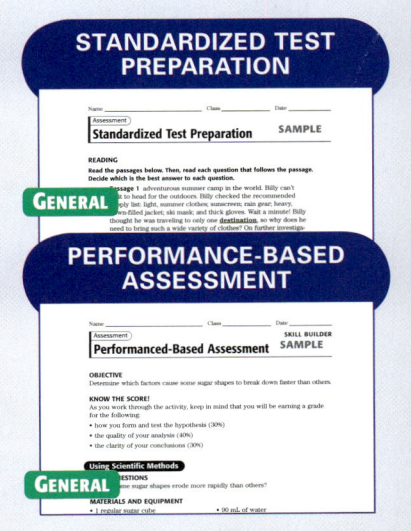

- **SECTION QUIZ** — GENERAL (ALSO IN SPANISH)
- **SECTION REVIEW** — GENERAL (ALSO IN SPANISH)
- **CHAPTER REVIEW** — GENERAL (ALSO IN SPANISH)
- **CHAPTER TEST A** — GENERAL (ALSO IN SPANISH)
- **CHAPTER TEST B** — ADVANCED
- **CHAPTER TEST C** — SPECIAL NEEDS
- **STANDARDIZED TEST PREPARATION** — GENERAL
- **PERFORMANCE-BASED ASSESSMENT** — GENERAL

Chapter 16 • Chapter Resources   479D

16 Chapter Enrichment

This Chapter Enrichment provides relevant and interesting information to expand and enhance your presentation of the chapter material.

Section 1

Water in the Air

Earth's Water Cycle

- The atmosphere contains only about 0.001% of the total volume of water on the planet (about 1.46×10^9 km^3).
- The rate at which water evaporates into Earth's atmosphere is about 5.1×10^{17} L per year.
- About 78% of all precipitation falls over Earth's oceans. Of the 22% that falls on land, about 65% returns to the air by evaporation.

Clouds

- Clouds may be composed of water droplets, ice crystals, or a combination of the two. For example, cirrus clouds are made of only ice crystals; stratus clouds are made of only water droplets; and altostratus clouds are mixtures of ice and liquid water. Cumulonimbus clouds, which produce snowflakes and hail, consist of water droplets near the bottom of the clouds and ice crystals in the upper parts of the clouds.

Is That a Fact!
◆ The largest hailstone ever recorded fell on Coffeyville, Kansas, on September 3, 1970. The hailstone was the size of a softball and weighed 0.75 kg.

Precipitation

- Due to differences in condensation rates within the cloud, not all of the millions of droplets of water that make up a cloud are the same size. Larger drops collide and merge with smaller drops to form raindrops.

Section 2

Air Masses and Fronts

Fronts

- As a warm front approaches, the first clouds to appear in the sky are the high clouds: cirrus, cirrostratus, and cirrocumulus. As the warm front moves closer, medium-height clouds, then low clouds appear. As the warm front arrives, the temperature and air pressure drop. In the Northern Hemisphere, winds generally blow from the northeast. Nimbostratus clouds bring drizzly precipitation, which may fall within 24 hours of the first cloud sighting.

- When a cold front enters an area, cumulonimbus clouds can produce thunderstorms, heavy rain, or snow along the front. After the cold front passes through an area, winds change direction and barometric pressure rises. Behind the cold front, temperatures usually fall, which brings cool, clear weather to the area.

Section 3

Severe Weather

Tornadoes

- Meteorologists rate tornado intensity using the Fujita Tornado Intensity Scale. An F0 tornado is a relatively weak storm that may damage chimneys, tree branches, and billboard signs. An F1 tornado is a moderate storm that can peel the surfaces off roofs, overturn mobile homes, and push moving cars off roads. F2 and F3 tornadoes cause considerable to severe damage by tearing roofs off houses, overturning railroad cars, and uprooting mature trees. An F4 tornado is a devastating storm that levels houses and other buildings and tosses cars into the air. The most severe tornado is an F5 tornado, which can lift houses off their foundations and carry them great distances. An F5 tornado can also carry cars over 100 m and strip the bark off trees.

Hurricanes

- On the Saffir-Simpson Scale, hurricanes fall into five categories. Category 1 hurricanes have sustained winds between 74 and 95 km/h and usually cause relatively minimal damage. Category 2 hurricanes cause moderate damage with winds ranging between 96 and 110 km/h. Category 3 hurricanes cause extensive damage with winds that blow between 111 and 130 km/h. Category 4 hurricanes have sustained winds between 131 and 155 km/h. Category 5 hurricanes, like Hurricane Andrew, which struck Florida in 1992, have sustained winds of more than 155 km/h. Category 5 hurricanes are classified as catastrophic storms.

Is That a Fact!

- A hurricane is called a *willy-willy* in Australia, a *taino* in Haiti, a *baguio* in the Philippines, and a *cordonazo* in western Mexico.

- The *trends method* involves determining high- and low-pressure areas, gauging the velocity of weather fronts, and locating areas of clouds and precipitation. A forecaster then uses these data to predict where these weather phenomena will be in the future. This method of weather prediction works well only when weather systems maintain constant velocities for a long period of time.

- The *climatology method* involves averaging weather data that have accumulated over many years to make a forecast. This method is accurate when weather patterns are similar to those expected for a given time of year.

- The *numerical weather-prediction (NWP)* method uses complex computer programs to generate models of probable air temperature, barometric pressure, wind velocity, and precipitation. A meteorologist then analyzes how he or she thinks the features predicted by the computer will interact to produce the day's weather. Despite its flaws, the NWP method is one of the most reliable methods available.

Section 4

Forecasting the Weather

Weather-Prediction Methods

- One of the simplest methods of weather prediction, the *persistence method*, assumes that the atmospheric conditions at the time of a weather forecast will not change in the near future. This method is fairly accurate in areas where weather patterns change very slowly, such as in southern California, where summer weather typically changes very little from day to day. Other methods are described below.

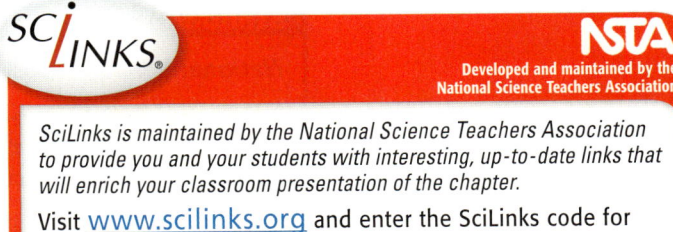

SciLinks is maintained by the National Science Teachers Association to provide you and your students with interesting, up-to-date links that will enrich your classroom presentation of the chapter.

Visit www.scilinks.org and enter the SciLinks code for more information about the topic listed.

Topic: The Water Cycle
SciLinks code: HSM1626

Topic: Severe Weather
SciLinks code: HSM1383

Topic: Air Masses and Fronts
SciLinks code: HSM0032

Topic: Forecasting the Weather
SciLinks code: HSM0606

Chapter 16 • Chapter Enrichment   479F

Overview

This chapter introduces some fundamental principles of meteorology and weather forecasting. Students learn about relative humidity, clouds, air masses and fronts, severe weather, and weather forecasting.

Assessing Prior Knowledge

Students should be familiar with the following topics:
- the water cycle
- characteristics of the atmosphere

Identifying Misconceptions

Students may think that weather forecasting is extremely complicated. Point out that the science of meteorology relies on a few simple concepts, such as relative humidity, simple gas laws, and the movement of air masses. The tools needed to forecast weather are inexpensive and easy to use. If students become familiar with these tools and concepts, they will understand the basic science of meteorology. As you teach this chapter, work as a class every day to forecast the next day's weather. Review the predictions at the beginning of each class. Forecasts should improve as students learn more about weather.

16

Understanding Weather

SECTION 1 Water in the Air 482

SECTION 2 Air Masses and Fronts 490

SECTION 3 Severe Weather 496

SECTION 4 Forecasting the Weather 504

Chapter Lab 508
Chapter Review 510
Standardized Test Preparation 512
Science in Action 514

About the PHOTO

Flamingos in the bathroom? This may look like someone's idea of a practical joke, but in fact, it's a practical idea! These flamingos reside at the Miami-Metro Zoo in Florida. They were put in the bathroom for protection against the incredibly dangerous winds of Hurricane Floyd in September of 1999.

PRE-READING ACTIVITY

FOLDNOTES **Four-Corner Fold**
Before you read the chapter, create the FoldNote entitled "Four-Corner Fold" described in the **Study Skills** section of the Appendix. Label the flaps of the four-corner fold with "Water in the air," "Air masses and fronts," "Severe weather," and "Forecasting the weather." Write what you know about each topic under the appropriate flap. As you read the chapter, add other information that you learn.

Standards Correlations

National Science Education Standards

The following codes indicate the National Science Education Standards that correlate to this chapter. The full text of the standards is at the front of the book.

Chapter Opener
UCP 2; SAI 1; SPSP 3, 4; ES 1f, 1i, 1j

Section 1 Water in the Air
UCP 2, 3; SAI 1; SPSP 3; ES 1f, 1i, 1j; *LabBook:* UCP 3; SAI 1

Section 2 Air Masses and Fronts
HNS 3; ES 1j

Section 3 Severe Weather
SPSP 3, 4; ES 1i, 1j

Section 4 Forecasting the Weather
SPSP 3, 4; ES 1i, 1j; *LabBook:* SAI 1; ST 1

Chapter Lab
UCP 2, 3; SAI 1, 2; ST 1; HNS 2

Chapter Review
UCP 1; ST 2; SPSP 3, 4, 5; ES 1f, 1i, 1j

Science in Action
ST 2; SPSP 3, 5; HNS 1, 3

480 Chapter 16 • Understanding Weather

START-UP ACTIVITY

MATERIALS
FOR EACH GROUP
- beaker (2)
- container, clear plastic
- cooking oil (500 mL)
- water (500 mL)

Teacher's Notes: Students should be able to distinguish the oil from the water when the two liquids are poured together. If not, try the experiment again using water with food coloring.

Answers
1. The oil rises to the top and sits on the surface of the water.
2. Answers may vary.
3. Sample answer: The warm air mass would be pushed up by the cold air mass.

START-UP ACTIVITY

Meeting of the Masses

In this activity, you will model what happens when two air masses that have different temperature characteristics meet.

Procedure
1. Pour **500 mL of water** into a **beaker**. Pour **500 mL of cooking oil** into a **second beaker**. The water represents a dense cold air mass. The cooking oil represents a less dense warm air mass.
2. Predict what would happen to the two liquids if you tried to mix them.
3. Pour the contents of both beakers into a **clear, plastic, rectangular container** at the same time from opposite ends of the container.
4. Observe the interaction of the oil and water.

Analysis
1. What happens when the liquids meet?
2. Does the prediction that you made in step 2 of the Procedure match your results?
3. Using your results, hypothesize what would happen if a cold air mass met a warm air mass.

Chapter Starter Transparency
Use this transparency to help students begin thinking about the types of conditions that produce tornadoes.

CHAPTER RESOURCES

Technology
- **Transparencies**
  - Chapter Starter Transparency *READING SKILLS*
- **Student Edition on CD-ROM**
- **Guided Reading Audio CD**
  - English or Spanish
- **Classroom Videos**
  - Brain Food Video Quiz

Workbooks
- **Science Puzzlers, Twisters & Teasers**
  - Understanding Weather *GENERAL*

Chapter 16 • Understanding Weather **481**

SECTION 1

Focus

Overview
This section discusses the water cycle, relative humidity, types of clouds, and forms of precipitation.

🔔 Bellringer
Place a glass of ice water and a glass of warm water on your desk. Ask students: "Why do water drops form on the cold glass? Where does the water come from? Why are there no water drops on the warm glass?"

Motivate

Group Activity — GENERAL

Air Molecules Divide the class in half. Half of the students will pretend to be air molecules; half will pretend to be water molecules. Ask the "air molecules" to stand four feet apart in a square grid. Then, have the "water molecules" stand between the air molecules without touching anyone. Tell students that they are modeling a warm air mass. Cool the air mass by moving the air molecules closer together so that eventually they are holding hands. As the temperature drops, the water molecules will be expelled as "precipitation." Finally, ask the air molecules to stand with their shoulders touching to show how a cold air mass expels the water molecules. **LS Kinesthetic**

SECTION 1

READING WARM-UP

Objectives
- Explain how water moves through the water cycle.
- Describe how relative humidity is affected by temperature and levels of water vapor.
- Describe the relationship between dew point and condensation.
- List three types of cloud forms.
- Identify four kinds of precipitation.

Terms to Learn
weather
humidity
relative humidity
condensation
cloud
precipitation

READING STRATEGY

Paired Summarizing Read this section silently. In pairs, take turns summarizing the material. Stop to discuss ideas that seem confusing.

CHAPTER RESOURCES

Chapter Resource File
- Lesson Plan
- Directed Reading A **BASIC**
- Directed Reading B **SPECIAL NEEDS**

Technology
- Transparencies
  - Bellringer
  - The Water Cycle

Water in the Air

What will the weather be this weekend? Depending on what you have planned, knowing the answer to this question could be important. A picnic in the rain can be a mess!

Have you ever wondered what weather is? **Weather** is the condition of the atmosphere at a certain time and place. The condition of the atmosphere is affected by the amount of water in the air. So, to understand weather, you need to understand how water cycles through Earth's atmosphere.

The Water Cycle

Water in liquid, solid, and gaseous states is constantly being recycled through the water cycle. The *water cycle* is the continuous movement of water from sources on Earth's surface—such as lakes, oceans, and plants—into the air, onto and over land, into the ground, and back to the surface. The movement of water through the water cycle is shown in **Figure 1**.

✓ **Reading Check** What is the water cycle? (See the Appendix for answers to Reading Checks.)

Figure 1 The Water Cycle

Condensation occurs when water vapor cools and changes from a gas to a liquid. Clouds form by this process.

Evaporation occurs when liquid water changes into water vapor, which is a gas.

Precipitation occurs when rain, snow, sleet, or hail falls from the clouds onto Earth's surface.

Runoff is water, usually from precipitation, that flows across land and collects in rivers, streams, and eventually the ocean.

Answer to Reading Check
The water cycle is the continuous movement of water from Earth's oceans and rivers into the atmosphere, into the ground, and back into the oceans and rivers.

482 Chapter 16 • Understanding Weather

Amount of Water Vapor Air Can Hold at Various Temperatures

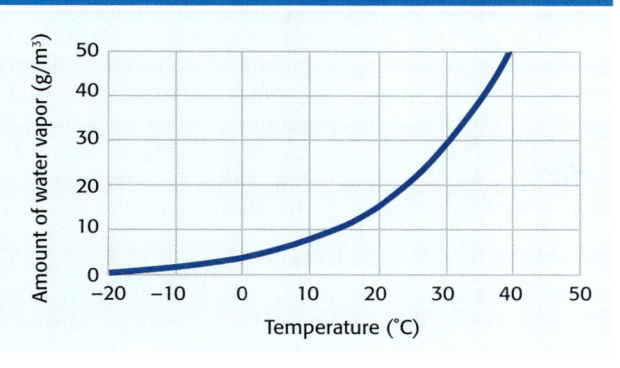

Figure 2 This graph shows that as air gets warmer, the amount of water vapor that the air can hold increases.

Humidity

As water evaporates from lakes, oceans, and plants, it becomes *water vapor,* or moisture in the air. Water vapor is invisible. The amount of water vapor in the air is called **humidity**. As water evaporates and becomes water vapor, the humidity of the air increases. The air's ability to hold water vapor changes as the temperature of the air changes. **Figure 2** shows that as the temperature of the air increases, the air's ability to hold water vapor also increases.

Relative Humidity

One way to express humidity is through relative humidity. **Relative humidity** is the amount of water vapor in the air compared with the maximum amount of water vapor that the air can hold at a certain temperature. So, relative humidity is given as a percentage. When air holds all of the water that it can at a given temperature, it is said to be *saturated.* Saturated air has a relative humidity of 100%. But how do you find the relative humidity of air that is not saturated? If you know the maximum amount of water vapor that air can hold at a given temperature and the actual amount of water vapor in the air, you can calculate the relative humidity.

Suppose that 1 m³ of air at a certain temperature can hold 24 g of water vapor. However, you know that the air actually contains 18 g of water vapor. You can calculate the relative humidity by using the following formula:

$$\frac{\text{actual water vapor content (g/m}^3\text{)}}{\text{saturation water vapor content (g/m}^3\text{)}} \times 100 = \text{relative humidity (\%)}$$

$$\frac{18 \text{ g/m}^3}{24 \text{ g/m}^3} = 75\%$$

weather the short-term state of the atmosphere, including temperature, humidity, precipitation, wind, and visibility

humidity the amount of water vapor in the air

relative humidity the ratio of the amount of water vapor in the air to the maximum amount of water vapor the air can hold at a set temperature

MATH PRACTICE

Relative Humidity
Assume that 1 m³ of air at 25°C contains 11 g of water vapor. At this temperature, the air can hold 24 g/m³ of water vapor. Calculate the relative humidity of the air.

Teach

Demonstration — BASIC

Water in Air Use two small, identical sponges and a beaker of water to demonstrate air's ability to hold water. Explain that one of the dry sponges represents warm, dry air. Like the dry sponge, warm, dry air can absorb water because there is space available. Dip the second sponge into the beaker, and put the sponge on a table. Lead students to conclude that this sponge represents saturated air; there is no room for any more water. Squeezing the sponge represents the way condensation would occur if the air mass were cooled.

Ask students why their hair dries faster if they blow dry their hair on a warm air setting rather than a cool air setting. (Students should conclude that the warm air setting will cause water to evaporate faster and therefore would dry hair faster.) **English Language Learners**
LS Visual/Verbal

Answer to Math Practice

(11 g/m³ ÷ 24 g/m³) × 100 = 46%

CONNECTION to Life Science — ADVANCED

Hair Hygrometer When the air is humid, hair becomes frizzy. Hair is made of a protein called *keratin.* Each hair fiber has a scaly outer cuticle, which you can feel by running your fingers up and down a single hair. The scales allow moisture to enter the inner part of the hair fiber. When the air is humid, hair absorbs moisture and becomes longer and frizzy. Hair dries out and becomes shorter when the air is dry. Because humidity can cause hair length to change by as much as 2.5%, a device called a *hair hygrometer* can very accurately measure changes in humidity. Have students design and build their own hair hygrometers. Plans for making a hair hygrometer are available on the Internet. Note: This project will not work on very short hair. **LS Kinesthetic**

Section 1 • Water in the Air 483

Teach, continued

ACTIVITY — GENERAL

Sentence Completion After students have read this page, have them complete the following sentences:

- If the humidity is low, a _____ amount of water will evaporate from a wet-bulb thermometer and the _____ between the wet-bulb reading and the dry-bulb reading of the psychrometer will be high. **(large, temperature difference)**

- If the dry bulb reads 10°C, and the difference between the thermometers is 8°C, the relative humidity is _____. **(15%)**

Verbal

Cultural Awareness — GENERAL

Hopi Rainmakers Have students research the rainmakers in Hopi Indian culture. Students might find out about *Leenangkatsina*, whose flute brings rain; *Qaleetaqa*, who carries lightning and a bull-roarer to bring rain; and *Si'o Sa'lakwmana* or *Pawtiwa*, both of whom bring rain and mist to villages. **Interpersonal**

Answer to Reading Check
A psychrometer is used to measure relative humidity.

INTERNET ACTIVITY

For another activity related to this chapter, go to **go.hrw.com** and type in the keyword **HZ5WEAW**.

Factors Affecting Relative Humidity

Two factors that affect relative humidity are amount of water vapor and temperature. At constant temperature and pressure, as the amount of water vapor in air changes, the relative humidity changes. The more water vapor there is in the air, the higher the relative humidity is. If the amount of water vapor in the air stays the same but the temperature changes, the relative humidity changes. The relative humidity decreases as the temperature rises and increases as the temperature drops.

Measuring Relative Humidity

A *psychrometer* (sie KRAHM uht uhr) is an instrument that is used to measure relative humidity. A psychrometer consists of two thermometers, one of which is a wet-bulb thermometer. The bulb of a wet-bulb thermometer is covered with a damp cloth. The other thermometer is a dry-bulb thermometer.

The difference in temperature readings between the thermometers indicates the amount of water vapor in the air. The larger the difference between the two readings is, the less water vapor the air contains and thus the lower the humidity is. **Figure 3** shows how to use a table of differences between wet-bulb and dry-bulb readings to determine relative humidity.

✓ **Reading Check** What tool is used to measure relative humidity?

Figure 3 Determining Relative Humidity

Find the relative humidity by locating the column head that is equal to the difference between the wet-bulb and dry-bulb readings. Then, locate the row head that equals the temperature reading on the dry-bulb thermometer. The value that lies where the column and row intersect equals the relative humidity. You can see a psychrometer below.

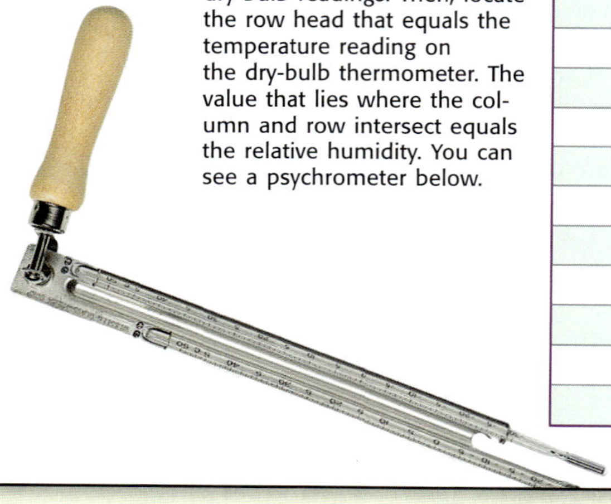

Dry-bulb reading (°C)	Relative Humidity (%) Difference between wet-bulb reading and dry-bulb reading (°C)							
	1	2	3	4	5	6	7	8
0	81	64	46	29	13			
2	84	68	52	37	22	7		
4	85	71	57	43	29	16		
6	86	73	60	48	35	24	11	
8	87	75	63	51	40	29	19	8
10	88	77	66	55	44	34	24	15
12	89	78	68	58	48	39	29	21
14	90	79	70	60	51	42	34	26
16	90	81	71	63	54	46	38	30
18	91	82	73	65	57	49	41	34
20	91	83	74	66	59	51	44	37

INCLUSION Strategies

- **Learning Disabled**   • **Attention Deficit Disorder**

Have student groups make a pyschrometer. Give each group two identical thermometers, gauze, tape, water, a rubber band, and an 8 1/2 in. × 11 in. piece of cardboard. Ask each group to wrap the gauze around the bulb of a thermometer and attach it firmly with the rubber band. Next, have students wet the gauze. Then, have students place the thermometers side by side with the bulbs hanging over the edge of a desk. Students should tape the thermometers securely to the desk. Have students use the cardboard to carefully fan the thermometers until the temperature of the wet-bulb thermometer stops decreasing. Have students subtract the wet-bulb temperature from the dry-bulb temperature and record the difference. Then, have students determine the relative humidity of the air in the classroom using **Figure 3**. **Kinesthetic**

484 Chapter 16 • Understanding Weather

How a Wet-Bulb Thermometer Works

A wet-bulb thermometer works differently than a dry-bulb thermometer, which measures only air temperature. As air passes over the wet-bulb thermometer, the water in the cloth evaporates. As the water evaporates, the cloth cools. If the humidity is low, the water will evaporate more quickly and the temperature reading on the wet-bulb thermometer will drop. If the humidity is high, only a small amount of water will evaporate from the cloth of the wet-bulb thermometer and the change in temperature will be small.

Reading Check Explain how a wet-bulb thermometer works.

Condensation

You have probably seen water droplets form on the outside of a glass of ice water, as shown in **Figure 4**. Where did those water drops come from? The water came from the surrounding air, and droplets formed as a result of condensation. **Condensation** is the process by which a gas, such as water vapor, becomes a liquid. Before condensation can occur, the air must be saturated, which means that the air must have a relative humidity of 100%. Condensation occurs when saturated air cools.

Dew Point

Air can become saturated when water vapor is added to the air through evaporation. Air can also become saturated when it cools to its dew point. The *dew point* is the temperature at which a gas condenses into a liquid. At its dew point, air is saturated. The ice in the glass of water causes the air surrounding the glass to cool to its dew point.

Before water vapor can condense, though, it must have a surface to condense on. In the case of the glass of ice water, water vapor condenses on the outside of the glass.

Figure 4 Condensation occurred when the air next to the glass cooled to its dew point.

condensation the change of state from a gas to a liquid

Quick Lab

Out of Thin Air

1. Pour **room-temperature water** into a **plastic container,** such as a drinking cup, until the water level is near the top of the cup.
2. Observe the outside of the container, and record your observations.
3. Add **one or two ice cubes** to the container of water.
4. Watch the outside of the container for any changes.
5. What happened to the outside of the container?
6. What is the liquid on the container?
7. Where did the liquid come from? Explain your answer.

Discussion — GENERAL

What Dew You Think Have students decide if the following statements are true or false:

- Condensation is the process in which a liquid changes to a gas. (false)
- Dew point is the temperature to which air must cool before it becomes saturated. (true)
- The dew you observe on grass forms on hot, cloudy, windless nights. (false)

LS Verbal

Answer to Reading Check

The bulb of a wet-bulb thermometer is covered with moistened material. The bulb cools as water evaporates from the material. If the air is dry, more water will evaporate from the material, and the temperature recorded by the thermometer will be low. If the air is humid, less water will evaporate from the material, and the temperature recorded by the thermometer will be higher.

Answers to Quick Lab

5. Liquid droplets formed on the outside of the container.
6. The liquid is water.
7. The air next to the cup cooled to below its dew point, and water vapor condensed on the cup.

Cultural Awareness — GENERAL

Chinese Meteorology Dating back to 1216 BCE, Chinese meteorological records have helped modern climatologists determine long-term global climate patterns. To measure humidity, Chinese meteorologists dried pieces of charcoal in an oven and weighed them. The charcoal was then left outside to absorb moisture from the atmosphere and weighed again. The difference between the two weights accurately indicated the humidity. Have students test this method with a balance and some pieces of charcoal. Students can also design their own experiment to measure humidity and share the experiment with the class. **LS** Kinesthetic

Section 1 • Water in the Air

Teach, continued

READING STRATEGY — GENERAL

Sequencing After students read this page, have them arrange the following steps in a logical order:

- Water vapor condenses on smoke, dust, salt, and other small particles suspended in the air. (4)
- The relative humidity of the air increases. (2)
- Warm air rises and cools. (1)
- Air eventually becomes saturated. (3)
- Millions of tiny drops of liquid water collect to form a cloud. (5)

LS Logical

Debate — ADVANCED

Cloud Seeding Meteorologists sometimes use a technique known as *cloud seeding* to try to cause or increase precipitation. Have groups of students research this technique and write a position paper about it. After students have gathered their information, have small groups debate the pros and cons of artificially stimulating precipitation. **LS Verbal**

Figure 5 Three Forms of Clouds

Cumulus clouds look like piles of cotton balls.

Stratus clouds are not as tall as cumulus clouds, but they cover more area.

Cirrus clouds are made of ice crystals.

cloud a collection of small water droplets or ice crystals suspended in the air, which forms when the air is cooled and condensation occurs

CONNECTION TO Language Arts

Cloud Clues Did you know that the name of a cloud actually describes the characteristics of the cloud? For example, the word *cumulus* comes from the Latin word meaning "heap." A cumulus cloud is a puffy, white cloud, which could be described as a "heap" of clouds. Use a dictionary or the Internet to find the word origins of the names of the other cloud types you learn about in this section.

Clouds

Have you ever wondered what clouds are and how they form? A **cloud** is a collection of millions of tiny water droplets or ice crystals. Clouds form as warm air rises and cools. As the rising air cools, it becomes saturated. When the air is saturated, the water vapor changes to a liquid or a solid, depending on the air temperature. At temperatures above freezing, water vapor condenses on small particles in the air and forms tiny water droplets. At temperatures below freezing, water vapor changes to a solid to form ice crystals. Clouds are classified by form, as shown in **Figure 5,** and by altitude.

Cumulus Clouds

Puffy, white clouds that tend to have flat bottoms are called *cumulus clouds* (KYOO myoo luhs KLOWDZ). Cumulus clouds form when warm air rises. These clouds generally indicate fair weather. However, when these clouds get larger, they produce thunderstorms. Thunderstorms come from a kind of cumulus cloud called a *cumulonimbus cloud* (KYOO myoo loh NIM buhs KLOWD). Clouds that have names that include *-nimbus* or *nimbo-* are likely to produce precipitation.

Stratus Clouds

Clouds called *stratus clouds* (STRAYT uhs KLOWDZ) are clouds that form in layers. Stratus clouds cover large areas of the sky and often block out the sun. These clouds can be caused by a gentle lifting of a large body of air into the atmosphere. *Nimbostratus clouds* (NIM boh STRAYT uhs KLOWDZ) are dark stratus clouds that usually produce light to heavy, continuous rain. *Fog* is a stratus cloud that has formed near the ground.

Homework — BASIC

Cloud Models On a poster board, have students use cotton balls to make models of different types of clouds at different altitudes. Students should create labels to describe the clouds and the types of weather with which they are associated.
English Language Learners
LS Visual/Intrapersonal

MISCONCEPTION ALERT

Contrails What appears to be white smoke from an airplane's engine is not smoke at all. Condensation trails, or contrails, form as the combustion of the aircraft's fuel forms water vapor which condenses and freezes along the airplane's exhaust tail. A thick contrail that will not dissipate is a sign that a frontal system is approaching.

---

486 Chapter 16 • Understanding Weather

Cirrus Clouds

As you can see in **Figure 5,** *cirrus clouds* (SIR uhs KLOWDZ) are thin, feathery, white clouds found at high altitudes. Cirrus clouds form when the wind is strong. If they get thicker, cirrus clouds indicate that a change in the weather is coming.

Clouds and Altitude

Clouds are also classified by the altitude at which they form. **Figure 6** shows two altitude groups used to describe clouds and the altitudes at which they form in the middle latitudes. The prefix *cirro-* is used to describe clouds that form at high altitudes. For example, a cumulus cloud that forms high in the atmosphere is called a *cirrocumulus cloud*. The prefix *alto-* describes clouds that form at middle altitudes. Clouds that form at low altitudes do not have a specific prefix to describe them.

Reading Check At what altitude does an altostratus cloud form?

Figure 6 Cloud Types Based on Form and Altitude

High Clouds Because of the cold temperatures at high altitude, high clouds are made up of ice crystals. The prefix *cirro-* is used to describe high clouds.

Middle Clouds Middle clouds can be made up of both water drops and ice crystals. The prefix *alto-* is used to describe middle clouds.

Low Clouds Low clouds are made up of water drops. There is no specific prefix used to describe low clouds.

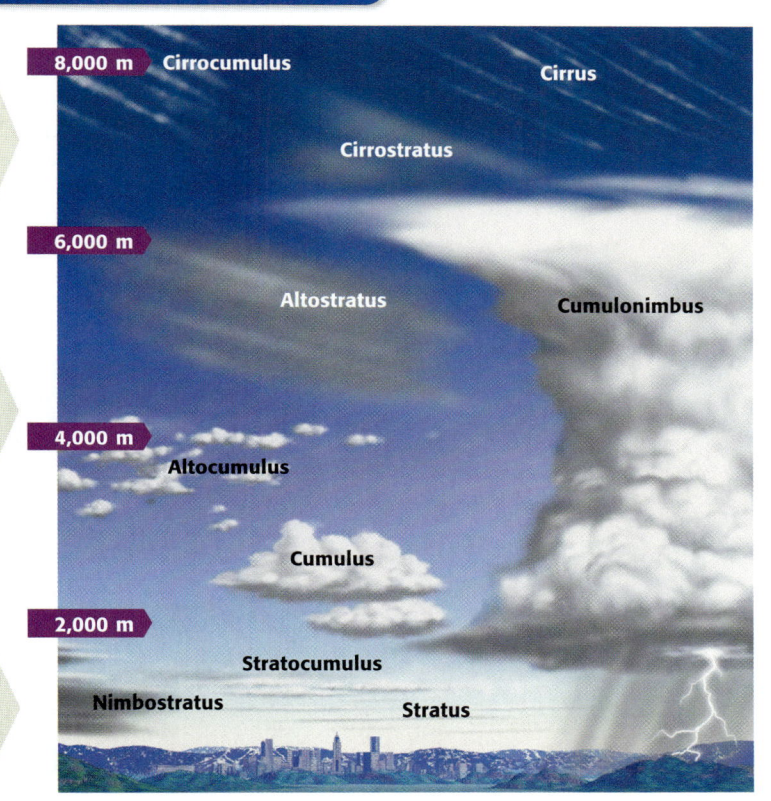

- 8,000 m — Cirrocumulus, Cirrus, Cirrostratus
- 6,000 m — Altostratus, Cumulonimbus
- 4,000 m — Altocumulus
- 2,000 m — Cumulus, Stratocumulus, Nimbostratus, Stratus

Answer to Reading Check
Altostratus clouds form at middle altitudes.

CHAPTER RESOURCES

Technology

Transparencies
- Cloud Types Based on Form and Altitude

ACTIVITY — BASIC

Naming Clouds Challenge students to use the adjectives and word parts used to classify clouds to generate a list of possible cloud types. Students should describe or illustrate the differences between each type of cloud. Students' lists should include the following names: *cirrus, cirrostratus, cirrocumulus, altocumulus, altostratus, stratus, stratocumulus, nimbostratus, cumulus,* and *cumulonimbus*
LS Verbal

CONNECTION ACTIVITY
Language Arts — GENERAL

Recording Observations
Recording descriptive and useful observations of clouds is an essential skill in amateur meteorology. Show students examples of good and bad cloud descriptions, and discuss the factors that make scientific observations useful. When describing clouds, students should consider these questions: Do the clouds appear close to the ground or high up? Are they white, light gray, or dark gray? Are they flat and sheetlike, rounded and fluffy, or thin and wispy? Are the clouds distinct? Have students make several entries in their **science journal** that describe the clouds they observe over a period of a week. Entries should include both descriptions and sketches, and students should write a weather forecast based on the clouds observed each day.
LS Intrapersonal/Visual

Section 1 • Water in the Air

Close

Reteaching — BASIC
Concept Mapping Have students construct a concept map using section concepts and terms. Tell students that their map should explain the relative location of clouds in the atmosphere and should describe how they form. **Visual**

Quiz — GENERAL
1. If an air mass is cooled and the amount of humidity in the air mass stays the same, does the relative humidity of the air mass increase or decrease? (It increases.)
2. What causes dew? (At night and in the early morning, the air cools and it can hold less moisture. Dew is water that condenses from the air in the early morning.)
3. How does hail form? (Hail forms when raindrops are carried to the tops of clouds by updrafts. The raindrops freeze and become hail. The hail grows larger as it is repeatedly covered with layers of freezing water.)

Alternative Assessment — ADVANCED
Story Have students write a short story that describes the travels of a water molecule from the moment it evaporates from the sea to the moment it returns to the sea. Students can also include illustrations with their stories. **Verbal**

Figure 7 *Snowflakes are six-sided ice crystals that can be several millimeters to several centimeters in size.*

precipitation any form of water that falls to the Earth's surface from the clouds

Figure 8 *The impact of large hailstones can damage property and crops. The inset photograph shows layers inside of a hailstone, which reveal how it formed.*

Precipitation
When water from the air returns to Earth's surface, it returns as precipitation. **Precipitation** is water, in solid or liquid form, that falls from the air to Earth. There are four major forms of precipitation—rain, snow, sleet, and hail.

Rain
The most common form of precipitation is *rain*. A cloud produces rain when the water drops in the cloud become large enough to fall. A water drop in a cloud begins as a droplet that is smaller than the period at the end of this sentence. Before such a water drop falls as rain, it must become about 100 times its original size.

Sleet and Snow
Sleet forms when rain falls through a layer of freezing air. The rain freezes in the air, which produces falling ice. *Snow* forms when temperatures are so cold that water vapor changes directly to a solid. Snow can fall as single ice crystals or can join to form snowflakes, as shown in **Figure 7**.

Hail
Balls or lumps of ice that fall from clouds are called *hail*. Hail forms in cumulonimbus clouds. When updrafts of air in the clouds carry raindrops high in the clouds, the raindrops freeze and hail forms. As hail falls, water drops coat it. Another updraft of air can send the hail up again. Here, the water drops collected on the hail freeze to form another layer of ice on the hail. This process can happen many times. Eventually, the hail becomes too heavy to be carried by the updrafts and so falls to Earth's surface, as shown in **Figure 8**.

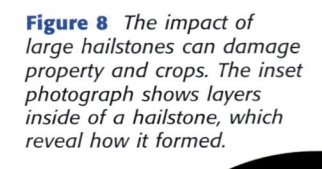

Homework — ADVANCED
Weather Journal Two centuries ago, Emerson wrote that the sky is the "daily bread of our eyes." Careful observation of the sky remains an important skill. Encourage students to keep a daily journal of weather observations for at least a week. To help motivate students, have them consider writing their journal from the perspective of a 19th-century farmer. Each entry should describe the weather conditions at two times of the day and once at night. Based on their observations, students should predict the next day's weather. Students should note cloud types, wind direction, and temperature changes. Encourage students to go beyond the data they could find in a weather report and incorporate qualitative observations of the world around them. **Visual/Intrapersonal**

SECTION Review

Summary

- Weather is the condition of the atmosphere at a certain time and place. Weather is affected by the amount of water vapor in the air.
- The water cycle describes the movement of water above, on, and below Earth's surface.
- Humidity describes the amount of water vapor in the air. Relative humidity is a way to express humidity.
- When the temperature of the air cools to its dew point, the air has reached saturation and condensation occurs.
- Clouds form as air cools to its dew point. Clouds are classified by form and by the altitude at which they form.
- Precipitation occurs when the water vapor that condenses in the atmosphere falls back to Earth in solid or liquid form.

Using Key Terms

1. In your own words, write a definition for each of the following terms: *relative humidity, condensation, cloud,* and *precipitation.*

Understanding Key Ideas

2. Which of the following clouds is most likely to produce light to heavy, continuous rain?
   a. cumulus cloud
   b. cumulonimbus cloud
   c. nimbostratus cloud
   d. cirrus cloud

3. How is relative humidity affected by the amount of water vapor in the air?

4. What does a relative humidity of 75% mean?

5. Describe the path of water through the water cycle.

6. What are four types of precipitation?

Critical Thinking

7. **Applying Concepts** Why are some clouds formed from water droplets, while others are made up of ice crystals?

8. **Applying Concepts** How can rain and hail fall from the same cumulonimbus cloud?

9. **Identifying Relationships** What happens to relative humidity as the air temperature drops below the dew point?

Interpreting Graphics

Use the image below to answer the questions that follow.

10. What type of cloud is shown in the image?
11. How is this type of cloud formed?
12. What type of weather can you expect when you see this type of cloud? Explain.

SciLinks
Developed and maintained by the National Science Teachers Association
For a variety of links related to this chapter, go to www.scilinks.org
Topic: The Water Cycle
SciLinks code: HSM1626

CONNECTION to Physical Science — GENERAL

Water Molecules Explain that a water molecule has a positive end and a negative end. Opposite charges attract, so the positive end of one water molecule attracts the negative end of another. This attraction helps explain why small water droplets that collide are able to form relatively large raindrops.

CHAPTER RESOURCES

Chapter Resource File
- Section Quiz GENERAL
- Section Review GENERAL
- Vocabulary and Section Summary GENERAL
- Datasheet for Quick Lab

Answers to Section Review

1. Sample answer: Relative humidity is the amount of water vapor the air contains compared with the maximum amount it can hold at a given temperature. Condensation is a process that occurs when air reaches its saturation point. A cloud is a mass of air that contains millions of condensed water droplets. Precipitation is solid or liquid water that falls from a cloud.
2. c
3. If the amount of water vapor in the air increases, the relative humidity also increases.
4. The air contains 75% of the maximum amount of water it can hold at a given temperature.
5. Sample answer: Water evaporates from the Earth's surface and rises into the atmosphere. The air cools as it rises. As the air cools, water condenses and falls as precipitation. The precipitation falls to the Earth.
6. rain, snow, sleet, and hail
7. Sample answer: Clouds that form at high altitudes are usually colder than clouds that form at lower altitudes. The cold, high-altitude clouds can be composed of ice crystals.
8. Sample answer: Cumulonimbus clouds can be very tall. Rain can form at the bottom of the cloud, and hail can form near the top of the cloud.
9. As the air temperature drops below the dew point, relative humidity increases to the saturation point, and condensation occurs.
10. a cumulus cloud
11. Cumulus clouds form when warm, moist air rises.
12. Sample answer: Cumulus clouds usually indicate fair weather. However, when cumulus clouds grow large, they can become cumulonimbus clouds, which often produce thunderstorms.

Section 1 • Water in the Air 489

SECTION 2

Focus

Overview
In this section, students learn about air masses and the ways that they affect weather in the United States. Students also learn about fronts—the boundaries between air masses.

🔔 Bellringer
Ask students to write down as many different qualities of air as possible. (Students might note that air can be humid or dry, can be hot or cold, or can have high pressure or low pressure.) Tell students that the air they are breathing now was hundreds of miles away yesterday. Ask them to think about what caused that air to move. Explain that air masses tend to flow from areas of high pressure to areas of low pressure, just as the air inside a balloon escapes when the balloon is punctured.

Motivate

Discussion — GENERAL
Air Masses and You Have students use **Figure 1** to determine which type of air mass is mainly responsible for the weather in your area. Have students describe the general temperatures and humidity typical of your area. Have students compare their results with information in this section. **LS** Visual

---

SECTION 2

READING WARM-UP

Objectives
- Identify the four kinds of air masses that influence weather in the United States.
- Describe the four major types of fronts.
- Explain how fronts cause weather changes.
- Explain how cyclones and anticyclones affect the weather.

Terms to Learn
air mass   cyclone
front   anticyclone

READING STRATEGY

Reading Organizer As you read this section, make a table comparing cold, warm, occluded, and stationary fronts.

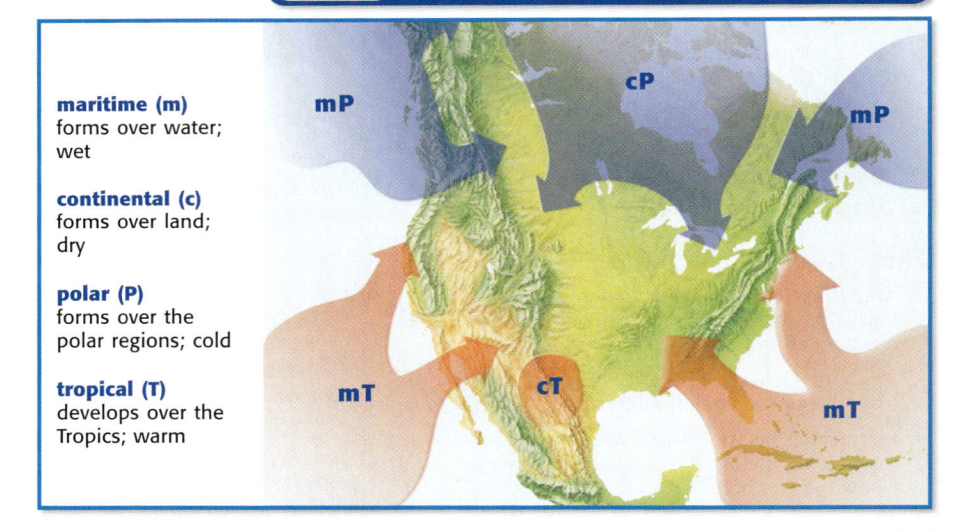

CHAPTER RESOURCES

Chapter Resource File
- Lesson Plan
- Directed Reading A BASIC
- Directed Reading B SPECIAL NEEDS

Technology
- Transparencies
  • Bellringer

Air Masses and Fronts

Have you ever wondered how the weather can change so quickly? For example, the weather may be warm and sunny in the morning and cold and rainy by afternoon.

Changes in weather are caused by the movement and interaction of air masses. An **air mass** is a large body of air where temperature and moisture content are similar throughout. In this section, you will learn about air masses and their effect on weather.

Air Masses

Air masses are characterized by their moisture content and temperature. The moisture content and temperature of an air mass are determined by the area over which the air mass forms. These areas are called *source regions*. An example of a source region is the Gulf of Mexico. An air mass that forms over the Gulf of Mexico is warm and wet because this area is warm and has a lot of water that evaporates. There are many types of air masses, each of which is associated with a particular source region. The characteristics of these air masses are represented on maps by a two-letter symbol, as shown in **Figure 1**. The first letter indicates the moisture content that is characteristic of the air mass. The second letter represents the temperature that is characteristic of the air mass.

Figure 1 Air Masses That Affect Weather in North America

maritime (m) forms over water; wet

continental (c) forms over land; dry

polar (P) forms over the polar regions; cold

tropical (T) develops over the Tropics; warm

Homework — GENERAL
Researching Weather Lore Have students research weather lore at the library or on the Internet to find out if the stories have a scientific basis. For example, students could research the saying, "Red sky at night, sailors delight; red sky at morning, sailors take warning." **LS** Intrapersonal/Logical

---

490   Chapter 16 • Understanding Weather

Figure 2 Cold air masses that form over the North Atlantic Ocean can bring severe weather, such as blizzards, in the winter.

Cold Air Masses

Most of the cold winter weather in the United States is influenced by three polar air masses. A continental polar (cP) air mass forms over northern Canada, which brings extremely cold winter weather to the United States. In the summer, a cP air mass generally brings cool, dry weather.

A maritime polar (mP) air mass that forms over the North Pacific Ocean is cool and very wet. This air mass brings rain and snow to the Pacific Coast in the winter and cool, foggy weather in the summer.

A maritime polar air mass that forms over the North Atlantic Ocean brings cool, cloudy weather and precipitation to New England in the winter, as shown in **Figure 2**. In the summer, the air mass brings cool weather and fog.

Warm Air Masses

Four warm air masses influence the weather in the United States. A maritime tropical (mT) air mass that develops over warm areas in the Pacific Ocean is milder than the maritime polar air mass that forms over the Pacific Ocean.

Other maritime tropical air masses develop over the warm waters of the Gulf of Mexico and the Atlantic Ocean. These air masses move north across the East Coast and into the Midwest. In the summer, they bring hot and humid weather, hurricanes, and thunderstorms, as shown in **Figure 3**. In the winter, they bring mild, often cloudy weather.

A continental tropical (cT) air mass forms over the deserts of northern Mexico and the southwestern United States. This air mass moves northward and brings clear, dry, and hot weather in the summer.

✓ **Reading Check** What type of air mass contributes to the hot and humid summer weather in the midwestern United States? (*See the Appendix for answers to Reading Checks.*)

air mass a large body of air where temperature and moisture content are constant throughout

Figure 3 Warm air masses that develop over the Gulf of Mexico bring thunderstorms in the summer.

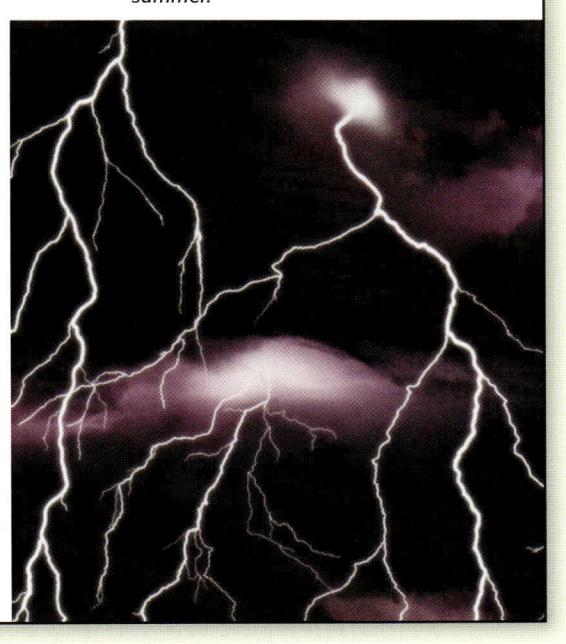

Teach

Demonstration —— GENERAL

Density Students may have a difficult time understanding how hot and cold air masses stay separated as they move. Tell students that air at different temperatures has different densities. In this respect, air behaves much like water. To demonstrate how temperature can separate liquid masses, fill a large beaker or jar with hot water and a small beaker with cold water. Add several drops of blue food coloring to the cold water to make it visible. Slowly pour the cold water down the side of the beaker or jar. Encourage students to describe and explain what they observe. **LS Visual**

Answer to Reading Check
A maritime tropical air mass causes hot and humid summer weather in the midwestern United States.

MISCONCEPTION ALERT

Humid Air Is Lighter Than Dry Air
People often assume that humid air is heavier than dry air. Actually, humid air rises like a balloon because it is less dense than dry air at the same pressure and temperature. The reason is that water molecules are lighter than N_2 and O_2, the main constituents of air. The more water vapor there is in a mass of air, the more N_2 and O_2 is displaced. In general, when humidity increases, air becomes less dense and rises. As an air mass rises, it cools. The water vapor condenses, and the air mass eventually sinks. In addition to the lower density of water vapor, humid air is also generally warmer than dry air. Warm air is less dense than cool air. If water vapor were heavier than air, clouds would form only at the Earth's surface.

Section 2 • Air Masses and Fronts

Teach, continued

Cultural Awareness — GENERAL

Local Weather Local weather patterns are heavily influenced by air masses, which tend to bring predictable weather. All cultures have names for familiar weather patterns. For example, in Tunisia, Africa, weather forecasters often predict "hot and *chili*" conditions. This forecast may not make sense to people elsewhere, but to a Tunisian, *chili* refers to a hot wind blowing from the North African desert. Similarly, in parts of the eastern United States, people refer to the hot, dry, and relatively windless weeks of August as the "dog days" of summer. Have interested students research the names and characteristics of typical weather patterns in other countries. **LS Interpersonal**

Figure 4 Fronts That Affect Weather in North America

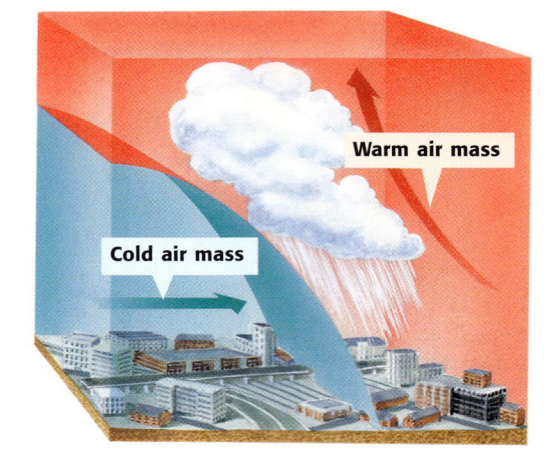

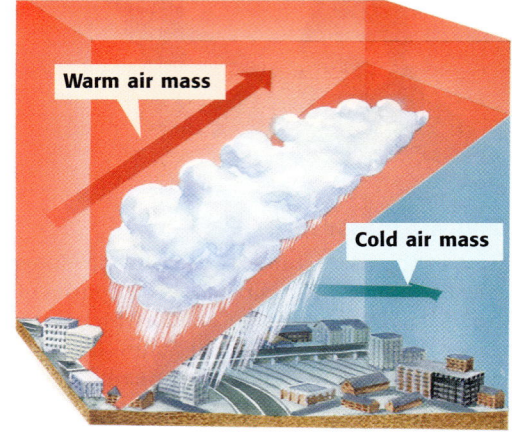

Cold Front

Warm Front

front the boundary between air masses of different densities and usually different temperatures

Fronts

Air masses that form from different areas often do not mix. The reason is that the air masses have different densities. For example, warm air is less dense than cold air. So, when two types of air masses meet, warm air generally rises. The area in which two types of air masses meet is called a **front**. The four kinds of fronts—cold fronts, warm fronts, occluded fronts, and stationary fronts—are shown in **Figure 4**. Fronts are associated with weather in the middle latitudes.

Cold Front

A cold front forms where cold air moves under warm air, which is less dense, and pushes the warm air up. Cold fronts can move quickly and bring thunderstorms, heavy rain, or snow. Cooler weather usually follows a cold front because the air mass behind the cold front is cooler and drier than the air mass that it is replacing.

Warm Front

A warm front forms where warm air moves over cold, denser air. In a warm front, the warm air gradually replaces the cold air. Warm fronts generally bring drizzly rain and are followed by clear and warm weather.

CONNECTION to History — GENERAL

WWI and Meteorology During World War I, European nations stopped broadcasting weather reports, fearing that they would be used by advancing enemy troops. This left nonaligned countries such as Norway to develop their own meteorology program. Norwegian meteorologists responded by forming the famous Bergen School, which greatly advanced the field of meteorology. They discovered that air masses formed from source regions and found that these masses traveled with the winds. Influenced by the war, the meteorologists described air masses using military terms. They imagined Europe as a battleground where different air masses fought like armies trying to advance on each other. The boundary between the air masses, where the "battle" occurs, was called the *front*.

492 Chapter 16 • Understanding Weather

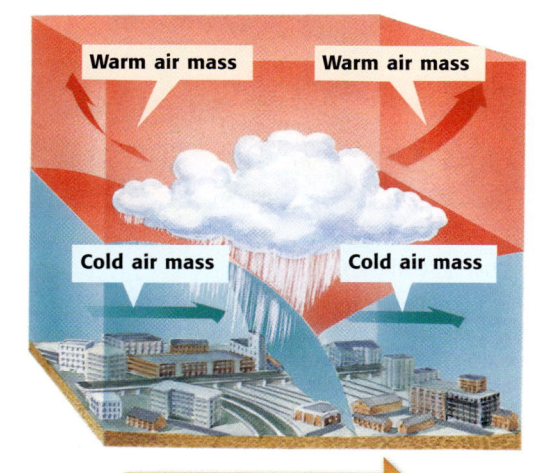

Occluded Front

Warm air mass | **Warm air mass**
Cold air mass | **Cold air mass**
Direction of front

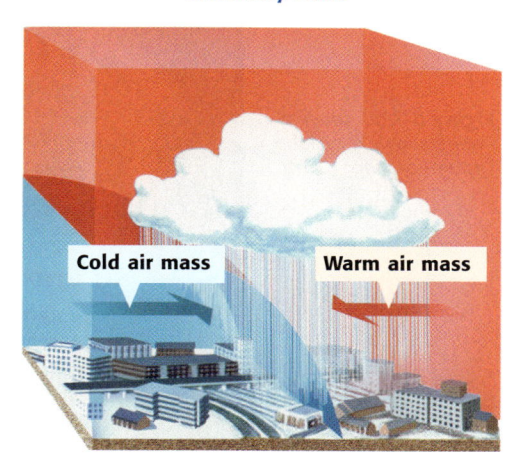

Stationary Front

Cold air mass | **Warm air mass**

Occluded Front

An occluded front forms when a warm air mass is caught between two colder air masses. The coldest air mass moves under and pushes up the warm air mass. The coldest air mass then moves forward until it meets a cold air mass that is warmer and less dense. The colder of these two air masses moves under and pushes up the warmer air mass. Sometimes, though, the two colder air masses mix. An occluded front has cool temperatures and large amounts of rain and snow.

Reading Check What type of weather would you expect an occluded front to produce?

Stationary Front

A stationary front forms when a cold air mass meets a warm air mass. In this case, however, both air masses do not have enough force to lift the warm air mass over the cold air mass. So, the two air masses remain separated. This may happen because there is not enough wind to keep the air masses pushing against each other. A stationary front often brings many days of cloudy, wet weather.

Answer to Reading Check
An occluded front produces cool temperatures and large amounts of rain.

CONNECTION to Physical Science — GENERAL

Specific Heat Water has a very high *specific heat,* which means that a great deal of thermal energy is needed to increase the temperature of water. Thus, water heats and cools very slowly. Rock, on the other hand, has a very low specific heat, so it heats rather quickly. For this reason, areas of high pressure (anticyclones) form over bodies of water, and areas of low pressure (cyclones) form over landmasses during the summer months. Because water tends to retain heat and rock tends to lose heat quickly, cyclones tend to form over bodies of water and anticyclones tend to form over landmasses during the winter months.

ACTIVITY — BASIC

Using Maps Have students collect the daily weather maps from a newspaper for 1 week. Have students locate the high and low pressure systems on the map and track the movement of these systems. Ask students to analyze the types of weather that are associated with the pressure systems. At the end of the week, ask students to predict the weather for their area for the next week according to the position and movement of the high- and low-pressure systems.
LS Visual

CHAPTER RESOURCES

Technology

Transparencies
• Cold and Warm Fronts
• Occluded and Stationary Fronts

Section 2 • Air Masses and Fronts

Close

Reteaching — BASIC

Section Outline Have students copy the section headings and then create an outline that includes at least two points for each heading. Students can use their outline as a study guide.

LS Visual/Verbal

Quiz — GENERAL

1. What type of weather is associated with a continental polar air mass in the summer? (cool and dry)
2. What is the area called over which an air mass forms? (source region)
3. Explain how a cold front develops. (A cold front develops when a cold air mass moves under a warm air mass, which forces the warmer air upward.)
4. What kind of weather is associated with a stationary front? (The weather will probably be cloudy and rainy as long as the front lies over an area. After the front passes, the weather will usually clear up.)

Alternative Assessment — GENERAL

United States Air Masses Have students list five places in the United States that they have visited or would like to visit and the air masses that affect the weather in those places.

LS Intrapersonal

Figure 5 This satellite image shows a cyclone system forming.

cyclone an area in the atmosphere that has lower pressure than the surrounding areas and has winds that spiral toward the center

anticyclone the rotation of air around a high-pressure center in the direction opposite to Earth's rotation

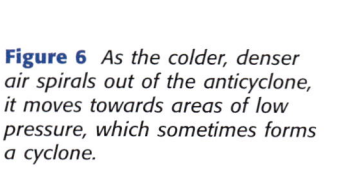

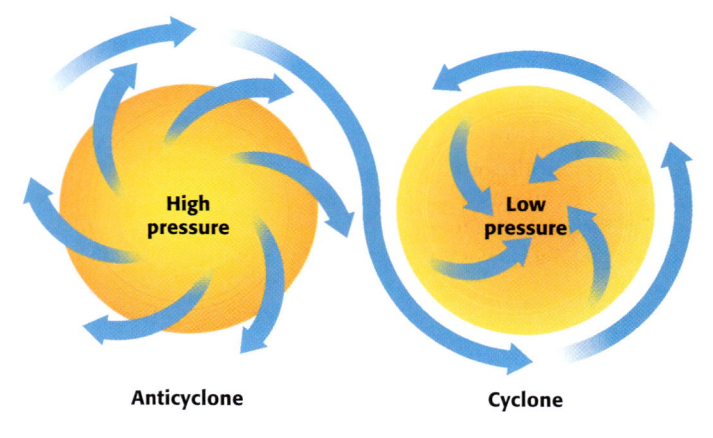

Figure 6 As the colder, denser air spirals out of the anticyclone, it moves towards areas of low pressure, which sometimes forms a cyclone.

Air Pressure and Weather

You may have heard a weather reporter on TV or radio talking about areas of low pressure and high pressure. These areas of different pressure affect the weather.

Cyclones

Areas that have lower pressure than the surrounding areas do are called **cyclones**. Cyclones are areas where air masses come together, or converge, and rise. **Figure 5** shows a satellite image of the formation of a cyclone system.

Anticyclones

Areas that have high pressure are called **anticyclones**. Anticyclones are areas where air moves apart, or diverges, and sinks. The sinking air is denser than the surrounding air, and the pressure is higher. Cooler, denser air moves out of the center of these high-pressure areas toward areas of lower pressure. **Figure 6** shows how wind can spiral out of an anticyclone and into a cyclone.

High pressure — Anticyclone
Low pressure — Cyclone

CONNECTION to Life Science — GENERAL

Aching Joints and Air Pressure Why do people complain of aching joints before a thunderstorm? A study found that nearly 75% of arthritis sufferers felt more pain in their joints when air pressure was falling. Although this effect has been thoroughly documented, there is no definitive evidence of why it occurs.

Cyclones, Anticyclones, and Weather

You have learned what cyclones and anticyclones are. So, now you might be wondering how do cyclones and anticyclones affect the weather? As the air in the center of a cyclone rises, it cools and forms clouds and rain. The rising air in a cyclone causes stormy weather. In an anticyclone, the air sinks. As the air sinks, it gets warmer and absorbs moisture. The sinking air in an anticyclone brings dry, clear weather. By keeping track of cyclones and anticyclones, meteorologists can predict the weather.

✓ **Reading Check** Describe the different types of weather that a cyclone and an anticyclone can produce.

CONNECTION TO Astronomy

Storms on Jupiter Cyclones and anticyclones occur on Jupiter, too! Generally, cyclones on Jupiter appear as dark ovals, and anticyclones appear as bright ovals. Jupiter's Great Red Spot is an anticyclone that has existed for centuries. Research the existence of cyclones and anticyclones on other bodies in our solar system.

SECTION Review

Summary

- Air masses are characterized by moisture content and temperature.
- A front occurs where two air masses meet.
- Four major types of fronts are cold, warm, occluded, and stationary fronts.
- Differences in air pressure cause cyclones, which bring stormy weather, and anticyclones, which bring dry, clear weather.

Using Key Terms

For each pair of terms, explain how the meanings of the terms differ.

1. *front* and *air mass*
2. *cyclone* and *anticyclone*

Understanding Key Ideas

3. What kind of front forms when a cold air mass displaces a warm air mass?
   a. a cold front
   b. a warm front
   c. an occluded front
   d. a stationary front
4. What are the major air masses that influence the weather in the United States?
5. What is one source region of a maritime polar air mass?
6. What are the characteristics of an air mass whose two-letter symbol is cP?
7. What are the four major types of fronts?
8. How do fronts cause weather changes?
9. How do cyclones and anticyclones affect the weather?

Math Skills

10. A cold front is moving toward the town of La Porte at 35 km/h. The front is 200 km away from La Porte. How long will it take the front to get to La Porte?

Critical Thinking

11. **Applying Concepts** How do air masses that form over the land and ocean affect weather in the United States?
12. **Identifying Relationships** Why does the Pacific Coast have cool, wet winters and warm, dry summers? Explain.
13. **Applying Concepts** Which air masses influence the weather where you live? Explain.

For a variety of links related to this chapter, go to www.scilinks.org
Topic: Air Masses and Fronts
SciLinks code: HSM0032

Answer to Reading Check

An anticyclone can produce dry, clear weather.

Answers to Section Review

1. Sample answer: An air mass is a large body of air that has a similar temperature and moisture level throughout. A front is a boundary between two air masses.
2. Sample answer: A cyclone is an area of low pressure with winds that spiral toward the center. An anticyclone is an area of high pressure with winds that flow outward.
3. a
4. continental polar, maritime polar, maritime tropical, and continental tropical
5. Sample answer: The North Pacific Ocean is one source region for maritime polar air masses.
6. A cP air mass is very cold and dry. It forms over areas near the poles, such as northern Canada.
7. The major types of fronts are cold fronts, warm fronts, stationary fronts, and occluded fronts.
8. Fronts are boundaries between air masses. When a front occurs, air masses of different temperature and humidity interact. The interactions of air masses cause weather changes.
9. The rising air of a cyclone often causes stormy weather. The sinking air of an anticyclone often causes dry, clear weather.
10. 200 km × 35 km/h = 5.7 h
11. Sample answer: Air masses that form over land have less moisture than those that form over the ocean. The amount of moisture carried in both types of air masses affects the amount of precipitation that the United States receives. Air masses that form over the ocean generally bring precipitation.
12. Sample answer: The Pacific Coast has cool, wet winters because it is affected by a maritime polar air mass during the winter. Summers on the Pacific Coast are warm and dry because the weather is influenced by a dry continental air mass.
13. Answers may vary.

CHAPTER RESOURCES

Chapter Resource File
- Section Quiz GENERAL
- Section Review GENERAL
- Vocabulary and Section Summary GENERAL

SECTION 3

Focus

Overview
In this section, students will learn about severe weather. The section explores thunderstorms, tornadoes, and hurricanes. Students learn about the causes of severe weather and about severe weather safety.

🔔 Bellringer
Have students write a one-paragraph description of a thunderstorm. Ask them to describe the weather conditions immediately before, during, and after a thunderstorm. Ask students to describe how the storm affects each of their senses.

Motivate

Demonstration — GENERAL

Modeling Thunder Inflate a balloon with air, and tie it closed. Explain that thunder occurs when lightning superheats air, which causes the gases to expand rapidly. The air in the balloon is under pressure, so it will also expand rapidly if the pressure is suddenly released. The rapid expansion of air causes vibrations that we hear as sound. Hold up a pin or needle, pause, and pop the balloon with a flourish.
LS Kinesthetic

SECTION 3

READING WARM-UP

Objectives
- Describe how lightning forms.
- Describe the formation of thunderstorms, tornadoes, and hurricanes.
- Describe the characteristics of thunderstorms, tornadoes, and hurricanes.
- Explain how to stay safe during severe weather.

Terms to Learn
thunderstorm   tornado
lightning   hurricane
thunder

READING STRATEGY
Reading Organizer As you read this section, create an outline of the section. Use the headings from the section in your outline.

thunderstorm a usually brief, heavy storm that consists of rain, strong winds, lightning, and thunder

---

Severe Weather

CRAAAACK! BOOM! What made that noise? You didn't expect it, and it sure made you jump.

A big boom of thunder has probably surprised you at one time or another. And the thunder was probably followed by a thunderstorm. A thunderstorm is an example of severe weather. *Severe weather* is weather that can cause property damage and sometimes death.

Thunderstorms

Thunderstorms can be very loud and powerful. **Thunderstorms**, such as the one shown in **Figure 1**, are small, intense weather systems that produce strong winds, heavy rain, lightning, and thunder. Thunderstorms can occur along cold fronts. But thunderstorms can develop in other places, too. There are only two atmospheric conditions required to produce thunderstorms: warm and moist air near Earth's surface and an unstable atmosphere. The atmosphere is unstable when the surrounding air is colder than the rising air mass. The air mass will continue to rise as long as the surrounding air is colder than the air mass.

When the rising warm air reaches its dew point, the water vapor in the air condenses and forms cumulus clouds. If the atmosphere is extremely unstable, the warm air will continue to rise, which causes the cloud to grow into a dark, cumulonimbus cloud. Cumulonimbus clouds can reach heights of more than 15 km.

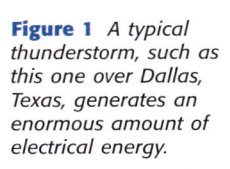

Figure 1 A typical thunderstorm, such as this one over Dallas, Texas, generates an enormous amount of electrical energy.

CHAPTER RESOURCES

Chapter Resource File
- Lesson Plan
- Directed Reading A BASIC
- Directed Reading B SPECIAL NEEDS

Technology
- Transparencies
  - Bellringer
  - LINK TO PHYSICAL SCIENCE How Lightning Forms

MISCONCEPTION ALERT

"The Same Place Twice" Inform students that the old saying, "Lightning never strikes twice in the same place," is not true. Lightning has struck the same place, and even the same person, more than once. Ray Sullivan, a retired national park ranger, has been hit seven times by lightning. Luckily, he has survived the strikes.

---

496 Chapter 16 • Understanding Weather

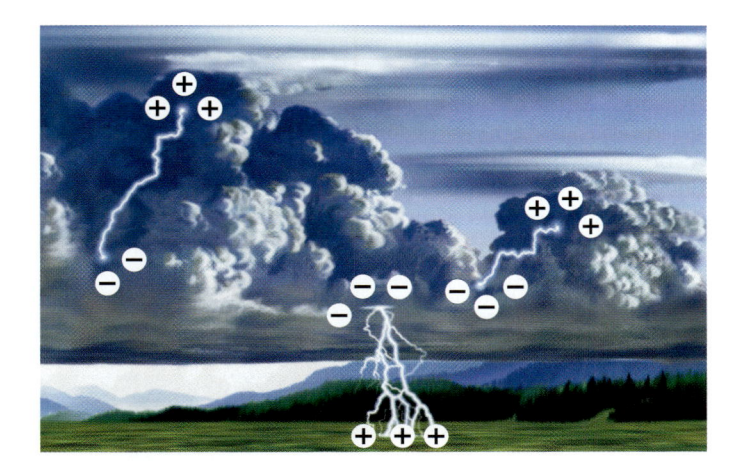

Figure 2 *The upper part of a cloud usually carries a positive electric charge, while the lower part of the cloud carries mainly negative charges.*

Lightning

Thunderstorms are very active electrically. **Lightning** is an electric discharge that occurs between a positively charged area and a negatively charged area, as shown in **Figure 2**. Lightning can happen between two clouds, between Earth and a cloud, or even between two parts of the same cloud. Have you ever touched someone after scuffing your feet on the carpet and received a mild shock? If so, you have experienced how lightning forms. While you walk around, friction between the floor and your shoes builds up an electric charge in your body. When you touch someone else, the charge is released.

When lightning strikes, energy is released. This energy is transferred to the air and causes the air to expand rapidly and send out sound waves. **Thunder** is the sound that results from the rapid expansion of air along the lightning strike.

Severe Thunderstorms

Severe thunderstorms can produce one or more of the following conditions: high winds, hail, flash floods, and tornadoes. Hailstorms damage crops, dent the metal on cars, and break windows. Flash flooding that results from heavy rains causes millions of dollars in property damage annually. And every year, flash flooding is a leading cause of weather-related deaths.

Lightning, as shown in **Figure 3**, happens during all thunderstorms and is very powerful. Lightning is responsible for starting thousands of forest fires each year and for killing or injuring hundreds of people a year in the United States.

✓ **Reading Check** What is a severe thunderstorm? (*See the Appendix for answers to Reading Checks.*)

lightning an electric discharge that takes place between two oppositely charged surfaces, such as between a cloud and the ground, between two clouds, or between two parts of the same cloud

thunder the sound caused by the rapid expansion of air along an electrical strike

Figure 3 *Lightning often strikes the tallest object in an area, such as the Eiffel Tower in Paris, France.*

Teach

CONNECTION ACTIVITY
Math — GENERAL

How Far Is the Storm? To find the distance of a thunderstorm in kilometers, count the number of seconds between a lightning flash and the thunder and divide that number by 3. Ask students, "If you see a lightning flash and then hear thunder 21 s later, how far away is a storm?" (7 km) "How far is the storm if the time difference is 9 s?" (3 km) "7 s?" (2.3 km) **LS Logical**

CONNECTION to
Physical Science — GENERAL

Lightning Strikes Lightning can heat the air to 33,000°C, more than five times the temperature of the sun's surface. On average, 10 million bolts of lightning strike the Earth every day. Lightning strikes happen because the air currents in a thunderstorm separate charged particles of water and ice. Negatively charged particles tend to accumulate near the bottom of a cloud. When the charge overcomes the electric resistance of the air, lightning strikes. Use the teaching transparency entitled "How Lightning Forms" to illustrate how lightning forms. **LS Visual**

Is That a Fact!

The color of lightning can indicate atmospheric conditions. Blue lightning indicates hail, red lightning indicates rain, yellow or orange lightning indicates dust, and white lightning indicates low humidity.

Answer to Reading Check

A severe thunderstorm is a thunderstorm that produces high winds, hail, flash floods, or tornadoes.

Section 3 • Severe Weather

Teach, continued

INCLUSION Strategies

- Hearing Impaired
- Attention Deficit Disorder
- Developmentally Delayed

Students will make a model of a tornado in a plastic bottle. Organize students into groups of three or four students. Give each group a clear, plastic 2 L soda bottle, water, salt, a teaspoon, liquid detergent and food coloring. Ask each group to fill the bottle with water up to 1 in. from the top and then add 1 tsp of salt. Next, have students cover the bottle and shake it until the salt has dissolved. Add a drop of liquid detergent and a drop of food coloring. Tell students to cover the bottle tightly, and move the bottle in a swirling motion. Ask students to record what they observe in their **science journal**.
LS Kinesthetic

CONNECTION ACTiViTY Real World — GENERAL

Lightning Safety Students may be surprised to learn that, on average, lightning kills more people in the United States than tornadoes or hurricanes do. Discuss lightning safety tips with students, and have students create a poster showing what to do during a thunderstorm.
LS Visual/Verbal

tornado a destructive, rotating column of air that has very high wind speeds, is visible as a funnel-shaped cloud, and touches the ground

Tornadoes

Tornadoes happen in only 1% of all thunderstorms. A **tornado** is a small, spinning column of air that has high wind speeds and low central pressure and that touches the ground. A tornado starts out as a funnel cloud that pokes through the bottom of a cumulonimbus cloud and hangs in the air. The funnel cloud becomes a tornado when it makes contact with Earth's surface. **Figure 4** shows how a tornado forms.

Figure 4 How a Tornado Forms

❶ Wind moving in two directions causes a layer of air in the middle to begin to spin like a roll of toilet paper.

❷ The spinning column of air is turned to a vertical position by strong updrafts of air in the cumulonimbus cloud. The updrafts of air also begin to spin.

❸ The spinning column of air moves to the bottom of the cumulonimbus cloud and forms a funnel cloud.

❹ The funnel cloud becomes a tornado when it touches the ground.

BRAIN FOOD

Tornado Formation Most tornadoes develop from thunderstorms at the leading edge of a cold front. Ask students to think about why this is so. (The cool air wedges under the warm air, which may result in wind moving in opposite directions. This movement may cause a layer of air to spin. Rapidly rising warm air can turn the spinning layer into a vertical funnel.) **LS Verbal**

WEIRD SCIENCE

People have reported seeing "naked" chickens after tornadoes strike rural areas. A likely explanation is that tornadoes cause chickens to shed their feathers, or molt. Chickens often molt when attacked. As the chickens molt, the strong tornadic winds blow their feathers off.

498 Chapter 16 • Understanding Weather

Figure 5 *The tornado that hit Kissimmee, Florida, in 1998 had wind speeds of up to 416 km/h.*

Twists of Terror

About 75% of the world's tornadoes occur in the United States. Most of these tornadoes happen in the spring and early summer when cold, dry air from Canada meets warm, moist air from the Tropics. The size of a tornado's path of destruction is usually about 8 km long and 10 to 60 m wide. Although most tornadoes last only a few minutes, they can cause a lot of damage. Their ability to cause damage is due to their strong spinning winds. The average tornado has wind speeds between 120 and 180 km/h, but rarer, more violent tornadoes can have spinning winds of up to 500 km/h. The winds of tornadoes have been known to uproot trees and destroy buildings, as shown in **Figure 5**. Tornadoes are capable of picking up heavy objects, such as mobile homes and cars, and hurling them through the air.

hurricane a severe storm that develops over tropical oceans and whose strong winds of more than 120 km/h spiral in toward the intensely low-pressure storm center

Hurricanes

A large, rotating tropical weather system that has wind speeds of at least 120 km/h is called a **hurricane,** shown in **Figure 6**. Hurricanes are the most powerful storms on Earth. Hurricanes have different names in different parts of the world. In the western Pacific Ocean, hurricanes are called *typhoons*. Hurricanes that form over the Indian Ocean are called *cyclones*.

Most hurricanes form in the areas between 5° and 20° north latitude and between 5° and 20° south latitude over warm, tropical oceans. At higher latitudes, the water is too cold for hurricanes to form. Hurricanes vary in size from 160 to 1,500 km in diameter and can travel for thousands of kilometers.

✓ Reading Check What are some other names for hurricanes?

Figure 6 *This photograph of Hurricane Fran was taken from space.*

CONNECTION to History — GENERAL

Hurricanes and American History Hurricanes played a significant role in early American history. In 1609, a fleet of ships with settlers from England who were bound for Virginia was blown off course by a hurricane. Some of the ships landed in Bermuda instead, and the settlers started the first European colony there. Stories of the storm and the shipwrecks may have inspired William Shakespeare to write *The Tempest*.

Homework — ADVANCED

Disaster Plan Have students find out how to protect themselves during a thunderstorm, tornado, or hurricane. Using their findings, students should draw up a disaster plan for severe weather. The plan should include general information as well as things that might be specific to their family, such as what to do with the family pet(s), how to assist a person who uses a wheelchair or walker, and so on. Suggest that students review the plan with their family. **LS Intrapersonal**

Is That a Fact!

Before 1950, hurricanes were named or identified by their latitude and longitude. In the 1950s, meteorologists began assigning names to hurricanes. Today, the names are assigned in advance for 6-year cycles. The names are submitted by countries potentially in the paths of hurricanes and approved by the World Meteorological Organization.

Answer to Reading Check

Hurricanes are also called *typhoons* or *cyclones*.

Section 3 • Severe Weather

Teach, continued

ACTIVITY — GENERAL

Weather and Energy
Tell students that creating severe weather takes a lot of energy. Have them research the relationship between energy and storm formation. For example, as a warm air mass rises, energy from water condensation helps fuel hurricanes. The energy released by a typical hurricane in 1 day is equal to detonating four hundred 20-megaton hydrogen bombs. Challenge students to research these concepts in books, magazines, and the Internet and to compile their findings into a short report. **LS Intrapersonal**

Group ACTIVITY — GENERAL

Hurricane Newscast Have students work in groups to learn about a hurricane of their choosing. Have students find out where the storm formed, what path it followed, what damage it did, and how people recovered from the damage. Ask students to focus on the people involved in the hurricane, from the meteorologists to relief workers. Have groups present the information they gathered as a series of simulated newscasts. **LS Auditory/Interpersonal** Co-op Learning

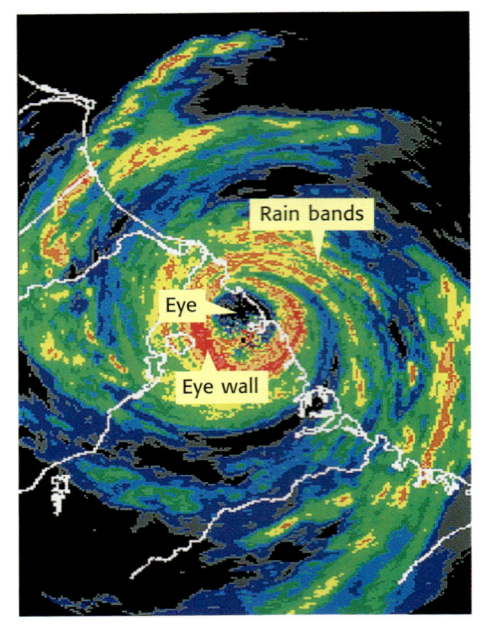

How a Hurricane Forms

A hurricane begins as a group of thunderstorms moving over tropical ocean waters. Winds traveling in two different directions meet and cause the storm to spin. Because of the Coriolis effect, the storm turns counterclockwise in the Northern Hemisphere and clockwise in the Southern Hemisphere.

A hurricane gets its energy from the condensation of water vapor. Once formed, the hurricane is fueled through contact with the warm ocean water. Moisture is added to the warm air by evaporation from the ocean. As the warm, moist air rises, the water vapor condenses and releases large amounts of energy. The hurricane continues to grow as long as it is over its source of warm, moist air. When the hurricane moves into colder waters or over land, it begins to die because it has lost its source of energy. **Figure 7** and **Figure 8** show two views of a hurricane.

✓ **Reading Check** Where do hurricanes get their energy?

Figure 7 The photo above gives you a bird's-eye view of a hurricane.

Figure 8 Cross Section of a Hurricane

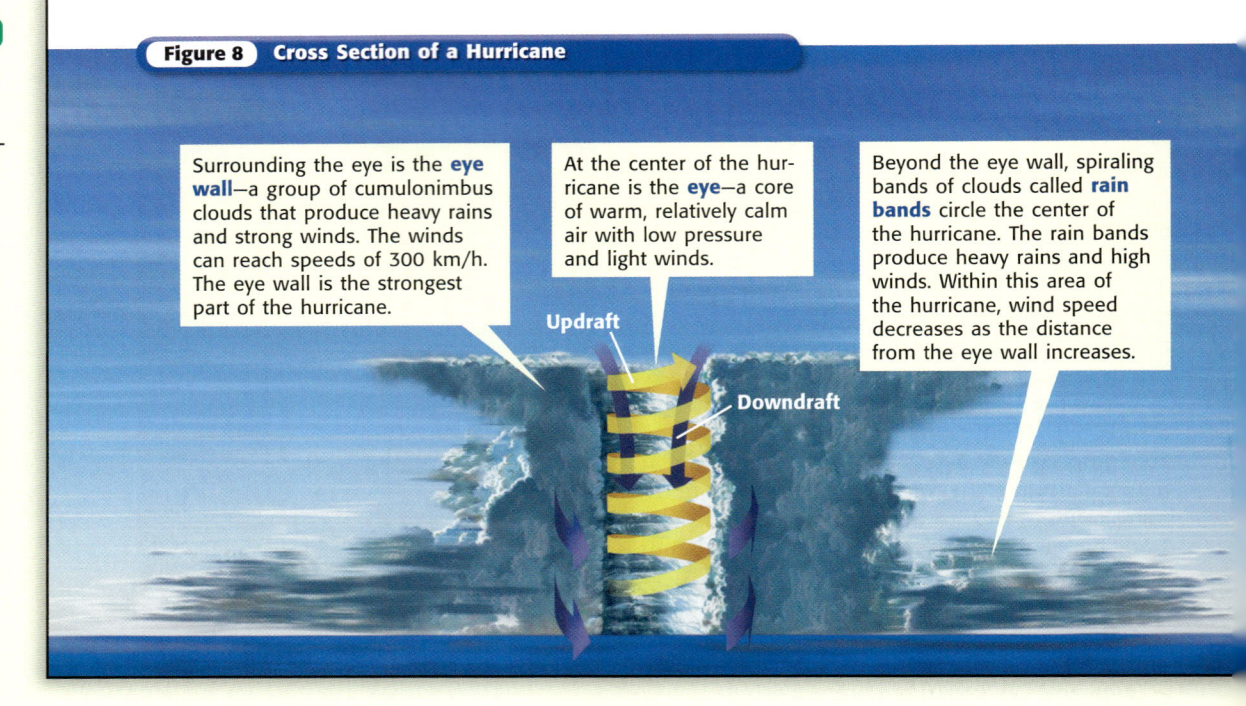

Surrounding the eye is the **eye wall**—a group of cumulonimbus clouds that produce heavy rains and strong winds. The winds can reach speeds of 300 km/h. The eye wall is the strongest part of the hurricane.

At the center of the hurricane is the **eye**—a core of warm, relatively calm air with low pressure and light winds.

Beyond the eye wall, spiraling bands of clouds called **rain bands** circle the center of the hurricane. The rain bands produce heavy rains and high winds. Within this area of the hurricane, wind speed decreases as the distance from the eye wall increases.

Answer to Reading Check
Hurricanes get their energy from the condensation of water vapor.

500 Chapter 16 • Understanding Weather

Damage Caused by Hurricanes

Hurricanes can cause a lot of damage when they move near or onto land. Wind speeds of most hurricanes range from 120 to 150 km/h. Some can reach speeds as high as 300 km/h. Hurricane winds can knock down trees and telephone poles and can damage and destroy buildings and homes.

While high winds cause a great deal of damage, most hurricane damage is caused by flooding associated with heavy rains and storm surges. A *storm surge* is a wall of water that builds up over the ocean because of the strong winds and low atmospheric pressure. The wall of water gets bigger as it nears the shore, and it reaches its greatest height when it crashes onto the shore. Depending on the hurricane's strength, a storm surge can be 1 to 8 m high and 65 to 160 km long. Flooding causes tremendous damage to property and lives when a storm surge moves onto shore, as shown in **Figure 9**.

Severe Weather Safety

Severe weather can be very dangerous, so it is important to keep yourself safe. One way to stay safe is to turn on the radio or TV during a storm. Your local radio and TV stations will let you know if a storm has gotten worse.

Thunderstorm Safety

Lightning is one of the most dangerous parts of a thunderstorm. Lightning is attracted to tall objects. If you are outside, stay away from trees, which can get struck down. If you are in the open, crouch down. Otherwise, you will be the tallest object in the area! Stay away from bodies of water. If lightning hits water while you are in it, you could be hurt or could even die.

Figure 9 A hurricane's storm surge can cause severe damage to homes near the shoreline.

SCHOOL to HOME

Natural Disaster Plan

WRITING SKILL Every family should have a plan to deal with weather emergencies. With a parent, discuss what your family should do in the event of severe weather. Together, write up a plan for your family to follow in case of a natural disaster. Also, make a disaster supply kit that includes enough food and water to last several days.

CONNECTION ACTIVITY
Meteorology — ADVANCED

Hurricane Tracking Meteorologists know where to look for hurricanes. Most hurricanes originate in an area called the *doldrums*, a narrow zone near the equator, and move in a curved path like a parabola. People have been tracking hurricanes for more than 50 years. New instruments, such as radar and geosynchronous weather satellites, allow meteorologists to track building pressure systems and make predictions about the path a tropical storm or a hurricane may take. U.S. military aircraft have even been used for informational reconnaissance, flying into hurricanes to measure wind velocities and direction, pressure, thermal structure, and the location of the eye. The ability to identify potential storm threats allows communities in the path of a hurricane time to prepare for the storm or to evacuate to safety. The National Hurricane Center monitors and stores information on hurricanes. Have students track a hurricane and write an autobiography of a hurricane from its birth to its death.
LS Verbal

MISCONCEPTION ALERT

Tropical Storm or Hurricane? Students may be confused by the terms *tropical storm* and *hurricane*. The difference between a hurricane and a tropical storm is wind speed. To qualify as a tropical storm, the wind speed must be at least 63 km/h but no greater than 119 km/h. If wind speed is greater than 119 km/h, the storm is considered to be a hurricane.

Section 3 • Severe Weather

Close

Reteaching — BASIC
Comparing Severe Weather
Have students work in pairs or small groups to design a poster that compares and contrasts thunderstorms, tornadoes, and hurricanes. Then, have the groups display their posters around the classroom. **LS Visual**

Quiz — GENERAL

1. What is the relationship between lightning and thunder? (Lightning is an electric discharge that forms between clouds or between a cloud and the ground. The air around the lightning bolt expands rapidly to produce sound waves that we call *thunder*.)
2. Explain why tornadoes often destroy buildings in their paths. (A tornado's strong winds often destroy buildings in the tornado's path.)
3. Why do hurricanes not form over land? (A hurricane gets its energy from the evaporation of enormous volumes of water in warm, moist air. These volumes of water are not present over landmasses.)

Alternative Assessment — GENERAL
Concept Mapping Have students make a severe-weather concept map. Tell them that their map should illustrate how thunderstorms, tornadoes, and hurricanes form and what their characteristics are. **LS Visual**

Figure 10 During a tornado warning, it is best to protect yourself by crouching against a wall and covering the back of your head and neck with your hands or a book.

Figure 11 These store owners are boarding up their windows to protect the windows from strong winds during a hurricane.

Tornado Safety
Weather forecasters use watches and warnings to let people know about tornadoes. A *watch* is a weather alert that lets people know that a tornado may happen. A *warning* is a weather alert that lets people know that a tornado has been spotted.

If there is a tornado warning for your area, find shelter quickly. The best place to go is a basement or cellar. Or you can go to a windowless room in the center of the building, such as a bathroom, closet, or hallway, as **Figure 10** shows. If you are outside, lie down in a large, open field or a deep ditch.

Flood Safety
An area can get so much rain that it begins to flood. So, like tornadoes, floods have watches and warnings. However, little warning can usually be given. A flash flood is a flood that rises and falls very suddenly. The best thing to do during a flood is to find a high place to wait out the flood. You should always stay out of floodwaters. Even shallow water can be dangerous if it is moving fast.

Hurricane Safety
If a hurricane is in your area, your local TV or radio station will keep you updated on its condition. People living on the shore may be asked to evacuate the area. If you live in an area where hurricanes strike, your family should have a disaster supply kit that includes enough water and food to last several days. To protect the windows in your home, you should cover them with plywood, as shown in **Figure 11**. Most important, you must stay indoors during the storm.

Science Bloopers

Native Meteorologists The Seminole Indians of Florida have used their own observations of nature to successfully predict severe weather. In one instance, their observations of plants and animals indicated that a hurricane was approaching. Although the weather bureau predicted the storm would miss the area, the Seminoles evacuated—and were spared the storm's destruction. In another instance, meteorologists were so sure of their predictions of a hurricane approaching that heavy equipment was moved away from the endangered area so that it would be available later to help relief efforts. The Seminoles thought otherwise and remained in the area. The hurricane never reached Florida.

SECTION Review

Summary

- Thunderstorms are intense weather systems that produce strong winds, heavy rain, lightning, and thunder.
- Lightning is a large electric discharge that occurs between two oppositely charged surfaces. Lightning releases a great deal of energy and can be very dangerous.
- Tornadoes are small, rotating columns of air that touch the ground and can cause severe damage.
- A hurricane is a large, rotating tropical weather system. Hurricanes cause strong winds and can cause severe property damage.
- In the event of severe weather, it is important to stay safe. Listening to your local TV or radio station for updates and remaining indoors and away from windows are good rules to follow.

Using Key Terms

Complete each of the following sentences by choosing the correct term from the word bank.

hurricane   storm surge
tornado   lightning

1. Thunderstorms are very active electrically and often cause ___.
2. A ___ forms when a funnel cloud pokes through the bottom of a cumulonimbus cloud and makes contact with the ground.

Understanding Key Ideas

3. The safest thing to do if you are caught outdoors during a tornado is to
   a. stay near buildings and roads.
   b. head for an open area.
   c. seek shelter near a large tree.
   d. None of the above
4. Describe how tornadoes form.
5. At what latitudes do hurricanes usually form?
6. What is lightning? What happens when lightning strikes?

Critical Thinking

7. **Applying Concepts** What items do you think you would need in a disaster kit? Explain.
8. **Identifying Relationships** What happens to a hurricane as it moves over land? Explain.

Interpreting Graphics

Use the diagram below to answer the questions that follow.

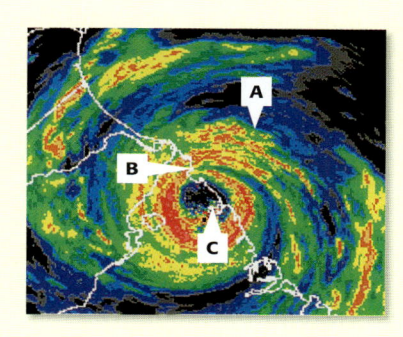

9. Describe what is happening at point C.
10. What is point B?
11. What kind of weather can you expect at point A?

Answers to Section Review

1. lightning
2. tornado
3. b
4. A tornado develops when wind traveling in two different directions causes the air in the middle to rotate. The rotating column of air is turned upright by updrafts that begin spinning with it. The rotating air works its way down to the bottom of the cloud and forms a funnel cloud. When the funnel cloud touches the ground, it is called a *tornado*.
5. Most hurricanes form between 5° and 20° latitude in both hemispheres.
6. Lightning is a large electric discharge that occurs between two oppositely charged surfaces. When lightning strikes, the air expands rapidly, causing thunder.
7. Answers may vary.
8. When a hurricane moves over land, it begins to lose energy because there is less warm, moist air over land.
9. Point C is the eye of the hurricane, which is an area of warm, relatively calm air with low pressure and light winds.
10. Point B is the eye wall. It is composed of a group of cumulonimbus clouds that produce very strong winds.
11. Point A is in the rain band. In the rain band, winds can be strong and rain can be heavy.

CHAPTER RESOURCES

Chapter Resource File
- Section Quiz GENERAL
- Section Review GENERAL
- Vocabulary and Section Summary GENERAL
- Reinforcement Worksheet BASIC
- SciLinks Activity GENERAL

Section 3 • Severe Weather

SECTION 4

Focus

Overview
This section introduces instruments used to forecast and report the weather, such as thermometers, barometers, weather balloons, and radar. Students will also learn how meteorologists use weather maps to depict the data they gather.

🔔 Bellringer
Pose this question to students: "If you did not have the benefit of the weather forecast on the news, radio, or television, how would you forecast the weather?" (Answers will vary. Possible answers include observing the sky and noticing the direction and intensity of the winds.)

Motivate

Demonstration — GENERAL

Air Pressure and Barometers
Low pressure usually indicates stormy weather, and high pressure usually indicates clear weather. If possible, show students a barometer, and tell them that barometers are still widely used in weather forecasting. Show students how to read a barometer and how to use the movable pointer to track if air pressure is increasing or decreasing. **English Language Learners**
LS Visual

SECTION 4

READING WARM-UP

Objectives
- Describe the different types of instruments used to take weather measurements.
- Explain how radar and weather satellites help meteorologists forecast the weather.
- Explain how to interpret a weather map.

Terms to Learn
thermometer
barometer
anemometer

READING STRATEGY

Reading Organizer As you read this section, make a table comparing the different instruments used to collect weather data.

Figure 1 Weather balloons carry radio transmitters that send measurements to stations on the ground.

CHAPTER RESOURCES

Chapter Resource File
- Lesson Plan
- Directed Reading A BASIC
- Directed Reading B SPECIAL NEEDS

Technology
- Transparencies
  - Bellringer

Forecasting the Weather

You watch the weather forecast on the evening news. The news is good—there's no rain in sight. But how can the weather forecasters tell that it won't rain?

Weather affects how you dress and how you plan your day, so it is important to get accurate weather forecasts. But where do weather reporters get their information? And how do they predict the weather? A *weather forecast* is a prediction of weather conditions over the next 3 to 5 days. A *meteorologist* is a person who observes and collects data on atmospheric conditions to make weather predictions. In this section, you will learn how weather data are collected and shown.

Weather-Forecasting Technology

To accurately forecast the weather, meteorologists need to measure various atmospheric conditions, such as air pressure, humidity, precipitation, temperature, wind speed, and wind direction. Meteorologists use special instruments to collect data on weather conditions both near and far above Earth's surface.

High in the Sky

Weather balloons carry electronic equipment that can measure weather conditions as high as 30 km above Earth's surface. Weather balloons, such as the one in **Figure 1,** carry equipment that measures temperature, air pressure, and relative humidity. By tracking the balloons, meteorologists can also measure wind speed and direction.

✓ **Reading Check** How do meteorologists gather data on atmospheric conditions above Earth's surface? (*See the Appendix for answers to Reading Check.*)

Answer to Reading Check
Meteorologists use weather balloons to collect atmospheric data above Earth's surface.

---

504 Chapter 16 • Understanding Weather

Figure 2 Meteorologists use these tools to collect atmospheric data.

Windsock

Thermometer

Anemometer

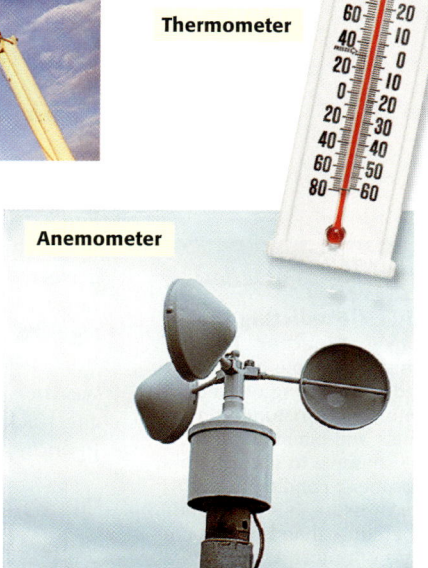

Measuring Air Temperature and Pressure

A tool used to measure air temperature is called a **thermometer.** Most thermometers use a liquid sealed in a narrow glass tube, as shown in **Figure 2.** When air temperature increases, the liquid expands and moves up the glass tube. As air temperature decreases, the liquid shrinks and moves down the tube.

A **barometer** is an instrument used to measure air pressure. A mercurial barometer consists of a glass tube that is sealed at one end and placed in a container full of mercury. As the air pressure pushes on the mercury inside the container, the mercury moves up the glass tube. The greater the air pressure is, the higher the mercury will rise.

Measuring Wind Direction

Wind direction can be measured by using a windsock or a wind vane. A windsock, shown in **Figure 2,** is a cone-shaped cloth bag open at both ends. The wind enters through the wide end and leaves through the narrow end. Therefore, the wide end points into the wind. A wind vane is shaped like an arrow with a large tail and is attached to a pole. As the wind pushes the tail of the wind vane, the wind vane spins on the pole until the arrow points into the wind.

Measuring Wind Speed

An instrument used to measure wind speed is called an **anemometer.** An anemometer, as shown in **Figure 2,** consists of three or four cups connected by spokes to a pole. The wind pushes on the hollow sides of the cups and causes the cups to rotate on the pole. The motion sends a weak electric current that is measured and displayed on a dial.

thermometer an instrument that measures and indicates temperature

barometer an instrument that measures atmospheric pressure

anemometer an instrument used to measure wind speed

CONNECTION to Life Science — GENERAL

Feeling the Pressure Although airplane cabins are pressurized, passengers still feel the pressure change as the plane climbs and descends. Middle ear barotrauma is an earache caused by a difference in pressure between the air and a person's middle ear. The eustachian tube, a passageway between the middle ear and the throat, fails to open wide enough to equalize the pressure. Chewing gum, yawning, or swallowing often alleviates the condition.

MISCONCEPTION ALERT

High Noon and Midnight Students may think that the lowest and highest temperatures occur in the middle of the night and in the middle of the day. Actually, the lowest temperatures usually occur around sunrise because the Earth's surface has radiated thermal energy all night. The highest temperatures usually occur in the late afternoon.

Teach

CONNECTION ACTIVITY Real World — GENERAL

Weather Watchers Before sophisticated weather forecasts, people learned to carefully observe the world around them for evidence of changing weather. These clues can be found everywhere. Have groups of students research and test these and other observations.

- Birds fly higher when fair weather is coming. (They fly high to avoid the increased air resistance of a high pressure air mass.)

- Heavy dew condenses early in fair night air. If there is little or no dew, the chance for rain is good.

- Halos form around the sun or moon as light shines through ice particles in the clouds of an advancing rainstorm.

- As a pre-rain low pressure front moves in, odors trapped in objects by high pressure air masses are suddenly released.

- Ants travel in lines when rain is coming and scatter when the weather is clear.

- Robins sing high in fair weather and sing low if rain is approaching.

- Flying insects swarm before a rain; they bite the most when the air is moist.

- Clouds lower as a low pressure system approaches. This signals that a storm is coming.

- Swallows and bats fly lowest when air pressure decreases before a storm. Their sensitive ears are more comfortable when these animals are flying close to the ground (where air pressure is highest).

LS Intrapersonal Co-op Learning

Section 4 • Forecasting the Weather

Close

Reteaching — BASIC
Temperature Versus Pressure
Ask students what the difference is between a thermometer and a barometer. (A thermometer is sealed at both ends, so temperature is the only factor affecting the liquid. A barometer is open to the air at one end and subject to changes in air pressure.) Have students build models of each using two straws, colored water, clay for sealing the ends of the straws, and a paper cup. **LS Kinesthetic**

Quiz — GENERAL

1. What advantage do weather satellites have over ground-based weather stations? (Satellites can gather weather data at different altitudes and can track large systems better than land-based instruments can.)

2. Why are so many station models used to gather weather data in the United States? (The United States is very large, and Earth's atmosphere is constantly changing. Data from many stations help make forecasts more accurate.)

Alternative Assessment — GENERAL
Making a Weather Map Have students use the weather report from their local newspaper over a 1-week period to construct a picture of local weather conditions. Then, tell students to analyze their findings by applying what they have learned in this chapter. **LS Visual**

Figure 3 Using Doppler radar, meteorologists can predict a tornado up to 20 minutes before it touches the ground.

CONNECTION TO Biology
WRITING SKILL **Predicting the Weather** Throughout history, people have predicted approaching weather by interpreting natural signs. Animals and plants are usually more sensitive to changes in atmospheric conditions, such as air pressure, humidity, and temperature, than humans are. To find out more about natural signs, research this topic at the library or on the Internet. Write a short paper on your findings to share with the class.

Is That a Fact!
Bats use the Doppler effect to locate prey and to navigate. Bats emit high-frequency sounds that bounce off objects. If the objects are moving, then the wave frequency changes. If the frequency does not change, then the bat knows the object is stationary.

Radar and Satellites
Radar is used to find the location, movement, and amount of precipitation. It can also detect what form of precipitation a weather system is carrying. You might have seen a kind of radar called *Doppler radar* used in a local TV weather report. **Figure 3** shows how Doppler radar is used to track precipitation. *Weather satellites* that orbit Earth provide the images of weather systems that you see on TV weather reports. Satellites can track storms and measure wind speeds, humidity, and temperatures at different altitudes.

Weather Maps
In the United States, the National Weather Service (NWS) and the National Oceanic and Atmospheric Administration (NOAA) collect and analyze weather data. The NWS produces weather maps based on information gathered from about 1,000 weather stations across the United States. On these maps, each station is represented by a station model. A *station model* is a small circle that shows the location of the weather station. As shown in **Figure 4**, surrounding the small circle is a set of symbols and numbers, which represent the weather data.

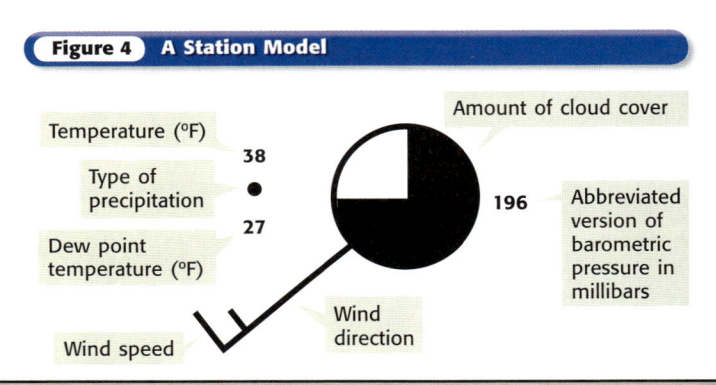

Figure 4 A Station Model

- Temperature (°F): 38
- Type of precipitation
- Dew point temperature (°F): 27
- Wind speed
- Wind direction
- Amount of cloud cover
- 196 Abbreviated version of barometric pressure in millibars

CONNECTION ACTiViTY
Math — GENERAL

Temperature Conversion Have students use the formulas below to convert 32°F, 72°F, and 5°F into degrees Celsius. Then, have students convert 100°C, 45°C, and 21°C into degrees Fahrenheit.

$$°C = (°F - 32) \times 5/9$$

$$°F = (°C \times 9/5) + 32$$

(0°C, 22.2°C, −15°C; 212°F, 113°F, 69.8°F)
LS Logical

---

506 Chapter 16 • Understanding Weather

Reading a Weather Map

Weather maps that you see on TV include lines called *isobars*. Isobars are lines that connect points of equal air pressure. Isobars that form closed circles represent areas of high or low pressure. These areas are usually marked on a map with a capital *H* or *L*. Fronts are also labeled on weather maps, as you can see on the weather map in **Figure 5**.

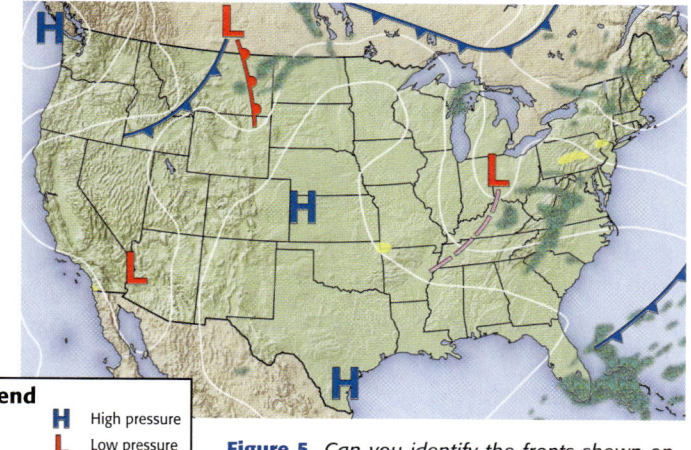

Legend
- Cold front
- Warm front
- Low pressure trough
- Isobar
- H High pressure
- L Low pressure
- Rain
- Fog

Figure 5 Can you identify the fronts shown on the weather map?

SECTION Review

Summary

- Meteorologists use several instruments, such as weather balloons, thermometers, barometers, anemometers, windsocks, weather vanes, radar, and weather satellites, to forecast the weather.
- Station models show the weather conditions at various points across the United States.
- Weather maps show areas of high and low pressure as well as the location of fronts.

Using Key Terms

1. In your own words, write a definition for each of the following terms: *thermometer, barometer,* and *anemometer*.

Understanding Key Ideas

2. Which of the following instruments measures air pressure?
   a. thermometer
   b. barometer
   c. anemometer
   d. windsock

3. How does radar help meteorologists forecast the weather?

4. What does a station model represent?

Math Skills

5. If it is 75°F outside, what is the temperature in degrees Celsius? (Hint: °F = (°C × 9/5) + 32)

Critical Thinking

6. **Applying Concepts** Why would a meteorologist compare a new weather map with one that is 24 h old?

7. **Making Inferences** In the United States, why is weather data gathered from a large number of station models?

8. **Making Inferences** How might several station models from different regions plotted on a map help a meteorologist?

SciLinks
For a variety of links related to this chapter, go to www.scilinks.org
Topic: Forecasting the Weather
SciLinks code: HSM0606

Answers to Section Review

1. Sample answer: A thermometer is a device used to measure temperature. A barometer is an instrument used to measure atmospheric pressure. An anemometer is an instrument used to measure wind speed.
2. b
3. Sample answer: Radar can detect the location, movement, and amount of precipitation.
4. A station model represents the location of a weather station and the weather data collected there.
5. 75 °F = (°C × 9/5) + 32
   °C = (75 − 32) ÷ 9/5
   °C = 43 ÷ 1.8
   °C = 23.9°C
6. Answers may vary. Sample answer: Meteorologists would compare a new weather map with one 24 h old to see how fast a front is moving.
7. Sample answer: Because the United States is very large, a large number of station models help give a more complete picture of weather and make weather forecasts more accurate.
8. Sample answer: Several station models plotted on a map would help a meteorologist get a better visual representation of what the weather is doing across the United States.

CHAPTER RESOURCES

Chapter Resource File
- Section Quiz GENERAL
- Section Review GENERAL
- Vocabulary and Section Summary GENERAL
- Critical Thinking ADVANCED

Workbooks
- Math Skills for Science
  - Using Temperature Scales GENERAL

Section 4 • Forecasting the Weather

Inquiry Lab

Boiling Over!

Teacher's Notes

Time Required
One 45-minute class period

Lab Ratings
EASY —————— HARD

Teacher Prep 🧪
Student Set-Up 🧪🧪🧪
Concept Level 🧪🧪
Clean Up 🧪🧪

MATERIALS
The materials listed on the student page are enough for a group of 3–4 students.

Safety Caution
Remind students to review all safety cautions and icons before beginning this lab activity.

Preparation Notes
Begin the activity by leading a discussion of how thermometers work. Have students observe a regular thermometer. Ask students what parts make a thermometer work. (the bulb, a tube, and air in the tube)

Using Scientific Methods
Inquiry Lab

OBJECTIVES
Construct a device that uses water to measure temperature.
Calibrate the new device by using a mercury thermometer.

MATERIALS
- bottle, plastic
- can, aluminum soda
- card, index, 3 in. × 5 in.
- clay, modeling (1 lb)
- container, yogurt, with lid
- cup, plastic-foam, large (2)
- film canister
- food coloring, red (1 bottle)
- funnel, plastic or paper cone
- gloves, heat-resistant
- hot plate
- ice, cube (5 or 6)
- pan, aluminum pie
- pitcher
- plastic tubing, 5 mm diameter, 30 cm long
- ruler, metric
- straw, plastic, inflexible, clear (1)
- tape, transparent (1 roll)
- thermometer, Celsius
- water, tap

SAFETY

Boiling Over!

Safety Industries, Inc., would like to produce and sell thermometers that are safer than mercury thermometers. The company would like your team of inventors to design a thermometer that uses water instead of mercury. The company will offer a contract to the team that creates the best design of a water thermometer. Good luck!

Ask a Question
① What causes the liquid in a thermometer to rise? How can I use this information to make a thermometer?

Form a Hypothesis
② Brainstorm with a classmate to design a thermometer that uses only water to measure temperature. Sketch your design. Write a one-sentence hypothesis that describes how your thermometer will work.

Test the Hypothesis
③ Following your design, build a thermometer by using only materials from the materials list. Like a mercury thermometer, your thermometer needs a bulb and a tube. However, the liquid in your thermometer will be water.

④ To test your design, place the aluminum pie pan on a hot plate. Use the pitcher to carefully pour water into the pan until the pan is half full. Turn on the hot plate, and heat the water.

⑤ Put on your safety goggles and heat-resistant gloves, and carefully place the "bulb" of your thermometer in the hot water. Observe the water level in the tube. Does the water level rise?

⑥ If the water level does not rise, change your design as necessary and repeat steps 3–5. When the water level in your thermometer does rise, sketch the design of this thermometer as your final design.

⑦ After you decide on your final design, you must calibrate your thermometer by using a laboratory thermometer. Tape an index card to your thermometer's tube so that the part of the tube that sticks out from the "bulb" of your thermometer touches the card.

CLASSROOM TESTED & APPROVED

Daniel Bugenhagen
Yutan Jr.–Sr. High
Yutan, Nebraska

CHAPTER RESOURCES

Chapter Resource File
- Datasheet for Chapter Lab
- Lab Notes and Answers

Technology
Classroom Videos
- Lab Video

LabBook

- Watching the Weather
- Let It Snow!
- Gone with the Wind

Chapter 16 • Understanding Weather

8. Place the plastic funnel or the cone-shaped paper funnel into a plastic-foam cup. Carefully pour hot water from the pie pan into the funnel. Be sure that no water splashes or spills.

9. Place your thermometer and a laboratory thermometer in the hot water. As your thermometer's water level rises, mark the level on the index card. At the same time, observe and record the temperature of the laboratory thermometer, and write this value beside your mark on the card.

10. Repeat steps 8–9 using warm tap water.

11. Repeat steps 8–9 using ice water.

12. Draw evenly spaced scale markings between your temperature markings on the index card. Write the temperatures that correspond to the scale marks on the index card.

Analyze the Results

1. **Analyzing Results** How well does your thermometer measure temperature?

Draw Conclusions

2. **Drawing Conclusions** Compare your thermometer design with other students' designs. How would you change your design to make your thermometer measure temperature better?

3. **Applying Conclusions** Take a class vote to see which design should be used by Safety Industries. Why was this thermometer design chosen? How did it differ from other designs in the class?

CHAPTER RESOURCES

Workbooks

- **Whiz-Bang Demonstrations**
  - It's Raining Again GENERAL
  - When Air Bags Collide GENERAL
- **Inquiry Labs**
  - When Disaster Strikes BASIC
- **EcoLabs & Field Activities**
  - Rain Maker or Rain Faker? ADVANCED
- **Long-Term Projects & Research Ideas**
  - A Storm on the Horizon ADVANCED
- **Calculator-Based Labs**
  - Relative Humidity ADVANCED

Lab Notes

A water thermometer has a receptacle containing water and air and a tube protruding from the receptacle. A trick to getting the water thermometer to work well is to allow a lot of air in the "bulb" because air expands more than water. As the air heats, it expands and pushes the water upward in the tube. One way to build such a thermometer is to put a straw in a soda can and seal the opening of the can with modeling clay so that water can escape only by moving upward, out of the straw. It is important that students' thermometers are tightly sealed. A sample design is shown below.

Analyze the Results

1. Answers may vary. Accept all reasonable responses.

Draw Conclusions

2. Answers may vary. Accept all reasonable responses.

3. Accept all reasonable responses.

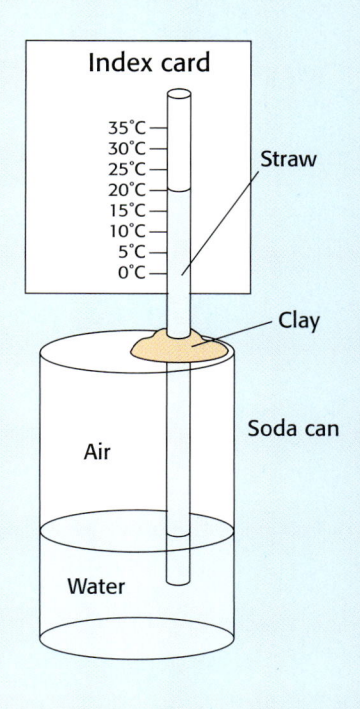

Chapter 16 • Chapter Lab

Chapter Review

Assignment Guide

Section	Questions
1	1, 2, 7–12, 17, 21, 29–32
2	3, 4, 13–14, 18, 19
3	5, 15, 20, 22–28
4	6, 16
2 and 3	24
2 and 4	33, 34

ANSWERS

Using Key Terms

1. Relative humidity is the amount of water vapor the air contains relative to the maximum amount it can hold at a given temperature. Dew point is the temperature to which air must cool to be saturated.
2. Condensation is the change of state from a gas to a liquid. Precipitation is water that falls from the atmosphere to the Earth.
3. An air mass is a large body of air that has the same moisture and temperature throughout. A front is the boundary between two different air masses.
4. Lightning is a large electric discharge that occurs between two oppositely charged surfaces. Thunder is the sound that results from the rapid expansion of air along a lightning strike.
5. A tornado is a small, rotating column of air with high wind speed that touches the ground. A hurricane is a large, rotating tropical weather system with wind speeds equal to or greater than 119 km/h.
6. A barometer is an instrument used to measure air pressure. An anemometer is an instrument used to measure wind speed.

Chapter Review

USING KEY TERMS

For each pair of terms, explain how the meanings of the terms differ.

1. *relative humidity* and *dew point*
2. *condensation* and *precipitation*
3. *air mass* and *front*
4. *lightning* and *thunder*
5. *tornado* and *hurricane*
6. *barometer* and *anemometer*

UNDERSTANDING KEY IDEAS

Multiple Choice

7. The process in which water changes from a liquid to gas is called
   a. precipitation.
   b. condensation.
   c. evaporation.
   d. water vapor.

8. What is the relative humidity of air at its dew point?
   a. 0%
   b. 50%
   c. 75%
   d. 100%

9. Which of the following is NOT a type of condensation?
   a. fog
   b. cloud
   c. snow
   d. dew

10. High clouds made of ice crystals are called ___ clouds.
    a. stratus
    b. cumulus
    c. nimbostratus
    d. cirrus

11. Large thunderhead clouds that produce precipitation are called ___ clouds.
    a. nimbostratus
    b. cumulonimbus
    c. cumulus
    d. stratus

12. Strong updrafts within a thunderhead can produce
    a. snow.
    b. rain.
    c. sleet.
    d. hail.

13. A maritime tropical air mass contains
    a. warm, wet air.
    b. cold, moist air.
    c. warm, dry air.
    d. cold, dry air.

14. A front that forms when a warm air mass is trapped between cold air masses and is forced to rise is a(n)
    a. stationary front.
    b. warm front.
    c. occluded front.
    d. cold front.

15. A severe storm that forms as a rapidly rotating funnel cloud is called a
    a. hurricane.
    b. tornado.
    c. typhoon.
    d. thunderstorm.

16. The lines connecting points of equal air pressure on a weather map are called
    a. contour lines.
    b. highs.
    c. isobars.
    d. lows.

Short Answer

17. Explain the relationship between condensation and dew point.

Understanding Key Ideas

7. c	12. d
8. d	13. a
9. c	14. c
10. d	15. b
11. b	16. c

17. Air must cool to a temperature below its dew point before condensation can occur.
18. Stationary fronts generally bring many days of cloudy, wet weather.
19. An air mass that forms over the Gulf of Mexico is warm and wet.

Chapter 16 • Understanding Weather

18 Describe the conditions along a stationary front.

19 What are the characteristics of an air mass that forms over the Gulf of Mexico?

20 Explain how a hurricane develops.

21 Describe the water cycle, and explain how it affects weather.

22 List the major similarities and differences between hurricanes and tornadoes.

23 Explain how a tornado forms.

24 Describe an interaction between weather and ocean systems.

25 What is a station model? What types of information do station models provide?

26 What type of technology is used to locate and measure the amount of precipitation in an area?

27 List two ways to keep yourself informed during severe weather.

28 Explain why staying away from flood-water is important even when the water is shallow.

CRITICAL THINKING

29 Concept Mapping Use the following terms to create a concept map: *evaporation, relative humidity, water vapor, dew, psychrometer, clouds,* and *fog*.

30 Making Inferences If both the air temperature and the amount of water vapor in the air change, is it possible for the relative humidity to stay the same? Explain.

31 Applying Concepts What can you assume about the amount of water vapor in the air if there is no difference between the wet- and dry-bulb readings of a psychrometer?

32 Identifying Relationships Explain why the concept of relative humidity is important to understanding weather.

INTERPRETING GRAPHICS

Use the weather map below to answer the questions that follow.

33 Where are thunderstorms most likely to occur? Explain your answer.

34 What are the weather conditions in Tulsa, Oklahoma? Explain your answer.

---

20. A hurricane begins as a group of thunderstorms moving over tropical ocean waters. Winds traveling in two different directions collide, which causes the storm to rotate over an area of low pressure. The hurricane is fueled by the condensation of water vapor.

21. The water cycle is the continuous movement of water from the Earth's surface, to the air, and back to the surface. Weather is affected by evaporation, condensation, and precipitation of water in the air.

CHAPTER RESOURCES

Chapter Resource File
- Chapter Review GENERAL
- Chapter Test A GENERAL
- Chapter Test B ADVANCED
- Chapter Test C SPECIAL NEEDS
- Vocabulary Activity GENERAL

Workbooks
- Study Guide
- Assessment resources are also available in Spanish.

---

22. Sample answer: Both begin as a result of thunderstorms and are centered around low pressure. Hurricanes occur over water, and tornadoes generally occur over land.

23. Cold, dry air meets warm, moist air and starts to spin. Updrafts of air turn the spinning column vertical. The column moves to the bottom of the cloud and becomes a funnel cloud. A funnel cloud becomes a tornado when it touches the ground.

24. Sample answer: Evaporating ocean water fuels hurricanes in tropical regions.

25. Sample answer: A station model represents the location of a weather station and shows temperature, precipitation, wind direction, and other data.

26. Radar is used to find the location, movement, and amount of precipitation.

27. Sample answer: Turn the TV and radio to local stations for weather information.

28. Sample answer: Even shallow water can be dangerous if it is moving quickly.

Critical Thinking

29. An answer to this exercise can be found at the end of this book.

30. Sample answer: If air temperature rises, then the air can hold more water. If vapor content in the air also increases, then relative humidity could stay the same.

31. Sample answer: It can be assumed that the relative humidity is 100% because no water evaporated.

32. Sample answer: Precipitation can occur only when the air is saturated, which is when the relative humidity is 100%.

Interpreting Graphics

33. Thunderstorms are most likely to occur in Chicago because a cold front is approaching.

34. Tulsa is experiencing a stationary front and is probably receiving drizzly precipitation.

Standardized Test Preparation

Teacher's Note

To provide practice under more realistic testing conditions, give students 20 minutes to answer all of the questions in this Standardized Test Preparation.

MISCONCEPTION ALERT

Answers to the standardized test preparation can help you identify student misconceptions and misunderstandings.

READING

Passage 1
1. B
2. H
3. D

TEST DOCTOR

Question 3: Students may think that all the answer choices could be correct. It is true that violent tornadoes can destroy paved roads, damage crops, and damage homes. However, the question asks for a characteristic of violent storms. Answers A, B, and C list things a tornado can do, which are actions, not characteristics. The only answer that describes a characteristic of violent tornadoes is answer D.

Passage 2
1. C
2. F
3. B

Standardized Test Preparation

READING

Read each of the passages below. Then, answer the questions that follow each passage.

Passage 1 In May 1997, a springtime tornado <u>wreaked</u> havoc on Jarrell, Texas. The Jarrell tornado was a powerful tornado, whose wind speeds were estimated at more than 410 km/h. The winds of the twister were so strong that they peeled the asphalt from paved roads, stripped fields of corn bare, and destroyed an entire neighborhood. Some tornadoes, such as the one that struck the town of Jarrell, are classified as violent tornadoes. Only 2% of the tornadoes that occur in the United States are categorized as violent tornadoes. Despite the fact that these types of tornadoes do not occur often, 70% of all tornado-related deaths are a result of violent tornadoes.

1. In the passage, what does the word *wreaked* mean?
   A smelled
   B caused
   C prevented
   D removed

2. Which of the following can be concluded from the passage?
   F Tornadoes often hit Jarrell, Texas.
   G Most tornadoes fall into the violent category.
   H The tornado that hit Jarrell was a rare type of tornado.
   I Tornadoes always happen during the spring.

3. Which of the following **best** describes a characteristic of violent tornadoes?
   A Violent tornadoes destroy paved roads.
   B Violent tornadoes damage crops.
   C Violent tornadoes damage homes.
   D Violent tornadoes have extremely strong winds.

Passage 2 Water evaporates into the air from Earth's surface. This water returns to Earth's surface as <u>precipitation</u>. Precipitation is water, in solid or liquid form, that falls from the air to Earth. The four major types of precipitation are rain, snow, sleet, and hail. The most common form of precipitation is rain.

A cloud produces rain when the cloud's water drops become large enough to fall. A raindrop begins as a water droplet that is smaller than the period at the end of this sentence. Before a water drop falls as rain, it must become about 100 times this beginning size. Water drops get larger by joining with other water drops. When the water drops become too heavy, they fall as precipitation.

1. In this passage, what does *precipitation* mean?
   A acceleration
   B haste
   C water that falls from the atmosphere to Earth
   D separating a substance from a solution as a solid

2. What is the main idea of the second paragraph?
   F Rain occurs when the water droplets in clouds become large enough to fall.
   G Raindrops are very small at first.
   H Water droplets join with other water droplets to become larger.
   I Rain is a form of precipitation.

3. According to the passage, which step happens last in the formation of precipitation?
   A Water droplets join.
   B Water droplets fall to the ground.
   C Water droplets become heavy.
   D Water evaporates into the air.

TEST DOCTOR

Question 1: Both answers C and D are correct definitions for the word "precipitation." However, in this paragraph precipitation is defined as water returning to Earth's surface, so only answer C is correct.

512 Chapter 16 • Understanding Weather

INTERPRETING GRAPHICS

Use each diagram below to answer the question that follows each diagram.

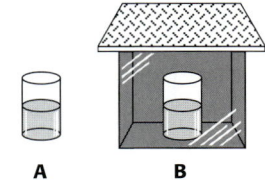

A   **B**

1. During an experiment, the setup shown in the diagram above is maintained for 72 h. Which of the following is the most likely outcome?
   A Beaker A will hold less water than beaker B will.
   B The amount of water in beaker A and beaker B will stay the same.
   C The amount of water in beaker A and beaker B will change by about the same amount.
   D Beaker B will hold less water than beaker A will.

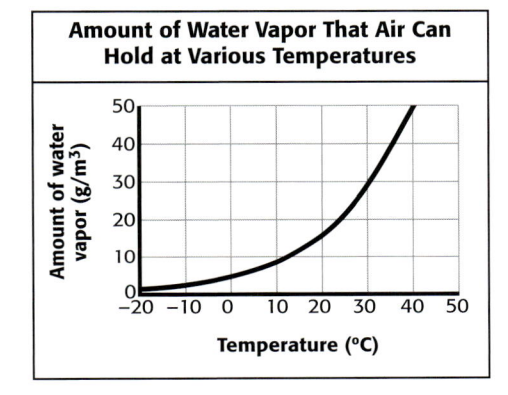

Amount of Water Vapor That Air Can Hold at Various Temperatures

2. Look at the line graph above. Which statement is consistent with the line graph?
   F The ability of air to hold moisture increases as temperature increases.
   G The ability of air to hold moisture decreases as temperature increases.
   H The ability of air to hold moisture decreases and then increases as temperature increases.
   I The ability of air to hold moisture stays the same regardless of temperature.

MATH

Read each question below, and choose the best answer.

1. The speed of light is 3.00×10^8 m/s. What is another way to express this measure?
   A 3,000,000,000 m/s
   B 300,000,000 m/s
   C 3,000,000 m/s
   D 300,000 m/s

2. A hurricane is moving 122 km/h. How long will it take to hit the coast, which is 549 km away?
   F 4.2 h
   G 4.5 h
   H 4.8 h
   I 5.2 h

3. A front is moving 15 km/h in an easterly direction. At that rate, how far will the front travel in 12 h?
   A 0.8 km
   B 1.25 km
   C 27 km
   D 180 km

4. On average, 2 out of every 100 tornadoes are classified as violent tornadoes. If there are 400 tornadoes in 1 year, which is the best prediction of the number of tornadoes that will be classified as violent tornadoes during that year?
   F 2
   G 4
   H 8
   I 16

5. The air temperature in the morning was 27°C. During the day, a front moved into the region and caused the temperature to drop to 18°C. By how many degrees did the temperature drop?
   A 1°C
   B 9°C
   C 11°C
   D 19°C

INTERPRETING GRAPHICS
1. A
2. F

TEST DOCTOR

Question 2: Some students may have difficulty interpreting graphs. To help students understand trends in graphs, have them choose two places on the curved line in the graph. It is best if students choose points that are easy to evaluate, such as points where grid lines cross. On this graph, students could choose the points where $x = 10$, $y = 10$ and $x = 30$, $y = 30$. Then, ask students to notice that when one number increased, the other also increased.

MATH
1. B
2. G
3. D
4. H
5. B

TEST DOCTOR

Question 4: This question asks students to evaluate a ratio. Students may have difficulty deciding which numbers should go together when comparing the ratio. Tell students to look for the words *out of* as a clue about which numbers are part of the same fraction in a ratio. In this case, "2 out of every 100 tornadoes" would indicate a fraction of 2/100. Then, the question can be interpreted as "How many tornadoes out of 400 are violent?" This interpretation produces a fraction of x/400.

CHAPTER RESOURCES

Chapter Resource File
- Standardized Test Preparation GENERAL

State Resources

For specific resources for your state, visit **go.hrw.com** and type in the keyword **HSMSTR**.

Chapter 16 • Standardized Test Preparation

Science in Action

Science Fiction

Background

Ray Bradbury is one of the world's most celebrated writers. He was born in the small town of Waukegan, Illinois, in 1920. He and his family moved several times and eventually ended up in Los Angeles. There he began a writing career that has spanned more than 60 years!

Bradbury has earned top honors in the field of literature, including the World Fantasy Award for lifetime work and the Grand Master Award from Science Fiction Writers of America. An unusual honor came when an astronaut named a crater on the moon Dandelion Crater after Ray Bradbury's novel *Dandelion Wine*.

Weird Science

CONNECTION ACTIVITY
History — BASIC

Have students research a list of traditional weather signs. Once a class list is compiled, begin keeping a weather log. Students should record observations, make a prediction, and then check their predictions the following day.

Science in Action

Science Fiction

"All Summer in a Day" by Ray Bradbury

It is raining, just as it has been for seven long years. For the people who live on Venus, constant rain is a fact of life. But today is a special day—a day when the rain stops and the sun shines. This day comes once every seven years. At school, the students have been looking forward to this day for weeks. But Margot longs to see the sun even more than the others do. The reason for her longing makes the other kids jealous, and jealous kids can be cruel. What happens to Margot? Find out by reading Ray Bradbury's "All Summer in a Day" in the *Holt Anthology of Science Fiction*.

Language Arts ACTIVITY

WRITING SKILL What would living in a place where it rained all day and every day for seven years be like? Write a short story describing what your life would be like if you lived in such a place. In your story, describe what you and your friends would do for fun after school.

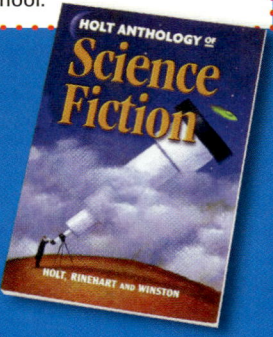

Weird Science

Can Animals Forecast the Weather?

Before ways of making sophisticated weather forecasts were developed, people observed animals and insects for evidence of changing weather. By observing the behavior of certain animals and insects, you, too, can detect changing weather! For example, did you know that birds fly higher when fair weather is coming? And a robin's song is high pitched in fair weather and low pitched as rain approaches. Ants travel in lines when rain is coming and scatter when the weather is clear. You can tell how hot the weather is by listening for the chirping of crickets—crickets chirp faster as the temperature rises!

Math ACTIVITY

To estimate the outdoor temperature in degrees Fahrenheit, count the number of times that a cricket chirps in 15 s and add 37. If you count 40 chirps in 15 s, what is the estimated temperature?

Answer to Language Arts Activity
Answers may vary. Accept any reasonable answer.

Answer to Math Activity
40 chirps + 37 = 77°F

Careers

Cristy Mitchell

Meteorologist Predicting floods, observing a tornado develop inside a storm, watching the growth of a hurricane, and issuing flood warnings are all in a day's work for Cristy Mitchell. As a meteorologist for the National Weather Service, Mitchell spends each working day observing the powerful forces of nature. When asked what made her job interesting, Mitchell replied, "There's nothing like the adrenaline rush you get when you see a tornado coming!"

Perhaps the most familiar field of meteorology is weather forecasting. However, meteorology is also used in air-pollution control, weather control, agricultural planning, and even criminal and civil investigations. Meteorologists also study trends in Earth's climate.

Meteorologists such as Mitchell use high-tech tools—computers and satellites—to collect data. By analyzing such data, Mitchell is able to forecast the weather.

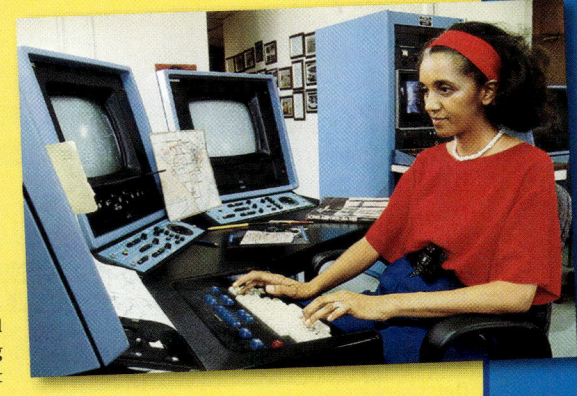

Social Studies ACTIVITY

An almanac is a type of calendar that contains various information, including weather forecasts and astronomical data, for every day of the year. Many people used almanacs before meteorologists started to forecast the weather on TV. Use an almanac from the library to find out what the weather was on the day that you were born.

Current Science

To learn more about these Science in Action topics, visit **go.hrw.com** and type in the keyword **HZ5WEAF**.

Check out Current Science® articles related to this chapter by visiting **go.hrw.com**. Just type in the keyword **HZ5CS16**.

People in Science
CONNECTION ACTIVITY
Forensic Science — ADVANCED

Have students research how meteorology is used to help with criminal investigations. Have students write a report and present their findings to the class. Then, have students work in small groups to write a scene in which a crime has been committed and is solved using meteorological information.

Homework — GENERAL

Have students watch their local weather forecasts for 1 week and then write a forecast of their own, using terminology they have picked up from watching the news. Have interested students act out their forecast for the class using a pointer and a display of a United States map.

Answer to Social Studies Activity
Answers may vary. Accept any well-supported answer.

Chapter 16 • Science in Action

17 Climate
Chapter Planning Guide

Compression guide: To shorten instruction because of time limitations, omit Section 2.

OBJECTIVES	LABS, DEMONSTRATIONS, AND ACTIVITIES	TECHNOLOGY RESOURCES
PACING • 90 min pp. 516–525 **Chapter Opener**	SE Start-up Activity, p. 517 GENERAL	OSP Parent Letter ■ GENERAL CD Student Edition on CD-ROM CD Guided Reading Audio CD ■ TR Chapter Starter Transparency* VID Brain Food Video Quiz
Section 1 What is Climate? • Explain the difference between weather and climate. • Identify five factors that determine climates. • Identify the three climate zones of the world.	TE Connection Activity Math, p. 519 GENERAL TE Activity Modeling the Earth and Sun, p. 520 ◆ BASIC SE Quick Lab A Cool Breeze, p. 521 GENERAL CRF Datasheet for Quick Lab* TE Connection Activity Geography, p. 521 ADVANCED SE School-to-Home Activity Using a Map, p. 522 GENERAL SE Skills Practice Lab Biome Business, p. 542 GENERAL CRF Datasheet for Chapter Lab* SE Skills Practice Lab For the Birds, p. 755 GENERAL CRF Datasheet for LabBook* LB Whiz-Bang Demonstrations How Humid Is It?* GENERAL	CRF Lesson Plans* TR Bellringer Transparency* TR The Seasons* TR The Circulation of Warm and Cold Air* TR The Earth's Land Biomes* VID Lab Videos for Earth Science
PACING • 45 min pp. 526–529 **Section 2 The Tropics** • Locate and describe the tropical zone. • Describe the biomes found in the tropical zone.	TE Activity Country Profile, p. 526 GENERAL TE Connection Activity Life Science, p. 527 GENERAL SE Science in Action Math, Social Studies, and Language Arts Activities, pp. 548–549 GENERAL	CRF Lesson Plans* TR Bellringer Transparency* TR LINK TO LIFE SCIENCE Gas Exchange in Leaves* CRF SciLinks Activity* GENERAL
PACING • 45 min pp. 530–535 **Section 3 Temperate and Polar Zones** • Locate and describe the temperate zone and the polar zone. • Describe the different biomes found in the temperate zone and the polar zone. • Explain what a microclimate is.	TE Activity Camp Climate, p. 530 GENERAL TE Demonstration Mock Permafrost, p. 533 ◆ GENERAL SE School-to-Home Activity Your Biome, p. 534 GENERAL LB Calculator-Based Labs What Causes the Seasons?* ◆ ADVANCED SE Connection to Physics Hot Roofs!, p. 535 ◆ GENERAL	CRF Lesson Plans* TR Bellringer Transparency*
PACING • 45 min pp. 536–541 **Section 4 Changes in Climate** • Describe how the Earth's climate has changed over time. • Summarize four different theories that attempt to explain why the Earth's climate has changed. • Explain the greenhouse effect and its role in global warming.	TE Demonstration The Greenhouse Effect, p. 536 ◆ GENERAL TE Activity Ancient Climates, p. 537 ADVANCED TE Activity Volcanic Eruptions, p. 538 GENERAL TE Connection Activity Real World, p. 539 ADVANCED SE School-to-Home Activity Reducing Pollution, p. 541 GENERAL LB Long-Term Projects & Research Ideas Sun-Starved in Fairbanks* ADVANCED	SE Internet Activity, p. 537 GENERAL CRF Lesson Plans* TR Bellringer Transparency* TR The Milankovitch Theory*

PACING • 90 min

CHAPTER REVIEW, ASSESSMENT, AND STANDARDIZED TEST PREPARATION

CRF Vocabulary Activity* ■ GENERAL
SE Chapter Review, pp. 544–545 GENERAL
CRF Chapter Review* ■ GENERAL
CRF Chapter Tests A* ■ GENERAL, B* ADVANCED, C* SPECIAL NEEDS
SE Standardized Test Preparation, pp. 546–547 GENERAL
CRF Standardized Test Preparation* GENERAL
CRF Performance-Based Assessment* GENERAL
OSP Test Generator GENERAL
CRF Test Item Listing* GENERAL

Online and Technology Resources

go.hrw.com — Visit go.hrw.com for a variety of free resources related to this textbook. Enter the keyword **HZ5CLM**.

Holt Online Learning — Students can access interactive problem-solving help and active visual concept development with the *Holt Science and Technology* Online Edition available at **www.hrw.com**.

Guided Reading Audio CD Also in Spanish
A direct reading of each chapter for auditory learners, reluctant readers, and Spanish-speaking students.

Science Tutor CD-ROM
Excellent for remediation and test practice.

KEY							
SE	Student Edition	CRF	Chapter Resource File	SS	Science Skills Worksheets	*	Also on One-Stop Planner
TE	Teacher Edition	OSP	One-Stop Planner	MS	Math Skills for Science Worksheets	◆	Requires advance prep
		LB	Lab Bank	CD	CD or CD-ROM	■	Also available in Spanish
		TR	Transparencies	VID	Classroom Video/DVD		

SKILLS DEVELOPMENT RESOURCES	SECTION REVIEW AND ASSESSMENT	STANDARDS CORRELATIONS
SE Pre-Reading Activity, p. 516 GENERAL OSP Science Puzzlers, Twisters & Teasers GENERAL		National Science Education Standards SAI 1
CRF Directed Reading A* ■ BASIC, B* SPECIAL NEEDS CRF Vocabulary and Section Summary* ■ GENERAL SE Reading Strategy Discussion, p. 518 GENERAL TE Inclusion Strategies, p. 522 ◆	SE Reading Checks, pp. 518, 520, 522, 523, 524 GENERAL TE Homework, p. 523 TE Reteaching, p. 524 BASIC TE Quiz, p. 524 GENERAL TE Alternative Assessment, p. 524 GENERAL SE Section Review,* p. 525 ■ GENERAL CRF Section Quiz* ■ GENERAL	SAI 1; SPSP 1, 3; ES 1f, 1j, 3d; *Chapter Lab:* SAI 1; SPSP 2 *LabBook:* UCP 2, 3; SAI 1; ST 1
CRF Directed Reading A* ■ BASIC, B* SPECIAL NEEDS CRF Vocabulary and Section Summary* ■ GENERAL SE Reading Strategy Reading Organizer, p. 526 GENERAL SE Connection to Social Studies Living in the Tropics, p. 527 GENERAL SE Connection to Biology Animal and Plant Adaptations, p. 528 GENERAL MS Math Skills for Science Rain-Forest Math* GENERAL SS Science Skills Finding Useful Sources* GENERAL	SE Reading Checks, pp. 526, 529 GENERAL TE Reteaching, p. 528 BASIC TE Quiz, p. 528 GENERAL TE Alternative Assessment, p. 528 GENERAL SE Section Review,* p. 529 ■ GENERAL CRF Section Quiz* ■ GENERAL	UCP 2, 3; SAI 1, 2; ST 1; SPSP 2; HNS 1, 3
CRF Directed Reading A* ■ BASIC, B* SPECIAL NEEDS CRF Vocabulary and Section Summary* ■ GENERAL SE Reading Strategy Reading Organizer, p. 530 GENERAL TE Inclusion Strategies, p. 532 CRF Reinforcement Worksheet A Tale of Three Climates* BASIC	SE Reading Checks, pp. 530, 532, 535 GENERAL TE Homework, p. 533 ADVANCED TE Reteaching, p. 534 BASIC TE Quiz, p. 534 GENERAL TE Alternative Assessment, p. 534 GENERAL SE Section Review,* p. 535 ■ GENERAL CRF Section Quiz* ■ GENERAL	SAI 1, 2; SPSP 2; HNS 1, 3
CRF Directed Reading A* ■ BASIC, B* SPECIAL NEEDS CRF Vocabulary and Section Summary* ■ GENERAL SE Reading Strategy Paired Summarizing, p. 536 GENERAL SE Connection to Astronomy Sunspots, p. 539 GENERAL SE Math Practice The Ride to School, p. 540 GENERAL CRF Critical Thinking Cyberspace Heats Up* ADVANCED SS Science Skills Understanding Bias* GENERAL	SE Reading Checks, pp. 537, 538, 541 GENERAL TE Reteaching, p. 540 BASIC TE Quiz, p. 540 GENERAL TE Alternative Assessment, p. 540 GENERAL SE Section Review,* p. 541 ■ GENERAL CRF Section Quiz* ■ GENERAL	UCP 2, 3; SAI 1, 2; ST 2; SPSP 3, 4, 5; HNS 1; ES 1k, 2a

One-Stop Planner® CD-ROM

This convenient CD-ROM includes:
- Lab Materials QuickList Software
- Holt Calendar Planner
- Customizable Lesson Plans
- Printable Worksheets
- ExamView® Test Generator

CNN Student News

cnnstudentnews.com

Find the latest news, lesson plans, and activities related to important scientific events.

SciLinks NSTA

www.scilinks.org

Maintained by the **National Science Teachers Association.** See Chapter Enrichment pages for a complete list of topics.

Current Science®

Check out *Current Science* articles and activities by visiting the HRW Web site at **go.hrw.com.** Just type in the keyword **HZ5CS17T.**

Classroom Videos

- **Lab Videos** demonstrate the chapter lab.
- **Brain Food Video Quizzes** help students review the chapter material.
- **CNN Videos** bring science into your students' daily life.

Chapter 17 • Chapter Planning Guide

17 Chapter Resources

Visual Resources

CHAPTER STARTER TRANSPARENCY

BELLRINGER TRANSPARENCIES

TEACHING TRANSPARENCIES

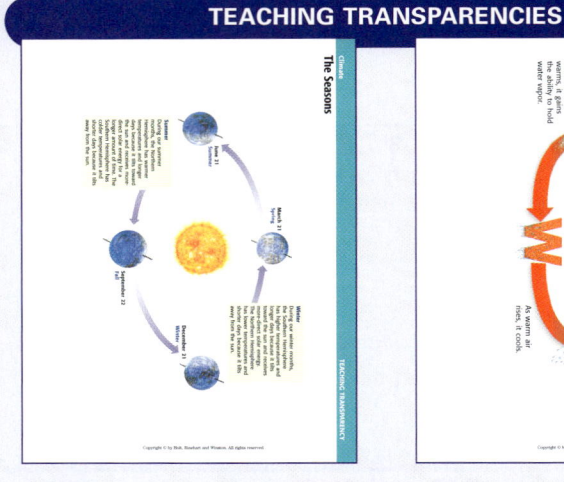

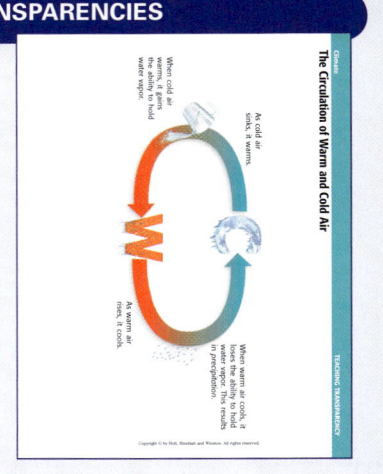

TEACHING TRANSPARENCIES

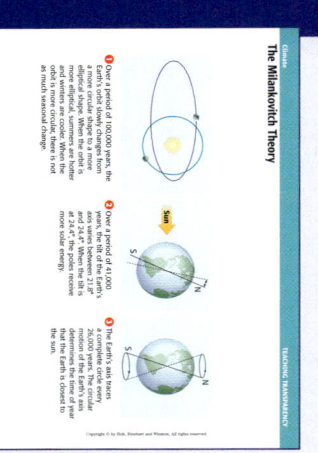

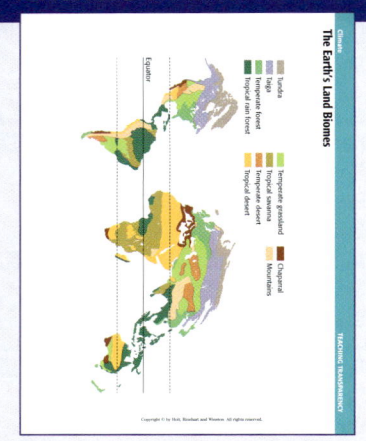

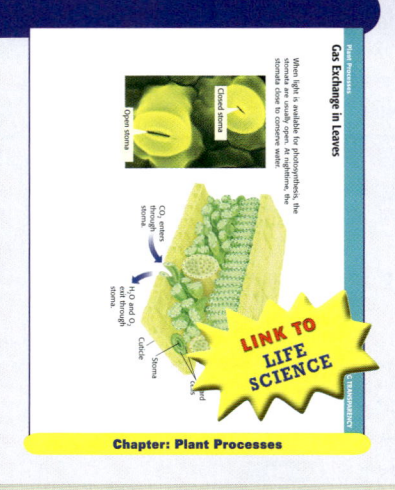

CONCEPT MAPPING TRANSPARENCY

Planning Resources

LESSON PLANS

PARENT LETTER

TEST ITEM LISTING

One-Stop Planner® CD-ROM

This CD-ROM includes all of the resources shown here and the following time-saving tools:

- Lab Materials QuickList Software
- Customizable lesson plans
- Holt Calendar Planner
- The powerful ExamView® Test Generator

515C Chapter 17 • Climate

For a preview of available worksheets covering math and science skills, see pages T26–T33. All of these resources are also on the One-Stop Planner®.

Meeting Individual Needs

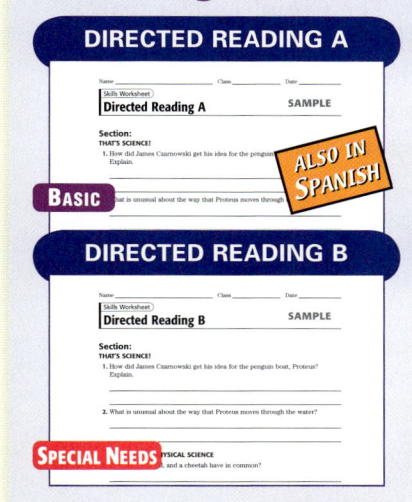

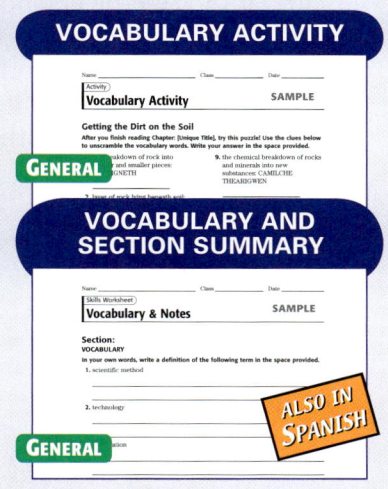

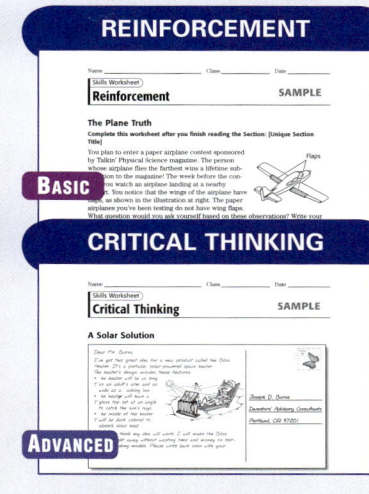

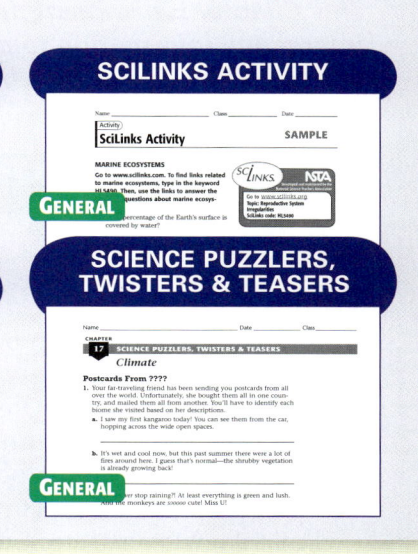

- **DIRECTED READING A** — BASIC / ALSO IN SPANISH
- **VOCABULARY ACTIVITY** — GENERAL
- **REINFORCEMENT** — BASIC
- **SCILINKS ACTIVITY** — GENERAL
- **DIRECTED READING B** — SPECIAL NEEDS
- **VOCABULARY AND SECTION SUMMARY** — GENERAL / ALSO IN SPANISH
- **CRITICAL THINKING** — ADVANCED
- **SCIENCE PUZZLERS, TWISTERS & TEASERS** — GENERAL

Labs and Activities

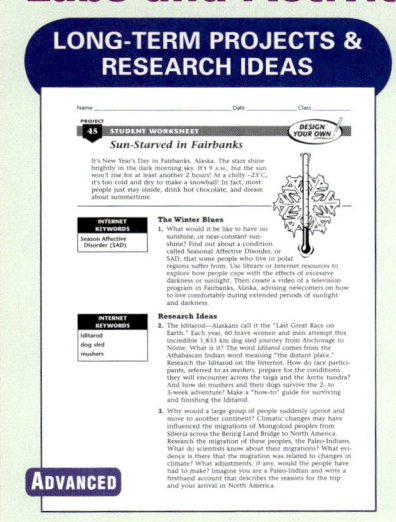

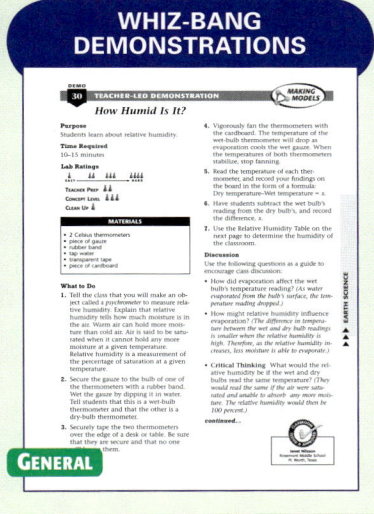

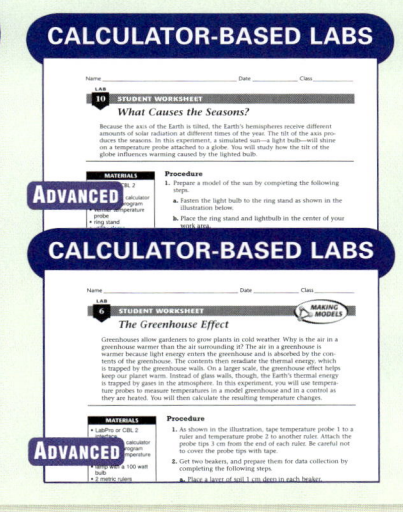

- **LONG-TERM PROJECTS & RESEARCH IDEAS** — ADVANCED
- **WHIZ-BANG DEMONSTRATIONS** — GENERAL
- **CALCULATOR-BASED LABS** — ADVANCED
- **DATASHEETS FOR QUICKLABS**
- **CALCULATOR-BASED LABS** — ADVANCED
- **DATASHEETS FOR CHAPTER LABS**
- **DATASHEETS FOR LABBOOK**

Review and Assessments

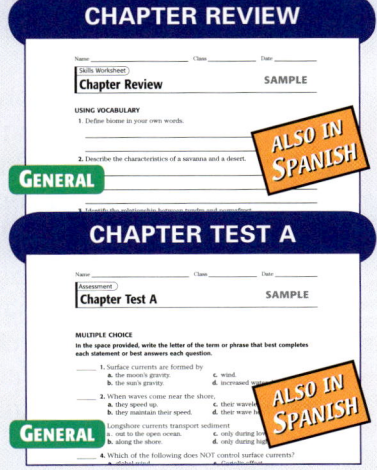

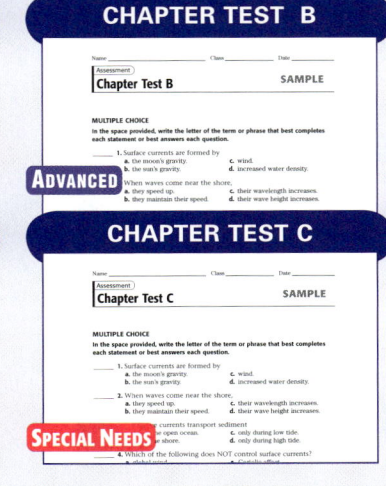

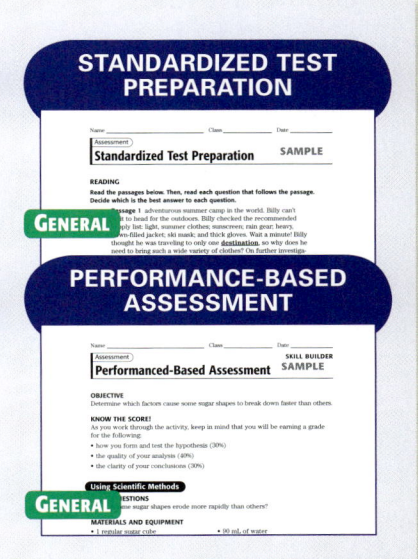

- **SECTION QUIZ** — GENERAL / ALSO IN SPANISH
- **CHAPTER REVIEW** — GENERAL / ALSO IN SPANISH
- **CHAPTER TEST B** — ADVANCED
- **STANDARDIZED TEST PREPARATION** — GENERAL
- **SECTION REVIEW** — GENERAL / ALSO IN SPANISH
- **CHAPTER TEST A** — GENERAL / ALSO IN SPANISH
- **CHAPTER TEST C** — SPECIAL NEEDS
- **PERFORMANCE-BASED ASSESSMENT** — GENERAL

Chapter 17 • Chapter Resources 515D

17 Chapter Enrichment

This Chapter Enrichment provides relevant and interesting information to expand and enhance your presentation of the chapter material.

Section 1

What Is Climate?

Climatology

- The study of climate can be traced back to Greek scientists of the sixth century BCE. In fact, the word *climate* comes from the Greek word *klíma*, meaning "an inclination" of the sun's rays. Climatology can be divided into three branches—global climatology, regional climatology, and physical climatology. Global climatology investigates the general circulation of wind and water currents around the Earth. Regional climatology studies the characteristic weather patterns and related phenomena of a particular region. Physical climatology analyzes statistics concerning climatic factors such as temperature, moisture, wind, and air pressure.

Global Winds

- Global winds are patterns of air circulation that travel across the Earth. These winds include the trade winds, the prevailing westerlies, and the polar easterlies.

- In both hemispheres, the trade winds blow from 30° latitude to the equator. The Coriolis effect makes the trade winds curve to the right in the Northern Hemisphere, moving northeast to southwest. In the Southern Hemisphere, the trade winds curve to the left and move from southeast to northwest.

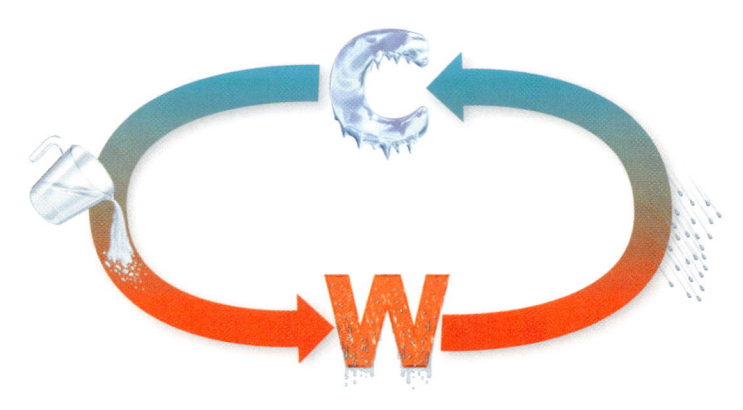

- The prevailing westerlies are found in both the Northern and Southern Hemispheres between 30° and 60° latitude. In the Northern Hemisphere, the westerlies blow from the southwest to the northeast. In the Southern Hemisphere, they blow from the northwest to the southeast.

- The polar easterlies extend from the poles to 60° latitude in both hemispheres. The polar easterlies blow from the northeast to the southwest in the Northern Hemisphere. In the Southern Hemisphere, these winds blow from the southeast to the northwest.

Section 2

The Tropics

Climate Classification

- Because climate is a complicated and somewhat abstract concept, more than 100 classification models have been devised, which vary according to the data on which the classifications are based. For instance, there have been attempts to classify climates according to factors such as soil formation, rock weathering, and even effects on human comfort!

- In 1966, Werner Terjung, an American geographer, developed a physiological climate classification. This system categorized climates according to their effects on people's comfort levels. The system focused on four factors that might affect human comfort—temperature, relative humidity, wind speed, and solar radiation.

515E Chapter 17 • Climate

Section 3

Temperate and Polar Zones

The Köppen System

- The most widely used climate classification system is the Köppen system. This system, named for Wladimir Köppen, the German botanist and climatologist who developed it, uses vegetation regions and average weather statistics to classify local climates. Each vegetation region is characterized by the natural vegetation that is predominant there. Critics have found fault with the Köppen system because it considers only average monthly temperatures and precipitation, ignoring other factors, such as winds, cloud cover, and daily temperature extremes.

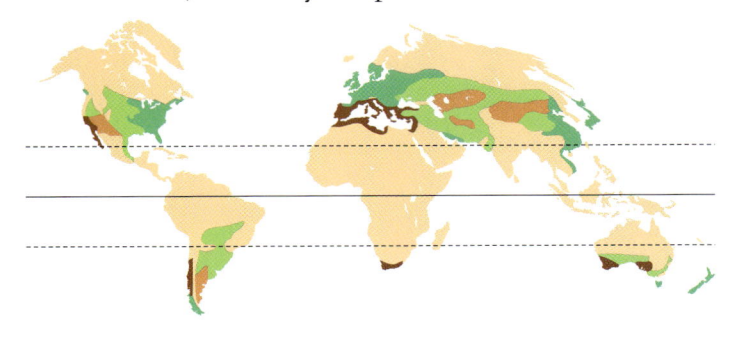

Section 4

Changes in Climate

Pangaea

- In 1620, the British philosopher Francis Bacon noted that Africa and South America looked as if they could fit together like puzzle pieces. But it was not until the early 20th century that the German meteorologist Alfred Wegener proposed a theory that all the continents were once one landmass. Wegener's hypothesis was supported by the existence of similar plant and animal fossils on different continents. Although his theory was initially ridiculed, Wegener was vindicated after World War II when sea-floor spreading and a mechanism for continental drift were discovered.

Is That a Fact!

◆ *Pangaea*, the name Wegener gave to the supercontinent, is Greek for "all Earth."

The Greenhouse Effect

- Gases such as water vapor, carbon dioxide and methane are known as greenhouse gases because they absorb and reradiate thermal energy in Earth's atmosphere. Greenhouse gases are necessary for life on Earth because they keep Earth's average temperature at 15°C. Without them, Earth would be frozen; the average temperature would be about –18°C.

Is That a Fact!

◆ Burning 1 gal of gasoline can produce 9 kg of carbon dioxide.

SciLinks is maintained by the National Science Teachers Association to provide you and your students with interesting, up-to-date links that will enrich your classroom presentation of the chapter.

Visit www.scilinks.org and enter the SciLinks code for more information about the topic listed.

Topic: What Is Climate?
SciLinks code: HSM1659

Topic: Climates of the World
SciLinks code: HSM0302

Topic: Modeling Earth's Climate
SciLinks code: HSM0976

Topic: Changes in Climate
SciLinks code: HSM0252

Chapter 17 • Chapter Enrichment **515F**

Overview
Tell students that this chapter describes different climates around the world and the factors that influence climate. This chapter also explains how climate can change over time.

Assessing Prior Knowledge
Students should be familiar with the following topics:
- weather patterns
- latitudes of the Earth

Identifying Misconceptions
Students may think that the Earth is farther away from the sun during winter and closer to the sun in the summer. Point out that the seasons are caused by the Earth's tilt, not by the distance between the Earth and the sun. Students may also think that the only factor that influences climate is a location's distance from the equator. Explain that this chapter will introduce many factors that influence climate.

17 Climate

SECTION 1	What Is Climate?	518
SECTION 2	The Tropics	526
SECTION 3	Temperate and Polar Zones	530
SECTION 4	Changes in Climate	536

Chapter Lab 542
Chapter Review 544
Standardized Test Preparation ... 546
Science in Action 548

About the PHOTO
Would you like to hang out on this ice with the penguins? You probably would not. You would be shivering, and your teeth would be chattering. However, these penguins feel comfortable. They have thick feathers and lots of body fat to keep them warm. Like other animals, penguins have adapted to their climate, which allows them to live comfortably in that climate. So, you will never see one of these penguins living comfortably on a hot, sunny beach in Florida!

PRE-READING ACTIVITY
FOLDNOTES **Pyramid** Before you read the chapter, create the FoldNote entitled "Pyramid" described in the **Study Skills** section of the Appendix. Label the sides of the pyramid with "Tropical climate," "Temperate climate," and "Polar climate." As you read the chapter, define each climate zone, and write characteristics of each climate zone on the appropriate pyramid side.

Standards Correlations

National Science Education Standards
The following codes indicate the National Science Education Standards that correlate to this chapter. The full text of the standards is at the front of the book.

Chapter Opener
SAI 1

Section 1 What Is Climate?
SAI 1; SPSP 1, 3; ES 1j, 3d

Section 2 The Tropics
SAI 2; HNS 1, 3; SPSP 2; *LabBook:* UCP 2, 3; SAI 1; ST 1

Section 3 Temperate and Polar Zones
SAI 1, 2; HNS 1, 3; SPSP 2

Section 4 Changes in Climate
UCP 2, 3; SAI 1, 2; ST 2; SPSP 3, 4, 5; HNS 1; ES 1k, 2a; *LabBook:* UCP 2, 3; SAI 1

Chapter Lab
SAI 1, UCP 2

Chapter Review
UCP 2; SAI 1; ES 1d, 1f, 1j, 3d

Science in Action
SPSP 5; HNS 1, 2

516 Chapter 17 • Climate

START-UP ACTIVITY

What's Your Angle?

Try this activity to see how the angle of the sun's solar rays influences temperatures on Earth.

Procedure

1. Place a **lamp** 30 cm from a **globe**.
2. Point the lamp so that the light shines directly on the globe's equator.
3. Using **adhesive putty**, attach a **thermometer** to the globe's equator in a vertical position. Attach **another thermometer** to the globe's North Pole so that the tip points toward the lamp.
4. Record the temperature reading of each thermometer.
5. Turn on the lamp, and let the light shine on the globe for 3 minutes.
6. After 3 minutes, turn off the lamp and record the temperature reading of each thermometer again.

Analysis

1. Was there a difference between the final temperature at the globe's North Pole and the final temperature at the globe's equator? If so, what was it?
2. Explain why the temperature readings at the North Pole and the equator may be different.

START-UP ACTIVITY

MATERIALS

FOR EACH GROUP
- adhesive putty
- globe
- lamp
- thermometers (2)

Safety Caution: Remind students to review all safety cautions and icons before beginning this lab activity. Students should not touch the lamp's bulb while it is on or immediately after it has been turned off.

Teacher's Notes: If you have time, encourage students to repeat the experiment, positioning one thermometer at the equator and one at the South Pole. Have students compare their results.

Answers

1. yes; The final temperature at the globe's North Pole was cooler than the final temperature at the globe's equator.
2. The temperature readings at the North Pole and the equator are different because the globe's equator received more direct energy from the lamp than the globe's North Pole received.

Chapter Starter Transparency
Use this transparency to help students begin thinking about the relationship between elevation and climate.

CHAPTER RESOURCES

Technology

- **Transparencies**
  - Chapter Starter Transparency   READING SKILLS
- **Student Edition on CD-ROM**
- **Guided Reading Audio CD**
  - English or Spanish
- **Classroom Videos**
  - Brain Food Video Quiz

Workbooks

- **Science Puzzlers, Twisters & Teasers**
  - Climate   GENERAL

Chapter 17 • Climate   **517**

SECTION 1

Focus

Overview
In this section, students will learn the difference between weather and climate. They will examine how latitude, prevailing winds, geography, and ocean currents affect an area's climate. Finally, students will learn about the three major climate zones of the world.

🔔 Bellringer
Have students imagine that they have entered a contest for a free trip to a place that has a perfect climate. To win, they must describe their idea of a perfect climate in 25 words or less.

Motivate

Discussion — GENERAL
Latitude and Climate Ask students to find locations on a United States or world map where they would like to visit. Write the locations and their latitudinal positions on the board. Review with students that latitude is the distance north or south from the equator, expressed in degrees. Ask students to help you list some observations about the climate in each location. Make sure students notice the relationship between latitude and climate. **LS Verbal**

SECTION 1

READING WARM-UP

Objectives
- Explain the difference between weather and climate.
- Identify five factors that determine climates.
- Identify the three climate zones of the world.

Terms to Learn
- weather
- climate
- latitude
- prevailing winds
- elevation
- surface current
- biome

READING STRATEGY
Discussion Read this section silently. Write down questions that you have about this section. Discuss your questions in a small group.

CHAPTER RESOURCES

Chapter Resource File
- Lesson Plan
- Directed Reading A BASIC
- Directed Reading B SPECIAL NEEDS

Technology
- Transparencies
  - Bellringer

What Is Climate?

Suppose you receive a call from a friend who is coming to visit you tomorrow. To decide what clothing to bring, he asks about the current weather in your area.

You step outside to see if rain clouds are in the sky and to check the temperature. But what would you do if your friend asked you about the climate in your area? What is the difference between weather and climate?

Climate Vs. Weather

The main difference between weather and climate is the length of time over which both are measured. **Weather** is the condition of the atmosphere at a particular time. Weather conditions vary from day to day and include temperature, humidity, precipitation, wind, and visibility. **Climate**, on the other hand, is the average weather condition in an area over a long period of time. Climate is mostly determined by two factors—temperature and precipitation. Different parts of the world can have different climates, as shown in **Figure 1**. But why are climates so different? The answer is complicated. It includes factors in addition to temperature and precipitation, such as latitude, wind patterns, mountains, large bodies of water, and ocean currents.

✓ **Reading Check** How is climate different from weather? (*See the Appendix for answers to Reading Checks.*)

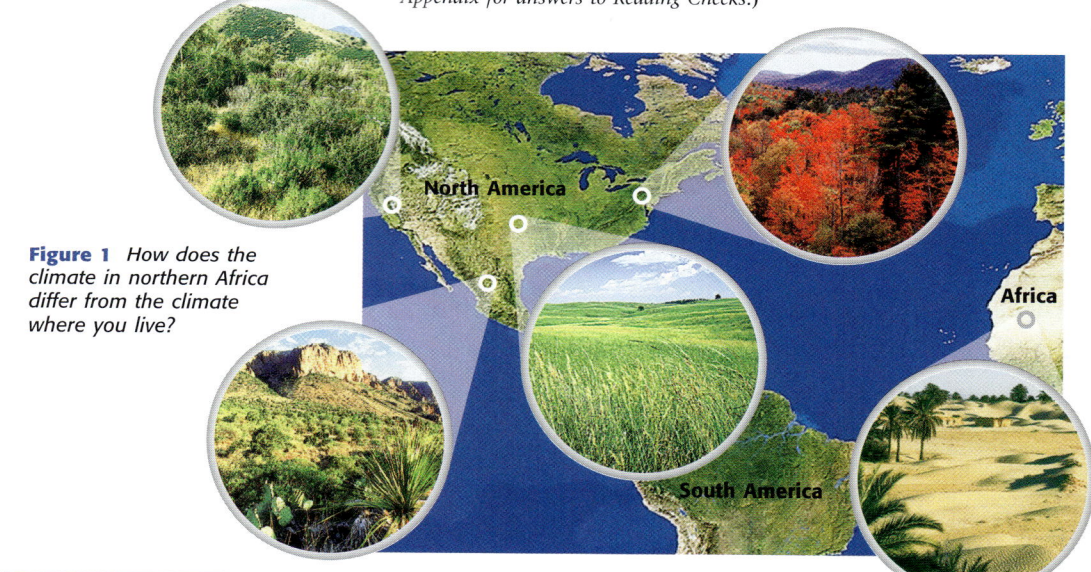

Figure 1 How does the climate in northern Africa differ from the climate where you live?

Answer to Reading Check
Climate is the average weather condition in an area over a long period of time. Weather is the condition of the atmosphere at a particular time.

---

518 Chapter 17 • Climate

Latitude

Think of the last time you looked at a globe. Do you recall the thin, horizontal lines that circle the globe? Those lines are called lines of latitude. **Latitude** is the distance north or south, measured in degrees, from the equator. In general, the temperature of an area depends on its latitude. The higher the latitude is, the colder the climate tends to be. One of the coldest places on Earth, the North Pole, is 90° north of the equator. However, the equator, at latitude 0°, is usually hot.

As shown in **Figure 2,** if you were to take a trip to different latitudes in the United States, you would experience different climates. For example, the climate in Washington, D.C., which is at a higher latitude, is different from the climate in Texas.

Solar Energy and Latitude

Solar energy, which is energy from the sun, heats the Earth. The amount of direct solar energy a particular area receives is determined by latitude. **Figure 3** shows how the curve of the Earth affects the amount of direct solar energy at different latitudes. Notice that the sun's rays hit the equator directly, at almost a 90° angle. At this angle, a small area of the Earth's surface receives more direct solar energy than at a lesser angle. As a result, that area has high temperatures. However, the sun's rays strike the poles at a lesser angle than they do the equator. At this angle, the same amount of direct solar energy that hits the area at the equator is spread over a larger area at the poles. The result is lower temperatures at the poles.

Figure 2 Winter in south Texas (top) is different from winter in Washington D.C. (bottom).

weather the short-term state of the atmosphere, including temperature, humidity, precipitation, wind, and visibility

climate the average weather condition in an area over a long period of time

latitude the distance north or south from the equator; expressed in degrees

Figure 3 The sun's rays strike the Earth's surface at different angles because the surface is curved.

Teach

CONNECTION ACTIVITY
Math — GENERAL

Circumference of the Earth
Each degree or line of latitude is approximately 111 km apart, and 180 lines of latitude circle the Earth. Have students calculate the circumference of the Earth from pole to pole.

(111 km × 180 lines = 19,980 km from North Pole to South Pole, then multiply by 2 to get 39,960 km—the total distance around the Earth)
LS Logical

Cultural Awareness — GENERAL

Charles Edward Anderson
Charles Edward Anderson was the first African American to receive a doctorate in meteorology. Anderson began his career in meteorology during World War II. He was a captain in the United States Air Force and served as a weather officer for the Tuskegee Airmen Regiment. He earned his doctorate in 1960 from the Massachusetts Institute of Technology. His work focused on cloud physics, the forecasting of severe storms, and weather on other planets.

Cultural Awareness — GENERAL

Weather Folklore Weather and climate have inspired a great number of rhymes, greetings, sayings, and other folklore. Here is one example you may have heard: "Red skies at night, sailors delight. Red skies in morning, sailors take warning." In the hot, wet climate of Venezuela, indigenous people sometimes greet each other by saying, "How have the mosquitoes used you?" Russia's cold climate inspired the saying, "There's no bad weather, only bad clothing." Invite students to interview friends and relatives or research weather and climate folklore in another country. Have students share their findings with the class. **LS** Interpersonal

Section 1 • What Is Climate? **519**

Teach, continued

Group Activity — BASIC

Modeling the Earth and Sun
Ask two volunteers to act as the Earth and the sun. Give the "sun" a flashlight and the "Earth" a globe with a half-meridian mounting. Turn off the lights, and have the volunteers sit on the floor. Ask the "sun" to shine the flashlight on the globe, and ask the "Earth" to slowly spin the globe counterclockwise. Have the class notice which parts of the globe are most exposed to the light. Next, have the "Earth" slowly make a complete revolution around the "sun" while rotating the globe at the same time. Make sure that the volunteer always keeps the axis of the globe oriented in the same direction. Stop the "Earth" at each season so that students can observe the flashlight's rays on the two hemispheres. If necessary, repeat this activity with other volunteers.

LS Kinesthetic/Visual Co-op Learning

Seasons and Latitude

In most places in the United States, the year consists of four seasons. But there are places in the world that do not have such seasonal changes. For example, areas near the equator have approximately the same temperatures and same amount of daylight year-round. Seasons happen because the Earth is tilted on its axis at a 23.5° angle. This tilt affects how much solar energy an area receives as Earth moves around the sun. **Figure 4** shows how latitude and the tilt of the Earth determine the seasons and the length of the day in a particular area.

✔ **Reading Check** Why is there less seasonal change near the equator?

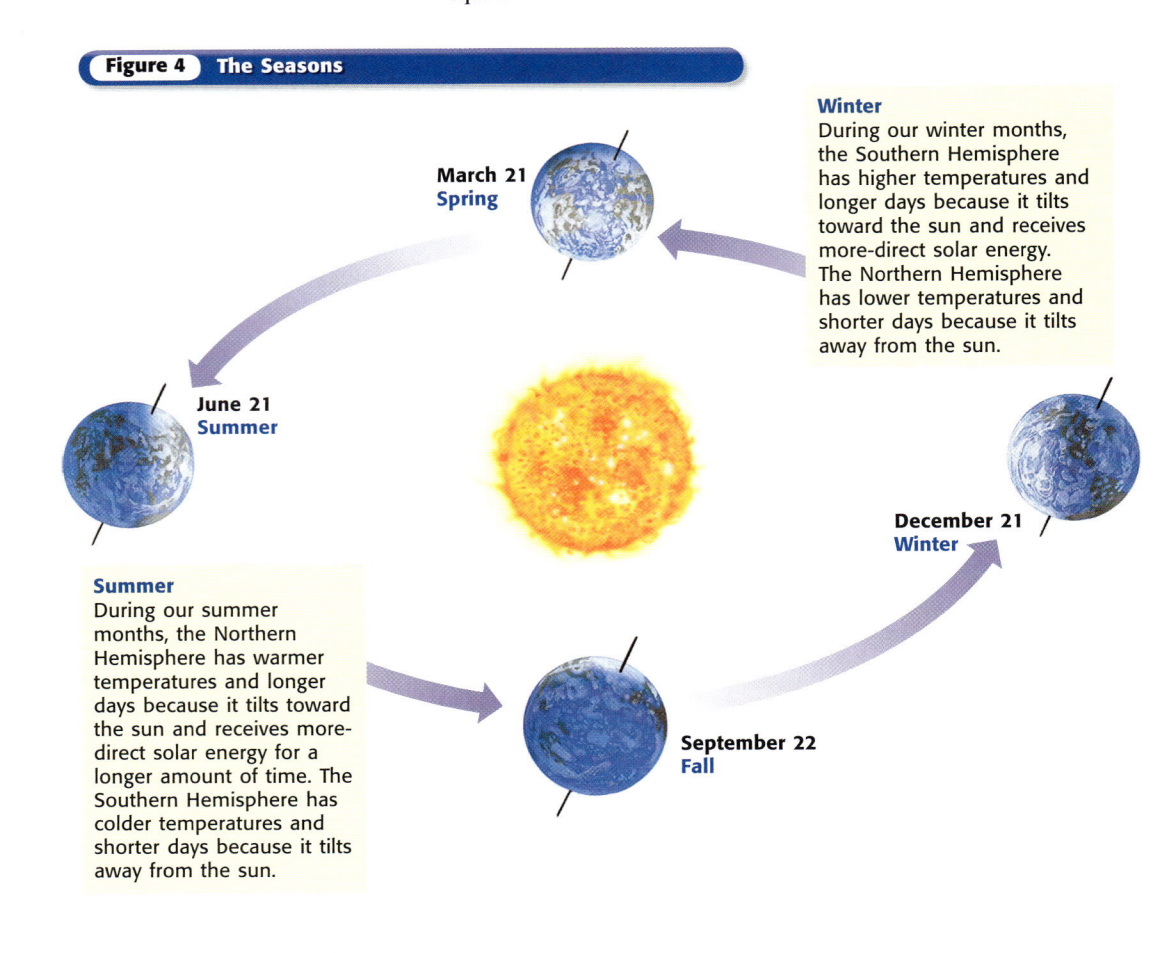

Figure 4 The Seasons

March 21 Spring

June 21 Summer

September 22 Fall

December 21 Winter

Winter
During our winter months, the Southern Hemisphere has higher temperatures and longer days because it tilts toward the sun and receives more-direct solar energy. The Northern Hemisphere has lower temperatures and shorter days because it tilts away from the sun.

Summer
During our summer months, the Northern Hemisphere has warmer temperatures and longer days because it tilts toward the sun and receives more-direct solar energy for a longer amount of time. The Southern Hemisphere has colder temperatures and shorter days because it tilts away from the sun.

Answer to Reading Check
Locations near the equator have less seasonal variation because the tilt of the Earth does not change the amount of energy these locations receive from the sun.

CHAPTER RESOURCES

Technology

 Transparencies
  • The Seasons
  • The Circulation of Warm and Cold Air

Figure 5 The Circulation of Warm Air and Cold Air

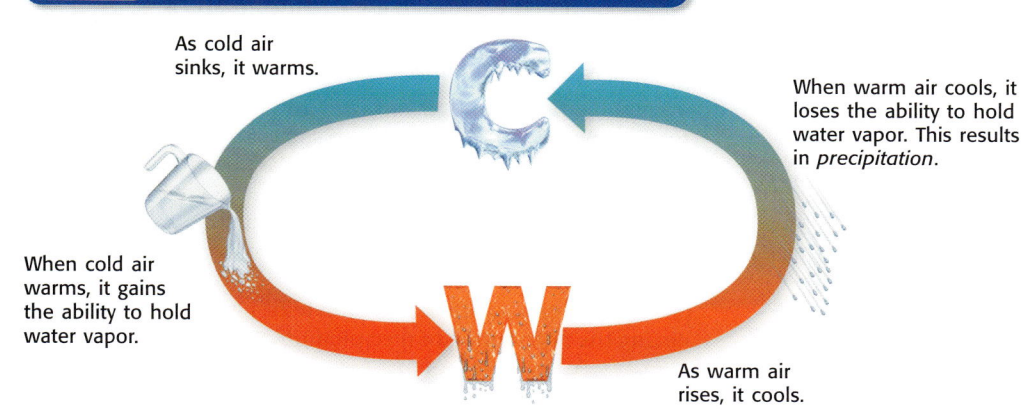

As cold air sinks, it warms.

When warm air cools, it loses the ability to hold water vapor. This results in *precipitation*.

When cold air warms, it gains the ability to hold water vapor.

As warm air rises, it cools.

Prevailing Winds

Winds that blow mainly from one direction are **prevailing winds**. Before you learn how the prevailing winds affect climate, take a look at **Figure 5** to learn about some of the basic properties of air.

Prevailing winds affect the amount of precipitation that a region receives. If the prevailing winds form from warm air, they may carry moisture. If the prevailing winds form from cold air, they will probably be dry.

The amount of moisture in prevailing winds is also affected by whether the winds blow across land or across a large body of water. Winds that travel across large bodies of water absorb moisture. Winds that travel across land tend to be dry. Even if a region borders the ocean, the area might be dry. **Figure 6** shows an example of how dry prevailing winds can cause the land to be dry though the land is near an ocean.

prevailing winds winds that blow mainly from one direction during a given period

Figure 6 The Sahara Desert, in northern Africa, is extremely dry because of the dry prevailing winds that blow across the continent.

Quick Lab

A Cool Breeze

1. Hold a **thermometer** next to the top edge of a **cup** of **water** containing two **ice cubes**. Record the temperature next to the cup.
2. Have your lab partner fan the surface of the cup with a **paper fan**. Record the temperature again. Has the temperature changed? Why or why not?

Quick Lab

MATERIALS

FOR EACH GROUP
- cup
- ice cubes (2)
- paper fan
- thermometer
- water

Answers
2. Sample answer: yes; The temperature dropped after we fanned the surface of the cup. The air traveling across the cup's surface was cooled by the ice, thereby changing the air temperature.

CONNECTION ACTIVITY
Geography — ADVANCED

Monsoons Monsoons are recurrent global weather patterns that dramatically affect the populations, economies, and environments of South Asia. The wet summer monsoon usually begins mid-June, when temperatures rise sharply in Asia's interior and cause the air above the land to warm and rise. This movement creates a low pressure area that draws warm, moist air inland from the Indian and Pacific Oceans. This moisture-laden air cools as it moves across the continent, causing heavy rains, thunderstorms, and flooding to occur. The heaviest rains occur where this air mass meets the foothills of the Himalayas. During the winter, the interior of Asia cools rapidly. This cool, dense air creates an immense high-pressure center, which forces cool, dry air to flow outward toward the oceans. As the air mass travels, it warms and becomes even drier. Warm, dry winters result. Encourage students to write a report about the effect of monsoons on South Asia. **LS Intrapersonal**

Section 1 • What Is Climate? **521**

Teach, continued

Answer to School-to-Home Activity
Mountain ranges in the United States are the Sierra Nevada, the Rocky Mountains, and the Appalachian Mountains; yes; Climate varies from one side of the mountain range to the other, so one side is densely vegetated and the other side is much drier and less vegetated. The prevailing winds blow from the side with the most vegetation.

Using the Figure — BASIC

Wet Winds Remind students that winds traveling across large bodies of water, such as the ocean, absorb moisture. Have students study **Figure 7**. The inset photographs were taken in California's Sierra Nevada mountain range. Ask students to examine the photographs closely and describe as many details as possible. Then ask students to consider which side of the mountain is likely to be closer to a large body of water. (the left side) **LS Visual** — English Language Learners

Answer to Reading Check
The atmosphere becomes less dense and loses its ability to absorb and hold thermal energy at higher elevations.

School to Home

Using a Map
With your parent, use a physical map to locate the mountain ranges in the United States. Does climate vary from one side of a mountain range to the other? If so, what does this tell you about the climatic conditions on either side of the mountain? From what direction are the prevailing winds blowing?

ACTIVITY

Mountains

Mountains can influence an area's climate by affecting both temperature and precipitation. Kilimanjaro is the tallest mountain in Africa. It has snow-covered peaks year-round, even though it is only about 3° (320 km) south of the equator. Temperatures on Kilimanjaro and in other mountainous areas are affected by elevation. **Elevation** is the height of surface landforms above sea level. As the elevation increases, the ability of air to transfer energy from the ground to the atmosphere decreases. Therefore, as elevation increases, temperature decreases.

Mountains also affect the climate of nearby areas by influencing the distribution of precipitation. **Figure 7** shows how the climates on two sides of a mountain can be very different.

✓ **Reading Check** Why does the atmosphere become cooler at higher elevations?

Figure 7 Mountains block the prevailing winds and affect the climate on the other side.

The Wet Side
Mountains force air to rise. The air cools as it rises, releasing moisture as snow or rain. The land on the windward side of the mountain is usually green and lush because the wind releases its moisture.

The Dry Side
After dry air crosses the mountain, the air begins to sink. As the air sinks, it is warmed and absorbs moisture. The dry conditions created by the sinking, warm air usually produce a desert. This side of the mountain is in a *rain shadow*.

INCLUSION Strategies

- Developmentally Delayed
- Hearing Impaired
- Learning Disabled

Organize students into small groups. Give each group a clear plastic rectangular pan, a paper cup, hot water, and cold water. Have students poke 10 holes into the sides of the paper cup and tape the cup to the corner of the pan. Fill the pan two-thirds full with cold water. Have students put three drops of food coloring into the hot water and pour it into the paper cup. Have students record and explain their observations. (Students will observe the colored water diffuse through the holes in the cup. The hot water will not mix very much with the cold water. Most of the hot water will "float" on top. Explain that hot and cold air move in similar ways as hot and cold water do.) **LS Kinesthetic** — English Language Learners

522 Chapter 17 • Climate

Large Bodies of Water

Large bodies of water can influence an area's climate. Water absorbs and releases heat slower than land does. Because of this quality, water helps to moderate the temperatures of the land around it. So, sudden or extreme temperature changes rarely take place on land near large bodies of water. For example, the state of Michigan, which is surrounded by the Great Lakes, has more-moderate temperatures than other places at the same latitude. The lakes also increase the moisture content of the air, which leads to heavy snowfall in the winter. This "lake effect" can cause 350 inches of snow to drop in one year!

Ocean Currents

The circulation of ocean surface currents has a large effect on an area's climate. **Surface currents** are streamlike movements of water that occur at or near the surface of the ocean. **Figure 8** shows the pattern of the major ocean surface currents.

As surface currents move, they carry warm or cool water to different locations. The surface temperature of the water affects the temperature of the air above it. Warm currents heat the surrounding air and cause warmer temperatures. Cool currents cool the surrounding air and cause cooler temperatures. The Gulf Stream current carries warm water northward off the east coast of North America and past Iceland. Iceland is an island country located just below the Arctic Circle. The warm water from the Gulf Stream heats the surrounding air and creates warmer temperatures in southern Iceland. Iceland experiences milder temperatures than Greenland, its neighboring island. Greenland's climate is cooler because Greenland is not influenced by the Gulf Stream.

Reading Check Why does Iceland experience milder temperatures than Greenland?

elevation the height of an object above sea level

surface current a horizontal movement of ocean water that is caused by wind and that occurs at or near the ocean's surface

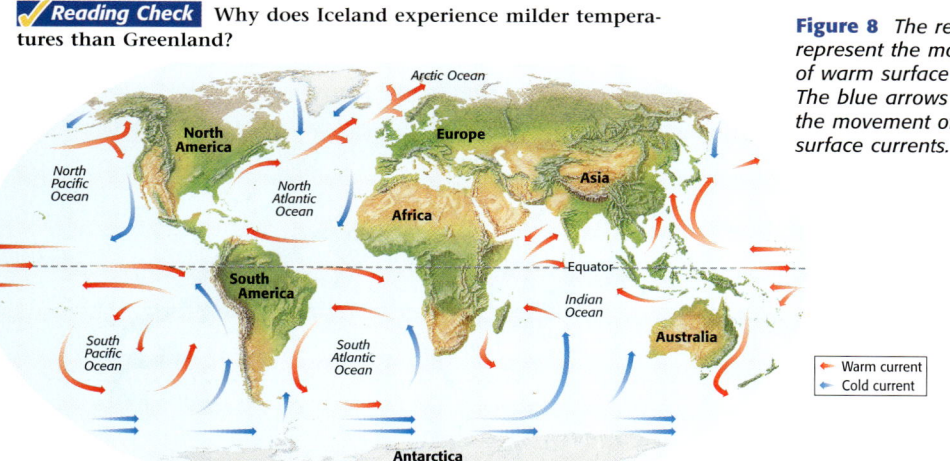

Figure 8 The red arrows represent the movement of warm surface currents. The blue arrows represent the movement of cold surface currents.

Homework — ADVANCED

Using Maps Have students look at a map and find cities that are at about the same latitude in a single continent. For example, Guadalajara and Tampico, in Mexico, are at about the same latitude, as are San Francisco, California, and Wichita, Kansas. Students should research the annual rainfall and temperature for each city. They can create a bar graph showing the differences in rainfall for each city, and students should attempt to explain the patterns they notice by identifying physical features on the map. If their data contradict what they have learned in this section, ask them to suggest explanations. **LS Visual**

Answer to Reading Check

The Gulf Stream current carries warm water past Iceland, which heats the air and causes milder temperatures.

SCIENCE HUMOR

Western and eastern Oregon have very different climates because the Cascades divide the state. Oregonians living east of the Cascades complain, "It's so dry, the jackrabbits carry canteens." West of the Cascades, people say, "It's so wet, folks don't tan, they rust!"

Is That a Fact!

Large lakes, such as the Great Lakes, in the United States and Canada, and Lake Victoria, in Africa, affect local climates. This phenomenon, called the *lake effect,* helps keep the surrounding land cooler in the summer and warmer in the winter.

Section 1 • What Is Climate?

Close

Reteaching — BASIC

Climate Factors Ask volunteers to list on the board the factors that influence climate. (temperature, precipitation, latitude, wind patterns, mountains, large bodies of water, and ocean currents) Ask students to describe how these factors influence climate. Have volunteers take turns writing these descriptions under each heading. **LS Verbal**

Quiz — GENERAL

1. Why are the poles colder than the equator? (The sun's rays strike the Earth's surface at a less direct angle at the poles than at the equator, so solar energy is spread over a larger area.)

2. Is precipitation more likely when the prevailing winds are formed from warm air or from cold air? (warm air)

Alternative Assessment — GENERAL

Climate Game Organize students into teams to play a climate game show. Have each team write 10 questions about material in the section. Have one team ask questions to the other teams. Have the other teams "buzz in" to answer the questions. **LS Verbal/Interpersonal**

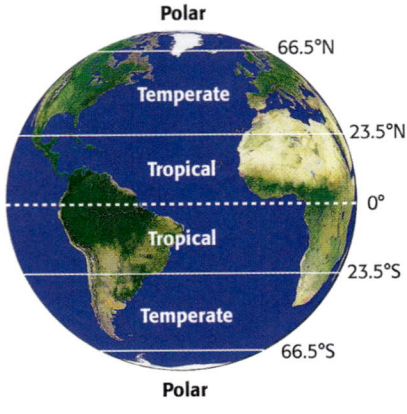

Figure 9 The three major climate zones are determined by latitude.

biome a large region characterized by a specific type of climate and certain types of plant and animal communities

Climates of the World

Have you seen any polar bears in your neighborhood lately? You probably have not. That's because polar bears live only in very cold arctic regions. Why are the animals in one part of the world so different from the animals in other parts? One of the differences has to do with climate. Plants and animals that have adapted to one climate may not be able to live in another climate. For example, frogs would not be able to survive at the North Pole.

Climate Zones

The Earth's three major climate zones—tropical, temperate, and polar—are shown in **Figure 9.** Each zone has a temperature range that relates to its latitude. However, in each of these zones, there are several types of climates because of differences in the geography and the amount of precipitation. Because of the various climates in each zone, there are different biomes in each zone. A **biome** is a large region characterized by a specific type of climate and certain types of plant and animal communities. **Figure 10** shows the distribution of the Earth's land biomes. In which biome do you live?

Reading Check What factors distinguish one biome from another biome?

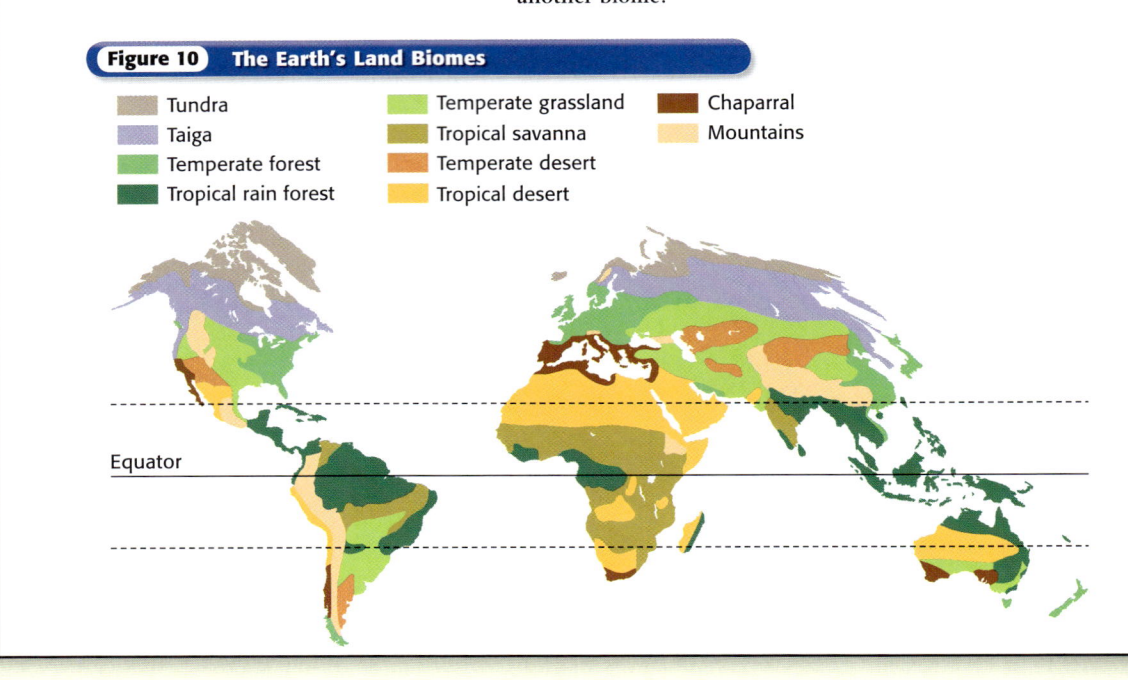

Figure 10 The Earth's Land Biomes

- Tundra
- Taiga
- Temperate forest
- Tropical rain forest
- Temperate grassland
- Tropical savanna
- Temperate desert
- Tropical desert
- Chaparral
- Mountains

Answer to Reading Check
Each biome has a different climate and different plant and animal communities.

Chapter 17 • Climate

SECTION Review

Summary

- Weather is the condition of the atmosphere at a particular time. This condition includes temperature, humidity, precipitation, wind, and visibility.
- Climate is the average weather condition in an area over a long period of time.
- The higher the latitude, the cooler the climate.
- Prevailing winds affect the climate of an area by the amount of moisture they carry.
- Mountains influence an area's climate by affecting both temperature and precipitation.
- Large bodies of water and ocean currents influence the climate of an area by affecting the temperature of the air over the water.
- The three climate zones of the world are the tropical zone, the temperate zone, and the polar zone.

Using Key Terms

1. In your own words, write a definition for each of the following terms: *weather, climate, latitude, prevailing winds, elevation, surface currents,* and *biome*.

Understanding Key Ideas

2. Which of the following affects climate by causing the air to rise?
   a. mountains
   b. ocean currents
   c. large bodies of water
   d. latitude

3. What is the difference between weather and climate?

4. List five factors that determine climates.

5. Explain why there is a difference in climate between areas at 0° latitude and areas at 45° latitude.

6. List the three climate zones of the world.

Critical Thinking

7. **Analyzing Relationships** How would seasons be different if the Earth did not tilt on its axis?

8. **Applying Concepts** During what months does Australia have summer? Explain.

Interpreting Graphics

Use the map below to answer the questions that follow.

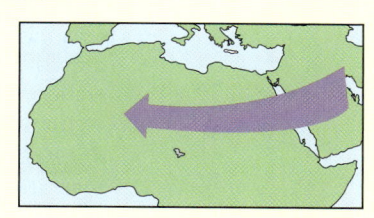

9. Would you expect the area that the arrow points to to be moist or dry? Explain your answer.

10. Describe how the climate of the same area would change if the prevailing winds traveled from the opposite direction. Explain how you came to this conclusion.

SciLinks / NSTA
Developed and maintained by the National Science Teachers Association
For a variety of links related to this chapter, go to www.scilinks.org
Topic: What Is Climate?
SciLinks code: HSM1659

Answers to Section Review

1. Sample answer: Weather is the condition of the atmosphere at a certain time. Climate is the average weather in an area over a long period of time. Latitude is the distance in degrees north or south of the equator. Prevailing winds are winds that blow mainly in one direction. Elevation is the height of surface landforms above sea level. Surface currents are streamlike movements of water that occur at or near the surface of the ocean. A biome is a large region characterized by a specific type of climate and certain types of plants and animals.

2. a

3. Weather is the condition of the atmosphere at a particular time. Climate is the average weather of a given area.

4. latitude, prevailing winds, mountains, large bodies of water, and ocean currents

5. Areas at different latitudes receive different amounts of solar energy because the Earth's surface is curved, and because the Earth is tilted on its axis.

6. tropical zone, temperate zone, and polar zone

7. If the Earth were not tilted on its axis, there would be no seasons.

8. Australia has summer during December, January, February, and March. This is because Australia is in the Earth's Southern Hemisphere, and the Southern Hemisphere is tilted away from the sun during these months.

9. dry

10. Accept all reasonable answers. If the prevailing winds blew from the Atlantic ocean, the area would have a wet climate with plenty of precipitation.

CHAPTER RESOURCES

Chapter Resource File
- Section Quiz GENERAL
- Section Review GENERAL
- Vocabulary and Section Summary GENERAL
- Datasheet for Quick Lab

Technology
Transparencies
- The Earth's Land Biomes

Section 1 • What Is Climate? **525**

SECTION 2

Focus

Overview
In this section, students learn the location and the characteristics of the tropical climate zone and the different biomes that are found in this climate.

🔔 Bellringer
Ask students to describe the differences between a deer and a camel. Where would they find these animals? Ask students to think about how climate influences the animals that live in certain areas.

Motivate

ACTIVITY — GENERAL

Writing **Country Profile** Have each student choose a country in the tropics to focus on for this section. Students should record the area's latitude and geographic characteristics. Tell students to find pictures from magazines or the Internet of the people, plants, and animals that live in the country. Then have students use the pictures to create a poster of the country they chose. Students should include information on average monthly rainfall and temperature. **LS Visual**

SECTION 2

READING WARM-UP

Objectives
- Locate and describe the tropical zone.
- Describe the biomes found in the tropical zone.

Terms to Learn
tropical zone

READING STRATEGY
Reading Organizer As you read this section, make a table comparing *tropical rain forests, tropical savannas,* and *tropical deserts.*

The Tropics

Where in the world do you think you could find a flying dragon gliding above you from one treetop to the next?

Don't worry. This flying dragon, or tree lizard, is only about 20 cm long, and it eats only insects. With winglike skin flaps, the flying dragon can glide from one treetop to the next. But, you won't find this kind of animal in the United States. These flying dragons live in Southeast Asia, which is in the tropical zone.

The Tropical Zone

The region that surrounds the equator and that extends from about 23.5° north latitude to 23.5° south latitude is called the **tropical zone.** The tropical zone is also known as the Tropics. Latitudes in the tropical zone receive the most solar radiation. Temperatures are therefore usually hot, except at high elevations.

Within the tropical zone, there are three major types of biomes—tropical rain forest, tropical desert, and tropical savanna. These three biomes have high temperatures. But they differ in the amount of precipitation, soil characteristics, vegetation, and kinds of animals. **Figure 1** shows the distribution of these biomes.

✓ **Reading Check** At what latitudes would you find the tropical zone? *(See the Appendix for answers to Reading Checks.)*

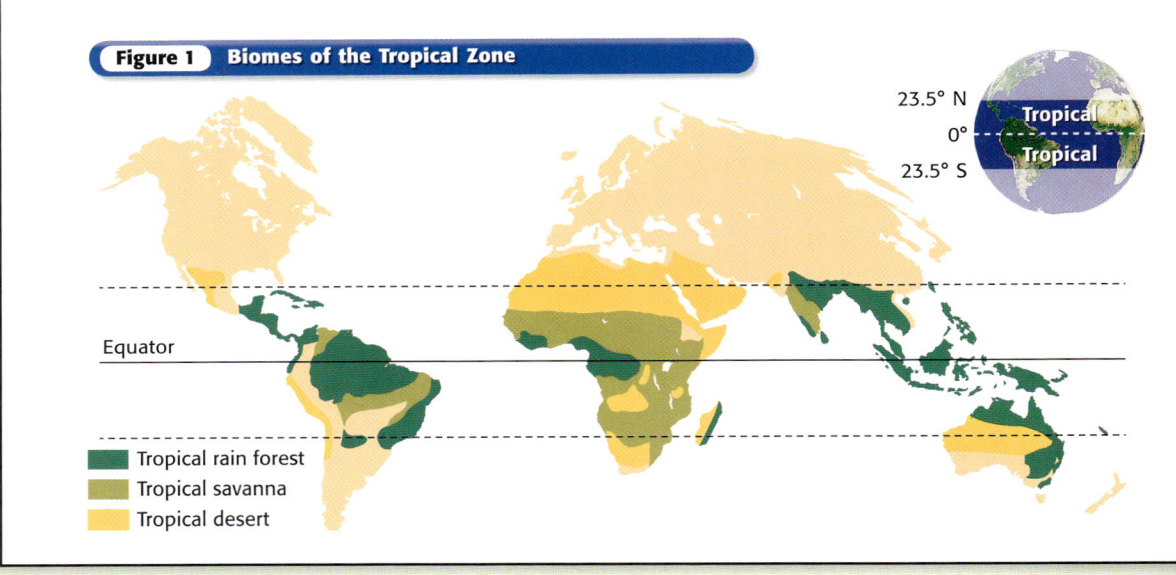

Figure 1 Biomes of the Tropical Zone

- Tropical rain forest
- Tropical savanna
- Tropical desert

CHAPTER RESOURCES

Chapter Resource File
- Lesson Plan
- Directed Reading A **BASIC**
- Directed Reading B **SPECIAL NEEDS**

Technology
Transparencies
- Bellringer
- **LINK TO LIFE SCIENCE** Gas Exchange in Leaves

Workbooks
Math Skills for Science
- Rainforest Math **GENERAL**

Answer to Reading Check
You would find the tropical zone from 23.5° north latitude to 23.5° south latitude.

526 Chapter 17 • Climate

Tropical Rain Forest
- Average Temperature Range 25°C to 28°C (77°F to 82°F)
- Average Yearly Precipitation 200 cm or more
- Soil Characteristics thin and nutrient poor

Figure 2 In tropical rain forests, many of the trees form above-ground roots that provide extra support for the trees in the thin, nutrient-poor soil.

Tropical Rain Forests

Tropical rain forests are always warm and wet. Because they are located near the equator, they receive strong sunlight year-round. So, there is little difference between seasons in tropical rain forests.

Tropical rain forests contain the greatest number of animal and plant species of any biome. Animals found in tropical rain forests include monkeys, parrots, tree frogs, tigers, and leopards. Plants found in tropical rain forests include mahogany, vines, ferns, and bamboo. But in spite of the lush vegetation, shown in **Figure 2**, the soil in rain forests is poor. The rapid decay of plants and animals returns nutrients to the soil. But these nutrients are quickly absorbed and used by the plants. The nutrients that are not immediately used by the plants are washed away by the heavy rains. The soil is left thin and nutrient poor.

tropical zone the region that surrounds the equator and that extends from about 23.5° north latitude to 23.5° south latitude

CONNECTION TO Social Studies

WRITING SKILL **Living in the Tropics** The tropical climate is very hot and humid. People who live in the Tropics have had to adapt to feel comfortable in that climate. For example, in the country of Samoa, some people live in homes that have no walls, which are called *fales*. Fales have only a roof, which provides shade. The openness of the home allows cool breezes to flow through the home. Research other countries in the Tropics. See how the climate influences the way the people live in those countries. Then, in your **science journal**, describe how the people's lifestyle helps them adapt to the climate.

WEIRD SCIENCE

In addition to having land biomes, Earth has marine biomes. However, marine biomes are less influenced by latitude than they are by water depth. Some of the animals that inhabit the deeper biomes have very interesting adaptations. For example, the anglerfish, which lives in total darkness uses a luminescent "lure" that trails from the fish's jaw and attracts prey within reach of its enormous, sharp teeth.

Teach

MISCONCEPTION ALERT

It's a Jungle Out There The popular image of a tropical rain forest is of dense jungle undergrowth. However, this type of growth occurs only where new growth has taken over, along rivers or in areas that humans have cleared. Most rainforests do not look like what students see in movies. Students may also confuse rain forests with forests in monsoon-climate regions. While rain forests have a fairly steady rate of precipitation, monsoon forests have a rainy season and a dry season. Rainfall during the rainy season may be measured in meters. During the dry season, the monsoon forest may receive little or no rainfall for many months. In fact, many monsoon-forest plants have some of the same adaptations for dry conditions that desert plants have.

CONNECTION ACTIVITY
Life Science — GENERAL

Transpiration Rain forests actually "recycle" much of their rain. In the Amazon rain forest, about three-quarters of all rainfall comes from the evaporation of water and the process of transpiration (the release of water through leaf pores, or stomata). Use the teaching transparency entitled "Gas Exchange in Leaves" to discuss this process. Ask students to determine how much rain is "recycled" if an Amazon rain forest gets 650 cm of rain annually. **(488 cm)**
LS Logical

Section 2 • The Tropics

Close

Reteaching — BASIC
Concept Mapping Have students create a concept map that shows how each of the three biomes in the tropical zone is influenced by precipitation and temperature. **LS** Visual

Quiz — GENERAL
1. What are three biomes in the tropical zone? (tropical rain forest, tropical savannas, and tropical deserts)
2. What do all tropical biomes have in common? (They are all between 23.5° north latitude and 23.5° south latitude.)

Alternative Assessment — GENERAL

Building a Biome Tell students that they are going to create an imaginary biome. Tell them to write the characteristics of their biome on a sheet of paper. Students should include the biome's annual precipitation, average temperature, topography, and latitude. When students have finished creating their imaginary biomes, ask them to write down the types of organisms that they think would inhabit their biomes. If students want, they can make drawings of some of the imaginary organisms. Invite students to share their work with the class. **LS** Intrapersonal

---

Tropical Savanna
- Average Temperature Range 27°C to 32°C (80°F to 90°F)
- Average Yearly Precipitation 100 cm
- Soil Characteristics generally nutrient poor

Figure 3 The grass of a tropical savanna can be as tall as 5 m.

Tropical Savannas

Tropical savannas, or grasslands, are composed of tall grasses and a few scattered trees. The climate is usually very warm. Tropical savannas have a dry season that lasts four to eight months and that is followed by short periods of rain. Savanna soils are generally nutrient poor. However, grass fires, which are common during the dry season, leave the soils nutrient enriched. An African savanna is shown in **Figure 3**.

Many plants have adapted to fire and use it to promote development. For example, some species need fire to break open their seeds' outer skin. Only after this skin is broken can each seed grow. For other species, heat from the fire triggers the plants to drop their seeds into the newly enriched soil.

Animals that live in tropical savannas include giraffes, lions, crocodiles, and elephants. Plants include tall grasses, trees, and thorny shrubs.

CONNECTION TO Biology

WRITING SKILL **Animal and Plant Adaptations** Animals and plants adapt to the climate in which they live. These adaptations cause certain animals and plants to be unique to particular biomes. For example, the camel, which is unique to the desert, has adapted to going for long periods of time without water. Research other animals or plants that live in the Tropics. Then, in your **science journal**, describe the characteristics that help them survive in the Tropics.

Is That a Fact!
The world's largest desert, the Sahara, covers more than 9 million square kilometers—about the size of the United States. In contrast, the largest desert in the United States is the Mojave Desert. It covers 38,900 km², which is nearly twice the size of New Jersey.

CONNECTION to Real World — GENERAL

Desertification Deserts are expanding at an accelerating rate. In the last 100 years, the estimated area of land occupied by deserts rose from 9.4% to 23.3%. Many factors have contributed to this phenomenon, including climatic shifts, overgrazing, and overuse of the land through inefficient agricultural practices. As a class, find out what is being done to stop desertification in western Africa and other areas of the world.

Tropical Deserts

A desert is an area that receives less than 25 cm of rainfall per year. Because of this low yearly rainfall, deserts are the driest places on Earth. Desert plants, such as those shown in **Figure 4**, are adapted to survive in places that have little water. Animals such as rats, lizards, snakes, and scorpions have also adapted to survive in these deserts.

There are two kinds of deserts—hot deserts and cold deserts. Hot deserts are caused by cool, sinking air masses. Many hot deserts, such as the Sahara, in Africa, are tropical deserts. Daily temperatures in tropical deserts often vary from very hot daytime temperatures (50°C) to cool nighttime temperatures (20°C). Because of the dryness of deserts, the soil is poor in organic matter, which is needed for plants to grow.

Reading Check What animals would you find in a tropical desert?

Tropical Desert
- Average Temperature Range 16°C to 50°C (61°F to 120°F)
- Average Yearly Precipitation 0–25 cm
- Soil Characteristics poor in organic matter

Figure 4 Plants such as succulents have fleshy stems and leaves to store water.

SECTION Review

Summary

- The tropical zone is located around the equator, between 23.5° north and 23.5° south latitude.
- Temperatures are usually hot in the tropical zone.
- Tropical rain forests are warm and wet. They have the greatest number of plant and animal species of any biome.
- Tropical savannas are grasslands that have a dry season.
- Tropical deserts are hot and receive little rain.

Using Key Terms

1. In your own words, write a definition for the term *tropical zone*.

Understanding Key Ideas

2. Which of the following tropical biomes has less than 50 cm of precipitation a year?
   a. rain forest   c. grassland
   b. desert   d. savanna

3. What are the soil characteristics of a tropical rain forest?

4. In what ways have savanna vegetation adapted to fire?

Math Skills

5. Suppose that in a tropical savanna, the temperature was recorded every hour for 4 h. The recorded temperatures were 27°C, 28°C, 29°C, and 29°C. Calculate the average temperature for this 4 h period.

Critical Thinking

6. **Analyzing Relationships** How do the tropical biomes differ?

7. **Making Inferences** How would you expect the adaptations of a plant in a tropical rain forest to differ from the adaptations of a tropical desert plant? Explain.

8. **Analyzing Data** An area has a temperature range of 30°C to 40°C and received 10 cm of rain this year. What biome is this area in?

For a variety of links related to this chapter, go to www.scilinks.org
Topic: Climates of the World
SciLinks code: HSM0302

Answer to Reading Check

Answers may vary. Sample answer: rats, lizards, snakes, and scorpions

CHAPTER RESOURCES

Chapter Resource File
- Section Quiz GENERAL
- Section Review GENERAL
- Vocabulary and Section Summary GENERAL
- Reinforcement Worksheet BASIC
- SciLinks Activity GENERAL

Answers to Section Review

1. Sample answer: The tropical zone is the climate region that surrounds the equator and that extends from about 23.5° north latitude to 23.5° south latitude.
2. b
3. thin and nutrient poor
4. Some savanna plant species need fire to break open their seeds' outer skin in order to grow. Also, for other plant species, the heat from the fire triggers the plant to drop its seeds into the newly enriched soil.
5. 27°C + 28°C + 29°C + 29°C = 113°C
   113°C ÷ 4 = 28.25°C
6. Sample answer: Tropical biomes differ in the amount of precipitation they receive, the average temperature range, soil characteristics, vegetation, and kinds of animals.
7. Sample answer: A plant in a tropical rain forest would have to adapt to an environment that received a large amount of rain that would leach nutrients from the soil. A plant in a tropical desert would have to adapt to a very hot, dry environment.
8. tropical desert

Section 2 • The Tropics   529

SECTION 3

Focus

Overview
In this section, students will learn the location and the characteristics of the temperate climate zone and the polar climate zone. They will also learn about microclimates and about different biomes that are found in these climate zones.

🔔 Bellringer
Tell students that they are taking a trip to the North Pole. In order to pack, they need to know what the climate is like. Have students write a description of what they would expect the climate to be like at the North Pole.

Motivate

Group Activity — GENERAL
Camp Climate Have groups write a brochure for a summer camp in a temperate biome of their choice. Suggest that they include information about the environment that will entice people to come and helpful tips about how to prepare for the area's climate.
LS Visual Co-op Learning

SECTION 3

READING WARM-UP

Objectives
- Locate and describe the temperate zone and the polar zone.
- Describe the different biomes found in the temperate zone and the polar zone.
- Explain what a microclimate is.

Terms to Learn
temperate zone
polar zone
microclimate

READING STRATEGY
Reading Organizer As you read this section, create an outline of the section. Use the headings from the section in your outline.

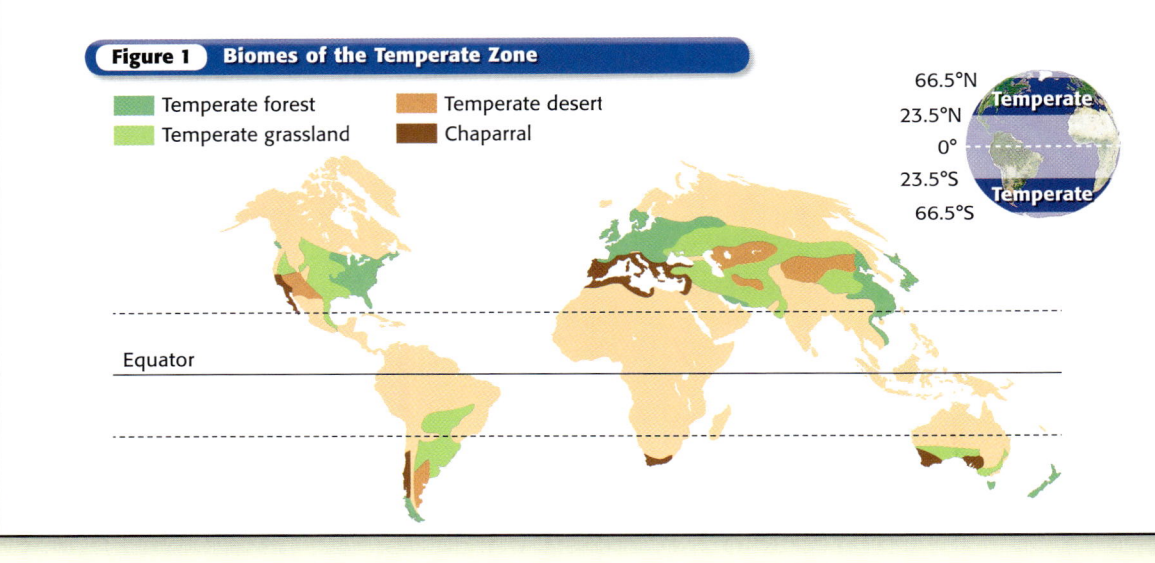

CHAPTER RESOURCES

Chapter Resource File
- Lesson Plan
- Directed Reading A BASIC
- Directed Reading B SPECIAL NEEDS

Technology
- Transparencies
  - Bellringer

Temperate and Polar Zones

Which season is your favorite? Do you like the change of colors in the fall, the flowers in the spring, or do you prefer the hot days of summer?

If you live in the continental United States, chances are you live in a biome that experiences seasonal change. Seasonal change is one characteristic of the temperate zone. Most of the continental United States is in the temperate zone, which is the climate zone between the Tropics and the polar zone.

The Temperate Zone
The climate zone between the Tropics and the polar zone is the **temperate zone.** Latitudes in the temperate zone receive less solar energy than latitudes in the Tropics do. Because of this, temperatures in the temperate zone tend to be lower than in the Tropics. Some biomes in the temperate zone have a mild change of seasons. Other biomes in the country can experience freezing temperatures in the winter and very hot temperatures in the summer. The temperate zone consists of the following four biomes—temperate forest, temperate grassland, chaparral, and temperate desert. Although these biomes have four distinct seasons, the biomes differ in temperature and precipitation and have different plants and animals. **Figure 1** shows the distribution of the biomes found in the temperate zone.

✓ **Reading Check** Where is the temperate zone? (See the Appendix for answers to Reading Checks.)

Figure 1 Biomes of the Temperate Zone

- Temperate forest
- Temperate grassland
- Temperate desert
- Chaparral

66.5°N
23.5°N
0°
23.5°S
66.5°S

Answer to Reading Check
The temperate zone is located between the Tropics and the polar zone.

530   Chapter 17 • Climate

Temperate Forest
- Average Temperature Range 0°C to 28°C (32°F to 82°F)
- Average Yearly Precipitation 76 to 250 cm
- Soil Characteristics very fertile, organically rich

Temperate Forests

The temperate forest biomes tend to have high amounts of rainfall and seasonal temperature differences. Summers are often warm, and winters are often cold. Animals such as deer, bears, and foxes live in temperate forests. **Figure 2** shows deciduous trees in a temperate forest. *Deciduous* describes trees that lose their leaves at the end of the growing season. The soils in deciduous forests are usually fertile because of the high organic content from decaying leaves that drop every winter. Another type of tree found in the temperate forest is the evergreen. *Evergreens* are trees that keep their leaves year-round.

Figure 2 Deciduous trees have leaves that change color and drop when temperatures become cold.

temperate zone the climate zone between the Tropics and the polar zone

Temperate Grasslands

Temperate grasslands, such as those shown in **Figure 3**, are regions that receive too little rainfall for trees to grow. This biome has warm summers and cold winters. Examples of animals that are found in temperate grasslands include bison in North America and kangaroo in Australia. Grasses are the most common kind of plant found in this biome. Because grasslands have the most-fertile soils of all biomes, much of the grassland has been plowed to make room for croplands.

Figure 3 At one time, the world's grasslands covered about 42% of Earth's total land surface. Today, they occupy only about 12% of the Earth's total land surface.

Temperate Grassland
- Average Temperature Range −6°C to 26°C (21°F to 78°F)
- Average Yearly Precipitation 38 to 76 cm
- Soil Characteristics most-fertile soils of all biomes

Teach

CONNECTION ACTIVITY
Life Science — GENERAL

Writing **Fragmentation** The settlement of humans in temperate forests around the world has greatly fragmented these areas. Much of the temperate forest has been converted to agricultural land or has been logged. Fragmentation has a negative impact on many plants and animals that have certain habitat requirements. In fact, fragmentation has led to the extinction of many species. The temperate forest is also vulnerable to air pollution resulting from industrial activity. Acid precipitation has damaged forests, either killing the trees or making them more susceptible to disease. Have students write a persuasive essay explaining the importance of conserving Earth's temperate forests. **LS** Intrapersonal

---

MISCONCEPTION ALERT

Temperate Rain Forest You don't need to travel to the Tropics to find a rain forest. Western Washington State is home to the largest temperate rain forest in the world. Moss-covered trees more than 500 years old stand 60 m tall and are 5 m in diameter. The ground is covered by ferns, moss, salmon-berries, and the thorny Hercules'-club. The growth is not as diverse as in the tropical forests, but it is every bit as lush. The forest receives 380 cm of rain each year! Have students find out more about this remarkable ecosystem and the efforts to preserve it.

Section 3 • Temperate and Polar Zones

Teach, continued

CONNECTION to Social Studies — GENERAL

Harvesting Fog Chile's arid northern desert land is one of the driest places on Earth. It receives so little rainfall that the yearly average is listed as "immeasurable." Surprisingly, people live there. They get drinking water by harvesting the fog. The village of Chungungo has built 75 fog-catching nets that supply 11,000 L of clean water per day. The nets, which look like giant volleyball nets, are positioned in the hills above the town. As the mountain fog passes through the nets, beads of water collect and are channeled to a pipeline that supplies the village with water. Scientists believe that this technology could be used in 30 other countries to supply safe and inexpensive water for drinking and agriculture.

Answer to Reading Check
Temperate deserts are cold at night because low humidity and cloudless skies allow energy to escape.

Chaparral
- Average Temperature Range 11°C to 26°C (51°F to 78°F)
- Average Yearly Precipitation 48 to 56 cm
- Soil Characteristics rocky, nutrient-poor soils

Figure 4 Some plant species found in chaparral require fire to reproduce.

Figure 5 The Great Basin Desert is in the rain shadow of the Sierra Nevada.

Temperate Desert
- Average Temperature Range 1°C to 50°C (34°F to 120°F)
- Average Yearly Precipitation 0 to 25 cm
- Soil Characteristics poor in organic matter

Chaparrals
Chaparral regions, as shown in **Figure 4,** have cool, wet winters and hot, dry summers. Animals, such as coyotes and mountain lions live in chaparrals. The vegetation is mainly evergreen shrubs. These shrubs are short, woody plants with thick, waxy leaves. The waxy leaves are adaptations that help prevent water loss in dry conditions. These shrubs grow in rocky, nutrient-poor soil. Like tropical-savanna vegetation, chaparral vegetation has adapted to fire. In fact, some plants, such as chamise, can grow back from their roots after a fire.

Temperate Deserts
The temperate desert biomes, like the one shown in **Figure 5,** tend to be cold deserts. Like all deserts, cold deserts receive less than 25 cm of precipitation yearly. Examples of animals that live in temperate deserts are lizards, snakes, bats, and toads. And the types of plants found in temperate deserts include cacti, shrubs, and thorny trees.

Temperate deserts can be very hot in the daytime. But, unlike hot deserts, they are often very cold at night. This large change in temperature between day and night is caused by low humidity and cloudless skies. These conditions allow for a large amount of energy to heat the Earth's surface during the day. However, these same characteristics allow the energy to escape at night. This causes temperatures to drop. You probably rarely think of snow and deserts together. But temperate deserts often receive light snow during the winter.

✓ Reading Check Why are temperate deserts cold at night?

INCLUSION Strategies

- Behavior Control Issues
- Visually Impaired
- Gifted and Talented

Organize students into small groups. Assign each group two biomes to categorize. Groups will need their textbook, additional resource books such as an encyclopedia, two large sheets of paper, various magazines to cut pictures from, and glue. For each biome, ask each group to record on paper the definition, a description with a picture, typical plants or animals that live in the biome, one or two locations of the biome, and something unique about this biome. For extra credit, ask students to hypothesize how geography may affect the climate of the locations they chose. Have groups share with the rest of the class what they documented. **LS Visual/Kinesthetic**

---

532 Chapter 17 • Climate

Figure 6 Biomes of the Polar Zone

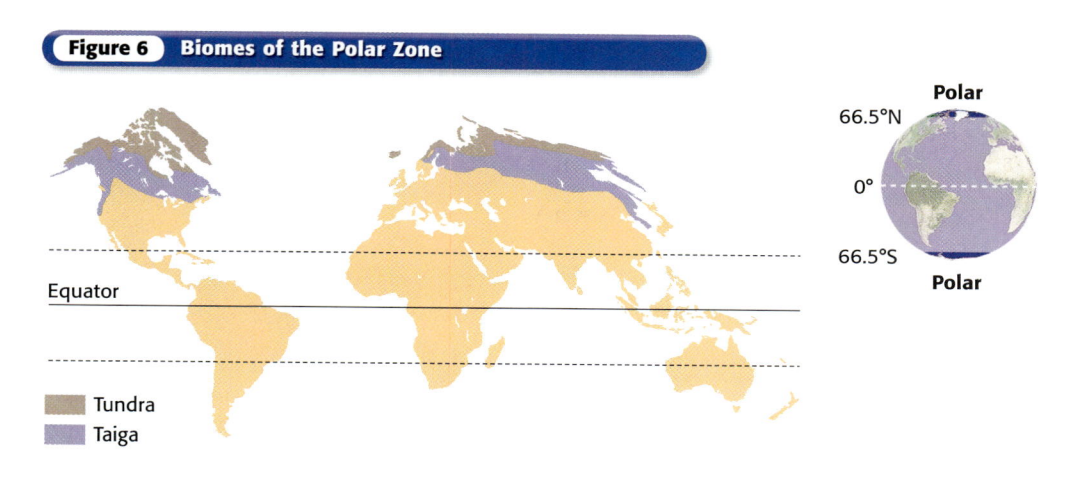

- Tundra
- Taiga

The Polar Zone

The climate zone located at the North or South Pole and its surrounding area is called the **polar zone**. Polar climates have the coldest average temperatures of all the climate zones. Temperatures in the winter stay below freezing. The temperatures during the summer remain cool. **Figure 6** shows the distribution of the biomes found in the polar zone.

polar zone the North or South Pole and its surrounding area

Tundra

The tundra biome, as shown in **Figure 7**, has long, cold winters with almost 24 hours of night. It also has short, cool summers with almost 24 hours of daylight. In the summer, only the top meter of soil thaws. Underneath the thawed soil lies a permanently frozen layer of soil, called *permafrost*. This frozen layer prevents the water in the thawed soil from draining. Because of the poor drainage, the upper soil layer is muddy. This muddy layer of soil makes a great breeding ground for insects, such as mosquitoes. Many birds migrate to the tundra during the summer to feed on the insects. Other animals that live in the tundra are caribou, reindeer, and polar bears. Plants in this biome include mosses and lichens.

Tundra
- Average Temperature Range –27°C to 5°C (–17°F to 41°F)
- Average Yearly Precipitation 0 to 25 cm
- Soil Characteristics frozen

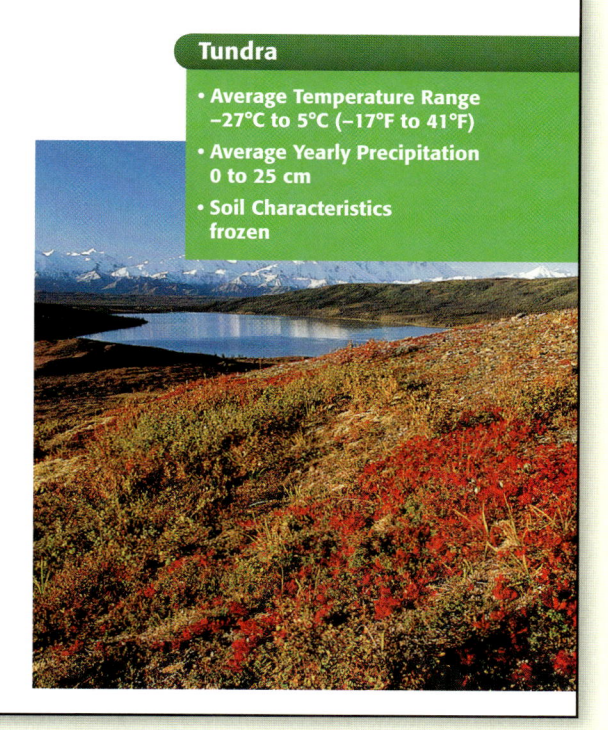

Figure 7 In the tundra, mosses and lichens cover rocks.

MISCONCEPTION ALERT

Tundra Students may think that the tundra is a relatively small and barren portion of the world. Actually, one-tenth of the Earth's land is tundra, and about 600 species of plants are native to the biome. Ninety-nine percent of those plants are perennials—the growing season is too short for annuals, which need time to produce flowers and seeds.

WEIRD SCIENCE

Lichens are organisms that thrive in the polar zone. Some lichens in the Arctic have been determined to be 4,500 years old. To protect themselves from the cold, some lichens live 2 cm inside rocks! Despite their ability to survive in extremely harsh arctic conditions, most lichens have an extremely low tolerance for sulfur dioxide in air pollution. As a result, they are usually not found in industrialized areas.

Demonstration — GENERAL

Mock Permafrost Prepare for the demonstration by punching five holes in the bottom of two coffee cans and filling each can one-third full with potting soil. Slowly add water to one can until it begins to drain through the bottom. The soil should be moist but not saturated. Allow the excess water to drain, and pack the soil firmly. Place that can in a freezer for 6 to 8 hours. Bring the two cans to class, and have students gather at a sink. Hold the can with the unfrozen soil over the sink, and slowly pour a glass of water onto the soil. Repeat with the frozen can. Discuss with students why muddy or "marshy" areas form in the frozen soil and why the soil did not drain. **LS** Visual

Homework — ADVANCED

Graphing Have students construct a bar graph that compares the average yearly precipitation ranges for the six biomes discussed in this section. Have students use their graph to determine which biomes receive the most rain, which biomes receive the least rain, and which biome has the widest variation in annual precipitation. Suggest that students obtain yearly precipitation records for their local region and compare these records with the information in their graph. Students may also be able to construct their graph on a computer or graphing calculator. **LS** Visual/Logical

Section 3 • Temperate and Polar Zones

Close

Reteaching — BASIC
Temperate Versus Polar Ask students to take out two pieces of paper. On one piece of paper, have students write "temperate zone." On the other piece of paper, have students write "polar zone." Have students write all the characteristics of each climate zone on its respective paper. Then have students share what they wrote with the class. Compile a class list on the board. **LS Logical**

Quiz — GENERAL
1. Can a climate zone contain more than one biome?
(A climate zone may contain several different biomes.)
2. What is a microclimate?
(a small area that has unique climate characteristics)

Alternative Assessment — GENERAL
Climate Zone Organizers Help students learn the characteristics of each of the nine biomes by having them make a graphic organizer for each climate zone. Have students match the appropriate biomes with each climate zone. Each graphic organizer should contain information about the biomes' temperature, precipitation, soil, plants, and animals. Students can also include magazine photographs that show plants and animals that inhabit each biome. **English Language Learners** **LS Visual**

Taiga
- Average Temperature Range –10°C to 15°C (14°F to 59°F)
- Average Yearly Precipitation 40 to 61 cm
- Soil Characteristics acidic

Figure 8 *The taiga, such as this one in Washington, have mostly evergreens for trees.*

microclimate the climate of a small area

School to Home
WRITING SKILL **Your Biome** With your parents, explore the biome in the area where you live. What kinds of animals and plants live in your area? Write a one-page paper that describes the biome and why the biome of your area has its particular climate.
ACTIVITY

Taiga (Northern Coniferous Forest)
Just south of the tundra lies the taiga biome. The taiga, as shown in **Figure 8**, has long, cold winters and short, warm summers. Animals commonly found here are moose, bears, and rabbits. The majority of the trees are evergreen needle-leaved trees called *conifers*, such as pine, spruce, and fir trees. The needles and flexible branches allow these trees to shed heavy snow before they can be damaged. Conifer needles are made of acidic substances. When the needles die and fall to the soil, they make the soil acidic. Most plants cannot grow in acidic soil. Because of the acidic soil, the forest floor is bare except for some mosses and lichens.

Microclimates
The climate and the biome of a particular place can also be influenced by local conditions. **Microclimate** is the climate of a small area. The alpine biome is a cold biome found on mountains all around the world. The alpine biome can even be found on mountains in the Tropics! How is this possible? The high elevation affects the area's climate and therefore its biome. As the elevation increases, the air's ability to transfer heat from the ground to the atmosphere by conduction decreases, which causes temperatures to decrease. In winter, the temperatures are below freezing. In summer, average temperatures range from 10°C to 15°C. Plants and animals have had to develop special adaptations to live in this severe climate.

Answer to School-to-Home Activity
Answers may vary. Students should recognize different plants and animals found in their area. Encourage students to use field guides and the Web sites of local parks to identify plants and animals. Students should also be able to describe the climate of their biome and explain why their biome has this particular climate, based on latitude, prevailing winds, mountains, bodies of water, and ocean currents.

Cities

Cities are also microclimates. In a city, temperatures can be 1°C to 2°C warmer than the surrounding rural areas. Have you ever walked barefoot on a black asphalt street on a hot summer day? Doing so burns your feet because buildings and pavement made of dark materials absorb solar radiation instead of reflecting it. There is also less vegetation in a city to take in the sun's rays. This absorption and re-radiation of heat by buildings and pavement heats the surrounding air. In turn, the temperatures rise.

Reading Check Why do cities have higher temperatures than the surrounding rural areas?

CONNECTION TO Physics

Hot Roofs! Scientists studied roofs on a sunny day when the air temperature was 13°C. They recorded roof temperatures ranging from 18°C to 61°C depending on color and material of the roof. Place thermometers on outside objects that are made of different types of materials and that are different colors. Please stay off the roof! Is there a difference in temperatures?

SECTION Review

Summary

- The temperate zone is located between the Tropics and the polar zone. It has moderate temperatures.
- Temperate forests, temperate grasslands, and temperate deserts are biomes in the temperate zone.
- The polar zone includes the North or South Pole and its surrounding area. The polar zone has the coldest temperatures.
- The tundra and the taiga are biomes within the polar zone.

Using Key Terms

1. In your own words, write a definition for the term *microclimate*.

Complete each of the following sentences by choosing the correct term from the word bank.

temperate zone   polar zone
microclimate

2. The coldest temperatures are found in the ___.

3. The ___ has moderate temperatures.

Understanding Key Ideas

4. Which of the following biomes has the driest climate?
   a. temperate forests
   b. temperate grasslands
   c. chaparrals
   d. temperate deserts

5. Explain why the temperate zone has lower temperatures than the Tropics.

6. Describe how the latitude of the polar zone affects the climate in that area.

7. Explain why the tundra can sometimes experience 24 hours of daylight or 24 hours of night.

8. How do conifers make the soil they grow in too acidic for other plants to grow?

Math Skills

9. Texas has an area of about 700,000 square kilometers. Grasslands compose about 20% of this area. About how many square kilometers of grassland are there in Texas?

Critical Thinking

10. **Identifying Relationships** Which biome would be more suitable for growing crops, temperate forest or taiga? Explain.

11. **Making Inferences** Describe the types of animals and vegetation you might find in the Alpine biome.

For a variety of links related to this chapter, go to www.scilinks.org
Topic: Modeling Earth's Climate
SciLinks code: HSM0976

Answer to Reading Check

Cities have higher temperatures than the surrounding rural areas because buildings and pavement absorb solar radiation instead of reflecting it.

CHAPTER RESOURCES

Chapter Resource File
- Section Quiz GENERAL
- Section Review GENERAL
- Vocabulary and Section Summary GENERAL
- Reinforcement Worksheet BASIC

Workbooks
- Science Skills
  - Finding Useful Sources GENERAL

Answers to Section Review

1. Sample answer: A microclimate is the climate of a small area.
2. polar zone
3. temperate zone
4. d
5. The temperate zone has lower temperatures than the Tropics because it is located at a higher latitude.
6. Because the polar zone is at a higher latitude than the other climate zones, it receives less direct solar energy and therefore has lower temperatures.
7. The Earth is tilted so that during the summer, high latitudes are pointed toward the sun. Therefore, polar regions receive 24 hours of daylight each day. In the winter, the Earth is tilted so that high latitudes are pointed away from the sun. Therefore, polar regions experience 24 hours of night each day.
8. The needles of conifers are acidic. When the needles fall to the ground, they make the soil acidic, which makes it difficult for many other plants to grow.
9. 700,000 km^2 × 0.20 = 140,000 km^2
10. Sample answer: A temperate forest would be better for growing crops than the taiga because the soil in the forest is very fertile and organically rich. The taiga would be a difficult place to grow crops because the soil is acidic from the conifer needles.
11. Students should choose plants and animals that are adapted to very cold climates in the mountains. Sample answer: mountain goat, snow leopard, moss

Section 3 • Temperate and Polar Zones

SECTION 4

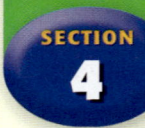

Focus

Overview
In this section, students will learn how the Earth's climate has changed in the past. Students will learn about different causes of climate change. Students will also learn about the greenhouse effect and its role in global warming.

Bellringer
Have students imagine that the climate of the area where they live has changed, so it is now warmer than it used to be. Have students write down five different ways they think the area would be affected by warmer temperatures.

Motivate

Demonstration — GENERAL
The Greenhouse Effect Tell students that the glass windows in a greenhouse are similar to the Earth's atmosphere. The glass allows radiant energy to enter but prevents thermal energy from escaping. Have students place a thermometer in a plastic bag on a sunny windowsill. Place another thermometer next to the plastic bag. After 30 minutes, have a student read the two thermometers and compare the difference in temperature.
English Language Learners
LS Kinesthetic

SECTION 4

READING WARM-UP

Objectives
- Describe how the Earth's climate has changed over time.
- Summarize four different theories that attempt to explain why the Earth's climate has changed.
- Explain the greenhouse effect and its role in global warming.

Terms to Learn
ice age
global warming
greenhouse effect

READING STRATEGY

Paired Summarizing Read this section silently. In pairs, take turns summarizing the material. Stop to discuss ideas that seem confusing.

ice age a long period of climate cooling during which ice sheets cover large areas of Earth's surface; also known as a glacial period

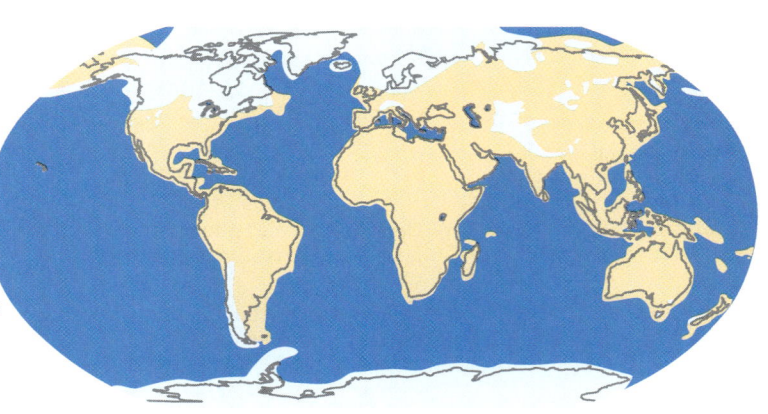

Figure 1 During glacial periods, ice sheets (as shown in light blue), cover a larger portion of the Earth.

CHAPTER RESOURCES

Chapter Resource File
- Lesson Plan
- Directed Reading A BASIC
- Directed Reading B SPECIAL NEEDS

Technology
Transparencies
- Bellringer
- The Milankovitch Theory

Changes in Climate

As you have probably noticed, the weather changes from day to day. Sometimes, the weather can change several times in one day! But have you ever noticed the climate change?

On Saturday, your morning baseball game was canceled because of rain, but by that afternoon the sun was shining. Now, think about the climate where you live. You probably haven't noticed a change in climate, because climates change slowly. What causes climatic change? Studies indicate that human activity may cause climatic change. However, natural factors also can influence changes in the climate.

Ice Ages

The geologic record indicates that the Earth's climate has been much colder than it is today. In fact, much of the Earth was covered by sheets of ice during certain periods. An **ice age** is a period during which ice collects in high latitudes and moves toward lower latitudes. Scientists have found evidence of many major ice ages throughout the Earth's geologic history. The most recent ice age began about 2 million years ago.

Glacial Periods

During an ice age, there are periods of cold and periods of warmth. These periods are called glacial and interglacial periods. During *glacial periods,* the enormous sheets of ice advance. As they advance, they get bigger and cover a larger area, as shown in **Figure 1**. Because a large amount of water is frozen during glacial periods, the sea level drops.

---

536   Chapter 17 • Climate

Interglacial Periods

Warmer times that happen between glacial periods are called *interglacial periods*. During an interglacial period, the ice begins to melt and the sea level rises again. The last interglacial period began 10,000 years ago and is still happening. Why do these periods occur? Will the Earth have another glacial period in the future? These questions have been debated by scientists for the past 200 years.

Motions of the Earth

There are many theories about the causes of ice ages. Each theory tries to explain the gradual cooling that begins an ice age. This cooling leads to the development of large ice sheets that periodically cover large areas of the Earth's surface.

The *Milankovitch theory* explains why an ice age isn't just one long cold spell. Instead, the ice age alternates between cold and warm periods. Milutin Milankovitch, a Yugoslavian scientist, proposed that changes in the Earth's orbit and in the tilt of the Earth's axis cause ice ages. His theory is shown in **Figure 2**. In a 100,000 year period, the Earth's orbit changes from elliptical to circular. This changes the Earth's distance from the sun. In turn, it changes the temperature on Earth. Changes in the tilt of the Earth also influence the climate. The more the Earth is tilted, the closer the poles are to the sun.

Reading Check What are the two things Milankovitch says causes ice ages? (*See the Appendix for answers to Reading Checks.*)

INTERNET ACTIVITY

For another activity related to this chapter, go to **go.hrw.com** and type in the keyword **HZ5CLMW**.

Figure 2 The Milankovitch Theory

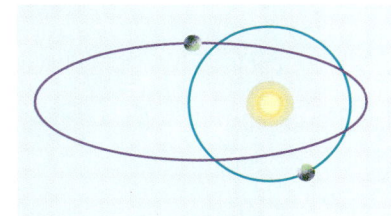

❶ Over a period of 100,000 years, the Earth's orbit slowly changes from a more circular shape to a more elliptical shape and back again. When Earth's orbit is elliptical, Earth receives more energy from the sun. When its orbit is more circular, Earth receives less energy from the sun.

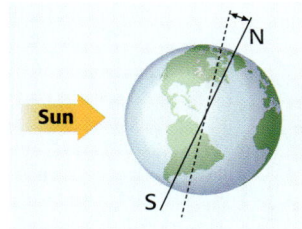

❷ Over a period of 41,000 years, the tilt of the Earth's axis varies between 22.2° and 24.5°. When the tilt is at 24.5°, the poles receive more solar energy.

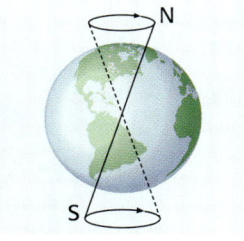

❸ The Earth's axis traces a complete circle every 26,000 years. The circular motion of the Earth's axis determines the time of year that the Earth is closest to the sun.

Teach

ACTIVITY — ADVANCED

Ancient Climates Have students find out why scientists study the dust concentrations and gas composition of glacial ice in places such as Antarctica and Greenland. In an oral or written presentation, have students explain why these and other data provide evidence about the last glacial period and other ice ages.
LS Verbal/Intrapersonal

Answer to Reading Check
Changes in the Earth's orbit and the tilt of the Earth's axis are the two things that Milankovitch says cause ice ages.

MISCONCEPTION ALERT

Ice Ages and Glacial Periods Students may be confused about the difference between an ice age and a glacial period. An ice age is the gradual cooling of the planet over thousands of years. During this time, glaciers repeatedly spread outward from the Earth's poles toward the equator. Ice ages are characterized by glacial periods (when glaciers spread) and interglacial periods (when glaciers retreat). Glacial periods can happen rather quickly—often in less than 30 years. Ice cores indicate that sudden glaciation periods could be caused by changes in major ocean currents or by volcanic eruptions. Currently, we are in an interglacial period of an ice age.

Section 4 • Changes in Climate

Teach, continued

ACTIVITY — GENERAL

Volcanic Eruptions
Have students research and write a short report on a large volcanic eruption. Reports should include where the volcano is located, what damage the eruption caused, and what the eruption's long-term effects were. **LS Intrapersonal**

CONNECTION to Geology — GENERAL

Climate Change Due to Plate Tectonics Tectonic activity will continue to rearrange the Earth's continents in the future. Europe and North America will continue to spread apart, allowing greater circulation between the Arctic and Atlantic Oceans. At the same time, Antarctica will move away from the South Pole. Ask students to imagine that they have been transported 50 million years into the future. How is the Earth different in terms of the events just described? Have students create a story or comic about the Earth of the distant future. (Sample answer: Earth will be much warmer. The sea level will be higher because ocean currents will reach both polar regions, warming them. Antarctica will no longer be an icebound continent. Additionally, the continents will be rearranged, and some of today's prominent geographic features, such as the Rocky Mountains, will be significantly eroded.)
LS Intrapersonal/Visual

Figure 3 Much of Pangaea—the part that is now Africa, South America, India, Antarctica, Australia, and Saudi Arabia—was covered by continental ice sheets.

Plate Tectonics

The Earth's climate is further influenced by plate tectonics and continental drift. One theory proposes that ice ages happen when the continents are positioned closer to the polar regions. About 250 million years ago, all the continents were connected near the South Pole in one giant landmass called *Pangaea*, as shown in **Figure 3**. During this time, ice covered a large area of the Earth's surface. As Pangaea broke apart, the continents moved toward the equator, and the ice age ended. During the last ice age, many large landmasses were positioned in the polar zones. Antarctica, northern North America, Europe, and Asia were covered by large sheets of ice.

Volcanic Eruptions

Many natural factors can affect global climate. Catastrophic events, such as volcanic eruptions, can influence climate. Volcanic eruptions send large amounts of dust, ash, and smoke into the atmosphere. Once in the atmosphere, the dust, smoke, and ash particles act as a shield. This shield blocks the sun's rays, which causes the Earth to cool. **Figure 4** shows how dust particles from a volcanic eruption block the sun.

✓ **Reading Check** How can volcanoes change the climate?

Figure 4 Volcanic Dust in the Atmosphere

Volcanic eruptions, such as the 1980 eruption of Mount St. Helens, as shown at right, produce dust that reflects sunlight.

Answer to Reading Check
Dust, ash, and smoke from volcanic eruptions block the sun's rays, which causes the Earth to cool.

Figure 5 Some scientists believe that a 10 km chunk of rock smashed into the Earth 65 million years ago, which caused the climatic change that resulted in the extinction of dinosaurs.

Asteroid Impact

Imagine a rock the size of a car flying in from outer space and crashing in your neighborhood. This rock, like the one shown in **Figure 5,** is called an asteroid. An *asteroid* is a small, rocky object that orbits the sun. Sometimes, asteroids enter our atmosphere and crash into the Earth. What would happen if an asteroid 1 km wide, which is more than half a mile long, hit the Earth? Scientists believe that if an asteroid this big hit the Earth, it could change the climate of the entire world.

When a large piece of rock slams into the Earth, it causes debris to shoot into the atmosphere. *Debris* is dust and smaller rocks. This debris can block some of the sunlight and thermal energy. This would lower average temperatures, which would change the climate. Plants wouldn't get the sunlight they needed to grow, and animals would find surviving difficult. Scientists believe such an event is what caused dinosaurs to become extinct 65 million years ago when a 10 km asteroid slammed into the Earth and changed the Earth's climate.

The Sun's Cycle

Some changes in the climate can be linked to changes in the sun. You might think that the sun always stays the same. However, the sun follows an 11-year cycle. During this cycle, the sun changes from a solar maximum to a solar minimum. During a solar minimum, the sun produces a low percentage of high-energy radiation. But when the sun is at its solar maximum, it produces a large percentage of high-energy radiation. This increase in high-energy radiation warms the winds in the atmosphere. This change in turn affects climate patterns around the world.

CONNECTION TO Astronomy

Sunspots Sunspots are dark areas on the sun's surface. The number of sunspots changes with the sun's cycle. When the cycle is at a solar maximum, there are many sunspots. When the cycle is at a solar minimum, there are fewer sunspots. If the number of sunspots was low in 1997, in what year will the next low point in the cycle happen?

CONNECTION to Language Arts — GENERAL

Roots of Words Have students look up the Latin and Greek roots of key terms and note the common roots. For example, the Spanish equivalent of *atmosphere* is *atmosfera,* derived from the Greek root *atmos* (vapor) and the Latin *sphaira* (sphere or ball). Provide English language learners with translations of the key terms in this section, or have them consult the Spanish glossary. **English Language Learners**
LS Intrapersonal

Answer to Connection to Astronomy
The sun has an 11-year cycle. If the solar minimum occurred in 1997, the next solar minimum would be in 2008.

CONNECTION ACTIVITY Real World — ADVANCED

Reducing CO₂ Emissions Fossil fuels, which release carbon dioxide into the air, are often used to heat water. So, washing clothes in cold water instead of hot water can reduce the amount of carbon dioxide released into the atmosphere. For example, a household that uses cold water to do two loads of laundry a week releases about 225 kg *less* carbon dioxide into the atmosphere each year. Have students calculate what the annual reduction in released carbon dioxide would be if the family of every student in the class used cold water for two loads of laundry a week. LS Logical

Cultural Awareness — GENERAL

Ancient Chinese Meteorology Predicting climatic changes is difficult because weather data have been accurately recorded for less than 200 years. However, the meteorological records of the Chinese date back to 1216 BCE. While these records do not indicate temperature, they do record rainfall, sleet, snow, humidity, and wind direction. The records also include comments on unusually warm or cool temperatures. Have interested students research the reasons for collecting the data and find out how the data are used today.

Section 4 • Changes in Climate 539

Close

Reteaching — BASIC

Changing Climate Ask students to describe the climate in their area. Then review the factors that might affect the climate. Have students describe how each factor would affect the climate in their area.

LS Intrapersonal

Quiz — GENERAL

1. Why does the sea level fall during glacial periods? (because much of Earth's water is frozen during a glacial period)

2. How might a major volcanic eruption have brought about an ice age? (Dust, smoke, and ash from a volcanic eruption entered the atmosphere and acted as a shield, blocking out many of the sun's rays and causing the Earth to cool.)

3. How might global warming affect coastal areas? (The warmer temperatures could cause polar icecaps to melt, which would raise the sea level and cause flooding in coastal areas.)

Alternative Assessment — GENERAL

Climate Collage Have students make a collage about global cooling or warming. They can include images of how they think the Earth would appear and descriptions of the likely causes of climate change.

English Language Learners

LS Visual

MATH PRACTICE

The Ride to School

1. The round-trip distance from your home to school is 20 km.
2. You traveled from home to school and from school to home 23 times in a month.
3. The vehicle in which you took your trips travels 30 km/gal.
4. If burning 1 gal of gasoline produces 9 kg of carbon dioxide, how much carbon dioxide did the vehicle release during the month?

global warming a gradual increase in the average global temperature

greenhouse effect the warming of the surface and lower atmosphere of Earth that occurs when carbon dioxide, water vapor, and other gases in the air absorb and trap thermal energy

Answer to Math Practice

10 km × 2 = 20 km/day
20 km/day × 23 trips = 460 km/mo
460 km ÷ 30 km/gal = 15.3 kg CO_2

Global Warming

A gradual increase in the average global temperature that is due to a higher concentration of gases, such as carbon dioxide in the atmosphere, is called **global warming.** To understand how global warming works, you must first learn about the greenhouse effect.

Greenhouse Effect

The Earth's natural heating process, in which gases in the atmosphere trap thermal energy, is called the **greenhouse effect.** The car in **Figure 6** shows how the greenhouse effect works. The car's windows stop most of the thermal energy from escaping, and the inside of the car gets hot. On Earth, instead of glass stopping the thermal energy, atmospheric gases absorb the thermal energy. When this happens, the thermal energy stays in the atmosphere and keeps the Earth warm. Many scientists believe that the rise in global temperatures is due to an increase of carbon dioxide, an atmospheric gas. Most evidence shows that the increase in carbon dioxide is caused by the burning of fossil fuels.

Another factor that may add to global warming is the clearing of forests. In many countries, forests are being burned to clear land for farming. Burning of the forests releases more carbon dioxide. Because plants use carbon dioxide to make food, destroying the trees decreases a natural way of removing carbon dioxide from the atmosphere.

Figure 6 Sunlight streams into the car through the clear, glass windows. The seats absorb the radiant energy and change it into thermal energy. The energy is then trapped in the car.

Answer to School-to-Home Activity

Sample answer: The city could pass legislation that requires all vehicle emissions to be below a certain standard. The city could provide incentives for car pooling. The city could also improve the public transportation system and create more public transportation routes.

540 Chapter 17 • Climate

Consequences of Global Warming

Many scientists think that if the global temperature continues to rise, the ice caps will melt and cause flooding. Melted ice-caps would raise the sea level and flood low-lying areas, such as the coasts.

Areas that receive little rainfall, such as deserts, might receive even less because of increased evaporation. Desert animals and plants would find surviving harder. Warmer and drier climates could harm crops in the Midwest of the United States. But farther north, such as in Canada, weather conditions for farming could improve.

Reading Check How would warmer temperatures affect deserts?

SCHOOL to HOME

Reducing Pollution
Your city just received a warning from the Environmental Protection Agency for exceeding the automobile fuel emissions standards. Discuss with your parent ways that the city can reduce the amount of automobile emissions.

ACTIVITY

SECTION Review

Summary

- The Earth's climate experiences glacial and interglacial periods.
- The Milankovitch theory states that the Earth's climate changes as its orbit and the tilt of its axis change.
- Climate changes can be caused by volcanic eruptions, asteroid impact, the sun's cycle, and by global warming.
- Excess carbon dioxide is believed to contribute to global warming.

Using Key Terms

1. Use the following term in a sentence: *ice age*.
2. In your own words, write a definition for each of the following terms: *global warming* and *greenhouse effect*.

Understanding Key Ideas

3. Describe the possible causes of an ice age.
4. Which of the following can cause a change in the climate due to dust particles?
   a. volcanic eruptions
   b. plate tectonics
   c. solar cycles
   d. ice ages
5. How has the Earth's climate changed over time?
6. What might have caused the Earth's climate to change?
7. Which period of an ice age are we in currently? Explain.
8. Explain how the greenhouse effect warms the Earth.

Math Skills

9. After a volcanic eruption, the average temperature in a region dropped from 30° to 18°C. By how many degrees Celsius did the temperature drop?

Critical Thinking

10. **Analyzing Relationships** How will the warming of the Earth affect agriculture in different parts of the world? Explain.
11. **Predicting Consequences** How would deforestation (the cutting of trees) affect global warming?

For a variety of links related to this chapter, go to www.scilinks.org
Topic: Changes in Climate
SciLinks code: HSM0252

Answer to Reading Check

The deserts would receive even less rainfall, making it harder for plants and animals in the desert to survive.

CHAPTER RESOURCES

Chapter Resource File
- Section Quiz GENERAL
- Section Review GENERAL
- Vocabulary and Section Summary GENERAL
- Critical Thinking ADVANCED

Workbooks
- Science Skills
  • Understanding Bias GENERAL

Answers to Section Review

1. Sample answer: Milankovitch theorized that ice ages were caused by changes in the Earth's orbit and changes in the tilt of the Earth's axis.
2. Sample answer: Global warming is the gradual increase in the average global temperature due to a higher concentration of greenhouse gases in the atmosphere. The greenhouse effect is the warming of the surface and lower atmosphere of the Earth that occurs when carbon dioxide, water vapor, and other gases in the air absorb and trap thermal energy.
3. Ice ages could be caused by changes in the Earth's orbit, in the tilt of the Earth's axis, by plate tectonics, volcanic eruptions, or asteroid impacts.
4. a
5. The Earth has experienced periods of cold and warm temperatures called glacial and interglacial periods.
6. The Earth's climate may have changed because of the change in the Earth's orbit, a change in the tilt of the Earth's axis, plate tectonics, volcanic eruptions, impact from a large asteroid, the sun's cycle, and global warming.
7. We are in an interglacial period. Ice sheets are melting instead of advancing.
8. The greenhouse effect occurs when gases in the atmosphere trap thermal energy and warm the Earth.
9. $30°C - 18°C = 12°C$
10. Sample answer: Global warming might improve farming at higher latitudes. Closer to the equator, an increase in evaporation and less rainfall might make growing crops difficult.
11. Answers may vary. Sample answer: Trees store carbon, so deforestation could cause carbon dioxide levels in the air to increase, which might increase global warming.

Section 4 • Changes in Climate

Skills Practice Lab

Biome Business

Teacher's Notes

Time Required
One 45-minute class period

Lab Ratings

EASY —————— HARD

Teacher Prep 🧪
Student Set-Up 🧪
Concept Level 🧪🧪
Clean Up 🧪

MATERIALS
Note that student groups will need a general map to identify their biome location.

Preparation Notes
Remind students not to use seasonal terms such as *spring* and *fall* because some of the biomes in the Southern Hemisphere may experience seasons that are opposite from the seasons of the Northern Hemisphere.

Skills Practice Lab

OBJECTIVES

Interpret data in a climatograph.

Identify the biome for each climatograph.

- Tundra
- Taiga
- Temperate forest
- Tropical rain forest
- Temperate grassland
- Tropical savanna
- Temperate desert
- Tropical desert
- Chaparral
- Mountains

Biome Business

You have just been hired as an assistant to a world-famous botanist. You have been provided with climatographs for three biomes. A *climatograph* is a graph that shows the monthly temperature and precipitation of an area in a year.

You can use the information provided in the three graphs to determine what type of climate each biome has. Next to the climatograph for each biome is an unlabeled map of the biome. Using the maps and the information provided in the graphs, you must figure out what the environment is like in each biome. You can find the exact location of each biome by tracing the map of the biome and matching it to the map at the bottom of the page.

Procedure

1. Look at each climatograph. The shaded areas show the average precipitation for the biome. The red line shows the average temperature.

2. Use the climatographs to determine the climate patterns for each biome. Compare the map of each biome with the map below to find the exact location of each biome.

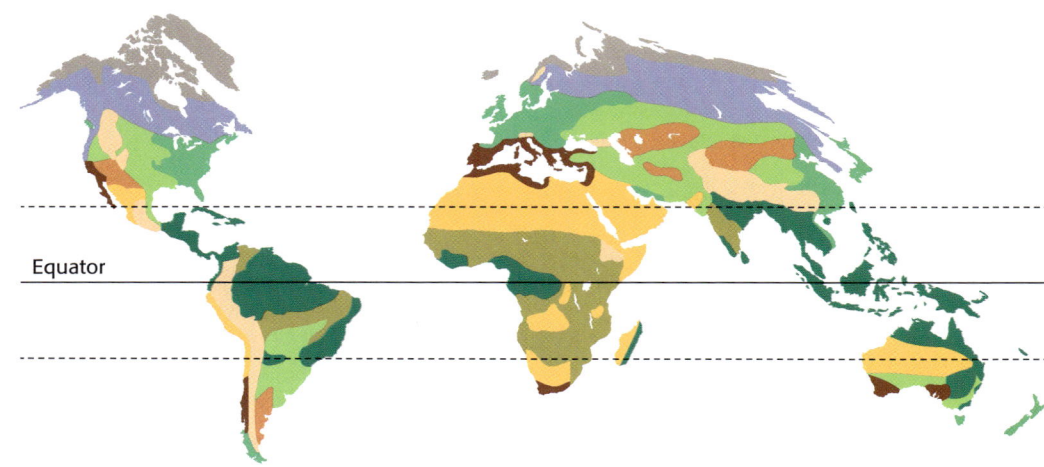

Equator

David Sparks
Redwater Jr. High
Redwater, Texas

CHAPTER RESOURCES

Chapter Resource File
- Datasheet for Chapter Lab
- Lab Notes and Answers

Technology

Classroom Videos
- Lab Video

LabBook
- Global Impact
- For the Birds

542   Chapter 17 • Climate

Analyze Results

1. **Analyzing Data** Describe the precipitation patterns of each biome by answering the following questions:
   a. In which month does the biome receive the most precipitation?
   b. Do you think that the biome is dry, or do you think that it is wet from frequent rains?

2. **Analyzing Data** Describe the temperature patterns of each biome by answering the following questions:
   a. In the biome, which months are warmest?
   b. Does the biome seem to have temperature cycles, like seasons, or is the temperature almost always the same?
   c. Do you think that the biome is warm or cold? Explain.

Draw Conclusions

3. **Drawing Conclusions** Name each biome.
4. **Applying Conclusions** Where is each biome located?

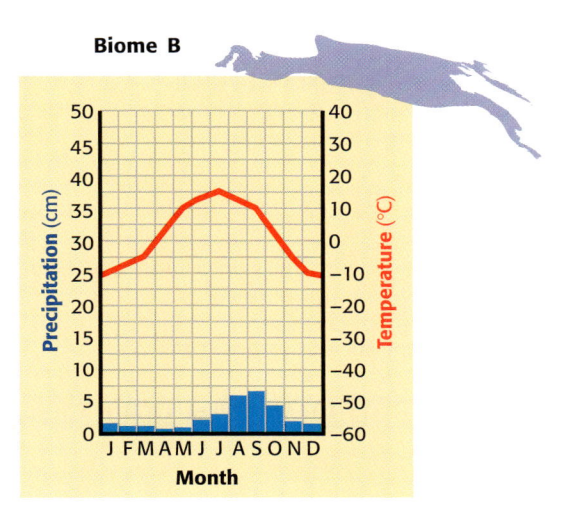

Biome A

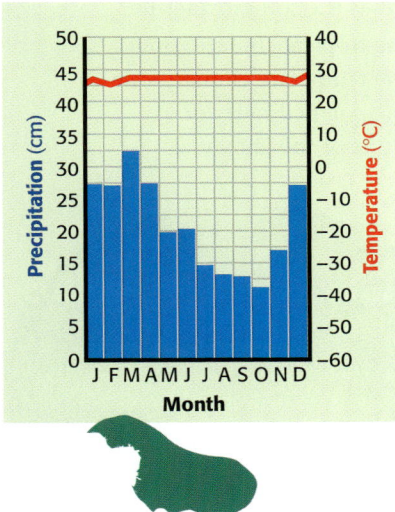

Biome B

Biome C

Analyze the Results

1. a. In Biome A, the rain is heaviest in March. In Biome B, the rain is heaviest in September. In Biome C, the rain is heaviest in May.
   b. Biome A is very wet. Biomes B and C are relatively dry, but some months are rainier than others.

2. a. Biome A has a relatively constant temperature throughout the year. Biomes B and C experience their warmest months from June to August.
   b. Biome A has a constant temperature throughout the year. Biomes B and C experience temperature cycles.
   c. Biome A is warm, and the temperature is high year-round. Biome B has a cooler climate, and the climatograph shows cooler temperatures year-round. Biome C has a moderate climate in the early and late months of the year, but the temperature is quite hot in the middle months of the year.

Draw Conclusions

3. Biome A is a tropical rain forest. Biome B is a taiga. Biome C is a temperate grassland.
4. Biome A is located on the western coast of Africa, near the equator. Biome B is located in northern Asia. Biome C is located in the midwestern United States.

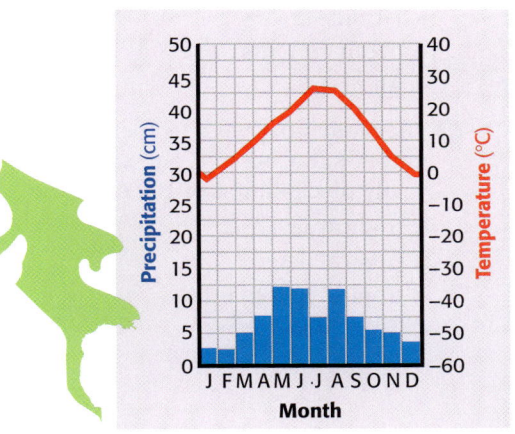

CHAPTER RESOURCES
Workbooks

- **Whiz-Bang Demonstrations**
  - How Humid Is it? GENERAL
- **Long-Term Projects & Research Ideas**
  - Sun-Starved in Fairbanks ADVANCED
- **Calculator-Based Labs**
  - The Greenhouse Effect ADVANCED
  - What Causes the Seasons? ADVANCED

Chapter 17 • Chapter Lab

Chapter Review

Assignment Guide

SECTION	QUESTIONS
1	1, 6, 9, 12, 13, 18–20, 24–26
2	7
3	2, 8, 14, 15, 23
4	10, 16, 21,
1 and 2	3
1 and 4	4, 5, 17
2 and 3	11, 22

ANSWERS

Using Key Terms

1. Sample answer: A biome is one large region characterized by a specific type of climate, and the tropical zone is an even larger region, consisting of several biomes.
2. Sample answer: Weather is the condition of the atmosphere at a particular time, and climate is the average weather condition of an area.
3. Sample answer: The temperate zone is between the Tropics and the polar zone. The polar zone includes the North and South Poles and their surrounding areas.
4. global warming
5. microclimate

Understanding Key Ideas

6. d
7. a
8. b
9. c
10. c
11. b

Chapter Review

USING KEY TERMS

For each pair of terms, explain how the meanings of the terms differ.

1. *biome* and *tropical zone*
2. *weather* and *climate*
3. *temperate zone* and *polar zone*

Complete each of the following sentences by choosing the correct term from the word bank.

    biome   microclimate
    ice age   global warming

4. One factor that could add to ___ is an increase in pollution.
5. A city is an example of a(n) ___.

UNDERSTANDING KEY IDEAS

Multiple Choice

6. Which of the following is a factor that affects climate?
   a. prevailing winds
   b. latitude
   c. ocean currents
   d. All of the above

7. The biome that has a temperature range of 28°C to 32°C and an average yearly precipitation of 100 cm is the
   a. tropical savanna.
   b. tropical desert.
   c. tropical rain forest.
   d. None of the above

8. Which of the following biomes is NOT found in the temperate zone?
   a. temperate forest
   b. taiga
   c. chaparral
   d. temperate grassland

9. In which of the following is the tilt of the Earth's axis considered to have an effect on climate?
   a. global warming
   b. the sun's cycle
   c. the Milankovitch theory
   d. asteroid impact

10. Which of the following substances contributes to the greenhouse effect?
    a. smoke
    b. smog
    c. carbon dioxide
    d. All of the above

11. In which of the following climate zones is the soil most fertile?
    a. the tropical climate zone
    b. the temperate climate zone
    c. the polar climate zone
    d. None of the above

---

12. Higher latitudes receive less solar radiation because the sun's rays strike the Earth's surface at a less direct angle. This spreads the same amount of solar energy over a larger area, resulting in lower temperatures.

13. The amount of precipitation an area receives can depend on whether the region's prevailing winds form from a warm air mass or from a cold air mass. If the winds form from a warm air mass, they will probably carry moisture. If the winds form from a cold air mass, they will probably be dry. Precipitation is more likely to occur when the prevailing winds are warm and moist.

14. Answers may vary. Sample answer: Alpine biomes on tropical mountains are examples of a microclimate. Less dense air at higher elevations retains less thermal energy and less precipitation than air at lower elevations.

15. The tundras and deserts receive very little precipitation.

16. Carbon dioxide is a greenhouse gas. Deforestation decreases the amount of trees, which naturally recycle carbon dioxide in the atmosphere. If the trees are burned, carbon dioxide will be released into the atmosphere, and global warming will increase.

544 Chapter 17 • Climate

Short Answer

12. Why do higher latitudes receive less solar radiation than lower latitudes do?

13. How does wind influence precipitation patterns?

14. Give an example of a microclimate. What causes the unique temperature and precipitation characteristics of this area?

15. How are tundras and deserts similar?

16. How does deforestation influence global warming?

CRITICAL THINKING

17. **Concept Mapping** Use the following terms to create a concept map: *global warming, deforestation, changes in climate, greenhouse effect, ice ages,* and *the Milankovitch theory.*

18. **Analyzing Processes** Explain how ocean surface currents cause milder climates.

19. **Identifying Relationships** Describe how the tilt of the Earth's axis affects seasonal changes in different latitudes.

20. **Evaluating Conclusions** Explain why the climate on the eastern side of the Rocky Mountains differs drastically from the climate on the western side.

21. **Applying Concepts** What are some steps you and your family can take to reduce the amount of carbon dioxide that is released into the atmosphere?

22. **Applying Concepts** If you wanted to live in a warm, dry area, which biome would you choose to live in?

23. **Evaluating Data** Explain why the vegetation in areas that have a tundra climate is sparse even though these areas receive precipitation that is adequate to support life.

INTERPRETING GRAPHICS

Use the diagram below to answer the questions that follow.

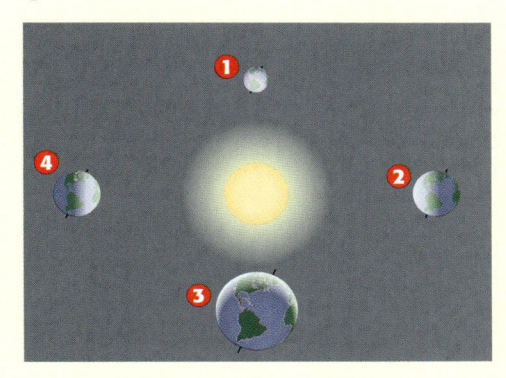

24. At what position—1, 2, 3, or 4—is it spring in the Southern Hemisphere?

25. At what position does the South Pole receive almost 24 hours of daylight?

26. Explain what is happening in each climate zone in both the Northern and Southern Hemispheres at position 4.

Critical Thinking

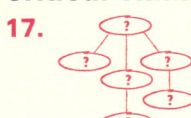

17. An answer to this exercise can be found at the end of this book.

18. Sample answer: Warm surface currents heat the surrounding air. A warm surface current might bring warmer temperatures to an area of land at a higher latitude that might normally be colder.

19. Sample answer: Due to the Earth's tilt, higher latitudes in the Northern Hemisphere receive more solar energy in June, July, and August, causing summer during that period. Because the Southern Hemisphere is tilted away from the sun during these months, higher latitudes in that hemisphere receive less direct solar energy, which causes winter.

20. Sample answer: The climate differs on each side of the Rocky Mountains because the mountains affect the distribution of precipitation. The western side receives more precipitation because, as the warm air is forced to rise, it releases precipitation. As the dry air crosses the mountain, it sinks, warming and absorbing moisture. Therefore, the eastern side is much warmer and drier.

21. Sample answer: conserve electricity, use public transportation, and plant trees

22. tropical savanna or tropical desert

23. Tundra soil is frozen for most of the year. In the summer, only the top meter thaws. The frozen soil underneath prevents the water from properly draining, which makes it difficult for some vegetation to grow.

Interpreting Graphics

24. 3
25. 2
26. In the tropical zone, temperatures are warm. The temperate zone in the Northern Hemisphere is experiencing summer. The temperate zone in the Southern Hemisphere is experiencing winter. The polar zone in the Northern Hemisphere is experiencing almost 24 hours of daylight. The polar zone in the Southern Hemisphere is experiencing almost 24 hours of night.

CHAPTER RESOURCES

Chapter Resource File
- Chapter Review GENERAL
- Chapter Test A GENERAL
- Chapter Test B ADVANCED
- Chapter Test C SPECIAL NEEDS
- Vocabulary Activity GENERAL

Workbooks
- Study Guide
- Assessment resources are also available in Spanish.

Chapter 17 • Chapter Review 545

Standardized Test Preparation

Teacher's Note

To provide practice under more realistic testing conditions, give students 20 minutes to answer all of the questions in this Standardized Test Preparation.

MISCONCEPTION ALERT

Answers to the standardized test preparation can help you identify student misconceptions and misunderstandings.

READING
Passage 1
1. C
2. G
3. C

TEST DOCTOR

Question 1: Some students may think the word *decipher* means "to question" or to "calculate" because students may relate these words to how scientists use computers to determine why climate changes, which is discussed in the passage.

Question 3: This fact is mentioned in the sentence: "For example, 6,000 years ago today's desert in North Africa was grassland and shallow lakes." If students chose A, they may not have realized that the climate of North Africa has changed.

Passage 2
1. C
2. F
3. A

Standardized Test Preparation

READING

Read each of the passages below. Then, answer the questions that follow each passage.

Passage 1 Earth's climate has gone through many changes. For example, 6,000 years ago today's desert in North Africa was grassland and shallow lakes. Hippopotamuses, crocodiles, and early Stone Age people shared the shallow lakes that covered the area. For many years, scientists have known that Earth's climate has changed. What they didn't know was why it changed. Today, scientists can use supercomputers and complex computer programs to help them find the answer. Now, scientists may be able to <u>decipher</u> why North Africa's lakes and grasslands became a desert. And that information may be useful for predicting future heat waves and ice ages.

1. In this passage, what does *decipher* mean?
   A to question
   B to cover up
   C to explain
   D to calculate

2. According to the passage, which of the following statements is true?
   F Scientists did not know that Earth's climate has changed.
   G Scientists have known that Earth's climate has changed.
   H Scientists have known why Earth's climate has changed.
   I Scientists know that North Africa was always desert.

3. Which of the following is a fact in the passage?
   A North African desert areas never had lakes.
   B North American desert areas never had lakes.
   C North African desert areas had shallow lakes.
   D North Africa is covered with shallow lakes.

Passage 2 El Niño, which is Spanish for "the child," is the name of a weather event that occurs in the Pacific Ocean. Every 2 to 12 years, the interaction between the ocean surface and atmospheric winds creates El Niño. This event influences weather patterns in many regions of the world. For example, in Indonesia and Malaysia, El Niño meant <u>drought</u> and forest fires in 1998. Thousands of people in these countries suffered respiratory ailments caused by breathing the smoke from these fires. Heavy rains in San Francisco created extremely high mold-spore counts. These spores caused problems for people who have allergies. In San Francisco, the spore count in February is usually between 0 and 100. In 1998, the count was often higher than 8,000.

1. In this passage, what does *drought* mean?
   A windy weather
   B stormy weather
   C long period of dry weather
   D rainy weather

2. What can you infer about mold spores from reading the passage?
   F Some people in San Francisco are allergic to mold spores.
   G Mold spores are only in San Francisco.
   H A higher mold-spore count helps people with allergies.
   I The mold-spore count was low in 1998.

3. According to the passage, which of the following statements is true?
   A El Niño causes droughts in Indonesia and Malaysia.
   B El Niño occurs every year.
   C El Niño causes fires in San Francisco.
   D El Niño last occurred in 1998.

TEST DOCTOR

Question 1: If students chose B, they may think that *drought* means "stormy weather" because heavy rains were mentioned in the passage. However, droughts are long periods of dry weather.

Chapter 17 • Climate

INTERPRETING GRAPHICS

The chart below shows types of organisms in an unknown biome. Use the chart below to answer the questions that follow.

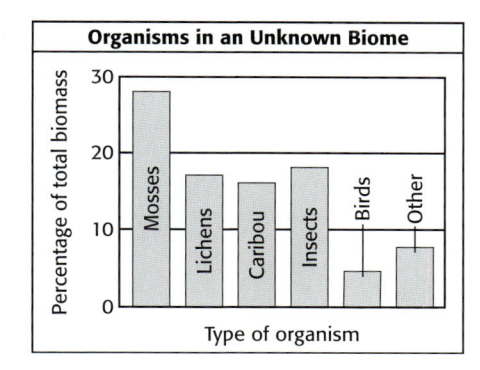

Organisms in an Unknown Biome

(Bar graph showing Percentage of total biomass vs. Type of organism: Mosses ~28%, Lichens ~17%, Caribou ~16%, Insects ~18%, Birds ~4%, Other ~8%)

1. *Biomass* is a term that means "the total mass of all living things in a certain area." The graph above shows the relative percentages of the total biomass for different plants and animals in a given area. What type of biome does the graph represent?
   A rain forest
   B chaparral
   C tundra
   D taiga

2. Approximately what percentage of biomass is made up of caribou?
   F 28%
   G 25%
   H 16%
   I 5%

3. Approximately what percentage of biomass is made up of lichens and mosses?
   A 45%
   B 35%
   C 25%
   D 16%

MATH

Read each question below, and choose the best answer.

1. In a certain area of the savanna that is 12 km long and 5 km wide, there are 180 giraffes. How many giraffes are there per square kilometer in this area?
   A 12
   B 6
   C 4
   D 3

2. If the air temperature near the shore of a lake measures 24°C and the temperature increases by 0.055°C every 10 m traveled away from the lake, what would the air temperature 1 km from the lake be?
   F 5°C
   G 25°C
   H 29.5°C
   I 35°C

3. In a temperate desert, the temperature dropped from 50°C at noon to 37°C by nightfall. By how many degrees Celsius did the noon temperature drop?
   A 13°C
   B 20°C
   C 26°C
   D 50°C

4. Earth is tilted on its axis at a 23.5° angle. What is the measure of the angle that is complementary to a 23.5° angle?
   F 66.5°
   G 67.5°
   H 156.5°
   I 336.5°

5. After a volcanic eruption, the average temperature in a region dropped from 30°C to 18°C. By what percentage did the temperature drop?
   A 30%
   B 25%
   C 40%
   D 15%

INTERPRETING GRAPHICS
1. C
2. H
3. A

TEST DOCTOR

Question 3: Letter A is the total percentage of biomass for lichens and mosses. If students chose D, they chose the percentage of biomass only for lichens.

MATH
1. D
2. H
3. C
4. H
5. C

TEST DOCTOR

Question 2: If students chose B, they probably did not convert 1 km to meters before calculating how much the temperature increased.

Question 4: If students chose I, they subtracted 23.5° from 360°. Students should subtract 23.5° from 180° to get the supplementary angle, which is H, 156.5°.

CHAPTER RESOURCES

Chapter Resource File
• Standardized Test Preparation GENERAL

State Resources
For specific resources for your state, visit go.hrw.com and type in the keyword HSMSTR.

Chapter 17 • Standardized Test Preparation

Science in Action

Scientific Debate

Debate — GENERAL

Organize the class into two teams. Have each team research global warming. After their research is complete, have each team prepare a position paper which states and supports their stance on the issues central to global warming. Using their position papers, have the teams engage in a debate about global warming. **LS** Interpersonal

Science, Technology, and Society

ACTIVITY — GENERAL

Have students design a model of an ice core. Have students fill a plastic foam cup one-third full with water. Place the cup of water in the freezer overnight. Add about 2 cm of water to the cup of frozen water. Then sprinkle ashes into the water to simulate the debris released from a volcanic eruption. Have the students put the cup in the freezer overnight again. Students may continue to add layers to their ice core to simulate conditions such as acid rain. Make sure students record each layer and mark the layer on the plastic foam cup. When the cup is filled, have students carefully remove the ice from the cup and analyze their findings. **LS** Kinesthetic

---

Science in Action

Scientific Debate

Global Warming

Many scientists believe that pollution from burning fossil fuels is causing temperatures on Earth to rise. Higher average temperatures can cause significant changes in climate. These changes may make survival difficult for animals and plants that have adapted to a biome.

However, other scientists believe that there isn't enough evidence to prove that global warming exists. They argue that any increase in temperatures around the world can be caused by a number of factors other than pollution, such as the sun's cycle.

Language Arts ACTIVITY

WRITING SKILL Read articles that present a variety of viewpoints on global warming. Then, write your own article supporting your viewpoint on global warming.

Science, Technology, and Society

Ice Cores

How do scientists know what Earth's climate was like thousands of years ago? Scientists learn about Earth's past climates by studying ice cores. An ice core is collected by drilling a tube of ice from glaciers and polar ice sheets. Layers in the ice core contain substances that landed in the snow during a particular year or season, such as dust from desert storms, ash from volcanic eruptions, and carbon dioxide from pollution. By studying the layers of the ice cores, scientists can learn what factors influenced the past climates.

Math ACTIVITY

An area has an average yearly rainfall of 20 cm. In 1,000 years, if the average yearly rainfall decreases by 6%, what would the new average yearly rainfall be?

Answer to Language Arts Activity
Students should supply articles with a variety of viewpoints on global warming.

Answer to Math Activity
20 cm × 0.06 = 1.2 cm
20 cm − 1.2 cm = 18.8 cm

People in Science

Mercedes Pascual

Climate Change and Disease Mercedes Pascual is a theoretical ecologist at the University of Michigan. Pascual has been able to help the people of Bangladesh save lives by using information about climate changes to predict outbreaks of the disease cholera. Cholera can be a deadly disease that people usually contract by drinking contaminated water. Pascual knew that in Bangladesh, outbreaks of cholera peak every 3.7 years. She noticed that this period matches the frequency of the El Niño Southern Oscillations, which is a weather event that occurs in the Pacific Ocean. El Niño affects weather patterns in many regions of the world, including Bangladesh. El Niño increases the temperatures of the sea off the coast of Bangladesh. Pascual found that increased sea temperatures lead to higher numbers of the bacteria that cause cholera. In turn, more people contract cholera. But because of the research conducted by Pascual and other scientists, the people of Bangladesh can better predict and prepare for outbreaks of cholera.

Social Studies ACTIVITY

WRITING SKILL Research the effects of El Niño. Write a report describing El Niño and its affect on a country other than Bangladesh.

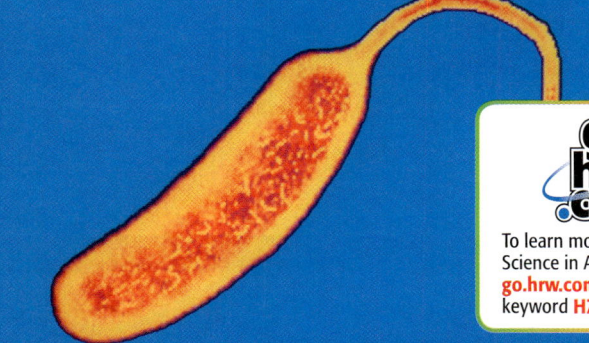

go.hrw.com
To learn more about these Science in Action topics, visit **go.hrw.com** and type in the keyword **HZ5CLMF**.

Current Science
Check out Current Science® articles related to this chapter by visiting **go.hrw.com**. Just type in the keyword **HZ5CS17**.

People in Science
Teaching Strategy — GENERAL
Tell students that cholera is caused by a bacterium that infects the intestines and causes diarrhea and vomiting. If the infection is severe, death may result from dehydration. Encourage students to find out more about cholera, the areas where it is most prevalent, and the ways that it can be controlled. **LS** Intrapersonal

Answer to Social Studies Activity
Many areas of the world are affected by El Niño. For example, El Niño causes droughts in Southeast Asia. Students may also find that El Niño affects the rate of other diseases such as dengue fever and malaria.

UNIT 7 TIMELINE

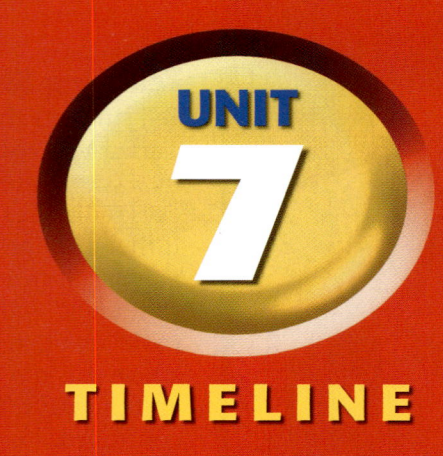

Astronomy

In this unit, you will learn about the science of astronomy. Long before science was called science, people looked up at the night sky and tried to understand the meaning of the twinkling lights above. Early astronomers charted the stars and built calendars based on the movement of the sun, moon, and planets. Today, scientists from around the world have come together to place a space station in orbit around the Earth. This timeline shows some of the events that have occurred throughout human history as scientists have come to understand more about our planet's "neighborhood" in space.

1054
Chinese and Korean astronomers record the appearance of a supernova, an exploding star. Strangely, no European observations of this event have ever been found.

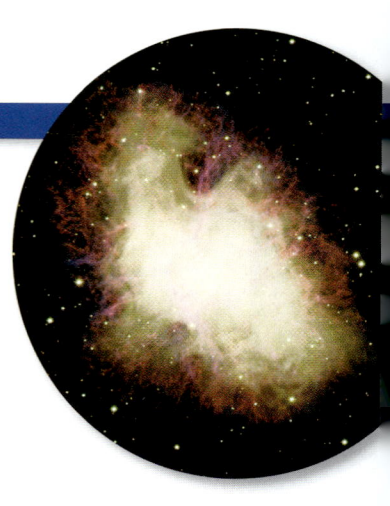

The Crab Nebula

1924
An astronomer named Edwin Hubble confirms the existence of other galaxies.

Andromeda Nebula

1983
Sally Ride becomes the first American woman to travel in space.

1582
Ten days are dropped from October as the Julian calendar is replaced by the Gregorian calendar.

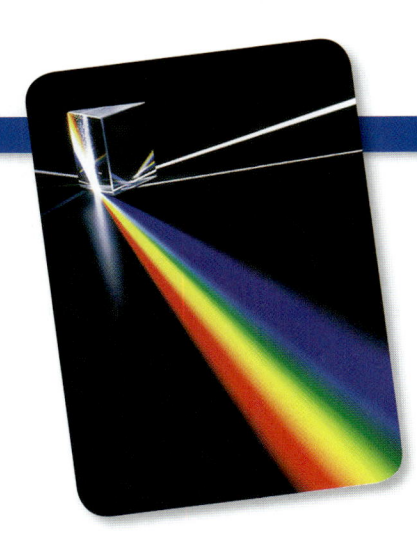

1666
Using a prism, Isaac Newton discovers that white light is composed of different colors.

1898
The War of the Worlds, by H. G. Wells, is published.

1958
The National Aeronautics and Space Administration (NASA) is established to oversee the exploration of space.

1970
Apollo 13 is damaged shortly after leaving orbit. The spacecraft's three astronauts navigate around the moon to return safely to the Earth.

1977
Voyager 1 and *Voyager 2* are launched on missions to Jupiter, Saturn, and beyond. Now more than 10 billion kilometers away from the Earth, they are still sending back information about space.

Voyager 2

1992
Astronomers discover the first planet outside the solar system.

1998
John Glenn becomes the oldest human in space. His second trip into space comes 36 years after he became the first American to orbit the Earth.

2003
Astronomers discover three distant quasars that date back to a time when the universe was only 800 million years old. It takes light 13 billion years to reach Earth from the farthest of the three quasars.

Astronomy 551

18 Studying Space
Chapter Planning Guide

Compression guide: To shorten instruction because of time limitations, omit the Chapter Lab.

OBJECTIVES	LABS, DEMONSTRATIONS, AND ACTIVITIES	TECHNOLOGY RESOURCES
PACING • 90 min pp. 552–557 **Chapter Opener**	SE Start-up Activity, p. 553 GENERAL	OSP Parent Letter ■ GENERAL CD Student Edition on CD-ROM CD Guided Reading Audio CD ■ TR Chapter Starter Transparency* VID Brain Food Video Quiz
Section 1 Astronomy: The Original Science • Identify the units of a calendar. • Describe two early ideas about the structure of the universe. • Describe the contributions of Brahe, Kepler, Galileo, Newton, and Hubble to modern astronomy.	TE Activity Naming the Months, p. 554 GENERAL TE Group Activity Astronomy Debate, p. 555 ADVANCED TE Connection Activity Real World, p. 557 BASIC	CRF Lesson Plans* TR Bellringer Transparency*
PACING • 90 min pp. 558–563 **Section 2 Telescopes** • Compare refracting telescopes with reflecting telescopes. • Explain how the atmosphere limits astronomical observations, and explain how astronomers overcome these limitations. • List the types of electromagnetic radiation that astronomers use to study objects in space.	TE Activity Making a Waterdrop Lens, p. 558 GENERAL TE Demonstration Mystery of the Floating Penny, p. 559 GENERAL TE Demonstration Electromagnetic Spectrum, p. 561 BASIC SE Connection to Physics Detecting Infrared Radiation, p. 562 GENERAL TE Group Activity Reflecting Telescopes, p. 562 GENERAL SE Skills Practice Lab Through the Looking Glass, p. 572 ◆ GENERAL CRF Datasheet for Chapter Lab* LB Whiz-Bang Demonstrations Refraction Action* ◆ GENERAL	CRF Lesson Plans* TR Bellringer Transparency* TR Refracting and Reflecting Telescopes* TR LINK TO PHYSICAL SCIENCE How Your Eyes Work; How a Camera Works* TR The Electromagnetic Spectrum* CRF SciLinks Activity* GENERAL VID Lab Videos for Earth Science
PACING • 45 min pp. 564–571 **Section 3 Mapping the Stars** • Explain how constellations are used to organize the night sky. • Describe how the altitude of a star is measured. • Explain how the celestial sphere is used to describe the location of objects in the sky. • Compare size and scale in the universe, and explain how red shift indicates that the universe is expanding.	SE Quick Lab Using a Sky Map, p. 565 GENERAL CRF Datasheet for Quick Lab* TE Group Activity Classroom Planetarium, p. 565 ADVANCED TE Activity A Compass on Your Wrist, p. 566 GENERAL TE Connection Activity Real World, p. 566 BASIC TE Group Activity Space Science Exploration, p. 566 GENERAL TE Activity SpaceLog, p. 567 GENERAL TE Connection Activity Math, p. 568 GENERAL TE Connection Activity Math, p. 569 GENERAL SE Science in Action Math, Social Studies, and Language Arts Activities, pp. 578–579 GENERAL SE Skills Practice Lab The Sun's Yearly Trip Through the Zodiac, p. 758 ◆ GENERAL CRF Datasheet for LabBook* LB Inquiry Labs Constellation Prize* ◆ ADVANCED LB Long-Term Projects & Research Ideas Celestial Inspiration* ADVANCED	CRF Lesson Plans* TR Bellringer Transparency* TR Spring Constellations in the Northern Hemisphere* TR Zenith, Altitude, and Horizon* TR The Celestial Sphere* TR From Home Plate to 10 Million Light Years Away* SE Internet Activity, p. 568 GENERAL

PACING • 90 min

CHAPTER REVIEW, ASSESSMENT, AND STANDARDIZED TEST PREPARATION
- CRF Vocabulary Activity* GENERAL
- SE Chapter Review, pp. 574–575 GENERAL
- CRF Chapter Review* ■ GENERAL
- CRF Chapter Tests A* ■ GENERAL, B* ADVANCED, C* SPECIAL NEEDS
- SE Standardized Test Preparation, pp. 576–577 GENERAL
- CRF Standardized Test Preparation* GENERAL
- CRF Performance-Based Assessment* GENERAL
- OSP Test Generator GENERAL
- CRF Test Item Listing* GENERAL

Online and Technology Resources

Visit **go.hrw.com** for a variety of free resources related to this textbook. Enter the keyword **HZ5OBS**.

Holt Online Learning
Students can access interactive problem-solving help and active visual concept development with the *Holt Science and Technology* Online Edition available at **www.hrw.com**.

Guided Reading Audio CD
Also in Spanish
A direct reading of each chapter for auditory learners, reluctant readers, and Spanish-speaking students.

Science Tutor CD-ROM
Excellent for remediation and test practice.

Chapter 18 • Studying Space

KEY

SE Student Edition	**CRF** Chapter Resource File	**SS** Science Skills Worksheets	***** Also on One-Stop Planner
TE Teacher Edition	**OSP** One-Stop Planner	**MS** Math Skills for Science Worksheets	**♦** Requires advance prep
	LB Lab Bank	**CD** CD or CD-ROM	**■** Also available in Spanish
	TR Transparencies	**VID** Classroom Video/DVD	

SKILLS DEVELOPMENT RESOURCES	SECTION REVIEW AND ASSESSMENT	STANDARDS CORRELATIONS
SE Pre-Reading Activity, p. 552 GENERAL **OSP** Science Puzzlers, Twisters & Teasers* GENERAL		**National Science Education Standards** UCP 3; SAI 1
CRF Directed Reading A* ■ BASIC, B* SPECIAL NEEDS **CRF** Vocabulary and Section Summary* ■ GENERAL **SE** Reading Strategy Reading Organizer, p. 554 GENERAL **TE** Inclusion Strategies, p. 555 ♦ **CRF** Reinforcement Worksheet Stella Star, Ace Reporter* BASIC	**SE** Reading Checks, pp. 555, 556 GENERAL **TE** Reteaching, p. 556 BASIC **TE** Quiz, p. 556 GENERAL **TE** Alternative Assessment, p. 556 GENERAL **SE** Section Review,* p. 557 ■ GENERAL **CRF** Section Quiz* ■ GENERAL	UCP 2; SAI 2; SPSP 5; HNS 1, 2, 3; ES 3a, 3b, 3c
CRF Directed Reading A* ■ BASIC, B* SPECIAL NEEDS **CRF** Vocabulary and Section Summary* ■ GENERAL **SE** Reading Strategy Mnemonics, p. 558 GENERAL **TE** Reading Strategy Prediction Guide, p. 559 BASIC **TE** Inclusion Strategies, p. 560	**SE** Reading Checks, pp. 558, 560, 563 GENERAL **TE** Reteaching, p. 562 BASIC **TE** Quiz, p. 562 GENERAL **TE** Alternative Assessment, p. 562 GENERAL **SE** Section Review,* p. 563 ■ GENERAL **CRF** Section Quiz* ■ GENERAL	ST 2; SPSP 5; HNS 1, 3; *Chapter Lab:* SAI 1; ST 1
CRF Directed Reading A* ■ BASIC, B* SPECIAL NEEDS **CRF** Vocabulary and Section Summary* ■ GENERAL **SE** Reading Strategy Paired Summarizing, p. 564 GENERAL **CRF** Critical Thinking Through the Eyes of a Telescope* ADVANCED	**SE** Reading Checks, pp. 565, 567, 568, 570 GENERAL **TE** Homework, p. 567 GENERAL **TE** Reteaching, p. 570 BASIC **TE** Quiz, p. 570 GENERAL **TE** Alternative Assessment, p. 570 GENERAL **TE** Homework, p. 570 GENERAL **SE** Section Review,* p. 571 ■ GENERAL **CRF** Section Quiz* ■ GENERAL	UCP 3; SAI 1; ST 2; SPSP 5; HNS 1; *LabBook:* UCP 2; SAI 1; HNS 1; ES 3b

One-Stop Planner® CD-ROM

This convenient CD-ROM includes:
- Lab Materials QuickList Software
- Holt Calendar Planner
- Customizable Lesson Plans
- Printable Worksheets
- ExamView® Test Generator

CNN Student News

cnnstudentnews.com

Find the latest news, lesson plans, and activities related to important scientific events.

SciLinks NSTA

www.scilinks.org

Maintained by the **National Science Teachers Association.** See Chapter Enrichment pages for a complete list of topics.

Current Science®

Check out *Current Science* articles and activities by visiting the HRW Web site at **go.hrw.com.** Just type in the keyword **HZ5CS18T**.

Classroom Videos

- **Lab Videos** demonstrate the chapter lab.
- **Brain Food Video Quizzes** help students review the chapter material.
- **CNN Videos** bring science into your students' daily life.

Chapter 18 • Chapter Planning Guide

18 Chapter Resources

Visual Resources

CHAPTER STARTER TRANSPARENCY

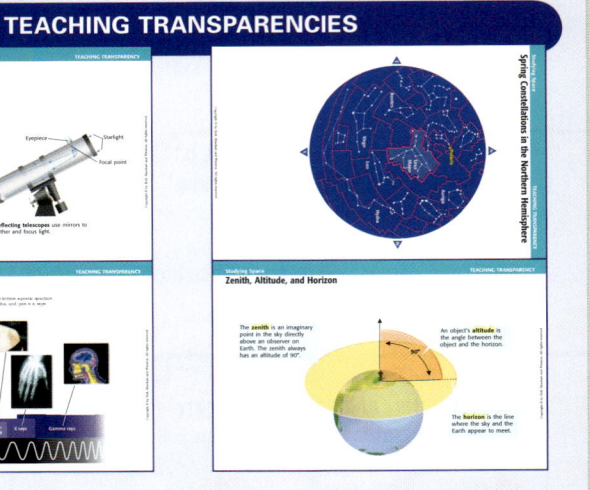

BELLRINGER TRANSPARENCIES

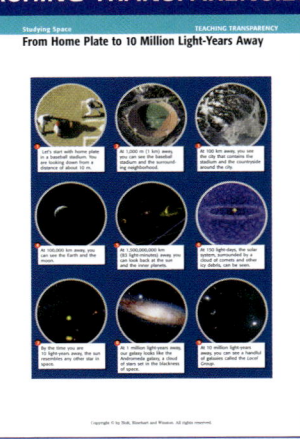

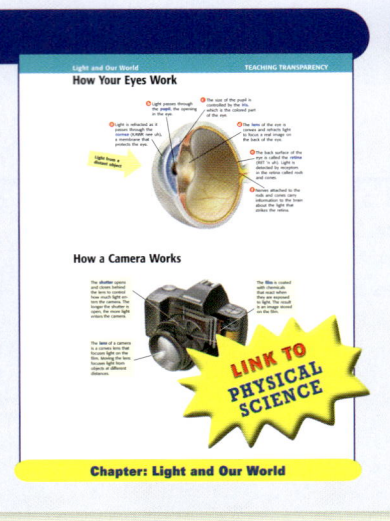

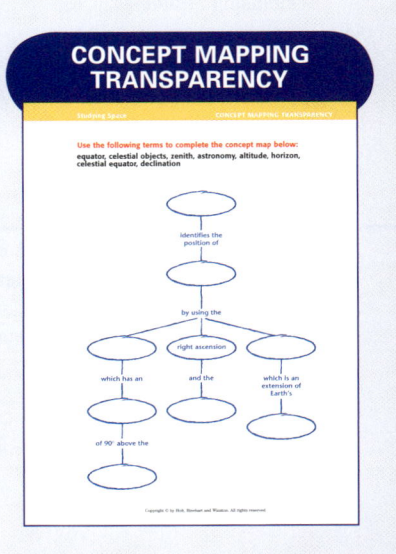

TEACHING TRANSPARENCIES
- Refracting and Reflecting Telescopes
- The Electromagnetic Spectrum
- Spring Constellations in the Northern Hemisphere
- Zenith, Altitude, and Horizon

TEACHING TRANSPARENCIES
- The Celestial Sphere
- From Home Plate to 10 Million Light-Years Away
- How Your Eyes Work / How a Camera Works — LINK TO PHYSICAL SCIENCE — Chapter: Light and Our World

CONCEPT MAPPING TRANSPARENCY

Planning Resources

LESSON PLANS

PARENT LETTER — ALSO IN SPANISH

TEST ITEM LISTING

One-Stop Planner® CD-ROM

This CD-ROM includes all of the resources shown here and the following time-saving tools:

- Lab Materials QuickList Software
- Customizable lesson plans
- Holt Calendar Planner
- The powerful ExamView® Test Generator

551C Chapter 18 • Studying Space

For a preview of available worksheets covering math and science skills, see pages T26–T33. All of these resources are also on the One-Stop Planner®.

Meeting Individual Needs

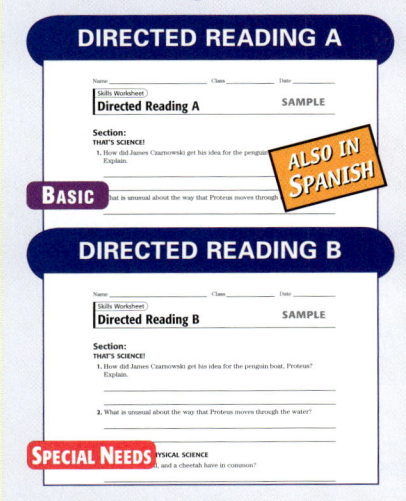

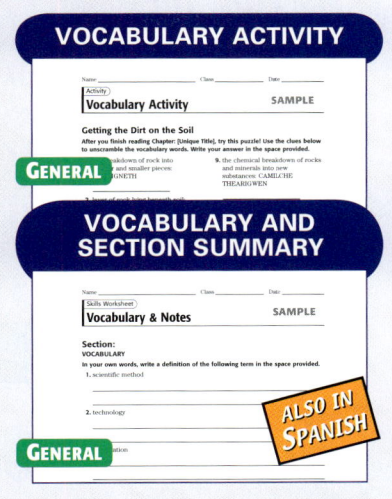

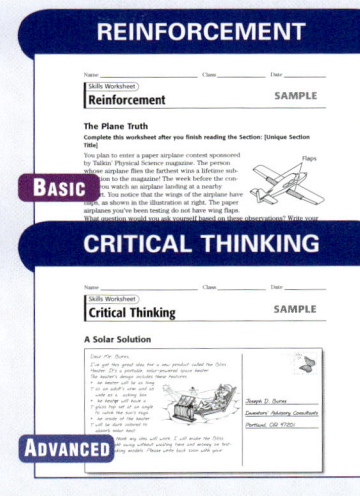

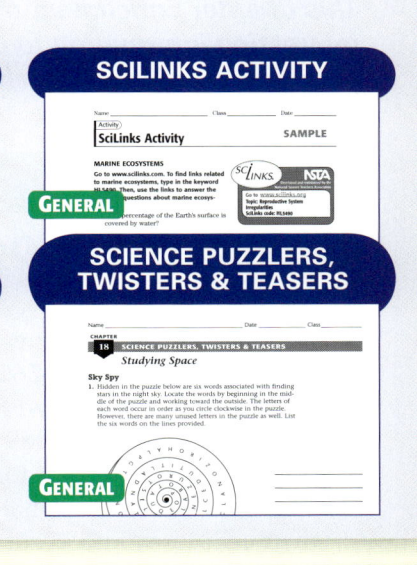

- **DIRECTED READING A** — BASIC (ALSO IN SPANISH)
- **DIRECTED READING B** — SPECIAL NEEDS
- **VOCABULARY ACTIVITY** — GENERAL
- **VOCABULARY AND SECTION SUMMARY** — GENERAL (ALSO IN SPANISH)
- **REINFORCEMENT** — BASIC
- **CRITICAL THINKING** — ADVANCED
- **SCILINKS ACTIVITY** — GENERAL
- **SCIENCE PUZZLERS, TWISTERS & TEASERS** — GENERAL

Labs and Activities

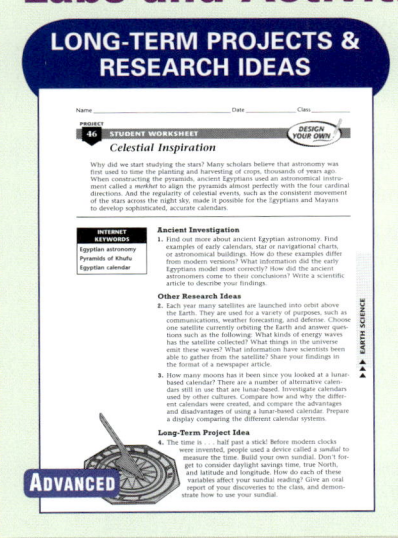

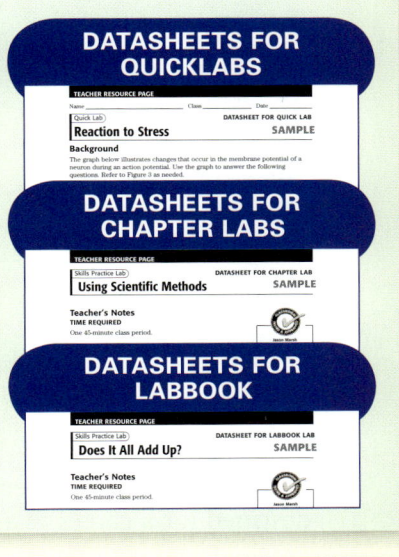

- **LONG-TERM PROJECTS & RESEARCH IDEAS** — ADVANCED
- **WHIZ-BANG DEMONSTRATIONS** — GENERAL
- **INQUIRY LABS** — ADVANCED
- **DATASHEETS FOR QUICKLABS**
- **DATASHEETS FOR CHAPTER LABS**
- **DATASHEETS FOR LABBOOK**

Review and Assessments

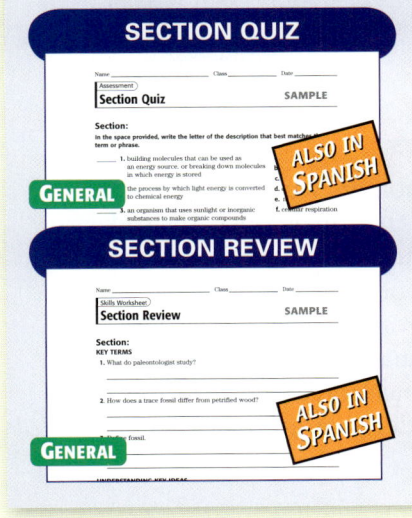

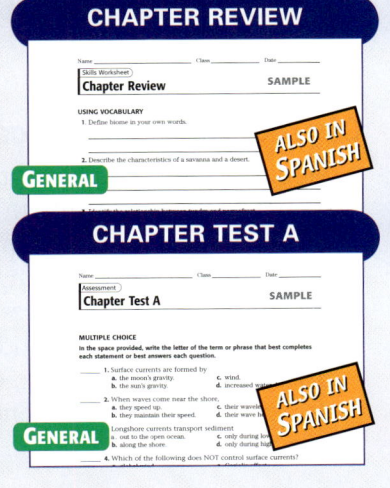

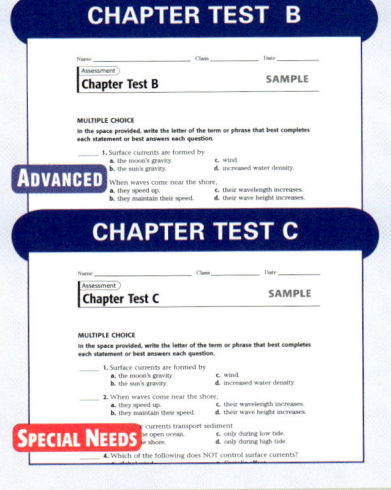

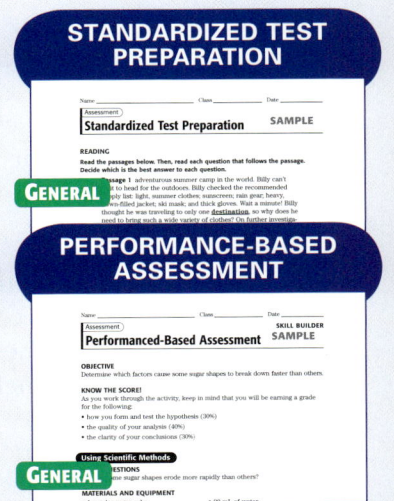

- **SECTION QUIZ** — GENERAL
- **SECTION REVIEW** — GENERAL (ALSO IN SPANISH)
- **CHAPTER REVIEW** — GENERAL
- **CHAPTER TEST A** — GENERAL (ALSO IN SPANISH)
- **CHAPTER TEST B** — ADVANCED
- **CHAPTER TEST C** — SPECIAL NEEDS
- **STANDARDIZED TEST PREPARATION** — GENERAL
- **PERFORMANCE-BASED ASSESSMENT** — GENERAL

Chapter 18 • Chapter Resources **551D**

18 Chapter Enrichment

This Chapter Enrichment provides relevant and interesting information to expand and enhance your presentation of the chapter material.

Section 1

Astronomy: The Original Science

Mayan Calendars

- The Maya of Central America used two calendars—a ceremonial calendar of 260 days and an astronomical calendar of 360 days, divided into 18 months of 20 days each. To make it a full 365 days, the Maya created an additional 5-day month for religious ceremony. These interlocking calendars enabled the Maya to predict when eclipses would occur and when Venus would rise.

The Herschel Family

- By the time William Herschel was 36, he seemed destined for a career as a musician. He was a gifted organist and conducted an orchestra in Bath, England. But Herschel had a great interest in stargazing, and he began to devote more of his time to astronomy. Finding the available telescopes to be inadequate, he set up his own forge and mirror-grinding shop to make large-mirror telescopes. His telescopes were of extremely high quality and power and surpassed even those used at the Royal Observatory, in Greenwich at that time.

- William Herschel was joined by his sister Caroline, and soon the two were conducting systematic telescopic surveys of the skies. In addition to discovering Uranus, William Herschel developed new observational techniques; made important discoveries about nebulas, star clusters, and double stars; and contributed immeasurably to the cataloging of stars.

Is That a Fact!

◆ Caroline Herschel made many significant discoveries and is considered to be the first modern female astronomer. She discovered eight comets and three nebulas. In 1828, Britain's Astronomical Society awarded her a gold medal for her collaborations with her brother.

Section 2

Telescopes

Linking Radio Telescopes

- To improve image resolution and detect very faint emissions, international teams of astronomers sometimes link telescopes from opposite sides of the world. Recently, scientists have taken this technique a step further with the Very Long Baseline Interferometry (VLBI) Space Observatory Program. In this program, astronomers from around the world link their ground-based radio telescopes with a radio telescope that is orbiting the Earth. Each time two telescopes link, they function as a single telescope that has a width 2.5 times the diameter of the Earth!

Charge Coupled Devices

- Modern professional astronomers who use optical telescopes rarely look through their telescopes. Instead, they view images on computer monitors. Most modern optical telescopes are equipped with a semiconductor detector known as a *charge coupled detector* (CCD), which converts the individual light particles (photons) from celestial objects into electrons. The electrons are detected, counted, and rendered as an image on a computer screen.

Chapter 18 • Studying Space

Gamma-Ray Telescopes

- Gamma-ray telescopes are designed to detect gamma rays, which behave more like "bullets of energy" than waves. To detect this type of radiation, a gamma-ray telescope is equipped with a particle detector that collects data resulting from the collision of a gamma-ray photon and an atom. The data can be used to determine both the energy of the ray and the direction of the ray's source. The gamma-ray telescope aboard the *Compton Gamma-ray Observatory* (launched in 1991) has detected objects known as *gamma-ray bursters*, which are brilliant, brief flashes of tremendous energy that last no more than a few minutes and then disappear.

Is That a Fact!

◆ The *Hubble Space Telescope*'s resolution and sensitivity are so acute that the telescope could detect the light from a firefly 16,000 km away!

Section 3

Mapping the Stars

Sky Maps

- Some star maps show what the night sky looks like during a particular season in the Northern or Southern Hemisphere. These star maps are circular, and their edges represent the horizon. They are labeled with cardinal directions, and a "+" represents the zenith. Stars are represented by dots—the larger a dot is, the brighter the star is. To use the map, a stargazer should hold the map overhead and orient it according to the cardinal directions.

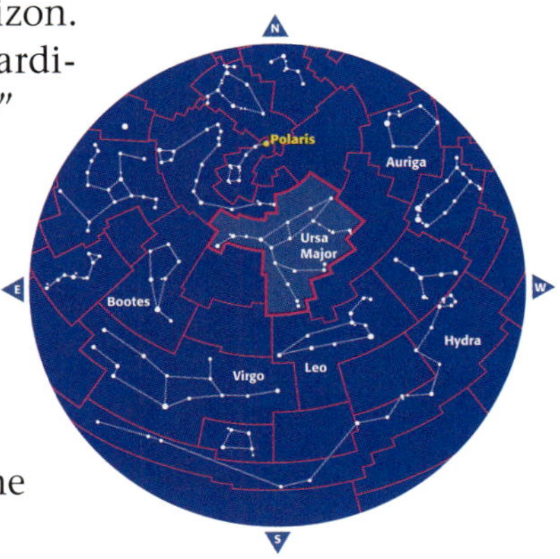

The Messier Catalog

- The *Messier Catalog* (1784) is one of the most well known astronomical catalogs. It was compiled by the French astronomer Charles Messier, whom King Louis XV dubbed the "comet ferret." Through the small telescopes available to Messier, comets looked like indistinct blotches. Many of Messier's blurred blotches weren't comets, however, but star clusters, nebulae, and galaxies. After he realized his mistake, Messier began to compile a catalog of these "noncomets" to spare other comet seekers the frustration that he experienced.

Is That a Fact!

◆ Messier's catalog of more than 100 star clusters, nebulae, and galaxies is widely used today by amateur astronomers with small telescopes. The catalog numbers are still used by professional astronomers. The objects on Messier's list, such as the Crab nebula and the Pleiades, retain their Messier designations, M1 and M45, respectively.

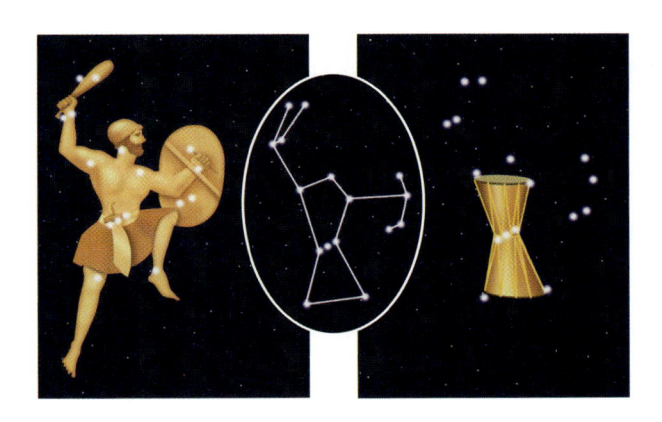

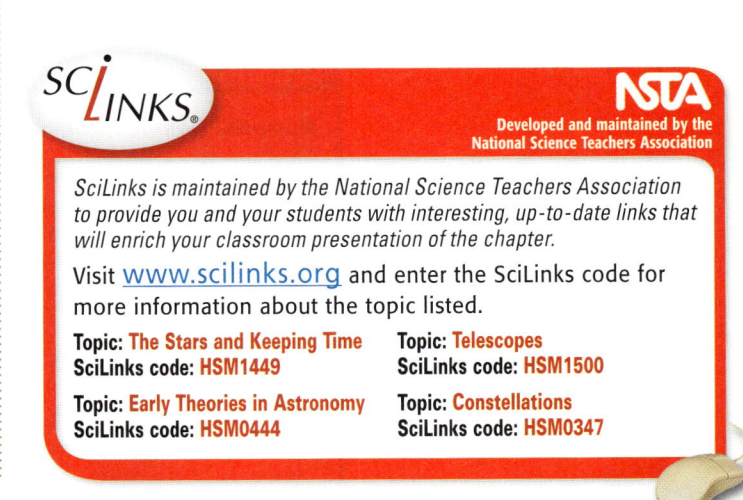

SciLinks is maintained by the National Science Teachers Association to provide you and your students with interesting, up-to-date links that will enrich your classroom presentation of the chapter.

Visit www.scilinks.org and enter the SciLinks code for more information about the topic listed.

Topic: The Stars and Keeping Time
SciLinks code: HSM1449

Topic: Telescopes
SciLinks code: HSM1500

Topic: Early Theories in Astronomy
SciLinks code: HSM0444

Topic: Constellations
SciLinks code: HSM0347

Overview

This chapter introduces some fundamental concepts in astronomy. Students learn about the early history of astronomy and early theories about the structure of the universe. The chapter then introduces optical and non-optical telescopes. The chapter also discusses how the location of stars and other objects in the sky is described. The chapter concludes with a discussion of distance and scale in the universe.

Assessing Prior Knowledge

Students should be familiar with the following topics:

- the solar system is composed of planets and one star
- Newton's law of universal gravitation

Identifying Misconceptions

Students may confuse the apparent movement of stars and other objects in the sky with the actual movement of these objects. As you discuss this chapter, it may be useful to compare apparent and actual movement with phenomena that students are familiar with. For example, compare astronomic observations with observations that students might make from a moving car or a Ferris wheel.

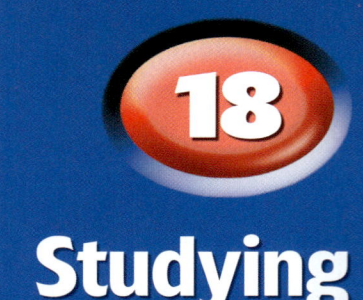

18 Studying Space

SECTION 1	Astronomy: The Original Science	554
SECTION 2	Telescopes	558
SECTION 3	Mapping the Stars	564

Chapter Lab 572
Chapter Review 574
Standardized Test Preparation 576
Science in Action 578

About the PHOTO

This time-exposure photograph was taken at an observatory located high in the mountains of Chile. As the night passed, the photograph recorded the stars as they circled the southern celestial pole. Just as Earth's rotation causes the sun to appear to move across the sky during the day, Earth's rotation also causes the stars to appear to move across the night sky.

PRE-READING ACTIVITY

FOLDNOTES

Three-Panel Flip Chart
Before you read the chapter, create the FoldNote entitled "Three-Panel Flip Chart" described in the **Study Skills** section of the Appendix. Label the flaps of the three-panel flip chart with "Astronomy," "Telescopes," and "Mapping the stars." As you read the chapter, write information you learn about each category under the appropriate flap.

Standards Correlations

National Science Education Standards

The following codes indicate the National Science Education Standards that correlate to this chapter. The full text of the standards is at the front of the book.

Chapter Opener
UCP 3; SAI 1

Section 1 Astronomy: The Original Science
UCP 2; SAI 2; SPSP 5; HNS 1, 2, 3; ES 3a, 3b, 3c

Section 2 Telescopes
ST 2; SPSP 5; HNS 1, 3

Section 3 Mapping the Stars
UCP 3; SAI 1; ST 2; SPSP 5; HNS 1; *LabBook:* UCP 2; SAI 1; HNS 1; ES 3b

Chapter Lab
SAI 1; ST 1

Chapter Review
SPSP 5; HNS 1; ES 3b, 3c

Science in Action
SAI 1; SPSP 5; HNS 1

552 Chapter 18 • Studying Space

START-UP ACTIVITY

MATERIALS

For Each Student
- paper clip
- protractor
- straw, soda
- thread, 15 cm

Teacher's Notes: Remind students that when the term *altitude* is used in astronomy, it does not denote height or elevation but rather the angle between an object, the horizon, and the observer.

Answers

1. Answers may vary. As a student moves closer to an object, the object's altitude should increase.
2. Answers may vary. A similar method could be used to measure the altitude of a star. One advantage of an astrolabe is that it allows an observer to precisely measure the altitude of an object. One disadvantage of an astrolabe is that the measurement depends on the location of the observer and the time that the measurement is taken.

START-UP ACTIVITY

Making an Astrolabe

In this activity, you will make an astronomical device called an *astrolabe* (AS troh LAYB). Ancient astronomers used astrolabes to measure the location of stars in the sky. You will use the astrolabe to measure the angle, or altitude, of an object.

Procedure

1. Tie one end of a **piece of thread** that is 15 cm long to the center of the straight edge of a **protractor**. Attach a **paper clip** to the other end of the string.
2. Tape a **soda straw** lengthwise along the straight edge of the protractor. Your astrolabe is complete!
3. Go outside, and hold the astrolabe in front of you.
4. Look through the straw at a distant object, such as a treetop. The curve of the astrolabe should point toward the ground.
5. Hold the astrolabe still, and carefully pinch the string between your thumb and the protractor. Count the number of degrees between the string and the 90° marker on the protractor. This angle is the altitude of the object.

Analysis

1. What is the altitude of the object? How would the altitude change if you moved closer to the object?
2. Explain how you would use an astrolabe to find the altitude of a star. What are the advantages and disadvantages of this method of measurement?

Chapter Starter Transparency
Use this transparency to help students begin thinking about the significance of space-based observatories.

CHAPTER RESOURCES

Technology

- **Transparencies**
  - Chapter Starter Transparency — READING SKILLS
- **Student Edition on CD-ROM**
- **Guided Reading Audio CD**
  - English or Spanish
- **Classroom Videos**
  - Brain Food Video Quiz

Workbooks

- **Science Puzzlers, Twisters & Teasers**
  - Studying Space GENERAL

Chapter 18 • Studying Space   **553**

SECTION 1

Focus

Overview
This section describes how the units of the calendar are based on the movements of bodies in space. Students will also explore the development of the science of astronomy.

Bellringer
Have students suppose that they need to explain the concepts of a year, a month, and a day to a small child. For each concept, have students illustrate the motion of the Earth and the moon. Students should write a caption describing each illustration.

Motivate

ACTIVITY — GENERAL

Naming the Months The lunar calendar of the Natchez peoples of the Mississippi River Valley reflected the seasonal rhythms of their culture. The names of the months in their calendar—strawberry month, peach month, maize month, turkey month, and chestnut month—reflect the hunter-gatherer nature of their society. Ask students if they can identify the time period that corresponds to each Natchez month. **LS Verbal**

SECTION 1

READING WARM-UP

Objectives
- Identify the units of a calendar.
- Describe two early ideas about the structure of the universe.
- Describe the contributions of Brahe, Kepler, Galileo, Newton, and Hubble to modern astronomy.

Terms to Learn
astronomy   month
year   day

READING STRATEGY

Reading Organizer As you read this section, make a flowchart of the development of astronomy.

astronomy the study of the universe

year the time required for the Earth to orbit once around the sun

---

Astronomy: The Original Science

Imagine that it is 5,000 years ago. Clocks and modern calendars have not been invented. How would you tell the time or know what day it is? One way to tell the time is to study the movement of stars, planets, and the moon.

People in ancient cultures used the seasonal cycles of the stars, planets, and the moon to mark the passage of time. For example, by observing these yearly cycles, early farmers learned the best times of year to plant and harvest various crops. Studying the movement of objects in the sky was so important to ancient people that they built observatories, such as the one shown in **Figure 1**. Over time, the study of the night sky became the science of astronomy. **Astronomy** is the study of the universe. Although ancient cultures did not fully understand how the planets, moons, and stars move in relation to each other, their observations led to the first calendars.

Our Modern Calendar

The years, months, and days of our modern calendar are based on the observation of bodies in our solar system. A **year** is the time required for the Earth to orbit once around the sun. A **month** is roughly the amount of time required for the moon to orbit once around the Earth. (The word *month* comes from the word *moon*.) A **day** is the time required for the Earth to rotate once on its axis.

Figure 1 This building is located at Chichén Itzá in the Yucatán, Mexico. It is thought to be an ancient Mayan observatory.

CHAPTER RESOURCES

Chapter Resource File
- Lesson Plan
- Directed Reading A BASIC
- Directed Reading B SPECIAL NEEDS

Technology
- Transparencies
  - Bellringer

SCIENCE HUMOR

Q: What did Copernicus say about Ptolemy's theory of an Earth-centered universe?

A: Ptolemy another one!

Who's Who of Early Astronomy

Astronomical observations have given us much more than the modern calendar that we use. The careful work of early astronomers helped people understand their place in the universe. The earliest astronomers had only oral histories to learn from. Almost everything they knew about the universe came from what they could discover with their eyes and minds. Not surprisingly, most early astronomers thought that the universe consisted of the sun, the moon, and the planets. They thought that the stars were at the edge of the universe. Claudius Ptolemy (KLAW dee uhs TAHL uh mee) and Nicolaus Copernicus (NIK uh LAY uhs koh PUHR ni kuhs) were two early scientists who influenced the way that people thought about the structure of the universe.

month a division of the year that is based on the orbit of the moon around the Earth

day the time required for Earth to rotate once on its axis

Ptolemy: An Earth-Centered Universe

In 140 CE, Ptolemy, a Greek astronomer, wrote a book that combined all of the ancient knowledge of astronomy that he could find. He expanded ancient theories with careful mathematical calculations in what was called the *Ptolemaic theory*. Ptolemy thought that the Earth was at the center of the universe and that the other planets and the sun revolved around the Earth. Although the Ptolemaic theory, shown in **Figure 2,** was incorrect, it predicted the motions of the planets better than any other theory at the time did. For over 1,500 years in Europe, the Ptolemaic theory was the most popular theory for the structure of the universe.

Figure 2 According to the Ptolemaic theory, the Earth is at the center of the universe.

Copernicus: A Sun-Centered Universe

In 1543, a Polish astronomer named Copernicus published a new theory that would eventually revolutionize astronomy. According to his theory, which is shown in **Figure 3,** the sun is at the center of the universe, and all of the planets—including the Earth—orbit the sun. Although Copernicus correctly thought that the planets orbit the sun, his theory did not replace the Ptolemaic theory immediately. When Copernicus's theory was accepted, major changes in science and society called the *Copernican revolution* took place.

✓ **Reading Check** What was Copernicus's theory? (See the Appendix for answers to Reading Checks.)

Figure 3 According to Copernicus's theory, the sun is at the center of the universe.

Teach

INCLUSION Strategies

- Attention Deficit Disorder
- Learning Disabled
- Hearing Impaired

Have students play a card game that will help them organize the astronomers described in this section. Organize students in groups of three to five students. Give students a deck of cards that has the names of Ptolemy, Copernicus, Brahe, Kepler, Galileo, Newton, and Hubble on separate cards. Give students a second deck of cards that is a different color. Each card in this deck should have five facts about one of the astronomers in the first deck. Ask each group to place the name cards face up in a row. The fact cards should be placed in a pile face down. Then, in turn, each team member should draw a card, read it aloud, and attempt to place it under the correct name. If a student is unable to match the facts with the correct name, his or her team members may help. The game is complete when all fact cards are matched with the correct name cards. At the end of class, hand out a paper copy of the facts and names. **LS Verbal/Interpersonal**

Answer to Reading Check
Copernicus believed in a sun-centered universe.

Group ACTIVITY — Advanced

Astronomy Debate Have teams role-play a debate between Ptolemy, Copernicus, Brahe, Kepler, and Newton. Suggest that students prepare for the debate by researching how each scientist formed his theories. For example, Copernicus used mathematics to analyze the observations made by earlier astronomers, and he made few personal observations. Ptolemy, on the other hand, was a keen observer, but he could reconcile his theory with his observations only by developing a complex but inaccurate system to explain the apparent motion of the planets. Encourage students to research the lives of these scientists and base their positions on the scientists' ideas. When students are role-playing, remind them that each scientist based his theories on his own observations and the theories of scientists who came before him. **LS Logical** Co-op Learning

Section 1 • Astronomy: The Original Science

Close

Reteaching — BASIC

Astronomy Review Have student work in groups to choose an astronomer described in this section and spend ten minutes summarizing the contributions of the astronomer chosen. Have groups present their summaries to the class. **LS Interpersonal**

Quiz — GENERAL

1. What was Copernicus's theory about the structure of the universe? (Copernicus argued that the sun is at the center of the universe and that all planets revolve around the sun.)
2. How did Newton's theories explain why planets orbit the sun and why moons orbit planets? (Newton explained that the force of gravity keeps the planets and moons in orbit.)

Alternative Assessment — GENERAL

Timeline Have students make an illustrated timeline that describes 10 events important to the development of modern astronomy. Encourage students to use reference materials to research timeline entries. **LS Visual**

Answer to Reading Check

Newton's law of gravity helped explain why the planets orbit the sun and moons orbit planets.

Figure 4 Brahe (upper right) used a mural quadrant, which is a large quarter-circle on a wall, to measure the positions of stars and planets.

Tycho Brahe: A Wealth of Data

In the late-1500s, Danish astronomer Tycho Brahe (TIE koh BRAW uh) used several large tools, including the one shown in **Figure 4**, to make the most detailed astronomical observations that had been recorded so far. Brahe favored a theory of an Earth-centered universe that was different from the Ptolemaic theory. Brahe thought that the sun and the moon revolved around the Earth and that the other planets revolved around the sun. While his theory was not correct, Brahe recorded very precise observations of the planets and stars that helped future astronomers.

Johannes Kepler: Laws of Planetary Motion

After Brahe died, his assistant, Johannes Kepler, continued Brahe's work. Kepler did not agree with Brahe's theory, but he recognized how valuable Brahe's data were. In 1609, after analyzing the data, Kepler announced that all of the planets revolve around the sun in elliptical orbits and that the sun is not in the exact center of the orbits. Kepler also stated three laws of planetary motion. These laws are still used today.

Galileo: Turning a Telescope to the Sky

In 1609, Galileo Galilei became one of the first people to use a telescope to observe objects in space. Galileo discovered craters and mountains on the Earth's moon, four of Jupiter's moons, sunspots on the sun, and the phases of Venus. These discoveries showed that the planets are not "wandering stars" but are physical bodies like the Earth.

Isaac Newton: The Laws of Gravity

In 1687, a scientist named Sir Isaac Newton showed that all objects in the universe attract each other through gravitational force. The force of gravity depends on the mass of the objects and the distance between them. Newton's law of gravity explained why all of the planets orbit the most massive object in the solar system—the sun. Thus, Newton helped explain the observations of the scientists who came before him.

✓ **Reading Check** How did the work of Isaac Newton help explain the observations of earlier scientists?

SCIENTISTS AT ODDS

Tycho Brahe Tycho Brahe was eccentric and contrary. As a young man, he insulted a fellow student and was challenged to a duel. During the duel, part of his nose was sliced off, and for the rest of his life, he wore a metal nose prosthesis. Brahe was also a notoriously bad landlord. He cheated and abused the peasants who worked for him. It's not surprising that given his bad temperament, Brahe withheld vital information from his assistant, Johannes Kepler. Although Brahe's family fought Kepler for years, Kepler finally gained access to Brahe's observations after Brahe's death. These observations helped prove that the planets revolve around the sun in elliptical orbits.

Modern Astronomy

The invention of the telescope and the description of gravity were two milestones in the development of modern astronomy. In the 200 years following Newton's discoveries, scientists made many discoveries about our solar system. But they did not learn that our galaxy has cosmic neighbors until the 1920s.

Edwin Hubble: Beyond the Edge of the Milky Way

Before the 1920s, many astronomers thought that our galaxy, the Milky Way, included every object in space. In 1924, Edwin Hubble proved that other galaxies existed beyond the edge of the Milky Way. His data confirmed the beliefs of some astronomers that the universe is much larger than our galaxy. Today, larger and better telescopes on the Earth and in space, new models of the universe, and spacecraft help astronomers study space. Computers, shown in **Figure 5,** help process data and control the movement of telescopes. These tools have helped answer many questions about the universe. Yet new technology has presented questions that were unthinkable even 10 years ago.

Figure 5 *Computers are used to control telescopes and process large amounts of data.*

SECTION Review

Summary

- Astronomy, the study of the universe, is one of the oldest sciences.
- The units of the modern calendar—days, months, and years—are based on observations of objects in space.
- Ptolemaic theory states that the Earth is at the center of the universe.
- Copernican theory states that the sun is at the center of the universe.
- Modern astronomy has shown that there are billions of galaxies.

Using Key Terms

1. Use each of the following terms in a separate sentence: *year, day, month,* and *astronomy.*

Understanding Key Ideas

2. What happens in 1 year?
   a. The moon completes one orbit around the Earth.
   b. The sun travels once around the Earth.
   c. The Earth revolves once on its axis.
   d. The Earth completes one orbit around the sun.

3. What is the difference between the Ptolemaic and Copernican theories? Who was more accurate: Ptolemy or Copernicus?

4. What contributions did Brahe and Kepler make to astronomy?

5. What contributions did Galileo, Newton, and Hubble make to astronomy?

Math Skills

6. How many times did Earth orbit the sun between 140 CE, when Ptolemy introduced his theories, and 1543, when Copernicus introduced his theories?

Critical Thinking

7. **Analyzing Relationships** What advantage did Galileo have over earlier astronomers?

8. **Making Inferences** Why is astronomy such an old science?

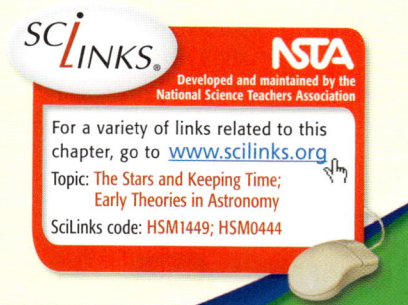

SciLinks
Developed and maintained by the National Science Teachers Association
For a variety of links related to this chapter, go to www.scilinks.org
Topic: The Stars and Keeping Time; Early Theories in Astronomy
SciLinks code: HSM1449; HSM0444

Answers to Section Review

1. Sample answer: A year is the amount of time Earth takes to complete one orbit around the sun. A day is the amount of time Earth takes to complete one rotation on its axis. A month is based on the phases of the moon. Astronomy is the study of the universe.

2. d

3. Ptolemy believed that the Earth was at the center of the universe and that the planets and the sun revolved around the Earth. Copernicus believed that the planets revolved around the sun. Copernicus was more accurate.

4. Answers may vary. Brahe recorded very accurate observations of the movement of bodies in the solar system. Kepler used Brahe's data to create an accurate solar system model and to develop the laws of planetary motion.

5. Answers may vary. Galileo proved that planets, moons, and the sun were physical bodies, like Earth. Newton formulated the law of gravity, which helped explain planetary motions. Hubble proved that galaxies exist outside our own galaxy.

6. $1{,}543 - 140 = 1{,}403$ times

7. Galileo used a telescope to study the night sky. The telescope enabled him to discover that planets and moons are physical bodies.

8. Answers may vary. Astronomy is an old science because studying the stars, moon, and sun has been important to timekeeping, navigation, and religious ceremonies for a very long time.

CONNECTION ACTIVITY
Real World — BASIC

Binocular Astronomy The power of the telescope Galileo used to discover Jupiter's moons was equivalent to that of most modern binoculars. Have students determine when Jupiter is visible from where they live, and have them use a sky chart to locate Jupiter in the night sky. If Jupiter is not visible, encourage students to use binoculars to observe the moon and to sketch its surface features. **LS** Visual/Intrapersonal

CHAPTER RESOURCES

Chapter Resource File
- Section Quiz GENERAL
- Section Review GENERAL
- Vocabulary and Section Summary GENERAL
- Reinforcement Worksheet BASIC

Section 1 • Astronomy: The Original Science

SECTION 2

Focus

Overview
In this section, students will learn how reflecting and refracting telescopes work. The section discusses the electromagnetic spectrum and the use of non-optical telescopes to detect invisible radiation.

Bellringer
Ask students to write a brief answer to the following questions: "Have you ever bent or slowed down light? How?" (Students may mention wearing glasses or looking through a microscope.)

Motivate

ACTIVITY — GENERAL

Making a Waterdrop Lens Give pairs of students a 6 cm × 6 cm piece of plastic wrap, and have each pair place the plastic wrap over some print on a newspaper. Put a drop of water on each piece of plastic. Have students note what shape the drop is and how the drop magnifies the newsprint. Tell students that the rounded, or *convex*, waterdrop is a very simple lens that is similar in principle to the kinds of lenses used in some telescopes. **LS Visual/Kinesthetic**

SECTION 2

READING WARM-UP

Objectives
- Compare refracting telescopes with reflecting telescopes.
- Explain how the atmosphere limits astronomical observations, and explain how astronomers overcome these limitations.
- List the types of electromagnetic radiation that astronomers use to study objects in space.

Terms to Learn
telescope
refracting telescope
reflecting telescope
electromagnetic spectrum

READING STRATEGY

Mnemonics As you read this section, create a mnemonic device to help you remember the characteristics of each type of radiation in the electromagnetic spectrum.

CHAPTER RESOURCES

Chapter Resource File
- Lesson Plan
- Directed Reading A BASIC
- Directed Reading B SPECIAL NEEDS

Technology
- Transparencies
  - Bellringer
  - Refracting and Reflecting Telescopes

Telescopes

What color are Saturn's rings? What does the surface of the moon look like? To answer these questions, you could use a device called a telescope.

For professional astronomers and amateur stargazers, the telescope is the standard tool for observing the sky. A **telescope** is an instrument that gathers electromagnetic radiation from objects in space and concentrates it for better observation.

Optical Telescopes

Optical telescopes, which are the most common type of telescope, are used to study visible light from objects in the universe. Without using an optical telescope, you can see at most about 3,000 stars in the night sky. Using an optical telescope, however, you can see millions of stars and other objects.

An optical telescope collects visible light and focuses it to a focal point for closer observation. A *focal point* is the point where the rays of light that pass through a lens or that reflect from a mirror converge. The simplest optical telescope has two lenses. One lens, called the *objective lens*, collects light and forms an image at the back of the telescope. The bigger the objective lens is, the more light the telescope can gather. The second lens is located in the eyepiece of the telescope. This lens magnifies the image produced by the objective lens. **Figure 1** shows how much more of the moon you can see by using an optical telescope.

✓ **Reading Check** What are the functions of the two lenses in an optical telescope? (*See the Appendix for answers to Reading Checks.*)

Figure 1 By using telescopes, people can study objects such as the moon in greater detail.

Answer to Reading Check
The objective lens collects light and forms an image at the back of the telescope. The eyepiece magnifies the image produced by the objective lens.

---

558 Chapter 18 • Studying Space

Figure 2 Refracting and Reflecting Telescopes

Refracting telescopes use lenses to gather and focus light.

Reflecting telescopes use mirrors to gather and focus light.

Refracting Telescopes

Telescopes that use lenses to gather and focus light are called **refracting telescopes.** As shown in **Figure 2,** a refracting telescope has an objective lens that bends light that passes through it and focuses the light to be magnified by an eyepiece. Refracting telescopes have two disadvantages. First, lenses focus different colors of light at slightly different distances, so images cannot be perfectly focused. Second, the size of a refracting telescope is also limited by the size of the objective lens. If the lens is too large, the glass sags under its own weight and images are distorted. These limitations are two reasons that most professional astronomers use reflecting telescopes.

Reflecting Telescopes

A telescope that uses a curved mirror to gather and focus light is called a **reflecting telescope.** Light enters the telescope and is reflected from a large, curved mirror to a flat mirror. As shown in **Figure 2,** the flat mirror focuses the image and reflects the light to be magnified by the eyepiece.

One advantage of reflecting telescopes is that the mirrors can be very large. Large mirrors allow reflecting telescopes to gather more light than refracting telescopes do. Another advantage is that curved mirrors are polished on their curved side, which prevents light from entering the glass. Thus, any flaws in the glass do not affect the light. A third advantage is that mirrors can focus all colors of light to the same focal point. Therefore, reflecting telescopes allow all colors of light from an object to be seen in focus at the same time.

telescope an instrument that collects electromagnetic radiation from the sky and concentrates it for better observation

refracting telescope a telescope that uses a set of lenses to gather and focus light from distant objects

reflecting telescope a telescope that uses a curved mirror to gather and focus light from distant objects

CONNECTION to Physical Science — GENERAL

Cones and Rods The human retina contains receptors called *cones* and *rods,* which perceive different wavelengths of light. Cones are found in the central part of the retina and perceive color. Rods, located at the outer part of the retina, perceive only black and white. When little light is present, rods are more sensitive than cones. For this reason, stargazers sometimes look at objects by using their peripheral vision rather than looking at an object straight on. This method takes advantage of the rods' ability to detect faint objects in the sky. Encourage interested students to use a telescope, binoculars, or their unaided eyes to test this technique.

Teach, continued

INCLUSION Strategies

- Learning Disabled
- Attention Deficit Disorder
- Behavior Control Issues

Have students model the electromagnetic spectrum to gain a better understanding of the different wave types. Organize students into seven groups. Assign each group one wave type to research. If possible, make reference books available. Have groups write down important facts about their wave type. Groups can present their findings in the order of the waves in the electromagnetic spectrum. After all groups have finished presenting, ask them to assemble themselves in the order of the electromagnetic spectrum. The following day, hand out a matrix that includes the important facts that each group contributed.

LS Interpersonal/Kinesthetic

Co-op Learning

Answer to Reading Check

The motion of air pollution, water vapor, and light pollution distort the images produced by optical telescopes.

Figure 3 *The Keck Telescopes are in Hawaii. The 36 hexagonal mirrors in each telescope (shown in the inset) combine to form a light-reflecting surface that is 10 m across.*

Figure 4 *The Hubble Space Telescope has produced very clear images of objects in deep space.*

Very Large Reflecting Telescopes

In some very large reflecting telescopes, several mirrors work together to collect light and focus it in the same area. The Keck Telescopes in Hawaii, shown in **Figure 3**, are twin telescopes that each have 36 hexagonal mirrors that work together. Linking several mirrors allows more light to be collected and focused in one spot.

Optical Telescopes and the Atmosphere

The light gathered by telescopes on the Earth is affected by the atmosphere. The Earth's atmosphere causes starlight to shimmer and blur due to the motion of the air above the telescope. Also, light pollution from large cities can make the sky look bright. As a result, an observer's ability to view faint objects is limited. Astronomers often place telescopes in dry areas to avoid moisture in the air. Mountaintops are also good locations for telescopes because the air is thinner at higher elevations. In addition, mountaintops generally have less air pollution and light pollution than other areas do.

✓ **Reading Check** How does the atmosphere affect the images produced by optical telescopes?

Optical Telescopes in Space

To avoid interference by the atmosphere, scientists have put telescopes in space. Although the mirror in the *Hubble Space Telescope*, shown in **Figure 4**, is only 2.4 m across, this optical telescope can detect very faint objects in space.

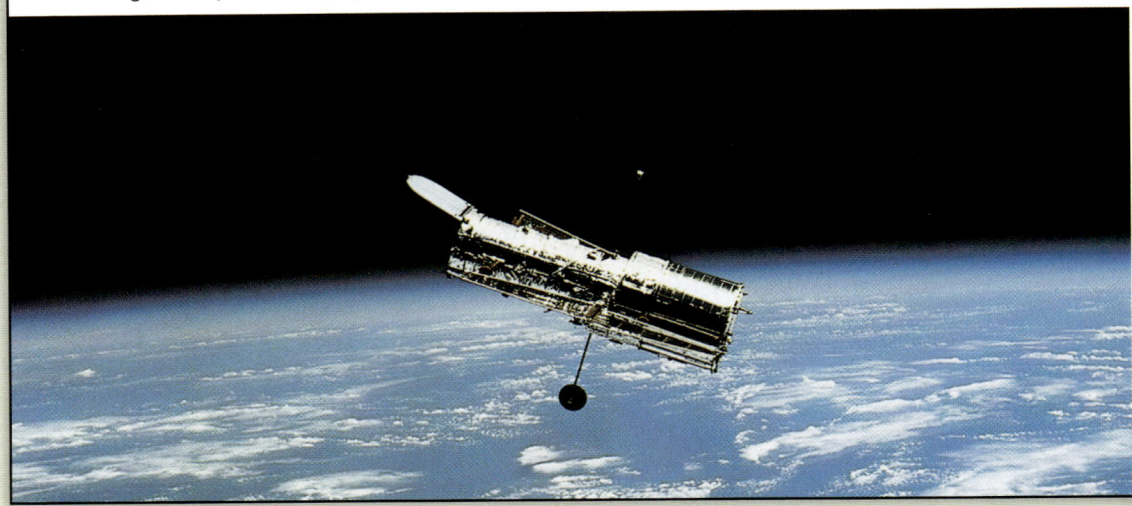

Science Bloopers

Hubble Mirror Flaws When the *Hubble Space Telescope* was deployed in 1990, it became immediately apparent that the telescope was not operating correctly—images transmitted back to Earth were blurred. A minute flaw was discovered in the telescope's main mirror. The mirror had been ground about 0.0002 cm (about one-fiftieth of the width of a human hair) flatter than it should have been. Although much of the image distortion was corrected with computer processing, the telescope was much less powerful than scientists originally hoped it would be. During a 1993 repair mission, space shuttle astronauts placed on the telescope a number of corrective devices that made the telescope fully operational.

560 Chapter 18 • Studying Space

The Electromagnetic Spectrum

For thousands of years, humans have used their eyes to observe stars and planets. But scientists eventually discovered that visible light, the light that we can see, is not the only form of radiation. In 1852, James Clerk Maxwell proved that visible light is a part of the electromagnetic spectrum. The **electromagnetic spectrum** is made up of all of the wavelengths of electromagnetic radiation.

Detecting Electromagnetic Radiation

Each color of light is a different wavelength of electromagnetic radiation. Humans can see radiation from red light, which has a long wavelength, to blue light, which has a shorter wavelength. But visible light is only a small part of the electromagnetic spectrum, as shown in **Figure 5**. The rest of the electromagnetic spectrum—radio waves, microwaves, infrared light, ultraviolet light, X rays, and gamma rays—is invisible. The Earth's atmosphere blocks most invisible radiation from objects in space. In this way, the atmosphere functions as a protective shield around the Earth. Radiation that can pass through the atmosphere includes some radio waves, microwaves, infrared light, visible light, and some ultraviolet light.

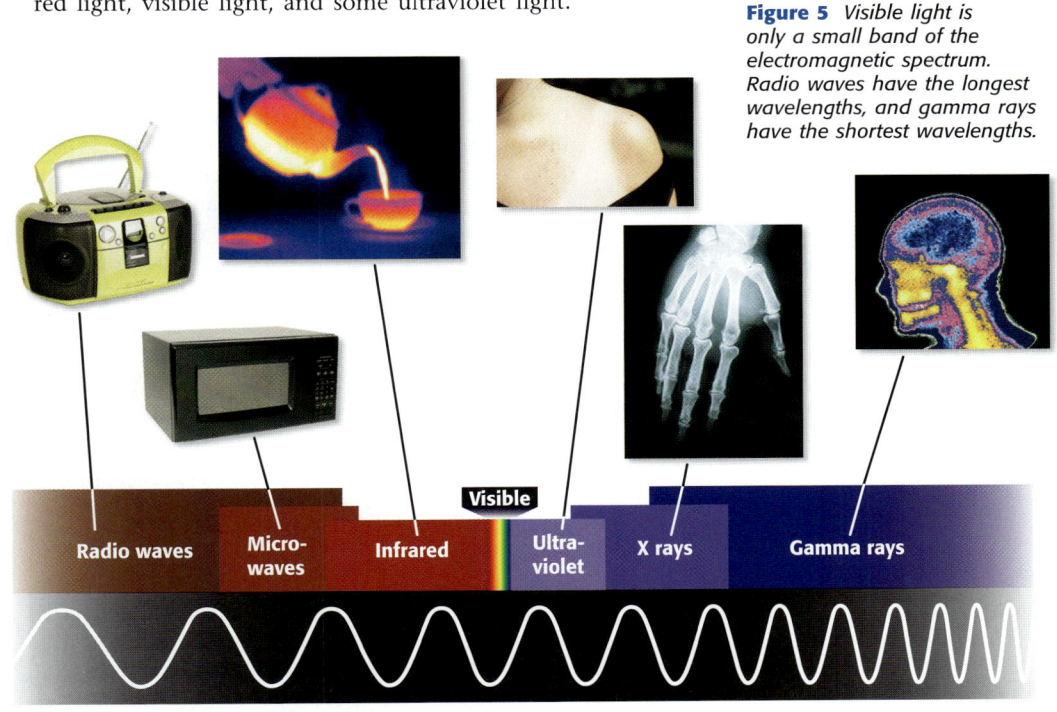

electromagnetic spectrum all of the frequencies or wavelengths of electromagnetic radiation

Figure 5 Visible light is only a small band of the electromagnetic spectrum. Radio waves have the longest wavelengths, and gamma rays have the shortest wavelengths.

Demonstration — BASIC
Electromagnetic Spectrum
To help students comprehend how little of the electromagnetic spectrum is visible to the human eye, show them a photograph of a piano keyboard. Tell students that the part of the electromagnetic spectrum that humans can see is comparable to one key on the piano. **English Language Learners**
LS Visual

CONNECTION to Physical Science — ADVANCED

Bug Eyes Use the transparency "How Your Eyes Work; How a Camera Works" to compare human eyes and cameras. Human eyes can detect only visible light, but some organisms have eyes more like nonoptical telescopes. Insects, such as bees, can see ultraviolet radiation. Flowers, in turn, have ultraviolet patterns that direct bees to their center. Have interested students find out what it is like to look at the world through the eyes of a bee or an ant. Encourage students to find out about experimental telescope designs that are modeled after the eyes of animals. One example of an X-ray telescope is the Lobster Eye Telescope.

BRAIN FOOD

Although the sun appears to be yellowish in color, it is radiating energy across the electromagnetic spectrum. When a space-based X-ray telescope is used to observe the sun, the sun appears nearly black, but the solar atmosphere above sunspots appear brilliantly active with magnetic storms and solar flares that release X rays.

CHAPTER RESOURCES
Technology
- Transparencies
  - The Electromagnetic Spectrum
  - **LINK TO PHYSICAL SCIENCE** How Your Eyes Work; How a Camera Works

WEIRD SCIENCE

Shortly after Marconi invented the radio in the 1890s, people became interested in listening for messages from intelligent life in the universe. In 1901, a reward of 100,000 francs was offered to the first person to communicate with aliens.

Section 2 • Telescopes

Close

Reteaching — BASIC
Optical Telescope Review
Reproduce **Figure 2** on the board, but omit labels or lines indicating the path of light in the telescopes. Ask student volunteers to help you indicate the path of light in each telescope and to add the labels shown in the figure. **LS Visual**

Quiz — GENERAL
1. What limits the size and magnification of a refracting telescope? (If the objective lens is too large, gravity will cause the glass to sag, which distorts the image.)
2. What is the advantage of linking radio telescopes? (When radio telescopes are linked together, they act as a very large unit and are more powerful. Scientists can then make observations that show extremely fine details of distant objects.)

Alternative Assessment — GENERAL
Writing Letters Have students imagine that they are trying to gather support for building the largest radio-telescope array ever. Have them write a persuasive letter describing how radio telescopes differ from optical telescopes and how building such a large array could further our understanding of the universe. Students should include a diagram showing how their array would collect signals from a wide area. **LS Intrapersonal**

Group Activity — GENERAL
Reflecting Telescopes Students can construct a simple reflecting telescope. Instruct students to turn off the lights and place a makeup mirror (a curved, focusing mirror) near a window so that the moon and some stars are reflected in it. One student should hold a hand mirror in front of the makeup mirror so that he or she can see a reflection of the makeup mirror in the hand mirror. Then, the other student should use a magnifying lens to view the reflection in the hand mirror. **LS Kinesthetic/Visual**

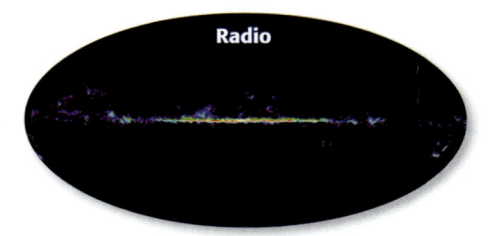

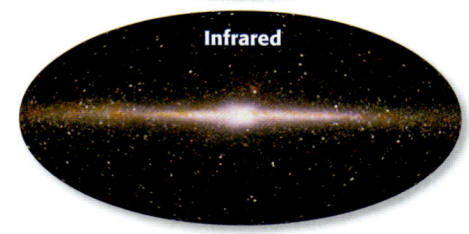

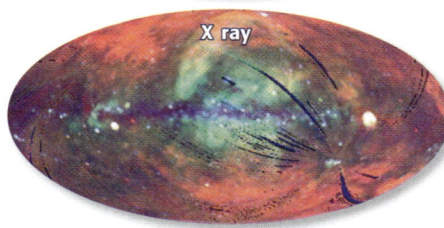

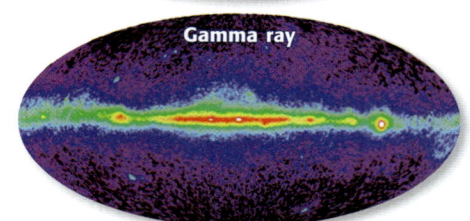

Figure 6 Each image shows the Milky Way as it would appear if we could see other wavelengths of electromagnetic radiation.

(Radio, Infrared, X ray, Gamma ray)

Nonoptical Telescopes
To study invisible radiation, scientists use nonoptical telescopes. Nonoptical telescopes detect radiation that cannot be seen by the human eye. Astronomers study the entire electromagnetic spectrum because each type of radiation reveals different clues about an object. As **Figure 6** shows, our galaxy looks very different when it is observed at various wavelengths. A different type of telescope was used to produce each image. The "cloud" that goes across the image is the Milky Way galaxy.

Radio Telescopes
Radio telescopes detect radio waves. Radio telescopes have to be much larger than optical telescopes because radio wavelengths are about 1 million times longer than optical wavelengths. Most radio radiation reaches the ground and can be detected both during the day and night. The surface of radio telescopes does not have to be as flawless as the lenses and mirrors of optical telescopes. In fact, the surface of a radio telescope does not have to be solid.

Linking Radio Telescopes
Astronomers can get more detailed images of the universe by linking radio telescopes together. When radio telescopes are linked together, they work like a single giant telescope. For example, the Very Large Array (VLA) consists of 27 radio telescopes that are spread over 30 km. Working together, the telescopes function as a single telescope that is 30 km across!

CONNECTION TO Physics
Detecting Infrared Radiation In this activity, you will replicate Sir William Herschel's discovery of invisible infrared radiation. First, paint the bulbs of three thermometers black. Place a sheet of white paper inside a tall cardboard box. Tape the thermometers parallel to each other, and place them inside the box. Cut a small notch in the top of the box, and position a small glass prism so that a spectrum is projected inside the box. Arrange the thermometers so that one is just outside the red end of the spectrum, with no direct light on it. After 10 min, record the temperatures. Which thermometer recorded the highest temperature? Explain why. **ACTIVITY**

Answer to Connection to Physics
The thermometer that was placed just outside of the visible spectrum recorded the highest temperature, because infrared radiation is warmer than visible light. (Note: A detailed procedure and diagrams of this experiment are available on the Internet.)

Chapter 18 • Studying Space

Nonoptical Telescopes in Space

Because most electromagnetic waves are blocked by the Earth's atmosphere, scientists have placed ultraviolet telescopes, infrared telescopes, gamma-ray telescopes, and X-ray telescopes in space. The *Chandra X-Ray Observatory*, a space-based telescope that detects X rays, is illustrated in **Figure 7**. X-ray telescopes in space can be much more sensitive than optical telescopes. For example, NASA has tested an X-ray telescope that can detect an object that is the size of a frisbee on the surface of the sun. If an optical telescope had a similar power, it could detect a hair on the head of an astronaut on the moon!

Reading Check Why are X-ray telescopes placed in space?

Figure 7 The Chandra X-Ray Observatory *can detect black holes and some of the most distant objects in the universe.*

SECTION Review

Summary

- Refracting telescopes use lenses to gather and focus light.
- Reflecting telescopes use mirrors to gather and focus light.
- Astronomers study all wavelengths of the electromagnetic spectrum, including radio waves, microwaves, infrared light, visible light, ultraviolet light, X rays, and gamma rays.
- The atmosphere blocks most forms of electromagnetic radiation from reaching the Earth. To overcome this limitation, astronomers place telescopes in space.

Using Key Terms

For each pair of terms, explain how the meanings of the terms differ.

1. *refracting telescope* and *reflecting telescope*
2. *telescope* and *electromagnetic spectrum*

Understanding Key Ideas

3. How does the atmosphere affect astronomical observations?
   a. It focuses visible light.
   b. It blocks most electromagnetic radiation.
   c. It blocks all radio waves.
   d. It does not affect astronomical observations.
4. Describe how reflecting and refracting telescopes work.
5. What limits the size of a refracting telescope? Explain.
6. What advantages do reflecting telescopes have over refracting telescopes?
7. List the types of radiation in the electromagnetic spectrum, from the longest wavelength to the shortest wavelength. Then, describe how astronomers study each type of radiation.

Math Skills

8. A telescope's light-gathering power is proportional to the area of its objective lens or mirror. If the diameter of a lens is 1 m, what is the area of the lens? (Hint: $area = 3.1416 \times radius^2$)

Critical Thinking

9. **Applying Concepts** Describe three reasons why Hawaii is a good location for a telescope.
10. **Making Inferences** Why doesn't the surface of a radio telescope have to be as flawless as the surface of a mirror in an optical telescope?
11. **Making Inferences** What limitation of a refracting telescope could be overcome by placing the telescope in space?

For a variety of links related to this chapter, go to www.scilinks.org

Topic: Telescopes
SciLinks code: HSM1500

Answer to Reading Check

because the atmosphere blocks most X-ray radiation from space

Answers to Section Review

1. Sample answer: A refracting telescope uses lenses to gather and focus light. A reflecting telescope uses mirrors to gather and focus light.
2. A telescope is an instrument that is used to observe electromagnetic radiation. The electromagnetic spectrum consists of all of the wavelengths of electromagnetic radiation.
3. b
4. A refracting telescope has an objective lens that gathers and focuses light. Another lens in the eyepiece magnifies the image produced by the objective lens. A reflecting telescope has a large curved mirror that reflects light to a flat mirror. A lens in the eyepiece magnifies the image reflected from the flat mirror for observation.
5. The size of the objective lens limits the size of a refracting telescope. If the lens is too large, it sags and distorts images.
6. Answers may vary. Reflecting telescopes can be more powerful than refracting telescopes because reflecting telescopes are not limited by the size of the objective lens. Also, mirrors reflect all wavelengths of light to the same focal point, and lenses focus different wavelengths at slightly different distances.
7. radio waves, microwaves, infrared, visible light, ultraviolet, X rays, gamma rays; Astronomers use reflecting and refracting telescopes to study visible light, and special nonoptical telescopes to study the other forms of electromagnetic radiation.
8. 3.1416×0.25 m^2 = 0.79 m^2
9. Hawaii has little light pollution. Air pollution is also minimal. In addition, Hawaii has many tall volcanoes, some of which are good sites for observatories.
10. The surface of a radio telescope does not have to be as flawless as the surface of a mirror in an optical telescope because radio waves are much larger than visible light waves.
11. The atmosphere distorts radiation passing through it, and light pollution can limit an astronomer's ability to see faint objects. In addition, Earth's gravity causes the objective lens to sag, which distorts images. Placing a telescope in space can solve these problems.

CHAPTER RESOURCES

Chapter Resource File
- Section Quiz GENERAL
- Section Review GENERAL
- Vocabulary and Section Summary GENERAL
- Critical Thinking ADVANCED
- SciLinks Activity GENERAL

Section 2 • Telescopes

SECTION 3

Focus

Overview

This section discusses constellations and their significance to ancient and modern astronomers. Students will learn how to use a sky map to find stars in the night sky. The section also explains how the celestial sphere helps astronomers describe the location of stars. The section defines *light-year* and concludes with a discussion of the size and scale of the universe.

🔔 Bellringer

Ask students if it is possible to determine the direction of the North Pole by looking at the stars. Have students explain their answers in their **science journal.**

Motivate

Discussion — GENERAL

Naming Constellations Ask students to think of other possible names for the constellation in **Figure 1.** Discuss why people such as farmers, poets, and astronomers have been inspired to name and identify constellations. As an extension, ask students to observe the night sky at home and name their own constellations. Students can write a legend about their constellation and share a sketch of it with the class. **LS Verbal/Visual**

SECTION 3

READING WARM-UP

Objectives
- Explain how constellations are used to organize the night sky.
- Describe how the altitude of a star is measured.
- Explain how the celestial sphere is used to describe the location of objects in the sky.
- Compare size and scale in the universe, and explain how red shift indicates that the universe is expanding.

Terms to Learn
constellation   horizon
zenith   light-year
altitude

READING STRATEGY

Paired Summarizing Read this section silently. In pairs, take turns summarizing the material. Stop to discuss ideas that seem confusing.

CHAPTER RESOURCES

Chapter Resource File
- Lesson Plan
- Directed Reading A BASIC
- Directed Reading B SPECIAL NEEDS

Technology
- Transparencies
  - Bellringer
  - Spring Constellations in the Northern Hemisphere

Mapping the Stars

Have you ever seen Orion the Hunter or the Big Dipper in the night sky? Ancient cultures linked stars together to form patterns that represented characters from myths and objects in their lives.

Today, we can see the same star patterns that people in ancient cultures saw. Modern astronomers still use many of the names given to stars centuries ago. But astronomers can now describe a star's location precisely. Advances in astronomy have led to a better understanding of how far away stars are and how big the universe is.

Patterns in the Sky

When people in ancient cultures connected stars in patterns, they named sections of the sky based on the patterns. These patterns are called *constellations*. **Constellations** are sections of the sky that contain recognizable star patterns. Understanding the location and movement of constellations helped people navigate and keep track of time.

Different civilizations had different names for the same constellations. For example, where the Greeks saw a hunter (Orion) in the northern sky, the Japanese saw a drum, as shown in **Figure 1.** Today, different cultures still interpret the sky in different ways, but astronomers have agreed on the names and locations of the constellations.

Figure 1 The ancient Greeks saw Orion as a hunter, but the Japanese saw the same set of stars as a drum.

Is That a Fact!

The International Astronomical Union has standardized the boundaries of the 88 constellations so that the total area of the celestial sphere can be classified according to the constellations. Thus, the constellations fit together like a jigsaw puzzle that surrounds the Earth.

---

564 Chapter 18 • Studying Space

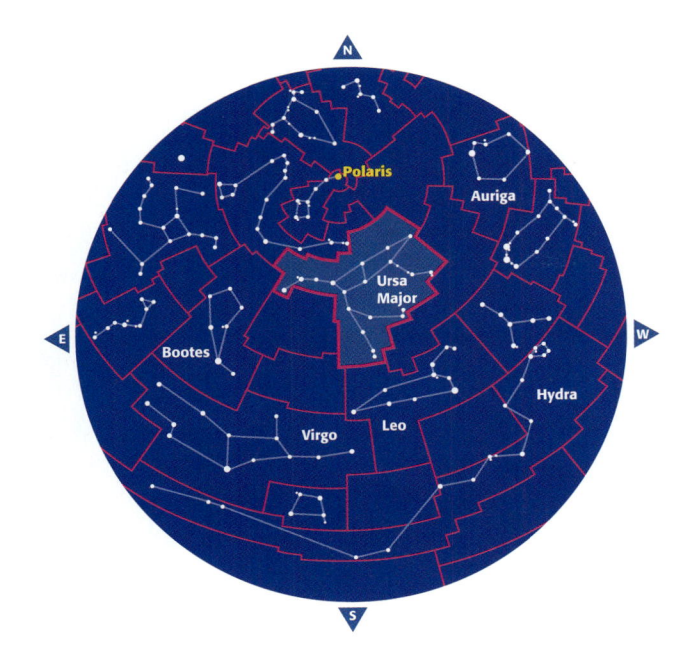

Figure 2 This sky map shows some of the constellations in the Northern Hemisphere at midnight in the spring. Ursa Major (the Great Bear) is a region of the sky that includes all of the stars that make up that constellation.

constellation a region of the sky that contains a recognizable star pattern and that is used to describe the location of objects in space

Constellations Help Organize the Sky

When you think of constellations, you probably think of the stick figures made by connecting bright stars with imaginary lines. To an astronomer, however, a constellation is something more. As you can see in **Figure 2,** a constellation is a region of the sky. Each constellation shares a border with neighboring constellations. For example, in the same way that the state of Texas is a region of the United States, Ursa Major is a region of the sky. Every star or galaxy is located within 1 of 88 constellations.

Seasonal Changes

The sky map in **Figure 2** shows what the midnight sky in the Northern Hemisphere looks like in the spring. But as the Earth revolves around the sun, the apparent locations of the constellations change from season to season. In addition, different constellations are visible in the Southern Hemisphere. Thus, a child in Chile can see different constellations than you can. Therefore, this map is not accurate for the other three seasons or for the Southern Hemisphere. Sky maps for summer, fall, and winter in the Northern Hemisphere appear in the Appendix of this book.

✓ **Reading Check** Why are different constellations visible in the Northern and Southern Hemispheres? *(See the Appendix for answers to Reading Checks.)*

Quick Lab

Using a Sky Map

1. Hold your **textbook** over your head with the cover facing upward. Turn the book so that the direction at the bottom of the sky map is the same as the direction you are facing.
2. Notice the locations of the constellations in relation to each other.
3. If you look up at the sky at night in the spring, you should see the stars positioned as they are on your map.
4. Why are *E* and *W* on sky maps the reverse of how they appear on land maps?

Teach

Cultural Awareness — ADVANCED

Greek Constellations Many of the names of constellations are derived from Greek and Roman mythology. Have groups research the mythology of Cepheus, Cassiopeia, Perseus, Pegasus, Hercules, or the Hydra. Groups can write a skit to retell the myth for the class. Then, have groups use a star map to locate their constellation.
LS Interpersonal/Verbal

Quick Lab

MATERIALS
For Each Student
• textbook

Answer
4. The directions are reversed because sky maps are made to be looked at upside down.

Answer to Reading Check
Different constellations are visible in the Northern and Southern Hemispheres because different portions of the sky are visible from the Northern and Southern Hemispheres.

Group Activity — ADVANCED

Classroom Planetarium Organize the class into groups of four. Assign each group a different season, and have the groups locate a sky map for that season. Have students copy the map with tracing paper and mark the stars that form constellations and any other celestial objects. Then, have groups place a sheet of aluminum foil over a piece of cardboard and tape the tracing paper on top. Have students use a pencil to carefully poke small holes through the tracing paper and aluminum. Students can create larger holes to show planets and other bright objects. After students remove the tracing paper, have them locate the constellations and prepare a guided tour of the night sky in their season. To begin the tour, place the aluminum-foil transparencies on an overhead projector in a dark room. Be sure to cover the lighted surface of the projector completely.

Safety Caution: Be sure to check the projector periodically for overheating.

As groups give their tours, they can highlight individual constellations by using a piece of colored cellophane. **LS Visual**

Section 3 • Mapping the Stars

Teach, continued

ACTIVITY — GENERAL

A Compass on Your Wrist Tell students that a watch that has an hour hand can be used to tell direction during the daytime. Have students hold a watch horizontally such that the hour hand (the shorter hand) points directly at the sun. If they halve the distance between the hour hand and the 12 with a toothpick, the toothpick will be pointing south. Ask students how they would adapt this method to work in the Southern Hemisphere. **LS Kinesthetic/Logical**

CONNECTION ACTIVITY
Real World — BASIC

Measuring the Sky with Your Hands Amateur astronomers can measure the sky by using their hands. If you extend your arm and make a fist that begins at the horizon, you can gauge roughly 10°. If you open your hand and align your little finger with the horizon, you have marked off 20°. **English Language Learners**
LS Kinesthetic

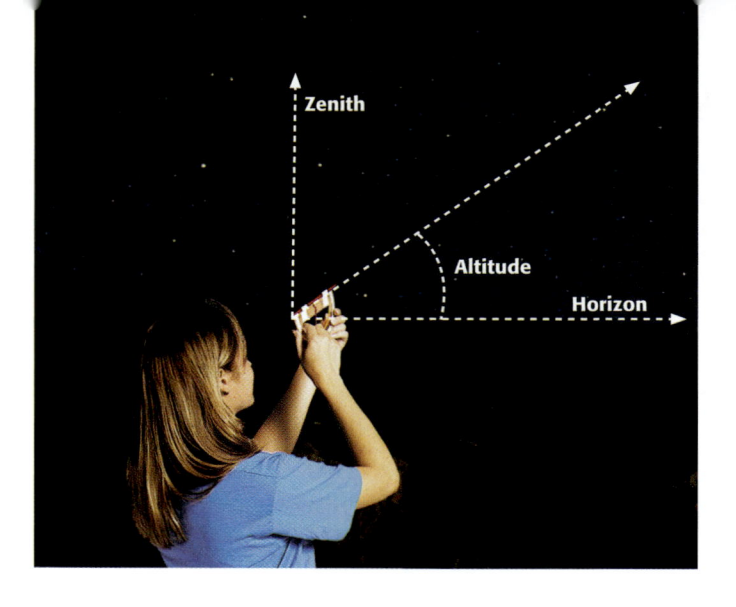

Figure 3 Using an astrolabe, you can determine the altitude of a star by measuring the angle between the horizon and a star. The altitude of any object depends on where you are and when you look.

zenith the point in the sky directly above an observer on Earth

altitude the angle between an object in the sky and the horizon

horizon the line where the sky and the Earth appear to meet

The **zenith** is an imaginary point in the sky directly above an observer on Earth. The zenith always has an altitude of 90°.

Finding Stars in the Night Sky

Have you ever tried to show someone a star by pointing to it? Did the person miss what you were seeing? If you use an instrument called an *astrolabe*, shown in **Figure 3,** you can describe the location of a star or planet. To use an astrolabe correctly, you need to understand the three points of reference shown in **Figure 4**. This method is useful to describe the location of a star relative to where you are. But if you want to describe a star's location in relation to the Earth, you need to use the celestial sphere, shown in **Figure 5**.

Figure 4 Zenith, Altitude, and Horizon

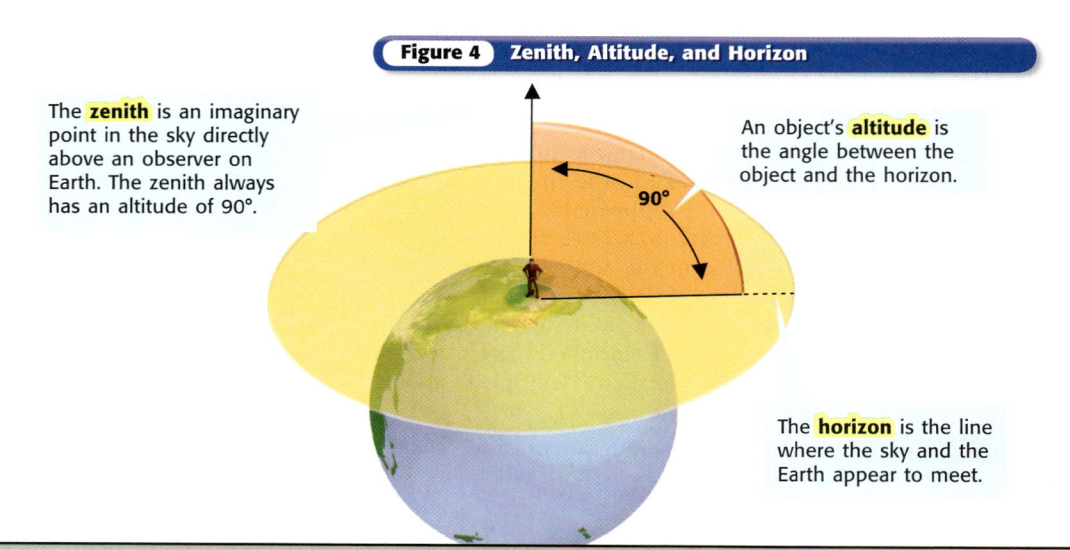

An object's **altitude** is the angle between the object and the horizon.

The **horizon** is the line where the sky and the Earth appear to meet.

MISCONCEPTION ALERT

Altitude Students may be confused by the term *altitude* when it is used in astronomy. Point out that altitude does not denote height or elevation but rather the angle between an object, the horizon, and the observer. As the Earth rotates, the altitude of the stars changes. The altitude of an object is also affected by the location of the observer.

Group ACTIVITY — GENERAL

Space Science Exploration Engage the class in a space science Internet orientation. There are hundreds of well-maintained Web sites with stunning images from all over the universe. Students will be excited to find these images and share them with the class.
LS Interpersonal

---

566 Chapter 18 • Studying Space

Figure 5 The Celestial Sphere

To talk to each other about the location of a star, astronomers must have a common method of describing a star's location. The method that astronomers have invented is based on a reference system known as the *celestial sphere*. The celestial sphere is an imaginary sphere that surrounds the Earth. Just as we use latitude and longitude to plot positions on Earth, astronomers use right ascension and declination to plot positions in the sky. *Right ascension* is a measure of how far east an object is from the *vernal equinox*, the location of the sun on the first day of spring. *Declination* is a measure of how far north or south an object is from the celestial equator.

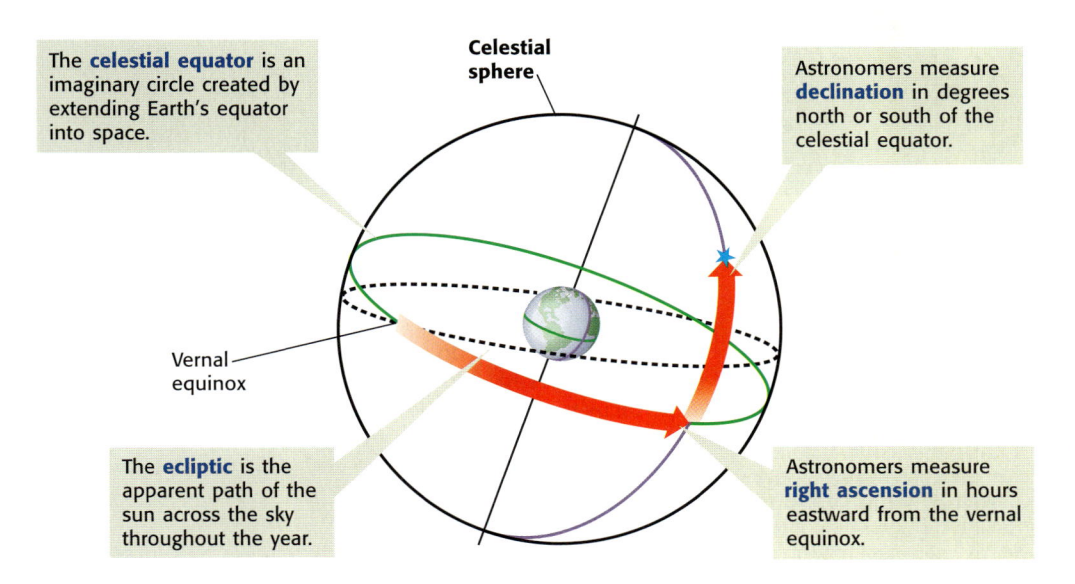

The **celestial equator** is an imaginary circle created by extending Earth's equator into space.

Celestial sphere

Astronomers measure **declination** in degrees north or south of the celestial equator.

Vernal equinox

The **ecliptic** is the apparent path of the sun across the sky throughout the year.

Astronomers measure **right ascension** in hours eastward from the vernal equinox.

The Path of Stars Across the Sky

Just as the sun appears to move across the sky during the day, most stars and planets rise and set throughout the night. This apparent motion is caused by the Earth's rotation. As the Earth spins on its axis, stars and planets appear to move. Near the poles, however, stars are circumpolar. *Circumpolar stars* are stars that can be seen at all times of year and all times of night. These stars never set, and they appear to circle the celestial poles. You also see different stars in the sky depending on the time of year. Why? The reason is that as the Earth travels around the sun, different areas of the universe are visible.

✓ **Reading Check** How is the apparent movement of the sun similar to the apparent movement of most stars during the night?

CHAPTER RESOURCES

Technology

📦 **Transparencies**
• Zenith, Altitude, and Horizon
• The Celestial Sphere

ACTIVITY — GENERAL

📁 **SpaceLog** As students read this chapter, have them keep a SpaceLog at home. Encourage them to observe the night sky for 10 minutes every night and record their observations. Students can annotate their SpaceLog with photographs and magazine or newspaper articles that relate to what they are learning in this chapter.
LS Intrapersonal

Homework — GENERAL

Locating Polaris The Big Dipper is an easily recognizable group of stars that can be seen from the mid-northern latitudes all year. If students are unfamiliar with the Big Dipper, draw it on the board or show them a picture of it. Ask students to use a star chart to locate the Big Dipper on a clear night. After students have located the Big Dipper, they can easily find Polaris (the North Star). The two stars that make up the front of the dipper bowl point directly toward Polaris. To find Polaris, students should estimate the distance between the two stars that make up the front of the bowl. Students can pinpoint the North Star by extending from the front two stars of the bowl an imaginary line that is 5 times the length of that distance.

Answer to Reading Check

The apparent movement of the sun and stars is caused by the Earth's rotation on its axis.

Section 3 • Mapping the Stars

Teach, continued

MISCONCEPTION ALERT

The Distance of Stars A common misconception is that each star in a constellation is the same distance from Earth. In fact, most of the stars in a constellation are not near each other in space. They appear to be near each other because of our perspective from Earth. If Earth were in a different location, we would see the same stars in different patterns or might see different stars altogether.

CONNECTION ACTIVITY
Math — GENERAL

Calculating a Light-Year
The textbook indicates that the distance light travels in a year is 9.46 trillion kilometers. Have students verify this distance by doing the calculation themselves. Ask students to calculate the distance light travels in 1 day. (approximately 26 billion kilometers) **LS Logical**

Answer to Reading Check
9.46 trillion kilometers

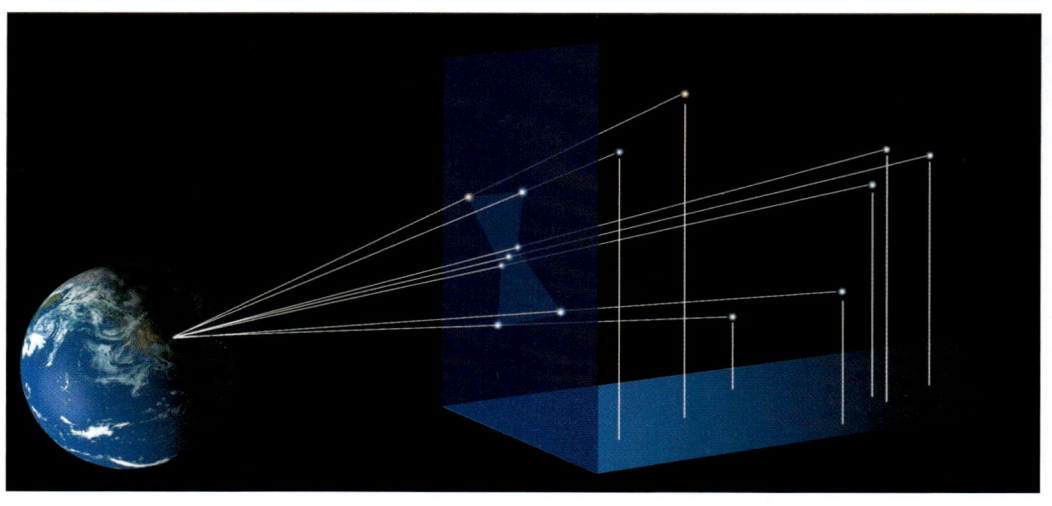

Figure 6 While the stars in the constellation Orion may appear to be near each other when they are seen from Earth, they are actually very far apart.

light-year the distance that light travels in one year; about 9.46 trillion kilometers

INTERNET ACTIVITY
For another activity related to this chapter, go to **go.hrw.com** and type in the keyword **HZ5OBSW**.

The Size and Scale of the Universe
Imagine looking out the window of a moving car. Nearby trees appear to move more quickly than farther trees do. Objects that are very far away do not appear to move at all. The same principle applies to stars and planets. In the 1500s, Nicolaus Copernicus noticed that the planets appeared to move relative to each other but that the stars did not. Thus, he thought that the stars must be much farther away than the planets.

Measuring Distance in Space
Today, we know that Copernicus was correct. The stars are much farther away than the planets are. In fact, stars are so distant that a new unit of length—the light-year—was created to measure their distance. A **light-year** is a unit of length equal to the distance that light travels in 1 year. One light-year is equal to about 9.46 trillion kilometers! The farthest objects we can observe are more than 10 billion light-years away. Although the stars may appear to be at similar distances from Earth, their distances vary greatly. For example, **Figure 6** shows how far away the stars that make up part of Orion are.

✓ **Reading Check** How far does light travel in 1 year?

Considering Scale in the Universe
When you think about the universe and all of the objects it contains, it is important to consider scale. For example, stars appear to be very small in the night sky. But we know that most stars are a lot larger than Earth. **Figure 7** will help you understand the scale of objects in the universe.

CONNECTION to
History — GENERAL

The North Star in History Polaris has not always been the North Star. Nearly 5,000 years ago, a faint star named Thuban in the constellation Draco held that honor. Because the Earth wobbles on its axis, the location of the north celestial pole changes on a 25,780-year cycle. Some theories argue that the Great Pyramid of Giza was built such that its main passageway aligned with Thuban. Because Thuban did not appear to move in the night sky, it symbolized immortality. In 12,000 years, Vega will replace Polaris as the pole star.

Figure 7 From Home Plate to 10 Million Light-Years Away

1. Let's start with home plate in a baseball stadium. You are looking down from a distance of about 10 m.

2. At 1,000 m (1 km) away, you can see the baseball stadium and the surrounding neighborhood.

3. At 100 km away, you see the city that contains the stadium and the countryside around the city.

4. At 100,000 km away, you can see the Earth and the moon.

5. At 1,500,000,000 km (83 light-minutes) away, you can look back at the sun and the inner planets.

6. At 150 light-days, the solar system, surrounded by a cloud of comets and other icy debris, can be seen.

7. By the time you are 10 light-years away, the sun resembles any other star in space.

8. At 1 million light-years away, our galaxy looks like the Andromeda galaxy, a cloud of stars set in the blackness of space.

9. At 10 million light-years away, you can see a handful of galaxies called the *Local Group*.

Is That a Fact!

The *Hubble Space Telescope* has relayed the first detailed images of distant galaxies. These images have led astronomers to think that there may be 10 times the number of galaxies in the universe than previously thought. Students will enjoy finding images from the *Hubble Space Telescope* on the Internet and sharing them with the class.

CHAPTER RESOURCES

Technology

Transparencies
- From Home Plate to 10 Million Light-Years Away

Discussion — ADVANCED

Expanding Universe Students may assume that because the universe is expanding, every star they see is moving away from Earth. Point out that the only stars visible with the unaided eye are the ones in our galaxy, which is not expanding. The Milky Way is not expanding for the same reason that our solar system is not expanding— gravity holds moving bodies in orbit. The Milky Way and the Andromeda galaxies are part of the Local Group, a galaxy cluster of 30 galaxies. The galaxies that make up a galaxy cluster are also held together by gravity. The expansion of the universe occurs as galaxy clusters move apart from one another.

If the expansion of the universe were compared to baking a chocolate chip cookie, the chocolate chips would represent galaxy clusters. As the cookie bakes, the chocolate chips do not change in size; however, as the dough expands, the space between the chocolate chips increases. **LS Logical**

CONNECTION ACTIVITY
Math — GENERAL

Scientific Notation Have students convert the following numbers to or from scientific notation:

1,200 (1.2×10^3)

150,000 (1.5×10^5)

3.2×10^6 (3,200,000)

790,000,000 (7.9×10^8)

5.6×10^{12} (5,600,000,000,000)

LS Logical

Section 3 • Mapping the Stars

Close

Reteaching — BASIC
Section Outlines Have students create an outline of this section by using the headings and subheadings. **LS Intrapersonal**

Quiz — GENERAL
1. What is the celestial equator? (an imaginary circle extending from Earth's equator into space)
2. Why is using the celestial sphere a better way to indicate the position of a star than using altitude is? (Altitude is dependent on an observer's location and the time of night. The celestial sphere is a coordinate system that uses the Earth as a reference.)

Alternative Assessment — GENERAL
Celestial Guidebook Have groups of students develop for the novice stargazer a guidebook that includes a glossary of astronomical terms. Encourage students to include diagrams, illustrations, and analogies to help clarify their entries. **English Language Learners** **LS Interpersonal**

Answer to Reading Check
One might conclude that all of the galaxies are traveling toward the Earth and that the universe is contracting.

Figure 8 As an object moves away from an observer at a high speed, the light from the object appears redder. As the object moves toward the observer, the light from the object appears bluer.

The Doppler Effect
Have you ever noticed that when a driver in an approaching car blows the horn, the horn sounds higher pitched as the car approaches and lower pitched after the car passes? This effect is called the *Doppler effect*. As shown in **Figure 8,** the Doppler effect also occurs with light. If a light source, such as a star or galaxy, is moving quickly away from an observer, the light emitted looks redder than it normally does. This effect is called *redshift*. If a star or galaxy is moving quickly toward an observer, its light appears bluer than it normally does. This effect is known as *blueshift*.

An Expanding Universe
After discovering that the universe is made up of many other galaxies like our own, Edwin Hubble analyzed the light from galaxies and stars to study the general direction that objects in the universe are moving. Hubble soon made another startling discovery—the light from all galaxies except our close neighbors is affected by redshift. This means that galaxies are rapidly moving apart from each other. In other words, because all galaxies except our close neighbors are moving apart, the universe must be expanding. **Figure 9** shows evidence of redshift recorded by the *Hubble Space Telescope* in 2002.

✓ **Reading Check** What logical conclusion could be made if the light from all of the galaxies were affected by blueshift?

Figure 9 The galaxy that is cut off at the bottom of this image is moving away from us at a much slower speed than the other galaxies are. Distant galaxies are visible as faint disks.

Homework — GENERAL
Observing Stars Over a week or two, have students use a sky map to identify some of the brighter stars and planets in the night sky. Even if students live in a city, they should be able to locate Betelgeuse, Rigel, and Sirius in winter. In addition, they may be able to spot Venus, Mars, or Jupiter. Students should keep an observer's log in which they record the date; time; sky conditions; instruments used, if any (binoculars are an excellent aid, if available); descriptions and names of objects observed; and drawings of constellations. Students can supplement their logs with astronomical research on the objects that they observe. If possible, have students compare their logs in class. **LS Intrapersonal/Visual**

SECTION Review

Summary

- Astronomers use constellations to organize the sky.
- Altitude, or the angle between an object and the horizon, can be used to describe the location of an object in the sky.
- The celestial sphere is an imaginary sphere that surrounds the Earth. Using the celestial sphere, astronomers can accurately describe the location of an object without reference to an observer.
- A light-year is the distance that light travels in 1 year.
- The Doppler effect causes the light emitted by objects that are moving away from an observer to appear to shift toward the red end of the spectrum. Objects moving toward an observer are shifted to the blue end of the spectrum.
- Observations of redshift and blueshift indicate that the universe is expanding.

Using Key Terms

The statements below are false. For each statement, replace the underlined term to make a true statement.

1. Zenith is the angle between an object and the horizon.
2. The distance that light travels in 1 year is called a light-meter.

Understanding Key Ideas

3. Stars appear to move across the night sky because of
   a. the rotation of Earth on its axis.
   b. the movement of the Milky Way galaxy.
   c. the movement of stars in the universe.
   d. the revolution of Earth around the sun.
4. How do astronomers use the celestial sphere to plot a star's exact position?
5. How do constellations relate to patterns of stars? How are constellations like states?
6. Why are different sky maps needed for different times of the year?
7. What are redshift and blueshift? Why are these effects useful in the study of the universe?

Critical Thinking

8. **Applying Concepts** Light from the Andromeda galaxy is affected by blueshift. What can you conclude about this galaxy?
9. **Making Comparisons** Explain how Copernicus concluded that stars were farther away than planets. Draw a diagram showing how this principle applies to another example.

Interpreting Graphics

The diagram below shows the altitude of Star A and Star B. Use the diagram below to answer the questions that follow.

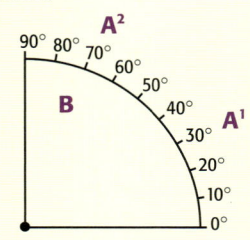

10. What is the approximate altitude of star B?
11. In 4 h, star A moved from A^1 to A^2. How many degrees did the star move each hour?

Answers to Section Review

1. Altitude
2. light-year
3. a
4. The celestial sphere is a coordinate system that uses the Earth as a reference. Declination indicates how far north or south from the celestial equator an object is. Right ascension indicates how far east or west from the vernal equinox an object is.
5. Constellations are patterns of stars. They are similar to states because both are regions of a much larger area. Like states, constellations share borders with each other.
6. Different sky maps are needed for different times of the year because as the Earth orbits the sun, different stars become visible.
7. Redshift occurs when an object is moving rapidly away from an observer. Light emitted from the object appears to be shifted toward the red end of the spectrum. Blueshift occurs when an object is moving rapidly toward an observer. Light emitted from the object appears to be shifted toward the blue end of the spectrum. Redshifts are also found in distant galaxies, which is the result of an expanding universe.
8. Students should conclude that the Andromeda galaxy is moving toward us.
9. Copernicus concluded that the stars were farther away than the planets because the planets moved more quickly than stars throughout the year. The effect is similar to how nearby objects observed from the window of a moving car appear to move more quickly than distant objects.
10. about 70°
11. 40° ÷ 4 h = 10° per hour (Note that this question is intended to help students sharpen basic math skills and that the actual movement of stars is much more complex.)

CHAPTER RESOURCES

Chapter Resource File
- Section Quiz GENERAL
- Section Review GENERAL
- Vocabulary and Section Summary GENERAL

Section 3 • Mapping the Stars

Skills Practice Lab

Through the Looking Glass

Teacher's Notes

Time Required
One 45-minute class period

Lab Ratings
EASY → HARD

Teacher Prep 🧪🧪
Student Set-Up 🧪🧪🧪
Concept Level 🧪🧪
Clean Up 🧪

MATERIALS
The materials listed on the student page are enough for a group of 2 or 3 students.

Safety Caution
Remind students to review all safety cautions and icons before beginning this lab activity. Students should never look at the sun through their telescopes. Caution students not to focus sunlight through their telescopes because a fire could start.

Skills Practice Lab

Through the Looking Glass

Have you ever looked toward the horizon or up into the sky and wished that you could see farther? Do you think that a telescope might help you see farther? Astronomers use huge telescopes to study the universe. You can build your own telescope to get a glimpse of how these enormous, technologically advanced telescopes help astronomers see distant objects.

OBJECTIVES
Construct a simple model of a refracting telescope.
Observe distant objects by using your telescope.

MATERIALS
- clay, modeling (1 stick)
- convex lens, 3 cm in diameter (2 of different focal length)
- lamp, desk
- paper, white (1 sheet)
- ruler, metric
- scissors
- tape, masking (1 roll)
- toilet-paper tube, cardboard
- wrapping paper tube, cardboard

SAFETY

Procedure

1. Use modeling clay to form a base that holds one of the lenses upright on your desktop. When the lights are turned off, your teacher will turn on a lamp at the front of the classroom. Rotate your lens so that the light from the lamp passes through the lens.

2. Hold the paper so that the light passing through the lens lands on the paper. To sharpen the image of the light on the paper, slowly move the paper closer to or farther from the lens. Hold the paper in the position in which the image is sharpest.

3. Using the metric ruler, measure the distance between the lens and the paper. Record this distance.

Preparation Notes
One week before the activity, ask students to collect wrapping-paper and toilet-paper cardboard tubes to bring to class. Obtain two double-convex lenses.

You may wish to experiment with the lenses before class to determine their focal length. If you add another lens to the telescope, you can make the image right side up, but light is lost as it passes through the third lens.

CHAPTER RESOURCES

Chapter Resource File
- Datasheet for Chapter Lab
- Lab Notes and Answers

Technology

Classroom Videos
- Lab Video

LabBook
- The Sun's Yearly Trip Through the Zodiac

4. How far is the paper from the lens? This distance, called the *focal length*, is the distance that the paper has to be from the lens for the image to be in focus.

5. Repeat steps 1–4 using the other lens.

6. Measuring from one end of the long cardboard tube, mark the focal length of the lens that has the longer focal length. Place a mark 2 cm past this line toward the other end of the tube, and label the mark "Cut."

7. Measuring from one end of the short cardboard tube, mark the focal length of the lens that has the shorter focal length. Place a mark 2 cm past this line toward the other end of the tube, and label the mark "Cut."

8. Shorten the tubes by cutting along the marks labeled "Cut." Wear safety goggles when you make these cuts.

9. Tape the lens that has the longer focal length to one end of the longer tube. Tape the other lens to one end of the shorter tube. Slip the empty end of one tube inside the empty end of the other tube. Be sure that there is one lens at each end of this new, longer tube.

10. Congratulations! You have just constructed a telescope. To use your telescope, look through the short tube (the eyepiece) and point the long end at various objects in the room. You can focus the telescope by adjusting its length. Are the images right side up or upside down? Observe birds, insects, trees, or other outside objects. Record the images that you see. **Caution:** NEVER look directly at the sun! Looking directly at the sun could cause permanent blindness.

Analyze the Results

1. **Analyzing Results** Which type of telescope did you just construct: a refracting telescope or a reflecting telescope? What makes your telescope one type and not the other?

2. **Identifying Patterns** What factor determines the focal length of a lens?

Draw Conclusions

3. **Evaluating Results** How would you improve your telescope?

Background

Begin the activity by discussing the components of a telescope. Simple telescopes, such as the one Galileo made, consist of two lenses and a tube. For the telescope to provide a clear image, the tube should be as long as the total of the focal lengths of the two lenses. Some students may have difficulty knowing when the image is in focus. Explain to these students that they should focus the light bulb's filament on the paper.

Analyze the Results

1. Sample answer: We just constructed a refracting telescope. Refracting telescopes use lenses. Reflecting telescopes use mirrors and lenses.

2. Answers may vary. Students should notice that the size and shape of a lens determine the focal length of the lens.

Draw Conclusions

3. Answers may vary. Accept all reasonable responses.

CHAPTER RESOURCES

Workbooks

Whiz-Bang Demonstrations
• Refraction Action GENERAL

Inquiry Labs
• Constellation Prize ADVANCED

Long-Term Projects & Research Ideas
• Celestial Inspiration ADVANCED

CLASSROOM TESTED & APPROVED

Michael E. Kral
West Hardin Middle School
Cecilia, Kentucky

Chapter Review

Assignment Guide

SECTION	QUESTIONS
1	6, 8–9, 18, 20
2	2, 5, 7, 14, 16, 19
3	3, 10–13, 15, 17, 21–22
1 and 3	4
1, 2, and 3	1

ANSWERS

Using Key Terms

1. Sample answer: A year is the amount of time Earth takes to complete one orbit around the sun. A month is based on the phases of the moon. A day is the amount of time Earth takes to rotate once on its axis. Astronomy is the study of the universe. The electromagnetic spectrum is made up of all forms of electromagnetic radiation. A constellation is a region of the sky that contains a recognizable pattern of stars. Altitude is the angle between an observer, the horizon, and an object in the sky.

2. Sample answer: Refracting telescopes use lenses to magnify and focus an image, and reflecting telescopes use mirrors to magnify and focus an image.

3. Sample answer: The zenith is a point in the sky that is directly above an observer. The horizon is the line where the Earth and the sky appear to meet.

Chapter Review

USING KEY TERMS

1. Use each of the following terms in a separate sentence: *year, month, day, astronomy, electromagnetic spectrum, constellation,* and *altitude.*

For each pair of terms, explain how the meanings of the terms differ.

2. *reflecting telescope* and *refracting telescope*

3. *zenith* and *horizon*

4. *year* and *light-year*

UNDERSTANDING KEY IDEAS

Multiple Choice

5. Which of the following answer choices lists types of electromagnetic radiation from longest wavelength to shortest wavelength?
   a. radio waves, ultraviolet light, infrared light
   b. infrared light, microwaves, X rays
   c. X rays, ultraviolet light, gamma rays
   d. microwaves, infrared light, visible light

6. The length of a day is based on the amount of time that
   a. Earth takes to orbit the sun one time.
   b. Earth takes to rotate once on its axis.
   c. the moon takes to orbit Earth one time.
   d. the moon takes to rotate once on its axis.

7. Which of the following statements about X rays and radio waves from objects in space is true?
   a. Both types of radiation can be observed by using the same telescope.
   b. Separate telescopes are needed to observe each type of radiation, but both telescopes can be on Earth.
   c. Separate telescopes are needed to observe each type of radiation, but both telescopes must be in space.
   d. Separate telescopes are needed to observe each type of radiation, but only one of the telescopes must be in space.

8. According to ___, Earth is at the center of the universe.
   a. the Ptolemaic theory
   b. Copernicus's theory
   c. Galileo's theory
   d. None of the above

9. Which scientist was one of the first scientists to successfully use a telescope to observe the night sky?
   a. Brahe   c. Hubble
   b. Galileo   d. Kepler

10. Astronomers divide the sky into
    a. galaxies.   c. zeniths.
    b. constellations.   d. phases.

11. ___ determines which stars you see in the sky.
    a. Your latitude
    b. The time of year
    c. The time of night
    d. All of the above

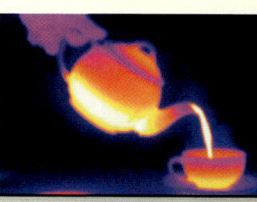

4. Sample answer: A year is the amount of time Earth takes to complete one orbit around the sun. A light-year is the distance that light travels in one year.

Understanding Key Ideas

5. d	10. b
6. b	11. d
7. d	12. a
8. a	13. b
9. b	14. c

574 Chapter 18 • Studying Space

12. The altitude of an object in the sky is the object's angular distance
    a. above the horizon.
    b. from the north celestial pole.
    c. from the zenith.
    d. from the prime meridian.

13. Right ascension is a measure of how far east an object in the sky is from
    a. the observer.
    b. the vernal equinox.
    c. the moon.
    d. Venus.

14. Telescopes that work on Earth's surface include all of the following EXCEPT
    a. radio telescopes.
    b. refracting telescopes.
    c. X-ray telescopes.
    d. reflecting telescopes.

Short Answer

15. Explain how right ascension and declination are similar to latitude and longitude.

16. How does a reflecting telescope work?

CRITICAL THINKING

17. **Concept Mapping** Use the following terms to create a concept map: *right ascension, declination, celestial sphere, degrees, hours, celestial equator,* and *vernal equinox.*

18. **Making Inferences** Why was seeing objects in the sky easier for people in ancient cultures than it is for most people today? What tools help modern people study objects in space in greater detail than was possible in the past?

19. **Making Inferences** Because many forms of radiation from space do not penetrate Earth's atmosphere, astronomers' ability to detect this radiation is limited. But how does the protection of the atmosphere benefit humans?

20. **Analyzing Ideas** Explain why the Ptolemaic theory seems logical based on daily observations of the rising and setting of the sun.

INTERPRETING GRAPHICS

Use the sky map below to answer the questions that follow. (Example: The star Aldebaran is located at about 4 h, 30 min right ascension, 16° declination.)

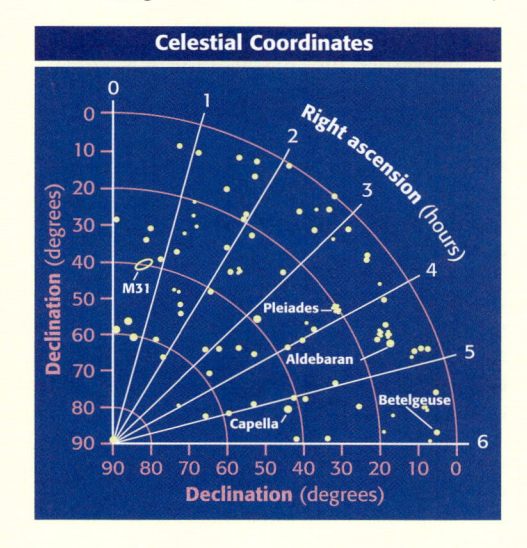

Celestial Coordinates

21. What object is located near 5 h, 55 min right ascension, and 7° declination?

22. What are the celestial coordinates for the Andromeda galaxy (M31)? Round off the right ascension to the nearest half-hour.

---

15. Sample answer: Right ascension and declination are similar to latitude and longitude because both are coordinate systems that use Earth as a reference point.

16. A reflecting telescope uses a large mirror to gather and focus light. A second mirror, located in front of the focal point, directs light toward an eyepiece for observation.

Critical Thinking

17. An answer to this exercise can be found at the end of this book.

18. Sample answer: There was not as much light and air pollution in the past as there is now, so fewer stars are visible to the unaided eye now. Tools such as telescopes help modern people study objects in space in greater detail.

19. Sample answer: The Earth's atmosphere protects humans from many forms of harmful radiation. It also traps thermal energy to make Earth warm enough for life.

20. Sample answer: Daily observations of the sun would indicate that the sun is moving. Every day, the sun rises and sets. From this observation, it would be logical but incorrect to conclude that the sun rotates around the Earth.

Interpreting Graphics

21. Betelgeuse
22. 0 h, 30 min right ascension, 40° declination

CHAPTER RESOURCES

Chapter Resource File
- Chapter Review GENERAL
- Chapter Test A GENERAL
- Chapter Test B ADVANCED
- Chapter Test C SPECIAL NEEDS
- Vocabulary Activity GENERAL

Workbooks
- Study Guide
  • Assessment resources are also available in Spanish.

Chapter 18 • Chapter Review   575

Standardized Test Preparation

Teacher's Note

To provide practice under more realistic testing conditions, give students 20 minutes to answer all of the questions in this Standardized Test Preparation.

MISCONCEPTION ALERT

Answers to the standardized test preparation can help you identify student misconceptions and misunderstandings.

READING

Passage 1
1. C
2. H
3. A

TEST DOCTOR

Question 1: Students may choose answer D because 1,800 is divisible by 4, but it is also divisible by 100 and is not divisible by 400.

Passage 2
1. C
2. F

Standardized Test Preparation

READING

Read each of the passages below. Then, answer the questions that follow each passage.

Passage 1 In the early Roman calendar, a year had exactly 365 days. The calendar worked well until people realized that the seasons were beginning and ending later each year. To fix this problem, Julius Caesar developed the Julian calendar based on a 365.25-day calendar year. He added 90 days to the year 46 BCE and added an extra day every 4 years. A year in which an extra day is added to the calendar is called a *leap year*. In the mid-1500s, astronomers determined that there are actually 365.2422 days in a year, so Pope Gregory XIII developed the Gregorian calendar. He dropped 10 days from the year 1582 and restricted leap years to years that are divisible by 4 but not by 100 (except for years that are divisible by 400). Today, most countries use the Gregorian calendar.

1. According to the passage, which of the following years is a leap year?
   A 46 BCE
   B 1582
   C 1600
   D 1800

2. How long is a year?
   F 365 days
   G 365.224 days
   H 365.2422 days
   I 365.25 days

3. Why did Julius Caesar change the early Roman calendar?
   A to deal with the fact that the seasons were beginning and ending later each year
   B to compete with the Gregorian calendar
   C to add an extra day every year
   D to shorten the length of a year

Passage 2 The earliest known evidence of astronomical observations is a group of stones near Nabta in southern Egypt that is between 6,000 and 7,000 years old. According to archeoastronomers, some of the stones are positioned such that they would have lined up with the sun during the summer solstice 6,000 years ago. The summer solstice occurs on the longest day of the year. At the Nabta site, the noonday sun is at its zenith (directly overhead) for about three weeks before and after the summer solstice. When the sun is at its zenith, upright objects do not cast shadows. For many civilizations in the Tropics, the zenith sun has had ceremonial significance for thousands of years. The same is probably true for the civilizations that used the Nabta site. Artifacts found at the site near Nabta suggest that the site was created by African cattle herders. These people probably used the site for many purposes, including trade, social bonding, and ritual.

1. In the passage, what does *archeoastronomer* mean?
   A an archeologist that studies Egyptian culture
   B an astronomer that studies the zenith sun
   C an archeologist that studies ancient astronomy
   D an astronomer that studies archeologists

2. Why don't upright objects cast a shadow when the sun is at its zenith?
   F because the sun is directly overhead
   G because the summer solstice is occurring
   H because the sun is below the horizon
   I because the sun is at its zenith on the longest day of the year

TEST DOCTOR

Question 1: Students may choose answer D because the word archeoastronomer combines the words *archeology* and *astronomy*. Explain that because the prefix is *archeo-*, an archeoastronomer is an archeologist.

576 Chapter 18 • Studying Space

INTERPRETING GRAPHICS

The diagram below shows a galaxy moving in relation to four observers. The concentric circles illustrate the Doppler effect at each location. Use the diagram below to answer the questions that follow.

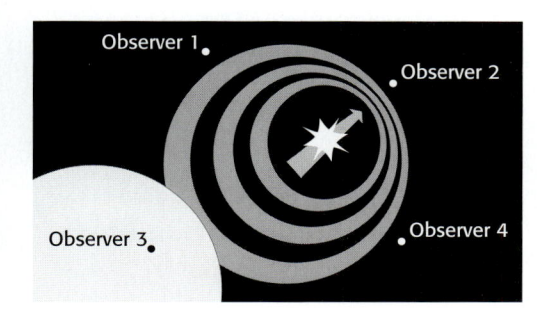

1. Which of the following observers would see the light from the galaxy affected by redshift?
   A observers 1 and 2
   B observer 3
   C observers 3 and 4
   D observers 1 and 4

2. Which of the following observers would see the light from the galaxy affected by blueshift?
   F observer 1
   G observers 2 and 4
   H observers 3 and 4
   I observer 2

3. How would the wavelengths of light detected by observer 4 appear?
   A The wavelengths would appear shorter than they really are.
   B The wavelengths would appear longer than they really are.
   C The wavelengths would appear unchanged.
   D The wavelengths would alternate between blue and red.

MATH

Read each question below, and choose the best answer.

1. If light travels 300,000 km/s, how long does light reflected from Mars take to reach Earth when Mars is 65,000,000 km away?
   A 22 s
   B 217 s
   C 2,170 s
   D 2,200 s

2. Star A is 8 million kilometers from star B. What is this distance expressed in meters?
   F 0.8 m
   G 8,000 m
   H 8×10^6 m
   I 8×10^9 m

3. If each hexagonal mirror in the Keck Telescopes is 1.8 m across, how many mirrors would be needed to create a light-reflecting surface that is 10.8 m across?
   A 3.2
   B 5
   C 6
   D 6.2

4. If the altitude of a star is 37°, what is the angle between the star and the zenith?
   F 143°
   G 90°
   H 53°
   I 37°

5. You are studying an image made by the *Hubble Space Telescope*. If you observe 90 stars in an area that is 1 cm², which of the following estimates is the best estimate for the number of stars in 15 cm²?
   A 700
   B 900
   C 1,200
   D 1,350

INTERPRETING GRAPHICS

1. B
2. I
3. C

TEST DOCTOR

Question 2: Remind students that blueshift occurs when an object is moving toward an observer at a high speed. Based on this information, observer 2 is the only reasonable choice.

MATH

1. B
2. I
3. C
4. H
5. D

TEST DOCTOR

Question 2: Remind students that 1,000 m = 1 km. If students chose answer H, they probably converted 8 million kilometers to scientific notation but may have forgotten that the answer should be expressed in meters. Remind students to read every question in a standardized test at least twice.

Chapter 18 • Standardized Test Preparation

Science in Action

Science Fiction

Background
Lawrence Watt-Evans's memorable characters and stories have earned him high honors in the fields of science fiction and fantasy writing. Readers of *Asimov's Science Fiction* magazine nominated "Why I Left Harry's All-Night Hamburgers" for the best short story of 1987. The next year, that story earned Watt-Evans the Hugo Award and was nominated for the Nebula Award. Two years later, another story, "Windwagon Smith and the Martians," captured an Asimov's Reader's Choice Award. Check out that story in *Crosstime Traffic*, a collection of short stories that Watt-Evans published in 1992.

Science, Technology, and Society

Background
Light pollution can be reduced by fitting lights with "full cut-off fixtures," which are reflector shields that direct light downward. Another simple solution to reduce light pollution is to aim spotlights down rather than up. People can also reduce light pollution and save energy by using motion sensor lights. Timer-controlled lighting is another effective remedy to reduce light pollution.

Science in Action

Science Fiction

"Why I Left Harry's All-Night Hamburgers" by Lawrence Watt-Evans

The main character was 16, and he needed to find a job. So, he began working at Harry's All-Night Hamburgers. His shift was from midnight to 7:30 A.M. so that he could still go to school. Harry's All-Night Hamburgers was pretty quiet most nights, but once in a while some unusual characters came by. For example, one guy came in dressed for Arctic weather even though it was April. Then there were the folks who parked a very strange vehicle in the parking lot for anyone to see. The main character starts questioning the visitors, and what he learns startles and fascinates him. Soon, he's thinking about leaving Harry's. Find out why when you read "Why I Left Harry's All-Night Hamburgers," in the *Holt Anthology of Science Fiction*.

Social Studies ACTIVITY

WRITING SKILL The main character in the story learns that Earth is a pretty strange place. Find out about some of the places mentioned in the story, and create an illustrated travel guide that describes some of the foreign places that interest you.

Science, Technology, and Society

Light Pollution
When your parents were your age, they could look up at the night sky and see many more stars than you can now. In a large city, seeing more than 50 stars or planets in the night sky can be difficult. Light pollution is a growing—or you could say "glowing"—problem. If you have ever seen a white glow over the horizon in the night sky, you have seen the effects of light pollution. Most light pollution comes from outdoor lights that are excessively bright or misdirected. Light pollution not only limits the number of stars that the average person can see but also limits what astronomers can detect. Light pollution affects migrating animals, too. Luckily, there are ways to reduce light pollution. The International Dark Sky Association is working to reduce light pollution around the world. Find out how you can reduce light pollution in your community or home.

Math ACTIVITY

A Virginia high school student named Jennifer Barlow started "National Dark Sky Week." If light pollution is reduced for 1 week each year, for what percentage of the year would light pollution be reduced?

Answer to Social Studies Activity
Answers may vary.

Answer to Math Activity
1 week ÷ 52 weeks × 100 = 1.9%

People in Science

Neil deGrasse Tyson

Star Writer When Neil deGrasse Tyson was nine years old, he visited a planetarium for the first time. Tyson was so affected by the experience he decided at that moment to dedicate his life to studying the universe. Tyson began studying the stars through a telescope on the roof of his apartment building. This interest led Tyson to attend the Bronx High School of Science, where he studied astronomy and physics. Tyson's passion for astronomy continued when he was a student at Harvard. However, Tyson soon realized that he wanted to share his love of astronomy with the public. So, today Tyson is America's best-known astrophysicist. When something really exciting happens in the universe, such as the discovery of evidence of water on Mars, Tyson is often asked to explain the discovery to the public. He has been interviewed hundreds of times on TV programs and has written several books. Tyson also writes a monthly column in the magazine *Natural History*. But writing and appearing on TV isn't even his day job! Tyson is the director of the Hayden Planetarium in New York—the same planetarium that ignited his interest in astronomy when he was nine years old!

Language Arts Activity

WRITING SKILL Be a star writer! Visit a planetarium or find a Web site that offers a virtual tour of the universe. Write a magazine-style article about the experience.

To learn more about these Science in Action topics, visit **go.hrw.com** and type in the keyword **HZ5OBSF.**

Current Science Check out Current Science® articles related to this chapter by visiting go.hrw.com. Just type in the keyword **HZ5CS18.**

People in Science

ACTIVITY — GENERAL

If there is an observatory, a planetarium, or a local astronomy club in your area, plan a field trip for the class. A cloudless night is best. Afterward, have students record their thoughts and observations in their **science journal.**

Answer to Language Arts Activity
Answers may vary.

Chapter 18 • Science in Action 579

19 Stars, Galaxies, and the Universe
Chapter Planning Guide

Compression guide: To shorten instruction because of time limitations, omit the Chapter Lab.

OBJECTIVES	LABS, DEMONSTRATIONS, AND ACTIVITIES	TECHNOLOGY RESOURCES
PACING • 90 min pp. 580–589 **Chapter Opener**	SE Start-up Activity, p. 581 ◆ GENERAL	OSP Parent Letter ■ GENERAL CD Student Edition on CD-ROM CD Guided Reading Audio CD ■ TR Chapter Starter Transparency* VID Brain Food Video Quiz
Section 1 Stars • Describe how color indicates the temperature of a star. • Explain how a scientist can identify a of star's composition. • Describe how scientists classify stars. • Compare absolute magnitude with apparent magnitude. • Identify how astronomers measure distances from Earth to stars. • Describe the difference between the apparent motion and the actual motion of stars.	TE Demonstration Light Pollution, p. 582 ◆ BASIC SE Connection to Physics Fingerprinting Cars, p. 583 GENERAL TE Demonstration Color Indicates Temperature, p. 583 GENERAL SE Connection to Biology Rods, Cones, and Stars, p. 584 GENERAL SE School-to-Home Activity Stargazing, p. 585 GENERAL TE Connection Activity Math, p. 586 GENERAL SE Quick Lab Not All Thumbs!, p. 587 GENERAL SE Skills Practice Lab Red Hot, or Not?, p. 604 ◆ GENERAL CRF Datasheet for Chapter Lab* SE Skills Practice Lab I See the Light!, p. 752 GENERAL CRF Datasheet for LabBook* LB Whiz-Bang Demonstrations Where Do the Stars Go?* BASIC	CRF Lesson Plans* TR Bellringer Transparency* TR Finding the Distance to Stars with Parallax* CRF SciLinks Activity* GENERAL VID Lab Videos for Earth Science
PACING • 45 min pp. 590–595 **Section 2 The Life Cycle of Stars** • Describe different types of stars. • Describe the quantities that are plotted in the H-R diagram. • Explain how stars at different stages in their life cycle appear on the H-R diagram.	SE Connection to Astronomy Long Live the Sun, p. 591 GENERAL TE Activity Researching Red Giants, p. 591 ADVANCED TE Group Activity Star Cycle, p. 592 GENERAL TE Activity Using the H-R Diagram, p. 593 BASIC TE Connection Activity Language Arts, p. 593 BASIC	CRF Lesson Plans* TR Bellringer Transparency* TR The H-R Diagram A* TR The H-R Diagram B* TE Internet Activity, p. 593 GENERAL
PACING • 45 min pp. 596–599 **Section 3 Galaxies** • Identify three types of galaxies. • Describe the contents and characteristics of galaxies. • Explain why looking at distant galaxies reveals what young galaxies looked like.	SE Connection to Language Arts Alien Observer, p. 597 GENERAL SE Science in Action Math, Social Studies, and Language Arts Activities, pp. 610–611 GENERAL	CRF Lesson Plans* TR Bellringer Transparency*
PACING • 45 min pp. 600–603 **Section 4 Formation of the Universe** • Describe the big bang theory. • Explain evidence used to support the big bang theory. • Describe the structure of the universe. • Describe two ways scientists calculate the age of the universe. • Explain what will happen if the universe expands forever.	TE Activity The Expanding Universe, p. 600 ◆ GENERAL LB Long-Term Projects & Research Ideas Contacting the Aliens* ADVANCED	CRF Lesson Plans* TR Bellringer Transparency* TR LINK TO PHYSICAL SCIENCE The Doppler Effect*

PACING • 90 min

CHAPTER REVIEW, ASSESSMENT, AND STANDARDIZED TEST PREPARATION
CRF Vocabulary Activity* GENERAL
SE Chapter Review, pp. 606–607 GENERAL
CRF Chapter Review* ■ GENERAL
CRF Chapter Tests A* ■ GENERAL, B* ADVANCED, C* SPECIAL NEEDS
SE Standardized Test Preparation, pp. 608–609 GENERAL
CRF Standardized Test Preparation* GENERAL
CRF Performance-Based Assessment* GENERAL
OSP Test Generator GENERAL
CRF Test Item Listing* GENERAL

Online and Technology Resources

Visit **go.hrw.com** for a variety of free resources related to this textbook. Enter the keyword **HZ5UNV**.

Holt Online Learning
Students can access interactive problem-solving help and active visual concept development with the *Holt Science and Technology* Online Edition available at **www.hrw.com**.

Guided Reading Audio CD
Also in Spanish
A direct reading of each chapter for auditory learners, reluctant readers, and Spanish-speaking students.

Science Tutor CD-ROM
Excellent for remediation and test practice.

KEY

SE Student Edition	**CRF** Chapter Resource File	**SS** Science Skills Worksheets
TE Teacher Edition	**OSP** One-Stop Planner	**MS** Math Skills for Science Worksheets
	LB Lab Bank	**CD** CD or CD-ROM
	TR Transparencies	**VID** Classroom Video/DVD

* Also on One-Stop Planner
♦ Requires advance prep
■ Also available in Spanish

SKILLS DEVELOPMENT RESOURCES	SECTION REVIEW AND ASSESSMENT	STANDARDS CORRELATIONS
SE Pre-Reading Activity, p. 580 `GENERAL` **OSP** Science Puzzlers, Twisters & Teasers `GENERAL`		National Science Education Standards UCP 1, 2
CRF Directed Reading A* ■ `BASIC`, B* `SPECIAL NEEDS` **CRF** Vocabulary and Section Summary* ■ `GENERAL` **SE** Reading Strategy Prediction Guide, p. 582 `GENERAL` **TE** Reading Strategy Mnemonics, p. 583 `GENERAL` **TE** Inclusion Strategies, p. 585 ♦ **SE** Math Practice Starlight, Star Bright, p. 586 `GENERAL` **MS** Math Skills for Science Arithmetic with Positive and Negative Numbers* `GENERAL` **MS** Math Skills for Science Distances in Space* `GENERAL`	**SE** Reading Checks, pp. 582, 584, 586, 587, 588 `GENERAL` **TE** Reteaching, p. 588 `BASIC` **TE** Quiz, p. 588 `GENERAL` **TE** Alternative Assessment, p. 588 `GENERAL` **SE** Section Review,* p. 589 ■ `GENERAL` **CRF** Section Quiz* ■ `GENERAL`	UCP 1, 3; SAI 1, 2; SPSP 5; *Chapter Lab:* UCP 1, 3; SAI 1, 2; ST 1; *LabBook:* UCP 2, 3; SAI 1, 2
CRF Directed Reading A* ■ `BASIC`, B* `SPECIAL NEEDS` **CRF** Vocabulary and Section Summary* ■ `GENERAL` **SE** Reading Strategy Paired Summarizing, p. 590 `GENERAL` **CRF** Reinforcement Worksheet Diagramming the Stars* `BASIC`	**SE** Reading Checks, pp. 591, 595 `GENERAL` **TE** Reteaching, p. 594 `BASIC` **TE** Quiz, p. 594 `GENERAL` **TE** Alternative Assessment, p. 594 `GENERAL` **SE** Section Review,* p. 595 ■ `GENERAL` **CRF** Section Quiz* ■ `GENERAL`	UCP 1, 2, 3, 5; SAI 1; HNS 1, 2
CRF Directed Reading A* ■ `BASIC`, B* `SPECIAL NEEDS` **CRF** Vocabulary and Section Summary* ■ `GENERAL` **SE** Reading Strategy Reading Organizer, p. 596 `GENERAL` **TE** Inclusion Strategies, p. 597	**SE** Reading Checks, pp. 596, 598, 599 `GENERAL` **TE** Reteaching, p. 598 `BASIC` **TE** Quiz, p. 598 `GENERAL` **TE** Alternative Assessment, p. 598 `ADVANCED` **SE** Section Review,* p. 599 ■ `GENERAL` **CRF** Section Quiz* ■ `GENERAL`	UCP 1, 5; SAI 1; ST 1, 2; HNS 1, 2; SPSP 5
CRF Directed Reading A* ■ `BASIC`, B* `SPECIAL NEEDS` **CRF** Vocabulary and Section Summary* ■ `GENERAL` **SE** Reading Strategy Prediction Guide, p. 600 `GENERAL` **CRF** Critical Thinking Fleabert and the Amazing Watermelon Seed* `ADVANCED`	**SE** Reading Checks, pp. 601, 602, 603 `GENERAL` **TE** Reteaching, p. 602 `BASIC` **TE** Quiz, p. 602 `GENERAL` **TE** Alternative Assessment, p. 602 `GENERAL` **SE** Section Review,* p. 603 ■ `GENERAL` **TE** Homework, p. 603 `ADVANCED` **CRF** Section Quiz* ■ `GENERAL`	UCP 1, 2, 3, 5; SAI 1

One-Stop Planner® CD-ROM

This convenient CD-ROM includes:
- Lab Materials QuickList Software
- Holt Calendar Planner
- Customizable Lesson Plans
- Printable Worksheets
- ExamView® Test Generator

CNN Student News

cnnstudentnews.com

Find the latest news, lesson plans, and activities related to important scientific events.

SciLinks NSTA

www.scilinks.org

Maintained by the National Science Teachers Association. See Chapter Enrichment pages for a complete list of topics.

Current Science®

Check out *Current Science* articles and activities by visiting the HRW Web site at **go.hrw.com.** Just type in the keyword **HZ5CS19T.**

Classroom Videos

- **Lab Videos** demonstrate the chapter lab.
- **Brain Food Video Quizzes** help students review the chapter material.
- **CNN Videos** bring science into your students' daily life.

Chapter 19 • Chapter Planning Guide

19 Chapter Resources

Visual Resources

- **CHAPTER STARTER TRANSPARENCY**
- **BELLRINGER TRANSPARENCIES**
- **TEACHING TRANSPARENCIES**
- **TEACHING TRANSPARENCIES**
- **CONCEPT MAPPING TRANSPARENCY**

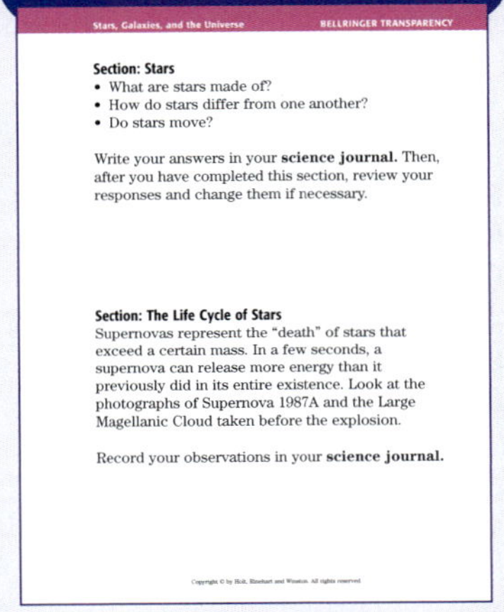

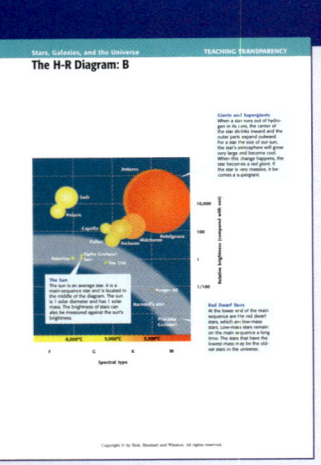

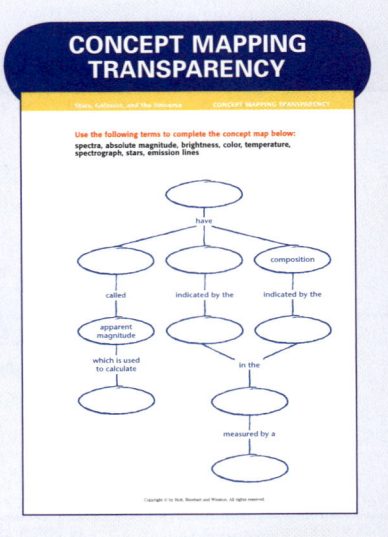

Planning Resources

- **LESSON PLANS**
- **PARENT LETTER** (ALSO IN SPANISH)
- **TEST ITEM LISTING**

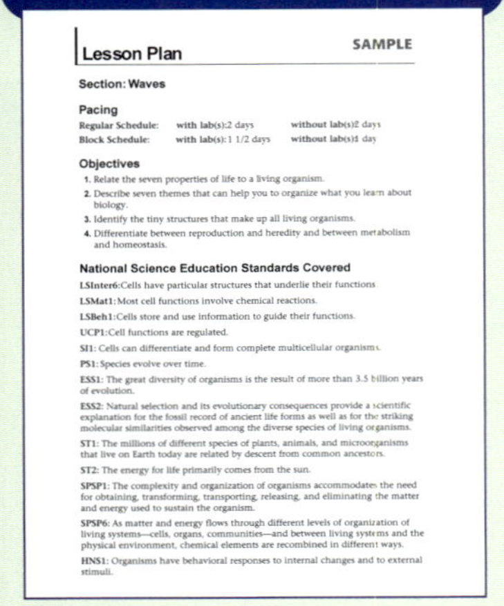

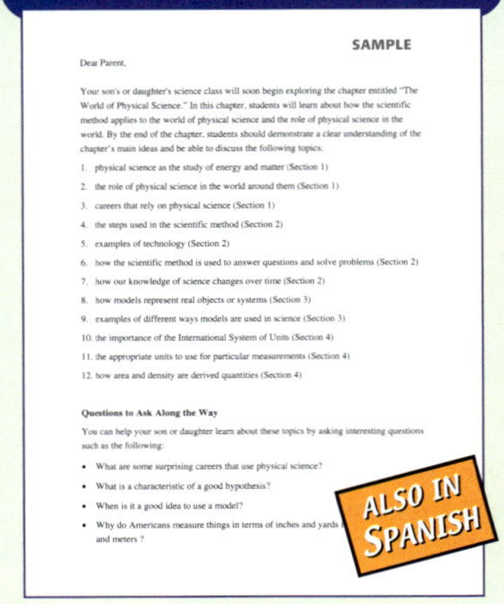

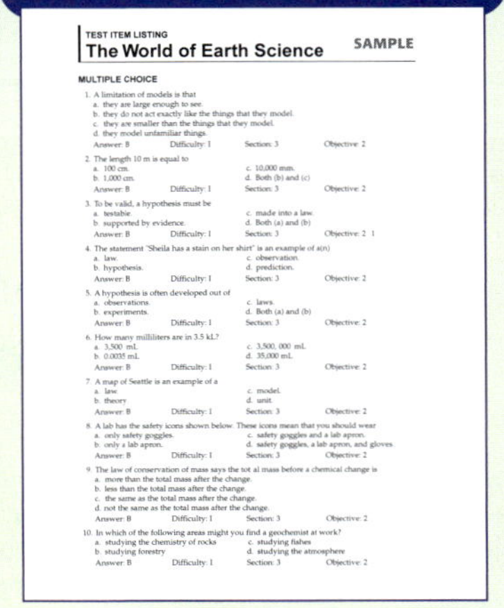

One-Stop Planner® CD-ROM

This CD-ROM includes all of the resources shown here and the following time-saving tools:

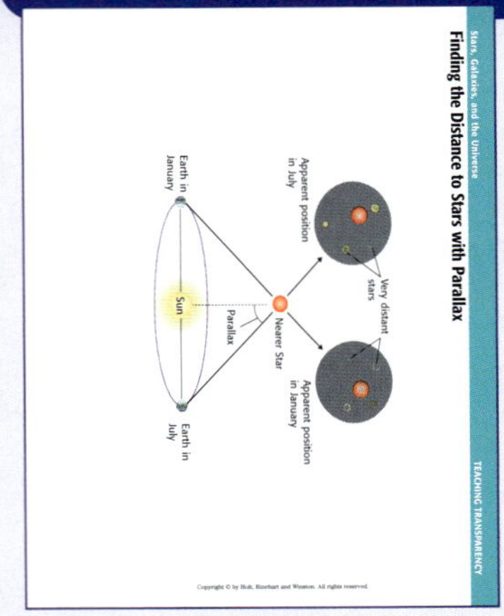

- Lab Materials QuickList Software
- Customizable lesson plans
- Holt Calendar Planner
- The powerful ExamView® Test Generator

579C Chapter 19 • Stars, Galaxies, and the Universe

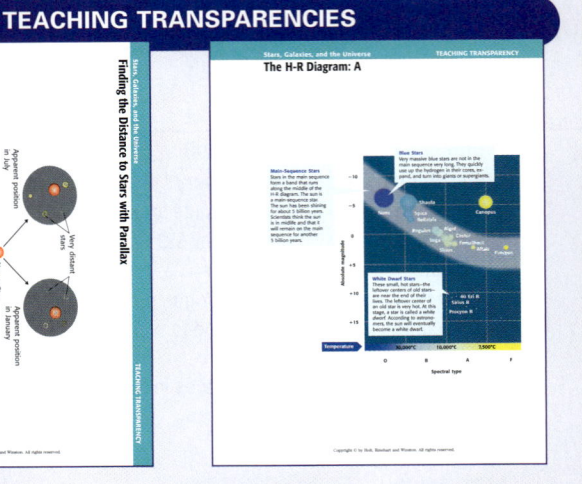

For a preview of available worksheets covering math and science skills, see pages T26–T33. All of these resources are also on the One-Stop Planner®.

Meeting Individual Needs

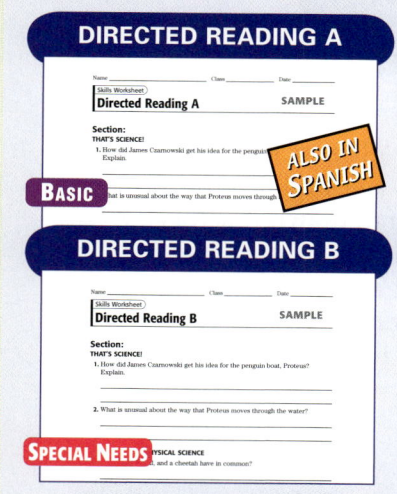

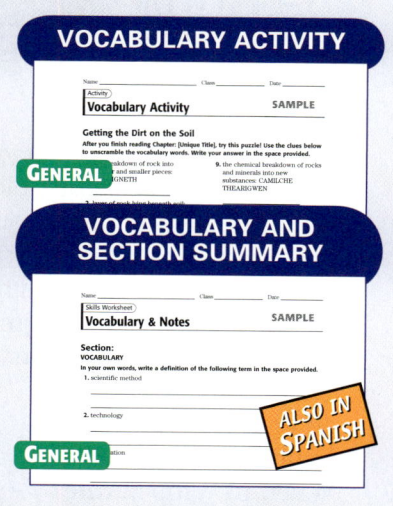

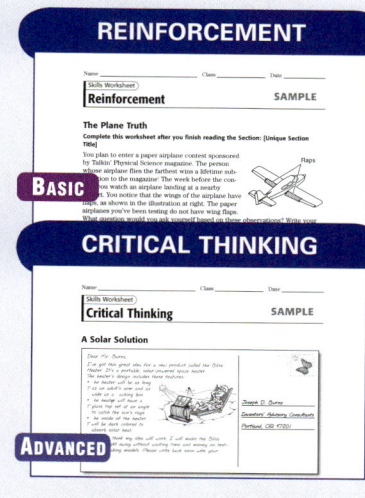

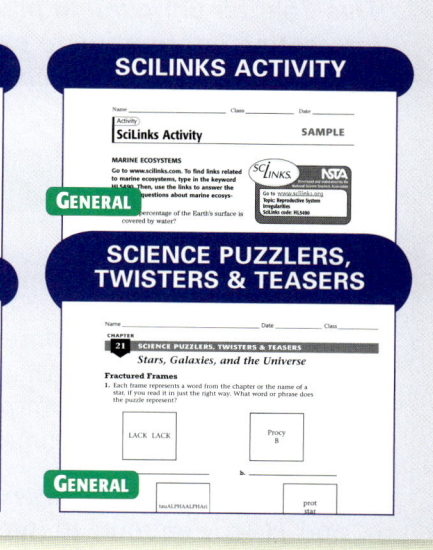

- **DIRECTED READING A** — BASIC (ALSO IN SPANISH)
- **VOCABULARY ACTIVITY** — GENERAL
- **REINFORCEMENT** — BASIC
- **SCILINKS ACTIVITY** — GENERAL
- **DIRECTED READING B** — SPECIAL NEEDS
- **VOCABULARY AND SECTION SUMMARY** — GENERAL (ALSO IN SPANISH)
- **CRITICAL THINKING** — ADVANCED
- **SCIENCE PUZZLERS, TWISTERS & TEASERS** — GENERAL

Labs and Activities

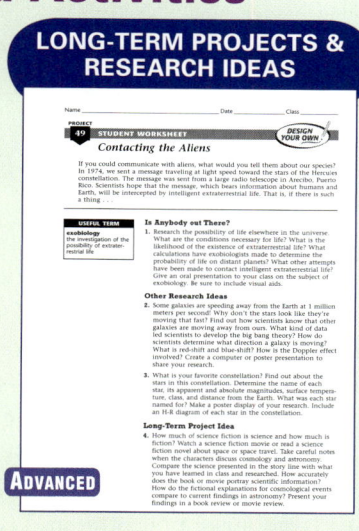

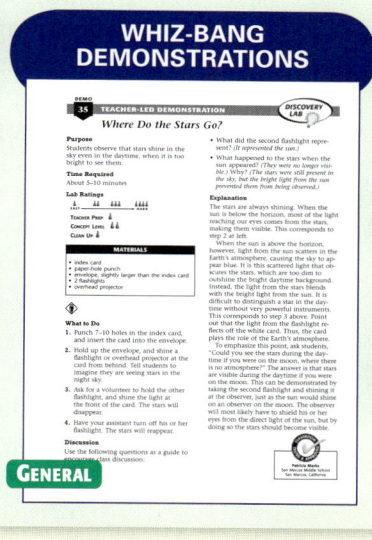

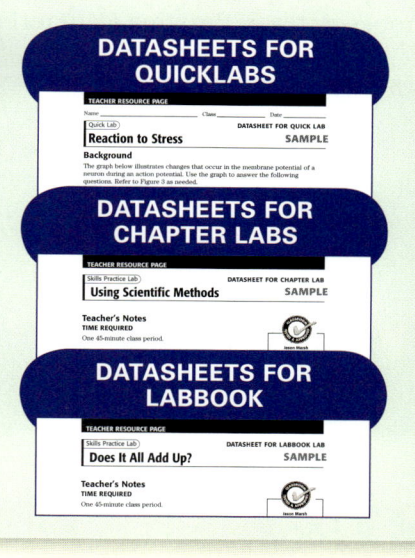

- **LONG-TERM PROJECTS & RESEARCH IDEAS** — ADVANCED
- **WHIZ-BANG DEMONSTRATIONS** — GENERAL
- **DATASHEETS FOR QUICKLABS**
- **DATASHEETS FOR CHAPTER LABS**
- **DATASHEETS FOR LABBOOK**

Review and Assessments

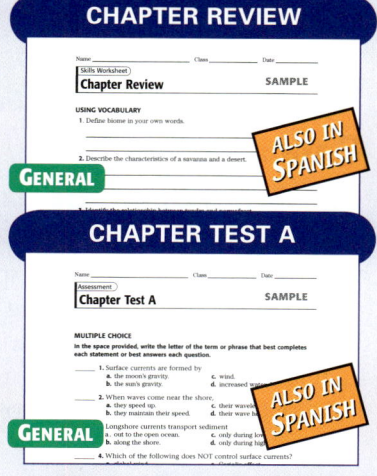

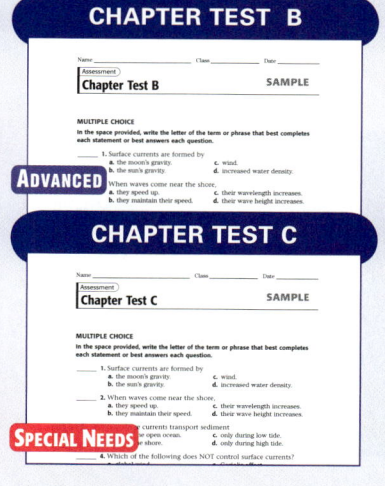

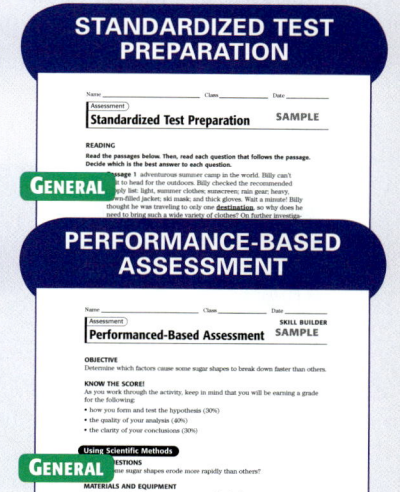

- **SECTION QUIZ** — GENERAL (ALSO IN SPANISH)
- **CHAPTER REVIEW** — GENERAL (ALSO IN SPANISH)
- **CHAPTER TEST B** — ADVANCED
- **STANDARDIZED TEST PREPARATION** — GENERAL
- **SECTION REVIEW** — GENERAL (ALSO IN SPANISH)
- **CHAPTER TEST A** — GENERAL (ALSO IN SPANISH)
- **CHAPTER TEST C** — SPECIAL NEEDS
- **PERFORMANCE-BASED ASSESSMENT** — GENERAL

Chapter 19 • Chapter Resources 579D

19 Chapter Enrichment

This Chapter Enrichment provides relevant and interesting information to expand and enhance your presentation of the chapter material.

Section 1

Stars

Space Distances

- After the sun, the star closest to Earth is Proxima Centauri, located more than 4 light-years away. To walk an equivalent distance, a person would have to walk around the Earth more than 944 million times!

- Four space probes—*Voyagers 1* and *2* and *Pioneers 10* and *11*—are en route to interstellar space. They are traveling at a rate of approximately 40,000 km/h. Even at this astounding speed, it would take 150,000 years for the probes to reach Proxima Centauri.

Is That a Fact!

◆ The Big Dipper is not a constellation; it is an asterism, a familiar pattern of stars that may or may not be part a constellation. The Big Dipper is part of the constellation known as *Ursa Major*, or Big Bear.

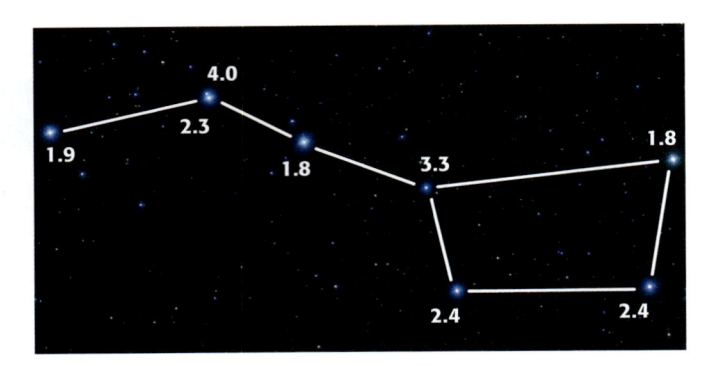

Section 2

The Life Cycle of Stars

The Birth of a Star

- Like humans, stars undergo a life cycle that consists of birth, infancy, maturity, old age, and death. In space, clouds of gas and dust abound; drawn together by gravity, they eventually form a protostar. This fledgling star gives off no visible light and must undergo many changes before it is recognizable as a star. In a process that takes millions of years, the protostar contracts. This shrinkage causes an enormous buildup of pressure and heat. When its temperature reaches about 10 million degrees Celsius, the protostar stops contracting and the process of nuclear fusion begins. Once this hydrogen-fusing process is initiated, the star is born!

Is That a Fact!

◆ From the time our sun emerged as a protostar, it took about 10 million years to become a main-sequence star. A star with one-tenth the mass of the sun would mature in 100 million years, and a star with 3 times the mass of the sun would mature in 1 million years. Stars that have large mass are hotter and take less time to mature than stars that have less mass.

Section 3

Galaxies

Observing Spiral Galaxies

- Most spiral galaxies appear very thin when seen edge-on. The thickness of the spiral disk is only about one-fifth to one-twentieth the width of the disk. When seen edge-on, spiral galaxies resemble a fried egg. The relative size and shape of the bulge are important clues to determining the type of galaxy.

579E Chapter 19 • Stars, Galaxies, and the Universe

How Many Stars Are in a Galaxy?

- To estimate the number of stars in a galaxy, astronomers consider the sun as one unit of mass. Large spiral galaxies, for example, have a mass of 1 billion to 1 trillion solar masses. Dwarf elliptical galaxies have only a few million solar masses, about one-thousandth the mass of a spiral galaxy. Giant elliptical galaxies have more mass than large spiral galaxies do.

Is That a Fact!

◆ The word *galaxy* comes from the Greek word *gala*, meaning "milk." The visible portion of our galaxy looks like a milky cloud in the night sky.

Section 4

Formation of the Universe

Top-Down or Bottom-Up?

- No one is certain how large-scale structures in the universe emerged. Some scientists support the top-down theory. This theory explains that areas of the universe that contained large-scale objects (the size of clusters and super-clusters) were the first to collapse into gaseous, pancake-like shapes. Galaxies condensed from these structures.

- Other scientists support the bottom-up theory. This theory argues that areas of the universe that had small-scale objects (the size of galaxies or smaller) were the first to form. Because of the gravitational forces, these areas aggregated into clusters and superclusters.

Life on Other Planets?

- Many scientists believe that our galaxy alone contains hundreds of millions of planets similar to Earth. These planets may be able to support carbon-based life.

Is That a Fact!

◆ The William Herschel telescope on La Palma in the Canary Islands is one of the world's biggest optical telescopes. With its 4.2 m mirror, it could detect a single candle burning 160,000 km away.

SciLinks is maintained by the National Science Teachers Association to provide you and your students with interesting, up-to-date links that will enrich your classroom presentation of the chapter.

Visit www.scilinks.org and enter the SciLinks code for more information about the topic listed.

Topic: Stars
SciLinks code: HSM1448

Topic: Supernova
SciLinks code: HSM1482

Topic: Galaxies
SciLinks code: HSM0632

Topic: Structure of the Universe
SciLinks code: HSM1469

Overview
Tell students that this chapter will help them learn about the characteristics and life cycles of stars. Students will also learn about types of galaxies, and the structure of the universe.

Assessing Prior Knowledge
Students should be familiar with the following topics:
- the history of astronomy
- the size and scale of the universe

Identifying Misconceptions
As students learn about the expansion of the universe, some of them may think that the expansion of the universe is caused by the expansion of the particles rather than an increase in the space between the particles. Students are also often confused by the terms *mass* and *volume* and often define both as "the amount of matter." It may be helpful to review the definitions of *matter, mass,* and *volume* before teaching the material about universal expansion.

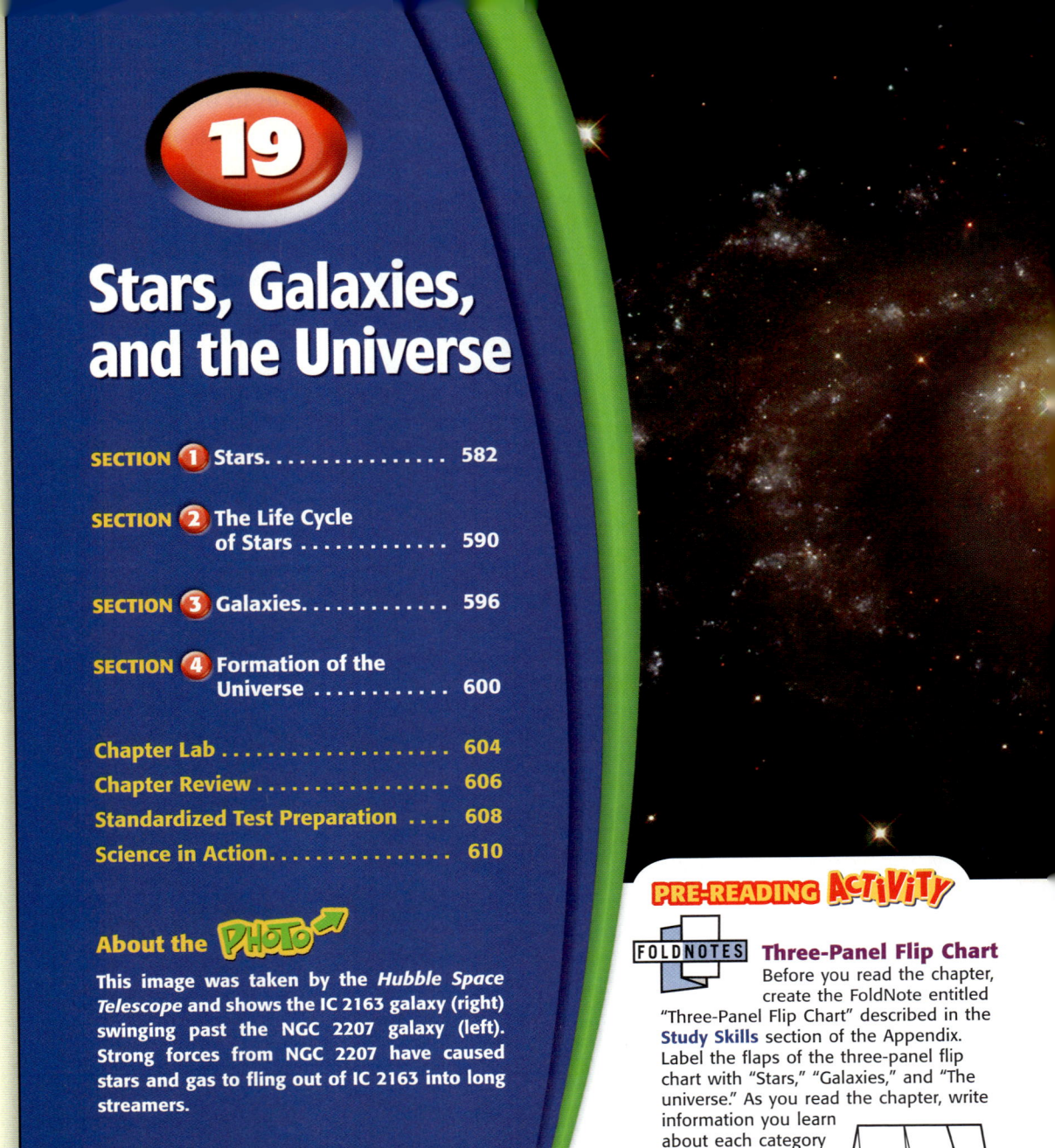

19
Stars, Galaxies, and the Universe

SECTION 1	Stars	582
SECTION 2	The Life Cycle of Stars	590
SECTION 3	Galaxies	596
SECTION 4	Formation of the Universe	600

Chapter Lab 604
Chapter Review 606
Standardized Test Preparation 608
Science in Action 610

About the PHOTO
This image was taken by the *Hubble Space Telescope* and shows the IC 2163 galaxy (right) swinging past the NGC 2207 galaxy (left). Strong forces from NGC 2207 have caused stars and gas to fling out of IC 2163 into long streamers.

PRE-READING ACTIVITY
FOLDNOTES **Three-Panel Flip Chart**
Before you read the chapter, create the FoldNote entitled "Three-Panel Flip Chart" described in the **Study Skills** section of the Appendix. Label the flaps of the three-panel flip chart with "Stars," "Galaxies," and "The universe." As you read the chapter, write information you learn about each category under the appropriate flap.

Standards Correlations

National Science Education Standards
The following codes indicate the National Science Education Standards that correlate to this chapter. The full text of the standards is at the front of the book.

Chapter Opener
UCP 1, 2

Section 1 Stars
UCP 1, 3; SAI 1; SPSP 5; *LabBook:* UCP 2, 3; SAI 1

Section 2 The Life Cycle of Stars
UCP 1, 2, 3, 5; SAI 1; HNS 1, 2

Section 3 Galaxies
UCP 1, 5; SAI 1; ST 1, 2; HNS 1, 2; SPSP 5

Section 4 Formation of the Universe
UCP 1, 2, 3, 5; SAI 1

Chapter Lab
UCP 1, 3; SAI 1, 2; ST 1

Chapter Review
UCP 1, 2, 3, 5; SAI 1; ST 2; HNS 1, 2

Science in Action
UCP 1, 2, 3; HNS 1, 2, 3

580 Chapter 19 • Stars, Galaxies, and the Universe

START-UP ACTIVITY

MATERIALS

FOR EACH GROUP
- glitter (any color)
- glass jar, 1 qt
- spoon, wooden
- water

Teacher's Notes: Use glass jars that are clear on all sides so that it is easy for students to view the swirling galaxies.

Answers

1. The water should make a swirling, spiral motion after being stirred.
2. The motion of the glitter should appear to be similar to the galaxies in the photo.
3. Answers may vary.

START-UP ACTIVITY

Exploring the Movement of Galaxies in the Universe

Not all galaxies are the same. Galaxies can differ by size, shape, and how they move in space. In this activity, you will explore how the galaxies in the photo move in space.

Procedure

1. Fill a **one-quart glass jar** three-fourths of the way with **water**.
2. Take a pinch of **glitter**, and sprinkle it on the surface of the water.
3. Quickly stir the water with a **wooden spoon**. Be sure to stir the water in a circular pattern.
4. After you stop stirring, look at the water from the sides of the jar and from the top of the jar.

Analysis

1. What kind of motion did the water make after you stopped stirring the water?
2. How is the motion similar to the galaxies in the photo?
3. Make up a name that describes the galaxies in the photo.

Chapter Starter Transparency
Use this transparency to help students begin thinking about studying the universe.

CHAPTER RESOURCES

Technology

Transparencies
- Chapter Starter Transparency

READING SKILLS

Student Edition on CD-ROM

Guided Reading Audio CD
- English or Spanish

Classroom Videos
- Brain Food Video Quiz

Workbooks

Science Puzzlers, Twisters & Teasers
- Stars, Galaxies, and the Universe GENERAL

Chapter 19 • Stars, Galaxies, and the Universe

SECTION 1

Focus

Overview
This section discusses the classification of stars by their color, composition, and brightness. This section also explores how apparent magnitude differs from absolute magnitude and how apparent motion of the stars differs from actual motion of stars.

🔔 Bellringer
On the board, write the following questions: "What are stars made of? How do stars differ from one another? Do stars move?" Have students review their responses after completing this section.

Motivate

Demonstration —GENERAL
Light Pollution Demonstrate how ambient light affects the number of visible stars by using a slide projector, a piece of aluminum foil, and a flashlight. Poke small holes in the foil, and in a dark room, project light through the foil. Ask students to count the stars. Then, shine the flashlight on the screen, and ask students to count the stars again. Discuss with students some artificial sources of light pollution. **LS Visual**

SECTION 1

Stars

Do you remember the children's song "Twinkle, Twinkle Little Star"? In the song, you sing "How I wonder what you are!" Well, what are stars? And what are they made of?

Most stars look like faint dots of light in the night sky. But stars are actually huge, hot, bright balls of gas that are trillions of kilometers away from Earth. How do astronomers learn about stars when the stars are too far away to visit? Astronomers study starlight!

READING WARM-UP

Objectives
- Describe how color indicates the temperature of a star.
- Explain how a scientist can identify a of star's composition.
- Describe how scientists classify stars.
- Compare absolute magnitude with apparent magnitude.
- Identify how astronomers measure distances from Earth to stars.
- Describe the difference between the apparent motion and the actual motion of stars.

Terms to Learn
spectrum
apparent magnitude
absolute magnitude
light-year
parallax

READING STRATEGY
Prediction Guide Before reading this section, write the title of each heading in this section. Next, under each heading, write what you think you will learn.

Color of Stars
Look at the flames on the candle and the Bunsen burner shown in **Figure 1**. Which flame is hottest? How can you tell? Although red and yellow may be thought of as "warm" colors and blue may be thought of as a "cool" color, scientists consider red and yellow to be cool colors and blue to be a warm color. For example, the blue flame of the Bunsen burner is much hotter than the yellow flame of the candle.

If you look carefully at the night sky, you might notice the different colors of some stars. Betelgeuse (BET uhl JOOZ), which is red, and Rigel (RIE juhl), which is blue, are the stars that form two corners of the constellation Orion, shown in **Figure 1**. Because these two stars are different colors, we can conclude that they have different temperatures.

✓ **Reading Check** Which star is hotter, Betelgeuse or Rigel? Explain your answer. (*See the Appendix for answers to Reading Checks.*)

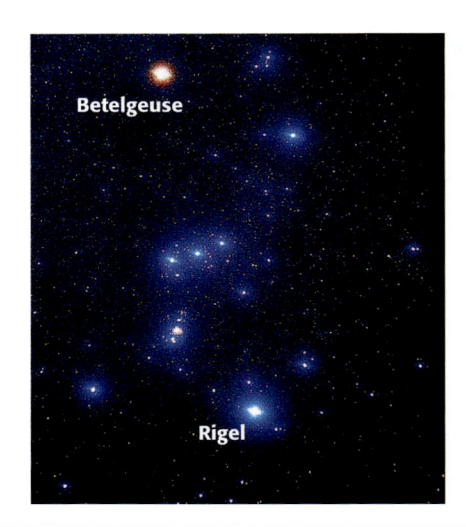

Figure 1 *In the same way that we know the blue flame of the Bunsen burner is hotter than the yellow flame of the candle, astronomers know that Rigel is hotter than Betelgeuse.*

CHAPTER RESOURCES

Chapter Resource File
- Lesson Plan
- Directed Reading A BASIC
- Directed Reading B SPECIAL NEEDS

Technology
- Transparencies
  • Bellringer

Answer to Reading Check
Rigel is hotter than Betelgeuse because blue stars are hotter than red stars.

---

582 Chapter 19 • Stars, Galaxies, and the Universe

Composition of Stars

A star is made up of different elements in the form of gases. The inner layers of a star are very dense and hot. But the outer layers of a star, or a star's atmosphere, are made up of cool gases. Elements in a star's atmosphere absorb some of the light that radiates from the star. Because different elements absorb different wavelengths of light, astronomers can tell what elements a star is made of from the light they observe from the star.

The Colors of Light

When you look at white light through a glass prism, you see a rainbow of colors called a **spectrum.** The spectrum consists of millions of colors, including red, orange, yellow, green, blue, indigo, and violet. A hot, solid object, such as the glowing wire inside a light bulb, gives off a *continuous spectrum*—a spectrum that shows all the colors. However, the spectrum of a star is different. Astronomers use an instrument called a *spectrograph* to break a star's light into a spectrum. The spectrum gives astronomers information about the composition and temperature of a star. To understand how to read a star's spectrum, think about something more familiar—a neon sign.

Making an ID

Many restaurants use neon signs to attract customers. The gas in a neon sign glows when an electric current flows through the gas. If you were to look at the sign with a spectrograph, you would not see a continuous spectrum. Instead, you would see *emission lines*. Emission lines are lines that are made when certain wavelengths of light, or colors, are given off by hot gases. When an element emits light, only some colors in the spectrum show up, while all the other colors are missing. Each element has a unique set of bright emission lines. Emission lines are like fingerprints for the elements. You can see emission lines for four elements in **Figure 2**.

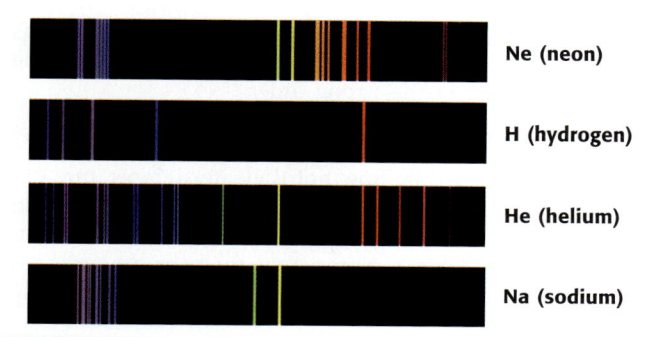

CONNECTION TO Physics

WRITING SKILL **Fingerprinting Cars** Police use spectrographs to "fingerprint" cars. Car makers put trace elements in the paint of cars. Each make of car has a special paint and thus its own combination of trace elements. When a car is in a hit-and-run accident, police officers can identify the make of the car by the paint left behind. Using a spectrograph to identify a car is one of many scientific methods that police use to solve crimes. Solving crimes by using scientific equipment and methods is part of a science called *forensic science*. Research the topic of forensic science. In your **science journal,** write a short paragraph about the other scientific methods that forensic scientists use to solve crimes.

spectrum the band of color produced when white light passes through a prism

Figure 2 Neon gas produces a unique set of emission lines, as do the elements hydrogen, helium, and sodium.

Ne (neon)
H (hydrogen)
He (helium)
Na (sodium)

MISCONCEPTION ALERT

Planets and Stars Sometimes, differentiating between stars and planets in the night sky is difficult. If an object twinkles, it's probably a star. Because of their proximity to Earth, planets appear as tiny disks shining with a steady light. Venus is an easy planet to spot—it can often be seen shining brightly in the west, immediately after the sun sets. Venus can also be seen in the morning, accompanying the rising sun. Venus is then called "the morning star." Although stars appear to twinkle in the sky, they actually shine with a steady light. They appear to twinkle because their light is distorted when it passes through Earth's atmosphere. If you were standing on the moon, where there is not an atmosphere, the stars would appear to shine steadily.

Teach

Answer to Connection to Physics
Suggest that students use the Internet or library resources to research the other scientific methods that forensic scientists use to solve crimes.

READING STRATEGY — GENERAL

Mnemonics Many people remember the colors of the spectrum by using the name **ROY G. BIV,** which stands for **R**ed, **O**range, **Y**ellow, **G**reen, **B**lue, **I**ndigo, and **V**iolet. **LS Verbal**

English Language Learners

Demonstration — GENERAL

MATERIALS
- beaker (2)
- Bunsen burner (2)
- tripod (2)
- water

Color Indicates Temperature Students may have trouble understanding how the color of a star indicates the star's temperature. Light two Bunsen burners. Adjust one burner so that it has a yellow flame and the other burner so that it has a bluish white flame. Place a beaker half-filled with water on a tripod over each flame, and have students time how long the water in each beaker takes to boil. Ask students to discuss other examples in which the color of an object indicates the object's temperature. **LS Visual**

Section 1 • Stars 583

Teach, continued

CONNECTION to Physical Science—ADVANCED

Learning About Spectra
When electrons become excited or absorb enough energy, they are boosted to a higher energy level. When the electrons return to their normal energy level, they release energy at specific wavelengths. The specific wavelength emitted depends on the amount of energy that the electron releases when it returns to its normal energy level. This wavelength is unique to each element. By studying the wavelengths emitted from a substance, scientists can determine the elements that are present in that substance. Have students research the elements and compounds that scientists studying starlight have found, and have students use colored pencils to reproduce some of the spectra in their **science journal**.
LS Interpersonal

Answer to Connection to Biology
Rods are good at distinguishing shades of light and dark and at distinguishing shape and movement. Cones are good for distinguishing colors. However, cones do not work well in low light. For this reason, distinguishing star colors is difficult.

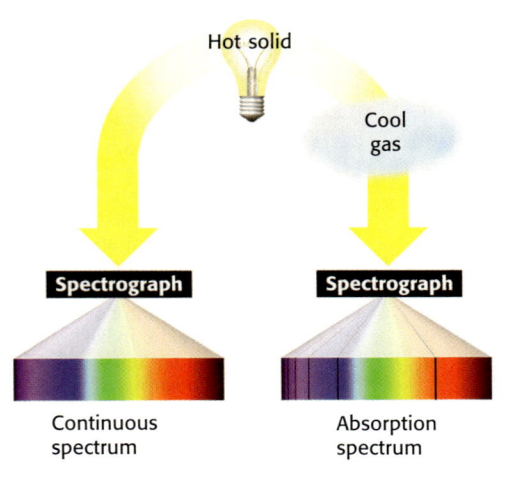

Figure 3 *A continuous spectrum (left) shows all colors while an absorption spectrum (right) absorbs some colors. Black lines appear in the spectrum where colors are absorbed.*

CONNECTION TO Biology
Rods, Cones, and Stars
WRITING SKILL Have you ever wondered why it's hard to see the different colors of stars? Our eyes are not sensitive to colors when light levels are low. There are two types of light-sensitive cells in the eye: rods and cones. Research the functions of rods and cones. In your **science journal**, write a paragraph that explains why we can't see colors well in low light.

Science Bloopers
The composition of the sun has been the subject of much speculation. In the 19th century, some scientists thought that the sun was made of pure anthracite, because coal was one of the best heat-generating fuels of the time. But given the energy output of the sun, coal would have lasted only about 10,000 years. It took the discovery of radiation and nuclear energy for scientists to develop the current model of the sun's composition and structure.

Trapping the Light—Cosmic Detective Work
Like an element that is charged by an electric current, a star also produces a spectrum. However, while the spectrum of an electrically charged element is made of bright emission lines, a star's spectrum is made of dark emission lines. A star's atmosphere absorbs certain colors of light in the spectrum, which causes black lines to appear.

Identifying Elements Using Dark Lines
Because a star's atmosphere absorbs colors of light instead of emitting them, the spectrum of a star is called an *absorption spectrum*. An absorption spectrum is produced when light from a hot solid or dense gas passes through a cooler gas. Therefore, a star gives off an absorption spectrum because a star's atmosphere is cooler than the inner layers of the star. The black lines of a star's spectrum represent places where less light gets through. **Figure 3** compares a continuous spectrum and an absorption spectrum. What do you notice about the absorption spectrum that is different?

The pattern of lines in a star's absorption spectrum shows some of the elements that are in the star's atmosphere. If a star were made of one element, we could easily identify the element from the star's absorption spectrum. But a star is a mixture of elements and all the different sets of lines for a star's elements appear together in its spectrum. Sorting the patterns is often a puzzle.

✓**Reading Check** What does a star's absorption spectrum show?

Classifying Stars
In the 1800s, astronomers started to collect and classify the spectra of many stars. At first, letters were assigned to each type of spectra. Stars were classified according to the elements of which they were made. Later, scientists realized that the stars were classified in the wrong order.

Differences in Temperature
Stars are now classified by how hot they are. Temperature differences between stars result in color differences that you can see. For example, the original class O stars are blue—the hottest stars. Look at **Table 1**. Notice that the stars are arranged in order from highest temperature to lowest temperature.

Answer to Reading Check
A star's absorption spectrum indicates some of the elements that are in the star's atmosphere.

Table 1 Types of Stars

Class	Color	Surface temperature (°C)	Elements detected	Examples of stars
O	blue	above 30,000	helium	10 Lacertae
B	blue-white	10,000–30,000	helium and hydrogen	Rigel, Spica
A	blue-white	7,500–10,000	hydrogen	Vega, Sirius
F	yellow-white	6,000–7,500	hydrogen and heavier elements	Canopus, Procyon
G	yellow	5,000–6,000	calcium and other metals	the sun, Capella
K	orange	3,500–5,000	calcium and molecules	Arcturus, Aldebaran
M	red	less than 3,500	molecules	Betelgeuse, Antares

Differences in Brightness

With only their eyes to aid them, early astronomers created a system to classify stars based on their brightness. They called the brightest stars in the sky *first-magnitude* stars and the dimmest stars *sixth-magnitude* stars. But when they began to use telescopes, astronomers were able to see many stars that had been too dim to see before. Rather than replace the old system of magnitudes, they added to it. Positive numbers represent dimmer stars, and negative numbers represent brighter stars. For example, by using large telescopes, astronomers can see stars as dim as 29th magnitude. And the brightest star in the night sky, Sirius, has a magnitude of -1.4. The Big Dipper, shown in **Figure 4**, contains both bright stars and dim stars.

Figure 4 *The Big Dipper contains both bright stars and dim stars. What is the magnitude of the brightest star in the Big Dipper?*

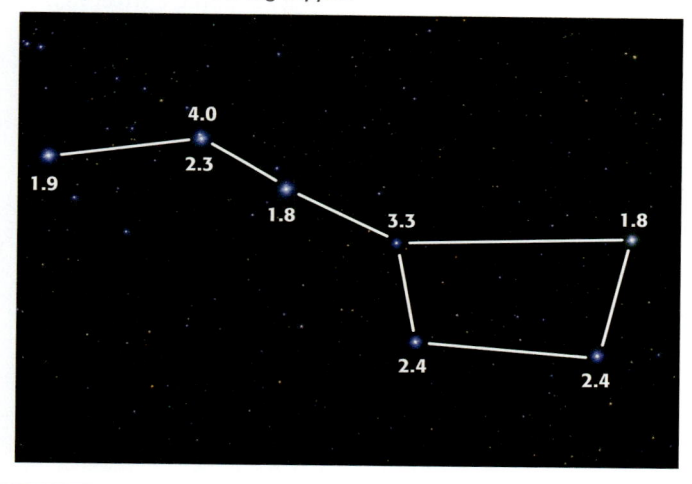

SCHOOL to HOME

Stargazing

WRITING SKILL Someone looking at the night sky in a city would not see as many stars as someone looking at the sky in the country. With a parent, research why this is true. Try to find a place near your home that would be ideal for stargazing. If you find one, schedule a night to stargaze. Write down what you see in the night sky.

ACTIVITY

Is That a Fact!

The brightness of astronomical objects that are not stars is also measured in star magnitudes. For example, Venus shines with an apparent magnitude of −4.6, while the full moon shines with an apparent magnitude of −12.5. With practice, the human eye can discern differences in brightness to one-tenth of a magnitude!

INCLUSION Strategies

- Learning Disabled
- Attention Deficit Disorder
- Gifted and Talented

Organize students into small teams that will create a mnemonic device to help them remember star classification. Next, hand out one deck of star cards comprising star classes and a second deck of star cards comprising the colors, surface temperatures, elements detected, and examples of stars. Ask each team to match each star class with the appropriate attributes.

LS Interpersonal

Using the Table — BASIC

Star Types Draw students' attention to **Table 1**. Have students explain how the stars are arranged (from the hottest to the coolest), and have them identify the hottest and the coolest stars. (The hottest is 10 Lacertae; the coolest are Betelgeuse and Antares.)

Have students locate our sun on the table and describe its temperature relative to the temperatures of other stars. (The sun is a class G star and has a surface temperature of 5,500°C.)

Be sure that students notice that the temperature of a star indicates the elements detected in star's spectrum. **LS** Visual

CONNECTION to History — GENERAL

Early Systems of Star Classification Hipparchus, a second-century Greek astronomer, developed the first system for star classification. His system divided the stars into six categories based on their apparent brightness. He called the stars that appeared brightest *first magnitude* and called the faintest stars *sixth magnitude*. When telescopes were invented, people learned that many stars were brighter than first-magnitude stars. By the 18th century, scientists decided that a star of a specific magnitude would be about 2.5 times brighter than a star of the previous magnitude. The brightest stars were reclassified to have negative magnitudes.

Section 1 • Stars **585**

Teach, continued

Discussion — BASIC

Magnitude Scale You may wish to draw a number line on the board to show students how the magnitude scale works. Explain how stars were originally classified on a scale of 1 to 6. Later, as advances in technology enabled the discovery of brighter and fainter stars, the scale was expanded. **LS Visual**

CONNECTION ACTIVITY
Math — GENERAL

Apparent Magnitude Encourage students to compare the apparent magnitude of stars. Point out that if two stars differ by a magnitude of 1, the brighter star is 2.5 times brighter than the dimmer star. Tell students that the star Rigel has an apparent magnitude of 0.18, while Pollux has an apparent magnitude of 1.16. Have students calculate how much brighter Rigel appears than Pollux. (1.16 − 0.18 = 0.98); (0.98 × 2.5 = approximately 2.5; Students should find that Rigel appears about 2.5 times brighter than Pollux.) **LS Logical**

Answer to Reading Check

Apparent magnitude is the brightness of a light or star.

Figure 5 You can estimate how far away each street light is by looking at its apparent brightness. Does this process work when estimating the distance of stars from Earth?

apparent magnitude the brightness of a star as seen from the Earth

absolute magnitude the brightness that a star would have at a distance of 32.6 light-years from Earth

MATH PRACTICE

Starlight, Star Bright
Magnitude is used to show how bright one object is compared with another object. Every five magnitudes is equal to a factor of 100 times in brightness. The brightest blue stars, for example, have an absolute magnitude of −10. The sun has an absolute magnitude of about +5. How much brighter is a blue star than the sun? Because each five magnitudes is a factor of 100 and the blue star is 15 magnitudes greater than the sun, the blue star must be 100 × 100 × 100, or 1,000,000 (1 million), times brighter than the sun!

How Bright Is That Star?

If you look at a row of street lights, such as those shown in **Figure 5,** do they all look the same? Of course not! The nearest ones look bright, and the farthest ones look dim.

Apparent Magnitude

The brightness of a light or star is called **apparent magnitude.** If you measure the brightness of a street light with a light meter, you will find that the light's brightness depends on the square of the ratio between the light and the light meter. For example, a light that is 10 m away from you will appear 4 (2 × 2, or 2^2) times brighter than a light that is 20 m away from you. The same light will appear 9 (3 × 3, or 3^2) times brighter than a light that is 30 m away. But unlike street lights, some stars are brighter than other stars because of their size or energy output, not because of their distance from Earth. So, how can you tell how bright a star is and why?

✓ Reading Check What is apparent magnitude?

Absolute Magnitude

Astronomers use a star's apparent magnitude and its distance from Earth to calculate its absolute magnitude. **Absolute magnitude** is the actual brightness of a star. If all stars were the same distance away, their absolute magnitudes would be the same as their apparent magnitudes. The sun, for example, has an absolute magnitude of +4.8, which is ordinary for a star. But because the sun is so close to Earth, the sun's apparent magnitude is −26.8, which makes it the brightest object in the sky.

MISCONCEPTION ALERT

Negative Numbers Are Brighter
Students may think that stars that have negative absolute magnitude values are fainter than those stars that have positive values. Point out that *decreasing* values indicate *increasing* brightness.

CHAPTER RESOURCES

Technology
- **Transparencies**
  • Finding the Distance to Stars with Parallax

Workbooks
- **Math Skills for Science**
  • Arithmetic with Positive and Negative Numbers **GENERAL**

---

586 Chapter 19 • Stars, Galaxies, and the Universe

Figure 6 Measuring a Star's Parallax

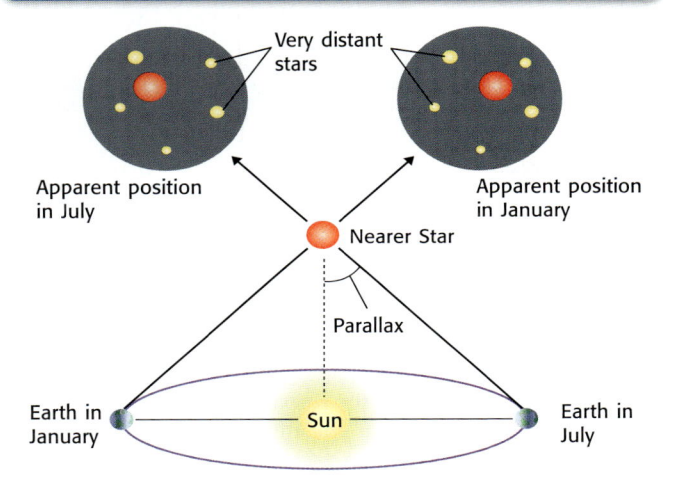

Very distant stars

Apparent position in July

Apparent position in January

Nearer Star

Parallax

Earth in January

Sun

Earth in July

light-year the distance that light travels in one year; about 9.5 trillion kilometers

parallax an apparent shift in the position of an object when viewed from different locations

Distance to the Stars

Because stars are so far away, astronomers use light-years to measure the distances from Earth to the stars. A **light-year** is the distance that light travels in one year. Obviously, it would be easier to give the distance to the North Star as 431 light-years than as 4,080,000,000,000,000 km. But how do astronomers measure a star's distance from Earth?

Stars near the Earth seem to move, while more-distant stars seem to stay in one place as Earth revolves around the sun, as shown in **Figure 6**. A star's apparent shift in position is called **parallax**. Notice that the location of the nearer star in **Figure 6** seems to shift in relation to the pattern of more-distant stars. This shift can be seen only through telescopes. Astronomers use parallax and simple trigonometry (a type of math) to find the actual distance to stars that are close to Earth.

Reading Check What is a light-year?

Motions of Stars

As you know, daytime and nighttime are caused by the Earth's rotation. The Earth's tilt and revolution around the sun cause the seasons. During each season, the Earth faces a different part of the sky at night. Look again at **Figure 6**. In January, the Earth's night side faces a different part of the sky than it faces in July. This is why you see a different set of constellations at different times of the year.

Quick Lab

Not All Thumbs!

1. Hold your thumb in front of your face at arm's length.
2. Close one eye, and focus on an **object** some distance behind your thumb.
3. Slowly turn your head side to side a small amount. Notice how your thumb seems to be moving compared with the background you are looking at.
4. Now, move your thumb in close to your face, and move your head the same amount. Does your thumb seem to move more?

MISCONCEPTION ALERT

The Constellations Change Over Time
Students may think that the constellations have always looked the same from Earth. Point out that our solar system and the stars in our galaxy are moving at different speeds as they revolve around the Milky Way. Thus, 100,000 years ago, the constellations looked much different than they do today.

Answer to Reading Check
A light-year is the distance that light travels in 1 year.

CONNECTION to History — GENERAL

Aristarchus of Samos The Greek astronomer Aristarchus of Samos came up with a method for calculating the distance of heavenly bodies more than 2,200 years ago. He calculated that the moon was much smaller than the sun and therefore much closer to Earth than previously thought. He also suggested that the known planets revolved around the sun and that the stars were very far away. Ironically, Aristarchus was ridiculed for his theory of a sun-centered universe, and his ideas were dismissed by other philosophers of the time. **LS Verbal**

Quick Lab

Teacher's Note: Explain the concept of parallax by asking students to imagine that they are in a car traveling on a road lined with trees. Ask students to imagine looking out of the window and to describe the apparent motion of the trees. (Students may answer that the trees closest to the car appear to move faster than those farther away do.) Tell students that they can determine the distance to a tree or a star by measuring the apparent motion of the tree or star.

Answers
4. Students should notice that their thumb seems to move more when their thumb is closer to their face.

Section 1 • Stars **587**

Close

Reteaching — BASIC
Classifying the Stars Ask students to describe the different ways in which scientists classify stars. **LS** Verbal

Quiz — GENERAL
1. How is the distance from Earth to a star measured? (Scientists determine the distance to a star by using parallax and trigonometry.)
2. How is the apparent movement of the stars in the night sky different from the movement of the stars within a constellation? (The stars in the night sky rise and set as Earth rotates. All of the stars in a constellation are moving relative to one another. It takes thousands of years to observe their movement.)

Alternative Assessment — GENERAL
Illustrating Parallax Have students make an illustration of the phenomenon of parallax in their **science journal**. Then, have students explain their illustration to a partner.
LS Intrapersonal/Interpersonal

Figure 7 As Earth rotates on its axis, the stars appear to rotate around Polaris.

The Apparent Motion of Stars

Because of Earth's rotation, the sun appears to move across the sky. Likewise, if you look at the night sky long enough, the stars also appear to move. In fact, at night you can observe that the whole sky is rotating above us. Look at **Figure 7.** All the stars you see appear to rotate around Polaris, the North Star, which is almost directly above Earth's North Pole. Because of Earth's rotation, all of the stars in the sky appear to make one complete circle around Polaris every 24 h.

The Actual Motion of Stars

You now know that the apparent motion of the sun and stars in our sky is due to Earth's rotation. But each star is also moving in space. Because stars are so distant, however, their actual motion is hard to see. If you could put thousands of years into one hour, a star's movement would be obvious. **Figure 8** shows how familiar star patterns slowly change their shapes.

✓ **Reading Check** Why is the actual motion of stars hard to see?

Figure 8 Over time, the shapes of star patterns, such as the Big Dipper and other groups, change.

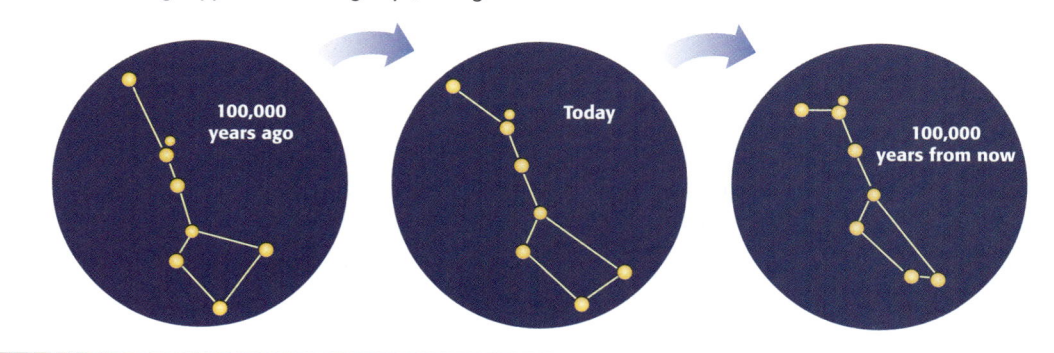

100,000 years ago → Today → 100,000 years from now

Answer to Reading Check
The actual motion of stars is hard to see because the stars are so distant.

588 Chapter 19 • Stars, Galaxies, and the Universe

SECTION Review

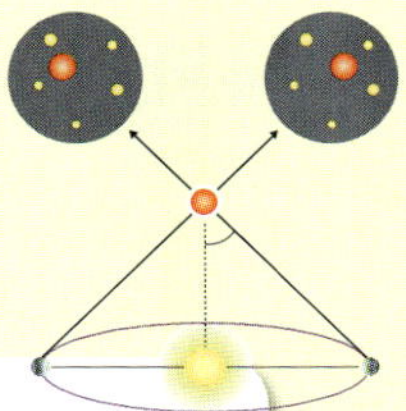

Summary

- The color of a star depends on its temperature. Hot stars are blue. Cool stars are red.
- The spectrum of a star shows the composition of a star.
- Scientists classify stars by temperature and brightness.
- Apparent magnitude is the brightness of a star as seen from Earth.
- Absolute magnitude is the measured brightness of a star at a distance of 32.6 light-years.
- Astronomers use parallax and trigonometry to measure distances from Earth to stars.
- Stars appear to move because of Earth's rotation. However, the actual motion of stars is very hard to see because stars are so distant.

Using Key Terms

1. Use the following terms in the same sentence: *apparent magnitude* and *absolute magnitude*.
2. Use each of the following terms in a separate sentence: *spectrum, light-year,* and *parallax.*

Understanding Key Ideas

3. When you look at white light through a glass prism, you see a rainbow of colors called a
   a. spectograph.
   b. spectrum.
   c. parallax.
   d. light-year.
4. Class F stars are
   a. blue.
   b. yellow.
   c. yellow-white.
   d. red.
5. Describe how scientists classify stars.
6. Explain how color indicates the temperature of a star.

Critical Thinking

7. **Applying Concepts** If a certain star displayed a large parallax, what could you say about the star's distance from Earth?
8. **Making Comparisons** Compare a continuous spectrum with an absorption spectrum. Then, explain how an absorption spectrum can identify a star's composition.
9. **Making Comparisons** Compare apparent motion with actual motion.

Interpreting Graphics

10. Look at the two figures below. How many hours passed between the first image and the second image? Explain your answer.

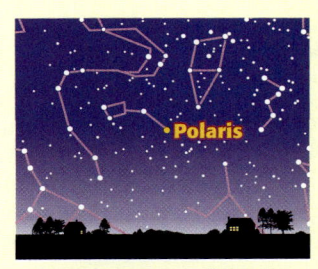

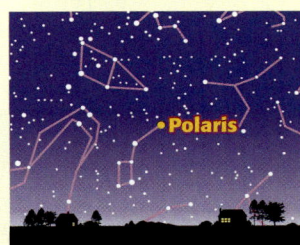

Answers to Section Review

1. Sample answer: Apparent magnitude is the brightness of a star as seen from Earth, whereas absolute magnitude is the measured brightness of a star at a distance of 32.6 light-years.
2. Sample answer: A spectrum is the band of color produced when white light passes through a prism. A light-year is the distance that light travels in one year. Parallax is an apparent shift in the position of an object when the object is viewed from different locations.
3. b
4. c
5. Scientists classify stars by temperature and brightness.
6. Astronomers have determined that the color of a star is the direct result of its temperature. For example, hot stars are blue, and cool stars are red.
7. The star would be relatively close to Earth.
8. A continuous spectrum is a spectrum that shows all colors. An absorption spectrum is produced when light from a hot solid or dense gas passes through a cooler gas. Stars give off an absorption spectrum. The pattern of lines in a star's absorption spectrum shows some of the elements that are in the star's atmosphere and therefore identifies the star's composition.
9. The apparent motion of stars is due to Earth's rotation. The actual motion, or true motion of stars, is very hard to see because stars are so distant from Earth.
10. About 6 hours have passed. The stars would make a complete circle (360°) in 24 h. In the figures, they have turned 90°, which is 1/4 of 360°. Therefore, 24 h × 1/4 = 6 h.

CHAPTER RESOURCES

Chapter Resource File
- Section Quiz GENERAL
- Section Review GENERAL
- Vocabulary and Section Summary GENERAL
- Critical Thinking ADVANCED
- SciLinks Activity GENERAL
- Datasheet for Quick Lab

Section 1 • Stars   589

SECTION 2

Focus

Overview
This section discusses the life cycle of stars. It also explores how the H-R diagram shows the relationship between a star's surface temperature and absolute magnitude. Finally, this section discusses how stars can become supernovas, neutron stars, pulsars, or black holes.

🔔 Bellringer
Display photographs of Supernova 1987A and a photograph of the Large Magellanic Cloud taken before the explosion. Explain that supernovas represent the "death" of stars that exceed a certain mass. In a few seconds, a supernova can release more energy than it previously released in its entire existence.

SECTION 2

The Life Cycle of Stars

Some stars exist for billions of years. But how are they born? And what happens when a star dies?

Because stars exist for billions of years, scientists cannot observe a star throughout its entire life. Therefore, scientists have developed theories about the life cycle of stars by studying them in different stages of development.

READING WARM-UP

Objectives
- Describe different types of stars.
- Describe the quantities that are plotted in the H-R diagram.
- Explain how stars at different stages in their life cycle appear on the H-R diagram.

Terms to Learn
red giant   supernova
white dwarf   neutron star
H-R diagram   pulsar
main sequence   black hole

READING STRATEGY

Paired Summarizing Read this section silently. In pairs, take turns summarizing the material. Stop to discuss ideas that seem confusing.

The Beginning and End of Stars

A star enters the first stage of its life cycle as a ball of gas and dust. Gravity pulls the gas and dust together into a sphere. As the sphere becomes denser, it gets hotter and the hydrogen changes to helium in a process called *nuclear fusion*.

As stars get older, they lose some of their material. Stars usually lose material slowly, but sometimes they can lose material in a big explosion. Either way, when a star dies, much of its material returns to space. In space, some of the material combines with more gas and dust to form new stars.

Different Types of Stars

Stars can be classified by their size, mass, brightness, color, temperature, spectrum, and age. Some types of stars include *main-sequence stars*, *giants*, *supergiants*, and *white dwarf stars*. A star can be classified as one type of star early in its life cycle and then can be classified as another star when it gets older. For example, the star shown in **Figure 1** has reached the final stage in its life cycle. It has run out of fuel, which has caused the central parts of the star to collapse inward.

Figure 1 This star (center) has entered the last stage of its life cycle.

CHAPTER RESOURCES

Chapter Resource File
- Lesson Plan
- Directed Reading A BASIC
- Directed Reading B SPECIAL NEEDS

Technology
- Transparencies
  • Bellringer

CONNECTION to Astronomy — ADVANCED

The *Hubble Space Telescope* From its orbit around the Earth, the *Hubble Space Telescope* has photographed newborn stars emerging from huge pillars of dense gas and dust. Some of these events occurred about 7,000 light-years away in the Eagle Nebula. The largest of these pillars photographed by the telescope is an estimated 10 trillion kilometers long. Have students find these images on the Internet and discuss them during class. **LS Verbal**

590 Chapter 19 • Stars, Galaxies, and the Universe

Main-Sequence Stars

After a star forms, it enters the second and longest stage of its life cycle known as the main sequence. During this stage, energy is generated in the core of the star as hydrogen atoms fuse into helium atoms. This process releases an enormous amount of energy. The size of a main-sequence star will change very little as long as the star has a continuous supply of hydrogen atoms to fuse into helium atoms.

Giants and Supergiants

After the main-sequence stage, a star can enter the third stage of its life cycle. In this third stage, a star can become a red giant. A **red giant** is a star that expands and cools once it uses all of its hydrogen. Eventually, the loss of hydrogen causes the center of the star to shrink. As the center of the star shrinks, the atmosphere of the star grows very large and cools to form a red giant or a red supergiant, as shown in **Figure 2**. Red giants can be 10 or more times bigger than the sun. Supergiants are at least 100 times bigger than the sun.

Reading Check What is the difference between a red giant star and a red supergiant star? *(See the Appendix for answers to Reading Checks.)*

Figure 2 The red supergiant star Antares is shown above. Antares is located in the constellation of Scorpius.

red giant a large, reddish star late in its life cycle

white dwarf a small, hot, dim star that is the leftover center of an old star

White Dwarfs

In the final stages of a star's life cycle, a star that has the same mass as the sun or smaller can be classified as a white dwarf. A **white dwarf** is a small hot star that is the leftover center of an older star. A white dwarf has no hydrogen left and can no longer generate energy by fusing hydrogen atoms into helium atoms. White dwarfs can shine for billions of years before they cool completely.

CONNECTION TO Astronomy

WRITING SKILL **Long Live the Sun** Our sun probably took about 10 million years to become a main-sequence star. It has been shining for about 5 billion years. In another 5 billion years, our sun will burn up most of its hydrogen and expand to become a red giant. When this change happens, the sun's diameter will increase. How will this change affect Earth and our solar system? Use the Internet or library resources to find out what might happen as the sun gets older and how the changes in the sun might affect our solar system. Gather your findings, and write a report on what you find out about the life cycle the sun.

Answer to Reading Check

A red giant star is a star that expands and cools once it uses most of its hydrogen. As the center of a star continues to shrink, a red giant star can become a red supergiant star.

Motivate

Discussion — GENERAL

Star Characteristics Ask students to hypothesize how a star's magnitude, temperature, mass, density, and composition are related. (A star's mass and density affect its temperature, composition, and magnitude.) By learning about types of stars, students will learn how to determine a star's age. When its nuclear fuel begins to be used up, the star changes. Throughout their life cycles, stars vary in magnitude, temperature, mass, density, and composition. **LS** Verbal

Teach

ACTIVITY — ADVANCED

Researching Red Giants Encourage students to research what happens as a red giant or supergiant ages. Direct them to focus on the physical changes that occur in an aging star and to prepare a brief report or poster describing the reactions that allow an old star to spend several million years alternately approaching and receding from the main sequence. (Reports and posters should include the following information: As a red giant or supergiant ages, its helium core contracts and grows hotter, while its burning hydrogen mantle expands and cools. As a result, the star grows bigger and brighter. When the core reaches a temperature of 100 million degrees Celsius, its helium converts to carbon through nuclear fusion. Over the next several million years, the star alternately approaches and recedes from the main sequence.) **LS** Intrapersonal

Section 2 • The Life Cycle of Stars

Teach, continued

Using the Figure — BASIC

Star Magnitudes Remind students that the lower the magnitude of a star is, the brighter the star is. By looking at the H-R diagram, students should be able to identify the sun as a main-sequence, yellowish dwarf star with medium brightness and a surface temperature of almost 6,000°C. Have students describe other stars in the diagram in a similar manner. **LS** Visual/Logical

Group Activity — GENERAL

Star Cycle Divide the class into small groups, and provide each group with a piece of newsprint paper and markers. Direct each group to use these materials to create a flowchart describing the life of a star. Encourage students to refer to the H-R diagram as they work. Their chart should indicate that stars (1) form when gas and dust are drawn together by gravity and nuclear fusion begin, (2) enter the main sequence when they mature, and (3) may then become red giants, supergiants, or eventually white dwarfs. Have students label their charts and write a descriptive caption for each stage. **LS** Interpersonal/Visual

H-R diagram Hertzsprung-Russell diagram, a graph that shows the relationship between a star's surface temperature and absolute magnitude

A Tool for Studying Stars

In 1911, a Danish astronomer named Ejnar Hertzsprung (IE nawr HUHRTS sproong) compared the brightness and temperature of stars on a graph. Two years later, American astronomer Henry Norris Russell made some similar graphs. Although these astronomers used different data, they had similar results. The combination of their ideas is now called the Hertzsprung-Russell diagram, or H-R diagram. The **H-R diagram** is a graph that shows the relationship between a star's surface temperature and its absolute magnitude. Over the years, the H-R diagram has become a tool for studying the lives of stars. It shows not only how stars are classified by brightness and temperature but also how stars change over time.

Blue Stars Very massive blue stars are not in the main sequence very long. They quickly use up the hydrogen in their cores, expand, and turn into giants or supergiants.

Main-Sequence Stars Stars in the main sequence form a band that runs along the middle of the H-R diagram. The sun is a main-sequence star. The sun has been shining for about 5 billion years. Scientists think the sun is in midlife and that it will remain on the main sequence for another 5 billion years.

White Dwarf Stars These small, hot stars—the leftover centers of old stars—are near the end of their lives. The leftover center of an old star is very hot. At this stage, a star is called a *white dwarf*. According to astronomers, the sun will eventually become a white dwarf.

WEIRD SCIENCE

When the core from a star that is the size of the sun becomes a white dwarf that is the size of Earth, the white dwarf is much denser than our planet. In fact, a teaspoon of the matter that makes up a white dwarf would weigh several metric tons on Earth!

Is That a Fact!

Most of the stars near our solar system are not as bright as the sun. How do we know this fact? When the 100 stars nearest to Earth are arranged on the H-R diagram, we can see that almost all of them fall in the region of the red dwarfs. The sun is a brighter, type G main-sequence star.

Reading the H-R Diagram

The modern H-R diagram is shown below. Temperature is given along the bottom of the diagram and absolute magnitude, or brightness, is given along the left side. Hot (blue) stars are located on the left, and cool (red) stars are on the right. Bright stars are at the top, and dim stars are at the bottom. The brightest stars are 1 million times brighter than the sun. The dimmest stars are 1/10,000 as bright as the sun. The diagonal pattern on the H-R diagram where most stars lie, is called the **main sequence.** A star spends most of its lifetime in the main sequence. As main-sequence stars age, they move up and to the right on the H-R diagram to become giants or supergiants and then down and to the left to become white dwarfs.

main sequence the location on the H-R diagram where most stars lie

Giants and Supergiants

When a star runs out of hydrogen in its core, the center of the star shrinks inward and the outer parts expand outward. For a star the size of our sun, the star's atmosphere will grow very large and become cool. When this change happens, the star becomes a *red giant*. If the star is very massive, it becomes a supergiant.

The Sun
The sun is an average star. It is a main-sequence star and is located in the middle of the diagram. The sun is 1 solar diameter and has 1 solar mass. The brightness of stars can also be measured against the sun's brightness.

Red Dwarf Stars

At the lower end of the main sequence are the red dwarf stars, which are low-mass stars. Low-mass stars remain on the main sequence a long time. The stars that have the lowest mass are among the oldest stars in the universe.

ACTIVITY — BASIC

Using the H-R Diagram Have students locate where on the H-R diagram each of the stars in the table below would be found.

	Magnitude	Temperature
Star A	+10	10,000°C
Star B	−2	5,000°C
Star C	+3	7,000°C
Star D	−9	3,500°C

Ask students the following questions:

- Which star is a giant? (B)
- Which star is a white dwarf? (A)
- Which star is a supergiant? (D)
- Which star is most like the sun? (C)

LS Verbal/Visual

CONNECTION ACTIVITY
Language Arts — BASIC

Star Crossword Puzzles Divide the class into small groups, and challenge each group to create a crossword puzzle using the vocabulary and concepts from this section. Have students in each group work together to write clues and to construct the puzzle. Then allow groups to exchange and solve the puzzles.
LS Interpersonal   English Language Learners

INTERNET ACTIVITY
Sequence Board — GENERAL

For an Internet activity related to this chapter, have students go to **go.hrw.com** and type in the keyword **HZ5UNVW**.

CHAPTER RESOURCES

Technology

- **Transparencies**
  - The H-R Diagram: A
  - The H-R Diagram: B

Section 2 • The Life Cycle of Stars   **593**

Close

Reteaching — BASIC
Autobiography of the Stars
Have students write a brief autobiography of each type of star and then read their autobiography to the class. **LS Verbal**

Quiz — GENERAL

1. What information does the H-R diagram give us? (It indicates the relationship between a star's temperature and the star's brightness, which indicates the star's age.)

2. What is a supernova? (the explosion of a massive star at the end of its life)

3. What is a neutron star? How is it different from a pulsar? (A neutron star is the compressed core of a star that became a supernova. A pulsar is a spinning neutron star.)

Alternative Assessment — GENERAL

Writing **1987A** Have students research the astral events of 1987, known as the "year of the supernova." Have them prepare a brief report and share their findings with the class. (Reports should include the following information: In 1987, for the first time in almost 400 years, people on Earth witnessed the death of a star without using a telescope. The supernova was located in a satellite galaxy of the Milky Way called the *Large Magellanic Cloud* and was visible only from the Southern Hemisphere.) **LS Interpersonal**

When Stars Get Old

Although stars may stay on the main sequence for a long time, they don't stay there forever. Average stars, such as the sun, become red giants and then white dwarfs. However, stars that are more massive than the sun may explode with such intensity that they become a variety of strange objects such as supernovas, neutron stars, pulsars, and black holes.

Supernovas

Massive blue stars use their hydrogen much faster than stars like the sun do. Therefore, blue stars generate more energy than stars like the sun do, which makes blue stars very hot and blue! And compared with other stars, blue stars don't have long lives. At the end of its life, a blue star may explode in a large, bright flash called a *supernova*. A **supernova** is a gigantic explosion in which a massive star collapses. The explosion is so powerful that it can be brighter than an entire galaxy for several days. The ringed structure shown in **Figure 3** is the result of a supernova explosion.

Neutron Stars and Pulsars

After a supernova occurs, the materials in the center of a supernova are squeezed together to form a new star. This new star is about two times the mass of the sun. The particles inside the star's core are forced together to form neutrons. A star that has collapsed under gravity to the point at which all of its particles are neutrons is called a **neutron star.**

If a neutron star is spinning, it is called a **pulsar.** A pulsar sends out a beam of radiation that spins very rapidly. The beam is detected on Earth by radio telescopes as rapid clicks, or pulses.

supernova a gigantic explosion in which a massive star collapses and throws its outer layers into space

neutron star a star that has collapsed under gravity to the point that the electrons and protons have smashed together to form neutrons

pulsar a rapidly spinning neutron star that emits rapid pulses of radio and optical energy

Figure 3 Explosion of a Supernova

Supernova 1987A was the first supernova visible to the unaided eye in 400 years. The first image shows what the original star must have looked like only a few hours before the explosion. Today, the star's remains form a double ring of gas and dust, as shown at right.

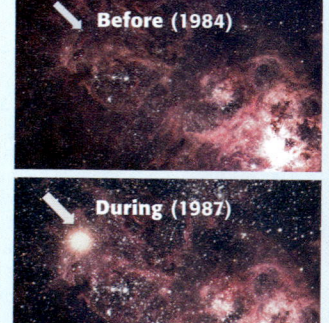

Before (1984)

During (1987)

After (Hubble Space Telescope close-up, 1994)

SCIENCE HUMOR

When pulsars were first recorded, their regular pulses of energy were unlike anything else in the universe. Astronomers first thought that the pulses might be signals transmitted by intelligent beings. Jokingly, pulsars were called *LGM*—an acronym for *Little Green Men*.

Black Holes

Sometimes the leftovers of a supernova are so massive that they collapse to form a black hole. A **black hole** is an object that is so massive that even light cannot escape its gravity. So, it is called a *black hole*. A black hole doesn't gobble up other stars like some movies show. Because black holes do not give off light, locating them is difficult. If a star is nearby, some gas or dust from the star will spiral into the black hole and give off X rays. These X rays allow astronomers to detect the existence of black holes.

black hole an object so massive and dense that even light cannot escape its gravity

✓ **Reading Check** What is a black hole? How do astronomers detect the presence of black holes?

SECTION Review

Summary

- New stars form from the material of old stars that have gone through their lives.
- Types of stars include main-sequence stars, giants and supergiants, and white dwarf stars.
- The H-R diagram shows the brightness of a star in relation to the temperature of a star. It also shows the life cycle of stars.
- Most stars are main-sequence stars.
- Massive stars become supernovas. Their cores can change into neutron stars or black holes.

Using Key Terms

For each pair of terms, explain how the meanings of the terms differ.

1. *white dwarf* and *red giant*
2. *supernova* and *neutron star*
3. *pulsar* and *black hole*

Understanding Key Ideas

4. The sun is a
   a. white dwarf.
   b. main-sequence star.
   c. red giant.
   d. red dwarf.
5. A star begins as a ball of gas and dust pulled together by
   a. black holes.
   b. electrons and protons.
   c. heavy metals.
   d. gravity.
6. Are blue stars young or old? How can you tell?
7. In main-sequence stars, what is the relationship between brightness and temperature?
8. Arrange the following stages in order of their appearance in the life cycle of a star: white dwarf, red giant, and main-sequence star. Explain your answer.

Math Skills

9. The sun's present radius is 700,000 km. If the sun's radius increased by 150 times, what would its radius be?

Critical Thinking

10. **Applying Concepts** Given that there are more low-mass stars than high-mass stars in the universe, do you think there are more white dwarfs or more black holes in the universe? Explain.
11. **Analyzing Processes** Describe what might happen to a star after it becomes a supernova.
12. **Evaluating Data** How does the H-R diagram explain the life cycle of a star?

SciLINKS
Developed and maintained by the National Science Teachers Association
For a variety of links related to this chapter, go to www.scilinks.org
Topic: Supernova
SciLinks code: HSM1482

Answer to Reading Check

A black hole is an object that is so massive that even light cannot escape its gravity. A black hole can be detected when it gives off X rays.

Answers to Section Review

1. Sample answer: White dwarfs are small, hot, dim stars that are leftover centers of old stars. Red giants are large, reddish stars that are in the third stage of their life cycles.
2. Sample answer: A supernova is a gigantic explosion in which a massive star collapses and throws its outer layers into space. A neutron star is a massive star that has collapsed under gravity to the point that the electrons and protons have become neutrons.
3. Sample answer: A pulsar is a rapidly spinning neutron star that emits rapid pulses of radio and optical energy. A black hole is an object that is so massive and dense that even light cannot escape its gravity.
4. b
5. d
6. Blue stars are young. They use up their hydrogen quickly and become supernovas before they get old.
7. In the main sequence, hotter stars are usually brighter.
8. The order would be main-sequence star, red giant, and white dwarf. As a main-sequence star runs out of fuel, its core shrinks and its atmosphere expands. It then becomes a red giant. After the red giant loses its outer layers, its core remains as a white dwarf.
9. 700,000 km × 150 = 105,000,000 km
10. There are more white dwarfs. White dwarfs are the remains of average-sized stars that grow old. Only very massive stars become black holes.
11. After a star becomes a supernova, it could become a neutron star, a pulsar, or a black hole.
12. The H-R diagram explains the life cycle of a star, because a star can be plotted on the diagram at any point during its life cycle. The H-R diagram plots stars according to their magnitude and temperature. Therefore, as a star goes through its life cycle, it can be plotted in different locations as its magnitude and temperature change.

CHAPTER RESOURCES

Chapter Resource File
- Section Quiz GENERAL
- Section Review GENERAL
- Vocabulary and Section Summary GENERAL
- Reinforcement Worksheet BASIC

Section 2 • The Life Cycle of Stars

SECTION 3

Focus

Overview

This section discusses the differences between the three types of galaxies: spiral, elliptical, and irregular. Students will learn that galaxies have features known as *nebulas, open clusters,* and *globular clusters.* Finally, students will learn how scientists study the origin of galaxies.

Bellringer

Show students a photograph of a spiral galaxy. Discuss the evidence that indicates that the galaxy is rotating. Ask students the following questions: "What other objects that look similar have you seen? Do they rotate?" **English Language Learners**
LS **Visual/Verbal**

Motivate

Discussion — GENERAL

Star Factory Galaxies can be thought of as star factories. Ask students to identify the raw materials used by the "factory" to produce stars. (clouds of gas and dust) Have students describe how stars are assembled. (The gases and dust are drawn together by gravity.) Discuss whether star formation is an ongoing process. (Establish that the process is ongoing because of the abundance of raw materials.) LS **Verbal**

SECTION 3

READING WARM-UP

Objectives
- Identify three types of galaxies.
- Describe the contents and characteristics of galaxies.
- Explain why looking at distant galaxies reveals what young galaxies looked like.

Terms to Learn
galaxy
nebula
globular cluster
open cluster
quasar

READING STRATEGY

Reading Organizer As you read this section, make a table comparing the different types of galaxies.

galaxy a collection of stars, dust, and gas bound together by gravity

CHAPTER RESOURCES

Chapter Resource File
- Lesson Plan
- Directed Reading A BASIC
- Directed Reading B SPECIAL NEEDS

Technology
- Transparencies
- Bellringer

Galaxies

Your complete address is part of a much larger system than your street, city, state, country, and even the planet Earth. You also live in the Milky Way galaxy.

Large groups of stars, dust, and gas are called **galaxies**. Galaxies come in a variety of sizes and shapes. The largest galaxies contain more than a trillion stars. Astronomers don't count the stars, of course. They estimate how many sun-sized stars the galaxy might have by studying the size and brightness of the galaxy.

Types of Galaxies

There are many different types of galaxies. Edwin Hubble, the astronomer for whom the *Hubble Space Telescope* is named, began to classify galaxies, mostly by their shapes, in the 1920s. Astronomers still use the galaxy classification that Hubble developed.

Spiral Galaxies

When someone says the word *galaxy,* most people probably think of a spiral galaxy. *Spiral galaxies,* such as the one shown in **Figure 1,** have a bulge at the center and spiral arms. The spiral arms are made up of gas, dust, and new stars that have formed in these denser regions of gas and dust.

Reading Check What are two characteristics of spiral galaxies? What makes up the arms of a spiral galaxy? (See the Appendix for answers to Reading Checks.)

Figure 1 Types of Galaxies

▼ **Spiral Galaxy**
The Andromeda galaxy is a spiral galaxy that looks similar to what our galaxy, the Milky Way, is thought to look like.

Answer to Reading Check

Spiral galaxies have a bulge at the center and spiral arms. The arms of spiral galaxies are made up of gas, dust, and new stars.

---

596 Chapter 19 • Stars, Galaxies, and the Universe

The Milky Way

It is hard to tell what type of galaxy we live in because the gas, dust, and stars keep astronomers from having a good view of our galaxy. Observing other galaxies and making measurements inside our galaxy, the Milky Way, has led astronomers to think that our solar system is in a spiral galaxy.

Elliptical Galaxies

About one-third of all galaxies are simply massive blobs of stars. Many look like spheres, and others are more stretched out. Because we don't know how they are oriented, some of these galaxies could be cucumber shaped, with the round end facing our galaxy. These galaxies are called *elliptical galaxies*. Elliptical galaxies usually have very bright centers and very little dust and gas. Elliptical galaxies contain mostly old stars. Because there is so little free-flowing gas in an elliptical galaxy, few new stars form. Some elliptical galaxies, such as M87, shown in **Figure 1,** are huge and are called *giant elliptical galaxies*. Other elliptical galaxies are much smaller and are called *dwarf elliptical galaxies*.

CONNECTION TO Language Arts

WRITING SKILL **Alien Observer** As you read earlier, it's hard to tell what type of galaxy we live in because the gas, dust, and stars keep us from having a good view. But our galaxy might look different to an alien observer. Write a short story describing how our galaxy would look to an alien observer in another galaxy.

Irregular Galaxies

When Hubble first classified galaxies, he had a group of leftovers. He named the leftovers "irregulars." *Irregular galaxies* are galaxies that don't fit into any other class. As their name suggests, their shape is irregular. Many of these galaxies, such as the Large Magellanic Cloud, shown in **Figure 1,** are close companions of large spiral galaxies. The large spiral galaxies may be distorting the shape of these irregular galaxies.

▼ **Elliptical Galaxy**
Unlike the Milky Way, the galaxy known as M87 has no spiral arms.

▼ **Irregular Galaxy**
The Large Magellanic Cloud, an irregular galaxy, is located within our galactic neighborhood.

SCIENTISTS AT ODDS

The Shapley-Curtis Debate When the American astronomer Harlow Shapley mapped globular clusters, he found that they form an enormous spherical system surrounding the Milky Way and that Earth was not at the center of the galaxy. This discovery sparked a heated astronomical debate over whether other spiral nebulas in the distant universe are part of our galaxy or are separate "island universes," or distant galaxies. This discussion led to the 1920 Shapley-Curtis debate at the National Academy of Sciences. The debate was resolved in 1924, when observations by Edwin Hubble showed that these nebulas were so far away that they must be distinct galaxies.

Teach

INCLUSION Strategies

- *Learning Disabled*
- *Visually Impaired*
- *Gifted and Talented*

Organize students into small teams to play a galaxy quiz game. Each team should choose a category that relates to a heading in the section and then write five questions and answers for the category on separate index cards. The difficulty and point value of the questions should increase incrementally. Review each team's questions and answers before you start the game. If a team cannot answer a question, the team should work with another team to answer the question. If teams cooperate, they should share the points earned. When the game is over, hand out a review sheet that contains the questions and answers.
LS Interpersonal

BRAIN FOOD

Colliding Galaxies
Sometimes, entire galaxies collide and form new galaxies. Scientists theorize that these collisions result in elliptical or irregular galaxies. The Milky Way and our closest neighboring spiral galaxy, Andromeda, are moving toward each other at 500,000 km/h. Even at this speed, the galaxies will not collide for another 5 billion years.

Section 3 • Galaxies   **597**

Close

Reteaching — BASIC

Types of Galaxies Help students differentiate between the types of galaxies by having them divide a large sheet of paper into thirds and draw a spiral, an ellipse, and an irregular shape. Have students describe the galaxy type under each drawing. **English Language Learners**
LS Visual

Quiz — GENERAL

1. What is a nebula? (A nebula is an enormous cloud of gas and dust in space.)
2. What are open clusters? (They are groups of a few hundred to a few thousand stars that form when great amounts of gas and dust come together.)

Alternative Assessment — ADVANCED

Interstellar Medium Tell students that the material that exists between a galaxy's stars is called *interstellar medium*. Ask them to hypothesize what makes up interstellar medium. (Students should recognize that nebulas—giant clouds of gas and dust—make up interstellar medium.)

Challenge students to compare irregular, spiral, and elliptical galaxies and to determine how much interstellar medium each galaxy has. (Irregular and spiral galaxies have more interstellar medium than elliptical galaxies have.) LS Verbal

---

nebula a large cloud of dust and gas in interstellar space; a region in space where stars are born or where stars explode at the end of their lives

globular cluster a tight group of stars that looks like a ball and contains up to 1 million stars

open cluster a group of stars that are close together relative to surrounding stars

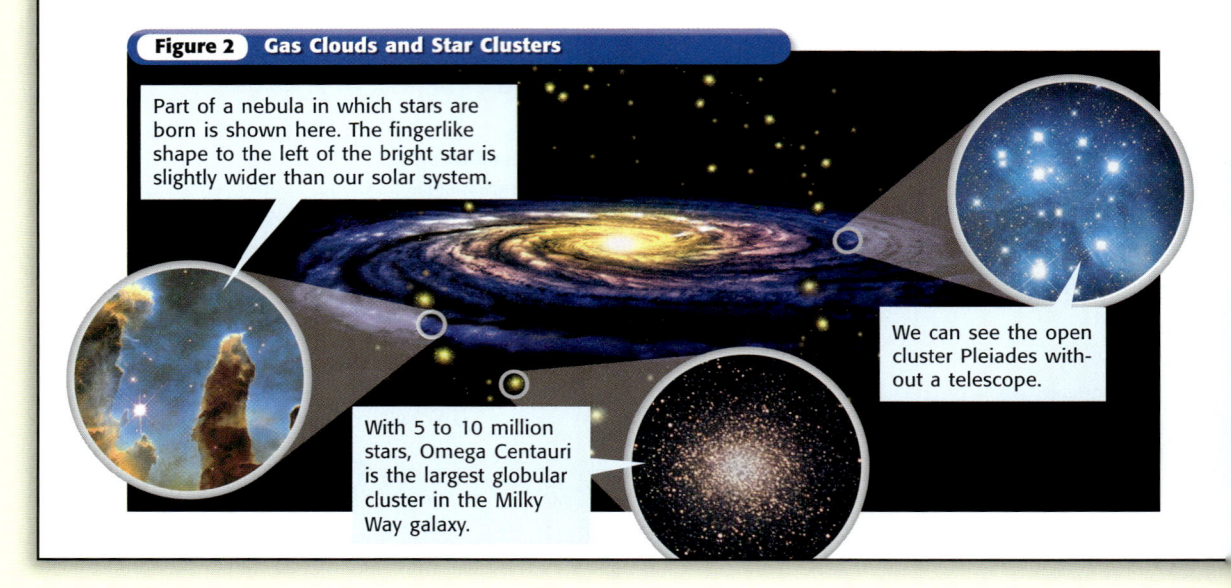

Answer to Reading Check

A globular cluster is a tight group of up to 1 million stars that looks like a ball. An open cluster is a group of closely grouped stars that are usually located along the spiral disk of a galaxy.

Contents of Galaxies

Galaxies are composed of billions of stars and some planetary systems, too. Some of these stars form large features, such as gas clouds and star clusters, as shown in **Figure 2**.

Gas Clouds

The Latin word for "cloud" is *nebula*. In space, **nebulas** (or nebulae) are large clouds of gas and dust. Some types of nebulas glow, while others absorb light and hide stars. Still, other nebulas reflect starlight and produce some amazing images. Some nebulas are regions in which new stars form. **Figure 2** shows part of the Eagle nebula. Spiral galaxies usually contain nebulas, but elliptical galaxies contain very few.

Star Clusters

Globular clusters are groups of older stars. A **globular cluster** is a group of stars that looks like a ball, as shown in **Figure 2**. There may be up to one million stars in a globular cluster. Globular clusters are located in a spherical *halo* that surrounds spiral galaxies such as the Milky Way. Globular clusters are also common near giant elliptical galaxies.

Open clusters are groups of closely grouped stars that are usually located along the spiral disk of a galaxy. Newly formed open clusters have many bright blue stars, as shown in **Figure 2**. There may be a few hundred to a few thousand stars in an open cluster.

✓ **Reading Check** What is the difference between a globular cluster and an open cluster?

Figure 2 Gas Clouds and Star Clusters

Part of a nebula in which stars are born is shown here. The fingerlike shape to the left of the bright star is slightly wider than our solar system.

With 5 to 10 million stars, Omega Centauri is the largest globular cluster in the Milky Way galaxy.

We can see the open cluster Pleiades without a telescope.

Is That a Fact!

Earth is about two-thirds of the distance from the center of the Milky Way to the edge of the Milky Way. Our solar system revolves around the galaxy every 200 million years. The last time the solar system was in its current position was during the Triassic period, when dinosaurs first appeared on Earth!

---

598 Chapter 19 • Stars, Galaxies, and the Universe

Origin of Galaxies

Scientists investigate the early universe by observing objects that are extremely far away in space. Because it takes time for light to travel through space, looking through a telescope is like looking back in time. Looking at distant galaxies reveals what early galaxies looked like. This information gives scientists an idea of how galaxies change over time and may give them insight about what caused the galaxies to form.

Quasars

Among the most distant objects are quasars. **Quasars** are starlike sources of light that are extremely far away. They are among the most powerful energy sources in the universe. Some scientists think that quasars may be caused by massive black holes in the cores of some galaxies. **Figure 3** shows a quasar that is 6 billion light-years away.

Reading Check What are quasars? What do some scientists think quasars might be?

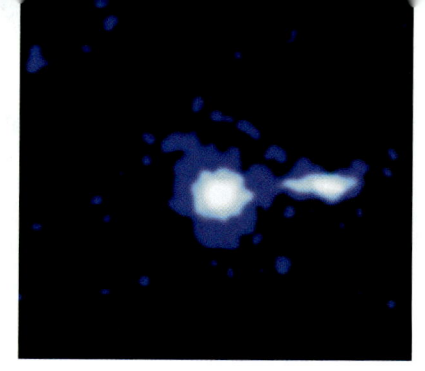

Figure 3 The quasar known as PKS 0637-752 is as massive as 10 billion suns.

quasar a very luminous, starlike object that generates energy at a high rate; quasars are thought to be the most distant objects in the universe

SECTION Review

Summary

- Edwin Hubble classified galaxies according to their shape including spiral, elliptical, and irregular galaxies.
- Some galaxies consist of nebulas and star clusters.
- Nebulas are large clouds of gas and dust. Globular clusters are tightly grouped stars. Open clusters are closely grouped stars.
- Scientists look at distant galaxies to learn what early galaxies looked like.

Using Key Terms

1. Use the following terms in the same sentence: *nebula, globular cluster,* and *open cluster.*

Understanding Key Ideas

2. Arrange the following galaxies in order of decreasing size: spiral, giant elliptical, dwarf elliptical, and irregular.

3. All of the following are shapes used to classify galaxies EXCEPT
   a. elliptical.
   b. irregular.
   c. spiral.
   d. triangular.

Critical Thinking

4. **Making Comparisons** Describe the difference between an elliptical galaxy and a globular cluster.

5. **Identifying Relationships** Explain how looking through a telescope is like looking back in time.

Math Skills

6. The quasar known as PKS 0637-752 is 6 billion light-years away from Earth. The North Star is 431 light-years away from Earth. What is the ratio of the distances in kilometers these two celestial objects are from Earth? (Hint: One light-year is equal to 9.46 trillion km.)

For a variety of links related to this chapter, go to www.scilinks.org
Topic: Galaxies
SciLinks code: HSM0632

Answer to Reading Check
Quasars are starlike sources of light that are extremely far away. Some scientists think that quasars may be the core of young galaxies that are in the process of forming.

Answers to Section Review

1. Sample answer: Nebulas, globular clusters, and open clusters are features of galaxies.
2. giant elliptical, spiral, irregular, dwarf elliptical
3. d
4. Sample answer: Elliptical galaxies usually have very bright centers and very little gas and dust. A globular cluster is a tight group of stars within a galaxy that looks like a ball and contains up to 1 million stars.
5. Looking through a telescope is like looking back in time because the light that you see through the telescope took a very long time to travel through space and reach your eye. Therefore, looking at distant galaxies reveals what early galaxies looked like.
6. The quasar is 6 billion light-years $\times$ 9.46 trillion km/light-year = 5.676×10^{22} km away from Earth; The North Star is 431 light-years $\times$ 9.46 trillion km/light-year = 4.08×10^{15} km away from Earth; ratio is about 6×10^{22} km: 4×10^{15} km = 6 million km: 4 km or 3 million km: 2 km

CHAPTER RESOURCES

Chapter Resource File
- Section Quiz GENERAL
- Section Review GENERAL
- Vocabulary and Section Summary GENERAL

Section 3 • Galaxies

SECTION 4

Focus

Overview
This section discusses the study of cosmology. Students will learn about the big bang theory and about evidence that supports the theory. Finally, they will learn about the structure of the universe.

🔔 Bellringer
Have students examine **Figure 1** and describe, in writing, the differences between the images. The first image represents the initial explosion, and the following images represent the expansion of the universe and the formation of the galaxies.

Motivate

ACTIVITY — GENERAL
The Expanding Universe Have students draw several dots on an uninflated balloon with a permanent marker and label the dots with letters. Ask students to measure the distances between the dots. Then, have students blow up their balloon and tie the end. Have students measure the distances between the dots again. Ask students to explain how this model represents the expansion of the universe. (As the universe expands, the distance between every star and galaxy increases.) **LS** Visual/Verbal

---

SECTION 4

READING WARM-UP

Objectives
- Describe the big bang theory.
- Explain evidence used to support the big bang theory.
- Describe the structure of the universe.
- Describe two ways scientists calculate the age of the universe.
- Explain what will happen if the universe expands forever.

Terms to Learn
cosmology
big bang theory

READING STRATEGY
Prediction Guide Before reading this section, write the title of each heading in this section. Next, under each heading, write what you think you will learn.

cosmology the study of the origin, properties, processes, and evolution of the universe

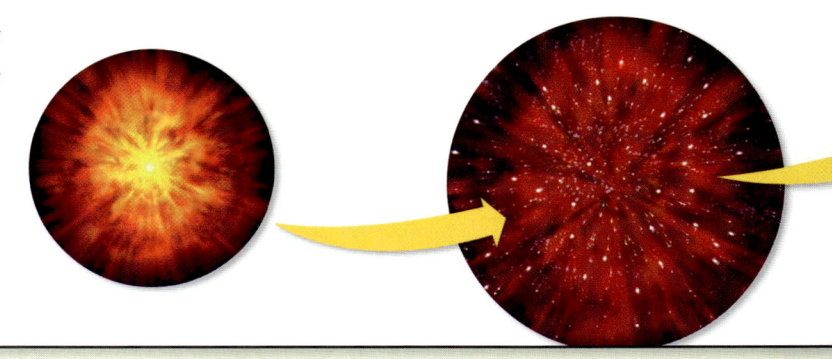

Figure 1 Some astronomers think the big bang caused the universe to expand in all directions.

CHAPTER RESOURCES

Chapter Resource File
- Lesson Plan
- Directed Reading A BASIC
- Directed Reading B SPECIAL NEEDS

Technology
- Transparencies
  - Bellringer
  - LINK TO PHYSICAL SCIENCE The Doppler Effect
  - The Big Bang Theory

Formation of the Universe

Imagine explosions, bright lights, and intense energy. Does that scene sound like an action movie? This scene could also describe a theory about the formation of the universe.

The study of the origin, structure, and future of the universe is called **cosmology**. Like other scientific theories, theories about the beginning and end of the universe must be tested by observations or experiments.

Universal Expansion
To understand how the universe formed, scientists study the movement of galaxies. Careful measurements have shown that most galaxies are moving apart.

A Raisin-Bread Model
To understand how the galaxies are moving, imagine a loaf of raisin bread before it is baked. Inside the dough, each raisin is a certain distance from every other raisin. As the dough gets warm and rises, it expands and all of the raisins begin to move apart. No matter which raisin you observe, the other raisins are moving farther away from it. The universe, like the rising bread dough, is expanding. Think of the raisins as galaxies. As the universe expands, the galaxies move farther apart.

The Big Bang Theory
With the discovery that the universe is expanding, scientists began to wonder what it would be like to watch the formation of the universe in reverse. The universe would appear to be contracting, not expanding. All matter would eventually come together at a single point. Thinking about what would happen if all of the matter in the universe were squeezed into such a small space led scientists to the big bang theory.

⚠ MISCONCEPTION ALERT

Distances in Space Students may have difficulty understanding that because of the great distances between Earth and stars, the light that they see was emitted from the stars in the distant past. If a star is 100 light-years away from Earth, the star's light takes 100 years to travel from the star to Earth.

---

600 Chapter 19 • Stars, Galaxies, and the Universe

A Tremendous Explosion

The theory that the universe began with a tremendous explosion is called the **big bang theory.** According to the theory, 13.7 billion years ago all the contents of the universe was compressed under extreme pressure, temperature, and density in a very tiny spot. Then, the universe rapidly expanded, and matter began to come together and form galaxies. **Figure 1** illustrates what the big bang might have looked like.

Cosmic Background Radiation

In 1964, two scientists using a huge antenna accidentally found radiation coming from all directions in space. One explanation for this radiation is that it is *cosmic background radiation* left over from the big bang. To understand the connection between the big bang theory and cosmic background radiation, think about a kitchen oven. When an oven door is left open after the oven has been used, thermal energy is transferred throughout the kitchen and the oven cools. Eventually, the room and the oven are the same temperature. According to the big bang theory, the thermal energy from the original explosion was distributed in every direction as the universe expanded. This cosmic background radiation now fills all of space.

Reading Check Explain the relationship between cosmic background radiation and the big bang theory. (*See the Appendix for answers to Reading Checks.*)

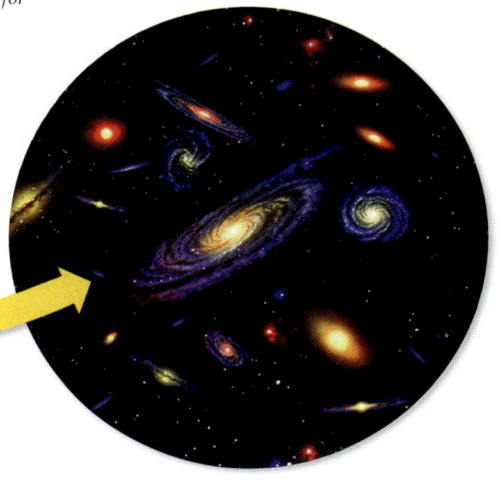

big bang theory the theory that states the universe began with a tremendous explosion 13.7 billion years ago

Teach

CONNECTION to Physical Science—GENERAL

Red Shift Ask students if they have ever noticed how the siren of an ambulance sounds higher in pitch when the ambulance is approaching than when it is receding. Students may be surprised to learn that a similar effect occurs with light. Scientists can observe that the light emitted by galaxies that are moving away from us is shifted to the red end of the spectrum. This shift occurs because as galaxies move away, the waves appear to have longer wavelengths. This phenomenon is caused by the Doppler effect. Because the light from all distant galaxies is red shifted, scientists can conclude that the universe is expanding. Use the teaching transparency called "The Doppler Effect" to show how the Doppler effect works with sound waves.
LS Visual

Answer to Reading Check
Cosmic background radiation is radiation that is left over from the big bang. After the big bang, cosmic background radiation was distributed everywhere and filled all of space.

MISCONCEPTION ALERT

The Big Bang Theory Make sure that students realize that according to the big bang theory, the big bang was not an explosion that happened "somewhere in space." Space and time did not exist before the big bang;—they came into being with the big bang. Just before expansion, the universe was compressed into an infinitely dense mass. There was no "space" outside this mass. Thus, we are not receding away from the bang; rather, the explosion continues to expand. We aren't moving away from the point of the big bang because the big bang is happening everywhere.

Section 4 • Formation of the Universe **601**

Close

Reteaching — BASIC
The Big Bang Theory Ask students to explain the big bang theory in their own words.
LS Verbal

Quiz — GENERAL
1. What is cosmic background radiation? (It is the radiation that comes from all directions in space and is left over from the big bang.)
2. How old is the universe? (13.7 billion years old)

Alternative Assessment — GENERAL
Universal Address Have students use reference materials to find out their universal address:

   Name
   Street address
   City, State
   Country
   Continent
   Planet
   Solar system
   Galaxy
   Galaxy group
   Galaxy cluster
   Local supercluster
   The universe

LS Verbal

Structure of the Universe

From our home on Earth, the universe stretches out farther than astronomers can see with their most advanced instruments. The universe contains a variety of objects. But these objects in the universe are not simply scattered through the universe in a random pattern. The universe has a structure that is loosely repeated over and over again.

A Cosmic Repetition

Every object in the universe is part of a larger system. As illustrated in **Figure 2,** a cluster or group of galaxies can be made up of smaller star clusters and galaxies. Galaxies, such as the Milky Way, can include planetary systems, such as our solar system. Earth is part of our solar system. Although our solar system is the planetary system that we are most familiar with, other planets have been detected in orbit around other stars. Scientists think that planetary systems are common in the universe.

How Old Is the Universe?

One way scientists can calculate the age of the universe is to measure the distance from Earth to various galaxies. By using these distances, scientists can estimate the age of the universe and predict its rate of expansion.

Another way to estimate the age of the universe is to calculate the ages of old, nearby stars. Because the universe must be at least as old as the oldest stars it contains, the ages of the stars provide a clue to the age of the universe.

Reading Check What is one way that scientists calculate the age of the universe?

Figure 2 Every object in the universe is part of a larger system. Earth is part of our solar system, which is in turn part of the Milky Way galaxy.

Answer to Reading Check
One way to calculate the age of the universe is to measure the distance from Earth to various galaxies.

Cultural Awareness — GENERAL

Milky Way Legends Many cultures have created legends about the Milky Way. The ancient Chinese believed that the Milky Way was a heavenly silver river, while early Scandinavians thought it was the path that souls took to reach heaven. Native American legends say that the stars of the Milky Way were campfires that guided souls to paradise.

A Forever Expanding Universe

What will happen to the universe? As the galaxies move farther apart, they get older and stop forming stars. The farther galaxies move apart from each other, the less visible to us they will become. The expansion of the universe depends on how much matter the universe contains. Scientists predict that if there is enough matter, gravity could eventually stop the expansion of the universe. If the universe stops expanding, it could start collapsing to its original state. This process would be a reverse of what might have happened during the big bang.

However, scientists now think that there may not be enough matter in the universe, so the universe will continue to expand forever. Therefore, stars will age and die, and the universe will probably become cold and dark after many billions of years. Even after the universe becomes cold and dark, it will continue to expand forever.

Reading Check If the universe expanded to the point at which gravity stopped the expansion, what would happen? What will happen if the expansion of the universe continues forever?

CONNECTION TO Physics

WRITING SKILL **Origin of the Universe** The big bang theory is one scientific theory about the origin of the universe. Use library resources to research these other scientific theories. In your **science journal**, describe in your own words the different theories of the origin of the universe. Use charts or tables to examine and evaluate these differences.

SECTION Review

Summary

- Observations show that the universe is expanding.
- The big bang theory states that the universe began with an explosion about 13.7 billion years ago.
- Cosmic background radiation helps support the big bang theory.
- Scientists use different ways to calculate the age of the universe.
- Scientists think that the universe may expand forever.

Using Key Terms

1. In your own words, write a definition for the following terms: *cosmology* and *big bang theory*.

Understanding Key Ideas

2. Describe two ways scientists calculate the age of the universe.

3. The expansion of the universe can be compared to
   a. cosmology.
   b. raisin bread baking in an oven.
   c. thermal energy leaving an oven as the oven cools.
   d. bread pudding.

4. How does cosmic background radiation support the big bang theory?

5. What do scientists think will eventually happen to the universe?

Math Skills

6. The North Star is 4.08×10^{12} km from Earth. What is this number written in its long form?

Critical Thinking

7. **Applying Concepts** Explain how every object in the universe is part of a larger system.

8. **Analyzing Ideas** Why do scientists think that the universe will expand forever?

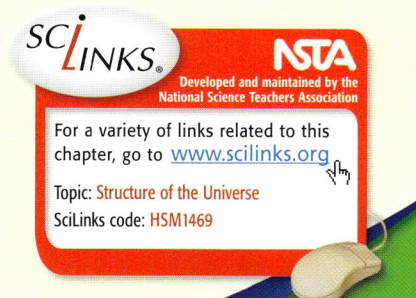

SciLinks For a variety of links related to this chapter, go to www.scilinks.org
Topic: Structure of the Universe
SciLinks code: HSM1469

Homework — ADVANCED

Age of the Universe Remind students that one way to determine the age of the universe is to divide the distance to other galaxies by the speed at which those galaxies appear to be moving away from us. Scientists now think that the universe is 13.7 billion years old. Have students consider how many light-years away a celestial object would be if it existed during the formation of the universe. (It would be 13.7 billion light-years away.) **Logical**

CHAPTER RESOURCES

Chapter Resource File
- Section Quiz GENERAL
- Section Review GENERAL
- Vocabulary and Section Summary GENERAL
- Critical Thinking ADVANCED

Answers to Section Review

1. Sample answer: The study of the origin, structure, and future of the universe is called *cosmology*. The theory that the universe began with a tremendous explosion is called the *big bang theory*.

2. One way that scientists calculate the age of the universe is by measuring the distance from Earth to various galaxies. Another way to estimate the age of the universe is to calculate the ages of old, nearby stars.

3. b

4. Cosmic background radiation supports the big bang theory because measurements show that cosmic background radiation is distributed everywhere in the universe, which is what the big bang theory predicts.

5. Scientists think that the universe may continue to expand forever. Therefore, stars will die and the universe will eventually become a cold and dark place after billions of years, because the fusion process will gradually cause stars to die out.

6. 4,080,000,000,000 km

7. Sample answer: Every object in the universe is part of a larger system because the universe has a structure that is loosely repeated. For example, a cluster or group of galaxies can be made up of smaller star clusters and galaxies.

8. Scientists think that the universe will expand forever because they think that there may not be enough matter to produce the gravitational attraction needed to counteract expansion.

Answer to Reading Check

If gravity stops the expansion of the universe, the universe might collapse. If the expansion of the universe continues forever, stars will age and die and the universe will eventually become cold and dark.

Section 4 • Formation of the Universe

Skills Practice Lab

Red Hot, or Not?

Teacher's Notes

Time Required
One 45-minute class period

Lab Ratings
EASY → HARD

Teacher Prep 🧪🧪
Student Set-Up 🧪🧪
Concept Level 🧪
Clean Up 🧪

MATERIALS

The materials listed on this page are enough for a group of 3 to 4 students.

Safety Caution
Remind students to review all safety cautions and icons before beginning this lab activity. Be sure that the students disconnect the wires at each step. If left connected, the wires can get very hot.

Lab Notes
Students may find that holding the wires to the light bulb is difficult. If so, you may use a light socket. Any miniature incandescent light bulb can be used as the flashlight bulb.

Using Scientific Methods
Skills Practice Lab

OBJECTIVES

Discover what the color of a glowing object reveals about the temperature of the object.

Describe how the color and temperature of a star are related.

MATERIALS

- battery, D cell (2)
- battery, D cell, weak
- flashlight bulb
- tape, electrical
- wire, insulated copper, with ends stripped, 20 cm long (2)

SAFETY

Red Hot, or Not?

When you look at the night sky, some stars are brighter than others. Some are even different colors. For example, Betelgeuse, a bright star in the constellation Orion, glows red. Sirius, one of the brightest stars in the sky, glows bluish white. Astronomers use color to estimate the temperature of stars. In this activity, you will experiment with a light bulb and some batteries to discover what the color of a glowing object reveals about the temperature of the object.

Ask a Question

1. How are the color and temperature of a star related?

Form a Hypothesis

2. On a sheet of paper, change the question above into a statement that gives your best guess about the relationship between a star's color and temperature.

Kathy McKee
Hoyt Middle School
Des Moines, Iowa

CHAPTER RESOURCES

Chapter Resource File
- Datasheet for Chapter Lab
- Lab Notes and Answers

Technology
- Classroom Videos
  - Lab Video

LabBook
- I See the Light!

---

604 Chapter 19 • Stars, Galaxies, and the Universe

Test the Hypothesis

3. Tape one end of an insulated copper wire to the positive pole of the weak D cell. Tape one end of the second wire to the negative pole.

4. Touch the free end of each wire to the light bulb. Hold one of the wires against the bottom tip of the light bulb. Hold the second wire against the side of the metal portion of the bulb. The bulb should light.

5. Record the color of the filament in the light bulb. Carefully touch your hand to the bulb. Observe the temperature of the bulb. Record your observations.

6. Repeat steps 3–5 with one of the two fresh D cells.

7. Use the electrical tape to connect two fresh D cells so that the positive pole of the first cell is connected to the negative pole of the second cell.

8. Repeat steps 3–5 using the fresh D cells that are taped together.

Analyze the Results

1. **Describing Events** What was the color of the filament in each of the three trials? For each trial, compare the bulb temperature to the temperature of the bulb in the other two trials.

2. **Analyzing Results** What information does the color of a star tell you about the star?

3. **Classifying** What color are stars that have relatively high surface temperatures? What color are stars that have relatively low surface temperatures?

Draw Conclusions

4. **Applying Conclusions** Arrange the following stars in order from highest to lowest surface temperature: Sirius, which is bluish white; Aldebaran, which is orange; Procyon, which is yellow-white; Capella, which is yellow; and Betelgeuse, which is red.

Analyze the Results

1. With the weaker cell, the filament should glow with a dull red color. The filament glows bright red or orange with the stronger cell. With two fresh D cells, the filament becomes almost white. The temperature increases as more cells—or if fresh cells—are used.

2. Cooler objects emit red light. As an object becomes hotter, its color gradually changes from red to orange to white. Therefore, the color of the light emitted from the stars helps scientists determine the surface temperatures of stars.

3. Stars that have relatively high surface temperatures are white or blue. Stars that have relatively low surface temperatures are red or orange.

Draw Conclusions

4. The order of the stars from highest to lowest surface temperature is as follows: Sirius, Procyon, Capella, Aldebaran, and Betelgeuse.

CHAPTER RESOURCES

Workbooks

- **Whiz-Bang Demonstrations**
  - Where Do the Stars Go? BASIC
- **Long-Term Projects & Research Ideas**
  - Contacting the Aliens ADVANCED

Chapter 19 • Chapter Lab

Chapter Review

Assignment Guide

Section	Questions
1	1, 4, 5, 7–10, 13–14, 17, 19, 21
2	12, 16, 18
3	2, 3
4	6, 11, 15, 20
1, 3	22–24

ANSWERS

Using Key Terms

1. a light-year
2. Open clusters
3. elliptical galaxies
4. spectrum

Understanding Key Ideas

5. c
6. d
7. c
8. a
9. d
10. Scientists classify stars by temperature and magnitude.
11. Sample answer: The universe has a structure that is loosely repeated over and over again. Every object in the universe is part of a larger system. For example, a group of galaxies can include planetary systems, such as our solar system.

Chapter Review

USING KEY TERMS

The statements below are false. For each statement, replace the underlined term to make a true statement.

1. The distance that light travels in space in 1 year is called <u>apparent magnitude</u>.
2. <u>Globular clusters</u> are groups of stars that are usually located along the spiral disk of a galaxy.
3. Galaxies that have very bright centers and very little dust and gas are called <u>spiral galaxies</u>.
4. When you look at white light through a glass prism, you see a rainbow of colors called a <u>supernova</u>.

UNDERSTANDING KEY IDEAS

Multiple Choice

5. A scientist can identify a star's composition by looking at
   a. the star's prism.
   b. the star's continuous spectrum.
   c. the star's absorption spectrum.
   d. the star's color.

6. If the universe expands forever,
   a. the universe will collapse.
   b. the universe will repeat itself.
   c. the universe will remain just as it is today.
   d. stars will age and die and the universe will become cold and dark.

7. The majority of stars in our galaxy are
   a. blue stars.
   b. white dwarfs.
   c. main-sequence stars.
   d. red giants.

8. Which of the following is used to measure the distance between objects in space?
   a. parallax   c. zenith
   b. magnitude   d. altitude

9. Which of the following stars would be seen as the brightest star?
   a. Alcyone, which has an apparent magnitude of 3
   b. Alpheratz, which has an apparent magnitude of 2
   c. Deneb, which has an apparent magnitude of 1
   d. Rigel, which has an apparent magnitude of 0

Short Answer

10. Describe how scientists classify stars.
11. Describe the structure of the universe.
12. Explain how stars at different stages in their life cycle appear on the H-R diagram.
13. Explain the difference between the apparent motion and actual motion of stars.
14. Describe how color indicates the temperature of a star.
15. Describe two ways that scientists calculate the age of the universe.

---

12. Sample answer: After a star forms, it enters the second and longest stage of its life cycle, known as the *main sequence*. The main sequence is the diagonal pattern on the H-R diagram where most stars lie. After the main sequence, a star can enter the third stage of its life cycle and become a red giant star. Red giants are located on the upper-right part of the H-R diagram because these stars are very massive. In the final stages of a star's life cycle, a star can become a white dwarf. White dwarfs are located in the lower-left part of the H-R diagram because they are extremely hot but dim.

13. The apparent motion of stars, or how the stars appear to move, is due to Earth's rotation. The actual motion of stars is very hard to see because the stars are very distant.

14. Stars that have different temperatures have different colors. For example, blue stars are much hotter than red stars are.

15. Two ways that scientists calculate the age of the universe are by measuring the distance from Earth to various galaxies and by calculating the ages of old, nearby stars.

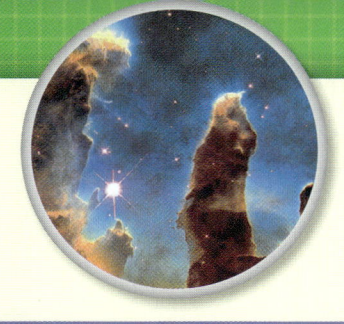

CRITICAL THINKING

16. Concept Mapping Use the following terms to create a concept map: *main-sequence star*, *nebula*, *red giant*, *white dwarf*, *neutron star*, and *black hole*.

17. Evaluating Conclusions While looking through a telescope, you see a galaxy that doesn't appear to contain any blue stars. What kind of galaxy is it most likely to be? Explain your answer.

18. Making Comparisons Explain the differences between main-sequence stars, giant stars, supergiant stars, and white dwarfs.

19. Evaluating Data Why do astronomers use absolute magnitudes to plot stars? Why don't astronomers use apparent magnitudes to plot stars?

20. Evaluating Sources According to the big bang theory, how did the universe begin? What evidence supports this theory?

21. Evaluating Data If a certain star displayed a large parallax, what could you say about the star's distance from Earth?

INTERPRETING GRAPHICS

The graph below shows Hubble's law, which relates how far galaxies are from Earth and how fast they are moving away from Earth. Use the graph below to answer the questions that follow.

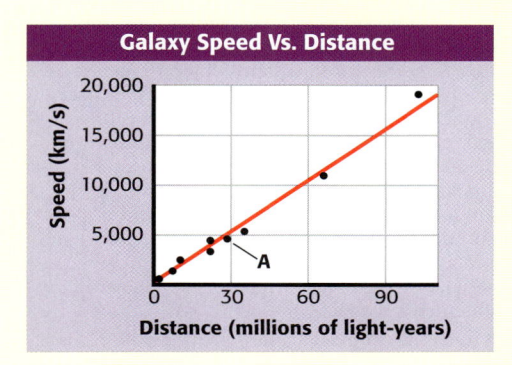

Galaxy Speed Vs. Distance

22. Look at the point that represents galaxy A in the graph. How far is galaxy A from Earth, and how fast is it moving away from Earth?

23. If a galaxy is moving away from Earth at 15,000 km/s, how far is the galaxy from Earth?

24. If a galaxy is 90,000,000 light-years from Earth, how fast is it moving away from Earth?

CHAPTER RESOURCES

Chapter Resource File
- Chapter Review GENERAL
- Chapter Test A GENERAL
- Chapter Test B ADVANCED
- Chapter Test C SPECIAL NEEDS
- Vocabulary Activity GENERAL

Workbooks

Study Guide
- Assessment resources are also available in Spanish.

Critical Thinking

16. An answer to this exercise can be found at the end of this book.

17. The galaxy is most likely an elliptical galaxy because it lacks the gas and dust needed for star formation. Blue stars are young stars.

18. Sample answer: Main-sequence stars are stars that are in the second stage of their life cycle. Red giant stars are large, reddish stars that are late in their life cycle. Red super-giant stars are similar to red giant stars but are much larger. White dwarf stars are small, hot, dim stars that are the left-over centers of old stars.

19. Absolute magnitude is a physical property of the star. Apparent magnitude varies according to a star's distance and absolute magnitude.

20. According to the big bang theory, the universe began with an explosion of matter and energy. Scientists can support this theory because they have shown that all distant galaxies are moving apart from all other galaxies.

21. The star would be relatively close to Earth.

Interpreting Graphics

22. The galaxy is about 30 million light-years away from Earth, and its speed is about 5,000 km/s.

23. The galaxy is almost 90 million light-years away from Earth.

24. The galaxy is moving at about 15,000 km/s.

Chapter 19 • Chapter Review **607**

Standardized Test Preparation

Teacher's Note

To provide practice under more realistic testing conditions, give students 20 minutes to answer all of the questions in this Standardized Test Preparation.

MISCONCEPTION ALERT

Answers to the standardized test preparation can help you identify student misconceptions and misunderstandings.

READING

Passage 1
1. C
2. G
3. C

➕ TEST DOCTOR

Question 2: Answer G is correct because according to the passage, quasars appear as tiny pinpoints of light, but they emit a large amount of energy. Answer F is incorrect because quasars are not the same as galaxies. Answer H is incorrect because the passage does not state that quasars can be viewed only by using an optical telescope. Although scientists do not yet understand exactly how quasars can emit so much energy, answer I is incorrect because the passage does not state that quasars will never be understood.

Passage 2
1. D
2. H

Standardized Test Preparation

READING

Read each of the passages below. Then, answer the questions that follow each passage.

Passage 1 Quasars are some of the most puzzling objects in the sky. If viewed through an optical telescope, a quasar appears as a small, dim star. Quasars are the most distant objects that have been observed from Earth. But many quasars are hundreds of times brighter than the brightest galaxy. Because quasars are so far away from Earth and yet are very bright, they most likely emit a large amount of energy. Scientists do not yet understand exactly how quasars can emit so much energy.

1. Based on the passage, which of the following statements is a fact?
   A Quasars, unlike galaxies, include billions of bright objects.
   B Galaxies are brighter than quasars.
   C Quasars are hundreds of times brighter than the brightest galaxy.
   D Galaxies are the most distant objects observed from Earth.

2. Based on the information in the passage, what can the reader conclude?
   F Quasars are the same as galaxies.
   G Quasars appear as small, dim stars, but they emit a large amount of energy.
   H Quasars can be viewed only by using an optical telescope.
   I Quasars will never be understood.

3. Why do scientists think that quasars emit a large amount of energy?
   A because quasars are the brightest stars in the universe
   B because quasars can be viewed only through an optical telescope
   C because quasars are very far away and are still bright
   D because quasars are larger than galaxies

Passage 2 If you live away from bright outdoor lights, you may be able to see a faint, narrow band of light and dark patches across the sky. This band is called the Milky Way. Our galaxy, the Milky Way, consists of stars, gases, and dust. Between the stars of the Milky Way are clouds of gas and dust called interstellar matter. These clouds provide materials that form new stars.

Every star that you can see in the night sky is a part of the Milky Way, because our solar system is inside the Milky Way. Because we are inside the galaxy, we cannot see the entire galaxy. But scientists can use astronomical data to create a picture of the Milky Way.

1. In the passage, what does the term *interstellar matter* mean?
   A stars in the Milky Way
   B the Milky Way
   C a narrow band of light and dark patches across the sky
   D the clouds of gas and dust between the stars in the Milky Way

2. Based on the information in the passage, what can the reader conclude?
   F The Milky Way can be seen in the night sky near a large city.
   G The entire Milky Way can be seen all at once.
   H Every star that is seen in the night sky is a part of the Milky Way.
   I Scientists have no idea what the entire Milky Way looks like.

➕ TEST DOCTOR

Question 2: Answer F is incorrect because according to the passage, the Milky Way galaxy can usually be seen in the night sky if you are away from bright outdoor lights. Answer G is incorrect because the second paragraph indicates that we cannot see the entire Milky Way galaxy. Answer H is correct because this fact is mentioned in the second paragraph. Answer I is incorrect because the second paragraph mentions that scientists use astronomical data to create pictures of the Milky Way.

608 Chapter 19 • Stars, Galaxies, and the Universe

INTERPRETING GRAPHICS

The graph below shows the relationship between a star's age and mass. Use the graph below to answer the questions that follow.

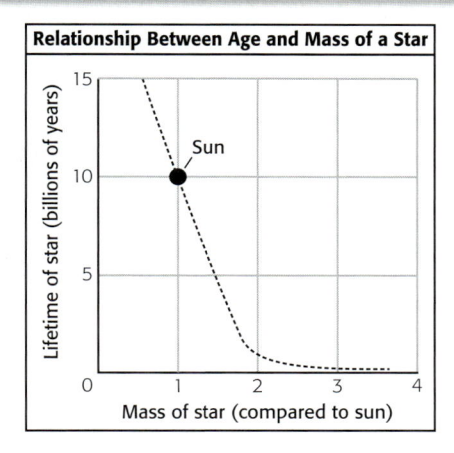

Relationship Between Age and Mass of a Star

[Graph: x-axis "Mass of star (compared to sun)" from 0 to 4; y-axis "Lifetime of star (billions of years)" from 0 to 15; curve decreasing steeply, with point labeled "Sun" at (1, 10)]

1. How long does a star that has 1.2 times the mass of the sun live?
   - A 10 billion years
   - B 8 billion years
   - C 6 billion years
   - D 5 billion years

2. How long does a star that has 2 times the mass of the sun live?
   - F 4 billion years
   - G 1 billion years
   - H 10 billion years
   - I 5 billion years

3. If the sun's mass was reduced by half, how long would the sun live?
   - A 2 billion years
   - B 8 billion years
   - C 10 billion years
   - D more than 15 billion years

4. According to the graph, how long is the sun predicted to live?
   - F 15 billion years
   - G 10 billion years
   - H 5 billion years
   - I 2 billion years

MATH

Read each question below, and choose the best answer.

1. How many kilometers away from Earth is an object that is 8 light-years away from Earth? (Hint: One light-year is equal to 9.46 trillion kilometers.)
   - A 77 trillion kilometers
   - B 76 trillion kilometers
   - C 7.66 trillion kilometers
   - D 7.6 trillion kilometers

2. An astronomer observes two stars of about the same temperature and size. Alpha Centauri B is about 4 light-years away from Earth, and Sigma 2 Eridani A is about 16 light-years away from Earth. How many times as bright as Sigma 2 Eridani A does Alpha Centauri B appear? (Hint: One light-year is equal to 9.46 trillion kilometers.)
   - F 2 times as bright
   - G 4 times as bright
   - H 16 times as bright
   - I 32 times as bright

3. Star A is 5 million kilometers from Star B. What is this distance expressed in meters?
   - A 0.5 m
   - B 5,000 m
   - C 5×10^6 m
   - D 5×10^9 m

4. In the vacuum of space, light travels 3×10^8 m/s. How far does light travel in 1 h in space?
   - F 3,600 m
   - G 1.80×10^{10} m
   - H 1.08×10^{12} m
   - I 1.08×10^{16} m

5. The mass of the known universe is about 10^{23} solar masses, which is 10^{50} metric tons. How many metric tons is one solar mass?
   - A 10^{27} solar masses
   - B 10^{27} metric tons
   - C 10^{73} solar masses
   - D 10^{73} metric tons

INTERPRETING GRAPHICS

1. B
2. G
3. D
4. G

TEST DOCTOR

Question 1: Answer B is correct because when 1.2 is located on the *x*-axis, the student will find that the star will live for approximately 8 billion years. Answer A is incorrect because the star would have to be almost the same mass as the sun to live for approximately 10 billion years. Answers C and D are incorrect because they apply to a star that is closer to 1.5 times the mass of the sun.

MATH

1. B
2. H
3. D
4. H
5. B

TEST DOCTOR

Question 1: When 9.46 trillion kilometers is multiplied by 8 light-years, the product is 75.68 trillion kilometers. When this answer is rounded to the nearest whole number, the answer equals 76 trillion kilometers. Therefore, answer B is correct. Answer A is too high, and answers C and D are 10 times too low.

CHAPTER RESOURCES

Chapter Resource File
- Standardized Test Preparation GENERAL

State Resources

For specific resources for your state, visit **go.hrw.com** and type in the keyword **HSMSTR**.

Chapter 19 • Standardized Test Preparation **609**

Science in Action

Weird Science

Background
Scientists theorize that two types of stars can turn into black holes. When an extremely large star (about 8 to 25 times as massive as the sun) runs out of fuel and dies, it usually explodes as a supernova. A star that is more than 25 times as massive as the sun may collapse without exploding. If the core of either type of star is at least 3 times as massive as the sun, it is predicted that the core will collapse under its own gravity and become a black hole.

Scientific Discoveries

Discussion — GENERAL
Scientists think that Eta Carinae could become a supernova at anytime. Review the definition of *supernova* with students, and then ask them, "If Eta Carinae becomes a supernova, would life on this planet be threatened?" Then, ask them why or why not. (Answers may vary. At a distance of more than 8,000 light-years from our solar system, Eta Carinae is not close enough to threaten us. However, it's explosion would be seen from Earth.)

Science in Action

Weird Science

Holes Where Stars Once Were
An invisible phantom lurks in space, ready to swallow everything that comes near it. Once trapped in its grasp, matter is stretched, torn, and crushed into oblivion. Does this tale sound like a horror story? Guess again! Scientists call this phantom a *black hole*. As a star runs out of fuel, it cools and eventually collapses under the force of its own gravity. If the collapsing star is massive enough, it may shrink to become a black hole. The resulting gravitational attraction is so strong that even light cannot escape! Many astronomers think that black holes lie at the heart of many galaxies. Some scientists suggest that there is a giant black hole at the center of our own Milky Way.

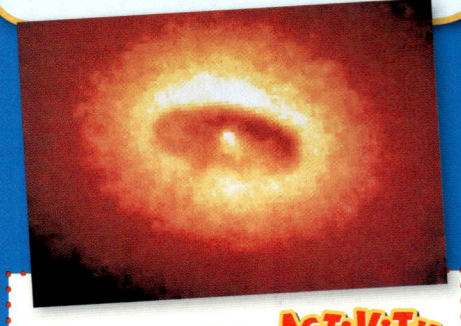

Language Arts ACTIVITY

WRITING SKILL Can you imagine traveling through a black hole? Write a short story that describes what you would see if you led a space mission to a black hole.

Scientific Discoveries

Eta Carinae: The Biggest Star Ever Discovered
In 1841, Eta Carinae was the second-brightest star in the night sky. Why is this observation a part of history? Eta Carinae's brightness is historic because before 1837, Eta Carinae wasn't even visible to the naked eye! Strangely, a few years later Eta Carinae faded again and disappeared from the night sky. Something unusual was happening to Eta Carinae, and scientists wanted to know what it was. As soon as scientists had telescopes with which they could see far into space, they took a closer look at Eta Carinae. Scientists discovered that this star is highly unstable and prone to violent outbursts. These outbursts, the last of which was seen in 1841, can be seen on Earth. Scientists also discovered that Eta Carinae is 150 times as big as our sun and about 4 million times as bright. Eta Carinae is the biggest and brightest star ever found!

Math ACTIVITY

If Eta Carinae is 8,000 light-years from our solar system, how many kilometers is Eta Carinae from our solar system? (Hint: One light-year is equal to 9.46 trillion kilometers.)

Answer to Language Arts Activity
To help students with their short story, suggest that they use the Internet or library resources to read more about black holes.

Answer to Math Activity
9,460,000,000,000 km × 8,000 light-years = approximately 7.57×10^{16} km away from our solar system

Careers

Jocelyn Bell-Burnell

Astrophysicist Imagine getting a signal from far out in space and not knowing what or whom it's coming from. That's what happened to astrophysicist Jocelyn Bell-Burnell. Bell-Burnell is known for discovering pulsars, objects in space that emit radio waves at short, regular intervals. But before she and her advisor discovered that the signals came from pulsars, they thought that the signals may have come from aliens!

Born in 1943 in Belfast, Northern Ireland, Jocelyn Bell-Burnell became interested in astronomy at an early age. At Cambridge University in 1967, Bell-Burnell, who was a graduate student, and her advisor, Anthony Hewish, completed work on a huge radio telescope designed to pick up signals from quasars. Bell-Burnell's job was to operate the telescope and analyze its chart paper recordings on a graph. Each day, the telescope recordings used 29.2 m of chart paper! After a month, Bell-Burnell noticed that the recordings showed a few "bits of scruff"—very short, pulsating radio signals—that she could not explain. Bell-Burnell and Hewish struggled to find the source of the mysterious signal. They checked the equipment and began eliminating possible sources of the signal, such as satellites, television, and radar. Shortly after finding the first signal, Bell-Burnell discovered a second. The second signal was similar to the first but came from a different position in the sky. By January 1968, Bell-Burnell had discovered two more pulsating signals. In March of 1968, her findings that the signals were from a new kind of star were published and amazed the scientific community. The scientific press named the newly discovered stars *pulsars*.

Today, Bell-Burnell is a leading expert in the field of astrophysics and the study of stars. She is currently head of the physics department at the Open University, in Milton Keynes, England.

Social Studies ACTIVITY

Use the Internet or library resources to research historical events that occurred during 1967 and 1968. Find out if the prediction that the signals from pulsars were coming from aliens affected historical events during this time.

Current Science

Check out Current Science® articles related to this chapter by visiting go.hrw.com. Just type in the keyword **HZ5CS19**.

To learn more about these Science in Action topics, visit **go.hrw.com** and type in the keyword **HZ5UNVF**.

Careers

Background

One of the most fascinating properties of neutron stars is their incredible mass. Most neutron stars are only about 10 to 16 km in diameter, but their mass can be equal to the mass of our sun. The mass of a neutron star is so great that if you could stand on its surface and drop a coin, the coin would hit the ground at half the speed of light.

Discussion —— GENERAL

Controversial Nobel Prize The discovery of the pulsar is a very important part of the history of astrophysics. In 1967, Sir Martin Ryle and Tony Hewish, from the Cavendish Laboratory in Cambridge, England, were jointly awarded the Nobel Prize in physics. Hewish was recognized for his discovery of pulsars. This Nobel Prize announcement sparked a public controversy because some people thought that Hewish should have shared the Nobel Prize with Bell-Burnell. Have students do some research to find out what Bell-Burnell's reaction was to the controversy. Then, have a class discussion on the topic. Encourage students to share their opinions about the controversy.

Answer to Social Studies Activity

To help students conduct research, suggest that they look at the front-page sections or science sections of major newspapers during 1967 and 1968. Students may also find information or news stories that were featured in mainstream news and science magazines during 1967 and 1968.

Chapter 19 • Science in Action

20 Formation of the Solar System
Chapter Planning Guide

Compression guide: To shorten instruction because of time limitations, omit the Chapter Lab.

OBJECTIVES	LABS, DEMONSTRATIONS, AND ACTIVITIES	TECHNOLOGY RESOURCES
PACING • 90 min pp. 612–617 **Chapter Opener**	SE Start-up Activity, p. 613 GENERAL	OSP Parent Letter ■ GENERAL CD Student Edition on CD-ROM CD Guided Reading Audio CD ■ TR Chapter Starter Transparency* VID Brain Food Video Quiz
Section 1 A Solar System Is Born • Explain the relationship between gravity and pressure in a nebula. • Describe how the solar system formed.	TE Group Activity The Solar System, p. 614 GENERAL TE Activity Modeling Planetesimal Formation, p. 616 ◆ BASIC SE Connection to Language Arts Eyewitness Account, p. 617 GENERAL LB Whiz-Bang Demonstrations Can You Vote on Venus?* GENERAL	CRF Lesson Plans* TR Bellringer Transparency*
PACING • 45 min pp. 618–623 **Section 2 The Sun: Our Very Own Star** • Describe the basic structure and composition of the sun. • Explain how the sun generates energy. • Describe the surface activity of the sun, and identify how this activity affects Earth.	TE Demonstration Observing Sunspots, p. 618 ◆ GENERAL TE Connection Activity Math, p. 619 GENERAL SE Connection to Chemistry Atoms, p. 620 GENERAL TE Group Activity Escape from the Sun, p. 620 ADVANCED TE Connection Activity Math, p. 621 BASIC TE Connection Activity History, p. 621 GENERAL SE Skills Practice Lab How Far Is the Sun?, p. 634 ◆ GENERAL CRF Datasheet for Chapter Lab*	CRF Lesson Plans* TR Bellringer Transparency* TR The Structure and Atmosphere of the Sun* TR Fusion of Hydrogen in the Sun* TR LINK TO PHYSICAL SCIENCE The Periodic Table of the Elements* CRF SciLinks Activity* GENERAL VID Lab Videos for Earth Science
PACING • 45 min pp. 624–629 **Section 3 The Earth Takes Shape** • Describe the formation of the solid Earth. • Describe the structure of the Earth. • Explain the development of Earth's atmosphere and the influence of early life on the atmosphere. • Describe how the Earth's oceans and continents formed.	TE Discussion Earth's Atmosphere, p. 624 GENERAL SE Connection to Environmental Science The Greenhouse Effect, p. 626 GENERAL TE Activity Rings Around Our Planet, p. 626 GENERAL TE Internet Activity Researching New Planets, p. 626 ADVANCED SE School-to-Home Activity Comets and Meteors, p. 627 GENERAL	CRF Lesson Plans* TR Bellringer Transparency* TR Formation of Earth's Layers* SE Internet Activity, p. 629 GENERAL
PACING • 45 min pp. 630–633 **Section 4 Planetary Motion** • Explain the difference between rotation and revolution. • Describe three laws of planetary motion. • Describe how distance and mass affect gravitational attraction.	TE Activity Measuring Ellipses, p. 630 GENERAL TE Connection Activity Language Arts, p. 631 GENERAL SE Quick Lab Staying in Focus, p. 632 GENERAL CRF Datasheet for Quick Lab* LB Long-Term Projects & Research Ideas A Two-Sun Solar System* ADVANCED	CRF Lesson Plans* TR Bellringer Transparency* TR Earth's Rotation and Revolution* TR Ellipse* TR Gravity and the Motion of the Moon*

PACING • 90 min

CHAPTER REVIEW, ASSESSMENT, AND STANDARDIZED TEST PREPARATION

CRF Vocabulary Activity* GENERAL
SE Chapter Review, pp. 636–637 GENERAL
CRF Chapter Review* ■ GENERAL
CRF Chapter Tests A* ■ GENERAL, B* ADVANCED, C* SPECIAL NEEDS
SE Standardized Test Preparation, pp. 638–639 GENERAL
CRF Standardized Test Preparation* GENERAL
CRF Performance-Based Assessment* GENERAL
OSP Test Generator GENERAL
CRF Test Item Listing* GENERAL

Online and Technology Resources

Visit **go.hrw.com** for a variety of free resources related to this textbook. Enter the keyword **HZ5SOL**.

Holt Online Learning
Students can access interactive problem-solving help and active visual concept development with the Holt Science and Technology Online Edition available at **www.hrw.com**.

Guided Reading Audio CD
Also in Spanish
A direct reading of each chapter for auditory learners, reluctant readers, and Spanish-speaking students.

Science Tutor CD-ROM
Excellent for remediation and test practice.

Chapter 20 • Formation of the Solar System

KEY

SE	Student Edition	**CRF**	Chapter Resource File	**SS**	Science Skills Worksheets	*****	Also on One-Stop Planner
TE	Teacher Edition	**OSP**	One-Stop Planner	**MS**	Math Skills for Science Worksheets	♦	Requires advance prep
		LB	Lab Bank	**CD**	CD or CD-ROM	■	Also available in Spanish
		TR	Transparencies	**VID**	Classroom Video/DVD		

SKILLS DEVELOPMENT RESOURCES	SECTION REVIEW AND ASSESSMENT	STANDARDS CORRELATIONS
SE Pre-Reading Activity, p. 612 GENERAL OSP Science Puzzlers, Twisters & Teasers* GENERAL		National Science Education Standards UCP 1, 2; SAI 2; ES 3b
CRF Directed Reading A* ■ BASIC, B* SPECIAL NEEDS CRF Vocabulary and Section Summary* ■ GENERAL SE Reading Strategy Reading Organizer, p. 614 GENERAL TE Inclusion Strategies, p. 615 ♦ MS Math Skills for Science Density* GENERAL CRF Critical Thinking A Balooney Universe* ADVANCED	SE Reading Checks, pp. 615, 617 GENERAL TE Reteaching, p. 616 BASIC TE Quiz, p. 616 GENERAL TE Alternative Assessment, p. 616 GENERAL TE Homework, p. 616 ADVANCED SE Section Review,* p. 617 ■ GENERAL CRF Section Quiz* ■ GENERAL	UCP 1, 2, 4; ST 2; HNS 2, 3; SPSP 5; ES 3a, 3b, 3c
CRF Directed Reading A* ■ BASIC, B* SPECIAL NEEDS CRF Vocabulary and Section Summary* ■ GENERAL SE Reading Strategy Reading Organizer, p. 618 GENERAL CRF Reinforcement Worksheet Stay on the Sunny Side* GENERAL	SE Reading Checks, pp. 619, 621, 622 GENERAL TE Reteaching, p. 622 BASIC TE Quiz, p. 622 GENERAL TE Alternative Assessment, p. 622 ADVANCED SE Section Review,* p. 623 ■ GENERAL CRF Section Quiz* ■ GENERAL	ST 2; SPSP 5; HNS 1, 2, 3; ES 3a; *Chapter Lab:* UCP 2, 3, 5; SAI 1, 2; ST 1; SPSP 5; HNS 1; ES 3a
CRF Directed Reading A* ■ BASIC, B* SPECIAL NEEDS CRF Vocabulary and Section Summary* ■ GENERAL SE Reading Strategy Discussion, p. 624 GENERAL TE Inclusion Strategies, p. 625 MS Math Skills for Science Reducing Fraction to Lowest Terms* GENERAL CRF Reinforcement Worksheet Third Rock from the Sun* GENERAL	SE Reading Checks, pp. 624, 626, 628 GENERAL TE Homework, p. 627 GENERAL TE Reteaching, p. 628 BASIC TE Quiz, p. 628 GENERAL TE Alternative Assessment, p. 628 GENERAL SE Section Review,* p. 629 ■ GENERAL CRF Section Quiz* ■ GENERAL	UCP 2, 4; SAI 1; ES 2b
CRF Directed Reading A* ■ BASIC, B* SPECIAL NEEDS CRF Vocabulary and Section Summary* ■ GENERAL SE Reading Strategy Paired Summarizing, p. 630 GENERAL SE Math Practice Kepler's Formula, p. 631 GENERAL	SE Reading Checks, pp. 631, 632 GENERAL TE Reteaching, p. 632 BASIC TE Quiz, p. 632 GENERAL TE Alternative Assessment, p. 632 GENERAL SE Section Review,* p. 633 ■ GENERAL CRF Section Quiz* ■ GENERAL	UCP 1, 2, 3; SAI 1, 2; ST 2; SPSP 5; HNS 1, 2, 3; ES 3b

One-Stop Planner® CD-ROM

This convenient CD-ROM includes:
- Lab Materials QuickList Software
- Holt Calendar Planner
- Customizable Lesson Plans
- Printable Worksheets
- ExamView® Test Generator

CNN Student News

cnnstudentnews.com

Find the latest news, lesson plans, and activities related to important scientific events.

SciLinks NSTA

www.scilinks.org

Maintained by the **National Science Teachers Association.** See Chapter Enrichment pages for a complete list of topics.

Current Science®

Check out *Current Science* articles and activities by visiting the HRW Web site at **go.hrw.com.** Just type in the keyword **HZ5CS20T.**

Classroom Videos

- **Lab Videos** demonstrate the chapter lab.
- **Brain Food Video Quizzes** help students review the chapter material.
- **CNN Videos** bring science into your students' daily life.

Chapter 20 • Chapter Planning Guide

20 Chapter Resources

Visual Resources

CHAPTER STARTER TRANSPARENCY

BELLRINGER TRANSPARENCIES

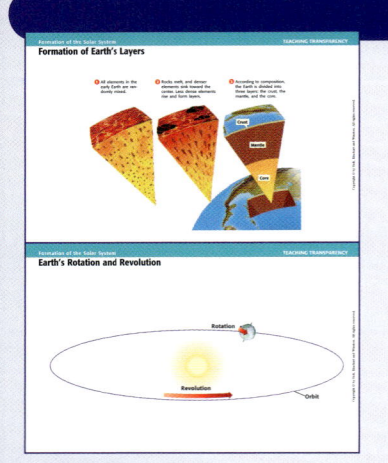

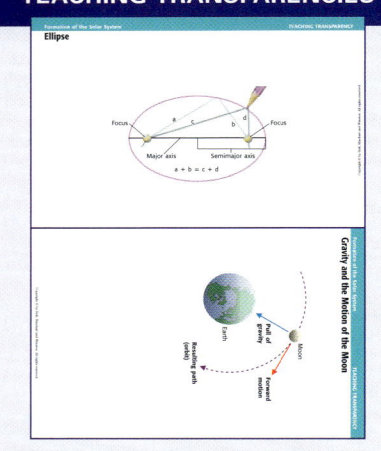

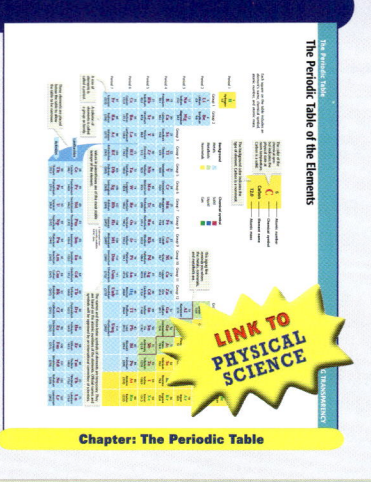

TEACHING TRANSPARENCIES
- The Structure and Atmosphere of the Sun
- Fusion of Hydrogen in the Sun

TEACHING TRANSPARENCIES
- Formation of Earth's Layers
- Earth's Rotation and Revolution
- Ellipse
- Gravity and the Motion of the Moon
- The Periodic Table of the Elements (LINK TO PHYSICAL SCIENCE — Chapter: The Periodic Table)

CONCEPT MAPPING TRANSPARENCY

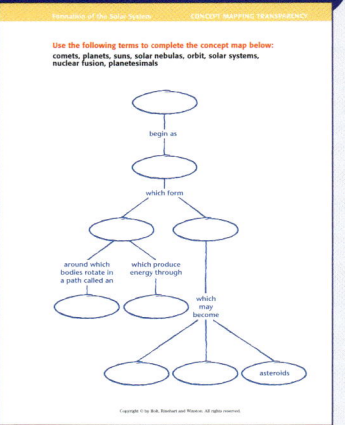

Planning Resources

LESSON PLANS

PARENT LETTER (ALSO IN SPANISH)

TEST ITEM LISTING

One-Stop Planner® CD-ROM

This CD-ROM includes all of the resources shown here and the following time-saving tools:
- Lab Materials QuickList Software
- Customizable lesson plans
- Holt Calendar Planner
- The powerful ExamView® Test Generator

611C Chapter 20 • Formation of the Solar System

For a preview of available worksheets covering math and science skills, see pages T26–T33. All of these resources are also on the One-Stop Planner®.

Meeting Individual Needs

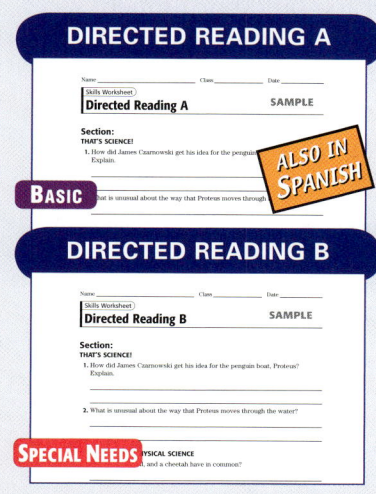

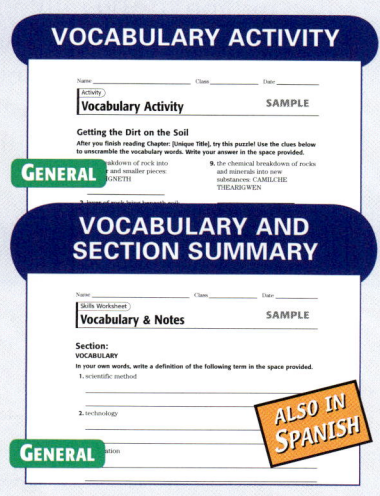

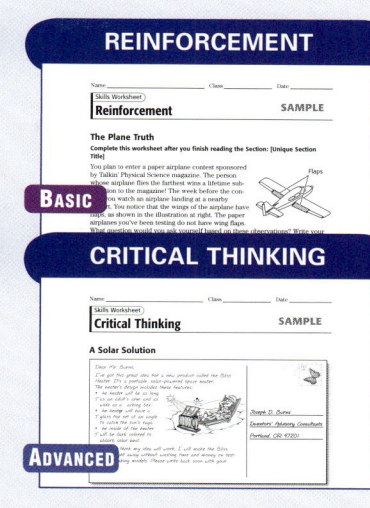

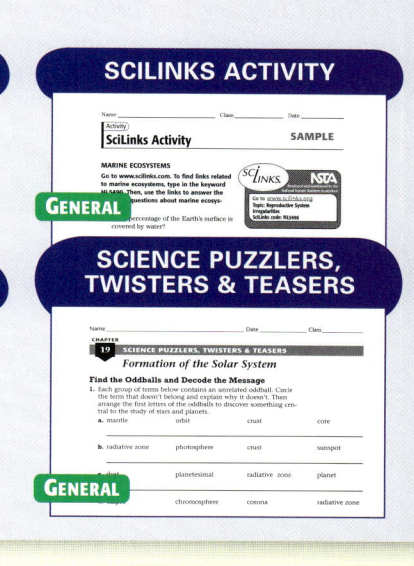

- **DIRECTED READING A** — BASIC — ALSO IN SPANISH
- **DIRECTED READING B** — SPECIAL NEEDS
- **VOCABULARY ACTIVITY** — GENERAL
- **VOCABULARY AND SECTION SUMMARY** — GENERAL — ALSO IN SPANISH
- **REINFORCEMENT** — BASIC
- **CRITICAL THINKING** — ADVANCED
- **SCILINKS ACTIVITY** — GENERAL
- **SCIENCE PUZZLERS, TWISTERS & TEASERS** — GENERAL

Labs and Activities

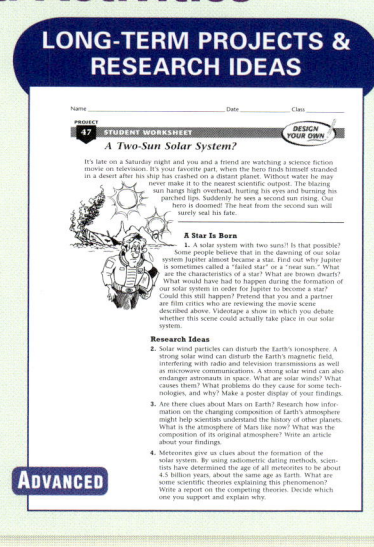

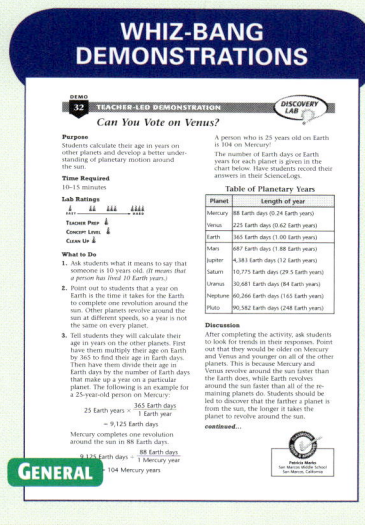

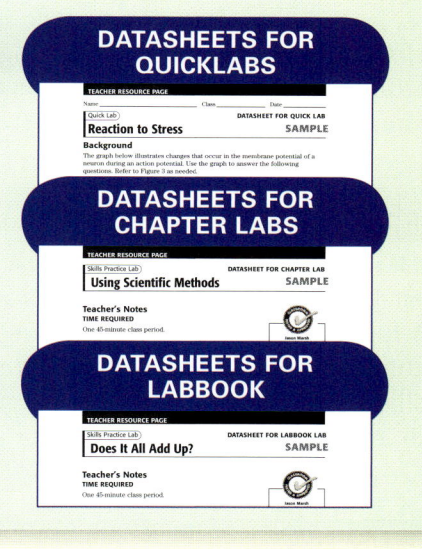

- **LONG-TERM PROJECTS & RESEARCH IDEAS** — ADVANCED
- **WHIZ-BANG DEMONSTRATIONS** — GENERAL
- **DATASHEETS FOR QUICKLABS**
- **DATASHEETS FOR CHAPTER LABS**
- **DATASHEETS FOR LABBOOK**

Review and Assessments

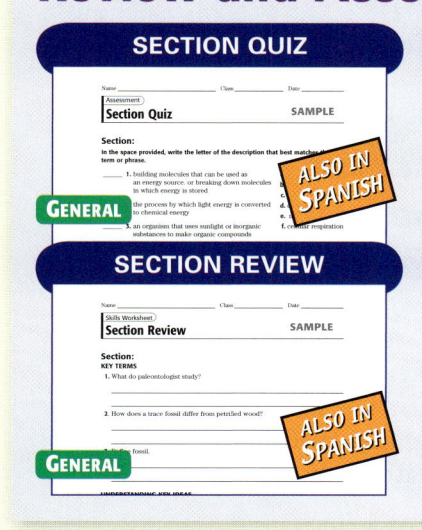

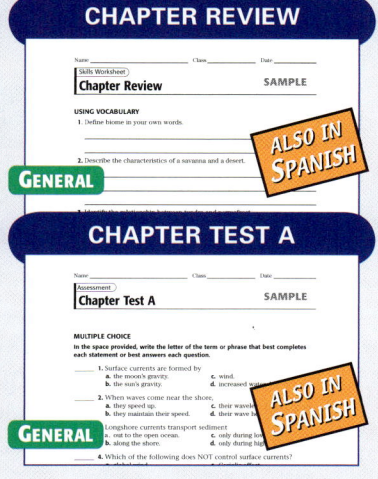

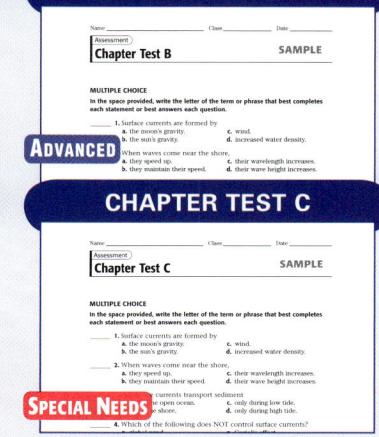

- **SECTION QUIZ** — GENERAL — ALSO IN SPANISH
- **SECTION REVIEW** — GENERAL — ALSO IN SPANISH
- **CHAPTER REVIEW** — GENERAL — ALSO IN SPANISH
- **CHAPTER TEST A** — GENERAL — ALSO IN SPANISH
- **CHAPTER TEST B** — ADVANCED
- **CHAPTER TEST C** — SPECIAL NEEDS
- **STANDARDIZED TEST PREPARATION** — GENERAL
- **PERFORMANCE-BASED ASSESSMENT** — GENERAL

Chapter 20 • Chapter Resources   611D

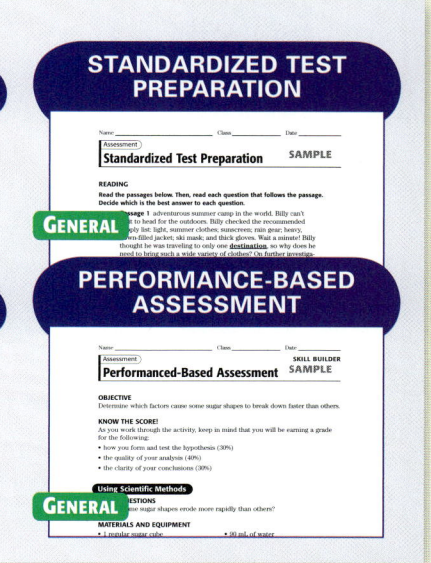

Chapter Enrichment

This Chapter Enrichment provides relevant and interesting information to expand and enhance your presentation of the chapter material.

Section 1

A Solar System Is Born

A Computer Model of Planet Building

- The Planetary Science Institute in Tucson, Arizona, produced a computer program in the late 1970s to test hypotheses about the formation of planetesimals and planets. The program has given credence to the theory that particle collisions within a swirling, collapsing nebula could have led to the creation of our solar system. The program simulates the motion of particles at various distances from the sun and tracks the results of collisions based on actual physical and mechanical properties, such as gas drag and particle speed. Run with various starting conditions, the program shows small particles aggregating into numbers of larger bodies and the eventual production of a system of planets.

Is That a Fact!

◆ A typical star begins life when fusion reactions start (at about 10 million degrees Celsius). It can burn steadily for billions of years by converting hydrogen to helium in its core. As the hydrogen runs out, the core collapses and heats up. The star's atmosphere expands and cools, and the star becomes a red giant.

High-Mass Stars: Live Fast and Die Young

- Stars that have a mass similar to that of our sun have a life cycle of 10 billion to 11 billion years. High-mass stars, which have a mass at least 10 times that of our sun, actually burn up much quicker than the sun—in 5 million to 100 million years—and burn much brighter than the sun. When a high-mass star runs out of fuel, its core collapses, and the star becomes a supernova. A supernova explosion is one of the most spectacular events in the universe.

Section 2

The Sun: Our Very Own Star

The Sunspot Cycle

- The increasing and decreasing number of sunspots in an 11-year cycle appears to be driven by the magnetic field in the sun's surface layers. The field seems to "wind up" much as a rubber band does (perhaps because of the difference in the rate of rotation between the sun's poles and its equator). This process intensifies the magnetic field; therefore, more sunspots appear, and the sun becomes much more active.

- Solar flares and Coronal Mass Ejections (CMEs) occur at places on the sun that are most active. CMEs can contain a trillion kg of solar material and can propagate from the sun to the Earth at speeds of 1000km/s. Despite the great distance between the sun and Earth, solar flares and CMEs can disrupt TV programs, damage satellites, and endanger astronauts.

Section 3

The Earth Takes Shape

Evidence of Earth's Origins

- Many different sciences have contributed to our understanding of Earth's origin. Much remains to be discovered through computer models and the study of meteorites and other planets. The following evidence has shaped the current scientific theories about the formation of Earth and its atmosphere:

Chapter 20 • Formation of the Solar System

- The oldest rocks on Earth are about 4 billion years old. Some of the oldest rocks are sedimentary in origin, so we know that oceans must have existed early in the history of Earth.

- The sun was about 30% less luminous when Earth was forming. We know this from the study of how hydrogen fusion reactions work.

- Earth must have had a dense atmosphere with greenhouse gases early in its life, or Earth would have been too cold to have liquid oceans.

- The oldest fossils of primitive life are stromatolites, blue-green algae colonies that originated between 3.7 billion and 3.4 billion years ago. Simple life-forms may have appeared on Earth before this time.

- Blue-green algae release oxygen as a byproduct of photosynthesis. Evidence from the oxidation of minerals in the rock record indicates that oxygen started to appear in significant concentrations in Earth's atmosphere between 2.5 billion and 2.0 billion years ago.

- Some of the water that formed the oceans came from the early Earth's interior and was released by outgassing during the differentiation process. As Earth heated and differentiated, water that was chemically bound in minerals was carried to the surface of the planet along with magma. Water vapor was then released to form the early atmosphere. Even at current rates of volcanism, the water vapor released from lava flows would be more than enough to fill Earth's oceans in about a billion years.

Section 4

Planetary Motion

The Orbit of Comets

- Orbits represent the entire path of an orbiting body. A planet or asteroid orbit has an elliptical shape. Scientists observe that near the sun comets seem to have a parabolic orbit (shaped like an open-ended ellipse). This shape may indicate that comets come from the outer reaches of the solar system. Scientists theorize that some comets originate in an enormous spherical cloud surrounding the solar system. This region, named the *Oort cloud*, may contain 100 billion comets. The gravitational pull of another object can knock a comet out of the Oort cloud, after which the comet's orbit brings it into the inner solar system.

Is That a Fact!

- Although Kepler's laws of motion and Newton's law of gravity were formulated over 300 years ago, space scientists and engineers still use the laws to plan and calculate the flight paths of artificial satellites orbiting the Earth.

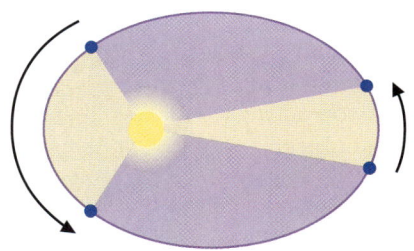

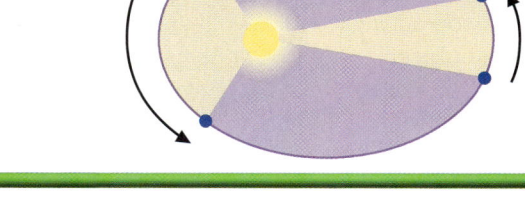

SciLinks is maintained by the National Science Teachers Association to provide you and your students with interesting, up-to-date links that will enrich your classroom presentation of the chapter.

Visit www.scilinks.org and enter the SciLinks code for more information about the topic listed.

Topic: Planets
SciLinks code: HSM1152

Topic: The Oceans
SciLinks code: HSM1069

Topic: The Sun
SciLinks code: HSM1477

Topic: Kepler's Laws
SciLinks code: HSM0827

Topic: Layers of the Earth
SciLinks code: HSM0862

Overview

Tell students that this chapter will help them learn about how the solar system formed. The chapter also describes the processes that formed the sun and Earth. Finally, the chapter discusses the laws related to planetary motion.

Assessing Prior Knowledge

Students should be familiar with the following topics:
- the scale of the universe
- the life cycle of stars
- the contents of galaxies

Identifying Misconceptions

As students learn about the action of gravity, some of them may characterize it as an action of "holding." Students may also confuse gravity with atmospheric pressure, and they may describe gravity as something that keeps things from floating away. Remind students that gravity does not require air and that gravity does not stop acting on an object when the object has finished falling. Also, when teaching about the formation of the solar system, remind students that gravity is present in space.

20 Formation of the Solar System

SECTION 1	A Solar System Is Born	614
SECTION 2	The Sun: Our Very Own Star	618
SECTION 3	The Earth Takes Shape	624
SECTION 4	Planetary Motion	630

Chapter Lab 634
Chapter Review 636
Standardized Test Preparation 638
Science in Action 640

About the PHOTO

The Orion Nebula, a vast cloud of dust and gas that is 35 trillion miles wide, is part of the familiar Orion constellation. Here, swirling clouds of dust and gas give birth to systems like our own solar system.

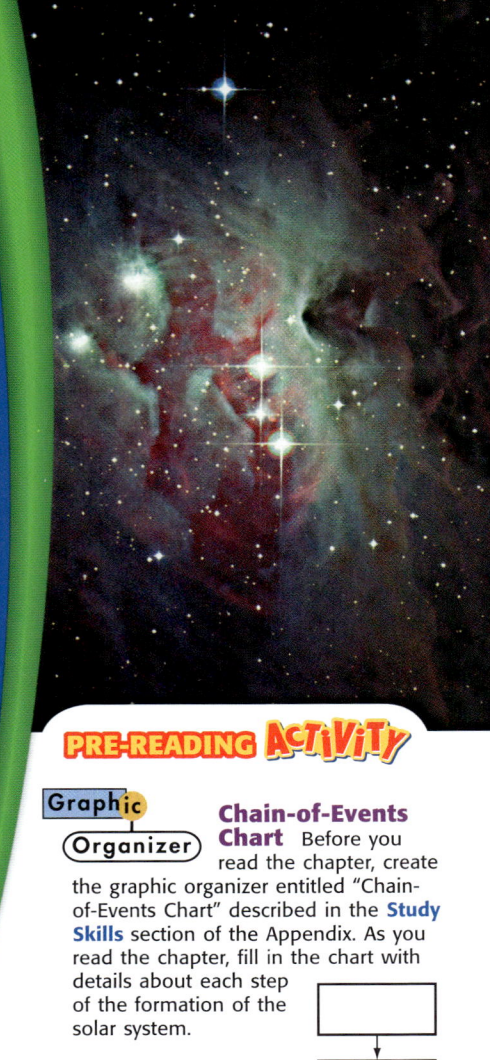

PRE-READING ACTIVITY

Graphic Organizer

Chain-of-Events Chart Before you read the chapter, create the graphic organizer entitled "Chain-of-Events Chart" described in the **Study Skills** section of the Appendix. As you read the chapter, fill in the chart with details about each step of the formation of the solar system.

Standards Correlations

National Science Education Standards

The following codes indicate the National Science Education Standards that correlate to this chapter. The full text of the standards is at the front of the book.

Chapter Opener
UCP 1, 2; SAI 2; ES 3b

Section 1 A Solar System Is Born
UCP 1, 2, 4; ST 2; HNS 2, 3; SPSP 5; ES 3a, 3b, 3c

Section 2 The Sun: Our Very Own Star
ST 2; SPSP 5; HNS 1, 2, 3; ES 3a

Section 3 The Earth Takes Shape
UCP 2, 4; SAI 1; ES 2b

Section 4 Planetary Motion
UCP 1, 2, 3; SAI 1, 2; ST 2; SPSP 5; HNS 1, 2, 3; ES 3b

Chapter Lab
UCP 2, 3, 5; SAI 1, 2; ST 1; SPSP 5; HNS 1; ES 3a

Chapter Review
UCP 1, 2, 4, SAI 1, 2; SPSP 5; HNS 2, 3; ES 2b; 3a, 3b, 3c

Science in Action
UCP 1, 2; SAI 2; ST 2; SPSP 5; HNS 1, 2, 3

START-UP ACTIVITY

MATERIALS
FOR EACH STUDENT
- book
- paper, notebook (2 sheets)

Teacher's Notes: You might point out to students that when David Scott performed his experiment on the moon's surface, he paid homage to Galileo. While Galileo did predict that the mass of an object does not affect the rate at which the object falls, it is uncertain whether Galileo demonstrated this theory by dropping cannonballs of different masses from the Leaning Tower of Pisa.

Answers
1. Sample answer: Both pieces of paper should reach the bottom at the same time. They should fall at the same rate as the book. Gravity causes all objects to fall at the same rate regardless of their mass.
2. Sample answer: The crumpled piece of paper should reach the floor first. Although gravity pulled both pieces toward the floor, the crumpled piece of paper hit the ground first because it fell with less air resistance than the flat piece of paper did.

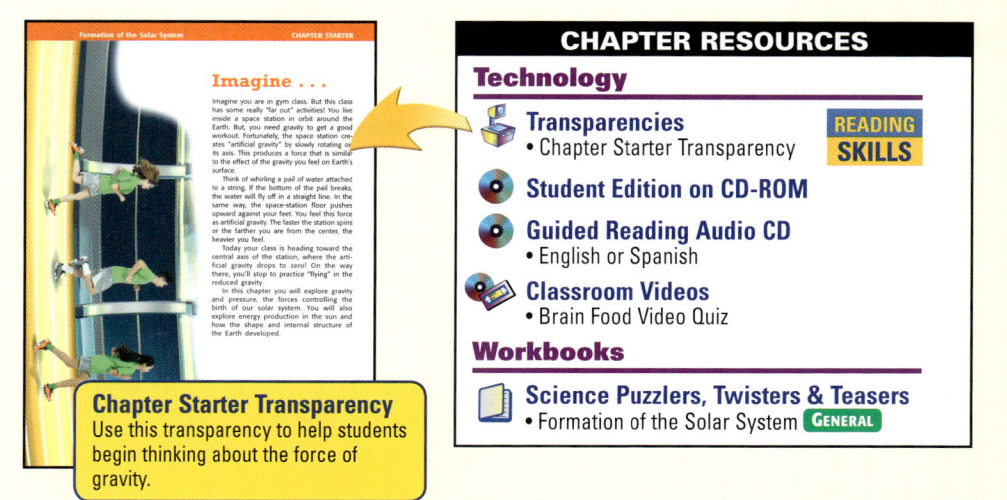

START-UP ACTIVITY

Strange Gravity

If you drop a heavy object, will it fall faster than a lighter one? According to the law of gravity, the answer is no. In 1971, *Apollo 15* astronaut David Scott stood on the moon and dropped a feather and a hammer. Television audiences were amazed to see both objects strike the moon's surface at the same time. Now, you can perform a similar experiment.

Procedure
1. Select **two pieces of identical notebook paper.** Crumple one piece of paper into a ball.
2. Place the flat piece of paper on top of a **book** and the paper ball on top of the flat piece of paper.
3. Hold the book waist high, and then drop it to the floor.

Analysis
1. Which piece of paper reached the bottom first? Did either piece of paper fall slower than the book? Explain your observations.
2. Now, hold the crumpled paper in one hand and the flat piece of paper in the other. Drop both pieces of paper at the same time. Besides gravity, what affected the speed of the falling paper? Record your observations.

Chapter Starter Transparency
Use this transparency to help students begin thinking about the force of gravity.

CHAPTER RESOURCES

Technology
- **Transparencies**
  - Chapter Starter Transparency **READING SKILLS**
- **Student Edition on CD-ROM**
- **Guided Reading Audio CD**
  - English or Spanish
- **Classroom Videos**
  - Brain Food Video Quiz

Workbooks
- **Science Puzzlers, Twisters & Teasers**
  - Formation of the Solar System **GENERAL**

Chapter 20 • Formation of the Solar System

SECTION 1

Focus

Overview
This section describes the formation of the solar system. It also describes the role that gravity and pressure played in the formation of the solar system.

Bellringer
Write the following question on the board: "Could astronauts land on a star in the same way that they landed on the moon?" (Sample answer: No, stars are composed of gas, not solid rock like the moon is. Stars are also a lot hotter than the moon is!)

Motivate

Group Activity — GENERAL

The Solar System Display a poster of the solar system. Have student groups brainstorm a list of facts they know about the solar system and some questions that they want to answer. Ask each group to study the display and note the following: what a planet's orbit looks like and how planets close to the sun differ from those far away from the sun. Discuss students' observations and hypotheses.
LS Visual **English Language Learners**

SECTION 1

READING WARM-UP

Objectives
- Explain the relationship between gravity and pressure in a nebula.
- Describe how the solar system formed.

Terms to Learn
nebula
solar nebula

READING STRATEGY

Reading Organizer As you read this section, make a flowchart of the steps of the formation of a solar system.

nebula a large cloud of gas and dust in interstellar space; a region in space where stars are born or where stars explode at the end of their lives

Figure 1 The Horsehead Nebula is a cold, dark cloud of gas and dust. But observations suggest that it is also a site where stars form.

CHAPTER RESOURCES

Chapter Resource File
- Lesson Plan
- Directed Reading A BASIC
- Directed Reading B SPECIAL NEEDS

Technology
- Transparencies
- Bellringer

A Solar System Is Born

As you read this sentence, you are traveling at a speed of about 30 km/s around an incredibly hot star shining in the vastness of space!

Earth is not the only planet orbiting the sun. In fact, Earth has eight fellow travelers in its cosmic neighborhood. The solar system includes a star we call the sun, nine planets, and many moons and small bodies that travel around the sun. For almost 5 billion years, planets have been orbiting the sun. But how did the solar system come to be?

The Solar Nebula

All of the ingredients for building planets, moons, and stars are found in the vast, seemingly empty regions of space between the stars. Just as there are clouds in the sky, there are clouds in space. These clouds are called nebulas. **Nebulas** (or nebulae) are mixtures of gases—mainly hydrogen and helium—and dust made of elements such as carbon and iron. Although nebulas are normally dark and invisible to optical telescopes, they can be seen when nearby stars illuminate them. So, how can a cloud of gas and dust such as the Horsehead Nebula, shown in **Figure 1,** form planets and stars? To answer this question, you must explore two forces that interact in nebulas—gravity and pressure.

Gravity Pulls Matter Together

The gas and dust that make up nebulas are made of matter. The matter of a nebula is held together by the force of gravity. In most nebulas, there is a lot of space between the particles. In fact, nebulas are less dense than air! Thus, the gravitational attraction between the particles in a nebula is very weak. The force is just enough to keep the nebula from drifting apart.

Answer to Reading Check
The solar nebula is the cloud of gas and dust that formed our solar system.

614 Chapter 20 • Formation of the Solar System

Figure 2 Gravity and Pressure in a Nebula

❶ Gravity causes the particles in a nebula to be attracted to each other.

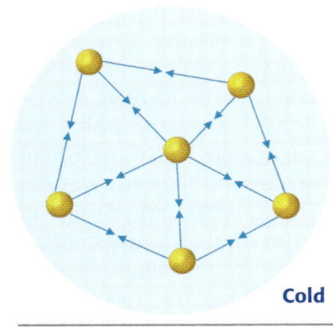

❷ As particles move closer together, collisions cause pressure to increase and particles are pushed apart.

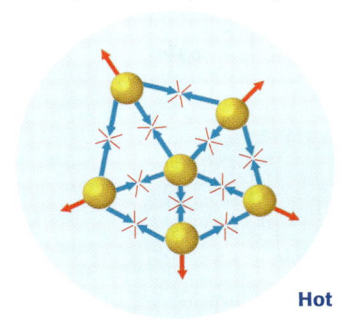

❸ If the inward force of gravity is balanced by outward pressure, the nebula becomes stable.

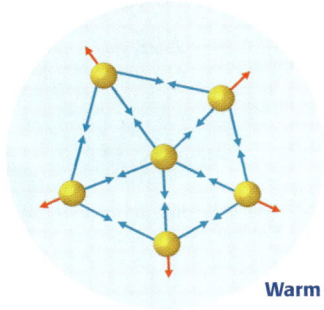

Cold   Hot   Warm

Pressure Pushes Matter Apart

If gravity pulls on all of the particles in a nebula, why don't nebulas slowly collapse? The answer has to do with the relationship between temperature and pressure in a nebula. *Temperature* is a measure of the average kinetic energy, or the energy of motion, of the particles in an object. If the particles in a nebula have little kinetic energy, they move slowly and the temperature of the cloud is very low. If the particles move fast, the temperature of the cloud is high. As particles move around, they sometimes crash into each other. As shown in **Figure 2,** these collisions cause particles to push away from each other, which creates *pressure*. If you have ever blown up a balloon, you understand how pressure works—pressure keeps a balloon from collapsing. In a nebula, outward pressure balances the inward gravitational pull and keeps the cloud from collapsing.

Upsetting the Balance

The balance between gravity and pressure in a nebula can be upset if two nebulas collide or a nearby star explodes. These events compress, or push together, small regions of a nebula called *globules*, or gas clouds. Globules can become so dense that they contract under their own gravity. As the matter in a globule collapses inward, the temperature increases and the stage is set for stars to form. The **solar nebula**—the cloud of gas and dust that formed our solar system—may have formed in this way.

solar nebula the cloud of gas and dust that formed our solar system

✓ **Reading Check** What is the solar nebula? (*See the Appendix for answers to Reading Checks.*)

Teach

Using the Figure — BASIC
Forces in a Nebula Have students refer to the three steps in **Figure 2** as they explain the force that pulls particles together (gravity) and the force that pushes particles apart (pressure due to the collision of particles). Be sure that students understand the role of temperature in a nebula. (As temperature increases, particles speed up, collisions increase, and pressure increases.) **LS** Visual

Discussion — BASIC
Reaching Equilibrium Have volunteers describe in their own words an example of a system that is in equilibrium because opposing forces of gravity (pulling) and pressure (pushing) balance one another. (Sample answer: One example is a person sitting in a chair. Gravity pulls down with a force equal to the force with which the chair pushes up.) **LS** Verbal

CONNECTION to Physical Science — GENERAL

Writing **Gas Laws** Discuss with students how Boyle's and Charles's laws help us understand the formation of the solar system.

- Boyle's law: At a constant temperature, the volume of a gas is inversely proportional to the pressure.
- Charles's law: At constant pressure, the volume of a gas is directly proportional to the temperature.

Review with students the difference between inverse and direct relationships, and have them give examples. Ask students to explain, in writing, why the temperature of a nebula increases as the nebula becomes denser. **LS** Verbal

---

INCLUSION Strategies

- Learning Disabled
- Attention Deficit Disorder
- Behavioral Control Issues

Have students model what the very early solar system would have looked like as predicted by the accretion theory. Provide each group of students with a bucket, a stirring stick, a basin for collecting used water, and 15 mL of vermiculite. Tell students to fill the bucket 3/4 full with water and pour the vermiculite on top of the water. Next, have them stir the mixture vigorously in a circular motion. When a funnel-shaped pattern is produced, have students stop and remove the stirring stick. Ask students to describe and draw what they observe in their **science journal.** Then, ask students the following: "Why did the vermiculite eventually slow down and stop? Why didn't the same thing happen to our solar system?" **LS** Visual/Kinesthetic

Section 1 • A Solar System Is Born **615**

Close

Reteaching — BASIC

Stages of Formation Draw four large squares on the board, and label them as follows: "The solar nebula," "The nebula collapsing," "The planetesimals form," and "The sun and planets form." Sketch each stage of solar system formation in the appropriate square. Have students use arrows and phrases to indicate changes in temperature and the balance between gravity and pressure.
LS Visual

Quiz — GENERAL

1. Why does the center of a collapsing nebula form a star? (High temperature causes pressure to become so intense between the crowded particles that atoms fuse and give off large amounts of energy.)

2. How do planets form? (Particles swirling in a cloud of dust and gas stick together and form planetesimals, which accumulate more matter and eventually form planets.)

Alternative Assessment — GENERAL

Explaining How the Solar System Formed Have students write a story in their **science journal** that would explain to a 17th-century astronomer how the sun and the planets formed. A 17th-century astronomer would not know nebulas or planetesimals by their current names. Students should share their stories with the class.

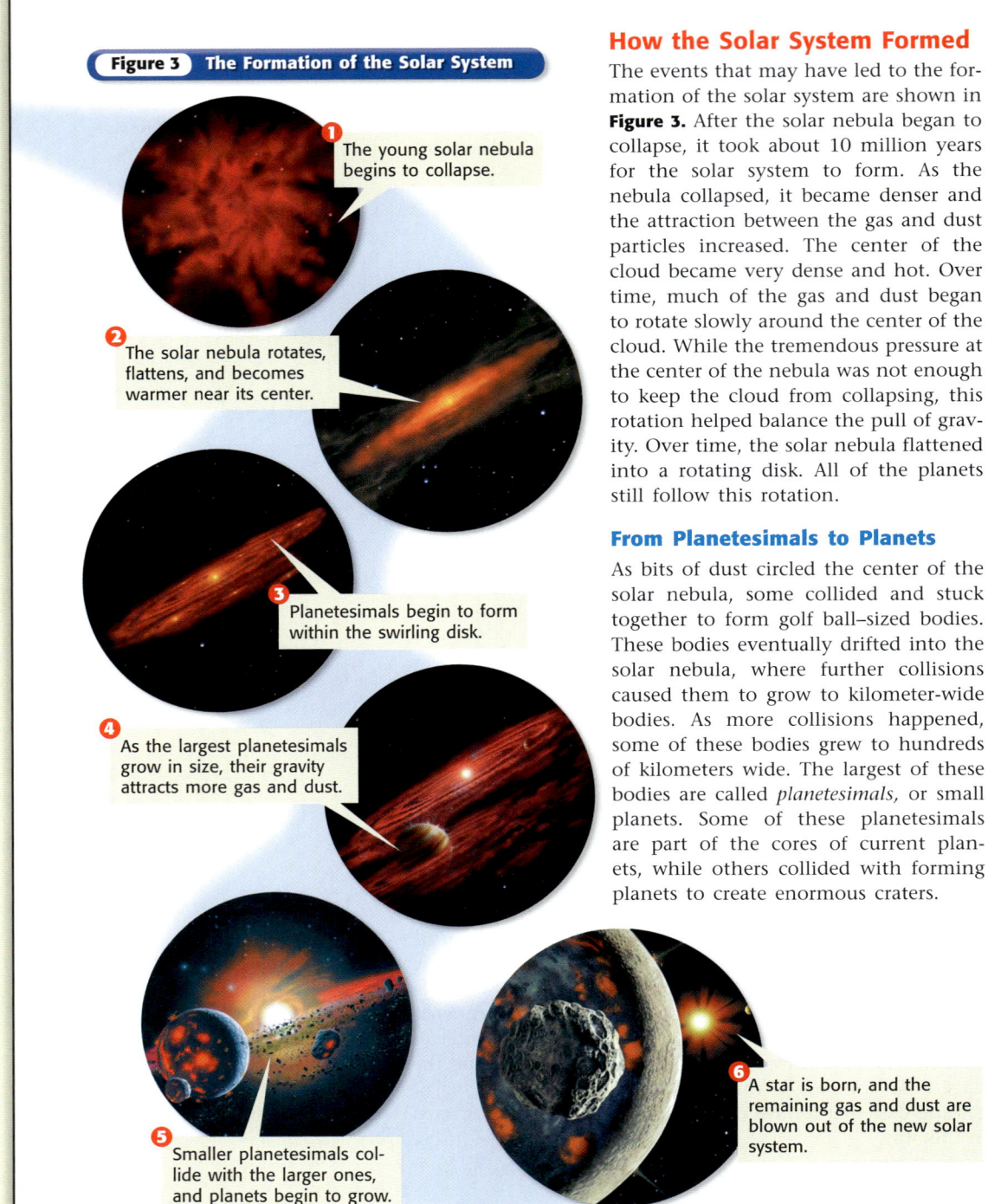

Figure 3 The Formation of the Solar System

1. The young solar nebula begins to collapse.
2. The solar nebula rotates, flattens, and becomes warmer near its center.
3. Planetesimals begin to form within the swirling disk.
4. As the largest planetesimals grow in size, their gravity attracts more gas and dust.
5. Smaller planetesimals collide with the larger ones, and planets begin to grow.
6. A star is born, and the remaining gas and dust are blown out of the new solar system.

Activity — BASIC

Modeling Planetesimal Formation Have students work in pairs. Each pair will need a couple of sheets of wax paper and a small spray bottle containing some water tinted by food coloring. Have students spray a little water on a sheet of wax paper. As students observe the wax paper after each spray, they will see large drops form. Discuss whether this model of planetesimal formation is accurate, and note how gravity, rather than surface tension, causes planetesimals to form. **LS** Visual

How the Solar System Formed

The events that may have led to the formation of the solar system are shown in **Figure 3.** After the solar nebula began to collapse, it took about 10 million years for the solar system to form. As the nebula collapsed, it became denser and the attraction between the gas and dust particles increased. The center of the cloud became very dense and hot. Over time, much of the gas and dust began to rotate slowly around the center of the cloud. While the tremendous pressure at the center of the nebula was not enough to keep the cloud from collapsing, this rotation helped balance the pull of gravity. Over time, the solar nebula flattened into a rotating disk. All of the planets still follow this rotation.

From Planetesimals to Planets

As bits of dust circled the center of the solar nebula, some collided and stuck together to form golf ball–sized bodies. These bodies eventually drifted into the solar nebula, where further collisions caused them to grow to kilometer-wide bodies. As more collisions happened, some of these bodies grew to hundreds of kilometers wide. The largest of these bodies are called *planetesimals*, or small planets. Some of these planetesimals are part of the cores of current planets, while others collided with forming planets to create enormous craters.

Homework — ADVANCED

Preparing a Presentation Have students find information about the asteroid belt, the Kuiper belt, the Oort cloud, and comets. Ask students to explain one or more of these phenomena using the steps shown in **Figure 3.** Encourage students to find a creative way to present their findings.
LS Visual/Interpersonal

Gas Giant or Rocky Planet?

The largest planetesimals formed near the outside of the rotating solar disk, where hydrogen and helium were located. These planetesimals were far enough from the solar disk that their gravity could attract the nebula gases. These outer planets grew to huge sizes and became the gas giants—Jupiter, Saturn, Uranus, and Neptune. Closer to the center of the nebula, where Mercury, Venus, Earth, and Mars formed, temperatures were too hot for gases to remain. Therefore, the inner planets in our solar system are made mostly of rocky material.

Reading Check Which planets are gas giants?

The Birth of a Star

As the planets were forming, other matter in the solar nebula was traveling toward the center. The center became so dense and hot that hydrogen atoms began to fuse, or join, to form helium. Fusion released huge amounts of energy and created enough outward pressure to balance the inward pull of gravity. At this point, when the gas stopped collapsing, our sun was born and the new solar system was complete!

CONNECTION TO Language Arts

WRITING SKILL **Eyewitness Account** Research information on the formation of the outer planets, inner planets, and the sun. Then, imagine that you witnessed the formation of the planets and sun. Write a short story describing your experience.

SECTION Review

Summary

- The solar system formed out of a vast cloud of gas and dust called the *nebula*.
- Gravity and pressure were balanced until something upset the balance. Then, the nebula began to collapse.
- Collapse of the solar nebula caused heating at the center, while planetesimals formed in surrounding space.
- The central mass of the nebula became the sun. Planets formed from the surrounding materials.

Using Key Terms

1. In your own words, write a definition for each of the following terms: *nebula* and *solar nebula*.

Understanding Key Ideas

2. What is the relationship between gravity and pressure in a nebula?
   a. Gravity reduces pressure.
   b. Pressure balances gravity.
   c. Pressure increases gravity.
   d. None of the above

3. Describe how our solar system formed.

4. Compare the inner planets with the outer planets.

Math Skills

5. If the planets, moons, and other bodies make up 0.15% of the solar system's mass, what percentage does the sun make up?

Critical Thinking

6. **Evaluating Hypotheses** Pluto, the outermost planet, is small and rocky. Some scientists argue that Pluto is a captured asteroid, not a planet. Use what you know about how solar systems form to evaluate this hypothesis.

7. **Making Inferences** Why do all of the planets go around the sun in the same direction, and why do the planets lie on a relatively flat plane?

SCLINKS Developed and maintained by the National Science Teachers Association

For a variety of links related to this chapter, go to www.scilinks.org
Topic: The Planets
SciLinks code: HSM1152

Answer to Reading Check
Jupiter, Saturn, Uranus, and Neptune

CHAPTER RESOURCES

Chapter Resource File
- Section Quiz GENERAL
- Section Review GENERAL
- Vocabulary and Section Summary GENERAL
- Critical Thinking ADVANCED

Answers to Section Review

1. Sample answer: A nebula is a large cloud of gas and dust in interstellar space. The solar nebula is the cloud of gas and dust that formed our solar system.

2. b

3. Sample answer: After the balance between gravity and pressure became unbalanced in the solar nebula, it began to collapse. The solar nebula became denser, and the attraction between the gas and dust particles increased. This attraction caused the center of the nebula to become dense and hot. As bits of dust circled the center, some collided to form planetesimals. The central mass of the nebula became the sun, and the planetesimals that continued to circle the sun eventually formed the planets.

4. The inner planets, Mercury, Venus, Earth, and Mars, formed closer to the sun where temperatures were too hot for gases to remain. So, the inner planets are made of mostly rocky material. The outer planets, Jupiter, Saturn, Uranus, and Neptune, formed farther away from the sun and are partially made up of gases. Pluto, the outermost planet, is not a gas giant.

5. $100\% - 0.15\% = 99.85\%$

6. Answers may vary.

7. Sample answer: The planets formed from the flattened disk of the nebula, which rotated. The dust and gas that formed the planets rotated in the same direction that the nebula was spinning.

Section 1 • A Solar System Is Born

SECTION 2

Focus

Overview
This section describes the structure of the sun. It discusses the early theories about the source of the sun's energy and why nuclear fusion is the accepted theory today.

🔔 Bellringer
Have students write about the following quotation by Henry Thoreau: "The sun is but a morning star."

Motivate

Demonstration — GENERAL

Observing Sunspots Clamp a pair of binoculars in a ring stand, and cut a hole in a piece of cardboard that fits around the eyepiece of one binocular lens. Darken the classroom, and orient the binoculars toward the sun. Hold a mirror in the shadow of the cardboard, and project an image of the sun onto a wall. Focus the image, and have students identify sunspots and other features of the sun.

Safety Caution: Make sure that students do not look at the sun through the binoculars. Also, caution students never to look directly at the sun. **LS Visual**

SECTION 2

READING WARM-UP

Objectives
- Describe the basic structure and composition of the sun.
- Explain how the sun generates energy.
- Describe the surface activity of the sun, and identify how this activity affects Earth.

Terms to Learn
nuclear fusion
sunspot

READING STRATEGY

Reading Organizer As you read this section, create an outline of the section. Use the headings from the section in your outline.

The Sun: Our Very Own Star

Can you imagine what life on Earth would be like if there were no sun? Without the sun, life on Earth would be impossible!

Energy from the sun lights and heats Earth's surface. Energy from the sun even drives the weather. Making up more than 99% of the solar system's mass, the sun is the dominant member of our solar system. The sun is basically a large ball of gas made mostly of hydrogen and helium held together by gravity. But what does the inside of the sun look like?

The Structure of the Sun

Although the sun may appear to have a solid surface, it does not. When you see a picture of the sun, you are really seeing through the sun's outer atmosphere. The visible surface of the sun starts at the point where the gas becomes so thick that you cannot see through it. As **Figure 1** shows, the sun is made of several layers.

Figure 1 The Structure and Atmosphere of the Sun

The **corona** forms the sun's outer atmosphere.

The **chromosphere** is a thin region below the corona, only 30,000 km thick.

The **photosphere** is the visible part of the sun that we can see from Earth.

The **convective zone** is a region about 200,000 km thick where gases circulate.

The **radiative zone** is a very dense region about 300,000 km thick.

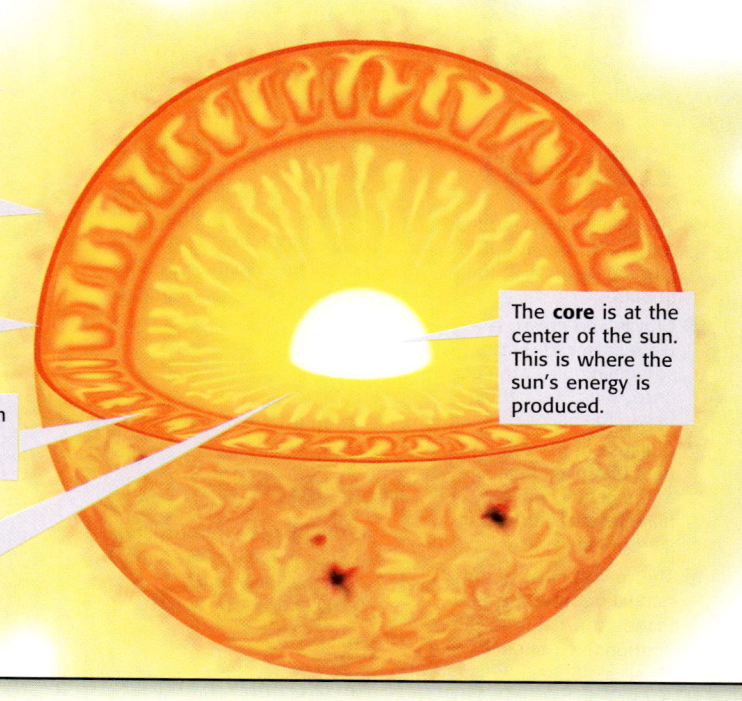

The **core** is at the center of the sun. This is where the sun's energy is produced.

CHAPTER RESOURCES

Chapter Resource File
- Lesson Plan
- Directed Reading A **BASIC**
- Directed Reading B **SPECIAL NEEDS**

Technology
- Transparencies
  - Bellringer
  - The Structure and Atmosphere of the Sun

Is That a Fact!

In 1868, a French astronomer named Pierre Janssen and an English astronomer named Norman Lockyer independently detected in the chromosphere of the sun a new element that was unknown on Earth. The new element, called helium (named after *helios*, the Greek word for "sun"), was not discovered on Earth until 1895.

---

618 Chapter 20 • Formation of the Solar System

At first, some type of burning fuel was thought to be the source of the sun's energy.

A shrinking sun was another explanation for solar energy.

Figure 2 Ideas about the source of the sun's energy have changed over time.

Energy Production in the Sun

The sun has been shining on Earth for about 4.6 billion years. How can the sun stay hot for so long? And what makes it shine? **Figure 2** shows two theories that were proposed to answer these questions. Many scientists thought that the sun burned fuel to generate its energy. But the amount of energy that is released by burning would not be enough to power the sun. If the sun were simply burning, it would last for only 10,000 years.

Burning or Shrinking?

It eventually became clear to scientists that burning wouldn't last long enough to keep the sun shining. Then, scientists began to think that gravity was causing the sun to slowly shrink. They thought that perhaps gravity would release enough energy to heat the sun. While the release of gravitational energy is more powerful than burning, it is not enough to power the sun. If all of the sun's gravitational energy were released, the sun would last for only 45 million years. However, fossils that have been discovered prove that dinosaurs roamed the Earth more than 65 million years ago, so this couldn't be the case. Therefore, something even more powerful than gravity was needed.

✓ **Reading Check** Why isn't energy from gravity enough to power the sun? (See the Appendix for answers to Reading Checks.)

Cultural Awareness — GENERAL

Ancient Beliefs About the Sun
Ancient cultures imagined the sun as a god. The Greeks called their sun god *Helios* and depicted him driving a flaming chariot across the sky. For the Egyptians, *Ra* was a sun god and the creator and controller of the universe. The Japanese considered their emperor to be a descendant of their sun goddess, *Amaterasu*.

WEIRD SCIENCE

Even though the temperature of the sun's corona can reach 2 million K, particles in the corona are so far apart that they don't transfer much thermal energy. A space shuttle could enter the sun's corona and not burn up, despite the high temperature. However, the space shuttle would quickly absorb electromagnetic radiation, which would be very destructive to the space shuttle.

Teach

Using the Figure — GENERAL

The Structure of the Sun Refer students to **Figure 1,** and have them find dictionary definitions for the name of each layer of the sun and write an additional caption that explains why each name is appropriate for a particular layer. **English Language Learners**
LS Intrapersonal

CONNECTION ACTIVITY
Math ———————— GENERAL

Graphing Have students create a graph that shows the differences in the temperature (in kelvins) of the sun's layers from the core to the corona. The data for the graph are as follows:
- core: 15,000,000 K
- radiative and convective zone: 4,000,000 K
- photosphere: 6,000 K
- chromosphere: 7,000 K
- corona: 1,000,000 K

LS Visual/Logical

Answer to Reading Check

Energy from gravity is not enough to power the sun, because if all of the sun's gravitational energy were released, the sun would last for only 45 million years.

Section 2 • The Sun: Our Very Own Star **619**

Teach, continued

Answer to Connection to Chemistry

nitrogen: 7 protons, 7 neutrons, and 7 electrons; oxygen: 8 protons, 8 neutrons, and 8 electrons; and carbon: 6 protons, 6 neutrons, and 6 electrons

Group Activity — ADVANCED

Escape from the Sun Have groups of students create a board game to model the movement of energy in the sun. Students should begin by making a game board out of poster board. The board should accurately illustrate the structure of the sun from the core to the corona. Then, have students create a series of index cards containing questions and answers about the sun. Explain to students the following objectives of the game: "A player begins the game as a proton and attempts to "collide" with another proton in the sun's core. A player "collides" when he or she correctly answers a question. Players will continue through each step of the fusion process by correctly answering more questions. Players then leave the core as energy and continue traveling to the convective and radiative zones by correctly answering more questions. The object of the game is to reach Earth's surface as infrared, UV, or visible light energy."

LS Verbal/Interpersonal

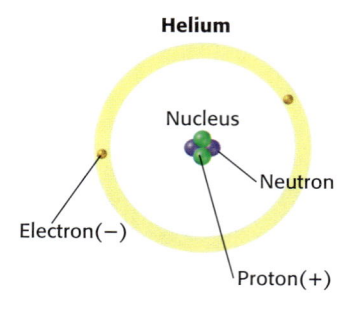

Helium

(Diagram labels: Nucleus, Neutron, Proton(+), Electron(−))

nuclear fusion the combination of the nuclei of small atoms to form a larger nucleus; releases energy

CONNECTION TO Chemistry

Atoms An atom consists of a nucleus surrounded by one or more electrons. Electrons have a negative charge. In most elements, the atom's nucleus is made up of two types of particles: *protons,* which have a positive charge, and *neutrons,* which have no charge. The protons in the nucleus are usually balanced by an equal number of electrons. The number of protons and electrons gives the atom its chemical identity. A helium atom, shown at left, has two protons, two neutrons, and two electrons. Use a Periodic Table to find the chemical identity of the following atoms: nitrogen, oxygen, and carbon.

Nuclear Fusion

At the beginning of the 20th century, Albert Einstein showed that matter and energy are interchangeable. Matter can change into energy according to his famous formula: $E = mc^2$. (E is energy, m is mass, and c is the speed of light.) Because c is such a large number, tiny amounts of matter can produce a huge amount of energy. With this idea, scientists began to understand a very powerful source of energy.

Nuclear fusion is the process by which two or more low-mass nuclei join together, or fuse, to form another nucleus. In this way, four hydrogen nuclei can fuse to form a single nucleus of helium. During the process, energy is produced. Scientists now know that the sun gets its energy from nuclear fusion. Einstein's equation, shown in **Figure 3,** changed ideas about the sun's energy source by equating mass and energy.

Figure 3 Einstein's equation changed ideas about the sun's energy source by equating mass and energy.

$$E = mc^2$$

CONNECTION to Physical Science — GENERAL

Star Stuff Stars are the crucibles in which the heavy elements of the universe are forged. As generations of stars are born, grow old, and re-form, heavy elements have become more abundant in the universe. The calcium in our bones and the iron in our blood originated in stars—we are made of "star stuff." The big bang produced mainly hydrogen and helium, the fuel that powers stars. All other elements in the universe are produced during the life cycle of stars. Our sun is massive enough to create elements as heavy as oxygen, and more-massive stars can produce elements as heavy as sodium. Elements heavier than iron are synthesized only when extremely massive supergiants become supernovas. Use the teaching transparency entitled "The Periodic Table of the Elements" to discuss the types of elements produced by stars. **LS Verbal/Visual**

Fusion in the Sun

During fusion, under normal conditions, the nuclei of hydrogen atoms never get close enough to combine. The reason is that they are positively charged. Like charges repel each other, as shown in **Figure 4**. In the center of the sun, however, the temperature and pressure are very high. As a result, the hydrogen nuclei have enough energy to overcome the repulsive force, and hydrogen fuses into helium, as shown in **Figure 5**.

The energy produced in the center, or core of the sun takes millions of years to reach the sun's surface. The energy passes from the core through a very dense region called the *radiative zone*. The matter in the radiative zone is so crowded that the light and energy are blocked and sent in different directions. Eventually, the energy reaches the *convective zone*. Gases circulate in the convective zone, which is about 200,000 km thick. Hot gases in the convective zone carry the energy up to the *photosphere,* the visible surface of the sun. From there, the energy leaves the sun as light, which takes only 8.3 min to reach Earth.

Reading Check What causes the nuclei of hydrogen atoms to repel each other?

Figure 4 Like charges repel just as similar poles on a pair of magnets do.

Figure 5 Fusion of Hydrogen in the Sun

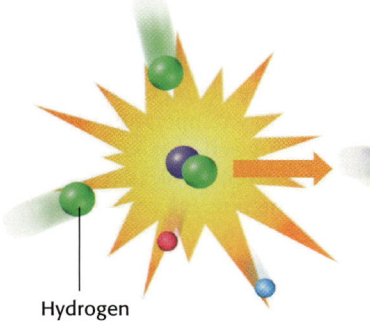

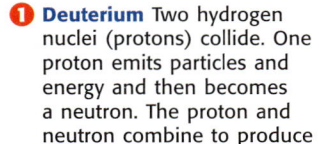

Hydrogen

Gamma ray

❶ **Deuterium** Two hydrogen nuclei (protons) collide. One proton emits particles and energy and then becomes a neutron. The proton and neutron combine to produce a heavy form of hydrogen called *deuterium*.

❷ **Helium-3** Deuterium combines with another hydrogen nucleus to form a variety of helium called *helium-3*. More energy, as well as gamma rays, is released.

❸ **Helium-4** Two helium-3 atoms then combine to form ordinary helium-4, which releases more energy and a pair of hydrogen nuclei.

CONNECTION ACTIVITY
Math — BASIC

Graphing Density Density is a measure of the amount of matter in a specific volume of space. Have students create a bar graph comparing the densities of different planets given in the table below, and have students answer the questions that follow.

Planet	Mean Density
Mercury	5.43 g/cm^3
Venus	5.20 g/cm^3
Earth	5.52 g/cm^3
Mars	3.93 g/cm^3
Jupiter	1.32 g/cm^3
Saturn	0.69 g/cm^3
Uranus	1.32 g/cm^3
Neptune	1.64 g/cm^3
Pluto	2.05 g/cm^3

- How many times denser than Jupiter is Mercury?
  (5.43 ÷ 1.32 = 4.11)
- How many times denser than Saturn is Earth?
  (5.52 ÷ 0.69 = 8.00)

LS Visual/Logical

Answer to Reading Check
The nuclei of hydrogen atoms repel each other because they are positively charged and like charges repel each other.

CONNECTION ACTIVITY
History — GENERAL

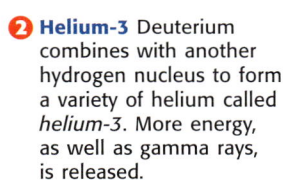

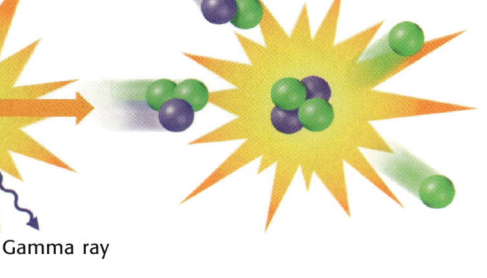

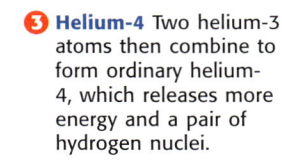

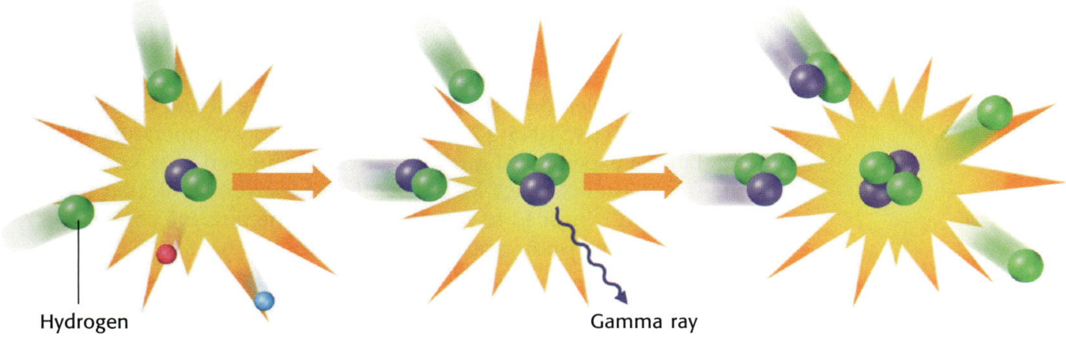

Gerard Peter Kuiper Gerard Peter Kuiper (KIE puhr) lived from 1902 to 1973 and is often called the *father of modern planetary science.* Kuiper made discoveries about Saturn and its largest moon, Titan, as well as discoveries about Mars, Uranus, Neptune, Pluto, and Jupiter. Have students find out more about his discoveries. **LS** Interpersonal

CHAPTER RESOURCES
Technology

Transparencies
- Fusion of Hydrogen in the Sun
- **LINK TO PHYSICAL SCIENCE** The Periodic Table of the Elements

Close

Reteaching — BASIC
The Layers of the Sun's Atmosphere Have students create a mnemonic device to help them remember the layers of the sun's atmosphere. **LS Verbal**

Quiz — GENERAL
1. How do you know that gravity does not produce the sun's energy? (If all of the sun's gravitational energy were released, the sun would last only 45 million years. The solar system is at least 4.6 billion years old.)
2. How does energy produced by nuclear fusion move from the sun's core to space? (It moves very slowly through the radiative zone, circulates through the convective zone, passes through the photosphere, and leaves the sun as light.)

Alternative Assessment — ADVANCED
Energy Transfer Have students explain how energy released from the collision of two protons in the sun's core warms a car seat on Earth. Students should account for the following: nuclear fusion, the movement of energy through the radiative and convective zones, Earth's atmosphere, and the amount of time this process takes. **LS Verbal**

Figure 6 Sunspots mark cooler areas on the sun's surface. They are related to changes in the magnetic properties of the sun.

sunspot a dark area of the photosphere of the sun that is cooler than the surrounding areas and that has a strong magnetic field

Figure 7 This graph shows the number of sunspots that have occurred each year since Galileo's first observation in 1610.

Solar Activity
The photosphere is an ever-changing place. Thermal energy moves from the sun's interior by the circulation of gases in the convective zone. This movement of energy causes the gas in the photosphere to boil and churn. This circulation, combined with the sun's rotation, creates magnetic fields that reach far out into space.

Sunspots
The sun's magnetic fields tend to slow down the activity in the convective zone. When activity slows down, areas of the photosphere become cooler than surrounding areas. These cooler areas show up as sunspots. **Sunspots** are cooler, dark spots of the photosphere of the sun, as shown in **Figure 6.** Sunspots can vary in shape and size. Some sunspots can be as large as 50,000 miles in diameter.

The numbers and locations of sunspots on the sun change in a regular cycle. Scientists have found that the sunspot cycle lasts about 11 years. Every 11 years, the amount of sunspot activity in the sun reaches a peak intensity and then decreases. **Figure 7** shows the sunspot cycle since 1610, excluding the years 1645–1715, which was a period of unusually low sunspot activity.

✓ **Reading Check** What are sunspots? What causes sunspots to occur?

Climate Confusion
Scientists have found that sunspot activity can affect the Earth. For example, some scientists have linked the period of low sunspot activity, 1645–1715, with the very low temperatures that Europe experienced during that time. This period is known as the "Little Ice Age." Most scientists, however, think that more research is needed to fully understand the possible connection between sunspots and Earth's climate.

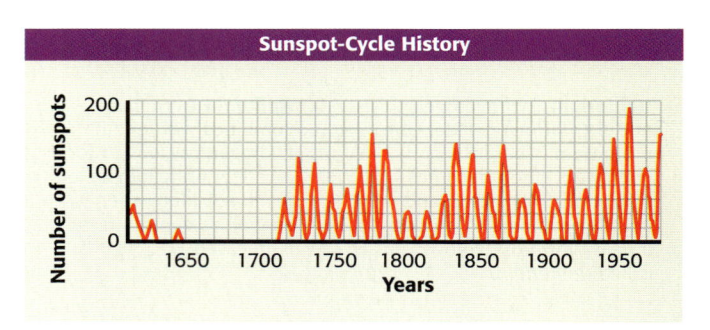

Answer to Reading Check
Sunspots are cooler, dark spots on the sun. Sunspots occur because when activity slows down in the convective zone, areas of the photosphere become cooler.

---

622 Chapter 20 • Formation of the Solar System

Solar Flares

The magnetic fields that cause sunspots also cause solar flares. *Solar flares,* as shown in **Figure 8,** are regions of extremely high temperature and brightness that develop on the sun's surface. When a solar flare erupts, it sends huge streams of electrically charged particles into the solar system. Solar flares can extend upward several thousand kilometers within minutes. Solar flares are usually associated with sunspots and can interrupt radio communications on Earth and in orbit. Scientists are trying to find ways to give advance warning of solar flares.

Figure 8 *Solar flares are giant eruptions on the sun's surface.*

SECTION Review

Summary

- The sun is a large ball of gas made mostly of hydrogen and helium. The sun consists of many layers.
- The sun's energy comes from nuclear fusion that takes place in the center of the sun.
- The visible surface of the sun, or the photosphere, is very active.
- Sunspots and solar flares are the result of the sun's magnetic fields that reach space.
- Sunspot activity may affect Earth's climate, and solar flares can interact with Earth's atmosphere.

Using Key Terms

1. In your own words, write a definition for each of the following terms: *sunspot* and *nuclear fusion*.

Understanding Key Ideas

2. Which of the following statements describes how energy is produced in the sun?
   a. The sun burns fuels to generate energy.
   b. As hydrogen changes into helium deep inside the sun, a great deal of energy is made.
   c. Energy is released as the sun shrinks because of gravity.
   d. None of the above

3. Describe the composition of the sun.

4. Name and describe the layers of the sun.

5. In which area of the sun do sunspots appear?

6. Explain how sunspots form.

7. Describe how sunspots can affect the Earth.

8. What are solar flares, and how do they form?

Math Skills

9. If the equatorial diameter of the sun is 1.39 million kilometers, how many kilometers is the sun's radius?

Critical Thinking

10. **Applying Concepts** If nuclear fusion in the sun's core suddenly stopped today, would the sky be dark in the daytime tomorrow? Explain.

11. **Making Comparisons** Compare the theories that scientists proposed about the source of the sun's energy with the process of nuclear fusion in the sun.

SCLINKS. NSTA
Developed and maintained by the National Science Teachers Association

For a variety of links related to this chapter, go to www.scilinks.org
Topic: The Sun
SciLinks code: HSM1477

Answers to Section Review

1. Sample answer: A sunspot is a dark area of the photosphere of the sun that is cooler than the surrounding areas. Nuclear fusion occurs when the nuclei of small atoms combine to form a larger nucleus.

2. b

3. The sun is a large ball of gas made mostly of hydrogen and helium held together by gravity.

4. The corona forms the sun's outer atmosphere. The chromosphere is below the corona and is only 30,000 km thick. The photosphere is the visible part of the sun that we can see from Earth. The convective zone is a region about 200,000 km thick where gases circulate. The radiative zone is a very dense region about 300,000 km thick. The core is at the center of the sun, and it is where the sun's energy is produced.

5. Sunspots appear as cool, dark spots of the photosphere of the sun.

6. The sun's magnetic fields slow down the activity in the convective zone, which causes areas of the photosphere to become cooler. Sunspots are the dark, cooler spots on the sun.

7. Scientists think that a period of less sunspot activity may cause lower temperatures on Earth.

8. Solar flares are regions of extremely high temperature and brightness that develop on the sun's surface. Solar flares are caused by the sun's magnetic fields, which are caused by the movement of energy in the sun.

9. 1,390,000 km ÷ 2 = 695,000 km

10. No, it would take millions of years for the last energy made in the core to reach the surface of the sun.

11. In the 19th century, some scientists thought that the sun burned fuel to generate its energy. Other scientists thought that gravity was causing the sun to slowly shrink and release energy. Finally, with the help of Albert Einstein's equation, $E = mc^2$, the process of nuclear fusion was defined. Nuclear fusion is the combination of the nuclei of small atoms to form a large nucleus. The result of nuclear fusion is the release of energy. The fusion of hydrogen into helium in the sun generates a large amount of energy and therefore is the source of the sun's energy.

CHAPTER RESOURCES

Chapter Resource File
- Section Quiz GENERAL
- Section Review GENERAL
- Vocabulary and Section Summary GENERAL
- Reinforcement Worksheet BASIC
- SciLinks Activity GENERAL

Section 2 • The Sun: Our Very Own Star

SECTION 3

Focus

Overview

This section explores Earth's formation. Students will learn how Earth's atmosphere, oceans, and continents developed and how our atmosphere sustains life today.

🔔 Bellringer

Tell students that Earth is about 4.6 billion years old. The first fossil evidence of life on Earth has been dated between 3.7 billion and 3.4 billion years ago. Have students write a paragraph describing what Earth might have been like during the first billion years of its existence.

Motivate

Discussion — GENERAL

Earth's Atmosphere Tell students that gases released from Earth's molten surface helped create Earth's first atmosphere. Explain that the gases in our atmosphere are held by gravity, and ask students to speculate why there is very little hydrogen or helium atoms in our atmosphere if these are the most abundant elements in the universe. (These gases are so light that Earth's gravity cannot trap them.) **LS** Visual

---

SECTION 3

READING WARM-UP

Objectives
- Describe the formation of the solid Earth.
- Describe the structure of the Earth.
- Explain the development of Earth's atmosphere and the influence of early life on the atmosphere.
- Describe how the Earth's oceans and continents formed.

Terms to Learn
crust
mantle
core

READING STRATEGY

Discussion Read this section silently. Write down questions that you have about this section. Discuss your questions in a small group.

The Earth Takes Shape

In many ways, Earth seems to be a perfect place for life.

We live on the third planet from the sun. The Earth, shown in **Figure 1,** is mostly made of rock, and nearly three-fourths of its surface is covered with water. It is surrounded by a protective atmosphere of mostly nitrogen and oxygen and smaller amounts of other gases. But Earth has not always been such an oasis in the solar system.

Formation of the Solid Earth

The Earth formed as planetesimals in the solar system collided and combined. From what scientists can tell, the Earth formed within the first 10 million years of the collapse of the solar nebula!

The Effects of Gravity

When a young planet is still small, it can have an irregular shape, somewhat like a potato. But as the planet gains more matter, the force of gravity increases. When a rocky planet, such as Earth, reaches a diameter of about 350 km, the force of gravity becomes greater than the strength of the rock. As the Earth grew to this size, the rock at its center was crushed by gravity and the planet started to become round.

The Effects of Heat

As the Earth was changing shape, it was also heating up. Planetesimals continued to collide with the Earth, and the energy of their motion heated the planet. Radioactive material, which was present in the Earth as it formed, also heated the young planet. After Earth reached a certain size, the temperature rose faster than the interior could cool, and the rocky material inside began to melt. Today, the Earth is still cooling from the energy that was generated when it formed. Volcanoes, earthquakes, and hot springs are effects of this energy trapped inside the Earth. As you will learn later, the effects of heat and gravity also helped form the Earth's layers when the Earth was very young.

✓ **Reading Check** What factors heated the Earth during its early formation? (*See the Appendix for answers to Reading Checks.*)

Figure 1 When Earth is seen from space, one of its unique features—the presence of water—is apparent.

CHAPTER RESOURCES

Chapter Resource File
- Lesson Plan
- Directed Reading A BASIC
- Directed Reading B SPECIAL NEEDS

Technology
- Transparencies
  - Bellringer
  - Formation of Earth's Layers

Answer to Reading Check

During Earth's early formation, planetesimals collided with the Earth. The energy of their motion heated the planet.

---

624 Chapter 20 • Formation of the Solar System

How the Earth's Layers Formed

Have you ever watched the oil separate from vinegar in a bottle of salad dressing? The vinegar sinks because it is denser than oil. The Earth's layers formed in much the same way. As rocks melted, denser materials, such as nickel and iron, sank to the center of the Earth and formed the core. Less dense materials floated to the surface and became the crust. This process is shown in **Figure 2**.

The **crust** is the thin, outermost layer of the Earth. It is 5 to 100 km thick. Crustal rock is made of materials that have low densities, such as oxygen, silicon, and aluminum. The **mantle** is the layer of Earth beneath the crust. It extends 2,900 km below the surface. Mantle rock is made of materials such as magnesium and iron and is denser than crustal rock. The **core** is the central part of the Earth below the mantle. It contains the densest materials (nickel and iron) and extends to the center of the Earth—almost 6,400 km below the surface.

crust the thin and solid outermost layer of the Earth above the mantle

mantle the layer of rock between the Earth's crust and core

core the central part of the Earth below the mantle

Figure 2 The Formation of Earth's Layers

1. All materials in the early Earth are randomly mixed.
2. Rocks melt, and denser materials sink toward the center. Less dense elements rise and form layers.
3. According to composition, the Earth is divided into three layers: the crust, the mantle, and the core.

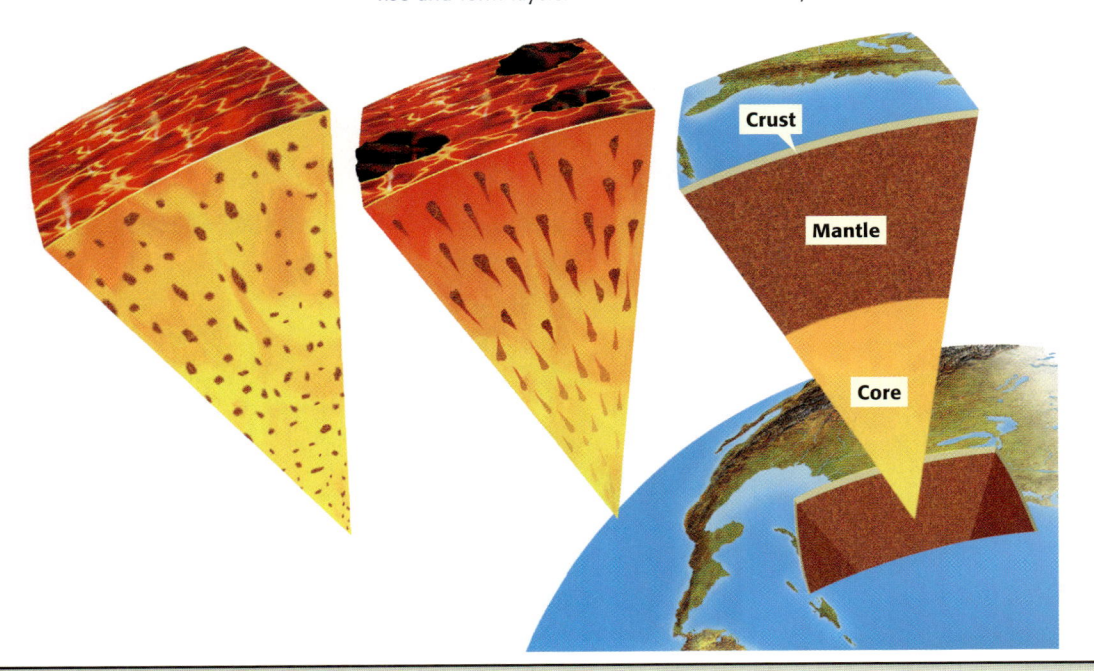

Science Bloopers

Impact Craters Impact craters have left scars on planets and moons throughout the solar system. In 1826, an eccentric Bavarian astronomer named Franz von Paula Gruithuisen was one of the first scientists to suggest that lunar craters were caused by meteorite impacts. However, he also asserted that other lunar features were built by a race of moon creatures called *Selenites*, and his theory of crater formation was not taken seriously. Students will enjoy reading and reporting on other imaginative descriptions of the moon by authors such as Jules Verne. Even astronomer Johannes Kepler wrote about creatures living on the moon in his book *The Dream*.

Teach

CONNECTION to Geology — ADVANCED

Comparing Mars and Earth's Core Earth's core is 33% of Earth's mass. Although the planet Mars is approximately the same volume as Earth's core, the mass of Mars is only 11% of Earth's mass. Ask students to compare the density of Mars with the density of Earth's core and to explain the differences they note. (Mars is less dense than Earth's core. Mars is composed of a smaller core and lighter materials than Earth's core is.) **LS** Verbal

CONNECTION to Language Arts — GENERAL

Science Fiction Have students read "Desertion" by Clifford Simak in the *Holt Anthology of Science Fiction*. **LS** Intrapersonal

INCLUSION Strategies

- Learning Disabled
- Attention Deficit Disorder

Have students model the interior of the early Earth. Organize students into groups of three or four and give each group 50 mL of water, a 150 mL container, 50 mL of cooking oil, and a spoon. Ask students to pour 50 mL of water into the container. Then, have them add 50 mL of cooking oil to the water. Ask students to stir the mixture vigorously. Have students stop stirring, and ask them to let the mixture stand for a few minutes. Then, ask students how the mixture models the interior of the early Earth. **LS** Visual/Kinesthetic

Section 3 • The Earth Takes Shape

Teach, continued

ACTIVITY — GENERAL

Rings Around Our Planet The rings of ice and rock that circle Jupiter, Saturn, Uranus, and Neptune may have formed through collisions between small bodies as they passed these planets. But Earth is also developing a system of rings. These rings are not moon debris, however, but debris from satellites and space missions. Have interested students research the problem of orbiting space trash and the proposed solutions to clean it up. **LS Intrapersonal**

INTERNET ACTIVITY
Math — ADVANCED

Researching New Planets
In 1991, Alexander Wolszczan discovered the first extra-solar planets orbiting a pulsar called *PSR B1257+12* in the constellation Virgo. A pulsar is the remains of a star that has exploded as a supernova. The masses of the three planets are 0.02, 4.3, and 3.9 times the mass of Earth. Wolszczan carefully measured the rotation of the pulsar and detected slight changes caused by the gravity from the three planets. Astronomers do not know how these three planets formed or how the planets survived the explosion of their parent star. Have students do research on the Internet for explanations about these extra-solar planets and to report to the class any additional planets that have

CONNECTION TO Environmental Science

WRITING SKILL

The Greenhouse Effect Carbon dioxide is a greenhouse gas. Greenhouse gases are gases that absorb thermal energy and radiate it back to Earth. This process is called the greenhouse effect because the gases function like the walls and roof of a greenhouse, which allow solar energy to enter but prevent thermal energy from escaping. Do research to find the percentage of carbon dioxide that is thought to make up Earth's early atmosphere. Write a report, and share your findings with your class.

Figure 3 This artwork is an artist's view of what Earth's surface may have looked like shortly after the Earth formed.

SCIENCE HUMOR

Q: Have you heard about the new restaurant on the moon?
A: great food, lousy atmosphere

Formation of the Earth's Atmosphere

Today, Earth's atmosphere is 78% nitrogen, 21% oxygen, and about 1% argon. (There are tiny amounts of many other gases.) Did you know that the Earth's atmosphere did not always contain the oxygen that you need to live? The Earth's atmosphere is constantly changing. Scientists think that the Earth's earliest atmosphere was very different than it is today.

Earth's Early Atmosphere

Scientists think that Earth's early atmosphere was a mixture of gases that were released as Earth cooled. During the final stages of the Earth's formation, its surface was very hot—even molten in places—as shown in **Figure 3**. The molten rock released large amounts of carbon dioxide and water vapor. Therefore, scientists think that Earth's early atmosphere was a steamy mixture of carbon dioxide and water vapor.

✓ **Reading Check** Describe Earth's early atmosphere.

Answer to Reading Check
Scientists think that the Earth's early atmosphere was a steamy mixture of carbon dioxide and water vapor.

Earth's Changing Atmosphere

As the Earth cooled and its layers formed, the Earth's atmosphere changed again. This atmosphere probably formed from volcanic gases. Volcanoes, such as the one in **Figure 4,** released chlorine, nitrogen, and sulfur in addition to large amounts of carbon dioxide and water vapor. Some of this water vapor may have condensed to form the Earth's first oceans.

Comets, which are planetesimals made of ice, also may have contributed to this change of Earth's atmosphere. As comets crashed into the Earth, they brought in a range of elements, such as carbon, hydrogen, oxygen, and nitrogen. Comets also may have brought some of the water that helped form the oceans.

The Role of Life

How did this change of Earth's atmosphere become the air you are breathing right now? The answer is related to the appearance of life on Earth.

Ultraviolet Radiation

Scientists think that ultraviolet (UV) radiation, the same radiation that causes sunburns, helped produce the conditions necessary for life. Because UV light has a lot of energy, it can break apart molecules in your skin and in the air. Today, we are shielded from most of the sun's UV rays by Earth's protective ozone layer. But Earth's early atmosphere probably did not have ozone, so many molecules in the air and at Earth's surface were broken apart. Over time, this material collected in the Earth's waters. Water offered protection from the effects of UV radiation. In these sheltered pools of water, chemicals may have combined to form the complex molecules that made life possible. The first life-forms were very simple and did not need oxygen to live.

Figure 4 As this volcano in Hawaii shows, a large amount of gas is released during an eruption.

SCHOOL to HOME
Comets and Meteors
What is the difference between a comet and a meteor? With a parent, research the difference between comets and meteors. Then, find out if you can view meteor showers in your area!
ACTIVITY

Debate — GENERAL
Life on Earth: Could It Happen Again? Ask students to imagine that life on Earth is completely destroyed. Encourage students to debate whether life could evolve again in our current atmosphere. Students should consider conditions on primitive Earth as well as the requirements for life as we know it. **LS Verbal**

CONNECTION to Life Science — GENERAL
The Presence of Oxygen If the early Earth had contained a lot of oxygen in its atmosphere, the chemical processes that gave rise to life probably would not have occurred! Oxygen is very reactive; it combines with other elements readily. High levels of oxygen would have prevented organic molecules from combining, which would have stopped the development of early forms of life.

Homework — GENERAL
Poster Project Have students create a series of drawings and captions to show how Earth's atmosphere first formed and how it changed over time. Encourage students to use creative approaches, such as comic-strips, to communicate the concepts. **LS Intrapersonal**

Answer to School-to-Home Activity
A comet is a small body of ice, rock, and cosmic dust that follows an elliptical orbit around the sun and that gives off gas and dust in the form of a tail as it passes close to the sun. A meteor is a bright streak of light that results when a meteoroid burns up in the Earth's atmosphere.

Is That a Fact!
Earth is growing heavier by thousands of metric tons every year. Microscopic dust constantly filters through the atmosphere from space and lands on our planet. You can look at these so-called micrometeroids by collecting rainwater that has dropped directly into a glass. You can use a microscope to search and view round, dark particles from the rainwater sediment—more than likely, the particles are from space!

MISCONCEPTION ALERT
Meteors and Meteorites Students may think that large meteors threaten Earth. Movies and films have popularized the notion that large meteors threaten Earth and could cause widespread destruction. Although several tons of meteoroid material enters Earth's atmosphere each day, most pieces have a mass of only a few milligrams. The largest meteors that reach Earth's surface are called meteorites.

Section 3 • The Earth Takes Shape

Close

Reteaching — BASIC

Changing Earth's Composition
Ask students to choose one step in the development of Earth's composition and then eliminate it. Then, ask them to describe what the composition of Earth's atmosphere would be like if this step had not occurred. **Verbal**

Quiz — GENERAL

1. How did oxygen become abundant in Earth's atmosphere? (Billions of years ago, life-forms evolved that produced oxygen as a byproduct of photosynthesis; eventually oxygen levels increased.)

2. How has the relationship between ozone and life on Earth changed since Earth's early atmosphere? (The absence of ozone in Earth's early atmosphere allowed molecules to be broken apart by UV radiation. These molecules combined to form the complex molecules that gave rise to life. The ozone layer protects life on Earth from the harmful effects of UV radiation.)

Alternative Assessment — GENERAL

Earth Quiz Game Have students write facts about each stage of Earth's development on 3 in. × 5 in. cards. Mix the cards as a deck. Students should form teams and play a quiz game. Teams earn points by assigning the correct fact to the correct stage of Earth's development. **Intrapersonal**

The Source of Oxygen

Sometime before 3.4 billion years ago, organisms that produced food by photosynthesis appeared. *Photosynthesis* is the process of absorbing energy from the sun and carbon dioxide from the atmosphere to make food. During the process of making food, these organisms released oxygen—a gas that was not abundant in the atmosphere at that time. Scientists think that the descendants of these early life-forms are still around today, as shown in **Figure 5**.

Photosynthetic organisms played a major role in changing Earth's atmosphere to become the mixture of gases you breathe today. Over the next hundreds of millions of years, more and more oxygen was added to the atmosphere. At the same time, carbon dioxide was removed. As oxygen levels increased, some of the oxygen formed a layer of ozone in the upper atmosphere. This ozone blocked most of the UV radiation and made it possible for life, in the form of simple plants, to move onto land about 2.2 billion years ago.

Reading Check How did photosynthesis contribute to Earth's current atmosphere?

Formation of Oceans and Continents

Scientists think that the oceans probably formed during Earth's second atmosphere, when the Earth was cool enough for rain to fall and remain on the surface. After millions of years of rainfall, water began to cover the Earth. By 4 billion years ago, a global ocean covered the planet.

For the first few hundred million years of Earth's history, there may not have been any continents. Given the composition of the rocks that make up the continents, scientists know that these rocks have melted and cooled many times in the past. Each time the rocks melted, the heavier elements sank and the lighter ones rose to the surface.

Figure 5 *Stromatolites, mats of fossilized algae (left), are among the earliest evidence of life. Blue-green algae (right) living today are thought to be similar to the first life-forms on Earth.*

Answer to Reading Check

When photosynthetic organisms appeared on Earth, they released oxygen into the Earth's atmosphere. Over several million years, more and more oxygen was added to the atmosphere, which helped form Earth's current atmosphere.

The Growth of Continents

After a while, some of the rocks were light enough to pile up on the surface. These rocks were the beginning of the earliest continents. The continents gradually thickened and slowly rose above the surface of the ocean. These scattered young continents did not stay in the same place, however. The slow transfer of thermal energy in the mantle pushed them around. Approximately 2.5 billion years ago, continents really started to grow. And by 1.5 billion years ago, the upper mantle had cooled and had become denser and heavier. At this time, it was easier for the cooler parts of the mantle to sink. These conditions made it easier for the continents to move in the same way that they do today.

INTERNET ACTIVITY

For another activity related to this chapter, go to **go.hrw.com** and type in the keyword **HZ5SOLW**.

SECTION Review

Summary

- The effects of gravity and heat created the shape and structure of Earth.
- The Earth is divided into three main layers based on composition: the crust, mantle, and core.
- The presence of life dramatically changed Earth's atmosphere by adding free oxygen.
- Earth's oceans formed shortly after the Earth did, when it had cooled off enough for rain to fall. Continents formed when lighter materials gathered on the surface and rose above sea level.

Using Key Terms

1. Use each of the following terms in a separate sentence: *crust*, *mantle*, and *core*.

Understanding Key Ideas

2. Earth's first atmosphere was mostly made of
   a. nitrogen and oxygen.
   b. chlorine, nitrogen, and sulfur.
   c. carbon dioxide and water vapor.
   d. water vapor and oxygen.

3. Describe the structure of the Earth.

4. Why did the Earth separate into distinct layers?

5. Describe the development of Earth's atmosphere. How did life affect Earth's atmosphere?

6. Explain how Earth's oceans and continents formed.

Critical Thinking

7. **Applying Concepts** How did the effects of gravity help shape the Earth?

8. **Making Inferences** How would the removal of forests affect the Earth's atmosphere?

Interpreting Graphics

Use the illustration below to answer the questions that follow.

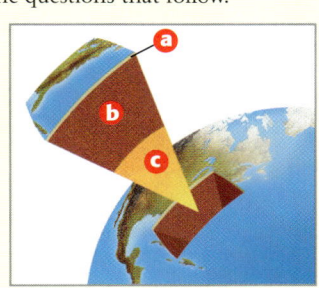

9. Which of the layers is composed mostly of the elements magnesium and iron?

10. Which of the layers is composed mostly of the elements iron and nickel?

SciLinks
Developed and maintained by the National Science Teachers Association

For a variety of links related to this chapter, go to www.scilinks.org
Topic: The Layers of the Earth; The Oceans
SciLinks code: HSM0862; HSM1069

Answers to Section Review

1. Sample answer: The crust is the thin and solid outermost layer of Earth above the mantle. The mantle is the layer of rock between Earth's crust and core. The core is below the mantle and is the central part of Earth.

2. c

3. Earth is divided into three layers: the crust, the mantle, and the core. The crust is the thin, outermost layer; the mantle is the layer of Earth beneath the crust; and the core is the central and densest part of Earth.

4. As rocks melted inside Earth, denser materials sank to the center of Earth, and less dense materials floated to the surface.

5. Sample answer: Scientists think that Earth's first atmosphere contained carbon dioxide and water vapor. Later, volcanoes added carbon dioxide, water vapor, chlorine, nitrogen, and sulfur. Comets brought water, carbon, hydrogen, nitrogen, and oxygen. Solar energy created new chemicals that led to the formation of living organisms. These organisms greatly changed the composition of the atmosphere by adding oxygen.

6. Scientists think that the oceans formed when Earth was cool enough for rain to fall and remain on the surface. After millions of years of rainfall, water began to cover Earth and eventually formed the global ocean. Earth's continents formed as heavy elements sank close to the core of Earth and light elements rose to Earth's surface. The light elements were light enough to pile up on the surface and began to form the earliest continents. These continents gradually thickened and slowly rose above the surface of the ocean.

7. When Earth was still a young planet, it had an irregular shape. But as Earth gained more matter, gravity became greater than the strength of the rock. Therefore, the rock at the center of Earth was crushed by gravity and Earth started to become round.

8. Answers may vary. Deforestation on a large scale would allow more carbon dioxide to accumulate in the atmosphere. As carbon dioxide increased, oxygen levels would likely decrease.

9. b

10. c

CHAPTER RESOURCES

Chapter Resource File
- Section Quiz GENERAL
- Section Review GENERAL
- Vocabulary and Section Summary GENERAL
- Reinforcement Worksheet BASIC

Section 3 • The Earth Takes Shape 629

SECTION 4

Focus

Overview
In this section, students will learn about planetary orbits and about Kepler's laws of planetary motion. The section discusses how Newton's law of universal gravitation helped explain the discoveries of Kepler.

Bellringer
Ask students to create a mnemonic device to help them differentiate between planetary rotation and revolution. For example, they might link the long *a* sound in *rotation* with the fact that Earth makes one rotation in a *day*. The following rhyme may also help them remember: As we rotate, we spin about our axis and live a day. A revolution is a voyage around the sun, and a year will pass away.

Motivate

ACTIVITY — GENERAL

Measuring Ellipses Have students use a ruler to measure segments *a*, *b*, *c*, and *d* in **Figure 2** and then determine if *a* + *b* = *c* + *d*. The illustration shows the string at two distinct points in its description of an ellipse. **LS** Visual/Interpersonal

---

SECTION 4

READING WARM-UP

Objectives
- Explain the difference between rotation and revolution.
- Describe three laws of planetary motion.
- Describe how distance and mass affect gravitational attraction.

Terms to Learn
rotation
orbit
revolution

READING STRATEGY

Paired Summarizing Read this section silently. In pairs, take turns summarizing the material. Stop to discuss ideas that seem confusing.

rotation the spin of a body on its axis

orbit the path that a body follows as it travels around another body in space

revolution the motion of a body that travels around another body in space; one complete trip along an orbit

---

Planetary Motion

Why do the planets revolve around the sun? Why don't they fly off into space? Does something hold them in their paths?

To answer these questions, you need to go back in time to look at the discoveries made by the scientists of the 1500s and 1600s. Danish astronomer Tycho Brahe (TIE koh BRAH uh) carefully observed the positions of planets for more than 25 years. When Brahe died in 1601, a German astronomer named Johannes Kepler (yoh HAHN uhs KEP luhr) continued Brahe's work. Kepler set out to understand the motions of planets and to describe the solar system.

A Revolution in Astronomy

Each planet spins on its axis. The spinning of a body, such as a planet, on its axis is called **rotation**. As the Earth rotates, only one-half of the Earth faces the sun. The half facing the sun is light (day). The half that faces away from the sun is dark (night).

The path that a body follows as it travels around another body in space is called the **orbit**. One complete trip along an orbit is called a **revolution**. The amount of time a planet takes to complete a single trip around the sun is called a *period of revolution*. Each planet takes a different amount of time to circle the sun. Earth's period of revolution is about 365.25 days (a year), but Mercury orbits the sun in only 88 days. **Figure 1** illustrates the orbit and revolution of the Earth around the sun as well as the rotation of the Earth on its axis.

Figure 1 *A planet rotates on its own axis and revolves around the sun in a path called an* orbit.

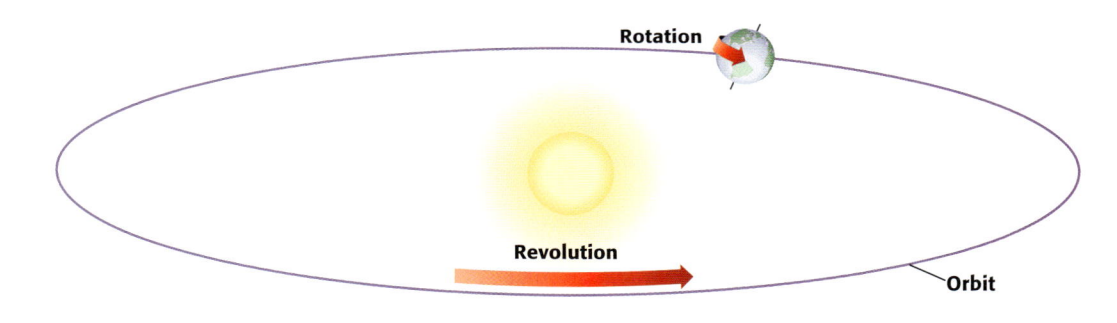

CHAPTER RESOURCES

Chapter Resource File
- Lesson Plan
- Directed Reading A BASIC
- Directed Reading B SPECIAL NEEDS

Technology
- Transparencies
  - Bellringer
  - Earth's Rotation and Revolution
  - Ellipse

MISCONCEPTION ALERT

The Seasons Students may think that Earth's elliptical orbit brings it closer to the sun in the summer. The shape of Earth's orbit does not cause the seasons; the seasons are caused by Earth's tilt on its axis. In the summer, the Northern Hemisphere is tilted toward the sun. In the winter, the Northern Hemisphere is tilted away from the sun. Earth is actually closest to the sun during the Northern Hemisphere's winter.

Chapter 20 • Formation of the Solar System

Figure 2 Parts of an Ellipse

a + b = c + d

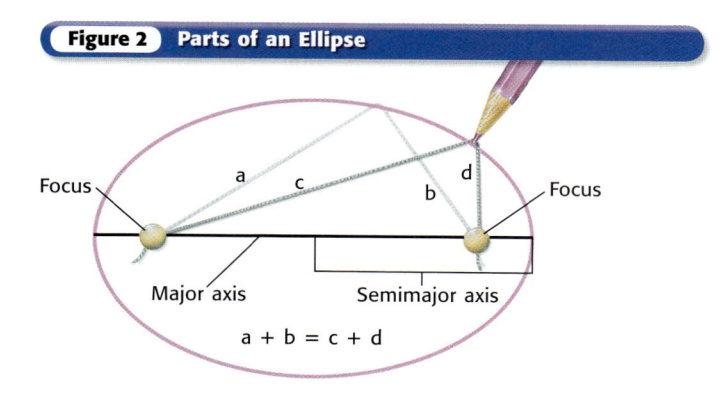

Kepler's First Law of Motion

Kepler's first discovery came from his careful study of Mars. Kepler discovered that Mars did not move in a circle around the sun but moved in an elongated circle called an *ellipse*. This finding became Kepler's first law of motion. An ellipse is a closed curve in which the sum of the distances from the edge of the curve to two points inside the ellipse is always the same, as shown in **Figure 2**. An ellipse's maximum length is called its *major axis*. Half of this distance is the *semimajor axis*, which is usually used to describe the size of an ellipse. The semimajor axis of Earth's orbit—the maximum distance between Earth and the sun—is about 150 million kilometers.

Kepler's Second Law of Motion

Kepler's second discovery, or second law of motion, was that the planets seemed to move faster when they are close to the sun and slower when they are farther away. To understand this idea, imagine that a planet is attached to the sun by a string, as modeled in **Figure 3**. When the string is shorter, the planet must move faster to cover the same area.

Kepler's Third Law of Motion

Kepler noticed that planets that are more distant from the sun, such as Saturn, take longer to orbit the sun. This finding was Kepler's third law of motion, which explains the relationship between the period of a planet's revolution and its semimajor axis. Knowing how long a planet takes to orbit the sun, Kepler was able to calculate the planet's distance from the sun.

✓ **Reading Check** Describe Kepler's third law of motion. *(See the Appendix for answers to Reading Checks.)*

MATH PRACTICE

Kepler's Formula
Kepler's third law can be expressed with the formula

$$P^2 = a^3$$

where P is the period of revolution and a is the semimajor axis of an orbiting body. For example, Mars's period is 1.88 years, and its semimajor axis is 1.523 AU. Thus, $1.88^2 = 1.523^3 = 3.53$. Calculate a planet's period of revolution if the semimajor axis is 5.74 AU.

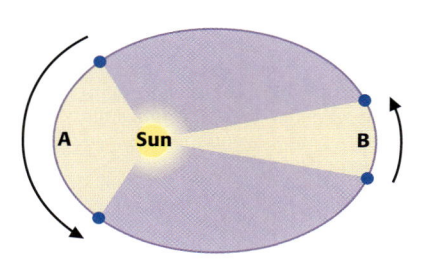

Figure 3 According to Kepler's second law, to keep the area of A equal to the area of B, the planet must move faster in its orbit when it is closer to the sun.

Science Bloopers

Discovery of Elliptical Orbits
Johannes Kepler was obsessed with trying to describe the geometric harmony of the universe. He believed that there were five perfect geometric solids that fit precisely between the six known planets and that this pattern contained the divine meaning of the solar system. Although Kepler was wrong, his efforts to prove this idea enabled him to discover the elliptical orbit of the planets.

Teach

CONNECTION to Astronomy — GENERAL

The Moon's Orbit Every second, the moon travels 1 km in its orbit. During that second, it also falls about 1.4 mm toward Earth. Because of the moon's velocity and the pull of gravity, it travels along a path that follows the curved surface of Earth. This condition, known as *free fall*, keeps the moon in orbit around Earth. Explain to students that the condition of free fall does not mean that there is no gravity. Earth's gravity acts on the moon in the same way it acts on an apple that falls out of a tree. The difference is that the moon, unlike the apple, is moving forward faster than it is falling. **LS Verbal**

Answer to Math Practice
$a^3 = 5.74^3 = 189.12$; Because $a^3 = P^2$, the planet's period of revolution, P, can be found by taking the square root of a^3; $P^2 = 189.12 = 13.75$.

CONNECTION ACTIVITY
Language Arts — GENERAL

Why Do Planets Orbit? Kepler described the orbits of planets, but Newton showed *why* planets orbit. Have students use the following laws to compose a letter to Kepler explaining planetary orbits.

- Every object in the universe attracts every other object in the universe with a force that is dependent on the object's mass and the inverse square of the distance between the objects.

- An object remains in a state of rest or motion unless acted on by an outside force.

LS Intrapersonal

Answer to Reading Check
Kepler's third law of motion states that planets that are farther away from the sun take longer to orbit the sun.

Section 4 • Planetary Motion **631**

Close

Reteaching — BASIC
Comparing Kepler and Newton Have students compare the work of Kepler and Newton. Have students explain how Kepler's discoveries are related to Newton's discoveries and vice versa.
LS Verbal

Quiz — GENERAL

1. Place the nine planets in order by the time it takes each to orbit the sun from fastest to slowest. (Since Kepler's third law states that the farther a planet is from the sun, the longer the planet takes to orbit the sun, the order of the planets in distance from the sun is the same as the order of the planets in terms of orbital period around the sun from fastest to slowest.)

2. If the semimajor axis of Earth's orbit is 150 million kilometers, what is its major axis? (300 million kilometers)

Alternative Assessment — GENERAL
The Laws of Motion and Gravity Have students reproduce **Figures 2, 3, 4,** and **5** in their **science journal.** Students should write an explanation of each diagram in their own words. Have students exchange illustrations and quiz each other. **LS Interpersonal**

Quick Lab

Staying in Focus

1. Take a **short piece of string,** and pin both ends to a **piece of paper** by using **two thumbtacks.**
2. Keeping the string stretched tight at all times, use a **pencil** to trace the path of an ellipse.
3. Change the distance between the thumbtacks to change the shape of the ellipse.
4. How does the position of the thumbtacks (foci) affect the ellipse?

Newton to the Rescue!
Kepler wondered what caused the planets closest to the sun to move faster than the planets farther away. However, he never found an answer. Sir Isaac Newton finally put the puzzle together when he described the force of gravity. Newton didn't understand why gravity worked or what caused it. Even today, scientists do not fully understand gravity. But Newton combined the work of earlier scientists and used mathematics to explain the effects of gravity.

The Law of Universal Gravitation
Newton reasoned that an object falls toward Earth because Earth and the object are attracted to each other by gravity. He discovered that this attraction depends on the masses of the objects and the distance between the objects.

Newton's *law of universal gravitation* states that the force of gravity depends on the product of the masses of the objects divided by the square of the distance between the objects. The larger the masses of two objects and the closer together the objects are, the greater the force of gravity between the objects. For example, if two objects are moved twice as far apart, the gravitational attraction between them will decrease by 2 × 2 (a factor of 4), as shown in **Figure 4.** If two objects are moved 10 times as far apart, the gravitational attraction between them will decrease by 10 × 10 (a factor of 100).

Both Earth and the moon are attracted to each other. Although it may seem as if Earth does not orbit the moon, Earth and the moon actually orbit each other.

✓ Reading Check Explain Newton's law of universal gravitation.

Figure 4 *If two objects are moved twice as far apart, the gravitational attraction between them will be 4 times less.*

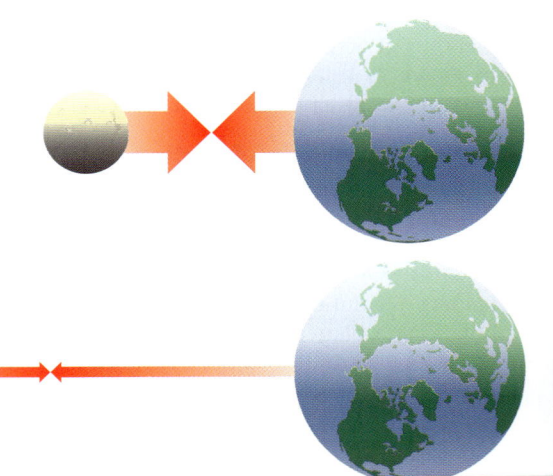

Answer to Reading Check
Newton's law of universal gravitation states that the force of gravity depends on the product of the masses of the objects divided by the square of the distance between the objects.

Quick Lab
Safety Caution: Students should use care with thumbtacks to avoid injuring themselves or damaging the surface on which they work. Have them put a piece of cardboard under their sheet of paper.

Answers
4. The closer together the foci are, the more circular the ellipse is.

Orbits Falling Down and Around

If you drop a rock, it falls to the ground. So, why doesn't the moon come crashing into the Earth? The answer has to do with the moon's inertia. *Inertia* is an object's resistance in speed or direction until an outside force acts on the object. In space, there isn't any air to cause resistance and slow down the moving moon. Therefore, the moon continues to move, but gravity keeps the moon in orbit, as **Figure 5** shows.

Imagine twirling a ball on the end of a string. As long as you hold the string, the ball will orbit your hand. As soon as you let go of the string, the ball will fly off in a straight path. This same principle applies to the moon. Gravity keeps the moon from flying off in a straight path. This principle holds true for all bodies in orbit, including the Earth and other planets in our solar system.

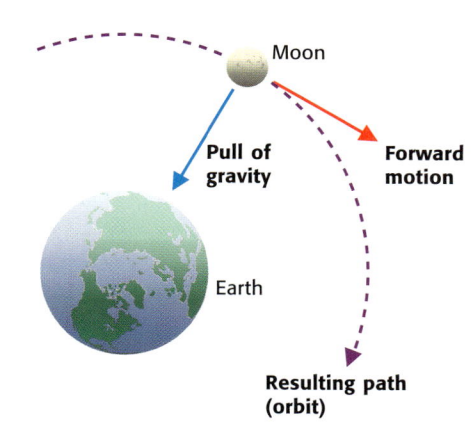

Figure 5 *Gravity causes the moon to fall toward the Earth and changes a straight-line path into a curved orbit.*

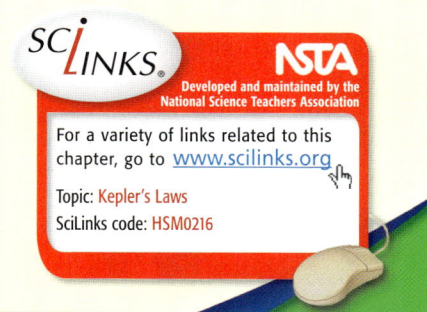

SECTION Review

Summary

- Rotation is the spinning of a planet on its axis, and revolution is one complete trip along an orbit.
- Planets move in an ellipse around the sun. The closer they are to the sun, the faster they move. The period of a planet's revolution depends on the planet's semimajor axis.
- Gravitational attraction decreases as distance increases and as mass decreases.

Using Key Terms

1. In your own words, write a definition for each of the following terms: *revolution* and *rotation*.

Understanding Key Ideas

2. Kepler discovered that planets move faster when they
   a. are farther from the sun.
   b. are closer to the sun.
   c. have more mass.
   d. rotate faster.

3. On what properties does the force of gravity between two objects depend?

4. How does gravity keep a planet moving in an orbit around the sun?

Math Skills

5. The Earth's period of revolution is 365.25 days. Convert this period of revolution into hours.

Critical Thinking

6. **Applying Concepts** If a planet had two moons and one moon was twice as far from the planet as the other, which moon would complete a revolution of the planet first? Explain your answer.

7. **Making Comparisons** Describe the three laws of planetary motion. How is each law related to the other laws?

Topic: Kepler's Laws
SciLinks code: HSM0216

Section 4 • Planetary Motion

Skills Practice Lab

How Far Is the Sun?

Teacher's Notes

Time Required
One 45-minute class period

Lab Ratings
EASY →→→→ HARD

Teacher Prep 🧪🧪
Student Set-Up 🧪
Concept Level 🧪🧪🧪🧪
Clean Up 🧪

MATERIALS
The materials listed on the student page are enough for a group of 2 to 3 students.

Safety Caution
Remind students to review all safety cautions and icons before beginning this lab activity. Also, caution students never to look directly at the sun.

Preparation Notes
Conduct this activity on a sunny day. This lab works best in the late afternoon because the sun is lower in the sky. The sunlight should shine through the window as close to perpendicular to the window as possible. You may want to lower the blinds so that the sunlight will pass through a narrow opening. Sample data are provided in the table at the top of the next page.

Using Scientific Methods
Skills Practice Lab

OBJECTIVES
Create a solar-distance measuring device.
Calculate the Earth's distance from the sun.

MATERIALS
- aluminum foil, 5 cm × 5 cm
- card, index
- meterstick
- poster board
- ruler, metric
- scissors
- tape, masking
- thumbtack

SAFETY

How Far Is the Sun?
It doesn't slice, it doesn't dice, but it can give you an idea of how big our universe is! You can build your very own solar-distance measuring device from household items. Amaze your friends by figuring out how many metersticks can be placed between the Earth and the sun.

Ask a Question
1. How many metersticks could I place between the Earth and the sun?

Form a Hypothesis
2. Write a hypothesis that answers the question above.

Test the Hypothesis
3. Measure and cut a 4 cm × 4 cm square from the middle of the poster board. Tape the foil square over the hole in the center of the poster board.

4. Using a thumbtack, carefully prick the foil to form a tiny hole in the center. Congratulations! You have just constructed your very own solar-distance measuring device!

5. Tape the device to a window facing the sun so that sunlight shines directly through the pinhole. **Caution:** Do not look directly into the sun.

6. Place one end of the meterstick against the window and beneath the foil square. Steady the meterstick with one hand.

7. With the other hand, hold the index card close to the pinhole. You should be able to see a circular image on the card. This image is an image of the sun.

8. Move the card back until the image is large enough to measure. Be sure to keep the image on the card sharply focused. Reposition the meterstick so that it touches the bottom of the card.

Daniel Bugenhagen
Yutan Jr.–Sr. High
Yutan, Nebraska

CHAPTER RESOURCES
Chapter Resource File
- Datasheet for Chapter Lab
- Lab Notes and Answers

Technology
- Classroom Videos
  - Lab Video

---

634 Chapter 20 • Formation of the Solar System

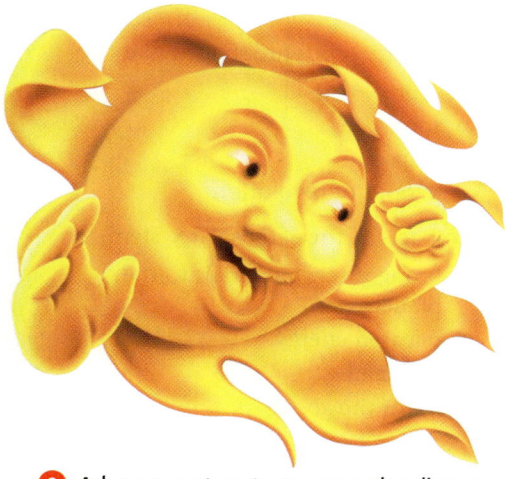

Distance from hole to image (cm)	Diameter of image (cm)
214 cm	2 cm

Background
On the board, draw the diagram at the bottom of this page and explain that this activity uses triangles and proportions to find the distance to the sun. Because the sun forms the image on the paper, there must be a proportionate relationship between the triangles in the diagram. The hole divides the proportions, so the distance between the image and the hole is related to the distance between the sun and the hole.

9 Ask your partner to measure the diameter of the image on the card by using the metric ruler. Record the diameter of the image in millimeters.

10 Record the distance between the window and the index card by reading the point at which the card rests on the meterstick.

11 Calculate the distance between Earth and the sun by using the following formula:

$$\text{distance between the sun and Earth} = \text{sun's diameter} \times \frac{\text{distance to the image}}{\text{image's diameter}}$$

1 cm = 10 mm
1 m = 100 cm
1 km = 1,000 m

(Hint: The sun's diameter is 1,392,000,000 m.)

Analyze the Results
1 **Analyzing Results** According to your calculations, how far from the Earth is the sun? Don't forget to convert your measurements to meters.

Draw Conclusions
2 **Evaluating Data** You could put 150 billion metersticks between the Earth and the sun. Compare this information with your result in step 11. Do you think that this activity was a good way to measure the Earth's distance from the sun? Support your answer.

Analyze the Results
1. Answers may vary. Based on the sample data, the sun is 148,944,000,000 m from Earth. The sun is actually 149,600,000,000 m from Earth.

Draw Conclusions
2. Answers may vary. Accept all well-supported answers. According to the sample data, the calculated value was within 0.5% of the actual value. So, this activity is generally a good way to measure the distance from Earth to the sun.

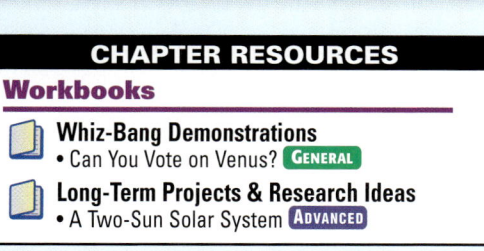

CHAPTER RESOURCES
Workbooks
- **Whiz-Bang Demonstrations**
  • Can You Vote on Venus? GENERAL
- **Long-Term Projects & Research Ideas**
  • A Two-Sun Solar System ADVANCED

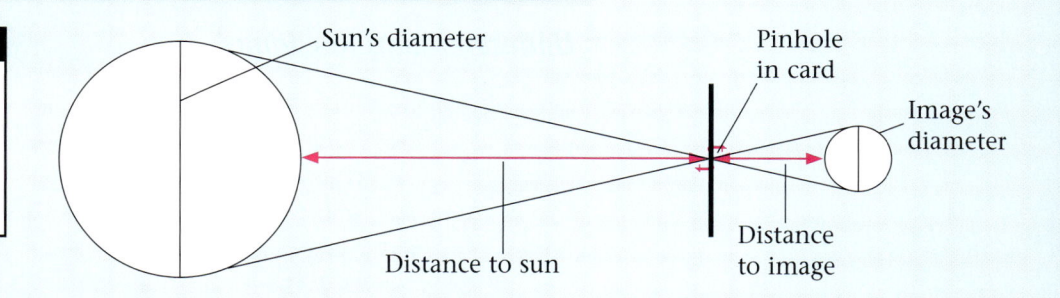

Sun's diameter — Pinhole in card — Image's diameter — Distance to sun — Distance to image

Chapter 20 • Chapter Lab

Chapter Review

Assignment Guide

Section	Questions
1	1, 3, 10, 15, 18
2	6, 16, 19
3	2, 4, 8, 11, 13–14, 17, 22
4	5, 7, 9, 12, 21, 23–26
1 and 2	20

ANSWERS

Using Key Terms

1. nebula
2. mantle
3. Sample answer: A nebula is a large cloud of gas and dust in interstellar space. The solar nebula is the cloud of gas and dust that formed our solar system.
4. Sample answer: The crust is the outermost layer of Earth. The mantle is the layer of rock between Earth's crust and core.
5. Sample answer: Rotation is the spin of a body on its axis. Revolution is the motion of a body that travels around another body in space.
6. Sample answer: Nuclear fusion is the combination of the nuclei of small atoms to form a large nucleus. A sunspot is a dark area of the photosphere of the sun that is cooler than the surrounding areas and that has a strong magnetic field.

Chapter Review

USING KEY TERMS

Complete each of the following sentences by choosing the correct term from the word bank.

nebula   crust
mantle   solar nebula

1. A ___ is a large cloud of gas and dust in interstellar space.
2. The ___ lies between the core and the crust of the Earth.

For each pair of terms, explain how the meanings of the terms differ.

3. *nebula* and *solar nebula*
4. *crust* and *mantle*
5. *rotation* and *revolution*
6. *nuclear fusion* and *sunspot*

UNDERSTANDING KEY IDEAS

Multiple Choice

7. To determine a planet's period of revolution, you must know its
   a. size.
   b. mass.
   c. orbit.
   d. All of the above

8. During Earth's formation, materials such as nickel and iron sank to the
   a. mantle.
   b. core.
   c. crust.
   d. All of the above

9. Planetary orbits are shaped like
   a. orbits.
   b. spirals.
   c. ellipses.
   d. periods of revolution.

10. Impacts in the early solar system
    a. brought new materials to the planets.
    b. released energy.
    c. dug craters.
    d. All of the above

11. Organisms that photosynthesize get their energy from
    a. nitrogen.   c. the sun.
    b. oxygen.   d. water.

12. Which of the following planets has the shortest period of revolution?
    a. Pluto   c. Mercury
    b. Earth   d. Jupiter

13. Which gas in Earth's atmosphere suggests that there is life on Earth?
    a. hydrogen   c. carbon dioxide
    b. oxygen   d. nitrogen

14. Which layer of the Earth has the lowest density?
    a. the core
    b. the mantle
    c. the crust
    d. None of the above

15. What is the measure of the average kinetic energy of particles in an object?
    a. temperature   c. gravity
    b. pressure   d. force

Understanding Key Ideas

7. c
8. b
9. c
10. d
11. c
12. c
13. b
14. c
15. a

16. Sample answer: A sunspot is a dark area of the photosphere of the sun that is cooler than the surrounding areas and that has a strong magnetic field. A solar flare is a region of extremely high temperature and brightness that develops on the sun's surface.

17. Sample answer: Scientists think that the oceans formed during Earth's second atmosphere, when Earth was cool enough for rain to fall and stay on the surface. After millions of years of rainfall, water began to cover Earth and formed a global ocean. The continents formed after the first few hundred million years and are made up of rocks that have melted and cooled many times.

18. Sample answer: Pressure and gravity may have become unbalanced in the solar nebula because of an external force, such as a collision of the solar nebula with another nebula or force from a nearby exploding star. This type of force was strong enough to overcome the pressure of the nebula and trigger its collapse.

636   Chapter 20 • Formation of the Solar System

Short Answer

16. Compare a sunspot with a solar flare.

17. Describe how the Earth's oceans and continents formed.

18. Explain how pressure and gravity may have become unbalanced in the solar nebula.

19. Define *nuclear fusion* in your own words. Describe how nuclear fusion generates the sun's energy.

CRITICAL THINKING

20. Concept Mapping Use the following terms to create a concept map: *solar nebula, solar system, planetesimals, sun, photosphere, core, nuclear fusion, planets,* and *Earth*.

21. Making Comparisons How did Newton's law of universal gravitation help explain the work of Johannes Kepler?

22. Predicting Consequences Using what you know about the relationship between living things and the development of Earth's atmosphere, explain how the formation of ozone holes in Earth's atmosphere could affect living things.

23. Identifying Relationships Describe Kepler's three laws of motion in your own words. Describe how each law relates to either the revolution, rotation, or orbit of a planetary body.

INTERPRETING GRAPHICS

Use the illustration below to answer the questions that follow.

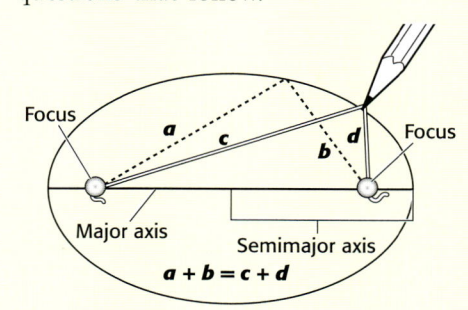

$a + b = c + d$

24. Which of Kepler's laws of motion does the illustration represent?

25. How does the equation shown above support the law?

26. What is an ellipse's maximum length called?

Critical Thinking

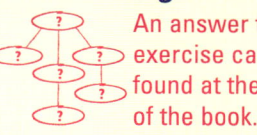

20. An answer to this exercise can be found at the end of the book.

21. Sample answer: Kepler could describe planetary orbits, but he could not explain why planets stay in their orbits. Newton's law of gravitation explained why the planets orbit the sun.

22. Sample answer: The ozone layer shielded Earth from most of the sun's harmful UV radiation and allowed more-complex life-forms to develop. If the ozone layer is damaged, some types of organisms could be threatened.

23. Sample answer: Kepler's first law of motion states that a planet revolves around the sun in an elliptical orbit. Kepler's second law of motion states that planets move faster when they are closer to the sun and slower when they are farther from the sun. Kepler's third law explains the relationship between the period of a planet's revolution and its semimajor axis. Planets that are farther from the sun have a longer period of revolution.

Interpreting Graphics

24. Kepler's first law of motion

25. Sample answer: The equation supports the law by allowing us to determine distances between a planet and the sun as the planet orbits the sun.

26. major axis

---

19. Sample answer: Nuclear fusion occurs when the nuclei of small atoms combine to form a larger nucleus. In the core of the sun, the temperature and pressure are very high. Therefore, hydrogen nuclei, which would normally repel each other, have enough energy to overcome this repulsive force and fuse into helium. This fusion process generates the sun's energy.

CHAPTER RESOURCES

Chapter Resource File
- Chapter Review GENERAL
- Chapter Test A GENERAL
- Chapter Test B ADVANCED
- Chapter Test C SPECIAL NEEDS
- Vocabulary Activity GENERAL

Workbooks

Study Guide
- Assessment resources are also available in Spanish.

Chapter 20 • Chapter Review

Standardized Test Preparation

Teacher's Note

To provide practice under more realistic testing conditions, give students 20 minutes to answer all of the questions in this Standardized Test Preparation.

MISCONCEPTION ALERT

Answers to the standardized test preparation can help you identify student misconceptions and misunderstandings.

READING

Passage 1
1. C
2. G
3. D

TEST DOCTOR

Question 1: Answer C is correct because the passage states this fact in the last sentence. Students may incorrectly choose answers A, B, or D because these proper nouns also occur in the passage.

Standardized Test Preparation

READING

Read each of the passages below. Then, answer the questions that follow each passage.

Passage 1 You know that you should not look at the sun, right? But how can we learn anything about the sun if we can't look at it? We can use a solar telescope! About 70 km southwest of Tucson, Arizona, is Kitt Peak National Observatory, where you will find three solar telescopes. In 1958, Kitt Peak was chosen from more than 150 mountain sites to be the site for a national observatory. Located in the Sonoran Desert, Kitt Peak is on land belonging to the Tohono O'odham Indian nation. On this site, the McMath-Pierce Facility houses the three largest solar telescopes in the world. Astronomers come from around the globe to use these telescopes. The largest of the three, the McMath-Pierce solar telescope, produces an image of the sun that is almost 1 m wide!

1. Which of the following is the largest telescope in the world?
    A Kitt Peak
    B Tohono O'odham
    C McMath-Pierce
    D Tucson

2. According to the passage, how can you learn about the sun?
    F You can look at it.
    G You can study it by using a solar telescope.
    H You can go to Kitt Peak National Observatory.
    I You can study to be an astronomer.

3. Which of the following is a fact in the passage?
    A One hundred fifty mountain sites contain solar telescopes.
    B Kitt Peak is the location of the smallest solar telescope in the world.
    C In 1958, Tucson, Arizona, was chosen for a national observatory.
    D Kitt Peak is the location of the largest solar telescope in the world.

Passage 2 Sunlight that has been focused can produce a great amount of thermal energy—enough to start a fire. Now, imagine focusing the sun's rays by using a magnifying glass that is 1.6 m in diameter. The resulting heat could melt metal. If a <u>conventional</u> telescope were pointed directly at the sun, it would melt. To avoid a meltdown, the McMath-Pierce solar telescope uses a mirror that produces a large image of the sun. This mirror directs the sun's rays down a diagonal shaft to another mirror, which is 50 m underground. This mirror is adjustable to focus the sunlight. The sunlight is then directed to a third mirror, which directs the light to an observing room and instrument shaft.

1. In this passage, what does the word *conventional* mean?
    A special
    B solar
    C unusual
    D ordinary

2. What can you infer from reading the passage?
    F Focused sunlight can avoid a meltdown.
    G Unfocused sunlight produces little energy.
    H A magnifying glass can focus sunlight to produce a great amount of thermal energy.
    I Mirrors increase the intensity of sunlight.

3. According to the passage, which of the following statements about solar telescopes is true?
    A Solar telescopes make it safe for scientists to observe the sun.
    B Solar telescopes don't need to use mirrors.
    C Solar telescopes are built 50 m underground.
    D Solar telescopes are 1.6 m in diameter.

Passage 2
1. D
2. H
3. A

TEST DOCTOR

Question 1: Answer D is correct because the word *conventional* usually means "not unusual or extreme." The word *conventional* is used in the passage to compare an ordinary telescope with a solar telescope. Remind students that if they are asked to infer the meaning of a word in a passage, they should substitute each answer choice for the underlined word and reread the sentence to determine the correct answer choice.

638 Chapter 20 • Formation of the Solar System

INTERPRETING GRAPHICS

The diagram below models the moon's orbit around the Earth. Use the diagram below to answer the questions that follow.

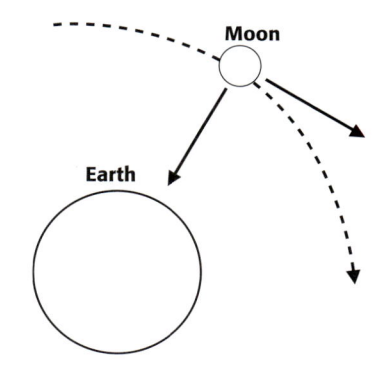

1. Which statement best describes the diagram?
   A Orbits are straight lines.
   B The force of gravity does not affect orbits.
   C Orbits result from a combination of gravitational attraction and inertia.
   D The moon moves in three different directions depending on its speed.

2. In which direction does gravity pull the moon?
   F toward the Earth
   G around the Earth
   H away from the Earth
   I toward and away from the Earth

3. If the moon stopped moving, what would happen?
   A It would fly off into space.
   B It would continue to orbit the Earth.
   C It would stay where it is in space.
   D It would move toward the Earth.

MATH

Read each question below, and choose the best answer.

1. An astronomer found 3 planetary systems in the nebula that she was studying. One system had 6 planets, another had 2 planets, and the third had 7 planets. What is the average number of planets in all 3 systems?
   A 3
   B 5
   C 8
   D 16

2. A newly discovered planet has a period of rotation of 270 Earth years. How many Earth days are in 270 Earth years?
   F 3,240
   G 8,100
   H 9,855
   I 98,550

3. A planet has seven rings. The first ring is 20,000 km from the center of the planet. Each ring is 50,000 km wide and 500 km apart. What is the total radius of the ring system from the planet's center?
   A 353,000 km
   B 373,000 km
   C 373,500 km
   D 370,000 km

4. If you bought a telescope for $87.75 and received a $10 bill, two $1 bills, and a quarter as change, how much money did you give the clerk?
   F $100
   G $99
   H $98
   I $90

INTERPRETING GRAPHICS

1. C
2. F
3. D

TEST DOCTOR

Question 2: Answer F is correct because the pull of gravity (shown by the arrow from the moon to Earth) causes the moon to be pulled toward Earth. Students may choose answer G because the orbit of the moon around Earth makes it appear as though the moon is being pulled around Earth. Answers H and I are incorrect because Earth's gravity does not pull the moon away from Earth.

MATH

1. B
2. I
3. B
4. F

TEST DOCTOR

Question 3: Answer B is the correct answer because 20,000 km + (500 km × 6) + (50,000 km × 7) = 373,000 km. Students may choose answer A if they did not include the 20,000 km distance from the center of the planet to the first ring. Students may choose answer C if they added an additional 500 km. Students may choose answer D if they did not include the distance between the rings.

CHAPTER RESOURCES

Chapter Resource File
- Standardized Test Preparation GENERAL

State Resources
For specific resources for your state, visit **go.hrw.com** and type in the keyword **HSMSTR**.

Chapter 20 • Standardized Test Preparation

Science in Action

Science, Technology, and Society

Background
The McMath-Pierce solar telescope has a 91.5 m focal length. Such a long focal length allows scientists to see the details on a sunspot. The facility that houses the telescope looks like an upside-down V. The vertical side of this V is 30 m tall and contains the heliostat. The sun strikes the heliostat, which is a large, flat, rotating mirror. After sunlight strikes the heliostat, it travels 50 m underground to another mirror, which reflects it back to the observation room. In the observation room, the light is broken down into its different wavelengths by a spectrograph.

Scientific Discoveries

Homework —— GENERAL

Giant Molecular Clouds Giant molecular clouds can send comets into orbit from the Oort cloud. Ask students to research giant molecular clouds and write a report about what they are, how often they interact with the Oort cloud, and what happens to the Oort cloud after it interacts with giant molecular clouds.

Science in Action

Science, Technology, and Society

Don't Look at the Sun!
How can we learn anything about the sun if we can't look at it? The answer is to use a special telescope called a *solar telescope*. The three largest solar telescopes in the world are located at Kitt Peak National Observatory near Tucson, Arizona. The largest of these telescopes, the McMath-Pierce solar telescope, creates an image of the sun that is almost 1 m wide! How is the image created? The McMath-Pierce solar telescope uses a mirror that is more than 2 m in diameter to direct the sun's rays down a diagonal shaft to another mirror, which is 152 m underground. This mirror is adjustable to focus the sunlight. The sunlight is then directed to a third mirror, which directs the light to an observing room and instrument shaft.

Math ACTIVITY

The outer skin of the McMath-Pierce solar telescope consists of 140 copper panels that measure 10.4 m × 2.4 m each. How many square meters of copper were used to construct the outer skin of the telescope?

Scientific Discoveries

The Oort Cloud
Have you ever wondered where comets come from? In 1950, Dutch astronomer Jan Oort decided to find out where comets originated. Oort studied 19 comets. He found that none of these comets had orbits indicating that the comets had come from outside the solar system. Oort thought that all of the comets had come from an area at the far edge of the solar system. In addition, he believed that the comets had entered the planetary system from different directions. These conclusions led Oort to theorize that the area from which comets come surrounds the solar system like a sphere and that comets can come from any point within the sphere. Today, this spherical zone at the edge of the solar system is called the *Oort Cloud*. Astronomers believe that billions or even trillions of comets may exist within the Oort Cloud.

Social Studies ACTIVITY

WRITING SKILL Before astronomers understood the nature of comets, comets were a source of much fear and misunderstanding among humans. Research some of the myths that humans have created about comets. Summarize your findings in a short essay.

Answer to Math Activity
10.4 m × 2.4 m × 140 copper panels = 3,494.4 m² of copper

Answer to Social Studies Activity
Suggest that students use library resources or the Internet to research myths about comets.

640 Chapter 20 • Formation of the Solar System

People in Science

Subrahmanyan Chandrasekhar

From White Dwarfs to Black Holes You may be familiar with the *Chandra X-Ray Observatory*. Launched by NASA in July 1999 to search for x-ray sources in space, the observatory is the most powerful x-ray telescope that has ever been built. However, you may not know how the observatory got its name. The *Chandra X-Ray Observatory* was named after the Indian American astrophysicist Subrahmanyan Chandrasekhar (SOOB ruh MAHN yuhn CHUHN druh SAY kuhr).

One of the most influential astrophysicists of the 20th century, Chandrasekhar was simply known as "Chandra" by his fellow scientists. Chandrasekhar made many contributions to physics and astrophysics. The contribution for which Chandrasekhar is best known was made in 1933, when he was a 23-year-old graduate student at Cambridge University in England. At the time, astrophysicists thought that all stars eventually became planet-sized stars known as *white dwarfs*. But from his calculations, Chandrasekhar believed that not all stars ended their lives as white dwarfs. He determined that the upper limit to the mass of a white dwarf was 1.4 times the mass of the sun. Stars that were more massive would collapse and would become very dense objects. These objects are now known as *black holes*. Chandrasekhar's ideas revolutionized astrophysics. In 1983, at the age of 73, Chandrasekhar was awarded the Nobel Prize in physics for his work on the evolution of stars.

Language Arts ACTIVITY

WRITING SKILL Using the Internet or another source, research the meaning of the word *chandra*. Write a paragraph describing your findings.

To learn more about these Science in Action topics, visit **go.hrw.com** and type in the keyword **HZ5SOLF**.

Current Science Check out Current Science® articles related to this chapter by visiting go.hrw.com. Just type in the keyword **HZ5CS20**.

Answer to Language Arts Activity
The word *chandra* means "moon" in Sanskrit. Students should indicate in their paragraph how the word *chandra* relates to the feature.

People in Science

ACTIVITY — GENERAL

Chandrasekhar's Achievements Most of the work that Chandrasekhar received a Nobel Prize for was completed in the 1930s. Have students research Chandrasekhar's other accomplishments in astrophysics. Have students research the other areas of astronomy and physics that Chandrasekhar studied. Have students share their findings with the class.

Chapter 20 • Science in Action

21 A Family of Planets
Chapter Planning Guide

Compression guide: To shorten instruction because of time limitations, omit Section 1.

OBJECTIVES	LABS, DEMONSTRATIONS, AND ACTIVITIES	TECHNOLOGY RESOURCES
PACING • 90 min pp. 642–647 **Chapter Opener**	SE Start-up Activity, p. 643 GENERAL	OSP Parent Letter ■ GENERAL CD Student Edition on CD-ROM CD Guided Reading Audio CD ■ TR Chapter Starter Transparency* VID Brain Food Video Quiz
Section 1 The Nine Planets • List the planets in the order in which they orbit the sun. • Explain how scientists measure distances in space. • Describe how the planets in our solar system were discovered. • Describe three ways in which the inner planets and outer planets differ.	TE Connection Activity Math, p. 645 GENERAL SE Model-Making Lab Why Do They Wander?, p. 762 GENERAL LB Long-Term Projects & Research Ideas What Did You See, Mr. Messier?* ADVANCED	CRF Lesson Plans* TR Bellringer Transparency* SE Internet Activity, p. 646 GENERAL CRF SciLinks Activity* GENERAL
PACING • 90 min pp. 648–653 **Section 2 The Inner Planets** • Explain the difference between a planet's period of rotation and period of revolution. • Describe the difference between prograde and retrograde rotation. • Describe the individual characteristics of Mercury, Venus, Earth, and Mars. • Identify the characteristics that make Earth suitable for life.	TE Activity Your Age in Venusian Years, p. 648 GENERAL TE Connection Activity Math, p. 651 GENERAL SE Connection to Physics Boiling Point on Mars, p. 652 GENERAL SE Inquiry Lab Create a Calendar, p. 674 GENERAL LB Whiz-Bang Demonstrations Crater Creator* ◆ BASIC LB Whiz-Bang Demonstrations Space Snowballs* ◆ BASIC LB Labs You Can Eat Meteorite Delight* ◆ ADVANCED	CRF Lesson Plans* TR Bellringer Transparency* TR The Inner Planets; The Outer Planets* VID Lab Videos for Earth Science
PACING • 45 min pp. 654–659 **Section 3 The Outer Planets** • Explain how gas giants are different from terrestrial planets. • Describe the individual characteristics of Jupiter, Saturn, Uranus, Neptune, and Pluto.	SE School-to-Home Activity Surviving Space, p. 659 GENERAL SE Science in Action Math, Social Studies, and Language Arts Activities, pp. 680–681 GENERAL TE Connection Activity Fine Arts, p. 658 GENERAL	CRF Lesson Plans* TR Bellringer Transparency* CD Interactive Explorations CD-ROM Space Case GENERAL
PACING • 45 min pp. 660–667 **Section 4 Moons** • Describe the current theory of the origin of Earth's moon. • Explain what causes the phases of Earth's moon. • Describe the difference between a solar eclipse and a lunar eclipse. • Describe the individual characteristics of the moons of other planets.	TE Activity Lunar Ice, p. 660 GENERAL TE Activity Modeling the Earth and Moon, p. 662 GENERAL TE Connection Activity Language Arts, p. 662 BASIC SE Quick Lab Clever Insight, p. 663 GENERAL TE Connection Activity Math, p. 663 GENERAL SE Model-Making Lab Eclipses, p. 764 GENERAL SE Skills Practice Lab Phases of the Moon, p. 765 GENERAL	CRF Lesson Plans* TR Bellringer Transparency* TR **LINK TO PHYSICAL SCIENCE** Two Motions Combine to Form Projectile Motion* TR Formation of the Moon* TR Phases of the Moon* TR Solar Eclipse; Lunar Eclipse*
PACING • 45 min pp. 668–673 **Section 5 Small Bodies in the Solar System** • Explain why comets, asteroids, and meteoroids are important to the study of the formation of the solar system. • Describe the similarities of and differences between asteroids and meteoroids. • Explain how cosmic impacts may affect life on Earth.	TE Demonstration Modeling Comets, p. 668 ◆ GENERAL SE Connection to Language Arts Interplanetary Journalist, p. 669 GENERAL TE Activity Meteors Made Simple, p. 671 BASIC SE Connection to Biology Mass Extinctions, p. 672 GENERAL	CRF Lesson Plans* TR Bellringer Transparency*

PACING • 90 min

CHAPTER REVIEW, ASSESSMENT, AND STANDARDIZED TEST PREPARATION
- CRF Vocabulary Activity* GENERAL
- SE Chapter Review, pp. 676–677 GENERAL
- CRF Chapter Review* ■ GENERAL
- CRF Chapter Tests A* ■ GENERAL, B* ADVANCED, C* SPECIAL NEEDS
- SE Standardized Test Preparation, pp. 678–679 GENERAL
- CRF Standardized Test Preparation* GENERAL
- CRF Performance-Based Assessment* GENERAL
- OSP Test Generator GENERAL
- CRF Test Item Listing* GENERAL

Online and Technology Resources

Visit **go.hrw.com** for a variety of free resources related to this textbook. Enter the keyword **HZ5FAM**.

Holt Online Learning
Students can access interactive problem-solving help and active visual concept development with the *Holt Science and Technology* Online Edition available at **www.hrw.com**.

Guided Reading Audio CD
Also in Spanish
A direct reading of each chapter for auditory learners, reluctant readers, and Spanish-speaking students.

Science Tutor CD-ROM
Excellent for remediation and test practice.

KEY			
SE Student Edition	CRF Chapter Resource File	SS Science Skills Worksheets	* Also on One-Stop Planner
TE Teacher Edition	OSP One-Stop Planner	MS Math Skills for Science Worksheets	♦ Requires advance prep
	LB Lab Bank	CD CD or CD-ROM	■ Also available in Spanish
	TR Transparencies	VID Classroom Video/DVD	

SKILLS DEVELOPMENT RESOURCES	SECTION REVIEW AND ASSESSMENT	STANDARDS CORRELATIONS
SE Pre-Reading Activity, p. 642 GENERAL OSP Science Puzzlers, Twisters & Teasers GENERAL		National Science Education Standards SAI 1; HNS 1, 3; ES 3a
CRF Directed Reading A* ■ BASIC, B* SPECIAL NEEDS CRF Vocabulary and Section Summary* GENERAL SE Reading Strategy Paired Summarizing, p. 644 GENERAL SS Science Skills Grasping Graphing* GENERAL CRF Critical Thinking Martian Holiday* ADVANCED CRF Reinforcement Worksheet The Planets of Our Solar System* BASIC TE Inclusion Strategies, p. 646	SE Reading Checks, pp. 645, 647 GENERAL TE Reteaching, p. 646 BASIC TE Quiz, p. 646 GENERAL TE Alternative Assessment, p. 646 GENERAL SE Section Review,* p. 647 ■ GENERAL CRF Section Quiz* ■ GENERAL	UCP 1, 3; SAI 1; ST 2; SPSP 5; HNS 1, 3; ES 1c, 3a, 3b, 3c; *LabBook:* UCP 2; SAI 1; ST 1
CRF Directed Reading A* ■ BASIC, B* SPECIAL NEEDS CRF Vocabulary and Section Summary* GENERAL SE Reading Strategy Reading Organizer, p. 648 GENERAL	SE Reading Checks, pp. 649, 650, 652 GENERAL TE Homework, p. 649 ADVANCED TE Reteaching, p. 652 BASIC TE Quiz, p. 652 GENERAL TE Alternative Assessment, p. 652 GENERAL SE Section Review,* p. 653 ■ GENERAL CRF Section Quiz* ■ GENERAL	UCP 1, 3; SAI 1; ST 2; SPSP 5; HNS 1, 3; ES 1c, 3a, 3b; *Chapter Lab:* UCP 1, 2; SAI 1, 2; ST 1; ES 3b
CRF Directed Reading A* ■ BASIC, B* SPECIAL NEEDS CRF Vocabulary and Section Summary* GENERAL SE Reading Strategy Prediction Guide, p. 654 GENERAL TE Reading Strategy Prediction Guide, p. 656 GENERAL	SE Reading Checks, pp. 655, 657 GENERAL TE Reteaching, p. 658 BASIC TE Quiz, p. 658 GENERAL TE Alternative Assessment, p. 658 ADVANCED SE Section Review,* p. 659 ■ GENERAL CRF Section Quiz* ■ GENERAL	UCP 1, 3; SAI 1; ST 2; SPSP 5; HNS 1, 3; ES 1c, 3a, 3b
CRF Directed Reading A* ■ BASIC, B* SPECIAL NEEDS CRF Vocabulary and Section Summary* ■ GENERAL SE Reading Strategy Reading Organizer, p. 660 GENERAL TE Reading Strategy Prediction Guide, p. 661 GENERAL CRF Reinforcement Worksheet Lunar and Solar Eclipses* BASIC	SE Reading Checks, pp. 661, 663, 664, 665, 666 GENERAL TE Homework, p. 664 GENERAL TE Reteaching, p. 666 BASIC TE Quiz, p. 666 GENERAL TE Alternative Assessment, p. 666 GENERAL SE Section Review,* p. 667 ■ GENERAL CRF Section Quiz* ■ GENERAL	UCP 1, 3; SAI 1; HNS 1, 3; ES 3a, 3b, 3c; *LabBook:* UCP 2; SAI 1; ST 1; ES 1a, 3b
CRF Directed Reading A* ■ BASIC, B* SPECIAL NEEDS CRF Vocabulary and Section Summary* ■ GENERAL SE Reading Strategy Discussion, p. 668 GENERAL TE Inclusion Strategies, p. 671	SE Reading Checks, pp. 669, 671, 672 GENERAL TE Homework, p. 669 GENERAL TE Reteaching, p. 672 BASIC TE Quiz, p. 672 GENERAL TE Alternative Assessment, p. 672 GENERAL SE Section Review,* p. 673 ■ GENERAL CRF Section Quiz* ■ GENERAL	UCP 1; ES 2a, 3a, 3b

One-Stop Planner® CD-ROM

This convenient CD-ROM includes:
- Lab Materials QuickList Software
- Holt Calendar Planner
- Customizable Lesson Plans
- Printable Worksheets
- ExamView® Test Generator

CNN Student News

cnnstudentnews.com

Find the latest news, lesson plans, and activities related to important scientific events.

SciLinks NSTA

www.scilinks.org

Maintained by the **National Science Teachers Association**. See Chapter Enrichment pages for a complete list of topics.

Current Science®

Check out *Current Science* articles and activities by visiting the HRW Web site at **go.hrw.com.** Just type in the keyword **HZ5CS21T.**

Classroom Videos

- **Lab Videos** demonstrate the chapter lab.
- **Brain Food Video Quizzes** help students review the chapter material.
- **CNN Videos** bring science into your students' daily life.

Chapter 21 • Chapter Planning Guide

21 Chapter Resources

Visual Resources

CHAPTER STARTER TRANSPARENCY

BELLRINGER TRANSPARENCIES

TEACHING TRANSPARENCIES

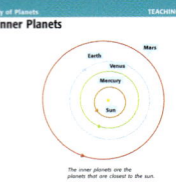

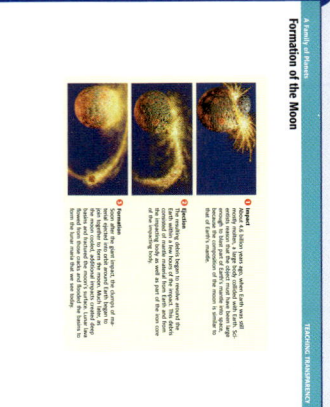

TEACHING TRANSPARENCIES

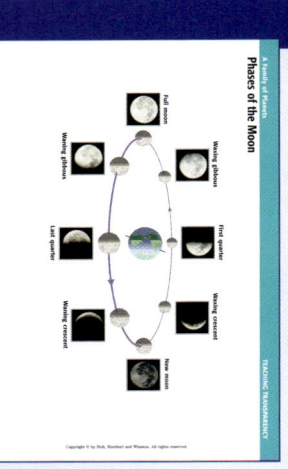

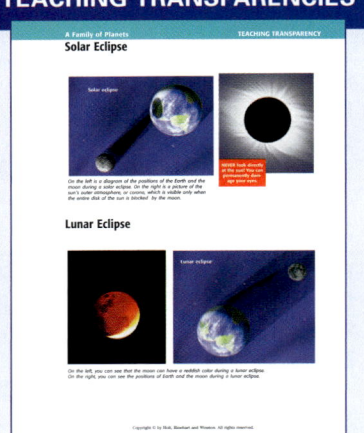

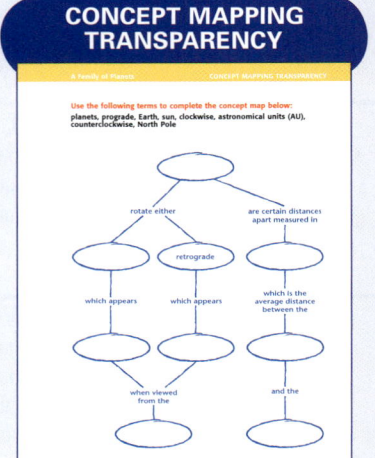

CONCEPT MAPPING TRANSPARENCY

Planning Resources

LESSON PLANS

PARENT LETTER — ALSO IN SPANISH

TEST ITEM LISTING

One-Stop Planner® CD-ROM

This CD-ROM includes all of the resources shown here and the following time-saving tools:

- **Lab Materials QuickList Software**
- **Customizable lesson plans**
- **Holt Calendar Planner**
- **The powerful ExamView® Test Generator**

641C Chapter 21 • A Family of Planets

For a preview of available worksheets covering math and science skills, see pages T26–T33. All of these resources are also on the One-Stop Planner®.

Meeting Individual Needs

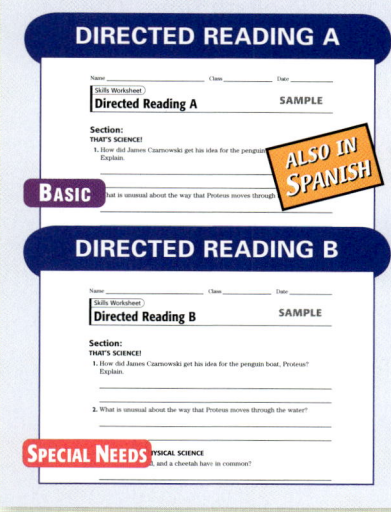

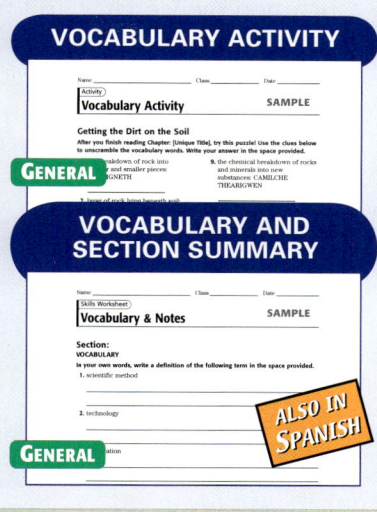

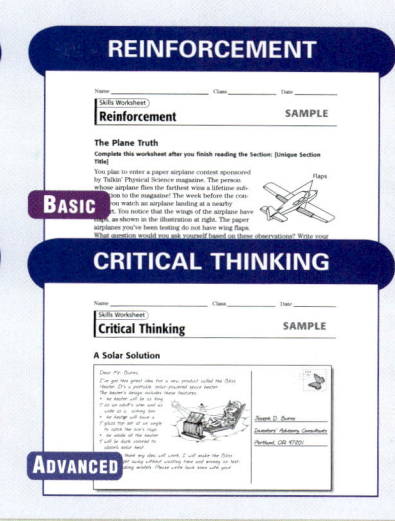

- **DIRECTED READING A** — BASIC (Also in Spanish)
- **DIRECTED READING B** — SPECIAL NEEDS
- **VOCABULARY ACTIVITY** — GENERAL
- **VOCABULARY AND SECTION SUMMARY** — GENERAL
- **REINFORCEMENT** — BASIC
- **CRITICAL THINKING** — ADVANCED (Also in Spanish)
- **SCILINKS ACTIVITY** — GENERAL
- **SCIENCE PUZZLERS, TWISTERS & TEASERS** — GENERAL

Labs and Activities

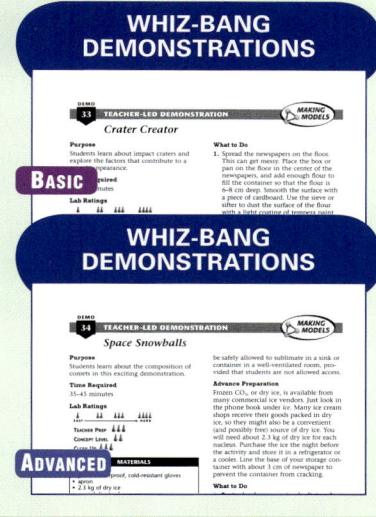

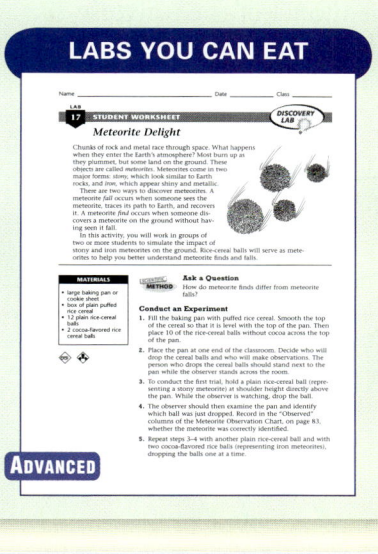

- **LONG-TERM PROJECTS & RESEARCH IDEAS** — ADVANCED
- **WHIZ-BANG DEMONSTRATIONS** — BASIC
- **WHIZ-BANG DEMONSTRATIONS** — ADVANCED
- **LABS YOU CAN EAT** — ADVANCED
- **DATASHEETS FOR QUICK LABS**
- **DATASHEETS FOR CHAPTER LABS**
- **DATASHEETS FOR LABBOOK**

Review and Assessments

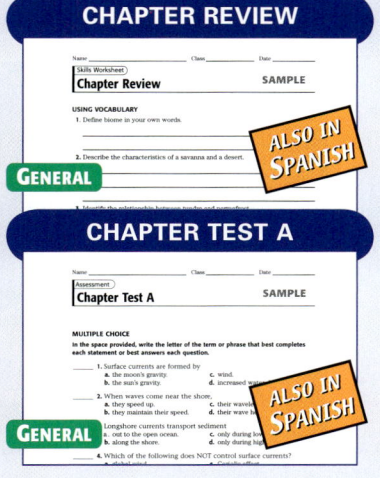

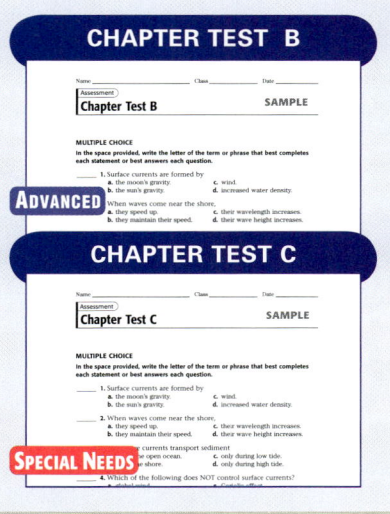

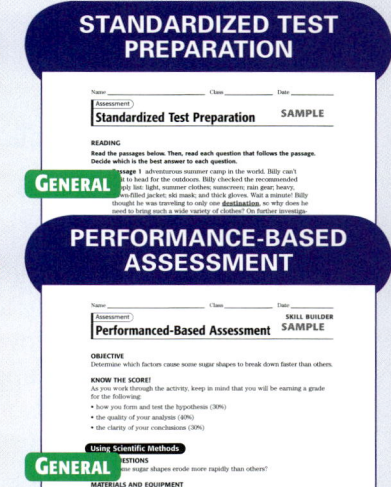

- **SECTION QUIZ** — GENERAL (Also in Spanish)
- **SECTION REVIEW** — GENERAL (Also in Spanish)
- **CHAPTER REVIEW** — GENERAL (Also in Spanish)
- **CHAPTER TEST A** — GENERAL (Also in Spanish)
- **CHAPTER TEST B** — ADVANCED
- **CHAPTER TEST C** — SPECIAL NEEDS
- **STANDARDIZED TEST PREPARATION** — GENERAL
- **PERFORMANCE-BASED ASSESSMENT** — GENERAL

Chapter 21 • Chapter Resources **641D**

21 Chapter Enrichment

This Chapter Enrichment provides relevant and interesting information to expand and enhance your presentation of the chapter material.

Section 1

The Nine Planets

Ptolemy

- In the second century CE, the astronomer Claudius Ptolemy formulated an elaborate scientific theory of a geocentric universe. He argued that everything in the universe revolves around Earth's center. In Ptolemy's model, the stars moved in a rotating sphere, and the motion of the planets, moons, and comets was explained by a series of large and small circles turning inside one another. Although Ptolemy's theories about the mechanism of planetary movement were later rejected, his basic model of the universe remained the predominant scientific theory until the work of Copernicus, Galileo, and Kepler from around 1500 to 1650.

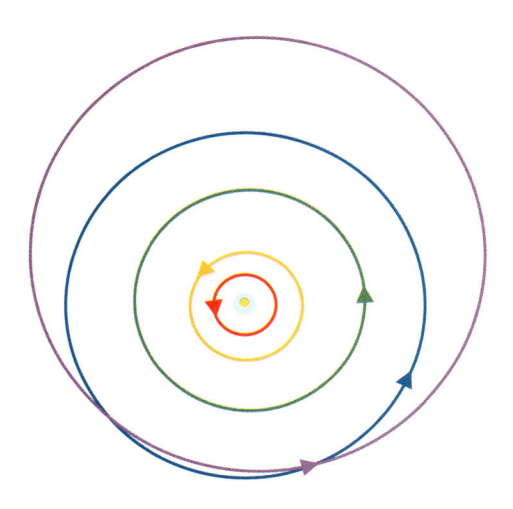

Section 2

The Inner Planets

A Day on Mercury

- Imagine waking up in the middle of winter just before dawn to find the outside temperature a frigid −173°C! As you watch the sun slowly rise over the next several days, you notice that it appears 3 times as big as it does from Earth. You also notice that the sky is black. The reason is that Mercury has an extremely thin atmosphere that doesn't scatter blue light as Earth's atmosphere does. Forty-four Earth days later, it would be noon on Mercury and the middle of summer. The temperature would be a broiling 427°C. The range of Mercury's surface temperatures is more extreme than that of any other planet in the solar system.

Is That a Fact!

♦ The planet Mercury has been known and studied for more than 2,000 years. Its wanderings may have been noted by Hypatia (415–370 BCE), an Egyptian mathematician and philosopher and the first known female astronomer. Hypatia was a student of Plato.

Section 3

The Outer Planets

Which Is Last?

- Pluto is not always the farthest planet from the sun. Pluto's orbit around the sun takes 248 Earth years to complete. Because its orbit is highly elliptical, Pluto spends about 20 years of its orbit closer to the sun than Neptune does. The last time that Pluto was closer to the sun than Neptune was occurred between 1979 and 1999. The next time will be in the 23rd century.

641E Chapter 21 • A Family of Planets

Section 4

Moons
Earth Tides

- As the moon revolves around the Earth, it causes tides—even on land! The distance from Earth's center to its surface increases by a few centimeters as the moon passes overhead. This change is not as noticeable as ocean tides, but it can be detected by very sensitive instruments.

Is That a Fact!

- Four moons in the solar system are larger than Earth's moon: Jupiter's Ganymede, Callisto, and Io and Saturn's Titan. Earth's moon is special because it is very large relative to the planet it orbits. Pluto's moon, Charon, however, is more than half the size of Pluto.

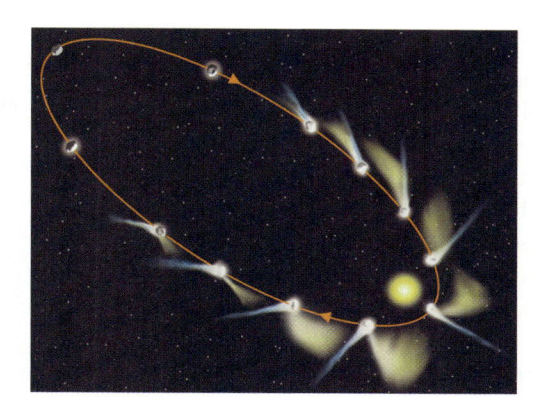

The Kuiper Belt

- To explain the source of short-period comets (comets with periods shorter than 200 years), the Dutch American astronomer Gerard Kuiper proposed in 1949 that a belt of icy bodies must lie beyond the orbits of Pluto and Neptune. Kuiper argued that comets were icy planetesimals that formed during the condensation of our solar nebula. Because the icy bodies are so far from any large planet's gravitational field (30 AU to 100 AU), they can remain on the fringe of the solar system. Some theorists speculate that the large moons Triton and Charon were once members of the Kuiper belt before they were captured by Neptune and Pluto. These moons and short-period comets have similar physical and chemical properties.

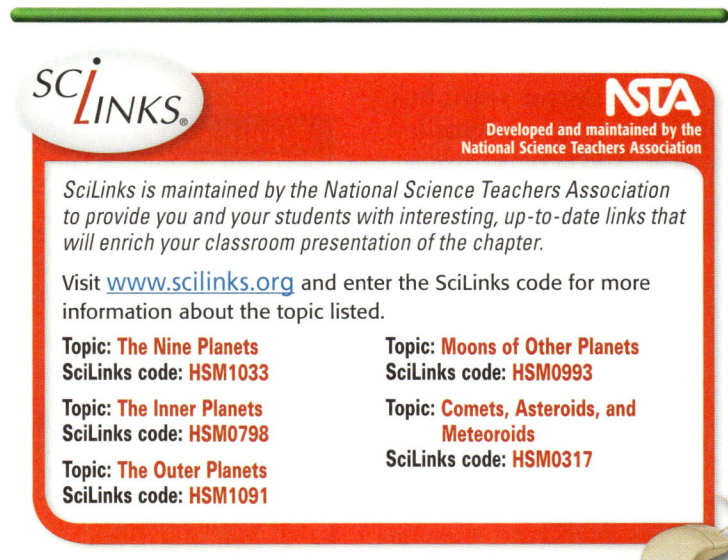

Section 5

Small Bodies in the Solar System
The Oort Cloud

- To explain the origin of comets, a Dutch astronomer named Jan Oort suggested in the 1950s that a spherical cloud of comets surrounds the solar system. He estimated that the cloud is 40,000 to 100,000 astronomical units (AU) from the sun and that it may contain trillions of icy bodies.

SciLinks is maintained by the National Science Teachers Association to provide you and your students with interesting, up-to-date links that will enrich your classroom presentation of the chapter.

Visit www.scilinks.org and enter the SciLinks code for more information about the topic listed.

Topic: **The Nine Planets**
SciLinks code: **HSM1033**

Topic: **The Inner Planets**
SciLinks code: **HSM0798**

Topic: **The Outer Planets**
SciLinks code: **HSM1091**

Topic: **Moons of Other Planets**
SciLinks code: **HSM0993**

Topic: **Comets, Asteroids, and Meteoroids**
SciLinks code: **HSM0317**

Overview

This chapter introduces the planets in the solar system. Students will learn about the differences between the inner planets and the outer planets. Students will also learn about moons and smaller bodies of the solar system, such, as comets, asteroids, and meteoroids.

Assessing Prior Knowledge

Students should be familiar with the following topics:
- methods of studying space
- stars
- the formation of the solar system

Identifying Misconceptions

Students may not understand that the mass and volume of planets varies greatly. Students may benefit from a comparison of the relative mass, volume, and location of the sun and planets. Point out that in terms of mass, the solar system has two main bodies—the sun and Jupiter. The sun makes up more than 99.5% of the mass in the solar system. Jupiter has one-thousandth the mass of the sun but is roughly 317 times more massive than Earth, and Jupiter's volume is 1,321 times the volume of Earth. As you teach this chapter, encourage students to make other such comparisons.

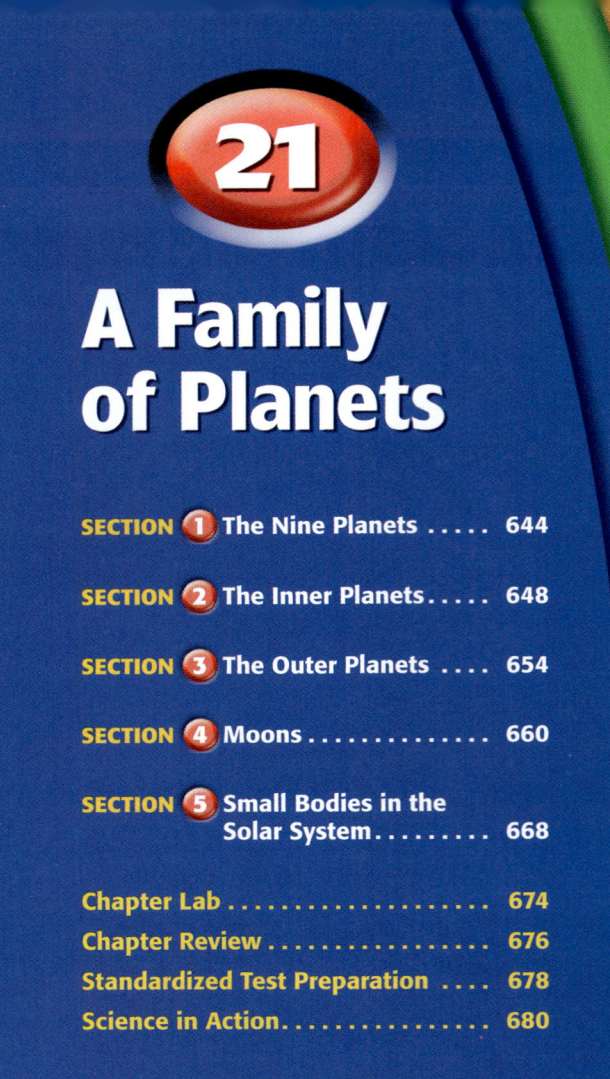

21
A Family of Planets

SECTION 1 The Nine Planets 644

SECTION 2 The Inner Planets 648

SECTION 3 The Outer Planets 654

SECTION 4 Moons 660

SECTION 5 Small Bodies in the Solar System 668

Chapter Lab 674
Chapter Review 676
Standardized Test Preparation 678
Science in Action 680

About the PHOTO

These rich swirls of color may remind you of a painting you might see in an art museum. But this photograph is of the planet Jupiter. The red swirl, called the Great Red Spot, is actually a hurricane-like storm system that is 3 times the diameter of Earth!

PRE-READING ACTIVITY

FOLDNOTES **Booklet** Before you read the chapter, create the FoldNote entitled "Booklet" described in the **Study Skills** section of the Appendix. Label each page of the booklet with a name of a planet in our solar system. As you read the chapter, write what you learn about each planet on the appropriate page of the booklet.

Standards Correlations

National Science Education Standards

The following codes indicate the National Science Education Standards that correlate to this chapter. The full text of the standards is at the front of the book.

Chapter Opener
SAI 1; HNS 1, 3; ES 3a

Section 1 The Nine Planets
UCP 1, 3; SAI 1; ST 2; SPSP 5; HNS 1, 3; ES 1c, 3a, 3b, 3c; LabBook: UCP 2; SAI 1; ST 1

Section 2 The Inner Planets
UCP 1, 3; SAI 1; ST 2; SPSP 5; HNS 1, 3; ES 1c, 3a, 3b

Section 3 The Outer Planets
UCP 1, 3; SAI 1; ST 2; SPSP 5; HNS 1, 3; ES 1c, 3a, 3b

Section 4 Moons
UCP 1, 3; SAI 1; HNS 1, 3; ES 3a, 3b, 3c; LabBook: UCP 2; SAI 1; ST 1; ES 1a, 3b

Section 5 Small Bodies in the Solar System
UCP 1; ES 2a, 3a, 3b

642 Chapter 21 • A Family of Planets

START-UP ACTIVITY

MATERIALS

FOR EACH GROUP
- chalk
- chalkboard
- meterstick

Teacher's Notes: The solar and planetary data presented in this chapter are the most current data available at the time of publication. Because of the vast size of the solar system, instrument limitations, and differences in methods of gathering data, the values given have varying margins of error. As measuring precision increases, these values are updated. Therefore, other sources may show different values for the same statistics.

Answer
1. The inner four planets are closer together than the outer planets are.

START-UP ACTIVITY

Measuring Space
Do the following activity to get a better idea of your solar neighborhood.

Procedure
1. Use a **meterstick** and some **chalk** to draw a line 2 m long on a **chalkboard.** Draw a large dot at one end of the line. This dot represents the sun.
2. Draw smaller dots on the line to represent the relative distances of each of the planets from the sun, based on information in the table.

Analysis
1. What do you notice about how the planets are spaced?

Planet	Distance from sun	
	Millions of km	Scaled to cm
Mercury	57.9	2
Venus	108.2	4
Earth	149.6	5
Mars	227.9	8
Jupiter	778.4	26
Saturn	1,424.0	48
Neptune	2,827.0	97
Uranus	4,499.0	151
Pluto	5,943.0	200

Chapter Lab
UCP 1, 2; SAI 1, 2; ES 3b

Chapter Review
UCP 1, 2, 3; SAI 1, 2; ES 1a, 3a, 3b, 3c

Science in Action
UCP 1, 2, SAI 2; ST 2; SPSP 5; HNS 1; ES 3a, 3b, 3c

Chapter Starter Transparency
Use this transparency to help students begin thinking about why planets were called "wanderers" by the Greeks.

CHAPTER RESOURCES

Technology
- **Transparencies**
  - Chapter Starter Transparency
- **Student Edition on CD-ROM**
- **Guided Reading Audio CD**
  - English or Spanish
- **Classroom Videos**
  - Brain Food Video Quiz

READING SKILLS

Workbooks
- **Science Puzzlers, Twisters & Teasers**
  - A Family of Planets GENERAL

Chapter 21 • A Family of Planets **643**

SECTION 1

Focus

Overview
This section describes the scale of the solar system, the discovery of the planets, and planetary motion. The section also introduces the differences between the inner and outer planets.

Bellringer
To introduce this chapter, assign each student a planet to research. Tell students to create a poster that features the planet and includes a cross section of the planet's interior. Students should provide factual information and mythology about the planet in their poster.

Motivate

Discussion — GENERAL

Solar System Questions
Display the posters that the students made for the Bellringer activity. Have students list questions they want to answer about the planets. Pool students' questions to form one list. Read the list aloud for the class, and have students propose possible answers to the questions. Then, list the questions on a bulletin board. Leave space for answers, and have students fill in the answers as they study this chapter. **LS Visual/Verbal**

SECTION 1

READING WARM-UP

Objectives
- List the planets in the order in which they orbit the sun.
- Explain how scientists measure distances in space.
- Describe how the planets in our solar system were discovered.
- Describe three ways in which the inner planets and outer planets differ.

Terms to Learn
astronomical unit

READING STRATEGY

Paired Summarizing Read this section silently. In pairs, take turns summarizing the material. Stop to discuss ideas that seem confusing.

The Nine Planets

Did you know that planets, when viewed from Earth, look like stars to the naked eye? Ancient astronomers were intrigued by these "stars" which seemed to wander in the sky.

Ancient astronomers named these "stars" planets, which means "wanderers" in Greek. These astronomers knew planets were physical bodies and could predict their motions. But scientists did not begin to explore these worlds until the 17th century, when Galileo used the telescope to study planets and stars. Now, scientists have completed more than 150 successful missions to moons, planets, comets, and asteroids in our cosmic neighborhood.

Our Solar System

Our *solar system*, shown in **Figure 1**, includes the sun, the planets, and many smaller objects. In some cases, these bodies may be organized into smaller systems of their own. For example, the Saturn system is made of the planet Saturn and the several moons that orbit Saturn. In this way, our solar system is a combination of many smaller systems.

Figure 1 *These images show the relative diameters of the planets and the sun.*

Mercury 4,879 km
Venus 12,104 km
Earth 12,756 km
Mars 6,794 km
Sun 1,392,000 km
Jupiter 142,984 km

CHAPTER RESOURCES

Chapter Resource File
- Lesson Plan
- Directed Reading A BASIC
- Directed Reading B SPECIAL NEEDS

Technology
- Transparencies
  - Bellringer

Chapter 21 • A Family of Planets

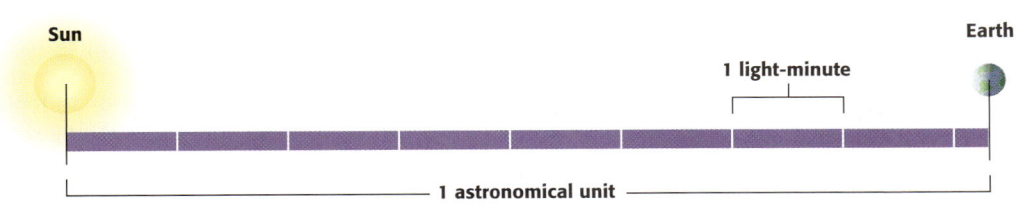

Figure 2 One astronomical unit equals about 8.3 light-minutes.

Measuring Interplanetary Distances

One way that scientists measure distances in space is by using the astronomical unit. One **astronomical unit** (AU) is the average distance between the sun and Earth, or approximately 150,000,000 km. Another way to measure distances in space is by using the speed of light. Light travels at about 300,000 km/s in space. This means that in 1 s, light travels 300,000 km.

In 1 min, light travels nearly 18,000,000 km. This distance is also called a *light-minute*. Look at **Figure 2**. Light from the sun takes 8.3 min to reach Earth. So, the distance from Earth to the sun, or 1 AU, is 8.3 light-minutes. Distances in the solar system can be measured in light-minutes and light-hours.

astronomical unit the average distance between the Earth and the sun; approximately 150 million kilometers (symbol, AU)

Reading Check How far does light travel in 1 s? (*See the Appendix for answers to Reading Checks.*)

Saturn 120,536 km
Uranus 51,118 km
Neptune 49,528 km
Pluto 2,390 km

Teach

Using the Figure — GENERAL

A Sense of Scale The images of the planets and the sun in **Figure 1** are shown to scale. Ask students to use a ruler to estimate how many Earths would fit side by side along the diameter of Jupiter. (Answers may vary, but students should determine that about 10 Earths would fit within the diameter of Jupiter.) **LS** Visual/Kinesthetic

MISCONCEPTION ALERT

Scale in Diagrams Tell students that the diameters of Earth and the sun are not to scale in **Figure 2**. If they were, the sun would be a little less than 2 mm across, and Earth would be too small to see. The lengths of the light-minute and the AU, however, are to scale. Ask students why the AU is the average distance between the Earth and sun. (The Earth's orbit is elliptical. Therefore, the distance between the Earth and the sun is continuously changing.) **LS** Logical

Answer to Reading Check
Light travels about 300,000 km/s.

CONNECTION ACTIVITY
Math — GENERAL

Calculating Distances If light travels 18 million kilometers in 1 min, how far away is Earth from the sun if sunlight takes 8.3 min to reach Earth?
(18,000,000 km/min × 8.3 min = 149,400,000 km)
How far is Mercury from the sun if sunlight takes 3.2 min to reach its surface?
(18,000,000 km/min × 3.2 min = 57,600,000 km)
Remind students that these numbers are rounded. **LS** Logical

Section 1 • The Nine Planets **645**

Close

Reteaching — BASIC

Planetary Review On the board or an overhead transparency, draw a diagram of the solar system that shows the orbit of each planet. Ask students to help you indicate which planet occupies each orbital path. **LS Visual**

Quiz — GENERAL

1. Which planets are part of the inner solar system? (Mercury, Venus, Earth, and Mars)

2. If a rocket could travel at the speed of light, how far would it go in 15 min? (18,000,000 km/min × 15 min = 270,000,000 km)

3. Why are the inner planets known as the *terrestrial planets*? (because their surfaces are dense and rocky)

Alternative Assessment — GENERAL

Build a Mobile Ask students to create a mobile or diorama of the planets. The mobile should have the planets in order, and their sizes should be in correct proportion to one another. As students learn more about the planets, they should add facts about each planet to their mobile. **LS Visual/Kinesthetic**

INTERNET ACTIVITY

For another activity related to this chapter, go to **go.hrw.com** and type in the keyword **HZ5FAMW**.

The Discovery of the Solar System

Up until the 17th century, the universe was thought to have only eight bodies. These bodies included the planets Earth, Mercury, Venus, Mars, Jupiter, and Saturn, the sun, and the Earth's moon. These bodies are the only ones that can be seen from Earth without using a telescope.

After the telescope was invented in the 17th century, however, more discoveries were made. By the end of the 17th century, nine more large bodies were discovered. These bodies were moons of Jupiter and Saturn.

By the 18th century, the planet Uranus, along with two of its moons and two more of Saturn's moons, was discovered. In the 19th century, Neptune, as well as moons of several other planets, was discovered. Finally, in the 20th century, the ninth planet, Pluto, was discovered.

The Inner and Outer Solar Systems

The solar system is divided into two main parts: the inner solar system and the outer solar system. The inner solar system contains the four planets that are closest to the sun. The outer solar system contains the planets that are farthest from the sun.

The Inner Planets

The planets of the inner solar system, shown in **Figure 3**, are more closely spaced than the planets of the outer solar system. The inner planets are also known as the *terrestrial planets* because their surfaces are dense and rocky. However, each of the inner planets is unique.

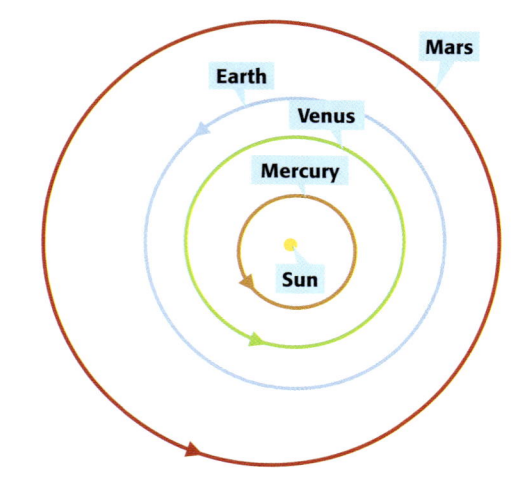

Figure 3 The inner planets are the planets that are closest to the sun.

INCLUSION Strategies

- Learning Disabled
- Developmentally Delayed
- Visually Impaired

Organize students into small teams to play a planetary quiz game. Each team should choose a category that relates to a heading in the section. Have students write five questions and answers for the category on separate index cards. The difficulty and point value of the questions should increase incrementally. Review each team's questions and answers. Play the game by allowing teams to ask questions to another team. If a team cannot answer a question, the team should work with another team to find the answer. If teams cooperate, they should share the points earned. When the game is over, hand out a review sheet that contains all the questions with corresponding answers. **English Language Learners LS Verbal**

Chapter 21 • A Family of Planets

The Outer Planets

The planets of the outer solar system include Jupiter, Saturn, Uranus, Neptune, and Pluto. The outer planets are very different from the inner planets, as you will soon find out.

Unlike the inner planets, the outer planets, except for Pluto, are large and are composed mostly of gases. Because of this, Jupiter, Saturn, Uranus, and Neptune are known as gas giants. The atmospheres of these planets blend smoothly into the denser layers of their interiors. The icy planet Pluto is the only planet of the outer solar system that is small, dense, and rocky. You can see a diagram of the outer solar system in **Figure 4.**

Reading Check Which planets are in the outer solar system?

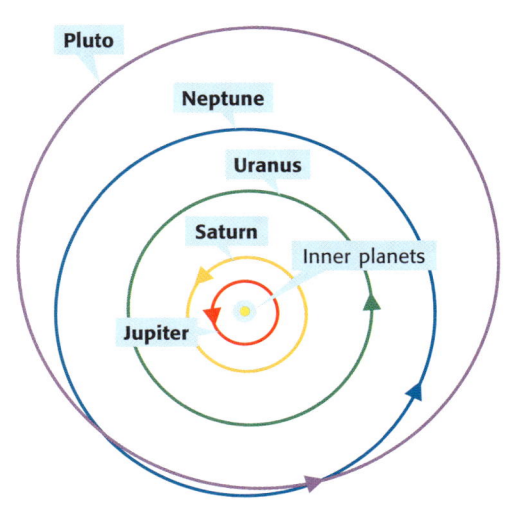

Figure 4 The planets of the outer solar system are the farthest from the sun.

SECTION Review

Summary

- In the order in which they orbit the sun, the nine planets are Mercury, Venus, Earth, Mars, Jupiter, Saturn, Uranus, Neptune, and Pluto.
- Two ways in which scientists measure distances in space are to use astronomical units and to use light-years.
- The inner planets are spaced more closely together, are smaller, and are rockier than the outer planets.

Using Key Terms

1. In your own words, write a definition for the term *astronomical unit*.

Understanding Key Ideas

2. When was the planet Uranus discovered?
   a. before the 17th century
   b. in the 18th century
   c. in the 19th century
   d. in the 20th century

3. The invention of what instrument helped early scientists discover more bodies in the solar system?

4. Which of the nine planets are included in the outer solar system?

5. Describe how the inner planets are different from the outer planets.

Math Skills

6. If Venus is 6.0 light-minutes from the sun, what is Venus's distance from the sun in astronomical units?

Critical Thinking

7. **Analyzing Methods** The distance between Earth and the sun is measured in light-minutes, but the distance between Pluto and the sun is measured in light-hours. Explain why.

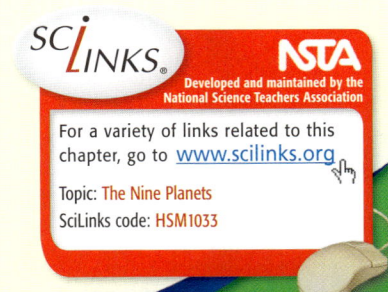

Answers to Section Review

1. Sample answer: An astronomical unit is the average distance from the Earth to the sun.
2. b
3. the telescope
4. Jupiter, Saturn, Uranus, Neptune, and Pluto
5. Sample answer: The surfaces of the inner planets are dense and rocky. Except for Pluto, the outer planets are extremely large and composed mostly of gases. Pluto is the only outer planet that is small, dense, and rocky.
6. Use a ratio to calculate the relationship between the distance from Venus to the sun in light-minutes and in astronomical units.

   6 light-minutes ÷ X AU = 8.3 light-minutes ÷ 1 AU

   This fraction reduces to X = 6 light-minutes ÷ 8.3 light-minutes

   X = 0.7 AU

7. Sample answer: Pluto is so far from the sun that expressing this distance in light-minutes would require a very large number. The distance is measured in light-hours, which is a smaller number than light-minutes.

Answer to Reading Check

Jupiter, Saturn, Uranus, Neptune, and Pluto are in the outer solar system.

CHAPTER RESOURCES

Chapter Resource File
- Section Quiz GENERAL
- Section Review GENERAL
- Vocabulary and Section Summary GENERAL
- SciLinks Activity GENERAL

Technology
- Transparencies
  - The Inner Planets; The Outer Planets

Workbooks
- Math Skills for Science
  - A Shortcut for Multiplying Large Numbers GENERAL

Section 1 • The Nine Planets

SECTION 2

Focus

Overview
This section teaches students about the four inner planets of the solar system: Mercury, Venus, Earth, and Mars.

🔔 Bellringer
Have students create a mnemonic device to help them remember the order of the planets:

Mercury, **V**enus, **E**arth, **M**ars, **J**upiter, **S**aturn, **U**ranus, **N**eptune, **P**luto

Example: My very eccentric mother just sent us nine pigs.

Motivate

ACTIVITY — GENERAL

Your Age in Venusian Years
Tell students that Venus is the second-brightest object in the night sky. Venus is often called the *morning star* or the *evening star* because it is visible only at dawn or dusk. Also, the planet rotates much more slowly than Earth does. A Venusian day is longer than a Venusian year! A Venusian year is 224 Earth days long, but a Venusian day is 243 Earth days long. Have students calculate their age in Venusian years. (A 10-year-old student is 3,656 days old: 3,656 Earth days ÷ 224 Earth days/Venusian year = 16.3 Venusian years old.)
LS Logical

SECTION 2

READING WARM-UP

Objectives
- Explain the difference between a planet's period of rotation and period of revolution.
- Describe the difference between prograde and retrograde rotation.
- Describe the individual characteristics of Mercury, Venus, Earth, and Mars.
- Identify the characteristics that make Earth suitable for life.

Terms to Learn
terrestrial planet
prograde rotation
retrograde rotation

READING STRATEGY

Reading Organizer As you read this section, create an outline of the section. Use the headings from the section in your outline.

terrestrial planet one of the highly dense planets nearest to the sun; Mercury, Venus, Mars, and Earth

---

The Inner Planets

In the inner solar system, you will find one of the hottest places in our solar system as well as the only planet known to support life.

The inner planets are also called **terrestrial planets** because, like Earth, they are very dense and rocky. The inner planets are smaller, denser, and rockier than the outer planets. In this section, you will learn more about the individual characteristics of Mercury, Venus, Earth, and Mars.

Mercury: Closest to the Sun

If you visited the planet Mercury, shown in **Figure 1,** you would find a very strange world. For one thing, on Mercury you would weigh only 38% of what you weigh on Earth. The weight you have on Earth is due to surface gravity, which is less on less massive planets. Also, because of Mercury's slow rotation, a day on Mercury is almost 59 Earth days long! The amount of time that an object takes to rotate once is called its *period of rotation*. So, Mercury's period of rotation is almost 59 Earth days long.

A Year on Mercury

Another curious thing about Mercury is that its year is only 88 Earth days long. As you know, a *year* is the time that a planet takes to go around the sun once. The motion of a body orbiting another body in space is called *revolution*. The time an object takes to revolve around the sun once is called its *period of revolution*. Every 88 Earth days, or 1.5 Mercurian days, Mercury revolves once around the sun.

Figure 1 This image of Mercury was taken by the *Mariner 10* spacecraft on March 24, 1974, from a distance of 5,380,000 km.

Mercury Statistics

Distance from sun	3.2 light-minutes
Period of rotation	58 days, 19 h
Period of revolution	88 days
Diameter	4,879 km
Density	5.43 g/cm^3
Surface temperature	−173°C to 427°C
Surface gravity	38% of Earth's

CHAPTER RESOURCES

Chapter Resource File
- Lesson Plan
- Directed Reading A BASIC
- Directed Reading B SPECIAL NEEDS

Technology
- Transparencies
  - Bellringer

---

648 Chapter 21 • A Family of Planets

Venus Statistics	
Distance from sun	6.0 light-minutes
Period of rotation	243 days, 16 h (R)*
Period of revolution	224 days, 17 h
Diameter	12,104 km
Density	5.24 g/cm^3
Surface temperature	464°C
Surface gravity	91% of Earth's

*R = retrograde rotation

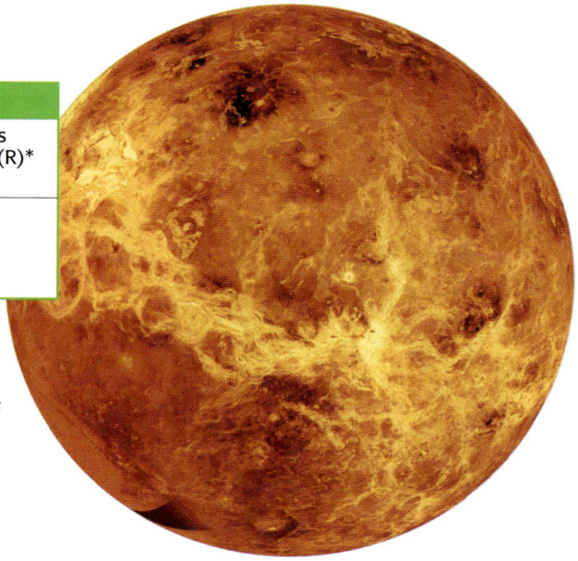

Figure 2 *This image of Venus was taken by Mariner 10 on February 5, 1974. The uppermost layer of clouds contains sulfuric acid.*

Venus: Earth's Twin?

Look at **Figure 2.** In many ways, Venus is more like Earth than any other planet. Venus is only slightly smaller, less massive, and less dense than Earth. But in other ways, Venus is very different from Earth. On Venus, the sun rises in the west and sets in the east. The reason is that Venus and Earth rotate in opposite directions. Earth is said to have **prograde rotation** because it appears to spin in a *counterclockwise* direction when it is viewed from above its North Pole. If a planet spins in a *clockwise* direction, the planet is said to have **retrograde rotation.**

The Atmosphere of Venus

Of the terrestrial planets, Venus has the densest atmosphere. Venus's atmosphere has 90 times the pressure of Earth's atmosphere! The air on Venus is mostly carbon dioxide, but the air is also made of some of the most destructive acids known. The carbon dioxide traps thermal energy from sunlight in a process called the *greenhouse effect.* The greenhouse effect causes Venus's surface temperature to be very high. At 464°C, Venus has the hottest surface of any planet in the solar system.

Mapping Venus's Surface

Between 1990 and 1992, the *Magellan* spacecraft mapped the surface of Venus by using radar waves. The radar waves traveled through the clouds and bounced off the planet's surface. Data gathered from the radar waves showed that Venus, like Earth, has volcanoes.

Reading Check What technology was used to map the surface of Venus? (*See the Appendix for answers to Reading Checks.*)

prograde rotation the counterclockwise spin of a planet or moon as seen from above the planet's North Pole; rotation in the same direction as the sun's rotation

retrograde rotation the clockwise spin of a planet or moon as seen from above the planet's North Pole

Homework — ADVANCED

Using Maps Most of the features of Venus are named after female scientists, female historical figures, and goddesses. Many of Mercury's craters are named after artists and musicians, and most craters of the moon are named after famous scientists. Have students use maps of the inner planets to learn more about their features and the origin of their names. **LS Visual**

Answer to Reading Check
Radar technology was used to map the surface of Venus.

Teach

CONNECTION to Environmental Science — GENERAL

Writing **Atmospheric Change** The concentration of carbon dioxide in Venus's atmosphere causes a severe greenhouse effect. As a result, surface temperatures on Venus are hot enough to melt lead. Could an increased greenhouse effect cause Earth's atmosphere to become more like Venus's? Earth's current atmosphere is primarily nitrogen and oxygen. CO_2 levels in our atmosphere have risen steadily since the Industrial Revolution. Have students write a short story describing how Earth's atmosphere could become more like Venus's atmosphere. Ask students to describe how life on Earth would change. **LS Verbal**

MISCONCEPTION ALERT

Variations in Brightness Students may believe that the planets always have the same brightness. Actually, planets appear brighter when they are closer to Earth. For example, as Mars and Earth orbit the sun, the distance between the two planets varies from about 75 million kilometers to about 375 million kilometers. This difference in distance causes the apparent brightness of Mars to vary by a factor of 25.

Section 2 • The Inner Planets

Teach, continued

Discussion — BASIC

Defining Terms Ask students what an oasis is. (An oasis is a hospitable place in an otherwise inhospitable area.) Discuss with students why Earth is referred to in the text as an *oasis*. Tell them to focus on the importance of Earth's distance from the sun and the presence of large amounts of liquid water on Earth's surface. Earth's mass also plays an important role because the mass "holds" the gases that constitute Earth's life-sustaining atmosphere around the Earth.
LS Verbal

MISCONCEPTION ALERT

The World Is Not Round
Earth is not a perfect sphere. The diameter of Earth as measured from the North Pole to the South Pole is 44 km less than the diameter as measured at the equator. None of the other planets or stars is perfectly spherical either. Therefore, all of the planetary diameters given in this chapter are equatorial diameters.

Figure 3 Earth is the only planet known to support life.

Earth: An Oasis in Space

As viewed from space, Earth is like a sparkling blue oasis in a black sea of stars. Constantly changing weather patterns create the swirls of clouds that blanket the blue and brown sphere we call home. Look at **Figure 3**. Why did Earth have such good fortune, while its two nearest neighbors, Venus and Mars, are unsuitable for life as we know it?

Water on Earth

Earth formed at just the right distance from the sun. Earth is warm enough to keep most of its water from freezing. But unlike Venus, Earth is cool enough to keep its water from boiling away. Liquid water is a vital part of the chemical processes that living things depend on for survival.

The Earth from Space

The picture of Earth shown in **Figure 4** was taken from space. You might think that the only goal of space exploration is to make discoveries beyond Earth. But the National Aeronautics and Space Administration (NASA) has a program to study Earth by using satellites in the same way that scientists study other planets. This program is called the Earth Science Enterprise. Its goal is to study the Earth as a global system that is made of smaller systems. These smaller systems include the atmosphere, land, ice, the oceans, and life. The program will also help us understand how humans affect the global environment. By studying Earth from space, scientists hope to understand how different parts of the global system interact.

✓ **Reading Check** What is the Earth Science Enterprise?

Earth Statistics

Distance from sun	8.3 light-minutes
Period of rotation	23 h, 56 min
Period of revolution	365 days, 6 h
Diameter	12,756 km
Density	5.52 g/cm^3
Surface temperature	−13°C to 37°C
Surface gravity	100% of Earth's

Figure 4 This image of Earth was taken on December 7, 1972, by the crew of the *Apollo 17* spacecraft while on their way to the moon.

WEIRD SCIENCE

The Earth and its moon revolve around the sun like a "double planet." They can be thought of as the unequal ends of a barbell. The center of gravity for the Earth-moon system, called the *barycenter*, is actually 1,700 km below the Earth's surface. The barycenter is what follows the curved line of Earth's orbit. The moon and the Earth wobble around this center of gravity as they circle the sun.

Answer to Reading Check

Earth Science Enterprise is a NASA program that uses satellites to study Earth's atmosphere, land, oceans, life, and ice. This program will help scientists understand how humans affect the environment and how different parts of the global system interact.

---

650 Chapter 21 • A Family of Planets

Mars Statistics	
Distance from sun	12.7 light-minutes
Period of rotation	24 h, 40 min
Period of revolution	1 year, 322 days
Diameter	6,794 km
Density	3.93 g/cm^3
Surface temperature	−123°C to 37°C
Surface gravity	38% of Earth's

Mars: Our Intriguing Neighbor

Mars, shown in **Figure 5,** is perhaps the most studied planet in the solar system other than Earth. Much of our knowledge of Mars has come from information gathered by spacecraft. *Viking 1* and *Viking 2* landed on Mars in 1976, and *Mars Pathfinder* landed on Mars in 1997.

The Atmosphere of Mars

Because of its thinner atmosphere and greater distance from the sun, Mars is a cold planet. Midsummer temperatures recorded by the *Mars Pathfinder* range from −13°C to −77°C. Martian air is so thin that the air pressure on the surface of Mars is about the same as it is 30 km above Earth's surface. This distance is about 3 times higher than most planes fly! The air pressure is so low that any liquid water would quickly boil away. The only water found on the surface of Mars is in the form of ice.

Figure 5 *This Viking orbiter image shows the eastern hemisphere of Mars. The large circular feature in the center is the impact crater Schiaparelli, which has a diameter of 450 km.*

Water on Mars

Even though liquid water cannot exist on Mars's surface today, there is strong evidence that it existed there in the past. **Figure 6** shows an area on Mars with features that might have resulted from deposition of sediment in a lake. This finding means that in the past Mars might have been a warmer place and had a thicker atmosphere.

Figure 6 *The origin of the features shown in this image is unknown. The features might have resulted from deposition of sediment in a lake.*

CONNECTION ACTIVITY
Math — GENERAL

Making Graphs Have students use the planetary statistics tables to make a comparative graph of each planet's distance to the sun and average surface temperature. Challenge students to draw conclusions about the relationship between the two statistics. Is there a linear relationship between the two? **(no)** Why is Mercury colder than Venus even though Mercury is almost 3 light-minutes closer to the sun? **(Unlike Venus, Mercury does not have an atmosphere dense enough to trap solar radiation.)** **LS** Logical

BRAIN FOOD

Retrograde Motion As Mars moves eastward through Earth's night sky, Mars appears to gradually slow to a stop and then reverse its direction for several weeks. Then, it resumes its normal west-to-east motion through the sky. This curious looped path puzzled astronomers in the past. Today, we know that Earth passes Mars as the two planets orbit the sun; thus, Mars seems to move backward for a time. This movement is called *retrograde motion,* not to be confused with *retrograde rotation.*

Science Bloopers

Giovanni Schiaparelli (1835–1910), an Italian astronomer, studied Mars in the late 1800s. He thought that he saw straight lines crisscrossing the surface of the red planet. He called these lines *canali.* In Italian, *canali* means "channels," but the word was erroneously translated to English as "canals." Partly because of this misconception, for nearly 100 years, many people believed that Mars had supported at some time in its past intelligent beings that had built canals. This belief was disproved in the 1960s when a spacecraft sent to Mars did not find any canals.

Section 2 • The Inner Planets

Close

Reteaching — BASIC
Planetary Data Table Have students create a table summarizing the data in this section. (Answers may vary. Answers could include a row for each planet and columns for distance from the sun, period of rotation, period of revolution, diameter, density, surface temperature, and surface gravity.)
LS Logical

Quiz — GENERAL
Have students complete the following sentences:

1. The counterclockwise spin of a planet or moon as seen from above the planet's North Pole is ____. (prograde rotation)

2. The space probes that have been sent to Mars are ____, ____, ____, and ____. (*Viking 1, Viking 2, Mars Pathfinder,* and *Mars Express Orbiter*)

Alternative Assessment — GENERAL
Adaptations for Space Ask students to think about the conditions to which hypothetical life-forms on Mercury, Venus, or Mars would need to adapt. Have students draw a poster that show an imaginary organism for each planet. Students should include a description of adaptations that the life-forms have developed to live on each planet. **LS Verbal**

CONNECTION TO Physics

WRITING SKILL **Boiling Point on Mars** At sea level on Earth's surface, water boils at 100°C. But if you try to boil water on top of a high mountain, you will find that the boiling point is lower than 100°C. Do some research to find out why. Then, in your own words, explain why liquid water cannot exist on Mars, based on what you learned.

Where Is the Water Now?
Mars has two polar icecaps made of both frozen water and frozen carbon dioxide. But the polar icecaps do not have enough water to create a thick atmosphere or rivers. Looking closely at the walls of some Martian craters, scientists have found that the debris around the craters looks as if it were made by the flow of mud rather than by dry soil. In this case, where might some of the "lost" Martian water have gone? Many scientists think that it is frozen beneath the Martian soil.

Martian Volcanoes
Mars has a rich volcanic history. Unlike Earth, where volcanoes exist in many places, Mars has only two large volcanic systems. The largest, the Tharsis region, stretches 8,000 km across the planet. The largest mountain in the solar system, Olympus Mons, is an extinct shield volcano similar to Mauna Kea on the island of Hawaii. Mars not only is smaller and cooler than Earth but also has a slightly different chemical makeup. This makeup may have kept the Martian crust from moving around as Earth's crust does. As a result, the volcanoes kept building up in the same spots on Mars. Images and data sent back by probes such as the *Sojourner* rover, shown in **Figure 7,** are helping to explain Mars's mysterious past.

Reading Check What characteristics of Mars may explain why Mars has only two large volcanic systems?

Figure 7 The *Sojourner* rover, part of the Mars Pathfinder mission, is shown here creeping up to a rock named Yogi to measure its composition. The solar panel on the rover's back collected the solar energy used to power the rover's motor.

Answer to Reading Check
Mars' crust is chemically different from Earth's crust, so the Martian crust does not move. As a result, volcanoes build up in the same spots on Mars.

652 Chapter 21 • A Family of Planets

Missions to Mars

Scientists are still intrigued by the mysteries of Mars. Several recent missions to Mars were launched to gain a better understanding of the Martian world. **Figure 8** shows the *Mars Express Orbiter*, which was launched by the European Space Agency (ESA) in 2003, and was designed to help scientists determine the composition of the Martian atmosphere and Martian climate. Also, in 2003, NASA launched the Twin Rover mission to Mars. These exploration rovers are designed to gather information that may help scientists determine if life ever existed on Mars. In addition, information collected by these rovers may help scientists prepare for human exploration on Mars.

Figure 8 *The Mars Express Orbiter will help scientists study Mars's atmosphere.*

SECTION Review

Summary

- A period of rotation is the length of time that an object takes to rotate once on its axis.
- A period of revolution is the length of time that an object takes to revolve around the sun.
- Mercury is the planet closest to the sun. Of all the terrestrial planets, Venus has the densest atmosphere. Earth is the only planet known to support life. Mars has a rich volcanic history and shows evidence of once having had water.

Using Key Terms

1. In your own words, write a definition for the term *terrestrial planet*.

For the pair of terms below, explain how the meanings of the terms differ.

2. *prograde rotation* and *retrograde rotation*

Understanding Key Ideas

3. Scientists believe that the water on Mars now exists as
   a. polar icecaps.
   b. dry riverbeds.
   c. ice beneath the Martian soil.
   d. Both (a) and (c)

4. List three differences between and three similarities of Venus and Earth.

5. What is the difference between a planet's period of rotation and its period of revolution?

6. What are some of the characteristics of Earth that make it suitable for life?

7. Explain why the surface temperature of Venus is higher than the surface temperatures of the other planets in our solar system.

Math Skills

8. Mercury has a period of rotation equal to 58.67 Earth days. Mercury's period of revolution is equal to 88 Earth days. How many times does Mercury rotate during one revolution around the sun?

Critical Thinking

9. **Making Inferences** What type of information can we get by studying Earth from space?

10. **Analyzing Ideas** What type of evidence found on Mars suggests that Mars may have been a warmer place and had a thicker atmosphere?

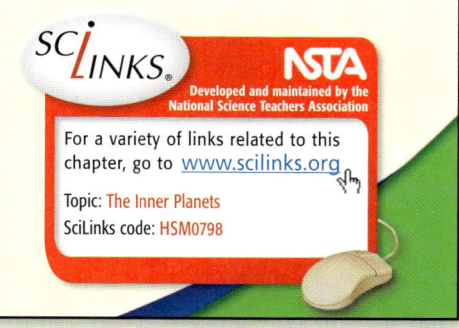

SCI LINKS — Developed and maintained by the National Science Teachers Association

For a variety of links related to this chapter, go to www.scilinks.org
Topic: The Inner Planets
SciLinks code: HSM0798

CHAPTER RESOURCES

Chapter Resource File
- Section Quiz GENERAL
- Section Review GENERAL
- Vocabulary and Section Summary GENERAL
- Critical Thinking ADVANCED

Answers to Section Review

1. Sample answer: A terrestrial planet is a planet that has a solid, rocky surface.

2. Answers may vary. Answers should indicate that prograde rotation is counterclockwise and retrograde rotation is clockwise when viewed from above the planet's North Pole.

3. d

4. Sample answer: Unlike Earth, Venus has retrograde rotation, Venus's surface temperature is very hot, and Venus's atmosphere is very dense. Also, Venus's atmosphere contains destructive acids. Similarities between Earth and Venus include size, density, mass, and surface gravity.

5. Answers may vary. Answers should indicate that the period of rotation is the amount of time a planet takes to spin on its axis. The period of revolution is amount of time the planet takes to make one trip around the sun.

6. Sample answer: Earth is warm enough to keep most of its water from freezing and cool enough to keep its water from boiling away. Living things depend on liquid water for survival.

7. The surface temperature of Venus is high because of a severe greenhouse effect.

8. 1.5 rotations per revolution (88 days/revolution ÷ 58.67 days/rotation = 1.5 rotations/revolution)

9. Answers may vary. Sample answer: We can learn about Earth's systems and how they interact.

10. Answers may vary. Sample answer: Some features on Mars might have resulted from the deposition of sediment in a lake. For this reason, some scientists think that Mars might have been a warmer place and had a thicker atmosphere in the past. If Mars had not been warmer and had a thicker atmosphere, a lake would not have formed.

Section 2 • The Inner Planets

SECTION 3

Focus

Overview
This section teaches students about the atmosphere and characteristics of the outer planets: Jupiter, Saturn, Uranus, Neptune, and Pluto.

Bellringer
All planets with atmospheres have weather. Jupiter's Great Red Spot appears to be very similar to a hurricane system on Earth, but it has lasted for centuries, driven by the planet's internal thermal energy. Have students write and tape-record a humorous but accurate weather forecast for one of the planets with an atmosphere.

Motivate

Discussion — GENERAL

Almost a Star Some astronomers think of Jupiter as a small star that never reached maturity. The *Galileo* probe found that the relative amounts of hydrogen and helium in Jupiter's atmosphere are very similar to those in the sun. However, Jupiter's 30,000°C core temperature is not high enough to initiate the fusion reactions that occur in the sun's core. **LS Verbal**

SECTION 3

READING WARM-UP

Objectives
- Explain how gas giants are different from terrestrial planets.
- Describe the individual characteristics of Jupiter, Saturn, Uranus, Neptune, and Pluto.

Terms to Learn
gas giant

READING STRATEGY

Prediction Guide Before reading this section, write the title of each heading in this section. Next, under each heading write what you think you will learn.

gas giant a planet that has a deep, massive atmosphere, such as Jupiter, Saturn, Uranus, or Neptune

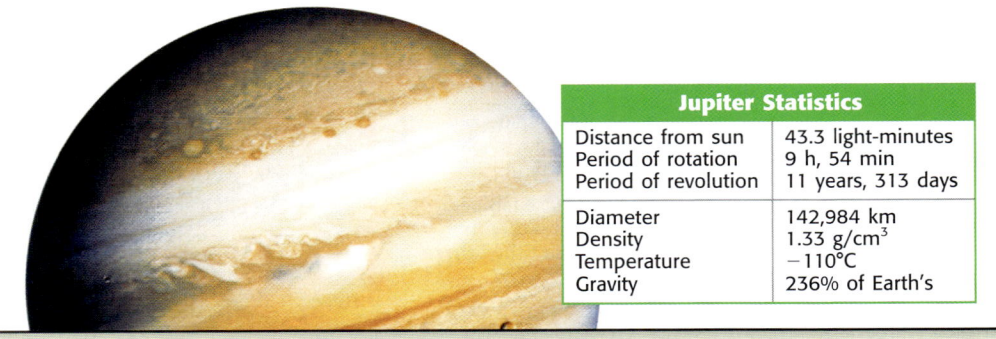

Figure 1 This *Voyager 2* image of Jupiter was taken at a distance of 28.4 million kilometers. Io, one of Jupiter's largest moons, can also be seen in this image.

CHAPTER RESOURCES

Chapter Resource File
- Lesson Plan
- Directed Reading A BASIC
- Directed Reading B SPECIAL NEEDS

Technology
- Transparencies
  • Bellringer

The Outer Planets

What do all the outer planets except for Pluto have in common?

Except for Pluto, the outer planets are very large planets that are made mostly of gases. These planets are called gas giants. **Gas giants** are planets that have deep, massive atmospheres rather than hard and rocky surfaces like those of the inner planets.

Jupiter: A Giant Among Giants

Jupiter is the largest planet in our solar system. Like the sun, Jupiter is made mostly of hydrogen and helium. The outer part of Jupiter's atmosphere is made of layered clouds of water, methane, and ammonia. The beautiful colors you see in **Figure 1** are probably due to small amounts of organic compounds. At a depth of about 10,000 km into Jupiter's atmosphere, the pressure is high enough to change hydrogen gas into a liquid. Deeper still, the pressure changes the liquid hydrogen into a liquid, metallic state. Unlike most planets, Jupiter radiates much more energy into space than it receives from the sun. The reason is that Jupiter's interior is very hot. Another striking feature of Jupiter is the Great Red Spot, a storm system that is more than 400 years old and is about 3 times the diameter of Earth!

NASA Missions to Jupiter

NASA has sent five missions to Jupiter. These include two Pioneer missions, two Voyager missions, and the recent Galileo mission. The *Voyager 1* and *Voyager 2* spacecraft sent back images that revealed a thin, faint ring around Jupiter. The Voyager missions also gave us the first detailed images of Jupiter's moons. The *Galileo* spacecraft reached Jupiter in 1995 and sent a probe into Jupiter's atmosphere. The probe sent back data on Jupiter's composition, temperature, and pressure.

Jupiter Statistics	
Distance from sun	43.3 light-minutes
Period of rotation	9 h, 54 min
Period of revolution	11 years, 313 days
Diameter	142,984 km
Density	1.33 g/cm^3
Temperature	−110°C
Gravity	236% of Earth's

CONNECTION to Meteorology — GENERAL

Wind Advisory Saturn has the most violent winds of any planet in our solar system. At Saturn's equator, the wind blows at nearly 1,700 km/h (approximately 1,000 mph)—not exactly good weather for playing outside.

---

654 Chapter 21 • A Family of Planets

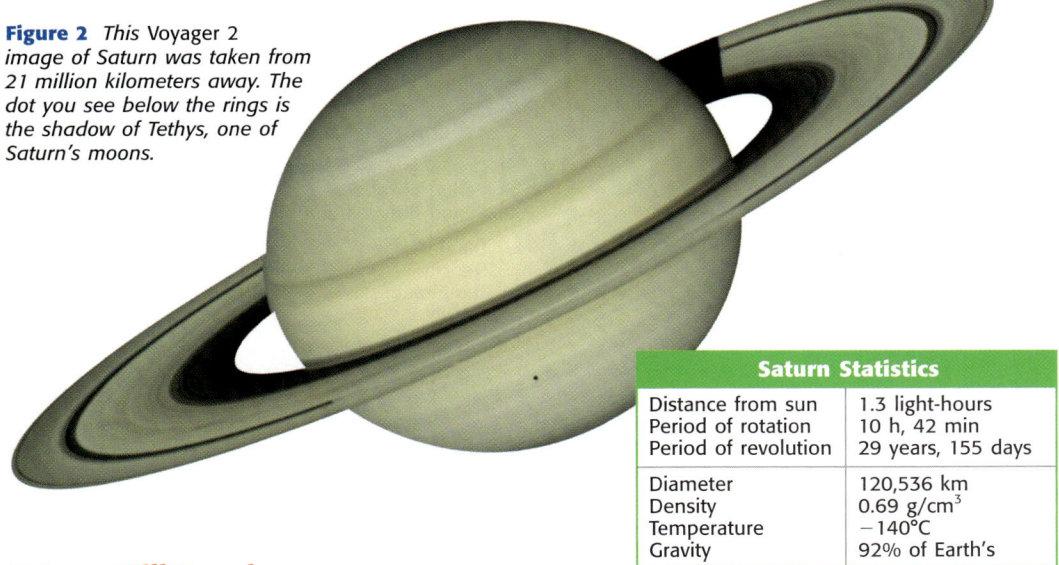

Figure 2 *This Voyager 2 image of Saturn was taken from 21 million kilometers away. The dot you see below the rings is the shadow of Tethys, one of Saturn's moons.*

Saturn Statistics	
Distance from sun	1.3 light-hours
Period of rotation	10 h, 42 min
Period of revolution	29 years, 155 days
Diameter	120,536 km
Density	0.69 g/cm^3
Temperature	−140°C
Gravity	92% of Earth's

Saturn: Still Forming

Saturn, shown in **Figure 2,** is the second-largest planet in the solar system. Saturn has roughly 764 times the volume of Earth and is 95 times more massive than Earth. Its overall composition, like Jupiter's, is mostly hydrogen and helium. But methane, ammonia, and ethane are found in the upper atmosphere. Saturn's interior is probably much like Jupiter's. Also, like Jupiter, Saturn gives off much more energy than it receives from the sun. Scientists think that Saturn's extra energy comes from helium falling out of the atmosphere and sinking to the core. In other words, Saturn is still forming!

The Rings of Saturn

Although all of the gas giants have rings, Saturn's rings are the largest. Saturn's rings have a total diameter of 272,000 km. Yet, Saturn's rings are only a few hundred meters thick. The rings are made of icy particles that range in size from a few centimeters to several meters wide. **Figure 3** shows a close-up view of Saturn's rings.

✓ **Reading Check** What are Saturn's rings made of? *(See the Appendix for answers to Reading Checks.)*

NASA's Exploration of Saturn

Launched in 1997, the *Cassini* spacecraft is designed to study Saturn's rings, moons, and atmosphere. The spacecraft is also designed to return more than 300,000 color images of Saturn.

Figure 3 *The different colors in this Voyager 2 image of Saturn's rings show differences in the rings' chemical composition.*

Answer to Reading Check
Saturn's rings are made of icy particles ranging in size from a few centimeters to several meters wide.

WEIRD SCIENCE

Although Saturn's composition is similar to Jupiter's, Saturn appears less colorful. The reason is that Saturn's colder atmosphere causes thick, white ammonia clouds to condense and block our view.

Teach

Using the Table — GENERAL
Density Have students compare the density of Saturn with the densities of other planets, including Earth. Then, have them compare the density of Saturn with the density of water. What conclusions can they draw from this information? (Answers may vary. Sample answer: If Saturn were put in an ocean large enough, Saturn would float.) **LS** Logical

Using the Figure — ADVANCED
Equatorial Bulges Ask students to measure the polar diameter and the equatorial diameter of Saturn in **Figure 2,** and ask them to hypothesize why Saturn appears to bulge around its equator. Tell students that there are two clues in the table "Saturn Statistics." Point out that Saturn's low density (0.69 g/cm^3) and fast period of rotation (10 h, 42 min) cause the gaseous planet to bulge along its equator. **LS** Logical/Kinesthetic

MISCONCEPTION ALERT

Gas Giants Statistics for the gas giants do not include the word *surface* because it is thought that the gas giants do not have a definite surface. Temperature, diameter, and gravity measurements will vary depending on where the surface is measured. The surfaces of the gas giants are sometimes defined as the level of the atmosphere at which the pressure is 1 bar (~1 atm). The values listed in this book are for the 1-bar level.

Section 3 • The Outer Planets

Teach, continued

READING STRATEGY — GENERAL

Prediction Guide Before students read this page, ask them whether each of the following statements is true or false.

- Uranus was discovered in the 18th century. (true)
- Uranus's axis of rotation is almost parallel to the planet's orbit around the sun. (true)

LS Verbal

Using the Figure — GENERAL

Axial Tilt Using **Figure 5,** point out that because Uranus has an axial tilt of 82°, its poles point toward the sun during part of its year. (For simplicity, the figure shows the angle between the pole and the plane of orbit.) In contrast, Earth's 23° tilt means that like the poles of most planets, Earth's poles never point directly toward the sun. Students can simulate these axial tilts using a globe and an object to represent the sun. As students revolve around the sun, have them tilt the globe to represent the axial tilts of Venus (3°), Earth, and Uranus. Point out the times that Uranus's poles point toward the sun.

LS Kinesthetic   Co-op Learning

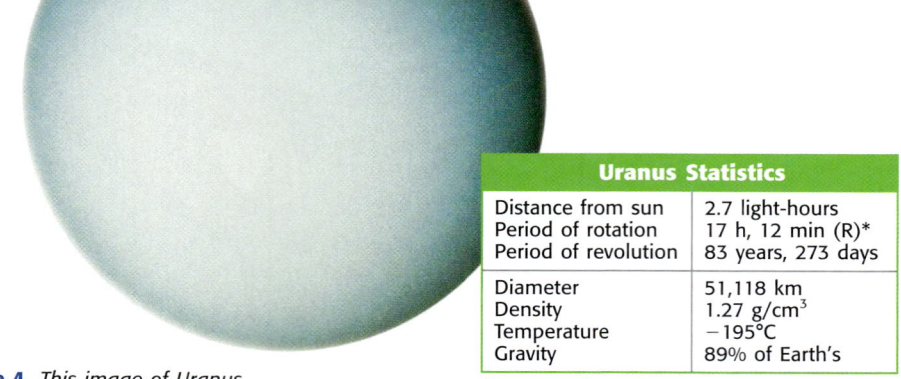

Figure 4 This image of Uranus was taken by Voyager 2 at a distance of 9.1 million kilometers.

Uranus Statistics	
Distance from sun	2.7 light-hours
Period of rotation	17 h, 12 min (R)*
Period of revolution	83 years, 273 days
Diameter	51,118 km
Density	1.27 g/cm³
Temperature	–195°C
Gravity	89% of Earth's

*R = retrograde rotation

Uranus: A Small Giant

Uranus (YOOR uh nuhs) was discovered by the English amateur astronomer William Herschel in 1781. The atmosphere of Uranus is mainly hydrogen and methane. Because these gases absorb the red part of sunlight very strongly, Uranus appears blue-green in color, as shown in **Figure 4.** Uranus and Neptune have much less mass than Jupiter, but their densities are similar. This suggests that their compositions are different from Jupiter's. They may have lower percentages of light elements and a greater percentage of water.

A Tilted Planet

Unlike most other planets, Uranus is tipped over on its side. So, its axis of rotation is tilted by almost 90° and lies almost in the plane of its orbit, as shown in **Figure 5.** For part of a Uranus year, one pole points toward the sun while the other pole is in darkness. At the other end of Uranus's orbit, the poles are reversed. Some scientists think that early in its history, Uranus may have been hit by a massive object that tipped the planet over.

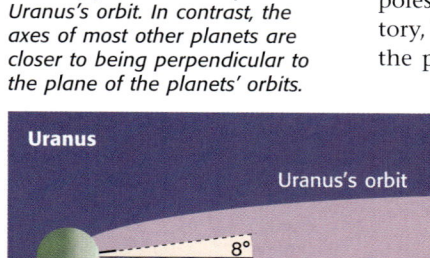

Figure 5 Uranus's axis of rotation is tilted so that the axis is nearly parallel to the plane of Uranus's orbit. In contrast, the axes of most other planets are closer to being perpendicular to the plane of the planets' orbits.

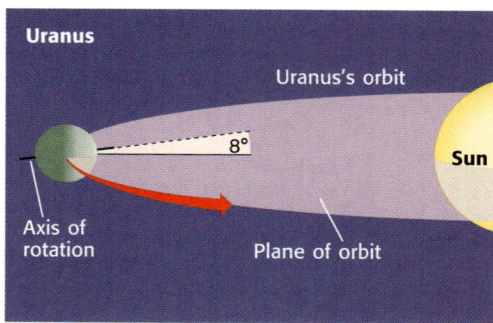

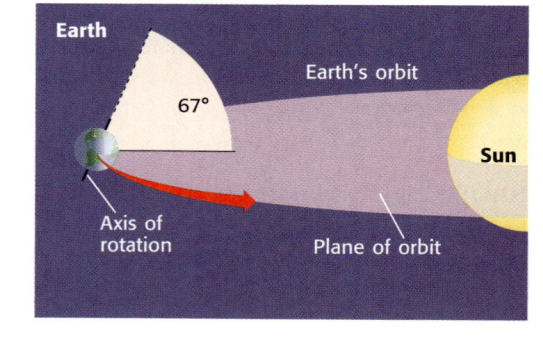

Science Bloopers

Uranus was discovered in 1781 by an English music teacher named William Herschel. Herschel originally named the planet *Georgium Sidus,* Latin for "George's Star," after England's King George III. No one outside England liked the name. A few years later, an astronomer named J. E. Bode suggested the name *Uranus* to continue the tradition of naming the planets after Greek or Roman gods.

Is That a Fact!

Measuring Tilt The *obliquity* values for planets, which also measure the tilt of a planet's axis, are greater than 90° for planets with retrograde rotation. These planets are thought to have tipped over after colliding with other massive bodies shortly after they formed. In essence, their "rotational north poles" now point "south" in space. For this reason, the obliquity values for Venus, Uranus, and Pluto are 177°, 98°, and 123°, respectively.

656 Chapter 21 • A Family of Planets

Neptune: The Blue World

Irregularities in the orbit of Uranus suggested to early astronomers that there must be another planet beyond it. They thought that the gravity of this new planet pulled Uranus off its predicted path. By using the predictions of the new planet's orbit, astronomers discovered the planet Neptune in 1846. Neptune is shown in **Figure 6.**

The Atmosphere of Neptune

The *Voyager 2* spacecraft sent back images that provided much new information about Neptune's atmosphere. Although the composition of Neptune's atmosphere is similar to that of Uranus's atmosphere, Neptune's atmosphere has belts of clouds that are much more visible. At the time of *Voyager 2*'s visit, Neptune had a Great Dark Spot like the Great Red Spot on Jupiter. And like the interiors of Jupiter and Saturn, Neptune's interior releases thermal energy to its outer layers. This release of energy helps the warm gases rise and the cool gases sink, which sets up the wind patterns in the atmosphere that create the belts of clouds. *Voyager 2* images also revealed that Neptune has a set of very narrow rings.

Reading Check What characteristic of Neptune's interior accounts for the belts of clouds in Neptune's atmosphere?

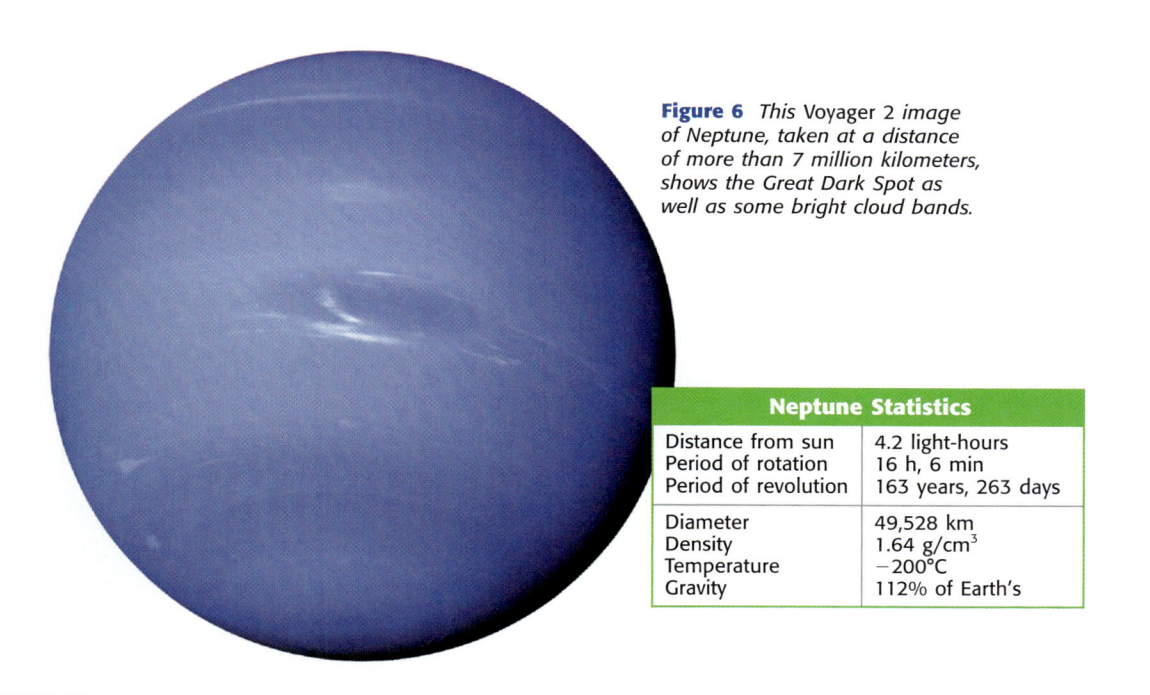

Figure 6 This *Voyager 2* image of Neptune, taken at a distance of more than 7 million kilometers, shows the Great Dark Spot as well as some bright cloud bands.

Neptune Statistics	
Distance from sun	4.2 light-hours
Period of rotation	16 h, 6 min
Period of revolution	163 years, 263 days
Diameter	49,528 km
Density	1.64 g/cm³
Temperature	−200°C
Gravity	112% of Earth's

Discussion — ADVANCED

Discovering Neptune Point out that Neptune was discovered in 1846 by the British astronomer John Adams and the French astronomer Joseph Leverrier. They found discrepancies in Uranus's motion that could not be explained by its gravitational interactions with the sun and the other known planets. Using Newton's laws of motion and gravity, the astronomers accurately predicted Neptune's position. Ask students how they think deviations in one planet's orbit could indicate the presence of an unknown planet. (Answers may vary. Sample answer: The gravitational pull of an undiscovered planet would pull the known planet off its predicted path.) **LS** Verbal

Answer to Reading Check

Neptune's interior releases energy to its outer layers, which creates belts of clouds in Neptune's atmosphere.

CONNECTION to Environmental Science — GENERAL

Global Warming Since the *Voyager* spacecraft passed Neptune's moon Triton in 1989, scientists have noticed an interesting trend in Triton's atmosphere. Images from the *Hubble Space Telescope* taken in 1998 indicate that Triton is going through a rapid period of global warming. As Triton warms, frozen nitrogen on its surface melts and contributes nitrogen gas to its thin atmosphere. This process has happened so rapidly that the atmospheric pressure of Triton has doubled in less than 10 years! Scientists hope to use the global-warming trends on Triton to understand warming patterns on Earth. Ask students to discuss what they would expect to happen to Triton's atmosphere in the next 10 years. (Answers may vary. Sample answer: Triton's surface nitrogen will melt and contribute to the atmosphere, causing it to become even thicker and trap more heat. The atmospheric pressure will double again.) **LS** Verbal

Section 3 • The Outer Planets

Close

Reteaching — BASIC
Planetary Quiz Have students write at least two characteristics of each planet on the back of separate index cards. Then, have them exchange index cards with a partner and try to guess the identity of each planet. **LS Verbal**

Quiz — GENERAL
1. Which of the outer planets have retrograde rotation? (Uranus and Pluto)
2. Which of the outer planets has the shortest period of rotation? (Jupiter)

Alternative Assessment — GENERAL
Planetary Postcards Ask students to write a postcard as if they were a tourist on an outer planet of their choice. Students should describe the weather, the view, the gravity, and other features, but they should not name the planet that they are visiting. Have students "mail" the postcards to a partner and then ask the partner to try to determine which planet the tourist is visiting. If the partner guesses incorrectly, the tourist should send another postcard describing more details about the planet. If the partner guesses correctly, the tourist can move to another planet. Have partners continue this game until they have both visited all five of the outer planets. **LS Kinesthetic/Visual**

Figure 7 *This Hubble Space Telescope image is one of the clearest ever taken of Pluto (left) and its moon, Charon (right).*

Pluto Statistics	
Distance from sun	5.4 light-hours
Period of rotation	6 days, 10 h (R)*
Period of revolution	248 years, 4 days
Diameter	2,390 km
Density	1.75 g/cm³
Surface temperature	−225°C
Surface gravity	6% of Earth's

*R = retrograde rotation

Pluto: The Mystery Planet
Further study of Neptune showed some irregularities in Neptune's orbit. This finding led many scientists to believe there was yet another planet beyond Neptune. The mystery planet was finally discovered in 1930.

A Small World
The mystery planet, now called Pluto, is the farthest planet from the sun. Less than half the size of Mercury, Pluto is also the smallest planet. Pluto's moon, Charon (KER uhn), is more than half its size! In fact, Charon is the largest satellite relative to its planet in the solar system. **Figure 7** shows Pluto and Charon together. From Earth, it is hard to separate the images of Pluto and Charon because the bodies are so far away. **Figure 8** shows how far from the sun Pluto and Charon really are. From Pluto, the sun looks like a very distant bright star.

From calculations of Pluto's density, scientists know that Pluto must be made of rock and ice. Pluto is covered by frozen nitrogen, but Charon is covered by frozen water. Scientists believe Pluto has a thin atmosphere of methane.

Figure 8 *An artist's view of the sun and Charon from Pluto shows just how little light and heat Pluto receives from the sun.*

CONNECTION ACTIVITY
Fine Arts — GENERAL
Alien Horizons Have students choose a planet and imagine what the sky would look like from their planet. Have students make a poster showing the view from their planet. Students could include moons, rings, or the sun in their illustration. Display the artwork in the class. **LS Visual**

A True Planet?

Because Pluto is so small and is so unusual, some scientists think that it should not be classified as a planet. In fact, some scientists agree that Pluto could be considered a large asteroid or comet—large enough to have its own satellite. However, because Pluto was historically classified as a planet, it most likely will remain so.

Pluto is the only planet that has not been visited by a NASA mission. However, plans are underway to visit Pluto and Charon in 2006. During this mission, scientists hope to learn more about this unusual planet and map the surface of both Pluto and Charon.

School to Home
Surviving Space

WRITING SKILL Imagine it is the year 2150 and you are flying a spacecraft to Pluto. Suddenly, your systems fail, giving you only one chance to land safely. You can't head back to Earth. With a parent, write a paragraph explaining which planet you would choose to land on.

SECTION Review

Summary

- Jupiter is the largest planet in our solar system. Energy from the interior of Jupiter is transferred to its exterior.
- Saturn is the second-largest planet and, in some ways, is still forming as a planet.
- Uranus's axis of rotation is tilted by almost 90°.
- Neptune has a faint ring, and its atmosphere contains belts of clouds.
- Pluto is the smallest planet, and its moon, Charon, is more than half its size.

Using Key Terms

1. In your own words, write a definition for the term *gas giant*.

Understanding Key Ideas

2. The many colors of Jupiter's atmosphere are probably caused by _____ in the atmosphere.
   a. clouds of water
   b. methane
   c. ammonia
   d. organic compounds

3. Why do scientists claim that Saturn, in a way, is still forming?

4. Why does Uranus have a blue green color?

5. What is unusual about Pluto's moon, Charon?

6. What is the Great Red Spot?

7. Explain why Jupiter radiates more energy into space than it receives from the sun.

8. How do the gas giants differ from the terrestrial planets?

9. What is so unusual about Uranus's axis of rotation?

Math Skills

10. Pluto is 5.5 light-hours from the sun. How far is Pluto from the sun in astronomical units? (Hint: 1 AU = 8.3 light-minutes)

11. If Jupiter is 43.3 light-minutes from the sun and Neptune is 4.2 light-hours from the sun, how far from Jupiter is Neptune?

Critical Thinking

12. **Evaluating Data** What conclusions can your draw about the properties of a planet just by knowing how far it is from the sun?

13. **Applying Concepts** Why isn't the word *surface* included in the statistics for the gas giants?

For a variety of links related to this chapter, go to www.scilinks.org
Topic: The Outer Planets
SciLinks code: HSM1091

Answers to Section Review

1. Sample answer: A gas giant is a planet that has a deep, massive atmosphere.
2. d
3. Sample answer: Helium is currently falling out of Saturn's atmosphere and sinking to its core. So, scientists think that Saturn is still forming.
4. The atmosphere of Uranus is mainly hydrogen and methane gases, which absorb red light, making Uranus appear blue green.
5. Charon is the largest satellite relative to its planet in the solar system.
6. Sample answer: The Great Red Spot is a storm system on Jupiter that is more than 400 years old and is about 3 times the diameter of Earth.
7. Jupiter radiates energy because Jupiter's interior is very hot.
8. Sample answer: Gas giants are much larger and more massive than terrestrial planets, and gas giants have deep, massive atmospheres rather than hard, rocky surfaces.
9. Sample answer: Uranus is tipped over on its side. Uranus's axis of rotation is tilted so that it lies almost in plane with its orbit. Each pole points toward the sun for part of Uranus's year.
10. about 40 AU (5.5 light-hours × 60 min/h = 330 light-minutes; 330 light-minutes ÷ 8.3 light-minutes/AU = 39.8 AU)
11. 208.7 light-minutes (4.2 light-hours × 60 min/h = 252 light-minutes; 252 light-minutes − 43.3 light-minutes = 208.7 light-minutes)
12. Answers may vary. Planets farther from the sun tend to have lower surface temperatures, they are spaced farther apart, their period of revolution is much longer than that of the inner planets, and they are more likely to be gas giants. (This pattern does not necessarily apply to other solar systems.)
13. Sample answer: Gas giants have no definite surface. Their atmosphere blends smoothly into the dense layers of their interior.

CHAPTER RESOURCES

Chapter Resource File
- Section Quiz GENERAL
- Section Review GENERAL
- Vocabulary and Section Summary GENERAL

Technology
- Interactive Explorations CD-ROM
- Space Case GENERAL

Workbooks
- Science Skills
  - Grasping Graphing GENERAL

Section 3 • The Outer Planets

SECTION 4

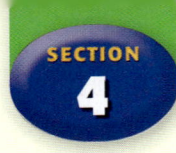

Focus

Overview
In this section, students learn about Earth's moon and the major moons of the other planets in the solar system.

🔔 Bellringer
The first astronauts to land on the moon were quarantined after their mission. NASA wanted to make sure that the astronauts didn't bring back any disease-causing organisms from the moon. Ask students to discuss whether or not they think this would be possible.

Motivate

ACTIVITY — GENERAL

Lunar Ice The 1998 Lunar Prospector mission showed that there could be water on our moon. The craters near the poles may contain as much as 300 million metric tons of ice! The ice can exist only in the permanently shadowed regions of the moon's poles; elsewhere, daytime temperatures can reach 134°C. Have students illustrate a lunar base, including a description of how lunar pioneers could obtain liquid water. **LS Visual**

SECTION 4

READING WARM-UP

Objectives
- Describe the current theory of the origin of Earth's moon.
- Explain what causes the phases of Earth's moon.
- Describe the difference between a solar eclipse and a lunar eclipse.
- Describe the individual characteristics of the moons of other planets.

Terms to Learn
satellite
phase
eclipse

READING STRATEGY

Reading Organizer As you read this section, make a table comparing solar eclipses and lunar eclipses.

Moons

If you could, which moon would you visit? With volcanoes, craters, and possible underground oceans, the moons in our solar system would be interesting places to visit.

Natural or artificial bodies that revolve around larger bodies such as planets are called **satellites.** Except for Mercury and Venus, all of the planets have natural satellites called *moons*.

Luna: The Moon of Earth

Scientists have learned a lot from studying Earth's moon, which is also called *Luna*. The lunar rocks brought back during the Apollo missions were found to be about 4.6 billion years old. Because these rocks have hardly changed since they formed, scientists know the solar system itself is about 4.6 billion years old.

The Surface of the Moon

As you can see in **Figure 1,** the moon's history is written on its face. The surfaces of bodies that have no atmospheres preserve a record of almost all of the impacts that the bodies have had. Because scientists now know the age of the moon, they can count the number of impact craters to find the rate of cratering since the birth of our solar system. By knowing the rate of cratering, scientists are able to use the number of craters on any body to estimate how old the body's surface is. That way, scientists don't need to bring back rock samples.

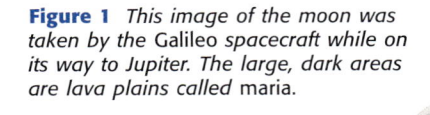

Figure 1 *This image of the moon was taken by the* Galileo *spacecraft while on its way to Jupiter. The large, dark areas are lava plains called* maria.

Moon Statistics	
Period of rotation	27 days, 9 hours
Period of revolution	27 days, 7 hours
Diameter	3,475 km
Density	3.34 g/cm³
Surface temperature	−170 to 134°C
Surface gravity	16% of Earth's

CHAPTER RESOURCES

Chapter Resource File
- Lesson Plan
- Directed Reading A BASIC
- Directed Reading B SPECIAL NEEDS

Technology

Transparencies
- Bellringer
- **LINK TO PHYSICAL SCIENCE** How an Orbit Is Formed; Projectile Motion
- Formation of the Moon

MISCONCEPTION ALERT

An Optical Illusion Students may think the moon is larger when it is close to the horizon. The moon appears larger because the observer's reference point is the skyline. The same phenomenon makes the sun appear larger. Challenge students to devise a way to verify this for themselves. Caution them not to look directly at the sun.

---

660   Chapter 21 • A Family of Planets

Lunar Origins

Before scientists had rock samples from the moon, there were three popular explanations for the moon's formation: (1) The moon was a separate body captured by Earth's gravity, (2) the moon formed at the same time and from the same materials as the Earth, and (3) the newly formed Earth was spinning so fast that a piece flew off and became the moon.

When rock samples of the moon were brought back from the Apollo mission, the mystery was solved. Scientists found that the composition of the moon was similar to that of Earth's mantle. This evidence from the lunar rock samples supported the third explanation for the moon's formation.

The current theory is that a large, Mars-sized object collided with Earth while the Earth was still forming, as shown in **Figure 2.** The collision was so violent that part of the Earth's mantle was blasted into orbit around Earth to form the moon.

Reading Check What is the current explanation for the formation of the moon? (See the Appendix for answers to Reading Checks.)

satellite a natural or artificial body that revolves around a planet

Figure 2 Formation of the Moon

❶ Impact
About 4.6 billion years ago, when Earth was still mostly molten, a large body collided with Earth. Scientists reason that the object must have been large enough to blast part of Earth's mantle into space, because the composition of the moon is similar to that of Earth's mantle.

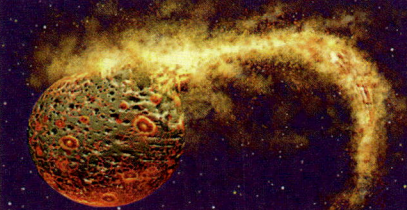

❷ Ejection
The resulting debris began to revolve around the Earth within a few hours of the impact. This debris consisted of mantle material from Earth and from the impacting body as well as part of the iron core of the impacting body.

❸ Formation
Soon after the giant impact, the clumps of material ejected into orbit around Earth began to join together to form the moon. Much later, as the moon cooled, additional impacts created deep basins and fractured the moon's surface. Lunar lava flowed from those cracks and flooded the basins to form the lunar maria that we see today.

Answer to Reading Check
The moon formed from a piece of Earth's mantle, which broke off during a collision between Earth and a large object.

Teach

READING STRATEGY — GENERAL

Prediction Guide Before students read this page, ask the following questions: "Where did the moon come from?" and "What evidence is there to support this theory?" As students read the rest of this section, have them construct a chart that describes some of the major moons in our solar system. **LS Logical**

CONNECTION to Physics — ADVANCED

Orbital Motion Every second, the moon travels 1 km in its orbit, but during that second, it also falls about 14 mm toward the Earth. Because of the moon's velocity and the pull of gravity, the moon travels along a path that follows the curved surface of the Earth. This condition, known as *free fall,* keeps the moon in orbit around the Earth. Explain to students that the condition of free fall, or weightlessness, does not mean that there is no gravity. The Earth's gravity acts on the moon in the same way gravity acts on an apple that falls from a tree. The difference is that the moon, unlike the apple, is moving forward much, much faster than it is falling. Use the transparency entitled "Projectile Motion" to help students understand the moon's orbit. **LS Logical**

Section 4 • Moons

Teach, continued

ACTIVITY — GENERAL

Modeling the Earth and Moon
Pick three volunteers. One will be the moon, another will be Earth, and the third will be the sun. Have the sun stand 5 m from Earth and hold a bright flashlight. Instruct the moon to stand 1 m away from Earth. Tell the moon to slowly orbit Earth, keeping his or her face turned toward Earth. Have the sun turn on the flashlight and point the light toward Earth and the moon. Darken the room. Ask students:

- How much of the moon is lit by the flashlight? (half)
- When the moon is between Earth and the sun, what phase is the moon in? (new)

As the moon moves around Earth, ask the students which phase is being demonstrated by the moon's motion and the pattern of light on the moon.
English Language Learners
LS Visual/Kinesthetic

CONNECTION ACTIVITY
Language Arts — BASIC

Which Is Waxing? Students may have a difficult time remembering how to tell whether the moon is *waxing* or *waning*. To help students remember, have them develop a mnemonic device such as the following: "Light on the left is leaving, light on the right is returning." (Note: This statement is true only when you are studying a diagram of the moon's orbit.) **LS Verbal**

phase the change in the sunlit area of one celestial body as seen from another celestial body

Figure 3 The positions of the moon, sun, and Earth determine which phase the moon is in. The photo insets show how the moon looks from Earth at each phase.

Phases of the Moon

From Earth, one of the most noticeable aspects of the moon is its continually changing appearance. Within a month, the moon's Earthward face changes from a fully lit circle to a thin crescent and then back to a circle. These different appearances of the moon result from its changing position relative to Earth and the sun. As the moon revolves around Earth, the amount of sunlight on the side of the moon that faces Earth changes. The different appearances of the moon due to its changing position are called **phases.** The phases of the moon are shown in **Figure 3**.

Waxing and Waning

When the moon is *waxing,* the sunlit fraction that we can see from Earth is getting larger. When the moon is *waning,* the sunlit fraction is getting smaller. Notice in **Figure 3** that even as the phases of the moon change, the total amount of sunlight that the moon gets remains the same. Half the moon is always in sunlight, just as half the Earth is always in sunlight. But because the moon's period of rotation is the same as its period of revolution, on Earth you always see the same side of the moon. If you lived on the far side of the moon, you would see the sun for half of each lunar day, but you would never see the Earth!

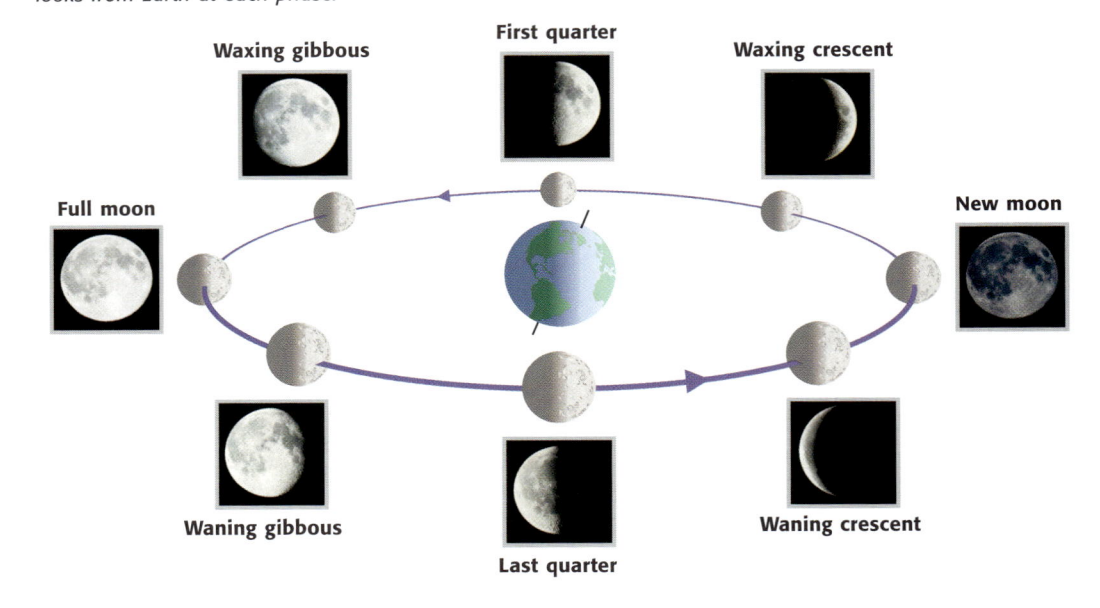

Waxing gibbous — First quarter — Waxing crescent
Full moon — New moon
Waning gibbous — Last quarter — Waning crescent

CHAPTER RESOURCES
Technology
Transparencies
• Phases of the Moon

Is That a Fact!
Waxing means "growing," and *waning* means "shrinking." In the first quarter of a lunar phase, the moon is one-quarter of the way through its cycle of phases. At this point, sunlight is shining on the right half of the moon. During the last quarter, sunlight is shining on the left half of the moon.

Chapter 21 • A Family of Planets

Solar eclipse

NEVER look directly at the sun! You can permanently damage your eyes.

Eclipses

When the shadow of one celestial body falls on another, an **eclipse** occurs. A *solar eclipse* happens when the moon comes between Earth and the sun and the shadow of the moon falls on part of Earth. A *lunar eclipse* happens when Earth comes between the sun and the moon and the shadow of Earth falls on the moon.

Solar Eclipses

Because the moon's orbit is elliptical, the distance between the moon and the Earth changes. During an *annular eclipse*, the moon is farther from the Earth. The disk of the moon does not completely cover the disk of the sun. A thin ring of the sun shows around the moon's outer edge. When the moon is closer to the Earth, the moon appears to be the same size as the sun. During a *total solar eclipse*, the disk of the moon completely covers the disk of the sun, as shown in **Figure 4**.

✓ **Reading Check** Describe what happens during a solar eclipse.

Figure 4 On the left is a diagram of the positions of the Earth and the moon during a solar eclipse. On the right is a picture of the sun's outer atmosphere, or corona, which is visible only when the entire disk of the sun is blocked by the moon.

eclipse an event in which the shadow of one celestial body falls on another

Quick Lab

Clever Insight

1. Cut out a circle of **heavy, white paper**. This circle will represent Earth.
2. Find **two spherical objects** and **several other objects** of different shapes.
3. Hold up each object in front of a **lamp** (which represents the sun) so that the object's shadow falls on the white paper circle.
4. Rotate your objects in all directions, and record the shapes of the shadows that the objects make.
5. Which objects always cast a curved shadow?

CONNECTION ACTIVITY
Math — GENERAL

The Geometry of an Eclipse
To better understand the uniqueness of a solar eclipse on Earth, have students calculate the following:

- What is the ratio of the moon's diameter (3,476 km) to the sun's diameter (1,392,000 km)? (1:400)
- What is the ratio of their distances from Earth if the moon is about 384,000 km from Earth and the sun is about 150,000,000 km from Earth? (1:390)

Help students understand that although the sun is 400 times larger than the moon, because Earth is nearly 400 times closer to the moon than to the sun, the moon is able to completely block our view of the sun.
LS Logical

Cultural Awareness — ADVANCED

Naming the Full Moon
Students may be surprised to learn that every full moon has a name. The most familiar moon is the harvest moon, which occurs in the fall. Have students find out about the names of the full moons, such as the hunter's moon or the sap moon, and report on the origins of the names. **LS** Verbal

---

Quick Lab

Safety Caution: Strongly caution students against looking directly at the sun (especially through binoculars or a telescope). Explain that doing so can result in permanent damage to their eyes or even blindness.

Answer

5. Spherical objects always cast a curved shadow.

Answer to Reading Check
During a solar eclipse, the moon blocks out the sun and casts a shadow on Earth.

Section 4 • Moons

Teach, continued

BRAIN FOOD

Why Are Moons Round?
Like planets, most moons are spherical in shape. Why aren't some moons square, tube shaped, or pyramidal? The force of gravity and the origin of celestial bodies have something to do with the answer. As the mass of an object increases, the gravitational force that it exerts also increases. When a rocky object reaches a diameter of about 350 km, the gravitational force becomes greater than the strength of the material, and the moon starts to become spherical.

Homework — GENERAL

NASA in the News NASA is planning several missions to explore the moons of different planets. Have students select one of NASA's projects and find out what was discovered or what NASA hopes to find. Have students imagine that they are reporters assigned to the project. Have them write a newspaper article with the details of the project. **LS Verbal**

Figure 5 On the left, you can see that the moon can have a reddish color during a lunar eclipse. On the right, you can see the positions of Earth and the moon during a lunar eclipse.

Lunar Eclipses

As shown in **Figure 5**, the view during a lunar eclipse is spectacular. Earth's atmosphere acts like a lens and bends some of the sunlight into the Earth's shadow. When sunlight hits the particles in the atmosphere, blue light is filtered out. As a result, most of the remaining light that lights the moon is red.

The Tilted Orbit of the Moon

You may be wondering why you don't see solar and lunar eclipses every month. The reason is that the moon's orbit around Earth is tilted—by about 5°—relative to the orbit of Earth around the sun. This tilt is enough to place the moon out of Earth's shadow for most full moons and Earth out of the moon's shadow for most new moons.

✓ **Reading Check** Explain why you don't see solar and lunar eclipses every month.

The Moons of Other Planets

The moons of the other planets range in size from very small to as large as terrestrial planets. All of the gas giants have multiple moons, and scientists are still discovering new moons. Some moons have very elongated, or elliptical, orbits, and some moons even orbit their planet backward! Many of the very small moons may be captured asteroids. As scientists are learning from recent space missions, moons may be some of the most bizarre and interesting places in the solar system!

CHAPTER RESOURCES

Technology

Transparencies
• Solar Eclipse; Lunar Eclipse

Answer to Reading Check

We don't see solar and lunar eclipses every month because the moon's orbit around Earth is tilted.

The Moons of Mars

Mars's two moons, Phobos and Deimos, are small, oddly shaped satellites. Both moons are very dark. Their surface materials are much like those of some asteroids—large, rocky bodies in space. Scientists think that these two moons are asteroids caught by Mars's gravity.

The Moons of Jupiter

Jupiter has dozens of moons. The four largest moons—Ganymede, Callisto, Io, and Europa—were discovered in 1610 by Galileo. They are known as the *Galilean satellites*. The largest moon, Ganymede, is even larger than the planet Mercury! Many of the smaller moons probably are captured asteroids.

The Galilean satellite closest to Jupiter is Io, a truly bizarre world. Io is caught in a gravitational tug of war between Jupiter and Io's nearest neighbor, the moon Europa. This constant tugging stretches Io a little and causes it to heat up. As a result, Io is the most volcanically active body in the solar system!

Recent pictures of the moon Europa, shown in **Figure 6,** support the idea that liquid water may lie beneath the moon's icy surface. This idea makes many scientists wonder if life could have evolved in the underground oceans of Europa.

Figure 6 *Europa, Jupiter's fourth largest moon, might have liquid water beneath the moon's icy surface.*

The Moons of Saturn

Like Jupiter, Saturn has dozens of moons. Most of these moons are small bodies that are made mostly of frozen water but contain some rocky material. The largest satellite, Titan, was discovered in 1655 by Christiaan Huygens. In 1980, the *Voyager 1* spacecraft flew past Titan and discovered a hazy orange atmosphere, as shown in **Figure 7.** Earth's early atmosphere may have been much like Titan's is now. In 1997, NASA launched the *Cassini* spacecraft to study Saturn and its moons, including Titan. By studying Titan, scientists hope to learn more about how life began on Earth.

Figure 7 *Titan is Saturn's largest moon.*

✓ Reading Check How can scientists learn more about how life began on Earth by studying Titan?

CONNECTION to Life Science — ADVANCED

Is There Life Out There? Life as we know it requires liquid water. If liquid water exists on other planets or their moons, it is possible that there are also living organisms there. Scientists have been studying a group of organisms called *extremophiles* for clues about what extraterrestrial life might be like. Extremophiles are organisms that live in extreme environments, such as deep-ocean volcanic vents, hot springs, or highly acidic or basic environments. Scientists hope that studying these organisms will help in their search for life elsewhere in the solar system. Some of the most likely places to search for evidence of life are Mars and some of the moons of Jupiter. Have interested students find out about the status of NASA projects that are searching for extraterrestrial life and about organisms classified as extremophiles. **LS Verbal**

Answer to Reading Check
Because Titan's atmosphere is similar to the atmosphere on Earth before life evolved, scientists can study Titan's atmosphere to learn about the conditions under which life began.

Is That a Fact!

Io, one of Jupiter's moons, is well known for the volcanoes on its surface. These volcanoes regularly erupt yellow and red clouds of sulfur up to 300 km above the surface!

Section 4 • Moons

Close

Reteaching — BASIC
Modeling Eclipses Have students describe the location of the moon in relation to Earth and the sun during solar and lunar eclipses. Have them demonstrate the positions using paper cutouts to represent the sun, the moon, and Earth.
LS **Verbal/Visual**

Quiz — GENERAL

1. What characteristic of Earth's moon supports the current theory of its formation? (The moon has a composition similar to that of Earth's mantle.)

2. Why doesn't a solar eclipse occur every month? (because the moon's orbit around Earth is titled, which places Earth out of the moon's shadow for most new moons)

3. What is the difference between an annular eclipse and a total solar eclipse? (During an annular eclipse, the moon is farther from Earth and doesn't completely cover the disk of the sun. During a total solar eclipse, the moon completely covers the sun.)

Alternative Assessment — GENERAL

Moon Mission Have students research the moons of a planet other than Earth and write a short paper about them. LS **Verbal**

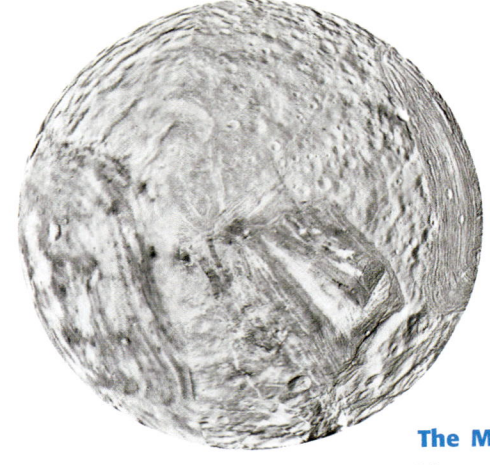

Figure 8 This Voyager 2 image shows Miranda, the most unusual moon of Uranus. Its patchwork terrain indicates that it has had a violent history.

The Moons of Uranus

Uranus has several moons. Like the moons of Saturn, Uranus's largest moons are made of ice and rock and are heavily cratered. The small moon Miranda, shown in **Figure 8**, has some of the strangest features in the solar system. Miranda's surface has smooth, cratered plains as well as regions that have grooves and cliffs. Scientists think that Miranda may have been hit and broken apart in the past. Gravity pulled the pieces together again, leaving a patchwork surface.

The Moons of Neptune

Neptune has several known moons, only one of which is large. This large moon, Triton, is shown in **Figure 9**. It revolves around the planet in a *retrograde*, or "backward," orbit. This orbit suggests that Triton may have been captured by Neptune's gravity. Triton has a very thin atmosphere made mostly of nitrogen gas. Triton's surface is mostly frozen nitrogen and methane. *Voyager 2* images reveal that Triton is geologically active. "Ice volcanoes," or geysers, eject nitrogen gas high into the atmosphere. The other moons of Neptune are small, rocky worlds much like the smaller moons of Saturn and Jupiter.

The Moon of Pluto

Pluto's only known moon, Charon, was discovered in 1978. Charon's period of revolution is the same as Pluto's period of rotation—about 6.4 days. So, one side of Pluto always faces Charon. In other words, if you stood on the surface of Pluto, Charon would always occupy the same place in the sky. Charon's orbit around Pluto is tilted relative to Pluto's orbit around the sun. As a result, Pluto, as seen from Earth, is sometimes eclipsed by Charon. But don't hold your breath; this eclipse happens only once every 120 years!

✓**Reading Check** How often is Pluto eclipsed by Charon?

Figure 9 This Voyager 2 image shows Neptune's largest moon, Triton. The polar icecap currently facing the sun may have a slowly evaporating layer of nitrogen ice, adding to Triton's thin atmosphere.

Answer to Reading Check
Pluto is eclipsed by Charon every 120 years.

SECTION Review

Summary

- Scientists reason that the moon formed from the debris that was created after a large body collided with Earth.
- As the moon revolves around Earth, the amount of sunlight on the side of the moon changes. Because the amount of sunlight on the side of the moon changes, the moon's appearance from Earth changes. These changes in appearance are the phases of the moon.
- A solar eclipse happens when the shadow of the moon falls on Earth.
- A lunar eclipse happens when the shadow of Earth falls on the moon.
- Mars has 2 moons: Phobos and Deimos.
- Jupiter has dozens of moons. Ganymede, Io, Callisto, and Europa are the largest.
- Saturn has dozens of moons. Titan is the largest.
- Uranus has several moons.
- Neptune has several moons. Triton is the largest.
- Pluto has 1 known moon, Charon.

Using Key Terms

Complete each of the following sentences by choosing the correct term from the word bank.

satellite   eclipse

1. A(n) ____, or a body that revolves around a larger body, can be either artificial or natural.
2. A(n) ____ occurs when the shadow of one body in space falls on another body.

Understanding Key Ideas

3. Which of the following is a Galilean satellite?
   a. Phobos
   b. Deimos
   c. Ganymede
   d. Charon
4. Describe the current theory for the origin of Earth's moon.
5. What is the difference between a solar eclipse and a lunar eclipse?
6. What causes the phases of Earth's moon?

Critical Thinking

7. **Analyzing Methods** How can astronomers use the age of a lunar rock to estimate the age of the surface of a planet such as Mercury?
8. **Identifying Relationships** Charon stays in the same place in Pluto's sky, but the moon moves across Earth's sky. What causes this difference?

Interpreting Graphics

Use the diagram below to answer the questions that follow.

9. What type of eclipse is shown in the diagram?
10. Describe what is happening in the diagram.
11. Make a sketch of the type of eclipse that is not shown in the diagram.

SciLinks
Developed and maintained by the National Science Teachers Association
For a variety of links related to this chapter, go to www.scilinks.org
Topic: Moons of Other Planets
SciLinks code: HSM0993

CHAPTER RESOURCES

Chapter Resource File
- Section Quiz GENERAL
- Section Review GENERAL
- Vocabulary and Section Summary GENERAL
- Reinforcement Worksheet BASIC
- Datasheet for Quick Lab

Answers to Section Review
1. satellite
2. eclipse
3. c
4. The current theory for the origin of the moon is that a large, Mars-sized body collided with Earth during Earth's formation. The collision ejected part of Earth's mantle into orbit around Earth. This material became the moon.
5. Sample answer: During a lunar eclipse, Earth comes between the sun and the moon, and Earth's shadow falls on the moon. During a solar eclipse, the moon comes between Earth and the sun, and the moon's shadow falls on Earth.
6. Lunar phases result from the moon's changing position relative to Earth and the sun. As the moon orbits Earth, the amount of sunlight on the side of the moon that faces Earth changes.
7. Answers may vary. Sample answer: Dating the lunar rock will determine the age of the moon. Then, scientists can compare the amount of cratering on the moon's surface with the amount of cratering on Mercury's surface to estimate the age of Mercury.
8. Sample answer: Charon's period of revolution is about the same as Pluto's period of rotation. So, Charon remains in a fixed position in Pluto's sky. The moon's period of revolution is not the same as Earth's period of rotation, so the moon moves across Earth's sky.
9. a solar eclipse
10. The moon is between Earth and the sun. The moon is casting a shadow on Earth. As viewed from Earth, the sun would be obscured by the moon.
11. Sketches should illustrate a lunar eclipse.

Section 4 • Moons

SECTION 5

Focus

Overview
This section explores the minor bodies of the solar system, including comets, asteroids, and meteoroids.

Bellringer
Ask students if scientists have ever brought extraterrestrial material to Earth. (The only samples came from the moon missions.) Then, point out that scientists have studied rocks from Mars and other parts of the solar system. Ask students how scientists obtained these rocks. (The rocks are meteorites.)

Motivate

Demonstration — GENERAL

Modeling Comets To simulate a comet and its tail, mix 2 cups of water, 2 tbsp of dirt, and a few pebbles in a container. While wearing protective gloves, crush 2 cups of dry ice in a plastic bag. Slowly pour the liquid mixture into the bag, mixing constantly. Mold this mixture to produce a model comet. Spread plastic over your work area, and place the comet on top of an inverted foam cup. Use a hair dryer to simulate the solar wind that produces a comet's tail when a comet approaches the sun.
LS Visual/Kinesthetic

SECTION 5

READING WARM-UP

Objectives
- Explain why comets, asteroids, and meteoroids are important to the study of the formation of the solar system.
- Describe the similarities of and differences between asteroids and meteoroids.
- Explain how cosmic impacts may affect life on Earth.

Terms to Learn
comet   meteoroid
asteroid   meteorite
asteroid belt   meteor

READING STRATEGY

Discussion Read this section silently. Write down questions that you have about this section. Discuss your questions in a small group.

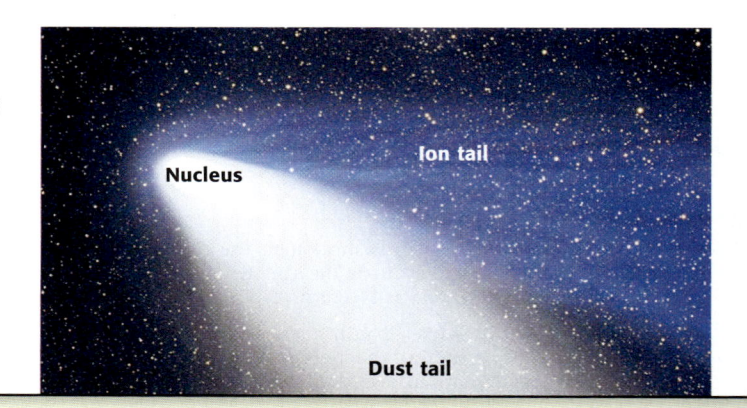

Figure 1 This image shows the physical features of a comet when it is close to the sun. The nucleus of a comet is hidden by brightly lit gases and dust.

CHAPTER RESOURCES

Chapter Resource File
- Lesson Plan
- Directed Reading A BASIC
- Directed Reading B SPECIAL NEEDS

Technology
- Transparencies
- Bellringer

Small Bodies in the Solar System

Imagine you are traveling in a spacecraft to explore the edge of our solar system. You see several small bodies, as well as the planets and their satellites, moving through space.

The solar system contains not only planets and moons but other small bodies, including comets, asteroids, and meteoroids. Scientists study these objects to learn about the composition of the solar system.

Comets

A small body of ice, rock, and cosmic dust loosely packed together is called a **comet**. Some scientists refer to comets as "dirty snowballs" because of their composition. Comets formed in the cold, outer solar system. Nothing much has happened to comets since the birth of the solar system 4.6 billion years ago. Comets are probably left over from the time when the planets formed. As a result, each comet is a sample of the early solar system. Scientists want to learn more about comets to piece together the history of our solar system.

Comet Tails

When a comet passes close enough to the sun, solar radiation heats the ice so that the comet gives off gas and dust in the form of a long tail, as shown in **Figure 1**. Sometimes, a comet has two tails—an *ion tail* and a *dust tail*. The ion tail is made of electrically charged particles called *ions*. The solid center of a comet is called its *nucleus*. Comet nuclei can range in size from less than half a kilometer to more than 100 km in diameter.

Is That a Fact!

Comets are fairly fragile; some break apart on their own, or the gravity of a planet can pull them apart. For example, comet Shoemaker-Levy 9 broke apart when it passed too close to Jupiter. When Shoemaker-Levy 9 returned in 1994, fragments of the comet crashed into Jupiter's atmosphere. Some of the fragments generated explosions that produced fireballs larger than Earth.

668 Chapter 21 • A Family of Planets

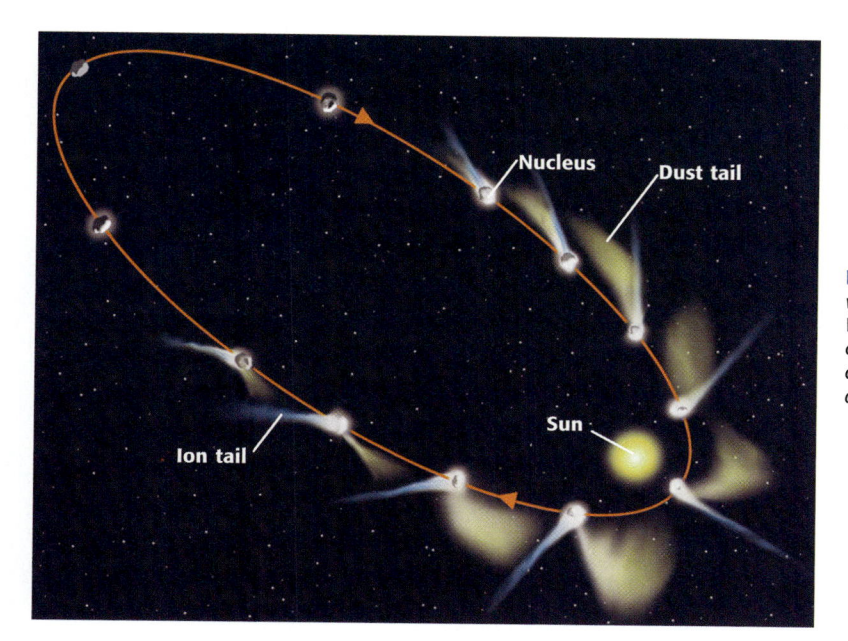

Figure 2 Comets have very elongated orbits. When a comet gets close to the sun, the comet can develop one or two tails.

Comet Orbits

The orbits of all bodies that move around the sun are ellipses. *Ellipses* are circles that are somewhat stretched out of shape. The orbits of most planets are close to perfect circles, but the orbits of comets are very elongated.

Notice in **Figure 2** that a comet's ion tail always points away from the sun. The reason is that the ion tail is blown away from the sun by *solar wind*, which is also made of ions. The dust tail tends to follow the comet's orbit around the sun. Dust tails do not always point away from the sun. When a comet is close to the sun, its tail can extend millions of kilometers through space!

Comet Origins

Where do comets come from? Many scientists think that comets come from the Oort (AWRT) cloud, a spherical region that surrounds the solar system. When the gravity of a passing planet or star disturbs part of this cloud, comets can be pulled toward the sun. Another recently discovered region where comets exist is the Kuiper (KIE puhr) belt, which is the region outside the orbit of Neptune.

Reading Check From which two regions do comets come? (See the Appendix for answers to Reading Checks.)

comet a small body of ice, rock, and cosmic dust that follows an elliptical orbit around the sun and that gives off gas and dust in the form of a tail as it passes close to the sun

CONNECTION TO Language Arts

WRITING SKILL **Interplanetary Journalist** In 1994, the world watched in awe as parts of the comet Shoemaker-Levy 9 collided with Jupiter, which caused enormous explosions. Imagine you were an interplanetary journalist who traveled through space to observe the comet during this time. Write an article describing your adventure.

Teach

BRAIN FOOD

Comets Versus Asteroids In the past, the primary distinction between a comet and an asteroid was that comets have ice and asteroids do not. The development of sophisticated telescopes and remote-sensing instruments has challenged this distinction. There is evidence that some asteroids may contain ice and that some asteroids develop comet tails. Also, some comets have stopped producing tails and are beginning to look more like asteroids! In general, comets contain enough ice to become "active" and develop a tail, and asteroids do not. Asteroids range in size from a few kilometers to about 1,000 km across, but comet nuclei are rarely larger than 100 km.

Homework — GENERAL

Concept Mapping Have students create a concept map using at the vocabulary terms from this section. Tell them that their map should illustrate logical connections between the terms they choose.
LS Logical/Visual

Answer to Reading Check
Comets come from the Oort cloud and the Kuiper belt.

MISCONCEPTION ALERT

Comet Tails Students may be surprised to learn that comets don't have a tail during most of their orbit. Only when they near the sun do they warm up and release a tail made of gas and dust. The comet nucleus has an irregular shape. Sometimes, gas leaves the comet's surface unevenly in "jets." These jets can act like miniature rocket engines, pushing a comet off course and making it difficult to find during its next orbit.

Section 5 • Small Bodies in the Solar System

Teach, continued

BRAIN FOOD

Tracking Asteroids The orbits of some asteroids cross Earth's orbit. Every few million years, one of these asteroids hits the Earth. If an asteroid is larger than 10 km across, its impact can have catastrophic global effects. In the first few seconds of an impact event, both the impactor and part of the target become liquid, and an impact crater forms. Shock waves spread out from the site, and debris is ejected high into the atmosphere. About 65 million years ago, a large asteroid struck Earth on the Yucatán Peninsula. This event may have led to the mass extinction of the dinosaurs. The collision of comet Shoemaker-Levy 9 with Jupiter in 1994 led NASA to devote more of its resources to finding and tracking asteroids whose orbits cross Earth's. Have students find out more about NASA's asteroid-tracking program.

asteroid a small, rocky object that orbits the sun, usually in a band between the orbits of Mars and Jupiter

asteroid belt the region of the solar system that is between the orbits of Mars and Jupiter and in which most asteroids orbit

Asteroids

Small, rocky bodies that revolve around the sun are called **asteroids**. They range in size from a few meters to more than 900 km in diameter. Asteroids have irregular shapes, although some of the larger ones are spherical. Most asteroids orbit the sun in the asteroid belt. The **asteroid belt** is a wide region between the orbits of Mars and Jupiter. Like comets, asteroids are thought to be material left over from the formation of the solar system.

Types of Asteroids

The composition of asteroids varies depending on where they are located within the asteroid belt. In the outermost region of the asteroid belt, asteroids have dark reddish brown to black surfaces. This coloring may indicate that the asteroids are rich in organic material. Asteroids that have dark gray surfaces are rich in carbon. In the innermost part of the asteroid belt are light gray asteroids that have either a stony or metallic composition. **Figure 3** shows three asteroids: Hektor, Ceres, and Vesta.

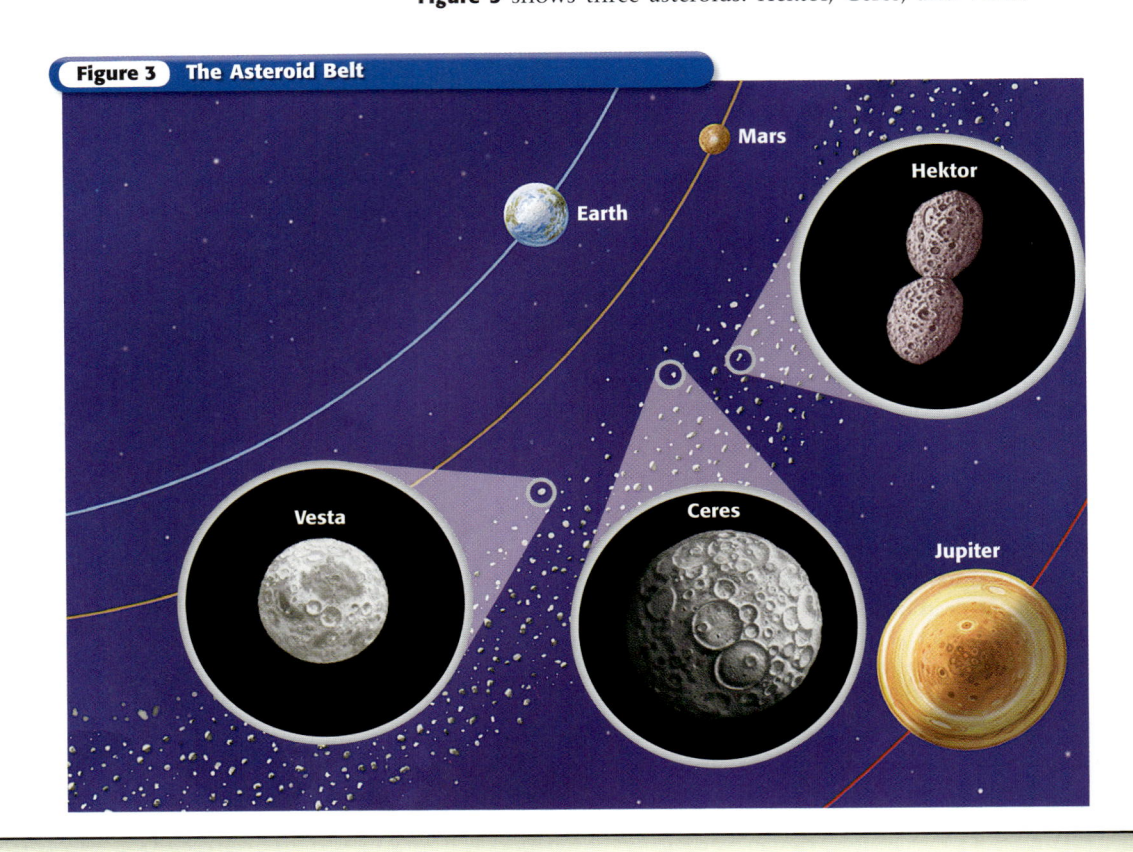

Figure 3 The Asteroid Belt

WEIRD SCIENCE

In 1908, an object thought to be a comet about 60 m in diameter exploded less than 10 km above a remote part of Siberia. The blast flattened trees in an area greater than 2,000 km². The crater has never been found.

Meteoroids

Meteoroids are similar to but much smaller than asteroids. A **meteoroid** is a small, rocky body that revolves around the sun. Most meteoroids are probably pieces of asteroids. A meteoroid that enters Earth's atmosphere and strikes the ground is called a **meteorite.** As a meteoroid falls into Earth's atmosphere, the meteoroid moves so fast that its surface melts. As the meteoroid burns up, it gives off an enormous amount of light and thermal energy. From the ground, you see a spectacular streak of light, or a shooting star. A **meteor** is the bright streak of light caused by a meteoroid or comet dust burning up in the atmosphere.

meteoroid a relatively small, rocky body that travels through space

meteorite a meteoroid that reaches the Earth's surface without burning up completely

meteor a bright streak of light that results when a meteoroid burns up in the Earth's atmosphere

Meteor Showers

Many of the meteors that we see come from very small (dust-sized to pebble-sized) rocks. Even so, meteors can be seen on almost any night if you are far enough away from a city to avoid the glare of its lights. At certain times of the year, you can see large numbers of meteors, as shown in **Figure 4.** These events are called *meteor showers*. Meteor showers happen when Earth passes through the dusty debris that comets leave behind.

Types of Meteorites

Like their asteroid relatives, meteorites have different compositions. The three major types of meteorites—stony, metallic, and stony-iron meteorites—are shown in **Figure 5.** Many of the stony meteorites probably come from carbon-rich asteroids. Stony meteorites may contain organic materials and water. Scientists use meteorites to study the early solar system. Like comets and asteroids, meteorites are some of the building blocks of planets.

Reading Check What are the major types of meteorites?

Figure 4 Meteors are the streaks of light caused by meteoroids as they burn up in Earth's atmosphere.

Figure 5 Three Major Types of Meteorites

Stony meteorite rocky material

Metallic meteorite iron and nickel

Stony-iron meteorite rocky material, iron, and nickel

Answer to Reading Check
The major types of meteorites are stony, metallic, and stony-iron meteorites.

SCIENTISTS AT ODDS

What Are Meteorites? As late as the 1800s, scientists were skeptical that meteorites originate in space—despite records from the Chinese, Romans, and Greeks describing stones falling from the sky. In 1803, meteorites fell in France. A physicist documented the event, finally convincing scientists that meteorites fall from the sky.

INCLUSION Strategies

- Hearing Impaired
- Developmentally Delayed

List the terms *meteoroid, meteor,* and *meteorite* on the board. For each of the terms, have students define the word, use it in a sentence, and draw an illustration. (A meteoroid is a small rocky body that orbits the sun. A meteor is the bright streak of light that we see when a meteoroid enters Earth's atmosphere. A meteorite is a meteoroid that does not burn up completely and lands on the Earth's surface.)

Verbal/Visual — English Language Learners

ACTIVITY — GENERAL

Collecting Micrometeorites
Earth's atmosphere is constantly bombarded with microscopic meteorites that are too small to burn up. These micrometeorites float in the atmosphere and eventually settle to the ground. The best time to collect micrometeorites is after a meteor shower. Clean a small glass dish, and place it outside to collect rainwater. If you live in an area with little rain, fill the dish with distilled water and place it outside for several days. Place a small, strong magnet in a small plastic bag, and sweep the covered magnet slowly through the water, along the bottom and sides of the dish. Place the covered magnet in a second pan of distilled water, and remove the magnet, shaking the bag in the water to dislodge any particles. Evaporate the water over a hot plate, and drag a magnetized needle across the sides and bottom of the dish. Tap the needle onto a microscope slide, and examine the sediment with a microscope—any rounded and pitted metallic particles are probably micrometeorites. **Kinesthetic**

Section 5 • Small Bodies in the Solar System

Close

Reteaching — BASIC
Draw a diagram of a comet on the board. Ask volunteers to label the parts and to describe the composition of each part.
LS Visual/Kinesthetic — English Language Learners

Quiz — GENERAL
Have students complete the following sentences:

1. ____ are small bodies of ice and cosmic dust. (Comets)
2. Most asteroids in our solar system are found between ____ and ____. (Mars, Jupiter)
3. ____ are meteoroids that fall to Earth. (Meteorites)

Alternative Assessment — GENERAL

Field Guide to the Solar System Have students create an illustrated field guide to small bodies in our solar system. The guide should incorporate all of the vocabulary used in this section as well as drawings, diagrams, and explanations for each object they include. **LS Visual** — English Language Learners

---

CONNECTION TO Biology

WRITING SKILL **Mass Extinctions** Throughout Earth's history, there have been times when large numbers of species suddenly became extinct. Many scientists think that these mass extinctions may have been caused by impacts of large objects on Earth. However, other scientists are not so sure. Use the Internet or another source to research this idea. In your **science journal**, write a paragraph describing the different theories scientists have for past mass extinctions.

Figure 6 The surface of the moon preserves a record of billions of years of cosmic impacts.

WEIRD SCIENCE

In 1954, Mrs. E. Hulitt Hodge, of Alabama, was struck by a meteorite as she was taking her afternoon nap. Bruised, but not badly injured, she is one of only two people known to have been struck by a meteorite.

The Role of Impacts in the Solar System

An impact happens when an object in space collides with another object in space. Often, the result of such a collision is an impact crater. Many planets and moons have visible impact craters. In fact, several planets and moons have many more impact craters than Earth does. Planets and moons that do not have atmospheres have more impact craters than do planets and moons that have atmospheres.

Look at **Figure 6**. Earth's moon has many more impact craters than the Earth does because the moon has no atmosphere to slow objects down. Fewer objects strike Earth because Earth's atmosphere acts as a shield. Smaller objects burn up before they ever reach the surface. Also, most craters left on Earth are no longer visible because of weathering, erosion, and tectonic activity.

Future Impacts on Earth?

Most objects that come close to Earth are small and usually burn up in the atmosphere. However, larger objects are more likely to strike Earth's surface. Scientists estimate that impacts that are powerful enough to cause a natural disaster might happen once every few thousand years. An impact that is large enough to cause a global catastrophe is estimated to happen once every few hundred thousand years, on average.

✓ Reading Check How often do large objects strike Earth?

Answer to Reading Check
Large objects strike Earth every few thousand years.

The Torino Scale

The Torino scale is a system that allows scientists to rate the hazard level of an object moving toward Earth. The object is carefully observed and then assigned a number from the scale. The scale ranges from 0 to 10. Zero indicates that the object has a very small chance of striking Earth. Ten indicates that the object will definitely strike Earth and cause a global disaster. The Torino scale is also color coded. White represents 0, and green represents 1. White and green objects rarely strike Earth. Yellow represents 2, 3, and 4 and indicates a higher chance that objects will hit Earth. Orange, which represents 5, 6, and 7, refers to objects highly likely to hit Earth. Red refers to objects that will definitely hit Earth.

SECTION Review

Summary

- Studying comets, asteroids, and meteoroids can help scientists understand more about the formation of the solar system.
- Asteroids are small bodies that orbit the sun. Meteoroids are similar to but smaller than asteroids. Most meteoroids come from asteroids.
- Most objects that collide with Earth burn up in the atmosphere. Large impacts, however, may cause a global catastrophe.

Using Key Terms

For each pair of terms, explain how the meanings of the terms differ.

1. *comet* and *asteroid*
2. *meteor* and *meteorite*

Understanding Key Ideas

3. Which of the following is NOT a type of meteorite?
   a. stony meteorite
   b. rocky-iron meteorite
   c. stony-iron meteorite
   d. metallic meteorite

4. Why is the study of comets, asteroids, and meteoroids important in understanding the formation of the solar system?

5. Why do a comet's two tails often point in different directions?

6. How can a cosmic impact affect life on Earth?

7. What is the difference between an asteroid and a meteoroid?

8. Where is the asteroid belt located?

9. What is the Torino scale?

10. Describe why we see several impact craters on the moon but few on Earth.

Math Skills

11. The diameter of comet A's nucleus is 55 km. If the diameter of comet B's nucleus is 30% larger than comet A's nucleus, what is the diameter of comet B's nucleus?

Critical Thinking

12. **Expressing Opinions** Do you think the government should spend money on programs to search for asteroids and comets that have Earth-crossing orbits? Explain.

13. **Making Inferences** What is the likelihood that scientists will discover an object belonging in the red category of the Torino scale in the next 500 years? Explain your answer.

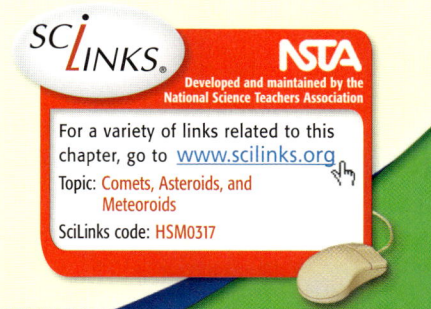

Answers to Section Review

1. Sample answer: A comet is a small body of ice, rock, and dust that forms a tail when it passes close to the sun. An asteroid is a small, rocky body that does not have much ice and does not form a tail.

2. Sample answer. A meteor is a streak of light that results when a meteoroid burns up in Earth's atmosphere. A meteorite is a meteoroid that reaches Earth's surface without burning up completely.

3. b

4. Sample answer: Comets, asteroids, and meteoroids represent the leftover building blocks of the solar system. Studying these bodies will help scientists learn about the composition of the solar system.

5. A comet's ion tail is blown away from the sun by the solar wind, but its dust tail is not. So, a comet's two tails may point in different directions.

6. Answers may vary. Sample answer: A cosmic impact can change the global climate, causing plants and animals not suited to the new climate to die.

7. Sample answer: Meteoroids are similar to asteroids but are much smaller.

8. The asteroid belt is located between Mars and Jupiter.

9. The Torino scale is a system that enables scientists to rate the hazard level of an object moving toward Earth.

10. Answers may vary. Answers should include that most objects burn up in Earth's atmosphere before striking Earth's surface. The moon does not have an atmosphere to slow objects down. In addition, erosion and plate tectonics cause the surface features of Earth to change.

11. 71.5 km
    (55 km × 0.30 = 16.5 km; 55 km + 16.5 km = 71.5 km)

12. Sample answer: yes; Tracking asteroids and comets with Earth-crossing orbits is important because doing so could help people prepare for a possible disaster.

13. Answers may vary. Sample answer: Because large impacts occur every few thousand years, it is somewhat likely that scientists will discover a red-category object in the next 500 years.

CHAPTER RESOURCES

Chapter Resource File
- Section Quiz GENERAL
- Section Review GENERAL
- Vocabulary and Section Summary GENERAL

Inquiry Lab

Create a Calendar

Teacher's Notes

Time Required
One 45-minute class period

Lab Ratings
EASY —————→ HARD

Teacher Prep 🧪🧪
Student Set-Up 🧪
Concept Level 🧪🧪🧪
Clean Up 🧪

MATERIALS
The materials listed on the student page are enough for a group of 2 or 3 students.

Preparation Notes
This activity will require math skills. As a class, you may need to review how to multiply fractions.

As an extension activity, students may research the rotation and revolution of other planets. Students can then create a calendar for one of the other planets.

Using Scientific Methods
Inquiry Lab

Create a Calendar

Imagine that you live in the first colony on Mars. You have been trying to follow the Earth calendar, but it just isn't working anymore. Mars takes almost 2 Earth years to revolve around the sun—almost 687 Earth days to be exact! That means that there are only two Martian seasons for every Earth calendar year. On Mars, in one Earth year, you get winter and spring, but the next year, you get only summer and fall! And Martian days are longer than Earth days. Mars takes 24.6 Earth hours to rotate on its axis. Although they are similar, Earth days and Martian days just don't match. You need a new calendar!

OBJECTIVES

Create a calendar based on the Martian cycles of rotation and revolution.

Describe why it is useful to have a calendar that matches the cycles of the planet on which you live.

MATERIALS
- calculator (optional)
- marker
- pencils, assorted colors
- poster board
- ruler, metric

Ask a Question

1. How can I create a calendar based on the Martian cycles of rotation and revolution that includes months, weeks, and days?

Form a Hypothesis

2. Write a few sentences that answer your question.

Test the Hypothesis

3. Use the following formulas to determine the number of Martian days in a Martian year:

$$\frac{687 \text{ Earth days}}{1 \text{ Martian year}} \times \frac{24 \text{ Earth hours}}{1 \text{ Earth day}} = \text{Earth hours per Martian year}$$

$$\text{Earth hours per Martian year} \times \frac{1 \text{ Martian day}}{24.6 \text{ Earth hours}} = \text{Martian days per Martian year}$$

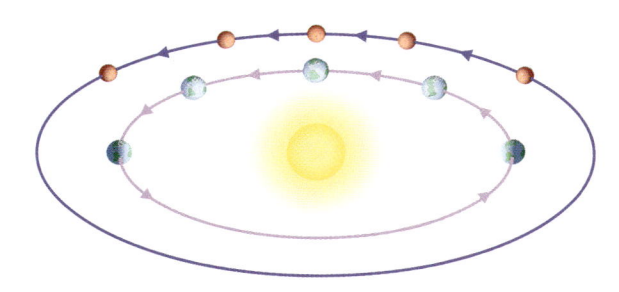

Michael E. Kral
West Hardin Middle School
Cecilia, Kentucky

CHAPTER RESOURCES

Chapter Resource File
- Datasheet for Chapter Lab
- Lab Notes and Answers

Technology
- Classroom Videos
  - Lab Video

LabBook
- Why Do They Wander?
- Phases of the Moon
- Eclipses

674 Chapter 21 • A Family of Planets

4. Decide how to divide your calendar into a system of Martian months, weeks, and days. Will you have a leap day, a leap week, a leap month, or a leap year? How often will it occur?

5. Choose names for the months and days of your calendar. Explain why you chose each name. If you have time, explain how you would number the Martian years. For instance, would the first year correspond to a certain Earth year?

6. Follow your design to create your own calendar for Mars. Construct your calendar by using a computer to help organize your data. Draw the calendar on your piece of poster board. Make sure it is brightly colored and easy to follow.

7. Present your calendar to the class. Explain how you chose your months, weeks, and days.

Analyze the Results

1. **Analyzing Results** What advantages does your calendar design have? Are there any disadvantages to your design?

2. **Classifying** Which student or group created the most original calendar? Which design was the most useful? Explain.

3. **Analyzing Results** What might you do to improve your calendar?

Draw Conclusions

4. **Evaluating Models** Take a class vote to decide which design should be chosen as the new calendar for Mars. Why was this calendar chosen? How did it differ from the other designs?

5. **Drawing Conclusions** Why is it useful to have a calendar that matches the cycles of the planet on which you live?

Test the Hypothesis

7. Accept all reasonable responses. Students should have used the formula in the procedure to calculate the number of days in a Martian year. There are 670.24 Martian days in a Martian year. Students should explain the system they used for grouping Martian days into weeks and months.

Analyze the Results

1. Accept all reasonable responses. Sample answer: A calendar with a leap year that has one extra day every four Martian years would be less confusing than having leap days with extra hours every year.

2. Accept all reasonable responses.

3. Accept all reasonable responses. Sample answer: An improvement might be to divide the Martian year into 10 months with 67 days per month. Students may suggest simplifying their design

Draw Conclusions

4. Accept all reasonable responses.

5. Accept all reasonable responses. Sample answer: It would be difficult to keep track of the changing seasons of a planet using a calendar that doesn't match the period of revolution of the planet.

CHAPTER RESOURCES

Workbooks

- **Whiz-Bang Demonstrations**
  - Crater Creator BASIC
  - Space Snowballs BASIC
- **Labs You Can Eat**
  - Meteorite Delight ADVANCED
- **Long-Term Projects & Research Ideas**
  - What Did You See, Mr. Messier? ADVANCED

Chapter Review

Assignment Guide

Section	Questions
1	1, 4, 12–13
2	6, 11, 16–18
3	26
4	7, 19-20, 22, 24–25
5	2-3, 5, 15
2 and 3	9–10, 14, 27–28
2, 3, and 4	8, 23
2, 3, 4, and 5	21

ANSWERS

Using Key Terms

1. Sample answer: The terrestrial planets are the small, rocky planets of the inner solar system. The gas giants are the large, gaseous planets of the outer solar system.
2. Sample answer: Asteroids are small bodies made of rocky material, and comets are small bodies made of ice, rock, and cosmic dust.
3. Sample answer: A meteor is a streak of light that results from a meteoroid burning up in the atmosphere. A meteorite is a meteoroid that has passed through the atmosphere and struck the ground.
4. astronomical unit
5. meteoroid
6. prograde
7. satellite

Understanding Key Ideas
8. d
9. d
10. a
11. d
12. Mercury, Venus, Earth, Mars, Jupiter, Saturn, Uranus, Neptune, and Pluto
13. Sample answer: The inner planets are small, rocky, and closely spaced. The outer planets are large, gaseous, and far apart.
14. Sample answer: The gas giants are the large, gaseous planets of the outer solar system. In contrast, the terrestrial planets are the small, rocky planets of the inner solar system.
15. Asteroids are small bodies made of rocky material. Meteoroids are similar to asteroids, only much smaller.
16. The period of rotation is how long a planet takes to complete a turn on its axis. The period of revolution is how long a planet takes to orbit the sun.

Chapter Review

USING KEY TERMS

For each pair of terms, explain how the meanings of the terms differ.

1. *terrestrial planet* and *gas giant*
2. *asteroid* and *comet*
3. *meteor* and *meteorite*

Complete each of the following sentences by choosing the correct term from the word bank.

astronomical unit	meteorite
meteoroid	prograde
retrograde	satellite

4. The average distance between the sun and Earth is 1 ___.
5. A small rock in space is called a(n) ___.
6. When viewed from above its north pole, a body that moves in a counter-clockwise direction is said to have ___ rotation.
7. A(n) ___ is a natural or artificial body that revolves around a planet.

UNDERSTANDING KEY IDEAS

Multiple Choice

8. Of the following, which is the largest body?
   a. the moon
   b. Pluto
   c. Mercury
   d. Ganymede

9. Which of the following planets have retrograde rotation?
   a. the terrestrial planets
   b. the gas giants
   c. Mercury, Venus, and Uranus
   d. Venus, Uranus, and Pluto

10. Which of the following planets does NOT have any moons?
    a. Mercury
    b. Mars
    c. Uranus
    d. None of the above

11. Why can liquid water NOT exist on the surface of Mars?
    a. The temperature is too high.
    b. Liquid water once existed there.
    c. The gravity of Mars is too weak.
    d. The atmospheric pressure is too low.

Short Answer

12. List the names of the planets in the order the planets orbit the sun.
13. Describe three ways in which the inner planets are different from the outer planets.
14. What are the gas giants? How are the gas giants different from the terrestrial planets?
15. What is the difference between asteroids and meteoroids?
16. What is the difference between a planet's period of rotation and period of revolution?

---

676 Chapter 21 • A Family of Planets

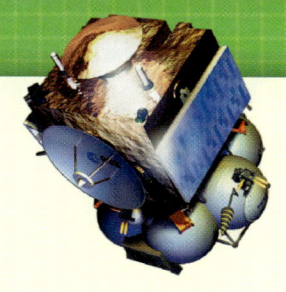

17. Explain the difference between prograde rotation and retrograde rotation.

18. Which characteristics of Earth make it suitable for life?

19. Describe the current theory for the origin of Earth's moon.

20. What causes the phases of the moon?

CRITICAL THINKING

21. **Concept Mapping** Use the following terms to create a concept map: *solar system, terrestrial planets, gas giants, moons, comets, asteroids,* and *meteoroids.*

22. **Applying Concepts** Even though we haven't yet retrieved any rock samples from Mercury's surface for radiometric dating, scientists know that the surface of Mercury is much older than that of Earth. How do scientists know this?

23. **Making Inferences** Where in the solar system might scientists search for life, and why?

24. **Analyzing Ideas** Is the far side of the moon always dark? Explain your answer.

25. **Predicting Consequences** If scientists could somehow bring Europa as close to the sun as the Earth is, 1 AU, how do you think Europa would be affected?

26. **Identifying Relationships** How did variations in the orbit of Uranus help scientists discover Neptune?

INTERPRETING GRAPHICS

The graph below shows density versus mass for Earth, Uranus, and Neptune. Mass is given in Earth masses—the mass of Earth is equal to 1 Earth mass. The relative volumes for the planets are shown by the size of each circle. Use the graph below to answer the questions that follow.

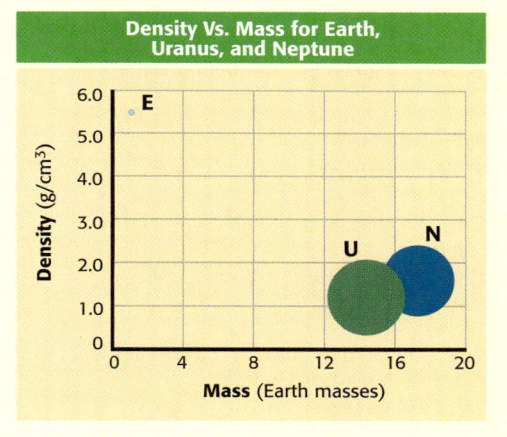

Density Vs. Mass for Earth, Uranus, and Neptune

(Graph showing Density (g/cm³) on y-axis from 0 to 6.0, Mass (Earth masses) on x-axis from 0 to 20. E at mass ~1, density ~5.5; U at mass ~14, density ~1.5; N at mass ~17, density ~1.8)

27. Which planet is denser, Uranus or Neptune? How can you tell?

28. You can see that although Earth has the smallest mass, it has the highest density of the three planets. How can Earth be the densest of the three when Uranus and Neptune have so much more mass than Earth does?

---

17. Prograde rotation is counterclockwise when viewed from a planet's North Pole. Retrograde rotation is clockwise when viewed from a planet's North Pole.

18. Sample answer: The presence of liquid water makes Earth suitable for life. Earth's atmosphere also regulates temperature on Earth.

19. The current theory is that a collision with a Mars-sized object blasted part of Earth's mantle into space. This material formed the moon.

CHAPTER RESOURCES

Chapter Resource File
- Chapter Review GENERAL
- Chapter Test A GENERAL
- Chapter Test B ADVANCED
- Chapter Test C SPECIAL NEEDS
- Vocabulary Activity GENERAL

Workbooks
- Study Guide
- Assessment resources are also available in Spanish.

---

20. Answers may vary. Sample answer: As Earth and the moon revolve together around the sun, the side of the moon facing Earth gets varying amounts of sunlight.

Critical Thinking

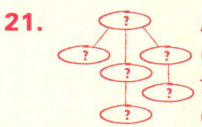

21. An answer to this exercise can be found at the end of this book.

22. Sample answer: Mercury's surface is covered with impact craters that record the planet's history. Earth's surface has only a few craters, indicating that the rocks on Earth's surface are continually recycled.

23. Sample answer: The search for life should include areas where liquid water is present because life as we know it depends on liquid water for survival.

24. Sample answer: no; The far side of the moon gets as much sunlight as the near side. As the moon revolves around Earth, the moon also rotates.

25. Answers will vary. If Europa were closer to the sun, it would heat up considerably. Europa is made mostly of ice, so much of its surface might melt to form oceans and an atmosphere.

26. Sample answer: Neptune's gravitational field prevented Uranus from following its predicted orbit. The irregular orbit of Uranus indicated to scientists that there was something, probably a planet, beyond Uranus.

Interpreting Graphics

27. Neptune is denser. It has a higher density value on the chart. (Neptune has a smaller volume and more mass, giving it a greater density than Uranus.)

28. The masses of Neptune and Uranus occupy a much larger volume than the mass of Earth does. (Density is the amount of mass that exists within a given volume of space.)

Chapter 21 • Chapter Review **677**

Standardized Test Preparation

Teacher's Note

To provide practice under more realistic testing conditions, give students 20 minutes to answer all of the questions in this Standardized Test Preparation.

MISCONCEPTION ALERT

Answers to the standardized test preparation can help you identify student misconceptions and misunderstandings.

READING

Passage 1
1. D
2. F
3. B

TEST DOCTOR

Question 2: None of the answers provided have been specifically stated in the passage. However, students should infer from the statement "After years of observing the sky" that Greek astronomers were both patient and observant.

Passage 2
1. D
2. F

Standardized Test Preparation

READING

Read each of the passages below. Then, answer the questions that follow each passage.

Passage 1 Imagine that it is 200 BCE and you are an apprentice to a Greek astronomer. After years of observing the sky, the astronomer knows all of the constellations as well as the back of his hand. He shows you how the stars all move together—the whole sky spins slowly as the night goes on. He also shows you that among the thousands of stars in the sky, some of the brighter ones slowly change their position relative to the other stars. He names these stars *planetai*, the Greek word for "wanderers." Building on the observations of the ancient Greeks, we now know that the *planetai* are actually planets, not wandering stars.

1. Which of the following did the ancient Greeks know to be true?
   A All planets have at least one moon.
   B The planets revolve around the sun.
   C The planets are much smaller than the stars.
   D The planets appear to move relative to the stars.

2. What can you infer from the passage about the ancient Greek astronomers?
   F They were patient and observant.
   G They knew much more about astronomy than we do.
   H They spent all their time counting stars.
   I They invented astrology.

3. What does the word *planetai* mean in Greek?
   A planets
   B wanderers
   C stars
   D moons

Passage 2 To explain the source of short-period comets (comets that have a relatively short orbit), the Dutch-American astronomer Gerard Kuiper proposed in 1949 that a belt of icy bodies must lie beyond the orbits of Pluto and Neptune. Kuiper argued that comets were icy planetesimals that formed from the condensation that happened during the formation of our galaxy. Because the icy bodies are so far from any large planet's gravitational field (30 to 100 AU), they can remain on the fringe of the solar system. Some theorists speculate that the large moons Triton and Charon were once members of the Kuiper belt before they were captured by Neptune and Pluto. These moons and short-period comets have similar physical and chemical properties.

1. According to the passage, why can icy bodies remain at the edge of the solar system?
   A The icy bodies are so small that they naturally float to the edge of the solar system.
   B The icy bodies have weak gravitational fields and therefore do not orbit individual planets.
   C The icy bodies are short-period comets, which can reside only at the edge of the solar system.
   D The icy bodies are so far away from any large planet's gravitational field that they can remain at the edge of the solar system.

2. According to the passage, which of the following best describes the meaning of the word *planetesimal*?
   F a small object that existed during the early development of the solar system
   G an extremely tiny object in space
   H a particle that was once part of a planet
   I an extremely large satellite that was the result of a collision of two objects

TEST DOCTOR

Question 2: Several of the choices may seem as if they could be correct. However, only one of the phrases most completely describes the underlined term. Answer F most fully defines planetesimals.

Chapter 21 • A Family of Planets

INTERPRETING GRAPHICS

Use the diagrams below to answer the questions that follow.

Planet A 115 craters/km²

Planet B 75 craters/km²

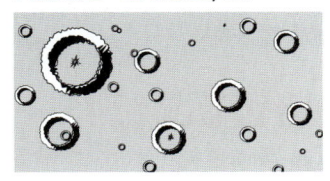

Planet C 121 craters/km²

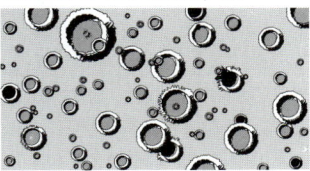

Planet D 97 craters/km²

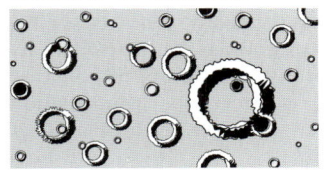

1. According to the information above, which planet has the oldest surface?
   - **A** planet A
   - **B** planet B
   - **C** planet C
   - **D** planet D

2. How many more craters per square kilometer are there on planet C than on planet B?
   - **F** 46 craters per square kilometer
   - **G** 24 craters per square kilometer
   - **H** 22 craters per square kilometer
   - **I** 6 craters per square kilometer

MATH

Read each question below, and choose the best answer.

1. Venus's surface gravity is 91% of Earth's. If an object weighs 12 N on Earth, how much would it weigh on Venus?
   - **A** 53 N
   - **B** 13 N
   - **C** 11 N
   - **D** 8 N

2. Earth's overall density is 5.52 g/cm³, while Saturn's density is 0.69 g/cm³. How many times denser is Earth than Saturn?
   - **F** 8 times
   - **G** 9 times
   - **H** 11 times
   - **I** 12 times

3. If Earth's history spans 4.6 billion years and the Phanerozoic eon was 543 million years, what percentage of Earth's history does the Phanerozoic eon represent?
   - **A** about 6%
   - **B** about 12%
   - **C** about 18%
   - **D** about 24%

4. The diameter of Venus is 12,104 km. The diameter of Mars is 6,794 km. What is the difference between the diameter of Venus and the diameter of Mars?
   - **F** 5,400 km
   - **G** 5,310 km
   - **H** 4,890 km
   - **I** 890 km

INTERPRETING GRAPHICS
1. C
2. F

TEST DOCTOR

Question 2: Remind students to use the data provided above the graphic rather than try to count craters themselves.

MATH
1. C
2. F
3. B
4. G

TEST DOCTOR

Question 1: Remind students that to find the percentage of a number, they should multiply the number by the percentage, written as a decimal. Therefore, students should multiply 12 by 0.91 to find weight on Venus.

CHAPTER RESOURCES

Chapter Resource File
- Standardized Test Preparation GENERAL

State Resources

For specific resources for your state, visit **go.hrw.com** and type in the keyword **HSMSTR**.

Chapter 21 • Standardized Test Preparation **679**

Science in Action

Science Fiction
Background
In 1934, Stanley Weinbaum published his first science fiction story, "A Martian Odyssey." Before becoming a writer, Weinbaum studied chemical engineering. During the Great Depression, Weinbaum gave up his science career to be a writer. Sadly, less than two years after his first story was published, Stanley Weinbaum died of cancer. Although his list of works is short, many people consider him among the best science fiction writers.

Discuss the author's description of Io. Ask students, "How does the author's description compare with what we now know about Io?" Have students use the story as inspiration to write their own description of a human colony on one of Jupiter's moons.

Scientific Debate
Background
In many ways, Pluto resembles Neptune's moon Triton. Pluto and Triton are similar in size, and both rotate in a direction counter to that of the other planets. Some scientists believe that there was a collision between Pluto and Triton and that the force of the collision ejected Pluto from the Neptune system.

Science in Action

Science Fiction
"The Mad Moon" by Stanley Weinbaum

The third largest moon of Jupiter, called Io, can be a hard place to live. Grant Calthorpe is finding this out the hard way. Although living comfortably is possible in the small cities at the polar regions of Io, Grant has to spend most of his time in the moon's hot and humid jungles. Grant treks into the jungles of Io to gather ferva leaves so that they can be converted into useful medications for humans. During Grant's quest, he encounters loonies and slinkers, and he has to avoid blancha, a kind of tropical fever that causes hallucinations, weakness, and vicious headaches. Without proper medication a person with blancha can go mad or even die. In "The Mad Moon," you'll discover a dozen adventures with Grant Calthorpe as he struggles to stay alive—and sane.

Language Arts ACTIVITY
WRITING SKILL Read "The Mad Moon" by Stanley Weinbaum. Write a short story describing the adventures that you would have on Io if you were chosen as Grant Calthorpe's assistant.

Scientific Debate
Is Pluto a Planet?

Is it possible that Pluto isn't a planet? Some scientists think so! Since 1930, Pluto has been included as one of the nine planets in our solar system. But observations in the 1990s led many astronomers to refer to Pluto as an object, not a planet. Other astronomers disagree with this change. Astronomers that refer to Pluto as an object do not think that it fits well with the other outer planets. Unlike the other outer planets, which are large and gaseous, Pluto is small and made of rock and ice. Pluto also has a very elliptical orbit that is unlike its neighboring planets. Astronomers that think Pluto is a planet point out that Pluto, like all other planets, has its own atmosphere and its own moon, called Charon. These and other factors have fueled a debate as to whether Pluto should be classified as a planet.

Math ACTIVITY
How many more kilometers is Earth's diameter compared to Pluto's diameter if Earth's diameter is 12,756 km and Pluto's diameter is 2,390 km?

Answer to Language Arts Activity
Accept any reasonable answer that demonstrates that students have completed their assigned reading.

Answer to Math Activity
10,366 km (12,756 km − 2,390 km = 10,366 km)

680 Chapter 21 • A Family of Planets

Careers

Adriana C. Ocampo

Planetary Geologist Sixty-five million years ago, in what is now Mexico, a giant meteor at least six miles wide struck Earth. The meteor made a hole nine miles deep and over 100 miles wide. The meteor sent billions of tons of dust into Earth's atmosphere. This dust formed thick clouds. After forming, these clouds may have left the planet in total darkness for six months, and the temperature near freezing for ten years. Some scientists think that this meteor crash and its effect on the Earth's climate led to the extinction of the dinosaurs. Adriana Ocampo studies the site in Mexico made by the crater known as the Chicxulub (cheeks OO loob) impact crater. Ocampo is a planetary geologist and has been interested in space exploration since she was young. Ocampo's specialty is studying "impact craters." "Impact craters are formed when an asteroid or a comet collides with the Earth or any other terrestrial planet," explains Ocampo. Ocampo visits crater sites around the world to collect data. She also uses computers to create models of how the impact affected the planet. Ocampo has worked for NASA and has helped plan space exploration missions to Mars, Jupiter, Saturn, and Mercury. Ocampo currently works for the European Space Agency (ESA) and is part of the team getting ready to launch the next spacecraft that will go to Mars.

Social Studies Activity

Research information about impact craters. Find the different locations around the world where impact craters have been found. Make a world map that highlights these locations.

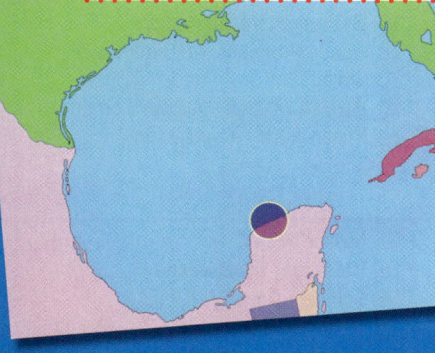

The circle on the map shows the site in Mexico made by the Chicxulub impact crater.

go.hrw.com
To learn more about these Science in Action topics, visit go.hrw.com and type in the keyword **HZ5FAMF**.

Current Science
Check out Current Science® articles related to this chapter by visiting go.hrw.com. Just type in the keyword **HZ5CS21**.

Careers

Group Activity — GENERAL

Disaster Preparation Organize the class into groups of three or four students. Ask each group to discuss what the results might be if another large meteor were to strike the Earth. Have each group create a disaster plan to prepare for such an event. Tell students to include in their plan strategies for protecting the biodiversity of the planet. (Note: Remind students that it is unlikely that such a disaster will occur within their lifetime.) (Answers might include developing a way to maintain warmth on the planet and preventing water from freezing. Answers might also include preserving animal and plant species by freezing their DNA for cloning in the future, when the planet warms up again.)

Answer to Social Studies Activity
Answers may vary. Students may include locations such as Barringer Meteorite Crater (also known as "Meteor Crater") near Flagstaff, Arizona; and Clearwater East and West Craters located in Quebec, Canada.

22 Exploring Space
Chapter Planning Guide

Compression guide: To shorten instruction because of time limitations, omit the Chapter Lab.

OBJECTIVES	LABS, DEMONSTRATIONS, AND ACTIVITIES	TECHNOLOGY RESOURCES
PACING • 120 min pp. 682–687 **Chapter Opener**	SE Start-up Activity, p. 683 ◆ GENERAL	OSP Parent Letter ■ GENERAL CD Student Edition on CD-ROM CD Guided Reading Audio CD ■ TR Chapter Starter Transparency* VID Brain Food Video Quiz
Section 1 Rocket Science • Outline the development of rocket technology. • Describe how a rocket accelerates. • Explain the difference between orbital velocity and escape velocity.	TE Demonstration Expanding Gas, p. 684 ◆ GENERAL TE Connection Activity History, p. 685 GENERAL TE Connection Activity Language Arts, p. 685 GENERAL SE Skills Practice Lab Water Rockets Save the Day!, p. 706 ◆ GENERAL CRF Datasheet for Chapter Lab* LB Whiz-Bang Demonstrations Rocket Science* ◆ GENERAL	CRF Lesson Plans* TR Bellringer Transparency* TR 40 Years of NASA* TR How a Rocket Works* VID Lab Videos for Earth Science
PACING • 45 min pp. 688–693 **Section 2 Artificial Satellites** • Identify the first satellites. • Compare low Earth orbits with geostationary orbits. • Explain the functions of military, communications, and weather satellites. • Explain how remote sensing from satellites has helped us study Earth as a global system.	TE Connection Activity Real World, p. 688 ADVANCED SE Quick Lab Modeling LEO and GEO, p. 689 GENERAL CRF Datasheet for Quick Lab* SE School-to-Home Activity Tracking Satellites, p. 691 GENERAL SE Connection to Environmental Science Space Junk, p. 692 GENERAL LB Inquiry Labs Crash Landing* ◆ BASIC	CRF Lesson Plans* TR Bellringer Transparency* TR GEO and LEO* TR Landsat Data*
PACING • 45 min pp. 694–699 **Section 3 Space Probes** • Describe five discoveries made by space probes. • Explain how space-probe missions help us better understand the Earth. • Describe how NASA's new strategy of "faster, cheaper, and better" relates to space probes.	TE Activity Design Your Own Space Mission, p. 694 ADVANCED TE Activity Designing a Mission Patch, p. 695 GENERAL TE Connection Activity History, p. 696 GENERAL TE Connection Activity History, p. 697 GENERAL SE Connection to Social Studies Cosmic Message in a Bottle, p. 698 GENERAL LB Long-Term Projects & Research Ideas Space Voyage* ADVANCED	CRF Lesson Plans* TR Bellringer Transparency* TR Space Probes in the Outer Solar System* TR **LINK TO PHYSICAL SCIENCE** Forming Positive and Negative Ions*
PACING • 45 min pp. 700–705 **Section 4 People in Space** • Summarize the history and future of human spaceflight. • Explain the benefits of crewed space programs. • Identify five "space-age spinoffs" that are used in everyday life.	TE Demonstration O-Ring Failure, p. 701 ◆ BASIC SE Connection to Biology Effects of Weightlessness, p. 702 GENERAL TE Group Activity Skylab Results, p. 702 GENERAL SE Connection to Social Studies Oral Histories, p. 703 GENERAL SE Model-Making Lab Reach for the Stars, p. 766 GENERAL CRF Datasheet for Lab Book* LB Inquiry Labs Space Fitness* ◆ ADVANCED LB EcoLabs & Field Activities There's a Space for Us* ◆ GENERAL	CRF Lesson Plans* TR Bellringer Transparency* CRF SciLinks Activity* GENERAL

PACING • 90 min

CHAPTER REVIEW, ASSESSMENT, AND STANDARDIZED TEST PREPARATION
- CRF Vocabulary Activity* GENERAL
- SE Chapter Review, pp. 708–709 GENERAL
- CRF Chapter Review* GENERAL
- CRF Chapter Tests A* GENERAL, B* ADVANCED, C* SPECIAL NEEDS
- SE Standardized Test Preparation, pp. 710–711 GENERAL
- CRF Standardized Test Preparation* GENERAL
- CRF Performance-Based Assessment* GENERAL
- OSP Test Generator GENERAL
- CRF Test Item Listing* GENERAL

Online and Technology Resources

go.hrw.com — Visit go.hrw.com for a variety of free resources related to this textbook. Enter the keyword HZ5EXP.

Holt Online Learning — Students can access interactive problem-solving help and active visual concept development with the *Holt Science and Technology* Online Edition available at www.hrw.com.

Guided Reading Audio CD — Also in Spanish. A direct reading of each chapter for auditory learners, reluctant readers, and Spanish-speaking students.

Science Tutor CD-ROM — Excellent for remediation and test practice.

KEY

SE Student Edition	**CRF** Chapter Resource File	**SS** Science Skills Worksheets	✱ Also on One-Stop Planner
TE Teacher Edition	**OSP** One-Stop Planner	**MS** Math Skills for Science Worksheets	◆ Requires advance prep
	LB Lab Bank	**CD** CD or CD-ROM	■ Also available in Spanish
	TR Transparencies	**VID** Classroom Video/DVD	

SKILLS DEVELOPMENT RESOURCES	SECTION REVIEW AND ASSESSMENT	STANDARDS CORRELATIONS
SE Pre-Reading Activity, p. 682 GENERAL **OSP** Science Puzzlers, Twisters & Teasers GENERAL		National Science Education Standards UCP 2, 3; SAI 1; ST 1
CRF Directed Reading A✱ ■ BASIC, B✱ SPECIAL NEEDS **CRF** Vocabulary and Section Summary✱ ■ GENERAL **SE** Reading Strategy Discussion, p. 684 GENERAL **TE** Inclusion Strategies, p. 687 **CRF** Reinforcement Worksheet Ronnie Rocket✱ BASIC	**SE** Reading Checks, pp. 684, 686 GENERAL **TE** Homework, p. 685 GENERAL **TE** Reteaching, p. 686 BASIC **TE** Quiz, p. 686 GENERAL **TE** Alternative Assessment, p. 686 GENERAL **SE** Section Review,✱ p. 687 ■ GENERAL **CRF** Section Quiz✱ ■ GENERAL	UCP 2, 3; HNS 1, 3; *Chapter Lab:* SAI 1; ST 1
CRF Directed Reading A✱ ■ BASIC, B✱ SPECIAL NEEDS **CRF** Vocabulary and Section Summary✱ ■ GENERAL **SE** Reading Strategy Reading Organizer, p. 688 GENERAL **TE** Inclusion Strategies, p. 689 **SE** Math Practice Triangulation, p. 690 GENERAL	**SE** Reading Checks, pp. 689, 691, 693 GENERAL **TE** Reteaching, p. 692 BASIC **TE** Quiz, p. 692 GENERAL **TE** Alternative Assessment, p. 692 GENERAL **SE** Section Review,✱ p. 693 ■ GENERAL **CRF** Section Quiz✱ ■ GENERAL	UCP 2, 3; SAI 1; ST 2; SPSP 5
CRF Directed Reading A✱ ■ BASIC, B✱ SPECIAL NEEDS **CRF** Vocabulary and Section Summary✱ ■ GENERAL **SE** Reading Strategy Reading Organizer, p. 694 GENERAL **TE** Reading Strategy Paired Summarizing, p. 695 GENERAL **CRF** Critical Thinking Spacecraft R' Us✱ ADVANCED **CRF** Reinforcement Worksheet Probing Space✱ BASIC	**SE** Reading Checks, pp. 695, 696, 698 GENERAL **TE** Reteaching, p. 698 BASIC **TE** Quiz, p. 698 GENERAL **TE** Alternative Assessment, p. 698 GENERAL **SE** Section Review,✱ p. 699 ■ GENERAL **CRF** Section Quiz✱ ■ GENERAL	UCP 5; ST 2
CRF Directed Reading A✱ ■ BASIC, B✱ SPECIAL NEEDS **CRF** Vocabulary and Section Summary✱ ■ GENERAL **SE** Reading Strategy Reading Organizer, p. 700 GENERAL **TE** Reading Strategy Prediction Guide, p. 701 GENERAL	**SE** Reading Checks, pp. 701, 703, 705 GENERAL **TE** Homework, p. 702 GENERAL **TE** Reteaching, p. 704 BASIC **TE** Quiz, p. 704 GENERAL **TE** Alternative Assessment, p. 704 GENERAL **TE** Homework, p. 704 GENERAL **SE** Section Review,✱ p. 705 ■ GENERAL **CRF** Section Quiz✱ ■ GENERAL	UCP 5; ST 2; SPSP 5; HNS 1, 3; *LabBook:* UCP 2; SAI 1; ST 1, 2

One-Stop Planner® CD-ROM

This convenient CD-ROM includes:
- Lab Materials QuickList Software
- Holt Calendar Planner
- Customizable Lesson Plans
- Printable Worksheets
- ExamView® Test Generator

CNN Student News

cnnstudentnews.com

Find the latest news, lesson plans, and activities related to important scientific events.

SciLinks NSTA

www.scilinks.org

Maintained by the **National Science Teachers Association**. See Chapter Enrichment pages for a complete list of topics.

Current Science®

Check out *Current Science* articles and activities by visiting the HRW Web site at **go.hrw.com.** Just type in the keyword **HZ5CS22T.**

Classroom Videos

- **Lab Videos** demonstrate the chapter lab.
- **Brain Food Video Quizzes** help students review the chapter material.
- **CNN Videos** bring science into your students' daily life.

Chapter 22 • Chapter Planning Guide

Chapter 22 Chapter Resources

Visual Resources

- **CHAPTER STARTER TRANSPARENCY**
- **BELLRINGER TRANSPARENCIES**
- **TEACHING TRANSPARENCIES**
- **TEACHING TRANSPARENCIES**
- **CONCEPT MAPPING TRANSPARENCY**

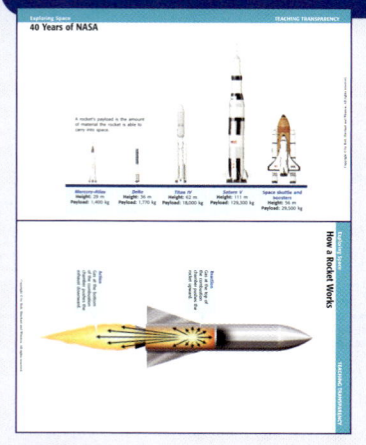

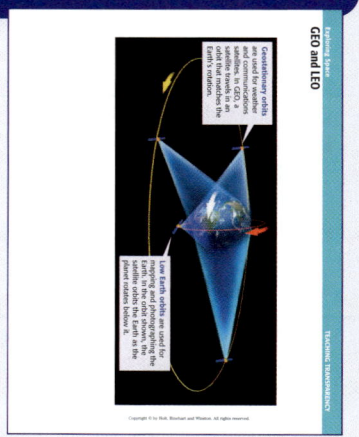

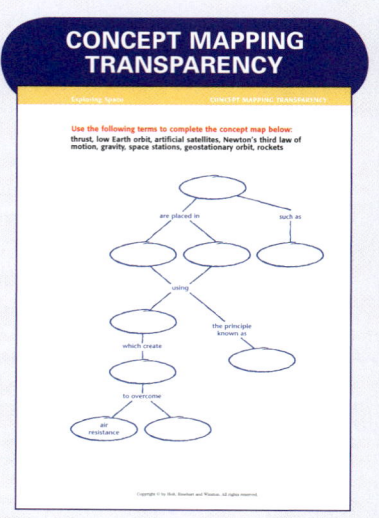

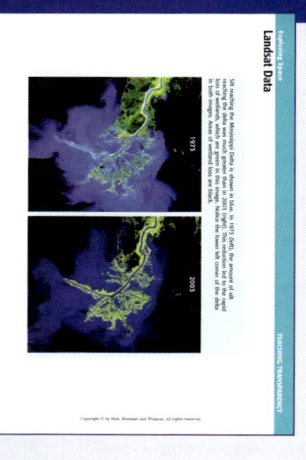

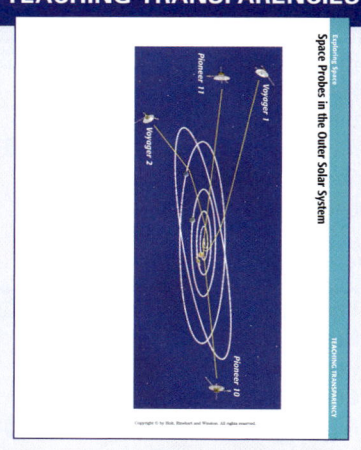

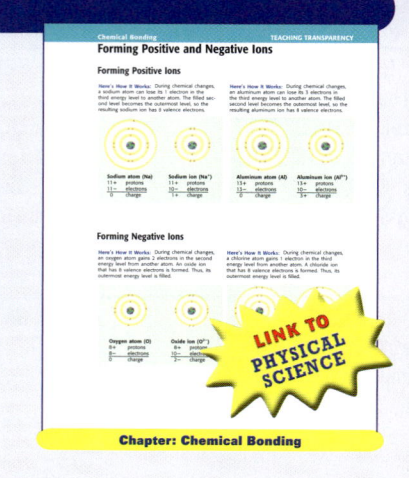

Planning Resources

- **LESSON PLANS**
- **PARENT LETTER** — *ALSO IN SPANISH*
- **TEST ITEM LISTING**
- **One-Stop Planner® CD-ROM**

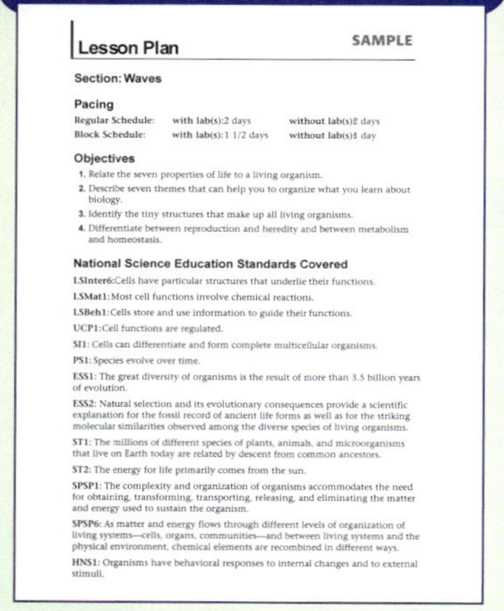

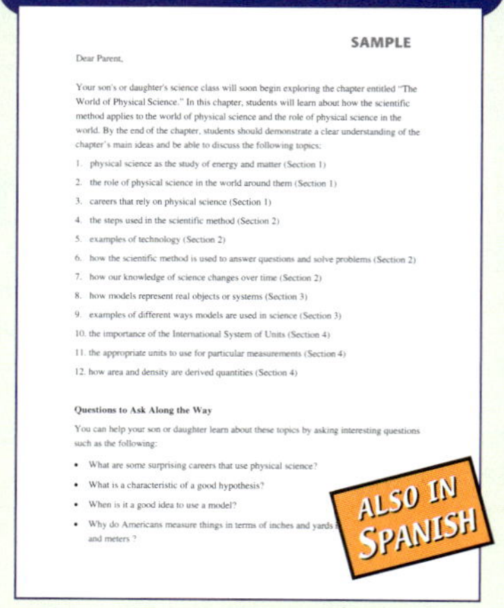

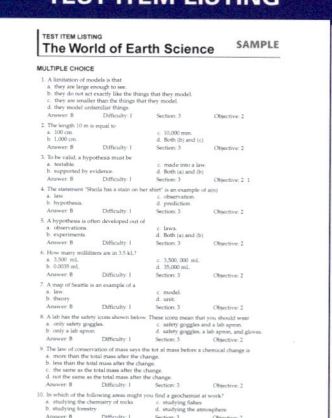

This CD-ROM includes all of the resources shown here and the following time-saving tools:

- Lab Materials QuickList Software
- Customizable lesson plans
- Holt Calendar Planner
- The powerful ExamView® Test Generator

681C Chapter 22 • Exploring Space

For a preview of available worksheets covering math and science skills, see pages T26–T33. All of these resources are also on the One-Stop Planner®.

Meeting Individual Needs

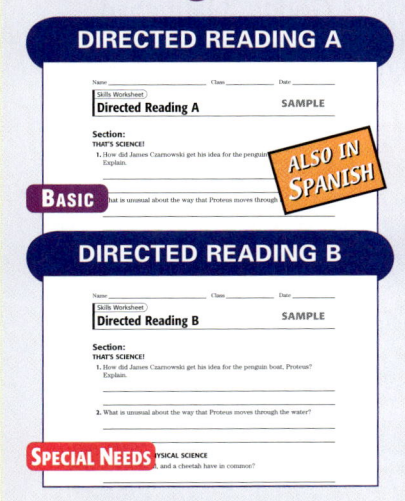

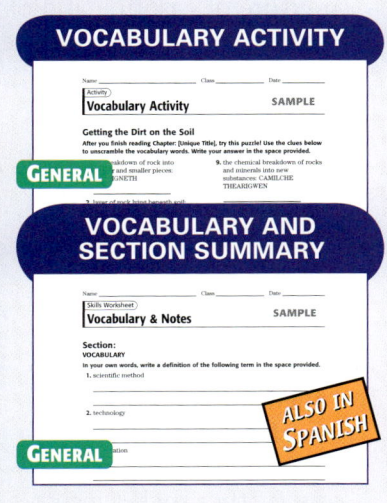

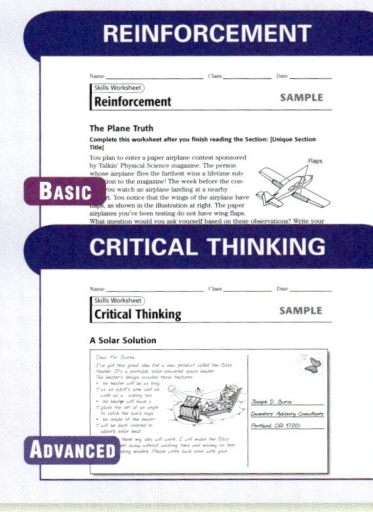

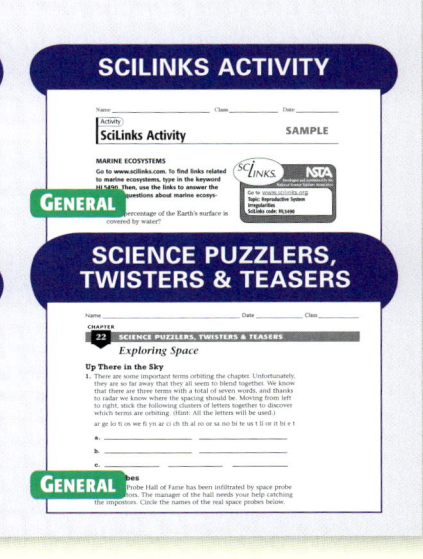

- **DIRECTED READING A** (Basic) — *Also in Spanish*
- **DIRECTED READING B** (Special Needs)
- **VOCABULARY ACTIVITY** (General)
- **VOCABULARY AND SECTION SUMMARY** (General) — *Also in Spanish*
- **REINFORCEMENT** (Basic)
- **CRITICAL THINKING** (Advanced)
- **SCILINKS ACTIVITY** (General)
- **SCIENCE PUZZLERS, TWISTERS & TEASERS** (General)

Labs and Activities

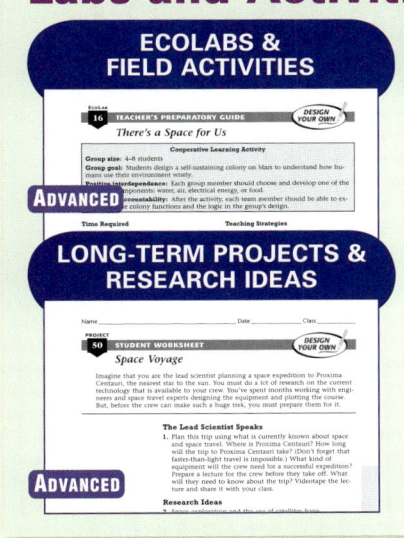

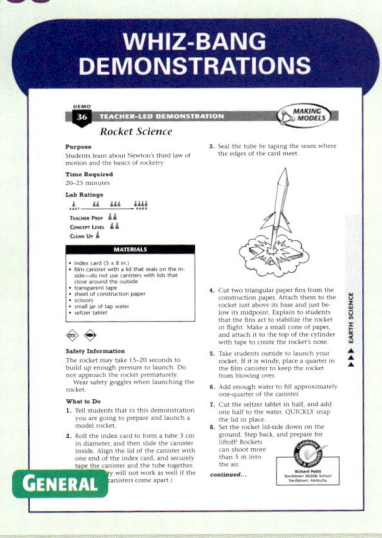

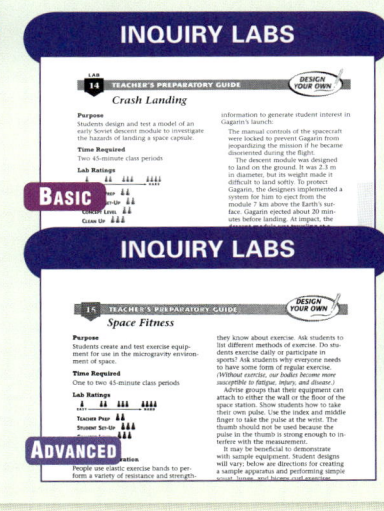

- **ECOLABS & FIELD ACTIVITIES** (Advanced)
- **LONG-TERM PROJECTS & RESEARCH IDEAS** (Advanced)
- **WHIZ-BANG DEMONSTRATIONS** (General)
- **INQUIRY LABS** (Basic)
- **INQUIRY LABS** (Advanced)
- **DATASHEETS FOR QUICK LABS**
- **DATASHEETS FOR CHAPTER LABS**
- **DATASHEETS FOR LABBOOK**

Review and Assessments

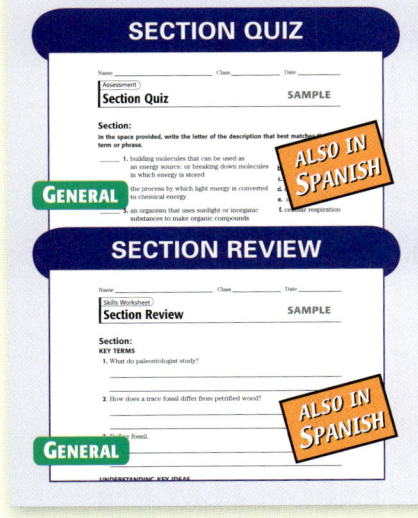

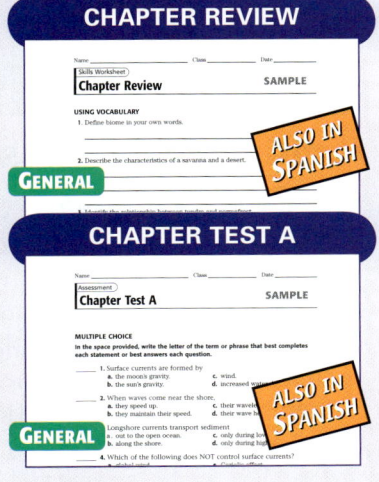

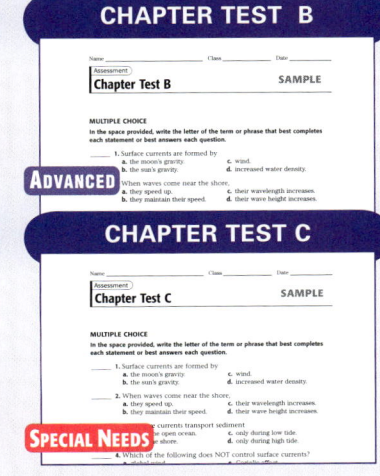

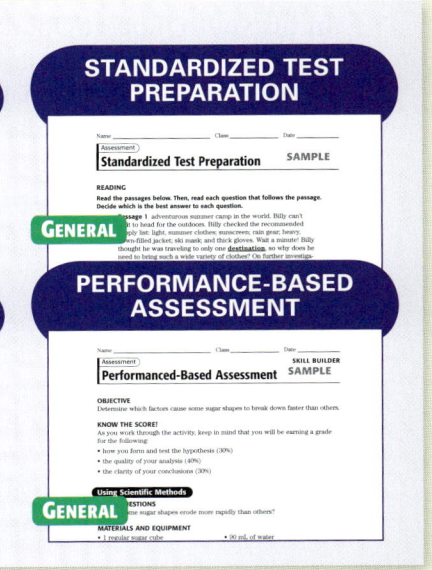

- **SECTION QUIZ** (General) — *Also in Spanish*
- **SECTION REVIEW** (General) — *Also in Spanish*
- **CHAPTER REVIEW** (General) — *Also in Spanish*
- **CHAPTER TEST A** (General) — *Also in Spanish*
- **CHAPTER TEST B** (Advanced)
- **CHAPTER TEST C** (Special Needs)
- **STANDARDIZED TEST PREPARATION** (General)
- **PERFORMANCE-BASED ASSESSMENT** (General)

Chapter 22 • Chapter Resources **681D**

22 Chapter Enrichment

This Chapter Enrichment provides relevant and interesting information to expand and enhance your presentation of the chapter material.

Section 1

Rocket Science

Konstantin Tsiolkovsky (1857–1935)

- As a youth, Konstantin Tsiolkovsky, the father of rocket theory, demonstrated a keen interest in science and mathematics. At age 9, a bout of scarlet fever left him partially deaf, and he spent much of his time studying on his own. After studying chemistry, astronomy, mathematics, and mechanics in Moscow, Tsiolkovsky got a job in 1876 as a mathematics teacher in a community north of Moscow. There, he continued his scientific pursuits. In 1903, Tsiolkovsky published the article "Exploration of Cosmic Space by Means of Reaction Devices," the culmination of years of theorization about the use of rocket engines for space travel.

- In later years, Tsiolkovsky elaborated on his earlier theories, developing a theory of rocket propulsion and anticipating a number of technologies used in contemporary space exploration, including multistage boosters and the use of chemical propellants to achieve enough thrust to overcome Earth's gravity.

Robert Goddard (1882–1945)

- In his youth, Robert Goddard was an enthusiastic reader of science fiction tales of space travel, and at an early age he wrote a paper titled "The Navigation of Space." In 1912, Goddard developed a mathematical theory of rocket propulsion. He achieved a major breakthrough in 1915, when he proved that rocket engines would work in a vacuum and thus could be used for space travel.

- In 1919, Goddard published his research in the landmark paper "A Method of Reaching Extreme Altitudes," in which he argued that rockets could be used to escape Earth's gravity. Some people found Goddard's theories ludicrous. *The New York Times,* for example, scoffed at Goddard and questioned his scientific qualifications. Undeterred, Goddard continued to design and experiment with rockets. In 1926, using a liquid fuel mixture of gasoline and oxygen, Goddard launched his first liquid-fueled rocket, which ascended to a height of nearly 13 m in 2.5 sec.

- In 1929, Goddard launched his first rocket to carry scientific instruments. The rocket rose about 30 m and then crashed to Earth, where it caught fire. People living nearby called the state fire marshal, who banned Goddard from doing any further rocket tests in Massachusetts. With a Guggenheim grant of $50,000, Goddard set up a test site in an unpopulated area outside of Roswell, New Mexico. He launched increasingly complex rockets that featured innovations such as steering systems, fuel pumps, and cooling mechanisms.

Is That a Fact!

◆ When Goddard died in 1945, his immense contributions to rocket technology were still relatively unknown. By 1960, however, the U.S. Department of Defense and NASA had fully recognized Goddard's achievements and paid his estate $1 million for the use of his 214 patented rocket-componentry designs. A year later, NASA named the Goddard Space Flight Center in Greenbelt, Maryland, in his honor.

Section 2

Artificial Satellites

The Echo Satellites

- The United States launched its first communications satellite, *Echo I,* into orbit on August 12, 1960. Surprisingly simple in its design, *Echo I* consisted of an aluminum-coated plastic balloon that inflated to a diameter of 30 m when it reached orbit. From a low Earth orbit, *Echo I* reflected radio signals back to Earth until 1968.

Chapter 22 • Exploring Space

For background information about teaching strategies and issues, refer to the *Professional Reference for Teachers*.

Is That a Fact!
◆ The *Echo II* satellite was part of the first cooperative space effort between the United States and the Soviet Union. A radio signal from an observatory in England was reflected off *Echo II* and was received in the Soviet Union.

Section 3
Space Probes
Soviet Lunar Probes
- Although Soviet cosmonauts never landed on the moon, their Luna space probes gathered a remarkable amount of lunar data using robotics and remotely controlled devices. In 1966, *Luna 9* became the first space probe to make a soft landing on the moon (previous probes crash-landed, and one shot past the moon into space). On impact, *Luna 9*'s egg-shaped instrument capsule rolled itself upright and automatically stabilized itself with four spring-loaded mechanisms. *Luna 9* sent the first television images of the lunar landscape back to Earth.

- Perhaps the most impressive of the Soviets' lunar space probes were *Luna 17* and *Luna 18*, which carried the eight-wheeled, heavy-duty lunar rovers *Lunokhod 1* and *2*. From Earth, the vehicles were directed around treacherous craters to cover vast expanses of the moon's surface. The rovers took photos, collected soil samples, and carried out other tests. *Lunokhod 1* traveled over the moon's surface for 11 months.

Section 4
People in Space
The Daily Routine Aboard Skylab
- Measuring 36 m long and 6.6 m high, *Skylab* was luxuriously large in comparison with previous space stations and had both working quarters and a living space. The living area included private sleeping quarters, a galley, a shower, and a suction toilet. Crew members carried out hundreds of astronomical and medical experiments.

- Astronauts were required to document everything they ate; measure the girth of their limbs, waists, and necks to check for muscle-tone loss; and wear electrodes while exercising so that their vital signs could be monitored. Astronauts did enjoy diversions such as "astrobatics"; in fact, *Skylab* astronaut Charles "Pete" Conrad commented, "We never went anywhere straight. We always did a somersault or a flip on the way."

Is That a Fact!
◆ By the time of the *Skylab* missions, the infamous spacebars and tubes of gooey "spacefood" had been replaced with more-palatable frozen, canned, and dehydrated foods. With more than 80 food items to choose from, a crew might whip up a breakfast of scrambled eggs, sausage, strawberries, bread and jam, orange juice, and coffee and finish out the day with a dinner of filet mignon, potato salad, and ice cream.

SCILINKS
Developed and maintained by the National Science Teachers Association

SciLinks is maintained by the National Science Teachers Association to provide you and your students with interesting, up-to-date links that will enrich your classroom presentation of the chapter.

Visit www.scilinks.org and enter the SciLinks code for more information about the topic listed.

Topic: Rocket Technology
SciLinks code: HSM1323

Topic: History of NASA
SciLinks code: HSM0745

Topic: Artificial Satellites
SciLinks code: HSM0101

Topic: Space Probes
SciLinks code: HSM1432

Topic: Space Exploration and Space Stations
SciLinks code: HSM1430

Chapter 22 • Chapter Enrichment   681F

22

Overview
This chapter discusses the development of rocket science. Students will learn about rockets, satellites, space probes, and space stations. In addition, the chapter discusses how the political climate after WWII led to the space race.

Assessing Prior Knowledge
Students should be familiar with the following topics:
- Newton's third law of motion
- the movement of bodies in the solar system

Identifying Misconceptions
Students may have some questions about the benefits of the space program. As students explore the concepts in this chapter, help them assess how developments in space technology benefit humanity. Many students also have misconceptions about rocket propulsion. Rockets do not move by pushing against air in the atmosphere. The reaction to the force and direction of the exhaust causes a rocket to move. Thus, rockets can accelerate in the vacuum of space, where there is nothing to push against. In fact, rockets accelerate more efficiently in space, where there is no friction. The Start-Up Activity will help address this misconception.

22
Exploring Space

SECTION 1	Rocket Science	684
SECTION 2	Artificial Satellites	688
SECTION 3	Space Probes	694
SECTION 4	People in Space	700

Chapter Lab 706
Chapter Review 708
Standardized Test Preparation 710
Science in Action 712

About the PHOTO
Although the astronauts in the photo appear to be motionless, they are orbiting the Earth at almost 28,000 km/h! The astronauts reached orbit—about 300 km above the Earth's surface—in a space shuttle. Space shuttles are the first vehicles in a new generation of reusable spacecraft. They have opened an era of space exploration in which missions to space are more common than ever before.

PRE-READING ACTIVITY

Graphic Organizer — **Chain-of-Events Chart** Before you read the chapter, create the graphic organizer entitled "Chain-of-Events Chart" described in the **Study Skills** section of the Appendix. As you read the chapter, fill in the chart with a timeline that describes the exploration of space from the theories of Konstantin Tsiolkovsky to the future of space exploration.

Standards Correlations

National Science Education Standards
The following codes indicate the National Science Education Standards that correlate to this chapter. The full text of the standards is at the front of the book.

Chapter Opener
UCP 2; SAI 1

Section 1 Rocket Science
UCP 2, 3; HNS 1, 3

Section 2 Artificial Satellites
UCP 3, 4; SAI 1; ST 2; SPSP 5; HNS 3

Section 3 Space Probes
UCP 5; ST 2

Section 4 People in Space
UCP 4, 5; SAI 1; ST 2; SPSP 5; HNS 1, 3; LabBook: SAI 1; ST 1, 2

Chapter Lab
SAI 1; ST 1

Chapter Review
SAI 1; ST 2; HNS 1, 2, 3; SPSP 5

Science in Action
SPSP 5; HNS 1

682 Chapter 22 • Exploring Space

START-UP ACTIVITY

MATERIALS

FOR EACH GROUP
- balloon, large
- drinking straw
- meterstick
- poster board
- tape
- thread, 2 m

Teacher's Note: Discuss the limitations of using a balloon to model a launch vehicle. If the balloon were to "launch" something, what improvements should be made? (Students may suggest that the balloon would need to be more powerful and able to sustain thrust for a longer period of time. In addition, the balloon would need a steering or guidance device.)

Answers

1. Sample answer: The balloon traveled the same distance. The poster board did not affect the distance the balloon traveled because the balloon did not push off the poster board.

2. Sample answer: The balloon moved because of Newton's third law of motion. As air left the balloon, the balloon reacted by moving in the opposite direction. Hot gases escape from the bottom of a rocket, and the rocket reacts by moving in the opposite direction. Rockets do not push off a launch pad.

START-UP ACTIVITY

Balloon Rockets

In this activity you will launch a balloon "rocket" to learn about how rockets move.

Procedure

1. Insert a **2 m thread** through a **drinking straw**, and tie it between two objects that won't move, such as **chairs**. Make sure that the thread is tight.

2. Inflate a **large balloon**. Do not tie the neck of the balloon closed. Hold the neck of the balloon closed, and **tape** the balloon firmly to the straw, parallel to the thread.

3. Move the balloon to one end of the thread, and then release the neck of the balloon. Use a **meterstick** to record the distance the balloon traveled.

4. Repeat steps 2–3. This time, hold a piece of **poster board** behind the balloon.

Analysis

1. Did the poster board affect the distance that the balloon traveled? Explain your answer.

2. Newton's third law of motion states that for every action there is an equal and opposite reaction. Apply this idea and your observations of the balloon to explain how rockets accelerate. Do rockets move by "pushing off" a launch pad? Explain your answer.

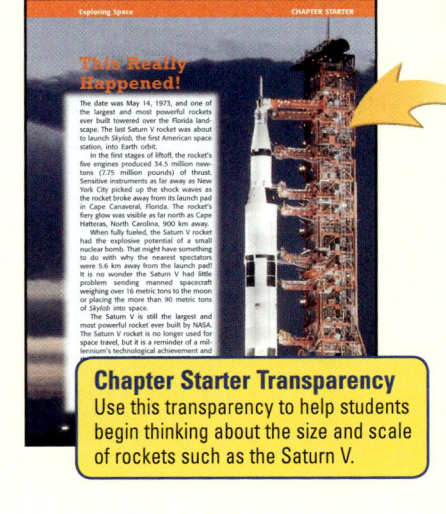

CHAPTER RESOURCES

Technology

- **Transparencies**
  - Chapter Starter Transparency **READING SKILLS**
- **Student Edition on CD-ROM**
- **Guided Reading Audio CD**
  - English or Spanish
- **Classroom Videos**
  - Brain Food Video Quiz

Workbooks

- **Science Puzzlers, Twisters & Teasers**
  - Exploring Space GENERAL

Chapter Starter Transparency
Use this transparency to help students begin thinking about the size and scale of rockets such as the Saturn V.

Chapter 22 • Exploring Space **683**

SECTION 1

Focus

Overview
This section discusses the development of rocket technology and the establishment of NASA. The section also discusses the principles of rocket propulsion.

🔔 Bellringer
Ask students, "Why can't a commercial airplane be used for space exploration?" (Jet engines rely on air for propulsion and for fuel combustion, and there is no air in space. Commercial airplanes cannot carry enough fuel for space exploration, their engines are not powerful enough to escape Earth's gravity, and they cannot withstand the extreme cold of space or the heat of reentry into Earth's atmosphere.)

Motivate

Demonstration — GENERAL
Expanding Gas Attach a pre-stretched balloon over the mouth of a plastic bottle, and put the bottle in a bucket of hot water. Explain that as the gases in the balloon become hot, they expand and cause the balloon to inflate. The expansion of hot gases is powerful enough to launch rockets into space. As hot gases escape through the rocket nozzle, the rocket reacts by moving in the opposite direction—skyward. **LS Visual**

SECTION 1

READING WARM-UP

Objectives
- Outline the development of rocket technology.
- Describe how a rocket accelerates.
- Explain the difference between orbital velocity and escape velocity.

Terms to Learn
rocket   thrust
NASA

READING STRATEGY
Discussion Read this section silently. Write down questions that you have about this section. Discuss your questions in a small group.

Figure 1 Robert Goddard is known as the father of modern rocketry.

CHAPTER RESOURCES
Chapter Resource File
- Lesson Plan
- Directed Reading A BASIC
- Directed Reading B SPECIAL NEEDS

Technology
- Transparencies
  • Bellringer

Rocket Science

If you could pack all of your friends in a car and drive to the moon, it would take about 165 days to get there. And that doesn't include stopping for gas or food!

The moon is incredibly far away, and years ago people could only dream of traveling into space. The problem was that no machine could generate enough force to overcome Earth's gravity and reach outer space. But about 100 years ago, a Russian high school teacher named Konstantin Tsiolkovsky (KAHN stuhn TEEN TSI uhl KAHV skee) proposed that machines called *rockets* could take people to outer space. A **rocket** is a machine that uses escaping gas to move. Tsiolkovsky stated, "The Earth is the cradle of mankind. But one does not have to live in the cradle forever." Rockets would become the key to leaving the cradle of Earth and starting the age of space exploration.

The Beginnings of Rocket Science
Tsiolkovsky's inspiration came from the imaginative stories of Jules Verne. In Verne's book *From the Earth to the Moon*, characters reached the moon in a capsule shot from an enormous cannon. Although this idea would not work, Tsiolkovsky proved—in theory—that rockets could generate enough force to reach outer space. He also suggested the use of liquid rocket fuel to increase a rocket's range. For his vision and careful work, Tsiolkovsky is known as the father of rocket theory.

A Boost for Modern Rocketry
Although Tsiolkovsky proved scientifically that rockets could reach outer space, he never built any rockets himself. That task was left to American physicist and inventor Robert Goddard, shown in **Figure 1**. Goddard launched the first successful liquid-fuel rocket in 1926. Goddard tested more than 150 rocket engines, and by the time of World War II, Goddard's work began to interest the United States military. His work drew much attention because of a terrifying new weapon that the German army had developed.

✓ **Reading Check** How did Tsiolkovsky and Goddard contribute to the development of rockets? (*See the Appendix for answers to Reading Checks.*)

Answer to Reading Check
Tsiolkovsky helped develop rocket theory. Goddard developed the first rockets.

684 Chapter 22 • Exploring Space

From Rocket Bombs to Rocket Ships

Toward the end of World War II, Germany developed a new weapon known as the V-2 rocket. The V-2 rocket, shown in **Figure 2**, could deliver explosives from German military bases to London—a distance of about 350 km. The V-2 rocket was developed by a team led by Wernher von Braun, a young Ph.D. student whose research was supported by the German military. But in 1945, near the end of the war, von Braun and his entire research team surrendered to the advancing Americans. The United States thus gained 127 of the best German rocket scientists. With this gain, rocket research in the United States boomed in the 1950s.

The Birth of NASA

The end of World War II marked the beginning of the *Cold War*—a long period of political tension between the United States and the Soviet Union. The Cold War was marked by an arms race and by competition in space technology. In response to Soviet advances in space, the U.S. government formed the National Aeronautics and Space Administration, or **NASA**, in 1958. NASA combined all of the rocket-development teams in the United States. Their cooperation led to the development of many rockets, including those shown in **Figure 3**.

Figure 2 *The V-2 rocket is the ancestor of all modern rockets.*

rocket a machine that uses escaping gas from burning fuel to move

NASA the National Aeronautics and Space Administration

Figure 3 — 40 Years of NASA Rockets

A rocket's payload is the amount of material the rocket is able to carry into space.

Mercury-Atlas	Delta	Titan IV	Saturn V	Space shuttle and boosters
Height: 29 m	Height: 36 m	Height: 62 m	Height: 111 m	Height: 56 m
Payload: 1,400 kg	Payload: 1,770 kg	Payload: 18,000 kg	Payload: 129,300 kg	Payload: 29,500 kg

Cultural Awareness — GENERAL

Diversity in Space Many nations have taken an active role in space exploration. China launched its first satellite in 1970, and by late 1980, it was launching Western communications satellites in its advanced booster rockets. Also, in 2003, China launched its first Taikonaut (the Chinese term for "astronaut"). Before achieving launch capability in 1980, India had a number of satellites launched by the United States and the Soviet Union. An Indian astronaut took part in a *Soyuz* visit to the *Salyut 7* space station in 1984. In 1993, Brazil launched its first satellite. The satellite measures air pollution and collects data from 500 sensors along the Amazon River basin. Encourage interested students to find out more about the space programs of other countries. **LS** Intrapersonal

Teach

CONNECTION to History — GENERAL

The Cold War Make sure students understand that the term *cold war* describes a period of tense or strained political relations without actual military aggression. You might explain to students that after World War II, the United States and its allies followed very different political and economic policies from the Soviet Union and its allies. The two powers viewed each other with suspicion and fear. Both countries responded by spending tremendous amounts of money to increase their military strength. An arms race led to the proliferation of nuclear weapons, which increased tensions further with the fear that nuclear war could destroy all of humanity. For both sides, space exploration became a yardstick of national superiority and played an important role in the development of military weapons.

CONNECTION ACTIVITY Language Arts — GENERAL

Science Fiction? The works of Jules Verne inspired both Goddard and Tsiolkovsky to develop rocket theory. Have students read sections from Jules Verne's *From the Earth to the Moon* or *Around the Moon*. Have them compare Verne's descriptions of spaceships with this section and summarize their thoughts in a written book report. Students may also research the influence of H. G. Wells on the development of space science. **LS** Intrapersonal

Section 1 • Rocket Science **685**

Close

Reteaching — BASIC

Rocket Review Reproduce **Figure 4** on the board, and have student volunteers add descriptive labels that explain the action and reaction that accelerates a rocket. **LS Visual**

Quiz — GENERAL

1. How did NASA contribute to the United States' rocket program? (NASA coordinated the efforts of many rocket research teams, which led to the rapid development of a variety of rocket designs.)

2. How does Newton's third law of motion apply to rocket propulsion? (Newton's law states that for every action there is an equal and opposite reaction. When hot gases rush out of the bottom of a rocket, the rocket moves in the opposite direction.)

Alternative Assessment — GENERAL

Poster Project Have students make a series of sketches that show the evolution of rocket design. Encourage students to use poster board so that they can make scale models to compare the size of the spacecraft. Have students write a brief description of each spacecraft.
LS Visual/Intrapersonal

Answer to Reading Check

Rockets carry oxygen so that their fuel can be burned.

---

thrust the pushing or pulling force exerted by the engine of an aircraft or rocket

Figure 4 Rockets move according to Newton's third law of motion.

Reaction
Gas at the top of the combustion chamber pushes the rocket upward.

Action
Gas at the bottom of the combustion chamber pushes the exhaust downward.

How Rockets Work

If you are sitting in a chair that has wheels and you want to move, you would probably push away from a table or kick yourself along with your feet. Many people think that rockets move in a similar way—by pushing off of a launch pad. But if rockets moved in this way, how would they accelerate in the vacuum of space where there is nothing to push against?

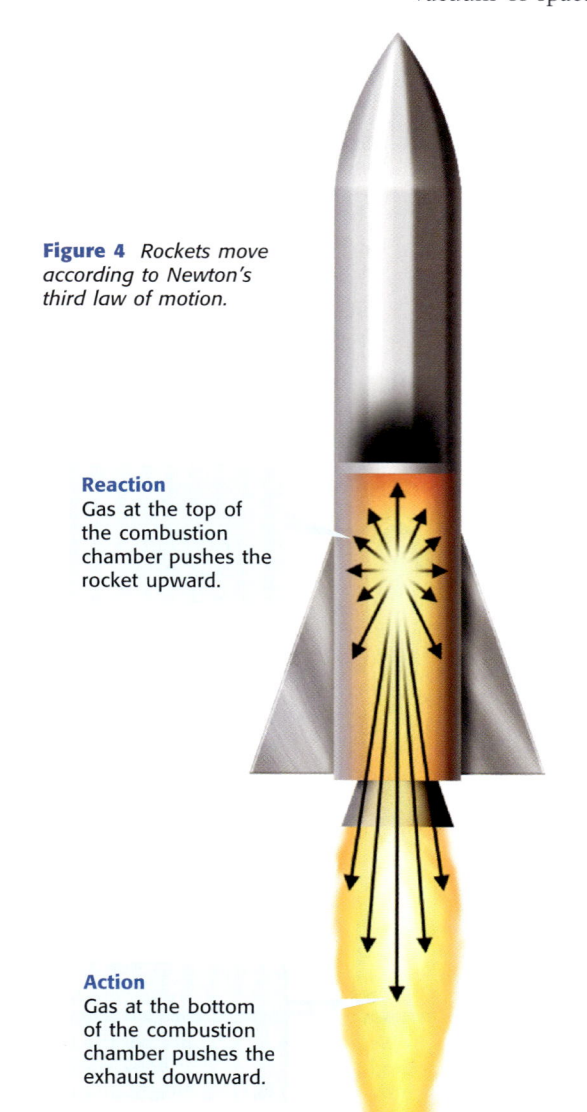

For Every Action . . .

As you saw in the Start-Up Activity, the balloon moved according to Newton's third law of motion. This law states that for every action there is an equal and opposite reaction. For example, the air rushing backward from a balloon (the action) results in the forward motion of the balloon (the reaction). Rockets work in the same way. In fact, rockets were once called *reaction devices*.

However, in the case of rockets, the action and the reaction may not be obvious. The mass of a rocket—including all of the fuel it carries—is much greater than the mass of the hot gases that come out of the bottom of the rocket. But because the exhaust gases are under extreme pressure, they exert a huge amount of force. The force that accelerates a rocket is called **thrust**. Look at **Figure 4** to learn more about how rockets work.

You Need More Than Rocket Fuel

Rockets burn fuel to provide the thrust that propels them. In order for something to burn, oxygen must be present. Although oxygen is plentiful at the Earth's surface, there is little or no oxygen in the upper atmosphere and in outer space. For this reason, rockets that go into outer space must carry enough oxygen with them to be able to burn their fuel. The space shuttles, for example, carry hundreds of thousands of gallons of liquid oxygen. This oxygen is needed to burn the shuttle's rocket fuel.

✓ **Reading Check** Why do rockets carry oxygen in addition to fuel?

CONNECTION to Physical Science — ADVANCED

Velocity Versus Speed It is important for students to understand the difference between velocity and speed. Speed is the rate at which an object moves. An object's velocity is the speed the object travels in a particular direction. Think of velocity as the rate of change in an object's position. This distinction is very important in rocket science. For example, rockets are always launched in the direction that Earth rotates. At the equator, Earth has a rotational velocity of nearly 0.5 km/s east. In other words, standing still, a rocket travels 0.5 km/s east, so, to reach orbital velocity, it has to increase its horizontal velocity by only an additional 7.5 km/s. As an extension, show students the following locations on a world map: Cape Canaveral, Florida (28.5°N), and the ESA Spaceport in Korou, French Guiana (5°N). Ask students to explain why NASA chose a launch site in Florida, rather than a launch site in Maine or Alaska. (The Earth's rotational velocity is greatest at the equator, so rockets launched from areas close to the equator get the greatest boost possible.)

686 Chapter 22 • Exploring Space

How to Leave the Earth

The gravitational pull of the Earth is the main factor that a rocket must overcome. As shown in **Figure 5**, a rocket must reach a certain *velocity*, or speed and direction, to orbit or escape the Earth.

Orbital Velocity and Escape Velocity

For a rocket to orbit the Earth, it must have enough thrust to reach orbital velocity. *Orbital velocity* is the speed and direction a rocket must travel in order to orbit a planet or moon. The lowest possible speed a rocket may go and still orbit the Earth is about 8 km/s (17,927 mi/h). If the rocket goes any slower, it will fall back to Earth. For a rocket to travel beyond Earth orbit, the rocket must achieve escape velocity. *Escape velocity* is the speed and direction a rocket must travel to completely break away from a planet's gravitational pull. The speed a rocket must reach to escape the Earth is about 11 km/s (24,606 mi/h).

Suborbital velocity less than 8 km/s
Orbital velocity about 8 km/s
Escape velocity about 11 km/s

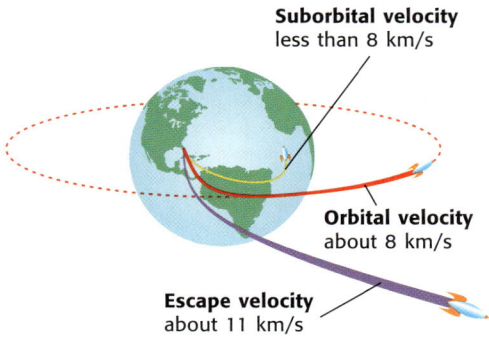

Figure 5 *A rocket must travel very fast to escape the gravitational pull of the Earth.*

SECTION Review

Summary

- Tsiolkovsky and Goddard were pioneers of rocket science.
- The outcome of WWII and the political pressures of the Cold War helped advance rocket science.
- Rockets work according to Newton's third law of motion—for every action there is an equal and opposite reaction.
- Rockets need to reach different velocities to attain orbit and to escape a planet's gravitational attraction.

Using Key Terms

1. Use each of the following terms in a separate sentence: *rocket, thrust,* and *NASA*.

Understanding Key Ideas

2. What factor must a rocket overcome to reach escape velocity?
   a. Earth's axial tilt
   b. Earth's gravity
   c. the thrust of its engines
   d. Newton's third law of motion

3. Describe the contributions of Tsiolkovsky and Goddard to modern rocketry.

4. Use Newton's third law of motion to describe how rockets work.

5. What is the difference between orbital and escape velocity?

6. How did the Cold War accelerate the U.S. space program?

Math Skills

7. If you travel at 60 mi/h, it takes about 165 days to reach the moon. Approximately how far away is the moon?

Critical Thinking

8. **Applying Concepts** How do rockets accelerate in space?

9. **Making Inferences** Why does escape velocity vary depending on the planet from which a rocket is launched?

For a variety of links related to this chapter, go to www.scilinks.org
Topic: Rocket Technology
SciLinks code: HSM1323

Answers to Section Review

1. Sample answers: A rocket is a vehicle that uses thrust provided by escaping gas to move. Thrust is the force that accelerates a rocket. NASA was established in 1958 to combine the efforts of rocket development teams in the United States.

2. b

3. Tsiolkovsky is known as the father of rocket theory because he proved, in theory, that rockets could be used to reach space. Robert Goddard is known as the father of modern rocketry because he developed and tested hundreds of rocket designs, and he built the first liquid-fuel rocket.

4. Answers may vary. Rocket engines use the pressure of expanding gas to generate thrust. Newton's third law of motion explains why rockets move in a direction opposite to the direction of the escaping gas.

5. Orbital velocity is the speed and direction an object must travel to stay in orbit around a body in space. Escape velocity is the speed and direction that an object must travel to break away from a planet's or moon's gravitational attraction.

6. Answers may vary. World War II led to an arms race between the United States and the Soviet Union, which encouraged competition between the two superpowers to achieve superiority in space.

7. 165 days × 24 h/day = 3,960 h
   3,960 h × 60 mi/h = 237,600 mi
   (Students may note that the moon's distance from the Earth varies and that the average distance is about 239,000 mi. To travel this distance at the rate described would take nearly 166 days.)

8. Rockets accelerate in space using Newton's third law of motion.

9. Escape velocity varies because the surface gravity of each planet depends on both the mass of the planet and the distance of the rocket from the center of the planet.

INCLUSION Strategies

- **Learning Disabled**

How can a gas move a heavy, solid rocket? Ask students to imagine a cannon shooting a cannonball. The cannon recoils backward at a much slower speed and in the opposite direction of the cannonball. When a rocket is launched, hot gases rush out of the exhaust nozzle at high speeds. The rocket reacts by moving upward at a slower speed. **LS Logical**

CHAPTER RESOURCES

Chapter Resource File

- Section Quiz GENERAL
- Section Review GENERAL
- Vocabulary and Section Summary GENERAL
- Reinforcement Worksheet BASIC

Technology

- Transparencies
  - How a Rocket Works

Section 1 • Rocket Science

SECTION 2

Focus

Overview

This section discusses the different kinds of satellites and satellite orbits. Students learn how remote sensing devices have helped us understand Earth as a global system.

🔔 Bellringer

Ask students to write two paragraphs describing the ways satellite technology affects their lives. (Students might mention the Global Positioning System, satellite television, satellite phones, or accurate weather forecasts.)

Motivate

CONNECTION ACTIVITY
Real World — ADVANCED

TV Satellites Write the following information on the board, and ask students to use a globe to find the location of the geostationary communications satellites that relay the signals of their favorite television shows. Note that this information changes often because satellites are moved to different orbits.

- ABC uses *Telstar-5* at 97°E.
- CBS uses *Telstar-6* at 93°W.
- Discovery Channel and ESPN use *Galaxy-5* at 125°W.
- The Weather Channel uses *Satcom-C3* at 131°W.

SECTION 2

READING WARM-UP

Objectives
- Identify the first satellites.
- Compare low Earth orbits with geostationary orbits.
- Explain the functions of military, communications, and weather satellites.
- Explain how remote sensing from satellites has helped us study Earth as a global system.

Terms to Learn
artificial satellite
low Earth orbit
geostationary orbit

READING STRATEGY

Reading Organizer As you read this section, make a table comparing the advantages and disadvantages of low Earth orbits and geostationary orbits.

Figure 1 A model of Sputnik 1, the first satellite to orbit the Earth, is shown below. It started a revolution in modern life that led to technology such as the Global Positioning System.

CHAPTER RESOURCES

Chapter Resource File
- Lesson Plan
- Directed Reading A **BASIC**
- Directed Reading B **SPECIAL NEEDS**

Technology
- Transparencies
  - Bellringer
  - GEO and LEO

Artificial Satellites

You are watching TV, and suddenly a weather bulletin interrupts your favorite show. There is a HURRICANE WARNING! You grab a cell phone and call your friend—the hurricane is headed straight for where she lives!

In the story above, the TV show, the weather bulletin, and perhaps even the phone call were all made possible by artificial satellites orbiting thousands of miles above Earth! An **artificial satellite** is any human-made object placed in orbit around a body in space.

There are many kinds of artificial satellites. Weather satellites provide continuous updates on the movement of gases in the atmosphere so that we can predict weather on Earth's surface. Communications satellites relay TV programs, phone calls, and computer data. Remote-sensing satellites monitor changes in the environment. Perhaps more than the exploration of space, satellites have changed the way we live.

The First Satellites

The first artificial satellite, *Sputnik 1*, was launched by the Soviets in 1957. **Figure 1** shows a model of *Sputnik 1*, which orbited for 57 days before it fell back to Earth and burned up in the atmosphere. Two months later, *Sputnik 2* carried the first living being into space—a dog named Laika. The United States followed with the launch of its first satellite, *Explorer 1*, in 1958. The development of new satellites increased quickly. By 1964, communications satellite networks were able to send messages around the world. Today, thousands of satellites orbit the Earth, and more are launched every year.

CONNECTION to Physical Science — GENERAL

Satellite Orbits Tell students that the orbit of satellites is determined by three major variables: gravity, velocity, and altitude (the distance above Earth). The force of gravity pulls satellites toward the Earth, so satellites must have a velocity great enough to remain in orbit. The closer a satellite is to Earth, the faster it must travel to remain in orbit. The result of these three variables is a curved path. **LS** Logical

---

688 Chapter 22 • Exploring Space

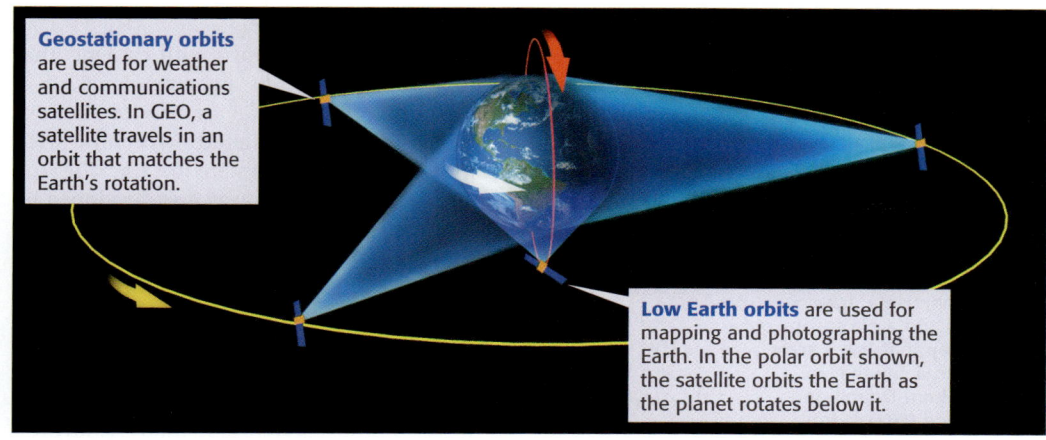

Geostationary orbits are used for weather and communications satellites. In GEO, a satellite travels in an orbit that matches the Earth's rotation.

Low Earth orbits are used for mapping and photographing the Earth. In the polar orbit shown, the satellite orbits the Earth as the planet rotates below it.

Figure 2 Low Earth orbits are in the upper reaches of Earth's atmosphere, while geostationary orbits are about 36,000 km from Earth's surface.

Choosing Your Orbit

Satellites are placed in different types of orbits, as shown in **Figure 2**. All of the early satellites were placed in **low Earth orbit** (LEO), which is a few hundred kilometers above the Earth's surface. A satellite in LEO moves around the Earth very quickly and can provide clear images of Earth. However, this motion can place a satellite out of contact much of the time.

Most communications satellites and weather satellites orbit much farther from Earth. In this orbit, called a **geostationary orbit** (GEO), a satellite travels in an orbit that exactly matches the Earth's rotation. Thus, the satellite is always above the same spot on Earth. Ground stations are in continuous contact with these satellites so that TV programs and other communications will not be interrupted.

✓ **Reading Check** What is the difference between GEO and LEO? (See the Appendix for answers to Reading Checks.)

artificial satellite any human-made object placed in orbit around a body in space

low Earth orbit an orbit less than 1,500 km above the Earth's surface

geostationary orbit an orbit that is about 36,000 km above the Earth's surface and in which a satellite is above a fixed spot on the equator

Quick Lab

Modeling LEO and GEO

1. Use a **length of thread** to measure 300 km on the scale of a **globe**.
2. Use another **length of thread** to measure 36,000 km on the globe's scale.
3. Use the short thread to measure the distance of LEO from the surface of the globe and the long thread to measure the distance of GEO from the surface of the globe.
4. Your teacher will turn off the lights. One student will spin the globe, while other students will hold **penlights** at LEO and GEO orbits.
5. Was more of the globe illuminated by the penlights in LEO or GEO?
6. Which orbit is better for communications satellites? Which orbit is better for spy satellites?

Quick Lab

Teacher's Notes: The contrast between the LEO and GEO orbits will be dramatic. Students may need help measuring 36,000 km on the globe's scale. One easy way to do this is to have students choose a cylindrical object such as a pen or a magic marker. Have them wrap a length of thread once around the pen and, on the thread, mark the circumference with another pen. Then, have students measure this length on the globe's scale. (The circumference of the pen tested equaled 1,000 km.) Then, students should divide 36,000 by the unit length (in this case, 1,000 km). Thus, 36 wraps around the pen will equal 36,000 km on the globe's scale.

Answers

5. Penlights in GEO illuminated more of the globe.
6. GEO is better for communications satellites. LEO is better for spy satellites.

Teach

INCLUSION Strategies

- Developmentally Delayed
- Hearing Impaired
- Learning Disabled

This activity is best performed in a gym or outside. Have five students sit at arm's length in a circle. This circle will simulate the Earth. Then, have the remainder of the class encircle the Earth in a circle that is 15 paces away from the Earth's "surface." These students are satellites. Show students a length of string, and tell them that the string represents a satellite signal. Explain that a student on Earth must send a signal to a student on the other side of the Earth, and the string cannot pass through the Earth. Have students brainstorm a way to use the satellites and ground stations to relay the signal. Have students practice sending several signals, and then ask them to summarize the activity in their **science journal** and include two questions that they have about satellite orbits. (Note: For advanced students, try turning off the lights and using mirrors and a flashlight or laser pointer instead of string. If you use a laser pointer, make sure that students use eye protection.)

LS Kinesthetic/Interpersonal

Answer to Reading Check
Answers may vary. LEO is much closer to the Earth than GEO.

Section 2 • Artificial Satellites **689**

Teach, continued

Answer to Math Practice
Atlanta, Georgia

Teacher's Notes: Students may need help measuring the distances on the map's scale. Show them how to use a piece of scrap paper with a straight-edge to measure the distances needed to adjust the compass.

Other Options: Roswell, New Mexico, is about 690 km from Oklahoma City, Oklahoma, 1,070 km from Salt Lake City, and 1,175 km from Monroe, Louisiana.

Discussion — ADVANCED

Polar Orbits Satellites such as those in the Landsat program are deployed in polar orbits; that is, they orbit Earth from pole to pole. Have students find out why polar orbits are best for mapping purposes. (One reason is that as the Landsat satellites orbit the Earth, the Earth rotates beneath them. In this way, the satellites can survey the entire planet without changing their orbit.)

Ask students to write a brief explanation of the advantages of polar orbits and draw a diagram showing the path a satellite in a polar orbit would take. **LS Visual**

MATH PRACTICE

Triangulation
GPS uses the principle of triangulation. To practice triangulation, use a drawing compass and a photocopy of a U.S. map that has a scale. Try to find a city that is 980 km from Detroit and Miami, and 950 km from Baltimore. For each city named, adjust the compass to the correct distance on the map's scale. Then, place the compass point on the city's location. Draw a circle with a radius equal to the given distance. Where do the circles overlap? Once you have solved this riddle, write one for a friend!

ACTIVITY

Military Satellites

Some satellites placed in LEO are equipped with cameras that can photograph the Earth's surface in amazing detail. It is possible to photograph objects as small as this book from LEO. While photographs taken by satellites are now used for everything from developing real estate to tracking the movements of dolphins, the technology was first developed by the military. Because satellites can take very detailed photos from hundreds of kilometers above the Earth's surface, they are ideal for defense purposes. The United States and the Soviet Union developed satellites to spy on each other right up to the end of the Cold War. **Figure 3,** for example, is a photo of San Francisco taken by a Soviet spy satellite in 1989. Even though the Cold War is over, spy satellites continue to play an important role in the military defense of many countries.

The Global Positioning System

In the past, people invented very complicated ways to keep from getting lost. Now, for less than $100, people can find out their exact location on Earth by using a Global Positioning System (GPS) receiver. GPS is another example of military satellite technology that has become a part of everyday life. The GPS consists of 27 solar-powered satellites that continuously send radio signals to Earth. From the amount of time it takes the signals to reach Earth, the hand-held receiver can calculate its distance from the satellites. Using the distance from four satellites, a GPS receiver can determine a person's location with great accuracy.

Figure 3 This photo was taken in 1989 by a Soviet spy satellite in LEO about 220 km above San Francisco. Can you identify any objects on the ground?

WEIRD SCIENCE

Geostationary satellites generally have a life span of 5 to 13 years. Because there are a limited number of locations in GEO, "dead" satellites must be disposed of in some way. Currently, satellites use their remaining propellant to navigate into a higher "graveyard orbit." Once in a graveyard orbit, a dead satellite circles Earth every 2 to 5 days and does not interfere with operating satellites in geostationary orbits.

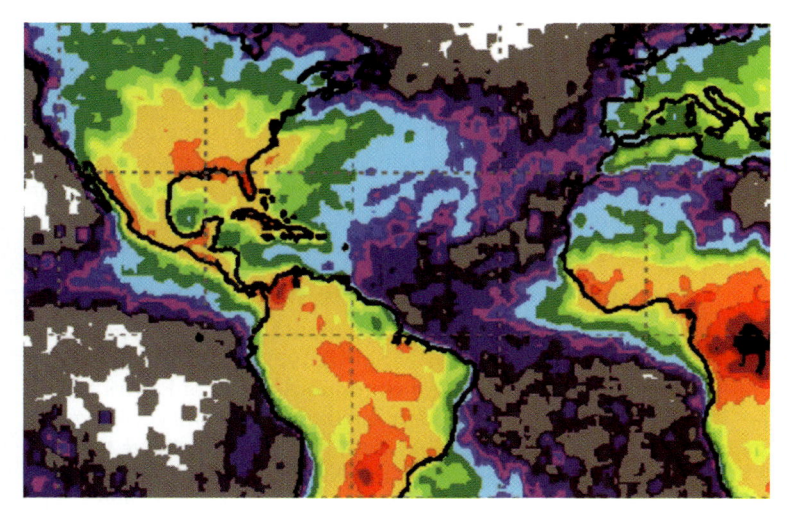

Figure 4 This map shows average annual lightning strikes around the world. Red and black indicate a high number of strikes. Cooler colors, such as purple and blue, indicate fewer strikes.

Weather Satellites

It is hard to imagine life without reliable weather forecasts. Every day, millions of people make decisions based on information provided by weather satellites. Weather satellites in GEO provide a big-picture view of the Earth's atmosphere. These satellites constantly monitor the atmosphere for the "triggers" that lead to severe weather conditions. Weather satellites in GEO created the map of world lightning strikes shown in **Figure 4.** Weather satellites in LEO are usually placed in polar orbits. Satellites in polar orbits revolve around the Earth in a north or south direction as the Earth rotates beneath them. These satellites, which orbit between 830 km and 870 km above the Earth, provide a much closer look at weather patterns.

Communications Satellites

Many types of modern communications use radio waves or microwaves to relay messages. Radio waves and microwaves are ideal for communications because they can travel through the air. The problem is that the Earth is round, but the waves travel in a straight line. So how do you send a message to someone on the other side of the Earth? Communications satellites in GEO solve this problem by relaying information from one point on Earth's surface to another. The signals are transmitted to a satellite and then sent to receivers around the world. Communications satellites relay computer data, and some television and radio broadcasts.

Reading Check How do communications satellites relay information from one point on Earth's surface to another?

School to Home

Tracking Satellites

A comfortable lawn chair and a clear night sky are all you need to track satellites. Just after sunset or before sunrise, satellites in LEO are easy to track. They look like slow-moving stars, and they generally move in a west to east direction. With a little practice, you should be able to find one or two satellites a minute. A pair of binoculars will help you get a closer look. Satellites in GEO are difficult to see because they do not appear to move. You and a parent can find out more about how to track specific satellites and space stations on the Internet.

ACTiViTY

CONNECTION to Physical Science—GENERAL

The Heat of Reentry What causes objects to heat up as they enter the atmosphere? People generally assume that friction from high-speed collisions with air molecules generates this heat. Actually, friction plays a minor role relative to pressure. As an object, such as a spacecraft, enters our atmosphere, the object compresses a layer of air about a meter deep beneath it. Imagine a snowplow pushing a mound of snow before it. As the layer of air beneath the spacecraft reaches tremendous pressures, thermal energy is transferred to the surface of the spacecraft by conduction, which causes the surface to glow red-hot. If students have ever inflated a bike tire using a well-oiled pump, they have observed this effect: the repeated compression of air causes the pump to become hot. For this reason, LEO satellites orbit in the outer reaches of Earth's atmosphere at a point where air pressure is insignificant.
LS Logical

Answer to Reading Check
Information from one location is transmitted to a communications satellite. The satellite then sends the information to another location on Earth.

Notes for School-to-Home Activity:
Satellites do not produce their own light; they reflect sunlight and "Earthshine" off their surfaces. The best time to view satellites is about an hour after sunset or an hour before sunrise. Encourage students to lie on the ground or sit in a reclining chair and scan the skies for satellites. Students can use binoculars if binoculars are available. A satellite will look like a star moving across the sky in a straight line. The star will fade out of sight before it reaches the horizon because it will be in Earth's shadow. Satellites can be seen moving from west to east or from pole to pole. Geosynchronous satellites are difficult to detect because they do not appear to move and because they are so far away. There are many Web sites that will help you determine the location of satellites and other objects in orbit, including the space shuttles and the *International Space Station*.

Section 2 • Artificial Satellites **691**

Close

Reteaching — BASIC

Orbital Review Have a student draw a diagram of GEO and LEO orbital paths. Ask students to help you add direction arrows that indicate the movement of satellites and the rotation of the Earth. Students should also help you fill in information about each orbit and the types of satellites that are placed in each orbit. Then, erase the information, and ask students to answer questions such as the following: "I want to place a spy satellite in an orbit in which the Earth rotates beneath it. What type of orbit should I use?" (polar LEO)
LS Visual

Quiz — GENERAL

1. What was the name of the first satellite to be placed in orbit, and what nation launched it? (The Soviet Union launched *Sputnik 1*.)
2. What is a geostationary orbit? (In a geostationary orbit, a satellite travels at a speed that matches the rotational speed of Earth. A satellite completes an orbit in the same time that Earth completes one rotation.)

Alternative Assessment — GENERAL

Satellite News Have each student bring in one article about a discovery made by a satellite using remote sensing. Have students share the articles with the class. **LS Verbal**

CONNECTION TO Environmental Science

WRITING SKILL **Space Junk** After more than 40 years of space launches, Earth orbits are getting cluttered with "space junk." The United States Space Command—a new branch of the military—tracks more than 10,000 pieces of debris. Left uncontrolled, this debris may become a problem for space vehicles in the future. Write a creative illustrated proposal to clean up space junk.

Remote Sensing and Environmental Change

Using satellites, scientists have been able to study the Earth in ways that were never before possible. Satellites gather information by *remote sensing*. Remote sensing is the gathering of images and data from a distance. Remote-sensing satellites measure light and other forms of energy that are reflected from Earth. Some satellites use radar, which bounces high-frequency radio waves off the Earth and measures the returned signal.

Landsat: Monitoring the Earth from Orbit

One of the most successful remote-sensing projects is the Landsat program, which began in 1972 and continues today. It has given us the longest continuous record of Earth's surface as seen from space. Landsat satellites gather images in several wavelengths—from visible light to infrared. **Figure 5** shows Landsat images of part of the Mississippi Delta. One image was taken in 1973, and the other was taken in 2003. The two images reveal a pattern of environmental change over a 30-year period. The main change is a dramatic reduction in the amount of silt that is reaching the delta. A comparison of the images also reveals a large-scale loss of wetlands in the bottom left of the delta in 2003. The loss of wetlands affects plants and animals living on the delta and the fishing industry.

Figure 5 The Loss of Wetlands in the Mississippi Delta

Silt reaching the Mississippi Delta is shown in blue. In 1973 (left), the amount of silt reaching the delta was much greater than in 2003 (right). This reduction led to the rapid loss of wetlands, which are green in this image. Notice the lower left corner of the delta in both images. Areas of wetland loss are black.

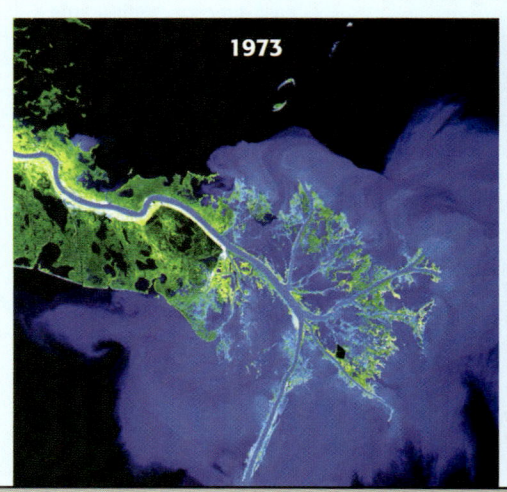

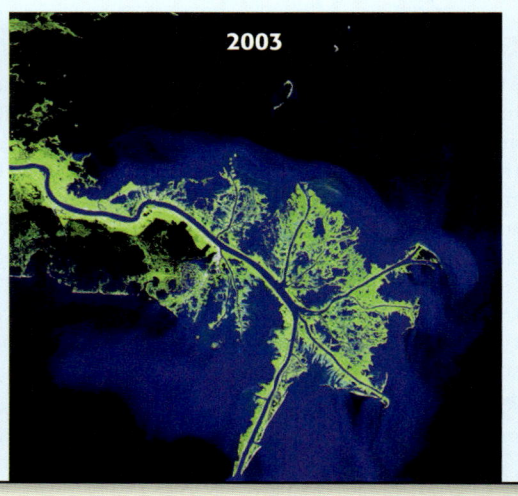

Cultural Awareness — GENERAL

INTELSAT INTELSAT is an international not-for-profit communications satellite representing more than 140 nations. Decisions about the system's upkeep and future are reached by consensus among the member nations. INTELSAT satellites relay telephone calls, television broadcasts, and other telecommunications data. During the 1998 Winter Olympics, INTELSAT linked people from China, Germany, South Africa, the United States, Australia, and Japan to form an international 2,000-member chorus. Have groups of students work together to write a proposal to launch a satellite that would benefit the global community. **LS Interpersonal**

A New Generation of Remote-Sensing Satellites

The Landsat program has produced millions of images that are used to identify and track environmental change on Earth. Satellite remote sensing allows scientists to perform large-scale mapping, look at changes in patterns of vegetation growth, map the spread of urban development, and study the effect of humans on the global environment. In 1999, NASA launched *Terra 1*, the first satellite in NASA's Earth Observing System (EOS) program. Satellites in the EOS program are designed to work together so that they can gather integrated data on environmental change on the land, in the atmosphere, in the oceans, and on the icecaps.

Reading Check What is unique about the EOS program?

INTERNET ACTIVITY

For another activity related to this chapter, go to **go.hrw.com** and type in the keyword **HZ5EXPW**.

SECTION Review

Summary

- *Sputnik 1* was the first artificial satellite. *Explorer 1* was the first U.S. satellite.
- Low Earth orbits are used for making detailed images of the Earth.
- Geostationary orbits are used for communications, navigation, and weather satellites.
- Satellites with remote sensing technology have helped us understand the Earth as a global system.

Using Key Terms

1. Use each of the following terms in a separate sentence: *artificial satellite, low Earth orbit,* and *geostationary orbit.*

Understanding Key Ideas

2. In a low Earth orbit, the speed of a satellite is
   a. slower than the rotational speed of the Earth.
   b. equal to the rotational speed of the Earth.
   c. faster than the rotational speed of the Earth.
   d. None of the above

3. What was the name of the first satellite placed in orbit?

4. List three ways that satellites benefit human society.

5. What was the *Explorer 1*?

6. Explain the differences between LEO and GEO satellites.

7. How does the Global Positioning System work?

8. How do communications satellites relay signals around the curved surface of Earth?

Math Skills

9. The speed required to reach Earth orbit is 8 km/s. What does this equal in *meters per hour*?

Critical Thinking

10. **Applying Concepts** The *Hubble Space Telescope* is located in LEO. Does the telescope move faster or slower around the Earth compared with a geostationary weather satellite? Explain.

11. **Applying Concepts** To triangulate your location on a map, you need to know your distance from three points. If you knew your distance from two points, how many possible places could you occupy?

SCLINKS

NSTA
Developed and maintained by the National Science Teachers Association

For a variety of links related to this chapter, go to www.scilinks.org
Topic: Artificial Satellites
SciLinks code: HSM0101

Answer to Reading Check

Satellites in the EOS program are designed to work together so that many different types of data can be integrated.

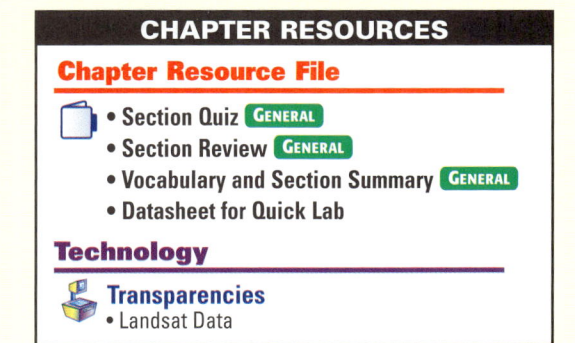

CHAPTER RESOURCES

Chapter Resource File
- Section Quiz GENERAL
- Section Review GENERAL
- Vocabulary and Section Summary GENERAL
- Datasheet for Quick Lab

Technology
- Transparencies
  - Landsat Data

Answers to Section Review

1. Sample answer: Artificial satellites are used for communications and for studying the Earth. Because the satellite was placed in low Earth orbit, it could make very detailed images of the Earth's surface. Communications satellites are placed in geostationary orbits.

2. c

3. *Sputnik 1*

4. Answers may vary. Students could note that satellites relay communications, help make accurate weather forecasts, and study environmental change using remote sensing.

5. *Explorer 1* was the first satellite launched by the United States.

6. Answers may vary. LEO is much closer to the Earth than GEO. Satellites in LEO are often used for studying the Earth in detail. Satellites in GEO are often used for communications and navigation.

7. The Global Positioning System uses a network of 27 satellites that sends signals to the Earth. A GPS receiver interprets the signals from four satellites and determines the location of the user based on the amount of time it takes the signals to reach the receiver. Using that information, the receiver can determine the position of the user using triangulation.

8. Answers may vary. Students should note that a signal is sent to a satellite in GEO. Then, the satellite transmits the signal back to a ground station on Earth.

9. 8,000 m/s × 3,600 s/h = 28,800,000 m/h

10. The *Hubble Space Telescope* will orbit faster than a satellite in GEO because objects in LEO orbit at a much faster speed than objects in GEO.

11. If you knew your distance from two points on a map, you could be in two possible locations.

Section 2 • Artificial Satellites

SECTION 3

Focus

Overview

This section describes some of the discoveries made by the earliest space probes. Students will also learn about the data gathered by recent probes that have visited the inner and outer planets. Finally, this section describes how NASA's strategy of "faster, cheaper, and better" relates to space probes.

Bellringer

Ask students to consider the following questions: "Does exploring other planets benefit us here on Earth? Why or why not?"

Motivate

ACTIVITY — GENERAL

Design Your Own Space Mission Have students imagine that they could send a space probe anywhere in the solar system. In their **science journal,** have students write a paragraph about where they would send their probe, what kind of instruments it would carry, what kind of data it would collect, and what its primary mission would be. Invite volunteers to read their paragraphs to the class and elaborate on their choices. **LS Verbal/Visual**

SECTION 3

READING WARM-UP

Objectives
- Describe five discoveries made by space probes.
- Explain how space-probe missions help us better understand the Earth.
- Describe how NASA's new strategy of "faster, cheaper, and better" relates to space probes.

Terms to Learn
space probe

READING STRATEGY

Reading Organizer As you read this section, make a concept map showing the space probes, the planetary bodies they visited, and their discoveries.

space probe an uncrewed vehicle that carries scientific instruments into space to collect scientific data

CHAPTER RESOURCES

Chapter Resource File
- Lesson Plan
- Directed Reading A BASIC
- Directed Reading B SPECIAL NEEDS

Technology
- Transparencies
- Bellringer

Space Probes

What does the surface of Mars look like? Does life exist anywhere else in the solar system?

To answer questions like these, scientists send space probes to explore the solar system. A **space probe** is an uncrewed vehicle that carries scientific instruments to planets or other bodies in space. Unlike satellites, which stay in Earth orbit, space probes travel away from the Earth. Space probes are valuable because they can complete missions that would be very dangerous and expensive for humans to undertake.

Visits to the Inner Solar System

Because Earth's moon and the inner planets are much closer than the other planets and moons in the solar system, they were the first to be explored by space probes. Let's take a closer look at some missions to the moon, Venus, and Mars.

Luna and Clementine: Missions to the Moon

Luna 1, the first space probe, was launched by the Soviets in 1959 to fly past the moon. In 1966, *Luna 9* made the first soft landing on the moon's surface. During the next 10 years, the United States and the Soviet Union completed more than 30 lunar missions. Thousands of images of the moon's surface were taken. In 1994, the United States probe *Clementine* discovered that craters of the moon may contain water left by comet impacts. In 1998, the *Lunar Prospector* confirmed that frozen water exists on the moon. This ice would be very valuable to a human colony on the moon.

Missions to the Moon

Luna 9 (U.S.S.R)
Launched: January 1966
Purpose: to land the first spacecraft on the moon

Clementine (U.S.)
Launched: January 1994
Purpose: to map the composition of the moon's surface

Is That a Fact!

As a rocket moves away from Earth, gravitational pull and air resistance decrease. In addition, the rocket's mass decreases as the rocket burns fuel. Thus, rockets accelerate as they travel from Earth's surface. The space shuttle accelerates from 0 km/h to 27,000 km/h in a little more than 8 min!

---

694 Chapter 22 • Exploring Space

Venera 9: The First Probe to Land on Venus

The Soviet probe *Venera 9* was the first probe to land on Venus. The probe parachuted into Venus's atmosphere and transmitted images of the surface to Earth. *Venera 9* found that the surface temperature and atmospheric pressure on Venus are much higher than on Earth. The surface temperature of Venus is an average of 464°C—hot enough to melt lead! *Venera 9* also found that the chemistry of the surface rocks on Venus is similar to that of Earth rocks. Perhaps most important, *Venera 9* and earlier missions revealed that Venus has a severe greenhouse effect. Scientists study Venus's atmosphere to learn about the effects of increased greenhouse gases in Earth's atmosphere.

The Magellan Mission: Mapping Venus

In 1989, the United States launched the *Magellan* probe, which used radar to map 98% of the surface of Venus. The radar data were transmitted back to Earth where computers used the data to generate three-dimensional images like the one shown in **Figure 1**. The Magellan mission showed that, in many ways, the geology of Venus is similar to that of Earth. Venus has features that suggest plate tectonics occurs there, as it does on Earth. Venus also has volcanoes, and some of them may be active.

✔ **Reading Check** What discoveries were made by *Magellan*? (*See the Appendix for answers to Reading Checks.*)

Missions to Venus

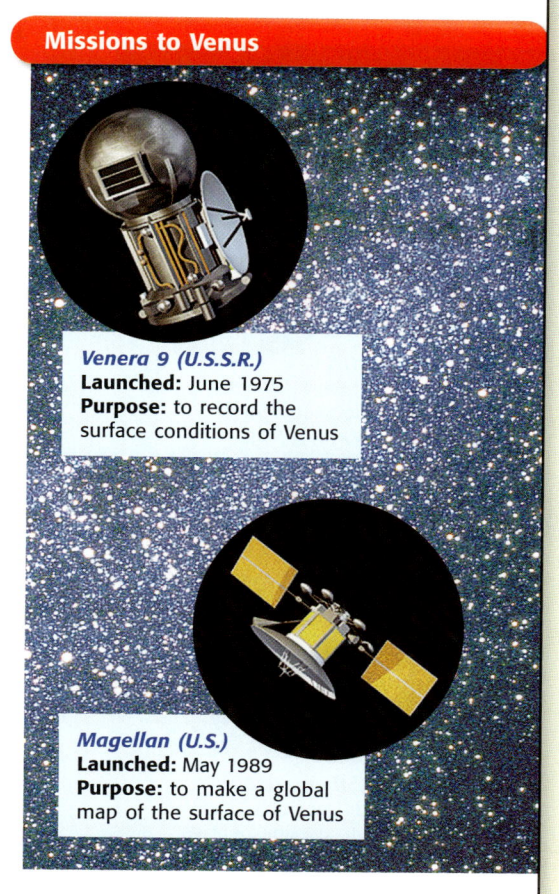

Venera 9 (U.S.S.R.)
Launched: June 1975
Purpose: to record the surface conditions of Venus

Magellan (U.S.)
Launched: May 1989
Purpose: to make a global map of the surface of Venus

Figure 1 This false-color image of volcanoes on the surface of Venus was made with radar data transmitted to Earth by *Magellan*.

Science Bloopers

Life on Venus? For the first half of the 20th century, a popular theory suggested that every planet had once supported life or would support it in the future. The theory was based on the idea that the sun has gradually cooled since its formation. Thus, Mars had once harbored life; it was currently Earth's turn, and Venus would be next. Some scientists thought that Venus might already be home to primitive life-forms equivalent to those of Earth's Cambrian period. However, the 1962 *Mariner 2* flyby showed that the surface temperature of Venus was a constant 464°C. We also know now that the sun is hotter now than when it formed 4.5 billion years ago.

Teach

READING STRATEGY — GENERAL

Paired Summarizing Group students into pairs, and have them read silently about space probes in this section. Then, have one student summarize the mission and discoveries of each space probe. The other student should listen to the retelling and point out any inaccuracies or facts that were left out. **LS Interpersonal**

Using the Figure — BASIC

Probe Design Have students study the images of space probes in this section. Then, have students design and draw their own version of a space probe. Have them outline their probe's mission and give the probe an appropriate name. **LS Visual** **English Language Learners**

ACTIVITY — GENERAL

Designing a Mission Patch Astronauts Gordon Cooper and Charles "Pete" Conrad, members of the 1965 Gemini 5 mission, began a NASA tradition by designing a patch to be worn on their spacesuits that symbolized the purpose of their mission. As students read about the space-probe missions described in the section, have them choose one mission and then create a patch design that commemorates the purpose and accomplishments of that mission. Students might also include a motto on their patches. Patch designs are available on NASA's Web site. **LS Intrapersonal**

Answer to Reading Check

The Magellan mission showed that, in many ways, the surface of Venus is similar to the surface of Earth.

Section 3 • Space Probes **695**

Teach, continued

CONNECTION to Physical Science — GENERAL

Gravity Assists *Voyagers 1* and *2*, *Galileo*, *Ulysses*, and *Cassini* have used a maneuver called a *gravity assist* to explore the solar system. In a gravity assist, spacecraft make use of a planet's gravitational pull to accelerate, slow down, or change direction. Accomplishing such maneuvers using gravity is a triumph of Newtonian physics and saves a tremendous amount of fuel. A slingshot analogy is sometimes used to describe gravity assists because of the way the spacecraft swings around the planet and is released, slingshotting out into space in a new flight path. *Voyagers 1* and *2* gained momentum with gravity assists from Jupiter and Saturn. *Voyager 2* also gained momentum with gravity assists from Uranus and Neptune. The *Ulysses* space probe obtained a gravity assist from Jupiter that sent it into a highly inclined trajectory, which eventually placed it in a polar orbit around the sun.

Missions to Mars

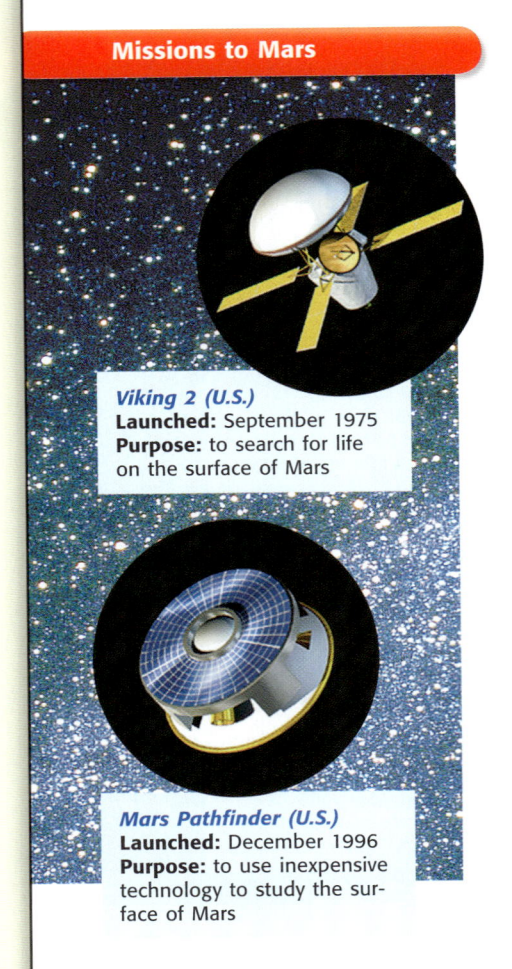

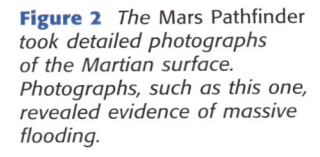

Viking 2 (U.S.)
Launched: September 1975
Purpose: to search for life on the surface of Mars

Mars Pathfinder (U.S.)
Launched: December 1996
Purpose: to use inexpensive technology to study the surface of Mars

Figure 2 *The* Mars Pathfinder *took detailed photographs of the Martian surface. Photographs, such as this one, revealed evidence of massive flooding.*

CONNECTION ACTIVITY
History — GENERAL

Writing **The United Nations Outer Space Treaty** On January 23, 1967, the United Nations Outer Space Treaty was signed. The treaty guarantees all nations the freedom to explore and use space. The treaty emphasizes a humanistic and pacifist philosophy, which governs the actions of countries as they explore outer space, the moon, and other objects in space. Have students research this treaty and outline its major points. **LS Intrapersonal**

The Viking Missions: Exploring Mars

In 1975, the United States sent a pair of probes—*Viking 1* and *Viking 2*—to Mars. The surface of Mars is more like the Earth's surface than that of any other planet. For this reason, one of the main goals of the Viking missions was to look for signs of life. The probes contained instruments designed to gather soil and test it for evidence of life. However, no hard evidence was found. The Viking missions did find evidence that Mars was once much warmer and wetter than it is now. This discovery led scientists to ask even more questions about Mars. Did the Martian climate once support life? Why and when did the Martian climate change?

The Mars Pathfinder Mission: Revisiting Mars

More than 20 years later, in 1997, the surface of Mars was visited again by a NASA space probe. The goal of the Mars Pathfinder mission was to show that Martian exploration is possible at a much lower cost than the Viking missions. The probe sent back detailed images of dry water channels on the planet's surface. These images, such as the one shown in **Figure 2**, suggest that massive floods flowed across the surface of Mars relatively recently in the planet's past. The *Mars Pathfinder* successfully landed on Mars and deployed the *Sojourner* rover. *Sojourner* traveled across the surface of Mars for almost three months, collecting data and recording images. The European Space Agency and NASA have many more Mars missions planned for the near future. These missions will pave the way for a crewed mission to Mars that may occur in your lifetime!

✓ **Reading Check** What discoveries were made by the Mars Pathfinder mission?

Answer to Reading Check

The Mars Pathfinder mission found evidence suggesting that water once flowed across the surface of Mars.

696 Chapter 22 • Exploring Space

Visits to the Outer Solar System

The planets in the outer solar system—Jupiter, Saturn, Uranus, Neptune, and Pluto—are very far away. Probes such as those described below can take 10 years or more to complete their missions.

Pioneer and Voyager: To Jupiter and Beyond

The *Pioneer 10* and *Pioneer 11* space probes were the first to visit the outer planets. Among other things, these probes sampled the *solar wind*—the flow of particles coming from the sun. The Pioneer probes also found that the dark belts on Jupiter provide deep views into Jupiter's atmosphere. In 1983, *Pioneer 10* became the first probe to travel past the orbit of Pluto, the outermost planet.

The Voyager space probes were the first to detect Jupiter's faint rings, and *Voyager 2* was the first probe to fly by the four gas giants—Jupiter, Saturn, Uranus, and Neptune. The paths of the Pioneer and Voyager space probes are shown in **Figure 3**. Today, they are near the solar system's edge and some are still sending back data.

The Galileo Mission: A Return to Jupiter

The *Galileo* probe arrived at Jupiter in 1995. While *Galileo* itself began a long tour of Jupiter's moons, it sent a smaller probe into Jupiter's atmosphere to measure its composition, density, temperature, and cloud structure. *Galileo* gathered data about the geology of Jupiter's major moons and Jupiter's magnetic properties. The moons of Jupiter proved to be far more exciting than the earlier Pioneer and Voyager images had suggested. *Galileo* discovered that two of Jupiter's moons have magnetic fields and that one of its moons, Europa, may have an ocean of liquid water under its icy surface.

Missions to the Outer Solar System

Pioneer 10 (U.S.)
Launched: March 1972
Purpose: to study Jupiter and the outer solar system

Galileo (U.S.)
Launched: October 1989
Purpose: to study Jupiter and its moons

Figure 3 The Orbits of the *Pioneer* and *Voyager* Probes

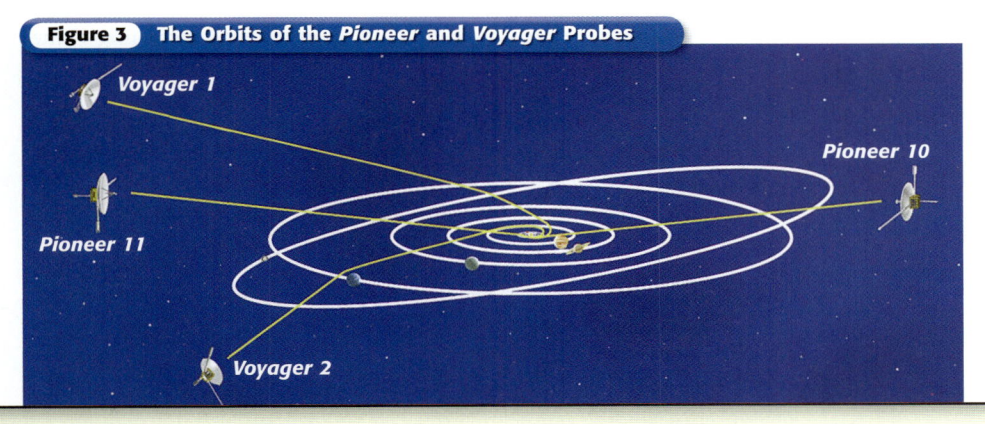

CHAPTER RESOURCES

Technology

Transparencies
• Space Probes in the Outer Solar System

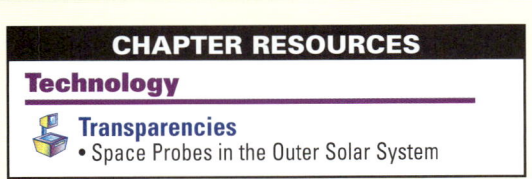

CONNECTION ACTIVITY
History — GENERAL

The Voyager Probes When the Voyager space probes were launched in 1977, each carried two gold-plated phonograph records with a variety of sounds and music intended as a message for intelligent life in the universe. The probes also carried a variety of images and written messages. Share the following list with students, and discuss the kinds of historical, scientific, and cultural information that the Voyagers carry:

- greetings from Earth spoken in 55 languages, ranging from ancient Sumerian to English
- printed messages from U.S. President Jimmy Carter and U.N. Secretary General Kurt Waldheim
- the sound of surf, wind, thunder, birdcalls, cricket chirps, and a whale song
- musical selections ranging from bagpipe music from Azerbaijan to "Johnny B. Goode" by Chuck Berry
- a diagram of the solar system
- anatomical drawings of a man and a woman
- a variety of images, ranging from the Great Wall of China to rush-hour traffic in India to a house in New England

A complete description of the contents of the Voyager probes can be found on NASA's Web site using the keyword "Golden Record."

Note: Some pictures, such as a photograph of a nursing mother, may be inappropriate for children. You may want to print selected photographs for students.

LS Visual/Auditory

Close

Reteaching — BASIC

Space Probe Profiles Have students create a poster of each space probe that includes pictures of the probe and information about its mission and discoveries. **LS Visual**

Quiz — GENERAL

1. How is a space probe different from an artificial satellite? (A space probe carries scientific instruments to other bodies in space. Probes do not orbit Earth. Students may also note that some probes become satellites of other planets.)

2. What was the main goal of the Viking missions? (to look for signs of life on Mars)

Alternative Assessment — GENERAL

Debate: Faster, Cheaper, and Better? Some scientists think that traditional space probe projects are obsolete. These projects are expensive and require considerable support staff to receive and interpret the data. Others feel that large, complex probes are the best way to explore the solar system. Larger probes can carry more equipment and can gather more information than smaller, cheaper probes. Have students form two groups to research this debate. Student groups should present their findings as if they were NASA scientists going before Congress to secure funding for their projects. **LS Verbal**

Figure 4 This artist's view shows the *Huygens* probe parachuting to the surface of Saturn's moon Titan. Saturn and *Cassini* are in the background.

The Cassini Mission: Exploring Saturn's Moons

In 1997, the *Cassini* space probe was launched on a seven-year journey to Saturn where it will make a grand tour of Saturn's moons. As shown in **Figure 4**, a smaller probe, called the *Huygens* probe, will detach itself from *Cassini* and descend into the atmosphere of Saturn's moon Titan. Scientists are interested in Titan's atmosphere because it may be similar to the Earth's early atmosphere. Titan's atmosphere may reveal clues about how life developed on Earth.

Faster, Cheaper, and Better

The early space probe missions were very large and costly. Probes such as *Voyager 2* and *Galileo* took years to develop. Now, NASA has a vision for missions that are "faster, cheaper, and better." One new program, called Discovery, seeks proposals for smaller science programs. The first six approved Discovery missions include sending small space probes to asteroids, landing on Mars again, studying the moon, and returning comet dust to Earth.

Stardust: Comet Detective

Launched in 1999, the *Stardust* space probe is the first probe to focus only on a comet. The probe will arrive at the comet in 2004 and gather samples of the comet's dust tail. It will return the samples to Earth in 2006. For the first time, pure samples from beyond the orbit of the moon will be brought back to Earth. The comet dust should help scientists better understand how the solar system formed.

✓ **Reading Check** What is the mission of the *Stardust* probe?

CONNECTION TO Social Studies

Cosmic Message in a Bottle When the Voyager space probes were launched in 1977, they carried a variety of messages intended for alien civilizations that might find them. In addition to greetings spoken in 55 different languages, a variety of songs, nature sounds, a diagram of the solar system, and photographs of life on Earth were included. Find out more about the message carried by the Voyager missions, and then create your own cosmic message in a bottle. **ACTIVITY**

Notes for Connection to Social Studies: Have students consider these questions: What important events or discoveries have occurred since 1977? What information would you consider most important? What kinds of music or images would you want aliens to know about? How would you design an intelligible message for alien civilizations?

Answer to Reading Check
The mission of the Stardust probe is to gather samples from a comet's tail and return them to Earth.

CONNECTION to Physical Science — GENERAL

Ion Propulsion In *Deep Space 1*, xenon gas is bombarded with electrons to create ions. Positive ions are drawn toward a high voltage grid and are expelled at 30 km/s. This may sound fast, but the thrust generated by *Deep Space 1* is 10,000 times weaker than that generated by a typical space probe. Although the thrust is equivalent to the weight of one sheet of paper on Earth, the probe gradually accelerates to incredible speeds over many months.

Deep Space 1: Testing Ion Propulsion

Another NASA project is the New Millennium program. Its purpose is to test new technologies that can be used in the future. *Deep Space 1*, shown in **Figure 5**, is the first mission of this program. It is a space probe with an ion-propulsion system. Instead of burning chemical fuel, an ion rocket uses charged particles that exit the vehicle at high speed. An ion rocket follows Newton's third law of motion, but it does so using a unique source of propulsion. Ion propulsion is like sitting on the back of a truck and shooting peas out of a straw. If there were no friction, the truck would gradually accelerate to tremendous speeds.

Figure 5 Deep Space 1 uses a revolutionary type of propulsion—an ion rocket.

SECTION Review

Summary

- Exploration with space probes began with missions to the moon. Space probes then explored other bodies in the inner solar system.
- Space-probe missions to Mars have focused on the search for signs of water and life.
- The Pioneer and Voyager programs explored the outer solar system.
- Space probe missions have helped us understand Earth's formation and environment.
- NASA's new strategy of "faster, cheaper, and better" seeks to create space-probe missions that are smaller than those of the past.

Using Key Terms

The statements below are false. For each statement, replace the underlined term to make a true statement.

1. <u>Luna 1</u> discovered evidence of water on the moon.
2. <u>Venera 9</u> helped map 98% of Venus's surface.
3. <u>Stardust</u> uses ion propulsion to accelerate.

Understanding Key Ideas

4. What is the significance of the discovery of evidence of water on the moon?
   a. Water is responsible for the formation of craters.
   b. Water was left by early space probes.
   c. Water could be used by future moon colonies.
   d. The existence of water proves that there is life on the moon.
5. Describe three discoveries that have been made by space probes.
6. How do missions to Venus, Mars, and Titan help us understand Earth's environment?

Math Skills

7. Traveling at the speed of light, signals from *Voyager 1* take about 12 h to reach Earth. The speed of light is about 299,793 km/s, how far away is the probe?

Critical Thinking

8. **Making Inferences** Why did we need space probes to discover water channels on Mars and evidence of ice on Europa?
9. **Expressing Opinions** What are the advantages of the new Discovery program over the older space-probe missions, and what are the disadvantages?
10. **Applying Concepts** How does *Deep Space 1* use Newton's third law of motion to accelerate?

SciLinks — Developed and maintained by the National Science Teachers Association
For a variety of links related to this chapter, go to www.scilinks.org
Topic: Space Probes
SciLinks code: HSM1342

CONNECTION to Physical Science — GENERAL

Forming Ions *Deep Space 1* carried 81 kg of xenon gas propellant, which is enough to operate the thruster at one-half throttle for more than 20 months. Use the teaching transparency "Forming Positive and Negative Ions" to show students how the xenon ions that propel the probe are formed.

CHAPTER RESOURCES

Chapter Resource File
- Section Quiz GENERAL
- Section Review GENERAL
- Vocabulary and Section Summary GENERAL
- Reinforcement Worksheet BASIC
- Critical Thinking ADVANCED

Technology

Transparencies
- LINK TO PHYSICAL SCIENCE Forming Positive and Negative Ions

Answers to Section Review

1. *Clementine* or *Lunar Prospector*
2. *Magellan*
3. *Deep Space 1*
4. c
5. Sample answer: The Viking missions sent images of dry water channels on the surface of Mars. *Venera 9* recorded information about the surface and atmosphere of Venus. *Galileo* discovered that two of Jupiter's moons have magnetic fields.
6. Venus and Mars have surface features that are similar to Earth's. In addition, the high levels of CO_2 in Venus's atmosphere produce a severe greenhouse effect. This may help us understand the greenhouse effect on Earth. The atmosphere of Titan may be similar to Earth's early atmosphere. Studying Titan's atmosphere may provide clues about how life developed on Earth.
7. 299,793 km/s × 60 s/min = 17,987,580 km/min
   17,987,580 km/min × 60 min/h = 1,079,254,800 km/h
   1,079,254,800 km/h × 12 h = 12,951,057,600 km
8. Answers may vary. Students should note that the conditions on Mars and Europa are extreme and that the danger and expense of sending humans there is great. These places are also too distant to be seen clearly by a telescope on Earth's surface or in orbit around Earth.
9. Sample answer: The Discovery program seeks to produce results quickly and inexpensively. The disadvantages may be that missions may fail because of cost-cutting. Also, probes in the Discovery program may not gather as much data as larger probes do.
10. *Deep Space 1* accelerates by expelling very small charged particles at a high speed. The probe reacts by moving forward.

Section 3 • Space Probes

SECTION 4

Focus

Overview

This section explores the political rivalry that led to the Apollo program. The section discusses how reusable space shuttles have revolutionized space travel and research. Students also learn about *Skylab*, *Mir*, and the *International Space Station*.

🔔 Bellringer

Ask students to write a letter from a space station orbiting Earth. They should describe the station, their mission, and their day-to-day lives.

Motivate

Discussion — GENERAL

A "Walk" on the Moon Read students *Apollo 12* astronaut Alan Bean's description of his 1969 moon walk:

> "After pushing off on one foot, there will be a long wait until you land on the other, exactly like running in slow motion.... As you run, you'll feel as if you're leaping long, impossible distances. And in fact you are."

This and other quotes from Apollo astronauts may help students experience the excitement of space exploration by humans.
LS Verbal

SECTION 4

READING WARM-UP

Objectives
- Summarize the history and future of human spaceflight.
- Explain the benefits of crewed space programs.
- Identify five "space-age spinoffs" that are used in everyday life.

Terms to Learn
space shuttle
space station

READING STRATEGY

Reading Organizer As you read this section, make a flowchart that shows the events of the space race.

People in Space

One April morning in 1961, a rocket stood on a launch pad in a remote part of the Soviet Union. Inside, a 27-year-old cosmonaut named Yuri Gagarin sat and waited. He was about to do what no human had done before—travel to outer space. No one knew if the human brain would function in space or if he would be instantly killed by radiation.

On April 12, 1961, Yuri Gagarin, shown in **Figure 1,** became the first human to orbit Earth. The flight lasted 108 minutes. An old woman, her granddaughter, and a cow were the first to see Gagarin as he safely parachuted back to Earth, but the news of his success was quickly broadcast around the world.

The Race Is On

The Soviets were first once again, and the Americans were concerned that their rivals were winning the space race. Therefore, on May 25, 1961, President Kennedy announced, "I believe that the nation should commit itself to achieving the goal, before this decade is out, of landing a man on the moon and returning him safely to the Earth. No single project in this period will be more impressive to mankind, or more important for the long range exploration of space."

Kennedy's speech took everyone by surprise—even NASA's leaders. Go to the moon? We had not even reached orbit yet! In response to Kennedy's challenge, a new spaceport called Kennedy Space Center was built in Florida and Mission Control was established in Houston, Texas. In February 1962, John Glenn became the first American to orbit the Earth.

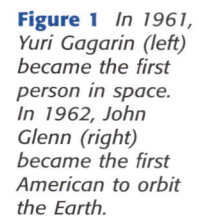

Figure 1 In 1961, Yuri Gagarin (left) became the first person in space. In 1962, John Glenn (right) became the first American to orbit the Earth.

CHAPTER RESOURCES

Chapter Resource File
- Lesson Plan
- Directed Reading A BASIC
- Directed Reading B SPECIAL NEEDS

Technology
- Transparencies
  - Bellringer

CONNECTION to Life Science — GENERAL

The Smallest Astronauts During the second crewed mission to the moon (*Apollo 12*, November 14–24, 1969), astronauts retrieved some pieces of the space probe *Surveyor*. Amazingly, the pieces of *Surveyor* harbored bacteria from Earth that survived for 2 1/2 years in the moon's dry, near-vacuum environment!

---

700 Chapter 22 • Exploring Space

"The Eagle Has Landed"

Seven years later, on July 20, 1969, Kennedy's challenge was met. The world watched on television as the *Apollo 11* landing module—the *Eagle,* shown in **Figure 2**—landed on the moon. Neil Armstrong became the first human to set foot on a world other than Earth. This moment forever changed the way we view ourselves and our planet. The Apollo missions also contributed to the advancement of science. *Apollo 11* returned moon rocks to Earth for study. Its crew also put devices on the moon to study moonquakes and the solar wind.

The Space Shuttle

The Saturn V rockets, which carried the Apollo astronauts to the moon, were huge and very expensive. They were longer than a football field, and each could be used only once. To save money, NASA began to develop the space shuttle program in 1972. A **space shuttle** is a reusable space vehicle that takes off like a rocket and lands like an airplane.

The Space Shuttle Gets off the Ground

Columbia, the first space shuttle, was launched on April 12, 1981. Since then, NASA has completed more than 100 successful shuttle missions. If you look at the shuttle *Endeavour* in **Figure 3,** you can see its main parts. The orbiter is about the size of an airplane. It carries the astronauts and payload into space. The liquid-fuel tank is the large red column. Two white solid-fuel booster rockets help the shuttle reach orbit. Then they fall back to Earth along with the fuel tank. The booster rockets are reused, the fuel tank is not. After completing a mission, the orbiter returns to Earth and lands like an airplane.

Reading Check What are the main parts of the shuttle? (*See the Appendix for answers to Reading Checks.*)

Shuttle Tragedies

On January 28, 1986, the booster rocket on the space shuttle *Challenger* exploded just after takeoff, killing all seven of its astronauts. On board was Christa McAuliffe, who would have been the first teacher in space. Investigations found that cold weather on the morning of the launch had caused rubber gaskets in the solid fuel booster rockets to stiffen and fail. The failure of the gaskets led to the explosion. The shuttle program resumed in 1988. In 2003, however, the space shuttle *Columbia* exploded as it reentered the atmosphere. All seven astronauts onboard were killed. These disasters emphasize the dangers of space exploration that continue to challenge scientists and engineers.

Figure 2 *Neil Armstrong took this photo of Edwin "Buzz" Aldrin as Aldrin was about to become the second human to set foot on the moon.*

space shuttle a reusable space vehicle that takes off like a rocket and lands like an airplane

Figure 3 *The space shuttles are the first reusable space vehicles.*

SCIENCE HUMOR

As *Apollo 11* approached the moon, a special mechanism kept it rotating slowly. Had the spacecraft not been rotating, the side exposed to the sun would have quickly overheated. The Apollo astronauts comically referred to this rotisserie-like movement as the "barbecue mode." When Neil Armstrong hopped off the ladder onto the moon's surface and made his historic speech, he bungled his line. The astronaut meant to say, "One small leap for *a* man, one giant leap for mankind." This flub inspired numerous jokes, including one by Apollo astronaut Pete Conrad, who was known for his sense of humor. As the relatively short astronaut stepped onto the moon, he joked, "Whoopie! Man, that may have been a small one for Neil, but that's a long one for me." When the poet Joseph Brodsky won the Nobel Prize for literature in 1987, he quipped, "A big step for me, a small one for mankind."

Teach

READING STRATEGY — GENERAL

Prediction Guide Have students predict whether the following statements are true or false:

- There is only one space shuttle. (false)
- Both the United States and the Soviet Union have launched space stations. (true)
- Many nations are collaborating on an international space station. (true)

LS Logical

Demonstration — BASIC

O-Ring Failure The day of the Challenger disaster was unseasonably cold for Florida, with temperatures below freezing. The investigation that followed the tragedy traced the explosion to the failure of O-ring seals that were designed to prevent hot exhaust gases from leaking out of the spacecraft's rocket boosters. Due to the cold temperatures, the rings had stiffened and failed to seal effectively. As a result, one of the rocket boosters leaked, which led to a catastrophic explosion 73 s after liftoff. To replicate physicist Richard Feynman's dramatic demonstration of how the cold weather contributed to the O-ring failure, pass a rubber gasket from a hardware store around class. Allow students to note the gasket's pliability. Then, place the gasket in a glass of ice water for a minute. Pass the gasket around again, and allow students to examine how inflexible the gasket became.

LS Kinesthetic

Answer to Reading Check

the orbiter, the liquid-fuel tank, and the solid-fuel booster rockets

Section 4 • People in Space

Teach, continued

Debate — GENERAL

Space Exploration: Does the Expense Outweigh the Benefits? Encourage students to debate the costs of space exploration versus the potential benefits to humankind. Students should recognize that although space exploration is very expensive, measuring or predicting how much could be gained by exploration is difficult. The space industry also employs many people, including scientists, engineers, and support personnel. On the other hand, there are many problems on Earth, such as hunger, disease, homelessness, and illiteracy. **LS** Verbal

Group Activity — GENERAL

Skylab Results Have students find out about the experiments conducted on *Skylab* or *Mir*. Groups should focus on biological, medical, space manufacturing, or astronomical experiments. Have groups share their findings in an oral presentation. **LS** Verbal

Figure 4 As this illustration shows, space planes may provide transportation to outer space and around the world.

space station a long-term orbiting platform from which other vehicles can be launched or scientific research can be carried out

CONNECTION TO Biology

Effects of Weightlessness When a human body stays in space for long periods of time without having to work against gravity, the bones lose mass and muscles become weaker. Find out about the exercises to reduce the loss of bone mass used by astronauts aboard the *International Space Station*. Create an "Astronaut Exercise Book" to share with your friends.

ACTIVITY

Space Planes: The Shuttles of the Future?

NASA is working to develop advanced space systems, such as a space plane. This craft will fly like a normal airplane, but it will have rocket engines for use in space. Once in operation, space planes, such as the one shown in **Figure 4**, may lower the cost of getting material to LEO by 90%. Private companies are also becoming interested in developing space vehicles for commercial use and to make space travel cheaper, easier, and safer.

Space Stations—People Working in Space

A long-term orbiting platform in space is called a **space station**. On April 19, 1971, the Soviets became the first to successfully place a space station in orbit. A crew of three Soviet cosmonauts conducted a 23-day mission aboard the station, which was called *Salyut 1*. By 1982, the Soviets had put up seven space stations. Because of this experience, the Soviet Union became a leader in space-station development and in the study of the effects of weightlessness on humans. Their discoveries will be important for future flights to other planets—journeys that will take years to complete.

Skylab and *Mir*

Skylab, the United States' first space station, was a science and engineering lab used to conduct a wide variety of scientific studies. These studies included experiments in biology and space manufacturing and astronomical observations. Three different crews spent a total of 171 days on *Skylab* before it was abandoned. In 1986, the Soviets began to launch the pieces for a much more ambitious space station called *Mir* (meaning "peace"). Astronauts on *Mir* conducted a wide range of experiments, made many astronomical observations, and studied manufacturing in space. After 15 years, *Mir* was abandoned and it burned up in the Earth's atmosphere in 2001.

WEIRD SCIENCE

As astronaut William Pogue exercised on *Skylab*, his sweat "just sort of slithered around" instead of pooling on the floor beneath him, he reported. After exercising, he corralled the hovering sweat with a towel so that it wouldn't interfere with the spacecraft's equipment!

The *International Space Station*

The *International Space Station (ISS)*, the newest space station, is being constructed in LEO. Russia, the United States, and 14 other countries are designing and building different parts of the station. **Figure 5** shows what the *ISS* will look like when it is completed. The *ISS* is being built with materials brought up on the space shuttles and by Russian rockets. The United States is providing lab modules, the supporting frame, solar panels, living quarters, and a biomedical laboratory. The Russians are contributing a service module, docking modules, life-support and research modules, and transportation to and from the station. Other components will come from Japan, Canada, and several European countries.

Reading Check What contributions are the Americans and Russians making to the *ISS*?

Research on the *International Space Station*

The *ISS* will provide many benefits—some of which we cannot predict. What scientists do know is that it will be a unique, space-based facility to perform space-science experiments and to test new technologies. Much of the space race involved political and military rivalry between the Soviet Union and the United States. Hopefully, the *ISS* will promote cooperation between countries while continuing the pioneering spirit of the first astronauts and cosmonauts.

CONNECTION TO Social Studies

Oral Histories The exciting times of the Apollo moon missions thrilled the nation. Interview adults in your community about their memories of those times. Prepare a list of questions first, and have your questions and contacts approved by your teacher. If possible, use a tape recorder or video camera to record the interviews. As a class, create a library of your oral histories for future students.

ACTIVITY

Figure 5 When the International Space Station *is completed, it will be about the size of a soccer field and will weigh about 500 tons.*

MISCONCEPTION ALERT

Weightlessness in Space
Students may presume that astronauts experience weightlessness because there is no gravity in space. Astronauts in a typical orbit 296 km above Earth are still affected by Earth's gravity; in fact, gravity is what keeps the spacecraft in orbit. The reason the astronauts have the sensation of weightlessness is that they are in a constant state of free fall as they orbit Earth. This apparent weightlessness is similar to what sky divers experience when they jump from airplanes. By ascending and diving repeatedly, NASA's "Vomit Comet" airplane can produce a similar effect. Students may be interested in learning more about astronaut training on the "Vomit Comet."

Answer to Reading Check
The Russians are supplying a service module, docking modules, life-support and research modules, and transportation to and from the station. The Americans are providing lab modules, the supporting frame, solar panels, living quarters, and a biomedical laboratory.

SCIENCE HUMOR

The news that *Skylab* would re-enter the atmosphere and plummet to Earth generated mild panic among some people. Despite NASA's assurances that the debris would fall in oceans or unpopulated areas, a few quick profits were made from the sale of hard hats billed as "*Skylab* Survival Kits." Much of the debris fell into the Indian Ocean, but some charred fragments were found strewn across the Australian Outback, which prompted Australian officials to present the United States with a $400 fine for littering!

Section 4 • People in Space

Close

Reteaching — BASIC

Space Timeline As a class, make a timeline on the board that shows major events in the history of space exploration. Have students help you add notes that are related to concepts in the section.

LS Interpersonal

Quiz — GENERAL

1. What kind of vehicle has been proposed that would make space travel cheaper?
   (a space plane)
2. What is a space station?
   (It is a long-term orbiting platform from which science and technology research can be conducted by resident astronauts.)

Alternative Assessment — GENERAL

People in Space Science

Have a round-table discussion in which students impersonate the following people after having researched their lives and careers:

Robert Goddard, Konstantin Tsiolkovsky, Yuri Gagarin, John Glenn, Rita Mae Jemison, Valentina Tereshkova, Arnaldo Tamayo-Mendez, Alexi Leonov, Edward White, Chuck Yeager, Helen Sharman

Have students discuss the history of the space program and then speculate on future developments.

LS Interpersonal Co-op Learning

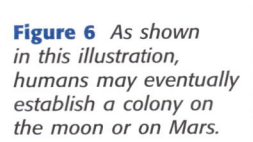

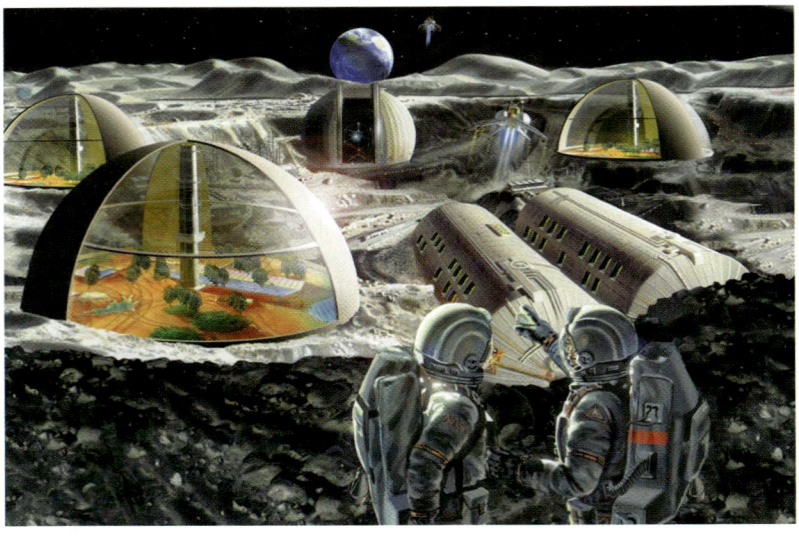

Figure 6 As shown in this illustration, humans may eventually establish a colony on the moon or on Mars.

To the Moon, Mars, and Beyond

We may eventually need resources beyond what Earth can offer. Space offers many such resources. For example, a rare form of helium is found on the moon. If this helium could be used in nuclear fusion reactors, it would produce no radioactive waste! A base on the moon similar to the one shown in **Figure 6** could be used to manufacture materials in low gravity or in a vacuum. A colony on the moon or on Mars could be an important link to bringing space resources to Earth. It would also be a good base for exploring the rest of the solar system. The key will be to make these missions economically worthwhile.

The Benefits of the Space Program

Space exploration is expensive, and it has cost several human lives since the time that Yuri Gagarin and John Glenn first left the Earth more than 40 years ago. We have visited the moon, and we have sent probes outside the solar system. So why should we continue to explore space? There are many answers to this question. Space exploration has expanded our scientific knowledge of everything from the most massive stars to the smallest particles. Life-saving technologies have also resulted from the space missions. For example, artificial heart pumps use a turbine developed to pump fuel in the space shuttles. NASA's aerogel, shown in **Figure 7,** may become an energy-saving replacement for windows in the future. All of the scientific benefits of the space programs cannot be predicted. However, the exploration of space is also a challenge to human courage and a quest for new knowledge of ourselves and the universe.

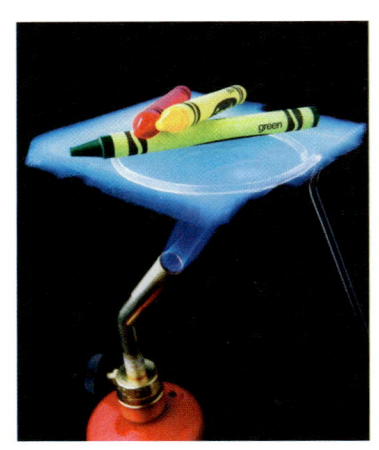

Figure 7 Aerogel is the lightest solid on Earth. Aerogel is only 3 times heavier than air, and has 39 times the insulating properties of the best fiberglass insulation.

Homework — GENERAL

Space-Age Spinoff Comic Books Encourage students to research the development of a few of the spinoffs listed in **Table 1**. Students may also find out about other spinoffs of their choice. Then, have students write and illustrate a space-age spinoff comic book that describes how a few spinoffs were developed and how the technology made its way into our daily lives. **LS Visual**

Space-Age Spinoffs

Technologies that were developed for the space programs but are now used in everyday life are called space-age spinoffs. There are dozens of examples of common items that were first developed for the space programs. Cordless power tools, for example, were first developed for use on the moon by the Apollo astronauts. Hand-held cameras that were developed to study the heat emitted from the space shuttle are used by firefighters to detect dangerous hot spots in fires. A few other examples of space-age spinoffs are shown in **Table 1.**

Reading Check What are space-age spinoffs?

Table 1 **Space-Age Spinoffs**

smoke detectors
bar coding on merchandise
pacemakers
artificial heart pumps
land mine removal devices
medical lasers
fire fighting equipment
invisible braces
video game joysticks
ear thermometers

SECTION Review

Summary

- In 1961, the Soviet cosmonaut Yuri Gagarin became the first person in space. In 1969, Neil Armstrong became the first person on the moon.
- During the 1970s, the United States focused on developing the space shuttle. The Soviets focused on developing space stations.
- The United States, Russia, and 14 other countries are currently developing the *International Space Station.*
- There have been many scientific, economic, and social benefits of the space programs.

Using Key Terms

1. Use each of the following terms in a separate sentence: *space shuttle* and *space station.*

Using Key Ideas

2. What is the main difference between the space shuttles and other space vehicles?
    a. The space shuttles are powered by liquid rocket fuel.
    b. The space shuttles take off like a plane and land like a rocket.
    c. The space shuttles are reusable.
    d. The space shuttles are not reusable.
3. Describe the history and future of human spaceflight. How was the race to explore space influenced by the Cold War?
4. Describe five "space-age spinoffs."
5. How will space stations help in the exploration of space?
6. In the 1970s, what was the main difference in the focus of the space programs in the United States and in the Soviet Union?

Math Skills

7. When it is fueled, a space shuttle has a mass of about 2,000,000 kg. About 80% of that mass is fuel and oxygen. Calculate the mass of a space shuttle's fuel and oxygen.

Critical Thinking

8. **Making Inferences** Why did the United States stop sending people to the moon after the Apollo program ended?
9. **Expressing Opinions** Imagine that you are a U.S. senator reviewing NASA's proposed budget. Write a two-paragraph position statement expressing your opinion about increasing or decreasing funding for NASA.

SciLinks
Developed and maintained by the National Science Teachers Association
For a variety of links related to this chapter, go to www.scilinks.org
Topic: Space Exploration and Space Stations
SciLinks code: HSM1340

Answer to Reading Check

Space-age spinoffs are technologies that were developed for the space program but are now used in everyday life.

Answers to Section Review

1. Sample answer: NASA has completed more than 100 successful space shuttle missions. The International Space Station is being built with the help of many nations.
2. c
3. Answers may vary. Students should note that Cold War tensions greatly accelerated the space programs of the United States and the Soviet Union.
4. Answers may vary. Students can describe any of the space-age spinoffs that are described in the text or in Table 1.
5. Answers may vary. Space stations will serve as refueling, construction, and research stations.
6. Answers may vary. The United States was mainly focused on space shuttle development, while the Soviet Union was focused on space station development.
7. 2 million kg × 0.80 = 1.6 million kg
8. Answers may vary. After the Apollo program, the United States focused on developing a reusable space shuttle.
9. Answers may vary. Accept any well-supported answer. Students may describe the technology that has come from the space program to support increasing NASA funding. Students may also support a position to decrease funding based on the expense of the space program and the tragedies that have occurred.

CHAPTER RESOURCES

Chapter Resource File
- Section Quiz GENERAL
- Section Review GENERAL
- Vocabulary and Section Summary GENERAL
- SciLinks Activity GENERAL

Section 4 • People in Space

Inquiry Lab

Water Rockets Save the Day!

Teacher's Notes

Time Required
Two 45-minute class periods

Lab Ratings
EASY —————— HARD

Teacher Prep 🧪🧪🧪
Student Set-Up 🧪🧪🧪
Concept Level 🧪🧪
Clean Up 🧪🧪

MATERIALS
The materials listed in this lab are best for groups of 3 or 4.

Safety Caution
Remind students to review all safety cautions and icons before beginning this lab activity. Make sure that students are several meters away from the launch site when the rockets are being launched.

Using Scientific Methods
Inquiry Lab

OBJECTIVES
Predict which design features would improve a rocket's flight.

Design and build a rocket that includes your design features.

Test your rocket design, and evaluate your results.

MATERIALS
- bottle, soda, 2 L
- clay, modeling
- foam board
- rocket launcher
- scissors
- tape, duct
- watch or clock that indicates seconds
- water

SAFETY

Water Rockets Save the Day!

Imagine that for the big Fourth of July celebration, you and your friends had planned a full day of swimming, volleyball, and fireworks at the lake. You've just learned, however, that the city passed a law that bans all fireworks within city limits. But you do not give up so easily on having fun. Last year at summer camp, you learned how to build water rockets. And you have kept the launcher in your garage since then. With a little bit of creativity, you and your friends are going to celebrate with a splash!

Ask a Question
1. What is the most efficient design for a water rocket?

Form a Hypothesis
2. Write a hypothesis that provides a possible answer to the question above.

Test the Hypothesis
3. Decide how your rocket will look, and then draw a sketch.

4. Using only the materials listed, decide how to build your rocket. Write a description of your plan, and have your teacher approve your plan. Keep in mind that you will need to leave the opening of your bottle clear. The bottle opening will be placed over a rubber stopper on the rocket launcher.

5. Fins are often used to stabilize rockets. Do you want fins on your water rocket? Decide on the best shape for the fins, and then decide how many fins your rocket needs. Use the foam board to construct the fins.

6. Your rocket must be heavy enough to fly in a controlled manner. Consider using clay in the body of your rocket to provide some additional weight and stability.

7. Pour water into your rocket until the rocket is one-third to one-half full.

8. Your teacher will provide the launcher and will assist you during blastoff. Attach your rocket to the launcher by placing the opening of the bottle on the rubber stopper.

Preparation Notes

Each student or group of students will need a 2 L soda bottle to construct their rocket. You can ask students a week or two ahead of time to save any 2 L soda bottles they have at home. Water rockets require a launcher that you will need to make or purchase in advance. Launchers are the key to a successful and safe liftoff. They can be purchased at most hobby shops or from Science Kit®. You can expect to spend at least $20 for a launcher or launcher kit at a hobby shop. You need only one launcher for your class. When buying a launcher, make sure the launcher is compatible with the size of your water-rocket bottle. This lab is a popular activity, and water-bottle rocket hobbyists have posted detailed information on the Internet.

706 Chapter 22 • Exploring Space

9 When the rocket is in place, clear the immediate area and begin pumping air into your rocket. Watch the pump gauge, and take note of how much pressure is needed for liftoff. **Caution:** Be sure to step back from the launch site. You should be several meters away from the bottle when you launch it.

10 Use the watch to time your rocket's flight. How long was your rocket in the air?

11 Make small changes in your rocket design that you think will improve the rocket's performance. Consider using different amounts of water and clay or experimenting with different fins. You may also want to compare your design with those of your classmates.

Analyze the Results

1 **Describing Events** How did your rocket perform? If you used fins, do you think they helped your flight? Explain your answer.

2 **Explaining Results** What do you think propelled your rocket? Use Newton's third law of motion to explain your answer.

3 **Analyzing Results** How did the amount of water in your rocket affect the launch?

Draw Conclusions

4 **Drawing Conclusions** What modifications made your rocket fly for the longest time? How did the design help the rockets fly so far?

5 **Evaluating Results** Which group's rocket was the most stable? How did the design help the rocket fly straight?

6 **Making Predictions** How can you improve your design to make your rocket perform even better?

Analyze the Results

1. Answers may vary. Fins might help stabilize the rocket when it is in flight.
2. Answers may vary. Students should note that the water in the bottle was under pressure. When the rocket was released, the water escaped out of the opening. The bottle reacted by moving in the opposite direction—upward.
3. Answers may vary. Water is the propellant for the rocket. Pressurized air provides the force to launch the rocket. The amount of water in a rocket determines how much space air can occupy. The ideal rocket should expel all of the water at the maximum pressure.

Draw Conclusions

4. Answers may vary. Modifying the fins, adjusting the water-to-air ratio, increasing the air pressure inside the rocket, and changing the amount of modeling clay used should affect the duration of the rocket's flight.
5. Answers may vary.
6. Answers may vary.

CHAPTER RESOURCES

Chapter Resource File
- Datasheet for Chapter Lab
- Lab Notes and Answers

Technology
- Classroom Videos
  - Lab Video

LabBook
- Reach for the Stars

CHAPTER RESOURCES

Workbooks
- Whiz-Bang Demonstrations
  - Rocket Science GENERAL
- Inquiry Labs
  - Crash Landing ADVANCED
  - Space Fitness ADVANCED
- EcoLabs & Field Activities
  - There's a Space for Us GENERAL
- Long-Term Projects & Research Ideas
  - Space Voyage ADVANCED

CLASSROOM TESTED & APPROVED

Alyson Mike
East Valley Middle School
East Helena, Montana

Chapter 22 • Chapter Lab

Chapter Review

Assignment Guide

Section	Questions
1	6–7, 16, 21–22, 24–27
2	1, 3, 8–10, 17, 19
3	4–7, 11, 13–15
4	12, 18, 23
3 and 4	2
1, 2, 3, and 4	20

ANSWERS

Using Key Terms

1. Sample answer: A geostationary orbit is about 36,000 km above the Earth's surface. In order to maintain GEO, satellites must orbit at a speed that exactly matches the speed of Earth's rotation. LEO is less than 1,500 km above the Earth's surface. To remain in LEO, satellites must travel much faster than the Earth rotates.

2. Sample answer: A space probe is a vehicle that carries scientific instruments to planets or other bodies in space. Space probes do not carry people. A space station is a long-term orbiting platform with scientific research labs and living quarters for astronauts.

3. Sample answer: An artificial satellite is any human-made object placed in orbit around a body in space. A moon is a natural satellite of a planet.

4. thrust
5. oxygen

Understanding Key Ideas

6. c
7. c
8. d
9. b
10. a
11. c
12. c
13. d
14. d
15. c

Chapter Review

USING KEY TERMS

For each pair of terms, explain how the meanings of the terms differ.

1. *geostationary orbit* and *low Earth orbit*
2. *space probe* and *space station*
3. *artificial satellite* and *moon*

Complete each of the following sentences by choosing the correct term from the word bank.

    escape velocity   oxygen
    nitrogen   thrust

4. The force that accelerates a rocket is called ___.
5. Rockets need to have ___ in order to burn fuel.

UNDERSTANDING KEY IDEAS

Multiple Choice

6. Whose rocket research team surrendered to the Americans at the end of World War II?
   a. Konstantin Tsiolkovsky's
   b. Robert Goddard's
   c. Wernher von Braun's
   d. Yuri Gargarin's

7. Rockets work according to Newton's
   a. first law of motion.
   b. second law of motion.
   c. third law of motion.
   d. law of universal gravitation.

8. The first artificial satellite to orbit the Earth was
   a. *Pioneer 4.*   c. *Voyager 2.*
   b. *Explorer 1.*   d. *Sputnik 1.*

9. Communications satellites are able to transfer TV signals between continents because communications satellites
   a. are located in LEO.
   b. relay signals past the horizon.
   c. travel quickly around Earth.
   d. can be used during the day and night.

10. GEO is a better orbit for communications satellites because satellites that are in GEO
    a. remain in position over one spot.
    b. have polar orbits.
    c. do not revolve around the Earth.
    d. orbit a few hundred kilometers above the Earth.

11. Which space probe discovered evidence of water at the moon's south pole?
    a. *Luna 9*
    b. *Viking 1*
    c. *Clementine*
    d. *Magellan*

12. When did humans first set foot on the moon?
    a. 1959   c. 1969
    b. 1964   d. 1973

13. Which of the following planets has not yet been visited by space probes?
    a. Venus   c. Mars
    b. Neptune   d. Pluto

708 Chapter 22 • Exploring Space

14 Which of the following space probes has left our solar system?
 a. *Galileo*
 b. *Magellan*
 c. *Viking 10*
 d. *Pioneer 10*

15 Based on space-probe data, which of the following is the most likely place in our solar system to find liquid water?
 a. the moon
 b. Mercury
 c. Europa
 d. Venus

Short Answer

16 Describe how Newton's third law of motion relates to the movement of rockets.

17 What is one disadvantage that objects in LEO have?

18 Why did the United States develop the space shuttle?

19 How does data from satellites help us understand the Earth's environment?

CRITICAL THINKING

20 Concept Mapping Use the following terms to create a concept map: *orbital velocity, thrust, LEO, artificial satellites, escape velocity, space probes, GEO,* and *rockets.*

21 Making Inferences What is the difference between speed and velocity?

22 Applying Concepts Why must rockets that travel in outer space carry oxygen with them?

23 Expressing Opinions What impact has space research had on scientific thought, on society, and on the environment?

INTERPRETING GRAPHICS

The diagram below illustrates suborbital velocity, orbital velocity, and escape velocity. Use the diagram below to answer the questions that follow.

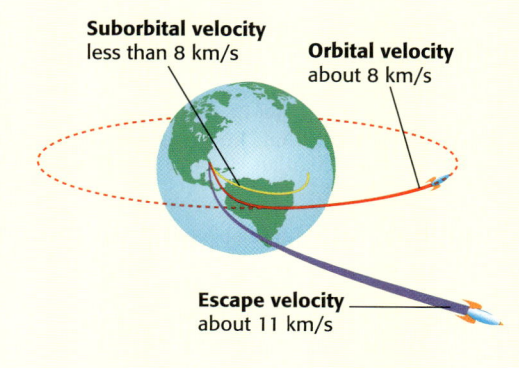

Suborbital velocity less than 8 km/s
Orbital velocity about 8 km/s
Escape velocity about 11 km/s

24 Could a rocket traveling at 6 km/s reach orbital velocity?

25 If a rocket traveled for 3 days at the minimum escape velocity, how far would the rocket travel?

26 How much faster would a rocket traveling in orbital velocity need to travel to reach escape velocity?

27 If the escape velocity for a planet was 9 km/s, would you assume that the mass of the planet was more or less than the mass of Earth?

Critical Thinking
20. An answer to this exercise can be found at the end of this book.
21. Speed is a measure of how fast an object travels. Velocity is the speed and direction an object travels.
22. Rockets must carry oxygen with them because there is no oxygen in outer space. Without oxygen, rocket fuel cannot burn.
23. Answers may vary. Students should note that space research has helped develop many areas of human knowledge, including medicine, physics, engineering, biology, geology, and astronomy. The space program is also a challenge to human courage and can promote international cooperation and peace. Students may also mention space-age spinoffs. Finally, space probes enable us to study the atmospheres and surfaces of other bodies in the solar system. Scientists use these data to understand changes in Earth's environment.

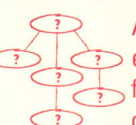

Interpreting Graphics
24. no
25. 60 s/min × 60 min/h × 24 h/day × 3 days = 259,200 s
259,200 s × 11 km/s = 2,851,200 km
26. 11 km/s − 8 km/s = 3 km/s A rocket traveling in orbital velocity would need to travel 3 km/s faster to reach escape velocity.
27. If a planet's escape velocity was 9 km/s, the planet's mass would be less than the mass of Earth.

16. Answers may vary. Sample answer: Newton's third law of motion states that for every action, there is an equal reaction in the opposite direction. As the gases escape through the rocket nozzle, the rocket reacts by moving in the opposite direction.
17. Answers may vary. One disadvantage of LEO is that a satellite cannot maintain constant communication with a ground station.
18. Answers may vary. One reason the United States developed the space shuttle was to have a reusable space vehicle that would be less expensive than the Apollo rockets.
19. Answers may vary.

CHAPTER RESOURCES
Chapter Resource File
- Chapter Review GENERAL
- Chapter Test A GENERAL
- Chapter Test B ADVANCED
- Chapter Test C SPECIAL NEEDS
- Vocabulary Activity GENERAL

Workbooks
Study Guide
• Assessment resources are also available in Spanish.

Standardized Test Preparation

Teacher's Note
To provide practice under more realistic testing conditions, give students 20 minutes to answer all of the questions in this Standardized Test Preparation.

MISCONCEPTION ALERT

Answers to the standardized test preparation can help you identify student misconceptions and misunderstandings.

READING

Passage 1
1. C
2. H
3. B

TEST DOCTOR

Question 1: Students may be confused by the fact that none of the answer options come directly from the passage. They may think none of the answers are correct. Tell students that the main idea of a paragraph is not always stated in the paragraph. In this case, students would need to choose the best answer that most fully encompasses the main idea of the paragraph.

Standardized Test Preparation

READING
Read each of the passages below. Then, answer the questions that follow each passage.

Passage 1 One of the strange things about living in space is free fall, the reduced effect of gravity. Everything inside the *International Space Station* that is not fastened down will float! The engineers who designed the space station have come up with some <u>intriguing</u> solutions to this problem. For example, each astronaut sleeps in a sack similar to a sleeping bag that is fastened to the module. The sack keeps the astronauts from floating around while they sleep. Astronauts shower with a hand-held nozzle. Afterward, the water droplets are vacuumed up. Other problems that are being studied include how to prepare and serve food, how to design an effective toilet, and how to dispose of waste.

1. What is the main idea of the passage?
   A There is no gravity in space.
   B Astronauts will stay aboard the space station for long periods of time.
   C Living in free fall presents interesting problems.
   D Sleeping bags are needed to keep astronauts warm in space.

2. Which of the following is a problem mentioned in the passage?
   F how to dissipate the heat of reentry
   G how to maintain air pressure
   H how to serve food
   I how to listen to music

3. Which of the following words is the best antonym for *intriguing*?
   A authentic
   B boring
   C interesting
   D unsolvable

Passage 2 In 1999, the crew of the space station *Mir* tried to place a large, umbrella-like mirror in orbit. The mirror was designed to reflect sunlight to Siberia. The experiment failed because the crew was unable to unfold the mirror. If things had gone as planned, the beam of reflected sunlight would have been 5 to 10 times brighter than the light from the moon! If the first space mirror had worked, Russia was planning to place many more mirrors in orbit to lengthen winter days in Siberia, extend the growing season, and even reduce the amount of electricity needed for lighting. Luckily, the experiment failed. If it had succeeded, the environmental effects of extra daylight in Siberia would have been catastrophic. Astronomers were concerned that the mirrors would cause light pollution and obstruct their view of the universe. Outer space should belong to all of humanity, and any project of this kind, including placing advertisements on the moon, should be banned.

1. Which of the following is a statement of opinion?
   A Astronomers were concerned about the effects of the space mirror.
   B Outer space should belong to all of humanity.
   C The experiment failed because the mirror could not unfold.
   D Russia was planning to place many more mirrors in orbit.

2. What can you infer about the location of Siberia?
   F It is near the equator.
   G It is closer to the equator than it is to the North Pole.
   H It is closer to the North Pole than it is to the equator.
   I It is the same distance from the equator as it is from the North Pole.

Passage 2
1. B
2. H

TEST DOCTOR

Question 2: This question may be difficult for students because they must infer information that is not stated in the passage. Emphasize that some standardized test questions may ask students to make inferences. In this case, students must infer that Siberia is closer to the North Pole than it is to the equator, because the passage discusses a strategy to provide more solar energy for the region. Areas that are close to the poles receive less solar energy than areas close to the equator do.

710 Chapter 22 • Exploring Space

INTERPRETING GRAPHICS

The diagram below shows the location of satellites in LEO and GEO. Use the diagram below to answer the questions that follow.

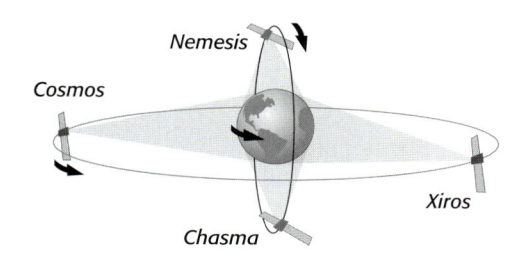

(Diagram showing Earth with satellites labeled Nemesis, Cosmos, Chasma, and Xiros)

1. Which satellites are always located over the same spot on Earth?
   A *Xiros* and *Chasma*
   B *Xiros* and *Cosmos*
   C *Nemesis* and *Cosmos*
   D *Chasma* and *Nemesis*

2. Which satellites are likely to be spy satellites?
   F *Xiros* and *Cosmos*
   G *Xiros* and *Chasma*
   H *Chasma* and *Nemesis*
   I *Nemesis* and *Cosmos*

3. Which satellites are likely to be communications satellites?
   A *Chasma* and *Nemesis*
   B *Nemesis* and *Cosmos*
   C *Xiros* and *Cosmos*
   D *Xiros* and *Chasma*

4. Which satellites are traveling in an orbit that is 90° with respect to the direction of Earth's rotation?
   F *Nemesis* and *Cosmos*
   G *Xiros* and *Chasma*
   H *Nemesis* and *Chasma*
   I *Xiros* and *Cosmos*

MATH

Read each question below, and choose the best answer.

1. To escape Earth's gravity, a rocket must travel at least 11 km/s. About how many hours would it take to get to the moon at this speed? (On average, the moon is about 384,500 km away from Earth.)
   A 1 h
   B 7 h
   C 8 h
   D 10 h

2. The Saturn V launch vehicle, which carried the Apollo astronauts into space, had a mass of about 2.7 million kilograms and carried about 2.5 million kilograms of propellant. What percentage of Saturn V's mass was propellant?
   F 9.25%
   G 9%
   H 92.5%
   I 90%

3. Scientists discovered that when a person is in orbit, bone mass in the lower hip and spine is lost at a rate of 1.2% per month. At that rate, how long would it take for 7.2% of bone mass to be lost?
   A 4 months
   B 6 months
   C 7.2 months
   D 8 months

4. The space shuttle can carry 25,400 kg of cargo into orbit. Assume that the average astronaut has a mass of 75 kg and that each satellite has a mass of 4,300 kg. If a shuttle mission is already carrying 9,000 kg of equipment and 10 astronauts, how many satellites can the shuttle carry?
   F 2
   G 3
   H 4
   I 5

INTERPRETING GRAPHICS

1. B
2. H
3. C
4. H

TEST DOCTOR

Question 4: Students may not know what a 90° angle is. Tell students that a 90° angle makes up the corner of a square, or, in this case, a cross.

MATH

1. D
2. H
3. B
4. G

TEST DOCTOR

Question 2: To derive the percentage, students should divide 2.5 million kilograms by 2.7 million kilograms and then multiply by 100. Students might get an answer of 108% if they divide 2.7 by 2.5 and then multiply by 100. If students accidentally multiply by 10, they will get answer F, 9.25%.

Question 4: This question requires several steps. First, students must find the total weight of the cargo plus astronauts. Multiplying 75 times 10 to get 750 gives the weight of the astronauts. Adding 750 to 9,000 will give the weight of the cargo plus astronauts, which is 9,750. Now, students must subtract this weight from 25,400 to find the amount that the shuttle can still hold. Finally, dividing this amount by 4,300 will give students the number of satellites that will fit on the shuttle. Remind students to ignore the remainder in this situation, because the question is asking about whole satellites.

CHAPTER RESOURCES

Chapter Resource File
• Standardized Test Preparation GENERAL

State Resources
For specific resources for your state, visit go.hrw.com and type in the keyword HSMSTR.

Science in Action

Science, Technology, and Society

ACTIVITY — GENERAL

Privatized Space Exploration
Many space technology innovations are made by private companies and individuals. Several awards are currently offered for the first private group to launch an inexpensive rocket into space. Ask students to find out more about the role of private companies in the future of space exploration, and suggest that they learn about experimental projects such as the *Roton* rocket. **LS Intrapersonal**

Weird Science

Discussion — GENERAL

The volunteers at the Flashline Mars Arctic Research Station (FMARS) have already learned many things that will help NASA prepare for a trip to Mars. For example, they learned that they can use much less water if they skip a few baths. Also, it is important to have backup equipment and to travel in groups. Have students discuss other ideas that might help NASA plan for a trip to Mars.

Science in Action

Science, Technology, and Society

Mission to Mars
In spring 2003, two cutting-edge NASA rovers were sent on a mission to Mars. When they reach their destination, they will parachute through the thin Martian atmosphere and land on the surface. First, the rovers will use video and infrared cameras to look around. Then, for at least 92 Earth days (90 Martian days), the rovers will explore the surface of Mars. They will gather geologic evidence of liquid water because liquid water may have enabled Mars to support life in the past. Each rover will carry five scientific tools and a Rock Abrasion Tool, or "RAT," which will grind away rock surfaces to expose the rock interiors for scientific tests. Stay tuned for more news from Mars!

Language Arts ACTIVITY

Watch for stories about this mission in newspapers and magazines. If you read about a discovery on Mars, bring a copy of the article to share with your class. As a class, compile a scrapbook entitled "Mars in the News."

Weird Science

Flashline Mars Arctic Research Station
If you wanted to visit a place on Earth that is like the surface of Mars, where would you go? You might head to an impact crater on Devon Island, close to the Arctic circle. The rugged terrain and harsh weather there resemble what explorers will find on Mars, although Mars has no breathable air and is a lot colder. In the summer, volunteers from the Mars Society live in an experimental base in the crater and test technology that might be used on Mars. The volunteers try to simulate the experience of explorers on Mars. For example, the volunteers wear spacesuits when they go outside, and they explore the landscape by using rovers. They even communicate with the outside world using types of technology likely to be used on Mars. These dedicated volunteers have already made discoveries that will help NASA plan a crewed mission to Mars!

Social Studies ACTIVITY

A Mars mission could require astronauts to endure nearly two years of extreme isolation. Research how NASA would prepare astronauts for the psychological pressures of a mission to Mars.

Answer to Language Arts Activity
Answers may vary. Scrapbooks may include pictures taken by the Mars rovers and NASA press releases. Students can edit and publish their findings in a *Mars Tribune* newspaper to be distributed to other classes or posted on the Internet.

Answer to Social Studies Activity
Answers may vary. Popular science magazines, such as *Discover*, have published articles concerning the psychological pressures of a Mars mission.

712   Chapter 22 • Exploring Space

Careers

Franklin Chang-Diaz

Astronaut You have to wear a suit, but the commute is not too long. In fact, it is only about eight and a half minutes, and what a view on your way to work! Astronauts, such as Franklin Chang-Diaz, have one of the most exciting jobs on Earth—or in space. Chang-Diaz has flown on seven space shuttle missions and has completed three space walks. Since the time he became an astronaut in 1981, Chang-Diaz has spent more than 1,601 hours (66 days) in space.

Chang-Diaz was born in San Jose, Costa Rica. He earned a degree in mechanical engineering in 1973 and received a doctorate in applied plasma physics from the Massachusetts Institute of Technology (MIT) in 1977. His work in physics attracted the attention of NASA, and he began training at the Johnson Space Center in Houston, Texas. In addition to doing research on the space shuttle, Chang-Diaz has worked on developing plasma propulsion systems for long space flights. He has also helped create closer ties between astronauts and scientists by starting organizations such as the Astronaut Science Colloquium Program and the Astronaut Science Support Group. If you want to find out more about what it takes to be an astronaut, look on NASA's Web site.

Math Activity

If 1 out of 120 people interviewed by NASA is selected for astronaut training, how many people will be selected for training if 10,680 people are interviewed?

As this mission patch shows, Chang-Diaz flew on the 111th space shuttle mission.

To learn more about these Science in Action topics, visit go.hrw.com and type in the keyword **HZ5EXPF.**

Current Science
Check out Current Science® articles related to this chapter by visiting go.hrw.com. Just type in the keyword **HZ5CS22.**

Careers

Teaching Strategy —GENERAL
There are a number of resources available on the Internet for students interested in becoming astronauts. Have teams of students research different aspects of this exciting career and present their findings to the class.

Answer to Math Activity
10,680 ÷ 120 = 89

Science Humor

Astronaut Jerry Linenger listed the following skills on his astronaut application: woodworking, drafting, carpentry, small-engine repair, electrical wiring, sprinkling-system installation, heavy cement work, plumbing, and bricklaying. After spending time on *Mir*, he joked, "With the exception of the cement work and bricklaying, all of these skills proved indispensable on *Mir*."

LabBook

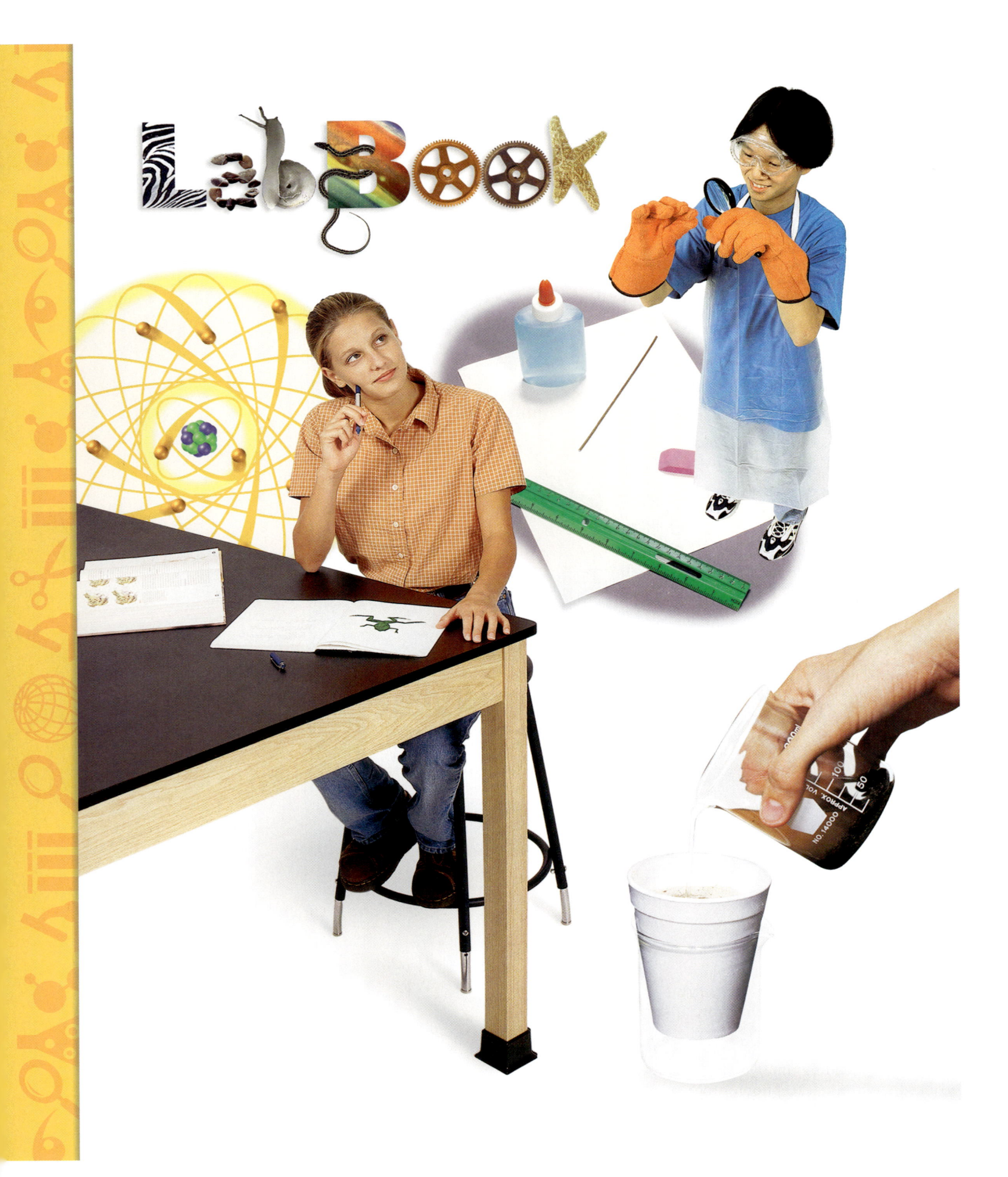

714 LabBook

Contents

CHAPTER 2 Maps as Models of the Earth
- **Inquiry** Orient Yourself! 716
- **Skills Practice** Topographic Tuber 718

CHAPTER 3 Minerals of the Earth's Crust
- **Skills Practice** Mysterious Minerals 720

CHAPTER 4 Rocks: Mineral Mixtures
- **Skills Practice** Crystal Growth 722
- **Model Making** Metamorphic Mash 725

CHAPTER 5 Energy Resources
- **Skills Practice** Power of the Sun 726

CHAPTER 7 Plate Tectonics
- **Model Making** Oh, the Pressure! 728

CHAPTER 8 Earthquakes
- **Skills Practice** Earthquake Waves 731

CHAPTER 9 Volcanoes
- **Skills Practice** Some Go "Pop," Some Do Not 733

CHAPTER 10 Weathering and Soil Formation
- **Skills Practice** Great Ice Escape 735

CHAPTER 11 The Flow of Fresh Water
- **Skills Practice** Clean Up Your Act 736

CHAPTER 12 Agents of Erosion and Deposition
- **Model Making** Dune Movement 740
- **Skills Practice** Creating a Kettle 741

CHAPTER 13 Exploring the Oceans
- **Skills Practice** Investigating an Oil Spill 742

CHAPTER 14 The Movement of Ocean Water
- **Model Making** Turning the Tides 744

CHAPTER 15 The Atmosphere
- **Skills Practice** Go Fly a Bike! 746

CHAPTER 16 Understanding Weather
- **Skills Practice** Watching the Weather 748
- **Skills Practice** Let It Snow! 751
- **Model Making** Gone with the Wind 752

CHAPTER 17 Climate
- **Skills Practice** Global Impact 754
- **Skills Practice** For the Birds 755

CHAPTER 18 Studying Space
- **Skills Practice** The Sun's Yearly Trip Through the Zodiac 758

CHAPTER 19 Stars, Galaxies, and the Universe
- **Skills Practice** I See the Light! 760

CHAPTER 21 A Family of Planets
- **Model Making** Why Do They Wander? 762
- **Model Making** Eclipses 764
- **Skills Practice** Phases of the Moon 765

CHAPTER 22 Exploring Space
- **Model Making** Reach for the Stars 766

LabBook

LabBook

Inquiry Lab

Orient Yourself!

Teacher's Notes

Time Required

Two 45-minute class periods: one period to learn the use of a compass and the second to follow the orienteering course

Lab Ratings

EASY ———→ HARD

Teacher Prep 🧪🧪🧪
Student Set-Up 🧪
Concept Level 🧪🧪🧪
Clean Up 🧪

MATERIALS

The materials listed on the student page are enough for a group of 3 to 4 students.

Inquiry Lab

Orient Yourself!

You have been invited to attend an orienteering event with your neighbors. In orienteering events, participants use maps and compasses to find their way along a course. There are several control points that each participant must reach. The object is to reach each control point and then the finish line. Orienteering events are often timed competitions. In order to find the fastest route through the course, the participants must read the map and use their compass correctly. Being the fastest runner does not necessarily guarantee finishing first. You also must choose the most direct route to follow.

Your neighbors participate in several orienteering events each year. They always come home raving about how much fun they had. You would like to join them, but you will need to learn how to use your compass first.

MATERIALS

- compass, magnetic
- course map
- pencils (or markers), colored (2)
- ruler

Procedure

1. Together as a class, go outside to the orienteering course your teacher has made.

2. Hold your compass flat in your hand. Turn the compass until the N is pointing straight in front of you. (The needle in your compass will always point north.) Turn your body until the needle lines up with the N on your compass. You are now facing north.

3. Regardless of which direction you want to face, you should always align the end of the needle with the N on your compass. If you are facing south, the needle will be pointing directly toward your body. When the N is aligned with the needle, the S will be directly in front of you, and you will be facing south.

4. Use your compass to face east. Align the needle with the N. Where is the E? Turn to face that direction. You are facing east when the needle and the N are aligned and the E is directly in front of you.

5. In an orienteering competition, you will need to know how to determine which direction you are traveling. Now, face any direction you choose.

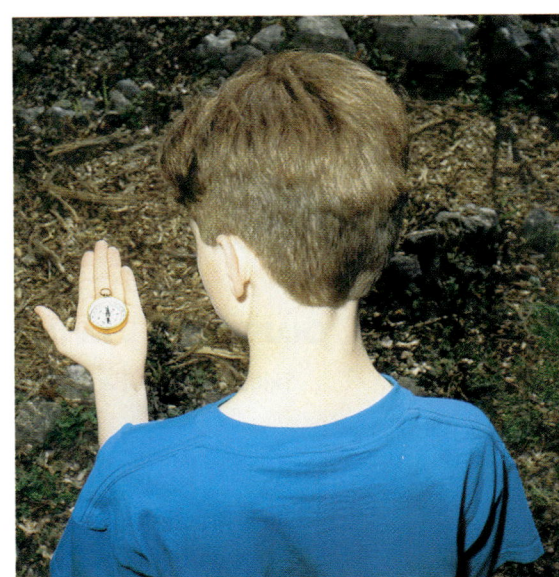

Preparation Notes

Find a suitable outdoor location for a simple orienteering course, and choose five control points for students to map. For example, you may wish to use several pieces of equipment in the playground, the flagpole, a tree, and a small hill. Be sure to mark each control point with either a specific color or a code word that students can collect or note on their maps when they reach each point.

Next, draw a map that includes the control points and the cardinal directions. Label a sixth spot as the starting point. Each group of students will need a copy of this map. Before groups begin exploring the orienteering course, have students perform steps 2–6 individually. An entire class period may be required for students to feel confident using a compass.

716 Chapter 2 • LabBook

6. Do not move, but rotate the compass to align the needle on your compass with the N. What direction are you facing? You are probably not facing directly north, south, east, or west. If you are facing between north and west, you are facing northwest. If you are facing between north and east, you are facing northeast.

7. Find a partner or partners to follow the course your teacher has made. Get a copy of the course map from your teacher. It will show several control points. You must stop at each one. You will need to follow this map to find your way through the course. Find and stand at the starting point.

8. Face the next control point on your map. Rotate your compass to align the needle on your compass with the N. What direction are you facing?

9. Use the ruler to draw a line on your map between the two control points. On your map, write the direction between the starting point and the next control point.

10. Walk toward the control point. Keep your eyes on the horizon, not on your compass. You might need to go around an obstacle, such as a fence or a building. Use the map to find the easiest way around.

11. Next to the control point symbol on your map, record the color or code word you find at the control point.

12. Repeat steps 8–11 for each control point. Follow the points in order as they are labeled. For example, determine the direction from control point 1 to control point 2. Be sure to include the direction between the final control point and the starting point.

Analyze the Results

1. The object of an orienteering competition is to arrive at the finish line first. The maps provided at these events do not instruct the participants to follow a specific path. In one form of orienteering, called *score orienteering,* competitors may find the control points in any order. Look at your map. If this course were used for a score-orienteering competition, would you change your route? Explain.

Draw Conclusions

2. If there is time, follow the map again. This time, use your own path to find the control points. Draw this path and the directions on your map in a different color. Do you believe this route was faster? Why?

Applying Your Data

Do some research to find out about orienteering events in your area. The Internet and local newspapers may be good sources for the information. Are there any events that you would like to attend?

David Jones
Andrew Jackson Middle School
Cross Lanes, West Virginia

CHAPTER RESOURCES

Chapter Resource File
- Datasheet for LabBook
- Lab Notes and Answers

Analyze the Results

1. Answers may vary. Students should realize that the path shown on the map did not instruct them to follow the most direct route. They should propose a more direct route to follow. Their proposal should include the direction from one control point to the next.

Draw Conclusions

2. This route should be faster. Students should realize that in an orienteering event, participants generally need to determine the quickest route. Some students may also realize that the quickest route is not necessarily the most direct. For example, there may be obstacles in the way (such as hills or lakes) that could slow participants down. Orienteering maps include these landmarks.

Chapter 2 • LabBook

LabBook Skills Practice Lab

Topographic Tuber

Teacher's Notes

Time Required
One 45-minute class period

Lab Ratings
EASY ——————→ HARD

Teacher Prep 🧪🧪
Student Set-Up 🧪
Concept Level 🧪🧪🧪
Clean Up 🧪🧪

MATERIALS
The materials listed on the student page are enough for groups of 2 to 3 students. Modeling clay may be used in place of the potatoes.

Preparation Notes

It may be easier for students to see the waterline if you add a few drops of food coloring to the water before they add it to the container. Before the activity, select several oddly shaped root vegetables from your local grocery store. Choose vegetables that have varied contour and shape. Sweet potatoes, for example, are available year-round and have many irregular shapes. If you cannot find naturally occurring root vegetables that have odd shapes, shape potatoes with a knife and peeler. You will then need to cut the potatoes in half lengthwise.

Using Scientific Methods
Skills Practice Lab

Topographic Tuber

Imagine that you live on top of a tall mountain and often look down on the lake below. Every summer, an island appears. You call it Sometimes Island because it goes away again during heavy fall rains. This summer, you begin to wonder if you could make a topographic map of Sometimes Island. You don't have fancy equipment to make the map, but you have an idea. What if you place a meterstick with the 0 m mark at the water level in the summer? Then, as the expected fall rains come, you could draw the island from above as the water rises. Would this idea really work?

MATERIALS
- container, clear plastic storage, with transparent lid
- marker, transparency
- paper, tracing
- potato, cut in half
- ruler, metric
- water

Ask a Question
1. How do I make a topographic map?

Form a Hypothesis
2. Write a hypothesis that is a possible answer to the question above. Describe the method you would use.

Test the Hypothesis
3. Place a mark at the storage container's base. Label this mark "0 cm" with a transparency marker.

4. Measure and mark 1 cm increments up the side of the container until you reach the top of the container. Label these marks "1 cm," "2 cm," "3 cm," and so on.

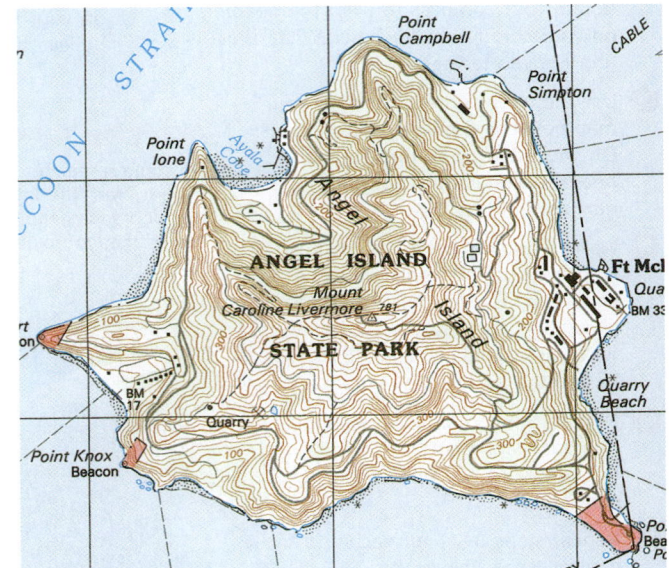

5. The scale for your map will be 1 cm = 10 m. Draw a line 2 cm long in the bottom right-hand corner of the lid. Place hash marks at 0 cm, 1 cm, and 2 cm. Label these marks "0 m," "10 m," and "20 m."

6. Place the potato, flat side down, in the center of the container.

7. Place the lid on the container, and seal it.

Lab Notes

Only islands that are at sea level begin at an elevation of 0 m. In order to calculate the elevation of an island that forms in a lake, you must also consider the elevation of the lake.

---

718 Chapter 2 • LabBook

8. Viewing the potato from above, use the transparency marker to trace the outline of the potato where it rests on the bottom of the container. The floor of the container corresponds to the summer water level in the lake.

9. Label this contour "0 m." (For this activity, assume that the water level in the lake during the summer is the same as sea level.)

10. Pour water into the container until it reaches the line labeled "1 cm."

11. Again, place the lid on the container, and seal it. Part of the potato will be sticking out above the water. Viewing the potato from above, trace the part of the potato that touches the top of the water.

12. Label the elevation of the contour line you drew in step 11. According to the scale, the elevation is 10 m.

13. Remove the lid. Carefully pour water into the container until it reaches the line labeled "2 cm."

14. Place the lid on the container, and seal it. Viewing the potato from above, trace the part of the potato that touches the top of the water at this level.

15. Use the scale to calculate the elevation of this line. Label the elevation on your drawing.

16. Repeat steps 13–15, adding 1 cm to the depth of the water each time. Stop when the potato is completely covered.

17. Remove the lid, and set it on a tabletop. Place tracing paper on top of the lid. Trace the contours from the lid onto the paper. Label the elevation of each contour line. Congratulations! You have just made a topographic map!

Analyze the Results

1. What is the contour interval of this topographic map?

2. By looking at the contour lines, how can you tell which parts of the potato are steeper?

3. What is the elevation of the highest point on your map?

Draw Conclusions

4. Do all topographic maps have a 0 m elevation contour line as a starting point? How would this affect a topographic map of Sometimes Island? Explain your answer.

5. Would this method of measuring elevation be an effective way to make a topographic map of an actual area on Earth's surface? Why or why not?

Applying Your Data

Place all of the potatoes on a table or desk at the front of the room. Your teacher will mix up the potatoes as you trade topographic maps with another group. By reading the topographic map you just received, can you pick out the matching potato?

Analyze the Results

1. The contour interval of the topographic map is 10 m.
2. Steeper parts of the potato will have contour lines that are closer together.
3. Answers may vary. Elevation is indicated by numbers on the contour lines.

Draw Conclusions

4. Sample answer: no; Topographic maps do not necessarily start with a 0 m elevation contour line. It is possible to make a topographic map of Sometimes Island showing its contours, but it is impossible to know the island's elevation above sea level.
5. Sample answer: no; Flooding an island is not an effective way of mapping it.

Michael E. Kral
West Hardin Middle School
Cecilia, Kentucky

CHAPTER RESOURCES

Chapter Resource File
- Datasheet for LabBook
- Lab Notes and Answers

LabBook

Skills Practice Lab

Mysterious Minerals

Teacher's Notes

Time Required
One 45-minute class period

Lab Ratings
EASY →→→ HARD

Teacher Prep 🧪🧪
Student Set-Up 🧪🧪
Concept Level 🧪🧪
Clean Up 🧪

MATERIALS
The materials listed on the student page are sufficient for each student. Students may also work in groups of 3 to 4. You will need one streak plate per student or group. A class should be able to share 3 to 5 streak plates.

Safety Caution
Remind students to review all safety cautions and icons before beginning this lab activity. Students need to be careful with glass microscope slides. Broken slides are likely to have sharp edges. Caution students not to taste the mineral samples.

Skills Practice Lab

Mysterious Minerals

Imagine sitting on a rocky hilltop, gazing at the ground below you. You can see dozens of different types of rocks. How can scientists possibly identify the countless variations? It's a mystery!

In this activity, you'll use your powers of observation and a few simple tests to determine the identities of rocks and minerals. Take a look at the Mineral Identification Key on the next page. That key will help you use clues to discover the identity of several minerals.

MATERIALS
- gloves, protective
- iron filings
- minerals, samples
- slides, microscope, glass
- streak plate

SAFETY

Procedure

1. On a separate sheet of paper, create a data chart like the one below.

2. Choose one mineral sample, and locate its column in your data chart.

3. Follow the Mineral Identification Key to find the identity of your sample. When you are finished, record the mineral's name and primary characteristics in the appropriate column in your data chart. **Caution:** Put on your safety goggles and gloves when scratching the glass slide.

4. Select another mineral sample, and repeat steps 2 and 3 until your data table is complete.

Analyze the Results

1. Were some minerals easier to identify than others? Explain.

2. A streak test is a better indicator of a mineral's true color than visual observation is. Why isn't a streak test used to help identify every mineral?

3. On a separate sheet of paper, summarize what you learned about the various characteristics of each mineral sample you identified.

Mineral Summary Chart

Characteristics	1	2	3	4	5	6
Mineral name						
Luster						
Color			DO NOT WRITE IN BOOK			
Streak						
Hardness						
Cleavage						
Special properties						

Preparation Notes
Explain to students that they are not determining the absolute hardness of the mineral samples. Instead, they are comparing the hardness of the samples with that of glass.

Your sample minerals should include pyrite, galena, hematite, magnetite, orthoclase (feldspar), quartz, muscovite, gypsum, hornblende (amphibole), garnet, biotite, and graphite.

Lab Notes
Each test in this lab tells the student more about the sample and narrows the possibilities. For example, the fact that a particular mineral sample does not have a streak eliminates hematite as a possibility but indicates that quartz is a possibility.

- It is possible for minerals that are softer than glass to leave a mark on glass. If the glass wipes clean and no scratch remains, then students will know that the mineral is softer than glass.

- Garnet is typically red, but it can also be pale green.

720   Chapter 3 • LabBook

Mineral Identification Key

1. **a.** If your mineral has a metallic luster, **GO TO STEP 2.**
   b. If your mineral has a nonmetallic luster, **GO TO STEP 3.**

2. **a.** If your mineral is black, **GO TO STEP 4.**
   b. If your mineral is yellow, it is **PYRITE.**
   c. If your mineral is silver, it is **GALENA.**

3. **a.** If your mineral is light in color, **GO TO STEP 5.**
   b. If your mineral is dark in color, **GO TO STEP 6.**

4. **a.** If your mineral leaves a red-brown line on the streak plate, it is **HEMATITE.**
   b. If your mineral leaves a black line on the streak plate, it is **MAGNETITE.** Test your sample for its magnetic properties by holding it near some iron filings.

5. **a.** If your mineral scratches the glass microscope slide, **GO TO STEP 7.**
   b. If your mineral does not scratch the glass microscope slide, **GO TO STEP 8.**

6. **a.** If your mineral scratches the glass slide, **GO TO STEP 9.**
   b. If your mineral does not scratch the glass slide, **GO TO STEP 10.**

7. **a.** If your mineral shows signs of cleavage, it is **ORTHOCLASE FELDSPAR.**
   b. If your mineral does not show signs of cleavage, it is **QUARTZ.**

8. **a.** If your mineral shows signs of cleavage, it is **MUSCOVITE.** Examine this sample for twin sheets.
   b. If your mineral does not show signs of cleavage, it is **GYPSUM.**

9. **a.** If your mineral shows signs of cleavage, it is **HORNBLENDE.**
   b. If your mineral does not show signs of cleavage, it is **GARNET.**

10. **a.** If your mineral shows signs of cleavage, it is **BIOTITE.** Examine your sample for twin sheets.
    b. If your mineral does not show signs of cleavage, it is **GRAPHITE.**

Applying Your Data

Using your textbook and other reference books, research other methods of identifying different types of minerals. Based on your findings, create a new identification key. Give the key and a few sample minerals to a friend, and see if your friend can unravel the mystery!

Analyze the Results

1. Students will find that some minerals required fewer steps to identify than others. For example, pyrite and galena are identified in two steps. Students may also find that they recognize some of the minerals and that the identification key is there merely to verify the identity.
2. For a mineral to leave a streak on the streak plate, the plate must be harder than the mineral. Therefore, extremely hard minerals do not leave a streak. Also, some minerals that are softer than a streak plate leave behind a colorless streak.
3. Answers will vary.

Applying Your Data

Scientists test minerals for their density, crystal form, reaction to acids, optical properties, fluorescence, and radioactivity. Students should create an identification key that is very similar to the one provided in the lab, but their key should include different characteristics.

CLASSROOM TESTED & APPROVED

David Jones
Andrew Jackson Middle School
Cross Lanes, West Virginia

CHAPTER RESOURCES

Chapter Resource File
- Datasheet for LabBook
- Lab Notes and Answers

LabBook
Skills Practice Lab

Crystal Growth

Teacher's Notes

Time Required
Two 45-minute class periods

Lab Ratings

EASY —————— HARD

Teacher Prep 🧪🧪
Student Set-Up 🧪🧪🧪
Concept Level 🧪🧪
Clean Up 🧪🧪

MATERIALS

The materials listed are enough for a group of 4 to 5 students working cooperatively. Using a higher proportion of magnesium sulfate crystals to water will take significantly longer.

Safety Caution

Remind students to review all safety cautions and icons before beginning this lab activity.

Preparation Notes

Samples of igneous rocks may be obtained locally or through various science supply catalogs.

Using Scientific Methods
Skills Practice Lab

Crystal Growth

Magma forms deep below the Earth's surface at depths of 25 km to 160 km and at extremely high temperatures. Some magma reaches the surface and cools quickly. Other magma gets trapped in cracks or magma chambers beneath the surface and cools very slowly. When magma cools slowly, large, well-developed crystals form. But when magma erupts onto the surface, it cools more quickly. There is not enough time for large crystals to grow. The size of the crystals found in igneous rocks gives geologists clues about where and how the rocks formed.

In this experiment, you will demonstrate how the rate of cooling affects the size of crystals in igneous rocks by cooling crystals of magnesium sulfate at two different rates.

Ask a Question

1. How does temperature affect the formation of crystals?

Form a Hypothesis

2. Suppose you have two solutions that are identical in every way except for temperature. How will the temperature of a solution affect the size of the crystals and the rate at which they form?

Test the Hypothesis

3. Put on your gloves, apron, and goggles.

4. Fill the beaker halfway with tap water. Place the beaker on the hot plate, and let it begin to warm. The temperature of the water should be between 40°C and 50°C.
   Caution: Make sure the hot plate is away from the edge of the lab table.

5. Examine two or three crystals of the magnesium sulfate with your magnifying lens. On a separate sheet of paper, describe the color, shape, luster, and other interesting features of the crystals.

6. On a separate sheet of paper, draw a sketch of the magnesium sulfate crystals.

MATERIALS

- aluminum foil
- basalt
- beaker, 400 mL
- gloves, heat-resistant
- granite
- hot plate
- laboratory scoop, pointed
- magnesium sulfate ($MgSO_4$) (Epsom salts)
- magnifying lens
- marker, dark
- pumice
- tape, masking
- test tube, medium-sized
- thermometer, Celsius
- tongs, test-tube
- watch (or clock)
- water, distilled
- water, tap, 200 mL

SAFETY

Gordon Zibelman
Drexel Hill Middle School
Drexel Hill, Pennsylvania

7 Use the pointed laboratory scoop to fill the test tube about halfway with the magnesium sulfate. Add an equal amount of distilled water.

8 Hold the test tube in one hand, and use one finger from your other hand to tap the test tube gently. Observe the solution mixing as you continue to tap the test tube.

9 Place the test tube in the beaker of hot water, and heat it for approximately 3 min. **Caution:** Be sure to direct the opening of the test tube away from you and other students.

10 While the test tube is heating, shape your aluminum foil into two small boatlike containers by doubling the foil and turning up each edge.

11 If all the magnesium sulfate is not dissolved after 3 min, tap the test tube again, and heat it for 3 min longer. **Caution:** Use the test-tube tongs to handle the hot test tube.

12 With a marker and a piece of masking tape, label one of your aluminum boats "Sample 1," and place it on the hot plate. Turn the hot plate off.

13 Label the other aluminum boat "Sample 2," and place it on the lab table.

14 Using the test-tube tongs, remove the test tube from the beaker of water, and evenly distribute the contents to each of your foil boats. Carefully pour the hot water in the beaker down the drain. Do not move or disturb either of your foil boats.

15 Copy the table below onto a separate sheet of paper. Using the magnifying lens, carefully observe the foil boats. Record the time it takes for the first crystals to appear.

Crystal-Formation Table			
Crystal formation	Time	Size and appearance of crystals	Sketch of crystals
Sample 1			
Sample 2		DO NOT WRITE IN BOOK	

Lab Notes

Some volcanic rocks contain both large and small crystals because the magma cooled for a period of time before erupting. This period of time was long enough for some minerals to crystallize but too short for other minerals to form.

CHAPTER RESOURCES

Chapter Resource File
- Datasheet for LabBook
- Lab Notes and Answers

Chapter 4 • LabBook

Analyze the Results

1. Answers may vary. A correct prediction would state that a cool solution will produce crystals more quickly than a warm solution. A correct prediction would also state that the crystals produced in a warm solution will be much larger than those produced in a cool solution.

2. Because the original crystals were small, students may conclude that they formed quickly.

Draw Conclusions

4. Accept all reasonable sketches.

5. See the chart at the bottom of this page.

Communicating Your Data

Volcanic rocks that form in the air as the result of a violent volcanic eruption would cool quickly and have small crystals. Volcanic rocks that form from lava oozing out of a volcano would cool more slowly and have larger crystals.

---

16 If crystals have not formed in the boats before class is over, carefully place the boats in a safe place. You may then record the time in days instead of in minutes.

17 When crystals have formed in both boats, use your magnifying lens to examine the crystals carefully.

Analyze the Results

1 Was your prediction correct? Explain.

2 Compare the size and shape of the crystals in Samples 1 and 2 with the size and shape of the crystals you examined in step 5. How long do you think the formation of the original crystals must have taken?

Draw Conclusions

3 Granite, basalt, and pumice are all igneous rocks. The most distinctive feature of each is the size of its crystals. Different igneous rocks form when magma cools at different rates. Examine a sample of each with your magnifying lens.

4 Copy the table below onto a separate sheet of paper, and sketch each rock sample.

5 Use what you have learned in this activity to explain how each rock sample formed and how long it took for the crystals to form. Record your answers in your table.

Igneous Rock Observations

	Granite	Basalt	Pumice
Sketch			
How did the rock sample form?		DO NOT WRITE IN BOOK	
Rate of cooling			

Communicating Your Data

Describe the size and shape of the crystals you would expect to find when a volcano erupts and sends material into the air and when magma oozes down the volcano's slope.

Igneous Rock Observations

	Granite	Basalt	Pumice
How did the rock sample form?	the slow cooling of magma beneath the Earth's surface	the quick cooling of lava on the Earth's surface	ejected magma from a volcano during a violent eruption
Rate of cooling	cools slowly; large crystals	cools quickly; small crystals	cools very quickly; very small or no crystals

Model-Making Lab

Metamorphic Mash

Metamorphism is a complex process that takes place deep within the Earth, where the temperature and pressure would turn a human into a crispy pancake. The effects of this extreme temperature and pressure are obvious in some metamorphic rocks. One of these effects is the reorganization of mineral grains within the rock. In this activity, you will investigate the process of metamorphism without being charred, flattened, or buried.

MATERIALS

- cardboard (or plywood), very stiff, small pieces
- clay, modeling
- knife, plastic
- sequins (or other small flat objects)

SAFETY

Procedure

1. Flatten the clay into a layer about 1 cm thick. Sprinkle the surface with sequins.
2. Roll the corners of the clay toward the middle to form a neat ball.
3. Carefully use the plastic knife to cut the ball in half. On a separate sheet of paper, describe the position and location of the sequins inside the ball.
4. Put the ball back together, and use the sheets of cardboard or plywood to flatten the ball until it is about 2 cm thick.
5. Using the plastic knife, slice open the slab of clay in several places. Describe the position and location of the sequins in the slab.

Analyze the Results

1. What physical process does flattening the ball represent?
2. Describe any changes in the position and location of the sequins that occurred as the clay ball was flattened into a slab.

Draw Conclusions

3. How are the sequins oriented in relation to the force you put on the ball to flatten it?
4. Do you think the orientation of the mineral grains in a foliated metamorphic rock tells you anything about the rock? Defend your answer.

Applying Your Data

Suppose you find a foliated metamorphic rock that has grains running in two distinct directions. Use what you have learned in this activity to offer a possible explanation for this observation.

CHAPTER RESOURCES

Chapter Resource File
- Datasheet for LabBook
- Lab Notes and Answers

Dwight Patton
Carrol T. Welch Middle School
Horizon City, Texas

LabBook
Model-Making Lab

Metamorphic Mash

Teacher's Notes

Time Required
One 45-minute class period

Lab Ratings
EASY ———— HARD

Teacher Prep
Student Set-Up
Concept Level
Clean Up

MATERIALS

The materials listed on the student page are enough for 1 student.

Safety Caution

Remind students to review all safety cautions and icons before beginning this lab activity.

Procedure

3. The sequins should be lying in a random pattern. Any layering is the result of rolling the ball.
5. The sequins are all horizontal.

Analyze the Results

1. It represents the pressure that creates metamorphic rock.
2. Before the ball was flattened, the sequins were in a random pattern. Once the ball was flattened, they lined up perpendicular to the pressure.

Draw Conclusions

3. The sequins are aligned perpendicular to the force.
4. Because the grains line up at right angles to the pressure, they are perpendicular to the strongest stress.

Applying Your Data

Answers may vary. Sample answer: Two pressures acting on the rock at different times must have pushed on the rock in different directions.

Chapter 4 • LabBook 725

Skills Practice Lab

Power of the Sun

Teacher's Notes

Time Required
One or two 45-minute class periods

Lab Ratings

EASY ———————— HARD

Teacher Prep 🧪🧪
Student Set-Up 🧪
Concept Level 🧪🧪
Clean Up 🧪

MATERIALS
The materials listed on the student page are enough for a group of 2 to 3 students.

Safety Caution
Remind students to review all safety cautions and icons before beginning this lab activity. Instruct students to not look directly at the sun. Also, caution them not to squeeze the aluminum too hard around the thermometer so that the thermometer is not crushed. Tell students not to force the thermometers through the holes if the holes are too small.

Skills Practice Lab

Power of the Sun

The sun radiates energy in every direction. Like the sun, the energy radiated by a light bulb spreads out in all directions. But how much energy an object receives depends on how close that object is to the source. As you move farther from the source, the amount of energy you receive decreases. For example, if you measure the amount of energy that reaches you from a light and then move three times farther away, you will discover that nine times less energy will reach you at your second position. Energy from the sun travels as light energy. When light energy is absorbed by an object it is converted into thermal energy. Power is the rate at which one form of energy is converted to another, and it is measured in watts. Because power is related to distance, nearby objects can be used to measure the power of far-away objects. In this lab you will calculate the power of the sun using an ordinary 100-watt light bulb.

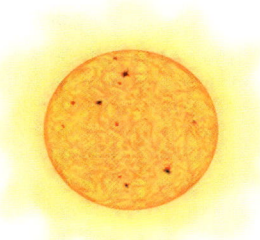

MATERIALS
- aluminum strip, 2 × 8 cm
- calculator, scientific
- clay, modeling
- desk lamp with a 100 W bulb and removable shade
- gloves, protective
- marker, black permanent
- mason jar, cap, and lid with hole in center
- pencil
- ruler, metric
- thermometer, Celsius
- watch (or clock) that indicates seconds

SAFETY

Procedure

1. Gently shape the piece of aluminum around a pencil so that it holds on in the middle and has two wings, one on either side of the pencil.

2. Bend the wings outward so that they can catch as much sunlight as possible.

3. Use the marker to color both wings on one side of the aluminum strip black.

4. Remove the pencil and place the aluminum snugly around the thermometer near the bulb. **Caution:** Do not press too hard—you do not want to break the thermometer! Wear protective gloves when working with the thermometer and the aluminum.

5. Carefully slide the top of the thermometer through the hole in the lid. Place the lid on the jar so that the thermometer bulb is inside the jar, and screw down the cap.

6. Secure the thermometer to the jar lid by molding clay around the thermometer on the outside of the lid. The aluminum wings should be in the center of the jar.

7. Read the temperature on the thermometer. Record this as room temperature.

8. Place the jar on a windowsill in the sunlight. Turn the jar so that the black wings are angled toward the sun.

9. Watch the thermometer until the temperature reading stops rising. Record the temperature.

10. Remove the jar from direct sunlight, and allow it to return to room temperature.

11. Remove any shade or reflector from the lamp. Place the lamp at one end of a table.

12. Place the jar about 30 cm from the lamp. Turn the jar so that the wings are angled toward the lamp.

Preparation Notes
Prepare the lids by punching a hole in the center of each lid with a nail and hammer. Flatten the jagged edges against the inside of the lid with the hammer. Each hole should be big enough to accommodate a thermometer. Cut 2 cm × 8 cm strips of aluminum from the bottom of a pie plate. Make sure there are no sharp burrs left on the edges of the strips. Before beginning this lab, you may wish to review the concept of ratios with students.

726 Chapter 5 • LabBook

13. Turn on the lamp, and wait about 1 minute.

14. Move the jar a few centimeters toward the lamp until the temperature reading starts to rise. When the temperature stops rising, compare it with the reading you took in step 9.

15. Repeat step 14 until the temperature matches the temperature you recorded in step 9.

16. If the temperature reading rises too high, move the jar away from the lamp and allow it to cool. Once the reading has dropped to at least 5°C below the temperature you recorded in step 9, you may begin again at step 12.

17. When the temperature in the jar matches the temperature you recorded in step 9, record the distance between the center of the light bulb and the thermometer bulb.

Analyze the Results

1. The thermometer measured the same amount of energy absorbed by the jar at the distance you measured to the lamp. In other words, your jar absorbed as much energy from the sun at a distance of 150 million kilometers as it did from the 100 W light bulb at the distance you recorded in step 17.

2. Use the following formula to calculate the power of the sun (be sure to show your work):

$$\frac{\text{power of the sun}}{(\text{distance to the sun})^2} = \frac{\text{power of the lamp}}{(\text{distance to the lamp})^2}$$

Hint: $(\text{distance})^2$ means that you multiply the distance by itself. If you found that the lamp was 5 cm away from the jar, for example, the $(\text{distance})^2$ would be 25.

Hint: Convert 150,000,000 km to 15,000,000,000,000 cm.

3. Review the discussion of scientific notation in the Math Refresher found in the Appendix at the back of this book. You will need to understand this technique for writing large numbers in order to compare your calculation with the actual figure. For practice, convert the distance to the sun given above in step 2 of Analyze the Results to scientific notation.

15,000,000,000,000 cm = $1.5 \times 10^?$ cm

Draw Conclusions

4. The sun emits 3.7×10^{26} W of power. Compare your answer in step 2 with this value. Was this a good way to calculate the power of the sun? Explain.

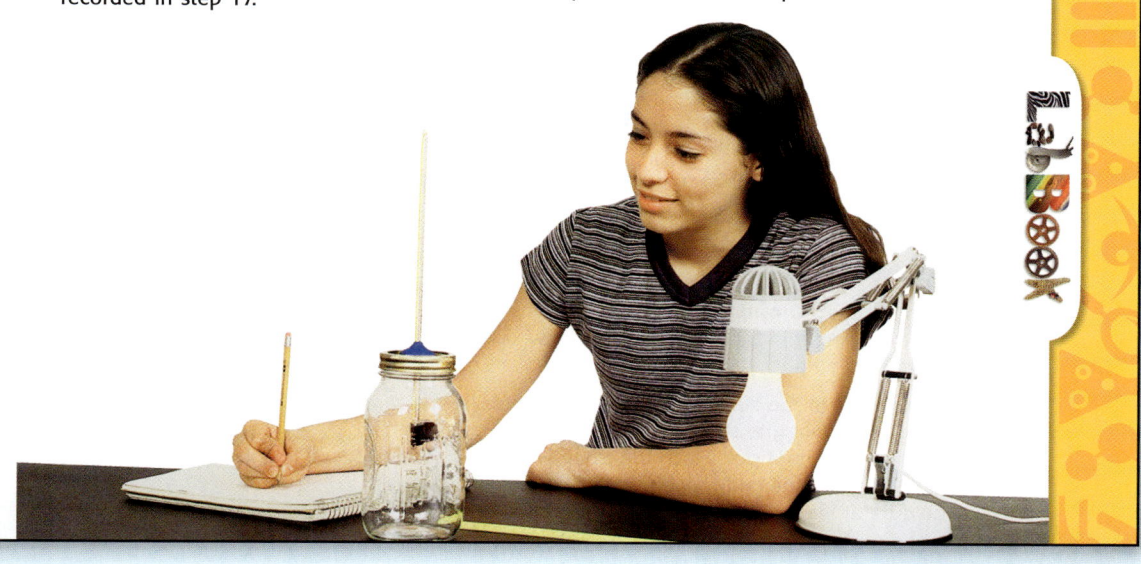

Analyze the Results

2. Answers may vary. Ask students to show their calculations.

3. 15,000,000,000,000 cm = 1.5×10^{13} cm

Draw Conclusions

4. Answers may vary. If students performed the lab correctly, their numbers should be close to 3.7×10^{26} W.

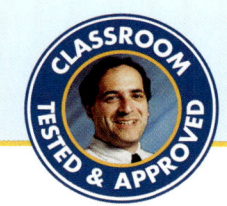

CHAPTER RESOURCES

Chapter Resource File
- Datasheet for LabBook
- Lab Notes and Answers

Gordon Zibelman
Drexel Hill Middle School
Drexel Hill, Pennsylvania

Chapter 5 • LabBook

Model-Making Lab

Oh, the Pressure!

Teacher's Notes

Time Required
One 45-minute class period

Lab Ratings

EASY ——————→ HARD

Teacher Prep 🧪🧪🧪
Student Set-Up 🧪🧪
Concept Level 🧪🧪🧪
Clean Up 🧪🧪🧪

MATERIALS

The materials listed on the student page are enough for a group of 3 to 4 students.

Safety Caution

Remind students to review all safety cautions and icons before beginning this lab activity.

Lab Notes

Homemade modeling dough may be substituted for modeling clay in this activity. In step 6, students may find it easier to trim each layer of clay with the plastic knife before stacking the layers together.

Using Scientific Methods

Model-Making Lab

Oh, the Pressure!

When scientists want to understand natural processes, such as mountain formation, they often make models to help them. Models are useful in studying how rocks react to the forces of plate tectonics. A model can demonstrate in a short amount of time geological processes that take millions of years. Do the following activity to find out how folding and faulting occur in the Earth's crust.

MATERIALS

- can, soup (or rolling pin)
- clay, modeling, 4 colors
- knife, plastic
- newspaper
- pencils, colored
- poster board, 5 cm × 5 cm squares (2)
- poster board, 5 cm × 15 cm strip

SAFETY

Ask a Question

1. How do synclines, anticlines, and faults form?

Form a Hypothesis

2. On a separate piece of paper, write a hypothesis that is a possible answer to the question above. Explain your reasoning.

Test the Hypothesis

3. Use modeling clay of one color to form a long cylinder, and place the cylinder in the center of the glossy side of the poster-board strip.

4. Mold the clay to the strip. Try to make the clay layer the same thickness all along the strip; you can use the soup can or rolling pin to even it out. Pinch the sides of the clay so that the clay is the same width and length as the strip. Your strip should be at least 15 cm long and 5 cm wide.

Daniel Bugenhagen
Yutan Jr.–Sr. High
Yutan, Nebraska

CLASSROOM TESTED & APPROVED

728 Chapter 7 • LabBook

5. Flip the strip over on the newspaper your teacher has placed across your desk. Carefully peel the strip from the modeling clay.

6. Repeat steps 3–5 with the other colors of modeling clay. Each person should have a turn molding the clay. Each time you flip the strip over, stack the new clay layer on top of the previous one. When you are finished, you should have a block of clay made of four layers.

7. Lift the block of clay, and hold it parallel to and just above the tabletop. Push gently on the block from opposite sides, as shown below.

8. Use the colored pencils to draw the results of step 6. Use the terms *syncline* and *anticline* to label your diagram. Draw arrows to show the direction that each edge of the clay was pushed.

9. Repeat steps 3–6 to form a second block of clay.

10. Cut the second block of clay in two at a 45° angle as seen from the side of the block.

Preparation Notes

Homemade Modeling Dough (optional) The night before the activity, prepare enough modeling dough for each class, using the recipe below. The recipe provides enough dough for each group. Combine the following ingredients in a large saucepan over low heat in the order that they are listed:

- 2 cups cold water
- $\frac{1}{3}$ cup cooking oil
- 1 cup salt
- 4 tsp cream of tartar
- 2 cups flour
- food coloring

Constantly stir the mixture until the modeling dough forms a ball. Turn the modeling dough out onto a floured surface. Use a ruler to divide the dough into fourths. When the dough cools slightly, add 15–20 drops of food coloring to each quarter. Fold and knead to evenly distribute the color throughout the dough. Place the dough in an airtight container, such as an 8 oz yogurt container. If you freeze it, the modeling dough will last for months.

Just before the activity, cover all workspaces with newspaper, and secure the newspapers in place. If the dough gets dry, rinse your hands and continue to mold the dough.

CHAPTER RESOURCES

Chapter Resource File
- Datasheet for LabBook
- Lab Notes and Answers

Chapter 7 • LabBook

Lab Notes

Students should realize that stress is equivalent to pressure or force. Explain to them that rocks can undergo stress without deforming. When the stress becomes too great, the rocks become folded or faulted. This deformation is also called *strain*. Stress and the result of stress (strain) are two different concepts.

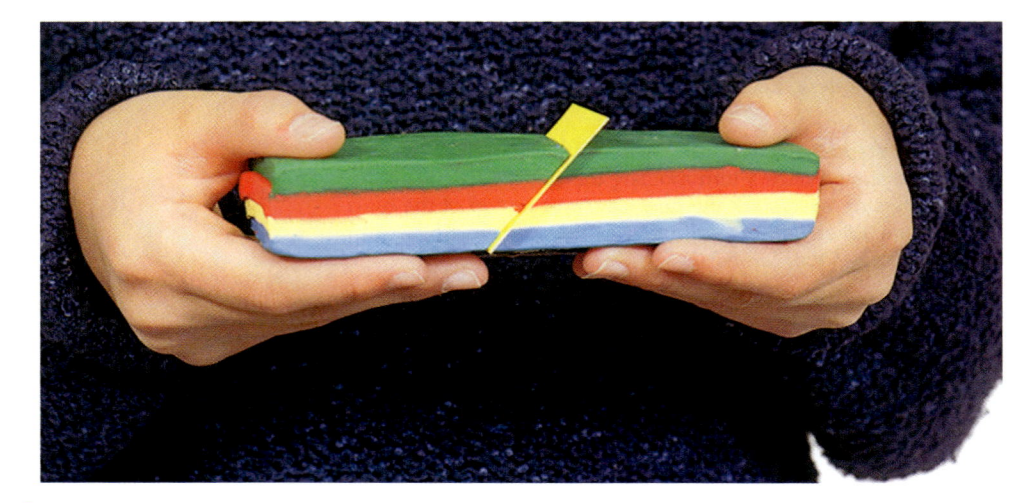

11. Press one poster-board square on the angled end of each of the block's two pieces. The poster board represents a fault. The two angled ends represent a hanging wall and a footwall. The model should resemble the one in the photograph above.

12. Keeping the angled edges together, lift the blocks, and hold them parallel to and just above the tabletop. Push gently on the two blocks until they move. Record your observations.

13. Now, hold the two pieces of the clay block in their original position, and slowly pull them apart, allowing the hanging wall to move downward. Record your observations.

Analyze the Results

1. What happened to the first block of clay in step 7? What kind of force did you apply to the block of clay?

2. What happened to the pieces of the second block of clay in step 12? What kind of force did you apply to them?

3. What happened to the pieces of the second block of clay in step 13? Describe the forces that acted on the block and the way the pieces of the block reacted.

Draw Conclusions

4. Summarize how the forces you applied to the blocks of clay relate to the way tectonic forces affect rock layers. Be sure to use the terms *fold, fault, anticline, syncline, hanging wall, footwall, tension,* and *compression* in your summary.

Analyze the Results

1. The first block got shorter and taller. The layers of clay became folded due to compression.
2. One of the pieces (the hanging wall) slid above the other piece (the footwall) due to compression.
3. One of the pieces (the footwall) moved up relative to the other piece (the hanging wall) as tension was released.

Draw Conclusions

4. The conclusion should be a complete summary of this activity, indicating the direction of pressure at each step. Any diagrams should be correctly labeled, and students should demonstrate a good understanding of the terms *fold, fault, anticline, syncline, hanging wall, footwall, tension,* and *compression*.

Skills Practice Lab

Earthquake Waves

The energy from an earthquake travels as seismic waves in all directions through the Earth. Seismologists can use the properties of certain types of seismic waves to find the epicenter of an earthquake.

P waves travel more quickly than S waves and are always detected first. The average speed of P waves in the Earth's crust is 6.1 km/s. The average speed of S waves in the Earth's crust is 4.1 km/s. The difference in arrival time between P waves and S waves is called *lag time*.

In this activity, you will use the S-P-time method to determine the location of an earthquake's epicenter.

MATERIALS
- calculator (optional)
- compass
- ruler, metric

SAFETY

Procedure

1. The illustration below shows seismographic records made in three cities following an earthquake. These traces begin at the left and show the arrival of P waves at time zero. The second set of waves on each record represents the arrival of S waves.

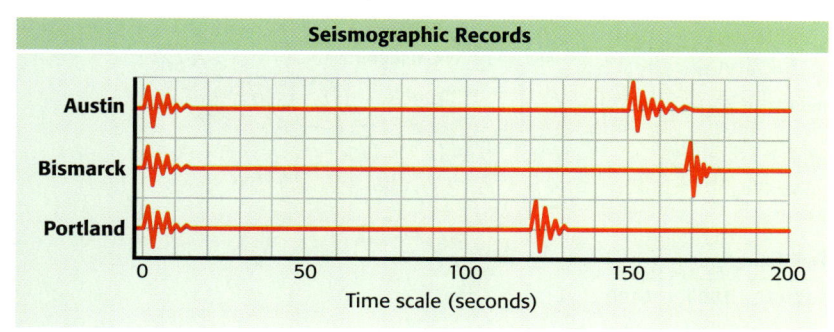

Seismographic Records

(Austin, Bismarck, Portland traces; Time scale 0–200 seconds)

2. Copy the data table on the next page.

3. Use the time scale provided with the seismographic records to find the lag time between the P waves and the S waves for each city. Remember that the lag time is the time between the moment when the first P wave arrives and the moment when the first S wave arrives. Record this data in your table.

4. Use the following equation to calculate how long it takes each wave type to travel 100 km:

   100 km ÷ *average speed of the wave* = *time*

CHAPTER RESOURCES

Chapter Resource File
- Datasheet for LabBook
- Lab Notes and Answers

Janel Guse
West Central Middle School
Hartford, South Dakota

LabBook

Skills Practice Lab

Earthquake Waves

Teacher's Notes

Time Required
One 45-minute class period

Lab Ratings
EASY ——————————→ HARD

Teacher Prep
Student Set-Up
Concept Level
Clean Up

MATERIALS
The materials listed on the student page are enough for 2 students.

Safety Caution
Remind students to review all safety cautions and icons before beginning this lab activity.

Preparation Notes
Be sure that students understand in step 6 how to calculate the distance from each city to the epicenter of the earthquake. These distances must be correct to accurately determine the epicenter of the earthquake on the map.

Emphasize to students that the circles on the map must intersect or come very close to intersecting in order to determine the epicenter of the earthquake. If the circles do not come close to intersecting, tell students that they must check their calculations.

Chapter 8 • LabBook 731

Procedure

3. Austin: 150 s
Bismarck: 168 s
Portland: 120 s

6. Austin: 1,875 km; Bismarck: 2,100 km; Portland: 1,500 km

Analyze the Results

1. San Diego, California

Draw Conclusions

2. Sample answer: Seismologists require at least three intersecting circles to determine the epicenter of an earthquake. The first two circles intersect in two places. When a third circle is used, all three circles intersect in only one place near the epicenter.

---

5 To find lag time for earthquake waves at 100 km, subtract the time it takes P waves to travel 100 km from the time it takes S waves to travel 100 km. Record the lag time.

6 Use the following formula to find the distance from each city to the epicenter:

$$\text{distance} = \frac{\text{measured lag time (s)} \times 100 \text{ km}}{\text{lag time for 100 km (s)}}$$

In your data table, record the distance from each city to the epicenter.

7 Trace the map below onto a separate sheet of paper.

8 Use the scale to adjust your compass so that the radius of a circle with Austin at the center is equal to the distance between Austin and the epicenter of the earthquake.

Epicenter Data Table		
City	Lag time (seconds)	Distance to the epicenter (km)
Austin, TX		
Bismarck, ND	DO NOT WRITE IN BOOK	
Portland, OR		

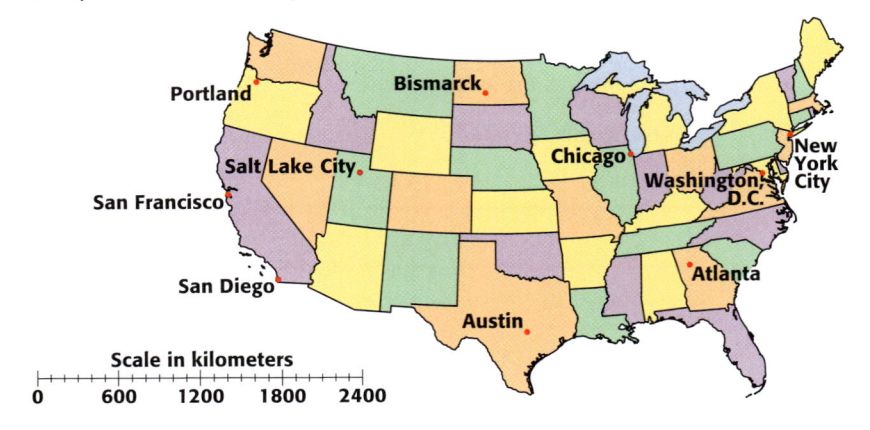

9 Put the point of your compass at Austin on your copy of the map, and draw a circle.

10 Repeat steps 8 and 9 for Bismarck and Portland. The epicenter of the earthquake is located near the point where the three circles meet.

Analyze the Results

1 Which city is closest to the epicenter?

Draw Conclusions

2 Why do seismologists need measurements from three different locations to find the epicenter of an earthquake?

Skills Practice Lab

Some Go "Pop," Some Do Not

Volcanic eruptions range from mild to violent. When volcanoes erupt, the materials left behind provide information to scientists studying the Earth's crust. Mild, or nonexplosive, eruptions produce thin, runny lava that is low in silica. During nonexplosive eruptions, lava simply flows down the side of the volcano. Explosive eruptions, on the other hand, do not produce much lava. Instead, the explosions hurl ash and debris into the air. The materials left behind are light in color and high in silica. These materials help geologists determine the composition of the crust underneath the volcanoes.

MATERIALS
- paper, graph (1 sheet)
- pencils (or markers), red, yellow, and orange
- ruler, metric

Procedure

1. Copy the map below onto graph paper. Take care to line the grid up properly.

2. Locate each volcano from the list on the next page by drawing a circle with a diameter of about 2 mm in the proper location on your copy of the map. Use the latitude and longitude grids to help you.

3. Review all the eruptions for each volcano. For each explosive eruption, color the circle red. For each quiet volcano, color the circle yellow. For volcanoes that have erupted in both ways, color the circle orange.

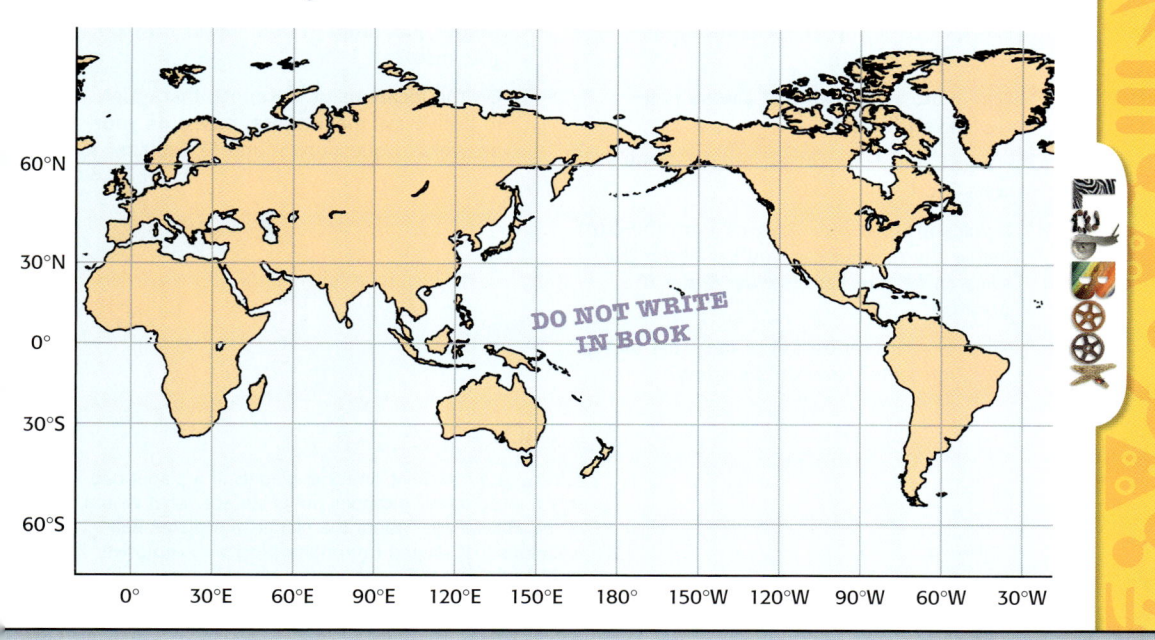

C. John Graves
Monforton Middle School
Bozeman, Montana

Lab Notes

In a very simple way, this lab models how the composition of magma can evolve. For example, basaltic (mafic) magma can evolve into granitic (felsic) magma through chemical differentiation processes. Scientists often use measurements of trace elements in the resulting rock to "fingerprint" the source of magma from which volcanic rocks formed.

Skills Practice Lab

Some Go "Pop," Some Do Not

Teacher's Notes

Time Required
One 45-minute class period

Lab Ratings
EASY → HARD
Teacher Prep 🧪🧪
Student Set-Up 🧪
Concept Level 🧪🧪🧪
Clean Up 🧪

MATERIALS
The materials listed on the student page are enough for 1 student. Students may wish to use tracing paper in step 1.

Preparation Notes

Students should be aware that volcanoes with a high water and silica content tend to erupt explosively. They should use this information to analyze the data in this activity. You may also wish to inform students that, in general, quietly erupting volcanoes are derived from basaltic magma, and explosively erupting volcanoes are derived from granitic magma. Remind students that oceanic crust is basaltic and low in silica, and continental crust is granitic and high in silica.

Students may need some practice finding locations by using latitude and longitude. If necessary, guide them through the steps needed to locate the first volcano on the chart.

Chapter 9 • LabBook   **733**

Analyze the Results

1. Nonexplosive volcanoes are usually located on oceanic crust.
2. Explosive volcanoes are usually located on continental crust.
3. Volcanoes that erupt in both ways are usually located near boundaries between oceanic and continental crusts.
4. The crust under the oceans must be low in silica. Students may also know that the crust is likely to be made of basalt.
5. Continental crust is generally high in silica. Students may also know that the crust is likely to be made of granite.

Draw Conclusions

6. The volcanoes that erupt in both ways must be near the boundary between the oceanic crusts and the continental crusts. The crust must have both basalt and granite.
7. The volcanoes that erupt in both ways are located near the boundaries between continents and oceans. Students should understand that two different crusts must meet in these areas and that both granitic (felsic) and basaltic (mafic) magma is generated.

Volcanic Activity Chart

Volcano name	Location	Description
Mount St. Helens	46°N 122°W	An explosive eruption blew the top off the mountain. Light-colored ash covered thousands of square kilometers. Another eruption sent a lava flow down the southeast side of the mountain.
Kilauea	19°N 155°W	One small eruption sent a lava flow along 12 km of highway.
Rabaul caldera	4°S 152°E	Explosive eruptions have caused tsunamis and have left 1–2 m of ash on nearby buildings.
Popocatépetl	19°N 98°W	During one explosion, Mexico City closed the airport for 14 hours because huge columns of ash made it too difficult for pilots to see. Eruptions from this volcano have also caused damaging avalanches.
Soufriere Hills	16°N 62°W	Small eruptions have sent lava flows down the hills. Other explosive eruptions have sent large columns of ash into the air.
Long Valley caldera	37°N 119°W	Explosive eruptions have sent ash into the air.
Okmok	53°N 168°W	Recently, there have been slow lava flows from this volcano. Twenty-five hundred years ago, ash and debris exploded from the top of this volcano.
Pavlof	55°N 161°W	Eruption clouds have been sent 200 m above the summit. Eruptions have sent ash columns 10 km into the air. Occasionally, small eruptions have caused lava flows.
Fernandina	42°N 12°E	Eruptions have ejected large blocks of rock from this volcano.
Mount Pinatubo	15°N 120°E	Ash and debris from an explosive eruption destroyed homes, crops, and roads within 52,000 km² around the volcano.

Analyze the Results

1. According to your map, where are volcanoes that always have nonexplosive eruptions located?
2. Where are volcanoes that always erupt explosively located?
3. Where are volcanoes that erupt in both ways located?
4. If volcanoes get their magma from the crust below them, what can you say about the silica content of Earth's crust under the oceans?
5. What is the composition of the crust under the continents? How do we know?

Draw Conclusions

6. What is the source of materials for volcanoes that erupt in both ways? How do you know?
7. Do the locations of volcanoes that erupt in both ways make sense, based on your answers to questions 4 and 5? Explain.

Applying Your Data

Volcanoes are present on other planets. If a planet had only nonexplosive volcanoes on its surface, what would we be able to infer about the planet? If a planet had volcanoes that ranged from nonexplosive to explosive, what might that tell us about the planet?

Applying Your Data

Answers should reflect the idea that the crust on planets with nonexplosive volcanoes must be low in silica compared to the crust on Earth. Students may also realize that planets that have only nonexplosive volcanoes must have basaltic crust. If a planet has all three types of volcanoes, it must have both basaltic and granitic crusts.

CHAPTER RESOURCES

Chapter Resource File

- Datasheet for LabBook
- Lab Notes and Answers

Using Scientific Methods
Skills Practice Lab

Great Ice Escape

Did you know that ice acts as a natural wrecking ball? Even rocks don't stand a chance against the power of ice. When water trapped in rock freezes, a process called *ice wedging* occurs. The water volume increases, and the rock cracks to "get out of the way." This expansion can fragment a rock into several pieces. In this exercise, you will see how this natural wrecker works, and you will try to stop the great ice escape.

Ask a Question

1. If a plastic jar is filled with water, is there a way to prevent the jar from breaking when the water freezes?

Form a Hypothesis

2. Write a hypothesis that is a possible answer to the question above. Explain your reasoning.

Test the Hypothesis

3. Fill three identical jars to overflowing with water, and close two of them securely.
4. Measure the height of the water in the unsealed container. Record the height.
5. Tightly wrap one of the closed jars with tape, string, or other items to reinforce the jar. These items must be removable.
6. Place all three jars in resealable sandwich bags, and leave them in the freezer overnight. (Make sure the open jar does not spill.)
7. Remove the jars from the freezer, and carefully remove the wrapping from the reinforced jar.
8. Did your reinforced jar crack? Why or why not?
9. What does each jar look like? Record your observations.
10. Record the height of the ice in the unsealed jar. How does the new height compare with the height you measured in step 4?

Analyze the Results

1. Do you think it is possible to stop the ice from breaking the sealed jars? Why or why not?
2. How could ice wedging affect soil formation?

MATERIALS

- bags, sandwich resealable (3)
- freezer
- jars, hard plastic with screw-on lids, such as spice containers (3)
- ruler, metric
- tape, strings, rubber bands, and other items to bind or reinforce the jars
- water

SAFETY

CHAPTER RESOURCES

Chapter Resource File
- Datasheet for LabBook
- Lab Notes and Answers

CLASSROOM TESTED & APPROVED

David M. Sparks
Redwater Junior High School
Redwater, Texas

Analyze the Results

1. Sample answer: no; The expanding ice cannot be confined. If it can shatter a rock, it can break plastic.
2. Sample answer: Ice wedging breaks up large rocks into smaller pieces that are further weathered chemically and physically. The processes of weathering create soil.

LabBook
Skills Practice Lab

Great Ice Escape

Teacher's Notes

Time Required
Two 45-minute class periods

Lab Ratings
EASY ——— HARD

Teacher Prep 🧪🧪🧪
Student Set-Up 🧪🧪
Concept Level 🧪
Clean Up 🧪🧪

MATERIALS
The materials listed on the student page are enough for 1 to 3 students.

Safety Caution
Remind students to review all safety cautions and icons before beginning this lab activity. Warn them that when a plastic jar cracks, the pieces could be very sharp.

Preparation Notes
You should perform this lab ahead of time in order to make certain that your plastic jars will break.

Test the Hypothesis
8. Answers may vary.
9. Sample answer: Ice is protruding from the top of the unsealed jar. Both sealed jars are cracked. The unwrapped jar cracked more severely.
10. Answers may vary, students should observe that the height of the water has increased.

Chapter 10 • LabBook **735**

LabBook

Skills Practice Lab

Clean Up Your Act

Teacher's Notes

Time Required
Two 45-minute class periods

Lab Rating
EASY →→→ HARD

Teacher Prep 🧪🧪🧪
Student Set-Up 🧪🧪🧪
Concept Level 🧪🧪
Clean Up 🧪🧪🧪

MATERIALS
The materials listed on the student page are enough for a group of 4 to 5 students. To keep results consistent with all lab groups, each group should have the same-size gravel and the same-size sand. Also, the layers of sand and gravel should be the same dimensions in each group.

Safety Caution
Remind students to review all safety cautions and icons before beginning this lab activity. Caution students not to taste any of the liquids in this lab.

Using Scientific Methods
Skills Practice Lab

Clean Up Your Act

When you wash dishes, the family car, the bathroom sink, or your clothes, you wash them with water. But have you ever wondered how water gets clean? Two major methods of purifying water are filtration and evaporation. In this activity, you will use both of these methods to test how well they remove pollutants from water. You will test detritus (decaying plant matter), soil, vinegar, and detergent. Your teacher may also ask you to test other pollutants.

Form a Hypothesis

1 Form a hypothesis about whether filtration and evaporation will clean each of the four pollutants from the water and how well they might do it. Then, use the procedures below to test your hypothesis.

Part A: Filtration
Filtration is a common method of removing various pollutants from water. Filtration requires very little energy—gravity pulls water down through the layers of filter material. See how well this energy-efficient method works to clean your sample of polluted water.

Test the Hypothesis

2 Put on your gloves and goggles. Use scissors to carefully cut the bottom out of the empty soda bottle.

3 Using a small nail and hammer, carefully punch four or five small holes through the plastic cap of the bottle. Screw the plastic cap onto the bottle.

4 Turn the bottle upside down, and set its neck in a ring on a ring stand, as shown on the next page. Put a handful of gravel into the inverted bottle. Add a layer of activated charcoal, followed by thick layers of sand and gravel. Place a 400 mL beaker under the neck of the bottle.

5 Fill each of the large beakers with 1,000 mL of clean water. Set one beaker aside to serve as the control. Add three or four spoonfuls of each of the following pollutants to the other beaker: detritus, soil, household vinegar, and dishwashing detergent.

6 Copy the table on the next page, and record your observations for each beaker in the columns labeled "Before cleaning."

7 Observe the color of the water in each beaker.

8 Use a hand lens to examine the water for visible particles.

MATERIALS

Part A
- charcoal, activated
- goggles
- gravel
- hammer and small nail
- sand
- scissors
- soda bottle, plastic, with cap, 2 L

Part B
- bag, plastic sandwich, sealable
- flask, Erlenmeyer
- gloves, heat-resistant
- hot plate
- ice
- stopper, rubber, one-hole, with a glass tube
- tubing, plastic, 1.5 m

Parts A and B
- beaker, 400 mL
- beaker, 1,000 mL (2)
- detergent, dishwashing
- detritus (grass and leaf clippings)
- hand lens
- pH test strips
- ring stand with ring
- soil
- spoons, plastic (2)
- vinegar, household
- water, 2,000 mL

SAFETY

Kenneth Creese
White Mountain Jr. High
Rock Springs, Wyoming

9. Smell the water, and note any unusual odors.
10. Stir the water in each beaker rapidly with a plastic spoon, and check for suds. Use a different spoon for each sample.
11. Use a pH test strip to find the pH of the water.
12. Gently stir the clean water, and then pour half of it through the filtration device.
13. Observe the water in the collection beaker for color, particles, odors, suds, and pH. Be patient. It may take several minutes for the water to travel through the filtration device.
14. Record your observations in the appropriate "After filtration" column in your table.
15. Repeat steps 12–14 using the polluted water.

Analyze the Results

1. How did the color of the polluted water change after the filtration? Did the color of the clean water change?
2. Did the filtration method remove all of the particles from the polluted water? Explain.
3. How much did the pH of the polluted water change? Did the pH of the clean water change? Was the final pH of the polluted water the same as the pH of the clean water before cleaning? Explain.

Results Table

	Before cleaning (clean water)	Before cleaning (polluted water)	After filtration (clean water)	After filtration (polluted water)	After evaporation (clean water)	After evaporation (polluted water)
Color						
Particles						
Odor			DO NOT WRITE IN BOOK			
Suds						
pH						

Preparation Notes

Varying the thickness of the layers can contribute to a variation in the results. Specify the thickness of each layer so that the results between groups are comparable. The layers could be the following dimensions: 7 cm of gravel, 2.5 cm of charcoal, 10 cm of sand, and 10 cm of gravel. You may adjust the layers according to your class size or the size of the bottles.

For variation, try different sizes of gravel or different textures of sand. Both will affect how many particles travel through the filter. If you place a few drops of food coloring in the water, students can watch the progress of the water as it passes through the filter.

You may decide that it is easier and safer for you to perform step 2 of Part A, cutting the soda bottles, before class. You may also wish to perform steps 2–5 of Part B ahead of time. Some students may find it difficult to attach the plastic tubing to the glass tube or to slide the glass tube into the rubber stopper.

CHAPTER RESOURCES

Chapter Resource File
- Datasheet for LabBook
- Lab Notes and Answers

Chapter 11 • LabBook

Part A
Analyze the Results

1. Sample answer: The filtered water was lighter in color than the unfiltered water. The water was still not as clear as the clean water; The color of the clean water stayed about the same.

2. Sample answer: no; The filtration method did not remove all of the particles from the polluted water; Many of the particles passed through the filter, but there were fewer particles than before the filtration.

3. Sample answer: The pH of the water changed slightly; The final pH of the polluted water was not the same as that of the clean water. After the polluted water was filtered, its pH was still slightly more acidic than that of the clean water.

Part B
Analyze the Results

1. Sample answer: After the evaporation process, the polluted water was clear. The color of the clean water did not change.

2. Sample answer: No particles were visible in the treated water after the evaporation method; The particles in the polluted water were left behind when the water evaporated.

3. Answers may vary, depending on the clean-water source. Generally, the pH of the two samples should be very close or the same.

Part B: Evaporation

Cleaning water by evaporation is more expensive than cleaning water by filtration. Evaporation requires more energy, which can come from a variety of sources. In this activity, you will use an electric hot plate as the energy source. See how well this method works to clean your sample of polluted water.

Form a Hypothesis

1. Write a hypothesis about which method you think will work better for water purification. Explain your reasoning.

Test the Hypothesis

2. Fill an Erlenmeyer flask with about 250 mL of the clean water, and insert the rubber stopper and glass tube into the flask.

3. Wearing goggles and gloves, connect about 1.5 m of plastic tubing to the glass tube.

4. Set the flask on the hot plate, and run the plastic tubing up and around the ring and down into a clean, empty 400 mL collection beaker.

5. Fill the sandwich bag with ice, seal the bag, and place the bag on the ring stand. Be sure the plastic bag and the tubing touch, as shown below.

6. Bring the water in the flask to a slow boil. As the water vapor passes by the bag of ice, the vapor will condense and drip into the collection beaker.

7. Observe the water in the collection beaker for color, particles, odor, suds, and pH. Record your observations in the "After evaporation" column in your data table.

8. Repeat steps 2–7 using the polluted water.

Analyze the Results

1. How did the color of the polluted water change after evaporation? Did the color of the clean water change after evaporation?

2. Did the evaporation method remove all of the particles from the polluted water? Explain.

3. How much did the pH of the polluted water change? Did the pH of the final clean water change? Was the final pH of the polluted water the same as the pH of the clean water before it was cleaned? Explain.

738 Chapter 11 • LabBook

Draw Conclusions: Parts A and B

4. Which method—filtration or evaporation—removed the most pollutants from the water? Explain your reasoning.

5. Describe any changes that occurred in the clean water during this experiment.

6. What do you think are the advantages and disadvantages of each method?

7. Explain how you think each material (sand, gravel, and charcoal) used in the filtration system helped clean the water.

8. List areas of the country where you think each method of purification would be the most and the least beneficial. Explain your reasoning.

Applying Your Data

Do you think either purification method would remove oil from water? If time permits, repeat your experiment using several spoonfuls of cooking oil as the pollutant.

Filtration is only one step in the purification of water at water treatment plants. Research other methods used to purify public water supplies.

Parts A and B
Draw Conclusions

4. Sample answer: The evaporation method removed the most pollutants from the water; The pollutants were left behind when the water evaporated.

5. Sample answer: The clean water picked up some particles as it traveled through the filter. The water was not as clean after the filtration as it had been before the filtration.

6. Sample answer: The advantages of the filtration method are that: it is easy to do, it can treat large amounts of water, and it works relatively quickly. The filtration method doesn't remove all of the pollutants, however.

   The evaporation method removed more of the pollutants, but it is time consuming and expensive, particularly with large volumes of water.

7. Sample answer: The sand filtered out some of the larger particles and some of the soap. The gravel also removed the large particles. The charcoal removed most of the smaller particles, the odors, and some of the soap.

8. Answers may vary.

Applying Your Data

- Oil is removed from the water in both methods. The filtration method is relatively quicker than the evaporation method.

- Other methods of water purification include reverse osmosis, settling ponds, chemical additives such as chlorine, and other filtration layers. Students may also find out about bioremediation and the use of bacteria and plants to clean polluted water.

Chapter 11 • LabBook

Model-Making Lab

Dune Movement

Teacher's Notes

Time Required
30 minutes

Lab Ratings
EASY —————— HARD

Teacher Prep 🧪
Student Set-Up 🧪🧪
Concept Level 🧪
Clean Up 🧪🧪

MATERIALS
The materials listed on the student page are enough for 2 students.

Safety Caution
Remind students to review all safety cautions and icons before beginning this lab activity.

Preparation Notes
You might want to have students do this activity outside, in an area where an electrical outlet is available.

Analyze the Results
1. Answers may vary. A typical answer would be about 0.5 to 1.0 cm.
2. Answers may vary. A typical answer would be about 5 to 10 cm.

Model-Making Lab

Dune Movement

Wind moves the sand by a process called *saltation*. The sand skips and bounces along the ground in the same direction as the wind is blowing. As sand is blown across a beach, the dunes change. In this activity, you will investigate the effect wind has on a model sand dune.

Procedure

1. Use the marker to draw and label vertical lines 5 cm apart along one side of the box.
2. Fill the box about halfway with sand. Brush the sand into a dune shape about 10 cm from the end of the box.
3. Use the lines you drew along the edge of the box to measure the location of the dune's peak to the nearest centimeter.
4. Slide the box into the paper bag until only about half the box is exposed, as shown below.
5. Put on your safety goggles and filter mask. Hold the hair dryer so that it is level with the peak of the dune and about 10–20 cm from the open end of the box.
6. Turn on the hair dryer at the lowest speed, and direct the air toward the model sand dune for 1 min.
7. Record the new location of the model dune.
8. Repeat steps 5 and 6 three times. After each trial, measure and record the location of the dune's peak.

Analyze the Results

1. How far did the dune move during each trial?
2. How far did the dune move overall?

Draw Conclusions

3. How might the dune's movement be affected if you were to turn the hair dryer to the highest speed?

Applying Your Data

Flatten the sand. Place a barrier, such as a rock, in the sand. Position the hair dryer level with the top of the sand's surface. How does the rock affect the dune's movement?

MATERIALS
- bag, paper, large enough to hold half the box
- box, cardboard, shallow
- hair dryer
- marker
- mask, filter
- ruler, metric
- sand, fine

SAFETY

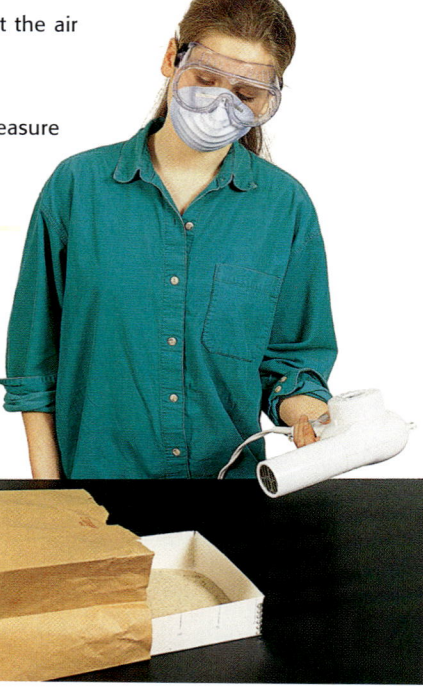

CHAPTER RESOURCES

Chapter Resource File
- Datasheet for LabBook
- Lab Notes and Answers

CLASSROOM TESTED & APPROVED

Larry Tackett
Andrew Jackson Middle School
Cross Lanes, West Virginia

Draw Conclusions

3. Answers may vary. The sand could be blown until it hits the bag, or the dune could move farther. Students may also have predicted that more sand would be blown out of the box.

Applying Your Data

The dune forms on the downwind side of the barrier. The rock slows the migration of the dune.

Using Scientific Methods

Skills Practice Lab

Creating a Kettle

As glaciers recede, they leave huge amounts of rock material behind. Sometimes receding glaciers form moraines by depositing some of the rock material in ridges. At other times, glaciers leave chunks of ice that form depressions called *kettles*. As the ice melts, these depressions may form ponds or lakes. In this activity, you will discover how kettles are formed by creating your own.

MATERIALS
- ice, cubes of various sizes (4–5)
- ruler, metric
- sand
- tub, small

Ask a Question
1. How are kettles formed?

Form a Hypothesis
2. Write a hypothesis that could answer the question above.

Test the Hypothesis
3. Fill the tub three-quarters full with sand.
4. Describe the size and shape of each ice cube.
5. Push the ice cubes to various depths in the sand.
6. Put the tub where it won't be disturbed overnight.
7. Closely observe the sand around the area where you left each ice cube.
8. What happened to the ice cubes?
9. Use a metric ruler to measure the depth and diameter of the indentation left by each ice cube.

Analyze the Results
1. How does this model relate to the size and shape of a natural kettle?
2. In what ways are your model kettles similar to real ones? How are they different?

Draw Conclusions
3. Based on your model, what can you conclude about the formation of kettles by receding glaciers?

CHAPTER RESOURCES

Chapter Resource File
- Datasheet for LabBook
- Lab Notes and Answers

CLASSROOM TESTED & APPROVED

Janel Guse
West Central Middle School
Hartford, South Dakota

Skills Practice Lab

Creating a Kettle

Teacher's Notes

Time Required
One 45-minute class period plus 30 minutes during a second day

Lab Ratings
EASY ———————— HARD

Teacher Prep
Student Set-Up
Concept Level
Clean Up

MATERIALS
The materials listed on the student page are enough for a group of 4 to 5 students.

Analyze the Results
1. Sample answer: The model is similar. The simulated kettle is the size of the ice cube. A real kettle hole is the size of the block of ice that breaks off a glacier. Its shape is determined by the shape of the ice.

2. Sample answer:
Similarities: The ice cube in the lab melted slowly to form a depression. Similarly, blocks of ice left behind by glaciers melt slowly to form kettles.
Differences: The materials and debris surrounding the model hole are different from those surrounding a real kettle. In addition, the shape of a real kettle would not be as uniform as the shape of the model hole.

Draw Conclusions
3. Answers may vary. Accept all reasonable responses. Kettles form from the slow melting of ice left behind when a glacier recedes.

Chapter 12 • LabBook 741

Skills Practice Lab

Investigating an Oil Spill

Teacher's Notes

Time Required
One 45-minute class period

Lab Ratings
EASY ←——————→ HARD

Teacher Prep 🧪🧪🧪
Student Set-Up 🧪
Concept Level 🧪🧪
Clean Up 🧪🧪🧪

MATERIALS
The materials listed on the student page are sufficient for a group of 2 to 4 students. You may also choose to perform this activity as a demonstration to limit the use of machine oil.

Safety Caution
Remind students to review all safety cautions and icons before beginning this lab activity. Machine oil releases a strong odor. Use it only in well-ventilated areas.

Preparation Notes
Light machine oil may be replaced by cooking oil to demonstrate the same principle. If you choose to use machine oil, be sure there is sufficient ventilation in your classroom.

Using Scientific Methods
Skills Practice Lab

Investigating an Oil Spill
Have you ever wondered why it is important to recycle motor oil rather than pour it down the drain or sewer? Or have you ever wondered why a seemingly small oil spill can cause so much damage? The reason is that a little oil goes a long way.

Observing Oil and Water
Maybe you've heard the phrase "Oil and water don't mix." Oil dropped in water will spread out thinly over the surface of the water. In this activity, you'll learn how far a drop of oil can spread.

Ask a Question
1. How far will one drop of oil spread in a pan of water?

Form a Hypothesis
2. Write a hypothesis that could answer the question above.

Test the Hypothesis
3. Use a pipet to place one drop of oil into the middle of a pan of water. **Caution:** Machine oil is poisonous. Wear goggles and gloves. Keep materials that have contacted oil out of your mouth and eyes.

4. Observe what happens to the drop of oil for the next few seconds. Record your observations.

5. Using a metric ruler, measure the diameter of the oil slick to the nearest centimeter.

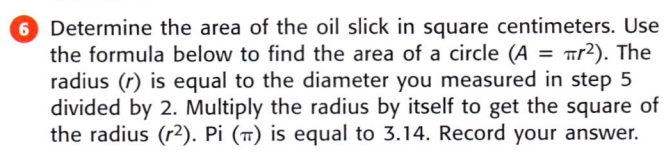

6. Determine the area of the oil slick in square centimeters. Use the formula below to find the area of a circle ($A = \pi r^2$). The radius (r) is equal to the diameter you measured in step 5 divided by 2. Multiply the radius by itself to get the square of the radius (r^2). Pi (π) is equal to 3.14. Record your answer.

Example
If your diameter is 10 cm,
$r = 5$ cm, $r^2 = 25$ cm^2, $\pi = 3.14$

$A = \pi r^2$
$A = 3.14 \times 25$ cm^2
$A = 78.5$ cm^2

MATERIALS
- calculator (optional)
- gloves, protective
- goggles
- graduated cylinder
- oil, light machine, 15 mL
- pan, large, at least 22 cm in diameter
- pipet
- ruler, metric
- water

SAFETY

CLASSROOM TESTED & APPROVED

David Sparks
Redwater Jr. High
Redwater, Texas

Analyze the Results

1. What happened to the drop of oil when it came in contact with the water?
2. What total surface area was covered by the oil slick? (Show your calculations.)

Draw Conclusions

3. What can you conclude about the density of oil compared with the density of water?

Finding the Number of Drops in a Liter

"It's only a few drops," you may think as you spill something toxic on the ground. But those drops eventually add up. Just how many drops does it take to make a difference? In this activity, you'll learn just what an impact a few drops can have.

Procedure

1. Using a clean pipet, count the number of water drops it takes to fill the graduated cylinder to 10 mL. Be sure to add the drops slowly so you get an accurate count.
2. Since there are 1,000 mL in a liter, multiply the number of drops in 10 mL by 100. The result is the number of drops in a liter.

Analyze the Results

1. How many drops of water from your pipet did it take to fill a 1 L container?
2. What would happen if someone spilled 4 L of oil into a lake?

Applying Your Data

Can you devise a way to clean the oil from the water? Get permission from your teacher before testing your cleaning method.

Do you think oil behaves the same way in ocean water? Devise an experiment to test your hypothesis.

CHAPTER RESOURCES

Chapter Resource File
- Datasheet for LabBook
- Lab Notes and Answers

Disposal Information

Always follow federal, state, and local guidelines when disposing of oil. Pour cooking oil into a container of sand, and put it in the trash.

Analyze the Results

1. When the drop of oil touched the water, the oil spread out. This may surprise some students, who might expect the two substances to mix or the oil to sink.
2. Answers may vary. Students should show their work to illustrate that they understand the mathematical principles involved.

Draw Conclusions

3. Sample answer: This experiment shows that oil is less dense than water. For this reason, oil floats on water.

Analyze the Results

1. Answers may vary. The answer depends on the number of drops the students count in 10 mL of water. They should show their work to illustrate that they understand the mathematical principles involved.
2. The oil would spread to cover a large area. Students will not be able to determine the exact area for such an oil slick, but they should understand that the oil will spread significantly and pollute much of the lake.

Applying Your Data

- Answers may vary. One possibility is to use detergent to change the surface tension and remove the oil.
- To test the behavior of oil in ocean water, students could repeat the activity, using cold salt water instead of tap water. They could also rock the pan back and forth to simulate waves.

Chapter 13 • LabBook

LabBook

Model-Making Lab

Turning the Tides

Teacher's Notes

Time Required
One 45-minute class period

Lab Ratings
EASY —————— HARD

Teacher Prep 🧪🧪
Student Set-Up 🧪🧪🧪
Concept Level 🧪🧪🧪
Clean Up 🧪

MATERIALS
The materials listed on the student page are enough for a group of 2 to 4 students.

Safety Caution
Remind students to review all safety cautions and icons before beginning this lab activity. Students should wear safety goggles. Be sure that students have enough space to spin the system.

Model-Making Lab

Turning the Tides

Daily tides are caused by two "bulges" on the ocean's surface—one on the side of the Earth facing the moon and the other on the opposite side of the Earth. The bulge on the side facing the moon is caused by the moon's gravitational pull on the water. But the bulge on the opposite side of the Earth is slightly more difficult to explain. Whereas the moon pulls the water on one side of the Earth, the combined rotation of the Earth and the moon "pushes" the water on the opposite side of the Earth. In this activity, you will model the motion of the Earth and the moon to investigate the tidal bulge on the side of Earth facing away from the moon.

Procedure

1. Draw a line from the center of each disk along the folds in the cardboard to the edge of the disk. This line is the radius.

2. Place a drop of white glue on one end of the dowel. Lay the larger disk flat, and align the dowel with the line for the radius you drew in step 1. Insert about 2.5 cm of the dowel into the edge of the disk.

3. Add a drop of glue to the other end of the dowel, and push that end into the smaller disk, again along its radius. The setup should look like a large, two-headed lollipop, as shown below. This setup is a model of the Earth-moon system.

4. Staple the string to the edge of the large disk on the side opposite the dowel. Staple the cardboard square to the other end of the string. This smaller piece of cardboard represents the Earth's oceans that face away from the moon.

5. Place the tip of the pencil at the center of the large disk, as shown in the figure on the next page, and spin the model. You may poke a small hole in the bottom of the disk with your pencil, but DO NOT poke all the way through the cardboard. Record your observations. **Caution:** Be sure you are at a safe distance from other people before spinning your model.

MATERIALS
- cardboard, 1 cm × 1 cm piece
- corrugated cardboard, one large and one small, with centers marked (2 disks)
- dowel, $\frac{1}{4}$ in. in diameter and 36 cm long
- glue, white
- pencil, sharp
- stapler with staples
- string, 5 cm length

SAFETY

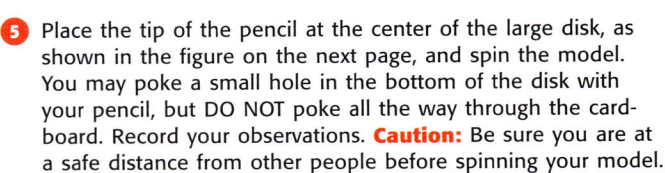

Preparation Notes

You will need to put a mark at the center of all of the cardboard disks. Students will need to draw the radius of the circle from the center to the edge of the disk. Encourage students to draw this line along the corrugations of the cardboard. Otherwise, several other steps will be made more difficult.

The cardboard disks are not to scale with the Earth and moon. They are used to show how a two-body system, such as the Earth-moon system, rotates. The disks must be different sizes. The large disks could be 10 cm in diameter, and the smaller disks could be 5 cm in diameter.

744 Chapter 14 • LabBook

6 Now, find your model's center of mass. The center of mass is the point at which the model can be balanced on the end of the pencil. (Hint: It might be easier to find the center of mass by using the eraser end. Then, use the sharpened end of the pencil to balance the model.) This balance point should be just inside the edge of the larger disk.

7 Place the pencil at the center of mass, and spin the model around the pencil. Again, you may wish to poke a small hole in the disk. Record your observations.

Analyze the Results

1 What happened when you tried to spin the model around the center of the large disk? This model, called the Earth-centered model, represents the incorrect view that the moon orbits the center of the Earth.

2 What happened when you tried to spin the model around its center of mass? This point, called the *barycenter,* is the point around which both the Earth and the moon rotate.

3 In each case, what happened to the string and cardboard square when the model was spun?

Draw Conclusions

4 Which model—the Earth-centered model or the barycentric model—explains why the Earth has a tidal bulge on the side opposite the moon? Explain.

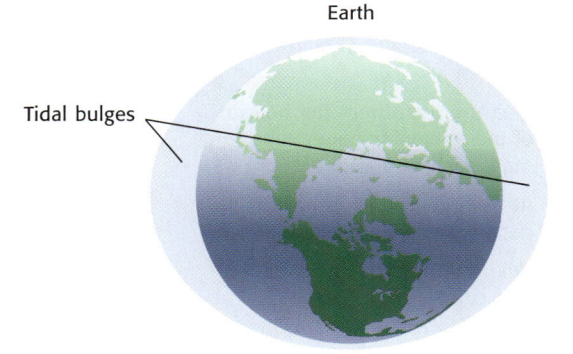

Moon

Earth

Tidal bulges

Analyze the Results

1. Answers may vary. Sample answer: When I tried to spin the model around the center of the large disk, I could not get the model to balance on the pencil.

2. Answers may vary. Sample answer: I was able to balance the model at the barycenter. The model spun, and the small piece of cardboard on the string swung outward.

3. Answers may vary. Sample answer: The cardboard square hung down when I tried to swing the model around the center of the large disk. I was unable to make the model spin. When I spun the model around its barycenter, the square swung away from the model.

Draw Conclusions

4. Sample answer: The barycentric model explains why the Earth has a bulge on the side opposite the moon. The side of the Earth opposite the side facing the moon acts in much the same way the small square of cardboard does in this model. As the Earth-moon system rotates, the side of the Earth facing away from the moon bulges outward.

Tracy Jahn
Berkshire Jr.-Sr. High
Canaan, New York

CHAPTER RESOURCES

Chapter Resource File
- Datasheet for LabBook
- Lab Notes and Answers

Chapter 14 • LabBook

Skills Practice Lab

Go Fly a Bike!

Teacher's Notes

Time Required
One 45-minute class period

Lab Ratings
EASY —————— HARD

Teacher Prep ▲
Student Set-Up ▲▲▲
Concept Level ▲▲
Clean Up ▲▲

MATERIALS
The materials listed on the student page are enough for a group of 3 to 4 students.

Safety Caution
Remind students to review all safety cautions and icons before beginning this lab activity.

Preparation Notes
Conduct this activity on a day when the wind is blowing but not when the wind speed is greater than 50 km/h. Use straight, plastic straws. Before the activity, explain that an *anemometer* is a device that measures wind speed. It works because the wind pushes the cups at the same speed that the wind is moving.

Using Scientific Methods
Skills Practice Lab

Go Fly a Bike!

Your friend Daniel just invented a bicycle that can fly! Trouble is, the bike can fly only when the wind speed is between 3 m/s and 10 m/s. If the wind is not blowing hard enough, the bike won't get enough lift to rise into the air, and if the wind is blowing too hard, the bike is difficult to control. Daniel needs to know if he can fly his bike today. Can you build a device that can estimate how fast the wind is blowing?

Ask a Question
1. How can I construct a device to measure wind speed?

Form a Hypothesis
2. Write a possible answer for the question above. Explain your reasoning.

Test the Hypothesis
3. Cut off the rolled edges of all five paper cups. They will then be lighter so that they can spin more easily.
4. Measure and place four equally spaced markings 1 cm below the rim of one of the paper cups.
5. Use the hole punch to punch a hole at each mark so that the cup has four equally spaced holes. Use the sharp pencil to carefully punch a hole in the center of the bottom of the cup.
6. Push a straw through two opposite holes in the side of the cup.
7. Repeat step 5 for the other two holes. The straws should form an X.
8. Measure 3 cm from the bottom of the remaining paper cups, and mark each spot with a dot.
9. At each dot, punch a hole in the paper cups with the hole punch.
10. Color the outside of one of the four cups.

MATERIALS
- clay, modeling
- cups, paper, small (5)
- hole punch
- marker, colored
- pencil, sharp, with an eraser
- ruler, metric
- scissors
- stapler, small
- straws, straight plastic (2)
- tape, masking
- thumbtack
- watch (or clock) that indicates seconds

SAFETY

Terry J. Rakes
Elmwood Jr. High
Rogers, Arkansas

11 Slide a cup on one of the straws by pushing the straw through the punched hole. Rotate the cup so that the bottom faces to the right.

12 Fold the end of the straw, and staple it to the inside of the cup directly across from the hole.

13 Repeat steps 11–12 for each of the remaining cups.

14 Push the tack through the intersection of the two straws.

15 Push the eraser end of a pencil through the bottom hole in the center cup. Push the tack as far as it will go into the end of the eraser.

16 Push the sharpened end of the pencil into some modeling clay to form a base. The device will then be able to stand up without being knocked over, as shown at right.

17 Blow into the cups so that they spin. Adjust the tack so that the cups can freely spin without wobbling or falling apart. Congratulations! You have just constructed an anemometer.

18 Find a suitable area outside to place the anemometer vertically on a surface away from objects that would obstruct the wind, such as buildings and trees.

19 Mark the surface at the base of the anemometer with masking tape. Label the tape "starting point."

20 Hold the colored cup over the starting point while your partner holds the watch.

21 Release the colored cup. At the same time, your partner should look at the watch or clock. As the cups spin, count the number of times the colored cup crosses the starting point in 10 s.

Analyze the Results

1 How many times did the colored cup cross the starting point in 10 s?

2 Divide your answer in step 21 by 10 to get the number of revolutions in 1 s.

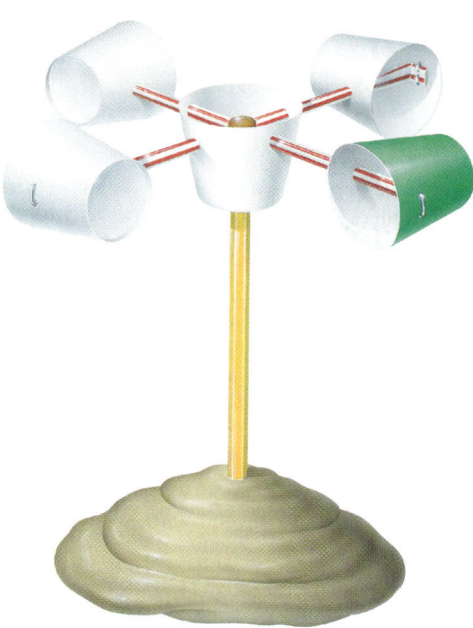

3 Measure the diameter of your anemometer (the distance between the outside edges of two opposite cups) in centimeters. Multiply this number by 3.14 to get the circumference of the circle made by the cups of your anemometer.

4 Multiply your answer from step 3 by the number of revolutions per second (step 2). Divide that answer by 100 to get wind speed in meters per second.

5 Compare your results with those of your classmates. Did you get the same results? What could account for any slight differences in your results?

Draw Conclusions

6 Could Daniel fly his bicycle today? Why or why not?

Analyze the Results
1. Answers may vary, depending on the wind speed.
2. Answers may vary according to each student's response to question 1.
3. Answers may vary according to the length of the straws and the size of the cups used.
4. Answers may vary.
5. Each group's anemometer should provide similar results. Differences may be caused by inconsistent wind speed. If students did not answer question 1 accurately, their results will be slightly different from those of other groups.

Draw Conclusions
6. If the wind speed is between 3 m/s and 10 m/s, Daniel could fly his bicycle. Otherwise, the weather would be too windy or too still for the bicycle to work.

CHAPTER RESOURCES

Chapter Resource File
- Datasheet for LabBook
- Lab Notes and Answers

Chapter 15 • LabBook

LabBook

Skills Practice Lab

Watching the Weather

Teacher's Notes

Time Required
One 45-minute class period

Lab Ratings

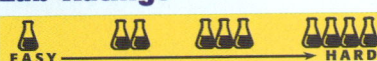

EASY → HARD

Teacher Prep 🧪
Student Set-Up 🧪
Concept Level 🧪🧪
Clean Up 🧪

MATERIALS
The only material required in this lab is a pencil. Have students complete the lab individually.

Skills Practice Lab

Watching the Weather

Imagine that you own a private consulting firm that helps people plan for big occasions, such as weddings, parties, and celebrity events. One of your duties is making sure the weather doesn't put a damper on your clients' plans. In order to provide the best service possible, you have taken a crash course in reading weather maps. Will the celebrity golf match have to be delayed on account of rain? Will the wedding ceremony have to be moved inside so the blushing bride doesn't get soaked? It is your job to say yea or nay.

MATERIALS
- pencil

Procedure

1. Study the station model and legend shown on the next page. You will use the legend to interpret the weather map on the final page of this activity.

2. Weather data is represented on a weather map by a station model. A station model is a small circle that shows the location of the weather station along with a set of symbols and numbers around the circle that represent the data collected at the weather station. Study the table below.

Weather-Map Symbols

Weather conditions	Cloud cover	Wind speed (mph)
•• Light rain	○ No clouds	◎ Calm
∴ Moderate rain	◐ One-tenth or less	3–8
⁞ Heavy rain	◔ Two- to three-tenths	9–14
, Drizzle	◑ Broken	15–20
✶✶ Light snow	◕ Nine-tenths	21–25
✶✶✶ Moderate snow	● Overcast	32–37
⚡ Thunderstorm	⊗ Sky obscured	44–48
∽ Freezing rain	**Special Symbols**	55–60
∞ Haze	▲▲▲▲ Cold front	66–71
≡ Fog	⌒⌒⌒ Warm front	
	H High pressure	
	L Low pressure	
	🌀 Hurricane	

Gordon Zibelman
Drexel Hill Middle School
Drexel Hill, Pennsylvania

Station Model

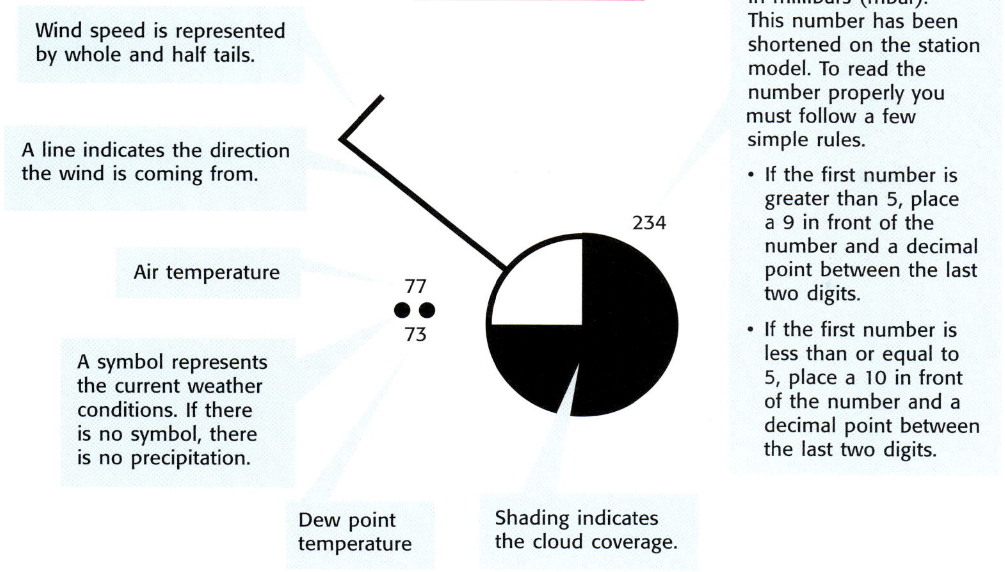

Wind speed is represented by whole and half tails.

A line indicates the direction the wind is coming from.

Air temperature

A symbol represents the current weather conditions. If there is no symbol, there is no precipitation.

Dew point temperature

Shading indicates the cloud coverage.

Atmospheric pressure in millibars (mbar). This number has been shortened on the station model. To read the number properly you must follow a few simple rules.

- If the first number is greater than 5, place a 9 in front of the number and a decimal point between the last two digits.

- If the first number is less than or equal to 5, place a 10 in front of the number and a decimal point between the last two digits.

Interpreting Station Models

The station model below is for Boston, Massachusetts. The current temperature in Boston is 42°F, and the dew point is 39°F. The barometric pressure is 1011.0 mbar. The sky is overcast, and there is moderate rainfall. The wind is coming from the southwest at 15–20 mph.

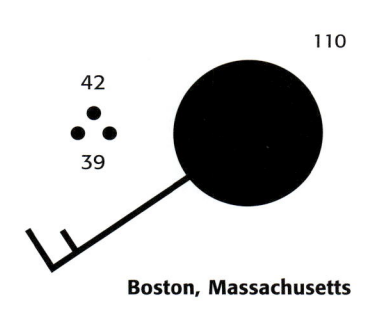

Boston, Massachusetts

Lab Notes

You may want to go over the different weather symbols with students and discuss how to convert the abbreviated form of atmospheric pressure to its actual measure. Before the lab, have students review the different kinds of fronts. Students may enjoy creating a weather report based on the weather report provided in this lab. Students can present this report to the class as a "live" studio show or through a videotape they create in their own time.

CHAPTER RESOURCES

Chapter Resource File
- Datasheet for LabBook
- Lab Notes and Answers

Chapter 16 • LabBook

Analyze the Results

1. It's the winter. A cold front is coming through. Temperatures are low where the cold front has passed.

2. The temperature is 42°F. The dewpoint is 36°F. There is broken cloud cover, the wind is from the northwest at 3–8 mph, and the barometric pressure is 1,024.6 mb.

3. As the cold front approaches, the wind is generally from the south, temperatures are warmer and the barometric pressure is low. As the cold front passes, the wind is from the northwest, temperatures are much cooler, and the pressure rises.

Draw Conclusions

4. The temperature is 45°F. The barometric pressure is 965.4 mb, the dewpoint is 38°F, the sky is obscured, there is a thunderstorm, and the wind is from the south at 21–25 mph.

Analyze the Results

1. Based on the weather for the entire United States, what time of year is it? Explain your answer.

2. Interpret the station model for Salem, Oregon. What is the temperature, dew point, cloud coverage, wind direction, wind speed, and atmospheric pressure? Is there any precipitation? If so, what kind?

3. What is happening to wind direction, temperature, and pressure as the cold front approaches? as it passes?

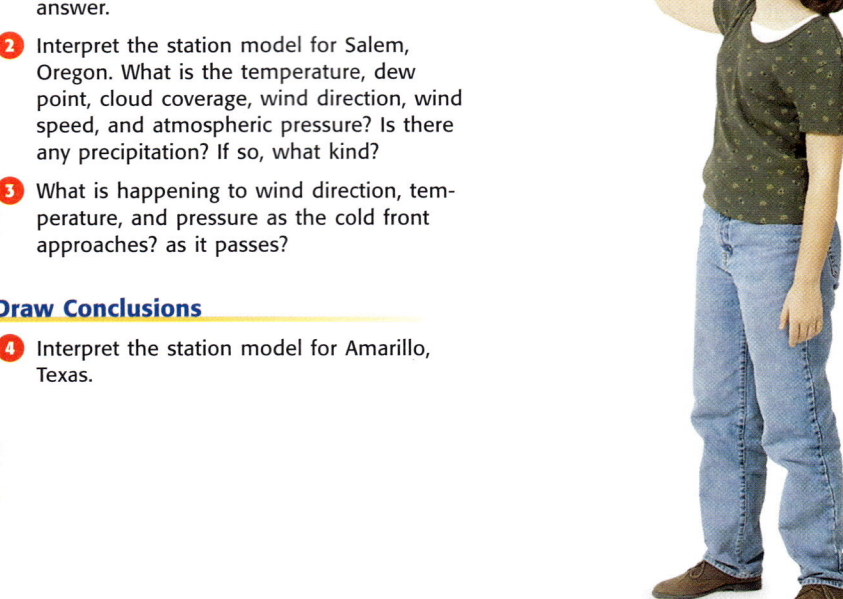

Draw Conclusions

4. Interpret the station model for Amarillo, Texas.

Skills Practice Lab

Let It Snow!

Although an inch of rain might be good for your garden, 7 cm or 8 cm could cause an unwelcome flood. But what about snow? How much snow is too much? A blizzard might drop 40 cm of snow overnight. Sure it's up to your knees, but how does this much snow compare with rain? This activity will help you find out.

MATERIALS

- beaker, 100 mL
- gloves, heat-resistant
- graduated cylinder
- hot plate
- ice, shaved, 150 mL
- ruler, metric

SAFETY

Procedure

1. Pour 50 mL of shaved ice into your beaker. Do not pack the ice into the beaker. This ice will represent your snowfall.
2. Use the ruler to measure the height of the snow in the beaker.
3. Turn on the hot plate to a low setting. **Caution:** Wear heat-resistant gloves and goggles when working with the hot plate.
4. Place the beaker on the hot plate, and leave it there until all of the snow melts.
5. Pour the water into the graduated cylinder, and record the height and volume of the water.
6. Repeat steps 1–5 two more times.

Analysis

1. What was the difference in height before and after the snow melted in each of your three trials? What was the average difference?
2. Why did the volume change after the ice melted?
3. What was the ratio of snow height to water height?
4. Use the ratio you found in step 3 of the Analysis to calculate how much water 50 cm of this snow would produce. Use the following equation to help.

$$\frac{\text{measured height of snow}}{\text{measured height of water}} = \frac{50 \text{ cm of snow}}{? \text{ cm of water}}$$

5. Why is it important to know the water content of a snowfall?

Applying Your Data

Shaved ice isn't really snow. Research to find out how much water real snow would produce. Does every snowfall produce the same ratio of snow height to water depth?

CHAPTER RESOURCES

Chapter Resource File
- Datasheet for LabBook
- Lab Notes and Answers

CLASSROOM TESTED & APPROVED

Walter Woolbaugh
Manhattan School System
Manhattan, Montana

LabBook

Skills Practice Lab

Let It Snow!

Teacher's Notes

Time Required
One 45-minute class period

Lab Ratings

EASY ———————————→ HARD

Teacher Prep 🧪
Student Set-Up 🧪🧪
Concept Level 🧪
Clean Up 🧪

MATERIALS

The materials listed on the student page are enough for a group of 3 to 4 students.

Safety Caution

Remind students to review all safety cautions and icons before beginning this lab activity.

Analyze the Results

1. Answers may vary according to the water content of the ice or snow sample.
2. The volume changed because the water changed from a solid to a liquid.
3. Answers may vary.
4. Answers may vary
5. Sample answer: The water content of a snowfall—whether it is relatively wet or relatively dry—affects how much flooding may occur as the snow melts. A "wetter" snow has more water per volume and may cause more flooding than a "drier" snow.

Applying Your Data

Every snowfall does not produce the same ratio of snow height to water depth. The ratio of snow height to water depth is dependent on several variables, including whether the snow is wet or dry.

Chapter 16 • LabBook **751**

LabBook
Model-Making Lab

Gone with the Wind

Teacher's Notes

Time Required
One 45-minute class period

Lab Ratings
EASY → HARD

Teacher Prep 🧪🧪
Student Set-Up 🧪🧪
Concept Level 🧪🧪
Clean Up 🧪

MATERIALS
The materials listed on the student page are enough for a group of 2 to 3 students.

Safety Caution
Remind students to review all safety cautions and icons before beginning this lab activity.

Preparation Notes
You might want to watch your local weather station in order to schedule this experiment on a windy day. Use a magnetic compass to find magnetic north. Then, use masking tape or chalk to mark the sidewalk or parking lot with an arrow pointing toward magnetic north. Before the activity, ask students if they have ever seen a weather vane. Also, have them list several reasons why knowing the wind direction might be helpful.

Using Scientific Methods
Model-Making Lab

Gone with the Wind

Pilots at the Fly Away Airport need your help—fast! Last night, lightning destroyed the orange windsock. This windsock helped pilots measure which direction the wind was blowing. But now the windsock is gone with the wind, and an incoming airplane needs to land. The pilot must know which direction the wind is blowing and is counting on you to make a device that can measure wind direction.

MATERIALS
- card, index
- compass, drawing
- compass, magnetic
- pencil, sharpened
- plate, paper
- protractor
- rock, small
- ruler, metric
- scissors
- stapler
- straw, straight plastic
- thumbtack (or pushpin)

SAFETY

Ask a Question
1. How can I measure wind direction?

Form a Hypothesis
2. Write a possible answer to the question above.

Test the Hypothesis
3. Find the center of the plate by tracing around its edge with a drawing compass. The pointed end of the compass should poke a small hole in the center of the plate.
4. Use a ruler to draw a line across the center of the plate.
5. Use a protractor to help you draw a second line through the center of the plate. This new line should be at a 90° angle to the line you drew in step 4.
6. Moving clockwise, label each line "N," "E," "S," and "W."
7. Use a protractor to help you draw two more lines through the center of the plate. These lines should be at a 45° angle to the lines you drew in steps 4 and 5.

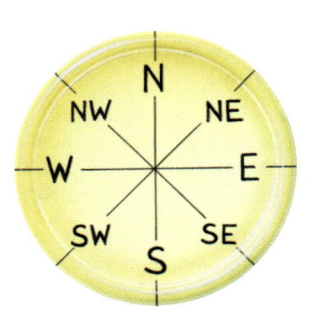

CLASSROOM TESTED & APPROVED

Walter Woolbaugh
Manhattan School System
Manhattan, Montana

752 Chapter 16 • LabBook

⑧ Moving clockwise from *N,* label these new lines "NE," "SE," "SW," and "NW." The plate now resembles the face of a magnetic compass. The plate will be the base of your wind-direction indicator. It will help you read the direction of the wind at a glance.

⑨ Measure and mark a 5 cm × 5 cm square on an index card, and cut out the square. Fold the square in half to form a triangle.

⑩ Staple an open edge of the triangle to the straw so that one point of the triangle touches the end of the straw.

⑪ Hold the pencil at a 90° angle to the straw. The eraser should touch the balance point of the straw. Push a thumbtack or pushpin through the straw and into the eraser. The straw should spin without falling off.

⑫ Find a suitable area outside to measure the wind direction. The area should be clear of trees and buildings.

⑬ Press the sharpened end of the pencil through the center hole of the plate and into the ground. The labels on your paper plate should be facing the sky, as shown on this page.

⑭ Use a compass to find magnetic north. Rotate the plate so that the *N* on the plate points north. Place a small rock on top of the plate so that the plate does not turn.

⑮ Watch the straw as it rotates. The triangle will point in the direction the wind is blowing.

Analyze the Results

❶ From which direction is the wind coming?

❷ In which direction is the wind blowing?

Draw Conclusions

❸ Would this be an effective way for pilots to measure wind direction? Why or why not?

❹ What improvements would you suggest to Fly Away Airport to measure wind direction more accurately?

Applying Your Data

Use this tool to measure and record wind direction for several days. What changes in wind direction occur as a front approaches? as a front passes?

Review magnetic declination in the chapter entitled "Maps as Models of the Earth." How might magnetic declination affect your design for a tool to measure wind direction?

Analyze the Results

1. Answers may vary.
2. Answers may vary.

Draw Conclusions

3. Answers may vary. Accept all reasonable responses.
4. Answers may vary. Accept all reasonable responses.

Applying Your Data

Answers may vary. (Wind direction varies according to the type of front that is moving through.)

Sample answer: You have to adjust the weather vane to account for the difference between magnetic north and true north. The adjustment will vary depending on where you live.

CHAPTER RESOURCES

Chapter Resource File
- Datasheet for LabBook
- Lab Notes and Answers

Chapter 16 • LabBook

LabBook

Skills Practice Lab

Global Impact

Teacher's Notes

Time Required
One 45-minute class period

Lab Ratings

EASY → HARD

Teacher Prep 🧪
Student Set-Up 🧪🧪🧪
Concept Level 🧪🧪
Clean Up 🧪

MATERIALS
The materials listed on the student page are enough for 1 student.

Preparation Notes
This activity requires graphing skills. Students may need a review of graphing, analyzing data from a graph, and calculating the slope of a graph.

Analyze the Results
1. Students will notice that temperatures fluctuated over the last 100 years but have increased in the last 30 years.
2. Sample answer: The larger the sample size, the more precise your analysis will be. The average temperature for a certain year might not be representative for the entire decade. There were very few similarities among the graphs.

Skills Practice Lab

Global Impact

For years, scientists have debated the topic of global warming. Is the temperature of the Earth actually getting warmer? In this activity, you will examine a table to determine if the data indicate any trends. Be sure to notice how much the trends seem to change as you analyze different sets of data.

MATERIALS
- pencils, colored (4)
- ruler, metric

Procedure

1. The table below shows average global temperatures recorded over the last 100 years.

2. Draw a graph. Label the horizontal axis "Time." Mark the grid in 5-year intervals. Label the vertical axis "Temperature (°C)," with values ranging from 13°C to 15°C.

3. Starting with 1900, use the numbers in red to plot the temperature in 20-year intervals. Connect the dots with straight lines.

4. Using a ruler, estimate the average slope for the temperatures. Draw a red line to represent the slope.

5. Using different colors, plot the temperatures at 10-year intervals and 5-year intervals on the same graph. Connect each set of dots, and draw the average slope for each set.

Analyze the Results

1. Examine your completed graph, and explain any trends you see in the graphed data. Was there an increase or a decrease in average temperature over the last 100 years?

2. What similarities and differences did you see between each set of graphed data?

Draw Conclusions

3. What conclusions can you draw from the data you graphed in this activity?

4. What would happen if your graph were plotted in 1-year intervals? Try it!

Average Global Temperatures

Year	°C	Year	°C	Year	°C	Year	°C	Year	°C	Year	°C
1900	14.0	1917	13.6	1934	14.0	1951	14.0	1968	13.9	1985	14.1
1901	13.9	1918	13.6	1935	13.9	1952	14.0	1969	14.0	1986	14.2
1902	13.8	1919	13.8	1936	14.0	1953	14.1	1970	14.0	1987	14.3
1903	13.6	1920	13.8	1937	14.1	1954	13.9	1971	13.9	1988	14.4
1904	13.5	1921	13.9	1938	14.1	1955	13.9	1972	13.9	1989	14.2
1905	13.7	1922	13.9	1939	14.0	1956	13.8	1973	14.2	1990	14.5
1906	13.8	1923	13.8	1940	14.1	1957	14.1	1974	13.9	1991	14.4
1907	13.6	1924	13.8	1941	14.1	1958	14.1	1975	14.0	1992	14.1
1908	13.7	1925	13.8	1942	14.1	1959	14.0	1976	13.8	1993	14.2
1909	13.7	1926	14.1	1943	14.0	1960	14.0	1977	14.2	1994	14.3
1910	13.7	1927	14.0	1944	14.1	1961	14.1	1978	14.1	1995	14.5
1911	13.7	1928	14.0	1945	14.0	1962	14.0	1979	14.1	1996	14.4
1912	13.7	1929	13.8	1946	14.0	1963	14.0	1980	14.3	1997	14.4
1913	13.8	1930	13.9	1947	14.1	1964	13.7	1981	14.4	1998	14.5
1914	14.0	1931	14.0	1948	14.0	1965	13.8	1982	14.1	1999	14.5
1915	14.0	1932	14.0	1949	13.9	1966	13.9	1983	14.3	2000	14.5
1916	13.8	1933	13.9	1950	13.8	1967	14.0	1984	14.1	2001	14.5

CHAPTER RESOURCES

Chapter Resource File
- Datasheet for LabBook
- Lab Notes and Answers

Janel Guse
West Central Middle School
Hartford, South Dakota

Draw Conclusions

3. Sample answer: You can conclude that a larger data set gives you a more complete picture of what is happening. Global temperatures have gradually increased in the last 100 years.

4. Sample answer: Global temperatures would appear to fluctuate more.

754 Chapter 17 • LabBook

Using Scientific Methods
Skills Practice Lab

For the Birds

You and a partner have a new business building birdhouses. But your first clients have told you that birds do not want to live in the birdhouses you have made. The clients want their money back unless you can solve the problem. You need to come up with a solution right away!

You remember reading an article about microclimates in a science magazine. Cities often heat up because the pavement and buildings absorb so much solar radiation. Maybe the houses are too warm! How can the houses be kept cooler?

You decide to investigate the roofs; after all, changing the roofs would be a lot easier than building new houses. In order to help your clients and the birds, you decide to test different roof colors and materials to see how these variables affect a roof's ability to absorb the sun's rays.

One partner will test the color, and the other partner will test the materials. You will then share your results and make a recommendation together.

MATERIALS
- cardboard (4 pieces)
- paint, black, white, and light blue tempera
- rubber, beige or tan
- thermometers, Celsius (4)
- watch (or clock)
- wood, beige or tan

SAFETY

Part A: Color Test

Ask a Question

1. What color would be the best choice for the roof of a birdhouse?

Form a Hypothesis

2. Write down the color you think will keep a birdhouse coolest.

Test the Hypothesis

3. Paint one piece of cardboard black, another piece white, and a third light blue.

4. After the paint has dried, take the three pieces of cardboard outside, and place a thermometer on each piece.

5. In an area where there is no shade, place each piece at the same height so that all three receive the same amount of sunlight. Leave the pieces in the sunlight for 15 min.

6. Leave a fourth thermometer outside in the shade to measure the temperature of the air.

7. Record the reading of the thermometer on each piece of cardboard. Also, record the outside temperature.

CHAPTER RESOURCES
Chapter Resource File
- Datasheet for LabBook
- Lab Notes and Answers

Larry Tackett
Andrew Jackson Middle School
Cross Lanes, West Virginia

LabBook
Skills Practice Lab

For the Birds

Teacher's Notes

Time Required
One 45-minute class period

Lab Ratings
EASY —————— HARD

Teacher Prep
Student Set-Up
Concept Level
Clean Up

MATERIALS
The materials listed on the student page are enough for a group of 4 to 5 students.

Safety Caution
Remind students to review all safety cautions and icons before beginning this lab activity.

Part A
Analyze the Results
1. Sample answer: no, The thermometers recorded different temperatures. The black and blue pieces of cardboard, particularly the black one, caused the temperature to increase.
2. Sample answer: The temperature of the black cardboard was much higher than the outside temperature. Students should find that the temperature of the other colors was also different from the outside temperature.

Part A
Draw Conclusions
3. Answers may vary. Accept all reasonable responses.

Analyze the Results
1. Did each of the three thermometers record the same temperature after 15 min? Explain.
2. Were the temperature readings on each of the three pieces of cardboard the same as the reading for the outside temperature? Explain.

Draw Conclusions
3. How do your observations compare with your hypothesis?

Part B: Material Test
Ask a Question
1. Which material would be the best choice for the roof of a birdhouse?

Form a Hypothesis
2. Write down the material you think will keep a birdhouse coolest.

Test the Hypothesis
3. Take the rubber, wood, and the fourth piece of cardboard outside, and place a thermometer on each.
4. In an area where there is no shade, place each material at the same height so that they all receive the same amount of sunlight. Leave the materials in the sunlight for 15 min.
5. Leave a fourth thermometer outside in the shade to measure the temperature of the air.
6. Record the temperature of each material. Also, record the outside temperature. After you and your partner have finished your investigations, take a few minutes to share your results.

Analyze the Results

1. Did each of the thermometers on the three materials record the same temperature after 15 min? Explain.

2. Were the temperature readings on the rubber, wood, and cardboard the same as the reading for the outside temperature? Explain.

Draw Conclusions

3. How do your observations compare with your hypothesis?

4. Which material would you use to build the roofs for your birdhouses? Why?

5. Which color would you use to paint the new roofs? Why?

Applying Your Data

Make three different-colored samples for each of the three materials. When you measure the temperatures for each sample, how do the colors compare for each material? Is the same color best for all three materials? How do your results compare with what you concluded in steps 4 and 5 under Draw Conclusions of this activity? What's more important, color or material?

Part B
Analyze the Results

1. Sample answer: no, The temperatures were different. The temperature of the rubber was higher than that of the other two materials.

2. Sample answer: no, The temperature of the rubber was higher than the outside temperature. Accept all other reasonable answers for the other materials.

Part B
Draw Conclusions

3. Answers may vary. Accept all reasonable answers.

4. Sample answer: The wood would be the coolest. The cardboard would be a possible alternative.

5. Sample answer: The white roof would be the coolest. A light blue roof would be a possible alternative.

Applying Your Data

Answers may vary. Accept all reasonable interpretations of the data collected.

Chapter 17 • LabBook

Skills Practice Lab

The Sun's Yearly Trip Through the Zodiac

Teacher's Notes

Time Required
Two 45-minute class periods

Lab Ratings
EASY → HARD

Teacher Prep 🧪🧪🧪
Student Set-Up 🧪🧪
Concept Level 🧪🧪🧪
Clean Up 🧪

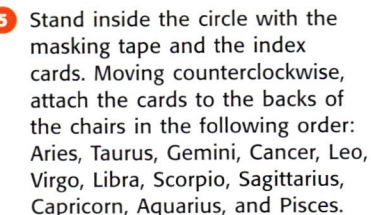

MATERIALS

The materials listed on the student page are enough for a group of 12 students. However, you may choose to use this activity as a demonstration for the entire class.

Preparation Notes
One week before the activity, collect large cardboard boxes. Designate a large, clear area for the activity, such as a gym, cafeteria, playground, or large classroom. You may wish to get a basketball from the physical education instructor, or ask students to bring basketballs from home. Folding chairs work best for this activity because of their portability.

Review the terms *clockwise* and *counterclockwise* to ensure consistency of student results.

Using Scientific Methods
Skills Practice Lab

The Sun's Yearly Trip Through the Zodiac

During the course of a year, the sun appears to move through a circle of 12 constellations in the sky. The 12 constellations make up a "belt" in the sky called the *zodiac*. Each month, the sun appears to be in a different constellation. The ancient Babylonians developed a 12-month calendar based on the idea that the sun moved through this circle of constellations as it revolved around the Earth. They believed that the constellations of stars were fixed in position and that the sun and planets moved past the stars. Later, Copernicus developed a model of the solar system in which the Earth and the planets revolve around the sun. But how can Copernicus's model of the solar system be correct when the sun appears to move through the zodiac?

MATERIALS
- ball, inflated
- box, cardboard, large
- cards, index (12)
- chairs (12)
- tape, masking (1 roll)

Ask a Question
1. If the sun is at the center of the solar system, why does it appear to move with respect to the stars in the sky?

Form a Hypothesis
2. Write a possible answer to the question above. Explain your reasoning.

Test the Hypothesis
3. Set the chairs in a large circle so that the backs of the chairs all face the center of the circle. Make sure that the chairs are equally spaced, like the numbers on the face of a clock.

4. Write the name of each constellation in the zodiac on the index cards. You should have one card for each constellation.

5. Stand inside the circle with the masking tape and the index cards. Moving counterclockwise, attach the cards to the backs of the chairs in the following order: Aries, Taurus, Gemini, Cancer, Leo, Virgo, Libra, Scorpio, Sagittarius, Capricorn, Aquarius, and Pisces.

6. Use masking tape to label the ball "Sun."

7. Place the large, closed box in the center of the circle. Set the roll of masking tape flat on top of the box.

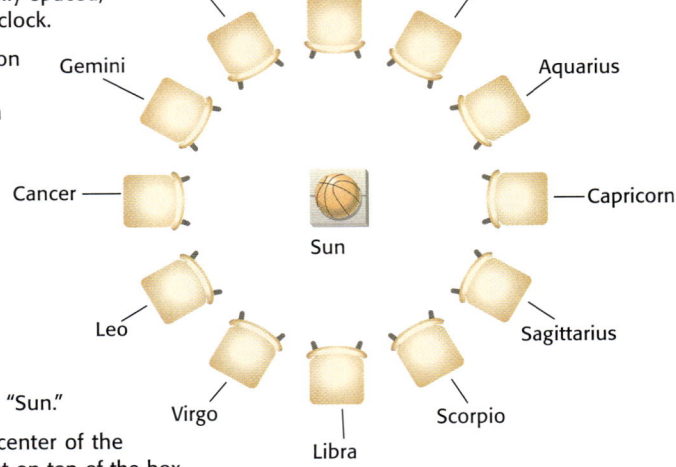

Joseph W. Price
H. M. Browne Junior High
Washington, D.C.

758 Chapter 18 • LabBook

8. Place the ball on top of the roll of masking tape so that the ball stays in place.

9. Stand inside the circle of chairs. You will represent the Earth. As you move around the ball, you will model the Earth's orbit around the sun. Notice that even though only the "Earth" is moving, as seen from the Earth, the sun appears to move through the entire zodiac!

10. Stand in front of the chair labeled "Aries." Look at the ball representing the sun. Then, look past the ball to the chair at the opposite side of the circle. Where in the zodiac does the sun appear to be?

11. Move to the next chair on your right (counterclockwise). Where does the sun appear to be? Is it in the same constellation? Explain your answer.

12. Repeat step 10 until you have observed the position of the sun from each chair in the circle.

Analyze the Results

1. Did the sun appear to move through the 12 constellations, even though the Earth was orbiting around the sun? How can you explain this apparent movement?

Draw Conclusions

2. How does Copernicus's model of the solar system explain the apparent movement of the sun through the constellations of the zodiac?

CHAPTER RESOURCES

Chapter Resource File
- Datasheet for LabBook
- Lab Notes and Answers

Background
Begin the activity by asking students if they are familiar with the constellations of the zodiac. Have they seen them depicted in a list or in a circle? How did the mythology of the zodiac begin? (The 12 familiar signs of the zodiac were adopted by the Babylonians about 3,000 years ago. The word *zodiac* means "circle," and the Babylonians thought that the sun and the planets moved in a circle through 12 fixed constellations in the night sky.)

Ask each student group to list as many zodiac constellations as they can remember. (The constellations and their corresponding signs are as follows: Aries, the ram; Taurus, the bull; Gemini, the twins; Cancer, the crab; Leo, the lion; Virgo, the virgin; Libra, the scales; Scorpio, the scorpion; Sagittarius, the hunter; Capricorn, the mountain goat; Aquarius, the water bearer; and Pisces, the fish.)

Analyze the Results
1. When students stand in front of a chair, the sun appears to be in the constellation opposite the chair. As they move outside the circle counterclockwise, the sun appears to shift through the constellations counterclockwise. As the Earth (the student) orbits the sun (the ball), the sun never appears in the same constellation because of the Earth's perspective relative to the fixed constellations.

Draw Conclusions
2. In Copernicus's heliocentric model of the solar system, the Earth orbits the sun. As the Earth moves around the sun, the position of the sun in relation to the constellations changes.

Chapter 18 • LabBook

LabBook
Skills Practice Lab

I See the Light!

Teacher's Notes

Time Required
One to two 45-minute class periods

Lab Ratings

EASY ——————— HARD

Teacher Prep 🧪🧪
Student Set-Up 🧪🧪🧪
Concept Level 🧪🧪🧪🧪
Clean Up 🧪

MATERIALS

The materials listed on the student page are enough for a group of 1 to 2 students.

Safety Caution

Remind students to review all safety cautions and icons before beginning this lab activity. Remind students to be careful about traffic hazards around your school's flagpole.

Using Scientific Methods
Skills Practice Lab

I See the Light!

How do you find the distance to an object you can't reach? You can do it by measuring something you can reach, finding a few angles, and using mathematics. In this activity, you'll practice measuring the distances of objects here on Earth. When you get used to it, you can take your skills to the stars!

Ask a Question

1. How can you measure the distance to a star?

Form a Hypothesis

2. Write a hypothesis that might answer this question. Explain your reasoning.

Test the Hypothesis

3. Draw a line 4 cm away from the edge of one side of the piece of poster board. Fold the poster board along this line.

4. Tape the protractor to the poster board with its flat edge against the fold, as shown in the photo below.

5. Use a pencil to carefully punch a hole through the poster board along its folded edge at the center of the protractor.

6. Thread the string through the hole, and tape one end to the underside of the poster board. The other end should be long enough to hang off the far end of the poster board.

7. Carefully punch a second hole in the smaller area of the poster board halfway between its short sides. The hole should be directly above the first hole and should be large enough for the pencil to fit through. This hole is the viewing hole of your new parallax device. This device will allow you to measure the distance of faraway objects.

8. Find a location that is at least 50 steps away from a tall, narrow object, such as the school's flagpole or a tall tree. (This object will represent background stars.) Set the meterstick on the ground with one of its long edges facing the flagpole.

9. Ask your partner, who represents a nearby star, to take 10 steps toward the flagpole, starting at the left end of the meterstick. You will be the observer. When you stand at the left end of the meterstick, which represents the location of the sun, your partner's nose should be lined up with the flagpole.

MATERIALS
- calculator, scientific
- meterstick
- pencil, sharp
- poster board, 16 × 16 cm
- protractor
- ruler, metric
- scissors
- string, 30 cm
- tape measure, metric
- tape, transparent

SAFETY

Viewing hole

Preparation Notes

Students may need an introduction to angles and the use of protractors. Be sure they understand how to use protractors *before* you perform this activity. Explain that astronomers use trigonometry, which is the measurement of triangles, to calculate distances to nearby stars. By using the TAN function on a calculator, students can find the length of the unknown leg of the triangle formed by the sun, Earth, and a star. If students are unfamiliar with the TAN function, they may prefer to use the table provided.

Angle	Tangent	Angle	Tangent
1°	0.0175	6°	0.1051
2°	0.0349	7°	0.1228
3°	0.0524	8°	0.1405
4°	0.0699	9°	0.1584
5°	0.0875	10°	0.1763

10 Move to the other end of the meterstick, which represents the location of Earth. Does your partner appear to the left or right of the flagpole? Record your observations.

11 Hold the string so that it runs straight from the viewing hole to the 90° mark on the protractor. Using one eye, look through the viewing hole along the string, and point the device at your partner's nose.

12 Holding the device still, slowly move your head until you can see the flagpole through the viewing hole. Move the string so that it lines up between your eye and the flagpole. Make sure the string is taut, and hold it tightly against the protractor.

13 Read and record the angle made by the string and the string's original position at 90° (count the number of degrees between 90° and the string's new position).

14 Use the measuring tape to find and record the distance from the left end of the meterstick to your partner's nose.

15 Now, find a place outside that is at least 100 steps away from the flagpole. Set the meterstick on the ground as before, and repeat steps 9–14.

Analyze the Results

1 The angle you recorded in step 13 is called the *parallax angle*. The distance from one end of the meterstick to the other is called the *baseline*. With this angle and the length of your baseline, you can calculate the distance to your partner.

2 To calculate the distance (*d*) to your partner, use the following equation:

$$d = b/\tan A$$

In this equation, *A* is the parallax angle, and *b* is the length of the baseline (1 m). (Tan *A* means the tangent of angle *A*, which you will learn more about in math classes.)

3 To find *d*, enter 1 (the length of your baseline in meters) into the calculator, press the division key, enter the value of *A* (the parallax angle you recorded), then press the tan key. Finally, press the equals key.

4 Record this result. It is the distance in meters between the left end of the meterstick and your partner. You may want to use a table like the one below.

5 How close is this calculated distance to the distance you measured?

6 Repeat steps 1–3 under Analyze the Results using the angle you found when the flagpole was 100 steps away.

Draw Conclusions

7 At which position, 50 steps or 100 steps from the flagpole, did your calculated distance better match the actual distance as measured?

8 What do you think would happen if you were even farther from the flagpole?

9 When astronomers use parallax, their "flagpoles" are distant stars. Might this affect the accuracy of their parallax readings?

Distance by Parallax Versus Measuring Tape		
	At 50 steps	At 100 steps
Parallax angle		
Distance (calculated)		
Distance (measured)		

Lab Notes

If the school's flagpole is not in a convenient spot, a tall tree or lamppost will work. If students have difficulty keeping the device still while moving their head, you might have them try steadying the device on a tripod or on the end of a meterstick.

Some students may have difficulty understanding the relationship between measuring stars with parallax and the parallax effects on measurements (for example, reading a dial off to the side can give a different value). The viewing hole in the parallax device used in this activity reduces such errors. Thus, the parallax effect in this activity measures only faraway distances.

Students should realize that as the distance to a reference point (such as a flagpole or background stars) increases, the angle measured by the parallax device becomes closer to the actual parallax angle. Therefore, students should find that their calculation of the distance to their partner should be more accurate when they move 100 steps from the tree. They should also realize that astronomers use the "fixed stars," which are essentially at optical infinity, as a reference.

CHAPTER RESOURCES

Chapter Resource File
- Datasheet for LabBook
- Lab Notes and Answers

Susan Gorman
North Ridge Middle School
North Richmond Hills, Texas

Analyze the Results

5. Answers may vary but should approximate the actual distance given in meters.

6. Answers may vary due to differences in technique.

Draw Conclusions

7. At 100 steps, the distance calculated should be closer to the distance measured.

8. Accuracy should increase.

9. Their calculations should be very close to the actual distance (if it could be measured).

LabBook

Model-Making Lab

Why Do They Wander?

Teacher's Notes

Time Required
This activity will take approximately 30 minutes. But it may take as much as one 45-minute class period to instruct students on how to use a compass.

Lab Ratings

EASY ————————— HARD

Teacher Prep 🧪🧪
Student Set-Up 🧪
Concept Level 🧪🧪🧪
Clean Up 🧪

MATERIALS
The materials listed on the student page are enough for 1 to 2 students. The compasses, rulers, and colored pencils may be shared among several groups.

Safety Caution
Remind students to review all safety cautions and icons before beginning this lab activity.

Preparation Notes
Students may need instruction on how to use a drawing compass. This activity works best when students work individually or in pairs. Each group will need a compass, a piece of white paper, and a metric ruler.

Using Scientific Methods

Model-Making Lab

Why Do They Wander?

Before the discoveries of Nicholas Copernicus in the early 1500s, most people thought that the planets and the sun revolved around the Earth and that the Earth was the center of the solar system. But Copernicus observed that the sun is the center of the solar system and that all the planets, including Earth, revolve around the sun. He also explained a puzzling aspect of the movement of planets across the night sky.

If you watch a planet every night for several months, you'll notice that it appears to "wander" among the stars. While the stars remain in fixed positions relative to each other, the planets appear to move independently of the stars. Mars first travels to the left, then back to the right, and then again to the left.

In this lab, you will make your own model of part of the solar system to find out how Copernicus's model of the solar system explained this zigzag motion of the planets.

MATERIALS
- compass, drawing
- paper, white
- pencils, colored
- ruler, metric

SAFETY

Ask a Question

❶ Why do the planets appear to move back and forth in the Earth's night sky?

Form a Hypothesis

❷ Write a possible answer to the question above.

Test the Hypothesis

❸ Use the compass to draw a circle with a diameter of 9 cm on the paper. This circle will represent the orbit of the Earth around the sun. (Note: The orbits of the planets are actually slightly elliptical, but circles will work for this activity.)

❹ Using the same center point, draw a circle with a diameter of 12 cm. This circle will represent the orbit of Mars.

❺ Using a blue pencil, draw three parallel lines diagonally across one end of your paper, as shown at right. These lines will help you plot the path Mars appears to travel in Earth's night sky. Turn your paper so the diagonal lines are at the top of the page.

Lab Notes

Plan View Versus Sky View: It is important to note that the circles represent a plan view of part of the solar system, and the diagonal lines represent a view of the apparent motion of Mars in Earth's night sky. Students are asked to jump from line to line as they draw their dots in order to show them the apparent path of Mars in the sky.

Note on Scale: Notice that, according to the drawing, it appears that for less than half of its orbit, Mars travels more than a year of Earth's time. In fact, an Earth year is actually more than half of a Martian year. Mars's period of revolution is 1.88 Earth years. The drawing on this page is not to scale in this respect; if it were to scale, the wandering motion of the planets could not be depicted on one page.

762 Chapter 21 • LabBook

6. Place 11 dots 2.5 cm apart from each other on your Earth orbit. Number the dots 1 through 11. These dots will represent Earth's position from month to month.

7. Now, place 11 dots along the top of your Mars orbit 0.5 cm apart from each other. Number the dots as shown. These dots will represent the position of Mars at the same time intervals. Notice that Mars travels slower than Earth.

8. Draw a green line to connect the first dot on Earth's orbit to the first dot on Mars's orbit. Extend this line to the first diagonal line at the top of your paper. Place a green dot where the green line meets the first blue diagonal line. Label the green dot "1."

9. Now, connect the second dot on Earth's orbit to the second dot on Mars's orbit, and extend the line all the way to the first diagonal at the top of your paper. Place a green dot where this line meets the first blue diagonal line, and label this dot "2."

10. Continue drawing green lines from Earth's orbit through Mars's orbit and finally to the blue diagonal lines. Pay attention to the pattern of dots you are adding to the diagonal lines. When the direction of the dots changes, extend the green line to the next diagonal line, and add the dots to that line instead.

11. When you are finished adding green lines, draw a red line to connect all the green dots on the blue diagonal lines in the order you drew them.

Analyze the Results

1. What do the green lines connecting points along Earth's orbit and Mars's orbit represent?

2. What does the red line connecting the dots along the diagonal lines look like? How can you explain this?

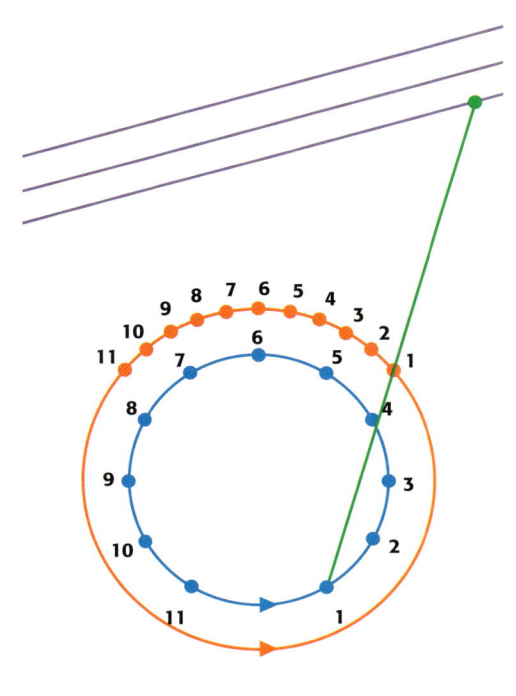

Draw Conclusions

3. What does this demonstration show about the motion of Mars?

4. Why do planets appear to move back and forth across the sky?

5. Were the Greeks justified in calling the planets *wanderers*? Explain.

Analyze the Results

1. The green lines connecting Earth's orbit and Mars's orbit represent the students' line of sight as they stand on Earth and look at Mars.

2. Sample answer: The red line along the diagonals changed direction at the fifth and seventh points; This happened because Mars was behind Earth in its orbit. To a person on Earth, Mars would seem to have changed direction at those moments.

Draw Conclusions

3. Sample answer: When Earth catches up to Mars, Mars appears to reverse its direction. As Earth passes Mars, Mars appears to revert to its original direction.

4. Sample answer: Planets appear to move back and forth because they travel around the sun at different speeds and at different distances. When the Earth overtakes a slower planet, such as Mars, that planet appears to move backward in Earth's sky.

5. Sample answer: Although the planets do not actually wander, it does appear as if they do to people on Earth. Students may consider this enough justification for calling the planets wanderers. Accept all well-supported responses.

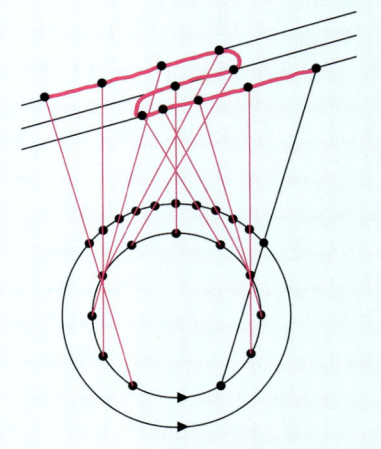

CHAPTER RESOURCES

Chapter Resource File
- Datasheet for LabBook
- Lab Notes and Answers

CLASSROOM TESTED & APPROVED

Joseph W. Price
H. M. Browne Junior High
Washington, D.C.

MISCONCEPTION ALERT

The apparent motion of Mars illustrated in this lab is called *retrograde motion*. It should not be confused with retrograde orbit or retrograde rotation. In addition, this lab does not accurately portray the actual *positions* of Earth and Mars during their orbits; it merely shows how their relative positions change.

Chapter 21 • LabBook 763

LabBook

Model-Making Lab

Eclipses

Teacher's Notes

Time Required
One 45-minute class period

Lab Ratings
EASY → HARD

Teacher Prep 🧪
Student Set-Up 🧪🧪
Concept Level 🧪🧪🧪
Clean Up 🧪

MATERIALS
The materials listed on the student page are enough for each student or for students working in groups of 2 to 3.

Analyze the Results

1. The flashlight represents the sun.
2. Step 4 modeled a lunar eclipse, as viewed from Earth.
3. Step 4 modeled a solar eclipse, as viewed from the moon.
4. Step 5 modeled a solar eclipse, as viewed from Earth.
5. Step 5 modeled an eclipse of Earth, as viewed from the moon.

6. There would be a lunar and a solar eclipse each month. This reason is that the model shows Earth and the moon orbiting in exactly the same plane around the sun. However, the planes are usually above or below the shadow of the other, so an eclipse does not always occur.

Model-Making Lab

Eclipses

As the Earth and the moon revolve around the sun, they both cast shadows into space. An eclipse occurs when one planetary body passes through the shadow of another. You can demonstrate how an eclipse occurs by using clay models of planetary bodies.

MATERIALS
- clay, modeling
- flashlight, small
- paper, notebook (1 sheet)
- ruler, metric

Procedure

1. Make two balls out of the modeling clay. One ball should have a diameter of about 4 cm and will represent the Earth. The other should have a diameter of about 1 cm and will represent the moon.

2. Place the two balls about 15 cm apart on the sheet of paper. (You may want to prop the smaller ball up on folded paper or on clay so that the centers of the two balls are at the same level.)

3. Hold the flashlight approximately 15 cm away from the large ball. The flashlight and the two balls should be in a straight line. Keep the flashlight at about the same level as the clay. When the whole class is ready, your teacher will turn off the lights.

4. Turn on your flashlight. Shine the light on the larger ball, and sketch your model. Include the beam of light in your drawing.

5. Move the flashlight to the opposite side of the paper. The flashlight should now be approximately 15 cm away from the smaller clay ball. Repeat step 4.

Analyze the Results

1. What does the flashlight in your model represent?
2. As viewed from Earth, what event did your model represent in step 4?
3. As viewed from the moon, what event did your model represent in step 4?
4. As viewed from Earth, what event did your model represent in step 5?
5. As viewed from the moon, what event did your model represent in step 5?
6. According to your model, how often would solar and lunar eclipses occur? Is this accurate? Explain.

CHAPTER RESOURCES

Chapter Resource File
- Datasheet for LabBook
- Lab Notes and Answers

CLASSROOM TESTED & APPROVED

Joseph W. Price
H. M. Browne Junior High
Washington, D.C.

Skills Practice Lab

Phases of the Moon

It's easy to see when the moon is full. But you may have wondered exactly what happens when the moon appears as a crescent or when you cannot see the moon at all. Does the Earth cast its shadow on the moon? In this activity, you will discover how and why the moon appears as it does in each phase.

Procedure

1. Place your globe near the light source. Be sure that the north pole is tilted toward the light. Rotate the globe so that your state faces the light.

2. Using the ball as your model of the moon, move the moon between the Earth (the globe) and the sun (the light). The side of the moon that faces the Earth will be in darkness. Write your observations of this new-moon phase.

3. Continue to move the moon in its orbit around the Earth. When part of the moon is illuminated by the light, as viewed from Earth, the moon is in the crescent phase. Record your observations.

4. If you have time, you may draw your own moon-phase diagram.

Analyze the Results

1. About 2 weeks after the new moon appears, the entire moon is visible in the sky. Move the ball to show this event.

2. What other phases can you add to your diagram? For example, when does the quarter moon appear?

3. Explain why the moon sometimes appears as a crescent to viewers on Earth.

MATERIALS
- ball, plastic-foam
- globe, world
- light source

SAFETY

CHAPTER RESOURCES

Chapter Resource File
- Datasheet for LabBook
- Lab Notes and Answers

Joseph W. Price
H. M. Browne Junior High
Washington, D.C.

LabBook

Skills Practice Lab

Phases of the Moon

Teacher's Notes

Time Required
One 45-minute class period

Lab Ratings
EASY — HARD

Teacher Prep 🧪🧪
Student Set-Up 🧪🧪
Concept Level 🧪
Clean Up 🧪

MATERIALS
The materials listed on the student page are enough for a group of 3 to 4 students. You can use a lamp or a flashlight as the light source.

Analyze the Results

1. At full moon, Earth is between the sun and the moon. To represent this phase, students should move the plastic-foam ball to the opposite side of the globe from the light source.

2. In the model, students should move the plastic-foam ball one-quarter of the way around the globe and three-quarters of the way around the globe. These positions represent the first-quarter phase and last-quarter phase.

3. Sample answer: As the moon continues to move in its orbit around Earth, part of its illuminated half becomes visible. When a sliver of the moon is visible from Earth, the moon enters a crescent phase.

Chapter 21 • LabBook

Model-Making Lab

Reach for the Stars

Teacher's Notes

Time Required
Two 45-minute class periods

Lab Ratings

EASY —————— HARD

Teacher Prep
Student Set-Up
Concept Level
Clean Up

MATERIALS
The materials listed on the student page are enough for 3 to 4 students.

Safety Caution
Remind students to review all safety cautions and icons before beginning this lab activity.

Using Scientific Methods
Model-Making Lab

Reach for the Stars

Have you ever thought about living and working in space? Well, in order for you to do so, you would have to learn to cope with the new environment and surroundings. At the same time that astronauts are adjusting to the topsy-turvy conditions of space travel, they are also dealing with special tools used to repair and build space stations. In this activity, you will get the chance to model one tool that might help astronauts work in space.

MATERIALS
- ball, plastic-foam
- box, cardboard
- hole punch
- paper brads (2)
- paper clips, jumbo (2)
- ruler, metric
- scissors
- wire, metal

SAFETY

Ask a Question

1. How can I build a piece of equipment that models how astronauts work in space?

Form a Hypothesis

2. Write a possible answer for the question above. Describe a possible tool that would help astronauts work in space.

Test the Hypothesis

3. Cut three strips from the cardboard box. Each strip should be about 5 cm wide. The strips should be at least 20 cm long but not longer than 40 cm.

CLASSROOM TESTED & APPROVED

Alyson Mike
East Valley Middle School
East Helena, Montana

766 Chapter 22 • LabBook

4. Punch holes near the center of each end of the three cardboard strips. The holes should be about 3 cm from the end of each strip.

5. Lay the strips end to end along your table. Slide the second strip toward the first strip so that a hole in the first strip lines up with a hole in the second strip. Slip a paper brad through the holes, and bend its ends out to attach the cardboard strips.

6. Use another brad to attach the third cardboard strip to the free end of the second strip. Now, you have your mechanical arm. The paper brads create joints where the cardboard strips meet.

7. Straighten the wire, and slide it through the hole in one end of your mechanical arm. Bend about 3 cm of the wire in a 90° angle so that it will not slide back out of the hole.

8. Now, try to move the arm by holding the free ends of the cardboard and wire. The arm should bend and straighten at the joints. If it is difficult to move your mechanical arm, adjust the design. Consider loosening the brads, for example.

9. Your mechanical arm now needs a hand. Otherwise, it won't be able to pick things up! Straighten one paper clip, and slide it through the hole where you attached the wire in step 7. Bend one end of the paper clip to form a loop around the cardboard and the other end to form a hook. You will use this hook to pick things up.

10. Bend a second paper clip into a U shape. Stick the straight end of this paper clip into the foam ball. Leave the ball on your desk.

11. Move your mechanical arm so that you can lift the foam ball. The paper-clip hook on the mechanical arm will have to catch the paper clip on the ball.

Analyze the Results

1. Did you have any trouble moving the mechanical arm in step 8? What adjustments did you make?

2. Did you have trouble picking up the foam ball? What might have made picking up the ball easier?

Draw Conclusions

3. What improvements could you make to your mechanical arm that might make it easier to use?

4. How would a tool like this one help astronauts work in space?

Applying Your Data

Adjust the design for your mechanical arm. Can you find a way to lift objects other than the foam ball? For example, can you lift heavier objects or objects that do not have a loop attached? How?

Research the tools that astronauts use on space stations and on the space shuttle. How do their tools help them work in the special conditions of space?

Analyze the Results

1. Answers may vary. Students may have loosened the paper brads.

2. Answers may vary. Altering the paper-clip loop on the ball or changing the shape of the hook on the arm could make the task easier.

Draw Conclusions

3. Answers may vary. Students may suggest using different materials, changing the length of different arm segments, or mounting the arm on a secure base.

4. Answers may vary. This device could help astronauts manipulate objects outside a spacecraft without having to go on a spacewalk. Also, if the arm were mechanized, it could allow astronauts to move massive objects with precision.

Applying Your Data

Answers may vary.

CHAPTER RESOURCES

Chapter Resource File

- Datasheet for LabBook
- Lab Notes and Answers

Contents

Reading Check Answers 769
Study Skills 776
SI Measurement 782
Temperature Scales 783
Measuring Skills 784
Scientific Methods 785
Making Charts and Graphs 787
Math Refresher 790
Periodic Table of the Elements 794
Physical Science Refresher 796
Physical Science Laws and Equations 798
Properties of Common Minerals 800
Sky Maps 802

Reading Check Answers

Chapter 1 The World of Earth Science

Section 1
Page 7: Four areas of oceanography are physical oceanography, biological oceanography, geological oceanography, and chemical oceanography.

Page 9: Astronomers study stars, asteroids, planets, and everything else in space.

Page 11: Cartographers make maps.

Section 2
Page 12: Scientists begin to learn about things by asking questions.

Page 15: Scientists create graphs and tables to organize and summarize their data.

Page 16: It is important for the scientific community to review new evidence so that scientists can evaluate and question the evidence for accuracy.

Section 3
Page 19: The big bang theory is an explanation of the creation of the universe.

Page 21: A climate model is complicated because there are so many variables that affect climate.

Section 4
Page 22: The International System of Units was developed to create a standard measurement system.

Page 25: Before you start a science investigation, obtain your teacher's permission and read the lab procedures carefully.

Chapter 2 Maps as Models of the Earth

Section 1
Page 37: A reference point is a fixed place on the Earth's surface from which direction and location can be described.

Page 38: True north is the direction to the geographic North Pole.

Page 40: lines of longitude

Section 2
Page 42: Distortions are inaccuracies produced when information is transferred from a curved surface to a flat surface.

Page 45: Azimuthal and conic projections are similar because they are both ways to represent the curved surface of the Earth on a flat map. Azimuthal projections show the surface of a globe transferred to a flat plane, whereas conic projections show the surface of a globe transferred to a cone.

Page 46: Every map should have a title, a compass rose, a scale, the date, and a legend.

Page 48: A GIS stores information in layers.

Section 3
Page 51: An index contour is a darker contour line that is usually every fifth line. Index contours make it easier to read a map.

Chapter 3 Minerals of the Earth's Crust

Section 1
Page 67: An element is a pure substance that cannot be broken down into simpler substances by ordinary chemical means. A compound is a substance made of two or more elements that have been chemically bonded.

Page 68: Answers may vary. Silicate minerals contain a combination of silicon and oxygen; nonsilicate minerals do not contain a combination of silicon and oxygen.

Section 2
Page 71: A mineral's streak is not affected by air or water, but a mineral's color may be affected by air or water.

Page 72: Scratch the mineral with a series of 10 reference minerals. If the reference mineral scratches the unidentified mineral, the reference mineral is harder than the unidentified mineral.

Section 3
Page 77: Surface mining is used to remove mineral deposits that are at or near the Earth's surface. Subsurface mining is used to remove mineral deposits that are too deep to be removed by surface mining.

Page 79: Sample answer: Gemstones are nonmetallic minerals that are valued for their beauty and rarity rather than for their usefulness.

Chapter 4 Rocks: Mineral Mixtures

Section 1
Page 90: Types of rocks that have been used by humans to construct buildings include granite, limestone, marble, sandstone, and slate.

Page 94: Rock within the Earth is affected by temperature and pressure.

Page 95: The minerals that a rock contains determine a rock's composition.

Page 96: Fine-grained rocks are made of small grains, such as silt or clay particles. Medium-grained rocks are made of medium-sized grains, such as sand. Coarse-grained rocks are made of large grains, such as pebbles.

Section 2
Page 99: Felsic rocks are light-colored igneous rocks rich in aluminum, potassium, silicon, and sodium. Mafic rocks are dark-colored igneous rocks rich in calcium, iron, and magnesium.

Page 101: New sea floor forms when lava that flows from fissures on the ocean floor cools and hardens.

Section 3
Page 103: Halite forms when sodium and chlorine ions become so concentrated in sea water that halite crystallizes from the sea-water solution.

Page 105: Ripple marks are the marks left by wind and water waves on lakes, seas, rivers, and sand dunes.

Appendix **769**

Section 4
Page 107: Regional metamorphism occurs when pressure builds up in rock that is buried deep below other rock formations or when large pieces of the Earth's crust collide. The increased pressure can cause thousands of square miles of rock to become deformed and chemically changed.

Page 108: An index mineral is a metamorphic mineral that forms only at certain temperatures and pressures and therefore can be used by scientists to estimate the temperature, pressure, and depth at which a rock undergoes metamorphosis.

Page 109: Increased heat and pressure cause metamorphic rocks to change from fine-grained rocks, such as slate and phyllite, to coarse-grained rocks, such as schist and gneiss.

Page 111: Deformation causes metamorphic structures, such as folds.

Chapter 5 Energy Resources
Section 1
Page 123: A renewable resource is a natural resource that can be replaced at the same rate at which the resource is used.

Page 125: Answers may vary. Sample answer: newspapers, plastic containers, and cardboard boxes.

Section 2
Page 127: Natural gas is most often used for heating and for generating electrical energy.

Page 128: Coal was most commonly used to power trains.

Page 130: Lignite has a higher carbon content than peat does.

Page 131: Natural gas and petroleum are removed from the Earth by drilling wells into rock that contains petroleum and natural gas.

Page 132: The sulfur dioxide released from the burning coal combines with moisture in the air to produce acid rain.

Section 3
Page 135: Fusion produces few dangerous wastes.

Page 136: The energy of fossil fuels comes from the sun.

Page 138: Hydroelectric energy is renewable because water is constantly recycled.

Page 140: Geothermal power plants obtain energy from the Earth by pumping steam and hot water from wells drilled into the rock.

Chapter 6 The Rock and Fossil Record
Section 1
Page 153: Catastrophists believed that all geologic change occurs rapidly.

Page 154: A global catastrophe can cause the extinction of species.

Section 2
Page 157: Geologists use the geologic column to interpret rock sequences and to identify layers in puzzling rock sequences.

Page 159: An unconformity is a surface that represents a missing part of the geologic column.

Page 160: A disconformity is found where part of a sequence of parallel rock layers is missing. A nonconformity is found where horizontal sedimentary rock layers lie on top of an eroded surface of igneous or metamorphic rock. Angular unconformities are found between horizontal sedimentary rock layers and rock layers that have been tilted or folded.

Section 3
Page 163: A half-life is the time it takes one-half of a radioactive sample to decay.

Page 164: strontium-87

Section 4
Page 166: An organism is caught in soft, sticky tree sap, which hardens and preserves the organism.

Page 168: A mold is a cavity in rock where a plant or an animal was buried. A cast is an object created when sediment fills a mold and becomes rock.

Page 170: To fill in missing information about changes in organisms in the fossil record, paleontologists look for similarities between fossilized organisms or between fossilized organisms and their closest living relatives.

Page 171: *Phacops* can be used to establish the age of rock layers because *Phacops* lived during a relatively short, well-defined time span and is found in rock layers throughout the world.

Section 5
Page 173: approximately 2 billion years

Page 174: The geological time scale is a scale that divides Earth's 4.6 billion–year history into distinct intervals of time.

Page 176: The Mesozoic era is known as the *Age of Reptiles* because reptiles, including the dinosaurs, were the dominant organisms on land.

Chapter 7 Plate Tectonics
Section 1
Page 191: The crust is the thin, outermost layer of the Earth. It is 5 km to 100 km thick and is mainly made up of the elements oxygen, silicon, and aluminum. The mantle is the layer between the crust and core. It is 2,900 km thick, is denser than the crust, and contains most of the Earth's mass. The core is the Earth's innermost layer. The core has a radius of 3,430 km and is made mostly of iron.

Page 192: The five physical layers of the Earth are the lithosphere, asthenosphere, mesosphere, outer core, and inner core.

Page 195: Although continental lithosphere is less dense than oceanic lithosphere is, continental lithosphere has a greater mass because of its greater thickness and will displace more asthenosphere than oceanic lithosphere.

Page 196: Answers may vary. A seismic wave traveling through a solid will go faster than a seismic wave traveling through a liquid.

Section 2
Page 198: Similar fossils were found on landmasses that are very far apart. The best explanation for this phenomenon is that the landmasses were once joined.

Page 201: The molten rock at mid-ocean ridges contains tiny grains of magnetic minerals. The minerals align with the Earth's magnetic field before the rock cools and hardens. When the Earth's magnetic field reverses, the orientation of the mineral grains in the rocks will also change.

Section 3
Page 203: A transform boundary forms when two tectonic plates slide past each other horizontally.

Page 204: The circulation of thermal energy causes changes in density in the asthenosphere. As rock is heated, it expands, becomes less dense, and rises. As rock cools, it contracts, becomes denser, and sinks.

Section 4
Page 206: Compression can cause rocks to be pushed into mountain ranges as tectonic plates collide at convergent boundaries. Tension can pull rocks apart as tectonic plates separate at divergent boundaries.

Page 208: In a normal fault, the hanging wall moves down. In a reverse fault, the hanging wall moves up.

Page 210: Folded mountains form when rock layers are squeezed together and pushed upward.

Chapter 8 Earthquakes
Section 1
Page 225: During elastic rebound, rock releases energy. Some of this energy travels as seismic waves that cause earthquakes.

Page 227: Earthquake zones are usually located along tectonic plate boundaries.

Page 229: Surface waves travel more slowly than body waves but are more destructive.

Section 2
Page 231: Seismologists determine an earthquake's start time by comparing seismograms and noting differences in arrival times of P and S waves.

Page 232: Each time the magnitude increases by 1 unit, the amount of ground motion increases by 10 times.

Section 3
Page 235: With a decrease of one unit in earthquake magnitude, the number of earthquakes occurring annually increases by about 10 times.

Page 236: Retrofitting is the process of making older structures more earthquake resistant.

Page 238: You should crouch or lie face down under a table or desk.

Chapter 9 Volcanoes
Section 1
Page 251: Nonexplosive eruptions are common, and they feature relatively calm flows of lava. Explosive eruptions are less common and produce large, explosive clouds of ash and gases.

Page 252: Because silica-rich magma has a high viscosity, it tends to trap gases and plug volcanic vents. This causes pressure to build up and can result in an explosive eruption.

Page 254: Volcanic bombs are large blobs of magma that harden in the air. Lapilli are small pieces of magma that harden in the air. Volcanic blocks are pieces of solid rock erupted from a volcano. Ash forms when gases in stiff magma expand rapidly and the walls of the gas bubbles shatter into tiny glasslike slivers.

Section 2
Page 256: Eruptions release large quantities of ash and gases, which can block sunlight and cause global temperatures to drop.

Page 258: Calderas form when a magma chamber partially empties and the roof overlying the chamber collapses.

Section 3
Page 261: Volcanic activity is common at tectonic plate boundaries because magma tends to form at plate boundaries.

Page 263: When a tectonic plate subducts, it becomes hotter and releases water. The water lowers the melting point of the rock above the plate, causing magma to form.

Page 264: According to one theory, a rising body of magma, called a mantle plume, causes a chain of volcanoes to form on a moving tectonic plate. According to another theory, a chain of volcanoes forms along cracks in the Earth's crust.

Chapter 10 Weathering and Soil Formation
Section 1
Page 279: Wind, water, and gravity can cause abrasion.

Page 280: Answers may vary. Sample answer: ants, worms, mice, coyotes, and rabbits.

Page 283: Oxidation occurs when oxygen combines with an element to form an oxide.

Section 2
Page 285: As the surface area increases, the rate of weathering also increases.

Page 286: Warm, humid climates have higher rates of weathering because oxidation happens faster when temperatures are higher and when water is present.

Page 287: Mountains weather faster because they are exposed to more wind, rain, and ice, which are agents of weathering.

Section 3
Page 288: Soil is formed from parent rock, organic material, water, and air.

Page 291: Heavy rains leach precious nutrients into deeper layers of soil, resulting in a very thin layer of topsoil.

Page 292: Temperate climates have the most productive soil.

Section 4
Page 294: Soil provides nutrients to plants, houses for animals, and stores water.

Appendix **771**

Page 297: They restore important nutrients to the soil and provide cover to prevent erosion.

Chapter 11 The Flow of Fresh Water
Section 1
Page 308: The Colorado River eroded the rock over millions of years.

Page 310: A divide is the boundary that separates drainage areas, whereas a watershed is the area of land that is drained by a water system.

Page 311: An increase in a stream's gradient and discharge can cause the stream to flow faster.

Page 313: A mature river erodes its channel wider rather than deeper. It is not steep and has fewer falls and rapids. It also has good drainage and more discharge than a youthful river does.

Page 314: Rejuvenated rivers form when the land is raised by tectonic forces.

Section 2
Page 317: Deltas are made of the deposited load of the river, which is mostly mud.

Page 319: The flow of water can be controlled by dams and levees.

Section 3
Page 320: The zone of aeration is located underground. It is the area above the water table.

Page 322: The size of the recharge zone depends on how permeable rock is at the surface.

Page 323: A well must be deeper than the water table for it to be able to reach water.

Page 324: Deposition is the process that causes the formation of stalactites and stalagmites.

Section 4
Page 326: Nonpoint-source pollution is the hardest to control.

Page 329: Less than 8% of water in our homes is used for drinking.

Page 330: Drip irrigation systems deliver small amounts of water directly to the roots of the plant so that the plant absorbs the water before it can evaporate or runoff.

Page 331: Answers may vary. Sample answer: taking shorter showers, avoiding running water while brushing your teeth, and using the dishwasher only when it is full.

Chapter 12 Agents of Erosion and Deposition
Section 1
Page 343: The amount of energy released from breaking waves causes rock to break down, eventually forming sand.

Page 345: Large waves are more capable of moving large rocks on a shoreline because they have more energy than normal waves do.

Page 346: Beach material is material deposited by waves.

Section 2
Page 349: Deflation hollows form in areas where there is little vegetation.

Page 351: Dunes move in the direction of strong winds.

Section 3
Page 352: Alpine glaciers form in mountainous areas.

Page 357: A till deposit is made up of unsorted material, while stratified drift is made up of sorted material.

Section 4
Page 359: A slump is the result of a landslide in which a block of material moves downslope over a curved surface.

Page 360: A lahar is caused by the eruption of an ice-covered volcano, which melts ice and causes a hot mudflow.

Chapter 13 Exploring the Oceans
Section 1
Page 375: The first oceans began to form sometime before 4 billion years ago as the Earth cooled enough for water vapor to condense and fall as rain.

Page 376: Coastal water in places with hotter, drier climates has a higher salinity because less fresh water runs into the ocean in drier areas and because heat increases the evaporation rate.

Page 378: Parts of the ocean along the equator are warmer because they receive more sunlight per year.

Page 380: If the ocean did not release thermal energy so slowly, the air temperature on land would vary greatly from above 100°C during the day to below 100°C at night.

Section 2
Page 383: Satellite photos from *Seasat* send images of the ocean back to Earth. These images allow scientists to measure the direction and speed of ocean currents. Satellite photos and information from *Geosat* have been used to measure slight changes in the height of the ocean's surface.

Page 384: 64,000 km; on the ocean floor

Page 385: continental shelf, continental slope, and continental rise

Page 386: It is unique because some organisms living around the vent do not rely on photosynthesis for energy.

Section 3
Page 389: The tough shells of clams and oysters protect the organisms against strong waves and harsh sunlight.

Page 391: crabs, sponges, worms, and sea cucumbers

Page 392: The neritic zone contains the largest concentration of marine life in the ocean because it receives more sunlight than the other zones in the ocean.

Section 4
Page 395: Fish farms can help reduce overfishing because the fish are raised instead of fished directly out of the ocean.

Page 396: Nonrenewable resources are resources that cannot be replenished. Oil and natural gas are nonrenewable resources.

Page 397: Desalination plants are most likely to be built in drier parts of the world, and where governments can afford to buy expensive equipment. Most desalination plants are in the Middle East, where the fuel needed to run the plants is relatively inexpensive.

Page 399: Wave energy would be a good alternative energy resource because it is a clean and renewable resource.

Section 5
Page 401: One effect of trash dumping is that plastic materials may harm and kill marine animals because these animals may mistake the trash for food.

Page 403: An oil tanker that has two hulls can prevent an oil spill, because if the outer hull is damaged, the inner hull will prevent oil from spilling into the ocean.

Page 405: The U.S. Marine Protection, Research, and Sanctuaries Act prohibits the dumping of any material that would affect human health or welfare, the marine environment or ecosystems, or businesses that depend on the ocean.

Chapter 14 The Movement of Ocean Water
Section 1
Page 416: Heyerdahl theorized that the inhabitants of Polynesia originally sailed from Peru on rafts powered only by the wind and ocean currents. Heyerdahl proved his theory by sailing from Peru to Polynesia on a raft powered only by wind and ocean currents.

Page 418: The Earth's rotation causes surface currents to move in curved paths rather than in straight lines.

Page 419: The three factors that form a pattern of surface currents on Earth are global winds, the Coriolis effect, and continental deflections.

Page 420: Density causes variations in the movement of deep currents.

Section 2
Page 423: Cold-water currents keep coastal climates cooler than inland climates all year long.

Page 425: Answers may vary. Sample answer: It is important to study El Niño because El Niño can greatly affect organisms and land. One way that scientists study El Niño is through a network of buoys located along the equator. These buoys record information that helps scientists predict when an El Niño is likely to occur.

Section 3
Page 426: The lowest point of a wave is called a *trough*.

Page 428: Deep-water waves become shallow-water waves as they move toward the shore and reach water that is shallower than one-half their wavelength.

Page 431: A storm surge is a local rise in sea level near the shore and is caused by strong winds from a storm, such as a hurricane. Storm surges are difficult to study because they disappear as quickly as they form.

Section 4
Page 432: The gravity of the moon pulls on every particle of the Earth.

Page 434: A tidal range is the difference between levels of ocean water at high tide and low tide.

Chapter 15 The Atmosphere
Section 1
Page 448: Water can be liquid (rain), solid (snow or ice), or gas (water vapor).

Page 450: The troposphere is the layer of turning or change. The stratosphere is the layer in which gases are layered and do not mix vertically. The mesosphere is the middle layer. The thermosphere is the layer in which temperatures are highest.

Page 452: The thermosphere does not feel hot because air molecules are spaced far apart and cannot collide to transfer much thermal energy.

Section 2
Page 455: Cold air is more dense than warm air, so cold air sinks and warm air rises. This produces convection currents.

Page 457: A greenhouse gas is a gas that absorbs thermal energy in the atmosphere.

Section 3
Page 459: Sinking air causes areas of high pressure because sinking air presses down on the air beneath it.

Page 460: the westerlies

Page 463: At night, the air along the mountain slopes cools. This cool air moves down the slopes into the valley and produces a mountain breeze.

Section 4
Page 464: Sample answer: smoke, dust and sea salt

Page 467: Answers may vary. Acid precipitation may decrease the soil nutrients that are available to plants.

Page 468: Powdered lime is used to counteract the effects of acidic snowmelt from snow that accumulated during the winter.

Page 470: Allowance trading establishes allowances for a certain type of pollutant. Companies are permitted to release their allowance of the pollutant, but if they exceed the allowance, they must buy additional allowances or pay a fine.

Chapter 16 Understanding Weather
Section 1
Page 482: The water cycle is the continuous movement of water from Earth's oceans and rivers into the atmosphere, into the ground, and back into the oceans and rivers.

Page 484: A psychrometer is used to measure relative humidity.

Page 485: The bulb of a wet-bulb thermometer is covered with moistened material. The bulb cools as water evaporates from the material. If the air is dry, more water will evaporate from the material, and the temperature recorded by the thermometer will be low. If the air is humid, less water will evaporate from the material, and the temperature recorded by the thermometer will be higher.

Page 487: Altostratus clouds form at middle altitudes.

Section 2
Page 491: A maritime tropical air mass causes hot and humid summer weather in the midwestern United States.

Page 493: An occluded front produces cool temperatures and large amounts of rain.

Page 495: An anticyclone can produce dry, clear weather.

Section 3
Page 497: A severe thunderstorm is a thunderstorm that produces high winds, hail, flash floods, or tornadoes.
Page 499: Hurricanes are also called *typhoons* or *cyclones.*
Page 500: Hurricanes get their energy from the condensation of water vapor.

Section 4
Page 504: Meteorologists use weather balloons to collect atmospheric data above Earth's surface.

Chapter 17   Climate
Section 1
Page 518: Climate is the average weather condition in an area over a long period of time. Weather is the condition of the atmosphere at a particular time.
Page 520: Locations near the equator have less seasonal variation because the tilt of the Earth does not change the amount of energy these locations receive from the sun.
Page 522: The atmosphere becomes less dense and loses its ability to absorb and hold thermal energy, at higher elevations.
Page 523: The Gulf Stream current carries warm water past Iceland, which heats the air and causes milder temperatures.
Page 524: Each biome has a different climate and different plant and animals communities.

Section 2
Page 526: You would find the tropical zone from 23.5° north latitude to 23.5° south latitude.
Page 529: Answers may vary. Sample answer: rats, lizards, snakes, and scorpions.

Section 3
Page 530: The temperate zone is located between the Tropics and the polar zone.
Page 532: Temperate deserts are cold at night because low humidity and cloudless skies allow energy to escape.
Page 535: Cities have higher temperatures than the surrounding rural areas because buildings and pavement absorb solar radiation instead of reflecting it.

Section 4
Page 537: Changes in the Earth's orbit and the tilt of the Earth's axis are the two things that Milankovitch says cause ice ages.
Page 538: Dust, ash, and smoke from volcanic eruptions block the sun's rays, which causes the Earth to cool.
Page 541: The deserts would receive less rainfall, making it harder for plants and animals in the desert to survive.

Chapter 18   Studying Space
Section 1
Page 555: Copernicus believed in a sun-centered universe.
Page 556: Newton's law of gravity helped explain why the planets orbit the sun and moons orbit planets.

Section 2
Page 558: The objective lens collects light and forms an image at the back of the telescope. The eyepiece magnifies the image produced by the objective lens.
Page 560: The motion of air, air pollution, water vapor, and light pollution distort the images produced by optical telescopes.
Page 563: because the atmosphere blocks most X-ray radiation from space

Section 3
Page 565: Different constellations are visible in the Northern and Southern Hemispheres because different portions of the sky are visible from the Northern and Southern hemispheres.
Page 567: The apparent movement of the sun and stars is caused by the Earth's rotation on its axis.
Page 568: 9.46 trillion kilometers
Page 570: One might conclude that all of the galaxies are traveling toward the Earth and that the universe is contracting.

Chapter 19   Stars, Galaxies, and the Universe
Section 1
Page 582: Rigel is hotter than Betelgeuse because blue stars are hotter than red stars.
Page 584: A star's absorption spectrum indicates some of the elements that are in the star's atmosphere.
Page 586: Apparent magnitude is the brightness of a light or star.
Page 587: A light-year is the distance that light travels in 1 year.
Page 588: The actual motion of stars is hard to see because the stars are so distant.

Section 2
Page 591: A red giant star is a star that expands and cools once it uses all of its hydrogen. As the center of a star continues to shrink a red giant star can become a red supergiant star.
Page 595: A black hole is an object that is so massive that even light cannot escape its gravity. A black hole can be detected when it gives off X rays.

Section 3
Page 596: Spiral galaxies have a bulge at the center and spiral arms. The arms of spiral galaxies are made up of gas, dust, and new stars.
Page 598: A globular cluster is a tight group of up to 1 million stars that looks like a ball. An open cluster is a group of closely grouped stars that are usually located along the spiral disk of a galaxy.
Page 599: Quasars are starlike sources of light that are extremely far away. Some scientists think that quasars may be the core of young galaxies that are in the process of forming.

Section 4
Page 601: Cosmic background radiation is radiation that is left over from the big bang. After the big bang, cosmic background radiation was distributed everywhere and filled all of space.
Page 602: One way to calculate the age of the universe is to measure the distance from Earth to various galaxies.

Page 603: If gravity stops the expansion of the universe, the universe might collapse. If the expansion of the universe continues forever, stars will age and die and the universe will eventually become cold and dark.

Chapter 20 Formation of the Solar System
Section 1
Page 615: The solar nebula is the cloud of gas and dust that formed our solar system.

Page 617: Jupiter, Saturn, Uranus, and Neptune

Section 2
Page 619: Energy from gravity is not enough to power the sun, because if all of the sun's gravitational energy were released, the sun would last for only 45 million years.

Page 621: The nuclei of hydrogen atoms repel each other because they are positively charged and like charges repel each other.

Page 622: Sunspots are cooler, dark spots on the sun. Sunspots occur because when activity slows down in the convective zone, areas of the photosphere become cooler.

Section 3
Page 624: During Earth's early formation, planetesimals collided with the Earth. The energy of their motion heated the planet.

Page 626: Scientists think that the Earth's first atmosphere was a steamy mixture of carbon dioxide and water vapor.

Page 628: When photosynthetic organisms appeared on Earth, they released oxygen into the Earth's atmosphere. Over several million years, more and more oxygen was added to the atmosphere, which helped form Earth's current atmosphere.

Section 4
Page 631: Kepler's third law of motion states that planets that are farther away from the sun take longer to orbit the sun.

Page 632: Newton's law of universal gravitation states that the force of gravity depends on the product of the masses of the objects divided by the square of the distance between the objects.

Chapter 21 A Family of Planets
Section 1
Page 645: Light travels about 300,000 km/s.

Page 647: Jupiter, Saturn, Uranus, Neptune, and Pluto are in the outer solar system.

Section 2
Page 649: Radar technology was used to map the surface of Venus.

Page 650: Earth's global system includes the atmosphere, the oceans, and the biosphere.

Page 652: Mars' crust is chemically different from Earth's crust, so the Martian crust does not move. As a result, volcanoes build up in the same spots on Mars.

Section 3
Page 655: Saturn's rings are made of icy particles ranging in size from a few centimeters to several meters wide.

Page 657: Neptune's interior releases energy to its outer layers, which creates belts of clouds in Neptune's atmosphere.

Section 4
Page 661: The moon formed from a piece of Earth's mantle, which broke off during a collision between Earth and a large object.

Page 663: During a solar eclipse, the moon blocks out the sun and casts a shadow on Earth.

Page 664: We don't see solar and lunar eclipses every month because the moon's orbit around Earth is tilted.

Page 665: Because Titan's atmosphere is similar to the atmosphere on Earth before life evolved, scientists can study Titan's atmosphere to learn how life began.

Page 666: Pluto is eclipsed by Charon every 120 years.

Section 5
Page 669: Comets come from the Oort cloud and the Kuiper belt.

Page 671: The major types of meteorites are stony, metallic, and stony-iron meteorites.

Page 672: Large objects strike Earth every few thousand years.

Chapter 22 Exploring Space
Section 1
Page 684: Tsiolkovsky helped develop rocket theory. Goddard developed the first rockets.

Page 686: Rockets carry oxygen so that their fuel can be burned.

Section 2
Page 689: Answers may vary. LEO is much closer to the Earth than GEO.

Page 691: Information from one location is transmitted to a communications satellite. The satellite then sends the information to another location on Earth.

Page 693: Satellites in the EOS program are designed to work together so that many different types of data can be integrated.

Section 3
Page 695: The Magellan mission showed that, in many ways, the surface of Venus is similar to the surface of Earth.

Page 696: The Mars Pathfinder mission found evidence suggesting that water once flowed across the surface of Mars.

Page 698: The mission of the Stardust probe is to gather samples from a comet's tail and return them to Earth.

Section 4
Page 701: the orbiter, the liquid-fuel tank, and the solid-fuel booster rockets

Page 703: The Russians are supplying a service module, docking modules, life-support and research modules, and transportation to and from the station. The Americans are providing lab modules, the supporting frame, solar panels, living quarters, and a biomedical laboratory.

Page 705: Space-age spinoffs are technologies that were developed for the space program but are now used in everyday life.

Study Skills

FoldNote Instructions

Have you ever tried to study for a test or quiz but didn't know where to start? Or have you read a chapter and found that you can remember only a few ideas? Well, FoldNotes are a fun and exciting way to help you learn and remember the ideas you encounter as you learn science!

FoldNotes are tools that you can use to organize concepts. By focusing on a few main concepts, FoldNotes help you learn and remember how the concepts fit together. They can help you see the "big picture." Below you will find instructions for building 10 different FoldNotes.

Pyramid

1. Place a sheet of paper in front of you. Fold the lower left-hand corner of the paper diagonally to the opposite edge of the paper.
2. Cut off the tab of paper created by the fold (at the top).
3. Open the paper so that it is a square. Fold the lower right-hand corner of the paper diagonally to the opposite corner to form a triangle.
4. Open the paper. The creases of the two folds will have created an X.
5. Using scissors, cut along one of the creases. Start from any corner, and stop at the center point to create two flaps. Use tape or glue to attach one of the flaps on top of the other flap.

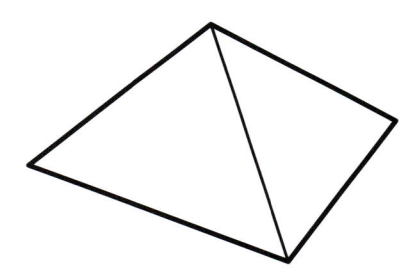

Double Door

1. Fold a sheet of paper in half from the top to the bottom. Then, unfold the paper.
2. Fold the top and bottom edges of the paper to the crease.

Booklet

1. Fold a sheet of paper in half from left to right. Then, unfold the paper.
2. Fold the sheet of paper in half again from the top to the bottom. Then, unfold the paper.
3. Refold the sheet of paper in half from left to right.
4. Fold the top and bottom edges to the center crease.
5. Completely unfold the paper.
6. Refold the paper from top to bottom.
7. Using scissors, cut a slit along the center crease of the sheet from the folded edge to the creases made in step 4. Do not cut the entire sheet in half.
8. Fold the sheet of paper in half from left to right. While holding the bottom and top edges of the paper, push the bottom and top edges together so that the center collapses at the center slit. Fold the four flaps to form a four-page book.

Layered Book

1. Lay one sheet of paper on top of another sheet. Slide the top sheet up so that 2 cm of the bottom sheet is showing.
2. Hold the two sheets together, fold down the top of the two sheets so that you see four 2 cm tabs along the bottom.
3. Using a stapler, staple the top of the FoldNote.

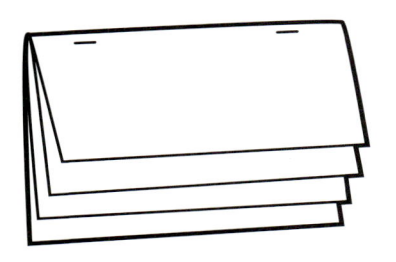

Appendix

Key-Term Fold

1. Fold a sheet of lined notebook paper in half from left to right.

2. Using scissors, cut along every third line from the right edge of the paper to the center fold to make tabs.

Four-Corner Fold

1. Fold a sheet of paper in half from left to right. Then, unfold the paper.

2. Fold each side of the paper to the crease in the center of the paper.

3. Fold the paper in half from the top to the bottom. Then, unfold the paper.

4. Using scissors, cut the top flap creases made in step 3 to form four flaps.

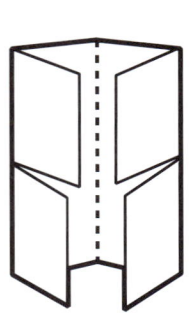

Three-Panel Flip Chart

1. Fold a piece of paper in half from the top to the bottom.

2. Fold the paper in thirds from side to side. Then, unfold the paper so that you can see the three sections.

3. From the top of the paper, cut along each of the vertical fold lines to the fold in the middle of the paper. You will now have three flaps.

778　Appendix

Table Fold

1. Fold a piece of paper in half from the top to the bottom. Then, fold the paper in half again.
2. Fold the paper in thirds from side to side.
3. Unfold the paper completely. Carefully trace the fold lines by using a pen or pencil.

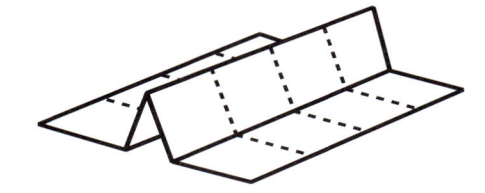

Two-Panel Flip Chart

1. Fold a piece of paper in half from the top to the bottom.
2. Fold the paper in half from side to side. Then, unfold the paper so that you can see the two sections.
3. From the top of the paper, cut along the vertical fold line to the fold in the middle of the paper. You will now have two flaps.

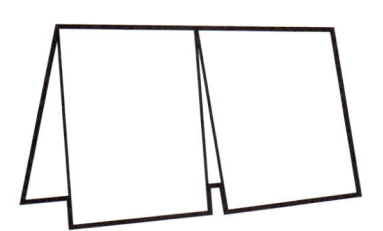

Tri-Fold

1. Fold a piece a paper in thirds from the top to the bottom.
2. Unfold the paper so that you can see the three sections. Then, turn the paper sideways so that the three sections form vertical columns.
3. Trace the fold lines by using a pen or pencil. Label the columns "Know," "Want," and "Learn."

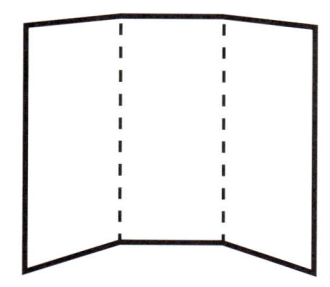

Graphic Organizer Instructions

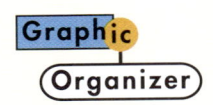

Have you ever wished that you could "draw out" the many concepts you learn in your science class? Sometimes, being able to *see* how concepts are related really helps you remember what you've learned. Graphic Organizers do just that! They give you a way to draw or map out concepts.

All you need to make a Graphic Organizer is a piece of paper and a pencil. Below you will find instructions for four different Graphic Organizers designed to help you organize the concepts you'll learn in this book.

Spider Map

1. Draw a diagram like the one shown. In the circle, write the main topic.

2. From the circle, draw legs to represent different categories of the main topic. You can have as many categories as you want.

3. From the category legs, draw horizontal lines. As you read the chapter, write details about each category on the horizontal lines.

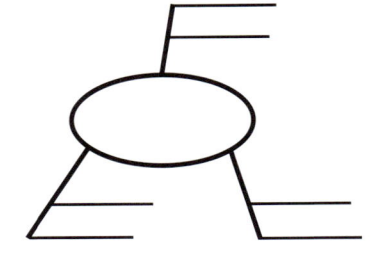

Comparison Table

1. Draw a chart like the one shown. Your chart can have as many columns and rows as you want.

2. In the top row, write the topics that you want to compare.

3. In the left column, write characteristics of the topics that you want to compare. As you read the chapter, fill in the characteristics for each topic in the appropriate boxes.

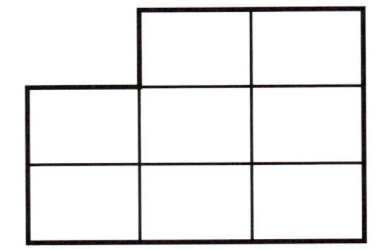

Chain-of-Events-Chart

1. Draw a box. In the box, write the first step of a process or the first event of a timeline.

2. Under the box, draw another box, and use an arrow to connect the two boxes. In the second box, write the next step of the process or the next event in the timeline.

3. Continue adding boxes until the process or timeline is finished.

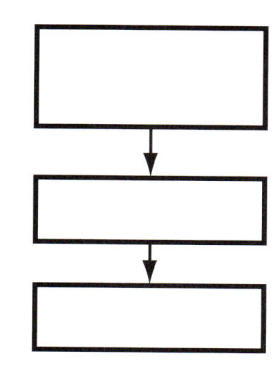

Concept Map

1. Draw a circle in the center of a piece of paper. Write the main idea of the chapter in the center of the circle.

2. From the circle, draw other circles. In those circles, write characteristics of the main idea. Draw arrows from the center circle to the circles that contain the characteristics.

3. From each circle that contains a characteristic, draw other circles. In those circles, write specific details about the characteristic. Draw arrows from each circle that contains a characteristic to the circles that contain specific details. You may draw as many circles as you want.

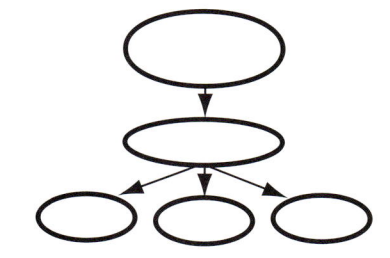

Appendix

SI Measurement

The International System of Units, or SI, is the standard system of measurement used by many scientists. Using the same standards of measurement makes it easier for scientists to communicate with one another.

SI works by combining prefixes and base units. Each base unit can be used with different prefixes to define smaller and larger quantities. The table below lists common SI prefixes.

SI Prefixes

Prefix	Symbol	Factor	Example
kilo-	k	1,000	kilogram, 1 kg = 1,000 g
hecto-	h	100	hectoliter, 1 hL = 100 L
deka-	da	10	dekameter, 1 dam = 10 m
		1	meter, liter, gram
deci-	d	0.1	decigram, 1 dg = 0.1 g
centi-	c	0.01	centimeter, 1 cm = 0.01 m
milli-	m	0.001	milliliter, 1 mL = 0.001 L
micro-	μ	0.000 001	micrometer, 1 μm = 0.000 001 m

SI Conversion Table

SI units	From SI to English	From English to SI
Length		
kilometer (km) = 1,000 m	1 km = 0.621 mi	1 mi = 1.609 km
meter (m) = 100 cm	1 m = 3.281 ft	1 ft = 0.305 m
centimeter (cm) = 0.01 m	1 cm = 0.394 in.	1 in. = 2.540 cm
millimeter (mm) = 0.001 m	1 mm = 0.039 in.	
micrometer (μm) = 0.000 001 m		
nanometer (nm) = 0.000 000 001 m		
Area		
square kilometer (km^2) = 100 hectares	1 km^2 = 0.386 mi^2	1 mi^2 = 2.590 km^2
hectare (ha) = 10,000 m^2	1 ha = 2.471 acres	1 acre = 0.405 ha
square meter (m^2) = 10,000 cm^2	1 m^2 = 10.764 ft^2	1 ft^2 = 0.093 m^2
square centimeter (cm^2) = 100 mm^2	1 cm^2 = 0.155 in.^{2}	1 in.^{2} = 6.452 cm^2
Volume		
liter (L) = 1,000 mL = 1 dm^3	1 L = 1.057 fl qt	1 fl qt = 0.946 L
milliliter (mL) = 0.001 L = 1 cm^3	1 mL = 0.034 fl oz	1 fl oz = 29.574 mL
microliter (μL) = 0.000 001 L		
Mass		
kilogram (kg) = 1,000 g	1 kg = 2.205 lb	1 lb = 0.454 kg
gram (g) = 1,000 mg	1 g = 0.035 oz	1 oz = 28.350 g
milligram (mg) = 0.001 g		
microgram (μg) = 0.000 001 g		

Temperature Scales

Temperature can be expressed by using three different scales: Fahrenheit, Celsius, and Kelvin. The SI unit for temperature is the kelvin (K).

Although 0 K is much colder than 0°C, a change of 1 K is equal to a change of 1°C.

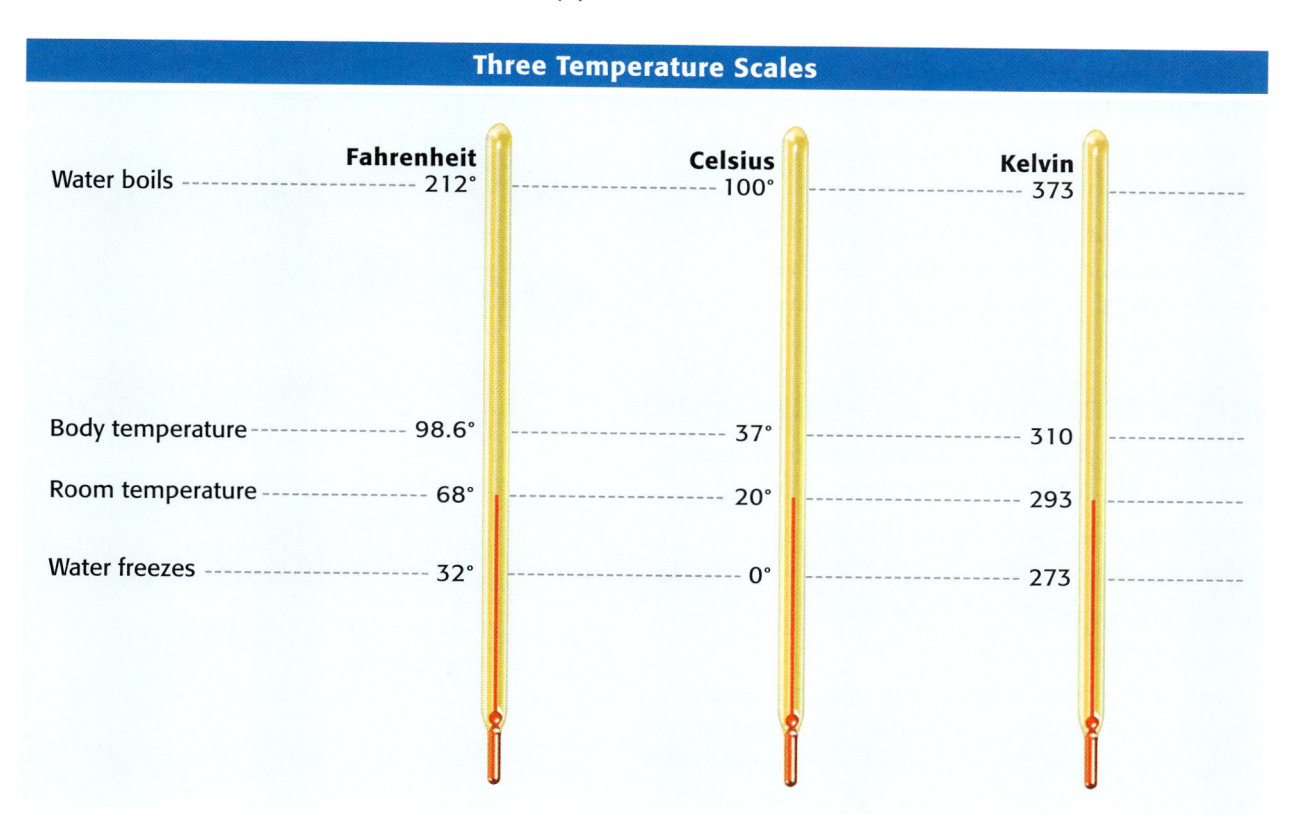

Three Temperature Scales

	Fahrenheit	Celsius	Kelvin
Water boils	212°	100°	373
Body temperature	98.6°	37°	310
Room temperature	68°	20°	293
Water freezes	32°	0°	273

Temperature Conversions Table

To convert	Use this equation:	Example
Celsius to Fahrenheit °C → °F	$°F = \left(\frac{9}{5} \times °C\right) + 32$	Convert 45°C to °F. $°F = \left(\frac{9}{5} \times 45°C\right) + 32 = 113°F$
Fahrenheit to Celsius °F → °C	$°C = \frac{5}{9} \times (°F - 32)$	Convert 68°F to °C. $°C = \frac{5}{9} \times (68°F - 32) = 20°C$
Celsius to Kelvin °C → K	$K = °C + 273$	Convert 45°C to K. $K = 45°C + 273 = 318 K$
Kelvin to Celsius K → °C	$°C = K - 273$	Convert 32 K to °C. $°C = 32K - 273 = -241°C$

Measuring Skills

Using a Graduated Cylinder

When using a graduated cylinder to measure volume, keep the following procedures in mind:

1. Place the cylinder on a flat, level surface before measuring liquid.
2. Move your head so that your eye is level with the surface of the liquid.
3. Read the mark closest to the liquid level. On glass graduated cylinders, read the mark closest to the center of the curve in the liquid's surface.

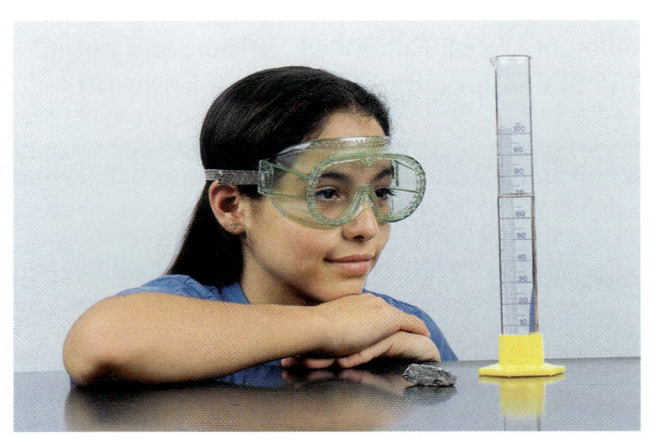

Using a Meterstick or Metric Ruler

When using a meterstick or metric ruler to measure length, keep the following procedures in mind:

1. Place the ruler firmly against the object that you are measuring.
2. Align one edge of the object exactly with the 0 end of the ruler.
3. Look at the other edge of the object to see which of the marks on the ruler is closest to that edge. (Note: Each small slash between the centimeters represents a millimeter, which is one-tenth of a centimeter.)

Using a Triple-Beam Balance

When using a triple-beam balance to measure mass, keep the following procedures in mind:

1. Make sure the balance is on a level surface.
2. Place all of the countermasses at 0. Adjust the balancing knob until the pointer rests at 0.
3. Place the object you wish to measure on the pan. **Caution:** Do not place hot objects or chemicals directly on the balance pan.
4. Move the largest countermass along the beam to the right until it is at the last notch that does not tip the balance. Follow the same procedure with the next-largest countermass. Then, move the smallest countermass until the pointer rests at 0.
5. Add the readings from the three beams together to determine the mass of the object.
6. When determining the mass of crystals or powders, first find the mass of a piece of filter paper. Then, add the crystals or powder to the paper, and remeasure. The actual mass of the crystals or powder is the total mass minus the mass of the paper. When finding the mass of liquids, first find the mass of the empty container. Then, find the combined mass of the liquid and container. The mass of the liquid is the total mass minus the mass of the container.

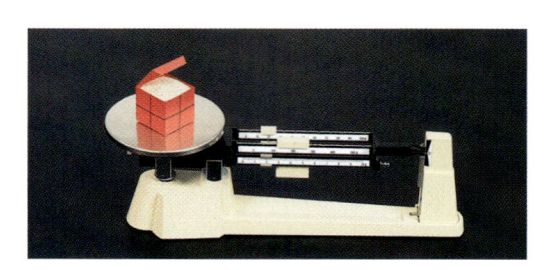

Scientific Methods

The ways in which scientists answer questions and solve problems are called **scientific methods.** The same steps are often used by scientists as they look for answers. However, there is more than one way to use these steps. Scientists may use all of the steps or just some of the steps during an investigation. They may even repeat some of the steps. The goal of using scientific methods is to come up with reliable answers and solutions.

Six Steps of Scientific Methods

1 Ask a Question

Good questions come from careful **observations.** You make observations by using your senses to gather information. Sometimes, you may use instruments, such as microscopes and telescopes, to extend the range of your senses. As you observe the natural world, you will discover that you have many more questions than answers. These questions drive investigations.

Questions beginning with *what, why, how,* and *when* are important in focusing an investigation. Here is an example of a question that could lead to an investigation.

Question: How does acid rain affect plant growth?

2 Form a Hypothesis

After you ask a question, you need to form a **hypothesis.** A hypothesis is a clear statement of what you expect the answer to your question to be. Your hypothesis will represent your best "educated guess" based on what you have observed and what you already know. A good hypothesis is testable. Otherwise, the investigation can go no further. Here is a hypothesis based on the question, "How does acid rain affect plant growth?"

Hypothesis: Acid rain slows plant growth.

The hypothesis can lead to predictions. A prediction is what you think the outcome of your experiment or data collection will be. Predictions are usually stated in an if-then format. Here is a sample prediction for the hypothesis that acid rain slows plant growth.

Prediction: If a plant is watered with only acid rain (which has a pH of 4), then the plant will grow at half its normal rate.

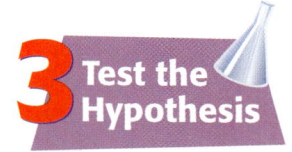

3 Test the Hypothesis

After you have formed a hypothesis and made a prediction, your hypothesis should be tested. One way to test a hypothesis is with a controlled experiment. A **controlled experiment** tests only one factor at a time. In an experiment to test the effect of acid rain on plant growth, the **control group** would be watered with normal rain water. The **experimental group** would be watered with acid rain. All of the plants should receive the same amount of sunlight and water each day. The air temperature should be the same for all groups. However, the acidity of the water will be a variable. In fact, any factor that is different from one group to another is a **variable.** If your hypothesis is correct, then the acidity of the water and plant growth are *dependant variables.* The amount a plant grows is dependent on the acidity of the water. However, the amount of water each plant receives and the amount of sunlight each plant receives are *independent variables.* Either of these factors could change without affecting the other factor.

Sometimes, the nature of an investigation makes a controlled experiment impossible. For example, the Earth's core is surrounded by thousands of meters of rock. Under such circumstances, a hypothesis may be tested by making detailed observations.

4 Analyze the Results

After you have completed your experiments, made your observations, and collected your data, you must analyze all the information you have gathered. Tables and graphs are often used in this step to organize the data.

Appendix **785**

5 Draw Conclusions

After analyzing your data, you can determine if your results support your hypothesis. If your hypothesis is supported, you (or others) might want to repeat the observations or experiments to verify your results. If your hypothesis is not supported by the data, you may have to check your procedure for errors. You may even have to reject your hypothesis and make a new one. If you cannot draw a conclusion from your results, you may have to try the investigation again or carry out further observations or experiments.

6 Communicate Results

After any scientific investigation, you should report your results. By preparing a written or oral report, you let others know what you have learned. They may repeat your investigation to see if they get the same results. Your report may even lead to another question and then to another investigation.

Scientific Methods in Action

Scientific methods contain loops in which several steps may be repeated over and over again. In some cases, certain steps are unnecessary. Thus, there is not a "straight line" of steps. For example, sometimes scientists find that testing one hypothesis raises new questions and new hypotheses to be tested. And sometimes, testing the hypothesis leads directly to a conclusion. Furthermore, the steps in scientific methods are not always used in the same order. Follow the steps in the diagram, and see how many different directions scientific methods can take you.

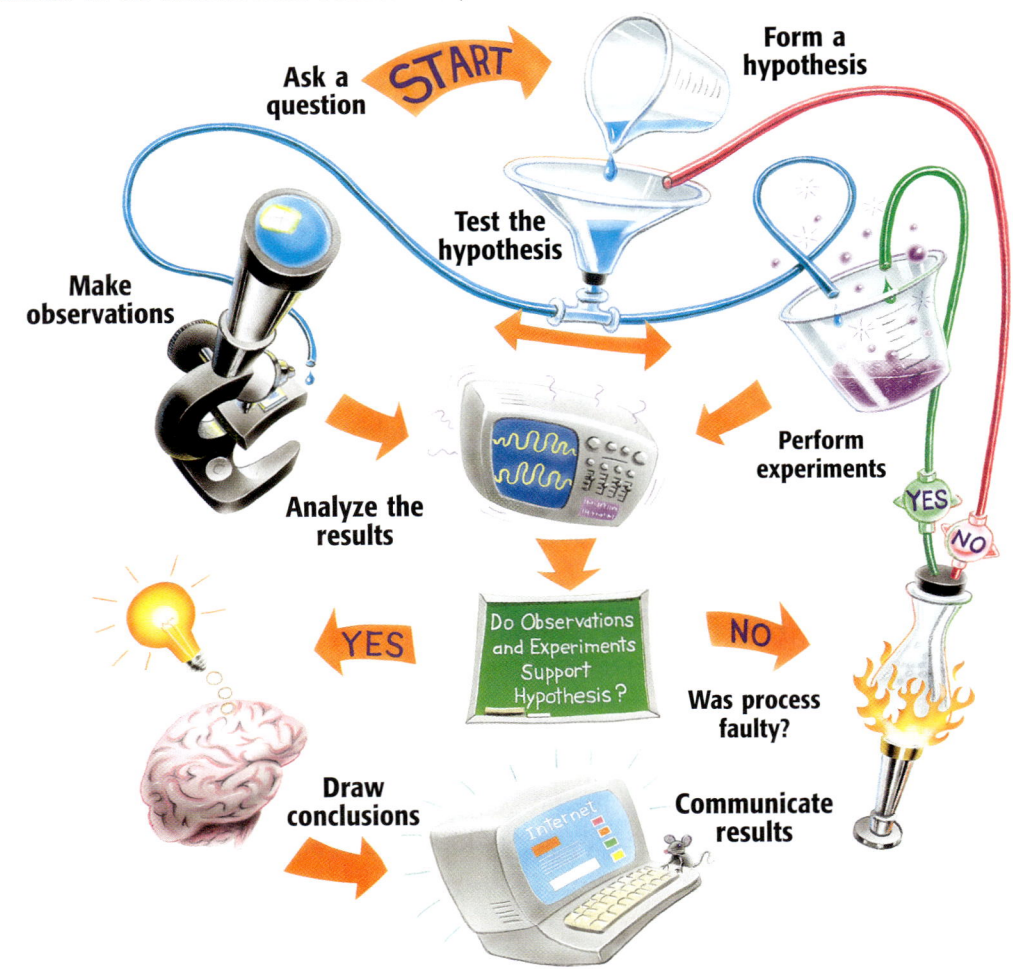

START — Ask a question — Form a hypothesis — Test the hypothesis — Make observations — Perform experiments — Analyze the results — Do Observations and Experiments Support Hypothesis? — YES → Draw conclusions — NO → Was process faulty? — Communicate results

786   Appendix

Making Charts and Graphs

Pie Charts

A pie chart shows how each group of data relates to all of the data. Each part of the circle forming the chart represents a category of the data. The entire circle represents all of the data. For example, a biologist studying a hardwood forest in Wisconsin found that there were five different types of trees. The data table at right summarizes the biologist's findings.

| Wisconsin Hardwood Trees ||
Type of tree	Number found
Oak	600
Maple	750
Beech	300
Birch	1,200
Hickory	150
Total	3,000

How to Make a Pie Chart

1 To make a pie chart of these data, first find the percentage of each type of tree. Divide the number of trees of each type by the total number of trees, and multiply by 100.

$$\frac{600 \text{ oak}}{3{,}000 \text{ trees}} \times 100 = 20\%$$

$$\frac{750 \text{ maple}}{3{,}000 \text{ trees}} \times 100 = 25\%$$

$$\frac{300 \text{ beech}}{3{,}000 \text{ trees}} \times 100 = 10\%$$

$$\frac{1{,}200 \text{ birch}}{3{,}000 \text{ trees}} \times 100 = 40\%$$

$$\frac{150 \text{ hickory}}{3{,}000 \text{ trees}} \times 100 = 5\%$$

2 Now, determine the size of the wedges that make up the pie chart. Multiply each percentage by 360°. Remember that a circle contains 360°.

20% × 360° = 72°   25% × 360° = 90°
10% × 360° = 36°   40% × 360° = 144°
5% × 360° = 18°

3 Check that the sum of the percentages is 100 and the sum of the degrees is 360.

20% + 25% + 10% + 40% + 5% = 100%
72° + 90° + 36° + 144° + 18° = 360°

4 Use a compass to draw a circle and mark the center of the circle.

5 Then, use a protractor to draw angles of 72°, 90°, 36°, 144°, and 18° in the circle.

6 Finally, label each part of the chart, and choose an appropriate title.

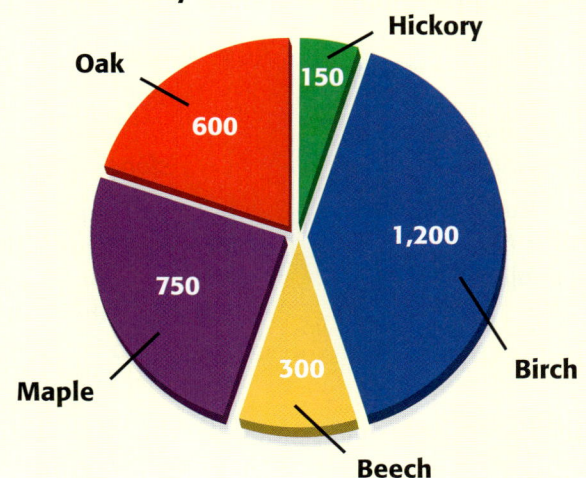

A Community of Wisconsin Hardwood Trees

Appendix **787**

Line Graphs

Line graphs are most often used to demonstrate continuous change. For example, Mr. Smith's students analyzed the population records for their hometown, Appleton, between 1900 and 2000. Examine the data at right.

Because the year and the population change, they are the *variables*. The population is determined by, or dependent on, the year. Therefore, the population is called the **dependent variable,** and the year is called the **independent variable.** Each set of data is called a **data pair.** To prepare a line graph, you must first organize data pairs into a table like the one at right.

Population of Appleton, 1900–2000

Year	Population
1900	1,800
1920	2,500
1940	3,200
1960	3,900
1980	4,600
2000	5,300

How to Make a Line Graph

1. Place the independent variable along the horizontal (*x*) axis. Place the dependent variable along the vertical (*y*) axis.
2. Label the *x*-axis "Year" and the *y*-axis "Population." Look at your largest and smallest values for the population. For the *y*-axis, determine a scale that will provide enough space to show these values. You must use the same scale for the entire length of the axis. Next, find an appropriate scale for the *x*-axis.
3. Choose reasonable starting points for each axis.
4. Plot the data pairs as accurately as possible.
5. Choose a title that accurately represents the data.

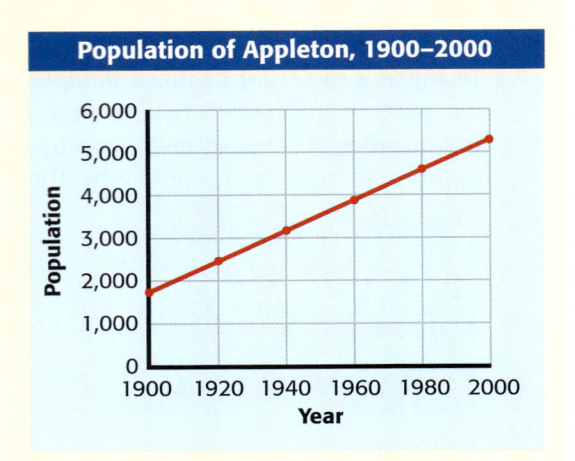

How to Determine Slope

Slope is the ratio of the change in the *y*-value to the change in the *x*-value, or "rise over run."

1. Choose two points on the line graph. For example, the population of Appleton in 2000 was 5,300 people. Therefore, you can define point *a* as (2000, 5,300). In 1900, the population was 1,800 people. You can define point *b* as (1900, 1,800).
2. Find the change in the *y*-value.
 (*y* at point *a*) − (*y* at point *b*) =
 5,300 people − 1,800 people =
 3,500 people
3. Find the change in the *x*-value.
 (*x* at point *a*) − (*x* at point *b*) =
 2000 − 1900 = 100 years
4. Calculate the slope of the graph by dividing the change in *y* by the change in *x*.

$$\text{slope} = \frac{\text{change in } y}{\text{change in } x}$$

$$\text{slope} = \frac{3,500 \text{ people}}{100 \text{ years}}$$

slope = 35 people per year

In this example, the population in Appleton increased by a fixed amount each year. The graph of these data is a straight line. Therefore, the relationship is **linear.** When the graph of a set of data is not a straight line, the relationship is **nonlinear.**

Using Algebra to Determine Slope

The equation in step 4 may also be arranged to be

$y = kx$

where y represents the change in the y-value, k represents the slope, and x represents the change in the x-value.

$$slope = \frac{change\ in\ y}{change\ in\ x}$$

$$k = \frac{y}{x}$$

$$k \times x = \frac{y \times x}{x}$$

$$kx = y$$

Bar Graphs

Bar graphs are used to demonstrate change that is not continuous. These graphs can be used to indicate trends when the data cover a long period of time. A meteorologist gathered the precipitation data shown here for Hartford, Connecticut, for April 1–15, 1996, and used a bar graph to represent the data.

Precipitation in Hartford, Connecticut April 1–15, 1996

Date	Precipitation (cm)	Date	Precipitation (cm)
April 1	0.5	April 9	0.25
April 2	1.25	April 10	0.0
April 3	0.0	April 11	1.0
April 4	0.0	April 12	0.0
April 5	0.0	April 13	0.25
April 6	0.0	April 14	0.0
April 7	0.0	April 15	6.50
April 8	1.75		

How to Make a Bar Graph

1 Use an appropriate scale and a reasonable starting point for each axis.

2 Label the axes, and plot the data.

3 Choose a title that accurately represents the data.

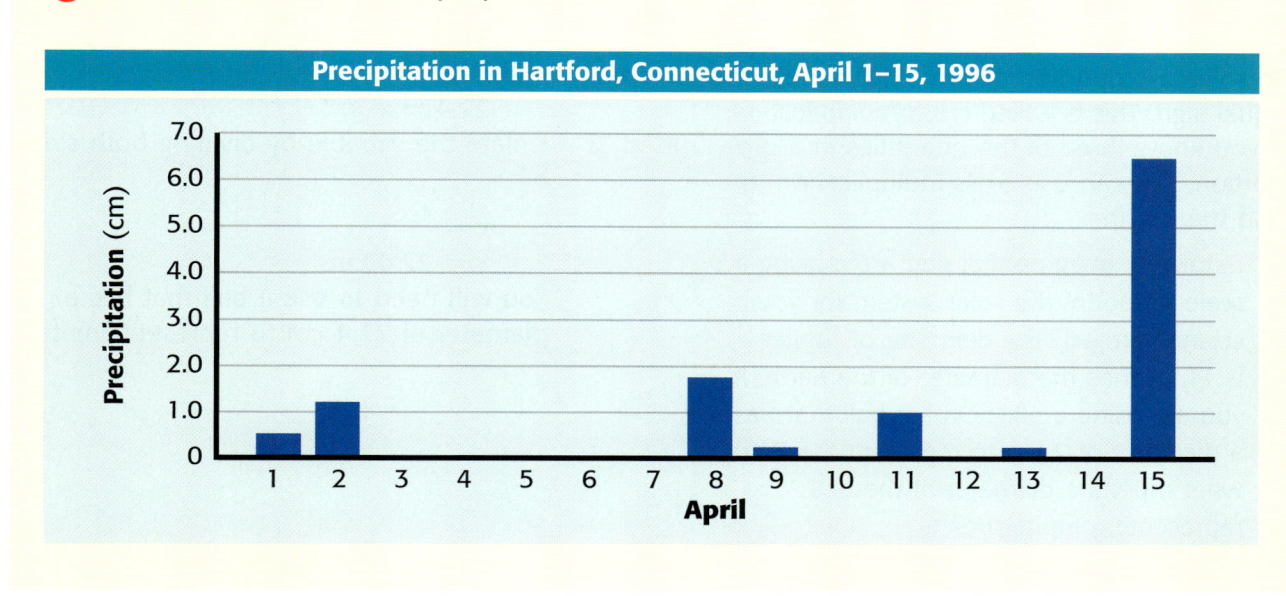

Precipitation in Hartford, Connecticut, April 1–15, 1996

Appendix **789**

Math Refresher

Science requires an understanding of many math concepts. The following pages will help you review some important math skills.

Averages

An **average,** or **mean,** simplifies a set of numbers into a single number that *approximates* the value of the set.

Example: Find the average of the following set of numbers: 5, 4, 7, and 8.

Step 1: Find the sum.
$$5 + 4 + 7 + 8 = 24$$

Step 2: Divide the sum by the number of numbers in your set. Because there are four numbers in this example, divide the sum by 4.
$$\frac{24}{4} = 6$$

The average, or mean, is **6.**

Ratios

A **ratio** is a comparison between numbers, and it is usually written as a fraction.

Example: Find the ratio of thermometers to students if you have 36 thermometers and 48 students in your class.

Step 1: Make the ratio.
$$\frac{36 \text{ thermometers}}{48 \text{ students}}$$

Step 2: Reduce the fraction to its simplest form.
$$\frac{36}{48} = \frac{36 \div 12}{48 \div 12} = \frac{3}{4}$$

The ratio of thermometers to students is **3 to 4,** or $\frac{3}{4}$. The ratio may also be written in the form 3:4.

Proportions

A **proportion** is an equation that states that two ratios are equal.
$$\frac{3}{1} = \frac{12}{4}$$

To solve a proportion, first multiply across the equal sign. This is called *cross-multiplication.* If you know three of the quantities in a proportion, you can use cross-multiplication to find the fourth.

Example: Imagine that you are making a scale model of the solar system for your science project. The diameter of Jupiter is 11.2 times the diameter of the Earth. If you are using a plastic-foam ball that has a diameter of 2 cm to represent the Earth, what must the diameter of the ball representing Jupiter be?
$$\frac{11.2}{1} = \frac{x}{2 \text{ cm}}$$

Step 1: Cross-multiply.
$$\frac{11.2}{1} \times \frac{x}{2}$$
$$11.2 \times 2 = x \times 1$$

Step 2: Multiply.
$$22.4 = x \times 1$$

Step 3: Isolate the variable by dividing both sides by 1.
$$x = \frac{22.4}{1}$$
$$x = 22.4 \text{ cm}$$

You will need to use a ball that has a diameter of **22.4** cm to represent Jupiter.

Percentages

A **percentage** is a ratio of a given number to 100.

Example: What is 85% of 40?

Step 1: Rewrite the percentage by moving the decimal point two places to the left.
0.85

Step 2: Multiply the decimal by the number that you are calculating the percentage of.
0.85 × 40 = 34

85% of 40 is **34.**

Decimals

To **add** or **subtract decimals,** line up the digits vertically so that the decimal points line up. Then, add or subtract the columns from right to left. Carry or borrow numbers as necessary.

Example: Add the following numbers: 3.1415 and 2.96.

Step 1: Line up the digits vertically so that the decimal points line up.

$$\begin{array}{r} 3.1415 \\ + \ 2.96 \\ \hline \end{array}$$

Step 2: Add the columns from right to left, and carry when necessary.

$$\begin{array}{r} \overset{1\ \ 1}{3.1415} \\ + \ 2.96 \\ \hline 6.1015 \end{array}$$

The sum is **6.1015.**

Fractions

Numbers tell you how many; **fractions** tell you *how much of a whole*.

Example: Your class has 24 plants. Your teacher instructs you to put 5 plants in a shady spot. What fraction of the plants in your class will you put in a shady spot?

Step 1: In the denominator, write the total number of parts in the whole.

$$\frac{?}{24}$$

Step 2: In the numerator, write the number of parts of the whole that are being considered.

$$\frac{5}{24}$$

So, $\frac{5}{24}$ of the plants will be in the shade.

Reducing Fractions

It is usually best to express a fraction in its simplest form. Expressing a fraction in its simplest form is called *reducing* a fraction.

Example: Reduce the fraction $\frac{30}{45}$ to its simplest form.

Step 1: Find the largest whole number that will divide evenly into both the numerator and denominator. This number is called the *greatest common factor* (GCF).

Factors of the numerator 30:
1, 2, 3, 5, 6, 10, **15,** 30

Factors of the denominator 45:
1, 3, 5, 9, **15,** 45

Step 2: Divide both the numerator and the denominator by the GCF, which in this case is 15.

$$\frac{30}{45} = \frac{30 \div 15}{45 \div 15} = \frac{2}{3}$$

Thus, $\frac{30}{45}$ reduced to its simplest form is $\frac{2}{3}$.

Adding and Subtracting Fractions

To **add** or **subtract fractions** that have the **same denominator,** simply add or subtract the numerators.

Examples:

$$\frac{3}{5} + \frac{1}{5} = ? \text{ and } \frac{3}{4} - \frac{1}{4} = ?$$

Step 1: Add or subtract the numerators.

$$\frac{3}{5} + \frac{1}{5} = 4 \text{ and } \frac{3}{4} - \frac{1}{4} = 2$$

Step 2: Write the sum or difference over the denominator.

$$\frac{3}{5} + \frac{1}{5} = \frac{4}{5} \text{ and } \frac{3}{4} - \frac{1}{4} = \frac{2}{4}$$

Step 3: If necessary, reduce the fraction to its simplest form.

$$\frac{4}{5} \text{ cannot be reduced, and } \frac{2}{4} = \frac{1}{2}.$$

To **add** or **subtract fractions** that have **different denominators,** first find the least common denominator (LCD).

Examples:

$$\frac{1}{2} + \frac{1}{6} = ? \text{ and } \frac{3}{4} - \frac{2}{3} = ?$$

Step 1: Write the equivalent fractions that have a common denominator.

$$\frac{3}{6} + \frac{1}{6} = ? \text{ and } \frac{9}{12} - \frac{8}{12} = ?$$

Step 2: Add or subtract the fractions.

$$\frac{3}{6} + \frac{1}{6} = \frac{4}{6} \text{ and } \frac{9}{12} - \frac{8}{12} = \frac{1}{12}$$

Step 3: If necessary, reduce the fraction to its simplest form.

The fraction $\frac{4}{6} = \frac{2}{3}$, and $\frac{1}{12}$ cannot be reduced.

Multiplying Fractions

To **multiply fractions,** multiply the numerators and the denominators together, and then reduce the fraction to its simplest form.

Example:

$$\frac{5}{9} \times \frac{7}{10} = ?$$

Step 1: Multiply the numerators and denominators.

$$\frac{5}{9} \times \frac{7}{10} = \frac{5 \times 7}{9 \times 10} = \frac{35}{90}$$

Step 2: Reduce the fraction.

$$\frac{35}{90} = \frac{35 \div 5}{90 \div 5} = \frac{7}{18}$$

Dividing Fractions

To **divide fractions,** first rewrite the divisor (the number you divide by) upside down. This number is called the *reciprocal* of the divisor. Then multiply and reduce if necessary.

Example:

$$\frac{5}{8} \div \frac{3}{2} = ?$$

Step 1: Rewrite the divisor as its reciprocal.

$$\frac{3}{2} \rightarrow \frac{2}{3}$$

Step 2: Multiply the fractions.

$$\frac{5}{8} \times \frac{2}{3} = \frac{5 \times 2}{8 \times 3} = \frac{10}{24}$$

Step 3: Reduce the fraction.

$$\frac{10}{24} = \frac{10 \div 2}{24 \div 2} = \frac{5}{12}$$

Scientific Notation

Scientific notation is a short way of representing very large and very small numbers without writing all of the place-holding zeros.

Example: Write 653,000,000 in scientific notation.

Step 1: Write the number without the place-holding zeros.
653

Step 2: Place the decimal point after the first digit.
6.53

Step 3: Find the exponent by counting the number of places that you moved the decimal point.
6.53000000
The decimal point was moved eight places to the left. Therefore, the exponent of 10 is positive 8. If you had moved the decimal point to the right, the exponent would be negative.

Step 4: Write the number in scientific notation.
6.53×10^8

Area

Area is the number of square units needed to cover the surface of an object.

Formulas:

area of a square = side × side
area of a rectangle = length × width
area of a triangle = $\frac{1}{2}$ × base × height

Examples: Find the areas.

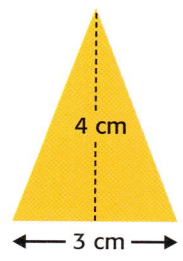

Triangle
area = $\frac{1}{2}$ × base × height
area = $\frac{1}{2}$ × 3 cm × 4 cm
area = **6 cm²**

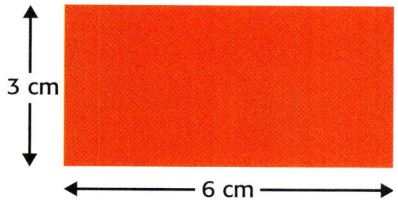

Rectangle
area = length × width
area = 6 cm × 3 cm
area = **18 cm²**

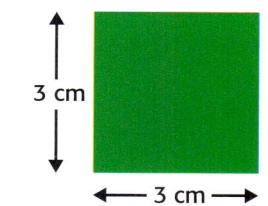

Square
area = side × side
area = 3 cm × 3 cm
area = **9 cm²**

Volume

Volume is the amount of space that something occupies.

Formulas:

volume of a cube = side × side × side

volume of a prism = area of base × height

Examples: Find the volume of the solids.

Cube
volume = side × side × side
volume = 4 cm × 4 cm × 4 cm
volume = **64 cm³**

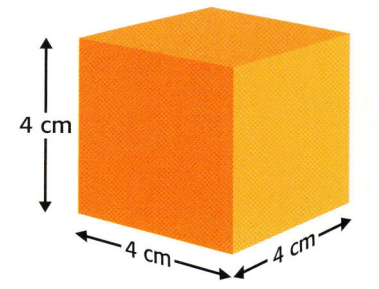

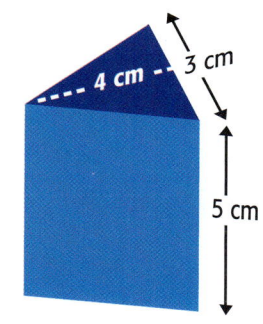

Prism
volume = area of base × height
volume = (area of triangle) × height
volume = ($\frac{1}{2}$ × 3 cm × 4 cm) × 5 cm
volume = 6 cm² × 5 cm
volume = **30 cm³**

Appendix

Periodic Table of the Elements

Each square on the table includes an element's name, chemical symbol, atomic number, and atomic mass.

The color of the chemical symbol indicates the physical state at room temperature. Carbon is a solid.

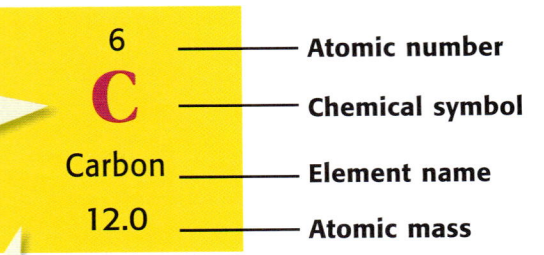

6	— Atomic number
C	— Chemical symbol
Carbon	— Element name
12.0	— Atomic mass

The background color indicates the type of element. Carbon is a nonmetal.

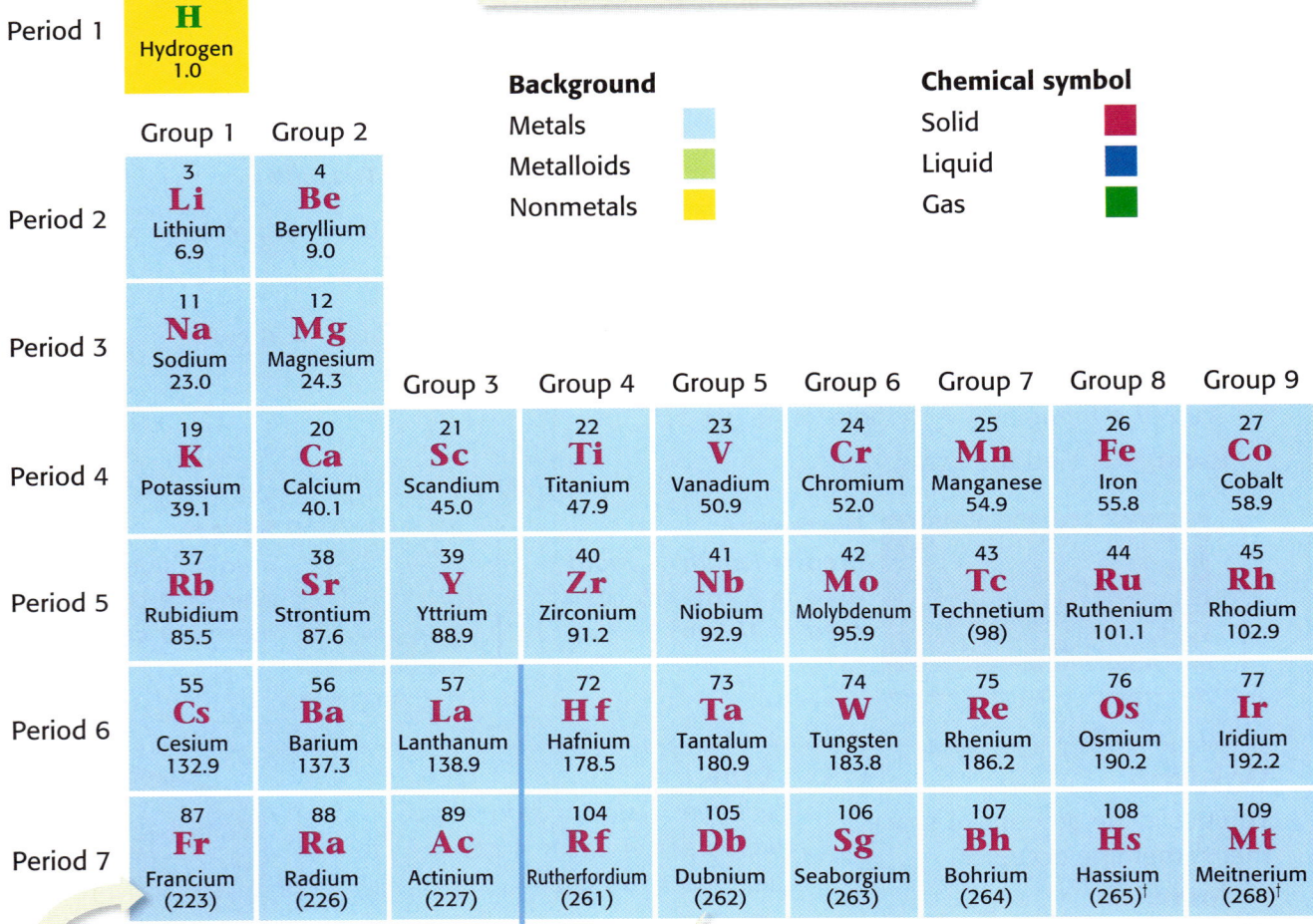

Background
- Metals
- Metalloids
- Nonmetals

Chemical symbol
- Solid
- Liquid
- Gas

Period 1: 1 **H** Hydrogen 1.0

	Group 1	Group 2		Group 3	Group 4	Group 5	Group 6	Group 7	Group 8	Group 9
Period 2	3 **Li** Lithium 6.9	4 **Be** Beryllium 9.0								
Period 3	11 **Na** Sodium 23.0	12 **Mg** Magnesium 24.3								
Period 4	19 **K** Potassium 39.1	20 **Ca** Calcium 40.1		21 **Sc** Scandium 45.0	22 **Ti** Titanium 47.9	23 **V** Vanadium 50.9	24 **Cr** Chromium 52.0	25 **Mn** Manganese 54.9	26 **Fe** Iron 55.8	27 **Co** Cobalt 58.9
Period 5	37 **Rb** Rubidium 85.5	38 **Sr** Strontium 87.6		39 **Y** Yttrium 88.9	40 **Zr** Zirconium 91.2	41 **Nb** Niobium 92.9	42 **Mo** Molybdenum 95.9	43 **Tc** Technetium (98)	44 **Ru** Ruthenium 101.1	45 **Rh** Rhodium 102.9
Period 6	55 **Cs** Cesium 132.9	56 **Ba** Barium 137.3		57 **La** Lanthanum 138.9	72 **Hf** Hafnium 178.5	73 **Ta** Tantalum 180.9	74 **W** Tungsten 183.8	75 **Re** Rhenium 186.2	76 **Os** Osmium 190.2	77 **Ir** Iridium 192.2
Period 7	87 **Fr** Francium (223)	88 **Ra** Radium (226)		89 **Ac** Actinium (227)	104 **Rf** Rutherfordium (261)	105 **Db** Dubnium (262)	106 **Sg** Seaborgium (263)	107 **Bh** Bohrium (264)	108 **Hs** Hassium (265)†	109 **Mt** Meitnerium (268)†

A row of elements is called a *period*.

A column of elements is called a *group* or *family*.

Values in parentheses are of the most stable isotope of the element.

† Estimated from currently available IUPAC data.

These elements are placed below the table to allow the table to be narrower.

Lanthanides

| 58 **Ce** Cerium 140.1 | 59 **Pr** Praseodymium 140.9 | 60 **Nd** Neodymium 144.2 | 61 **Pm** Promethium (145) | 62 **Sm** Samarium 150.4 |

Actinides

| 90 **Th** Thorium 232.0 | 91 **Pa** Protactinium 231.0 | 92 **U** Uranium 238.0 | 93 **Np** Neptunium (237) | 94 **Pu** Plutonium (244) |

Appendix

Topic: **Periodic Table**
Go To: **go.hrw.com**
Keyword: **HN0 PERIODIC**
Visit the HRW Web site for updates on the periodic table.

This zigzag line reminds you where the metals, nonmetals, and metalloids are.

			Group 13	Group 14	Group 15	Group 16	Group 17	Group 18
								2 **He** Helium 4.0
			5 **B** Boron 10.8	6 **C** Carbon 12.0	7 **N** Nitrogen 14.0	8 **O** Oxygen 16.0	9 **F** Fluorine 19.0	10 **Ne** Neon 20.2
Group 10	Group 11	Group 12	13 **Al** Aluminum 27.0	14 **Si** Silicon 28.1	15 **P** Phosphorus 31.0	16 **S** Sulfur 32.1	17 **Cl** Chlorine 35.5	18 **Ar** Argon 39.9
28 **Ni** Nickel 58.7	29 **Cu** Copper 63.5	30 **Zn** Zinc 65.4	31 **Ga** Gallium 69.7	32 **Ge** Germanium 72.6	33 **As** Arsenic 74.9	34 **Se** Selenium 79.0	35 **Br** Bromine 79.9	36 **Kr** Krypton 83.8
46 **Pd** Palladium 106.4	47 **Ag** Silver 107.9	48 **Cd** Cadmium 112.4	49 **In** Indium 114.8	50 **Sn** Tin 118.7	51 **Sb** Antimony 121.8	52 **Te** Tellurium 127.6	53 **I** Iodine 126.9	54 **Xe** Xenon 131.3
78 **Pt** Platinum 195.1	79 **Au** Gold 197.0	80 **Hg** Mercury 200.6	81 **Tl** Thallium 204.4	82 **Pb** Lead 207.2	83 **Bi** Bismuth 209.0	84 **Po** Polonium (209)	85 **At** Astatine (210)	86 **Rn** Radon (222)
110 **Ds** Darmstadtium (269)†	111 **Uuu** Unununium (272)†	112 **Uub** Ununbium (277)†		114 **Uuq** Ununquadium (285)†				

The names and three-letter symbols of elements are temporary. They are based on the atomic numbers of the elements. Official names and symbols will be approved by an international committee of scientists.

| 63 **Eu** Europium 152.0 | 64 **Gd** Gadolinium 157.2 | 65 **Tb** Terbium 158.9 | 66 **Dy** Dysprosium 162.5 | 67 **Ho** Holmium 164.9 | 68 **Er** Erbium 167.3 | 69 **Tm** Thulium 168.9 | 70 **Yb** Ytterbium 173.0 | 71 **Lu** Lutetium 175.0 |
| 95 **Am** Americium (243) | 96 **Cm** Curium (247) | 97 **Bk** Berkelium (247) | 98 **Cf** Californium (251) | 99 **Es** Einsteinium (252) | 100 **Fm** Fermium (257) | 101 **Md** Mendelevium (258) | 102 **No** Nobelium (259) | 103 **Lr** Lawrencium (262) |

Appendix

Physical Science Refresher

Atoms and Elements

Every object in the universe is made up of particles of some kind of matter. **Matter** is anything that takes up space and has mass. All matter is made up of elements. An **element** is a substance that cannot be separated into simpler components by ordinary chemical means. This is because each element consists of only one kind of atom. An **atom** is the smallest unit of an element that has all of the properties of that element.

Atomic Structure

Atoms are made up of small particles called subatomic particles. The three major types of subatomic particles are **electrons, protons,** and **neutrons.** Electrons have a negative electric charge, protons have a positive charge, and neutrons have no electric charge. The protons and neutrons are packed close to one another to form the **nucleus.** The protons give the nucleus a positive charge. Electrons are most likely to be found in regions around the nucleus called **electron clouds.** The negatively charged electrons are attracted to the positively charged nucleus. An atom may have several energy levels in which electrons are located.

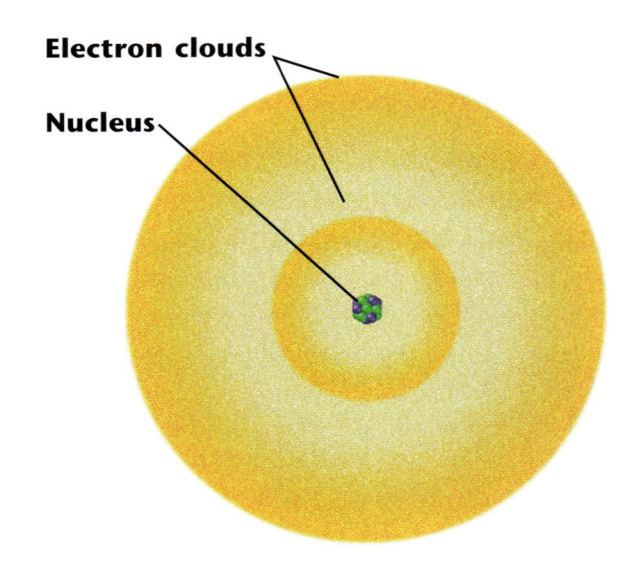

Atomic Number

To help in the identification of elements, scientists have assigned an **atomic number** to each kind of atom. The atomic number is the number of protons in the atom. Atoms with the same number of protons are all the same kind of element. In an uncharged, or electrically neutral, atom there are an equal number of protons and electrons. Therefore, the atomic number equals the number of electrons in an uncharged atom. The number of neutrons, however, can vary for a given element. Atoms of the same element that have different numbers of neutrons are called **isotopes.**

Periodic Table of the Elements

In the periodic table, the elements are arranged from left to right in order of increasing atomic number. Each element in the table is in a separate box. An uncharged atom of each element has one more electron and one more proton than an uncharged atom of the element to its left. Each horizontal row of the table is called a **period.** Changes in chemical properties of elements across a period correspond to changes in the electron arrangements of their atoms. Each vertical column of the table, known as a **group,** lists elements with similar properties. The elements in a group have similar chemical properties because their atoms have the same number of electrons in their outer energy level. For example, the elements helium, neon, argon, krypton, xenon, and radon all have similar properties and are known as the noble gases.

Electron clouds

Nucleus

796 Appendix

Molecules and Compounds

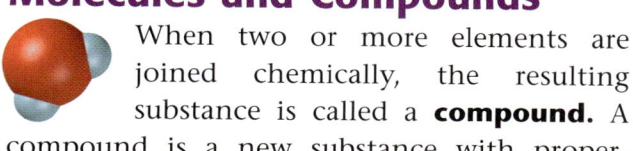

When two or more elements are joined chemically, the resulting substance is called a **compound**. A compound is a new substance with properties different from those of the elements that compose it. For example, water, H₂O, is a compound formed when hydrogen (H) and oxygen (O) combine. The smallest complete unit of a compound that has the properties of that compound is called a **molecule**. A chemical formula indicates the elements in a compound. It also indicates the relative number of atoms of each element present. The chemical formula for water is H₂O, which indicates that each water molecule consists of two atoms of hydrogen and one atom of oxygen. The subscript number after the symbol for an element indicates how many atoms of that element are in a single molecule of the compound.

Acids, Bases, and pH

An ion is an atom or group of atoms that has an electric charge because it has lost or gained one or more electrons. When an acid, such as hydrochloric acid, HCl, is mixed with water, it separates into ions. An **acid** is a compound that produces hydrogen ions, H+, in water. The hydrogen ions then combine with a water molecule to form a hydronium ion, H_3O^+. A **base**, on the other hand, is a substance that produces hydroxide ions, OH⁻, in water.

To determine whether a solution is acidic or basic, scientists use pH. The **pH** is a measure of the hydronium ion concentration in a solution. The pH scale ranges from 0 to 14. The middle point, pH = 7, is neutral, neither acidic nor basic. Acids have a pH less than 7; bases have a pH greater than 7. The lower the number is, the more acidic the solution. The higher the number is, the more basic the solution.

Chemical Equations

A chemical reaction occurs when a chemical change takes place. (In a chemical change, new substances with new properties are formed.) A chemical equation is a useful way of describing a chemical reaction by means of chemical formulas. The equation indicates what substances react and what the products are. For example, when carbon and oxygen combine, they can form carbon dioxide. The equation for the reaction is as follows: $C + O_2 \rightarrow CO_2$.

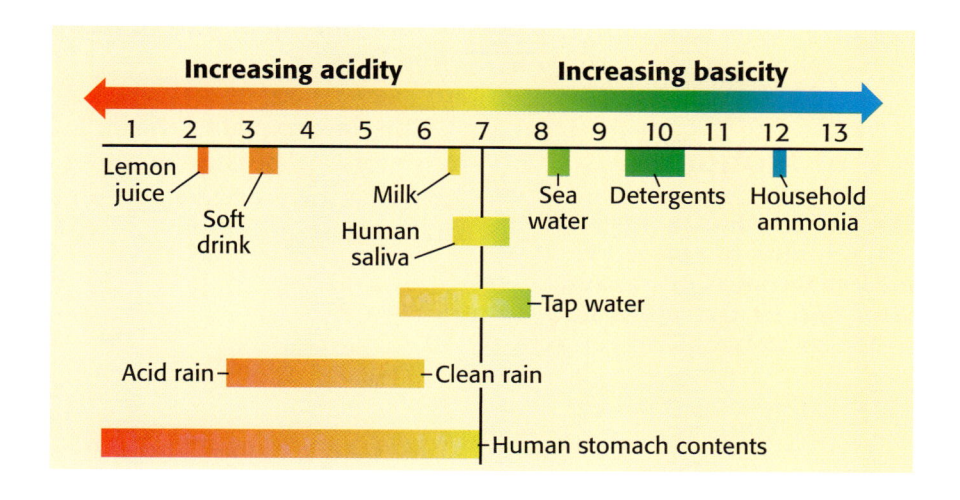

Increasing acidity ← 1 2 3 4 5 6 7 8 9 10 11 12 13 → **Increasing basicity**

- Lemon juice
- Soft drink
- Milk
- Human saliva
- Sea water
- Detergents
- Household ammonia
- Tap water
- Acid rain — Clean rain
- Human stomach contents

Physical Science Laws and Equations

Law of Conservation of Energy

The law of conservation of energy states that energy can be neither created nor destroyed.

The total amount of energy in a closed system is always the same. Energy can be changed from one form to another, but all of the different forms of energy in a system always add up to the same total amount of energy no matter how many energy conversions occur.

Law of Universal Gravitation

The law of universal gravitation states that all objects in the universe attract each other by a force called *gravity*. The size of the force depends on the masses of the objects and the distance between objects.

The first part of the law explains why a bowling ball is much harder to lift than a table-tennis ball. Because the bowling ball has a much larger mass than the table-tennis ball does, the amount of gravity between the Earth and the bowling ball is greater than the amount of gravity between the Earth and the table-tennis ball.

The second part of the law explains why a satellite can remain in orbit around the Earth. The satellite is carefully placed at a distance great enough to prevent the Earth's gravity from immediately pulling the satellite down but small enough to prevent the satellite from completely escaping the Earth's gravity and wandering off into space.

Newton's Laws of Motion

Newton's first law of motion states that an object at rest remains at rest and an object in motion remains in motion at constant speed and in a straight line unless acted on by an unbalanced force.

The first part of the law explains why a football will remain on a tee until it is kicked off or until a gust of wind blows it off.

The second part of the law explains why a bike rider will continue moving forward after the bike comes to an abrupt stop. Gravity and the friction of the sidewalk will eventually stop the rider.

Newton's second law of motion states that the acceleration of an object depends on the mass of the object and the amount of force applied.

The first part of the law explains why the acceleration of a 4 kg bowling ball will be greater than the acceleration of a 6 kg bowling ball if the same force is applied to both.

The second part of the law explains why the acceleration of a bowling ball will be larger if a larger force is applied to the bowling ball.

The relationship of acceleration (a) to mass (m) and force (F) can be expressed mathematically by the following equation:

$$acceleration = \frac{force}{mass}, \text{ or } a = \frac{F}{m}$$

This equation is often rearranged to the form

$$force = mass \times acceleration$$
or
$$F = m \times a$$

Newton's third law of motion states that whenever one object exerts a force on a second object, the second object exerts an equal and opposite force on the first.

This law explains that a runner is able to move forward because of the equal and opposite force that the ground exerts on the runner's foot after each step.

Useful Equations

Average speed

$$\text{average speed} = \frac{\text{total distance}}{\text{total time}}$$

Example: A bicycle messenger traveled a distance of 136 km in 8 h. What was the messenger's average speed?

$$\frac{136 \text{ km}}{8 \text{ h}} = 17 \text{ km/h}$$

The messenger's average speed was **17 km/h.**

Average acceleration

$$\text{average acceleration} = \frac{\text{final velocity} - \text{starting velocity}}{\text{time it takes to change velocity}}$$

Example: Calculate the average acceleration of an Olympic 100 m dash sprinter who reaches a velocity of 20 m/s south at the finish line. The race was in a straight line and lasted 10 s.

$$\frac{20 \text{ m/s} - 0 \text{ m/s}}{10 \text{ s}} = 2 \text{ m/s/s}$$

The sprinter's average acceleration is **2 m/s/s south.**

Net force

Forces in the Same Direction

When forces are in the same direction, add the forces together to determine the net force.

Example: Calculate the net force on a stalled car that is being pushed by two people. One person is pushing with a force of 13 N northwest, and the other person is pushing with a force of 8 N in the same direction.

$$13 \text{ N} + 8 \text{ N} = 21 \text{ N}$$

The net force is **21 N northwest.**

Forces in Opposite Directions

When forces are in opposite directions, subtract the smaller force from the larger force to determine the net force. The net force will be in the direction of the larger force.

Net force (continued)

Example: Calculate the net force on a rope that is being pulled on each end. One person is pulling on one end of the rope with a force of 12 N south. Another person is pulling on the opposite end of the rope with a force of 7 N north.

$$12 \text{ N} - 7 \text{ N} = 5 \text{ N}$$

The net force is **5 N south.**

Density

$$\text{density} = \frac{\text{mass}}{\text{volume}}$$

Example: Calculate the density of a sponge that has a mass of 10 g and a volume of 40 cm^3.

$$\frac{10 \text{ g}}{40 \text{ cm}^3} = \frac{0.25 \text{ g}}{\text{cm}^3}$$

The density of the sponge is **0.25 g/cm^3.**

Pressure

Pressure is the force exerted over a given area. The SI unit for pressure is the pascal, whose symbol is Pa.

$$\text{pressure} = \frac{\text{force}}{\text{area}}$$

Example: Calculate the pressure of the air in a soccer ball if the air exerts a force of 10 N over an area of 0.5 m^2.

$$\text{pressure} = \frac{10 \text{ N}}{0.5 \text{ m}^2} = \frac{20 \text{ N}}{\text{m}^2} = 20 \text{ Pa}$$

The pressure of the air inside the soccer ball is **20 Pa.**

Concentration

$$\text{concentration} = \frac{\text{mass of solute}}{\text{volume of solvent}}$$

Example: Calculate the concentration of a solution in which 10 g of sugar is dissolved in 125 mL of water.

$$\frac{10 \text{ g of sugar}}{125 \text{ mL of water}} = \frac{0.08 \text{ g}}{\text{mL}}$$

The concentration of this solution is **0.08 g/mL.**

Properties of Common Minerals

Silicate Minerals

Mineral	Color	Luster	Streak	Hardness
Beryl	deep green, pink, white, bluish green, or yellow	vitreous	white	7.5–8
Chlorite	green	vitreous to pearly	pale green	2–2.5
Garnet	green, red, brown, black	vitreous	white	6.5–7.5
Hornblende	dark green, brown, or black	vitreous	none	5–6
Muscovite	colorless, silvery white, or brown	vitreous or pearly	white	2–2.5
Olivine	olive green, yellow	vitreous	white or none	6.5–7
Orthoclase	colorless, white, pink, or other colors	vitreous	white or none	6
Plagioclase	colorless, white, yellow, pink, green	vitreous	white	6
Quartz	colorless or white; any color when not pure	vitreous or waxy	white or none	7

Nonsilicate Minerals

Native Elements

Mineral	Color	Luster	Streak	Hardness
Copper	copper-red	metallic	copper-red	2.5–3
Diamond	pale yellow or colorless	adamantine	none	10
Graphite	black to gray	submetallic	black	1–2

Carbonates

Mineral	Color	Luster	Streak	Hardness
Aragonite	colorless, white, or pale yellow	vitreous	white	3.5–4
Calcite	colorless or white to tan	vitreous	white	3

Halides

Mineral	Color	Luster	Streak	Hardness
Fluorite	light green, yellow, purple, bluish green, or other colors	vitreous	none	4
Halite	white	vitreous	white	2.0–2.5

Oxides

Mineral	Color	Luster	Streak	Hardness
Hematite	reddish brown to black	metallic to earthy	dark red to red-brown	5.6–6.5
Magnetite	iron-black	metallic	black	5.5–6.5

Sulfates

Mineral	Color	Luster	Streak	Hardness
Anhydrite	colorless, bluish, or violet	vitreous to pearly	white	3–3.5
Gypsum	white, pink, gray, or colorless	vitreous, pearly, or silky	white	2.0

Sulfides

Mineral	Color	Luster	Streak	Hardness
Galena	lead-gray	metallic	lead-gray to black	2.5–2.8
Pyrite	brassy yellow	metallic	greenish, brownish, or black	6–6.5

Density (g/cm³)	Cleavage, Fracture, Special Properties	Common Uses
2.6–2.8	1 cleavage direction; irregular fracture; some varieties fluoresce in ultraviolet light	gemstones, ore of the metal beryllium
2.6–3.3	1 cleavage direction; irregular fracture	
4.2	no cleavage; conchoidal to splintery fracture	gemstones, abrasives
3.0–3.4	2 cleavage directions; hackly to splintery fracture	
2.7–3	1 cleavage direction; irregular fracture	electrical insulation, wallpaper, fireproofing material, lubricant
3.2–3.3	no cleavage; conchoidal fracture	gemstones, casting
2.6	2 cleavage directions; irregular fracture	porcelain
2.6–2.7	2 cleavage directions; irregular fracture	ceramics
2.6	no cleavage; conchoidal fracture	gemstones, concrete, glass, porcelain, sandpaper, lenses
8.9	no cleavage; hackly fracture	wiring, brass, bronze, coins
3.5	4 cleavage directions; irregular to conchoidal fracture	gemstones, drilling
2.3	1 cleavage direction; irregular fracture	pencils, paints, lubricants, batteries
2.95	2 cleavage directions; irregular fracture; reacts with hydrochloric acid	no important industrial uses
2.7	3 cleavage directions; irregular fracture; reacts with weak acid; double refraction	cements, soil conditioner, whitewash, construction materials
3.0–3.3	4 cleavage directions; irregular fracture; some varieties fluoresce	hydrofluoric acid, steel, glass, fiberglass, pottery, enamel
2.1–2.2	3 cleavage directions; splintery to conchoidal fracture; salty taste	tanning hides, salting icy roads, food preservation
5.2–5.3	no cleavage; splintery fracture; magnetic when heated	iron ore for steel, pigments
5.2	no cleavage; splintery fracture; magnetic	iron ore
3.0	3 cleavage directions; conchoidal to splintery fracture	soil conditioner, sulfuric acid
2.3	3 cleavage directions; conchoidal to splintery fracture	plaster of Paris, wallboard, soil conditioner
7.4–7.6	3 cleavage directions; irregular fracture	batteries, paints
5	no cleavage; conchoidal to splintery fracture	sulfuric acid

Sky Maps

Spring

Summer

Constellations

1. Ursa Minor
2. Draco
3. Cepheus
4. Cassiopeia
5. Auriga
6. Ursa Major
7. Bootes
8. Hercules
9. Cygnus
10. Perseus
11. Gemini
12. Cancer
13. Leo
14. Serpens
15. Sagitta
16. Pegasus
17. Pisces

802 Appendix

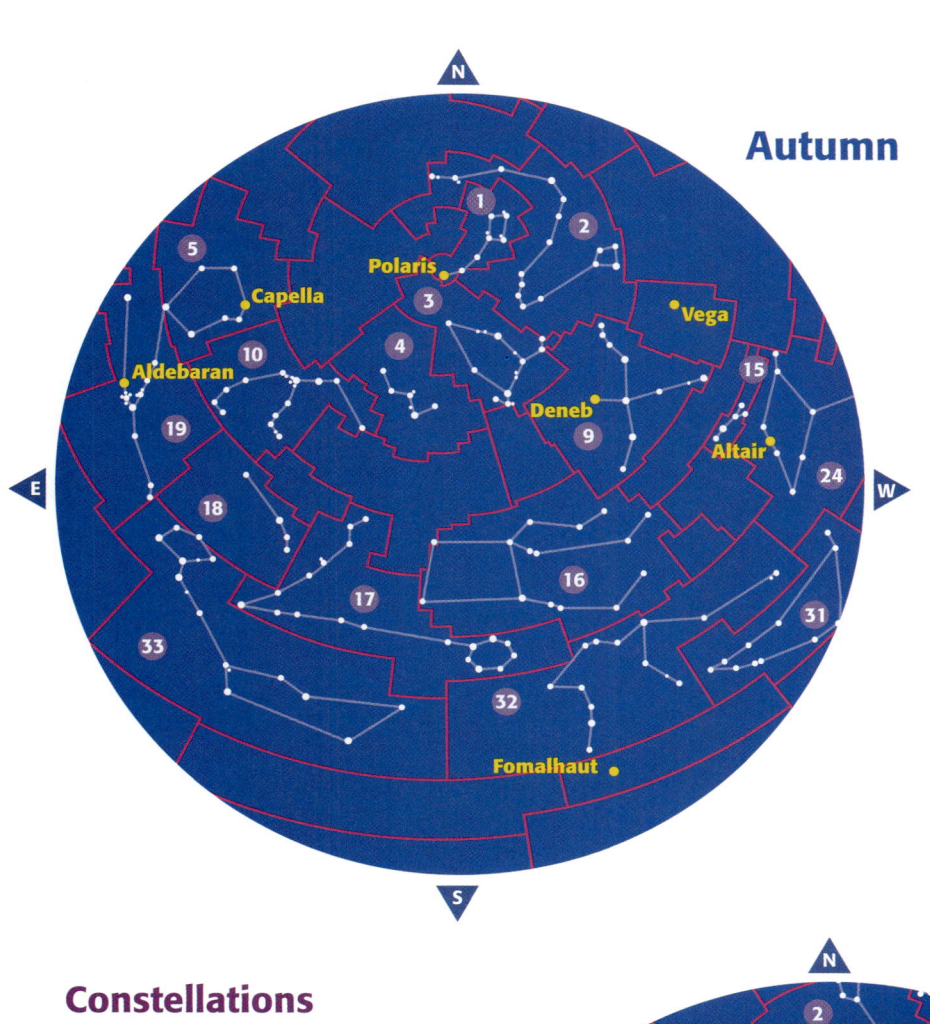

Autumn

Constellations
18 Aries
19 Taurus
20 Orion
21 Virgo
22 Libra
23 Ophiuchus
24 Aquila
25 Lepus
26 Canis Major
27 Hydra
28 Corvus
29 Scorpius
30 Sagittarius
31 Capricornus
32 Aquarius
33 Cetus
34 Columba

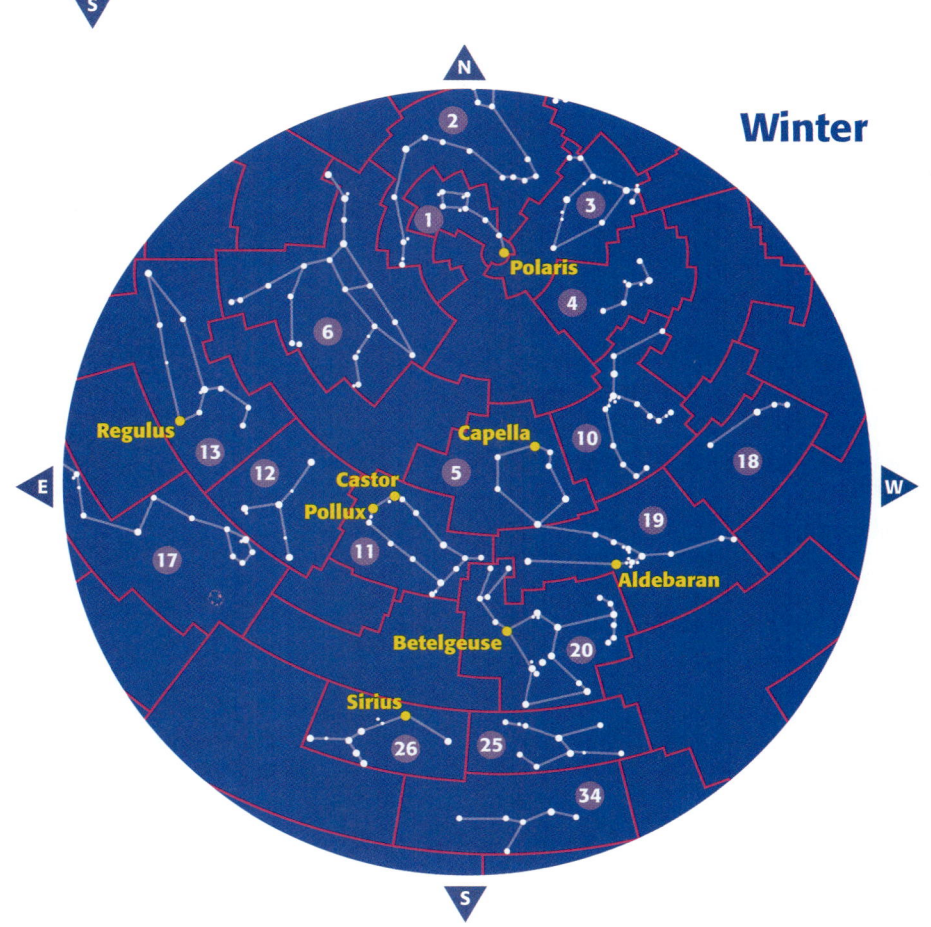

Winter

Appendix **803**

Glossary

A

abrasion the grinding and wearing away of rock surfaces through the mechanical action of other rock or sand particles (279, 349)

absolute dating any method of measuring the age of an event or object in years (162)

absolute magnitude the brightness that a star would have at a distance of 32.6 light-years from Earth (586)

abyssal plain a large, flat, almost level area of the deep-ocean basin (384)

acid precipitation rain, sleet, or snow that contains a high concentration of acids (132, 281, 467)

air mass a large body of air where temperature and moisture content are similar throughout (490)

air pollution the contamination of the atmosphere by the introduction of pollutants from human and natural sources (464)

air pressure the measure of the force with which air molecules push on a surface (449)

alluvial fan a fan-shaped mass of material deposited by a stream when the slope of the land decreases sharply (318)

altitude the angle between an object in the sky and the horizon (566)

anemometer an instrument used to measure wind speed (505)

anticyclone the rotation of air around a high-pressure center in the direction opposite to Earth's rotation (494)

apparent magnitude the brightness of a star as seen from the Earth (586)

aquifer a body of rock or sediment that stores groundwater and allows the flow of groundwater (321)

area a measure of the size of a surface or a region (24)

artesian spring a spring whose water flows from a crack in the cap rock over the aquifer (323)

artificial satellite any human-made object placed in orbit around a body in space (688)

asteroid a small, rocky object that orbits the sun, usually in a band between the orbits of Mars and Jupiter (670)

asteroid belt the region of the solar system that is between the orbits of Mars and Jupiter and in which most asteroids orbit (670)

asthenosphere the soft layer of the mantle on which the tectonic plates move (192)

astronomical unit the average distance between the Earth and the sun; approximately 150 million kilometers (symbol, AU) (645)

astronomy the study of the universe (9, 554)

atmosphere a mixture of gases that surrounds a planet or moon (448)

azimuthal projection (az uh MYOOTH uhl proh JEK shuhn) a map projection that is made by moving the surface features of the globe onto a plane (45)

B

barometer an instrument that measures atmospheric pressure (505)

beach an area of the shoreline made up of material deposited by waves (346)

bedrock the layer of rock beneath soil (288)

benthic environment the region near the bottom of a pond, lake, or ocean (389)

benthos the organisms that live at the bottom of the sea or ocean (388)

big bang theory the theory that states that the universe began with a tremendous explosion about 13.7 billion years ago (601)

biomass organic matter that can be a source of energy; the total mass of the organisms in a given area (139)

biome a large region characterized by a specific type of climate and certain types of plant and animal communities (524)

black hole an object so massive and dense that even light cannot escape its gravity (595)

C

caldera a large, semicircular depression that forms when the magma chamber below a volcano partially empties and causes the ground above to sink (258)

cast a type of fossil that forms when sediments fill in the cavity left by a decomposed organism (168)

catastrophism a principle that states that geologic change occurs suddenly (153)

channel the path that a stream follows (311)

chemical energy the energy released when a chemical compound reacts to produce new compounds (136)

chemical weathering the process by which rocks break down as a result of chemical reactions (281)

cleavage the splitting of a mineral along smooth, flat surfaces (71)

climate the average weather conditions in an area over a long period of time (518)

cloud a collection of small water droplets or ice crystals suspended in the air, which forms when the air is cooled and condensation occurs (486)

coal a fossil fuel that forms underground from partially decomposed plant material (128)

comet a small body of ice, rock, and cosmic dust that follows an elliptical orbit around the sun and that gives off gas and dust in the form of a tail as it passes close to the sun (668)

composition the chemical makeup of a rock; describes either the minerals or other materials in the rock (95)

compound a substance made up of atoms of two or more different elements joined by chemical bonds (67)

compression stress that occurs when forces act to squeeze an object (206)

condensation the change of state from a gas to a liquid (485)

conic projection a map projection that is made by moving the surface features of the globe onto a cone (44)

constellation a region of the sky that contains a recognizable star pattern and that is used to describe the location of objects in space (564)

continental drift the hypothesis that states that the continents once formed a single landmass, broke up, and drifted to their present locations (198)

continental rise the gently sloping section of the continental margin located between the continental slope and the abyssal plain (384)

continental shelf the gently sloping section of the continental margin located between the shoreline and the continental slope (384)

continental slope the steeply inclined section of the continental margin located between the continental rise and the continental shelf (384)

contour interval the difference in elevation between one contour line and the next (51)

contour line a line that connects points of equal elevation (50)

convection the transfer of thermal energy by the circulation or movement of a liquid or gas (455)

convergent boundary the boundary formed by the collision of two lithospheric plates (203)

core the central part of the Earth below the mantle (191, 627)

Coriolis effect the apparent curving of the path of a moving object from an otherwise straight path due to the Earth's rotation (418, 460)

cosmology the study of the origin, properties, processes, and evolution of the universe (600)

crater a funnel-shaped pit near the top of the central vent of a volcano (258)

creep the slow downhill movement of weathered rock material (361)

crust the thin and solid outermost layer of the Earth above the mantle (190, 625)

crystal a solid whose atoms, ions, or molecules are arranged in a definite pattern (67)

cyclone an area in the atmosphere that has lower pressure than the surrounding areas and has winds that spiral toward the center (494)

cylindrical projection (suh LIN dri kuhl proh JEK shuhn) a map projection that is made by moving the surface features of the globe onto a cylinder (43)

D

day the time required for Earth to rotate once on its axis (554)

deep current a streamlike movement of ocean water far below the surface (419)

deflation a form of wind erosion in which fine, dry soil particles are blown away (349)

deformation the bending, tilting, and breaking of the Earth's crust; the change in the shape of rock in response to stress (225)

delta a fan-shaped mass of material deposited at the mouth of a stream (317)

density the ratio of the mass of a substance to the volume of the substance (25, 72)

deposition the process in which material is laid down (91, 316)

desalination (DEE SAL uh NAY shuhn) a process of removing salt from ocean water (397)

differential weathering the process by which softer, less weather resistant rocks wear away and leave harder, more weather resistant rocks behind (284)

divergent boundary the boundary between two tectonic plates that are moving away from each other (203)

divide the boundary between drainage areas that have streams that flow in opposite directions (310)

dune a mound of wind-deposited sand that keeps its shape even though it moves (350)

E

eclipse an event in which the shadow of one celestial body falls on another (663)

elastic rebound the sudden return of elastically deformed rock to its undeformed shape (225)

electromagnetic spectrum all of the frequencies or wavelengths of electromagnetic radiation (561)

element a substance that cannot be separated or broken down into simpler substances by chemical means (66)

elevation the height of an object above sea level (50, 522)

El Niño a change in the surface water temperature in the Pacific Ocean that produces a warm current (424)

eon (EE AHN) the largest division of geologic time (175)

epicenter the point on Earth's surface directly above an earthquake's starting point, or focus (230)

epoch (EP uhk) a subdivision of a geologic period (175)

equator the imaginary circle halfway between the poles that divides the Earth into the Northern and Southern Hemispheres (39)

era a unit of geologic time that includes two or more periods (175)

erosion the process by which wind, water, ice, or gravity transports soil and sediment from one location to another (91, 295, 308)

extinction the death of every member of a species (175)

extrusive igneous rock rock that forms as a result of volcanic activity at or near the Earth's surface (101)

F

fault a break in a body of rock along which one block slides relative to another (208)

floodplain an area along a river that forms from sediments deposited when the river overflows its banks (318)

focus the point along a fault at which the first motion of an earthquake occurs (230)

folding the bending of rock layers due to stress (207)

foliated describes the texture of metamorphic rock in which the mineral grains are arranged in planes or bands (109)

fossil the remains or physical evidence of an organism preserved by geological processes (166)

fossil fuel a nonrenewable energy resource formed from the remains of organisms that lived long ago (126)

fracture the manner in which a mineral breaks along either curved or irregular surfaces (71)

front the boundary between air masses of different densities and usually different temperatures (492)

G

galaxy a collection of stars, dust, and gas bound together by gravity (596)

gap hypothesis a hypothesis that is based on the idea that a major earthquake is more likely to occur along the part of an active fault where no earthquakes have occurred for a certain period of time (235)

gas giant a planet that has a deep, massive atmosphere, such as Jupiter, Saturn, Uranus, or Neptune (654)

gasohol a mixture of gasoline and alcohol that is used as a fuel (139)

geologic column an arrangement of rock layers in which the oldest rocks are at the bottom (157)

geologic time scale the standard method used to divide the Earth's long natural history into manageable parts (174)

geology the study of the origin, history, and structure of the Earth and the processes that shape the Earth (6)

geostationary orbit an orbit that is about 36,000 km above the Earth's surface and in which a satellite is above a fixed spot on the equator (689)

geothermal energy the energy produced by heat within the Earth (140)

glacial drift the rock material carried and deposited by glaciers (356)

glacier a large mass of moving ice (352)

global warming a gradual increase in average global temperature (457, 540)

globular cluster a tight group of stars that looks like a ball and contains up to 1 million stars (598)

greenhouse effect the warming of the surface and lower atmosphere of Earth that occurs when water vapor, carbon dioxide, and other gases absorb and reradiate thermal energy (456, 540)

H

half-life the time needed for half of a sample of a radioactive substance to undergo radioactive decay (163)

hardness a measure of the ability of a mineral to resist scratching (72)

horizon the line where the sky and the Earth appear to meet (566)

hot spot a volcanically active area of Earth's surface far from a tectonic plate boundary (264)

H-R diagram **H**ertzsprung-**R**ussell diagram, a graph that shows the relationship between a star's surface temperature and absolute magnitude (592)

humidity the amount of water vapor in the air (483)

humus dark, organic material formed in soil from the decayed remains of plants and animals (290)

hurricane a severe storm that develops over tropical oceans and whose strong winds of more than 120 km/h spiral in toward the intensely low-pressure storm center (499)

hydroelectric energy electrical energy produced by falling water (138)

hypothesis (hie PAHTH uh sis) an explanation that is based on prior scientific research or observations and that can be tested (14)

I

ice age a long period of climate cooling during which ice sheets cover large areas of Earth's surface; also known as a *glacial period* (536)

index contour on a map, a darker, heavier contour line that is usually every fifth line and that indicates a change in elevation (51)

index fossil a fossil that is found in the rock layers of only one geologic age and that is used to establish the age of the rock layers (170)

intrusive igneous rock rock formed from the cooling and solidification of magma beneath the Earth's surface (100)

isobar a line that is drawn on a weather map and that connects points of equal pressure (507)

isotope an atom that has the same number of protons (or the same atomic number) as other atoms of the same element do but that has a different number of neutrons (and thus a different atomic mass) (162)

J

jet stream a narrow belt of strong winds that blow in the upper troposphere (462)

L

landslide the sudden movement of rock and soil down a slope (359)

La Niña a change in the eastern Pacific Ocean in which the surface water temperature becomes unusually cool (424)

latitude the distance north or south from the equator; expressed in degrees (39, 519)

lava plateau a wide, flat landform that results from repeated nonexplosive eruptions of lava that spread over a large area (259)

leaching the removal of substances that can be dissolved from rock, ore, or layers of soil due to the passing of water (290)

lightning an electric discharge that takes place between two oppositely charged surfaces, such as between a cloud and the ground, between two clouds, or between two parts of the same cloud (497)

light-year the distance that light travels in one year; about 9.46 trillion kilometers (568, 587)

lithosphere the solid, outer layer of the Earth that consists of the crust and the rigid upper part of the mantle (192)

load the materials carried by a stream; *also* the mass of rock overlying a geological structure (312)

loess (LOH ES) very fertile sediments of quartz, feldspar, hornblende, mica, and clay deposited by the wind (350)

longitude the distance east and west from the prime meridian; expressed in degrees (40)

longshore current a water current that travels near and parallel to the shoreline (429)

low earth orbit an orbit that is less than 1,500 km above the Earth's surface (689)

luster the way in which a mineral reflects light (70)

M

magma chamber the body of molten rock that feeds a volcano (252)

magnetic declination the difference between the magnetic north and the true north (38)

main sequence the location on the H-R diagram where most stars lie; it has a diagonal pattern from the lower right (low temperature and luminosity) to the upper left (high temperature and luminosity) (593)

mantle the layer of rock between the Earth's crust and core (191, 625)

map a representation of the features of a physical body such as Earth (36)

mass a measure of the amount of matter in an object (24)

mass movement a movement of a section of land down a slope (358)

mechanical weathering the breakdown of rock into smaller pieces by physical means (278)

mesosphere the strong, lower part of the mantle between the asthenosphere and the outer core (193); *also* the layer of the atmosphere between the stratosphere and the thermosphere and in which temperature decreases as altitude increases (451)

meteor a bright streak of light that results when a meteoroid burns up in the Earth's atmosphere (671)

meteorite a meteoroid that reaches the Earth's surface without burning up completely (671)

meteoroid a relatively small, rocky body that travels through space (671)

meteorology the scientific study of the Earth's atmosphere, especially in relation to weather and climate (8)

meter the basic unit of length in the SI (symbol, m) (23)

microclimate the climate of a small area (534)

mid-ocean ridge a long, undersea mountain chain that forms along the floor of the major oceans (385)

mineral a naturally formed, inorganic solid that has a definite chemical structure (66)

model a pattern, plan, representation, or description designed to show the structure or workings of an object, system, or concept (18)

mold a mark or cavity made in a sedimentary surface by a shell or other body (168)

month a division of the year that is based on the orbit of the moon around the Earth (554)

mudflow the flow of a mass of mud or rock and soil mixed with a large amount of water (360)

N

NASA the **N**ational **A**eronautics and **S**pace **A**dministration (685)

natural gas a mixture of gaseous hydrocarbons located under the surface of the Earth, often near petroleum deposits; used as a fuel (127)

natural resource any natural material that is used by humans, such as water, petroleum, minerals, forests, and animals (122)

neap tide a tide of minimum range that occurs during the first and third quarters of the moon (434)

nebula a large cloud of gas and dust in interstellar space; a region in space where stars are born or where stars explode at the end of their lives (598, 614)

nekton all organisms that swim actively in open water, independent of currents (388)

neutron star a star that has collapsed under gravity to the point that the electrons and protons have smashed together to form neutrons (594)

nonfoliated describes the texture of metamorphic rock in which the mineral grains are not arranged in planes or bands (110)

nonpoint-source pollution pollution that comes from many sources rather than from a single, specific site (326, 400)

nonrenewable resource a resource that forms at a rate that is much slower than the rate at which it is consumed (123)

nonsilicate mineral a mineral that does not contain compounds of silicon and oxygen (68)

nuclear energy the energy released by a fission or fusion reaction; the binding energy of the atomic nucleus (134)

nuclear fusion the combination of the nuclei of small atoms to form a larger nucleus; releases energy (620)

O

ocean current a movement of ocean water that follows a regular pattern (416)

oceanography the scientific study of the sea (7)

ocean trench a steep and long depression in the deep-sea floor that runs parallel to a chain of volcanic islands or a continental margin (385)

open cluster a group of stars that are close together relative to surrounding stars (598)

orbit the path that a body follows as it travels around another body in space (630)

ore a natural material whose concentration of economically valuable minerals is high enough for the material to be mined profitably (76)

P

paleontology the scientific study of fossils (154)

parallax an apparent shift in the position of an object when viewed from different locations (587)

parent rock a rock formation that is the source of soil (288)

pelagic environment in the ocean, the zone near the surface or at middle depths, beyond the sublittoral zone and above the abyssal zone (392)

period a unit of geologic time into which eras are divided (175)

permeability the ability of a rock or sediment to let fluids pass through its open spaces, or pores (321)

petroleum a liquid mixture of complex hydrocarbon compounds; used widely as a fuel source (127)

phase the change in the sunlit area of one celestial body as seen from another celestial body (662)

plankton the mass of mostly microscopic organisms that float or drift freely in freshwater and marine environments (388)

plate tectonics the theory that explains how large pieces of the Earth's outermost layer, called *tectonic plates,* move and change shape (202)

point-source pollution pollution that comes from a specific site (326, 401)

polar easterlies prevailing winds that blow from east to west between 60° and 90° latitude in both hemispheres (460)

polar zone the North or South Pole and the surrounding region (533)

porosity the percentage of the total volume of a rock or sediment that consists of open spaces (321)

precipitation any form of water that falls to the Earth's surface from the clouds (488)

prevailing winds winds that blow mainly from one direction during a given period (521)

prime meridian the meridian, or line of longitude, that is designated as 0° longitude (40)

prograde rotation the counterclockwise spin of a planet or moon as seen from above the planet's North Pole; rotation in the same direction as the sun's rotation (649)

pulsar a rapidly spinning neutron star that emits rapid pulses of radio and optical energy (594)

P wave a seismic wave that causes particles of rock to move in a back-and-forth direction (228)

Q

quasar a very luminous, starlike object that generates energy at a high rate; quasars are thought to be the most distant objects in the universe (599)

R

radiation the transfer of energy as electromagnetic waves (454)

radioactive decay the process in which a radioactive isotope tends to break down into a stable isotope of the same element or another element (162)

radiometric dating a method of determining the age of an object by estimating the relative percentages of a radioactive (parent) isotope and a stable (daughter) isotope (163)

recharge zone an area in which water travels downward to become part of an aquifer (322)

reclamation the process of returning land to its original condition after mining is completed (77)

recycling the process of recovering valuable or useful materials from waste or scrap; the process of reusing some items (125)

red giant a large, reddish star late in its life cycle (591)

reflecting telescope a telescope that uses a curved mirror to gather and focus light from distant objects (559)

refracting telescope a telescope that uses a set of lenses to gather and focus light from distant objects (559)

relative dating any method of determining whether an event or object is older or younger than other events or objects (156)

relative humidity the ratio of the amount of water vapor in the air to the maximum amount of water vapor the air can hold at a set temperature (483)

relief the variations in elevation of a land surface (51)

remote sensing the process of gathering and analyzing information about an object without physically being in touch with the object (47)

renewable resource a natural resource that can be replaced at the same rate at which the resource is consumed (123)

retrograde rotation the clockwise spin of a planet or moon as seen from above the planet's North Pole (649)

revolution the motion of a body that travels around another body in space; one complete trip along an orbit (630)

rift valley a long, narrow valley that forms as tectonic plates separate (385)

rift zone an area of deep cracks that forms between two tectonic plates that are pulling away from each other (262)

rock a naturally occurring solid mixture of one or more minerals or organic matter (90)

rock cycle the series of processes in which a rock forms, changes from one type to another, is destroyed, and forms again by geological processes (90)

rocket a machine that uses escaping gas from burning fuel to move (684)

rock fall the rapid mass movement of rock down a steep slope or cliff (359)

rotation the spin of a body on its axis (630)

S

salinity a measure of the amount of dissolved salts in a given amount of liquid (376)

saltation the movement of sand or other sediments by short jumps and bounces that is caused by wind or water (348)

satellite a natural or artificial body that revolves around a planet (660)

scientific methods a series of steps followed to solve problems (13)

sea-floor spreading the process by which new oceanic lithosphere forms as magma rises toward the surface and solidifies (200)

seamount a submerged mountain on the ocean floor that is at least 1,000 m high and that has a volcanic origin (385)

seismic gap an area along a fault where relatively few earthquakes have occurred recently but where strong earthquakes have occurred in the past (235)

seismic wave a wave of energy that travels through the Earth and away from an earthquake in all directions (228)

seismogram a tracing of earthquake motion that is created by a seismograph (230)

seismograph an instrument that records vibrations in the ground and determines the location and strength of an earthquake (230)

seismology (siez MAHL uh jee) the study of earthquakes (224)

septic tank a tank that separates solid waste from liquids and that has bacteria that break down the solid waste (329)

sewage treatment plant a facility that cleans the waste materials found in water that comes from sewers or drains (328)

shoreline the boundary between land and a body of water (342)

silicate mineral a mineral that contains a combination of silicon, oxygen, and one or more metals (68)

smog photochemical haze that forms when sunlight acts on industrial pollutants and burning fuels (132)

soil a loose mixture of rock fragments, organic material, water, and air that can support the growth of vegetation (288)

soil conservation a method to maintain the fertility of the soil by protecting the soil from erosion and nutrient loss (294)

soil structure the arrangement of soil particles (289)

soil texture the soil quality that is based on the proportions of soil particles (289)

solar energy the energy received by the Earth from the sun in the form of radiation (136)

solar nebula the cloud of gas and dust that formed our solar system (615)

space probe an uncrewed vehicle that carries scientific instruments into space to collect scientific data (694)

space shuttle a reusable space vehicle that takes off like a rocket and lands like an airplane (701)

space station a long-term orbiting platform from which other vehicles can be launched or scientific research can be carried out (702)

spectrum the band of colors produced when white light passes through a prism (583)

spring tide a tide of increased range that occurs two times a month, at the new and full moons (434)

storm surge a local rise in sea level near the shore that is caused by strong winds from a storm, such as those from a hurricane (431)

strata layers of rock (singular, *stratum*) (102)

stratification the process in which sedimentary rocks are arranged in layers (105)

stratified drift a glacial deposit that has been sorted and layered by the action of streams or meltwater (357)

stratosphere the layer of the atmosphere that is above the troposphere and in which temperature increases as altitude increases (451)

streak the color of the powder of a mineral (71)

subsidence (suhb SIED'ns) the sinking of regions of the Earth's crust to lower elevations (212)

sunspot a dark area of the photosphere of the sun that is cooler than the surrounding areas and that has a strong magnetic field (622)

supernova a gigantic explosion in which a massive star collapses and throws its outer layers into space (594)

superposition a principle that states that younger rocks lie above older rocks if the layers have not been disturbed (156)

surface current a horizontal movement of ocean water that is caused by wind and that occurs at or near the ocean's surface (417, 523)

S wave a seismic wave that causes particles of rock to move in a side-to-side direction (228)

swell one of a group of long ocean waves that have steadily traveled a great distance from their point of generation (430)

T

tectonic plate a block of lithosphere that consists of the crust and the rigid, outermost part of the mantle (194)

telescope an instrument that collects electromagnetic radiation from the sky and concentrates it for better observation (558)

temperate zone the climate zone between the Tropics and the polar zone (530)

temperature a measure of how hot (or cold) something is; specifically, a measure of the average kinetic energy of the particles in an object (24)

tension stress that occurs when forces act to stretch an object (206)

terrestrial planet one of the highly dense planets nearest to the sun; Mercury, Venus, Mars, and Earth (648)

texture the quality of a rock that is based on the sizes, shapes, and positions of the rock's grains (96)

theory an explanation that ties together many hypotheses and observations (20)

thermal conduction the transfer of energy as heat through a material (455)

thermometer an instrument that measures and indicates temperature (505)

thermosphere the uppermost layer of the atmosphere, in which temperature increases as altitude increases (452)

thrust the pushing or pulling force exerted by the engine of an aircraft or rocket (686)

thunder the sound caused by the rapid expansion of air along an electrical strike (497)

thunderstorm a usually brief, heavy storm that consists of rain, strong winds, lightning, and thunder (496)

tidal range the difference in levels of ocean water at high tide and low tide (434)

tide the periodic rise and fall of the water level in the oceans and other large bodies of water (432)

till unsorted rock material that is deposited directly by a melting glacier (356)

topographic map (TAHP uh GRAF ik MAP) a map that shows the surface features of Earth (50)

tornado a destructive, rotating column of air that has very high wind speeds, is visible as a funnel-shaped cloud, and touches the ground (498)

trace fossil a fossilized mark that is formed in soft sediment by the movement of an animal (168)

trade winds prevailing winds that blow northeast from 30° north latitude to the equator and that blow southeast from 30° south latitude to the equator (460)

transform boundary the boundary between tectonic plates that are sliding past each other horizontally (203)

tributary a stream that flows into a lake or into a larger stream (310)

tropical zone the region that surrounds the equator and that extends from about 23° north latitude to 23° south latitude (526)

troposphere the lowest layer of the atmosphere, in which temperature decreases at a constant rate as altitude increases (451)

true north the direction to the geographic North Pole (38)

tsunami a giant ocean wave that forms after a volcanic eruption, submarine earthquake, or landslide (430)

U

unconformity a break in the geologic record created when rock layers are eroded or when sediment is not deposited for a long period of time (159)

undertow a subsurface current that is near shore and that pulls objects out to sea (429)

uniformitarianism a principle that states that geologic processes that occurred in the past can be explained by current geologic processes (153)

uplift the rising of regions of the Earth's crust to higher elevations (212)

upwelling the movement of deep, cold, and nutrient-rich water to the surface (423)

V

vent an opening at the surface of the Earth through which volcanic material passes (252)

volcano a vent or fissure in the Earth's surface through which magma and gases are expelled (250)

volume a measure of the size of a body or region in three-dimensional space (23)

W

water cycle the continuous movement of water from the ocean to the atmosphere to the land and back to the ocean (309, 379)

watershed the area of land that is drained by a water system (310)

water table the upper surface of underground water; the upper boundary of the zone of saturation (320)

weather the short-term state of the atmosphere, including temperature, humidity, precipitation, wind, and visibility (482, 518)

weathering the process by which rock materials are broken down by the action of physical or chemical processes (278)

westerlies prevailing winds that blow from west to east between 30° and 60° latitude in both hemispheres (460)

whitecap the bubbles in the crest of a breaking wave (430)

white dwarf a small, hot, dim star that is the leftover center of an old star (591)

wind the movement of air caused by differences in air pressure (458)

wind power the use of a windmill to drive an electric generator (137)

Y

year the time required for the Earth to orbit once around the sun (554)

Z

zenith the point in the sky directly above an observer on Earth (566)

Spanish Glossary

A

abrasion/abrasión proceso por el cual las superficies de las rocas se muelen o desgastan por medio de la acción mecánica de otras rocas y partículas de arena (279, 349)

absolute dating/datación absoluta cualquier método que sirve para determinar la edad de un suceso u objeto en años (162)

absolute magnitude/magnitud absoluta el brillo que una estrella tendría a una distancia de 32.6 años luz de la Tierra (586)

abyssal plain/llanura abisal un área amplia, llana y casi plana de la cuenca oceánica profunda (384)

acid precipitation/precipitación ácida lluvia, aguanieve o nieve que contiene una alta concentración de ácidos (132, 281, 467)

air mass/masa de aire un gran volumen de aire que tiene una temperatura y contenido de humedad similar en toda su extensión (490)

air pollution/contaminación del aire la contaminación de la atmósfera debido a la introducción de contaminantes provenientes de fuentes humanas y naturales (464)

air pressure/presión del aire la medida de la fuerza con la que las moléculas del aire empujan contra una superficie (449)

alluvial fan/abanico aluvial masa de materiales rocosos en forma de abanico, depositados por un arroyo cuando la pendiente del terreno disminuye bruscamente (318)

altitude/altitud el ángulo que se forma entre un objeto en el cielo y el horizonte (566)

anemometer/anemómetro un instrumento que se usa para medir la rapidez del viento (505)

anticyclone/anticiclón la rotación del aire alrededor de un centro de alta presión en dirección opuesta a la rotación de la Tierra (494)

apparent magnitude/magnitud aparente el brillo de una estrella como se percibe desde la Tierra (586)

aquifer/acuífero un cuerpo rocoso o sedimento que almacena agua subterránea y permite que fluya (321)

area/área una medida del tamaño de una superficie o región (24)

artesian spring/manantial artesiano un manantial en el que el agua fluye a partir de una grieta en la capa de rocas que se encuentra sobre el acuífero (323)

artificial satellite/satélite artificial cualquier objeto hecho por los seres humanos y colocado en órbita alrededor de un cuerpo en el espacio (688)

asteroid/asteroide un objeto pequeño y rocoso que se encuentra en órbita alrededor del Sol, normalmente en una banda entre las órbitas de Marte y Júpiter (670)

asteroid belt/cinturón de asteroides la región del Sistema Solar que está entre las órbitas de Marte y Júpiter, en la que la mayoría de los asteroides se encuentran en órbita (670)

asthenosphere/astenosfera la capa blanda del manto sobre la que se mueven las placas tectónicas (192)

astronomical unit/unidad astronómica la distancia promedio entre la Tierra y el Sol; aproximadamente 150 millones de kilómetros (símbolo: UA) (645)

astronomy/astronomía el estudio del universo (9, 554)

atmosphere/atmósfera una mezcla de gases que rodea un planeta o una luna (448)

azimuthal projection/proyección azimutal una proyección cartográfica que se hace al transferir las características de la superficie del globo a un plano (45)

B

barometer/barómetro un instrumento que mide la presión atmosférica (505)

beach/playa un área de la costa formada por materiales depositados por las olas (346)

bedrock/lecho de roca la capa de rocas que está debajo del suelo (288)

benthic environment/ambiente béntico la región que se encuentra cerca del fondo de una laguna, lago u océano (389)

benthos/benthos los organismos que viven en el fondo del mar o del océano (388)

big bang theory/teoría del Big Bang la teoría que establece que el universo comenzó con una tremenda explosión hace aproximadamente 13.7 mil millones de años (601)

biomass/biomasa materia orgánica que puede ser una fuente de energía; la masa total de los organismos en un área determinada (139)

biome/bioma una región extensa caracterizada por un tipo de clima específico y ciertos tipos de comunidades de plantas y animales (524)

black hole/hoyo negro un objeto tan masivo y denso que ni siquiera la luz puede salir de su campo gravitacional (595)

C

caldera/caldera una depresión grande y semicircular que se forma cuando se vacía parcialmente la cámara de magma que hay debajo de un volcán, lo cual hace que el suelo se hunda (258)

cast/molde un tipo de fósil que se forma cuando un organismo descompuesto deja una cavidad que es llenada por sedimentos (168)

catastrophism/catastrofismo un principio que establece que los cambios geológicos ocurren súbitamente (153)

channel/canal el camino que sigue un arroyo (311)

chemical energy/energía química la energía que se libera cuando un compuesto químico reacciona para producir nuevos compuestos (136)

chemical weathering/desgaste químico el proceso por medio del cual las rocas se fragmentan como resultado de reacciones químicas (281)

cleavage/exfoliación el agrietamiento de un mineral en sus superficies lisas y planas (71)

climate/clima las condiciones promedio del tiempo en un área durante un largo período de tiempo (518)

cloud/nube un conjunto de pequeñas gotitas de agua o cristales de hielo suspendidos en el aire, que se forma cuando el aire se enfría y ocurre condensación (486)

coal/carbón un combustible fósil que se forma en el subsuelo a partir de materiales vegetales parcialmente descompuestos (128)

comet/cometa un cuerpo pequeño formado por hielo, roca y polvo cósmico que sigue una órbita elíptica alrededor del Sol y que libera gas y polvo, los cuales forman una cola al pasar cerca del Sol (668)

composition/composición la constitución química de una roca; describe los minerales u otros materiales presentes en ella (95)

compound/compuesto una substancia formada por átomos de dos o más elementos diferentes unidos por enlaces químicos (67)

compression/compresión estrés que se produce cuando distintas fuerzas actúan para estrechar un objeto (206)

condensation/condensación el cambio de estado de gas a líquido (485)

conic projection/proyección cónica una proyección cartográfica que se hace al transferir las características de la superficie del globo a un cono (44)

constellation/constelación una región del cielo que contiene un patrón reconocible de estrellas y que se utiliza para describir la ubicación de los objetos en el espacio (564)

continental drift/deriva continental la hipótesis que establece que alguna vez los continentes formaron una sola masa de tierra, se dividieron y se fueron a la deriva hasta terminar en sus ubicaciones actuales (198)

continental rise/elevación continental la sección del margen continental que tiene un ligero declive, ubicada entre el talud continental y la llanura abisal (384)

continental shelf/plataforma continental la sección del margen continental que tiene un ligero declive, ubicada entre la costa y el talud continental (384)

continental slope/talud continental la sección del margen continental que tiene una gran inclinación, ubicada entre la elevación continental y la plataforma continental (384)

contour interval/distancia entre las curvas de nivel la diferencia en elevación entre una curva de nivel y la siguiente (51)

contour line/curva de nivel una línea que une puntos que tienen la misma elevación (50)

convection/convección la transferencia de energía térmica mediante la circulación o el movimiento de un líquido o gas (455)

convergent boundary/límite convergente el límite que se forma debido al choque de dos placas de la litosfera (203)

core/núcleo la parte central de la Tierra, debajo del manto (191, 627)

Coriolis effect/efecto de Coriolis la desviación aparente de la trayectoria recta que experimentan los objetos en movimiento debido a la rotación de la Tierra (418, 460)

cosmology/cosmología el estudio del origen, propiedades, procesos y evolución del universo (600)

crater/cráter una depresión con forma de embudo que se encuentra cerca de la parte superior de la chimenea central de un volcán (258)

creep/arrastre el movimiento lento y descendente de materiales rocosos desgastados (361)

crust/corteza la capa externa, delgada y sólida de la Tierra, que se encuentra sobre el manto (190, 625)

crystal/cristal un sólido cuyos átomos, iones o moléculas están ordenados en un patrón definido (67)

cyclone/ciclón un área de la atmósfera que tiene una presión menor que la de las áreas circundantes y que tiene vientos que giran en espiral hacia el centro (494)

cylindrical projection/proyección cilíndrica una proyección cartográfica que se hace al transferir las características de la superficie del globo a un cilindro (43)

D

day/día el tiempo que se requiere para que la Tierra rote una vez sobre su eje (554)

deep current/corriente profunda un movimiento del agua del océano que es similar a una corriente y ocurre debajo de la superficie (419)

deflation/deflación una forma de erosión del viento en la que se mueven partículas de suelo finas y secas (349)

deformation/deformación el proceso de doblar, inclinar y romper la corteza de la Tierra; el cambio en la forma de una roca en respuesta a la tensión (225)

delta/delta un depósito de materiales rocosos en forma de abanico ubicado en la desembocadura de un río (317)

density/densidad la relación entre la masa de una substancia y su volumen (25, 72)

deposition/deposición el proceso por medio del cual un material se deposita (91, 316)

desalination/desalación (o desalinización) un proceso de remoción de sal del agua del océano (397)

differential weathering/desgaste diferencial el proceso por medio cual las rocas más suaves y menos resistentes al clima se desgastan y las rocas más duras y resistentes al clima permanecen (284)

divergent boundary/límite divergente el límite entre dos placas tectónicas que se están separando una de la otra (203)

divide/división el límite entre áreas de drenaje que tienen corrientes que fluyen en direcciones opuestas (310)

dune/duna un montículo de arena depositada por el viendo que conserva su forma incluso cuando se mueve (350)

E

eclipse/eclipse un suceso en el que la sombra de un cuerpo celeste cubre otro cuerpo celeste (663)

elastic rebound/rebote elástico ocurre cuando una roca deformada elásticamente vuelve súbitamente a su forma no deformada (225)

electromagnetic spectrum/espectro electromagnético todas las frecuencias o longitudes de onda de la radiación electromagnética (561)

element/elemento una substancia que no se puede separar o descomponer en substancias más simples por medio de métodos químicos (66)

elevation/elevación la altura de un objeto sobre el nivel del mar (50, 522)

El Niño/El Niño un cambio en la temperatura del agua superficial del océano Pacífico que produce una corriente caliente (424)

eon/eón la mayor división del tiempo geológico (175)

epicenter/epicentro el punto de la superficie de la Tierra que queda justo arriba del punto de inicio, o foco, de un terremoto (230)

epoch/época una subdivisión de un período geológico (175)

equator/ecuador el círculo imaginario que se encuentra a la mitad entre los polos y divide a la Tierra en los hemisferios norte y sur (39)

era/era una unidad de tiempo geológico que incluye dos o más períodos (175)

erosion/erosión el proceso por medio del cual el viento, el agua, el hielo o la gravedad transporta tierra y sedimentos de un lugar a otro (91, 295, 308)

extinction/extinción la muerte de todos los miembros de una especie (175)

extrusive igneous rock/roca ígnea extrusiva una roca que se forma como resultado de la actividad volcánica en la superficie de la Tierra o cerca de ella (101)

F

fault/falla una grieta en un cuerpo rocoso a lo largo de la cual un bloque se desliza respecto a otro (208)

floodplain/llanura de inundación un área a lo largo de un río formada por sedimentos que se depositan cuando el río se desborda (318)

focus/foco el punto a lo largo de una falla donde ocurre el primer movimiento de un terremoto (230)

folding/plegamiento fenómeno que ocurre cuando las capas de roca se doblan debido a la compresión (207)

foliated/foliada término que describe la textura de una roca metamórfica en la que los granos de mineral están ordenados en planos o bandas (109)

fossil/fósil los restos o las pruebas físicas de un organismo preservados por los procesos geológicos (166)

fossil fuel/combustible fósil un recurso energético no renovable formado a partir de los restos de organismos que vivieron hace mucho tiempo (126)

fracture/fractura la forma en la que se rompe un mineral a lo largo de superficies curvas o irregulares (71)

front/frente el límite entre masas de aire de diferentes desidades y, normalmente, diferentes temperaturas (492)

G

galaxy/galaxia un conjunto de estrellas, polvo y gas unidos por la gravedad (596)

gap hypothesis/hipótesis del intervalo una hipótesis que se basa en la idea de que es más probable que ocurra un terremoto importante a lo largo de la parte de una falla activa donde no se han producido terremotos durante un determinado período de tiempo (235)

gas giant/gigante gaseoso un planeta con una atmósfera masiva y profunda, como por ejemplo, Júpiter, Saturno, Urano o Neptuno (654)

gasohol/gasohol una mezcla de gasolina y alcohol que se usa como combustible (139)

geologic column/columna geológica un arreglo de las capas de roca en el que las rocas más antiguas están al fondo (157)

geologic time scale/escala de tiempo geológico el método estándar que se usa para dividir la larga historia natural de la Tierra en partes razonables (174)

geology/geología el estudio del origen, historia y estructura del planeta Tierra y los procesos que le dan forma (6)

geostationary orbit/órbita geoestacionaria una órbita que está a aproximadamente 36,000 km de la superficie terrestre, en la que un satélite permanece sobre un punto fijo en el ecuador (689)

geothermal energy/energía geotérmica la energía producida por el calor del interior de la Tierra (140)

glacial drift/deriva glacial el material rocoso que es transportado y depositado por los glaciares (356)

glacier/glaciar una masa grande de hielo en movimiento (352)

global warming/calentamiento global un aumento gradual de la temperatura global promedio (457, 540)

globular cluster/cúmulo globular un grupo compacto de estrellas que parece una bola y contiene hasta un millón de estrellas (598)

greenhouse effect/efecto de invernadero el calentamiento de la superficie y de la parte más baja de la atmósfera, el cual se produce cuando el vapor de agua, el dióxido de carbono y otros gases absorben y vuelven a irradiar la energía térmica (456, 540)

H

half-life/vida media el tiempo que tarda la mitad de la muestra de una substancia radiactiva en desintegrarse por desintegración radiactiva (163)

hardness/dureza una medida de la capacidad de un mineral de resistir ser rayado (72)

horizon/horizonte la línea donde parece que el cielo y la Tierra se unen (566)

hot spot/mancha caliente un área volcánicamente activa de la superficie de la Tierra que se encuentra lejos de un límite entre placas tectónicas (264)

H-R diagram/diagrama H-R diagrama de Hertzsprung-Russell; una gráfica que muestra la relación entre la temperatura de la superficie de una estrella y su magnitud absoluta (592)

humidity/humedad la cantidad de vapor de agua que hay en el aire (483)

humus/humus material orgánico obscuro que se forma en la tierra a partir de restos de plantas y animales en descomposición (290)

hurricane/huracán tormenta severa que se desarrolla sobre océanos tropicales, con vientos fuertes que soplan a más de 120 km/h y que se mueven en espiral hacia el centro de presión extremadamente baja de la tormenta (499)

hydroelectric energy/energía hidroeléctrica energía eléctrica producida por agua en caída (138)

hypothesis/hipótesis una explicación que se basa en observaciones o investigaciones científicas previas y que se puede probar (14)

I

ice age/edad de hielo un largo período de tiempo frío durante el cual grandes áreas de la superficie terrestre están cubiertas por capas de hielo; también conocido como período glacial (536)

index contour/índice de las curvas de nivel en un mapa, la curva de nivel que es más gruesa y oscura, la cual normalmente se encuentra cada quinta línea e indica un cambio en la elevación (51)

index fossil/fósil guía un fósil que se encuentra en las capas de roca de una sola era geológica y que se usa para establecer la edad de las capas de roca (170)

intrusive igneous rock/roca ígnea intrusiva una roca formada a partir del enfriamiento y solidificación del magma debajo de la superficie terrestre (100)

isobar/isobara una línea que se dibuja en un mapa meteorológico y conecta puntos de igual presión (507)

isotope/isótopo un átomo que tiene el mismo número de protones (o el mismo número atómico) que otros átomos del mismo elemento, pero que tiene un número diferente de neutrones (y, por lo tanto, otra masa atómica) (162)

J

jet stream/corriente en chorro un cinturón delgado de vientos fuertes que soplan en la parte superior de la troposfera (462)

L

landslide/derrumbamiento el movimiento súbito hacia abajo de rocas y suelo por una pendiente (359)

La Niña/La Niña un cambio en el océano Pacífico oriental por el cual el agua superficial se vuelve más fría que de costumbre (424)

latitude/latitud la distancia hacia el norte o hacia el sur del ecuador; se expresa en grados (39, 519)

lava plateau/meseta de lava un accidente geográfico amplio y plano que se forma debido a repetidas erupciones no explosivas de lava que se expanden por un área extensa (259)

leaching/lixiviación la remoción de substancias que pueden disolverse de rocas, menas o capas de suelo debido al paso del agua (290)

lightning/relámpago una descarga eléctrica que ocurre entre dos superficies que tienen carga opuesta, como por ejemplo, entre una nube y el suelo, entre dos nubes o entres dos partes de la misma nube (497)

light-year/año luz la distancia que viaja la luz en un año; aproximadamente 9.46 trillones de kilómetros (568, 587)

lithosphere/litosfera la capa externa y sólida de la Tierra que está formada por la corteza y la parte superior y rígida del manto (192)

load/carga los materiales que lleva un arroyo; también, la masa de rocas que recubre una estructura geológica (312)

loess/loess sedimentos muy fértiles de cuarzo, feldespato, hornblenda, mica y arcilla depositados por el viento (350)

longitude/longitud la distancia hacia el este y hacia el oeste del primer meridiano; se expresa en grados (40)

longshore current/corriente de ribera una corriente de agua que se desplaza cerca de la costa y paralela a ella (429)

low earth orbit/órbita terrestre baja una órbita ubicada a menos de 1,500 km sobre la superficie terrestre (689)

luster/brillo la forma en que un mineral refleja la luz (70)

M

magma chamber/cámara de magma la masa de roca fundida que alimenta un volcán (252)

magnetic declination/declinación magnética la diferencia entre el norte magnético y el norte verdadero (38)

main sequence/secuencia principal la ubicación en el diagrama H-R donde se encuentran la mayoría de las estrellas; tiene un patrón diagonal de la parte inferior derecha (baja temperatura y luminosidad) a la parte superior izquierda (alta temperatura y luminosidad) (593)

mantle/manto la capa de roca que se encuentra entre la corteza terrestre y el núcleo (191, 625)

map/mapa una representación de las características de un cuerpo físico, tal como la Tierra (36)

mass/masa una medida de la cantidad de materia que tiene un objeto (24)

mass movement/movimiento masivo un movimiento hacia abajo de una sección de terreno por una pendiente (358)

mechanical weathering/desgaste mecánico el rompimiento de una roca en pedazos más pequeños mediante medios físicos (278)

mesosphere/mesosfera la parte fuerte e inferior del manto que se encuentra entre la astenosfera y el núcleo externo (193); *también,* la capa de la atmósfera que se encuentra entre la estratosfera y la termosfera, en la cual la temperatura disminuye al aumentar la altitud (451)

meteor/meteoro un rayo de luz brillante que se produce cuando un meteoroide se quema en la atmósfera de la Tierra (671)

meteorite/meteorito un meteoroide que llega a la superficie de la Tierra sin quemarse por completo (671)

meteoroid/meteoroide un cuerpo rocoso relativamente pequeño que viaja en el espacio (671)

meteorology/meteorología el estudio científico de la atmósfera de la Tierra, sobre todo en lo que se relaciona al tiempo y al clima (8)

meter/metro la unidad fundamental de longitud en el sistema internacional de unidades (símbolo: m) (23)

microclimate/microclima el clima de un área pequeña (534)

mid-ocean ridge/dorsal oceánica una larga cadena submarina de montañas que se forma en el suelo de los principales océanos (385)

mineral/mineral un sólido natural e inorgánico que tiene una estructura química definida (66)

model/modelo un diseño, plan, representación o descripción cuyo objetivo es mostrar la estructura o funcionamiento de un objeto, sistema o concepto (18)

mold/molde una marca o cavidad hecha en una superficie sedimentaria por una concha u otro cuerpo (168)

month/mes una división del año que se basa en la órbita de la Luna alrededor de la Tierra (554)

mudflow/flujo de lodo el flujo de una masa de lodo o roca y suelo mezclados con una gran cantidad de agua (360)

N

NASA/NASA la Administración Nacional de Aeronáutica y del Espacio (685)

natural gas/gas natural una mezcla de hidrocarburos gaseosos que se encuentran debajo de la superficie de la Tierra, normalmente cerca de los depósitos de petróleo, y los cuales se usan como combustible (127)

natural resource/recurso natural cualquier material natural que es utilizado por los seres humanos, como agua, petróleo, minerales, bosques y animales (122)

neap tide/marea muerta una marea que tiene un rango mínimo, la cual ocurre durante el primer y el tercer cuartos de la Luna (434)

nebula/nebulosa una nube grande de gas y polvo en el espacio interestelar; una región en el espacio donde las estrellas nacen o donde explotan al final de su vida (598, 614)

nekton/necton todos los organismos que nadan activamente en las aguas abiertas, de manera independiente de las corrientes (388)

neutron star/estrella de neutrones una estrella que se ha colapsado debido a la gravedad hasta el punto en que los electrones y protones han chocado unos contra otros para formar neutrones (594)

nonfoliated/no foliada término que describe la textura de una roca metamórfica en la que los granos de mineral no están ordenados en planos ni bandas (110)

nonpoint-source pollution/contaminación no puntual contaminación que proviene de muchas fuentes, en lugar de provenir de un solo sitio específico (326, 400)

nonrenewable resource/recurso no renovable un recurso que se forma a una tasa que es mucho más lenta que la tasa a la que se consume (123)

nonsilicate mineral/mineral no-silicato un mineral que no contiene compuestos de sílice y oxígeno (68)

nuclear energy/energía nuclear la energía liberada por una reacción de fisión o fusión; la energía de enlace del núcleo atómico (134)

nuclear fusion/fusión nuclear combinación de los núcleos de átomos pequeños para formar un núcleo más grande; libera energía (620)

O

ocean current/corriente oceánica un movimiento del agua del océano que sigue un patrón regular (416)

oceanography/oceanografía el estudio científico del mar (7)

ocean trench/fosa oceánica una depresión empinada y larga del suelo marino profundo, paralela a una cadena de islas volcánicas o al margen continental (385)

open cluster/conglomerado abierto un grupo de estrellas que se encuentran juntas respecto a las estrellas que las rodean (598)

orbit/órbita la trayectoria que sigue un cuerpo al desplazarse alrededor de otro cuerpo en el espacio (630)

ore/mena un material natural cuya concentración de minerales con valor económico es suficientemente alta como para que el material pueda ser explotado de manera rentable (76)

P

paleontology/paleontología el estudio científico de los fósiles (154)

parallax/paralaje un cambio aparente en la posición de un objeto cuando se ve desde lugares distintos (587)

parent rock/roca precursora una formación rocosa que es la fuente a partir de la cual se origina el suelo (288)

pelagic environment/ambiente pelágico en el océano, la zona ubicada cerca de la superficie o en profundidades medias, más allá de la zona sublitoral y por encima de la zona abisal (392)

period/período una unidad de tiempo geológico en la que se dividen las eras (175)

permeability/permeabilidad la capacidad de una roca o sedimento de permitir que los fluidos pasen a través de sus espacios abiertos o poros (321)

petroleum/petróleo una mezcla líquida de compuestos hidrocarburos complejos; se usa ampliamente como una fuente de combustible (127)

phase/fase el cambio en el área iluminada de un cuerpo celeste según se ve desde otro cuerpo celeste (662)

plankton/plancton la masa de organismos en su mayoría microscópicos que flotan o se encuentran a la deriva en ambientes de agua dulce o marina (388)

plate tectonics/tectónica de placas la teoría que explica cómo se mueven y cambian de forma las placas tectónicas, que son grandes porciones de la capa más externa de la Tierra (202)

point-source pollution/contaminación puntual contaminación que proviene de un lugar específico (326, 401)

polar easterlies/vientos polares del este vientos preponderantes que soplan de este a oeste entre los 60° y los 90° de latitud en ambos hemisferios (460)

polar zone/zona polar el Polo Norte y el Polo Sur y la región circundante (533)

porosity/porosidad el porcentaje del volumen total de una roca o sedimento que está formado por espacios abiertos (321)

precipitation/precipitación cualquier forma de agua que cae de las nubes a la superficie de la Tierra (488)

prevailing winds/vientos prevalecientes vientos que soplan principalmente de una dirección durante un período de tiempo determinado (521)

prime meridian/meridiano de Greenwich el meridiano, o línea de longitud, que se designa como longitud 0° (40)

prograde rotation/rotación progresiva el giro en contra de las manecillas del reloj de un planeta o de una luna según lo vería un observador ubicado encima del Polo Norte del planeta; rotación en la misma dirección que la rotación del Sol (649)

pulsar/pulsar una estrella de neutrones que gira rápidamente y emite pulsaciones rápidas de energía radioeléctrica y óptica (594)

P wave/onda P una onda sísmica que hace que las partículas de roca se muevan en una dirección de atrás hacia delante (228)

Q

quasar/cuasar un objeto muy luminoso, parecido a una estrella, que genera energía a una gran velocidad; se piensa que los cuásares son los objetos más distantes del universo (599)

R

radiation/radiación la transferencia de energía en forma de ondas electromagnéticas (454)

radioactive decay/desintegración radiactiva el proceso por medio del cual un isótopo radiactivo tiende a desintegrarse y formar un isótopo estable del mismo elemento o de otro elemento (162)

radiometric dating/datación radiométrica un método para determinar la edad de un objeto estimando los porcentajes relativos de un isótopo radiactivo (precursor) y un isótopo estable (hijo) (163)

recharge zone/zona de recarga un área en la que el agua se desplaza hacia abajo para convertirse en parte de un acuífero (322)

reclamation/restauración el proceso de hacer que la tierra vuelva a su condición original después de que se terminan las actividades de explotación minera (77)

recycling/reciclar el proceso de recuperar materiales valiosos o útiles de los desechos o de la basura; el proceso de reutilizar algunas cosas (125)

red giant/gigante roja una estrella grande de color rojizo que se encuentra en una etapa avanzada de su vida (591)

reflecting telescope/telescopio reflector un telescopio que utiliza un espejo curvo para captar y enfocar la luz de objetos lejanos (559)

refracting telescope/telescopio refractante un telescopio que utiliza un conjunto de lentes para captar y enfocar la luz de objetos lejanos (559)

relative dating/datación relativa cualquier método que se utiliza para determinar si un acontecimiento u objeto es más viejo o más joven que otros acontecimientos u objetos (156)

relative humidity/humedad relativa la proporción de la cantidad de vapor de agua que hay en el aire respecto a la cantidad máxima de vapor de agua que el aire puede contener a una temperatura dada (483)

relief/relieve las variaciones en elevación de una superficie de terreno (51)

remote sensing/teledetección el proceso de recopilar y analizar información acerca de un objeto sin estar en contacto físico con el objeto (47)

renewable resource/recurso renovable un recurso natural que puede reemplazarse a la misma tasa a la que se consume (123)

retrograde rotation/rotación retrógrada el giro en el sentido de las manecillas del reloj de un planeta o de una luna según lo vería un observador ubicado encima del Polo Norte del planeta (649)

revolution/revolución el movimiento de un cuerpo que viaja alrededor de otro cuerpo en el espacio; un viaje completo a lo largo de una órbita (630)

rift valley/fosa tectónica un valle largo y estrecho que se forma cuando se separan las placas tectónicas (385)

rift zone/zona de rift un área de grietas profundas que se forma entre dos placas tectónicas que se están alejando una de la otra (262)

rock/roca una mezcla sólida de uno o más minerales o de materia orgánica que se produce de forma natural (90)

rock cycle/ciclo de las rocas la serie de procesos por medio de los cuales una roca se forma, cambia de un tipo a otro, se destruye y se forma nuevamente por procesos geológicos (90)

rocket/cohete un aparato que para moverse utiliza el gas de escape que se origina a partir de la combustión (684)

rock fall/desprendimiento de rocas el movimiento rápido y masivo de rocas por una pendiente empinada o un precipicio (359)

rotation/rotación el giro de un cuerpo alrededor de su eje (630)

S

salinity/salinidad una medida de la cantidad de sales disueltas en una cantidad determinada de líquido (376)

saltation/saltación el movimiento de la arena u otros sedimentos por medio de saltos pequeños y rebotes debido al viento o al agua (348)

satellite/satélite un cuerpo natural o artificial que gira alrededor de un planeta (660)

scientific methods/métodos científicos una serie de pasos que se siguen para solucionar problemas (13)

sea-floor spreading/expansión del suelo marino el proceso por medio del cual se forma nueva litosfera oceánica a medida que el magma se eleva hacia la superficie y se solidifica (200)

seamount/montaña submarina una montaña sumergida que se encuentra en el fondo del océano, la cual tiene por lo menos 1,000 m de altura y cuyo origen es volcánico (385)

seismic gap/brecha sísmica un área a lo largo de una falla donde han ocurrido relativamente pocos terremotos recientemente, pero donde se han producido terremotos fuertes en el pasado (235)

seismic wave/onda sísmica una onda de energía que viaja a través de la Tierra y se aleja de un terremoto en todas direcciones (228)

seismogram/sismograma una gráfica del movimiento de un terremoto elaborada por un sismógrafo (230)

seismograph/sismógrafo un instrumento que registra las vibraciones en el suelo y determina la ubicación y la fuerza de un terremoto (230)

seismology/sismología el estudio de los terremotos (224)

septic tank/tanque séptico un tanque que separa los desechos sólidos de los líquidos y que tiene bacterias que descomponen los desechos sólidos (329)

sewage treatment plant/planta de tratamiento de residuos una instalación que limpia los materiales de desecho que se encuentran en el agua procedente de cloacas o alcantarillas (328)

shoreline/orilla el límite entre la tierra y una masa de agua (342)

silicate mineral/mineral silicato un mineral que contiene una combinación de sílice, oxígeno y uno o más metales (68)

smog/esmog bruma fotoquímica que se forma cuando la luz solar actúa sobre contaminantes industriales y combustibles (132)

soil/suelo una mezcla suelta de fragmentos de roca, material orgánico, agua y aire en la que puede crecer vegetación (288)

soil conservation/conservación del suelo un método para mantener la fertilidad del suelo protegiéndolo de la erosión y la pérdida de nutrientes (294)

soil structure/estructura del suelo la organización de las partículas del suelo (289)

soil texture/textura del suelo la cualidad del suelo que se basa en las proporciones de sus partículas (289)

solar energy/energía solar la energía que la Tierra recibe del Sol en forma de radiación (136)

solar nebula/nebulosa solar la nube de gas y polvo que formó nuestro Sistema Solar (615)

space probe/sonda espacial un vehículo no tripulado que lleva instrumentos científicos al espacio con el fin de recopilar información científica (694)

space shuttle/transbordador espacial un vehículo espacial reutilizable que despega como un cohete y aterriza como un avión (701)

space station/estación espacial una plataforma orbital de largo plazo desde la cual pueden lanzarse otros vehículos o en la que pueden realizarse investigaciones científicas (702)

spectrum/espectro la banda de colores que se produce cuando la luz blanca pasa a través de un prisma (583)

spring tide/marea muerta una marea de mayor rango que ocurre dos veces al mes, durante la luna nueva y la luna llena (434)

storm surge/marea de tempestad un levantamiento local del nivel del mar cerca de la costa, el cual es resultado de los fuertes vientos de una tormenta, como por ejemplo, los vientos de un huracán (431)

strata/estratos capas de roca (102)

stratification/estratificación el proceso por medio del cual las rocas sedimentarias se acomodan en capas (105)

stratified drift/deriva estratificada un depósito glacial que ha formado capas debido a la acción de los arroyos o de las aguas de ablación (357)

stratosphere/estratosfera la capa de la atmósfera que se encuentra encima de la troposfera y en la que la temperatura aumenta al aumentar la altitud (451)

streak/veta el color del polvo de un mineral (71)

subsidence/hundimiento del terreno el hundimiento de regiones de la corteza terrestre a elevaciones más bajas (212)

sunspot/mancha solar un área oscura en la fotosfera del Sol que es más fría que las áreas que la rodean y que tiene un campo magnético fuerte (622)

supernova/supernova una explosión gigantesca en la que una estrella masiva se colapsa y lanza sus capas externas hacia el espacio (594)

superposition/superposición un principio que establece que las rocas más jóvenes se encontrarán sobre las rocas más viejas si las capas no han sido alteradas (156)

surface current/corriente superficial un movimiento horizontal del agua del océano que es producido por el viento y que ocurre en la superficie del océano o cerca de ella (417, 523)

S wave/onda S una onda sísmica que hace que las partículas de roca se muevan en una dirección de lado a lado (228)

swell/mar de leva un grupo de olas oceánicas grandes que se han desplazado una gran distancia desde el punto en el que se originaron (430)

T

tectonic plate/placa tectónica un bloque de litosfera formado por la corteza y la parte rígida y más externa del manto (194)

telescope/telescopio un instrumento que capta la radiación electromagnética del cielo y la concentra para mejorar la observación (558)

temperate zone/zona templada la zona climática ubicada entre los trópicos y la zona polar (530)

temperature/temperatura una medida de qué tan caliente (o frío) está algo; específicamente, una medida de la energía cinética promedio de las partículas de un objeto (24)

tension/tensión estrés que se produce cuando distintas fuerzas actúan para estirar un objeto (206)

terrestrial planet/planeta terrestre uno de los planetas muy densos que se encuentran más cerca del Sol; Mercurio, Venus, Marte y la Tierra (648)

texture/textura la cualidad de una roca que se basa en el tamaño, la forma y la posición de los granos que la forman (96)

theory/teoría una explicación que relaciona muchas hipótesis y observaciones (20)

thermal conduction/conducción térmica la transferencia de energía en forma de calor a través de un material (455)

thermometer/termómetro un instrumento que mide e indica la temperatura (505)

thermosphere/termosfera la capa más alta de la atmósfera, en la cual la temperatura aumenta a medida que la altitud aumenta (452)

thrust/empuje la fuerza de empuje o arrastre ejercida por el motor de un avión o cohete (686)

thunder/trueno el sonido producido por la expansión rápida del aire a lo largo de una descarga eléctrica (497)

thunderstorm/tormenta eléctrica una tormenta fuerte y normalmente breve que consiste en lluvia, vientos fuertes, relámpagos y truenos (496)

tidal range/rango de marea la diferencia en los niveles del agua del océano entre la marea alta y la marea baja (434)

tide/marea el ascenso y descenso periódico del nivel del agua en los océanos y otras masas grandes de agua (432)

till/arcilla glaciárica material rocoso desordenado que deposita directamente un glaciar que se está derritiendo (356)

topographic map/mapa topográfico un mapa que muestra las características superficiales de la Tierra (50)

tornado/tornado una columna destructiva de aire en rotación cuyos vientos se mueven a velocidades muy altas; se ve como una nube con forma de embudo y toca el suelo (498)

trace fossil/fósil traza una marca fosilizada que se forma en un sedimento blando debido al movimiento de un animal (168)

trade winds/vientos alisios vientos preponderantes que soplan hacia el noreste a partir de los 30° de latitud norte hacia el ecuador y que soplan hacia el sureste a partir de los 30° de latitud sur hacia el ecuador (460)

transform boundary/límite de transformación el límite entre placas tectónicas que se están deslizando horizontalmente una sobre otra (203)

tributary/afluente un arroyo que fluye a un lago o a otro arroyo más grande (310)

tropical zone/zona tropical la región que rodea el ecuador y se extiende desde aproximadamente 23° de latitud norte hasta 23° de latitud sur (526)

troposphere/troposfera la capa inferior de la atmósfera, en la que la temperatura disminuye a una tasa constante a medida que la altitud aumenta (451)

true north/norte verdadero la dirección al Polo Norte geográfico (38)

tsunami/tsunami una ola gigante del océano que se forma después de una erupción volcánica, terremoto submarino o desprendimiento de tierras (430)

U

unconformity/disconformidad una ruptura en el registro geológico, creada cuando las capas de roca se erosionan o cuando el sedimento no se deposita durante un largo período de tiempo (159)

undertow/resaca un corriente subsuperficial que está cerca de la orilla y que arrastra los objetos hacia el mar (429)

uniformitarianism/uniformitarianismo un principio que establece que es posible explicar los procesos geológicos que ocurrieron en el pasado en función de los procesos geológicos actuales (153)

uplift/levantamiento la elevación de regiones de la corteza terrestre a elevaciones más altas (212)

upwelling/surgencia el movimiento de las aguas profundas, frías y ricas en nutrientes hacia la superficie (423)

V

vent/chimenea una abertura en la superficie de la Tierra a través de la cual pasa material volcánico (252)

volcano/volcán una chimenea o fisura en la superficie de la Tierra a través de la cual se expulsan magma y gases (250)

volume/volumen una medida del tamaño de un cuerpo o región en un espacio de tres dimensiones (23)

W

water cycle/ciclo del agua el movimiento continuo del agua: del océano a la atmósfera, de la atmósfera a la tierra y de la tierra al océano (309, 379)

watershed/cuenca hidrográfica el área del terreno que es drenada por un sistema de agua (310)

water table/capa freática el nivel más alto del agua subterránea; el límite superior de la zona de saturación (320)

weather/tiempo el estado de la atmósfera a corto plazo que incluye la temperatura, la humedad, la precipitación, el viento y la visibilidad (482, 518)

weathering/meteorización el proceso por el cual se desintegran los materiales que forman las rocas debido a la acción de procesos físicos o químicos (278)

westerlies/vientos del oeste vientos preponderantes que soplan de oeste a este entre 30° y 60° de latitud en ambos hemisferios (460)

whitecap/cabrillas las burbujas de la cresta de una ola rompiente (430)

white dwarf/enana blanca una estrella pequeña, caliente y tenue que es el centro sobrante de una estrella vieja (591)

wind/viento el movimiento de aire producido por diferencias en la presión barométrica (458)

wind power/potencia eólica el uso de un molino de viento para hacer funcionar un generador eléctrico (137)

Y

year/año el tiempo que se requiere para que la Tierra le dé la vuelta al Sol una vez (554)

Z

zenith/cenit el punto del cielo situado directamente sobre un observador en la Tierra (566)

Index

Boldface page numbers refer to illustrative material, such as figures, tables, margin elements, photographs, and illustrations.

A

aa lava, 253, **253**
abrasion, 279, **279**, 298–299, 349, **349**
absolute dating, 162, **162**
　radioactive decay, 162–163, **162**
　radiometric dating, 163–165, **163, 164, 165**
absolute magnitude, 585, 586, **586**, 592, **592–593**
absorption spectrum, 584, **584**
abyssal plains, **384**, 385
abyssal zone, 391, **391**
acceleration, 798, 799
acidification, 467
acid precipitation, 281, **281**, 467–468, **467, 468**
　aquatic ecosystems and, 468, **468**
　effects on forests, 467, **467**
　from fossil fuels, 132, **132**
　weathering from, 281
acids, 797. See also pH
acid shock, 468
active tendon systems, **237**
active volcanoes, 264. See also volcanoes
adaptations, **528**, 529, 532
adding decimals, 791
adding fractions, 792
Adopt-a-Beach program, 404, **404**
aeration, zone of, 320, **320**
aerogels, **704**
aftershocks, **236**
agents of weathering, 278, 281
Age of Mammals (Cenozoic era), **174**, 177, **177**
Age of Reptiles (Mesozoic era), **174**, 176, **176**
ages
　geologic time scale, 174–177
　ice, 536–538, **536, 537, 538**
　of the universe, 602
agriculture, water use by, 330, **330**
air, weathering from, 283, **283**. See also acid precipitation
air masses, 490–495, **491**
　cold, 491, **491, 492–493**
　fronts and, 492–493, **492–493, 507**

source regions, 490, **490**
　warm, 491, **491, 492–493**
air pollution, 464–471
　acid precipitation from, 281, 467–468, **467, 468**
　awareness of, **470**
　cleaning up, 469–470, **469, 470**
　human health and, 469, **469**
　human sources of, 466, **466**
　indoor, 466, **466**
　lab on, **467**
　ozone hole and, 468, **468**
　particulate testing of, **467**
　plants and, **466**
　primary pollutants, 464, **464**
　secondary pollutants, 465, **465**
　smog, 132, **132**, 465, **465**
air pressure, 449, **449**. See also atmosphere
　calculation of, 799
　isobars, 507, **507**
　lab on, 471–472
　measurement of, 505, **505**
　pressure belts, 459, **459**
　sea breezes and, 462, **462**
　land breezes and, 462, **462**
　weather and, 494–495, **494**
Alaska Volcano Observatory, 273
alcohol, as fuel, 139, **139**
Aldrin, Edwin "Buzz," **701**
algae, 442, **628**
alkalinity, 327, **327**
Allowance Trading System, 470
"All Summer in a Day," 514
alluvial fans, 318, **318**
alpine glaciers, 352, **352**, 354, **354, 355**
alpines, 534
Alps, 210
alternative energy resources, 134–141
　biomass, 139, **139**
　fission, 134–135, **134, 135**
　fuel cells, 136, **136**
　fusion, 135, **135**, 149
　gasohol, 139, **139**
　geothermal, 140, **140**
　hydroelectric, 138, **138**, 148
　solar, 136–137, **136, 137**
　wind, 137, **137**
altitude, 565, **566**
　atmosphere and, 451, **451**
　clouds and, 487, **487**
　star location from, 566, **566**
altocumulus clouds, **487**
altostratus clouds, **487**
aluminum, 68, **69**, 77, **78**
Alvin, 7, 386

amber, 166, **166**
ammonia, **466**
ammonites, 168, **168**, 169, **169**
Andes Mountains, **210**
Andrew, Hurricane, 8, **8, 458**
Andromeda galaxy, **596**
anemometers, 505, **505**
angle of repose, 358, **358**
angler fish, **393**
angular unconformities, 160, **160**
anhydrite, **800–801**
animals
　earthquake prediction by, 246
　magnetite in, 68
　weather forecasting by, **506**, 514
　weathering by, 280, **280**
Ankarana National Park, 338
annular eclipses, 663, **663**
Antarctica, 353, 468, **468**
Antarctic Bottom Water, 420
anthracite, 130, **130**
anticlines, 207, **207**
anticyclones, 494–495, **494, 495**
ants, weather and, 514
apatite, **72**
Apollo missions, 660, 701
Appalachian Mountains, 210, **210**
apparent magnitude, 585, 586, **586**
aqualung, 413
aquamarines, 79
aquatic ecosystems, 468, **468, 692**. See also marine life
aquifers, 321–322, **321, 322**, 330, **330**. See also groundwater
aragonite, **800–801**
Archean Eon, **174**, 175
arctic climates, 293, **293**
area, 24, **24**
　of squares or rectangles, 24, **24**, 793
　surface, 285, **285**
　of triangles, 793
　units of, **782**
Arecibo radio telescope, 562
arêtes, **355**
argon, **164**
Armstrong, Neil, 701, **701**
artesian formations, 323, **323**
artesian springs, 322–323, **323**
artifacts, American Indian, **15**
artificial reefs, 412
artificial satellites, 688–693, **689, 691**
　communications, 691
　earliest, 688, **688**
　lab on, **689**
　military, 690, **690**
　observing, **691**

824 Index

orbits of, 664, 688, **688,** 689, **689,** 798
remote sensing, 47, **47,** 692–693, **692**
weather, 506, 691
ash, volcanic, 251, **253,** 254
asphalt, fossils in, 167
asteroid belt, 670, **670**
asteroids, 670, **670.** *See also* impacts
 captured, 665
 climate change and, 539, **539**
 strikes by, 118, 154, **154,** 176
asthenosphere, **192–193,** 195, 202, **202,** 204
astrolabes, 566, **566**
astronauts, 700, **700, 701,** 713
astronomical units (AUs), 645, **645**
astronomy, 9, **9,** 554–705, **554**
 ancient, 555–556, **556**
 big bang theory, 19, 600–601, **600–601**
 calendars and, 554, **554,** 674–675
 constellations, 564–565, **564, 565, 568, 802–803**
 Doppler effect, 570, **570**
 Kepler's laws of planetary motion, 631, **631**
 labs on, **562,** 572–573, **632,** 634–635
 modern, 557, **557**
 nebulae, 598, **598,** 614–616, **614, 615**
 nonoptical telescopes, 561–563, **561, 562, 563**
 optical telescopes, 558–560, **558, 559, 560**
 orbits, 630–631, **630, 631,** 669, **669**
 size and scale of universe, 568, **568,** 569
 solar system formation, 614–617, **616**
 star location, 564–571, **566, 567, 802–803**
astrophysicists, 611, 641
Atlantic Ocean
 Gulf Stream, 422, **422**
 Mid-Atlantic Ridge, 262
 North Atlantic Deep Water, 420
 surface currents in, **417, 418, 419**
atmosphere, 448–471, **448**
 acid precipitation, 467–468, **467, 468**
 anticyclones and, 494–495, **494, 495**
 causes of winds, 458–460, **459, 460**
 composition of, 448, **448,** 626

cyclones and, 494–495, **494, 495**
effect of life on, 627–628
effect of ocean on, 380
energy in, 454–457, **454, 455, 456, 457**
formation of, 626–628, **626, 627**
global warming and, 457
greenhouse effect, 456, **456,** 540, **540**
heating of, 454–457
of Jupiter, 654
labs on, **467,** 471–472
layers of, 450–453, **450, 451, 452, 453**
of Mars, 651
of Neptune, 657, **657**
ozone hole in, 468, **468**
pressure and temperature in, 449, **449, 458–463,** 471–472, 505
pressure belts in, 459, **459**
primary and secondary pollutants in, 464–465, **464, 465**
relative humidity in, 483–484, **483, 484**
of Saturn, 655
on Venus, 649, **649**
atomic number, 796
atoms, 67, **67,** 195, **195,** 796
 particles in, **620**
 structure of, 796
AUs (astronomical units), 645, **645**
auroras, 453, **453**
average acceleration, 799
averages, 790
average speed, 799
axis of Earth
 climate change and, 537, **537**
 as reference point, 37, **37**
 seasons and, 520, **520**
azimuthal projections, 45, **45**

B

balances, 784
Ballard, Robert, **386**
balloons, weather, 504, **504**
Bamberger, J. David, 305, **305**
Bangladesh, 549
bar graphs, 789
barium, **134**
barometers, 471–472, 505, **505**
barrier spits, 347, **347**
basalt, 96, **96**
base isolators, **237**
bases, 797
batholiths, 100, **100**
bathyal zone, 390, **390**

bathymetric profiles, **382–383,** 406–407
bats, **324**
Bay of Fundy, **435**
beaches, 346, **346,** 401. *See also* shorelines
Becquerel, Henri, 162
bed load, **312**
bedrock, 288, **288**
Begay, Fred, 149, **149**
Bell-Burnell, Jocelyn, 611
benthic environment, 389–391, **389, 390, 391**
benthos, 388, **388, 389**
beryl, **78,** 87, **800–801**
beryllium, **78**
Betelgeuse, 582, **582**
bicycles, **78,** 470, **470**
big bang theory, 19, 600–601, **600–601**
Big Dipper, **585, 588**
biological oceanographers, 7
biomass, 139, **139**
biomes, 524, **524**
 alpine, 534
 chaparral, **530,** 532, **532**
 taiga, **533,** 534, **534**
 temperate desert, **530,** 532, **532**
 temperate forest, 292, **292, 530,** 531, **531**
 temperate grassland, **530,** 531, **531**
 tropical desert, **526,** 529, **529**
 tropical rain forest, 291, **291,** 304, 526, **526, 527, 527**
 tropical savanna, **526,** 528, **528**
 tundra, 533, **533**
biotite, **68**
birds, weather and, 514
bituminous coal, 130, **130**
Blackfooted Penguins, 132, **132**
black gold, 127. *See also* petroleum
black holes, **594,** 595, 610, 641
black smokers, 7, **7,** 391, **391**
blocks, volcanic, **254**
blocky lava, 253, **253**
blue-green algae, **628**
blueshift, 570, **570**
blue stars, 592, **592**
Bluestein, Howard, 8
body seismic waves, 228, **228**
body temperature, 24, **24, 783**
bombs, volcanic, **254**
booklet instructions (FoldNote), 777, **777**
boundaries, plate, 202–203, **202–203.** *See also* plate tectonics
 compression at, 206
 earthquakes at, 224, 226, **226–227**
 fault types at, 226
 mid-ocean ridges at, **203**

Index **825**

boundaries (continued)
  mountain formation at, 210–211, **210, 211**
  rift zones at, 212, **212**
  types of, 202–203, **202–203**
  volcanoes at, 261–263, **261, 262, 263**
brachiopods, **104**
Bradbury, Ray, 514
Brazil Current, 418, **418**
breakers, 428, **428**. *See also* waves, ocean
brightness, of stars, 585–586, **585, 586, 592–593**
British Isles, 422, **422**
  warm-water currents and, 422, **422**
  tidal bores in, 435
bromine, 68, **69**
Bryce Canyon, **94**
buildings, earthquakes and, 236–238, **236, 237,** 240–241
burial mounds, 164, **164**
Burnell, Jocelyn Bell, 611
burrows, fossil, 168
bush pilots, 479
butane, 127
butterflies, **110**

C

calcite, **69, 72, 74, 78, 800–801**
calcium, 68, **69**
calderas, 258, **258**
calendars, 554, **554,** 674–675
California Current, 423, **423**
Callisto, 665
Calthorpe, Grant, 680
Calypso, 413
Cambrian period, **174,** 175, **175**
Canada, 435, **435,** 541
Canyonlands National Park, **314**
Cape Cod, 347, **347**
carats, 79
carbon
  carbon-14 dating method, 165
  in coal, 130, **130**
  in diamonds, **72, 78, 79, 800–801**
  in minerals, **68, 74, 800–801**
carbonates, 69, 74, 800–801
carbon-14 dating method, 165
carbon dioxide
  in the early atmosphere, 626
  as greenhouse gas, 457, 540, **626**
  as predictor of volcanic eruptions, 266–267
  on Venus, 649

carbon monoxide, **466**
cardinal directions, 37, **37**
Carlsbad Caverns (New Mexico), 282, **282, 324**
cars
  air pollution from, 465, **465,** 470
  fingerprinting of, **583**
  fuel cell, **136**
  greenhouse effect in, 540, **540**
  hybrid, 148
cartography, 11. *See also* maps
Carver, George Washington, 297, **297**
Cassini mission, 655, 665, 698, **698**
Castro, Cristina, 443
casts, 168, **168**
catastrophism, 153, **153**
cave formations
  from acids in groundwater, 282, **282, 324**
  forests in, 338
  sea caves, **344**
  sinkholes, 325, **325**
  from underground erosion, 324–325, **324**
  underwater, 6, **6**
celestial equator, **567**
celestial sphere, 566, **567**
cells, convection, 459, **459**
Celsius scale, **22,** 24, **24,** 783
cementation, **92**
Cenozoic era, **174,** 177, **177**
centimeters (cm), **22,** 23, **782**
Ceres, 670, **670**
CFCs (chlorofluorocarbons), 468
chain-of-events chart instructions (Graphic Organizer), 781, **781**
Challenger, HMS, 406
Chandrasekhar, Subrahmanyan, 641, **641**
Chandra X-Ray Observatory, 563, **563,** 641
Chang-Diaz, Franklin, 713
channels, 311, **311**
chaparral, **530,** 532, **532**
Charon, 658–659, **658,** 666
chemical energy, 136, **136**
chemical equations, 797
chemical oceanographers, 7
chemical reactions, **73**
chemical sedimentary rock, 103
chemical weathering, 280, 281–283, **281, 282, 283**
Chernobyl nuclear release, 135
Chiappe, Luis, 166
Chichén Itzá observatory, **554**
Chicxulub impact crater, 681
China, tidal bores in, 435
chlorine
  as indoor air pollutant, **466**
  in minerals, 67, **67,** 69
  in ocean, 376, **376**
  in water treatment, 328, **328**

chlorite, **108, 800–801**
chlorofluorocarbons (CFCs), 468
cholera, 339, 549
chromosphere, **618**
cinder cone volcanoes, 257, **257**
circle graphs, 787
circumference, 36, 54–55
circumpolar stars, 567
cirques, **355**
cirrocumulus clouds, 487, **487**
cirrus clouds, **486,** 487, **487**
cities, microclimates in, 535, **535**
clastic sedimentary rock, 103, **103**
clay, **289**
Clean Air Act of 1970, 469
Clean Water Act of 1972, 405
cleavage, 71, **71,** 801
Clemens, Samuel, **313**
Clementine missions, 694, **694**
climate, 518–541, **518.** *See also* biomes; climate change; weather
  adaptations to, **528,** 529, 532
  arctic, 293, **293**
  bodies of water and, 523
  in cities, 535, **535**
  climatographs, 542–543
  desert, 292, **292**
  effect of oceans on, 380, **380**
  El Niño and, 424–425, **424,** 443, 549
  grasslands, 292, **292**
  greenhouse effect and, 456, **456,** 540, **540, 626**
  Gulf Stream and, 422, **422,** 523, **523**
  in ice ages, 536–538, **536, 537, 538**
  ice cores and, 548
  labs on, **521,** 542–543
  La Niña and, 424–425, **424,** 443, 549
  latitude and, 519, **519**
  microclimates, 534–535, **534, 535**
  mountains and, 522, **522**
  polar zones, 533–534, **533, 534**
  prevailing winds and, 521, **521**
  seasons and, 520, **520**
  soil and, 291–293, **291, 292, 293**
  sunspot cycle and, 539, **539,** 622–623, **622**
  surface currents and, 422–425, **422, 423, 424,** 523, **523**
  temperate forests, 292, **292**
  temperate zones, 530–532, **530, 531, 532**
  tropical rain forests, 291, **291,** 304, 526, **526,** 527, **527**
  tropical zone, 526–529, **526, 527, 528, 529**

weather compared to, 518, **518**
weathering and, 286, **286**
zone distribution, 524, **524**
climate change
    asteroid impacts and, 539, **539**
    evidence from fossil record, 169
    evidence from ice cores, 548
    in glacial periods, 536, **536**
    global warming and, 457, 540–541, **540,** 548
    in interglacial periods, **527,** 537
    mathematical models of, 21, **21**
    Milankovitch theory of, 537, **537**
    plate tectonics and, 538, **538**
    volcanic eruptions and, 256, **256,** 538, **538**
climate models, 21, **21**
climatographs, 542–543
clouds, 486–488, **486, 487, 496, 498**
coal, 128, **128**
    acid precipitation from, 132
    coal-burning power plants, 128, **128,** 469, **469**
    formation of, 130, **130**
    location of, 131, **131**
    mining of, 76, 132
    types of, 130, **130**
coal-burning power plants, 128, **128,** 469, **469**
coarse-grained texture, 96, **96,** 99, **99**
coastal cleanups, 404, **404**
Colbert, Edwin, **155**
cold air masses, 491, **491, 492–493**
cold fronts, 492, **492**
cold-water currents, 419, **419,** 423, **423.** See also surface currents
Coleridge, Samuel Taylor, 392
collisions, plate, **202**
color, of minerals, 70, **70,** 79, **800**
Colorado River, 173
colors
    of common minerals, 70, **70,** 79, **800**
    seeing, **584**
    in spectrum, 583
    of stars, 582, **582, 585,** 592, **592**
    temperature and, 604–605
Columbia River Plateau, **259**
Columbia (shuttle), 701
Colwell, Rita, 339
comets, 668, **669.** See also impacts
    atmosphere and, 627
    exploration of, 698
    meteors and, **627**
    from the Oort cloud, 640
    orbits of, 669, **669**
    origins of, 669
    tails, 668, **668, 669**
communications satellites, 691

compaction, **92**
comparison table instructions (Graphic Organizer), 780, **780**
compasses, **37,** 38, **38**
compass rose, **46**
composite volcanoes, 257, **257**
composition, 95, **95**
    of the atmosphere, 448, **448,** 626
    of the Earth, 190–191, **190, 191**
    of igneous rock, 99, **99**
    of limestone, **95**
    of magma, 98, **98,** 252
    of metamorphic rock, 108, **108**
    of sedimentary rock, 103–104, **104**
    of stars, 583–584, **583, 584, 585**
compounds, 67, **67,** 797
compression, 206, **206,** 208, **208,** 210
concentration, 799
concept map instructions (Graphic Organizer), 781, **781**
conceptual models, 19
conchoidal fractures, **71, 801**
condensation, **309, 379, 482,** 485, **485**
conduction, in the atmosphere, **454–455,** 455
conglomerate, **96, 103**
conic projections, 44, **44**
conifers, 534
conservation of energy, law of, 798
conservation of resources, 124–125, **125, 322,** 331
conservation of soil, 294–297, **294, 295, 296, 297**
constellations, 564–565, **564, 565, 568, 802–803.** See also stars
contact metamorphism, 106, **106**
continental-continental boundaries, 203
continental-continental collisions, **202**
continental crust, 190, **190,** 195, **195, 202**
continental deflections, 418, **418**
Continental Divide, 310, **310**
continental drift hypothesis, 198–199, **198, 199,** 221. See also plate tectonics
continental glaciers, 353–354, **354**
continental-oceanic boundaries, 203
continental-oceanic collisions, **202**
continental polar (cP) air mass, **490,** 491
continental rises, **384,** 385
continental shelves, **384,** 385
continental slopes, **384,** 385
continental tropical (cT) air mass, **490,** 491
continents, formation of, 628–629

continuous spectrum, 583
contour intervals, 51, **51**
contour lines, 50, **50,** 53
contour plowing, 296, **296**
control groups, 786
controlled experiments, 14, 786
convection, 455, **455**
    in the atmosphere, **454–455,** 455
    cells, 459, **459**
    currents, **419,** 455, **455**
    in plate tectonics, **204,** 214–215
    in the sun, **618,** 621
convection cells, 459, **459**
convection currents, **419,** 455, **455**
convective zone, in the sun, **618,** 621
convergent boundaries, 202 **202,** 203, **203**
    compression at, 206
    magma formation at, 263, **263**
    mountain formation at, 210–211, **210, 211**
convergent motion, **227**
conversion table, for units, **782, 783**
Copernican revolution, 555
Copernicus, Nicolaus, 555, **555,** 568
copper
    formation of, **75**
    in minerals, **69**
    mining of, 76
    properties of, **800–801**
    uses of, 78, **78**
coprolites, 168
coral reefs, 104, **104, 424**
corals, 104, **104,** 390, **390**
core, of the Earth, 190–191, **191, 192–193,** 625, **625**
core, of the sun, **618**
core sampling, 26–27
Coriolis effect, 417–418, **418,** 460, **460**
corn, gasohol from, 139, **139**
corona, **618**
corundum, **69, 72**
cosmic background radiation, 601, **601**
cosmology, 600, **600**
Cousteau, Jacques, 413
cover crops, **296,** 297, **297**
cP (continental polar) air mass, **490,** 491
craters, impact, **258,** 681
craters, volcanic, 258, **258**
creep, 361, **361**
crests, wave, 426, **426**
Cretaceous period, **174**
crickets, 514
crop rotation, 297, **297**
cross braces, **237**
cross-multiplication, 790
crude oil, 127. See also petroleum

Index **827**

crust, of the Earth, 190, **190**, 625, **625**
 formation of, 625, **625**
 tectonic plates and, 195, **195, 202**
 thickness of, **191**
crystalline structure, 66, **66**, 67, **67**
crystals, 67, **67**
cT (continental tropical) air mass, **490**, 491
cubes, volume formula for, 793
cubic meters, **22**, 23
Cullinan diamond, **79**
cumulonimbus clouds, 486, **487, 488, 498**
cumulus clouds, 486, **486, 487**
currents, ocean, 416–425, **416**
 climate and, 422–423, **422, 423,** 523, **523**
 convection, **419**, 455, **455**
 deep, 419–420, **420, 421**
 El Niño and, 424–425, **424**, 443, 549
 Heyerdahl's explorations of, 416, **416**
 La Niña and, 424–425, **424**
 longshore, 429, **429**
 surface, 417–419, **417, 418, 419, 421** (see also surface currents)
 tracking, 442
 upwelling and, 423, **423**
cyclones, 494–495, **494, 495,** 499. See also hurricanes
cylindrical projections, 43, **43**

D

dams, flood control, 319
Darwin, Charles, **153**
data pairs, **591**, 788
dates, on maps, **46**
dating methods
 absolute, 162–165, **162, 163, 164, 165**
 fossils and, 170–171, **170, 171**
 relative, 156–161, **156, 157, 158, 159, 160**
daughter isotopes, **162**, 163
Davis, William Morris, 313
days, 554, **554**
Death Valley, 292, **292, 318**
debris, 539
deciduous trees, 531, **531**
decimals, 791
declination, **567**
deep currents, 419–420, **420, 421**
Deep Flight, 386, **386**
Deep Space 1, 699, **699**
deep-water waves, 428, **428**

deep zone, oceanic, **377**
deflation, 349, **349**
deflation hollows, 349
deforestation, **291**
deformation, 111, 206, **206**, 225, **225**
degrees, of latitude and longitude, 39, **39,** 40, **40, 41**
Deimos, 665
deltas, 317, **317, 692**
Denali Highway (Alaska), **293**
density, **24**, 25, 72, **72**
 calculation of, 25, 799
 formation of Earth's layers and, 625, **625**
 lab on, 80–81
 of minerals, 72, 81, **801**
 ocean currents and, 419–420, **420, 421**
 of population, **20**
 of the thermosphere, 452
dependent variables, 788
deposition, 94, **94**, 316, **316,** 342–361
 by glaciers, 356–357, **356, 357**
 on land, 318–319, **318, 319**
 placer deposits, 317, **317**
 unconformities in, 159–160, **159, 160**
 underground, 324–325, **324, 325,** 338
 in water, 316–317, **316, 317**
 by waves, 346–347, **346, 347**
 by wind, 350–351, **350, 351**
desalination, 397, **397**
desertification, 295
deserts
 desert pavement, 349
 dust from, 304
 lab on, **349**
 soil in, 292, **292**
 temperate, **530,** 532, **532**
 tropical, **526,** 529, **529**
deuterium, **135,** 621
Devils Tower, **284**
Devonian period, **174**
dew point, 485
diamonds, **72, 78, 79, 800–801**
differential weathering, 284, **284**
dikes, 100, **100**
Dinosaur National Monument, 172, **172**
dinosaurs
 extinction of, 154, **154,** 177, 539
 feathered, 184
 fossil excavations, 33
 fossils, 168, **168,** 172, **172,** 184
 Seismosaurus hallorum, 12, **12, 16, 17**
 use of scientific methods on, 13–17

directions
 cardinal, 37, **37**
 compasses, **37,** 38, **38**
 latitude and, 39, **39,** 40, **41**
 longitude and, 40, **40, 41**
 reference points for, 37, **37**
 true north and magnetic declination, 38–39, **38, 39**
disaster planning, 238–239, **501**
discharge, from rivers, 311, 313
disconformities, 160, **160**
Discovery program, 698
diseases, **20,** 339, 549
dissolved load, **312**
dissolved oxygen (DO), 327
dissolved solids, 376, **376**
distance
 gravity and, 632, **632**
 lab on, 634–635
 in light-years, 568, **568,** 587, **587**
distortions, map, 42, **42**
divergent boundaries, 202, **203**
 mid-ocean ridges at, 203, **203,** 262, **262**
 motion of, **203**
 rift zones at, 212, **212**
 tension at, 206
divergent motion, in earthquakes, **227**
divides, 310, **310**
dividing fractions, 792
DNA, mammoth, 184
DO (dissolved oxygen), 327
doldrums, 461, **461**
dolomite, **74**
dolphins, 392, **392**
Doppler effect, 570, **570**
Doppler radar, 506, **506**
dormant volcanoes, 264. See also volcanoes
double-door instructions (FoldNote), 776, **776**
double-hulled tankers, 403, **403**
drainage basins, 310, **310**
drain fields, 329
drift nets, 394, **394**
drip irrigation, 330, **330**
dripstone columns, 324, **324**
droughts, 424
dunes, 350–351, **350, 351**
dung, as fuel, 139, **139**
Dust Bowl, **350**
dust tails, 668, **668, 669**
dust transport, 304
dwarf elliptical galaxies, 597
dwarf stars, **592**

E

Eagle lander, 701, **701**
Eagle nebula, **598**

Earth. *See also* history of Earth
　absolute dating and, 162, 165, **162, 163, 164, 165**
　axis of, 37, **37**
　composition of, 190–191, **190, 191**
　distance from sun, 634–635
　escape velocity from, 687, **687**
　formation of, 624–625, **624, 625**
　gravitational attraction with the moon, 632, **632**
　magnetic field of, 200–201, **200, 201**
　models of, 20, **20, 192**
　ocean and continent formation on, 628–629
　physical structure of, **192–193**
　planetary statistics on, **650**
　rotation of, 588
　size of, 36, 54–55, **644**
　from space, 650, **650**
　as a sphere, 36, 37
　tectonic plates and, 195, **195**
Earth Observing System (EOS) program, 693
earthquake hazard, 234, **234**
earthquakes, 224–239
　buildings and, 236–238, **236, 237,** 240–241
　causes of, 225–226, **225, 226**
　divergent motion, 227
　earthquake hazard, 234, **234**
　elastic rebound in, 225, **225**
　faults and, 224, 226–227, **226–227**
　focus, 230, **230**
　forecasting, 235–236, **235, 236,** 246
　Kobe, **236**
　labs on, **228,** 240–241
　locations of, 224, **224, 234, 235**
　Loma Prieta, 236, **236**
　methods of locating, 230–231, **230, 231**
　New Madrid, **232**
　observatories, 246
　preparation for, 238–239, **238**
　San Francisco, 233, **233,** 240
　seismic gaps in, 235–236, **235, 236**
　seismic waves in, 228–229, **228, 229**
　strength and magnitude of, 232–233, **232, 233, 235**
　tsunamis and, 247
　from volcanoes, 264
　zones, 227
Earth Science Enterprise, 650
earthy luster, **70**
East African Rift, **212**
Easter Island, 118
eclipses, 663–664, **663**

ecliptic, **567**
ecologists, 10, 549
ecology, 10
ecosystems. *See also* biomes
　acid precipitation and, 467–468, **467, 468**
　aquatic, 468, **692**
　remote sensing of, 692–693, **692**
　study of, 10
Edmontosaurus, 33
Effigy Mounds National Monument, 164, **164**
Einstein, Albert, 620, **620**
Eisner, Vladimir, **167**
elastic deformation, 225, **225**
elastic rebound, 225, **225**
Eldfell eruption (Iceland), 272
electrical energy
　from fossil fuels, 126, **126,** 128, **128**
　from geothermal energy, 140, **140**
　in satellite photo of U.S., **126**
　in thunderstorms, 496–497, **496, 497**
electromagnetic spectrum, 561, **561**
electromagnetic waves, 454
electron clouds, 796
electrons, **620,** 796
elements, 66, **66,** 796
　emission and absorption spectra of, 583–584, **583, 584**
　formation of, 595
　periodic table of, **794–795**
　in stars, **585**
elevation, 50, **50,** 522, **522**
　climate and, 522, **522**
　weathering and, 287, **287**
ellipses, 631, **631, 632**
elliptical galaxies, 597, **597**
El Niño, 424–425, **424,** 443, 549
emeralds, 79, 87
emission lines, 583–584, **583**
Enchanted Rock (Texas), **100**
Endeavour, 701, **701**
energy, 122–141. *See also* energy resources
　in the atmosphere, 454–457, **454, 455, 456, 457**
　chemical, 136, **136**
　electrical, 126, **126,** 128, **128,** 140
　from fission, 134–135, **134, 135**
　from fusion, 135, **135,** 149, 593, 620–621
　geothermal, 140, **140,** 338
　greenhouse effect and, 456, **456**
　hydroelectric, 138, **138,** 148
　law of conservation of, 798
　from matter, 620, **620**
　from the oceans, 398–399, **398**

　production in the sun, 619–621, **619, 620, 621**
　solar, 136–137, **136, 137,** 519
　thermal, 452, **452,** 455, **455,** 601
　in thunderstorms, 496–497, **496, 497**
　tidal, 398, **398**
　units of, 134
　wave, 342–343, **343,** 399
energy resources. *See also* fossil fuels
　biomass, 139, **139**
　coal, 76, 128, **128,** 469 (*see also* coal)
　conserving, 124–125, **125, 322**
　fission, 134–135, **134, 135**
　fuel cells, 136, **136**
　fusion, 135, **135,** 149
　gasohol, 139, **139**
　geothermal, 140, **140,** 338
　hydroelectric, 138, **138,** 148
　labs on, **129,** 142–143
　natural gas, 127, **127**
　from oceans, 396, **396,** 398–399, **398**
　petroleum, 127, **127**
　pollution from, 132, **132**
　renewable vs. nonrenewable, 123, **123**
　solar, 136–137, **136, 137**
　wind power, 137, **137**
English units, **782**
environmental science, 10, **10**
Eocene epoch, **174**
eons, geologic, **174,** 175, **175**
EOS (Earth Observing System) program, 693
epicenters, 230, **230, 231**
epochs, geologic, **174,** 175, **175**
equal-area projections, 45, **45**
equator, 39, **39**
　celestial, **567**
　measuring circumference at, 54–55
　rising air at, 458, 459
eras, geologic, **174,** 175, **175**
Eratosthenes, 36, 54–55
erosion, 94, **94,** 295, **295,** 308, **308,** 342–361. *See also* deposition
　angle of repose and, 358, **358**
　deposition by waves, 346–347, **346, 347**
　deposition in water, 316–317, **316, 317**
　deposition on land, 318–319, **318, 319**
　effect of gravity on, 358–361, **358, 359, 360, 361**
　by glaciers, 352–357, **352, 353, 354, 355, 356, 357**
　labs on, **349,** 362–363

Index **829**

erosion (continued)
　　load and, 312, **312**
　　from ocean waves, 343, 344–345, **344–345**
　　from overgrazing, 305
　　from rivers, 308, **308**, 311–312, **311, 312**
　　rock cycle and, **91–92**, 92–93, **93,** 94
　　of shorelines, 342–347
　　of soil, 295, **295**
　　stages of rivers and, 313, **313**
　　unconformities and, 159–160, **159, 160**
　　underground, 324–325, **324, 325,** 338
　　wind, 279, **279,** 348–351, **348, 349, 350**
eruptions
　　climate change and, 256, **256,** 538, **538**
　　explosive, 251, **251,** 252, **252,** 254
　　gas release from, 264, 627, **627**
　　lab on, 266–267
　　lava flows from, 101, **101,** 250, **250, 251**
　　magma in, 252, **252**
　　nonexplosive, 250, **250,** 253
　　predicting, 264–265, 266–267
　　pyroclastic flows from, 253–255, **254**
　　water in, 252, 263, **263**
escape velocity, 687, **687**
Eta Carinae, 610, **610**
Europa, 665, 697
European Space Agency (ESA), 653, 681
evaporation
　　mineral formation from, **74**
　　of ocean water, 376, **379,** 397, **397, 420**
　　in the water cycle, **309,** 379, 482
evergreen trees, 531, 534
expansion of the universe, 570, 600–603
experimental groups, 786
experiments, controlled, 14
Explorer 1, 688
extinctions, 175–177, **175,** 539, **672**
　　of dinosaurs, 154, **154,** 177, 539
extinct volcanoes, 264
extrusive igneous rock, 101, **101**
Exxon Valdez oil spill, 402–403, **402, 403**
eyes, of hurricanes, **500**
eyes, rods and cones in, **584**
eye wall, **500**

F

Fahrenheit scale, 24, **24,** 783
fales, 527
fault-block mountains, 211, **211**
fault blocks, 208, **208,** 210, 212, **212**
faults, 208, **208**
　　earthquakes and, 224, 226–227, **226–227**
　　effect on rock layers, 158, **158**
　　normal and reverse, 208–209, **208, 209,** 211, **211, 226,** 227
　　in rift zones, 212, **212**
　　strike-slip, 209, **209,** 226, **226**
　　types of, 226, **226–227**
feathered dinosaurs, 184
feldspar, **68, 75**
felsic rocks, 99, **99**
fine-grained texture, 96, **96,** 99, **99**
fingerprinting cars, **583**
first law of motion, Newton's, 798
fish, raining, 32
fish farming, 395, **395**
fishing, 394–395, **394, 395,** 412
fission, 134–135, **134, 135**
fissures, 101
flash floods, 319
Flashline Mars Arctic Research Station (FMARS), 712
flexible pipes, **237**
FLIP (Floating Instrument Platform), 32
flood plains, 314, **314,** 318–319, **318, 319**
floods, safety during, 502
fluorescence, **73**
fluorine, 68, **69**
fluorite, **69, 72, 800–801**
FMARS (Flashline Mars Arctic Research Station), 712
focus, earthquake, 230, **230**
fog, 486
folded mountains, 207, **207,** 210, **210**
folding, 158, **158,** 207, **207**
FoldNote instructions, 776–778, **776, 777, 778**
folds, 111, **111**
foliated rock, 109, **109**
Folk, Robert L., 119, **119**
fool's gold (pyrite), 70, **75,** 80–81, **800–801**
footwalls, 208–209, **208**
force, net, 799
forecasting earthquakes, 235–236, **235, 236,** 246
forecasting weather, 504–507, **504, 505, 506, 507,** 514
forensic science, **583**

forests
　　acid precipitation and, 467, **467**
　　cave formations in, 338
　　deforestation, **291**
　　northern coniferous, **533,** 534, **534**
　　temperate, 292, **292, 530,** 531, **531**
　　tropical rain, 291, **291,** 526, **526,** 527, **527**
formaldehyde, **466**
fossil fuels, 126–133, **126.** *See also* energy resources
　　coal, 76, 128, **128,** 469 (*see also* coal)
　　formation of, 129–130, **129, 130**
　　lab on, **129**
　　location of, 131, **131**
　　natural gas, 127, **127,** 129, **129,** 131
　　obtaining, 131, **131**
　　petroleum, 127, **127,** 129, **129,** 131–132
　　problems with, 132, **132,** 548
fossiliferous limestone, 104, **104**
fossils, 166–171, **166**
　　absolute dating of, 162–165, **162, 163, 164, 165**
　　casts, 168, **168**
　　dinosaur, 33, 168, **168,** 172, **172,** 184
　　fossilized organisms, 166–167, **166, 167**
　　frozen, 167, **167,** 184
　　geologic time and, 172–173, **172, 173**
　　index, 170–171, **170–171**
　　information from, 169–170
　　labs on, **157, 169,** 178–179
　　limestone from, 104, **104**
　　mineral replacement in, 167
　　molds, 168, **168**
　　record, 173, **173**
　　relative dating of, 156–161, **156, 157, 158, 159, 160**
　　trace, 168, **168**
four-corner fold instructions (FoldNote), 778, **778**
fractionation, **127**
fractions, 791
fracture, mineral, 71, **71, 801**
Fran, Hurricane, **499**
France, tidal bores in, 435
Frank landslide of 1903, 368
freezing, ocean currents and, **420**
freezing points, **24,** 98, **783**
friction, permeability and, 321, **321**
frogs, raining, 32
Fronk, Robert, 6
fronts, air, 492–493, **492–493,** 507
frost action, 278, **278**
frozen fossils, 167, **167,** 184
fuel cells, 136, **136**

830 Index

Fuji, Mount, 257, **257**
fusion, 620, **620**
    energy production from, 135, **135,** 149, 593, 620–621
    in star formation, 593, 617
    study of, 149
    in the sun, 617, 620–621, **621**

G

gabbro, **99**
Gagarin, Yuri, 700, **700**
Gagnan, Emile, 413
galactic halos, 598
galaxies, 596–599, **596**
    contents of, 598, **598**
    Doppler effect and, 570, **570**
    Hubble's discoveries of, 557, 570
    Milky Way galaxy, **562,** 597, **597**
    origin of, 599, **599**
    types of, 596–597, **596–597**
galena
    formation of, **75**
    properties of, **69,** 80–81, **800–801**
    uses of, **78**
Galilean satellites, 665
Galileo, 9, 556
Galileo missions, 654, **660,** 697, **697**
gamma ray telescopes, **562,** 563
Ganymede, 665
gap hypothesis, 235–236, **235, 236**
garnets, **74, 108, 800–801**
gases, volcanic, 264, 627, **627**
gas giants, 654, **654**
gasohol, 139, **139**
gasoline, **400**
GCF (greatest common factor), 791
Geiger counters, **73**
gemstones, 79, **79,** 87
GEO (geostationary orbit), 689, **689,** 691
geocaching, 60
geochemistry, 10, **10**
geochemists, 10, **10**
geographic information systems (GIS), 11, 48, **48**
geography, 11
geological oceanographers, 7
geologic column, 157, **157,** 178–179
geologic time
    fossil record and, 173, **173**
    geologic time scale, 174–177, **174, 175**
    lab on, **157**
    rock record and, 172–173
geologic time scale, 174–177, **174, 175**

geology, 6, **6,** 152–155
    historical, 152–155
Geosat, 383, **383**
geostationary orbit (GEO), 689, **689,** 691
geothermal energy, 140, **140,** 338
The Geysers power plant, 140
giant elliptical galaxies, 597
giant squids, 412
giant stars, 591, **593**
gibbous moon, 662, **662**
gibbsite, **78**
Gillette, David D., 13–16, **14, 15, 17**
GIS (geographic information systems), 11, 48, **48**
glacial drift, 356–357, **356, 357**
glacial horns, **355**
glacial periods, 536, **536**
glaciers, 352, **352**
    alpine, 352, **352,** 354, **354, 355**
    continental, 353–354, **354**
    deposits from, 356–357, **356, 357**
    glacial periods, 536, **536**
    lab on, 362–363
    landforms carved by, 354, **354, 355**
    movement of, 353, **354**
    in North America, **353**
    pressure and melting rate of, 363
    Lost Squadron and, 368
Glenn, John, 700, **700**
global positioning system (GPS), 48, **48**
    geocaching using, 60
    predicting volcanic eruptions with, 265
    solar-powered satellites in, 690
    tracking tectonic plate motion with, 205, **205**
global warming, 457, **457,** 540–541, **540,** 548
global winds, 417, **417, 418,** 460–461, **461**
globes, 42
globular clusters, 598, **598**
globules, in nebulas, 615
Glossopteris fossils, **198**
gneiss, 109, **109**
Gobi Desert, dust from, 304
Goddard, Robert, 684, **684**
gold
    formation of, **75**
    mineral composition of, 67, **67**
    mining of, 76, 317, **317**
    properties of, **69,** 72, 81
    uses of, 78, **78**
Gondwana, 199, **199**
Gould, Stephen J., 154
GPS (global positioning system), 48, **48**
    geocaching using, 60

    predicting volcanic eruptions using, 265
    solar-powered satellites in, 690
    tracking tectonic plate motion with, 205, **205**
gradients, 311, **311,** 313
graduated cylinders, **23,** 784
grams (g), **22,** 24, **782**
Grand Canyon National Park, 173, 308, **308**
granite, 95, **95,** 278, 281
Graphic Organizer instructions, 779–781, **779, 780, 781**
graphite, **74,** 800–801
graphs, **591,** 787–789
grasslands
    temperate, 292, **292,** 530, 531, **531**
    tropical savanna, **526,** 528, **528**
gravity
    erosion and, 358–361, **358, 359, 360, 361**
    escape velocity and, 687, **687**
    formation of Earth and, 624–625, **624, 625**
    mass and, 632–633, **632, 633**
    in nebulas, 614–615, **615**
    Newton's law of universal gravitation, 632–633, **632, 633,** 798
    orbits and, 556, 632–633, **632, 633**
    in the sun, 619
    tides and, 432–434, **432, 433, 434**
Great Basin Desert, **532**
Great Dark Spot (Neptune), **657**
greatest common factor (GCF), 791
Great Red Spot (Jupiter), **495,** 654
greenhouse effect, 456, **456,** 540, **540**
    carbon dioxide and, 457, 540, **626**
    global warming and, 457, **457,** 540, **540**
    habitability of Earth and, 456, **456**
    on Venus, 649
Greenland, climate of, 523
Green River formation, 173, **173**
ground moraines, **356**
groundwater
    acids in, 282, **282**
    aquifers, 321–322, **321, 322,** 330, **330**
    labs on, **321, 327,** 332–333
    location of, 320, **320**
    recharge zones for, 322, **322**
    springs and wells, 322–323, **323**
    underground erosion and deposition by, 324–325, **324, 325,** 338

groundwater (continued)
    water table, 320, **320**, 322, **322**
groups, in the periodic table, 796
Gulf Stream
    climate and, 422, **422**, 523, **523**
    location of, **380**, 417
    as surface current, **417**, **419**
    temperature regulation by, 380, **380**
gypsum
    formation of, **74**
    properties of, **69**, **72**, **800–801**
    uses of, 78, **78**

H

habitat, soil as, 294, 305
habitat restoration, 305, **305**
HABs (harmful algal blooms), 442
hadal zone, 391, **391**
Hadean Eon, **174**, 175
hadrosaurs, 185
hail, 488, **488**
half-lives, dating by using, **163**, 163–165
halides, **69**, **800–801**
halite
    as chemical sedimentary rock, 103
    formation of, **74**
    properties of, **71**, **73**, **800–801**
    structure of, 67, **67**
    uses of, **78**
Hallucigenia, 175, **175**
halos, galactic, 598
hanging valleys, **355**
hanging walls, 208–209, **208**
hardness, mineral, 72, **72**, **800**
harmful algal blooms (HABs), 442
Haughton Crater, 712
headlands, **345**
health, air pollution and, 469, **469**
heat (thermal energy). *See also* temperature
    in the atmosphere, 452, **452**
    from the big bang, 601
    conduction and convection of, 455, **455**
    in the formation of the Earth, 624
    in metamorphism, 94
hectares, **782**
Hektor, 670, **670**
helium
    atomic structure of, **620**
    emission lines of, **583**
    isotopes of, **621**
    on the moon, 704
    from nuclear fusion, **135**, **621**
hematite, 71, **71**, **74**, **800–801**
Hendrickson, Sue, 33

Henson, Matthew, 61
herbicides, **400**
Herschel, William, 656
Hertzsprung, Ejnar, 591
Hertzsprung-Russell diagram (H-R diagram), 591–592, **591**, **592–593**
Heyerdahl, Thor, 416, **416**
    Kon Tiki and, **416**
high tides, 433, **433**
Hill, Jamie, 87
Himalayas, 210
historical geology, 152–155
history of Earth, 152–177
    absolute dating and, 162–165, **162**, **163**, **164**, **165**
    catastrophism and, 153, **153**
    fossils and, 166–171, **166**, **167**, **168**, **169**, **170**
    in modern geology, 154, **154**
    paleontology and, 155, **155**
    relative dating and, 156–161, **156**, **157**, **158**, **159**, **160**
    uniformitarianism and, 152–153, **152**, **153**
HMS *Challenger*, 406
holdfasts, 389
Holocene epoch, **174**
Hood, Mount, 257
horizon, 566, **566**
horizons, soil, 290, **290**
hornblende, **800–801**
horns, glacial, **355**
Horsehead Nebula, 614, **614**
horse latitudes, 461, **461**
hot spots, 263–264, **264**
hot springs, 323
hot-water solutions, **75**
H-R diagram (Hertzprung-Russell diagram), 591–592, **591**, **592–593**
Hubble, Edwin, 557, 570, 596–597
Hubble Space Telescope, 560, **560**, 570, 596
human population growth, **19**, 20
humidity, 286, 483–485, **483**, **484**
humpback whales, 443
humus, 290, **290**
hurricanes, 499, **499**
    Andrew, 8, **8**, 458
    damage from, 501, **501**
    formation and structure of, **500**, 501, **501**
    Fran, 499
    typhoons, cyclones, and, 499
    winds in, **500**, 501
Hutton, James, 152–153, **152**, **153**
Huygens, Christian, 665
Huygens probe, 698
hybrid cars, 148, 470
hydrocarbons, 127, **128**. *See also* fossil fuels

hydroelectric energy, 138, **138**, 148
hydrogen
    emission lines of, **583**
    fusion of, 621, **621**
    ions of, 797
    isotopes of, **135**, **621**
    in stars, **590**
hydronium ions, 797
hydrothermal vents, 7, **7**, 386, 391
hydroxide ions, 797
hypersoar jets, 478
hypotheses (singular, *hypothesis*), 14–15, **14**, 785–786

I

ice ages, 536–538, **536**, **537**, **538**
icebergs, **353**
ice cores, 548
Iceland, 262, 272, 523
ice shelves, **353**
ice volcanoes, 666
ice wedging, 278, **278**, 286, **286**
ichthyosaurs, 185
igneous rock, 98–101
    composition and texture of, 99, **99**
    extrusive, 101, **101**
    formation of, 98, **98**
    intrusive, 100, **100**
    in the rock cycle, **91–92**, 92–93, **93**
ilmenite, **78**
impacts
    craters from, 681
    extinctions from, 154, **154**, 176, 539, **539**
    formation of the moon from, 661, **661**
    in the future, 672
    role of, 672, **672**
    shock metamorphism from, 118
    Torino Scale, 673
impermeability, 321, **321**
Inca Ice Maiden, 369
independent variables, 788
index contours, 51, **51**
index fossils, 170–171, **170**, **171**
index minerals, 108, **108**
indoor air pollution, 466, **466**
inertia, orbits and, 633, **633**
infiltration, 289
infrared radiation, 456, **456**, 562
infrared satellite images, 265
inner core, **192–193**
inner planets, 646, **646**. *See also* Earth
    Earth, 650, **650**
    Mars, **644**, 651–653, **651**, **652**, **653**

Mercury, 630, **644,** 648, **648**
Venus, **644,** 649, **649,** 695, **695**
intensity of earthquakes, 233, **233**
    Modified Mercalli Intensity Scale and, 233
interglacial periods, **527,** 537
International Dark Sky Association, 578
International Space Station (ISS), 703, **703**
intertidal zone, 389, **389**
intrusions, 158, **158**
intrusive igneous rock, 100, **100**
Io, **654,** 665, **665,** 680
iodine, 68, **69**
ionosphere, 453, **453**
ion rockets, 699, **699**
ions, 453, **453,** 668
ion tails, 668, **668, 669**
iron
    in minerals, 68, **69**
    rust, 283, **283**
    uses of, **78**
irregular galaxies, 597, **597**
irrigation, 330, **330**
isobars, 507, **507**
isotopes, 162, **162,** 796
    absolute dating using, 162–163, **162, 163,** 165
    of carbon, 165
    of helium, **621**
    of hydrogen, **135,** 621
    parent and daughter, **162,** 163
Israel, agriculture in, **330**
ISS (International Space Station), 703, **703**

J

JASON II, 387
JASON project, **386**
jets, hypersoar, 478
jet skis, nonpoint-source pollution and, **400**
jet streams, 462, **462**
joules, 134
Jupiter
    as gas giant, 654
    Great Red Spot, **495,** 654
    missions to, 697, **697**
    moons of, 665, **665**
    relative size of, **644**
    statistics on, **654**
    storms on, **495**
Jurassic period, **174**

K

Kamchatka, crater in, **258**
Kanamori, Hiroo, 247
karst features, 282, **282**
Keck Telescopes, 560, **560**
kelp, 395, **395**
Kelvin, Thomas, 86
kelvins (K), **22,** 24, **783**
Kepler, Johannes, 556, **556,** 630–631, **631**
Kepler's laws of planetary motion, 631, **631**
ketchup, acids in, **282**
kettles, 357, **357**
key-term fold instructions (FoldNote), 778, **778**
Kilimanjaro, Mount, 522
kilograms (kg), **22,** 24, **782**
kilometers (km), **22, 782**
Kitt Peak National Observatory, 640
Kobe (Japan), earthquake of 1995, **236**
Kon Tiki, **416**
krypton, **134**
Kuiper belt, 669
Kuskowin River, **311**
Kuwait, desalination in, **397**

L

La Brea asphalt deposits, 167
lahars, 360, **360**
lake ecosystems, 468
lakes, kettle, 357, **357**
land breezes, 462, **462**
land degradation, 295
Landsat program, 692–693, **692**
landslides, 359, **359,** 368
La Niña, 424–425, **424**
lapilli, **254**
Large Magellanic Cloud, 597, **597**
lateral moraines, **356**
latitude, 39, **39,** 519, **519**
    climate zones and, 524, **524**
    seasons and, 520, **520**
    solar energy and, 519, **519**
    used to find location, 40, **41**
Laurasia, 199, **199**
lava
    from fissures, 101
    flows, 101, **101,** 250, **250,** 251
    types of, 253, **253,** 272
lava fountains, **250**
lava plateaus, 101, 259, **259**
law of conservation of energy, 798
law of universal gravitation, 632–633, **632, 633,** 798
laws of motion, Newton's, 686, **686, 707,** 798
layered book instructions (FoldNote), 777, **777**

leaching, **290**
lead, **69, 164**
least common denominator (LCD), 792
legends, map, **46,** 52, **52**
length, units of, **22,** 23, **782**
lenses, telescope, 558–559, **559**
LEO (low Earth orbit), **689,** 689–691
levees, 319
lichens, 282, **282,** 533
life
    in the benthic environment, 389–391, **389, 390, 391**
    classification of, 388, **388**
    effects on atmosphere, 627–628
    in the neritic zone, 392, **392**
    in the oceanic zone, 393, **393**
    origins in the ocean, 627–628, **628**
    in the pelagic environment, 392, **392**
    upwelling and, 423–424, **423**
light
    absorption lines, 584, **584**
    continuous spectrum, 583
    electromagnetic spectrum, 561, **561**
    emission lines, 583–584, **583**
    lab on, **562**
    pollution, 578
    visible, 561, **561**
light-minutes, 645, **645**
lightning, 497, **497,** 501, 691
light pollution, 578
light-years, 568, **568,** 587, **587**
lignite, 130, **130**
limestone
    from bacteria, 118
    caves in, 282, **282**
    composition of, **95**
    formation of, **74**
    fossiliferous, 104, **104**
    weathering of, 298–299
line graphs, 788–789
liquids, volume measurements of, 23, **23,** 784
liters (L), **22,** 23, **782**
lithosphere, **192–193**
    at mid-ocean ridges, 200, **200**
    tectonic plates and, 195, 202–204, **202–203, 204**
Little Ice Age, 623
load, stream, 312, **312**
Local Group, **569**
local winds, 462–463, **462, 463**
loess, 350, **350**
Loma Prieta earthquake of 1989, 236, **236**
longitude, 40, **40,** 41
long period seismic waves, 247

longshore currents, 346–347, **346,** 429, **429**
Los Angeles, air pollution in, 465, **465**
Lost Squadron, 368
low Earth orbit (LEO), **689,** 689–691
low tides, 433, **433**
Luna (moon of Earth)
    eclipses of, 663–664, **663**
    effect on tides, 432–433, **432, 433**
    formation of, 661, **661**
    gravitational attraction with the Earth, 632, **632**
    missions to, 694
    orbit of, 633, **633,** 664
    phases of, 662, **662**
    statistics on, **660**
    surface of, 660
Luna missions, 694, **694**
lunar eclipses, 663–664, **663**
lunar phases, 662, **662**
Lunar Prospector, 694
luster, 70, **70, 800**
Lyell, Charles, 153, **153**

M

M87 galaxy, 597, **597**
"The Mad Moon," 680
mafic rocks, 99, **99**
Magellan missions, 649, 695, **695**
magma
    chambers, 252, **252,** 258, **258**
    composition of, 98, **98,** 252
    contact metamorphism and, 106, **106**
    at divergent boundaries, 262, **262**
    formation of, 260–261, **260, 263, 263**
    in lava flows, 101, **101**
    at mid-ocean ridges, 200, **200**
    mineral formation from, **75**
    in the rock cycle, **91, 93**
    temperature of, **262**
    in undersea volcanic vents, **191**
    in volcanic eruptions, 252, **252**
magma chambers, 252, **252,** 258, **258**
magnesium, **68**
magnetic declination, 38–39, **38, 39**
magnetic fields, polarity of, 200–201, **200, 201**
magnetic poles, 38, **38,** 200, **200**
magnetic reversals, 200–201, **200, 201**
magnetism, in minerals, **68, 73**

magnetite
    in animals, **68**
    formation of, **74–75**
    properties of, **73, 800–801**
    uses of, **78**
magnitude, earthquake, 232, **232, 235**
magnitudes, star, 585–586, **586, 592–593**
main-sequence stars, 590, **590,** 592, **592–593**
major axis, 631, **631**
Mammals, Age of (Cenozoic era), **174,** 177, **177**
mammoths, 167, **167,** 184
manganese nodules, 398, **398**
mantle, 191, **191,** 625, **625**
    composition of, 191
    formation of, 625, **625**
    magma formation in, 261
    plumes, 264, **264**
mapmaking, 11, 47–48, **47, 48**
maps, 36, **36**
    of the ancient world, **36**
    azimuthal projections, 45, **45**
    cartography, 11
    conic projections, 44, **44**
    cylindrical projections, 43, **43**
    distortions in, 42, **42**
    equal-area projections, 45, **45**
    labs on, **38,** 54–55, **565**
    latitude on, 39, **39,** 40, **41**
    legends, **46,** 52, **52**
    longitude on, 40, **40, 41**
    magnetic declination on, 38–39, **38, 39**
    mapmaking, 11, 47–48, **47, 48**
    Mercator projections, 43, **43**
    sky, 565, **565, 802–803**
    topographic, 50–53, **50, 51, 52**
    weather, 506–507, **506, 507**
marble, 110, **110**
maria, lunar, **660**
marine biologists, 443
marine life
    in the benthic environment, 389–391, **389, 390, 391**
    classification of, 388, **388**
    in the neritic zone, 392, **392**
    in the oceanic zone, 393, **393**
    in the pelagic environment, 392, **392**
    upwelling and, 423–424, **423**
Marine Protection Act of 1972, 405
maritime polar (mP) air mass, **490,** 491
maritime tropical (mT) air mass, **490,** 491
Mars
    atmosphere of, 651
    missions to, 651–653, **653,** 696, **696,** 712

    moons of, 665
    relative size of, **644**
    statistics on, **651**
    volcanoes on, 652
    water on, 651–652, **651**
Mars Express, 712
Mars Express Orbiter, 653
Mars Pathfinder, 651, **652,** 696, **696**
Mars Society, 712
mass, 24, **24**
    gravity and, 632–633, **632, 633**
    measurement of, 784
    of stars, 641
    units of, **22,** 24, **782**
mass dampers, **237**
mass extinctions, 539, 672, **672**
mass movement, 358, **358.** *See also* deposition; erosion
    angle of repose and, 358, **358**
    rapid, 359, **359**
    slow, 361, **361**
masses, air, 490–495
mathematical ecologists, 549
mathematical models, 19, **19,** 21, **21**
math refresher, 790–793
matter, 620, **620,** 796
Mauna Kea, 257, **257**
Maxwell, James Clerk, 561
May, Lizzie and Kevin, 185
McAuliffe, Christa, 701
McMath-Pierce solar telescope, 640
mean, 790
meanders, **313,** 316
measurements, 22–25
    of mass, 784
    of relative humidity, 484, **484**
    of the size of the Earth, 54–55
    tools for, 784
    using hands, **23**
    of volumes, 23, **23**
mechanical weathering, 278–280, **278, 279, 280**
Medea, 387
medial moraines, **356**
medium-grained texture, 96, **96**
megaplumes, 220
megawatts (MWe), 134
melting points, 98, **98**
Mercator, Gerardus, 44
Mercator projections, 43, **43**
Mercury (planet), 630, **644,** 648, **648**
Mercury-Atlas rockets, **685**
meridians (longitude), 40, **40, 41**
Mesosaurus fossils, 198
mesosphere, **192–193, 450,** 451, **451**
Mesozoic era, **174,** 176, **176**
metallic minerals, 70, **70,** 78
"The Metal Man," 86

metamorphic rock, 106–111
　composition of, 108, **108**
　foliated, 109, **109**
　lab on, **107**
　metamorphism and, **92,** 106, **106,** 118
　nonfoliated, 110, **110**
　origins of, **74,** 106–107, **106, 107**
　in the rock cycle, **91–92,** 92–93, **93,** 94
　structures in, 111, **111**
　textures of, 109–110, **109, 110**
metamorphism, **92,** 106, **106,** 118
metamorphosis, biological, **110**
meteorites, 671, **671**
meteoroids, 671, **671**
meteorologists, 8, **21,** 504, 515
meteorology, 8, **8,** 21, **21,** 515
meteors, **627,** 671, **671**
meteor showers, 671
meters (m), **22,** 23, **23, 782**
metersticks, 784, **784**
methane, 127
metric rulers, 784, **784**
metric tons, 24
mica
　biotite, **68**
　formation of, **74,** 75
　muscovite, **108, 800–801**
　properties of, 68, 71, **800–801**
microclimates, 534–535, **534, 535**
microscopes, 119
Mid-Atlantic Ridge, 262
mid-ocean ridges, 385, **385**
　divergent boundaries at, 203, **203,** 262, **262**
　lithosphere at, 200, **200**
　magma at, 200, **200**
　magnetic reversals at, 200–201, **200, 201**
　megaplumes at, 220
　ocean floor structure and, 385, **385**
　ridge push at, **204**
　sea-floor spreading at, 200, **200**
Milankovitch, Milutin, 537
Milankovitch theory, 537, **537**
military satellites, 690, **690**
Milky Way galaxy, **562,** 597, **597**
millimeters (mm), **22, 782**
mineral replacement, 167, **167**
minerals, 66–69. *See also names of individual minerals*
　alignment during metamorphism, 106, **106**
　atoms in, 67, **67**
　chemical reaction and, 68
　cleavage and fracture in, 71, **71**
　color of, 70, **70,** 79, **800**
　compounds in, 67, **67**
　crystals, 67, **67**
　density of, 72, 80–81

　as dissolved load, **312**
　formation of, **74–75**
　flourescence of, **73**
　fracture, 71, **71, 801**
　gemstones, 79, **79,** 87
　hardness of, 72, **72, 800**
　identification of, 70–73, **70, 71, 72, 73**
　index, 108, **108**
　labs on, **72,** 80–81
　luster of, 70, **70, 800**
　magnetic, **68, 73**
　metallic, 70, **70,** 78
　mining of, 76–77, **76, 77,** 317, **317**
　nonmetallic, 70, **70,** 78
　nonsilicate, 68, **68, 69**
　from the ocean floor, 398, **398**
　optical properties of, 68, **73**
　properties of common, **73, 800–801**
　radioactivity of, 68, **73**
　recycling, **77**
　silicate, 68, **68, 69**
　streak of, 71, **71, 800**
　structure of, 66, **66**
　taste of, 68
　uses of, 78–79, **78, 801**
mining
　of coal, 76, 132
　of copper, 76
　of gold, 76, 317, **317**
　of minerals, 76–77, **76, 77,** 317, **317**
　of salt, 86
　strip, 76, 131
　subsurface, 77, **77**
　surface, 76, **76,** 131
Miocene epoch, **174**
Miranda, 666, **666**
mirrors, telescope, 559, **559**
Mir space station, 702, **702**
Mississippian period, **174**
Mississippi River
　delta, 317, **317, 692**
　flood plains, 314, **314,** 318–319, **318, 319**
　Huckleberry Finn and, **313**
　watershed of, 310, **310**
Mitchell, Cristy, 515
moai of Easter Island, 118
models, 18, **19**
　choosing, 20, **20**
　conceptual, 19
　of the Earth, 20, **20,** 192
　lab on, 214–215
　mathematical, 19, **19,** 21, **21**
　physical, 18, **18**
　raisin-bread, 600
　of the solar system, 555–556, **555**
　station, 506, **506**

Modified Mercalli Intensity Scale, 233
Mohs hardness scale, 72, **72**
molds, 168, **168**
molecules, 797
mollusks, limestone from, 104, **104**
monoclines, 207, **207**
months, 554, **554**
Mont-St-Michel, **433**
Monument Valley (Arizona), **102**
moon (moon of Earth)
　eclipses, 663–664, **663**
　effect on tides, 432–433, **432, 433**
　formation of, 661, **661**
　gravitational attraction of, 632, **632**
　missions to, 694, **694**
　orbit of, 633, **633,** 664
　phases of, 662, **662**
　statistics on, **660**
　surface of, 660
moons, of other planets, 660–667
moraines, 356, **356**
mosses, **533**
motion, Newton's laws of, 686, **686, 707,** 798
mountains
　breezes in, 463
　climate and, 522, **522**
　fault-block, 211, **211**
　folded, 207, **207,** 210, **210**
　volcanic, 211
　weathering in, 287, **287**
mP (maritime polar) air mass, **490,** 491
mT (maritime tropical) air mass, **490,** 491
mud cracks, 105
mudflows, 360, **360**
multiplying fractions, 792
muscovite mica, **108, 800–801**

N

nannobacteria, 119
National Aeronautics and Space Administration (NASA), 650, 681
National Oceanic and Atmospheric Administration (NOAA), 425, 506
National Weather Service (NWS), 506, **506,** 515
Native Americans, 149
native elements, 67, **69**
natural gas, 127, **127**
　formation of, 129, **129**
　location of, 131, **131**
　as a nonrenewable resource, 396, **396**

natural resources, 122–125. *See also* energy resources; fossil fuels; ocean resources
　conservation of, 124–125, **125, 322,** 331
　examples of, **122**
　habitat restoration, 305, **305**
　renewable vs. nonrenewable, 123, **123,** 396
　soil conservation, 294–297, **294, 295, 296, 297**
Navajos, 149
Neal, Tina, 273
neap tides, 434, **434**
near-infrared telescopes, **562**
nebulas, 598, **598,** 614, **614**
　examples of, **598, 614**
　formation of, 614–615, **615**
　solar, 615–616, **616**
necks, volcanic, **100**
nekton, 388, **388, 389**
neon emission lines, 583–584, **583**
Neptune
　atmosphere of, 657, **657**
　discovery of, 646
　Great Dark Spot, **657**
　moons of, 666, **666**
　relative size of, **644**
　statistics on, **657**
neritic zone, 392, **392**
net force, 799
neutrons, **620,** 796
neutron stars, 594, **594**
Newfoundland, 422
New Madrid earthquakes of 1812, **232**
New Millennium program, 699
Newton, Sir Isaac
　contributions to astronomy, 556
　first law of motion, 798
　law of universal gravitation, 632–633, **632, 633,** 798
　second law of motion, 798
　third law of motion, 686, 798
nickel, **69**
Nile Delta, 317, **317**
nimbostratus clouds, 486, **487**
nitrates, 327, **327**
nitrogen, in the atmosphere, 448, **448**
nitrogen oxides, **466**
NOAA (National Oceanic and Atmospheric Administration), 425, 506
noble gases, 796
nodules, 398, **398**
nonconformities, 160, **160**
nondeposition, rock record and, 159, **159**
nonexplosive eruptions, 250, **250,** 253

nonfoliated metamorphic rock, 110, **110**
nonlinear relationships, 788
nonmetallic minerals, 70, **70,** 78
nonoptical telescopes, 561–563, **561, 562, 563**
nonpoint-source pollution, 326, **326,** 400, **400**
nonrenewable resources, 123, **123,** 396, **396.** *See also* energy resources; fossil fuels
nonsilicate minerals, 68, **68, 69**
normal faults, 208, **208, 209,** 211, **211**
normal polarity, **200**
North Atlantic Deep Water, 420
North Pole, **37,** 38, **38,** 61, **200**
no-till farming, 296, **296**
nuclear energy, 134, **134**
　fission, 134–135, **134, 135**
　fusion, 135, **135,** 149, 593, 620–621 (*see also* nuclear fusion)
　radioactive wastes from, 135
　in the sun, 617, 620–621, **620, 621**
nuclear fusion, 620, **620**
　energy production from, 135, **135,** 149, 593, 620–621
　in star formation, 593, 617
　study of, 149
　in the sun, 617, 620–621, **620, 621**
nuclear wastes, 135
nucleus, atomic, 796
nucleus, cometary, 668, **668**
nutrients
　in ocean currents, 423, **423**
　in soil, 290, 291–293, **294,** 304
NWS (National Weather Service), 506, **506,** 515

O

objective lenses, 558
observations, 15, 785
Ocampo, Adriana C., 681
occluded fronts, 493, **493**
ocean currents, 416, **416**
　climate and, 422–423, **422, 423,** 523, **523**
　convection and, **419,** 455, **455**
　deep, 419–420, **420, 421**
　El Niño and, 424–425, **424,** 443, 549
　Heyerdahl's explorations of, 416, **416**
　La Niña and, 424–425, **424**
　longshore, 429, **429**

　surface, 417–419, **417, 418, 419, 421** (*see also* surface currents)
　tracking, 442
　upwelling and, 423, **423**
oceanic crust
　continental crust and, 190, **190**
　magnetic reversals in, 201, **201**
　plate tectonics and, 195, **195, 202**
oceanic-oceanic boundaries, 203
oceanic-oceanic collisions, **202**
oceanic zone, 393, **393**
oceanography, 7, **7, 15**
ocean resources, 394–399
　fresh water and desalination, 397, **397**
　living, 394–395, **394, 395,** 412
　minerals, 398, **398**
　oil and gas, 396, **396**
　pollution and, 400–405, **400, 401, 402, 403, 404**
　protecting, 404–405, **404**
　tidal and wave energy, 398–399, **398**
oceans, 374–405, 414–435. *See also* ocean currents; ocean resources; ocean water; waves, ocean
　divisions of global ocean, 374, **374**
　energy resources from, 396, **396,** 398–399, **398**
　evaporation, 376, **379,** 397, **397, 420**
　floor, 382–385, **382, 383, 384–385,** 385, 406–407
　formation of, 375, 628–629
　as global thermostat, 380, **380**
　hydrothermal vents in, 7, **7,** 386, 391
　labs on, **397,** 406–407
　life in, 388–393, **388, 389, 390, 391**
　living resources from, 394–395, **394, 395**
　megaplumes in, 220
　mineral resources in, 398, **398**
　pollution of, 400–405, **400, 401, 402, 403, 404**
　protecting, 404–405, **404**
　recent history of, 375, **375**
　sea-floor spreading in, 199–201, **200, 201**
　submarine volcanoes in, **378, 385**
　temperature zones in, 377–378, **377, 378**
　tides and, 432–435, **433, 434, 435, 436**
　trenches, 385, **385**

836 Index

underwater vessels in, 386–387, **386**
water cycle and, 379, **379**
water movement in, 377, **377**
ocean trenches, 385, **385**
ocean water. *See also* ocean currents; shorelines; waves, ocean
characteristics of, 376–378, **376, 377, 378**
desalination of, 397, **397**
labs on, **397, 429,** 436–437
salinity of, 376–377, **376, 377**
surface height of, 383, **383**
surface temperature changes in, 378, **378**
temperature with depth in, 377–378, **377, 378,** 436–437
water cycle and, 379, **379**
octopuses, **390**
Ogallala aquifer, 330, **330**
oil resources, 396, **396, 400.** *See also* petroleum
oil spills, 132, **132,** 402–403, **402, 403**
Old Faithful, 258
Oligocene epoch, **174**
olivine, **800–801**
Olympus Mons, 652
Omega Centauri globular cluster, **598**
Oort, Jan, 640
Oort cloud, 640, 669
open clusters, 598, **598**
open-ocean waves, 430, **430**
open-pit mining, 76, **76**
optical properties of minerals, 68, **73**
optical telescopes, 9, 558–560, **558, 559, 560**
orbital velocity, 687, **687**
orbits, 630–631, **630**
comet, 669, **669**
geostationary, 689, **689,** 691
gravity and, 556, 632–633, **632, 633**
Kepler's laws of planetary motion, 631, **631**
lab on, **632**
low Earth, 689–691, **689**
of moon, 633, **633,** 664
Newton's law of universal gravitation, 632–633, **632, 633**
revolution and rotation, 630, **630**
satellite, 664, 688, **688,** 689, **689,** 798
Ordovician period, **174**
ore, 76, **76**
organic material, soil, 290, **290**

organic sedimentary rock, 103–104, **104**
Orion constellation, 564, **564,** 568
orthoclase, **72, 800–801**
outer core, **192–193**
outer planets, 647, **647**
Jupiter, **495, 644,** 654, **654,** 665
missions to, 655, 697–698, **697, 698**
Neptune, **644,** 646, 657, **657,** 666
Pluto, **644,** 646, 658–659, **658,** 680
Saturn, **644,** 655, **655,** 697
Uranus, **644,** 646, 656, **656,** 666
outwash plains, 357, **357**
overfishing, 394
overgrazing, 305
oxidation, weathering from, 283, **283,** 286, **286**
oxides, **69, 800–801**
oxygen
in the atmosphere, 448, **448**
dissolved, 327
in the early atmosphere, 626–628
in minerals, 68, **68,** 69
from photosynthesis, 628, **628**
rocket engines and, 686
ozone, as air pollutant, 465, **465**
ozone hole, 468, **468**
ozone layer, **450,** 451, 627–628

P

Pacific Ocean
coastal climate and, 523
El Niño and, 424–425, **424,** 443, 549
La Niña and, 424–425, **424**
surface currents in, **419,** 423, **423**
surface temperature changes in, **378**
pahoehoe lava, 253, **253**
Painted Desert, **349**
Paleocene epoch, **174**
paleontologists, 6, 33, **155,** 185
paleontology, 155, **155.** *See also* fossils
Paleozoic era, **174,** 176, **176**
Paneok, Ellen, 479
Pangaea, 199, **199, 375,** 538, **538**
Panthalassa, **199, 375**
parallax, 587, **587**
parallels (latitude), 39, **39,** 40, **41**
parent isotopes, **162,** 163
parent rock, 288, **288**
Paricutín, 257, **257**
particle size, porosity and, 321, **321**

particulates, testing for, **467**
Pascual, Mercedes, 549
payload, **685**
pearly luster, **70**
Peary, Lt. Robert E., 61
peat, 130, **130**
pegmatites, **75,** 87
pelagic environment, 392–393, **392, 393**
Pele's Hair, 272
penguins, 132, **132**
Pennsylvanian period, **174**
Penzias, Arno, **601**
percentages, 791
percolation, **309**
periodic table of the elements, **794–795,** 796
period of revolution, 630, 648
period of rotation, 648
periods, geologic, **174,** 175, **175**
periods, glacial, 536, **536**
periods, in the periodic table, 796
permafrost, 533
permeability, 129, **129,** 321–322, **321**
permeable rocks, 129, **129**
Permian period, **174**
permineralization, 167
pesticides, **400**
petrification, 167
petroleum, 127, **127**
crude oil, 127
formation of, 129, **129**
location of, 131, **131**
as a nonrenewable resource, 396, **396**
obtaining, 131, **131**
oil spills, 132, **132**
petrologists, 119
pH
alkalinity and, 327, **327**
of precipitation, 281, **281**
scale, 797, **797**
of soil, 291
weathering of rocks and, 281, **281**
Phacops, 171, **171**
Phanerozoic Eon, **174,** 175
phases of the moon, 662, **662**
Phobos, 665
photosphere, **618,** 621
photosynthesis, 628, **628**
phyllite, 109, **109**
physical models, 18, **18**
physical oceanographers, 7
phytoplankton, 388, **388**
pillow lava, 253, **253**
Pinatubo, Mount, 255, **255,** 256, **256**
Pioneer 10, 697, **697**
Pioneer 11, 697, **697**

Index **837**

placer deposits, 317, **317**
plagioclase, **800–801**
planetariums, 579
planetary geologists, 681
planetary motion, 630–633
    Kepler's laws of, 631, **631**
    Newton's law of universal gravitation, 632–633, **632, 633**
    Newton's laws of motion, 686, **686, 707,** 798
    revolution and rotation, 630, **630**
planetary systems, 602
planetesimals, 616–617, **616**
planets, 644–659
    Earth, 650, **650** (see also Earth)
    formation of, 616–617, **616**
    inner and outer, 646–647, **646, 647**
    Jupiter, **644,** 654, **654,** 665, 697
    Kepler's laws of planetary motion, 630–631, **630, 631**
    labs on, **663,** 674–675
    Mars, **644,** 651–653, **651, 652, 653** (see also Mars)
    Mercury, 630, **644,** 648, **648**
    moons of, 664–666, **665, 666**
    Neptune, **644,** 646, **657,** 657, 666
    Newton's law of universal gravitation, 632–633, **632, 633,** 798
    observations by Galileo, 556
    origin of term, 644
    Pluto, **644,** 646, 658–659, **658,** 680
    Saturn, **644,** 655, **655,** 697–698, **697**
    Uranus, **644,** 646, 656, **656, 666**
    Venus, **644,** 649, **649, 695,** 695
plankton, 388, **388, 389**
plants, 280, **280, 466,** 628, **628**
plastic deformation, 225, **225**
plastic pollution, 401, **401**
plate tectonics, 202, **203**
    causes of plate motion, 204, **204**
    climate change and, 538, **538**
    composition of the Earth and, 190–191, **190, 191**
    continental drift hypothesis, 198–199, **198, 199,** 221
    deformation and, 206, **206**
    earthquakes and, 224, **224,** 226–227, **226–227**
    faulting and, 208–209, **208, 209**
    folding and, 207, **207**
    hot spots and, 263, **264**
    labs on, **195, 209,** 214–215
    magnetic reversals and, 200–201, **200, 201**
    mountain building and, 210–211, **210, 211**
    physical structure and, **192–193**
    plate boundaries, 202–203, **202–203,** 261–263, **261, 262, 263**
    rivers and, 314, **314**
    sea-floor spreading and, 199–201, **200, 201**
    subsidence, 212, **212**
    tectonic plates, 194–195, **194, 195**
    theory of, 202–205
    tracking motion of, 205, 220
    tsunamis and, 247
    uplift and subsidence and, 212, **212**
    volcanoes and, 261–263, **261, 262, 263**
Pleiades, **598**
Pleistocene epoch, **174**
Pliocene epoch, **174**
Pluto, **644,** 646, 658–659, **658,** 680
plutons, **75,** 100, **100**
point-source pollution, 326, 401–403, **401, 402, 403**
polar easterlies, 460, **460, 461**
polarity of Earth's magnetic field, 200–201, **200, 201**
polar orbits, 691
polar zones, 533–534, **533, 534**
poles of the Earth, **37,** 38, **38, 458,** 459
pollution
    air, 464–471, **464, 465, 466, 468** (see also air pollution)
    from fossil fuels, 132, **132**
    light, 578
    nonpoint-source, 326, **326,** 400–403, **400, 401, 402, 403**
    point-source, 326, **326,** 400–403, **400, 401, 402, 403**
    ocean, 400–405, **400, 401, 402, 403, 404**
    oil spills, 132, **132,** 402–403, **402, 403**
    primary and secondary pollutants, 464–465, **464, 465**
    sludge dumping, 402, **402**
    thermal, 327
    trash dumping, 401, **401**
    water, 124, 326–327, **326, 327,** 339
Pompeii, 260
pond ecosystems, 468
population growth, human, **19, 20**
porosity, 321, **321**
potassium, 68, **69**
potassium-argon dating method, 164
power plants
    coal-burning, 128, **128,** 469, **469**
    fission, 134–135, **134, 135**

geothermal, 140, **140,** 338
hydroelectric, 138, **138,** 148
precipitation, **482,** 488, **488**
    acid, 281, **281,** 467–468, **467, 468**
    El Niño and, 424–425, **424**
    of fish and frogs, 32
    La Niña and, 424–425, **424**
    prevailing winds and, 521, **521**
    in rain shadows, **522, 532**
    in temperate biomes, **531, 532**
    in tropical biomes, **527, 528, 529**
    types of, 488, **488**
    in the water cycle, **309, 379, 482**
prefixes, unit, 782, **782**
pressure
    air, 449, **449,** 459, **462,** 471–472 (see also air pressure)
    calculation of, 799
    magma formation and, 98, **98,** 260, **260**
    in metamorphism, 94, 106
    in nebulas, 615, **615**
pressure belts, 459, **459**
prevailing winds, 521, **521**
primary pollutants, 464–465, **464, 465**
primary treatment, 328, **328**
primary waves, 228, **228**
prime meridian, 40, **40**
principle of superposition, 156–157, **156,** 178
prisms, volume formula for, 793
probes, space, 694–699
prograde rotation, 649, **649**
projections, map, 43–45, **43, 44, 45**
propane, 127, **128**
proportions, 790
Proterozoic eon, **174,** 175
protons, **620,** 796
Providence Canyon, 295, **295**
psychrometers, 484, **484**
Ptolemaic theory, 555, **555**
Ptolemy, Claudius, 555, **555**
pulsars, 594, **594,** 611
pumice, 252
pupal stage, **110**
P waves, 228, **228**
pyramid instructions (FoldNote), 776, **776**
pyrite, 70, **75,** 80–81, **800–801**
pyroclastic flows, 253–255, **254, 255**
pyroclastic material, 253–254, **254**
pyrrhotite, 73
Pytheas, 432

Q

quarries, 76
quartz
 conchoidal fractures in, **71**
 formation of, **75**
 properties of, **68,** 70, **72, 800–801**
 uses of, **78**
quartzite, 110, **110**
quasars, 599, **599**
Quaternary period, **174,** 175

R

radar, 47, 60, 649
radar zoology, 478
radiation, 454, **454**
 in the atmosphere, 454, **454–455**
 cosmic background, 601, **601**
 infrared, 456, **456, 562**
 ultraviolet, 451, 468, 563, 627–628
radiation balance, **454–455,** 456
radiative zone, **618,** 621
radioactive decay, 162–163, **162**
radioactive wastes, 135
radioactivity of minerals, 68, **73**
radiometric dating, 163–165, **163, 164, 165**
radio telescopes, 9, **9,** 562, **562,** 611
radium, **73**
rain, 488, **488**
 acid, 281, **281,** 467–468, **467**
 El Niño and, 424–425, **424**
 of fish and frogs, 32
 La Niña and, 424–425, **424**
 prevailing winds and, 521, **521**
 in rain shadows, **522, 532**
 in temperate biomes, **531, 532**
 in tropical biomes, **527, 528, 529**
 types of, 488, **488**
 in the water cycle, **309, 379, 482**
rain bands, **500**
raindrop impressions, 105
Rainier, Mount, 257
rain shadows, **522, 532**
raisin-bread model of expansion, 600
ratios, 790
raw sewage, 402
reaction devices, 686
rebound, elastic, 212
recharge zones, 322, **322**
reclamation, of mines, 77, **77**
record keeping, 15
recrystallization, 110
recycling, 125, **125**
recycling minerals, **77**
red dwarf stars, **593**
red giants, 591, **591, 593**
Redoubt, Mount, **251**
redshifts, 570, **570**
red tides, 442
reducing fractions, 791
reefs, artificial, 412
reference points, 37, **37**
refineries, 127, **127**
reflecting telescopes, 559–560, **559, 560**
refracting telescopes, 559, **559**
regional metamorphism, 106, **106**
Reinhard, Johan, 369
rejuvenated rivers, 314, **314**
relative dating, 156–161, **156**
 disturbed rock layers and, 158, **158**
 geologic column and, 157, **157**
 principle of superposition and, 156–157, **156,** 178
 rock-layer puzzles, 161, **161**
 unconformities and, 159–160, **159–160**
relative humidity, 483–484, **483, 484**
relief, on topographic maps, 51, **51**
remote sensing, 47, **47,** 692–693, **692**
renewable resources, 123, **123,** 396, **396.** See also energy resources
Reptiles, Age of (Mesozoic era), **174,** 176, **176**
residual soil, 288, **288**
resinous luster, **70**
resources, natural, 122–125, **123.** See also energy resources; fossil fuels; ocean resources
 conservation of, 124–125, **125, 322,** 331
 examples of, **122**
 habitat restoration, 305, **305**
 renewable vs. nonrenewable, 123, **123,** 396, **396**
 soil conservation, 294–297, **294, 295, 296, 297**
restoration, habitat, 305, **305**
retrofitting, 236
retrograde revolution, 666
retrograde rotation, 649, **649, 658**
reverse faults, 208, **208, 209,** 226, **227**
reverse polarity, **200**
revolution, of bodies in the solar system, 630, **630,** 648
rhyolite, **99**
Richter, Charles, 232
Richter magnitude scale, 232, **232, 235**
ridge push, **204**
rift valleys, 385, **385**
rift zones, 212, **212,** 262, **262,** 385
Rigel, 582, **582**
right ascension, **567**
"The Rime of the Ancient Mariner," **392**
Ring of Fire, 211, 261, **261**
rings, planetary, 654–655, **655**
ripple marks, 104, **104**
rivers, 308–319
 acid precipitation and, 468
 deltas, 317, **317,** 692
 deposition in water, 316–317, **316, 317**
 deposition on land, 318–319, **318, 319**
 discharge from, 311
 erosion from, 308, **308,** 311, **311**
 flooding by, 318–319, **318, 319**
 load in, 312, **312**
 stages of, 313–314, **313, 314**
 watersheds, 310, **310**
river systems, 310, **310**
robotic vessels, 387
rock, 90–111. See also minerals; names of individual rocks; weathering
 absolute dating of, 162–165, **162, 163, 164, 165**
 bedrock, 288, **288**
 classification of, 95–96
 collections, **108**
 composition of, 95, **95**
 in continents, 629
 in Earth's layers, 625, **625**
 factors that disturb rock layers, 158, **158**
 folding, 207, **207**
 formation of, **74–75**
 fossils in, 162–166, **163, 164, 165, 166**
 igneous, **92,** 98–101, **98, 99, 100**
 labs on, **107,** 112–113, **129**
 lunar, 660–661
 mafic, 99, **99**
 metamorphic, **74, 92,** 106–111, **106, 107** (see also metamorphic rock)
 parent, 288, **288**
 permeable, 129, **129**
 relative dating of, 156–161, **156, 157, 158, 159, 160**
 rock cycle, 90–97, **90, 91–92, 93**
 sedimentary, **91–92,** 102–104, **102, 103, 104,** 156
 subsidence of, 212, **212**
 texture of, 96, **96**
 uplift of, 212, **212**
 uses of, 90, **90**
rock cycle, 90–97, **90, 91–92, 93**
rocket fuel, 686

Index **839**

rockets, definition of, 685, **685**
rocket science
 beginnings of, 684, **684**
 birth of NASA, 685, **685**
 development of, 684–687
 how rockets work, 686, **686**
 ion propulsion, 699, **699**
 orbital and escape velocities, 687, **687**
 water rockets, 706–707
 World War II and the development of, 685, **685**
rock falls, 359, **359**
rock salt, 67, **67**
Rocky Mountains, **207**
room temperature, **783**
rotation, planetary, 630, **630,** 648–649, **649,** 656
rubidium-strontium dating method, 164
rubies, 79
runoff, **309,** 482
Russell, Henry Norris, 591
rust, 283, **283**

S

safety, 22–25, 501–502, **502**
safety symbols, **25**
SAFOD (San Andreas Fault Observatory at Depth), 246
Saglet Fjord (Labrador), **111**
Sahara Desert, **521,** 529
salinity, 376–377, **376, 377,** 419, **420**
saltation, 348, **348**
salts
 desalination, 397, **397**
 mining of, 86
 salinity of ocean water, 376–377, **376, 377,** 419, **420**
 sodium chloride, 103, 376, **376**
 in soils, 292, **292**
Salyut 1, 702
Samoa, **527**
San Andreas Fault, 203, 209, **225,** 236, **236**
San Andreas Fault Observatory at Depth (SAFOD), 246
San Andreas Fault Zone, 227
sand, 289, 346, **346**
sandbars, 347, **347**
sandstone, 96, **96,** 102–103, **102**
San Francisco, earthquake of 1906, 233, **233,** 240
Santa Ana wind, **463**
sapphires, 79
Sargasso Sea, **377**
satellite images, 383, **383**
satellite laser ranging (SLR), 220

satellites, 660, **660.** *See also* moon
 moons of other planets, 660–667, **665, 666**
satellites, artificial, 688–693
 communications, 691
 earliest, 688, **688**
 lab on, 689
 military, 690, **690**
 observing, 691
 orbits for, 664, 688, **688,** 689, **689**
 remote sensing by, 47, **47,** 692–693, **692**
 weather, 506, 691
saturated air, 483
saturation, zone of, 320, **320**
Saturn
 atmosphere of, 655
 missions to, 655, 697–698, **697, 698**
 moons of, 665, **665**
 relative size of, **644**
 rings of, 655, **655**
 statistics, 655
Saturn V rockets, **685,** 701
Saudi Arabia, desalination in, 397
scale, of a map, **46**
scanning electron microscopes, 118
Schiaparelli crater, **651**
schist, 109, **109**
scientific methods, 12–17, **13,** 26–27
 analyzing results, 15, 786
 asking questions, 13, 785
 communicating results, 16, 786
 drawing conclusions, 16, 786
 forming hypotheses, 14, 785
 summary of steps in, **13,** 785–786
 testing hypotheses, 14–15, 785–786
scientific models, 18–21, **19**
 choosing, 20, **20**
 climate models, 21, **21**
 conceptual, 19
 of the Earth, 20, **20, 192**
 lab on, 214–215
 mathematical, 19, **19,** 21, **21**
 physical, 18, **18**
 of the solar system, 555–556, **555**
 station, 506, **506**
scientific notation, 793
scientific theories, 20, **20**
sea anemones, **389**
sea arches, **344**
sea breezes, 462, **462**
sea caves, **344**
sea cliffs, **344**
sea-floor spreading, 199–201, **200, 201**
seamounts, 385, **385**

seasons, 520, **520,** 565, **802–803**
sea stacks, **344**
seaweed, 389, 395, **395**
secondary pollutants, 465, **465**
secondary treatment, 328, **328**
secondary waves, 228, **228**
second law of planetary motion, Kepler's, 631, **631**
second law of motion, Newton's, 798
sediment. *See also* deposition; erosion
 deposition in water, 316–317, **316, 317**
 deposition process and, 94, **94**
 erosion process and, 94, **94**
 formation of rock from, 102
sedimentary rock, 102–105
 composition of, 103–104, **104**
 lab on, 112–113
 metamorphism of, 94, 109
 origins of, 102, **102**
 in the rock cycle, **91–92,** 92–94, 93
 stratification of, 104, **104,** 156
 texture of, 96, **96,** 103
seismic gaps, 235–236, **235, 236**
seismic waves, 228, **228**
 in earthquakes, 228–229, **228, 229**
 elastic rebound and, 225, **225**
 lab on, **228**
 long period, 247
seismograms, 230
seismographs, 230, **230, 231**
seismologists, 6, 247
seismology, 224, **225.** *See also* earthquakes
Seismosaurus hallorum, 12, **12, 16, 17**
semimajor axis, 631, **631**
SEMs (scanning electron microscopes), 118
septic tanks, 329, **329**
sewage sludge dumping, 402, **402**
sewage treatment plants, 328, **328**
shale, 103, 109, **109**
shallow-water waves, 428, **428**
shamal, **463**
Shasta, Mount, 257
shellfish, toxins in, 442
shield volcanoes, 257, **257**
shock metamorphism, 118
Shoemaker-Levy 9 comet, **669**
shore currents, 429, **429**
shorelines, 342, **342**
 beaches, 346, **346,** 401
 dunes, 350–351, **350, 351**
 erosion of, 342–347
 landforms at, **344–345**
 wave energy and, 342–343, **343**
 wave trains and, 343, **343**

840 Index

Shuttle Imaging Radar system, 60
Siberian mammoths, 167, **167,** 184
Siccar Point (Scotland), **153**
silica, 78, 252
silicate minerals, 68, **68, 69**
silicon, 68, **68**
silky luster, **70**
sills, 100, **100**
silt, **289**
siltstone, **96,** 103
Silurian period, **174**
silver, 67, **69,** 78, **78,** 81
sinkholes, 325, **325,** 338
Sinosauropteryx, 184
sirocco, **463**
SI units, 22–25, **22, 23, 24,** 782
Skylab, 702
sky maps, 565, **565, 802–803**
slab pull process, **204**
slate, 109, **109**
sleet, 488
slip faces, 351
slopes, of graphs, 788–789
SLR (satellite laser ranging), 220
sludge dumping, 402, **402**
slump, 359
smog, 132, **132,** 465, **465**
snow, 488, **488**
sodium, 67, **67,** 68, **69, 583**
sodium chloride, 103, 376, **376.** *See also* halite
soil, 288, **288**
   in arctic climates, 293, **293,** 534
   conservation of, 294–297, **294, 295, 296, 297**
   creep of, 361, **361**
   in deserts, 292, **292**
   fertility of, 290, 291–293, **294,** 304
   horizons, 290, **290**
   importance of, 294–295, **294**
   patterns on, 304
   pH, 291
   residual, 288, **288**
   source of, 288, **288**
   in temperate biomes, 292, **292,** 531–532
   texture and structure of, 289, **289**
   in tropical biomes, 291, **291,** 304, 527, 528
soil conservation, 294–297, **294**
   contour plowing and terracing, 296, **296**
   cover crops and crop rotation, 297, **297**
   importance of, 294–295, **294**
   restoration in, 305
   soil erosion and, 295, **295**
soil erosion, 295, **295**
soil formation, 288–297
soil structure, 289, **289**

soil texture, 289, **289**
Sojourner rover, **652,** 696
solar activity, 539, **539,** 622–623, **622, 623**
solar collectors, 137, **137**
solar eclipse, 663, **663**
solar energy, 136, **136**
   in the atmosphere, 454–457, **454–455, 456, 457**
   electricity and heating from, 136–137, **136, 137**
   latitude and, 519, **519**
solar flares, 623, **623**
solar nebulas, 615–616, **615, 616**
solar system. *See also* Earth; planets; sun
   ancient models of, 555–556, **555**
   asteroids, 118, **154,** 670, **670**
   comets, 627, 640, 668–669, **668, 669**
   discovery of, 646
   formation of, 614–617, **616**
   impacts in, 118, 539, 672–673, **672,** 681
   inner and outer planets, 646–647, **646, 647**
   labs on, **632,** 634–635
   meteoroids, 671, **671**
   moon of Earth, 660–664, **660, 661, 662, 663, 664**
   moons of other planets, 660, 664–666, **665, 666**
   Oort cloud, 640, 669
   planetary motion, 630–633, **630, 631, 632, 633**
   sizes and distances, 644, **644–645**
solar telescopes, 640
solar wind, 669
solvents, **466**
sonar, 382, **382–383**
source regions, 490, **490**
South American plate, 195, **195, 210**
South Pole, **37,** 38, **38, 200**
space exploration. *See also* space probes and missions
   benefits of, 704–705, **704, 705**
   of comets, 698
   inner solar system missions, 694–696, **694, 695, 696,** 712
   labs on, **689,** 706–707
   outer solar system missions, 697–698, **697, 698**
   race to the moon, 700–701, **700, 701**
   rocket science, 684–687, **684, 685, 686, 687**
   space colonies, 704, **704**
   space junk, **692**
   space planes, 702, **702**

space shuttles and boosters, **685,** 686, 701–702, **701**
space stations, 702–703, **702, 703**
spinoffs from, 704, **704, 705**
space probes and missions, 694–699, **694.** *See also* space exploration
   Apollo missions, 660, 701
   Cassini mission, 655, 665, 698, **698**
   Clementine missions, 694, **694**
   Deep Flight, 386, **386**
   Deep Space 1, 699, **699**
   Galileo missions, 654, **660,** 697, **697**
   Luna missions, 694, **694**
   Magellan missions, 649, 695, **695**
   Mars Pathfinder, 651, **652,** 696, **696**
   Pioneer missions, 697, **697**
   Sojourner, **652,** 696
   Sputnik 1, 688, **688**
   Sputnik 2, 688, **688**
   Stardust space probe, 698
   Twin Rover mission, 653
   Venera 9, 695, **695**
   Viking missions, 651, 696, **696**
   Voyager missions, 654, 655, **655,** 656, 657, **657, 666,** 697, **697**
space shuttles and boosters, **685,** 686, **700,** 701–702, **701**
space stations, 702–703, **702, 703**
specific gravity, 72, 81
spectra (singular, *spectrum*), **583,** 583–584, **583, 584**
spectrographs, 583–584, **584**
speed
   average, 799
   of glaciers, **354**
   of waves, 427, **427**
sphalerite, **78**
spider map Graphic Organizers, 780, **780**
spinoffs from space programs, **704,** 705, **705**
spiral galaxies, 596, **596**
springs, 322–323, **323**
spring tides, 434, **434**
S-P time method, 231, **231**
Sputnik 1, 688, **688**
Sputnik 2, 688, **688**
squids, giant, 412
stalactites, 6, **6,** 324, **324**
stalagmites, 6, **6,** 324, **324**
star clusters, 598, **598**
Stardust space probe, 698
starfish, **389**
stars, 582–595. *See also* galaxies
   apparent and absolute magnitude, 585–586, **586,** 592, **592–593**

Index   **841**

stars (continued)
  circumpolar, 567
  classification of, 584–585, **585**
  color of, 582, **582, 585**, 592, **592**
  composition of, 583–584, **583, 584, 585, 590**
  in constellations, 564–565, **564, 565, 802–803**
  distance to, 568, **568, 569**, 587, **587**
  Doppler effects from, 570, **570**
  elements in, **585**
  Eta Carinae, 610, **610**
  formation of, 593, 616–617, **616**
  giants, 591, **593**
  in Hertzsprung-Russell diagram, 591–592, **591, 592–593**
  labs on, **565, 587**
  life cycle of, 590–595, **590, 591, 592–593, 594**
  locating, 564–571, **566, 567, 802–803**
  magnitudes, 585–586, **586, 592–593**
  main-sequence, 590, **590, 592–593**
  mass of, 641
  motion of, 587–588, **588**
  neutron stars and pulsars, 594, **594**
  number of, 9, **9**
  parallax and, 587, **587**
  path across sky, 567
  red dwarf, **593**
  star clusters, 598, **598**
  supergiants, 591, **593**
  supernovas, 594, **594**
  white dwarf, 590–591, **590, 591, 592**, 641
stationary fronts, 493, **493**
station models, 506, **506**
St. Helens, Mount, **251**, 257, 538, **538**
stocks, **100**
storms
  hurricanes, 8, **8, 458**, 499–501, **499, 500, 501**
  on Jupiter, **495**
  thunderstorms, 486, 491, **491, 496–497, 496, 497, 501, 691**
  tornadoes, 8, **8**, 32, 498, **498, 499, 499**, 502, **502**
storm surges, 431, **431**, 501, **501**
strata, (singular, *stratum*) 102, **102**, 104
stratification, 104, **104**, 105, **105**, 156, **156**
stratified drift, 357, **357**
stratocumulus clouds, **487**
stratosphere, **450**, 451, **451**
stratovolcanoes, 257, **257**
stratus clouds, 486, **486, 487**
streak, 71, **71, 800**
streak plates, 71

stream discharge, 311
stream ecosystems, 468. *See also* rivers
streams, 316–319
stress, 206, **206, 207**, 261
strike-slip faults, 209, **209**, 226, **226**
strip mining, 76, 131
stromatolites, **628**
strontium, 164
subduction zones
  at convergent boundaries, 202, **202**, 203, **203**
  magma formation at, 260–261, **260**, 263, **263**
  mountain building and, 210–211
  sea-floor spreading towards, 200
sublittoral zone, 390, **390**
submarine volcanoes, **378**, 385
submetallic luster, 70, **70**
suborbital velocity, 687, **687**
subsidence, 212, **212**
subsurface mining, 77, **77**
subtracting decimals, 791
subtracting fractions, 792
succulents, **529**
Sue (fossil dinosaur), 33
sulfates, **69, 800–801**
sulfides, **69, 800–801**
sulfur, 68, **69**, 75
sulfuric acid, 649, **649**
sun, 618–623
  age of, 619
  distance from Earth, 634–635
  eclipses of, 663–664, **663**
  formation of, 616–617, **616**
  fusion in, 617, 620–621, **620, 621**
  gravity and, 619
  in H-R diagram, **593**
  radiation from, 454
  size of, **644**
  solar activity, 539, **539**, 622–623, **622, 623**
  solar telescopes, 640
  solar wind, 669
  structure of, 618, **618**
  theories of energy production in, 619, **619**
  tides and, 434, **434**
sunspots, 539, **539**, 622–623, **622**
supergiants, 591, **593**
supernovas, 594, **594**
superposition, principle of, 156–157, **156**, 178
surf, 428, **428**. *See also* waves, ocean
surface area–to-volume ratio, 285, **285**
surface coal mining, 76, **76**, 131
surface currents, 417, **417**, 523, **523**. *See also* ocean currents
  in Atlantic Ocean, **417**, 418, 419

  climate and, 422–423, **422, 423**, 523, **523**
  cold-water, 419, **419**, 423, **423**
  continental deflections, 418, **418**
  Coriolis effect and, 418, **418**
  deep currents and, **421**
  El Niño and, 424–425, **424**, 443, 549
  global winds and, 417, **417**
  La Niña and, 424–425, **424**
  shore currents, 429, **429**
  upwelling and, 423, **423**
  warm-water, 419, **419, 421**, 422, **422**
surface waves, seismic, 228–229, **229**
surface zone, oceanic, **377**
Surtsey, 262
suspended load, **312**
S waves, 228, **228**
swells, 430, **430**
symbols, safety, **25**
synclines, 207, **207**

T

table fold instructions (FoldNote), 779, **779**
taiga, **533**, 534, **534**
talc, **72**, **74**
Tambora, Mount, 256
tar pits, 167
tectonic plates, 194, **194**. *See also* plate tectonics
  causes of motion of, 204, **204**
  close-up of, 195, **195**
  earthquakes at boundaries of, 224, **224**, 226, **226–227**
  fault types at boundaries of, 226, **226–227**
  labs on, **195**, 214–215
  lithosphere and, 195, 202–204, **202–203, 204**
  map of, 194, **194**
  tracking motion of, 205, **205**
  types of tectonic boundaries, 202–203, **202–203**
  volcanoes at boundaries of, 261–263, **261, 262, 263**
telescopes, 558–563, **559**
  atmospheric effects on, 560
  electromagnetic spectrum and, 561, **561**
  importance to astronomy, 9, **9**
  lab on, 572–573
  nonoptical, 561–563, **561, 562, 563**
  optical, 9, 558–560, **558, 559, 560**
  radio, 9, **9**, 562, **562**, 611
  reflecting, 559–560, **559, 560**
  refracting, 559, **559**

solar, 640
in space, 560, **560,** 570, 596
temperate deserts, **530,** 532, **532**
temperate forests, 292, **292, 530,** 531, **531**
temperate grasslands, 292, **292, 530,** 531, **531**
temperate zone, 530–532, **530, 531, 532**
temperature, 24, **24**
  in the atmosphere, **449,** 450, 452
  body, 24, **24,** 783
  color and, 604–605
  deep currents and, **420**
  in Earth formation, 624
  in H-R diagram, **592–593**
  labs on, **7, 521,** 604–605
  magma formation and, 98–99, **98, 99,** 260, **260**
  of metamorphism, 106
  in nebulas, 615
  in the ocean, 377–378, **377, 378,** 380, **380**
  relative humidity and, 483–484, **483**
  star classification by, 584, **585**
  surface currents and, 378, **378,** 419, **419,** 424–425
  in temperate biomes, **531,** 532
  thermometers, 24, **24,** 505, **505,** 508–509
  in tropical biomes, **527, 528, 529**
  units of, **22, 783**
  weathering and, 286, **286**
tension, at plate boundaries, 206, **206,** 210, 211
temperate zones, 530–535, **531, 532**
terminal moraines, **356**
Terra I, 693
terraces, wave-cut, 345
terracing, 296, **296,** 314, **314**
terrestrial planets, 646, **646,** 648, **648**
  Earth, 650, **650** (*see also* Earth)
  Mars, **644,** 651–653, **651, 652, 653**
  Mercury, 630, **644,** 648, **648**
  Venus, **644,** 649, **649,** 695, **695**
Tertiary period, **174,** 175
Tethys, **655**
Tetons, 211, **211**
texture, 96, **96**
  of igneous rock, 99, **99**
  of metamorphic rock, 109–110, **109, 110**
  of sedimentary rock, 96, **96,** 103
  of soil, 289, **289**
thermal energy
  in the atmosphere, 452, **452**

from the big bang, 601
conduction and convection of, 455, **455**
in the formation of the Earth, 624
in metamorphism, 94
thermal pollution, 327
thermocline, **377**
thermometers, 505, **505**
  labs on, **7,** 508–509, **521**
  temperature scales on, **22,** 24, **24, 783**
  use in weather forecasting, 505, **505**
  water, 508–509
  wet-bulb, 484–485, **484**
thermosphere, **450,** 452, **452**
third law of motion, Newton's, 686, 798
Three Gorges dam (China), 149
three-panel flip chart instructions (FoldNote), 778, **778**
thrust, 686, **686**
thunder, 497, **497**
thunderstorms, 496, **496**
  air masses and, 491, **491**
  cumulus clouds and, 486
  lightning in, 497, **497,** 501, **691**
  safety during, 501
  severe, 496–497, **496, 497**
tidal bores, 435, **435**
tides, 432–435, **432**
  effect of moon on, 432–433, **432, 433**
  high and low, 432–433, **432, 433**
  red, 442
  tidal energy, 398, **398**
  tidal range, 434–435, **434, 435**
  timing of, 433, **433**
  topography and, 435, **435**
till, 356, **356**
tilting, 158, **158**
tiltmeters, 265
time scale, geologic, 174–177, **174, 175**
Titan, 665, **665,** 698
Titanic, **353**
titanium, **78**
titles, map, **46**
topaz, **72, 75,** 79
topographic maps, 50–53, **50, 51, 52**
topsoil, 290, **290**
Torino Scale, 673
tornadoes, 32, 498, **498**
  damage from, 499, **499**
  formation of, 498, **498**
  safety during, 502, **502**
  tornado chasers, 8, **8**
Torrington, John, **167**
tourmaline, **75,** 79
trace fossils, 168, **168**

tracks, fossil, 168, **168**
trade winds, 460, **460, 461**
transform boundaries, 202–203, **203**
transform motion, **226**
transported soil, 288, **288**
trash dumping, 401, **401**
Treasure oil spill, 132, **132**
trees, 531, **531,** 534
Trefry, John, 7
triangulation, **690**
Triassic period, **174**
tributaries, 310, **310**
tri-fold instructions (FoldNote), 778
trilobites, 171, **171**
triple-beam balances, 784
tritium, **135**
Triton, 666, **666**
tropical deserts, **526,** 529, **529**
tropical rain forests
  climate of, 526, **526,** 527, **527**
  deforestation of, **291**
  soil in, 291, **291,** 304
tropical savannas, **526,** 528, **528**
tropical zone, 526–529, **526, 527, 528, 529**
the Tropics, 526–529
tropites, 170, **170**
troposphere, **450,** 451, **451,** 452
troughs, wave, 426, **426**
true north, 38, **38**
Tsiolkovsky, Konstantin, 684
tsunamis, 247, 430, **430**
tube worms, 7, **7,** 391, **391**
tundra, 533, **533**
turbines, wind, **122,** 137, **137**
Twain, Mark, **313**
Twin Rover mission, 653
two-panel flip chart instructions (FoldNote), 778, **778**
Tycho Brahe, 556, **556,** 630
typhoons, 499. *See also* hurricanes
Tyrannosaurus rex, 33
Tyson, Neil deGrasse, 579

U

Ubar, lost city of, 60
ultraviolet (UV) radiation, 451, 468, 563, 627–628
unconformities, 159–160, **159, 160**
underground deposits, 324–325, **324, 325,** 338
underground erosion, 324–325, **324, 325,** 338
underground water, 320–325
undersea volcanic vents, **191**
undertow, 429, **429**
underwater caves, 6, **6**
underwater vessels, 386–387, **386**

Index **843**

uniformitarianism, 152–153, **152, 153**
United States Geological Survey (USGS), 50, **50,** 52, **52**
units
   astronomical, 645, **645**
   conversion table, **782,** 783
   of energy, 134
   of length, **22,** 23, **782**
   of mass, **22,** 24, **782**
   prefixes for, 782, **782**
   of temperature, **22, 783**
   of volume, **22,** 23, **782**
universal gravitation, Newton's law of, 632–633, **632, 633,** 798
universe
   age of, 602
   ancient models of, 555–556, **555, 556**
   expansion of, 570, 600–603
   formation of, 600–603, **600–601**
   size and scale of, 568, **568,** 569
   structure of, 602, **602**
uplift, **91,** 94, 212, **212**
upwelling, 423, **423**
Ural Mountains, 210
uranium, **73,** 134–135, **134**
uranium-lead dating method, 164
Uranus
   axis of rotation of, 656, **656**
   discovery of, 646
   moons of, 666, **666**
   relative size of, **644**
   statistics on, **656**
Ursa Major constellation, 565, **565**
USGS (United States Geological Survey), 50, **50,** 52, **52**
U-shaped valleys, **355**
UV (ultraviolet) radiation, 451, 468, 563, 627–628

V

valley breezes, 463
valley glaciers, 352, **352**
vanes, wind, 505
variables, 14, 786
Venera 9, 695, **695**
ventifacts, **279**
ventilation, 466
vents
   hydrothermal, 7, **7,** 386, 391
   volcanic, **191,** 252, **252**
Venus, **644,** 649, **649,** 695, **695**
vernal equinox, **567**
Verne, Jules, 684
Very Large Array (VLA), 562
Vesta, 670, **670**
Vesuvius, Mount, 260
Viking missions, 651, 696, **696**

visible light, 561, **561**
vitreous luster, **70**
VLA (Very Large Array), 562
volcanic ash, 251, 253, **254**
volcanic blocks, **254**
volcanic bombs, **254**
volcanic mountains, 211
volcanic necks, **100**
volcanic vents, undersea, **191,** 252, **252**
volcanoes, 250–265, **250**
   active, 264
   calderas, 258, **258**
   climate change and, 256, **256,** 538, **538**
   craters, 258, **258**
   differential weathering in, 284, **284**
   dormant, 264
   explosive eruptions of, 251, **251,** 252, **252, 254**
   extinct, 264
   formation of magma in, 260–261, **260,** 263, **263**
   gas release from, 264, 627, **627**
   at hot spots, 263, **264**
   ice, 666
   internal structure of, 252, **252**
   labs on, **254, 261,** 266–267
   lava flows from, 101, **101,** 250, **250, 251**
   lava plateaus from, 259, **259**
   lava types from, 253, **253,** 272
   magma, **191,** 252, **252** (*see also* magma)
   on Mars, 652
   nonexplosive eruptions of, 250, **250,** 253
   physical models of, 18, **18**
   at plate boundaries, 261–263, **261, 262, 263**
   predicting eruptions of, 264–265, 266–267
   pyroclastic flows from, 253–255, **254, 255**
   submarine, **378, 385**
   types of, 257, **257**
   on Venus, 649, **649**
volcanologists, 6, 273
volume, 23, **23**
   formulas for, 793
   units of, **22,** 23, **782**
von Braun, Wernher, 685
Vostok, Lake, 338
Voyager missions
   to Jupiter, 654, 697
   to Neptune, 657, **657,** 666
   to the outer solar system, 697, **697**
   to Saturn, 655, **655**
   to Uranus, **656,** 666
V-2 rockets, 685, **685**

W

waning moon, 662, **662**
warm air masses, 491, **491, 492–493**
warm fronts, 492, **492**
warm-water currents, 419, **419, 421,** 422, **422**
water. *See also* groundwater; ocean water
   agricultural use of, 330, **330**
   boiling point of, **24,** 652, **783**
   climate and, 523
   from comets, 627
   conservation of, **322,** 331
   density of, 72
   drinkable, 326
   on Europa, 665
   filters, 339
   freezing point of, **24, 783**
   fresh, 308–331
   household use of, 326, 329, **329,** 331
   hydroelectric energy from, 138, **138,** 148
   industrial use of, 330
   labs on, **321, 327,** 332–333
   on Mars, 651–652, **651,** 712
   pollution, 124, 326–327, **326, 327,** 339
   quality, 327
   river deposition and, 316–319, **316, 317, 318**
   river stages and, 313–314, **313, 314**
   river systems and, 310, **310**
   rockets, 706–707
   in soils, 295
   in thermometers, 508–509
   treatment, 328–329, **328, 329**
   underground, 320–325
   usage, 326–331
   vapor, 448, 483, **483**
   in volcanic eruptions, 252, 263, **263**
   water cycle, 309, **309,** 332–333, 379, **379,** 482, **482**
   weathering by, 279, **279,** 281, **281,** 286
water conservation, **322,** 331
water cycle, 309, **309,** 332–333, 379, **379,** 482, **482**
water filters, 339
water rockets, 706–707
watersheds, 310, **310**
waterspouts, 32
water table, 320, **320,** 322, **323**
water thermometers, 508–509

water vapor, 448, 483, **483**
water wheels, 138, **138,** 142–143
Watt-Evans, Lawrence, 578
wave-cut terraces, 345
wave energy, 342–343, **343,** 399
wave height, 426, **426**
wavelengths, 426–428, **426, 427, 428**
wave periods, 427, **427**
waves, ocean, 426–431
    breakers, 428, **428**
    deep-water and shallow-water, 428, **428**
    energy of, 342–343, **343,** 399
    formation and movement of, 427, **427**
    lab on, **429**
    longshore currents, 429, **429**
    open-ocean, 430, **430**
    parts of, 426, **426**
    periods, 343, **343**
    shore currents, 429, **429**
    speed of, 427, **427**
    storm surges, 431, **431,** 501, **501**
    wave-cut terraces, **345**
    wave deposits, 346–347, **346, 347**
    wave trains, 343, **343**
wave speed, 427, **427**
wave troughs, 426, **426**
waxing moon, 662, **662**
waxy luster, **70**
weather, 482–507, **483,** 518, **518.** *See also* climate
    air masses and, 490–491, **490, 491**
    anticyclones, 494–495, **494, 495**
    birds and, 514
    clouds and, 486–488, **486, 487**
    condensation and, **309,** 482, 485, **485**
    cyclones, 494–495, **494, 495**
    forecasting, 504–507, **504, 505, 506, 507,** 514
    fronts and, 492–493, **492–493, 507**
    humidity and, 483–485, **483, 484**
    hurricanes, 499–501, **499, 500, 501**
    labs on, **485,** 508–509
    precipitation, **482,** 488, **488**
    safety during severe, 501–502, **502**
    thunderstorms, 486, 491, **491,** 496–497, **496, 497**
    tornadoes, **8,** 32, 498–499, **498, 499**
    water cycle and, 482, **482**
weather balloons, 504, **504**

weather forecasting
    animal and plant signs in, **506,** 514
    meteorologists, 8, **8,** 504, 515
    technology for, 504–505, **504, 505**
    weather maps, 506–507, **506, 507**
    weather satellites in, 506, 691
weathering, 278–287, **278.** *See also* soil
    chemical, 280, 281–283, **281, 282, 283**
    climate and, 286, **286**
    differential, 284, **284**
    elevation and, 287, **287**
    labs on, **282,** 298–299
    mechanical, 278–280, **278, 279, 280**
    from organisms, 282
    from oxidation, 283, **283,** 286, **286**
    patterns from, 304
    in the rock cycle, **91,** 93, **93**
    surface area and, 285, **285**
weather maps, 506–507, **506, 507**
weather satellites, 506, 691
Wegener, Alfred, 198–199, 221
weightlessness, 702, **702**
Weinbaum, Stanley, 680
wells, 323, **323**
westerlies, 460, **460, 461**
wet-bulb thermometers, 484–485, **484**
wetland ecosystems, **692**
whales, humpback, 443
whitecaps, 430, **430**
white dwarf stars, 590–591, **590, 591, 592,** 641
"Why I Left Harry's All-Night Hamburgers," 578
Wieliczka salt mine, 86
Williamson, Jack, 86
Wilson, Robert, **601**
wind erosion, 279, **279,** 348–351, **348, 349, 350**
wind power, 137, **137**
winds, 458–463, **458**
    causes of, 458–460, **458, 459, 460**
    Coriolis effect on, 417–418, **418,** 460, **460**
    deposition by, 350–351, **350, 351**
    direction, measurement of, 505, **505**
    global, 417, **417, 418,** 460–461, **461**
    in hurricanes, **500,** 501
    in jet streams, 462, **462**
    local, 462–463, **462, 463**
    prevailing, 521, **521**

    solar, 669
    in storms, **458**
    trade, 460, **460, 461**
wind socks, 505, **505**
wind turbines, **122,** 137, **137**
wind vanes, 505
woolly mammoths, 167, **167,** 184
world population growth, **19**

X

X-ray telescopes, **562,** 563, **563,** 641

Y

years, 554, **554,** 630
Yellowstone National Park, 258, **313**
Yoho National Park, **169**

Z

zenith, 566, **566**
zone of aeration, 320, **320**
zone of saturation, 320, **320**
zoology, radar, 478
zooplankton, 388, **388**

Acknowledgments
continued from page ii

Joel S. Leventhal, Ph.D.
Emeritus Scientist
U.S. Geological Survey
Lakewood, Colorado

Madeline Micceri Mignone, Ph.D.
Assistant Professor
Natural Science
Dominican College
Orangeburg, New York

Sten Odenwald, Ph.D.
Astronomer
NASA Goddard Space Flight Center and Raytheon ITSS
Greenbelt, Maryland

Kenneth K. Peace
Manager of Transportation
WestArch Coal, Inc.
St. Louis, Missouri

Kenneth H. Rubin, Ph.D.
Associate Professor
Department of Geology & Geophysics
University of Hawaii at Manoa
Honolulu, Hawaii

Dork Sahagian, Ph.D.
Research Professor
Department of Earth Sciences
Institute for the Study of Earth, Oceans, and Space
University of New Hampshire
Durham, New Hampshire

Daniel Z. Sui, Ph.D.
Professor
Department of Geography
Texas A&M University
College Station, Texas

Colin D. Sumrall, Ph.D.
Lecturer of Paleontology
Earth and Planetary Sciences
The University of Tennessee
Knoxville, Tennessee

Vatche P. Tchakerian, Ph.D.
Professor
Department of Geography & Geology
Texas A&M University
College Station, Texas

Peter W. Weigand, Ph.D.
Professor Emeritus
Department of Geological Sciences
California State University
Northridge, California

Teacher Reviewers

Diedre S. Adams
Physical Science Instructor
Science Department
West Vigo Middle School
West Terre Haute, Indiana

Laura Buchanan
Science Teacher and Department Chairperson
Corkran Middle School
Glen Burnie, Maryland

Robin K. Clanton
Science Department Head
Berrien Middle School
Nashville, Georgia

Randy Dye, M.S.
Middle School Science Department Head
Earth Science
Wood Middle School
Waynesville School District #6, Missouri

Meredith Hanson
Science Teacher
Westside Middle School
Rocky Face, Georgia

James Kerr
Oklahoma Teacher of the Year 2002–2003
Oklahoma State Department of Education
Union Public Schools
Tulsa, Oklahoma

Laura Kitselman
Science Teacher and Coordinator
Loudoun Country Day School
Leesburg, Virginia

Deborah L. Kronsteiner
Teacher
Science Department
Spring Grove Area Middle School
Spring Grove, Pennsylvania

Jennifer L. Lamkie
Science Teacher
Thomas Jefferson Middle School
Edison, New Jersey

Sally M. Lesley
ESL Science Teacher
Burnet Middle School
Austin, Texas

Susan H. Robinson
Science Teacher
Oglethorpe County Middle School
Lexington, Georgia

Marci L. Stadiem
Department Head
Science Department
Cascade Middle School, Highline School District
Seattle, Washington

Lab Development

Kenneth E. Creese
Science Teacher
White Mountain Junior High School
Rock Spring, Wyoming

Linda A. Culp
Science Teacher and Department Chair
Thorndale High School
Thorndale, Texas

Bruce M. Jones
Science Teacher and Department Chair
The Blake School
Minneapolis, Minnesota

Shannon Miller
Science and Math Teacher
Llano Junior High School
Llano, Texas

Robert Stephen Ricks
Special Services Teacher
Department of Classroom Improvement
Alabama State Department of Education
Montgomery, Alabama

James J. Secosky
Science Teacher
Bloomfield Central School
Bloomfield, New York

Lab Testing

Barry L. Bishop
Science Teacher and Department Chair
San Rafael Junior High
Ferron, Utah

Daniel Bugenhagen
Science Teacher and Department Chair
Yutan Jr.–Sr. high
Yutan, Nebraska

Kenneth Creese
Science Teacher
White Mountain Junior High
Rock Springs, Wyoming

Susan Gorman
Science Teacher
North Ridge Middle School
North Richmond Hills, Texas

C. John Graves
Science Teacher
Monforton Middle School
Bozeman, Montana

Janel Guse
Science Teacher and Department Chair
West Central Middle School
Hartford, South Dakota

Norman Holcomb
Science Teacher
Marion Local Schools
Maria Stein, Ohio

Tracy Jahn
Science Teacher
Berkshire Jr–Sr. High
Canaan, New York

David Jones
Science Teacher
Andrew Jackson Middle School
Cross Lanes, West Virginia

Michael E. Kral
Science Teacher
West Hardin Middle School
Cecilia, Kentucky

Kathy McKee
Science Teacher
Hoyt Middle School
Des Moines, Iowa

Alyson, Mike
Science Teacher
East Valley Middle School
East Helena, Montana

Jan Nelson
Science Teacher
East Valley Middle School
East Helena, Montana

Dwight Patton
Science Teacher
Carrol T. Welch Middle School
Horizon City, Texas

Joseph Price
Chairman—Science Department
H.M. Browne Junior High
Washington, D.C.

Terry J. Rakes
Science Teacher
Elmwood Junior High
Rogers, Arkansas

Helen Schiller
Science Teacher
Northwood Middle School
Taylors, South Carolina

Bert Sherwood
Science Teacher
Socorro Middle School
El Paso, Texas

David M. Sparks
Science Teacher
Redwater Junior High School
Redwater, Texas

Larry Tackett
Science Teacher and Department Chair
Andrew Jackson Middle School
Cross Lanes, West Virginia

Walter Woolbaugh
Science Teacher
Manhattan School System
Manhattan, Montana

Gordon Zibelman
Science Teacher
Drexel Hill Middle School
Drexel Hill, Pennsylvania

Answer Checking
Catherine Podeszwa
Duluth, Minnesota

Feature Development
Katy Z. Allen
Hatim Belyamani
John A. Benner
David Bradford
Jennifer Childers
Mickey Coakley
Susan Feldkamp
Jane Gardner
Erik Hahn
Christopher Hess
Deena Kalai
Charlotte W. Luongo, MSc
Michael May
Persis Mehta, Ph.D.
Eileen Nehme, MPH
Catherine Podeszwa
Dennis Rathnaw
Daniel B. Sharp
John Stokes
April Smith West
Molly F. Wetterschneider

Staff Credits

Editorial
Robert Todd, *Vice President, Editorial Science*
Debbie Starr, *Managing Editor*
Leigh Ann García, *Senior Editor*

Editorial Development Team
Jen Driscoll
Amy Fry
Angela Hemmeter
Shari Husain
Bill Rader
Jim Ratcliffe

Copyeditors
Dawn Marie Spinozza, *Copyediting Manager*
Anne-Marie De Witt
Jane A. Kirschman
Kira J. Watkins

Editorial Support Staff
Mary Anderson
Suzanne Krejci
Shannon Oehler

Online Products
Bob Tucek, *Executive Editor*
Wesley M. Bain

Design
Book Design
Kay Selke, *Director of Book Design*
Sonya Mendeke, *Designer*
Mercedes Newman, *Designer*
Holly Whittaker, *Project Administrator*

Media Design
Richard Metzger, *Design Director*
Chris Smith, *Senior Designer*

Image Acquisitions
Curtis Riker, *Director*
Jeannie Taylor, *Photo Research Manager*
Andy Christiansen, *Photo Researcher*
Elaine Tate, *Art Buyer Supervisor*
Angela Boehm, *Senior Art Buyer*

Design New Media
Edwin Blake, *Director*
Kimberly Cammerata, *Design Manager*
Michael Rinella, *Senior Designer*

Cover Design
Bill Smith Studio

Publishing Services
Carol Martin, *Director*

Graphic Services
Bruce Bond, *Director*
Jeff Bowers, *Graphic Services Manager*
JoAnn Stringer, *Senior Graphics Specialist II*
Cathy Murphy, *Senior Graphics Specialist*
Nanda Patel, *Graphics Specialist*
Katrina Gnader, *Graphics Specialist*

Technology Services
Laura Likon, *Director*
Juan Baquera, *Technology Services Manager*
Lana Kaupp, *Senior Technology Services Analyst*
Margaret Sanchez, *Senior Technology Services Analyst*
Sara Buller, *Technology Services Analyst*
Patty Zepeda, *Technology Services Analyst*
Jeff Robinson, *Ancillary Design Manager*

New Media
Armin Gutzmer, *Director*
Melanie Baccus, *New Media Coordinator*
Lydia Doty, *Senior Project Manager*
Cathy Kuhles, *Technical Assistant*
Marsh Flournoy, *Quality Assurance Analyst*
Tara F. Ross, *Senior Project Manager*

Production
Eddie Dawson, *Production Manager*
Sherry Sprague, *Senior Production Coordinator*
Suzanne Brooks, *Production Coordinator*

Teacher Edition
Alicia Sullivan
David Hernandez
April Litz

Manufacturing and Inventory
Wilonda Ieans
Ivania Quant Lee

Ancillary Development and Production
General Learning Communications,
Northbrook, Illinois

Credits

Abbreviations used: (t) top, (c) center, (b) bottom, (l) left, (r) right, (bkgd) background

PHOTOGRAPHY

Front Cover (tl), Paul & Lindamarie Ambrose/Getty Images; (tr), NASA Goddard Space Flight Center. Image by Reto Stöckli (land surface, shallow water, clouds). Enhancements by Robert Simmon (ocean color, compositing, 3D globes, animation). Data and technical support: MODIS Land Group; MODIS Science Data Support Team; (cr), Larry Landolfi/Photo Researchers, Inc.; (c), Steve Niedirf Photography/Getty Images; (bl), Corel; (owl), Kim Taylor/Bruce Coleman

Skills Practice Lab Teens Sam Dudgeon/HRW

Connection to Astrology Corbis Images; **Connection to Biology** David M. Phillips/Visuals Unlimited; **Connection to Chemistry** Digital Image copyright © 2005 PhotoDisc; **Connection to Environment** Digital Image copyright © 2005 PhotoDisc; **Connection to Geology** Letraset Phototone; **Connection to Language Arts** Digital Image copyright © 2005 PhotoDisc; **Connection to Meteorology** Digital Image copyright © 2005 PhotoDisc; **Connection to Oceanography** © ICONOTEC; **Connection to Physics** Digital Image copyright © 2005 PhotoDisc

Table of Contents iii (t), Sam Dudgeon/HRW; iii (b), NASA; iv (t), Howard B. Bluestein; iv (b), Tom Pantages Photography; v (tl), E. R. Degginger/Color-Pic, Inc.; v (green), Dr. E.R. Degginger/Bruce Coleman Inc.; v (purple), Mark A. Schneider/Photo Researchers, Inc.; v, CORBIS Images/HRW; vi, Laurent Gillieron/Keystone/AP/Wide World Photos; vi (b), The G.R. "Dick" Roberts Photo Library; viii (t), National Geographic Image Collection/Robert W. Madden; viii (b), Bob Krueger/Photo Researchers, Inc.; ix (t), Glenn M. Oliver/Visuals Unlimited; ix (b) Tom Bean/CORBIS; x (t), Stuart Westmorland/CORBIS; xi (t), Goddard Space Flight Center Scientific Visualization Studio/NASA; xi (b), NASA; xii (tl), Index Stock; xii (c), MSFC/NASA; xii (bl), Peter Van Steen/HRW; xiii (t), Bill & Sally Fletcher/Tom Stack & Associates; xiii (b), NASA/TSADO/Tom Stack & Associates; xiv (t), NASA/Peter Arnold, Inc.; xv; Sam Dudgeon/HRW, xvi, Victoria Smith/HRW; xviii, xix, xx, xxii, Victoria Smith/HRW; xxvi, Sam Dudgeon/HRW; xxvii (t), John Langford/HRW; xxvii (b), xxviii (t, bl), Sam Dudgeon/HRW; xxviii (bl), Stephanie Morris/HRW; xxix (tl), Sam Dudgeon/HRW; xxix (tr), Jana Birchum/HRW; xxix (b), Sam Dudgeon/HRW

Unit One 2 (tl), Ed Reschke/Peter Arnold, Inc.; 2 (c), Francois Gohier; 2 (b), Smithsonian Air and Space Museum; 2 (tl), T.A. Wiewandt/DRK Photo; 3 (tl), Uwe Fink/University of Arizona, Department of Planetary Sciences, Lunar & Planetary Laboratory; 3 (tr), Hulton Archive/Getty Images; 3 (stone), Adam Woolfitt/British Museum/Woodfin Camp & Assocites, Inc.; 3, (volcano), K. Segerstrom/USGS; 3 (bl), NASA; 3 (br), Iziko Museums of Cape Town

Chapter One 4-5, © Louie Psihoyos/psihoyos.com; 6, James W. Rozzi; 7, Woods Hole Oceanographic Institute; 8 (t), Marit Jentof-Nilsen and Fritz Hasler/NASA Goddard Laboratory for Atmospheres; 8 (b), Howard B. Bluestein; 9, Jean Miele/Corbis Stock Market; 10 (bl, br), Andy Christiansen/HRW; 10, Mark Howard/Westfall Eco Images; 11, Annie Griffiths Belt/CORBIS; 14, Dr. David Gillette; 17, Paul Fraughton/HRW; 18 (r), Jim Sugar Photography/CORBIS; 18 (l), Sam Dudgeon/HRW; 20 (l), AKG Photo, London; 20 (r), Image Copyright ©2005 PhotoDisc, Inc.; 21, Andy Newman/AP/Wide World Photos; 23 (l, r), Peter Van Steen/HRW; 26, Victoria Smith/HRW; 29 (b), Andy Christiansen/HRW; 29 (l), Peter Van Steen/HRW; 32 (tl), Scripps Institution of Oceanography; 32 (tr), The Stuart News, Carl Rivenbark/AP/Wide World Photos; 33, AFP/CORBIS; 33 (b), AFP/CORBIS

Chapter Two 34-35, JPL/NASA; 36, Royal Geographical Society, London ,UK./The Bridgeman Art Library; 37 (t), Sam Dudgeon/HRW; 37 (b), Tom Pantages Photography; 38, Sam Dudgeon/HRW; 42 (bl, br), Andy Christiansen/HRW; 46, Texas Department of Transportaion; 47, Spaceimaging.com/Getty Images/NewsCom; 48 (bl, bc, br), Strategic Planning Office, City of Seattle; 48 (tl), HO/NewsCom; 49, Andy Christiansen/HRW; 50, USGS; 51 (tl), USGS; 51 (tr), USGS; 52, USGS; 55, Sam Dudgeon/HRW ; 57, USGS; 57 (br), Strategic Planning Office, City of Seattle; 60 (r), JPL/NASA; 60 (l), Victoria Smith/HRW; 61 (r), Bettman/CORBIS; 61 (bl), Layne Kennedy/CORBIS

Unit Two 62 (tl), Science Photo Library/Photo Researchers, Inc; 62 (c), Francois Gohier; 62 (bl), © UPI/ Bettmann/CORBIS; 62 (br), Thomas Laird/Peter Arnold, Inc; 63 (tl), Science VU/Visuals Unlimited; 63 (tr), SuperStock; 63 (cl), AP/Wide World Photos; 63 (cr), NASA/Image State; 63 (br), File/AP/Wide World Photos

Chapter Three 64-65, Terry Wilson; 66, Sam Dudgeon/HRW; 67, Dr. Rainer Bode/Bode-Verlag Gmb; 68 (tr), Victoria Smith/HRW; 68 (bc), Sam Dudgeon/HRW; 68 (tl), Sam Dudgeon/HRW; 69, (copper), E. R. Degginger/Color-Pic, Inc.; 69, (calcite), E. R. Degginger/Color-Pic, Inc.; 69, (fluorite), E. R. Degginger/Color-Pic, Inc.; 69, (corundum), E. R. Degginger/Color-Pic, Inc.; 69, (gypsum), SuperStock; 69, (galena), Visuals Unlimited/Ken Lucas; 70, (vitreous), Biophoto Associates/Photo Researchers, Inc.; 70, (waxy), Biophoto Associates/Photo Researchers, Inc.; 70, (silky), Dr. E.R. Degginger/Bruce Coleman Inc.; 70, (submetallic), John Cancalosi 1989/DRK Photo; 70 (bl), Kosmatsu Mining Systems; 70, (resinous), Charles D. Winters/Photo Researchers, Inc.; 70, (pearly), Victoria Smith/HRW; 70, (metallic), Victoria Smith/HRW; 70, (earthy), Sam Dudgeon/HRW; 71 (tr, c, bl), Sam Dudgeon/HRW; 71, Tom Pantages; 72, (1), Visuals Unlimited/Ken Lucas; 72, (3), Visuals Unlimited/Dane S. Johnson; 72, (7), Carlyn Iverson/Absolute Science Illustration and Photography; 72, (8), Mark A. Schneider/Visuals Unlimited; 72, (9), Charles D. Winters/Photo Researchers, Inc.; 72, (10), Bard Wrisley; 72, (5), Biophoto Associates/Photo Researchers, Inc.; 72, (6), Victoria Smith/HRW; 72, (4), Mark A. Schneider/Photo Researchers, Inc.; 72, (2), Sam Dudgeon/HRW; 73 (tc), Sam Dudgeon/HRW; 73 (tr), Sam Dudgeon/HRW, Courtesy Science Stuff, Austin, TX; 73 (br), Tom Pantages Photography; 73 (bc), Sam Dudgeon/HRW; 73 (tl), Mark A. Schneider/Photo Researchers, Inc.; 73 (tl), Mark A. Schneider/Photo Researchers, Inc.; 73 (bl), 74 (t), Sam Dudgeon/HRW; 74 (bl), Victoria Smith/HRW Photo, Courtesy Science Stuff, Austin, TX; 74 (c), Breck P. Kent; 75 (br), Sam Dudgeon/HRW; 75 (c), Breck P. Kent; 75 (t), Visuals Unlimited/Ken Lucas; 76 (br), Wernher Krutein; 77, Stewart Cohen/Index Stock Photography, Inc.; 78, Digital Image copyright © 2005 PhotoDisc; 79, Historic Royal Palaces; 80 (c), Russell Dian/HRW; 80 (b), 81 (tr), Sam Dudgeon/HRW; 82, Digital Image copyright © 2005 PhotoDisc; 83 (b), E. R. Degginger/Color-Pic, Inc.; 86 (t), Stephan Edelbroich; 87 (t), Will & Dennie McIntyre/McIntyre Photography; 87 (b), Mark Schneider/Visuals Unlimited

Chapter Four 88-89, Tom Till; 90 (bl), Michael Melford/Getty Images/The Image Bank; 90 (br), Joseph Sohm; Visions of America/CORBIS; 91, CORBIS Images/HRW; 94 (t), Joyce Photographics/Photo Researchers, Inc.; 94 (l), Pat Lanza/Bruce Coleman Inc.; 94 (r), Sam Dudgeon/HRW ; 94 (b), James Watt/Animals Animals/Earth Scenes; 94 (l), Pat Lanza/Bruce Coleman Inc.; 95, (granite), Pat Lanza/Bruce Coleman Inc.; 95, (mica), E. R. Degginger/Color-Pic, Inc.; 95, (aragonite), Breck P. Kent; 95, (limestone), Breck P. Kent; 95, (calcite), Mark Schneider/Visuals Unlimited; 95, (feldspar), Mark Schneider/Visuals Unlimited; 95, (quartz), Digital Image copyright © 2005 PhotoDisc; 96 (tl), Sam Dudgeon/HRW; 96 (tc), Dorling Kindersley; 96 (tr, br), Breck P. Kent; 96 (bl), E. R. Degginger/Color-Pic, Inc.; 97, Joseph Sohm; Visions of America/CORBIS; 98 (l), E. R. Degginger/Color-Pic, Inc.; 99 (tr, tl, bl), Breck P. Kent; 99 (br), Victoria Smith/HRW; 101, J.D. Griggs/USGS; 102, CORBIS Images/HRW; 103, (conglomerate), Breck P. Kent; 103, (siltstone), Sam Dudgeon/HRW; 103, (sandstone), Joyce Photographics/Photo Researchers, Inc.; 103, (shale), Sam Dudgeon/HRW; 104 (tl), Stephen Frink/Corbis; 104 (br), Breck P. Kent; 104 (bc), David Muench/CORBIS; 105, Franklin P. OSF/Animals Animals/Earth Scenes; 106, George Wuerthner; 108, (calcite), Dane S. Johnson/Visuals Unlimited; 108, (quartz), Carlyn Iverson/Absolute Science Illustration and Photography; 108, (hematite), Breck P. Kent; 108, (garnet), Breck P. Kent/Animals Animals/Earth Scenes; 108, (chlorite), Sam Dudgeon/HRW; 108, (mica), Tom Pantages; 109, (shale), Ken Karp/HRW; 109, (slate), Sam Dudgeon/HRW; 109, (phyllite), Sam Dudgeon/HRW; 109, (gneiss), Breck P. Kent; 109, (schist), Sam Dudgeon/HRW; 110 (tl), E. R. Degginger/Color-Pic, Inc.; 110 (bl), Ray Simmons/Photo Researchers, Inc; 110 (tr), The Natural History Museum, London; 110 (br), Breck P. Kent; 111, Jim Wark/Airphoto; 113 (t), Sam Dudgeon/HRW; 113 (b), James Tallon; 118 (l), Wolfgang Kaehler/CORBIS; 118 (tr), Dr. David Kring/Science Photo Library/Photo Researchers, Inc.; 119 (r), James Miller/Courtesy Robert Folk, Department of Geological Sciences, University of Texas at Austin; 119 (l), Dr. Philppa Uwins, Whistler Research PTY/SPL/Photo Researchers, Inc.; 120 (inset), Roger Ressmeyer/CORBIS;

Chapter Five 120-121 (inset), Novovitch/Liaison/Getty Images; 122 (tc), Andy Christiansen/HRW; 122 (tl), John Blaustein/Liaison/Getty Images; 122 (tr), Mark Lewis/Getty Images/Stone; 123 (tl), James Randklev/Getty Images/Stone; 123 (b), Ed Malles/Liaison/Newsmakers/Getty Images; 123 (tr), Myrleen Furgusson Cate/PhotoEdit; 124, Victoria Smith/HRW; 126, Data courtesy Marc Imhoff of NASA/GSFC and Christopher Elvidge of NOAA/NGDC. Image by Craig Mayhew and Robert Simmon, NASA/GSFC.; 127 (b), John Zoiner; 127 (t), Mark Green/Getty Images/Taxi; 128, John Zoiner; 130, 2, Paolo Koch/Photo Researchers, Inc.; 130, 1, Horst Schafer/Peter Arnold, Inc.; 130, 3, Brian Parker/Tom Stack & Associates; 130, 4, C. Kuhn/Getty Images/The Image Bank; 131 (br), Alberto Incrocci/Getty Images/The Image Bank; 132 (inset), ©1994 NYC Parks Photo Archive/Fundamental Photographs; 132 (tl), © 1994 Kristen Brochman/Fundamental Photographs; 132, Martin Harvey; 135 (tr), Tom Myers/Photo Researchers, Inc; 136 (t), Laurent Gillieron/Keystone/AP/Wide World Photos; 137 (b), Terry W. Eggers/CORBIS; 138 (t), Craig Sands/National Geographic Image Collection/Getty Images; 138 (b), Caio Coronel/Reuters/NewsCom; 139, G.R. Roberts Photo Library; 141, Laurent Gillieron/Keystone/AP/Wide World Photos; 143, Sam Dudgeon/HRW; 144, HRW; 145; 132, Martin Harvey; 148 (t), Junko Kimura/Getty Images; 148 (b), STR/AP/Wide World Photos; 149 (t), Courtesy of Los Alamos National Laboratories; 149 (b), Corbis Images

848 Credits

Chapter Six 150, National Geographic Image Collection/Jonathan Blair, Courtesy Hessian Regional Museum, Darmstadt, Germany; 153, GeoScience Features Picture Library; 155, Museum of Northern Arizona; 156 (l), Sam Dudgeon/HRW; 156 (r), Andy Christiansen/HRW; 158 (tl), Fletcher & Baylis/Photo Researchers, Inc.; 158 (tr), Ken M. Johns/Photo Researchers, Inc.; 158 (bl), Glenn M. Oliver/Visuals Unlimited; 158 (br), Francois Gohier/Photo Researchers, Inc.; 163, Sam Dudgeon/HRW; 164, Tom Till/DRK Photo; 165, Courtesy Charles S. Tucek/University of Arizona at Tucson; 166, Howard Grey/Getty Images/Stone; 167, Francis Latreille/Nova Productions/AP/Wide World Photos; 168 (b), The G.R. "Dick" Roberts Photo Library; 168 (t), © Louie Psihoyos/psihoyos.com; 169 (l), Brian Exton; 169 (r), Chip Clark/Smithsonian; 170 (l), ; 171, Thomas R. Taylor/Photo Researchers, Inc.; 172, James L. Amos/CORBIS; 173 (tl), Tom Till Photography; 173 (fish), Tom Bean/CORBIS; 173 (leaf), James L. Amos/CORBIS; 173 (turtle), Layne Kennedy/CORBIS; 173 (fly), Ken Lucas/Visuals Unlimited; 175, Chip Clark/Smithsonian; 176 (t), Neg. no. 5793 Courtesy Dept. of Library Services., American Museum of Natural History; 176 (b), Neg. no. 5799 Courtesy Department of Library Services., American Museum of Natural History; 177, Neg. no. 5801 Courtesy Department of Library Services, American Museum of Natural History; 178, Jonathan Blair/CORBIS; 180 (b), The G.R. "Dick" Roberts Photo Library; 181 (fly), Ken Lucas/Visuals Unlimited; 184 (tl), Beth A. Keiser/AP/Wide World Photos; 184 (tr), Jonathan Blair/CORBIS; 185, Courtesy Kevin C. May

Unit Three 186 (tl), Charles Scribner's Sons NY, 1906; 186 (bl), USGS/NASA/Science Source/Photo Researchers, Inc.; 187 (tl), Getty Images/Taxi; 187 (tr), Culver Pictures Inc.; 187 (c), Lambert/Hulton Archive/Getty Images; 187 (cr), Steve Winter/National Geographic Society; 187 (cl), Randy Duchaine/Corbis Stock Market; 187 (b), Robotics Institute Carnegie Mellon University

Chapter Seven 188-189, James Balog/Getty Images/Stone; 191 (t), James Wall/Animals Animals/Earth Scenes; 194, Bruce C. Heezen and Marie Tharp; 205 (tc), ESA/CE/Eurocontrol/Science Photo Library/Photo Researchers, Inc.; 205 (tr), NASA; 206 (bl, br), Peter Van Steen/HRW; 207 (bc), Visuals Unlimited/SylvesterAllred; 207 (br), G.R. Roberts Photo Library; 209 (tl), Tom Bean; 209 (tr), Landform Slides; 210, Jay Dickman/CORBIS; 211 (b), Michele & Tom Grimm Photography; 212, Y. Arthus-B./Peter Arnold, Inc.; 213, Peter Van Steen/HRW; 215, Sam Dudgeon/HRW; 220 (bl), NASA/Science Photo Library/Photo Researchers, Inc.; 220 (c), Ron Miller/Fran Heyl Associates; 220 (tr), Photo by S. Thorarinsson/Solar-Filma/Sun Film-15/3/courtesy of Edward T. Baker, Pacific Marine Environmental Laboratory, NOAA; 221 (r), Bettman/CORBIS

Chapter Eight 222-223, Robert Patrick/Sygma/CORBIS; 225, Roger Ressmeyer/CORBIS; 231, Earth Images/Getty Images/Stone; 233, Bettmann/CORBIS; 236, Michael S. Yamashita/CORBIS; 238, Paul Chesley/Getty Images/Stone; 240, NOAA/NGDC; 241, Sam Dudgeon/HRW; 243, Bettmann/CORBIS; 246, Sam Dudgeon/HRW; 246 (t), Courtesy Stephen H. Hickman, USGS; 247 (t), Todd Bigelow/HRW; 247 (b), Corbis Images

Chapter Nine 248-249, Carl Shaneff/Pacific Stock; 250 (bl), National Geographic Image Collection/Robert W. Madden; 250 (br), Ken Sakamoto/Black Star; 251 (b), Breck P. Kent/Animals Animals/Earth Scenes; 251, Joyce Warren/USGS Photo Library; 253 (tl), Tui De Roy/Minden Pictures; 253 (bl), B. Murton/Southampton Oceanography Centre/Science Photo Library/Photo Researchers, Inc.; 253 (tr), Visuals Unlimited/Martin Miller; 253 (br), Buddy Mays/CORBIS; 254 (t), Tom Bean/DRK Photo; 254 (tl), Francois Gohier/Photo Researchers, Inc.; 254, (tlc), Visuals Unlimited Inc./Glenn Oliver; 254, (tlb), E. R. Degginger/Color-Pic, Inc.; 255 (tr), Alberto Garcia/SABA/CORBIS; 255, Robert W. Madden/National Geographic Society; 256, Images & Volcans/Photo Researchers, Inc.; 257 (br), SuperStock; 257 (cr), SuperStock; 257 (tr), Roger Ressmeyer/CORBIS; 258 (t), Yann Arthus-Bertrand/CORBIS; 259 (t), Joseph Sohm; ChromoSohm Inc./CORBIS; 264 (bl), Robert McGimsey/USGS Alaska Volcano Observatory; 268 (tr), Alberto Garcia/SABA/CORBIS; 272 (bl), CORBIS; 272 (tr), Photo courtesy of Alan V. Morgan, Department of Earth Sciences, University of Waterloo; 272 (tc), © Sigurgeir Jonasson; Frank Lane Picture Agency/CORBIS; 273 (bl), Courtesy Christina Neal; 273 (r), Courtesy Alaska Volcano Observatory

Unit Four 274 (bl), Detail of The Age of Reptiles, a mural by Rudolph F. Zallinger. ©1996, 1975,1985,1989, Peabody Museum of Natural History, Yale University, New Haven, Connecticut, USA.; 274-275 (bc), Price, R.-Survi OSF/Animals Animals/Earth Scenes; 274 (c), Peter Essick/Aurora; 274 (bl), Tom Bean/CORBIS; 275 (tr), John Eastcott/YVA Momatiuk/DRK Photo; 275 (cl), Stock Montage, Inc.; 275 (cr), Tom Bean/Getty Images/Stone; 275 (br), Hong Kong Airport Authority/AP/Wide World Photos; 275 (inset), Corbis Images

Chapter Ten 276-277, Johny Sundby/Zuma Press/NewsCom; 278, SuperStock; 279 (tc), Visuals Unlimited/Martin G. Miller; 279 (tl), Ron Niebrugge/Niebrugge Images; 279 (tr), Grant Heilman/Grant Heilman Photography; 280 (t), John Sohlden/Visuals Unlimited; 282 (t), Laurence Parent; 282 (b), C. Campbell/Westlight/Corbis; 283, Bob Krueger/Photo Researchers, Inc.; 284 (b), B. Ross/Westlight/Corbis; 286 (bl), Digital Image copyright © 2005 EyeWire ; 286 (br), David Cumming; Eye Ubiquitous/CORBIS; 287, Corbis Images; 288, The G.R. "Dick" Roberts Photo Library; 291, Tom Bean/Getty Images/Stone; 292 (t), Bill Ross/Westlight/Corbis; 292 (b), Bruce Coleman, Inc.; 293, Lee Rentz/Bruce Coleman, Inc.; 294 (bl), Grant Heilman Photography, Inc.; 294 (br), Charlton Photos, Inc.; 295, Kevin Fleming/CORBIS; 296 (tr), Mark Lewis/ImageState; 296 (tl), Paul Chesley/Getty Images/Stone; 296 (br), Tom Hovland/Grant Heilman Photography, Inc.; 296 (bl), AgStockUsa; 297, Bettmann/CORBIS; 298 (bl), 299 Sam Dudgeon/HRW; 300, B. Ross/Westlight/Corbis; 301, Bob Krueger/Photo Researchers, Inc.; 304 (tr), M.A. Kessler/Earth Sciences Department, University of California at Santa Cruz; 304 (tl), © W. Ming/UNEP/Peter Arnold, Inc.; 305 (t), Michael Murphy/By permission of Selah, Bamberger Ranch; 305 (b), Michael Murphy/By permission of Selah, Bamberger Ranch;

Chapter Eleven 306-307, Owen Franklin/CORBIS; 308, Tom Bean/DRK Photo; 310, E.R.I.M./Stone; 311, Jim Wark/Peter Arnold; 311 (tl), Nancy Simmerman/Getty Images/Stone; 313, Frans Lanting/Minden Pictures; 313 (cr), Laurence Parent; 314 (t), The G.R. "Dick" Roberts Photo Library; 314, Galen Rowell/Peter Arnold, Inc.; 315 (t), Nancy Simmerman/Getty Images/Stone; 316, Glenn M. Oliver/Visuals Unlimited; 317 (t), The Huntington Library/SuperStock; 317 (b), Earth Satellite Corporation/Science Photo Library/Photo Researchers, Inc.; 318 (t), Visuals Unlimited/Martin G. Miller; 318 (b), Earth Satellite Corporation; 319, Jerry Laizure/AP/Wide World Photos; 324, Rich Reid/Animals Animals/Earth Scenes; 325, Leif Skoogfers/Woodfin Camp & Associates, Inc.; 326, Digital Image © 2005, Eyewire/Getty Images; 327, Morton Beebe/CORBIS; 331, Getty Images/Stone; 332, Victoria Smith/HRW; 334, Martin Harvey; Gallo Images/CORBIS; 335 (t), The Huntington Library/SuperStock; 335 (b), Jim Wark/Peter Arnold; 338 (t), David R. Parks; 338 (br), Martin Harvey; Gallo Images/CORBIS; 339 (tr), Photo by Sam Kittner, courtesy of Rita Colwell/National Science Foundation; 339 (b), Anwar Huq, UMBI

Chapter Twelve 341, John Kuntz/Reuters NewMedia Inc./CORBIS; 342, Aaron Chang/Corbis Stock Market; 343 (t), Tom Bean; 343 (b), CORBIS Images/HRW; 344 (tc), The G.R. "Dick" Roberts Photo Library; 344 (br), Jeff Foott/DRK Photo; 344 (bl), CORBIS Images/HRW; 345 (tl), Breck P. Kent; 345 (tr), John S. Shelton ; 346 (t), Don Herbert/Getty Images/Taxi; 346 (b), Jonathan Weston/ImageState; 346 (t), SuperStock; 347, InterNetwork Media/Getty Images; 349, Jonathan Blair/CORBIS; 350, Telegraph Colour Library/FPG International/Getty Images/Taxi; 352, Tom Bean/CORBIS; 354 (b), Getty Images/Stone; 354 (t), Visuals Unlimited/Glenn M. Oliver; 356, 357, Tom Bean; 358 (l), Sam Dudgeon/HRW; 358 (r), Sam Dudgeon/HRW Photo; 359 (b), Sebastian d'Souza/AFP/CORBIS; 359 (t), Jacques Jangoux/Getty Images/Stone; 360 (t), Jebb Harris/Orange County Register/SABA/CORBIS; 360 (b), Mike Harvey/Woodfin Camp & Associates; 361, Visuals Unlimited/John D. Cunningham; 362, Sam Dudgeon/HRW; 364, Tom Bean/CORBIS; 365, Aaron Chang/Corbis Stock Market; 368 (bl), Geological Survey of Canada, Photo #2002-581, Photographer Dr. Rejean Couture; 368, Charles H. Stites/The Lost Squadron Museum; 368 (t), Louis Sapienza/The Lost Squadron Museum; 369 (r), ©National Geographic Image Collection/ Marla Stenzel; 369 (l), Martin Mejia/AP/Wide World Photos

Unit Five 370 (tl), Herman Melville: Classics Illustrated/Kenneth Spencer Research Library; 370 (c), Peter Scoones/Woodfin Camp & Associates; 370 (bl), Mark Votier/Sygma/CORBIS; 370 (br), New York Aquarium/Wildlife Conservation Society; 371 (tr), National Air and Space Museum/Smithsonian; 371 (cl), Saola/Wallet-Rosenfeld/Liaison/Getty Images; 371 (cr), Hulton-Deutsch Collection/Corbis; 371 (bl), Jeremy Horner/CORBIS

Chapter Thirteen 372-373, Henry Wolcott/Getty Images/National Geographic; 374, Tom Van Sant, Geosphere Project/Planetary Visions/Science Photo Library; 378 (l), U.S. Navy; 378 (r), U.S. Navy; 380, Rosentiel School of Marine and Atmospheric Science, University of Miami; 381, Courtesy of Robert Cantor/Christian Grantham; 382 (l), W. Haxby, Lamont-Doherty Earth Observatory/ Science Photo Library/Photo Researchers, Inc.; 383 (t), NOAA/NSDS; 386 (r), James Wilson/Woodfin Camp & Associates; 386 (l), Norbert Wu; 389, Stuart Westmorland/CORBIS; 389, Stuart Westmorland/CORBIS; 390 (t), Mike Bacon/Tom Stack & Associates; 390 (b), James B. Wood; 391 (b), JAMESTEC; 392, Mike Hill/Getty Images/Photographer's Choice; 393, ©2005 Norbert Wu/www.norbertwu.com; 394, Joel W. Rogers; 395 (t), Breg Vaughn/Tom Stack & Associates; 395 (b), Gregory Ochocki/Photo Researchers, Inc.; 396, Terry Vine/Getty Images/Stone; 397, Steve Raymer/National Geographic Society Image Collection; 398 (tl), Institute of Oceanographic Sciences/NERC/Science Photo Library/Photo Researchers, Inc.; 398 (inset), Charles D. Winters/Photo Researchers, Inc.; 399, Gregory Ochocki/Photo Researchers, Inc.; 400 (r), Photo Edit; 400 (l), Andy Christiansen/HRW; 400 (c), Richard Hamilton Smith/CORBIS; 401 (t), E. R. Degginger/Color-Pic, Inc.; 401 (b), Fred Bavendam/Peter Arnold, Inc.; 402, Greenpeace International; 403 (t), Ben Osborne/Getty Images/Stone; 403 (b), Courtesy Mobil; 404 (l), Courtesy Texas General Land Office Adopt-A-Beach Program; 404 (r), Tony Amos; 405, Ben Osborne/Getty Images/Stone; 407, Sam Dudgeon/HRW; 408, ©2005 Norbert Wu/www.norbertwu.com; 412 (b), © Reuters NewMedia Inc./CORBIS; 412 (tr), ©Patricia Jordan/Peter Arnold, Inc.; 412 (tl), ©Aldo Brando/Peter Arnold, Inc.; 413 (r), HO/The Cousteau Society/Reuters Photo Archive/NewsCom; 413 (l), Parrot Pascal/Corbis Sygma

Credits **849**

Chapter Fourteen 414-415, Tom Salyer/Reuters NewMedia Inc./CORBIS; 416, Hulton Archive/Getty Images; 417 (r), Sam Dudgeon/HRW; 417 (t), Rosentiel School of Marine and Atmospheric Science, University of Miami; 424, Lacy Atkins/San Francisco Examiner/AP/Wide World Photos; 429 (b), CC Lockwood/Bruce Coleman, Inc.; 430 (tl), Darrell Wong/Getty Images/Stone; 430 (tr), August Upitis/Getty Images/Taxi; 435 (tl), VOSCAR/The Maine Photographer; 435 (tr), VOSCAR/The Maine Photographer; 436, Andy Christiansen/HRW; 442 (t), J.A.L. Cooke/Oxford Scientific Films/Animals Animals/Earth Scenes; 443 (t), Pacific Whale Foundation; 443 (b), Flip Nicklin/Minden Pictures

Unit Six 444 (t), Ronald Sheridan/Ancient Art & Architecture Collection; 444 (c), The Huntington Library, Art Collections, and Botanical Gardens, San Marino, California/SuperStock; 445 (tl), NASA; 445 (tr), Sam Dudgeon/HRW; 445 (cr), SuperStock; 445 (bc), Lawrence Livermore Laboratory/Photo Researchers, Inc.; 445, S.Feval/Le Matin/Corbis Sygma

Chapter Fifteen 446-447, Robert Holmes/CORBIS; 449, Peter Van Steen/HRW; 451 (t), SuperStock; 451 (b), NASA; 452, Image Copyright ©2005 PhotoDisc, Inc.; 453, Patrick J. Endres/Alaskaphotographics.com; 458, Terry Renna/AP/Wide World Photos; 459 (b), Moredun Animal Health Ltd./Science Photo Library/Photo Researchers, Inc.; 462 (t), NASA/Science Photo Library/Photo Researchers, Inc.; 464 (c), Argus Fotoarchiv/Peter Arnold, Inc.; 464 (r), David Weintraub/Photo Researchers, Inc; 464 (l), Digital Image copyright © 2005 PhotoDisc/Getty Images; 465 (bl), Steve Starr/CORBIS; 465 (r), Corbis Images; 467, Simon Fraser/SPL/Photo Researchers, Inc.; 468 (t), Goddard Space Flight Center Scientific Visualization Studio/NASA; 468 (b), Goddard Space Flight Center Scientific Visualization Studio/NASA; 469, Tampa Electric; 470, Francis Dean/The Image Works; 471, Tampa Electric; 472, 473, Sam Dudgeon/HRW; 475 (t), Goddard Space Flight Center Scientific Visualization Studio/NASA; 478 (b), James McInnis/Los Alamos National Laboratories; 478 (t), Jonathan Blair/CORBIS; 479 (r), Fred Hirschmann; 479 (bl), Fred Hirschmann

Chapter Sixteen 480-481, Tim Chapman/Miami Herald/NewsCom; 484, Sam Dudgeon/HRW; 485, Victoria Smith/HRW; 486 (tc), NOAA; 486 (tr), Joyce Photographics/Photo Researchers, Inc.; 486 (tl), Corbis Images; 488, Gene E. Moore; 488 (tl), Gerben Oppermans/Getty Images/Stone; 489 (c), Corbis Images; 489 (t), Victoria Smith/HRW; 491, Image Copyright ©2005 PhotoDisc, Inc.; 491 (t), Reuters/Gary Wiepert/NewsCom; 494, NASA; 496, William H. Edwards/Getty Images/The Image Bank; 497 (br), Jean-Loup Charmet/Science Photo Library/Photo Researchers, Inc.; 498 (all), Howard B. Bluestein/Photo Researchers, Inc.; 499 (t), Red Huber/Orlando Sentinel/SYGMA/CORBIS; 499 (b), NASA; 500 (tl), NASA/Science Photo Library/Photo Researchers, Inc.; 501, Dave Martin/AP/Wide World Photos; 502 (b), Joe Raedle/NewsCom; 502 (t), Will Chandler/Anderson Independent-Mail/AP/Wide World Photos; 503 (t), Jean-Loup Charmet/Science Photo Library/Photo Researchers, Inc.; 503 (c), NASA/Science Photo Library/Photo Researchers, Inc.; 504, Graham Neden/Ecoscene/CORBIS; 505, Sam Dudgeon/HRW; 505 (br), G.R. Roberts Photo Library; 505 (t), Guido Alberto Rossi/Getty Images/The Image Bank; 506, National Weather Service/NOAA; 510, Sam Dudgeon/HRW; 511 (tl), Corbis Images; 514 (tr), Lightscapes Photography, Inc./CORBIS; 511 (b), Joyce Photographics/Photo Researchers, Inc.; 515 (t), Michael Lyon; 515 (bl), Corbis Images

Chapter Seventeen 516-517, Steve Bloom Images; 518 (bkgd), Tom Van Sant, Geosphere Project/Planetary Visions/Science Photo Library/Photo Researchers, Inc.; 518 (tl), G.R. Roberts Photo Library; 518 (tr), Index Stock; 518 (c), Yva Momatiuk & John Eastcott; 518 (bl), Gary Retherford/Photo Researchers, Inc.; 518 (br), SuperStock; 519 (tr), CALLER-TIMES/AP/Wide World Photos; 519 (tc), Doug Mills/AP/Wide World Photos; 521 (b), Tom Van Sant, Geosphere Project/Planetary Visions/Science Photo Library/Photo Researchers, Inc.; 522 (bl), Larry Ulrich Photography; 522 (br), Paul Wakefield/Getty Images/Stone; 525, Index Stock; 526 (br), Tom Van Sant/Geosphere Project, Santa Monica/Science Photo Library/Photo Researchers, Inc.; 527 (tl), Carlos Navajas/Getty Images/The Image Bank; 527 (tr), Michael Fogden/Bruce Coleman, Inc.; 528, Nadine Zuber/Photo Researchers, Inc.; 529, Larry Ulrich Photography; 530 (br), Tom Van Sant/Geosphere Project, Santa Monica/Science Photo Library/Photo Researchers, Inc.; 531 (b), Tom Bean/Getty Images/Stone; 531 (t), CORBIS Images/HRW; 532 (b), Steven Simpson/Getty Images/FPG International; 532 (t), Fred Hirschmann; 533 (b), Harry Walker/Alaska Stock; 533 (tr), Tom Van Sant/Geosphere Project, Santa Monica/Science Photo Library/Photo Researchers, Inc.; 534, SuperStock; 538 (br), Roger Werth/Woodfin Camp & Associates; 539, D. Van Ravenswaay/Photo Researchers, Inc.; 544, Gunter Ziesler/Peter Arnold, Inc.; 545, SuperStock; 548, Roger Ressmeyer/CORBIS; 548 (b), Terry Brandt/Grant Heilman Photography, Inc.; 549 (t), Courtesy of The University of Michigan

Unit Seven 550 (t), Astronomical Society of Pacific/Peter Arnold, Inc; 550 (c), Warren Faidley/NASA/Image State; 550 (bl), NASA/JPL; 551 (tl), Alfred Pasieka/Peter Arnold, Inc.; 551 (tr), Hulton Archive/Getty Images; 551 (cl, bc), NASA; 551 (cr), NASA/JPL; 551 (paper), Hulton Archive/Getty Images

Chapter Eighteen 552-553, Roger Ressmeyer/CORBIS; 554, David L. Brown/Tom Stack & Associates; 556, The Bridgeman Art Library; 557, Roger Ressmeyer/Corbis; 558 (bl), Peter Van Steen/HRW; 558 (r), Fred Espenek; 560 (tl), Simon Fraser/Science Photo Library/Photo Researchers, Inc.; 560 (b), NASA; 560 (inset), Roger Ressmeyer/Corbis; 561 (radio), Sam Dudgeon/HRW; 561 (microwave) Sam Dudgeon/HRW; 561 (keyboard), Chuck O'Rear/Woodfin Camp & Associates, Inc.; 561 (sunburn), HRW; 561 (x-ray), David M. Dennis/Tom Stack & Associates; 561 (head), Michael Scott/Getty Images/Stone; 561 (tea), Tony McConnell/SPL/Photo Researchers, Inc.; 562 (gamma), NASA; 562 (radio), NASA; 562 (x-ray), NASA; 562 (infrared), NASA; 563, MSFC/NASA; 566, Peter Van Steen/HRW; 566 (bkgd), Frank Zullo/Photo Researchers, Inc.; 569 (tl), Jim Cummings/Getty Images/Taxi; 569 (tc), Mike Yamashita/Woodfin Camp/Picture Quest; 569 (tr), NASA; 569 (cr), Nozomi MSI Team/ISAS; 569 (bc), Jerry Lodriguss/Photo Researchers, Inc.; 569 (br), Tony & Daphne Hallas/Science Photo Library/Photo Researchers, Inc.; 570 (b), Jane C. Charlton, Penn State/HST/ESA/NASA; 570 (tc), NCAR/Tom Stack & Associates; 572, Peter Van Steen/HRW; 573, Peter Van Steen/HRW; 574 (t), MSFC/NASA; 574 (tea),Tony McConnell/SPL/Photo Researchers, Inc.; 578 (t), Craig Matthew and Robert Simmon/NASA/GSFC/DMSP; 579 (t), American Museum of Natural History; 579 (bl), Richard Berenholtz/CORBIS

Chapter Nineteen 580-581, NASA; 582 (bl), Phil Degginger/Color-Pic, Inc.; 582 (br), John Sanford/Astrostock; 583, Sam Dudgeon/HRW; 585, Roger Ressmeyer/CORBIS; 586, Andre Gallant/Getty Images/The Image Bank; 590, V. Bujarrabal (OAN, Spain), WFPC2, HST, ESA/ NASA ; 591, Royal Observatory, Edinburgh/SPL/Photo Researchers, Inc.; 594 (br), Dr. Christopher Burrows, ESA/STScI/NASA; 594, blt Anglo-Australian Telescope Board; 594 (bl), Anglo-Australian Telescope Board; 595, V. Bujarrabal (OAN, Spain), WFPC2, HST, ESA/ NASA ; 596, Bill & Sally Fletcher/Tom Stack & Associates; 597 (br), Dennis Di Cicco/Peter Arnold, Inc.; 597 (bl), David Malin/Anglo-Australian Observatory; 598 (bl), I M House/Getty Images/Stone; 598 (br), Bill &Sally Fletcher/Tom Stack & Associates; 598 (bc), Jerry Lodriguss/Photo Researchers, Inc; 599, NASA/CXC/Smithsonian Astrophysical Observatory; 604, Sam Dudgeon/HRW; 605, John Sanford/Photo Researchers, Inc.; 610 (bl), NASA; 610 (tr), Jon Morse (University of Colorado)/NASA; 611 (r), The Open University; 611 (bkgd), Dutlev Van Ravenswaay/SPL/Photo Researchers, Inc.

Chapter Twenty 612-613, Anglo-Australian Observatory/Royal Obs. Edinburgh; 614, David Malin/Anglo-Australian Observatory/Royal Observatory, Edinburgh; 622, NASA/Mark Marten/Photo Researchers, Inc. ; 623, NASA/TSADO/Tom Stack & Associates; 624, Earth Imaging/Getty Images/Stone; 627, SuperStock; 628 (l), Breck P. Kent/Animals Animals/Earth Scenes; 628 (r), John Reader/Science Photo Library/Photo Researchers, Inc; 630 (bc), Scott Van Osdol/HRW; 634, Sam Dudgeon/HRW; 636, Earth Imaging/Getty Images/Stone; 640 (b), NSO/NASA; 640 (tr), Jon Lomberg/Science Photo Library/Photo Researchers, Inc.; 640 (inset), David A. Hardy/Science Photo Library/Photo Researchers, Inc.; 641 (r), NASA/CXC/SAO/AIP/Niels Bohr Library; 641 (l), Corbis Sygma

Chapter Twenty One 642-643, NASA/CORBIS; 644 (Mercury), NASA; 644 (Venus), NASA/Peter Arnold, Inc; 644 (Earth), Paul Morrell/Getty Images/Stone; 644 (Mars), USGS/TSADO/Tom Stack & Associates; 644 (Jupiter), Reta Beebe (New Mexico State University)/NASA; 648, NASA/Mark S. Robinson; 649, NASA; 650 (b), NASA; 650 (tl), Frans Lanting/Minden Pictures; 651, World Perspective/Getty Images/Stone; 651 (b), 652 (b), 652 (inset), NASA; 653, ESA; 654, NASA/Peter Arnold, Inc.; 655 (t), 655 (b), 655 (Saturn), 655 (Uranus), 655, (Neptune), 655 (Pluto), 656 (t), 657, 658 (t), 660, NASA; 662 (moons), John Bova/Photo Researchers, Inc.; 663, Fred Espenek; 664 (tl), Jerry Lodriguss/Photo Researchers, Inc.; 665 (b), NASA; 666 (t), USGS/Science Photo Library/Photo Researchers, Inc.; 666 (b), World Perspective/Getty Images/Stone; 667 (t), NASA; 668, Bill & Sally Fletcher/Tom Stack & Associates; 671 (bc), Breck P. Kent/Animals Animals/Earth Scenes; 671 (bl), E.R. Degginger/Bruce Coleman Inc.; 671 (br), Ken Nichols/Institute of Meteorites/University of New Mexico; 671 (t), Dennis Wilson/Science Photo Library/Photo Researhers, Inc.; 672, NASA; 673, Ken Nichols/Institute of Meteorites/University of New Mexico; 676, NASA; 677, ESA; 677 (b), NASA; 680 (tr), Richard Murrin; 681 (t), NASA; 681 (bl), Mehau Kulyk/Science Photo Library/Photo Researchers, Inc.

Chapter Twenty Two 682, Smithsonian Institution/Lockhead Corportation/Courtesy of Ft. Worth Museum of Science and History; 684, NASA; 685 (tr), Hulton Archive/Getty Images; 688 (bl), Brian Parker/Tom Stack & Associates; 688 (br), Sam Dudgeon/HRW; 690, Aerial Images, Inc. and SOVINFORMSPUTNIK; 691, NASA Marshall/National Space Science and Technology Center; 692 (bl, br), USGS; 694 (bkgd), Jim Ballard/Getty Images/Stone; 695 (bl), JPL/TSADO/Tom Stack & Associates; 695 (bkgd), Jim Ballard/Getty Images/Stone; 696 (bkgd), Jim Ballard/Getty Images/Stone; 696 (b), NASA/JPL/Malin Space Station Systems; 697 (bkgd), Jim Ballard/Getty Images/Stone; 699, JPL/NASA; 700 (bl, br), Bettmann/CORBIS; 701 (t), NASA; 701 (br), Corbis Images; 702 (plane), NASA; 702 (bkgd), Telegraph Colour Library/Getty Images/Taxi; 703, NASA; 704 (b), JPL/NASA; 712 (bl), NASA; 712 (tr), Photo courtesy Robert Zubrin, Mars Society; 713 (tr, b), NASA

Lab Book/Appendix "LabBook Header", "L", Corbis Images; "a", Letraset Phototone; "b", and "B", HRW; "o", and "k", images ©2006 PhotoDisc/HRW; 714 (l, tr, br), Sam Dudgeon/HRW; 714 (c), Scott Van Osdol/HRW; 716, 717, Sam Dudgeon/HRW; 718, USGS; 719, Sam Dudgeon/HRW; 721 (tr), Victoria Smith/HRW, Courtesy of Science Stuff, Austin, TX; 721, (galena), Ken Lucas/Visuals Unlimited Inc.; 721 (cr), Charlie Winters/HRW; 721, 722, 723 (hematite, br), Sam Dudgeon/HRW; 724 (all), Andy Christiansen/HRW; 725, 727, Sam Dudgeon/HRW; 728, Tom Bean; 729, 730, Sam Dudgeon/HRW; 731, Andy Christiansen/HRW; 733 (tr), 735, Sam Dudgeon/HRW; 738, Victoria Smith/HRW; 739, Andy Christiansen/HRW; 740, 741, 742, Sam Dudgeon/HRW; 741, Sam Dudgeon/HRW; 745, Victoria Smith/HRW; 746, Sam Dudgeon/HRW; 749, Kuni Stringer/AP/Wide World Photos; 750, Victoria Smith/HRW; 751, Jay Malonson/AP/Wide World Photos; 753, 756, Sam Dudgeon/HRW; 757, Andy Christiansen/HRW; 758, Victoria Smith/HRW; 759, Peter Van Steen/HRW; 760, 761, 762, 764, 765, Sam Dudgeon/HRW; 766, NASA/Getty Images/Stone; 767, Sam Dudgeon/HRW

TEACHER EDITION CREDITS

3E (l), James W. Rozzi; 3F (l), AKG Photo, London; 3F (r), Image Copyright (c)2005 PhotoDisc, Inc.; 33E (t), Sam Dudgeon/HRW; 33E (b), HO/NewsCom; 33F (tl), Spaceimaging.com/Getty Images/NewsCom; 33F (bl), Strategic Planning Office, City of Seattle; 33F (r), USGS; 62E (bl), Mark A. Schneider/Photo Researchers, Inc.; 62E (br), Mark A. Schneider/Photo Researchers, Inc.; 63F (tr), Breck P. Kent; 63F (bl), Stewart Cohen/Index Stock Photography, Inc.; 63F (tl), Historic Royal Palaces; 87E (r), J.D. Griggs/USGS; 87E (aragonite), Breck P. Kent; 87E (limestone), Breck P. Kent; 87E (calcite), Mark Schneider/Visuals Unlimited; 87E (siltstone), Sam Dudgeon/HRW; 87E (sandstone), Dorling Kindersley; 87E (conglomerate), Breck P. Kent; 87F (tl), CORBIS Images/HRW; 87F (mica), Tom Pantages; 87F (chlorite), Sam Dudgeon/HRW; 87F (mica), Tom Pantages; 119E (tl), James Randklev/Getty Images/Stone; 119E (bl), Andy Christiansen/HRW; 119E (r), Mark Green/Getty Images/Taxi; 119F (bl), Laurent Gillieron/Keystone/AP/Wide World Photos; 119F (r), G.R. Roberts Photo Library; 149E (br), Tom Till/DRK Photo; 149F (t), (c) Louie Psihoyos/psihoyos.com; 149F (br), Ken Lucas/Visuals Unlimited; 221E (b), Michael S. Yamashita/CORBIS; 221F (tr), Paul Chesley/Getty Images/Stone; 247E (bl), (c)National Geographic Image Collection/ Robert W. Madden; 247E (tl), E. R. Degginger/Color-Pic, Inc.; 247F (l), Alberto Garcia/ SABA/CORBIS; 247F (r), Roger Ressmeyer/CORBIS; 275E (l), SuperStock; 275E (tr), Laurence Parent; 275E (br), Corbis Images; 275F (l), The G.R. "Dick" Roberts Photo Library; 275F (r), Mark Lewis/ImageState; 205E (l), Tom Bean/DRK Photo; 305E (r), Earth Satellite Corporation/Science Photo Library/Photo Researchers, Inc.; 305F (r), Getty Images/Stone; 339E (tl), Aaron Chang/Corbis Stock Market; 339E (bl), InterNetwork Media/Getty Images; 339E (r), Jonathan Blair/CORBIS; 339F (l), Tom Bean/CORBIS; 339F (r), Jebb Harris/Orange County Register/SABA/CORBIS; 371E (l), Tom Van Sant, Geosphere Project/Planetary Visions/Science Photo Library; 371E (br), James Wilson/Woodfin Camp & Associates; 371E (bl), Norbert Wu; 327F (l), Mike Hill/Getty Images/Photographer's Choice; 327F (r), Ben Osborne/Getty Images/Stone; 413E (bl), Hulton Archive/Getty Images; 413E (r), Sam Dudgeon/HRW; 413F (tl), Darrell Wong/Getty Images/Stone; 413F (tr), August Upitis/Getty Images/Taxi; 413F (br), VOSCAR/The Maine Photographer; 413F (br), VOSCAR/The Maine Photographer; 445E (b), NASA; 445F (bl), NASA/Science Photo Library/Photo Researchers, Inc.; 446F (r), Digital Image copyright (c) 2005 PhotoDisc/Getty Images; 479E (l), Gene E. Moore; 479E (br), Howard B. Bluestein/Photo Researchers, Inc.; 479E (t), NASA; 479F (br), Graham Neden/Ecoscene/CORBIS; 515E (tl), CALLER-TIMES/AP/Wide World Photos; 515E(tr), Doug Mills/AP/Wide World Photos; 515E (b), Tom Van Sant, Geosphere Project/Planetary Visions/Science Photo Library/Photo Researchers, Inc.; 479E (l), David L. Brown/Tom Stack & Associates; 479E (r), Simon Fraser/Science Photo Library/Photo Researchers, Inc.; 479E (inset), Roger Ressmeyer/Corbis; 479F (tl), MSFC/NASA; 579E (bl), Roger Ressmeyer/CORBIS; 579F (tl), Bill & Sally Fletcher/ Tom Stack & Associates; 579E (r), I M House/Getty Images/Stone; 579E (tl), John Sanford/Astrostock; 611E (bl), David Malin/Anglo-Australian Observatory/Royal Observatory, Edinburgh; 611F (tl), Earth Imaging/Getty Images/Stone; 641E (tr), NASA/Mark S. Robinson; 641F (br), Bill & Sally Fletcher/Tom Stack & Associates; 641F (bl), NASA; 681E (l), Hulton Archive/Getty Images; 681E (r), NASA; 681F (plane), NASA; 681F (plane bkgd), Telegraph Colour Library/Getty Images/Taxi

Credits **851**

Answers to Concept Mapping Questions

The following pages contain sample answers to all of the concept mapping questions that appear in the Chapter Reviews. Because there is more than one way to do a concept map, your students' answers may vary.

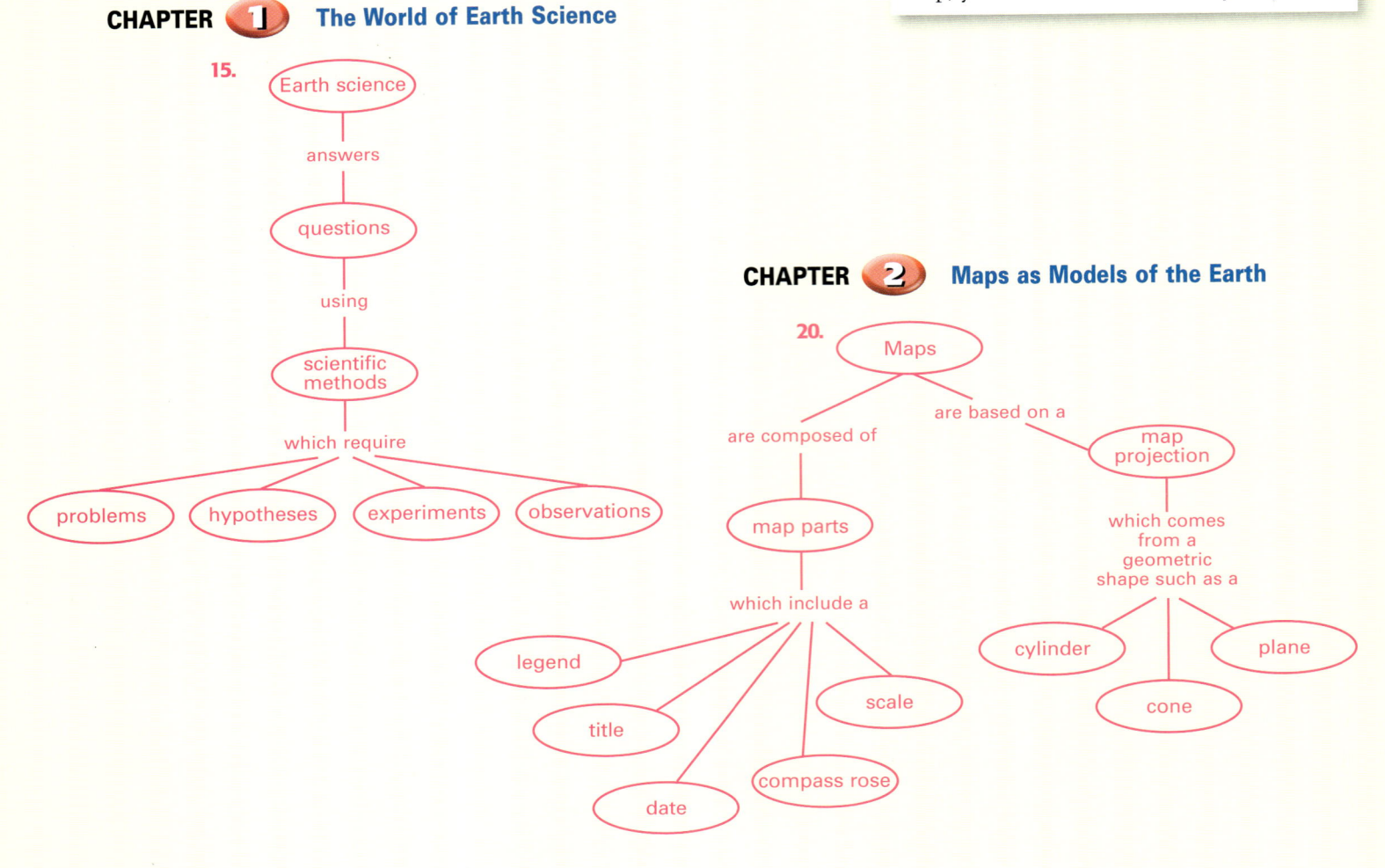

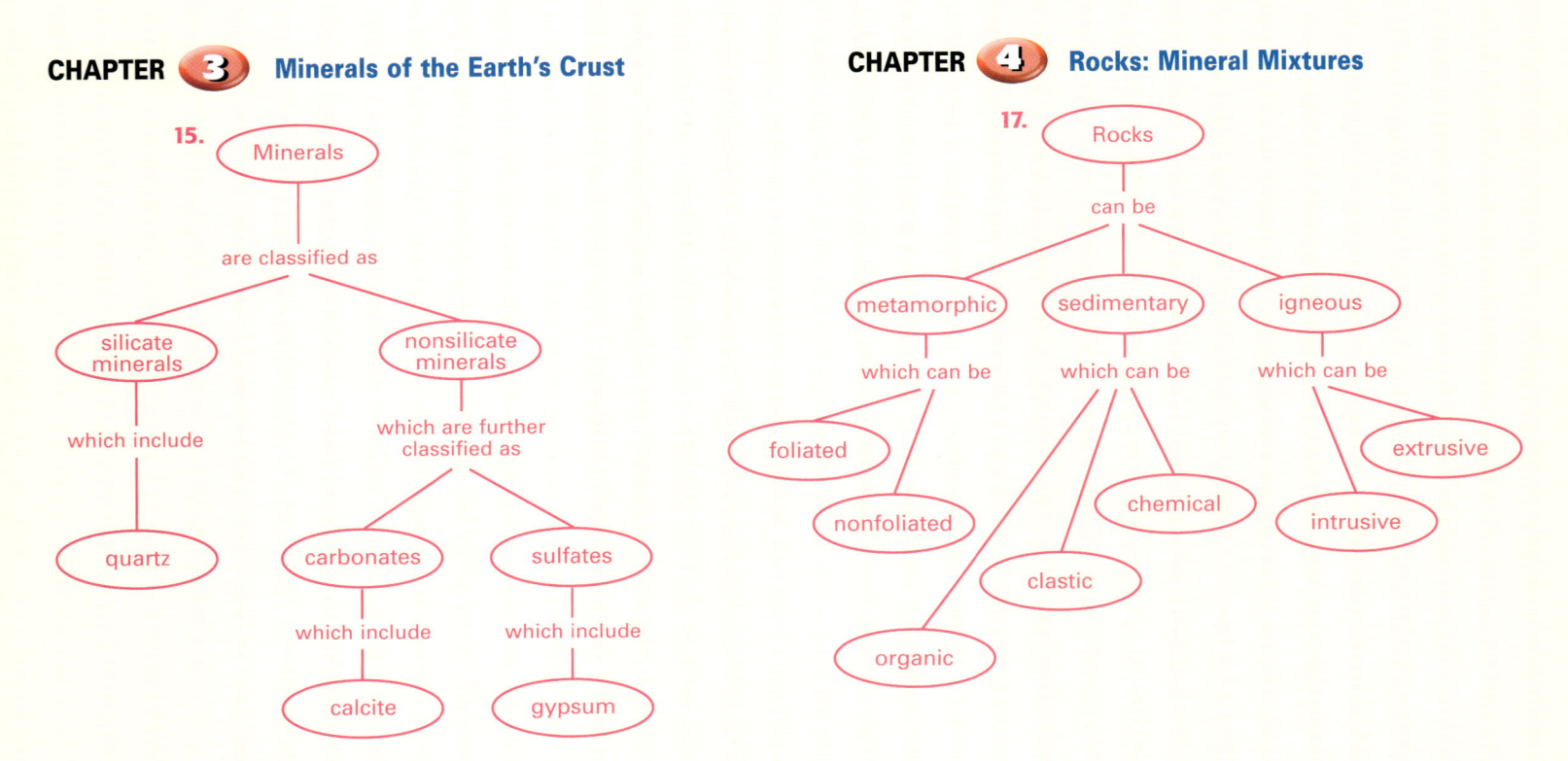

CHAPTER 1 — The World of Earth Science

15.

Earth science → answers → questions → using → scientific methods → which require:
- problems
- hypotheses
- experiments
- observations

CHAPTER 2 — Maps as Models of the Earth

20.

Maps
- are composed of → map parts → which include a:
  - legend
  - title
  - date
  - compass rose
  - scale
- are based on a → map projection → which comes from a geometric shape such as a:
  - cylinder
  - cone
  - plane

CHAPTER 3 — Minerals of the Earth's Crust

15.

Minerals → are classified as:
- silicate minerals → which include → quartz
- nonsilicate minerals → which are further classified as:
  - carbonates → which include → calcite
  - sulfates → which include → gypsum

CHAPTER 4 — Rocks: Mineral Mixtures

17.

Rocks → can be:
- metamorphic → which can be:
  - foliated
  - nonfoliated
- sedimentary → which can be:
  - clastic
  - chemical
  - organic
- igneous → which can be:
  - extrusive
  - intrusive

852 Concept Mapping Answers

CHAPTER 5 Energy Resources

16.

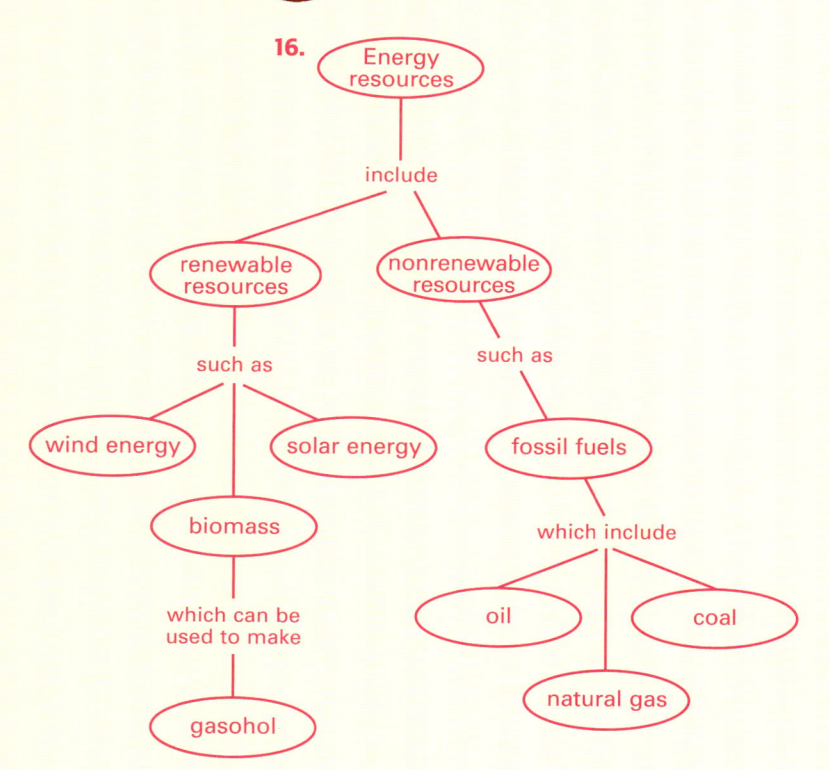

- Energy resources
  - *include*
    - renewable resources
      - *such as*
        - wind energy
        - solar energy
          - biomass
            - *which can be used to make*
              - gasohol
    - nonrenewable resources
      - *such as*
        - fossil fuels
          - *which include*
            - oil
            - coal
            - natural gas

CHAPTER 6 The Rock and Fossil Record

18.

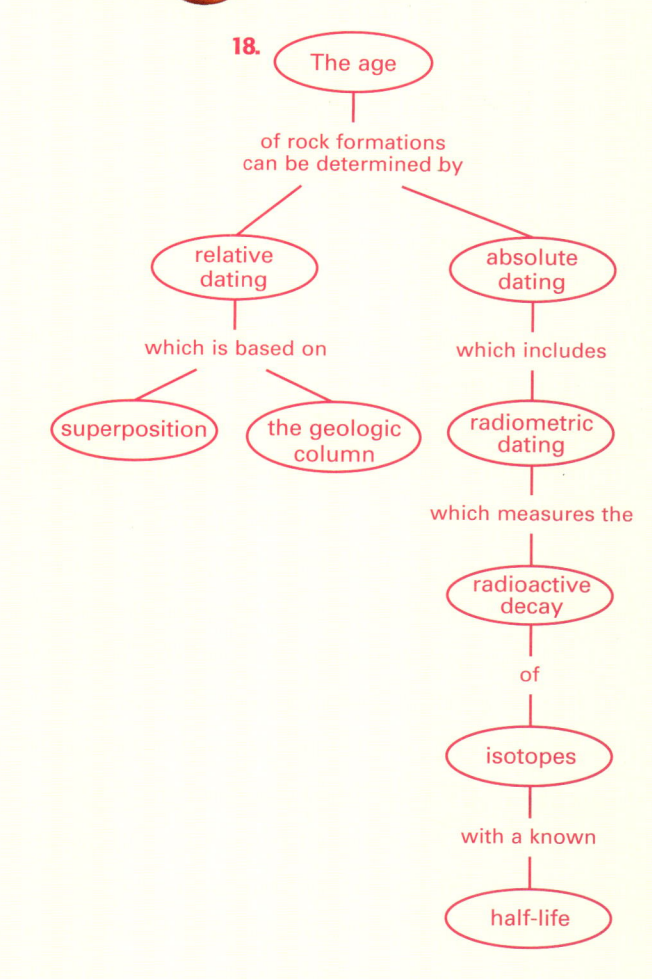

- The age
  - *of rock formations can be determined by*
    - relative dating
      - *which is based on*
        - superposition
        - the geologic column
    - absolute dating
      - *which includes*
        - radiometric dating
          - *which measures the*
            - radioactive decay
              - *of*
                - isotopes
                  - *with a known*
                    - half-life

CHAPTER 7 Plate Tectonics

17.

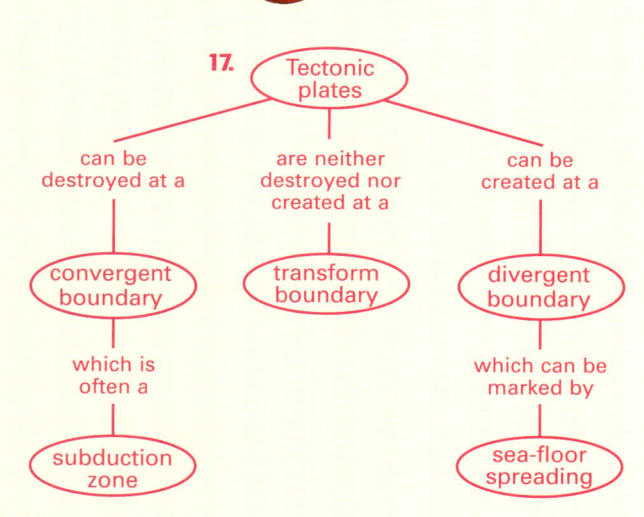

- Tectonic plates
  - *can be destroyed at a*
    - convergent boundary
      - *which is often a*
        - subduction zone
  - *are neither destroyed nor created at a*
    - transform boundary
  - *can be created at a*
    - divergent boundary
      - *which can be marked by*
        - sea-floor spreading

CHAPTER 8 Earthquakes

16.

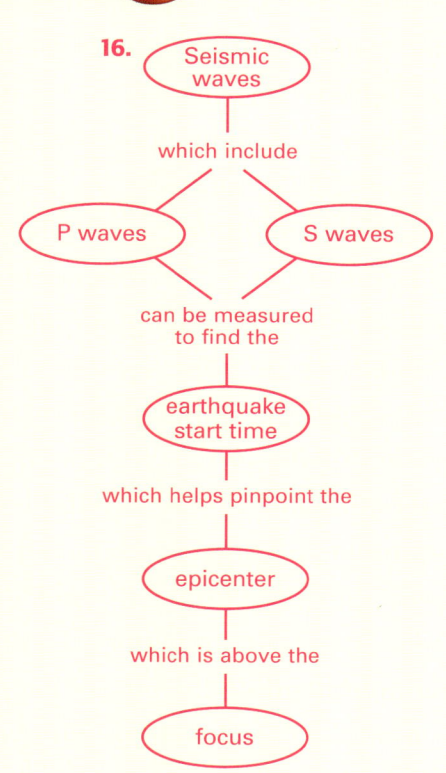

- Seismic waves
  - *which include*
    - P waves
    - S waves
  - *can be measured to find the*
    - earthquake start time
      - *which helps pinpoint the*
        - epicenter
          - *which is above the*
            - focus

Concept Mapping Answers **853**

CHAPTER 9 Volcanoes

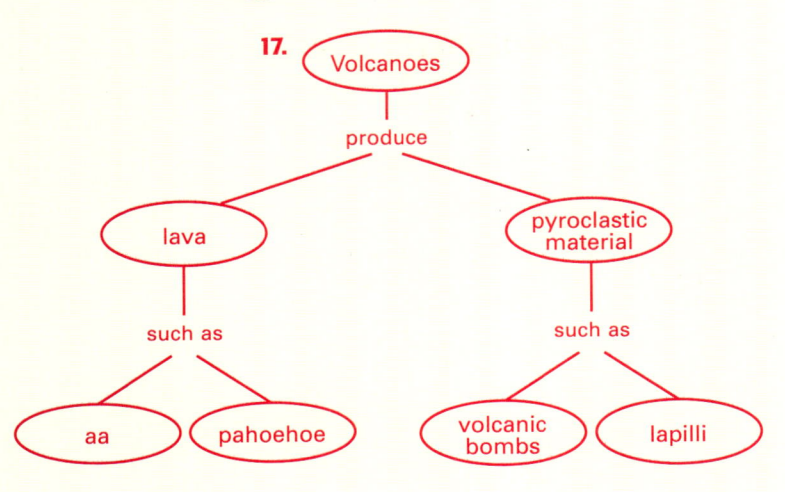

17.
- Volcanoes
  - produce
    - lava
      - such as: aa, pahoehoe
    - pyroclastic material
      - such as: volcanic bombs, lapilli

CHAPTER 10 Weathering and Soil Formation

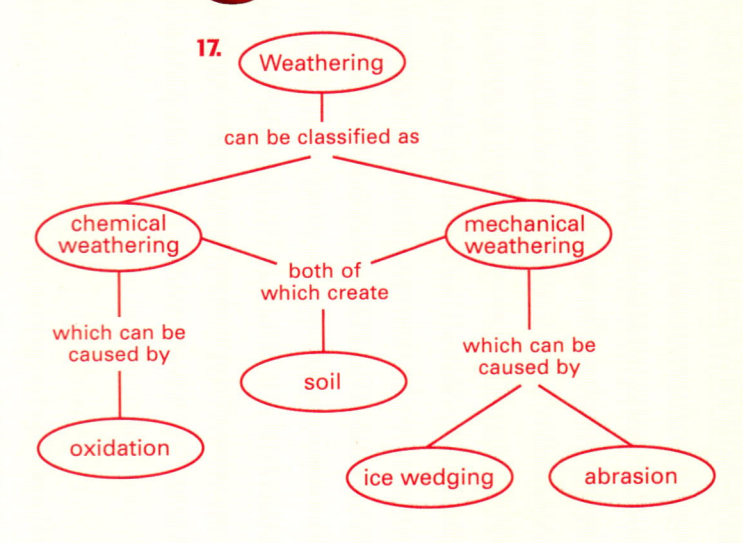

17.
- Weathering
  - can be classified as:
    - chemical weathering
      - which can be caused by: oxidation
    - mechanical weathering
      - which can be caused by: ice wedging, abrasion
  - both of which create: soil

CHAPTER 11 The Flow of Fresh Water

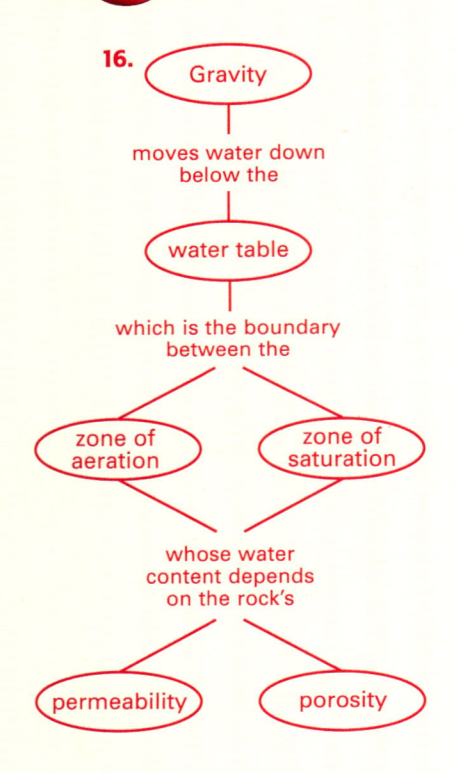

16.
- Gravity
  - moves water down below the: water table
    - which is the boundary between the: zone of aeration, zone of saturation
      - whose water content depends on the rock's: permeability, porosity

CHAPTER 12 Agents of Erosion and Deposition

20.
- Strong winds
  - cause:
    - saltation
      - which can form a: dune
    - deflation
      - which can form: desert pavement

CHAPTER 13 Exploring the Oceans

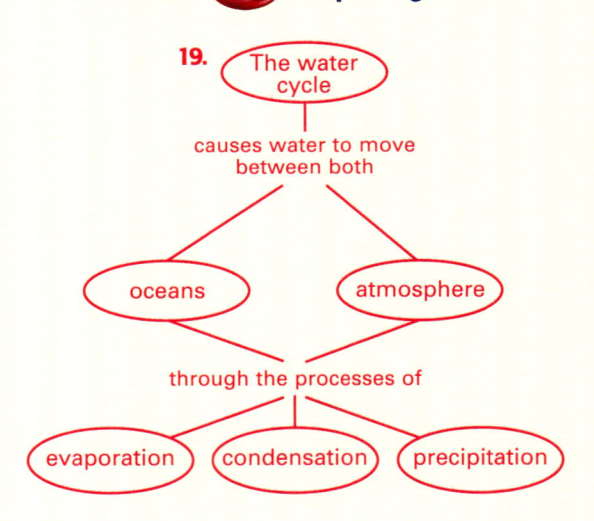

19.
- The water cycle
  - causes water to move between both: oceans, atmosphere
    - through the processes of: evaporation, condensation, precipitation

854 Concept Mapping Answers

CHAPTER 14 The Movement of Ocean Water

17. Types of ocean-water movement **include**:
- **tides**, which are created by sun's gravity and moon's gravity
- **deep currents**, which are created by increasing water density
- **surface currents**
- **waves**, which are created by wind

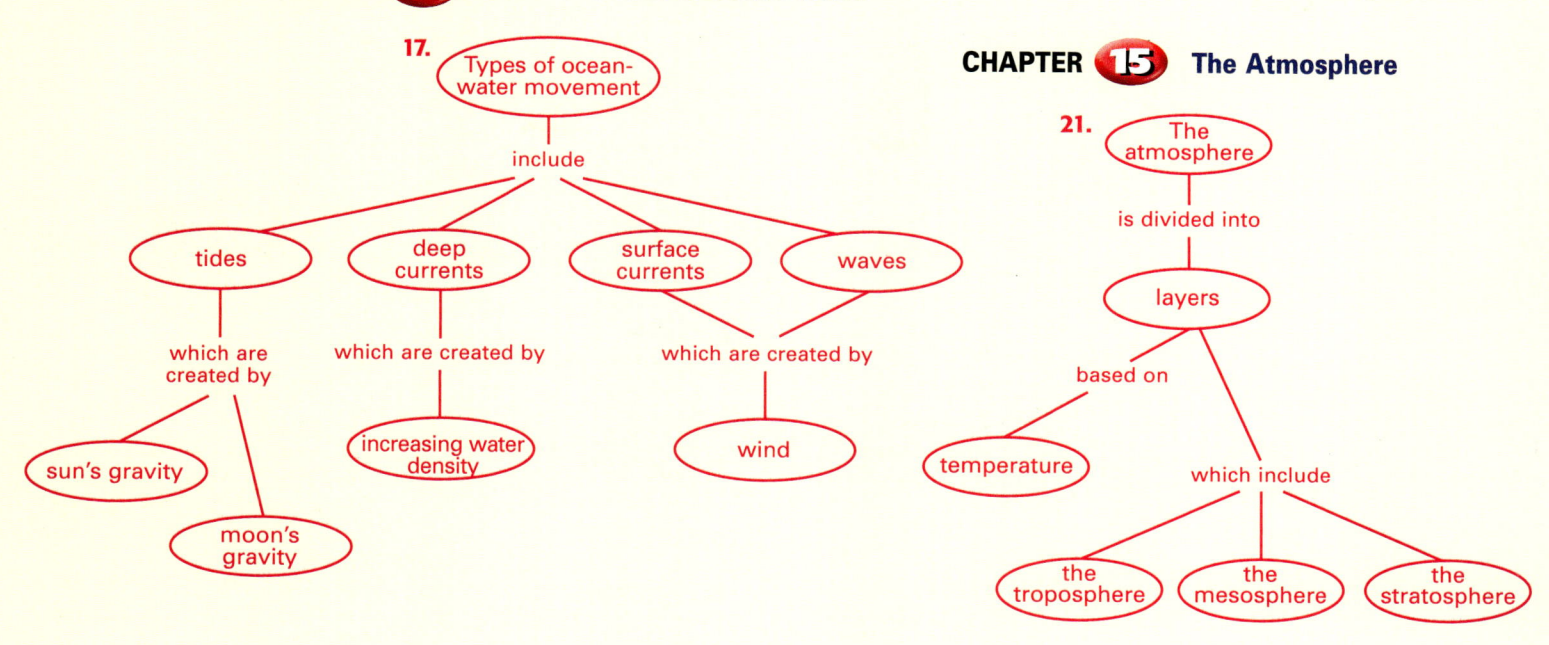

CHAPTER 15 The Atmosphere

21. The atmosphere **is divided into** layers **based on** temperature, **which include**:
- the troposphere
- the mesosphere
- the stratosphere

CHAPTER 16 Understanding Weather

29. Evaporation **increases** relative humidity,
- **which is a measure of** water vapor, **which condenses to form** dew, fog, clouds
- **which is measured with a** psychrometer

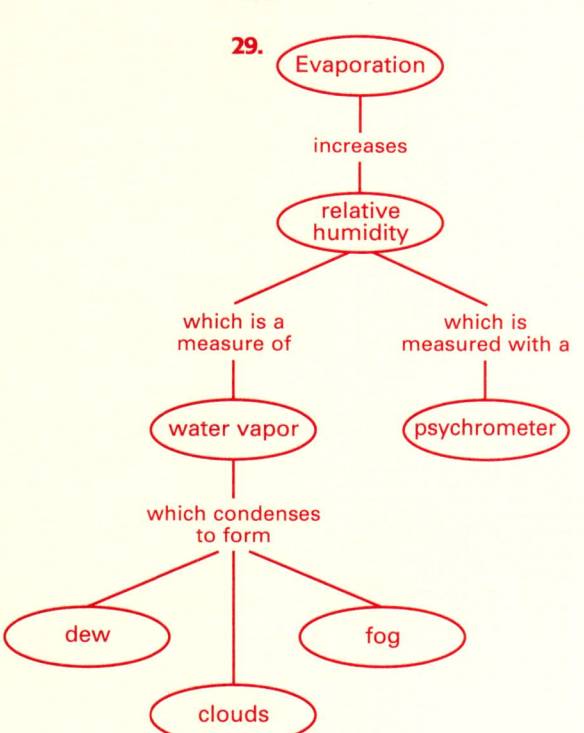

CHAPTER 17 Climate

17. Changes in climate, **such as**:
- global warming, **might be caused by** greenhouse effect, **which might be related to** deforestation
- ice ages, **might be explained by** Milankovitch theory

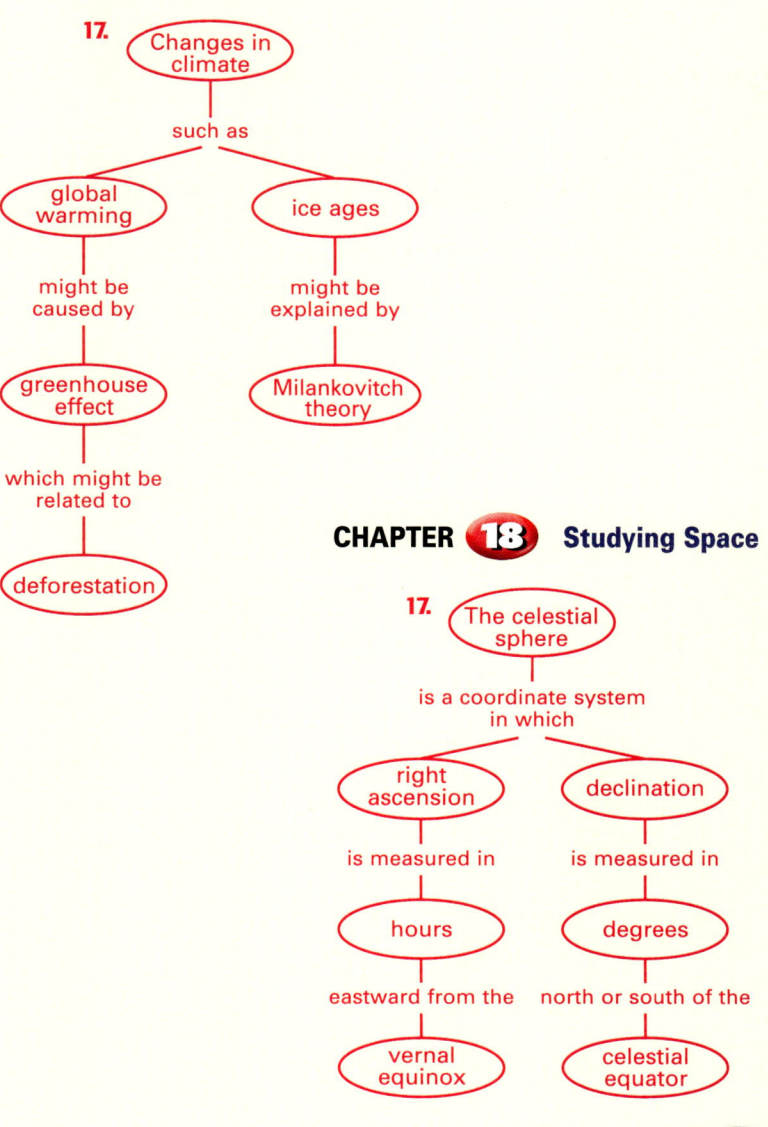

CHAPTER 18 Studying Space

17. The celestial sphere **is a coordinate system in which**:
- right ascension **is measured in** hours **eastward from the** vernal equinox
- declination **is measured in** degrees **north or south of the** celestial equator

CHAPTER 19 Stars, Galaxies, and the Universe

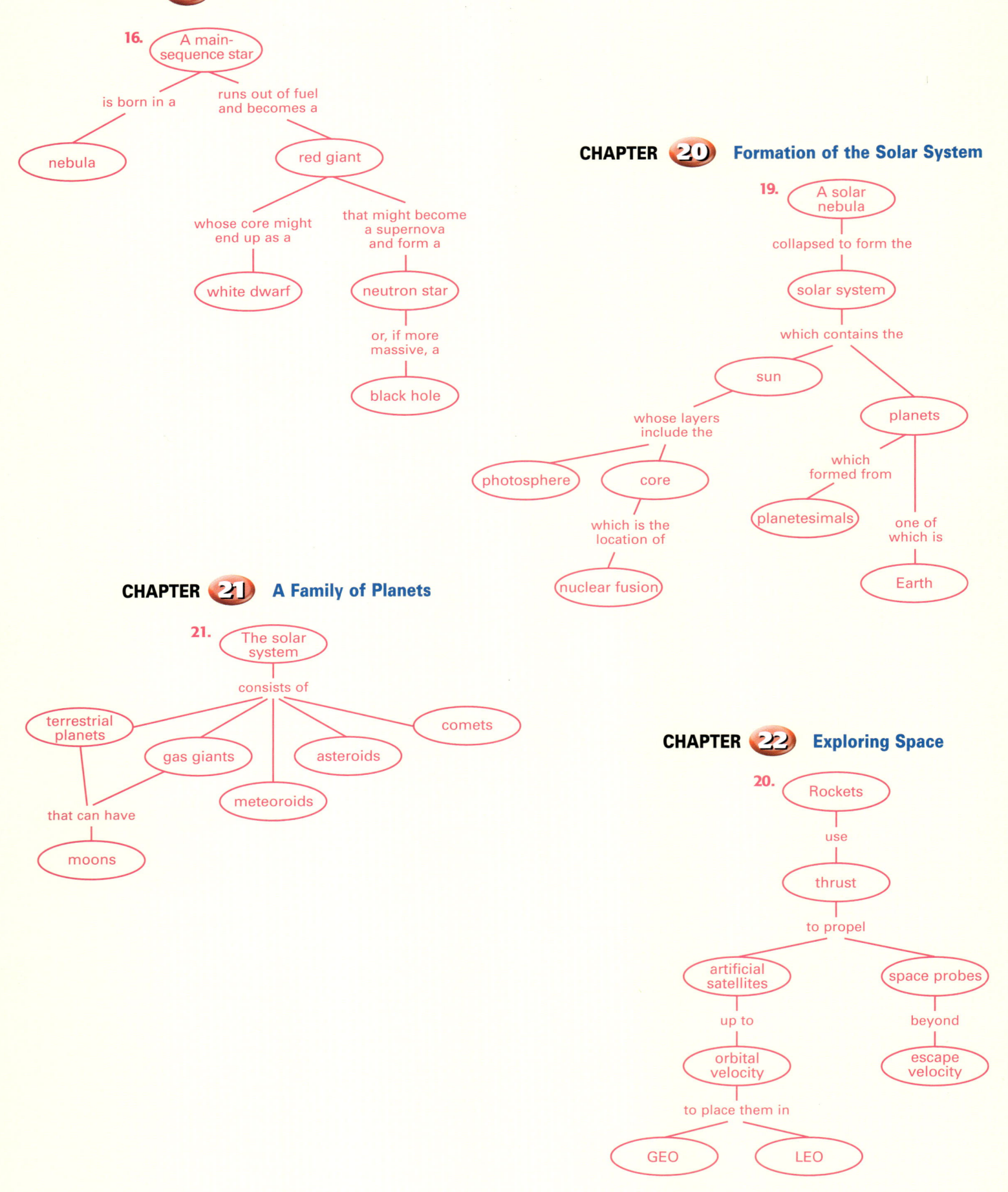

16.

- A main-sequence star
  - is born in a → **nebula**
  - runs out of fuel and becomes a → **red giant**
    - whose core might end up as a → **white dwarf**
    - that might become a supernova and form a → **neutron star**
      - or, if more massive, a → **black hole**

CHAPTER 20 Formation of the Solar System

19.

- A solar nebula
  - collapsed to form the → **solar system**
    - which contains the
      - **sun**
        - whose layers include the
          - **photosphere**
          - **core** — which is the location of → **nuclear fusion**
      - **planets**
        - which formed from → **planetesimals**
        - one of which is → **Earth**

CHAPTER 21 A Family of Planets

21.

- The solar system consists of
  - **terrestrial planets**
  - **gas giants**
  - **asteroids**
  - **comets**
  - **meteoroids**
  - that can have → **moons**

CHAPTER 22 Exploring Space

20.

- Rockets
  - use → **thrust**
    - to propel
      - **artificial satellites**
        - up to → **orbital velocity**
          - to place them in → **GEO**, **LEO**
      - **space probes**
        - beyond → **escape velocity**

856 Concept Mapping Answers

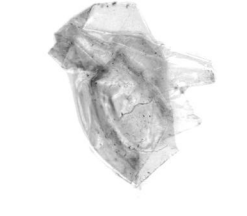